THE ENVIRONMENTAL RESOURCE HANDBOOK

2019/20

TENTH EDITION

THE ENVIRONMENTAL RESOURCE HANDBOOK

A Universal Reference Book

GREY HOUSE PUBLISHING

PUBLISHER: Leslie Mackenzie
EDITORIAL DIRECTOR: Laura Mars
STATISTICS EDITOR: David Garoogian

PRODUCTION MANAGER & COMPOSITION: Kristen Hayes
MARKETING DIRECTOR: Jessica Moody

A Sedgwick Press Book
Grey House Publishing, Inc.
4919 Route 22
Amenia, NY 12501
518.789.8700
Fax: 845.373.6390
www.greyhouse.com
books@greyhouse.com

First edition published 2001
Tenth edition published 2019

Printed in Canada

The environmental resource handbook. – 10th Ed. (2019/20)

Spine title: ERH

1. Environmental protection – United States – Directories. 2. Environmental agencies – United States –Directories. 3. Conservation of natural resources – Societies, etc. – Directories. 4. Nature conservation –Societies, etc. – Directories. 5. Environmental protection – United States – Bibliography. 6. Conservation of natural resources – Bibliography. 7. Nature conservation – Bibliography. I. Grey House Publishing, Inc.

II. Title: ERH.GE20.E5861 363'7 – dc21

RC108 .C645 616' .0025'73 96-640803

ISBN: 978-1-64265-268-0

Table of Contents

Introduction

This tenth edition of *The Environmental Resource Handbook* offers immediate access to a unique combination of more than 6,300 resources and 350 statistical and ranking charts, tables and maps, all revised with the most current information available.

Recognized as a "must-have resource" for environmentalists, educators, researchers and students of environmental studies, this new edition is comprehensive and thoughtfully arranged for easy and efficient use. We've added more than 200 new listings and updated thousands, with current email addresses, and key contacts—providing multiple ways to reach exactly who you need. In addition to the thousands of resources and statistics, this edition includes two valuable front matter reports:

Annual Energy Outlook 2019 with Projections to 2050

Distributed by the U.S. Energy Information Administration, this 96-page report provides long-term energy projections in easy-to-understand bulleted text with dozens of charts and graphs. It was developed using an integrated model that captures interactions of economic changes and energy supply, demand and prices.

Science to Protect Public Health and the Environment

This 30-page research program overview 2016-2019, by the EPA's Office of Research and Development, focuses on the connections between a healthy and sustainable environment and healthy people, and recognizes these main challenges: rising global temperature; record-breaking drought; balancing the level of nutrients in our environment; and chemical exposure.

Section One: Resources

Includes 15 major chapters from **Associations** to **Green Product Catalogs,** and 68 subchapters that further organize the wealth of information in this handbook by specific environmental issues from **Air & Climate** to **Water Resources**.

1. Associations & Organizations disseminate information, host seminars, provide educational literature and promote studies. These listings are defined by both national categories and state listings.

2. Awards & Honors list organizations that recognize education and business professionals for excellence in environmental sciences.

3. Conferences & Trade Shows include large conventions, as well as small, specialized conferences. The listings in this section include who, what, when, where and why.

4. Consultants offer information on environmental consulting services – including hazardous material screening, construction requirements, and habitat conservation.

5. Environmental Health addresses health issues, both general and pediatric, caused by the environment. These listings are divided into three sections: **General Environmental Associations; Pediatric Health Associations**; and **Pediatric Health Publications.**

6. Environmental Law offers resources that offer legal solutions and advocacy that are needed when environmental issues turn into legal ones.

7. Financial Resources include grants, foundations and scholarships that offer financing for educational programs, research and environmental clean-up programs.

8. Government Agencies & Programs list Federal and State agencies. This section ends with a separate by-state list of National Forests, Parks, and Refuges.

9. Publications include books and periodicals that focus on the environment as a business, course of study, subject of activism, and scientific research. These listings are divided into three sections: **Individual Publications**; **Environmental Library Collections;** and **Publishers**.

10. Research Centers helps those looking to research environmental issues. The centers listed here are divided into two categories – those that operate within universities, and those that are run by commercial corporations.

11. Educational Programs are divided into two sections – public and private educational institutions, and workshops and camps. These listings offer environmental educational experiences in a wide variety of specific topics for beginning students, professionals new to the work force, and seasoned environmentalists.

12. Industry Web Sites, Online Databases and **Videos** offer ways to connect electronically to environmental resources.

13. Green Product Catalogs lists the best companies for environmentally friendly products for home, office and everything in between, from tree-free paper to cruelty-free aromatherapy products.

Section Two: Statistics & Rankings

Hundreds of tables and charts in this section comprise dozens of main topics from **Agriculture** to **UV Index,** plus valuable **Green Metro Area Rankings.** This section includes the most current data available, as well as a variety of maps, graphs, and pie charts to make the information as accessible as possible.

> *"...Some charts document consumption and production back to the 1940s and will prove valuable to researchers seeking to identify broader trends."*
>
> **Library Journal**

You will find a great number of state statistics and rankings, making it easy to compile environmental snapshots by state, as well as to compare individual states, counties, and regions of the country. This section is designed to show which communities are taking an active role in protecting our environment and preserving our natural resources. This section helps complete the picture for those doing research, conducting business, or providing education and consulting services. Specific material is listed in the Table of Contents.

Section Three: Appendices

- **Abbreviations & Acronyms**, provided by the Environmental Protection Agency, contains listings that identify and define the political and educational language of the industry.
- **Glossary of Terms**, also from the EPA, defines thousands of commonly used environmental terms in non-technical language.

Section Four: Indexes

- **Entry**: Lists all entries alphabetically, identified by record number.
- **Geographic**: Lists entries alphabetically by state.
- **Subject**: Facilitates search of resources and statistics by environmental categories.

In addition to this print directory, *The Environmental Resource Handbook* is available for subscription on G.O.L.D, Grey House OnLine Databases. This gives you immediate access to the most valuable US environmental contacts, plus offers easy-to-use keyword searches, organization type and subject searches, hotlinks to web sites and emails, and so much more. Call 800-562-2139 for a free trial of the new G.O.L.D OnLine Database, or visit http://gold.greyhouse.com for more information.

User Guide

Descriptive listings in *The Environmental Resource Handbook (ERH)* are organized into 15 chapters and 68 subchapters. You will find the following types of listings throughout the book:

- Associations & Organizations
- Conferences & Trade Shows
- Print & Electronic Media
- Foundations
- Government Agencies
- Research Centers
- Educational Programs
- Catalogs

Below is a sample listing illustrating the kind of information that is or might be included in an Association entry. Each numbered item of information is described in the paragraphs on the following page.

12345 **Water Environment Association of South Central US**
1762 South Major Drive
Suite 200
New Orleans, LA 98087

800-000-0000
058-884-0709
058-884-0568

info@wenvi.com
www.wenvi.com

Barbara Pierce, Executive Director
Diane Watkins, Marketing Director
Robert Goldfarb, Administrative Assistant
Ann Klein, Wastewater Consultant

The mission of the Association is to develop and disseminate information concerning waste quality management and the nature, collection, treatment, and disposal of wastewater. The Association publishes information, including a monthly magazine, manages a web site, and offers workshops and consultation on health and legal issues. A variety of educational programs are offered throughout the year on the history, ecology and culture of local rivers and streams, both on site, and in community schools.

Founded 1964

18 pages

Monthly

User Key

Record Number: Entries are listed alphabetically within each category and numbered, sequentially. Entry numbers, rather than page number, are used in the indexes to refer to listings.

Title: Formal name of company or association. Where association names are completely capitalized, the listing will appear at the beginning of the alphabetized section.

Address: Location or permanent address of the association.

Toll-Free Number: This is listed when provided by the association.

Phone Number: The listed phone number is usually for the main office of the association, but may also be for the sales, marketing, or public relations office as provided.

Fax Number: This is listed when provided by the association.

E-Mail: This is listed when provided, and is generally the main office e-mail.

Web Site: This is listed when provided.

Key Personnel: Names and titles of department heads of the association.

Association Description: This paragraph contains a brief description of the association and their services.

Year Founded: The year in which the association was established or founded. If there has been a name change, the founding date is usually for the earliest name under which it was known.

Number of Pages: Number of pages if the listing is a publication.

Frequency: How often it is published if it is a publication.

Annual Energy Outlook 2019

with projections to 2050

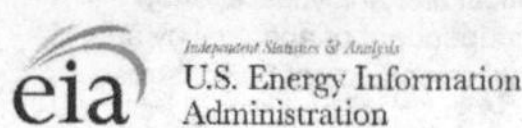

#AEO2019

January 24, 2019
www.eia.gov/aeo

Annual Energy Outlook 2019
with projections to 2050

January 2019

U.S. Energy Information Administration
Office of Energy Analysis
U.S. Department of Energy
Washington, DC 20585

This publication is on the Web at:
www.eia.gov/aeo

This report was prepared by the U.S. Energy Information Administration (EIA), the statistical and analytical agency within the U.S. Department of Energy. By law, EIA's data, analyses, and forecasts are independent of approval by any other officer or employee of the United States Government. The views in this report therefore should not be construed as representing those of the Department of Energy or other federal agencies.

The Annual Energy Outlook provides long-term energy projections for the United States

- Projections in the *Annual Energy Outlook 2019* (AEO2019) are not predictions of what will happen, but rather modeled projections of what may happen given certain assumptions and methodologies.
- The AEO is developed using the National Energy Modeling System (NEMS), an integrated model that captures interactions of economic changes and energy supply, demand, and prices.
- Energy market projections are subject to much uncertainty because many of the events that shape energy markets as well as future developments in technologies, demographics, and resources cannot be foreseen with certainty. To illustrate the importance of key assumptions, AEO2019 includes a Reference case and six side cases that systematically vary important underlying assumptions.
- More information about the assumptions used in developing these projections will be available shortly after the release of the AEO2019.
- The AEO is published to satisfy the Department of Energy Organization Act of 1977, which requires the Administrator of the U.S. Energy Information Administration to prepare annual reports on trends and projections for energy use and supply.

U.S. Energy Information Administration #AEO2019 | www.eia.gov/aeo

What is the Reference case?

- The AEO2019 Reference case represents EIA's best assessment of how U.S. and world energy markets will operate through 2050, based on many key assumptions. For instance, the Reference case projection assumes improvement in known energy production, delivery, and consumption technology trends.
- The economic and demographic trends reflected in the Reference case reflect current views of leading economic forecasters and demographers.
- The Reference case generally assumes that current laws and regulations that affect the energy sector, including laws that have end dates, are unchanged throughout the projection period. This assumption is important because it permits EIA to use the Reference case as a benchmark to compare policy-based modeling.
- The potential impacts of proposed legislation, regulations, or standards are not included in the AEO2019 cases.
- The Reference case should be interpreted as a reasonable baseline case that can be compared with the cases that include alternative assumptions.

U.S. Energy Information Administration #AEO2019 | www.eia.gov/aeo

What are the side cases?

- The side cases in AEO2019 show the effect that changing important model assumptions have on the projections when compared with the Reference case.
- Two AEO2019 side cases are the High and Low Oil Price cases, which represent international conditions outside the United States that could collectively drive prices to extreme, sustained deviations from the Reference case price path.
- Additional AEO2019 side cases are the High and Low Oil and Gas Resource and Technology cases, where production costs and resource availability within the United States are varied, allowing for more or less production at given world oil and natural gas prices.
- The two AEO2019 side cases that vary the effects of economic assumptions on energy consumption are the High and Low Economic Growth cases, which modify population growth and productivity assumptions throughout the projection period to yield higher or lower compound annual growth rates for U.S. gross domestic product than in the Reference case.

U.S. Energy Information Administration #AEO2019 | www.eia.gov/aeo

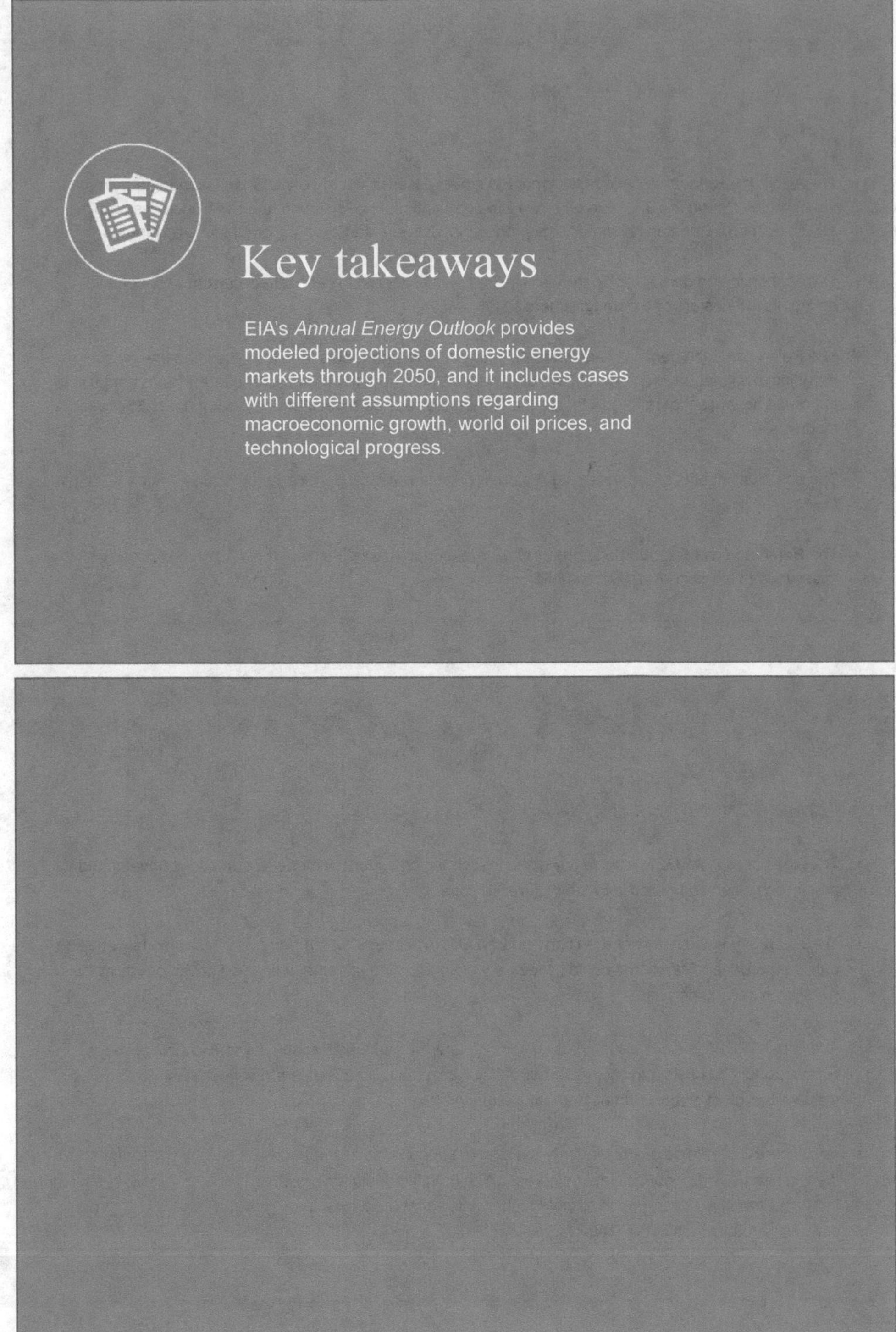
Key takeaways
EIA's *Annual Energy Outlook* provides modeled projections of domestic energy markets through 2050, and it includes cases with different assumptions regarding macroeconomic growth, world oil prices, and technological progress.

Key takeaways from the Reference case

- The United States becomes a net energy exporter in 2020 and remains so throughout the projection period as a result of large increases in crude oil, natural gas, and natural gas plant liquids (NGPL) production coupled with slow growth in U.S. energy consumption.
- Of the fossil fuels, natural gas and NGPLs have the highest production growth, and NGPLs account for almost one-third of cumulative U.S. liquids production during the projection period.
- Natural gas prices remain comparatively low during the projection period compared with historical prices, leading to increased use of this fuel across end-use sectors and increased liquefied natural gas exports.
- The power sector experiences a notable shift in fuels used to generate electricity, driven in part by historically low natural gas prices. Increased natural gas-fired electricity generation; larger shares of intermittent renewables; and additional retirements of less economic existing coal and nuclear plants occur during the projection period.
- Increasing energy efficiency across end-use sectors keeps U.S. energy consumption relatively flat, even as the U.S. economy continues to expand.

The United States becomes a net energy exporter after 2020 in the Reference case—

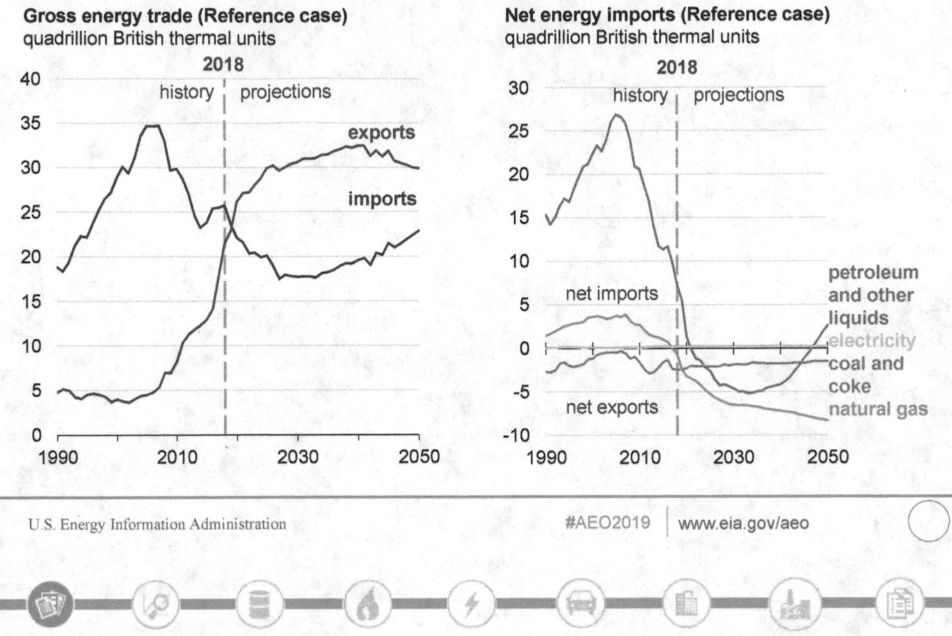

—but the United States continues to import and export throughout the projection period

- The United States has been a net energy importer since 1953, but continued growth in petroleum and natural gas exports results in the United States becoming a net energy exporter by 2020 in all cases.

- In the Reference case, the United States becomes a net exporter of petroleum liquids after 2020 as U.S. crude oil production increases and domestic consumption of petroleum products decreases. Near the end of the projection period, the United States returns to being a net importer of petroleum and other liquids on an energy basis as a result of increasing domestic gasoline consumption and falling domestic crude oil production in those years.

- The United States became a net natural gas exporter on an annual basis in 2017 and continued to export more natural gas than it imported in 2018. In the Reference case, U.S. natural gas trade, which includes shipments by pipeline from and to Canada and to Mexico as well as exports of liquefied natural gas (LNG), will be increasingly dominated by LNG exports to more distant destinations.

- The United States continues to be a net exporter of coal (including coal coke) through 2050 in the Reference case, but coal exports are not expected to increase because of competition from other global suppliers closer to major world markets.

U.S. Energy Information Administration #AEO2019 | www.eia.gov/aeo

Production of U.S. crude oil and natural gas plant liquids continues to grow through 2025 in the Reference case—

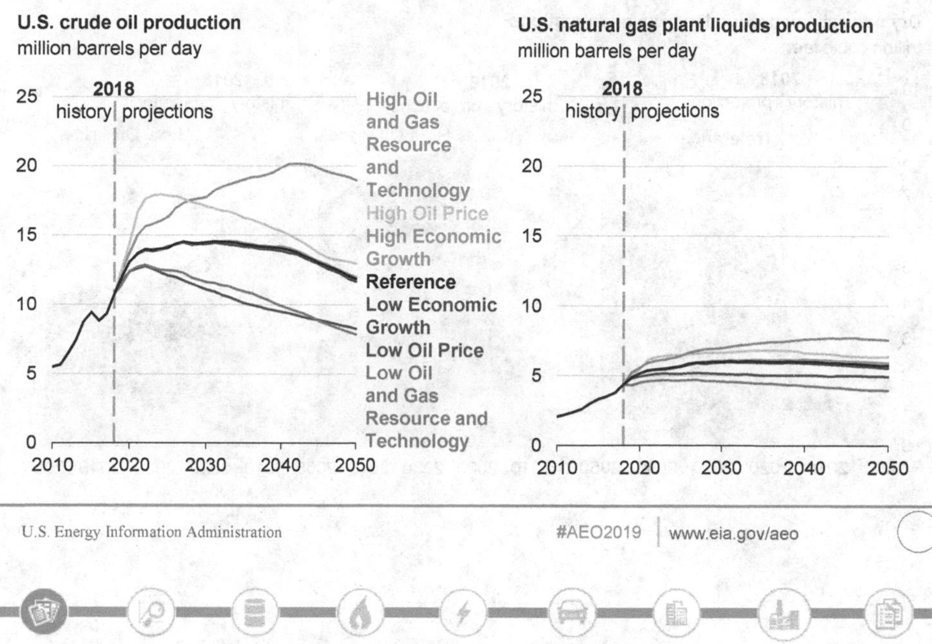

—and natural gas plant liquids comprise nearly one-third of cumulative 2019–2050 U.S. liquids production

- In the Reference case, U.S. crude oil production continues to set annual records through 2027 and remains greater than 14.0 million barrels per day (b/d) through 2040. Lower 48 onshore tight oil development continues to be the main source of growth in total U.S. crude oil production.
- The continued development of tight oil and shale gas resources supports growth in natural gas plant liquids (NGPL) production, which reaches 6.0 million b/d by 2029 in the Reference case.
- The High Oil and Gas Resource and Technology case represents a potential upper bound for crude oil and NGPL production, as additional resources and higher levels of technological advancement result in continued growth in crude oil and NGPL production. In the High Oil Price case, high crude oil prices lead to more drilling in the near term, but cost increases and fewer easily accessible resources decrease production of crude oil and NGPL.
- Conversely, under conditions with fewer resources, lower levels of technological advancement, and lower crude oil prices, the Low Oil and Gas Resource and Technology case and the Low Oil Price case represent potential lower bounds for domestic crude oil and NGPL production. Changes in economic growth have little impact on domestic crude oil and NGPL production.

The United States continues to produce large volumes of natural gas from oil formations, even with relatively low oil prices—

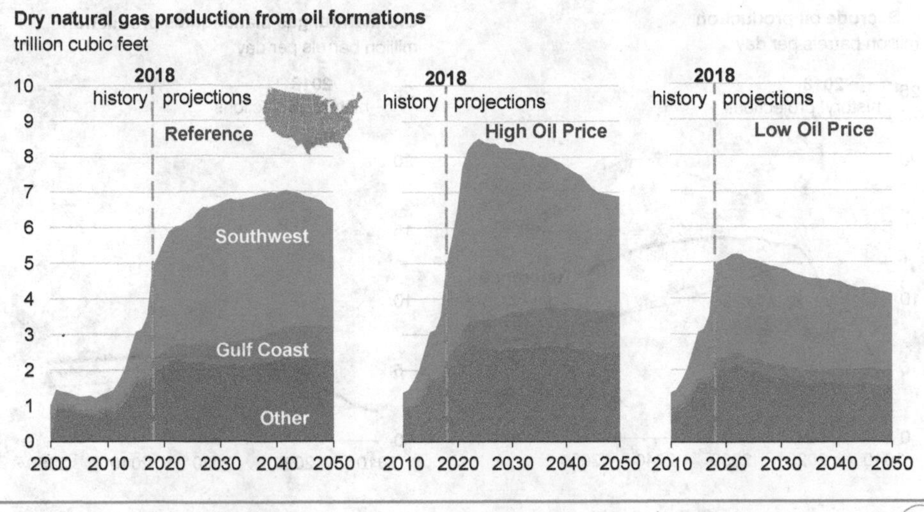

—putting downward pressure on natural gas prices

- The percentage of dry natural gas production from oil formations increased from 8% in 2013 to 17% in 2018 and remains near this percentage through 2050 in the Reference case.
- Growth in drilling in the Southwest region, particularly in the Wolfcamp formation in the Permian basin, is the main driver for natural gas production growth from tight oil formations.
- The Low Oil Price case, with the U.S. crude oil benchmark West Texas Intermediate (WTI, Cushing, Oklahoma) price at $58 per barrel or lower, is the only case in which natural gas production from oil formations is lower in 2050 than at current levels.
- The level of drilling in oil formations primarily depends on crude oil prices rather than natural gas prices. Increased natural gas production from oil-directed drilling puts downward pressure on natural gas prices throughout the projection period.

U.S. net exports of natural gas continue to grow in the Reference case—

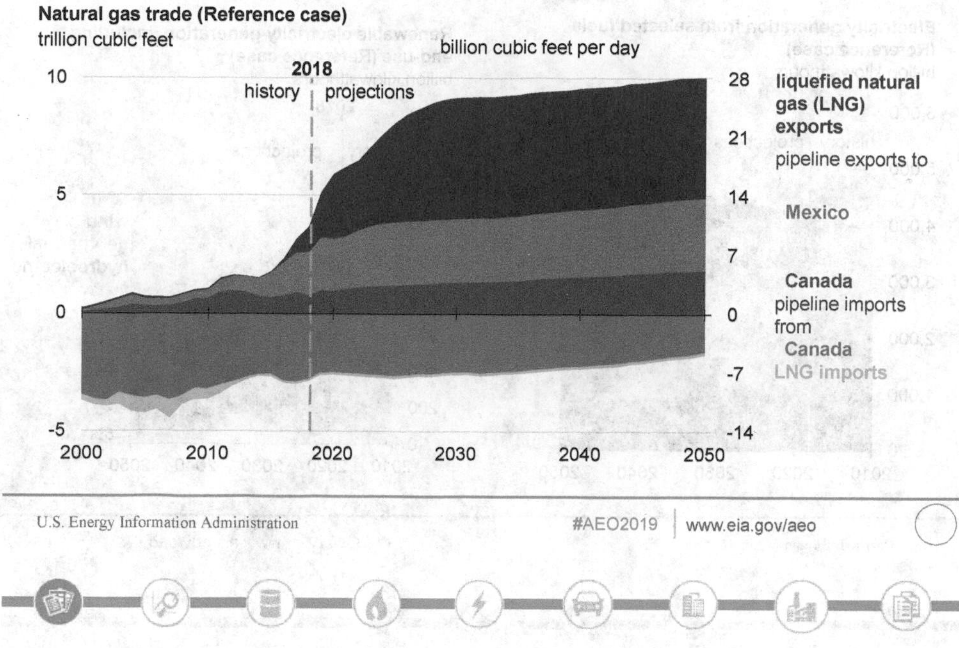

U.S. Energy Information Administration

—as liquefied natural gas becomes an increasingly significant export

- In the Reference case, U.S. liquefied natural gas (LNG) exports and pipeline exports to Canada and to Mexico increase until 2030 and then flatten through 2050 as relatively low, stable natural gas prices make U.S. natural gas competitive in North American and global markets.

- After LNG export facilities currently under construction are completed by 2022, U.S. LNG export capacity increases further. Asian demand growth allows U.S. natural gas to remain competitive there. After 2030, U.S. LNG is no longer as competitive because additional suppliers enter the global LNG market, reducing LNG prices and making additional U.S. LNG export capacity uneconomic.

- Increasing natural gas exports to Mexico are a result of more pipeline infrastructure to and within Mexico, resulting in increased natural gas-fired power generation. By 2030, Mexican domestic natural gas production begins to displace U.S. exports.

- As Canadian natural gas faces competition from relatively low-cost U.S. natural gas, U.S. imports of natural gas from Western Canada continue to decline from historical levels. U.S. exports of natural gas to Eastern Canada continue to increase because of its proximity to U.S. natural gas resources in the Marcellus and Utica plays and because of recent additions to pipeline infrastructure.

U.S. Energy Information Administration #AEO2019 | www.eia.gov/aeo

Electricity generation from natural gas and renewables increases, and the shares of nuclear and coal generation decrease—

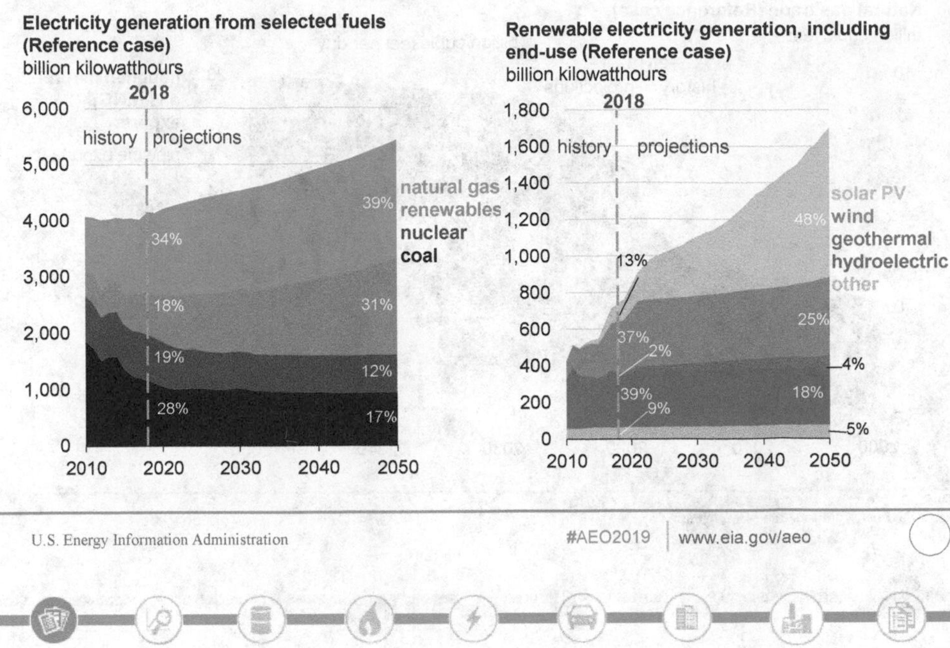

—as lower natural gas prices and declining costs of renewable capacity make these fuels increasingly competitive

- The continuing decline in natural gas prices and increasing penetration of renewable electricity generation have resulted in lower wholesale electricity prices, changes in utilization rates, and operating losses for a large number of baseload coal and nuclear generators.
- Generation from both coal and nuclear is expected to decline in all cases. In the Reference case, from a 28% share in 2018, coal generation drops to 17% of total generation by 2050. Nuclear generation declines from a 19% share of total generation in 2018 to 12% by 2050. The share of natural gas generation rises from 34% in 2018 to 39% in 2050, and the share of renewable generation increases from 18% to 31%.
- Assumptions of declining costs and improving performance make wind and solar increasingly competitive compared with other renewable resources in the Reference case. Most of the wind generation increase occurs in the near term, when new projects enter service ahead of the expiration of key federal production tax credits.
- Solar Investment Tax Credits (ITC) phase down after 2024, but solar generation growth continues because the costs for solar continue to fall faster than for other sources.

End-use activities grow, and energy intensities decrease in all sectors in the Reference case—

Indexed end-use demand drivers and energy intensities by sector (2018–50) (Reference case)

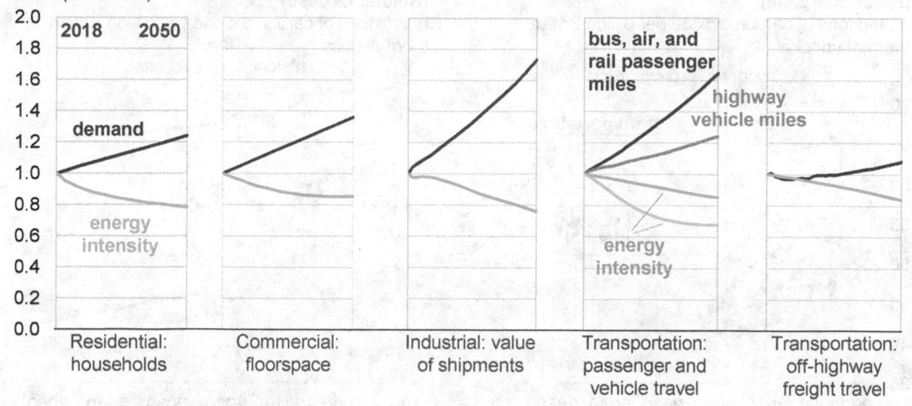

Note: Energy intensities are a lighter shade of the same color as the respective demand, and they are calculated as energy used per unit of respective demand.

—offsetting each other to limit energy consumption growth

- Delivered U.S. energy consumption grows across all major end-use sectors, with electricity and natural gas growing fastest. However, increases in efficiency, represented by declines in energy intensity (the amount of energy consumed per unit of potential demand), partially offset growth in total U.S. energy consumption across all end-use sectors.

- The end-use sectors have different representative metrics for demand used to estimate energy intensity—number of households for the residential sector, floorspace for the commercial sector, industrial value of shipments for the industrial sector, and travel metrics for the transportation sector.

- Transportation travel is measured in three ways, depending on the mode: highway vehicle miles (light- and heavy-duty vehicles), passenger miles (bus, passenger rail, and air), and off-highway freight ton-miles (freight rail, air, and domestic shipping).

- The steepest decline in energy intensity is in the transportation sector, with the level of energy used per highway vehicle-mile traveled declining by 32% from 2018 to 2050 as a result of increasingly stringent fuel economy and energy efficiency standards for light- and heavy-duty vehicles.

Across end-use sectors, carbon dioxide intensity declines with changes in the fuel mix—

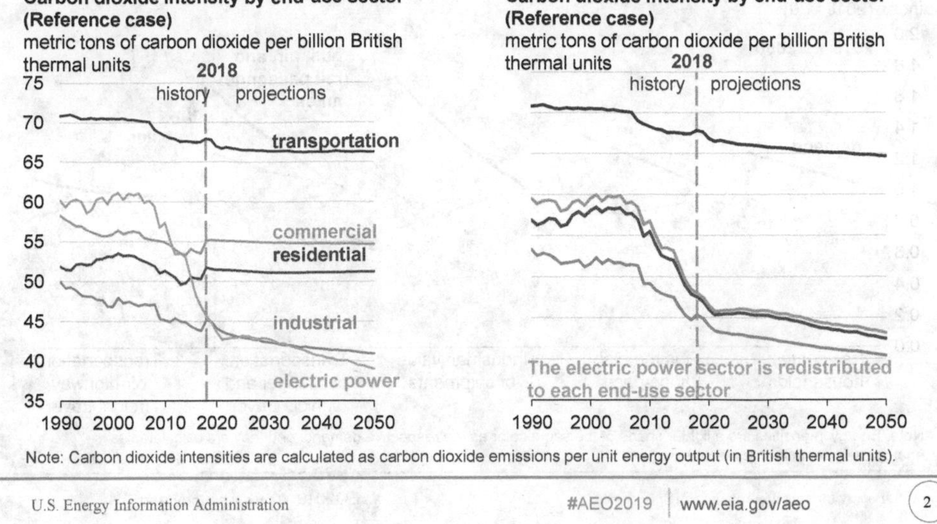

Note: Carbon dioxide intensities are calculated as carbon dioxide emissions per unit energy output (in British thermal units).

—despite overall increases in energy consumption

- Carbon dioxide (CO2) intensity can vary greatly depending on the mix of fuels the end-use sectors consume. Historically, the industrial sector has had the lowest CO2 intensity, as measured by CO2 emissions per British thermal unit (Btu). The transportation sector historically has had the highest CO2 intensity, which continues in the projection because carbon-intensive petroleum remains the dominant fuel used in vehicles throughout the projection period.

- The generation fuel mix in the electric power sector has changed since the mid-2000s, with lower generation from high-carbon intensive coal and higher generation from natural gas and carbon-free renewables, such as wind and solar. This change resulted in the overall CO2 intensity of the electric power sector declining by 25% from the mid-2000s to 2018 and continuing to decline through 2050.

- Accounting for the CO2 emissions from the electricity sector in the end-use sectors that consume the electricity results in larger declines in CO2 intensity across those sectors for all AEO2019 cases. In the Reference case, the CO2 intensities of the residential and commercial sectors decline less than 1% when only their direct CO2 intensities are counted. When the electric power sector energy is distributed to the end-use sectors, the residential and commercial sectors decline by 11% and 10%, respectively, while the industrial sector declines by 11%. Transportation carbon intensity declines by 5%.

Policy, technology, and economics affect the mix of U.S. fuel consumption—

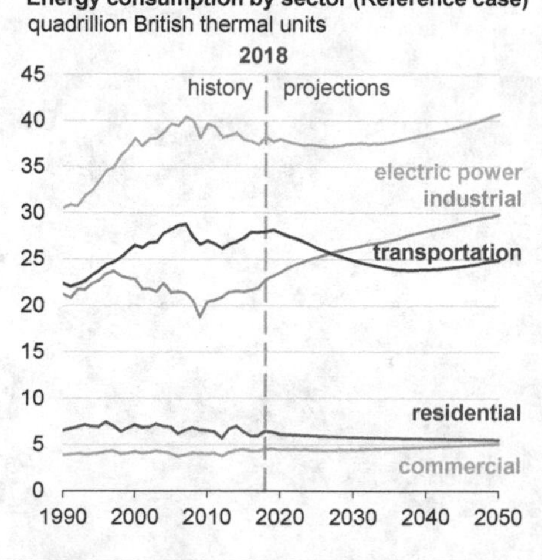

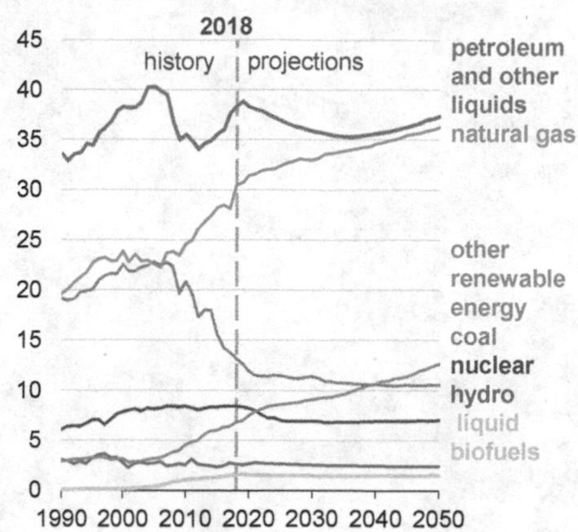

U.S. Energy Information Administration #AEO2019 | www.eia.gov/aeo 7

—which affects energy consumption patterns throughout the projection period

- In all cases, non-hydroelectric renewables consumption grows the most (on a percentage basis). Implementing policies at the state level (renewable portfolio standards) and at the federal level (production and investment tax credits) has encouraged the use of renewables. Growing renewable use has driven down the costs of renewables technologies (wind and solar photovoltaic), further supporting their expanding adoption by the electric power and buildings sectors.

- Natural gas consumption rises as well, driven by projected low natural gas prices. In the Reference case, the industrial sector becomes the largest consumer of natural gas starting in the early 2020s. This sector will expand the use of natural gas as feedstock in the chemical industries and as lease and plant fuel, for industrial heat and power, and for liquefied natural gas production. Natural gas consumption for electric power also increases significantly in the power sector in response to low natural gas prices and to installing lower cost natural gas-fired combined-cycle generating units.

- The transportation sector is the largest consumer of petroleum and other liquids, particularly motor gasoline and distillate fuel oil. Current fuel economy standards stop requiring additional efficiency increases in 2025 for light-duty vehicles and in 2027 for heavy-duty vehicles, but travel continues to rise, and as a result, consumption of petroleum and other liquids increases later in the projection period.

U.S. Energy Information Administration #AEO2019 | www.eia.gov/aeo

"Annual Energy Outlook 2019," U.S. Energy Information Administration. To read the full report please see: https://www.eia.gov/outlooks/aeo.

EPA
United States
Environmental Protection
Agency
EPA 601/K-15/007 | November 2015 | www.epa.gov/research
Science to Protect
Public Health and the Environment
EPA RESEARCH PROGRAM OVERVIEW
2016–2019
Office of Research and Development
Overview: Science for a Sustainable Future

Introduction

The United States has made tremendous progress in environmental protection, and we now have cleaner air and water, waste sites restored to useful purposes, and safer consumer products. For more than four decades, EPA research has informed policies and led to impacts that define environmental progress. EPA research provided the evidence and assessments that led the Agency to ban the use of lead in gasoline, protecting an entire generation of children from hazardous lead exposure. EPA research illuminated the critical link between secondhand tobacco smoke and serious health impacts, findings that turned the tide so that smoking is no longer permitted in many public spaces, reducing the risks for all.

EPA researchers continue to build on this progress by delivering new scientific understanding and technologies to help solve the complex environmental challenges affecting our health, environment and economy.

This document provides an overview of EPA's research programs within the Office of Research and Development. This critically important work is providing the science needed to address the biggest problems facing environmental science, the Agency, and the world. This cutting-edge and innovative research portfolio is connecting the dots in an unprecedented and integrated way by characterizing problems up front, recognizing the inherent connections between a healthy and sustainable environment and healthy people, and working across historical media-specific lines with an understanding that problems aren't isolated to just air or water or land, but in fact, cut across those domains. Environmental challenges include:

- Rising global average temperature is associated with widespread changes in weather patterns which can impact people's lives. Many areas have seen changes in rainfall, resulting in more frequent and intense flooding and drought events, as well as more frequent and severe heat waves. These events can cause loss of life, injury, and property damage, and can disrupt basic services such as transportation, electrical power and water supply. (See text box, Our Changing Climate.)
- Much of the western U.S. is facing record-setting drought with mountain snowpack levels at or near their lowest levels on record. In addition to greatly reducing water supplies, drought contributes to increased incidence of wildfires and forest disease, leading to loss of life and property damage, air pollution health effects, habitat destruction, and potential impacts to water quality.

- Nutrients, such as nitrogen and phosphorus, are polluting our waterways, creating another difficult environmental and human health issue affecting local and regional economies. We face a serious challenge—to achieve the beneficial level of nutrients in the environment to enhance food production and other services, while protecting human and ecosystem health.

- Tens of thousands of chemicals are currently used, but only a small fraction have been thoroughly evaluated for potential risks to human health, wildlife and the environment. We know very little about people's real life exposures to most of these chemicals; in particular we lack data about exposures during critical stages of life and development.

- Many communities are disproportionately overburdened by pollution. We need to better understand the impacts of chemical and non-chemical stressors in causing disparities in health effects and how to help communities improve resilience to disasters.

Advances in science and technology, including social sciences, can help us address these and other complex challenges. EPA's portfolio of research for 2016–2019 builds on the research program from 2012–2016[1] and is designed to advance our understanding of the complex relationships between human activities and their impacts on public health and the environment. This overview of EPA research summarizes:

Research Organization and Support for EPA Strategic Plan

Guiding Principles for EPA Research

Highlights of EPA Strategic Research Action Plans

Our Changing Climate

Over the past century, the large amounts of carbon dioxide and other greenhouse gases released into the atmosphere have been the most important cause of recent climate change. The earth's average temperature has risen by 1.4° F, and if no action is taken to reduce emissions, the average temperature will rise another 2–11.5° F over the next hundred years*. EPA's 2015 Report on the Environment says that, among other impacts, future global warming is projected to produce more severe droughts in the southwestern U.S.

*Melillo, Jerry M., Terese (T.C.) Richmond, and Gary W. Yohe, Eds., 2014: Climate Change Impacts in the United States: The Third National Climate Assessment. U.S. Global Change Research Program, 841 pp. doi:10.7930/J0Z31WJ2.

[1]U.S. Environmental Protection Agency (2012). *Science for a Sustainable Future, EPA Research Program Overview 2012-2016.* Available at: http://www2.epa.gov/research/science-sustainable-future-epa-research-program-overview-2012-2016-0.

Research Organization and Support for EPA Strategic Plan

EPA science is anchored in the priorities of the Agency. EPA's *FY 2014–2018 EPA Strategic Plan*[2] states, "Sustainable, innovative approaches grounded in science—the underpinning of the EPA's decision making—are instrumental to solving today's environmental challenges. Now more than ever EPA's leadership as a pre-eminent science and research institution is essential."

To embrace the critical need for science leadership, EPA's Office of Research and Development (ORD), the science arm of the Agency, has established six highly integrated and transdisciplinary national research programs that closely align with the Agency's strategic goals (2014–2018) and cross-Agency strategies (see Figure 1).

The six programs are:

- Air, Climate, and Energy (ACE)
- Chemical Safety for Sustainability (CSS)
- Homeland Security Research Program (HSRP)
- Human Health Risk Assessment (HHRA)
- Safe and Sustainable Water Resources (SSWR)
- Sustainable and Healthy Communities (SHC)

Each research program engages EPA program and regional offices and outside partners and stakeholders to identify the research priorities that are important for achieving EPA's strategic goals and objectives.

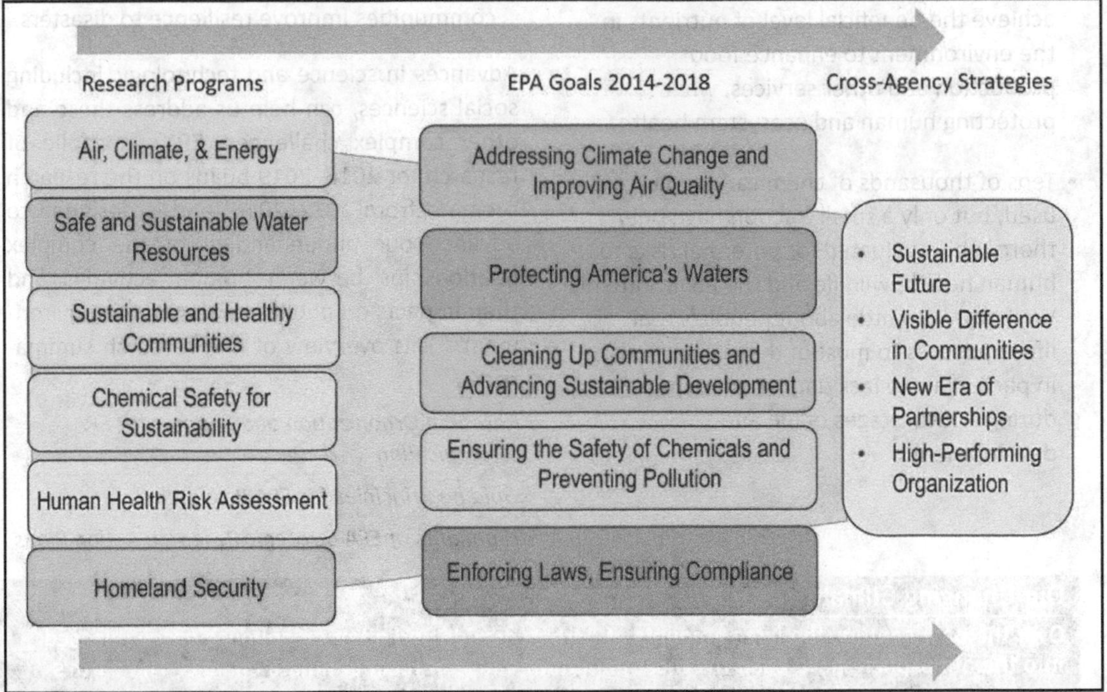

Figure 1. ORD's Six Research Programs Aligned with EPA Strategic Plan. The EPA Office of Research and Development's six national research programs are closely aligned with EPA Strategic Goals and Cross-Agency Strategies. Research in any one program also helps the Agency achieve multiple goals.

[2]U.S. Environmental Protection Agency (2014). *FY 2014–2018 EPA Strategic Plan*. Available at: http://www2.epa.gov/planandbudget/strategicplan.

EPA staff scientists and engineers conduct research in laboratories and research facilities at 14 locations across the country. Overall resources for ORD in fiscal year 2015 included $521 million and 1755 employees. EPA staff are joined by a network of collaborators, partners, fellows, and grantees. For example, scientists in the research laboratories collaborate with scientists in EPA regional offices on projects addressing specific regional concerns. Grantees and fellows compete from across the nation to receive funding from EPA's Science to Achieve Results (STAR) extramural research program. EPA is one of 11 federal agencies that participate in the Small Business Innovative Research (SBIR) program, enacted in 1982 to strengthen the role of small businesses in federal research and development, create jobs, and promote technological innovation.[3]

[3]See http://www2.epa.gov/research-grants

EPA continues to experiment with initiatives to foster innovation and creativity in research. Staff are exploring scientific competitions and challenges, citizen science and crowd-sourcing, public-private partnerships, and other activities that promote innovative thinking and sustainable solutions. For example, the "Pathfinder Innovation Projects" internal agency competition offers EPA scientists an opportunity to win seed funding for out-of-the-box ideas that could be "game-changers" for environmental protection.

Guiding Principles for EPA Research

Several principles guide the design and implementation of EPA research programs. They are: Protect Public Health and Advance Sustainability; Ensure Science Quality and Transparency; Achieve Broad Impact; Innovate; Inform Decisions and Actions; Seek Collaboration; and Support High-Performing Workforce. Completed and ongoing research activities that illustrate these principles are highlighted below.

Protect Public Health and Advance Sustainability

Protecting public health is one of EPA's fundamental goals. EPA research uses a systems approach to understand what causes environmental problems, and to design solutions that benefit health, the environment, and the economy—all of which are interconnected. Systems approaches help advance understanding of the complex relationships between human health and the environment, and this knowledge leads to progress in achieving sustainability—meeting today's needs without compromising the ability of future generations to meet their needs. One example of current research:

- **Clean energy future:** natural gas is playing a key role in reducing carbon emissions, creating jobs, and providing a domestic source of energy. EPA's research on the potential drinking water impacts of the development of America's shale gas resources is helping ensure that responsible development will benefit the economy, energy security, and the environment.

Ensure Science Quality and Transparency

Given the stakes of environmental decisions, it is imperative that EPA produce and rely on high quality science. Whether it's a community determining the safety of reusing precious water for a variety of purposes, a national policy under scrutiny by the Supreme Court, or an enforcement action requiring an industry to revamp its processes to prevent toxic emissions, the science and technology underlying these important decisions must be of the highest quality and accessible to the public. EPA's commitment to quality science includes a rigorous peer review policy, publishing results in peer-reviewed journals, and review by external scientific committees such as the National Academy of Sciences and EPA's Science Advisory Board and Board of Scientific Counselors. Our commitment to transparency includes public access to EPA's publications and supporting scientific data.

- **Scientific advice:** Each research program benefits from the advice of a dedicated subcommittee of EPA's Board of Scientific Counselors with ongoing engagement throughout the duration of the 2016-2019 research program. EPA recognizes that its sound, high quality research will be used not only by the Agency, but also by other federal, state and local agencies, private companies and organizations around the world.

Achieve Broad Impact

EPA's research addresses environmental problems of national and international significance and strives to produce scientific results that are timely and solution-oriented. For example:

- **Climate change:** EPA research contributed evidence that provided the scientific foundation for EPA to move forward with regulations to reduce greenhouse gas emissions from stationary sources. Groundbreaking research on the role of black carbon in climate change is helping decision makers assess benefits of reducing these emissions on a global to local scale. This work, together with other air quality research, such as studies on cookstoves, has global impact affecting billions of people.

The World Health Organization estimates that exposure to smoke from traditional cookstoves and open fires leads to 4.3 million deaths each year. EPA research helps to improve air quality, protect public health and slow climate change.[4]

- **Streams and wetlands impact water quality:** Smaller water bodies play an important role in the health of larger downstream waterways such as rivers and lakes, as described in an extensive EPA state-of-the-science report[5]. The report provided the science behind the 2015 Clean Water Rule that clarified the jurisdiction of the Clean Water Act, protecting the streams and wetlands that form the foundation of the nation's water resources.

- **Clean air:** Over the last 45 years, air quality in the U.S. has improved dramatically. EPA's National Ambient Air Quality Standards are the highest impact regulations, ensuring U.S. air quality that prevents thousands of heart attacks and premature deaths, and millions of cases of respiratory illness, such as bronchitis and asthma. Every five years, EPA reviews the standards for air pollutants such as particulate matter, ozone, and nitrogen oxides. The standards often face legal challenges, including cases that are decided by the U.S. Supreme Court. EPA depends on the sound, peer-reviewed scientific research and assessments that characterize the health, ecological and welfare effects from exposure to these pollutants.

EPA's CMAQ Model is a powerful computational tool used by EPA and states for air quality management. The National Weather Service uses the model to produce daily U.S. forecasts for ozone air quality. CMAQ is also used by states to assess implementation actions needed to attain National Ambient Air Quality Standards.

[4]World Health Organization: Household Air Pollution and Health, Fact Sheet No. 292, March 2014 http://www.who.int/mediacentre/factsheets/fs292/en/

[5]US EPA (2015) Connectivity of Streams and Wetlands to Downstream Waters: A Review and Synthesis of the Scientific Evidence (Final Report) http://cfpub.epa.gov/ncea/risk/recordisplay.cfm?deid=296414

Innovate

Fostering creativity and stimulating transformational change can solve complex problems in new and innovative ways. Sometimes, it's the advent of technological advances in other fields that can be applied to an environmental problem. Examples include:

- **Rapid, automated chemical testing:** Agency researchers and their partners are revolutionizing the assessment of potential risks to humans and the environment from exposures to chemicals and forging a new generation of predictive capabilities, technologies and solutions. New tools enable rapid screening of chemicals for adverse effects, using very small amounts of chemicals in laboratory test samples, high-throughput robotics, and automated analysis.
- **Satellite data for water monitoring:** A team of scientists from EPA, NASA and the U.S. Geological Survey used satellites to monitor and assess water quality and harmful algal blooms in lakes, reservoirs and estuaries. This new approach can provide early warning to environmental and public health agencies to prepare for action.

Inform Decisions and Actions

EPA relies on sound science to inform decisions that affect communities across the nation. To ensure research is relevant, ORD works very closely with EPA partners to define the most pressing environmental problems, research needs, and data gaps. EPA research is intended to be accessible and meet both near- and long-term science needs. Significant research efforts focus on developing the science that serves as the foundation for environmental regulations. Providing technical support to help with more immediate local issues continues to be of great value to EPA regions. ORD is also poised in times of crisis, such as chemical spills, explosions or other potentially hazardous releases into the environment, to make its laboratories and technical experts available to provide immediate assistance to the on-site decision makers. Research plans and products are peer-reviewed to ensure transparency of methods and results. For EPA research to be relevant and accessible, it also has to be translated and delivered such that it can be of real value to the end users. The clients for EPA research range from scientists to policymakers, lawyers, and the general public. Examples include:

- **Asbestos assessment in Region 8:** EPA and federal partners assessed the risk to public health from asbestos-contaminated vermiculite in Libby, MT. This assessment informs risk management decisions, including the ongoing clean-up and remediation activities in the Libby community. These activities have reduced the asbestos outdoor air concentrations in Libby, making the air quality in Libby similar to other Montana cities and reducing risks of cancer and respiratory disease from asbestos.
- **Reducing stormwater runoff:** Stormwater flowing from paved streets, parking lots, and building rooftops can accumulate chemicals and other pollutants that can adversely affect water quality. Green infrastructure, which includes approaches such as rain gardens, porous pavement, and green roofs, can alleviate flooding and protect water quality. EPA's National Stormwater Calculator is a desktop application that estimates reductions in stormwater runoff for various green infrastructure options, and it is a practical and easy-to-use tool for local decision makers such as urban planners, landscape architects, site developers and homeowners.

EPA green infrastructure researchers provide key tools, such as the National Stormwater Calculator, to address stormwater management.

Seek Collaboration

EPA science has even greater impact through strong collaboration with public health and environmental partners. ORD works collaboratively across its research programs and also develops partnerships within EPA and with external organizations to accomplish its work. Partners include scientists, engineers, decision makers, risk managers, and other experts in EPA program and regional offices, other federal agencies, state and local governments, and other research organizations. Developing scientific tools and information jointly with partners, and soliciting feedback from EPA partners and outside stakeholders, helps ensure that research results are meaningful and that research products are tailored to meet the needs of decision makers at the federal, state and local levels.

- **Children's environmental health:** Children's environmental health research involves many disciplines, such as reproductive and developmental health, genetics, exposure science, sociology, and pediatrics, and requires coordination and collaboration across EPA research programs, laboratories and centers. In a long-running partnership with the National Institute of Environmental Health Sciences, EPA supports university-based, multi-disciplinary research centers dedicated to children's health[6]. These centers have provided the foundational science for understanding environmental health impacts on children and have contributed evidence supporting policy decisions related to air pollution, pesticides and endocrine-disrupting chemicals.
- **Homeland security:** Multiple agencies are involved in responding to environmental disasters, including terrorist incidents. EPA regularly collaborates with other federal agencies to conduct joint research and operational activities. For example, a recent full-scale test operation focused on sampling, decontamination and waste management for a facility contaminated with simulated anthrax spores. EPA's partners in the effort included the U.S. Departments of Homeland Security, Health and Human Services, Justice, Defense, and Energy.

EPA partnered with the U.S. Department of Health and Human Services on a campaign to promote heart health.

Support High-Performing Workforce

EPA's research organization is unique in its breadth of expertise and science leadership to address multifaceted environmental issues. Engineering, environmental health, ecology, computer science, and meteorology are just a few examples of the many scientific and technical fields represented. Multidisciplinary research is encouraged so that scientists can work together across many different areas of expertise. As science evolves, so do the areas of expertise needed to maintain highly relevant and outstanding research. EPA's Office of Research and Development developed a workforce strategy to address the critical expertise gaps in the next three to five years and to serve as a guide for future hiring decisions. Social science is just one area of expertise needed for research planned in the next several years.

[6]NIEHS/EPA Children's Environmental Health and Disease Prevention Research Centers http://www2.epa.gov/research-grants/niehsepa-childrens-environmental-health-and-disease-prevention-research-centers

Strategic Research Action Plans 2016–2019

EPA has developed six Strategic Research Action Plans, one for each of the national research programs. The plans describe the research vision, objectives, topics, and expected accomplishments. Each explains the programs' efforts to collaborate with EPA partners and stakeholders. Involving those who rely on EPA research, from staff to senior managers, in setting priorities and following research progress through to translation is vital to program success and ultimate impact.

Integrating across the six programs is a particular focus for the 2016–2019 plans. Many environmental issues cut across the six programs. ORD puts special emphasis on ensuring that research on cross-cutting issues is coordinated and collaborative. Embracing such integration ensures that the work is designed to tackle the increasingly complex nature of environmental challenges and threats.

In addition, because of their Agency-wide prominence, four key topic areas have been selected for focused and active integration across the six national programs: climate change, children's environmental health, nitrogen and co-pollutants, and environmental justice (see Figure 2). Each of these efforts is described in a cross-cutting research roadmap led by one of the research programs. The roadmaps describe ongoing research and also help inform the national research programs' strategic planning activities. EPA program and regional office partners provide instrumental input that helps shape ORD's investment in these cross-cutting topics. The research programs work together to address additional important cross-cutting issues, such as community resilience and integrating new data streams into risk assessment.

Highlights from the six Strategic Research Action plans, including examples of research planned for the years 2016–2019 and examples of research collaboration on cross cutting issues, are summarized in the following pages.

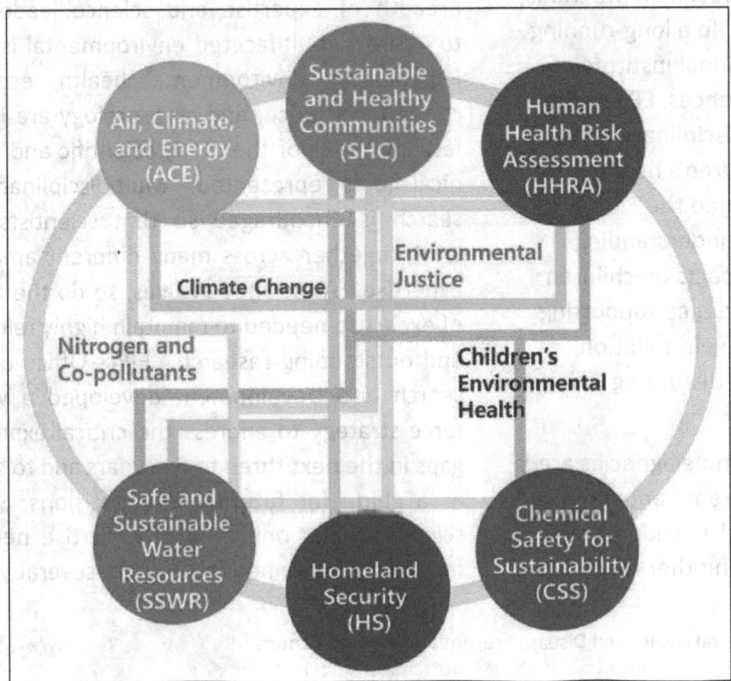

Figure 2. Integration across the six national research programs and four roadmap topics.

Air, Climate, and Energy

The Air, Climate, and Energy (ACE) research program builds upon 40 years of achievement in air pollution research that has led to landmark outcomes—including visibly cleaner air, healthier communities, and longer life expectancies. Looking forward, we understand that air quality and climate are inextricably linked, and global climate change is adversely affecting public health and the environment in many areas of the country. Energy production and use have major impacts on both air quality and climate with conventional energy options generally representing the major source of air pollution emissions, including greenhouse gases.

ACE research will directly advance EPA's strategic goal to address climate change and improve air quality. The ACE program continues to fulfill Clean Air Act requirements by providing scientific support to decision makers on individual air pollutants of concern. However, we all breathe mixtures of air and are not often exposed to air pollutants one at a time. As a result, ACE research is also focused on assessing impacts of exposures to a combination of many pollutants in the air, analyzing approaches for preventing and reducing emissions of pollutants including greenhouse gases, and helping communities, states, and regions respond to the impacts of changes in climate and air quality.

By addressing air, climate, and energy issues in an integrated way, the ACE research program provides the scientific results and innovative technologies that are needed to take action on climate change and improve air quality.

The ACE program has brought together scientists from a broad range of disciplines including atmospheric and climate science, air and water quality, environmental health, exposure, ecology, economics, and more. These scientists and engineers work collaboratively with those who use and depend upon our research—EPA policy makers, state, local and regional officials and external stakeholders—to ensure the ACE program is responsive and relevant to the greatest needs. By working together to articulate highest priority problems and research, the ACE program is focused on three main objectives:

1) **Assess Impacts**
Develop and apply methods to assess the impacts and effects of air pollution exposure and climate change at individual, community, regional, and global scales.

2) **Prevent and Reduce Emissions**
Provide the science needed to develop and evaluate approaches to prevent and reduce harmful air emissions. The data and methods resulting from this research can be used to analyze the full life cycle impacts of new and existing technologies and assess the sustainability of various energy choices.

Research Challenges

We breathe a mixture of air pollutants. Current scientific understanding of environmental and health risks of air pollution is based on single pollutants.

The effects of climate change on air, water and ecosystems will vary by region and locality. Helping communities prepare for climate change requires scientific data across a range of geographic scales, not currently available.

Energy choices have trade-offs, but the health and environmental risks and benefits of new technologies and approaches are not well understood.

Social, behavioral, and economic factors influence the effectiveness of air quality and climate policies, and methods are lacking to address all factors together.

3) **Respond to Changes in Climate and Air Quality**
   Provide modeling and monitoring tools and information to help government agencies and communities prepare for impacts to air, water, and land from climate change. While reducing greenhouse gas emissions is a critical part of minimizing future climate change, it is also necessary to adapt to the environmental impacts caused by unavoidable changes in climate.

The ACE program will continue to provide direct technical assistance to its EPA partners in the program offices and regions; provide research needed for immediate policy or regulatory action; and anticipate and develop the science needed for decisions in the coming decade. As the lead for the cross-cutting issue of climate change research, the ACE program works closely with scientists from other federal programs and across EPA, including the other five research programs (see text box). EPA is one of 13 departments and agencies that contribute to the U.S. Global Change Research Program (USGCRP)[7], which coordinates federal climate change research. ACE research is of interest to scientists and environmental managers all over the world.

2016–2019 ACE Strategic Research Action Plan: Research Examples

The ACE program encompasses research related to air quality monitoring, modeling, public health, climate change and energy sustainability. Examples of this research for 2016-2019 are described below.

Next Generation Air Pollution Monitoring

Historically, approaches for monitoring air pollution generally use expensive, complex, stationary equipment, which limits who collects data, what data are collected and how data are accessed. This landscape is changing rapidly with the emergence of lower-cost, easy-to-use, portable air pollution monitors (e.g., sensors) that provide high-resolution data in near real time and may be used by state and local agencies, research scientists, regulated facilities, communities and individuals for a range of different purposes. ORD collaborates with EPA programs and regions, states and federal partners on this research.

Agency scientists will continue to evaluate and utilize versatile, next-generation air monitoring technologies in novel ways, such as mounted to vehicles or applied along fence lines.

Global Climate Change Research Roadmap

EPA's mission to safeguard the environment and protect human health puts the Agency at the forefront of federal efforts to mitigate and prepare for climate change impacts to air, water, land, ecosystems, and human health. Highlighting the unique role that EPA plays, the Climate Change Research Roadmap illustrates how EPA's research will: improve the understanding of the interactions between climate change and the environment; evaluate the resulting impacts on human health and welfare; develop strategies to prepare for and respond to these impacts; and ensure that such responses promote sustainability and avoid further, unintended adverse impacts. The Roadmap illustrates the coordination and integration of research related to climate change across the six national research programs (ACE, CSS, HHRA, HSRP, SHC and SSWR), responding to the needs of EPA's Office of Air and Radiation, Office of Water, Office of Solid Waste and Emergency Response, Office of Policy, Office of Children's Health Protection and the EPA regional offices.

[7]See http://www.globalchange.gov/

Working with the industrial community and other partners, they are providing spatial and temporal data useful for assessing both air pollution source emissions and ambient air quality around facilities and areas of high interest, such as energy production and processing plants, industrial facilities, agricultural operations, landfills, brownfields and waste water treatment operations.

EPA researchers are advancing next generation mobile air quality monitors.

EPA researchers designed and installed solar-powered, community-based air monitoring systems ("Village Green Benches") to explore real-world applications of next-generation air monitors, and develop new approaches for harnessing the proliferation of new data they are generating.

EPA-supported Air, Climate, and Energy Research Centers

Through the highly-competitive Science to Achieve Results (STAR) grants program, EPA will fund the fourth-generation of air research centers, now the Air, Climate, and Energy Research Centers, a network of university-based, multidisciplinary consortia. Center researchers are focusing on the challenges faced by different regions of the country in achieving and sustaining air quality as climate change continues. Local conditions can be highly variable, including differences in emission sources, topography, climate, meteorology, demographics, and socioeconomic and cultural patterns. Researchers are improving understanding of how these social, economic, environmental and other factors affect regional differences in the mix and magnitude of air pollution. Results will inform policy makers on the development of innovative approaches that enhance the effectiveness of air pollution control strategies and achieve the greatest public health benefits.

Helping to Protect Local Air Quality in a Changing Climate

As part of their efforts to protect public health, states across the nation rely on EPA's Community Multi-scale Air Quality Model (CMAQ) to help predict changes to air quality as a result of proposed actions to meet clean air standards. But while that system has proved invaluable for more than a decade, a new challenge has emerged: climate change. EPA modelers are developing new frameworks for incorporating critical data across multiple scales, down-scaling global climate meteorological projections to expand CMAQ's powerful capabilities for calculating local and regional air quality projections. The work will support air quality managers who must consider how changes in climate would affect their state efforts to achieve clean air.

Public-Private Research Partnership: Health Effects of Air Pollution

Through a long-term partnership, EPA and the motor vehicle industry jointly fund the Health Effects Institute, which sponsors independent, peer-reviewed research on the health impacts of motor vehicle emissions. For 2015-2020, the Institute is focusing on research to inform decisions on air quality and on climate-driven technology. The program has four core program elements: (1) addressing the continuing challenges of multipollutant science; (2) accountability and transparency; (3) assessing emerging fuels and technologies; and (4) global health.

EPA and the Health Effects Institute are developing the next generation of tools and scientific information to examine the combined effects of air pollution on human health and the relationship between air quality and climate change.

Safe and Sustainable Water Resources

Water is one of our Nation's most precious resources. The United States uses about 400 billion gallons of water each day. We depend upon it for our lives and our livelihoods, for healthy ecosystems and a robust economy. Yet a host of challenges threaten the safety and sustainability of our water resources, including biological and chemical contaminants, aging water-system infrastructure, demands of the energy, agriculture and manufacturing sectors, population change, climate change, extreme weather events and homeland security threats.

To address these challenges, EPA's Safe and Sustainable Water Resources (SSWR) research program is using an integrated, systems approach to develop scientific and technological solutions to protect human health and to protect and restore watersheds and aquatic ecosystems.

The research directly advances EPA's strategic goal "Protecting America's Waters" and provides scientific and technical support to meet

Research Challenges

Excess levels of nutrients and sediment remain the Nation's largest contributor to water-quality deterioration. The rate at which water bodies are newly listed for water-quality impairment exceeds the pace that restored waters are removed from the list. Surplus nutrients cause widespread damage to aquatic ecosystems and impact public health.

Sustainability of groundwater, with regard to drawdown, recharge, and increasing potential of contamination, is a growing concern.

Current drinking water and water treatment systems are inadequate to meet future needs.

Many water systems are outdated and inefficient, losing trillions of gallons of treated water each year because of pipe leaks and breaks.

Stormwater overflows in combined sewer systems send billions of gallons of untreated sewage into lakes and rivers.

Changes in population, land use, climate and extreme events will affect water resources and aquatic ecosystems.

Agency obligations enforcing key legislative mandates, including the Clean Water Act and the Safe Drinking Water Act.

SSWR scientists have worked closely with partners from EPA programs and regional offices, as well as federal and state agencies, public and private stakeholders and the scientific community to identify research priorities. Four main objectives guide the SSWR research program:

1) **Address Complex Chemical and Microbial Pollutants**
   Develop new methods for detecting, quantifying, monitoring, and treating complex chemical and microbial pollutants. This research focuses on new and emerging contaminants that threaten human health and aquatic ecosystems, providing scientific and engineering guidance to strengthen drinking water and water quality standards.

2) **Transform the Concept of 'Waste' to 'Resource'**
   Develop innovative water treatment technologies and green infrastructure techniques to tap current streams of wastewater for resources. Through this research, stormwater runoff as well as wastewater from homes and industries has the potential to become a source for certain, closely defined ("fit-for-purpose") water use, and as a source for recovering energy, nutrients, metals and other valuable substances.

3) **Quantify the Benefits of Water Quality**
   Clean water and healthy ecosystems provide many services that are currently undervalued. By developing models and tools to estimate the economic benefits of water-quality improvements, this research will aid in the protection or restoration of water quality.

4) **Translate Research into Real-world Solutions**
   Move results out of the lab and into the hands of end users who can use those applications to sustainably manage water resources and infrastructure.

As the lead for the cross-cutting issue of nitrogen and co-pollutants research, the SSWR program works closely with scientists from other research programs, EPA program and regional offices and other federal agencies (see text box).

Nitrogen and Co-pollutants Research Roadmap

Excess nutrients in water are causing widespread damage to aquatic systems and impacting public health. Significant, sustainable reductions in nutrients must be economically efficient, socially acceptable, environmentally sound, adaptable to climate change, land-use and demographic changes, and permanent. These requirements can be met only through integrated research that informs the systematic collective, adaptive management of nutrients across air, land, and water. To achieve that, SSWR is leading a collaboration on nitrogen and co-pollutants research across multiple media and spatial scales. The Nitrogen and Co-pollutant Roadmap is a collaboration among ORD's research programs (ACE, HHRA, SHC, and SSWR), EPA's Office of Water, EPA's Office of Air and Radiation, and EPA's Regional Offices. The roadmap provides a cross-media, integrated, multi-disciplinary approach to sustainably manage reactive nitrogen and co-pollutant (in particular phosphorus, but also sulfur, sediments) loadings to air, surface and ground water to reduce adverse impacts on the environment and human health.

2016–2019 SSWR Strategic Research Action Plan: Research Examples

SSWR research focuses on high-priority, current and long-term water resource challenges identified in partnership with EPA program and regional office partners and other partners and stakeholders. Examples of research for 2016-19 are described below.

Addressing Harmful Algal Blooms

Human activities appear to be increasing the frequency of harmful algal blooms — the rapid overgrowth of certain types of toxin-containing algae and cyanobacteria. The proliferation of such organisms can pose risks to human health by contaminating recreational waters and drinking water supplies. EPA researchers are developing predictive capabilities, analytical methods, and remote sensing techniques to detect blooms. EPA works with partners at NASA, NOAA and USGS to use data collected by satellites. That and other innovative work will provide stakeholders and decision makers with improved scientific information and tools to effectively assess and manage harmful algal blooms and associated toxicity events.

NASA satellite image of harmful algal bloom striking Lake Erie in the summer of 2014, resulting in a "do not drink" water advisory for the entire City of Toledo, OH.

Green Infrastructure in Communities

For many cities, stormwater management remains one of the greatest challenges to meeting water quality standards. Local communities can realize cost savings and many other benefits by using green infrastructure—natural and engineered techniques that increase the capacity of local watersheds to absorb stormwater runoff and seasonal snow and ice melt. EPA researchers are developing a green infrastructure classification framework, and advancing research to test and refine sophisticated tools, models, and screens that incorporate multiple community-based parameters, including the evaluation of financial strategies and economic costs. Results will help communities effectively use innovative green infrastructure techniques to meet their goals for minimizing stormwater discharge and mitigating combined sewer overflow events. Green infrastructure can potentially improve water quality, while providing other benefits such as additional green space in urban settings and recharging ground water supplies.

Green roofs can be used effectively to reduce stormwater runoff from commercial, industrial, and residential buildings.

Reducing Risks from Water Treatment Disinfection By-products

The presence and potential health effects of by-products from chemical water treatment, known as disinfection by-products, are a concern for water treatment facilities and public health officials. EPA researchers are tapping recent technical advances in integrated toxicological and chemical characterization studies (see more in the Chemical Safety for Sustainability section of this document) to advance the understanding of the joint impacts of initial source water quality and the choice of disinfection techniques and technologies. Results will advance water treatment techniques and better protect public health.

EPA researchers are helping water quality treatment facilities reduce risks from disinfection by-products.

Sustainable and Healthy Communities

How do communities meet their day-to-day needs without compromising the ability of their children and future generations to one day meet their own? And more specifically, how can we take action to protect our shared environment—air, water, land, and ecosystems—in ways that are economically viable, beneficial to human health and well-being, and socially just?

The Sustainable and Healthy Communities (SHC) research program is developing the knowledge, data, and tools to answer those questions. The program is focused on providing scientifically sound information to EPA program and regional offices and U.S. communities to

Quantifying National Water Quality Benefits

The long-term sustainability of water quantity and quality depends on better assessing the value of clean, abundant water that contributes to human health, recreation, food production and other environmental services. Without that understanding, the degradation of water quality due to chemical and microbial contaminants, including nutrients, will continue to outpace water quality improvements. ORD and EPA policy partners are advancing national water quality benefit-cost analyses and modeling tools that will build the capacity for estimating the economic benefits of water quality improvements. These resources include a new generation of studies that will identify market and non-market values associated with water quality, and will identify useful metrics for linking water quality models to economic valuation.

Research Challenges

Communities need information to make decisions on infrastructure, land use, transportation, and waste management that meet short-term priorities while minimizing impacts to, and maximizing benefits for long-term public health and community prosperity.

The complex and dynamic interactions of social, economic, and environmental trade-offs are not well understood, nor incorporated into usable, accessible tools and models.

Information is limited on linkages between human health and well-being, ecosystems, local economies, and disproportionate environmental burden.

inform decisions that produce more sustainable outcomes for our environment, society, and economy.

The SHC program is strongly aligned with advancing EPA's strategic goal, "Cleaning Up Communities and Advancing Sustainable Development," and the cross-agency strategies of "Working Toward a Sustainable Future" and "Working to Make a Visible Difference in Communities." The program is also helping the Agency implement key recommendations made by the National Research Council (NRC) in its reports *Sustainability and the US EPA* and *Sustainability for the Nation*[8]. The NRC explicitly recommends adopting a sustainability framework that requires a comprehensive approach for incorporating sustainability into decisions and actions.

Traditional methods for evaluating environmental impacts typically focus on one pollutant or one type of activity. To better evaluate effects of policies or programs, SHC focuses on incorporating environmental science into more holistic approaches (such as health impact assessment) that consider the interaction of environmental, social and economic factors on the health of a population. SHC is partnering with EPA regional offices and communities to apply these methods to help solve complex community issues.

SHC research is focused on many of our nation's most pressing problems, including: contaminated sites and revitalizing communities, oil spill response and clean up, and shifting the paradigm from disposal of waste to reuse of materials and resource management.

Collectively, the SHC research program delivers information and tools needed to support and inform decisions that advance outcomes that sustain a healthy environment, society, and economy. Four broad research objectives guide that work:

1) **Support Community Decisions**
   Assist decision makers through the development of information, methods and tools incorporating decision science, citizen science, spatial analysis, cause-and-effect modeling, and sustainability assessments. These resources help decision makers frame different options, increase community-engagement, and identify potential solutions that promote a more sustainable future.

2) **Develop Tools and Metrics to Identify, Monitor, and Track the Links between Human Well-being and the Environment**
   Explore ecosystem services, natural and built environments, and the interactions of chemical and nonchemical environmental factors to better understand how environmental conditions provide a foundation for human well-being. SHC researchers and their partners are developing metrics, including indicators and indices (combinations of indicators), that communities can use to better assess and predict the environmental, public health, and economic implications of decision alternatives. A particular emphasis is on identifying the links between the environment and disproportionate impacts on vulnerable groups and lifestages.

[8]National Research Council (2011). *Sustainability and the U.S. EPA*. National Academies Press: Washington, DC.
National Research Council (2013). *Sustainability for the Nation*. National Academies Press: Washington, DC.

3) **Research and Technical Support for Environmental Clean Up, Mitigation, and Restoration, and for Advancing Sustainable Development**
Help community stakeholders improve the efficiency and effectiveness of addressing contaminated sediments, land, and ground water, and resultant vapor intrusion. The program also provides and evaluates standards, products, data, and approaches to prevent, characterize, and clean up environmental releases of petroleum and other fuel products. SHC methods, models, tools, and data are designed to enhance sustainable materials management.

4) **Develop and Apply a Sustainability Assessment and Management Toolbox**
Provide community stakeholders with a suite of tools that, when used together, produce a full accounting that links environmental decisions with human well-being. The "Sustainability Toolbox" can be used to identify and characterize the costs, benefits, and potential tradeoffs of different decisions as they relate to social (including public health), economic, and environmental outcomes.

As the lead for developing the cross-cutting roadmap for environmental justice research, the SHC program works closely with EPA's Office of Environmental Justice and the five other national research programs (see text box).

Environmental Justice Research Roadmap

EPA has long recognized that environmental risks are often greater for low income and minority communities. The impacts on communities at higher risk are influenced not only by differential exposures due to close proximity to sources of harmful chemicals, but also by interactions with non-chemical stressors that may impact effects posed by exposures to environmental contaminants. Disproportionate impacts can also arise from enhanced susceptibilities, as well as from the lack of sufficient health services or benefits. Communities may suffer from inadequate physical and economic infrastructures, such as poor housing, lack of transportation, and inadequate water systems. SHC is the lead on the Environmental Justice Research roadmap to promote sustainable, healthy communities by providing state-of-the-science tools and information that can be used to characterize and mitigate environmental and health inequities. The program will collaborate with the other programs in ORD (ACE, HHRA, SSWR, HSRP and CSS) and EPA partners, including the Office of Solid Waste and Emergency Response, the Office of Environmental Justice, and the Office of Children's Health Protection, on research to advance EPA's EJ 2020 Action Agenda.

2016–2019 SHC Strategic Research Action Plan: Research Examples

SHC is developing information and tools to offer solutions to community-based decision makers within and outside the Agency. Examples of research planned for the 2016-19 timeframe are described below.

Making the Connection: Developing Environmental Indicators and Indices to Inform Decision Making and Track Progress

Local communities face multiple and sometimes conflicting priorities when it comes to balancing immediate goals with long-term needs and stability. To help them meet those challenges, EPA researchers are developing a suite of environmental indicators to characterize current conditions across a host of environmental media, particularly as they connect to human well-being. For example, the indices and indexes inform EPA's Report on the Environment[9], an easily accessible, on-line resource that presents the best available indicators of national trends in environmental and human health conditions. Other searchable databases allow users to find the appropriate metrics for different decision contexts, such as land use, materials management, community revitalization, or commercial, residential, or transportation planning.

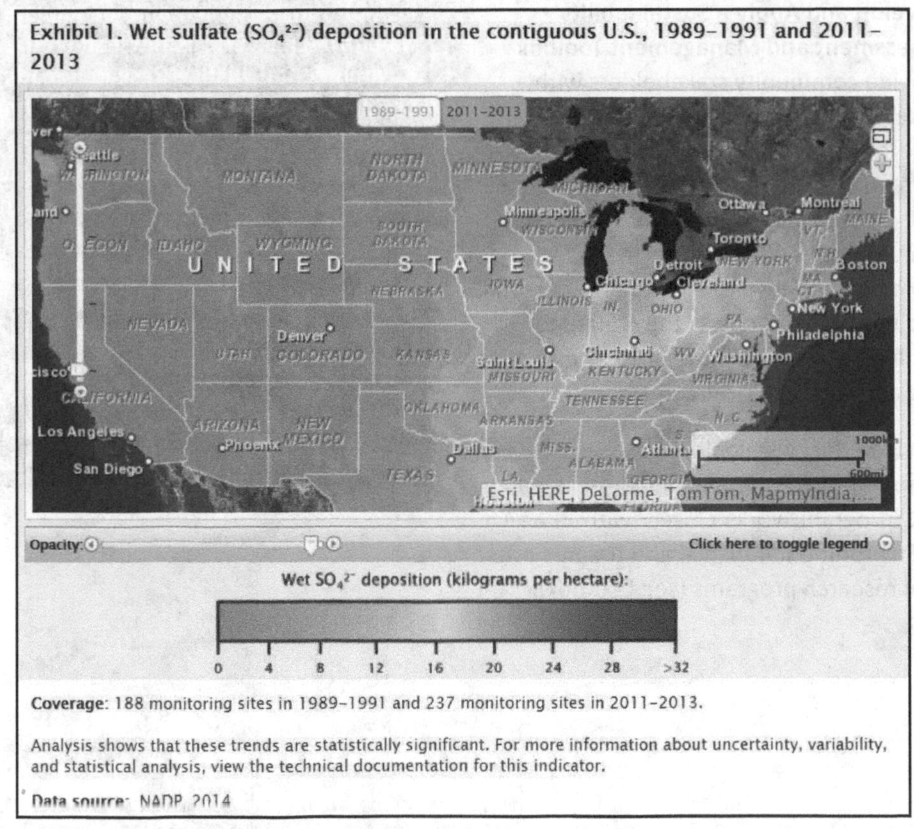

Exhibit 1. Wet sulfate (SO_4^{2-}) deposition in the contiguous U.S., 1989–1991 and 2011–2013

Coverage: 188 monitoring sites in 1989–1991 and 237 monitoring sites in 2011–2013.

Analysis shows that these trends are statistically significant. For more information about uncertainty, variability, and statistical analysis, view the technical documentation for this indicator.

Data source: NADP, 2014

Indicators of national environmental and human health trends are readily accessible from EPA's Report on the Environment[10].

[9,10]EPA's Report on the Environment, http://cfpub.epa.gov/roe/

Helping Communities Identify the Benefits of Ecosystems

An important goal of the SHC research program is to help community stakeholders and national decision makers assess, and predict effects due to the interactions between people and the natural environment. EPA is conducting research to identify the benefits that local communities derive from the natural environment, "community-based ecosystem goods and services." For example, natural wetlands help purify water and provide flood control, but these benefits are hard to quantify. There are a whole host of resources like wetlands that provide important goods and services that are often undervalued. The research includes the identification and inventory of ecosystem goods and services at multiple geographic scales, approaches communities can use to measure those benefits, and the development of a library of ecological production models. Researchers are also advancing the understanding of how climate change and other major drivers and stressors affect the production, delivery, and benefits of ecosystem goods and services.

EPA led a multi-agency collaboration on the first-ever report on wetland ecological condition as part of its National Aquatic Resources Surveys.

Helping Address Contaminated Sites

SHC plays a major role in advancing techniques and technologies to help communities and others remediate and rehabilitate Superfund and other contaminated sites, including addressing challenges sparked by hazardous materials reaching groundwater, which can lead to contamination of drinking water and vapor intrusion—when volatile organic compounds and other gases migrate from underlying water and soil into the air of homes and other buildings. Examples of this work include improving the application and interpretation of high-resolution groundwater characterization technologies, advancing the long-term evaluation of the use of permeable reactive barriers for the treatment of groundwater contamination, novel vapor intrusion studies using real-time observations and modeling scenarios, and the continued operation of three technical support centers focused on site characterization and monitoring, engineering and groundwater issues at contaminated sites.

EPA is providing innovative science solutions for contaminated sites, while restoring and protecting the environment and public health from exposure to environmental chemicals and toxins.

Supporting EPA Regional Science Needs

SHC sponsors collaborative projects in communities across the country, taking advantage of unique opportunities to apply new research tools, gaining immediate feedback, and improving the design and delivery of research results as they are used more widely to make a difference in communities. SHC's Regional Sustainable Environmental Sciences Research program unites problem-solvers from the Office of Research and Development directly with experts from each of the Agency's ten regional offices located across the country.

Examples of regional projects include: *Engaging Communities and Citizen Science to Assess and Address Children's Environmental Health from Transit and Air Pollution; Improving Public Health through Urban and Roadside Vegetation;* and *Using Ecosystem Services Assessment and Health Impact Assessments as Part of a Stakeholder-driven Approach to Storm Recovery: Long Island Case Study.*

EPA's EnviroAtlas: A Mapping Tool to Assess the Benefits of Nature

EPA researchers are expanding EnviroAtlas, a collection of interactive tools and resources that allow users to explore and visualize the many benefits people receive from nature in ways that are immediately applicable to decision-making and planning. The dynamic resource combines multiple ecosystem-based data sets, sophisticated geographic information systems, and visualization tools to present fine-scaled, multilayered maps and other resources that people can download and use to inform decisions to keep their communities healthy and resilient. Development plans for EnviroAtlas extend out to 2017, incorporating updates, additional data, analytical tools, and increased functionality as they become available.

Using EnviroAtlas, many types of users can access, view, and analyze diverse information to better understand how various decisions can affect an array of ecological and human health outcomes.

Chemical Safety for Sustainability

Chemicals are a lynchpin of the American economy. Moving toward sustainability requires innovation to design, produce, and use chemicals in safer ways.

The challenges faced in today's chemical environment are formidable. Tens of thousands of chemicals are currently in use and hundreds more are introduced into the market every year. Many of these chemicals have not been thoroughly evaluated for potential hazard to human health, wildlife and the environment, particularly when considering the consequences of use over a chemical's life cycle (from production to disposal). Current toxicity testing methods focus on evaluating hazard from exposures to individual chemicals and are expensive and time consuming. Characterizing exposures to multiple chemicals, and understanding their impacts across the life cycle of products, further amplifies the challenge. Innovative methods to assess hazard and exposure, and to integrate this information to assess risk, are needed to make better-informed, more-timely decisions about chemicals.

To address these challenges, the Chemical Safety for Sustainability (CSS) research program is leading development of innovative science to support safe and sustainable selection, design, and use of chemicals and materials required to promote human and ecological wellbeing, as well as to protect vulnerable species, lifestages, and populations. The ultimate goal is to enable EPA to address impacts of existing chemicals, anticipate impacts of new chemicals and materials, and evaluate complex interactions of chemical and biological systems.

Research Challenges

Thousands of chemicals have not been evaluated and new chemicals are continually being developed and introduced into commerce.

Chemical substitutions and other alternatives designed to solve one environmental health problem may have unintended consequences.

The real-world is inherently more complicated than current experimental models of toxicology can depict.

Decision-makers need demonstrated solutions to translate new information into action.

The research strategy guiding the work was developed in partnership with EPA program and regional offices, and with input from other federal agencies, states, public and private stakeholders, and the global scientific community. The research program recognizes that transformative approaches are needed to improve the information used in chemical evaluations. CSS science is strategically scoped with four integrated research topics to support Agency priorities.

1) **Chemical Evaluation**
   Advancing cutting-edge methods to provide data for risk-based evaluation of both existing chemicals and emerging materials.

2) **Life Cycle Analytics**
   Exploring new ways to evaluate risks to human and ecological health across the lifecycle of manufactured chemicals, materials and products. CSS methods will efficiently evaluate alternatives and support more sustainable chemical design and use.

3) **Complex System Science**
Adopting a systems-based approach to examine complex chemical-biological interactions and predict potential for adverse outcomes resulting from exposures to chemicals.

4) **Translation and Delivery**
Promoting web-based tools, data, and applications to support chemical safety evaluations and related decisions. CSS engages Agency partners and stakeholders to ground truth the transparency, access, relevance, and applicability of our research.

As the lead for the cross-cutting issue of children's environmental health, the CSS program works with scientists from the other research programs and from EPA program and regional offices, to identify research priorities and coordinate research (see text box).

Children's Environmental Health Research Roadmap

Public concern about the potential role of environmental factors on children's health including asthma, autism spectrum disorder, and childhood obesity is increasing. To date, research in this area has been limited and recent studies are difficult to evaluate and interpret. The Children's Environmental Health Research roadmap presents ORD's vision for providing integrated, cutting-edge science required for EPA actions to promote children's environmental health and wellbeing. It recognizes that EPA has a unique mandate to focus on understanding the role of exposure to environmental stressors on health impacts during early life and across the course of development. The Children's Environmental Health Research Roadmap is a collaboration among ORD's research programs (ACE, CSS, HSRP, HHRA, SHC, and SSWR), EPA's Office of Children's Health Protection, Office of Air and Radiation, and Office of Solid Waste and Emergency Response.

2016–2019 CSS Strategic Research Action Plan: Research Examples

The CSS program maps out innovative research that will transform how scientists and policy makers assess the safety of chemicals and exposure to them. Working closely with EPA partners to conduct case studies of new approaches improves the quality of the science and confidence in the methods. Examples of CSS research for 2016-2019 are described below.

Accelerating the Pace of Data-driven Chemical Evaluations

Driven by limitations of current chemical testing methods, EPA needs very rapid and efficient methods to prioritize, screen, and evaluate chemical safety for thousands of compounds. The ToxCast research program generates data and predictive models on a large number of chemicals using high-throughput screening methods and computational toxicology approaches that are increasing the pace and decreasing the cost of chemical screening.

ToxCast uses robotics technology to screen chemicals for potential toxicity, developing a cost-effective approach for prioritizing the thousands of chemicals that need toxicity testing.

While ToxCast measures changes in biological activity, ExpoCast uses related high-throughput estimates to assess exposure, another key aspect of assessing risk. ExpoCast and new approaches known as *non-targeted measurement methods* are being developed and deployed to more rapidly generate much-needed exposure information on several thousand chemicals, including data on chemicals not expected to be found in environmental samples. Together, this multi-year effort is generating an unprecedented volume of exposure and toxicology data and making it publicly available. Moving forward, researchers will assess how to apply these data from the very start to a range of applications including: chemical screening and priority setting for more in-depth studies of health hazard; human or ecological risk assessments; and the design of safe chemicals.

Shifting the Paradigm of Toxicity Characterization

Traditionally, toxicological testing for chemical exposure has focused on observing health outcomes such as disease and death. Using systems science, CSS research will identify early indicators, or "tipping points" of adversity or biological harm associated with chemical exposures, and build predictive models that are public health protective. To facilitate this research, ORD is funding four university-based centers. The centers will develop cell models for high-priority biological systems such as the brain, liver, kidney, testis, breast tissue, heart and neurovascular, and evaluate them for use in research into the interactions of chemicals with key biological processes. This innovative work will provide new biological insight into how tissues and organs function during chemical exposures and illuminate when and how those "tipping points" occur. Scientists will use the data to develop advanced computational models of how organs and tissues respond to chemicals, and use the models to evaluate predictive models of human disease or response.

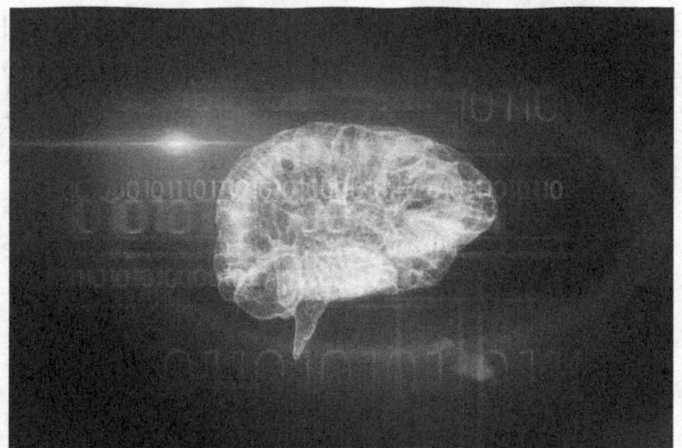

EPA is advancing and supporting innovative science to model the brain and other high-priority biological systems.

Transforming Ecological Risk Assessments

EPA uses a tiered ecological risk assessment process for registering and regulating chemical compounds. Chemicals determined to present an appreciable risk based on first tier screening with minimal data are subject to higher-level assessments that provide quantitative estimates. For the vast majority of chemicals and species, little or no data exist and refined assessments must rely on modeled estimates of exposure and effects. The Ecological Modeling project area will advance efficient methods to improve risk assessments with limited data availability, as well as more complex approaches where data are more abundant. Research will also focus on developing and evaluating ecological models for endangered species and wildlife populations exposed to pesticides. The ability to apply models with varying complexities and data requirements will enhance EPA capacity to protect sensitive ecosystems and species.

This work will provide demonstrated ecological risk assessment tools that reduce uncertainty for high priority and methodologically challenging chemicals. The resulting decision framework for using models of various complexities and data requirements appropriate for the assessment will enhance EPA's capacity to protect sensitive ecosystems and species.

Integrating Life Cycle Thinking

To make sustainable decisions it is important to understand the broad range of impacts to human health and the environment associated with a chemical or product throughout the life cycle. CSS is developing efficient tools that will help consider, among the broad range of impacts, the potential for exposures to human and ecological species across the chemical life cycle where limited data are available. Scientists are developing approaches to efficiently evaluate environmental and human health impacts and identifying metrics to quantify tradeoffs between risks and other sustainability factors. By bringing together two of ORD's leading disciplines, exposure science and life cycle assessment, this project is transforming how scientists in the broader community are attacking these same challenges. Research in this area will be focused on how to operationalize sustainability analysis for chemical safety evaluation by leveraging and extending methods in life cycle assessment and exposure modeling to incorporate metrics of human and ecological risk.

Human Health Risk Assessment

Every day, EPA and diverse stakeholders must make decisions to protect human health and the environment from the known or potential adverse effects of exposure to environmental pollutants. Such decisions span a large regulatory landscape and require different types of environmental pollutant risk information: evaluating data on new chemicals entering the market; characterizing potential public and environmental health impacts during emergency situations; screening and prioritizing chemicals for monitoring at Superfund sites and in the air and water; evaluating health and ecological effects data to derive benchmark estimates; and interpreting and integrating different lines of evidence to support decisions to establish, retain or revise national standards.

EPA's Human Health Risk Assessment (HHRA) research program is designed to provide robust and responsive risk assessment support for a wide range of risk management decisions aimed at protecting human health and the environment. The HHRA program provides an essential portfolio of risk assessment products and undertakes targeted and innovative development of new approaches to advance risk analysis.

Research Challenges

Decision makers need timely and robust scientific risk evaluations that include an ever-expanding number of exposure scenarios and environmental contaminants.

Current risk assessment methods must continually modernize and accelerate the application of scientific advances in molecular biology and computational sciences.

Communities need technical support to assess urgent environmental contamination issues, assess exposures to multiple pollutants and address cumulative risk concerns.

The HHRA program addresses the Strategic Goals in the Fiscal Year 2014–2018 EPA Strategic Plan: "Addressing Climate Change and Improving Air Quality"; "Protecting America's Waters"; "Cleaning Up Communities and Advancing Sustainable Development"; and "Ensuring the Safety of Chemicals and Preventing Pollution." In addition, HHRA research supports the cross-agency strategies "Working Toward a Sustainable Future" and "Making a Visible Difference in Communities."

The HHRA research program adapts and evolves as needed. The program adjusts in response to EPA needs, new scientific opportunities, and new challenges and needs in the risk assessment and management arenas. To help partners and stakeholder gain confidence in the application of new approaches, projects in the program are targeted at characterizing the utility of emerging science and tools to improve risk assessments. Program researchers regularly engage EPA and external partners and stakeholders to solicit feedback and ensure that assessments are conducted in open, transparent ways.

The three main HHRA program objectives support the vision of protecting public health and the environment by providing state-of-the-science chemical assessments, refining risk assessment approaches, advancing innovative applications and providing stakeholder engagement.

1) **Characterize Risks**
   Efficiently support a range of decision making with an agile, fit-for-purpose portfolio of robust and responsive assessment products that characterize risks and potential impacts to human health and the environment.

2) **Advance and Refine Assessment Approaches**
   Refine risk assessments by identifying critical issues and advancing analytical approaches and applications to incorporate new science, methods and technologies.

3) **Enhance and Engage**
   Enhance data access and management systems to support transparency and efficiency; provide outreach and engage stakeholders to ensure support, training, and tailoring of assessment priorities and products.

Cross Program Collaboration: Incorporating New Data Streams into Health and Environmental Risk Assessments

The HHRA and CSS programs are working together to evaluate how the new data emerging from computational toxicology can be used effectively in risk assessment. Characterizing the utility of these new data and tools for improving risk assessment will build both stakeholder confidence in and capacity for their application, and thereby accelerate their acceptance in regulatory decision making. Projects in the HHRA program include case studies demonstrating several new approaches applied to different classes of chemicals, various endpoints and toxicities, and with varying degrees of supporting evidence.

2016–2019 HHRA Strategic Research Action Plan: Research Examples

The HHRA program provides a course of action for delivering direct scientific and technical support on risk assessment. Examples from the 2016–2019 research program are described below.

Integrated Science Assessments (ISAs)

The HHRA program regularly develops ISAs as a major component of its research portfolio. The ISAs evaluate and synthesize the most policy-relevant science for reviewing the National Ambient Air Quality Standards (NAAQS), set by EPA for six principal pollutants: ozone, particulate matter, carbon monoxide, sulfur dioxide, nitrogen oxides and lead. Called *criteria pollutants*, these are derived from numerous sources and are considered harmful to public health and the environment. Because each ISA communicates critical science judgments, it forms the scientific foundation for the review of the NAAQS. The ISAs are developed on a five-year cycle, in response to regulatory requirements, and are vetted through a rigorous peer review process.

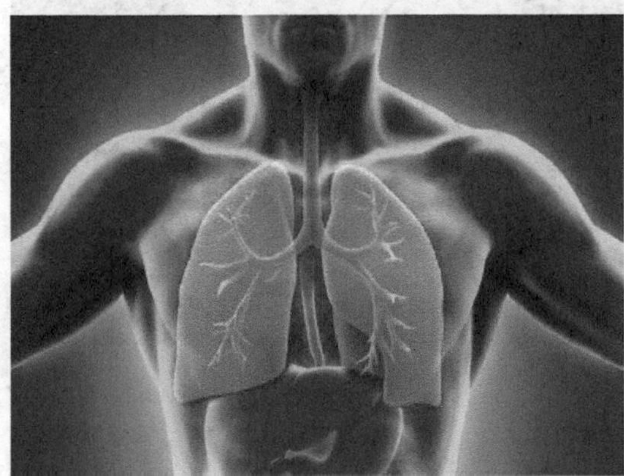

Integrated Risk Information System

Under the Integrated Risk Information System (IRIS) program, EPA evaluates scientific information on health effects that may result from exposure to environmental contaminants. The web-accessible IRIS database provides health effects information on more than 550 chemical substances, and these scientific evaluations support EPA decisions related to air and water pollution, Superfund cleanups, and other regulatory activities. For 2016–2019, the IRIS program is focused on implementing a series of recommendations from the National Research Council to improve the process for developing IRIS assessments, including enhancing stakeholder engagement. Additionally, the IRIS program is embarking on an effort to review and update older assessments in the database. Together, the ongoing improvements will continue to strengthen the IRIS program and increase transparency and productivity.

Cumulative Risk Assessment

To address the desire of communities to understand and conduct local or "place-based" risk assessments, EPA scientists are developing methods to integrate and evaluate impacts of chemical and non-chemical stressors on human health and the environment. Cumulative risk assessment requires understanding key biological, social, spatial, temporal and environmental factors and how they contribute to disproportionate risk. Research may include scenario-specific case studies in collaboration with regional partners. Advances in cumulative risk assessment will support communities in addressing environmental justice concerns.

Homeland Security

Recent major disasters in the United States (Hurricane Sandy, the Deepwater Horizon oil spill, the Oklahoma tornados, avian influenza, and the West Virginia water contamination incident) and abroad (Fukushima nuclear power plant accident) illustrate the critical need for rapid recovery after all types of disasters. The U.S. Government has recognized that preparing for and responding to most disasters, man-made or natural, have common elements.

The mission of EPA's Homeland Security Research Program (HSRP) is to conduct research and deliver scientific products that advance the Agency's homeland security responsibilities in ways that also help communities become resilient to disasters.

To guide that work, HSRP researchers work closely with Agency partners and stakeholders, including emergency response professionals and water utilities, to understand their most important gaps in the science and technology needed for decontamination and resiliency. This work directly supports EPA strategic goals to protect America's waters and clean up communities.

HSRP uses a systems approach to develop methodologies, strategies, and tools to support water security and wide area contamination after disasters. The program has two primary objectives:

1) **Improve Water Utilities' Abilities to Prepare for and Respond to Incidents that Threaten Public Health**
   Disasters are likely to impact water utilities' ability to function. To build resilience, HSRP develops modeling tools that support the design and operation of water systems to decrease their vulnerability to disasters. HSRP also builds tools, technologies and data to support post-incident responses including decontamination of infrastructure and treatment of contaminated water.

2) **Advance EPA's Capabilities to Respond to Wide Area Contamination Incidents**
   Terrorist incidents or natural disasters can result in wide area contamination with chemical, biological, radiological and nuclear agents or materials. HSRP develops cost effective and efficacious cleanup strategies and methods to enable recovery of the contaminated area including cleanup approaches and waste management strategies and tools.

Research Challenges

Environmental disasters due to intentional or natural causes can result in the loss of human life and create long-term injury to social, economic, and environmental systems.

Devising and adapting methods and technologies to effectively respond to and recover from these incidents requires understanding the complex and evolving nature of the incident and subsequent response activities.

2016–2019 HSRP Strategic Research Action Plan: Research Examples

From preparing for terrorist threats that could impair our air, water, land and infrastructure to responding to natural disasters and industrial accidents, HSRP addresses EPA's environmental priorities. Examples of research for 2016–2019 are described below.

The Water Security Test Bed: Advancing Water Security in Real-World Scenarios

EPA and research partners designed and constructed a replica of a municipal drinking water piping system at the Department of Energy's Idaho National Laboratory, part of efforts to advance decontamination techniques beyond laboratory and field-scale studies. Experiments at the newly constructed facility will allow researchers to conduct the first evaluations of technologies and techniques for monitoring and decontaminating drinking water systems under real-world conditions; tests will include in-line contaminant detectors, decontamination methodologies (including automatic flushing), and wash water treatment methodologies. EPA researchers will also be leading the development of water systems modeling tools.

Water security test bed at the Idaho National Laboratory.

Decontamination Technologies for Wide Area Contamination Events

Recent catastrophic events such as the Fukushima Daiichi incident following the earthquake and ensuing tsunami in Japan clearly demonstrate the need for decontamination and remediation techniques that can be effective across large areas (single building to entire neighborhoods), and a diversity of environments (from soil and vegetation to manmade structures). HSRP is developing and improving decontamination engineering processes to facilitate implementation of technologies in the field and provide information to assist in scaling up of such methodologies to improve resiliency. For example, Agency researchers are developing risk reduction and self-help remediation methods for use after a contamination incident involving a wide area anthrax or radiological contamination incident.

EPA supports its responders' ability to characterize site contamination by developing sampling protocols, sample preparation methods, and analytical methods for chemicals, biotoxins, microbial pathogens, and radiological agents.

Sampling Strategy for Anthrax

Any large-scale contamination event involving the bacteria responsible for anthrax (*B. anthracis*) will require extensive environmental sampling to inform remediation and decision support regarding the potential for re-inhabiting areas and buildings. HSRP scientists have reviewed and assessed traditional sampling strategies, and are developing innovative new strategy options to support responses, such as modeling tools to support air sampler placement after a wide area outdoor release of *B. anthracis*.

Cross Program Collaboration: Community Resilience

Increasing the resilience of communities to changing climate, declining ecosystem goods and services, and man-made or natural environmental disasters is an area of interest in all of EPA's national research programs. HSRP is facilitating research coordination in this area as it continues to grow over 2016-2019.

As a part of these research efforts, HSRP is developing indicators of community environmental resilience. By highlighting strengths and weaknesses, these indicators will support communities' efforts to improve their resilience to disasters and help focus research on building tools and technologies needed to minimize the impact of disasters and to improve post-disaster adaptation. HSRP will collaborate with the other programs in ORD (ACE, SHC, HHRA, and SSWR) to develop these indicators and the tools that facilitate their use by communities.

Science to Protect Public Health and the Environment

EPA research is strategically designed to deliver the scientific and engineering solutions the nation—and the world—need to meet today's complex environmental and human health challenges, while advancing a more sustainable and resilient future. Together, its six national research programs—Air, Climate, and Energy; Safe and Sustainable Water Resources; Sustainable and Healthy Communities; Chemical Safety for Sustainability; Human Health Risk Assessment; and Homeland Security Research—are laying the foundation for new ways of looking at and solving environmental problems. The cross-cutting roadmaps are demonstrating the value of interdisciplinary research that spans media-specific lines in recognition that in the real world, environmental problems don't stop at the borders of land, air or water. EPA research is forging a path to the future while building on a forty-year legacy of scientific achievement and leadership. Beginning with framing problems up front with input from partners and stakeholders, EPA research is using innovative, interdisciplinary, and integrative solutions that transcend traditional boundaries. It's connecting the dots between a healthy ecosystem and healthy people, and working across media to solve problems in an unprecedented way. EPA research closes the loop by translating research findings to partners and stakeholders and assisting those who use our data, tools, and models. This model of science-based, problem-driven research designed to inform solutions will drive change in the scientific community and the way we address the nation's most challenging environmental problems today and tomorrow.

"Science to Protect Public Health and the Environment – EPA Research program Overview, 2016-2019." Office of Research and Development, United States Environmental Protection Agency, November 2015.

https://www.epa.gov/research/science-protect-public-health-and-environment-epa-research-program-overview-2016-2019. Accessed June 4, 2019.

Associations & Organizations

National: Air & Climate

1 **Air & Waste Management Association**
Koppers Building
436 Seventh Avenue, Suite 2100
Pittsburgh, PA 15219
412-232-3444
800-270-3444
Fax: 412-232-3450
info@awma.org
www.awma.org
Professional development organization providing a forum for the exchange of information, networking, public education, and outreach to over 5,000 environmental professionals in 65 countries.
Founded: 1907
Stephanie Glyptis, Executive Director
Tracy Fedkoe, Director, Marketing

2 **American Clean Skies Foundation**
1875 Connecticut Ave NW
Suite 705
Washington, DC 20009
202-361-3701
info@cleanskies.org
www.cleanskies.org
Independent non-profit works for cleaner energy in the transportation and electric power sectors.
Founded: 2007
Gregory C. Staple, Chief Executive Officer

3 **American Meteorological Society**
45 Beacon St
Boston, MA 02108-3693
617-227-2425
Fax: 617-742-8718
amsinfo@ametsoc.org
www.ametsoc.org
Professional organization disseminates information about the atmospheric, oceanic and hydrologic sciences.
Founded: 1919 13,000 members
Keith L. Seitter, Executive Director
Wendy Abshire, Director, Education

4 **Center for Clean Air Policy**
750 First St NE
Suite 1025
Washington, DC 20002
202-408-9260
Fax: 202-408-8896
ccap.org
Climate and air quality think tank.
Founded: 1985
Allison Bender-Corbett, Executive Director
Stecey Davis, Director, Policy & Programs

5 **Citizens' Climate Lobby**
1330 Orange Ave
Suite 309
Coronado, CA 92118
619-437-7142
citizensclimatelobby.org
Citizens' Climate Lobby is a non-profit, non-partisan, grassroots advocacy organization focused on national policies to address climate change.
Founded: 2007
Marshall Saunders, Founder & President
Mark Reynolds, Executive Director

6 **Clean Air Council**
135 S 19th Street
Suite 300
Philadelphia, PA 19103
215-567-4004
Fax: 215-567-5791
cleanair.org
Seeks to protect and defend the right to a healthy environment through education, community initiatives, government intervention, and enforcement of relevant environmental laws.
Founded: 1967
Joseph Otis Minott, Executive Director
Eric Cheung, Deputy Director

7 **Climate Institute**
1201 New York Avenue
Suite 400
Washington, DC 20005
202-552-0163
info@climate.org
climate.org
The Climate Institute seeks to implement innovative and practical solutions to climate change by supporting and collaborating with private, nonprofit and government organizations.
Founded: 1986
Mark Goldberg, Chief Executive Officer
Mike MacCracken, Chief Scientist

8 **Conservation International**
2011 Crystal Dr
Suite 500
Arlington, VA 22202
703-341-2400
800-429-5660
www.conservation.org
CI promotes sustainable development and the conservation of earth's ecosystems as keys to solving climate change.
Peter Seligmann, Chair
M. Sanjayan, Chief Executive Officer

9 **Environment America**
1543 Wazee Street
Suite 410
Denver, CO 80202
303-801-0581
800-401-6511
membership@environmentamerica.org
environmentamerica.org
A nonprofit organization dedicated to educating the public on environmental issues through research reports, news conferences, interviews with reporters, op-ed pieces, letters to the editor and more; and to promote sensible solutions.
Ed Johnson, President
Andre Delattre, Chief Operating Officer

10 **Environmental Defense Fund (EDF)**
257 Park Avenue South
New York, NY 10010
212-505-2100
Fax: 212-505-2375
www.edf.org
Dedicated to protecting the environmental rights of all people, including future generations. Among these rights are clean air, clean water, healthy, nourishing food and a flourishing ecosystem. Advocates solutions based on science,even when it leads in unfamiliar directions. Works to create solutions that win lasting political, economic and social support because they are bipartisan, efficient and fair.
Founded: 1967
Fred Krupp, President
Catherine Nardone, Chief Development Officer

11 **Institute for Global Environmental Strategies**
3033 Wilson Blvd
Suite 700
Arlington, VA 22201
703-312-0823
info@strategies.org
www.strategies.org
IGES is an earth and space science educator.
Nancy Colleton, President
Rusty Low, Chief Scientist

12 **Institute of Clean Air Companies (ICAC)**
2200 Wilson Boulevard
Suite 310
Arlington, VA 22201
571-858-3707
Fax: 703-243-8696
icacinfo@icac.com
www.icac.com
Organization of manufacturers of air pollution monitoring and control systems.
Founded: 1960
Clare Schulzki, Executive Director
Haley Armstrong, Director, Policy & Programs

13 **International Center for Arid and Semiarid Land Studies**
Texas Tech University
International Affairs
601 Indiana Ave
Lubbock, TX 79409-5004
806-742-3667
Fax: 806-742-1286
oia.reception@ttu.edu
www.depts.ttu.edu/international
Interdisciplinary study of arid and semiarid environments from international perspective.
Founded: 1966
Gad Perry, Contact

14 **International Research Institute for Climate and Society**
61 Route 9W 845-680-4468
Monell Building info@iri.columbia.edu
Palisades, NY 10964-1000 iri.columbia.edu
The International Research Institute for Climate and Society (IRI) aims to enhance society's capability to understand, anticipate and manage the impacts of climate in order to improve human welfare and the environment, especially indeveloping countries. This goal is conducted through strategic and applied research and education.
Lisa Goddard, Director
Haresh Bhojwani, Special Advisor

15 **National Association of Clean Air Agencies**
444 N Capitol St NW 202-624-7864
Suite 307 *Fax:* 202-624-7863
Washington, DC 20001 4cleanair@4cleanair.org
www.4cleanair.org
National, non-partisan, non-profit association of air pollution control agencies.
Miles Keogh, Executive Director
Nancy Kruger, Deputy Director

National: Business & Education

16 **ASTM International**
100 Barr Harbor Dr 610-832-9500
PO Box C700 877-909-2786
West Conshohocken, PA 19428-2959 *Fax:* 610-832-9555
service@astm.org
www.astm.org
One of the world's largest, and earliest, international standards developing organizations.
Founded: 1898 30K members
Katharine E. Morgan, President
John Pace, Senior Vice President

17 **American Association of Zoo Keepers**
8476 E Speedway Blvd 520-298-9688
Suite 204 www.aazk.org
Tucson, AZ 85710-1728
Membership association for animal care professionals, fostering professional development and advancing animal care, animal welfare and conservation.

18 **American Chemical Society**
1155 16th St NW 614-447-3776
Washington, DC 20036 800-333-9511
service@acs.org
www.acs.org
The American Chemical Society aims to promote a positive public perception and understanding of chemistry and the chemical sciences through public outreach programs and public awareness campaigns; involve the Society's 150,000+ membersin improving the public's perception of chemistry.
Founded: 1876
Thomas M. Connelly Jr., Executive Director & CEO
LaTrease E. Garrison, EVP, Education

19 **American Chemistry Council**
700 Second St NE 202-249-7000
Washington, DC 20002 *Fax:* 202-249-6100
www.americanchemistry.com
Industry organization working to enable a more sustainable future, through advocacy, member engagement, communications, and scientific research.
Founded: 1872
Calvin M. Dooley, President & CEO
Raymond J. O'Bryan, CFO & CAO

20 **American Federation of Teachers**
555 New Jersey Ave NW 202-879-4400
Washington, DC 20001 *Fax:* 202-879-4597
www.aft.org
Founded to represent the economic, social and professional interests of classroom teachers.
Founded: 1916 1.7 million members
Randi Weingarten, President
Lorretta Johnson, Secretary-Treasurer

21 **American Forest & Paper Association**
1101 K Street NW 202-463-2700
Suite 700 info@afandpa.org
Washington, DC 20005 www.afandpa.org
The national trade association of the forest, paper, and wood products industry, seeking to advance public policies, and to promote a strong and sustainable forest products industry both in the US and internationally.
Founded: 1993
Donna Harman, President & CEO
Samuel Kerns, VP, Administration & CFO

22 **American National Standards Institute**
1899 L Street NW 202-293-8020
11th Floor *Fax:* 202-293-9287
Washington, DC 20036 info@ansi.org
www.ansi.org
The Institute's mission is to enhance both the global competitivness of US business and the US quality of life by promoting and facilitating voluntary consensus standards and conformity assessment systems, and safeguarding their integrity.
Founded: 1918 3.5 million members
Joe Bhatia, President & CEO
James McCabe, Sr. Dir., Standards

23 **American Public Works Association**
1200 Main St 816-472-6100
Suite 1400 800-848-2792
Kansas City, MO 64105-2100 *Fax:* 816-472-1610
www.apwa.net
An international educational and professional association of public agencies, private sector companies, and individuals dedicated to providing high quality public works goods and services.
Founded: 1937 30,000 members
Scott Grayson, Executive Director
Becky Stein, Director, Education

24 **Association for Educational Communications and Technology**
320 W 8th Street 812-335-7675
Suite 101 877-677-2328
Bloomington, IN 47404-3745 aect@aect.org
www.aect.org
Professional association of educators seeking to improve instruction through technology.
Phillip Harris, Executive Director
Larry Vernon, Director, Electronic Service

25 **Association of American Geographers**
1710 16th Street NW 202-234-1450
Washington, DC 20009-3198 *Fax:* 202-234-2744
gaia@aag.org
www.aag.org
Nonprofit, educational society advancing the theory, methods and practice of geography.
Founded: 1904
Douglas Richardson, Executive Director
Zan Dodson, Director, Research

26 **Association of Environmental and Resource Economists (AERE)**
222 S Westmonte Drive 407-774-7880
Suite 111 *Fax:* 407-774-6440
Washington, DC 32714 info@aere.org
www.aere.org
Offers a way to exhange ideas, stimulate research, and promote graduate training in resource and environmental economics. Members come from academic institutions, the public sector, and private industry.
Founded: 1979 Over 1,000 members
Daniel J. Phaneuf, President
Amy W. Ando, Vice President

27 **Association of Federal Wildlife Officers**
theafwo@gmail.com
www.nwroa.org
Dedicated to the protection of wildlife, the enforcement of federal wildlife law, the fostering of cooperation and communication among federal wildlife officers, and the perpetuation, enhancement and defense of the wildlife enforcementprofession.
Jane Whaley, President
Amanda Posick, Vice President

28 **Association of State Wetland Managers (ASWM)**
32 Tandberg Trail 207-892-3399
Suite 2A *Fax:* 207-894-7992
Windham, ME 04062 jeanne.christie@aswm.org
www.aswm.org
Nonprofit organization dedicated to the protection and restoration of the nation's wetlands. ASWM's goal is to help public and private wetland decision-makers utilize the best possible scientific information and techniques in wetlanddelineation, assessment, mapping, planning, regulation, acquisition, restoration and other management.
Founded: 1983
Marla J. Stelk, Executive Director
Brenda Zollitsch, Senior Policy Analyst

29 **Association of Zoos and Aquariums (AZA)**
8403 Colesville Road 301-562-0777
Suite 710 *Fax:* 301-562-0888
Silver Spring, MD 20910-3314 membership@aza.org
www.aza.org
Nonprofit organization dedicated to the advancement of accredited zoos and aquariums in the areas of animal care, wildlife conservation, education and science.
Founded: 1924
Dan Ashe, President & CEO
Kris Vehrs, Executive Director

30 **Bank Information Center**
1023 15th Street NW 202-737-7752
10th floor info@bankinformationcenter.org
Washington, DC 20005 www.bankinformationcenter.org
The Bank Information Center partners with civil society to help countries influence the World Bank and other international financial institutions to promote social and economic justice and ecological sustainability.
Elana Berger, Executive Director
Ladd Connell, Director, Environment

31 **Biotechnology Industry Organization (BIO)**
1201 Maryland Avenue NW 202-962-9200
Suite 900 *Fax:* 202-488-6301
Washington, DC 20024 info@bio.org
www.bio.org
The mission of BIO is to be the champion of biotechnology and the advocate for its member organizations-both large and small.
Founded: 1993
James C. Greenwood, President & CEO
Tom DiLenge, President, Advocacy

32 **Bureau of Land Management (BLM)**
U.S. Department of the Interior
1849 C Street NW 202-208-3801
Room 5665 *Fax:* 202-208-5242
Washington, DC 20240 www.blm.gov
The mission of the Bureau of Land Management is to ensure the sustainability and diversity of the public lands for the use and enoyment of present and future generations. The Bureau offers environmental education, news about theactivities of the Bureau, events, and regulations.
Founded: 1946
Michael Nedd, Deputy Director, Operations
Casey Hammond, Principal Deputy

33 **Business for Social Responsibility (BSR)**
5 Union Square W 212-370-7707
6th Floor *Fax:* 646-758-8150
New York, NY 10003 connect@bsr.org
www.bsr.org
Works with its global network of more than 250 member companies to develop sustainable business strategies and solutions through consulting, research and cross-sector collaboration.
Founded: 1992
Aron Cramer, President & CEO
Laura Gitman, Chief Operating Officer

34 **Center for Environmental Philosophy**
University of North Texas
1704 W Mulberry 940-565-2727
Suite 370 *Fax:* 940-565-4439
Denton, TX 76201 cep@unt.edu
www.cep.unt.edu
The Center for Environmental Philosophy, a non-profit organization affiliated with the University of North Texas, is responsible for the publication of the Environmental Ethics journal, as well as the training and promotion of researchin environmental ethics through workshops and conferences.
Founded: 1989
Eugene C. Hargrove, President
Jan Dickson, Secretary-Treasurer

35 **Center for the Study of Carbon Dioxide and Global Change**
PO Box 25697 480-966-3719
Tempe, AZ 85285-5697 center@co2science.org
www.co2science.org
Also known as CO2 Science, the Center reviews articles, books and other educational materials, attempting to separate reality from rhetoric in the debate that surrounding the subject of carbon dioxide and global change. The Centermaintains on-line intructions on how to conduct CO2 enrichment and depletion experiments in its Global Change Laboratory.
Craig D. Idso, Chair & Founder
Frederick D. Palmer, Senior Fellow

36 **Ceres**
99 Chauncy Street 617-247-0700
6th Floor info@ceres.org
Boston, MA 02111 www.ceres.org
Ceres is a sustainability non-profit organization working with investors and companies to build leadership and drive solutions throughout the economy. Through networks and advocacy, Ceres tackles international sustainabilitychallenges, including climate change, water scarcity and pollution, and inequitable workplaces.
Founded: 1989
Mindy S. Lubber, President & CEO
Dawn M. Martin, Chief Program Officer

37 **Chelonian Research Institute**
402 South Central Avenue 407-365-6347
Oviedo, FL 32765 chelonianri@gmail.com
chelonianri.org
Dedicated to the study and conservation of turtles and tortoises worldwide. One of the world's leading institutions on the research and conversation of turtles. The 10-acre campus includes offices, a library and a museum to be enjoyedby reseachers, students and dignitaries, as well as the public.
Founded: 1997
Dr. Peter C.H. Pritchard, Founder

38 **Chlorine Institute**
1300 Wilson Boulevard 703-894-4140
Suite 525 *Fax:* 703-894-4130
Arlington, VA 22209 info@cl2.com
www.chlorineinstitute.org
Exists to support the chlor-alkali industry and serve the public by fostering continuous improvements to safety and the protection of human health and the environment connected with the production, distribution and use of chlorine,sodium and potassium hydroxides, and sodium hypochlorite; and the distribution and use of hydrogen chloride.
Founded: 1924 196 Members
Frank Reiner, President
Robyn Kinsley, VP, Transportation

39 Corps Network
1275 K Street NW 202-737-6272
Suite 1050 *Fax:* 202-737-6277
Washington, DC 20005 msprenkel@corpsnetwork.org
A proud advocate and representative of the nation's Service and Conservation Corps. The number one goal is to sustain and grow the Corps movement. The Corps Network's member Service and Conservation Corps operate in 42 state and theDistrict of Columbia. Over 26,000 Corps members, ages 16-25, contribute and generate more than 16 million hours of service annually.
Founded: 1985
Mary Ellen Sprinkel, President & CEO
Marie Walker, Chief Operating Officer

40 Council of Producers and Distributors of Agrotechnology
1730 Rhode Island Ave NW 202-386-7407
Suite 812 *Fax:* 202-386-7409
Washington, DC 20036 ghalvorson@cpda.com
cpda.com
Serves as an advocate for suppliers of agricultural adjuvant and inert ingredients, including sell tank-mix adjuvants, pesticides, & other agrotechnology products.
Founded: 1987
Gary Halvorson, President

41 Council of State Governments (CSG)
1776 Avenue of the States 859-244-8000
Lexington, KY 40511 *Fax:* 859-244-8001
www.csg.org
A region-based forum that fosters the exchange of insights and ideas to help state officials shape public policy. CSG serves the executive, judicial and legislative branches of state government through leadership education, researchand information services.
Founded: 1933
David Akins, Executive Director/CEO
Gov. Ricardo Rossello, National President

42 Earth First!
PO Box 1112 541-244-1533
Grants Pass, OR 97528 collective@earthfirstjournal.org
earthfirstjournal.org
Earth First! was first created in response to a compromising and increasingly corporate environmental community. Earth First! publish Earth First! Journal. Earth First! Journal highlights radical environmental movements and causes.Earth First! pride themselves on being a grassroots organization fighting to saves lives and the evironment, including tactics such as civil disobedience and monkeywrenching.
Founded: 1979

43 EarthShare
7735 Old Georgetown Road 800-875-3863
Suite 900 *Fax:* 240-333-0301
Bethesda, MD 20814 info@earthshare.org
www.earthshare.org
Mission is to engage individuals and organization in creating a healthy and sustainable environment.
Founded: 1988
Deb Furry, Interim CEO
Mary MacDonald, Sr. VP, Business Development

44 Ecological Society of America
1990 M Street NW 202-833-8773
Suite 700 *Fax:* 202-833-8775
Washington, DC 20036 esahq@esa.org
www.esa.org
To promote ecological science by improving communication among ecologists; raise the public's level of awareness of the importance of ecological science; increase the resources available for the conduct of ecological science.
Founded: 1915 Over 9,000 members
Catherine O'Riordan, Executive Director
Elizabeth Biggs, Chief Financial Officer

45 Environmental Council of the States
1250 H Street NW 202-266-4920
Suite 850 *Fax:* 202-266-4937
Washington, DC 20005 ecos@ecos.org
www.ecos.org
National non-profit and non-partisan association of state and territorial environmental agency leaders. Its purpose is to improve human health and the environment through improving the capabilities of regional environmental agencies.
Founded: 1993
Don Welsh, Executive Director
Carolyn Hanson, Deputy Director

46 Environmental Media Association (EMA)
8909 W Olympic Boulevard 323-556-2790
Suite 200 ema@ema-online.org
Beverly Hills, CA 90211 www.green4ema.org
Dedicated to the broadcast of balanced news about the environment. Through celebrity role modeling, campaign work, year-round programs and annual events EMA looks to promote environmental progress and innovation.
Founded: 1989
Debbie Levin, Chief Executive Officer
Paul Sposare, Executive Director

47 Federation of Environmental Technologists (FET)
W175 N11081 Stonewood Drive 262-437-1700
Suite 203 *Fax:* 262-437-1702
Germantown, WI 53022 info@fetinc.org
www.fetinc.org
A nonprofit organization formed to assist industry in interpretation of and compliance with environmental regulations. FET provides education on regulatory compliance and technological advancements to its members, and otherenvironmental professionals, through training, professional development, and networking.
Founded: 1982 600-700 Members
Jeffrey Nettesheim, Chair/Director
Cheryl Moran, President/Director

48 Forestry Conservation Communications Association (FCAA)
424 E. Middle Street 717-398-0812
Rear Unit 844-458-0298
Gettysburg, PA 17325 *Fax:* 717-778-4237
info@fcca-usa.org
fcca-usa.org
National organization serving all public safety two-way radio licensees by locating suitable frequencies within designated areas, coordinating licensing with the FCC, and protecting them once approved.
Ralph Haller, Executive Director
Michelle Fink, Natl. Frequency Coordinator

49 Get America Working!
1700 N Moore Street info@getamericaworking.org
Arlington, VA 22209-1921 www.getamericaworking.org
A nonprofit national organization striving to create millions of jobs through structural changes in the US economy.
Hon. William Drayton, Chair
Steve Kent, Contact

50 Global Environmental Management Initiative (GEMI)
1200 G Street NW 202-296-7449
Suite 350 www.gemi.org
Washington, DC 20005
Organization of companies dedicated to environment health and safety and sustainability, through the sharing of information and resources.
Founded: 1990
Steve Hellem, Executive Director
Kellen Mahoney, Program Manager

51 Green America
1612 K Street NW 800-584-7336
Suite 600 *Fax:* 202-331-8166
Washington, DC 20006 info@greenamerica.org
www.greenamerica.org
Formerly known as Co-op America, Green America seeks to foster social justice and environmental sustainability through harnessing economic power.
Founded: 1982
Alisa Gravitz, President & CEO
Russ Gaskin, Sr. Dir., Strategic Design

52 Green Seal
1001 Connecticut Avenue NW 202-872-6400
Suite 827 *Fax:* 202-872-4324
Washington, DC 20036-5525 greenseal@greenseal.org
www.greenseal.org
An independent nonprofit organization dedicated to safeguarding the environment and transforming the marketplace by promoting the manufacture, purchase, and use of environmentally responsible products and services.
Founded: 1989
Doug Gatlin, Chief Executive Officer
Mary B. Swanson, VP, Certification

53 Greenpeace USA
702 H Street NW 202-462-1177
Suite 300 800-722-6995
Washington, DC 20001 *Fax:* 202-462-4507
info@wdc.greenpeace.org
www.greenpeace.org
Greenpeace is an independent, international organization dedicated to using peaceful protest and communication to draw attention to environmental issues, and to promote solutions.
Founded: 1971
Annie Leonard, Executive Director
Nathan Santry, Actions Director

54 H. John Heinz III Center for Science, Economics and the Environment
900 17th Street NW 202-737-6307
Suite 700 info@heinzctr.org
Washington, DC 20006 www.heinzctr.org
The Center is a nonpartisan, nonprofit institute dedicated to improving the scientific and economic foundation for environmental policy through multisectoral collaboration. The Heinz Center fosters collaboration among industry,environmental organizations, academia, and all levels of government in each of its program areas.
Founded: 1995
Conn Nugent, President
Matthew Grason, Fundraising Coordinator

55 Halogenated Solvents Industry Alliance, Inc. (HSIA)
3033 Wilson Boulevard 703-875-0683
Suite 700 info@hsia.org
Arlington, VA 22201 www.hsia.org
The mission is to represent the users and producers of chlorinated solvents - trichloroethylene, perchloroethylene and methylene chloride. To promote the continued safe use of these products and the use of sound science in assessingtheir potential health effects.
Founded: 1980
Faye Graul, Executive Director
Christopher Bevan, PhD, DABT, Dir., Scientific Programs

56 Honor the Earth
607 Main Avenue 218-375-3200
PO Box 63 info@honorearth.org
Callaway, MN 56521 www.honorearth.org
Honor the Earth is a Native-led organization, addressing the two primary needs of the Native environmental movement: the need to break the geographic and political isolation of Native communities and the need to increase financialresources for organizing and change.
Founded: 1993
Winona LaDuke, Executive Director
Nicolette Slagle, Research Director

57 Household and Consumer Products Association
1667 K Street NW 202-872-8110
Suite 300 info@theHCPA.org
Washington, DC 20006 www.thehcpa.org
Formerly known as the Consumer Specialty Products Association (CSPA), the HCPA is a trade association representing companies that sell products intended for cleaning, protecting, maintaining, and disinfecting dwellings and commercial environments.
Founded: 1914 220 members
Stephen J. Caldeira, President & CEO
Rick Peluso, Sr. VP & CFO

58 Institute for Earth Education (IEE)
PO Box 115 304-832-6404
Greenville, WV 24945 *Fax:* 304-832-6077
info@ieetree.org
www.ieetree.org/iee
The IEE develops and disseminates instructional programs aimed at helping people live more lightly, harmoniously, and joyously with the natural world, through three pillars: interpretation, education, and contemplation.
Founded: 1974

59 Institute of Clean Air Companies (ICAC)
2200 Wilson Boulevard 571-858-3707
Suite 310 *Fax:* 703-243-8696
Arlington, VA 22201 icacinfo@icac.com
www.icac.com
Organization of manufacturers of air pollution monitoring and control systems.
Founded: 1960
Clare Schulzki, Executive Director
Haley Armstrong, Director, Policy & Programs

60 Institute of Environmental Sciences and Technology (IEST)
1827 Walden Office Square 847-981-0100
Suite 400 *Fax:* 847-981-4130
Schaumburg, IL 60173 information@iest.org
www.iest.org
An international professional society that serves the environmental sciences in the areas of contamination control in electronics manufacturing and pharmaceutical processes, design, test and evaluation of commercial and militaryequipment and product reliability issues.
Founded: 1953
Angela McKay, Executive Director
Heather Wooden, Coordinator, Education

61 Institute of Hazardous Materials Management (IHMM)
9210 Corporate Blvd. 301-984-8969
Suite 470 *Fax:* 301-984-1516
Rockville, MD 20850 info@ihmm.org
www.ihmm.org
A nonprofit organization that protects the environment and the public's health and safety through the administration of credentials recognizing professionals who have demonstrated a high level of knowledge, expertise, and excellence inthe management of hazardous materials.
Founded: 1984
Gene Guilford, Executive Director
Patricia Buley, Director, Certification

62 Interstate Mining Compact Commission (IMCC)
445A Carlisle Drive 703-709-8654
Herndon, VA 20170 *Fax:* 703-709-8655
bbotsis@imcc.isa.us
imcc.isa.us
A multi-state governmental organization that represents the natural resource interests of its members. They work closely with several Federal agencies such as Office of Surface Mining Reclamation and Enforcement, US EPA and US Bureauof Land Management.
Founded: 1970
Tom Clarke, Executive Director
Ryan Ellis, Director, Regulatory

63 Jane Goodall Institute
1595 Spring Hill Road 703-682-9220
Suite 550 *Fax:* 703-682-9312
Vienna, VA 22182 www.janegoodall.org
A nonprofit corporation founded to concentrate on research, education and conservation of wildlife, pursuant to the life work of Jane Goodall. Offices are located across the world.
Jane Goodall, Ph.D., DBE, Founder
Tammy Palmer, Interim Executive Director

64 Land Improvement Contractors of America (LICA)
3080 Ogden Avenue 630-548-1984
Suite 300 *Fax:* 630-548-9189
Lisle, IL 60532 nlica@aol.com
www.licanational.com
Organization composed primarily of small contractors whose activities related to the conservation, use and improvement of land and water resources ranging from grading, excavating, paving, landscaping, wetland development, drainage,and site preparation. Strives to improve the climate within which members conduct their businesses by working for better legislation and regulations.
Founded: 1950
Gerald Biuso, Sr., Chief Executive Officer
John Peterson, Director, Govt. Relations

65 National Association for Environmental Management (NAEM)
1612 K Street NW 202-986-6616
Suite 1002 800-391-6236
Washington, DC 20006 *Fax:* 202-530-4408
programs@naem.org
www.naem.org
Provides peer-to-peer networking for EHS managers; develop EHS professionals as leaders; advance the integration of EHS into business as a value driver; and promote the growth and implementation of EHS management systems worldwide; so,as to offer tangible benefits to the regulated entity and other stakeholders.
Founded: 1990
Carol Singer Neuvelt, Executive Director
Virginia Hoekenga, Deputy Director

66 National Association of Biology Teachers (NABT)
PO Box 3363 703-264-9696
Warrenton, VA 20188 888-501-6228
Fax: 202-962-3939
office@nabt.org
www.nabt.org
Includes more than 3,000 educators who share experience and expertise with colleagues from around the globe; keep up with trends and developments; and grow professionally. The NABT empowers educators to provide the best biology andlife science education for all students.
Founded: 1938
Sharon Gusky, President
Jaclyn Reeves-Pepin, Executive Director

67 National Association of Environmental Professionals (NAEP)
2150 N 107th Street 206-209-5286
Suite 205 *Fax:* 206-367-8777
Seattle, WA 98133 office@naep.org
www.naep.org
NAEP is a multidisciplinary association dedicated to the advancement of environmental professionals in the US and abroad, and a forum for current information on environmental planning, research, and management.
Krystina Toscas, Executive Director
Makenna Wallingford, Marketing & Communications

68 National Conference of State Legislatures (NCSL)
7700 East First Place 303-364-7700
Denver, CO 80230 800-659-2656
Fax: 303-364-7800
ncslnet-admin@ncsl.org
www.ncsl.org
The National Conference of State Legislatures serves the legislators and staffs of the nation's 50 states and its commonwealths and territories. NCSL is a bipartisan organization with three objectives: to improve the quality andeffectiveness of state legislatures; to foster interstate communications and cooperation; and to ensure states a strong cohesive voice in the federal system.
Founded: 1975
Robin Vos, President
Jon Heining, Staff Chair

69 National Council for Science and the Environment
740 15th Street NW 202-530-5810
Suite 900 ncse@ncseglobal.org
Washington, DC 20005 www.ncseglobal.org
National non-profit organization working to improve the scientific basis for making decisions on environmental issues. The Council promotes a new crosscutting approach to environmental science that integrates interdisciplinaryresearch, scientific assessment, environmental education and communication of science-based information to decision makers and the public.
Founded: 1990
Michelle Wyman, Executive Director
Erica Goldman, PhD, Director, Scientific Policy

70 National Energy Foundation (NEF)
4516 South 700 East 801-327-9500
Suite 100 800-616-8326
Salt Lake City, UT 84107 *Fax:* 801-908-5400
nef1.org
A non-profit educational organization dedicated to the development, dissemination and implementation of supplemental educational materials and programs primarily related to the environment, conservation, science, energy, water andnatural resources.
Founded: 1976
Elissa Richards, President & CEO
Anne Lowe, Vice-President, Operations

71 National Environmental Education Foundation (NEEF)
4301 Connecticut Avenue NW 202-833-2933
Suite 160 www.neefusa.org
Washington, DC 20008-2326
Provides objective environmental information and education to help Americans live better. Environmental education programs include those tailored to the adult public, for health professionals, and in the schools.
Meri-Margaret Deoudes, President & CEO
Sara Espinoza, Vice President, Programs

72 National FFA Organization
6060 FFA Drive 888-332-2668
PO Box 68960 *Fax:* 800-366-6556
Indianapolis, IN 46268-0960 www.ffa.org
The organization (formerly Future Farmers of America) is dedicated to making a positive difference in the lives of young people by developing their potential for premier leadership, personal growth and career success throughagricultural education.
Founded: 1928
Mark Poeschl, Chief Executive Officer
Dave Schapker, Chief Financial Officer

73 National Geographic Society
1145 17th Street NW 800-373-1717
Washington, DC 20036 givinginfo@ngs.org
www.nationalgeographic.org
Seeks to inspire people to care about the planet. Programs support scientific fieldwork and expeditions; encourage geography education for students; and promote natural and cultural conservation.
Founded: 1888
Tracy R. Wolstencroft, President & CEO
Jonathan Baillie, Chief Scientist

74 **National Governors Association (NGA)**
444 North Capitol Street 202-624-5300
Suite 267 *Fax:* 202-624-5313
Washington, DC 20001 info@nga.org
www.nga.org
The Association works closely with the administration and Congress on state and federal policy issues, serves as a vehicle for sharing knowledge of innovative programs among states, and provides technical assistance and consultantservices to governors on a wide range of management and policy issues. Part of the organization is the Center for Best Practices which undertakes demonstration projects and provides anticipatory research on important policy issues.
Founded: 1908
Nikki Guilford, Interim Executive Director
Matt Simeon, Director, External Affairs

75 **National Network of Forest Practitioners (NNFP)**
8 North Court Street 740-593-8733
Suite 411
Athens, OH 45701
Promotes the mutual well-being of workers, rural communities and forests by supporting individuals and groups that build sustainable relationships between forests and people.

76 **National Parent Teachers Association**
1250 N. Pitt Street 703-518-1200
Alexandria, VA 22314 800-307-4782
Fax: 703-836-0942
info@pta.org
www.pta.org
Part of the mission of the National PTA is to support and speak on behalf of children and youth in the school, in the community and before governmental bodies and other organizations. School Construction and Environmental Health is oneof the program focuses where the National PTA aims to ensure that facilities are free from health and environmental hazards.
Nathan R. Monell, Executive Director
Mary Pat King, Director, Education

77 **National Religious Partnership for the Environment**
110 Maryland Avenue, NE 212-532-7436
Suite 203 *Fax:* 413-253-1414
Washington, DC 20002 nrpe@nrpe.org
www.nrpe.org
The mission of the National Religious Partnership for the Environment is to permanently integrate issues of environmental sustainability andjustice across all aspects of organized religious life.
Cassandra Carmichael, Executive Director
Rev. Michael McClain, Outreach Coordinator

78 **National Waste & Recycling Association (NWRA)**
1550 Crystal Drive 202-244-4700
Suite 804 800-424-2869
Arlington, VA 22202 *Fax:* 202-966-4824
info@wasterecycling.org
wasterecycling.org
Formerly known as the Environmental Industry Associations, which oversaw the National Solid Wastes Management Association and the Waste and Equipment Technology Association. This trade association represents private-sector companies inNorth America that provide solid, hazardous and medical waste collection, recycling and disposal services, and companies that provide professionals and consulting services to the waste services industry.
Founded: 1962
Darrell K. Smith, President & CEO
Kevin Kraushaar, Sr. VP, Government Affairs

79 **Nature's Classroom**
19 Harrington Road 508-248-2741
Charlton, MA 01507 800-433-8375
Fax: 508-248-2745
info@naturesclassroom.org
naturesclassroom.org
Nature's Classroom is a residential environmental education program, at 12 sites in New York and New England. They give students, and teachers, the chance to experience education from another perspective, outside the walls of theclassroom. After spending time in Nature's Classroom, living and learning together, students develop a sense of community, a confidence in themselves and an appreciation for others that carries over to the school community.
Dr. John Santos, Director

80 **Netcentric Campaigns**
202-770-0767
info@greenmediatoolshed.org
www.netcentriccampaigns.org
Netcentric Campaigns transforms advocacy for foundations and non-profits by building networks of people to move change forward.
Founded: 2000
Marty Kearns, Executive Director
Krishna Roy, Senior Strategy Advisor

81 **Noise Free America**
P.O. Box 2754 877-664-7366
Chapel Hill, NC 27515 director@noisefree.org
www.noisefree.org
A national non-profit organization aimed at reducing noise pollution in the community. Their main focus is on noises from airplaines and helicopters, road vehicles, lawn and garden equipment, music, sports stadiums, and other sources.
Founded: 2001

82 **North American Association for Environmental Education (NAAEE)**
1725 DeSales Street NW 202-419-0412
Suite 401 *Fax:* 202-419-0415
Washington, DC 20036 info@naaee.org
www.naaee.org
A professional association that promotes excellence in environmental education and serves environmental educators for the purpose of achieving environmental literacy to allow present and future generations to benefit from a safe andhealthy environment.
Founded: 1971 16,000 members
Judy Braus, Executive Director
Sarah Bodor, Director, Policy

83 **Orion Society**
187 Main Street 413-528-4422
Great Barrington, MA 01230 888-909-6568
orionmagazine.org
A nonprofit organization supported by donations from individuals, families and foundations, and corporate and government grants. Mission is to inform, inspire, and engage individuals and grassroots organizations in becoming asignificant cultural force for healing nature and community. Publishes Orion Magazine, among other publications.
Founded: 1992
H. Emerson Blake, Executive Director
Madeline Miller, Strategic Director

84 **Pew Charitable Trusts**
2005 Market Street 215-575-9050
Suite 2800 *Fax:* 215-575-4939
Philadelphia, PA 19103-7077 info@pewtrusts.org
www.pewtrusts.org
Pew uses an analytical approach to solve international challenges, by improving public policy, informing the public, and bettering civic life.
Rebecca W. Rimel, President & CEO
Janice Bogash, Senior Vice President

85 **Public Citizen**
1600 20th Street NW 202-588-1000
Washington, DC 20009 member@citizen.org
www.citizen.org
A consumer advocacy organization founded to represent consumer interests in Congress, the executive branch, and the courts.
Founded: 1971
Robert Weissman, President
Margrete Strand Rangnes, Executive Vice President

86 Public Employees for Environmental Responsibility (PEER)
962 Wayne Avenue 202-265-7337
Suite 610 *Fax:* 202-265-4192
Silver Spring, MD 20910-4453 info@peer.org
www.peer.org

A national nonprofit alliance of local, state and federal scientists, law enforcement officers, land managers and other professionals dedicated to upholding environmental laws and values.
Tim Whitehouse, Executive Director
Kyla Bennett, Director, Science Policy

87 Renew The Earth (RTE)
8 Robin Ann Lane 518-797-3377
Westerlo, NY 12193 susancaumont@renew-the-earth.org
renew-the-earth.org

Promotes an exchange of ideas, information, and action across the globe in an effort to move away from fossil fuels, and embrace sustainable energy and water.
Founded: 1989
Susan Caumont, President
Dennis Irwin, Secretary

88 Renewable Fuels Association (RFA)
16024 Manchester Road 202-289-3835
Suite 101 *Fax:* 202-289-7519
Ellisville, MO 63011 info@ethanolrfa.org
www.ethanolrfa.org

The national trade association for the US ethanol industry, promotes policies, regulations and research and development initiative that will lead to the increased production and use of fuel ethanol.
Founded: 1981
Geoff Cooper, President & CEO
Robert White, VP, Industry Relations

89 Roger Tory Peterson Institute of Natural History
311 Curtis Street 716-665-2473
Jamestown, NY 14701 info@rtpi.org
rtpi.org

Nature education organization that works on the national level, with an audience of primarily adults who are interested in gaining skills for educating young people about the natural world. RTPI also houses the life's work of RogerTory Peterson.
Founded: 1984
Joni Blackman, Chief Operations Officer
Linda Pierce, Director, Development

90 Silicones Environmental, Health and Safety Center
American Chemistry Council (ACC)
700 2nd Street NE 202-249-7000
Washington, DC 20002 *Fax:* 202-249-6100
sehsc@americanchemistry.com
sehsc.americanchemistry.com

An organization of North America silicone chemical producers and importers. It promotes the safe use of silicones through product stewardship and environmental, health and safety research. It focuses on coordinating research andsubmitting it for peer review through independent advisory boards and publication of peer-reviewed literature.
Karluss Thomas, Executive Director

91 Smithsonian Institution
Smithsonian Information
SI building, Room 153, MRC 010 202-633-1000
PO Box 37012 866-868-7774
Washington, DC 20013-7012 info@si.edu
www.si.edu

Independent trust instrumental of the United States holding more than 154 million artifacts and specimens in its trust for the public interest and knowledge. Also a center for research dedicated to public education, national service,and scholarship in the arts, sciences, and history.
Founded: 1846
Dr. David J. Skorton, Secretary
Cathy Helm, Inspector General

92 Society of American Foresters (SAF)
10100 Laureate Way 301-897-8720
Bethesda, MD 20814-2198 866-897-8720
Fax: 301-897-3690
membership@safnet.org
www.eforester.org

To advance the science, education, technology, and practice of forestry; to enhance the competency of its members; to establish professional excellence; and to use the knowledge, skills, and conservation ethic of the profession toensure the continued health and use of forest ecosystems present and future of availability of forest resources to benefit society.
Founded: 1900
Terry Baker, Chief Executive Officer
Louise Murgia, Chief Operating Officer

93 Society of Chemical Manufacturers and Affiliates (SOCMA)
1400 Crystal Drive 571-348-5100
Suite 630 *Fax:* 571-348-5138
Arlington, VA 22202 info@socma.com
www.socma.com

International trade association serving small and mid-sized batch chemical manufacturers, striving for safe, sustainable and environmentally sound operations.
Founded: 1921
Jennifer L. Abril, President & CEO
Paul J. Hirsh, Sr. VP, Industry Development

94 Student Pugwash USA
2711 Ordway Steeet NW 202-794-6928
Suite 203 contact@spusa.org
Washington, DC 20008-5036 www.spusa.org

Promotes social responsibility in science and technology. Prepare science, technology and policy students to make social responsibility a guiding focus of their academic and professional endeavors.
Founded: 1979
Jeff Porten, Chair
Joshua Foster, Secretary

95 U.S. Global Change Research Program
1800 G St NW 202-223-6262
Suite 9100 *Fax:* 202-223-3065
Washington, DC 20006 www.globalchange.gov

The U.S. Global Change Research Program (USGCRP) was established by Congress to organize federal research into studying forces that affect global environment, be they human or natural.
Founded: 1989
Michael Kuperberg, Executive Director
Nico Adams, Chief of Operations

96 United Nations Environment Programme New York Office
2 UN Plaza, Room DC2-803 212-963-8210
323 E. 44th Street *Fax:* 212-963-7341
New York, NY 10017 unepnyo@un.org
www.unenvironment.org/regions/north-america/new-york-office

Provides leadership and to encourage partnership in caring for the environment by inspiring, informing, and enabling nations and peoples to improve their quality of life without compromising that of future generations.
Founded: 1972
Satya S. Tripathi, Director

97 Welder Wildlife Foundation
10429 Welder Wildlife 361-364-2643
PO Box 1400 *Fax:* 361-364-2650
Sinton, TX 78387 welderwildlife.org

A private nonprofit organization that conducts research and education in the fields of wildlife management and conservation, and other closely related fields.
Founded: 1954
Terry Blankenship, Director
Selma Glasscock, Assistant Director

National: Design & Architecture

98 ABS Group
American Bureau of Shipping
1701 City Plaza Drive 281-673-2800
Spring, TX 77389 *Fax:* 281-877-5946
info@abs-group.com
www.abs-group.com
A subsidiary of American Bureau of Shipping offering risk management, safety, quality and environmental consulting and certification services to a wide range of industries and companies throughout the world.
Founded: 1990
Ryan Moody, President & CEO
David F. Montague, Sr. VP, Safety & Compliance

99 American Society of Landscape Architects (ASLA)
636 Eye Street NW 202-898-2444
Washington, DC 20001-3736 888-999-2752
Fax: 202-898-1185
info@asla.org
www.asla.org
To advance the field of landscape architecture through advocacy, communication, education, and fellowship.
Founded: 1899
Nancy Somerville, CEO & EVP
Susan Cahill-Aylward, Director, Information

100 Associated General Contractors of America (AGC)
2300 Wilson Boulevard 703-548-3118
Suite 300 800-242-1767
Arlington, VA 22201 *Fax:* 703-548-3119
info@agc.org
www.agc.org
Advocates for and on behalf of the construction industry. Priorities include health and safety, and energy and the environment, with dedicated environmental resources available to members.
26,000 member firms
Stephen Sandherr, Chief Executive Officer
Jeff Shoaf, Chief Operating Officer

101 Environmental Design Research Association (EDRA)
651-379-7306
Fax: 651-290-2266
headquarters@edra.org
www.edra.org
Advances and disseminates behavior and design research toward improving understanding of the relationships between people and their environments.
Founded: 1968
Linda Nubani, Chair
Chingwen Cheng, Secretary

102 Green Building Initiative (GBI)
7805 SW 40th Avenue 503-274-0448
Suite 80010 info@thegbi.org
Portland, OR 97219 thegbi.org
Nonprofit organization dedicated to accelerating the adoption of building practices that result in energy-efficient, healthier and environmentally sustainable buildings.
Founded: 2004
Vicki Worden, President
Megan Baker, Director, Engagement

103 Land Improvement Contractors of America (LICA)
3080 Ogden Avenue 630-548-1984
Suite 300 *Fax:* 630-548-9189
Lisle, IL 60532 nlica@aol.com
www.licanational.com
Organization composed primarily of small contractors whose activities related to the conservation, use and improvement of land and water resources ranging from grading, excavating, paving, landscaping, wetland development, drainage,and site preparation. Strives to improve the climate within which members conduct their businesses by working for better legislation and regulations.
Founded: 1950
Gerald Biuso, Sr., Chief Executive Officer
John Peterson, Director, Govt. Relations

104 Rocky Mountain Institute
Innovation Center
22830 Two Rivers Road 970-927-3851
Basalt, CO 81621 *Fax:* 970-927-3420
www.rmi.org
An independent, entrepreneurial, nonprofit think and do tank. Envisage a world thriving, verdant, and secure, for all.
Jules Kortenhorst, President & CEO
Amory Lovins, Chief Scientist

105 U.S. Green Building Council (USGBC)
2101 L Street NW 202-742-3792
Suite 500 800-795-1747
Washington, DC 20037 education@usgbc.org
usgbc.org
USGBC is a nonprofit organization that promotes sustainability in buildings design, construction, and operation. They work in collaboration with industry experts, market research publications and LEED professional credentials.
Founded: 1993
Mahesh Ramanujam, President & CEO
David Witek, Sr. VP, Enterprise Operation

National: Disaster Preparedness & Response

106 Cultural Survival
2067 Massachusetts Avenue 617-441-5400
Cambridge, MA 02140 culturalsurvival@cs.org
www.culturalsurvival.org
Provides a worldwide connection for a better global environment through effective letter-writing campaigns. Empowers people of all ages, cultures, and nationalities to protect the environment by creating partnerships for effectivecitizen action.
Founded: 1972
Mark Camp, Interim Executive Director
Denielle DeLuca, Manager, Advocacy

107 Disaster Recovery Institute International (DRI)
119 West 23rd Street 866-542-3744
Suite 704 drii.org
New York, NY 10011
DRI International is the non-profit that helps organizations prepare for and recover from disasters. DRI also serves continuity professionals through conferencing, outreach, and volunteerism.
Founded: 1988
Chloe Demrovsky, President
Traci O'Neal, Sr. Director, Operations

108 International Association for Disaster Preparedness and Response (DERA)
PO Box 797 info@disasters.org
Longmont, CO 80502 www.disasters.org
Nonprofit association aiming to connect individuals and organizations involved in all aspects of emergency management.
Founded: 1962

109 International Association of Emergency Managers (IAEM)
201 Park Washington Court 703-538-1795
Falls Church, VA 22046-4527 *Fax:* 703-241-5603
info@iaem.com
iaem.com
Nonprofit educational organization dedicated to Emergency Management and representing those professionals whose goals are saving lives and protecting property and the environment during emergencies and disasters.
Marty Shaub, USA President

110 **International Association of Wildland Fire**
1418 Washburn Street 406-531-8264
Missoula, MT 59801 888-440-4293
execdir@iawfonline.org
www.iawfonline.org
A professional association representing members of the global wildland fire community. It facilitates communication and provides leadership for the wildland fire community.
Alen Slijepcevic, President
Toddi A. Steelman, Vice-President

111 **National Association of Flood and Stormwater Management Agencies (NAFSMA)**
PO Box 56764 202-289-8625
Washington, DC 20040 *Fax:* 202-530-3389
info@nafsma.org
www.nafsma.org
NAFSMA is an organization of public agencies whose function is the protection of lives, property and economic activity from the adverse impacts of storm and flood waters. The mission of the association is to advocate public policy,encourage technologies and conduct education programs which facilitate and enhance the achievement of the public service functions of its members.
Founded: 1978
Janet Bly, President
Mark Pestrella, Vice President

112 **National Council on Radiation Protection and Measurements (NCRP)**
7910 Woodmont Avenue 301-657-2652
Suite 400 *Fax:* 301-907-8768
Bethesda, MD 20814-3095 ncrp@ncrponline.org
ncrponline.org
The Council seeks to formulate and widely disseminate information, guidance and recommendations on radiation protection and measurements which represent the consensus of leading scientific thinking.
Founded: 1964
Laura J. Atwell, Director, Operations
John D. Boice, Jr., Director, Science

113 **National Emergency Management Association (NEMA)**
www.nemaweb.org
Nonprofit, nonpartisan association seeking to improve the country's ability to handle all types of emergencies, disasters, and national security threats.
Founded: 1974
Brad Richy, President
Sima Merick, Vice President

114 **National Fire Protection Association (NFPA)**
1 Batterymarch Park 617-770-3000
Quincy, MA 02169-7471 800-344-3555
Fax: 800-593-6372
www.nfpa.org
Reduces the worldwide burden of fire and other hazards on the quality of life by providing and advocating consensus codes and standards, research, training and education.
Founded: 1896 50,000 members
Jim Pauley, President
Christian Dubay, VP, Codes & Standards

115 **Natural Hazards Center**
University of Colorado Boulder
1440 15th Street 303-735-5844
Boulder, CO 80302 *Fax:* 303-492-2151
hazctr@colorado.edu
hazards.colorado.edu
Advances and communicates knowledge on hazards mitigation and disaster preparedness, response, and recovery. Using an all-hazards and interdisciplinary framework, the Center fosters information sharing and integration of activitiesamong researchers, practitioners, and policy makers from around the world; supports and conducts research; and provides educational opportunities for the next generation of hazards scholars and professionals.
Founded: 1976
Lori Peek, Director
Jason Van Horn, Program Manager

116 **Safety Equipment Institute (SEI)**
1307 Dolley Madison Boulevard 703-442-5732
Suite 3A *Fax:* 703-442-5756
McLean, VA 22101 Info@SEInet.org
www.seinet.org
A private, nonprofit organization established to administer the first non-governmental, third-party certification program to test and certify a broad range of safety equipment products.
Founded: 1981
Patricia A. Gleason, President
Tricia Hock, Dir., Program Development

National: Energy & Transportation

117 **Alliance to Save Energy**
1850 M St NW 202-857-0666
Suite 610 www.ase.org
Washington, DC 20036
This organization is a nonprofit collective of business, government, environmental and consumer leaders with the mission of promoting energy efficiency worldwide to achieve a healthier economy, environment and greater energy security.
Founded: 1977
Jason Hartke, President
Daniel Bresette, Vice President, Policy

118 **American Clean Skies Foundation**
1875 Connecticut Ave NW 202-361-3701
Suite 705 info@cleanskies.org
Washington, DC 20009 www.cleanskies.org
Independent non-profit works for cleaner energy in the transportation and electric power sectors.
Founded: 2007
Gregory C. Staple, Chief Executive Officer

119 **American Coal Ash Association (ACAA)**
38800 Country Club Drive 720-870-7897
Farmington Hills, MI 48331 *Fax:* 720-870-7889
info@acaa-usa.org
www.acaa-usa.org
Mission is to advance the management and use of coal combustion products in ways that are environmentally responsible, technically sound, commercially competitive and more supportive of a sustainable global community.
Thomas Adams, Executive Director
Alyssa Barto, Member Liaison

120 **American Council for an Energy-Efficient Economy (ACEEE)**
529 14th Street NW 202-507-4000
Suite 600 *Fax:* 202-429-2248
Washington, DC 20045-1000 industry@aceee.org
aceee.org
A nonprofit organization dedicated to advancing energy efficiency by promoting policies, programs, technologies and sustainable living. ACEEE employs a number of strategies to accomplish this goal, such as conducting technical andpolicy assessments, advising governments, publishing books, holding conferences, generating research reports and more.
Founded: 1980
Steven Nadel, Executive Director
Maggie Molina, Senior Director, Policy

121 **American Gas Association (AGA)**
400 North Capitol Street NW 202-824-7000
Suite 450 *Fax:* 202-824-7115
Washington, DC 20001 tburleson@aga.org
www.aga.org

The Association represents over 200 local energy companies responsible for delivering natural gas throughout the United States.
Founded: 1918
James P. Torgerson, Chair
Ken A. Harbert, President & CEO

122 American Petroleum Institute (API)
200 Massachusetts Avenue NW 202-682-8000
Suite 1100 www.api.org
Washington, DC 20005-5571
API is the major national trade association representing all aspects of America's oil and natural gas industry. With over 600 corporate members (including producers, refiners, pipeline operators, and service companies) the associationoffers a broad range of programs including advocacy, research and statistics, certification, operating standards, and education.
Founded: 1919
Jack Gerard, President & CEO
Kyle Isakower, Vice President

123 American Public Power Association
2451 Crystal Drive 202-467-2900
Suite 1000 www.publicpower.org
Arlington, VA 22202-4804
Provides the nation with more than 2,000 community-owned electric utilities serving over 48 million Americans. It is a nonprofit organization. APPA aims to advance the public policy interests of its members and consumers throughservices that create reliable, affordable electricity while keeping environmental health in mind.
Founded: 1940
Sue Kelly, President & CEO
Michael Hyland, Sr. VP, Engineering Services

124 American Solar Energy Society (ASES)
2525 Arapahoe Ave 303-443-3130
Suite E4-253 info@ases.org
Boulder, CO 80302 www.ases.org
National organization dedicated to advancing the use of solar energy for the benefit of US citizens and the global environment. The organization promotes this goal by offering education, events and resources to communities.
Founded: 1954
Carly Rixham, Executive Director
Carly Cipolla, Director, Operations

125 Association of Energy Engineers (AEE)
3168 Mercer University Drive 770-447-5083
Atlanta, GA 30341 *Fax:* 770-446-3969
info@aeecenter.org
www.aeecenter.org
Nonprofit professional society that promotes the scientific and educational interests of those in the energy industry. The association offers conferences, journals, books and certification programs in support of sustainabledevelopment.
Founded: 1977 18,000 members
Bill Kent, Executive Director
Michael Hewson, Creative Director

126 CECA Solutions
2737 Devonshire Place NW www.cecarf.org
Suite 102
Washington, DC 20008
Formerly the Consumer Energy Council of America, CECA Solutions is an organization in the US focusing on supporting clean, affordable energy services for consumers.
Founded: 1973
Rich Aiken, President
Ellen Berman, Chief Executive Officer

127 Citizens' Climate Lobby
1330 Orange Ave 619-437-7142
Suite 309 citizensclimatelobby.org
Coronado, CA 92118
Citizens' Climate Lobby is a non-profit, non-partisan, grassroots advocacy organization focused on national policies to address climate change.
Founded: 2007
Marshall Saunders, Founder & President
Mark Reynolds, Executive Director

128 Clean Fuels Development Coalition (CFDC)
4641 Montgomery Avenue 301-718-0077
Suite 350 *Fax:* 301-718-0606
Bethesda, MD 20814 CFDCInc@aol.com
www.cleanfuelsdc.org
Aims to support the production and use of fuels helping to reduce air pollution and oil imports.
Douglas Durante, Executive Director

129 Compressed Gas Association (CGA)
14501 George Carter Way 703-788-2700
Suite 103 *Fax:* 703-961-1831
Chantilly, VA 20151 cga@cganet.com
www.cganet.com
Mission is to promote the safe manufacture, transportation, storage, transfilling, and disposal of industrial and medical gases and their containers. Strategies employed by the CGA include developing standards and practices, workingwith other organizations, providing safety training and more.
Founded: 1913 110 member firms
Rich Gottwald, President & CEO

130 Energy Efficiency Global Alliance
1850 M St NW 202-857-0666
Suite 610 lvanwie@ase.org
Washington, DC 20036 eeglobalalliance.org
An initiative of the Alliance to Save Energy, the EE Global Alliance aims to make energy efficiency an integral part of international conversations on energy, climate, and the economy.
Founded: 1977
Jason Hartke, President
Laura Van Wie McGrory, VP, Strategic Initiatives

131 Energy-Efficient Codes Coalition (EECC)
Alliance to Save Energy
1850 M St NW 202-857-0666
Suite 610 energyefficientcodes.org
Washington, DC 20036
Established by the Alliance to Save Energy, the EECC is an group of building sector advocates and other supporters who aim to improve the International Energy Conservation Code in 2021 in terms of energy efficiency.
Founded: 2007
Jason Hartke, President
Daniel Bresette, Vice President, Policy

132 Environment America
1543 Wazee Street 303-801-0581
Suite 410 800-401-6511
Denver, CO 80202 membership@environmentamerica.org
environmentamerica.org
A nonprofit organization dedicated to educating the public on environmental issues through research reports, news conferences, interviews with reporters, op-ed pieces, letters to the editor and more; and to promote sensible solutions.
Ed Johnson, President
Andre Delattre, Chief Operating Officer

133 Institute for Energy and Environmental Research (IEER)
PO Box 5324 301-509-6843
Takoma Park, MD 20913 www.ieer.org
IEER's aim is to provide scientific information about environmental issues in an easy to understand format for use by activists, policy-makers, journalists and the public. The educational material covers emissions-free energy systems,energy equity, energy democracy, nuclear weapons security and more.
Founded: 1987
Arjun Makhijani, President
Lois Chalmers, Consulting Librarian

134 **International Association for Energy Economics (IAEE)**
28790 Chagrin Boulevard 216-464-5365
Suite 350 iaee@iaee.org
Cleveland, OH 44122 www.iaee.org
A non-profit, professoinal organization that provides an interdisciplinary forum for the exchage of ideas, experiences and issues among professionals interested in the field of energy economics. Conferences are held in North Americaand internationally.
Founded: 1977
David L. Williams, Executive Director
Jean-Michael Glachant, VP, Communications

135 **Interstate Oil and Gas Compact Commission**
900 NE 23rd Street 405-525-8380
PO Box 53127 *Fax:* 405-525-3592
Oklahoma City, OK 73152 iogcc.ok.gov
A multi-state government agency that maximizes oil and natural gas resources in order to protect the nation's health, safety, and environment.
Founded: 1935
Lori Wrotenbery, Executive Director
Amy Childers, Projects Manager

136 **LUMEN Coalition**
Alliance to Save Energy
1850 M St NW 202-857-0666
Suite 610 lumennow.org
Washington, DC 20036
Standing for Lighting Understanding for a More Efficient Nation, the LUMEN Coalition is a consortium of individuals and organizations dedicated to helping consumers make energy efficient lighting choices.
Jason Hartke, President
Daniel Bresette, Vice President, Policy

137 **Midwest Energy Efficiency Alliance (MEEA)**
20 N Wacker Drive 312-587-8390
Suite 1301 mwalliance.org
Chicago, IL 60606
Collaborative network advancing energy efficiency in the Midwest for sustainable economic development and environmental stewardship.
Stacey Paradis, Executive Director
William Angelos, Deputy Director

138 **NW Energy Coalition**
811 1st Avenue 206-621-0094
Suite 305 *Fax:* 206-621-0097
Seattle, WA 98104 nwec@nwenergy.org
www.nwenergy.org
The Coalition promotes renewable energy development, energy conservation, consumer protection, low-income energy assistance, and fish and wildlife restoration.
Founded: 1981
Nancy Hirsh, Executive Director
Joni Bosh, Senior Policy Associate

139 **National Energy Foundation (NEF)**
4516 South 700 East 801-327-9500
Suite 100 800-616-8326
Salt Lake City, UT 84107 *Fax:* 801-908-5400
nef1.org
A non-profit educational organization dedicated to the development, dissemination and implementation of supplemental educational materials and programs primarily related to the environment, conservation, science, energy, water andnatural resources.
Founded: 1976
Elissa Richards, President & CEO
Anne Lowe, Vice-President, Operations

140 **Northwest Energy Efficiency Alliance (NEEA)**
421 SW 6th Avenue 503-688-5400
Suite 600 800-411-0834
Portland, OR 97204 *Fax:* 503-688-5447
www.neea.org
A non-profit organization working to maximize energy efficiency in the Pacific Northwest through the acceleration and adoption of energy-efficient products, services, and practices.
Susan Stratton, Executive Director
Susan Hermenet, Director, Research

141 **Northwest Power and Conservation Council**
851 SW 6th Avenue 503-222-5161
Suite 1100 800-452-5161
Portland, OR 97204 *Fax:* 503-820-2370
info@nwcouncil.org
www.nwcouncil.org
Develops and maintains a regional power plan and a fish and wildlife program to balance the Northwest's environment and energy needs.
Founded: 1980
Jennifer Anders, Chair
Richard Devlin, Vice Chair

142 **Renewable Fuels Association (RFA)**
16024 Manchester Road 202-289-3835
Suite 101 *Fax:* 202-289-7519
Ellisville, MO 63011 info@ethanolrfa.org
www.ethanolrfa.org
The national trade association for the US ethanol industry, promotes policies, regulations and research and development initiative that will lead to the increased production and use of fuel ethanol.
Founded: 1981
Geoff Cooper, President & CEO
Robert White, VP, Industry Relations

143 **Rocky Mountain Institute**
Innovation Center
22830 Two Rivers Road 970-927-3851
Basalt, CO 81621 *Fax:* 970-927-3420
www.rmi.org
An independent, entrepreneurial, nonprofit think and do tank. Envisage a world thriving, verdant, and secure, for all.
Jules Kortenhorst, President & CEO
Amory Lovins, Chief Scientist

144 **Western Electricity Coordinating Council (WECC)**
155 North 400 West 801-883-6879
Suite 200 877-937-9722
Salt Lake City, UT 84103 support@wecc.org
www.wecc.org
Promotes bulk power system reliability in the Western Interconnection, and is responsible for compliance monitoring and enforcement. It also oversees reliability planning and assessments.
Founded: 1967
Kris Hafner, Chair
Steve Goodwill, Staff Liaison

National: Environmental Engineering

145 **American Academy of Environmental Engineers & Scientists (AAEES)**
147 Old Solomons Island Road 410-266-3311
Suite 303 *Fax:* 410-266-7653
Annapolis, MD 21401 www.aaees.org
Dedicated to excellence in the practice of environmental engineering and science by providing professional opportunities for students and protecting the environment and public health.
Founded: 1955
Burk Kalweit, Executive Director
J. Sammi Olmo, Manager, Special Projects

146 **American Institute of Chemical Engineers (AIChE)**
120 Wall Street 203-702-7660
FL 23 800-242-4363
New York, NY 10005-4020 *Fax:* 203-775-5177
www.aiche.org

The world's leading organization for chemical engineering professionals. Provides resources, leadership and career development opportunities for members.
Founded: 1908 60,000 members
Monty Alger, President

147 **American Institute of Chemists**
315 Chestnut Street 215-873-8224
Philadelphia, PA 19106-2702 *Fax:* 215-629-5224
info@theaic.org
www.theaic.org
To advance the chemical sciences by establishing high professional standards of practice and to emphasize the professional, ethical, economic, and social status of its members for the benefit of society as a whole.
Founded: 1923
Dr. David M. Manuta, President
Dr. Jerry Jasinski, Chairman

148 **American Society for Engineering Education**
1818 N Street NW 202-331-3500
Suite 600 *Fax:* 202-265-8504
Washington, DC 20036-2479 board@asee.org
asee.org
Nonprofit organization of individuals and institutions committed to furthering education in engineering and engineering technology.
Founded: 1893
Norman Fortenberry, Executive Director
Adrianne Triolio, Managing Director, Admin.

149 **American Society of Agricultural and Biological Engineers (ASABE)**
2950 Niles Road 269-429-0300
St Joseph, MI 49085 *Fax:* 269-429-3852
hq@asabe.org
www.asabe.org
An educational and scientific organization dedicated to the advancement of agricultural, food, and biological systems, with members in more than 100 countries.
Founded: 1907
Sue E. Nokes, President
Darrin J. Drollinger, Executive Director

150 **American Society of Civil Engineers (ASCE)**
1801 Alexander Bell Drive 703-295-6300
Reston, VA 20191 800-548-2723
customercare@asce.org
www.asce.org
Represents members of the civil engineering profession worldwide, and aims to protect and restore the natural environment.
Founded: 1852 150,000 Members
K.N. Gunalan, President
Thomas W. Smith III, Executive Director

151 **American Society of Safety Engineers (ASSP)**
520 N. Northwest Hwy 847-699-2929
Park Ridge, IL 60068 *Fax:* 847-768-3434
customerservice@asse.org
www.asse.org
The oldest and largest professional safety organization whose members are dedicated to creating safer work environments and protecting people, property, and the environment.
Founded: 1911 38,000 Members
Jennifer McNelly, Chief Executive Officer
Tim Fisher, Standards

152 **American Society of Sanitary Engineering (ASSE)**
18927 Hickory Creek Drive 708-995-3019
Suite 220 info@asse-plumbing.org
Mokena, IL 60448 www.asse-plumbing.org
A nonprofit organization that is comprised of individuals and sustaining members who represent all disciplines of the plumbing industry.
Founded: 1906
Tom Palkon, Executive Director
Scott Hamilton, Senior Director

153 **Association for Environmental Health and Sciences Foundation**
150 Fearing Street 413-549-5170
Suite 21 *Fax:* 413-549-0579
Amherst, MA 01002 paul@aehs.com
www.aehsfoundation.org
The AEHS Foundation was created to facilitate communication among professionals concerned with soil protection and water assessment.
Founded: 2009 600 members
Paul Kostecki, Executive Director
Ed Calabrese, Editor-in-Chief

154 **Association of Energy Engineers (AEE)**
3168 Mercer University Drive 770-447-5083
Atlanta, GA 30341 *Fax:* 770-446-3969
info@aeecenter.org
www.aeecenter.org
Nonprofit professional society that promotes the scientific and educational interests of those in the energy industry. The association offers conferences, journals, books and certification programs in support of sustainabledevelopment.
Founded: 1977 18,000 members
Bill Kent, Executive Director
Michael Hewson, Creative Director

155 **Association of Environmental Engineering and Science Professors (AEESP)**
AEESP Business Office 202-640-6591
1211 Connecticut Ave NW, Suite 650 *Fax:* 217-355-9232
Washington, DC 20036 bschorr@aeesp.org
www.aeesp.org
The association is made up of professors who provide education in the sciences and technologies of environmental protection.
Founded: 1963
Karl G. Linden, President
Brian Schorr, Business Contact

156 **Environmental and Engineering Geophysical Society (EEGS)**
1391 Speer Blvd. 303-531-7517
Suite 450 staff@eegs.org
Denver, CO 80204 www.eegs.org
An applied scientific organization that promotes the science of geophysics as it is applied to environmental and engineering problems.
Founded: 1992 650 Members
Kathie Barstnar, Executive Director
Jackie Jacoby, Managing Director

157 **Institute of Noise Control Engineering (INCE-USA)**
11130 Sunrise Valley Drive 703-234-4124
Suite 350 *Fax:* 703-435-4390
Reston, VA 20191 ibo@inceusa.org
www.inceusa.org
A non-profit professional organization that promotes noise control solutions to environmental, product, machinery, industrial and other noise problems.
Joseph M. Cuschieri, Executive Director
Beatrice Barry, Business Manager

158 **National Ground Water Association (NWGA)**
601 Dempsey Road 614-898-7791
Westerville, OH 43081 800-551-7379
Fax: 614-898-7786
ngwa@ngwa.org
www.ngwa.org
Works to provide and protect the world's ground water resources; enhance the skills and credibility of all ground water professionals; develop and exchange industry knowledge and promote the ground water industry and understanding ofground water resources.
Founded: 1948
Scott King, President

159 **National Registry of Environmental Professionals (NREP)**
PO Box 2099 224-277-8594
Glenview, IL 60025-6099 *Fax:* 847-724-4223
customerservice@nrep.org
www.nrep.org
The NREP are dedicated to enhancing the recognition of those who possess the education and experience as qualified environmental and safety professionals.
Founded: 1987 15,000 Members
Christopher A. Young, Executive Director

160 **NatureServe**
2511 Richmond Highway 703-908-1800
Suite 930 *Fax:* 703-229-1670
Arlington, VA 22202 info@natureserve.org
www.natureserve.org
Provides the scientific basis for conservation action. Collects and manages local information on plants, animals and ecosystems and develops related information products, data management tools and conservation services.
Sean O'Brien, President & CEO
Healy Hamilton, Chief Scientist

National: Environmental Health

161 **Action on Smoking and Health (ASH)**
1250 Connecticut Avenue NW 202-659-4310
7th Floor *Fax:* 202-289-7166
Washington, DC 20036 info@ash.org
ash.org
Organized to use the power of the law to protect the rights of nonsmokers. Emphasis is placed on legal efforts to protect nonsmokers and to get courts to support the rights of nonsmokers. Also conducts educational and awarenesscampaigns regarding the problem of smoking and the rights of nonsmokers.
Laurent Huber, Executive Director
Chris Bostic, Deputy Director, Policy

162 **American Academy of Environmental Medicine (AAE)**
6505 E. Central Avenue 316-684-5500
Suite 296 *Fax:* 316-684-5709
Wichita, KS 67206 defox@aaemonline.org
www.aaemonline.org
The Academy focuses on the study of interactions between human individuals and their environment, and the environmental impact on human health. The Academy is comprised primarily of medical professionals who sponsor publications,seminars and courses. A newsletter and journal are among the organization's publications.
De Rodgers-Fox, Executive Director

163 **American Association of Poison Control Centers (AAPCC)**
515 King Street 800-222-1222
Suite 510 info@aapcc.org
Alexandria, VA 22314 www.aapcc.org
A nonprofit national organization that represents the poison control centers of the United States and the interests of poison prevention and treatment of poisoning.
Founded: 1958
Steve Kaminski, Executive Director
Leslie Sandler, VP, Certification

164 **American Board of Environmental Medicine (ABEM)**
65 Wehrle Drive 716-833-2213
Buffalo, NY 14225 *Fax:* 716-833-2244
www.americanboardofenvironmentalmedicine.org
To establish and maintain the educational and testing criteria for board certification to ensure optimal standard and quality of the environmental physician.
Dr. Phil Ranhein, President

165 **American Board of Industrial Hygiene (ABIH)**
6005 W St Joseph Highway 517-321-2638
Suite 300 *Fax:* 517-321-4624
Lansing, MI 48917 abih@abih.org
www.abih.org
Certifies professionals in the practice of industrial hygiene. Responsible for ensuring high-quality certification application and examination processes, certifcation maintenance and ethics governance and enforcement.
Ulric K. Chung, Chief Executive Officer
Ron Drafta, Examination Contact

166 **American College of Occupational and Environmental Medicine (ACOEM)**
25 NW Point Blvd 847-818-1800
Suite 700 *Fax:* 847-818-9266
Elk Grove Village, IL 60007-1030 www.acoem.org
Made up of physicians in industry, government, academia, private practice and the military, who promote the health of workers through preventive medicine, clinical care, research and education.
Bill Bruce, Executive Director
Lucy Free, Director, Governance

167 **American Council on Science and Health**
1995 Broadway 212-362-7044
Suite 202 866-905-2694
New York, NY 10023-5882 *Fax:* 212-362-4919
acsh@acsh.org
www.acsh.org
A consumer education consortium concerned with issues related to food, nutrition, chemicals, pharmaceuticals, lifestyle, the environment and health.
Founded: 1978
Josh Bloom, Acting President
Alex Berezow, VP, Scientific Affairs

168 **American Industrial Hygiene Association (AIHA)**
3141 Fairview Park Drive 703-849-8888
Suite 777 *Fax:* 703-207-3561
Falls Church, VA 22042 infonet@aiha.org
www.aiha.org
To promote the highest quality of occupational and environmental health and safety within the workplace and the community through advocacy and the provision of services and tools to enhance the professional practice of our members.
Lawrence D. Sloan, Chief Executive Officer
Peter Hanley, Managing Dir., Technology

169 **American Society for Environmental History (ASEH)**
UIC Department of History
601 S Morgan Street dspatz@aseh.net
MC 198 aseh.net
Chicago, IL 60607-7109
Promotes historical research and education on environmental matters, as a means of better understanding human interactions with the natural world. Affiliated with the Forest History Society, which co-publishes the Environmental Historyjournal.
David Spatz, Executive Director

170 **Association for Environmental Health and Sciences Foundation**
150 Fearing Street 413-549-5170
Suite 21 *Fax:* 413-549-0579
Amherst, MA 01002 paul@aehs.com
www.aehsfoundation.org
The AEHS Foundation was created to facilitate communication among professionals concerned with soil protection and water assessment.
Founded: 2009 600 members
Paul Kostecki, Executive Director
Ed Calabrese, Editor-in-Chief

171 **Association of Occupational and Environmental Clinics (AOEC)**
1010 Vermont Ave. NW 202-347-4976
#513 888-347-2632
Washington, DC 20005 *Fax:* 202-347-4950
aoec@aoec.org
www.aoec.org
Non-profit organization of over 60 clinics and 250 individuals, committed to improving the practice of occupational and environmental health through information sharing and collaborative research.
Founded: 1987 $500/Year
Ingrid Denis, Program Coordinator
Katherine H Kirkland, Executive Director

172 **Beyond Pesticides**
701 E Street SE 202-543-5450
Suite 200 *Fax:* 202-543-4791
Washington, DC 20003 info@beyondpesticides.org
www.beyondpesticides.org
Beyond Pesticides works with allies in protecting public health and the environment to lead the transition to a world free of toxic pesticides.
Jay Feldman, Executive Director
Drew Toher, Director, Policy

173 **Bonneville Environmental Foundation**
1500 SW 1st Avenue 503-248-1905
Suite 885 866-233-8247
Portland, OR 97201 *Fax:* 503-248-1908
info@b-e-f.org
www.b-e-f.org
Strives to protect the globe against climate change and the degradation of world freshwater resources through products, programs, and custom solutions for businesses.
Founded: 1998
Angus Duncan, Founder & President
Todd Reeve, Chief Executive Officer

174 **Center for Health, Environment and Justice (CHEJ)**
7139 Shreve Road 703-237-2249
Falls Church, VA 22046 *Fax:* 703-237-8389
info@chej.org
www.chej.org
Works to build healthy communities, with social justice, economic well-being, and democratic governance.
Founded: 1981
Sharon Franklin, Chief of Operations
Stephen Lester, Science Director

175 **Commonweal**
PO Box 316 415-868-0970
Bolinas, CA 94924 commonweal@commonweal.org
www.commonweal.org
A health and environment research institute that conducts programs that contribute to human and ecosystem health. The Commonweal Health and Environment Program focuses on environmental contaminants.
Founded: 1976
Michael Lerner, President & Co-Founder
Arlene Allsman, Chief Operating Officer

176 **Corporate Accountability International**
10 Milk Street 617-695-2525
Suite 610 800-688-8797
Boston, MA 00210 *Fax:* 617-695-2626
info@corporateaccountability.org
www.corporateaccountability.org
Aims to stop large corporations from damaging democracy, human rights, and the environment.
Founded: 1977
Patti Lynn, Executive Director
Melissa Hale Woodman, Dir., Strategic Partnerships

177 **Environmental Action**
294 Washington Street 800-401-6511
Suite 500 environmental-action.org
Boston, MA 02108
Engages in activisim around environmental concerns, with an emphasis on holding corporations and members of the government accountable.
Founded: 1970

178 **Environmental Defense Fund (EDF)**
257 Park Avenue South 212-505-2100
New York, NY 10010 *Fax:* 212-505-2375
www.edf.org
Dedicated to protecting the environmental rights of all people, including future generations. Among these rights are clean air, clean water, healthy, nourishing food and a flourishing ecosystem. Advocates solutions based on science,even when it leads in unfamiliar directions. Works to create solutions that win lasting political, economic and social support because they are bipartisan, efficient and fair.
Founded: 1967
Fred Krupp, President
Catherine Nardone, Chief Development Officer

179 **Environmental Hazards Management Institute (EHMI)**
10 New Market Road 603-868-1496
Durham, NH 03821 *Fax:* 603-868-1547
info@ehmi.org
www.ehmi.org
An independent, nonprofit organization dedicated to understanding enhancement and preservation of the environment. A catalyst for informed environmental decision making by gathering, refining, and disseminating objective information toall stakeholders with emphasis on the role played by individuals and communities of individuals.
Founded: 1979
Alan John Borner, Founder & CEO

180 **Environmental Information Association (EIA)**
6935 Wisconsin Avenue 301-961-4999
Suite 306 888-343-4342
Chevy Chase, MD 20815-6112 *Fax:* 301-961-3094
info@eia-usa.org
www.eia-usa.org
A nonprofit organization dedicated to providing environmental information to individuals, members, and industry. They specialize in the dissemination of information about the abatement of asbestos and lead based paint, and about safetyand health issues, analytical issues and environmental site assessments.
Brent Kynoch, Managing Director
Kelly Rutt, Director, Development

181 **Friends of the Earth**
1100 15th Street NW 202-783-7400
11th Floor 877-843-8687
Washington, DC 20005 *Fax:* 202-783-0444
foe@foe.org
www.foe.org
National nonprofit advocacy organization dedicated to protecting the planet from environmental degradation; preserving biological, cultural and ethnic diversity, and empowering citizens to have an influential voice in decisionsaffecting the quality of their environment and their lives.
Founded: 1969
Erich Pica, President
Michelle Chan, Vice-President, Programs

182 **Group Against Smog & Pollution (GASP)**
1133 South Braddock Avenue 412-924-0604
Suite 1A info@gasp-pgh.org
Edgewood, PA 15218 gasp-pgh.org
The Group Against Smog and Pollution is a nonprofit organization dedicated to the improvement of air quality through public meetings, engagement with the press, educational events, permit reviews, and other means.
Founded: 1969
Rachel Fillipini, Executive Director
Suzanne Seppi, Project Manager

183 **Holistic Management International (HMI)**
5941 Jefferson St. NE 505-842-5252
Suite B *Fax:* 505-843-7900
Albuquerque, NM 87109 hmi@holisticmanagement.org
www.holisticmanagement.org
Seeks to help farmers, ranchers, and pastoralists enhance the efficiency, natural health, productivity and profitability of the land; increase natural annual profits; provide a framework for stakeholders to work together toward acommon future; and enable development agencies working with marginalized farmers or pastoral people to break the cycle of food and water insecurity.
Founded: 1984
Ann Adams, Executive Director
Kathy Harris, Director, Programs

184 **International Society of Environmental Forensics**
150 Fearing Street 413-549-5170
Suite 21 *Fax:* 413-549-0579
Amherst, MA 01002 www.environmentalforensics.org
The society aims to provide training on environmental contamination of areas of air, water, soil, and biota. Also publishes the journal Environmental Forensics.

185 **National Center for Healthy Housing (NCHH)**
10320 Little Patuxent Parkway 410-992-0712
Suite 500 www.centerforhealthyhousing.org
Columbia, MD 21044
Formerly known as the National Center for Lead-Safe Housing, it deveops and promotes practical methods to protect children fron environmental health hazards in homes while preserving affordable housing.
Founded: 1992
Amanda L. Reddy, Executive Director
Michelle Harvey, Chief Operating Officer

186 **National Environmental Health Association (NEHA)**
720 S Colorado Boulevard 303-756-9090
Suite 1000-N *Fax:* 303-691-9490
Denver, CO 80246-1926 staff@neha.org
www.neha.org
Represents all of environmental health and protection from terrorism and all-hazards preparedness, to food safety and protection and on site wastewater systems. Over 4,500 members and the profession are served by the associationthrough its Journal of Environmental Health, Annual Education Conference and Exhibition credentialing programs, research and development activities and other services.
Founded: 1937
David T. Dyjack, Executive Director

187 **National Environmental Health Science and Protection Accreditation Council (EHAC)**
PO Box 66057 206-522-5272
Burien, WA 98166 executive.director@nehspac.org
nehspac.org
Promotes a high quality education for persons studying environmental health science and protection; promotes commonality in coverage of basic concepts of environmental health science and protection education; and promotes undergraduatecurricula of a quality and content compatible with admission prerequisites of graduate programs in environmental health science and protection.
Leslie D. Mitchell, Executive Director

188 **Physicians for Social Responsibility (PSR)**
1111 14th St., NW 202-667-4260
Suite 700 *Fax:* 202-667-4201
Washington, DC 20005 psrnatl@psr.org
www.psr.org
A non-profit advocacy organization that is the medical and public health voice for policies to prevent nuclear war and proliferation and to slow, stop and reverse global warming and toxic degradation of the environment.
Jeff Carter, Executive Director
Barbara Gottlieb, Dir., Environment & Health

189 **Second Nature Inc.**
18 Tremont Street 617-722-0036
Suite 608 *Fax:* 617-259-1734
Boston, MA 02108 info@secondnature.org
www.secondnature.org
Dedicated to advancing our quality of life by demostrating the close links between human health and the environment. The center's goal is to make the relationship of environment to human health an integral part of medical education.
Timothy Carter, President
Michele Madia, Director, Programs

190 **Soil Health Institute**
2803 Slater Road 919-230-0303
Suite 115 soilhealthinstitute.org
Morrisville, NC 27560
The Soil Health Institue is an independent, nonprofit organization focused on fundamental and applied research and ensuring its adoption.
Founded: 2013
C. Wayne Honeycutt, President & CEO

191 **Way of Nature Spiritual Fellowship**
PO Box 268 520-730-8271
Crestone, CO 81131 info.wayofnature@gmail.com
www.sacredpassage.com
Way of Nature is now a global fellowship of people of all ages and nationalities. Founded by John P. Milton, Milton has guided thousands of people into the wilderness, sharing with them different ways to connect with nature on a deepand spiritual level.
John P. Milton, President

National: Gaming & Hunting

192 **American Bass Association**
12340 Seal Beach Blvd. 714-423-4532
Suite B120 info@americanbass.com
Seal Beach, CA 90740 www.americanbass.co
American Bass develops programs to protect and improve the environment and natural resources while providing high value to sponsors and advertisers through quality run events and promotions. They are also involved in stocking bass inpublic lakes, planting trees, protection of natural spawning and juvenile fish.
Founded: 1983
David Plotnik, President & Founder

193 **American Birding Association (ABA)**
93 Clinton Street 302-838-3660
Suite ABA; PO Box 744 800-850-2473
Delaware City, DE 19706 *Fax:* 302-838-3651
info@aba.org
www.aba.org
The Association represents the interests of birdwatchers and helps birders increase their knowledge and skills of birding. ABA also contributes to bird conservation and promotes field-birding skills through meetings, workshops,equipment, and guided involvement in birding, promoting national and international birders networks and publications.
Founded: 1969
Jeffrey A. Gordon, President & CEO
John Lowry, Marketing & Advertising

194 **American Eagle Foundation**
PO Box 333 865-429-0157
Pigeon Forge, TN 37868 800-232-4537
Fax: 865-429-4743
eaglemail@eagles.org
www.eagles.org
Not-for-profit organization of concerned citizens and professionals who develop and conduct bald eagle and environmental recovery programs in the United States and assist private, state and federal projects that do the same.
Founded: 1985
Jim Marietta, President
Spencer Williams, Chief Operations Officer

195 **American Fisheries Society (AFS)**
425 Barlow Place 301-897-8616
Suite 110 *Fax:* 301-897-8096
Bethesda, MD 20814-2144 main@fisheries.org
www.fisheries.org
Promotes the research and management of fisheries resources, is dedicated to the advancement of fisheries sciences and professionals, and the sustainability of aquatic ecosystems.
Founded: 1870 8,000 Members
Douglas Austen, Executive Director
Daniel Cassidy, Deputy Executive Director

196 **American Humane Association**
1400 16th Street NW 800-227-4645
Suite 360 info@americanhumane.org
Washington, DC 20036 www.americanhumane.org
The American Humane Association is committed to preventing cruelty,abuse, neglect and exploitation of children and animals and to assure that their interests and well-being are fully, effectively, and humanely guaranteed by an awareand caring society.
Founded: 1877
Robin R. Ganzert, President/CEO
Jack Hubbard, Chief Operating Officer

197 **American Medical Fly Fishing Association (AMFFA)**
PO Box 768 570-769-7375
Lock Haven, PA 17745 www.amffa.org
The Association began with the idea of combining professional medical interests with the interest of fly fishing to promote conservation of the natural resources as pertains to the sport and support the causes and efforts orientedtowards these intersts.
Founded: 1969 $35 annually
Veryl F. Frye MD, Secretary-Treasurer

198 **American Pheasant and Waterfowl Society (APWS)**
7153 Piney Island Road jantrader62@gmail.com
Chincoteague, VA 23336 www.apwsbirds.com
To promote the rights and interest of the members to keep and rear upland aquatic and ornamental birds while collecting pertinent and scientific data and information relating to these rights.
Founded: 1936 $25/Year
Eugene Goss, President
E.T. Trader, Treasurer

199 **American Society of Ichthyologists and Herpetologists (ASIH)**
810 E 10th Street 785-865-9405
Lawrence, KA 66044 800-627-0326
asih@allenpress.com
www.asih.org
ASIH is dedicated to the scientific study of fishes, amphibians and reptiles. Its mission is to increase knowledge about these organisms through publications, conferences, and symposia, and to encourage young scientists who will makefuture advances in these fields.
Founded: 1913
Chris Beachy, President
Prosanta Chakrabarty, Secretary

200 **American Society of Mammalogists (ASM)**
PO Box 4973 785-550-6904
Topeka, KS 66604 cclassi@mammalsociety.org
www.mammalsociety.org
Established for the purpose of promoting interest in the conservation, education and resource management of mammals.
Founded: 1919 2,500 Members
Enrique P. Lessa, President
Cody Thompson, Program Director

201 **Animal Welfare Institute (AWI)**
900 Pennsylvania Ave SE 202-337-2332
Washington, DC 20003 *Fax:* 202-446-2131
awi@awionline.org
www.awionline.org
AWI works to alleviate the suffering inflicted on animals by humans including factory farming, experimentation, commercial whaling, as well as the impact on endangered species and their habitat.
Founded: 1951
Nadia Adawi, Executive Director
Nancy Glaney, Director, Government Affairs

202 **Association of Federal Wildlife Officers**
theafwo@gmail.com
www.nwroa.org
Dedicated to the protection of wildlife, the enforcement of federal wildlife law, the fostering of cooperation and communication among federal wildlife officers, and the perpetuation, enhancement and defense of the wildlife enforcementprofession.
Jane Whaley, President
Amanda Posick, Vice President

203 **Birds of Prey Foundation**
2290 South 104th Street 303-460-0674
Broomfield, CO 80020 raptor@birds-of-prey.org
www.birds-of-prey.org
Fosters compassion and seeks protecton for injured and orphaned raptors such as eagles, hawks, falcons and owls, and improves the quality of care through education, observation, and invention.
Founded: 1981
Heidi Bucknam, Executive Director

204 **Boone and Crockett Club**
250 Station Drive 406-542-1888
Missoula, MT 59801 888-840-4868
Fax: 406-542-0784
bcclub@boone-crockett.org
www.boone-crockett.org
Organization founded by Theodore Roosevelt with the vision of establishing a coalition of dedicated conservationists and sportsmen to provide leadership in the issues affecting hunting, wildlife and wildlife habitat.
Founded: 1887
Tony A. Schoonen, Chief of Staff
Justin Spring, Director, Big Game Records

205 **Born Free USA**
8737 Colesville Road 301-448-1407
Suite 715 info@bornfreeusa.org
Silver Spring, MD 20910 www.bornfreeusa.org
A national animal advocacy nonprofit organization established to advocate for the protection of animals from cruelty and exploitation. Its primary campaign areas include: farmed animals, companion animals, compassionate consumerism,wildlife protection, and animals used in entertainment. Also operates a 186-acre primate sanctuary. Merged with the Animal Protection Institute in 2007.
Founded: 2002
Angela Grimes, Chief Executive Officer
Garrett Johnson, Director, Communications

206 **Cetacean Society International**
PO Box 330298 860-313-0711
West Hartford, CT 06133-0298 info@csiwhalesalive.org
www.csiwhalesalive.org
All-volunteer, nonprofit conservation, educational and research organization to benefit whales, dolphins, porpoises and the marine environment. Promotes education and conservation programs, including whale and dolphin watching, andnoninvasive, benign research. Website gives access to a newsletter archive, and a whale adoption program.
Founded: 1974
David Kaplan, President
George A. Upton, Vice-President

207 **Ducks Unlimited (DU)**
One Waterfowl Way 901-758-3825
Memphis, TN 38120 800-453-8257
www.ducks.org

The mission is to fulfill the annual life cycle needs of North American waterfowl by protecting, enhancing, restoring and managing important wetlands and associated uplands.
Founded: 1937
Rogers Hoyt, Jr., President
Dale Hall, CEO

208 **EcoHealth Alliance**
460 West 34th Street 212-380-4460
17th Floor *Fax:* 212-380-4465
New York, NY 10001-2320 homeoffice@ecohealthalliance.org
www.ecohealthalliance.org
Works in the United States and worldwide to save threatened species from extinction, safeguard human health from the emergence of diesease, and promote conservation by protecting ecosystems.
Founded: 1971
Peter Daszak, President
William Karesh, EVP, Health & Policy

209 **Friends of the Australian Koala Foundation**
112 East 17th Street 212-967-8200
Suite #1W *Fax:* 212-967-7292
New York, NY 10003 akf@savethekoala.com
www.savethekoala.com
The AFK is a non profit organization dedicated to the conservation, management, research, and community education of koalas and their habitat.
Founded: 1986
Deborah Tabart, CEO, Chair
Lorraine O'Keefe, Director

210 **Friends of the Earth**
1100 15th Street NW 202-783-7400
11th Floor 877-843-8687
Washington, DC 20005 *Fax:* 202-783-0444
foe@foe.org
www.foe.org
National nonprofit advocacy organization dedicated to protecting the planet from environmental degradation; preserving biological, cultural and ethnic diversity, and empowering citizens to have an influential voice in decisionsaffecting the quality of their environment and their lives.
Founded: 1969
Erich Pica, President
Michelle Chan, Vice-President, Programs

211 **Fund for Animals**
1255 23rd Street NW 866-482-3708
Suite 460 info@fundforanimals.org
Washington, DC 20037 www.fundforanimals.org
The Fund for Animals was founded by author/humanitarian Cleveland Amory and in 2005 merged with The Humane Society of the United States. It is dedicated to protecting animals and providing veterinary and rehabilitative needs.
Founded: 1967
Melissa Seide Rubin, President
G. Thomas Waite III, Treasurer

212 **Game Conservancy USA**
49 Locust Ave 203-966-4187
Suite 104 *Fax:* 203-661-7997
New Canaan, CT 06840 info@gcusa.org
www.gcusa.org
Seeks to increase support for research of the conservation of game and wildlife habitats in the US and UK through an expanding membership base.
Ronald N. Beck, President
Robert Hatch, Director

213 **Hawk Migration Association of North America (HMANA)**
28916 Millbrook Road info@hmana.org
Farmington Hills, MI 48334 www.hmana.org
To conserve raptor populations through the scientific study, enjoyment and appreciation of raptor migration.
Founded: 1974
Carolyn Hoffman, Chair
Jane Ferreyra, Executive Director

214 **HawkWatch International**
2240 South 900 East 801-484-6808
Salt Lake City, UT 84106 800-726-4295
Fax: 801-484-6810
hwi@hawkwatch.org
hawkwatch.org
HawkWatch International is a non-profit organization that works to protect raptors and their environment through scientific research and public education.
Founded: 1986
Nikki Wayment, Executive Director
Christina Castellano, Director, Development

215 **Humane Society of the United States (HSUS)**
1255 23rd Street, NW 202-452-1100
Suite 450 866-720-2676
Washington, DC 20037 www.humanesociety.org
HSUS is the nation's largest animal-protection organization. It is dedicated to promoting the humane treatment of animals, to foster respect, understanding, and compassion for all creatures.
Founded: 1954
Kitty Block, President & CEO
G. Thomas Waite III, Chief Operating Officer

216 **International Association for Bear Research and Management (IBA)**
University Hall 907-459-7238
Room 309 *Fax:* 907-451-9723
Missoula, MT 59812 alexander.kopatz@bearbiology.org
www.bearbiology.com
A volunteer, nonprofit organization open to professional biologists, wildlife managers and others dedicated to the conservation of all species of bears. Supports the scientific management of bears through research and distribution ofinformation.
Founded: 1968 550+ members
Andreas Zedrosser, President
Alexander Kopatz, Secretary

217 **International Hunter Education Association (IHEA-USA)**
800 East 73rd Avenue 303-430-7233
Unit 3 *Fax:* 303-430-7236
Denver, CO 80229 www.ihea-usa.org
Operates programs across the U.S. teaching hunting and shooting safety and responsibility. Courses cover firearm safety, bowhunting, wildlife management, field care, responsible hunting, landowner relations, wildlife identification,and more. Affiliated with the Association of Fish and Wildlife Agencies and local state fish and hunter education programs.
Founded: 1949 $30 annually
Marisa Lee Futral, President
David Allen, Executive Director

218 **International Wild Waterfowl Association (IWWA)**
500 Sylvian Heights Park Way 252-826-3186
P.O Box 11 *Fax:* 425-397-8136
Scotland Neck, NC 27874 info@shwpark.com
www.wildwaterfowl.org
Committed to protecting and enhancing wild waterfowl habitats. Supports the captive breeding and restoration of endangered species, and the establishment and maintenance of genetically diverse and disease-free captive populations ofendangered waterfowl.
Founded: 1958
Ian Gereg, President
Anne Lemenager, Secretary

219 **International Wildlife Conservation Society (IWCS)**
PO Box 802 310-344-7057
Pacific City, OR 97135 cathy@internationalwildlife.org
www.internationalwildlife.org
The Society has created a Wildlife Reserve that provides habitat to a variety of mammals, birds, fish and reptiles. The Society continues to increase the awareness of wildlife conservation, preservation and research.
Founded: 1968
Cathy Griffin, Contact

220 **International Wolf Center**
1396 Highway 169 218-365-4695
Ely, MN 55731-8129 *Fax:* 218-365-3318
www.wolf.org
The International Wolf Center advances the survival of the wolf populations by teaching the public about wolves and their relationship to wildlands and humans for the benefit of their future.
Founded: 1985
Lori Schmidt, Wolf Curator
April Wamhoff, Manager, Office & Facility

221 **Last Chance Forever**
PO Box 460993 210-499-4080
San Antonio, TX 78246-0993 *Fax:* 210-499-4305
info@lastchanceforever.org
www.lastchanceforever.org
Dedicated to the rehabilitation of sick, injured and orphaned birds of prey, scientific investigation, and educating the public.
Founded: 1978
John A. Karger, Executive Director, Founder
Kelly Rayner, Volunteer Contact

222 **Livestock Conservancy**
33 Hillsboro St 919-542-5704
PO Box 477 info@livestockconservancy.org
Pittsboro, NC 27312 livestockconservancy.org
Protects the genetic diversity of livestock and poultry species through the conservation of endangered breeds.
Founded: 1977
Allison Martin, Executive Director
Jeannette Beranger, Senior Program Manager

223 **Muskies, Inc.**
PO Box 1509 888-710-8286
Waukesha, WI 53187-1509 www.muskiesinc.org
Supports growth and interest in the sport of muskie fishing. Works to protect existing fisheries, to develop new fisheries, and to support conservation practices and research.
Founded: 1966 6,000+ members
Jim Ashton, President

224 **NAWEOA - Conservation Law Enforcement**
Leaf River, IL
Organization of wildlife conservation law enforcement officers, promoting professionalism and excellence through training, networking, and professional recognition.
8,000+ members
Shawn Farrell, President
Steve Beltran, Secretary-Treasurer

225 **National Bison Association (NBA)**
8690 Wolff Ct. 303-292-2833
Suite 200 *Fax:* 303-845-9081
Westminster, CO 80031 info@bisoncentral.com
www.bisoncentral.com
A nonprofit association which promotes the preservation, production and marketing of bison. Activities and services serve to better inform and educate the general public about bison and to create and sustainable future for theindustry.
Founded: 1995 1,100+ members
Dave Carter, Executive Director
Jim Matheson, Assistant Director

226 **National Endangered Species Act Reform Coalition (NESARC)**
1050 Thomas Jefferson Street NW 202-333-7481
6th Floor *Fax:* 202-338-2416
Washington, DC 20007 nesarc@vnf.com
www.nesarc.org
Dedicated to promoting effective legislative and administrative improvements to the ESA that protect fish, wildlife and plant populations as well as responsible land, water and resource management.
Jordan A. Smith, Executive Director
Joseph B. Nelson, Lead Counsel

227 **National Rifle Association of America (NRA)**
11250 Waples Mill Road 800-672-3888
Fairfax, VA 22030 www.nra.org
Gun rights organization that serves to protect the Second Amendment rights of Americans as well as offer firearm educational programs.
Founded: 1871 5 million+ members
Carolyn Meadows, President
Wayne LaPierre, Chief Executive Officer

228 **National Shooting Sports Foundation (NSSF)**
11 Mile Hill Road 203-426-1320
Newtown, CT 06470-2359 *Fax:* 203-426-1087
www.nssf.org
Leading trade association of the firearms and recreational shooting sports industry. The NSSF manages a variety of programs designed to promote a better understanding of and a more active participaqtion in the shooting sports.
Founded: 1961
Stephen L. Sanetti, President & CEO
Hugh C. Wiley, COO

229 **National Trappers Association (NTA)**
2815 Washington Avenue 812-277-9670
Bedford, IN 47421 866-680-8727
Fax: 812-277-9672
ntaheadquarters@nationaltrappers.com
www.nationaltrappers.com
To promote conservation, legislation and administrative procedures; to save and faithfully defend from waste the natural resources of the United States; to promote environmental education programs; and to promote a continued annual furharvest using the best tools.
Founded: 1959
Chris McAllister, President
John Daniel, Vice President

230 **National Walking Horse Association (NWHA)**
PO Box 7111 859-252-6942
Jacksonville, NC 28540 office@nwha.com
www.nwha.com
An alliance of people committed to preserving and fostering the natural abilities and welfare of the Walking Horse while improving the lives of horses and people by encouraging responsibility and sportsmanship.
Amy Spinelli, President
Kimberly O'Connor, Chief Administrative Officer

231 **National Wildlife Federation**
11100 Wildlife Center Drive 800-822-9919
Reston, VA 20190 www.nwf.org
The National Wildlife Federation is the largest member-supported conservation group, uniting individuals, organizations, businesses and government to protect wildlife, wild places and the environment.
Founded: 1936
Collin O'Mara, President & CEO
Mustafa Santiago Ali, VP, Environmental Justice

232 **Native American Fish and Wildlife Society**
8515 Pearl Street 303-466-1725
Suite 203 866-890-7258
Thornton, CO 80229 *Fax:* 303-466-5414
Fax: 866-889-4956
klynch@nafws.org
www.nafws.org
A Native American non-profit organization assisting with the conservation, protection, and enhancement of fish and wildlife resources through conferences, training, summer youth programs and information dissemination.
Founded: 1983
Julie Thorstsenson, Executive Director
Elveda Martinez, President of the Board

233 North American Bear Center
1926 Highway 169 218-365-7879
PO Box 161 877-365-7879
Ely, MN 55731 info@bear.org
bear.org
To advance the long-term survival of bears by replacing misconceptions with scientific facts about their role in ecosystems and their relations with humans.
Lynn Rogers, Chair
Joe Edlund, Vice Chair

234 North American Native Fishes Association
info@nanfa.org
www.nanfa.org
NANFA is dedicated to the enjoyment, study and conservation of the continent's native fishes. Strives to disseminate knowledge about fishes and their habitats and to promote the conservation and the restoration of natural habitats.
Fritz Rohde, President
Brian Zimmerman, Vice President

235 Organization of Wildlife Planners
517-284-6199
wildlifeplanners@gmail.com
www.wildlifeplanners.org
A professional organization concerned with the management and future of government agencies that manage fish and wildlife populations and habitat. The purpose of OWP is to improve the management of fish and wildlife agencies.
Founded: 1978
Ann LeClaire-Mitchell, President
Shawna Wilson, Organization Manager

236 PAWS Wildlife Rehabilitation Center & Hospital
15305 44th Avenue West 425-787-2500
PO Box 1037 *Fax:* 425-742-5711
Lynnwood, WA 98087 www.paws.org/wildlife
Rehabilitating injured and orphaned wildlife, provides shelter and adoption for animals. PAWS educates people to recognize the intrinsic value of animals and make choices that demonstrate compassion and respect.
Founded: 1967
Annette Laico, Chief Executive Officer
James J. Marshall-Ward, Chief Operating Officer

237 Pacific Whale Foundation
300 Maalaea Road 808-249-8811
612 Front St, Lahaina, HI 800-942-5311
Wailuku, HI 96793 www.pacificwhale.org
Mission is to promote appreciation, understanding and protection of whales, dolphins, coral reefs, and the planet's oceans by educating the public from a scientific perspective about the marine environment. Offers ocean ecotoursthrough PacWhale Eco-Adventures.
Founded: 1980
Eric Brown, PhD, MS, Chair
Kristie Wrigglesworth, Executive Director

238 People for the Ethical Treatment of Animals (PETA)
501 Front Street 757-622-7382
Norfolk, VA 23510 *Fax:* 757-622-0457
info@peta.org
www.peta.org
PETA is the largest animal rights organization in the world. Dedicated to establishing and protecting the rights of all animals. Operates under the principal that animals are not ours to eat, wear, experiment on, or use forentertainment.
Founded: 1980
Ingrid Newkirk, President
Tracy Reiman, Executive Vice President

239 Pheasants Forever
1783 Buerkle Circle 651-773-2000
St. Paul, MN 55110 877-773-2070
contact@pheasantsforever.org
www.pheasantsforever.org
A nonprofit organization dedicated to the protection and enhancement of pheasant and other wildlife populations in North America. This mission is carried out through habitat improvement, land management, public awareness, andeducation.
Founded: 1982 149,000 Members
Tim Kessler, Chair
Howard K. Vincent, President & CEO

240 Pope and Young Club
PO Box 548 507-867-4144
Chatfield, MN 55923 admin@pope-young.org
www.pope-young.org
The Club advocates and encourages responsible bowhunting by promoting quality, fair chase hunting, and sound conservation practices.
Founded: 1961
Jim Williams, President
Jason Rounsaville, Executive Director

241 Purple Martin Conservation Association
301 Peinsula Drive 814-833-7656
Suite 6 webadmin@purplemartin.org
Erie, PA 16505 www.purplemartin.org
Nonprofit organization devoted to the scientific study of purple martins, their biology, and habitat requirements.
Founded: 1987
Larry Melcher, Chair
Joe Siegrist, President & CEO

242 RedRover
PO Box 188890 202-452-1100
Sacramento, CA 95818 *Fax:* 916-378-5098
info@RedRover.org
redrover.org
Provides temporary emergency shelter, resources, financial help, and emotional support for animals and people in crisis.
Founded: 1987
Nicole Forsyth, President & CEO
Karly Noel, VP, Operations & Education

243 Safari Club International (SCI)
4800 West Gates Pass Road 520-620-1220
Tucson, AZ 85745-9490 888-486-8724
Fax: 520-622-1205
www.safariclub.org
A leader in wildlife conservation, hunter education, and protecting the freedom to hunt.
Paul Babaz, President
Michael Roqueni, Director, Membership

244 Scientists Center for Animal Welfare (SCAW)
2660 NE Highway 20 301-345-3500
Suite 610-115 *Fax:* 541-383-4655
Bend, OR 97701 info@scaw.com
www.scaw.com
A nonprofit educational association of individuals whose mission is to promote humane care, use, and management of animals involved in research, testing or education in laboratory, agricultural, wildlife or other settings.
Founded: 1978
Randall J. Nelson, PhD, President
Paul G. Braunschweiger, Vice President

245 Sea Shepherd Conservation Society
PO Box 8626 212-220-2302
Alexandria, VA 22306 *Fax:* 818-279-0707
info@seashepherd.org
www.seashepherd.org
This organization is committed to mammal protection and conservation with an immediate goal of shutting down illegal whaling and sealing operations, poaching, shark finning, unlawful habitat destruction, and violations of establishedlaws in the world's oceans.
Founded: 1977
David Hance, Chief Operating Officer
Capt. Lockhart MacLean, Director, Ship Operations

246 **Society of Tympanuchus Cupido Pinnatus (SCTP)**
PO Box 320487 414-559-4278
Franklin, WI 53132 sharptailpoint@earthlink.net
www.prairiegrouse.org/stcp.html
The oldest organization dedicated to conserving and restoring native prairie grouse populations in North America.
Founded: 1961
Peter D. Ziegler, President
Greg Septon, Executive Director

247 **Trout Unlimited**
PO Box 7400 703-522-0200
Woolly Bugger, WV 25438-7400 800-834-2419
Fax: 703-284-9400
trout@tu.org
www.tu.org
This organization seeks to conserve, protect and restore North America's trout and salmon fisheries and their watersheds.
Founded: 1959 300,000 members
Chris Wood, President & CEO
Elizabeth Maclin, Executive Vice President

248 **Trumpeter Swan Society (TSS)**
12615 Rockford Road 763-441-1994
Plymouth, MN 55441-1248 *Fax:* 763-557-4943
ttss@trumpeterswansociety.org
www.trumpeterswansociety.org
Private, nonprofit organization dedicated to assuring the vitality and welfare of wild Trumpeter Swan populations, and to restoring the species to as much of its former range as possible.
Founded: 1968
Carey Smith, President
Margaret Smith, Executive Director

249 **Turtle Island Restoration Network**
9255 Sir Francis Drake Blvd 415-663-8590
Olema, CA 94950 800-859-7283
info@seaturtles.org
www.seaturtles.org
Fights to protect endangered sea turtle populations in ways that meet the ecological needs of the sea turtles and the oceans and inland watersheds that sustain them.
Founded: 1989
Donna Howe, Board Chair
Todd Steiner, Executive Director

250 **US Sportsmen's Alliance**
801 Kingsmill Parkway 614-888-4868
Columbus, OH 43229 *Fax:* 614-888-0326
info@sportsmensalliance.org
www.sportsmensalliance.org
The US Sportsmen's Alliance is a national nonprofit association that protects hunting, fishing and trapping and scientific wildlife management programs.
Founded: 1978
Evan Heusinkveld, President & CEO
Sean Curran, Vice President, Development

251 **Waterfowl USA**
PO Box 500 803-637-5767
Oak Forest, IL 60452 nwfusa@yahoo.com
www.waterfowlusa.org
National nonprofit conservation organization dedicated to using funds for local and state waterfowl projects.
Founded: 1983
Mark Judge, President
Tabatha Cloutier, Executive Director

252 **Whitetails Unlimited (WTU)**
2100 Michigan Street 920-743-6777
PO Box 720 800-274-5471
Sturgeon Bay, WI 54235 *Fax:* 920-743-4658
www.whitetailsunlimited.com
A national nonprofit conservation organization that dedicates their resources to the betterment of the white-tail deer and its environment.
Founded: 1982
Jeffrey Schinkten, President
Peter J. Gerl, Executive Director

253 **Wild Sheep Foundation (WSF)**
412 Pronghorn Trail 406-404-8750
Bozeman, MT 59718 800-653-6297
info@wildsheepfoundation.org
www.wildsheepfoundation.org
The Foundation's mission is to promote and enhance populations of indigenous wild sheep in North America, and to fund programs for the professional management of these populations.
Founded: 1977
Gray Thornton, President & CEO
Kevin Hurley, VP, Conservation

254 **Wilderness Society**
1615 M Street NW 800-843-9453
Washington, DC 20036 action@tws.org
www.wilderness.org
Conservation organization working to protect the nation's shared wildlands and to inspire Americans to care for the wilderness.
Founded: 1935
Jamie Williams, President
Melyssa Watson, Executive Director

255 **Xerces Society for Invertebrate Conservation**
628 NE Broadway 503-232-6639
Suite 200 855-232-6639
Portland, OR 97232 *Fax:* 503-233-6794
info@xerces.org
www.xerces.org
An international non profit organization dedicated to protecting biological diversity through inverterate conservation. Core programs focus on endangered species, protecting pollinators and watershed health.
Founded: 1971
Scott Hoffman Black, Executive Director
Denise Ledgerwood, Director, Grants

National: Habitat Preservation & Land Use

256 **Aldo Leopold Foundation**
E13701 Levee Road 608-355-0279
PO Box 77 *Fax:* 608-356-7309
Baraboo, WI 53913-0077 mail@aldoleopold.org
www.aldoleopold.org
Nonprofit organization that works to promote the philosophy of Aldo Leopold and the land ethic he so eloquently defined in his writing. The foundation actively integrates programs on land stewardship, environmental education andscientific research to promote care of natural resources and have an ethical relationship between people and land.
Founded: 1982
Buddy Huffaker, Executive Director
Jennifer Farnum, Director, Development

257 **American Birding Association (ABA)**
93 Clinton Street 302-838-3660
Suite ABA; PO Box 744 800-850-2473
Delaware City, DE 19706 *Fax:* 302-838-3651
info@aba.org
www.aba.org
The Association represents the interests of birdwatchers and helps birders increase their knowledge and skills of birding. ABA also contributes to bird conservation and promotes field-birding skills through meetings, workshops,equipment, and guided involvement in birding, promoting national and international birders networks and publications.
Founded: 1969
Jeffrey A. Gordon, President & CEO
John Lowry, Marketing & Advertising

258 American Cave Conservation Association (ACCA)
119 E Main Street 270-786-1466
PO Box 409 hiddenrivercave@gmail.com
Horse Cave, KY 42749 hiddenrivercave.com
A national nonprofit association dedicated to the protection of caves, karstlands and groundwater. The ACCA operates the American Cave Museum and Karst Center, an educational center that includes the American Cave Museum and HiddenRiver Cave.
Founded: 1978
David G. Foster, Executive Director
Peggy A Nims, Education Director

259 American Eagle Foundation
PO Box 333 865-429-0157
Pigeon Forge, TN 37868 800-232-4537
Fax: 865-429-4743
eaglemail@eagles.org
www.eagles.org
Not-for-profit organization of concerned citizens and professionals who develop and conduct bald eagle and environmental recovery programs in the United States and assist private, state and federal projects that do the same.
Founded: 1985
Jim Marietta, President
Spencer Williams, Chief Operations Officer

260 American Fisheries Society (AFS)
425 Barlow Place 301-897-8616
Suite 110 *Fax:* 301-897-8096
Bethesda, MD 20814-2144 main@fisheries.org
www.fisheries.org
Promotes the research and management of fisheries resources, is dedicated to the advancement of fisheries sciences and professionals, and the sustainability of aquatic ecosystems.
Founded: 1870 8,000 Members
Douglas Austen, Executive Director
Daniel Cassidy, Deputy Executive Director

261 American Geosciences Institute (AGI)
4220 King Street 703-379-2480
Alexandria, VA 22302-1502 *Fax:* 703-379-7563
agi@americangeosciences.org
www.americangeosciences.org
Provides information services to geoscientists, serves as a voice of shared interests in the profession, plays a major role in strengthening geoscience education, and strives to increase public awareness of the vital role thegeosciences play in society's use of resources and interaction with the environment.
Founded: 1948
Allyson K. Anderson Book, Executive Director
Christopher Keane, Geoscience Contact

262 American Institute of Fishery Research Biologists (AIFRB)
NMFS Science & Technology
1315 East West Highway www.aifrb.org
Silver Spring, MD 20910
A professional organization that pusrues the conservation and proper utlization of fishery resources. In dedication to the cause AIFRB develops and promotes advancements in the theory, practice and application of fishery biology andrelated sceinces.
Founded: 1951
Kim Anthony, President
Mary Blasius, Executive Secretary

263 American Littoral Society
18 Hartshorne Drive 732-291-0055
Suite 1 *Fax:* 732-291-3551
Highlands, NJ 07732 www.littoralsociety.org
Environmental organization concerned about issues that affect the littoral zone: that area on the beach between low and high tide. The American Littoral Society is a national, nonprofit, public-interest organization comprised of over6,000 professional and amateur naturalists.
Tim Dillingham, Executive Director
Nicole Haines, Education Director

264 American Public Gardens Association (APGA)
351 Longwood Road 610-708-3010
Kennett Square, PA 19348 *Fax:* 610-444-3594
info@publicgardens.org
publicgardens.org
Formerly the American Association of Botanical Gardens and Arboreta. APGA is committed to increasing the knowledge of public garden professionals through information sharing, professional development, education, research and plantconservation.
Founded: 1940
Casey Sclar, PhD, Executive Director
Joan Thomas, Director, External Relations

265 American Shore and Beach Preservation Association (ASBPA)
5460 Beaujolais Lane 239-489-2616
Fort Myers, FL 33919 *Fax:* 239-362-9771
derek.brockbank@asbpa.org
asbpa.org
Dedicated to preserving, protecting and enhancing the beaches, shores and other coastal resources of America, recognizing their important quality-of-life assets.
Founded: 1926
Derek Brockbank, Executive Director
Nicole Elko, PhD, Science Director

266 American Society of Ichthyologists and Herpetologists (ASIH)
810 E 10th Street 785-865-9405
Lawrence, KA 66044 800-627-0326
asih@allenpress.com
www.asih.org
ASIH is dedicated to the scientific study of fishes, amphibians and reptiles. Its mission is to increase knowledge about these organisms through publications, conferences, and symposia, and to encourage young scientists who will makefuture advances in these fields.
Founded: 1913
Chris Beachy, President
Prosanta Chakrabarty, Secretary

267 Animal Welfare Institute (AWI)
900 Pennsylvania Ave SE 202-337-2332
Washington, DC 20003 *Fax:* 202-446-2131
awi@awionline.org
www.awionline.org
AWI works to alleviate the suffering inflicted on animals by humans including factory farming, experimentation, commercial whaling, as well as the impact on endangered species and their habitat.
Founded: 1951
Nadia Adawi, Executive Director
Nancy Glaney, Director, Government Affairs

268 Antarctic and Southern Ocean Coalition (ASCO)
1320 19th Street, NW 202-234-2480
5th Floor info@asoc.org
Washington, DC 20036 www.asoc.org
ASOC is a collaborative effort by conservation organizations from around the world to defend the integrity of Antarctic and Southern Ocean ecosystems from encroaching human activities. Responsible for national and inernationalcampaigns to protect the biological diversity and pristine wilderness of Antarctica, including its oceans and marine life.
Founded: 1978
Claire Christian, Executive Director
Eli Webster, Operations Manager

269 Association for Conservation Information (ACI)
1085 Lake Road www.aci-net.org
Panton, VT 05491
Nonprofit association of information and education professionals representing state, federal and Canadian agencies and private conservation organizations.
Jennifer Wisniewski, President
Judy Stokes Weber, Treasurer

270 **Association of Consulting Foresters (ACF)**
376 McLaws Circle 703-548-0990
Suite 1A *Fax:* 703-548-6395
Williamsburg, VA 23185 membership@acf-foresters.org
www.acf-foresters.org
To protect the public welfare and property in the practice of forestry. To raise the professional standards and work of ACF Consultants and all other consulting foresters. To develop and expand the services of ACF Consultants.
Founded: 1948
Shannon M. McCabe, Executive Director
Lucy Firebaugh, Coordinator, Member Services

271 **Association of Field Ornithologists (AFO)**
Florida Atlantic University
777 Glades Road 561-297-3333
Boca Raton, FL 33431-0991 dgawlik@fau.edu
afonet.org
Society of professional and amateur ornithologists dedicated to the scientific study and dissemination of information about birds in their natural habitats. Especially active in bird-banding and development of field techniques.Encourages participation of amateurs in research, and emphasizes conservation biology of birds.
Founded: 1922
Dan Ardia, President
Dale Gawlik, Secretary

272 **Association of Great Lakes Outdoor Writers (AGLOW)**
PO Box 548 877-472-4569
Knox, IN 46534 aglowinfo.org
Dedicated to communicating the outdoor experience in word and image. AGLOW provide grants, scholarships and awards to writers and students who promote the outdoors in their own work.
Josh Lantz, President
Mark C. Smith, Executive Director

273 **Association of State Wetland Managers (ASWM)**
32 Tandberg Trail 207-892-3399
Suite 2A *Fax:* 207-894-7992
Windham, ME 04062 jeanne.christie@aswm.org
www.aswm.org
Nonprofit organization dedicated to the protection and restoration of the nation's wetlands. ASWM's goal is to help public and private wetland decision-makers utilize the best possible scientific information and techniques in wetlanddelineation, assessment, mapping, planning, regulation, acquisition, restoration and other management.
Founded: 1983
Marla J. Stelk, Executive Director
Brenda Zollitsch, Senior Policy Analyst

274 **Bat Conservation International**
500 North Capital of Texas Highway 512-327-9721
Building 1 800-538-2287
Austin, TX 78746 www.batcon.org
Dedicated to preserving and restoring bat populations and habitats around the world. Uses a non-confrontational approach to educate the public about the ecological and economic value of bats, advance scientific knowledge about bats andthe ecosystems that rely on them and preserve critical bat habitats through win-win solutions that benefit both humans and bats.
Founded: 1982
Mike Daulton, Executive Director
Kevin Pierson, Chief Conservation Officer

275 **Big Thicket Association (BTA)**
700 North Street 409-790-5399
Suite 79 director@bigthicket.org
Beaumont, TX 77701 www.bigthicket.org
Formed to save remnants of the once extensive historic Big Thicket forests with its remarkable diversity. by establising the Big Thicket National Preserve, a preserve that is now designated as one of America's Ten Most EndangeredNational Parks.
Founded: 1964
Bruce Walker, Executive Director

276 **Birds of Prey Foundation**
2290 South 104th Street 303-460-0674
Broomfield, CO 80020 raptor@birds-of-prey.org
www.birds-of-prey.org
Fosters compassion and seeks protecton for injured and orphaned raptors such as eagles, hawks, falcons and owls, and improves the quality of care through education, observation, and invention.
Founded: 1981
Heidi Bucknam, Executive Director

277 **Blue Frontier**
PO Box 19367 202-387-8030
Washington, DC 20036 *Fax:* 202-234-5176
bluefront.org
The Blue Frontier is a nonprofit organization working towards preserving oceans and marine wildlife by providing resources to other organizations and communities.
Founded: 2003
David Helvarg, Executive Director
Eleanor Kewlow, Sr. Communications Advisor

278 **BlueVoice.org**
10 Sunnfish Drive contact@bluevoice.org
St. Augustine, FL 32080 bluevoice.org
BlueVoice.org is an ocean conservation organization seeking to protect dolphins, save the whales, and other marine mammals and to raise popular awareness about toxic chemicals in the oceans.
Founded: 2000
Hardy Jones, Executive Director

279 **Boone and Crockett Club**
250 Station Drive 406-542-1888
Missoula, MT 59801 888-840-4868
Fax: 406-542-0784
bcclub@boone-crockett.org
www.boone-crockett.org
Organization founded by Theodore Roosevelt with the vision of establishing a coalition of dedicated conservationists and sportsmen to provide leadership in the issues affecting hunting, wildlife and wildlife habitat.
Founded: 1887
Tony A. Schoonen, Chief of Staff
Justin Spring, Director, Big Game Records

280 **Brotherhood of the Jungle Cock**
MD bojcmd.wordpress.com
A member based organization focused on upholding the traditions of angling and fishing in Maryland's Hunting Creek. Campfire, an annual event, takes place to pass on to the youth of today the knowledge, skills and love for angling andthe outdoors. The parent chapter is located in Maryland with new chapters located in Michigan, New York, Ohio, Pennsylvania and Virginia.
Founded: 1938 $25/Year
Steve Lewis, President
Bosley Wright, Executive Vice-President

281 **Camp-Fire Club of America**
230 Camp Fire Road www.campfireclub.com
Chappaqua, NY 10514
A wildlife and habitat conservation organization created over 100 years ago to bring together hunters, anglers, explorers, and naturalists in an effort to promote fellowship in the outdoors, and the furthering of sports and wildlifeconservation.
Founded: 1897

282 **Canyonlands Field Institute**
1320 South Highway 191 435-259-7750
PO Box 68 800-860-5262
Moab, UT 84532 info@cfimoab.org
cfimoab.org
To increase understanding of, connection to and care for the Colorado Plateau, expand perception of and appreciation for the beauty and integrity of the natural world, improve the quality of field oriented, experiential teaching andlearning for students and

adults and to encourage individuals to be involved in the care of their own home places.
Founded: 1984
Karla VanderZanden, Executive Director
Dave Montgomery, Operations Manager

283 Carrying Capacity Network
PO Box 457
San Francisco, CA 94104
carryingcapacity.org
An information exchange network. Interests include resource conservation, population stabilization and environmental protection.

284 Center for Humans and Nature
20 N. Wacker Drive
Suite 2807
Chicago, IL 60606
312-629-5060
Fax: 312-629-5061
www.humansandnature.org
Works to explore and promote human responsibilities in relation to nature.
Founded: 2003
Brooke Parry Hecht, President
Gavin Van Horn, Director, Conservation

285 Center for Plant Conservation (CPC)
15600 San Pasqual Valley Road
Escondido, CA 92027-7000
760-796-5686
info@saveplants.org
www.saveplants.org
The CPC is a consortium of 50+ American botanical gardens and arboreta whose mission is to conserve and restore the rare native plants of the US To meet this end, they are involved in plant conservation, research and education. Thissite includes information about the National Collection of Endangered Plants, which is maintained by the group.
John R. Clark, PhD, President & CEO
Joyce Maschinski, PhD, VP, Conservation & Science

286 Center for Wildlife Information
406-239-2315
cfwi@cfwi.org
www.centerforwildlifeinformation.org
A resource that provides information on ways to interact and enjoy wildlife safely and responsibly. The objective is to reduce conflcits between humans and wildlife, in particular with bears, alligators and cougars.
Chuck Bartlebaugh, Contact

287 Center for the Study of Tropical Birds
210-214-9292
Fax: 210-828-9732
admin@cstbinc.org
www.cstbinc.org
Devoted to the conservation of neotropical birdlife through collaborative programs of research and education. PDF copies of Center publications are available on request.
Jack Eitniear, President/Chair
Thomas Rueckle, Treasurer

288 Conservation International
2011 Crystal Dr
Suite 500
Arlington, VA 22202
703-341-2400
800-429-5660
www.conservation.org
CI promotes sustainable development and the conservation of earth's ecosystems as keys to solving climate change.
Peter Seligmann, Chair
M. Sanjayan, Chief Executive Officer

289 Conservation Management Institute
Virginia Tech
1900 Kraft Drive
Suite 250
Blacksburg, VA 24061
540-231-7348
Fax: 540-231-8825
cmiinfo@vt.edu
www.cmi.vt.edu
To better address multi-disciplinary research questions that affect conservation management effectiveness in Virginia, North America and the world. Faculty from research institutions work collaboratively on projects ranging fromendangered species propagation to natural resource-based satellite imagery interpretation.
Founded: 2000
Scott D. Klopfer, Executive Director

290 Counterpart International
2345 Crystal Drive
Suite 301
Arlington, VA 22202
571-447-5700
Fax: 703-412-5035
communications@counterpart.org
www.counterpart.org
Promotes socioeconomics, health care, biodiversity, and natural resource management in over 60 countries.
Ann Hudock, President & CEO
Derek Hodkey, Chief Operating Officer

291 Defenders of Wildlife
1130 17th Street NW
Washington, DC 20036
202-682-9400
800-385-9712
Fax: 202-682-1331
memberservices@defenders.org
www.defenders.org
Dedicated to the protection of all native wild animals and plants in their natural communities. Focus is placed on the accelerating rate of extinction of species and the associated loss of biological diversity, and habitat alterationand destruction.
Jamie Rappaport Clark, President & CEO
Shawn Cantrell, VP, Field Conservation

292 Delta Wildlife
433 Stoneville Road
PO Box 276
Stoneville, MS 38776
662-686-3370
Fax: 662-686-3382
trey@deltawildlife.org
deltawildlife.org
Recognizing the need for an agressive, but reasonable effort to develop wildlife, in 1990, one-hundred agri-business leaders, representing every country in Mississippi Delta, had the vision and dedication to form Delta Wildlife so theyand others could do more for conservation.
Trey Cooke, Executive Director
Liz Brown, Director, Marketing

293 Department of Fisheries, Wildlife and Conservation Biology (FWCB)
University of Minnesota
2003 Upper Buford Circle
135 Skok Hall
St. Paul, MN 55108
612-624-3600
Fax: 612-301-1852
myfwcb@unm.edu
fwcb.cfans.umn.edu
Fosters a high quality natural environment by contributing to the management, protection, and sustainable use of fisheries and wildlife resources through teaching, research and outreach.
Founded: 1972
Susan Galatowitsch, Professor & Head

294 Desert Fishes Council (DFC)
1447 Edgecliff Drive
Sandy, UT 84092
dfc-excomm@utlists.utexas.edu
www.desertfishes.org
The mission of the Desert Fishes Council is to preserve the biological integrity of desert aquatic ecosystems and their associated life forms, to hold symposia to report related research and management endeavors, and to effect rapiddissemination of information concerning activities of the Council and its members.
Founded: 1969
Krissy Wilson, President
Phil Pister, Executive Secretary

295 Desert Tortoise Council (DTC)
4654 East Avenue S
Suite 257B
Palmdale, CA 93552
info@deserttortoise.org
www.deserttortoise.org
The Council is a private, nonprofit organization made up of hundreds of professionals, and lay-persons from all walks of life, from across the United States, and several continents. These people come together from a shared fascinationwith wild desert tortoises and environments they depend upon.
Founded: 1976
Ken MacDonald, Chair
Becky Jones, Corresponding Secretary

296 **Dragonfly Society of the Americas (DSA)**
president@dragonflysocietyamericas.org
www.dragonflysocietyamericas.org
The Dragonfly Society of the Americas was organized in 1988. It is a nonprofit society whose purpose is to encourage scientific research, habitat preservation and aesthetic enjoyment of Odonata (dragon flies.)
Founded: 1988 $15/Year
Melissa Sanchez Herrera, President
Michael Moore, Secretary

297 **Ducks Unlimited (DU)**
One Waterfowl Way 901-758-3825
Memphis, TN 38120 800-453-8257
www.ducks.org
The mission is to fulfill the annual life cycle needs of North American waterfowl by protecting, enhancing, restoring and managing important wetlands and associated uplands.
Founded: 1937
Rogers Hoyt, Jr., President
Dale Hall, CEO

298 **Eagle Nature Foundation Ltd.**
300 East Hickory Street 815-594-2306
Apple River, IL 61001 *Fax:* 815-594-2305
eaglenature.tni@juno.com
eaglenature.com
A non-profit organization dedicated to the preservation of the bald eagle, America's national symbol, and other endangered species from extinction and to increase public awareness of unique endangered plants and animals. They monitorbald eagle and other endangered species populations, strive to preserve habitiat essential to their survival, and develops materials for schools to inform students about the needs of the bald eagle.
Founded: 1995
Terrence N. Ingram, Founder/President
Susan Ertmer, Vice President

299 **Earth Ecology Foundation (EEF)**
4175 S. Decatur 702-778-9930
Las Vegas, NV 89103 erikwunstell@aol.com
www.westvegas.com/earth_ecology_foundation.html
Exploring natural and human environments by imagining futuristic ecological technolgies, and encouraging discoveries in theoretical physics and applies sciences.
Founded: 1980
Erik Wunstell, Director

300 **Earth Island Institute**
2150 Allston Way 510-859-9100
Suite 460 *Fax:* 510-859-9091
Berkeley, CA 94704-1375 donorinquiry@earthisland.org
www.earthisland.org
A nonprofit, public interest, membership organization that supports people who are creating solutions to protect the shared planet.
Founded: 1982
David Phillips, Executive Director
Susan Kamprath, Director, Operations

301 **Earthworks**
1612 K Street NW 202-887-1872
Suite 904 info@earthworks.org
Washington, DC 20006 earthworks.org
Earthworks carries out research and publishes reports on the environmental impacts of mining, as well as promoting sustainable solutions.
Jennifer Krill, Executive Director
Lauren Pagel, Director, Policy

302 **EcoHealth Alliance**
460 West 34th Street 212-380-4460
17th Floor *Fax:* 212-380-4465
New York, NY 10001-2320 homeoffice@ecohealthalliance.org
www.ecohealthalliance.org
Works in the United States and worldwide to save threatened species from extinction, safeguard human health from the emergence of diesease, and promote conservation by protecting ecosystems.
Founded: 1971
Peter Daszak, President
William Karesh, EVP, Health & Policy

303 **Endangered Species Coalition**
PO Box 65195 240-353-2765
Washington, DC 20035 www.endangered.org
Seeks to stop human-caused species extinctions, to protect and restore habitats, and help at-risk species recover.
Leda Huta, Executive Director
David Robinson, Dir., Env. Education

304 **Endangered Wolf Center**
PO Box 760 636-938-5900
Eureka, MO 63025 info@endangeredwolfcenter.org
www.endangeredwolfcenter.org
A private nonprofit conservation organization dedicated to the preservation of the wolf and other endangered canids through education, research and captive breeding.
Founded: 1971
Jermiah Dellas, Chair
Ginny Busch, Executive Director

305 **Ford Foundation Center for Social Justice**
320 E 43rd Street 212-573-5000
New York, NY 10017 *Fax:* 212-351-3677
www.fordfoundation.org
Concerned with natural resource preservation. Provides funding for environmental projects throughout the world.
Francisco G. Cigarroa, Chair
Darren Walker, President

306 **Forest History Society**
2925 Academy Road 919-682-9319
Durham, NC 27705-9311 *Fax:* 919-682-2349
steven.anderson@foresthistory.org
www.foresthistory.org
A nonprofit educational institution that links the past to the future by identifying, collecting, preserving, interpreting and disseminating information on the history of people, forests and their related resources.
Founded: 1946
Steven Anderson, President
Janet Askew, Assistant Director

307 **Forest Stewards Guild**
2019 Galisteo Street 505-983-8992
Suite N7 *Fax:* 505-986-0798
Santa Fe, NM 87505 info@forestguild.org
foreststewardsguild.org
Promotes excellence in forest stewardship, supports foresters and related professionals, and educates and advocates about the challenges of forest conservation.
Zander Evans, Executive Director
Eytan Krasilovsky, Deputy Director

308 **Friends of Acadia**
43 Cottage Street 207-288-3340
PO Box 45 800-625-0321
Bar Harbor, ME 04609 info@friendsofacadia.org
www.friendsofacadia.org
The mission of Friends of Acadia is to preserve and protect the outstanding natural beauty, ecological vitality and cultural distinctiveness of Acadia National Park and the surrounding communities. Their methods are: raises and donatesprivate funds to park and communities; advocates before legislatures and agencies; counters threats to park; and represents users in betterment of its operations.
Founded: 1986
David MacDonald, President & CEO
Stephanie Clement, Director, Conservation

309 **Friends of the Sea Otter**
PO Box 223260
Carmel, CA 93922
831-915-3275
info@seaotters.org
www.seaotters.org

Nonprofit organization dedicated to the protection of a threatened species, the Southern Sea Otter, as well as Sea Otters throughout their north pacific range, and all sea otter habitat.
Jennifer Covert, Chair
Cassie Pais, Administrator

310 **Game Conservancy USA**
49 Locust Ave
Suite 104
New Canaan, CT 06840
203-966-4187
Fax: 203-661-7997
info@gcusa.org
www.gcusa.org

Seeks to increase support for research of the conservation of game and wildlife habitats in the US and UK through an expanding membership base.
Ronald N. Beck, President
Robert Hatch, Director

311 **Garden Club of America (GCA)**
14 East 60th Street
3rd Floor
New York, NY 10022
212-753-8287
Fax: 212-753-0134
gca@gcamerica.org
www.gcamerica.org

Seeks to stimulate the knowledge and love of gardening, to share the advantages of association by means of educational meetings, conferences, correspondence and publications, and to restore, improve, and protect the quality of theenvironment through educational programs and action in the fields of conservation and civic improvement. Has 201 member clubs.
Founded: 1913 18,000 members
Anne Neal Petri, President

312 **George Wright Society**
PO Box 65
Hancock, MI 49930-0065
906-487-9722
info@georgewright.org
www.georgewrightsociety.org

Concerned with the preservation and management of parks, protected areas, and cultural sites.
Founded: 1980
David Reynolds, President
David Harmon, Executive Director

313 **Global Coral Reef Alliance (GCRA)**
37 Pleasant Street
Cambridge, MA 02139
857-285-3745
info@globalcoral.org
www.globalcoral.org

A nonprofit organization for the protection and sustainable management of coral reef.
Founded: 1990
Thomas J Goreau, PhD, President

314 **Gopher Tortoise Council**
PO Box 241
Safety Harbor, FL 34695
www.gophertortoisecouncil.org

Formed by a group of biologists and others concerned about the range-wide decline of the gopher tortoise.
Founded: 1978
Ericha Shelton-Nix, Co-Chair
Betsoe Rothermel, Co-Chair

315 **Grand Canyon Trust**
2601 N. Fort Valley Road
Flagstaff, AZ 86001
928-774-7488
888-428-5550
Fax: 928-774-7570
info@grandcanyontrust.org
www.grandcanyontrust.org

The mission of The Grand Canyon Trust is to protect and restore the canyon country of the Colorado Plateau. The vision for this unique region 100 years from now is of a landscape still characterized by vast open spaces, dominated bywildness and healthy and restored natural ecosystems.
Founded: 1985
Ethan Aumack, Executive Director
Travis Bruner, Director, Conservation

316 **Grassland Heritage Foundation (GHF)**
PO Box 394
Shawnee Mission, KS 66201
785-748-0955
ghf@grasslandheritage.org
www.grasslandheritage.org

Nonprofit membership organization dedicated to prairie preservation and education.
Founded: 1976
Sue Holcomb, President
Kim Bellemere, Coordinator, Education

317 **Great Bear Foundation**
PO Box 1616
Haines, AK 99827
907-766-2024
gbf@greatbear.org
www.greatbear.org

The Foundation was established to promote conservation of wild bears and their natural habitat worldwide.
Founded: 1981
Frank Tyro, PhD, President
Shannon Donahue, Executive Director

318 **HawkWatch International**
2240 South 900 East
Salt Lake City, UT 84106
801-484-6808
800-726-4295
Fax: 801-484-6810
hwi@hawkwatch.org
hawkwatch.org

HawkWatch International is a non-profit organization that works to protect raptors and their environment through scientific research and public education.
Founded: 1986
Nikki Wayment, Executive Director
Christina Castellano, Director, Development

319 **Humane Society of the United States (HSUS)**
1255 23rd Street, NW
Suite 450
Washington, DC 20037
202-452-1100
866-720-2676
www.humanesociety.org

HSUS is the nation's largest animal-protection organization. It is dedicated to promoting the humane treatment of animals, to foster respect, understanding, and compassion for all creatures.
Founded: 1954
Kitty Block, President & CEO
G. Thomas Waite III, Chief Operating Officer

320 **Hummingbird Society**
6560 State Route 179
Suite 124
Sedona, AZ 86351
928-284-2251
800-529-3699
Fax: 928-284-2251
info@hummingbirdsociety.org
www.hummingbirdsociety.org

Nonprofit corporation organized for the purpose of encouraging international understanding and conservation of hummingbirds by publishing and disseminating information, promoting and supporting scientific study, and protecting habitat.
Founded: 1996
Cletus Toschlog, President
Dr. Robert L. Gell, Vice-President

321 **Inland Bird Banding Association (IBBA)**
11114 Harrison Road
Rockton, IL 61072
president@ibbainfo.org
www.ibbainfo.org

An organization for all individuals interested in the serious study of birds, their life history, ecology, and conservation.
Founded: 1922
Linda Tossing, President
Mike Eickman, Treas. & Membership Sec.

322 **Institute for Conservation Leadership**
7000 Carroll Avenue
Suit 200-14
Takoma Park, MD 20912
301-888-6401
Fax: 301-270-0610
info@icl.org
www.icl.org

The mission of this Institute is to train and empower volunteer leaders and to build volunteer institutions that protect and conserve the Earth's environment. They lend a helping hand to dedicated partners in pursuit of a better worldfor everyone.
Dianne Russell, President
Sarah Clark, Senior Associate

323 International Association for Bear Research and Management (IBA)
University Hall
Room 309
Missoula, MT 59812
907-459-7238
alexander.kopatz@bearbiology.org
www.bearbiology.com
A volunteer organization open to professional biologists, wildlife managers and others dedicated to the conservation of all species of bears. Supports the scientific management of bears through research and distribution of information.
Founded: 1968 550+ members
Andreas Zedrosser, President
Alexander Kopatz, Secretary

324 International Bird Rescue
PO Box 2171
Long Beach, CA 90801
707-207-0380
Fax: 707-207-0395
gifts@bird-rescue.org
www.bird-rescue.org
Dedicated to mitigating the human impact on aquatic birds and other wildlife worldwide. The Rescue provides emergency response and planning, wildlife rehabilitation, research and education.
Founded: 1971
J.D. Bergeron, Executive Director
Rebecca Duerr, PhD, Research Director

325 International Crane Foundation (ICF)
E11376 Shady Lane Road
PO Box 447
Baraboo, WI 53913
608-356-9462
info@savingcranes.org
www.savingcranes.org
Works worldwide to conserve cranes and the wetland and grasslands communities on which they depend. Dedicated to providing experience, knowledge, and inspiration to involve people in resolving threats to these ecosystems.
Founded: 1973
George Archibald, Co-Founder
Rich Beilfuss, President & CEO

326 International Erosion Control Association (IECA)
3033 S Parker Road
Suite 410
Aurora, CO 80014
303-640-7554
800-220-3153
Fax: 866-308-3087
info@ieca.org
www.ieca.org
An organization dedicated to minimizing accelerated soil erosion. IECA offers an annual conference, chapter events, training courses as well as a variety of topic-specific publications and a quarterly newsletter.
Founded: 1972
Samantha Roe, Executive Director
Joanna Fetherolf, Director, Education

327 International Fund for Animal Welfare (IFAW)
290 Summer Street
Yarmouth, MA 02675
508-744-2000
800-932-4329
Fax: 508-744-2009
info@ifaw.org
www.ifaw.org
Aims to improve the welfare of wild and domestic animals throughout the world by reducing commercial exploitation of animals in distress, primarily by motivating the public to prevent cruelty to animals and promoting animal welfare andconservation policies that advance the well-being of both animals and people.
Azzedine Downes, President & CEO
Faye Cuevas, Esq., Senior Vice President

328 International SeaKeepers Society
255 Aragon Avenue
Third Floor
Coral Gables, FL 33134
786-924-6209
media@seakeepers.org
seakeepers.org
The International SeaKeepers Society promotes oceanographic research, conservation, and education through direct involvement with the yachting community. SeaKeepers enables the yachting community to take full advantage of their uniquepotential to advance marine sciences and to raise awareness about global ocean issues.
Richard Snow, President/CEO
Carolyn Ruth Robinson, Operations & Administration

329 International Society for the Protection of Mustangs and Burros (ISPMB)
PO Box 435
Rapid City, SD 57709
605-430-2088
ispmb@ispmb.org
www.ispmb.org
Dedicated to preserving wild horses/burros and their habitats. They also run a rescue program and purchase slaughter bound wild horses and burros, placing them in permanent loving homes, or transporting entire herds of horses.
Founded: 1960
Karen Sussman, President

330 International Society of Limnology (SIL)
www.limnology.org
To further the study and understanding of all aspects of limnology. Promotes and communicates new and emerging knowledge among limnologists to advance the understanding of inland aquatic ecosystems and their management.
Founded: 1922
Prof. Yves Prairie, President
Tamar Zohary, General Secretary-Treasurer

331 International Union for Conservation of Nature (IUCN)
1630 Connecticut Avenue NW
3rd Floor, Suite 300
Washington, DC 20009
202-387-4826
+41-22-9990000
Fax: 202-387-4823
Fax: +41-22-9990002
deborah.good@iucn.org
www.iucn.org
Membership union of government and civil organizations dedicated to furthering human progress, economic development, and nature conservation.
Founded: 1948 1,300 member orgs
Grethel Aguilar, Acting Director General
Deborah Good, U.S. Membership Contact

332 International Wild Waterfowl Association (IWWA)
500 Sylvian Heights Park Way
P.O Box 11
Scotland Neck, NC 27874
252-826-3186
Fax: 425-397-8136
info@shwpark.com
www.wildwaterfowl.org
Committed to protecting and enhancing wild waterfowl habitats. Supports the captive breeding and restoration of endangered species, and the establishment and maintenance of genetically diverse and disease-free captive populations ofendangered waterfowl.
Founded: 1958
Ian Gereg, President
Anne Lemenager, Secretary

333 International Wildlife Conservation Society (IWCS)
PO Box 802
Pacific City, OR 97135
310-344-7057
cathy@internationalwildlife.org
www.internationalwildlife.org
The Society has created a Wildlife Reserve that provides habitat to a variety of mammals, birds, fish and reptiles. The Society continues to increase the awareness of wildlife conservation, preservation and research.
Founded: 1968
Cathy Griffin, Contact

334 International Wildlife Rehabilitation Council (IWRC)
PO Box 3197
Eugene, OR 97403
866-871-1869
Fax: 408-876-6153
info@theiwrc.org
theiwrc.org
A nonprofit organization that works to enhance the integrity of native wildlife systems and conserve biological diversity world-

wide, through rehabilitation of wildlife, support of rehabilitators, public education and advocacy.
Founded: 1972
Adam Grogan, President
Amanda Kamps, Vice President

335 Island Conservation
2100 Delaware Avenue 831-359-4787
Suite 1 info@islandconservation.org
Santa Cruz, CA 95060 www.islandconservation.org
Island Conservation look to maintain wildlife by removing invasive species from islands. Islands across the world are where biodiversity and species exstinction is the greatest.
Founded: 1994
Karen Poiani, Chief Executive Officer
Doug Bragdon, Chief Operations Officer

336 Izaak Walton League of America (IWLA)
707 Conservation Lane 301-548-0150
Gaithersburg, MD 20878 info@iwla.org
www.iwla.org
The mission is to conserve, maintain, protect and restore the soil, forest water and other natural resources of the United States and other lands; to promote means and opportunities for the education of the public with respect to suchresources and their enjoyment and wholesome utilization.
Founded: 1922 41,000 members
Scott Kovarovics, Executive Director
Jared Mott, Director, Conservation

337 Lady Bid Johnson Wildflower Center
4801 La Crosse Avenue 512-232-0200
Austin, TX 78739 www.wildflower.org
The State Botanic Garden and Arboretum of Texas as of 2017, the Center uses native plants to restore and create sustainable landscapes.
Founded: 1982
Patrick Newman, Executive Director
Andrea DeLong-Amaya, Director, Horticulture

338 Lighthawk
PO Box 913239 970-797-9355
Denver, CO 80291 info@lighthawk.org
www.lighthawk.org
Nonprofit organization addressing critical environmental issues by providing an aerial perspective on areas of concern in the US, Canada and Central America. Using small aircrafts, they fly partner organizations, elected officials,industry and media representatives, activists, and indigenous groups over protected and threatened regions.
Founded: 1979
Terri Watson, Chief Executive Officer
Bob Francella, Chief Advancement Officer

339 Marin Conservation League (MCL)
175 N. Redwood Drive 415-485-6257
Suite 135 *Fax:* 415-485-6259
San Rafael, CA 94903 mcl@conservationleague.org
www.conservationleague.org
The Marin Conservation League is an a nonprofit organization founded in 1934 to preserve, protect and enhance the natural assets of Marin County for all people. MCL is Marin's oldest, locally based environmental organization,championing a sound balance between the needs of Marin's citizens and its beautiful and fragile environment.
Founded: 1934
Linda Novy, President
Holly Smith, Office Manager

340 Marine Conservation Alliance (MCA)
360-626-1140
Fax: 206-260-3639
marineconservationalliance@gmail.com
marineconservationalliance.org
Seeks to provide proactive management of ecosystems and fisheries to ensure sustainable seafood providers.
Rebecca Skinner, President
Anne Vanderhoeven, Vice President

341 Marine Conservation Institute
4010 Stone Way N 206-686-1455
Suite 210 *Fax:* 206-686-1460
Seattle, WA 98103-8099 info@marine-conservation.org
marine-conservation.org
Nonprofit organization dedicated to ensuring permanent protection for the ocean's survival. The Institute works with scientists, politicians, government officials and other organizations to identify key threats to areas in marineecosystems and build workable solutions.
Founded: 1996
Lance Morgan, President
Michael Gravitz, Dir., Policy & Legislation

342 Mountain Lion Foundation
PO Box 1896 916-442-2666
Sacramento, CA 95812 info@mountainlion.org
www.mountainlion.org
A national nonprofit conservation and education organization dedicated to protecting the mountain lion, its habitat and the wildlife that shares that habitat.
Founded: 1986
Lynn Cullens, Executive Director
Melissa Brown, Coordinator, Membership

343 Mustangs of America Foundation (MAF)
1895 Crockett Lane 775-790-0207
Gardnerville, NV 89410 MustangUpRanch@cs.com
www.mustangsofamericafoundation.org
Dedicated to promoting mustang and burro adoption, training, facilitating public education, rescue and prevention of cruelty to animals. MAF is committed to working with the Bureau of Land Management, Department of Agriculture andother nonprofit organizations to increase the number of successful adoptions by providing information and education to the public about adoption, rescue and training programs.
Lynda Sanford, Director/Secretary

344 National Association of Conservation Districts (NACD)
509 Capitol Court NE 202-547-6223
Washington, DC 20002-4937 *Fax:* 202-547-6450
info@nacdnet.org
www.nacdnet.org
A non-governmental, nonprofit organization representing 3000 local soil and water conservation districts as well as the 17,000 that serve on their governing boards. Among its goals are: provide useful information to the districts andtheir state associations; represent them as a national unified voice; analyze programs and policy issues that have an impact on local districts; and offer needed and cost-effective services.
Founded: 1946
Jeremy Peters, Chief Executive Officer
Laura Demmel, Director, Development

345 National Audubon Society (NAS)
225 Varick Street 212-979-3196
7th Floor 844-428-3826
New York, NY 10014 *Fax:* 212-979-3188
audubon@emailcustomerservice.com
www.audubon.org
The National Audubon Society is one of the oldest, largest, and most powerful nature appreciation and conservation organizations in the country. NAS works on a broad range of concerns related to the protection of the world'secosystems; preserving wetlands, population planning, eliminating acid rain and reducing air pollution, promoting environmental justice, and protecting water quality.
Founded: 1905
David Yarnold, President & CEO
Stephen Meyer, Chief Operations Officer

346 National Audubon Society: Project Puffin
311 Main Street 207-596-5566
Rockland, ME 04841 877-478-3346
puffin@audubon.org
projectpuffin.audubon.org

Established to learn how to restore puffins to historic nesting islands in the Gulf of Maine. Although puffins are abundant in Newfoundland, Iceland and Britain, they are rare in Maine. Project Puffin has a year round staff of sixwhich increases to include more than 50 biologists and researchers during the seabird breeding season in spring and summer.
Founded: 1973
Stephen W. Kress, Executive Director
Tiffany Huenefeldt, Managing Director

347 National Fish and Wildlife Foundation (NFWF)
1133 15th Street, NW 202-857-0166
Suite 1000 *Fax:* 202-857-0162
Washington, DC 20005 info@nfwf.org
www.nfwf.org
Nonprofit organization dedicated to the conservation of fish, wildlife, and plants and the habitats on which they depend. Among its goals are species habitat protection, environmental education, public policy development, naturalresource management, habitat and ecosystem rehabilitation and restoration, and leadership training for conservation professionals.
Founded: 1984
Jeff Trandahl, CEO & Executive Director
Holly Bamford, PhD, Chief Conservation Officer

348 National Forest Foundation
Fort Missoula Road 406-542-2805
Building 27, Suite 3 *Fax:* 406-542-2810
Missoula, MT 59804 mmitsos@nationalforests.org
www.nationalforests.org
The official nonprofit partner of the USDA Forest Service. To accept and administer private contributions, undertaking activities that further the purposes for which the National Forest System was established and conductingeducational, technical, and other activities that support the multiple use, research, and forestry programs administered by the Forest Service.
Mary Mitsos, President
Sheree Bombard, Director, Administration

349 National Garden Clubs
4401 Magnolia Avenue 314-776-7574
St. Louis, MO 63110 800-550-6007
Fax: 314-776-5108
headquarters@gardenclub.org
www.gardenclub.org
Nonprofit educational organization with its headquarters in St. Louis, Missouri, US. It is composed of 50 State Garden Clubs and the National Capital Area, 5,000 member garden clubs and 165,000 members. In addition, NGC proudlyrecognizes 200 Internationl Affiliates from Canada to Mexico and South America.
Founded: 1891
Gay Austin, President
Michelle Austin, Executive Director

350 National Grange
1616 H Street NW 202-628-3507
Washington, DC 20006 888-447-2643
Fax: 202-347-1091
info@nationalgrange.org
www.nationalgrange.org
The Grange is a family based community organization with a special interest in agriculture and rural America, as well as in legislative efforts regarding these issues.
Founded: 1867
Betsy Huber, President
Burton Eller, Legislative Director

351 National Military Fish and Wildlife Association (NMFWA)
www.nmfwa.org
NMFWA recognizes the critical need for enhanced awareness of natural resource conservation requirements to provide for both long term sustainability of resource diversity and the successful accomplishment of the military trainingmission on public lands. Members include biologists, botanists, ecologists, range conservationists, foresters, cultural resource managers and law enforcement agents.
Founded: 1983
Nicole Olmsted, President
Janet Johnson, Vice President

352 National Park Foundation (NPF)
1110 Vermont Avenue, NW 202-796-2500
Suite 200 888-467-2757
Washington, DC 20005 *Fax:* 202-796-2509
ask-npf@nationalparks.org
www.nationalparks.org
Mission is to strengthen the connection between the American people and their National Parks by raising private funds, making strategic grants, creating innovative parnerships and increasing public awareness.
Will Shafroth, President & CEO
Dieter Fenkart-Froeschl, Chief Operating Officer

353 National Park Trust (NPT)
401 E. Jefferson Street 301-279-7275
Suite 207 www.parktrust.org
Rockville, MD 20850
Builds awareness and appreciation for American national parks and other public lands and waters.
Founded: 1983
Grace Lee, Executive Director
Erin Mezgar, Chief Development Officer

354 National Parks Conservation Association (NPCA)
777 6th Street NW 202-223-6722
Suite 700 800-628-7275
Washington, DC 20001-3723 npca@npca.org
www.npca.org
The National Parks Conservation Association is the voice of the American people fighting to safeguard the scenic beauty, wildlife, and historical and cultural treasures of their American homeland.
Founded: 1919
Theresa Pierno, President & CEO
Robin Martin McKenna, Executive Vice President

355 National Recreation and Park Association (NRPA)
22377 Belmont Ridge Road 800-626-6772
Ashburn, VA 20148-4501 customerservice@nrpa.org
www.nrpa.org
The NRPA is a national nonprofit organization devoted to advancing park, recreation and conservation efforts that enhance the quality of life for all Americans. The Association works to extend social, health, cultural and economicbenefits of parks and recreation through its network of 60,000 recreation and park professionals and civic leaders. NRPA encourages recreation initiatives for youth in high-risk environments.
Founded: 1965
Kristine Stratton, President & CEO
Richard Dolesh, VP, Strategic Initiatives

356 National Speleological Society (NSS)
6001 Pulaski Pike 256-852-1300
Huntsville, AL 35810-1122 nss@caves.org
caves.org
Founded for the purpose of advancing the study, conservation, exploration, and knowledge of caves. 10,000 members in 250 chapters (known as grottos) conduct regular meetings to bring cavers trogether within their general area tocoordinate activities which may include mapping, cleaning and investigating sensitive caves.
Geary Schindel, President
Scott Engel, Executive Vice President

357 National Trust for Historic Preservation
2600 Virginia Avenue NW 202-588-6000
Suite 1100 800-944-6847
Washington, DC 20037 *Fax:* 202-588-6038
info@savingplaces.org
savingplaces.org

Provides leadership, education, resources and advocacy to save America's diverse historic places and revitalize its communities.
Founded: 1949
Paul Edmondson, President & CEO
Katherine Malone-France, Chief Preservation Officer

358 **National Wildlife Federation**
11100 Wildlife Center Drive 800-822-9919
Reston, VA 20190 www.nwf.org
The National Wildlife Federation is the largest member-supported conservation group, uniting individuals, organizations, businesses and government to protect wildlife, wild places and the environment.
Founded: 1936
Collin O'Mara, President & CEO
Mustafa Santiago Ali, VP, Environmental Justice

359 **National Wildlife Refuge Association**
1001 Connecticut Avevenue NW 202-417-3803
Suite 905 nwra@refugeassociation.org
Washington, DC 20036 refugeassociation.org
The National Wildlife Refuge Association is the only conservation organization solely dedicated to protecting and enhancing the National Wildlife Refuge System, the world's largest network of lands and waters set aside for wildlifeconservation.
Founded: 1975
Rebecca Rubin, Chair
Geoffrey Haskett, President

360 **National Wildlife Rehabilitators Association (NWRA)**
2625 Clearwater Road 320-230-9920
Saint Cloud, MN 56301 www.nwrawildlife.org
Nonprofit international membership organization committed to promoting and improving the integrity and professionalism of wildlife rehabilitation and contributing to the preservation of natural ecosystems.
Founded: 1982
Michele Goodman, President
Deb Dohrmann, Central Office Manager

361 **National Woodland Owners Association (NWOA)**
374 Maple Avenue East 703-255-2700
Suite 310 www.nwoa.net
Vienna, VA 22180
NWOA is independent of the forest products industry and forestry agencies. They work with all organizations to promote non-industrial forestry and the best interests of woodland owners.
Founded: 1983
Dick Couter, Chair
Keith A. Argow, President

362 **Natural Areas Association (NAA)**
PO Box 594 724-995-8466
Ligonier, PA 15658 info@naturalareas.org
naturalareas.org
Seeks to advance the preservation of natural diversity; to inform, unite and support persons engaged in identifying, protecting, managing, and studying natural areas and biological diversity across landscapes and ecosystems.
Founded: 1978
Lisa Smith, Executive Director
Amy Willis, Operations Manager

363 **Natural Resources Defense Council (NRDC)**
40 West 20th Street 212-727-2700
11th Floor *Fax:* 212-727-1773
New York, NY 10011 nrdcinfo@nrdc.org
www.nrdc.org
The NRDC focuses on issues impacting climate change, ocean pollution, water management and treatment, clean energy, and the conservation of wildlife.
Founded: 1970
Rhea Suh, President
Mitchell Bernard, Chief Counsel

364 **Neighborhood Parks Council**
1663 Mission Street 415-621-3260
Suite 320 *Fax:* 415-703-0889
San Francisco, CA 94103 feedback@sfparksalliance.org
www.sfparksalliance.org
Neighborhood Parks Council (NPC) advocates for a superior, equitable and sustainable park and recreation system. NPC provides leadership and support to park users through community-driven stewardship, education, planning and research.
Founded: 1996
Drew Becher, CEO

365 **Nicodemus Wilderness Project**
PO Box 40712 mail@wildernessproject.org
Albuquerque, NM 87196-0712 www.wildernessproject.org
The Nicodemus Wilderness Project was founded because of the need for environmental restoration, stewardship, and projection of neglected public lands.
Robert K. Dudley, PhD, President/Executive Director
Yih Ming Hsu, VP, Program Manager

366 **North American Bluebird Society (NABS)**
PO Box 7844 513-300-8714
Bloomington, IN 47407 info@nabluebirdsociety.org
www.nabluebirdsociety.org
Nonprofit conservation, education and research organization, promotes the recovery of the bluebirds and other native cavity-nesting bird species. NABS supports conservation through such continent wide programs as the TranscontinentalBluebird Trail and the NABS Nestbox Approval Process. NABS also produces award-winning educational materials.
Founded: 1977
Bernie Daniel, President
Kevin Conway, 1st Vice President

367 **North American Crane Working Group (NACWG)**
E-11376 Shady Lane Road www.nacwg.org
PO Box 447
Baraboo, WI 53913
NACWG is an organization of professional biologists, aviculturists, land managers and other interested individuals dedicated to the conservation of cranes and their habitats in North America. They sponsor a North American CraneWorkshop every 3-4 years, promulgates technical information including a published Proceedings of a North American Workshop and a semi-annual newsletter, address conservation issues affecting cranes and their habitat, promote appropriate research oncrane conservation.
Founded: 1987
Richard Urbanek, President
Sammy King, Vice President

368 **North American Falconers Association (NAFA)**
7828 Hood Street www.n-a-f-a.com
Fort Worth, TX 76135
Provides communication among and disseminates relevant information to interested members; scientific study of raptorial species, their care, welfare and training; promotes conservation of the birds of prey and an appreciation of theirvalue in nature and in wildlife conservation programs; urges recognition of falconry as a legal field sport; and establishs traditions which will aid, perpetuate and further the welfare of falconry and raptors it employs.
Founded: 1961
Sheldon Nicolle, President
Brandi Nickerson, Membership Secretary

369 **North American Grouse Partnership (NAGP)**
1670 N 1/2 Road NAGP@grousepartners.org
Fruita, CO 81521 www.grousepartners.org
Promotes the conservation of grouse and their natural habitats.
Founded: 1999
Steve Belinda, Executive Director

370 **North American Native Fishes Association**
info@nanfa.org
www.nanfa.org
NANFA is dedicated to the enjoyment, study and conservation of the continent's native fishes. Strives to disseminate knowledge

about fishes and their habitats and to promote the conservation and the restoration of natural habitats.
Fritz Rohde, President
Brian Zimmerman, Vice President

371 **North American Wildlife Park Foundation: Wolf Park**
4004 East 800 North 765-567-2265
Battle Ground, IN 47920 *Fax:* 765-567-4299
wolfpark@WolfPark.org
wolfpark.org
Nonprofit organization with a mission to improve public understanding of wolves and the value they provide to the environment.
Founded: 1972
Holly Jaycox, President
Pat Goodmann, Senior Animal Curator

372 **Ocean Alliance**
32 Horton Street 978-281-2814
Gloucester, MA 01930 info@whale.org
whale.org
Ocean Alliance is a nonprofit organization dedicated to increasing public awareness of the importance of whale and ocean health through research and public education.
Founded: 1971
Iain Kerr, Chief Executive Officer
Roger Payne, PhD, President

373 **Oceanic Preservation Society (OPS)**
336 Bon Air Center info@opsociety.org
Suite 384 opsociety.org
Greenbrae, CA 94904
The Oceanic Preservation Society is dedicated to the conservation of marine ecosystems and promote advocacy through the use of film, photography, social media, and collaboration.
Louie Psihoyos, Founder & CEO
Samara Stein, Chief Operating Officer

374 **Open Space Institute**
1350 Broadway 212-290-8200
Suite 201 *Fax:* 212-244-3441
New York, NY 10018 webmaster@osiny.org
www.openspaceinstitute.org
Protects land for public benefit and supports the efforts of citizen activists working to improve environmental regulations in their communities.
Christopher J. Elliman, President & CEO
Robert K. Anderberg, Sr. VP & General Counsel

375 **Openlands**
25 East Washington Street 312-863-6250
Suite 1650 *Fax:* 312-863-6251
Chicago, IL 60602 info@openlands.org
openlands.org
Openlands is one of the nation's oldest and most successful metropolitan conservation organizations, having helped secure, protect, and provide public access to more than 55,000 acres of land for parks, forest preserves, wildliferefuges, land and water greenway corridors, and urban gardens in the Chicago region.
Founded: 1963
Carrie C. McNally, Chair
Gerald W. Adelmann, President & CEO

376 **Ozark Society**
PO Box 2914 501-679-2935
Little Rock, AR 72203 ospres@ozarksociety.net
www.ozarksociety.net
Regional conservation organization dedicated to preserving the rivers, wilderness and unique natural areas of the Ozark-Ouachita region and its associated bottom land habitat.
Founded: 1962
David Peterson, President
Lucas Parsch, Vice-President

377 **Pacific Marine Mammal Center**
20612 Laguna Canyon Road 949-494-3050
Laguna Beach, CA 92651 info@pacificmmc.org
www.pacificmmc.org
Formerly Friends of the Sea Lion Marine Mammal Center, Pacific Marine Mammal Center is a nonprofit organization staffed by dedicated volunteers and funded by donations. Its mission is to rescue, medically treat and rehabilitate sealsand sea lions that are stranded along Orange County, California beaches due to injury and illness; release healthly animals back to their natural habitat; and increase public awareness of the marine environment through education and research.
Peter Chang, Chief Executive Officer
Keith Matassa, Dir., Conservation Programs

378 **Panthera**
8 West 40th Street 646-786-0400
18th Floor info@panthera.org
New York, NY 10018 panthera.org
Panthera is an international nonprofit organization devoted to the conservation of the world's 40 wild cat species and their ecosystems.
Founded: 2006
Fred Launay, PhD, President & CEO
John Goodrich, PhD, Chair & Chief Scientist

379 **Partners in Parks**
PO 362 714-393-8506
Tustin, CA 92781 www.partnersinparks.org
Organizes and directs volunteers for work in city parks and trails. Outdoor work can be as simple as litter pick-up to trail cleaning and tree planting.
Founded: 1988

380 **Peregrine Fund**
5668 W Flying Hawk Lane 208-362-3716
Boise, ID 83709 *Fax:* 208-362-2376
tpf@peregrinefund.org
www.peregrinefund.org
The Peregrine Fund was founded to restore the Peregrine Falcon, which was removed from the U.S. Endangered Species List in 1999. That success has encouraged the organization to expand its focus and apply its experience andunderstanding to raptor conservation efforts on behalf of 87 species in 61 countries worldwide, including the California Condor and Aplomado Falcon in the United States. The organization is non-political, solution-oriented, and hands-on.
Founded: 1970
Rick Watson, PhD, President & CEO
Munir Virani, PhD, Vice President, Conservation

381 **Pheasants Forever**
1783 Buerkle Circle 651-773-2000
St. Paul, MN 55110 877-773-2070
contact@pheasantsforever.org
www.pheasantsforever.org
A nonprofit organization dedicated to the protection and enhancement of pheasant and other wildlife populations in North America. This mission is carried out through habitat improvement, land management, public awareness, andeducation.
Founded: 1982 149,000 Members
Tim Kessler, Chair
Howard K. Vincent, President & CEO

382 **Point Blue Conservation Science**
3820 Cypress Drive 707-781-2555
Suite 11 *Fax:* 707-765-1685
Petaluma, CA 94954 pointblue@pointblue.org
pointblue.org
Point Blue's mission is to conserve birds, other wildlife and ecosystems through science, partnerships, and outreach.
Founded: 1965
Manuel Oliva, Chief Executive Officer
Grant Ballard, PhD, Chief Science Officer

383 **Prairie Grouse Technical Council**
North American Grouse Partnership
1670 N 1/2 Road NAGP@grousepartners.org
Fruita, CO 81521 www.grousepartners.org/pgtc

The Prairie Grouse Technical Council is an organization of people who appreciate and enjoy grouses and their habitats. The group meets in odd numbered years.
Steve Belinda, Executive Director, NAGP

384 Project AWARE
301541 Tomas 949-858-7657
Suite 200 projectaware.org
Rancho Santa Margarita, CA 92688
Nonprofit organization dedicated to engaging divers and activists around the world in marine conservation with a focus on sharks and marine debris.
Founded: 1992
Danna Moore, Director, Global Operations
Ian Campbell, Associate Director

385 Public Lands Alliance (PLA)
2401 Blueridge Ave 301-946-9475
Suite 303 *Fax:* 301-946-9478
Silver Spring, MD 20902 publiclandsalliance.org
Formely known as Association of Partners for Public Lands (APPL), Public Lands Alliance work to create understanding and appreciation for America's public lands by partnering with nonprofit organizations.
Founded: 1977
Dan Puskar, President & CEO
Jocelyn Boss, Manager, Development

386 Public Lands Foundation (PLF)
PO Box 7226 703-935-0916
Arlington, VA 22207-0226 866-985-9636
Fax: 888-204-9814
info@publicland.org
publicland.org
National nonprofit membership organization that advocates and works for the retention of America's National System of Public Lands (NSPL) in public hands, professionally and sustainably managed by the Bureau of Land Management (BLM)for responsible use and enjoyment by everyone.
Founded: 1987
Ed Shepard, President
Don Simpson, Vice-President

387 Quail Forever
1783 Buerkle Circle 651-209-4981
St. Paul, MN 55110 866-457-8245
contact@quailforever.org
www.quailforever.org
Quail Forever is a division of Pheasant Forever. Quail Forever is a grassroots, volunteer, membership-based organization that sets out to preserve and replenish quail habitats and quail populations acros North America.
Founded: 2005 $35 annually
Howard K. Vincent, President & CEO

388 Rainforest Alliance
125 Broad Street 212-677-1900
9th Floor *Fax:* 212-677-2187
New York, NY 10004 info@ra.org
www.rainforest-alliance.org
Dedicated to tropical forest conservation for the benefit of the global community. Rainforest Alliance works with farmers, foresters and tourism entrepreneurs. Through education and training they believe they can show people how tominimize environmental impact, while earning a stable income.
Founded: 1987
Han De Groot, Chief Executive Officer
Alex Morgan, Chief Markets Officer

389 Raptor Education Foundation (REF)
PO Box 200400 303-680-8500
Denver, CO 80220 *Fax:* 720-685-9988
raptor2@usaref.org
www.usaref.org
Raptors refer to birds with hoooked beakes; eagles, hawks, falcons and owls are all raptors. REF provides environmental literacy to schools, corporations, conventions and gatherings of all sizes, including consulting services. They uselive, non-releasable raptors in their seminars and programs to better demonstrate environmental concepts. Their raptor sanctuary in Colorado is the state's most comprehensive resource for all things related to eagles, hawks, falcons, owls, andvultures.
Founded: 1980
Peter Reshetniak, Chair
Marie Bolster, Vice President

390 Rare
1310 North Courthouse Road 703-522-5070
Suite 110 *Fax:* 703-522-5027
Arlington, VA 22201 info@rare.org
www.rare.org
Rare is an organization that focuses on the things that are working in environmental conservation. Rare's methodology revolves around locally-led solutions, bright spots, and repeats them in communities around the globe.
Founded: 1973
Brett Jenks, President & CEO
Anna Bartlett, Chief of Staff

391 Ruffed Grouse Society
451 McCormick Road 412-262-4044
Coraopolis, PA 15108 888-564-6747
rgs@ruffedgrousesociety.org
www.ruffedgrousesociety.org
The Ruffed Grouse Society's role in conservation of wildlife habitat is to enhance the environment for the Ruffed Grouse, American Woodcock, and other forest wildlife that require or utilize thick, young forests.
Founded: 1961
Benjamin C. Jones, President & CEO
Tracy M. Greene, Director, Headquarters

392 Save the Dunes Council
444 Barker Road 219-879-3564
Michigan City, IN 46360 *Fax:* 219-872-4875
office@savedunes.org
savedunes.org
Maintains and restores the integrity and quality of the natural environment of the Indiana Dunes region. Their work led to the establishment of the Indiana Dunes National Lakeshore in 1966; the group continues to work on a wide varietyof issues concerning the Dunes and the environmental quality of the area.
Founded: 1952
Natalie Johnson, Executive Director
Cathy Martin, Program Manager

393 Save the Manatee Club (SMC)
500 N Maitland Avenue 407-539-0990
Suite 210 800-432-5646
Maitland, FL 32751 *Fax:* 407-539-0871
membership@savethemanatee.org
www.savethemanatee.org
Nonprofit organization established by US Senator Bob Graham and singer/songwriter Jimmy Buffett so the general public could participate in conservation efforts to save endangered manatees from extinction. The purpose of SMC is topromote public awareness and education; fund manatee research, rescue, and rehabilitation efforts; lobby for the protection of manatees and their habitat, and take appropriate legal action.
Founded: 1981
Patrick Rose, Executive Director
Tonya Higgins, Director, Development

394 Scenic America
727 15th Street NW 202-792-1300
Suite 1100 max.ashburn@scenic.org
Washington, DC 20005-6029 www.scenic.org
A national nonprofit organization dedicated solely to protecting natural beauty and distinctive community character. They provide technnical assistance across the nation and through their state affiliates on scenic byways, billboardand sign control, context sensitive highway design, wireless telecommunications tower location, transportation enhancements, and other scenic

conservation. Scenic's number one goal is to build a citizen movement for scenic conservation througheducation.
Mark Falzone, President
Max Ashburn, Director, Communciations

395 Sea Turtle Conservancy
4581 NW 6th Street
Suite A
Gainesville, FL 32609
352-373-6441
Fax: 352-375-2449
stc@conserveturtles.org
www.conserveturtles.org
Strives to ensure the survival of sea turtles within the Wider Caribbean basin and Atlantic through research, education, training, advocacy and protection of habitats. CCC was the first marine turtle conservation organization in theworld, and has more than 40 years of experience in national and international sea turtle conservation, research and educational endeavors.
Founded: 1959
Landon T. Clay, Chair
Laura Forte, President

396 Seacology
1623 Solano Avenue
Berkeley, CA 94707
510-559-3505
Fax: 510-559-3506
islands@seacology.org
seacology.org
Seacology is a nonprofit organization whose mission is to work with islanders around the world to protect threatened ecosystems and help their local communities.
Founded: 1991
Duane Silverstein, Executive Director
Mary Rudolph, Program Manager

397 Secore International
4673 Northwest Parkway
Hilliard, OH 43026
614-969-3150
info@secore.org
secore.org
Secore International is a nonprofit organization dedicated to the protection and restorarion of coral reefs.
Dirk Petersen, Founder & Executive Director
Kara Rising, Administrative Manager

398 Sierra Club
2101 Webster Street
Suite 1300
Oakland, CA 94612
415-977-5500
Fax: 510-208-3140
information@sierraclub.org
www.sierraclub.org
Seeks to advance the preservation and protection of the natural environment by empowering the citizenry with charitable resources to further the cause of environmental protection.
Founded: 1892
Michael Brune, Executive Director
Jennifer Trahan, Chief Operating Officer

399 Smithsonian Institution
Smithsonian Information
SI building, Room 153, MRC 010
PO Box 37012
Washington, DC 20013-7012
202-633-1000
866-868-7774
info@si.edu
www.si.edu
Independent trust instrumental of the United States holding more than 154 million artifacts and specimens in its trust for the public interest and knowledge. Also a center for research dedicated to public education, national service,and scholarship in the arts, sciences, and history.
Founded: 1846
Dr. David J. Skorton, Secretary
Cathy Helm, Inspector General

400 Snow Leopard Trust
4649 Sunnyside Avenue North
Suite 325
Seattle, WA 98103
206-632-2421
Fax: 206-632-3967
info@snowleopard.org
www.snowleopard.org
The trust is dedicated to the conservation of the endangered Snow Leopard and its mountain ecosystem. Since its founding by Helen Freeman, ISLT has worked on more than 100 projects with local people throughout Central Asia. Focus is onsmall, creative and sustainable programs to make conservation happen now and in the future. Has hosted snow leopard symposia and developed the Snow Leopard Information Management System. This allows for range-wide comparison and sharing ofinformation.
Founded: 1981
Michael Despines, Executive Director
Chardutt Mishra, Dir., Science & Conservation

401 Society for Conservation Biology (SCB)
1133 15th Street, NW
Suite 300
Washington, DC 20005
202-384-4133
Fax: 855-523-6070
info@conbio.org
conbio.org
International professional organization dedicated to promoting the scientific study of the phenomena that affect the maintenance, loss, and restoration of biological diversity. The Society's membership comprises a wide range of peopleinterested in the conservation and study of biological diversity: resource managers, educators, government and private conservation workers, and students make up the more than 5,000 members world-wide.
Founded: 1986
Debborah Luke, PhD, Executive Director
Shona Gilliland Foster, Dir., Research Fellowships

402 Society for Marine Mammalogy
c/o Kathleen Moore
290 Summer Street
Yarmouth Port, MA 02675
admin@marinemammalscience.org
www.marinemammalscience.org
Seeks to evaluate and promote the educational, scientific and managerial advancement of marine mammal science. Gathers and disseminates to members of the Society, the public and private institutions, scientific, technical andmanagement information through publications and meetings. Provides scientific information, as required, on matters related to the conservation and management of marine mammal resources.
Founded: 1981
Charles Littnan, President
Tara M. Cox, Secretary

403 Sonoran Institute
100 N Stone Avenue
Suite 400
Tucson, AZ 85701
520-290-0828
Fax: 520-290-0969
tbullington@sonoraninstitute.org
www.sonoraninstitute.org
Nonprofit organization that works collaboratively with local people and interests to conserve and restore important natural landscapes in western North America, engaging partners such as landowners, public land managers, local leaders,commuunity residents and nongovernmental organizations. Community Stewardship is an innovative approach to conservation.
Founded: 1990
Stephanie Sklar, Chief Executive Officer
Michael Blimes, Director, Development

404 Tall Timbers Research Station
13093 Henry Beadel Drive
Tallahassee, FL 32312
850-893-4153
Fax: 850-668-7781
bpalmer@talltimbers.org
talltimbers.org
Dedicated to protecting wildlands and preserving natural habitats. Promotes public education on the importance of natural disturbances to the environment and the subsequent need for wildlife and land management. Conducts fire ecologyresearch and other biological research programs through the Tall Timbers Research Station. Operates a museum.
Founded: 1958
William E. Palmer, President & CEO
Crystal Davis, Director, Development

405 The International Osprey Foundation (TIOF)
PO Box 250
Sanibel, FL 33957
tiof@ospreys.com
www.ospreys.com
Nonprofit corporation dedicated to the continuing recovery and preservation of the osprey, others in the raptor family, wildlife and the environment as a whole. Conducts monitoring activities and accumulates data specific to thebreeding activities of the osprey population. Publishes newsletter, issues grants for researchers whose studies involve environmental concerns. Directs and

participates in all areas of wildlife and habitat maintenance and restoration.
Founded: 1981
Susan Tucker, Acting President

406 **The Mountain Institute (TMI)**
1725 I Street NW 202-234-4050
Suite 300 summit@mountain.org
Washington, DC 20006 www.mountain.org
Objectives are to conserve high priority mountain eco-systems; increase environmentally and culturally sustainable livelihoods for mountain communities; and promote support for mountain cultures and issues through advocacy, educationand outreach.
Founded: 1972
Edie Farwell, Acting Executive Director
Erin Gleeson, Associate Director

407 **Theodore Roosevelt Conservation Partnership (TRCP)**
529 14th Street NW 202-639-8727
Suite 500 *Fax:* 202-639-8728
Washington, DC 20045 info@trcp.org
www.trcp.org
Mission to preserve America's quality places to hunt and fish. TRCP supports federal policy and funding solutions by uniting its partners and making the voices of American sportsmen and women heard.
Founded: 1991
Whit Fosburgh, President & CEO
Christy Plumer, Chief Conservation Officer

408 **Tread Lightly!**
500 N Marketplace Drive 801-627-0077
Suite 240 800-966-9900
Centerville, UT 84014 *Fax:* 801-990-9807
treadlightly@treadlightly.org
www.treadlightly.org
National nonprofit organization dedicated to proactively protecting recreation access and opportunities through education and stewardship.
Founded: 1985
Keith Gordon, Executive Director
Danielle L. Fowles, Assistant Director

409 **Trees for Life**
3006 W St Louis 316-945-6929
Wichita, KS 67203-5129 *Fax:* 316-945-0909
info@treesforlife.org
www.treesforlife.org
Empowers people by demonstrating that in helping each other, they can unleash extraordinary power that impacts lives. By planting fruit trees in developing countries, Trees for Life protect the environment and provide a low-cost,self-renewing source of food for a large number of people. Activities include three elements: education, health and environment.
Founded: 1984
Balbir S. Mathur, President & Founder
Jeffrey Faus, Assistant to President

410 **Trout Unlimited**
PO Box 7400 703-522-0200
Woolly Bugger, WV 25438-7400 800-834-2419
Fax: 703-284-9400
trout@tu.org
www.tu.org
This organization seeks to conserve, protect and restore North America's trout and salmon fisheries and their watersheds.
Founded: 1959 300,000 members
Chris Wood, President & CEO
Elizabeth Maclin, Executive Vice President

411 **Trumpeter Swan Society (TSS)**
12615 Rockford Road 763-441-1994
Plymouth, MN 55441-1248 *Fax:* 763-557-4943
ttss@trumpeterswansociety.org
www.trumpeterswansociety.org
Private, nonprofit organization dedicated to assuring the vitality and welfare of wild Trumpeter Swan populations, and to restoring the species to as much of its former range as possible.
Founded: 1968
Carey Smith, President
Margaret Smith, Executive Director

412 **Trust for Public Land**
101 Montgomery Street 415-495-4014
Suite 900 800-714-5263
San Francisco, CA 94104 www.tpl.org
National nonprofit land conservation organization working to protect land for human enjoyment and well-being.
Founded: 1972
Diane Regas, President & CEO
Adrian Benepe, Sr. VP/Dir., Nat'l Programs

413 **Turtle Island Restoration Network**
9255 Sir Francis Drake Blvd 415-663-8590
Olema, CA 94950 800-859-7283
info@seaturtles.org
www.seaturtles.org
Fights to protect endangered sea turtle populations in ways that meet the ecological needs of the sea turtles and the oceans and inland watersheds that sustain them.
Founded: 1989
Donna Howe, Board Chair
Todd Steiner, Executive Director

414 **United Nations Environment Programme New York Office**
2 UN Plaza, Room DC2-803 212-963-8210
323 E. 44th Street *Fax:* 212-963-7341
New York, NY 10017 unepnyo@un.org
www.unenvironment.org/regions/north-america/new-york-office
Provides leadership and to encourage partnership in caring for the environment by inspiring, informing, and enabling nations and peoples to improve their quality of life without compromising that of future generations.
Founded: 1972
Satya S. Tripathi, Director

415 **Waitt Institute**
PO Box 1948 858-551-4437
La Jolla, CA 92038-1948 waittinstitute.org
The Waitt Institute endeavors to ensure ecologically, economically, and culturally sustainable use of ocean resources. The Institute partners with governments committed to developing and implementing comprehensive, science-based,community-driven solutions for sustainable ocean management. They aim to benefit coastal communities while restoring fish populations and habitats.
Kathryn Mengerink, PhD, Executive Director
Tamara Marshall, Director, Operations & Legal

416 **Waterfowl USA**
PO Box 500 803-637-5767
Oak Forest, IL 60452 nwfusa@yahoo.com
www.waterfowlusa.org
National nonprofit, conservation organization dedicated to using funds for local and state waterfowl projects.
Founded: 1983
Mark Judge, President
Tabatha Cloutier, Executive Director

417 **Western Hemisphere Shorebird Reserve Network (WHSRN)**
PO Box 1770 207-721-9040
Manomet, MA 02345 whsrn@manomet.org
www.whsrn.org
Voluntary, community-based coalition of 106 sites across the US and other countries in the Western Hemisphere that have joined together to protect, restore and manage critical wetland habitats for migratory birds.
Rob P. Clay, Director
Laura Chamberlin, Assistant Director

418 **Western Society of Naturalists**
PO Box 247 secretariat@wsn-online.org
Bodega Bay, CA 94923 www.wsn-online.org
A scientific society with a strong focus on ecology, evolution, natural history and marine biology. Its members are predominantly from the west coast. The society organizes one or two meetings each year for its members.
Founded: 1916
Danielle Zacherl, President
Andrew Brooks, Treasurer

419 **Whitetails Unlimited (WTU)**
2100 Michigan Street 920-743-6777
PO Box 720 800-274-5471
Sturgeon Bay, WI 54235 *Fax:* 920-743-4658
www.whitetailsunlimited.com
A national nonprofit conservation organization that dedicates their resources to the betterment of the white-tail deer and its environment.
Founded: 1982
Jeffrey Schinkten, President
Peter J. Gerl, Executive Director

420 **Wild Oceans**
PO Box 258 703-777-0037
Waterford, VA 20197 wildoceans.org
Wild Oceans (formerly the National Coalition for Marine Conservation or NCMC) is a nonprofit organization dedicated to the protection of fish by bringing conservation-minded fishermen and pro-fishing environmentalists together topromote a broad, ecosystems approach to fisheries management.
Founded: 1973
Ken Hinman, President
Pam Lyons Gromen, Executive Director

421 **Wilderness Society**
1615 M Street, NW 202-833-2300
Washington, DC 20036 800-843-9453
action@tws.org
wilderness.org
Protects the wilderness and inspires Americans to care for the wild places. Devoted to protecting the nation's well-known icons and hidden gems, because the wilderness provides clean air and water; abundant wildlife; havens forrecreation, solitude and sources of renewable energy; and vital natural resources.
Founded: 1935
David Churchill, Chair
Jamie Williams, President

422 **Wilderness Watch**
PO Box 9175 406-542-2048
Missoula, MT 59807 wild@wildernesswatch.org
wildernesswatch.org
Leading the nation as an organization whose sole focus in the preservation and proper stewardship of lands and rivers included in the National Wilderness Preservation System (NWPS). Established out of the concern that already existingWilderness and rivers are largely ignored.
Founded: 1989
George Nickas, Executive Director
Clare Mack, Policy Director

423 **Wildlife Action**
405 N Main Street 843-464-8473
PO Box 866 800-753-2264
Mullins, SC 29574 *Fax:* 843-464-8859
wlaceo@bellsouth.net
www.wildlifeaction.com
Raises public awareness about wildlife habitat, security, protection and management; protects the rivers and wetlands from unnecessary destruction and development and works to reduce poaching, trespassing and other illegal outdooractivities.
Founded: 1977
Rivers Anderson, National President
John Watson, National VP

424 **Wildlife Conservation Society (WCS)**
2300 Southern Boulevard 718-220-5100
Bronx, NY 10460 *Fax:* 718-220-2685
www.wcs.org
WCS is at work in 16 priority regions across Africa, Latin America and North America, protecting wild landscapes that are home to a variety of species from butterflies to tigers. They uniquely combine the resources of wildlife parks inNew York with field projects around the globe to inspire care for nature, provide leadership in environmental eduation, and help sustain our planet's biological diversity.
Founded: 1895
Cristian Samper, PhD, President & CEO
Robert G. Menzi, Executive VP & COO

425 **Wildlife Disease Association (WDA)**
c/o Allen Press, Inc.
PO Box 7065 785-865-9404
Lawrence, KS 66044-7065 800-627-0326
Fax: 785-843-6153
wda@allenpress.com
www.wildlifedisease.org
Acquires, disseminates and applies knowledge of the health and diseases of wild animals in relation to their biology, conservation and interactions with human and domestic animals.
Founded: 1952
Dave Jessup, Executive Manager
Christopher Lapine, Association Manager

426 **Wildlife Forever**
5350 Hwy 61 N 763-253-0222
Suite 7 www.wildlifeforever.org
White Bear Lake, MN 55110
Wildlife Forever conserves America's wildlife heritage through preservation of habitat, conservation education and management of fish and wildlife.
Founded: 1987
Douglas H. Grann, President & CEO

427 **Wildlife Habitat Council**
8737 Colesville Road 301-588-8994
Suite 800 whc@wildlifehc.org
Silver Spring, MD 20910 www.wildlifehc.org
Nonprofit group of corporations, conservations, and individuals dedicated to protecting and enhancing wildlife habitat.
Founded: 1998
Margaret O'Gorman, President
Josiane Bonneau, Sr. Dir., Conservation

428 **Wildlife Management Institute (WMI)**
1440 Upper Bermudian Road 717-677-4480
Gardners, PA 17324 info@wildlifemgt.org
wildlifemanagement.institute
Private, nonprofit, scientific and educational organization committed to the conservation, enhancement and professional management of North America's wildlife and other natural resources.
Founded: 1911
Steven Williams, PhD, President & Project Manager
Scot Williamson, Vice President

429 **Wildlife Society**
425 Barlow Place 301-897-9770
Suite 200 tws@wildlife.org
Bethesda, MD 20814 wildlife.org
Nonprofit scientific and educational organization that serves professionals such as government agencies, academia, industry, and non-government organizations in all areas related to the conservation of wildlife and natural resourcesmanagement.
Founded: 1937
Gary C. White, PhD, President
Carol L. Chambers, PhD, Vice President

430 **Wilson Ornithological Society**
Biology Dept., Hobart & William Smith Colleges
Geneva, NY 14456 734-764-0457
deutschlande@hws.edu
wilsonsociety.org

Global organization of people interested in birds.
Founded: 1888
Mark Deutschlander, President
Jameson Chace, 1st Vice-President

431 **Wolf Education and Research Center (WERC)**
PO Box 12604 888-422-1110
Portland, OR 97212 info@wolfcenter.org
www.wolfcenter.org
Dedicated to providing public education concerning the gray wolf and its habitat in the Northern Rocky Mountains. Provides the public with the rare opportunity to observe and learn about wolves in their natural habitat.

432 **Wolf Haven International**
3111 Offut Lake Road SE 360-264-4695
Tenino, WA 98589 800-448-9653
Fax: 360-264-4639
info@wolfhaven.org
wolfhaven.org
Conserves and protects wolves and their habitat. They are nationally and internationally certified sanctuary for captive-born and displaced wolves. Wolf Haven offers a variety of educational programs in English and Spanish about wolvesand the value of all wildlife. Guided 50-minute sanctuary visits offer guests an opportunity to learn more about wolves and their role in the wild.
Founded: 1982
Diane Gallegos, Executive Director
Linda Saunders, Director, Conservation

433 **World Bird Sanctuary**
125 Bald Eagle Ridge Road 636-225-4390
Valley Park, MO 63088 *Fax:* 636-861-3240
info@worldbirdsanctuary.org
www.worldbirdsanctuary.org
Seeks to preserve the earth's biological diversity and to secure the future of threatened bird species in their natural environment, through education, propagation, field studies and rehabilitation.
Dawn Griffard, Executive Director
Roger Holloway, Deputy Director

434 **World Forestry Center (WFC)**
4033 SW Canyon Road 503-228-1367
Portland, OR 97221 *Fax:* 503-228-4608
www.worldforestry.org
They educate and inform people about the world's forests and trees and their importance to all life, in order to promote a balanced and sustainable future. The WFC also operates a museum in Portland, OR, with local, national, andinternational programs and three demonstration forests.
Founded: 1964
Joseph Furia, Executive Director
Darlene Boles, Financial Director

435 **World Wildlife Fund (WWF)**
1250 24th Street NW 202-293-4800
PO Box 97180 800-225-5993
Washington, DC 20037 *Fax:* 202-293-9211
membership@wwfus.org
www.worldwildlife.org
Dedicated to protecting endangered species and their habitats through field work, advocacy, policy engagement, pioneering work and education. The largest multinational conservation organization in the world. WWF works in 100 countriesand is supported by more than 1 million members in the US and almost 5 million members globally.
Founded: 1960
Carter Roberts, President & CEO
Nik Sekhran, Chief Conservation Officer

436 **Xerces Society for Invertebrate Conservation**
628 NE Broadway 503-232-6639
Suite 200 855-232-6639
Portland, OR 97232 *Fax:* 503-233-6794
info@xerces.org
www.xerces.org
An international non profit organization dedicated to protecting biological diversity through inverterate conservation. Core programs focus on endangered species, protecting pollinators and watershed health.
Founded: 1971
Scott Hoffman Black, Executive Director
Denise Ledgerwood, Director, Grants

National: Recycling & Pollution Prevention

437 **Acoustical Society of America (ASA)**
1305 Walt Whitman Road 516-576-2360
Suite 300 *Fax:* 631-923-2875
Melville, NY 11747-4300 asa@acousticalsociety.org
acousticalsociety.org
For years the society has been involved in studies of noise as far as measurements, effects, and ways of reducing noise to improve the human environment.
Founded: 1929
Susan Fox, Executive Director
Elaine Moran, Director, Operations

438 **Air & Waste Management Association**
Koppers Building 412-232-3444
436 Seventh Avenue, Suite 2100 800-270-3444
Pittsburgh, PA 15219 *Fax:* 412-232-3450
info@awma.org
www.awma.org
Professional development organization providing a forum for the exchange of information, networking, public education, and outreach to over 5,000 environmental professionals in 65 countries.
Founded: 1907
Stephanie Glyptis, Executive Director
Tracy Fedkoe, Director, Marketing

439 **Association of Battery Recyclers (ABR)**
www.associationofbatteryrecyclers.com
Aims to keep members abreast of environmental, health, and safety requirements that affect the industry. The association meets two times a year and membership consists of recyclers of lead-acid batteries and their components,manufacturers and environmental consulting services.
Founded: 1984

440 **Association of State and Territorial Solid Waste Management Officials (ASTSWMO)**
1101 17th Street NW 202-640-1060
Suite 707 *Fax:* 202-331-3254
Washington, DC 20036 daniar@astswmo.org
www.astswmo.org
Seeks to enhance and promote effective state and territorial waste management programs, and affect national waste management policies.
Founded: 1974
Dania Rodriguez, Executive Director
Kerry Callahan, Senior Program Manager

441 **Citizens' Climate Lobby**
1330 Orange Ave 619-437-7142
Suite 309 citizensclimatelobby.org
Coronado, CA 92118
Citizens' Climate Lobby is a non-profit, non-partisan, grassroots advocacy organization focused on national policies to address climate change.
Founded: 2007
Marshall Saunders, Founder & President
Mark Reynolds, Executive Director

442 **College & University Recycling Coalition (CURC)**
curc3r.org
Nonprofit organization dedicated to helping higher education institutions facilitate the exchange of technical knowledge and best practices on recycling and waste reduction programs. CURC represents a community of over 900 recyclingand sustainability professionals in higher education led by a Board of Directors made

up of recycling, zero waste and sustainability managers in North America.
Brittany Morra, Chair
Eric Halvarson, Program Coordinator

443 Container Recycling Institute (CRI)
4361 Keystone Avenue 310-559-7451
Culver City, CA 90232 info@container-recycling.org
www.container-recycling.org
Nonprofit organization that studies and promotes policies and programs that increase recovery and recycling of beverage containers, and shift the social and environmental costs associated with manufacturing, recycling and disposal ofcontainer and packaging waste from government and taxpayers to producers and consumers.
Founded: 1991
Susan V. Collins, President
Karen Hilsberg, Project Manager

444 Environmental Technology Council (ETC)
1112 16th Street NW 202-783-0870
Suite 420 *Fax:* 202-737-2038
Washington, DC 20036 www.etc.org
Trade association of commercial environmental firms the recycle, treat and dispose of industrial and hazardous wastes; and firms involved in cleanup of contaminated sites.
Founded: 1982
David Case, Executive Director

445 Global Links
700 Trumbull Drive 412-361-3424
Pittsburgh, PA 15205 *Fax:* 412-875-6150
globallinks.org
Global Links is a medical relief and development organization dedicated to supporting health improvement initiatives in resource-poor communities and promoting environmental stewardship in the US healthcare system. The organization iscommited to environmental and sustainable practices and ensures recycling and reuse of medical surplus and deliver them to resource-poor communities.
Founded: 1989
Angela Garcia, Executive Director
Matt Fuller, Director, Operations

446 Institute of Clean Air Companies (ICAC)
2200 Wilson Boulevard 571-858-3707
Suite 310 *Fax:* 703-243-8696
Arlington, VA 22201 icacinfo@icac.com
www.icac.com
Organization of manufacturers of air pollution monitoring and control systems.
Founded: 1960
Clare Schulzki, Executive Director
Haley Armstrong, Director, Policy & Programs

447 Institute of Noise Control Engineering (INCE-USA)
11130 Sunrise Valley Drive 703-234-4124
Suite 350 *Fax:* 703-435-4390
Reston, VA 20191 ibo@inceusa.org
www.inceusa.org
A non-profit professional organization that promotes noise control solutions to environmental, product, machinery, industrial and other noise problems.
Joseph M. Cuschieri, Executive Director
Beatrice Barry, Business Manager

448 Institute of Scrap Recycling Industries (ISRI)
1250 H Street 202-662-8500
Suite 400 *Fax:* 202-626-0900
Washington, DC 20005 isri@isri.org
www.isri.org
Membership is made up of manufacturers and processors, brokers and industrial consumers of scrap commodities, including ferrous and nonferrous metals, paper, electronics, rubber, plastics, glass and textiles. ISRI's associate membersinclude equipment and service providers to the scrap recycling industry.
Robin Wiener, President
David Wagger, Chief Scientist

449 Kids Against Pollution (KAP)
8096 Boonville Road 315-942-4492
Boonville, NY 13309 contact@kids-against-pollution.org
www.kids-against-pollution.org
Nonprofit organization of active youth dedicated to solving and preventing pollution problems through educational projects and events in order to protect children's health and the planet.
Founded: 1987

450 Manufacturers of Emission Controls Association (MECA)
2200 Wilson Boulevard 202-296-4797
Suite 310 *Fax:* 202-331-1388
Arlington, VA 22201 asantos@meca.org
www.meca.org
Offers current and relevant technical information on emission control technology thereby facilitating strong state, federal and local air quality programs that promote public health, environmental quality and industrial progress.
Founded: 1976
Rasto Brezny, Executive Director
Michael Geller, Deputy Director

451 Municipal Waste Management Association (MWMA)
1620 I Street NW 202-293-7330
Washington, DC 20006 info@usmayors.org
www.usmayors.org/mwma
MWMA promotes operational efficiencies, facilitates information, fosters innovation and promotes legislation advocacy around Superfund, brownfields redevlopment, clean air and water and waste energy regulations.
Founded: 1982
Paul F. Alcantar, President
Lori M.K. Kahikina, 1st Vice-President

452 NORA An Association of Responsible Recyclers
7250 Heritage Village Plaza 703-753-4277
Suite 201 *Fax:* 703-753-2445
Gainesville, VA 20155 sparker@noranews.org
www.noranews.org
A trade association that represents more than 325 leading companies in the liquid recycling industry. It defends and promotes the liquid recycling industry and business.
Founded: 1985
Scott D. Parker, Executive Director
Casey Parker, Associate Director

453 National Association for PET Container Resources (NAPCOR)
3440 Toringdon Way 980-265-2353
Suite 250 www.napcor.com
Charlotte, NC 28277
A trade association that helps communities establish recycling programs and conducts promotional and educational activities to promote PET plastic container recycling. The members of NAPCOR are manufacturers of polyester resins andbottles.
Founded: 1987
Darrel Collier, Executive Director
Kate Eagles, Project Director

454 National Association of Clean Air Agencies
444 N Capitol St NW 202-624-7864
Suite 307 *Fax:* 202-624-7863
Washington, DC 20001 4cleanair@4cleanair.org
www.4cleanair.org
National, non-partisan, non-profit association of air pollution control agencies.
Miles Keogh, Executive Director
Nancy Kruger, Deputy Director

455 National Center for Electronics Recycling (NCER)
161 Studio Lane 304-699-1008
Vienna, WV 26105 jlinnell@electronicsrecycling.org
electronicsrecycling.org
Nonprofit organization dedicated to the development and enhancement of a national infrastructure for the recycling of used electronics in the U.S. through the coordination of initiatives, participation in pilot projects to advance andencourage electron-

ics recycling, and the development of programs that reduce the burden of government through private management of electronics recycling systems.
Founded: 2005
Jason Linnell, Executive Director
Heather Smith, Senior Manager

456 **National Council for Air and Stream Improvements (NCASI)**
1513 Walnut Street 919-941-6400
Suite 200 administrator@ncasi.org
Cary, NC 27511 www.ncasi.org
The Council is a technical organization devoted to finding solutions to environmental protection problems in the manufacture of pulp, paper, and wood products in industrial forestry.
Founded: 1943
Dirk J. Krouskop, President
Tammerah D. Garren, VP, Business Affairs

457 **National Recycling Coalition, Inc. (NRC)**
PO Box 731 303-907-8609
Erie, CO 80516 nrcexecdirector@gmail.com
nrcrecycles.org
Nonprofit advocacy group with members from all aspects of the waste reduction, reuse and recycling industries. It is dedicated to the advancement and improvement of recycling, waste prevention, composting and reuse.
Founded: 1978
David Keeling, President
Stephen Bantillo, Executive Vice President

458 **National Waste & Recycling Association (NWRA)**
1550 Crystal Drive 202-244-4700
Suite 804 800-424-2869
Arlington, VA 22202 *Fax:* 202-966-4824
info@wasterecycling.org
wasterecycling.org
Formerly known as the Environmental Industry Associations, which oversaw the National Solid Wastes Management Association and the Waste and Equipment Technology Association. This trade association represents private-sector companies inNorth America that provide solid, hazardous and medical waste collection, recycling and disposal services, and companies that provide professionals and consulting services to the waste services industry.
Founded: 1962
Darrell K. Smith, President & CEO
Kevin Kraushaar, Sr. VP, Government Affairs

459 **Noise Free America**
P.O. Box 2754 877-664-7366
Chapel Hill, NC 27515 director@noisefree.org
www.noisefree.org
A national non-profit organization aimed at reducing noise pollution in the community. Their main focus is on noises from airplaines and helicopters, road vehicles, lawn and garden equipment, music, sports stadiums, and other sources.
Founded: 2001

460 **Noise Pollution Clearinghouse**
PO Box 1137 888-200-8332
Montpelier, VT 05601-1137 npc@nonoise.org
www.nonoise.org
National nonprofit organization with extensive online noise related resources. Creates more civil cities and more natural rural and wilderness areas by reducing noise pollution at the source.

461 **Physicians for Social Responsibility (PSR)**
1111 14th St., NW 202-667-4260
Suite 700 *Fax:* 202-667-4201
Washington, DC 20005 psrnatl@psr.org
www.psr.org
A non-profit advocacy organization that is the medical and public health voice for policies to prevent nuclear war and proliferation and to slow, stop and reverse global warming and toxic degradation of the environment.
Jeff Carter, Executive Director
Barbara Gottlieb, Dir., Environment & Health

462 **Public Citizen**
1600 20th Street NW 202-588-1000
Washington, DC 20009 member@citizen.org
www.citizen.org
A consumer advocacy organization founded to represent consumer interests in Congress, the executive branch, and the courts.
Founded: 1971
Robert Weissman, President
Margrete Strand Rangnes, Executive Vice-President

463 **Secondary Materials and Recycled Textiles Association (SMART)**
3465 Box Hill Corp. Center Drive 443-640-1050
Suite H *Fax:* 410-569-3340
Abingdon, MD 21009 smartinfo@kingmgmt.org
www.smartasn.org
Represents the interests of companies dealing with pre-consumer and post-consumer recycable textile materials. This material includes fibers, remnants, recycled clothing and shoes, and other related materials. SMART members alsomanufacture and distribute industrial and commercial wipers.
Founded: 1932
Jackie King, Executive Director
Jessica Franken, Director, Government Affairs

464 **Solid Waste Association of North America (SWANA)**
1100 Wayne Avenue 800-467-9262
Suite 650 *Fax:* 301-589-7068
Silver Spring, MD 20910 info@swana.org
swana.org
Professional organization for the advancement of responsible solid waste management.
Founded: 1965
David Biderman, Executive Director & CEO
Sara Bixby, Deputy Executive Director

465 **Southeast Recycling Development Council (SERDC)**
638 Spartanburg Hwy will.sagar@serdc.org
Suite 70-152 serdc.org
Hendersonville, NC 28792
Nonprofit dedicated to unite industry, government, and non-government organizations to promote sustainable recycling in the Southeast.
Will Sagar, Executive Director
Nicole Smith, Chair

466 **Steel Recycling Institute (SRI)**
680 Andersen Drive 412-922-2772
Pittsburgh, PA 15220 www.steelsustainability.org
The Steel Recycling Institute, a unit of the American Iron and Steel Institute, is an industry association that promotes and sustains the recycling of all steel products. The SRI educates the solid waste industry, government, bussinesand ultimately the consumer about the benefit of steel's infinite recycling cycle.
Founded: 1988

467 **Zero Waste USA**
672 Robinson Road 707-321-7883
Sebastopol, CA 95472 www.grrn.org
Formerly known as the GrassRoots Recycling Network, they are a national network of waste reduction activists and recycling professionals calling for Zero Waste in the United States.
Rick Anthony, Board President
Portia Sinnott, Program Director

National: Sustainable Development

468 **Alliance for Sustainability**
2801 21st Avenue S 612-250-0389
Suite 100 sean@afors.org
Minneapolis, MN 55407 www.afors.org
The Mission of the Alliance is to bring about personal, organizational and planetary sustainability through support of projects

that are ecologically sound, economically viable, socially just and humane.
Founded: 1983
Terry Gips, President
Sean Gosiewski, Executive Director

469 American Forest Foundation (AFF)
2000 M Street NW 202-765-3660
Suite 550 *Fax:* 202-827-7924
Washington, DC 20036 info@forestfoundation.org
www.forestfoundation.org
Nonprofit conservation and education organization that strives to ensure the sustainability of America's family forests for present and future generations. The vision is to create a future where North American forests are sustained bythe public which understands and values the social, economic, and environmental benefits they provide to the communities, the nation, and the world.
Founded: 1982
Tom Martin, President & CEO
Rita Hite, EVP, Woodlands & Policy

470 American Forests
1220 L Street NW 202-737-1944
Suite 750 *Fax:* 202-737-2457
Washington, DC 20005 info@americanforests.org
www.americanforests.org
Works to protect, restore and enhance the natural capital of trees and forests. Healthy forest filter water, remove air pollution, catch carbon, and provide homes for wildlife.
Founded: 1875
Jad Daley, President & CEO
Peter Hutchins, Chief Operations Officer

471 American Planning Association (APA)
205 N Michigan Avenue 312-431-9100
Suite 1200 *Fax:* 312-786-6700
Chicago, IL 60601-5927 www.planning.org
Nonprofit public interest and research organization representing 30,000 practicing officials, and citizens involved with urban and rural planning issues. Sixty-five percent of APA's members are employed by state and local governmentagencies. These members are involved, on a day-to-day basis, in formulating planning policies and preparing land use regulations.
Joel Albizo, Chief Executive Officer
Ann Simms, COO & CFO

472 American Society of Agronomy (ASA)
5585 Guilford Road 608-273-8080
Madison, WI 53711-5801 membership@agronomy.org
www.agronomy.org
Dedicated to development of agricultural interests in harmony with environmental and human values. The society supports scientific, educational and professional activities that enhance communication and technology transfer amongagronomists and those in related disciplines on topics of local, regional, national and international significance.
Sylvie M. Brouder, President
Ellen G.M. Bergfeld, Chief Executive Officer

473 Ancient Forest International (AFI)
PO Box 1850 707-923-4475
Redway, CA 95560 *Fax:* 707-923-4475
afi@ancientforests.org
www.ancient-forests.org
Ancient Forest International has been instrumental in the protection of primary forests around the world. With the help of its international ancient forest network, AFI develops opportunities for wildlands philanthropists andcommunities to work together to acquire and protect strategic and invaluable forestlands.
Founded: 1989

474 Association of Fish and Wildlife Agencies (AFWA)
1100 First Street, NE 202-838-3474
Suite 825 *Fax:* 202-350-9869
Washington, DC 20002 info@fishwildlife.org
www.fishwildlife.org
Representing North America's fish and wildlife agencies, they advance science-based management with the goal to conserve fish and wildlife and the habitats they depend on. The Association represents its state agency members on CapitolHill and before the Administration creating a clear and collective voice.
Founded: 1902
Ron Regan, Executive Director
Patricia Allen, Director, Communications

475 CONCERN
PO Box 5892 concern@sustainable.org
Washington, DC 20016 www.sustainable.org
CONCERN is a national nonprofit environmental education organization with a focus on sustainable communities. CONCERN disseminates examples of successful initiatives, offers numerous resources and guidelines for action, serves as aclearinghouse for information and collaborates with others to carry out its programs. Through its Sustainable Communities Network CONCERN seeks to increase public understanding of and participation in initatives that are environmentally and sociallysound.
Founded: 1970

476 Center for Clean Air Policy
750 First St NE 202-408-9260
Suite 1025 *Fax:* 202-408-8896
Washington, DC 20002 ccap.org
Climate and air quality think tank.
Founded: 1985
Allison Bender-Corbett, Executive Director
Stecey Davis, Director, Policy & Programs

477 Center for Ecoliteracy
David Brower Center
2150 Allston Way 510-845-4595
Suite 270 info@ecoliteracy.org
Berkeley, CA 94704-1377 www.ecoliteracy.org
Dedicated to fostering a profound understanding of the natural world, grounded in direct experience that leads to sustainable patterns of living.
Founded: 1995
Adam Kesselman, Executive Director
Karen Brown, Creative Director

478 Conservation Fund
1655 N Fort Myer Drive 703-525-6300
Suite 1300 *Fax:* 703-525-4610
Arlington, VA 22209-3199 webmaster@conservationfund.org
www.conservationfund.org
Forges partnerships to protect America's legacy of land and water resources. Through land acquisition, community initiatives and leadership training, the Fund and its partners demonstrate sustainable conservation solutions emphasizingthe integration of economic and environmental goals.
Founded: 1985
Lawrence A. Selzer, President & CEO
Holly Cannon, Executive Vice President

479 CropLife America (CLA)
1156 15th Street NW 202-296-1585
Washington, DC 20005 info@croplifeamerica.org
www.croplifeamerica.org
CLA promotes the environmentally sound use of crop protection products for the economical production of safe, high-quality food, fiber and renewable fuel.
Founded: 1933
Christopher Novak, President & CEO
Beau Greenwood, Executive Vice President

480 Earth Island Institute
2150 Allston Way 510-859-9100
Suite 460 *Fax:* 510-859-9091
Berkeley, CA 94704-1375 donorinquiry@earthisland.org
www.earthisland.org

A nonprofit, public interest, membership organization that supports people who are creating solutions to protect the shared planet.
Founded: 1982
David Phillips, Executive Director
Susan Kamprath, Director, Operations

481 Environmental and Energy Study Institute (EESI)
1020 19th Street NW 202-628-1400
Suite 650 *Fax:* 202-204-5244
Washington, DC 20036 info@eesi.org
www.eesi.org
Nonprofit organization dedicated to promoting environmentally sustainable societies. EESI believes meeting this goal requires transitions to social and economic patterns that sustain people, the environment and the natural resourcesupon which present and future generations depend. Offers a variety of publications.
Founded: 1984
Carol Werner, Executive Director
Susan Williams, Director, Development

482 Forest History Society
2925 Academy Road 919-682-9319
Durham, NC 27705-9311 *Fax:* 919-682-2349
steven.anderson@foresthistory.org
www.foresthistory.org
A nonprofit educational institution that links the past to the future by identifying, collecting, preserving, interpreting and disseminating information on the history of people, forests and their related resources.
Founded: 1946
Steven Anderson, President
Janet Askew, Assistant Director

483 Friends of the Earth
1100 15th Street NW 202-783-7400
11th Floor 877-843-8687
Washington, DC 20005 *Fax:* 202-783-0444
foe@foe.org
www.foe.org
National nonprofit advocacy organization dedicated to protecting the planet from environmental degradation; preserving biological, cultural and ethnic diversity, and empowering citizens to have an influential voice in decisionsaffecting the quality of their environment and their lives.
Founded: 1969
Erich Pica, President
Michelle Chan, Vice-President, Programs

484 Global Cities
One Rockefeller Plaza 212-618-6345
Suite 1134 info@globalcities.org
New York, NY 10020 www.globalcities.org
A Program of Bloomberg Philanthropies, Global Cities aims to connect cities around the world in an information-sharing network, to address common issues.
Marjorie B. Tiven, Founder

485 Holistic Management International (HMI)
5941 Jefferson St. NE 505-842-5252
Suite B *Fax:* 505-843-7900
Albuquerque, NM 87109 hmi@holisticmanagement.org
www.holisticmanagement.org
Seeks to help farmers, ranchers, and pastoralists enhance the efficiency, natural health, productivity and profitability of the land; increase natural annual profits; provide a framework for stakeholders to work together toward acommon future; and enable development agencies working with marginalized farmers or pastoral people to break the cycle of food and water insecurity.
Founded: 1984
Ann Adams, Executive Director
Kathy Harris, Director, Programs

486 Institute for Agriculture and Trade Policy (IATP)
2105 First Avenue South 612-870-0453
Minneapolis, MN 55404 *Fax:* 612-870-4846
info@iatp.org
www.iatp.org
IATP works locally and globally at the intersection of policy and practice to ensure fair and sustainable food, farm and trade systems.
Founded: 1980
Juliette Majot, Executive Director
Colleen Borgendale, Director, Communications

487 Institute for Sustainable Communities
535 Stone Cutters Way 802-229-2900
Montpelier, VT 05602 *Fax:* 802-229-2919
isc@sustain.org
www.iscvt.org
Promotes sustainable environmental practices in the US and around the world. It leads transformative communtiy-driven projects for environmental problem solving and other challenges.
Founded: 1991
George Hamilton, President
Steve Nicholas, Vice Presdient

488 International Society of Arboriculture (ISA)
270 Peachtree Street NW 678-367-0981
Suite 1900 888-472-8733
Atlanta, GA 30303 *Fax:* 240-547-1795
isa@isa-arbor.com
www.isa-arbor.com
Through research, technology, and education ISA is able to promote the professional practice of arboriculture and foster a greater public awareness of the benefits of trees.
Founded: 1924
Caitlyn Pollihan, Executive Director
Eduardo Aliskevich, Dir., Educational Products

489 Interstate Mining Compact Commission (IMCC)
445A Carlisle Drive 703-709-8654
Herndon, VA 20170 *Fax:* 703-709-8655
imcc.isa.us
A multi-state governmental organization that represents the natural resource interests of its members. They work closely with several Federal agencies such as Office of Surface Mining Reclamation and Enforcement, US EPA and US Bureauof Land Management.
Founded: 1970
Tom Clarke, Executive Director
Ryan Ellis, Director, Regulatory

490 Kids for Saving Earth Worldwide
37955 Bridge Road 763-559-1234
North Branch, MN 55056 *Fax:* 651-674-5005
kse@kidsforsavingearth.org
www.kidsforsavingearth.org
A nonprofit organization inspired by Clinton Hill, who died at the young age of eleven. The organization dreams of a healthy planet and provides "Education into Action" curriculum to thousands of teachers, parents and kids to helpinspire envirnmnetal awareness.
Tessa Hill, President

491 Land Institute
2440 E Water Well Road 785-823-5376
Salina, KS 67401 info@landinstitute.org
landinstitute.org
Nonprofit organization working to develop science-based alternatives to current destructive agricultural practices. In particular, they are focused on advancing perennial grain crops and polyculture farming solutions, instead of heavychemical application and petroleum consumption.
Founded: 1976
Fred Iutzi, President
Tim Crews, Director, Research

492 Land Trust Alliance
1250 H Street NW 202-638-4725
Suite 600 *Fax:* 202-638-4730
Washington, DC 20055 info@lta.org
www.landtrustalliance.org
The Land Trust Alliance is a national conservation organization that works to influence the conservation movement, by promoting voluntary land conservation across the country and providing

resources, leadership and training to thenation's 1,200+ non-profit, grassroots land trusts, helping them to protect important open spaces.
Founded: 1982
Andrew Bowman, President & CEO
Wendy Jackson, Executive Vice President

493 Manomet
125 Manomet Point Road 508-224-6521
PO Box 1770 *Fax:* 508-224-9220
Plymouth, MA 02345 info@manomet.org
www.manomet.org
Manomet aims to conserve natural resources for the benefit of wildlife and human populations. Through research and collaboration, Manomet builds science-based, cooperative solutions to environmental problems.
Founded: 1970
John Hagan, President
Cheryl T. Botieri, VP, Mission Advancement

494 Manufacturers of Emission Controls Association (MECA)
2200 Wilson Boulevard 202-296-4797
Suite 310 *Fax:* 202-331-1388
Arlington, VA 22201 asantos@meca.org
www.meca.org
Offers current and relevant technical information on emission control technology thereby facilitating strong state, federal and local air quality programs that promote public health, environmental quality and industrial progress.
Founded: 1976
Rasto Brezny, Executive Director
Michael Geller, Deputy Director

495 Mountain Research and Development (MRD)
810 E 10th Street mrd-journal@peertrack.net
Lawrence, KS 66044 www.mrd-journal.org
MRD is devoted to preserving mountains and their surrounding lowlands where communities are often marginalized. Through peer-reviewed, interdisciplinary, disciplinary and transdisciplinary research MRD are strengthening networks withinthe mountain community. Their content is all available through open access.
Thomas Breu, Editor-in-chief
David Molden, Editor-in-chief

496 National Association of State Departments of Agriculture (NASDA)
4350 North Fairfax Drive 202-296-9680
Suite 910 nasda@nasda.org
Arlington, VA 22203 www.nasda.org
Objectives include growing and enhancing agricultural practices and procedures by forging partnerships and creating consensuses to achieve sound policy outcomes.
Founded: 1916
Barb Glenn, Chief Executive Officer
Aline Delucia, Sr. Dir., Public Policy

497 National Association of State Land Reclamationists (NASLR)
186 Enterprise Drive 814-342-8116
Phlipsburg, PA 16866 jmeitrott@pa.gov
naslr.org
With its beginnings in Illinois, NASLR holds anuual conferences across America. NASLR sponsors awards and programs in the pursuit to support the reclamation lands and waters across America.
Founded: 1972
Danielle Duhe, President
Jeff Meitrott, Secretary-Treasurer

498 National Environmental Development Association Clean Air Project (NEDA/CAP)
www.nedacap.org
Coalition of manufacturing companies with operations across the U.S., seeking to address issues with the Clean Air Act.

499 National FFA Organization
6060 FFA Drive 888-332-2668
PO Box 68960 *Fax:* 800-366-6556
Indianapolis, IN 46268-0960 www.ffa.org
The organization (formerly Future Farmers of America) is dedicated to making a positive difference in the lives of young people by developing their potential for premier leadership, personal growth and career success throughagricultural education.
Founded: 1928
Mark Poeschl, Chief Executive Officer
Dave Schapker, Chief Financial Officer

500 National Forestry Association
374 Maple Avenue East www.nationalforestry.net
Suite 310
Vienna, VA 22180
Referral program linking private forest owners with professional foresters.
Founded: 1981

501 National Gardening Association
www.garden.org
The mission of the National Gardening Association is to sustain and renew the fundamental links between people, plants and the earth. NGA achieves its mission through youth and community gardening programs, industry research, freegardening information and memberships.
Founded: 1971
Dave Whitinger, Executive Director
Trish Whitinger, Chief Operating Officer

502 National Mining Association (NMA)
101 Constitution Avenue NW 202-463-2600
Suite 500 East *Fax:* 202-463-2666
Washington, DC 20001 nma.org
The mission of the National Mining Association is to create and maintain a broad base of political support in Congress, the Administration and the media for the mining industry of the US. In doing so, a secondary goal is to help thenation and the world realize the full promise and potential of the natural resources derived from America's mining industry.
Founded: 1917
Hal Quinn, President & CEO
Rich Nolan, Sr. VP, Government Affairs

503 Native Forest Council (NFC)
1455 E Briarcliff Lane 541-688-2600
Eugene, OR 97402 *Fax:* - - 6
info@forestcouncil.org
forestcouncil.org
Aims to provide visionary leadership and to ensure the integrity of public land ecosystems without compromising people or forests.
Founded: 1987
Timothy Hermach, President & Founder

504 Native Seeds/SEARCH
3061 N Campbell Avenue 520-622-5561
Tucson, AZ 85719 info@nativeseeds.org
www.nativeseeds.org
Promotes the use of ancient crops and their wild relatives by gathering, safeguarding, and distributing their seeds, while sharing benefits with tradtional communities. Works to preserve knowledge about their uses. Through research,training, and community education, works to protect biodiversity and to celebrate cultural diversity.
Founded: 1983
Joy Hought, Executive Director
Glenn Wagner, Manager, Operations

505 Negative Population Growth (NPG)
2861 Duke Street 703-370-9510
Suite 36 *Fax:* 703-370-9514
Alexandria, VA 22314 npg@npg.org
www.npg.org
Leader in the movement for a sound population policy and advocates a smaller and truly sustainable population through volun-

tary incentives for smaller families and reduced immigration levels.
Founded: 1972
Donald Mann, President
Craig Lewis, Executive Vice President

506 Old-Growth Forest Network
PO Box 21 410-251-1800
Easton, MD 21601 joan@oldgrowthforest.net
oldgrowthforest.net
Old-Growth Forest Network is a non-profit organization dedicated to the preservation of ancient forests, and connecting people with those forests. They also educate about the importance of unlogged forests.
Founded: 2013
Joan Maloof, Executive Director
Susan Barnett, Administrative Assistant

507 PCI Media
777 United Nations Plaza 212-687-3366
5th Floor *Fax:* 212-661-4188
New York, NY 10017 info@pcimedia.org
www.pcimedia.org
PCI's mission is to work creatively with the media and other organizations to motivate individuals and communities to make choices that influence population trends encouraging sustainable development and environmental protection.
Founded: 1985
Sean Southey, President
David Andrews, Director, Development

508 Pacific Institute
654 13th Street 510-251-1600
Preservation Park *Fax:* 510-251-2203
Oakland, CA 94612 info@pacinst.org
pacinst.org
Nonprofit policy research group, bringing knowledge to power on issues of environmental, economical development, and international peace and security.
Founded: 1987
Jason Morrison, President
Heather Cooley, Director, Research

509 Pinchot Institute for Conservation
1400 16th Street NW 202-797-6580
Suite 350 pinchot@pinchot.org
Washington, DC 20036 www.pinchot.org
Strives to advance conservation and sustainable natural resource management by developing innovative, practical, and broadly-supported solutions to conservation challenges and opportunities. This is accomplished through nonpartisanresearch, education and technical assistance.
Founded: 1963
William C. Price, President
Alex Andrus, Director, External Affairs

510 Population Connection
2120 L Street NW 202-332-2200
Suite 500 800-767-1956
Washington, DC 20037 *Fax:* 202-332-2302
info@populationconnection.org
www.populationconnection.org
National nonprofit organization working to slow population growth and achieve a sustainable balance between the Earth's people and its resources. They seek to protect the environment and ensure a high quality of life for present andfuture generations.
Founded: 1965
John Seager, President & CEO
Pamela Wasserman, Sr. VP, Education

511 Population Institute
105 2nd Street NE 202-544-3300
Washington, DC 20002 *Fax:* 202-544-0068
info@populationinstitute.org
www.populationinstitute.org
The Population Institute is the World's largest independent non-profit, educational organization dedicated exclusively to achieving a more equitable balance between the worlds population, environment, and resources. The Institute uses avariety of resources and programs to bring its concerns about the consequences of rapid poulation growth to the forefront of the national agenda.
Founded: 1969
Robert Walker, President
William Ryerson, Chair & CEO

512 Population Reference Bureau
1875 Connecticut Avenue NW 202-483-1100
Suite 520 800-877-9881
Washington, DC 20009-5728 *Fax:* 202-328-3937
popref@prb.org
www.prb.org
PRB informs policymakers, educators, the media, and concerned citizens working in the public interest around the world through a broad range of activities, including publications, information services, seminars and workshops, andtechnical support. They work with both public-sector and private-sector partners.
Founded: 1929
Jeffrey Jordan, President/CEO
James Scott, CFO/COO

513 Population Resource Center
15 Roszel Road 609-452-2822
Princeton, NJ 08540 *Fax:* 609-452-0010
www.prcdc.org
The mission of the Population Resource Center is to promote the use of accurate population data and sound, objective analysis of these data in the making of public policy.
Founded: 1985
Jane S De Lung, President
Linda Rosen, Director of Policy Analysis

514 Population: Environment Balance
1629 K Street NW 202-955-5700
Suite 300 800-866-8269
Washington, DC 20006 *Fax:* 202-955-6161
info@balance.org
www.balance.org
Population Environment Balance is a national, nonprofit membership organization dedicated to maintaing the quality of the United States population stabilization.
Founded: 1973
Aaron Beckwith, Vice President

515 Population: Environmental Council
1629 K Street NW 202-955-5700
Suite 300 *Fax:* 202-955-6161
Washington, DC 20006 info@balance.org
www.balance.org
Population-Environment Balance is dedicated to public education regarding the adverse effects of population growth on the environment. Founded in 1973, Population-Environment Balance has 8,800 members. It advocates measures that wouldencourage population stabilization.
Founded: 1973
Aaron Beckwith, Vice President

516 Quebec-Labrador Foundation (QFL)
4 South Main Street 978-356-0038
Ipswich, MA 01938 *Fax:* 978-268-5310
qlf@qlf.org
www.qlf.org
A not-for-profit corporation in the United States and a registered Charity in Canada. QLF exissts to support the rural communities and environment of eastern Canada and New England and to create models for stewardship of naturalresources and cultural heritage that can be applied worldwide.
Founded: 1961
Elizabeth Alling, President & CEO
Brett Mitchell, Senior Vice-President

517 Rainforest Relief
PO Box 8451 917-543-4064
Jersey City, NJ 07308 info@rainforestrelief.org
www.rainforestrelief.org

Rainforest Relief works to end the loss of the world's tropical and temperate rainforests by reducing the demand for materials for which rainforests are destroyed. These include rainforest woods such as mohogany, lauan and cedar,agricultural products such as bananas, chocolate, coffee and cut flowers, and mining products such as petroleum, gold, aluminum and copper. Rainforest relief works through research, education and non-violent direct action campaigns.
Founded: 1989

518 **Renew The Earth (RTE)**
8 Robin Ann Lane 518-797-3377
Westerlo, NY 12193 susancaumont@renew-the-earth.org
renew-the-earth.org
Promotes an exchange of ideas, information, and action across the globe in an effort to move away from fossil fuels, and embrace sustainable energy and water.
Founded: 1989
Susan Caumont, President
Dennis Irwin, Secretary

519 **Renewable Fuels Association (RFA)**
16024 Manchester Road 202-289-3835
Suite 101 *Fax:* 202-289-7519
Ellisville, MO 63011 info@ethanolrfa.org
www.ethanolrfa.org
The national trade association for the US ethanol industry, promotes policies, regulations and research and development initiative that will lead to the increased production and use of fuel ethanol.
Founded: 1981
Geoff Cooper, President & CEO
Robert White, VP, Industry Relations

520 **Rural Advancement Foundation International USA (RAFI USA)**
PO Box 640 919-542-1396
274 Pittsboro Elementary School Road rafiusa.org
Pittsboro, NC 27312
RAFI USA is a nonprofit organization promoting community, equity and sustainability for family farmers and rural communities. Our headquarters serves as a model for green building. In addition to daylighting, solar and energyconservation features, the building showcases the use of salvaged materials from the deconstruction of an 1830s farmhouse.
Founded: 1990
Edna Rodriguez, Executive Director
Sally Lee, Associate Director

521 **Save America's Forests**
4 Library Court SE 202-544-9219
Washington, DC 20003 *Fax:* 202-544-7462
webmaster@saveamericasforests.org
www.saveamericasforests.org
A nationwide campaign to end clearcutting and protect and restore America's wild and natural forests. A coalition of groups through America working together to protect local forests, national forests and forests throughout the world.
Founded: 1994
Carl Ross, Executive Director

522 **Society for Ecological Restoration (SER)**
1133 15th Street NW 202-299-9518
Suite 300 info@ser.org
Washington, DC 20005 www.ser.org
SER is dedicated to reversing the damage done to aquatic, marine and terrestrial environments and restoring the earth for the benefit of humans and nature. Restoration embraces the interrelationships between nature and culture byengaging all sectors of society and enabling full and effective participation.
Founded: 1988
Bethanie Walder, Executive Director
Levi Wickwire, Program Manager

523 **Society of American Foresters (SAF)**
10100 Laureate Way 301-897-8720
Bethesda, MD 20814-2198 866-897-8720
Fax: 301-897-3690
membership@safnet.org
www.eforester.org
Seeks to advance the science, education, technology, and practice of forestry; to enhance the competency of its members; to establish professional excellence; and to use the knowledge, skills, and conservation ethic of the professionto ensure the continued health and use of forest ecosystems present and future of availability of forest resources to benefit society.
Founded: 1900
Terry Baker, Chief Executive Officer
Louise Murgia, Chief Operating Officer

524 **Society of Chemical Manufacturers and Affiliates (SOCMA)**
1400 Crystal Drive 571-348-5100
Suite 630 *Fax:* 571-348-5138
Arlington, VA 22202 info@socma.com
www.socma.com
International trade association serving small and mid-sized batch chemical manufacturers, striving for safe, sustainable and environmentally sound operations.
Founded: 1921
Jennifer L. Abril, President & CEO
Paul J. Hirsh, Sr. VP, Industry Development

525 **Soil Science Society Of America (SSSA)**
5585 Guilford Road 608-273-8080
Madison, WI 53711-5801 *Fax:* 608-273-2021
membership@soils.org
soils.org
International scientific society that fosters the transfer of knowledge and practices to sustain global soils. The Society provides information about soils in relation to crop production, environmental quality, ecosystemsustainability, bioremediation, waste management, recycling, and wise land use.
Founded: 1936
Ellen Bergfeld, PhD, Chief Executive Officer
Chris Boomsma, Director, Education

526 **Southface Energy Institute**
241 Pine Street NE 404-872-3549
Atlanta, GA 30308 *Fax:* 404-872-5009
info@southface.org
www.southface.org
An environmental nonprofit working to promote sustainable homes, workplaces and communities through education, research, advocacy and technical assistance.
Founded: 1978
Barry R. Goldman, Chair
Andrea Pinabell, President

527 **Sustainable Forestry Initiative**
2121 K Street, NW 202-596-3450
Suite 750 *Fax:* 202-596-3451
Washington, DC 20037 info@sfiprogram.org
sfiprogram.org
SFI is an independent, nonprofit organization dedicated to sustainable forest management across the United States and Canada.
Kathy Abusow, President/CEO
Nadine Block, Chief of Operations

528 **United Nations Environment Programme New York Office**
2 UN Plaza, Room DC2-803 212-963-8210
323 E. 44th Street *Fax:* 212-963-7341
New York, NY 10017 unepnyo@un.org
www.unenvironment.org/regions/north-america/new-york-office
Provides leadership and to encourage partnership in caring for the environment by inspiring, informing, and enabling nations and peoples to improve their quality of life without compromising that of future generations.
Founded: 1972
Satya S. Tripathi, Director

529 **World Environment Center**
734 15th Street NW 202-312-1370
Suite 720 *Fax:* 202-637-2411
Washington, DC 20005 info@wec.org
www.wec.org

The World Environment Center is an independent, global non-profit, non-advocacy organization that advances sustainable development worldwide through the business practices of member companies and in partnership with governments,multi-lateral organizations, private sector organizations, universities and other stakeholders.
Founded: 1974
Francisco Su rez Hern ndez, Chair
Dr. Terry F. Yosie, President/CEO

530 **Worldwatch Institute**
1400 16th Street NW 202-745-8092
Suite 430 *Fax:* 202-478-2534
Washington, DC 20036 worldwatch@worldwatch.org
www.worldwatch.org

The Worldwatch Institute is an independent, nonprofit environmental research organization in Washington DC. Its mission is to foster a sustainable society in which human needs are met in ways that do not threaten the health of thenatural environment or future generations. To this end, this Institute conducts interdisciplinary research on emerging global issues, the results of which are published and disseminated to decision-makers and the media.
Founded: 1974
Ed Groark, Acting Interim President
Barbara Fallin, Director, Finance

National: Travel & Tourism

531 **American Hiking Society (AHS)**
8605 Second Avenue 301-565-6704
Silver Spring, MD 20910 800-972-8608
Fax: 301-565-6704
info@americanhiking.org
americanhiking.org

AHS is a recreation based conservation organization working to cultivate a nation of hikers dedicated to establishing, protecting, and maintaning foot trails in America. The more than 10,000 individual members and hiking club memberscontribute to this national effort.
Founded: 1976
Jack Hess, Chair
Kathryn Van Waes o, Executive Director

532 **American Recreation Coalition (ARC)**
1200 G Street NW 202-682-9530
Suite 650 *Fax:* 202-682-9529
Washington, DC 20005-3832 bnasta@funoutdoors.com
www.funoutdoors.com

Washington based nonprofit that partners public and private organizations to enhance and protect outdoor recreational opportunities and resources. ARC also monitors legislative and regulatory proposals that influence recreation.
Founded: 1979
Derrick Crandall, President
Ben Nasta, Director, Communications

533 **American Whitewater**
PO Box 1540 828-586-1930
Cullowhee, NC 28723 866-262-8429
Fax: 828-586-2840
info@americanwhitewater.org
www.americanwhitewater.org

Restores rivers adversely affected by hydropower dams, eliminates water degradation, improves public land management and protects public access to rivers for responsible recreational use.
Founded: 1954
Courtney Wilton, President
Christopher Hest, Vice-President

534 **Association of Outdoor Recreation and Education**
1100 North Main Street 810-299-2782
Suite 101 *Fax:* 810-299-3436
Ann Arbor, MI 48104 nationaloffice@aore.org
aore.org

The Association of Outdoor Recreation and Education (AORE) is a nonprofit organization serving the needs of recreation and education professionals.AORE promotes ecologically sound stewardship of the natural environment and serves as acollective voice for its members regarding topics of regional and national concern.
Jeannette Stawski, Executive Director
Lance Haynie, President

535 **Association of Zoos and Aquariums (AZA)**
8403 Colesville Road 301-562-0777
Suite 710 *Fax:* 301-562-0888
Silver Spring, MD 20910-3314 membership@aza.org
www.aza.org

Nonprofit organization dedicated to the advancement of accredited zoos and aquariums in the areas of animal care, wildlife conservation, education and science.
Founded: 1924
Dan Ashe, President & CEO
Kris Vehrs, Executive Director

536 **Federation of Western Outdoor Clubs (FWOC)**
1864 SE Anspach Street 503-653-1394
Oak Grove, OR 97267 sylviamilne@msn.com
www.federationofwesternoutdoorclubs.org

The Federation is composed of organizations that engage in hiking, camping, birding and other similar activities that rely on an outdoor environment where natural conditions predominate. Organizations in the West that have suchprograms, and that have an active interest in protecting the natural environment are invited to affiliate.
Founded: 1932
George Milne, President
Jan Walker, Vice-President

537 **Green Hotels Association**
1611 Mossy Stone Drive 713-789-8889
Houston, TX 77242-0212 *Fax:* 713-789-9786
green@greenhotels.com
www.greenhotels.com

Bringing together hotels that are interested in environmental issues by informing its members of the latest green and environmentally friendly procedurs and products that help hotels save money and time, and preserve the environment.
Founded: 1993
Patricia Griffin, President/Founder

538 **Lighthawk**
PO Box 913239 970-797-9355
Denver, CO 80291 info@lighthawk.org
www.lighthawk.org

Nonprofit organization addressing critical environmental issues by providing an aerial perspective on areas of concern in the US, Canada and Central America. Using small aircrafts, they fly partner organizations, elected officials,industry and media representatives, activists, and indigenous groups over protected and threatened regions.
Founded: 1979
Terri Watson, Chief Executive Officer
Bob Francella, Chief Advancement Officer

539 **National Association of State Outdoor Recreation Liaison Officers (NASORLO)**
University of Missouri
105 H, ABNR Building 573-353-2702
Columbia, MO 65211 *Fax:* 573-882-9526
nasorlo@gmail.com
www.nasorlo.org

An association representing the states and territories as a liason to the National Park Service. Their primary objective is to promote

and advocate for the State Assistance program of the Land and Water Conservation Fund.
Lauren Imgrund, President
Doug Eiken, Executive Director

540 National Council of State Tourism Directors (NCSTD)
U.S. Travel Association
1100 New York Avenue NW 202-408-2147
Suite 450
Washington, DC 20005
NCSTD represents all U.S. states, territories and districts providing a voice on critical public policy, offering learning opportunities to furhter the professionalism and effectiveness of state tourism offices, facilitating internaland external communication and supporting domestic and international marketing efforts.
Jim Hagen, Chair
Duane Parrish, Vice Chair

541 North Country Trail Association
229 East Main Street 616-897-5987
Lowell, MI 49331 866-445-3628
Fax: 616-897-6605
hq@northcountrytrail.org
northcountrytrail.org
The North Country Trail Association (NCTA) unites individuals, affiliated trail groups, local chapters, corporate sponsors and others linked in support of building and maintaining the North Country National Scenic Trail, and tellingits story.
Ruth Dorrough, President
Jaron Nyhof, First Vice-President

542 Outdoor Industry Association
4909 Pearl East Circle 303-443-353
Suite 300 *Fax:* 303-444-3284
Boulder, CO 80301 info@outdoorindustry.org
outdoorindustry.org
The Outdoor Industry Association is a membership-driven trade organization for the outdoor recreation industry.
Amy Roberts, Executive Director
Travis Campbell, President

543 Pacific Crest Trail Association
1331 Garden Highway 916-285-1846
Sacramento, CA 95833 *Fax:* 916-285-1865
info@pcta.org
pcta.org
PCTA is a nonprofit organization singularly focused on preserving , protecting, and promoting the Pacific Crest Trail.
Liz Bergeron, Executive Director
John E. Crawford, Board Chair

544 Rails-to-Trails Conservancy
2121 Ward Court NW 202-331-9696
5th Floor 866-202-9788
Washington, DC 20037 *Fax:* 202-223-9257
www.railstotrails.org
A nonprofit organization working with communities to preserve unused rail corridors by transforming them into trails, enhancing the health of American's environment, economy, neighborhoods and people.
Founded: 1986
Keith Laughlin, President
Cindy Dickerson, COO

545 Safari Club International (SCI)
4800 West Gates Pass Road 520-620-1220
Tucson, AZ 85745-9490 888-486-8724
Fax: 520-622-1205
www.safariclub.org
A leader in wildlife conservation, hunter education, and protecting the freedom to hunt.
Paul Babaz, President
Michael Roqueni, Director, Membership

546 Society of Health and Physical Educators (SHAPE)
1900 Association Drive 703-476-3400
Reston, VA 20191-1598 800-213-7193
Fax: 703-476-9527
www.shapeamerica.org
SHAPE America serves recreation professionals, practitioners, educators and students by encouraging and facilitating healthy living through physical activity.
Founded: 2005
Fran Cleland, President
Judy LoBianco, President-Elect

547 Society of Outdoor Recreation Professionals (SORP)
PO Box 221 814-927-8212
Marienville, PA 16239 *Fax:* 814-927-6659
brenda@recpro.org
www.recpro.org
Dedicated to serving the outdoor recreation profession. Acts as the nation's leading association of outdoor recreation and related professionals who strive to protect natural and cultural resources. SORP uses research, planning,management and policy development to meets its mission to serve outdoor recreatio professionals.
Founded: 1983
Rachel Franchina, President
Maren Murphy, VP of Operation

548 Wilderness Education Association (WEA)
PO Box 601 740-607-9759
Dresden, OH 43821 nationaloffice@weainfo.org
www.weainfo.org
WEA provides professional instruction, leadership training and wilderness travel. Promoting safe, ethical and professional wilderness leaders.
Founded: 1977
Kelli McMahan, President
Francois Guilleux, President-Elect

National: Water Resources

549 Adopt A Stream Foundation (AASF)
Northwest Stream Center 425-316-8592
600 - 128th Street SE *Fax:* 425-338-1423
Everett, WA 98208 aasf@streamkeeper.org
www.streamkeeper.org
The mission of the AASF is to teach people how to become stewards of their watersheds. This mission is carried out by conducting classes, producing environmental education materials, and providing local communities stream and wetlandrestoration technical assistance.
Founded: 1985
Daryl Williams, President
Tom Murdoch, Executive Director

550 Alliance for Water Efficiency
33 N LaSalle Street 773-360-5100
Suite 2275 866-730-A4WE
Chicago, IL 60602 *Fax:* 773-345-3636
allianceforwaterefficiency.org
The Alliance for Water Efficiency is a nonprofit organization dedicated to the efficient and sustainable use of water. It provides information and assistance on water conservation efforts.
Pete DeMarco, Chair
Kirk Stinchcombe, Vice Chair

551 American Canal Society
117 Main Street 610-691-0956
Freemansburg, PA 18017 www.americancanals.org
Dedicated to historic canal research, preservation, restoration, and parks, this organization educates the public on canal history, activities, and problems. Their mission is to promote the wise use of the nation's canal resources;they carry this out through the publication of regional canal guides and the creation of commit-

tees focusing on various issues related to resoration and maintenance of canals.
Founded: 1972
Michael Riley, President
Charles Derr, Secretary & Treasurer

552 **American Ground Water Trust**
50 Pleasant Street 603-228-5444
Suite 2 800-423-7748
Concord, NH 03301 *Fax:* 603-228-6557
trustinfo@agwt.org
agwt.org

A not-for-profit education organization. Promotes opportunity, cooperation and action among individuals, groups and organizations in order to educate the public and further its mission: to protect ground water, promote public awarenessof the environment and economic importance of groundwater, and provide accurate information to assist public participation in water resources decisions.
Founded: 1986
David Kill, Chair
Andrew Stone, Executive Director

553 **American Rivers**
1101 14th Street NW 202-347-7550
Suite 1400 877-347-7550
Washington, DC 20005 feedback@americanrivers.org
www.americanrivers.org

American Rivers is an organization that uses advocacy and field work to accomplish their mission of protecting and restoring the nation's rivers. They work with local river advocates, business and agricultural interests, recreationgroups, and others to accomplish their goals.
Founded: 1973
William Robert Irwin, President
Kimberley Milligan, Chair

554 **American Shore and Beach Preservation Association (ASBPA)**
5460 Beaujolais Lane 239-489-2616
Fort Myers, FL 33919 *Fax:* 239-362-9771
derek.brockbank@asbpa.org
asbpa.org

Dedicated to preserving, protecting and enhancing the beaches, shores and other coastal resources of America, recognizing their important quality-of-life assets.
Founded: 1926
Derek Brockbank, Executive Director
Nicole Elko, PhD, Science Director

555 **American Sportfishing Association (ASA)**
1001 North Fairfax Street 703-519-9691
Suite 501 *Fax:* 703-519-1872
Alexandria, VA 22314 info@asafishing.org
asafishing.org

A sportsfishing trade association that advocates for the promotion and protection of the industry. Their mission is to ensure that the industry remains strong and prosperous, and to safeguard the conservation, economic, and socialvalues of sportfishing in America.
Founded: 1933
Glenn Hughes, President
Joyce Anderson-Logan, Executive Assistant

556 **American Water Resources Association (AWRA)**
P.O. Box 2663 540-687-8390
Woodbridge, VA 22195 *Fax:* 540-687-8395
info@awra.org
www.awra.org

AWRA advances water resources research, planning, development, management and education. AWRA takes a balanced, professional approach to solving water resources challenges by establishing discourse between physical, biological, andsocial scientists, engineers, and other persons concerned with water resources.
Founded: 1964
Dresden Farrand, Executive VP & CEO
Michael J. Kowalski, Director of Operations

557 **American Water Works Association (AWWA)**
6666 W Quincy Avenue 303-794-7711
Denver, CO 80235 800-926-7337
Fax: 303-347-0804
www.awwa.org

The AWWA is an international, nonprofit, scientific, and educational society that carries out the mission of assuring the effective management of water by providing water solutions. They offer education to water professionals, advocatefor safe and sustainable water, and educate the public on water resource management.
Founded: 1881
David B. LaFrance, CEO
Paula I. MacIlwaine, Deputy CEO

558 **Association of Metropolitan Water Agencies (AMWA)**
1620 I Street NW 202-331-2820
Suite 500 *Fax:* 202-785-1845
Washington, DC 20006 info@amwa.net
www.amwa.net

AMWA works with Congress and federal agencies to protect public health through federal laws and regulations with the goal of representing the interests of metropolitan water systems. The organization also offers programs, publications,and services to water suppliers.
Founded: 1981
Diane VanDe Hei, Chief Executive Officer
Michael Arceneaux, Chief Operating Officer

559 **Association of State Floodplain Managers (ASFPM)**
8301 Excelsior Drive 608-828-3000
Madison, WI 53717 *Fax:* 608-828-6319
asfpm@floods.org
www.floods.org

ASFPM is an organization of professionals involved in floodplain management, flood hazard mitigation, the National Flood Insurance Program, and flood preparedness, warning and recovery.
Founded: 1976
Chad Berginnis, Executive Director
Ingrid D. Wadsworth, Deputy Director

560 **Association of State Wetland Managers (ASWM)**
32 Tandberg Trail 207-892-3399
Suite 2A *Fax:* 207-894-7992
Windham, ME 04062 jeanne.christie@aswm.org
www.aswm.org

Nonprofit organization dedicated to the protection and restoration of the nation's wetlands. ASWM's goal is to help public and private wetland decision-makers utilize the best possible scientific information and techniques in wetlanddelineation, assessment, mapping, planning, regulation, acquisition, restoration and other management.
Founded: 1983
Marla J. Stelk, Executive Director
Brenda Zollitsch, Senior Policy Analyst

561 **CEDAM International**
2 Fox Road 914-271-5365
Croton-on-Hudson, NY 10520 susansammon@gmail.com
cedarinternational.com

Conservation, Education, Diving, Awareness and Marine research International is a nonprofit organization dedicated to the understanding, protection and preservation of the world's marine resources.They continue to offer the LloydBridges Scholarship which allows teachers and educators to have a chance to participate in a REEF field survey.
Founded: 1967
Susan Sammon, Director

562 **Center for Coastal Studies**
5 Holway Avenue 508-487-3623
Provincetown, MA 02657 800-900-3622
ccs@coastalstudies.org
coastalstudies.org

Private nonprofit organization for research, conservation and education in the coastal and marine environments.
Founded: 1976
Bill Bonn, Chair
Richard Delaney, President/CEO

563 Center for Marine Conservation (CMC)

2029 K Street, NW — 202-429-5609
Washington, DC 20006 — 800-519-1541
Fax: 202-872-0619
www.cmc-ocean.org

The mission of the CMC is to protect ocean ecosystems and conserve the global abundance and diversity of marine wildlife. Through sciencebased advocacy, research and public education, CMC informs, inspires and empowers people to speakand act for the oceans.
Roger Rufe Jr, President
Thomas J Tepper, Senior VP Operations

564 Center for Watershed Protection

3290 North Ridge Road — 410-461-8323
Suite 290 — *Fax:* 410-461-8324
Ellicott City, MD 21043 — center@cwp.org
www.cwp.org

The center is a nonprofit 501(c)3 organization dedicated to finding new ways to protect and restore the nation's streams, lakes, rivers and estuaries. The center publishes numerous technical publications on all aspects of watershedprotection, including stormwater management, watershed planning and better site design. Publications are available online.
Founded: 1992
Carlton G. Epps, Sr., President
Hye Yeong Kwon, Executive Director

565 Clean Water Action

1444 I Street NW — 202-895-0420
Suite 400 — *Fax:* 202-895-0438
Washington, DC 20005 — www.cleanwateraction.org

National citizens' organization working for clean, safe and affordable water, prevention of health-threatening pollution, creation of environmentally-safe jobs and businesses, and empowerment of people to make democracy work.Organizes strong grassroots groups, coalitions and campaigns to protect the environment, health, economic well-being and community quality of life.
Founded: 1972
Robert Wendelgass, President/CEO

566 Clean Water Fund

1444 I Street — 202-895-0420
Suite 400 — *Fax:* 202-895-0438
Washington, DC 20005 — www.cleanwaterfund.org

Brings diverse communities together to work for changes that improve our lives, promoting sensible solutions for people and the environment.
Founded: 1972
Robert Wendelgass, President/CEO

567 Clean Water Network

1200 New York Avenue NW — 202-298-2421
Suite 400 — *Fax:* 202-289-1060
Washington, DC 20005 — www.cleanwaternetwork.org

A nonprofit network of over 1,000 organizations that deal with clean water issues covered by the Clean Water Act. Our member organizations consist of a variety of organizations representing environmentalists, family farmers, recreationanglers, commercial fishermen, surfers, boaters, faith communities, labor unions and civic associations. We publish a monthly newsletter and various reports.
Natalie Roy, Executive Director

568 Coastal Conservation Association

6919 Portwest — 713-626-4234
Suite 100 — 800-201-3474
Houston, TX 77024 — *Fax:* 713-626-5852
ccantl@joincca.org
www.joincca.org

A national nonprofit organization of 17 coastal state chapters dedicated to the conservation and preservation of marine resources.
Founded: 1977
Patrick D. Murray, President
Robert G. Hayes, Vice-President

569 Coastal Society

PO Box 3590 — 757-565-0999
Williamsburg, VA 23187-3590 — *Fax:* 757-565-0922
coastalsoc@aol.com
www.thecoastalsociety.org

Organization of private sector, academic, government professionals and students dedicated to actively addressing emerging coastal issues by fostering dialogue, forging partnerships and promoting communication and education.
Founded: 1975
Lewis Lawrence, President
Megan D. Bailiff, President-Elect

570 Cook Inletkeeper

3734 Ben Walters Lane — 907-235-4068
Homer, AK 99603 — 888-694-6538
Fax: 907-235-4069
inletkeeper.org

Dedicated to protecting the vast Cook Inlet watershed and the life it sustains; it is a community-based nonprofit organization that combines education, advocacy and science to reach this goal.
Founded: 1995
Bob Shavelson, Executive Director
Sue Mauger, Science Director

571 Coral Reef Alliance

1330 Broadway — 510-370-0500
Suite 1602 — info@coral.org
Oakland, CA 94612 — coral.org

Unites and empowers communities to save coral reefs. Provides tools, education and inspiration to residents of coral reef destinations to support local projects that benefit both reefs and people.
Founded: 1994
Dr. Michael Webster, Executive Director
Dr. Madhavi Colton, Program Director

572 Earth Island Institute

2150 Allston Way — 510-859-9100
Suite 460 — *Fax:* 510-859-9091
Berkeley, CA 94704-1375 — donorinquiry@earthisland.org
www.earthisland.org

A nonprofit, public interest, membership organization that supports people who are creating solutions to protect the shared planet.
Founded: 1982
David Phillips, Executive Director
Susan Kamprath, Director, Operations

573 Ecological Society of America

1990 M Street NW — 202-833-8773
Suite 700 — *Fax:* 202-833-8775
Washington, DC 20036 — esahq@esa.org
www.esa.org

To promote ecological science by improving communication among ecologists; raise the public's level of awareness of the importance of ecological science; increase the resources available for the conduct of ecological science.
Founded: 1915 Over 9,000 members
Catherine O'Riordan, Executive Director
Elizabeth Biggs, Chief Financial Officer

574 Environment America

1543 Wazee Street — 303-801-0581
Suite 410 — 800-401-6511
Denver, CO 80202 — membership@environmentamerica.org
environmentamerica.org

A nonprofit organization dedicated to educating the public on environmental issues through research reports, news conferences,

interviews with reporters, op-ed pieces, letters to the editor and more; and to promote sensible solutions.
Ed Johnson, President
Andre Delattre, Chief Operating Officer

575 **Environmental Defense Fund (EDF)**
257 Park Avenue South 212-505-2100
New York, NY 10010 *Fax:* 212-505-2375
www.edf.org
Dedicated to protecting the environmental rights of all people, including future generations. Among these rights are clean air, clean water, healthy, nourishing food and a flourishing ecosystem. Advocates solutions based on science,even when it leads in unfamiliar directions. Works to create solutions that win lasting political, economic and social support because they are bipartisan, efficient and fair.
Founded: 1967
Fred Krupp, President
Catherine Nardone, Chief Development Officer

576 **Freshwater Society**
2424 Territorial Road 651-313-5800
Suite B *Fax:* 651-666-2569
St. Paul, MN 55114 freshwater@freshwater.org
freshwater.org
Founded by the late Dick Gray, the late Hib Hill and Dr. Richard Caldecott, the Freshwater Society sets out to promote the conservation, protection and restoration of all freshwaterresources across the United States.
Founded: 1968
Rick Bateson, Chair
Steve Woods, Executive Directors

577 **Gaia Institute**
440 City Island Avenue 718-885-1906
Bronx, NY 10464 *Fax:* 718-885-0882
thegaiainstitute.org
Named after the Gaia hypothesis, the Gaia Institute believes the planet's well-being is connected to the activities of organisms. The Gaia Institute partners with eager and bright people who are creating new solutions in greentechnology.
Founded: 1972
Paul Mankiewicz, Executive Director

578 **Global Water Policy Project (GWPP)**
107 Larkspur Drive info@globalwaterpolicy.org
Amherst, MA 01002 www.globalwaterpolicy.org
Global Water Policy Projects aims to promote the preservation and sustainable use of Earth's fresh water through research, writing, outreach, and public speaking.
Founded: 1994
Sandra Postel, Founder/Director

579 **Groundwater Foundation**
3201 Pioneers Boulevard 402-434-2740
Suite 105 800-858-4844
Lincoln, NE 68502 *Fax:* 402-434-2742
info@groundwater.org
www.groundwater.org
The Groundwater Foundation is a nonprofit organization that is dedicated to informing the public about one of our greatest hidden resources, groundwater. Since 1985, our programs and publications present the benefits everyone receivesfrom groundwater and the risks that threaten groundwater quality. We make learning about groundwater fun and understandable for kids and adults alike.
Founded: 1985
Andy Belenger, President
Jane Grffin, Vice-President

580 **International Association for Environmental Hydrology (IAEH)**
2607 Hopeton Drive 201-984-7583
San Antonio, TX 78230 *Fax:* 703-564-8581
hydroweb@gmail.com
www.hydroweb.com
IAEH tries to share its knowledge and expertise in hydrology and to provide a source of inexpensive tools and resources for hydrologists all over the world.

581 **International Desalination Association (IDA)**
94 Central Street, Suite 200 978-887-0410
PO Box 387 *Fax:* 978-887-0411
Topsfield, MA 01983 info@idadesal.org
idadesal.org
IDA is committed to the development and promotion of the appropriate use of desalination and desalination technology worldwide. We endeavor to carry out these goals by encouraging research and development, exchanging, promoting communication and disseminating information.
Founded: 1972
Dr. Emilio Gabbrielli, President
Shannon McCarthy, 1st Vice-President

582 **International Rivers**
2054 University Avenue 510-848-1155
Suite 300 *Fax:* 510-848-1008
Berkeley, CA 94704-2644 contact@internationalrivers.org
www.internationalrivers.org
International Rivers works with an international network of dam-affected people, grassroots organizations, environmentalists, human rights advocates and others who are committed to stopping destructive river projects and promotingbetter options.
Founded: 1985
Scott Spann, Chair
Kate Horner, Executive Director

583 **Interstate Council on Water Policy (ICWP)**
505 North Ivy Street 573-303-6644
Arlington, VA 22220-1707 www.icwp.org
The ICWP is the national organization of state and regional water resource management agencies. It provides a means to exchange information, ideas, and experience and to work with Federal agencies which share water managementresponsibilities. In paricular, ICWP focuses on water quality and water quantity issues, and on the dynamic interface state and Federal roles.
Founded: 1959
Dru Buntin, Chair
Ryan Mueller, Executive Director

584 **Marine Technology Society**
1100 H Street NW 202-717-8705
Suite LL 100 *Fax:* 202-347-4302
Washington, DC 20005 membership@mtsociety.org
www.mtsociety.org
Addresses coastal zone management, marine mineral and energy resources, marine environmental protection, and ocean engineering issues.
Founded: 1963
Kevin Traver, Executive Director

585 **National Association of Clean Water Agencies (NACWA)**
1816 Jefferson Place NW 202-833-2672
Washington, DC 20036 *Fax:* 888-267-9505
info@nacwa.org
www.nacwa.org
The NACWA is a recognized leader in environmental policy and a technical resource on water quality and ecosystem protection issues. It represents the interests of the country's wastewater treatment agencies and true environmentalpractioners.
Raymond J. Marshall, President
Adam Krantz, CEO

586 **National Association of Flood and Stormwater Management Agencies (NAFSMA)**
PO Box 56764 202-289-8625
Washington, DC 20040 *Fax:* 202-530-3389
www.nafsma.org
NAFSMA is an organization of public agencies whose function is the protection of lives, property and economic activity from the adverse impacts of storm and flood waters. The mission of the association is to advocate public policy,encourage technologies

and conduct education programs which facilitate and enhance the achievement of the public service functions of its members.
Founded: 1978
Janet Bly, President
Mark Pestrella, Vice President

587 National Boating Federation
PO Box 4111 — *Fax:* 866-239-2070
Annapolis, MD 21403-4111 — info@n-b-f.org
www.n-b-f.org
Nonprofit, volunteer organization that represents over 2 million of America's boaters. It is an alliance of yacht and boating clubs, recreational boating organizations and includes associate and individual members.
Founded: 1966
Keith Christopher, President
Ed Payne, Vice-President

588 National Council for Air and Stream Improvements (NCASI)
1513 Walnut Street — 919-941-6400
Suite 200 — administrator@ncasi.org
Cary, NC 27511 — www.ncasi.org
The Council is a technical organization devoted to finding solutions to environmental protection problems in the manufacture of pulp, paper, and wood products in industrial forestry.
Founded: 1943
Dirk J. Krouskop, President
Tammerah D. Garren, VP, Business Affairs

589 National Ground Water Association (NWGA)
601 Dempsey Road — 614-898-7791
Westerville, OH 43081 — 800-551-7379
Fax: 614-898-7786
ngwa@ngwa.org
www.ngwa.org
Works to provide and protect the world's ground water resources; enhance the skills and credibility of all ground water professionals; develop and exchange industry knowledge and promote the ground water industry and understanding ofground water resources.
Founded: 1948
Scott King, President

590 National Institutes for Water Resources
niwr@mail.wvu.edu
niwr.info
The National Institutes for Water Resources is a network of Research Institutes in every state. They conduct basic and applied research to solve water problems unique to their area. The regulations laid out by the Water ResourcesResearch Act provide a unified focus for the federal and non-federal components of the Institute Program.
John Tracy, Secretary-Treasurer
Alexander G. Fernald, President

591 National Water Center
Eureka Springs, AR — 479-244-0985
lwater@nationalwatercenter.org
www.nationalwatercenter.org
Strives to look at water with the broadest ideas of ecological balance and harmony. Support appropriate technology, bioregionalism, composting toilets, dowsing, ecology, flow forms, stream monitoring, vibrational water, watershedplanning.

592 National Water Resources Association (NWRA)
4 E Street Southeast — 202-698-0693
Washington, DC 20003 — nwra@nwra.org
www.nwra.org
The NWRA consists of individuals and groups, such as irrigation districts, canal companies and conservancy districts, municipalities and the public in general, who are interested in water resource development projects. It now hasabout 5,000 members.
Founded: 1932
Ron Thompson, President
Ian Lyle, Vice-President

593 National Watershed Coalition
PO Box 566 — 405-627-0670
Pawnee, OK 74058 — nwchdqtrs@sbcglobal.net
A nonprofit Coalition made up of national, regional, state, and local organizations, associations, and individuals, that advocate dealing with natural resource problems and issues using watersheds as the planning and implementationunit.
Founded: 1989

594 National Waterways Conference
1100 North Glebe Road — 703-224-8007
Suite 1010 — *Fax:* 866-371-1390
Arlington, VA 22201 — info@waterways.org
www.waterways.org
Coalition of trade and regional associations that have an interest in national waterways policy issues.
Founded: 1960
Amy W. Larson, President
Carole Wright, Dir., Internal Operations

595 North American Lake Management Society (NAMLS)
PO Box 5443 — 608-233-2836
Madison, WI 53705-0443 — info@nalms.org
www.nalms.org
NAMLS's focus is on lake management for a wide variety of uses, but they are also involved with other issues on a watershed level: land, streams, wet lands, and estuaries. The society forges partnerships among citizens, scientists andprofessionals to foster the management and protection of lakes and reservoirs.
Founded: 1980
Frank Wilhelm, President
Frank Browne, President-Elect

596 Ocean Champions
202 San Jose Avenue — 831-462-2539
Capitola, CA 95010 — *Fax:* 831-462-2542
info@oceanchampions.org
www.oceanchampions.org
Environmental organization connected to a political action committee focused solely on oceans and ocean wildlife. Ocean Champions works to build a broad, bipartisan base of supporters to create a strong group of people who willchampion policy that supports ocean conservation.
Founded: 2003
Michael Sutton, Chair
David Wilmot, Ph.D., President/Co-Founder

597 Ocean Conservancy
1300 19th Street NW — 202-429-5609
8th Floor — 800-519-1541
Washington, DC 20036 — oceanconservancy.org
By working with millions of volunteers of all ages, from all around the world, Ocean Conservancy is able to organize International Coastal Cleanup.
Founded: 1972
Andreas Merkl, President
Janis Searles Jones, CEO

598 Ocean Foundation
1320 19th Street NW — 202-887-8996
Washington, DC 20036 — info@oceanfdn.org
www.oceanfdn.org
The Ocean Foundation sets out to aid in every way possible the preservation and strengthening of ocean environmnets around the world. Workig with donors to get resources out to marine conservation intiatives is one of the many ways TheOcean Foundation works to preserve the oceans.
Mark J. Spalding, Chair/President
Karen Muir, Vice-President

599 Oceana USA
1350 Connecticut Avenue NW — 202-833-3900
5th Floor — 877-762-3262
Washington, DC 20036 — *Fax:* 202-833-2070
info@oceana.org
usa.oceana.org
Established by a group of leading foundations with the mission to achieve measurable change by conducting specific, sci-

ence-based campaigns with fixed deadlines and articulated goals. Oceana is an international, nonprofit organizationwith chapters all over the world.
Founded: 2001
Simon Sidamon-Eristoff, Chair
Keith Addis, President

600 Oceanic Society
PO Box 844 415-256-9604
Ross, CA 94957 800-326-7491
www.oceanic-society.org
Founded for the protection of the marine environment, environmental education and conservation-based field research.
Founded: 1969
Zachary Rabinor, Chair
Roderic Mast, President/CEO

601 River Network
PO Box 21387 303-736-2724
Boulder, CO 80308 info@rivernetwork.org
www.rivernetwork.org
River Network is a national nonprofit organization for citizen groups working for river and watershed protection. Thier mission is to help people understand, protect and restore rivers and their watersheds. They provide conservationpartners with with information training, consultation, grants, referrals to other service organizations and networking opportunities.
Founded: 1988
Lynn Boaddus, Chair
Nicole Silk, President

602 Safina Center
80 North Country Road 631-675-1984
Setauket, NY 11733 admin@safinacenter.org
safinacenter.org
Formerly Blue Ocean Institute, the Safiina Center, named after its founder is inspired to do great work in the sciences by fostering relationships with science communicators and bringing forward discussion about the planet's ecologicalconcerns.
Founded: 2003
B. Eric Graham, Chair
Dr. Carl Safina, Founder/President

603 Scientific Committee on Oceanic Research (SCOR)
University of Delaware
Newark, DE 19716 secretariat@scor-int.org
www.scor-int.org
SCOR is an international nonprofit organization whose purpose is to encourage international cooperation in ocean research.
Founded: 1957
Edward R. Urban Jr., Executive Director

604 Seacoast Anti-Pollution League (SAPL)
PO Box 1136 603-431-5089
Portsmouth, NH 03802 sapl.info@comcast.net
saplnh.org
A nonprofit environmental group that monitor threats to public health and safety, wildlife, and ecosystems in the community.
Founded: 1969
Doug Bogen, Executive Director

605 Society for Freshwater Science (SFS)
Stroud Water Research Center
970 Spencer Road 610-268-2153
Avondale, PA 19311 webeditor@freshwater-science.org
www.freshwater-science.org
Previously North American Benthological Society, SFS specializes in stream insect ecology along with other scientific endeavors including; environmental impact assessments; taxonomy of microbes, algae, invertebrates and fish; carbonand nutrient dynamics; watershed dynamics; hydrology and geomorphology; conservation and restoration.
Founded: 1953

606 Soil and Water Conservation Society
945 SW Ankeny Road 515-289-2331
Ankeny, IA 50023-9723 800-THE-SOIL
Fax: 515-289-1227
swcs@swcs.org
www.swcs.org
Their mission is to foster the science and art of natural resource conservation. Their work targets the conservation of soil, water, and related natural resources.
Founded: 1943
Clare Lindahl, CEO
Rex Martin, President

607 Steamboaters
PO Box 41266 541-688-4980
Eugene, OR 97404 *Fax:* 541-607-3763
steamboaters@hotmail.com
www.steamboaters.org
Nonprofit organization dedicated to work to restore the North Umpqua river system's wild fish stocks, particularly steelhead, to a sustainable level that is consistent with optimum natural population levels. Protect, preserve andrestore fish habitat, including adequate and consistent flows of high quality water in the North Umpqua and its tributaries.
Founded: 1975
Tim Goforth, President
Jeff Dose, Vice-President

608 Surfrider Foundation
942 Calle Negocio 949-492-8170
Suite 350 *Fax:* 949-492-8142
San Clemente, CA 92673 info@surfrider.org
www.surfrider.org
A nonprofit organization that works to protect the world's oceans, waves and beaches. The organization largely focuses on issues such as; water quality, beach access, beach and surf spot preservation and sustaining marine and coastalecosystems.
Founded: 1984
Dr. Chad Nelsen, CEO
Michelle Kremer, COO

609 Water Environment Federation (WEF)
601 Wythe Street 703-684-2400
Alexandria, VA 22314-1304 800-666-0206
www.wef.org
A nonprofit technical and educational organization with members from varied disciplines who work toward the WEF vision of preservation and enhancement of the global water environment.
Founded: 1928
Rick Warner, P.E., President
Jenny Hartfelder, P.E., PMP, President-Elect

610 Water Quality Association (WQA)
4151 Naperville Road 630-505-0160
Lisle, IL 60532-3696 *Fax:* 630-505-9637
www.wqa.org
Nonprofit international trade association representing the water treatment industry. Members include manufacturers, suppliers, dealers and distributors of water quality improvement products and services.
Founded: 1974
Pauli Undesser, Executive Director
Scott Parker, Associate Exective Director

611 Water Resources Congress
2300 Claredon Boulevard 703-525-4881
Suite 404 *Fax:* 703-527-1693
Arlington, VA 22201
Kathleen A Phelps, Executive Director

612 Watershed Management Group
1137 N Dodge Blvd 520-396-3266
Tuscon, AZ 85716 *Fax:* 520-300-6700
watershedmg.org

Watershed Management Group (WMG) is a nonprofit organization that develops community-based solutions to ensure the long-term prosperity of people and health of the environment.
Founded: 2002
Bill Wilkening, President
Jennifer Mills, Treasurer

613 Western Hemisphere Shorebird Reserve Network (WHSRN)
PO Box 1770 207-721-9040
Manomet, MA 02345 whsrn@manomet.org
www.whsrn.org
Voluntary, community-based coalition of 106 sites across the US and other countries in the Western Hemisphere that have joined together to protect, restore and manage critical wetland habitats for migratory birds.
Rob P. Clay, Director
Laura Chamberlin, Assistant Director

614 Wild Oceans
PO Box 258 703-777-0037
Waterford, VA 20197 wildoceans.org
Wild Oceans (formerly the National Coalition for Marine Conservation or NCMC) is a nonprofit organization dedicated to the protection of fish by bringing conservation-minded fishermen and pro-fishing environmentalists together topromote a broad, ecosystems approach to fisheries management.
Founded: 1973
Ken Hinman, President
Pam Lyons Gromen, Executive Director

615 Wildlands Conservancy
3701 Orchid Place 610-965-4397
Emmaus, PA 18049 info@wildlandspa.org
www.wildlandspa.org
Wildlands Conservancy is a nonprofit organization dedicated to preserving precious lands, restoring rivers, maintaining healthy waterways, teaching the community about nature and caring for orphaned or injured wildlife.
Founded: 1973
Lona Farr, Chair
Christopher M. Kocher, President

616 World Aquaculture Society (WAS)
143 JM Parker Coliseum 225-578-3137
Baton Rouge, LA 70803 *Fax:* 225-578-3493
carolm@was.org
www.was.org
The World Aquaculture Society is an international nonprofit society, whose commitment to excellence in science, technology, education and information exchange, contribute to progressive and sustainable development of aquaculturethroughout the world.
Founded: 1970
Dr. William Daniels, President
Dr. Maria Celia Portella, President-Elect

Alabama

617 Alabama Association of Soil & Water Conservation Committee
100 North Union Street 334-242-2620
PO Box 304800 *Fax:* 334-242-0551
Montgomery, AL 36104 debra.brooks@swcc.alabama.gov
www.alconservationdistricts.gov
The committee is committed to conserving Alabama's natural resources to promote healthy soil, fishable and drinkable water, sustainable forests, and clean air for prosperous farming industries and quality of life for Alabama citizens.
Founded: 1937
William E. Puckett, PhD, Executive Director
Charles A. Holmes, Chairman

618 Alabama Environmental Council
4330 1st St Avenue S 205-252-7581
Birmingham, AL 35222 info@aeconline.org
www.aeconline.org
The AEC gives voice to those interested in protecting the rights to have a clean and safe environment. Their efforts are focused towards sustainable living through reducing the impacts of global warming, educating through environmentalliteracy and recycling.
Founded: 1967
Julie Danley, President
Laney DeJonge, Vice President

619 Alabama National Safety Council: Birmingham
2125 Data Office Drive 205-328-7233
Suite 102 800-457-7233
Birmingham, AL 35244 *Fax:* 205-328-1467
info@nsc.org
www.nsc.org/Pages/Alabama.aspx
The National Safety Council eliminates preventable deaths at work, in homes, communities and on the road through leadership, research, education and advocacy. Provides training, conferences, workshops, consultations newletters, updatesand safety support materials.
Founded: 1913
Donny Ward, Executive Director
Janet Froetscher, President, CEO

620 Alabama Solar Association
PO Box 143 256-650-5120
Huntsville, AL 35804-143 *Fax:* 256-650-5119
isimon1027@aol.com
al-solar.wixsite.com/a-s-a
A non-profit organization advocating and promoting green, renewable and solar energy conservation.
Doug Elgin, President
Al Orilion, Founder

621 Alabama Waterfowl Association
1346 Country Road #11
Scottsboro, AL 35768
205-259-2509
www.sites.google.com/site/alabamawaterfowlassociation
Dedicated to increasing waterfowl populations, natural wetland and upland waterways. AWA networks with other state waterfowl associations in the North American Waterfowl Federation for wetlands conservation.
Founded: 1989
Jerry Davis, CEO
Gary Benefield, Executive Director

622 Alabama Wildlife Federation
3050 Lanark Rd 334-285-4550
Millbrook, AL 36054 800-822-9453
Fax: 334-285-4959
awf@alabamawildlife.org
www.alabamawildlife.org
Mission is to promote the conservation of Alabama's wildlife and natural resources, as a basis for the social and economic prosperity, through responsible use and stewardship of wildlife, forests, fish, soils, water and air.
Founded: 1935
Angus R. Cooper, President
Ed Leigh McMillan, Vice President

623 American Lung Association of Alabama
1678 Montgomery Highway 205-603-1540
Suite 104-355 alaal@LungSE.org
Birmingham, AL 35216 www.lung.org
The American Lung Association of Alabama works to prevent lung disease and promote lung health; offering a wide variety of lung health services to the people of Alabama.
Martha C. Bogdan, Executive VP, Southeast
Willie L. Bythwood, Jr, CFO

624 American Society of Landscape Architects: Alabama Chapter
202-898-2444
888-999-2752
Fax: 202-898-1185
info@asla.org
www.alabamaasla.com
The professional association representing landscape architects who lead, educate and participate in the careful stewardship, planning, and artful design of cultural and natural environments.
Lois S. Mash, President
Jane Reed Ross, President-Elect

625 BASS Anglers Sportsman Society
3500 Blue Lake Drive
Suite 330
Birmingham, AL 35243
334-272-9530
877-227-7872
Fax: 334-270-7148
bassmaster@emailcustomerservice.com
www.bassmaster.com
B.A.S.S. is dedicated to enhancing the sport of bass fishing by advocating for access, conservation and youth fishing.
Founded: 1967
Gary Jones, Federation Director

626 National Safety Council: Tennessee Valley Office
2042 Beltline Road SW
Building A, Suite 110
Decatur, AL 35601
256-308-1133
Fax: 256-308-1161
alabama@nsc.org
Conducts safety, health and environmental efforts at the community level in order to eliminate preventable deaths at work, in homes, communities and on the road.
Donny Ward, Executive Director

627 Sierra Club: Alabama Chapter
4075 Lawson Gap Rd
Boaz, AL 35956-6507
256-572-0400
jonathonmeeks@gmail.com
www.sierraclub.org/alabama
The Alabama Chapter of the Sierra Club fights for clean water, educates the public and creates political action to protect Alabama's wilderness to make Alabama a cleaner and safer place.
Founded: 1908 3,000 Members
Loren Blackford, President
Susana Reyes, Vice President

Alaska

628 Alaska Conservation Alliance
810 N St #203
P.O Box 100660
Anchorage, AK 99501-3271
907-258-6171
Fax: 907-258-6177
info@akvoice.org
nwtoxiccommunities.org
Statewide non-profit organization whose primary mission is to protect Alaska's natural environment through voter education, engagement and advocacy.
Founded: 1997
Kate Troll, Principal Officer

629 Alaska Natural Resource & Outdoor Education
200 W. 34th Street
Suite 1007
Anchorage, AK 99503
907-292-1772
Fax: 907-207-1795
anroeak@gmail.com
www.anroe.net
Mission is to promote and implement excellence in natural resource, outdoor, and environmental education for Alaskans.
Founded: 1986
Marilyn Sigman, President
Elizabeth Trowbridge, Treasurer

630 Alaska Wildlife Alliance
PO Box 202022
Anchorage, AK 99520
907-277-0897
Fax: 907-277-7423
info@akwildlife.org
www.akwildlife.org
Advocates for scientifically managed and healthy ecosystems to protect wildlife for present and future generations.
Founded: 1978
Ed Schmitt, President
Richard Hoskins, Vice President

631 American Lung Association of Alaska
500 W Intl Airport Rd A
Anchorage, AK 99518
907-664-6400
Fax: 907-565-5587
marge.stoneking@lung.org
www.aklung.org
Promoting lung health awareness amd preventing lung diseases in Alaska.
Founded: 1934
Kathryn A. Forbes, CPA, Chair
John F. Emanuel, JD, Vice Chair

632 American Lung Association of Alaska: Fairbanks
529 6th Avenue
Suite 203
Fairbanks, AK 99701
907-891-7451
maegan.weltzin@lung.org
www.aklung.org

633 American Lung Association of Alaska: Wasilla
1075 S Check Street
Suite 205
Wasilla, AK 99654
907-891-7445
ashley.peltier@lung.org
www.aklung.org

634 American Society of Landscape Architects: Alaska Chapter
800 F St
PO Box 196650
Anchorage, AK 99519
907-343-8368
888-999-2752
Fax: 907-343-8088
aslaak.web@gmail.com
www.akasla.org
Supports the knowledge and practice of landscape architecture as a means to protect and enhance the natural and built environments of Alaska.
Founded: 1978
Ed Leonetti, President
Eliza Cink, Vice President, Interior

635 Audubon Alaska
431 West 7th Avenue
Suite 101
Anchorage, AK 99501
907-276-7034
Fax: 907-276-5069
audubonalaska@audubon.org
ak.audubon.org
Working to conserve Alaska's natural ecosystems, birds, wildlife, and their habitats by using science to identify conservation priorities and support conservation actions and policies.
Founded: 1977
David Yarnold, President & CEO
Natalie Dawson, VP & Executive Director

636 Bureau of Land Management
222 West 7th Ave #13
Anchorage, AK 99513
907-271-5960
Fax: 907-271-3684
AK_AKSO_Public_Room@blm.gov
www.blm.gov/alaska
The Bureau of Land Management in Alaska focuses on land transfer, energy development, Trans-Alaska pipeline system and fire management.
Mark Spencer, District Manager
Bonnie Million, Field Manager

637 National Wildlife Federation Alaska Regional Center
750 W. 2nd Avenue
Anchorage, AK 99501
206-285-8707
800-937-2026
Fax: 206-285-8698
www.nwf.org/pacific-region/alaska.aspx
Focuses on global warming, renewable energy, wildlife, sustainable tourism and youth education.
Founded: 1988
Beth Pratt, Director
Jennifer Murck, Manager

638 **Northern Alaska Environmental Center**
830 College Road 907-452-5021
Fairbanks, AK 99701-1535 *Fax:* 907-452-3100
info@northern.org
www.northern.org

Promotes conservation of the environment in Interior and Arctic Alaska through advocacy, education, and sustainable resource stewardship.
Founded: 1971
Elisabeth Dabney, Executive Director
Frank Williams, President

639 **Sierra Club Alaska Chapter**
750 W 2nd Ave 907-258-6807
Suite 100 *Fax:* 907-258-6807
Anchorage, AK 99501 dan.ritzman@sierraclub.org
www.sierraclub.org/alaska

The Alaska Chapter of the Sierra Club works to protect the Last Frontier from the damage of logging and drilling. It strives for renewable energy, sustainable use of resources, preservation of wild places, and the smart growth of urbanareas.
Founded: 1892
Dan Ritzman, Program Director
Yasuhiro Ozuru, Chair

640 **Trustees for Alaska**
1026 W 4th Avenue 907-276-4244
Suite 201 *Fax:* 907-276-7110
Anchorage, AK 99501 ecolaw@trustees.org
www.trustees.org

A public interest law firm that provides legal counsel to sustain and protect Alaska's natural environment.
Founded: 1974
Chase Hensel, Chair
Victoria Clark, Executive Director

641 **Wildlife Society: Alaska Chapter**
1271 Lowbush Lane 907-456-8682
Fairbanks, AK 99709 *Fax:* 907-257-2774
twsalaska@gmail.com
www.wildlife.org/alaska

A nonprofit organization of professional wildlife biologists dedicated to excellence in conserving wildlife and their habitats and wildlife sterwardship through science and education.
Founded: 1971
Scott Brainerd, President
Nate Svoboda, President-Elect

Arizona

642 **American Lung Association of Arizona**
102 West McDowell Rd 602-258-7505
2819 East Boradway Blvd 800-586-4872
Phoenix, AZ 85003 *Fax:* 877-276-2108
AZInfo@Lungs.org
www.lung.org

The mission of the American Lung Association is to prevent lung disease and promote lung health.
Founded: 1912
Lynn Rosenbach, Chair, CEO
Susan Cordier, COO

643 **American Lung Association of Arizona: Tucson**
2819 East Broadway Bouelvard 520-323-1812
Tucson, AZ 85716 AZInfo@Lungs.org
www.lung.org/about-us/local-associations/arizona.html

644 **Arizona ASLA: American Society of Landscape Architects**
PO Box 28393 602-258-8668
Tempe, AZ 85285 *Fax:* 602-273-6814
www.azasla.org

The Arizona state affiliate of the American Society of Landscape Architects are dedicated to educate and participate in the planning and design of cultural and natural environments.
Rick Campbell, President
Laura Paty, President Elect

645 **Arizona Automotive Recyclers Association**
1030 E. Baseline Rd. 480-609-3999
#105-1025 admin@aara.com
Tempe, AZ 85283 www.aara.com

A group of automotive recyclers that are committed to serving Arizona with quality recycled auto parts, to help customers, communities and the environment.
Founded: 1910
Mike Pierson Jr, President
Leroy Liebermann, Secretary/Treasurer

646 **Arizona BASS Chapter Federation**
P.O Box 11448 480-304-1033
Chandler, AZ 85248 *Fax:* 480-773-7019
info@azbassfederation.com
www.azbassfederation.com

Bass fishing tournament organization, facilitators of recruiting youth fishers and help conserve natural habitats.
Founded: 1972
Gregory Krueger, President
Steven Boyce, Vice President

647 **Arizona Chapter, National Safety Council**
1606 West Indian School Road 602-264-2394
Phoenix, AZ 85015-5232 *Fax:* 602-277-5485
main@acnsc.org
www.acnsc.org

To protect life and promote health through accident and injury prevention at home, work, school and on the road.
Founded: 1949
John Keeler, President
Margaret Cather, Executive Director

648 **Arizona Recycling Coalition**
24 West Camelback Road 408-254-1922
Suite A-492 info@arizonarecyclingcoalition.org
Phoenix, AZ 85013 arizonarecyclingcoalition.org

The Arizona Recycling Coalition (AzRC) is a membership-based, non-profit organization dedicated to promoting waste reuse, reduction and recycling throughout Arizona and our southwestern region.
Alana Levine, Chairperson
Terry Gellenbeck, Vice-Chair

649 **Arizona Solar Energy Industries Association**
Solar Energy Industries Association
2122 W. Lone Cactus Dr 602-559-4769
Suite 2 info@ariseia.org
Phoenix, AZ 85027 www.ariseia.org

A non-profit trade organization that aims to deploy solar energy technologies in an ethical manner.
Founded: 1997
Tom Harris, President
Court Rich, Vice President

650 **Arizona Water Well Association**
950 E. Baseline Rd. 480-609-3999
#104-1025 *Fax:* 480-609-3939
Tempe, AZ 85283 admin@azwwa.org
www.azwwa.org

Promotes protection and wise development of underground water resources.
Founded: 1957
Nate Little, President
David Williams, President Elect

651 **Arizona-Sonora Desert Museum**
2021 N Kinney Road 520-883-2702
Tucson, AZ 85743 *Fax:* 520-883-2500
info@desertmuseum.org
www.desertmuseum.org

Museum, zoo, botanical garden, art gellery and aquarium. Also helps to conserve the Sonoran Desert.
Founded: 1952
Craig Ivanyi, Executive Director
Holly Swangstu, Art Institute Director

652 **Center for Biological Diversity**
PO Box 710 520-623-5252
Tucson, AZ 85702-0710 866-357-3349
Fax: 520-623-9797
center@biologicaldiversity.org
www.biologicaldiversity.org
Works through science, law and creative media to secure a future for all species on the brink of extinction.
Marcey Olajos, Chair
Kieran Suckling, Exe. Dir., Co-Founder

653 **Sierra Club: Arizona Chapter**
514 W. Roosevelt St 602-253-8633
Phoenix, AZ 85003 grand.canyon.chapter@sierraclub.org
www.sierraclub.org/arizona
The Grand Canyon Chapter utilizes conservation, political and legislative activism, administrative work and outings to protect the state and its natural resources.
Founded: 1965
Jim Vaaler, Chair
Sandy Bahr, Outreach Director

Arkansas

654 **American Fisheries Society: Fish Administration Section**
AR afsfisheriesadministration.wordpress.com
Represents members who administer state, federal, and provincial fishery agencies and fisheries programs, as well as encouraging information exchange.
Jim Fredericks, President
Jason Olive, Secretary-Treasurer

655 **American Society of Landscape Architects: Arkansas Chapter**
P.O. Box 3343 202-898-2444
Fayetteville, AR 72702 800-999-2752
Fax: 202-898-1185
www.arasla.org
Promotes the profession of landscappe architecture and advances the practive through advocacy, education, communication and fellowship.
Founded: 1899
Allison Thurmond Quinlan, President
Alan Ostner, Treasurer

656 **Arkansas Association of Conservation Districts**
101 East Capitol 501-682-2915
Suite 350 *Fax:* 501-682-3991
Little Rock, AR 72201 rockyharrell@sbcglobal.net
www.aracd.org
The Arkansas Association of Conservation Districts assists the conservation districts of Arkansas in their efforts to serve the soil and water conservation needs of the people of Arkansas.
Founded: 1937
Debbie Moreland, Program Administrator
Martha Manley, President

657 **Arkansas Environmental Federation**
415 N. McKinley St 501-374-0263
Suite 835 *Fax:* 501-374-8752
Little Rock, AR 72205 cmiller@environmentark.org
www.environmentark.org
The AEF is a non-profit education association that provides training for environmental professionals and advocates with a focus on practical laws and regulations based on science, a teamwork approach to compliance, waste minimizationand pollution prevention.
Founded: 1967
Tom Fox, President
Kelley Crouch, President-Elect

658 **Arkansas Respiratory Health Association**
211 Natural Resources Drive 501-224-5864
Little Rock, AR 72205 800-880-5864
Fax: 501-224-5645
www.arkresp.org
Mission of the Arkansas Respiratory Health Association is to prevent lung disease and promote lung health through education, advocacy and research.

659 **Sierra Club: Arkansas Chapter**
1308 West 2nd St 501-301-8280
Little Rock, AR 72201 glen.hooks@sierraclub.org
www.sierraclub.org/arkansas
To practice and promote responsible use of the earth's ecosystems and resources; educate the public to protect and restore the quality of the natural environment. The Arkansas Chapter focuses on protecting the wilderness of Arkansasand clean energy and water.
Founded: 1982
Loren Blackford, President
Susana Reyes, Vice President

California

660 **American Lung Association of California**
American Lung Association
333 Hegenberger Rd 510-638-5864
Suite 450 *Fax:* 510-638-8984
Oakland, CA 94621 cainfo@lung.org
www.lung.org/about-us/local-associations/california.html
Focuses on lung cancer, air quality, lung diesease, the elimination of tobacco and related diseases and fundraising.
Founded: 1904
Stephen R. O'Kane, Secretary, Treasurer
Cheryl A. Calhoun, Managing Director

661 **American Lung Association of California: Bakersfield**
2025 Westwind Drive
Suite C 661-847-4700
Bakersfield, CA 93301 maria.jaime@lung.org
www.lung.org/about-us/local-associations/california.html

662 **American Lung Association of California: Chico**
25 Jan Court 530-345-5864
Chico, CA 95928 shelly.brantley@lung.org
www.lung.org/about-us/local-associations/california.html

663 **American Lung Association of California: Fresno**
1680 W Shaw Avenue 559-772-3307
Fresno, CA 93711 justina.felix@lung.org
www.lung.org/about-us/local-associations/california.html

664 **American Lung Association of California: Los Angeles**
3325 Wilshire Boulevard
Suite 900 213-384-5864
Los Angeles, CA 90010 ana.martinez@lung.org
www.lung.org/about-us/local-associations/california.html

665 **American Lung Association of California: Orange County**
513 E 1st Street 714-835-5864
Suite B www.lung.org/about-us/local-associations/california.html
Tustin, CA 92780

666 **American Lung Association of California: Sacramento**
1531 I St 916-554-5864
Sacramento, CA 95814 cainfo@lung.org
www.lung.org/about-us/local-associations/california.html

667 American Lung Association of California: San Berardino
441 Mac Kay Drive 909-884-5864
San Bernardino, CA 92408 clarissa.mprales@lung.org
www.lung.org/about-us/local-associations/california.html

668 American Lung Association of California: San Diego
2020 Camino Del Rio N
Suite 200 619-297-3901
San Diego, CA 92108 ellen.sherwood@lung.org
www.lung.org/about-us/local-associations/california.html

669 American Rivers: California Region: Fairfax
2150 Allston Way 510-809-8010
Suite 320 outreach@americanrivers.org
Berkeley, CA 94704 www.americanrivers.org
American Rivers is the only national organization standing up for healthy rivers so communities can thrive.
Founded: 1973
Bob Irvin, President
Chris Williams, Senior V.P, Conservation

670 American Rivers: California Region: Nevada City
120 Union St 530-478-0206
Nevada City, CA 95959 *Fax:* 530-478-5849
outreach@americanrivers.org
www.americanrivers.org
The conservation organization stands up for healthy rivers so communities can thrive. American Rivers protects and restores America's rivers for the benefit of people, wildlife and nature.
Founded: 1973 65,000 Members
Bob Irvin, President
Chris Williams, Senior V.P, Conservation

671 American Society of Landscape Architects: Northern California Chapter
3130 Balfour Road 415-974-5490
Suite D #275 *Fax:* 415-543-2112
Brentwood, CA 94513 www.asla-ncc.org
To advance the profession of Landscape Architecture for the public's appreciation and awareness.
Founded: 1899
Elizabeth Boults, President
Carolyne Orazi, President-Elect

672 American Society of Landscape Architects: San Diego Chapter
1050 Rosecrans St 619-283-8818
Suite B *Fax:* 619-222-8154
San Diego, CA 92106 aslasd@sbcglobal.net
www.asla-sandiego.org
To lead, educate and participate in the careful stewardship, planning and artful design of cultural and natural environments.
Nate Magnusson, President
Michael D. Brennan, President Elect

673 American Society of Landscape Architects: Sierra Chapter
1400 S St 916-447-7400
Suite 100 *Fax:* 916-447-8270
Sacramento, CA 95811 www.asla-sierra.org
Strives for the advancement of knowledge, education and skill in the art and science of landscape architecture.
Jessica McWilliams, President
Andrew Wickham, President-Elect

674 American Society of Landscape Architects: Southern California Chapter
360 E. First St 714-838-3615
Suite 371 877-378-6726
Tustin, CA 92780 *Fax:* 714-730-6296
vphillipy@socal-asla.org
www.socal-asla.org
Promotes landscape architecture through knowledge, ecducation, communication, advocacy and skill.
Duane Border, President
Pamela Brief, President Elect

675 Asian Pacific Environmental Network
426 17th St 510-834-8920
Suite 500 *Fax:* 510-834-8926
Oakland, CA 94612 info@apen4ej.org
www.apen4ej.org
The Asian Pacific Environmental Network (APEN) empowers low-income Asian Pacific Islander (API) communities to take action on environmental and social justice issues. APEN builds organizations in dis-empowered API communities todevelop lasting capacity and to achieve solutions to problems affecting people's lives.
Founded: 1991
Nayantara Mehta, Board Chair
Joanne Kim, Board Vice Chair

676 Bio Integral Resource Center
PO Box 7414 510-524-2567
Berkeley, CA 94707 *Fax:* 510-524-1758
birc@igc.org
www.birc.org
The goal of the Bio Integral Resources Center is to reduce pesticide use by educating the public about effective, less toxic alternatives for pest problems.
Founded: 1979
Dr. William Quarles, Executive Director

677 Breathe California Golden Gate Public Health Partnership
1 Sutter St 650-994-5868
Suite 225 *Fax:* 415-445-3000
San Francisco, CA 94014 info@ggbreathe.org
www.ggbreathe.org
Breathe California fights lung disease, advocates for clean air and advances public health through grassroots education, advocacy and services.
Founded: 1908
Tanya Stevenson, President/CEO
Elias Trevino, Vice President, Operations

678 Breathe California Of Los Angeles County
5858 Wilshire Blvd 323-935-8050
Suite 300 *Fax:* 323-935-1873
Los Angeles, CA 90036 info@breathela.org
www.breathela.org
Dedicated to providing communities in Los Angeles County with the resources needed to promote clean air initiatives through its continued commitment to research, education and advocacy.
Founded: 1903
Steven L. Bryson, Esq., Chair
Fernando Del Rio, Chair Elect

679 Breathe California of the Bay Area: Alameda, Santa Clara And San Benito Counties
1469 Park Ave 408-998-5865
San Jose, CA 95126 *Fax:* 408-998-0578
info@lungsrus.org
www.lungsrus.org
Fights lung disease and works with communities to promote lung health.
Founded: 1904
Scott McLarty, Chair
Abhay Tewari, Founder, CEO

680 California Academy of Sciences Library
55 Music Concourse Drive 415-379-8000
Golden Gate Park *Fax:* 415-321-8633
San Francisco, CA 94118 info@calacademy.org
www.calacademy.org
The California Academy of Sciences is dedicated to exploring, explaining, and sustaining life on Earth. Includes an aquarium, natural history museum, planetarium and rainforest.
Founded: 1853
Jonathan Foley, PhD, Executive Director
Mike McGee, Chief Financial Officer

681 California Air Resources Board
State of California

1001 I St
PO Box 2815
Sacramento, CA 95814
916-322-2990
800-242-4450
Fax: 916-445-5025
helpline@arb.ca.gov
www.arb.ca.gov

The California ARB is the state agency charged with coordinating efforts to attain and maintain ambient air quality standards, conduct research into the causes and solutions to air pollution and its health impacts. Their mission is topromote and protect public health, welfare and ecological resources.

Founded: 1967
Mary D. Nichols, Chairman
Sandra Berg, Vice Chair

682 California Association of Environmental Health
3700 Chaney Court
Carmichael, CA 95608
530-676-0715
Fax: 530-676-0515
justin@ccdeh.com
www.ccdeh.com

Environmental Health Departments provide the delivery of Local Environmental Health Programs.

Justin Malan, Executive Director
Sheryl Baldwin, CCDEH Manager

683 California Association of Resource Conservation Districts
801 K St, MS 14-15
Sacramento, CA 95814
916-457-7904
Fax: 916-457-7934
info@carcd.org
www.carcd.org

CARCD is a voluntary association whose primary purpose is to enhance the effectiveness of local Resource Conservation Districts (RCDs) so as to implement strong and locally-led conservation efforts of natural resources and agriculturein California.

Karen Buhr, Executive Director
Paul Williams, President

684 California BASS Federation
13350 Racquet Court
Poway, CA 92064
858-748-9459
californiabassorg@gmail.com
www.californiabass.org

Dedicated to promoting bass fishing through youth, conservation, public awareness, and local support. Regional tournaments are held throughout California.

Founded: 1969
Scott Sweet, President
Larry Wilson, VP

685 California Birth Defects Monitoring Program
1615 Capitol Ave
Sacramento, CA 95814
916-558-1784
Fax: 916-650-0305
mchinet@cdph.ca.gov
www.cdph.ca.gov/Programs/CFH/DGDS/Pages/cbdmp/about.aspx

The California Birth Defects Monitoring Program is a public health program devoted to finding the causes of birth defects in order to prevent them.

Founded: 1982
Karen L. Smith, Director
Kate Clayton, Health Promotion, Chief

686 California Certified Organic Farmers
2155 Delaware Avenue
Suite 150
Santa Cruz, CA 95060
831-423-2263
Fax: 831-423-4528
ccof@ccof.org
www.ccof.org

Promotes and supports organic food and agriculture through an organic certification program, trade support, producer and consumer education, and political advocacy.

Founded: 1973
Phil LaRocca, Chair
Malcolm Ricci, Vice Chair

687 California Council for Environmental and Economic Balance
101 Mission St
Suite 1440
San Francisco, CA 94105
415-512-7890
Fax: 415-512-7897
cceeb@cceeb.org
www.cceeb.org

A coalition of California business, labor and public leaders that strive to make environmental and economic balance a reality.

Founded: 1976
Walter McGuire, Chairman
Jerry Secundy, President/CEO

688 California Renewable Fuels Council
1516 Ninth St
MS-29
Sacramento, CA 95814-5512
916-654-4287
844-421-6229
renewable@energy.ca.gov
www.energy.ca.gov/renewables

As part of the California Energy Commission, the California Renewable Fuels Council is committed to reducing energy costs and the environmental impacts of energy use.

Founded: 2002
Robert B. Weisenmiller, Chair
Kourtney Vaccaro, Chief Counsel

689 California Resource Recovery Association
915 L Street
Suite C-216
Sacramento, CA 95814
916-441-2772
ccra.com

The California Resource Recovery Association (CRRA) is California's statewide recycling association dedicated to achieving environmental sustainability in and beyond California through Zero Waste strategies including productstewardship, waste prevention, reuse, recycling and composting.

Founded: 1974
Jenna Abbott, Executive Director
Rob Hilton, Conference Program Chair

690 California Solar Energy Industries Association
1107 9th St
Suite 820
Sacramento, CA 95814
916-228-4567
Fax: 707-374-4767
info@calseia.org
www.calseia.org

Promotes the expanding use of solar technologies in California and the growth of the solar industry.

Founded: 1977
Ed Murray, President
Jeanine Cotter, Vice President

691 California State University East Bay
California State University
California State University
25800 Carlos Bee Blvd
Hayward, CA 94542
510-885-3000
Fax: 510-885-4747
www.csueastbay.edu

The University's mission is to provide an academically rich, multicultural learning experience that prepares its students to realize their goals, pursue meaningful lifework, and to be socially responsible contributors to theircommunities.

Leroy M. Morishita, President
Bill Johnson, Vice President

692 California Trappers Association (CTA)
907 Holmes Flat Road
Redcrest, CA 95525
707-772-4259
www.californiatrappers.com

CTA's primary concern is California's fur bearing mammals and small predatory mammals.

Founded: 1863
John Clark, President
James C Schmerker Jr, Vice President

693 California Waterfowl Association
1346 Blue Oaks Blvd
Roseville, CA 95678
916-648-1406
Fax: 916-648-1665
www.calwaterfowl.org

A statewide nonprofit organization whose principal objectives are the preservation, protection, and enhancement of California's waterfowl resources, wetlands, and associated hunting heritage.

Founded: 1945
John Carlson Jr., President
Rob Plath, Chair

694 **California Wildlife Foundation**
428 13th St 510-763-0211
Suite 10A *Fax:* 510-268-9948
Oakland, CA 94612 info@californiawildlifefoundation.org
www.californiawildlifefoundation.org
Committed to protecting the state's wildlife species by acquiring, restoring, and managing sufficient habitat to sustain healthy populations over time.
Founded: 1990
Ellen Maldonado, Secretary
James Lightbody, Treasurer

695 **Californians for Population Stabilization (CAPS)**
P.O Box 90409 805-564-6626
Santa Barbara, CA 93101 *Fax:* 805-564-6636
info@capsweb.org
www.capsweb.org
A nonprofit, public interest organization that works to protect California's environment and quality of life by stabilizing the population.
Founded: 1986
Ben Zuckerman, President
Judith F. Smith, Vice President

696 **Central California Safety Council**
6004 N. El Dorado St 209-472-7233
Stockton, CA 95207-4349 www.californiasafety.org
To promote health and safety at home, in travel and in the workplace. Provides community health and safety programs, information and educational materials on health and safety-related topics and products.
Founded: 1934
Lynndee Riley, Secretary

697 **Colorado River Board of California**
770 Fairmont Ave 818-500-1625
Suite 100 *Fax:* 818-543-4685
Glendale, CA 91203-1068 crb@crb.ca.gov
www.crb.ca.gov
Established to protect California's rights and interests in the resources provided by the Colorado River and to represent California in discussions and negotiations regarding the Colorado River and its management.
Founded: 1937
Christopher Harris, Executive Director

698 **Communities for a Better Environment (CBE)**
6325 Pacific Blvd. 323-826-9771
Suite 300 *Fax:* 323-588-7079
Huntington Park, CA 90255 www.cbecal.org
Works to achieve environmental health and justice in California by building grassroots power in and with communities of color and working-class communities.
Darryl Molina Sarmiento, Executive Director
Julia May, Senior Scientist

699 **Concerned Citizens of South Central Los Angeles**
4707 South Central Avenue 323-846-2500
PO Box 11337 *Fax:* 323-846-2508
Los Angeles, CA 90011 info@ccscla.org
www.ccscla.org
The mission of the Concerned Citizens of South Central Los Angeles is to fight for social, economic and environmental justice and to encourage resident participation in the process.
Founded: 1985
Robin Cannon, President
Noreen McClendon, Executive Director & VP

700 **Desert Tortoise Preserve Committee**
Tortoise T-R-A-C-K-S
4067 Mission Inn Ave 951-683-3872
Riverside, CA 92501 *Fax:* 951-683-6949
dtpc@pacbell.net
www.tortoise-tracks.org
A non-profit organization formed to promote the welfare of the desert tortoise in its native wild state.
Founded: 1974
Ron Berger, President
Robert Wood, Vice President

701 **Environmental Defense Center**
906 Garden St 805-963-1622
Santa Barbara, CA 93101 *Fax:* 805-962-3152
EDC@EnvironmentalDefenseCenter.org
www.environmentaldefensecenter.org
The Environmental Defense Center is a nonprofit, public interest organization that provides legal, educational and advocacy support to advance the environmental quality of California's south central coast.
Founded: 1977
Judy Pirkowitsch, President
Dave Davis, Vice President

702 **Environmental Health Coalition**
2727 Hoover Ave 619-474-0220
Suite 202 *Fax:* 619-474-1210
National City, CA 91950 ehc@environmentalhealth.org
www.environmentalhealth.org
Uses social change strategies to achieve environmental and social justice. Organizes and advocates to protect public health and the environment threatened by toxic pollution.
Founded: 1980
Margaret Godshalk, President
Enrique Medina, Vice President

703 **Environmental Health Network**
PO Box 1155 415-541-5075
Larkspur, CA 94977-1155 fdadockets@oc.fda.gov
www.ehnca.org
Nonprofit, volunteer organization, whose main goal is to promote public awareness of environmental sensitivities and causative factors. EHN's focus is on issues of access and developments relating to the health and welfare of theenvironmentally sensitive.
Connie Barker, Board President
Cyndi Norwitz, Board Vice President

704 **Environmental Protection Information Center**
145 G Street 707-822-7711
Suite A *Fax:* 707-822-7712
Arcata, CA 95521 epic@wildcalifornia.org
wildcalifornia.org
The Environmental Protection Information Center (EPIC) advocates for science-based protection and restoration of Northwest California's forests, using an integrated, science-based approach, combining public education, citizen advocacy,and strategic litigation.
Founded: 1977
Shawnee Alexandri, President
Robert Shearer, Vice President

705 **Friends of the River**
1418 20th St 916-442-3155
Suite 100 888-464-2477
Sacramento, CA 95811 *Fax:* 916-442-3396
info@friendsoftheriver.org
www.friendsoftheriver.org
Friends of the River is dedicated to preserving and restoring California's rivers, streams and watersheds as well as advocating for sustainable water management.
Founded: 1973
Eric Wesselman, Executive Director
John Yost, Treasurer

706 **Get Oil Out**
PO Box 23625 805-965-1519
Santa Barbara, CA 93121 www.getoilout.org
A Santa Barbara public group dedicated to the protection of the Santa Barbara Channel and coastline from the environmental, economic and esthetic impact of oil development. The organization was formed in response to a 1969 accidentthat blackened the

beaches, poisoned the ocean's water and killed many creatures that depend on clean water for survival.
Founded: 1969
Michael T. Lyons, President

707 Heal the Bay
1444 9th St 310-451-1500
Santa Monica, CA 90401 *Fax:* 310-496-1902
A nonprofit organization dedicated to protecting Santa Monica Bay and all Southern California coastal waters and watersheds.
Founded: 1985
Shelley Luce, President, CEO
Sarah Abramson Sikich, Vice President

708 Hopland Research and Extension Center
4070 University Road 707-744-1424
Hopland, CA 95449 *Fax:* 707-744-1040
karodrigues@ucanr.edu
hrec.ucanr.edu
The Hopland Research and Extension Center (HREC) is a multi-disciplinary research and education facility for agriculture and natural resources in the North Coast region run by the University of California.
Founded: 1951
Kimberly A. Rodriques, Director

709 Institute of International Education
Institute of International Education
530 Bush St 415-362-6520
Suite 1000 *Fax:* 415-392-4667
San Francisco, CA 94108 iiesf@iie.org
www.iie.org
An independent non-profit organization that works to advance international education and access to education worldwide.
Founded: 1919
Allen E. Goodman, President, CEO
Mary Karam McKey, Director

710 League to Save Lake Tahoe
2608 Lake Tahoe Blvd 530-541-5388
South Lake Tahoe, CA 96150 *Fax:* 530-541-5454
www.keeptahoeblue.org
Focused on the preservation and restoration of the Tahoe Basin's waters, forests, wildlife and landscape for present and future generations.
Founded: 1957
Ash Daggs, President
David Brandenburger, Vice President

711 Marine Mammal Center
2000 Bunker Rd 415-289-7325
Fort Cronkite *Fax:* 415-289-7333
Sausalito, CA 94965-2619 info@tmmc.org
www.marinemammalcenter.org
Veterinary research hospital and educational center dedicated to the rescue and rehabilitation of ill and injured marine mammals.
Founded: 1975
Dr. Jeffrey R. Boehm, Executive Director
Marci Davis, CFO

712 Mendocino County Resource Conservation District
410 Jones Street 707-462-3664
Suite C-3 mcrcd.org
Ukiah, CA 95482
The Mendocino County Resource Conservation District is a nonprofit organization that helps communities voluntarily conserve, protect, and restore wild and working landscapes in Mendocino County. They provide technical assistance,education and outreach programs, monitoring and assessment services, and funding opportunities to help land managers improve the long-term stewardship of the county's natural resource base.
Dave Koball, Chair
Craig Blencowe, Vice Chair

713 Mendocino Land Trust
P.O. Box 1094 707-962-0470
330 N. Franklin Street, Suite 7 admin@mendocinolandtrust.org
Fort Bragg, CA 95437 mendocinolandtrust.org
The mission of the Mendocino Land Trust is to conserve important natural resources of Mendocino County including working farmlands and forests, wildlife habitat, open space, scenic vistas, watersheds, and to facilitate public access.
Founded: 1976
Terry Gross, President
Richard Strom, Vice President

714 Mendocino Wildlife Association
45090 Little Lake Street 707-357-5693
Mendocino, CA 95460 707-984-6363
mendowildlife.com
Mendocino Wildlife Association (MWA) is a non-profit organization dicated to public education about wildlife, using non-lethal wildlife management practices, and wildlife rescue and rehabilitation.
Traci Pellar, Administrator

715 NorCal Solar/Northern California Solar Energy Society
PO Box 3008 510-592-7136
Berkeley, CA 94703 info@norcalsolar.org
www.norcalsolar.org
A non-profit educational organization whose mission is to accelerate the use of solar energy technology through the exchange of information.
Founded: 1974
Eric Larson, President

716 Northcoast Environmental Center
415 I St 707-822-6918
Arcata, CA 95521 *Fax:* 707-822-6980
nec@yournec.org
www.yournec.org
A nonprofit educational organization devoted to conserving and protecting the terrestrial, aquatic and marine ecosystems of Northern California. Their goal is to promote the importance of the relations between people and the biosphere.
Founded: 1971
Larry Glass, President
Dan Sealy, Vice-President

717 Outdoor Programs
University of California San Francisco
Milberry Union 125 West 415-476-1115
500 Parnassus Ave *Fax:* 415-502-5887
San Francisco, CA 94143-0234 outdoors@cls.ucsf.edu
campuslifeservices.ucsf.edu/fitnessrecreation
Paddling, hiking, climbing, aquatics, personal training, and pilates available for students, families in the UCSF community and the public.
Founded: 1970
Kirk McLaughlin, Outdoor Programs Manager
Colleen Massey, Mission Bay Prog. Supervisor

718 Pesticide Action Network North America
161 Telegraph Ave 510-788-9020
Suite 1200 panna@panna.org
Oakland, CA 94612 www.panna.org
Pesticide Action Network North America advocates the adoption of ecologically sound practices in place of hazardous pesticide use in order to create a thriving food system.
Founded: 1984
Denise O'Brien, President
Virginia Nesmith, Vice President

719 Pesticide Education Center
PO Box 225279 415-391-8511
San Francisco, CA 94122-5279 *Fax:* 415-391-9159
pec@igc.org
To educate the public about the health effects of exposure to pesticides in the home, community and at work.
Founded: 1988
Marion Moses, President

720 Rainforest Action Network
425 Bush St 415-398-4404
Suite 300 *Fax:* 415-398-2732
San Francisco, CA 94108 ran@ran.org
www.ran.org
Rainforest Action Network works to protect the Earth's rainforest and support the rights of their inhabitants through education, grassroots organizing and non-violent direct action.
Founded: 1985
Anna Hawken, Chair
James D. Gollin, President

721 Redwood Empire Solar Living Association
c/o Solar Living Institute
P.O Box 836 707-472-2450
Hopland, CA 95449 *Fax:* 707-472-2498
sli@solarliving.org
www.solarliving.org
The Solar Living Institute promotes sustainable living through environmental education. Offers professional solar training and a wide array of sustainability courses.
Founded: 1998
John Schaeffer, President
Karen Kallen, Executive Director

722 San Diego Renewable Energy Society (SDRES)
PO Box 927203 sdres.org
San Diego, CA 92192
Dedicated to increasing the use of renewable and sustainable energy technologies in San Diego County.
Jamaal Knight, Chairman
Jake Lincoln, Treasurer

723 San Francisco Parks Alliance
1663 Mission Street 415-621-3260
Suite 320 *Fax:* 415-703-0889
San Francisco, CA 94103 feedback@sfparksalliance.org
www.sfparksalliance.org
Nonprofit organization supports park improvements through donations and investments, as well as engaging with city government.
Founded: 1996
Drew Becher, Chief Executive Officer

724 Save San Francisco Bay Association
1330 Broadway 510-463-6850
Suite 1800 *Fax:* 510-463-6851
Oakland, CA 94612-2519 info@saveSFbay.org
www.savesfbay.org
Save the Bay works to protect and restore the San Francisco Bay from pollution, fill, shoreline destruction and fresh water diversion.
Founded: 1961
David Lewis, Executive Director
Samuel N. Luoma, Chair

725 Scenic California
CA 510-883-0390
Fax: 510-883-0391
www.scenic.org
Nonprofit organization dedicated to protecting natural beauty and distinctive community character through scenic conservation.
Mark Falzone, President
Ronald L. Fleming, Chair

726 Sierra Club: Angeles Chapter
3250 Wilshire Blvd 213-387-4287
Suite 660 *Fax:* 213-387-5383
Los Angeles, CA 90010-1904 info@angeles.sierraclub.org
To advance the preservation and protection of the natural environment by empowering the citizenry with charitable resources to further the cause of environmental protection.
Founded: 1920
Loren Blackford, President
Susana Reyes, Vice President

727 Sierra Club: Kern Kaweah Chapter
PO Box 3357 661-496-6585
Bakersfield, CA 93385-3357 harold.wood@sierraclub.org
www.kernkaweah.sierraclub.org
To advance the preservation and protection of the natural environment by empowering democratically-based grassroots organizations, with charitable resources to further the cause of environmental protection.
Founded: 1952
Loren Blackford, President
Susana Reyes, Vice President

728 Sierra Club: Loma Prieta Chapter
3921 East Bayshore Rd 650-390-8411
Suite 204 *Fax:* 650-390-8497
Palo Alto, CA 94303 loma.prieta.chapter@sierraclub.org
www.lomaprieta.sierraclub.org
To advance the preservation and protection of the natural environment by empowering the citizenry with charitable resources to further the cause of environmental protection.
Founded: 1933
James Eggers, Chapter Director
Barbara Kelsey, Chapter Coordinator

729 Sierra Club: Los Padres Chapter
PO Box 31241 805-965-9719
Santa Barbara, CA 93130-1241 davidgold4@aol.com
www.lospadres.sierraclub.org
To advance the preservation and protection of the natural environment by empowering the citizenry with charitable resources to further the cause of environmental protection.
Loren Blackford, President
Susana Reyes, Vice President

730 Sierra Club: Mother Lode Chapter
909 12th St 916-557-1100
Suite 202 *Fax:* 916-557-9669
Sacramento, CA 95814 info@mlc.sierraclub.org
www.sierraclub.org/mother-lode
Focused on tackling issues regarding fracking, the management of wolf populations, protecting old growth forests, forest clearcutting, climate change, and water management.
Dyane Osorio, Chapter Director
Andy Sawyer, Chair

731 Sierra Club: Redwood Chapter
55A Ridgeway Ave 707-544-7651
PO Box 466 *Fax:* 707-544-9861
Santa Rosa, CA 95402 www.redwood.sierraclub.org
The Redwood Chapter contends with climate change, works for sustainable communities, and defends land, water and wildlife while creating opportunities for the exploration and enjoyment.
Victoria Brandon, Chair
Ed Robey, Vice Chair

732 Sierra Club: San Diego Chapter
8304 Clairemont Mesa Blvd 858-569-6005
Suite 101 *Fax:* 619-299-1742
San Diego, CA 92111 san-diego.chapter@sierraclub.org
www.sandiego.sierraclub.org
To advance the preservation and protection of the natural environment by empowering the citizenry with charitable resources to further the cause of environmental protection.
11,000 Members
Loren Blackford, President
Susana Reyes, Vice President

733 Sierra Club: San Francisco Bay Chapter
2530 San Pablo Ave 510-848-0800
Suite I *Fax:* 510-345-2518
Berkeley, CA 94702-2000 info@sfbaysc.org
www.sanfranciscobay.sierraclub.org
To advance the preservation and protection of the natural environment by empowering the citizenry with charitable resources to further the cause of environmental protection.
Founded: 1924
Igor Tregub, Chair
Jennifer Ong, Vice Chair

734 **Sierra Club: San Gorgonio Chapter**
P.O Box 5452 951-684-6203
Riverside, CA 92517 *Fax:* 951-684-6172
ruizmaryann@gmail.com
www.sangorgonio.sierraclub.org
Advocates for the San Bernardino Mountains and forests, energy conservation, habitat and land use preservation and the congestion of urban cities and inland valleys.
Mary Ann Ruiz, Chair
Kim Floyd, Conservation Chair

735 **Sierra Club: Tehipite Chapter**
PO Box 5396 559-229-4031
Fresno, CA 93755-5396 robertsturner52@gmail.com
www.tehipite.sierraclub.org
To advance the preservation and protection of the natural environment by empowering the citizenry with charitable resources to further the cause of environmental protection.
Bruce Gray, Chapter Chair
Trudy Tucker, Vice Chair

736 **Sierra Club: Ventana Chapter**
PO Box 5667 831-624-8032
Carmel, CA 93921 *Fax:* 831-624-3371
chapter@ventana.sierraclub.org
www.ventana.sierraclub.org
Committed to protecting 127 miles of coastline, hundreds of thousands of acres of wild lands and dwindling water supplies.
Joel Weinstein, Chair
Scott Waltz, Vice Chair

737 **Society for the Conservation of Bighorn Sheep**
PO Box 94182 310-339-4677
Pasadena, CA 91109 sheepsociety.com
Strives for the full restoration of the California Desert Bighorn to its habitat and the establishment of self-sustaining populations.
Founded: 1964
Steve Marschke, President
Bob Burke, 1st Vice President

738 **Southern California Chapter: American Solar Energy Society**
P.O Box 2532 714-794-7795
Seal Beach, CA 90740 info@ocrenewables.org
www.ocrenewables.org
The official local chapter of the American Solar Energy Society (ASES). Provides the SoCal community a local resource to learn about solar energy, energy efficiency and sustainability.
Adam Plesniak, Managing Director
Mike Kilroy, Associate Director

739 **Southwestern Herpetologists Society**
PO Box 7469 818-503-2052
Van Nuys, CA 91409 peggywu@ca.rr.com
www.swhs.org
Promotes the conservation of repitiles and amphibians while educating the public about the role of reptiles and amphibians in the natural world.
Founded: 1954
Wes Pollock, President
Grayson Kent, Vice President

740 **The Nature Conservancy: California**
201 Mission St 4th Fl 415-777-0487
San Francisco, CA 94105-1832 *Fax:* 415-777-0244
nature.org/california
Protects California's important lands and waters with a focus on freshwater, climate change, renewable energy, oceans and migratory birds.
Mark R. Tercek, President/CEO
Thomas J. Tierney, Chairman

741 **TreePeople**
12601 Mulholland Drive 818-753-4600
Beverly Hills, CA 90210 *Fax:* 818-753-4635
info@treepeople.org
www.treepeople.org
Seeks to inspire the people of Los Angeles to take personal responsibility for their environment, training and supporting them as they plant and care for trees and improve the neighborhoods in which they live, work and play. Througheducation, planting projects, policy development and research, the organization is helping lead the promotion of integrated urban watershed management.
Founded: 1973
Andy Lipkis, President & Founder
Cindy Montanez, Chief Executive Officer

742 **Trees Foundation**
PO Box 2202 707-923-4377
Redway, CA 95560 *Fax:* 707-923-4427
www.treesfoundation.org
Aims to restore the ecology of California's North Coast through funding community-based efforts.
Founded: 1991
Susan Barsotti, President
Kerry Reynolds, Organizational Director

743 **Urban Habitat Program**
Presido Station
2000 Franklin St 510-839-9510
Oakland, CA 94612 *Fax:* 510-788-5406
info@urbanhabitat.org
www.urbanhabitat.org
Dedicated to building a multicultural majority that provides urban environmental leadership in order to create socially just, ecologically sustainable communities in the Bay Area.
Founded: 1989
Joe Brooks, Board Chair
Tamar Dorfman, Board Treasurer

744 **Western Occupational and Environmental Medical Association**
575 Market St 415-764-4918
Suite 2125 *Fax:* 415-764-4915
San Francisco, CA 94105 woema@woema.org
www.woema.org
To represent and be a resource to members in the profession and practice of occupational and environmental medicine and to enhance their efforts to promote and improve health in the workplace.
Founded: 1941
Scott C. Levy, Chairman
Robert C. Blink, President

745 **Yellowstone Grizzly Foundation**
2515 Wilshire Blvd 307-734-8643
5006 Coolidge Ave, Culver City www.grizzlypeople.com
Santa Monica, CA 90403
A non-profit organization dedicated to the conservation of the threatened grizzly bear and their wilderness habitat in the greater Yellowstone Ecosystem.
Louisa Willcox, President
Timothy Treadwell, Founder

Colorado

746 **American Lung Association of Colorado**
5600 Greenwood Plaza Boulevard 303-388-4327
Suite 100 COInfo@lungs.org
Greenwood Village, CO 80111-2316
www.lung.org/about-us/local-associations/colorado.html
Works to prevent lung disease and to promote lung health by fighting for cleaner air.
Founded: 1904
Cheryl A. Calhoun, Managing Director
Linn P. Bilingsley, Vice President

747 **American Society of Landscape Architects: Colorado Chapter**
PO Box 200822 303-748-0321
Denver, CO 80220 *Fax:* 303-220-5833
info@aslacolorado.org
www.aslacolorado.org

Serves as the state professional society representing landscape architects in Colorado and Wyoming. Promotes the landscape architecture profession and advances the practice through advocacy, education, communication and networking.
Founded: 1973
Brian Nicholson, President
Craig Stoffel, President-Elect

748 Aspen Global Change Institute
104 Midland Ave 970-925-7376
Suite 205 *Fax:* 970-925-7097
Basalt, CO 81621 www.agci.org
A Colorado nonprofit dedicated to furthering the understanding of Earth systems and global environmental change through interdisciplinary science meetings, publications and educational programs.
Dr. Marty Hoffert, Chairman
Ken Caldeira, Vice President

749 Association of Midwest Fish and Game Law Enforcement Officers
Division of Wildlife
6060 Broadway 303-291-7223
Denver, CO 80216 secretary@midwestgamewarden.org
www.midwestgamewarden.org
Lead group among wildlife enforcement organizations in the development and maintenance of training for field officers that protects the resource and benefit citizens.
Founded: 1944
Bob Thompson, Executive Secretary
Bill Hale, Audit Committee

750 B.A.S.S Nation: Colorado Chapter
4485 Enchanted Circle North 719-597-2304
Colorado Springs, CO 80917 info@coloradobassnation.com
www.coloradobassnation.com
Stimulates public awareness of bass fishing as a major sport and to offer the Colorado Department of Wildlife and other organizations moral and political support and encouragement.
Audrey McKenney, President
Jack Chaney, Vice President

751 Colorado Association of Conservation Districts
P.O. Box 1175 719-686-0020
Lamar, CO 81052 executivedirector4cacd@gmail.com
www.coloradoacd.org
Colorado's 76 conservation districts ensure the health, safety and general welfare of the citizens through the conservation of natural resources and a responsible conservation ethic.
Don McBee, President
Anthony Lobato, Vice President

752 Colorado Forestry Association
P.O Box 270132 970-531-9421
Ft. Collins, CO 80527 walt.bigkid@gmail.com
www.coloradoforestry.org
Strives for the renewal of forests through conservation, management, forestry legislation, public education and the creation of forest reserves.
Founded: 1884
Walt Plese, President
Ed Olmstead, Treasurer

753 Colorado Renewable Energy Society
430 Myrtle St 303-806-5317
Fort Collins, CO 80521 info@cres-energy.org
www.cres-energy.org
Nonprofit membership organization that works for the advancement of cost-effective energy efficient and renewable energy technologies for economic development.
Founded: 1996
Alex Blackmer, Board President
Janna West-Heiss, Vice President

754 Colorado Safety Association
1114 West 7th Ave 303-373-1937
Suite 150 800-727-0519
Denver, CO 80204 *Fax:* 303-373-1955
melodye@coloradosafety.org
www.coloradosafety.org
Not-for-profit educational organization specializing in occupational safety and health issues.
Founded: 1968
Liz Couture, Executive Director
Chris Baker, Program Director

755 Colorado Solar Energy Industries Association
1536 Wynkoop St 303-333-7342
Suite 104 *Fax:* 303-604-6988
Denver, CO 80202 info@coseia.org
www.coseia.org
Promote the use of solar energy technologies to improve the environment and create a sustainable future.
Founded: 1989
Taylor Henderson, President
Todd Stewart, Vice President

756 Colorado Trappers Association
PO Box 397 970-268-5554
Empire, CO 80438 Dan@coloradoridacritter.com
www.coloradotrapper.com
An organization dedicated to promoting wildlife education and management, and upholding the ideals of their unique trapping heritage.
Founded: 1975
Dan Gates, President, Director
Joe Herrman, Vice President

757 Colorado Water Congress
1580 Logan St 303-837-0812
Suite 700 *Fax:* 303-526-3864
Denver, CO 80203 info@cowatercongress.org
www.cowatercongress.org
Protects and conserves Colorado's water resources by means of advocacy and education.
Founded: 1958
Sam Susuras, President
Erin Wilson, Vice President

758 Colorado Wildlife Federation
1410 Grant St 303-987-0400
Suite C-313 *Fax:* 303-987-0200
Denver, CO 80203 cwfed@coloradowildlife.org
www.coloradowildlife.org
Promotes the conservation, management and sustainable use of Colorado's wildlife and wildlife habitats through education and advocacy.
Founded: 1953
Suzanne O'Neill, Executive Director
Kent Ingram, Chair

759 Keystone Center and Keystone Science School
Keystone Center & Science School
1053 Soda Ridge Rd 970-468-2098
Keystone, CO 80435 *Fax:* 970-262-0152
salexander@keystone.org
www.keystonescienceschool.org
Strives to develop creative problem-solving processes and to provide qualified science education through hands-on inquiry of the natural world for youth and adults.
Founded: 1975
Ellen Reid, Executive Director
Douglas D. Sims, Chairman

760 National Wildlife Federation: Rocky Mountain Regional Center
303 E 17th Ave 303-786-8001
Suite 15 800-822-9919
Denver, CO 80203 *Fax:* 303-786-8911
www.nwf.org/Rocky-Mountain-Region.aspx

Protects and restores wildlife habitat on tribal lands, conserves iconic Western species, fights climate change and water issues and inspire new generations.
Meaghan Olwell, Operations Manager
Brian Kurzel, Regional Executive Director

761 **Sierra Club: Rocky Mountain Chapter**
1536 Wynkoop Street 303-861-8819
Suite 312 *Fax:* 303-449-6520
Denver, CO 80202 rocky.mountain.chapter@sierraclub.org
www.sierraclub.org/colorado
Works directly on activism and advocacy with a grassroots, citizen-based leadership to protect Colorado and engages with the public through a leadership outings program.
Jim Alexee, Chapter Director
Bryce Carter, Conservation Program Manager

762 **The Nature Conservancy: Colorado Field Office**
2424 Spruce St 303-444-2950
Boulder, CO 80302 *Fax:* 303-444-2986
colorado@tnc.org
www.nature.org/colorado
The mission of the Nature Conservancy is to preserve plants, animals and natural communities that represent the diversity of life on Earth.
Founded: 1965
Mark R. Tercek, President/CEO
Thomas J. Tierney, Chairman

Connecticut

763 **American Association in Support of Ecological Initiatives**
45 Wyllys Avenue 860-685-2000
Middletown, CT 06459 *Fax:* 860-347-8459
admission@wesleyan.edu
www.wesleyan.edu
AASEI is a US 501 nonprofit organization which supports international environmental initiatives in Russian Nature Reserves. In cooperation with Russia and foreign scientists, students, and universities, AASEI organizes scientificresearch projects, academic internships, work camps, environmental exchanges, and eco-tourism. Our aim is to provide practical support to Russian Reserves, expand opportunities for international scientific research, and promote internationalunderstanding.
Founded: 1994
Michael S. Roth, President
Brendan Sweeney, President

764 **American Lung Association of Connecticut**
45 Ash Street 860-289-5401
East Hartford, CT 06108-3272 800-586-4872
Fax: 860-289-5405
info@lungne.org
www.lung.org/about-us/local-associations/connecticut.html
The American Lung Association of Connecticut offers a wide variety of lung health services to the people of Connecticut.
Founded: 1904
Kim Lacina, National VP, Marketing
Harold P. Wimmer, President, CEO

765 **American Society of Landscape Architects: Connecticut Chapter**
PO Box 209197 800-878-1474
New Haven, CT 06520 executivedirector@ctasla.org
www.ctasla.org
As a chapter of the American Society of Landscape Architects (ASLA), it aims to lead, educate and participate in the careful stewardship, wise planning, and artful design of cultural and natural environments.
275 Members
Jeffrey H. Mills, Executive Director

766 **Connecticut Audubon Society**
314 Unquowa Road 203-259-0416
Fairfield, CT 06824 *Fax:* 203-254-7673
fairfield@ctaudubon.org
www.ctaudubon.org
A statewide, nonprofit, membership organization dedicated to conserving the Connecticut environment through science-based education and adocacy focused on the state's bird populations and habitats. Each year, through school programs,teacher training workshops, youth activities, adult and family trips, community events and legislative initiatives, the Society reaches more than 200,000 people.
Founded: 1898
Nelson North, Executive Director
Tom Andersen, Director, Communications

767 **Connecticut Botanical Society**
PO Box 9004 860-246-2077
New Haven, CT 06532-0004 yyih@wesleyan.edu
www.ct-botanical-society.org
A group of amateur and professional botanists who share an interest in the plants and habitats of Connecticut and the surrounding region. The goals are to increase knowledge of the state's flora, to accumulate a permanent botanicalrecord, and to promote conservation and public awareness of the state's rich natural heritage.
Founded: 1903 $15/Year
David Yih, President
Susan Robinson, Secretary

768 **Connecticut Forest & Park Association**
16 Meriden Road 860-346-2372
Rockfall, CT 06481-2372 *Fax:* 860-347-7463
info@ctwoodlands.org
www.ctwoodlands.org
The Connecticut Forest & Park Association (CFPA) is a nonprofit organization dedicated to connecting people to the land in order to protect forests, parks, walking trails, and open spaces in Connecticut.
Founded: 1895
Eric Lukingbeal, President
Starr Sayres, Vice President

769 **Connecticut Fund for the Environment & Save the Sound**
900 Chapel Street 203-787-0646
Upper Mezzanine *Fax:* 203-787-0246
New Haven, CT 06510 protect@cfenv.org
www.ctenvironment.org
A nonprofit legal champion for the environment and water of the regiom. The CFE merged with Save the Sound and utilizes law, science and education to better air and water quality, control toxic contamination, minimize the adverseimpacts of highways and traffic congestion, protect public water supplies, and preserve the open space and wetlands so crucial to both the state's citizens and its wildlife.
Founded: 1978
Donald S. Strait, President
Curt Johnson, Executive Director

770 **Friends of Animals**
777 Post Road 203-656-1522
Suite 205 800-321-7387
Darien, CT 06820 *Fax:* 203-656-0267
info@friendsofanimals.org
www.friendsofanimals.org
A non-profit, international animal advocacy organization that works to cultivate a respectful view of non-human animals, free-living and domestic.
Founded: 1957
Priscilla Feral, President
Donna Berlanda, VP, Administration

771 **Sierra Club: Connecticut Chapter**
PO Box 270595 860-236-4405
West Hartford, CT 06127 connecticut.chapter@sierraclub.org
www.connecticut.sierraclub.org

To advance the preservation and protection of the natural environment by empowering the citizenry with charitable resources to further the cause of environmental protection.
Founded: 1972
Samantha Dynowski, State Director
Dennis Desmarais, Chair, Communications

772 **The Berkshire-Litchfield Environmental Council**
PO Box 668, The Roraback Building 860-824-7247
115 Main Street wml61@comcast.net
North Canaan, CT 06018 www.berklitchfieldenviro.org
The Berkshire-Litchfield Environmental Council (BLEC) is a group of citizens acting together as an advocate for the natural environment, to promote an understanding of both the environmental and economic needs, and of the preservationand conservation issues, within the bioregion.
Founded: 1970
Ellery Sinclair, Executive Secretary
B.Blake Levitt, Communications Director

District of Columbia

773 **American Lung Association Of the District of Columbia**
1331 Pennsylvania Avenue NW 202-747-5541
Suite 1425 lhale@lunginfo.org
Washington, DC 20004 www.lung.org/about-us/local-associations/washington.html
The American Lung Association of the District of Columbia works to prevent lung disease and promote lung health. Offering a wide variety of lung health services to the people of the District of Columbia.

774 **American Rivers**
1101 14th Street NW 202-347-7550
Suite 1400 877-347-7550
Washington, DC 20005 feedback@americanrivers.org
www.americanrivers.org
American Rivers is an organization that uses advocacy and field work to accomplish their mission of protecting and restoring the nation's rivers. They work with local river advocates, business and agricultural interests, recreationgroups, and others to accomplish their goals.
Founded: 1973
William Robert Irwin, President
Kimberley Milligan, Chair

775 **American Society of Landscape Architects: Potomac Chapter**
Washington, DC 202-827-7380
info@potomacasla.org
www.potomacasla.org
As a chapter of the American Society of Landscape Architects (ASLA), it aims to lead, educate and participate in the careful stewardship, wise planning, and artful design of cultural and natural environments. The Potomac Chapter of theALSA represents nearly 400 landscape architects and affiliates in the Greater Washington DC metro area.
Mike Casey, President, ASLA
Susan Newman, Executive Director

776 **Casey Trees**
3030 12th Street NE 202-833-4010
Washington, DC 20017 *Fax:* 202-833-4092
friends@caseytrees.org
caseytrees.org
A nonprofit, working to restore, enhance and protect the tree canopy of Washington D.C. Working with public and private affiliates, Casey Trees plants, maintains, monitors and advocates for the trees of Washington D.C.
Founded: 2002
Mark Buscaino, Executive Director
Omolara Fatiregun, COO

777 **Environmental Working Group**
1436 U Street NW 202-667-6982
Suite 100 www.ewg.org
Washington, DC 20009
The Environmental Working Group is a leading content provider for public interest groups and concerned citizens who are campaigning to protect the environment.
Founded: 1993
Ken Cook, President
Monica Amarelo, Director, Communications

778 **Resources for the Future**
1616 P Street NW 202-328-5000
Suite 600 *Fax:* 202-939-3460
Washington, DC 20036 info@rff.org
www.rff.org
Resource for the Future (RFF) is a nonprofit and nonpartisan organization that conducts independent research and analysis, rooted primarily in economics, to help leaders make decisions and policies regarding natural resources and theenvironment.
Founded: 1952
Richard G. Newell, President & CEO
Peter Nelson, Director, Communications

779 **Sierra Club: DC Chapter**
50 F Street NW 202-675-2391
Washington, DC 20001 washingtondc.chapter@sierraclub.org
dc.sierraclub.org
The more than 3,600 members of the DC Chapter are actively involved in local conservation and political efforts in conjunction with the national Sierra Club mission.
Rebekah Whilden, Chapter Organizer
Mark Rodeffer, Chair

780 **The Climate Reality Project**
750 9th Street NW www.climaterealityproject.org
Suite 520
Washington, DC 20001
The Climate Reality Project, is a nonprofit organization dedicated to the education and advocacy of climate change. Formerly known as the Alliance for Climate Protection, The Climate Reality Project is working to cause a global shiftaway from fossil fuels towards renewable resources
Founded: 2011
Ken Berlin, President & CEO
Stacie Paxton Cobos, Senior VP, Communications

Delaware

781 **American Lung Association of Delaware**
630 Churchmans Road 302-737-6414
Suite 202 www.lung.org/about-us/local-associations/delaware.html
Newark, DE 19702
The American Lung Association of Delaware works to prevent lung disease and promote lung health. Offering a wide variety of lung health services to the people of Delaware.
Deborah Brown, Executive VP, Mid-Atlantic

782 **American Lung Association of Delaware: Dover**
422 S Governor's Avenue 302-737-6414
Dover, DE 19904 www.lung.org/about-us/local-associations/delaware.html

783 **Atlantic Flyaway Council**
Division of Fish and Wildlife
89 Kings Highway 302-739-5295
Dover, DE 19901 *Fax:* 302-739-6157
www.flyways.us/flyways/atlantic
Committed to the preservation and advancement of waterfowl.
Founded: 1948
William C Wagner II, Chairman

784 **B.A.S.S Nation: Delaware Chapter**
DE
302-698-9257
800-463-6062
Fax: 720-302-1230
delawarebass1@verizon.net
www.delawarebassnation.com
The Delaware Chapter of BASS Nation works to stimulate public awareness of bass fishing as a major sport and encourages sportsmanship, courtesy and boating safety at all levels. The Chapter promotes the full adherence to allconservation codes, adequate water quality standards and legal enforcement of existing regulatory standards.
Founded: 1975
Ron Horton, President
Shawn Taylor, Vice President

785 **Delaware Greenways**
1910 Rockland Road
302-655-7275
Wilmington, DE 19803
info@delawaregreenways.org
www.delawaregreenways.org
Delaware Greenways promotes, protects and advocates for the development of outdoor trails, byways and natural open spaces.
Founded: 1989
Mary Roth, Executive Director
Leslie Hubbard, Marketing & Communication

786 **Delaware Nature Society**
Delaware Nature Society
PO Box 700
302-239-2334
Hockessin, DE 19707
dnsinfo@delawarenaturesociety.org
www.delawarenaturesociety.org
Delaware Nature Society (DNS) works to improve the environment through conservation, advocacy and education. DNS manages over 2,000 acres of land, including four nature preserves, and operates three educational nature centers, it isthe state affiliate of the National Wildlife Federation.
Founded: 1964
Brian Winslow, Executive Director
Ginger North, Director, Conservation

787 **National Association of Conservation Districts: Delaware**
NACD Headquarters
509 Capitol Court NE
202-547-6223
Washington, DC 20002-4937
Fax: 202-547-6450
www.nacdnet.org/state/delaware
The National Association of Conservation Districts (NACD) is the nonprofit organization that represents America's 3,000 conservation districts. Conservation districts are local units of government established under state law to carryout natural resource management programs and protection of land and water resources at the local level.
Robert Emerson, State Association President

788 **Sierra Club: Delaware Chapter**
100 West 10th Street
302-468-4550
Suite 106
delaware.chapter@sierraclub.org
Wilmington, DE 19801
delaware.sierraclub.org
The Delaware Chapter of the Sierra Club works to protect the Delaware River, Delaware's wetlands including critical habitat areas and the coastal zone.
Jamie Watts, Membership Committee Chair
Dee Durham, Vice Chair

Florida

789 **American Fisheries Society: Agriculture Economics Section**
University of California
PO Box 240
352-392-4991
Gainsville, FL 32611
Fax: 352-392-3646
adams@fred.ifas.ufl.edu
Committed to the preservation and advancement of Florida's natural resources.
Charles Adams, President

790 **American Lung Association of Florida**
6852 Belfort Oaks Place
904-743-2933
Jacksonville, FL 32216
alaf@lungse.org
www.lung.org/about-us/local-associations/florida.html
The American Lung Association of Florida works to prevent lung disease and promote lung health. Offering a wide variety of lung health services to the people of Florida.
Martha C. Bogdan, Executive VP, Southeast

791 **American Lung Association of Florida: Fort Lauderdale**
2020 South Andrews Avenue
954-524-4657
Fort Lauderdale, FL 33316-3430
alafsouth@lungse.org
www.lung.org/about-us/local-associations/florida.html
Martha C. Bogdan, Executive VP, Southeast

792 **American Lung Association of Florida: Fort Meyers**
PO Box 07142
239-908-2680
Fort Meyers, FL 33919
alafgcfm@lungse.org
www.lung.org/about-us/local-associations/florida.html
Martha C. Bogdan, Executive VP, Southeast

793 **American Lung Association of Florida: Orlando**
851 Outer Road
407-425-5864
Orlando, FL 32814-6652
central@lungse.org
www.lung.org/about-us/local-associations/florida.html
Martha C. Bogdan, Executive VP, Southeast

794 **American Lung Association of Florida: Palm Beach & Treasure Coast**
2701 North Australian Avenue
561-659-7644
Suite 100
alafse@lungse.org
West Palm Beach, FL 33407-4526
www.lung.org/about-us/local-associations/florida.html
Martha C. Bogdan, Executive VP, Southeast

795 **American Lung Association of Florida: Tampa**
100 South Ashley Drive
813-712-2307
Suite 275
alafgc@lungse.org
Tampa, FL 33603-1652
www.lung.org/about-us/local-associations/florida.html
Martha C. Bogdan, Executive VP, Southeast

796 **American Society of Landscape Architects: Florida Chapter**
1390 Timberlane Road
850-222-6000
Tallahassee, FL 32312
www.flasla.org
The Florida Chapter of the American Society of Landscape Architects(FLASLA), is a nonprofit association representing the landscape architecture profession throughout the state of Florida.
Founded: 1959
Deena Bell Llewellyn, President

797 **Association of Battery Recyclers**
PO Box 290286
813-626-6151
Tampa, FL 33687
Fax: 813-622-8388
www.americasbatteryrecyclers.com
To keep members abreast of environmental, health, and safety requirements that affect our industry.
Founded: 1984
Earl Cornette, President
Joyce Morales Caramella, Secretary

798 **Audubon of Florida**
Travenier Science Center
4500 Biscayne Blvd
305-371-6399
Suite 205
Fax: 305-371-6398
Miami, FL 33137
fl.audubon.org
The science center is the research arm of the Everglades Campaign. The mission of Audubon of Florida is to ensure the restoration and conservation of the Greater Everglades Ecosystem in order to achieve an ecologically and economicallysustainable South Florida. Our Everglades Conservation office has a five-part program including science, education, advocacy, outreach and grassroots action.
Founded: 1938
Eric Draper, Executive Director
Victoria Johnston, Donor Relations Manager

799 **Citizens for Scenic Florida**
4401 Emerson Street 904-396-0037
Suite 10 *Fax:* 904-744-2940
Jacksonville, FL 32207 www.scenicflorida.org
Citizens for Scenic Florida is a nonprofit corporation that enhances, protects and preserves the visual environment of Florida as mandated by the Scenic Beauty clause of the Florida Constitution.
Bill Jonson, President
Trudy Barker, Vice Chairman & Executive VP

800 **Fish & Wildlife Foundation of Florida**
2574 Seagate Drive
Suite 100 850-922-1066
Tallahassee, FL 32301 800-988-4889
info@wildlifeflorida.org
www.fishwildlifeflorida.org
Working closely with Florida Fish and Wildlife Conservation Commission, the Fish & Wildlife Foundation of Florida is a nonprofit organization that is dedicated to providing assistance, funding and promotional support for the habitatsand resources of Florida's fish and wildlife.
Founded: 1994
Andy Walker, President & CEO
Will Bradford, CFO

801 **Florida Center for Environmental Studies**
3200 College Avenue 954-236-1104
Building DW, Rm. 311 cpolsky@fau.edu
Davie, FL 33458 www.ces.fau.edu
Represents the ten state universities and the major private universities in regard to environmental studies and research.
Founded: 1995
Dr. Colin Polsky, Director
Dr. John D. Baldwin, Associate Director

802 **Florida Defenders of the Environment**
309 State Road 26 352-475-1119
Melrose, FL 32666 floridadefenders@gmail.com
www.fladefenders.org
The Florida Defenders of the Environment work to protect freshwater resources, conserve public lands and provide environmental education.
Founded: 1969
Jim Gross, Executive Director
Tracy Marinello, Executive Assistant

803 **Florida Environmental Health Association**
P.O. Box 350356 407-790-0347
Jacksonville, FL 32235 Contact_Us@feha.org
www.feha.org
The Florida Environmental Health Association, Inc (FEHA) is a nonprofit group of over 500 professionals that promotes and protects the health of Florida's resident and visitors. The FEHA is an affiliate of the National EnvironmentalHealth Association, Inc.
Founded: 1967
Trisha Dall, Director
Michael Crea, President

804 **Florida Forestry Association**
402 East Jefferson Street 850-222-5646
Tallahassee, FL 32301 *Fax:* 850-222-6179
info@forestfla.org
www.floridaforest.org
A statewide membership organization, the Florida Forestry Association advocates and promotes the responsible and sustainable use of Florida's forest resources.
Founded: 1923
Alan Shelby, Executive VP
Debbie Bryant, Director, Member Services

805 **Florida Keys Wild Bird Rehabilitation Center**
Mission Wild Bird
92080 Overseas Highway 305-852-4486
Tavernier, FL 33070 *Fax:* 305-852-3186
info@keepthemflying.org
www.keepthemflying.org
The Florida Keys Wild Bird Center is a nonprofit conservation organization dedicated to the rescue, rehabilitation, and release of native and migratory wild birds that have been harmed or displaced. The Florida Keys Wild Bird Centerprovides or locates a humane shelter for birds that cannot be released and educates the public on the importance of coexistence with all wild bird species.
Founded: 1988
Jordan Budnik, Executive Director
Shylyn Pierce, Manager, Wildlife Rehab

806 **Florida Oceanographic Society**
890 NE Ocean Boulevard 772-225-0505
Stuart, FL 34996 mperry@floridaocean.org
floridaocean.org
Florida Oceanographic Society is a non-profit organization with a mission to inspire environmental stewardship of Florida's coastal ecosystems through education, research and advocacy.
Founded: 1964
Mark D. Perry, Executive Director
Allen Herskowitz, Chairman

807 **Florida Ornithological Society**
www.fosbirds.org
The Florida Ornithological Society (FOS) promotes field ornithology and facilitates contact between ameteur and professional ornithologists.
Founded: 1972
Adam Kent, President
Emilynne Angell, Vice President

808 **Florida Public Interest Research Group**
3110 1st Avenue North 727-431-9686
Suite 2K 800-838-6554
St. Petersburg, FL 33713 info@floridapirg.org
www.floridapirg.org
Statewide, nonprofit, public interest advocacy organization that focuses primarily on environmental and consumer protection.
Steve Blackledge, Director, Pubic Health
Ed Mierzwinski, Consumer Program Director

809 **Florida Renewable Energy Association**
PO Box 560272 407-710-8705
Orlando, FL 32856-272 freainformation@gmail.com
www.cleanenergyflorida.org
The Florida Renewable Energy Association (FREA), is a nonprofit organization that promotes the development of clean renewable energy in Florida through public education, political advocacy, and individual networking opportunities. FREAis the Florida Chapter of the American Solar Energy Society (ASES).
Founded: 2006 $30/Year
Bill Young, President
Mehdi Zeyghami, Vice President

810 **Florida Solar Energy Industries Association**
2555 Porter Lake Drive 407-339-2010
Suite 106 800-426-5899
Sarasota, FL 34240 *Fax:* 941-366-7433
wendy@FlaSEIA.org
www.flaseia.org
The Florida Solar Energy Industries Association (FlaSEIA) is a nonprofit professional association of companies, dedicated to protecting and promoting the interests of Florida's solar energy industry.
Founded: 1977
Wendy Parker Barsell, Executive Director
Michelle D'Aiuto, Membership Coordinator

811 **Florida Trail Association**
5415 SW 13th Street 352-378-8823
Gainesville, FL 32608 fta@floridatrail.org
www.floridatrail.org
The Florida Trail Association (FTA) develops, maintains, protects and promotes a network of hiking trails across the state. With 18 statewide chapters, the FTA provides environmental edu-

cation and opportunities for the public toparticipate in outdoor recreation.
Founded: 1964
Janet Akerson, Administrative Director
Alex Stigliano, Trail Program Director

812 **International Association for Hydrogen Energy**
5794 SW 40 Street
303
Miami, FL 33155
info@iahe.org
www.iahe.org
The International Association for Hydrogen Energy promotes the use of hydrogen energy as the global clean energy source. The Association works to achieve this goal by exchanging hydrogen energy information through publications andinternational workshops.
Founded: 1974
T. Nejat Veziroglu, President
John W. Sheffield, Executive Vice President

813 **International Game Fish Association**
300 Gulf Stream Way
Dania Beach, FL 33004
954-927-2628
Fax: 954-924-4299
hq@igfa.org
www.igfa.org
The International Game Fish Association is a nonprofit organization committed to the conservation of game fish and the promotion of responsible, ethical angling practices through science, education, rulemaking and record keeping.
Founded: 1939
Rob Kramer, President
Michael J. Myatt, COO

814 **Keep Florida Beautiful**
3324 Charleston Road
Tallahassee, FL 32309
keepflbeautiful@gmail.com
www.keepfloridabeautiful.org
Keep Florida Beautiful (KFB) is Florida's largest volunteer-based community action and education organization. With more than 40 county and city affiliates, KFB is working to educate people about recycling and litter reduction. KFB isthe state affiliate of Keep America Beautiful (KAB).
Kim Brunson, Chair
Mary Jean Yon, Executive Director

815 **National Wildlife Federation: Everglades Project**
PO Box 1583
Merrifield, VA 22116-1583
239-643-4111
800-822-9919
Fax: 239-643-5130
adamsk@nwf.org
www.nwf.org
To advocate and support restoration of the greater Everglades ecosystem and protection of the western Everglades through planning, education and management activities. To re-create a more natural hydrologic flow through the greaterEverglades that ensures the long-term viability of native habitats, threatened and endangered species and associated wildlife.
Founded: 1934
Kathy Hadley, Chair
Collin O'Mara, President

816 **Reef Relief**
631 Greene Street
Key West, FL 33040
305-294-3100
Fax: 305-293-9515
reefrelief@gmail.com
www.reefrelief.org
Reef relief is a nonprofit membership organization, dedicated to protecting, preserving and improving Florida's coral reef. Through education, advocacy and eco-tourism, the organization works to increase awareness about coral reefecosystems.
Founded: 1987
Bob Cardenas, President & CEO
Tricia Coyne, Vice President

817 **Sanibel-Captiva Conservation Foundation**
3333 Sanibel-Captiva Road
Sanibel, FL 33957
239-472-2329
sccf@sccf.org
www.sccf.org
The Sanibel - Captiva Conservation Foundation (SCCF) is committed to the conservation of coastal habitats and aquatic resources on Sanibel and Captiva and it surrounding watershed. The SCCF is known as a land trust and is the largestprivate landowner on Sanibel Island managing over 1,200 acres of land on Sanibel with another 600 acres on Captiva Island.
Founded: 1967
Erick Lindblad, Executive Director
Karen Nelson, Communications Coordinator

818 **Seaside Seabird Sanctuary**
18328 Gulf Boulevard
Indian Shores, FL 33785
727-391-6211
800-406-3400
Fax: 727-399-2923
www.seabirdsanctuary.com
The sanctuary is the largest wild bird hospital in the United States dedicated to the rescue, repair, rehabilitation and hopeful release of sick and injured native birds. Over 600 birds permanently reside at our beachfront sanctuary.We are open free of charge to the public 365 days a year. Tours and educational programs are available.
Founded: 1971
Brian Max Tharp, Business Manager
Eddie Gayton, Operations Manager

819 **Sierra Club: Florida Chapter**
1990 Central Avenue
St. Petersburg, FL 33712
727-824-8813
frank.jackalone@sierraclub.org
florida.sierraclub.org
Comprising of 16 Club Groups across the state, the Florida Chapter of the Sierra Club promotes and practices the responsible use of Florida's ecosystems and natural resources.
35,200 Members
Mark Walters, Chair
Kristine Cunningham, Vice Chair

820 **Society of Environmental Toxicology and Chemistry**
SETAC North America
229 South Baylen Street
2nd Floor
Pensacola, FL 32502
850-469-1500
Fax: 888-296-4136
setac@setac.org
www.setac.org
The Society of Environmental Toxicology and Chemistry (SETAC), is a global nonprofit professional society, that promotes the development of principles and practices designed to protect, enhance and manage a sustainable environment.SETAC provides a forum for scientists, managers and other professionals to exchange information and ideas, for the development and application of multidisciplinary scientific principles in order to manage and conserve natural resources.
Founded: 1979 6,000 Members
Greg E. Schiefer, Executive Director

821 **South Florida Chapter, National Safety Council**
4171 West Hillsborro Boulevard
Suite 5
Coconut Creek, FL 33073
954-422-5757
800-392-5101
Fax: 954-418-9290
Not-for-profit, non-governmental, public service organization dedicated to the safety and health of the Broward, Dade, Palm Beach and surrounding communities.
Michael Walters, VP Operations

822 **Tallahassee Museum of History and Natural Science**
3945 Museum Drive
Tallahassee, FL 32310
850-575-8684
Fax: 850-574-8243
www.tallahasseemuseum.org
The Tallahassee Museum, is a 52-acre nonprofit outdoor museum. Combining a natural habitat zoo of indigenous wildlife, collection of historical building and artifacts and an environmental science center, the museum is dedicated topromoting the knowledge and understanding of the Big Bend's cultural history and natural environment.
Founded: 1957
Russell S. Daws, President/CEO
Rebekka K. Wade, Director, Finance

Georgia

823 **Agency for Toxic Substances and Disease Registry**
Centers for Disease Control and Prevention
4770 Buford Highway NE 770-488-0706
Atlanta, GA 30341-3717 800-232-4636
Fax: 770-488-1544
www.atsdr.cdc.gov
This agency provides leadership and direction to programs and activities designed to protect both the public and workers from exposure or adverse health effects of hazardous substances in storage sites or released in fires, explosions,or transportation accidents. The agency also collects, maintains, analyzes and disseminates information relating to serious diseases, mortality and human exposure to toxic or hazardous substances.
Founded: 1985
Patrick Breysse, Director
Christopher M Reh, Associate Director

824 **American Academy of Sanitarians**
GA 678-518-4028
gnoonan@charter.net
www.sanitarians.org
The American Academy of Sanitarians (AAS) is dedicated to improving the environmental health status of individuals through the certification process of environmental health professionals. The AAS works to elevate the standards, improvethe practice of and promote ethical conduct among sanitarians in all fields of environmental health. Certification is open to any persons who have attained high professional stature through leadership and accomplishment in the field of environmentalhealth.
Founded: 1966
Gary P. Noonan, Executive Secretary-Teasurer

825 **American Lung Association of Georgia**
2452 Spring Road SE 770-434-5864
Smyrna, GA 30080 alaga@lungse.org
www.lung.org/about-us/local-associations/georgia.html
The American Lung Association of Georgia works to prevent lung disease and promote lung health. Offering a wide variety of lung health services to the people of Georgia.
Martha C. Bogdan, Executive VP, Southest

826 **American Society of Landscape Architects: Georgia Chapter**
PO Box 18622 202-898-2444
Atlanta, GA 31126 www.gaasla.org
The Georgia Chapter of the American Society of Landscape Architects (ASLA) represents over 450 landscape architects and affiliates across the state, who are dedicated to the promotion of the landscape profession through advocacy,education and communication.
450 Members
Ben Kent, Section Chair
Matt Cherry, President

827 **Center for a Sustainable Coast**
221 Mallery Street 912-506-5088
Suite B *Fax:* 912-638-3615
St. Simons Island, GA 31522 susdev@gate.net
www.sustainablecoast.org
A nonprofit member organization that works to improve, protect, conserve and promote the responsible use of Georgia's coastal resources.
Founded: 1997
Steve Willis, President
David Kyler, Executive Director

828 **Centers for Disease Control and Prevention**
1600 Clifton Road 800-232-4636
Atlanta, GA 30329-4027 www.cdc.gov
To promote health and quality of life by preventing and controlling disease, injury and disability. The CDC seeks to accomplish its mission by working with partners throughout the nation and world to monitor health; detect andinvestigate health problems; conduct research to enhance prevention; develop and advocate sound public health policies; implement prevention strategies; promote healthy behaviors; foster safe and healthful environments and provide leadership andtraining.
Founded: 1946
Brenda Fitzgerald, Director
Sherri A. Berger, COO

829 **Chattahoochee Riverkeeper**
3 Puritan Mill 404-352-9828
916 Joseph E. Lowery Boulevard NW *Fax:* 404-352-8676
Atlanta, GA 30318 www.chattahoochee.org
An nonprofit environmental advocacy organization dedicated to the protection preservation and restoration of the Chattahoochee River, its lakes and tributaries. The Chattahoochee Riverkeeper (CRK) is part of the internationalWaterkeeper Alliance.
Founded: 1994 7,200 Members
Juliet Cohen, Executive Director
Chris Manganiello, Water Policy Director

830 **Coastal Conservation Association of Georgia**
Coastal Conservation Association
2807-A Roger Lacey Avenue 912-660-8440
Savannah, GA 31404 www.ccaga.org
A state affiliate of the Coastal Conservation Association (CCA), the Georgia Chapter is a nonprofit association dedicated to promoting the preservation, conservation, restoration and protection of the marine fisheries and habitats ofthe Georgia coast both onshore and offshore, for the benefit and responsible utilization by the general public.
Founded: 1986
Tom Rood, State Chairman
Ron Winders, Secretary

831 **Coosa River Basin Initiative**
408 Broad Street 706-232-2724
Rome, GA 30161 *Fax:* 706-235-9066
jcook@coosa.org
www.coosa.org
Cossa River Basin Initiative (CRBI) also known as the Upper Cossa Riverkeeper, is a nonprofit grassroots organization working to inform and empower citizens to become involved in creating a clean, healthy and economically viable CoosaRiver Basin. The CRBI is also a member of the International Waterkeeper Alliance, which works to enforce the Clean Water Act, the Georgia Water Coalition and Alabama Rivers Alliance.
Founded: 1992 3,000 Members
Joe Cook, Communication Coordinator
Jesse Demonbruen-Chapman, Executive Director

832 **Council of State and Territorial Epidemiologists (CSTE)**
CSTE National Office
2872 Woodcock Boulevard 770-458-3811
Suite 250 *Fax:* 770-458-8516
Atlanta, GA 30341 fellowship@cste.org
www.cste.org
The Council of State and Territorial Epidemiologists (CSTE) is an organization of epidemiologists working to advance public health policy, epidemiologic capacity and the establishment of more effective relationships among state andother health agencies. The CTSE provides education, information, and developmental support of practicing epidemiologists. It also provides technical advice and assistance to partner and federal public health organizations.
Founded: 1992
Jeff Engel, Executive Director
Shundra Clinton, Member Services Coordinator

833 **EarthShare Georgia**
715 Peachtree Street NE 404-873-3173
Suites 100 & 200 *Fax:* 404-873-3135
Atlanta, GA 30308 info@earthsharega.org
www.earthsharega.org
EarthShare Georgia works to protect, conserve, and enhance air, land, and water quality by connecting people to trusted nonprofit

organizations dedicated to creating a healthy and sustainable environment.
Founded: 1992
Madeline L. Reamy, Executive Director
Trecinia Wiggins, Development Manager

834 Environment Georgia
108 E. Ponce De Leon Avenue 404-370-1764
Suite 210 800-401-6511
Decatur, GA 30030 www.environmentgeorgia.org
Environment Georgia is a citizen advocacy group of Environment America. Through research and education, Environment Georgia is dedicated to conserving the air, water and land of Georgia.
Jennette Gayer, Director

835 Forest Landowners Association
3300 Highlands Parkway 404-325-2954
Suite 200 800-325-2954
Smyrna, GA 30082 *Fax:* 404-325-2955
info@forestlandowners.com
www.forestlandowners.com
The Forest Landowners Association (FLA) advocates and promotes the rights of all private landowners. The FLA provides its members with education, information and national grassroots advocacy enabling them to maintain their forestlands.
Founded: 1941
Scott Rowland, President
Scott P. Jones, CEO

836 Georgia Association of Conservation District
PO Box 1134 706-542-3065
Ringgold, GA 30736 info@gacd.us
www.gacd.us
Representing 40 Soil and Water Conservation Districts in Georgia, the Georgia Association of Conservation Districts (GACD) is a nonprofit organization dedicated to advocating for the conservation of Georgia's natural resources. Throughleadership and a unified strategic direction GACD works to conserve, support partner agencies, sustain Georgia's land and educate the public across the state.
Woody Snell, President
Marty McLendon, Vice-President

837 Georgia Association of Water Professionals
1655 Enterprise Way 770-618-8690
Marietta, GA 30067 *Fax:* 770-618-8695
www.gawp.org
Georgia Association of Water Professionals (GAWP) is a nonprofit organization focused on providing education and training opportunities for people working in the water and wastewater industr.
Pam Burnett, Executive Director
Susana Lanier, Member Services

838 Georgia Conservancy
230 Peachtree Street NW 404-876-2900
Suite 1250 *Fax:* 404-872-9229
Atlanta, GA 30303 mail@gaconservancy.org
www.georgiaconservancy.org
The Georgia Conservancy is a statewide member organization committed to the conservation of Georgia's natural resources.
Founded: 1967
Robert Ramsay, President
Monica Thornton, Vice President

839 Georgia Environmental Health Association
397 Eastman Highway 706-595-5478
Hawkinsville, GA 31036 www.geha-online.org
A non-profit, professional organization, dedicated to promoting, supporting, training, and registering individuals working in environmental health fields throughout government, academia, industry and business.
$25/Year
Jessica Baldour, Secretary
Angie Corder, President

840 Georgia Solar Energy Association
1199 Euclid Ave 404-522-4775
Atlanta, GA 30307 admin@gasolar.org
www.gasolar.org
The Georgia Solar Energy Association (GA Solar), is a nonprofit organization comprised of solar energy experts working to support the development of the solar industry in Georgia through advocacy, education and outreach.
Founded: 2002
Don Moreland, Chair
Norene Quinn, Executive Director

841 Georgia Trappers Association
9969 GA Highway 102 W info@gatrappersassoc.com
Mitchell, GA 30820 www.gatrappersassoc.com
The Georgia Trappers Association (GTA) promotes the education and growth of hunting,fishing and trapping while maintaining the highest standards of sportsmanship. The GTA encourages public conservation, protection, restoration andmanagement of the environment.
$25/Year
Dan Eaton, President
Brian Igou, Executive Director

842 Georgia Wildlife Federation
11600 Hazelbrand Road 770-787-7887
Covington, GA 30014 *Fax:* 770-787-9229
info@gwf.org
www.gwf.org
As Georgia's oldest and largest member supported conservation organization, Georgia Wildlife Federation (GWF), is working to encourage the protection, restoration and rehabilitation of Georgia's water, wildlife, forests and fields.
Founded: 1936
Mike Worley, President & CEO
DeAnna Harris, Conservation & Outreach Mngr

843 Human Ecology Action League (HEAL)
PO Box 509 HEALNatnl@aol.com
Stockbridge, GA 30281 www.healnatl.org
The Human Ecology Action League Inc (HEAL) is a nonprofit organization committed to serving those whose health has been adversely affected by environment exposures; to provide information to those who are concerned about the healtheffects of chemicals; and to alert the general public about the potential dangers of chemicals
Founded: 1977

844 Mountain Conservation Trust of Georgia
104 North Main Street 706-253-4077
Suite B3 conserve@mctga.org
Jasper, GA 30143 www.mctga.org
The Mountain Conservation Trust of Georgia (MCT) is an accredited land trust focused on the permanent conversation of the natural resources and scenic beauty of the North Georgia foothills and mountains.
Founded: 1991
George Kimberly, Executive Director
Jessica Pfiel, Office Manager

845 National Wildlife Federation: Southeast Regional Center
730 Peachtree Street NE 404-876-8733
Suite 1000 queenc@nwf.org
Atlanta, GA 30308 www.nwf.org
The Southeast Regional Center of the National Wildlife Federation, covers 7 states, Puerto Rico and the U.S. Virgin Islands. The center is dedicated to restoring and rehabilitating Longleaf pine forest and the Gulf of Mexico.
Carly Queen, Campus Field Coordinator

846 Sierra Club: Georgia Chapter
743 E College Avenue 404-607-1262
Suite B georgia.chapter@sierraclub.org
Decatur, GA 30030 georgia.sierraclub.org

The Georgia Chapter of the Sierra Club, is a grassroots environmental organization in the state dedicated to forest protection, transportation and clean energy.
45,000 Members
Ted Terry, Chapter Director
Jessica Morehead, Chapter Coordinator

847 The Nature Conservancy: Georgia Chapter
100 Peachtree NW 404-873-6946
Suite 2250 *Fax:* 404-873-6984
Atlanta, GA 30303 comment@tnc.org
www.nature.org
The Georgia Chapter of The Nature Conservancy, works to protect Georgia's woods, water and coast. It manages 15 nature preserves and more than 338,000 acres of land and water.
Founded: 1951
Mark R. Tercek, President/CEO
Thomas J. Tierney, Chairman

848 Trees Atlanta
225 Chester Avenue SE 404-522-4097
Atlanta, GA 30316 www.treesatlanta.org
Trees Atlanta is a nationally recognized nonprofit citizens' group committed to protecting and improving Atlanta's urban forest through planting trees, conservation and education.
Founded: 1985
Connie Veates, Co-Executive Director & COO
Greg Levine, Co-Executive Director & CPO

Hawaii

849 American Lung Association Of Hawaii
810 Richards Street 808-537-5966
Suite 750 bev.stewart@lung.org
Honolulu, HI 96813 www.ala-hawaii.org
The American Lung Association of Hawaii works to prevent lung disease and promote lung health. Offering a wide variety of lung health services to the people of Hawaii.
Allison Hickey, Exec. VP, Mountain Pacific
Tony Peterson, CFO

850 American Society of Landscape Architects: Hawaii Chapter
1253 South Beretania Street #3006 www.hawaiiasla.org
Honululu, HI 96814
The Hawaii Chapter of the American Society of Landscape Architects, is a nonprofit association representing the landscape architecture profession throughout the state of Hawaii.
Grace Zheng, President
Rachel Katzman, Secretary

851 Earth Trust
Windward Environmental Center
1118 Manuawili Road 415-662-3264
Kailua, HI 96734 *Fax:* 206-202-3893
info@earthtrust.us
www.earthtrust.org
Earth Trust is a nonprofit organization focused on solving global environmental issues through advocacy and innovative strategy.
Founded: 1976
Don White, President

852 Greenpeace Foundation
Windward Environmental Center
1118 Manawili Road 415-689-9931
Kailua, HI 96734 *Fax:* 206-202-3893
email@gpfdn.com
www.greenpeacefoundation.org
Greenpeace Foundation is a nonprofit organization committed to the advocacy of species conservation and biodiversity; with a focus is on the marine ecosystem and how human interaction changes it. The Foundation is dedicated to solvingand preventing environmental crises.
Founded: 1976

853 Hawaii Association of Conservation Districts
Po Box 1411 808-214-5388
Wailuku, HI 96793 hacdhawaii@gmail.com
www.nacdnet.org/hawaii
The state chapter of the National Association of Conservation Districts, the Hawaii Association of Conservation Districts (HCAD), works to conserve the Soil and Water Conservation Districts of Hawaii.
Founded: 1954
Michelle Watkins, State Executive Director
Brenda lokepa-Moses, State President

854 Hawaii Nature Center
875 Iao Valley Road 808-244-6500
Wailuku, HI 96793 hncinfo@hawaiinaturecenter.org
www.hawaiinaturecenter.org
The Hawaii Nature Center is a private nonprofit organization specializing in environmental education field program for children, adults and families. Its mission is to foster awareness appreciation and understanding of Hawaii andencourage wise stewardship of the Islands. The Nature Center provides full day field trips for more than 15,000 students on two islands each year and features an interactive nature museum at its field site on Maui.
Founded: 1981
Dee Dee Letts, President
Jeeyun Lee, Executive Director

855 Sierra Club: Hawaii Chapter
1164 Bishop Street 808-538-6616
Suite 1512 hawaii.chapter@sierraclub.org
Honolulu, HI 96813 www.hi.sierraclub.org
The Hawaii Chapter of the Sierra Club is one of the oldest grassroots environmental organization in the islands. It is made up of a four regional groups, that work toward water security, energy independence, food security, a zero wastefuture and the defense of special places.
Founded: 1968 16,000 Members
Marti Townsend, Director
Kirsten Fujitani, Communications Coordinator

856 The Nature Conservancy: Hawaii Chapter
923 Nuuanu Avenue 808-537-4508
Honolulu, HI 96817 hawaii@tnc.org
www.nature.org
The Hawaii Chapter of the Nature Conservancy, is a nonprofit organization focused on climate change, coral reefs, forests and invasive species. With over 200,000 acres of natural land and 10 conservancy preserves, the Hawaii Chapterworks to protect the threatened species that are native to the state of Hawaii.
Grady Timmons, Directo, Communications
Evelyn Wight, Senior Communications Mngr

Idaho

857 American Lung Association of Idaho
1412 W Idaho Street 208-345-5864
Suite 100 liz.hall@lung.org
Boise, ID 83702 www.lung.org/about-us/local-associations/idaho.html
The American Lung Association of Idahon works to prevent lung disease and promote lung health. Offering a wide variety of lung health services to the people of Idaho.
Allison Hickey, Exec. VP, Mountain Pacific
Tony Peterson, CFO

858 American Society of Landscape Architects: Idaho/Montana Chapter
PO Box 8224 208-321-2389
Boise, ID 83707 *Fax:* 208-321-4819
tottens@amsidaho.com
www.idmtasla.org
As a chapter of the American Society of Landscape Architects(ASLA), it aims to lead, educate and participate in the careful stewardship, wise planning, and artful design of cultural and natural environments.
Jay Gibbons, President
Jennie Meinershagen, VP of Montana

859 Idaho Association of Soil Conservation Districts
55 SW 5th Avnue 208-895-8928
Suite 100 *Fax:* 208-888-4586
Meridian, ID 83642 benjamin@amgidaho.com
www.iascd.org
Provides action at the local level for promoting wise and beneficial conservation of natural resources with emphasis on soil and water.
Founded: 1944
Kit Tillotson, President
Benjamin Kelly, Executive Director

860 Idaho Conservation League
710 North 6th Street 208-345-6933
Boise, ID 83702 *Fax:* 208-344-0344
icl@wildidaho.org
www.idahoconservation.org
The Idaho Conservation League (ICL) works to preserve Idaho's clean water, wilderness and quality of life through citizen action, public education, and professional advocacy.
Founded: 1973
Rick Johnson, Executive Director
Justin Hayes, Program Director

861 Northwest Management, Inc.
233 E. Palouse River Drive 208-883-4488
PO Box 9748 nwmanage@nmi2.com
Moscow, ID 83843 www.consulting-foresters.com
Northwest Management Inc. is a leader in forest and environmental management, with expertise in forestry, wildfire, water resources, hazard management and planning.
Founded: 1983
Vincent Corrao, President & CEO
Brock Purvis, Forest Inventory Manager

862 Sierra Club: Idaho Chapter
503 W Franklin Street 208-384-1023
Boise, ID 83702 zack.waterman@sierraclub.org
idaho.sierraclub.org
The Idaho Chapter of the Sierra Club works to secure the permanent protection of wildlands and endangered species in Idaho and advocates for the use of clean energy sources.
Zack Waterman, Chapter Director
Casey Mattoon, Conservation Coordinator

Illinois

863 Alliance for the Great Lakes
150 N Michigan Avenue 312-939-0838
Suite 700 alliance@greatlakes.org
Chicago, IL 60601 www.greatlakes.org
Dedicated to the preservation and restoration of the Great Lakes. The Alliance for the Great Lakes, formerly known as the Lake Michigan Federation, uses advocacy, volunteering, education and research to ensure the health and safety ofthe Great Lakes.
Founded: 1970
Joel Brammeier, President & CEO
Stephanie Smith, VP, Operations

864 American Fisheries Society: North Central Division: Illinois Chapter
IL JT-Lamer@wiu.edu
www.illinoisamericanfisheriessociety.weebly.com
The Illinois Chapter of the American Fisheries Society, is part of the American Fisheries Society (AFS) North Central Division. Working to further to the goals of the AFS through research, education, and professional development, thechapter is committed to the conservation, development, and wise use of fishery resources, and the global protection and sustainability of aquatic ecosystems.
Jim Lamer, President
Phil Willink, Secretary

865 American Lung Association of Illinois
55 W Wacker
Suite 800 312-781-1100
Chicago, IL 60601 info@lungil.org
www.lung.org/about-us/local-associations/illinois.html
The American Lung Association of Illinois works to prevent lung disease and promote lung health. Through education, advocacy, support and campaigns, such as Smokefree Illinois; the Association offers a wide variety of lung healthservices to the people Illinois.
Kristen Young, Executive Director, Chicago
Lewis Bartfield, Executive VP, Upper Midwest

866 American Lung Association of Illinois: Springfield
3000 Kelly Lane 217-787-5864
Springfield, IL 62711 info@lungil.org
www.lung.org/about-us/local-associations/illinois.html
Lewis Bartfield, Executive VP, Upper Midwest

867 American Society of Landscape Architects: Illinois Chapter
PO Box 4566 630-833-4516
Oak Brook, IL 60522-4566 www.il-asla.org
The Illinois Chapter of the American Society of Landscape Architects, is a nonprofit association representing the landscape architecture profession throughout the state of Illinois.
Susan Ragaishis, Executive Director
John Pizzo, President

868 Association of Illinois Soil and Water Conservation Districts
4285 North Walnut Street 217-744-3414
Springfield, IL 62707 *Fax:* 217-744-3420
www.aiswcd.org
The Association of Illinois Soil and Water Conservation Districts (AISWCD) is a grassroots organization committed to reprsenting and empowering the 97 soil and water conservation districts of Illinois.
Founded: 1948
Kelly Thompson, Executive Director
Steve Stierwalt, President

869 Chicago Chapter: National Safety Council
1121 Spring Lake Drive 630-285-1121
Suite 100 800-621-7615
Itasca, IL 60143-3201 *Fax:* 630-285-1434
customerservice@nsc.org
www.chicago.nsc.org
The National Safety Council saves lives by preventing injuries and deaths at work, in homes and communities, and on the roads through leadership, research, education and advocacy.
Jeffrey J. Woodbury, NSC Board Chairman
Deborah Hersman, President & CEO

870 Chicago Zoological Society
Brookfield Zoo 708-688-8000
3300 Golf Road bzadmin@brookfieldzoo.org
Brookfield, IL 60513 www.czs.org/Chicago-Zoological-Society
The Chicago Zoological Society is a nonprofit operating out of Brookfield Zoo. The society is committed to inspiring conservation leadership by connecting people with wildlife and nature.
Founded: 1934
Stuart D. Strahl, President & CEO
Richar G. Gamble, COO

871 Environmental Education Association of Illinois
Enivronmental Education Association of Illinois
Anita Purves Nature Center EEAssociation.Illinois@gmail.com
1505 N. Broadway www.eeai.net
Urbana, IL 61801
The Environment Education Association of Illinois (EEAI), is nonprofit association focused on the advancement of environmental education throughout the state. The EEAI is the Illinois affiliate of the North American Association forEnvironmental Education (NAAEE).
Jennifer Tariq, President
Kirsten Hope Walker, Treasurer

872 **Great Lakes Sport Fishing Council**
PO Box 297 630-941-1351
Elmhurst, IL 60126 www.great-lakes.org
The Great Lakes Sport Fishing council is a nonprofit confederation of organizations and individuals representing the Great Lakes region. Dedicated to the advocacy of the present and future state of sport fishing, the council promotes,protects and conserves the regions aquatic resources.
Founded: 1971 325,000 Members
Dan Thomas, President
Robert Mitchell, Vice President

873 **Illinois Association of Environmental Professionals**
9575 West Higgins Road info@iaepnetwork.org
Suite 600 www.iaepnetwork.org
Rosemont, IL 60018
A nonprofit organization focused on enhnacing environmental awareness and quality for the businesses, communities and citizens of Illinois.
Founded: 1975
Caroline Levenda, President
Larry Falbe, VP

874 **Illinois Audubon Society**
IL 217-544-2473
www.illinoisaudubon.org
The Illinois Audubon Society (IAS), is a member organization with 16 chapters throughout the state. The IAS is dedicated to the preservation of Illinois wildlife and the habitats which support them.
Founded: 1897 $25/Year
Jim Herkert, Executive Director
Jodie Owen, Accounts Manager

875 **Illinois Environmental Council**
230 Broadway 217-544-5954
Suite 150 *Fax:* 217-544-5958
Springfield, IL 62701 iec@ilenviro.org
www.ilenviro.org
Known as the IEC, the Illinois Environmental Council is made up of the Illinois Environmental Council Education Fund and the Illinois Environmental Council. The Education Fund provides education, outreach and a forum forenvironmentalists and the Council serves as the voice for the environmental community of Illinois. The IEC represents 60 environmental and community organizations and close to 300 individuals from across the state.
Founded: 1975
Jennifer Walling, Executive Director
Matt Steffen, Director, Communications

876 **Illinois Prairie Path**
P.O. Box 1086 630-752-0120
Wheaton, IL 60187 info@ipp.org
www.ipp.org
The Illinois Prairie Path (IPP), is a nonprofit corporation working to preserve, enhance and advocate for the Illinois Prairie Path. The path was the first successful U.S. "rails-to-trails" path, in which the abandoned route ofChicago's Aurora and Elgin Electric rail line was converted to a public path, starting the "rails-to-trails" movement of the 1960's. The IPP is for non-motorized public use.
Founded: 1963

877 **Illinois Recycling Association**
PO Box 6957 708-358-0050
Villa Park, IL 60181 info@illinoisrecycles.org
www.illinoisrecycles.org
A collective voice for waste management in the state of Illinois, the Illinois Recycling Association (IRA) is a nonprofit organization consisting of municipal, county, and state recycling coordinators. The IRA is dedicated to theadvocacy of the responsible use of resources through the promotion of waste reduction, re-use and recycling.
Founded: 1980 100 Members
Kris Kaar, President

878 **Illinois Solar Energy Association**
C/O Shamrock Electirc
1281 E Brummel Avenue 312-376-8245
Elk Grove Village, IL 60007 *Fax:* 630-420-1517
contactisea@illinoissolar.org
www.illinoissolar.org
The Illinois Solar Energy Association (ISEA) is a nonprofit organization using education and advocacy to promote the widespread use of solar and other renewable energy sources.
Founded: 1975
Nicola Brown, Program Development
Lesley McCain, Executive Director

879 **Iowa-Illinois Safety Council**
1501 42nd Street 515-276-4724
Suite 100 800-568-2495
West Des Moines, IA 50266 *Fax:* 515-276-8038
iiscadmin@iisc.org
www.iisc.org
The Iowa-Illinois Safety Council (IISC) is a nonprofit resource organization that helps business and industry with safety, health and environmental programs. As of 1980, the IISC is a chapter of the National Safety Council.
Founded: 1953 1,000 Members
Adam Lathrop, Executive Director
Dawn Gunderson, Director, Communications

880 **Midwest Pesticide Action Center**
35 E Upper Wacker Drive 773-878-7378
Suite 1200 general@pesticideaction.org
Chicago, IL 60601 www.midwestpesticideaction.org
Working at the local, state and regional level, the Midwest Pesticide Action Center, uses advocacy, education, and outreach to reduce the health risks and environmental impact of pesticides and promote safer alternatives.
Founded: 1994
Ruth Kerzee, Executive Director
Ryan Anderson, Program Manager

881 **Natural Land Institute (NLI)**
320 South 3rd Street 815-964-6666
Rockford, IL 61104 *Fax:* 815-964-6661
info@naturalland.org
www.naturalland.org
Nonprofit organization dedicated to preserving land and natural diversity for future generations, and helping residents of northern Illinois conserve the land they cherish.
Founded: 1958
Kerry Leigh, Executive Director
Jill Kennay, Assistant Director

882 **Prairie Rivers Network**
1902 Fox Drive 217-344-2371
Suite G *Fax:* 217-344-2381
Champaign, IL 61820 info@prairierivers.org
www.prairierivers.org
Working at a local, state and federal level, Prairie Rivers Networks champions the protection, conservation and restoration of rivers and lakes; promoting healthy waterways and safe drinking water for people, fish and wildlife.
Founded: 1967
Jon McNussen, President
Carol Hays, Executive Director

883 **Respiratory Health Association**
1440 W Washington Boulevard 312-243-2000
Chicago, IL 60607 888-880-5864
Fax: 312-243-3954
info@lungchicago.org
www.lungchicago.org
The Respiratory Health Association (RHA) works to prevent lung disease, promote clean air and help people live better. Through education, research and policy change, the RHA is a public health leader in metropolitan Chicago with afocus on asthma, COPD, lung cancer, tobacco control and air quality.
Founded: 1906
Beth Ritter Ruback, Director, Communications
Joel Africk, President & CEO

884 **Sierra Club: Illinois Chapter**
70 E Lake Street 312-251-1680
Suite 1500 *Fax:* 312-251-1780
Chicago, IL 60601 illinois.sierraclub.org
With 14 local groups, the Illinois Chapter of the Sierra Club encompasses the entire state of Illinois plus a small part of Iowa. In conjunction with the National Sierra Club's mission, the Illinois Chapter protects and promotes cleanenergy, air and water.
Founded: 1959
Jack Darin, Chapter Director
Kady McFadden, Deputy Director

885 **The Nature Conservancy: Illinois Chapter**
8 S Michigan Avenue 312-580-2100
Suite 900 *Fax:* 312-346-5606
Chicago, IL 60603 illinois@tnc.org
www.nature.org/illinois
The mission of The Nature Conservancy is to conserve the lands and waters on which all life depends. They work in all 50 states and more than 70 countries, with their work addressing critical conservation issues through strategies thataim to improve water quality, address the effects of climate change, create resilient cities, and allow both people and nature to thrive.
Founded: 1957
Michelle Carr, State Director
Georgie Geraghty, Deputy Director

Indiana

886 **Acres Land Trust**
1802 Chapman Road 260-637-2273
PO Box 665 *Fax:* 260-637-2273
Huntertown, IN 46748 acres@acreslandtrust.org
www.acreslandtrust.org
Acres Land Trust is the largest and oldest local land trust, covering 32 counties across northeast Indiana and Michigan. Dedicated to the protecting, promotion, and education of local land. Acres Land Trust acquires, owns, manages andprotects the working land, forests, wetlands, native grasslands, unique geological formations and habitats of the rare, threatened and endangered species of Indiana.
Founded: 1960
Steven Hammer, President
Jason Kissel, Executive Director

887 **American Fisheries Society: North Central Division: Indiana Chapter**
IN bmiller2@dnr.in.gov
www.indianaafs.org
The Indiana Chapter of the American Fisheries Society (IAFS), is part of the American Fisheries Society (AFS) North Central Division. Working to further to the goals of the AFS through research, education, and professional development,the chapter is committed to the conservation, development, and wise use of fishery resources in Indiana.
Ben Miller, President
Briana Ciara, Secretary & Treasurer

888 **American Lung Association of Indiana**
115 West Washington Street 317-819-1181
Suite 1180 South info@lungin.org
Indianapolis, IN 46204
www.lung.org/about-us/local-associations/indiana.html
The American Lung Association of Indiana works to prevent lung disease and promote lung health. Through education, advocacy,and campaigns, such as the Indiana Tuberculosis Education program; the Association offers a wide variety oflung health services to the people Illinois.
Tanya Husain, Executive Director, Indiana
Lewis Bartfield, Executive VP, Upper Midwest

889 **American Society of Landscape Architects: Indiana Chapter**
PO Box 441195 office@inasla.org
Indianapolis, IN 46244-1195 www.inasla.org
As a chapter of the American Society of Landscape Architects(ASLA), it aims to lead, educate and participate in the careful stewardship, wise planning, and artful design of cultural and natural environments.
Founded: 1972 200 Members
April Westcott, President
Jon Ruble, VP

890 **Conservation Technology Information Center**
3495 Kent Avenue 765-494-9555
Suite L100 *Fax:* 765-463-4106
West Lafayette, IN 47906 ctic@ctic.org
Conservation Technology Information Center (CTIC) is dedicated the promotion and provision of information on technologies and sustainable agricultural systems that conserve and enhance soil, water, air and wildlife resources.
Chad Watts, Executive Director
Tammy Taylor, Director, Operations

891 **Dj Case & Associates**
317 E Jefferson Boulevard 574-258-0100
Mishawaka, IN 46545 info@djcase.com
www.djcase.com
Specializing in conservation and natural resources communication, DJ Case & Associates is made up of social scientists, biologists, strategic communication planners, storytellers, video producers and web application developers.Working with state, federal and private natural resource agencies, DJ Case & Associates are dedicated to implementing positive, measurable and effective communication using conservation engagement and digital tools.
Founded: 1986
Dave Case, President
Phil Seng, Vice President

892 **Indiana Audubon Society**
3499 S Bird Sanctuary Road 765-827-5109
Connersville, IN 47331 president@indianaaudubon.org
indianaaudubon.org
The Indiana Audubon Society (IAS) is dedicated to stimulating interest in and promoting the protection of resident and migrant bird species and their habitats, both in Indiana and other regions. The organization also strives to supporteducational efforts to assist future generations in continuing this tradition.
Founded: 1898
Brad Bumgardner, Executive Director
Jeff Canada, Board President

893 **Indiana State Trappers Association**
ISTA C/O Ms. Georgia Gifford Treasurer
921 S Locke Street 765-438-3630
Kokomo, IN 46901 www.indianatrappers.org
The Indiana State Trappers Association (ISTA) is a public charity working to conserve Indiana's fur resources, preserve the rights, history and heritage of trappers, educate those interested in trapping and increasing public awarenessof trapping issues and benefits.
Fred Philips, President
Tom Setser, VP

894 **Indiana Water Environment Association**
8909 Purdue Road 317-686-2664
Suite 130 *Fax:* 317-686-2672
Indianapolis, IN 46268 kylee@indianawea.org
www.indianawea.org
The Indiana Water Environment Association is dedicated to perserving and protecting Indiana's waterways through the education of it members and the general public. The Indiana Water Environment Association is an affiliate of the WaterEnvironment Federation (WEF).
$35/Year
Kylee Dycus, Association Coordinator
Julia Whitson, Executive Director

895 **Indiana Woodland Steward**
IN steward1@inwoodlands.org
www.inwoodlands.org

The Indiana Woodland Steward is made up of 11 member organizations with the purpose of promoting the wise use of Indiana's forest resources.
Dan Shaver, President
Lynn Andrews, Treasurer

896 **Sierra Club: Indiana Chapter**
1100 W 42nd Street 317-822-3750
Suite 140 sierra@netdirect.net
Indianapolis, IN 46208 www.hoosier.sierraclub.org
To advance the preservation and protection of the natural environment by empowering the citizenry with charitable resources to further the cause of environmental protection.
Founded: 1975 8,000 Members
Loren Blackford, President
Susana Reyes, Vice President

897 **The Wildlife Society: Indiana Chapter**
IN www.intws.org
The Indiana Chapter of the the Wildlife Society is dedicated to enhancing the ability of wildlife professionals, conserve diversity, sustained productivity and ensuring the responsible use of wildlife resources.
Founded: 1968 $12 for Membership

Iowa

898 **ASLA Iowa Chapter**
200 W. 2nd Avenue 515-442-2451
Indianola, IA 50125 *Fax:* 866-442-6751
ia-asla@assocserv.com
www.iaasla.org
The chapter organizes educational and social activities for its more than 155 members.
Laura Peters, President
Jim Harbaugh, President Elect

899 **American Fisheries Society: North Central Division: Iowa Chapter**
IA jonathan.meerbeek@dnr.iowa.gov
The Iowa Chapter of the American Fisheries Society, is part of the American Fisheries Society (AFS) North Central Division. Working to further to the goals of the AFS through research, education, and professional development; the IowaChapter is a scientific and professional society focused on the encouragement of exchanging information by members working in, living in or have an interest in the state of Iowa.
Founded: 1969
Jonathan Meerbeek, President
Ryan Hupfeld, Secretary & Treasurer

900 **American Lung Association of Iowa**
2530 73rd Street 515-309-9507
Des Moines, IA 50322 info@lungia.org
www.lung.org/about-us/local-associations/iowa.html
The American Lung Association of the Iowa works to prevent lung disease and promote lung health. Offering a wide variety of lung health services to the people of Iowa.
Micki Sandquist, Executive Director, Iowa
Lewis Bartfield, Executive VP, Upper Midwest

901 **American Society of Landscape Architects: Iowa Chapter**
200 W. 2nd Avenue 515-442-2451
Indianola, IA 50125 *Fax:* 866-442-6751
ia-asla@assocserv.com
www.iaasla.org
The chapter organizes educational and social activities for its more than 155 members.
Founded: 1899
Laura Peters, President
Jim Harbaugh, President Elect

902 **B.A.S.S Nation: Iowa Chapter**
IA 319-393-1481
bobgarman@aol.com
www.iabass.com
The Iowa Chapter of BASS Nation is dedicated to the promotion of the sport of bass fishing, fishing tournaments and conservation initiatives to preserve the states natural resources.
Bob Garman, President
Harry Heines, Vice President

903 **Indian Creek Nature Center**
6665 Otis Road SE 319-362-0664
Cedar Rapids, IA 52403 *Fax:* 319-362-2876
naturecenter@indiancreeknaturecenter.org
www.indiancreeknaturecenter.org
A private nonprofit organization open to the public. The Nature Center provides about 300 acres of natural land and provides an array of educational programs.
Founded: 1973
John Myers, Executive Director
Dana Wood, Office Manager

904 **Iowa Academy of Science**
Iowa Academy of Science
BRC 50 319-273-2581
University of Northern Iowa *Fax:* 319-273-2807
Cedar Falls, IA 50614-0508 iascience@uni.edu
www.scienceiniowa.org
Iowa Academy of Science is a professional scientific organization.
Founded: 1875
Craig Johnson, Executive Director
Cory Davis, Office Manager

905 **Iowa Association of Soil and Water Conservation District Commissioners**
945 SW Ankeny Road 515-289-8300
Suite A www.cdiowa.org
Ankeny, IA 50023
Bernie Bolton, Secretary

906 **Iowa Native Plant Society**
Iowa State University
Botany Department, 341A Bessey Hall 515-294-9499
Iowa State University *Fax:* 515-294-1337
Ames, IA 50011 pubmaster@iastate.edu
www.public.iastate.edu
An organization of amateur and professional botanists and native plant enthusiasts who are interested in the scientific, educational and cultural aspects, as well as the preservation and conservation of the native plants of Iowa. TheSociety was organized in 1995 to create a forum where plant enthusiasts, gardners and professional botanists could exchange ideas and coordinate activities such as field trips, work shops, and restoration of natural areas.
Larissa Mottl, President
Connie Mutel, Vice President

907 **Iowa Prairie Network**
IA www.iowaprairienetwork.org
The Iowa Prairie Network is a grass-roots, volunteer, non-profit, organization that is dedicated to the preservation of Iowa's prairie heritage.
Mark Wilson, President
Jon Judson, Vice President

908 **Iowa Renewable Fuels Association**
5505 NW 88th Street 515-252-6249
100 *Fax:* 515-225-0781
Johnston, IA 50131-2948 info@IowaRFA.org
www.iowarfa.org
Brings together ethanol and biodiesel producers to promote the development and growth of the state's renewable fuels industry through education and infrastructure development.
Brian Cahill, President
Monte Shaw, Executive Director

909 Iowa Trappers Association
Gene Purdy 641-682-3937
122 2nd Street *Fax:* 641-682-9092
Fontanelle, IA 50846 hightoweria@aol.com
www.iowatrappers.com
Craig Sweet, President
Randy Mitchell, Vice President

910 Iowa Wildlife Rehabilitators Association
328 Main Street 515-233-1379
Suite 208 www.iowawildlifecenter.org
Ames, IA 50010
Terry VanDeWalle, President
Marlene Ehresman, Executive Director

911 Iowa-Illinois Safety Council
1501 42nd Street 515-276-4724
Suite 100 800-568-2495
West Des Moines, IA 50266 *Fax:* 515-276-8038
iiscadmin@iisc.org
www.iisc.org
The Iowa-Illinois Safety Council (IISC) is a nonprofit resource organization that helps business and industry with safety, health and environmental programs. As of 1980, the IISC is a chapter of the National Safety Council.
1,000 Members
Adam Lanthrop, Executive Director
Dawn Gunderson, Director, Communications

912 Macbride Raptor Project
309 S. Madison Street 319-335-9293
Iowa City, IA 52242 *Fax:* 319-398-4493
rec-services@uiowa.edu
www.macbrideraptorproject.org
A nonprofit organization jointly sponsored by the University of Iowa and Kirkwood Community College. The project has two main facilities, the educational display facility and rehabilitation flight cage at the Macbride NatureRecreational Area and the medical clinic on the Kirkwood Campus.
Founded: 1985
Jodeane Cancilla, Project Coordinator
Brian Baxter, Senior Associate Director

913 Practical Farmers of Iowa
1615 Golden Aspen Drive 515-232-5661
Suite 101 *Fax:* 515-232-5649
Ames, IA 50010 info@practicalfarmers.org
www.practicalfarmers.org
Practical Farmers of Iowa was founded in 1985 as an organization for farmers. We use farmer-led investigation and information sharing to help farmers practice an agriculture that benefits both the land and people.
Founded: 1985
Sally Worley, Executive Director
Debra Boekholder, Membership & Event Asst.

914 Sierra Club: Iowa Chapter
3839 Merle Hay Road 515-277-8868
Suite 280 iowa.chapter@sierraclub.org
Des Moines, IA 50310 iowa.sierraclub.org
To advance the preservation and protection of the natural environment by empowering the citizenry with charitable resources to further the cause of environmental protection.
Founded: 1972
Loren Blackford, President
Susana Reyes, Vice President

915 Soil and Water Conservation Society
945 SW Ankeny Road 515-289-2331
Ankeny, IA 50023-9723 800-THE-SOIL
Fax: 515-289-1227
swcs@swcs.org
www.swcs.org
Their mission is to foster the science and art of natural resource conservation. Their work targets the conservation of soil, water, and related natural resources.
Founded: 1943
Clare Lindahl, CEO
Rex Martin, President

916 State of Iowa Woodlands Associations
204 Park Rd 515-233-1161
Iowa City, IA 52246 *Fax:* 515-233-1131
Al Wagner, President
Chuck Semler, VP

917 The Nature Conservancy: Iowa Chapter
505 5th Ave 515-244-5044
Suite 930 800-628-6860
Des Moines, IA 50309 *Fax:* 515-244-8890
iowa@tnc.org
nature.org
To preserve the plants, animals and natural communities that represent the diversity of life on Earth by protecting the lands and waters they need to survive.
Founded: 1951
Jan Glendening, State Director

Kansas

918 American Fisheries Society: North Central Division: Kansas Chapter
KS josh.jagels@ksoutdoors.com
www.ksfisheries.org
The Kansas Chapter of the American Fisheries Society, is part of the American Fisheries Society (AFS) North Central Division. Working to further to the goals of the AFS through research, education, and professional development, thechapter is committed to the conservation, development, and wise use of fishery resources, and protection and sustainability of aquatic ecosystems.
Founded: 1975 $10/Year
Josh Jagels, President
Eric Johnson, Secretary

919 American Lung Association of Kansas
8400 W 110th Street
Suite 130 913-353-9165
Overland Park, KS 66210 kansas@lung.org
www.lung.org/about-us/local-associations/kansas.html
The American Lung Association of Kansas works to prevent lung disease and promote lung health through direct assistance, education programs, advocacy and research.
Linda Crider, Executive Director, Kansas
Lewis Bartfield, Executive VP, Upper Midwest

920 Arkansas River Compact Administration
KS www.co-ks-arkansasrivercompactadmin.org
The Arkansas River Compact Administration (ARCA), is a committee that settles disputes over the Arkansas River between Arkansas and Colorado.
James Rizzuto, Chairman
Randy Hayzlett, Vice-Chairman

921 Audubon of Kansas
210 Southwind Place 785-537-4385
Manhattan, KS 66503 *Fax:* 785-537-4395
aok@audubonofkansas.org
www.audubonofkansas.org
The Audubon of Kansas, Inc (AOK) is a nonprofit grassroots statewide organization. The AOK is dedicated to promoting the appreciation and stewardship of the ecosystems of Kansas, with a focus on birds, wildlife, prairies and otherhabitats.
Founded: 1999
Ron Klataske, Executive Director
Monica Goss, Director, Development

922 B.A.S.S Nation: Kansas Chapter
KS joelbassman87@yahoo.com
www.ksbassnation.com

Kansas BASS Nation works to stimulate public awareness of bass fishing as a major sport and encourages sportsmanship, courtesy and boating safety at all levels. Kansas BASS Nation promotes the full adherence to all conservation codes,adequate water quality standards and legal enforcement of existing regulatory standards.
Evan Hartnett, Director
Joel Porter, President

923 **Heartland Renewable Energy Society**
9844 Georgia Avenue 913-299-4474
Kansas City, KS 66109 info@heartlandrenewable.org
www.heartlandrenewable.org
As a chapter of the American Solar Energy Society, the Heartland Renewable Energy Society (HRES) is a volunteer based organization working to support and further develop the use of renewable energy and energy efficient techniques inbusiness. HRES promotes businesses using renewable energy and educates the public about clean, safe and renewable energy.
Founded: 2000
Craig Wolfe, President
Shauna Zahner, Secretary

924 **Kansas Academy of Science**
KS 785-231-1010
sam.leung@washburn.edu
www.kansasacademyscience.org
The Kansas Academy of Science (KAS) is dedicated to encouraging science and science education in the State of Kansas. KAS is a member of the National Association of Academies of Science and is affiliated with the American Associationfor the Advancement of Science and the US National Academy of Science.
Founded: 1868
David McKenzie, President
Sam Leung, Secretary

925 **Kansas Association for Conservation and Environmental Education**
2610 Claflin Road 785-532-1902
Manhattan, KS 66502-2743 *Fax:* 785-532-3305
info@kacee.org
www.kacee.org
The Kansas Assocaition for Conservation and Environmental Education (KACEE) is a statewide nonprofit dedicated to promoting quality sound, non-brased environmental education in Kansas through professional development and technicalassistance.
Melissa Arthur, Director, Operations
Laura Downey, Executive Director

926 **Kansas Native Plant Society**
Kansas Native Plant Society
R.L McGregor Herbarium 785-864-3453
2045 Constant Avenue email@ksnps.org
Lawrence, KS 66047-3729 www.kansasnativeplantsociety.org
Formerly known as the Kansas Wildflower Society, the Kansas Native Plant Society (KNPS) is a nonprofit organization working to encourage awareness and appreciation of the states native plants, their habitats and landscapes througheducation, stewardship and scientific knowledge.
Founded: 1978
Dwight Platt, President
Cynthia Ford, Secretary

927 **Kansas Natural Resources Council**
PO Box 2635 785-840-8104
Topeka, KS 66601 lerick@ksu.edu
www.knrc.weebly.com
A nonprofit, member organization the Kansas Natural Resource Council (KNRC) is dedicated to educating Kansans about the natural resources of the state and advocating for the wise use and conservation of these natural resources. KNRCprotects the quality of the water and air of Kansas.
Founded: 1981
Larry Erickson, President
Sharon Ashworth, Program Manager

928 **Kansas Rural Center**
4021 SW 10th Street 866-579-5469
#337 info@kansasruralcenter.org
Topeka, KS 66604 www.kansasruralcenter.org
Kansas Rural Center Inc. (KRC), is a nonprofit organization committed to promoting the long-term health of the land and the people of Kansas through community based research, education and advocacy. By working directly with Kansasfarmers, communities and leaders, KRC seeks to advance a sustainable farm and food system that is ecologically sound, economically viable and socially just in the state.
Founded: 1979
Mary Fund, Executive Director
Natalie Fullerton, Project Director

929 **Kansas Wildscape Foundation**
2500 W 6th 785-843-9453
Suite G 866-655-4377
Lawrence, KS 66049 *Fax:* 785-843-6379
charlieblack@sunflower.com
www.kansaswildscape.org
The Kansas Wildscape Foundation is a private, nonprofit organization working to conserve the land and wild species of the state. Wildscape promotes outdoor recreation and public land use, through projects such as the Kansas WetlandsEducational Center, the Cabins Project and the Milford Wetlands Restoration.
Founded: 1991
Charlie Black, Executive Director
Debbie Brandt, Director, Member Services

930 **Safety and Health Council of Western Missouri& Kansas**
5829 Troost Avenue 816-842-5223
Kansas City, MO 64110 *Fax:* 816-842-6226
shc@safetycouncilmoks.com
www.safetycouncilmoks.com
A private nonprofit community service organization dedicated to preventing unintentional injuries where ever they occur through education and outreach
Julian H. Harvey, President
H.L. Goodwin, Secretary & Treasurer

931 **Sierra Club: Kansas Chapter**
9844 Georgia Avenue 913-707-3296
Kansas City, KS 66109 info@kansas.sierraclub.org
kansas.sierraclub.org
To advance the preservation and protection of the natural environment by empowering the citizenry with charitable resources to further the cause of environmental protection.
Loren Blackford, President
Susana Reyes, Vice President

932 **The Wildlife Society: Kansas Chapter**
Kansas State University
205 Ackert 758-532-0978
Manhattan, KS 66506 justin.hamilton@ksoutdoors.com
www.wildlife.org/kansas-chapter
The Kansas Chapter of The Wildlife Society provides an avenue for professionals in wildlife management and natural resource fields a way to connect and work with their peers, in order to further advance professional natural resourcemanagment.
$10/Year
Justin Hamilton, President
Kent Fricke, Secretary & Treasurer

Kentucky

933 **American Lung Association of Kentucky**
4100 Churchman Avenue 502-363-2652
Louisville, KY 40215 barry.gottschalk@lung.org
www.lung.org/about-us/local-associations/kentucky.html
The American Lung Association of Kentucky works to prevent lung disease and promote lung health through direct assistance, education programs, advocacy and research.
Patricia J. Volz, VP, Communication
Barry Gottschalk, Executive VP, Midland States

934 **American Society of Landscape Architects: Kentucky Chapter**
KY www.kyasla.com
The Kentucky Chapter seeks to represent and further the aims and policies of the American Society of Landscape Architects as they fall within the domain of the Chapter.
John Swontosky, Trustee
Josh DeSpain, President

935 **Friends of Land Between The Lakes**
345 Maintenance Road 800-455-5897
Murray, KY 42211 information@friendsoflbl.org
www.friendsoflbl.org
Friends of Land Between The Lakes is a private nonprofit organization that provides educational programs at the Woodlands Nature Station, Golden Pond Planetarium and Observatory, and The Homeplace 1850's Working Farm. Friends of LandBetween The Lakes is a partner of the Forest Service at the Land Between the Lakes National Recreation Area.
John Rufli, Executive Director
Jim Taylor, Director, Operations

936 **Kentucky Association for Environmental Education**
PO Box 1208 programs@kaee.org
Frankfort, KY 40602 www.kaee.org
The first affiliate of the North American Association for Environment Education, the Kentucky Association for Environment Education (KAEE) is nonprofit, professional membership organization and of the country's oldest association. KAEEis dedicated to the promotion of excellence in environmental education through the support and networking the the states environmental educators.
Ashley Hoffman, Executive Director
Brittany Wray, Operations Coordinator

937 **Kentucky Audubon Council**
KY president@kentuckyaudubon.org
www.kentuckyauduboncouncil.org
The Kentucky Audubon Council is an organization acting as the facilitator for the Audubon chapters in the state, including: the Central Kentucky, Daviess County, Frankfort, Jackson Purchase, Little River and Louisville Audubon Society.The council is comprised of a member from each chapter and is actively working to conserve and restore natural ecosystems with a focus on birds, other wildlife and their habitats.
Angela Myers, President
Robin Antenucci, VP

938 **Kentucky Audubon Council: Central Kentucky Audubon Society**
KY 859-299-9421
president@centralkentuckyaudubon.org
www.centralkentuckyaudubon.org
The Central Kentucky Audubon Society serves 10 central Kentucky counties and promotes conservation education and awareness.
Founded: 1968 $20/Year
Tony Brusate, President
David Lang, VP

939 **Kentucky Audubon Council: Daviess County Audubon Society**
Owensboro, KY 42303 270-926-2202
dcas@daviessaudubon.net
www.daviessaudubon.net
The Daviess County Audubon Society works to support the mission of the National Audubon Society and is involved in community outreach and education.
David Stratton, President
Mike Henshaw, Director, Program

940 **Kentucky Audubon Council: Frankfort Audubon Society**
844-428-3826
FrankfortAudubonChapter@gmail.com
www.sites.google.com/site/frankfortaudubon/
The Frankfort Audubon Society works to connect people with nature through education and wildlife conservation.
Robin Antenucci, President
Don Stosberg, Treasurer

941 **Kentucky Audubon Council: Jackson Purchase Audubon Society**
Office or Chapter J59
www.audubon.org/location/jackson-purchase-audubon-society
Paducah, KY 42001

942 **Kentucky Audubon Council: Little River Audubon Society**
Office or Chapter J61
PO Box 352 www.audubon.org/location/little-river-audubon-society
Hopkinsville, KY 42240

943 **Kentucky Audubon Council: Louisville Audubon Society**
PO Box 22162 louisvilleaudubon@gmail.com
Louisville, KY 40222 www.louisvilleaudubon.org
Kathy Dennis, President
Charon Morales, VP

944 **Kentucky Department of Fish & Wildlife Resources**
1 Sportsman's Lane 800-858-1549
Frankfort, KY 40601 info.center@ky.gov
fw.ky.gov
The Kentucky Department of Fish & Wildlife Resources is dedicated to the conservation and enhancement of fish and wildlife resources. The Department provides education and opportunities for hunting, fishing, trapping, boating and otherwildlife related activities.
Dr. Johathan W. Gassett, Commissioner

945 **Kentucky Resources Council**
PO Box 1070 502-875-2428
Frankfort, KY 40602 *Fax:* 502-875-2845
FitzKRC@aol.com
www.kyrc.org
The Kentucky Resource Council (KRC) is a nonprofit member organization committed to protecting the states natural resources and promoting healthy communities by providing legal and technical guidance to individuals, communities andorganizations.
Founded: 1982
Tom Fitzgerald, Director

946 **Scenic Kentucky**
PO Box 23317 502-574-3768
Louisville, KY 40223-0317 *Fax:* 502-489-5278
info@scenickentucky.org
www.scenickentucky.org
Scenic Kentucky is the state affiliate of Scenic America dedicated to protecting, preserving and enhancing the scenic character of the state. Working at the local, state and federal level, Scenic Kentucky uses advocacy to protect thescenic heritage of the Commonwealth of Kentucky.
Paul Bergmann, Executive Director
Marlene Grissom, President

947 **Sierra Club: Kentucky Chapter**
PO Box 1368 859-444-4338
Lexington, KY 40588-1368 kentucky.sierraclub.org
To advance the preservation and protection of the natural environment by empowering the citizenry with charitable resources to further the cause of environmental protection.
Founded: 1968
Loren Blackford, President
Susana Reyes, Vice President

948 **The Nature Conservancy: Kentucky Chapter**
114 Woodland Ave 859-259-9655
Lexington, KY 40502 *Fax:* 859-259-9678
kentucky@tnc.org
www.nature.org

In conjunction with the mission of the Nature Conservancy, the Kentucky Chapter protects 50,000 acres of private and public land across the state, including 18 miles of public use nature trail.
David Phemister, State Director
Lisa Morris, Office Manager

Louisiana

949 American Lung Association of Louisiana
2325 Severn Avenue
Suite 8 504-828-5864
Metairie, LA 70001-6918 alala@lungse.org
www.lung.org/about-us/local-associations/louisiana.html
The American Lung Association of Louisiana works to prevent lung disease and promote lung health through direct assistance, education programs, advocacy and research.
Martha C. Bogdan, Executive VP, Southeast
Willie L. Bythwood, Jr, CFO

950 American Society of Landscape Architects: Louisiana Chapter
541 South Eugene Street www.lcasla.org
Baton Rouge, LA 70806
As the Louisiana Chapter of the American Society of Landscape Architects (LCASLA), it aims to lead, educate and participate in the careful stewardship, wise planning, and artful design of cultural and natural environments. The LCASLArepresents landscape architects from across the state and provides its members with networking, social and volunteer opportunities.
150 Members
Shannon Blakeman, Trustee
Michael Petty, Secretary

951 B.A.S.S Nation: Louisiana Chapter
603 Terri Drive 985-785-9069
Luling, LA 70070 kevgobear@cox.net
www.louisianabass.com
The Louisiana Chapter of BASS Nation is dedicated to the promotion of the sport of bass fishing, fishing tournaments and conservation initiatives to preserve the states natural resources.
Kevin Gaubert, President
Tracy Noble, VP

952 Calcasieu Parish Animal Control & Protection Department
5500-A Swift Plant Road 337-721-3730
Lake Charles, LA 70615 *Fax:* 337-721-4188
cpas@cppj.net
www.cppj.net/services/animal-services-and-adoption
The Calcasieu Parish Animal Control & Protection Department provides education and intervention surrounding public and animal safety. The Department is dedicated to preventing animal abuse and neglect.
Nathan Areno, Director
Jerry Roy, Operations Supervisor

953 LACD: Louisiana Association of Conservation Districts
825 Kaliste Saloom Road 337-262-5777
Brandywine III, Suite 220 *Fax:* 337-262-5486
Lafayette, LA 70508 www.laconservationdistricts.org
The Louisiana Association of Conservation Districts(LACD) is charged with the conservation and regulation of the states oil, gas, and lignite resources.

954 LACD: Monroe
24 Accent Drive 318-362-3111
Suite 104 *Fax:* 318-362-5227
Monroe, LA 71202 www.laconservationdistricts.org

955 LACD: Shreveport
1525 Fairfield Avenue 318-676-7585
Suite 668 *Fax:* 318-676-7486
Shreveport, LA 71101-4327 www.laconservationdistricts.org

956 Louisiana Wildlife Federation
337 S Acadian Thruway 225-344-6707
Baton Rouge, LA 70806 *Fax:* 225-344-6707
lwf@lawildlifefed.org
www.lawildlifefed.org
The Louisiana Wildlife Federation (LWF) is a statewide, nonprofit conservation education and advocacy organization dedicated to the restoration, preservation, and development of birds, fish, game, forestry, wild flowers and wildliferesources of the state.
Founded: 1940
Rebecca Triche, Executive Director
Stacy Ortego, Outreach Coordinator

957 National Safety Council: ArkLaTex Chapter
8101 Kingston Road 318-687-7550
Suite 107 800-595-7550
Shreveport, LA 71108 *Fax:* 318-687-7298
info@nscaltchapter.org
www.nscaltchapter.org
The National Safety Council: ArkLaTex Chapter is a nonprofit corporation that advocates and offers compliance training on safety, health, and environmental issues, with a heavy emphasis on industrial requirements, occupationaltraining, First Aid/CPR, OSHA and supervisor development. The ArkLaTex Chapter is the regional chapter of the National Safety Council.
Larry Holbert, President & CEO
Dana Gunn, Director, Operations

958 Sierra Club: Delta Chapter of Louisiana
PO Box 52503 337-298-8380
Lafayette, LA 70505 hrmartin2sc@gmail.com
www.sierraclub.org/louisiana
The Delta Chapter is comprised of 5 regional groups working to conserve Louisiana's environment through lobbying efforts, education campaigns and the protection of the Atchafalaya Basin.
3,000 Members
Martin Haywood, Chair
Diana Morgan, Vice Chair

959 Sierra Club: New Orleans/Gulf of Mexico Regional Office
716 Adams Street 504-861-4834
New Orleans, LA 70118 *Fax:* 504-861-4441
darryl.malek-wiley@sierraclub.org
www.sierraclub.org/louisiana
Daryl Malek-Wiley, Regional Representative
Grace Morris, Conservation Organizer

960 The Nature Conservancy: Louisiana Chapter
PO Box 4125 225-338-1040
Baton Rouge, LA 70821 lafo@tnc.org
www.nature.org
The Louisiana Chapter of the Nature Conservancy works to conserve the natural resources of the state with multiple locations and the management of 5 nature preserves.

961 The Nature Conservancy: Louisiana Chapter: Cypress Island
PO Box 317 337-342-2475
Breaux Bridge, LA 70517 www.nature.org

962 The Nature Conservancy: Louisiana Chapter: Grande Isle
PO Box 675 985-787-3599
Grand Isle, LA 70358 www.nature.org

963 The Nature Conservancy: Louisiana Chapter: New Orleans
320 Hammond Highway 504-831-9689
Suite 404 www.nature.org
Metairie, LA 70005

964 The Nature Conservancy: Louisiana Chapter: Northeast Louisiana
4276 Front Street 318-412-0472
Winnsboro, LA 71295 www.nature.org

965 The Nature Conservancy: Louisiana Chapter: Southwest Louisiana
12 Williamsburg Street 337-480-9393
Lake Charles, LA 70605 www.nature.org

966 The Nature Conservancy: Louisiana Chapter: Northshore Field Office
PO Box 1657 985-809-1414
Abita Springs, LA 70420 www.nature.org

967 The Nature Conservancy: Louisiana Chapter: Northwest Louisiana
PO Box 72299 318-560-5725
Bossier City, LA 71125 www.nature.org

968 The Wildlife Society: Louisiana Chapter
LA 70808 www.wildlife.org/tag/louisiana
The LouisianaCchapter of the the Wildlife Society,is a nonprofit scientific and educational organization that serves professionals such as government agencies, academia, industry and non-government organizations in all areas related tothe conservation of wildlife and natural resources management.

969 Tulane Environment Law Clinic
6329 Freret Street 504-865-5789
New Orleans, LA 70118 *Fax:* 504-862-8721
www.tulane.edu/~telc/
Part of Tulane University's Law School, the Tulane Environmental Law Clinic was founded in order to offer students real world experience in representing clients in order to resolve disputes under state and federal environmental laws.The Clinic is Louisiana's premier public interest environmental legal services organization, providing free legal representation and community outreach to community organizations, lower-income individuals and local governments.
Founded: 1989
Lisa Lavie Jordan, Director
Corinne Van Dalen, Clinic Instructor

Maine

970 American Lung Association of Maine
122 State Street 207-622-6394
Augusta, ME 04330 info@lungne.org
www.lung.org/about-us/local-associations/maine.html
The American Lung Association of Maine works to prevent lung disease and promote lung health through direct assistance, education programs, advocacy and research.
Jeff Seyler, Executive VP, Northeast
Adam Shuster, CFO

971 Atlantic Salmon Federation
PO Box 807 506-529-4581
Calais, ME 04619-0807 506-529-1033
800-565-5666
Fax: 506-529-1070
Fax: 506-529-4438
savesalmon@asf.ca
www.asf.ca
The Atlantic Salmon Federation is an international nonprofit organization that promotes the conservation and wise management of wild Atlantic salmon and their habitat.
Bill Taylor, President & CEO
Robert Otto, COO

972 Maine Association of Conservation Commissions
665 Western Avenue 207-623-1217
Manchester, ME 04351 fws319@aol.com
www.meaccme.org
The Maine Association of Conservation Commissions is committed to connecting the communities of Maine to the natural resources of the state, including its water, woods and wildlife.
Founded: 1973
Robert C Cummings, Executive Director
Marcel Polak, Cons. Resource Advisor

973 Maine Association of Conservation Districts
Portland, ME 207-878-0857
tomgordon@avportland.com
www.maineconservationdistricts.com
Reprsenting Maine's 16 Soil & Water Conservation disitrcts. The Maine Association of Conservation Districts, works to strengthn the states ability to conserve natural resources.
Founded: 1949
Andy Reed, President
Steve Follette, Vice President

974 Maine Audubon
20 Gilsland Farm Road 207-781-2330
Falmouth, ME 04105 *Fax:* 207-781-0974
info@maineaudubon.org
maineaudubon.org
Maine Audubon works to conserve Maine's wildlife and wildlife habitat by engaging people of all ages in education, conservation and action.
Founded: 1843
Andrew Beahm, Executive Director
Eric Topper, Director of Education

975 Maine Coast Heritage Trust
1 Bowdoin Mill Island 207-729-7366
Suite 201 *Fax:* 207-729-6863
Topsham, ME 04086 info@mcht.org
www.mcht.org
Maine Coast Heritage Trust (MCHT) is a statewide nonprofit organization working to conserve and promote the natural places of Maine. Through land trusts, communities,and partnerships MCHT protects over 146,000 acres of land and morethan 322 costal islands
Founded: 1970
Tim Glidden, President
Richard Knox, Director, Communications

976 Maine Coast Heritage Trust: Aldermere Farm
70 Russel Avenue 207-236-2739
Rockport, ME 04856 *Fax:* 207-230-2582
info@mcht.org
www.mcht.org
Tim Glidden, President
Richard Knox, Director, Communications

977 Maine Coast Heritage Trust: Downeast Field Office
13A Willow Street 207-259-5040
East Machias, ME 04630 info@mcht.org
www.mcht.org
Tim Glidden, President
Richard Knox, Director, Communications

978 Maine Coast Heritage Trust: Mount Desert Island
PO Box 669 201-244-5100
Mount Desert, ME 04660 *Fax:* 207-244-5200
info@mcht.org
www.mcht.org
Tim Glidden, President
Richard Knox, Director, Communications

979 Maine Woodland Owners
153 Hospital Street 207-626-0005
PO Box 836 877-467-9626
Augusta, ME 04332-0836 info@mainewoodlandowners.org
www.swoam.org
Formerly known as the Small Woodland Owners Association of Maine, the Woodland Owners of Maine, is a nonprofit organization working to promote the stewardship of Maine's woodland resources and provide information for better forestmanagement. Maine Woodland Owners is a statewide organization with 10 regional chapters.
Founded: 1975
Thomas C. Doak, Executive Director
Bill S. Williams, Deputy Executive Director

980 **Sierra Club: Maine Chapter**
44 Oak Street 207-761-5616
Suite 301 *Fax:* 207-773-6690
Portland, ME 04101-3936 maine.chapter@sierraclub.org
maine.sierraclub.org
To advance the preservation and protection of the natural environment by empowering the citizenry with charitable resources to further the cause of environmental protection.
Loren Blackford, President
Susana Reyes, Vice President

Massachusetts

981 **Alternatives for Community & Environment**
2201 Washington Street 617-442-3343
Suite 302 *Fax:* 617-442-2425
Roxbury, MA 02119 info@ace-ej.org
www.ace-ej.org
The Alternatives for Community & Environment organization works to support and build the communities of color and lower income communities in New England by pursuing systematic change in order to eliminate environmental racism,classism and achieve environmental justice.
Founded: 1994
Sue Heilman, Interim Executive Director
Lee Matsueda, Political Director

982 **American Fisheries Society: Bioengineering Section**
c/o U.S. Fish and Wildlife Service
Hadley, MA 01035 413-253-8303
jessica_pica@fws.gov
units.fisheries.org/bes
The Bioengineering Section focuses on techniques and impacts of fisheries bioengineering, and improved communication between biologists, engineers, and other professionals.
Founded: 1979
Dan Giza, President
Jessica E. Pica, Treasurer/Secretary

983 **American Lung Association of Massachusetts**
14 Beacon Street 781-890-4262
Suite 717 info@lungne.org
Boston, MA 02108 www.lung.org/about-us/local-associations/massachusetts.html
The American Lung Association of Massachusetts works to prevent lung disease and promote lung health; offering a wide variety of lung health services to the people of Massachusetts.
Jeff Seyler, Executive VP, Northeast
Adam Shuster, CFO

984 **American Lung Association of Massachusetts: Framingham**
1661 Worcester Road
Suite 301 781-890-4262
Framingham, MA 01701 info@lungne.org
www.lung.org/about-us/local-associations/massachusetts.html
Jeff Seyler, Executive VP, Northeast
Adam Shuster, CFO

985 **American Lung Association of Massachusetts: Springfield**
393 Maple Street 413-737-3506
Springfield, MA 01105 info@lungne.org
www.lung.org/about-us/local-associations/massachusetts.html
Jeff Seyler, Executive VP, Northeast
Adam Shuster, CFO

986 **Boston Society of Landscape Architects**
PO Box 262047 chapteroffice@bslanow.org
Boston, MA 02196 www.bslaweb.org
The Boston Society of Landscape Architects (BSLA) is the state affiliate of the American Society of Landscape Architects, it is the oldest and largest chapter of the ASLA. The BSLA is focused on supporting the success of its membersand their supporters through member benefits, career and skill development and scholarship programs.
Founded: 1913
Chris Moyles, President
Jeanne Lukenda, Trustee

987 **Earthwatch Institute**
114 Western Avenue 978-461-0081
Boston, MA 02134 800-776-0188
Fax: 978-461-2332
info@earthwatch.org
earthwatch.org
Earthwatch Institute is an international environmental conservation organization, dedicated to scientific field research and education in the promotion and creation of a sustainable environment. Working with the general public,scientists, communities, educators, students and other organizations, Earthwatch has over 50 scientific research expeditions in over 40 countries focused on ocean health, climate change, habitat and ecosystems, and cultural heritage.
Founded: 1971
Kristen Kusek, COO, Comm.& Development
Scott Kania, CEO, United States

988 **Environmental League of Massachusetts**
14 Beacon Street 617-742-2553
Suite 714 *Fax:* 617-742-9656
Boston, MA 02108 info@environmentalleague.org
www.environmentalleague.org
The Environmental League of Massachusetts (ELM) is a nonprofit educational and advocacy organization. ELM focuses its resources on the state level and works to combat climate change and protect the land, water and public health ofMassachusetts.
Founded: 1898
Elizabeth Turnbull, President
Nancy Goodman, VP, Policy

989 **Mass Audubon**
208 South Great Road 781-259-9500
Lincoln, MA 01773 mass_audubon@massaudubon.org
www.massaudubon.org
Mass Audubon is the largest nonprofit nature conservation in Massachusetts, it works to protect nature for the people and wildlife of the state. Through education and advocacy, the Mass Audubon is protecting over 37,000 acres of land,including the habitats of over 150 endangered and threatened native species.
Founded: 1896 125,000 Members
Gary Clayton, President
Bancroft Poor, VP, Operations

990 **Massachusetts Association of Conservation Commissions**
10 Juniper Road 617-489-3930
Belmont, MA 02478 staff@maccweb.org
www.maccweb.org
The Massachusetts Association of Conservation Commissions (MACC) is a statewide, nonprofit organization dedicated to the protection of Massachusetts natural resources by supporting Conservation Commissions. Through education andadvocacy, MACC provides training and assistance for more than 2,000 conservation commissioners protecting wetlands, open space and biological diversity across the state.
Founded: 1961
Eugene B. Benson, Executive Director
Michele Girard, Associate Director

991 **Massachusetts Association of Conservation Districts**
319 Littleton Road 978-692-9395
Suite 205 *Fax:* 978-392-1305
Westford, MA 01886 jobbagymacd@gmail.com
www.massacd.wordpress.com
The Massachusetts Association of Conservation Districts (MACD) represents the 14 conservation districts of the state. MACD works to protect wildlife, restore habitats, conserve soil and improve the water quality of Massachusetts.
Jane Obbagy, Executive Director
Joseph Smith, President

992 **Massachusetts Environmental Education Society**
c/O Environmental Business Council
375 Harvard Street
Suite 2
Brookline, MA 02446
info@massmees.org
www.massmees.org

The Massachusetts Environmental Education Society (MEES) is committed to the promotion, preservation, and improvement of environmental education in the state and region. MEES provides tools to environmental educators, including accessto online resources, professional development through an annual conference and social media connection.
Founded: 1977
Ann Gisinger, President
Erin Kelly, Treasurer

993 **Massachusetts Forest Alliance**
249 Lakeside Avenue
Marlborough, MA 01752-4503
617-455-9918
nletoile@massforestalliance.org
www.massforestalliance.net

The Massachusetts Forest Alliance (FLA) represents and advocates for citizens and businesses who support a strong, sustainable forest economy. Working on a local, regional and state level the FLA promotes the understanding of forestmanagement, provides educational opportunities for landowners, foresters, timber harvesters and public officials and ensures a sensible legal and regulatory environment.
Founded: 2012
Nathan L'Etoile, Executive Director
Gregory Cox, Program Director

994 **Massachusetts Public Interest Research Group**
294 Washington St
Suite 500
Boston, MA 02108
617-292-4800
800-838-6554
www.masspirg.org

Massachusetts Public Interest Research Group (MASSPIRG) is a statewide, nonprofit, public interest advocacy organization; that focuses primarily on environmental, health, safety, financial and consumer protection.
Founded: 1972
Janet Domenitz, Executive Director
Deirdre Cummings, Legislative Director

995 **Massachusetts Trappers Association**
c/o Marie Barras
PO Box 476
Leominster
, MA 01453
www.masstrappers.com

The Massachusetts Trappers Association works to perserve, promote and educate on the tradition of fur harvesting.

996 **Massachusetts Water Pollution Control Association**
PO Box 60
Rochdale, MA 01542
774-276-9722
Fax: 774-670-9956
mwpca2011@yahoo.com
www.mwpca.org

The Massachusetts Water Pollution Control Association (MWPCA) is a nonprofit organization that provides education, training, and promotes the exchange of information among operators and water quality professionals.
Founded: 1965
Lynn Foisy, Executive Director
Tom Azevedo, Program Coordinator

997 **Mount Grace Land Conservation Trust**
1461 Old Keene Road
Athol, MA 01331
978-248-2043
Fax: 978-248-2053
landtrust@mountgrace.org
www.mountgrace.org

The Mount Grace Land Trust is a regional land trust serving 23 towns in Worcester and Franklin counties. The Trust protects natural, agricultural, and scenic areas through the promotion and encouragement of stewardship.
Founded: 1986 1,200 Members
Leigh Youngblood, Executive Director
David Graham Wolf, Deputy Director

998 **New England Water Environment Association**
10 Tower Office Park
Suite 601
Woburn, MA 01801-2155
781-939-0908
Fax: 781-939-0907
mail@newea.org
www.newea.org

A not-for-profit organization whose objective is the advancement of fundamental knowledge and technology of design, construction, operation and management of waste treatment works and other water pollution contral activities anddedication to the preservation of water quality and water resources.
Founded: 1929
Mary Barry, Executive Director
Janice Moran, Program Coordinator

999 **Northeast Sustainable Energy Association**
50 Miles Street
Greenfield, MA 01301
413-774-6051
Fax: 413-774-6053
nesea@nesea.org
www.nesea.org

The Northeast Sustainable Energy Association (NESA) is the region's leading membership organization promoting the use of sustainable energy in the built environment.
Founded: 1974
Jennifer Marrapese, Executive Director
Miriam Aylward, Director,Program Development

1000 **Save the Harbor/Save the Bay**
Boston Fish Pier
212 Northern Avenue
Suite 304 West
Boston, MA 02210
617-451-2860
Fax: 617-451-0496
info@savetheharbor.org
www.savetheharbor.org

Save the Harbor/Save the Bay is nonprofit public interest organization using education and advocacy to restore and protect the Boston Harbor, Massachusetts Bay and the marine environment.
Founded: 1986
Joseph P. Newman, Chairman
Mark Chrisos, Vice Chair

1001 **Sierra Club: Massachusetts Chapter**
10 Milk Street
Suite 417
Boston, MA 02108-4600
617-423-5775
Fax: 617-423-5858

To advance the preservation and protection of the natural environment by empowering the citizenry with charitable resources to further the cause of environmental protection.
Cathy Ann Buckley, Chair
Elisa Campbell, Vice Chair

1002 **Walden Woods Project**
The Thoreau Institue at Walden Woods
44 Baker Farm Road
Lincoln, MA 01773-3004
781-259-4700
Fax: 781-259-4710
wwproject@walden.org
www.walden.org

The Walden Woods Project is a nonprofit organization committed to preserving the land, literature, and legacy of Henry David Thoreau through conservation, education, research and advocacy.
Founded: 1990
Don Henley, Founder
Kathi Anderson, Executive Director

Maryland

1003 **Alliance for the Chesapeake Bay**
501 Sixth Street
Annapolis, MD 21403
443-949-0575
Fax: 443-949-0673
contact@allianceforthebay.org
www.allianceforthebay.org

The Alliance for the Chesapeake Bay leads and supports local collaborative action in order to restore and protect Chesapeake Bay and its surrounding watershed. The Alliance has programs in all 6 Chesapeake Bay watershed states and theDistrict of Colum-

bia, that work to restore, conserve, and clean up local rivers and streams.
Founded: 1971
Al Todd, Executive Director
Lou Etgen, Deputy & State Director

1004 American Fisheries Society: Marine Fisheries Section
NOAA, Office of Science and Technology
1315 East-West Highway 301-427-8100
12th Floor mfs.fisheries.org
Silver Spring, MD 20910
Provides expertise to AFS and domestic and international organizations on maintaining healthy and diverse marine ecosystems.
Rick Methot, President
Patrick Lynch, Secretary-Treasurer

1005 American Lung Association of Maryland
211 East Lombard Street #260 804-302-5740
Baltimore, MD 21202 lungmd@lunginfo.org
www.lung.org/about-us/local-associations/maryland.html
The American Lung Association of Maryland works to prevent lung disease and promote lung health through direct assistance, education programs, advocacy and research.
Deborah Brown, Executive VP, Mid-Atlantic
Joy Meyer, VP, Community Impact

1006 American Society of Landscape Architects: Maryland Chapter
Baltimore, MD www.marylandasla.org
The Maryland Chapter of the American Society of Landscape Architects (MDASLA), is a nonprofit association representing the landscape architecture profession throughout the state of Maryland.
Founded: 1972 370 Members
Larissa Torres, President
Jennifer Kirschnick, Exectuive Director

1007 Audubon Naturalist Society
Woodend Sanctuary
8940 Jones Mill Road 301-652-9188
Chevy Chase, MD 20815 www.anshome.org
Through education, advocacy and outdoor experiences, the Audubon Naturalist Society (ANS) works to inspire the community of the greater Washington, DC region to appreciate, understand and protect the natural environment.
Founded: 1897
Lisa Alexander, Executive Director
Jacky Wershbale, Director, Development

1008 B.A.S.S Nation: Maryland Chapter
MD 410-426-2343
teamroger@aol.com
www.mdbass.com
Dedicated to the promotion of the sport of bass fishing. The Maryland BASS nation is comprised of 50 bass fishing clubs organized into four separate regions.
Roger Trageser, President
Denis Schanberger, Secrtary

1009 Center for Chesapeake Communities
192 Duke Of Gloucester Street 410-267-8595
Annapolis, MD 21401 *Fax:* 410-267-8597
Technical assistance on environmental, land use, energy and water quality issues for local government in Chesapeake Bay Watershed.
Gary Allen, Executive Director

1010 Chesapeake Bay Environmental Center
600 Discovery Lane 410-827-6694
PO Box 519 jwink@bayrestoration.org
Grasonville, MD 21638 www.bayrestoration.org
The Chesapeake Bay Environmental Center (CBEC) is a nonprofit membership organization dedicated to the promotion of stewardship and sustainability through environmental education and habitat restoration. The CBEC is an environmentcenter located on a 510 acre wildlife habitat surrounded by the Chesapeake Bay, where research, education, and restoration of the Bay occurs.
Founded: 1979
Judy Wink, Executive Director
Vicki Paulas, Assistant Director

1011 Chesapeake Bay Foundation
Philip Merrill Environmental Center
6 Herndon Avenue 410-268-8816
Annapolis, MD 21403 888-728-3229
Fax: 410-268-6687
chesapeake@cbf.org
www.cbf.org
Through education, advocacy and litigation, the Chesapeake Bay Foundation (CBF) is the largest nonprofit, independent conservation organization, dedicated solely to the protection and restoration of Chesapeake Bay and its watersheds.
Founded: 1967
Alison Prost, Executive Director, Maryland
Tom Zopler, Assitant Director, Media

1012 Chesapeake Wildlife Heritage, Inc.
CWH and Western Maryland Division
c/o Ned Gerber 410-822-5100
1201 Parson Island Road *Fax:* 443-249-3428
Chester, MD 21619-2866 info@cheswildlife.org
www.cheswildlife.org
Dedicated to designing, restoring, and managing wildlife habitat and establishing a more sustainable agriculture through direct action, education and research in partnership with private and public landowners.
Founded: 1980
John E. (Ned) Gerber, Director
Ralph V. Partlow III, President & Treasurer

1013 Eastern Shore Land Conservancy
114 S Washington Street 410-690-4603
Suite 101 info@eslc.org
Easton, MD 21601 www.eslc.org
Eastern Shore Land Conservancy (ESLC) is a private, nonprofit organization committed to preserving and sustaining the communities of Eastern Shore, their lands and water. Through the promotion of sound land use, planning and ESLC LandProtection Program, the ESLC has protected nearly 60,000 acres of the regions natural habitats and farmland.
Founded: 1990
Robert Etgen, Executive Director
Laura Sanford, Director of Advancement

1014 Institute of Hazardous Materials Management (IHMM)
9210 Corporate Blvd. 301-984-8969
Suite 470 *Fax:* 301-984-1516
Rockville, MD 20850 info@ihmm.org
www.ihmm.org
A nonprofit organization that protects the environment and the public's health and safety through the administration of credentials recognizing professionals who have demonstrated a high level of knowledge, expertise, and excellence inthe management of hazardous materials.
Founded: 1984
Gene Guilford, Executive Director
Patricia Buley, Director, Certification

1015 Maryland Association of Soil Conservation Districts
209 Jarman Branch Drive 443-262-8491
Centreville, MD 21617 *Fax:* 410-956-0161
lindsay.mdag@gmail.com
www.mascd.net
The Maryland Association of Soil Conservation Districts (MASCD) is a nonprofit organization representing the 24 soil and water conservation districts of the state. The MASCD provides a forum for training, policy-making and the exchangeof information while promoting the practical and effective use of soil and water.
Founded: 1956
Danielle Bauer, Program Assitant
Lindsay Thompson, Executive Director

1016 Maryland Native Plant Society
PO Box 4877 info@mdflora.org
Silver Spring, MD 20914 www.mdflora.org
Through education, research, advocacyand service activities the Maryland Native Plant Society, promotes awareness, appreciation, and conservation of the states native plants and their habitats.
Founded: 1992
Kristen Johnson, President
Karyn Molines, VP

1017 Maryland Recyclers Network
c/o Mariner Management 443-741-8740
PO Box 1046 *Fax:* 301-238-4579
Laurel, MD 20725 info@marylandrecyclingnetwork.org
www.marylandrecyclingnetwork.org
The Maryland Recycling Network (MRN) serves as an educational resource providing information regarding the 3 "R's" to professionals in the recycling industry and the public through a combination of programs, advocacy activities andtechnical assitance the MRN promotes the sustainable reduction, reuse and recycling in Maryland.
Peter Houstle, Executive Director
Brian Ryerson, President

1018 Multiple Chemical Sensitivity Referral and Resources
MD 410-889-6666
adonnay@mcsrr.org
www.mcsrr.org
A non-profit organization engaged in professional outreach, patient support and public advocacy devoted to the diagnosis, treatment, accommodation and prevention of Multiple Chemical Sensitivity disorders.
Albert Donnay MHS, Co-Founder/Exe. Director

1019 Rachel Carson Council
8600 Irvington Avenue 301-214-2400
Bethesda, MD 20817 office@rachelcarsoncouncil.org
rachelcarsoncouncil.org
An association seeking to inform and advise the public about the effects of pesticides that threaten the health, welfare, and survival of living organisms and biological systems. Special attention is given to the areas of globalclimate change, renewable energy, toxic chemicals and sustainable food.
Founded: 1965
Roger Christie, Chairman
Robert K. Musil, Ph.D., President & CEO

1020 Sierra Club: Maryland Chapter
7338 Baltimore Avenue 301-277-7111
#102 *Fax:* 301-277-6699
College Park, MD 20740 josh.tulkin@sierraclub.org
maryland.sierraclub.org
To advance the preservation and protection of the natural environment by empowering the citizenry with charitable resources to further the cause of environmental protection.
Founded: 1865
Baird Straughan, Chair
Josh Tulkin, State Director

1021 The Nature Conservancy: Maryland/DC Chapter
425 Barlow Plae 301-897-8570
Suite 100 800-628-6860
Bethesda, MD 20814 *Fax:* 301-897-0858
www.nature.org/maryland
The Maryland/DC Chapter of The Nature Conservancy uses advocacy and on the ground conservation work to protect the region's natural resources. Primarily focused on clean water and climate resilience, the Maryland/DC Chapter manages75,000 acres of private and public lands, including 13 nature preserves.
Mark Bryer, Acting Executive Director
Severn Smith, Director, Comm. & Marketing

1022 The Wildlife Society: Maryland - Delaware Chapter
MD 20814 301-897-9770
Fax: 301-530-2471
mddechapter@gmail.com
www.mddechapter.wixsite.com/mdde
The Maryland-Delaware Chapter is a local membership organization of The Wildlife Society, the Chapter is dedicated to the promotion and development of sound stewardship of wildlife resources and the surrounding environment.
Founded: 1977 80 Members
Jennifer Murrow, President
Trevor Michaels, Vice President

1023 White Lung Association
MD www.whitelung.org
A nonprofit organization dedicated to the education of the public to the hazards of asbestos exposure. Has developed programs of public education and consults with victims of asbestos exposure, school boards, building owners,government agencies and others interested in identifying asbestos hazards and developing control programs.

Michigan

1024 American Fisheries Society: North Central Division: Michigan Chapter
MI keiperw@michigan.gov
The Michigan Chapter of the American Fisheries Society, is part of the American Fisheries Society (AFS) North Central Division, it is a professional organization comprised of around 400 members from different fishery backgrounds.Working to further to the goals of the AFS through research, education, and professional development, the Chapter's primary focus is to provide a forum for the discussion of fishery issues and raise awareness regarding aquatic resources in Michigan.
Founded: 1973 $10/ Year
Justin Chiotti, President
William Keiper, Secretary & Treasurer

1025 American Fisheries Society: Physiology Section
Biology Dept., Nothern Michigan University
1401 Presque Isle Avenue jileonar@nmu.edu
Marquette, MI 49855 mfs.fisheries.org
Dedicated to improving communication between researchers and professionals involved in the science of fish physiology. Publishes a newsletter and holds workshops and symposia.
Chris Myrick, President
Jill B.K. Leonard, Secretary-Treasurer

1026 American Lung Association of Michigan
1475 E 12 Mile Road 248-784-2000
Madison Heights, MI 48071 midland@lung.org
www.lung.org/about-us/local-associations/michigan.html
The American Lung Association of Michigan works to prevent lung disease and promote lung health through direct assistance, education programs, advocacy and research.
Patricia J. Volz, VP, Communication
Barry Gottschalk, Executive VP, Midland States

1027 American Lung Association of Michigan: Flint
PO Box 966
Grand Blanc, MI 48480 800-586-4872
www.lung.org/about-us/local-associations/michigan.html
Barry Gottschalk, Executive VP, Midlant States
Patricia J. Volz, VP, Communication

1028 American Society of Landscape Architects: Michigan Chapter
1000 W St Joseph Highway 517-485-4116
Suite 200 *Fax:* 517-485-9408
Lansing, MI 48915 manager@michiganasla.org
www.michiganasla.org
The Michigan Chapter of the American Society of Landscape Architects (MiASLA), is a nonprofit association representing the landscape architecture profession throughout the state of Michigan. Through advocacy, education, communicationand fellowship, the MiASLA promotes and advances the profession of landscape architecture.
330 Members
Ben Baker, President
Dana Hernalsteen, VP, Membership

1029 B.A.S.S Nation: Michigan Chapter
MI 248-909-5750
webtech@michiganbass.net
www.michiganbassnation.com
Dedicated to the promotion of the sport of bass fishing. The Michigan BASS Nation is focused on building youth programs, fishing tournaments and conservation initiatives to preserve the states natural resources.
Founded: 1973 600 Members
Paul Rambo, President
Jason Hurst, Director, Membership

1030 Ecology Center
339 E Liberty Street 734-663-2400
Suite 300 info@ecocenter.org
Ann Arbor, MI 48104 www.ecocenter.org
Through education, the Ecology Center educates consumers, advocates for clean energy and provides services in the promotion of an environment, food and products that are safe and healthy.
Founded: 1970
Katy Adams, Education Director
Mike Garfield, Director

1031 Great Lakes Commission
Eisenhower Corporate Park
2805 S Industrial Highway 734-971-9135
Suite 100 *Fax:* 734-971-9150
Ann Arbor, MI 48104-6791 www.glc.org
A binational public agency dedicated to the use, management and protection of the water, land and other natural resources of the Great Lakes-St Lawrence system.
Founded: 1955
Jon W. Allan, Chair
John Linc Stine, Vice Chair

1032 Great Lakes Renewable Energy Association
MI 313-655-7945
info@glrea.org
www.glrea.org
The Great Lakes Renewable Energy Association (GLREA), is a nonprofit member association that represents individuals, organizations, and businesses that support the use and expansion of clean and renewable energy, such as wind and solarin Michigan. GLREA uses education, training and advocacy to promote the increased use of renewable energy.
Founded: 1991
Dave Konkle, President
Sarah Mulkoff, VP

1033 Michigan Association of Conservation Districts
3001 Coolidge Road 517-324-5274
Suite 250 *Fax:* 517-324-4435
East Lansing, MI 48823 lori.phalen@macd.org
www.macd.org
A nonprofit, non-governmental organization the Michigan Association of Conservation Districts (MACD) represents and provides services to Michigan's 78 Conservation Districts. Working at a state level with legislators, agencies andspecial interest groups, MACD advocates for the management and conservation of the states natural resources.
Lori Phalen, Executive Director
Angela Sandusky, Coordinator

1034 Michigan Forest Association
15851 S US 27 517-816-7879
Suite 16 info@michiganforests.org
Lansing, MI 48906-1987 www.michiganforests.org
The Michigan Forest Association (MFA) is a nonprofit organization that represents and educates Michigan forest owners and citizens about forest management and sustainability.
Founded: 1972
Debra Huff, Executive Director
Lisa Parker, Associate Director

1035 Michigan United Conservation Clubs
2101 Wood Street 517-371-1041
Lansing, MI 48912 muccpolicy@mucc.org
www.mucc.org
The largest statewide conservation organization in the United States, Michigan United Conservation Clubs, is a nonprofit working to conserve Michigan's natural resources and outdoor heritage. Through its membership of over 40,000hunters, anglers, conservationists and 200 local clubs, Michigan United Conservation Clubs uses advocacy, education and on the ground work to conserve, protect, and enhance Michigan's natural resources.
Founded: 1937
Ron Burris, President
Dan Eichinger, Executive Director

1036 Midwest Association of Fish & Wildlife Agencies
PO Box 30028 517-284-6367
Lansing, MI 48909 www.mafwa.org
The Midwest Association of Fish & Wildlife Agencies (MAFWA) is an organization made up of 13 state and 3 Midwest fish and wildlife agencies. MAFWA works to provide a forum for the exchange of information and ideas and initiate actionto protect and conserve fish and wildlife resources of the Midwest.
Founded: 1934
Jim Douglas, President
Terry Steinwand, First VP

1037 National Wildlife Federation: Great Lakes Regional Center
213 W Liberty 734-769-3351
Suite 200 greatlakes@nwf.org
Ann Arbor, MI 48104 www.nwf.org/greatlakes
The Great Lakes Regional Center of the National Wildlife Federation works to protect and restore the Great Lakes for the people and wildlife dependant upon them.
Founded: 1982
Anna Brunner, Communications Coordinator
Mike Shriberg, Regional Executive Director

1038 Scenic Michigan
445 E Mitchell Street 231-347-4929
Petoskey, MI 49770 *Fax:* 231-347-1185
info@scenicmichigan.org
www.scenicmichigan.org
The state affiliate of Scenic America, Scenic Michigan works to preserve and enhance the aesthetic amenities of the state. Primarily a grassroots organization, Scenic Michigan uses education, legislature and lobbying to improvecommunity appearance.
Founded: 1996
Abby Dart, Executive Director
Jim Lagowski, President

1039 Sierra Club: Michigan Chapter
109 E Grand River Avenue 517-484-2372
Lansing, MI 48906-4348 Contact.Us@michigan.sierraclub.org
www.michigan.sierraclub.org
With 10 regional volunteer groups and conservation committees, the Michigan Chapter of the Sierra Club is dedicated to the promotion of better environmental stewardship in the state. The Michigan Chapter is focused on the longevity ofnatural resources and works to preserve and enhance the quality of water and air in Michigan communities and promotes the use of renewable energy sources.
Founded: 1967 150,000 Members
Cecilla J. Garcia, Administrative Assitant
Gail Philbin, State Director

1040 The Nature Conservancy: Michigan Chapter
101 East Grand River Avenue 517-316-0300
Lansing, MI 48906 *Fax:* 517-316-9886
michigan@tnc.org
www.nature.org/michigan
The Michigan Chapter of the Nature Conservancy is dedicated to protecting the land and water, including the Great Lakes, of the state. Through the development of broad and innovative strategies that can be applied to large naturalenvironment systems, the Michigan Chapter has been able to put these strategies into effect throughout the 20 nature preserves the chapter manages.
Founded: 1952
Danielle Basgall, Conservation Coordinator
Sharon Mascola, Office Manager

1041 The Wildlife Society: Michigan Chapter
MI www.michigantws.wixsite.com/mitws
The state chapter of The Wildlife Society, it works to promote the sound stewardship of Michigan's wildlife and environmental resources and increase the appreciation of wildlife.
Founded: 1982
Lori Sargent, Secretary & Treasurer
Sonja Christensen, President

1042 Wildflower Association of Michigan
Lansing, MI www.wildflowersmich.org
The Wildflower Association of Michigan (WAM) is a nonprofit, membership based organization that encourages the preservation and restoration of Michigan's native plants through advocacy and the education of Michigan's citizens.
Founded: 1986
Chad Hughson, President
Trish Hacker-Hennig, 1st Vice President

Minnesota

1043 American Fisheries Society: North Central Division: Minnesota Chapter
MN pgafs2012@gmail.com
The Minnesota Chapter of the American Fisheries Society (MNAFS), is part of the American Fisheries Society (AFS) North Central Division. Working to further to the goals of the AFS through research, education, and professionaldevelopment, the chapter is committed to the conservation, development, and wise use of fishery resources, and protection and sustainability of aquatic ecosystems.
Founded: 1967 $10/ Year
Paul Glander, President
Calub Shavlik, Secretary & Treasurer

1044 American Lung Association in Minnesota
490 Concordia Avenue 651-227-8014
Saint Paul, MN 55103 info@lungmn.org
www.lung.org/about-us/local-associations/minnesota.html
The American Lung Association of Minnesota works to prevent lung disease and promote lung health. Through education, advocacy,and campaigns, such as Teens Against Tobacco Use (TATU); the Association offers a wide variety of lung healthservices to the people Minnesota.
Lewis Bartfield, Executive VP, Upper Midwest
Greg Voss, Executive Dir. Minnesota

1045 American Lung Association of Minnesota: Duluth
424 W Superior Street 218-726-4721
Suite 202 info@lungmn.org
Duluth, MN 55802 www.lung.org/about-us/local-associations/minnesota.html
Lewis Bartfield, Executive VP, Upper Midwest
Greg Voss, Executive Dir. Minnesota

1046 American Society of Landscape Architects: Minnesota Chapter
International Market Square
275 Market Street 612-339-0797
Suite 54 *Fax:* 612-338-7981
Minneapolis, MN 55405-1627 info@asla-mn.org
www.asla-mn.org
The Minnesota Chapter of the American Society of Landscape Architects (ASLA-MN) represents over 300 landscape architects and affiliates across the state, who are dedicated to the promotion of the landscape profession through advocacy,education and communication.
David Motzenbecker, President
Nicole Peterson, Director, Communications

1047 B.A.S.S Nation: Minnesota Chapter
MN 55349 218-390-9973
www.mnbfn.org
Minnesota BASS Nation works to stimulate public awareness of bass fishing as a major sport and encourages sportsmanship, courtesy and boating safety at all levels. Minnesota BASS Nation promotes the full adherence to all conservationcodes, adequate water quality standards and legal enforcement of existing regulatory standards.
Peter Perovich, President
Mark Gomez, VP

1048 Minnesota Association of Soil and Water Conservation Districts
Soil and Water Conservation Districts
255 Kellogg Boulevard East 651-690-9028
Suite 101 *Fax:* 651-690-9065
St. Paul, MN 55101 www.maswcd.org
The Minnesota Association of Soil and Water Conservation Districts (MASWCD) is a nonprofit organization representing Minnesota soil and water conservation districts. MASWCD is committed to maintaining a positive, results-oriented relationship with rule making agencies, partners and legislators; expanding education opportunities for the districts so they may carry out effective conservation programs.
Founded: 1952
LeAnn Buck, Executive Director
Sheila Vanney, Assitant Director

1049 Minnesota Conservation Federation
542 Snelling Avenue 651-690-3077
#104 info@mncf.org
Saint Paul, MN 55116 www.mncf.org
The Minnesota Conservation Federation (MCF) is an organization of dedicated hunters, anglers and other environmentally conscious individuals, working to educate and promote the enjoyment of, and ethical use of Minnesota's naturalresources. The MCF is an affiliate of the National Wildlife Federation.
Joe Hoffmann, President
Gary Botzek, Executive Director

1050 Minnesota Ground Water Association
4779 126th Street N office@mgwa.org
White Bear Lake, MN 55110 www.mgwa.org
The Minnesota Ground Water Association (MGWA) is a nonprofit, volunteer organization dedicated to the promotion and encouragement of scientific and public policy regarding ground water. MGWA provides a forum for ground waterprofessionals and educates the public about ground water.
Founded: 1982
Ellen Considine, President
Andrew Retzler, Secretary

1051 Minnesota Renewable Energy Society
2928 5th Avenue South 612-308-4757
Minneapolis, MN 55408 info@mnRenewables.org
www.mnrenewables.org
A nonprofit, member-run organization the Minnesota Renewable Energy Society (MRES) promotes, advocates and encourages the use of renewable energy in Minnesota.
Founded: 1978
Kitty (Kitrina) Stratton, Director
Mark Weber, Director

1052 Parks and Trails Council of Minnesota
275 E 4th Street 651-726-2457
Suite 250 800-944-0707
St. Paul, MN 55101-1626 *Fax:* 651-726-2458
info@parksandtrails.org
www.parksandtrails.org
Parks and Trails Council of Minnesota seeks to aquire, protect andsustain long-term statewide land.
Founded: 1954
Julie Gugin, President
Bob Biersheid, Vice President

1053 Raptor Center
University Of Minnesota
College of Veterinary Medicine 612-624-4745
1920 Fitch Avenue *Fax:* 612-624-8740
St.Paul, MN 55108 raptor@umn.edu
www.raptor.cvm.umn.edu
Specializes in the medical care, rehabilitation, and conservation of eagles, hawks, owls and falcons. In addition to treating approxminately 800 birds a year, the internationally known pro-

gram reaches more than 240,000 people each yearthrough public education programs and events, provides training in avian medicine and surgery for veterinarians from around the world, and identifies emerging issues related to raptor health and populations.
Founded: 1974
Dr Julia Ponder, Executive Director
Lori Arent, Clinic Manager

1054 **Sierra Club: North Star Chapter**
2327 East Franklin Avenue 612-659-9124
Suite 1 *Fax:* 612-659-9129
Minneapolis, MN 55406-1024 north.star.chapter@sierraclub.org
www.sierraclub.org/minnesota
In conjunction with the national mission of the Sierra Club, the North Star Chapter is the leading volunteer organizations working to protect and preserve Minnesota's environment.
Margaret Levin, State Director
Alexis Boxer, Associate Organizing Rep.

1055 **The Nature Conservancy: Minnesota Chapter**
1101 West River Parkway 612-331-0750
Suite 200 *Fax:* 612-331-0770
Minneapolis, MN 55415-1291 minnesota@tnc.org
www.nature.org/minnesota
The Minnesota Chapter of The Nature Conservancy uses science to implement effective environmental strategies in order to protect and conserve the over 50 nature preserves in the state.
Founded: 1958
Wendy Bennet, Chair
Jack Dempsey, Vice Chair

1056 **The Nature Conservancy: Minnesota Chapter: Central Minnesota**
7163 Bear Road 218-575-3032
Cushing, MN 56443-1291 *Fax:* 218-212-1320
minnesota@tnc.org
www.nature.org/minnesota
Wendy Bennet, Chair
Jack Dempsey, Vice Chair

1057 **The Nature Conservancy: Minnesota Chapter: Mississippi River**
PO Box 422 612-867-3140
Brainerd, MN 56401-1291 minnesota@tnc.org
www.nature.org/minnesota
Wendy Bennet, Chair
Jack Dempsey, Vice Chair

1058 **The Nature Conservancy: Minnesota Chapter: Northeast Minnesota**
394 Lake Avenue S 218-727-6119
Suite 308 *Fax:* 218-727-0882
Duluth, MN 55802-1291 minnesota@tnc.org
www.nature.org/minnesota
Wendy Bennet, Chair
Jack Dempsey, Vice Chair

1059 **The Nature Conservancy: Minnesota Chapter: Tallgrass Aspen Parkland**
202 N Main Street 218-436-3455
PO Box 139 *Fax:* 218-436-3454
Karlstad, MN 56732 minnesota@tnc.org
www.nature.org/minnesota
Wendy Bennet, Chair
Jack Dempsey, Vice Chair

1060 **The Nature Conservancy: Minnesota Chapter:Northern Tallgrass Prairie Ecoregion**
15337 28th Avenue S 218-498-2679
Glyndon, MN 56547-9561 *Fax:* 218-498-2325
minnesota@tnc.org
www.nature.org/minnesota
Wendy Bennet, Chair
Jack Dempsey, Vice Chair

Mississippi

1061 **American Lung Association of Mississippi**
438 Kathrine Drive
Suite C 601-206-5810
Flowood, MS 39232 alams@lungse.org
www.lung.org/about-us/local-associations/mississippi.html
The American Lung Association of Mississippi works to prevent lung disease and promote lung health through direct assistance, education programs, advocacy and research.
Martha C. Bogdan, Executive VP, Southeast
Willie L. Bythwood, Jr, CFO

1062 **American Lung Association of Mississippi: Bay St. Louis**
7060 Stennis Airport Road 228-282-2622
Kiln, MS 39556 alams@lungse.org
www.lung.org/about-us/local-associations/mississippi.html
Martha C. Bogdan, Executive VP, Southeast
Willie L. Bythwood, Jr, CFO

1063 **American Lung Association of Mississippi: Biloxi**
1141 Bayview Avenue 228-282-2622
Biloxi, MS 39530 alams@lungse.org
www.lung.org/about-us/local-associations/mississippi.html
Martha C. Bogdan, Executive VP, Southeast
Willie L. Bythwood, Jr, CFO

1064 **American Lung Association of Mississippi: Pascagoula**
4502 Lt. Eugene J Manure Drive 678-478-0314
Pascagoula, MS 39581 alams@lungse.org
www.lung.org/about-us/local-associations/mississippi.html
Martha C. Bogdan, Executive VP, Southeast
Willie L. Bythwood, Jr, CFO

1065 **American Society of Landscape Architects: Mississippi Chapter**
MS ahoops601@gmail.com
www.msasla.wordpress.com
The Mississippi Chapter of the American Society of Landscape Architects, is a nonprofit association representing the landscape architecture profession throughout the state of Mississippi.
Jim Jackson, President
Alan Hoops, Advocacy Chair

1066 **Mississippi Flyway**
MI
The Mississippi Flyway Council works to coordinate the management of migratory game birds and their resources to ensure longevity. The Council is composed of representatives from Alabama, Arkansas, Indiana, Illinois, Iowa, Kentucky,Louisiana, Michigan, Minnesota, Mississippi, Missouri, Ohio, Tennessee, and Wisconsin,and the Canadian provinces of Saskatchewan, Manitoba and Ontario.
Founded: 1952
Ed Penny, Mississippi Representative

1067 **Mississippi Wildlife Federation**
517 Cobblestone Court 601-605-1790
Suite 2 *Fax:* 601-605-1794
Madison, MS 39110-7570 www.mswildlife.org
The Mississippi Wildlife Federation works to advance the protection of wildlife in Mississippi, the conservation of natural resources and the environmental quality of hunting, fishing and outdoor recreation.
Founded: 1946
Brad Young, Executive Director
Melanie Starnes, Office Manager

1068 **Sierra Club: Mississippi Chapter**
921 North Congress Street 601-624-3503
Jackson, MS 39202 louie.miller@sierraclub.org
mississippi.sierraclub.org
The Mississippi Chapter of the Sierra Club is comprised of three regional groups. The Chapter works in coordination with the mis-

sion of the National Sierra Club to protect and conserve the natural resources of Mississippi.
Louie Miller, State Director

1069 The Crosby Arboretum
P.O. Box 1639 — 601-799-2311
Picayune, MS 39466 — *Fax:* 601-799-2372
drackett@ext.msstate.edu
www.crosbyarboretum.msstate.edu
Owned by Mississippi State University and operated the MSU Extension Service, The Crosby Arboretum is dedicated to education the public about the environment they live in. The Arboretum preserves, protects and displays plants native tothe Pearl River Drainage Basin ecosystem of Mississippi and Louisiana, providing research opportunities and offering cultural, scientific and recreational programs.
Founded: 1986
Patricia Drackett, Director
Kimberly Johnson, Customer Service

Missouri

1070 American Fisheries Society: North Central Division: Missouri Chapter
MO — gregndonna8286@gmail.com
www.moafs.org
The Missouri Chapter of the American Fisheries Society (MOAFS), is part of the AFS' North Central Division. MOAFS works to further to the goals of the AFS and is committed to the conservation, development, and wise use of fisheryresources and the distribution and exchange of information pertaining to aquatic sciences.
Greg Pitchford, President
Alex Prentice, Treasurer

1071 American Lung Association of Missouri
7745 Carondelet Avenue — 314-645-5505
Suite 305 — missouri@lung.org
Clayton, MO 63105-3196 — www.lung.org/about-us/local-associations/missouri.html
The American Lung Association of Missouri works to prevent lung disease and promote lung health through direct assistance, education programs, advocacy and research.
Angela Wiseman, Executive Director, Missouri
Lewis Bartfield, Executive VP, Upper Midwest

1072 American Society of Landscape Architects: Prairie Gateway Chapter
Center for Architecture & Design:c/O PGASLA
1801 McGee Street — 816-421-1054
Suite 100 — president@pgasla.org
Kansas City, MO 64108 — www.pgasla.org
The Prairie Gateway Chapter of The American Society of Landscape Architects (PGASLA) represents those in the landscape architecture profession throughout Kansas and Western Missouri. The PGASLA is dedicated to the promotion of thelandscape architecture profession through advocacy, education and communication with its members working to enhance natural and built environments.
Christopher Cline, President
Chad Weinand, VP, Communications

1073 American Society of Landscape Architects: St. Louis Chapter
St. Louis, MO 63105 — 314-206-4313
exdir@stlouisasla.org
www.stlouisasla.org
The St. Louis Chapter of the American Society of Landscape Architects represents the eastern half of Missouri. Through advocacy, education and communication the chapter is dedicated to the promotion of the landscape architectureprofession in the St. Louis region.
Cory Murner, President
Chris Sanders, VP, Membership

1074 Audubon Society of Missouri
2101 W Broadway — webmaster@mobirds.org
PO Box 122 — www.mobirds.org
Columbia, MO 65203-1261
The Audubon Society of Missouri is dedicated to the preservation and protection of birds and other wildlife; to education and appreciation of the natural world; and to effective wildlife and habitat conservation practices.
Founded: 1990
Mark Haas, President
Bill Eddelman, VP

1075 Missouri Forest Products Association
505 East State Street — 573-634-3252
Jefferson City, MO 65101 — laura@moforest.org
www.moforest.org
The Missouri Forest Products Association (MFA) serves and promotes the forest products industry in the state, advocating for the sustainable management of Missouri's forests. The MFA represents the primary and secondary wood industry,suppliers and service industries, loggers, and landowners.
Founded: 1970 300 Members
Brian Brookshire, Executive Director
Laura Brookshire, Communications Manager

1076 Missouri Prairie Foundation
PO Box 200 — 888-843-6739
Columbia, MO 65205 — info@moprairie.com
www.moprairie.org
A nonprofit organization dedicated to the permanent protection of prairie habitat. The Missouri Prairie Foundation works with public and private partners to protect and restore prairie and native grassland communities through landacquisition, management, education and research.
Founded: 1966
Carol Davit, Executive Director
Dorris Sherrick, President

1077 Missouri Public Interest Research Group
10 S Euclid Ave — 314-454-1713
Suite H — info@mopirg.org
Saint Louis, MO 63108 — www.mopirg.org
The Missouri Public Interest Research Group (MoPIRG) is a statewide, nonprofit, public interest advocacy organization that uses investigative research, media exposes, grassroots organization and litigation to inform, represent andeducate the public. MoPIRG focuses primarily on environmental, health, safety, financial and consumer protection.
Founded: 1972
Kathryn Lee, Digital Campaigner
Ed Mierzwinski, Consumer Program Director

1078 Missouri Stream Team
2901 W Truman Boluevard — 800-781-1989
Jefferson City, MO 65109 — streamteam@mdc.mo.gov
www.mostreamteam.org
Part of the Missouri Department of Conservation, the Missouri Stream Team endeavours to conserve the 110,000 miles of Missouri's streams through education, stewardship and advocacy. By partnering with citizens, the Stream Team is ableto execute campaigns and on the ground action work to protect Missouri's streams and watersheds.
Founded: 1989
Chris Riggert, Stream Team, Coordinator
Sherry Fischer, Streams & Watershed Chief

1079 Scenic Missouri
607 Dougherty Terrace Drive — info@scenicmo.org
Ballwin, MO 63021 — scenicmo.org
Scenic Missouri is a statewide, nonprofit dedicated to protecting, preserving and enhancing the scenic character of the state. Scenic Missouri provides education and technical services to communities throughout the state to assist inaesthetic issues.
John Hock, President
Karl Kruse, Director, Emeritus

1080 Sierra Club: Missouri Chapter
2818 Sutton Boulevard 314-644-1011
St. Louis, MO 63143 800-628-5333
missouri.chapter@sierraclub.org
missouri.sierraclub.org
To advance the preservation and protection of the natural environment by empowering the citizenry with charitable resources to further the cause of environmental protection.
Jim Turner, Chair
Carolyn Amparan, Vice Chair

1081 Society for Environmental Geochemistry and Health
MO 573-341-4831
Fax: 303-556-4822
seghwebmaster@gmail.com
www.segh.net
The Society for Environmental Geochemistry and Health (SEGH) provides a forum for scientists from various disciplines, to work together in order to understand the interaction between the geochemical environment and the health ofplants, animals, and humans.
Founded: 1971
Chaosheng Zhang, President
Anthea Brown, Treasurer

Montana

1082 Alternative Energy Resources Organization (AERO)
PO Box 1558 406-443-7272
Helena, MT 59621 aero@aeromt.org
aeromt.org
A nonprofit organization dedicated to promoting sustainable living in Montana by nuturing individuals and communities through programs that support sustainable agriculture, renewable energy and access to healthy food.
Founded: 1974
Jenn Battles, Executive Director
Jackie Heinert, Coordinator, Food Systems

1083 American Lung Association of Montana
936 S 2nd Street West 406-214-5700
Missoula, MT 59801 ronni.flannery@lung.org
www.lung.org/about-us/local-associations/montana.html
The American Lung Association of Montana works to prevent lung disease and promote lung health through direct assistance, education programs, advocacy and research.
Allison Hickey, Exec. VP, Mountain Pacific
Tony Peterson, CFO

1084 Chemical Injury Information Network
PO Box 301 406-547-2255
White Sulphur Springs, MT 59645 *Fax:* 406-547-2455
chemicalinjury@ciin.org
www.ciin.org
A nonprofit support and advocacy organization, the Chemical Injury Information Network (CIIN) deals with Multiple Chemical Sensitivities (MCS). CIIN is run by the chemically injured for the benefit of the chemically injured andprimarily focuses on education, research and support of the chemically injured.
Founded: 1990

1085 Craighead Institute
201 S Wallace Avenue 405-585-8705
Suite B2D info@craigheadresearch.org
Bozeman, MT 59715 craigheadresearch.org
The Craighead Institute, formerly Craighead Environmental Research Institute, is an applied science and research organization dedicated to the designing and managing research projects to help conserve the Northern Rockies.
Founded: 1964
Frank Lance Craighead, PhD, Executive Director
Brent Brock, Research Associate

1086 Foundation for Research on Economics & the Environment (FREE)
PO Box 555 406-585-1776
Gallatin Gateway, MT 59730 www.free-eco.org
FREE mission is to advance conservation and environmental values consistent with individuals freedom and responsibility. The Foundation's intellectual entrepreneurs develop environmental policies featuring private property rights,market incentives, and voluntary organizations. FREE achieves its mission by working with leaders in universities, businesses, environmental groups, government, the media, and think tanks.
John A. Baden, Chairman
John A. Von Kannon, VP

1087 Greater Yellowstone Coalition
215 South Wallace Avenue 406-586-1593
Bozeman, MT 59715 800-775-1834
Fax: 406-556-2839
gyc@greateryellowstone.org
www.greateryellowstone.org
The Greater Yellowstone Coalition works to permanently protect the 4.5 million acres in the Greater Yellowstone Ecosystem. With offices in Montana, Wyoming and Idaho, the Greater Yellowstone Coalition engages in local, regional andnational efforts to protect the land, water, and wildlife found within the Greater Yellowstone Ecosystem.
Founded: 1983
Caroline Byrd, Executive Director
Scott Christensen, Director, Conservation

1088 Montana Association of Conservation Districts
1101 11th Avenue 406-443-5711
Helena, MT 59601 *Fax:* 406-443-0174
mail@macdnet.org
www.macdnet.org
The Montana Association of Conservation Districts represents the 58 conservation districts of the state. The Association works to protect the natural resources of the state, conserve soil and improve the water quality of Montana. TheMontana Association of Conservation Districts works with the National Association of Conservation Districts to advocate legislature on a federal and congressional level.
Founded: 1942
Elena Evansm, Executive Director
Jeff Tiberi, Director, Policy

1089 Montana Audubon
P.O. Box 595 406-443-3949
Helena, MT 59624 *Fax:* 406-443-7144
info@mtaudubon.org
www.mtaudubon.org
Founded in 1976, Montana Audubon is an independent, statewide conservation organization whose mission is to promote appreciation, knowledge, and conservation of Montana's native birds, other wildlife, and natural ecosystems, and tosafeguard biological diversity for current and future generations. They seek to create an environment in which all of Montana's native bird species have healthy, sustainable populations ensured by long-term habitat security.
Founded: 1976
Larry Berrin, Executive Director
Norane Freistadt, Development Director

1090 Montana Environmental Information Center
P.O. Box 1184 406-443-2520
Helena, MT 59624 *Fax:* 406-443-2507
meic@meic.org
www.meic.org
The Montana Environmental Information Center (MEIC) is a nonprofit, environmental advocacy organization dedicated to protection and restoration of Montana's natural environment. MEIC works to monitor and contribute to the environmental decisions and activities of the government on a state, local and federal level, educate individuals and assist individuals and other nonprofit organizations in the conservation of Montana's natural environment.
Founded: 1973 5,000 Members
James Jensen, Executive Director

1091 **Montana Land Reliance**
324 Fuller Avenue 406-443-7027
PO Box 355 *Fax:* 406-443-7061
Helena, MT 59624-0355 info@mtlandreliance.org
www.mtlandreliance.org
Working with private landowners, the Montana Land Reliance (MLR) is dedicated to the permanent protection of Montana's agricultural lands, fish, wildlife and open space. The MLR has conserved over 958, 000 acres of land in over 820voluntary easement agreements across the state.
Founded: 1978
Rock Ringling, Managing Director
Lois Delger-DeMars, Managing Director

1092 **Montana Wildlife Federation**
PO Box 1175 406-458-0227
Helena, MT 59601 800-517-7256
Fax: 406-458-0373
mwf@mtwf.org
www.montanawildlife.com
The Montana Wildlife Federation (MWF), is the oldest and largest conservation organization in the state. Comprised of state and national members, including 15 local affiliate clubs, the MWF is committed to the conservation of Montana'swild rivers, natural lands, fish, wildlife and public access outdoor recreation land.
Founded: 1936
Dave Chadwick, Executive Director
Nick Gevock, Director, Conservation

1093 **Rocky Mountain Elk Foundation**
5705 Grant Creek 406-523-4500
PO Box 8249 800-225-5355
Missoula, MT 59808 www.rmef.org
Committed to conserving, restoring and enhancing natural habitats; promoting the sound management of wild, free-ranging elk, which may be hunted or otherwise enjoyed; fostering cooperation among federal, state, tribal and privateorganizations and individuals in wildlife management and habitat conservation; and educating members and the public about habitat conservation, the value of hunting, hunting ethics and wildlife management.
Founded: 1984
M David Allen, President & CEO
Rod Triepke, COO

1094 **Sierra Club: Montana Chapter**
PO Box 7201 406-549-1142
Missoula, MT 59807 sierraclubmt@gmail.com
montana.sierraclub.org
The Montana Chapter of the Sierra Club is made up of 4 local groups in Missoula, Bozeman, Helena and Billings. The Chapter works in conjunction with the Sierra Club's national efforts and is committed to addressing the environmentalissues of the state.
Jonathan Matthews, Chair
David Merrill, Senior Organizing

1095 **The Wildlife Society: Montana Chapter**
MT mttws.secretary@gmail.com
www.wildlife.org/montana-chapter
The Montana Chapter of The Wildlife Society works to serve and represent wildlife life professionals in all areas of wildlife conservation and management in the state of Montana.
Founded: 1962
Kelvin Johnson, President
Dan Bachen, Secretary

Nebraska

1096 **American Fisheries Society: North Central Division: Nebraska Chapter**
NE mike.archer@Nebraska.gov
The Nebraska Chapter of the American Fisheries Society, is part of the American Fisheries Society (AFS) North Central Division, it is a professional organization with its members coming from diverse fishery backgrounds. Working tofurther to the goals of the AFS through research, education, and professional development, the chapter is committed to the conservation, development, and wise use of fishery resources, and protection and sustainability of aquatic ecosystems.
Founded: 1970 $10/ Year
Mike Archerr, President
Dave Adams, Secretary & Treasurer

1097 **American Lung Association of Nebraska**
8990 West Dodge
Suite 226 402-502-4950
Omaha, NE 68114 info@lungnb.org
www.lung.org/about-us/local-associations/nebraska.html
The American Lung Association of Nebraska works to prevent lung disease and promote lung health through direct assistance, education programs, advocacy and research.
Julia McCarville, Executive Director, Nebraska
Lewis Bartfield, Executive VP, Upper Midwest

1098 **American Society of Landscape Architects: Great Plains Chapter**
NE Regan.Pence@LRA-INC.com
www.gpcasla.org
Representing Nebraska, North Dakota and South Dakota, the Great Plains Chapter of the American Landscape Society works to expand the profession of landscape architecture in these states. The Chapter advocates and provides professionaleducational and developmental programs for its members
Regan Pence, President
Chad Kucker, Secretary & Treasurer

1099 **B.A.S.S Nation: Nebraska Chapter**
NE 402-563-2297
jlcitta@nppd.com
www.nebraskabass.com
Dedicated to the promotion of the sport of bass fishing. The Nebraska Chapter of BASS Nation also known as Nebraska BASS federation, is focused on building youth programs, fishing tournaments and conservation initiatives to preservethe states natural resources.
Joe Citta Jr., President
Dave Knuth, Vice President

1100 **Nebraska Association of Resource Districts**
601 S 12th Street 402-471-7670
Suite 201 *Fax:* 402-471-7677
Lincoln, NE 68508 nard@nrdnet.org
www.nrdnet.org
The Nebraska Association of Resources Districts (NARD) is the trade association representing Nebraska's 23 Natural Resource Districts. NARD works to assist in the coordination of Nebraska's Natural Resource Districts, in order toprovide a collective voice for state and federal policies and to further enhance conservation and improvement efforts in the state.
Dean E. Edson, Executive Director
Jeanne Dryburgh, Office Manager

1101 **Nebraska Wildlife Federation**
PO Box 81437 402-477-1008
Lincoln, NE 68501 Info@NebraskaWildlife.org
www.nebraskawildlife.org
A statewide, nonprofit membership organization dedicated wildlife and wild places through environmental education, fish and wild life conservation, and public policy. The Nebraska Wildlife Federation is the state affiliate of TheNational Wildlife Federation.
J.J. Johnson, President
Duane Hovorka, Executive Director

1102 **Sierra Club: Nebraska Chapter**
PO Box 4664 www.sierraclub.org/nebraska
Omaha, NE 68104-664
The Nebraska Chapter of the Sierra Club is made up of the MoValley Group and Bluestem Group and is working in the state to fulfill the goals of the National Sierra Club.
3,000 Members
Candy Bless, Chapter Chair
David Corbin, Chapter Vice Chair

1103 **The Nature Conservancy: Nebraska Chapter**
1007 Leavenworth Street 402-342-0282
Omaha, NE 68102 *Fax:* 402-342-0474
nebraska@tnc.org
www.nature.org/nebraska
The Nebraska Chapter of The Nature Conservancy works to to preserve the plants, animals and natural communities of Nebraska by protecting the lands and waters needed to sustain these ecosystems.
Founded: 1915
Mace Hack, State Director
Katie Torpy Carroll, Operations Coordinator

1104 **The Nature Conservancy: Nebraska Chapter: Derr House**
13650 South Platte River Drive 308-583-2294
Wind River, NE 68883 *Fax:* 308-583-0102
nebraska@tnc.org
www.nature.org/nebraska
Nelson Winkle, Prserve Management Assistant
Mace Hack, State Director

1105 **The Nature Conservancy: Nebraska Chapter: Eastern Nebraska Project Office**
1228 L Street 402-694-4191
PO Box 438 *Fax:* 402-694-4191
Aurora, NE 68818 nebraska@tnc.org
www.nature.org/nebraska
Chris Helzer, Director, Science
Mardell Jasnowski, Operations Assistant

1106 **The Nature Conservancy: Nebraska Chapter: Niobrara Valley Preserve**
42269 Morel Road 402-722-4440
Johnstown, NE 69214 *Fax:* 402-722-4203
nebraska@tnc.org
www.nature.org/nebraska
Rich Walters, Jr., Director, Stewardship
Mace Hack, State Director

1107 **The Nature Conservancy: Nebraska Chapter: Platte River Project Office**
112 W 8th Street 308-784-5336
PO Box 144 *Fax:* 308-784-5326
Cozad, NE 69130 nebraska@tnc.org
www.nature.org/nebraska
Jacob Fritton, Irrigation Coordinator
Mace Hack, State Director

1108 **The Wildlife Society: Nebraska Chapter**
NE www.wildlife.org/nebraska
The Nebraska Chapter of the Wildlife Society (NE-TWS) is a professional organzation of biologists, educators, and administrators working in the field of wildlife management. NE-TWS is dedicated to the promotion of sound stewardship ofwildlife resource and habitats in Nebraska.
Founded: 1966
Matt Steffl, President
Melvin Nenneman, Secretary

Nevada

1109 **American Lung Association of Nevada**
3552 West Cheyenne Avenue 702-431-6333
Suite 130 nvinfo@lungs.org
Las Vegas, NV 89032-8920 www.lung.org/about-us/local-associations/nevada.html
The American Lung Association of Nevada works to prevent lung disease and promote lung health. Through direct assistance, advocacy and education programs, such as Addressing COPD in Nevada; the Association offers a wide variety of lunghealth services to the people Nevada.
Bill Pfeifer, Executive VP, Southwest
Kristina Crawford, Executive Director

1110 **American Society of Landscape Architects: Nevada Chapter**
PO Box 97986 info@nvasla.com
Las Vegas, NV 89193 www.nvasla.com
The Nevada Chapter of the American Society of Landscape Architects (NVASLA) is dedicated to the continuous education of its members and the public in the service of promoting sound stewardship of the environment.
Laura Miller, President
Nicole Hoffmann, Association Assitant

1111 **Nevada Wildlife Federation**
PO Box 71238 775-677-0927
Reno, NV 89570 *Fax:* 775-885-0405
nvwf@nvwf.org
www.nvwf.org
The Nevada Wildlife Federation (NvWF) is an all volunteer organization dedicated to sustaining Nevada's natural resources for the states wildlife. The NvWF is an affiliate of the National Wildlife Federation.
Robert Gaudet, President
Tammi Gaudet, Treasurer

1112 **Sierra Club: Toiyabe Chapter**
PO Box 8096 toiyabe.chapter@gmx.com
Reno, NV 89507 nevada.sierraclub.org
The Toiyabe Chapter of the Sierra Club is the largest grassroots conservation organization of the region. Made of the 4 local groups, the Great Basin Group, Range of Light Group, Southern Nevada Group and the Tahoe Area Group, theChapter is primarily focused on the conservation of water, public lands, and wilderness, the promotion of renewable energy and environmental legislation in Nevada.
David Von Seggern, Chapter Chair
David Gibson, Chapter Vice Chair

1113 **Solar NV**
817 S Main St *Fax:* 702-507-0093
Las Vegas, NV 89101 contact@solarnv.org
www.solarnv.org
Solar NV is a nonprofit, volunteer organization dedicated to the promotion, education and use of solar and renewable energy in Nevada. Solar NV is the Southern Nevada chapter of the American Solar Energy Society.
Founded: 2004 $24/Year

1114 **Sunrise Sustainable Resources Group**
PO Box 19074 775-348-7192
Reno, NV 89511 president@sunrisenevada.org
Empowers Nevadans to use resources responsibly through education, advocacy and community.
Founded: 1996
KC Mares, President
Roger Jacobson, VP

1115 **Tahoe Regional Planning Agency**
128 Market Street 775-588-4547
PO Box 5310 *Fax:* 775-588-4527
Stateline, NV 89449 trpa@trpa.org
www.trpa.org
Tahoe Regional Planning Agency (TRPA) was the first bi-state environmental planning agency in the United States. Leading through cooperative efforts TRPA is dedicated to the preservation, restoration and the enhancement of the uniquenatural and human environments in the Lake Tahoe Region.
Joanne Marchetta, Executive Director
John Hester, COO

New Hampshire

1116 **American Lung Association of New Hampshire**
Cove Workspace
36 Maplewood Avenue 603-369-3977
Portsmouth, NH 03801 info@lungne.org
www.lung.org/about-us/local-associations/new-hampshire.html

The American Lung Association of New Hampshire works to prevent lung disease and promote lung health; offering a wide variety of lung health services to the people of New Hampshire.
Jeff Seyler, Executive VP, Northeast
Adam Shuster, CFO

1117 B.A.S.S Nation: New Hampshire Chapter
235 Ridgeview Road 603-529-2642
Weare, NH 03281 www.nhbassfednation.com
Dedicated to the promotion of the sport of bass fishing.The New Hampshire Chapter of BASS Nation is focused on building youth programs, fishing tournaments and conservation initiatives to preserve the states natural resources.
John Foster, President
Brian Emerson, Secretary & Webmaster

1118 Breathe New Hampshire
145 Hollis Street 603-669-2411
Unit C 800-835-8647
Manchester, NH 03101 *Fax:* 603-645-6220
info@breathenh.org
www.breathenh.org
A nonprofit organization, Breather New Hampshire, is dedicated to the elimination of lung disease and the improvement in the quality of life for those living with lung disease in the state. Through educational programs, advocacy, andresearch, Breathe New Hampshire is focused on the issues related to lung health, including tobacco use, COPD, asthma, air quality and lung cancer.
Founded: 1916
Daniel Fortin, President/CEO
Allyssa Thompson, Director, Programs

1119 New Hampshire Association of Conservation Commissions
54 Portsmouth Street 603-224-7867
Concord, NH 03301 *Fax:* 603-228-0423
info@nhacc.org
www.nhacc.org
The New Hampshire Association of Conservation Commissions is a private, nonprofit association of 216 Conservation Commissions. Its purpose is to foster conservation and appropriate use of New Hampshire's natural resources by providingassistance to conservation commissions, facilitating communication and cooperation among commissions, and helping to create a climate in which commissions can be successful.
Founded: 1970
Rep. Michele Peckham, President
Barbara Richter, Executive Director

1120 New Hampshire Association of Conservation Districts
PO Box 2311 603-796-2615
Concord, NH 03302-2311 *Fax:* 603-796-2600
nhenvirothon@gmail.com
www.nhacd.net
The New Hampshire Association of Conservation Districts (NHACD) works collaboratively with county districts, federal, state and local nonprofit agencies to conserve, protect and promote the responsible use of New Hampshire's naturalresources. The NHACD, provides statewide coordination and representation for the Conservation Districts of New Hampshire.
Founded: 1946
Sue Kessler, NH Envirothon Coordinator
Lisa M. Morin, Soil Judging Coordinator

1121 New Hampshire Audubon
84 Silk Farm Road 603-224-9909
Concord, NH 03301 *Fax:* 603-226-0902
nha@nhaudubon.org
www.nhaudubon.org
A statewide, nonprofit membership organization dedicated to the conservation of wildlife and habitat throughout the New Hampshire. The New Hampshire Audubon (NHA) offers environmental education, convservation, land protection andenviornmental policy programs. The NHA is independent of the National Audubon Society.
Founded: 1914
Doug Bechtel, President
Shelby Bernier, Director, Education

1122 New Hampshire Lakes Association
14 Horseshoe Pond Lane 603-226-0299
Concord, NH 03301 *Fax:* 603-224-9442
info@nhlakes.org
www.nhlakes.org
The New Hampshire Lake Association (NH LAKES) is a member supported, nonprofit organization dedicated to the protection of the states 1,000 lakes.
Founded: 1992
Tom O'Brien, President
Erin Grichen, Membership Coordinator

1123 New Hampshire Wildlife Federation
54 Portsmouth Street 603-224-5953
Concord, NH 03301 ed@nhwf.org
www.nhwf.org
Through education, legislation, conservation, community organizations and affiliates, the New Hampshire Wildlife Federation promotes and protects hunting, fishing, trapping and the conservation and access to fish and wildlife habitats.The New Hampshire Wildlife Federation is an affiliate of the National Wildlife Federation.
Founded: 1933
James Morse, President
Ron Sowa, Executive Director

1124 Northeast Resource Recovery Association
2101 Dover Road 603-736-4401
Epsom, NH 03234 800-223-0150
Fax: 603-736-4402
info@nrra.net
www.nrra.net
The Northeast Resource Recovery Association is a pro-active nonprofit working with its membership to make their recycling programs strong, efficient, and financially successful by providing cooperative marketing, cooperativepurchasing, education and networking opportunities; developing innovative recycling programs; creating sustainable alternatives to reduce the volume and toxicity of the waste, and educating and informing local officials about recycling and solidwaste issues.
Founded: 1981
Duncan P. Watson, President
John Hurd, Vice President

1125 The Nature Conservancy: New Hampshire Chapter
22 Bridge Street 603-224-5853
4th Floor *Fax:* 603-228-2459
Concord, NH 03301 kelly.buchanan@tnc.org
www.nature.org/newhampshire
The New Hampshire Chapter of The Nature Conservancy, works to protect New Hampshire's lands and natural resources. Through science based projects and conservation efforts, the chapter protects 280,000 acres of the states naturalresources.
Founded: 1961
Mark Zankel, State Director
Kelly Buchanan, Operations Assistant

1126 The Nature Conservancy:New Hampshire Chapter:Great Bay Office
112 Bay Road 603-659-2678
Newmarket, NH 03857 *Fax:* 603-659-2729
kelly.buchanan@tnc.org
www.nature.org/newhampshire
Mark Zankel, State Director
Kelly Buchanan, Operations Assistant

1127 The Nature Conservancy:New Hampshire Chapter:Northern New Hampshire Office
24 Reporter Court, 2nd Floor 603-356-8833
PO Box 310 *Fax:* 603-356-2434
North Conway, NH 03860 kelly.buchanan@tnc.org
www.nature.org/newhampshire
Mark Zankel, State Director
Kelly Buchanan, Operations Assistant

New Jersey

1128 **American Bass Association of Eastern Pennsylvania & New Jersey**
NJ
abapanj@gmail.com
www.bestbassteams.com
The American Bass Association of PA & NJ is dedicated to the promotion of bass fishing as a major sport, to conserve the future of fishing through the protection and enhancement of fishery resources and to introduce fishing to Americanyouth.
Founded: 1974
Fred Eurick, President
Mark Dilatush, VP

1129 **American Lung Association of New Jersey**
PO Box 10188,37214 908-685-8040
Newark, NJ 07101 Klsky@lunginfo.org
www.lung.org/about-us/local-associations/new-jersey.html
The American Lung Association of New Jersey works to prevent lung disease and promote lung health; offering a wide variety of lung health services to the people of New Jersey.
Deborah Brown, Executive VP, Mid-Atlantic
Joy Meyer, VP, Community Impact

1130 **American Society of Landscape Architects: New Jersey Chapter**
414 River View Plaza 609-393-7500
Trenton, NJ 08611-3420 *Fax:* 609-393-9891
www.njasla.org
As the New Jersey Chapter of the American Society of Landscape Architects (NJASLA), it aims to lead, educate and participate in the careful stewardship, wise planning, and artful design of cultural and natural environments. The NJASLArepresents landscape architects from across the state and provides its members with networking, social and volunteer opportunities.
Founded: 1901
John M. Thomas, President

1131 **Association of New Jersey Environmental Commissions**
Morris County Cultural Center
300 Mendham Road 973-539-7547
PO Box 157 *Fax:* 973-539-7713
Mendham, NJ 07945 info@anjec.org
www.anjec.org
The Association of New Jersey Environmental Commissions (ANJEC) promotes the responsible and sustainable use of New Jersey's natural resources and the protection of the states environmental health. ANJEC is a statewide, nonprofitorganization.
Jennifer M. Coffey, Executive Director
Elizabeth Ritter, Deputy Director

1132 **B.A.S.S Nation: New Jersey Chapter**
NJ 201-584-9387
rjrjob@verizon.net
www.njbassnation.org
The New Jersey BASS Nation is the state affiliate of BASS Nation, the New Jersey chapter works to provide an association between anglers for the advancement and promotion of sport bass fishing.
Founded: 1917
Randy Baran, President
Billy Tyger, Vice President

1133 **Clean Ocean Action**
18 Hartshorne Dr 732-872-0111
Suite 2 *Fax:* 732-872-8041
Highlands, NJ 07732 info@cleanoceanaction.org
www.cleanoceanaction.org
COA staff research pollution in the New York Bight then organize campaigns to clean up and protect the waters of the New York and New Jersey coasts.
Founded: 1984
Cindy Zipf, Executive Director

1134 **Environmental and Occupational Health Science Institute**
Rutgers University
170 Frelinghuysen Road 848-445-0200
Piscataway, NJ 08854 *Fax:* 732-445-0131
info@eohsi.rutgers.edu
eohsi.rutgers.edu
Sponsors research, education and service programs in a setting that fosters interaction among experts in environmental health, toxicology, occupational health, exposure assessment, public policy and health education. The Institute alsoserves as an unbiased source of expertise about environmental problems for communities, employers and government in all areas of occupational and environmental health, toxicology and risk assessment.
Kenneth Reuhl, Interim Director
Howard Kipen, Associate Director

1135 **New Jersey Environmental Lobby**
204 W State Street njel@earthlink.net
Trenton, NJ 08608
The New Jersey Environmental Lobby (NJEL) is a nonpartisan, independent organization committed to lobbying on behalf of the environment. Primarily focused on environmental efforts in New Jersey, such as the expansion of mass transitand legislature for the control of single use plastic bags, the NJEL collaborates with other organizations to advocate and educate for the conservation of New Jersey's environment.
Founded: 1969
Anne O. Poole, President
Noemi de la Puente, Executive Director

1136 **New Jersey Public Interest Research Group**
104 Bayard St. 609-394-8155
6th Floor info@njpirg.org
New Brunswick, NJ 08901 www.njpirg.org
The New Jersey Public Interest Research Group (NJPIRG) is a statewide, nonprofit, public interest advocacy organization that uses investigative research, media exposes, grassroots organization and litigation to inform, represent andeducate the public. NJPIRG focuses primarily on environmental, health, safety, financial and consumer protection.
Dan Xie, Organizing Director
Ed Mierzeinkski, Consumer Program Director

1137 **New York/New Jersey Trail Conference**
600 Ramapo Valley Road 201-512-9348
Mahwah, NJ 07430-1199 office@nynjtc.org
www.nynjtc.org
A federation of 104 hiking clubs and environmental organizations and 10,000 individuals dedicated to building and maintaining marked hiking trails and protecting related open spaces in the bi-state region.
Edward Goodell, Executive Director
Joshua Howard, Deputy Executive Director

1138 **Passaic River Coalition**
330 Speedwell Avenue 973-532-9830
Morristown, NJ 07960 *Fax:* 973-889-9172
www.passaicriver.org
A nonprofit organization, the Passaic River Coalition (PRC) is dedicated to the preservation and protection of the Passaic River and its watersheds. The PRC focuses on improvements in land-water resource management and public healthissues by advising citizens, environmental organizations, governments and businesses.
Founded: 1969
Laurie Howard, Chair
Russell Furnari, Treasurer

1139 **Sierra Club: New Jersey Chapter**
145 West Hanover Street 609-656-7612
Trenton, NJ 08618 *Fax:* 609-656-7618
jeff.tittel@SierraClub.org
newjersey.sierraclub.org
The New Jersey Chapter of the Sierra Club is comprised of 12 regional groups. The Chapter works in coordination with the mis-

sion of the National Sierra Club to protect and conserve the natural resources of New Jersey.
20,000 Members
Jeff Tittel, Senior Chapter Director
Toni Granato, Program Assistant

1140 Unexpected Wildlife Refuge
PO Box 765 856-697-3541
Newfield, NJ 08344-0765 *Fax:* 856-697-5081
manager@unexpectedwildliferefuge.org
www.unexpectedwildliferefuge.org
Providing sanctuary for animals and plants indigenous to New Jersey Pinelands.
Nedim C. Buyukmihci, President & Secretary
Darwin Sawyer, Vice Presdient

New Mexico

1141 American Lung Association of New Mexico
5911 Jefferson Stree NE 800-586-4872
Albuquerque, NM 87109 NMInfo@lungs.org
www.lung.org/about-us/local-associations/new-mexico.html
The American Lung Association of New Mexico works to prevent lung disease and promote lung health; offering a wide variety of lung health services to the people of New Mexico.
Terry Huertaz, Executive Director
Kathy Moseley, Program Manager

1142 American Society of Landscape Architects: New Mexico
NM jlent@asla.org
www.nmasla.org
The New Mexico Chapter of the American Society of Landscape Architects (NMASLA), is a nonprofit association representing the landscape architecture profession throughout the state of New Mexico.
Julia Lent, Director, Chapter Services
Justin Weathermon, President

1143 New Mexico Association of Conservation Districts
163 Trail Canyon Road 505-981-2400
Carlsbad, NM 88220 *Fax:* 505-981-2400
conserve@hughes.net
www.nmacd.org
The New Mexico Association of Conservation Districts (NMACD), is a private nonprofit organization working with New Mexico Legislature, Congressional Delegations, and related governmental agencies to provide statewide coordination andrepresentation for the 48 Soil and Water Conservation Districts of New Mexico.
Founded: 1946
Debbie Hughes, Executive Director
Mary Lou Ballard, Executive Assistant

1144 New Mexico Rural Water Association
8336 Washington Place NE 505-884-1031
Albuquerque, NM 87113 800-819-9893
Fax: 505-884-1032
info@nmrwa.org
www.nmrwa.org
A state affiliate of the National Rural Water Association, the New Mexico Rural Water Association (NMRWA) is a nonprofit organization committed to ensuring communities have safe drinking water and wastewater services . NMRWA offerson-site technical assistance and specialized training.
Bill Conner, Executive Director
Jose E. Terrones, President

1145 New Mexico Solar Energy Association
PO Box 3434 505-246-0400
Albuquerque, NM 87190 info@NMSolar.org
www.nmsolar.org
New Mexico Solar Energy Association (NMSEA) is a nonprofit, educational organization. Made of up 7 regional chapters, the NMSEA promotes the use of clean and renewable energy and sustainability in New Mexico.
Founded: 1972
Jim DesJardins, Chapter Leader

1146 New Mexico Solar Energy Association: Alamgordo Chapter
Alamgordo, NM ronnoffley@gmail.com
www.nmsolar.org/alamagordo/
Ron Offley, Chapter Leader

1147 New Mexico Solar Energy Association: Las Vegas Chapter
Las Vegas, NM lgoding@hughes.net
www.nmsolar.org/las-vegas-chapter/
Also known as Sustainable Las Vegas
Lloyd Goding, Chapter Leader
Cheryl Zebrowski, Chapter Secretary

1148 New Mexico Solar Energy Association: Los Alamos Chapter
Los Alamos, NM ekarenp@gmail.com
www.nmsolar.org/los-alamos-chapter/
Also known as the Los Alamos Sustainable Energy Network.
Karen Paramanandam, Chapter President

1149 New Mexico Solar Energy Association: Santa Fe Chapter
Santa Fe, NM cjpavel@me.com
www.nmsolar.org/santa-fe-chapter
Claudia Pavel, Chapter Contact

1150 New Mexico Solar Energy Association: Silver City Chapter
Silver City, NM laimansmith@gmail.com
www.nmsolar.org/silver-city-chapter
Lydia Aiman-Smith, Chapter Co-President
Mike Sauber, Chapter Co-President

1151 New Mexico Solar Energy Association: Taps Chapter
Taos, NM 575-758-5338
greenbuilderstaos@gmail.com
www.nmsolar.org/taos-chapter
Scott Evans, Chapter President

1152 Sierra Club: Rio Grande Chapter
142 Truman NE 505-243-7767
Albuquerque, NM 87108 *Fax:* 505-243-7771
nmsierraclub.org
To advance the preservation and protection of the natural environment by empowering the citizenry with charitable resources to further the cause of environmental protection.
Founded: 1892
John Buchser, Chair
Norma McCallan, Vice Chair

1153 The Nature Conservancy: New Mexico Chapter
212 E Marcy Street 505-988-3867
Santa Fe, NM 87501 *Fax:* 505-988-4095
nm@tnc.org
www.nature.org
The New Mexico Chapter of The Nature Conservancy, works to protect New Mexico's land, water and wildlife. The New Mexico Chapter protects more than 1.4 million acres of land, including 6 nature preserves.
Founded: 1951
Priscilla Ornelas, Director, Operations
Terry Sullivan, State Director

1154 The Wildlife Society: New Mexico Chapter
NM twsnewmexico@gmail.com
www.wildlife.org/nm-chapter/

The New Chapter of The Wildlife Society works to serve and represent wildlife life professionals in all areas of wildlife conservation and management in the state of New Mexico.
$8/Year
Scott Carleton, Chapter President
Dan Collins, Treasurer

New York

1155 **Adirondack Council**
103 Hand Avenue, Suite 3 518-873-2240
PO Box D-2 info@adirondackcouncil.org
Elizabethtown, NY 12932 www.adirondackcouncil.org
Through cooperative collaboration, the Adirondacks Council uses science, the law and knowledge of political decision making in order to educate and motivate the public to protect the Adirondack Park.
Founded: 1975
William C. Janeway, Executive Director
Diane W. Fish, Deputy Director

1156 **Adirondack Council: Albany Office**
342 Hamilton Street 518-432-1770
First Floor info@adirondackcouncil.org
Albany, NY 12210 www.adirondackcouncil.org
William C. Janeway, Executive Director
Diane W. Fish, Deputy Director

1157 **Adirondack Mountain Club**
814 Goggins Road 518-668-4447
Lake George, NY 12845-1738 800-395-8080
Fax: 518-668-3746
info@adk.org
www.adk.org
The Adirondack Mountain Club (ADK) is composed of 27 regional chapters spanning through the state, dedicated to the protection and responsible recreational use of the New York State's wildlands and water.
Founded: 1922 30,000 Members
Neil Woodworth, Executive Director
Wes Lampman, COO

1158 **American Lung Association of New York**
21 West 38th Street 212-889-3370
3rd Floor info@lungne.org
New York, NY 10018 www.lung.org/about-us/local-associations/new-york.html
The American Lung Association of New York works to prevent lung disease and promote lung health through direct assistance, education programs, advocacy and research.
Jeff Seyler, Executive VP, Northeast
Adam Shuster, CFO

1159 **American Lung Association of New York: Albany**
418 Broadway 518-465-2013
1st Floor info@lungne.org
Albany, NY 12207 www.lung.org/about-us/local-associations/new-york.html
Jeff Seyler, Executive VP, Northeast
Adam Shuster, CFO

1160 **American Lung Association of New York: Hauppauge**
700 Veterans Memorial Highway 631-265-3848
Hauppauge info@lungne.org
Albany, NY 11788 www.lung.org/about-us/local-associations/new-york.html
Jeff Seyler, Executive VP, Northeast
Adam Shuster, CFO

1161 **American Lung Association of New York: Rochester**
1595 Elmwood Avenue 585-442-4260
Rochester, NY 14620 info@lungne.org
www.lung.org/about-us/local-associations/new-york.html
Jeff Seyler, Executive VP, Northeast
Adam Shuster, CFO

1162 **American Lung Association of New York: White Plains**
237 Mamaroneck Avenue
Suite 205 585-442-4260
White Plains, NY 10605 info@lungne.org
www.lung.org/about-us/local-associations/new-york.html
Jeff Seyler, Executive VP, Northeast
Adam Shuster, CFO

1163 **American Society of Landscape Architects: New York Upstate Chapter**
The Rivers Organization 585-586-6906
P.O. Box 227 asla@riversorg.com
East Rochester, NY 14445 www.nyuasla.org
The New York Upstate Chapter of the American Society of Landscape Architects is a nonprofit association representing the landscape architecture profession throughout Upstate New York. The Chapter is dedicated to the promotion of thelandscape architecture profession through advocacy, education and communication.
Founded: 1954 16,000
Nick Schwartz, President
Rick Rivers, Chapter Executive Director

1164 **American Society of Landscape Architects: New York Chapter**
205 East 42nd Street 212-269-2984
14th Floor director@aslany.org
New York, NY 10017 www.nyasla.org
The New York Chapter of the American Society of Landscape Architects (ASLA-NY) is a nonprofit association representing the landscape architecture profession throughout 5 New York City boroughs, Nassau and Suffolk counties on LongIsland, and Westchester, Putnam, Dutchess, Orange, and Rockland counties. The Chapter is dedicated to the promotion of the landscape architecture profession through advocacy, education and communication.
Founded: 1914 500 Members
Jennifer Nitzky, President
Kathy Shea, Executive Director

1165 **Catskill Forest Association**
43469 State Highway 28 845-586-3054
PO Box 336 *Fax:* 845-586-4071
Arkville, NY 12406 cfa@catskill.net
www.catskillforest.org
Catskill Forest Association, Inc. is dedicated to protecting the health and environmental well being of the forests and the forests ecosystem, through knowledge promotion, understanding forest ecology, promotion of long-term forestmanagement and education of the public in a six-country region in Central New York State.
Founded: 1982
Ryan Trapani, Director, Forest Operations
Kathy Fox, Office Administrator

1166 **Clean Ocean Action**
18 Hartshorne Dr 732-872-0111
Suite 2 *Fax:* 732-872-8041
Highlands, NJ 07732 info@cleanoceanaction.org
www.cleanoceanaction.org
COA staff research pollution in the New York Bight then organize campaigns to clean up and protect the waters of the New York and New Jersey coasts.
Founded: 1984
Cindy Zipf, Executive Director

1167 **Cornell Lab of Ornithology**
159 Sapsucker Woods Road 607-254-2437
Ithaca, NY 14850 800-843-2473
www.birds.cornell.edu
The Cornell Lab of Ornithology is a nonprofit environmental organization concerned with the study, appreciation and conservation of birds. Using scientific knowledge and technological innovation, the Cornell Lab has become a worldleader in advancing the understanding of nature and engaging people of all ages in

learning about birds and protecting the planet. The Cornell Lab is a unit of Cornell University.
Founded: 1915
John Fitzpatrick, Executive Director
Ron Rohrbaugh, Assitant Director

1168 Great Camp Sagamore
Sagamore Road 315-354-5311
PO Box 40 info@greatcampsagamore.org
Raquette Lake, NY 13436 www.greatcampsagamore.org
A nonprofit corporation dedicated to the stewardship of Great Camp Sagamore, and its use for educational and interpretive purposes.
Founded: 1973
Garet D. Livermore, Executive Director
Frances Parent, Associate Director

1169 Hudsonia Limited
30 Campus Road 845-758-7053
PO Box 5000 *Fax:* 845-758-7033
Annandale, NY 12504 www.hudsonia.org
Hudsonia Ltd., is a nonprofit, non advocacy, public interest organization. Hudsonia is committed to research, education, and technical assistance in the environmental sciences; helping people and professionals makes the most informeddecision regarding the environment and natural resources based on the available data
Founded: 1981
Erik Kiviat PhD, Executive Director
Robert E. Schmidt PhD, Associate Director

1170 In Our Backyards
540 President Street 917-464-4515
1st Floor hello@ioby.org
Brooklyn, NY 11215 www.ioby.org
Strives to deepen civic engagement in cities by connecting individuals directly to community-led, crowdfunded projects in their neighborhoods.
Founded: 2008
Erin Barnes, Co-Founder & Exec. Director
Brandon Whitney, Co-Founder & COO

1171 New York Association of Conservation Districts
415 W Morris Street blanche_13335@yahoo.com
Bath, NY 14810 www.nyacd.org
The New York Association of Conservation Districts (NYACD) provides statewide coordination and representation for the Soil and Water Conservation Districts of New York. The NYACD provides a platform for relationships, networking,advocacy, training, and education and promotes the wise use of soil, water and natural resources throughout the state.
Founded: 1958
Dan Farrand, President
Blanche Hurlbutt, Executive Director

1172 New York Forest Owners Association
PO Box 541 800-836-3566
Lima, NY 14485 info@nyfoa.org
www.nyfoa.org
The New York Forest Owners Association (NYFOA) is a nonprofit organization comprised of 10 regional chapters working to promote sustainable forestry and improved stewardship of privately owned woodlands across the state.
Charles Stackhouse, President
Liana Gooding, Office Administrator

1173 New York Healthy Schools Network
NY 518-462-0632
info@healthyschools.org
www.healthyschools.org
Healthy Schools Network is a nonprofit, responsible for the start of the national healthy school environments movement. The Healthy Schools Network supports collaborative research, policy development, and systemic reform for thepromotion of a healthier school environment for children.
Founded: 1995
Chip Halverson, President
Linda Mendonca, VP

1174 New York State Department of Environmental Conservation
625 Broadway contact@dec.ny.gov
Albany, NY 12233-1 www.dec.ny.gov
The New York State Department of Environmental Conservation (DEC) protects, improves and conserves the state's land, water, air, fish, wildlife and other resources to enhance the health, safety and welfare of the people and theiroverall economic and social well-being.
Founded: 1970
Kenneth Lynch, Exec. Deputy Commissione
Basil Seggos, Commissioner

1175 New York State Ornithological Association
NYSOA, Inc.
PO Box 296 president1@nybirds.org
Somers, NY 10589 www.nybirds.org
Formerly the Federation of New York State Birds, the New York State Ornithological Association (NYSOA) is dedicated to the documentation and protection of New York State's birds and their habitats and to the promotion of interest inand appreciation of birds.
Joan Collins, President
Andy Mason, Treasurer

1176 New York Turtle and Tortoise Society
1214 W Boston Post Road www.nytts.org
PO Box 267
Mamaroneck, NY 10543
A nonprofit organization dedication to the conservation, preservation of habitat, and the promotion of proper husbandry and captive propagation of turtles and tortoises.
Founded: 1970

1177 New York Water Environment Association
525 Plum Street 315-422-7811
Suite 102 877-556-9932
Syracuse, NY 13204 *Fax:* 315-422-3851
pcr@nywea.org
www.nywea.org
The New York Water Environment Association is a nonprofit educational association dedicated to the development and dissemination of information concerning water quality management and the nature, collection, treatment, and disposal ofwastewater.
Founded: 1929 2,500 Members
Paul McGarvey, President
Geoffrey Baldwin, President Elect

1178 Parks and Trails New York
29 Elk Street 518-434-1583
Albany, NY 12207 *Fax:* 518-427-0067
ptny@ptny.org
www.ptny.org
The only organization working statewide to protect New York's parks and help communities create new parks. A non-profit organization whose mission is to expand, protect and promote a network of parks, trails, and open spaces throughoutour state for use and enjoyment by all.
Founded: 1985
A. Joseph Scott, Chairman
Richard H. Remmer, Vice Chairman

1179 Riverkeeper
20 Secor Road 800-217-4837
Ossining, NY 10562 info@riverkeeper.org
www.riverkeeper.org
Riverkeeper works to protect the environmental, recreational, and commercial integrity of the Hudson River and its tributaries. Riverkeeper is a global leader in water keeper programs and is New York's clean water advocate.
Founded: 1966
Deborah Brown, Chief of Staff
Paul Gallay, President

1180 Scenic Hudson
1 Civic Center Plaza 845-473-4440
Suite 200 *Fax:* 845-473-2648
Poughkeepsie, NY 12601 info@scenichudson.org
www.scenichudson.org
Scenic Hudson works to protect and restore the Hudson River. Through land preservation, citizen-based advocacy, and the creation of parks; Scenic Hudson is the largest environmental organization focused on the Hudson River Valley,preserving 40,000 acres and creating or enhancing 65 parks in the region.
Founded: 1963
Steve Rosenberg, Senior VP
Ned Sullivan, President

1181 Selikoff Clinical Center for Occupational & Environmental Medicine
Mount Sinai School of Medicine
Department of Community Medicine 212-241-6500
1 Gustave Levy Place, Box 1043 *Fax:* 212-241-6696
New York, NY 10029-6574 www.mssm.edu/cpm
Internationally respected diagnostic referral center and an important interface between the research programs of the Division of Environmental Health Science and populations exposed to environmental hazards.

1182 Sierra Club: Atlantic Chapter
744 Broadway 518-426-9144
Albany, NY 12207 atlantic.chapter@sierraclub.org
www.atlantic2.sierraclub.org
The Atlantic Chapter applies the principles of the national Sierra Club to the environmental issues facing New York State.
Rogers Downs, Director, Conservation
Caitlin Ferrante, Program Manager

1183 Sierra Club: New York City Chapter
NY info@nyc.sierraclub.org
www.nyc.sierraclub.org
The New York City Chapter applies the principles of the national Sierra Club to the environmental issues facing New York City.
Founded: 1892
Allison Tupper, Chair
Bonnie Lane Webber, Vice Chair

1184 The Nature Conservancy: New York Chapter
195 New Karner Road 518-690-7850
Suite 200 *Fax:* 518-869-2332
Albany, NY 12205 natureny@tnc.org
www.nature.org/newyork
In conjunction with the mission of the The Nature Conservancy, which started in New York, the New York Chapter protects more than 815,000 acres of land across the state. This chapter was the first state chapter to establish acomprehensive program for fresh water, oceans and cities.
Founded: 1955 90,000 Members

1185 The Nature Conservancy: New York Chapter: Long Island The Center for Conservation
142 Route 114 631-329-7689
PO Box 5125 *Fax:* 631-329-0215
East Hampton, NY 11937 natureny@tnc.org
www.nature.org/newyork

1186 The Nature Conservancy: New York Chapter: Adirondacks
Adirondack Land Trust
PO Box 65 518-576-2082
Keene Valley, NY 12943 adirondacks@tnc.org
www.nature.org/newyork
Tim Barnett, VP, Special Programs
Dirk Bryan, Director, Conservation

1187 The Nature Conservancy: New York Chapter: Central & Western New York
274 N Goodman Street 585-546-8030
Suite B261 *Fax:* 585-546-7825
Rochester, NY 14607 natureny@tnc.org
www.nature.org/newyork
Jim Howe, Executive Director
Darran Crabtree, Director, Conservation

1188 The Nature Conservancy: New York Chapter: Long Island Uplands Farm Sanctuary
250 Lawrence Hill Road 631-367-3225
Cold Spring Harbor, NY 11724 *Fax:* 631-367-4715
natureny@tnc.org
www.nature.org/newyork

1189 The Nature Conservancy: New York Chapter: New York City
322 8th Avenue 212-997-1880
16th Floor *Fax:* 212-997-8451
New York, NY 10001 natureny@tnc.org
www.nature.org/newyork

1190 Tug Hill Tomorrow Land Trust
1 Thompson Park 315-779-8240
PO Box 6063 thtomorr@northnet.org
Watertown, NY 13601 www.tughilltomorrowlandtrust.org
A regional, private, nonprofit organization, Tug Hill Tomorrow Land Trust works to protect the 2,100 square mile region. Tug Hill Tomorrow Land Trust uses publications, education, and community programs to increase the awareness,appreciation, and conservation of the Tug Hill region land.
Founded: 1991
Linda Garrett, Executive Director
Lianna Lee, Manager, Communications

1191 Waterkeeper Alliance
180 Maiden Lane 212-747-0622
Suite 603 info@waterkeeper.org
New York, NY 10038 www.waterkeeper.org
The Waterkeeper Alliance provides global coordination and networking for local waterkeeper organizations and affiliates. A nonprofit organization, the Waterkeeper Alliance works to conserve, protect, and promote water quality fordrinkable, fishable, and swimmable water.
Marc Yaggi, Executive Director
Mary Beth Postman, Deputy Director

1192 West Harlem Environmental Action
1854 Amsterdam Avenue 212-961-1000
2nd Floor *Fax:* 212-961-1015
New York, NY 10031 info@weact.org
www.weact.org
A nonprofit, community-based, environmental organization dedicated to building community power to help end environmental racism and improve environmental health, protection and policy in communities of color and low incomeneighborhoods.
Peggy M Shepard, Executive Director
Cecill D. Corbin-Mark, Deputy Director

North Carolina

1193 American Lung Association of North Carolina
514 Daniels Street 919-792-1641
Suite 109 alanc-r@lungse.org
Raleigh, NC 27605 www.lungnc.org
The American Lung Association of North Carolina works to prevent lung disease and promote lung health through direct assistance, education programs, advocacy and research.
Martha C. Bogdan, Executive VP, South East
Willie L. Bythwood, Jr, CFO

1194 **American Lung Association of North Carolina: Charlotte**
401 Hawthrone Lane 980-237-6611
Suite 110 #298 alanc@lungse.org
Charlotte, NC 28204 www.lungnc.org
Martha C. Bogdan, Executive VP, South East
Willie L. Bythwood, Jr, CFO

1195 **American Society of Landscape Architects: North Carolina Chapter**
c/o Blue Star Services
5201 Albemarle Drive 919-215-3117
Oriental, NC 28571 manager@ncasla.org
www.ncasla.org
The North Carolina Chapter of the American Society of Landscape Architects (NCASLA) is a nonprofit association representing the landscape architecture profession throughout North Carolina. The Chapter is dedicated to the promotion ofthe landscape architecture profession through advocacy, education and communication.
Founded: 1899
Debora Steenson, Chapter Co-Manager
George Steenson, Chapter Co-Manager

1196 **Carolina Bird Club**
1809 Lakepark Drive 910-791-9034
Raleigh, NC 27612 *Fax:* 910-791-7228
hq@carolinabirdclub.org
www.carolinabirdclub.org
A nonprofit education and scientific association, open to anyone interested in the study and conservation of wildlife, particularly birds. Through its website, publications, meetings, workshops, trips, and partnerships, the CarolinaBird Club supports the birding community in the Carolinas.
Founded: 1937
Christine Stoughton-Root, President
Paul Dayer, Treasurer

1197 **Environmental Educators of North Carolina**
PO Box 4904 919-250-1050
Chapel Hill, NC 27515-4904 *Fax:* 919-250-1058
communicationseenc@gmail.com
www.eenc.org
A nonprofit organization, dedicated to promoting excellence, professional development, and to facilitate networking opportunities, in order to foster greater environmental education among the community and environmental educators.
Founded: 1987
Jonathan Marchal, President
Chris Goforth, Communications Chair

1198 **NC Sustainable Energy Association**
4800 Six Forks Road 919-832-7601
Suite 300 info@energync.org
Raleigh, NC 27609 www.energync.org
Composed of individuals, businesses, government, and nonprofits, the NC Sustainable Energy Association (NCSEA) is a nonprofit membership organization working to change policy and market development to create clean energy jobs, economicopportunities, and affordable energy in North Carolina.
Founded: 1978
Ivan Urlaub, Executive Director
Ward Lenz, Director, Development

1199 **North Carolina Association of Soil & Water Conservation Districts**
PO Box 27943 919-715-6104
Raleigh, NC 27611 ncaswcd@gmail.com
www.ncaswcd.org
An independent nonpartisan conservation organization created to represent the interests of 96 local soil and water conservation districts and the 492 district supervisors who direct their local district's conservation programs.
Founded: 1944
Chris Hogan, President
Dietrich Kilpatrick, First Vice President

1200 **North Carolina Coastal Federation**
3609 N.C. 24 Ocean 252-393-8185
Newport, NC 28570 *Fax:* 252-393-7508
nccf@nccoast.org
www.nccoast.org
Working with citizens to safeguard the state's coastal rivers, creeks, sounds and beaches. The state's only nonprofit organization focused exclusivley on protecting and restoring the coast of Nort Carolina through education, advocacy,and habitat preservation and restoration.
Founded: 1982
Todd Miller, Executive Director
Lauren Kolodij, Deputy Director

1201 **North Carolina Coastal Federation: Northeast Office**
637 Harbor Road 252-473-1607
PO Box 276 *Fax:* 252-473-2402
Wanchese, NC 27981 nccf@nccoast.org
www.nccoast.org
Founded: 1982
Todd Miller, Executive Director
Lauren Kolodij, Deputy Director

1202 **North Carolina Coastal Federation: Southeast Office**
Wrightsville Beach Historic Square
309 W Salisbury Street 910-509-2838
Wrightsville Beach, NC 28480 *Fax:* 910-509-2840
nccf@nccoast.org
www.nccoast.org
Founded: 1982
Todd Miller, Executive Director
Lauren Kolodij, Deputy Director

1203 **North Carolina Museum of Natural Sciences**
11 W Jones Street 919-707-9800
Raleigh, NC 27601 www.naturalsciences.org
The North Museum of Natural Sciences, is a free admission museum working to highlight the interdependent relationship between the natural environment and humanity.
Founded: 1985
Angela Baker-James, Executive Director
Emlyn Koster, Director

1204 **North Carolina Native Plant Society**
PO Box 10815 jean@ncwildflower.org
Greensboro, NC 27404 www.ncwildflower.org
A nonprofit organization dedicated to the promotion, enjoyment and conservation of North Carolina's native plants and their habitats through education, protection, and propagation.
Founded: 1951
Jean Woods, President
John Clarke, VP

1205 **Sierra Club: North Carolina Chapter**
19 W. Hargett Street 919-833-8467
Suite 210 www.sierraclub.org/north-carolina
Raleigh, NC 27601
The North Carolina Chapter of the Sierra Club, is composed of 12 local groups that work to advocate across the state in order to protect the land and environment of North Carolina.
Founded: 1970 70,000 Members
Molly Diggins, State Director
Margaret Lillard, Communications Coordinator

1206 **Southeastern Association of Fish and Wildlife Agencies**
27 Sylwood Place 601-668-6916
Jackson, MS 39209 crayhopkins@bellsouth.net
www.seafwa.org
The Southeastern Association of Fish and Wildlife Agencies (SEAFWA) is an organization whose members are the state agencies with primary responsibility for management and protection of the fish and wildlife resources in 15 states.
Curtis R. Hopkins, Executive Secretary
Alvin Taylor, President

1207 **The Wildlife Society: North Carolina Chapter**
NC admin@nctws.org
www.nctws.org/wordpress
The North Carolina Chapter of The Wildlife Society works to serve and represent wildlife life professionals in all areas of wildlife conservation and management in the state of North Carolina.
Founded: 1983
Colleen Olfenbuttel, President
Brandon Sherrill, Treasurer

North Dakota

1208 **American Fisheries Society: North Central Division: Dakota Chapter**
ND Steven.Chipps@sdstate.edu
www.dakota.fisheries.org
The Dakota Chapter of the American Fisheries Society, is part of the American Fisheries Society (AFS) North Central Division. The Dakota Chapter works to further to the goals of the AFS and is committed to the conservation,development, and wise use of fishery resources, the chapter provides several annual awards to fishery professionals, conservation groups, and students.
Steve Chipps, President
Michael Johnson, Secretary & Treasurer

1209 **American Lung Association in North Dakota**
212 North 2nd Street 701-223-5613
Bismarck, ND 58501 info@lungnd.org
www.lung.org/about-us/local-associations/north-dakota.html
The American Lung Association of North Dakota works to prevent lung disease and promote lung health through direct assistance, education programs, advocacy and research.
Penny Fena, Chief Mission Officer
Lewis Bartfield, Executive VP,Upper Midwest

1210 **American Society of Landscape Architects: Great Plains Chapter**
NE Regan.Pence@LRA-INC.com
www.gpcasla.org
Representing North Dakota, South Dakota, and Nebraska the Great Plains Chapter of the American Landscape Society works to expand the profession of landscape architecture in these states. The Chapter advocates and provides professionaleducational and developmental programs for its members
Regan Pence, President
Chad Kucker, Secretary & Treasurer

1211 **International Association for Impact Assessment**
1330 23rd Street South 701-297-7908
Suite C *Fax:* 701-297-7917
Fargo, ND 58103-3705 info@iaia.org
www.iaia.org
The International Association for Impact Assessment (IAIA) is an interdisciplinary society dedicated to developing international capacity to anticipate, plan and manage the consequences of development. IAIA seeks to ensure thatpolitical, environmental, social and technological dimensions of decisions are understood by those making them.
Founded: 1980
Jill Baker, Executive Director
Kayla Deitch, Administrative Assistant

1212 **North Dakota Association of Soil Conservation Districts**
3310 University Drive 701-223-8518
Bismarck, ND 58504 kathy@lincolnoakes.com
ndascd.org
The North Dakota Association of Soil Conservation Districts (NDASD) works to promote the widespread application of sound and practical soil and water conservation practices in the state.
Richard Knopp, President
Kathy Hendrickson, Association Secretary

Ohio

1213 **American Fisheries Society: North Central Division: Ohio Chapter**
OH kristin.arend@dnr.state.oh.us
The Ohio Chapter of the American Fisheries Society (OCAFS), is part of the American Fisheries Society (AFS) North Central Division. Working to further to the goals of the AFS through research, education, and professional development,the chapter is committed to the conservation, development, and wise use of fishery resources, and the protection and sustainability of aquatic ecosystems.
Founded: 1970 $10/ Year
Kristi Arend, President
Jo Ann Banda, Secretary & Treasurer

1214 **American Lung Association of Ohio**
4050 Executive Park Drive 513-985-3990
402 midland@lung.org
Cincinatti, OH 45241 www.lung.org/about-us/local-associations/ohio.html
The American Lung Association of Ohio works to prevent lung disease and promote lung health through direct assistance, advocacy and education programs. Due to the unique partnership between the American Lung Association of Ohio andpublic television stations in Daytona and Cincinnati, the ALA of Ohio established the project CAARE for care providers, dedicated to managing childhood asthma in daycare centers.
Barry Gottschalk, Executive VP, Midland States
Patricia J. Volz, VP, Communication

1215 **American Lung Association of Ohio: Columbus**
5900 Wilcox Place 614-279-1700
Dublin, OH 43016 midland@lung.org
www.lung.org/about-us/local-associations/ohio.html
Barry Gottschalk, Executive VP, Midland States
Patricia J. Volz, VP, Communication

1216 **American Lung Association of Ohio: Independence**
6100 Rockside Wood 216-524-5864
Suite 260 midland@lung.org
Independence, OH 44131 www.lung.org/about-us/local-associations/ohio.html
Founded: 1901
Barry Gottschalk, Executive VP, Midland States
Patricia J. Volz, VP, Communication

1217 **American Lung Association of Ohio: Sandusky**
PO Box 415 419-663-5864
Sandusky, OH 44871 pat.volz@lung.org
www.lung.org/about-us/local-associations/ohio.html
Barry Gottschalk, Executive VP, Midland states
Patricia J. Volz, VP, Communication

1218 **American Society of Landscape Architects: Ohio Chapter**
PO Box 776 info@ohioasla.org
Worthington, OH 43085 www.ohioasla.org
The Ohio Chapter of the American Society of Landscape Architects is a nonprofit association representing the landscape architecture profession throughout the state. The Chapter is dedicated to the promotion of the landscapearchitecture profession through advocacy, education and communication.
Ashley Solether, President
Eugenia M. Martin, Chapter Trustee

1219 **B.A.S.S Nation: Ohio Chapter**
OH www.ohiobassnation.com
The Ohio Chapter of BASS Nation is dedicated to the promotion of the sport of bass fishing, fishing tournaments and conservation initiatives to preserve the states natural resources.
Al Evans, President
Danny Ryan, VP

1220 **Cincinnati Nature Center**
4949 Tealtown Road 513-831-1711
Milford, OH 45150 cnc@cincynature.org
www.cincynature.org

To inspire passion for nature and promote environmentally responsible choices through experience and education. The Cincinnati Nature Center is 1,600 acres of forests, fields, streams and ponds.
Founded: 1965
Paul F. Haffner, Chair
Michael R. Mauch, Vice Chair

1221 Green Energy Ohio
7870 Olentangy River Road 614-985-6131
Suite 304 *Fax:* 614-888-9716
Columbus, OH 43235 geo@greenenergyohio.org
www.greenenergyohio.org
Green Energy Ohio is a statewide nonprofit that promotes the use of renewable energy and policies.
Barry Adler, Operations Coordinator
Jane Harf, Executive Director

1222 Holden Arboretum
9500 Sperry Road 440-946-4400
Kirtland, OH 44094 www.holdenarb.org
The Holden Arboretum is a living museum that covers over 3,600 acres. The Arboretum promotes the importance of a trees and woodlands and connecting with nature, allowing the public to walk through themed gardens, hiking trails, picnicareas, and receive guided tours.
Founded: 1931
Paul Abbey, Interim President & CEO
Patricia Roberts, VP, Operations

1223 League of Ohio Sportsmen
642 West Broad Street 614-224-8970
Columbus, OH 43215 *Fax:* 614-224-8971
president@leagueofohiosportsmen.org
www.leagueofohiosportsmen.org
Dedicated to supporting conservation, restoration, and education that promotes the wise use and enjoyment of our natural resources including wildlife management.
Founded: 1908
Larry Mitchell Sr, President
John Hobbs, Vice President

1224 Ohio Energy Project
200 E. Wilson Bridge Road 614-785-1717
Suite 320 *Fax:* 614-785-1731
Worthington, OH 43085 dyerkes@ohioenergy.org
www.ohioenergy.org
An nonproft organization, created by teachers for teachers that provides energy and energy efficiency education using current complete and unbiased information, as well as hands-on, engaging and innovative techniques.
Debby Yerkes, Executive Director
Sue Tenney, Education Coordinator

1225 Ohio Environmental Council
Chesapeake Warehouse
1145 Chesapeake Avenue 614-487-7506
Suite I *Fax:* 614-487-7510
Columbus, OH 43212 OEC@theOEC.org
www.theoec.org
Through legislative initiatives, legal action, science , and statewide partnerships the Ohio Environmental Council is dedicated to advocating for healthier air, land, and water in Ohio.
Jodi Segal, COO
Heather Taylor-Miles, Executive Director

1226 Ohio Federation of Soil and Water Conservation Districts
8995 E Main Street 614-784-1900
Reynoldsburg, OH 43068 www.ofswcd.org
Working to provide leadership and support to the board supervisors, soil and water conservation districts, and their partners through grassroots programs that promote natural resource stewardship.
Founded: 1943
Harold Neuenschwander, President
Bob Short, First VP

1227 Ohio Parks and Recreation Association
1069-A West Main Street 614-895-2222
Westerville, OH 43081 800-238-1108
Fax: 614-895-3050
opra@opraonline.org
www.opraonline.org
A nonprofit, public interest organization representing over 1,700 professionals and citizen board members involved in providing leisure facilities and opportunities to all Ohioans as well as the tourists who visit the state each year.Dedicated to the promotion of parks and recreation services for all Ohioans and the sound stewardship of Ohio's natural resources.
Founded: 1934
Woody Woodward, Executive Director
Mindy McInturf, Business Manager

1228 Sierra Club: Ohio Chapter
Columbus, OH www.sierraclub.org/ohio
To advance the preservation and protection of the natural environment by empowering the citizenry with charitable resources to further the cause of environmental protection.
Guy Marentette, Chapter Chair
Jen Miller, Chapter Director

1229 The Native Plant Society of Northeastern Ohio
OH www.nativeplantsocietyneo.org
As the Northeastern Chapter of The Ohio Native Plant Society, the chapter works to promote the conservation of Ohio's native plants and native plant communities through habitat protection.
Kathy Hanratty, President
Judy Barnhart, VP

1230 The Nature Conservancy: Ohio Chapter
6375 Riverside Drive 614-717-2770
Suite 100 877-862-6446
Dublin, OH 43017 ohio@tnc.org
www.nature.org/ohio
The Ohio Chapter of The Nature Conservancy is dedicated to protecting Ohio's streams, wetlands and forests. With more than 15 nature preserves and over 60,000 acres of natural land protected, The Nature Conservancy of Ohio works toconserve the natural resources across the state of Ohio.
Founded: 1958
Josh Knights, Executive Director
Julia Gehring, Conservation Coordinator

1231 The Nature Conservancy: Ohio Chapter: Coastal Programs Office
2900 Columbus Avenue 419-627-7564
Sadusky, OH 44870 877-862-6446
ohio@tnc.org
www.nature.org/ohio

1232 The Nature Conservancy: Ohio Chapter: Edge of Appalachia Preserve - Eulett Center
4274 Waggoner Riffle Road 937-544-2188
West Union, OH 45693 877-862-6446
ohio@tnc.org
www.nature.org/ohio

1233 The Nature Conservancy: Ohio Chapter: Grand Rivers Conservation Campus
3973 Callender Road 440-563-3081
Rock Creek, OH 44084 877-862-6446
ohio@tnc.org
www.nature.org/ohio

1234 The Nature Conservancy: Ohio Chapter: Northeast Ohio Coastal Project
416 West Prospect Street 847-641-1129
Painesville, OH 44077 877-862-6446
ohio@tnc.org
www.nature.org/ohio

1235 The Nature Conservancy: Ohio Chapter: Oak Openings Region
10420 Old State Line Road 419-867-1521
Swanton, OH 43558 877-862-6446
ohio@tnc.org
www.nature.org/ohio

1236 The Nature Conservancy: Ohio Chapter: Western Lake Erie Basin Agriculture Project Office
210 Clinton Street 614-570-0034
Defiance, OH 43512 877-862-6446
ohio@tnc.org
www.nature.org/ohio

1237 The Wildlife Society: Ohio Chapter
OH www.wildlife.org/ohio
The Ohio Chapter of The Wildlife Society works to serve and represent wildlife life professionals in all areas of wildlife conservation and management in the state of Ohio.
Geoff Westerfield, President
Gabe Karns, Secretary

Oklahoma

1238 American Lung Association of Oklahoma
730 Wilshire Boulevard 405-748-4674
Suite 105 www.lung.org/about-us/local-associations/oklahoma.html
Oklahoma City, OK 73116
The American Lung Association of Oklahoma works to prevent lung disease and promote lung health through direct assistance, education programs, advocacy and research.
Terri Bailey, Executive Director
Cassidy Fallik, Program Coordinator

1239 B.A.S.S Nation: Oklahoma Chapter
OK 580-761-8094
limit5mike@yahoo.com
www.okbassnation.com
The Oklahoma Chapter of BASS Nation works to stimulate public awareness of bass fishing as a major sport and encourages sportsmanship, courtesy and boating safety at all levels. The Chapter promotes the full adherence to allconservation codes, adequate water quality standards and legal enforcement of existing regulatory standards.
Founded: 1972
Mike Myers, President
Chuck Boso, Secretary

1240 Oklahoma Association of Conservation Districts
PO Box 2775 info@okconservation.org
Oklahoma City, OK 73101-2775 www.okconservation.org
Working to provide leadership, resources, and partnership opportunities for the 88 conservation districts and those who manage the land to enhance the natural resources of Oklahoma.
Founded: 1950
Jimmy Emmons, President
Sarah Blaney, Director

1241 Oklahoma Ornithological Society
OK www.okbirds.org
The Oklahoma Ornithological Society (OOS) is an independent, nonprofit educational organization, dedicated to the observation, study, and conservation of birds in Oklahoma.
Founded: 1951
Jimmy Woodard, President
Doug Wood, Secretary

1242 Sierra Club: Oklahoma Chapter
Oklahoma City, OK johnson.bridgwater@sierraclub.org
www.oklahoma.sierraclub.org
Composed of local groups from across the state, the Oklahoma Chapter of the Sierra Club organizes outdoor activities, social events, conservation activities, and education outreach efforts in support of the national Sierra Club'smission.
Founded: 1972 3,000 Members
Johnson Bridgwater, Chapter Director
Michael Belifuss, Chapter Chair

1243 The Nature Conservancy: Oklahoma Chapter
10425 South 82nd East Avenue 918-585-1117
Suite 104 *Fax:* 888-267-5904
Tulsa, OK 74133 www.nature.org/oklahoma
In conjunction with the mission of the The Nature Conservancy, the Oklahoma Chapter conserves nearly 100,00 acres land and unique biodiversity across the state.
Mike Fuhr, State Director
Ashley Dubriwny, Director, Operations

1244 The Nature Conservancy: Oklahoma Chapter: Oklahoma City
408 NW 7th Street 405-858-8557
Oklahoma City, OK 73102 *Fax:* 888-267-5904
www.nature.org/oklahoma
Katie Hawk, Director, Communications
Melissa Nagel Shackford, Director, Land Protection

Oregon

1245 American Lung Association of Oregon
16037 SW Upper Boones Ferry Road 503-924-4094
Suite 165 InfoMTP@lung.org
Tigard, OR 97224 www.lung.org/about-us/local-associations/oregon.html
The American Lung Association of Oregon works to prevent lung disease and promote lung health through direct assistance, education programs, advocacy and research.
Allison Hickey, Exec. VP, Mountain Pacific
Tony Peterson, CFO

1246 American Rivers: Pacific Northwest Region: Portland
317 SW Alder Street 503-827-8648
Suite 900 www.americanrivers.org/region/pacific
Portland, OR 97204
The Pacific Northwest Region of American Rivers works according to the mission of American Rivers, and promotes and applies innovative water and river management.
Founded: 1992

1247 American Society of Landscape Architects: Oregon Chapter
147 SE 102nd Avenue 503-227-6136
Portland, OR 97216 *Fax:* 503-253-9172
info@aslaoregon.org
www.aslaoregon.org
The Oregon Chapter of the American Society of Landscape Architects, is a nonprofit association representing the landscape architecture profession throughout the state of Oregon.
Andreas Stavropoulos, President
Jamie Hendrickson, VP Chapter Services

1248 Columbia Basin Fish and Wildlife Authority
851 SW Sixth Avenue, Suite 260 503-229-0191
Pacific Centre *Fax:* 503-229-0443
Portland, OR 97204 www.cbfish.org
A non-profit corporation to provide an opportunity for the Agencies and Tribes of the Pacific Northwest to become directly involved in the fiscal, administrative and managerial aspects of jointly funded activities.
Founded: 1993
Jann Eckman, President
Dave Statler, Vice President

1249 Ecotrust
Jean Vollum Natural Capital Center
721 NW 9th Avenue 503-227-6225
Portland, OR 97209 contact@ecotrust.org
www.ecotrust.org

Working to inspire innovative thinking that creates economic opportunity, social equity and environmental well-being.
Founded: 1991
Jeremy Barnicle, Executive Director
Laura Ford, Director, Communications

1250 Northwest Center for Alternatives to Pesticides
PO Box 1393 541-344-5044
Eugene, OR 97440 info@pesticide.org
www.pesticide.org
Protects the health of people and the environment by advancing alternatives to pesticides through research, education, and advocacy.
Founded: 1977
Tony Brand, President
Edward Winter, Chief Financial Officer

1251 Oregon Refuse and Recycling Association
727 Center Street NE, Suite 350 503-588-1837
PO Box 2186 800-527-7624
Salem, OR 97308 *Fax:* 503-399-7784
orrainfo@orra.net
www.orra.net
A 200 member voluntary association of solid waste management companies and businesses which specialize in offering equipment and services important to the industry. ORRA provides legislative advocacy, education, group insurance,meeting facilities and advice on regulatory matters to its memebers.
Founded: 1965
Kristan Mitchell, Executive Director
Kimera Coady, Executive Assistant

1252 Oregon State Public Interest Research Group
1536 SE 11th Avenue 503-231-4181
Suite A info@ospirg.org
Portland, OR 97214 www.ospirg.org
OSPIRG's mission is to deliver persistent, result-oriented public interest activism that protects consumers, encourages a fair, sustainable economy, and fosters responsive democratic government.
Founded: 1983
Dave Rosenfeld, Executive Director
Jesse Ellis O'Brien, Health Care Advocate

1253 Oregon Trout
65 SW Yamhill Street 503-222-9091
Suite 200 *Fax:* 503-222-9187
Portland, OR 97204 info@thefreshwatertrust.org
www.ortrout.org
A statewide non-profit organization headquartered in Portland, Oregon with satellite offices in Bandon, Bend, Corvallis and Medford. Oregon Trout works to restore freshwater health through innovation and education.
Founded: 1983
Joe S. Whitworth, President
Alan Horton, Managing Director

1254 Oregon Water Resources Congress
437 Union Street NE 503-363-0121
Salem, OR 97301 *Fax:* 503-371-4926
owrc_info@yahoo.com
www.owrc.org
To promote the protection and use of water rights and the wise stewarship of water resources.
Founded: 1912
April Snell, Executive Director
Ken Crick, Office Manager

1255 Oregon Wild
5825 N. Greeley Ave. 503-283-6343
Portland, OR 97217 *Fax:* 503-283-0756
info@oregonwild.org
www.oregonwild.org
Formerly Oregon Natural Resources Council, Oregon Wild works to protect and restore Oregon's wildlands, wildlife and waters as an enduring leagacy for all Oregonians.
Founded: 1974
Daniel Robertson, President
Brett Sommermeyer, VP

1256 Pacific Rivers Council
PO Box 10798 541-345-0119
Eugene, OR 97440 *Fax:* 541-345-0710
www.pacrivers.org
One of the most influential river conservation organizations in the United States. The mission is to protect and restore rivers, their watersheds, and native aquatic species.
Founded: 1987
Holly Spencer, Acting Executive Director

1257 Rising Tide North America
268 Bush St networking@risingtidenorthamerica.org
Box # 3717 www.risingtidenorthamerica.org
San Francisco, CA 94101
An international, all-volunteer, grassroots network of groups and individuals who organize locally, promote community-based solutions to the climate crisis and take direct action to confront the root causes of climate change.

1258 Sierra Club-Oregon Chapter
1821 SE Ankeny St 503-238-0442
Portland, OR 97214-1521 *Fax:* 503-238-6281
oregon.chapter@sierraclub.org
oregon.sierraclub.org
To advance the preservation and protection of the natural environment by empowering the citizenry with charitable resources to further the cause of environmental protection.
Amanda Caffall, Chair
Mary Fifield, Vice Chair

1259 Solar Oregon
1231 NW Hoyt St. 503-231-5662
Suite 402 info@SolarOregon.org
Portland, OR 97209 solaroregon.org
A non-profit membership organization providing public education and community outreach to encourage Oregonians to choose solar energy
Alan Scott, President
Lisa Logie, Executive Director

1260 University of Oregon Environmental Studies Program
5223 University of Oregon 541-346-5257
Eugene, OR 97403-5223 *Fax:* 541-346-5954
envs.uoregon.edu
Environmental Studies crosses the boundaries of traditional disciplines, challenging faculty and students to look at the relationship between humans and their environment from a new perspective. They are dedicated to gaining greaterunderstanding of the natural world from an ecological perspective; devising policy and behavior that address contemporary environmental problems; and promoting a rethinking of basic cultural premises, ways of structuring knowledge and the rootmetaphors of society.
Founded: 1983
Monica Guy, Office Manager
Mark Carey, Director, Env. Studies

1261 Wildlife Society
PO Box 2378 541-937-2131
Corvallis, OR 97339 *Fax:* 541-937-3401
To promote wise conservation and management of wildlife resources in Oregon by serving and representing wildlife professionals.
Mark Penninger, President

Pennsylvania

1262 Air & Waste Management Association
Koppers Building 412-232-3444
436 Seventh Avenue, Suite 2100 800-270-3444
Pittsburgh, PA 15219 *Fax:* 412-232-3450
info@awma.org
www.awma.org
Professional development organization providing a forum for the exchange of information, networking, public education, and outreach to over 5,000 environmental professionals in 65 countries.
Founded: 1907
Stephanie Glyptis, Executive Director
Tracy Fedkoe, Director, Marketing

1263 Alliance for the Chesapeake Bay
3310 Market Street 717-737-8622
Suite A *Fax:* 717-737-8650
Camp Hill, PA 17011 contact@allianceforthebay.org
www.allianceforthebay.org
Founded: 1971
David Bancroft, President

1264 American Bass Association of Eastern Pennsylvania & New Jersey
NJ abapanj@gmail.com
www.bestbassteams.com
The American Bass Association of PA & NJ is dedicated to the promotion of bass fishing as a major sport, to conserve the future of fishing through the protection and enhancement of fishery resources and to introduce fishing to Americanyouth.
Founded: 1974
Fred Eurick, President
Mark Dilatush, VP

1265 American Lung Association of Pennsylvania
3001 Old Gettysburg Road 717-541-5864
Camp Hill, PA 17011 ckillinger@lunginfo.org
www.lung.org/about-us/local-associations/pennsylvania.html
The American Lung Association of Pennsylvania works to prevent lung disease and promote lung health through direct assistance, education programs, advocacy and research.
Deborah Brown, Excutive VP, Mid-Atlantic
Joy Meyer, VP, Community Impact

1266 American Lung Association of Pennsylvania: Allentown
2200 W Hamilton Street 610-253-5060
Suite 318 kwerkheiser@lunginfo.org
Allentown, PA 18104 www.lung.org/about-us/local-associations/pennsylvania.html
Deborah Brown, Excutive VP, Mid-Atlantic
Joy Meyer, VP, Community Impact

1267 American Lung Association of Pennsylvania: Pittsburgh
810 River Avenue 412-321-4029
Suite 140 pschnarrs@lunginfo.org
Pittsburgh, PA 15212 www.lung.org/about-us/local-associations/pennsylvania.html
Deborah Brown, Excutive VP, Mid-Atlantic
Joy Meyer, VP, Community Impact

1268 American Lung Association of Pennsylvania: Plymouth Meeting & Scranton
527 Plymouth Road 610-941-9595
Suite 415 jkeith@lunginfo.org
Plymouth Meeting, PA 19462 www.lung.org/about-us/local-associations/pennsylvania.html
Deborah Brown, Excutive VP, Mid-Atlantic
Joy Meyer, VP, Community Impact

1269 American Rivers: Mid-Atlantic Region
1 Danker Avenue 518-482-2631
Albany, NY 12206 *Fax:* 518-482-2632
www.americanrivers.org
Stephanie Lindloff, Director

1270 American Society of Landscape Architects: Pennsylvania/Delaware Chapter
908 North Second Street 717-441-6041
Harrisburg, PA 19102 www.padeasla.org
Founded: 1899
Adam Supplee, President
John D Wanner, Executive Director

1271 Appalachian States Low-Level Radioactive Waste Commission
Rachel Carson State Office Building 410-537-3345
400 Market Street, 13th Floor *Fax:* 410-537-4133
Harrisburg, PA 17101 kmcginty@state.pa.us
www.dep.state.pa.us
The commission was ratified by Maryland, Delaware, Pennsylvania and West Virginia to assure intertstate cooperation for the proper packaging and transportation of low-level radioactive waste. Pennsylvania is the host state and handlesthe administrative duties of the commission at this time.
Founded: 1986
Kathleen A McGinty, Chair/Executive Director
Richard R Janati, Administrator

1272 Audubon Society of Western Pennsylvania at the Beechwood Farms Nature Reserve
614 Dorseyville Road 412-963-6100
Pittsburgh, PA 15238 *Fax:* 412-963-6761
aswp@aswp.org
www.aswp.org/
To inspire and educate the people of southwesterm Pennsylvania to be respectful and responsible stewards of the natural world.
Founded: 1916
Sally Tarhi, President
Jim Bonner, Executive Director

1273 B.A.S.S Nation: Pennsylvania Chapter
PA president@pabassnation.com
www.pabassnation.com
The Pennsylvania Chapter of BASS Nation is dedicated to the promotion of the sport of bass fishing, fishing tournaments and conservation initiatives to preserve the states natural resources.
Josh Giran, President
Derek Severns, VP

1274 Brandywine Conservancy
PO Box 141 610-388-2700
Chadds Ford, PA 19317 *Fax:* 610-388-1197
emc@brandywine.org
www.brandywineconservancy.org
The Conservancy is a nonprofit land and water conservation organization protecting natural resources in southeastern PA and northern DE. It provides conservation services to landowners, farmers and municipalities through acomprehensive approach to cutting-edge environmental planning and management. Through conservation easements, historic preservation, and water protection efforts, the Conservancy has been instrumental in permanently protecting more than 43,000 acresof land.
Founded: 1967
Joel E. Necowitz, Director of Finance
Andrew Stewart, Director of Marketing

1275 Global Education Motivators
9601 Germantown Avenue 215-248-1150
Philadelphia, PA 19118 877-451-7925
Fax: 215-248-7056
gem@chc.edu
A non-profit organization to help schools meet the complex challenges of living in a global society.
Founded: 1981
Wayne Jacoby, President
Sabrina Cusimano, Director of Programs

1276 Hawk Mountain Sanctuary Association
1700 Hawk Mountain Road 610-756-6961
Kempton, PA 19529 *Fax:* 601-756-4468
www.hawkmountain.org

To conserve birds of prey worldwide by providing leadership in raptor conservation science and education, and by maintaining Hawk Mountain Sanctuary as a model observation, research and education facility.
Wendy Mclean, Chairman
Frederick Beste, III, Vice Chairman

1277 **Nature Conservancy: Pennsylvania Chapter**
Nature Conservancy
2101 North Front Street 717-232-6001
Building # 1 Suite 200 866-298-1267
Harrisburg, PA 17110 *Fax:* 717-232-6061
pa_chapter@tnc.org
nature.org/wherewework/northamerica/states/pennsylvania
To preserve the plants, animals and natural communities that represent the diversity of life on Earth by protecting the lands and waters they need to survive.
Founded: 1951
Bill Kunze, State Director
Nels Johnson, Deputy State Director

1278 **Penn State Institutes of Energy and the Environment**
100 Land and Water Research Buildin 814-863-0291
University Park, PA 16802 *Fax:* 814-865-3378
www.environment.psu.edu
The mission is to expand Penn State's capacity to pursue the newest frontiers in energy and environmental research by encouraging cooperation across disciplines and the participation of local, state, federal and internationalstakeholders.
Tom Richard, Director
Jenni Evans, Acting Director

1279 **Pennsylvania Association of Accredited Environmental Laboratories**
316 Roosevelt Street 570-888-4768
Sayre, PA 18840 *Fax:* 570-882-8538
www.paael.org
A non-profit association of PA DEP accredited laboratories and related industry representatives which takes a leadership role in promoting the advancement of environmental laboratories by: providing educational opportunities,professional development, and a forum for information exchange; providing an arena for memebers to effectively interact with state and national regulatory agencies; and encouraging ethical conduct of environmental laboratories.
Founded: 1987
Twila Dixon, President
Judy Graves, Executive Director

1280 **Pennsylvania Association of Conservation Districts**
25 North Front Street 717-238-7223
Harrisburg, PA 17101 *Fax:* 717-238-7201
pacd@pacd.org
www.pacd.org
A nonprofit organization that supports, enhances and promotes Pennsylvania's Conservation Districts and their programs. PACd provides districts with education and information to help them in their work in land and water conservation.
Founded: 1950
Robert Maiden, Executive Director

1281 **Pennsylvania Environmental Council**
3915-917 Union Deposit Road 717-230-8044
Harrisburg, PA 17109 *Fax:* 717-230-8045
bhill@pecpa.org
www.pecpa.org
Protects and restores the natural and built environments through innovation, collaboration, education and advocacy.
Carol F. McCabe, Chair
Jolene Chinchilli, Vice Chair

1282 **Pennsylvania Forestry Association**
116 Pine Street 717-766-5371
5th Floor 800-835-8065
Harrisburg, PA 17101 thePFA@paforestry.org
pfa.cas.psu.edu
A broad-based citizens organization, provides leadership in sound forest management advice and education and promotes wise stewardship to private land owners, resulting in benefits for the resident of the Commonwealth.
Founded: 1886
Robert W. Piper, Jr., President
Gene F. Odato, Vice President

1283 **Pennsylvania Resources Council**
3606 Providence Road 610-353-1555
Newtown Square, PA 19073 *Fax:* 610-353-6257
infoeast@prc.org
www.prc.org
To promote conservation of our natural resources and protection of scenic beauty through public education and outreach in a collaborative effort with government agencies, business, charitable foundations and other nonprofitorganizations.
Founded: 1939
Tomlinson Fort, President
Robert Jondreau, Executive Director

1284 **Pocono Environmental Education Center**
538 Emery Road 570-828-2319
Dingsman Ferry, PA 18328-9614 *Fax:* 570-828-9695
peec@peec.org
www.peec.org
PEEC enhances environmental awareness, knowledge, and appreciation through hands-on experience in a natural outdoor classroom. Located in the Delaware Water Gap National Recreation Area, PEEC is open year-round and welcomes schoolgroups families, retreats, and volunteers.
Founded: 1972
Jeff Rosalsky, Executive Director
Dennis Miranda, Development Director

1285 **Rodale Institute**
611 Siegfriedale Road 610-683-1400
Kutztown, PA 19530-9320 *Fax:* 610-683-8548
info@rodaleinst.org
www.rodaleinstitute.org
Works with people worldwide to achieve a regenerative food system thaty renews environmental and human health working with the philosophy that healthy soil = healthy food = healthy people.
Mark Smallwood, Executive Director
Dr. Kristine Nichols, Chief Scientist

1286 **Sierra Club: Pennsylvania Chapter**
PO Box 606 717-232-0101
Harrisburg, PA 17108 *Fax:* 717-238-6330
pennsylvania.chapter@sierraclub.org
pennsylvania.sierraclub.org
Includes 10 local Sierra Club groups. Emphasis is on state environmental policy advocacy, outings, education and local environmental protection efforts.
Joanne Kilgour, Esq. , Director
Deb Nardone, Director

1287 **Western Pennsylvania Conservancy**
800 Waterfront Drive 412-288-2777
Pittsburgh, PA 15222 866-564-6972
Fax: 412-231-1414
info@paconserve.org
Protects, conserves and restores land and water for the diversity of the region's plants, animals and their ecosystems. Through science-based strategies, collaboration, leadership and recognition of the relationship between humankindand nature, WPC achieves tangible conservation outcomes for present and future generations.
Susan Fitzsimmons, Chairman
Stephen G Robinson, Vice Chairman

Rhode Island

1288 **American Lung Association of Rhode Island**
260 West Exchange Street
Suite 102 B 401-421-6487
Providence, RI 02903 info@lungne.org
www.lung.org/about-us/local-associations/rhode-island.html

The American Lung Association of Rhode Island works to prevent lung disease and promote lung health through direct assistance, education programs, advocacy and research.
Jeff Seyler, Executive VP, Northeast
Adam Shuster, CFO

1289 **American Society of Landscape Architects: Rhode Island Chapter**
www.riasla.org
The purpose shall be the advancement of knowledge, education, and skill in the art and science of landscape architecture as an instrument of service in the public welfare.
Jennifer Judge, President
Kurt Van Dexter, President-Elect

1290 **Audubon Society of Rhode Island**
12 Sanderson Road 401-949-5454
Smithfield, RI 02917 *Fax:* 401-949-5788
audubon@asri.org
www.asri.org
An independent, nonprofit, state organization dedicated to the conservation of wildlife habitat, the education of young and old about natural ecosystems and the need to preserve them, and advocacy in order to promote continued effortsat preserving our natural heritage.
Founded: 1897
Cynthia J. Warren, Esq., President
Deborah Linnell , VP

1291 **Nature Conservancy: Rhode Island Chapter**
159 Waterman Street 401-331-7110
Providence, RI 02906 *Fax:* 401-273-4902
ri@tnc.org
www.nature.org
An international nonprofit organization dedicated to preserving the plants, animals and natural communities that represent the diversity of life on Earth by protecting the lands and waters they need to survive.
John Cook, Regional Managing Director

1292 **Sierra Club: Rhode Island Chapter**
42 Rice Street 401-521-4734
Providence, RI 02907 chair@risierraclub.org
rhodeisland.sierraclub.org
To advance the preservation and protection of the natural environment by empowering the citizenry with charitable resources to further the cause of environmental protection.
2500 Members
Dana Goodman, Chair
Peter Galvin, Treasurer

South Carolina

1293 **American Lung Association of South Carolina**
44-A Markfield Drive 843-556-8451
Charleston, SC 29407 *Fax:* 843-766-3294
costal@lungsc.org
www.lung.org/about-us/local-associations/south-carolina.html
The American Lung Association of South Carolina works to prevent lung disease and promote lung health through direct assistance, education programs, advocacy and research.
Martha C. Bogdan, Executive VP, Southeast
Willie L. Bythwood, Jr, CFO

1294 **American Lung Association of South Carolina: Upstate**
2030 North Church Place 864-764-1777
Spartanburg, SC 29303 upstate@lungsc.org
www.lung.org
Martha C. Bogdan, Executive VP, Southeast
Willie L. Bythwood, Jr, CFO

1295 **American Rivers: Southeast Region**
215 Pickens Street 803-771-7114
Columbia, SC 29205 *Fax:* 803-771-7580
www.americanrivers.org
Jeremy Diner, Clean Water Supply Associate
Ben Emanuel, Associate Dir, Water Supply

1296 **American Society of Landscape Architects: South Carolina Chapter**
7 Lafayette Place 843-681-6618
Hilton Head Island, SC 29926 *Fax:* 843-681-7086
www.scasla.org
Jesse McClung, President
Jamie Hairfield, President Elect

1297 **B.A.S.S Nation: South Carolina Chapter**
SC www.scbassfed.org
The South Carolina Chapter of BASS Nation is dedicated to the promotion of the sport of bass fishing, fishing tournaments and conservation initiatives to preserve the states natural resources
Randy Mosley, President
Chris Jones, VP

1298 **Carolina Recycling Association**
PO Box 1296 877-972-0007
Greenville, SC 29602 *Fax:* 919-545-9060
staff@cra-recycle.org
www.cra-recycle.org
Conserves resources by advancing waste reducation and recycling throughout the Carolinas
Founded: 1989
Amanda Kain, Board President
Harris Deloach III, Board VP

1299 **Friends of the Reedy River**
PO Box 9351 864-255-8946
Greensville, SC 29604 www.friendsofthereedyriver.org
The Reedy River is an economic and social resource for the community that impacts our quality of life. Maintaining and protecting its health, above and below the surface, is pivotal in maintaining the natural, social and economicalhealth of the Upstate of South Carolina.
Nikki Grumbine, President
Bob Lloyd, Vice President

1300 **Nature Conservancy: South Carolina Chapter**
2231 Devine Street, Suite 100 803-254-9049
P.O. Box 5475 *Fax:* 803-252-7134
Columbia, SC 29205 southcarolina@tnc.org
www.nature.org
To preserve the plants, animals and natural communities that represent the diversity of life on Earth by protecting the lands and waters they need to survive.
Mark Robertson, Executive Director
Serena Hunter, Director of Operations

1301 **Sierra Club: South Carolina Chapter**
1314 Lincoln Street 803-256-8487
Suite 211 *Fax:* 803-256-8448
Columbia, SC 29202 southcarolina.sierraclub.org
To advance the preservation and protection of the natural environment by empowering the citizenry with charitable resources to further the cause of environmental protection.
Kurt Henning, Chapter Coordinator

1302 **South Atlantic Fishery Management Council**
1314 Lincoln Street, Suite 211 803-256-8487
P O Box 2388 866-SAF-C 10
Columbia, SC 29201 *Fax:* 843-769-4520
safmc@safmc.net
www.safmc.net
Responsible for the conservation and management of fish stocks within the federal 200-mile limit of the Atlantic off the coasts of North Carolina, South Carolina, Georgia and east Florida to Key West.
Robert Mahood, Executive Director
Gregg Waugh, Deputy Executive Director

1303 **South Carolina Native Plant Society**
PO Box 1324 jeffbeacham@gmail.com
Greenville, SC 29602 www.scnps.org
A non-profit ograniization committed to the preservation and protection of native plant communities in South Carolina.
Jeff Beacham, President
Thomas Angell, Vice-President

1304 **South Carolina Solar Council**
PO Box 402 803-691-4576
Columbia, SC 29201 scsolarcouncil@gmail.com
www.scsolarcouncil.org
Todd Delello, Chairman
Ron Sebeczek, Treasurer

1305 **Southern Appalachian Botanical Society: Gastanea**
Newberry College
2100 College Street 803-321-5257
Newberry, SC 29108 *Fax:* 803-321-5636
charles.horn@newberry.edu
www.sabs.us
This is a professional organization for those interested in botanical research, especially in the areas of ecology, floristics and systematics. To this end, they publish a journal, CASTANEA, and a newsletter, CHINQUAPIN.
Founded: 1936
Charles Horn, President
Kunsiri Grubbs, Treasurer

South Dakota

1306 **American Fisheries Society: North Central Division: Dakota Chapter**
SD Steven.Chipps@sdstate.edu
The Dakota Chapter of the American Fisheries Society, is part of the American Fisheries Society (AFS) North Central Division. The Dakota Chapter works to further to the goals of the AFS and is committed to the conservation,development, and wise use of fishery resources, the chapter provides several annual awards to fishery professionals, conservation groups, and students.
Steve Chipps, President
Michael Johnson, Secretary & Treasurer

1307 **American Fisheries Society: Socioeconomics Section**
SDSU Dept. of Natural Resource Management
Box 2230 320-699-9221
Brookings, SD 57007 Aaron.Sundmark@sdstate.edu
units.fisheries.org/socioecon
Promotes the use of social science information in fisheries management.
Mackenzie Mazur, President
Aaron P. Sundmark, Secretary-Treasurer

1308 **American Lung Association of South Dakota**
490 Concordia Avenue 651-227-8014
St. Paul, MN 55103 info@lungsd.org
www.lung.org/about-us/local-associations/south-dakota.html
The American Lung Association of South Dakota works to prevent lung disease and promote lung health through direct assistance, education programs, advocacy and research.
Lewis Bartfield, Executive VP, Upper Midwest
Penny Fena, Chief Mission Officer

1309 **American Society of Landscape Architects: Great Plains Chapter**
NE Regan.Pence@LRA-INC.com
www.gpcasla.org
Representing South Dakota, North Dakota, and Nebraska the Great Plains Chapter of the American Landscape Society works to expand the profession of landscape architecture in these states. The Chapter advocates and provides professionaleducational and developmental programs for its members
Regan Pence, President
Chad Kucker, Secretary & Treasurer

1310 **Great Plains Native Plant Society**
P.O. Box 321 605-745-3397
Hermosa, SD 57744 *Fax:* 605-745-3397
info@gpnps.org
www.gpnps.org
The mission of the Society is to conduct scientific research regarding plants of the Great Plains of North America, and to disseminate this knowledge through the creation of one or more educational botanic gardens of plants of theGreat Plains. These gardens feature, but are not limited to, Barr's discoveries. The society also engages in educational activities that further public familiarity with plants of the Great Plains, their uses, and enjoyment.
Founded: 1984
Cindy Reed, President

1311 **Sierra Club: South Dakota Chapter**
PO Box 1624 605-348-1345
Rapid City, SD 57709 *Fax:* 605-348-1344
southdakota.sierraclub.org
To advance the preservation and protection of the natural environment by empowering the citizenry with charitable resources to further the cause of environmental protection.
Dana Loseke, Chair
Michelle Loseke, Secretary

1312 **South Dakota Association of Conservation Districts**
116 N Euclid Avenue 605-895-4099
Pierre, SD 57501 800-729-4099
www.sdconservation.org
Mission is to lead, represent and assist South Dakota's conservation districts in promoting a healthy environment. Specific areas of concern include wind and water erosion, water quality and quantity including preservation of theMissouri main stem dams, air quality, forestry, rangeland, wildlife and recreation.
Founded: 1942
Angela Ehlers, Executive Director
Karl Jensen, President

1313 **South Dakota Ornithologists Union**
Sioux Falls, SD 57105 www.sdou.org
To encourage the study of birds in South Dakota and to promote the study of orinthology by more closely uniting the students of this branch of natural science.
Founded: 1949
Kent C. Jensen, President
Scott Stolz, Vice President

1314 **South Dakota Wildlife Federation**
PO Box 7075 605-224-7524
Pierre, SD 57501 *Fax:* 605-224-7524
sdwf@mncomm.com
www.sdwf.org
Represents the interests of all South Dakotans in wildelife, outdoor recreation, natural resources, and a quality environment.
Founded: 1945
Rich Widman, President
Mark Widman, 1st Vice-President

1315 **Wildlife Society**
Box 218 605-854-9105
DeSmet, SD 57231 paul.coughlin@state.sd.us
A nonprofit scientific and educational organization that serves professionals such as government agencies, academia, industry, and non-government organizations in all areas related to the conservation of wildlife and natural resourcesmanagement.
Founded: 1937
Will Morlock, South Dakota State President

Tennessee

1316 **American Fisheries Society: Fisheries Information and Technology Section**
c/o Tennessee Tech University
Box 5114 knkey42@students.tntech.edu
Cookeville, TN 38505 units.fisheries.org/fits

Provides the fisheries community with expertise on new technology, including software and database systems. Sponsors technological workshops and symposia.
Paul Venturelli, President
Kayla Key, Secretary-Treasurer

1317 American Lung Association of Tennessee
1466 Riverside Drive 423-629-1098
Suite D Gail.Bost@lung.org
Chattanooga, TN 37406 www.lung.org/about-us/local-associations/tennessee.html
The American Lung Association of Tennessee is dedicated to preventing lung disease and promoting lung health through direct assistance, education programs, advocacy and research.
Barry Gottschalk, Executive VP, Midland States
Patricia J. Volz, VP, Communication

1318 American Lung Association of Tennessee: Nashville
One Vantage Way 615-329-1151
Suite C 120 Gail.Bost@lung.org
Nashville, TN 37228 www.lung.org/about-us/local-associations/tennessee.html
Barry Gottschalk, Executive VP, Midland States
Patricia J Vloz, VP, Communication

1319 American Society of Landscape Architects: Tennessee Chapter
hollie@tnasla.org
www.tnasla.org
Allen Jonest, President
Alisha Eley, President-Elect

1320 Environmental Toxicology Laboratory
PO Box 2008 865-574-9387
Oak Ridge, TN 37831 www.ornl.gov/content/environmental-toxicology-laboratory
Oak Ridge National Laboratory's Environmental Toxicology Laboratory provides toxicity testing for the DOE, DoD and other Federal agencies.
Mark Greeley Jr., Contact

1321 Kids for a Clean Environment
PO Box 158254 615-331-7381
Nashville, TN 37215 *Fax:* 615-333-9879
kidsface@mindspring.com
www.kidsface.org
Established to help children who wanted to learn more about the world in which they live, provide a way for children to be involved in the protection of nature and connect children with other children who share their concerns aboutglobal environmental issues.
Founded: 1989
Melissa Poe, Founder

1322 Nature Conservancy: Tennessee Chapter
2021 21st Avenue South 615-383-9909
Suite C-400 800-628-6860
Nashville, TN 37212 *Fax:* 615-383-9717
tennessee@tnc.org
www.nature.org
To preserve the plants, animals and natural communities that represent the diversity of life on Earth by protecting the lands and waters they need to survive.
Founded: 1951
Gina Hancock, State Director
Paul Kingsbury, Communications Manager

1323 Scenic Tennessee
45 Burris Court 615-758-8647
Mount Juliet, TN 37122 margedavis@comcast.net
The only organization in the state devoted exclusively to issues of scenic beauty.
Marge Davis Ph D, President
Jay Nevans, Vice President

1324 Sierra Club: Tennessee Chapter
3712 Ringgold Road 615-837-3773
#156 tennessee.sierraclub.org
Chattanooga, TN 37412-1638
To advance the preservation and protection of the natural environment by empowering the citizenry with charitable resources to further the cause of environmental protection.
Keven Routon, Chair
Angela Garrone, Vice Chair

1325 Tennessee Association of Conservation Districts
PO Box 107 731-764-2909
Hickory Valley, TN 38042 *Fax:* 731-658-6726
tnacd.org
Founded: 1982
Ray Weaver, President
John Leeman, Vice President

1326 Tennessee Citizens for Wilderness Planning
130 Tabor Road 865-481-0286
Oak Ridge, TN 37830 groton87@comcast.net
www.tcwp.org
Dedicated to achieving and perpetuating protection of natural lands and waters by means of public ownership, legislation, or cooperation of the private sector.
Founded: 1966
Jimmy Groton, President
Sandra Goss, Executive Director

1327 Tennessee Environmental Council
One Vantage Way 615-248-6500
Suite E-250 *Fax:* 615-248-6500
Nashville, TN 37228 tec@tectn.org
www.tectn.org
The mission of the Tennessee Environmental Council is to educate and advocate for the conservation and improvement of Tennessee's environment, communities, and public health.
Founded: 1970
Pat Van Ryckeghem, Chairman
Mary Mastin, Board Secretary

1328 Tennessee Woodland Owners Association
PO Box 1400 615-484-5535
Crossville, TN 38557 *Fax:* 915-484-1924
Robert Harrison, Secretary/Treasurer

1329 Wildlife Society
554 University Street 731-881-7000
PO Box 40747 mdodson@fs.fed.us
Martin, TN 38238 www.utm.edu/TN-TWS
A nonprofit scientific and educational organization that serves professionals such as government agencies, academia, industry, and non-government organizations in all areas related to the conservation of wildlife and natural resourcesmanagement.
Founded: 1968 $10/Year
Ed Warr, President
Tim White, President-Elect

Texas

1330 American Environmental Health Foundation
8345 Walnut Hill Lane 214-361-9515
Suite 225 800-428-2343
Dallas, TX 75231 *Fax:* 214-361-2534
aehf@aehf.com
www.aehf.com
The Environmental Health Foundation's mission is two-fold: to fund scientific and/or medical research into the causes of environmentally linked disease; and to educate the public about environmentally linked illness and how to preventexposure through lifestyle changes.
Founded: 1975
William Rea, Founder
David Hicks, Director

1331 American Lung Association of Texas
1349 Empire Central Drive 214-631-5864
Suite 280 TXInfo@lungs.org
Dallas, TX 75247 www.lung.org/about-us/local-associations/texas.html

The American Lung Association of Texas is dedicated to preventing lung disease and promoting lung health through direct assistance, education programs, advocacy and research.
Holly Torres, Executive Director
Kellye Stephens, Program Coordinator

1332 American Lung Association of Texas: Houston
2030 North Loop West 713-476-9882
Suite 250 TXInfo@lungs.org
Houston, TX 77018 www.lung.org/about-us/local-associations/texas.html
Katie Jones, Executive Director
Dr. Rubina Abrol, MD, Program Manager

1333 American Lung Association of Texas: San Antonio & Austin
8207 Callaghan Road 210-308-8978
Suite 140 TXInfo@lungs.org
San Antonio, TX 78230 www.lung.org/about-us/local-associations/texas.html
Bill Pfeifer, Executive VP, Southwest
Robbie Moore, Office Assistant

1334 American Society of Landscape Architects: Texas Chapter
P O Box 170125 512-627-4570
Austin, TX 78725 *Fax:* 512-249-9885
jennifer@texasasla.org
www.texasasla.org
Tim Bargainer, President
Jennifer Fontana,CAE, Executive Director

1335 Association of Texas Soil and Water Conservation Districts
4311 South 31st Street 254-773-2250
Suite 125 800-792-3485
Temple, TX 76502 *Fax:* 254-773-3311
The nonprofit organization attempts to make owners and operators of agricultural land aware of the need to conserve and protect the soil and water resources in Texas. It promotes SWCDs (soil and water conservation districts) througheducational, scientific, charitable, and religious activities.
Scott Buckles, President

1336 Big Bend Natural History Association
PO Box 196 432-477-2236
Big Bend National Park, TX 79834 *Fax:* 432-477-2234
info@bigbendbookstore.org
www.bigbendbookstore.org
The association's goal is to educate the public and increase their appreciation of the Big Bend Area. It conducts seminars, publishes and supplies books, maps and other materials.
Founded: 1956
Mike Boren, Executive Director

1337 Center for Environmental Philosophy
University of North Texas
1704 W Mulberry 940-565-2727
Suite 370 *Fax:* 940-565-4439
Denton, TX 76201 cep@unt.edu
www.cep.unt.edu
The Center for Environmental Philosophy, a non-profit organization affiliated with the University of North Texas, is responsible for the publication of the Environmental Ethics journal, as well as the training and promotion of researchin environmental ethics through workshops and conferences.
Founded: 1989
Eugene C. Hargrove, President
Jan Dickson, Secretary-Treasurer

1338 National Wildlife Federation Gulf States Natural Resource Center
44 East Avenue 512-610-7761
Suite 200 *Fax:* 512-476-9810
Austin, TX 78701 dayanandap@nwf.org
www.nwf.org
The focus of the four state region (TX, LA, OK, MO) is to restore clean rivers and estuaries, conserve wetlands and natural river systems, protect wildlife populations, promote sustainable land and water use, and educate the public onthese issues.
Praween Dayananda, Campus Field Coordinator
Lacey McCormick, Communications Manager

1339 Nature Conservancy: Texas
www.tnc.org/texas/
The Nature Conservancy of Texas conserves habitat for native wildlife, using science based research and a cooperative approach to protect the animals and plants that represent Texas' precious natural heritage.

1340 North Plains Groundwater Conservation District
603 E 1st Street 806-935-6401
PO Box 795 *Fax:* 806-935-6633
Dumas, TX 79029
Founded: 1949
Steven Walthour, General Manager
Casey Tice, Compliance Coordinator

1341 Scenic Texas
3015 Richmond Ave 713-629-0481
Suite 220 *Fax:* 713-629-0485
Houston, TX 77098 scenic@scenictexas.org
www.scenictexas.org
Scenic Texas is a nonprofit organization dedicated to the preservation and enhancement of the tstate's visual environemnt. It seeks and supports public policies which promote scenic conservation and beautification and limits harmfulactions to the visual environment.
Founded: 1967
Don Glendenning, President
Margaret Lloyd, Vice President

1342 Sierra Club: Lone Star Chapter
PO Box 1931 512-477-1729
Austin, TX 78767-1931 *Fax:* 512-477-8526
lonestar.chapter@sierraclub.org
texas.sierraclub.org
The Lone Star Chapter consists of over 25,000 members and serves as the grassroots communications center. The chapter also represents memebers as they fight at the state level to protect and conserve Texas' diverse natural heritage.
Founded: 1965
Reggie James, Director
Cyrus Reed, Conservation Director

1343 Texas Conservation Alliance
PO Box 822554 512-327-4119
Dallas, TX 75382-2554 TCA@TCAtexas.org
tconr.org
Formerly the Texas Committee on Natural Resources. A statewide conservation organization protecting native wildlife habitat and urging the wise and efficient use of natural resources.
Founded: 1970
Mack Turner, Chairman
Richard LeTourneau, Vice Chair

1344 Texas Environmental Health Association
PO Box 889 806-855-4277
Wolfforth, TX 79382 *Fax:* 806-855-4277
www.myteha.org
A professional nonprofit educational organization that was originally founded as the Texas Association of Sanitarians and then merged with the National Environmental Health Association and changed its name in 1971. TEHA provides aprofessional organization for Sanitarians and Environmental Health Professionals, designed to serve as the focal point for their education and professional status.
Founded: 1956
J. Victor Baldovinos, President
Russell O'Brien, President Elect

1345 Texas Solar Energy Society
PO Box 1447 512-326-3391
Austin, TX 78767 800-465-5049
Fax: 512-444-0333
info@txses.org
www.txses.org
Their mission is to increase the awareness of the potential of solar and other renewable energy applications and promote the wise use of these sustainable and non-polluting resources.
Lucy Stolzenburg, Executive Director
Scot Arey, Chairman

1346 Texas State Soil and Water Conservation Board (TSSWCB)
4311 South 31st Street 254-773-2250
Suite 125 800-792-3485
Temple, TX 76502 *Fax:* 254-773-3311
The state agency that administers Texas' soil and water conservation laws and coordinates conservation and nonpoint source pollution abatement programs through the State. The Board is composed of 7 members, 2 Governor appointed and 5landowners, from across Texas, and is the lead state agency for planning, management, and abatement of agricultural and silvicultural (forestry) nonpoint source pollution, and administers the Texas Brush Control Program. There are regional officesthroughout Texas.
Founded: 1939
Marty H. Graham, Chairman
Scott Buckles, Vice Chairman

1347 Texas Water Conservation Association
3755 S. Capital of Texas Highway 512-472-7216
Suite 105 *Fax:* 512-472-0537
Austin, TX 78704 admin@twca.org
www.twca.org
The Texas Water Conservation Association consists of water professionals and organizations in the state of Texas who represent river authorities, municipalities, navigation and flood control districts, drainage and irrigationdistricts, utility districts, municipalities, groundwater conservation districts, all kinds of water users, and general/environmental water interests.
Founded: 1944
Michael J. Baldovinos, President
Hope Wells, President-Elect

Utah

1348 American Fisheries Society: Water Quality Section
324 25th Street 801-625-5358
Ogden, UT 84401 *Fax:* 801-625-5756
glampman@fs.fed.us
Section objectives are to: maintain an association of persons involved in the protection of watersheds, water quality, and aquatic habitat, and the abatement of water pollution and aquatic habitat and water deterioration.
Gina Lampman, President

1349 American Lung Association Of Utah
3920 South 1100 East 801-484-4456
Suite 240 UTInfo@Lungs.org
Salt Lake City, UT 84124 www.lung.org/about-us/local-associations/utah.html
The American Lung Association of Utah is committed to preventing lung disease and promoting lung health, through education, research, and advocacy.
Founded: 1904
Bill Pfeifer, Executive VP, Southwest
Kelly Smith, Senior VP,Programs

1350 American Society of Landscape Architects: Utah Chapter
636 Eye Street NW 202-898-2444
Washington, DC 20001 888-999-2752
Fax: 202-898-1185
info@asla.org

1351 Grand Canyon Trust: Utah Office
390 Castle Creek Lane 435-259-5284
Moab, UT 84532 info@grandcanyontrust.org
www.grandcanyontrust.org
A regional, non-profit conservation organization that advocates for collaborative, common sense solutions to the significant problems affecting the natural resources of the greater Grand Canyon region of northern Arizona, as well asthe forests and red rock country of central and southern Utah.
Bill Hedden, Executive Director
Ethan Aumack, Conservation Director

1352 Jack H Berryman Institute
Utah State University 435-797-2436
5230 Old Main Hill NR 206 *Fax:* 435-797-1871
Logan, UT 84322-5271 www.berrymaninstitute.org
The Berryman Institute is a national organization based in the Department of Wildland Resources at Utah State University and the Department of Wildlife & Fisheries at Mississippi State University. The Berryman Institiute is dedicatedto improving human-wildlife relationships and resolving human-wildlife conflicts through teaching, research, and extension.
Dr. Terry A. Messmer, Director
Dr. Mike Conover, Editor in Chief

1353 Nature Conservancy: Utah Chapter
559 E South Temple 801-531-0999
Salt Lake City, UT 84102 *Fax:* 801-531-1003
utah@tnc.org
www.tnc.org/utah
To preserve the plants, animals and natural communities that represent the diversity of life on Earth by protecting the lands and waters they need to survive.
Founded: 1951
Dave Livermore, State Director
Ian Mathias, Marketing Manager

1354 Sierra Club: Utah Chapter
423 W 800 S STE A103 801-467-9294
Salt Lake City, UT 84101-4803 utah.chapter@sierraclub.org
utah.sierraclub.org
To advance the preservation and protection of the natural environment by empowering the citizenry with charitable resources to further the cause of environmental protection.
Founded: 1892
Marion Klaus, Chair
Leslie Hugo, Secretary

1355 Southern Utah Wilderness Alliance
425 East 100 South 801-486-3161
Salt Lake City, UT 84111 info@suwa.org
www.suwa.org
The mission is the preservation of the outstanding wilderness at the heartof the Colorado Plateau, and the mangement of these lands in their natural state for the benefit of all Americans.
Founded: 1983
Darrell Knuffke, Chair
Richard Ingebretsen, Vice-Chair & Secretary

1356 Utah Association of Conservation Districts
PO Box 4117 435-881-7688
Logan, UT 84323 www.uacd.org
A nonprofit corporation representing Utah's 38 soil conservation districts. Provides technicians and planners to design conservation projects for private landowners, staff to coordinate watershed and conservation district projects andconservation education outreach.
Bob Barry, President
Allen Henrie, Vice President

1357 Utah Association of Soil Conservation Districts
40 West Cache Valley Blvd. 435-753-6029
Building 8C *Fax:* 435-753-4037
Logan, UT 84341 www.uacd.org
William Rigby, Executive Board Member

1358 **Utah Division of Wildlife Resources**
1594 West North Temple 801-538-4700
Suite 2110 Box 146301 *Fax:* 801-538-4745
Salt Lake City, UT 84114-6301 wildlife.utah.gov
Serve people of Utah as trustee and guardian of the state's wildlife.

1359 **Utah Solar Energy Association**
7414 S State 801-566-5620
PO Box 25263 *Fax:* 801-566-0708
SLC, UT 84125 info@UTSOLAR.org
utsolar.org
Organized to promote the usage of renewable energy, with a focus on solar energy, through education, public outreach, participation in policy development and other activities to accomplish the goals of the organization.

Vermont

1360 **American Lung Association of Vermont**
372 Hurricane Lane 802-876-6500
Suite 101 info@lungne.org
Williston, VT 05495 www.lung.org/about-us/local-associations/vermont.html
The American Lung Association of Vermont is dedicated to preventing lung disease and promoting lung health through direct assistance, education programs, advocacy and research.
Jeff Seyler, Executive VP, Northeast
Adam Shuster, CFO

1361 **American Society of Landscape Architects: Vermont Chapter**
PO Box 1844 info@vtasla.org
Chester www.vtasla.org
Burlington, VT 05401
The chapter holds monthly meetings to encourage dialogue among practioners and members, collaborate with those in related fields, and embrace professional guidelines.
Scott Wunderle, President
Hannah Loope, President Elect

1362 **Bluebirds Across Vermont Project**
The Birdhouse Network
255 Sherman Hollow Road 802-434-3068
Green Mountain Abdubon Society *Fax:* 802-434-4686
Huntington, VT 05462 bluebirdhousing@ellijay.com
www.cornell.edu
Elizabeth Garrett, President

1363 **Conservation and Research Foundation**
PO Box 909 913-268-0076
Shelburne, VT 05482 *Fax:* 913-268-0076
www.conservationresearch.wordpress.com
Founded: 1953
Mary Wetzel, President
Myron Sopher, Treasurer

1364 **National Wildlife Federation Northeastern Natural Resource Center**
149 State Street 802-229-0650
Suite 1 800-822-9919
Montpelier, VT 05602 *Fax:* 802-229-4532
www.nwf.org
The Northeastern Field Office works with state-based affiliates and like-minded organizations to protect valuable woods, water and wildlife resources across New England through education, advocacy and research.
Curtis Fisher, Regional Executive Director
Catherine Bowes, Senior Manager

1365 **Northeast Recycling Council**
139 Main Street 802-254-3636
Suite 401 info@nerc.org
Brattleboro, VT 05301 www.nerc.org
NERC's mission is to To advance an environmentally sustainable economy by promoting source and toxicity reduction, recycling, and the purchasing of environmentally preferable products and services.
Robert Isner, President
Kaley Laleker, Vice President

1366 **Sierra Club: Vermont Chapter**
4 Saint Paul St. 802-229-6399
Montpelier, VT 05602 sierraclub.vt@gmail.com
vermont.sierraclub.org
To advance the preservation and protection of the natural environment by empowering the citizenry with charitable resources to further the cause of environmental protection.
Mark Nelson , Chair
David Ellenbogen, Vice-Chair

1367 **Vermont Association of Conservation Districts**
PO Box 566 802-496-5162
Waitsfield, VT 05673-2057 *Fax:* 802-329-2057
jill.arace@vacd.org
www.vacd.org
A non-profit organization of Vermont's 14 Conservation Districts whose mission is to help the Districts carry out natural resource oriented programs at the local level.
Jonathan Chamberlin, President
D. Jill Arace, Executive Director

1368 **Vermont Haulers and Recyclers Association**
PO Box 976 802-864-3615
Williston, VT 05495 *Fax:* 802-660-8553

1369 **Vermont Land Trust**
8 Bailey Avenue 802-223-5234
Montpelier, VT 05602 800-639-1709
Fax: 802-223-4223
info@vlt.org
www.vlt.org
One of the most effective land trusts in the country. Its primary focus is on permanently conserving productive, recreational, and scenic lands vital to Vermont's and rural economy and environment.
Founded: 1977
Gil Livingston, President
Rick Provost, Director of Finance

1370 **Vermont Public Interest Research Group**
141 Main Street 802-223-5221
Suite 6 *Fax:* 802-223-6855
Montpelier, VT 05602 vpirg@vpirg.org
www.vpirg.org
The largest nonprofit consumer and environmental advocacy organization in the state, with approximately 20,000 members and supporters. VPIRG's mission is to promote and protect the health of Vermont's people, environment andlocally-based economy by informing and mobilizing citizens statewide.
Founded: 1972
Paul Burns, Executive Director
Colleen Thomas, Associate Director

1371 **Vermont State-Wide Environmental Education Programs**
P.O. Box 412 802-985-8686
Lincoln, MA 00177 info@neeea.org
vermontsweep.org
Heather Durkel, Co-Chair
Jenna Guarino, Co-Chair

Virginia

1372 **American Bird Conservancy**
4249 Loudoun Ave 540-253-5780
PO Box 249 888-247-3624
The Plains, VA 20198-2237 *Fax:* 540-253-5782
www.abcbirds.org

A not-for-profit organization whose mission is to conserve native birds and their habitats throughout the Americas.
George H Fenwick, President
Warren F Cooke, Chairman

1373 American Dream
PO Box 797 301-891-3683
Suite 101 newdream@newdream.org
Charlottesville, VA 22902 www.newdream.org
New Dream empowers individuals, communities, and organizations to transform their consumption habits to improve the well-being of people and the planet.
Founded: 1997
Guinevere Higgins, Strategic Partnerships
Casey Williams, Operations & Outreach

1374 American Fisheries Society: International Fisheries Section
National Climate Change & Wildlife Science Center
12201 Sunrise Valley Drive 703-648-4097
MS-516, Room 21225B units.fisheries.org/ifs
Reston, VA 20192
Dedicated to AFS members with an interest in global fisheries science.
Abigail Lynch, President
Danielle Reich, Treasurer

1375 American Lung Association of Virginia
9702 Gayton Road,#110 804-302-5740
Richmond, VA 23238 kkoon@lunginfo.org
www.lung.org/about-us/local-associations/virginia.html
The American Lung Association of Virginia is dedicated to preventing lung disease and promoting lung health through direct assistance, education programs, advocacy and research.
Deborah Brown, Executive Director
Joy Meyer, VP, Community Impact

1376 American Society of Landscape Architects: Virginia Chapter
2415-B Westwood Avenue 804-523-2901
Richmond, VA 23230 *Fax:* 804-288-3551
mary.kidd@vaasla.org
www.vaasla.org
Founded: 1899
Barry Frankenfield, President
Jimmy Shepherd, President-Elect

1377 Arlington Outdoor Education Association
Phoebe Hall Knipling Outdoor Laboratory
PO Box 5646 703-228-7650
Arlington, VA 22205 *Fax:* 540-349-3336
arlingtonoutdoorlab@gmail.com
www.outdoorlab.org
Founded to own and operate the Phoebe Hall Knipling Outdoor Laboratory. Its primary purpose is to provide a facility and support a school program designed to give urban school children who live in Arlington, Virginia, an opportunity tolearn science, outdoor skills, arts and humanities in a natural setting.
Founded: 1967
Mike Nardolilli, President
Bob Schrider, Vice President

1378 Ashoka
1700 N Moore Street 703-527-8300
Suite 2000, 20th Floor *Fax:* 703-527-8383
Arlington, VA 22209 info@ashoka.org
www.ashoka.org
Strives to shape a global, entrepreneurial, competitive citizen sector: one that allows social entrepreneurs to thrive and enables the world's citizens to think and act as changemakers.
Bill Drayton, CEO/Chair
Diana Wells, President

1379 Association for Facilities Engineering
12801 Worldgate Drive 571-203-7171
Suite 500 *Fax:* 571-766-2142
Herndon, VA 20170 info@AFE.org
www.afe.org
The premier organization for facility engineers and maintenance personnel. Unites a large community of likeminded professionals for networking opportunities, knowledge-sharing, and support, as well as offers members a world variety ofeducational opportunities, training, and certification for career advancement.
Dennis M. Hydrick, President & Chairman
Wayne P. Saya, Sr., CPE, Executive Director

1380 Audubon Society of Northern Virginia
11100 Wildlife Center Drive 703-438-6008
Suite 100 info@audubonva.org
Reston, VA 20190 www.audubonva.org
To conserve and restore natural ecosystems. ASNV carries out conservation, education and advocacy programs throughout the region from Alexandria to Manassas in Fairfax, Prince William, Loudoun and Arlington counties, and beyond.
Founded: 1980
Terrence Liercke, President
Bill Brown, Treasurer

1381 Chesapeake Bay Foundation
Capitol Place
1108 E Main Street 804-780-1392
Suite 1600 *Fax:* 804-648-4011
Richmond, VA 23219 chesapeake@cbf.org
www.cbf.org
Founded: 1964
William C. Baker, President
Fay R. Nance, Chief Financial Officer

1382 Mid Atlantic Solar Energy Society
PO Box 3333 301-880-7045
Fairfax, VA 22038 info@mases.org
www.mases.org
Mid Atlantic Solar Energy Society (MASES) is a nonprofit organization working to further the development of, use of, and support solar energy. MASES is the regional chapter of the American Solar Energy Society and serves Maryland,Washington DC and Virginia, Delaware, New Jersey, Pennsylvania and West Virginia (Formerly known as Potomac Region Solar Energy Association (PRSEA)).
John Essig

1383 Nature Conservancy
4245 North Fairfax Drive 703-841-5300
Suite 100 800-628-6860
Arlington, VA 22203-1606 mlipford@tnc.org
www.nature.org
To preserve the plants, animals and natural communities that represent the diversity of life on Earth by protecting the lands and waters they need to survive.
Michael L Lipford, Executive Director

1384 Potomac Appalachian Trail Club
118 Park Street SE 703-242-0315
Vienna, VA 22180-4609 *Fax:* 703-242-0968
info@patc.net
www.patc.net
A volunteer-based organization, founded by the men and women who planned and built the Appalachian Trail. The Club now manages over 1000 miles of hiking trails in the Mid-Atlantic region, along with cabins, shelters, and hundreds ofacres of conserved land.
Founded: 1927
Brewster Thhackeray, Staff Director
Heidi Forrest, Management Coordinator

1385 Scenic Virginia
4 East Main Street 804-643-8439
Suite 2A *Fax:* 804-643-8438
Richmond, VA 23219 email@scenicvirginia.org
scenicvirginia.org
The sole statewide organization in the Commonwealth dedicated to the preservation, protection and enhancement of Virginia's scenic beauty and community character. Promotes and sponsors programs that enhance landscapes, promote tourismand economic development, encourage natural beauty in the environ-

ment, preserve historical and cultural resources, and improve community appearance.
Founded: 1998
Cecelia S Howell, Chair
Barry W Starke, President

1386 Sierra Club: Virginia Chapter
422 East Franklin Street 804-225-9113
Suite 302 *Fax:* 804-225-9114
Richmond, VA 23219 virginia.sierraclub.org
To advance the preservation and protection of the natural environment by empowering the citizenry with charitable resources to further the cause of environmental protection.
Glen Besa, Director
Eileen Levandoski, Assistant Director

1387 Spill Control Association of America
103 Oronoco Street 571-451-0433
Suite 200 info@scaa-spill.org
Alexandria, VA 22314 www.scaa-spill.org
Organized to actively promote the interests of all groups within the spill response community. The organization represents spill response contractors, manufacturers, distributors, consultants, instructors, government & traininginstitutions and corporation working in the industry.
Founded: 1973
Rick Lewis, President
Devon Grennan, Vice President

1388 Student Conservation Association
4245 North Fairfax Drive 703-524-2441
Suite 825 *Fax:* 603-543-1828
Arlington, VA 22203 dcinfo@thesca.org
www.thesca.org
To build the next generation of conservation leaders and inspire lifelong stewardship of our environment and communities by engaging young people in hands-on service to the land.
Founded: 1957
Martha H Talbot, Co-Founder
Elizabeth Titus Putnam, Founding President

1389 Teratology Society
1821 Michael Faraday Drive 703-438-3104
Suite 300 *Fax:* 703-438-3113
Reston, VA 20190 tshq@teratology.org
teratology.org/
A multidisciplinary scientific society founded in 1960, the members of which study the causes and biological processes leading to abnormal development and birth defects at the fundamental and clinical level, and appropriate measuresfor prevention.

1390 Virginia Association of Soil and Water Conservation Districts
7308 Hanover Green Drive 804-559-0324
Suite 100 *Fax:* 804-559-0325
Mechanicsville, VA 23111 info@vaswcd.org
www.vaswcd.org
The Virginia Association of Soil and Water Conservation Districts (VASWCD) is a private nonprofit association of 47 soil and water conservation districts in Virginia. It is a voluntary, nongovernmental association of Virginia'sdistricts that provides and promotes leadership in the conservation of natural resources through stewardship and education programs.
Founded: 1930
Steven Meeks, President
Kendall Elaine Tyree, Executive Director

1391 Virginia Conservation Network
409 East Main Street 804-644-0283
Suite 104 *Fax:* 804-644-0286
Richmond, VA 23219 www.vcnva.org
Devoted to advancing a common, environmentally sound vision for Virginia. The network's membership is comprised of more than 115 member organizations committed to protecting Virginia's natural resources.
Founded: 1990
Jacob Powell, Executive Director
Kelley Galownia, Communications Manager

1392 Virginia Forestry Association
3808 Augusta Avenue 804-278-8733
Richmond, VA 23230 *Fax:* 804-278-8774
vfa@vaforestry.org
www.vaforestry.org
VFA promotes stewardship and wise use of the Commonwealth's forestresources for the economic and environmental benefits of all Virginians. Membership consists of forest landowners, forest product businesses, forestry professionals, anda variety of individuals and groups who are concerned about the future and well-being of Virginia's forest resources.
Founded: 1943
John Carroll, President
Brad Fuller, Vice President

1393 Virginia Native Plant Society
400 Blandy Farm Lane 540-837-1600
Unit 2 *Fax:* 540-837-1523
Boyce, VA 22620 vnpsofa@shentel.net
www.vnps.org
A statewide organization with approximately 2000 members supported primarily by dues and contributions. The Society's programs emphasize public education, protection of endangered species, habitat preservation, and encouragement ofappropriate landscape use of natice plants.
Founded: 1982
Sally Anderson, President

1394 Virginia Waste Industries Association
508 Somerset Avenue 757-686-5960
Richmond, VA 23226 *Fax:* 757-686-0010
www.vwia.com
To promote the management of waste in a manner that is environmentally responsible, efficient, profitable, and ethical while benefiting the public and protecting the employees.
Mike Dobson, Manager

1395 Water Environment Federation
601 Wythe Street 703-684-2400
Alexandria, VA 22314-1994 800-666-0206
Fax: 703-684-2492
inquiry@wef.org
www.wef.org
A not-for-profit technical and educational organization with 32,000 individual members and 80 affiliated Member Associations representing and additional 50,000 water quality professionals throughout the world. WEF and its memberassociations proudly work to achieve our mission of preserving and enhancing the global water environment.
Founded: 1928
Rick Warner, President

Washington

1396 American Fisheries Society: Early Life History Section (ELHS)
Seattle, WA earlylifehistory.fisheries.org
Devoted to early life history of freshwater, estuarine, and marine fishes, and related subjects. Publishes a newsletter, Stages, and puts on an annual Larval Fish Conference.
Claire Paris, President
Alison Deary, Secretary

1397 American Lung Association of Washington
5601 6th Avenue 206-441-5100
Suite 460 InfoMTP@Lung.org
Seattle, WA 98108 www.lung.org/about-us/local-associations/washington.html
The American Lung Association of Washington works to prevent lung disease and promote lung health; offering a wide variety of lung health services to the people of Washington.
Allison Hickey, Exec. VP, Mountain Pacific
Tony Peterson, CFO

1398 American Rivers: Pacific Northwest
P.O. Box 1234 206-213-0330
Bellingham, WA 98227 877-347-7550
www.americanrivers.org
American Rivers protects and promotes rivers across the United States through national advocacy, innovative solutions and networking with strategic partners. The Pacific Northwest chapter focuses on the conservation of the coastalrivers of Washington and Oregon.
Founded: 1992
Wendy McDermott, Associate Director

1399 American Society of Landscape Architects: Washington Chapter
2150 N. 107th St. 206-443-9484
Suite 205 *Fax:* 206-367-8777
Seattle, WA 98133-9009 office@wasla.org
www.wasla.org
Mission is to lead, to educate and to participate in the careful stewardship, wise planning and artful design of our cultural and natural environments.
Founded: 1973
Laura Thompson, President
Dean W. Koonts, Treasurer

1400 Conservation Northwest
1208 Bay Street 360-671-9950
Suite 201 www.conservationnw.org
Bellingham, WA 98225-4301
A nonprofit organization protecting old-growth forests and other wildlands, connecting a larger landscape and vital natural habitats and restoring native wildlife.
Founded: 1988
Bill Donnelly, President
Lisa McShane, Vice President

1401 Environmental Education Association of Washington
Environmental Education Association of Washington
210 South Hudson Street info@e3washington.org
Seattle, WA 98134 www.e3washington.org
Dedicated to increasing the awareness of and support for environmental education in the state of Washington.
Founded: 1991
Ron Harris-White, President
Gillia Bakie, Foundation Manager

1402 Friends of Discovery Park
PO Box 99662 friendsdiscoverypark@gmail.com
Seattle, WA 98139 www.seattlediscoverypark.org
An all-volunteer group formed to defend the integrity of Discovery Park and to create and protect there an open space of quiet and tranquility, a sanctuary where the words of man are minimized.
Founded: 1970
Gary Gaffner, President
David Sinclair, Secretary/Treasurer

1403 Friends of the San Juans
PO Box 1344 360-378-2319
Friday Harbor, WA 98250 friends@sanjuans.org
www.sanjuans.org
Mission is to protect and preserve the San Juan Islands and Salish Sea for people and for nature.
Founded: 1979
San Olson, President
Stephanie Buffum, Executive Director

1404 Great Peninsula Conservancy
423 Pacific Ave 360-373-3500
Suite 401 info@greatpeninsula.org
Bremerton, WA 98337 www.greatpeninsula.org
The Great Peninsula Conservancy is a private nonprofit land trust dedicated to protecting the rural landscapes, natural habitat and open spaces of the Great Peninsula region.
Founded: 2000
Sandr S Bortner, Executive Director
Kate Kuhlman, Operations Director

1405 International Bicycle Fund
4887 Columbia Drive South 206-767-0848
Seattle, WA 98108-1919 ibike@ibike.org
www.ibike.org
A non-governmental, nonprofit, advocacy organization, promoting sustainable transport and international understanding. Major areas of activity are non-motorized urban planning, economic development, bike safety education, responsibletravel and bicycle tourism, and cross-cultural, educational programs.
Founded: 1983
David Mozer, President
John Dowlin, Executive Director

1406 Issaquah Alps Trails Club
PO Box 351 844-392-4282
Issaquah, WA 98027 contact@issaquahalps.org
www.issaquahalps.org
Mission is to act as custodian of the trails and the lush, open tree-covered mountaintops known as the Issaquah Alps. Offers free guided hikes and a voice for protection of our open spaces, trails, and quality of life.
Founded: 1979
Kirt Lenard, President
David Kappler, Vice President

1407 Mountaineers Conservation Division
The Mountaineers
7700 Sand Point Way NW 206-521-6000
Seattle, WA 98115 800-573-8484
Fax: 206-523-6763
info@mountaineers.org
www.mountaineers.org
Mission is to be the premier outdoor recreation club, dedicated to the responsible employment and protection of natural areas.
Founded: 1906
Geoff Lawrence, President
Lorna Corrigan, Vice President

1408 Nature Conservancy: Washington Chapter
74 Wall Street 206-343-4345
Seattle, WA 98121 800-964-0636
Fax: 206-343-5608
washington@tnc.org
www.washingtonnature.org
The Nature Conservancy in Washington is dedicated to sustaining and enhancing a healthy relationship between people and nature.
Founded: 1951
Mike Stevens, Director
Melissa Garvey, Deputy Director

1409 North Cascades Conservation Council
PO Box 95980 ncccinfo@northcascades.org
Seattle, WA 98145-2980 www.northcascades.org/wordpress
The North Cascades Conservation Council (NCCC) keeps government officials, environmental organizations and the general public informed about issues affecting the Greater North Cascade Ecosystem. Action is pursued through legislative,legal and public participation channels to protect the lands, waters, plants and wildlife.
Founded: 1957
Tom Hammond, President
Tom Brucker, Treasurer

1410 Olympic Park Associates
P.O. Box 27560 olympicparkassociates.org
Seattle, WA 98165-2560
An organization working to preseve Olympic Park's wilderness, beauty and spelndor.
Founded: 1948
Donna Osseward, President
John Bridge, Secretary

1411 Olympic Region Clean Air Agency
2940 Limited Lane
Olympia, WA 98502
360-539-7610
800-422-5623
Fax: 360-491-6308
info@orcaa.org
www.orcaa.org
A local government agency charged with regulatory and enforcement authority for air quality issues. It is one of the seven such regional air pollution control agencies in Washington State. The agency also administers laws andregulations regarding such programs as solid fuel burning devices, asbestos abatement, and open burning. ORCAA's jurisdiction: Clallam, Grays Harbor, Jefferson, Mason, Pacific and Thurston Counties.
Founded: 1968
Jim Cooper, Chairman
Cynthia Pratt, Vice Chair

1412 People for Puget Sound
1402 3rd Avenue
Suite 1400
Seattle, WA 98101
206-631-2600
info@wecprotects.org
www.pugetsound.org
People for Puget Sound is a regional citizen's organization founded to educate and involve people in protecting and restoring the land and waters of Puget Sound. People for Puget Sound's programs are based on partnership andcollaborations, scientific credibility, creative use of communications and technology, and a hands-on-style. The organization publishes a quarterly newsletter, and many scientific publications.
Founded: 1991
Joan Crooks, CEO
Rein Attemann, Advocacy Manager

1413 Sea Shepherd: Seattle Chapter
Seattle, WA
seattle@seashepherd.org
www.seashepherd.org
An international non-profit, marine wildlife conservation organization whose mission is to end the destruction of habitat and slaughter of wildlife in the world's oceans in order to conserve and protect ecosystems and species. TheSeattle Chapter focuses on Orcas, Salmon, whales, seals, birds and other marine life and ocean habitats of the Puget Sound and Salish Sea.
Founded: 1977
Paul Watson, President
Peter Rysman, Secretary / Treasurer

1414 Sierra Club: Cascade Chapter
180 Nickerson Street
Suite 202
Seattle, WA 98109
206-378-0114
Fax: 206-378-0034
cascade.chapter@sierraclub.org
cascade.sierraclub.org
To advance the preservation and protection of the natural environment by empowering the citizenry with charitable resources to further the cause of environmental protection.
Margie V Cleve, Chairman
Ken Gersten, Vice Chairman

1415 Solar Washington
PO Box 3832
Seattle, WA 98124
206-618-3620
www.solarwashington.org
A private not-for-profit 501(c)3 association of solar energy equipment manufacturers, system integrators, distributors, dealers, designers, consultants, students, and interested people
.
David Nicol, President
Robert Ransom, Vice President

1416 Student Conservation Association Northwest
1265 S Main Street
Suite 210
Seattle, WA 98144
412-325-1851
Fax: 206-324-4998
webmaster@thesca.org
www.thesca.org/
SCA is a national organization with regional offices in Seattle, Oakland, Pittsburg, Washington DC and headquartered in Charlestown NH. Our mission is to build the next generation of conservation leaders and inspire lifelongstewardship of our environment and communities by engaging young people in hands-on service to the land. We offer a wide range of internships and crew based programs for ages 16 years and up.
Founded: 1957
Dale M Penny, President/CEO
Jay A Satz, Vice President

1417 Washington Association of Conservation Districts
185 Beebe Road
Goldendale, WA 98620
509-773-5065
Fax: 509-773-5600
wacd@ncia.com
A non-profit organization representing Washington's 48 Conservation Districts, whos mission is to advance the purposes of Conservation Districts and their constituents by providing leadership, information, and representation.
Alan Stromberger, President
Mark Craven, Vice President

1418 Washington Environmental Council
1402 Third Avenue
Suite 1400
Seattle, WA 98101
206-631-2600
800-561-8294
Fax: 206-622-8113
wec@wecprotects.org
www.wecprotects.org
Protects what Washingtonians care about- our land and water, fish, and wildlife, and our special way of life. We engage the public and decision makers to improve and enforce protections for the health and well-being of our communities.
Founded: 1967
Jay Manning, President

1419 Washington Public Interest Research Group
1402 Third Avenue
Suite 715
Seattle, WA 98101
206-568-2854
800-213-7383
Fax: 206-568-2858
www.washpirg.org
When consumers are cheated or the voices of ordinary citizens are drowned out by special interest lobbyists, WashPIRG speaks up and takes action.
Steve Blackledge, Regional Director

1420 Washington Recreation and Park Association
2150 N 107th St
#205
Seattle, WA 98133
360-459-9396
888-459-0009
Fax: 206-367-8777
www.wrpatoday.org
A not-for-profit professional and public interest organization which is dedicated to enhancing and promoting parks, recreation and arts pursuits in Washington State.
Brad Case, President
Cheryl Fraser, President Elect

1421 Washington Refuse and Recycling Association
4160 6th Avenue SE
Suite 205
Lacey, WA 98503
360-943-8859
866-788-9772
Fax: 360-357-6958
www.wrra.org
Represents Washington's diverse and multifaceted solid waste handling industry, providing its members with general legal support, educational seminars, workshops, and representation before regulatory agencies and the Legislature.
Jay Alexander, President
Mark Wash, Vice-President

1422 Washington Toxics Coalition
4649 Sunnyside Avenue N
Suite 540
Seattle, WA 98103
206-632-1545
800-844-7233
Fax: 206-632-8661
webmaster@watoxics.org
www.watoxics.org
Washington Toxics Coalition protects public health and the environment by eliminating toxic pollution. WTC promotes alternatives, advocates policies, empowers communities, and educates people to create a healthy environment.
Founded: 1981
Jesseca Brand, President
Laurie Valeriano, Executive Director

1423 Washington Wilderness Coalition
305 North 83rd Street
Seattle, WA 98103
206-633-1992
800-627-0062
Fax: 206-633-1996
info@wawild.org
www.wawild.org
Mission is to preserve and restore wild areas of Washington State throuh citizen empowerment, support for grassroots community groups and advocacy and public education.
Founded: 1979
Roger Mellem, President
Doug North, Vice President

1424 Washington Wildlife Federation
PO Box 1656
Bellevue, WA 98009
206-769-5627
www.washingtonwildlife.org
To preserve, enhance, and perpetuate Washington's fish, wildlife and habitat through education and conservation programs.
Ronni McGlenn, President

West Virginia

1425 American Lung Association of West Virginia
2102 Kanawha Boulevard E
Charleston, WV 25311
304-342-6600
www.lung.org/about-us/local-associations/west-virginia.html
The American Lung Association of West Virginia works to prevent lung disease and promote lung health; offering a wide variety of lung health services to the people of West Virginia.
Deborah Brown, Executive VP, Mid-Atlantic
Joy Meyer, VP, Community Impact

1426 Sierra Club: West Virginia Chapter
PO Box 4142
Morgantown, WV 26504-4142
melwaggy@gmail.com
westvirginia.sierraclub.org
To advance the preservation and protection of the natural environment by empowering the citizenry with charitable resources to further the cause of environmental protection.
Jim Kotcon, Chair
Mel Waggy, Secretary

1427 West Virginia Department of Health and Human Resources
West Virginia Department of Health and Human Reso
One Davis Square
Suite 100 East
Charleston, WV 25301
304-558-0684
Fax: 304-558-1130
DHHRSecretary@wv.gov
www.dhhr.wv.gov
This organization provides life-saving services to West Virginia residents, and has a specific focus on protecting children in West Virginia.
Bill J. Crouch, Cabinet Secretary
Cynthia Dellinger, Assistant General Counsel

1428 West Virginia Forestry Association
1776 Parkersburg Road
PO Box 718
Ripley, WV 25271
304-372-1955
Fax: 304-372-1957
wvfa@wvfa.org
www.wvfa.org
The West Virginia Forestry Association is a non-profit organization funded by its membership. Our members include individuals and businesses involved in forest management, timber production and wood product manufacturing. Our membersare concerned with protecting the environment, as well as enhancing the future of West Virginia's forests through multiple-use management.
Mark Haddix, President
Dane Moore, First Vice President

1429 West Virginia Highlands Conservancy
P.O. Box 306
Charleston, WV 25321
info@wvhighlands.org
www.wvhighlands.org
One of the state's oldest environmental activist organizations. A coalition of recreational users of the West Virginia Highlands working together to address the host of environmental threats to the state.
Founded: 1967
Cynthia Ellis, President
Larry Thomas, Senior Vice President

1430 West Virginia Woodland Owners Association
374 Maple Avenue East
Suite 310
Vienna, VA 22180
703-255-2700
Fax: 703-281-9200
woodlandowners.org
A nonprofit membership organization started and continues to be operated exclusively by independent West Virginia woodland owners.
Keith Argow, President
Dick Courter, Chairman

Wisconsin

1431 American Fisheries Society: Genetics Section
c/o University of Wisconsin
Trainer Natural Resources Bldg.
Stevens Point, WI 54481
wes.larson@uwsp.edu
units.fisheries.org/genetics
Seeks to provide better understanding of genetics in aquatic sciences, fisheries management, and aquaculture.
Marlis Douglas, President
Wes Larson, Secretary-Treasurer

1432 American Fisheries Society: North Central Division: Wisconsin Chapter
WI
Secretary-treasurer@wi-afs.org
www.wi-afs.org
The Wisconsin Chapter of the American Fisheries Society , is part of the American Fisheries Society (AFS) North Central Division. Working to further to the goals of the AFS through research, education, and professional development, thechapter is committed to the conservation, development, and wise use of fishery resources, and the protection and sustainability of aquatic ecosystems.
Founded: 1969 $10/ Year
Derek Ogle, President
Ted Treska, Secretary & Treasurer

1433 American Lung Association of Wisconsin
13100 W Lisbon Road
Suite 700
Brookfield, WI 53005
262-703-4200
info@lungwi.org
www.lung.org/about-us/local-associations/wisconsin.html
The American Lung Association of Wisconsin works to prevent lung disease and promote lung health; offering a wide variety of lung health services to the people of Wisconsin.
Linda Witucki, Executive Directo, Wisconsin
Lewis Bartfield, Executive VP, Upper Midwest

1434 American Society of Landscape Architects: Wisconsin Chapter
11801 W. Silver Spring Drive
Suite 200
Milwaukee, WI 53225
414-930-1797
president@wiasla.com
www.wiasla.com
The Wisconsin state chapter supports professional development, visibility and network working opportunities in the field of landscape architecture.
Cody Axness, President
Jonathan Bronk, President-Elect

1435 Botanical Club of Wisconsin
Wisconsin Academy of Science, Arts, & Letters
8166 Highway 57
Baileys Harbor, WI 54202
botanicalclubofwisconsin@gmail.com
sites.google.com/site/botanicalclubofwisconsin
The Botanical Club serves the interests of amateurs and professionals working towards a common goal of learning more about the state's diverse vegitation.
Chris Tyrrell, Treasurer

1436 Central Wisconsin Environmental Station (CWES)
10186 County Road MM 715-346-2937
Amherst Junction, WI 54407 *Fax:* 715-346-2493
tquinn@uwsp.edu
www.uwsp.edu/cnr/cwes/
Mission is to foster the appreciation, understanding, skill development, and motivation needed to help build a sustainable balance between the environment, economy, and community.
Founded: 1975
Tom Quinn, Director
Sheri Trzebiatowski, Office Manager

1437 Midwest Renewable Energy Association
7558 Deer Road 715-592-6595
Custer, WI 54423 info@midwestrenew.org
www.midwestrenew.org
A non profit organization promoting renewable energy, energy efficiency, and sustainable living through education and demonstration. There are over 3200 active international members representing 39 states and 3 foreign countries.
Founded: 1990
Nick Hylla, Executive Director
Amiee Wetmore, Operations Director

1438 River Alliance of Wisconsin
147 S. Butler Street 608-257-2424
Suite 2 info@wisconsinrivers.org
Madison, WI 53703 www.wisconsinrivers.org
Mission is to advocate for the protection, enhancement and restoration of Wisconsin's rivers and watersheds.
Tamara Dean, Chair
Ronald G. Anderson, Vice Chair

1439 Sierra Club: John Muir Chapter
754 Williamson Street 608-256-0565
Madison, WI 53703 john.muir.chapter@sierraclub.org
wisconsin.sierraclub.org
The mission of the Sierra Club is to explore, enjoy, and protect the planet. The John Muir Chapter is Wisconsin's voice for the nation's largest grassroots environmental organization. Their members include 18,000 community members whofollow the footsteps of Wisconsin conservationists such as Sierra Club founder John Muir, Aldo Leopold, and Gaylord Nelson. They are inspired by Wisconsin's natural scenery, and work together to protect communities and the planet.
Founded: 1963
Jacinda Tessmann, Chapter Coordinator
Elizabeth Ward, Programs Coordinator

1440 Sixteenth Street Community Health Center
1032 South Cesar E Chavez Drive 414-672-1353
Milwaukee, WI 53204 www.sschc.org
The mission of the Sixteenth Street Community Health Center is to improve the health and well-being of Milwaukee's Near South Side residents by providing quality, family-based health care, health education and social services, freefrom linguistic, cultural and economic barriers.
Founded: 1969
Liz Claudio, VP of Operations
Julie B. Schuller, President/CEO

1441 Trees for Tomorrow Natural Resources Educational Center
519 Sheridan Street 715-479-6456
PO Box 609 *Fax:* 715-479-2318
Eagle River, WI 54521 learning@treesfortomorrow.com
www.treesfortomorrow.com
Accredited natural resource specialty school. Hosts workshops for middle/high school students during the school year. Workshops emphasize conservation, proper land management and environmental basics.
Founded: 1944
Kelley Knoerr, President
Bill O'Brion, Vice President

1442 Upper Mississippi River Conservation Committee
9053 Route 148 618-997-6869
Marion, IL 62959 neal_jackson@fws.gov
www.umrcc.org
An organization of natural resource managers from IL, IA, MN, MO, and WI, created to promote a continuing cooperation between conservation agencies on the Upper Mississippi River. This is accomplished through workshops, publicationsand annual meetings.
Founded: 1943
Neal Jackson, UMRCC Coordinator
Jeff Janvrin, Chair

1443 Wildlife Society
425 Barlow Place 301-897-9770
Suite 200 tws@wildlife.org
Bethesda, MD 20814 www.wildlife.org/Wisconsin/home
A nonprofit scientific and educational organization that serves professionals such as government agencies, academia, industry, and non-government organizations in all areas related to the conservation of wildlife and natural resourcesmanagement.
Bruce C. Thompson, President
Darren A. Millier, Vice President

1444 Wisconsin Association for Environmental Education
P.P. Box 418 715-570-2587
Stevens Point, WI 54481 admin@waee.org
www.waee.org
A non-profit organization that sponsors conferences, workshops, and gatherings to promote professional growth and networking opportunities in environmental studies.
Founded: 1975
Lynn Karbowski, Administor

1445 Wisconsin Association of Lakes
147 S. Butler Street 608-661-4313
Madison, WI 53703 info@wisconsinlakes.org
www.wisconsinlakes.org
The Wisconsin Association of Lakes is the only statewide nonprofit organization working exclusively to protect and enhance the quality of Wisconsin's 15,000 lakes.
Mary Knipper, President
Derek Kavanaugh, Vice President

1446 Wisconsin Land and Water Conservation Association
131 W. Wilson Street 608-441-2677
Suite 601 *Fax:* 608-441-2676
Madison, WI 53703 info@wisconsinlandwater.org
wisconsinlandwater.org
To assist county Land Conservation Committees and Departments with the protection, enhancement and sustainable use of Wisconsin's natural resources and to represent them through education and governmental interaction.
Jim VandenBrook, Executive Director
Kirsten Moore, Office Manager

1447 Wisconsin Society for Ornithology
654 W Hillcrest Road 414-416-3272
Apt 202 treasurer@wsobirds.org
Saukville, WI 53080 www.wsobirds.org
Emphasizes all of the many aspects of birding and to support the research and habitat protection necessary to preserve Wisconsin's birdlife.
Founded: 1939
Michael John Jaeger, President
Andy Cassini, Vice President

1448 Wisconsin Wildlife Federation
213 North Main Street 608-635-0600
P.O. Box 460 800-897-4161
Poynette, WI 53955 office@wiwf.org
www.wiwf.org
The mission of the Wisconsin Wildlife Federation is to conserve Wisconsin's wildlife, natural resources and outdoor sporting heritage through conservation education and advocating for strong conservation policies on state and nationallevels.
Bill Tollard, President
Gary Dieckd, First Vice President

1449 **Wisconsin Woodland Owners Association**
PO Box 285 715-346-4798
Stevens Point, WI 54481 wwoa@uwsp.edu
www.wisconsinwoodlands.org
The Wisconsin Woodland Owners Association is a nonprofit educational organization seeking to advance the interests of woodland owners and the cause of forestry; develop public appreciation for the value of Wisconsin's woodlands andtheir importance in the economy and overall welfare of the state; foster and encourage wise use and management of Wisconsin's woodlands for timber production, wildlife habitat and recreation; and to educate those interested in managing the woodlands.
Founded: 1979
Steven Ring, President
David Congos, Vice President

Wyoming

1450 **American Lung Association of Wyoming**
c/o American Lung Association
822 John Street 206-441-5100
Seattle, WA 98109 InfoMTP@Lung.org
www.lung.org/about-us/local-associations/wyoming.html
The American Lung Association of the Wyoming works to prevent lung disease and promote lung health; offering a wide variety of lung health services to the people of Wyoming.
Allison Hickey, Exec. VP, Mountain Pacific
Tony Peterson, CFO

1451 **Jackson Hole Conservation Alliance**
685 S. Cache Street 307-733-9417
PO Box 2728 info@jhalliance.org
Jackson, WY 83001 www.jhalliance.org
An organization dedicated to responsible land stewardship in Jackson Hole, Wyoming to ensure that human activities are in harmony with the area's irreplaceable wildlife, scenery and other natural resources.
Founded: 1979
Carter Cox, Development Director
Dawn Webster, Operations Manager

1452 **Nature Conservancy: Wyoming Chapter**
Nature Conservancy
258 Main Street 307-335-2120
Suite 200 *Fax:* 307-332-2974
Lander, WY 82520 pplatt@tnc.org
www.nature.org
The leading conservation organization working around the world to protect ecologically important lands and waters for nature and people.
Founded: 1950
Milward Simpson, State Director
Arlen Lancaster, Conservation Director

1453 **Powder River Basin Resource Council**
934 North Main Sreet 307-672-5809
Sheridan, WY 82801 *Fax:* 307-672-5800
info@powderriverbasin.org
www.powderriverbasin.org
Committed to the preservation and enrichment of Wyoming's agricultural heritage and rural lifestyle; the conservation of Wyoming's land, mineral, water and clean air resources, consistent with responsible use of those resources tosustain the vitality of present and future generations; the education and empowerment of Wyoming's citizens to raise a coherent voice in decisions. They are the only group in Wyoming that addresses both agricultural and conservation issues.
Bob LeResche, Chairman
Joyce Evans, Vice Chairman

1454 **Sierra Club: Wyoming Chapter**
PO Box 1736 307-742-0056
Laramie, WY 82501 *Fax:* 307-460-8046
connie.wilbert@sierraclub.org
www.wyoming.sierraclub.org
To advance the preservation and protection of the natural environment by empowering the citizenry with charitable resources to further the cause of environmental protection.
Founded: 1984
Connie Wilbert, Chapter Director
Lloyd Dorsey, Conservation Director

1455 **Western Association of Fish and Wildlife Agencies**
522 Notre Dame Court 307-631-4536
Cheyenne, WY 82009 *Fax:* 307-638-1470
larry.kruckenberg@wyo.gov
www.wafwa.org
The Western Association of Fish and Wildlife Agencies represents 23states and Canadian provinces and supports resource management to conserve wildlife.
Curt Melcher, President
Keith Sexton, 1st Vice President

1456 **Wyoming Association of Conservation Districts**
517 E 19th Street 307-632-5716
Cheyenne, WY 82001 *Fax:* 307-638-4099
bobbie.frank@conservewy.com
www.conservewy.com
Mission is to provide leadership for the conservation of Wyoming's soil and water resources; promote the controll of soil erosion; promote and protects the quality of Wyomings's waters; reduce siltation of stream channels andreservoirs; promote wise use of Wyoming's water and other natural resources; preserve and enhance wildlife habitat; protect the tax base and promote the health, safety and general welfare of the citzens of the state through a responsible conservationethic.
Founded: 1945
Bobbie Frank, Executive Director
Shaun Sims, President

1457 **Wyoming Native Plant Society**
P.O. Box 2449 wynps@wynps.org
Laramie, WY 82073 www.wynps.org
Goals are to encourage the appreciation and conservation of the native flora and plant communities of Wyoming through education, research, and communication.
Founded: 1981
Charmaine Delmatier, President
Katy Duffy, Vice President

1458 **Wyoming Wildlife Federation**
PO Box 1312 307-335-8633
Lander, WY 82520 800-786-5434
Fax: 307-335-8690
info@wyomingwildlife.org
www.wyomingwildlife.org
The Wyoming Wildlife Federation is Wyomings oldest and largest conservation group advocating sportsmen and sportswomen. The Federation's mission is to work for hunters, anglers and other wildlife enthusiasts to protect and enhancehabitat; propetuate quality hunting and fishing; protect citizens rights to use public lands and waters; and promote ethical hunting and fishing.
Founded: 1937
Dwayne Meadows, Executive Director
Joy Bannon, Field Director

Awards & Honors

Environmental

1459 Adirondack Council Conservationist of the Year
103 Hand Avenue 518-873-2240
P.O. Box D-2, Suite 3 877-873-2240
Elizabethtown, NY 12932 *Fax:* 518-873-6675
info@adirondackcouncil.org
www.adirondackcouncil.org
This is awarded to the individual or organization who has provided the greatest contribution towards protecting the health of Adirondack Park. The award is presented each year at the Council's Forever Wild Day, and winners receive aspecailly commissioned, museum-quality, hand-carved common loon in recognition of their achievements.

Ann E. Carmel, Chair
Kevin Arquit, Vice-Chair

1460 Aerospace Medical Association
Aerospace Medicine and Human Performance
320 S Henry Street 703-739-2240
Alexandria, VA 22314-3579 *Fax:* 703-739-9652
rrayman@asma.org
www.asma.org
AsMA is dedicated to uniting the world's professionals in aviation, space and environmental medicine; advancing the frontiers of aerospace medicineand ensuring the highest level of safety, health and performance of those involved inaerospace. AsMA offers a number of awards outstanding contributors to fields such as aerospace physiology, spatial disorientation, and longstanding education and development of Aerospace Medicine.

Jeffrey Sventek, Executive Director
Fredrick Bonato, Editor-in-Chief

1461 Air & Waste Management Association
Koppers Building 412-232-3444
436 Seventh Avenue, Suite 2100 800-270-3444
Pittsburgh, PA 15219 *Fax:* 412-232-3450
info@awma.org
www.awma.org
Professional development organization providing a forum for the exchange of information, networking, public education, and outreach to over 5,000 environmental professionals in 65 countries.

Stephanie Glyptis, Executive Director
Tracy Fedkoe, Director, Marketing

1462 Air Force Association
1501 Lee Highway 703-247-5800
Arlington, VA 22209-1198 800-727-3337
Fax: 703-247-5853
membership@afa.org
www.afa.org
The Air Force Association's mission is to advocate aerospace power and a strong national defense; to support the United States Air Force and Air Force Family; and to promote aerospace education to the American people. The associationhonors the outstanding achievements and contributions of men and women to the United States Air Force. They present over two dozen awards each year.

Kathy Hartness, Industry Relations

1463 Aldo Leopold Foundation
E13701 Levee Road 608-355-0279
PO Box 77 *Fax:* 608-356-7309
Baraboo, WI 53913-0077 mail@aldoleopold.org
www.aldoleopold.org
Nonprofit organization that works to promote the philosophy of Aldo Leopold and the land ethic he so eloquently defined in his writing. The foundation actively integrates programs on land stewardship, environmental education andscientific research to promote care of natural resources and have an ethical relationship between people and land. Teaches classes on environmental values and land care.

Buddy Huffaker, Executive Director
Jennifer Farnum, Director, Development

1464 American Association of Engineering Societies
1801 Alexander Bell Dr 202-296-2237
Reston, VA 20191 *Fax:* 202-296-1151
info@aaes.org
www.aaes.org
Multidisciplinary organization dedicated to advancing the knowledge, understanding and practice of engineering in the public interest. Its members represent the mainstream of US engineering-affecting over 1,000,000 engineers inindustry, government and education. Through its councils, commissions, committees and task forces, the AAES addresses questions relating to the engineering profession. AAES offer their members awards in celebration of their accomplishments inengineering and leadership.

Melissa Prelewicz, Ass. Executive Director

1465 American Chemical Society
American Chemical Society
1155 16th Street NW 614-447-3776
Washington, DC 20036 800-227-5558
webmaster@acs.org
www.chemistry.org
The American Chemical Society is a self-governed individual membership organization that consists of more than 158,000 members in the field of chemistry. The organizations provides a broad range of opportunities for peer intereactionand career development, regardless of professional or scientific interests. They also offer grants and scholarships and awards to honor achivements made in field.
Allison A. Campbell, President
Peter K. Dorhout, President-Elect

1466 American Conference of Governmental Industrial Hygienists
1330 Kemper Meadow Dr 513-742-2020
Cincinnati, OH 45240 *Fax:* 513-742-3355
mail@acgih.org
www.acgih.org
ACGIH is a member-based organization and community of professionals that advances worker health and safety through education and the development and dissemination of scientific and technical knowledge. The organization honors itsmembers with six awards each year for exceptional leadership and dedication.
Sheryl A. Milz, Chair
Alan Rossner, Treasurer

1467 American Forest and Paper Association
1101 K Street NW 202-463-2700
Suite 700 800-878-8878
Washington, DC 20005 info@afandpa.org
afandpa.org
The American Forest and Paper Association (AF&PA) is the national trade association of the forest, pulp, and paperboard wood products industry. The association represents member companies engaged in growing, harvesting and processingwood and wood fibers, manufacturing paper products from both virgin and recycled fiber, and producing engineered and traditional wood products. They offer the Sustainability Award to a group of exceptional individuals for their work in the field.
Linda Massman, Chairman
John Rooney, First Vice Chairman

1468 American Institute of Chemical Engineers (AIChE)
120 Wall Street 212-591-8100
FL 23 800-242-4363
New York, NY 10005-4020 *Fax:* 203-775-5177
awards@aiche.org
www.aiche.org/community/awards
A professional association of more than 60,000 members that provides leadership in advancing the chemical engineering profession. Fosters and disseminates chemical engineering knowledge,

supports the professional and personal growth ofits members, and applies the expertise of its members to address societal needs through the world. It offers over 60 awards including certificates, medals, scholarships, and more.

Monty Alger, President

1469 **American Institute of Mining, Metallurgical and Petroleum Engineers**
12999 East Adam Aircraft Circle 303-325-5185
Englewood, CO 80112 *Fax:* 888-702-0049
aime@aimehq.org
www.aimehq.org
Organized and operated exclusively to advance, record and disseminate significant knowledge of engineering and the arts and sciences involved in the production and use of minerals, metals, energy sources and materials. AIME funds 25awards, including medals and scholarships, every year to honor those who have contributed exceptional work to the AIME disciplines.
L. Michele Lawrie-Munro, Executive Director

1470 **American Nuclear Society**
555 North Kensington Ave 708-352-6611
La Grange Park, IL 60526 800-323-3044
Fax: 708-352-0499
nucleus@ans.org
www.ans.org
The American Nuclear Society is a not-for-profit, international, scientific and educational organization. It was established by a group of individuals who recognized the need to unify the professional activities within the diversefields of nuclear science and technology.
Robert N. Coward, President
Robert C. Fine, Executive Director

1471 **American Society for Environmental History (ASEH)**
UIC Department of History
601 S Morgan Street dspatz@aseh.net
MC 198 aseh.net
Chicago, IL 60607-7109
Promotes historical research and education on environmental matters, as a means of better understanding human interactions with the natural world. Affiliated with the Forest History Society, which co-publishes the Environmental Historyjournal. Offers numerous awards, fellowships, and other funding.
David Spatz, Executive Director

1472 **American Society of Civil Engineers (ASCE)**
1801 Alexander Bell Drive 703-295-6300
Reston, VA 20191 800-548-2723
customercare@asce.org
www.asce.org
The American Society of Civil Engineers represents more than 150,000 members of the civil engineering profession worldwide, and is America's oldest national engineering society. The organization funds over a hundred awards tocommemorate the achievements and contribution of its members in the field.
K.N. Gunalan, President
Thomas W. Smith III, Executive Director

1473 **American Society of Heating, Refrigerating and Air-Conditioning (ASHRAE)**
1791 Tullie Circle NE 404-636-8400
Atlanta, GA 30329 800-527-4723
Fax: 404-321-5478
ashrae@ashrae.org
www.ashrae.org
ASHRAE is an international organization of some 50,000 persons. ASHRAE fulfills its mission of advancing heating, ventilation, air conditioning and refrigeration to serve humanity and promote a sustainable world through reserach,standards writing, publishing and continuing education. The organization offers a number of awards and certificates in recognition of the dedication demonstrated by its members.

Jeff Littleton, Executive Vice President

1474 **American Sportfishing Association (ASA)**
1001 North Fairfax Street 703-519-9691
Suite 501 *Fax:* 703-519-1872
Alexandria, VA 22314 info@asafishing.org
asafishing.org
A sportsfishing trade association that advocates for the promotion and protection of the industry. Their mission is to ensure that the industry remains strong and prosperous, and to safeguard the conservation, economic, and socialvalues of sportfishing in America.

Glenn Hughes, President
Joyce Anderson-Logan, Executive Assistant

1475 **American Water Resources Association (AWRA)**
P.O. Box 2663 540-687-8390
Woodbridge, VA 22195 *Fax:* 540-687-8395
info@awra.org
www.awra.org
AWRA advances water resources research, planning, development, management and education. AWRA takes a balanced, professional approach to solving water resources challenges by establishing discourse between physical, biological, andsocial scientists, engineers, and other persons concerned with water resources.

Dresden Farrand, Executive VP & CEO
Michael J. Kowalski, Director of Operations

1476 **Association for Conservation Information (ACI)**
1085 Lake Road www.aci-net.org
Panton, VT 05491
ACI is a nonprofit association of information and education professionals representing state, federal and Canadian agencies and private conservation organizations. Provides natural resource, environmental, wildlife and otherinformation and education to the public through a variety of means, many of which are continental in scope. Each year, the association honors a group of indivudals who demonstrate excellence and innitiative in support of conservation work.
Jennifer Wisniewski, President
Judy Stokes Weber, Treasurer

1477 **Association of Conservation Engineers**
PO Box 180 conversationengineers@gmail.com
Jefferson City, MO 65109 www.conservationengineers.org
Association of conservation engineers and technicians who are working to conserve and improve the nation's natural heritage. It employs experts in the conservation of fish, wildlife, natural resource protection, parks, forests, andrecreation fields.

Holly Bentze, President
Natalie Little, President-Elect

1478 **Audubon Naturalist Society of Central Atlantic**
8940 Jones Mill Rd 301-652-9188
Chevy Chase, MD 20815 *Fax:* 301-951-7179
The Audubon Naturalist Society is an independent environmental education and conservation organization with over 10,000 members in the Washington DC area. The society offers a wide variety of natural history classes and campaigns forthe protection and renewal of the Mid-Atlantic regions natural resources. ANS grants the Paul Bartsch Award for distinguished contributions to natural history.

Leslie Catherwood, President
Paul D'Andrea, Vice President

1479 **Audubon Society of New Hampshire**
84 Silk Farm Rd 603-224-9909
Concord, NH 03301 *Fax:* 603-226-0902
asnh@nhaudubon.org
www.nhaudubon.org
The Audubon Society of New Hampshire, a nonprofit statewide membership organization, is dedicated to the conservation of wildlife and habitat throughout the state. Independent of the National Audubon Society, ASNH offers programs inwildlife con-

servation, land protection, environmental policy and environmental education.

Douglas A. Bechtel, President
Helen Dalbeck, Executive Director

1480 Audubon of Florida: Center for Birds of Prey

1101 Audubon Way 407-644-0190
Maitland, FL 32751 *Fax:* 407-644-8940
fl.audubon.org/chapters-centers/audubon-center-birds-prey

Audubon of Florida aims to conserve and restore natural ecosystems, focusing on birds and other wildlife for the benefit of humanity and the earth's biological diversity. The Center for Birds of Prey is dedicated to promoting astewardship ethic towards Florida's birds of prey and their habitats through medical rehabilitation, interactive education and practical research.

Katie Warner, Program Manager

1481 Botanical Society of America

PO Box 299 314-577-9566
St. Louis, MO 63166-0299 *Fax:* 314-577-9515
bsa-manager@botany.org
www.botany.org

This organization promotes botany, the field of basic science dealing with the study and inquiry into the form, function, reproduction, evolution, and the use of plants and their interactions within the biosphere. The society offers anumber of awards to scientists and students in both research and active field work, as well as grants and buseries.

Loren Rieseberg, President

1482 Chicago Community Trust

225 North Michigan Ave 312-616-8000
Suite 2200 *Fax:* 312-616-7955
Chicago, IL 60601 info@cct.org
www.cct.org

The Chicago Community Trust is a foundation that assists nonprofit organizations through the development of grants and other resources.

Terry Mazany, President/CEO
Michelle Hunter, Director of Strategy

1483 Connecticut River Watershed Council

15 Bank Row 413-772-2020
Greenfield, MA 00130 *Fax:* 413-772-2090
afisk@ctriver.org
www.ctriver.org

The Connecticut River Watershed Council (CRWC) is the only broad-based citizen advocate for the environmental well-being of the entire Connecticut River. Their mission is to promote improvement of water quality and the restoration,conservation, wise development and use of the natural resources of the Connecticut River watershed.

Andrew Fisk, Executive Director
Colleen Bent, Development Director

1484 Department of the Interior

1849 C Street NW 202-208-3100
Washington, DC 20240 feedback@ios.doi.gov
www.doi.gov

The Department of the Interior protects and manages the Nation's natural resources and cultural heritage, honoring its trust responsibilities to American Indians, Alaska Natives, and affiliated island communities. It also providesinformation about natural resources and hazards.

David Bernhardt, Secretary
Susan Combs, Assistant Secretary

1485 Ecological Society of America

1990 M Street NW 202-833-8773
Suite 700 *Fax:* 202-833-8775
Washington, DC 20036 awards@esa.org
www.esa.org

To promote ecological science by improving communication among ecologists; raise the public's level of awareness of the importance of ecological science; increase the resources available for the conduct of ecological science. Offersnumerous awards, as do its chapters.

Catherine O'Riordan, Executive Director
Alison Mize, Director, Public Affairs

1486 Environmental Protection Agency (EPA)

1200 Pennsylvania Avenue NW 202-564-4700
Washington, DC 20460 www.epa.gov

EPA's mission is to protect human health and to safeguard the natural environment - air, water and land - upon which life depends. This agency also ensures that communities, individuals, businesses, and governments have access toaccurate information about human health and environmental risks.

Andrew Wheeler, Administrator
Ryan Jackson, Chief of Staff

1487 Federal Aviation Administration

Office of Public Affairs
800 Independence Avenue SW 202-267-3883
Washington, DC 20591 *Fax:* 202-267-5047
www.faa.gov

The major roles of the Federal Aviation Administration (a part of the Department of Transportation) include regulation, development, and research in the areas of civil aviation, civil aeronautics, and U.S. commercial spacetransportation. The FAA funds awards for airport safety, aerospace medicine, and more.

Michael Huerta, Administrator
Dan Elwell, Deputy Administrator

1488 Fly Fishers International

5237 U.S. Highway 89 South 406-222-9369
Suite 11 *Fax:* 406-222-5823
Livingston, MT 59047 ceo@flyfishersinternational.org
www.flyfishersinternational.org

Fly Fishers International seeks to cultivate and advance the art science and sport of flyfishing; to promote conservation of recreational resources; to facilitate and improve the knowledge of fly fishing; and to elevate the standard ofintegrity, honor and courtesy of anglers. Each year, awards are given to various individuals and groups who exemplify the mission and values of the IFFF.

Len Zickler, President/CEO
Rhonda Sellers, Operations Manager

1489 Forest History Society

2925 Academy Road 919-682-9319
Durham, NC 27705-9311 *Fax:* 919-682-2349
steven.anderson@foresthistory.org
www.foresthistory.org

A nonprofit educational institution that links the past to the future by identifying, collecting, preserving, interpreting and disseminating information on the history of people, forests and their related resources. Offers an array ofawards, grants, and fellowships.

Steven Anderson, President
Janet Askew, Assistant Director

1490 Frank A Chambers Excellence in Air Pollution Award

Air and Waste Management Association
Koppers Building 412-232-3444
436 Seventh Avenue, Suite 2100 800-270-3444
Pittsburgh, PA 15219 *Fax:* 412-232-3450
info@awma.org
www.awma.org

This award is for outstanding achievement in the science and art of air pollution control. It requires accomplishment of a technical nature on the part of the recipient which is considered to be a major contribution to the science andart of air pollution control.

Stephanie Glyptis, Executive Director
Phoebe Gorges, Awards Coordinator

1491 **Garden Club of America National Awards**
14 East 60th Street 212-753-8287
3rd Floor *Fax:* 212-753-0134
New York, NY 10022 gca@gcamerica.org
www.gcamerica.org

Seeks to stimulate the knowledge and love of gardening, to share the advantages of association by means of educational meetings, conferences, correspondence and publications, and to restore, improve, and protect the quality of theenvironment through educational programs and action in the fields of conservation and civic improvement. Offers a range of medals, funds, and awards.
18,000 members
Anne Neal Petri, President

1492 **German Marshall Fund of the United States**
1744 R Street NW 202-683-2650
Washington, DC 20009 *Fax:* 202-265-1662
info@gmfus.org
www.gmfus.org

This organization seeks to stimulate the exchange of ideas and promote cooperation between the United States and Europe in the spirit of the postwar Marshall Plan. They recognizes excellence in leadership and innovation through theirawards, grants, and fellowship program.

Craig Kennedy, President

1493 **Golden Gate Audubon Society**
2530 San Pablo Avenue 510-843-2222
Suite G *Fax:* 510-843-5351
Berkeley, CA 94702 ggas@goldengateaudubon.org
goldengateaudubon.org

A conservation and education organization that seek to protect birds and wildlife and their natural habitat in San Francisco and East Bay.

Cindy Margulis, Executive Director
Hana DeBare, Communications Director

1494 **Goldman Environmental Foundation**
160 Pacific Avenue 415-249-5800
Suite 200 *Fax:* 415-772-9137
San Francisco, CA 94111 info@goldmanprize.org
www.goldmanprize.org

Goldman Environmental Prizes are awarded for sustained and important efforts to preserve the natural environment, including, but not limited to: protecting endangered ecosystems and species, combatting destructive development projects,promoting sustainability, influencing environmental policies and striving for environmental justice.

John D. Goldman, President
Susan R. Gelman, Vice President

1495 **Great Lakes Commission**
2805 S Industrial Highway 734-971-9135
Suite 100 *Fax:* 734-971-9150
Ann Arbor, MI 48104-6791 eschmidt@glc.org
www.glc.org

Binational agency that promotes the orderly, integrated and comprehensive development, use and conservation of the water and related natural resources of the Great Lakes basin and St Lawrence River. The Great Lakes Commission offersthe Sea Grant Fellowship which is a year-long position focusing on environmental quality and sustainable economic development in the Great Lakes region.

Jon W. Allan, Chair
John Linc Stine, Vice Chair

1496 **Green Watch**
Capital Research Center
1513 16th Street NW 202-483-6900
Washington, DC 20036 *Fax:* 202-483-6990
contact@capitalresearch.org
www.capitalresearch.org/gw

Green Watch is an online database and information clearinghouse providing factual information on over 500 nonprofit environmental groups. This free service identifies the location, leadership and membership of each profiled group.Green Watch also produces timely news reports and analyses of the environmental movement.
Terrence Scanlon, Chairman

1497 **Honorary Membership**
Air and Waste Management Association
Koppers Building 412-232-3444
436 Seventh Avenue, Suite 2100 800-270-3444
Pittsburgh, PA 15219 *Fax:* 412-232-3450
info@awma.org
www.awma.org

This honorary membership may be conferred upon persons who have attained eminence in some field related to Air and Waste management and have rendered valuable service to the Association of Air and Waste Management.
Stephanie Glyptis, Executive Director
Phoebe Gorges, Awards Coordinator

1498 **Institute of Environmental Sciences and Technology (IEST)**
1827 Walden Office Square 847-981-0100
Suite 400 *Fax:* 847-981-4130
Schaumburg, IL 60173 www.iest.org

An international professional society that serves the environmental sciences in the areas of contamination control in electronic manufacturing and pharmaceutical processes, design, test and evaluation of commercial and militaryequipment and product reliability issues. IEST recognizes outstanding achievements in technological advances, contamination control, and leadership through their awards program. They also offer scholarships and fellows.

Angela McKay, Executive Director
Heather Wooden, Coordinator, Education

1499 **International Desalination Association**
PO Box 387 978-887-0410
94 Central Street, Suite 200 *Fax:* 978-887-0411
Topsfield, MA 01983 info@idadesal.org
www.idadesal.org

IDA is committed to the development and promotion of the appropriate use of desalination and desalination technology worldwide. The association encourages research and development, promotes communication and disseminates information.

Dr. Emilio Gabbrielli, President
Shannon McCarthy, First Vice President

1500 **International Wildlife Film Festival: Media Center**
718 S Higgins Avenue 406-728-9380
Missoula, MT 59801 *Fax:* 406-728-2881
iwff@wildlifefilms.org
www.wildlifefilms.org

An organization showcasing the world's best wildlife films and television programs, providing educational resources and event seminars, workshops, field classes, film tours and many hands-on activities that emphasize the mostup-to-date, factual and ethical scienced based information. Their goal is to promote awareness, knowledge and understanding of wildlife, habitat, people and nature through the medium of film, television and media.
Mike Steinberg, Executive Director

1501 **Irrigation Association**
8280 Willow Oaks Corporate Drive 703-536-7080
Suite 400 *Fax:* 703-536-7019
Fairfax, VA 22031 webmaster@irrigation.org
www.irrigation.org

This associate seeks to improve the products and practices used to manage water resources and to help shape the worldwide business environment of the irrigation industry. Each year the Irrigation Association recognizes individuals andorganizations that have made significant contributions to the irrigation industry with the presentation of six awards.
Gregory R. Hunter, President
Warren S. Gorowitz, Vice President

1502 John Burroughs`Association
15 West 77th Street 212-769-5169
New York, NY 10024 lbreslof@amnh.org
research.amnh.org/burroughs

Each year a medal is awarded to the author of a distinguished book of natural history, a list of exceptional national history books for young readers is selected, and an outstanding nature essay is identified.

Jeff Walker, President
Dave Liddell, First Vice President

1503 Keep America Beautiful
1010 Washington Boulevard 203-659-3000
Stamford, CT 00690 *Fax:* 203-659-3001
info@kab.org
www.kab.org

Nonprofit organization whose network of local, statewide and international affiliate progams educates individuals about litter prevention and ways to reduce, reuse, recycle and properly manage wase materials. KAB recognizesachievements made by individuals, communities, and corperations in the field of environmental sustainability, innovation, litter prevention and more.

Carey Hamilton, Executive Director
Beth Buehler, Chief Operating Officer

1504 Keep North Carolina Beautiful
1663 Edgewood Drive 843-427-4969
Little River, NC 29566 nckab@carolina.rr.com
keepncbeautiful.org

Keep North Carolina Beautiful is a nonprofit public education organization dedicated to enhancing the natural beauty of North Carolina communities, improving waste handling practices and empowering individuals to take greaterresponsibility for improving community environments.

Brenda Ewadinger, Executive Director

1505 Lyman A Ripperton Award
Air and Waste Management Association
Koppers Building 412-232-3444
436 Seventh Avenue, Suite 2100 800-270-3444
Pittsburgh, PA 15219 *Fax:* 412-232-3450
info@awma.org
www.awma.org

Awarded for distinguished achievement as an educator in some field of air pollution control. Awarded to an individual, who by precept and example, has inspired students to achieve excellence in all their professional and socialendeavors.

Stephanie Glyptis, Executive Director
Phoebe Gorges, Awards Coordinator

1506 NSF International
789 North Dixboro Road 734-769-8010
P.O. Box 130140 800-673-6275
Ann Arbor, MI 48105 *Fax:* 734-769-0109
info@nsf.org
www.nsf.org

The National Sanitation Foundation is an independent, accredited organization providing a wide range of services around the world, including standards development, testing, certification, auditing, inspection, consulting, and training.Their mission is to be the leading global provider of health and safety risk management solutions.

Lori Bestervelt, Senior VP & CTO
Kevan P. Lawlor, President & CEO

1507 National Association of Conservation Districts (NACD)
509 Capitol Court, NE 202-547-6223
Washington, DC 20002-4937 *Fax:* 202-547-6450
awards@email.nacdnet.org
www.nacdnet.org

The association's annual Awards Program recognizes individuals and organizations for outstanding work and leadership in soil and water conservation. Awards include: NACD Friend of Conservation; Distinguished Service; President's;Excellence in Communications; District Excellence; and Collaborative Conservation.

Jeremy Peters, Chief Executive Officer
Rich Duesterhaus, Director, Projects

1508 National Audubon Society (NAS)
National Audubon Society
225 Varick Street 212-979-3196
7th Floor 844-428-3826
New York, NY 10014 *Fax:* 212-979-3188
audubon@emailcustomerservice.com
www.audubon.org

The mission of the National Audubon Society is to conserve and restore natural ecosystems, focusing on birds and other wildlife for the benefit of humanity and the earth's biological diversity. Awards include: the Callison Award, theRachel Carson Award, and the Audubon Photography Awards.

David Yarnold, President & CEO
Stephen Meyer, Chief Operations Officer

1509 National Bison Association
The National Bison Association
8690 Wolff Ct 303-292-2833
Suite 200 *Fax:* 303-845-9081
Westminster, CO 80031 info@bisoncentral.com
www.bisoncentral.com

A nonprofit association which promotes the preservation, production and marketing of bison. Activities and services serve to better inform andeducate the general public about bison and to create and sustainable future forthe industry.The association offers scholarships for university students persuing bison related studies.

Dave Carter, Executive Director
Jim Matheson, Assistant Director

1510 National Environmental, Safety And Health Training Association
584 Main Street 207-771-9020
South Portland, MN 04106 neshta@neshta.org
neshta.org

The National Environmental Training Assoication, is a nonprofit international organization of enviromental, health and safety, and other technical training professionals.

Myrtle I. Turner-Harris, Executive Director
Jeffery K. Dennis, President

1511 National Ocean Industries Association
National Ocean Industries Association
1120 G Street NW 202-347-6900
Suite 900 *Fax:* 202-347-8650
Washington, DC 20005 jwilliams@noia.org
www.noia.org

The National Ocean Industries Assoication represents all facets of the domestic offshore and related industries. More than 300 member companies are dedicated to the development of offshore oil and natural gas. Annual awards include theCulture of Safety Award and the Safety Practice Award.

Cindy Taylor, Chairman
Kevin Mcevoy, Vice Chairman

1512 National Press Club
National Press Club
529 14th Street NW 202-662-7500
13th Floor info@press.org
Washington, DC 20045 www.press.org

Professional organization of reporters, writers and newspeople employed by newspapers, wire services, magazines, radio and television stations, and other forms of news media. They publish a weekly newsletter. Awards include: ConsumerJournalism Award; Washington Regional Reporting Award; Arthur Rowse Award for Press Criticism; Edwin M. Hood Award for Diplomatic Correspondence; Newsletter Journalism Award; Joan M. Friedenberg Online Journalism Award; and eight more.

Jeffrey Ballou, President

1513 National Recreation and Park Association (NRPA)
22377 Belmont Ridge Road 800-626-6772
Ashburn, VA 20148-4501 info@nrpa.org
www.nrpa.org
The mission of the National Recreation and Park Association is to a advance parks, recreation and environmental conservation efforts that enhance the quality of life for all people. The association recognizes individual achievementswithin the field through scholarships and fellows, and awards including the Gold Medal Award for Excellence in Park and Recreation Management, the NRPA National Award, and induction into the NRPA Robert C. Crawford Hall of Fame.
Kristine Stratton, President & CEO
Richard Dolesh, VP, Strategic Initiatives

1514 National Recycling Coalition
National Recycling Coalition
1220 L St NW 202-618-2107
Suite 100-155 *Fax:* 202-789-1431
Washington, DC 20005 www.nrc-recycle.org
NRC is a not-for-profit organization dedicated to the advancement and improvement of recycling, source reduction, composting, and reuse by providing technical information, education, training, outreach, and advocacy services to itsmembers in order to conserve resources and benefits the environment. Awards include: NRCs's Lifetime Achievement Award; Bill Heenan Emerging Leader Award; Outstanding Recycling Organization; Outstanding Community or Government Program ; and threemore.
Bob Gedert, President
Marjie Griek, Vice President

1515 National Water Resources Association (NWRA)
4 E Street Southeast 202-698-0693
Washington, DC 20003 *Fax:* 202-698-0694
nwra@nwra.org
www.nwra.org
The NWRA consists of individuals and groups, such as irrigation districts, canal companies and conservancy districts, municipalities and the public in general, who are interested in water resource development projects. The NWRA offersseven awards for achievements within the field, including Distinguished Service Award, the Water Buffalo Award, the Lifetime Achievement Award, the President's Award, the John M. Sayre Award, Water Statesman Award, and the John F. Sullivan/G. ThomasChoules Award.

Ron Thompson, President
Ian Lyle, Vice-President

1516 National Wild Turkey Federation
770 Augusta Road 803-637-3106
PO Box 530 800-843-6983
Edgefield, SC 29824-530 *Fax:* 803-637-0034
nwtf@nwtf.net
www.nwtf.org/
The NWTF, an international nonprofit conservation and education organization dedicated to conserving wild turkeys and preserving hunting traditions. The NWTF funs over 30 different awards including invidual achievements in preservingheritage, communication, law enforecement, forest services, volunteering, wildlife preservation, education, and sportmenship.
Becky Humphries, CEO
Vern Ross, Chairman

1517 National Wildlife Federation
11100 Wildlife Center Drive 800-822-9919
Reston, VA 20190 www.nwf.org
The National Wildlife Federation represents the power and commitment of over five million members and supporters joined by affiliated wildlife organizations throughout the states and territories. The NWF honors three individuals everyyear at their annual luncheon through the Jay N. Ding Darling Conservation Award, Conservationist of the Year, and the National Conservation Achievement Award.
Collin O'Mara, President/CEO
Kathy Hadley, Chair

1518 National Wildlife Rehabilitators Association (NWRA)
2625 Clearwater Road 320-230-9920
Saint Cloud, MN 56301 www.nwrawildlife.org
Nonprofit international membership organization committed to promoting and improving the integrity and professionalism of wildlife rehabilitation and contributing to the preservation of natural ecosystems. Offers a number of grants,awards, and scholarships.

Michele Goodman, President
Deb Dohrmann, Central Office Manager

1519 Natural Resources Defense Council
40 West 20th Street 212-727-2700
11th Floor *Fax:* 212-727-1773
New York, NY 10011 nrdcinfo@nrdc.org
www.nrdc.org
The NRDC focuses on issues impacting climate change, ocean pollution, water management and treatment, clean energy, and the conservation of wildlife. The NRDC funds the the Growing Green Awards to celebrate America's most influentialleaders in sustainable food market.

Rhea Suh, President
Mitchell Bernard, Chief Counsel

1520 Nature Conservancy
4245 N Fairfax Drive 703-841-5300
Suite 100 800-628-6860
Arlington, VA 22203-1606 www.nature.org
The Nature Conservancy is an international, nonprofit organization dedicated to preserving plant life. animals and natural communities by protecting the lands and waters they need to survive. Awards funded by this organization includeConservation Leadership, Volunteer Excellence, and Special Recognition.
Mark R. Tercek, President/CEO
Thomas J. Tierney, Chairman

1521 New England Wildflower Society
180 Hemenway Road 508-877-7630
Framingham, MA 01701-2699 508-877-3658
Fax: 508-877-3658
information@newenglandwild.org
www.newenglandwild.org
New England Wild Flower Society is a recognized leader in native plant conservation. Its purpose is to promote the conservation of temperate North American plants through key programs-conservation and research, education, horticultureand habitat preservation. They publish two magazines annually. The society offers three awards: the Founder's Medal, the Regional Impact Award, and the Service to the Society Award.

Debbi Edelstein, Executive Director
Alan Smith, Chair, Board of Trustees

1522 New York Botanical Garden
2900 Southern Boulevard 718-817-8700
Bronx, NY 10458-5126 *Fax:* 718-562-8474
www.nybg.org
The Garden is one of the world's largest collection of plants, an educational center for gardening and horticulture, and an international center for plant research. The NYBG honors persons whose committment to botanical research isinfluencial with the Gold Medal.

Maureen Chilton, Chairman
Gregory Long, President

1523 North American Association for Environmental Education (NAAEE)
1725 DeSales Street NW 202-419-0412
Suite 401 *Fax:* 202-419-0415
Washington, DC 20036 info@naaee.org
www.naaee.org
The North American Association for Environmental Education is a network of professionals, students and volunteers working in the field of environmental education. NAAEE takes a cooperative, non-confrontational, scientifically-basedapproach to pro-

moting education about environmental issues. Awards funded by the NAAEE include: Walter E. Jeske Award, Rosa Parks and Grace Lee Boggs Outstanding Service, K-12 Educator of the Year, Outstanding Affiliate Organization; and more.

16,000 members

Judy Braus, Executive Director
Sarah Bodor, Director, Policy

1524 Outdoor Writers Association of America

615 Oak Street 406-728-7434
Suite 201 800-692-2477
Missoula, MT 59801 *Fax:* 406-728-7445
krhoades@owaa.org
www.owaa.org

The mission of the Outdoor Writers Association of America is to improve the professional skills of its members, encourage public enjoyment and conservation of natural resources, and be mentors for the next generation of professionaloutdoor communicators. It funds a number of scholarships and fellows; and honors its memebers' achievements with five awards, which include: the Excellence in Craft Award, the Outstanding Board Member award, the Ham Brown Award, and Jackie PfeifferMemorial Award.

Brett Prettyman, President
Phil Bloom, First Vice President

1525 Sea Grant Association

University Of Maine
PO Box 1950 608-262-0905
Ocean Springs, ME 03956-1950 jphurley@wisc.edu
www.sga.seagrant.org

SGA is a non-profit organization dedicated to furthering the Sea Grant program concept. SGA provides the mechanism for academic institutions to coordinate their activities, set program priorities at both the regional and nationallevel, and to be a unified voice for the institutions on issues of importance to the oceans and coasts. The association funds six awards, including: the Distinguished Service Award, the President's Award, and the Sea Grant Association Award.

James Hurley, President
Fredrika Moser, President-Elect

1526 Sierra Club

2101 Webster Street 415-977-5500
Suite 1300 *Fax:* 510-208-3140
Oakland, CA 94612 information@sierraclub.org
www.sierraclub.org

To advance the preservation and protection of the natural environment by empowering the citizenry with charitable resources to further the cause of environmental protection. The Sierra Club honors its volunteers and staff membersthrough its awards program. Awards include: the John Muir award, the Distinguished Achievement Award, the Special Service Award, the One-Club Award, The Roy Family Award for Environmental Partnership, and many more.

Michael Brune, Executive Director
Jesse Simons, National Program Director

1527 Society of American Foresters (SAF)

10100 Laureate Way 301-897-8720
Bethesda, MD 20814-2198 866-897-8720
Fax: 301-897-3690
membership@safnet.org
www.eforester.org

To advance the science, education, technology, and practice of forestry; to enhance the competency of its members; to establish professional excellence; and to use the knowledge, skills, and conservation ethic of the profession toensure the continued health and use of forest ecosystems present and future of availability of forest resources to benefit society. Awards are offered for communication, journalism, forest science, technoly, leadership, and outstanding achievments inforestry.

Terry Baker, Chief Executive Officer
Louise Murgia, Chief Operating Officer

1528 Society of American Travel Writers

7044 South 13th Street 414-908-4949
Oak Creek, WI 53154 *Fax:* 414-768-8001
satw@satw.org
www.satw.org

SATW is a professional association whose purpose is to promote responsible journalism, provide professional support and development for its members and encourage the conservation and preservation of travel resources worldwide. Awardsoffered by SATW include: the Lowell Thomas Award, the Marco Polo Status, the Phoenix Award, the Muster Photo Competition; as well as writing and photography awards.

Catharine Hamm, President
Barbara Ramsay, President-Elect

1529 Society of Petroleum Engineers

222 Palisades Creek Drive 972-952-9393
PO Box 833836 *Fax:* 972-952-9435
Richardson, TX 75080 spedal@spe.org
www.spe.org

This organization represents and serves managers, engineers, scientists and other professionals worldwide in the oil and gas industry. The SPE celebrates its members with over 30 awards, including: Anthony F. Lucas Technical LeadershipGold Medal, Drilling Engineering Award, Production and Operations Award, Distinguished Lifetime Achievement Award, Young Member Outstanding Service Award, Health, Safety, Security, Environment, and Social Responsibility Award, and many more.

Janeen Judah, President
Roland Moreau, VP, Finance

1530 Soil and Water Conservation Society

945 Sw Ankeny Road 515-289-2331
Ankeny, IA 50023-9723 800-THE-SOIL
Fax: 515-289-1227
swcs@swcs.org
www.swcs.org

Foster the science and the art of soil, water and related natural resource management to achieve sustainability. To promote and practice an ethic recognizing the interdependence of the people in the environment. Awards include afellowship, the Outstanding Service Award, the Commendation Award, the Conservation Research Award, the Hugh Hammond Bennett Award, the Harold-Kay Scholl Excellence in Conservation Award, and the Merit and Honor awards.

Clare Lindahl, CEO
Rex Martin, President

1531 Solar Energy Industries Association

600 14th Street NW 202-682-0556
Suite 400 *Fax:* 202-628-7779
Washington, DC 20005 info@seia.org
www.seia.org/

SEIA seeks to expand the use of solar technologies in the global marketplace. National members combined with chapter members in 22 states exceed 500 compines providing solar thermal and solar electric products and services. It honorsachievments in the field of solar energy with their annual Solar Champion Awards.

Abigail Ross Hopper, President
Tom Starrs, Chair

1532 Solid Waste Association of North America (SWANA)

1100 Wayne Avenue 800-467-9262
Suite 650 *Fax:* 301-589-7068
Silver Spring, MD 20910 info@swana.org
swana.org

Professional organization for the advancement of responsible solid waste management. Offers a range of awards and scholarships.

David Biderman, Executive Director & CEO
Sara Bixby, Deputy Executive Director

1533 **The Wildlife Society Awards**
5410 Grosvenor Lane 301-897-9770
Suite 200 *Fax:* 301-530-2471
Bethesda, MD 20814-2144 wildlife.org/engage/awards
TWS Awards Program honors individuals and groups who have made notable contributions to wildlife conservation. With more than a dozen awards in all, visit thieir website for full details and nomination information. Some included areAldo Leopold Memorial Award, Chapter of the Year Award, Distinguished Service Award, Caesar Kleberg Award For Excellence in Applied Wildlife Research, Donald H. Rusch Memorial Game Bird Research Scholarship, Wildlife Publication Awards, and more.

Bruce C. Thompson, President
Darren A. Miller, Vice President

1534 **Trout Unlimited**
PO Box 7400 703-522-0200
Woolly Bugger, WV 25438-7400 800-834-2419
Fax: 703-284-9400
trout@tu.org
www.tu.org
This organization seeks to conserve, protect and restore North America's trout and salmon fisheries and their watersheds. Trout Unlimited offer five awards including: State Council Award for Excellence, Gold and Silver Trout ChapterAwards, Mortensen Award for Outstanding Volunteer Leadership, Trout Conservation Award: Professional, Partner Organization/Business, Communications, and Distinguished Service Award: Conservation, Leadership, Communications, Youth Education, andVeteran's Services.
Chris Wood, President & CEO
Elizabeth Maclin, Executive Vice President

1535 **U.S. Army Corps of Engineers**
441 G Street NW 202-761-0011
Washington, DC 20314-1000 www.usace.army.mil
The U.S. Army Corps of Engineers manages and executes civil works programs, including research and development, planning, design, construction, operation and maintenance, and real estate activities related to rivers, harbors andwaterways; it further administers laws for protection and preservation of navigable waters and related resources such as wetlands, and assists in recovery from natural disasters.

Todd T Semonite, Chief of Engineers
Michael Wehr, Deputy Chief of Engineers

1536 **U.S. Department of Energy**
1000 Independence Ave SW 202-586-5000
Washington, DC 20585 www.energy.gov
The Department of Energy's goal is to foster a secure and reliable energy system that is environmentally and economically sustainable, to be a responsible steward of the nation's nuclear weapons and to support continued US leadershipin science and technology.

Rick Perry, Secretary of Energy
Dan Brouillette, Deputy Secretary of Energy

1537 **Underwater Society of America**
PO Box 628 650-583-8492
Daly City, CA 94017 *Fax:* 408-294-3496
www.underwater-society.org/
This organization focuses on diving, marine ecology, safety, legislation, and marine conservation. Awards include: the NOGI, The Regional Divers of the Year Award, and the Women Divers Hall of Fame.

Carol Rose, President

1538 **Washington Journalism Center**
P.O. Box 15603 202-296-8455
Washington, DC 20003-603 *Fax:* 808-588-365
terrymichael@wcpj.org
National Award for Environmental Reporting recognizes excellence in journalism and promoting awareness to environmental issues.

Joe Foote, President

1539 **Water Environment Federation**
601 Wythe Street 800-666-0206
Alexandria, VA 22314 *Fax:* 703-684-2400
inquiry@wef.org
www.wef.org
The Water Environment Federation (WEF) is a not-for-profit technical and educational organization with members from varied disciplines who work toward the preservation and enhancement of the global water environment. The Awards Programprovides an opportunity to recognize individuals and organizations that have made outstanding contributions to the water environment profession. Catergories include: graduate studies scholarships, environmental engineering, excellenence in safety andoperations.
Jenny Hartfelder, President-Elect
Rick Warner, President

1540 **Whooping Crane Conservation Association**
715 Earl Drive 337-234-6339
Lawrenceburg, TN 38464 www.whoopingcrane.com
To advance conservation, protection and propagation of the Whooping Crane population, to prevent its extinction, to establish and maintain a captive management program for the perpetuation of the species. The Whooping CraneConservation Award is for lifetime achievement through exceptional dedication and significant contributions to the conservation and/or collective knowledge of the whooping crane.
Walt Strugeon, President

1541 **Wild Sheep Foundation (WSF)**
412 Pronghorn Trail 406-404-8750
Bozeman, MT 59718 800-653-6297
info@wildsheepfoundation.org
www.wildsheepfoundation.org
The Foundation's mission is to promote and enhance populations of indigenous wild sheep in North America, and to fund programs for the professional management of these populations. Also offers awards in the following categories:Service Awards, Hunting Awards, and International Awards.

Gray Thornton, President & CEO
Kevin Hurley, VP, Conservation

1542 **Wilderness Society**
1615 M Street NW 800-843-9453
Washington, DC 20036 member@tws.org
www.wilderness.org
The Wilderness Society seeks to achieve clean air and water; and preserve forestry and ecosystems. Ansel Adams Conservation Award is presented to a current or former federal official who has shown exceptional commitment to the cause ofconservation and the fostering of an American land ethic. The The Robert Marshall Award is The Wilderness Society's highest award presented to a private citizen who has never held federal office but has devoted long-term service to and has had anotable influence.
Jamie Williams, President
Melyssa Watson, Executive Director

1543 **Willowbrook Wildlife Haven Preservation**
National Wildlife Rehabilitation Association
2625 Clearwater Road 320-230-9920
Suite 110 *Fax:* 320-230-3077
St. Cloud, MN 56301
The National Wildlife Rehabilitators Association is a nonprofit international membership organization committed to promoting and improving the integrity and professionalism of wildlife rehabilitation and contributing to thepreservation of natural ecosystems.
Elaine M. Thrune, President
Richard Grant, President Elect

1544 World Environment Center
734 15th Street NW 202-312-1370
Suite 720 *Fax:* 202-637-2411
Washington, DC 20005 info@wec.org
www.wec.org

The World Environment Center is an independent, global non-profit, non-advocacy organization that advances sustainable development worldwide through the business practices of member companies and in partnership with governments,multi-lateral organizations, private sector organizations, universities and other stakeholders. The Gold Medal Award is presented annually to a global company that has demonstrated a unique example of sustainability in business practice.

Francisco Su rez Hern ndez, Chair
Dr. Terry F. Yosie, President/CEO

1545 World Wildlife Fund (WWF)
1250 24th Street NW 202-293-4800
PO Box 97180 800-225-5993
Washington, DC 20037 *Fax:* 202-293-9211
membership@wwfus.org
www.worldwildlife.org

Dedicated to protecting endangered species and their habitats through field work, advocacy, policy engagement, pioneering work and education. The largest multinational conservation organization in the world. Awards funded by theorganization include: The Duke of Edinburgh Conservation, the International President's Award, WWF Award for Conservation Merit, the Gift to the Earth award, Leaders for a Living Planet, and External Recognition of WWF.

Carter Roberts, President & CEO
Nik Sekhran, Chief Conservation Officer

Conferences & Trade Shows

Environmental

1546 **AEE East Energy Conference and Expo**
Association of Energy Engineers
3168 Mercer University Drive 770-447-5083
Suite 420 *Fax:* 770-446-3969
Atlanta, GA 30341 info@aeecenter.org
east.aeecenter.org
The Association of Energy Engineers is a nonprofit professional society that promotes the scientific and educational interests of those in the energy industry. The association offers conferences, journals, books and certificationprograms in support of sustainable development.
April
Bill Kent, Executive Director
Connie Meadows, Conference Director

1547 **AEE West Energy Conference and Expo**
Association of Energy Engineers
3168 Mercer University Drive 770-447-5083
Suite 420 *Fax:* 770-446-3969
Atlanta, GA 30341 info@aeecenter.org
west.aeecenter.org
The Association of Energy Engineers is a nonprofit professional society that promotes the scientific and educational interests of those in the energy industry. The association offers conferences, journals, books and certificationprograms in support of sustainable development.
June
Bill Kent, Executive Director
Connie Meadows, Conference Director

1548 **AEE World Energy Conference and Expo**
Association of Energy Engineers
3168 Mercer University Drive 770-447-5083
Suite 420 *Fax:* 770-446-3969
Atlanta, GA 30341 info@aeecenter.org
world.aeecenter.org
The Association of Energy Engineers is a nonprofit professional society that promotes the scientific and educational interests of those in the energy industry. The association offers conferences, journals, books and certificationprograms in support of sustainable development.
September
Bill Kent, Executive Director
Connie Meadows, Conference Director

1549 **Air and Waste Management Association Annual Conference and Exhibition**
Koppers Building 412-232-3444
436 Seventh Avenue, Suite 2100 800-270-3444
Pittsburgh, PA 15219 *Fax:* 412-232-3450
info@awma.org
www.awma.org
Environmental professionals from all sectors of the economy including colleges, universities, natural resource manufacturing and process industries, consultants, local state, provincial, regional and federal governments, construction,utilities industries gather to work together to improve community health and protect the environment.
June
56 exhibits
Stephanie Glyptis, Executive Director
Cindy Fontanesi, Conference Planner

1550 **American Academy of Environmental Medicine Conference**
6505 E. Central Avenue 316-684-5500
Suite 296 *Fax:* 888-411-1206
Wichita, KS 67206 defox@aaemonline.org
aaemconference.com
Aims to support physicians and other professionals in serving the public through education about the interaction between humans and their environment, and to promote optimal health through prevention and safe, effective treatment ofthe causes, not the illness. Meetings are held in spring and fall.
35+ booths with 200 attendees and 35+ exhibits
De Rodgers-Fox, Executive Director

1551 **American Conference of Governmental Industrial Hygienists**
1330 Kemper Meadow Drive 513-742-2020
Cincinnati, OH 45240 *Fax:* 513-742-3355
mail@acgih.org
www.acgih.org
ACGIH is a charitable scientific organization that aims to advance occupational and environmental health through education and the development and dissemination of scientific and technical knowledge.
3,000 Members
90 booths
Sheryl A. Milz, Chair
Alan Rossner, Treasurer

1552 **American Industrial Hygiene Association Conference and Exposition**
3141 Fairview Park Drive 703-849-8888
Suite 777 *Fax:* 703-207-3561
Falls Church, VA 22042 infonet@aiha.org
www.aiha.org
AIHA promotes, protects and enhances industrial hygienists and other occupational health, safety and environmental professionals in their efforts to improve the health and well-being of workers, the community and the environment.
May
Lawrence D. Sloan, Chief Executive Officer
Bethany Blue Chirico, Managing Dir., Meetings

1553 **American Society for Environmental History Conference**
UIC Department of History
601 S Morgan Street dspatz@aseh.net
MC 198 aseh.net
Chicago, IL 60607-7109
Promotes historical research and education on environmental matters, as a means of better understanding human interactions with the natural world. Affiliated with the Forest History Society, which co-publishes the Environmental Historyjournal.
March-April
David Spatz, Executive Director

1554 **American Solar Energy Society Conference**
American Solar Energy Society
2525 Arapahoe Ave 303-443-3130
Ste E4-253 info@ases.org
Boulder, CO 80302 www.ases.org
The American Solar Energy Society (ASES) is natioal nonprofit organization dedicated to advancing the use of solar energy for the benefit of uS citizens and the global environment. The organization promotes this goal by offeringeducation, events and resources to communities.

Elaine Hebert, Chair
Lucas Dixon, Vice-Chair

1555 **American Water Resources Association Conference**
P.O. Box 2663 540-687-8390
Woodbridge, VA 22195 *Fax:* 540-687-8395
info@awra.org
www.awra.org
AWRA advances water resources research, planning, development, management and education. AWRA takes a balanced, professional approach to solving water resources challenges by establishing discourse between physical, biological, andsocial scientists, engineers, and other persons concerned with water resources.

Dresden Farrand, Executive VP & CEO
Michael J. Kowalski, Director of Operations

1556 Arkansas Association of Conservation Districts Annual Conference
101 East Capitol 501-682-2915
Suite 350 *Fax:* 501-682-3991
Little Rock, AR 72201 debbiepinreal@aol.com
www.aracd.org
Affiliated with the National Association of Conservation Districts.The AACD is dedicated to educating the public about conservation work.
November
Martha Manley, President
William Bailey, First Vice President

1557 Association for Conservation Information (ACI) Conference
1085 Lake Road www.aci-net.org
Panton, VT 05491
Nonprofit association of information and education professionals representing state, federal and Canadian agencies and private conservation organizations.
July
Jennifer Wisniewski, President
Judy Stokes Weber, Treasurer

1558 Atlantic States Marine Fisheries Commission Annual Meeting
150 N Highland Street 703-842-0740
Suite 200 A-N *Fax:* 703-842-0741
Arlington, VA 22201 info@asmfc.org
www.asmfc.org
The Atlantic States Marine Fisheries Commission serves as a deliberative body, coordinating the conservation and management of the states shared near shore fishery resources-marine, shell, and anadromous-for sustainable use.

Robert E. Beal, Executive Director
Tina L. Berger, Director of Communications

1559 Children's Environmental Health: Research, Practice, Prevention and Policy
110 Maryland Avenue NE 202-543-4033
Suite 404 *Fax:* 202-543-8797
Washington, DC 20002 cehn@cehn.org
www.cehn.org
Children's Environmental Health Network is a national nonprofit organization focused on environmental health. The work of the work focuses on promoting pediatric research, prevention and practice. The organization hosts a AnniversaryGala every year to raise awareness for the cause.
Nsedu Obot Witherspoon, Executive Director
Kristie Trousdale, Program Manager

1560 Civilian Conservation Corps Legacy
P.O. Box 341 540-984-8735
Edinburg, VA 22824 ccc@ccclegacy.org
www.ccclegacy.org
Provides educational programs to perserve the heritage of the California Conservation Corp alumni and their conservation efforts.
10 booths
Jean Martin, President

1561 Coastal Society Conference
PO Box 3590 757-565-0999
Williamsburg, VA 23187-3590 *Fax:* 757-565-0922
coastalsoc@aol.com
www.thecoastalsociety.org
The Coastal Society is an organization of private sector, academic, and government professionals and students dedicated to actively addressing emerging coastal issues by fostering dialogue, forging partnerships, and promotingcommunication and education.
Lewis Lawrence, President
Megan D. Bailiff, President-Elect

1562 Colorado Water Congress Annual Meeting
1580 Logan Street 303-837-0812
Suite 700 *Fax:* 303-526-3864
Denver, CO 80203 cwc@cowatercongress.org
www.cowatercongress.org
Protects and conserves Colorado's water resources by means of advocacy and education.
January
350 attendees and 9 exhibits
Sam Susuras, President
Erin Wilson, Vice President

1563 Connecticut Forest & Park Association Annual Meeting
16 Meriden Road 860-346-TREE
Rockfall, CT 06481-2372 info@ctwoodlands.org
www.ctwoodlands.org
The Connecticut Forest & Park Association (CFPA) is a nonprofit organization dedicated to connecting people to the land in order to protect forests, parks, walking trails, and open spaces in Connecticut.
Spring
Eric Lukingbeal, President
Starr Sayres, Vice President

1564 ESTECH Annual Meeting and Exposition
Institute of Environmental Sciences & Technology
1827 Walden Office Square 847-981-0100
Suite 400 *Fax:* 847-981-4130
Schaumburg, IL 60173 information@iest.org
www.iest.org
Meeting for professionals in the disciplines of reliability, availability, and maintainability engineering.
April
Angela McKay, Executive Director
Heather Wooden, Coordinator, Education

1565 Energy Efficiency Global Forum
Alliance to Save Energy
1850 M St NW 202-857-0666
Suite 610 eeglobalforum.org
Washington, DC 20036
EE Global is an international meeting of business executives, government leaders, and advocates concerned with energy efficiency. Hosted by the Alliance to Save Energy.
Courtney Galatioto, VP, Stakeholder Relations
Susanna Silvan, Manager, Events

1566 Federation of Environmental Technologists Annual Conference
W175 N11081 Stonewood Dr 262-437-1700
Ste 203 *Fax:* 262-437-1702
Germantown, WI 53022 info@fetinc.org
www.fetinc.org
A nonprofit organization formed to assist industry in interpretation of and compliance with environmental regulations. FET provides education on regulatory compliance and technological advancements to its members, and otherenvironmental professionals, through training, professional development, and networking.
October
200 attendees and 30 exhibits
Jeffrey Nettesheim, Chair/Director
Cheryl Moran, President/Director

1567 Forestry Conservation Communications Association Annual Meeting
424 E. Middle Street 717-398-0815
Rear Unit 844-458-0298
Gettysburg, PA 17325 *Fax:* 717-778-4237
info@fcca-usa.org
www.fcca-usa.org
National organization serving all public safety two-way radio licensees by locating suitable frequencies within designated areas, coordinating licensing with the FCC, and protecting them once approved.
Ralph Haller, Executive Director
Michelle Fink, Natl. Frequency Coordinator

1568 GlobalCon
Association of Energy Engineers
3168 Mercer University Drive 770-447-5083
Atlanta, GA 30340 *Fax:* 770-446-3969
info@aeecenter.org
www.globalconevent.com
Presented by the Association of Energy Engineers (AEE) the conference is designed to provide hands-on, up-to-the-minute information to improve energy management programs, and get up to speed on the current generation of innovativetechnologies.
Craig White, President
Albert Thumann, Executive Director

1569 Greenprints: Sustainable Communities by Design
Southface Energy Institute
241 Pine Street Northeast 404-872-3549
Atlanta, GA 30308 *Fax:* 404-872-5009
info@southface.org
www.southface.org
Southface promotes sustainable homes, workplaces and communities through education, research, advocacy and technical assistance. Greenprints is a conference and trade show produced by the Southface Energy Institute.
March
100 booths with 1200 attendees
Linda Bolan, Vice President
Barry R. Goldman, Chair

1570 HydroVision International
Pennwell Publications
501 S College Street 918-831-9160
Charlotte, SC 28202 888-299-8016
registration@pennwell.com
www.hydroevent.com
Hydrovision Int'l provides a week of informative hydropower focused meetings including perspectives on the role of hydropower and issues affecting hydro resources. It will also help participants develop a vision to meet challenges andensure the future sustainability of hydro.
Andrea Harner, Conference Manager
Elizabeth Ingram, Conference Committee Chair

1571 Institute of Environmental Sciences and Technology Fall Conference
1827 Walden Office Square 847-981-0100
Suite 400 *Fax:* 847-981-4130
Schaumburg, IL 60173 information@iest.org
www.iest.org
An international professional society that serves the environmental sciences in the areas of contamination control in electronics manufacturing and pharmaceutical processes, design, test and evaluation of commercial and militaryequipment and product reliability issues.
October - November
100 attendees
Angela McKay, Executive Director
Heather Wooden, Coordinator, Education

1572 Institute of Scrap Recycling Industries Convention and Exposition
1250 H Street 202-662-8500
Suite 400 *Fax:* 202-626-0900
Washington, DC 20005 isri@isri.org
www.isri.org
Membership is made up of manufacturers and processors, brokers and industrial consumers of scrap commodities, including ferrous and nonferrous metals, paper, electronics, rubber, plastics, glass and textiles. ISRI's associate membersinclude equipment and service providers to the scrap recycling industry.
April
Robin Wiener, President
David Wagger, Chief Scientist

1573 International Association for Energy Economics North American Conference
International Association for Energy Economics
28790 Chagrin Boulevard 216-464-5365
Suite 350 iaee@iaee.org
Cleveland, OH 44122 www.iaee.org
The IAEE is a nonprofit professional organization that provides a forum for the exchange of ideas and experiences among energy professionals. The conference attracts governmental, corporate, and academic energy decision-makers.
November
David L. Williams, Executive Director
Ronald D. Ripple, VP, Conferences

1574 International Conference on Solid Waste
Widener University, Civil Engineering
One University Place 610-499-4042
Chester, PA 19013-5792 *Fax:* 610-499-4461
solid.waste@widener.edu
solid-waste.org
An annual conference on solid waste technology and management. Over 150 speakers from 40 countries present their work.
March
Ronald L Mersky, Chair

1575 Larval Fish Conference
earlylifehistory.fisheries.org
Conference of the Early Life History section of the American Fisheries Society.
May - June
Claire Paris, President
Alison Deary, Secretary

1576 Maryland Recyclers Coalition Annual Conference
Maryland Recyclers Coalition
PO Box 1640 443-741-8740
Columbia, MD 21044 *Fax:* 301-238-4579
www.marylandrecyclingnetwork.org
MRC's mission is to promote sustainable reduction, reuse and recycling of materials otherwise destined for disposal and promote and increase buying products made with recycled material content. Maryland recycling and solid wastemanagement professionals gather each year to discuss topics such as changing waste management and recycling models, policy & regulation, commodities markets, new technologies & more.
June
Kemrey Kidd, President
Peter Houstle, Executive Director

1577 Massachusetts Association of Conservation Commissions Conference
10 Juniper Road 617-489-3930
Belmont, MA 02478 *Fax:* 617-489-3935
staff@maccweb.org
www.maccweb.org
MACC hosts an Annual Environmental Conference, the largest in New England, with over 40 workshops and nearly 50 exhibitors.
March
1100 attendees and 50 exhibits
Jennifer Carlino, Board President
Michael Howard, First Vice President

1578 Massachusetts Water Pollution Control Association Annual Conference
P.O. Box 60 774-276-9722
Rochdale, MA 01542 *Fax:* 774-670-9956
mwpca2011@yahoo.com
www.mwpca.org
The Massachusetts Water Pollution Control Association (MWPCA) is a non profit organization that provides education, training, and promote the exchange of information among operators and water quality professionals.
September
Bob Greene, President
Eric Smith, President-Elect

1579 Michigan Association of Conservation Districts Annual Meeting
3001 Coolidge Road 517-324-5274
Suite 250 *Fax:* 517-324-4435
East Lansing, MI 48823 macd@macd.org
www.macd.org
The Michigan Association of Conservation Districts is a non-governmental, non-profit organization, established to represent and provide services to Michigan's 76 Conservation Districts. The Association represents its members at thestate level by working with legislators, cooperating agencies, and special interest groups whose programs affect the care and management of Michigan's natural resources, especially on private lands.
November
Art Pelon, President
Lori Phalen, Executive Director

1580 Michigan Forest Association Annual Meeting
6120 South Clinton Trail 517-663-3423
Eaton Rapids, MI 48827 www.michiganforests.com
The Association seeks to promote good management on all forest land, to educate its members about good forest practices and stewardship of the land, and to inform the general public about forestry issues and the benefits of good forestmanagement.
Summer
William Botti, Executive Director

1581 Minnesota Association of Soil and Water Conservation Districts Annual Meeting
255 Kellogg Boulevard East 651-690-9028
Ste 101 *Fax:* 651-690-9065
St. Paul, MN 55101 www.maswcd.org
MASWCD is a nonprofit organization which exists to provide leadership and a common voice for Minnesota's soil and water conservation districts and to maintain a positive, results-oriented relationship with rule making agencies,partners and legislators; expanding education opportunities for the districts so they may carry out effective conservation programs.
December
Kurt Beckstorm, President
Roland Celevland, Vice President

1582 Montana Association of Conservation Districts Annual Meeting
1101 11th Avenue 406-443-5711
Helena, MT 59601 *Fax:* 406-443-0174
mail@macdnet.org
www.macdnet.org
The Montana Association of Conservation Districts provides assistance to the state's 58 conservation districts by helping local people match their needs with technical and financial resources.
November
Jeff Wivholm, President
Mark Suta, Vice President

1583 Montana Water Environment Association Annual Meeting
601 Wythe Street 800-666-0206
Alexandria, VA 22314 *Fax:* 703-684-2400
wef.org
A division of the Water Environment Federation, the Montana Water Environment Association (MWEA) is a non-profit organization dedicated to the preservation and enhancement of Montana's water environment. The Association is committed toadvancing science and education, disseminating technical information, increasing public understanding and promoting sound public policy in the water quality and water resources field.
Spring
Starr Sullivan, President
Herb Bartle, Vice-President

1584 NEHA Annual Educational Conference and Exhibition
National Environmental Health Association
720 S Colorado Boulevard 303-756-9090
Suite 1000-N *Fax:* 303-691-9490
Denver, CO 80246 staff@neha.org
www.neha.org
The NEHA AEC and Exhibition is a six-day educational event consisting of nine different environmental health and protection conferences and a two-day exhibition. It is the only conference that emcompasses all areas of environmentalhealth and protection, including, but not limited to: food protection, onsite wastewater, chemical and bioterrorism preparedness, indoor air quality, hazardous waste, and drinking water.
Late June-Early July
900 booths with 1300 attendees
David T. Dyjack, Executive Director

1585 NESEA BuildingEnergy Conference
50 Miles Street 413-774-6051
Greenfield, MA 01301 *Fax:* 413-774-6053
nesea@nesea.org
www.nesea.org
This conference is the oldest and largest regional building energy and renewable energy conference and trade show for practitioners in the Northeast.
March
4000 attendees and 150 exhibits
Martine Dion, Vice-Chair
Paul Eldrenkamp, Treasurer

1586 National Association of Environmental Professionals Conference
2150 N 107th Street 206-209-5286
Suite 205 *Fax:* 206-367-8777
Seattle, WA 98133 office@naep.org
www.naep.org
NAEP is a multidisciplinary association dedicated to the advancement of environmental professionals in the US and abroad, and a forum for current information on environmental planning, research, and management.
Krystina Toscas, Executive Director
Makenna Wallingford, Marketing & Communications

1587 National Conference of Local Environmental Health Administrators
University of Washington
1010 South Third Street 509-382-2181
Dayton, WA 99328 *Fax:* 360-382-2942
david_riggs@co.columbia.wa.us
depts.washington.edu/clehaweb
The NCLEHA's purpose is to provide a forum for local administrators to share common concerns and solutions to mutual problems, and to provide a professional organization for environmental health administrators, focused on the issuesand problems of local environmental health programs.
Dave Riggs, Chair

1588 National Environmental Balancing Bureau Meeting
National Environmental Balancing Bureau
8575 Grovemont Circle 301-977-3698
Gaithersburg, MD 20877 877-800-5147
Fax: 301-977-9589
tiffany@nebb.org
www.nebb.org
The NEBB is a nonprofit organization founded by contractors in the heating, ventilating and air conditioning (HVAC) industry. NEBB exists to help architects, engineers, building owners and contractors produce great buildings with HVACsystems that perform in ways they have visualized and designed.
Jim Kelleher, President
Donald E. Hill, President Elect

1589 National Environmental, Safety and Health Training Association
584 Main Street 207-771-9020
South Portland, MN 04106-1147 neshta@neshta.org
neshta.org
NESHTA is a non-profit international society for environmental, safety, health and other technical training and adult education professionals. NESHTA promotes trainer competency through

training and education standards, voluntarycertification, and peer networking. They partner with the National Partnership for Environmental Technology Education to host education and training conferences.

Myrtle I. Turner-Harris, President
Jeffery K. Dennis, Vice President

1590 National Recycling Congress Show
1220 L St NW 202-618-2107
Suite 100 *Fax:* 202-789-1431
Washington, DC 20005 www.nrc-recycle.org
The National Recycling Coalition, Inc. provides technical education, disseminates public information on selected recycling issues, shapes public and private policy on recycling and operates programs that encourage recycling markets andeconomic development.

Bob Gebert, President
Marjie Griek, Vice President

1591 National Solar Conference
2525 Arapahoe Ave 303-443-3130
Ste E4-253 *Fax:* 303-442-3212
Boulder, CO 80302 info@ases.org
www.ases.org
The event combines a premiere technical conference, plenary and forum sessions, a Renewable Energy Products and Services exhibit, workshops, tours and special events of interest to professionals and consumers. Hosted by the AmericanSolar Energy Society (ASES).
August
750 attendees and 75-100 exhibits
Carly Rixham, Executive Director
Carly Cipolla, Director, Operations

1592 National Water Resources Association Annual Conference
4 E Street Southeast 202-698-0693
Suite 4 *Fax:* 202-698-0694
Washington, DC 20003 nwra@nwra.org
www.nwra.org
The NWRA consists of individuals and groups, such as irrigation districts, canal companies and conservancy districts, municipalities and the publicin general, who are interested in water resource development projects. It now has about5,000 members.
Ron Thompson, President
Ian Lyle, Vice-President

1593 Natural Resources Districts Annual Conference
Nebraska Association of Resources Districts
601 South 12th Street 402-471-7670
Suite 201 *Fax:* 402-471-7677
Lincoln, NE 68508 nard@nrdnet.org
www.nrdnet.org
The Nebraska Association of Resources Districts (NARD) is the trade association for Nebraska's 23 Natural Resources Districts. Its mission is to coordinated effort to accomplish collectively what may not be accomplished individually toconserve, sustain, and improve our natural resources and environment.
September
Jim Bendfeldt, President
Larry Reynolds, Vice President

1594 New England Water Environment Association Annual Meeting
NEWEA
10 Tower Office Park 781-939-0908
Suite 601 *Fax:* 781-939-0907
Woburn, MA 00180-2155 mail@newea.org
www.newea.org
We are a regional member association of the Water Environmental Federation. We provide technical and education for the waste water industry.
150+ booths with 1500 attendees
Mary Barry, Executive Director
Janice Moran, Program Coordinator

1595 New Hampshire Association of Conservation Commissions Annual Meeting
54 Portsmouth Street 603-224-7867
Concord, NH 03301 info@nhacc.org
www.nhacc.org
The New Hampshire Association of Conservation Commissions is a private, non-profit association of municipal conservation commissions. Its purpose is to foster conservation and appropriate use of New Hampshire's natural resources byproviding assistance to conservation commissions, facilitating communication and cooperation among commissions, and helping to create a climate in which commissions can be successful.
November
Rep. Michele Peckham, President
Bruce Allen, Vice President

1596 New Jersey Society for Environmental Economic Development Annual Conference
222 West State Street 609-695-3481
Trenton, NJ 08608 *Fax:* 609-695-0151
www.njslom.org
Servicing the local municiple government and providing resources to improve the quality of living for its citizens.
November
16,000 attendees and 700+ exhibits
Albert B. Kelly, President
James Cassella, 1st Vice President

1597 New Jersey Water Environment Association Conference
Fair Lawn, NJ john.corkery@pumpingservices.com
www.njwea.org
The New Jersey Water Environment Association is a nonprofit educational organization dedicated to preserving and enhancing the water environment.

Francis Bonaccorso, President
John Corkery, Secretary

1598 New Mexico Association of Soil and Water Conservation Annual Conference
New Mexico Association Of Conservation Districts
163 Trail Canyon Road 575-981-2400
Carlsbad, NM 88220 conserve@hughes.net
www.nmacd.org
The mission of NMACD is to facilitate conservation of the natural resources in New Mexico by providing opportunities and quality support to local conservation districts through representation and leadership.
Fall
Jim Berlier, President
John Arrington, Vice President

1599 New York Water Environment Association Semi-Annual Conferences
Nywea
525 Plum Street 315-422-7811
Suite 102 877-556-9932
Syracuse, NY 13204 *Fax:* 315-422-3851
pcr@nywea.org
www.nywea.org
The New York Water Environment Association is a nonprofit educational association dedicated to the development and dissemination of information concerning water quality management and the nature, collection, treatment, and disposal ofwastewater.
2,500 Members
Winter and Summer
Paul McGarvey, President
Geoffrey Baldwin, President Elect

1600 North American Lake Management Society International Symposium
PO Box 5443 608-233-2836
Madison, WI 53705-0443 *Fax:* 608-233-3186
www.nalms.org
NAMLS's focus is on lake management for a wide variety of uses, but they are also involved with other issues on a watershed level:

land, streams, wet lands, and estuaries. The society forges partnerships among citizens, scientists andprofessionals to foster the management and protection of lakes and reservoirs.
October and November
100 booths with 850 attendees and 50 exhibits
Frank Wilhelm, President
Frank Browne, President-Elect

1601 North Carolina Association of Soil and Water Conservation Districts Annual Conference
Po Box 27943 919-715-6104
Raleigh, NC 27611 ncaswcd@gmail.com
www.ncaswcd.org

The association is an indepented, nonpartisan conservation organization presenting the interests of the 96 local soil and water conservation districts and the 492 district supervisors who direct their local district's conservationprograms.
January
Chris Hogan, President
Dietrich Kilpatrick, First Vice-President

1602 North Dakota Association of Soil Conservation Districts Annual Conference
Lincoln Oaks Nursurey
3310 University Drive 701-223-8575
Bismarck, ND 58504 *Fax:* 701-223-1291
bismarcknursery@lincolnoakes.com
www.lincolnoakes.com

The purpose of the North Dakota Association of Soil Conservation Districts is to further the widespread application of sound and practical soil and water conservation practices in North Dakota.
November
Bill Elhard, Nursery Manager
Shirley Christenson, Nursery Tech

1603 Northeast Recycling Council Conference
139 Main Street 802-254-3636
Suite 401 info@nerc.org
Brattleboro, VT 05301 www.nerc.org
NERC's mission is to To advance an environmentally sustainable economy by promoting source and toxicity reduction, recycling, and the purchasing of environmentally preferable products and services.
March and November
Robert Isner, President
Kaley Laleker, Vice President

1604 Northeast Resource Recovery Association Annual Conference
2101 Dover Road 603-736-4401
Epsom, NH 03234 800-223-0150
Fax: 603-736-4402
info@nrra.net
www.nrra.net

The Northeast Resource Recovery Association is a pro-active nonprofit working with its membership to make their recycling programs strong, efficient, and financially successful by providing cooperative marketing, cooperativepurchasing, education and networking opportunities; developing innovative recycling programs; creating sustainable alternatives to reduce the volume and toxicity of the waste, and educating and informing local officials about recycling and solidwaste issues.
June
Duncan P. Watson, President
John Hurd, Vice President

1605 Pacific Fishery Management Council Conferences
7700 Northeast Ambassador Place 503-820-2280
Suite 101 866-806-7204
Portland, OR 97220 *Fax:* 503-820-2299
pfmc.comments@noaa.gov
www.pcouncil.org

The Pacific Council has developed fishery management plans for salmon, groundfish and coastal species in the US Exclusive Economic Zone off the coast of Washington, Oregon and California.
5x year
Chuck Tracy, Executive Director
Mike Burner, Deputy Director

1606 Parks and Trails Council of Minnesota Annual Meeting
275 E 4th Street 651-726-2457
Suite 250 800-944-0707
St. Paul, MN 55101-1626 *Fax:* 651-726-2458
info@parksandtrails.org
www.parksandtrails.org

Parks and Trails Council of Minnesota seeks to aquire, protect and sustain long-term statewide land.
March
Julie Gugin, President
Bob Biersheid, Vice President

1607 Reliability and Maintainability Symposium (RAMS)
Institute of Environmental Sciences & Technology
1827 Walden Office Square 847-981-0100
Suite 400 *Fax:* 847-981-4130
Schaumburg, IL 60173 information@iest.org
www.iest.org

Conference for professionals in the fields of controlled environments, environmental testing, product reliability, and nanotechnology facilities.
January
Angela McKay, Executive Director
Heather Wooden, Coordinator, Education

1608 Renewable Energy Roundup & Green Living Fair
PO Box 1447 512-345-5446
Austin, TX 78767-1447 800-465-5049
info@txses.org
www.txses.org

Organized by the Texas Solar Energy Society and Texas Renewable Energy Industries Association featuring solutions to global warming such as rainwater harvesting, green and sustainable building, alternative transporation, and energyconservation.
September
Lucy Stolzenburg, Executive Director
Russel Smith, Event Coordinator

1609 Solar Cookers International World Conference
2400 22nd Street 916-455-4499
Suite 210 info@solarcookers.org
Sacramento, CA 95818 www.solarcookers.org
Solar Cookers International's mission is to spread solar thermal cooking technology to benefit people and environments.
James G. Moose, President
Monica Woods, Vice President

1610 South Dakota Association of Conservation Districts Conference
116 N Euclid Avenue 605-895-4099
Pierre, SD 57501 800-729-4099
www.sdconservation.org

Mission is to lead, represent and assist South Dakota's conservation districts in promoting a healthy environment. Specific areas of concern include wind and water erosion, water quality and quantity including preservation of theMissouri main stem dams, air quality, forestry, rangeland, wildlife and recreation.
September
Angela Ehlers, Executive Director
Karl Jensen, President

1611 South Dakota Environmental Health Association Annual Conference
State Department of Health
PO Box 2275A 605-773-3361
Pierre, SD 57007 800-738-2301
office@sdpublichealth.org
sdpublichealth.org

The South Dakota Public Health Association is the only trade association in South Dakota for public health professionals, whose

mission is to promote and protect the health of individuals, families and the communities.
April
Kimberly Wilson-Sweebe, President
Wyatt Pickner, Vice President

1612 Southeastern Association of Fish and Wildlife Agencies Annual Meeting
27 Sylwood Place 601-668-6916
Jackson, MS 39209 crayhopkins@bellsouth.net
www.seafwa.org
The SEAFWA conducts an annual conference each fall to provide a forum for presentation of information and exchange of ideas regarding the management and protection of fish and wildlife resources throughout the nation with emphasis onthe southeast.
October/November
Curtis R Hopkins, Executive Secretary
Alvin Taylor, President

1613 Symposium on the Application of Geophysics to Engineering and Environmental Problems
1391 Speer Blvd. 303-531-7517
Suite 450 staff@eegs.org
Denver, CO 80204 www.eegs.org
SAGEEP is the annual meeting of the Environmental and Engineering Geophysical Society, focused on the practical application of shallow geophysics.
Winter-Spring
350 attendees
Kathie Barstnar, Executive Director
Jackie Jacoby, Managing Director

1614 Take it Back
Raymond Communications
P.O. Box 4311 301-879-0628
Silver Spring, MD 20914-4311 circulation@raymond.com
www.raymond.com
Raymond Communications provides news and insight on environmental legislative and regulatory developments from around the world. Their Take It Back conferences focus on recycling and waste management programs.
250 attendees
Bruce Popka, President

1615 Texas Environmental Health Association Annual Education Conference
PO Box 889 806-855-4277
Wolfforth, TX 79382 *Fax:* 806-855-4277
www.myteha.org
TEHA provides a professional organization for Sanitarians and Environmental Health Professionals, designed to serve as the focal point for their education and professional status. They host educational meetings each year for membersand their guests and to promote the exchange of ideas and update techniques in the profession.
March
J. Victor Baldovinos, President
Russell O'Brien, President Elect

1616 Texas Water Conservation Association Annual Conference
3755 S. Capital of Texas Highway 512-472-7216
Suite 105 *Fax:* 512-472-0537
Austin, TX 78704 admin@twca.org
www.twca.org
The Texas Water Conservation Association consists of water professionals and organizations in the state of Texas who represent river authorities, municipalities, navigation and flood control districts, drainage and irrigationdistricts, utility districts, municipalities, groundwater conservation districts, all kinds of water users, and general/environmental water interests.
March
Michael J. Booth, President
Hope Wells, President-Elect

1617 Utah Association of Conservation Districts Annual Conference
PO Box 4117 435-881-7688
Logan, UT 84323 uacd.org
The Utah Association of Conservation Districts is a nonprofit corporation representing Utah's 38 soil conservation districts. By working with landowners, organizations and government, the conservation districts work through voluntary,incentive-based programs to protect soil, water quality and other natural resources.
November
Bob Barry, President
Allen Henrie, Vice President

1618 Virginia Association of Soil and Water Conservation Districts Annual Conference
7308 Hanover Green Drive 804-559-0324
Suite 100 *Fax:* 804-559-0325
Mechanicsville, VA 23111 info@vaswcd.org
www.vaswcd.org
The Virginia Association of Soil and Water Conservation Districts (VASWCD) is a private nonprofit association of 47 soil and water conservation districts in Virginia. It is a voluntary, nongovernmental association of Virginia'sdistricts that provides and promotes leadership in the conservation of natural resources through stewardship and education programs.
December
Steven Meeks, President
Kendall Elaine Tyree, Executive Director

1619 Virginia Forestry Association Annual Conference
3308 Augusta Avenue 804-278-8733
Richmond, VA 23230 *Fax:* 804-278-8774
www.vaforestry.org
VFA promotes stewardship and wise use of the Commonwealth's forest resources for the economic and environmental benefits of all Virginians. Membership consists of forest landowners, forest product businesses, forestry professionals,and a variety of individuals and groups who are concerned about the future and well-being of Virginia's forest resources.
Late Spring
John Hancock, President
Carl Garrison, Vice President

1620 WEFTEC Show
Water Environment Federation
601 Wythe Street 800-666-0206
Alexandria, VA 22314 *Fax:* 703-684-2400
inquiry@wef.org
www.wef.org
North America's largest annual water quality conference and exposition. The WEFTEC covers a wide spectrum of critical water quality issues.
Fall
16,000 attendees and 800+ exhibits
Rick Warner, President
Jenny Harfelder, President-Elect

1621 Waste Expo
Waste360
Las Vegas Convention Center 312-840-8408
3150 Paradise Road wasteexpo.com
Las Vegas, NV
This conference focuses on education and training on recycling programs and waste management, including topics such as bioplastics, composting, equipment leasing and financing, fire safety, food waste reduction, operating landfills,Zero Waste strategies and practices, and more.
April
Mark Hickey, Market Leader
Catherine E. Campfield, Show Coordinator

1622 West Virginia Forestry Association
1776 Parkersburg Road 304-372-1955
PO Box 718 *Fax:* 304-372-1957
Ripley, WV 25271 wvfa@wvfa.org
www.wvfa.org

The West Virginia Forestry Association is a non-profit organization funded by its membership. Our members include individuals and businesses involved in forest management, timber production and wood product manufacturing. Our membersare concerned with protecting the environment, as well as enhancing the future of West Virginia's forests through multiple-use management.
Summer
Mark Haddix, President
Dane Moore, First Vice President

1623 Western Association of Fish and Wildlife Agencies Annual Meeting
522 Notre Dame Court 307-631-4536
Cheyenne, WY 82009 *Fax:* 307-638-1470
www.wafwa.org
The Western Association of Fish and Wildlife Agencies represents 23 states and Canadian provinces and supports resource management to conserve wildlife.
July
Curt Melcher, President
Keith Sexton, 1st VP

1624 Western Forestry and Conservation Association Conference
4033 SW Canyon Road 503-226-4562
Portland, OR 97221 *Fax:* 503-226-2515
richard@westernforestry.org
westernforestry.org
Offers continuing education workshops and seminars for professional foresters throughout the west.
January/February
Richard Zabel, Executive Director

1625 Western Society of Naturalists Annual Meeting
PO Box 247 secretariat@wsn-online.org
Bodega Bay, CA 94923 www.wsn-online.org
Members include researchers, educators, academics and others with an interest in the area's biology, particularly its marine life.
November
Danielle Zacherl, President
Andrew Brooks, Treasurer

1626 Wildlife Habitat Council Conservation Conference
Wildlife Habitat Council
8737 Colesville Road 301-588-8994
Suite 800 whc@wildlifehc.org
Silver Spring, MD 20910 www.wildlifehc.org
Annual conference of the Wildlife Habitat Council, a nonprofit group of corporations, conservation organizations, and individuals dedicated to restoring and enhancing wildlife habitat.
Margaret O'Gorman, President
Josiane Bonneau, Sr. Dir., Conservation

1627 Wildlife Society Annual Conference
Wildlife Society
425 Barlow Place 301-897-9770
Suite 200 tws@wildlife.org
Bethesda, MD 20814 www.wildlife.org
Annual conference of wildlife professionals, organized by the Wildlife Society.
September
50 booths with 1400 attendees
Ed Thompson, Executive Director/CEO
Bruce C. Thompson, President

1628 Wisconsin Association for Environmental Education Annual Conference
2100 Main Street 715-346-0123
University of Wisconsin webmaster@uwsp.edu
Stevens Point, WI 54481-3897 www.uwsp.edu
WAEE is a statewide non-profit organization promoting responsible environmental action through education in the classroom and in the community. Each year WAEE hosts an Annual Conference where environmental educators from across thestate gather to learn from one another, meet others in the field.
Fall
Rebecca Franzen, Instructor

1629 Wisconsin Land and Water Conservation Association Annual Conference
131 W. Wilson St. 608-441-2677
Suite 601 *Fax:* 608-441-2676
Madison, WI 53703 info@wisconsinlandwater.org
wisconsinlandwater.org
To assist county Land Conservation Committees and Departments with the protection, enhancement and sustainable use of Wisconsin's natural resources and to represent them through education and governmental interaction.
December
Ken Dolata, Executive Director

1630 Wisconsin Woodland Owners Association Annual Conference
PO Box 285 715-346-4798
Stevens Point, WI 54481 wwoa@uwsp.edu
www.wisconsinwoodlands.org
The Wisconsin Woodland Owners Association is a nonprofit educational organization seeking to advance the interests of woodland owners and the cause of forestry; develop public appreciation for the value of Wisconsin's woodlands andtheir importance in the economy and overall welfare of the state; foster and encourage wise use and management of Wisconsin's woodlands for timber production, wildlife habitat and recreation; and to educate those interested in managing the woodlands.
October
Steven Ring, President
David Congos, Vice President

Consultants

Environmental

1631 **AAA Lead Consultants and Inspections Inc**
1307 West 6th Street 951-582-9071
Suite 134 aaalead@sbcglobal.net
Corona, CA 92882 aaalead.com
This organization offers quality consulting, inspections, monitoring and project design for lead based paint and other lead containing materials.

Michael Cohn, Chief Executive Officer

1632 **ABCO Construction Services**
6901 South Yosemite Street 303-220-8220
Suite 205 info@abco-corp.com
Centennial, CO 80112 www.abco-corp.com
Provides a full spectrum of engineering and environmental services pertaining to both new construction and existing buildings. Services include Property Condition Assessment Reports, Phase I Environmental Assessments, Quality ControlReports and other technical support services relating to buildings and building systems.
Joe Johnson, Owner & Manager

1633 **ABS Group Training**
American Bureau of Shipping
1701 City Plaza Drive 281-673-2800
Spring, TX 77389 *Fax:* 281-877-5946
info@abs-group.com
www.abs-group.com/training
A subsidiary of American Bureau of Shipping offering risk management, safety, quality and environmental consulting and certification services to a wide range of industries and companies throughout the world.

Ryan Moody, President & CEO
David F. Montague, Sr. VP, Safety & Compliance

1634 **ACC Environmental Consultants**
7977 Capwell Drive 510-638-8400
Suite 100 800-525-8838
Oakland, CA 94621 *Fax:* 510-638-8404
general@accenv.com
www.accenv.com
This organization is an employee-owned environmental and energy consulting firm, assisting companies and public agencies throughout California to identify and manage environmental hazards and comply with environmental policies. ACCoffers a number of services: asbestos consulting, site assessments for real estate businesses, emergency response services, and more.

Jim Wilson, President & CEO
Steve Jackson, Senior Project Manager

1635 **ACRT Environmental Specialists**
4500 Courthouse Boulevard 330-945-7500
Suite 150 800-622-2562
Stow, OH 44224 *Fax:* 330-945-7200
support@acrtinc.com
www.acrtinc.com
ACRT is an independent consulting service and training organization providing research and educational services relating to urban forestry, arboricultural, and horticultural fields. They prevent and resolve management challenges forutilities across the nation by moitoring and assessing systems for vegetation liabilities, storm preparedness, and more.

Michael B. Weidner, President & CEO
Todd Jones, Chief Operations Officer

1636 **ACV Enviro**
928 East Hazelwood Avenue 732-815-0220
Rahway, NJ 07065 800-777-4557
Fax: 732-815-9892
www.acvenviro.com
Provider of industrial and environmental waste management services: cleaning and maintenance, tank and oil processing, waste disposal, transportation and more.
Andrew Shackett, President & CEO
Kevin Sheppard, Chief Development Officer

1637 **ADS LLC**
340 The Bridge Street 256-430-6234
Suite 204 800-633-7246
Huntsville, AL 35806 *Fax:* 256-430-6615
adssales@idexcorp.com
www.adsenv.com
ADS LLC develops and provides technology-based hardware and software products and services for the water, wastewater, gas, and hydroelectric industries. They aim to help municipalities diagnose and correct wastewater infrastructureproblems. ADS pioneered the industry's first flow monitoring hardware and software products over 32 years ago.

Ramona Bolden Fether, Director, Human Resources

1638 **AECOS**
45-939 Kamehameha Highway 808-234-7770
Suite 104 *Fax:* 808-234-7775
Kaneohe, HI 96744 aecos@aecos.com
www.aecos.com
Environmental consulting firm providing the services of scientists and facilities in the environmental sciences to clients throughout the Pacific area. AECOS specializes in terrestrial and aquatic (both fresh water and marine) biologyand water quality, with expertise in analytical chemistry, oceanography, water pollution, and marine and fresh water ecology.
Eric B. Guinther, President
Susan Burr, Vice-President

1639 **AKT Peerless Environmental Services**
1709 Mount Vernon 800-985-7633
Suite B www.aktpeerless.com
Dunwoody, GA 30338
Provides environmental services to facilitate real estate transfer, development, and redevelopment. Services include phase I ESA, subsurface investigation, remediation, Brownfield's redevelopment and Brownfield's financial incentives.

Tony R. Anthony, Principal
Robert W. Lambdin, Senior VP, Operations

1640 **ALS Environmental**
10450 Stancliff Road 800-695-7222
Suite 210 www.caslab.com
Houston, TX 77099
Areas of expertise and services include environmental testing of air, water, soil, hazardous waste, sediments and tissues; process and quality control testing; analytical method development; sampling and mobile laboratory services; andconsulting and data management services.

Raj Naran, CEO & Managing Director
Bruce Phillips, Chair

1641 **AM Kinney**
150 E 4th Street 513-421-2265
Cincinnati, OH 45202 800-265-3682
hollowoodd@amkinney.com
www.amkinney.com
Provides creative and cost effective solutions in the planning, design and delivery of clients' projects. Areas covered include mechanical, electrical, structural, civil, industrial and chemical engineering, architectural design andconstruction management.

A.M. Kinney, Chairman & Owner
George L. Nielsen, Senior Architect

1642 **ANA-Lab Corporation**
2600 Dudley Road 903-984-0551
PO Box 9000 *Fax:* 903-984-5914
Kilgore, TX 75663 hr@ana-lab.com
www.ana-lab.com
ANA-Lab is an environmental testing laboratory providing analytical testing of wastewater, groundwater, and solid waste for a wide range of materials including heavy metals, pollutants, pesticides, and more.

Tobi Duckworth, President & CEO
Carolyn Rominger, Chief Financial Officer

1643 **ARCADIS**
630 Plaza Drive 720-344-3500
Suite 100 866-287-7373
Highlands Ranch, CO 80129 AUSInternet@arcadis.com
www.arcadis.com
A global, knowledge-driven service provider for the fields of infrastructure, environment, and buildings. ARCADIS offers feasibility studies, design, engineering, project management, implementation, and facility management services, aswell as legal and financial support.

Joachim Ebert, Chief Executive Officer
Darren English, Chief Financial Officer

1644 **Aarcher**
2635 Riva Road 410-897-9100
Suite 100 cschwartz@aarcherinc.com
Annapolis, MD 21401 www.aarcherinc.com
Aarcher provides environmental management, assessment and planning services nationwide. Services provided include environmental compliance audits, NEPA analysis and documentation, resource management planning, site assessment, plansand permits, and environmental liability assessment.

Craig J. Schwartz, President

1645 **Abacus Environment Inc**
5480 La Sierra Drive 214-363-0099
Dallas, TX 75231 *Fax:* 214-363-3919
kmoon@lgidallas.com
www.abacusae.com
Full service environmental and occupational safety and health consulting firm. Services include project management, indoor air quality and industrial hygiene, asbestos and lead project management, expert witness testimony, and allaspects of workplace safety.

Kiran Desai, Owner
John Klim, Operations Manager

1646 **Abonmarche Environmental**
95 West Main Street 269-927-2295
Benton Harbor, MI 49022 *Fax:* 269-927-4639
aci@abonmarche.com
www.abonmarche.com
Full-service architectural, engineering, land surveying and planning firm. Abonmarche's goal is to put their technical and creative knowledge towards helping clients create an ideal place.

Christopher Cook, President & CEO
John Linn, Chair

1647 **AccuTech Environmental Services**
43 West Front Street 732-739-6444
Suite D *Fax:* 732-739-0451
Keyport, NJ 07735
Manages environmental sampling and cleanup programs, provides environmental assessments, soil and groundwater remediation, and underwater storage tank management.

James Bartley, Owner

1648 **Acheron Engineering Services**
147 Main Street 207-368-5700
Newport, ME 04953 *Fax:* 207-368-5120
WBall@AcheronEngineering.com
www.acheronengineering.com
Provides solutions to uncommon engineering, environmental and geologic issues. Some services offered include water supply engineering, contingency plans, design, site planning, aquatic and terrestrial ecology, wastewater testing, labtesting and more.

William B. Ball, President
Kirk Ball, Project Engineer

1649 **Acumen Industrial Hygiene**
1032 Irving Street 415-242-6060
Suite 922 *Fax:* 415-242-6006
San Francisco, CA 94122 info@acumen-ih.com
www.acumen-ih.com
Offers hygiene consultation for industrial fields. Services include air and noise monitoring programs, injury and illness prevention programs, building inspections, hazardous materials investigation, employee safety training, and more.

Paul Spillane, Owner

1650 **Advanced Chemical Laboratories**
13704 Alma Avenue 310-756-6745
Gardena, CA 90249 info@advancedchemicallaboratories.com
www.advancedchemicallaboratories.com
An independent research laboratory specializing in the analysis of trace level organic and inorganic contaminants in soil, water, groundwater, and air.

Maryam Azad, Owner

1651 **Advanced Energy**
909 Capability Drive 919-857-9000
Suite 2100 advancedenergy.org
Raleigh, NC 27606
Advanced Energy is a nonprofit energy consulting firm that works with electric utilities, government, and public and private organizations in the residential, commercial and industrial, solar, and vehicle markets. They provide energyefficient services through research, testing, training, consulting and program design.

Bob Goodson, President & Director
Brian Coble, Senior Vice President

1652 **Advanced Resources International**
4501 Fairfax Drive 703-528-8420
Suite 910 *Fax:* 703-528-0439
Arlington, VA 22203 www.adv-res.com
Consulting, research and development firm providing services in the areas of unconventional gas, oil recovery, carbon capture, and utilization and storage.

Vello A. Kuuskraa, President
Jonathan R. Kelafant, Senior Vice President

1653 **Advanced Waste Management Systems**
6430 Hixson Pike 423-843-2206
P.O. Box 100 *Fax:* 423-843-2301
Hixson, TN 37343 info@awm.net
www.awm.net
Provides a wide range of environmental and engineering services to domestic and international clients such as governments, corporations, and private citizens. Some of these services include GHG verification, industrial wastemanagement, project management, and auditing.

Richard Ellis, Founder
Rob Ellis, Chair

1654 **Aegion Corporation**
17988 Edison Avenue 636-530-8000
St Louis, MO 63005 800-325-1159
www.aegion.com

A company that works to rehabilitate and strengthen infrastructure, including pipelines in the wastewater, water, energy, mining, and refining industries. They serve the municipal, oil and gas, industrial, mining, and structuralmarkets.

Charles Gordon, President & CEO
Stephanie Cuskley, Chair

1655 Aerosol Monitoring & Analysis, Inc.
1331 Ashton Road 410-684-3327
Hanover, MD 21076 *Fax:* 410-684-3384
www.amatraining.com
AMA provides industrial hygiene, environmental, and health & safety services to government agencies, institutions, building owners, property managers, architects, and engineers.
Todd M. Woerner, President
Joseph A. Coco, Senior Vice President

1656 Aguirre Roden
10670 N Central Expwy 972-788-1508
6th Floor *Fax:* 972-788-1583
Dallas, TX 75231 paguirre@AguirreRoden.com
www.aguirreroden.com
Aguirre Roden is an environmental engineering firm offering services such as architectural planning and design, plumbing, construction, and program management.

Gary Roden, President
Pedro Aguirre, Chief Executive Officer

1657 Air Sciences
150 Capital Drive 303-988-2960
Suite 320 air@airsci.com
Golden, CO 80401 airsci.com
Air Sciences provides consulting in air quality and environmental issues. Some of its work has included mineral extraction and refining, natural gas processing, chemical manufacturing, pesticide formulation, environmental compliance,fire emissions modeling, and more.

Kevin Lewis, President
Mark Schaaf, Vice President

1658 Aires Consulting Group
1550 Hubbard Avenue 630-879-3006
Batavia, IL 60510 800-247-3799
Fax: 630-879-3014
info@airesconsulting.com
www.airesconsulting.com
Offers services in occupational hygiene and safety, environmental engineering, and building sciences.

Rich Rapacki, Contact
Kevin Bannon, Contact

1659 Airtek Environmental Corporation
39-37 29th Street 718-937-3720
New York City, NY 11101 *Fax:* 718-937-3721
www.airtekenv.com
Team of environmental investigation and management professionals offering environmental consulting and testing services. These services include mold and bacteria testing, air quality testing, lead paint management, industrial hygiene,biosafety, industry training, and more.

Saad Zouak, President

1660 Alan Plummer Associates
1320 South University Drive 817-806-1700
Suite 300 *Fax:* 817-870-2536
Fort Worth, TX 76107 emcdonald@apaienv.com
www.apaienv.com
The mission of the organization is to uphold environmental stewardship. They study, plan, model, design, permit, and manage water and wastewater infrastructure during construction.

Chris Young, President & CEO
Steve Coonan, Chief Financial Officer

1661 All 4 Inc
2393 Kimberton Road 610-933-5246
P.O. Box 299 *Fax:* 610-933-5127
Kimberton, PA 19442 info@all4inc.com
www.all4inc.com
An environmental consulting company specializing in air quality services, primarily assisting clients with complex air permitting, air quality modeling, continuous monitoring systems, and regulation compliance.
Bill Straub, Chief Executive Officer
Kevin Hickey, Chief Operating Officer

1662 AllWest Environmental
2141 Mission Street 415-391-2510
Suite 100 info@allwest1.com
San Francisco, CA 94110 www.allwest1.com
Business-oriented consulting firm specializing in Environmental and Engineering sectors, offering expertise to the real estate industry. AllWest assists clients in understanding and managing potential environmental and buildingliabilites, and in advocating their interests through the discovery and mitigation process.

Marc Cunningham, President
Chris Marinescu, Vice President

1663 Allee, King, Rosen & Fleming
440 Park Avenue South 800-899-2573
7th Floor info@akrf.com
New York, NY 10016 www.akrf.com
Offers services in the areas of environmental regulations, engineering, planning, air quality, cultural resources, environmental impact assessment, natural resources, permits, compliance, site assessment, and more.

Debra Allee, Founder
Edward Applebome, Senior Vice President

1664 Allied Engineers
2303 Camino Ramon 925-867-4646
Suite 290 *Fax:* 925-867-4474
San Ramon, CA 94583 info@alliedengineersinc.com
www.alliedengineersinc.com
Provides consulting services in wastewater treatment and reclamation systems for communities and commercial developments.

Robert Dawyot, President
Vlasta Cejna, Vice President

1665 Alpha Omega Environmental Services Inc
933 31st Avenue NW 954-969-5906
Pompano Beach, FL 33069 866-969-6653
Fax: 954-969-5232
www.aomegagroup.com
Organization offering services for water damage mitigation, mold remediation, smoke and odor removal, hoarding clean up, emergency board ups or tarp, and other emergency needs.

1666 Alternative Futures Associates (AFA)
703-684-5880
Fax: 703-684-0640
futurist@altfutures.com
www.altfutures.com
Consulting firm specializing in helping private sector companies pan ahead, through discovering emerging issues and trends, creating forecasts, and developing scenarios.
Clem Bezold, Consultant
Yasemin Arikan, Consultant

1667 Alternative Resources
1732 Main Street 978-371-2054
Concord, MA 01742 info@alt-res.com
alt-res.com
Alternative Resources is an independent consulting firm providing management, engineering, environmental, economic and fi-

nancial solutions in the fields of water and wastewater treatment, solid waste management and renewable energygeneration.

James Osborn, President
Susan Higgins, Director

1668 American Archaeology Group LLC
PO Box 534 512-843-0135
Lampasas, TX 76550 *Fax:* 512-556-3373
Archaeological consulting firm offering archaeological investigations, historical research, and archival research during construction projects.

1669 American Engineering Testing
550 Cleveland Avenue North 651-659-9001
St. Paul, MN 55114 800-972-6364
dlarson@amengtest.com
www.amengtest.com
Provides engineering, testing and laboratory services for environmental, geotechnical and construction purposes.

Dan Larson, Chief Executive Officer
David Rettner, President

1670 American Petroleum & Environmental Consulting
2236 NW 164th Street 405-840-9327
Edmond, OK 73013
APEC is a petroleum and environmental consulting firm providing oil and gas exploration services.

Saleem Nizami, Founder

1671 Andco Environmental Processes
415 Commerce Drive 716-691-2100
Amherst, NY 14228 *Fax:* 716-691-2880
andco@localnet.com
Manufacturers of waste disposal treatment systems.
William Waytena, Chair

1672 Anderson Consulting Group
PO Box 407 610-918-7461
Downingtown, PA 19335 *Fax:* 610-918-9469
Anderson Consulting Group helps companies and public agencies to manage project development risk and reduce construction costs, while offering environmental and geotechnical services as well as engineering solutions tailored to theirneeds.

1673 Apollo Energy Systems
4100 North Powerline Road www.electricauto.com
Suite D3
Pompano Beach, FL 33073
Developer of environmentally friendly batteries, fuel cells and systems.

Robert Aronsson, Chair
Raymond Douglas, Chief Executive Officer

1674 Applied Ecological Services
17921 Smith Road 608-897-8641
Brodhead, WI 53520 *Fax:* 608-897-8486
info@appliedeco.com
www.appliedeco.com
AES is an ecological consulting, contracting and restoration firm providing services to foundations, government units, corporations and commercial and residential developers nationwide. Consultations are provided in the areas ofwetlands, natural resources, endangered species, site design, watershed planning and more.

Steven Apfelbaum, Founder & Chair
Steven Dischler, President & CEO

1675 Applied Geoscience and Engineering
150-C Love Road 610-777-5027
Reading, PA 19607 *Fax:* 610-777-4276
lmullis@appliedgeoscience.com
www.appliedgeoscience.com
Specializes in the areas of civil and geotechnical engineering, soils laboratory testing, site development, and construction testing. Provides consulting and engineering services to public and private sectors at various stages of aproject, such as site development, preliminary design, construction, and performance monitoring.

M. Ayub Iqbal, President
Drew M. Kurtz, Senior Geotechnical Engineer

1676 Applied Science Associates
3525 Piedmont Road NE 281-448-6188
Suite 520 asascience.com
Atlanta, GA 30305
Applied Science Associates is a division of the RPS Group, a company that offers advisory and management consulting, communications and creative services, and design development among other services.

David Balmos, Senior VP, RPS Houston
Peter Fearn, CEO, RPS North America

1677 Aqua Sierra
9094 US Highway 285 303-697-5486
Morrison, CO 80465-8950 *Fax:* 303-697-5069
info@aqua-sierra.com
www.aqua-sierra.com
Aqua Sierra offers consulting services for managing aquatic resources by combining a broad base of experience in all aspects of fisheries, aquatic ecology, and water quality management. Some of their services include water qualitytesting, wastewater treatment, aquatic treatment, lake and stream design, biofouling control, aquaculture and more.

Bill Logan, Chief Executive Officer
Kendra Holmes, President

1678 Aqua Survey
469 Point Breeze Road 908-788-8700
Flemington, NJ 08822 *Fax:* 908-788-9165
www.aquasurvey.com
Aqua Survey is a full service ecotoxicology company providing laboratory testing, field sampling and consulting services in the areas of sediment vibracoring, water quality, benthic grab sampling and taxonomy, toxicity identification,geophysical and hydrographic surveys, sediment toxicology and more.

Ken Hayes, President
Jon Doi, Executive Vice President

1679 Aqualogic
30 Devine Street 203-248-8959
North Haven, CT 06473 800-989-8959
Fax: 203-288-4308
waterservices@aqualogic.com
www.aqualogic.com
Provider of equipment for wastewater treatment, recovery, and process. Some of their products include carbon and particle filters, water filters, acid recovery systems and more.

Nick Papa, General Manager
Richard Heller, Sales Engineer

1680 Arctech
14100 Park Meadow Drive 703-222-0280
Chantilly, VA 20151 info@arctech.com
www.arctech.com
Arctech provides cost-effective solutions and products for the energy, environmental, and agriculture markets. These products help to create economical clean energy, clean water and environ-

ments, safer foods, effective waste managementprocesses, and the reduction of greenhouse gas emissions.

Daman Walia, President & CEO

1681 Ardea Consulting
10 1st Street 530-669-1645
Woodland, CA 95695 birdtox1@ardeacon.com
www.ardeacon.com
Ardea Consulting provides avian and wildlife toxicology and ecological risk assessments guidance to clients in order to provide technical solutions to environmental toxicology issues. Among its services are pesticide evaluations,wildlife and environmental sampling, project and research proposals, and more.

Joseph P. Sullivan, Senior Consultant

1682 Arro Consulting
108 West Airport Road
Lititz, PA 17543 717-569-7021
www.thearrogroup.com
Offers services in the areas of waste water management, planning, geosciences, environmental site assessments and more.

Brady L. Flaharty, President & COO
G. Matthew Brown, Chair & CEO

1683 Arro Laboratory
425 Caton Farm Road 815-727-5436
Crest Hill, IL 60431 www.arrolab.com
Provides environmental and chemical testing services for wastewater, drinking water, in addition to product quality control and process troubleshooting. They offer their services to manufacturers, municipalities, and design orengineering firms.

Joan Rolih, President

1684 Artemel International
218 North Lee Street 703-683-3838
Suite 316 *Fax:* 703-836-1370
Alexandria, VA 22314 aiusa@artemel.com
www.artemel.com
Artemel International offers project development, financial packaging, and project management facilitation in the energy, environmental, financial, and other sectors.

Engin Artemel, President

1685 Athena Enzyme Systems
1450 South Rolling Road 410-455-6319
Baltimore, MD 21227 888-892-8408
Fax: 410-455-1155
aesinfo@athenaes.com
www.athenaes.com
Athena Enzyme Systems investigates and develops proteins by manufacturing biotechnology for research, biopharmaceutical, and industrial uses. Products range in the fields of biochromatography, cell culture products, protein refolding reagents, and more.
Sheldon Broedel, Founder & CEO

1686 Atkins
4030 West Boy Scout Boulevard 813-282-7275
Suite 700 800-477-7275
Tampa, FL 33607 *Fax:* 813-281-7698
www.atkinsglobal.com/en-GB
A member of the SNC-Lavalin Group, Atkins is a design, engineering, and project management consultancy firm. They offer various products to help clients with software analysis, sustainable travel, flood risk assessments, and more.Their services span a wide range of sectors, from aerospace and energy to government and education.

Philip Hoare, President

1687 Atlantic Testing Laboratories
6431 US Highway 11 315-386-4578
Canton, NY 13617 *Fax:* 315-386-1012
WBell@AtlanticTesting.com
www.atlantictesting.com
ATL is a full-service engineering support firm offering environmental services, subsurface investigations, water-based services, geotechnical engineering, construction materials testing and engineering, special inspections,nondestructive testing, and more.

William J. Bell, Assistant VP, Operations
James A. Trathen, Operations Manager

1688 Atlas Environmental Engineering
3185 Airway Avenue 714-890-7129
Suite D-1 *Fax:* 714-890-7149
Costa Mesa, CA 92626 info@aeei.com
www.aeei.com
Atlas Environmental Engineering provides cost effective site assessments, investigations, risk-based corrective action plans, groundwater monitoring, soil remediation, and more.
Karl Kerner, Senior Engineer
Jasmine Senn, Technical Support

1689 Ayres Associates
3433 Oakwood Hills Parkway 715-834-3161
Eau Claire, WI 54701-7698 ayrescontact@ayresassociates.com
www.ayresassociates.com
Ayres Associates is an architectural/engineering consulting firm providing services in aerial mapping, architecture, land surveying, structural design, water resources, transportation engineering, environmental science, siteinspections, and more.

Jan Zander, Executive Vice President
Richard Schoenthaler, Chief Financial Officer

1690 BATTA Environmental Associates
6 Garfield Way 302-737-3376
Newark, DE 19713 800-862-2882
Fax: 302-737-5764
info@battaenv.com
www.battaenv.com
BATTA provides services in the scientific disciplines of geology, hydrogeology, civil and environmental engineering, chemistry, toxicology, health and safety, project design, and construction management. BATTA also offers lab testingfor asbestos, lead, and mold analysis.

Neeraj Batta, Vice President

1691 BJAAM Environmental
472 Elm Ridge Avenue 330-854-5300
P.O. Box 523 *Fax:* 330-854-5340
Canal Fulton, OH 44614 info@bjaam.com
bjaam.com
Environmental contracting company that provides services such as environmental remediation, general contracting services, grant procurement, and more.

Troy Schultz, President & CEO
Jeff Myers, Executive Vice President

1692 BMC Bulk
4321 State Route 7 330-831-4852
New Waterford, OH 44445 www.bmcbulk.com
Provides bulk transportation and disposal of solid waste to the oil, gas, steel, and waste management industries. Hauling capabilities include oil and gas, sand, water, drill cuttings, guar, and more.
Craig Stacy, President & CEO
Paul Wilson, Vice President

1693 BRC Acoustics & Audiovisual Design
1932 First Avenue 206-270-8910
Suite 620 800-843-4524
Seattle, WA 98101 *Fax:* 206-270-8690
brc@brcacoustics.com
www.brcacoustics.com

A Seattle-based acoustical and technology consulting firm serving public and private clients throughout the United States. Services include architectural and mechanical acoustics, vibration measurement and analysis, and noise contourmapping for environmental noise control projects.

Daniel C. Bruck, President
Roger Andrews, General Manager

1694 Bac-Ground
3216 Georgetown — 713-664-8452
Houston, TX 77005 — ebaca@bac-ground.com
www.bac-ground.com
Independent consultation service for groundwater pollution concerns. Bac-Ground offers water, soil, and waste material sampling, surface and borehole geophysical surveys, and aquifer tests.

Ernesto Baca, Owner

1695 Badger Laboratories
501 West Bell Street — 920-729-1100
Neenah, WI 54956 — 800-776-7196
Fax: 920-729-4945
information@badgerlabs.com
www.badgerlabs.com
Badger Laboratories and Engineering provides customers with analytical, engineering and technical services focusing on the environmental field. The labs specialize in the testing and sampling of drinking water, groundwater, wastewater,solids and hazardous waste.

Richard Larson, President
Jeff Wagner, Lab Manager

1696 Barco Enterprises
11200 Pulaski Highway — 410-335-0660
PO Box 0074 — 800-832-7538
White Marsh, MD 21162 — *Fax:* 410-335-0790
bart@barcoent.com
www.barcoenterprises.com
Offers cleaning and restoration services. Some services include asbestos and lead paint abatement; dry ice blasting; air conveyance system cleaning; mold remediation; fire, smoke, and water damage restoration; infrared inspections;concrete cutting and more.

Bart Harrison, President
John King, VP, Operations

1697 Barer Engineering
199 Main Street — 518-236-7070
Suite 600 — 800-878-2806
Burlington, VT 05401-8339 — *Fax:* 518-236-5796
info@barer.com
www.barer.com
Produces precision machine tools and fabricating equipments that assist in air pollution control. Products include turnmill centers, bed mills, horizontal boring mills, saws, and more.

David Barer, Contact

1698 Baron Analytical Laboratories
181 Research Drive — 203-874-5678
Suite 1 — kevin@baronlabsct.com
Milford, CT 06460 — baronlabsct.com
Provides testing and consulting services to clients in the chemical and consumer industries, hospitals, universities, and others. Some services include checking air quality for metals, solvents, and toxins. Types of materials testedinclude parmaceuticals, medical devices, cosmetic products and fragrances, plastic and polymers, speciality chemicals, rubber products and more.

Kevin Ovian, Director

1699 Barr Engineering Company
4300 Market Pointe Drive — 952-832-2600
Suite 200 — 800-632-2277
Minneapolis, MN 55435 — *Fax:* 952-832-2601
askbarr@barr.com
www.barr.com
Barr provides engineering, environmental, and information technology services to clients across the nation and around the world. Services include engineering support, natural resources management, site assessment, groundwater modeling,water quality control and more.
Jim Langseth, Vice President
Julie Macejkovic, Senior Civil Engineer

1700 Baxter and Woodman
8678 Ridgefield Road — 815-459-1260
Crystal Lake, IL 60012 — *Fax:* 815-455-0450
info@baxterwoodman.com
www.baxterwoodman.com
Provides services in the planning, design, and construction of public infrastructure. Focus is given to municipal technology, water preservation, wastewater treatment, road and highway development, environmental design, and more.

Joanna MacCallum, Marketing Manager
John P. Mick II, Division Manager, Illinois

1701 Beals and Thomas
144 Turnpike Road — 508-366-0560
Suite 210 — *Fax:* 508-366-4391
Southborough, MA 01772-2104 — mail@bealsandthomas.com
www.bealsandthomas.com
Beals and Thomas is a multidisciplinary consulting firm providing services to support the development and conservation of land and water resources throughout New England and the northeastern United States. Services include constructionplanning, waste management, water quality sampling, the issuing of permits, sustainable design, and more.

George Preble, President
Richard Kosian, Executive Vice President

1702 Becher-Hoppe Associates
330 North Fourth Street — 715-845-8000
Wausau, WI 54403-5417 — www.becherhoppe.com
Becher-Hoppe Associates is a consulting firm of engineers, architects, scientists, real estate specialists and surveyors. Services offered include airport, highway, municipal and facilities maintainance; solid waste and wastewatermanagement; agriculture management; and environmental projects.

Randy W. Van Natta, President
Bonnie L. Stange, Corporate Controller

1703 Benchmark Environmental Consultants
5220 McKinney Avenue — 214-888-6965
Suite 301 — benchmarkec.com
Dallas, TX 75205
An environmental consulting firm offering site assessments, subsurface and geotechnical investigations, environmental permitting and compliance, archaeological surveys, spill prevention and control, wetland delineations and surveys,and more.

Kelly Walker, President
Saundra Horton, Business Development

1704 Berkshire Hathaway Energy
666 Grand Avenue — 515-242-3022
P.O. Box 657 — info@berkshirehathawayenergyco.com
Des Moines, IA 50306-0657 — www.brkenergy.com
BHE offers services in energy efficiency, grid composition, and sustainability, among others. They strive to provide sustainable energy solutions to their clients by pursuing fossil fuel efficiency improvement projects.
Gregory E. Abel, Vice Chair
William J. Fehrman, President & CEO

1705 **Beta & Associates**
30 Macintosh Boulevard 416-736-1886
Unit 11 info@betaandassociates.ca
Concord, ZZ L4K-4P1 betaandassociates.ca
A professional organization which provides complete problem analysis, as well as engineering and design services for construction projects.

1706 **Bhate Environmental Associates**
1608 13th Avenue South 205-918-4000
Suite 300 *Fax:* 205-918-4050
Birmingham, AL 35205 www.bhate.com
Provides environmental, technical, and infrastructural services to the government and private industry. Services include environmental remediation and compliance, bulk fuels storage, construction services, demolition, and more.

Johnny Roberts, Chief Executive Officer
Sam Bhate, President

1707 **BioSpec Products**
P.O. Box 788 918-336-3363
Bartlesville, OK 74005 800-617-3363
Fax: 918-336-6060
info@biospec.com
biospec.com
Producers of laboratory scientific equipment. Products include homogenizers & cell disrupters, pulverizers, tissue dispersers and extraction tools, vials, and more.
Tim Hopkins, President

1708 **Biological Monitoring**
1800 Kraft Drive 540-953-2821
Suite 101 877-953-2821
Blacksburg, VA 24060 *Fax:* 540-951-1481
bmi@biomon.com
www.biomon.com
Offers consulting on issues related to water quality and toxicology. Amongs its services are ecological risk assessments, permit negotiations, toxicity reduction evaluations, and more.

David Gruber, President

1709 **Bison Engineering**
1400 11th Avenue 406-442-5768
Helena, MT 59601 *Fax:* 844-273-5270
www.bison-eng.com
Bison Engineering is an environmental consulting company offering services related to air quality compliance. Amongs its services are air quality permit application preparation, emissions testing, air quality and climate impactsevaluation, and more.

Christopher P. Hiltunen, President
Shain Chappell, Treasurer

1710 **Black and Veatch**
11401 Lamar Avenue 913-458-2000
Overland Park, KS 66211 www.bv.com
Consultants specializing in energy resources, water quality control, and communication techology. Services include asset management, data analysis, program and construction management, environmental consultancy, and more.

Steven L. Edwards, Chair & CEO
Ken Williams, Chief Financial Officer

1711 **Block Environmental**
23 Musick 949-455-0325
Suite 100 *Fax:* 949-455-1958
Irvine, CA 92618 eblock@blockenvironmental.com
blockenvironmental.com
A consulting firm specializing in environmental solutions, including investigating, assessing, and cleaning contaminated properties. Their main clients are purchasers of industrial and commercial properties.

Erik Block, Founder

1712 **Bollyky Associates**
31 Strawberry Hill Avenue 203-967-4223
Stamford, CT 06902 *Fax:* 203-967-4845
ljbbai@bai-ozone.com
www.bai-ozone.com
Engineering firm specializing in Ozone technology, water and wastewater treatment, treatability studies, and consulting services.
L Joseph Bollyky, President

1713 **Braun Intertec Corporation**
11001 Hampshire Avenue S 952-995-2000
Minneapolis, MN 55438 800-279-6100
Fax: 952-995-2020
bborth@braunintertec.com
braunintertec.com
An engineering firm providing consulting, management, and testing services to clients in the commercial, real estate, institutional, retail, financial, and government markets. Some services include environmental and geothermalconsulting, geospacial operations, construction materials testing, structures evaluation and more.

Jon Carlson, Chief Executive Officer
Robert Janssen, President

1714 **Breedlove, Dennis & Associates**
330 West Canton Avenue 407-677-1882
Winter Park, FL 32789 bda-inc.com
Offers environmental and natural resources consulting. Services include environmental impact assessments, aquatic resources analyses, endangered species mitigation, natural resource and wildlife management, wetland delineation, waterresources planning, landscape planning, analytical software, litigation support, and more.

W. Michael Dennis, President
W. Jeffrey Pardue, Vice President

1715 **Brinkerhoff Environmental Services**
1805 Atlantic Avenue 732-223-2225
Manasquan, NJ 08736 800-246-7358
Fax: 732-223-3666
info@brinkenv.com
brinkenv.com
Offers consulting services in the areas of environmental site assessments, site remediation, storage tank management, coastal development and permitting, hazardous materials, and more.
Laura Brinkerhoff, President & CEO
John Checchio, VP, Technical Services

1716 **Brown, Vence & Associates**
115 Sansome Street 415-434-0900
Suite 800 *Fax:* 415-956-6220
San Francisco, CA 94104 bvamail@brownvence.com
www.brownvence.com
A division of HDR, this company provides solid waste and energy management solutions with the aim of helping clients create efficient, environmentally sustainable, and publicly acceptable waste management and energy projects.

1717 **Buck, Seifert & Jost**
65 Oak Street 201-767-3111
Suite 201 800-245-1105
Norwood, NJ 07648-0415 *Fax:* 201-767-3178
bsjinc@bsjinc.com
www.bsjinc.com
Consultancy for the water and wastewater industries. Services include water supply treatment, industrial waste management, site development, permits, environmental planning and design, and more.

Ronald von Autenried, President
Jonelle R. von Autenried, Vice President & Treasurer

1718 Bureau Veritas
100 Northpointe Parkway 716-505-3300
Buffalo, NY 14228 800-277-3300
Fax: 716-505-3301
group.bureauveritas.com

Specializes in the testing, inspection and certification of workplace safety. Some of the industries served include marine, mining, oil and gas, transport and infrastructures, agriculture and food.

Didier Michaud-Daniel, Chief Executive Officer
Helen Bradley, Executive VP, HR

1719 Burk-Kleinpeter
4176 Canal Street 504-486-5901
New Orleans, LA 70119 *Fax:* 504-488-1714
www.bkiusa.com

A full service consulting firm providing services such as transportation systems, flood protection, wastewater management, electrical systems, environmental compliance consulting, and more.

Michael D. Chopin, President
J. W. Giardina, Jr., Chief Executive Officer

1720 Burns and McDonnell
9400 Ward Parkway 816-333-9400
Kansas City, MO 64114 www.burnsmcd.com

A multidisciplinary engineering, architectural, construction and environmental service firm. Services are offered in the areas of aviation, construction, environmental engineering, oil and gas, power, water, industrial management,transportation, and more.

Melissa Lavin-Hickey, Director of Marketing

1721 C&H Environmental Technical Services
P.O. Box 334 413-464-4815
Pittsfield, MA 01202 *Fax:* 413-499-4510
www.chenvironmental.com

Environmental consulting firm providing services in demolition projects, asbestos abatement, sediment assessment, landfill services, health and safety for wastewater facilities, and more.
Brude Eulian, Contact
Clint Kunzer, Contact

1722 CA Rich
17 Dupont Street 516-576-8844
Plainview, NY 11803 info@carichinc.com
carichinc.com

A consulting firm providing hydrogeologic and environmental engineering services. CA Rich also assists in the conception, development, design, implementation, documentation and defense of site evaluations and remedial action.

Charles A. Rich, Founder & President

1723 CBA Environmental Services
57 Park Lane 570-682-8742
Hegins, PA 17938 *Fax:* 570-682-8915
info@cbaenvironmental.com
www.cbaenvironmental.com

Provides environmental solutions from general plant maintenance and cleaning to large-scale soil remediation projects. Services also include groundwater treatment, storage tank management and training.

Bruce L. Bruso, President

1724 CEDA
567 W Lake Street 312-782-2332
Suite 1200 800-571-2332
Chicago, IL 60661 webmaster@cedaorg.net
www.cedaorg.net

CEDA offers programs and services in community and economic development, education, emergency assistance, employment and training, energy conservation and services, health and nutrition, and housing. Among their programs are housingservices, women, infances, and children (WIC) program, energy assistance programs, and more.
Harold T. Rice, President & CEO
Glen Ofenloch, Chief Financial Officer

1725 CIH Environmental Solutions
425 SW 17 Avenue 888-860-0101
Miami, FL 33135 info@cihenvironmental.com
www.cihenvironmental.com

Provides services in indoor air quality, industrial hygiene and mold/bacterial contaminations. Among their services are environmental and occupational assessments, and specialized training.

Armando Chamorro, President

1726 CIH Services
1859 Je To Lake Drive 317-590-4073
Avon, IN 46123 jhenseler@cih-services.com
www.cih-services.com

Offers services in indoor air quality and industrial hygiene. Services include occupational exposure monitoring, chemical exposure assessments, indoor air quality assessments, and more.
Joe Henseler, Sr. Industrial Hygienist

1727 CII Service
6767 Forrest Hill Avenue 804-320-1405
Suite 100 800-768-2545
Richmond, VA 23225 cii.richmond@ciiservice.com
www.ciiservice.com

Provides services in energy management, including HVAC services and comprehensive utility management to reduce energy costs.

Dorothy Thacker, Chair
Mark Woodcock, VP, Operations

1728 CK Environmental
1020 Turnpike Street 781-828-5200
Suite 8 888-253-0303
Canton, MA 02021 *Fax:* 781-828-5380
info@ckenvironmental.com
www.ckenvironmental.com

Purveyor of air quality testing in compliance with environmental policies. Services include continuous emissions monitoring systems and environmental consulting.
Michael Kelley, President & Cofounder
Stephen Phillips, Sr. Project Manager

1729 CRB Geological and Environmental Services
8744 SW 133rd Street 305-447-9777
Miami, FL 33176 www.crbgeo.com
Environmental consulting firm offering site assessments, treatment of waste water, air quality assessments, asbestos abatement, mold testing, and environmental permits.

Fred Baddour, Owner
Victor Rossinsky, Vice President

1730 CTI
28001 Cabot Drive 248-486-5100
Suite 250 *Fax:* 248-486-5050
Novi, MI 48377 info@cticompanies.com
www.cticompanies.com

Environmental engineering firm offering services in site remediation, environmental compliance, industrial hygiene, waste management, renewable energy, geotechnical engineering and more.

Morgan Subbarayan, Owner & President
Christopher Winkeljohn, Executive Vice President

1731 CZR Incorporated
825 S US Highway 1 561-747-7455
Suite 110 *Fax:* 561-747-7576
Jupiter, FL 33477-3902 czrinc@czr-inc.com
www.czr-inc.com

An environmental consulting firm that specializes in various scientific, planning, design, and management services. Some examples include water quality studies, aquatic and terrestrial biota sampling, environmental permitting,endangered and threatened species surveys, and more.

Susan Hudgens-Moore, President
Sam Cooper, Office Manager, Wilmington

1732 California Environmental Protection Agency
1001 I Street 916-323-2514
P.O. Box 2815 calepa.ca.gov
Sacramento, CA 95812-2815
The CalEPA's goals are to protect the environment, public health, and economic vitality. They accomplish these goals by implementing regulatory laws that focus on air, water, and soil quality as well as pesticide use and wastereduction.

Jared Blumenfeld, Secretary
Serena McIlwain, Undersecretary

1733 California GeoSystems
1545 Victory Boulevard 818-500-9533
2nd Floor *Fax:* 818-500-0134
Glendale, CA 91201 info@geosys1.com
www.geosys1.com
An organization made up of registered geologists, certified engineering geologists, and registered civil and geotechnical engineers, this company offers geotechnical environmental services such as site assessments, groundwatermonitoring, engineering investigations, soil sampling and more.
Vincent J. Carnegie, Licensed Principal
Steve S. Tsai, Licensed Principal

1734 Cambridge Environmental
CDM Smith
75 State Street 617-452-6180
Suite 701 www.cambridgeenvironmental.com
Boston, MA 02109
Consulting and research firm that assesses and works to minimize risks to health and the environment. Some services offered include interpretation of scientific studies and policies, data analysis, regulatory compliance, permitting andsafety checks.

Laura Green, President
Stephen Zemba, Senior Engineer

1735 Camiros Limited
411 South Wells Street 312-922-9211
Suite 400 info@camiros.com
Chicago, IL 60607 www.camiros.com
Camiros offers services in planning, zoning, urban design, economic development, and landscape architecture. The firm has drafted land use plans and zoning ordinances that pay careful attention to environmental issues.

Bill James, Principal
Arista Strungys, Principal

1736 Camo Pollution Control
1610 State Route 376 845-463-7310
Wappingers Falls, NY 12590
Producer of water purification and sewage treatment systems.
Cacchio Bob, President

1737 Canin Associates
500 Delaney Avenue 407-422-4040
Suite 404 *Fax:* 407-425-7427
Orlando, FL 32801 www.canin.com
Provides the environmental services of urban planning, landscape architecture, and building design.

Brian Canin, President
Myrna Canin, Vice President

1738 CannonDesign
2170 Whitehaven Road 716-773-6800
Grand Island, NY 14072 *Fax:* 716-773-5909
www.cannondesign.com
Provides informational services for sustainable development, promoting environmentally friendly engineering. Topics covered include renewable energy, clean water, and more.
Bradley A. Lukanic, Chief Executive Officer
Deb Sheehan, Executive Director

1739 Cape Environmental Management
500 Pinnacle Court 877-422-7350
Suite 100 800-488-4372
Norcross, GA 30071 pferroni@cape-inc.com
www.cape-inc.com
Consulting firm offering construction, environmental remediation, fabrication, and industrial services in the petroleum, chemical, power, aviation, and government sectors.

Fernando Rios, Chief Executive Officer
Chuck Payne, Quality Control Manager

1740 Capital Environmental Enterprises
3440 S Post Road 317-708-4813
Indianapolis, IN 46239 www.capenv.com
Environmental consulting professionals with a focus on asbestos, underground storage tank removal, material testing, and indoor air quality testing.
Davies Batterton, President

1741 Cardinal Environmental
3303 Paine Avenue 920-459-2500
Sheboygan, WI 53081 redbird@cardinalenvironmental.com
www.cardinalenvironmental.com
Environmental testing laboratory and environmental health and safety compliance consulting firm offering services in air permitting, asbestos inspections, health and safety training programs, industrial hygiene, wastewater sampling andmore.

Scott Hanson, President
Jennifer Beimel, Vice President

1742 Cardno ATC
10004 Park Meadows Drive 720-257-5800
Suite 300 *Fax:* 720-257-5801
Lone Tree, CO 80124 www.cardno.com
An infrastructure, environmental, and social development consulting firm offering services in environmental design, planning, software, construction management, material testing and more.
Ian Ball, Chief Executive Officer
Peter Barker, Chief Financial Officer

1743 Carpenter Environmental Associates
610 County Route 1 845-781-4844
Suite 2F mail@cea-enviro.com
Pine Island, NY 10969 www.ceaenviro.com
Provides environmental engineering and assessment services, including wastewater and storm water management, wetlands and ecological investigations, site assessments, environmental compliance and contingency planning, permittingservices, and litigation support.

Kim Bell Hosea, President
Janelle Robbins, Senior Scientist

1744 Carr Research Laboratory
251 W Central St 508-651-7027
Natick, MA 01760
Environmental consulting research laboratory providing wetlands delineation, wildlife habitat evaluation, groundwater impact study, soil testing, water quality monitoring and more.

Jerome Carr, President

1745 Cartier Group Environmental Solutions
P.O. Box 338 603-366-7356
Laconia, NH 03247 cartiergroup@metrocast.net

Offers environmental consulting for regulatory compliance, permitting, hazardous materials education and training, and site assessments.
Diane Cartier, Principal

1746 **Catlin Engineers and Scientists**
220 Old Dairy Road 910-452-5861
Wilmington, NC 28405 *Fax:* 910-452-7563
info@catlinusa.com
www.catlinusa.com
Specializes in providing quality services in the fields of environmental, civil, and geotechnical engineering. Services include evaluations of soil integrity, environmental assessment and permitting, subsurface investigations, andmore.

Richard Catlin, President
Cindy Liu, Sr. Geotechnical Engineer

1747 **Central States Environmental**
2206 Horns Mill Road SE 740-681-9902
Lancaster, OH 43130 800-837-8064
Fax: 740-681-1389
bbu@rrohio.com
www.bbuenvironmental.com
A division of BBU Environmental Services. Offers environmental clean-up contracting with services in transportation of hazardous and non-hazardous waste, oil and gas pipeline maintenance, and emergency spill response.
Steve Schmelzer, President

1748 **Challenge Environmental Systems**
2270 Worth Lane 479-927-1008
Suite D *Fax:* 479-927-1000
Springdale, AR 72764 mark@challenge-sys.com
challenge-sys.com
Challenge Environmental Systems manufactures environmental equipment for testing wastewater, soil and compost, biomethane potential, and more.
Mark Kuss, President

1749 **Chapman Engineering**
P.O. Box 1305 830-816-3311
Boerne, TX 78006 800-375-7747
Fax: 830-816-1753
info@chapmanengr.com
www.chapman.engineering
Offers environmental engineering services including pipeline corrosion assessment, environmental compliance, spill prevention and control, water pollution control, and more.

Cal Chapman, President
Mikes Ames, Vice President

1750 **Chelsea Group Limited**
733 Bishop Street 808-888-7148
Suite 181 info@ameresco.com
Honolulu, HI 96813 www.ameresco.com
A division of Ameresco, Chelsea Group specializes in consulting for the enhancement of building infrastructure, considering areas such as air quality, property condition, energy planning, and more.
George Benda, Founder, Chelsea Group
George P. Sakellaris, CEO, Ameresco

1751 **Chemical Data Management Systems**
6516 Trinity Court 925-551-7300
Suite 201 800-735-1761
Dublin, CA 94568 www.cdms.com
Provides a full range of hazardous material and OSHA regulatory compliance services, including implementing compliance programs, submitting necessary reports to all regulatory agencies, employee training, noise monitoring, spillprevention and more.

Michele McSweeney, CEO & Owner
Raschelle Mullette, Business Manager

1752 **Chicago Chem Consultants Corporation**
14 North Peoria Street 312-226-2436
Suite 2C *Fax:* 312-226-8886
Chicago, IL 60607-2609 info@chichem.com
www.chichem.com
Provides a range of risk protective environmental and engineering services, including energy management, chemical process design, forensics, equipment evaluation and more.

Jeffrey P. Perl, President
Stanley Yoslov, Senior Associate

1753 **Chubb Global Risk Advisors (CGRA)**
1133 Avenue of the Americas 212-827-4400
New York, NY 10036 www.chubb.com/us-en/
CGRA is an insurance company offering services in environmental consulting, including environmental compliance and management systems support. Services include compliance assessments, emergency preparedness and response, wastemanagement, air quality management, and more.

Evan G. Greenberg, CEO & Chair
John Keogh, COO & Executive VP

1754 **Clean Environments**
2800 NE Loop 410 512-444-9499
Suite 105 *Fax:* 210-349-1132
San Antonio, TX 78218
Environmental consulting firm offering mold and asbestos control services, including toxic lead and air quality tests.

Greg Shilts, President
Ray Keeble, Senior Project Manager

1755 **Clean World Engineering**
1737 S Naperville Road 630-260-0200
Suite 200
Wheaton, IL 60189
An environmental engineering firm specializing in developing practical solutions in compliance with environmental regulations. Services include asbestos and lead inspections, indoor air quality testing, site assessments, industrialhygiene, waste management and more.

Rita Kapur, President
Kathleen Wahl, Senior Project Manager

1756 **CleanAir Engineering**
500 West Wood Street 847-991-3300
Palatine, IL 60067-4929 800-553-5511
info@cleanair.com
www.cleanair.com
Environmental consulting firm for air quality management, emissions measurement, and thermal performance and efficiency determination. CleanAir Engineering also offers permitting services, process engineering, emergency responsemonitoring, and measurement and analytical services.

Allen Kephart, President & CEO
Anthony Milianti, Project Engineer

1757 **Cohen Group**
3 Waters Park Drive 650-349-9737
Suite 226 *Fax:* 650-349-3378
San Mateo, CA 94403-1169 www.thecohengroup.com
Provides a complete range of environmental health and safety services to businesses and governments, covering indoor air quality, asbestos, respiratory protection, industrial hygiene safety, and more.

Joel M. Cohen, President
Timothy Bormann, Vice President

1758 **Community Conservation**
120 Sunset Ridge Avenue 608-735-4717
Suite 114 www.communityconservation.org
Gays Mills, WI 54631

Works together with local rural people to aid in the protection of their wildlife and forests. Projects undertaken have been located in India, Belize, Peru, Wisconsin, and other places around the world, with an emphasis on primates andother species. The organization offers services such as project management, land use assessment, zoning plans, resource monitoring, publicity, and more.

Teri Allendorf, President
Joe Rising, Vice President

1759 Compass Environmental
1751 McCollum Parkway NW 770-499-7127
Kennesaw, GA 30144 *Fax:* 770-423-7402
www.compassenv.com
Offers services in asbestos control, indoor air quality investigations, industrial hygiene surveys and audits, and guidance in environmental regulatory compliance.
Eva M. Ewing, Senior Industrial Hygienist
William M. Ewing, Technical Director

1760 Comprehensive Environmental
41 Main Street 508-281-5160
Bolton, MA 01740 800-725-2550
Fax: 508-281-5136
adminassist@ceiengineers.com
ceiengineers.com
A civil engineering and environmental services company. Provides water and wastewater services, flood and drainage management, stormwater engineering, environmental compliance services, and more.
Eileen Pannetier, President
Richard Cote, Principal

1761 Conservtech Group
5875 Rickenbacker Road 323-867-9044
Commerce, CA 90040 *Fax:* 323-867-9045
bob@conservtechgroup.com
www.conservtechgroup.com
Offers solutions for environmental challenges through pollution control systems, site assessment, waste management services, civil engineering planning and design, air quality analysis, and more.

Robert MacDonald, President
Bruce Charest, Sr. Environmental Engineer

1762 Consultox
P.O. Box 1239 207-563-2300
Damariscotta, ME 04543 800-566-2301
Fax: 207-563-8990
www.consultox.com
Consultation services offered by a certified toxicologist in the areas of product safety, trade association representation, drug and cosmetic registration, litigation support, occupational safety assessment and more.

Richard A. Parent, President
Michael J. Siener, Information Systems Manager

1763 Continental Shelf Associates
8502 SW Kansas Avenue 772-219-3000
Stuart, FL 34997 *Fax:* 772-219-3010
csa@conshelf.com
www.conshelf.com
Multidisciplinary corporation that oversees various subsidiaries, each of which offers differing environmental services. Examples include marine surveys and consulting, strategic marketing services to ocean and offshore industries,subsea data and communications network development, and financial consulting.

Kevin Peterson, President & CEO
Dan White, Chief Technology Officer

1764 Converse Consultants
717 South Myrtle Avenue 626-930-1200
Monrovia, CA 91016 *Fax:* 626-930-1212
converse@converseconsultants.com
www.converseconsultants.com
Environmental consulting and engineering firm offering services in geotechnical engineering, materials testing, water resource management, environmental science, and laboratory services.

Hashmi S. Quazi, President & Chair
Ruben L. Romero, Chief Financial Officer

1765 Cook, Flatt & Strobel Engineers
2930 SW Woodside Drive 785-272-4706
Topeka, KS 66614 *Fax:* 785-272-4736
www.cfse.com
Consulting services for transportation, wastewater management, geotechnical engineering, site development, land planning, construction inspection, stormwater management, bridge design, and more.

Kenneth Blair, Chair
Robert Chambers, President

1766 Cornerstone Environmental, Health and Safety
880 Lennox Court 317-733-2637
Zionsville, IN 46077 800-285-2568
www.corner-enviro.com
Provides environmental and safety compliance services such as chemical management, IT software, employee safety training, regulatory compliance assessments, and more.

Mark Miller, President
Kevin Mallin, Senior Project Manager

1767 Corporate Environmental Advisors
21 E Main Street 800-358-7960
Suite 201 *Fax:* 508-835-8812
Westborough, MA 01581 info@cea-inc.com
cea-inc.com
Environmental consulting firm specializing in environmental compliance and engineering, health and safety training, hazardous building material assessments, and more.

Joseph S. Campisi, President
Adam Last, Principal Engineer

1768 Corrpro
7000 A Hollister 866-267-7776
Suite 300 www.corrpro.com
Houston, TX 77040
A subsidiary of Aegion Corporation, Corrpro is a cathodic protection engineering company that provides corrosion control materials and cost-effective services, including engineering, pipeline integrity, construction, and protectivecoating inspection.
Franco Piarulli, Sales, North Texas
Lee Zickefoose, Sales, South Texas

1769 Cultural Resource Consultants, International Archaeology & Ecology
P.O. Box 315 979-530-0331
Chappell Hill, TX 77426 info@culturalresource.com
www.culturalresource.com
Provides services for environmentally sensitive projects: archaeology investigations, permitting, computer graphics and mapping, mineral exploration and development, ground penetrating radar, land reclamation, mine development, andmore.

John Griggs, Sr. Principal Investigator
Robert B. d'Aigle, Sr. Principal Investigator

1770 D'Appolonia
701 Rodi Road 412-856-9440
2nd Floor *Fax:* 412-856-9535
Pittsburgh, PA 15235-4559 info@dappolonia.com
www.dappolonia.com
Provides engineering, scientific and construction management services for projects involving large civil works and special

earth/structure interaction issues. Some of the areas covered include power generation, mining, dams andwaterways, geophysics, forensic studies, and more.

Robert Shusko, President
Aaron Antell, Principal Engineer

1771 **DPRA**
10215 Technology Drive 865-777-3772
Suite 201 info@dpra.com
Knoxville, TN 37932-4304 www.dpra.com
Offers environmental consulting services as well as systems, software, and planning tools for businesses and government. Target areas include large-scale military operations, humanitarian support, environmental policies, and change ofmanagement.

Denis O'Keefe, Chief Executive Officer
Mary Carter, Executive Vice President

1772 **Datanet Engineering**
11416 Reisterstown Road 410-654-1800
Owings Mills, MD 21117 *Fax:* 410-654-3711
info@datanetengineering.com
www.datanetengineering.com
Provides services for the fuel systems industry: corrosion engineering, cathodic protection, construction and training, system installations, and more.

Andrew Cignatta, President
John V. Cignatta, VP & Principal Engineer

1773 **DeVany Industrial Consultant**
14507 NW 19th Avenue 360-546-0999
Vancouver, WA 98685 mdevany@earthlink.net
Provides a full custom range of safety and industrial hygiene services.
Mary DeVany, President

1774 **Detail Associates**
300 Grand Avenue 201-569-6708
Englewood, NJ 07631 *Fax:* 201-569-4378
www.daienviro.com
Environmental engineering firm offering consulting services in asbestos assessment, project management, lead surveys, air quality testing, ergonomic assessments, occupant complaint investigations, and more.

Stephen Jaraczewski, President

1775 **Duffield Associates**
5400 Limestone Road 302-239-6634
Wilmington, DE 19808 *Fax:* 302-239-8485
duffnet.com
Environmental consulting and engineering firm offering services in environmental, civil, water/wastewater, and geotechnical engineering, as well as field services, landscape architecture, traffic/ transportation consulting, and more.
Stacy Ziegler, Chief Executive Officer
Deirdre Smith, Chief Operating Officer

1776 **Dunn Development Corporation**
589 Sackett Street 718-388-9407
2nd Floor *Fax:* 718-388-0638
Brooklyn, NY 11217 info@dunndev.com
www.dunndev.com
Development consulting firm for affordable housing building projects. Dunn Development incorporates sustainable design and green building into their projects. Areas covered include property acquisition, building design, assetmanagement, construction supervision, and more.

Martin Dunn, President
Stephen Viafore, Finance Director

1777 **Durand & Anastas Environmental Strategies**
27 Prospect Street 617-860-2556
Marlborough, MA 01752 info@durandanastas.com
www.durandanastas.com
Provides consulting services in project planning, regulatory compliance, and public outreach and media service. The agency specializes in issues affecting inland resources, the coastal zone, and offshore waters.
Bob Durand, President
Chuck Anastas, Managing Partner

1778 **ESS Group**
404 Wyman Street 781-419-7696
Suite 375 info@essgroup.com
Waltham, MA 02451 www.essgroup.com
ESS is a multi-disciplinary environmental consulting and engineering firm offering services in the areas of energy generation and transmission, coastal engineering and marine sciences, water resources, natural resources, environmentalcompliance and more.

Charles Natale, President & CEO
Payson Whitney, VP, Chief Operating Officer

1779 **ETS Environmental Services**
1401 Municipal Road NW 540-265-0004
Roanoke, VA 24012-1309 *Fax:* 540-265-0131
jmck@etsi-inc.com
www.etsi-inc.com
ETS is a full-service fabric filter baghouse consulting and training firm specializing in air emissions control, testing, training, testimony and troubleshooting services.

John McKenna, Principal
Marc McKenna, President

1780 **Earth Science Associates**
4300 Long Beach Boulevard 562-428-3181
Suite 310 contactESA@earthsci.com
Long Beach, CA 90807 www.earthsci.com
Consulting and software development company serving the oil and gas industry, as well as government agencies and international organizations. Among its services are the GOM geographic information system (GIS) and its online component,GOMsmart.
John D. Grace, President

1781 **EcoLogic Systems**
7977 Capwell Drive 510-635-7400
Suite 150 800-223-0609
Oakland, CA 94621 *Fax:* 510-635-7402
sales@ecologicsystems.com
www.ecologicsystems.com
Developer of software for hazardous material management and environmental health and safety compliance. Some of their programs include asbestos inventory and document management, indoor air quality and analytical data management,employee health and safety records management, equipment maintenance management, and more.
Heather Sobky, Project Manager

1782 **Ecology and Environment**
368 Pleasant View Drive 716-684-8060
Lancaster, NY 14086 info@ene.com
www.ene.com
Ecology and Environment is an environmental science and engineering company providing environmental consulting services and litigation support. Areas covered include engineering, restoration, water treatment, regulatory compliance,permitting, environmental impact assessments, air and noise studies, field studies, and more.
Mike Morgante, Contact

1783 **Elinor Schwartz and Associates**
318 South Abingdon Street 703-920-5389
Arlington, VA 22204 *Fax:* 703-920-5402
es@elinorschwartz.com
Offering representation services for state agencies and providing research on natural resources, energy and environmental issues.
Elinor Schwartz, President

1784 EnSafe
5724 Summer Trees Drive 901-372-7962
Memphis, TN 38134 800-588-7962
Fax: 901-372-2454
www.ensafe.com
Provides consulting services such as the implementation of occupational health and safety programs, technological solutions, and environmental management systems meant to decrease accident frequency and accident costs.

Phil Coop, Chair
Don Bradford, President & CEO

1785 EnviroTest Laboratories
315 Fullerton Avenue 845-562-0890
Newburgh, NY 12550 *Fax:* 845-562-0841
customerservice@envirotestlaboratories.com
www.envirotestlaboratories.com
Laboratory testing for soil and water for municipal and industrial clients, with a staff of 28 professionals.

Samuel Cohen, Principal

1786 Environmental Compliance Consultants
1500 Post Road 907-644-0428
Anchorage, AK 99501 tim.nunberg@eccalaska.com
www.eccalaska.com
Environmental consultants offering services in waste management and environmental consulting. Services include overland hauling, medical waste disposal, sites investigation, industrial janitorial, and more.

Tim Nunberg, Contact

1787 Environmental HELP
P.O. Box 222320 661-260-2260
Santa Clarita, CA 91322-2320 800-750-0622
Fax: 661-253-3555
www.environmentalhelp.net
Offers consultation services for environmental health and safety compliance. Areas of expertise include environmental assessments and audits, granting permits, waste water management, and more.

BJ Atkins, President

1788 Environmental Resource Associates
16341 Table Mountain Parkway 303-431-8454
Golden, CO 80403 800-372-0122
Fax: 303-421-0159
info@eraqc.com
www.eraqc.com
A division of Waters Corporation, ERA provides products and consultation services for laboratories in the areas of water pollution, chemistry, microbiology, soil testing and more.

Brian Murphy, PR, Waters Corporation

1789 Environmental Resources Management
3352 128th Avenue 616-399-3500
Holland, MI 49424 *Fax:* 616-399-3777
www.erm.com
Provides environmental, health, safety, risk, and social consulting services, including sustainability planning, health and safety, risk assessment, data management, asset management, and environmental compliance.

Keryn James, Chief Executive Officer
David McArthur, Chief Operating Officer

1790 Environmental Risk Management
3702 S Expressway 281 956-383-6569
Edinburg, TX 78542-7023 *Fax:* 956-383-6568
office@enrisk.com
enriskpetsol.wordpress.com
Provides environmental consulting to South Texas. Services include Phase I, II and III environmental site assessments, leaking petroleum storage tank assessments and project management, underground fuel system assessments and remedialservices for environmental projects.

Mark Barron, President
Scott Boyd, Vice President

1791 Environmental Science Associates
550 Kearney Street 415-896-5900
Suite 800 *Fax:* 415-896-0332
San Francisco, CA 94108 www.esassoc.com
Environmental Science Associates is a consulting firm committed to helping clients meet the challenges of environmental projects, planning, assessment and regulatory compliance.

Leslie Moulton-Post, President
Albert Cuisinot, Chief Financial Officer

1792 Environmental Strategy Consultants
1528 Walnut Street 215-731-4200
Suite 500 *Fax:* 215-731-4207
Philadelphia, PA 19102 info@envirostrat.com
www.envirostrat.com
An environmental, health and safety management firm specializing in environmental and air quality consulting. Some services include air permitting application consulting and negotiation, EPA enforcement consulting, and environmentaloutsourcing services.

Lorna M. Velardi, President
Clark R. Baubles, Managing Director

1793 Enviroplan Consulting
155 Route 46 West 973-256-2200
Suite 109
Wayne, NJ 07470
Meteorological and air pollution consulting company specializing in the areas of air pollution consulting, including greenhouse gas emmissions; inventory development and mitigation; and meteorological monitoring programs.

Howard Ellis, President

1794 Epcon Industrial Systems
P.O. Box 7060 936-273-3300
The Woodlands, TX 77387 *Fax:* 936-273-4600
epcon@epconlp.com
www.epconlp.com
Provides a broad line of air pollution control products, finishing systems, and heat processing equipment. Along with their products, they provide installation, start-up assistance, maintenance, and operations training.

Aziz Jamaluddin, President & CEO
Tasha Jamaluddin, Managing Director

1795 FirstCarbon Solutions
250 Commerce 714-508-4100
Suite 250 888-826-5814
Irvine, CA 92602 *Fax:* 714-508-4110
www.firstcarbonsolutions.com
FirstCarbon Solutions offers consulting, data management, and software solutions to its clients. Examples of these services include environmental and compliance solutions in energy, air, and carbon management; environmental assessmentsand planning; supply and life cycle assessments; permitting and compliance; and software and data processing.

Robert Francisco, President, North America
Patrick Schultz, Senior VP & COO

1796 GBMc & Associates
219 Brown Lane 501-847-7077
Suite 215 www.gbmcassoc.com
Bryant, AK 72022
GBMc & Associates is a consulting firm providing strategic environmental services to industrial clients in the form of air permitting support, water quality and toxicity studies, storm water

management, environmental programdevelopment and reporting, and more.
Chuck Campbell, Principal & Sr. Engineer
Jonathan Brown, Project Manager

1797 GHD USA
1240 North Mountain Road 717-541-0622
Harrisburg, PA 17112 www.ghd.com
Offers engineering, architecture, environmental and construction services such as agricultural impact assessments, air quality monitoring, construction engineering, waste management, and more.

Rob Knott, Chair
Ashley Wright, Chief Executive Officer

1798 GZA GeoEnvironmental
249 Vanderbilt Avenue 781-278-3700
Norwood, MA 02062 *Fax:* 781-278-5701
www.gza.com
GZA provides consulting services in the geotechnical, environmental, water, ecological, and construction fields. They work with a variety of organizations, including industrial, commercial, financial, public service, and governmententities.

Enda P. Fahey, Chief Financial Officer
Patrick F. Sheehan, President & CEO

1799 Gabbard Environmental Services
7611 Hope Farm Road 260-493-2982
Fort Wayne, IN 46815-654 *Fax:* 260-493-4043
wdgabbard@aol.com
www.gabbardenvironmentalservices.com
Consulting services for environmental affairs such as permitting, compliance, hazardous material transportation, inspections and audits, employee safety training, indoor air quality checks, written programs, and more.
William D. Gabbard, President

1800 Geo-Marine Technology
101 South California Street 406-721-1599
Suite B *Fax:* 406-926-1379
Missoula, MT 59801 services@geomarinetech.com
www.geomarinetech.com
Provides reports for offshore construction projects to ensure safety on these projects. The company gathers and synthesizes data regarding oceanography, meteorology, human impacts, and geology, and summarizes concerns such as stormfrequency, shipping lanes, wind and swell vectors, and more.
John Rietman, President & Founder
Beau Pallister, Vice President

1801 Gradient Corporation
20 University Road 617-395-5000
Cambridge, MA 02138 gradientcorp.com
A consulting firm offering services in toxicology, epidemiology, contaminants, industrial hygiene, geographic information systems, environmental sciences and forensic chemistry.

Teresa S. Bowers, Principal
Barbara D. Beck, Principal

1802 Greeley-Polhemus Group
1310 Birmingham Road 610-793-9440
West Chester, PA 19382
Environmental consulting firm that has served clients in State and Federal agencies, as well as the private industry. Primary clients include the U.S. Army Corps of Engineers, as well as various Corps Districts throughout the U.S.

Maureen Polhemus, President & Owner

1803 Green Analytical Laboratories
75 Suttle Street 970-247-4220
Durango, CO 81303 *Fax:* 970-247-4227
Company that provides consulting and laboratory services to the environmental industries of Colorado, New Mexico, and West Texas. Services include water quality tests, groundwater monitoring, hazardous waste analysis, soil testing, andmore.

1804 Ground/Water Treatment & Technology
627 Mt. Hope Road 973-983-0901
Wharton, NJ 07885 800-770-0901
Fax: 973-983-0903
solutions@gwttllc.com
www.gwttllc.com
Offers bioremedial technology for rapid cleanup of soil and groundwater. Services include system design; civil, electrical, and mechanical site work; equipment fabrication and customization; dewatering; and maintenance of groundwatertreatment systems.

Robert Kunzel, Chief Program Officer
Matthew Phillips, VP, Sales & Marketing

1805 HATCH
4110 North Scottsdale Road 602-666-6800
Suite 360 *Fax:* 602-572-2601
Scottsdale, AZ 85251 www.hatch.com/en
Aims to optimize environmental protection, economic prosperity, social justice, and cultural vibrancy in communities. The organization spans over 150 countries and works in the metals, energy, infrastructure, digital, and investmentsmarket sectors.

1806 HDR
1917 67th Street S 402-399-1000
Omaha, NE 68106-2973 800-366-4411
Fax: 402-548-5015
www.hdrinc.com
Environmental engineering and consulting firm offering services such as site design, asset management, commissioning plans, funding, environmental remediation, impact analysis, compliance, natural resources management, permitting, andmore.

Eric L. Keen, Chair & CEO
Charles L. O'Reilly, Vice Chair & COO

1807 Harold I Zeliger PhD
41 Wildwood Drive 207-747-4040
Cape Elizabeth, ME 04107 hiz@zeliger.com
www.zeliger.com
Consultant offering expertise in occupational and environmental exposure to toxic and flammable chemicals, hazard communication, chemical formulating and processing and forensic investigations.

Harold I Zeliger, Ph.D, Principal

1808 Hart Crowser
3131 Elliott Avenue 206-324-9530
Suite 600 *Fax:* 206-328-5581
Seattle, WA 98121 www.hartcrowser.com
Hart Crowser provides a full range of services from initial site studies through regulatory permitting design and construction. Areas covered include environmental site assessments, biological surveys, regulatory strategy and support,geotechnical and environmental engineering, and oil and gas contamination support.

David Winter, President & CEO
Tony Bardana, Business Development

1809 Hasbrouck Geophysics
12 Woodside Drive 928-925-4424
Prescott, AZ 86305 *Fax:* 928-778-6320
jim@hasgeo.com
www.hasgeo.com
Consulting firm that specializes in the areas of groundwater, engineering, environment, and mining. Services offered include geophysical consulting; field supervision; data processing; surface, airborne, and borehole geophysicalmethods; radiometrics; and more.
Jim Hasbrouck, Principal

1810 HazMat Environmental Group
60 Commerce Drive 716-827-7200
Buffalo, NY 14218-1040 www.hazmatinc.com
Offers transportation services for hazardous and non-hazardous materials via tank trailers, vacuum trailers, roll-offs, truckload, and less-than-truckload vans. Also offers OSHA certification training and other training courses forenvironmental consulting, logistics, and tank trailer repair.
John Stewart, President
Donna Crosta, Safety Manager

1811 Heritage Environmental Services
6510 Telecom Drive 877-436-8778
Suite 400 www.heritage-enviro.com
Indianapolis, IN 46278
Provides environmental services such as emergency response, data management, industrial cleaning, site remediation, regulatory compliance training, hazardous waste management, waste disposal, and more.

Ken Price, Chair & CEO

1812 Hermann and Associates
4603 North Galena Road 309-687-5566
Peoria Heights, IL 61616 *Fax:* 309-687-0571
info@hermannassoc.com
www.hermannassoc.com
Consulting firm offering services in transportation and municipal engineering. Services include traffic studies, drainage studies and design, asbestos inspection and air quality sampling, roadway reconstruction, and more.
Alicia Hermann, Principal & Project Manager
Jeff Hermann, Senior Project Engineer

1813 Huff and Huff
915 Harger Road 630-684-9100
Suite 330 *Fax:* 630-684-9120
Oak Brook, IL 60523-1486 www.huffnhuff.com
A subsidiary of GZA, Huff and Huff is a consulting firm providing environmental, civil, and biological engineering services in the areas of natural resource assessments, wetlands, remediation, wastewater, stream surveys, siteassessments, air quality, underground storage tanks, hazardous waste management, and more.

Enda P. Fahey, CFO, GZA
Jim Huff, Senior Consultant

1814 Hydrogeologic
11107 Sunset Hills Road 703-478-5186
Suite 400 *Fax:* 703-471-4180
Reston, VA 20190 contact@hgl.com
www.hgl.com
Offers consulting services for environmental, infrastructure and natural resource challenges. Services offered include remediation, military munitions response, mining reclamation, water resource management and more.

Peter Huyakorn, President
Scott Schulein, Chief Operating Officer

1815 Infrastructure and Energy Alternatives (IEA)
6325 Digital Way 800-688-3775
Suite 460 iea.net
Indianapolis, IN 46278
IEA is an infrastructure construction company that specializes in energy and provides civil expertise. Their mission is to provide quality engineering and construction services to meet clients' ongoing infrastructure requirements.
JP Roehm, Chief Executive Officer
Andrew Layman, Chief Financial Officer

1816 Institute for Energy and Environmental Research (IEER)
PO Box 5324 301-509-6843
Takoma Park, MD 20913 www.ieer.org
IEER's aim is to provide scientific information about environmental issues in an easy to understand format for use by activists, policy-makers, journalists and the public. The educational material covers emissions-free energy systems,energy equity, energy democracy, nuclear weapons security and more. Consulting services are also provided.

Arjun Makhijani, President
Lois Chalmers, Consulting Librarian

1817 Integrated Chemistries
5731 Norwich Ave N 651-426-3224
Oak Park Heights, MN 55082 *Fax:* 651-426-3114
integratedchemistries.com
Develops cleaning and extraction systems for the decontamination of buildings and structures. The equipment targets hazardous and non-hazardous waste.

Jim Nash, Owner

1818 Integrated Environmental Management
118 North Peters Road 865-588-9180
Suite 178
Knoxville, TN 37923
Provides strategic consulting and services in the areas of radiation, radioactivity and the environment.

1819 International Cotton Advisory Committee
1629 K Street North West 202-463-6660
Suite 702 *Fax:* 202-463-6950
Washington, DC 20006-1635 secretariat@icac.org
www.icac.org
An organization with the mission of encouraging a healthy cotton economy by providing information about world cotton production, consumption, trade and stocks.

Rebecca Pandolph, Statistician
James Johnson, Chair, USA Division

1820 Interpoll Laboratories
4500 Ball Road NE 763-786-6020
Circle Pines, MN 55014 *Fax:* 763-786-7854
interpoll@interpoll-labs.com
www.interpoll-labs.com
Environmental laboratory offering stack testing, field services, pharmaceutical research, residential testing, and other laboratory services.

Dan Despen, President
Gregg Holman, VP & Laboratory Manager

1821 JJ Keller and Associates
3003 Breezewood Lane 877-564-2333
P.O. Box 368 *Fax:* 800-727-7516
Neenah, WI 54957 www.jjkeller.com
Offers services in regulatory compliance, best practices and training for environmental, safety, and transportation issues.

Rustin Keller, President & CEO
Dana Gilman, Chief Financial Officer

1822 James M Anderson and Associates
104 Oak Street 912-764-2002
P.O. Box 894 800-829-4250
Statesboro, GA 30459 *Fax:* 912-489-6635
www.georgiacarolinasurveyors.com
Land surveying company offering services such as construction planning, GPS surveying, mapping, wetland surveys, 3D machine control, and more.

James Anderson, Principle & Owner

1823 James W Sewall Company
136 Center Street 207-827-4456
P.O. Box 433 800-648-4202
Old Town, ME 04468-0433 *Fax:* 207-827-3641
www.sewall.com

Sewall provides services in forestry appraisal and inventory, aerial imagery, GIS consulting and engineering, natural resources mapping, and more.

George N. Campbell, President
Charles Nadeau, Chief Financial Officer

1824 John Zink Hamworthy Combustion
11920 East Apache 918-234-1800
Tulsa, OK 74116 800-755-4252
www.johnzink.com
Offers technologically advanced equipment and systems for the clean and efficient combustion of fossil fuels, chemical processing, automobile manufacturing, food processing, waste management, and more. Some equipment include process,boiler, and duct burners; flare systems; thermal oxidation; vapor control technolgy; and more.
Scott Fox, Vice President
Ryan McKenzie, Senior Project Manager

1825 Kimre Clean Air Technology
744 South West 1st Street 305-233-4249
Homestead, FL 33030 *Fax:* 305-233-8687
sales@kimre.com
www.kimre.com
Produces technology for cleaning air through pollution control features. Products include mist eliminators, scrubbers, liquid coalescers, drift eliminators and aerosol separation systems.

Mary R. Keenan, President
George C. Pedersen, CEO

1826 LA Weaver Company
308 East Jones Street 919-832-6242
Raleigh, NC 27601
Occupational and environmental safety consulting services.

Al Weaver, President

1827 LSI Industries
10000 Alliance Road 513-793-3200
Cincinnati, OH 45242 *Fax:* 513-984-1335
custsvc1.cin@lsi-industries.com
www.lsi-industries.com
Produces LED technology for energy-efficient lighting, as well as custom graphic products. Some of their products include printed graphics, illuminated menu boards and decorations, structural graphics, LED products, digital signagesystems, and more.

James A. Clark, President & CEO
Wilfred T. O'Gara, Chair

1828 Landau Associates
130 2nd Avenue S 425-778-0907
Edmonds, WA 98020 800-552-5957
Fax: 425-778-6409
info@landauinc.com
www.landauinc.com
Provides environmental engineering and geotechnical consulting services such as site assessment, hazardous materials assessment, water quality analysis, habitat restoration, geologic hazards assessment, permitting, air qualityanalyses, and more.

Jay Bower, President & CEO
Larry Beard, Senior Principal Engineer

1829 Logan Simpson
51 West Third 480-967-1343
Suite 450 *Fax:* 480-966-9232
Tempe, AZ 85281 logansimpson.com
Provides environmental consulting, landscape architecture design, cultural resources, and community planning to communities in the West.

Diane Simpson-Colebank, Principal, Planning & Design
Wayne Colebank, Principal, Clean Water

1830 Louis Berger Group
412 Mount Kemble Avenue 973-407-1000
P.O. Box 1946 *Fax:* 973-267-6468
Morristown, NJ 07962-1946 www.louisberger.com
Offers professional services in environmental engineering and infrastructure development. Services include program management, planning, environmental sciences, cultural resources, information services, economic and institutionaldevelopment, policy and management analysis, and construction management.

Thomas G. Lewis, President, U.S. Division
Jim Stamatis, Chief Executive Officer

1831 Louis DeFilippi
208 Edgewood Lane 847-925-8524
Palatine, IL 60067 louisdef@expertbiochemist.com
www.expertbiochemist.com
Independent consulting firm offering consulting services in biochemistry, biocatalysis, bioprocessing, and biotransformations. Services cover the topics of regulatory compliance and hazardous waste treatment.
Louis DeFilippi, President

1832 MSA Professional Services
4321 West College Avenue 920-545-2083
Suite 200 888-958-0803
Appleton, WI 54914 *Fax:* 920-757-2401
www.msa-ps.com
Specializes in community and land development projects, including water services, agricultural engineering, economic development, municipal infrastructure, transportation services, and more. Their mission is to improve how peopleinteract with their environment.
Gil Hantzsch, Chief Executive Officer
Mike Statz, Chief Operating Officer

1833 Marc Boogay Consulting Engineer
1584 Whispering Palm Drive 760-407-4000
Oceanside, CA 92056 *Fax:* 760-407-4004
marc@boogay.com
www.boogay.com
Consulting firm offering services such as environmental site assessments, underground storage tank studies, percolation testing and septic system design, storm water infiltration testing, and more.
Marc Boogay, Owner
Claudia Padilla, Engineering Technician

1834 McDermott International Inc
757 N Eldridge Parkway 281-870-5000
Houston, TX 77079 www.mcdermott.com
A global engineering, procurement, construction, and installation company that offers offshore oil and gas production systems, refinery process units, Air Quality Control Systems, industrial storage systems, and more.

David Dickson, President & CEO
Stuart Spence, Chief Financial Officer

1835 McVehil-Monnett Associates
9250 East Costilla Avenue 303-790-1332
Suite 630 *Fax:* 303-790-7820
Greenwood Village, CO 80112
Consulting firm providing services in air quality monitoring, permitting, litigation support, environmental management systems, compliance, and more. Industries served include the mining, oil and gas, electricity, and manufacturingindustries.

Bill Monnett, President
George McVehil, Principal

1836 Meteorological Evaluation Services Company
165 Broadway 631-691-3395
Amityville, NY 11701 *Fax:* 631-691-3550
www.mesamity.com

Provides air quality and meteorological consulting services, specializing in environmental information development, as well as air pollution, meteorological, and climatological concerns.

1837 Miceli Kulik Williams and Associates
39 Park Avenue 201-933-7809
Rutherford, NJ 07070 *Fax:* 201-933-8702
info@mkwla.com
www.mkwla.com
Offers complete services covering the various aspects of landscape architecture, site planning, and urban design. Present scope of work includes historic renovation, urban revitalization, landscape architecture, environmentalassessment, construction observation, and more.
John P. Williams, Principal
Allen E. Juba, Principal

1838 Michael Baker International
500 Grant Street 412-918-4000
Suite 5400 800-553-1153
Pittsburgh, PA 15219 www.mbakerintl.com
Michael Baker Corporation provides engineering and consulting services for its clients' infrastructural challenges worldwide. The firm's primary practice areas are aviation, environment, energy, architecture, transportation, water,land development, cost management, and more. With nearly 100 offices nationwide, Michael Baker is focused on providing services that span the complete life cycle of infrastucture.

Brian A. Lutes, President & CEO

1839 Micro-Bac International
3200 North Interstate Highway 35 512-310-9000
Round Rock, TX 78681-2410 inquiry@micro-bac.com
www.micro-bac.com
Develops and manufactures biological products for oil spill clean up; paraffin build-up in oil wells; agri-business waste; animal processing facility waste; restaurant grease traps; and other clean up projects.
Juan M. Morales, President
Sharon Ryan, Controller

1840 Midstream Farm LLC
20004 Sterling Creek Lane 804-749-8720
Rockville, VA 23146 804-317-0777
clem@usaclem.com
www.usaclem.com
An independent company owned by Clement Mesavage, Jr. that provides consulting services of tank and pipeline locations. He also provides environmental, health, safety, security, and product quality control services.
Clement Mesavage, Jr., Proprietor

1841 Mostardi Platt
888 Industrial Drive 630-993-2100
Elmhurst, IL 60126 888-802-6855
Fax: 630-993-9017
info@mp-mail.com
mostardiplatt.com
Offers solutions and strategies to assist clients with the compliance of environmental, health, and safety regulations, and to develop environmental programs that save long-term costs. Services include air emissions testing andmonitoring; continuous emissions systems and service; environmental health and safety; environmental assessment and remediation; permitting and consulting; and compliance management process.

Joseph J. Macak III, VP & Principal Consultant

1842 NORESCO United Technologies
1 Research Drive 508-614-1000
Suite 400C *Fax:* 508-836-9988
Westborough, MA 01581 www.noresco.com
Provides energy efficiency and sustainable design consulting services for building owners, architects and engineers. Services offered include energy auditing, commissioning and retro-commissioning, energy & daylighting modeling, LEED© certification consulting, and sustainability planning.
Neil Petchers, President & CEO
David G. Mannherz, Chief Financial Officer

1843 NSF International
789 North Dixboro Road 734-769-8010
P.O. Box 130140 800-673-6275
Ann Arbor, MI 48105 *Fax:* 734-769-0109
info@nsf.org
www.nsf.org
The National Sanitation Foundation is an independent, accredited organization providing a wide range of services around the world, including standards development, testing, certification, auditing, inspection, consulting, and training.Their mission is to be the leading global provider of health and safety risk management solutions.

Lori Bestervelt, Senior VP & CTO
Kevan P. Lawlor, President & CEO

1844 NTH Consultants
41780 Six Mile Road 248-553-6300
Suite 200 *Fax:* 248-324-5179
Northville, MI 48168 marketingdept@nthconsultants.com
www.nthconsultants.com
NTH Consultants has provided consulting engineering services to clients throughout the United States since 1968. They offer geotechnical engineering, environmental, and facilities engineering services.

Kevin B. Hoppe, President & CEO
Keith M. Swaffar, Executive Chair

1845 National Governors Association (NGA)
444 North Capitol Street 202-624-5300
Suite 267 *Fax:* 202-624-5313
Washington, DC 20001 www.nga.org/consulting
The Association works closely with the administration and Congress on state and federal policy issues, serves as a vehicle for sharing knowledge of innovative programs among states, and provides technical assistance and consultantservices to governors on a wide range of management and policy issues. Part of the organization is the Center for Best Practices which undertakes demonstration projects and provides anticipatory research on important policy issues.

Nikki Guilford, Interim Executive Director
Christie Aberman, Interim Dir., Consulting

1846 Natural Resources Consulting Engineers
131 Lincoln Avenue 970-224-1851
Suite 300 *Fax:* 970-224-1885
Fort Collins, CO 80524 office@nrce.com
www.nrce.com
NRCE is an engineering consulting firm that works in the civil, water resources, agricultural, and environmental fields. They offer a wide range of services, including surface water hydrology, agricultural and irrigation engineering,construction management, and more.

Woldezion Mesghinna, President
Assad Safadi, Senior Vice President

1847 Navigant
150 North Riverside Plaza 312-583-5700
Suite 2100 *Fax:* 312-276-8658
Chicago, IL 60606 www.navigant.com
Consulting firm offering services to the energy, financial, governmental, healthcare, and life sciences industries. Services include business process outsourcing, data analytics, operations consulting, and more.
Julie Howard, Chair & CEO
Stephen R. Lieberman, Executive VP & CFO

1848 **Network Environmental Systems**
1141 Sibley Street 916-353-2360
Folsom, CA 95630 800-637-2384
Fax: 916-353-2375
office@nesglobal.net
www.nesglobal.net

NES is an organization that provides environmental health and safety training and consulting; clan lab training; industrial hygiene; construction safety oversight; and storm water compliance services.

Jerry Bucklin, President & CEO
Donald Rothenbaum, Senior Vice President

1849 **Ninyo and Moore**
5710 Ruffin Road 858-576-1000
San Diego, CA 92123 800-427-0401
Fax: 858-576-9600
nminquiries@ninyoandmoore.com
www.ninyoandmoore.com

As a leading geotechnical and environmental sciences engineering and consulting firm, Ninyo & Moore provides specialized services to clients in both public and private sectors. The company was established to provide engineering, soiland materials testing, and inspection services to clients.

Avram Ninyo, Principal Engineer

1850 **Nordlund and Associates**
813 East Ludington Avenue 231-843-3485
Ludington, MI 49431 *Fax:* 231-843-7676
ludington@nordlundandassociates.com
www.nordlundandassociates.com

An organization of consulting engineers, surveyors, and environmental scientists offering planning, grant and/or loan application assistance, design, and construction supervision.

Holly A. Mulherin, President
James T. Nordlund, Jr., Vice President

1851 **Normandeau Associates**
25 Nashua Road 603-472-5191
Bedford, NH 03110 *Fax:* 603-472-7052
www.normandeau.com

Normandeau Associates is an employee owned natural resources management consulting and testing services firm that provides: permit assistance, water quality studies, aquatic and terrestrial ecology, property transfer site assessments,wetlands services, contamination studies and biological laboratory services.

Pam Hall, CEO & Chair
Robert Varney, President

1852 **Norton Associates**
6670 Huntley Lane N 774-244-1248
Naples, FL 34104 norton@designofmachinery.com
www.designofmachinery.com

Professor Norton and his associates provide engineering consulting services on a wide range of subjects. Areas of expertise include: cam design and analysis, linkage design and analysis, stress analysis, vibrations in machinery,dynamic signal analysis, machinery monitoring, and machine dynamic analysis. They also provide short courses in cam design.

Robert L. Norton, President

1853 **OCCU-TEC**
2604 NE Industrial Drive 816-231-5580
North Kansas City, MO 64117 800-950-1953
Fax: 816-231-5641
service@occutec.com
www.occutec.com

OCCU-TEC provides solutions to energy, environmental, training, and occupational health and safety challenges. Services offered include environmental management, learning solutions, fuel management, workplace safety, and sustainabilitysevices.

Skuli Gudmundsson, President & CEO
Duncan Heydon, Executive Vice President

1854 **OccuSafe**
14144 Regency Place 214-662-6005
Dallas, TX 75254 occusafe@occusafeinc.com
occusafeinc.com

OccuSafe is an industrial hygiene consulting firm specializing in the evaluation of employee exposures to chemicals and noise, and indoor air quality.

Gary Ticker, President

1855 **Occupational Health & Safety Management**
1117 Lafarge Avenue 303-665-8528
Louisville, CO 80027
Industrial hygiene and safety consulting firm.

Mary Ann Heaney, President

1856 **Occupational Safety and Health Consultants**
12000 6th Street East 727-345-1552
Saint Petersburg, FL 33706 *Fax:* 727-363-8151
webmaster@oshc.com
www.oshc.com

Offers training for industrial lift truck and forklift safety certification, as well as general safety, construction safety, fire protection, and expert witness services.

1857 **Occupational and Environmental Health Consultiing Service**
6877 Bonillo Drive 630-325-2083
Las Vegas, NV 89103 bobb@safety-epa.com
www.oehcs.com

A full service regulatory, safety, industrial hygiene, and environmental engineering consulting firm. OEHCS specializes in assisting all sizes of companies and corporations, from very small businesses up to Fortune 100 corporations.

Bob Brandys, President

1858 **Omega Waste Management**
957 Colusa Street 530-824-1890
P.O. Box 495 roconnor@omegawaste.com
Corning, CA 96021 www.omegawaste.com

A company that specializes in solid waste removal. Additionally, they offer grease rendering, landscaping, janitorial, snow clearance, and other services.

Robert O'Connor, President
Karen O'Connor, Chief Financial Officer

1859 **PACE Analytical Services**
1800 Elm Street SE 612-607-6400
Minneapolis, MN 55414 www.pacelabs.com

Sampling and analytical testing firm that offers inorganic, organic, and radiochemistry laboratory testing, as well as an Instrument Support Group to troubleshoot and repair laboratory equipment.

Steve A. Vanderboom, CEO
Michael R. Prasch, Executive VP & CFO

1860 **PAR Environmental Services**
1906 21st Street 916-739-8356
Sacramento, CA 95811 mlmaniery@yahoo.com
www.parenvironmental.com

Provides clients with services in Cultural Resources Management and Environmental Planning. The planning department works on transportation and public works projects across California, while the cultural department provides historicpreservation, architectural history, and archaeological services to clients.

Mary L. Maniery, Chief Executive Officer
James G. Maniery, Chief Financial Officer

1861 **PBR HAWAII**
1001 Bishop Street 808-521-5631
Suite 650 *Fax:* 808-523-1402
Honolulu, HI 96813 www.pbrhawaii.com

Offers services in landscape architecture, land planning, environmental studies, and graphic design. Projects range from specific

site designs to urban design studies and large scale land management.
Thomas S. Witten, Chair
Stan Duncan, President

1862 PBS Engineering and Environmental
4412 SW Corbett Ave 503-248-1939
Portland, OR 97239 *Fax:* 866-727-0140
contactpbs_portland@pbsenv.com
www.pbsenv.com
PBS provides professional engineering, environmental, industrial hygiene, planning, and surveying services. Areas of expertise include environmental engineering, geotechnical engineering, hazardous materials management, industrialhygiene services, natural resources studies, and safety training.

Guy Neal, President
Brian Stanford, Chief Operating Officer

1863 PEER Consultants
409 12th Street SW 202-478-2060
Suite 603 *Fax:* 202-554-1471
Washington, DC 20024 info@peercpc.com
www.peercpc.com
An environmental engineering consulting firm offering water and wastewater engineering, environmental engineering and sustainability sciences, and MRO products. They aim to provide sustainable and appropriate solutions to today'senvironmental problems.

Lilia A. Abron, President & CEO
Diana Tucker Harrison, CFO & COO

1864 PELA GeoEnvironmental
P.O. Box 2310 205-752-5543
Tuscaloosa, AL 35403 *Fax:* 205-752-4043
mlee@pela.com
www.pela.com
PELA GeoEnvironmental is an environmental consulting company that engages in local and international projects revolving around geology, hydrogeology, and contamination remediation. These projects include wastewater treatment facilitydesign, regulatory compliance assessments, roadway design, and site development.
James LaMoreaux, Vice President & Chair
James Lee, President & CFO

1865 PETRA Environmental Consultants
10550 North 6th Avenue 715-536-7870
Merrill, WI 54452 *Fax:* 715-536-7890
info@petraenvironmental.net
www.petraenvironmental.net
PETRA Environmental Consultants is an environmental and safety compliance management and consulting firm, with the mission of helping clients comply with the environmental and safety regulations affecting their facilities. The companyoffers a variety of services, from air emissions reporting to environmental management system development and implementation.
David Treis, VP & General Manager
Mark Glendenning, Chief Executive Officer

1866 Pacific Soils Engineering
13331 Garden Grove Boulevard 714-703-1347
Suite N *Fax:* 714-703-1898
Garden Grove, CA 92843 info@pacificsoils.com
pacificsoils.com
Geologic and geotechnical consulting firm that addresses various geological concerns, including site seismicity, groundwater hydrology, liquefaction potential, foundation design, and more.

1867 Parish and Weiner Inc
297 Knollwood Road 914-997-7200
Suite 315 *Fax:* 914-997-7201
White Plains, NY 10607 www.parishweiner.com
A planning, development, and traffic consultant firm that offers services in land planning, environmental impact studies, transportation and traffic studies, site planning, office location studies, and more.
Nat Parish, President

1868 Phase One
23282 Mill Creek Drive 800-524-8877
Suite 160 *Fax:* 800-774-2731
Laguna Hills, CA 92653 info@phasei.com
www.phasei.com
An environmental consulting practice offering services in property assessments for property transfers, leasing developments, special uses, and financing purposes. Founded in response to the business community's need for affordable andstandardized assessment reports that allow for practical real estate decisions.

Eric D. Kieselbach, President & CEO

1869 Planning Resources
913 Parkview Boulevard 630-668-3788
Lombard, IL 60148 pri@planres.com
www.planres.com
A company that specializes in community planning, landscape architecture, park and recreation planning, and transportation planning. They aim to embrace the challenge of creating economically, socially, and environmentally impactfulsite solutions with intentional planning and design.
Darrell Garrison, Principal & Director
Mike Tait, Principal & CFO

1870 Process Applications
2627 Redwing Road 215-493-9361
Suite 340 info@palpaperchem.com
Fort Collins, CO 80526 www.palpaperchem.com
Produces specialty performance chemicals for paper industry machines with the aim of ensuring efficient and productive machines with low energy costs.

Bob Hegg, President

1871 Professional Analytical and Consulting Services (PACS)
409 Meade Drive 724-457-6576
Coraopolis, PA 15108 800-367-2587
henry@pacslabs.com
www.pacslabs.com
Provides short courses in spectrocopy, chomatography, quality, safety, environment and management. Also provided are professional manuals, software products, laboratory testing and consulting services.

Henry Nowicki, PhD, President
Barbara Sherman, Manager, Operations

1872 Psomas
1500 Iowa Avenue 951-787-8421
Suite 210 info@psomas.com
Riverside, CA 92507 www.psomas.com
Psomas is a consulting engineering firm offering services in land development, water and natural resources, transportaion, public works, survey and information systems to public and private sector clients.

Ryan McLean, CEO & President
Loren Sokolow, Chief Financial Officer

1873 Qk4
1046 East Chestnut Street 502-585-2222
Louisville, KY 40204 info@qk4.com
www.qk4.com
The aim of Qk4 is to provide sustainable engineering solutions that meet their clients' needs. They offer services in transportation, structural, water and wastewater, and construction engineering, as well as surveying, landacqusition, and Native American services.

Taylor M. Kelly, President
Glen M. Kelly, Executive Vice President

1874 RDG Geoscience and Engineering
10360 Sapp Brothers Drive 402-894-2678
Omaha, NE 68138 888-260-0893
Fax: 402-894-9043
www.rdgge.com

An earth science and engineering consulting firm that has completed over 3000 projects throughout the mid-west and mountain west of the U.S. They serve large corporations and small businesses in the areas of geologic and sitecharacterization, environmental site assessments, civil engineering, and water resources.
Jon Gross, President
Robert Kalinski, Vice President

1875 RESPEC
3824 Jet Drive 605-394-6400
Rapid City, SD 57703 *Fax:* 605-394-6456
www.respec.com

RESPEC provides clients with technical and advisory services. They serve the mining and energy, water and environmental, and data and technology sectors, providing a range of products to meet their clients' needs.

Todd J. Kenner, President & CEO
Philip A. Welling, Treasurer & CFO

1876 RGA Environmental, A Terracon Company
10841 South Ridgeview Road 800-593-7777
Olathe, KS 66061 www.terracon.com
RGA Environmental, acquired by Terracon in 2014, operates as a Terracon Company that provides hazardous materials, industrial hygiene, safety, emergency response, litigation, and environmental construction management services toclients in the public and private sectors.

M. Gayle Packer, President, Terracon

1877 RMI LLC
625 Chapin Road 803-345-0200
Chapin, SC 29036 800-207-7278
cdicus@askrmi.com
askrmi.com

Provider of environmental, industrial, and waste management services. Among their capabilities are recycling, waste-to-energy, incineration, treatment, disposal, industrial, employee training, and safety supply services.
Chase Dicus, President
Richard Elliott, Vice President

1878 Ramboll
4350 North Fairfax Drive 703-516-2300
Suite 300 *Fax:* 703-516-2345
Arlington, VA 22203 americas.ramboll.com
An international organization that provides services across the markets of buildings, transport, planning and urban design, water, environment and health, energy, and management consulting.

Daniel Kelley, GM, U.S. Energy Operations
Nicole D'Souza, Head Of Communications, U.S.

1879 Raterman Group
9000 Crow Canyon Road 866-545-0111
Suite 364 *Fax:* 925-855-1233
Danville, CA 94506 susan@ratermangroup.com
www.ratermangroup.com

Provides services to clients in the construction, commercial, manufacturing, and public sectors. Examples of services include indoor air quality smapling, mold and moisture investigations, industrial hygiene surveillance, asbestosmanagement services, and more.

Susan Raterman, President

1880 Reclamation Services Unlimited
701 Temple Street 270-754-3976
Central City, KY 42330 800-204-4676
Fax: 270-754-4374
scardwel@muhlon.com
www.total-testing.com

Construction and consulting firm offering services for soils and aggregates, concrete and mortar, steel and welding, and asphalt installation needs. Job sizes range from small residential sites to military bases.

Sue Cardwell, Owner

1881 Redniss and Mead
22 1st Street 203-327-0500
Stamford, CT 06905 800-404-2060
Fax: 203-357-1118
info@rednissmead.com
www.rednissmead.com

Provides land use services to homeowners and developers, ranging from small residential projects to large commercial or institutional developments. The company is comprised of surveyors, civil engineers, and planning consultants whosemission is to allow clients to realize the greatest value from their properties.
Craig J. Flaherty, President & Senior Engineer
Brian P. McMahon, Principal

1882 Remtech Engineers
200 Cobb Parkway North 770-427-7766
Suite 208 800-377-3648
Marietta, GA 30062 *Fax:* 770-427-7001
training@remtech-eng.com
www.remtech-eng.com
Provides services in spill response, environmental remediation, hazardous waste management, industrial cleaning, environmental engineering and disaster response.

Mark D. Ryckman, Founder & CEO
Larry K. Seabolt, Vice President

1883 Resource Concepts Inc (RCI)
340 North Minnesota Street 775-883-1600
Carson City, NV 89703 info@rci-nv.com
www.rci-nv.com
RCI combines technical abilities and working relationships with regulatory agencies to produce project planning and permitting services. Among their capabilities are civil engineering services, natural resource planning, gelogic andgeotechnical services, environmental compliance, surveying, and water rights analysis.

John McLain, Principal Emeritus
Bruce Scott, Principal

1884 Resource Decisions
934 Diamond Street 415-282-5330
San Francisco, CA 94114 mfeldman@resourcedecisions.net
www.resourcedecisions.net
The primary mission of Resource Decisions is to assist clients in fostering the wise allocation of resources. To accomplish this mission, the company provides cost-benefit analysis, statistical analysis, non-market valuation, anregional input-output analysis.

Marvin Feldman, Principal

1885 Resource Technologies Corporation
204 East Calder Way 888-512-2721
Suite 205 *Fax:* 814-237-1769
State College, PA 16801 appraisals@resourcetec.com
www.resourcetec.com

RTC offers mineral appraisals for businesses or landowners who possess assets such as coal, oil and gas, aggregate, or specialty minerals. They provide GIS and digital mapping services, as well as industrial site appraisals, landappraisals, expert witness testimony, and more.
Jeffrey R. Kern, Senior Appraiser

1886 Reston Consulting Group (RCG)
462 Herndon Parkway 703-834-1155
Suite 203 *Fax:* 703-834-3086
Herndon, VA 20170 info@rcg.com
www.rcg.com
RCG provides IT services and solutions to government and commercial clients. They help major telecom carriers apply business

practices and technologies, supporting optical fiber, Internet, telephony, data, CATV, satellite, andterrestrial wireless networks.

Rosemarie Franz, Director

1887 Rizzo Associates
145 Corte Madera Town Center 415-290-1670
Suite 424 info@rizzoassociates.com
Corte Madera, CA 94925 www.rizzoassociates.com
A construction development management company that offers real estate strategy, retail program management, and construction management services to retail, restaurant, and residential clients.

1888 Robert B. Balter Company
18 Music Fair Road 410-363-1555
Owings Mills, MD 21117 *Fax:* 410-363-8073
info@balterco.com
www.balterco.com
A consulting company that offers geotechnical, geoenvironmental, and pavement engineering to public and private sector clients. They have coordinated and managed surveying, civil, and structural engineering projects in a diverse rangeof fields, from airports to water facilities.
Edward Balter, Principal

1889 Rockwood Environmental Services Corporation
50 Kearney Road 781-449-8740
Needham, MA 00249-2508 *Fax:* 781-449-8741
bwhite@rockwood-enviro.com
www.rockwood-enviro.com
Rockwood specializes in solving the problems of hazardous waste management and disposal for New England generators. By shipping wastes directly to ultimate disposal sites on a regular basis, Rockwood reduces current disposal costs andreduces long-term liability exposure.
William A White III, President

1890 Rodriguez, Villacorta and Weiss
8765 Springs Cypress 281-379-4005
Suite L#177 mbrooks@rvw.net
Spring, TX 77379 rvw.net/
Our mission is to provide cost-effective and thorough work product for claims services and loss control. Maximum integration of all in-house and affiliated expertise will guarantee prompt service, nurturing strong client relationshipsbased on dependability, trust and competence.
Richard Rodriguez, Principal Associate

1891 Roux Associates
209 Shafter Street 631 232 2600
Islandia, NY 11749 800-322-Roux
Fax: 631-232-9898
sales@rouxinc.com
www.rouxinc.com
Environmental Consulting and Management.

Steve Sadiker, Vice President
Doug Swanson, CEO/President

1892 S&ME Inc
2724 Discovery Drive 919-872-2660
Suite 120 800-849-2517
Raleigh, NC 27616 www.smeinc.com
Offers engineering, design, environmental sciences, and construction services in the industrial, government, facilities, commercial, landfill, energy, and transportation industries. Their aim is to provide clients with reliable qualitycontrol services.

Matt Ryan, President & CEO
Meredith Keyes, Chief Financial Officer

1893 SCS Engineers
3900 Kilroy Airport Way 562-426-9544
Suite 100 800-767-4727
Long Beach, CA 90806-6816 *Fax:* 562-427-0805
service@scsengineers.com
www.scsengineers.com
Delivers economically and environmentally sound solutions for solid waste management and site remediation projects throughout the world. Services provided include engineering, construction, and contract operations services to privateand public sector clients through a network of more than 70 offices and 800 professional staff working in the US and abroad.

Jim Walsh, President & CEO
Mike McLaughlin, Sr VP, Environmental Service

1894 SGS Accutest Laboratories
201 Route 17 North 201-508-3000
Rutherford, NJ 07070 *Fax:* 732-329-3499
www.accutest.com
Testing laboratory delivering legally defensible data and providing a full range of environmental analytical services to industrial, engineering/consulting and government clients throughout the United States. Testing includes analysisof water, soil, air, waste characterization, energetics and explosives.

Charles Tate, Director of Finance
Charles Hartke, Quality Assurance Director

1895 SGS Galson
6601 Kirkville Road 315-671-3926
East Syracuse, NY 13057 888-432-5227
www.sgsgalson.com
Offers consulting services in industrial hygiene analysis with the aim of preventing hazardous exposures in the workplace. Services offered include sampling and analysis as well as equipment rentals.

Lisa Swab, Operations Manager
Ron McMahan, Development Director

1896 SLC Consultants/Constructors
295 Mill Street 716-433-0776
Lockport, NY 14094 800-932-0157
Fax: 716-433-0802

1897 SLR Environmental Consultants
597-599 Industrial Drive 317-876-3940
Suite 211 americaswebenquiry@slrconsulting.com
Carmel, IN 46032 slrconsulting.com/na/
Environmental consulting firm offering solutions for issues relating to oil and gas, environmental engineering, mining, infrastructure and energy.
Graham Love, Non-Executive Chairman
Neil Penhall, CEO

1898 Safe at Work
2123 University Park Drive 517-349-8066
Suite 130 *Fax:* 517-349-7870
Okemos, MI 48864 support@safe-at-work.com
www.safe-at-work.com
Provides noise control, sound exposure, and hearing loss prevention services and software.

1899 Safina
953 N Plum Grove Road 847-605-8319
Suite A-1 *Fax:* 847-956-8619
Schaumburg, IL 60173 safinacenter.org
Environmental due diligence.

Sanjiv Pillai, General Manager

1900 Sambatek, Inc.
12800 Whitewater Drive 763-476-6010
Suite 300 *Fax:* 763-476-8532
Minnetonka, MN 55343 sambatek@sambatek.com
www.sambatek.com
The environmental services of Sambatek, Inc. help clients achieve compliance and reducing, or eliminate risks and excess costs while protecting the natural environment. They work closely with clients and communities to solveenvironmental challenges facing the business life cycle: asset development, due

diligence reviews, environmental permitting and site assessment, operations optimization, construction, and resoration reuse.

Todd Ullom, Client Service Manager
Elling Olson, Director, Marketing

1901 Schneider Instrument Company
8115 Camargo Road 513-561-6803
74226 Nordheim *Fax:* 513-527-4375
Cincinnati, OH 45243 schneidxcompany@aol.com
www.as-schneider.com

G L Schneider, Vice President

1902 SciComm
7735 Old Georgetown Road 301-652-1900
12th Floor www.scicomm.com
Bethesda, MD 20814
A professional services firm specializing in communications, engineering, environmental, and information management services. Organized to carry out the interest, expertise, and vision of co-founder Laura Chen and Dan Lewis.

Laura Chen, President

1903 SevernTrent Laboratories
4101 Shuffel Drive NW 866-785-5227
North Canton, OH 44720 webmaster@testamericainc.com
www.stl-inc.com
The two compaines merged as Wadsworth/Alert Laboratories in early 1980's and the core business focused on environmental testing, with a specialization in on-site and emergency response projects. Mobile Labs were placed as far north asMichigan, and south to Florida, east to New York, and west to Missouri.
James Hyman, CEO

1904 Shaw Environmental
2103 Research Forest Drive 832-513-1000
The Woodland, TX 77380 general@shawgrp.com
Hazardous waste remediation.
Ron Prann, Division Manager

1905 Shell Engineering and Associates
2403 West Ash Street 573-445-0106
Columbia, MO 65203 *Fax:* 573-445-0137
info@shellengr.com
www.shellengr.com
Shell Engineering provides services firm specializing in communications, engineering, environmental monitoring and engineering. Shell Engineering has completed hundreds of projects since 1975 throughout the United States, Canada.Centeral America, South America, Asia and Africa.
Harvey D Shell, CEO/Chairman
Charles A Shell, President

1906 Sierra Geological and Environmental Consultants
91 South Main Street 800-769-7437
PO Box 136 *Fax:* 616-678-5149
Kent City, MI 49330 info@sierraconsultants.net
www.sierraconsultants.net
A full service environmental consulting firm providing assessment, investigation, and cleanup services throughout Michigan and the Great Lakes States.

1907 Slakey and Associates
375 Village Square 925-254-4164
PO Box 944 *Fax:* 925-254-0679
Orinda, CA 94563
Consulting, civil, mechanical, environmental engineers with 40 years experience in indoor air quality, air pollution control. Design of systems and equipment for collection abatement of fugitive and source missions of dusts, odor andfumes. Industrial clients only.
Philip Slakey, President

1908 Slosky & Company
999 18th Street 303-825-1911
Suite 2400 S *Fax:* 303-892-3882
Denver, CO 80202-2499 Lslosky@slosky.com
www.slosky.com

Full service environmental consulting firm.

Leonard Slosky, President

1909 Snyder Research Company
330Twin Dolphin Drive 408-414-5950
Suite # 101 *Fax:* 408-275-6219
Redwood City, CA 94065 info@sdforum.org
www.sdforum.org

1910 Staunton-Chow Engineers
5 Pen Plaza 212-683-8865
23rd Floor *Fax:* 212-695-6307
New York, NY 10001 www.stauntonchow.com
Known widely as a small premiere multidisciplined engineering/architectural consulting firm providing professional services for new construction, repair, alterations, and maintenance for nearly 50 years.
Kin Chow, President

1911 Strata Environmental Services
110 Perimeter Park 517-676-6900
Suite E *Fax:* 517-676-8834
Knoxville, TN 37922 strata@acd.net
www.strataenv.com
Founded to provide consulting services in geosciences, engineering, air quality, water quality, regulatory compliance, and environmental due diligence.

Charles W. Ferst, CEO

1912 TECHRAD Environmental Services
8440 East Washington Street 405-528-7016
#207 800-375-7016
Chagrin Falls, OH 44023 *Fax:* 405-528-3346
www.testingpartners.com
Analytical laboratory, environmental site assessments, underground storage tank management and remediation, industrial hygiene, stormwater and hazardous waste management, asbestos consulting and analysis and regulatory compliance.
Edward M Wall, President/CEO

1913 THP
100 E Eighth Street 533-241-3222
Ste 300 *Fax:* 513-241-2981
Cincinnati, OH 45202-2129 www.thpltd.com
Engineering traffic and engineering planning consulting firm.
E James Miller, President

1914 Technos
10430 Northwest 31st Terrace 305-718-9594
Miami, FL 33172 *Fax:* 305-718-9621
A geologic and geophysical consulting firm specializing in subsurface site characterization for geotechnical, environmental, and groundwater projects.

Lynn Yuhr, President
Ron Kaufmann, VP

1915 Terracon Consultants, Inc.
10841 South Ridgeview Road 800-593-7777
Olathe, KS 66061 www.terracon.com
Terracon is a geotechnical, environmental, facilities, and materials engineering firm. The company's aim is to provide private and public clients the services they expect at both small- and large-scale projects. Terracon has served adiverse range of markets, including the agricultural, financial, federal, oil and gas, and telecommunications sectors.

M. Gayle Packer, President

1916 **Terranext**
1660 South Albion 303-399-6145
Suite 900 *Fax:* 303-399-6146
Denver, CO 80222 kmartin@terranext.net
www.terranext.net
Provides environmental consulting and engineering services. Focus areas include environmental remediation, science and consulting, environmental engineering, energy reduction and more.

Kim Martin, CPA, President & CEO
Christopher Kinn, P.G., Senior Geophysicist

1917 **Terryn Barill**
301 N Harrison 800-718-6690
Suite 484 *Fax:* 609-243-8703
Princeton, NJ 00854 terryn1@mail.com
Audits/assessments, training, implementation and facilitation.

1918 **Tetra Tech**
3475 East Foothill Boulevard 802-658-3890
Pasadena, CA 91107 *Fax:* 802-658-4247
ard@ardinc.com
www.tetratech.com
Provides consulting and engineering services with a focus on environment. Some of its services include assessment, data analytics, resource management, energy and developments, lab services, geotechnical engineering, constructionmanagement, water management, government consulting and more.

Dan L. Batrack, President & CEO
Steven M. Burdick, Chief Financial Officer

1919 **Theil Consulting**
1136 South Fort Thomas Avenue 859-781-2651
Fort Thomas, KY 41075 *Fax:* 859-781-2356
Experts in industrial process exhausts—especially submicron particles created by heat or other high energy in a process.
Greg Theil, Technical Director
Larry Olson, Sales Manager

1920 **Titan Corp. Ship and Aviation Engineering Group**
11955 Freedom Drive 703-434-4000
Reston, VA 20190 *Fax:* 703-434-5075
www.titan.com
TITAN provides a wide range of engineering and environmental services. Experience includes ISO 14001 and ISO 9000 series and its implementation, pollution prevention planning, hazardous materials/waste management, database management.
Gene W Ray, Chairman of the Board
Lawrence J Delaney, VP of Operations

1921 **Tradet Laboratories**
8 Industrial Park Drive 304-233-9060
Wheeling, WV 26003 *Fax:* 304-233-9063
info@tra-det.com
www.tra-det.com
Coal, analytical and environmental services.
G William Kald, President

1922 **Transviron**
1624 York Road 410-321-6961
Lutherville, MD 21093 *Fax:* 410-494-9321
transviron.com

1923 **Trinity Consultants**
12770 Merit Drive 972-661-8100
Suite 900 800-229-6655
Dallas, TX 75251 *Fax:* 972-385-9203
information@trinityconsultants.com
www.trinityconsultants.com
An environmental consulting company that assists industrial facilities with issues related to regulatory compliance and environmental management. Founded in 1974, this nationwide firm has particular expertise in air quality issues.Trinity also sells environmental software and professional education. T3, a Trinity Consultants Company, provides EH&S management information systems (EMIS) implementation and integration services.

Jay Hofmann, President/CEO
Dave Larsen, CFO

1924 **Troppe Environmental Consulting**
24 N. High Street 330-375-1900
Akron, OH 44308 *Fax:* 330-375-1904
Provides level I and level II assessments, water and oil testing, and amtm standards.
Fred Troppe, President

1925 **Versar**
6850 Versar Center 703-750-3000
Springfield, VA 22151 800-283-7727
Fax: 703-642-6807
info@versar.com
www.versar.com
Versar is a public-held, international professional services firm that applies technology, science, and management skills to enhance its customers' performance.
Anthony L Otten, CEO

1926 **Water and Air Research**
6821 SW Archer Road 352-372-1500
Gainesville, FL 32608 800-242-4927
Fax: 352-378-1500
www.waterandair.com
Mission is to be an international environmental consulting firm that achieves extraordinary results by partnering with clients that to make informed and responsible decisions regarding the environment.

William C Zegel, President
William Kinser, Director/Manager

1927 **Waypoint Analytical**
2790 Whitten Road 901-213-2400
Memphis, TN 38133 800-264-4522
Fax: 901-213-2440
supportttn@waypointanalytical.com
www.waypointanalytical.com
Agricultural laboratory group specializing in soil tests.
Michael Sterling, Chief Financial Officer

1928 **Weavertown Group Optimal Technologies**
2 Dorrington Road 724-746-4850
Carnegie, PA 15106 800-746-4850
Fax: 724-746-9024
www.weavertown.com
We are an environmental engineering and consulting firm.
Dawn Fuchs, President

1929 **Wenck Associates**
1800 Pioneer Creek Center 763-479-4200
PO Box 249 800-472-2232
Maple Plain, MN 55359 *Fax:* 763-479-4242
wenckmp@wenck.com
www.wenck.com
Our mission is to provide our customers strategic advice and technical excellence.

1930 **Weston Solutions, Inc**
1400 Weston Way 610-701-3000
Box 2653 800-7WE-STON
West Chester, PA 19380-903 *Fax:* 610-701-3186
contactweston@westonsolutions.com
www.westonsolutions.com
Weston is a leading infrastructure redevelopment services firm delivering integrated environmental engineering solutions to industry and government worldwide. With an emphasis on creating lasting economic value for its clients, thecompany provides services in site remediation, redevelopment, infrastructure operations and knowledge management.
George Mackenzie, Chairman
William L. Robertson, CEO/President

1931 **Wilcox Environmental Engineering**
1552 Main Street 317-472-0999
Suite 100 *Fax:* 317-472-0993
Speedway, IN 46224 info@wilcoxenv.com
www.wilcoxenv.com

Provides a full range of environmental services in the areas of engineering, geology, chemistry, environmental science, air analysis, industrial compliance and hygiene, and health and safety. Services include site investigation andcorrective action, solid and hazardous waste management and more.
Steve Wilcox, President
Jim Nance, VP, Industrial Services

1932 **Wood Group**
1979 Lakeside Parkway 770-688-2500
Suite 400 www.woodplc.com
Atlanta, GA 30084

Wood provides services at various stages of the asset life cycle. Their services are used in the oil, gas, and power markets, as well as the environment and infrastructure, clean energy, mining, nuclear, and general industrial sectors.
Robin Watson, Chief Executive Officer
David Kemp, Chief Financial Officer

1933 **Zapata Engineering, Blackhawk Division**
6302 Fairview Road 704-358-8240
Suite 600 888-529-7243
Charlotte, NC 28210 *Fax:* 704-358-8342
zapata@zapatainc.com
www.zapatainc.com

High quality geophysical contracting and consulting services over the full spectrum of geophysical technologies, and to apply the geophysical technologies to several cross-cutting areas of engineering and exploration.
Manuel L. Zapata, P.E., President

Environmental Health

Associations

1934 **ALS Environmental**
10450 Stancliff Road 800-695-7222
Suite 210 www.caslab.com
Houston, TX 77099
Areas of expertise and services include environmental testing of air, water, soil, hazardous waste, sediments and tissues; process and quality control testing; analytical method development; sampling and mobile laboratory services; andconsulting and data management services.

Raj Naran, CEO & Managing Director
Bruce Phillips, Chair

1935 **Acadia Environmental Society**
626 Old Students' Union Building 902-585-2149
Wolfville, NS B4P-2R6 *Fax:* 902-542-3901
Provides resources on environmental issues. The Society's goal is to encourage and help the Acadia community to adopt and maintain environmentally sound and sustainable practices.
Hillary Barter, Coordinator

1936 **Acid Rain Foundation**
11 Bay St 919-828-9443
Suite 1B *Fax:* 919-515-3593
Easton, MD 21601
James E. Price, President

1937 **Action on Smoking and Health (ASH)**
1250 Connecticut Avenue NW 202-659-4310
7th Floor *Fax:* 202-289-7166
Washington, DC 20036 info@ash.org
ash.org
Organized to use the power of the law to protect the rights of nonsmokers. Emphasis is placed on legal efforts to protect nonsmokers and to get courts to support the rights of nonsmokers. Also conducts educational and awarenesscampaigns regarding the problem of smoking and the rights of nonsmokers.
Laurent Huber, Executive Director
Chris Bostic, Deputy Director, Policy

1938 **Advanced Foods & Materials Network**
8911 Jubilee Rd E 519-822-6253
Suite 310 *Fax:* 519-824-8453
Summerland, BC V0H-1Z5
Canada's front line of research and development in the area of advanced foods and bio-materials, including new, low-cost antibiotics, improved frozen food quality, and fast healing wound dressings.
Dr. Larry Milligan, Chairman
Rickey Yada, Scientific Director

1939 **Agency for Toxic Substances and Disease Registry**
Centers for Disease Control and Prevention
4770 Buford Highway NE 770-488-0706
Atlanta, GA 30341-3717 800-232-4636
Fax: 770-488-1544
www.atsdr.cdc.gov
This agency provides leadership and direction to programs and activities designed to protect both the public and workers from exposure or adverse health effects of hazardous substances in storage sites or released in fires, explosions,or transportation accidents. The agency also collects, maintains, analyzes and disseminates information relating to serious diseases, mortality and human exposure to toxic or hazardous substances.

Patrick Breysse, Director
Christopher M Reh, Associate Director

1940 **Air & Waste Management Association**
Koppers Building 412-232-3444
436 Seventh Avenue, Suite 2100 800-270-3444
Pittsburgh, PA 15219 *Fax:* 412-232-3450
info@awma.org
www.awma.org
Professional development organization providing a forum for the exchange of information, networking, public education, and outreach to over 5,000 environmental professionals in 65 countries.

Stephanie Glyptis, Executive Director
Tracy Fedkoe, Director, Marketing

1941 **Alliance for Acid Rain Control and Energy Policy**
444 N Capitol Street 202-624-5475
Suite 602 *Fax:* 202-508-3829
Washington, DC 20001

1942 **Alternatives for Community and Environment**
2201 Washington Street 617-442-3343
Suite 302 *Fax:* 617-442-2425
Roxbury, MA 00211 info@ace-ej.org
www.ace-ej.org
ACE is a community-based, nonprofit, environmental justice, law and education center. ACE works in partnership with community groups from low income communities and communities of color to help them address their environmental andenvironmental heath issues by providing free legal, educational and organizing services.

Kalila Barnett, Executive Director
Eugene B Benson, Program Director

1943 **American Academy of Environmental Medicine (AAE)**
6505 E. Central Avenue 316-684-5500
Suite 296 *Fax:* 316-684-5709
Wichita, KS 67206 defox@aaemonline.org
www.aaemonline.org
The Academy focuses on the study of interactions between human individuals and their environment, and the environmental impact on human health. The Academy is comprised primarily of medical professionals who sponsor publications,seminars and courses. A newsletter and journal are among the organization's publications.
De Rodgers-Fox, Executive Director

1944 **American Association for the Support of Ecological Initiatives**
150 Coleman Road 860-346-2967
Middletown, CT 00645 *Fax:* 860-347-8459
Wwasch@wesleyan.edu
www.wesleyan.edu
AASEI is a US 501 nonprofit organization which suports international environmental initiatives in Russian Nature Reserves. In cooperation sith Russia and foreign scientists, students, and universities, AASEI organizes scientificresearch projects, academic internships, work camps, environmental exchanges, and eco-tourism. Our aim is to provide practical support to Russina Reserves, expand opportunities for international scientific research, and promote internationalunderstanding.
Brendan Sweeney, President/Founder
Stephanie Hitztaler, Executive Director

1945 **American Association of Poison Control Centers (AAPCC)**
515 King Street 800-222-1222
Suite 510 info@aapcc.org
Alexandria, VA 22314 www.aapcc.org
A nonprofit national organization that represents the poison control centers of the United States and the interests of poison prevention and treatment of poisoning.

Steve Kaminski, Executive Director
Leslie Sandler, VP, Certification

1946 **American Board of Environmental Medicine (ABEM)**
65 Wehrle Drive 716-833-2213
Buffalo, NY 14225 *Fax:* 716-833-2244
www.americanboardofenvironmentalmedicine.org
To establish and maintain the educational and testing criteria for board certification to ensure optimal standard and quality of the environmental physician.
Dr. Phil Ranhein, President

1947 **American Board of Industrial Hygiene (ABIH)**
6005 W St Joseph Highway 517-321-2638
Suite 300 *Fax:* 517-321-4624
Lansing, MI 48917 abih@abih.org
www.abih.org
Certifies professionals in the practice of industrial hygiene. Responsible for ensuring high-quality certification application and examination processes, certifcation maintenance and ethics governance and enforcement.
Ulric K. Chung, Chief Executive Officer
Ron Drafta, Examination Contact

1948 **American Cancer Society**
PO Box 22718 800-227-2345
Oklahoma, OK 73123-1718 www.cancer.org
The American Cancer Society is the nationwide, community-based, voluntary health organization dedicated to eliminating cancer as a major health problem by preventing cancer, saving lives, and diminishing suffering from cancer throughresearch, education, advocacy and service.
John R Seffrin PhD, CEO

1949 **American Chemistry Council**
700 Second St NE 202-249-7000
Washington, DC 20002 *Fax:* 202-249-6100
www.americanchemistry.com
Industry organization working to enable a more sustainable future, through advocacy, member engagement, communications, and scientific research.

Calvin M. Dooley, President & CEO
Raymond J. O'Bryan, CFO & CAO

1950 **American College of Occupational and Environmental Medicine (ACOEM)**
25 NW Point Blvd 847-818-1800
Suite 700 *Fax:* 847-818-9266
Elk Grove Village, IL 60007-1030 www.acoem.org
Made up of physicians in industry, government, academia, private practice and the military, who promote the health of workers through preventive medicine, clinical care, research and education.
Bill Bruce, Executive Director
Lucy Free, Director, Governance

1951 **American Conference of Governmental Industrial Hygienists**
1330 Kemper Meadow Drive 513-742-2020
Cincinnati, OH 45240 *Fax:* 513-742-3355
mail@acgih.org
www.acgih.org
ACGIH is a member-based organization and community of professionals that advances worker health and saftey through education and the development and dissemination of scientific and technical knowledge.
90 pages Magazine
Sheryl A. Milz, Chair
Alan Rossner, Treasurer

1952 **American Council on Science and Health**
1995 Broadway 212-362-7044
Suite 202 866-905-2694
New York, NY 10023-5882 *Fax:* 212-362-4919
acsh@acsh.org
www.acsh.org
A consumer education consortium concerned with issues related to food, nutrition, chemicals, pharmaceuticals, lifestyle, the environment and health.

Josh Bloom, Acting President
Alex Berezow, VP, Scientific Affairs

1953 **American Indian Environmental Office**
1200 Pennsylvania Avenue NW 202-564-0303
Washington, DC 20460 *Fax:* 202-564-0298
www.epa.gov/indian
Coordinates the US environmental Protection Agency-wide effort to strengthen public health and environmental protection in Indian Country, with a special emphasis on building Tribal capacity to administer their own environmentalprograms.
Felicia Wright, Acting Director

1954 **American Industrial Hygiene Association (AIHA)**
3141 Fairview Park Drive 703-849-8888
Suite 777 *Fax:* 703-207-3561
Falls Church, VA 22042 infonet@aiha.org
www.aiha.org
To promote the highest quality of occupational and environmental health and safety within the workplace and the community through advocacy and the provision of services and tools to enhance the professional practice of our members.
Lawrence D. Sloan, Chief Executive Officer
Peter Hanley, Managing Dir., Technology

1955 **American Institute of Biological Sciences**
1800 Alexander Bell Drive 703-674-2500
Suite 400 *Fax:* 703-674-2509
Reston, VA 20191 www.aibs.org
AIBS facilities communication and interactions among biologists, biological societies, and biological disciplines in order to serve and advance the interests of organismal and integrative biology in the broader scientific community andother components of society on issues related to research, education, and public policy.
Joseph Travis, President
Karen Schmaling, Vice President

1956 **American Lung Association**
55 W. Wacker Drive 212-315-8700
Suite 1150 *Fax:* 202-452-1805
Chicago, IL 60601 www.lungusa.org
The American Lung Association has been fighting lung disease in all its forms with emphasis on environmental health, asthma, and tobacco control. The work continues as they strive to make breathing easier for everyone througheducation, community service, advocacy and research programs.
Kathryn A. Forbes, Chair
John F. Emanuel, Vice Chair

1957 **American Medical Association**
330 N. Wabash Ave. 312-464-5000
Chicago, IL 60611-5885 800-621-8335
Fax: 312-464-4184
www.ama-assn.org
Mission: To promote the art and science of medicine and the betterment of public health.
Jmaes L. Madara, CEO/Executive Vice President

1958 **American Public Health Association**
800 I Street NW 202-777-2742
Washington, DC 20001 *Fax:* 202-777-2534
comments@apha.org
www.apha.org
Aims to protect all Americans and their communities from preventable, serious health threats and strives to assure community-based health promotion and disease prevention activities and preventive health services are universallyaccessible in the United States.

Georges C Benjamin, Executive Director
Kemi Oluwafemi, Finance & System Controller

1959 **American Society for Microbiology**
1752 N Street NW 202-737-3600
Washington, DC 20036-2904 *Fax:* 202-942-9333
service@asmusa.org
www.asm.org

A scientific society of individuals interested inthe microbiological sciences. The mission is to advance microbiological sciences through the pursuit of scientific knowledge and dissemination of the results of fundamental and appliedresearch.
43,000 Members
Lynn Enquist, President
Joseph M. Campos, Secretary

1960 **American Society of Safety Engineers (ASSP)**
520 N. Northwest Hwy 847-699-2929
Park Ridge, IL 60068 *Fax:* 847-768-3434
customerservice@asse.org
www.asse.org

The oldest and largest professional safety organization whose members are dedicated to creating safer work environments and protecting people, property, and the environment.
38,000 Members
Jennifer McNelly, Chief Executive Officer
Tim Fisher, Standards

1961 **Appalachian States Low-Level Radioactive Waste Commission**
Pennsylvania DEP/BRP 717-783-2300
400 Market Street, 13th Floor kmcginty@state.pa.us
Harrisburg, PA 17101 www.dep.state.pa.us

The commission was ratified by Maryland, Delaware, Pennsylvania and West Virginia to assure intertstate cooperation for the proper packaging and transportation of low-level radioactive waste. Pennsylvania is the host state and handlesthe administrative duties of the commission at this time.

Darrin Bodner, Executive Deputy Secretary
Chris Abruzzo, Acting Secretary

1962 **Asbestos Information Association of North America**
PO Box 2227 703-560-2980
Arlington, VA 22202 *Fax:* 703-560-2981
aiabjpigg@aol.com

The Asbestos Information Association/North America was founded in 1970 to represent the interest of the asbestos industry and to collect and disseminate information about asbestos and asbestos products, with emphasis on safety, health,and environmental issues. The Association appears before Federal regulatory bodies and works with Government agencies to develop and implement standards for worker protection.

Bob Pigg, President

1963 **Asian Pacific Environmental Network**
426 17th Street 510-834-8920
Suite 500 *Fax:* 510-834-8926
Oakland, CA 94612 info@apen4ej.org
www.apen4ej.org

The Asian Pacific Environmental Network (APEN) empowers low-income Asian Pacific Islander (API) communities to take action on environmental and social justice issues. APEN builds organizations in dis-empowered API communities todevelop lasting capacity of the community to achieve solutions to problems affecting people's lives.
Roger Kim, Executive Director
Rachel Shigekane, Board Secretary

1964 **Association for Environmental Health and Sciences Foundation**
150 Fearing Street 413-549-5170
Suite 21 *Fax:* 413-549-0579
Amherst, MA 01002 paul@aehs.com
www.aehsfoundation.org

The AEHS Foundation was created to facilitate communication among professionals concerned with soil protection and water assessment.
600 members
Paul Kostecki, Executive Director
Ed Calabrese, Editor-in-Chief

1965 **Association of American Pesticide Control Officials**
PO Box 466 302-422-8152
Milford, DE 19963 *Fax:* 302-422-2435
www.aapco.org

Organization formed to provide a rational forum and representation for state pesticide control officials in the development, implementation, and communication of parties and programs related to the sale, transport, application anddisposal of pesticide.

Jeff Comstock, President
Tim Drake, President-Elect

1966 **Association of Battery Recyclers**
PO Box 290286 813-626-6151
Tampa, FL 33687 *Fax:* 813-622-8388
info@batteryrecyclers.com
www.batteryrecyclers.com

The Association of Battery Recyclers is a non-profit trade association. ABR strives to keep its members abreast on environmental and health matters and also provides a means for communication with government officials on issuesaffecting the lead recycling industry.
Joyce Morales, Contact

1967 **Association of Occupational and Environmental Clinics (AOEC)**
1010 Vermont Ave. NW 202-347-4976
#513 888-347-2632
Washington, DC 20005 *Fax:* 202-347-4950
aoec@aoec.org
www.aoec.org

Non-profit organization of over 60 clinics and 250 individuals, committed to improving the practice of occupational and environmental health through information sharing and collaborative research.
$500/Year
Ingrid Denis, Program Coordinator
Katherine H Kirkland, Executive Director

1968 **Association of State and Territorial Health Officials**
2231 Crystal Drive 202-371-9090
Suite 450 *Fax:* 571-527-3189
Arlington, VA 22202 pjarris@astho.org
www.astho.org

Dedicated to formulating and influencing sound public health policy, and to assuring excellence in state-based public health practice.
Jewel Mullen, President
Edward Ehlinger, President-Elect

1969 **Asthma and Allergy Foundation of America**
8201 Corporate Drive 202-466-7643
Suite 1000 800-727-8462
Landover, MD 20785 *Fax:* 202-466-8940
info@aafa.org
www.aafa.org

AAFA provides practical information, community based services and support through a national network of chapters and support groups. AAFA develops health education, organizes state and national advocacy efforts and funds research tofind better treatments and cures.
William Mclin, M. Ed., President
Jacqui Vok, Programs & Services Director

1970 **Beyond Pesticides**
701 E Street SE 202-543-5450
Suite 200 *Fax:* 202-543-4791
Washington, DC 20003 info@beyondpesticides.org
www.beyondpesticides.org

Beyond Pesticides works with allies in protecting public health and the environment to lead the transition to a world free of toxic pesticides.
Jay Feldman, Executive Director
Drew Toher, Director, Policy

1971 Bio Integral Resource Center
PO Box 7414 510-524-2567
Berkeley, CA 94707 *Fax:* 510-524-1758
birc@igc.org
www.birc.org
The goal of the Bio Integral Resources Center is to reduce pesticide use by educating the public about effective, less toxic alternatives for pest problems.
Dr. William Quarles, Executive Director

1972 BlueGreen Alliance
1300 Godward Street NE 612-466-4479
Suite 2625 info@bluegreenalliance.org
Minneapolis, MN 55413 bluegreenalliance.org
The BlueGreen Alliance unites America's largest labor unions and its most influential environmental organizations to solve today's environmental challenges in ways that create and maintain quality jobs and build a stronger, fairereconomy.
Kim Glas, Executive Director
Eric Steen, Director of Communications

1973 Center for Health, Environment and Justice (CHEJ)
7139 Shreve Road 703-237-2249
Falls Church, VA 22046 *Fax:* 703-237-8389
info@chej.org
www.chej.org
Works to build healthy communities, with social justice, economic well-being, and democratic governance.
Sharon Franklin, Chief of Operations
Stephen Lester, Science Director

1974 Center for Science in the Public Interest
1220 L St. N. W. 202-332-9110
Suite 300 *Fax:* 202-265-4954
Washington, DC 20005 cspi@cspinet.org
www.cspinet.org
Mission: To provide useful, objective information to the public and policymakers and to conduct research on food, alcohol, health, the environment, and other issues related to science and technology; to represent the citizen'sinterests before regulatory, judicial and legislative bodies on food, alcohol, health, the environment, and other issues; and to ensure that science and technology are used for the public good and to encourage scientists to engage in public-interestactivities.
Michael F. Jacobson, Executive Director
Don Allen, Director of Finance

1975 Center for the Evaluation of Risks to Human Reproduction
110 Maryland Avenue NE 202-543-4033
Suite 402 *Fax:* 202-543-8797
Washington, DC 20002 cehn@cehn.org
The Center's mission includes the following: to provide timely and unbiased, scientifically sound assessments of reproductive health hazards associated with human exposure to naturally occurring and man-made chemicals; to make theseassessments readily available to the public, to state and federal agencies and to the scientific community; and to build an electronic resource for providing, or directing one to, information of public interest concerning human reproductive health.
Dr. Michael D Shelby

1976 Centers for Disease Control & Prevention
National Center for Environmental Health
1600 Clifton Road 800-232-4636
Atlanta, GA 30329-4027 *Fax:* 800-232-6348
www.cdc.gov/nceh
To provide national leadership, through science and service, to promote health and quality of life by preventing and controlling disease and death resulting from interactions between people and their environment.
Robin Ikeda, Director
Donna Knutson, Deputy Director

1977 Chemical Injury Information Network
PO Box 301 406-547-2255
White Sulphur Springs, MT 59645 *Fax:* 406-547-2455
chemicalinjury@ciin.org
www.ciin.org
Nonprofit tax-exempt support and advocacy organization run by the chemically injured for the benefit of the chemically injured. CIIN serves an international membership, and focuses primarily on eductaion, credible multiple sensitivityresearch and the empowerment of the chemically injured.
Cinthia Wilson, Executive Director
Al Gore, Vice President

1978 Chlorine Institute
1300 Wilson Boulevard 703-894-4140
Suite 525 *Fax:* 703-894-4130
Arlington, VA 22209 info@cl2.com
www.chlorineinstitute.org
Exists to support the chlor-alkali industry and serve the public by fostering continuous improvements to safety and the protection of human health and the environment connected with the production, distribution and use of chlorine,sodium and potassium hydoroxides, and sodium hypochlorite; and the distribution and use of hydrogen chloride.
196 Members
Frank Reiner, President
Robyn Kinsley, VP, Transportation

1979 Commonweal
PO Box 316 415-868-0970
Bolinas, CA 94924 commonweal@commonweal.org
www.commonweal.org
A health and environment research institute that conducts programs that contribute to human and ecosystem health. The Commonweal Health and Environment Program focuses on environmental contaminants.
Michael Lerner, President & Co-Founder
Arlene Allsman, Chief Operating Officer

1980 Communities for a Better Environment (CBE)
6325 Pacific Blvd. 323-826-9771
Suite 300 *Fax:* 323-588-7079
Huntington Park, CA 90255 www.cbecal.org
Works to achieve environmental health and justice in California by building grassroots power in and with communities of color and working-class communities.
Darryl Molina Sarmiento, Executive Director
Julia May, Senior Scientist

1981 Community-Based Hazard Management Program
George Perkins Marsh Institute
Clark University 508-793-7711
950 Main Street otaylor@clarku.edu
Worcester, MA 00161 www.clarku.edu
The Community-Based Hazardous Management Program (formerly the Childhood Cancer Research Institute) is engaged in capacity building in communities affected by nuclear weapons production and testing and also specializes in radiationhealth risk assessment and management.
Davis Baird, Vice President

1982 Cork Forest Conservation Alliance
565 Oxford Street 503-931-9690
Salem, OR 97302 info@corkforest.org
corkforest.org
The Cork Forest Conservation Alliance campaigns globally for the protection and preservation of the Mediterranean cork forests, its inhabitants and biodiversity, through education, direct

action, and partnerships with communities,businesses and governments.

Patrick Spencer, Executive Director

1983 **Corporate Accountability International**
10 Milk Street 617-695-2525
Suite 610 800-688-8797
Boston, MA 00210 *Fax:* 617-695-2626
info@corporateaccountability.org
www.corporateaccountability.org
Aims to stop large corporations from damaging democracy, human rights, and the environment.

Patti Lynn, Executive Director
Melissa Hale Woodman, Dir., Strategic Partnerships

1984 **Council of State and Territorial Epidemiologists (CSTE)**
2872 Woodcock Boulevard 770-458-3811
Suite 250 *Fax:* 770-458-8516
Atlanta, GA 30341 www.cste.org
CSTE promotes the effective use of epidemiologic data to guide public health practice and improve health. CSTE accomplishes this by supporting the use of effective public health surveillance and good epidemiologic practice throughtraining, capacity development, and peer consultation, developing standards for practice, and advocating for resources and scientifically based policy.
Joseph McLaughlin, President
Alfred DeMaria, Vice President

1985 **Dangerous Goods Advisory Council**
7501 Greenway Center Drive 202-289-4550
Suite 760 *Fax:* 202-289-4074
Greenbelt, MD 20770 info@dgac.org
www.hmac.org
DGAC, also known as the Hazardous Materials Advisory Council, promotes improvement in the safe transportation of hazardous materials/dangerous goods globally by: providing education, assistance, and information to the private andpublic sectors; through our unique status with regulatory bodies; and the adversity and technical strengths of our membership.

Vaughn Arthur, President
Barbara Lantry-Miller, Chairman

1986 **Department of Commerce: National Oceanic & Atmospheric Administration**
1401 Constitution Avenue NW www.noaa.gov
Room 5128
Washington, DC 20230
The mission of the NOAA is to understand changes in climate, weather, oceans and coasts; to share that knowledge and information with the public; and to foster the conservation and management of coastal and marine ecosystems. Theagency studies the structure and behaviour of the ocean, atmosphere, and related ecosystems.

Neil Jacobs, Assistant Secretary
Craig McLean, Chief Scientist

1987 **Earth Regeneration Society**
1442A Walnut Street 510-527-9716
57 www.newenergymovement.org
Berkeley, CA 94709
The Earth Regeneration Society does research and education on climate change, ozone, and pollution, and calls for full employment and full social support based on surival programs and national and international networking.
Alden Bryant, President

1988 **EarthSave International**
20555 Devonshire St. 415-234-0829
Suite 105 *Fax:* 818-337-1957
Chatsworth, CA 91311 info@earthsave.org
www.earthsave.org
Educates people on the powerful effects that our food choices have on the environment, our health, and all life on Earth, and supports people in moving toward a plant-based diet. Founded by John Robbins, author of Diet for a NewAmerica.

Patricia Carney, Executive Director

1989 **Environmental Defense Fund (EDF)**
257 Park Avenue South 212-505-2100
New York, NY 10010 *Fax:* 212-505-2375
www.edf.org
Dedicated to protecting the environmental rights of all people, including future generations. Among these rights are clean air, clean water, healthy, nourishing food and a flourishing ecosystem. Advocates solutions based on science,even when it leads in unfamiliar directions. Works to create solutions that win lasting political, economic and social support because they are bipartisan, efficient and fair.

Fred Krupp, President
Catherine Nardone, Chief Development Officer

1990 **Environmental Hazards Management Institute (EHMI)**
10 New Market Road 603-868-1496
Durham, NH 03821 *Fax:* 603-868-1547
info@ehmi.org
www.ehmi.org
An independent, nonprofit organization dedicated to understanding enhancement and preservation of the environment. A catalyst for informed environmental decision making by gathering, refining, and disseminating objective information toall stakeholders with emphasis on the role played by individuals and communities of individuals.

Alan John Borner, Founder & CEO

1991 **Environmental Health Coalition**
2727 Hoover Avenue 619-474-0220
Suite 202 *Fax:* 619-474-1210
National City, CA 91950 ehc@environmentalhealth.org
www.environmentalhealth.org
One of the oldest and most effective grassroots organizations in the US, using social change strategies to achive environmental and social justice. We believe that justice is accomplished by empowered communities acting together tomake social change. We organize and advocate to protect public health and the environment threatened by toxic pollution. EHC supports broad efforts that create a just society which foster a healthy and sustainable quality of life.
Margaret Godshalk, President
Enrique Medina, Vice President

1992 **Environmental Health Education Center**
655 West Lombard Street 410-706-1849
Room 665 *Fax:* 410-706-0295
Baltimore, MD 21201
Mission: Supporting nursing professionals seeking accurate, timely and credible scientific information on environmental health and nursing. The ultimate goal is to prevent environmental disease by increasing the numbers of nursingprofessionals who can recognize environmental etiologies and risk factors of disease, promote health through risk reduction and control strategies and empower individuals, families and communities through partnering, advocacy and education.
Nsedu Obot Witherspoon, MPH, Executive Director
Kristie Trousdale, MPH, Program Associate

1993 **Environmental Health Network**
PO Box 1155 415-541-5075
Larkspur, CA 94977-1155 www.ehnca.org
Nonprofit, volunteer organization, whose main goal is to promote public awareness of evironmental sensitivities and causative factors. EHN's focus is on issues of access and developments relating to the health and welfare of theenvironmentally sensitive.
Janet Harmon, Manager

1994 **Environmental Health Strategy Center**
565 Congress St. 207-699-5795
Suite 204 *Fax:* 207-699-5790
Portland, ME 00410 info@preventharm.org
www.preventharm.org
The Environmental Health Strategy Center works to protect human health by reducing exposure to toxic chemicals, expanding the use of safer alternatives, and building partnerships that focus on the environment as a public healthpriority.
Michael Belliveau, Executive Director
Jenny Rottman, Managing Director

1995 **Environmental Information Association (EIA)**
6935 Wisconsin Avenue 301-961-4999
Suite 306 888-343-4342
Chevy Chase, MD 20815-6112 *Fax:* 301-961-3094
info@eia-usa.org
www.eia-usa.org
A nonprofit organization dedicated to providing environmental information to individuals, members, and industry. They specialize in the dissemination of information about the abatement of asbestos and lead based paint, and about safetyand health issues, analytical issues and environmental site assessments.
Brent Kynoch, Managing Director
Kelly Rutt, Director, Development

1996 **Environmental Integrity Project**
1000 Vermont Avenue NW 202-296-8800
Suite 1100 *Fax:* 202-296-8822
Washington, DC 20005 info@environmentalintegrity.org
environmentalintegrity.org
The Environmental Integrity Project is a nonpartisan, nonprofit watchdog organization that advocates for effective enforcement of environmental laws comprised of former EPA enforcement attorneys, public interest lawyers, analysts,investigators, and community organizers.
John Dawes, President
Wesley P. Warren, Treasurer

1997 **Environmental Justice Resource Center**
223 James P. Brawley Drive SW 404-880-6911
Atlanta, GA 30314 *Fax:* 404-880-6909
ejrc@cau.edu
Since 1994, a research, policy and information clearinghouse on issues related to environmental justice, race and the environment, civil rights, facility siting, land use planning, brownfields, transportation equity, suburban sprawland Smart Growth. The overall goal of the center is to assist, support, train and educate people of color, students, professionals and grassroots community leaders with the goal of facilitating their inclusion into the mainstream of environmentaldecision-making.
Robert D Bullard PhD, Director

1998 **Environmental Mutagenesis and Genomics Society**
12627 San Jose Blvd 904-289-3410
Suite 202 bobbk@emgs-us.org
Jacksonville, FL 32223 www.emgs-us.org
The Environmental Mutagenesis and Genomics Society's mission is to foster scientific research and education on the causes and mechanistic bases of DNA damage and repair, mutagenesis, heritable effects, epigenetic alterations in genomefunction, and their relevance to disease; to promote the application and communication of this knowledge to genetic toxicology testing, risk assessment, and regulatory policy-making to protect human health and the environment.
Bob Bevans-Kerr, Executive Director
Thomas E. Wilson, President

1999 **Environmental Protection Agency (EPA)**
1200 Pennsylvania Avenue NW 202-564-4700
Washington, DC 20460 www.epa.gov
EPA's mission is to protect human health and to safeguard the natural environment - air, water and land - upon which life depends. This agency also ensures that communities, individuals, businesses, and governments have access toaccurate information about human health and environmental risks.
Andrew Wheeler, Administrator
Ryan Jackson, Chief of Staff

2000 **Environmental Resource Center**
471 Washington Ave. N 208-726-4333
PO Box 819 *Fax:* 208-726-1531
Ketchum, ID 83340 molly@ercsv.org
www.ercsv.org
An oraganization offering environmental education for the community.
Kingsley Murphy, Chair
Michael Schlatter, Treasurer

2001 **Environmental Resources Management**
3352 128th Avenue 616-399-3500
Holland, MI 49424 *Fax:* 616-399-3777
www.erm.com
Provides environmental, health, safety, risk, and social consulting services, including sustainability planning, health and safety, risk assessment, data management, asset management, and environmental compliance.
Keryn James, Chief Executive Officer
David McArthur, Chief Operating Officer

2002 **Environmental Safety**
1700 North Moore Street 703-527-8300
Suite 2000 (20th Floor) *Fax:* 703-527-8383
Arlington, VA 22209 info@ashoka.org
www.ashoka.org
Ashoka's mission is to shape a citizen sector that is entrepreneurial, productive and globally integrated, and to develop the profession of social entrepreneurship around the world. Ashoka identifies and invests in leading socialentrepreneurs-extraordinary individuals and unprecedented ideas for change in their communities-supporting the individual, idea and institution through all phases of their career. Once elected to Ashoka, Fellows benefit from being part of the globalfellowship for life.
Dr. Iman Bibars, Regional Director
Romanus Berg, CIO

2003 **Environmental Technology Council**
1112 16th Street NW 202-783-0870
Suite 420 *Fax:* 202-737-2038
Washington, DC 20036 www.etc.org
Trade association of commercial firms that recycle, treat and dispose of industrial and hazardous wastes; and firms involved in cleanup of contaminated sites.
David Case, Executive Director

2004 **Environmental Working Group**
1436 U Street Northwest 202-667-6982
Suite 100 *Fax:* 202-232-2592
Washington, DC 20009 www.ewg.org
Mission: To use the power of public information to protect public health and the environment
Ken Cook, President
Heather White, Executive Director

2005 **Environmental and Occupational Health Science Institute**
Rutgers University
170 Frelinghuysen Road 848-445-0200
Piscataway, NJ 00885 *Fax:* 732-445-0131
www.eohsi.rutgers.edu
Environmental and Occupational Health Sciences Institute sponsors research, education and service programs in a setting that fosters interaction among experts in environmental health, toxicology, occupational health, exposureassessment, public policy and health education. The Institute also serves as an unbiased source of expertise about environmental problems for communities, employers and government in all areas of occupational and environmental health, toxicology andrisk assessment.
Howard Kipen, M.D, MPH, Associate Director
Kenneth Reuhl PhD, Interim Director

2006 Food Safety and Inspection Service
Food Safety Education Office
1400 Independence Avenue SW — 202-720-7025
Washington, DC 20250-3700 — *Fax:* 202-205-0158
fsis.webmaster@usda.gov
www.fsis.usda.gov
The Food Safety and Inspection Services (FSIS) is the public health agency in the U.S. Department of Agriculture responsible for ensuring that the nation's commercial supply of meat, poultry, and egg products is safe, wholesome, andcorrectly labeled and packaged.
Alfred V. Almanza, Deputy Under Secretary
Carmen Rottenberg, Deputy Administrator

2007 Food and Drug Administration
US Department of Health and Human Services
10903 New Hampshire Avenue — 888-463-6332
Silver Spring, MD 20993 — www.fda.gov
The FDA is responsible for protecting the public health by assuring the safety, efficacy, and security of human and veterinary drugs, biological products, medical devices, our nation's food supply, cosmetics, and products that emitradiation.
Scott Gottlieb, Commissioner
Anna Abram, Deputy Commissioner

2008 Friends of the River
1418 20th Street — 916-442-3155
Suite 100 — 888-464-2477
Sacramento, CA 95811 — *Fax:* 916-442-3396
info@friendsoftheriver.org
www.friendsoftheriver.org
Friends of the River educates, organizes, and advocates to protect and restore California rivers, streams, and watersheds.
Corley Phillips, Chair
John Yost, Treasurer

2009 Halogenated Solvents Industry Alliance, Inc. (HSIA)
3033 Wilson Boulevard — 703-875-0683
Suite 700 — info@hsia.org
Arlington, VA 22201 — www.hsia.org
The mission is to represent the users and producers of chlorinated solvents - trichloroethylene, perchloroethylene and methylene chloride. To promote the continued safe use of these products and the use of sound science in assessingtheir potential health effects.

Faye Graul, Executive Director
Christopher Bevan, PhD, DABT, Dir., Scientific Programs

2010 Holistic Management International (HMI)
5941 Jefferson St. NE — 505-842-5252
Suite B — *Fax:* 505-843-7900
Albuquerque, NM 87109 — hmi@holisticmanagement.org
www.holisticmanagement.org
Seeks to help farmers, ranchers, and pastoralists enhance the efficiency, natural health, productivity and profitability of the land; increase natural annual profits; provide a framework for stakeholders to work together toward acommon future; and enable development agencies working with marginalized farmers or pastoral people to break the cycle of food and water insecurity.

Ann Adams, Executive Director
Kathy Harris, Director, Programs

2011 Human Ecology Action League (HEAL)
PO Box 509 — 770-389-4519
Stockbridge, GA 30281 — *Fax:* 770-389-4520
HEALNatnl@aol.com
www.healnatl.org
The Human Ecology Action League Inc (HEAL) is a nonprofit organization founded in 1977 to serve those whose health has been adversely affected by environment exposures; to provide information to those who are concerned about the healtheffects of chemicals; and to alert the general public about the potential dangers of chemicals. Referrals to local HEAL chapters and other support groups are available from the League.
John Heal, Contact

2012 Institute for Agriculture and Trade Policy (IATP)
2105 First Avenue South — 612-870-0453
Minneapolis, MN 55404 — *Fax:* 612-870-4846
info@iatp.org
www.iatp.org
IATP works locally and globally at the intersection of policy and practice to ensure fair and sustainable food, farm and trade systems.

Juliette Majot, Executive Director
Colleen Borgendale, Director, Communications

2013 Institute of Hazardous Materials Management (IHMM)
9210 Corporate Blvd. — 301-984-8969
Suite 470 — *Fax:* 301-984-1516
Rockville, MD 20850 — info@ihmm.org
www.ihmm.org
A nonprofit organization that protects the environment and the public's health and safety through the administration of credentials recognizing professionals who have demonstrated a high level of knowledge, expertise, and excellence inthe management of hazardous materials.

Gene Guilford, Executive Director
Patricia Buley, Director, Certification

2014 MCS Referral and Resources
618 Wyndhurst Avenue #2 — 410-889-6666
Baltimore, MD 21210 — *Fax:* 410-889-4944
adonnay@mcsrr.org
www.mcsrr.org
The mission of MCS Refferal and Resources is to further the diagnosis, treatment, accomodation and prevention of multiple chemical sensitivity (MCS) disorders.
Dr. Anne McCampbell

2015 Midwest Center for Environmental Science and Public Policy
One East Hazelwood Drive — 800-407-0261
Champaign, IL 61820 — glrppr@istc.illinois.edu
www.glrppr.org
A professional organization dedicated to promoting information exchange and networking to P2 professionals in the Great Lakes regions of the United States and Canada
Bob Iverson, Contact

2016 Midwest Pesticide Action Center
35 E Upper Wacker Drive — 773-878-7378
Suite 1200 — general@pesticideaction.org
Chicago, IL 60601 — www.midwestpesticideaction.org
Working at the local, state and regional level, the Midwest Pesticide Action Center, uses advocacy, education, and outreach to reduce the health risks and environmental impact of pesticides and promote safer alternatives.
Ruth Kerzee, Executive Director
Ryan Anderson, Program Manager

2017 Mount Sinai School of Medicine: Division of Environmental Health Science
Department of Community and Preventive Medicine
1 Gustave Levy Place — 212-241-6500
Box 1057 — *Fax:* 212-241-6696
New York, NY 10029-6574 — www.mssm.edu/cpm
The Division's ultimate goal is the protection of the public's health by understanding, elucidating and preventing diseases that arise from environmental exposures.
Philip J Landrigan M.D., Chair

2018 National Alliance for Hispanic Health
1501 16th Street NW — 202-387-5000
Washington, DC 20036 — *Fax:* 202-797-4353
www.hispanichealth.org
The mission of the National Alliance for Hispanic Health is to improve the health and well-being of Hispanics. Issues covered in-

clude the full range of health and human services issues, including environmental health.
Jane L. Delgado, President and CEO
Adolph P. Falcon, Senior Vice President

2019 National Association of City and County Health Officials
1100 17th Street NW 202-783-5550
Seventh Floor *Fax:* 202-783-1583
Washington, DC 20036 info@naccho.org
www.naccho.org
The National Association of County and City Health Officials is a nonprofit, membership organization serving all 3,000 local health departments nationwide. NACCHO is dedicated to improving the health of people and communities byassuring an effective local public health system. As the Voice of local public health officials at the national level, NACCHO is able to promote the local perspective on national health programs and policies.
Georgia Heise, President

2020 National Association of Physicians for the Environment
6410 Rockledge Drive 307-571-9790
Suite 412 *Fax:* 301-530-8910
Bethesda, MD 20817
The National Association of Physicians for the Environment works to involve physicians and other health care professionals, particularly through their geographic and medical specialty organizations, to deal with the impact ofpollutants on organs and systems of the human body.
Betty Farley, Executive Assistant

2021 National Cancer Institute
National Institutes of Health
BG 9609 MSC 9760 301-496-6641
9609 Medical Centre Drive 800-422-6237
Bethesda, MD 20892-9760 *Fax:* 301-496-0846
ncipressofficers@mail.nih.gov
www.cancer.gov
Leads the Nation's fight against cancer by supporting and conducting ground-breaking research in cancer biology, causation, prevention, detection, treatment and survivorship.
John E Niederhuber, Director
Joseph V. Simone, MD, Chairman

2022 National Capital Poison Center
3201 New Mexico Avenue NW 202-362-3867
Suite 310 800-222-1222
Washington, DC 20016 *Fax:* 202-362-8377
pc@poison.org
www.poison.org
This mission of the Poison Center is to prevent poisonings, save lives, and limit injury from poisoning. In addition, the Center decreases health care costs of poisoning cases. The Center provides 24-hour telephone guidance, teachingmaterials, and professional education.

2023 National Center for Disease Control and Prevention
1600 Clifton Road 404-639-3311
Atlanta, GA 30333-4027 800-232-4636
www.cdc.gov
Mission: To promote health and quality of life by preventing and controlling disease, injury, and disability.
Lynn Austin, Chief of Staff

2024 National Center for Environmental Health Strategies
1100 Rural Avenue 856-429-5358
Voorhees, NJ 00804 *Fax:* 856-816-8820
marylamielle@ncehs.org
www.ncehs.org/
Fosters the development of creative solutions to environmental health problems with a focus on indoor air quality, chemical sensitivites and environmental disabilities.
Mary Lamielle, Executive Director

2025 National Center for Healthy Housing (NCHH)
10320 Little Patuxent Parkway 410-992-0712
Suite 500 www.centerforhealthyhousing.org
Columbia, MD 21044
Formerly known as the National Center for Lead-Safe Housing, it deveops and promotes practical methods to protect children fron environmental health hazards in homes while preserving affordable housing.
Amanda L. Reddy, Executive Director
Michelle Harvey, Chief Operating Officer

2026 National Conference of Local Environmental Health Administrators
University of Washington
Department of Environmental Health 509-382-2181
1010 South Third Street *Fax:* 360-382-2942
Dayton, WA 99328 ctreser@u.washington.edu
depts.washington.edu/clehaweb
The NCLEHA's purpose is to provide a forum for local administrators to share common concerns and solutions to mutual problems, and to provide a professional organization for environmental health administrators, focused on the issuesand problems of local environmental health programs.
David Riggs, Chair
Charles D Treser, Treasurer

2027 National Conference of State Legislatures (NCSL)
7700 East First Place 303-364-7700
Denver, CO 80230 800-659-2656
Fax: 303-364-7800
ncslnet-admin@ncsl.org
www.ncsl.org
The National Conference of State Legislatures serves the legislators and staffs of the nation's 50 states and its commonwealths and territories. NCSL is a bipartisan organization with three objectives: to improve the quality andeffectiveness of state legislatures; to foster interstate communications and cooperation; and to ensure states a strong cohesive voice in the federal system.
Robin Vos, President
Jon Heining, Staff Chair

2028 National Education Association Health Information Network
1201 16th Street NW 202-822-7570
Suite 216 800-718-8387
Washington, DC 20036-3290 *Fax:* 202-822-7775
info@neahin.org
The National Education Association Health Information Network believes that sound public education must begin with school employees and students who are healthy and free of preventable diseases and supported with information, materialsand training opportunities that reaffirm these values.
Jim Bender, Executive Director
Annelise Cohon, Program Coordinator

2029 National Environmental Coalition of Native Americans
PO Box 988 918-342-3041
Claremore, OK 74018 noteno_84@hotmail.com
necona.indigenousnative.org
Nonprofit organization formed to educate Indians and Non-Indians about the health dangers of radioactivity and the transport of nuclear waste on America's rails and roads. Networks with environmentalists to develop grassrootscounter-movement to the efforts of the nuclear industry and develop Tribal nuclear free zones across the nation.
Grace Thorpe, President

2030 National Environmental Health Association (NEHA)
720 S Colorado Boulevard 303-756-9090
Suite 1000-N *Fax:* 303-691-9490
Denver, CO 80246-1926 staff@neha.org
www.neha.org
Represents all of environmental health and protection from terrorism and all-hazards preparedness, to food safety and protection and on site wastewater systems. Over 4,500 members and the

profession are served by the associationthrough its Journal of Environmental Health, Annual Education Conference and Exhibition credentialing programs, research and development activities and other services.

David T. Dyjack, Executive Director

2031 National Environmental Health Science and Protection Accreditation Council (EHAC)
PO Box 66057 206-522-5272
Burien, WA 98166 executive.director@nehspac.org
nehspac.org

Promotes a high quality education for persons studying environmental health science and protection; promotes commonality in coverage of basic concepts of environmental health science and protection education; and promotes undergraduatecurricula of a quality and content compatible with admission prerequisites of graduate programs in environmental health science and protection.
Leslie D. Mitchell, Executive Director

2032 National Institute of Environmental Health Sciences
NIEHS Central Receiving
105 T.W. Alexander Drive 919-541-3345
Building 110 *Fax:* 301-480-2978
Research Triangle Park, NC 27709 webcenter@niehs.nih.gov
www.niehs.nih.gov

NIEHS' mission is to research how the environment affects people in order to promote healthier lives, and to provide global leadership for research that improves public health. NIEHS accomplishes this mission by translating theirfindings into comprehensible information that can inform real-life individual and public health outcomes.

Linda S. Birnbaum, Director
Richard Woychik, Deputy Director

2033 National Pesticide Information Center Oregon State University
310 Weniger Hall 800-858-7378
Corvallis, OR 97331 *Fax:* 541-737-0761
npic.orst.edu

Provides objective, science-based information about a wide variety of pesticide-related topics, including: pesticide product information, information on the recognition and management of pesticide poisonings, toxicology andenvironmental chemistry. Highly trained specialists can also provide referrals for the following: investigation of pesticide incidents, emergency treatment information, safety information, health and environmental effects, and clean-up and disposalprocedures.
Jeff Jenkins, Director
Amy Hallman, Project Coordinator

2034 National Religious Partnership for the Environment
110 Maryland Avenue, NE 212-532-7436
Suite 203 *Fax:* 413-253-1414
Washington, DC 20002 www.nrpe.org

The mission of the National Religious Partnership for the Environment is to permanently integrate issues of environmental sustainability and justice across all aspects of organized religious life.
Cassandra Carmichael, Executive Director
Rev. Michael McClain, Outreach Coordinator

2035 National Safety Council
Environmental Health Center
1121 Spring Lake Dr. 202-293-2270
Suite 1210 800-621-7615
Itasca, IL 60143-3201 *Fax:* 630-285-1434
info@nsc.org
www.nsc.org

The Mission of the Environmental Health Center is to foster improved public understanding of significant health risk and challenges facing modern society. This goal reinforces the National Safety Council's commitment to increased andmore effective citizen involvement in safety, health and environmental decision-making.
Jeffrey Shavelson, Policy Analyst

2036 Natural Resources Defense Council
40 West 20th Street 212-727-2700
New York, NY 10011 *Fax:* 212-727-1773
nrdcinfo@nrdc.org
www.nrdc.org

The NRDC focuses on issues impacting climate change, ocean pollution, water management and treatment, clean energy, and the conservation of wildlife.
Rhea Suh, President
Mitchell Bernard, Chief Counsel

2037 Navy & Marine Corps Public Health Center
620 John Paul Jones Circle
Suite 1100 757-953-0700
Portsmouth, VA 23708-2103 NMCPHC-PAO@med.navy.mil
www.med.navy.mil/sites/nmcphc/Pages/Home.aspx

The Navy and Marine Corps Center for Public Health Services provides leadership and expertise to ensure mission readiness through disease prevention and health promotion in support of the National Military Strategy.

Todd L. Wagner, Commanding Officer
Robert Hawkins, Executive Officer

2038 Navy and Marine Corps Public Health Center
620 John Paul Jones Circle 757-953-0700
Suite 1100 ask-nmcphc@med.navy.mil
Portsmouth, VA 23708

The Navy and Marine Corps center for public health services that provides leadership and expertise to ensure mission readiness through disease prevention and health promotion in support of the National Military Strategy.
CAPT Bruce A Cohen MC USN, Commanding Officer
CAPT Mike Henderson MSC USN, Executive Officer

2039 Noise Pollution Clearinghouse
PO Box 1137 888-200-8332
Montpelier, VT 05601-1137 npc@nonoise.org
www.nonoise.org

National nonprofit organization with extensive online noise related resources. Creates more civil cities and more natural rural and wilderness areas by reducing noise pollution at the source.

2040 North American Association for Environmental Education (NAAEE)
1725 DeSales Street NW 202-419-0412
Suite 401 *Fax:* 202-419-0415
Washington, DC 20036 info@naaee.org
www.naaee.org

A professional association that promotes excellence in environmental education and serves environmental educators for the purpose of achieving environmental literacy to allow present and future generations to benefit from a safe andhealthy environment.
16,000 members
Judy Braus, Executive Director
Sarah Bodor, Director, Policy

2041 Northwest Coalition for Alternatives to Pesticides
PO Box 1393 541-344-5044
Eugene, OR 97440 *Fax:* 541-344-6923
info@pesticide.org
www.pesticide.org

The Northwest Coalition for Alternatives to Pesticides protects the health of people and the environment by advancing alternatives to pesticides.
Tony Brand, President
Kim Leval, Executive Director

2042 Novozymes North America Inc
77 Perry Chapel Church Road 919-494-3000
Franklinton, NC 27525 *Fax:* 919-494-3450
enzymesna@novozymes.com
www.novozymes.com/en

Novozymes is the biotech bases world leader in enzymes and microorganisms. Using nature's own technologies, they continu-

ously expand the frontiers of biological solutions to improve industrial performance everywhere.
Henrik Gurtler, CEO

2043 Occupational Safety and Health Administration: U.S. Department of Labor
Occupational Safety and Health Administration
200 Constitution Avenue NW 800-321-6742
Room N3626 www.osha.gov
Washington, DC 20210
OSHA's mission is to send all workers home healthy every day by enforcing safe working conditions and providing training, education, outreach, and assistance.

Loren Sweatt, Assistant Secretary
Krisann Pearce, Chief of Staff

2044 Pesticide Action Network North America
1611 Telegraph Avenue 510-788-9020
Suite 1200 www.panna.org
Oakland, CA 94612
Pesticide Action Network North American advocates the adoption of ecologically sound practices in place of hazardous pestices in place of pesticide use. PANNA works with more than 100 affiliated oragnizations in Canada, Mexico and US,as well as with Pesticide Action Network partners around the world to demand that development agencies and governments redirect support from pesticides to safe alternatives.

Susan Baker, President
Mary Brune, Vice President

2045 Physicians for Social Responsibility (PSR)
1111 14th St., NW 202-667-4260
Suite 700 *Fax:* 202-667-4201
Washington, DC 20005 psrnatl@psr.org
www.psr.org
A non-profit advocacy organization that is the medical and public health voice for policies to prevent nuclear war and proliferation and to slow, stop and reverse global warming and toxic degradation of the environment.
Jeff Carter, Executive Director
Barbara Gottlieb, Dir., Environment & Health

2046 Plastic Pollution Coalition
2150 Allston Way 323-936-3010
Suite 460 dianna@plasticpollutioncoalition.org
Berkeley, CA 94704 plasticpollutioncoalition.org
The Plastic Pollution Coalition is a nonprofit association dedicated to finding a sustainable solution for plastic pollution through strategic planing and global communication.

Dianna Cohen, Chief Executive Officer
Jane Patton, Managing Director

2047 Public Citizen
1600 20th Street NW 202-588-1000
Washington, DC 20009 member@citizen.org
www.citizen.org
A consumer advocacy organization founded to represent consumer interests in Congress, the executive branch, and the courts.

Robert Weissman, President
Margrete Strand Rangnes, Executive Vice-President

2048 Rachel Carson Center for Natural Resources
Churchill High School 541-687-3421
1850 Bailey Hill Road haberman@4j.lane.edu
Eugene, OR 97405 schools.4j.lane.edu/carson/
Offers an alternative to the traditional high school curriculum, providing students with experience, knowledge, and skills that relate to the natural environment.
Helen Haberman, Environmental Instructor
Tim Whitley, Director

2049 Rachel Carson Council
8600 Irvington Avenue 301-214-2400
Bethesda, MD 20817 office@rachelcarsoncouncil.org
rachelcarsoncouncil.org
Independent nonprofit scientific organization dedicated to protecting the environment against toxic and chemical threats, particularly those of pesticides.

Roger Christie, Chairman
Robert K. Musil, Ph.D., President & CEO

2050 Rene Dubos Center
The Rene Dubos Center 914-337-1636
279 Bronxville Road *Fax:* 914-771-5206
Bronxville, NY 10708
The Rene Dubos Center for Human Environments is a non-profit education and research organization focused on the social and humanistic aspects of environmental problems.
Ruth A Eblen, President

2051 Rodale Institute
611 Siegfriedale Road 610-683-1400
Kutztown, PA 19530-9320 *Fax:* 610-683-8548
info@rodaleinst.org
www.rodaleinstitute.org
The Institute offers creative opportunities and solutions that contribute to regenerating environmental and human health worldwide. Their mission statement is clear: The Rodale Institute works worldwide to achieve a regenerative foodsystem that improves environmental and human health.
Anthony Rodale, Chairman
Paul A. McGinley, Co-chairman

2052 Second Nature Inc.
18 Tremont Street 617-722-0036
Suite 608 *Fax:* 617-259-1734
Boston, MA 02108 info@secondnature.org
www.secondnature.org
Dedicated to advancing our quality of life by demostrating the close links between human health and the environment. The center's goal is to make the relationship of environment to human health an integral part of medical education.
Timothy Carter, President
Michele Madia, Director, Programs

2053 Silicones Environmental, Health and Safety Center
American Chemistry Council (ACC)
700 2nd Street NE 202-249-7000
Washington, DC 20002 *Fax:* 202-249-6100
sehsc@americanchemistry.com
sehsc.americanchemistry.com
An organization of North America silicone chemical producers and importers. It promotes the safe use of silicones through product stewardship and environmental, health and safety research. It focuses on coordinating research andsubmitting it for peer review through independent advisory boards and publication of peer-reviewed literature.
Karluss Thomas, Executive Director

2054 Society of Chemical Manufacturers and Affiliates (SOCMA)
1400 Crystal Drive 571-348-5100
Suite 630 *Fax:* 571-348-5138
Arlington, VA 22202 info@socma.com
www.socma.com
International trade association serving small and mid-sized batch chemical manufacturers, striving for safe, sustainable and environmentally sound operations.

Jennifer L. Abril, President & CEO
Paul J. Hirsh, Sr. VP, Industry Development

2055 Society of Environmental Toxicology and Chemistry
SETAC N America Office
229 South Baylen Street 850-469-1500
2nd Floor *Fax:* 850-469-4136
Pensacola, FL 32502 setac@setac.org
www.setac.org

Mission: To support the development of principles and practices for protection, enhancement and management of sustainable environmental quality and ecosystem integrity.
Greg Schiefer, Executive Director
Jason Anderson, IT Manager

2056 Teratology Society
1821 Michael Faraday Drive 703-438-3104
Suite 300 *Fax:* 703-483-3113
Reston, VA 20190 tshq@teratology.org
www.teratology.org
A multidisciplinary scientific society founded in 1960, the members of which study the causes and biological processes leading to abnormal development and birth defects at the fundamental and clinical level, and appropriate measuresfor prevention.
Tacey E.K. White, President
Sonja A. Rasmussen, Vice President

2057 The Natural Step
251 Bank Street 613-748-3001
Suite 526 *Fax:* 613-748-1649
Ottawa, ON K2P-1X3 info@naturalstep.ca
naturalstep.ca
The Natural Step is a Canadian nonprofit organization dedicated to science-based sustainable development, working internationally with other organizations, researchers, and local communities.
Tim Broadhead, Director
Karen Clarke-Whistler, Vice-Chair

2058 U.S. Consumer Product Safety Commission
4330 East West Highway 301-504-7978
Bethesda, MD 20814 800-638-2772
Fax: 301-504-0124
www.cpsc.gov
The U.S. Consumer Product Safety Commission (CPSC) is an independent federal regulatory agency that aims to protect the public against unreasonable risks of injuries and deaths associated with consumer products. CPSC protects consumersfrom products that pose a fire, electrical, chemical, or mechanical hazard.
Ann Marie Buerkle, Chair
Robert S. Adler, Commissioner

2059 U.S. Nuclear Regulatory Commission
US Nuclear Regulatory Commission 301-415-7000
Washington, DC 20555-0001 800-368-5642
oca_web@nrc.gov
www.nrc.gov
The Nuclear Regulatory Commission focuses on reactor safety oversight and liscense renewal of existing plants, materials safety oversight and liscencing, as well as high and low-level waste management.
Jeff Baran, Commissioner
Kristine L Svinicki, Chair

2060 US Public Interest Research Group
218 D Street SE 202-546-9707
1st Floor *Fax:* 202-546-2461
Washington, DC 20003 www.pirg.org
Mission: To deliver persistent, result-oriented public interest activism that protects our environment, encourages a fair, sustainable economy, and fosters responsive, democratic government.
Douglas H Phelps, President
Andre Delattre, Executive Director

2061 US-Mexico Border Health Association
211 N. Florence 915-532-1006
Suite101 866-785-9867
El Paso, TX 79901 *Fax:* 915-833-7840
www.borderhealth.org
Promotes public and individual health along the United States-Mexico border through reciprocal technical cooperation.
Rebeca Ramos, Interim Executive Director

2062 Water Environment Federation
601 Wythe Street 703-684-2400
Alexandria, VA 22314-1994 800-666-0206
Fax: 703-684-2492
inquiry@wef.org
www.wef.org
Nonprofit international membership organization that develops and disseminates technical information on the nature, collection, treatment and disposal of domestic and industrial wastewater.
Rick Warner, President
Jenny Hartfelder, President-Elect

2063 Western Forest Genetics Association
1731 Research Park 530-759-1742
Davis, CA 95618
The Western Forest Genetics Association (WFGA) comprises professionals, researchers, and students involved in forest genetics issues in the western US and Canada.
Jessia W. Wright, Vice President
Andrew D. Bower, Treasurer

2064 Western Occupational and Environmental Medical Association
575 Market Street 415-764-4918
Suite 2125 *Fax:* 415-764-4915
San Francisco, CA 94105 woema@woema.org
www.woema.org
The mission is to represent and be a resource to members in the profession and practice of occupational and environmental medicine and to enhance their efforts to promote and improve health in the workplace and the community.
Ellyn G. McIntosh, Chairman
Peter J. Vasquez, President

2065 White Lung Association
PO Box 1483 410-243-5864
Baltimore, MD 21203 *Fax:* 410-243-5234
www.whitelung.org
National nonprofit organization dedicated to the education of the public to the hazards of asbestos exposure. Has developed programs of public education and consults with victims of asbestos exposure, school boards, building owners,government agencies and others interested in identifying asbestos hazards and developing control programs.
James Fite, Executive Director

Pediatric Health: Associations

2066 Academic Pediatric Association
6728 Old McLean Village Drive 703-556-9222
McLean, VA 22101 *Fax:* 703-556-8729
info@academicpeds.org
www.academicpeds.org
The mission of the APA is to foster the health and well-being of children and their families by: promoting health services, education and research in general pediatrics; affecting public and governmental policies regarding issues vitalto child health and to education and research in general pediatrics; and supporting the professional growth and development of faculty in general pediatrics.
David Keller, MD, President
Connie Mackay, Executive Director

2067 Allergy and Asthma Network: Mothers of Asthmatics
8229 Boone Boulevard 800-878-4403
Suite 260 *Fax:* 703-288-5271
Vienna, VA 22182 www.allergyasthmanetwork.org
Our mission is to eliminate suffering and death due to asthma and allergies through education, advocacy, community outreach and research.
Nancy Sander, President
Mary McGowan, Executive Director

2068 American Academy of Pediatrics: Committee on Environment Health
141 NW Point Boulevard 847-434-4000
Elk Grove Villiage, IL 60007-1098 800-433-9016
Fax: 847-434-8000
www.aap.org
The AAP is commited to the attainment of optimal physical, mental and social health for all infants, children, and young adults. This mission will be accomplished by engaging in the following activities: professional education,advocacy for children and youth, advocacy for pediatricians, public education, membership service and research.
Sandra Hassink, President
Benard P. Dreyer, President Elect

2069 American Federation of Teachers
555 New Jersey Ave NW 202-879-4400
Washington, DC 20001 *Fax:* 202-879-4597
www.aft.org
Founded to represent the economic, social and professional interests of classroom teachers.
1.7 million members
Randi Weingarten, President
Lorretta Johnson, Secretary-Treasurer

2070 Association of Maternal and Child Health Program
2030 M Street 202-775-0436
Suite 350 *Fax:* 202-775-0061
Washington, DC 20036 www.amchp.org
AMCHP accomplishes its mission through the active participation of its members and vital partnerships with government agencies, families and advocates, health care purchasers and providers, academic and research professionals, andothers at the national, state and local levels.
Millie Jones, President
Lori Tremmel Freeman, Chief Executive Officer

2071 Childhood Lead Poisoning Prevention Program
Ohio Department of Health
246 N High Street 614-728-9454
Columbus, OH 43215 *Fax:* 614-728-6793
BCFHS@odh.ohio.gov
The mission of Ohio's Childhood Lead Poisoning Prevention Program is to eliminate childhood lead poisoning through screening, environmental inspection, abatement, education and case management.
Alvin D Jackson, Director

2072 Children's Defense Fund
25 E Street NW 800-233-1200
Washington, DC 20001 cdfinfo@childrensdefense.org
www.childrensdefense.org
Mission: To ensure every child a healthy start, a head start, a fair start, a safe start, and a moral start in life and successful passage to adulthood with the help of caring families and communities.
Marian Wright Edelman, President
Melanie Hartzog, Executive Director

2073 Children's Environmental Health Network
110 Maryland Avenue NE 202-543-4033
Suite 404 *Fax:* 202-543-8797
Washington, DC 20002 cehn@cehn.org
www.cehn.org/
Mission is to promote a healthy environment and to protect the fetus and child from environmental hazards. Three areas of concentration for the Network are education, research and policy. Network's goals are: to promote the developmentof sound public health and child-focused national policy; to stimulate prevention-oriented research; to educate health professionals, policymakers and community members in preventive strategies; and to elevate public awareness of environmentalhazards to children.
James R. Roberts, M.D., M.P.H, Chair
Dick J Batchelor, Vice Chair

2074 Children's Hopsital at Montefiore
111 E 210th Street 718-920-5016
Bronx, NY 10467 *Fax:* 718-920-4377
www.montefiore.org
The Montefiore Lead Poisoning Prevention Program addresses all aspects of childhood lead poisoning from diagnosis and treatment to education and research. Their mission is to treat lead-poisoned children and their families and toeducate families at risk, other medical providers and local, state and national legislators and policy makers.
Steven M Safyer, President & CEO
Philip O Ozuah, Chief Operating Officer

2075 Coalition for Clean Air
800 Wilshire Blvd. 213-223-6860
Suite 1010 *Fax:* 213-223-6862
Los Angelos, CA 90017 NICHOLAS@CCAIR.ORG
www.coalitionforcleanair.org
The Coalition for Clean Air is committed to restoring clean, healthy air to all of California and strengthening the environmental movement by promoting broad-based community involvement, advocating responsible public policy andproviding technical expertise.
Erik Neandross, Board Chair
Joseph K Lyou, Ph.D, President & CEO

2076 Genesis Fund/National Birth Defects Center: Pregnancy Environmental Hotline
1347 Main Street 781-890-4282
Second Floor 800-322-5014
Waltham, MA 00245 *Fax:* 781-487-2361
www.thegenesisfund.org
General information service that provides information regarding exposure to environmental factors during pregnancy and the effects on the developing fetus.
Matthew Hoffman, Chairman
Erica D Agostino, Executive Director

2077 Healthy Child Healthy World
8383 Wilshire Blvd 424-343-0020
Suite 800 *Fax:* 310-820-2070
Beverly Hills, CA 90211 info@healthychild.org
www.healthychild.org
Healthy Child Healthy World is dedicated to protecting the health and well being of children from harmful environmental exposures. We educate parents, support protective policies, and engage communities to make responsible decisions,simple everyday choices, and well-informed lifestyle improvements to create healthy environments where children and families can flourish.
Megan Boyle, Editorial Director
Kelly Herman, Program Director

2078 Healthy Mothers, Healthy Babies
4401 Ford Avenue 703-838-7552
Suite 300 *Fax:* 703-664-0485
Alexandria, VA 22302 info@hmhb.org
www.hmhb.org
Healthy Mothers, Healthy Babies is a coalition of national, state and local providers, advocates and administrators concerned about health of pregnant women, infants and families. The coalition serves as a forum for informationexchange and as a catalyst to encourage collaborative partnerships amoung its members and colleagues.
Janice Frey-Angel, CEO
Jennifer Sharp, Authorized Executive

2079 Healthy Schools Network
773 Madison Avenue 518-462-0632
Albany, NY 12208 202-543-7555
Fax: 518-462-0433
www.healthyschools.org
HSN is a nationally recognized state-based advocate for the protection of children's environmental health in schools. Engages in research, education, outreach, technical assistance and coalition building to create schols that areenvironmentally responsible to children, and to their communities. Publishes a quarterly news-

letter and maintains an Information Clearinghouse and Referral Service.

Chip Halverson, President
Laura Anderko, Vice President

2080 Institute of Medicine: Board on Children, Youth and Families
500 Fifth Street, NW 202-334-2000
Washington, DC 20001 *Fax:* 202-334-3829
bocyf@nas.edu
The Board on Children, Youth and Families addresses a variety of policy-relevant issues related to the health and development, of children, youth and families. It does so by convening experts to weigh in on matters from the perspectiveof the behavioral, social, and health sciences. The Board operates under the National Research Council and the Institute of Medicine of the National Academies.
Kimber Bogard, Director
Morgan Ford, Senior Program Officer

2081 Kids for Saving Earth Worldwide
37955 Bridge Road 763-559-1234
North Branch, MN 55056 *Fax:* 651-674-5005
kse@kidsforsavingearth.org
www.kidsforsavingearth.org
A nonprofit organization inspired by Clinton Hill, who died at the young age of eleven. The organization dreams of a healthy planet and provides "Education into Action" curriculum to thousands of teachers, parents and kids to helpinspire envirnmnetal awareness.
Tessa Hill, President

2082 Kids for a Clean Environment
PO Box 158254 615-331-7381
Nashville, TN 37215 *Fax:* 615-333-9879
kidsface@mindspring.com
www.kidsface.org
Mission: To provide information on environmental issues to children, to encourage and facilitate youth's involvement with effective environmental action and to recognize those efforts which result in the improvement of nature.
Melissa Poe, Founder

2083 March of Dimes Birth Defects Foundation
1275 Mamaroneck Avenue 914-997-4488
White Plains, NY 10605 www.marchofdimes.org
The mission of the March of Dimes Birth Defects Foundation is to improve the health of babies by preventing birth defects and reducing infant mortality. The March of Dimes carries out the mission through research, community service,education and advocacy.
Ann Umemoto, Associate Director

2084 National Institute of Child Health and Human Development
31 Center Drive 800-370-2943
Building 31, Room 2A32 *Fax:* 866-760-5947
Bethesda, MD 20892-2425 NICHDInformationresourcecenter@mail.nih.gov
www.nichd.nih.gov
National Institute of Child Health and Human Development conducts and supports basic, translational, and clinical research in the biomedical, behavioral, and social sciences related to child and maternal health, in medicalrehabilitation, and in the reproductive sciences.
Diana Bianchi, Director
John N. Kennedy, President

2085 National Parent Teachers Association
1250 N. Pitt Street 703-518-1200
Alexandria, VA 22314 800-307-4782
Fax: 703-836-0942
info@pta.org
www.pta.org
The mission of the National PTA is to support and speak on behalf of children and youth in the school, in the community and before governmental bodies and other organizations; to assist parents in developing the skills they need toraise and protect their children and to encourage parent and public involvement in the public schools.
Laura Bay, President
Jim Accomando, President Elect

2086 Office of Children's Health Protection
US Environmental Protection Agency
Ariel Rios Building 202-564-2188
1200 Pennsylvania Avenue NW *Fax:* 202-564-2733
Washington, DC 20460 www.epa.gov
The mission of the Office of Children's Health Protection is to make the protection of children's health a fundamental goal of public health and environmental protection in the United States.

Dr. Ruth A. Etzel, M.D., Ph.D, Director

2087 Oklahoma Childhood Lead Poisioning Prevention Program
Oklahoma Department of Health
1000 Northeast 10th Street 405-271-5600
Room 711 800-522-0203
Oklahoma, OK 73117-1299 *Fax:* 405-271-4971
oklppp@health.ok.gov
lpp.health.ok.gov
Mission: To reduce blood lead levels to below a level of concern in all Oklahomans.

Pediatric Health: Publications

2088 Child Health and the Environment
Oxford University Press
198 Madison Avenue 212-726-6000
New York, NY 10016 800-445-9714
Fax: 919-677-1303
custserv.us@oup.com
global.oup.com
A publication on environmental threats to child health. The first three chapters provide overviews of key children's environmental health issues as well as the role of environmental epidemiology and risk assessment in child healthprotection. Later chapters address the health affects of metal, PCBs, dioxins, pesticides, hormonally active agents, radiation, indoor and outdoor air pollution, and water contaminants.
416 pages
ISBN: 0-195135-59-8
Donald T Wigle, Author

2089 Children's Defense Fund
25 E Street NW 202-628-8787
Washington, DC 20001 800-233-1200
cdfinfo@childrensdefense.org
www.childrensdefense.org
Mission: To ensure every child a healthy start, a head start, a fair start, a safe start, and a moral start in life and successful passage to adulthood with the help of caring families and communities.
Marian Wright Edelman, President
Lori Wood, Vice President for Field

2090 Handbook of Pediatric Environmental Health
American Academy of Pediatrics
141 NW Point Boulevard 847-434-4000
Elk Grove Village, IL 60007-1098 800-433-9016
Fax: 847-434-8000
www.aap.org
The AAP is committed to the attainment of optimal physical, mental and social health for all infants, children, and young adults. This mission will be accomplished by engaging in the following activities: professional education,advocacy for children and youth, advocacy for pediatricians, public education, membership service and research.
723 pages
ISBN: 1-581100-29-9
Sandra Hassink, President
Benard P. Dreyer, President Elect

2091 Kids Count Data Book: State Profiles of Child Well-Being

701 St. Paul Street
Baltimore, MD 21202
410-547-6600
Fax: 410-547-6624
webmail@aecf.org
www.aecf.org/work/kids-count

Kids Count is national and state-by-state effort to provide makers and citizens with benchmarks of child well-being. It includes variables such as percentage of low birth-weight babies, child death rates, percentage of childern inpoverty, and percentage of children without health insurance.

Patrick McCarthy, President & CEO
Ryan Chao, Vice President

2092 Pesticides and the Immune System: Public Health Risks

10 G Street NE
Suite 800
Washington, DC 20002
202-729-7600
Fax: 202-729-7686
lzelin@wri.org
www.wri.org

Brings together for the frist time an extensive body of experimental and epidemiological research from around the world documenting the the effects of widely used pesticides on the immune system and the attendent health risks. In sodoing, it documents that pesticide-related health risks are much more serious than genrally known, especially in developing countries where exposure is widespread and infectious diseases take a heavy toll.

100 pages
ISBN: 1-569730-87-3

Andrew Steer, President & CEO
Manish Bapna, EVP/Managing Director

2093 Resource Guide on Children's Environmental Health

600 Grant Street
Suite 800
Denver, CO 80203
303-861-5165
Fax: 303-861-5315
www.cchn.org

The Children's Environmental Health Network has developed the Resource Guide on Childern's Environmental Health to assist community leaders, policy makers, health and environmental specialists, members of the advocacy community andmedia, and the general public in identifying and accessing key resources in childern's environmental health.

Annette Kowal, CEO
Polly Anderson, Chief Operating Officer

Environmental Law

Associations

2094 Atlantic States Legal Foundation
658 West Onondaga Street 315-475-1170
Syracuse, NY 13204 *Fax:* 315-475-6719
atlantic.states@aslf.org
www.aslf.org
Atlantic States Legal Foundation was established in 1982 to provide legal, technical, and organizational assistance on environment issues to citizen organizations (NGOs), individuals, local governments, and others.

Robin Chanay, Chair
Martha Loew, Vice Chair

2095 Business & Legals Reports
100 Winners Circle 860-510-0100
Suite 300 800-727-5257
Brentwood, TN 37027 *Fax:* 860-510-7220
service@blr.com
www.blr.com
Provides essential tools for safety and environmental compliance and training needs.
Guy Crossley, Chief Operating Officer
Dan Oswald, Chief Executive Officer

2096 Center for Community Action and Environmental Justice
PO Box 33124 951-360-8451
Riverside, CA 92519 *Fax:* 951-360-5950
Jean.k@ccaej.org
www.ccaej.org
The Center for Community Action and Environmental Justice serves as a resource center for community groups working on environmental justice issues.
Maggie Hawkins, President
Gwen D'Arcangelis, President-Elect

2097 Center for Health, Environment and Justice (CHEJ)
7139 Shreve Road 703-237-2249
Falls Church, VA 22046 *Fax:* 703-237-8389
info@chej.org
www.chej.org
Works to build healthy communities, with social justice, economic well-being, and democratic governance.

Sharon Franklin, Chief of Operations
Stephen Lester, Science Director

2098 Center for International Environmental Law
1350 Connecticut Avenue NW 202-785-8700
Suite 1100 *Fax:* 202-785-8701
Washington, DC 20036 info@ciel.org
www.ciel.org
The Center for International Environmental Law (CIEL) is a nonprofit organization working to use international law and institutions to protect the environment, promote human health, and ensure a just and sustainable society. We providea wide range of services including legal counsel, policy research, analysis, advocacy, education, training, and capacity building.
Carroll Muffett, President & CEO
Cameron Aishton, Administrator

2099 Center for Investigative Reporting
2927 Newbury Street 510-809-3160
Suite A *Fax:* 510-849-1813
Berkeley, CA 94703 center@cironline.org
The only independent, nonprofit organization in the country dedicated to investigative reporting in the public interest on a broad range of issues.
Tom Goldstein, President
Christa Scharfenberg, Acting Executive Director

2100 Communities for a Better Environment (CBE)
6325 Pacific Blvd. 323-826-9771
Suite 300 *Fax:* 323-588-7079
Huntington Park, CA 90255 www.cbecal.org
Works to achieve environmental health and justice in California by building grassroots power in and with communities of color and working-class communities.
Darryl Molina Sarmiento, Executive Director
Julia May, Senior Scientist

2101 Community Environmental Council
26 West Anapamu Street 805-963-0583
2nd Floor *Fax:* 805-962-9080
Santa Barbara, CA 93101 cecadmin@cecmail.org
www.cecsb.org
The Community Environmental Council is a nonprofit environmental organization headquartered in Santa Barbara, California. Our community involvement includes managing two recycling centers, a household hazardous waste facility, anurban farm, and three community gardens as well as the environmental education program Art From Scrap. In addition CEC provides research, technical assistance and education on local and statewide land use planning, and solid waste and integrated pestmanagement.
Dave Davis, President & CEO
Laura Burton Capps, Vice President

2102 Community Rights Counsel
1301 Connecticut Avenue NW 202-296-6889
Suite 502 *Fax:* 202-296-6895
Washington, DC 20036 crc@communityrights.org
www.communityrights.org
A nonprofit public interest law firm that was formed in 1997 to assist communities in protecting their health and welfare by regulating permissible land uses, and that provides strategic assistance to state and local governmentattorneys in defending land use laws.
Douglas T Kendall, Founder/Executive Director
Timothy J Dowling, Chief Counsel

2103 Conservation Law Foundation
62 Summer Street 617-350-0990
Boston, MA 00211 *Fax:* 617-350-4030
www.clf.org
A nonprofit, member-supported organization that works to solve the environmental problems that threaten the people, natural resources and communities of New England. CLF's advocates use law, economics and science to design andimplement strategies that conserve natural resources, protect public health and promote vital communities in our region.

Peter Shelley, Interim President
Priscilla Brooks, Vice President

2104 Earthjustice
50 California Street 415-217-2000
Suite 500 800-584-6460
San Francisco, CA 94111 *Fax:* 415-217-2040
info@earthjustice.org
www.earthjustice.org
Nonprofit public interest law firm dedicated to protecting the magnificent places, natural resources, and wildlife of this earth and to defending the right of all people to a healthy environment. It enforces and strengthensenvironmental laws on behalf of hundreds of organizations and communities.
Trip Van Noppen, President
Minna Jung, Vice President

2105 Environmental Defense Fund (EDF)
257 Park Avenue South 212-505-2100
New York, NY 10010 *Fax:* 212-505-2375
www.edf.org
Dedicated to protecting the environmental rights of all people, including future generations. Among these rights are clean air, clean water, healthy, nourishing food and a flourishing ecosystem. Advocates solutions based on science,even when it leads in unfamiliar directions. Works to create solutions that win lasting

political, economic and social support because they are bipartisan, efficient and fair.

Fred Krupp, President
Catherine Nardone, Chief Development Officer

2106 Environmental Law Alliance Worldwide
1877 Garden Avenue 541-687-8454
Eugene, OR 97403 *Fax:* 541-687-0535
elawus@elaw.org
www.elaw.org
E-LAW advocates serve low income communities around the world, helping citizens strengthen and enforce laws to protect communities from toxic pollution and environmental degradation.
Bern Johnson, Executive Director
Lori Maddox, Associate Director

2107 Environmental Law Institute
1730 M Street, NW 202-939-3800
Suite 700 *Fax:* 202-939-3868
Washington, DC 20036 law@eli.org
www.eli.org
Community Education and Training Program provides citizens and grassroots groups with information on environmental law and policy that can help them participate effectively in the decisions that impact public health and the environmentin their communities. Program's activities have included training courses on right-to-know laws and a series of workshops in demystifying the law, which focus on using the tools of public participation to address issues ranging from hazardous wasteto land use.

Scott Schang, President
Scott Fulton, President Elect

2108 Environmental Law and Policy Center
35 East Wacker Drive 312-673-6500
Suite 1600 ELPCinfo@ELPC.org
Chicago, IL 60601 elpc.org
Organization responsible for developing advocacy campaigns to protect environmental quality and ensure the availability of clean air, transportation, energy and water.

Daniel Levin, Chairman
Howard A Learner, President

2109 Environmental Law and Policy Center of the Midwest
35 E Wacker Drive 312-673-6500
Suite 1600 *Fax:* 312-795-3730
Chicago, IL 60601 www.elpc.org

Howard A. Learner, President/Executive Director
Kevin Brubaker, Deputy Director

2110 Environmental Support Center
PO Box 1816 202-331-9700
Alexandria, VA 22313 *Fax:* 202-331-8592
envirosupport@hotmail.com
www.envsc.org/
The mission of the Environmental Support Center is to promote the quality of the natural environment, human health, and community sustainability by increasing the organizational effectiveness of local, state, and regional organizationsworking on environmental issues and for environmental justice. To be eligible for assistance, your organization must be a local, state or regional nonprofit organization with a portion of its resources devoted to environmental issues.
Judy Hatcher, Interim Co-Director
Yudi Kidokoro, Chair

2111 Federation of Environmental Technologists (FET)
W175 N11081 Stonewood Drive 262-437-1700
Suite 203 *Fax:* 262-437-1702
Germantown, WI 53022 info@fetinc.org
www.fetinc.org
A nonprofit organization formed to assist industry in interpretation of and compliance with environmental regulations. FET provides education on regulatory compliance and technological advancements to its members, and otherenvironmental professionals, through training, professional development, and networking.
600-700 Members
Jeffrey Nettesheim, Chair/Director
Cheryl Moran, President/Director

2112 Getches-Wilkinson Center for Natural Resources, Energy, and The Environment
University of Colorado
2450 Kittredge Loop Road 303-492-8047
Boulder, CO 80309 *Fax:* 303-492-1297
gwc@colorado.edu
www.colorado.edu
To promote sustainability in the rapidly changing American West by informing and influencing natural resources policies, and decisions.
Alice Madden, Executive Director
Shaun LaBarre, Program Manager

2113 Greenpeace
702 H Street NW 202-884-7615
Suite 300 800-722-6995
Washington, DC 20001 info@WDC.greenpeace.org
www.Greenpeaceusa.org
Greenpeace is an independent campaigning organization which uses non-violent creative confrontation to expose global environmental problems, and to force solutions that are essential to a green and peaceful future.
Phil Radford, Executive Director
David Barre, Communication Director

2114 Harvard Environmental Law Society
Harvard Law School
1585 Massachusetts Avenue 617-495-3125
Cambridge, MA 00213 els@mail.law.harvard.edu
The Harvard Environmental Law Society was founded by three Harvard Law students who perceived a pressing need for the Law School, and the law in general, to respond more effectively to the nation's environmental problems. To this end,they created an organization that was committed to preparing students to creatively and intelligently use the law in the service of the environment.

Alice Cherry, Co-President
Kelsey Skaggs, Co-President

2115 Humane Society Legislative Fund
2100 L Street NW 202-676-2314
Suite 310 866-720-2676
Washington, DC 20037 humanesociety@hslf.org
www.hslf.org
Humane Society Legislative Fund (HSLF) is a social welfare organization. HSLF works to pass animal protection laws at the state and federal level, to educate the public about animal protection issues, and to support humane candidatesfor office.
Michael Markarian, President
Wayne Pacelle, Executive Vice President

2116 International Land Conservation Network
617-661-3016
landconservationnetwork.org
The International Land Conservation Network connects organizations around the world that focus on the conservation, management, and development of land and water resources. They provide research, training, information regardingfinance, law, organization, stewardship and regional capacity building.
Laura Johnson, Director
Jivan Sobrinho-Wheeler, Project Coordinator

2117 LandWatch Monterey County
PO Box 1876 831-759-2824
Salinas, CA 93902-1876 *Fax:* 831-759-2825
landwatch@mclw.org
www.landwatch.org
LandWatch is a nonprofit membership organization, founded in 1997. LandWatch works to promote and inspire sound land use

legislation at the city, country, and regional lands, through grass-roots community action.
Chris Fitz, President
Amy White, Executive Director

2118 League of Conservation Voters
1920 L Street NW 202-785-8683
Suite 800 *Fax:* 202-835-0491
Washington, DC 20036 seth_stein@lcv.org
www.lcv.org
Works to create a Congress more responsive to your environmental concerns. As the nonpartisan political voice for over nine million members of environmental and conservation groups, LCV is the only national environmental organizationdedicated full-time to educating citizens about the environmental voting records of Members of Congress.
Carol Browner, Chair
Gene Karpinski, President

2119 League of Women Voters of the United States
1730 M Street NW 202-429-1965
Suite 1000 *Fax:* 202-429-0854
Washington, DC 20036-4508 lwv@lwv.org
www.lwv.org
The League of Women Voters, a nonpartisan political organization, encourages the informed and active participation of citizens in government, works to increase understanding of major public policy issues and influences public policythrough education and advocacy.
Elisabeth MacNamara, President
Toni Larson, Vice President

2120 Legacy International
1020 Legacy Drive 540-297-5982
Bedford, VA 24523 *Fax:* 540-297-1860
mail@legacyintl.org
www.legacyintl.org
Creates environments where people can address personal, community, and global needs while developing skills and effective responses to change.Whether working with youths, corporate leaders, educational professionals, entrepreneurs, orindividuals on opposing sides of a conflict, our goal is the same. Programs provide experiences, skills, and strategies that enable people to build better lives for themselves and others around them.
J E Rash, President
Shanti Thompson, VP/Director of Training

2121 National Association of Conservation Districts League City Office
509 Capitol Ct NE 202-547-6223
Washington, DC 20002 *Fax:* 202-547-6450
www.nacdnet.org
To serve conservation districts by providing national leadership and a unified voice for natural resource conservation.
David Guenther, President
Jeremy Peters, Chief Executive Officer

2122 Natural Resources Defense Council (NRDC)
40 West 20th Street 212-727-2700
New York, NY 10011 *Fax:* 212-727-1773
nrdcinfo@nrdc.org
www.nrdc.org
The NRDC focuses on issues impacting climate change, ocean pollution, water management and treatment, clean energy, and the conservation of wildlife.
Rhea Suh, President
Mitchell Bernard, Chief Counsel

2123 New Mexico Environmental Law Center
1405 Luisa Street 505-989-9022
Suite 5 *Fax:* 505-989-3769
Santa Fe, NM 87505 nmelc@nmelc.org
www.nmenvirolaw.org
The New Mexico Environmental Law Center works to protect New Mexico's communities and their environments through public education, legislative initiatives, administrative negotiations and litigation.
Douglas Meiklejohn, Executive Director
Shelbie Knox, Development Officer

2124 Southern Environmental Law Center
201 W Main Street 434-977-4090
Suite 14 *Fax:* 434-977-1483
Charlottesville, VA 22902 selcva@selcva.org
www.southernenvironment.org
Dedicated to protecting the natural resources of Alabama, Georgia, North Carolina, South Carolina, Tennessee and Virginia. Works with more than 100 partner groups to safeguard southern forests, wetlands, coastal resources, rivers, airand water quality, wildlife habitat and rural landscapes through policy reform, public education, and direct legal action.
Dennis M. Crumpler, President
Rick Middleton, Executive Director

2125 Stanford Environmental Law Society
559 Nathan Abbott Way 650-723-4421
Stanford, CA 94305-8610 elj.stanford.edu/
Provides students with a unique set of opportunities to tap into structured programs or to create and pursue their own projects. Both organizations complement the Stanford Environmental and Natural Reources Law and Policy Program.
Zachary Fabish, Co-President
Craig Segall, Co-President

2126 Student Environmental Action Coalition
PO Box 31909 215-222-4711
Philadelphia, PA 19104 webteam@seac.org
Student and youth run national network of progressive organizations and individuals whose aim is to uproot environmental injustices through action and education. Works to create progressive social change on both the local and globallevels.
Matt Reitmann, Working Comte Coordinator

2127 US Public Interest Research Group
294 Washington St 617-747-4370
Suite 500 *Fax:* 202-546-2461
Boston, MA 00210 webmaster@pirg.org
www.uspirg.org
Mission: To deliver persistent, result-oriented public interest activism that protects our environment, encourages a fair, sustainable economy, and fosters responsive, democratic government.
Douglas H Phelps, President
Andre Delattre, Executive Director

2128 Western Environmental Law Center
1216 Lincoln Street 541-485-2471
Eugene, OR 97401 *Fax:* 541-485-2457
info@westernlaw.org
www.westernlaw.org
The Western Environmental Law Center is a non-profit public interest law firm that works to protect and restore western wildlands and advocates for healthy environments on behalf of communities throughout the West.
Lori Maddox, President
Karin P. Sheldon, Vice President

Publications

2129 A Guide to Environmental Law in Washington DC
Environmental Law Institute
1730 M Street, NW 202-939-3800
Suite 700 *Fax:* 202-939-3868
Washington, DC 20036 law@eli.org
www.eli.org
Community Education and Training Program provides citizens and grassroots groups with information on environmental law and policy that can help them participate effectively in the decisions that impact public health and the environmentin their communities. Program's activities have included training courses on right-to-know laws and a series of workshops in demystifying the

law, which focus on using the tools of public participation to address issues ranging from hazardous wasteto land use.
Scott Schang, President
Scott Fulton, President Elect

2130 Buying Green: Federal Purchasing Practices and the Environment
Government Printing Office
732 North Capitol Street NW 202-512-1800
Washington, DC 20401-0001 866-512-1800
Fax: 202-512-2104
ContactCenter@gpo.gov
www.gpo.gov
Jim Breadley, Deputy Director
Andrew M. Sherman, Cheif of Staff

2131 Clean Water Act Twenty Years Later
Island Press
2000 M Street NW 202-232-7933
Suite 650 *Fax:* 202-234-1328
Washington, DC 20036 info@islandpress.org
www.islandpress.org
333 pages
ISBN: 1-559632-65-8
Richard W Alder; Jessica C Landman; Diane Cameron, Author
Charles C. Savitt, President
David Miller, SVP/Editor

2132 Comparative Environmental Law and Regulation
Oceana Publications, Inc
198 Madison Avenue 800-334-4249
New York, NY 10016 *Fax:* 212-726-6476
oxfordonline@oup.com
www.oceanalaw.com
Key environmental laws, regulations and implementation systems and agencies of 37 countries from around the world.
2 vol pages Semi-Annual
ISBN: 0-379012-51-0
Nicholas A Robinson, Editor

2133 Environmental Defense Fund Solutions Newsletter
257 Park Avenue South 212-505-2100
New York, NY 10010 *Fax:* 212-505-2375
www.edf.org
Dedicated to protecting the environmental rights of all people, including future generations. Among these rights are clean air, clean water, healthy, nourishing food and a flourishing ecosystem. Advocates solutions based on science,even when it leads in unfamiliar directions. Works to create solutions that win lasting political, economic and social support because they are bipartisan, efficient and fair.

Fred Krupp, President
Catherine Nardone, Chief Development Officer

2134 Environmental Law and Compliance Methods
Oceana Publications, Inc
198 Madison Avenue 800-334-4249
New York, NY 10016 *Fax:* 212-726-6476
www.oceanalaw.com
Presents practical information tailored to professionals responsible for day-to-day compliance with the environmental laws of the US.
678 pages One Time
ISBN: 0-379214-26-1
Edward E Shea, Author

2135 Environmental Politics and Policy
Congressional Quarterly Press
1255 22nd Street NW 202-729-1800
Suite 400
Washington, DC 20037
366 pages
ISBN: 1-568028-78-4
Walker A Rosenbaum, Author

2136 Environmental Regulatory Glossary
Government Institutes
4 Research Place 301-921-2300
Suite 200 *Fax:* 301-921-0373
Rockville, MD 20850
623 pages
Thomas F P Sullivan, Author

2137 Insider's Guide to Environmental Negotiation
Lewis Publishers
PO Box 72264 229-432-1781
Albany, GA 31708 tlewis@lewispub.com
www.lewispub.com
242 pages
ISBN: 0-873715-09-8
Dale M Gorczynski, Author

2138 International Environmental Policy: From the Twentieth to the Twenty-First Century
Duke University Press
905 W Main Street, Ste 18-B 919-688-5134
Durham, NC 27701 888-651-0122
Fax: 919-688-2615
www.dukepress.com
496 pages
Ken Wissoker, Editor in Chief
Courtney Berger, Assistant Editor

2139 Making Development Sustainable: Redefining Institutions, Policy, and Economics
Island Press
2000 M Street NW 202-232-7933
Suite 650 *Fax:* 202-234-1328
Washington, DC 20036 info@islandpress.org
www.islandpress.org
362 pages
ISBN: 1-559632-13-5
Johan Holmberg, Author
Charles C. Savitt, President
David Miller, SVP/Editor

2140 Managing Planet Earth: Perspectives on Population, Ecology and the Law
Greenwood Publishing Group
130 Cremona Drive 805-968-1911
Santa Barbara, CA 93117 800-368-6868
Fax: 866-270-3856
CustomerService@abc-clio.com
www.abc-clio.com
184 pages
ISBN: 0-897892-16-X
Miguel A Santos, Author
Vince Burns, Vice President

2141 Natural Resources Policy and Law: Trends and Directions
Island Press; Natural Resources Law Center
2000 M Street NW 202-232-7933
Suite 650 *Fax:* 202-234-1328
Washington, DC 20036 info@islandpress.org
www.islandpress.org
255 pages
ISBN: 1-559632-46-1
Lawrence J MacDonnell; Sarah F Bates, Author
Charles C. Savitt, President
David Miller, SVP/Editor

2142 New Mexico Environmental Law Center: Green Fire Report
1405 Luisa Street 505-989-9022
Suite 5 *Fax:* 505-989-3769
Santa Fe, NM 87505 nmelc@nmelc.org
A publication from the organization dedicated to protecting New Mexico's natural environment and communities from pollution and degradation. Over 80 percent of our clients are indigenous

Native American or Hispanic and low income.Cases often include mining issues, growth impacts, water protection, air pollution, public lands protection or indigenous land claims. The organization is supported by grants from foundations, contributions from individuals and fees.

12 pages Quarterly
Douglas Meiklejohn, Executive Director
Shelbie Knox, Development Officer

2143 Oversight of Implementation of the Clean Air Act Amendments of 1990
Government Printing Office
1616 P Street NW 202-328-5000
Washington, DC 20036 *Fax:* 202-939-3460
contactcenter@gpo.gov
www.rff.org

ISBN: 0-160388-26-0
Dana Yanocha, Development Officer
Adrienne Young, Managing Editor

2144 Renewable Resource Policy: The Legal-Institutional Foundation
Island Press
2000 M Street NW 202-232-7933
Suite 650 *Fax:* 202-234-1328
Washington, DC 20036 info@islandpress.org
www.islandpress.org

572 pages
ISBN: 1-559632-25-9
Charles C. Savitt, President
David Miller, SVP/Editor

2145 Saving All the Parts: Reconciling Economics and the Endangered Species Act
Island Press
2000 M Street NW 202-232-7933
Suite 650 *Fax:* 202-234-1328
Washington, DC 20036 info@islandpress.org
www.islandpress.org

280 pages
ISBN: 1-559632-02-X
Rocky Barker, Author
Charles C. Savitt, President
David Miller, SVP/Editor

2146 Searching Out the Headwaters: Change and Rediscovery in Western Policy
Island Press
2000 M Street NW 202-232-7933
Suite 650 *Fax:* 202-234-1328
Washington, DC 20036 info@islandpress.org
www.islandpress.org

253 pages
ISBN: 1-559632-17-8
Sarah F Bates, et al, Author
Charles C. Savitt, President
David Miller, SVP/Editor

2147 Setting National Priorities: Policy for the Nineties
Brookings Institution
1775 Massachusetts Ave., NW 202-797-6000
Washington, DC 20036 800-275-1447
Fax: 202-797-6004
www.brookings.edu

Strobe Talbott, President
Martin S Indyk, Executive Vice President

2148 Trade and the Environment: Law, Economics and Policy
Island Press
2000 M Street NW 202-232-7933
Suite 650 *Fax:* 202-234-1328
Washington, DC 20036 info@islandpress.org
www.islandpress.org

333 pages
ISBN: 1-559632-67-4
Charles C. Savitt, President
David Miller, SVP/Editor

2149 Understanding Environmental Administration and Law
Island Press
2000 M Street NW 202-232-7933
Suite 650 *Fax:* 202-234-1328
Washington, DC 20036 info@islandpress.org
www.islandpress.org

239 pages
ISBN: 1-559634-74-X
Susan J Buck, Author
Charles C. Savitt, President
David Miller, SVP/Editor

Financial Resources

Foundations & Charities

2150 AMETEK Foundation
1100 Cassatt Road
PO Box 1764
Berwyn, PA 19312
610-647-2121
800-473-1286
Fax: 215-323-9337
webmaster@ametek.com
www.ametek.com

AMETEK is a global manufacturer of electronic insturments and electric motors. The AMETEK Foundation provides funding for community programs such as science education for children. The products made by this company supportenvironmental sustainability, the production of renewable fuels and solar energy.

Frank S. Hermance, Chairman
David A. Zapico, CEO

2151 ARCO Foundation
515 South Flower Street
Los Angeles, CA 90071
213-486-3342
www.southlandarchitecture.com

The foundation awards education grants both on the national and regional level. Education programs that are national in scope are funded through the headquarters located in Los Angeles. Regional grants are made to nonprofitorganizations in states where ARCO has facilities and personnel.

Russell Sakaguchi, Program Officer

2152 Abelard Foundation
2530 San Pable Avenue
Suite B
Berkeley, CA 94702
510-644-1904

A family foundation with a 40 year history of progressive funding. The foundation is committed to supporting grassroots social change organizations which engage in community organizing.

Leah Brumer, Executive Director

2153 Acid Rain Foundation
1410 Varsity Drive
Raleigh, NC 27606
919-828-9443
Fax: 919-515-3593

Designed to significantly reduce emissions responsible for acid deposition.

Dr. Harriet S Stubbs, Executive Director

2154 African Wildlife Foundation
1400 Sixteenth Street, NW
Suite 120
Washington, DC 20036
202-939-3333
888-494-5354
Fax: 202-939-3332
africanwildlife@awf.org
www.awf.org

The African Wildlife Foundation, together with the people of Africa, work to ensure the wildlife and wild lands of Africa will endure forever. The AFW is the leading international conservation organization focused soley on Africa. Webelieve that protecting Africa's wildlife and wild landscapes is the key to the future prosperity of Africa and its people.

Jef Dupain, Director
Fiesta Warinwa, Program Director

2155 Aldo Leopold Foundation
E13701 Levee Road
PO Box 77
Baraboo, WI 53913-0077
608-355-0279
Fax: 608-356-7309
mail@aldoleopold.org
www.aldoleopold.org

Nonprofit organization that works to promote the philosophy of Aldo Leopold and the land ethic he so eloquently defined in his writing. The foundation actively integrates programs on land stewardship, environmental education andscientific research to promote care of natural resources and have an ethical relationship between people and land.

Buddy Huffaker, Executive Director
Jennifer Farnum, Director, Development

2156 Amax Foundation
200 Park Avenue
New York, NY 10166
212-856-4250

Sonja Michaud, President

2157 American Association of Petroleum Geologists Foundation
1444 S. Boulder
Tulsa, OK 74119
918-584-2555
800-364-2274
Fax: 918-560-2665
info@aapg.org
www.aapg.org

News for explorationists of oil, gas and minerals as well as for geologists with environmental and water well concerns.

John R Hogg, President
Paul W Britt, President Elect

2158 American Electric Power
1 Riverside Plaza
Columbus, OH 43215-2372
614-716-1000
corpcomm@aep.com
www.aep.com

One of the largest electric utilities in the United States, delivering electricity to more then 5 million customers in 11 states. AEP ranks among the nations largest generators of electricity, owning more then 38,000 megawatts ofgenerating capacity in the US.

Nicholas K. Akins, President & CEO
Robert P. Powers, Executive Vice President

2159 American Forest Foundation (AFF)
2000 M Street NW
Suite 550
Washington, DC 20036
202-765-3660
Fax: 202-827-7924
info@forestfoundation.org
www.forestfoundation.org

Nonprofit conservation and education organization that strives to ensure the sustainability of America's family forests for present and future generations. The vision is to create a future where North American forests are sustained bythe public which understands and values the social, economic, and environmental benefits they provide to the communities, the nation, and the world.

Tom Martin, President & CEO
Rita Hite, EVP, Woodlands & Policy

2160 American Gas Foundation
400 North Capitol Street NW
Suite 450
Washington, DC 20001
202-824-7329
Fax: 202-824-9116
www.gasfoundation.org

Funds research into energy policy, intended for use by policy experts, government officials, the media, and others. Offers the $5 million Georgetown University Energy Prize.

Rick Murphy, Contact

2161 American Geosciences Institute Foundation (AGIF)
American Geosciences Institute
4220 King Street
Alexandria, VA 22302-1502
703-379-2480
Fax: 703-379-7563
agi@americangeosciences.org
www.americangeosciences.org

Charitable arm of the American Geological Institute, seeking funding and partnerships with other organizations, corporations, and individuals.

Daniel D. Domeracki, Chair
Alexandra Lowe Lees, Director, Development

2162 American Rivers
1101 14th Street NW
Suite 1400
Washington, DC 20005
202-347-7550
877-347-7550
feedback@americanrivers.org
www.americanrivers.org

American Rivers is an organization that uses advocacy and field work to accomplish their mission of protecting and restoring the nation's rivers. They work with local river advocates, business and agricultural interests, recreationgroups, and others to accomplish their goals.

William Robert Irwin, President
Kimberley Milligan, Chair

2163 **Amoco Foundation**
501 Westlake Park Boulevard 312-856-6306
Houston, TX 77079 bpconsum@bp.com
www.bp.com
The BP Amoco awards grants for education, primarily in the field of science and engineering, as well as community organizations in BP Amoco communities.
Dr. Brian Gilvary, CFO
Bernard Looney, COO Production

2164 **Andrew W. Mellon Foundation**
140 East 62nd Street 212-838-8400
New York, NY 10065 *Fax:* 212-888-4172
inquiries@mellon.org
www.mellon.org
The foundation concentrates most of its grantmaking in a few areas. Institutions and programs receiving support are often leaders in fields of Foundation activity, but they may also be promising newcomers, or in a position todemonstrate new ways of overcoming obstacles to achieve program goals.
Earl Lewis, President
Mariët Westermann, Vice President

2165 **Association of Environmental Engineering and Science Professors Foundation**
AEESP Business Office 202-640-6591
1211 Connecticut Ave NW, Suite 650 *Fax:* 217-355-9232
Washington, DC 20036 bschorr@aeesp.org
www.aeesp.org/awards
The AEESP Foundation provides numerous awards recognizing service, research, professional involvement, and teaching in environmental engineering and science.
Karl G. Linden, President
Brian Schorr, Business Contact

2166 **Asthma and Allergy Foundation of America**
8201 Corporate Drive 202-466-7643
Suite 1000 800-727-8462
Landover, MD 20785 *Fax:* 202-466-8940
info@aafa.org
www.aafa.org
Dedicated to improving the quality of life for people with asthma and allergies through education, advocacy and research.
Heidi Bayer, Chair
James Flood, Chair, Finance & Treasurer

2167 **Atherton Family Foundation**
827 Fort Street Mall 808-566-5524
Honolulu, HI 96813 888-731-3863
Fax: 808-521-6286
foundations@hcf-hawaii.org
www.athertonfamilyfoundation.org
The Atherton Family Foundation is now one of the largest endowed grantmaking private resource in the State of Hawaii, devoted exclusively to the support of charutabe activities. It perpetuates the philanthropic commitment expressedduring the lifetime of Juliette M. Atherton and Frank C. Atherton, and of the family who have followed them.
Judith M. Dawson, President
Frank C. Atherton, Vice President & Treasurer

2168 **Audubon Naturalist Society of the Central Atlantic States**
8940 Jones Mill Road 301-652-9188
Chevy Chase, MD 20815 *Fax:* 301-951-7179
contact@audubonnaturalist.org
www.audubonnaturalist.org
The Audubon Naturalist Society is an independent environmental education and conservation organization with over 10,000 members in the Washington DC area. The society offers a wide variety of natural history classes and campaigns forprotection and renewal of the Mid-Atlantic regions natural resources.
Lee Babcock, President
Leslie Catherwood, Vice President

2169 **BP America**
501 Westlake Park Boulevard 281-366-2000
Houston, TX 77079 bpconsum@bp.com
www.bp.com
The purpose is to provide products that satisfy human needs, fuel progress and economic growth and to maintain and invest in a sustainable environment.
Dr. Brian Gilvary, CFO
Bernard Looney, COO Production

2170 **Baltimore Gas & Electric Foundation**
PO Box 1475 410-265-4100
Baltimore, MD 21203 800-685-0123
Fax: 410-234-7123
corporate.communications@bge.com
www.bge.com
The mission is to safely, economically, reliably, and profitably deliver gas and electricity to our customers. The vision is to be a recognized leader in energy delivery by enhancing our customer's quality of life, our shareholdersvalue, and our team's well being.
Stephen J Woerner PE, President & COO
Calvin G Butler, Chief Executive Officer

2171 **Bauman Foundation**
2040 S Street, NW 202-328-2040
Washington, DC 20009 *Fax:* 202-328-2003
www.baumanfoundation.org
The Bauman Foundation was funded by the estate of Lionel R. Bauman, a New York City lawyer and businessman. He was a partner in the real estate development firm of Eugene M. Grant & Co. The foundation is managed by Lionel's daughter.Patricia Bauman.
Patricia Bauman, President
John Landrum Bryant, Vice President & Treasurer

2172 **Bay and Paul Foundations, The**
17 West 94th Street 212-663-1115
1st Floor *Fax:* 212-932-0316
New York, NY 10025 info@bayandpaul.org
www.bayandpaulfoundations.org
The Bay and Paul Foundations Inc. was formed in January 2005 by the merger of 2 foundations. The Bay Foundation and the Josephine Bay Paul and C. Michael Paul Foundation.
David Bury, Chairman
Fred Bay, President & CEO

2173 **Bear Conservation Fund (BCF)**
IBA
University Hall 907-223-3483
Room 309 www.bearbiology.com
Missoula, MT 59812
Charitable arm of the International Association for Bear Research and Management (IBA), funding priority research and solutions to bear conservation problems. Also partners with other institutions.

Julia Bevins, Chair

2174 **Blandin Foundation**
100 North Pokegama Avenue 218-326-0523
Grand Rapids, MI 55744 877-882-2257
Fax: 218-327-1949
www.blandinfoundation.org
Blandin Foundation is focused on the economic viability of rural Minnesota communities, as part of our mission to help strengthen rural Minnesota and the Grand Rapids area, our home.
Annette Kathy, President
Wade Fauth, Vice President

2175 Boise Cascade Corporation
1111 West Jefferson Street 208-384-6161
Suite 300 *Fax:* 208-384-7189
Boise, ID 83728-5389 www.bc.com
As we focus on delivering the best return for our investors, we can be trusted to do what we say and take responsibility for our actions, which we base on values and principles.
Duane McDougall, Chairman
Thomas Carlile, CEO

2176 Camp Fire Conservation Fund Inc.
PO Box 678 campfirefund@gmail.com
Millwood, NY 10546 www.campfirefund.org
The financial arm of the Camp-Fire Club of America, which is a wildlife and habitat conservation organization that has been around for over 100 years.
Avery Stirratt, President
Ben W. Koehler, Vice President

2177 Cape Branch Foundation
5 Independence Way 609-987-0300
Princeton, NJ 00854 *Fax:* 609-452-1024
A private foundation which provides grant support for higher education, museums, and land conservation in the New Jersey area. There are no grants to individuals.
Dorothy Frank, Partner

2178 Cargill Foundation
PO Box 9300 952-742-2546
Minneapolis, MN 55440-9300 800-227-4455
Fax: 952-742-7224
www.cargill.com
Cargill is an international provider of food, agricultural and risk management products and services. With 158,000 employees in 66 countries, the company is committed to using its knoweldge and experience to collaborate with customersto help them succeed.
Gregory R. Page, Chairman & CEO
David W MacLennan, President, COO & CFO

2179 Caribbean Conservation Corporation
4424 NW 13th Street 352-373-6441
Suite B-11 800-678-7853
Gainesville, FL 32609 *Fax:* 352-375-2449
stc@conserveturtles.org
www.conserveturtles.org
Caribbean Conservation Corporation is a nonprofit membership organization based in Gainesville. CCC was the first marine turtle conservation organization in the world, and has more than 40 years of experience in national andinternational sea turtle conservation, research and educational endeavors.
Landon T. Clay, Chairman
Laura Forte, President

2180 Carolyn Foundation
1917 Logan Avenue South 612-596-3266
Minneapolis, MN 55403 612-596-3279
Fax: 612-979-2670
berdahl@carolynfoundation.org
www.carolynfoundation.org
The Carolyn Foundation is a small general foundation. Please check out our website www.carolynfoundation.org for the most up-to-date information regarding funding priorities, guidelines and application process.
Becky Erdahl, Executive Director
Caroline Partoll, Administrator

2181 Caterpillar Foundation
501 Southwest Jefferson Avenue 309-675-1000
Peoria, IL 61630 888-614-4328
www.caterpillar.com
Provides funding and support from a corporate perspective. Formed in 1952, the Foundation has distributed almost $200 million to support education, health and human services, and civic, cultural, and environmental causes.
Doug Oberhalman, Chairman & CEO
Edward J Scott, Treasurer

2182 Charles Engelhard Foundation
645 5th Avenue 212-935-2430
7th Floor
New York, NY 10022
Provides funding to a wide range of causes including education, medical research, cultural institutions, and wildlife conservation.
Elaine Catterall, Secretary

2183 Chesapeake Bay Foundation
6 Herndon Avenue 410-268-8816
Annapolis, MD 21403 *Fax:* 410-268-6687
chesapeake@cbf.org
www.cbf.org
The only independent organization dedicated soley to restoring and protecting the Chesapeake Bay and its tributary rivers.
William C Baker, President
Katharene Snavely, Vice President, Development

2184 Chevron Corporation
6001 Bollinger Canyon Road 925-842-1000
San Ramon, CA 94583 chevweb@chevron.com
www.chevron.com
As a global enterprise that is highly competitive across all energy sectors, Chevron brings together a wealth of talent, shared values and a strong commitment to developing vital energy resources worldwide.
John S Watson, Chairman
Alexander B Cummings, Executive Vice President

2185 Clean Water Action
1444 Eye Street NW 202-895-0420
Suite 400 *Fax:* 202-895-0438
Washington, DC 20005 cwa@cleanwater.org
www.cleanwateraction.org
Clean Water Action is a national organization of diverse people and groups working together for clean water, protecting health, creating jobs and making democracy work.
David Tykulsker, Chair
Robert Wendelgass, President

2186 Collins Foundation
1618 SW 1st Avenue 503-227-7171
Suite 505 *Fax:* 503-295-3794
Portland, OR 97201 information@collinsfoundation.org
www.collinsfoundation.org
An independent private foundation, exists to improve, enrich and give greater expression to the religious, educational, cultural, and scientific endeavors in the state of Oregon and to assist in improving the quality of life in thestate.
Truman W. Collins Jr., President
Cynthia G Adams, Executive Vice President

2187 Compton Foundation
101 Montgomery Street 415-391-9001
Suite 850 *Fax:* 415-391-9005
San Francisco, CA 94104 info@comptonfoundation.org
www.comptonfoundation.org
Seeks to foster human and ecological security by addressing contemporary threats to these inalienable rights. We support responsible stewardship that respects the rights of future generations to a balanced and healthy ecology, bothpersonal and global, allowing for the full richness of human experience.
Rebecca DiDomenico, President
Rebecca DiDomenico, Vice President

2188 Conservation International
2011 Crystal Dr 703-341-2400
Suite 500 800-429-5660
Arlington, VA 22202 www.conservation.org

CI promotes sustainable development and the conservation of earth's ecosystems as keys to solving climate change.
Peter Seligmann, Chair
M. Sanjayan, Chief Executive Officer

2189 Conservation and Research Foundation
PO Box 909 913-268-0076
Shelburne, VT 05482 *Fax:* 913-268-0076
conservationresearch.wordpress.com
Dr Mary Wetzel, President
Philip M Lintilhac, Secretary

2190 Cooper Industries Foundation
1000 Eaton Boulevard 713-209-8400
Cleveland, OH 44122 *Fax:* 713-209-8982
www.cooperindustries.com
Cooper was primarily a one-market company, manufactguring power and compression equipment for the transmission of natural gas. Eventually broadening its product lines to include petroleum and industrial equipment, electrical powerequipment, automotive products tools and hardware.
Alexander M Cutler, Chairman & CEO
Kenneth F Davis, President, Vehicle Group

2191 Cricket Foundation
Exchange Place 617-570-1130
Suite 2200 *Fax:* 617-523-1231
Boston, MA 00210
Dedicated to improving the quality of life
George W Butterworth III, Counsel

2192 Curtis and Edith Munson Foundation
1320 19th Street 202-887-8992
Suite 500 *Fax:* 202-887-8987
Washington, DC 20036 info@munsonfdn.org
www.munsonfdn.org
Over the past 15 years, we have emphasized partnerships, collaborations, and seed funding for new projects and organizations within the framework of our programs as defined by our guidelines.
C Wolcott Henry III, President
Angel Braestrup, Executive Director

2193 Deer Creek Foundation
20701 N. MacArthur Blvd 314-241-3228
Edmond, OK 73012 dcsfoundation.org
Projects should focus on the preservation and advancement of majority rule in our society, including the protection of basic rights
Rich DiAngelo, President
Gerald Elrod, Vice President

2194 Defenders of Wildlife
1130 17th Street NW 202-682-9400
Washington, DC 20036 800-385-9712
Fax: 202-682-1331
defenders@mail.defenders.org
www.defenders.org
Dedicated to the protection of all native wild animals and plants in their natural communities. Focus is placed on what scientists consider two of the most serious environmental threats to the planet: the accelerating rate ofextinction of species and the associated loss of biological diversity, and habitat alteration and destruction. Long known for leadership on endangered species issues.
Jamie Rappaport Clark, President & CEO

2195 Dunspaugh-Dalton Foundation
1501 Venera Avenue 305-668-4192
Suite 312 *Fax:* 305-668-4247
Coral Gables, FL 33146 ddf@dunspaughdalton.org
www.dunspaughdalton.com
Supports educational, social, medical and cultural institutions in Florida, California and North Carolina.
Sarah Lane Bonner, President
Aexina H Lane, Vice President

2196 Earth Society Foundation
238 E 58th Street 212-832-3659
Suite 2400 *Fax:* 212-826-6213
New York, NY 10022 earthsociety1@hotmail.com
earthsocietyfoundation.org
Started the original Earth Day, which is devoted to peace, justice and the care of earth. It invites everyone to think and act as trustees of earth.
Thomas C Dowd, President
Helen Garland, Chairperson

2197 EarthShare
7735 Old Georgetown Road 800-875-3863
Suite 900 *Fax:* 240-333-0301
Bethesda, MD 20814 info@earthshare.org
www.earthshare.org
A nationwide network of America's leading non-profit environmental and conservation organizations; works to promote environmental education and charitable giving through workplace giving campaigns.
Deb Furry, Interim CEO
Mary MacDonald, Sr. VP, Business Development

2198 Echoing Green
462 Seventh Avenue 212-689-1165
Thirteenth Floor *Fax:* 212-689-9010
New York, NY 10001 info@echoinggreen.org
www.echoinggreen.org
Echoing Green is a global science venture fund that provides seed funding and support to visionary leaders with bold new ideas for social change.
David C Hodgson, Chairman
Maya Ajmera, Co-Chairman

2199 Edward John Noble Foundation
Po Box 954 203-438-5690
Ridgefield, CT 00687
EJ Noble Smith, Executive Director

2200 Energy Foundation
301 Battery Street 415-561-6700
5th Floor *Fax:* 415-561-6709
San Francisco, CA 94111 energyfund@ef.org
www.ef.org
The Energy Foundation is a partnership of major donors interested in solving the world's energy problems by promoting energy efficiency and renewable energy.

Eric Heitz, CEO & Co-Founder
Mark Burget, VP, Regional Director

2201 Environmental Engineering and Science Foundation (EESF)
AAEES
147 Old Solomons Island Road 410-266-3390
Suite 303 info@eesfoundation.org
Annapolis, MD 21401 www.eesfoundation.org
Established by the American Academy of Environmental Engineers and Scientists to be its tax-exempt vehicle for accepting donations, it supports work in the areas of chapter development, partnerships, and recognizing engineers andscientists through the Frederick G. Pohland Medal, W. Brewster Snow Award, and the W. Eckenfelder Memorial Fund.
Cecil Lue-Hing, President
Brian P. Flynn, Secretary-Treasurer

2202 Environmental Law Institute
1730 M Street, NW 202-939-3800
Suite 700 *Fax:* 202-939-3868
Washington, DC 20036 law@eli.org
www.eli.org
Provides information services, advice, publications, training courses, seminars, research programs and policy recommendations to engage and empower environmental leaders the world over.
Scott Schang, President
Scott Fulton, President Elect

2203 Exxon Education Foundation
225 E John W Carpenter Freeway 972-444-1000
Room 1429 www.exxon.com
Irving, TX 75062
It is ExxonMobil's longstanding belief that education is the key to progress, development and economic growth, and we are committed to being a responsible partner in the communities where we operate.
Leonard Fleischer, Mgr. Corporate Contributions

2204 First Hawaiian Foundation
999 S Bishop Street 808-525-7000
29th Floor www.fhb.com
Honolulu, HI 96813
First Hawaiian Foundation is the charitable arm of First Hawaiian Bank. The foundation funds educational opportunities, access to health care, services for children and youth, human service needs, and the many ways that the arts enrichour lives.
Herbert E Wolff, Secretary

2205 First Interstate Bank of Nevada Foundation
PO Box 11007 775-784-3844
Reno, NV 89520 www.firstinterstatebank.com
Kevin Day, President

2206 FishAmerica Foundation
1001 North Fairfax St. 703-519-9691
Suite 501 *Fax:* 703-519-1872
Alexandria, VA 22314 fafgrants@asafishing.org
www.fishamerica.org
Unites the sportfishing industry with conservation groups, government natural resource agencies, corporations, and charitable foundations to invest in fish and habitat conservation and research across the country.
Jeff Marble, Chairman
Patrick Egan, Grants Manager

2207 FishAmerica Foundation.
Grant Guidelines
1001 North Fairfax St. 703-519-9691
Suite 501 *Fax:* 703-519-1872
Alexandria, VA 22314 fafgrants@asafishing.org
www.fishamerica.org
The FishAmerica Foundation provides funding for local, hands-on projects to enhance fish populations, restore fisheries habitat, improve water quality, and advancing fisheries research in North America; thereby increasing theopportunity for sportfishing success.

Jeff Marble, Chairman
Patrick Egan, Grants Manager

2208 Ford Foundation Center for Social Justice
320 E 43rd Street 212-573-5000
New York, NY 10017 *Fax:* 212-351-3677
www.fordfoundation.org
Concerned with natural resource preservation. Provides funding for environmental projects throughout the world.
Francisco G. Cigarroa, Chair
Darren Walker, President

2209 Foundation to Support Animal Protection (FSAP)
501 Front Street 757-622-7382
Norfolk, VA 23510 *Fax:* 757-622-0457
info@peta.org
www.petafoundation.org
Also known as the PETA Foundation, it is the charitable arm of People for the Ethical Treatment of Animals. It provides general and administrative support services to PETA and other related animal protection organizations.

Ingrid Newkirk, President
Tracy Reiman, Executive Vice President

2210 Frost Foundation
511 Armijo 505-986-0208
Suite A info@frostfound.org
Santa Fe, NM 87501 www.frostfound.org
Created to be operated exclusively for educational, charitable and religious purposes. The foundation possesses all powers, rights, privileges, capacities and immunities which non profit corporations are authorized to possess.
Mary Amelia Whited-Howell, President
Philip B. Howell, Executive Vice President

2211 Fund for Animals
1255 23rd Street NW 866-482-3708
Suite 460 info@fundforanimals.org
Washington, DC 20037 www.fundforanimals.org
The Fund for Animals was founded by author/humanitarian Cleveland Amory and in 2005 merged with The Humane Society of the United States. It is dedicated to protecting animals and providing veterinary and rehabilitative needs.

Melissa Seide Rubin, President
G. Thomas Waite III, Treasurer

2212 Fund for Preservation of Wildlife and Natural Areas
Boston Safe Deposit and Trust Company
1 Boston Place 617-722-7340
Boston, MA 00210 *Fax:* 617-722-7129
Accounting services for mutual fund companies.
Sylvia Salas, Director

2213 George B Storer Foundation
220 South King Street 307-733-0800
Jackson, WY 83001 info@storerfoundation.org
storerfoundation.org
Provides support for higher education and social services, especially for the blind, youth organizations, conservation, hospitals, and cultural programs.
Peter Storer, Chairman
Elizabeth Storer, President & CEO

2214 Georgia Pacific Foundation
133 Peachtree Street NE 404-652-4000
Atlanta, GA 30303 www.gp.com
Invests in educational efforts that empower youth, and provide workers with job readiness training. We also invest in scholarships and technical programs that give workers the skills necessary for today's workplace.
Curley M Dossman, President
Michael E. Adams, SVP, Sourcing

2215 Geraldine R. Dodge Foundation
14 Maple Avenue 973-540-8442
Suite 400 *Fax:* 973-540-1211
Morristown, NJ 00796 info@grdodge.org
www.grdodge.org
The mission of the Geraldine R. Dodge Foundation is to support and encourage those educational, cultural, social and environmental values that contribute to making our society more humaine and our world more liveable.
Chris Daggett, President & CEO
Cynthia Evans, Chief Financial Officer

2216 Great Bear Foundation
PO Box 1616 907-766-2024
Haines, AK 99827 gbf@greatbear.org
www.greatbear.org
The Foundation was established to promote conservation of wild bears and their natural habitat worldwide.

Frank Tyro, PhD, President
Shannon Donahue, Executive Director

2217 Greensward Foundation
Po Box 610 Lenox Hill Station 917-655-9491
New York, NY 10021 help@echonyc.com
www.echonyc.com
The Greensward Foundation, through its local branches, celebrates and suppports our communities's public parks. We are nonprofit. We receive no public funding, subsisting entirely on private grants and member contributions.
Robert M Makla, Director

2218 HKH Foundation
275 Madison Avenue 212-682-7522
33rd Floor
New York, NY 10016
Gives a major portion of its funding to the Adirondack Historical Association. Additional funding is distributed to the disarmament and prevention of war, civil liberties and human rights, and environmental protection.
Harriet Barlow, Adv.

2219 Helen Clay Frick Foundation
7227 Reynolds Street 412-371-0600
PO Box 86190
Pittsburgh, PA 15208
Devoted to the interpretation of the life and times of Henry Clay Frick.
DeCoursey E McIntosh, Executive Director

2220 Henry L and Consuelo S Wenger Foundation
100 Renaissance Center 313-567-1212
Detroit, MI 48226
Shelly Raines, Principal Manager

2221 Hoffman-La Roche Foundation
340 Kingsland Street 973-235-5000
Nutley, NJ 00711
Hoffman-La Roche is the US prescription drug unit of the Roche Group, one of the world's leading research-oriented health care groups with core businesses in pharmaceuticals and diagnostics.
Dr Christoph Franz, Chairman
Dr Severin Schwan, CEO

2222 International Primate Protection League
PO Box 776 843-871-2280
Summerville, SC 29484 *Fax:* 843-871-7988
info@ippl.org
www.ippl.org/gibbon
An organization that works worldwide for the conservation and protection of apes and monkeys.

Dr Shirley McGreal, Executive Director
Barbara Allison, Office Manager

2223 Jessie Smith Noyes Foundation
122 East 42nd St. 212-684-6577
Suite 2501 *Fax:* 212-689-6549
New York, NY 10168 noyes@noyes.org
www.noyes.org
Promotes a sustainable and just social and natural system by supporting grassroots organizations and movements committed to this goal.

Victor DeLuca, President
Margaret Segall, Director of Administration

2224 John D and Catherine T MacArthur Foundation
140 S Dearborn Street 312-920-6285
Suite 1100 *Fax:* 312-920-6258
Chicago, IL 60603-5285 4answers@macfound.org
www.macfound.org
A private independent grantmaking institution dedicated to helping groups and individuals foster lasting improvement in the human condition.

Robert L Galluci, President

2225 Jules and Doris Stein Foundation
PO Box 30 323-276-2101
Beverly Hills, CA 90213
Founded the Jules Stein Eyes Institute at UCLA in the 1960's. Founded as a multidisciplinary center for vision science.
Linda L Valliant, Secretary

2226 Kangaroo Protection Foundation
1900 L Street NW 202-452-1100
Suite 526
Washington, DC 20036
Marian Newman, Program Director

2227 Keep America Beautiful
1010 Washington Boulevard 203-659-3000
Stamford, CT 00690 *Fax:* 203-659-3001
info@kab.org
www.kab.org
Nonprofit organization whose network of local, statewide and international affiliate programs educates individuals about litter prevention and ways to reduce, reuse, recycle and properly manage waste materials. Through partnershipsand strategic alliances with citizens, businesses and government, Keep America Beautiful's programs motivate millions of volunteers annually to clean up, beautify and improve their neighborhoods, thereby creating healthier and safer communityenvironments.
Carey Hamilton, Executive Director
Beth Buehler, Chief Operating Officer

2228 Kraft General Foods Foundation
Kraft Court 877-535-5666
Unit 2W 800-543-5335
Glenview, IL 60025 www.kraftfoods.com
Based on the values of innovation, quality, safety, respect, integrtity and openness. These values are what we stand for, the standard of conduct we hold ourselves to and our commitment to the people who work with us, invest in us andpurchase our products.
Pamela Hollie, Dir. Corporate Contributions

2229 Kroger Company Foundation
1014 Vine Street 513-762-4443
PO Box 1199 866-221-4141
Cincinnati, OH 45202-1100 www.kroger.com
Spans many states with store formats that include grocery and multi-department store, convenience stores and mall jewelry stores. We operate under nearly 2 dozen banners, all of which share the same belief in building strong local tiesand brand loyalty with our customers.
Paul Bernish, VP/Secretary

2230 Liz Claiborne Foundation
1441 Broadway Avenue
New York, NY 10018
Established to serve as the Company's center for charitable activiteis. Works to meet the needs of the communities where the major facilities of Liz Claiborne, Inc. are located. Projects focus primarily on helping disadvantaged womengain their self-sufficiency through job training and microenterprise development. The Foundation also provides ongoing support to many artistic and cultural institutions which enhance the livability of our communities.

Paul R Charron, Chairman of the Board/CEO
Angela J Ahrendts, Executive Vice President

2231 Liz Claiborne and Art Ortenberg Foundation
650 5th Avenue 212-333-2536
15th Floor *Fax:* 212-956-3531
New York, NY 10019 www.lcaof.org
The Foundation has 2 primary program interests: mitigation of conflict between the land and resources needs of local communities and conservation of biological diversity in rural landscapes outside of parks and reserves; implementationof relevant, field based scientific, technical and practical training programs for local people. The Foundation typically funds modest, carefully designed field activities-primarily in developing countries and the Northern Rockies.
James Murtaugh, Director
Jim Murtaugh, Program Director

2232 Louis and Anne Abrons Foundation
437 Madison Avenue 212-756-3376
New York, NY 10017 fdo.foundationcenter.org
Richard Abrons, President and Director

2233 Louisiana Land and Exploration Company
PO Box 60350 504-566-6500
New Orleans, LA 70160
One of the largest independent oil and gas exploration compaines in the United States. It operates a crude oil refinery and conducts

exploration and production operations in the United States and selected foreign countries.
Karen A Overson, Contributions Coordinator

2234 MNC Financial Foundation
10 Light Street 301-244-5000
PO Box 987-MS251001
Baltimore, MD 21203
Geeorge BP Ward Jr, Secretary/Treasurer
Alfred Lerner, Chairman

2235 Mark and Catherine Winkler Foundation
4900 Seminary Road 703-998-0400
Alexandria, VA 22311 *Fax:* 703-578-7899
Lynne Ball, Executive Director

2236 Mars Foundation
2156 Vail Avenue 515-480-6610
Williams, IA 50271 wcande@wcande.com
www.multiple-sclerosis-mf.org
The mission of the MARS foundation is to be committed to finding a cure for multiple sclerosis by funding medical research.
Roger G Best, Secretary

2237 Marshall and Ilsley Foundation
770 North Water Street 414-765-7835
Milwaukee, WI 53201
Provides comprehensive financial products and services and unparalleled customer service to personal, business, corporate and institutional customers nationwide.
Diana L Sebion, Secretary

2238 Mary Reynolds Babcock Foundation
2920 Reynolda Village 336-748-9222
Winston-Salem, NC 27106 *Fax:* 336-777-0095
www.mrbf.org
Our mission is to help people and places to move out of poverty and achieve greater social and economic justice.
Justin Maxson, Executive Director
Jennifer Barksdale, Finance Officer

2239 Max McGraw Wildlife Foundation
PO Box 9 847-741-8000
Dundee, IL 60118 *Fax:* 847-741-8157
www.mcgrawwildlife.org
The foundation's mission: education, research, and land management. Currently, the Foundation is invovled in over 15 research and land management projects through the Chicago region, including participation in the Chicago Wildernessinitiative. Situated on 1,225 acres, the Foundation property is managed by professional land management staff.
Stanley W Koenig, Executive Director
John Thompson, Director Research

2240 Max and Victoria Dreyfus Foundation
2233 Wisconsin Avenue NW 202-337-3300
Suite 414 *Fax:* 202-337-3302
Washington, DC 20007 info@mvdreyfusfoundation.org
www.mvdreyfusfoundation.org
A leading figure in the music publishing business, the Foundation's grantmaking supports organizations in the arts, education, health care, hospitals, social services, civic affairs, and religion.
Lucy Gioia, Administrative Assistant

2241 May Stores Foundation
611 Olive Street 314-342-6300
St. Louis, MO 63101 *Fax:* 314-342-4461
www.lordandtaylor.com
James Abrams, VP Corporate Communications

2242 McIntosh Foundation
15840 Meadows Wood Drive 202-720-7871
Wellington, FL 33414 *Fax:* 202-234-0745
mcf@aol.com
www.activistfacts.com
The McIntosh foundation began in 1949 who founded the Great Atlantic & Pacific Tea Company...later renamed A&P
Michael A McIntosh, President
Hunter H. McIntosh, Director

2243 NRA Foundation
National Rifle Association
11250 Waples Mill Road 877-672-4483
Fairfax, VA 22030 nraf@nrahq.org
www.nrafoundation.org
Charitable arm of the National Rifle Association, supporting firearm-related public interest activities, including firearm and hunting safety, marksmanship, and public education.
Wayne LaPierre, Trustee

2244 Nathan Cummings Foundation
475 Tenth Avenue 212-787-7300
14th Floor *Fax:* 212-787-7377
New York, NY 10018 contact@nathancummings.org
www.nathancummings.org
The Nathan Cummings Foundation is rooted in the Jewish tradition and committed to democratic values and social justice, including fairness, diversity, and community. They seek to build a socially and economically just society thatvalues nature and protects the ecological balance for future generations; promotes humane health care; and fosters arts and cultures that enriches communities.
Adam N. Cummings, Chair
Roberta Friedm Cummings, Vice Chair

2245 National Arbor Day Foundation
100 Arbor Avenue 402-474-5655
Nebraska City, NE 68410 888-448-7337
Fax: 402-474-0820
info@arborday.org
www.arborday.org
A nonprofit educational, environmental organization that helps people plant and care for trees. We are committed to tree-planting and environmental stewardsip. Newsletter free with $10.00 annual membership.
8 pages Bi-Monthly
John Rosenow, President
Gary Brienzo, Info. Coordinator

2246 National FFA Foundation
National Future Federation of America
6060 FFA Drive 317-802-6060
PO Box 68960 888-332-2668
Indianapolis, IN 46268-0960 www.ffa.org/national-ffa-foundation
Partners with individuals, industry, and organizations to raise funds for agricultural education. Supports numerous, awards, grants, and scholarships.
Mark Poeschl, Chief Executive Officer
Molly Ball, President

2247 National Fish and Wildlife Foundation (NFWF)
1133 15th Street, NW 202-857-0166
Suite 1000 *Fax:* 202-857-0162
Washington, DC 20005 info@nfwf.org
www.nfwf.org
Nonprofit organization dedicated to the conservation of fish, wildlife, and plants and the habitats on which they depend. Among its goals are species habitat protection, environmental education, public policy development, naturalresource management, habitat and ecosystem rehabilitation and restoration, and leadership training for conservation professionals.
Jeff Trandahl, CEO & Executive Director
Holly Bamford, PhD, Chief Conservation Officer

2248 National Forest Foundation
Fort Missoula Road 406-542-2805
Building 27, Suite 3 *Fax:* 406-542-2810
Missoula, MT 59804 mmitsos@nationalforests.org
www.nationalforests.org
The official nonprofit partner of the USDA Forest Service. To accept and administer private contributions, undertaking activities

that further the purposes for which the National Forest System was established and conductingeducational, technical, and other activities that support the multiple use, research, and forestry programs administered by the Forest Service.
Mary Mitsos, President
Sheree Bombard, Director, Administration

2249 National Geographic Society
1145 17th Street NW 800-373-1717
Washington, DC 20036 givinginfo@ngs.org
www.nationalgeographic.org
Seeks to inspire people to care about the planet. Programs support scientific fieldwork and expeditions; encourage geography education for students; and promote natural and cultural conservation.

Tracy R. Wolstencroft, President & CEO
Jonathan Baillie, Chief Scientist

2250 National Park Foundation (NPF)
1110 Vermont Avenue, NW 202-796-2500
Suite 200 888-467-2757
Washington, DC 20005 *Fax:* 202-796-2509
ask-npf@nationalparks.org
www.nationalparks.org
Mission is to strengthen the connection between the American people and their National Parks by raising private funds, making strategic grants, creating innovative parnerships and increasing public awareness.
Will Shafroth, President & CEO
Dieter Fenkart-Froeschl, Chief Operating Officer

2251 Nature Conservancy
4245 North Fairfax Drive 703-841-5300
Suite 100 800-628-6860
Arlington, VA 22203-1606 *Fax:* 703-841-1283
member@tnc.org
www.nature.org
The mission is to preserve plants, animals and natural communities that represent the diversity of life on Earth by protecting the lands and waters they need to survive.
John C Sawhill, President

2252 New England Biolabs Foundation
240 Country Road 978-998-7990
Ipswich, MA 00193 *Fax:* 978-356-3250
info@nebf.org
www.nebf.org
NEBF funds grass roots organizations in developing countries that focus on environmental issues and education.

Jessica Brown, Executive Director
David Comb, Trustees

2253 New York Times Company Foundation
620 Eighth Avenue 212-556-1982
New York, NY 10018 *Fax:* 212-556-3690
danielle.rhoades-ha@nytimes.com
www.nytco.com
This foundation provides funds to organizations that are involved in journalism, education, culture or environmentalism.
Danielle Rhoades Ha, Vice President
Eileen M. Murphy, SVP, Communications

2254 New-Land Foundation
1114 Avenue of the Americans 212-479-6086
46th Floor *Fax:* 212-841-6275
New York, NY 10036 www.rlch.org
Seeks to foster positive change throughout the global community through its grant making.

Robert Wolf, President

2255 Norcross Wildlife Foundation
Caller Box 611 212-362-4831
New York, NY 10024 *Fax:* 212-812-4783
www.norcrosswildlife.org
A place of refuge where all wildlife is encouraged not just to survive but also to proliferate naturally, and where certain species, now threatned with extinction, may again attain more normal distribution and benefit the public bytheir survival.
Angel Braestrup, Chair
Jennifer Grossman, Vice Chair

2256 Northwest Area Foundation
60 Plato Boulevard E 651-224-9635
Suite 400 *Fax:* 651-225-3881
St. Paul, MN 55107 info@nwaf.org
www.nwaf.org
Committed to helping communities reduce poverty for the long term.
Kevin Walker, President/CEO
Millie Acamovic, Vice President

2257 Oliver S and Jennie R Donaldson Charitable Trust
US Trust Company of New York
114 W 47th Street 212-852-3683
New York, NY 10036 *Fax:* 212-852-3377
Philantropic organization working to promote social change that contributes to a more just, sustainable and peaceful world.
Anne L Smith-Ganey, Secretary

2258 Overbrook Foundation
60 East 42nd Street 212-603-9996
Suite 565 *Fax:* 212-661-8664
New York, NY 10165 www.overbrook.org
The Overbrook Foundation strives to improve the lives of people by supporting projects that protect human and civil rights, advance the self-sufficiencey and well being of individuals and their communities, and conserve the naturalenvironment.
Aaron Labaree, Chair
Carolyn J. Cole, Vice Chair

2259 Pacific Whale Foundation
300 Maalaea Road 808-249-8811
612 Front St, Lahaina, HI 800-942-5311
Wailuku, HI 96793 www.pacificwhale.org
Mission is to promote appreciation, understanding and protection of whales, dolphins, coral reefs, and the planet's oceans by educating the public from a scientific perspective about the marine environment. Offers ocean ecotoursthrough PacWhale Eco-Adventures.

Eric Brown, PhD, MS, Chair
Kristie Wrigglesworth, Executive Director

2260 Patrick and Anna Cudahy Fund
70 E. Lake St., 312-422-1442
Suite 1120 *Fax:* 312-641-5736
Chicago, IL 60601 laurenkrieg@cudahyfund.org
cudahyfund.org
Types of support: general/operating support; continuing support; annual campaigns; building/renovation; equipment; program development; seed money; technical assistance; matching funds.
Lauren Krieg, Executive Director

2261 Pew Charitable Trusts
2005 Market Street 215-575-9050
Suite 2800 *Fax:* 215-575-4939
Philadelphia, PA 19103-7077 info@pewtrusts.org
www.pewtrusts.org
Pew uses an analytical approach to solve international challenges, by improving public policy, informing the public, and bettering civic life.
Rebecca W. Rimel, President & CEO
Janice Bogash, Senior Vice President

2262 Providence Journal Charitable Foundation
75 Fountain Street 401-277-7000
Providence, RI 02902 help@providencejournal.com
www.providencejournal.com
Focuses on offering local and regional news, information, advertising and interactive opportunities for our audience.
Phil Kukielski, Managing Editor
John Kostrzewa, Business Editor

2263 Public Lands Foundation (PLF)
PO Box 7226 703-935-0916
Arlington, VA 22207-0226 866-985-9636
Fax: 888-204-9814
info@publicland.org
publicland.org
National nonprofit membership organization that advocates and works for the retention of America's National System of Public Lands (NSPL) in public hands, professionally and sustainably managed by the Bureau of Land Management (BLM)for responsible use and enjoyment by everyone.

Ed Shepard, President
Don Simpson, Vice-President

2264 RARE Center for Tropical Bird Conservation
1529 Walnut Street 215-568-0420
Philadelphia, PA 19102
Works globally to equip people in the world's most threatened natural areas with the tools and motivation they need to care for their natural resources.
John Guarnaccia, Executive Director

2265 Rainforest Action Network
425 Bush Street 415-398-4404
Suite 300 *Fax:* 415-398-2732
San Francisco, CA 94108 answers@ran.org
www.ran.org
Rainforest Action Network works to protect the Earth's rainforests and support the rights of their inhabitants through education, grassroots organizing and non-violent direct action.
André Carothers, Board Chair
James D. Gollin, President

2266 Rainforest Alliance
125 Broad Street 212-677-1900
9th Floor *Fax:* 212-677-2187
New York, NY 10004 info@ra.org
www.rainforest-alliance.org
Dedicated to tropical forest conservation for the benefit of the global community. Rainforest Alliance works with farmers, foresters and tourism entrepreneurs. Through education and training they believe they can show people how tominimize environmental impact, while earning a stable income.

Han De Groot, Chief Executive Officer
Alex Morgan, Chief Markets Officer

2267 Raytheon Company
870 Winter Street 781-552-3000
Waltham, MA 00245 www.raytheon.com
Raytheon is a technology leader specializing in defense, homeland security, and other government markets throughout the world.
Thomas A Kennedy, Chairman/CEO
John D Harris, Vice President

2268 Richard Lounsberry Foundation
601 Thirteenth Street 202-872-8080
Suite 1030N *Fax:* 202-872-9292
Washington, DC 20005 foundation@rlounsbery.org
www.rlounsbery.org
Aims to enhance national strengths in science and technology through support programs in the areas of science and technology components of key US policy issues, elementary and secondary science and math education, historical studiesand contemporary assessments of key trends in the physical and biomedical sciences and start up assistance for establishing the infrastructure of research projects.
William Happer, Chairman
Jesse H Ausubel, Vice Chairman

2269 Rockefeller Brothers Foundation
475 Riverside Drive 212-812-4200
Suite 900 *Fax:* 212-812-4299
New York, NY 10115 communications@rbf.org
www.rbf.org
A philantrophic organization working to promote social change that contributes to a more just, sustainable and peaceful world. The Fund's programs are intended to develop leaders, strenghten institutions, engage citizens, buildcommunity, and foster partnerships that include government, business, and civil society.
Stephen Heintz, President
Judy Clark, Executive Director

2270 Rockefeller Family Fund
475 Riverside Drive 212-812-4252
Suite 900 *Fax:* 212-812-4299
New York, NY 10115 www.rffund.org
For thirty years, the Rockefeller Family Fund has worked at the cutting edge of advocacy in such areas as environmental protection, advancing the economic rights of women, and holding public and private institutions accountable fortheir actions.
David Kaiser, President
Wendy Gordon, Vice President

2271 SCI Foundation
4800 West Gates Pass Road 520-620-1220
Tucson, AZ 85745-9490 888-486-8724
Fax: 520-622-1205
scifoundation@firstforwildlife.org
safariclubfoundation.org
Charitable arm of Safari Club International, funding and directing wildlife conservation programs and outdoor education.
Laird Hamilton, Chief Executive Officer
Jordan Hasler, Director, Development

2272 Safari Club International Foundation
4800 West Gates Pass Road 520-620-1220
Tucson, AZ 85745-9450 800-377-5399
Fax: 520-622-1205
www.scifirstforhunters.org
Safari Club Internation Foundation is a charitable organization that funds and manages worldwide programs dedicated to wildlife conservation, outdoor education and humanitarian services.
Larry B Higgins, President
Paul D Babaz, Vice President

2273 Samuel Roberts Noble Foundation
2510 Sam Noble Parkway 508-223-5810
Ardmore, OK 73401 *Fax:* 508-224-6217
www.noble.org
One of the largest international offshore drilling contractors in the world.

Bill Buckner, President & CEO
Billy Cook, Senior Vice President

2274 Save the Redwoods League
111 Sutter Street 415-362-2352
11th Floor 888-836-0005
San Francisco, CA 94104 *Fax:* 415-362-7017
info@savetheredwoods.org
www.savetheredwoods.org
Guided by their science-based master plan to save redwoods throughout their natural ranges, the Leagues purchases priority pieces of land and donates or sells the property to government agencies for protection as parks and reserves.The league funds restoration, supports research to expand knowledge of redwood forest dynamics, and educates the public about redwoods and their ecosystems, in order to reconnect people with the peace and beauty of these wonders of the natural world.

James Larson, President
Melinda Thomas, Vice President

2275 Scherman Foundation
16 E 52nd Street 212-832-3086
Suite #601 *Fax:* 212-838-0154
New York, NY 10022 mpratt@scherman.org
www.scherman.org
The giving program of the Foundation emphasizes long-term general support, reflecting the director's commitment to sustained support for current grantees, and the belief that strong non-

profit leaders who are closest to the issues canbest decide on the most effective use of grant funds.

Karen R. Sollins, Chair
Mr Mike Pratt, President

2276 Sequoia Foundation
1250 Pacific Avenue 253-627-1634
Suite 870 *Fax:* 253-627-6249
Tacoma, WA 98402 grants@grantmakerconsultants.com
www.sequoiafound.org

A private non-profit organization dedicated to the identification and reduction of environmental threats to public health. We seek to support the efforts of local, state, national-and international-public health agencies in promotingand implimenting effective public health policy. This mission is achieved through research collaborations with local, state, federal, and international agencies, community-based organizations, and hospitals and universities.

John S. Petterson Ph.D., Executive Director
Pam Petree, Contracts Manager

2277 Sierra Club Foundation
85 Second Street 415-995-1780
Suite 750 *Fax:* 415-995-1791
San Francisco, CA 94105 foundation@sierraclub.org
www.sierraclubfoundation.org

To advance the preservation and protection of the natural environment by empowering the citizenry with charitable resources to further the cause of environmental protection.

Steven Berkenfeld, Chair
Allison Chin, Vice Chair

2278 Social Justice Fund NW
1904 Third Avenue 206-624-4081
Suite 806 *Fax:* 206-382-2640
Seattle, WA 98101 info@socialjusticefund.org
www.socialjusticefund.org

Progressive foundation dedicated to creating a more just society. Funds grass-roots community-based organizations in Idoho, Montana, Wyoming, Washington, and Oregon.

Jessan Hutchison-Quillian, Chair
Abel Valladares, Vice Chair

2279 Switzer Foundation New Hampshire Charitable Foundation
Po Box 293 207-338-5654
Belfast, ME 00491 800-464-6641
Fax: 603-225-1700
info@switzernetwork.org
www.switzernetwork.org

Identifies and nurtures environmental leaders who have the ability and determination to make a significant impact, and supports initiatives that will have direct and measurable results to improve environmental quality.

Judith Burrows, Director Student Aid
Joe Aldy, Assistant professor

2280 Texaco Foundation
2000 Westchester Avenue 914-701-0320
White Plains, NY 10650 www.texaco.com

The foundation focuses on early childhood education in math and science through its Early Notes (music) program and its Touch Science program, which supports scientific discovery through hands-on learning.

Maria Mike-Mayer, Secretary

2281 Threshold Foundation
Po Box 29903 415-561-6400
San Francisco, CA 94129-0903 *Fax:* 415-561-6401
threshold@tides.org
www.thresholdfoundation.org

A progressive foundation and a community of individuals united through wealth, mobilizing money, people and power to create a more just, joyful and sustainable world.

Terrence Meck, President
Reid Williams, Treasurer

2282 Times Mirror Foundation
202 W First Street 213-237-3945
Los Angeles, CA 90012 *Fax:* 213-237-2116

The Times Mirror Foundation, an affiliate of Tribune Company, is dedicated to supporting nonprofit organizations that measurably improve the quality of life in communities we serve. The Foundation focuses its support on programs thatimprove the quality of journalism, education and literacy, strengthen the fabric of the community, and enhance cultural appreciation and understanding.

Cassandra Malry, Treasurer

2283 Tinker Foundation Inc
55 E 59th Street 212-421-6858
New York, NY 10022 *Fax:* 212-223-3326
tinker@tinker.org
www.tinker.org

Endeavors to promote better understanding among the peoples of the US, Latin America, and Iberia. In the environmental policy program area, grants are awarded to to 501(c)(3) or equivalent organizations for projects addressingresource-based economic activities and for improving the formulation of effective environmental governance.

Renate Rennie, Chairman/President
Alan Stoga, Secretary

2284 Town Creek Foundation
121 N West Street 410-763-8171
Easton, MD 21601 *Fax:* 410-763-8172
info@towncreekfdn.org
www.towncreekfdn.org

A private philanthropic foundation dedicated to a sustainable environment

Stuart Clarke, Executive Director
Jennifer Stanley, President

2285 Trees Foundation
PO Box 2202 707-923-4377
Redway, CA 95560 *Fax:* 707-923-4427
www.treesfoundation.org

Aims to restore the ecology of California's North Coast through funding community-based efforts.

Susan Barsotti, President
Kerry Reynolds, Organizational Director

2286 True North Foundation
508 Westwood Drive 970-223-5285
Fort Collins, CO 80524 *Fax:* 970-495-0892

Committed to preventing damage to the natural systems, water, air, and land on which all life depends.

Kerry K Anderson, President

2287 Turner Foundation
133 Luckie Street NW 404-681-9900
2nd Floor *Fax:* 404-681-0172
Atlanta, GA 30303 www.turnerfoundation.org

This Foundation is committed to preventing damage to the natural systems, water, air and land, on which all life depends.

Ted Turner, Chairman
Laura Turner Seydel, Director

2288 US-Japan Foundation
145 East 32nd Street 212-481-8753
New York, NY 10016 *Fax:* 212-481-8762
info@us-jf.org
www.us-jf.org

Committed to promoting stronger ties between Americans and Japanese by supporting projects that foster mutual knowledge and education, deepen understanding, create effective channels of communication, and address common concerns in anincreasingly interdependent world.

James W. Lintott, Chairman
Dr. George R. Packard, President

2289 USF and G Foundation
100 Light Street 410-685-3047
Baltimore, MD 21202

2290 Union of Concerned Scientists
2 Brattle Square 617-547-5552
Cambridge, MA 00213-3780 *Fax:* 617-864-9405
ucs@ucsusa.org
www.ucsusa.org
The Union of Scientists is the leading science-based nonprofit organization working for a healthy environment and a safer world. Since 1969. we've used rigorous scientific analysis, innovative policy development, and tenacious citizenadvocacy to advance practical solutions for the environment.

James J. McCarthy, Chair
Peter A. Bradford, Vice Chair

2291 Unitarian Universalist Veatch Program at Shelter Rock
48 Shelter Rock Road 516-627-6560
Manhasset, NY 11030 *Fax:* 516-627-6596
uucsr@uucsr.org
www.uucsr.org
Supports Unitarian Universalist organizations that foster the growth and development of the denomination and that increase the involvement of Unitarian Universalists in social action and non-denominational organizations whose goalsreflect UU principles.
Ned Wight, Executive Director

2292 Victoria Foundation
31 Mulberry Street 973-792-9200
5th Floor *Fax:* 973-792-1300
Newark, NJ 00710 info@victoriafoundation.org
www.victoriafoundation.org
A private grantmaking institution. Since the early 1960's the Foundation's trustees have targeted giving to programs that impact the cycle of poverty in Newark, New Jersey.

Frank Alvarez, President
Margaret H. Parker, Vice President

2293 Vidda Foundation
250 West 57th Street 212-696-4052
Suite 1928 *Fax:* 212-889-7791
New York, NY 10107 www.vidda.org
The Vidda Foundation is a private non-operating foundation interested in supporting programs that will have lasting impact in the areas of conservation, education, healthcare, human services, and the arts.
Gerald E Rupp, Chairman
John A. Downey, MD

2294 Virginia Environmental Endowment
Three James Center
1051 East Cary Street 804-644-5000
PO Box 790 info@vee.org
Richmond, VA 23218-790 www.vee.org
Mission is to improve the quality of the environment by using its capital to encourage all sectors to work together to prevent pollution, conserve natural resources, and promote environmental literacy
Gerald P McCarthy, Executive Director

2295 W Alton Jones Foundation
232 East High Street 804-295-2134
Charlottesville, VA 22902 *Fax:* 804-295-1648
Helps to fund hundreds of environmental groups.
Dr. JP Meyers, Director

2296 Wallace Genetic Foundation
4910 Massachusetts Avenue NW 202-966-2932
Suite 221 *Fax:* 202-966-3370
Washington, DC 20016 wgfdn@aol.com
www.wallacegenetic.org
Committed to funding a variety of interests including agricultural research, preservation of farmland, ecology, conservation and sustainable development.
John D Murray, President
David W Douglas, Vice President, Treasurer

2297 Weeden Foundation
P.O. Box 606 914-864-1375
Bedford Hills, NY 10507-0606 *Fax:* 914-864-1377
info@weedenfoundation.org
www.weedenfoundation.org
A foundation dedicated to the protection of biodiversity through the financial support of conservation-centered organizations.

Norman Weeden, Ph.D., President
Don A. Weeden, Executive Director

2298 Wild Sheep Foundation (WSF)
412 Pronghorn Trail 406-404-8750
Bozeman, MT 59718 800-653-6297
info@wildsheepfoundation.org
www.wildsheepfoundation.org
The Foundation's mission is to promote and enhance populations of indigenous wild sheep in North America, and to fund programs for the professional management of these populations.

Gray Thornton, President & CEO
Kevin Hurley, VP, Conservation

2299 Wildlife Preservation Trust International
3400 West Girard Avenue 215-222-3636
Philadelphia, PA 19104 *Fax:* 215-222-2191
www.wildlifeconservationtrust.org
Empowers local conservation scientists worldwide to protect nature and safeguard ecosystem and human health.

Dr. Mary Pearl

2300 William Bingham Foundation
1111 Superior Avenue 216-363-6482
Suite 700 info@wbinghamfoundation.org
Cleveland, OH 44114 www.foundationcenter.org
Supports organizations in in education, science, health and human servces and the arts.
Kari Blakley, Grants Manager
Daniel L Horn, Secretary

2301 William H Donner Foundation
520 White Plains Road 914-524-0404
Suite 500 *Fax:* 914-524-0407
Tarrytown, NY 10591 donner.org
When we build let us...build forever. Let it not be for present delight nor for present alone. Let it be such work as our descendants will thank us for.
Timothy E Donner, President
Cristina Winsor, Vice President

2302 William Penn Foundation
Two Logan Square 11th Floor 215-988-1830
100 North 18th Street *Fax:* 215-988-1823
Philadelphia, PA 19103-2757 grants@williampennfoundation.org
www.williampennfoundation.org
To improve the quality of life in the greater Philadelphia region through efforts that foster rich cultural expression, strenghten children's futures, and deepen connections to nature and community. In partnerships with others, we workto advance a vital, just and caring community.
Janet Haas, Chair
Leonard C. Haas, Vice Chair

2303 William and Flora Hewlett Foundation
2121 Sand Hill Road 650-234-4500
Menlo Park, CA 94025 *Fax:* 650-234-4501
www.hewlett.org
The Foundation concentrates its resources on activities in education, environment, global development, performing arts and population. In addition, the Foundation has programs that make

grants to advance the field of philanthropy, andto support disadvantaged communities in the San Francisco Bay Area.
Stephen C Neal, Chairman
Larry D Kramer, President

2304 Winston Foundation for World Peace
2040 S Street, NW 202-483-4215
Washington, DC 20009 *Fax:* 202-483-4219
winstonfoun@igc.apc.org
John H. Adams, Director

2305 Wisconsin Energy Corporation Foundation
231 W. Michigan St. 414-221-2345
Milwaukee, WI 53203 *Fax:* 414-221-2554
www.wecenergygroup.com
Wisconsin Energy's principal business is providng electric and natural gas service to customers across Wisconsin and the Upper Peninsula of Michigan.
David L Hughes, Assistant Treasurer
Gale E Klappa, Chairman, President & CEO

2306 World Parks Endowment
1616 Place Street NW 202-939-3808
Suite 200 *Fax:* 202-939-3868
Washington, DC 20036 info@worldlandtrust.org
www.worldlandtrust.org
The World Parks Endowment provides the opportunity to buy rainforest land and establish new protected areas that conserve rainforests and other sites of high biodiversity value. Our projects target lands that conserve rare orendangered species, and are low price, so the minimum amount of the funds protect high priority areas.
John A Burton, Chief Executive Officer
Roger Wilson, Senior Conservationist

2307 World Research Foundation
P.O. Box 20828 928-284-3300
Sedona, AZ 86341 *Fax:* 928-284-3530
info@wrf.org
www.wrf.org
The purpose of the foundation is to locate, gather, codify, evaluate, classify and disseminate information dealing with health and the environment. All countries are contacted to collect the best information in an unbiased, neutral andindependent manner.
LaVerne Boeckmann, Vice President/Founder

2308 World Resources Institute
10 G Street, NE 202-729-7600
Suite 800 *Fax:* 202-729-7686
Washington, DC 20002 www.wri.org
An independent nonprofit organization with a staff of more than 100 scientists, economists, policy experts, business analysts, statistic analysists, mapmakers and communicators working to protect the Earth and improve people's lives.Our four goals are: protect the Earth's living systems, increase access to information, create sustainable enterprise and opportunity and reverse global warming.
James A Harmon, Chairman
Harriet C Babbitt, Vice Chairman

2309 World Society for the Protection of Animals
450 Seventh Avenue 646-783-2200
31st Floor 800-883-9772
New York, NY 10123 *Fax:* 212-564-4250
wspa@wspausa.org
www.wspa-usa.org
The world's largest alliance of animal welfare organization whose vision is a world where animal welfare matters and animal cruelty ends. We strive to bring about change from grassroots to government levels to benefit animals. WSPAsupports and develops high-profile campaigns, scientifically-backed projects and innovative education initiatives. Its work is recognized by the United Nations and Council of Europe.

Annie Lieberman, USA Executive Director
John Bowen, President

2310 World Wildlife Fund (WWF)
1250 24th Street NW 202-293-4800
PO Box 97180 800-225-5993
Washington, DC 20037 *Fax:* 202-293-9211
membership@wwfus.org
www.worldwildlife.org
Dedicated to protecting endangered species and their habitats through field work, advocacy, policy engagement, pioneering work and education. The largest multinational conservation organization in the world. WWF works in 100 countriesand is supported by more than 1 million members in the US and almost 5 million members globally.

Carter Roberts, President & CEO
Nik Sekhran, Chief Conservation Officer

2311 Xerces Society for Invertebrate Conservation
628 NE Broadway 503-232-6639
Suite 200 855-232-6639
Portland, OR 97232 *Fax:* 503-233-6794
info@xerces.org
www.xerces.org
Works with farmers, land managers, golf course staff, public agencies, and gardners to promote the conservation and recovery of native pollinator insects and their habitat.
Scott Hoffman Black, Executive Director
Denise Ledgerwood, Director, Grants

Scholarships

2312 Abundant Life Seed Foundation
930 Lawrence Street 425-385-5660
PO Box 772 *Fax:* 360-385-7455
Port Townsend, WA 98368 www.abundantlifeseed.org
A nonprofit organization dedicated to the preservation of rare, heirloom and native seeds. ALSF grows and distributes open-pollinated seeds and offers them for sale in an annual catalog. Seeds are also sent to people in need throughthe World Seed Fund. ALSF teaches seed saving through workshops, appreticeships and school programs.
Matthew Dillon, Executive Director
Elsa Golts, Board President

2313 Alexander Hollaender Distinguished Postdoctoral Fellowships
PO Box 117 865-576-3146
Oak Ridge, TN 37831-117 *Fax:* 865-241-2923
www.orau.gov/orise/contacts.htm
Prepares and distributes program literature to universities and laboratories across the country, accepts application, convenes a panel to make award recommendation, and issues stipend checks.
Andy Page, Director
Dan Standley, Director

2314 American Association for the Advancement of Science
1200 New York Avenue NW 202-326-6400
Washington, DC 20005 *Fax:* 202-289-4950
www.aaas.org
An international non-profit organization dedicated to advancing science around the world by serving as an educator, leader, spokesperson and professional association.
Gerald Fink, Chair
Geraldine Richmond, President

2315 American Geophysical Union Member Programs Division
2000 Florida Avenue NW 202-462-6900
Washington, DC 20009 800-966-2481
Fax: 202-328-0566
service@agu.org
membership.agu.org
Organized to represent the US in the International Research Council's International Union Of Geodesy and Geophysics and

to serve as the National Research Council Committee on Geophysics.
Eric A Davidson, Chair
Robin Elizabeth Bell, Vice Chair

2316 American Indian Science and Engineering Society
PO Box 9828 505-765-1052
Albuquerque, NM 87119-9828 *Fax:* 505-765-5608
info@aises.org
www.aises.org
The mission is to increase substantially the representation of American Indian and Alaskan Natives in engineering, science and other related technology disciplines.
Sarah Echohawk, CEO
Shirley LaCourse, Business Development Officer

2317 American Museum of Natural History
Central Park West at 79th Street 212-769-5100
New York, NY 10024-5192 *Fax:* 212-769-5427
www.amnh.org
Mission is to discover, interpret, and disseminate-through scientific research and education, knowledge about human cultures, the natural world, and the universe.
Lewis W Bernard, Chairman
Ellen V Futter, President

2318 American Nuclear Society
555 North Kensington Ave 708-352-6611
La Grange Park, IL 60526 800-323-3044
Fax: 708-352-0499
www.ans.org
Not-for-profit, international, scientific and educational organization. Established by a group of individuals who recognized the need to unify the professional activities within the diverse fields of nuclear science and technology.
Robert N. Coward, President
Robert C. Fine, Executive Director

2319 American Society of Naturalists
Queens College - CUNY
Department of Biology 718-997-3426
Flushing, NY 11367 asn@press.uchicago.edu
www.amnat.org
Purpose is to advance and to diffuse knowledge of organic evolution and other broad biological principals so as to enhance the conceptual unification of the biological sciences.
Ellen Ketterson, President

2320 American Sportfishing Association (ASA)
1001 North Fairfax Street 703-519-9691
Suite 501 *Fax:* 703-519-1872
Alexandria, VA 22314 info@asafishing.org
asafishing.org
A sportsfishing trade association that advocates for the promotion and protection of the industry. Their mission is to ensure that the industry remains strong and prosperous, and to safeguard the conservation, economic, and socialvalues of sportfishing in America.
Glenn Hughes, President
Joyce Anderson-Logan, Executive Assistant

2321 Apple Computer Earth Grants: Community Affairs Department
1 Infinite Loop 408-996-1010
Cupertino, CA 95014 800-692-7753
www.apple.com
Beverly Long, Program Manager

2322 Beldon Fund
99 Madison Avenue 212-616-5600
8th Floor 800-591-9595
New York, NY 10016 *Fax:* 212-616-5656
beldoninfo@yahoo.com
www.beldon.org
Mission is by supporting effective, nonprofit, advocacy organizations, the Beldon Fund seeks to build a national consensus to achieve and sustain a healthy planet.
John Hunting, Chair
Lael Stegall, Vice Chair

2323 Beldon II Fund: Old Kent Bank and Trust Company
99 Madison Avenue 212-616-5600
8th Floor 800-591-9595
New York, NY 10016 *Fax:* 212-616-5656
beldoninfo@yahoo.com
www.beldon.org
John R Hunting, Chair
Lael Stegall, Vice Chair

2324 Charles A. and Anne Morrow Lindbergh Foundation
PO Box 861 763-576-1596
Berkeley Springs, WV 25411 *Fax:* 763-576-1664
www.lindberghfoundation.org
Each year, the Charles A. and Anne Morrow Lindbergh Foundation provides grants to men and women whose individual initiative and work in a wide spectrum of disciplines furthers the Lindbergh's vision of a balance between the advance oftechnology and the perservation of the natural/human environment.
John Peterson, Chairman
Gregg E Maryniak, Vice Chairman

2325 Cousteau Society
4 East 27th Street 212-532-2588
New York, NY 10001 800-441-4395
Fax: 757-722-8185
communication@cousteau.org
www.cousteau.org
Mission is to educate people to understand, to love and to protect the water systems of the planet, marine and fresh water, for the wellbeing of future generations.
Francine Cousteau, President

2326 DRB Communications
1234 Summer Street 800-323-1550
Stamford, CT 00690 *Fax:* 203-324-7175
Robyn DeWolf

2327 Delmar Publishers Scholarship
National FAA Foundation
6060 FFA Drive 317-802-6060
PO Box 68960 *Fax:* 317-802-6061
Indianapolis, IN 46268
Carrie Powers, Contact

2328 Du Pont de Nemours and Company
1007 Market Street 302-774-2036
Room 8065 800-441-7515
Wilmington, DE 19898 www.dupont.com
Creating sustainable solutions essential to a better, safer, healthier, life for people everywhere.
Peter C Morrow, Mgr. Corporate Contributions

2329 Earth Island Institute-Brower Youth Awards
2150 Allston Way 510-859-9100
Suite 460 *Fax:* 510-859-9091
Berkeley, CA 94704-1375 bya@earthisland.org
www.earthisland.org
Incubates and supports over 30 projects working on environmental issues worldwide. Publishes quarterly Earth Island Journal. Project support programs help aspiring and veteran activists alike put ideas into action. Youth programincreases the visibility, effectiveness and influence of youth leadership in the environmental movement, inspiring other young people to work for the Earth.
David Phillips, Executive Director
Susan Kamprath, Director, Operations

2330 **Environmental Defense Fund (EDF)**
257 Park Avenue South 212-505-2100
New York, NY 10010 *Fax:* 212-505-2375
www.edf.org
Dedicated to protecting the environmental rights of all people, including future generations. Among these rights are clean air, clean water, healthy, nourishing food and a flourishing ecosystem. Advocates solutions based on science,even when it leads in unfamiliar directions. Works to create solutions that win lasting political, economic and social support because they are bipartisan, efficient and fair.

Fred Krupp, President
Catherine Nardone, Chief Development Officer

2331 **Environmental Grantmakers Association**
475 Riverside Drive 212-812-4310
Suite 960 *Fax:* 212-812-4311
New York, NY 10115 ega.org
Mission is to help member organizations become more effective environmental grantmakers through information sharing, collaboration and networking.
Scott Cullen, Chair
Paul Beaudet, Vice Chair

2332 **Environmental Protection Agency: Grants**
Environmental Protection Agency
1200 Pennsylvania Avenue NW 202-564-5315
Mail Code 3901 www.epa.gov/grants
Washington, DC 20460
EPA awards over $4 billion in grants each year. The organizations that receive funding range from non-profits to governments. The goal of EPA Grants is to help organizations achieve their environmental goals.
Kathleen Timmins, Suspension & Debarment
Sharon Wells, Equal Employment Officer

2333 **Environmental and Engineering Fellowship**
American Association for the Advancement
1333 H Street NW 202-326-6600
Washington, DC 20005 *Fax:* 202-289-4950
Aimed at postdoctoral to midcareer professionals from any discipline of science, engineering or any relevant interdisciplinary fields.

2334 **Financial Support for Graduate Work**
Women's Seamen's Friend Society of Connecticut
300 Boston Post Road 800-342-5864
West Haven, CT 00651 skaplan@newhaven.edu
www.newhaven.edu/academics/10844/
Restricted to Connecticut residents who are students at state maritime schools, or Connecticut residents majoring in Marine Sciences at any college or university or residents of any state majoring in Marine Sciences at a Connecticutcollege or university.
Steven H. Kaplan, President

2335 **Garden Club of America (GCA)**
14 East 60th Street 212-753-8287
3rd Floor *Fax:* 212-753-0134
New York, NY 10022 gca@gcamerica.org
www.gcamerica.org/scholarships
Seeks to stimulate the knowledge and love of gardening, to share the advantages of association by means of educational meetings, conferences, correspondence and publications, and to restore, improve, and protect the quality of theenvironment through educational programs and action in the fields of conservation and civic improvement. Offers 28 merit-based scholarships in 12 areas.
18,000 members
Anne Neal Petri, President

2336 **Geoffrey Schneider Travel Scholarship**
Association for Conservation Information
1085 Lake Road www.aci-net.org
Panton, VT 05491
Covers the conference registration fee and four nights' lodging so recipients can attend the Association for Conservation Information conference.
July
Jennifer Wisniewski, President
Judy Stokes Weber, Treasurer

2337 **German Marshall Fund of the United States**
1744 R Street NW 202-683-2650
Washington, DC 20009 *Fax:* 202-265-1662
info@gmfus.org
www.gmfus.org
A nonpartisan American public policy and grantmaking institution dedicated to promoting greater cooperation and understanding between the United States and Europe.
Craig Kennedy, President

2338 **Great Lakes Protection Fund**
1560 Sherman Avenue 847-425-8150
Suite 880 *Fax:* 847-424-9832
Evanston, IL 60201 info@glpf.org
www.glpf.org
A private non profit organization formed by the Govenors of the Great Lakes States. It is a permanent environmental endowdment that supports collaborative actions to improve the health of the Great Lakes ecosystem.
Russell Van Herik, Executive Director
J. David Rankin, Program Director

2339 **Harriet Evelyn Wallace Scholarship**
American Geological Institute
4220 King Street 703-379-2480
Alexandria, VA 22302-1502 *Fax:* 703-379-7563
agi@americangeosciences.org
www.americangeosciences.org
Open to all women pursuing a Master's or Doctoral degree in the geosciences.
Allyson K. Anderson Book, Executive Director
Geoff Camphire, Communications Contact

2340 **Hawk Mountain Sanctuary Association**
1700 Hawk Mountain Road 610-756-6961
Kempton, PA 19529 *Fax:* 610-756-4468
info@hawkmountain.org
www.hawkmountain.org/contact/contact-us~form.aspx
Mission is to conserve birds of prey worldwide by providing leadership in raptor conservation science and education, and my maintaining Hawk Mountain Sanctuary as a model observation, research and education facility.
Wendy Mclean, Chairman
Peter Bennett, Vice Chairman

2341 **Hazardous Waste Reduction Loan Program**
California Department of Commerce
1001 I Street 916-341-6181
PO Box 4025 www.calrecycle.ca.gov
Sacramento, CA 95812
Loans assist small business to redude waste generation or to reduce the hazardous properties of waste generated. Proceeds can only be used to finance hazardous waste equipment acquistion, installation and processes.
Scott Smithline, Director
Ken DaRosa, Chief Deputy Director

2342 **Heller Charitable and Educational Fund**
244 California Street 415-434-3160
San Francisco, CA 94111 *Fax:* 415-434-3807
Mission is to protect and improve the quality of life through support of programs in the environment, human health, education, and the arts.
Ruth B Heller, Correspondence Secretary

2343 **JM Kaplan Fund**
120 East 23rd Street 212-767-0630
5th Floor *Fax:* 212-767-0639
New York, NY 10010 info@jmkfund.org
www.jmkfund.org

Support for the arts, the environment, human rights, and a robust civil society. New interests emerged in programs to support New York City neighborhoods parks and libraries as well as historic preservation and municipal design work inLower Manhattan.
Peter Davidson, Chairman
Joan K. Davidson, President

2344 Jessie Ball duPont Religious, Charitable and Educational Fund
40 East Adams Street 904-353-0890
Suite 300 800-252-3452
Jacksonville, FL 32202-3302 *Fax:* 904-353-3870
contactus@dupontfund.org
www.dupontfund.org
A private grantmaking foundation limited in its giving to approximately 330 eligible organizations to which Mrs. duPont personnally contributed to in a five year period 1960-1964. The duPont fund accomplishes its mission by workingcreatively with these organizations and their partners.

Sherry Magill, PhD, President
Mark D. Constantine, Senior Vice President

2345 Johnson's Wax Fund
1525 Howe Street 800-494-4855
Racine, WI 53403 www.scjohnson.com
Through the SC Johnson Fund, in the US, we donate, on average, 5% pre-tax profits every year to increase local and global well-being. Our contributions are targeted to advancing the three legs of sustainability: economic vitality,social progress, and a healthy environmnet.

2346 Joint Oceanographic Institutions
1201 New York Avenue NW
Suite 400 202-232-3900
Washington, DC 20005 *Fax:* 202-265-4409
info@joiscience.org
oceanleadership.org
A consortium of 20 premier oceanographic research institutions that serves the US scientific community through management of large scale, global research programs in the fields of marine geology and geophysics and oceanography.
Steven Bohlen, President
Amy Castner, Executive Program Associate

2347 LSB Leakey Foundation
1003B O'Reilly Avenue 415-561-4646
San Francisco, CA 94129 *Fax:* 415-561-4647
info@leakeyfoundation.org
www.leakeyfoundation.org/
The mission of the Leakey Foundation is to increase scientific knowledge and public understanding of human origins and evolution.
Dr. Francis Brown, Co-Chairman
Dr. Richard G. Klein, Co-Chairman

2348 MJ Murdock Charitable Trust
703 Broadway 360-694-8415
Suite 710 *Fax:* 360-649-1819
Vancouver, WA 98660
The mission is to enrich the quality of life in the Pacific Northwest by providing grants organizations that seek to strenghten the region's educational and cultural base in creative and sustainable ways.
Steve Moore, Executive Director

2349 Mary Flagler Cary Charitable Trust
122 East 42nd Street 212-953-7700
Room 3505 *Fax:* 212-953-7720
New York, NY 10168 www.carytrust.org/
The Trust was established as a testamentary, charitable trust by the will of the late Mary Flagler Cary. The trustees have worked to use the assets of the Trust to carry forward Mrs. Cary's interests, and to elaborate on them in lightof new circumstances and needs. A major part of the Trust's assets continue to be devoted to special commitments relating to the origins of the Trust, especially the Institute of Ecosystem Studies at the Mary Flagler Cary Arboretum in Millbrook, NewYork.

2350 Maryland Sea Grant
University of Maryland
4321 Hardwick Road 301-405-7500
Suite 300 *Fax:* 301-314-5780
College Park, MD 20740 moser@mdsg.umd.edu
www.mdsg.umd.edu
Supports innovative marine research and education, with a special focus on the Chesapeake Bay.
Dr Fredrika Moser, Director

2351 National Academy of Sciences
500 Fifth Street, NW 202-334-2000
Washington, DC 20001 *Fax:* 202-334-2158
www.nasonline.org
The National Academy of Sciences (NAS) is an honorific society of distinguished scholars engaged in scientific and engineering research, dedicated to the furtherance of science and technology and to their use for the general welfare.
Ralph J. Cicerone, President
Diane Griffin, Vice President

2352 National Center for Atmospheric Research
PO Box 3000 303-497-1601
Boulder, CO 80307-3000 *Fax:* 303-497-1314
ncar.ucar.edu
NCAR provides the university research and teaching community with tools such as aircraft and radar to observe the atmosphere and with the technology and assistance to interpret and use these observations, including supercomputeraccess, computer models, and user support.
Michael Thompson, Interim President
Jim Hurrell, Director

2353 National Environmental Health Association NEHA/AAS Scholarships
720 S Colorado Boulevard 303-756-9090
Suite 1000-N *Fax:* 303-691-9490
Denver, CO 80246-1926 staff@neha.org
www.neha.org
Mission is to advance the environmental health and protection professional for the purpose of providing a healthful environment for all.
David T. Dyjack, Executive Director

2354 National Trappers Association (NTA)
2815 Washington Avenue 812-277-9670
Bedford, IN 47421 866-680-8727
Fax: 812-277-9672
ntaheadquarters@nationaltrappers.com
www.nationaltrappers.com
To promote conservation, legislation and administrative procedures; to save and faithfully defend from waste the natural resources of the United States; to promote environmental education programs; and to promote a continued annual furharvest using the best tools. Numerous scholarships are offered.

Chris McAllister, President
John Daniel, Vice President

2355 National Wildlife Rehabilitators Association (NWRA)
2625 Clearwater Road 320-230-9920
Saint Cloud, MN 56301 www.nwrawildlife.org
Nonprofit international membership organization committed to promoting and improving the integrity and professionalism of wildlife rehabilitation and contributing to the preservation of natural ecosystems. Offers a number of grants,awards, and scholarships.

Michele Goodman, President
Deb Dohrmann, Central Office Manager

2356 **Needmor Fund**
42 South Saint Clair Street 419-255-5560
Toledo, OH 43604-8736 *Fax:* 419-255-5561
www.needmorfund.org/
Mission is to work with others to bring about social justice. The Needmor Fund supposrt people who work together to change the social, economic or politcal conditions which bar their access to participation in a democratic society.
Abby Staranahan, Chair
Ken Rolling, Vice Chair

2357 **Nixon Griffis Fund for Zoological Research: New York Zoological Society**
Bronx Zoo
185th Street & Southern Boulevard 212-220-5152
Bronx, NY 10460 *Fax:* 212-220-7114
Supports research in zoology, conservation, and marine science. Grants lilmited to $3,000. Grants made four times a year. Applications reviewed by selected US zoo personnel.
John Behler, Contact

2358 **North American Loon Fund Grants**
PO Box 329 603-528-4711
Holderness, NH 03245 800-462-5666
The North American Loon Fund's mission is to promote the preservation of loons and their lake habitats through research, public education, and the involvement of people who share their lakes with loons.
Linda O'Bara, Director

2359 **Oak Ridge Institute Science & Engineering Education Division**
MC100-44 865-576-3146
PO Box 117 *Fax:* 865-241-2923
Oak Ridge, TN 37831-0117 communications@orau.org
www.orau.org
Strive to advance scientific research and education by creating mutually beneficial collaborative partnerships involving academe, government, and industry.
Andy Page, President & CEO
Eric Abelquist, Executive Vice President

2360 **Resources for the Future**
1616 P Street NW 202-328-5000
Suite 600 *Fax:* 202-939-3460
Washington, DC 20036 info@rff.org
www.rff.org
Resource for the Future (RFF) is a nonprofit and nonpartisan organization that conducts independent research and analysis, rooted primarily in economics, to help leaders make decisions and policies regarding natural resources and theenvironment.

Richard G. Newell, President & CEO

2361 **Solid Waste Association of North America (SWANA)**
1100 Wayne Avenue 800-467-9262
Suite 650 *Fax:* 301-589-7068
Silver Spring, MD 20910 info@swana.org
swana.org
Professional organization for the advancement of responsible solid waste management. Offers a range of awards and scholarships.

David Biderman, Executive Director & CEO
Sara Bixby, Deputy Executive Director

2362 **The Center for Environmental Biotechnology at the University of Tennessee at Knoxville**
1416 Circle Drive, 676 Dabney Hall 865-974-8080
Knoxville, TN 37996 *Fax:* 865-974-8086
cebweb@utk.edu
www.ceb.utk.edu
One of the nations oldest and largest university-based multidisciplinary research units devoted to environmental analysis. The CEB is a leader in the development of whole cell bioluminescent bioreporters for the detection of organicand inorganic pollutants including environmental endocrine disruptors and toxicants.
Gary S Sayler, Professor & Director
Lee Barham, Research Assistant

2363 **University of Colorado: Boulder**
Campus Box 216 303-492-1143
Boulder, CO 80309 *Fax:* 303-492-1149
www.colorado.edu
Recoginzed as one of the outstanding public universities in the United States. The Boulder campus has 5 colleges and 4 schools, offering 3,400 courses in about 150 areas of study.
Dr. Robert Sievers, Director

2364 **WERC Undergraduate Fellowships**
New Mexico State University 575-646-2038
Box 30001, MSC WERC 800-523-5996
Las Cruces, NM 88003 *Fax:* 505-646-4149
iee@nmsu.edu
www.ieenmsu.com/werc-2
WERC a consortium for environmental education and technology development. The consortium's mission is to develop the human resources and technologies needed to address environmental issues.
Abbas Ghassemi, Director
Barbara Valdez, Program Coordinator

2365 **Water Environment Federation**
601 Wythe Street 703-684-2492
Alexandria, VA 22314-1994 800-666-0206
inquiry@wef.org
www.wef.org
The Water Environment Federation (WEF) is a not-for-profit technical and educational organization with members from varied disciplines who work toward the preservation and enhancement of the global water environment.
Rick Warner, President
Jenny Hartfelder, President Elect

2366 **Weston Institute**
1400 Weston Way 610-701-3000
Po Box 2653 800-7WE-STON
West Chester, PA 19380 *Fax:* 610-701-3186
contactweston@westonsolutions.com
www.westonsolutions.com
A leading environmental and redevelopment firm focused on restoring efficiency to your essential resources: air, land, water, people, and facilities. We can help you develop solutions that maximize resource value and turn environmentalresponsibility into economic growth.
William L. Roberston, President/CEO

2367 **Wildlife Conservation Society (WCS)**
2300 Southern Boulevard 718-220-5100
Bronx, NY 10460 *Fax:* 718-220-2685
www.wcs.org/about-us/grants
WCS is at work in 16 priority regions across Africa, Latin America and North America, protecting wild landscapes that are home to a variety of species from butterflies to tigers. They uniquely combine the resources of wildlife parks inNew York with field projects around the globe to inspire care for nature, provide leadership in environmental eduation, and help sustain our planet's biological diversity. They offer scholarships, graduate programs, and grants.

Cristian Samper, PhD, President & CEO
Robert G. Menzi, Executive VP & COO

2368 **Women's Seamen's Friend Society of Connecticut**
P.O. Box 83100 203-777-2165
New Haven, CT 07868-3100 *Fax:* 203-777-5774
C. Marshall Davidson, Executive Director

2369 **Yale Institute for Biospheric Studies (YIBS)**
21 Sachem Street 203-432-9856
Rooms 132 and 136 *Fax:* 203-432-9927
New Haven, CT 00651 roserita.riccitelli@yale.edu
www.yale.edu/yibs

The Yale Institute for Biospheric Studies (YIBS) serves as a principal focus for Yale University's research and training efforts in the environmental sciences, and is committed to the teaching of environmental studies to futuregenerations. It provides physical and intellectual centers for research and education that address fundamental questions that will inform the ability to generate solutions to the biosphere's most critical environmental solutions.

Rose Rita Riccitelli, Assistant Director
Oswald Schmitz, Director

Government Agencies & Programs

Federal

2370 Acid Rain Program (ARP)
Clean Air Markets Division
1200 Pennsylvania Avenue NW 202-343-9620
Mail Code 6204M www.epa.gov/airmarkets/acid-rain-program
Washington, DC 20460
The Acid Rain Program is a part of the Clean Air Markets Division of the EPA and works toward emissions reductions of sulfur dioxide and nitrogen oxides, precursors of acid rain, from the power sector.

Reid Harvey, Director, Clean Air Markets

2371 Advisory Committee on Reactor Safeguards
US Nuclear Regulatory Commission
Washington, DC 20555-0001 301-415-7000
800-368-5642
Fax: 301-415-5575
www.nrc.gov
This committee's primary purposes are to review and report on safety studies and licenses; to advise the Commission on the hazards of proposed and existing production and utilization facilities; to initiate reviews of nuclear facilitysafety; and to advise in the areas of health physics and radiation protection.

Kristine L. Svinicki, Chair
Jeff Baran, Commissioner

2372 Advisory Council on Historic Preservation
401 F Street NW 202-517-0200
Suite 308 achp@achp.gov
Washington, DC 20001 www.achp.gov
The council's mission is to promote the preservation, improvement, and productive use of the nation's historic resources, and advise the President and Congress on national historic preservation policy.

John M. Fowler, Executive Director
Valerie Hauser, Director

2373 Agency for Toxic Substances and Disease Registry
Centers for Disease Control and Prevention
4770 Buford Highway NE 770-488-0706
Atlanta, GA 30341-3717 800-232-4636
Fax: 770-488-1544
www.atsdr.cdc.gov
This agency provides leadership and direction to programs and activities designed to protect both the public and workers from exposure or adverse health effects of hazardous substances in storage sites or released in fires, explosions,or transportation accidents. The agency also collects, maintains, analyzes and disseminates information relating to serious diseases, mortality and human exposure to toxic or hazardous substances.

Patrick Breysse, Director
Christopher M. Reh, Associate Director

2374 Agricultural Marketing Service
USDA Agricultural Marketing Service
1400 Independence Avenue SW 202-720-8998
Washington, DC 20250 AMSAdministratorOffice@ams.usda.gov
www.ams.usda.gov/nop
The AMS creates national and international marketing opportunities for US producers of food, and provides the agricultural industry with services that ensure the quality and abundance of wholesome food for consumers.

Bruce Summers, Administrator
Erin Morris, Associate Administrator

2375 American Farmland Trust
1150 Connecticut Ave NW 202-331-7300
Suite 600 800-431-1499
Washington, DC 20036 www.farmland.org
American Farmland Trust aims to stop the loss of productive farmland, and to promote sound farming practices that lead to a healthy environment and keeps farmers on the land.

John Piotti, President
Ashley Bovino, Chief Financial Officer

2376 American Indian Environmental Office
Environmental Protection Agency
1200 Pennsylvania Avenue NW 202-272-0167
Washington, DC 20460 www.epa.gov/indian
Coordinates the US Environmental Protection Agency-wide effort to strengthen public health and environmental protection in Indian Country, with a special emphasis on building Tribal capacity to administer their own environmentalprograms.
JoAnn K. Chase, Director

2377 American Membrane Technology Association
2409 SE Dixie Highway 772-463-0820
Stuart, FL 34996 custsrv@amtaorg.com
www.amtaorg.com.
AMTA's mission is to advocate for and educate on the application of membrane technology in order to create safe and affordable water supplies, and to treat municipal, industrial, agricultural and waste waters for future use.

Harold G. Fravel, Jr., Executive Director
Chris Owen, President

2378 Animal and Plant Health Inspection Service
4700 River Road 844-820-2234
Riverdale, MD 20737CustomerServiceCallCenter@aphis.usda.gov
www.aphis.usda.gov
This organization aims to protect the welfare and value of American agriculture and natural resources by regulating genetically engineered organisms, administering the Animal Welfare Act, and carrying out wildlife damage managementactivities using science-based standards.

Gregory Ibach, Under Secretary
Kevin Shea, Administrator

2379 Antarctic and Southern Ocean Coalition
1320 19th Street, NW 202-234-2480
5th Floor info@asoc.org
Washington, DC 20036 www.asoc.org
ASOC is a collaborative effort by conservation organizations from around the world to defend the integrity of Antarctic and Southern Ocean ecosystems from encroaching human activities. Responsible for national and inernationalcampaigns to protect the biological diversity and pristine wilderness of Antarctica, including its oceans and marine life.

Claire Christian, Executive Director
Eli Webster, Operations Manager

2380 Aquatic Nuisance Species Task Force
5275 Leesburg Pike 301-427-8041
Falls Church, VA 22041 david_hoskins@fws.gov
www.anstaskforce.gov/taskforce.php
An intergovernmental organization dedicated to preventing and controlling aquatic nuisance species. The task force monitors and researches aquatic nuisance species with the aim of preventing the introduction and dispersal of thesespecies in U.S. waters.

David Hoskins, Co-Chair
Jennifer Lukens, Co-Chair

2381 Argonne National Laboratory
9700 S Cass Avenue 630-252-2000
Lemont, IL 60439 www.anl.gov/

One of the US Department of Energy's largest research centers that develops and researches solutions in areas such as sustainable energy, environmental health, and national safety.

Tim Knewitz, Chief Financial Officer
Paul K. Kearns, Laboratory Director

2382 Atlantic States Marine Fisheries Commission
1050 North Highland Street 703-842-0740
Suite 200A-N *Fax:* 703-842-0741
Arlington, VA 22201 info@asmfc.org
www.asmfc.org
The Atlantic States Marine Fisheries Commission serves as a deliberative body, coordinating the conservation and management of the Atlantic states' shared near-shore fishery resources - marine, shell, and anadromous - for sustainableuse.

Robert E. Beal, Executive Director
Tina L. Berger, Director of Communications

2383 Board of Scientific Counselors
NIEHS
111 T.W. Alexander Drive 919-966-5215
Durham, NC 27709 kathleen_caron@med.unc.edu
www.niehs.nih.gov
Part of the National Institute of Environmental Health Sciences (NIEHS), the BSC evaluates the Division of Intramural (DIR) scientists, acting as an external peer review committee. The BSC examines different research programs'long-term objectives, accomplishments, innovation, and relevance to the NIEHS to ensure quality research.
10 members
Kathleen M. Caron, Chair

2384 Bureau of Economic Analysis
4600 Silver Hill Road 301-278-9004
Washington, DC 20233 CustomerService@bea.gov
www.bea.gov
The mission of The Bureau of Economic Analysis (BEA) is to promote a better understanding of the U.S. economy by providing timely, relevant, objective, and accurate economic accounts data through research, analysis, estimationmethodologies, and dissemination of statistics to both the public and business professionals.
Brian C. Moyer, Director
Mary Bohman, Deputy Director

2385 Bureau of Land Management (BLM)
U.S. Department of the Interior
1849 C Street NW 202-208-3801
Room 5665 *Fax:* 202-208-5242
Washington, DC 20240 www.blm.gov
The mission of the Bureau of Land Management is to ensure the sustainability and diversity of the public lands for the use and enjoyment of present and future generations. The Bureau offers environmental education, news about theactivities of the Bureau, events, and regulations.

Michael Nedd, Deputy Director, Operations
Casey Hammond, Principal Deputy

2386 Bureau of Land Management: Division of Fish and Wildlife Conservation
U.S. Department of the Interior
1849 C Street NW 202-208-3801
Room 5665 *Fax:* 202-208-5242
Washington, DC 20240 www.blm.gov/programs/fish-and-wildlife
This division of the Bureau of Land Management aims to promote the restoration, enhancement, and protection of fish, wildlife, and invertebrate species and their habitats. More than 3,000 species of wildlife live on BLM-managed lands.

Michael Nedd, Deputy Director, Operations
Casey Hammond, Principal Deputy

2387 Bureau of Land Management: Soil, Air, and Water Program
U.S. Department of the Interior
1849 C Street NW 202-208-3801
Room 5665 *Fax:* 202-208-5242
Washington, DC 20240 www.blm.gov/programs/natural-resources
This division of the BLM integrates soil, water, and air information with other disciplines to support the BLM's multiple use and sustained yield mission. Strategies of the program include implementing sustainable practices in soil,water, and air activities, as well as collaborating with partners in landscape restoration efforts.

Michael Nedd, Deputy Director, Operations
Casey Hammond, Principal Deputy

2388 Bureau of Land Management: Threatened and Endangered Species Program
U.S. Department of the Interior
1849 C Street NW 202-208-3801
Room 5665 *Fax:* 202-208-5242
Washington, DC 20240 www.blm.gov/programs/fish-and-wildlife
The Threatened and Endangered Species Program works to manage lands that provide a habitat for threatened and endangered species, helps to recover listed animal and plant species to remove them from the List of Threatened andEndangered Species, and collaborates with other federal agencies such as the U.S. Fish and Wildlife Service.

Michael Nedd, Deputy Director, Operations
Casey Hammond, Principal Deputy

2389 Bureau of Land Management: Wildlife Program
U.S. Department of the Interior
1849 C Street NW 202-208-3801
Room 5665 *Fax:* 202-208-5242
Washington, DC 20240 www.blm.gov/programs/fish-and-wildlife/wildlife
The BLM's Wildlife program helps support habitat maintenance and restoration to ensure the self-sustaining, abundant and diverse populations of wildlife on public lands. This program coordinates with other agencies, such as the U.S.Fish and Wildlife Service, in order to manage wildlife habitat.

Michael Nedd, Deputy Director, Operations
Casey Hammond, Principal Deputy

2390 Center for Environmental Finance: Environmental Finance Center Network (EFC)
U.S. Environmental Protection Agency
1200 Pennsylvania Ave NW 202-564-4700
Washington, DC 20460 ocfoinfo@epa.gov
www.epa.gov/waterfinancecenter/efcn
Part of the EPA's Water Infrastructure and Resiliency Finance Center, the EFC is a network of 8 university-based programs in ten EPA regions that delivers technical assistance and solutions to help manage costs of environmentalfinancing.

Andrew Wheeler, Administrator

2391 Centers for Disease Control and Prevention
National Center for Environmental Health
1600 Clifton Road 800-232-4636
Atlanta, GA 30329 www.cdc.gov/nceh
To provide national leadership, through science and service, to promote health and quality of life by preventing and controlling disease and death resulting from interactions between people and their environment.

Robert R. Redfield, Director
Anne Schuchat, Principal Deputy Director

2392 Chemical, Bioengineering, Environmental & Transport Systems
National Science Foundation
2415 Eisenhower Ave 703-292-5111
Alexandria, VA 22314 800-381-1532
engwebmaster@nsf.gov
www.nsf.gov/div/index.jsp?div=CBET
CBET supports research and education in the rapidly evolving fields of bioengineering and environmental engineering in areas

that involve the transformation or transport of matter and energy by chemical, thermal, or mechanical means.

Richard B. Dickinson, Division Director
Carole J. Read, Deputy Division Director

2393 Chesapeake Bay Critical Areas Commission
1804 West Street 410-260-3460
Annapolis, MD 21401 *Fax:* 410-974-5338
Lisa.Hoerger@maryland.gov
dnr.maryland.gov/criticalarea/Pages/default.aspx
Develops criteria used by local jurisdictions to develop individual Critical Area programs and amend local comprehensive plans, zoning ordinances and subdivision regulations. Programs are designed to address the unique characteristicsand needs of each county and municipality and together they represent a comprehensive land use strategy for preserving and protecting the Chesapeake Bay.

Charles Deegan, Chair

2394 Chief of Engineers Environmental Advisory Board
441 G Street NW 202-761-0011
Washington, DC 20314-1000 www.usace.army.mil
Serves the Armed Forces and the Nation by providing vital engineering services and capabilities, as a public service, across the full spectrum of operations; from peace to war; in support of national interests. Collaborates withpartners in order to gain advice on environmental issues facing the Corps of Engineers.
5 to 10 members
Once or twice a year
Rollin H. Hotchkiss, Chair
Mary C. Barber, Vice Chair

2395 Children's Health Protection Advisory Committee (CHPAC)
U.S. Environmental Protection Agency
1200 Pennsylvanie Avenue NW 202-564-2188
Mail Code 1107-T *Fax:* 202-564-2733
Washington, DC 20460 www.epa.gov/children
Advises, consults with and makes recommendations to EPA on issues associated with the development of regulations to address prevention of adverse health effects to children. The Committee also carries out related functions such ascollecting information and data to inform Agency decisions and serves to improve the breadth and depth of analyses related to the rules.
2 or 3 times a year
Ellen Braff-Guajardo, Senior Program Officer
Barbara Morrissey, Committee Chair

2396 Clean Air Scientific Advisory Committee
U.S. Environmental Protection Agency
1200 Pennsylvania Avenue NW 202-564-2050
Washington, DC 20460 www.epa.gov
The Clean Air Scientific Advisory Committee (CASAC) has a statutorily mandated responsibility to review and offer scientific advice on the air quality criteria and regulatory documents which form the basis for the National Ambient AirQuality Standards (NAAQS), which are currently lead, particulate matter (PM), ozone and other photochemical oxidants (O3), carbon monoxide (CO), nitrogen oxides (NOx) and sulfur oxides (SOx).

Aaron Yeow, Designated Federal Officer

2397 Clean Air Status and Trends Network (CASTNET)
U.S. Environmental Protection Agency
1200 Pennsylvania Avenue NW 202-564-4700
Washington, DC 20460 www.epa.gov/castnet
Esablished under the 1991 Clean Air Act Amendments, CASTNET is a national network that asseses trends in pollutant concentrations, atmospheric depositions, and ecological effect of changes in pollutant emissions.
Andrew Wheeler, Administrator

2398 Coast Guard
2703 Martin Luther King Jr Ave SE 202-372-2100
Washington, DC 20593-7318 www.uscg.mil
The core roles of the U.S. Coast Guard are to protect the public, the environment, and U.S. ecomonic and security interests in any maritime region in which those interests may be at risk, including international waters and America'scoasts, ports, and inland waterways.

Karl L. Schultz, Commandant
Charles W. Ray, Vice Commandant

2399 Coastal States Organization
444 N Capitol Street NW 202-508-3860
Suite 638 *Fax:* 202-508-3843
Washington, DC 20001 cso@coastalstates.org
www.coastalstates.org
The mission of the Coastal States Organization is to support the shared vision of the coastal states, commonwealths and territories for the protection, conservation, responsible use and sustainable economic development of the nation'scoastal and ocean resources.
Mary Munson, Executive Director
Bradley Watson, Deputy Director

2400 Committee on Agriculture, Nutrition, and Forestry
328A Russell Senate Office Building 202-224-2035
Washington, DC 20510 *Fax:* 202-228-2125
agriculture.senate.gov
The Committee aims to help establish, guide, and examine agricultural policies both in America and abroad. The Committee deals with trade, research, food stafety, nutrition, conservation, and commodity price and income supports.
2 times per month
Debbie Stabenow, Ranking Member
Pat Roberts, Chairman

2401 Committee on Commerce, Science, and Transportation
512 Dirksen Senate Building 202-224-1251
Washington, DC 20510 www.commerce.senate.gov
The Committee on Commerce, Science, and Transportation studies and reviews all matters relating to science and technology, oceans policy, transportation, communications, and comsumer affairs. It is comprised of 6 subcommittees thatoversee any issues under their jurisdiction.
25 members
Roger Wicker, Chair
Maria Cantwell, Ranking Member

2402 Committee on Energy and Natural Resources
304 Dirksen Senate Building 202-224-4971
Washington, DC 20510 *Fax:* 202-224-6163
energy.senate.gov
The Committee on Energy and Natural Resources considers, reports, and oversees legislation in areas such as energy resources, including regulation and conservation; nuclear energy; Indian affairs; territories and insular possessions;water resources; surface mining, Federal coal, oil, gas, and other mineral leasing.

Lisa Murkowski, Chairman
Joe Manchin, Ranking Member

2403 Committee on Environment and Public Works
410 Dirksen Senate Office Bldg 202-224-6176
Washington, DC 20510-6175 epw.senate.gov
This committee oversees the construction of Federal buildings, additions to the U.S. Capitol building and grounds, and the White House and its grounds. Additionally, the committee holds responsibility for developing highway systemsacross the nation, and creating new laws to achieve community economic development.

John Barrasso, Chair

2404 Committee on Natural Resources
US House of Representatives
1324 Longworth House Office Bldg. 202-225-6065
Washington, DC 20515 *Fax:* 202-225-4273
naturalresources.house.gov
The Committee on Natural Resources considers legislation regarding energy production, mineral lands and mining, public

lands, water, oceans, and wildlife. It also advocates for the Indigenous Peoples of the United States' rights ofsovereign authority over land and natural resources.
Raul M. Grijalva, Chair

2405 Committee on Oversight and Reform
2157 Rayburn House Office Building 202-225-5051
Washington, DC 20515 *Fax:* 202-225-4784
oversight.house.gov
The Committee acts as the voice for the taxpayers by ensuring the efficieny, effectiveness, and accountability of the federal government. It does this by investigating subjects within the Committee's legislative jurisdiction.
Jim Jordan, Ranking Member
Elijah Cummings, Chair

2406 Committee on Science, Space, and Technology
2321 Rayburn House Office Building 202-225-6375
Washington, DC 20515 *Fax:* 202-225-3895
science.house.gov
The Committee on Science, Space, and Technology deals with all research, development, demonstrations, and projects relating to environmental research, marine research, research and development in astronomics, exploration of outerspace, civil aviation research and development, and more.
Eddie Bernice Johnson, Chair
Frank Lucas, Ranking Member

2407 Committee on Small Business: House of Representatives
Small Business Committee
2361 Rayburn House Office Bldg. 202-225-4038
Washington, DC 20515 *Fax:* 202-225-7209
smallbusiness.house.gov
The Committee on Small Business protects and assists small businesses in matters of financial aid, regulatory flexibility, and paperwork reduction.Additionally, they advocate for fair and true tax relief for small businesses.
Nydia M. Velazquez, Chair

2408 Committee on Transportation and Infrastructure
U.S. House of Representatives
217 Ford House Office Building 202-224-3121
Washington, DC 20515 *Fax:* 202-225-6999
house.leases@mail.house.gov
transportation.house.gov
The Committee on Transportation and Infrastructure has jurisdiction over all modes of transportation, including aviation, maritime and waterborne transportation; federal agencies, including the Department of Transportation, the U.S.Coast Guard, and the Environmental Protection Agency. They also deal with clean water and waste water management, flood damage reduction, and hazardous materials transportation.
Sam Graves, Ranking Member
Peter A. DeFazio, Chair

2409 Cooperative Forestry Research Advisory Council
U.S. Forest Service
1400 Independence Ave SW 800-832-1355
Washington, DC 20250-0003 www.fs.fed.us/research/about/
The Forestry Research Advisory Council (FRAC) provides advice to the Secretary of Agriculture on the McIntire-Stennis Act of 1962, and deals with regional and national forestry research planning and coordination within Federal andState agencies, forestry schools, forest industries, and non-governmental organizations.
20 members
Anually
Nicole D. Cavender, Chair-Elect
John D. Alexander, Executive Director

2410 Council for the Conservation of Migratory Birds
U.S. Fish & Wildlife Service
1849 C Street NW 703-358-2220
Washington, DC 20240 800-344-9453
Fax: 703-358-1930
www.fws.gov/
The Council was created by the Secretary of the Interior to oversee the implementation of an Executive Order that deals with the responsibilities of Federal Agencies to protect migratory birds.
Gavin Shire, Chief
David Bernhardt, Secretary of the Interior

2411 Council on Environmental Quality
730 Jackson Place NW 202-395-5750
Washington, DC 20503 www.whitehouse.gov/ceq/
The Council on Environmental Quality coordinates federal environmental efforts and works closely with agencies and other White House offices in the development of environmental policies and initiatives.
Mary B. Neumayr, Chair

2412 Dangerous Goods Advisory Council
7501 Greenway Center Drive 202-289-4550
Suite 760 *Fax:* 202-289-4074
Greenbelt, MD 20770 info@dgac.org
www.dgac.org
DGAC is an international, nonprofit, educational organization that promotes safety in the transportation of hazardous materials and dangerous goods, including hazardous substances and hazardous wastes. The council carries out itsmission by educating and assisting the private and public sectors in transportation safety.
Annual
Vaughn Arthur, President
Del Billings, Technical Director

2413 Department of Agriculture: Agricultural Research Service (ARS)
Jamie L Whitten Building 202-720-3656
Room 302-A www.ars.usda.gov/
Washington, DC 20250
ARS is a scientific research agency that is part of the USDA. They conduct research to develop and transfer solutions to agricultural problems with the goal of enhancing the natural resource base and the environment, and sustaining acompetitive agricultural economy.
Chavonda Jacobs-Young, Administrator

2414 Department of Agriculture: Economic Research Service
United States Department of Agriculture
1400 Independance Ave SW 202-720-2791
Mail Stop 1800 www.ers.usda.gov
Washington, DC 20250-0002
The USDA's Economic Research Service anticipates trends and emerging issues in agriculture, food, and the environment, and conducts objective economic reasearch to inform the public.
Ephraim Leibtag, Administrator
Greg Pompelli, Associate Administrator

2415 Department of Agriculture: Fire and Aviation Management (F&AM)
Missoula Technology And Development Center
5785 Hwy 10 W 406-329-3900
Missoula, MT 59808 *Fax:* 406-329-3719
wo_mtdc_webmaster@fs.fed.us
www.fs.fed.us/t-d/programs/fire/
The F&AM program of the Technology and Development Program is a resource for fire managers and wildland firefighters. The goal of the program is to innovate equipment, systems, materials, and procedures needed by fire managers andfirefighters.
Vicki Christiansen, Chief
Lenise Lago, Associate Chief

2416 Department of Agriculture: Food Safety and Inspection Service
Jamie L Whitten Building

1400 Jefferson Dr SW 202-720-7025
Washington, DC 20024 *Fax:* 202-690-0550
www.fsis.usda.gov

The Food Safety and Inspection Service (FSIS) is the public health agency in the U.S. Department of Agriculture responsible for ensuring that the nation's commercial supply of meat, poultry, and egg products is safe, wholesome, andcorrectly labeled and packaged.

Carmen Rottenberg, Administrator
Paul Kiecker, Deputy Administrator

2417 Department of Agriculture: Forest Inventory and Analysis Program

USDA Forest Service
1400 Independence Avenue SW 703-605-4189
Washington, DC 20250-0003 800-832-1355
Fax: 703-605-5131
greams@fs.fed.us
www.fia.fs.fed.us

The Forest Inventory and Analysis Program (FIA) provides census information on the nation's forests. They provide information regarding the status and trends in forest area and location; the species, size, and health of trees; totaltree growth, mortality, and removals; and forest land ownership.

Michael Wilson, Program Manager, Interior
Dennis May, Program Manager, Northern

2418 Department of Agriculture: Forest Service

201 14th Street SW 202-205-8333
Washington, DC 20024 800-832-1355
www.fs.fed.us

The mission of the Department of Agriculture's Forest Service is to promote sustainable forest management and biodiversity conservation, and to help sustain the health and diversity of the nation's forests and grasslands.

Vicki Christiansen, Chief
Lenise Lago, Associate Chief

2419 Department of Agriculture: Forest Service Public Affairs

1249 S Vinnell Way 208-373-4100
Suite 200 www.fs.fed.us
Boise, ID 83709

The Public Affairs section of the USDA Forest Service keeps Senators, County Supervisors, and members of local service clubs informed on natural resource management. Their audience varies depending on the topics discussed, which rangefrom field briefings to controversial and complex resource issues.

Cecilia Seesholtz, Forest Supervisor

2420 Department of Agriculture: National Agricultural Statistics Service

USDA-NASS
1400 Independence Avenue SW 800-727-9540
Washington, DC 20250 www.nass.usda.gov

The National Agricultural Statistics Service aims to remain knowledgeable about the issues and requirements of the agricultural industry, public policy, and Federal programs so that they can provide timely, accurate, and usefulstatistics in service to U.S. agriculture.

Hubert Hamer, Administrator
Kevin Barnes, Associate Administrator

2421 Department of Agriculture: Research & Development

U.S. Forest Service
1400 Independence Ave SW 800-832-1355
Washington, DC 20250-0003 www.fs.fed.us/research

The Forest Service Research & Development team works to improve the health of the nation's forests and grasslands, and to research and promote the sustainbale management of the nation's forests and rangelands. R&D has identified coreresearch topics in the fields of biomass and bioenergy, climate change, nanotechnology, urban natural resources stewardship, and watershed management and restoration.

Andrew Liebhold, Senior Scientist
Daniel Williams, Senior Scientist

2422 Department of Agriculture: Research, Education, and Economics

U.S. Department of Agriculture
1400 Independence Avenue SW 202-720-5923
Room 214W *Fax:* 202-690-2842
Washington, DC 20250-0110 www.ree.usda.gov

The Research, Education, and Economics section of the USDA has federal leadership responsibility for the discovery of knowledge spanning the biological, physical, and social sciences, and involving agricultural research, economicanalysis, statistics, outreach, and higher education.

Scott Hutchins, Deputy Under Secretary
Chavonda Jacobs-Young, Administrator

2423 Department of Agriculture: State And Private Forestry

USDA Forest Service
1400 Independence Avenue SW 202-205-1657
Washington, DC 20250-0003 800-832-1355
www.fs.fed.us/spf

The S&PF division of the USDA connects people to resources and provides technical and financial assitance to landowners and resource managers in order to help sustain the nation's forests. This organization works with National Forests,Tribes, communities, and non-industrial private landowners.

Vicki Christiansen, Deputy Chief
Jane Darnell, Associate Deputy Chief

2424 Department of Agriculture: Water, Air, and Soil Research

US Forest Service Research & Development
1400 Independence Ave SW 800-832-1355
Washington, DC 20250-0003www.fs.fed.us/research/water-air-soil

This research builds on 100 years of research to better understand various interactions of weather patterns, changing land uses, and pollution levels on the nation's forests and their water, air, and soil resources.

Daniel Williams, Senior Scientist
Andrew Liebhold, Senior Scientist

2425 Department of Agriculture: Watershed Team

U.S. Forest Service
1400 Independence Ave SW 800-832-1355
Washington, DC 20250-1111 *Fax:* 703-605-1544
www.fs.fed.us

The Watershed Team leads programs dealing with watershed restoration, surface water, and groundwater to conserve and protect the soil, water and aquatic resources of national forests and grasslands.

Chris Carlson, Assistant Director
Penny Luehring, Program Leader

2426 Department of Commerce: National Oceanic & Atmospheric Administration

1401 Constitution Avenue NW www.noaa.gov
Room 5128
Washington, DC 20230

The mission of the NOAA is to understand changes in climate, weather, oceans and coasts; to share that knowledge and information with the public; and to foster the conservation and management of coastal and marine ecosystems. Theagency studies the structure and behaviour of the ocean, atmosphere, and related ecosystems.

Neil Jacobs, Assistant Secretary
Craig McLean, Chief Scientist

2427 Department of Commerce: National Ocean Service

1305 East West Highway 301-713-3066
Silver Spring, MD 20910 nos.info@noaa.gov
www.oceanservice.noaa.gov

The National Ocean Service works to observe, understand, and manage our nation's coastal and marine resources. The priorities of the service include safe and efficient transportation and commerce; preparedness and risk reduction; andstewardship, recreation, and tourism.

Nicole LeBoeuf, Assistant Administrator

2428 **Department of Energy: EM Site-Specific Advisory Board (EM SSAB)**
Office of Environmental Management
1000 Independence Ave SW 202-586-9928
Washington, DC 20585 David.Borak@em.doe.gov
www.energy.gov
The purpose of the EM SSAB is to directly involve stakeholders in EM cleanup discussions. The goal of the Board is to engage public input in cleanup decisions to ensure environmentally sound and safe cleanups.
David Borak, Designated Federal Officer

2429 **Department of Energy: Environmental Management Advisory Board (EMAB)**
Office of Environmental Management
1000 Independence Ave SW 202-586-9928
Washington, DC 20585 David.Borak@em.doe.gov
www.energy.gov
The mission of the Environmental Management Advisory Board is to provide advice, information and recommendations to the Assistant Secretary for Environmental Management regarding environmental restoration and waste management issues.The Board also advises the Environmental Management program on management practices.
David Borak, Designated Federal Officer

2430 **Department of Energy: Office of Electricity**
U.S. Department of Energy
1000 Independence Ave SW 202-586-1411
Washington, DC 20585 800-541-1625
Fax: 202-586-1472
OEwebmaster@hq.doe.gov
www.energy.gov/oe/office-electricity
The OE works to ensure that the Nation's energy is secure and reliable, and to develop new technologies that improve existing energy systems, bringing electricity into homes and businesses. The office also seeks to advance gridmodernization in energy infrastructure.

Patricia A. Hoffman, Deputy Assistant Secretary
Bruce J. Walker, Assistant Secretary

2431 **Department of Energy: Office of Energy Efficiency & Renewable Energy**
U.S. Department of Energy
1000 Independence Avenue SW 202-586-5000
Mail Stop EE-1 energy.gov/eere/transportation
Washington, DC 20585
The EERE researches how to make transportation cleaner and more efficient through green technology and alternative fuels. They do so by developing technologies to improve electric and other alternative-fuel vehicles, and producelow-carbon domestic transportation fuels.
Daniel Simmons, Assistant Secretary
Alex Fitzsimmons, Chief of Staff

2432 **Department of Energy: Office of Environmental Management**
U.S. Department of Energy 202-586-7709
1000 Independence Ave SW EM.WebContentManager@em.doe.gov
Washington, DC 20585 www.em.doe.gov
The Office of Environmental Management deals with the safe cleanup of decades worth of nuclear weapons development and nuclear energy research. The mission of the Office is to address the legacy of nuclear weapons that emerged duringthe Cold War.
Anne Marie White, Assistant Secretary
Jeff C. Griffin, Associate Principal Deputy

2433 **Department of Energy: Office of Fossil Energy**
U.S. Department of Energy
1000 Independence Ave SW 202-586-6660
Forrestal Building FECommunications@hq.doe.gov
Washington, DC 20585 energy.gov/fe/office-fossil-energy
This office is responsible for the research, development, and demonstration efforts on advanced carbon capture and storage technologies. They aim to develop technological solutions to sustainably develop the nation's oil and gasdomestic resources.

Steven Winberg, Assistant Secretary
Mark Maddox, Deputy Assistant Secretary

2434 **Department of Energy: Office of NEPA Policy and Compliance**
U.S. Department of Energy
1000 Independence Avenue SW 202-586-4600
Washington, DC 20585 800-472-2756
Fax: 202-586-7031
AskNEPA@hq.doe.gov
energy.gov/nepa/office-nepa-policy-and-compliance
This office serves as the contact point for NEPA matters for the US Department of Energy, and ensures that any proposed actions comply with NEPA requirements. It was created to foster general welfare in order to establish harmony withhumans and nature.

Brian Costner, Supervisor
Carrie Moeller Abravanel, Env. Protection Specialist

2435 **Department of Energy: Office of Nuclear Energy**
U.S. Department of Energy 202-586-5000
1000 Independence Avenue SW energy.gov/ne/office-nuclear-energy
Washington, DC 20585
The Office of Nuclear Energy's (NE) primary mission is to advance nuclear power as a resource capable of making major contributions in meeting the Nation's energy supply, environmental, and energy security needs.
Edward McGinnis, Assistant Secretary
Dennis Michael Miotla, Chief Operating Officer

2436 **Department of State: Bureau of Economic and Business Affairs**
U.S. Department of State
2201 C Street NW 202-647-7971
Washington, DC 20520 www.state.gov
The Bureau of Economic and Business Affairs works to create jobs for Americans at home while increasing economic opportunities overseas, with the goal of making America more secure. They ensure equality for American companies doingbusiness around the world, and attract foreign investors to create jobs in America.
Manisha Singh, Acting Under Secretary
Peter Haas, Assistant Secretary

2437 **Department of State: Bureau of Oceans and International Environment and Scientific Affairs**
U.S. Department of State
2201 C Street NW 202-647-1554
Washington, DC 20520 www.state.gov
OES coordinates U.S. international oceans, environmental and health policy, integrating U.S. domestic concerns with geopolitical concerns. OES promotes the full range of U.S. interests in the oceans to advance national security,facilitate commerce, manage fish resources, foster scientific understanding, and protect the marine environment through bilateral, regional and multilateral fora.

Marcia Bernicat, Principal Deputy
William Gibbons-Fly, Deputy Assistant Secretary

2438 **Department of State: Office of Conservation and Water**
U.S. Department of State
2201 C Street NW 202-647-4683
Washington, DC 20520 www.state.gov
Coordinates and leads the formulation of policies on conserving and sustainably managing ecosystems such as forests, wetlands, drylands, and coral reefs.
Christine Dawson, Director
Ari Nathan, Deputy Director

2439 **Department of State: Office of Global Change**
U.S. Department of State

2201 C Street NW 202-647-3984
Washington, DC 20520 ClimateComms@State.gov
www.state.gov/e/oes/climate/

Leads the US in a variety of international panels and forums, coordinates bilateral and regional partnerships on climate change, and U.S. foreign assistance on clean energy, adaptation, and sustainable landscapes. The Office alsorepresents the U.S. in climate negotiations on the international stage.

Trigg Talley, Director
Holly Kirking Loomis, Deputy Director

2440 Department of State: Office of Marine Conservation
U.S. Department of State
2201 C Street NW 202-647-2337
Washington, DC 20520 www.state.gov

The Office of Marine Conservation is responsible for U.S. policy on the conservation and management of living marine resources. The aim of this office is to ensure economic prosperity and security through sustainable fisheries.

David F. Hogan, Acting Office Director
Deirdre M. Warner-Kramer, Acting Deputy Director

2441 Department of Transportation: Federal Highway Administration
1200 New Jersey Avenue SE 202-366-4000
Washington, DC 20590 www.fhwa.dot.gov

The goal of the FHWA is to support governments across the nation in the design, construction, and maintenance of highway systems. They provide financial and technical aid to state and local governments to ensure safe roads andhighways.

Brandye Hendrickson, Deputy Administrator
Thomas D. Everett, Executive Director

2442 Department of Transportation: Federal Railroad Administration
1200 New Jersey Avenue SE 202-493-6014
Washington, DC 20590 FRAPA@dot.gov
www.fra.dot.gov

Created by the Department of Transportation Act in 1966, the FRA ensures the safe and efficient movement of people and goods in the present and future.

Ronald Batory, Administrator
Brett A. Jortland, Chief Counsel

2443 Department of Transportation: Federal Transit Administration
1200 New Jersey Avenue SE 202-366-4043
4th & 5th Floor, East Building 866-377-8642
Washington, DC 20590 www.fta.dot.gov

Provides financial and technical assitance to local public transit systems, and oversees safety measures. Partners with state and local governments to create and enhance public transportation systems.

Matthew Welbes, Executive Director
John Brennan, Chief Counsel

2444 Department of Transportation: Maritime Administration
1200 New Jersey Avenue SE 202-366-4000
Washington, DC 20590 www.maritime.dot.gov

This agency within the U.S. Department of Transportation seeks to promote the use of marine transportation and enhance its interaction with other segments of the transportation system. Additionally, it educates the public about theimportance of the maritime industry.

Mark H. Buzby, Administrator

2445 Department of Transportation: Office of Pipeline Safety
U.S. Department of Transportation
1200 New Jersey Avenue SE 202-366-4595
Washington, DC 20590 *Fax:* 202-366-4566
phmsa.pipelinesafety@dot.gov
www.phmsa.dot.gov/pipeline

To protect people and the environment from the risks of hazardous materials transportation by establishing national policies, enforcing standards, educating the public, and conducting research. The goal of the office is to ensure thesafe and reliable use of the nation's natural gas transportation system.

Alan Mayberry, Associate Administrator

2446 Department of the Interior
1849 C Street NW 202-208-3100
Washington, DC 20240 feedback@ios.doi.gov
www.doi.gov

The Department of the Interior protects and manages the Nation's natural resources and cultural heritage, honoring its trust responsibilities to American Indians, Alaska Natives, and affiliated island communities. It also providesinformation about natural resources and hazards.

David Bernhardt, Secretary
Susan Combs, Assistant Secretary

2447 Department of the Interior: National Park Service
1849 C Street NW 202-208-6843
Washington, DC 20240 www.nps.gov

The National Park Service aims to preserve the natural and cultural resources and values of the national park system for the benefit of the public. The Park Service cooperates with partners to extend the advantages of these resourcesthroughout the U.S. and internationally.

Dan Smith, Deputy Director
Chris Powell, Chief of Staff

2448 Department of the Interior: Bureau of Reclamation
1849 C Street NW 202-513-0501
Washington, DC 20240-0001 *Fax:* 202-513-0309
www.usbr.gov

The Bureau of Reclamation leads projects for the development of dams, powerplants, and canals in the western states. They are the second largest producer of hydroelectric power in the country, and strive to manage, develop, and protectwater resources to benefit the environment and the economy.

Brenda Burman, Commissioner
Shelby Hagenaur, Deputy Commissioner

2449 Department of the Interior: Division of Parks and Wildlife
U.S. Department of the Interior
1849 C Street NW 202-208-4344
Washington, DC 20240 www.doi.gov/solicitor/headquarters

The purpose of the division is to provide legal counsel on matters such as the administration of programs and activities of the National Park Service, the Fish and Wildlife Service, and the biological research functions of theGeological Survey. The division also engages in endangered species protection.

David Bernhardt, Secretary, DOI
Susan Combs, Assistant Secretary, DOI

2450 Department of the Interior: Office of the Solicitor
1849 C Street NW 202-208-4423
Washington, DC 20240 www.doi.gov/solicitor

The goal of the Office is provide legal counsel for the U.S. Department of the Interior, in order to fulfill the Department's wide-ranging mission. The Office also manages the Department's Ethics Office and resolves FOIA Appeals.

David Bernhardt, Sectretary, DOI
Susan Combs, Assistant Secretary, DOI

2451 Department of the Interior: Office of the Secretary
U.S. Department of the Interior
1849 C Street NW 202-208-3100
Washington, DC 20240 feedback@ios.doi.gov
www.doi.gov

The Secretary of the Interior is responsible for leading an agency of over 70,000 empolyees. The role of the Department of the Interior is to ensure responsible development of conventional and renewable energy supplies on public landsand waters. The

Department also upholds trust responsibilities to the federally recognized American Indian Tribes and Alaska Natives.
David Bernhardt, Secretary
Susan Combs, Assistant Secretary

2452 Department of the Interior: U.S. Fish & Wildlife Service
1849 C Street NW 202-208-3100
Washington, DC 20240 800-344-9453
www.fws.gov
The mission of the U.S. Fish & Wildlife Service is to work with others to conserve, protect and enhance fish, wildlife, plants and their habitats for the continuing benefit of the American people.

David Bernhardt, Secretary
Susan Combs, Assistant Secretary

2453 Department of the Interior: Wild Horse and Burro Program
Bureau of Land Management
1849 C Steet NW 202-208-3801
Room 5665 866-468-7826
Washington, DC 20240 *Fax:* 202-208-5242
wildhorse@blm.gov
www.blm.gov
The Wild Horse and Burro Program protects, manages, and controls wild horses and burros under the authority of the Wild Free-Roaming Horses and Burros Act of 1971 to ensure that healthy herds thrive on public rangelands.
Brian Steed, Deputy Director
Michael Nedd, Deputy Director, Operations

2454 Environmental Change and Security Program: Woodrow Wilson International Center for Scholars
1300 Pennsylvania Ave NW 202-691-4000
Washington, DC 20004-3027 www.wilsoncenter.org/ecsp
The ECSP provides specialists and interested individuals with a road-map to the myriad conceptions, activities and policy initiatives related to environment, population and security. The project pursues three basic topic: environmentalsecurity and peacebuilding; sustainabile development and climate resilience; and population dynamics. The program explores a wide range of environment related issues.

Thelma Duggin, Chair
Nathalie Rayes, Vice Chair

2455 Environmental Financial Advisory Board (EFAB)
U.S. Environmental Protection Agency
1200 Pennsylvania Avenue NW 202-564-1151
Washington, DC 20460 www.epa.gov/waterfinancecenter/efab
The EFAB provides advice to the Environmental Protection Agency's Administrator and program offices around the financial aspects of environmental protection. The primary goals of the EFAB are to lower the cost of environmentalprotection, increase private and public contribution in environmental services, and build state financial ability to meet environmental laws.

Aurel M. Arndt, Advisor
Yvette Downs, Chief Financial Officer

2456 Environmental Health Sciences Review Committee
P.O. Box 12233 984-287-3236
Mail Drop K3-03 *Fax:* 919-316-4606
Durham, NC 27709 bass@niehs.nih.gov
www.niehs.nih.gov

This Committee is part of the National Institute of Environmental Health Sciences (NIEHS), and is responsible for the scientific review of various grant mechanisms within the NIEHS. These include the Environmental Health Science P30Core Centers; Institutional National Research Service Award (T32); and career awards, among others.
21 members
Linda K. Bass, Scientific Review Officer
Peter Dedon, Associate Director

2457 Environmental Protection Agency (EPA)
1200 Pennsylvania Avenue NW 202-564-4700
Washington, DC 20460 www.epa.gov
EPA's mission is to protect human health and to safeguard the natural environment - air, water and land - upon which life depends. This agency also ensures that communities, individuals, businesses, and governments have access toaccurate information about human health and environmental risks.

Andrew Wheeler, Administrator
Ryan Jackson, Chief of Staff

2458 Environmental Protection Agency: Clean Air Markets Division
Environmental Protection Agency
1200 Pennsylvania Avenue NW 202-343-9620
Mail Code 6204M www.epa.gov/airmarkets
Washington, DC 20460
Through regulatory programs, The Clean Air Markets division aims to reduce air pollution from power plants that contribute to environmental problems such as acid rain, ozone and particle pollution, and interstate transport of airpollution.
Karen VanSickle, Contact, Air Markets
Paula Branch, Contact, General Accounts

2459 Environmental Protection Agency: Climate Change Research
U.S. EPA Research
109 Alexander Drive 202-343-9990
Durham, NC 27711 brown.ann@epa.gov
www.epa.gov

The EPA Climate Change Research involves assessing and addressing global climate change and the associated risks to human health and the environment.
Rebecca Dodder, Senior Physical Scientist

2460 Environmental Protection Agency: Federal Facilities Enforcement Office (FFEO)
U.S. Environmental Protection Agency
1200 Pennsylvania Avenue 202-564-7068
Mail Code 2261A leff.karin@epa.gov
Washington, DC 20460 www.epa.gov
Within the Office of Enforcement and Compliance Assurance, FFEO works with federal facilities to ensure their compliance with environmental pollution standards. The Office carries this out through inspections and enforcement under allenvironmental statutes.
Karin Leff, Director

2461 Environmental Protection Agency: Greenhouse Gas Reporting Program (GHGRP)
EPA Climate Change Division
1200 Pennsylvania Avenue NW 202-343-9876
Washington, DC 20460 www.epa.gov/ghgreporting
This program, a part of the Climate Change Division of the EPA, requires reporting of greenhouse gas data from large greenhouse gas emission sources, fuel and industrial gas suppliers, and CO2 injection sites. The data gathered canthen be used by businesses, states, cities, and communities to take a number of actions including tracking greenhouse gas emissions, minimized wasted energy, and identify opportunities to cut pollution.
Paul Gunning, Director, Climate Change

2462 Environmental Protection Agency: Immediate Office of the Assistant Administrator for Water
Environmental Protection Agency
1200 Pennsylvania Avenue 202-564-5700
Mail Code 4101M ross.davidp@epa.gov
Washington, DC 20460 www.epa.gov/aboutepa/about-office-water
Within the Office of Water, this division works with other parts of EPA on broad or emerging issues, and performs various policy communications, resources management, and operational functions in the National Water Program.
Dave Ross, Assistant Administrator
Dennis Lee Forsgren, Jr., Deputy Asst Administrator

2463 Environmental Protection Agency: Indoor Air Quality
U.S. EPA Office Of Radiation and Indoor Air
1200 Pennsylvania Avenue NW 202-564-4700
Mail Code 6609T www.epa.gov/indoor-air-quality-iaq
Washington, DC 20460
The mission of the Indoor Air Quality division of the EPA is to protect the public and the environment from the risks of radiation and indoor air pollution.
Laureen Burton, Executive Secretariat

2464 Environmental Protection Agency: Local Government Advisory Committee (LGAC)
Environmental Protection Agency
1200 Pennsylvania Avenue NW 202-564-5200
Washington, DC 20460 scales.wuanisha@epa.gov
www.epa.gov/ocir
Composed mainly of elected and appointed local officials, several state representatives, and environmental interest groups, this committee advises, consults with, and makes recommendations to EPA on matters related to theimplementation of federal environmental requirements by local governments.

Bob Dixson, Chair
Jeff White, Vice Chair

2465 Environmental Protection Agency: Office of Pollution Prevention and Toxics (OPPT)
Environmental Protection Agency
1200 Pennsylvania Avenue NW 202-564-3810
Mail Code 7401M www.epa.gov
Washington, DC 20460
Within the Office of Chemical Safety and Pollution Prevention, the mission of the OPPT is to evaluate the risks of chemicals, and to find ways of preventing pollution before it is released into the environment. The programs managed bythe OPPT fall under the Toxic Substances Control Act and the Pollution Prevention Act.
Jeffrey Morris, Director
Tala Henry, Director for Programs

2466 Environmental Protection Agency: Office of Science and Technology (OST)
Environmental Protection Agency
1200 Pennsylvania Avenue 202-566-0430
Mail Code 4301M www.epa.gov/aboutepa/about-office-water
Washington, DC 20460
Within the Office of Water, the role of OST is to develop recommended safe water quality levels for toxics, nutrients, and pathogens in collaboration with states, tribes, and other stakeholders. The Office also implements performancestandards relating to water pollution from industry.
Deborah Nagle, Director
Jeff Lape, Deputy Director

2467 Environmental Protection Agency: Office of Administration and Policy (OAP)
U.S. Environmental Protection Agency
1200 Pennsylvania Avenue 202-564-2530
Mail Code 2201A badalamente.mark@epa.gov
Washington, DC 20460 www.epa.gov
Within the Office of Enforcement and Compliance Assurance, OAP manages and coordinates policy and administrative services, including human resources, labor relations, budget, finances, contracts, and grants, among others.
Mark Badalamente, Director

2468 Environmental Protection Agency: Office of Air Quality Planning and Standards (OAQPS)
U.S. Environmental Protection Agency
1200 Pennsylvania Avenue NW 919-541-5616
C404-04 www.epa.gov
Washington, DC 20460
Within the Office of Air and Radiation, the mission of the Office of Air Quality Planning and Standards (OAQPS) is to preserve and improve air quality. They accomplish this mission by compiling and reviewing air pollution data,implementing regulations to reduce air pollution, and making information about air pollution available to the public.
Peter Tsirigotis, Director
Mike Koerber, Deputy Director

2469 Environmental Protection Agency: Office of Atmospheric Programs (OAP)
U.S. Environmental Protection Agency
1200 Pennsylvania Avenue NW 202-343-9140
Mail Code 6201A www.epa.gov
Washington, DC 20460
Within the Office of Air and Radiation, the role of OAP is to manage programs that address ozone layer protection, climate change, and regional air quality. Examples of the programs OAP runs include the Acid Rain Program and ENERGYSTAR.
Sarah Dunham, Director

2470 Environmental Protection Agency: Office of Children's Health Protection (OCHP)
Environmental Protection Agency
1200 Pennsylvania Avenue NW 202-564-2199
Mail Code 1107T *Fax:* 202-564-2733
Washington, DC 20460 www.epa.gov/children
The mission of this office is to make the protection of children's environmental health a fundamental goal of public health and environmental protection in the U.S. They accomplish their mission through involvement in EPA rulemakingregarding prenatal and childhood vulnerabilities.
Michael Firestone, Director

2471 Environmental Protection Agency: Office of Civil Enforcement (OCE)
U.S. Environmental Protection Agency
1200 Pennsylvania Avenue 202-564-2220
Mail Code 2201A kelley.rosemarie@epa.gov
Washington, DC 20460 www.epa.gov
Within the Office of Enforcement and Compliance Assurance, OCE provides legal support for civil and judicial cases and investigations in EPA regions. They hold the responsibility of planning and setting priorities for enforcementactivities, and developing national enforcement policy and guidance.
Rosemarie Kelley, Director

2472 Environmental Protection Agency: Office of Compliance (OC)
U.S. Environmental Protection Agency
1200 Pennsylvania Avenue 202-564-2280
Mail Code 2201A hindin.david@epa.gov
Washington, DC 20460 www.epa.gov
Within the Office of Enforcement and Compliance Assurance, OC establishes enforcement initiatives and ensures effective assessment of compliance in order to reduce noncompliance and environmental risk.
David Hindin, Director
John Dombrowski, Deputy Director

2473 Environmental Protection Agency: Office of Criminal Enforcement, Forensics and Training (OCEFT)
U.S. Environmental Protection Agency
1200 Pennsylvania Avenue 202-564-2480
Mail Code 2201A barnet.henry@epa.gov
Washington, DC 20460 www.epa.gov
Within the Office of Enforcement and Compliance Assurance, OCEFT provides technical and forensic services for civil and criminal investigations, including the investigation of environmental law violations.
Mark Barnet, Director
Pam Mazakas, Deputy Director

2474 Environmental Protection Agency: Office of Enforcement and Compliance Assurance (OECA)
U.S. Environmental Protection Agency
1200 Pennsylvania Avenue 202-564-2440
Mail Code 2201A www.epa.gov
Washington, DC 20460
The role of OECA is to implement civil and criminal enforcement relating to pollution problems, including water, air, and chemical

hazards. OECA works with states and tribal partners, and aims to advance community participation inorder to ensure environmental compliance.
Susan Bodine, Assistant Administrator

2475 Environmental Protection Agency: Office of Environmental Justice
Environmental Protection Agency
1200 Pennsylvania Avenue NW 202-564-2515
Mail Code 2201A 800-962-6215
Washington, DC 20460 ejhotline@epa.gov
www.epa.gov
The Office works to integrate environmental justice considerations into the EPA. It accomplishes this mission by coordinating EPA efforts to address the needs of vulnerable populations, and providing financial and technical assistanceto communities working to address environmental justice.

Marsha Minter, Associate Director
Doretta Reaves, Contact, Public Engagement

2476 Environmental Protection Agency: Office of Ground Water and Drinking Water
Environmental Protection Agency
1200 Pennsylvania Avenue 202-564-3750
Mail Code 4601M www.epa.gov/ground-water-and-drinking-water
Washington, DC 20460
The mission of the Ground Water and Drinking Water division of the EPA is to protect public health by ensuring safe drinking water and protecting ground water.
Jennifer McLain, Director
Yu-Ting Guilaran, Deputy Director

2477 Environmental Protection Agency: Office of Land and Emergency Management
1200 Pennsylvania Ave NW 202-272-0167
Washington, DC 20460 www.epa.gov
The Office of Land and Emergency Management (OLEM) develops guidelines for land disposal of hazardous waste, provides assistance in the establishment of safe waste management practices, supports the redevelopment of contaminated sites,and responds to abandoned and active hazardous waste sites.
Barry Breen, Assistant Administrator
Steven Cook, Deputy Assistant

2478 Environmental Protection Agency: Office of Pesticide Programs (OPP)
Environmental Protection Agency
1200 Pennsylvania Avenue NW 703-305-7090
Mail Code 7501P pesticidequestions@epa.gov
Washington, DC 20460 www.epa.gov
Within the Office of Chemical Safety and Pollution Prevention, OPP is in charge of regulating the manufacture and use of pesticides in the U.S. and establishes safety standards regarding these chemicals. Additionally, the Programensures public access to information about risk management associated with pesticides.
Rick P. Keigwin, Director
Edward Messina, Director for Programs

2479 Environmental Protection Agency: Office of Radiation and Indoor Air (ORIA)
U.S. Environmental Protection Agency
1200 Pennsylvania Avenue NW 202-343-9320
Mail Code 6608T www.epa.gov
Washington, DC 20460
Within the office of Air and Radiation, ORIA protects the public and the environment from the effects of radiation and indoor air pollution by collaborating with other departments of the EPA as well as federal, state, tribal, andnon-governmental organizations.
Jonathan Edwards, Director

2480 Environmental Protection Agency: Office of Science Coordination and Policy (OSCP)
Environmental Protection Agency
1200 Pennsylvania Avenue NW 202-564-1116
Mail Code 7201M www.epa.gov
Washington, DC 20460
The role of OSCP is to provide coordination, leadership, peer review, and synthesis of science and science policy within the Office of Chemical Safety and Pollution Prevention (OCSPP). They carry out hazard assessment and ensure soundscientific decisions are made in chemical management.
Hayley Hughes, Director

2481 Environmental Protection Agency: Office of Site Remediation Enforcement (OSRE)
U.S. Environmental Protection Agency
1200 Pennsylvania Avenue 202-564-5510
Mail Code 2251A mackey.cyndy@epa.gov
Washington, DC 20460 www.epa.gov
Within the Office of Enforcement and Compliance Assurance, OSRE enforces EPA's national hazardous waste cleanup programs by ensuring that those responsible for hazardous waste spills either clean up the site or reimburse EPA for itscleanup.
Cyndy Mackey, Director
Rafael DeLeon, Deputy Director

2482 Environmental Protection Agency: Office of Transportation and Air Quality (OTAQ)
U.S. Environmental Protection Agency
1200 Pennsylvania Avenue NW 202-564-1682
Mail Code 6401A www.epa.gov
Washington, DC 20460
Within the Office of Air and Radiation, the mission of OTAQ is to protect human health and the environment through the reduction of air pollution and greenhouse gas emissions. They aim to advance clean fuels and technology, andencourage sustainable business practices and travel choices.
Christopher Grundler, Director

2483 Environmental Protection Agency: Office of Wastewater Management (OWM)
Environmental Protection Agency
1200 Pennsylvania Avenue 202-564-0748
Mail Code 4201M www.epa.gov/aboutepa/about-office-water
Washington, DC 20460
Within the Office of Water, OWM promotes effective and responsible water use, wastewater treatment, disposal, and management through the regulations of the Clean Water Act. They aid with the restoration of watersheds, provideregulatory standards, and work with communities to protect water infrastructure.
Andrew Sawyers, Director
Martha Shimkin, Deputy Director

2484 Environmental Protection Agency: Office of Water
Environmental Protection Agency
1200 Pennsylvania Avenue NW 202-564-5700
Mail Code 4101M
Washington, DC 20460
The Office of Water is responsible for implementing the Clean Water Act and Safe Drinking Water Act. They also help to restore and maintain the health of oceans, watersheds, and aquatic ecosystems.
Dave Ross, Assistant Administrator
Dennis Lee Forsgren Jr., Deputy Asst Administrator

2485 Environmental Protection Agency: Office of Wetlands, Oceans and Watersheds (OWOW)
Environmental Protection Agency
1200 Pennsylvania Avenue 202-566-1146
Mail Code 4501T ow-owow-internet-comments@epa.gov
Washington, DC 20460 www.epa.gov/aboutepa/about-office-water
Within the Office of Water, OWOW was established to protect freshwater, estuarine, coastal, and ocean ecosystems. Their job is to regulate and monitor ocean dumping and vessel discharges in order to reduce debris in the ocean, and toregulate runoff pollution.
John Goodin, Director
Sandra Connors, Deputy Director

2486 Environmental Protection Agency: Resource Conservation and Recovery Act
Environmental Protection Agency
1200 Pennsylvania Avenue 202-564-4700
Washington, DC 20460 www.epa.gov/rcra

RCRA is a public law that gives EPA the authority to control hazardous and non-hazardous waste from the cradle-to-grave. This includes the generation, transportation, treatment, storage, and disposal of hazardous waste.

Barnes Johnson, Director
Kathleen Salyer, Deputy Director

2487 Environmental Protection Agency: Science Advisory Committee on Chemicals
Environmental Protection Agency
1200 Pennsylvania Ave NW 707-564-4700
Washington, DC 20460
The SACC provides scientific advice to the EPA on risk assessments, methodologies, and pollution prevention for chemicals regulated by the Toxic Substances Control Act (TSCA).
26 members
Kenneth Portier, Chair

2488 Environmental Protection Agency: Small Community Advisory Subcommittee (SCAS)
Environmental Protection Agency
1200 Pennsylvania Avenue NW 202-564-3781
Mail Code 1301-A Matthews.Demond@epa.gov
Washington, DC 20460 www.epa.gov/ocir
As an independently-appointed subcommittee of the Local Government Advisory Committee (LGAC) within the EPA, the SCAS advises the Administrator on environmental issues relating to the residents of smaller communities. Their goal is toensure that small communities in the U.S. have clean air, drinking water, waste disposal, and related services.

Demond Matthews, Designated Federal Officer

2489 Farm, Ranch, and Rural Communities Committee (FRRCC)
Federal Advisory Committee Management Division
1200 Pennsylvania Avenue NW 202-564-2294
Mail Code 1601M www.epa.gov/faca/frrcc
Washington, DC 20460
The FRRCC provides advice and recommendations to the Administrator on environmental issues and programs that impact, or are of concern to, farms, ranches, and rural communities.
Twice a year
Hema Subramanian, Designated Federal Officer

2490 Federal Aviation Administration
800 Independence Avenue SW 866-835-5322
Washington, DC 20591 www.faa.gov
The major roles of the Federal Aviation Administration (a part of the Department of Transportation) include regulation, development, and research in the areas of civil aviation, civil aeronautics, and U.S. commercial spacetransportation. The mission of the Administration is to provide a safe and efficient aerospace system.

Dan Elwell, Administrator
Carl Burleson, Deputy Administrator

2491 Federal Energy Regulatory Commission
888 1st Street NE 202-502-6088
Washington, DC 20426 866-208-3372
customer@ferc.gov
www.ferc.gov
FERC's mission is to ensure economically efficient, safe, and reliable energy for consumers. It is an independent agency that accomplishes its mission by regulating the interstate transmission of natural gas, oil, and electricity.
Cheryl A. LaFleur, Commissioner
Neil Chatterjee, Chair

2492 Federal Insecticide, Fungicide, and Rodenticide Act Scientific Advisory Panel (FIFRA SAP)
Office of Science Coordination and Policy
1200 Pennsylvanie Avenue NW 202-564-0103
Mail Stop 7201M knott.steven@epa.gov
Washington, DC 20460-0001 www.epa.gov/sap
Provides scientific advice regarding pesticides and pesticide-related issues and analyzes the effects of EPA's pesticide-related regulatory actions. The FIFRA SAP is includes biologists, staisticians, toxicologists, and other experts.

Robert E. Chapin, Chair
George B. Corcoran, Professor

2493 Food and Drug Administration
10903 New Hampshire Avenue 888-463-6332
Silver Spring, MD 20993-0002 www.fda.gov
Assures the safety, efficacy, and security of human and veterinary drugs, biological products, medical devices, our nation's food supply, cosmetics, and products that emit radiation, in order to protect public health. The FDA is alsoresponsible for advancing the public health by helping to speed innovations that make medicines and foods more effective, safer, and more affordable.

Norman E. Sharpless, Commissioner
Amy Abernethy, Deputy Commissioner

2494 Forest Health Protection
Forest Service-USDA
1400 Independance Avenue SW 202-649-1191
Stop Code 1110 *Fax:* 703-605-5353
Washington, DC 20250-1110 www.fs.fed.us/foresthealth/
Forest Health Protection is part of the U.S. Forest Service, and protects and improves the health of America's rural, wildland, and urban forests by providing technical assistance on forest health-related matters. The goal of ForestHealth Protection is to maintain, enhance, and restore healthy forest conditions.
Rick Cooksey, Acting Director
Shray Jackson, Administrative Assistant

2495 General Services Administration
1800 F Street, NW 844-472-4111
Washington, DC 20405 www.gsa.gov
The GSA's mission is to provide the best value in real estate, acqusition, and technology services to the government and the American people. They provide workplaces by constructing, managing, and preserving government buildings and bymanaging commercial real estate.

Emily W. Murphy, Administrator
Allison F. Brigati, Deputy Administrator

2496 Global Learning and Observations to Benefit the Environment
3300 Mitchell Lane 800-858-9947
Boulder, CO 80301 help@globe.gov
www.globe.gov
This program aims to provide students and the public internationally with scientific education, including the opportunity to participate in the scientific process. The mission of the program is to promote scientific education, enhanceenvironmental literacy, and promote scientific discovery.

Tony Murphy, Director
Travis Anderson, Data Scientist

2497 Good Neighbor Environmental Board (GNEB)
1200 Pennsylvania Avenue NW 202-564-2294
Mail Code 1601-M www.epa.gov/faca/gneb
Washington, DC 20460
GNEB is an independent federal advisory committee that reports to and advises the President and Congress about environmental and infrastructure isses and needs within the states contiguous to Mexico in order to improve the quality oflife of persons residing along the U.S. border.

Ann-Marie Gantner, Designated Federal Officer

2498 House Agriculture Committee
1301 Longworth House Office Bldg 202-225-2171
Washington, DC 20515 *Fax:* 202-225-8510
agriculture.house.gov

The House Agriculture Committee presently deals with issues such as farm economy, agricultural conservation, food transparency, agricultural innovation, and more.
Collin Peterson, Chairman
David Scott, Ranking Member

2499 House Committee on Energy & Commerce
2125 Rayburn House Office Building 202-225-2927
Washington, DC 20515
The oldest standing legislative committee in the U.S. House of Representatives, the Committee on Engery & Commerce is responsible for things such as evironmental quality, energy policy, and food and drug safety. The Committee on Energy& Commerce also oversees the Department of Energy and the Environmental Protection Agency, among others.
Frank Pallone Jr, Chair

2500 House Committee on Foreign Affairs
2170 Rayburn House Office Building 202-225-5021
Washington, DC 20515 *Fax:* 202-225-5393
foreignaffairs.house.gov
The Committee manages legislation regarding foreign policy, foreign assistance, trade promotion, export controls, foreign arms sales, student exchanges, international broadcasting, international law, and many other issues.
Eliot Engel, Chair
Michale McCaul, Ranking Member

2501 Installation Management Command
Public Affairs Office
2405 Gun Shed Road 210-466-1022
Houston, TX 78234-1223 home.army.mil/imcom/index.php
ICOM oversees the daily operations of various U.S. Army operations around the world. They are in charge of ensuring the safe housing, childcare services, and fire and police forces in army communities.
Bradley A. Becker, Commanding General
Melissa A. Judkins, Command Sergeant Major

2502 Institutional Biosafety Committee
NIEHS
111 T.W. Alexander Drive 919-541-3345
Durham, NC 27709 francesco.demayo@nih.gov
www.niehs.nih.gov
Established as part of the National Institute of Environmental Health Sciences (NIEHS), the IBC reviews various projects relating to recombinant DNA, RNAi, pathogens, human materials, and other potentially infectious substances. Itrepresents the community's interests regarding public health and environmental protection.
13 members
Francesco J. Demayo, Chair

2503 Institutional Review Board
P.O. Box 12233 984-287-4208
Mail Drop E1-06 resnikd@niehs.nih.gov
Durham, NC 27709 www.niehs.nih.gov
Part of the National Institute of Environmental Health Sciences (NIEHS), the IRB provides ethical and regulatory review of research that involves human subjects at the NIEHS. Their mission is to protect the rights, welfare, andwellbeing of human research subjects participating in NIEHS research.
11 members
David B. Resnik, Chair
Joan P. Packenham, Vice Chair

2504 Inter-American Foundation
1331 Pennsylvania Avenue NW 202-360-4530
Suite 1200 North www.iaf.gov
Washington, DC 20004
The Inter-American Foundation (IAF) is an independent foreign assistance agency of the United States government, working to promote equitable, responsive, and participatory self-help development in Latin America and the Caribbean.
Eddy Arriola, Chair
Juan Carlos Iturregui, Vice Chair

2505 Interagency Breast Cancer & Environmental Research Coordinating Committee
NIEHS
111 T.W. Alexander Drive 919-541-3345
Durham, NC 27709 www.niehs.nih.gov
Established as part of the National Institute of Environmental Health Sciences (NIEHS), the IBCERCC is composed of federal and nonfederal members who examine the current state of breast cancer and environment research. The Committeeprovides reports summarizing its findings and gives recomendations to expand efforts that mitigate the environmental causes of breast cancer.
19 members
Michele R. Forman, Chair
Alice Chang, President

2506 International Joint Commission
US Section
1717 H Street NW 202-632-2006
Suite 801 www.ijc.org
Washington, DC 20006
Prevents and resolves disputes between the United States and Canada, and pursues the common good of both countries as an independent and objective advisor to the two governments. The IJC focuses specifically on the lake and riversystems that border the two countries, ensuring the cooperation between nations in order to protect these waters.
Jane Corwin, Chair & US Commissioner
Henry Lickers, Canada Commissioner

2507 Manpower and Reserve Affairs
Department of Defense
1400 Defense Pentagon prhome.defense.gov/M-RA/
Washington, DC 20301-1400
This office provides guidance, direction, and oversight for the department on all matters pertaining to the environment, safety, and occupational health. They are responsible for implementing human resource solutions to ensure missionreadiness as well as the development and delivery of personnel policy.
Virginia Penrod, Assistant Secretary

2508 Marine Mammal Commission
4340 East West Highway 301-504-0087
Suite 700 *Fax:* 301-504-0099
Bethesda, MD 20814 mmc@mmc.gov
www.mmc.gov
Develops, reviews, and makes recommendations on domestic and international actions and policies with respect to marine mammal protection, conservation and with carrying out a research program. The primary objective is to ensure thatfederal programs are being administered in ways that maintain the health and stability of marine ecosystems and do not disadvantage marine mammal populations or species.
Daryl J. Boness, Chairman
Frances Gulland, Commissioner

2509 Marine Minerals Program
Bureau of Ocean Energy Management
1849 C Street NW 703-787-1851
Washington, DC 20240 MarineMinerals@boem.gov
www.boem.gov/Marine-Minerals-Program/
The MMP works with communities to address erosion along the Nation's coastal beaches, dunes, barrier islands, and wetlands. To achieve this mission, MMP leases sand, gravel, and shell resources from federal waters on the outerContinental Shelf (OCS) to ensure beach nourishment and restoration.
Walter Cruickshank, Director

2510 Marine Protected Areas Federal Advisory Committee
1305 East West Highway 301-713-7265
Silver Spring, MD 20910-3281 *Fax:* 301-713-3110
mpainfo@noaa.gov
marineprotectedareas.noaa.gov/fac/
The Marine Protected Areas (MPA) Federal Advisory Committee serves to advise the NOAA and the Department of the Interior on ways in which the nation can improve its marine protected areas.
3x year
Charles Wahle, Designated Federal Officer
John Anderson, Executive Director

2511 Migratory Bird Conservation Commission
5275 Leesburg Pike 703-358-1713
Mail Stop 3N053 *Fax:* 703-358-2223
Falls Church, VA 22041-3803 mbcc@fws.gov
www.fws.gov/refuges/realty/mbcc.html
The Migratory Bird Conservation Commission (MBCC) is responsible for considering and approving for acquistion areas of migratory bird habitat (other than waterfowl production areas) that have been submitted by regional offices andrecommended by the Secretary. The MBCC is composed of representatives from the Legislative and Executive Branches of government, and fixes the price at which such areas may be purchased or rented.
2x year
John Boozman, Member
A. Eric Alvarez, Secretary

2512 Mine Safety and Health Administration
201 12th Street S 202-693-9400
Suit 401 AskMSHA@dol.gov
Arlington, VA 22202-5450 www.msha.gov
The mission of the Mine Safety and Health Administration is to administer the provisions of the Federal Mine Safety and Health Act of 1977 and to enforce compliance with mandatory safety and health standards as means to eliminate fatalaccidents; to reduce the frequency and severity of nonfatal accidents; to minimize health hazards; and to promote improved safety and health conditions in the nation's mines. MSHA carries out the mandates of the Mine Act at all mining and mineralprocessing areas.

David G. Zatezalo, Assistant Secretary
Wayne D. Palmer, Deputy Assistant Secretary

2513 NOAA Fisheries
NOAA Fisheries Directorate
1315 East West Highway 301-427-8000
Silver Spring, MD 20910 www.fisheries.noaa.gov
The Fisheries division of the National Oceanic and Atmospheric Administration oversees the nation's ocean resources and their habitat. They work to ensure productive and sustainable fisheries, safe sources of seafood, and healthyecosystems.
Chris Oliver, Assistant Administrator
Samuel D. Raunch III, Deputy Assistant Admin.

2514 NOAA Office of National Marine Sanctuaries
1305 East West Highway 301-713-3125
11th Floor *Fax:* 301-713-0404
Silver Spring, MD 20910 sanctuaries@noaa.gov
sanctuaries.noaa.gov
The mission of the office is to serve as the trustee for the nation's system of marine protected areas. They aim to conserve, protect, and enhance the biodiversity, ecological integrity and cultural legacy of America's ocean and GreatLakes waters.

Elizabeth L. Cheney, Advisory Council Member
Charles Wahle, Advisory Committee Member

2515 NTSB Office of Administration
National Transportation Safety Board
490 L'Enfant Plaza SW 202-314-6000
Washington, DC 20594 www.ntsb.gov
The Office of Administration manages the support activities for the National Transportation Safety Board, including human resource management, labor relations, facilities management, and more. The Office consists of four divisions: Administrative Operations & Security, Acquisitions, Human Resources, and Safety.
Susan Kantrowitz, Director
Christopher Blumberg, Deputy Director

2516 NTSB Office of Administrative Law Judges
National Transportation Safety Board
490 L'Enfant Plaza SW 202-314-6000
Washington, DC 20594 www.ntsb.gov
The role of the National Transportation Safety Board's administrative law judges is to consider and issue decisions on appeals filed with the Board. The four judges currently serving on the Board also adjudicate expense claims underthe Equal Access to Justice Act.
Alfonso J. Montano, Chief Judge

2517 NTSB Office of Aviation Safety
National Transportation Safety Board
490 L'Enfant Plaza SW 202-314-6000
Washington, DC 20594 www.ntsb.gov
The Office of Aviation Safety investigates civil domestic air carrier, commuter, and air taxi accidents; out-of-country airline crashes that involve U.S. carriers; and aviation safety problems. Their mission is to prevent recurringaccidents and to improve aviation safety.
John DeLisi, Director
Dana Schulze, Deputy Director

2518 NTSB Office of Highway Safety
National Transportation Safety Board
490 L'Enfant Plaza SW 202-314-6000
Washington, DC 20594 www.ntsb.gov
The role of the Office of Highway Safety is to investigate crashes that highlight national safety issues. Some examples of these types of accidents are collapses of highway bridge structures, fatalaties on public transit, andcollisions at highway crossings. The Office carries out studies to identify underlying causes of crashes.
Robert Molloy, Director
Kristen Poland, Deputy Director

2519 NTSB Office of Marine Safety
National Transportation Safety Board
490 L'Enfant Plaza SW 202-314-6000
Washington, DC 20594 www.ntsb.gov
The Office of Marine Safety investigates marine accidents that occur in navigable waters, internal waters, or the territorial sea of the U.S., as well as accidents involving U.S. vessels internationally.
Brian Curtis, Director
Morgan Turrell, Deputy Director

2520 NTSB Office of Railroad, Pipeline and Hazardous Materials Investigations
National Transportation Safety Board
490 L'Enfant Plaza SW 202-314-6000
Washington, DC 20594 www.ntsb.gov
Made up of four divisions, this office investigates accidents involving railroads, pipelines, and the transportation of hazardous materials and informs the NTSB of their findings so that the NTSB can make safety recommendations tofederal and state regulatory industries, and a variety of other organizations and individuals.
Robert Hall, Director
Sandy Rowlett, Deputy Director

2521 NTSB Office of Research and Engineering
National Transportation Safety Board
490 L'Enfant Plaza SW 202-314-6000
Washington, DC 20594 www.ntsb.gov
This office provides support to accident investigations and conducts safety studies for all modes of transportation. There are four divisions that make up this office: the Safety Research Division, the Vehicle Performance Division, theVehicle Recorder Division, and the Materials Laboratory Division.
Barbara Czech, Deputy Director
Jim Ritter, Director

2522 NTSB Office of the Chief Information Officer
National Transportation Safety Board
490 L'Enfant Plaza SW 202-314-6000
Washington, DC 20594 www.ntsb.gov
This office develops programs and products for use by the National Transportation Safety Board and the public, and provides support for the Board's information systems. It is composed of the Computer Services Division, the SystemsSupport Division, the Records Management Division, the Enterprise Architecture Division, and the Information Technology Security Program.
Angel Santa, Chief Information Officer
Wanda Briggs, Deputy CIO

2523 National Advisory Environmental Health Sciences Council
P.O. Box 12233 919-541-3201
Mail Drop B2-01 *Fax:* 919-541-5136
Durham, NC 27709 birnbaumls@niehs.nih.gov
www.niehs.nih.gov
This council oversees matters relating to research, research support, training, and career development supported by the NIEHS. It advises the secretary of HHS, the director of NIH, and the director of the NIEHS on its findings.
21 members
3x year
Linda S. Birnbaum, Chair
Gwen W. Collman, Executive Secretary

2524 National Aeronautics and Space Administration
NASA Headquarters
300 E Street SW 202-358-0001
Suite 5R30 *Fax:* 202-358-4338
Washington, DC 20546 public-inquiries@hq.nasa.gov
www.nasa.gov
NASA conducts scientific research and innovations on topics such as aeronautics, human exploration, science, and space discovery. The vision of this organization is to expand knowledge for the benefit of humanity.

Jim Bridenstine, Administrator
Jim Morhard, Deputy Administrator

2525 National Association of State Foresters
444 N Capitol Street NW 202-624-5415
Suite 540 *Fax:* 202-624-5407
Washington, DC 20001 info@stateforesters.org
www.stateforesters.org/
The National Association of State Foresters provides management assistance and protection services for more than two thirds of America's forests. It is a non-profit organization comprised of forestry agency directors.

Jay Farrell, Executive Director
Robyn Whitney, Policy Director

2526 National Atmospheric Deposition Program (NADP)
Wisonsin State Laboratory of Hygiene
465 Henry Mall 608-263-9162
Madison, WI 53706 nadp.slh.wisc.edu
This program involves the cooperation of federal, state, tribal and local governmental agencies; educational institutions; private companies; and non-governmental agencies to measure atmospheric deposition and study its effects on theenvironment

Michael Olson, Program Coordinator

2527 National Cancer Institute: Divison of Cancer Epidemiology & Genetics
9609 Medical Center Drive 240-276-7150
MSC 9776 ncicontactdceg@mail.nih.gov
Bethesda, MD 20892 www.dceg.cancer.gov/about
The DCEG is a division of the National Cancer Institute that conducts research on cancer epdiemiology and genetics. The mission of this division is to uncover the causes of cancer and the means of its prevention.
Stephen J. Chanock, Director
Montserrat Garcia-Closes, Deptuy Director

2528 National Center for Health Statistics
Centers for Disease Control and Prevention
1600 Clifton Road 800-232-4636
Atlanta, GA 30329-4027 www.cdc.gov/nchs/
NCHS aims to provide statistical information in order to enhance the health of the population, and guide actions and policies related to public health.
Jennifer H. Madans, Acting Director
Amy Branum, Acting Associate Director

2529 National Centers for Environmental Information
151 Patton Avenue 828-271-4800
Asheville, NC 28801-5001 *Fax:* 828-271-4876
ncei.info@noaa.gov
www.ncei.noaa.gov/
Provides access to one of the most signifact archives of oceanic, atmospheric, and geophysical data, and also provides products and services to businesses, the government, and the general public.

Thomas R. Karl, Director

2530 National Council on Radiation Protection and Measurements (NCRP)
7910 Woodmont Avenue 301-657-2652
Suite 400 *Fax:* 301-907-8768
Bethesda, MD 20814-3095 ncrp@ncrponline.org
ncrponline.org
The Council seeks to formulate and widely disseminate information, guidance and recommendations on radiation protection and measurements which represent the consensus of leading scientific thinking.

Laura J. Atwell, Director, Operations
John D. Boice, Jr., Director, Science

2531 National Drinking Water Advisory Council
EPA Office of Ground and Drinking Water
1200 Pennsylvania Avenue NW 202-564-3750
Mail Code 4601M www.epa.gov/ndwac
Washington, DC 20460
This council was established under the Safe Drinking Water Act of 1974 and provides EPA with advice and recommendations related to the national drinking water program.

William Alley, Director, Science
Carrie M. Lewis, Chairperson Superintendant

2532 National Environmental Education Advisory Council
Office of Environmental Education
1200 Pennsylvania Avenue NW 202-564-2642
Mail Code 1704A education@epa.gov
Washington, DC 20460 www.epa.gov/education
Comprised of representatives from organizations other than the federal goverment, NEEAC provides the EPA with advice on environmental education and an understanding of the needs of schools, universities, state departments, andeducational organizations.
Javier Araujo, Designated Federal Officer

2533 National Environmental Justice Advisory Council
EPA Office of Environmental Justice
1200 Pennsylvania Avenue NW 202-564-2515
Mail Code 2201A 800-962-6215
Washington, DC 20460 environmental-justice@epa.gov
www.epa.gov/environmentaljustice
A federal advisory committee established to provide independent advice, consultation, and recommendations to the Administrator of the U.S. Environmental Protection Agency on matters related to environmental justice.

Richard Moore, Chair
Sylvia Orduno, Vice Chair

2534 **National Environmental Satellite, Data, and Information Service**
1335 East West Highway 301-713-3578
SSMC1, 8th Floor *Fax:* 301-713-1249
Silver Spring, MD 20910 John.Leslie@noaa.gov
www.nesdis.noaa.gov
The National Environmental Satellite, Data, and Information Service operates a national environmental satellite system. It acquires, stores and disseminates worldwide environmental data through its data centers.
Stephen Volz, Assistant Administrator
Mark S. Paese, Deputy Assistant Admin.

2535 **National Health Information Center (NHIC)**
U.S. Department of Health and Human Services
1101 Wootton Parkway *Fax:* 240-453-8281
Suit LL100 odphpinfo@hhs.gov
Rockville, MD 20852 www.health.gov/nhic
A health information referral line, NHIC links consumers and health professionals who have health questions to organizations best able to provide reliable health information. The main types of information provided by the Center areNational Health Observances, Federal Health Information Centers and Clearinghouses, and Toll-Free Numbers for Health Information.
Don Wright, Director

2536 **National Institute for Occupational Safety and Health (NIOSH)**
Patriots Plaza 1
395 E Street SW 800-232-4636
Suite 9200 *Fax:* 513-533-8347
Washington, DC 20201 www.cdc.gov/niosh
Ensures that safe and healthy working conditions for all working people are met, develops occupational safety and health standards, and conducts research to reduce worker illness and injury.
John Howard, Director
Frank Hearl, Chief of Staff

2537 **National Institute of Environmental Health Sciences**
NIEHS Central Receiving
105 T.W. Alexander Drive 919-541-3345
Building 110 *Fax:* 301-480-2978
Research Triangle Park, NC 27709 webcenter@niehs.nih.gov
www.niehs.nih.gov
NIEHS' mission is to research how the environment affects people in order to promote healthier lives, and to provide global leadership for research that improves public health. NIEHS accomplishes this mission by translating theirfindings into comprehensible information that can inform real-life individual and public health outcomes.

Linda S. Birnbaum, Director
Richard Woychik, Deputy Director

2538 **National Institute of Standards andTechnology (NIST)**
100 Bureau Drive 301-975-2000
Gaithersburg, MD 20899 inquiries@nist.gov
www.nist.gov
The NIST assists industries in the development of technology needed to improve product quality, modernize manufacturing processes, ensure product reliability, and facilitate rapid commercialization of products based on new scientificdiscoveries. NIST's primary mission is to promote U.S. economic growth by working with industries to develop and apply technology, measurements, and standards.

Walter G. Copan, Director
Kevin Kimball, Chief of Staff

2539 **National Institutes of Health**
9000 Rockville Pike 301-496-4000
Bethesda, MD 20892 NIHinfo@od.nih.gov
www.nih.gov
The National Institutes of Health conducts, supports and promotes biomedical research to improve the health of the American people by increasing the understanding of processes underlying human health, disability, and disease. Theinstitutes advance knowledge concerning the health effects of interactions between humans and the environment.
Francis S. Collins, Director
Lawrence A. Tabak, Principal Deputy Director

2540 **National Lead Information Center**
422 South Clifton Avenue 800-424-5323
Rochester, NY 14620 *Fax:* 585-232-3111
www.epa.gov/lead/pubs/nlic.htm
The National Lead Information Center (NLIC) provides information to the public and to professionals regarding lead hazards and their prevention. A branch of the EPA, NLIC receives funding from the Department of Housing and UrbanDevelopment.
Amanda Brylski, Contact, Region 1
Vickie Pane, Contact, Region 2

2541 **National Oceanic and Atmospheric Administration Research**
National Oceanic and Atmospheric Administration
1315 East West Highway 301-713-2458
Silver Spring, MD 20910 www.oar.noaa.gov
The Office of Oceanic and Atmospheric Research provides the research that results in better weather forecasts, longer warning lead times for natural disasters, new products from the sea, and greater understanding of our climate,atmosphere, and oceans.
Craig McLean, Assistant Administrator
Ko Barrett, Deputy Asst. Administrator

2542 **National Petroleum Council**
1625 K Street NW 202-393-6100
Suite 600 *Fax:* 202-331-8539
Washington, DC 20006 info@npc.org
www.npc.org
The purpose of the NPC is to represent the views of the oil and natural gas industries in advising, informing, and making recommendations to the Secretary of Energy with respect to any matter relating to oil and natural gas, or to theoil and gas industries submitted to it or approved by the Secretary. The NPC does not concern itself with trade practices, nor does it engage in any of the usual trade association activities.
2x year
Nicholas K. Akins, Chair
Robert Neal Anderson, President

2543 **National Science Foundation**
2415 Eisenhower Ave 703-292-5111
Alexandria, VA 22314 800-381-1532
info@nsf.gov
www.nsf.gov
It is the National Science Foundation's mission to promote the progress of science, and to advance national health, prosperity, and welfare. The foundation aims to enhance national security and to educate in order to sustain globalleadership.

F Fleming Crim, Chief Operating Officer
France A Cordova, Director

2544 **National Science Foundation Office of Polar Programs**
National Science Foundation
2415 Eisenhower Ave 703-292-8030
Alexandria, VA 22314 *Fax:* 703-292-9081
info@nsf.gov
www.nsf.gov/div/index.jsp?div=OPP
OPP promotes scientific research, engineering, and education in and about the polar regions. The program leads discoveries and understanding of polar systems and their global interactions to inform the nation and advance the welfare ofall people, and shares in the vision and goals expressed in NSF's strategic plan.
Pawnee C Maiden, Administrative Officer
Kelly K Falkner, Office Director

2545 **National Science and Technology Council (NSTC)**
Office of Science and Technology Policy
1650 Pennsylvania Avenue 202-456-4444
Washington, DC 20504 nstc@ostp.eop.gov

Established by Executive Order in 1993, this Cabinet-level Council aims to establish clear national goals for Federal science and technology investments, and to coordinate policies across the many entities that make up the Federalresearch and development enterprise.

Donald J. Trump, Chair, President of the US

2546 **National Transportation Safety Board (NTSB)**
National Transportation Safety Board
490 L'Enfant Plaza SW 202-314-6000
Washington, DC 20594 www.ntsb.gov
The mission of the NTSB is to make transportation safer through accident investigations, safety improvement advocacy, and reviewing pilots' and mariners' certification appeals. NTSB is an independent Federal agency that investigatesall civil aviation accidents, as well as significant railroad, highway, marine, and pipeline accidents.

Robert L. Sumwalt, Chair
Edward Benthall, Chief Financial Officer

2547 **National Urban and Community Forestry Advisory Council**
USDA Forest Service
1400 Independence Avenue SW 800-832-1355
Washington, DC 20250-1111 nucfac@fs.fed.us
www.fs.fed.us/managing-land/urban-forests/ucf
This council is a Congressionally designated advisory council that focuses on urban forestry and related issues to the Secretary of Agriculture. They were created by the 1990 Farm Bill to bring together various voices concerned aboutthe present and future health of America's urban forests.
2 or 3x year
Lance Davisson, Chair

2548 **Natural Resources Conservation Service**
1400 Independence Avenue SW 202-720-7246
Room 5105-A *Fax:* 202-720-7690
Washington, DC 20250 www.nrcs.usda.gov
Provides leadership to help people conserve, maintain, and improve America's natural resources and environment. NRCS is the technical delivery arm of USDA and provides conservation information, incentive programs and technicalassistance at the state and county levels. Their goals include boosting rural economies, increasing competitiveness of American agriculture, and improving the quality of air, soil, and habitat.

Matthew Lohr, Chief
Kevin Norton, Acting Associate Chief

2549 **Naval Sea Systems Command**
1333 Isaac Hull Avenue SE 202-781-0000
Washington Navy Yard, DC 20376 800-356-8464
Fax: 202-781-4495
www.navsea.navy.mil
The mission of NAVSEA is to design, build, deliver, and maintain ships for the U.S. Navy. The team of staff, directorates, and Program Executive Offices engineer, build, buy, and maintain ships and other combat systems the meet thenation's defense requirements.
Thomas Moore, Commander
Jim Smerchansky, Executive Director

2550 **Navy and Marine Corps Public Health Center**
620 John Paul Jones Circle 757-953-0700
Suite 1100 www.med.navy.mil/sites/nmcphc/Pages/Home.aspx
Portsmouth, VA 23708-2103
The Navy and Marine Corps Public Health Center provides resources of public health services to the Navy and Marine Corps. Through leadership and expertise, they strive to prevent disease and promote health in order to ensure missionreadiness.

Todd L. Wagner, Commander
Robert Hawkins, Deputy Commander

2551 **New Forests Project**
1001 North Carolina Avenue SE 202-285-4328
Washington, DC 20003 info-newforests@theintlcenter.org
www.newforestsproject.org/
The New Forests Project strives to protect, conserve, and enhance the health of the Earth's ecosystems along with the people depending on them, by supporting integrated grassroots efforts in agroforestry, reforestation, protection ofwatersheds, water and sanitation, and renewable energy initiatives.

Catalina Serna-Valencia, Executive Director
Lysette House, Program Officer

2552 **Occupational Safety and Health Administration: U.S. Department of Labor**
Occupational Safety and Health Administration
200 Constitution Avenue NW 800-321-6742
Room N3626 www.osha.gov
Washington, DC 20210
OSHA's mission is to send all workers home healthy every day by enforcing safe working conditions and providing training, education, outreach, and assistance.

Loren Sweat, Assistant Secretary
Krisann Pearce, Chief of Staff

2553 **Office Of Air and Radiation (OAR)**
Environmental Protection Agency
1200 Pennsylvania Avenue NW 202-564-7400
Mail Code 6101A www.epa.gov
Washington, DC 20460
The Office of Air and Radiation (OAR) is in charge of developing national programs, policies, and regulations to control air pollution and radiation exposure. Among their concerns are pollution prevention and energy efficiency,industrial air pollution, climate change, and acid rain.

Bill Wehrum, Assistant Administrator
Anne Idsal, Principal Deputy

2554 **Office of Chemical Safety and Pollution Prevention (OCSPP)**
U.S. Environmental Protection Agency
1200 Pennsylvania Avenue NW 202-564-2910
Mail Code 7101M www.epa.gov
Washington, DC 20460
OCSPP aims to protect Americans, their families, and the environment from risks related to pesticides and toxic chemicals. The goal of the Office is to reduce waste, save energy, and ensure safer schools, homes, and workplaces.
Alexandra Dapolito Dunn, Assistant Administrator
Nancy B. Beck, Principal Deputy

2555 **Office of Nuclear Material Safety and Safeguards**
U.S. Nuclear Regulatory Commission 301-415-7000
Washington, DC 20555-0001 800-368-5642
www.nrc.gov
The Office of Nuclear Materials Safety and Safeguards at the NRC is responsible for regulating activities to ensure safety and quality associated with the possession, processing, and handling of nuclear material. To ensure safety andsecurity, the Office implements a regulatory program which includes licensing, inspection, and events analysis
John W. Lubinski, Director
Scott W. Moore, Deputy Director

2556 **Office of Response and Restoration-NOAA**
National Oceanic and Atmospheric Administration
1305 East-West Highway 240-533-0391
Silver Spring, MD 20910 orr.webmaster@noaa.gov
response.restoration.noaa.gov
Protects coastal and marine resources, mitigates threats, reduces harm, restores ecological function and provides comprehensive solutions to environmental hazards caused by oil, chemicals and marine debris.

Dave Westerholm, Director

2557 Office of Risk Assessment and Cost-Benefit Analysis (ORACBA)

Office of the Chief Economist
Whitten Federal Building 202-720-8022
Room 4032, South Building *Fax:* 202-720-1815
Washington, DC 20024 msewadeh@oce.usda.gov
www.usda.gov/oce/risk_assessment

ORACBA's primary role is to ensure that major regulations proposed by USDA are based on sound scientific and economic analysis.

Linda C. Abbott, Director
Mark R. Powell, Risk Scientist

2558 Office of Science and Technology Policy

Eisenhower Executive Office Bldg 202-456-4444
1650 Pennsylvania Avenue www.whitehouse.gov/administration/eop/ostp
Washington, DC 20504

The Office of Science and Technology Policy serves as a source of scientific, engineering, and technological analysis and judgement for the President with respect to major policies, plans, and programs of the federal government. Incarrying out this mission, the office advises the President of scientific and technological considerations involved in areas of national concern, including the economy, national security, health, foreign relations, and the environment.

2559 Office of Surface Mining Reclamation and Enforcement

1849 C Street NW 202-208-2565
Washington, DC 20240 getinfo@osmre.gov
www.osmre.gov

Their mission is to carry out the requirments of the Surface Mining Control and Reclamation Act in cooperation with States and Tribes. Their primary objectives are to ensure that coal mines are operated in a manner that protectscitizens and the environment during mining and assures that the land is restored to beneficial use following mining, and to mitigate the effects of past mining by aggressively pursuing reclamation of abandoned coal mines.

Glenda Owens, Acting Director
Loraine Dawkins, Assistant to the Director

2560 Office of the Chief Economist

Whitten Federal Building 202-720-4164
Room 112A www.usda.gov/oce
Washington, DC 20024

The Office of the Chief Economist advises the Secretary on the economic implications of policies and programs affecting the US food and fiber systems and rural areas. The Chief Economist coordinates, reviews, and approves theDepartment's commodity and farm sector forecast.

Robert Johansson, Chief Economist
Warren Preston, Deputy Chief Economist

2561 Office of the General Counsel

Herbert C. Hoover Building
14th & Constitution Avenue NW 202-482-4772
Washington, DC 20230 GeneralCounsel@doc.gov
ogc.commerce.gov/

The Office of the General Counsel provides legal services for all programs, operations, and activities of the Department of Commerce, and is the chief legal officer for the Department. The Office's mission is to revitalize the economyand work towards sustainable U.S. leadership in a global economy.

Peter B. Davidson, General Counsel
Michelle O. McClelland, Assistant General Counsel

2562 Office of the Secretary of Energy

1000 Independence Avenue SW 202-586-5000
Washington, DC 20585 *Fax:* 202-586-4403
The.Secretary@hq.doe.gov
www.energy.gov

The Secretary of Energy provides the framework for a comprehensive and balanced national energy plan through the coordination and administration of the energy functions of the federal government. The Secretary is also responsible forensuring a safe and secure nuclear deterrent, carrying out envirnmental cleanup from the Cold War nuclear mission, and managing 17 National Laboratories.

Rick Perry, Secretary

2563 Office of the Secretary of Health and Human Services

Hubert H Humphrey Building
200 Independence Avenue SW 877-696-6775
Washington, DC 20201 www.hhs.gov

The Secretary of Health and Human Services advises the President on health, welfare, and income security plans, policies, and programs of the federal government.

Alex M. Azar, Secretary
Eric D. Hargan, Deputy Secretary

2564 Office of the U.S. Trade Representative

600 17th Street NW 202-395-2870
Washington, DC 20508 *Fax:* 202-395-4656
www.ustr.gov

The Office of the U.S. Trade Representative is responsible for the coordination and development of U.S. international trade, commodity, and direct investment policy. The head of the Office, the U.S. Trade Representative, is a Cabinetmember who advises the president on trade issues and negotiations.

Robert E. Lighthizer, U.S. Trade Representative
Jeff Gerrish, Deputy Trade Representative

2565 Peace Corps

Paul D. Coverdell Peace Corps
1111 20th Street NW 855-855-1961
Washington, DC 20526 www.peacecorps.gov

The goal of the Peace Corps is to help people of interested countries in meeting their need for trained men and women. They advocate for world peace and friendship by promoting a better understanding between Americans and other peoplesaround the world.

Josephine K. Olsen, Director
Michelle K. Brooks, Chief of Staff

2566 Pesticide Program Dialogue Committee (PPDC)

EPA: Office of Pesticide Programs
1200 Pennsylvania Avenue NW
Mail Code 7506C 703-347-0109
Washington, DC 20460 pesticidequestions@epa.gov
www.epa.gov/environmental-topics/chemicals-and-toxics-topics

This committee provides feedback to the EPA on various pesticide regulatory, policy, and program implementation issues. The committee consists of a diverse range of stakeholders and meets with the EPA on a regular basis.

2x year
Richard P. Keigwin, Jr., Director
Shannon Jewell, Designated Federal Officer

2567 Regional Haze Program

US EPA
109 TW Alexander Drive 202-564-4700
Research Triangle Park, NC 27709 www.epa.gov/visibility

This program enforces the Regional Haze Rule, which calls for state and federal agencies to work to improve visibility in 156 national parks and wilderness areas by developing and implementing air quality protection plans that helpreduce the lack of visibility caused by pollution.

Richard A. Wayland, Director, Air Quality

2568 Rural Utilities Service

USDA Rural Development
1400 Independence Avenue SW 202-720-9540
Room 5135 www.rd.usda.gov
Washington, DC 20250-3201

RUS administers programs that provide infrastructure to rural communities, including water and waste treatment, electric power, and telecommunications services. The goal of RUS is to expand economic opportunities and improve quality oflife for rural residents.

Chad Rupe, Acting Administrator
Curtis Anderson, Chief of Staff

2569 Saint Lawrence Seaway Development Corporation
US Department of Transportation
1200 New Jersey Avenue SE 202-366-0091
Suite W32-300 800-785-2779
Washington, DC 20590 *Fax:* 202-366-7147
slsdc@dot.gov
www.seaway.dot.gov

Saint Lawrence Seaway Development Corporation operates and maintains the Great Lakes/St. Lawrence System, which encompasses the St. Lawrence River and the five Great lakes. The mission of the Corporation is to improve and maintain thewaterways of this area to ensure safe, reliable, efficient, and environmentally responsible operations.

Wayne A. Williams, Chief of Staff
Craig H. Middlebrook, Deputy Administrator

2570 Science Advisory Board Environmental Protection Agency
Environmental Protection Agency
1200 Pennsylvania Avenue NW 202-564-2221
Mail Code 1400R *Fax:* 202-565-2098
Washington, DC 20460-4164 sab@epa.gov
www.epa.gov/sab

The SAB was established by Congress to provide independent scientific and engineering advice to the EPA Administrator on the technical basis for EPA regulations. SAB reviews and gives advice on scientific issues and EPA programs, andperforms special assignments as requested by Agency officials.

Thomas Armitage, Designated Federal Officer

2571 Senate Committee on Appropriations
Committee on Appropriations
The Capitol 202-224-7257
Room S-128 www.appropriations.senate.gov
Washington, DC 20510
The largest committee in the U.S. Senate, the Senate Committee on Appropriations writes the legislation that allocates federal funds to numerous goverment agencies, departments, and organizations. 12 subcomittees are tasked withcreating legislation to allocate funds to government agencies within their juristictions, hearing testimonies from goverment officials, and drafting spending plans for the fiscal year.
31 members
Richard Shelby, Chair
Patrick Leahy, Vice Chair

2572 Senate Committee on Foreign Relations
423 Dirksen Senate Office Building 202-224-4651
Washington, DC 20510-6225 Web_Inquiry@foreign.senate.gov
www.foreign.senate.gov
Established as one of the original ten standing committees, the theSenate Foreign Relations Committee develops and influences U.S. foreign policy, debates and reports treaties and legislation, holds jurisdiction over all diplomaticnominations, and assists in the negotiation of treaties.

James E. Risch, Chair
Bob Menendez, Ranking Member

2573 Smithsonian Tropical Research Institute
Smithsonian Institution Research Department
1100 Jefferson Drive 202-633-4014
Suite 3123 507-212-8000
Washington, DC 20013-7012 *Fax:* 202-786-2557
Fax: 507-212-8148
stri.si.edu
The STRI is a bureau of the Smithsonian Insititution based outside the US in Panama, and is dedicated to understanding biological diversity.

Matthew C. Larsen, Director
William Wcislo, Deputy Director

2574 The Aspen Institute
2300 N St NW 202-736-5800
Suite 700 *Fax:* 202-467-0790
Washington, DC 20037 www.aspeninstitute.org
An education and policy studies organization that seeks to foster intellectual inquiry, create diverse leadership, and provides a nonpartisan forum for solutions on vital public policy issues in a number of areas, including engergy andthe environment.

Dan Porterfield, President and CEO
Amy DeMaria, Executive Vice President

2575 U.S. Agency for International Development
Ronald Reagan Building 202-712-0000
Washington, DC 20523-1000 www.usaid.gov
Aids in the development of urban environmental programs, works toward ending extreme poverty, and promotes the development of democratic societies. Supports American prosperity through investments that expand markets for U.S. exports.

Mark Green, Administrator
Bonnie Glick, Deputy Administrator

2576 U.S. Army Corps of Engineers
441 G Street NW 202-761-0011
Washington, DC 20314-1000 www.usace.army.mil
The U.S. Army Corps of Engineers manages and executes civil works programs, including research and development, planning, design, construction, operation and maintenance, and real estate activities related to rivers, harbors andwaterways; it further administers laws for protection and preservation of navigable waters and related resources such as wetlands, and assists in recovery from natural disasters.

Todd T Semonite, Chief of Engineers
Michael Wehr, Deputy Chief of Engineers

2577 U.S. Consumer Product Safety Commission
4330 East West Highway 301-504-7978
Bethesda, MD 20814 800-638-2772
Fax: 301-504-0124
www.cpsc.gov
The U.S. Consumer Product Safety Commission (CPSC) is an independent federal regulatory agency that aims to protect the public against unreasonable risks of injuries and deaths associated with consumer products. CPSC protects consumersfrom products that pose a fire, electrical, chemical, or mechanical hazard.

Ann Marie Buerkle, Chair
Robert S. Adler, Commissioner

2578 U.S. Customs and Border Protection
1300 Pennsylvania Avenue NW 202-325-0150
Washington, DC 20229 202-325-8000
877-227-5511
www.cbp.gov
The mission of CBP is to safeguard the American homeland at and beyond its borders, while enhancing the Nation's global economic competitiveness by enabling legitimate trade and travel.

John P. Sanders, Acting Commissioner
Robert E. Perez, Deputy Commissioner

2579 U.S. Department Of Justice: Consumer Protection Branch
U.S Department of Justice
950 Pennsylvania Avenue NW 202-307-0066
Washington, DC 20530-0001 Civil.Feedback@usdoj.gov
www.justice.gov/civil/consumer-protection-branch
The Consumer Protection Branch is part of the Civil Division of the U.S. Department of Justice. This branch oversees the enforcement of legislation aimed to protect the health, safety, economic security, and identity integrity ofAmericans.
Gustav W Eyler, Branch Director
Jill P Furman, Deputy Branch Director

2580 U.S. Department of Agriculture
1400 Independence Avenue SW 202-720-2791
Washington, DC 20250 feedback@oc.usda.gov
www.usda.gov
The mission of the USDA is to enhance the quality of life for the American people by supporting production of agriculture, ensuring a safe, affordable, nutritious, and accessible food supply. The Department promotes agriculturalproduction that benefits Americans and others worldwide, and is interested in cnoservation of natural resources.
Sonny Perdue, Secretary

2581 U.S. Department of Education
400 Maryland Avenue SW 800-872-5327
Washington, DC 20202 www.ed.gov
The mission of ED is to strengthen the federal commitment to assuring access to equal educational opportunity for every individual; improve the coordination of federal education programs; establish policies on federal financial aid foreducation; and collect data on America's schools.
Betsy DeVos, Secretary

2582 U.S. Department of Housing and Urban Development
451 7th Street SW 202-708-1112
Washington, DC 20410 portal.hud.gov/hudportal/HUD
HUD's mission is to create strong, sustainable, inclusive communities and quality affordable homes for all, and is working towards strengthening the housing market to bolster the economy and protect consumers.
Ben Carson, Secretary
Brian Montgomery, Deputy Secretary

2583 U.S. Department of Housing and Urban Development Office of Lead Hazard Control & Healthy Homes
Office of Lead Hazard Control
451 7th Street SW 202-708-1112
Washington, DC 20410 www.hud.gov/program_offices/healthy_homes
The office provides funds to state and local governments to develop cost-effective ways to reduce lead-based hazards, enforces lead-based paint regulations, provides public outreach, and conducts studies to aid children and familiesfrom health/safety hazards in the home.
Martin Nee, Contact, Region 1
Sue Horowitz, Contact, Region 2

2584 U.S. Department of Justice: Environment and Natural Resources Division
U.S. Department of Justice
950 Pennsylvania Avenue NW 202-514-2701
Washington, DC 20530-0001 webcontentmgr.enrd@usdoj.gov
www.justice.gov/enrd
The ENRD oversees environmental and natural resources litigation. It is responsible for prosecuting violations of civil and criminal pollution control laws, defending environmental challenges to government programs, and representingthe US in the stewardship of the nation's natural resources and public lands.
Jeffrey Bossert Clark, Assistant Attorney General
Corinne V Snow, Chief of Staff

2585 U.S. Department of Justice: Environmental Crimes Section
U.S. Department of Justice
950 Pennsylvania Avenue NW 202-514-2701
Washington, DC 20530-0001 webcontentmgr.enrd@usdoj.gov
www.justice.gov/enrd/environmental-crimes-section
The Environmental Crimes Section of the Environment and Natural Resources Division consists of prosecutors and support staff who bring criminal cases against individuals and organizations that break environmental laws. The section'swork is affiliated with U.S. Attorney's Offices.
Jeffrey Bossert Clark, Assistant Attorney General
Corinne V Snow, Chief of Staff

2586 U.S. Department of Labor
200 Constitution Avenue NW 202-693-6000
Washington, DC 20210 866-487-2365
webmaster@dol.gov
www.dol.gov
The mission of the U.S. Department of Labour is to develop the welfare of wage earners, job seekers, and retirees of the nation. The Department also seeks to improve working conditions, advance opportunities for profitable employment,and assure work-related benefits and rights.
Alexander Acosta, Secretary
Molly E. Conway, Chief of Staff

2587 U.S. Department of Treasury
1500 Pennsylvania Avenue NW 202-622-2000
Washington, DC 20220 *Fax:* 202-622-6415
www.treasury.gov
The mission of the Department of Treasury is to maintain a strong economy and create economic and job opportunities by promoting economic growth and stability at home and abroad. They also seek to strengthen national security bycombating threats and protecting the integrity of the financial system, and manage the U.S. Government's finances and resources effectively.
Steven Mnuchin, Secretary
Justin Muzinich, Deputy Secretary

2588 U.S. Department of the Army: Office of Public Affairs
ATTN: Chief of Public Affairs
1500 Army Pentagon 703-220-9044
Washington, DC 20310-1500 *Fax:* 703-697-2159
www.army.mil
The mission of the Office of Public Affairs is to fulfill the Army's obligation to keep the American people and the Army informed. The Office helps to establish a strong American Army, including its readiness to conduct operations inpeacetime, conflict, and war.
Amy E. Hannah, Chief of Public Affairs
Michael P. Brady, Principal Deputy Chief

2589 U.S. Forest Service: Forest Legacy Program
1400 Independence Avenue SW 202-205-1618
Code 1123 800-832-1355
Washington, DC 20250 www.fs.fed.us/spf/coop/programs/loa/flp.shtml
The Forest Legacy Program is a federal program that supports state efforts to protect environmentally sensitive forest lands by encouraging the protection of privately owned forest lands, supporting property aquisition, and helpingstates carry out conservation plans.
Scott Stewart, Program Manager
Laurie Schoonhoven, Acting Assistant Director

2590 U.S. Geological Survey: Water Resources Mission Area
12201 Sunrise Valley Drive 703-648-4557
Reston, VA 20192 888-275-8747
water.usgs.gov/about_WRD.html
The goal of the USGS is to provide reliable scientific information for the better understanding of Earth. Within the USGS, the Water Resources Mission Area strives to monitor, assess, and deliver information regarding water use andavailability.
Donald Cline, Associate Director
William Guertal, Deputy Associate Director

2591 U.S. Geological Survey: Wetlands and Aquatic Research Center
700 Cajundome Boulevard 337-266-8500
Lafayette, LA 70506-3152 *Fax:* 337-266-8513
nwrcinfo@usgs.gov
www.nwrc.usgs.gov
The research center's mission is to develop and disseminate scientific information needed for understanding the ecology and values of the nation's wetlands and other aquatic and coastal eco-

systems, and to manage and restore wetland,coastal, and aquatic habitats and associated plant and animal communtities.

Thomas Doyle, Deputy Director
Kenneth Rice, Center Director

2592 U.S. Nuclear Regulatory Commission
US Nuclear Regulatory Commission 301-415-7000
Washington, DC 20555-0001 800-368-5642
oca_web@nrc.gov
www.nrc.gov

The Nuclear Regulatory Commission focuses on reactor safety oversight and liscense renewal of existing plants, materials safety oversight and liscencing, as well as high and low-level waste management.

Jeff Baran, Commissioner
Kristine L Svinicki, Chair

2593 U.S. Senate Committee on Small Business and Entrepreneurship
428A Russell Senate Office Building 202-224-5175
Washington, DC 20510 *Fax:* 202-224-5619
sbc.senate.gov

Composed of 10 Republican and 9 Democrat members, the Committee on Small Business Entrepreneurship refers to all proposed legislation, messages, petitions, memorials, and other matters relating to the Small Business Administration(SBA). They also investigate all problems of small business enterprises.
19 members
Marco Rubio, Chair
Ben Cardin, Ranking Member

2594 Urban and Community Forestry Program
USDA Forest Service
1400 Intependence Avenue SW
Washington, DC 20250-1111 800-832-1355
www.fs.fed.us/managing-land/urban-forests/ucf

The Urban and Community Forestry Program (UCF) is a cooperative program that focuses on the stewardship of urban natural resources by providing technical, financial, research, and educational services to local government, nonprofit organizations, community groups, educational institutions, and tribal governments.
Vicki Christiansen, Deputy Chief
Jan Davis, Assisstant Director

Alabama

2595 Agriculture and Industries Department
Pesticide Laboratory
1445 Federal Drive 334-240-7171
Montgomery, AL 36107 800-642-7761
www.agi.stste.al.us/

Mission: To provide timely, fair and expert regulatory control over product, business entities, movement, and application of goods and services for which applicable state and federal law exists and strive to protect and provide serviceto Alabama consumers.
John McMillan, Commissioner
Brett Hall, Deputy Commissioner

2596 Alabama Cooperative Extension System
224 Duncan Hall Annex 334-844-5270
Auburn University, AL 36849 *Fax:* 334-844-5276
webmaster@aces.edu
www.aces.edu

Operates as the primary outreach organization for the land-grant function of Alabama A&M University and Auburn University. Identifies statewide educational needs, audiences, and optimal educational programs that are delivered through anetwork of public and private partners supported by county, state, and federal governments.
Paul Waddy, Extension Coordinator

2597 Alabama Department of Environmental Management
1400 Coliseum Boulevard 334-271-7700
PO Box 301463 *Fax:* 334-271-7950
Montgomery, AL 36110-2400 webmaster@adem.state.al.us
www.adem.state.al.us

Alabama Department of Environmental Management is the state agency responsible for the adoption and fair enforcement of rules and regulations set to protect and improve the quality of Alabama's environment and the health of all itscitizens. Monitor environmental conditions in Alabama and recommend changes in state law or revise regulations as needed to respond appropriately to changing environmental conditions.

Lance LeFleur, Director
Marilyn G. Elliott, Deputy Director

2598 Alabama Forestry Commission
513 Madison Avenue 334-240-9300
Montgomery, AL 36104 *Fax:* 334-240-9390
www.forestry.state.al.us

Mission: To serve Alabama by protecting and sustaining our forest resources using professionally applied stewardship principles and education. We will ensure Alabama's forests contribute to abundant timber and wildlife, clean air andwater, and a healthy economy.
Tommy Thompson, Chair
Jerry Dwyer, Vice Chairman

2599 Conservation and Natural Resources Department
64 North Union Street 334-242-3486
Suite 468 *Fax:* 334-242-0999
Montgomery, AL 36130 www.outdooralabama.com
N.Gunter Guy Jr., Commissioner
Curtis Jones, Deputy Commissioner

2600 Environmental Protection Agency: National Air and Radiation Environmental Laboratory
540 S Morris Avenue 334-270-3400
Montgomery, AL 36115-2600 www.epa.gov/

The National Air and Radiation Environmental Laboratory is a comprehensive environmental laboratory, and provides services to a wide range of clients, including other EPA offices, Federal agencies, and, in somes cases, the privatesector. The mission is the commitment to developing and applying the most advanced methods for measuring environmental radioactivity and evaluating its risk to the public.
John Griggs, Director
Michael S. Clark, Deputy Director

2601 Geological Survey of Alabama, Agency of the State of Alabama
University of Alabama
420 Hackberry Lane 205-349-2852
P.O. Box 869999 *Fax:* 205-349-2861
Tuscaloosa, AL 35486-6999 info@gsa.state.al.us
www.gsa.state.al.us

To survey and investigate the mineral, energy, water, and biological resources of the state, to maintain adequate geological, topographic, hydrologic, and biologic databases, and to prepare maps and reports on the state's naturalresources to encourage the safe and prudent development of Alabama's natural resources while providing for the safety, health and well-being of all Americans.

Dr. Berry H. Tew Jr., State Geologist
Dr. Patrick O'Neil, Deputy Director

Alaska

2602 Alaska Cooperative Fish and Wildlife Research Unit
University of Alaska
209 Irving 1 907-474-7661
PO Box 757020 *Fax:* 907-474-7872
Fairbanks, AK 99775-7020 uaf-iab-akcfwru@alaska.edu
www.akcfwru.uaf.edu

The Alaska Unit is a part of a nationwide program created to foster college-level research and graduate student training in support of science-based management of fish and wildlife, and their habitats. The Unit exists by cooperativeagreement between the AK Department of Fish and Game, University of Alaska Fairbanks, US Geological Survey, Wildlife Management Institute, and US Fish and Wildlife Service. The Unit is staffed by 5 USGS scientists, who are also research faculty.

Kathleen Pearse, Administrative Assistant

2603 **Alaska Department of Fish and Game**
PO Box 115526 907-465-4100
1255 W. 8th Street www.adfg.alaska.gov
Juneau, AK 99811-5526
Aims to manage, protect, maintain and improve the fish, game and aquatic plant resources of Alaska. The primary goals are to ensure that Alaska's renwable fish and wildlife resources and their habitats are conserved and managed on thesustained yield prinicpal, and the use of development of these resources are in the best interest of the economy and well-being of the people of the state.
Cora Campbell, Commissioner
Sunny Haight, Director

2604 **Alaska Department of Public Safety**
5700 E Tudor Road 907-269-5511
Anchorage, AK 99507 www.dps.state.ak.us
Provides functions relative to the protection of life, property and wildlife resources.
Joseph A. Masters, Commissioner
Terry Vrabec, Deputy Commissioner

2605 **Alaska Division of Forestry: Central Office**
550 W 7th Avenue 907-269-8400
Suite 1260 *Fax:* 907-269-8901
Anchorage, AK 99501-3557 forestry.alaska.gov
Mission: To develop, conserve, and enhance Alaska's forests to provide a sustainable supply of forest resources for Alaskans.
Chris Maisch, State Forester/Director
Dean Brown, Deputy State Forester

2606 **Alaska Division of Forestry: Coastal Region Office**
2417 Tongass Ave 907-225-3070
Suite 213 *Fax:* 907-247-3070
Ketchikan, AK 99901 forestry.alaska.gov
Mission: To develop, conserve, and enhance Alaska's forests to provide a sustainable supply of forest resources for Alaskans.
Chris Maisch, State Forester/Director
Mike Curran, Regional Forester

2607 **Alaska Division of Forestry: Delta Area Office**
Mi. 267.5 Richardson Highway 907-895-4225
PO Box 1149 *Fax:* 907-895-2125
Delta Junction, AK 99737 forestry.alaska.gov
Mission: To develop, conserve, and enhance Alaska's forests to provide a sustainable supply of forest resources for Alaskans.
Chris Maisch, State Forester/Director
Dean Brown, Deputy State Forester

2608 **Alaska Division of Forestry: Fairbanks Area Office**
3700 Airport Way 907-451-2600
Fairbanks, AK 99709-4699 *Fax:* 907-458-6895
forestry.alaska.gov
Mission: To develop, conserve, and enhance Alaska's forests to provide a sustainable supply of forest resources for Alaskans.
Chris Maisch, State Forester/Director
Paul Maki, Acting Area Forester

2609 **Alaska Division of Forestry: Kenai/Kodiak Area Office**
42499 Sterling Highway 907-260-4200
Mi. 92.5 Sterling Hwy. *Fax:* 907-260-4205
Soldotna, AK 99669 forestry.alaska.gov
Mission: To develop, conserve, and enhance Alaska's forests to provide a sustainable supply of forest resources for Alaskans.
Chris Maisch, State Forester/Director
Hans Rinke, Area Forester

2610 **Alaska Division of Forestry: Mat-Su/Southwest Area Office**
101 Airport Road 907-761-6300
Palmer, AK 99645 *Fax:* 907-761-6319
forestry.alaska.gov
Mission: To develop, conserve, and enhance Alaska's forests to provide a sustainable supply of forest resources for Alaskans.
Chris Maisch, State Forester/Director
Rick Jandreau, Area Forester

2611 **Alaska Division of Forestry: Northern Region Office**
3700 Airport Way 907-451-2670
Fairbanks, AK 99709-4699 *Fax:* 907-451-2690
forestry.alaska.gov
Mission: To develop, conserve, and enhance Alaska's forests to provide a sustainable supply of forest resources for Alaskans.
Chris Maisch, State Forester/Director
Tim Dabney, Regional Forester

2612 **Alaska Division of Forestry: State Forester's Office**
550 W 7th Avenue 907-451-8463
Suite 1450 *Fax:* 907-451-8931
Anchorage, AK 99501-3566 forestry.alaska.gov
Mission: To develop, conserve, and enhance Alaska's forests to provide a sustainable supply of forest resources for Alaskans.
Chris Maisch, State Forester/Director
Dean Brown, Deputy State Forester

2613 **Alaska Division of Forestry: Tok Area Office**
Mile 123 Glenn Highway 907-883-1400
PO Box 10 *Fax:* 907-883-5135
Tok, AK 99780 forestry.alaska.gov
Mission: To develop, conserve, and enhance Alaska's forests to provide a sustainable supply of forest resources for Alaskans.
Chris Maisch, State Forester/Director
Jeff Hermanns, Area Forester

2614 **Alaska Division of Forestry: Valdez/Copper River Area Office**
Mile 110 Richardson Highway 907-822-5534
Box 185 *Fax:* 907-822-8600
Glennallen, AK 99588 forestry.alaska.gov
Mission: To develop, conserve, and enhance Alaska's forests to provide a sustainable supply of forest resources for Alaskans.
Chris Maisch, State Forester/Director
Gary Mullen, Area Forester

2615 **Alaska Health Project**
3601 C Street 907-276-2864
Suite 902 *Fax:* 907-279-3089
Anchorage, AK 99503-5923 AhelpRequest@Alaska.gov
www.ahelp.org
Provides information to professionals and the general public about occupational safety and health, hazardous materials management and waste reduction at work and in the community
Carl Hild, Executive Director
Valerie Davidson, Commissioner

2616 **Alaska Oil and Gas Conservation Commission**
333 W 7th Avenue 907-279-1433
Suite 100 *Fax:* 907-276-7542
Anchorage, AK 99501 aogcc.customer.svc@alaska.gov
www.doa.alaska.gov/ogc/
Protecting the oil and gas of Alaska.
Dan Seamount, Commissioner
John Norman, Commissioner

2617 **Alaska Resource Advisory Council**
Bureau of Land Management
222 W 7th Avenue 907-271-5555
Suite 13 *Fax:* 907-271-3684
Anchorage, AK 99513 www.blm.gov
A statewide resource advisory council that advises BLM on land management issues for 80 million acres of federal public lands in Alaska. Membership is comprised of representatives from industry, conservation, recreation, Alaska Nativeorganizations, an

elected offical, and the public at large. The council meets three times a year.

Thomas P Lonnie, BLM/AK State Director
Sharon Wilson, Alaska RAC Coordinator

2618 Anchorage Office: Alaska Department of Environmental Conservation
555 Cordova Street 907-269-7553
Anchorage, AK 99501-2617 *Fax:* 907-269-7649
Jennifer.Roberts@alaska.gov
www.dec.state.ak.us
The people and industries that operate in our state have both the corporate conscience and the technical ability to work with us on constuctive solutions to basic environmental management and public health issues. We anticipate,collaborate, negotiate, educate and communicate to address the most important environmental and public health risks to Alaska and Alaskans. Investigation, legislation, regulation and litigation are available tools, but not the first tools of choice.
Larry Hartig, Commissioner

2619 Cooperative Extension Service: University of Alaska Fairbanks
308 Tanana Loop 907-474-5211
Room 101 *Fax:* 907-474-2631
Fairbanks, AK 99775-6180 snre-web@alaska.edu
www.uaf.edu/coop-ext
Mission: To interpret and extend relevant research-based knowledge in an understandable and usable form; and to encourage the application of this knowledge to solve the problems and meet the challenges that face the people of Alaska;and, to bring the concerns of the community back to the university.
Pete Pinney, Interim Director

2620 Fairbanks Office: Alaska Department of Environmental Conservation
610 University Avenue 907-451-2125
Fairbanks, AK 99709-3643 *Fax:* 907-451-2362
tom.deruyter@alaska.gov
www.dec.state.ak.us
Nancy Sonafrank, Program Manager

2621 Juneau Office: Alaska Department of Environmental Conservation
410 Willoughby Avenue 907-465-5066
Suite 303 *Fax:* 907-465-5070
Juneau, AK 99811-1800 www.dec.state.ak.us
Larry Hartig, Commissioner

2622 Kenai Office: Alaska Department of Environmental Conservation
43335 Kalifornsky Beach Road 907-262-5210
Suite 11, Red Diamond Center *Fax:* 907-262-2294
Soldotna, AK 99669-9792 www.dec.state.ak.us
Kristin Ryan, Director

2623 Kodiak Office: Alaska Department of Environmental Conservation
PO Box 515 907-486-3350
Kodiak, AK 99615-515 *Fax:* 907-486-5032
www.dec.state.ak.us
Kristin Ryan, Director

2624 Natural Resources Department Public Affairs Information Office
550 West 7th Avenue 907-269-8400
Suite 1260 *Fax:* 907-269-8901
Anchorage, AK 99501-3557 www.dnr.alaska.gov
Kathy Johnson, Manager

2625 Palmer Office: Alaska Department of Environmental Conservation
500 S Alaska Street 907-747-3236
Suite A www.dec.state.ak.us
Palmer, AK 99645

2626 Sitka Office: Alaska Department of Environmental Conservation
901 Halibut Point Road 907-747-8614
Suite 3 *Fax:* 907-747-7419
Sitka, AK 99835-7106 www.dec.state.ak.us
Kristin Ryan, Director

2627 Subsistance Resource Commission Cape Krusenstern National Monument
National Park Service
PO Box 1029 907-442-3890
Kotzebue, AK 99752 *Fax:* 907-442-8316
www.nps.gov/cakr
Frank Hays, Superintendent

2628 Subsistence Resource Gates of the Artic National Park
National Park Service
National Park Service-Fairbanks HQ 907-457-5752
4175 Geist Road *Fax:* 907-455-0601
Fairbanks, AK 99709 www.nps.gov/gaar
Susan Holly, Administrative Assistant

2629 United States Department of the Army: US Army Corps of Engineers
441 G Street NW 202-761-0011
Washington, DC 20314-1000 www.usace.army.mil
Design and constructs military projects for the Army, Air Force, civil works and water resources development projects for coastal communities. Conducts military Real Estate transactions, is responsible for Emergency Operationsinvolving national emergency and natural disaster, and regulates development in navigable waters, and placement of fill material in waters and wetlands.
Thomas P. Bostick, Commanding General
Richard L. Stevens, Deputy Commanding General

Arizona

2630 Arizona Department of Agriculture: Animal Services Division
1688 West Adams Street 602-542-4373
Phoenix, AZ 85007 www.azda.gov/ASD/asd.htm
Mission: Protect consumers from contagious and infectious disease in livestock, poultry, commercially raised fish, meat, milk, and eggs; enforce laws concerning the movement, sale, importation, transport, slaughter, and theft oflivestock.
Donald Butler, Director

2631 Arizona Department of Environmental Quality
1110 West Washington Street 602-771-2300
Phoenix, AZ 85007 800-234-5677
www.azdeq.gov/
The Arizona Department of Environmental Quality was established in 1987 to preserve, protect and enhance the environmental and public health through the maintenance of air, land and water resources. The department oversees compliancewith state and federal environmental regulations and works with industry and local governments.
Henry R. Darwin, Director
Misael Cabrera, Deputy Director

2632 Arizona Game & Fish Department
5000 W. Carefree Highway 602-942-3000
Phoenix, AZ 85086-5000 azgfdportal.az.gov
Aims to conserve, enhance and restore Arizona's diverse wildlife resources and habitats through aggressive protection and management programs, and to provide wildlife resources and safe watercraft and off-highway vehicle recreation forthe enjoyment, appreciation, and use by present and future generations.
Larry D. Voyles, Director
Ty Gray, Deputy Director

2633 Arizona Game & Fish Department: Region I
2878 East White Mountain Blvd 928-367-4281
Pinetop, AZ 85935 azgfdportal.az.gov
Aims to conserve, enhance and restore Arizona's diverse wildlife resources and habitats through aggressive protection and management programs, and to provide wildlife resources and safe watercraft and off-highway vehicle recreation forthe enjoyment, appreciation, and use by present and future generations.
Larry D. Voyles, Director
Ty Gray, Deputy Director

2634 Arizona Game & Fish Department: Region II
3500 South Lake Mary Road 928-774-5045
Flagstaff, AZ 86005 azgfdportal.az.gov
Aims to conserve, enhance and restore Arizona's diverse wildlife resources and habitats through aggressive protection and management programs, and to provide wildlife resources and safe watercraft and off-highway vehicle recreation forthe enjoyment, appreciation, and use by present and future generations.
Larry D. Voyles, Director
Ty Gray, Deputy Director

2635 Arizona Game & Fish Department: Region III
5325 North Stockton Hill Road 928-692-7700
Kingman, AZ 86409 azgfdportal.az.gov
Aims to conserve, enhance and restore Arizona's diverse wildlife resources and habitats through aggressive protection and management programs, and to provide wildlife resources and safe watercraft and off-highway vehicle recreation forthe enjoyment, appreciation, and use by present and future generations.
Larry D. Voyles, Director
Ty Gray, Deputy Director

2636 Arizona Game & Fish Department: Region IV
9140 East 28th Street 928-342-0091
Yuma, AZ 85365 azgfdportal.az.gov
Aims to conserve, enhance and restore Arizona's diverse wildlife resources and habitats through aggressive protection and management programs, and to provide wildlife resources and safe watercraft and off-highway vehicle recreation forthe enjoyment, appreciation, and use by present and future generations.
Larry D. Voyles, Director
Ty Gray, Deputy Director

2637 Arizona Game & Fish Department: Region V
555 North Greasewood Road 520-628-5376
Tucson, AZ 85745 azgfdportal.az.gov
Aims to conserve, enhance and restore Arizona's diverse wildlife resources and habitats through aggressive protection and management programs, and to provide wildlife resources and safe watercraft and off-highway vehicle recreation forthe enjoyment, appreciation, and use by present and future generations.
Larry D. Voyles, Director
Ty Gray, Deputy Director

2638 Arizona Game & Fish Department: Region VI
7200 East University 480-981-9400
Mesa, AZ 85207
Aims to conserve, enhance and restore Arizona's diverse wildlife resources and habitats through aggressive protection and management programs, and to provide wildlife resources and safe watercraft and off-highway vehicle recreation forthe enjoyment, appreciation, and use by present and future generations.
Larry D. Voyles, Director
Ty Gray, Deputy Director

2639 Arizona Geological Survey
416 W Congress Street 520-770-3500
Suite 100 *Fax:* 520-770-3505
Tucson, AZ 85701-1381 web@azgs.az.gov
www.azgs.state.az.us

The Arizona Geological Survey aims to inform and advise the public about the geologic character of Arizona in order to foster understanding and prudent development of the State's land, water, mineral and energy resources.
M Lee Allison, Director
Cindy Castro, Fiscal Services Specialist

2640 Arizona State Parks
1300 West Washington 602-542-4174
Phoenix, AZ 85007 800-285-3703
Fax: 602-542-4188
azstateparks.com

Walter D. Armer Jr., Chair
Bryan Martyn, Executive Director

2641 Arizona Strip District-US Department of Interior Bureau of Land Management
345 E Riverside Drive 435-688-3200
St George, UT 84790-6714 *Fax:* 435-688-3528
www.blm.gov
Manages nearly 2 million acres in northwestern Arizona, including the Vermilion Cliffs National Monument.
Timothy J. Burke, District Manager
Lorraine Christian, Acting Field Manager

2642 Environmental and Analytical Chemistry Laboratory
Arizona Department of Health 602-542-1025
150 North 18th Avenue *Fax:* 602-542-0883
Phoenix, AZ 85007 piowebmaster@azdhs.gov
www.azdhs.gov
State public health laboratory both in chemistry and microbiology. Supports investigations into environmental contamination by analyzing water, soil, air, hazardous materials, food and miscellaneous items for the presence of hazardousand toxic chemicals. Microbiology tests for pathogens and/or indicator organisms.
Will Humble, Director

2643 Gila Box Riparian National Conservation Area BLM Safford District Office
711 14th Avenue 928-348-4400
Safford, AZ 85546 *Fax:* 928-348-4450
www.az.blm.gov
There are more than 14 million acres of public lands in Arizona that people have put in our trust. It's an awesome responsiblity, and one that we take very seriously. We don't try to do it alone. Every day, we work with people to helpmake sure we are doing what is right for Arizona's envrionment, wildlife, culture, and history... for the people who rely upon the land to earn a living or to manufacture the things which make our lives a little easier...and most importantly, forArizona's future.
Tim Shannon, District Manager
Scott Cooke, Field Manager

2644 Phoenix District Advisory Council: BLM
21605 North 7th Avenue 623-580-5500
Phoenix, AZ 85027-2929 *Fax:* 623-580-5580
www.az.blm.gov
Manages public lands and resources in central Arizona, and supports related statewide initiatives and functions to sustain their health, diversity and productivity while providing for customer service and meeting public demandresulting from the expanding Phoenix metropolitan area and growth of adjoining communities.
Mary D'Aversa, District Manager
Rem Hawes, Field Manager

Arkansas

2645 Arkansas Department of Parks and Tourism
One Capitol Mall 501-682-7777
Little Rock, AR 72201 www.arkansas.com
To provide optimum quality state park recreation facilities conveniently located and in sufficient quantity to meet the needs of all state citizens and visitors
Richard W. Davis, Executive Director

2646 Arkansas Fish and Game Commission
2 Natural Resources Drive 501-223-6300
Little Rock, AR 72205 800-364-4263
askAGFC@agfc.state.ar.us
www.agfc.com

The Arkansas Game and Fish Commission plays an important role in keeping The Natural State true to its name.
Ronald Pierce, Commissioner
Ty Patterson, Commissioner

2647 Arkansas Natural Heritage Commission
323 Center Street 501-324-9619
St. 1500 *Fax:* 501-324-9618
Little Rock, AR 72201 www.arkansasheritage.com/
The Arkansas Natural Heritage Commission (ANHC) is responsible for maintaining the most up-to-date and comprehensive source of information concerning the rare plant and animal species, and high-quality natural communities of Arkansas.
Mark Karnes, Chairman
Robert Bevis, Vice Chairman

2648 Arkansas State Plant Board
1 Natural Resources Drive 501-225-1598
Little Rock, AR 72205 *Fax:* 501-219-1697
www.plantboard.org
Mission: To protect and serve the citizens of Arkansas and the agricultural and business communities by providing information and unbiased enforcement of laws and regulations thus ensuring quality products and services.
Darryl Little, Director

2649 Department of Environmental Quality
5301 Northshore Drive 501-682-0744
North Little Rock, AR 72118-5317 888-233-0326
www.adeq.state.ar.us
Mission: To protect, enhance and restore the natural environment for the well-being of Arkansas.
Teresa Marks, Director

California

2650 American Cetacean Society
PO Box 1391 310-548-6279
San Pedro, CA 90733-1391 *Fax:* 310-548-6950
acsoffice@acsonline.org
www.acsonline.org
A non profit organization that is the oldest whale conservation group in the world. Founded to protect whales, dolphins, porpoises, and their habitats through public education, research grants, and conservation actions.

Diane Glim, President
Barbara Bennett, Secretary

2651 California Department of Education Office of Environmental Education
1430 North Street 916-319-0800
Suite 5602 www.cde.ca.gov
Sacramento, CA 95814
Mission: Guiding principles, goals, and objectives of the California Department of Education.
Tom Torlakson, Superintendent
Richard Zeiger, Chief Deputy Superintendent

2652 California Department of Fish and Game
1416 9th Street 916-445-0411
12th Floor Webmaster@wildlife.ca.gov
Sacramento, CA 95814 www.wildlife.ca.gov
Manages California's diverse fish, wildlife, and plant resources, and the habitats upon which they depend, for their ecological values and for their use and enjoyment by the public.
Charlton H. Bonham, Director
Thomas Gibson, General Counsel

2653 California Department of Water Resources
1416-9th Street 916-653-5791
Room 1104-1 *Fax:* 916-653-3310
Sacramento, CA 95814
Mission: To manage the water resources of California in cooperation with other agencies, to benefit the State's people, and to protect, restore, and enhance the natural and human environments.
Mark W. Cowin, Director
Laura King Moon, Deputy Director

2654 California Desert District Advisory Council Bureau of Land Management
California State Office
2800 Cottage Way 916-78 -400
Suite W-1623 *Fax:* 916-978-4416
Sacramento, CA 9582-1886 www.ca.blm.gov
Mission: To protect the natural, historic, recreation and economic riches, and scenic beauty of the California Desert.

2655 California Environmental Protection Agency
1001 I Street 916-323-2514
P.O. Box 2815 calepa.ca.gov
Sacramento, CA 95812-2815
The CalEPA's goals are to protect the environment, public health, and economic vitality. They accomplish these goals by implementing regulatory laws that focus on air, water, and soil quality as well as pesticide use and wastereduction.

Jared Blumenfeld, Secretary
Serena McIlwain, Undersecretary

2656 California Pollution Control Financing Authority
915 Capitol Mall, Room 457 916-654-5610
Sacramento, CA 95814 *Fax:* 916-657-4821
cpcfa@treasurer.ca.gov
www.treasurer.ca.gov/cpcfa

Bill Lockyer, Chairman
Renee Webster-Hawkins, Executive Director

2657 Department of Agriculture: Forest Service, Pacific Southwest Region
1323 Club Drive 707-562-8737
Vallejo, CA 94592 *Fax:* 707-562-9130
www.fs.fed.us/r5
The Pacific Southwest Region of the USDA Forest Service, otherwise known as Region 5, manages National and Private forests in California, Hawaii, and the U.S. Affiliated Pacific Islands.
Randy Moore, Regional Forester
Jeff Moulton, Regional Attorney

2658 Department of Agriculture: Research, Education, and Economics
U.S. Department of Agriculture
1400 Independence Avenue SW 202-720-5923
Room 214W *Fax:* 202-690-2842
Washington, DC 20250-0110 www.ree.usda.gov
The Research, Education, and Economics section of the USDA has federal leadership responsibility for the discovery of knowledge spanning the biological, physical, and social sciences, and involving agricultural research, economicanalysis, statistics, outreach, and higher education.
Scott Hutchins, Deputy Under Secretary
Chavonda Jacobs-Young, Administrator

2659 Energy Commission
1516 9th Street 916 651 1287
MS-29 www.energy.ca.gov
Sacramento, CA 95814-5512
Promoting Efficiency and Conservation, Supporting Cutting-Edge Research, and Developing Our Renewable Energy Resources
Robert B. Weisenmiller, Ph.D., Chair
Karen Douglas, Commissioner

2660 Environmental Protection Agency Region 9
75 Hawthorne Street 415-947-8000
San Francisco, CA 94105 866-EPA-WEST
r9.info@epa.gov
www.epa.gov/region09/
Region 9 covers Arizona, California, Hawaii, Nevada, the Pacific Islands subject to U.S. law, and approximately 140 Tribal Na-

tions. They work together with state, local, and tribal governments in the region to carry out the nation'senvironmental laws.
Mike Stoker, Regional Administrator
Deborah Jordan, Deputy Administrator

2661 **Environmental Protection Office: Hazard Identification**
Environmental Health Hazard Assessment Office
1001 Street 916-445-6900
Sacramento, CA 95814 *Fax:* 916-323-8803
P65Public.comments@oehha.ca.gov
www.oehha.ca.gov/prop65/hazard_ident/092812HID.html
The mission of the Office of Environmental Health Hazard Assessment (OEHHA) is to protect and enhance public health and the environment by objective scientific evaluation of risks posed by hazardous substances.
Sam Delson, Deputy Director
Laura August, Staff

2662 **Environmental Protection Office: Toxic Substance Control Department**
1001 I Street 916-323-9723
PO Box 806 800-728-6942
Sacramento, CA 95814-2828 *Fax:* 916-323-3215
webcoord@dtsc.ca.gov
www.dtsc.ca.gov
The Department's mission is to restore, protect and enhance the environment, to ensure public health, environmental quality and economic vitality by regulating hazardous waste, conducting and overseeing cleanups, and developing andpromoting pollution prevention.
Barbara A. Lee, Director
Miriam B. Ingenito, Chief Deputy Director

2663 **Golden Gate National Recreation Area**
Fort Mason 415-561-4700
Building 201 www.nps.gov/goga
San Francisco, CA 94123-22
The Golden Gate National Recreation Area (GGNRA) is the largest urban national park in the world. The total park area is 74,000 acres of land and water. Approximately 28 miles of coastline line within its boundaries. It is nearly twoand one-half times the size of San Francisco.
Frank Dean, General Superintendent
Aaron Roth, Deputy Superintendent

2664 **Inter-American Tropical Tuna Commission**
8601 La Jolla Shores Drive 858-546-7100
La Jolla, CA 92037-1508 *Fax:* 858-546-7133
webmaster@iattc.org
www.iattc.org/homeeng.htm
The IATTC, established by international convention in 1950, is responsible for the conservation and management of fisheries for tunas and other species taken by tuna-fishing vessels in the eastern Pacific Ocean. The IATTC also hassignificant responsibilities for the implementation of the International Dolphin Conservation Program (IDCP), and provides the Secretariat for that program.
Guillermo Compean, Director
Richard B. Deriso, Chief Scientist

2665 **InterEnvironment Institute**
PO Box 99 909-621-9018
Claremont, CA 91711 Mail@InterEnvironment.org
www.interenvironment.org
A forum for policy dialogue and research on California and international environmental issues.
Thaddeus C Trzyna, President
Michael Paparian, Secretary-Treasurer

2666 **Klamath Fishery Management Council US Fish & Wildlife Service**
1829 South Oregon Street 530-842-5763
Yreka, CA 96097 *Fax:* 530-842-4517
yreka@fws.gov
www.fws.gov/yreka/kfmc.htm
To manage harvests and ensure continued viable populations of anadromous fish in the Klamath Basin
Phil Detrich, Supervisor

2667 **Native American Heritage Commission**
1550 Harbor Blvd 916-373-3710
Suite 100 *Fax:* 916-373-5471
Sacramento, CA 95691 nahc@pacbell.net
www.nahc.ca.gov
The mission of the Native American Heritage Comm. is to provide protection to Native American burials from vandalism and inadvertent destruction, provide a procedure for the notification of most likely descendents regarding thediscovery of Native American human remains and associated grave goods, bring legal action to prevent severe and irreparable damage to sacred shrines, ceremonial sites, sanctified cemeteries and place of worship on pub. property, and maintain aninventory of sacred places.
Cynthia Gomez, Executive Secretary
James Ramos, Chair

2668 **Pesticide Regulation, Environmental Monitoring and Pesticide Management**
1001 I Street 916-445-4300
PO Box 4015 *Fax:* 916-324-1452
Sacramento, CA 95812-4015 cdprweb@cdpr.ca.gov
www.cdpr.ca.gov
Mission: Protect human health and the environment by regulating pesticide sales and use, and by fostering reduced-risk pest management.
Rudy Artau, Branch Chief
Charles Andrews, Associate Director

2669 **Resources Agency: California Coastal Commission**
45 Fremont Street 415-904-5250
Suite 2000 *Fax:* 415-904-5400
San Francisco, CA 94105 www.coastal.ca.gov
Mission: To protect, conserve, restore, and enhance environmental and human-based resources of the California coast and ocean for environmentally sustainable and prudent use by current and future generations.
Mary K. Shallenberger, Chair
Steve Kinsey, Vice Chairman

2670 **Resources Agency: California Conservation Corps**
1719 24th Street 916-341-3100
Sacramento, CA 95816 800-952-5627
Fax: 916-323-8922
www.ccc.ca.gov
Engages young men and women in meaningful work, public service educational activities that assist them in becoming more responsible citizens, while protecting and enhancing California's environment, human resources and communities.
David Muraki, Director
Jeffrey Schwarzchild, Chief Counsel

2671 **Resources Agency: State Coastal Conservancy**
1330 Broadway 510-286-1015
13th Floor *Fax:* 510-286-0470
Oakland, CA 94612-2530 dwayman@scc.ca.gov
www.scc.ca.gov
The Coastal Conservancy acts with others to preserve, protect and restore the resources of the California Coast.
Quarterly Magazine
Samuel Schuchat, Executive Officer
Mary Small, Deputy Executive Officer

2672 **Southwestern Low-Level Radioactive Waste Commission**
1731 Howe Ave #611 916-448-2390
Sacramento, CA 95825 *Fax:* 916-720-0144
kathydavis@swllrwcc.org
www.swllrwcc.org
The Southwestern Low-Level Radioactive Waste Commission is the governing body for the Southwestern Low-Level Radioactive Waste Disposal Compact, consisting of Arizona, California, North Dakota, and South Dakota. Created by public law100-712 in 1988, its key duties include controlling the importation and ex-

portation of low-level waste into and out of the region. The Commission has no authority over disposal facility siting, but can make recommendations and comments to ensure safedisposal.

Kathy A David, Executive Director

Colorado

2673 Bureau of Land Management (BLM)
U.S. Department of the Interior
1849 C Street NW 202-208-3801
Room 5665 *Fax:* 202-208-5242
Washington, DC 20240 www.blm.gov
The mission of the Bureau of Land Management is to ensure the sustainability and diversity of the public lands for the use and enjoyment of present and future generations. The Bureau offers environmental education, news about theactivities of the Bureau, events, and regulations.

Michael Nedd, Deputy Director, Operations
Casey Hammond, Principal Deputy

2674 Bureau of Land Management: Little Snake Field Office
Little Snake Field Office 970-826-5000
455 Emerson Street *Fax:* 970-526-5002
Craig, CO 81625 swiser@blm.gov
www.blm.gov
Encompasses 4.2 million acres of federal, state and private lands in Moffat, Routt, and Rio Blanco counties.
Wendy Reynolds, Field Manager

2675 Canon City District Advisory Council
Royal Gorge Field Office 719-269-8500
3028 East Main Street *Fax:* 719-269-8599
Canon City, CO 81212
This office administers over 680,000 surface acres of public land along the Front Range and 6.8 million sub-surface acres

2676 Cheyenne Mountain Zoological Park
4250 Cheyenne Mountain Zoo Road 719-633-9925
Colorado Springs, CO 80906 *Fax:* 719-633-2254
info@cmzoo.org
www.cmzoo.org
Mission: To foster an appreciation and respect for all living things. Actifely provide survival assistance for species in peril. Provide a high quality recreational experience. Be source of pride and economic strength.
Erica Meyer, PR Manager

2677 Colorado Department of Agriculture
305 Interlocken Parkway 303-239-4100
Suite 4000 *Fax:* 303-239-4125
Broomfield, CO 80021 vital.records@state.co.us
www.colorado.gov/ag
Mission: To strengthen and advance Colorado's agriculture industry; ensure a safe, high quality, and sustainable food supply; and protect consumers, the environment, and natural resources.
John R Stulp, Commisioner
Dr. Larry Wolk, Executive Director

2678 Colorado Department of Natural Resources
1313 Sherman Street 303-866-3311
Room 718 800-536-5308
Denver, CO 80203 *Fax:* 303-866-2115
dnr.edoassist@state.co.us
cdnr.us

Mike King, Executive Director
Bob Randall, Deputy Director

2679 Colorado Department of Natural Resources: Division of Water Resources
1313 Sherman Street 303-866-3581
Room 818 *Fax:* 303-866-3589
Denver, CO 80203 firstname.lastname@state.co.us
www.water.state.co.us
The Colorado Division of Water Resources is an agency of the State of Colorado, Department of Natural Resources, operating under the direction of specific state stautes, court decrees, and interstate compacts. The DWR is empowered toadminister all surface and ground water rights throughout the state and ensure that the doctrine of prior appropiation is enforced.
Dick Wolfe, State Engineer
Scott Cuthbertson, Assistant State Engineer

2680 Colorado Department of Public Health Environment Consumer Protection Division
4300 Cherry Creek Drive South 303-692-3620
Denver, CO 80246 *Fax:* 303-753-6809
www.cdphe.state.co.us/cp
The Consumer Protection Division assumes the responsiblity for protecting Colorado residents and visitors by prevention of a wide array of health hazards.

2681 Colorado Department of Public Health and Environment
4300 Cherry Creek Drive South 303-692-2000
Denver, CO 80246 800-886-7689
cdphe.information@state.co.us
www.cdphe.state.co.us
Mission: Committed to protecting and preserving the health and environment of the people of Colorado.
Dr. Larry Wolk, Executive Director/CMO
Karin McGowan, Deputy Executive Director

2682 Colorado River Basin Salinity Control Program
US Bureau of Land Reclamation
125 S State Street 801-524-3753
Room 7311 *Fax:* 801-524-3847
Salt Lake City, UT 84138-1147 kjacobson@usbr.gov
www.usbr.gov
The Colorado River and its tributaries provide municipal and industrial water to about 27 million people and irrigation to nearly four million acres of land in the US. The river also serves about 2.3 million people and 500,000 acres inMexico. The threat of salinity is a major concern in both the US and Mexico. Salinity affects agricultural, municipal and industrial water users. We work to control the salinity of the Colorado river and thereby to protect the land and people.

Kib Jacobson, Program Manager
Brad Parry, Program Coordinator

2683 Colorado State Forest Service
Colorado State University
5060 Campus Delivery 970-491-8660
Fort Collins, CO 80523-5060 *Fax:* 970-491-8645
CSFS_FortCollins@mail.colostate.edu
www.csfs.colostate.edu
Mission: To provide for the stewardship of forest resources and to reduce related risks to life, property and the environment for the benefit of present and future generations.
Boyd Lebeda, District Forester

2684 Environmental Protection Agency Region 8
1595 Wynkoop Street 303-312-6312
Denver, CO 80202-1129 800-227-8917
r8eisc@epa.gov
www.epa.gov/region8/
This region of the EPA represents the mountains and plains of Colorado, Montana, North Dakota, South Dakota, Utah, Wyoming, and 27 Tribal Nations.
Gregory Sopkin, Regional Administrator
Deb Thomas, Deputy Administrator

2685 Governors Office of Energy, Management and Conservation: Colorado
1580 Logan Street 303-866-2100
Suite 100 800-632-6662
Denver, CO 80203 *Fax:* 303-866-2930
geo@state.co.us
www.colorado.gov/pacific/energyoffice

Supports cost-effective programs, grants and partnerships that benefit Colorado's economic and natural environment.
Jeff Ackermann, Director
Nancey Steinheimer, Assistant to the Director

2686 Minerals Management Service/Minerals Revenue Management
PO Box 25165 303-231-3162
Denver, CO 80225
Mission: To manage the ocean energy and mineral resources on the Outer Continental Shelf and Federal and Indian mineral revenues to enhance public and trust benefits, promote responsible use, and realize fair value.
Randall B Luthi, Director

2687 Natural Resources Department: Air Quality Division
Department of the Interior
PO Box 25287 303-969-2070
Denver, CO 80225-287 *Fax:* 303-969-2822
christine_shaver@nps.gov
www.nature.nps.gov/air/who/npsStaff.cfm
To protect air quality and resources affected by air pollution under the NPS Organic Act and the Clean Air Act
Carol McCoy, Division Chief
Chris Havermann, Office Manager

2688 Natural Resources Department: Oil & Gas Conservation Commission
1120 Lincoln Street Suite 801 303-894-2100
Denver, CO 80203 *Fax:* 303-894-2109
dnr_dnr.ogcc@state.co.us
To foster the responsible development of Colorado's oil and gas natural resources
M. Lepore, Director
J. Missey, Executive Assistant

2689 Natural Resources Department: Wildlife Division
6060 Broadway 303-291-7227
Denver, CO 80216
Manages the state's 960 wildlife species. Regulates hunting and fishing activities by issuing licenses and enforcing regulations. Conducts research to improve wildlife management activities, provides technical assistance to private andother land owners concerning wildlife and habitat management and develops programs to protect and recover threatened and endangered species.
Mark B Konishi, Acting Director

2690 Office of Surface Mining Reclamation & Enforcement
1999 Broadway 303-293-5000
Suite 3320 *Fax:* 303-844-1546
Denver, CO 80202-3050 osm-wrWeb@osmre.gov
www.wrcc.osmre.gov/
Al Klein, Regional Director
Jeffrey Fleischman, Field Manager

2691 Rocky Mountain Low-Level Radioactive Waste Board
1313 Sherman Street 303-825-1912
6th Floor *Fax:* 303-892-3882
Denver, CO 80203-1264 sreynolds@rmllwb.us
www.cpw.state.co.us
Gary Baughman, Director
Leonard C. Slosky, Executive Director

2692 United States Forest Service: United States Department of Agriculture
740 Simms Street 202-205-8333
Golden, CO 80401 800-832-1355
www.fs.fed.us/r2
Mary Wagner, Associate Chief
Thomas L. Tidwell, Chief

Connecticut

2693 Connecticut Department of Agriculture
165 Capitol Avenue 860-713-2500
Hartford, CT 00610 *Fax:* 860-713-2514
www.ct.gov/doag/site/default.asp
Steven K Reviczky, Commissioner

2694 Connecticut Department of Environmental Protection
Department of Environmental Protection
79 Elm Street 860-424-3000
Hartford, CT 00610 dep.webmaster@po.state.ct.us
www.ct.gov/deep/site/default.asp
Mission: To conserve, improve and protect the natural resources and environment of the State of Connecticut in such a manner as to encourage the social and economic development of Connecticut while preserving the natural environmentand the life forms it supports in a delicate, interrelated and complex balance, to the end that the state may fulfill its responsibility as trustee of the environment for present and future generations.
Daniel C. Esty, Commissioner

2695 Connecticut Department of Public Health
410 Capitol Avenue 860-509-8000
PO Box 340308 www.ct.gov/dph/site/default.asp
Hartford, CT 00613
Has long recognized the adverse public health impact of environmental sources of lead in many of Connecticut's childern. Established dedicated staff to evaluate these environmental sources and began funding local programs in the1970's. The Childhood Lead Posioning Prevention Program has continued to be active in addressing this issue by implementing additional state and community programs, especially in towns that have been identified as high risk.
Jewell Mullen, Commissioner
Norma Gyle, Deputy Commissioner

District of Columbia

2696 District of Columbia State Extension Services
4200 Connecticut Avenue 202-274-5000
Building 352, Suite 322 *Fax:* 202-274-7130
Washington, DC 20008 alumni@udc.edu
www.udc.edu

Delaware

2697 Delaware Association of Conservation Districts
PO Box 242 302-739-9921
Dover, DE 19903-242 *Fax:* 302-739-6724
Martha.Pileggi@state.de.us
www.nacdnet.org
Coordinates the three state conservation districts.
Wendy Baker, President
Robert Emerson, Vice President

2698 Delaware Cooperative Extension
University of Delaware
531 South College Avenue 302-831-2504
113 Townsend Hall *Fax:* 302-831-6758
Newark, DE 19716-2103 mrodgers@udel.edu
www.extension.udel.edu
Contact person Janice A Seitz's title is Associate Dean for Extension and Outreach Director of Extension College of Agriculture and Natural Resources.
Michelle Rogers, Director
Alice Moore, Administrative Assistant

2699 Delaware Department of Agriculture
2320 S DuPont Highway 302-698-4500
Dover, DE 19901 800-282-8685
www.dda.delaware.gov

As part of the state government, the department's mission is to sustain and promote the viability of food, fiber and agricultural industries in Delaware through quality services that protect and enhance the environment, health andwelfare of the general public.
Ed Kee, Secretary
E. Austin Short, Deputy Secretary

2700 Delaware Department of Natural Resources and Environmental Control
DNREC
89 Kings Highway 302-739-9400
Dover, DE 19901 *Fax:* 302-739-3106
dnrec.alpha.delaware.gov
Protects and manages the state's vital natural resources, protects public health and safety, provides quality outdoor recreation, and serves and educates the citizens of the First State about the wise use, conservation and enhancementof Delaware's environment.
Collin O'Mara, Secretary

2701 Delaware Sea Grant Program
University of Delaware 302-831-8083
222 South Chapel Street www.deseagrant.org/
Newark, DE 19716-3530
Using Technology, Innovation, and Cooperation to Tackle Coastal Challenges
Nancy Targett, Director
Jennifer Adkins, Executive Director

2702 Department of the Interior: U.S. Fish & Wildlife Service - Delaware Bay Estate Project
Delaware Bay Estuary Project
2610 Whitehall Neck Road 302-653-9152
Smyrna, DE 19977-2910 *Fax:* 302-653-9421
R5ES_DPEP@fws.gov
www.fws.gov/delawarebay/
Delaware Bay Estate Project is a field office of the US Fish & Wildlife service's coastal program.
Gregory Breese, Project Leader
Richard McCorkle, Biologist

2703 Mid-Atlantic Fishery Management Council
800 North State Street 302-674-2331
Suite 201 *Fax:* 302-674-5399
Dover, DE 19901 contact@mafmc.org
www.mafmc.org
The Mid-Atlantic Fishery Management Council is responsible for management of fisheries in federal waters which occur predominantly off the mid-Atlantic coast.
Richard B. Robins, Chairman
Lee Anderson, Vice Chairman

Florida

2704 Department of Commerce National Oceanic & Atlantic Oceanographic & Meteorological Laboratory
4301 Rickenbacker Causeway 305-361-4420
Miami, FL 33149 *Fax:* 305-361-4449
www.aoml.noaa.gov
Robert M Atlas, Director
Dr. Molly Baringer, Deputy Director

2705 Fish & Wildlife Conservation Commission
620 South Meridian Street 850-488-4676
Tallahassee, FL 32399 www.myfwc.com/
Mission: Managing fish and wildlife resources for their long-term well-being and the benefit of the people.
Rodney Barreto, Chair

2706 Florida Department of Agriculture & Consumer Service
The Capitol, Pl 10 850-488-3022
400 South Monroe Street *Fax:* 850-488-7585
Tallahassee, FL 32399-800 www.freshfromflorida.com
Mission: To safeguard the public and support Florida's agriculture economy by: ensuring the safety and wholesomeness of food and other consumer products through inspection and testing programs; protecting consumers from unfair anddeceptive business practices and providing consumer information; assisting Florida's farmers and agriculture industries with the production and promotion of agriculture products; and conserving and protecting the state's agriculture and naturalresources.
Adam H. Putnam, Commissioner

2707 Florida Department of Environmental Protection
3900 Commonwealth Boulevard 850-245-2118
M.S. 49 *Fax:* 850-245-2128
Tallahassee, FL 32399-3000 www.dep.state.fl.us
Mission: To promote the efficient and effective operation of the Agency consistent with its Administratice and statutory responsibilities.
Rick Scott, Governor
Herschel Vinyard, Jr., Secretary

2708 Florida State Department of Health
2585 Merchants Row Blvd 850-245-4444
Tallahassee, FL 32399 www.doh.state.fl.us
Mission: To promote and protect the health and safety of all people in Florida through the delivery of quality public health services and the promotion of health care standards.
J. Martin Stubblefield, Deputy Secretary
Kim Barnhill, Chief of Staff

2709 Gulf of Mexico Fishery Management Council
2203 North Lois Avenue 813-348-1630
Suite 1100 888-833-1844
Tampa, FL 33607 *Fax:* 813-348-1711
gulfcouncil@gulfcouncil.org
www.gulfcouncil.org
The Gulf of Mexico Fishery management Council is one of eight regional Fishery Management Councils which were established by the Fishery conservation and Management Act in 1976 (now called the Magnuson-Stevens Fishery Conservation andMagnuson Act). The Council prepares fishery plans which are designed to manage fishery resources from where state waters end to the 200 mile limit of the Gulf of mexico.
Wayne E Swingle, Executive Director
Rick Leard, Deputy Executive Director

2710 Lee County Parks & Recreation
3410 Palm Beach Boulevard 239-533-7275
Fort Myers, FL 33916 *Fax:* 239-485-2300
LeeParks@leegov.com
www.leeparks.org/
Our mission is to provide safe, clean and functional Parks & Recreation facilities; to provide programs and services that add to the quality of life for all Lee County residents and visitors; to enhance tourism through special eventsand attractions. We are committed to fulfilling this mission through visionary leadership, individual dedication and the trustworthy use of available resources.
Dana Kasler, Director
Dana Kasler, Deputy Director

2711 Natural Resources Department: Recreation & Parks Division
3900 Commonwealth Boulevard 850-245-2157
Tallahassee, FL 32399 www.dep.state.fl.us/parks
Mission: To provide resource-based recreation while preserving, interpreting and restoring natural and cultural resources. Our goal is to help create a sense of place by showing park visitors the best of Florida's diverse natural andcultural heritage sites.
Donald V. Forgione, Director

2712 **Southwest Florida Water Management District**
2379 Broad Street 352-796-7211
Brookville, FL 34604-6899 800-423-1476
Fax: 352-754-6885
info@watermatters.org
www.swfwmd.state.fl.us
Manages the water and water-related resources within its boundaries. Maintains balance between the water needs of current and future users while protecting and maintaining the natural systems that provide the District with its existingand future water supply. The Conservation Projects Section, in the Resource Conservation and Development Department, is reponsible for managing water conservation, reclaimed water and other alternative source projects, and estimating future waterdemands.
Michael A. Babb, Chairman
Randall S. Maggard, Vice Chairman

Georgia

2713 **Board of Scientific Counselors: Agency for Toxic Substance and Disease Registry**
4770 Buford Hwy NE 800-232-4636
Atlanta, GA 30341 800-232-4636
Fax: 404-562-1790
www.atsdr.cdc.gov
Serves the public by using the best science, taking responsive public health actions, and providing trusted health information to prevent harmful exposures and diseases related to toxic substances

Robin Ikeda, Director
Thomas Sinks, Deputy Director

2714 **Georgia Department of Agriculture**
19 Martin Luther King Jr Drive SW 404-656-3600
Atlanta, GA 30334 800-282-5852
www.agr.georgia.gov
Mission: To provide excellence in services and regulatory functions, to protect and promote agriculture and consumer interests, and to ensure an abundance of safe food and fiber for Georgia, America and the world by usingstate-of-the-art technology and a professional workforce.
Gary W. Black, Commissioner
James Sutton, Chief Administration Officer

2715 **Georgia Department of Education**
205 Jesse Hill Jr. Drive SE 404-656-2800
Atlanta, GA 30334 *Fax:* 404-651-8737
askdoe@gadoe.org
www.gadoe.org
To function as a service oriented and policy driven agency that meets the needs of local school systems as they go about the business of preparing all students for college or a career in a safe and drug free environment where we ensurethat no chils is left behind.
Joel Thorton, Chief of Staff
Mike Buck, Chief Academic Officer

2716 **Georgia Department of Natural Resources: Historic Preservation Division**
2610 GA Hwy 155, SW 404-656-2840
Stockbridge, GA 30281 *Fax:* 770-389-7844
www.georgiashpo.org
To promote the preservation and use of historic places for a better Georgia.
Ray Luce, Director

2717 **Georgia Department of Natural Resources: Pollution Prevention Assistance Division**
2 Martin Luther King Jr. Drive 404-651-5120
SE Suite 1252 800-685-2443
Atlantic, GA 30334 *Fax:* 404-651-5130
www.gadnr.org/

Lauren Travis, Program Manager
David Gipson, Assistant Director

2718 **Georgia Sea Grant College Program**
University of Georgia
220 Marine Science Building 706-542-6009
Athens, GA 30602 *Fax:* 706-542-3652
www.georgiaseagrant.uga.edu
Goal is to better understand the complex interactions between the physical, chemical, biological and geological processes that are manifested in the area where land and sea come together, and to make that knowledge available and usefulto Georgia's citizens. Sea Grant strives to deepen our understanding of coastal and estuarine ecology, the critical role of fresh water interaction and to expand our knowledge of action beyond the marshes and estuaries and into the life of the riversand streams.
Charles Hopkinson, Director
David Bryant, Assistant Director

2719 **National Center for Environmental Health**
1600 Clifton Road 800-232-4636
Atlanta, GA 30329-4027 *Fax:* 770-488-7042
www.cdc.gov/nceh
Mission: Plans, directs, and coordinates a national program to maintain and improve the health of the American people by promoting a healthy environment and by preventing premature death and avoidable illness and disability caused bynon-infectious, non-occupational and related factors.
Robin Ikeda, Director

2720 **Natural Resource Department**
2 Martin Luther King Jr Drive SE 404-656-3500
Suite 1252 East Tower www.state.ga.us/dnr/
Atlanta, GA 30334
The mission of the Department of Natural Resources is to sustain, enhance, protect and conserve Georgia's natural, historic and cultural resources for present and future generations, while recognizing the importance of promoting thedevelopment of commerce and industry that utilize sound environmental practices.
Noel Holcomb, Commissioner

2721 **Natural Resources Department: Air Protection**
4244 International Parkway 404-363-7000
Suite 120 *Fax:* 404-363-7100
Atlanta, GA 30354 james.capp@dnr.state.ga.us
www.georgiaair.org
The Air Protection Branch helps provide Georgia's citizens with clean air and works closely with other branches of Georgia's Environmental Protection Division to assure compliance with environmental laws so that, in addition to clearair, we have clean water, healthy lives and productive land.
James A Capp, Branch Chief

2722 **Natural Resources Department: Coastal Resources Division**
1 Conservation Way 912-264-7218
Brunswick, GA 31520 *Fax:* 912-262-3143
www.coastalgadnr.org

Spud Woodward, Director
Brad Jane, Ecological Services Chief

2723 **Natural Resources Department: Environmental Protection Division**
2 Martin Luther King Jr Drive 404-657-5947
Suite 1152 East Tower 888-373-5947
Atlanta, GA 30334 askepd@gaepd.org
www.gaepd.org
Provides Georgia's citizens with clean air, clean water, healthy lives and productive land by assuring compliance with environmental laws and by assisting others to do their part for a better environment.
Judson H. Turner, Director

2724 **United States Department of the Army US Army Corps of Engineers**
US Army Engineer Distric 912-652-5279
100 W Oglethorpe Ave cesas-cco@usace.army.mil
Savannah, GA 31401 www.sas.usace.army.mil
Mission: To provide quality, responsive engineering services to the nation including: planning, designing, building and operating

water resources and other civil works projects; designing and managing the construction of militaryfacilities for the Army and Air Force; and providing design and construction management support for other defense and federal agencies.
Jeffrey M. Hall, District Commander
Ronald L Johnson, Deputy Commander

2725 Wassaw National Wildlife Refuge
1000 Business Center Drive 912-832-4608
Suite 10 savannahcoastal@fws.gov
Savannah, GA 31405 www.fws.gov/wassaw
The most primitive of Georgia's barrier islands, the 10,053 acre refuge, includes beaches with rolling dunes, live oak and slash pine woodlands, and vast salt marshes. The island supports rookeries for egrets and herons, and a varietyof leading birds are abundant in the summer months. Wassaw also provides prime nesting habitat for the loggerhead seaturtles. Refuge visitors may enjoy recreational activities such as birdwatching, beachocombing, hiking, and general nature studies.
Jane Griess, Project Leader
Kimberley Hayes, Refuge Manager

Hawaii

2726 Agriculture Department
1428 South King Street 808-973-9560
Honolulu, HI 96814 www.agricoop.nic.in/
Sandra Lee Kunimoto, Chair

2727 College of Tropical Agriculture and Human Resources
University of Hawaii
3050 Maile Way 808-956-8131
Gilmore 202 *Fax:* 808-956-9105
Honolulu, HI 96822 gallom@ctahr.hawaii.edu
www.ctahr.hawaii.edu/site/
Mission: Committed to the preparation of students and all citizens of Hawaii for life in the global community through research and educational programs supporting tropical agriculture systems that foster viable communities, adiversified economy, and a healthy environment.
Maria Gallo, Dean/Director
Wimmie Wong Lui, Assistant

2728 Department of Land and Natural Resources Division of Water Resource Management
1151 Punchbowl Street 808-587-0214
Room 227 *Fax:* 808-587-0219
Honolulu, HI 96813 dlnr.cwrm@hawaii.gov
www.dlnr.hawaii.gov
W. Roy Hardy, P.E., Deputy Director
William J. Aila, Chair

2729 Environmental Center
University of Hawaii
2500 Dole Street 808-956-7361
Krauss Annex 19 *Fax:* 808-956-3980
Honolulu, HI 96822 www.hawaii.edu/envctr
The Center's three areas of focus are education, research and service. The education function of the Center includes the administration of the Environmental Studies Major Equivalent and Certificate program. It fulfills its researchfunction by identifying and addressing environmentally related research needs, particularly those pertinent to Hawaii. The service function primarily involves the coordination and transfer of technical information from the University community togovernment agencies.
Charlotte Kato, Secretary

2730 Hawaii Department of Agriculture
1428 South King Street 808-973-9560
Honolulu, HI 96814 www.hawaii.gov/hdoa
Contains devisions such as: Administrative; Animal Industry; Marketing; Measurement Standards; and Plant Industry. Carries out programs to conserve, develop and utilize the agricultural resources of the state. Enforces laws, andformulates and enforces rules and regulation to further control the management of these resources.
Sandra Lee Kunimoto, Chairperson

2731 Hawaii Institute of Marine Biology University of Hawaii
PO Box 1346 808-236-7401
Kane'ohe, HI 96744 *Fax:* 808-236-7443
www.hawaii.edu/HIMB
Jo-Ann C Leong, Director

2732 Health Department: Environmental Quality Control
235 S Beretania Street 808-586-4185
Room 702 *Fax:* 808-586-4186
Honolulu, HI 96813 oeqc@doh.hawaii.gov
health.hawaii.gov
The office is tasked to implement Chapter 343, Hawaii Revised Statues and Title 11, Chapter 200. This is a systematic process to ensure consideration is given to the environmental consequences of actions proposed within our state. Thereview process offers many opportunities to prevent environmental degradation and protect human communities through decreased citizen involvement and informed decision making.
Virgina Pressler, M.D., Director

2733 State of Hawaii: Department of Land and Natural Resources
Kalanimoku Building 808-587-0400
1151 Punchbowl Street *Fax:* 808-587-0390
Honolulu, HI 96813 dlnr@hawaii.gov
www.hawaii.gov/dlnr
State agency.
Suzanne D. Case, Chairperson
Kekoa Kaluhiwa, First Deputy

2734 Water Resources Research Center University of Hawaii
2540 Dole Street 808-956-7847
Holmes Hall 283 *Fax:* 808-956-5044
Honolulu, HI 96822 wrrc@hawaii.edu
www.wrrc.hawaii.edu
The Water Resources Research Center was organized under the federal Water Resources Research Act of 1964. The Center is supported by university funds, external grants, contracts and a small annual federal grant. WRRC faculty coverthe areas of engineering, hydrology, microbiology, ecology, economics and zoology. Cooperating faculty come from numerous other disciplines. WRRC is open to consideration of any question related to water supply or water quality.
James Moncur, Director

Idaho

2735 Department of the Interior: Bureau of Land Management - Idaho
1387 South Vinnell Way 208-373-4000
Boise, ID 83709 blm_id_stateoffice@blm.gov
www.blm.gov/idaho
The BLM manages a variety of resources in Idaho with an emphasis on recreation, grazing and fire management on nearly 12 million acres of public lands (nearly 1/4 of the state's total land area).
John Ruths, State Director
Peter Ditton, Associate State Director

2736 Idaho Association of Soil Conservation Districts
55 SW 5th Ave 208-895-8928
Suite 100 *Fax:* 208-376-6858
Meridian, ID 83642 kent.foster@agri.idaho.gov
www.iascd.org

Provides action at the local level for promoting wise and beneficial conservation of natural resources with emphasis on soil and water.

Kit Tillotson, President
Billie J. Brown, Vice President

2737 Idaho Cooperative Extension
875 Perimeter Drive 208-885-5883
MS 2338 *Fax:* 208-885-6654
Moscow, ID 83844-2338 extension@uidaho.edu
www.uidaho.edu/extension/
Barbara Petty, Interim Director

2738 Idaho Department of Environmental Quality: Pocatello Regional Office
444 Hospital Way #300 208-236-6160
Pocatello, ID 83201 888-655-6160
Fax: 208-236-6168
www.state.id.us
Mission: To protect human health and preserve the quality of Idaho's air, land, and water for use and enjoyment today and in the future.
Toni Hardesty, Director

2739 Idaho Department of Environmental Quality: State Office
1410 North Hilton 208-373-0502
Boise, ID 83706 *Fax:* 208-373-0417
john.tippets@deq.idaho.gov
www.deq.idaho.gov
Mission: To protect human health and preserve the quality of Idaho's air, land, and water for use and enjoyment today and in the future.
John Tippets, Director
Jess Byrne, Deputy Director

2740 Idaho Department of Environmental Quality: Idaho Falls Regional Office
900 N Skyline 208-528-2650
Suite B 800-232-4635
Idaho Falls, ID 83402 *Fax:* 208-528-2695
www.state.id.us
Mission: To protect human health and preserve the quality of Idaho's air, land, and water for use and enjoyment today and in the future.
Toni Hardesty, Director

2741 Idaho Department of Fish & Game: Clearwater Region
3316 16th Street 208-799-5010
Lewiston, ID 83501 *Fax:* 208-799-5012
Mission: All wildlife, including all wild animals, wild birds, and fish, within the state of Idaho, is hereby declared to be the property of the state of Idaho.
Virgil Moore, Director
Sharon Kiefer, Deputy Director

2742 Idaho Department of Fish & Game: Headquarters
600 S Walnut Street 208-334-3700
PO Box 25 *Fax:* 208-334-2114
Boise, ID 83707 www.fishandgame.idaho.gov
Mission: All wildlife, including all wild animals, wild birds, and fish, within the state of Idaho, is hereby declared to be the property of the state of Idaho.
Virgil Moore, Director
Sharon Kiefer, Deputy Director

2743 Idaho Department of Fish & Game: Magic Valley Region
324 South 417 East 208-324-4359
Suite 1 *Fax:* 208-324-1160
Jerome, ID 83338 www.fishandgame.idaho.gov
Mission: All wildlife including all wild animals, wild birds, and fish, within the state of Idaho, is hereby declared to be the property of the state of Idaho.
Virgil Moore, Director
Sharon Kiefer, Deputy Director

2744 Idaho Department of Fish & Game: McCall
555 Deinhard Lane 208-634-8137
McCall, ID 83638 *Fax:* 208-634-4320
www.fishandgame.idaho.gov
Mission: All wildlife, including all wild animals, wild birds, and fish, within the state of Idaho, is hereby declared to be the property of the state of Idaho.
Virgil Moore, Director
Sharon Kiefer, Deputy Director

2745 Idaho Department of Fish & Game: Panhandle Region
2885 West Kathleen Avenue 208-769-1414
Coeur d'Alene, ID 83815 *Fax:* 208-769-1418
www.fishandgame.idaho.gov
Mission: All wildlife, including all wild animals, wild birds, and fish, within the state of Idaho, is hereby declared to be the property of the state of Idaho.
Virgil Moore, Director
Sharon Kiefer, Deputy Director

2746 Idaho Department of Fish & Game: Salmon Region
99 Highway 93 N 208-756-2271
PO Box 1336 *Fax:* 208-756-6274
Salmon, ID 83467 www.fishandgame.idaho.gov
Mission: All wildlife, including all wild animals, wild birds, and fish, within the state of Idaho, is hereby declared to be the property of the state of Idaho.
Virgil Moore, Director
Sharon Kiefer, Deputy Director

2747 Idaho Department of Fish & Game: Southeast Region
1345 Barton Road 208-232-4703
Pocatello, ID 83204 *Fax:* 208-233-6430
www.fishandgame.idaho.gov
Mission: All wildlife, including all wild animals, wild birds, and fish, within the state of Idaho, is hereby declared to be the property of the state of Idaho.
Virgil Moore, Director
Sharon Kiefer, Deputy Director

2748 Idaho Department of Fish & Game: Southwest Region
3101 S Powerline Road 208-465-8465
Nampa, ID 83686 *Fax:* 208-465-8467
www.fishandgame.idaho.gov
Mission: All wildlife, including all wild animals, wild birds, and fish, within the state of Idaho, is hereby declared to be the property of the state of Idaho.
Virgil Moore, Director
Sharon Kiefer, Deputy Director

2749 Idaho Department of Fish & Game: Upper Snake Region
4279 Commerce Circle 208-525-7290
Idaho Falls, ID 83401 *Fax:* 208-523-7604
www.fishandgame.idaho.gov
Mission: All wildlife, including all wild animals, wild birds, and fish, within the state of Idaho, is hereby decalred to be the property of the state of Idaho.
Virgil Moore, Director
Sharon Kiefer, Deputy Director

2750 Idaho Department of Lands
300 N 6th Street, Suite 103 208-334-0200
Po Box 83720 *Fax:* 208-334-3698
Boise, ID 83720-0050 public_records_request@idl.idaho.gov
www.idl.idaho.gov

Mission: To manage endowment trust lands to maximize long-term financial returns to the benficiary institutions and provide protection to Idaho's natural resources.
Tom Schultz, Director
Kathy Opp, Deputy Director

2751 **Idaho Department of State Parks and Recreation**
PO Box 83720 208-334-4199
Boise, ID 83720 *Fax:* 208-334-5232
Manages 27 state parks. We also run the registration program for snowmobiles, boats and off-highway vehicles. Money from registrations and other sources goes to develop and maintain trails, facilities and programs statewide for thepeople who use those vehicles.
Robert L Meinen, Director

2752 **Idaho Department of Water Resources**
322 E Front Street 208-287-4800
Boise, ID 83720-98 *Fax:* 208-287-6700
IDWRInfo@idwr.idaho.gov
www.idwr.idaho.gov/about/
Working for a controlled development and wise management of Idaho's resources. Documents and reports on topics of public interest such as drought, salmon, wilderness and the Snake River Basin.

Roger Chase, Chairman
Jeffrey Raybould, Vice Chair

2753 **Idaho Geological Survey**
University of Idaho
Morrill Hall 208-885-7991
3rd Floor *Fax:* 208-885-5826
Moscow, ID 83844-3014 igs@uidaho.edu
www.idahogeology.org

Roy M Breckenridge, Director
Kurt L Othberg, Director

2754 **Idaho State Department of Agriculture**
2270 Old Penitentiary Road 208-332-8500
Boise, ID 83712 *Fax:* 208-334-2170
info@agri.idaho.gov
www.agri.idaho.gov
Celia R Gould, Director
Brian Oakey, Deputy Director

2755 **Lands Department: Soil Conservation Commission**
Po Box 790 208-332-8650
Boise, ID 83701
Responsibilities of the Commission are: organize Districts and provide assistance, coordination, information and training to Disrict supervisors; ensure that Districts function legally and properly as local subdivisions of stategovernment; administer general funds appropriated by the Idaho Legislature to Districts so they can install resource conservation practices and provide technical assistance personnel to Districts administering water quality projects and conductingsoil surveys.
Jerry Nicolescu, Administrator

Illinois

2756 **Construction Engineering Research Laboratory**
US Army Engineer Research and Development Center
PO Box 9005 217-352-6511
Champaign, IL 61826 800-USA-CERL
www.erdc.usace.army.mil/Locations/CERL
CERL conducts research to support sustainable military installations. Research is directed toward increasing the Army's ability to more efficiently construct, operate and maintain its installations and ensure environmental quality andsafety at a reduced life-cycle cost. Excellent facilities support the Army's training, readiness, mobilization and sustainability missions.
Ilker Adiguzel, Director

2757 **Department of Natural Resources: Division of Education**
Illinois Department of Natural Resources
One Natural Resources Way 217-524-4126
Springfield, IL 62702-1271 *Fax:* 217-782-9552
valerie.keener@illinois.gov
www.dnr.illinois.gov
Responsible for the development and dissemination of educational programs and materials and for training in their use. The website provides contests for students, loan materials, education materials, and grant information, in additionto graduate program information, podcasts and workshops. Overall, an excellent resource for education professionals, parents, and students.
Valerie Keener, Administrator

2758 **Environmental Protection Agency Region 5**
77 W Jackson Boulevard 312-353-2000
Chicago, IL 60604 800-621-8431
r5hotline@epa.gov
www.epa.gov/region5
This region of the EPA represents Illinois, Indiana, Michigan, Minnesota, Ohio, Wisconsin, and 35 federally recognized Tribes. The issues handled by the region include environmental justice, the National Environmental Policy Act,public affairs, and children's health, among others.
Cathy Stepp, Regional Administrator

2759 **Environmental Protection Agency: Bureau of Water Illinois**
Environmental Protection Agency Illinois
1021 North Grand Avenue E 217-782-3397
Springfield, IL 62794-9276 EPA.ContactUs@illinois.gov
www2.illinois.gov/epa/Pages/default.aspx
The mission of the Bureau of Water at EPA Illinois is to ensure the safety of rivers, streams, and lakes for all uses required, including protection of aquatic life, drinking water supply, and fish consumption. The Bureau monitors thequality of Illinois' water resources, responds to citizen complaints, and oversees permits for community water supplies.
John J. Kim, Director
Laura Roche, Deputy Director

2760 **Illinois Conservation Foundation**
One Natural Resources Way 217-785-2003
Springfield, IL 62702 *Fax:* 217-785-8405
www.ilcf.org
Established by law, the ILCF is a volunteer group with a 13-member Board, chaired by the Director of the IL Dept of Natural Resources. The role of the ILCF and its partners is to preserve and enhance our precious natural resources bysupporting and fostering ecological, educational, and recreational programs for the benefit of all citizens of Illinois and for future generations.

Wayne Rosenthal, Chairman
Barbara Ducey, Secretary

2761 **Illinois Department of Agriculture Bureau of Land and Water Resources**
PO Box 19281 217-782-2172
Springfield, IL 62794-9281 *Fax:* 217-785-4505
www.agr.state.il.us
Charles A Hartke, Director

2762 **Illinois Department of Transportation**
2300 S Dirksen Parkway 217-782-7820
Springfield, IL 62764-1 www.idot.illinois.gov
Provides cost-effective, safe and efficient transportation for the people who live, work, visit and do business in Illinois, and ensures that the system supports the state's economic growth.
Ann L Schneider, Director
Vincent E Rangel, Deputy Director

2763 **Illinois Nature Preserves Commission**
One Natural Resources Way 217-785-8686
Springfield, IL 62702 *Fax:* 217-785-2438
kelly.neal@illinois.gov
www.dnr.illinois.gov

Assists private and public landowners in protecting high quality natral areas and habitats of endangered and threatened species through voluntary dedication or registration of such lands into the Illinois Nature Preserves Systems. TheCommission also provides leadership in the areas of stewardship, management and protection.

Donald R. Dann, Chair
Kelly L. Neal, Stewardship Project Manager

2764 United States Department of the Army US Army Corps of Engineers
US Army Engineer District
Clock Tower Building 309-794-5729
PO Box 2004 *Fax:* 309-794-5793
Rock Island, IL 61204 www.usace.army.mil
Thomas Bostick, Commanding General
Todd T. Semonite, Deputy Commanding General

Indiana

2765 Indiana Department of Natural Resources
402 West Washington Street 317-232-4020
Indianapolis, IN 46204 *Fax:* 317-232-8036
www.ai.org/dnr
Protects, enhances, preserves, and wisely uses natural, cultural, and recreational resources for the benefit of Indiana's citizens through professional leadership, management and education.
Robert E Carter, Director
Todd Tande, Deputy Director

2766 Indiana State Department of Agriculture, Soil Conservation
One North Capitol Avenue 317-232-8770
Suite 600 *Fax:* 317-232-1362
Indianapolis, IN 46204 www.in.gov/isda
Mission: To facilitate the protection and enhancement of Indiana's land and water.
Ted McKinney, Director
Melissa Rekeweg, Deputy Director

2767 Indiana State Department of Health
2 N Meridan Street 317-233-1325
Indianapolis, IN 46204 www.in.gov/isdh/
Mission: To support Indiana's economic prosperity and quality of life by promoting, protecting and providing for the health of Hoosiers in their communities.
Judith A Monroe, State Health Commissioner
Mary L Hill, Deputy State Health Commiss.

2768 Natural Resources Department: Fish & Wildlife
402 West Washington Street RMW273 317-232-4080
Indianapolis, IN 46204 *Fax:* 317-232-8150
dfw@dnr.in.gov
www.in.gov/dnr/fishwild
Mission: To professionally manage Indiana's fish and wildlife for present and future generations, balancing ecological, recreational, and economic benefits.

Iowa

2769 Iowa Association of County Conservation Boards
405 SW 3rd Street 515-963-9582
Suite 1 *Fax:* 515-963-9582
Ankeny, IA 50023 iaccb@ecity.net
www.ecity.net/iaccb
IACCB is a nonprofit organization assisting member county conservation boards in areas of board member education, public relations and legislation. The association's main purposes are to promote the objectives and supplement theactivities of conservation boards, exchange information, assist boards and members in program development and provide a unified voice in the legislature. IACCB is governed by a nine-member board elected by member counties.

2770 Iowa Department of Agriculture, and Land Stewardship Division of Soil Conservation
502 E 9th 515-281-5321
Wallace State Office Building *Fax:* 515-281-6170
Des Moines, IA 50319 www.iowaagriculture.gov/
The Division of Soil Conservation is responsible for state leadership in the protection and management of soil, water and mineral resources, assisting soil and water conservation districts and private landowners to meet theiragricultural and environmental protection needs.
Chuck Gipp, Director
Karen Fynaardt, Administrative Assistant

2771 Iowa Department of Natural Resources Administrative Services Division
502 E 9th Street 515-281-5918
Wallace Office Building *Fax:* 515-281-8895
Des Moines, IA 50319-34 www.iowadnr.com
Aims to manage, protect, conserve and develop Iowa's natural resources in cooperation with other public and private organizations and individuals, so that the quality of life for Iowans is significantly enhanced by the use, enjoymentand understanding of those resources.

2772 Iowa State Extension Services
2150 Beardshear Hall 515-294-6192
Ames, IA 55011-2031 *Fax:* 515-294-4715
jlpease@iastate.edu
www.extension.iastate.edu/
Dr James L Pease, Specialist

2773 Natural Resource Department
502 E 9th Street 515-281-5385
Des Moines, IA 50319-34 *Fax:* 515-281-8895
www.iowadnr.com
Mission: To conserve and enhance our natural resources in cooperation with individuals and organizations to improve the quality of life for Iowans and ensure a legacy for future generations.
Richard Leopold, Director
Liz Christiansen, Deputy Director

Kansas

2774 Emporia Research and Survey Office Kansas Department of Wildlife & Parks
1830 Merchant
512 SE 25th Ave 620-672-5911
1830 Merchant www.ksoutdoors.com
Emporia, KS 67124-1525
Randy Doll, Commissioner
Robert J. Wilson, Commissioner

2775 Environmental Protection Agency Region 7: Air & Radiation Division
11201 Renner Boulevard 913-551-7003
Lenexa, KS 66219 800-223-0425
www.epa.gov/region7/
This division is responsible for management of programs for air, hazardous waste, toxic substances, radiation and pollution prevention in Iowa, Kansas, Missouri, Nebraska, and Nine Tribal Nations. Under the Clean Air Act, the divisionaims to reduce emissions by working with federal agencies, state and local agencies, tribal governments, and the private sector.
Mark Smith, Director

2776 Health & Environment Department: Air & Radiation
1000 SW Jackson 785-296-1593
Suite 310 *Fax:* 785-296-8464
Topeka, KS 66612 jmitchell@kdheks.gov
www.kdheks.gov/bar
Mission: To protect the public from the harmful effects of radiation and air pollution and conserve the natural resources of the state by preventing damage to the environment from releases of radioactive materials or air contaminants.
Rick Bruneti, Director

2777 Health & Environment Department: Environment Division
1000 SW Jackson Street 785-296-1535
Suite 400 *Fax:* 785-296-8464
Topeka, KS 66612-1367 jmitchell@kdheks.gov
www.kdheks.gov/environment
The mission of the Division of Environment is the protection of the public health and environment. The division conducts regulatory programs involving public water supplies, industrial discharges, wastewater treatment systems, solidswaste landfills, hazardous waste, air emissions, radioactive materials, asbestos removal, refined petroleum storage tanks and other sources which impact the environment.
John Michtell, Director
Sam Brownback, Secretary

2778 Health & Environment Department: Waste Management
1000 SW Jackson 785-296-1600
Suite 320 *Fax:* 785-296-8909
Topeka, KS 66612-1366 www.kdheks.gov/waste
Regulates landfills, HHW, Hazardous Waste Permitting, Solid Waste Permitting, Public Outreach, Illegal Dumps.
John Michtell, Director
Sam Brownback, Secretary

2779 Kansas Cooperative Fish & Wildlife Research Unit
Kansas State University
205 Leasure Hall 785-532-6070
Manhattan, KS 66506 *Fax:* 785-532-7159
kscfwru@ksu.edu
www.k-state.edu/kscfwru
Unit Research contributes to understanding ecological systems within the Great Plains. Unit staff, collaborators, and graduate students conduct research with both natural and altered systems, particularly those impacted by agriculture.Unit projects investigate ways to maintain a rich diversity of endemic wild animals and habitats while meeting the needs of people. The Unit focuses on projects that involve graduate students, and the research needs of cooperators are given priority.
David Haukos, Leader
Jack Cully Jr, Assistant Leader

2780 Kansas Corporation Commission Conservation Division
266 N. Main St. 316-337-6200
Ste 220 *Fax:* 316-337-6211
Wichita, KS 67202-1513 www.kcc.state.ks.us
State of Kansas oilfield regulatory agency. The KCC is responsible for the preservation of Kansas' hydro and carbo resources, protection of corrullative right and the prevention and remediation of oil field pollution.
Shari Feist, Chair
Jay Scott Emler, Commissioner

2781 Kansas Department of Health & Environment
1000 SW Jackson Street 785-296-1500
Topeka, KS 66612 *Fax:* 785-368-6368
info@kdhe.state.ks.us
www.kdheks.gov
An organization dedicated to optimizing the promotion and protection of the health of Kansas through efficient and effective public health programs and services and through preservation, protection and remediation of natural resourcesof the environment.
Susan Brownback, Secretary
Aaron Dunkel, Deputy Secretary

2782 Kansas Department of Wildlife & Parks Region 2
300 SW Wanamaker Road 785-273-6740
Topeka, KS 66606 *Fax:* 785-273-6757
www.ksoutdoors.com/
Manages and promotes the wildlife and natural resources of Kansas. Administered by a secetary of Wildlife and Parks and is advised by a seven-member Wildlife and Parks Commission.
Randy Doll, Commissioner
Robert J. Wilson, Commissioner

2783 Kansas Department of Wildlife & Parks Region 3
1001 McArtor Drive 620-227-8609
Dodge City, KS 67801-6024 *Fax:* 620-227-8600
www.ksoutdoors.com/
Randy Doll, Commissioner
Robert J. Wilson, Commissioner

2784 Kansas Department of Wildlife & Parks Region 4
6232 E 29th Street N 316-683-8069
Wichita, KS 67220 www.ksoutdoors.com/
Randy Doll, Commissioner
Robert J. Wilson, Commissioner

2785 Kansas Department of Wildlife & Parks Region 5
1500 W 7th Street 620-431-0380
Po Box 777 *Fax:* 620-431-0381
Chanute, KS 66720-777 www.ksoutdoors.com/
This region is made up of 18 counties in the southeastern corner of the state. This area is dominated by the Osage Questas physiographic region, which is characterized by rolling grasslands, limestone bluffs, and heavily timberedbottomlands.
Randy Doll, Commissioner
Robert J. Wilson, Commissioner

2786 Kansas Department of Wildlife and Parks
512 SE 25th Avenue 620-672-5911
Topeka, KS 66612-1327 *Fax:* 620-672-2972
www.ksoutdoors.com
Randy Doll, Commissioner
Robert J. Wilson, Commissioner

2787 Kansas Geological Survey
University of Kansas
1930 Constant Avenue 785-864-3965
Lawrence, KS 66047-3724 *Fax:* 785-864-5317
webadmin@kgs.ku.edu
www.kgs.ku.edu
Conducts geological studies and research and collects, correlates, preserves and disseminates information leading to a better understanding of the geology of Kansas, with special emphasis on nautral resources of economic value, waterquality and quantity and geologic hazards. This information is published in books and maps both technical and educational and also provides computer programs and data bases derived from geologic investigations.
Rex C. Buchanan, Director & State Geologist

2788 Kansas Health & Environmental Laboratories
6810 SE Dwight Street 785-296-0801
Building 740 *Fax:* 785-296-1641
Topeka, KS 66620-1401 www.kdhe.state.ks.us/labs
Provides timely and accurate analytical information for public health benefit in Kansas and assures the quality of statewide laboratory sevices though certification and improvement programs.
Leo Hanning, Interim Director
N. Myron Gunsalus, Jr., Director

2789 Kansas Water Office
901 S Kansas Avenue 785-296-3185
Topeka, KS 66612 888-526-9283
Fax: 785-296-0878
kwo-info@kwo.ks.gov
www.kwo.org
Works to achieve proactive solutions for resource issues of the state and to ensure good quality water to meet the needs of the people and the environment of Kansas. Evaluates and develops public policies, coordinating the waterresource operations of agencies at all levels of government.
Tracy Streeter, Director
Earl Lewis, Assistant Director

2790 Pratt Operations Office Kansas Department of Wildlife & Parks
512 SE 25th Avenue 620-672-5911
Pratt, KS 67124 www.ksoutdoors.com
Randy Doll, Commissioner
Robert J. Wilson, Commissioner

Kentucky

2791 Attorney General's Office Civil and Environmental Law Division
700 Capitol Avenue 502-696-5300
Capitol Building, Suite 118
Frankfort, KY 40601
Jack Conway, Attorney General
Margaret Everson, Asst Deputy Attorney General

2792 Department for Energy Development & Independence
500 Mero Street 502-564-7192
12th Floor Capital Plaza Tower *Fax:* 502-564-7484
Frankfort, KY 40601 amanda.cook@ky.gov
www.energy.ky.gov
Provides leadership to maximize the benefits of energy effeciency and alternate energy through awareness, technology development, energy preparedness and new partnerships and resources.
Greg Guess, Director
John Davies, Deputy Commissioner

2793 Department for Environmental Protection
300 Fair Oaks Lane 502-564-0323
Frankfort, KY 40601 *Fax:* 502-564-4245
envhelp@ky.gov
www.dep.ky.gov
Mission: To protect and enhance Kentucky's environment. This mission is important because it has a direct impact on Kentucky's public health, our citizens' safety and the quality of Kentucky's valuable natural resources-ourenvironment.
Robert W Logan, Commisioner

2794 Division of Mine Reclamation and Enforcement
Two Hudson Hollow Road 502-564-2340
Frankfort, KY 40601 *Fax:* 502-564-5848
j.hamon@ky.gov
www.dmre.ky.gov
The Division of Mine Reclamation and Enforcement is responsible for inspecting all surface and underground coal mining permits in the state to assure compliance with the 1977 Federal Surface Mining Control Act. The DMRE is alsoresponsible for regulating and enforcing the surface mining reclamation laws for non-coal mining sites in the state, including limestone, sand, gravel, clay, shale and the surface effects of dredging river sand and gravel.

2795 Economic Development Cabinet: Community Development Department Brokerage Division
Old Capitol Annex 502-564-7140
300 West Broadway 800-626-2930
Frankfort, KY 40601 *Fax:* 502-564-3256
econdev@ky.gov
www.thinkkentucky.com
Responsible for encouraging job creation and retention, and new investment in the state
Larry Hayes, Secretary
Hollie Spade, Chief of Staff

2796 Environmental Protection Department: Waste Management Division
200 Fair Oaks Lane 502-564-6716
4th Floor *Fax:* 502-564-4049
Frankfort, KY 40601 waste@ky.gov
www.waste.ky.gov
Mission: To protect human health and the environment by minimizing adverse impacts on all citizens of the commonwealth through the development and implementation of fair, equitable and effective waste management programs.
Anthony Hatton, Director
Jon Maybriar, Assistant Director

2797 Environmental Protection Department: Water Division
200 Fair Oaks Lane 502-564-6716
4th Floor *Fax:* 502-564-4049
Frankfort, KY 40601 water@ky.gov
www.water.ky.gov
To manage, protect and enhance the quality of the Commonwealth's water resources for present and future generations through voluntary, regulatory and educational programs
Anthony Hatton, Director
Jon Maybriar, Assistant Director

2798 Fish and Wildlife Resources Department: Fisheries Division
1 Sportsman's Lane 502-564-3596
1 Sportsman's Lane 800-858-1549
Frankfort, KY 40601 *Fax:* 502-564-6501
info.center@ky.gov
www.fw.ky.gov
Mission: To conserve and enhance fish and wildlife resources and provide opportunity for hunting, fishing, trapping, boating and other wildlife related activities.
John Gassett, Commissioner
Benjy T Kinman, Fisheries Director

2799 Kentucky Department for Public Health
275 E Main Street 502-564-5497
Franfort, KY 40621 800-372-2973
Fax: 502-564-9523
www.chfs.ky.gov/dph
Stephanie Mayfield Gibson, Commissioner

2800 Kentucky Environmental and Public Protection Cabinet
500 Metro Street 502-564-3350
Capital Plaza Tower, 5th Floor *Fax:* 502-564-3354
Frankfort, KY 40601
Provides a safe, clean environment in the Commonwealth, while working with business and industry to help ensure adequate jobs and a strong economy.
Teresa J Hill, Secretary

2801 Kentucky State Cooperative Extension Services
University of Kentucky
S-107 Agricultural Science Bldg N 859-257-4302
Lexington, KY 40546-91 *Fax:* 859-257-3501
jimmy.henning@uky.edu
www.ca.uky.edu/ces
Jimmy Henning, Director
Gary Palmer, Assistant Director

2802 Kentucky State Nature Preserves Commission
801 Schenkel Lane 502-573-2886
Frankfort, KY 40601 *Fax:* 502-573-2355
naturepreserves@ky.gov
www.naturepreserves.ky.gov
Aims to protect Kentucky's natural heritage by identifying, acquiring and managing natural areas that represent the best known occurrences of rare native species and natural communities and working together to protect biologicaldiversity.
Don Dott, Director

2803 Natural Resources Department: Conservation Division
#2 Hudson Hollow 502-564-2320
Frankfort, KY 40601 *Fax:* 502-564-6079
www.conservation.ky.gov
Assists Kentucky's local conservation districts in the development and implementation of sound soil and water conservation programs to manage, enhance, and promote the wise use of the Commonwealth's natural resources.
Stephen A Coleman, Director

2804 Natural Resources Department: Division of Forestry
500 Mero Street 502-564-2674
Capital Plaza Tower *Fax:* 502-564-6553
Frankfort, KY 40601 www.eqc.ky.gov
Steve Coleman, Chairman
Amrita Gadson, Executive Director

2805 Natural Resources and Environment Protection Cabinet: Environmental Quality Commission
500 Mero Street 502-564-2674
Capital Plaza Tower eqc@ky.gov
Frankfort, KY 40601 www.eqc.ky.gov
To serve as an advisory board to the governor and other state officials on environmental matters
Steve Coleman, Chairman
Steve Coleman, Vice Chairman

2806 Tourism Cabinet: Parks Department
Capital Plaza Tower 22nd floor 502-564-4930
500 Metro Street 800-225-8747
Frankfort, KY 40601 www.kentuckytourism.com/stateparks
Mike Mangeot, Commissioner
Hank Phillips, Deputy Commissioner

Louisiana

2807 Agriculture & Forestry: Soil & Water Conservation
Louisiana Department of Agriculture and Forestry
5825 Florida Blvd 866-927-2476
Baton Rouge, LA 70821-3554 *Fax:* 225-922-2577
www.ldaf.state.la.us
To sustain and conserve water quality and soil stability on croplands, woodlands, grasslands, wetlands and waterways of Louisiana
Mike Strain, Commissioner
Brad Spicer, Assistant Commissioner

2808 Culture, Recreation and Tourism
PO Box 94361 225-342-8115
Baton Rouge, LA 70802 *Fax:* 225-342-3207
ltgov@crt.la.gov
www.crt.state.la.us
Desireé W. Honoré, Undersecretary
Shirley S Johnson, Executive Assistant

2809 Department of Natural Resources: Office of Mineral Resources
617 North Third Street 225-342-4615
PO Box 2827 *Fax:* 225-342-4527
Baton Rouge, LA 70821-2827 www.dnr.louisiana.gov/MIN/
Provides staff support to the State Mineral Board in granting and administering leases on state-owned lands and waterbottoms for the production and development of minerals, primarily oil and gas, for the purpose of optimizing revenueto the state from the royalties, bonuses and rentals generated therefrom.
Stacey Talley, Deputy Assistant Secretary

2810 Louisiana Department of Natural Resources
PO Box 94396 225-342-4500
Baton Rouge, LA 70804-9396 *Fax:* 225-342-5861
www.dnr.louisiana.gov/
To preserve and enhance the nonrenewable natural resources of the state, consisting of land, water, oil, gas, and other minerals, through conservation, regulation, management and development to ensure that the state of Louisianarealizes appropriate economic benefit from its asset base
Stephen Chustz, Secretary
Lori LeBlanc, Deputy Secretary

2811 Louisiana Cooperative Extension Services
101 J. Norman Efferson Hall 225-578-4161
110 LSU Union Square *Fax:* 225-578-4225
Baton Rouge, LA 70803-106 www.lsuagcenter.com/
To provide the people of Louisiana with research-based educational information that will improve their lives and economic well-being
Bill Richardson, Chancellor

2812 Louisiana Department of Natural Resources Office of Coastal Restoration and Management
617 North Third Street 225-342-7591
Baton Rouge, LA 70821 800-267-4019
Fax: 225-342-9439
www.dnr.louisiana.gov/
Develops, implements and monitors costal vegetated wetland restoration, creation and conservation measures. Preforms engineering, planning and monitoring functions essential to successful development and implementation of wetlandconservation and restoration plans and projects as directed by the Costal Wetlands Conservation and Restoration Plan.
Keith Lowell, Acting Assistant Secretary

2813 Natural Resources: Conservation Office
617 N 3rd Street 225-342-5540
PO Box 94275 *Fax:* 225-342-3705
Baton Rouge, LA 70802 www.dnr.louisiana.gov
Regulatory oil and gas agency, State of Louisiana.
James H Welsh, Commissioner of Conservation
Gary P Ross, Asst. Commissioner, Conserva

2814 Natural Resources: Injection & Mining Division
PO Box 94275 225-342-5515
Baton Rouge, LA 70804 *Fax:* 225-342-3094
Injection-Mining@la.gov
www.dnr.louisiana.gov
Has the responsibility for implementation of major environmental programs statutorily charged to the Office of Conservation. Administers a regulatory and permit program to protect underground sources of drinking water fromendangerment; is responsible for regulating exploration, development and surface mining operations for coal and lignite; and protection of state and private lands.
Joseph S Ball Jr, Director
Laurence Bland, Assistant Director

Maine

2815 Maine Cooperative Fish & Wildlife Research Unit
University of Maine
USGS Biological ResourcesDiscipline 207-581-2862
5755 Nutting Hall *Fax:* 207-581-2858
Orono, ME 00446
Mission: To facilitate and strengthen professional education and training of fisheries and wildlife scientists; carry out research programs of aquatic, mammalian, and avian organisms and their habitats; and disseminate research resultsthrough the appropriate media, especially peer-review scientific articles.
Dr Cyndy Loftin, Leader

2816 Maine Department Of Inland Fisheries & Wildlife
284 State Street 207-287-8000
41 State House Station *Fax:* 207-287-6395
Augusta, ME 00433-0041 www.maine.gov/ifw
The Department of Inland Fisheries & Wildlife was established to ensure that all species of wildlife and aquatic resources in the State of Maine are maintained and perpetuated for their intrinsic and ecological values, for theireconomic contribution, and for their recreational, scientific and educational use by the people of the State. The Department is also responsible for the establishment and enforcement of rules and regulations.
Chandler E. Woodcock, Commissioner
Andrea Erskine, Deputy Commissioner

2817 Maine Department of Environmental Protection: Augusta
17 State House Station 207-287-7688
28 Tyson Drive 800-452-1942
Augusta, ME 00433-17 *Fax:* 207-287-7826
www.maine.gov/dep
Responsible for environmental protection and regulation in the state of Maine. Engages in a wide range of activities, makes reccomendations to the Legistlature regarding measures to minimize and eliminate environmental pollution,grants licenses, initiates enforcement actions, and provides information and technical assistance.
Robert A. Foley, Chair
Alvin K. Ahlers, Director

2818 Maine Department of Conservation
22 State House Station 207-287-3200
Augusta, ME 00433 *Fax:* 207-287-2400
DACF@Maine.gov
www.maine.gov/doc
To oversee the management, development and protection of some of Maine's most special places: 17 million acres of forest land, 10.4 million acres of unorganized territory, 48 parks and historic sites and more than 590,000 acres ofpublic-reserved and non-reserved land
Walter E. Whitcomb, Commissioner

2819 Maine Department of Conservation: Ashland Regional Office
45 Radar Road 207-435-7963
Ashland, ME 00473 *Fax:* 207-435-7184
DACF@Maine.gov
www.maine.gov/doc
To oversee the management, development and protection of some of Maine's most special places: 17 million acres of forest land, 10.4 million acres of unorganized territory, 48 parks and historic sites and more than 590,000 acres ofpublic-reserved and non-reserved land
Don Cote, Compliance Investigator
Billie J. MacLean, Regional Representative

2820 Maine Department of Conservation: Bangor Regional Office
106 Hogan Road 207-941-4014
BMHI Complex *Fax:* 207-941-4222
Bangor, ME 00440 DACF@Maine.gov
www.maine.gov/doc
To oversee the management, development and protection of some of Maine's most special places: 17 million acres of forest land, 10.4 million acres of unorganized territory, 48 parks and historic sites and more than 590,000 acres ofpublic-reserved and non-reserved land

2821 Maine Department of Conservation: Bolton Hill Regional Office
22 State House Station 207-624-3700
Augusta, ME 00433-22 *Fax:* 207-287-8534
DACF@Maine.gov
www.maine.gov/doc
To oversee the management, development and protection of some of Maine's most special places: 17 million acres of forest land, 10.4 million acres of unorganized territory, 48 parks and historic sites and more than 590,000 acres ofpublic-reserved and non-reserved land
Walter E. Whitcomb, Commissioner

2822 Maine Department of Conservation: Bureau of Parks & Lands
22 State House Station 207-287-3821
2nd & 1st Floors *Fax:* 207-287-3823
Augusta, ME 00433-22 DACF@Maine.gov
www.maine.gov/doc
To oversee the management, development and protection of some of Maine's most special places: 17 million acres of forest land, 10.4 million acres of unorganized territory, 48 parks and historic sites and more than 590,000 acres ofpublic-reserved and non-reserved land
Walter E. Whitcomb, Commissioner

2823 Maine Department of Conservation: Entomology Laboratory
22 State House Station 207-287-2431
Augusta, ME 00433-22 *Fax:* 207-287-2432
DACF@Maine.gov
www.maine.gov/doc
To oversee the management, development and protection of some of Maine's most special places: 17 million acres of forest land, 10.4 million acres of unorganized territory, 48 parks and historic sites and more than 590,000 acres ofpublic-reserved and non-reserved land
Walter E. Whitcomb, Commissioner

2824 Maine Department of Conservation: Farmington Regional Office
129 Main Street 207-778-8231
PO Box 327 *Fax:* 207-778-5932
Farmington, ME 00493 DACF@Maine.gov
www.maine.gov/doc
To oversee the management, development and protection of some of Maine's most special places: 17 million acres of forest land, 10.4 million acres of unorganized territory, 48 parks and historic sites and more than 590,000 acres ofpublic-reserved and non-reserved land

2825 Maine Department of Conservation: Greenville Regional Office
43 Lakeview Street 207-695-2466
PO Box 1107 *Fax:* 207-695-2380
Greenville, ME 00444-1107 DACF@Maine.gov
www.maine.gov/doc
To oversee the management, development and protection of some of Maine's most special places: 17 million acres of forest land, 10.4 million acres of unorganized territory, 48 parks and historic sites and more than 590,000 acres ofpublic-reserved and non-reserved land
Keith Smith, Regional Representative

2826 Maine Department of Conservation: Hallowell Regional Office
Winthrop Street 207-624-6080
Stevens Complex *Fax:* 207-287-5081
Hallowell, ME 00433 DACF@Maine.gov
www.maine.gov/doc
To oversee the management, development and protection of some of Maine's most special places: 17 million acres of forest land, 10.4 million acres of unorganized territory, 48 parks and historic sites and more than 590,000 acres ofpublic-reserved and non-reserved land

2827 Maine Department of Conservation: Jonesboro Regional Office
Route 1A 207-434-2627
PO Box 130 *Fax:* 207-434-2624
Jonesboro, ME 00464 DACF@Maine.gov
www.maine.gov/doc
To oversee the management, development and protection of some of Maine's most special places: 17 million acres of forest land, 10.4 million acres of unorganized territory, 48 parks and historic sites and more than 590,000 acres ofpublic-reserved and non-reserved land

2828 Maine Department of Conservation: Land Use Regulation Commission
22 State House Station 207-287-2631
4th Floor *Fax:* 207-287-7439
Augusta, ME 00433-22 DACF@Maine.gov
www.maine.gov/doc
The Maine Land Use Regulation Commission meets monthly in various locations throughout the state to discuss jurisdiction-related issues and to act upon pending cases.
Walter E. Whitcomb, Commissioner

2829 Maine Department of Conservation: Millinocket Regional Office
191 Main Street 207-746-2244
East Millinocket, ME 00443 *Fax:* 207-746-2243
DACF@Maine.gov
www.maine.gov/doc

To oversee the management, development and protection of some of Maine's most special places: 17 million acres of forest land, 10.4 million acres of unorganized territory, 48 parks and historic sites and more than 590,000 acres ofpublic-reserved and non-reserved land
Marc Russell, Regional Representative

2830 Maine Department of Conservation: Old Town Regional Office
87 Airport Road 207-827-1800
PO Box 415 *Fax:* 207-827-6295
Old Town, ME 00446 DACF@Maine.gov
www.maine.gov/doc

To oversee the management, development and protection of some of Maine's most special places: 17 million acres of forest land, 10.4 million acres of unorganized territory, 48 parks and historic sites and more than 590,000 acres ofpublic-reserved and non-reserved land

2831 Maine Department of Conservation: Rangeley Regional Office
133 Fyfe Road 207-670-7493
PO Box 307 *Fax:* 207-864-5252
West Farmington, ME 00499 DACF@Maine.gov
www.maine.gov/doc

To oversee the management, development and protection of some of Maine's most special places: 17 million acres of forest land, 10.4 million acres of unorganized territory, 48 parks and historic sites and more than 590,000 acres ofpublic-reserved and non-reserved land
Sara Brusila, Regional Representative

2832 Maine Department of Environmental Protection: Presque Isle
744 Main Street 207-764-2105
Skyway Park 888-769-1053
Presque Isle, ME 00476 *Fax:* 207-764-2035
DACF@Maine.gov
www.maine.gov/doc

2833 Maine Department of Environmental Protection: Portland
17 State House Station 207-287-7688
28 Tyson Drive 888-769-1036
Augusta, ME 00433-17 *Fax:* 207-287-7826
www.maine.gov/dep

Robert A. Foley, Chair
Alvin K. Ahlers, Director

2834 Maine Natural Areas Program
22 State House Station 207-287-3200
Augusta, ME 00433-93 *Fax:* 207-287-2400
dacf@maine.gov
www.maine.gov/dacf

Mission: To ensure the maintenance of Maine's natural heritage for the benefit of present and future generations. MNAP facilitates informed decision-making in development planning, conservation, and natural resources management. TheProgram's success relies upon using consistent and objective methods to collect, organize, and interpret information.
Molly Docherty, Director

2835 Maine Sea Grant College Program
University of Maine
5784 York Complex 207-581-1435
The University of Maine *Fax:* 207-581-1426
Orono, ME 00446-5784 umseagrant@maine.edu
www.seagrant.umaine.edu

Paul Anderson, Director
Beth Bisson, Assistant Director

2836 Northeastern Forest Fire Protection Compact
P.O. Box 6192 207-968-3782
21 Parmenter Terrace *Fax:* 207-968-3782
China Village, ME 00492 info@nffpc.org
www.nffpc.org

The mandate of the Northeastern Forest Fire Protection Commission is to provide the means for its member states and provinces to cope with fires that might be beyond the capabilities of a singler member through infromation, technologyand resources sharing activities.
Tom Parent, Executive Director

2837 University of Maine Cooperative Extension Forestry & Wildlife Office
5741 Libby Hall 207-581-3188
Room 105 *Fax:* 207-581-3466
Orono, ME 00446-5741 extension@maine.edu
www.extension.umaine.edu/

Catherine Elliott, Wildlife Specialist
Les Hyde, Extension Educator

Massachusetts

2838 Connecticut River Salmon Association
16 Forest Road 860-519-7451
West Hartford, CT 06119 info@ctriversalmon.org
www.ctriversalmon.org

To support the effort to restore Atlantic salmon in the Connecticut River basin.

Tom Chrosniak, President
Richard Bell, Vice President

2839 Department of Agricultural Resources
251 Causeway Street 617-626-1700
Suite 500 *Fax:* 617-626-1850
Boston, MA 00211 dwebber@state.ma.us
www.mass.gov/eea/agencies/agr/

The Bureau of Animal Health focuses its efforts on ensuring the health and safety of the Commonwealth's domestic animals. Through diligent inspection, examination, licensing, quarantine, and enforcement of laws, regulations and ordersand the provision of technical assistance the Bureau promotes the welfare of companion and food-producing animals in Massachusetts.
John Lebeaux, Commissioner

2840 Department of Environmental Protection
100 Cambridge Street 617-626-1000
Suite 900 *Fax:* 617-626-4900
Boston, MA 00211 env.internet@state.ma.us
www.mass.gov/eea

The Department of Environmental Protection is the state agency responsible for ensuring clean air and water, the safe management of toxics and hazards, the recycling of solid and hazardous wastes, the timely cleanup of hazardous wastesites and spills, and the preservation of wetlands and coastal resources.
Arleen O'Donnell, Acting Commissioner

2841 Department of Fish & Game
251 Causeway Street 617-626-1500
Suite 400 *Fax:* 617-626-1505
Boston, MA 00211 www.wildlife.ca.gov/

The Department of Fish & Game works to preserve the state's natural resources and people's right to conservation of those resources, as protected by Article 97 of the Massachusetts Constitution. To carry out this mission, theDepartment exercises responsibility over the Commonwealth's marine and freshwater fisheries, wildlife species, plants, and natural communities, as well as the habitats that support them.
Mary B Griffin, Commissioner

2842 Environmental Affairs Bureau of Markets
251 Causeway Street 617-626-1750
Suite 500 *Fax:* 617-626-1850
Boston, MA 00211 www.massdfa.org/agricult.html

2843 Environmental Affairs: Hazardous Waste Facilities Site Safety Council
100 Cambridge Street 617-727-6629
Boston, MA 00220
www.environment.gov.za/branches/chemiclas_wastemanagement

2844 Environmental Protection Agency Region 1
5 Post Office Square 617-918-1011
Suite 100 888-372-7341
Boston, MA 02109-3912 www.epa.gov/region1
This region of the EPA covers the states of New England, as well as ten Tribal Nations. The goal of the region is to allow the people of New England to live in an environment that is healthier, cleaner, and more prosperous than adecade ago.
Deborah Szaro, Regional Administrator

2845 Environmental Protection Agency: Region 1 Air and Radiation Division
5 Post Office Square 888-372-7341
Suite 100 www.epa.gov/region1
Boston, MA 02109-3912
The Air and Radiation Division of Region 1 administers programs relating to air quality, including air grants, State and Federal Implementation Plans, and National Emission Standards for Hazardous Air Pollutants.
Lynne Hamjian, Director

2846 Executive Office of Energy & Environmental Affairs
Executive Office of Environmental Affairs
100 Cambridge Street 617-626-1000
Suite 900 *Fax:* 617-626-4900
Boston, MA 00211 env.internet@state.ma.us
www.mass.gov/envir/eoea.htm
Richard K. Sullivan, Secretary
Kathleen Baskin, Director of Water Policy

2847 Massachusetts Highway Department
10 Park Plaza 857-368-4636
Suite 4160 877-623-6846
Boston, MA 00211 *Fax:* 857-368-0601
www.massdot.state.ma.us/highway/Main.aspx
To deliver excellent customer service to people who travel in the Commonwealth, and provide our nation's safest and most reliable transportation system in a way that strengthens our economy and quality of life
Luisa Paiewonsky, Commissioner
Charlie Baker, Governor

2848 New England Interstate Water Pollution Control Commission
650 Suffolk Street 978-323-7929
Suite 410 *Fax:* 978-323-7919
Lowell, MA 00185 mail@neiwpcc.org
www.neiwpcc.org
The New England Interstate Water Pollution Control Commission, a nonprofit interstate agency established by an Act of Congress, serves and assist its members states individually and collectively by providing coordination, publiceducation, training and leadership in the management and protection of water quality in the New England Region and New York.
Peter LaFlamme, Chair
Yvonne Bolton, Vice Chairman

2849 United States Department of the Army US Army Corps of Engineers
696 Virginia Road 978-318-8220
Concord, MA 00174 *Fax:* 978-318-8821
www.usace.army.mil
Thomas Bostick, Commanding General
Todd T. Semonite, Deputy Commanding General

2850 Waquoit Bay National Estuarine Research Reserve
131 Waquoit Highway 508-457-0495
PO Box 3092 *Fax:* 617-727-5537
Waquoit, MA 00253 www.waquoitbayreserve.org
In 1979, The Commonwealth of Massachusetts designated Waquoit Bay as an Area of Critical Environment Concern (ACEC) in recognition of its significant natural resources. The designation provides a state-wide umbrella of protection andoversight under the exisiting regulations of different state agencies which include higher standards of protection for ACEC's. The Waquoit Bay ACEC includes parts of the Bay proper. Although the ACEC covers 2522 acres, including Washburn Island andSouth Cape Beach.
Alison Leschen, Reserve Manager
Sheri Proft, Fiscal Administrator

Maryland

2851 Chesapeake Bay Executive Council
410 Severn Avenue 410-267-5700
Suite 112 800-908-7229
Annapolis, MD 21403 *Fax:* 410-267-5777
www.chesapeakebay.net
The Chesapeake Bay Executive Council establishes the policy direction for the restoration and protection of the Chesapeake Bay and its living resources. A series of Directives, Agreements, and Amendments signed by the ExecutiveCouncil set goals and guide policy for the Bay restoration. The Council meets annually.
Nicholas DiPasquale, Chairman
Greg Barranco, Coordinator

2852 Interstate Commission on the Potomac River Basin
30 West Gude Drive 301-984-1908
Suite 450 *Fax:* 301-984-5841
Rockville, MD 20850 info@icprb.org
www.potomacriver.org
The Interstate Commission on the Potomac River Basin is an interstate compact agency established to help protect the Potomac River and its 14,670-square-mile watershed. Its mission is to enhance, protect, and conserve the water andassociated land resources of the Potomac River and its tributaries through regional and interstate cooperation.
Carlton Haywood, Executive Director
Bo Park, Administrative Officer

2853 Maryland Department of Agriculture
50 Harry S Truman Parkway 410-841-5700
Annapolis, MD 21401 800-492-5590
Fax: 410-841-5914
www.mda.state.md.us
Established on the basis of agriculture's growing importance and impact to the economy of the state. Many activities are regulatory in nature, others are assigned to a category of public service and some are educational or promotionalin scope. All are intended to provide the maximum protection possible for the consumer as well as promote the economic well-being of farmers, food and fiber processors and businesses engage in agricultural related operations.
Earl F Hance, Secretary

2854 Maryland Department of Agriculture: State Soil Conservation Committee
50 Harry S Truman Parkway 410-841-5863
Annapolis, MD 21401 *Fax:* 410-841-5736
www.mda.state.md.us
Bill Giese, Chair
Charles Rice, Vice Chairman

2855 Maryland Department of Health and Mental Hygiene
201 W Preston Street 410-767-6500
Baltimore, MD 21201 877-463-3464
Fax: 410-767-6489
dhmh.healthmd@maryland.gov
www.dhmh.maryland.gov
The Maryland Department of Health and Mental Hygiene's mission is to protect and promote health and prevent disease and injury. This is accomplished through the provision of population-based health services and core public health;assessment, assurance and policy development.
Joshua M. Sharfstein, Secretary

2856 Maryland Department of the Environment: Water Management Field Office
160 South Water Street 301-689-5756
Frostburg, MD 21532 *Fax:* 301-689-6544
www.mde.state.md.us
To restore and maintain the quality of the State's ground and surface waters, protect wetland habitats throughout the State, and manage the utilization of Maryland's mineral resources.
Scott Boylan, Program Chief
Tamara Davis, Manager

2857 Maryland Department of the Environment/Water Management: Nontidal Wetlands & Waterways
201 Baptist Street 410-713-3680
Suite 15 *Fax:* 410-713-3681
Salisbury, MD 21801 www.mde.state.md.us
Jay Bozman, Manager

2858 Maryland Department of the Environment: Air & Radiation Management Field Office
201 Baptist Street 410-713-3680
Suite 15 *Fax:* 410-713-3681
Salisbury, MD 21801 awilliams@mde.state.md.us
www.mde.state.md.us
Jay Bozman, Manager

2859 Maryland Department of the Environment: Air and Radiation Management Main Field Office
160 South Water Street 301-689-5756
Frostburg, MD 21532 *Fax:* 301-689-6544
www.mde.state.md.us
Tamara Davis, Manager

2860 Maryland Department of the Environment: Field Operations Office
416 Chinquapin Round Road 443-482-2700
Annapolis, MD 21401 www.mde.state.md.us
John Steinfort, Manager

2861 Maryland Department of the Environment: Main Office
1800 Washington Blvd 410-537-3000
Baltimore, MD 21230 800-633-6101
www.mde.state.md.us
To protect and restore the quality of Maryland's air, land, and water resources, while fostering economic development, healthy and safe communities, and quality environmental education for the benefit of the environment, public health,and future generations.
Robert Summers, Secretary
David Costello, Deputy Secretary

2862 Maryland National Capital Park & Planning Commission
6611 Kenilworth Avenue 301-454-1740
Riverdale, MD 20737 *Fax:* 301-454-1750
mcp-infocounter@mncppc-mc.org
www.mncppc.org
Is a bi-county agency empowered by the State of Maryland to acquire, develop, maintain and administer a regional system of parks withing Montgomery and Prince George's Counties, and to prepare and administer a general plan for thephysical development of the two counties.
Patricia Barney, Executive Director
Joseph Zimmerman, Secretary-Treasurer's Office

2863 NOAA Chesapeake Bay Office
410 Severn Avenue 410-267-5660
Suite 207-A *Fax:* 410-267-5666
Annapolis, MD 21403 www.chesapeakebay.noaa.gov
NOAA Chesapeake Bay Office works to help protect and restore the Chesapeake Bay through programs in fisheries management, habitat restoration, coastal observations, and education.
Sean Corson, Acting Director

Michigan

2864 Great Lakes Environmental Research Laboratory
4840 S. State Rd 734-741-2235
Ann Arbor, MI 48108-9719 *Fax:* 734-741-2055
www.glerl.noaa.gov
Conducts integrated, interdisciplinary environmental research in support of resource management and environmental services in coastal and estuarine waters with a special emphasis on the Great Lakes. Laboratory performs field,analytical, and laboratory investigations to improve understanding and prediction of coastal and estaurine processes and the interdependencies with the atmosphere and sediments.
Marie C. Colton, Director
John Bratton, Deputy Director

2865 Great Lakes Fishery Commission
2100 Commonwealth Boulevard 734-662-3209
Suite 100 *Fax:* 734-741-2010
Ann Arbor, MI 48105 info@glfc.org
www.glfc.org
The Great Lakes Fishery Commision was established by the Convention on Great Lakes Fisheries between Canada and the US in 1955. It has two major responsibilities: to develop coordinated programs of research on the Great Lakes and, onthe basis of the findings, to recommend measures which will permit the maximum sustained productivity in stocks of fish of common concern; and to formulate and implement a program to eradicate or minimize sea lampry populations in the Great Lakes.
Michael Hansen, Chairman
David Ullrich, Commissioner

2866 Michigan Department of Community Health
Capitol View Building 517-335-9030
201 Townsend Street 800-649-3777
Lansing, MI 48913 *Fax:* 517-335-8509
www.michigan.gov/mdch
A state agency which continually and diligently endeavors to prevent disease, prolong life and promote the public health.
James K. Haveman, Director
Angela Awrey, Deputy Director/ COO

2867 Michigan Department of Environmental Quality
525 W Allegan Street, 6th Floor 517-373-7917
PO Box 30473 800-662-9278
Lansing, MI 48909-7973 www.michigan.gov/deq
Promotes wise management of Michigan's air, land, and water resources to support a sustainable environment, healthy communities, and vibrant economy
Dan Wyant, Director
Jim Kasprzak, State Bureau Administrator

2868 Michigan Department of Natural Resources
PO Box 30028 517-241-7427
Lansing, MI 48909 *Fax:* 517-241-7428
www.michigan.gov/dnr
Committed to the conservation, protection, management, use and enjoyment of the state's natural and cultural resources for current and future generations
Keith Creagh, Director
Dennis Knapp, Chief of Staff

2869 Michigan State University Extension
Agriculture Hall 517-355-2308
Room 108 *Fax:* 517-355-6473
East Lansing, MI 48824 www.msue.msu.edu/msue/
Michigan State University Extension helps people improve their lives through an educational process that applies knowledge to critical issues, needs and opportunities.
Thomas G Coon, Director
Stephen B. Lovejoy, Associate Director

2870 Natural Resources: Wildlife Division
PO Box 30444 517-373-1263
Lansing, MI 48909-7944 *Fax:* 517-373-1547
www.michigan.gov/dnr

Committed to the conservation, protection, management, use and enjoyment of the state's natural and cultural resources for current and future generations
Keith Creagh, Director
Terry Minzey, Regional Supervisor

Minnesota

2871 Minnesota Board of Water & Soil Resources
520 Lafayette Road North 651-296-3767
St Paul, MN 55155 *Fax:* 651-297-5615
www.bwsr.state.mn.us
The Minnesota Board of Water and Soil Resources assists local governments to manage and conserve their irreplaceable water and soil resources.
Brian Napstad, Chairman of the Board
Tom Loveall, Co-Commissioner

2872 Minnesota Department of Agriculture
625 Robert Street North 651-201-6000
St Paul, MN 55155-2538 800-967-2474
Fax: 651-297-5522
www.mda.state.mn.us
The MDA's mission is to work toward a diverse ag industry that is profitable as well as environmentally sound; to protect the public health safety regarding food and ag products; and to ensure orderly commerce in agricultural and foodproducts. We have two major branches of the department to accomplish this mission: regulatory divisions and non-regulatory divisions.
Dave Frederickson, Commissioner
Jim Boerboom, Deputy Commissioner

2873 Minnesota Department of Natural Resources
500 Lafayette Road 651-296-6157
Box 21 888-646-6367
St. Paul, MN 55155-4040 *Fax:* 651-297-4946
www.dnr.state.mn.us
The DNR vision hinges on the concept of sustainability. To DNR, sustainability means protecting and restoring the natural environment while enhancing economic opportunity and community well-being. DNR endorsed ecosystem-basedmanagement as its method to achieve sustainability goals. Sustainability addresses three related elements: the environment, the economy and the community. The goal is to maintain all three elements in a healthy state indefinitely.
Tom Landwehr, Commissioner
Bob Meier, Policy/Government Relations

2874 Minnesota Environmental Quality Board
520 Lafayette Road North 651-757-2014
St Paul, MN 55155 *Fax:* 651-296-6334
www.eqb.state.mn.us
The mission of the Environmental Quality Board is to lead Minnesota environmental policy by responding to key issues, providing appropriate review and coordination, serving as a public forum and developing long-range strategies toenhance Minnesota's environmental quality. The Environmental Quality Board consists of 10 state agency commissioners or directors and five citizen members. It was established by the Minnesota Legislature in 1973.
Dave Frederickson, Chair
Brian Napstad, Vice Chair

2875 Minnesota Pollution Control Agency
520 Lafayette Road North 651-296-6300
St. Paul, MN 55155-4194 800-657-3864
Fax: 651-296-7923
www.pca.state.mn.us
Established in 1967 to protect Minnesota's environment through monitoring environmental quality and enforcing environmental regulations.
John Linc Stine, Commissioner
Michelle Beeman, Deputy Commissioner

2876 Minnesota Pollution Control Agency: Duluth
525 S Lake Avenue 218-723-4660
Suite 400 800-657-3864
Duluth, MN 55802 *Fax:* 218-723-4727
www.pca.state.mn.us
MPCA staff at Duluth and the other six agency offices: identify environmental problems through testing, monitoring, inspections and research; develop environmental priorities; set standards and propose rules to protect people and theenvironment; develop permits; provide technical assistance; respond to emergencies and encourage pollution prevention and sustainability.
Suzanne Hanson, Manager

2877 Minnesota Sea Grant College Program
University of Minnesota
144 Chester Park 218-726-8106
31 W College Street *Fax:* 218-726-6556
Duluth, MN 55812 seagr@d.umn.edu
www.seagrant.umn.edu
Minnesota Sea Grant is dedicated to providing the tools and technology for responsible management and policy decisions to maintain and enhance Lake Superior and Minnesota's inland aquatic economies and resources. We involveuniversities, federal and state agencies, the public and industry in a partnership to understand the complex nature of the multidisciplinary problems facing us, and then help in the development of the infrastructure necessary for innovativesolutions.
Jeffrey Gunderson, Acting Director
Judy Zomerfelt, Executive Secretary

2878 United States Department of the Army US Army Corps of Engineers
190 5th Street East 651-290-5200
Suite 401 *Fax:* 651-290-5752
St. Paul, MN 55101-1638 www.usace.army.mil
Deliver vital public and military engineering services; partnering in peace and war to strengthen our Nation's security, energize the economy and reduce risks from disasters
Thomas P. Bostick, Commanding General
Todd T. Semonite, Deputy Commanding General

Mississippi

2879 Gulf Coast Research Laboratory
703 E Beach Drive 228-872-4200
Ocean Springs, MS 39564 *Fax:* 228-872-4204
www.usm.edu/gcrl
Operates centers of excellence and national research and development programs in fisheries, geospatial technologies, marine aquaculture, environmental assessment and marine toxicology
Eric N. Powell, Director
Dr Jeffrey M Lotz, Chair

2880 Mississippi Alabama Sea Grant Consortium
703 East Beach Drive 228-818-8836
Ocean Springs, MS 39564 *Fax:* 228-818-8841
swanndl@auburn.edu
www.masgc.org
A federal state partnership that is dedicated to activities that foster the conservation and sustainable development of coastal and marine resources in Mississippi and Alabama.
Dr La Don Swann, Director
Stephen Sempier, Deputy Director

2881 Mississippi Department Agriculture & Commerce
121 North Jefferson Street 601-359-1100
Jackson, MS 39201 *Fax:* 601-354-6290
WebMaster@mdac.ms.gov
The mission of the Mississippi Department of Agriculture and Commerce is to regulate and promote agricultural-related businesses within the state and to promote Mississippi's products throughout both the state and the rest of the worldfor the benefit of all Mississippi citizens.
Cindy Hyde-Smith, Commissioner

2882 Mississippi Department of Environmental Quality
PO Box 2261 601-961-5171
Jackson, MS 39225 888-786-0661
charles-chisolm@deq.state.ms.us
www.deq.state.ms.us
Mission: To safeguard the health, safety, and welfare of present and future generations of Mississippians by conserving and improving our environment and fostering wise economic growth through focused research and responsibleregulation.
Trudy D Fisher, Executive Director
Martha Dairymple, Chairman

2883 Mississippi Department of Wildlife, Fisheries and Parks
1505 Eastover Drive 601-432-2400
Jackson, MS 39211 www.mdwfp.com
It is the mission of the Mississippi Department of Wildlife, Fisheries and Parks to conserve and enhance Mississippi's natural resources, to provide continuing outdoor recreational opportunities, to maintain the ecological integrityand aesthetic quality of the resources and to ensure socioeconomic and educational opportunities for present and future generations.
Jerry Munro, Chairman
Sam Polles, Executive Director

2884 Mississippi Forestry Commission
660 North Street 601-359-1386
Suite 300 *Fax:* 601-359-1349
Jackson, MS 39202 www.mfc.ms.gov
Mission: To provide active leadership in forest protection, forest management, forest inventory and effective forest information distribution, necessary for Mississippi's sustainable forset-based economy.
Floyd Hobbs, Chairman
Joseph E. Pettigrew, Vice Chair

2885 Mississippi State Department of Health Bureau of Child/Adolescent Health
570 East Woodrow Wilson Drive 601-576-7464
Post Office Box 1700 866-453-4948
Jackson, MS 39216 www.msdh.state.ms.us
The Mississippi Department of Health's mission is to promote and protect the health of the citizens of Missippi. Geographic focus: Missippi other organizational activies, not directed specifically toward children; advocacy, directservice delivery, education, organizing, regulation, social services
Sam Valentine, Director

2886 United States Department of the Army US Army Corps of Engineers
4155 Clay Street 601-631-5972
Vicksburg, MS 39180 www.usace.army.mil
Deliver vital public and military engineering services; partnering in peace and war to strengthen our Nation's security, energize the economy and reduce risks from disasters
Thomas P. Bostick, Commanding General
Todd T. Semonite, Deputy Commanding General

Missouri

2887 Missouri Conservation Department
3500 East Gans Road 573-815-7901
Columbia, MO 65201 *Fax:* 573-815-7902
mdc.mo.gov

2888 Missouri Department of Natural Resources
PO Box 176 573-751-3443
Jefferson City, MO 65102 800-361-4827
Fax: 573-751-7627
contact@dnr.mo.gov
www.dnr.mo.gov
The Department of Natural Resources preserves, protects and enhances Missouri's natural, cultural and energy resources and works to inspire their enjoyment and responsible use for present and future generations. Our staff work toensure that our state enjoys clean air to breathe, clean water for drinking and recreation and land that sustains a diversity of life.
Sara Parker Pauley, Director

2889 Natural Resources Department: Air Pollution Control
PO Box 176 573-751-4817
Jefferson City, MO 65102 800-334-6946
Fax: 573-751-8656
cleanair@dnr.mo.gov
www.dnr.mo.gov
Mission: To maintain the purity of Missouri's air to protect the health, general welfare and property of the people.
Jack Baker, Chairman
Gary Pendergrass, Vice Chair

2890 Natural Resources Department: Energy Center
PO Box 176 573-751-3443
Jefferson City, MO 65102 800-361-4827
Fax: 573-751-6860
energy@dnr.mo.gov
www.dnr.mo.gov
A nonregulatory state agency that works to protect the environment and stimulate the economy through energy efficiency and renewable energy resources and technologies.

2891 Natural Resources Department: Environmental Improvement and Energy Resources Authority
PO Box 744 573-751-4919
Jefferson City, MO 65102 *Fax:* 573-635-3486
eiera@dnr.mo.gov
www.dnr.mo.gov
A quasi-governmental agency that serves as the financing arm for the Missouri Department of Natural Resources.
Deron Cherry, Director
Andy Dalton, Director

2892 United States Department of the Army US Army Corps of Engineers
US Army Engineer District
601 E 12th Street 816-389-3486
Room 736 www.usace.army.mil
Kansas City, MO 64106
Deliver vital public and military engineering services; partnering in peace and war to strengthen our Nation's security, energize the economy and reduce risks from disasters
Thomas P. Bostick, Commanding General
Todd T. Semonite, Deputy Commanding General

Montana

2893 Butte District Advisory Council
106 N Parkmont 406-533-7600
Butte, MT 59702 *Fax:* 406-533-7660
mt_butte_fo@blm.gov
www.mt.blm.gov/bdo/

Jamie Conell, State Director
Theresa Hanley, Deputy State Director

2894 Crown of the Continent Research Learning Center - Glacier National Park
PO Box 128 406-888-7863
West Glacier, MT 59936 *Fax:* 406-888-7903
tara_carolin@nps.gov
www.nps.gov/rlc/crown/index.htm
Designed to increase the effectiveness and communication of research and science results in national parks through facilitating the use of parks for scientific inquiry, supporting science-informed decision making, communicating therelevance of and providing access to knowledge gained through scientific research, and promoting science literacy and resource stewardship

Tara Carolin, Director
Melissa Sladek, Science Comm Specialist

2895 Environmental Quality Council
State Capitol, Room 171 406-444-3742
PO Box 201704 *Fax:* 406-444-3971
Helena, MT 59620-1704 teverts@mt.gov
The EQC is a state legislative committee create by the 1971 Montana Environmental Policy Act. As outlined in MEPA, the EQC'S purpose is to encourage conditions under which people can coexist with nature in productive harmony. TheCouncil fulfills this purpose by assisting the Legislature in the development of natural resource and environmental policy, by conducting studies on related issues and by serving in an advisory capacity to the state's natural resource programs.

Jim Keane, Chairman
Duane Ankney

2896 Lewiston District Advisory Council Bureau of Land Management
920 Northeast Main Street 406-538-1900
PO Box 1160 *Fax:* 406-538-1904
Lewistown, MT 59457 www.blm.gov
Manages approximately 750,300 surface acres of public land scattered across eight counties in central Montana

2897 Montana Department of Agriculture
302 North Roberts 406-444-3144
Helena, MT 59620-0201 *Fax:* 406-444-5409
Mission: To protect producers and consumers and to enhance and develop agriculture and allied industries.
Ron de Yong, Acting Director

2898 Montana Natural Heritage Program
1515 East 6th Avenue 406-444-5354
Helena, MT 59620-1800 *Fax:* 406-444-0266
mtnhp@mt.gov
www.mtnhp.org
The Montana Natural Heritage Program is the state's source for information on the status and distribution of our native animals and plants, emphasizing species of concern and high quality habitats such as wetlands.
Allan Cox, Lead Program Manager
Darlene Patzer, Finance/Grants Administrator

2899 Natural Resources & Conservation Department
1625 11th Avenue 406-444-2074
Helena, MT 59601 *Fax:* 406-444-2684
www.dnrc.mt.gov
To help ensure that Montana's land and water resources provide benefits for present and future generations
John Tubbs, Director

Nebraska

2900 Central Interstate Low-Level Radioactive Waste Commission
PO Box 4770 402-476-8247
Lincoln, NE 68504-770 *Fax:* 402-476-8205
rita@cillrwcc.org
www.cillrwcc.org

Rita Houskie, Administrator

2901 Department of Agriculture: Natural Resources Conservation Service
National Soil Survey Center
100 Centennial Mall N Room 152 402-437-5499
Lincoln, NE 68508-3866 *Fax:* 402-437-5336
www.soils.usda.gov
Developing and maintaining soil survey data and information systems; assistance in planning regional work planning conferences; liaison to NCSS Regional Agriculture Experiment Station Soil Survey Committees; and technical coordinationat the national level
Jonathan W. Hempel, Director
Linda M. Bouc, Administrative Assistant

2902 Department of Natural Resources
301 Centennial Mall S 402-471-2341
PO Box 94676 *Fax:* 402-471-6876
Lincoln, NE 68509-4947 www.dnr.ne.gov
State Natural Resources Agency
Ann Saloman Bleed, Director
Brian P Dunnigan, Deputy Director

2903 Nebraska Department of Agriculture
301 Centennial Mall S 402-471-2341
PO Box 94947 800-831-0550
Lincoln, NE 68509-4947 *Fax:* 402-471-6876
agr.webmaster@nebraska.gov
www.nda.nebraska.gov
The Nebraska Department of Agriculture is a regulatory state agency.

Greg Ibach, Director
Mat Habrock, Assistant Director

2904 Nebraska Department of Environmental Quality
1200 N Street Suite 400 402-471-2186
PO Box 98922 *Fax:* 402-471-2909
Lincoln, NE 68509 www.deq.state.ne.us
Mission: To protect the quality of Nebraska's environment-our air, land, and water resources. Enforce regulations and provide assistance.

2905 Nebraska Ethanol Board
301 Centennial Mall S 402-471-2941
PO Box 94922 *Fax:* 402-471-2470
Lincoln, NE 68509 www.ne-ethanol.org
The Nebraska Ethanol Board assists ethanol producers with programs and strategies for marketing ethanol and related co-products. The Board supports organizations and policies that advocate the increased use of ethanol fuels, andadministers public information, education and ethanol research projects. The Board also assists companies and organizations in the development of ethanol production facilities in Nebraska.

Paul Kenney, Chair
Mike Thede, Vice Chair

2906 Nebraska Game & Parks Commission: Fisheries Division
2200 N 33rd Street 402-471-0641
PO Box 30370 *Fax:* 402-471-4992
Lincoln, NE 68503 Donna.Waller@nebraska.gov
www.outdoornebraska.ne.gov
Mission: Stewardship of the state's fish, wildlife, park, and outdoor recreation resources in the best long-term interests of the people and those resources
James Douglas, Director
Tim McCoy, Deputy Director

2907 Nebraska Games & Parks Commission
2200 North 33rd Street 402-471-0641
Lincoln, NE 68503 www.outdoornebraska.ne.gov
Mission: Stewardship of the state's fish, wildlife, park, and outdoor recreation resources in the best long-term interests of the people and those resources
James Douglas, Director
Tim McCoy, Deputy Director

2908 Nebraska Games & Parks: Wildlife Division
2200 N 33rd Street 402-471-0641
PO Box 30370 *Fax:* 402-471-4992
Lincoln, NE 68503 jim.douglas@nebraska.gov
www.outdoornebraska.gov
Mission: Stewardship of the state's fish, wildlife, park, and outdoor recreation resources in the best long-term interests of the people and those resources
James Douglas, Director
Tim McCoy, Deputy Director

2909 United States Department of the Army US Army Corps of Engineers
US Army Engineer District

215 N 17th Street 402-995-2417
Omaha, NE 68102-4978 *Fax:* 402-221-4626
www.usace.army.mil
Deliver vital public and military engineering services; partnering in peace and war to strengthen our Nation's security, energize the economy and reduce risks from disasters
Thomas P. Bostick, Commanding General
Todd T. Semonite, Deputy Commanding General

Nevada

2910 Bureau of Land Management (BLM)
U.S. Department of the Interior
1849 C Street NW 202-208-3801
Room 5665 *Fax:* 202-208-5242
Washington, DC 20240 www.blm.gov
The mission of the Bureau of Land Management is to ensure the sustainability and diversity of the public lands for the use and enjoyment of present and future generations. The Bureau offers environmental education, news about theactivities of the Bureau, events, and regulations.
Michael Nedd, Deputy Director, Operations
Casey Hammond, Principal Deputy

2911 Bureau of Reclamation - Great Plains Region
Great Plains Regional Office
PO Box 36900 406-247-7610
Billings, MT 59101 www.usbr.gov/gp/
One of five Bureau Reclamation Regions dedicated to the management and protection of water and related resources.
Michael Ryan, Regional Director

2912 Bureau of Reclamation - Lower Colorado Region
Lower Colorado Regional Office
PO Box 61470 702-293-8000
Boulder City, NV 89006 *Fax:* 702-293-8333
www.usbr.gov/lc/
One of five Bureau Reclamation Regions dedicated to the management and protection of water and related resources.
Terry Fulp, Regional Director

2913 Bureau of Reclamation - Mid-Pacific Region
Mid-Pacific Regional Office
Federal Office Building 916-978-5001
2800 Cottage Way *Fax:* 916-978-5005
Sacramento, CA 95825-1898 www.usbr.gov/mp/
One of five Bureau Reclamation Regions dedicated to the management and protection of water and related resources.
David Murillo, Regional Director

2914 Bureau of Reclamation - Pacific Northwest Region
Pacific Northwest Regional Office
1150 North Curtis Rd www.usbr.gov/pn/
Suite 100
Boise, ID 83706-1234
One of five Bureau Reclamation Regions dedicated to the management and protection of water and related resources.
Lorri Gray, Regional Director

2915 Bureau of Reclamation - Upper Colorado
Upper Colorado Regional Office
125 South State St ucpao@usbr.gov
Room 8100 www.usbr.gov/uc/
Salt Lake City, UT 84138-1147
One of five Bureau Reclamation Regions dedicated to the management and protection of water and related resources.
Brent Rhees, Regional Director

2916 Carson City Field Office Advisory Council
Bureau of Land Management
5665 Morgan Mill Road 775-885-6000
Carson City, NV 89701 *Fax:* 775-885-6147
ccfoweb@blm.gov
www.blm.gov
A Federal Land Management Agency.

2917 Conservation and Natural Resources Department
Wildlife Division, Conservation Education
901 South Stewart Street 775-684-2700
Suite1003 *Fax:* 775-684-2715
Carson City, NV 89701 www.dcnr.nv.gov
The Department of Conservation and Natural Resources (DCNR) is responsible for the establishment and administration of goals, objectives and priorities for the preservation of the State's natural resources.
Leo Drozdoff, Director
Kay Scherer, Deputy Director

2918 Conservation and Natural Resources: Water Resources Division
901 South Stewart Street 775-684-2800
Suite 2002 *Fax:* 775-684-2811
Carson City, NV 89701 www.water.nv.gov
To conserve, protect, manage and enhance the State's water resources for Nevada's citizens through the appropriation and reallocation of the public waters
Jason King, State Engineer
Tracy Taylor, Deputy

2919 Las Vegas Bureau of Land Management
4701 N Torrey Pines Drive 702-515-5000
Las Vegas, NV 89130
The Bureau of Land Management's mission is to help sustain the health, diversity and productivity of public lands so they can be used and enjoyed by both present and future generations.

2920 Nevada Bureau of Mines & Geology
University of Nevada
Mail Stop 178 775-784-6691
Reno, NV 89557 *Fax:* 775-784-1709
nbmg@unr.edu
www.nbmg.unr.edu
Research and public service unit of the University of Nevada and is the state geological survey
James E. Faulds, Director/State Geologist

2921 Nevada Department of Wildlife
1100 Valley Road 775-688-1500
Reno, NV 89512 *Fax:* 775-688-1207
ndowinfo@ndow.org
www.ndow.org
Responsible for the restoration and management of fish and wildlife resources, and the promotion of boating safety on Nevada's waters
Tony Wasley, Director
Rich Haskins, Deputy Director

2922 Nevada Natural Heritage Program
901 South Stewart Street 775-684-2900
Suite 5002 *Fax:* 775-684-2909
Carson City, NV 89701
The mission is to develop and maintain a cost-effective central information source and inventory of locations, biology, and status of all threatened, endangered, rare and at-risk plants and animals in Nevada.
Jennifer Newmark, Administrator
Jessica Sanders, Office Manager

2923 Tahoe Regional Planning Agency (TRPA) Advisory Planning Commission
PO Box 5310 775-588-4547
Stateline, NV 89449 *Fax:* 775-588-4527
trpa@trpa.org
www.trpa.org
The TRPA leads the cooperative effort to preserve, restore and enhance the natural and human environment of the Lake Tahoe Region. The Code of Ordinances regulates, among other things, land use, density, rate of growth, land coverage,excavation and scenic impacts. These regulations are designed to bring the region into compliance with the threshold standards established for water quality, air quality, soil conservation, wildlife habitat, vegetation, noise, recreation and scenicresources.
Joanne Marchetta, Executive Director
Marja Ambler, Management Assistant

New Hampshire

2924 **New Hampshire Department of Environmental Services**
29 Hazen Drive 603-271-3503
PO Box 95 *Fax:* 603-271-2867
Concord, NH 03302-0095
The New Hampshire Department of Environmental Services aims to protect, maintain and enhance environmental quality and public health in New Hampshire.
Tom Burack, Commissioner
Vicki V. Quiram, Assistant Commissioner

2925 **New Hampshire Fish and Game Department**
11 Hazen Drive 603-271-3421
Concord, NH 03301 *Fax:* 603-271-1438
info@wildlife.nh.gov
www.wildnh.com
As the guardian of the states fish, wildlife and marine resources, the department works with the public to: conserve, manage and protect these resources and their habitats; inform and advise the public about these resources; providethe public with opportunities to use and appreciate these resources.
Gelnn Normandeau, Executive Director
Tanya L Haskell, Administrative Assistant

2926 **New Hampshire State Conservation Committee**
PO Box 3907 603-271-1092
Concord, NH 03302 www.nh.gov/scc
Coordinates the work of the ten county conservation districts in the state of New Hampshire.
Jim Raynes, Chairman

2927 **Resources & Development Council: State Planning**
Department of Resources & Economic Development
172 Pembroke Road 603-271-2411
P.O. Box 1856 *Fax:* 603-271-2629
Concord, NH 03302-1856
Promoting the principles of smart growth at the state, regional, and local levels through the municipal and regional planning assistance program
Victoria Cimino, Director
Michele Zydel, Administrative Secretary

2928 **University of New Hampshire Cooperative Extension**
Taylor Hall 603-862-1520
59 College Road *Fax:* 603-862-1585
Durham, NH 03824 ce.webinfo@unh.edu
www.extension.unh.edu
The University of New Hampshire Cooperative Extension provides New Hampshire citizens with research-based education and information, enhancing their ability to make informed decisions that strengthen youth, families and communities,sustain natural resources, and improve the economy.
John Pike, Dean/Director
Lisa Townson, Assistant Director

New Jersey

2929 **New Jersey Department of Agriculture**
PO Box 330 609-292-3976
Trenton, NJ 00862 *Fax:* 609-292-3978
The New Jersey Department of Agriculture is an agency which oversees programs that serve virutally all New Jersey citizens. A major priority of the NJDA is to promote, protect and serve the Garden State's diverse agriculture andagribusiness industries.
Douglas H. Fisher, Secretary

2930 **New Jersey Department of Environmental Protection**
401 E State Street 609-777-3373
7th Floor, E Wing 866-337-5669
Trenton, NJ 00862 *Fax:* 609-292-7695
www.nj.gov/dep/
A state department dedicated to protecting New Jersey's air, land, water and natural resources.
Bob Martin, Commissioner
Irene Kropp, Deputy Commissioner

2931 **New Jersey Department of Environmental Protection: Site Remediation Program**
401 E State Street 609-292-1250
PO Box 420 *Fax:* 609-777-1914
Trenton, NJ 00862-0420 www.state.nj.us/dep/srp
Kenneth Kloo, Director
David Sweeney, Assistant Commissioner

2932 **New Jersey Division of Fish & Wildlife**
501 E State Street, 3rd Fl 609-292-2965
PO Box 420 *Fax:* 609-292-8207
Trenton, NJ 00862-0420 www.njfishandwildlife.com
Our mission is to protect and manage the state's fish and wildlife to maximize their long-term biological, recreation and economic values for all New Jerseyans.
David Chanda, Director
Larry Herrighty, Assistant Director of Operat

2933 **New Jersey Geological Survey**
PO Box 420 609-292-1185
Mail Code:29-01 *Fax:* 609-633-1004
Trenton, NJ 00862-0420 njgsweb@dep.state.nj.us
www.njgeology.org
State agency that maps, interprets and provides geoscience information to the public on geology and ground water resources.
Karl Muessig, State Geologist

2934 **New Jersey Pinelands Commission**
PO Box 7 609-894-7300
15 Springfield Road *Fax:* 609-894-7330
New Lisbon, NJ 00806 info@njpines.state.nj.us
www.state.nj.us/pinelands/
Mission: To preserve, protect, and enhance the natural and cultural resourcse of the Pinelands National Reserve, and to encourage compatible economic and other human activities consistent with that purpose.
Mark S. Lohbauer, Chairman
Nancy Wittenberg, Executive Director

New Mexico

2935 **Albuquerque Bureau of Land Management**
435 Montano Road NE 505-761-8700
Albuquerque, NM 87107-4935 *Fax:* 505-761-8911
www.nm.blm.gov
Ed Singleton, District Manager
Ernest J Chavez, Assistant District Manager

2936 **Attorney General**
Environmental Enforcement
PO Drawer 1508 505-827-6000
Santa Fe, NM 87504-1508 *Fax:* 505-827-5826
Gary King, Attorney General

2937 **Department of the Interior: U.S. Fish & Wildlife Service - New Mexico**
U.S. Fish & Wildlife Service
500 Gold Avenue SW 505-248-6911
P.O. Box 1306 RDLueders@fws.gov
Albuquerque, NM 87102-1306 www.fws.gov/southwest/
Aims to protect endangered and threatened species, migratory birds, freshwater fish and wildlife habitats in New Mexico; work with many other private and public partners to preserve and protect living resources of the New Mexicoecosystems.
Amy Lueders, Regional Director

2938 Energy, Minerals & Natural Resources: Energy Conservation & Management Division
1220 South Street 505-476-3310
Francis Drive www.emnrd.state.nm.us/ecmd/
Santa Fe, NM 87505
Encourages efficient energy use in New Mexico by offerin programs and information for state agencies, companies and induviduals.
Louise N. Martinez, Director

2939 Energy, Minerals and Natural Resources Department
1220 S St. Francis Drive 505-476-3200
Santa Fe, NM 87505 *Fax:* 505-476-3220
www.emnrd.state.nm.us
Mission is to provide leadership in the protection, conservation, management and responsible use of New Mexico's natural resources.
David Martin, Cabinet Secretary
Brett F. Woods, Deputy Cabinet Secretary

2940 New Mexico Bureau of Geology & Mineral Resources
801 Leroy Place 505-835-5420
Socorro, NM 87801-4796 *Fax:* 505-835-6333
scholle1@nmt.edu
www.geoinfo.nmt.edu
A service and research division of the New Mexico Institute of Mining and Technology. Acts as the geological survey of New Mexico.

Paul Bauer, Principal Geologist, Assoc.
Bruce Allen, Sr. Field Geologist

2941 New Mexico Cooperative Fish & Wildlife Research Unit
New Mexico University MSC 4901 505-646-6053
PO Box 30003 *Fax:* 505-646-1281
Las Cruces, NM 88003 www.coopunits.org/New_Mexico/
The New Mexico Research Unit conducts, research on problems of mutual concern to cooperators; graduate academic training; technical assistance in fish and wildlife management; and conservation education through publications, lectures,and demonstrations.
Colleen Caldwell, Leader
Louis Bender, Assistant Unit Leader

2942 New Mexico Department of Game & Fish
1 Wildlife Way 505-476-8000
Santa Fe, NM 87507 888-248-6866
ispa@state.nm.us
www.wildlife.state.nm.us
To conserve, regulate, propagate and protect the wildlife and fish within the state of New Mexico using a flexible management system that ensures sustainable use for public food supply, recreation and safety; and to provide foroff-highway motor vehicle recreation that recognizes cultural, historic, and resource values while ensuring public safety
Jim Lane, Director
Alexa Sandoval, Chief

2943 New Mexico Environment Department
1190 St. Francis Drive 505-827-2855
Suite N4050 800-219-6157
Santa Fe, NM 87505 www.nmenv.state.nm.us
The New Mexico Environment Department's mission is to provide the highest quality of life throughout the state by promoting a safe, clean, and productive environment.
Ryan Flynn, Cabinet Secretary
Butch Tongate, Deputy Secretary

2944 New Mexico Soil & Water Conservation Commission
163 Trail Canyon Road 505-646-2642
Carlsbad, NM 88242 *Fax:* 505-646-1540
acoleman@nmda.nmsu.edu
www.nmacd.org/state-agencies
Serves as the state entity providing guidance and policy direction to the local soil and water conservation districts.
Jim Berlier, President
John Arrington, Vice President

2945 Roswell District Advisory Council: Bureau of Land Management
2909 W 2nd Street 505-627-0272
Roswell, NM 88201-2019 *Fax:* 505-627-0276
Larry Ashley, Engine Module Leader

New York

2946 Adirondack Park Agency
1133 NYS Route 86 518-891-4050
PO Box 99 *Fax:* 518-891-3938
Ray Brook, NY 12977 www.apa.state.ny.us
Mission: To protect the public and private resources of the Park through the exercise of the powers and duties provided by law.
Leilani Ulrich, Chair
Richard Booth, Commissioner

2947 Department of Environmental Conservation
625 Broadway 518-402-8545
Albany, NY 12233-0001 800-847-7332
Fax: 518-402-8541
dpaeweb@gw.dec.state.ny.us
www.dec.ny.gov
Mission: To conserve, improve, and protect New York State's natural resources and environment, and control water, land and air pollution, in order to enhance the health, safety and welfare of the people of the state and their overalleconomic and social well being.
Joe Martens, Commissioner
Marc Gerstman, Executive Dep Commissioner

2948 Department of Environmental Conservation: Division of Air Resources
625 Broadway 518-402-8452
Albany, NY 12233-0001 DARWeb@gw.dec.state.ny.us
www.dec.ny.gov/about/644.html
Maintains and improves New York State air quality through research, permitting and enforcement.
Jared Snyder, Assistant Commissioner

2949 Department of Environmental Conservation: Division of Mineral Resources
625 Broadway 518-402-8076
3rd Floor *Fax:* 518-402-8060
Albany, NY 12233-0001 dmninfo@gw.dec.state.ny.us
www.dec.ny.gov/about/636.html
The Division of Mineral Resources is responsible for ensuring the environmentally sound, economic development of New York's non-renewable energy and mineral resources for the benefit of current and future generations. To carry out thismission, we regulate the extraction of oil and gas, and require the reclamation of land after mining.
Bradley J. Field, Director
Kathleen F. Sanford, Assistant Director

2950 New York Cooperative Fish & Wildlife Research Unit
Cornell University, Fernow Hall 607-255-2839
Natural Resources Department *Fax:* 607-255-1895
Ithaca, NY 14853-3001 dnrcru-mailbox@cornell.edu
www.coopunits.org/New_York/index.html
Pays particular attention to the resource problems and issues of the Northeastern States with New York as its focal point

William Fisher, Unit Leader
Mitchell Eaton, Assistant Leader

2951 New York Department of Health
Corning Tower 518-402-7500
Empire State Plaza *Fax:* 518-402-7509
Albany, NY 12237 www.health.state.ny.us
Working together and committed to excellence, we protect and promote the health of New Yorkers through prevention, science and the assurance of quality health care delivery.
Nirav R. Shah, Commissioner

2952 New York State Office of Parks, Recreation and Historic Preservation
Empire State Plaza 518-474-0456
Agency Building 1 www.nysparks.com
Albany, NY 12238
The agency operates 168 parks offering a wide variety of recreational, cultural and education activities, and 35 state historic sites; sponsors boating and snowmobiling, nature study and outreach programs; manages grant programs forboating and snowmobiling enforcement and aid to zoos, botanical gardens, aquariums; and administers funds for federal historical preservation and parks programs, the Environmental Protection Fund and the 1996 Clean Water/Clean Air Bond act.
Rose Harvey, Commissioner

2953 New York State Soil and Water Conservation Committee
10B Airline Drive 518-457-3738
Albany, NY 12235 *Fax:* 518-457-3412
www.nys-soilandwater.org
The New York State Soil and Water Conservation Committee is composed of voting and advisory members who represent a wide range of agricultural, environmental and other interests. The Committee operates through a network of partnershipsbetween state, federal and local agencies, as well as citizen interests and the private sector. The mission of the Committee is to develop and oversee and agricultural nonpoint source water quality program for New York State.
Michael Latham, Director
Brian Steinmuller, Assistant Director

2954 Tug Hill Tomorrow Land Trust
PO Box 6063 315-779-8240
Watertown, NY 13601 *Fax:* 315-782-6192
thtomorr@northnet.org
www.tughilltomorrowlandtrust.org
A regional, private, nonprofit founded by a group of Tug Hill residents to serve the region of 2,100 square miles serving portions of Jefferson, Lewis, Oneida & Oswego Counties. The mission is two-fold: increase awareness andappreciation of the Tug Hill Rgion through education; and to help retain the forest, farm, recreation, and wild land of the region through voluntary, private land protection efforts.

Bob Quinn, Chairman
George Bibbins, Vice Chair

2955 United States Department of the Army US Army Corps of Engineers
1776 Niagara Street 800-833-6390
Buffalo, NY 14207-3199 www.lrb.usace.army.mil
Delivers world class engineering solutions to the Great Lakes Region, the Army, and the Nation in order to ensure national security, environmental sustainability, water resource management, and emergency assistance during peace and war
LTC Karl D. Jansen, Commander and District Engin
MAJ Michael A. Busby, Deputy Commander

North Carolina

2956 Carolina Tiger Rescue
1940 Hanks Chapel Road 919-542-4684
Pittsboro, NC 27312 *Fax:* 919-542-4454
info@carolinatigerrescue.org
carolinatigerrescue.org
Is a wildlife sanctuary, offering unique opportunities to learn about these animals and their critical importance to our quality of life on Earth.
Pam Fulk, Executive Director
Amanda Byrne, IT Administrator

2957 Department of Agriculture & Consumer Services
2 West Edenton Street 919-707-3000
Raleigh, NC 27601 www.ncagr.com
Mission: To improve the state of agriculture in North Carolina by providing services to farmers and agribusinesses, and to serve the citizens of North Carolina by providing services and enforcing laws to protect consumers.
Steve Troxler, Commissioner

2958 North Carolina Board of Science and Technology
301 North Wilmington Street 919-715-0303
1326 Mail Service Center *Fax:* 919-733-8356
Raleigh, NC 27699-1326 tguffey@nccommerce.com
www.nccommerce.com
Encourages, promotes, and supports scientific, engineering, and industrial research applications in North Carolina.
John Hardin, Executive Director
Trudy Guffey, Executive Assistant

2959 North Carolina Department of Environment and Natural Resources
1601 Mail Service Center 919-733-4984
Raleigh, NC 27699-1601 877-623-6748
Fax: 919-715-3060
www.ncdenr.gov/web/guest
John E. Skvarla, III, Secretary
Lacy Presnell, General Counsel

2960 United States Department of the Army US Army Corps of Engineers
69 Darlington Avenue 910-251-4626
PO Box 1890 910-251-4185
Wilmington, NC 28403 www.saw.usace.army.mil
Provides quality planning, design, construction, and operations products and services to meet the needs of civilian and military customers.
Colonel Kevin Landers, Commander
Major R.J. Hughes, Deputy Commander

North Dakota

2961 Dakotas Resource Advisory Council: Department of the Interior
Bureau of Land Management
99 23rd Avenue West 701-227-7700
Suite A *Fax:* 701-227-7701
Dickinson, ND 58601 www.blm.gov
The Dakotas Council currently has 15 members. It is structured to provide a balance of membership by area of expertise, training, and experience. It consists of five individuals in each of three categories.

2962 ND Game and Fish Department
100 N Bismarck Expressway 701-328-6300
Bismarck, ND 58501-5095 *Fax:* 701-328-6352
ndgf@nd.gov
www.gf.nd.gov
To protect, conserve and enhance fish and wildlife populations and their habitats for sustained public consumptive and nonconsumptive use.
Terry Steinwand, Director
Scott Peterson, Deputy Director

2963 North Dakota Forest Service
307 First Street E 701-228-5422
Bottineau, ND 58318-1100 *Fax:* 701-228-5448
forest@nd.gov
www.nd.gov
The ND Forest Service administers forestry programs statewide. The agency operates a nursery at Towner specializing in the production of conifer tree stock. The nursery is the sole supplier of evergreen seedlings in North Dakota.Technial assistance relating to the management of private forest lands, state forest lands, urban and community forests, tree planting and wildland fire protection is provided by the agency. The ND Forest Service also owns and manages app. 13,278acres of state lands.

Larry Kotchman, State Forester
Kathy Wyman, Administrative Assistant

2964 **North Dakota Parks and Recreation Department**
1600 E Century Ave. 701-328-5357
Suite 3 *Fax:* 701-328-5363
Bismarck, ND 58503
The state government agency charged with managing North Dakota's state parks and recreation areas; the state's nature preserves and natural area programs; motorized and non-motorized trail programs; recreational grants and state-widerecreation planning; and state scenic byways program.

Douglass A Prchal, Director
Dorothy Streyle, Coordinator

Ohio

2965 **Division of Environmental Services**
Ohio EPA
8955 East Main Street 614-644-4247
Reynoldsburg, OH 43068 *Fax:* 614-644-4272
web.requests@epa.ohio.gov
www.epa.state.oh.us/des
The Division of Environmental Services provides biological and chemical data and technical assistance to other divisions within Ohio EPA, state and local agencies, and private entities in order to help monitor and protect human healthand the environment to ensure a high quality of life in Ohio.
Steve Roberts, Quality Assurance Supervisor
Jennifer Kraft, Chief

2966 **Lead Poisoning Prevention Program**
Ohio Department of Health
246 N High Street 614-466-5332
Columbus, OH 43215 877-532-3723
Fax: 614-728-6793
lead@odh.ohio.gov
The Lead Poisoning Prevention Program ensures the public receives safe and proper lead abatement, detection, and analytical services by requiring those services be conducted according to federal and state regulations, and by trainedand licensed personnel.
Chris Alexander, Program Supervisor
Pam Blais, Environmental Supervisor

2967 **Ohio Department of Natural Resources Division of Geological Survey**
2045 Morse Rd 614-265-6576
Bldg C *Fax:* 614-447-1918
Columbus, OH 43229-6693 geo.survey@dnr.state.oh.us
www.ohiodnr.com
Provides geologic information and services for responsible management of Ohio's natural resources. Geologic maps, reports and data files developed by the division can be used by individuals, educators, industry, business andgovernment.

Thomas J. Serenko, Division Chief
Mike P. Angle, Assistant Chief

2968 **Ohio Environmental Protection Agency**
50 W Town Street 614-644-3020
Suite 700 www.epa.state.oh.us
Columbus, OH 43215
The mission of the Ohio EPA is to protect the environment and public health by ensuring compliance with environmental laws and demonstrating leadership in environmental stewardship. They work to enforce standards for air, water, andwaste management, and help businesses minimize their waste at the source.

Laurie A. Stevenson, Director
Laura Factor, Assistant Director

2969 **Ohio Environmental Protection Agency: Division of Surface Water**
50 W Town Street 614-644-2001
Suite 700 *Fax:* 614-644-2745
Columbus, OH 43215 www.epa.state.oh.us/dsw
The mission of this division is to protect and enhance Ohio's water to ensure the health and safety of the population. They carry out this mission through the monitoring of aquatic environment, enforcement of laws, and provision oftechnical assistance.
Tiffani Kavalec, Division Chief
Brian Hall, Assistant Chief

2970 **Ohio River Valley Water Sanitation Commission**
5735 Kellogg Avenue 513-231-7719
Cincinnati, OH 45230 *Fax:* 513-231-7761
info@orsanco.org
www.orsanco.org
ORSANCO operates programs to improve water quality in the Ohio River and its tributaries, including: setting waste water discharge standards; performing biological assessment; monitoring for the chemical and physical properties of thewaterways; and conducting special surveys and studies. Also coordinates emergency response activities for spills or accidental discharges to the river and promotes public participating programs.
Kenneth Komoroski, Chairman
Toby Frevert, Vice-Chairman

2971 **Ohio Water Development Authority**
480 South High Street 614-466-5822
Columbus, OH 43215 *Fax:* 614-644-9964
www.owda.org
Provides financial assistance for environmental infrastructure from the sale of municipal revenue bonds through loans to local governments in Ohio and issuing Industrial Revenue Bonds for qualified projects. The vision of OWDA is tocontinue to provide assistance for environmental infrastructure by being responsive to the needs of local government agencies, enhancing the provision of financial and technical assistance and developing new financial assistance products for theprivate sector.

James P. Joyce, Chairman
Steve Grossman, Executive Director

Oklahoma

2972 **Oklahoma Department of Environmental Quality**
707 N Robinson 405-702-0100
PO Box 1677 800-869-1400
Oklahoma City, OK 73101-1677 *Fax:* 405-702-1001
www.deq.state.ok.us
Administers environmental laws considering both the economy of today and the environment of tomorrow.

2973 **Oklahoma Department of Health**
1000 Northeast 10th Street 405-271-5600
Oklahoma, OK 73117 800-522-0203
Fax: 405-271-6199
AskVR@health.ok.gov
www.ok.gov/triton
The Oklahoma State Department of Health is to protect and promote the health of citizens of Oklahoma and to prevent disease and injury, and to assure the conditions by which our citizens can be healthy.
Terry L. Cline, Commissioner

2974 **Salt Plains National Wildlife Refuge**
71189 Harper Road 580-626-4794
Jet, OK 73749 *Fax:* 580-626-4793
fw2_rw_saltplains@fws.gov
www.fws.gov/refuge/Salt_Plains
Provide quality habitat for migratory waterfowl
Debbie Pike, Park Ranger

2975 **Water Quality Division**
5225 N Shurtel 405-702-8100
Oklahoma City, OK 73118 800-869-1400
Fax: 405-810-1046
www.deq.state.ok.us/WQDNew

Larry Edmison, Director

Oregon

2976 **Burns District: Bureau of Land Management**
Department of the Interior
28910 Highway 20 West 541-573-4400
Hines, OR 97738 BLM_OR_BU_Mail@blm.gov
www.blm.gov

Dana Shuford, Manager
Melissa Towers, Administrative Officer

2977 **Department of Transportation**
355 Capitol St. NE 888-275-6368
Salem, OR 97301-3871 *Fax:* 503-986-3432
www.oregon.gov/odot
Mission: To provide a safe, efficient transportation system that supports economic opportunity and livable communities for Oregonians.
Pat Egan, Chairman
David Lohman, Commissioner

2978 **Eugene District: Bureau of Land Management**
Department of the Interior
3106 Pierce Parkway 541-683-6600
Suite E 888-442-3061
Springfield, OR 97477 *Fax:* 541-683-6981
OR_Eugene_Mail@blm.gov
www.blm.gov
The Eugene District manages several ecosystems ranging from coastal inlands to dense Douglas-fir, hemlock, and cedar forests. The wide variation in the lands managed by the District offers the perfect compromise between the urban parksin the cities and the high elevation recreation opportunities in the adjacent Willamette, Siuslaw and Umpqua National Forest.
Ginnie Grilley, Manager

2979 **Klamath River Compact Commission**
280 Main Street 541-882-4436
Klamath Falls, OR 97601-6331
Created by the Klamath River Compact in 1957, KRCC is a three member commission whose purpose, with respect to the water of the Klamath River Basin, is to faciliate and promote the orderly, integrated, and comprehensive developement,use, conservation and control of water for development of lands by irrigation, protection of fish and wildlife, domestic and industrial use, hydropower, navigation, and flood protection.

2980 **Lakeview District: Bureau of Land Management**
Department of the Interior
1301 South G Street 541-947-2177
Lakeview, OR 97630 *Fax:* 541-947-6399
BLM_OR_LV_Mailbox@blm.gov
www.blm.gov

2981 **Medford District: Bureau of Land Management**
3040 Biddle Road 541-618-2200
Medford, OR 97504 BLM_OR_MD_Mail@blm.gov
www.blm.gov
The Bureau of Land Management's Medford District oversees approximately 862,000 acres of scattered public lands between the Cascade and Siskiyou mountain ranges and from the Oregon/California border to Canyon Creek and southern DouglasCounty. This large land base is divided into four Resource Areas: Ashland, Butte Falls, Grants Pass and Glendale.

2982 **Oregon Department of Environmental Quality**
811 SW Sixth Avenue 503-229-5696
Portland, OR 97204-1390 800-452-4011
Fax: 503-229-6124
deq.info@deq.state.or.us
www.oregon.gov/deq
Mission: To be a leader in restoring, maintaining and enhancing the quality of Oregon's air, land and water.
Dick Pederson, Director
Joni Hammond, Deputy Director

2983 **Oregon Department of Fish and Wildlife**
4034 Fairview Industrial Drive SE 503-947-6000
Salem, OR 97303 800-720-6339
odfw.info@state.or.us
www.dfw.state.or.us
Commissioners formulate general state programs and policies concerning management and conservation of fish wildlife resources and establishes seasons, methods and bag limits for recreational and commercial take.
Roy Elicker, Director
David Lane, Deputy Administrator-Informa

2984 **Oregon Department of Forestry**
2600 State Street 503-945-7200
Salem, OR 97310 800-437-4490
Fax: 503-945-7212
www.oregon.gov/odf
Mission: To serve the people of Oregon by protecting, managing, and promoting stewardship of Oregon's forests to enhance environmental, economic, and community sustainability.
Doug Decker, State Forester
Paul Bell, Deputy State Forester

2985 **Oregon Department of Land Conservation and Development**
635 Capitol Street NE 503-373-0050
Suite 150 *Fax:* 503-378-5518
Salem, OR 97301-2540 www.oregon.gov/LCD
Mission: Support all of our partners in creating and implementing comprehensive plans that reflect and balance the statewide planning goals, the vision of citizens, and the interests of local, state, federal and tribal governments.
Jim Rue, Director
Caroline Maclaren, Deputy Director

2986 **Oregon Water Resource Department**
725 Summer Street Northeast 503-986-0900
Suite A *Fax:* 503-986-0904
Salem, OR 97301 webmaster@wrd.state.or.us
www.oregon.gov/owrd
Mission: To serve the public by practicing and promoting responsible water management through two key goals: to directly address Oregon's water supply needs; and to restore and protect streamflows and watersheds in order to ensure thelong-term sustainability of Oregon's ecosystems, economy, and quality of life.
Tom Byler, Director
Brenda Bateman, Public Information Officer

2987 **Prineville District: Bureau of Land Management**
Department of the Interior
3050 NE Third Street 541-416-6700
Prineville, OR 97754 *Fax:* 541-416-6798
BLM_OR_PR_Mail@blm.gov
www.blm.gov

Debbie Henderson-Norton, Manager
Steve Robertson, Associate Manager

2988 **Roseburg District: Bureau of Land Management**
Department of the Interior
777 NW Garden Valley Boulevard 541-440-4930
Roseburg, OR 97471 *Fax:* 541-440-4948
BLM_OR_RB_Mail@blm.gov
www.blm.gov
Public lands of the Roseburg District, located in southwestern Oregon, contain some of the most productive forests in the world. An important mainstay of the local economy, which acquires timber from both private and federal lands inthe region. The district is criss-crossed with streams and rivers that support sport fishing. With Interstate 5 running through the middle of the district, and east-west state highways connecting Crater Lake to the Pacfic coast, the district drawsmany tourists.

2989 **Salem District: Bureau of Land Management**
Department of the Interior

1717 Fabry Road Southeast 503-375-5646
Salem, OR 97306 *Fax:* 503-375-5622
BLM_OR_SA_Mail@blm.gov
www.blm.gov

BLM Mission: to sustain the health, diversity and productivity of the public lands for the use and enjoyment of present and future generations. Salem District manages 400,000 acres scattered across 13 counties. Seventy three percent ofOregon's population live within the boundries of this district. Their major focus is an ecosystem management approach involving many different disciplines. Salem employs 200 full-time employees working in forestry, land surveying, wildlife biology,hydrology, etc.

Aaron Horton, Manager
Don Hollenkamp, Associate Manager

2990 United States Department of the Army: US Army Corps of Engineers
US Army Engineer Division
PO Box 2946 503-808-5150
Portland, OR 97208 www.army.mil/

2991 Vale District: Bureau of Land Management
Department of the Interior
100 Oregon Street 541-473-3144
Vale, OR 97918 *Fax:* 541-473-6213
BLM_OR_VL_Mail@blm.gov
www.blm.gov

The Vale District of the Bureau of Land Management manages 4.9 million acres of public land in eastern Oregon. The mission of the BLM is to sustain the health, diversity, and productivity of the public lands for the use and enjoymentof present and future generations.

Dave Henderson, Manager
Larry Frazier, Associate Manager

Pennsylvania

2992 Allegheny National Forest
US Forest Service
4 Farm Colony Road 814-723-5150
Warren, PA 16365 *Fax:* 814-726-1465
r9_allegheny_nf@fs.fed.us
www.fs.fed.us/r9/allegheny

An organization dedicated to providing advice for development of the corridor management plan for the northern section of the Allegheny River that has been designated as a National Wild and Scenic River.

Erin Connelly, Forest Supervisor

2993 Childhood Lead Poisoning Prevention Program
Pennsylvania Department of Health
PO Box 90 717-783-8451
Harrisburg, PA 17108 *Fax:* 717-772-0323
www.cehn.org

The mission of the Pennsylvania Department of Health, Childhood Lead Poisoning Prevention Program is to make the citizens of the Commonwealth aware of the dangers of lead poisoning and to reduce the number of children who becomelead-poisoned.

2994 Citizens Advisory Council
Pennsylvania Department Environmental Protection
13th Floor, RCSOB 717-787-4527
PO Box 8459 *Fax:* 717-787-2878
Harrisburg, PA 17105-8549 mahughes@pa.gov

Advises the Department of Environmental Protection, the Governor and the General Assembly on environmental issues and the work of the Department.

Susan Wilson, Executive Director
Joyce Hatala, Chair

2995 Environmental Protection Agency Region 3
1650 Arch Street 215-814-5122
Philadelphia, PA 19103-2029 800-438-2474
www.epa.gov/region03

This region is responsible for federal environmental programs in Delaware, Maryland, Pennsylvania, Virginia, West Virginia and District of Columbia. Programs include air and water pollution control; toxic substances, pesticides, anddrinking water regulation; wetlands protection; hazardous waste management, hazardous waste dump site cleanup; and some aspects of radioactive materials regulation.

Cosmo Servidio, Regional Administrator

2996 Lacawac Sanctuary Foundation
94 Sanctuary Road 570-689-9494
Lake Ariel, PA 18436 *Fax:* 570-689-2017
info@lacawac.org
www.lacawac.org

A nature preserve and historic site in northeastern PA's Pocono Mountains. The main function is the protection of its natural areas and historic buildings, including the pristine glacial Lake Lacawac. Research space is available forvisiting researchers, and participants in the Pocono Comparative Lakes Program.

Craig Lukatch, President/Executive Director
Lesley Knoll, Director of Research & Edu

2997 Pennsylvania Department of Conservation and Natural Resources
Rachel Carson State Office Building 717-787-2869
400 Market Street, PO Box 8767 *Fax:* 717-772-9106
Harrisburg, PA 17105-8767 ra-askdcnr@state.pa.us
www.dcnr.state.pa.us

Mission: To maintain, improve and preserve state parks; to manage state forest lands to assure their long-term health, sustainability and economic use; to provide information on Pennsylvania's ecological and geological resources; andto administer grant and technical assistance programs that will benefit rivers conservation, trails and greenways, local recreation, regional heritage conservation and environmental education programs across Pennsylvania.

Ellen Ferretti, Secretary
Jennifer Stepulitis, Executive Secretary

2998 Pennsylvania Fish & Boat Commission: Northeast Region
5566 Main Road 570-477-5717
Sweet Valley, PA 18656 *Fax:* 570-477-3221
ra-needureach@pa.gov
www.fishandboat.com

Mission: To protect, conserve, and enhance the Commonwealth's aquatic resources and provide fishing and boating opportunities.

Steven M. Ketterer, President
G. Warren Elliott, Vice-President

2999 Pennsylvania Forest Stewardship Program
PO Box 8552 717-787-2106
Harrisburg, PA 17105 www.enr.gov.nt.ca/

Forest stewardship is a US Forest Service program with the goal of helping private landowners manage their lands for various objectives. Landowners participating in the Forest Stewardship Program work with a private forestry consultantto depelop a customized plan for their land and objectives. Studies show that landowners that work with professionals and follow their customized plan are more likely to engage in practices that sustain forest values.

3000 Pennsylvania Game Commission
2001 Elmerton Avenue 717-787-4250
Harrisburg, PA 17110-9797 *Fax:* 717-772-0542
www.pgc.state.pa.us

The Pennsylvania Game Commission has the specific responsibility of acting as steward of the Commonwealth's wild birds and wild animals for the benefit of present and future generations. In carrying out this state constitutionalmandate, the Pennsylvania Game Commission will: Protect, conserve and manage the diversity of wildlife and their habitats; Provide wildlife related education, services, and recreational opportunities for both consumptive and non-consumptive uses ofwildlife.

Thomas Boop, President
Roxane Palone, Vice President

3001 **Susquehanna River Basin Commission**
4423 North Front Street 717-238-0423
Harrisburg, PA 17110 *Fax:* 717-238-2436
srbc@srbc.net
www.srbc.net
The responsibility of SRBC is to enhance public welfare through comprehensive planning, water supply allocation & management of the water resources of the Susquehanna River Basin. The SRBC works to reduce damages caused by floods;provide for the reasonable & sustained development & use of surface & ground water for municipal, agricultural, recreational, commercial & industrial purposes; protect & restore fisheries, wetlands & aquatic habitat; protect water quality & instreamuses.
Paul O Swartz, Executive Director
Thomas W. Beauduy, Deputy Executive Director

3002 **United States Department of the Army US Army Corps of Engineers**
US Army Engineer District
1000 Liberty Avenue 412-395-7500
Pittsburgh, PA 15222-4186 *Fax:* 412-644-2811
www.usace.army.mil
Michael P Crall, District Engineer
Peter A Steinig, Deputy District Engineer

Rhode Island

3003 **Division of Parks and Recreation**
2321 Hartford Avenue 401-222-2632
Johnston, RI 02919 *Fax:* 401-934-6010
www.riparks.com
The objective of the Division of Parks & Recreation is to provide all Rhode Island Residents and Visitors the opportunity to enjoy a diverse mix of well-maintained, scenic, safe, accessible areas and facilities within our park systemand to offer a variety of outdoor recreational opportunities and programming which may benefit and enhance our Quality of Life.

3004 **Environmental Management: Division of Fish and Wildlife**
82 Smith Street 401-222-2357
Room 217 *Fax:* 401-222-1356
Providence, RI 02903-1120 www.sos.ri.gov
Agency manages the fish and wildlife resources of the State of Rhode Island inluding marine fisheries. The division has 60 employees and is located in 4 stations statwide.
Michael Lapisky, Chief

3005 **Rhode Island Department of Environmental Management**
235 Promenade Street 401-222-6800
Providence, RI 02908 www.dem.ri.gov
We are committed to preserving the quality of Rhode Island's environment, maintaining and safety of its residents and protecting the natural systems upon which life depends. Together with many partners, we offer assistance toindividuals, business and municipalities, conduct research, find solutions, and enforce laws created to protect the environment.
W Michael Sullivan, Director

3006 **Rhode Island Department of Evironmental Management: Forest Environment**
1037 Hartford Pike 401-647-4389
North Scituate, RI 02857 *Fax:* 401-647-3590
www.dem.ri.gov
Coordinates a statewide forest fire protection plan, provides forest fire protection on state lands, assists rural volunteer fire departments, and develops forest and wildlife management plans for private landowners who choose tomanage their property in ways that will protect these resources on their land. The program promotes public understanding of environmental conservation, enforces Department rules and regulations on DEM lands.
Catherine Sparks, Chief

3007 **Rhode Island Water Resources Board**
1 Capitol Hill 401-574-8400
3rd Floor *Fax:* 401-574-8401
Providence, RI 02908 www.wrb.state.ri.us
An executive agency of state government charged with managingther proper development, utilization and conservation of water resources. The primary responsibility is to ensure that sufficient water supply is available for present andfuture generations, apportioning available water to all areas of the state.
Daniel W Varin, Chairman
Juan Mariscal, General Manager

South Carolina

3008 **Blackbeard Island National Wildlife Refuge**
694 Beech Hill Lane 843-784-2468
Hardeeville, SC 29927 *Fax:* 843-784-2465
savannahcoastal@fws.gov
www.fws.gov/blackbeardisland
This Georgia barrier island's 5,618 acres includes maritime forest, saltmarsh, freshwater marsh, and beach habitat, 3,000 of which has been set aside as National wilderness of variety of recreational activities are availableyear-round, including wildlife observation, birdwatching, hiking and beachcombing.
Jane Griess, Project Leader
Kimberley Hayes, Refuge Manager

3009 **Department of Interior: U.S. Fish & Wildlife Service - South Carolina**
Clemson University
261 Lehotsky Hall 864-656-2432
Clemson, SC 29634 *Fax:* 864-656-1350
southeast@fws.gov
www.fws.gov/southeast
Cindy Dohner, Regional Director

3010 **Department of Parks, Recreation and Tourism**
1205 Pendleton Street 803-734-1700
Edgar A Brown Building 866-224-9339
Columbia, SC 29201 www.scprt.com
Mission: To learn more about our purpose, mission, and vision.
Pam Benjamin, Director of Human Resources

3011 **Office of Environmental Laboratory Certification**
PO Box 72 803-896-0970
State Park, SC 29147 *Fax:* 803-896-0850
We offer certification to any environmental laboratory wishing to analyze samples for South Carolina's Department of Health and Environmental Control [DHEC]. This scope of certification covers the Safe Drinking Water Act (SDWA), theClean Water Act (NPDES), and solid & hazardous wastes including RCRA and CERCLA requirements (SW846 methodologies).

3012 **South Atlantic Fishery Management Council**
4055 Faber Place Drive 843-571-4366
Suite 201 *Fax:* 843-769-4520
North Charleston, SC 29405 safmc@safmc.net
www.safmc.net
The South Atlantic Fishery Management Council is headquartered in Charleston, SC, and is responsible for the conservation and management of fish stocks within the 200-mile limit of the Atlantic off the coasts of North Carolina, SouthCarolina, Georgia, and east florida to Key West.
David M. Cupka, Chairman
Ben C. Hartig, Vice Chairman

3013 **South Carolina Department of Health and Environmental Control**
2600 Bull Street 803-898-3432
Columbia, SC 29201
Mission: We promote and protect the health of the public and the environment.

3014 South Carolina Department of Natural Resources
1000 Assembly Street 803-734-4007
Rembert C Dennis Building *Fax:* 803-734-4300
Columbia, SC 29201 webmaster@dnr.sc.gov
www.dnr.state.sc.us
Mission: To serve as the principal advocate for and steward of South Carolina's natural resources.
Glenn McFadden, Chairman
Cary L. Chastain, Vice Chairman

3015 South Carolina Forestry Commission
5500 Broad River Road 803-896-8800
Columbia, SC 29212 *Fax:* 803-798-8097
www.trees.sc.gov
The mission of the Forestry Commission is to protect, promote, enhance and nurture the forest lands of South Carolina in a manner consistent with achieving the greatest good for its citizens. Responsibilities extend to all forestlands, both rural and urban, and to all associated forest values and amenities including, but not limited to: timber, wildlife, water quality, air quality, soil protection, recreation and aesthetics.
Henry E Kodama, State Forester
Tom Patton, Deputy State Forester

3016 United States Department of the Army US Army Corps of Engineers
69A Hagood Avenue 843-329-8000
Charleston, SC 29403 *Fax:* 843-329-2332
CESAC-PAO@usace.army.mil
www.sac.usace.army.mil
The Charleston District (USACE), South Atlantic Division serves the citizens of South Carolina, the Region, and the Nation by providing quality water resources, value engineering/value management, environmental, and international andinteragency projects and services.
Lt. Col. Edward Chamberlayne, Commander
Maj. John O'Brien, Deputy Commander

South Dakota

3017 Attorney General's Office
1302East Highway 14 605-773-3215
Suite 1 *Fax:* 605-773-4106
Pierre, SD 57501-8501 atghelp@state.sd.us
www.atg.sd.gov
The Natural Resources Division of the South Dakota Attorney General's Office provides specialized legal counsel to state agencies in environmental, agricultural, financial, Indian law and natural resource matters. It focuses on (1)state boards and agencies which issue environmental, water, and agricultural permits and the lease of state mineral lands; (2) environmental litigation before boards and agencies and in the courts; and (3) jurisdictional disputes.
Marty J. Jackley, Attorney General

3018 Department of Environment & Natural Resources
523 E Capitol Avenue 605-773-3151
Pierre, SD 57501 *Fax:* 605-773-6035
denrinternet@state.sd.us
www.extension.psu.edu/natural-resources
Our mission is to provide environmental and natural resources assessment, financial assistance, and regulation in a customer service manner that protects the public health, conserves natural resources, preserves the environment andpromotes economic development.
Steven M. Pirner, Secretary of the Department

3019 Department of Wildlife and Fisheries Sciences
South Dakota State University
Box 2140b 605-688-6121
Brookings, SD 57007 *Fax:* 605-688-4515
terri.symens@sdstate.edu
www.sdstate.edu/nrm/
David Willis, Department Head
Nels Troelstrup, Assistant Department Head

3020 South Dakota Department of Game, Fish & Parks
523 E Capitol Avenue 605-773-3485
Pierre, SD 57501 *Fax:* 605-773-5842
wildinfo@state.sd.us
www.gfp.sd.gov
The purpose of the Department of Game, Fish and Parks is to perpetuate, conserve, manage, protect and enhance South Dakota's wildlife resources, parks and outdoor recreational opportunities for the use, benefit and enjoyment of thepeople of this state and its visitors, and to give the highest priority to the welfare of this states's wildlife and parks, and their environment, in planning and decisions.
Susie Knippling, Chairwoman
John Cooper, Vice Chair

3021 South Dakota Department of Health
600 E Capitol Avenue 605-773-3361
Pierre, SD 57501-2536 800-738-2301
Fax: 605-773-5683
DOH.info@state.sd.us
www.doh.sd.gov/
Mission: To prevent disease and promote health, ensure access to needed, high-quality health care, and to efficiently manage public health resources.
Kim Malsam Rysdon, Secretary
Joan Adam, Division Director, Administr

3022 South Dakota State Extension Services
South Dakota State University
Box 2207D 605-688-4792
Brookings, SD 57007 *Fax:* 605-688-6733
www.sdstate.edu/sdsuextension/index.cfm
Extension serves the people of South Dakota by helping them apply unbiased, scientific knowledge to improve their lives. Extension also offers educational information, programs, and services in response to local issues and needs.
Barry Dunn, Extension Director
Karla Trautman, Associate Director

Tennessee

3023 Obed Wild & Scenic River
PO Box 429 423-346-6294
Wartburg, TN 37887 *Fax:* 423-346-3362
rebecca_schapansky@nps.gov
www.nps.gov/obed/
Approximately 45 miles of wild and scenic river are comprised of the Obed River, Clear Creek, Daddy's Creek and Emory River. These water courses have cut rugged gorges leaving exciting whitewater gorges with bluffs as high as 500 feetabove the water.
Niki Stephanie Nicholas, Superintendent
Barbara Olmstead, Administrative Officer

3024 Tennessee Department of Agriculture
Ellington Agricultural Center 615-837-5103
Melrose Station, PO Box 40627 *Fax:* 615-837-5333
Nashville, TN 37204 TN.Agriculture@TN.gov
www.tennessee.gov/agriculture
Mission: To serve the citizens of Tennessee by promoting wise uses of our agriculture and forest resources, developing economic opportunities, and ensuring safe and dependable food and fiber.
Julius Johnson, Commissioner
Jai Templeton, Deputy Commissioner

3025 **Tennessee Department of Environment and Conservation**
401 Church Street 615-532-0109
L&C Annex, 1st Floor 888-891-8332
Nashville, TN 37243 ask.TDEC@tn.gov
Safeguarding the health and safety of Tennessee citizens from environmental hazards
Robert J. Martineau, Jr., Commissioner
Shari Meghreblian, Deputy Commissioner

3026 **Tennessee Valley Authority**
400 W Summit Hill Drive 865-632-2101
Knoxville, TN 37902-1499 tvainfo@tva.com
www.tva.gov
TVA generates prosperity in the Tennessee Valley by promoting economic development, supplying low-cost, reliable power and supporting a thriving river system.
Bill Johnson, President/CEO
Janet Hernin, Executive Vice President

3027 **United States Army Engineer District: Memphis**
167 N Main Street 901-544-4109
Memphis, TN 38103 800-317-4156
MemphisPAO@usace.army.mil
www.mvm.usace.army.mil
Provides flood control, navigation, environmental stewardship, emergency operations, and other authorized civil works to benefit the region and the Nation.
Col. Vernie L. Reichling, Jr., Commander
Lt. Col. Thomas Patton, Deputy Commander

3028 **University of Tennessee Extension**
2621 Morgan Circle 865-974-7114
121 Morgan Hall *Fax:* 865-974-1068
Knoxville, TN 37996 tlcross@utk.edu
Statewide educational organization that brings research-based information about agriculture, family and consumer sciences, and resource development to the people of Tennessee where they live and work.
Tim L. Cross, Dean
Shirley W. Hastings, Deputy Dean

3029 **Wildlife Resources Agency**
440 Hogan Rd 615-781-6500
Nashville, TN 37220 *Fax:* 615-741-4606
Ask.TWRA@tn.gov
www.state.tn.us/twra
The Tennessee Wildlife Resources Agency develops, manages and maintains sound programs of hunting, fishing, trapping, boating, and other wildlife related outdoor recreational activities.
Ed Carter, Executive Director

3030 **Wildlife Resources Agency: Fisheries Management Division**
440 Hogan Rd 615-781-6500
PO Box 40747 *Fax:* 615-781-6667
Nashville, TN 37220 Ask.TWRA@tn.gov
Ed Carter, Executive Director

Texas

3031 **Attorney General of Texas Natural Resources Division (NRD)**
300 W 15th Street 512-463-2100
PO Box 12548 *Fax:* 512-475-2994
Austin, TX 78711-2548 www.texasattorneygeneral.gov
The NRD represents the enviromental and energy agencies of the State of Texas in court. NRD's primary activity is the prosecution of lawsuits, referred by state agencies, that involve violations of the state's enviromental and naturalresources protection laws. NRD also defends permits issued by agencies uder those laws and defends challenges to the statues and regulations themselves.NRD also has primary enforcement responsibility for protecting the public's access to Texasbeaches.
Greg Abbott, Attorney General

3032 **Bureau of Economic Geology**
University of Texas at Austin
10100 Burnet Rd., Bldg 130 512-471-1534
Box X 888-839-4365
Austin, TX 78713-8924 *Fax:* 512-471-0140
begmail@beg.utexas.edu
www.beg.utexas.edu
The Bureau provides wide-ranging advisory, technical, informational, and research-based services to industries, nonprofit organizations, and Federal, State, and local agencies.
Scott W Tinker, Director
Jay Kipper, Associate Director

3033 **Chihuahuan Desert Research Institute**
43869 Hwy 118 432-364-2499
PO Box 905 *Fax:* 432-364-2686
Fort Davis, TX 79734 www.cdri.org
Conducts research on the Chihuahuan Desert.
Rick Herman, Executive Director Interim
Rusty Brockman, Vice chair

3034 **Environmental Protection Agency Region 6**
1201 Elm Street 214-665-2760
Suite 500 800-887-6063
Dallas, TX 75270-2102 www.epa.gov/region06
Region 6 encompasses the ecologically, demographically and economically diverse of states of Arkansas, Louisiana, New Mexico, Oklahoma and Texas, along with 66 tribal nations. The regional vision is to meet the environmental needs of achanging world.
David W. Gray, Regional Administrator
Erin E. Chancellor, Chief of Staff

3035 **Guadalupe: Blanco River Authority**
933 E Court Street 830-379-5822
Seguin, TX 78155 *Fax:* 830-379-9718
comments@gbra.org
www.gbra.org
Aims to conserve and protect the water resources of the Guadalupe River basin and make them available for beneficial use. Services include water and wastewater treatment, water quality testing, the management of water rights anddelivery of stored water, the production of electricity from seven hydroelectric plants and engineering design support.
Thomas Mathews, Chair
James Murphy, Executive Manager

3036 **Parks & Wildlife: Public Lands Division**
4200 Smith School Road 512-389-4800
Austin, TX 78744 800-792-1112
Fax: 512-389-4960
www.tpwd.state.tx.us
In 1963 the Parks Board merged with the game and Fish Commission to form the Texas Parks and Wildlife Department. The merger created the Parks Division, currently the Public Lands Division. In 1967 park acquisition and developmentincreased with the passage of a $75 million parks bond authorization and the dedication of a portion of the state's cigarette tax to the development of state and local parks.
Carter Smith, Executive Director
Joe Carter, Internal Affairs

3037 **Parks & Wildlife: Resource Protection Division**
4200 Smith School Road 512-389-4864
Austin, TX 78744 www.tpwd.state.tx.us
The Resource Protection Division protects Tezas fich, wildlife, plant and mineral resources from degradation or depletion. The division investigates any environmental contamination that may cause loss of fish or wildlife. It providesinformation and recommendations to other government agencies and participates in administrative and judicial proceedings concerning pollution

incidents, development, development projects and other actions that may affect fish and wildlife.
Carter Smith, Executive Director
Joe Carter, Internal Affairs

3038 Pecos River Commission
PO Box 969 432-729-3225
Marfa, TX 79843 *Fax:* 432-729-3224
tatecattle@sbcglobal.net
www.tceq.state.tx.us
The Pecos River Compact Commission administers the Pecos River Compact to ensure that Texas receives its equitable share of quality water from the Pecos River and its tributaries as appointed by the Compact. The Compact includes thestates of New Mexico and Texas.
Frederic Tate, Commissioner

3039 Rio Grande Compact Commission
P.O. Box 13087 915-834-7075
Ste. 560 *Fax:* 915-834-7080
Austin, TX 79843-3087
The Rio Grande Compact Commission administers the Rio Grande Compact to ensure that Texas receives its equitable share of quality water from the Rio Grande and its tributaries as appointed by the Compact. The Compact includes thestates of Colorado, New Mexico, and Texas.
Patrick R Gordon, Commisioner

3040 Sabine River Compact Commission
P.O. Box 13087 409-988-9428
Austin, TX 79843-3087 gary.gagnon@att.net
The Sabine River Compact Commission administers the Sabine River Compact to ensure that Texas receives its equitable share of quality water from the Sabine River and its tributaries as apportioned by the Compact. The Compact includesthe states of Texas and Louisiana.
Gary E Gagnon, Commissioner
Jerry F. Gipson, Commissioner

3041 Texas Animal Health Commission
2105 Kramer Lane 512-719-0700
Austin, TX 78758 800-550-8242
Fax: 512-719-0719
www.tahc.state.tx.us
TAHC works to keep pests from reoccurring as major livestock health hazards. Ultimately, the TAHC mission and role is the assurance of marketability and mobility of Texas livestock. TAHC works to sustain and continue to make a vitalcontribution to a wholesome and abundant supply of meat, eggs, and dairy products at affordable costs.
Dee Ellis, Executive Director
Gene Snelson, General Counsel

3042 Texas Cooperative Extension
Jack K Williams Administration Bldg 979-845-7800
Room 112, 7101 TAMU *Fax:* 979-845-9542
College Station, TX 77843
Edward G Smith, Director

3043 Texas Department of Agriculture
PO Box 12847 512-463-7476
Austin, TX 78711-2847 800-835-5832
Fax: 888-223-8861
Customer.Relations@TexasAgriculture.gov
www.texasagriculture.gov
TDA's mission is to partner with all Texans to make Texas the nation's leader in agriculture, fortify our economy, empower rural communities, promote healthy lifestyles, and cultivate winning strategies for rural, suburban and urbanTexas through exceptional service and the common threads of agriculture in our daily lives
Sid Miller, Commissioner
Jason Fearneyhough, Deputy Commissioner

3044 Texas Department of Health
1100 W 49th Street 512-776-7111
Austin, TX 78756-3199 888-963-7111
Fax: 512-458-7686
customer.service@dshs.state.tx.us
www.dshs.state.tx.us
The Texas Department of Health is the state government agency charged with protecting and promoting the health of the public.
David L. Lakey, Commissioner
Kirk Cole, Associate Commissioner

3045 Texas Forest Service
301 Tarrow 979-458-6606
Suite 364 *Fax:* 979-458-6610
College Station, TX 77840 texasforestservice.tamu.edu
The mission is to provide statewide leadership and professional assistance to assure the states's forest, tree and related natural resources are wisely used, nurtured, protected and perpetuated for the benefit of all Texans.
Thomas G. Boggus, Director

3046 Texas Natural Resource Conservation Commission
12100 Park 35 Circle 512-239-1000
Austin, TX 78753 *Fax:* 512-239-4430
www.tceq.state.tx.us/
The Texas Natural Resource Conservation Commission strives to keep our state's human and natural resources consistent with sustainable economic development. Our goal is clean air, clean water and the safe management of waste.

3047 Texas Parks & Wildlife Department
4200 Smith School Road 512-389-4800
Austin, TX 78744 800-792-1112
Fax: 512-389-4814
webcomments@tpwd.state.tx.us
www.tpwd.state.tx.us
Mission: To manage and conserve the natural and cultural resources of Texas and to provide hunting, fishing and outdoor recreation opportunities for the use and enjoyment of present and future generations.
Carter Smith, Executive Director
Joe Carter, Internal Affairs

3048 Texas State Soil and Water Conservation Board (TSSWCB)
4311 South 31st Street 254-773-2250
Suite 125 800-792-3485
Temple, TX 76502 *Fax:* 254-773-3311
www.tpwd.state.tx.us
The state agency that administers Texas' soil and water conservation laws and coordinates conservation and nonpoint source pollution abatement programs through the State. The Board is composed of 7 members, 2 Governor appointed and 5landowners, from across Texas, and is the lead state agency for planning, management, and abatement of agricultural and silvicultural (forestry) nonpoint source pollution, and administers the Texas Brush Control Program. There are regional officesthroughout Texas.

Marty H. Graham, Chairman
Scott Buckles, Vice-Chairman

3049 United States Department of the Army: US Army Corps of Engineers
819 Taylor Street 817-886-1306
Fort Worth, TX 76102-0300 www.usace.army.mil
Thomas Bostick, Commander
Richard Stevens, Deputy Chief Of Engineers

Utah

3050 Cedar City District: Bureau of Land Management
Department of the Interior

176 East D.L. Sargent Drive 435-865-3000
Cedar City, UT 84721 *Fax:* 435-865-3053
utccmail@blm.gov
www.blm.gov
Responsible for administering about 2.1 million acres of public lands located in Iron and Beaver counties in southwestern Utah
Todd S Christiansen, Field Manager

3051 Colorado River Basin Salinity Control Advisory Council: Upper Colorado Region
US Bureau of Reclamation
125 S State Street 801-524-3774
Room 6107 *Fax:* 801-524-3856
Salt Lake City, UT 84138 www.usbr.gov/uc
Rick Gold, Director

3052 Moab District: Bureau of Land Management
Department of the Interior
82 East Dogwood 435-259-2100
Moab, UT 84532 *Fax:* 435-259-2106
www.blm.gov
The BLM is committed to providing the highest possible level of access to its facilities, programs, services, and activities on the public lands for persons with disabilities
Maggie Wyatt, Manager

3053 Richfield Field Office: Bureau of Land Management
Department of the Interior
150 E 900 N 435-896-1500
Richfield, UT 84701 *Fax:* 435-896-1550
utrfmail@blm.gov
www.blm.gov
Cornell Christensen, Manager

3054 Salt Lake District: Bureau of Land Management
Department of the Interior
2370 S. Decker Lake Blvd 801-977-4300
West Valley City, UT 84119 www.blm.gov
The BLM administers public lands within a framework of numerous laws. The most comprehensive of these is the Federal Land Policy and Management Act of 1976. All Bureau policies, procedures and management actions must be consistent withFLPMA and the other laws that govern use of the public lands. It is their mission to sustain the health, diversity and productivity of the public lands for the use and enjoyment of present and future generations.
Glenn Carpenter, Manager

3055 Upper Colorado River Commission
355 S 400 E Street 801-531-1150
Salt Lake City, UT 84111-2969 *Fax:* 801-531-9750
dostler@ucrcommission.com
www.usbr.gov/uc/rm/amp/amwg/amwgbioALT_ostler.html
The Upper Colorado River Commission is an interstate compact administration agency created by the Upper Colorado River Basin Compact of 1948. Since its inception, the Commission (made up of Commissioners appointed by the Governor ofeach Upper Division State and one appointed by the President of the United States) has actively participated in the development, utilization and conservation of the water resources of the Colorado River Basin.
Don Ostler, Executive Director

3056 Utah Department of Agriculture and Food
350 N Redwood Road 801-538-7100
PO Box 146500 *Fax:* 801-538-7126
Salt Lake City, UT 84114-6500 agriculture@utah.gov
www.ag.utah.gov
The Utah Department of Agriculture and Food is one of the state's oldest agencies, overseeing dozens of legislatively mandated programs that promote the healthy growth of Utah agriculture, the conservation of natural resources and theprotection of food supply.
LuAnn Adams, Commissioner
Scott Ericson, Deputy Commissioner

3057 Utah Geological Survey
1594 W North Temple, Suite 3110 801-537-3300
PO Box 146100 *Fax:* 801-537-3400
Salt Lake City, UT 84114-6100 www.geology.utah.gov
The Utah Geological Survey is an applied scientific agency that creates, interprets and provides information about Utah's geologic environment, resources and hazards to promote safe, beneficial and wise use of land.
Bill Loughlin, Chair
Mark D. Bunnell, Co-Chair

3058 Utah Natural Resources: Water Resources Section
1594 W North Temple, Room 310 801-538-7230
Salt Lake City, UT 84116 *Fax:* 801-538-7229
Mission: Plan, conserve, develop and protect Utah's water resources.
N.Gawain Snow, Chairman
Jim Lemmon, Vice Chairman

3059 Utah Natural Resources: Wildlife Resource Division
1594 W N Temple, Suite 2110 801-538-4700
Salt Lake City, UT 84116 *Fax:* 801-538-4745
Mission: To serve the people of Utah as trustee and guardian of the state's wildlife and to ensure its future and values through management, protection, conservation and education.
Greg Sheehan, Director
Mike P. Fowlks, Deputy Director

3060 Utah State Department of Natural Resources: Division of Forestry, Fire, & State Lands
1594 W North Temple, Suite 3520 801-538-5555
PO Box 145703 *Fax:* 801-533-4111
Salt Lake City, UT 84114-5703 www.ffsl.utah.gov
The Division of Forestry, Fire & State Lands manages, sustains and strengthens Utah's forests, rangelands, sovereign lands and watersheds for its citizens and visitors
Dick Buehler, State Forester/Director
Brian Cottam, Deputy Director

3061 Vernal District: Bureau of Land Management
Department of the Interior
170 South 500 East 435-781-4423
Vernal, UT 84078 *Fax:* 435-781-4410
BLM_UT_Vernal_Comments@blm.gov
Bill Stringer, Manager

Vermont

3062 Department of Forests, Parks, and Recreation
1 National Life Drive 802-241-3670
Davis 2 *Fax:* 802-244-1481
Montpelier, VT 05620-3801 www.fpr.vermont.gov
Mission: To practice and encourage high quality stewardship of Vermont's environment by: monitoring and maintaining the health, integrity and diversity of important species, natural communities, and ecological processes; managingforests for sustainable use; providing and promoting opportunities for compatible outdoor recreation; and furnishing related information, education, and service.
Michael C. Snyder, Commissioner
Tracy Zeno, Executive Assistant

3063 Vermont Agency of Agriculture, Food and Markets
116 State Street 802-828-2430
Montpelier, VT 05620-2901 www.vermontagriculture.com
To facilitate, support and encourage the growth and viability of agriculture while protecting the working landscape, human health, animal health, plant health, consumers and the environment
Chuck Ross, Secretary
Jolinda LaClair, Deputy Secretary

3064 Vermont Agency of Natural Resources
1 National Life Drive, Davis 2 802-828-1294
Montpelier, VT 05620-3901 *Fax:* 802-244-1102
www.anr.state.vt.us

To draw from and build upon Vermonters' shared ethic of responsibility for our natural environment, an ethic that encompasses a sense of place, community and quality of life, and understanding that we are an integral part of theenvironment and that we must all be responsible stewards for this and future generations
Deb Markowitz, Secretary

3065 Vermont Department of Health
108 Cherry Street 802-863-7200
PO Box 70 800-464-4343
Burlington, VT 05402 *Fax:* 802-865-7754
www.healthvermont.gov
The Vermont Department of Health, the state's public health agency, works to protect and improve the health of our population through core public health functions. Core public health functions are those activities that lay thegroundwork for healthy communities.
Harry Chen MD, Commissioner

Virginia

3066 Commerce and Trade: Mines, Minerals and Energy Department
Depart. Mines, Minerals & Energy 804-692-3200
9th St Office Bldg, 202 North 9th Street *Fax:* 804-692-3200
Richmond, VA 23219 www.mme.state.va.us/
Mission: To enhance the development and conservation of energy and mineral resources in a safe and environmentally sound manner in order to support a more productive economy in Virginia.
George P. Willis, Director

3067 Conservation & Development of Public Beaches Board
Virginia Department of Conservation & Recreation
600 E. Main St., 24th Floor 804-786-2064
Richmond, VA 23219 pco@dcr.virginia.gov
Helps localities maintain and improve public beaches to enhance recreation for Virginia's citizens and visitors
Mark E. Smith, Chair
W. Bruce Wingo, Vice-Chairman

3068 Department of Conservation & Recreation: Division of Dam Safety
600 E. Main St., 24th Floor 804-786-6124
Richmond, VA 23219 *Fax:* 804-786-0536
pco@dcr.virginia.gov
www.dcr.virginia.gov
The program's purpose is to provide for safe design, construction, operation and maintenance of dams to protect public safety.
Mark E. Smith, Chair
W. Bruce Wingo, Vice-Chairman

3069 Division of Mineral Resources
Washington Building , 8th Floor 804-692-3200
1100 Bank Street *Fax:* 804-692-3237
Richmond, VA 23219 www.dmme.virginia.gov
Mission: To enhance the development and conservation of energy and mineral resources in a safe and environmentally sound manner to support a more productive economy in Virginia. DMR generates, collects, complies, and evaluates geologicdata, creates and publishes geologic maps and report, works cooperatively with other state and federal agencies, and is the primary source of information on geology, minerla and energy resources, and geologic hazards for both the mineral and energyindustries.
Ed Erb, Director

3070 Division of State Parks
Virginia Department of Conservation & Recreation
600 E. Main St., 24th Floor 804-786-6124
Richmond, VA 23219 800-933-7275
Fax: 804-786-9294
pco@dcr.virginia.gov
www.dcr.virginia.gov

3071 Secretary of Commerce and Trade
1111 East Broad Street 804-786-7831
PO Box 1475 *Fax:* 804-371-0250
Richmond, VA 23218 www.commerce.virginia.gov
The secretayr of Commerce and Trade oversees the economic, community, and workforce development of the Commonwealth. Each of the 13 Commerce and Trade agencies actively contributes to the Commonwealth's economic strength and highquality of life.
Maurice A. Jones, Sec of Commerce & Trade
Carry Roth, Deputy Secretary

3072 US Geological Survey
12201 Sunrise Valley Drive 703-648-4000
Reston, VA 20192 va.water.usgs.gov
Mission: The Unites States Geological Survey serves the Nation by providing reliable scientific information to describe and understand the Earth; minimize loss of life and property from natural disasters; manage water, biological,energy, and mineral resources; and enhance and protect our quality of life.
Mark D Myers, Director
Bob Doyle, Deputy Director

3073 Virginia Cooperative Fish & Wildlife Research Unit
Virginia Polytechnic Institute & State Unversity
106 Cheatham Hall 540-231-4934
Blacksburg, VA 24061 www.coopunits.org
A field station of the US Geological Survey, dedicated to research and management of fish and wildlife resources in Virginia and surrounding states. Expertise includes freshwater fish and mollusks and large game mammals. The unitincludes 3 research scientists.
Ken Williams, Chief
Jim Fleming, Supervisor

3074 Virginia Department of Environmental Quality
629 E Main Street 804-698-4000
PO Box 1105 800-592-5482
Richmond, VA 23218 *Fax:* 804-698-4500
www.deq.virginia.gov
Virginia's regulatory state agency for air, water waste management and coastal resources. The department is also the coordinating clearinghouse for environmental education and information; and maintains the state's gateway.
David K Paylor, Director
James Golden, Deputy Director

3075 Virginia Department of Game & Inland Fisheries: Wildlife Division
P.O. Box 90778 804-367-1000
Henrico, VA 23228-778 *Fax:* 804-367-9147
dgifweb@dgif.virginia.gov
www.dgif.virginia.gov
Bob Duncan, Executive Director
Angele Goff, Executive Assistant

3076 Virginia Department of Game & Inland Fisheries Fisheries Division
P.O. Box 90778 804-367-1000
Henrico, VA 23228-778 *Fax:* 804-367-9147
dgifweb@dgif.virginia.gov
www.dgif.virginia.gov
Bob Duncan, Executive Director
Angele Goff, Executive Assistant

3077 Virginia Department of Game and Inland Fisheries
P.O. Box 90778 804-367-1000
Henrico, VA 23228-778 *Fax:* 804-364-9147
dgifweb@dgif.virginia.gov
www.dgif.virginia.gov
To manage Virginia's wildlife and inland fish to maintain optimum population of all species to serve the needs of the commonwealth; to provide opportunity for all to enjoy wildlife, inland fish, boating and related outdoor recreation;to promote safety for persons and property in connection with boating, hunting and fishing.
Bob Duncan, Executive Director
Angele Goff, Executive Assistant

3078 **Virginia Department of Health Commissioners Office**
2001 Maywill Street 804-786-3561
Richmond, VA 23230 *Fax:* 804-786-4616
www.vdh.state.va.us

Cynthia C. Romero, Commissioner

3079 **Virginia Department of Mines, Minerals & Energy: Division of Mined Land Reclamation**
3405 Mountain Empire Road 276-523-8100
Big Stone Gap, VA 24219 *Fax:* 276-523-8148
www.dmme.virginia.gov
Responsible for ensuring the reclamation of land affected by surface and underground coal mining activity
Randy Casey, Director

3080 **Virginia Department of Mines, Minerals and Energy: Division of Mineral Resources**
900 Natural Resources Drive 434-951-6310
Ste. 400 *Fax:* 434-951-6325
Charlottesville, VA 22903 www.dmme.virginia.gov
Mission: To enhance the development and conservation of energy and mineral resources in a safe and environementally sound manner to support a more productive economy in Virginia.

3081 **Virginia Museum of Natural History**
21 Starling Avenue 276-634-4141
Martinsville, VA 24112 *Fax:* 276-634-4199
information@vmnh.virginia.gov
www.vmnh.net
We are a state museum of natural history with research scientists in marine biology, vertebrate and invertebrate paleontology, archaeology, earth sciences, entomology, and mammalogy. Creates education programs, exhibits, and fieldtrips focused on natural history and environmental issues. Its publishing division specializes in works by natural scientists and environmental educators in the US and abroad. Writing, editorial, and design services available for books, reports, textbooks, etc..
Joe Keiper, Executive Director
Gloria Niblett, Director of Administration

3082 **Virginia Sea Grant Program**
1208 Greate Road 804-684-7530
PO Box 1346 rickards@virginia.edu
Gloucester Point, VA 23062 www.virginia.edu
Virginia Sea Grant facilitates research, educational, and outreach activities promoting sustainable management of marine resources.
William DuPaul, Interim Director
Cynthia L Suchman, Assistant Director

Washington

3083 **Department of Commerce: Pacific Marine Environmental Laboratory**
7600 Sand Point Way NE 206-526-6239
Seattle, WA 98115 *Fax:* 206-526-6815
pmel.info@noaa.gov
www.pmel.noaa.gov
PMEL carries out interdisciplinary scientific investigations in oceanography and atmospheric science.
Christopher Sabine, Director
Dan Simon, Associate Director

3084 **Department of Fish and Wildlife**
1111 Washington Street SE 360-902-2200
Olympia, WA 98501 *Fax:* 360-902-2947
www.wdfw.wa.gov
To preserve, protect and perpetuate fish, wildlife and ecosystems while providing sustainable fish and wildlife recreational and commercial opportunities
Jim Unsworth, Director

3085 **Environmental Protection Agency Region 10**
1200 6th Avenue 206-553-1200
Suite 155 800-424-4372
Seattle, WA 98101 epa-seattle@epa.gov
www.epa.gov/r10earth
This region serves Alaska, Idaho, Oregon, Washington, and 271 tribal nations. Their mission is to engage in environmental protection efforts for these regions.
Chris Hladick, Regional Administrator

3086 **Julia Butler Hansen Refuge for the Columbian White-Tailed Deer**
46 Steamboat Slough Rd 360-795-3915
Cathlamet, WA 98612-566 *Fax:* 360-795-0803
willapa@fws.gov
www.fws.gov/refuge/julia_butler_hansen/
Offers critical habitat for the endangered Columbian white-tailed deer. The refuge also provides a wintering area for tundra swans, Canada geese, mallards, American wigeon and pintails. Deer and elk are easily observed and photographedfrom the country road that circles the mainland portion of the refuge. Evenings and mornings are the best time to spot animals. Open year-round. No fees charged.

3087 **Washington Cooperative Fish & Wildlife Research Unit**
University of Washington
Box 355020 206-543-6475
Seattle, WA 98195 washcoop@u.washington.edu
www.coopunits.org

Chris Grue, Unit Leader
David Beauchamp, Assistant Unit Leader

3088 **Washington Department of Ecology**
300 Desmond Drive 360-407-6000
Lacey, WA 98503 *Fax:* 360-407-6989
www.ecy.wa.gov
The mission is to protect, preserve and enhance Washington's environment and to promote the wise management of our air, land and water.

Maia D. Bellon, Director

3089 **Washington Department of Fish & Wildlife: Fish and Wildlife Commission**
600 Capitol Way N 360-902-2267
Olympia, WA 98501-1091 *Fax:* 360-902-2448
commission@dfw.wa.gov
www.wdfw.wa.gov/commission
The Fish and Wildlife Commission's primary role is to establish policy and direction for fish and wildlife species and their habitats in Washington and to monitor the Department's implementation of the goals, policies and objectivesestablished by the Commission. The Commission also classifies wildlife and establishes the basic rules and regulations governing the time, place, manner, and methods used to harvest or enjoy fish and wildlife.
Miranda Wecker, Chair
Bradley Smith, Vice Chair

3090 **Washington Department of Fish & Wildlife: Habitat Program**
600 Capitol Way N 360-902-2534
Olympia, WA 98501 *Fax:* 360-902-2946
habitatprogram@dfw.wa.gov
www.wdfw.wa.gov

Includes Maps and Digital Info Requests.
Phil Anderson, Director

3091 **Washington Department of Natural Resources: Southeast Region**
713 Bowers Road 509-925-8510
Ellensburg, WA 98926-9301 *Fax:* 509-925-8522
southeast.region@dnr.wa.gov
www.dnr.wa.gov
In partnership with citizens and governments, the Washington State DNR provides innovative leadership and expertise to en-

sure environmental protection, public safety, perpetual funding for schools and communities, and a rich quality oflife
Peter Goldmark, Commissioner

3092 Washington Dept. of Natural Resources: Northwest Division
919 North Township Street 360-856-3500
Sedro Woolley, WA 98284-9384 *Fax:* 360-856-2150
northwest.region@dnr.wa.gov
www.dnr.wa.gov
In partnership with citizens and governments, the Washington State DNR provides innovative leadership and expertise to ensure environmental protection, public safety, perpetual funding for schools and communities, and a rich quality oflife
Peter Goldmark, Commissioner

3093 Washington Dept. of Natural Resources: South Puget Sound Region
950 Farman Avenue North 360-825-1631
Enumclaw, WA 98022-9282 *Fax:* 360-825-1672
southpuget.region@dnr.wa.gov
www.dnr.wa.gov
In partnership with citizens and governments, the Washington State DNR provides innovative leadership and expertise to ensure environmental protection, public safety, perpetual funding for schools and communities, and a rich quality oflife
Peter Goldmark, Commissioner

3094 Washington Sea Grant Program
University of Washington
3716 Brooklyn Avenue NE 206-543-6600
Seattle, WA 98105-6716 *Fax:* 206-685-0380
seagrant@uw.edu
www.wsg.washington.edu/
Mission: Washington Sea Grant serves communities, industries and the people of Washington state, the Pacific Northwest and the nation through research, education and outreach by: identifying and addressing important marine issues;providing better tools for management of the marine environment and use of its resources; and initiating and supporting strategic partnerships within the marine community.
Penelope D Dalton, Director
Raechel Waters, Associate Director

3095 Washington State Parks & Recreation Commission: Eastern Region
7150 Cleanwater Drive SW 360-902-8844
PO Box 42650 infocent@parks.wa.gov
Olympia, WA 98504 www.parks.wa.gov
The Washington State Parks and Recreation Commission aquires, operates, enhances and protects a diverse system of recreational, cultural, historical, and natural sites. The Commission fosters outdoor recreation and education statewideto provide enjoyment and enrichment for all and a valued legacy to future generations.
Rex Derr, Director
Judy Johnson, Deputy Director

West Virginia

3096 Capitol Conservation District
418 Goff Mountain Road 304-759-0736
Suite 102 *Fax:* 304-776-5326
Cross Lanes, WV 25313 ccd@wvca.us
www.wvca.us
Walt Helmick, Commissioner
Daniel J. Robinson, Commissioner

3097 Gauley River National Recreation Area Advisory National Park Service
PO Box 246 304-465-0508
Glen Jean, WV 25846 *Fax:* 304-465-0591
katy_miller@nps.gov
www.nps.gov
Located in the southern West Virginia, New River Gorge National River was established in 1978 to conserve and protect 53 miles of the New River as a free-flowing waterway. This unit of the National Park System encompasses over 70,000acres of land along the New River between the towns of Hinton and Fayetteville. New River Gorge National River and Bluestone National Scenic River are both managed by our same office in Glen Jean, WV.
Lorrie Sprague, Public Information Officer

3098 West Virginia Cooperative Fish & Wildlife Research Unit USGS
322 Percival Hall West Virginia Un 304-293-3794
PO Box 6125 *Fax:* 304-293-4826
Morgantown, WV 26506-6125 wvcoop@wvu.edu
www.coopunits.org
Patricia Mazik, Unit Leader Fisheries
Petra Wood, Assistant Leader Wildlife

3099 West Virginia Department of Environmental Protection
WV Dpt of Environmental Protection 304-926-0440
601 57th Street South East *Fax:* 304-926-0446
Charleston, WV 25304 dhhrsecretary@wv.gov
www.wvdep.org
Promotes compliance with environmental policies in the areas of hazardous waste management, air quality, water pollution, underground storage tanks, dam safety, land reclamation and more.
Randy Huffman, Cabinet Secretary
Bill Crouch, Cabinet Secretary

3100 West Virginia Division of Natural Resources
324 4th Avenue 304-558-2754
South Charleston, WV 25303 *Fax:* 304-558-2768
www.wvdnr.gov
Frank Jezioro, Director
Harry F Price, Executive Secretary

3101 West Virginia Geological & Economic Survey
1 Mont Chateau Road 304-594-2331
Morgantown, WV 26508-8079 *Fax:* 304-594-2575
www.wvgs.wvnet.edu
Michael Hohn, Director/State Geologist
Earl Ray Tomblin, Governor

Wisconsin

3102 Great Lakes Indian Fish and Wildlife Commission
72682 Maple Street 715-682-6619
PO Box 9 *Fax:* 715-682-9294
Odanah, WI 54861 www.glifwc.org
Mission: To help ensure significant, off-reservation harvests while protecting the resources for generations to come.
James Zorn, Executive Administrator
Gerald DePerry, Deputy Administrator

3103 Natural Resources Department
101 S. Webster Street 888-936-7463
PO Box 7921 *Fax:* 608-261-4380
Madison, WI 53707-7921 www.dnr.wi.gov
Mission: To protect and enhance our natural resources; to provide a healthy, sustainable environment; to ensure the right of all people; to work with people; and to consider the future and generations to follow.
P Scott Hassett, Secretary

3104 Wisconsin Cooperative Fishery Research Unit
University of Wisconsin
College of Natural Resources 715-346-2178
Stevens Point, WI 54481 *Fax:* 715-346-3624
coopfish@uwsp.edu

3105 Wisconsin Department of Agriculture Trade & Cosumer Protection: Land & Water Resources Bureau
2811 Agriculture Drive 608-224-5012
PO Box 8911 *Fax:* 608-224-4615
Madison, WI 53708-8911 www.datcp.state.wi.us
Ben Brancel, Secretary

3106 Wisconsin Geological & Natural History Survey
University of Wisconsin Extension
3817 Mineral Point Road 608-262-1705
Madison, WI 53705 *Fax:* 608-262-8086
www.wisconsingeologicalsurvey.org
Mission: The survey conducts earth-science surveys, field studies, and research. We provide objective scientific information about the geology, mineral resources, water resources, soil, and biology of Wisconsin. We collect, interpret,disseminate, and archive natural resource information. We communicate the results of our activities through publications, technical talks, and responses to inquiries from the public.
William G. Batten, State Geologist & Director

3107 Wisconsin State Extension Services Community Natural Resources & Economic Development
University of Wisconsin Extension
432 N Lake Street 608-263-2781
Madison, WI 53706 *Fax:* 606-262-9166
www.uwex.edu/ces/
Rick Klemme, Dean

Wyoming

3108 Casper District: Bureau of Land Management
Department of the Interior
2987 Prospector Drive 307-261-7600
Casper, WY 82604 *Fax:* 307-261-7587
casper_wymail@blm.gov
www.blm.gov

3109 Environmental Quality Department
122 W 25th Street 307-777-7937
Herschler Building *Fax:* 307-777-7682
Cheyenne, WY 82002 keith.guille@wyo.gov
www.michigan.gov/deq
DEQ contributes to Wyoming's quality of life through a combination of monitoring, permitting, inspection, enforcement and restoration/remediation activities which protect, conserve and enhance the environment while supportingresponsible stewardship of our state's resources.
Todd Parfitt, Director

3110 Rock Springs Field Office: Bureau of Land Management
Department of the Interior
280 Highway 191 N 307-352-0256
Rock Springs, WY 82901 *Fax:* 307-352-0329
www.blm.gov
BLM's Rock Springs Field Office is a federal agency in the USA that manages over 3.6 million acres of public land surface and 3.5 million acres of public sub-surface minerals in the southwestern part of the great State of Wyoming. Forthese public lands, BLM administers a variety of programs including mineral exploration and development, wildlife habitat, outdoor recreation, wild horses, lifestock grazing and historic trails.

3111 Wyoming Cooperative Fish and Wildlife Research Unit
University of Wyoming
1000 East University Avenue 307-766-5415
Dept. 3166 *Fax:* 307-766-5400
Laramie, WY 82071 www.wyocoopunit.org/index.php/test/
Unit conducts fish and wildlife research for the state of Wyoming conservation, fish department and federal agencies.
Matthew K. Kauffman, Leader

3112 Wyoming State Board Of Land Commissioners
Herschler Building 3W 307-777-7331
122 West 25th Street *Fax:* 307-777-2980
Cheyenne, WY 82002 slfmail@wyo.gov
lands.wyo.gov
Manages all land sales, acquisitions and exchanges, agricultural and commercial leasing, recreations, natural resources and minerals management in the state of Wyoming.
Jason Crowder, Assistant Director
Benjamin Bump, Assistant Director

3113 Wyoming State Forestry Division
5500 Bishop Blvd 307-777-7586
Cheyenne, WY 82002-0060 *Fax:* 307-777-5986
slf-forestry@wyo.gov
www.wsfd.wyo.gov/
The Forestry Division's general reposnsibility and objectives are to promote and assist the multiple use management and protection of Wyoming's 270,000 acres of state and 1.9 million acres of private forest lands; to provide forestryassistance and information to landowners, industry, communities and public agencies; and to help provide rural, range, and forest land fire protection, equipment and training.
Bill Crasper, State Forester
Dan Perko, Deputy State Forester

3114 Wyoming State Geological Survey
PO Box 1347 307-766-2286
Laramie, WY 82073 *Fax:* 307-766-2605
wsgs-info@uwyo.edu
www.wsgs.uwyo.edu
The Wyoming State Geological Survey's mission is to promote the beneficial and environmentally sound use of Wyoming's vast geologic, mineral, and energy resources while helping to protect the public from geologic hazards.
Thomas Drean, Director
Kathy Olson, Administrative Officer

Alabama: US Forests, Parks, Refuges

3115 Bon Secour National Wildlife Refuge
12295 State Highway 180 251-540-7720
Gulf Shores, AL 36542 *Fax:* 251-540-7301
bonsecour@fws.gov
www.fws.gov/refuge/Bon_Secour
Gulf Shores offer nature enthusiasts much to explore. The Bon Secour NWR, which lies just 6 miles west of Gulf Shores, caters equally to the angler, the hiker and the birder. The refuge encourages guests to enjoy a leisurely hikethrough the grounds or a fishing excursion on the 40-acre fresh water Gator Lake. Pack a picnic lunch and your binoculars, park your blanket on one of the many secluded beaches and savor the scenery. Call 1-866-SEA TURTLE to report sea turtleactivity.

3116 Choctaw National Wildlife Refuge
PO Box 150 251-843-5238
Gilbertown, AL 36908 *Fax:* 251-843-2568
choctaw@fws.gov
www.fws.gov/choctaw
The objectives of the Refuge are: to manage habitat for wintering waterfowl, maintain habitat and provide protection for threatened and endangered species, manage wood duck nest boxes and brood rearing habitat, maintain wildlifediversity, manage forest to be productive bottomland hardwoods, and to provide wildlife dependent recreation.
Robert Dailey, Manager

3117 Little River Canyon National Preserve
4322 Little River Trail NE 256-845-9605
Suite 100 *Fax:* 256-997-9129
Fort Payne, AL 35967 sandra_arther@nps.gov
www.nps.gov
Little River flows for most of its length atop Lookout Mountain in northeast Alabama. The river and canyon systems are Appala-

chian Plateau landscapes, made up of forested uplands, waterfalls, canyon rims and bluffs, stream riffles andpools, boulders and sandstone cliffs. Natural resources and cultural heritage come together to tell the story of the preserve, a special place in the Southern Appalachians.

Steve Black, Superintendent
Cheri Killam-Bomhard, Facility Manager

3118 Wheeler National Wildlife Refuge Complex
2700 Refuge Headquarters Road 256-353-7243
Decatur, AL 35603 *Fax:* 256-340-9728
wheeler@fws.gov
www.fws.gov/wheeler/
The 35,000 acre wildlife refuge was established in 1938 The refuge is located between Decatur and Huntsville in the Tennessee River Valley of northern Alabama.
Dwight Cooley, Project Leader

3119 William B Bankhead National Forest
Bankhead Ranger District 205-489-5111
1070 Hwy 33 *Fax:* 205-489-3427
Double Springs, AL 35553 www.forestcamping.com/dow/southern/bankinfo.htm
The William B Bankhead national Forest covers 180,000 acres in Franklin, Winston and Lawrence counties. Within the forest are the 26,000 acre Sipsey Wilkderness and the Sipsey Wild and Scenic River, offering 61.4 miles of seasonalcanoeing.

Alaska: US Forests, Parks, Refuges

3120 Alagnak Wild River Katmai National Park
1000 Silver Street, Bldg. 603 907-246-3305
PO Box 245 *Fax:* 907-246-2116
King Salmon, AK 99613 www.nps.gov/alag
The Alagnak river offers 69 miles of outstanding white-water floating. The river is also noted for abundant wildlife and sport fishing for five species of salmon.

3121 Alaska Maritime National Wildlife Refuge
95 Sterling Highway 907-235-6546
Suite 1 *Fax:* 907-235-7783
Homer, AK 99603 alaskamaritime@fws.gov
www.fws.gov/refuge/alaska_maritime
To administer a national network of lands and waters for the conservation management and where appropiate, restoration of the fish, wildlife, and plant resources and their habitats within the US for the benefit of present and futuregeneration of Americans.
Steve Delehanty, Refuge Manager

3122 Alaska Peninsula National Wildlife Refuge
P.O. Box 298 907-246-3339
King Salmon, AK 99613 *Fax:* 907-246-6696
becharof@fws.gov
www.fws.gov/refuges/profiles

3123 Becharof National Wildlife Refuge
PO Box 277 907-246-3339
4 Bear Road *Fax:* 907-246-6696
King Salmon, AK 99613 becharof@fws.gov
becharof.fws.gov
Daryle Lons, Manager

3124 Chugach National Forest
161 East 1st Avenue 907-743-9500
Door 8 *Fax:* 907-743-9476
Anchorage, AK 99501 www.fs.fed.us/r10/chugach

3125 Denali National Park and Preserve
PO Box 9 907-683-2294
Denali Park, AK 99755-0009 *Fax:* 907-683-9612
denali_info@nps.gov
www.nps.gov/dena

3126 Innoko National Wildlife Refuge
101 Front Street 907-656-1231
P.O. Box 287 800-656-1231
Galena, AK 99741-287 *Fax:* 907-656-1708
innoko@fws.gov
www.fws.gov/refuge/innoko
The Innoko National Wildlife Refuge was established December 2, 1980, with the passage of the Alaska National Interest Lands Conservation Act. This 3.85 million acre refuge supports a large nesting waterfowl population, and is wellpopulated with moose, bear, and other animals, as well as a variety of game birds and neotropical bird species and is a relatively flat plain covering much of the drainage area of the Innoko and Iditarod rivers. The vegetation of the reguse is atransition zone.
Kenton Moos, Manager
Bob Rebarchik, Deputy Refuge Manager

3127 Izembek National Wildlife Refuge
Box 127 907-532-2445
MS 515 877-837-6332
Cold Bay, AK 99571-127 *Fax:* 907-532-2549
izembek@fws.gov
www.fws.gov/refuge/izembek/
Established to conserve fish, wildlife and habitats in their natural diversity including, waterfowl, shorebirds, other migratory birds, brown bears and salmon; to fulfill treaty obligations; to provide the opportunity for continuedsubsistence uses by local residents consistent with the purposes previously mentioned; and to ensure necessary water quality and quantity.

Nancy Hoffman, Wildlife Refuge Manager

3128 Kanuti National Wildlife Refuge
101 12th Avenue 907-456-0329
MS 555 Room 262 877-220-1853
Fairbanks, AK 99701 *Fax:* 907-456-0506
kanuti_refuge@fws.gov
www.fws.gov/refuge/kanuti/
Mike Spindler, Manager

3129 Katmai National Park and Preserve
PO Box 7 907-246-3305
King Salmon, AK 99613 *Fax:* 907-246-2116
www.nps.gov/katm

3130 Kenai Fjords National Park
PO Box 1727 907-422-0500
Seward, AK 99664 *Fax:* 907-422-0571
www.nps.gov/kefj
This park encompasses over 600,000 acres of wild coastal Alaska. The Harding Icefield dominates most of the park. This 300-square mile bowl of ice spills out into numerous glaciers at its edges. Tidewater glaciers and the amazingmarine wildlife of the park can be viewed from boat or air. Humpback whales, orca, many species of sea birds, Steller sea lions and other marine wildlife come here because of the rich variety of foods. Sea birds and sea lions also raise their youngon the rocky sites.

3131 Kenai National Wildlife Refuge
PO Box 2139 907-262-7021
Soldotna, AK 99669-2139 *Fax:* 907-487-2144
kenai@fws.gov
www.fws.gov/refuge/Kenai

3132 Kobuk Valley National Park
PO Box 1029 907-442-3890
Kotzebue, AK 99752 *Fax:* 907-442-8316
NWAK_superintendant@nps.gov
www.nps.gov/kova
Mission: Cooperative stewardship for the conservation and understanding of natural and cultural resources in Northwest Alaska.

3133 Kodiak National Wildlife Refuge
1390 Buskin River Road 907-487-2600
MS 559 888-408-3514
Kodiak, AK 99615 *Fax:* 907-487-2144
kodiak@fws.gov
www.fws.gov/refuge/kodiak/
Kodiak National Wildlife Refuge was established to conserve Kodiak brown bears, salmon, sea otters, sea lions, other marine mammals, and migratory birds; to fulfill treaty obligations; to provide for continued subsistence uses; and toensure necessary water quanlity and quantity.
Gary Wheeler, Manager
Jason Osles, Park Ranger

3134 Koyukuk and Nowitna National Wildlife Refuge
101 Front Street 907-656-1231
PO Box 287 800-656-1231
Galena, AK 99741-0287 *Fax:* 907-656-1708
r7kynwr@fws.gov
www.fws.gov/refuges/profiles/
Approximately 200 miles west of Fairbanks, the refuge lies within a solar basin encircled by rolling hills capped by alpine tundra. The Nowitna River, a nationally designated Wild River, bisects the refuge and forms a broad meanderingfloodplain. The river passes through a scenic 15 mile canyon with peaks up to 2,100 feet.
Kenton Moos, Manager

3135 Lake Clark National Park and Preserve
2181 Kachemak Dr. 907- 23- 790
Suite 236 *Fax:* 907-644-3810
Homer, AK 99603 www.nps.gov/lacl
Lake Clark National Park and Preserve was created to protect scenic beauty, populations of fish and wildlife, watersheds essential for red salmon, and the traditional lifestyle of local residents.
Dick Proenneke, Wilderness Steward

3136 Selawik National Wildlife Refuge
160 2nd Avenue 907-442-3799
PO Box 270 800-492-8848
Kotzebue, AK 99752 *Fax:* 907-442-3124
selawik@fws.gov
www.fws.gov/refuge/Selawik/contact.html
Selawik National Wildlife Refuge was established to conserve the Western Arctic caribou herd, waterfowl, shorebirds, other migratory birds, salmon, and sheefish; to fulfill treaty obligations; to provide for continued subsistence uses;and to ensure necessary water quality and quantity.
LeeAnne Ayres, Manager
Tina Moran, Deputy Refuge Manager

3137 Tetlin National Wildlife Refuge
PO Box 779 907-883-5312
Tok, AK 99780 *Fax:* 907-883-5747
tetlin@fws.gov
www.fws.gov/refuge/tetlin/

Shawn Bayless, Refuge Manager
Jerry Hill, Deputy Refuge Manager

3138 Togiak National Wildlife Refuge
PO Box 270 907-842-1063
MS 569 800-817-2538
Dillingham, AK 99576 *Fax:* 907-842-5402
togiak@fws.gov
www.fws.gov/refuge/togiak/
Established to conserve fish and wildlife populations and habitats in their natural diversity including salmon, marine birds, mammals, migrating birds and large mammals, to fulfill international treaty obligations; to provide forcontinued subsistence uses; and to ensure necessary water quality and quantity.
Paul Liedberg, Manager

3139 Tongass National Forest: Chatham Area
204 Siginaka Way 907-747-6671
Sitka, AK 99835-7316 *Fax:* 907-747-4331
www.fs.fed.us/r10/tongass
The Tongass National Forest is a forest of islands and trees and rain. It also abounds in animals and birds and fish, with unsurpassed scenery. It's a place where eagles are commonplace, most every road is a deer crossing, and bearsuse the trails too. The spirituality and scenery demands respect.
Fred Salinas, Forest Supervisor

3140 Tongass National Forest: Ketchikan Area
Federal Building 907-225-3101
648 Mission Street *Fax:* 907-228-6215
Ketchikan, AK 99901-6591 www.fs.fed.us/r10/tongass
The Tongass National Forest is a forest of islands and trees and rain. It also abounds in animals and birds and fish, with unsurpassed scenery. It's a place where eagles are commonplace, most every road is a deer crossing, and bearsuse the trails too. The Tongass is a wild place, where the natural world is a strong presence that nurtures spirituality and materially demands respect.

3141 Tongass National Forest: Stikine Area
123 Scow Bay Loop Road 907-772-3841
PO Box 309 *Fax:* 907-772-5895
Petersburg, AK 99833-0309 www.fs.fed.us/r10/tongass
The Tongass National Forest is a forest of islands and trees and rain. It also abounds in animals and birds and fish, with unsurpassed scenery. It's a place where eagles are commonplace, most every road is a deer crossing, and bearsuse the trails too. The Tongass is a wild place, where the natural world is a strong presence that nurtures spirituality and materially demands respect.

3142 Yukon Delta National Wildlife Refuge
807 Chief Eddie Hoffman Road 907-543-3151
PO Box 346 MS 535 *Fax:* 907-543-4413
Bethel, AK 99559 yukondelta@fws.gov
www.fws.gov/refuge/yukon_delta
Yukon Delta National Wildlife Refuge was established to conserce shorebirds, seabirds, whistling swans, emperor, white-fronted and Canada geese, black brant and other migratory birds, salmon, muskox, and marine mammals; to fulfilltreaty obligations; to provide for continued subsistence uses; and to ensure necessary water quality and quantity.
Michael Rearden, Manager

3143 Yukon Flats National Wildlife Refuge
101 12th Avenue 907-456-0440
Room 264 MS 575 800-531-0676
Fairbanks, AK 99701 *Fax:* 907-456-0447
yukonflats@fws.gov
www.fws.gov/refuge/yukon_flats/
Located about 100 air miles north of Fairbanks, encompassing about 12 million acres along the Yukon River. In the spring, millions of migrating birds converge on the refuge. With its 40,000 lakes and other wetlands, it has one of thehighest waterfowl nesting densities in North America for ducks, geese, sandhill cranes, loons, grebes and songbirds. Each year, the Yukon Flats is a major contributor to the migrations that occur along the North American flyways.
Robert Jess, Refuge Manager
Wennona Brown, Deputy Refuge Manager

3144 Yukon-Charley Rivers National Preserve
PO Box 167 907-547-2233
Eagle, AK 99738 *Fax:* 907-547-2247
www.nps.gov/yuch

Arizona: US Forests, Parks, Refuges

3145 Apache-Sitgreaves National Forest
PO Box 640 928-333-4301
Springerville, AZ 85938 *Fax:* 928-333-5966
www.fs.fed.us/r3/asnf
Taking care of the land while making the forest resources available to all shareholders. Resources include: high quality water, wilderness, and outdoor recreation; quality habitat for many plants and animals; wood for paper, homes, andhundreds of other uses; forage for wildlife and livestock; a source of minerals.
Chris Knopp, Forests Supervisor
Pam Baltimore, Public Affairs Officer

3146 Bill Williams River National Wildlife Refuge
60911 Highway 95 928-667-4144
Parker, AZ 85344 *Fax:* 928-667-3402
dick_gilbert@fws.gov
www.billwilliamsriver.org

Bill Williams River National Wildlife Refuge is located along the Bill Williams River in La Paz and Mojave Counties, Arizona, with the river as the dividing line between the two counties. The refuge was established in 1941 as part ofHavasu NWR as mitigation for the Boulder and Parker Dam projects. In 1993, the two refuges were seperated and the Bill W Unit became the Bill Williams River NWR.

Larry Voyles, Member
Dave Weedman, Member

3147 Buenos Aires National Wildlife Refuge
PO Box 109 520-823-4251
Sasabe, AZ 85633 *Fax:* 520-823-4247
Daniel_Peterson@fws.gov
www.fws.gov/refuge/Buenos_Aires

3148 Cabeza Prieta National Wildlife Refuge
1611 N 2nd Avenue 520-387-6483
Ajo, AZ 85321 *Fax:* 520-387-5359
cabezaprieta@fws.gov
Roger Di Rosa, Manager

3149 Chiricahua National Monument
12856 East Rhyolite Creek Road 520-824-3560
Wilcox, AZ 85643 *Fax:* 520-824-3421
www.nps.gov/chir

The monument is mecca for hikers and birders. At the intersection of the Chiricahuan and Sonoran deserts, and the southern Rocky Mountains and northern Sierra Madre in Mexico, Chiricahua plants and animals represents one of the premierareas for biological diversity in the northern hemisphere.

3150 Coconino National Forest
1824 South Thompson Street 928-527-3600
Flagstaff, AZ 86001 *Fax:* 928-527-3620
www.fs.fed.us/r3/coconino/

The Coconino National Forest is one of the most diverse National Forests in the country with landscapes ranging from the famous Red Rocks of Sedona to Ponderosa Pine Forests, to alpine tundra

3151 Coronado National Forest
300 W Congress Street 520-388-8300
Tucson, AZ 85701 www.fs.fed.us/r3/coronado

The Coronado National Forest covers 1,780,000 acres of southeastern Arizona and southwestern New Mexico. Elevations range from 3,000 feet to 10,720 feet in 12 widely scattered mountain ranges or sky islands that rise dramatically fromthe desert floor, supporting plant communities as biologically diverse as those encountered on a trip from Mexico to Canada. The views are spectacular from these mountains, and visitors may experience all four seasons during a single day's journey.
Jim Upchurch, Forest Supervisor

3152 Glen Canyon National Recreation Area
Glen Canyon NRA 928-608-6200
PO Box 1507 *Fax:* 928-608-6259
Page, AZ 86040 GLCA CHVC@nps.gov
www.nps.gov/glca

Glen Canyon National Recreation Area offers unparalleled opportunities for water-based & backcountry recreation. The recreation area stretches for hundreds of miles from Lees Ferry in Arizona to the Orange Cliffs of southern Utah,encompassing scenic vistas, geologic wonders, and a panorama of human history. Additionally, the controversy surrounding the construction of Glen Cayon Dam and the creation of Lake Powell contributed to the birth of modern day environmental movement.

3153 Grand Canyon National Park
PO Box 129 928-638-7888
Grand Canyon, AZ 86023 *Fax:* 928-638-7797
www.nps.gov/grca

3154 Imperial National Wildlife Refuge
PO Box 72217 928-783-3371
Yuma, AZ 85365 *Fax:* 928-783-0652
FW2_RW_Imperial@fws.gov

Imperial National Wildlife Refuge protects wildlife habitat along 30 miles of the lower Colorado River in Arizona and California, including the last unchannelized section before the river enters Mexico.
Elaine Johnson, Manager

3155 Kaibab National Forest
800 South Sixth Street 928-635-8200
Williams, AZ 86046 *Fax:* 928-635-8208
www.fs.fed.us/r3/kai/

3156 Kofa National Wildlife Refuge
9300 East 28th Street 928-783-7861
Yuma, AZ 85365 *Fax:* 928-783-8611
www.fws.gov/refuge/Kofa

Refuge dedicated to protecting the desert bighorn sheep and other native wildlife of Arizona.

Lydia Morton, Volunteer Coordinator

3157 Organ Pipe Cactus National Monument
10 Organ Pipe Drive 520-387-6849
Ajo, AZ 85321 orpi_information@nps.gov
www.nps.gov/orpi

Organ Pipe Cactus National Monument celebrates the life and landscape of the Sonoran Desert. Here, in this desert wilderness of plants and animals and dramatic mountains and plains scenery, you can drive a lonely road, hike abackcountry trail, camp beneath a clear desert sky, or just soak in the warmth and beauty of Southwest.

3158 Petrified Forest National Park
1 Park Road 928-524-6228
PO Box 2217 *Fax:* 928-524-3567
Petrified Forest, AZ 86028 PEFO_superintendant@nps.gov
www.nps.gov/pefo

Petrified Forest is a surprising land of scenic wonders and fascinating science. The park is located in northeast Arizona and features one of the world's largest and most colorful concentrations of petrified wood. Also included in thepark's 93,533 acres are the multihued badlands of the Chinle Formation known as the Painted Desert, historic structures, archeological sites and displays of 225 millio-year-old fossils.

3159 Prescott National Forest
344 S Cortez Street 928-443-8000
Prescott, AZ 86303 www.fs.fed.us/r3/prescott

This involves taking care of the land while making the forest resources available to all shareholders. Resources include high quality water, wilderness and outdoor recreation; quality habitat for many plants and animals; wood forpaper, homes and hundreds of other uses; forage for wildlife and livestock; and minerals.

3160 Saguaro National Park
3693 S Old Spanish Trail 520-733-5153
Tuscon, AZ 85730-5601 *Fax:* 520-733-5183
www.nps.gov/sagu

This unique desert is home to the most recognizable cactus in the world, the majestic saguaro. Visitors of all ages are fascinated and enchanted by these desert gaints, especially their many interesting and complex interrelationshipswith other desert life. With the average life span of 150 years, a mature saguaro may grow to the height of 50 feet and weigh over 10 tons.

3161 San Bernardino/Leslie Canyon National Refuge
PO Box 3509 520-364-2104
Douglas, AZ 85607 *Fax:* 520-364-2130
Bill Radke, Manager

3162 Sunset Crater Volcano National Monument
6400 N. Hwy 89 928-526-0502
Flagstaff, AZ 86004 *Fax:* 928-714-0565
www.nps.gov/sucr

Welcome to the Flagstaff Area National Monuments! There is something for everyone: prehistoic cliff dwellings at Walnut Canyon, the mountain scenery and geology of Sunset Crater Volcano, and the painted desert landscape and masonrypueblos of Wupatki National Monument. Here at Sunset Crater Volcano, amid lava and cinders, one can imagine a landscape still hot to the touch. Imagine the thoughts of the prehistoric people who lived here when the eruption occured.

3163 Tonto National Forest
2324 East McDowell Road 602-225-5200
Phoenix, AZ 85006 *Fax:* 602-225-5295
www.fs.fed.us/r3/tonto

The Tonto National Forest occupies about 2.8 million acres which generally lie northeast of Phoenix, Ariz., to the Mogollon Rim and east to the San Carlos and Fort Apache Indain Reservations. The west side approximately interstate 17which stretches north of Phoenix to Flagstaff. The lower elevations are of the Sonoran Desert type while the northern portion of the Forest is generally Pinon, Juniper, and Ponderosa Pine types.

3164 Walnut Canyon National Monument
6400 N. Hwy 89 928-526-1157
Flagstaff, AZ 86004 *Fax:* 928-526-4259
www.nps.gov/waca

Hike down into Walnut Canyon and walk in the footsteps of people who lived here over 900 years ago. Built under limestone overhangs, these dwellings were occupied from about 1100 to 1250. Look down into the canyon and imagine the creekrunning through. Visualize a woman hiking up from the bottom with a pot of water on her back. Imagine the men on the rim farming corn or hunting deer. Think of a cold winter night with your family huddled around the fire.

3165 Wupatki National Monument
25137 N Wupatki Loop 928-679-2365
Flagstaff, AZ 86004 *Fax:* 928-679-2349
www.nps.gov

Wupatki, comprised of big skies, open grassland, and desert scrub, with Painted Desert to the east and San Francisco Peaks to the west. A visit to this beautiful landscape will remind you what life was like in this region 900 yearsago.
Chuck Sypher, District Ranger

Arkansas: US Forests, Parks, Refuges

3166 Bald Knob National Wildlife Refuge
1439 Coal Chute Road 501-724-2458
Bald Knob, AR 72010 *Fax:* 501-724-2460
paul_provence@fws.gov
www.fws.gov/baldknob

The refuge facts established in 1993 has 14,800 acres and the location is in White County, Ar approximately two miles south of Bald Knob, AR on Coal Chute Road. It provides habitat for migratory waterfowl and other birds. And also forendangered species recreational and environmental education opportunities.
Bald Knob, Refuge Manager

3167 Buffalo National River
402 N Walnut 870-365-2700
Suite 136 *Fax:* 870-365-2701
Harrison, AR 72601 buff_information@nps.gov
www.nps.gov/buff

One of the few remaining unpolluted, free-flowing rivers in the lower 48 states offering both swift-running and placid stretches. The river encompasses 135 miles of the 150 mile long river. It begins as a trickle in the BostonMountains 15 miles above the park boundary. Following what is likely an ancient riverbed, the Buffalo cuts its way through massive limestone bluffs traveling eastward throug the Ozarks and into the Whtie River.

3168 Felsenthal National Wildlife Refuge
5531 Highway 82 West 870-364-3167
Crossett, AR 71635 *Fax:* 870-364-3757
felsenthal@fws.gov
www.fws.gov/refuge/felsenthal

65,000 acre national wildlife refuge with abuntant water resources - 15,000 acres, and vast bottomland hardwood forest that rises to the pine uplands.
Bernard J Petersen, Project Leader

3169 Greers Ferry National Fish Hatchery
349 Hatchery Road 501-362-3615
Heber Springs, AR 72543 *Fax:* 501-362-4007
greersferry@fws.gov
www.fws.gov/greersferry

Through self-guided tours at the hatchery, visitors can observe techniques of trout production, view information exhibits in the aquarium, and see trout in the outdoor raceways. Adjacent to the hatchery, visitors can camp at JFK Parkand trout fish the Little Red River. Nearby, the US Army Corps of Engineers has a visitor center, two mini-hiking trails and an overlook of Greers Ferry Dam. Greers Ferry Lake on the other side of the dam offers camping, swimming, fishing and otherwater sports.
Sherri Shoults, Hatchery Manager
Eric Thompson, Assistant Hatchery Manager

3170 Holla Bend National Wildlife Refuge
10448 Holla Bend Road 479-229-4300
Dardanelle, AR 72834 *Fax:* 479-229-4302
hollabend@fws.gov
www.fws.gov/refuge/holla_bend

Part of a system of over 475 national wildlife refuges located across the country. Administered by US Fish and Wildlife Service, this system of refuges, the finest in the world, protects important habitat needed to provide a home for awide variety of wildlife. These refuges also provide the public with valuable opportunities to see and learn about wildlife and to enjoy outdoor activities such as hunting and fishing. Holla Bend's main purpose is to provide a winter home for ducksand geese.
Durwin Carter, Manager

3171 Hot Springs National Park
101 Reserve Street 501-620-6715
Hot Springs, AR 71901 *Fax:* 501-624-3458
HOSP_Interpretation@nps.gov
www.nps.gov/hosp

The park protects eight historic bathhouses with the former luxurious Fordyce Bathhouse housing the park visitor center. The entire Bathhouse Row area is national Historic Landmark District that contains the grandest collection ofbathhouses of its kind in North America. By protecting the 47 hot springs and their watershed, the National Park Service continues to provide visitors with historic leisure activities such as hiking, picnicking and scenic drives.

Josie Fernandez, Superintendent
Mardi Arce, Deputy Superintendent

3172 Ouachita National Forest
100 Reserve Street 501-321-5202
PO Box 1270 *Fax:* 501-321-5305
Hot Springs, AR 71902 www.fs.usda.gov/ouachita/

Mission: To sustain the ecological health and productivity of lands and waters entrusted to our care and provide for human uses compatible with that goal. We understand that our greatest asset is the land, our greatest strength is ourworkforce, and our greatest challenge is achieving public understanding, trust, and confidence in all that we do.

3173 Overflow National Wildlife Refuge
3858 Highway 8 East 870-473-2869
Parkdale, AR 71661 *Fax:* 870-473-5191
www.fws.gov

Refuge objectives are to: provide a diversity of habitat types for migratory waterfowl and other birds; provide habitat and protection for the delisted bald eagle; provide opportunities for environmental and ecological research;provide a variety of recreational opportunities consistent with primary wildlife objectives; and expand the public's understanding of and appreciation for the environment with special emphasis on natural resources.

Lake Lewis, Manager

3174 Ozark-St. Francis National Forest
605 W Main Street 479-964-7200
Russleville, AR 72801 www.fs.usda.gov/osfnf
The Ozark-St. Francis National Forests are really two separate Forests with many differences. They are distinct in their own topographical, geological, biological, cultural and social differences, yet each makes up a part of theoverall National Forest system.
Judi Henry, Forest Supervisor

3175 Pond Creek National Wildlife Refuge
1958 Central Road 870-289-2126
Lockesburg, AR 71846 *Fax:* 870-289-2127
www.fws.gov
Pond Creek National Wildlife Refuge plans to: protect the area's wetland and bottomland hardwood hbitat for natural diversity of wildlife; provide habitat for neo-tropical migratory birds; provide wintering habitat for migratorywaterfowl; provide breeding and nesting habitat for wood ducks; and to provide opportunities for compatible public outdoor recreation.

Paul Gideon, Manager

3176 Wapanocca National Wildlife Refuge
178 Hammond Avenue Highway 42 East 870-343-2595
PO Box 279 *Fax:* 870-343-2416
Turrell, AR 72384 jared_nance@fws.gov
www.fws.gov/wapanocca/
The 5,484 acre refuge is an important stopover for waterfowl traveling the Mississippi Flyway and for songbirds as they migrate to and from Central and South America. The refuge is open to limited small and big game hunting. Auto tourroutes offers excellent wildlife observation, photography and hiking opportunities. An observation platform is located on the east side of the 600 acre Wapanocca Lake.

Jared Nance, Refuge Manager

3177 White River National Wildlife Refuge
57 South CC Camp Road 870-282-8200
PO Box 205 *Fax:* 870-282-8234
St Charles, AR 72140 whiteriver@fws.gov
www.fws.gov/whiteriver
Refuge objectives are to provide: optimum habitat for migratory birds; habitat and protection for endangered species: a natural diversity of wildlife common to the White River bottoms; opportunities and facilities for wildlife orientedrecreation and environmental education; cooperation with other water and land managing agencies and private interests to foster proper management of the White River Basin's resources; and preservation of appropriate wooded areas in their naturalcondition.
Keith Weaver, Project Leader

California: US Forests, Parks, Refuges

3178 Angeles National Forest
701 North Santa Anita Avenue 626-574-1613
Arcadia, CA 91006 *Fax:* 626-574-5207
www.fs.usda.gov/angeles/
The Angeles National Forest covers 650,000 acres and is the backyard playground to the huge metropolitan area of Los Angeles. The Los Angeles National Forest manages the watersheds eithin its boundaries to provide valuable water tosouthern California and to protect surrounding communities from catastrophics floods.
Tom Contreras, Forest Supervisor

3179 Bear Valley National Wildlife Refuge
4009 Hill Rd 916-667-2231
Tulelake, CA 96134 *Fax:* 916-667-3299
ron_cole@fws.gov
www.fws.gov
Refuge was established to protect a major winter night roost site for bald egales. The acquisition program was completed in 1991. Klamath Basin hosts the largest wintering popluation of blad eagles in the contiguous United States, withnumbers some years approaching 1,000. Refuge serves as one of serveral eagle roots in the Basin. It consists of large stands of old-growth tinmber, which protects the birds at night from the harsh winter weather.
Ron Cole, Refuge Manager

3180 Bitter Creek National Wildlife Refuge
Hopper Mountain NWR 805-644-5185
Po Box 5839 *Fax:* 805-644-1732
Ventura, CA 93005www.fws.gov/hoppermountain/BitterCreekNWR
The primary wildlife traditional feeding and roosting habitat for the California condor. Also provides habitat for the San Joaquin kit fox, golden eagle, Southern bald eagle and American peregrine falcon. 14,000 contiguous acres,mostly annual grasslands with some juniper and scrub oak with grass understory. Public use is severely limited because of the sensitive situation of the California condor. The refuge can be viewed from the Cerro Noroeste Road.
Dan Tappe, Refuge Manager

3181 Blue Ridge National Wildlife Refuge
Kern NWR 805-644-5185
PO Box 5839 Dan_Tappe@fws.gov
Ventura, CA 93005 www.fws.gov/refuge/blue_ridge/
Primary wildlife area is a traditional summer roosting site for the endangered Califorina condor. The habitat includes 897 acres of rugged mountains, rock outcroppings, chaparral and coniferous trees. The refuge is closed to publicaccess due to the sensitivity of California condors and its isolation and difficulty in access.
Dan Tappe, Refuge Manager

3182 Castle Rock National Wildlife Refuge
Humboldt Bay NWR 707-733-5406
PO Box 576 *Fax:* 707-733-1946
Loleta, CA 95551 www.fws.gov/refuge/castle_rock/
The Refuge is a 14-acre offshore rock with steep cliffs and sparse vegetation. It was established in 1981 to protect an important migration staging area of the threatened Aleutian Canada goose. Over 21,000 of these roost on the island,which contains the second largest seabird breeding colony in California. Haul-out for a variety of marine mammals, including California sea lion, Stellar sea lion and northern elephant seal. Not open to the public, but wildlife can be observed fromshore.

3183 Channel Islands National Park
1901 Spinnaker Drive 805-658-5730
Ventura, CA 93001 *Fax:* 805-658-5799
chis_interpretation@nps.gov
www.nps.gov
Encompasses five of the eight California Channel Islands and their ocean environment, preserving and protecting a wealth of natural and cultural resources. Marine life ranges from microscopic plankton to the blue whale, the largestanimal to live on Earth. Archeological and cultural resources span a period of more than 10,000 years of human habitation.

3184 Clear Lake National Wildlife Refuge
Klamath Basin NWR Complex 916-667-2231
Route 1 Box 74 *Fax:* 916-667-3299
Tulelake, CA 96134 klamathbasinrefuges.fws.gov
Clear Lake National Wildlife Refuge plans to: maintain habitat for endangered, threatened and sensitive species; provide and enhance habitat for fall and spring migrant waterfowl; protect native habitats and wildlife representativeofthe natural biological diversity of the Klamath Basin; integrate the maintenance of productive wetland habitats and sustainable agriculture; and to provide high quality wildlife-dependent visitor services.

3185 Cleveland National Forest
10845 Rancho Bernardo Road 858-673-6180
Suite 200 *Fax:* 858-673-6192
San Diego, CA 92127 www.fs.usda.gov/cleveland/

3186 Coachella Valley National Wildlife Refuge
906 W Siclair Road 760-348-5278
PO Box 120 *Fax:* 760-348-7245
Calipatria, CA 92233 christian_schoneman@fws.gov
www.fws.gov
Contains 13,000 acres consisting of palm oasis woodlands, perennial desert pools and blow-sand habitat. This habitat is critical for the Coachella Valley fringe-toed lizard (Uma inornata) and flat-tailed horned lizard. These threatenedspecies are restricted to the refuge dune system and a few other small areas. Also has the state's second largest grove of native fan palms and the Coachella milk-vetch, a species of special concern.
Christian Schoneman, Project Leader

3187 Death Valley National Park
PO Box 579 760-786-3200
Death Valley, CA 92328 *Fax:* 760-786-3246
deva_superintendant@nps.gov
www.nps.gov/deva/index.htm
Death Valley National Park has more than 3.3 million acres of spectacular desert scenery, interesting and rare desert wildlife, complex geology, undisturbed wilderness and sites of historical and cultural interest. The National ParkService is dedicated to the protection and preservation of this park's unique resources for everyone to enjoy now and for future generations.

3188 Delevan National Wildlife Refuge
Sacramento NWR Complex 530-934-2801
752 County Road 99W *Fax:* 530-934-7814
Willows, CA 95988 www.fws.gov/sacramentovalleyrefuges
Delevan NWR is part of the Sacramento NWR Complex and is located in the Sacramento Valley of north-central California. The refuge consists of nearly 5,800 acres comprised of seasonal marsh, permanent ponds, watergrass and uplands inColusa County.

3189 Devil's Postpile National Monument
PO Box 3999 760-934-2289
Mammoth Lakes, CA 93546 *Fax:* 760-934-4780
www.nps.gov/depo
The geologic formation that is the Postpile is the world's finest example of unusual columnar basalt. Its columns of lava, with their four to seven sides, display of honeycomb pattern of order and harmony. Another jewel in the Monumentis the San Joaquin River.

3190 Eldorado National Forest
100 Forni Road 530-622-5061
Placeville, CA 95667 *Fax:* 530-621-5297
www.fs.usda.gov/eldorado/
Situated near the California gold discovery site on the American River at Coloma, this forest still boast numerous gold-bearing rivers and streams.Fishing opportunities are abundant. Only 34 miles of waterways are stocked, theremainder contain resident trout. Winter sports are cross country ski, sonowmobile and snowshoe. Backcountry exploration takes place year round in the Desolation and Mokelumme wildernesses.
Kathy Hardy, Forest Supervisor

3191 Ellicott Slough National Wildlife Refuge
San Andreas Rd 510-792-0222
Watsonville, CA 94560 sfbaynwrc@fws.gov
www.fws.gov

3192 Havasu National Wildlife Refuge
317 Mesquite Ave 760-326-3853
Needles, CA 92363 *Fax:* 760-326-5745
linda_l_miller@fws.gov
Benjamin Tuggle, Regional Director

3193 Hopper Mountain National Wildlife Refuge
2493 Portola Rd. 805-644-5185
Suite A *Fax:* 805-644-1732
Ventura, CA 9300 hoppermountain@fws.gov
www.fws.gov/refuge/hopper_mountain
The area is a traditional feeding site for the endangered California condor. Condors use the area frequently from October through May. A variety of other birds occur during migration and year round. The habitat includes 2,471 acres ofgrassland, chaparral and coastal sage scrub. There is a small, 350 acre area of intact California black walnut groves, some of the last remaining in southern California.
Dan Tappe, Refuge Manager

3194 Inyo National Forest
317 Mesquite Avenue 760-326-3853
Suite 200 *Fax:* 760-326-5745
Needles, CA 9236 www.fws.gov
The Inyo National Forest is a unique and special area of public land located along the aestern edge of California and Sierra Nevada. Extending 165 miles along the California/Nevada border between Los Angeles and Reno, the Inyo Nationalforest includes 1.9 million acres of pristine lakes, fragile meadows, winding streams, rugged Sierra Nevada peaks, and arid Great Baisn Mountains. Elevations range frome 4,000 to 14,495 feet, providing diverse habitats that support vegetationpatterns ranging.

3195 Joshua Tree National Park
74485 National Park Drive 760-367-5500
Twentynine Palms, CA 92277-3597 *Fax:* 760-367-6392
JOTR_info@nps.gov
www.nps.gov/jotr
Joshua Tree National Park's 794,000 acres span the transition between the Mojave and Colorado deserts of Southern California. Proclaimed a National Monument in 1936 and a Biosphere Reserve in 1984, Joshua Tree was designated a NationalPark In 1994. The area possesses a rich human history and a pristine natural environment.

3196 Kern National Wildlife Refuge
PO Box 670 661-725-2767
Delano, CA 93216-0670 *Fax:* 661-725-6041
www.natureali.org/KNWR.htm
David Hardt, Manager

3197 Kings Canyon National Park
Sequoia & Kings Canyon National Park
47050 Generals Highway 559-565-3341
Three Rivers, CA 93271-9700 *Fax:* 559-565-3730
www.nps.gov/seki
Kings Canyon National Park, located in California's Sierra Nevada Mountains, is a park most famous for its pristine stands of Giant Sequoia trees. Visitors explore Grant Grove along a network of easy trails. For the more adventurous,longer trails including those in the remote Kings Canyon Backcountry provide a greater challenge.

3198 Klamath Basin National Wildlife Refuges
Tulelake, CA 96134 530-667-2231
Fax: 530-667-8337
r8kbwebmaster@fws.gov
www.fws.gov/klamathbasinrefuges/
The Klamath Basin National Wildlife Refuges Complex consists of six refuges in Northern California and Southern Oregon. The refuges support the largest concentration of migratory water fowl on the west coast and the largest winteringnumbers of bald eagles in the lower 48 states.
Ron Cole, Refuge Manager
Greg Austin, Assistant Refuge Manager

3199 Klamath National Forest
1711 South Main Street 530-842-6131
Yreka, CA 96097-9549 www.fs.usda.gov/klamath/
The Klamath National Forest covers an area of 1,700,000 acres located in Siskiyou County, Northern California and Jackson County, Oregon. The forest comprises some five wilderness ar-

eas, Marble Mountain, Russian Wilderness Area,Trinity Alps, Red Buttes Wilderness Area and Siskiyou Wilderness Area.
Peg Boland, Forest Supervisor
Patricia A Grantham, Deputy Forest Supervisor

3200 Lake Tahoe Basin Management Unit
35 College Drive 530-543-2600
S Lake Tahoe, CA 96150 *Fax:* 530-573-2693
www.fs.usda.gov/ltbmu/
Majestic sceenery and diverse recreation oppotunities draw millions of visitors to the Lake Tahoe Basin annually. Changing colors throughout the year afford a brilliant backdrop to the many available activities in all seasons. TheBasin is home to a rich diversity of plants and animals that can be viewed during walks at interpertive sites and on many forest trails.

3201 Lassen National Forest
2550 Riverside Drive 530-257-2151
Susanville, CA 96130 www.fs.usda.gov/lassen/
Lassen National Forest lies at the heart of a fascinating part of California, a crossroads of people and nature. This is where the Sierra Nevada, the Cascades, the Modoc Plateau and the Great Basin meet. Within Lassen National Forest,you can explore a lava tube or the land of Ishi, the last survivor of the Yahi Tana Native American tribe: watch prong-horn antelope glide across sage flats; drive four-wheel trails into granite country appointed with sapphire lakes or discoverwildflowers on foot.

3202 Lava Beds National Monument
1 Indian Well Headquarters 530-667-8113
Tulelake, CA 96134 *Fax:* 530-667-2737
LABE_SUperintendent@nps.gov
www.nps.gov/labe
Volcanic eruptions on the Medicine Lake shield volcano have created an incredibly rugged landscape punctuated by cinder cones, lava flows, spatter cones, lava tube caves and pit craters. During the Modoc War of 1872-1873, the ModocIndains used these tortuous lava flows to their advantage. Under the leadership of Captain Jack, the Modocs took refuge in Captain Jack's Stronghold, a natural lava fortress.

3203 Los Padres National Forest
6755 Hollister Avenue 805-968-6640
Suite 150 www.fs.usda.gov/lpnf/
Goleta, CA 93117
Los Padres National Forest encompasses nearly 2 million acres of the central coastal mountains of California.
Ken Heffner, Forest Supervisor
Ann Garland, Deputy Forest Supervisor

3204 Lower Klamath National Wildlife Refuge
4009 Hill Rd 530-667-2231
Box 74 r8kbwebmaster@fws.gov
Tulelake, CA 96134 www.fws.gov/refuge/lower_klamath
The objectives of the refuge are to: maintain habitat for endangered, threatened and sensitive species; provide and enhance habitat for fall and spring migrant waterfowl; protect native habitats and wildlife representative of thenatural biological diversity of the Klamath Basin; integrate the maintenance of productive wetland habitats and sustainable agriculture; provide high quality wildlife-dependent visitor services.

3205 Mendocino National Forest
825 North Humboldt Avenue 530-934-3316
Willows, CA 95988 mailroom_r5_mendocino@fs.fed.us
www.fs.usda.gov/mendocino/
The Mendocino national Forest was set aside by President Roosevelt in 1907. It was frist named the Stony Creek Reserve and then the Stony Creek National Forest. It was later named the California National Forest and in 1932 became theMendocino National Forest. The MNF straddles the eastern spur of the Coastal Mountain Range in northernwestern Califonia, just a three hour drive north of San Francisco and Sacramento.
Tom Contreras, Forest Supervisor

3206 Modoc National Forest
225 West 8th Street 530-233-5811
Alturas, CA 96101 *Fax:* 530-233-8709
www.fs.usda.gov/modoc/
A land of contrasts and unspoiled vaction-hideaway settings. Nestled in the extreme northeastern corner of California, The Modoc National Forest is 140 miles east of Redding on Highway 299, and 169 miles north of Reno, Nevada, viahighway 395. The Modoc National Forest features several mountain areas. The Warner Mountains, on its east, are the western edge of Great Basin Province, the Medicine Lake Highlands, to northwest, are a couthern spur of the Cascade Range.
Stanley G Sylva, Forest Supervisor

3207 Modoc National Wildlife Refuge
PO Box 1610 530-233-3572
Alturas, CA 96101-1610 *Fax:* 530-233-4143
modoc@fws.gov
www.fws.gov/refuge/modoc/
A 7,000+ acre refuge established to manage and protect migratory waterfowl.

Steve Clay, Refuge Manager
Sean Cross, Assistant Refuge Manager

3208 Pinnacles National Monument
5000 Highway 146 831-389-4485
Paicines, CA 95043 *Fax:* 831-389-4489
www.nps.gov/pinn
Rising out of the chaparral-covered Gabilan Mountains, east of central California's Salinas Valley, are the spectacular remains of an ancient volcano. Massive monoliths, spires, sheer-walled canyons and talus passages define millionsof years of erosion, faulting and tectonic plate movement is reowned for the beauty and variety of its spring wildflowers. Hiking, rock climbing, picnicing and sildlife observation can be enjoyed throughout the year.

3209 Pixley National Wildlife Refuge
Kern NWR 661-725-2767
Po Box 670 www.fws.gov
Delano, CA 93216
Pixley national Wildlife Refuge provides for the endangered San Joaquin kit fox, Tipton kangaroo rat, and blunt-nosed leopard lizard.

3210 Plumas National Forest
159 Lawrence Street 530-283-2050
Quincy, CA 95971-6025 *Fax:* 530-283-7746
www.fs.usda.gov/plumas/
The Plumas National Forest has fresh conifer forests, rugged cayons, crystal clear lakes, grassy meadows, trout filled streams and brilliant star-filled skies. Located where the Sierra Nevada and Cascade Mountain ranges meet, thisforest has more than 100 lakes, 1,000 miles of rivers and streams, and over a million acres of National Forest.
Alice Carlton, Forest Supervisor

3211 Redwood National Park
1111 2nd Street 707-465-7335
Crescent City, CA 95531 *Fax:* 707-464-1812
www.nps.gov/redw
The world's tallest living trees can found along the northern California coast. Of the coast redwood forests still around today, almost one half of them can be found within the projected boundaries of Redwood National and State Parks.In 1994, the National Park Service and the Caifornia State Parks joined forces to manage four parks: Redwood National, Jebediah Smith, Del Norte Coast, and Prairie Creek Redwoods State Parks collectively known as Redwood National and State Parks.

3212 Sacramento National Wildlife Refuge Complex
752 County Road 99 West 530-934-2801
Willows, CA 95988 *Fax:* 530-934-7814
sacramentovalleyrefuges@fws.gov
www.fws.gov
The Complex consists of five national wildlife refuges and three wildlife management areas that comprise over 35,000 acres of wetlands and uplands in the Sacramento Valley of California. In addition there are over 30,000 acres ofconservation easements in the Complex. The refuges and easements serve as resting and feeding areas for nearly half the migratory birds on the Pacific Flyway.

3213 **Salinas River National Wildlife Refuge**
PO Box 524 510-792-0222
Newark, CA 94560 www.fws.gov
367 acres of diverse habitats including ocean, beach, dunes, grassland, river, lagoon, and salt marsh.

3214 **San Bernardino National Forest**
602 South Tippecanoe Avenue 909-382-2600
San Bernardino, CA 92408 www.fs.usda.gov/sbnf/
In the San Bernardino Mountains, the forest service has developed an extensive network of campgrounds and dozens of picnic areas for families and groups who want to enjoy a day in the mountains. The forest offers camping, picnicking,fishing, boating, swimming, hiking, horseback riding and more. During the winter, visitors come to the forest to cross-contry and down ski, snowboard and snowmobile.
Jeanne Wade Evans, Forest Supervisor
Max Copenhagen, Deputy Forest Supervisor

3215 **San Francisco Bay National Wildlife Refuge Complex**
1 Marshlands Rd 510-792-0222
Fremont, CA 94555 sfbaynwrc@fws.gov
www.fws.gov/sfbayrefuges
The San Francisco Bay National Refuge Complex is a collection of seven National Wildlife Refuges administered by the US Fish and Wildlife Service-Antioch Dunes National Wildlife Refuge, Don Edwards San Francisco Bay National Wildliferefuge, Ellicott Slough National Wildlife Refuge, Farallon National Wildlife Refuge, Marin Islands National Wildlife Refuge, Salinas River National Wildlife Refuge, and San Pablo National Wildlife Refuge.

3216 **San Luis National Wildlife Refuge**
7376 S. Wolfsen Road 209-826-3508
PO Box 2176 *Fax:* 209-826-1445
Los Banos, CA 93635
Mission: Working with others, to conserve, protect and enhance fish, wildlife, and plants and their habitats for the continuing benefit of the American people.

3217 **San Pablo Bay National Wildlife Refuge**
7715 Lakeville Highway 707-769-4200
Petaluma, CA 94954
San Pablo Bay National Wildlife Refuge protects and preserves habitat critical to the survival of the endangered California clapper rail and salt marsh harvest mouse. The Refuge and surrounding San Pablo Bay area also provide winteringhabitat for millions of shorebirds and thousands of waterfowl, including the largest wintering population of canvasbacks on the west coast.
Francesca Demgen, President
Debra Green, Vice President

3218 **Santa Monica Mountains National Recreation**
401 West Hillcrest Drive 805-370-2301
Thousand Oaks, CA 91360 *Fax:* 805-370-2351
www.nps.gov/samo
Santa Monica Mountains rise above Los Angeles, widen to meet the curve of Santa Monica Bay and reach their highest peaks facing the ocean, forming a beautiful and multi-faceted landscape. Santa Monica Mountains National Recreation Areais a cooperative effort that joins federal, state and local park agencies with private preserves and landowners to protect the natural and cultural resources of this transverse mountain range and seashore.

3219 **Sequoia National Forest**
1839 South Newcomb Street 559-784-1500
Porterville, CA 93257 *Fax:* 559-781-4744
www.fs.usda.gov/sequoia/
The Sequoia National Forest is at the southern tip of the Sierra Nevada range. Its highest point is 12,432 foot Florence Peak in the Golden Trout Wilderness. The forest has five wildernesses, a scenic byway and four wild and scenicrivers. About 10,000 cows graze on the forest land. Camping, water sports, hiking, downhill and cross-country skiing and horseback riding are amoung the forest's many recreational activities.

3220 **Shasta-Trinity National Forest**
3644 Avtech Parkway 530-226-2500
Redding, CA 96002 *Fax:* 530-226-2470
www.fs.usda.gov/stnf/
J Sharon Heywood, Forest Supervisor

3221 **Sierra National Forest**
1600 Tollhouse Road 559-297-0706
Clovis, CA 93611 www.fs.usda.gov/sierra/
Edward C Cole, Forest Supervisor

3222 **Six Rivers National Forest**
1330 Bayshore Way 707-442-1721
Eureka, CA 95501 *Fax:* 707-442-9242
www.fs.usda.gov/srnf/
Six Rivers National Forest lies east of Redwood State and National Parks in northwestern California, and stretches southward from the Oregon border for about 140 miles.
Tyrone Kelley, Forest Supervisor
Will Metz, Deputy Forest Supervisor

3223 **Sonny Bono Salton Sea National Wildlife Refuge Complex**
906 W Sinclair Road 760-348-5278
Calipatria, CA 92233 saltonsea.fws.gov
The Refuge is composed of two disjunctive units, separated by 18 miles of private lands. Each unit contains managed wetland habitat, agricultural fields, and tree rows. The courses of the New and Alamo rivers run through the Refuge,providing freshwater inflow to the Salton Sea.

3224 **Stanislaus National Forest**
19777 Greenley Road 209-532-3671
Sonora, CA 95370 *Fax:* 209-533-1890
www.fs.usda.gov/stanislaus/
The Stanislaus National Forest, created on February 22, 1897, is among the oldest of the National Forests. It is named for the Stanislaus River whose headwaters rise within Forest boundaries. The Spanish explorer Gabriel Moraga namedthe river Our Lady of Guadalupe during an 1806 expedition. Later, the river was renamed in honor of Estanislao, an Indian leader.

3225 **Sutter National Wildlife Refuge**
Sacramento NWR Complex 530-934-2801
752 County Road 99W *Fax:* 530-934-7814
Willows, CA 95988 www.fws.gov

3226 **Tahoe National Forest**
631 Coyote Street 530-265-4531
Nevada City, CA 95959 www.fs.usda.gov/tahoe/
The Tahoe National Forest straddles the crest of the Sierra Nevada mountains in northern California, and encompasses a vast territory, from the golden foothills on the western slope to the high peaks of the Sierra crest.

3227 **Tijuana Slough National Wildlife Refuge**
Tijuana River NERR 619-575-2704
301 Caspian Way *Fax:* 619-575-6913
Imperial Beach, CA 91932 www.fws.gov
Established in 1980 to conserve and protect endangered and threatened fish, wildlife and plant species. Conservation of the light-footed clapper rail was the primary impetus for the creation of the refuge. The refuge is part of alarger unit called the Tijuana River National Estuarine Research Reserve, which is administered by the National Oceanographic and Atmospheric Administration.

3228 **Tule Lake National Wildlife Refuge**
4009 Hill Road 530-667-2231
Tulelake, CA 96134 *Fax:* 530-667-3299
The objectives of Tule Lake are to: maintain habitat for endangered, threatened and sensitive species; provide and enhance habitat for fall and spring migrant waterfowl; protect native habitats and wildlife representative of thenatural biological diversity of the Klamath Basin; integrate the maintenance of productive wetland habitats and sustainable agriculture; and ensure that the refuge agricultural practices confirm to the principles of integrated pest management.

3229 **Yosemite National Park**
PO Box 577 209-372-0200
Yosemite National Park, CA 95389 www.nps.gov
Yosemite National Park embraces a spectacular tract of mountain- and-valley scenery in the Sierra Nevada, which was set aside as a national park in 1890. The park harbors a grand collection of waterfalls, meadows, and forests thatinclude groves of giant sequoias, the world's largest living things. Highlights of the park include Yosemite Valley, and its high cliffs and waterfalls;Wawona's history center and historic hotel; the Mariposa Grove, which contains hundreds of ancientgiant sequoias.

Colorado: US Forests, Parks, Refuges

3230 **Alamosa/Monte Vista/ Baca National Wildlife Refuge Complex**
9383 El Rancho Lane 719-589-4021
Alamosa, CO 81101 *Fax:* 719-587-0595
alamosa@fws.gov
www.fws.gov/refuge/alamosa
The Valley extends over 100 miles from north to south and 50 miles from east to west, with dwarfing mountains in three directions. The surrounding mountains feed the arid valley with precious surface water, as well as replenish anexpansive underground reservoir. This liquid wealth has made two National Wildlife Refuges possible in the San Luis Valley: Alamosa and Monte Vista.

3231 **Arapaho National Wildlife Refuge**
953 JC Rd 32 970-723-8202
Walden, CO 80480 *Fax:* 970-723-8528
arapaho@fws.gov
www.fws.gov/refuge/Arapaho
Arapaho National Wildlife Refuge supports diverse wildlife habitats including sagebrush grassland uplands, grassland meadows, willow riparian areas, wetlands and mixed conifer and aspen woodland. This refuge is one in a system of over500 National Wildlife Refuges, a network of lands set aside and managed specifically for wildlife. It is administered by the US Fish and Wildlife Service.

3232 **Browns Park National Wildlife Refuge**
1318 Highway 318 970-365-3613
Maybell, CO 81640 *Fax:* 970-365-3614
brownspark@fws.gov
www.fws.gov/refuge/browns_park
The primary purpose of Browns Park Refuge is to provide high quality nesting and migration habitat for the Great Basin Canada Goose, ducks and other migratory birds. Before Flaming Gorge Dam was constructed in 1962, the Green Riverflooded annually, creating excellent waterfowl nesting, feeding and resting marshes in the backwater sloughs and old stream meanders. The dam stopped the flooding, eliminating much of this waterfowl habitat.

3233 **Colorado National Monument**
1750 Rim Rock Drive 970-858-3617
Fruita, CO 81521 *Fax:* 970-858-0372
COLM_Info@nps.gov
www.nps.gov/colm
Colorado National Monument consists of geological features including: towering red sandstone monoliths, deep sheer-walled canyons and a variety of wildlife.

3234 **Curecanti National Recreation Area**
102 Elk Creek 970-641-2337
Gunnison, CO 81230 *Fax:* 970-641-3127
CURE_Vis_Mail@nps.gov
www.nps.gov/cure
Three reservoirs, named for corresponding dams on the Gunnison River, form the heart of Curecanti National Recreation Area; Blue Mesa Reservoir, Morrow Point Reservoir and the Crystal Reservoir.

3235 **Dinosaur National Monument**
4545 East Highway 40 970-374-3000
PO Box 128 *Fax:* 970-374-3003
Dinosaur, CO 81610 www.nps.gov/dino
Dinosaur Monument protects a large deposit of fossil dinosaur bones that lived millons of years ago.

3236 **Florissant Fossil Beds National Monument**
PO Box 185 719-748-3253
Florissant, CO 80816 *Fax:* 719-748-3164
FLFO_Information@nps.gov
www.nps.gov/flfo
Huge petrified redwoods and incredibly detailed fossils of ancient insects and plants reveal a very different Colorado of long ago. A lake formed in the valley and the fine-grained sediments at its bottom became the final resting-placefor thousands of insects and plants. These sediments compacted into layers of shale and preserved the delicated details of these organisms as fossils.

3237 **Great Sand Dunes National Park & Preserve**
11999 Highway 150 719-378-6399
Mosca, CO 81146 *Fax:* 719-378-6310
www.nps.gov/grsa
These dunes are the tallest in North America, rising 750 feet from the valley floor. The dunes are home to some unique and spectacular species of flora and fauna. Besides a large variety of birds, there are quite a few species ofmammals that visit or reside within the dunes. Few reptiles are found here due to the high altitude.

3238 **Rio Grande National Forest**
1803 W US Highway 160 719-852-5941
Monte Vista, CO 81144 www.fs.usda.gov/riogrande
The Rio Grande National Forest is 1.86 million acres located in southwestern Colorado and remains one of the true undiscovered jewels of Colorado. The Continental Divide runs for 236 miles along most of the western border of theForest. The Forest present myraid ecosystems; from 7600-ft alpine desert to over 14,300-ft in the majestic Sangre de Cristo Wilderness on the eastern side.

3239 **Rocky Mountain National Park**
1000 Highway 36 970-586-1206
Estes Park, CO 80517 *Fax:* 970-586-1256
ROMO_informatin@nps.gov
www.nps.gov/romo

3240 **San Juan National Forest**
15 Burnett Court 970-247-4874
Durango, CO 81301 *Fax:* 970-385-1243
www.fs.usda.gov/sanjuan
San Jaun National Forest, a region of forested mountains, 14,000-foot peaks, scenic roads, geological wonders, hisoric and prehistoric communities, and a narrow-gauge railroad.
Mark Stiles, Forest Supervisor
Howard Sargent, Deputy Forest Supervisor

3241 **White River National Forest**
900 Grand Avenue 970-945-2521
PO Box 948 *Fax:* 970-945-3266
Glenwood Springs, CO 81602 www.fs.usda.gov/wps
The two and one quarter million acre White River National Forest is located in the heart of the Colorado Rocky Mountains, approximately two to four hours west of Denver on Interstate 70. The scenic beauty of the area, along with ampledeveloped and undeveloped recreation opportunities on the forest, accounts for the fact the White River consistently ranks as one of the top five Forests nationwide for total recreation use.

Connecticut: US Forests, Parks, Refuges

3242 **Stewart B McKinney National Wildlife Refuge**
733 Old Clinton Road 860-399-2513
Westbrook, CT 00649 *Fax:* 860-399-2515
fw5rw_sbmnwr@fws.gov
www.fws.gov/refuge/stewart_b_mckinney

Delaware: US Forests, Parks, Refuges

3243 **Bombay Hook National Wildlife Refuge**
2591 Whitehall Neck Road 302-653-6872
Smyrna, DE 19977 fw5rw_bhnwr@fws.gov
www.fws.gov/refuge/bombay_hook/
Stretching about eight miles along Delaware Bay and covering nearly 16,000 acres, Bombay Hook NWR was established as a refuge for migratory waterfowl. Today, the Refuge provides habitat for a diversity of wildlife. The refuge offersauto tours, walking trails, observation towers, and interpretive displays for the visiting public.

3244 **Prime Hook National Wildlife Refuge**
11978 Turkle Pond Road 302-684-8419
Milton, DE 19968 *Fax:* 302-684-8504
FW5RW_PHNWR@fws.gov
primehook.fws.gov
The Prime Hook National Wlidlife Refuge spans about 10,000 acres along the western Delaware Bay. The marshes of the refuge are ideal habitat for thousands of migrating ducks, geese, and shorebirds. The refuge is also home to woodlandand grassland birds, reptiles, amphibians, and mammals, including the endangered Delmarva Peninsula Fox Squirrel. Avid photographers can enjoy the beauty of wildlife from a photography blind and wheel-chair accessible observation platform.

District of Columbia: US Forests, Parks, Refuges

3245 **Battleground National Cemetery**
6625 Georgia Avenue, NW 202-426-6924
Washington, DC 20240 *Fax:* 202-426-1845
www.nps.gov
Battleground National Cemetery, located at 6625 Georgia Avenue NW, was established shortly after the Battle of Fort Stevens in the summer of 1864. The battle, which lasted two days (July 11-12, 1864) marked the defeat of General JubalA Early's Confederate campaign to launch an offensive action against the poorly defended Nation's Capital. Near the entrance are monuments commemorating those units which fought at Fort Stevens.

Florida: US Forests, Parks, Refuges

3246 **Arthur R Marshall Loxahatchee National Wildlife Refuge**
10216 Lee Road 561-734-8303
Boynton Beach, FL 33437 *Fax:* 561-369-7190
www.fws.gov/refuge/arm_loxahatchee
Welcome to the Arthur R. Marshall Loxahatchee National Wildlife Refuge, the last northernmost portion of the unique Everglades. With over 221 square miles of Everglades habitat, A.R.M. Loxahatchee National Wildlife Refuge is home tothe American alligator and the endangered Everglades snail kite. In any given year, as many as 257 species of birds may use the refuge's diverse wetland habitats.

3247 **Big Cypress National Preserve**
33100 Tamiami Trail East 239-695-1201
Ochopee, FL 34141 *Fax:* 239-695-3901
bob_degross@nps.gov
www.nps.gov/bicy
The 729,000 acre Big Cypress National Preserve was set aside to ensure the preservation, conservation, and protection of the natural scenic, floral and faunal, and recreational values of the Big Cypress Watershed. The importance ofthis watershed to the Everglades National Park was a major consideration for its establishment. The name Big Cypress refers to the large size of this area. Vast expanses of cypress strands span this unique landscape.

3248 **Biscayne National Park**
9700 SW 328 Street 305-230-7275
Homestead, FL 33033 *Fax:* 305-230-1190
BISC_Information@nps.gov
www.nps.gov/bisc
Turquoise waters, emerald islands and fish-bejeweled reefs make Biscayne National Park a paradise for wildlife-watching, snorkeling, diving, boating, fishing and other activities. Within the park boundaries are the longest stretch ofmangrove forest left on Florida's east coast, the clear shallow waters of Biscayne Bay, over 40 of the northernmost Florida Keys, and a spectacular living coral reef. Superimposed on all of this natural beauty is 10,000 years of human history.

3249 **Canaveral National Seashore**
212 South Washington Avenue 321-267-1110
Titusville, FL 32796 *Fax:* 321-264-2906
cana_resource_management@nps.gov
www.nbbd.com/godo/cns/
Canaveral National Seashore is a step into the past, protection for the present and a doorway into the future. The 100 Native American Archeological sites that are within our boundaries are evidence of past generations of people thatlived here. Canaveral National Seashore covers 57,000 acres and is the longest stretch (24 miles) of undeveloped beach on Florida's east coast. Fourteen endangered species make their home within Canaveral's boundaries.
Carol Clark, Superintendent

3250 **Chassahowitzka National Wildlife Refuge Complex**
1502 SE Kings Bay Drive 352-563-2088
Crystal River, FL 34429 *Fax:* 352-795-7961
chassahowitzka@fws.gov
chassahowitzka.fws.gov
A complex of 5 National Wildlife Refuges on the Gulf Coast of Florida including Crystal River NWR. Established in 1983 for the protection of the endangered West Indian manatee. Office hours are from 7:30 AM to 4:00 PM Monday thruFriday. The office is also open Saturdays and Sundays during the winter months (November 15 - March 31) please call the office at 352-563-2088 for more information.
James Kraus, Manager

3251 **Dry Torgus National Park & Everglades National Park**
P.O. Box 6208 305-242-7700
Key West, FL 33041 *Fax:* 305-242-7711
drto_information@nps.gov
www.nps.gov/drto
Recognized for its near-pristine natural resources including sea grass beds, fisheries, and sea turtle and nesting habit. The area also lays claim to a rich cultural heritage with a diverse array of themes. Fort Jefferson, on GardenKey, is the park's central cultural feature and one of the largest 19th century American masonry coastal forts.
Dan Kimball, Superintendent
Keith Whisenant, Deputy Superintendent

3252 **Egmont Key National Wildlife Refuge**
1502 SE Kings Bay Drive 352-563-2088
Crystal River, FL 34429 *Fax:* 352-795-7961
CrystalRiver@fws.gov
www.fws.gov/refuge/Egmont_Key
This barrier island refuge is approximately 350 acres and was established to provide nesting, feeding and resting habitat for brown pelicans and other migratory birds. The combined resources of the US Fish and Wildlife Service andFlorida Park Service provide protection for Egmont Key and its wildlife, as well as an enjoyable experience for the visitor.
James Kraus, Manager

3253 **Everglades National Park**
40001 State Road 9336 305-242-7700
Homestead, FL 33034-6733 *Fax:* 305-242-7711
EVER_Information@nps.gov
www.nps.gov/ever
The largest subtropical wilderness in the United States, boasts rare and endangered species. It has been designated a World Heri-

tage Site, international Biosphere Reserve, and Wetland of International Importance, significant to allpeople of the world.
Dan Kimball, Superintendent
Keith Whisenant, Deputy Superintendent

3254 Florida Panther National Wildlife Refuge
12085 SR 29 South 239-657-8001
Suite 300 *Fax:* 239-657-8002
Immokalee, FL 34142 floridapanther@fws.gov
www.fws.gov/floridapanther
Mission: To conserve and manage lands and waters in concert with other agency efforts within the Big Cypress Watershed, primarily for the Florida Panther, other endangered and threatened species, natural diversity, and culturalresources for the benefit of the American people.
Layne Hamilton, Manager

3255 Hobe Sound National Wildlife Refuge and Nature Center
13640 U.S. Highway 1 772-546-6141
PO Box 645 *Fax:* 772-545-7572
Hobe Sound, FL 33475-645 hobesound@fws.gov
www.fws.gov/refuge/hobe_sound
Refuge objectives are to: maintain and restore diverse habitats designed to achieve refuge purposes and wildlife population objectives; maintain viable diverse populations of native flora and fauna consistent with sound biologicalprinciples; manage natural and cultural resources through land protection and partnership; and develop and implement wildlife dependent recreation and environmental education that leads to enjoyable recreation experiences and a greater understandingof resources.

Margo Stahl, Refuge Manager
Debbie Fritz-Quincy, Nature Center Director

3256 JN Darling National Wildlife Refuge
1 Wildlife Drive 239-472-1100
Sanibel, FL 33957 *Fax:* 239-472-4061
dingdarling@fws.gov
www.fws.gov/dingdarling
The refuge on Sanibel Island is a subtropical barrier island in the Gulf of Mexico hemmed by mangrove trees, shallow bays and white sandy beaches. The 6,300-acre refuge is connected to the mainland by a three-mile causeway. Named in1967 for Jay Norwood (Ding) Darling, an editorial cartoonist, pioneer conservationist and originator of the federal Duck Stamp Program. Darling, who was the first director of what is now the US Fish and Wildlife Service, wintered on neighboringCaptiva Island.
Paul Leader, Project Ledaer
Joyce Palmer, Deputy Refuge Mnanager

3257 Lake Woodruff National Wildlife Refuge
2045 Mud Lake Road 904-985-4673
DeLeon Springs, FL 32130 *Fax:* 904-985-0926
lakewoodruff@fws.gov
www.fws.gov/lakewoodruff
Encompasses two large lakes offering sights of diverse habitats and a variety of wildlife. Fishing and boating are the primary recreational activities.
Harold Morrow, Project Leader

3258 National Key Deer Refuge
28950 Watson Blvd. 305-872-2239
Big Pine Key Plaza *Fax:* 305-872-2154
Big Pine Key, FL 33043 keydeer@fws.gov
www.fws.gov/refuge/National_Key_Deer_Refuge
Refuge objectives are: to protect and preserve Key deer and other wildlife resources in the Florida Keys; to conserve endangered and threatened fish, wildlife and plants; to provide habitat and protection for migratory birds; and toprovide opportunities for environmental education and public viewing of refuge wildlife and habitats.
Anne Morkill, Manager

3259 Pelican Island National Wildlife Refuge
1339 20th Street 772-562-3909
Vero Beach, FL 32960 *Fax:* 772-299-3101
pelicanisland@fws.gov
www.fws.gov/pelicanisland

Charlie Pelizza, Refuge Manager
Nick Wirwa, Refuge Manager

3260 St. Marks National Wildlife Refuge
1255 Lighthouse Road 850-925-6121
St Marks, FL 32355 saintmarks@fws.gov
www.fws.gov/saintmarks
Saint Marks National Wildlife Refuge is in Wakulla, Jefferson and Taylor counties along the Gulf coast of north Florida. The refuge is approximately 25 miles south of Tallahassee. The refuge encompasses 65,000 acres of divided tidalflats; and freshwater impoundments harbor a large variety of wildlife, including 434 verebrate species, excluding fish. Over quarter million vistors enjoy a variety of outdoor recreation opportunities annually.

3261 St. Vincent National Wildlife Refuge
3100 County Road 30A 850-653-8808
Port St. Joe, FL 32456 *Fax:* 850-653-9893
saintvincent@fws.gov
www.fws.gov/saintvincent
The historic St Vincent National Wildlife Refuge is a large barrier island, four miles wide and nine miles long. It was inhabited as early as 240A.D. and is known to have been visited by Franciscan friars in the early 1600s. Over itshistory, private landowners developed the island into a preserve housing Asian and African wildlife and an assortment in between. The US Fish and Wildlife Service purchased the island in 1968 bringing an end to the exotic jungle.
Monica Harris, Manager

3262 Timucuan Ecological & Historic Preserve
12713 Fort Caroline Road 904-221-5568
Jacksonville, FL 32225 *Fax:* 904-221-5248
www.nps.gov/timu
The 46,000 acre Timucuan Ecological and Historic Preserve was established to protect one of the last unspoiled coastal wetlands on the Atlantic Coast and to preserve historic and prehistoric sites within the area. The estuarineecosystem includes aslt marsh, coastal dunes, hardwood hammock, as well as salt, fresh, and brackish waters, all rich in native vegetation and animal life.

Barbara Goodman, Superintendent

Georgia: US Forests, Parks, Refuges

3263 Chattahoochee-Oconee National Forest
1755 Cleveland Highway 770-297-3000
Gainesville, GA 30501 *Fax:* 770-297-3011
www.fs.usda.gov/main/conf/
Together, these forest offer more than ten wilderness areas, six beaches, and thousands of acres of lakes and stream. The forest is real draw for history buffs, who can get absorbed in tracing events such as the Trail of Tears and manya Civil War battle.

3264 Cumberland Island National Seashore
101 Wheeler Street 912-882-4336
P.O. Box 1203 *Fax:* 912-882-2651
Saint Marys, GA 31558 www.nps.gov/cuis
Cumberland Island is 17.5 miles long and totals 36,415 acres of which 16,850 are marsh, mud flats, and todal crreks. Well know for its sea turtles, abundant shore bierds, dune fields, maritime forest, salt marshes, and historicstructures.

3265 Okefenokee National Wildlife Refuge
2700 Suwannee Canal Road 912-496-7836
Folkston, GA 31537 okefenokee@fws.gov
www.fws.gov/okefenokee
Okefenokee NWR was established in 1937 to preserve the 438,000 acre Okefenokee Swamp. Presently the refuge encompasses approximately 406,000 acres of which 353,000 are desig-

nated as Wilderness. Habitats include open wet prairies,cypress forests, scrub-shrub, oak hammocks and longleaf pine forests. The prosperity and survival of the swamp, and the species dependent on it, is directly tied to maintaining the integrity of complex ecological processes, including hydrology andfire.

Michael Lusk, Refuge Manager

3266 Piedmont National Wildlife Refuge
718 Juliette Road 478-986-5441
Hillsboro, GA 31038 *Fax:* 478-986-9646
piedmont@fws.gov
www.fws.gov/piedmont
35,000 acre national wildlife refuge with hiking trails, gravel roads throughout, wildlife drive, hunting and fishing opportunties, bird watching.

3267 Pinckney Island National Wild Refuge
Savannah Coastal Refuges
694 Beech Hill Lane 843-784-2468
Suite 10 *Fax:* 912-652-4385
Hardeeville, SC 29927 savannahcoastal@fws.gov
www.fws.gov/refuge/pinckney_island
A group of islands and small hammocks, the 4,053-acre refuge includes a variety of land types: saltmarsh, forestland, brushland, fallow fields and freshwater ponds. Pinckney, the largest of the refuge islands, is 3.8 miles long and1.75 miles across at its greatest width. Boaters who navigate the refuge's estuarine waters may view shore and wading birds, including the endangered wood stork, that feeds on mudflats, oysterbeds and shores.

3268 Savannah National Wildlife Refuge
694 Beech Hill Lane 843-784-2468
Suite 10 *Fax:* 912-652-4385
Hardeeville, SC 29927 savannacoastal@fws.gov
www.fws.gov/refuge/pinckney_island
Refuge objectives are to provide: a refuge and feeding ground for native birds and wild animals; habitat and protection for threatened and endangered plants and animals; habitat and sanctuary for migratory birds consistent with theobjectives of the Atlantic Flyway; habitats for other species of indigenous wildlife and fishery resources; management of furbearers, deer and other upland animals; and opportunities for environmental education, interpretation and recreation for thevisiting public.

Hawaii: US Forests, Parks, Refuges

3269 Haleakala National Park
PO Box 369 808-572-4400
Makawao, HI 96768 www.nps.gov/hale
The Park preserves the outstanding volcanic landscape of the upper slopes of Haleakala on the island of Maui and protects the unique and fragile ecosystems of Kipahulu Valley, the scenic pools along Oheo gulch, and many rare andendangered species. Haleakala National Park was designated an International Biosphere Reserve.

3270 Hawaii Volcanoes National Park
1 Crater Rim Drive 808-985-6000
PO Box 52 *Fax:* 808-985-6004
Hawaii National Park, HI 96718-52 www.nps.gov/havo
Established in 1916, this 333,000 acre National Park encompasses coastal lava plains, rain forests and deserts. It preserves and protects active volcanoes, rare and endangered plants and animals, and Hawaiian archeological sites.

3271 Huleia National Wildlife Refuge: Kauai
PO Box 1128 808-828-1413
Kilauea *Fax:* 808-828-6634
Kauai, HI 96754 jennifer_waipa@fws.gov
www.fws.gov/refuge/huleia/
Located on the southeast side of Kauai, lies adjacent to the famous Menehune Fish Pond, a registered National Historic Landmark. The Huleia Refuge is approximately 241 acres of wetlands which provides habitat for five endangeredHawaiian waterbirds.
Shannon Smith, Refuge Manager
Mike Mitchell, Deputy Refuge Manager

3272 James Campbell National Wildlife Refuge
Oahu Refuge Complex 808-637-6330
66-590 Kam Highway, Rm 2C *Fax:* 808-637-3578
Haleiwa, HI 96712 sylvia_pelissa@fws.gov
James Campbell NWR lies at the northernmost tip of Oahu near the community of Kahuku and serves as a strategic landfall for native and migratory birds coming from as far away as Alaska, Siberia, and Asia. The specific purpose of theRefuge is to provide habitat for Hawaii's four endemic, endangered waterbirds and other native wildlife, as well as migratory waterfowl and shorebirds. A total of 102 bird species have been documented on the Refuge since its creation.
Sylvia R Pelizza, Manager

3273 Kauai National Wildlife Refuge Complex
PO Box 1128 808-828-1413
Kilauea, HI 96754 *Fax:* 808-828-1414
Kauai is also known as the Garden Isle for its lush vegetation and spectacular waterfalls. It is the oldest of the Hawaiian islands chain and is approximately 553 square miles in size. The Kauai National Wildlife Refuge Complexconsists of Kilauea Point, Hanalei, and Huleia National Wildlife Refuges.

3274 Kealia Pond National Wildlife Refuge
300 Ala Moana Boulevard 808-792-9400
Room 3-122, Box 50088 *Fax:* 808-792-9580
Honolulu, HI 96850 www.fws.gov/pacificislands
Glynnis Nakai, Manager

3275 Kilauea Point National Wildlife Refuge
PO Box 1128 808-828-1413
Kilauea, HI 96754 *Fax:* 808-828-1414
This National Wildlife Refuge provides nesting habitat for seabirds; notably red-footed boobies, Laysan albatross and wedge-tailed shearwaters. The Refuge is also home to the historic Kilauea Point Lighthouse and native marine coastalplant communities. In winter, the 180 foot high precipice provides an ideal site for viewing humpback whales in offshore waters.
Mike Hawkes, Refuge Manager

3276 Oahu National Wildlife Refuge Complex
66-590 Kamehameha Highway 808-637-6330
Room 2C *Fax:* 808-637-3578
Haleiwa, HI 96712 www.fws.gov/pacificislands
Sylvia Pelizza, Manager

3277 Pearl Harbor National Wildlife Refuge
66-590 Kamehameha Highway 808-637-6330
Room 2C *Fax:* 808-637-3578
Haleiwa, HI 96712 www.fws.gov/pacificislands
Sylvia Pelizza, Manager

Idaho: US Forests, Parks, Refuges

3278 Bear Lake National Wildlife Refuge
322 North 4th St. 208-847-1757
Montpelier, ID 83254-1019 *Fax:* 208-847-1319
annette_deknijf@fws.gov
www.fws.gov/refuge/bear_lake/
18,000 acres of marsh and uplands north of Bear Lake proper. Approx 7 miles south of Montpelier. White-faced ibis, Franklin's gulls, sandhill cranes, lots of ducks, Canada geese, Trumpeter swans.

Annette deKnijf, Refuge Manager

3279 Boise National Forest
1249 S Vinnell Way 208-373-4100
Boise, ID 83709 r4_boise_info@fs.fed.us
www.fs.usda.gov/boise

The predominantly Ponderosa pine and Douglas fir ecosystem provides homes for fish and wildlife; fiber for wood and paper products; forage for cows and sheep; precious metals for industrial and personal use; and an unlimited menu ofyear round opportunities. The Boise National Forest also contains a number of unique sites, including the Experimental Forest, the Lucky Peak Nursery and Bogus Basin Ski Area.

3280 Camas National Wildlife Refuge Southeast Idaho Refuge Complex
2150 E 2350 N 208-662-5423
Hamer, ID 83425 www.fws.gov/pacific/refuges
Cama NWR is 36 miles north of Idaho Falls in southeast Idaho, in the Cama Creek floodplain. Elevation is 4,800 feet. About half of its acreage consists of lakes, ponds and marshlands; the remainder is grass sagebrush uplands, meadowsand farm fields. Camas Creek flows for 8 miles through the length of the refuge and is the source of water for many of the lakes and ponds. Tall cottonwood trees along the creek attract a wide variety of songbirds.

3281 Caribou-Targhee National Forest
1405 Hollipark Drive 208-524-7500
Idaho Falls, ID 83401 jjbennett@fs.fed.us
www.fs.usda.gov/ctnf
The Caribou National Forest was created to help preserve wilderness land in an area marked by mining activity and westward migration. The forest now covers more than 1 million acres in southeast Idaho, with small portions in Utah andWyoming. Several north-south mountain ranges of the Overthrust Belt dominate the landscape. Caribou National Park offers a wide variety of outdoor activities, including camping, hiking, fishing, climbing, skiing and horseback riding.
Larry Timchak, Supervisor
Lynn Ballard, Public Affairs

3282 Clearwater National Forest
903 3rd Street 208-935-2513
Kamiah, ID 83536 *Fax:* 208-476-8329
www.fs.usda.gov/nezperceclearwater/
The Clearwater National Forest covers 1.8 million acres from the jagged peaks of the Bitterroot Mountains in the east to the river canyons and rolling hills of the Palouse Prairie in the west. The North Fork of the Clearwater & theLochsa rivers provide miles of tumbling white water interspersed with quiet pools for migratory and resident fish. The mountains provide habitat for elk, moose, whitetail & mule deer, gray wolf, cougar, mountain goats, and many smaller mammals.
Tom Reilly, Forest Supervisor
Kimberly Nelson, Public Affairs

3283 Craters of the Moon National Monument & Preserve
PO Box 29 208-527-3257
Arco, ID 83213 *Fax:* 208-527-3073
www.nps.gov/crmo
A sea of lava flows with scattered islands of cinder cones and sagebrush characterizes this wierd and scenic landscape known as Craters of the Moon. Craters of the Moon National Monument and Preserve contains three young lava fieldscovering almost half a million acres. These remarkably well preserved volcanic features resulted from geologic events that appear to have happened yesterday and will likely continue tomorrow.

3284 Deer Flat National Wildlife Refuge
13751 Upper Embankment Road 208-467-9278
Nampa, ID 83686 *Fax:* 208-467-1019
deerflat@fws.gov
www.fws.gov/refuge/deer_flat/
One of the nation's oldest refuges. It includes the Lake Lowell sector and the Snake River Islands sector. The refuge provides a mix of wildlife habitats, including open waters, wetland edges around the lake, sagebrush uplands,grasslands and riparian forests. More than 250 birds and 30 mammals have been seen on the refuge, providing excellent wildlife observation and photography opportunities.

3285 Grays Lake National Wildlife Refuge
74 Grays Lake Road 208-574-2755
Wayan, ID 83285 www.fws.gov/pacific/refuges
Twenty-seven miles north of Soda Springs in southeast Idaho, the refuge lies in a high mountain valley at 6,400 feet. Grays Lake is actually a large, shallow marsh with dense vegetation and little open water. Most of the marshvegetation is bulrush and cattail. Adjacent lands are primarily wet meadows and grasslands.

3286 Idaho Panhandle National Forest
3815 Schreiber Way 208-765-7223
Coeur d'Alene, ID 83815 *Fax:* 208-765-7307
www.fs.usda.gov/ipnf/

3287 Kootenai National Wildlife Refuge
287 Westside Rd 208-267-3888
Bonners Ferry, ID 83805 *Fax:* 208-267-5570
fw1KootenaiNWR@fws.gov
www.fws.gov/refuge/kootenai
The 2,774 acre refuge is located in the northern panhandle of Idaho, and serves as a resting and feeding area for migratory birds.

3288 Minidoka National Wildlife Refuge
961 E Minidoka Dam 208-436-3589
Rupert, ID 83350 www.fws.gov/pacific/refuges
Lying 12 miles northeast of Rupert in the Snake River Valley in south-central Idaho, the refuge extends upstream about 25 miles from the Minidoka Dam along both shores of the Snake River and includes all of Lake Walcott. Over half therefuge is open water, with some small marsh area.

3289 Nez Perce National Forest
1005 Highway 13 208-983-1950
Grangeville, ID 83530 *Fax:* 208-983-4099
www.fs.fed.us/r1/nezperce
The Forest is best known for its wild character. Nearly half of the Forest is designated wilderness. It also sports two rivers popular with thrill-seeking floaters-the Selway and the Salmon.
Jane Cottrell, Forest Supervisor

3290 Payette National Forest
500 N Mission St Building 2 208-634-0700
McCall, ID 83638 www.fs.usda.gov/payette/
Payette National Forest spans over 2.3 million acres of some of west-central Idaho's most beautiful and diverse country. In one day you can travel from hot desert grasslands through cool conifer forests to snow-capped peaks. Thespecacular land is bordered by two of the deepest canyons in North America— the Salmon River Canyon On the north and Hells Canyon of the Sake River on the west. To the east lies 2.4 million-acre the largest Congressionally designated wilderness inthe lower 48 states.
Suzanne Rainville, Forest Supervisor

3291 Sawtooth National Forest
2647 Kimberly Road E 208-737-3200
Twin Falls, ID 83301-7976 *Fax:* 208-737-3236
www.fs.usda.gov/sawtooth/
The Sawtooth National Forest encompasses 2.1 million acres of some of the nation's most magnificent country. Managed and protected by the US Department of Agriculture's Forest Service, the Sawtooth National Forest is working, producingforest that has been providing goods and services to the American people since its establishment in 1905.
Jane Kollmeyer, Forest Supervisor

3292 Southeast Idaho National Wildlife Refuge Complex
4425 Burley Drive 208-237-6615
Suite A
Chubbuck, ID 83202

Illinois: US Forests, Parks, Refuges

3293 **Mark Twain National Wildlife Refuge Complex**
1704 N 24th Street 217-224-8580
Quincy, IL 62301 Dick_Steinbach@fws.gov
www.fws.gov/Midwest/planning/marktwain
Administrative office over five refuges; Port Louisa NWR, Great River NWR, Clarence Common NWR, Two Rivers NWR, and Middle Mississippi River NWR.
Richard Steinbach, Manager

3294 **Shawnee National Forest**
50 Highway 145 South 618-253-7114
Harrisburg, IL 62946 800-699-6637
Fax: 618-253-1060
www.fs.usda.gov/shawnee/
The Shawnee National Forest lies in the rough, unglaciated areas known as the Illinois Ozark and Shawnee Hills. The geology is spectacular and divergent, with numerous stone bluffs and overlooks transcending to lowland areas.
Rebecca Banker, Public Affairs

3295 **Upper Mississippi River National Wildlife & Fish Refuge: Savanna District**
Riverview Road 815-273-2732
Thomson, IL 61285 *Fax:* 815-273-2960
uppermississippiriver@fws.gov
www.fws.gov/refuge/upper_mississippi_river
The Upper Mississippi River National Wildlife and Fish Refuge covers nearly 240,000 acres and extends along 281 miles of the Mississippi River. This Refuge is home to a diverse collection of wildlife, including bald eagles, great blueherons, sandhill cranes and spectacular concentrations of waterfowl. Local residents and visitors enjoy a wide array of opportunties throughout the year such as fishing, hunting, wildlife observation, photography, interpretation and environmentaleducation.

Sabrina Chandler, Refuge Manager
Timothy Yager, Assistant Refuge Manager

Indiana: US Forests, Parks, Refuges

3296 **Indiana Dunes National Lakeshore**
1100 N Mineral Springs Road 219-926-7561
Porter, IN 46304 *Fax:* 219-395-1767
www.nps.gov/indu
Indiana Dunes National Lakeshore, authorized by Congress in 1996, is located approximately 50 miles southeast of Chicago, Illinois in the counties of Lake, Porter and LaPorte in Northwest Indiana. The national lakeshore runs for nearly25 miles along southern Lake Michigan, bordered by Michigan City, Indiana on the east and Gary on the west. The park contains approximately 15,000 acres, 2,182 of which are located in Indiana Dunes State Park managed by the Indiana Department ofNatural Resources.

Iowa: US Forests, Parks, Refuges

3297 **DeSoto National Wildlife Refuge**
1434 316th Lane 712-388-4800
Missouri Valley, IA 51555 *Fax:* 712-388-4808
DeSoto@fws.gov
www.fws.gov/refuge/desoto
DeSoto Refuge is located along the Missouri River, 25 miles north of Omaha, NE. Popular activities include fishing, picnicking, mushroom-picking, hiking, boating, and wildlife observation. Peak viewing of 500,000 waterfowl inmid-November. The DeSoto Visitor Center houses over 200,000 artifacts from the 1860's steamboat Bertrand.

Larry Klimek, Refuge Manager
Mindy Sheets, Assistant Refuge Manager

3298 **McGregor District Upper: Mississippi River National Wildlife & Fish Refuge**
PO Box 460 563-873-3423
McGregor, IA 52157 *Fax:* 563-873-3803
uppermississippiriver@fws.gov
www.fws.gov/midwest/uppermississippiriver

Sabrina Chandler, Refuge Manager
Timothy Yager, Assistant Refuge Manager

Kansas: US Forests, Parks, Refuges

3299 **Kirwin National Wildlife Refuge**
702 East Xavier Road 785-543-6673
Kirwin, KS 67644 kirwin@fws.gov
www.fws.gov/refuge/kirwin
Brad Krohn, Refuge Manager
Melisa Johnson, Budget Technician

Kentucky: US Forests, Parks, Refuges

3300 **Daniel Boone National Forest**
1700 Bypass Road 859-745-3100
Winchester, KY 40391 *Fax:* 859-744-1568
www.fs.usda.gov/dbnf/
The mission is to achive quality land management under the sustainable multiple-use management concept to meer the diverse need of people.

3301 **Mammoth Cave National Park**
1 Mammoth Cave Parkway 270-758-2180
PO Box 7 MACA_Park_information@nps.gov
Mammoth Cave, KY 42259 www.nps.gov/maca
Established to preserve the cave system, including Mammoth Cave, the scenic river valleys of the Green and Nolin Rivers, and a section of the hilly country of south central Kentucky. This is the longest recorded cave system in theworld with more than 360 miles explored and mapped. Established July 1, 1941. Designated a World Heritage Site October 27, 1981. Designated a Biosphere Reserve in 1990.
Patrick Reed, Superintendent
Bruce Powell, Deputy Superintendent

Louisiana: US Forests, Parks, Refuges

3302 **Atchafalaya National Wildlife Refuge**
PO Box 127 318-566-2251
Krotz Springs, LA 70750 www.fws.gov/atchafalaya
The State of Louisiana's Sherburne Wildlife Management Area is located in the upper third of the Atchafalaya River Basin between Interstate Highway 10 and US Highway 190. It covers approximately 11,780 acres and was established in 1983by the Louisiana Department of Wildlife and Fisheries. The area supervisor's headquaters is located east of Krotz Springs, Louisiana, on LA 975 approximately three miles south of US Highway 190.

3303 **Cameron Prairie National Wildlife Refuge**
3599 Bayou Black Drive 985-853-1078
Houma, LA 70630 *Fax:* 985-853-1079
southeastlouisianarefuges@fws.gov
The refuge contains 9,621 acres of fresh marsh, coastal prairie and old rice fields. East Cove Unit of the refuge contains 14,927 acres of brackish and salt marsh. Seasonal visitors include the Peregrine falcon, alligators, whitetailed deer, wading and shorebirds, ducks and geese and various migratory birds.
Glen Harris, Manager

3304 **Catahoula National Wildlife Refuge**
P.O. Box 120 318-992-5261
Rhinehart, LA 71363-201 *Fax:* 318-992-6023
catahoula@fws.gov
catahoula.fws.gov

The objectives of the refuge are: to provide wintering habitat for migratory waterfowl consistent with Mississippi Flyway objectives; to provide habitat and protection for endangered species; preserve bottomland hardwoods and providehabitat necessary for wildlife diversity; provide opportunities for environmental education, interpretation and wildlife oriented recreation.
Greg Harper, Manager

3305 D'Arbonne National Wildlife Refuge
11372 Highway 143 318-726-4400
Farmerville, LA 71363 *Fax:* 318-726-4667
northlarefuges@fws.gov
www.fws.gov/darbonne
The Refuge provides habitat for a diversity of migratory birds and resident wildlife species, provides habitat and protection for endangered species such as the bald eagle, wood stork and red-cockaded woodpecker and providesopportunities for wildlife-oriented recreation, environmental education and interpretation.

Kelby Ouchley, Manager

3306 Kisatchie National Forest
2500 Shreveport Highway 318-473-7160
Pineville, LA 71360-2009 www.fs.usda.gov/kisatchie
The Kisatchie National Forest has a lot to offer vistors, such as 355 miles of trails for hiking, camping, mountain biking, horseback riding, ORV riding. Other recreational opportunites include four lakes, an 8700 acre Wilderness anddozens of caming sites. The forest also provides opportunities to hunt and fish.

3307 Lacassine National Wildlife Refuge
209 Nature Road 337-774-5923
Lake Arthur, LA 70549 *Fax:* 337-774-9913
lacassine@fws.gov
www.fws.gov/swlarefugecomplex/lacassine
The nearly 35,000 acre refuge is mostly freshwater marsh habitat. It preserves one of the major wintering grounds for waterfowl in the US. Wintering populations of ducks and geese at Lacassine are among the largest in the NationalWildlife Refuge System. Portions of the refuge are open year-round from one hour before sunrise until one hour after sunset. Please consult refuge brochures or contact the refuge office for more details. A vicinity map and refuge map are available.
Larry Narcisse, Manager

3308 Sabine National Wildlife Refuge
3000 Holly Beach Highway 337-762-3816
Hackberry, LA 70645 *Fax:* 337-762-3780
sabine@fws.gov
www.fws.gov/sabine/
The objectives of the refuge is to provide habitat for migratory waterfowl and other birds, to preserve and enhance coastal marshes for fish and wildlife, and to provide outdoor recreation and environmental education for the public.

Don Voros, Project Manager
Terence Delaine, Refuge Manager

Maine: US Forests, Parks, Refuges

3309 Acadia National Park
20 McFarland Hill Drive 207-288-8800
PO Box 177 *Fax:* 208-288-8813
Bar Harbor, ME 00460-177 Acadia_Information@nps.gov
www.nps.gov/acad/faqs.htm
The purpose of the commission is to consult with the Secretary of the Interior, or his designee, on matters relating to the management and development of the park, including but not liited to the acquisition of lands and interests inlands and termination of rights of use and occupancy.

3310 Sunkhaze Meadows National Wildlife Refuge
PO Box 453 207-827-6138
Old Town, ME 00446 *Fax:* 207-827-6099
FriendsofSunkhazeNWR@gmail.com
www.sunkhaze.org
Sunkhaze Meadows NWR was established to protect a large peat bog and its associated wildlife. There are three divisions of the refuge, totalling 11,772 acres. The areas are open to wildlife-dependent recreation.

Maryland: US Forests, Parks, Refuges

3311 Antietam National Battlefield
PO Box 158 301-432-5124
Sharpsburg, MD 21782 *Fax:* 301-432-4590
www.nps.gov/anti

3312 Assateague Island National Seashore
7206 National Seashore Lane 410-641-1441
Berlin, MD 21811 *Fax:* 410-641-1099
www.nps.gov
Natural resource management and environmental education related to coastal resources in general and Assateague Island in particular.
Trish Kicklighter, Superintendent

3313 Patuxent Research Refuge
230 Bald Eagle Drive 301-497-5770
Laurel, MD 20724 *Fax:* 301-497-5515
Jennifer_Hill@fws.gov
www.fws.gov/refuge/Patuxent
One of over 500 refuges in the National Wildlife Refuge System, a network of lands and waters specifically for the protection of wildlife and wildlife habitat.
Brad Knudsen, Project Leader/Manager

Massachusetts: US Forests, Parks, Refuges

3314 Boston National Historical Park
Charleston Navy Yard 617-242-5642
Boston, MA 00212 *Fax:* 617-242-6006
www.nps.gov/bost
Boston National Historical Park tells the story of the events that led to the American Revolution and the Navy that kept the nation strong.

3315 Cape Cod National Seashore
99 Marconi Station Site Road 508-349-3785
Wellfleet, MA 00266 *Fax:* 508-349-9052
CACO_Superintendent@nps.gov
www.nps.gov
Cape Cod National Seashore comprises 43,604 acres of shoreline and upland landscape features, including a forty-mile long stretch of pristine sandy beach, dozens of clear, deep, freshwater kettle ponds, and upland scenes that depictevidence of how people have used the land. A variety of historic structures are within the boundary of the Seashore, including lighthouses, a lifesaving station, and numerous Cape Cod style houses.

3316 Great Meadows National Wildlife Refuge
73 Weir Hill Road 978-443-4661
Sudbury, MA 00177 *Fax:* 978-443-2898
fw5rw_emnwr@fws.gov
www.fws.gov/refuge/great_meadows
The Sudbury office serves as the headquarters for the eight refuge Eastern Massachusetts National Wildlife Refuge Complex. Public use opportunities are available at a number of the complex's refuges.
Libby Herland, Complex Manager

3317 Silvio O Conte National Fish & Wildlife Refuge
2 Avenue A 413-863-3676
Turners Falls, MA 00137 *Fax:* 802-962-5006
www.fws.gov/refuge/Silvio_O_Conte
The Connecticut River Watershed, 7.2 million acres in four states, is larger and more heavily populated than areas usually considered when creating a refuge. The refuge's purposes are also much broader than usual. The new scientificand social challenge of protecting natural diversity cannot be met by land acquistion alone. The refuge's primary action is to involve people of the watershed, especially landowners and land managers, in environmental education programs andcooperative management.

Michigan: US Forests, Parks, Refuges

3318 Hiawatha National Forest
2727 North Lincoln Road 906-786-4062
Escanaba, MI 49829 *Fax:* 906-789-3311
www.fs.fed.us/r9/forests/hiawatha
Located in the central and easter Upper Peninsula of Michigan, the firest affords visitors access to white sand, scenic beaches and relatively undeveloped shorelines along three of Americas's Inland Seas, Lake Superior, Michigan andHuron.

3319 Huron-Manistee National Forest
1755 S Mitchell Street 231-775-2421
Cadillac, MI 49601 800-821-6263
Fax: 231-775-5551
www.fs.usda.gov/hmnf/
The Huron-Manistee National Forest comprise almost a million acres of public lands extending across the northern lower peninsula of Michigan. The Huron-Manistee national Forest provide recreation opportunities for visitors, habitat forfish and wildlife, and resources for local industry.

3320 Ottawa National Forest
E6248 US Highway 2 906-932-1330
Ironwood, MI 49938 *Fax:* 906-932-0122
www.fs.usda.gov/ottawa/
The almost one million acres of the Ottawa National Forest are located in the western Upper Peninsula of Michigan. It extends from the south shore of Lake Superior down to Wisconsin and the Nicolet National Forest. The area is rich inwildlife viewing opportunities; topography in the northern portion is the most dramatic with breathtaking views of rolling hills dotted with lakes, rivers and spectacular waterfalls.

3321 Pictured Rocks National Lakeshore
N8391 Sand Point Road 906-387-2607
PO Box 40 *Fax:* 906-387-4025
Munising, MI 49862 www.nps.gov
Multicolored sandstone cliffs, beaches, and dunes, waterfalls, inland lakes, wildlife and the forest of Lake Superior shoreline beckon visitors to explore this 73,000+ acre park. Attractions include a lighthouse and former Coast Guardlife-saving stations along with old farmsteads and orchards. The park is a four season recreational destination where hiking, camping, hunting, nature study, and winter activities abound.

3322 Seney National Wildlife Refuge
1674 Refuge Entrance Road 906-586-9851
Seney, MI 49883 *Fax:* 906-586-3800
seney@fws.gov
www.fws.gov/refuge/seney
Seney National Wildlife Refuge was established as a refuge and breeding ground for migratory birds and other wildlife. Today, Seney supports a variety of wildlife, including protected and reintroduced species. Bald eagles, commonloons, and trumpeter swans are regularly seen during the summer months, especially June and July, when they are raising their young.

Sara Siekierski, Refuge Manager
Greg McClellan, Assistant Refuge manager

3323 Shiawassee National Wildlife Refuge
6975 Mower Road 989-777-5930
Saginaw, MI 48601 *Fax:* 989-777-9200
shiawassee@fws.gov
www.fws.gov/refuge/Shiawassee
The refuge is comprised of over 9400 acres of wetlands, uplands, and bottomland hardwood forests. Four rivers flow through. Over 12 miles of hiking trails, bank fishing sites, and two photography blinds are available. Environmentaleducation progrms are offered at Green Point Environmental Learning Center in Saginaw.

Steve Kahl, Manager
Ed DeVries, Assistant Manager

3324 Sleeping Bear Dunes National Lakeshore
9922 Front Street 231-326-5134
Empire, MI 49630 *Fax:* 231-326-5382
www.nps.gov/slbe
Sleeping Bear Dunes National Lakeshore encompasses a 60 km stretch of Lake Michigan's eastern coastline, as well as North and South Manitou Islands. The park was established primarily for its outstanding natural features, includingforests, beaches, dune formations and ancient glacial phenomena. The Lakeshore also contains many cultural features including an 1871 lighthouse, three former Life-Saving Service (Coast Guard) Stations and an extensive rural historic farm district.

Minnesota: US Forests, Parks, Refuges

3325 Agassiz National Wildlife Refuge
22996 290th Street Northeast 218-449-4115
Middle River, MN 56737-9653 *Fax:* 218-449-3241
agassiz@fws.gov
www.fws.gov/refuge/agassiz
The National Refuge provides resting, nesting and feeding habitat for waterfowl and other migratory birds. Agassiz NWR is designated a Globally Important Bird Area by the American Bird Conservancy. It protects endangered and threatenedspecies. It also provides for biodiversity, public opportunities for outdoor recreation and environmental education.
Margaret Anderson, Manager

3326 Big Stone National Wildlife Refuge
44843 County Road 19 320-273-2191
Odessa, MN 56276 *Fax:* 320-273-2231
BigStone@fws.gov
www.fws.gov/refuge/big_stone
Fig Stone NWR is one of more than 545 National Wildlife Refuges administered as part of the National Wildlife Refuge System by the US Fish and Wildlife Service. The Refuge now overlays 11,585.8 acres of the Minnesota River Valley inwestern Minnesota. A unique visual and geological feature of the Refuge is the red, lichen covered granite outcrops for which the Refuge was named. The Refuge offers an auto tour route, nature trails, wildlife observation, hunting and fishingopportunities.

Alice Hanley, Manager

3327 Chippewa National Forest
200 Ash Avenue Northwest 218-335-8600
Cass Lake, MN 56633 www.fs.fed.us/r9/chippewa/
The Chippewa was the first National Forest established east of the Mississippi. The Forest boundary encompasses 1.6 millon, of which over 666,618 acres are managed by the USDA Forest Service. Aspen, birch, pines, balsam fir and maplesblanket the uplands. Water is abundant, with over 1300 lakes, 923 miles of rivers and streams, and 400,000 acres of wetlands.
Robert M Harper, Forest Supervisor

3328 Crane Meadows National Wildlife Refuge
19502 Iris Road 320-632-1575
Little Falls, MN 56345 *Fax:* 320-632-5471
cranemeadows@fws.gov
www.fws.gov/refuge/crane_meadows

Crane Meadows National Wildlife Refuge was established in 1992 to preserve a large, natural wetland complex. The refuge is located in central Minnesota and serves as an important stop for many species of migrating birds.

3329 Detroit Lakes Wetland Management District
26624 N Tower Road 218-847-4431
Detroit Lakes, MN 56501 *Fax:* 218-847-4156
DetroitLakes@fws.gov
www.fws.gov/Midwest.detroitlakes/
The district covers approximately 6000 square miles. From east to west, these are: the Red River Valley floodplain, the glacial moraine/prairie pothole region, and the hardwood/coniferous forest. Land acquisition and managementefforts are focused in the prairie pothole region of the WMD, with a goal of providing habitat for nesting waterfowl.

Scott Kahan, Manager

3330 Mille Lacs National Wildlife Refuge
36289 State Highway 65 218-768-2402
McGregor, MN 55760 *Fax:* 218-768-3040
ricelake@fws.gov
www.fws.gov/refuge/mille_lacs
Comprised of two small islands in Mille Lacs Lake in central Minnesota. The islands are boulder and gravel outcrops for colonial nesting birds including common terns and ring-billed gulls.

Walt Ford, Manager

3331 Minnesota Valley National Wildlife Refuge
3815 American Blvd East 612-854-5900
Bloomington, MN 55425 *Fax:* 612-725-3279
minnesotavalley@fws.gov
www.fws.gov/refuge/minnesota_valley
Mission: To restore and manage the ecological communities of the Lower Minnesota River Valley and its watershed while providing environmental education and wildlife dependent recreation.
Thomas Larson, Manager

3332 Rice Lake National Wildlife Refuge
36289 State Highway 65 218-768-2402
McGregor, MN 55760 *Fax:* 218-768-3040
ricelakes@fws.gov
www.fws.gov/refuge/rice_lake
Walt Ford, Manager

3333 Rydell National Wildlife Refuge
17788 349th Street Southeast 218-687-2229
Erskine, MN 56535 *Fax:* 218-687-2225
dave_bennett@fws.gov
Dave Bennett, Manager

3334 Sherburne National Wildlife Refuge
17076 293rd Avenue 763-389-3323
Zimmerman, MN 55398 *Fax:* 763-389-3493
sherburne@fws.gov
Mission: To represent a diverse biological community characteristic of the transition zone between tallgrass prairie and forest.

3335 Superior National Forest
8901 Grand Avenue Place 218-626-4300
Duluth, MN 55808 *Fax:* 218-626-4398
www.fs.usda.gov/superior/
Located in northeastern tip of Minnesota, the Superior National Forest stretches 150 miles along the US-Canadian border, encompassing 3.85 million acres. This hilly deep pine forest is home to moose, wolves, black bears, loons andmigratory birds. More than 2,250 miles of stream flow within the forest, including the renowned Boundary Waters Canoe Area, where you can canoe, portage and camp in the spirit of the French Canadian voyagers of 200 years ago.

Jim Sanders, Forest Supervisor

3336 Tamarac National Wildlife Refuge
35704 County Highway 26 218-847-2641
Rochert, MN 56578 *Fax:* 218-847-9141
tamarac@fws.gov
www.fws.gov/refuge/tamarac
Established in 1938, Tamarac Refuge is dedicated to providing a breeding ground and sanctuary for migratory birds and other wildlife. Situated at a unique transitional zone where hardwood forest, boreal forest and tallgrass prairiemeets. Tamarac provides boundless opportunities for visitors to observe wildlife in their natural surroundings. Spring and fall migrations of songbirds and waterfowl can be spectacular. Their visitor center offers interpretive displays and programs.

3337 Voyageurs National Park
360 Highway 11 East 218-283-6600
International Falls, MN 56649 *Fax:* 218-285-7407
www.nps.gov/voya
The park lies in the southern part of the Canadian Shield, representing some of the oldest exposed rock formations in the world. This bedrock has been shaped and carved by at least four periods of glaciation. The topography of the parkis rugged and varied; rolling hills are interspersed between bogs, beaver ponds, swamps, islands, small lakes and four large lakes.

3338 Winona District National Wildlife Refuge Upper Mississippi River National Wildlife and Fish
51 E 4th Street 507-452-4232
Winona, MN 55987 *Fax:* 507-452-0851
uppermississippiriver@fws.gov
www.fws.gov/refuge/upper_mississippi_river
Refuge objectives are to: protect and preserve one of America's premier fish and wildlife areas; provide habitat for migratory birds, fish, plants and resident wildlife; protect and enhance habitat for endangered species; provideinterpretation, environmental education and wildlife-oriented recreational public use opportunities; and conserve a diversity of plant life.
Sabira Chandler, Refugee Manager
Timothy Yager, Asst. Refuge Manager

Mississippi: US Forests, Parks, Refuges

3339 Bienville National Forest
200 S. Lamar St. 601-965-1600
Suite 500-N www.fs.usda.gov/mississippi/
Jackson, MS 39201
The forest offers camping, picnicking, swimming, hiking, fishing and historic sites. Bienville boasts the largest known cluster of old growth pine forest in Mississippi in the 180-acre Bienville Pines Scenic Area. Here visitors canwander among towering loblolly and shortleaf pines, many more than two centuries old. The 23-mile Shockaloe Horse Trail, a national recreation trail, starts near the town of Forest.

3340 Mississippi Sandhill Crane National Wildlife Refuge
7200 Crane Lane 228-497-6322
Gautier, MS 39553 *Fax:* 228-497-5407
mississippisandhillcrane@fws.gov
www.fws.gov/refuge/mississippi_sandhill_crane
Located in southeast Mississippi in Jackson County, the refuge was established to protect the endangered Mississippi Sandhill Cranes and the wet pine savanna habitat they prefer. The refuge features exhibits, informational videos, anda walking trail where you can view carnivorous plants.

Jereme Phillips, Complex Manager
Danny Moss, Refuge Manager

3341 Noxubee National Wildlife Refuge
13723 Bluff Lake Road 662-323-5548
Brooksville, MS 39739 *Fax:* 662-323-6390
noxubee@fws.gov
Established in 1940 to protect and enhance habitat for the conservation of migratory birds, endangered species and other wildlife. The recreational and educational opportunities provided on the refuge help the public experience natureand learn how sound

management ensures that future generations continue to enjoy fish and wildlife and their habitats.

3342 Panther Swamp National Wildlife Refuge
12595 Mississippi Highway 149 662-836-3004
Yazoo City, MS 39194 *Fax:* 662-836-3009
yazoo@fws.gov
www.fws.gov/refuge/panther_swamp
Refuge objectives are: to provide resting, nesting and feeding habitat for waterfowl and other migratory birds; to provide habitat for resident wildlife; to protect endangered and threatened species; and to provide public useopportunities for outdoor recreation and environmental education.
Bo Sloan, Refuge Manager

Missouri: US Forests, Parks, Refuges

3343 Mark Twain National Forest
401 Fairgrounds Road 573-364-4621
Rollo, MO 65401 *Fax:* 573-364-6844
www.fs.fed.us/r9/forests/marktwain
The Mark Twain National forest is located in southern and centeral Missouri, and extends from the St Francois Mountains in the southeast to glades in the southwest, from the southwest, from the prairie lands the Missouri River to thenation's most ancient mountains in the south.

3344 Mingo National Wildlife Refuge
24279 State Highway 51 573-222-3589
Puxico, MO 63960 *Fax:* 573-222-6343
mingo@fws.gov
www.fws.gov/refuge/mingo
Established as a resting and wintering area for migratory waterfowl and other birds. The 21,592-acre Refuge contains approximately 15,000 acres of bottomland hardwood forest, 3,500 acres of marsh and water, 506 acres of cropland, 704acres of seasonally flooded impoundments, and 474 acres of grassy openings.

3345 Ozark National Scenic Riverways
404 Watercress Drive 573-323-4236
PO Box 490 *Fax:* 573-323-4140
Van Buren, MO 63965 ozar_superintendent@nps.gov
www.nps.gov/ozar
Missouri's largest National Park and America's first to preserve a free flowing river in its wild state. Covers some 80,000 acres along 134 miles of the Current and Jacks Fork Rivers. Staff provide elementary level environmentaleducation programs on natural history, with an emphasis on karst and water issues. Publishes More Than Skin Deep, a Teacher's Guide to Caves and Groundwater, a curriculum guide suitable for grades K-12.

3346 Swan Lake National Wildlife Refuge
16194 Swan Lake Avenue 660-856-3323
Sumner, MO 64681 *Fax:* 660-856-3687
john_benson@fws.gov
www.fws.gov/refuge/swan_lake

Steve Whitson, Project Director

Montana: US Forests, Parks, Refuges

3347 Beaverhead-Deerlodge National Forest
200 East Broadway 406-329-3511
P.O. Box 7669 *Fax:* 406-329-3347
Missoula, MT 59807-7669 www.fs.usda.gov/r1
Bruce Ramsey, Forest Supervisor
Thomas D Osen, District Ranger

3348 Benton Lake National Wildlife Refuge
922 Bootlegger Trail 406-727-7400
Great Falls, MT 59404 *Fax:* 406-727-7432
bentonlake@fws.gov
www.fws.gov/refuge/benton_lake
Kathleen Burchett, Project Leader
Robert F Johnson Jr, Deputy Manager

3349 Bighorn Canyon National Recreation Area
5 Avenue B 406-666-2412
PO Box 7458 *Fax:* 406-666-2415
Fort Smith, MT 59035-7458 www.nps.gov/bica
This dam, named after the famous Crow chairman Robert Yellowtail, harnessed the waters of the Bighorn River and turned this variable stream into a magnificent lake. The Afterbay Lake below the Yellowtail Dam is a good spot for troutfishing and wildlife viewing for ducks, geese and other animals. The Bighorn River below the Afterbay Dam is a world class trout fishing area. Bighorn Canyon National Recreation Area boasts breath-takign scenery, countless varieties of wildlife.

3350 Bitterroot National Forest
1801 N First Street 406-363-7100
Hamilton, MT 59840 *Fax:* 406-363-7106
rl_bitterroot_comments@fs.fed.us
www.fs.fed.us
The 1.6 million acre Bitterroot National Forest, in west central Montana and east central Idaho, is part of the Norther Rocky Mountains. National Forest land begins above the foothills of the Bitterroot River Valley in two mountainranges—the Bitterroot Mountains on the west and the Sapphire Mountains on the east side of the valley.

3351 Bowdoin National Wildlife Refuge: Refuge Manager
194 Bowdoin Auto Tour Road 406-654-2863
Malta, MT 59538 *Fax:* 406-654-2866
bowdoin@fws.gov
www.fws.gov/refuge/bowdoin
Bowdoin National Wildlife Refuge was established in 1936 as a migratory bird refuge. It is located in the short and mixed greens prairie region of North-central Montana and encompasses 15,551 acres.

3352 Custer National Forest
1310 Main Street 406-657-6200
Billings, MT 59105 *Fax:* 406-657-6222
www.fs.fed.us/r1/custer/
The Custer national Forest is made up of 1.2 million acres of high alpine mountain country, and small pockets of timbered buttes and grasslands scattered across two states, Montana and South Dakota.
Mary C Erickson, Acting Forest Supervisor
Chris C Worth, Deputy Forest Supervisor

3353 Flathead National Forest
650 Wolfpack Way 406-758-5208
Kalispell, MT 59901 *Fax:* 406-758-5379
www.fs.usda.gov/flathead/
The 2.3 million-acre Flathead national Forest is bordered by Canada to the north, Glacier National Park to the north and east and Clark National Forest to the east, the Lolo national Forest to the south, and the Kootenai NationalForest to the west.

3354 Gallatin National Forest
10 East Babcock Ave. 406-587-6701
PO Box 130 *Fax:* 406-587-6758
Bozeman, MT 59771 www.fs.usda.gov/main/custergallatin

3355 Helena National Forest
2880 Skyway Drive 406-449-5201
Helena, MT 59602 *Fax:* 406-449-5436
www.fs.usda.gov/helena/
The Helena National Forest offers close to one million acres of diverse landscapes and wildland opportunities. Located in west central Montana, the Helena National Forest boasts some of the most vivid glimpses into the past of thishistorically rich area.

3356 Kootenai National Forest
31374 Highway 2 West 406-293-6211
Libby, MT 59923-3022 *Fax:* 406-283-7709
www.fs.usda.gov/kootenai/
The Kootenai National Forest, conataining 2.2 million acres, is located in the extreme northwest corner of Montana, Bordered on the north by Canada and on the west by Idaho. Of the total acres, 50,384 are in the state of Idaho. Accessinto the forest is available from US highways 2 and 93, and Montana State Highways 37, 56, 200, and 508.
Paul Bradford, Forest Supervisor

3357 Lee Metcalf National Wildlife Refuge
4567 Wildfowl Lane 406-777-5552
Stevensville, MT 59870 *Fax:* 406-777-2489
lee_metcalf@fws.gov
www.fws.gov/refuge/lee_metcalf/
Mission is to manage habitat for a diversity of wildlife species with emphasis on migratory birds and endangered and threatened species.
Tom Reed, Manager
Kim Pennigton, Admin. Asst.

3358 Lewis & Clark National Forest
1101 15th Street N 406-791-7700
Great Falls, MT 59401 www.fs.usda.gov/lcnf
The 1.8 million acres of the Lewis and clark National Forest are scatteered into seven separate mountain ranges. The Forest is situated i west central Montana. The boundaries spread eastward from the rugged, mountainous ContinentalDivide onto the plains. When looking at a map, the National Forest System lands appear as islands of forest within oceans of prairie. Because of its wide-ranging land pattern, the forest is separated into two divisions: the Rocky Mountain and theJefferson.

3359 Lolo National Forest
24 Fort Missoula Road 406-329-3750
Missoula, MT 59804 www.fs.usda.gov/lolo/
Of the 15 National Forests in the Northern Region of the USDA Forest Service, the Lolo National Forest is estimated to be the third largest. It is located in western Montana. Several major tributaries to the Clark Fork River of theColumbia River Basin flow through the Forest. Its 2.1 million acres of diverse and spectacular mountainous country extend into seven counties.
Debbie Austin, Forest Supervisor
Paul Matter, District Ranger

3360 Medicine Lake National Wildlife Refuge Complex
223 North Shore Road 406-789-2305
Medicine Lake, MT 59247 *Fax:* 406-789-2350
medicinelake@fws.gov
www.fws.gov/refuge/medicine_lake
Medicine Lake National Wildlife Refuge is located on the heavily glaciated rolling plains of northeaster Montana, between Missouri River and the Canadian Border.

3361 National Bison Range
58355 Bisons Range Road 406-644-2211
Moiese, MT 59824 *Fax:* 406-644-2211
bisonrange@fws.gov
www.fws.gov/refuge/national_bison_range
The National Bison Range provides conservation of habitat for the American bison, as well as wildlife viewing for the public.

Jeff King, Project Leader
Bob Rebarchik, Deputy Project leader

3362 Red Rocks Lakes National Wildlife Refuge
27650B South Valley Road 406-276-3536
Lima, MT 59739 *Fax:* 406-276-3538
redrocks@fws.gov
www.fws.gov/refuge/red_rock_lakes
Primarily a high elevation mountain wetland-riparian area. Red Rock Creek flows through the upper end of the Centennial Valley, within which the Refuge lies, creating the impressive Upper Red Rock Lake, River Marsh and Lower Red RockLake marshlands. The rugged Centennial Mountains border the Refuge on the south, catching the snows of winter that replenish the Refuge's lakes and marshes.

Nebraska: US Forests, Parks, Refuges

3363 Crescent Lake National Wildlife Refuge
10630 Road 181 308-762-4893
Ellsworth, NE 69340 *Fax:* 308-762-7606
crescentlake@fws.gov
www.fws.gov/refuge/crescent_lake
Located in the panhandle of Western Nebraska, Crescent Lake consists of 45,818 acres of rolling sandhills interspersed with numberous shallow wetlands and lakes. Plant and animal species call Crescent Lake home, while visitors canparticipate in a variety of public use activities.

3364 Fort Niobrara National Wildlife Refuge
Fort Niobrara/Valentine NWR Complex
39983 Refuge Road 402-376-3789
Nebraska, NE 69201 *Fax:* 402-376-3217
fortniobrara@fws.gov
www.fws.gov/refuge/fort_niobrara
National Wildlife Refuge Complex includes Fort Niobrara NWR, Valentine NWR and Seier NWR. Complex lands include riverine, riparian, marshland, hand prairie, and sandhills prairie habitats.

Steven A Hicks, Project Leader

3365 Nebraska & Samuel R McKelvie National Forest
125 N Main Street 308-432-0300
Chadron, NE 69337 nnf_info@fs.fed.us
www.fs.usda.gov/nebraska
There is an unusual combination of the native ponderosa pine forest of the Nebraska and Samuel R. McKelvie National Forests and mixed grass prairies on the Buffalo Gap, Fort Pierre, and Oglala National Grasslands
Jane Darnell, Supervisor
Stephen Lenzo, Deputy Supervisor

Nevada: US Forests, Parks, Refuges

3366 Ash Meadows National Wildlife Refuge
610 Springs Meadows Road 775-372-5435
Amargosa Valley, NV 89020 *Fax:* 775-372-5436
Daniel_Balduini@fws.gov
www.fws.gov/refuge/ash_meadows/
Refuge staff are responsible for managing the 22,117 acre refuge, most of which is spring-fed wetland and alkaline desert upland The refuge area habitat for at least 24 plants and animals found nowhere else in the world. Four fishesand one plant are currently listed as endangered. Species found on the refuge include numerous endemic species, the greatest concentration in the US and the second greatest in all of North America.

Sharon McKelvey, Manager

3367 Desert National Wildlife Refuge Complex
16001 Corn Creek Road 702-879-6110
Las Vegas, NV 89124 www.fws.gov/refuge/desert
Established in 1936 for perpetuating the desert bighorn sheep. Two threatened, and twenty-nine species of concern can be found at the refuge. Wildlife observation is one of the most popular refuge activities. Big game hunting is verylimited, but also very popular. Bird watching is another popular activity. A growing program provides additional opportunities and students are able to earn college credits through an internship at the refuge.

3368 Great Basin National Park
100 Great Basin National Park 775-234-7331
Baker, NV 89311 *Fax:* 775-234-7269
www.nps.gov/grba
Great Basin National Park includes streams, lakes, alpine plants, abundant wildlife, a variety of forest types including groves of

ancient bristlecone pines, and numerous limestone caverns, including beatiful Lehman Caves.

3369 Humboldt-Toiyabe National Forest
100 Midas Canyon Road 775-964-2671
P.O. Box 130 *Fax:* 775-964-1451
Austin, NV 89310 www.fs.usda.gov/htnf/
The Humboldt-Toiyabe National Forest encompasses all of Nevada and the far Eastern edge of California. The Humboldt-Toiyabe is the largest forest in the lower 48 states.
Bill Dunkelberger, Forest Supervisor
Jack Isaacs, Deputy Forest Supervisor

3370 Lake Mead National Recreation Area (NRA)
601 Nevada Way 702-293-8990
Boulder City, NV 89005 *Fax:* 702-293-8936
LAME_Interpretation@nps.gov
www.nps.gov/lame
Lake Mead NRA, which includes Lake Mohave, offers a wealth of things to do and places to go year-round. Its huge lakes cater to boaters, swimmers, sunbathers and fishermen while its desert rewards hikers, wildlife photographers androadside sightseers. Three of America's four desert ecosystems: the Mojave, the Great Basin and the Sonoran Desert meet in here. As a result, this seemingly barren area contains a surprising variety of plants animals, some of which may be foundnowhere else.

3371 Moapa Valley National Wildlife Refuge
4701 N Torrey Pines Drive 702-515-5450
Las Vegas, NV 89130 *Fax:* 702-515-5460
To secure habitat for the endangered Moapa dace, a small fish commonly found throughout the headwaters of the Muddy River system
Amy Lavoie, Refuge Manager

3372 Pahranagat National Wildlife Refuge
PO Box 510 775-725-3417
Alamo, NV 89001 *Fax:* 775-725-3389
amy_lavoie@fws.gov
www.fws.gov/refuge/Pahranagat/
Refuge staff are responsible for managing the 5,380 acre refuge, a mixture of desert, open water, native grass meadows, cropland and marsh. The refuge provides habitat for migratory birds of the Pacific Flyway and several speciesabound at this desert oasis. Wildlife observation is one of the most popular refuge activities. Waterfowl and small game hunting are also very popular, as is bird watching. A growing program provides additional opportunities, including internshipsfor college students.
Rob Vinson, Refuge Manager
Annji Greenwood, Deputy Refuge Manager

3373 Stillwater National Wildlife Refuge Complex
1020 New River Parkway 775-423-5128
Suite 305 *Fax:* 775-423-0416
Fallon, NV 89406 stillwater@fws.gov
The Stillwater NWRC includes three National Wildlife Refuges: Anaho Island, Fallon, and Stillwater NWRs. They work to conserve American white pelican nesting colonies, as well as double crested cormorant, great blue heron, and gullnesting olonies. The Fallon NWR conserves large expanses of playa and native shrub/scrub high desert habitat within the Carson Sink of the Great Basin. Stillwater NWR conserves and manages a network of wetlands at the terminal end of the CarsonRiver.

New Hampshire: US Forests, Parks, Refuges

3374 Lake Umbagog National Wildlife Refuge
PO Box 240 603-482-3415
2756 Dam Road *Fax:* 603-482-3308
Errol, NH 03579 lakeumbagog@fws.gov
www.fws.gov/northeast/lakeumbagog/
Northern Forest refuge of New Hampshire and Maine provides long-term conservation of important wetland/upland habitats for wildlife, migratory birds and protected species.

3375 White Mountain National Forest
200 East Broadway 414-297-3600
P.O. Box 7669 *Fax:* 603-528-8783
Missoula, MT 59807-7669 www.fs.usda.gov/r9
The White Mountain National Forest is located in northern New Hampshire and southwestern Maine, and lies within Carroll, Coos, and Grafton Counties in New Hampshire, and Oxford County in Maine.
Tom Wagner, Forest Supervisor

New Jersey: US Forests, Parks, Refuges

3376 Cape May National Wildlife Refuge
24 Kimbles Beach Road 609-463-0994
Cape May Courthouse, NJ 00821 *Fax:* 609-463-1667
capemay@fws.gov
www.fws.gov/refuge/cape_may

3377 Great Swamp National Wildlife Refuge
241 Pleasant Plains Road 973-425-1222
Basking Ridge, NJ 00792 *Fax:* 973-425-7309
greatswamp@fws.gov
www.fws.gov/refuge/great_swamp
Swamp woodland, hardwood ridges, cattail marsh and grassland are typical of this approximately 7,800 acre refuge. The Swamp contains many large old oak and beach trees, stands of mountain laurel, mosses, ferns and species of many otherplants of both Northern and Southern botanical zones.
William Koch, Refuge Manager
Steve Henry, Deputy Refuge Manager

New Mexico: US Forests, Parks, Refuges

3378 Bitter Lake National Wildlife Refuge
4200 East Pine Lodge Road 505-622-6755
Roswell, NM 88201 *Fax:* 505-623-9039
steve_alvarez@fws.gov
www.fws.gov/refuge/bitter_lake/
Native grasses, sand dunes, brushy bottomlands, seven lakes and a red-rimmed plateau make up Bitter Lake National Wildlife Refuge, winter home for thousands of migratory birds. The Lakes on the refuge were formed within the ancientriver beds of the Pecos River. These lakes store about 1,000 acres of water at their highest levels, while nearby marshland, mudflats and the Pecos Rriver provide an additional 24,500 acres of habitat.
Floyd Truetken, Refuge Manager

3379 Bosque del Apache National Wildlife Refuge
1001 Highway 1 505-835-1828
P.O. Box 280 *Fax:* 505-835-0314
San Antonio, NM 87832 fw2_rw_bosque_del_apache@fws.gov
www.fws.gov/southwest/refuges/newmex/bosque/
Bosque del Apache NWR is located in south-central New Mexico, along the Rio Grande in the northern reach of the Chihuahuan Desert. Habitats include cottonwood forests, seasonally managed wetlands, farm fields, saltgrass meadows, anddesert uplands. The refuge features large concentrations of sandhill cranes, light geese, and migrating waterfowl in fall and winter, shorebirds and songbirds travel through in spring and fall, and hummingbirds are abundant in summer.

3380 Capulin Volcano National Monument National Park Service
46 Volcano Rd. 505-278-2201
PO Box 40 *Fax:* 505-278-2211
Capulin, NM 88414 www.nps.gov/cavo
Capulin Volcano is long extinct, and today the forested slopes provide habitat for mule deer, wild turkey, black bear and other wildlife. Abundant displays of wildflowers bloom on the mountain each summer. A two mile paved roadspiraling to the volcano

rim makes Capulin Volcano one of the most accessible volcanos in the world. Trails leading around the rim allow exploration of this classic cinder cone.

, Superintendent, Park Ranger

3381 **Carlsbad Caverns National Park**
3225 National Parks Highway 505-785-2232
Carlsbad, NM 88220 *Fax:* 505-785-2133
cave_park_information@nps.gov
www.nps.gov/cave

Established to preserve Carlsbad Cavern and numerous other caves within a Permian-age fossil reef, the park contains over 100 known caves, including Lechuguilla Cave-the nation's deepest limestone cave and third longest. CarlsbadCavern, with one of the world's largest underground chambers and countless formations, is highly accessible, with a variety of tours offered year-round.

John Benjamin, Superintendent
Chuck Barat, Deputy Superintendent

3382 **Carson National Park**
208 Cruz Alta Road 505-758-6200
Taos, NM 87571 *Fax:* 505-758-6213
mailroom_r3_carson@fs.fed.us
www.fs.usda.gov/carson

Some of the finest mountain scenery in the southwest is found in the 1.5 million acres covered by the Carson National Forest. Elevations rise from 6,000 feet to 13,161 feet. The scenic Sangre de Cristo Mountains include Wheeler Peak,the highest peak in New Mexico.

3383 **Cibola National Forest**
2113 Osuna Road Northeast Suite A 505-346-3900
Albuquerque, NM 87113 *Fax:* 505-346-3901
www.fs.fed.us/r3/cibola

Cibola, pronounced See'-bo-lah, is thought to be the original Zuni Indian name for their group of pueblos or tribal lands. Later, the Spanish interpreted the word to mean, buffalo. Valued for its recreation opportunities, naturalbeauty, timber, watersheds, water, forage, and wilderness resources, the forest is managed to give the American people the greatest benefits that can be produced on a permanent basis.

Elaine Kohrman, Forest Supervisor
Ruth Sutton, Public Affairs

3384 **El Malpais National Monument**
1900 E Santa Fe Avenue 505-876-2783
201 E Roosevelt *Fax:* 505-285-5661
Grants, NM 87020 Leslie_DeLong@nps.gov
www.nps.gov/elma/

This monument preserves 114,277 acres of which 109,260 acres are federal and 5,017 acres are private. Volcanic features such as lava flows, cinder cones, pressure ridges and complex lava tube systems dominate the landscape. Sandstonebluffs and mesas border the eastern side, providing to vast wilderness.

Douglas E Eury

3385 **Las Vegas National Wildlife Refuge**
Route 1 Box 399 505-425-3581
Las Vegas, NM 87701 *Fax:* 505-454-8510
www.fws.gov/refuge/Las_Vegas

8,672 acres consisting of native grassland, cropland, marshes, ponds, forested canyons, and streams.

Joe B Rodriguez, Manager

3386 **Lincoln National Forest**
3463 Las Palomas Rd. 575-434-7200
Alamogordo, NM 88310 *Fax:* 575-434-7218
www.fs.fed.us/r3/lincoln/

The Lincoln consists of three ranger districts: Sacramento, Smokey Bear and Guadalupe

Travis Moseley, Forest Supervisor
Karla Eldridge, Administrative Officer

3387 **Maxwell National Wildlife Refuge**
168 Lake 13 Road 575-375-2331
PO Box 276 *Fax:* 575-375-2331
Maxwell, NM 87728 fw2_rw_maxwell@fws.gov
www.fws.gov/refuge/maxwell/

At an altitude of 6,050 feet, the refuge is made up of more than 3,000 acres of gently rolling prairie, playa lakes and farmland for waterfowl. Rangeland and reclaimed farmland on the refuge are made up of a variety of grassesincluding blue grama, galleta, sand dropseed, threeawn and buffalo grass, as well as fourwing saltbush and cactus. Several lakes provide approximately 700 acres of roosting and feeding habitat for waterfowl. Supports waterfowl nesting and is alsobeneficial to shore birds.

Leann Wilkins, Refuge Manager

3388 **San Andres National Wildlife Refuge**
5686 Santa Gertrudis Dr. 505-382-5047
Las Cruces, NM 88012 *Fax:* 505-382-5454
lorie_hardin@fws.gov
www.fws.gov/southwest/refuges/newmex/sanandres/index.html

Refuge not open to the public due to its location within the boundaries of U.S. Department of Army, White Sands Missile Range. Primary emphasis has been focused on restoring a remnant population of desert bighorn sheet (OvisCanadensis Mexicana)

Kevin Cobble, Refuge Manager

3389 **Sevilleta National Wildlife Refuge**
PO Box 1248 505-864-4021
Socorro, NM 87801 *Fax:* 505-864-7761
Jeannine_Kimble@fws.gov
www.fws.gov/refuge/sevilleta/

Home to over 1200 species of plants, 89 species of mammals, 225 species of birds and 15 species of amphibians. More commonly seen species include mule deer, coyotes, pronghorns, red-tailed hawks, northern harriers, western diamondbackrattlesnakes, roadrunners, sandhill cranes and many different types of waterfowl and migrating shorebirds. Bobcats, elk, bighorn sheep and an occasional mountain lion also roam the hillsides.

Kathy Granillo, Manager
Renee Robichaud, Deputy Refuge Manager

3390 **White Sands National Monument**
PO Box 1086 505-479-6124
Holloman Air Force Base, NM 88330 *Fax:* 505-479-4333
whsa_interpretation@nps.gov
www.nps.gov/whsa/

White Sands National Mounment preserves a major portion of this gypsum dune field, along with the plants and animals that have successfully adapted to this constantly changing environment.

Dennis L Ditmanson

New York: US Forests, Parks, Refuges

3391 **Fire Island National Seashore**
120 Laurel Street 631-687-4750
Patchogue, NY 11772-3596 *Fax:* 631-289-4898
fiis_interpretation@nps.gov
www.nps.gov/fiis/

There are 32 miles of sandy beaches and saltwater marshes, a sunken forest of 300 year old holly trees, hiking trails, a wilderness area and many other sites on the Fire Island National Seashore.

Michael T Reynolds, Superintendent
K Christopher Soller, Superintendent

3392 **Gateway National Recreation Area**
210 New York Avenue 718-354-4606
Staten Island, NY 10305 *Fax:* 718-354-4764
carole_silano@nps.gov
www.nps.gov/gate/

Gateway NRA is a 26,000 acre recreation area located in the heart of the New York metropolitan area. The park extends through

three New York City boroughs and into northern New Jersey. Parks sites offer a variety of recreationopportunities, along with a chance to explore many significant cultural resources.
Kevin Buckley, Supt

3393 Iroquois National Wildlife Refuge
1101 Casey Road 585-948-5445
Basom, NY 14013 *Fax:* 585-948-9538
iroquois@fws.gov
www.fws.gov/refuge/iroquois/
Iroquois National Wildlife Refuge lies within the rural township of Alabama, New York, midway between Buffalo and Rochester. Part of what the locals call the Alabama Swamps, its 10,818 acres of freshwater marshes, and hardwood swampsbounded by woods, forest, pastures and wet meadows, serve the habitat needs of many animals as a major stopover for migrating birds and as a year-round residence.
Robert Lamayr, Refuge Manager

3394 Montezuma National Wildlife Refuge
3395 Routes 5 & 20 East 315-568-5987
Seneca Falls, NY 13148 *Fax:* 315-568-8835
andrea_vanbeusichem@fws.gov
www.fws.gov/r5mnwr
Montezuma is the premiere refuge in New York State. View bald eagles year-round. Spring and fall bring tens of thousands of migrating ducks and geese. View Shaebirds in early spring and late summer. May and June are great for warblerwatching. Volunteer opportunities available Spring- Fall.
Tom Jasikoff, Manager
Andrea VanBeusichem, Visitor Services Manager

3395 Seatuck National Wildlife Refuge: Long Island National Wildlife Refuge Complex
340 Smith Road 631-286-0485
Shirley, NY 11967 *Fax:* 516-581-2003
R5RW_STKNWR@fws.gov
www.fws.gov/refuge/Seatuck
Located along the southern shore of Long Island, the Refuge consists of half salt marsh and half freshwater wetlands, ponds and sparsely wooded areas. It is part of the larger Great South Bay, which is a significant coastal habitat formigrating birds. Limited recreation includes viewing wildlife and bird watching.
Charles Stenvall, Manager

3396 Target Rock National Wildlife Refuge Long Island National Wildlife Refuge Complex
340 Smith Road 631-286-0485
Shirley, NY 11967 *Fax:* 516-286-4003
www.fws.gov/refuge/target_rock
The refuge was established in 1967. It consists of mixed upland forest, a half mile of rocky beach, a brackish and several vernal ponds. The offshore, beach and pond habitats provide foraging areas for piping plover, winteringwaterfowl and fish species.

North Carolina: US Forests, Parks, Refuges

3397 Alligator River National Wildlife Refuge
PO Box 1969 252-473-1131
Manteo, NC 27954 *Fax:* 252-473-1668
alligatorriver@fws.gov
www.fws.gov/alligatorriver
Provide habitat and protection for endangered species such as red wolves, red-cockaded woodpeckers, and American alligators
Mike Bryant, Refuge Manager
Scott Lanier, Deputy Refuge Manager

3398 Cape Hatteras National Seashore
1401 National Park Drive 252-473-2111
Manteo, NC 27954 *Fax:* 252-473-2595
CAHA_Information@nps.gov
www.nps.gov/caha/
A thin broken strand of islands curves out into the Atlantic Ocean and then back again in a sheltering embrace of North Carolina's mainland coast and its offshore sounds. These are the Outer Banks of North Carolina. Today their longstretches of beach, sand dunes, marshes and woodlands are set aside as Cape Hatteras National Seashore.
Lawrence A Belli, Superintendent

3399 Cape Lookout National Seashore
131 Charles Street 252-728-2250
Harkers Island, NC 28531 *Fax:* 252-728-2160
CALO_information@nps.gov
www.nps.gov/calo
The seashore is a 56 mile long section of the Outer Banks of North Carolina running from Ocracoke Inlet on the northeast to Beafort Inlet on the southeast. The four undeveloped barrier island, make up the seashore- North Core Banks,South Core Banks, Middle Core Banks and Shackleford Banks- may seem barren and isolated but they offer many natural and historical features that can make a visit very rewarding.
Robert A Vogel, Superintendent
Donna O Tiptor, Administrative Officer

3400 Cedar Island National Wildlife Refuge
85 Mattamuskeet Road 252-926-4021
Swan Quarter, NC 27885 *Fax:* 252-926-1743
mattamuskeet@fws.gov
www.fws.gov/refuge/cedar_island
Provide habitat and protection for endangered species such as American alligators and brown pelicans
Peter Campbell, Refuge Manager
Jerry Fringeli, Deputy Refuge Manager

3401 Currituck National Wildlife Refuge
316 Marsh Causeway 919-429-3100
PO Box 39 *Fax:* 919-429-3185
Knotts Island, NC 27950-0039 mackayisland@fws.gov
www.fws.gov/refuge/currituck/
The purpose of the Refuge is to preserve and protect a portion of the Outer Banks habitat for wintering waterfowl, endangered species, other migratory birds, and native wildlife

3402 Mattamuskeet National Wildlife Refuge
85 Mattamuskeet Road 919-926-4021
Box N-2 mattamuskeet@fws.gov
Swan Quarter, NC 27885 www.fws.gov/refuges
Located in eastern North Carolina in Hyde County, the Mattamuskeet Refuge consists of more than 50,000 acres of water, marsh, timber and crop lands. The refuge's most significant feature is lake Mattamuskeet, the largest natural lakein North Carolina. The lake is 18 miles long and five to 6 miles wide, encompassing approximately 40,000 acres, but averages 2 feet in depth.
Don Temple, Manager

3403 Nantahala National Forest
160-A Zillicoa Street 828-257-4200
Asheville, NC 28801 *Fax:* 828-257-4263
www.fs.usda.gov/recarea/nfsnc
The National Forests of North Carolina include four national forests covering 1.2 million acres from the mountains to the sea. The Nantahala is located in the Appalachians of southwest North Carolina. The Nantahala is the largest ofthe four forests, totaling 528,541 acres. The Nantahala sits adjacent to Great Smokey Mountains National Park.

3404 Pea Island River National Wildlife Refuge
PO Box 1969 252-473-1131
Manteo, NC 27954 *Fax:* 252-473-1668
alligatorriver@fws.gov
www.fws.gov/peaisland
Provide nesting, resting, and wintering habitat for migratory birds, including the greater snow geese and other migratory wa-

terfowl, shorebirds, wading birds, raptors, and neotropical migrants
Mike Bryant, Refuge Manager
Scott Lanier, Deputy Refuge Manager

3405 Pee Dee National Wildlife Refuge
5770 U.S. Hwy. 52 North 704-694-4424
Wadesboro, NC 28170 *Fax:* 704-694-6570
fw4_rw_pee_dee@fws.gov
www.fws.gov/peedee/
Refuge objectives are to: provide habitat for migratory waterfowl and song birds; to provide habitat and protection for an endangered species, the red-cockaded woodpecker; to provide recreation, environmental education andinterpretation for the public; to engage in dynamic partnering.
J.D Bricken, Refuge Manager
Greg Walmsley, Assistant Refuge Manager

3406 Pocosin Lakes National Wildlife Refuge
205 South Ludington Dr 252-796-3004
PO Box 329 *Fax:* 252-796-3010
Columbia, NC 27925 pocosinlakes@fws.gov
www.fws.gov/pocosinlakes/
The 112,000 acre refuge was established to protect and ehnhance a unique habitat called a pocosin and contains a variety of wildlife including endangered species such as the red wolf, bald eagle, peregrine falcon and red-cockadedwoodpecker as well as natural vegetation and scenic areas.

Howard Philips, Refuge Manager
David Kitts, Deputy Manager

3407 Roanoke River National Wildlife Refuge
114 W Water Street 252-794-3808
PO Box 430 *Fax:* 252-794-3780
Windsor, NC 27983 roanokeriver@fws.gov
www.fws.gov/roanokeriver/
Refuge objectives are: to provide habitat for migratory waterfowl, neo-tropical migrants and other birds; to provide migrating, spawning and nursery habitat for anadromous fish; (i.e. blueback herring, alewife, hickory shad and stripedbass); to enhance and protect forested wetlands consisting of bottomland hardwoods and swamps; to protect and manage for endangered and threatened wildlife; and to provide recreation and environmental education for the public

Matt Connolly, Refuge Manager
Jean Richer, Biologist

3408 Swanquarter National Wildlife Refuge
85 Mattamuskeet Road 252-926-4021
Swan Quarter, NC 27885 *Fax:* 252-926-1743
mattamuskeet@fws.gov
www.fws.gov/swanquarter/
Provide habitat for endangered species such as bald eagles, peregrine falcons, and American alligators.
Peter Campbell, Refuge Manager
Jerry Fringeli, Deputy Refuge Manager

North Dakota: US Forests, Parks, Refuges

3409 Crosby Wetland Management District
10100 Hwy 42 NW 701-965-6488
Crosby, ND 58730 crosbywetlands@fws.gov
Previously a part of the Des Lacs NWR Complex, the Crosby WMD includes of 17,000 acres of Waterfowl Production Areas (WPAs), numerous grassland and wetland easment contracts, and the 3,219 acre Lake Zahl NWR.
Tim K Kessler, WMD Manager

3410 Des Lacs National Wildlife Refuge
42000 520th Street NW 701-385-4046
Kenmare, ND 58746 *Fax:* 701-385-3214
deslacs@fws.gov
www.fws.gov/refuge/des_lacs/
Previously a part of the old Des Lacs NWR complex, the Des Lacs NWR is a smaller parcel that is home to wildlife and water fowl. The Lakes no longer encompass the the wetlands that are part of Crosby Wetlands district.

3411 Devils Lake Wetland Management District
221 2nd Street NW 701-662-8611
Suite #2 *Fax:* 701-662-8612
Devils Lake, ND 58301 devilslake@fws.gov
www.fws.gov/refuge/devils_lake_wmd/
Located in the heart of the Prairie Pothole Region of the US. The northeastern North Dakota counties of Towner, Cavalier, Pembina, Benson, Ramsey, Walsh, Nelson and Grand Forks are included in the District. Managed by the US Fish andWildlife Service, the district provides wetland areas needed by waterfowl in the spring and summer for nesting and feeding. Hundreds of thousands of waterfowl also use these wetlands in the spring and fall for feeding and resting during longmigratory flights.
Roger Hollevoet, Project Leader
Jim Alfonso, Deputy Project leader

3412 Lake Ilo National Wildlife Refuge
489 102 Avenue SW 701-548-8110
Dunn Center, ND 58626 *Fax:* 701-548-8108
lakeilo@fws.gov
www.fws.gov/lakeilo
Located near the center of Dunn County in west central North Dakota, the refuge habitat is made up of native prairie, planted grasslands and wetlands. The uplands are characterized by gently sloping hills and terraces with creeks andan occasional slough. The average rainfall of 16.8 inches supports a prairie environment with a climate of hot dry summers, occasional thunderstorms and cold winters.

Kory Richardson, Refuge Manager

3413 Long Lake National Wildlife Refuge
12000 353rd Street 56 701-387-4397
Moffit, ND 58560 *Fax:* 701-387-4767
longlake@fws.gov
www.fws.gov/refuge/long_lake/
The Refuge is about 18 miles long and contains 22,300 acres. The Refuge attracts a diversity and abundance of animals and waterfowl, both resident and migratory. Over 200 species of birds use the Refuge for breeding, rearing theiryoung and as a migratory stop. Long Lake Refuge is open for birdwatching, fishing, photography, boating, hiking and regulated hunting.

3414 Lostwood National Wildlife Refuge
8315 Highway 8 701-848-2722
Kenmare, ND 58746-9046 *Fax:* 701-848-2702
Lostwood@fws.gov
www.fws.gov/refuge/lostwood/
Lies in the highly productive pothole region that produces more ducks than any other region in the lower 48 states. The refuge is a land of rolling hills mantled in short-grass and mixed with grass prairie interspersed with numerouswetlands. Established to preserve a unique wildlife habitat, Lostwood is an important link in our nation's system of more than 410 wildlife refuges.

3415 Theodore Roosevelt National Park
315 Second Avenue 701-623-4466
PO Box 7 *Fax:* 701-623-4840
Medora, ND 58645-0007 susan_reece@nps.gov
www.nps.gov/thro/
Here in the North Dakota badlands, where many of his personal concerns first gave rise to his later environmental efforts, Roosevelt is remembered with a national park that bears his name and honors the memory of this greatconservationist. Theodore Roosevelt NAtional Park is colorful North Dakota badlands and is home to a variety of plants and animals, including bison, prairie dogs, and elk.

Ohio: US Forests, Parks, Refuges

3416 Cuyahoga Valley National Park
15610 Vaughn Road 216-524-1497
Brecksville, OH 44141 800-445-9667
Fax: 440-546-5989
cuva_canal_visitor_center@nps.gov
www.nps.gov/cuva

Cuyahoga Valley National Park protects 33,000 acres along the Cuyahoga River between Cleveland and Akron, Ohio. Managed by the National Park Service, CVNP combines cultural, historical, recreational and natural activities in onesetting. Visitors can hike, bike, birdwatch, golf, fish, ski, ride Cuyahoga Valley Scenic Railroad, explore the history of the Ohio and Erie Canal on a 20 mile section of the Towpath Trail, and attend national park ranger-guided programs, concerts,art exhibits and more.
Mary Pat Doorley, Media contact

3417 Ottawa National Wildlife Refuge
14000 W State Route 2 419-898-0014
Oak Harbor, OH 43449 *Fax:* 419-898-7895
ottawa@fws.gov
www.fws.gov/refuge/ottawa

Refuge objectives are: to restore optimum acreage to a natural floodplain condition; to improve and restore wetland habitat, to improve fishery and wildlife resources, to provide for biodiversity; and to provide public opportunitiesfor outdoor recreation and environmental education.
Dan Frisk, Refuge Manager

Oklahoma: US Forests, Parks, Refuges

3418 Deep Fork National Wildlife Refuge
21844 S. 250 Road 918-652-0456
PO Box 816 *Fax:* 918-652-3427
Okmulgee, OK 74447 lori_jones@fws.gov

Protecting important wetlands along the Deep Fork River, Deep Fork National Wildlife Refuge in eastern Oklahoma is a newcomer to the National Wildlife Refuge System. Established in 1993, the 9,000 acre refuge is subject to flooding atleast once a year. This flooding results in excellent conditions for waterfowl, including mallard, blue-winged teal, shoveler, pintail and wood ducks.
Darrin B Unruh, Manager

3419 Little River National Wildlife Refuge
PO Box 340 405-584-6211
Broken Bow, OK 74728 *Fax:* 405-584-2034
www.fws.gov/refuge/little_river/

13,000 acres of bottomland hardwoods within the floodplain of Little River.
Berlin A Heck, Manager

3420 Oklahoma Bat Caves National Wildlife Refuge
16602 CR 465 918-773-5251
Colcord, OK 74338 *Fax:* 918-773-5252
shea_hammond@fws.gov
www.fws.gov/refuge/ozark_plateau/

The endangered status of wildlife species and the delicate (and hazardous) nature of the habitat precludes any recreational use. Approved studies can be done under proper supervision.
Shea Hammond, Deputy Refuge Manager

3421 Optima National Wildlife Refuge
20834 east 940 Road 580-664-2205
Butler, OK 73625-5001 *Fax:* 580-664-2206
washita@fws.gov
www.fws.gov/refuge/optima

Located in the middle of the Oklahoma panhandle, the 4,333-acre refuge is made up of grasslands and wooded bottomland on the Coldwater Creek arm of the Army Corps of Engineers Optima Reservoir Project.

Daniel Moss, Refuge Manager

3422 Sequoyah National Wildlife Refuge
107993 S. 4520 Rd 918-773-5251
Vian, OK 74962-9304 *Fax:* 918-773-5598
www.fws.gov/refuge/Sequoyah

Sequoyah National Wildlife Refuge is home to wildlife as unique as the bald eagle and as elusive as the bobcat
Jeff Haas, Refuge Manager
Scott Gilje, Assistant Refuge Manager

3423 US Fish & Wildlife Service Tishomingo National Wildlife Refuge
12000 S Refuge Road 580-371-2402
Tishomingo, OK 73460 *Fax:* 580-371-9312
fw2_rw_tishomingo@fws.gov
www.fws.gov/refuge/tishomingo

The 16,464-acre Refuge lies at the upper Washita arm of Lake Texoma and is administered for the benefit of migratory waterfowl in the Central Flyway. It offers a variety of aquatic habitats for wildlife. The murky water of theCumberland Pool provides abundant nutrients for innumerable microscopic plants and animals. Seasonally flooded flats and willow shallows lying at the Pool's edge also provide excellent wildlife habitat.
Kris Patton, Refuge Manager

3424 Washita National Wildlife Refuge
20834 E 0940 Road 405-664-2205
Butler, OK 73625-5001 *Fax:* 580-664-2206
washita@fws.gov
www.fws.gov/refuge/washita/

Provides habitat for migrating/wintering waterfowl. Endangered species managed include the bald eagle, whooping crane, and interior least tern.
Jon M Brock, Manager

Oregon: US Forests, Parks, Refuges

3425 Ankeny National Wildlife Refuge
2301 Wintel Road 503-327-2444
2301 Wintel Road *Fax:* 541-757-4450
Jefferson, OR 97352-9758 willamettevalley@fws.gov
www.fws.gov/refuges

Refuge's primary management goal is to provide vital wintering habitat for dusky Canada geese. The refuge includes flat to gently rolling land near the confluence of the Willamette and Sanitiam rivers. The refuge's fertile farmedfields, hedgerows, forests, and wetlands provide a variety of wildlife habitats. the refuge is open to limited opportunites for wildlife-oriented education and recreation. Ducks, geese, and swans are commonly seen in refuge fields and ponds throughthe fall and winter.

3426 Bandon Marsh National Wildlife Refuge
83673 North Bank Lane 541-347-1470
2127 SE Marine Science Drive *Fax:* 541-347-9376
Bandon, OR 97411 oregoncoast@fws.gov
www.fws.gov/refuge/bandon_marsh/

3427 Baskett Slough National Wildlife Refuge
Western Oregon NWR Complex 503-757-7236
26208 Finley Refuge Road www.fws.gov/refuge/baskett_slough/
Corvallis, OR 97333

Includes 2,492 acres typical of Willamette Valley's irrigated hillsides, oak-covered knolls and grass fields. Wetlands include Morgan Lake and Baskett Slough. The refuge's objective is the protection and management of winteringhabitat for dusky Canada geese. Several species of waterfowl, herons, hawks, quail , shorebirds, mourning doves, woodpeckers and a variety of songbirds frequent the area, as well as mammals, amphibians and reptiles. Recreation includes observation,study and photography.
Richard Guadagno, Manager

3428 Cape Meares National Wildlife Refuge
2127 SE Marine Science Drive 541-867-4550
26208 Finley Refuge Road oregoncoast@fws.gov
Newport, OR 97365 www.fws.gov/refuge/cape_meares/

3429 **Cold Springs National Wildlife Refuge**
PO Box 239 541-992-3232
Umatilla, OR 97882 gary_hagedorn@fws.gov
Cold Springs NWR lies in sharp contrast with the arid desert surroundings of northeastern Oregon. The refuge, a tree-lined reservoir, lies 7 miles east of the agricultural community of Hermiston. The variety of refuge habitats attractsan abundance of wildlife. Cold Springs supports peak populations of over 45,000 winter waterfowl comprised mainly of mallards and Canada geese.

3430 **Columbia River Gorge National Scenic Area**
902 Wasco Avenue 541-386-2333
Waucoma Center, Suite 200 www.fs.fed.us/r6/columbia/
Hood River, OR 97031
The Columbia River Gorge is a espaectacular river canyon cutting the only sea-level route through the Cascade Mountain Range. It's 80 miles long and to 4,00 feet deep with the north canyon walls in Washington State and the south canyonwalls in Oregon State.

3431 **Crater Lake National Park**
Highway 62 541-594-3000
PO Box 7 *Fax:* 541-594-3010
Crater Lake, OR 97604 www.nps.gov
During the summer, visitors may navigate the Rim Drive around the lake, enjoy boat tours, stay in the historic Crater Lake Lodge Camp or hike some of the park's various trails. The winter brings some of the heaviest snowfall in thecountry, averaging 533 inches per year. Although park facilities mostly close for the snow season, visitors may view the lake during fair weather, enjoy cross-country skiing, and participate in weekend snowshoe hikes.
Dave Morris, Supt

3432 **Deschutes National Forest**
63095 Deschutes Market Road 541-383-5300
Bend, OR 97701 *Fax:* 541-383-5531
www.fs.usda.gov/main/deschutes
Scenic backdrop of volcanic attraction, evergreen forest, mountain lakes, caves, desert areas and alpine meadows.

3433 **Fremont Winema National Forest**
1301 South G Street 541-947-2151
Lakeview, OR 97630 *Fax:* 541-947-6399
www.fs.usda.gov/fremont-winema
Located in Oregon's Outback, the forest provides the self reliant recreationist the opportunity to discover nature in a rustic environment.

3434 **Malheur National Forest**
431 Patterson Bridge Road 541-575-1731
PO Box 909 jtrosclair02@fs.fed.us
John Day, OR 97845 www.fs.usda.gov/malheur/
The 1,460,000 acre Malheur National Forest is located in the blue Mountains of Eastern Oregon. The diverse and beautiful scenery of the forest includes high desert grasslands, sage and juniper, pine, fir and other tree species, and thehidden gem of alpine lakes and meadows. Elevations vary from about 4000feet (1200 meters) to the 9038 foot (2754 meters) top Strawberry Mountain. The Strawberry Mountain range extends east to west through the center of the forest.
Bonnie J Wood, Forest Supervisor

3435 **Malheur National Wildlife Refuge**
36391 Sodhouse Lane 541-493-2612
Princeton, OR 97721 *Fax:* 541-493-2405
tim_bodeen@fws.gov
www.fws.gov/refuge/malheur
Tim Bodeen, Manager

3436 **McKay Creek National Wildlife Refuge**
Umatilla NWR Complex 503-922-3232
PO Box 239
Umatilla, OR 97882

3437 **Mount Hood National Forest**
16400 Champion Way 503-668-1700
Sandy, OR 97055 *Fax:* 503-668-1641
www.fs.usda.gov/mthood/
Located 20 miles east of the city of Portland and the northern Willamette River valley, Mt Hood National Forest extends south from the strikingly beautiful Columbia River Gorge across more than sixty miles of forested mountains, lakesand streams to OlAllie Scienic Area, a high lake basin under the slopes of Mt Jefferson. Our many visitors enjoy fishing, caming, boating and hiking in the summer, hunting in the fall, skiing and other snow sports in the winter.

3438 **National Park Service: John Day Fossil Beds National Monument**
32651 Highway 19 541-987-2333
Kimberly, OR 97845-9701 *Fax:* 541-987-2336
joda_interpretation@nps.gov
www.nps.gov/joda
Within the heavily eroded volcanic deposits of the scenic John Day Fossil Basin is a great diversity of well-preserved plant and animal fossils. This remarkably complete record spans more than 40 of the 65 million years of the CenozoicEra (the Age of Mammals). The monument was established in 1975.
John Fiedor, Chief Visitor Services

3439 **Ochoco National Forest**
1220 SW 3rd Ave 503-808-2468
Portland, OR 97204 *Fax:* 541-416-6695
www.fs.fed.us/r6/centraloregon
With a total of almost 1,500 square miles, the Ochoco National Forest is endowed with vast natural resources, scenic grandeur and tremendous recreation opportunities. People are drawn to the Ochoco for its majestic ponderosa pinestands, picturesque rimrock vantage points, deep canyons, unique geologic formations, abundant wildlife and plentiful sunshine.

3440 **Oregon Caves National Monument**
19000 Caves Highway 541-592-2100
Cave Junction, OR 97523 *Fax:* 541-592-3981
www.nps.gov/orca
Oregan Caves National Monument is small in size, 480 acres, but rich in diversity. Above ground, the monument encompasses a remnant old-growth coniferous forest. It harbors a fantastic array of plants, and a Douglas-fir tree with thewildest known girth in Oregon. Three hiking trails access this forest. Below ground is an active marble cave created by natural forces over hundreds of thousands of years in one of the world's most diverse geologic realms.
Vicki Snitzler, Superintendent

3441 **Oregon Coastal Refuges**
2127 SE OSU Drive 541-867-4550
Newport, OR 97365 *Fax:* 541-867-4551
oregoncoast@fws.gov
575 acres of rocks and islands located offshore along the length of the Oregon coast. Most of the refuge is included in the Oregon Islands Wilderness.
Nancy Morrissey, Manager

3442 **Oregon Islands National Wildlife Refuge**
c/o Oregon Coast NWR Complex 541-867-4550
2127 SE Marine Science Drive *Fax:* 541-867-4551
Newport, OR 97365 oregoncoast@fws.gov
www.fws.gov/refuge/oregon_islands/
575 acres of rocks and islands located offshore along the length of the Oregon coast. Most of the refuge is included in the Oregon Islands Wilderness.

3443 **Rogue River National Forest**
3040 Biddle Road 541-858-2200
Medford, OR 97504 *Fax:* 541-858-2220
www.fs.fed.us/r6/rogue
Rob MacWhorter, Forest Supervisor
Tracy Tophooven, Deputy Forest Supervisor

3444 Sheldon National Wildlife Refuge
US Fish and Wildlife Service- Pacific Region
20995 Rabbit Hill Road 503-947-3315
PO Box 111 *Fax:* 503-947-4414
Lakeview, OR 97630 Sheldon-Hart@fws.gov
www.fws.gov/sheldonhartmtn/sheldon/
Provide habitat for pronghorn antelope, the primary species, and populations of native secondary species (e.g., mule deer, sage-grouse, and song birds) in such numbers as may be necessary to maintain a balanced wildlife population
Brian Day, Manager
John Kasbohm, Project Leader

3445 Siskiyou National Forest
3040 Biddle Road 866-296-3823
Medford, OR 9750 *Fax:* 541-471-6514
www.fs.usda.gov/rogue-siskiyou/
The Siskiyou National Forest embodies the most complex soils, geology, landscape, and plant communities in the Pacific Northwest. World-class rivers, biological diversity, fisheries, and complex watersheds rank the Siskiyou high in theNation as an outstanding resource.
Roy Bergstrom, District Ranger

3446 Siuslaw National Forest
3200 SW Jefferson Way 541-750-7000
Corvallis, OR 97331 *Fax:* 541-750-7234
www.fs.usda.gov/siuslaw
The Siuslaw National Forest encompasses one of the most productive and diverse landscapes in the world from fertile soils, which support tall stands of Douglas fir, western hemlock and Sitka spruce forests laced with miles of riversand streams, to miles of open sand dunes. These rich settings from habitats for a broad array of plants and animals and provide endless opportunities for learning.
Jerry Ingersoll, Forest Supervisor

3447 Three Arch Rocks National Wildlife Refuge
Western Oregon NWR Complex 541-867-4550
2127 SE Marine Science Drive oregoncoast@fws.gov
Newport, OR 97365 www.fws.gov/refuge/three_arch_rocks/
Large numbers of nesting common murres, tufted puffins, and Brandt's and pelagic cormorants use the area. Northern and California seal lions and harbor seals.

3448 Umatilla National Forest
72510 Coyote Road 541-278-3716
Pendleton, OR 97801 www.fs.usda.gov/umatilla
The Umatilla National Forest, located in the Blue Mountains of southeast Wasington and northeast Oregon, covers 1.4 million acres of diverse landscapes and plant communities. The forest has some mountainous terrain, but most of theforest consists of v-shaped valleys separated by narrow ridges or plateaus.
Kevin Martin, Forest Supervisor

3449 Umpqua National Forest
2900 NW Stewart Parkway 541-957-3200
PO Box 1008 *Fax:* 541-957-3495
Roseburg, OR 97471 jcaplan@fs.fed.us
www.fs.usda.gov/umpqua/
The Umpqua National Forest covers nearly one million acres and is located in the western slopes of the Cascades in Southwest Oregon. The forest encommpasses a diverse area of rugged peaks, high rolling meadows, sparkling rivers andlakes and deep canyons producing a wealth of water resources, timber, forage, minerals, wildlife and outdoor recreation opportunities.
Kelly Miller, Information Assistant

3450 Wallowa-Whitman National Forest
1500 Dewey Avenue 541-523-6391
PO Bos 907 *Fax:* 541-523-1315
Baker, OR 97814 www.fs.usda.gov/wallowa-whitman/
The Wallowa-Whitman National Forest contains 2.3 million acres ranging in elevation from 875 feet in Hells Canyon, to 9845 feet in the Eagle Cap Wilderness. Our varied forests are managed as sustainable ecosystems providing cleanwater, wildlife habitat and valuable forest products. For things to do and places to be, the Wallowa-Whitman is the setting for a variety of year-round recreation. You are welcome at the Wallowa-Whitman National Forest.

3451 William L Finley National Wildlife Refuge
26208 Finley Refuge Road 503-757-7236
Corvallis, OR 97333 www.fws.gov/refuge/william_l_finley/
Primary objective for the refuge is the protection and management of wintering habitat for dusky Canada geese. In addition to geese, other migratory and resident animals use refuge lands

3452 Winema National Forest
1301 South G Street 541-947-2151
Lakeview, OR 97630 *Fax:* 541-883-6709
www.fs.usda.gov/fremont-winema
The 1.1 million acre Winema National Forest lies on the eastern slopes of the Cascade Mountain Range in South Central Oregon, an area noted for its year-round sunshine. The Forest borders Crater Lake National Park near the crest of theCascades and stretches eastward into the Klamath River Basin. Near the floor of the Basin the Forest gives way to vast marshes and meadows assoicated with Upper Klamath Lake and the Williamson River.

Pennsylvania: US Forests, Parks, Refuges

3453 Allegheny National Forest
4 Farm Colony Road 814-723-5150
Warren, PA 16365-6100 *Fax:* 814-726-1465
r9_allegheny_nf@fs.fed.us
www.fs.usda.gov/allegheny/
An organization dedicated to providing advice for development of the corridor management plan for the northern section of the Allegheny River that has been designated as a National Wild and Scenic River.
Erin Connelly, Forest Supervisor

3454 Delaware National Scenic River: Delaware Water Gap National Recreation Area
Delaware Water Gap National Recreation Area
HQ River Road - Route 209 570-588-2435
Bushkill, PA 18324 *Fax:* 570-588-2780
www.nationalparksgallery.com/

3455 Erie National Wildlife Refuge
11296 Wood Duck Lane 814-789-3585
Guys Mills, PA 16327 *Fax:* 814-789-2909
erie@fws.gov
www.fws.gov/refuge/erie/
A haven for migratory birds consisting of two divisions: the Sugar Lake Division and the Seneca Division. Refuge management objectives include: providing waterfowl and other migratory birds with nesting, feeding, brooding, and restinghabitat; providing habitat to support a diversity of other wildlife species; and enhancing opportunities for wildlife-oriented public recreation and environmental education.

Patty Nagel, Deputy Refuge Manager

3456 Gettysburg National Military Park
1195 Baltimore Pike, Suite 100 717-334-1124
Gettysburg, PA 17325-2804 *Fax:* 717-334-1891
gett_superintendant@nps.gov
www.nps.gov/gett/index.htm
A unit of the national park service preserving 6000 acres of Gettysburg battlefield, and the Soldiers' National Cemetery, site of Lincoln's Gettysburg Address.

3457 John Heinz National Wildlife Refuge at Tinicum
8601 Lindbergh Boulevard 215-365-3118
Philadelphia, PA 19153 *Fax:* 215-365-2846
JohnHeinzNWR@fws.gov
www.fws.gov/refuge/John_Heinz
The John Heinz National Wildlife Refuge at Tinicum is administered by the Department of Interior's U.S. Fish and Wildlife Service and is located in Philadelphia and Delaware Counties, Pennsylvania. The refuge protects the last 200acres of freshwater

tidal marsh in Pennsylvania. The refuge has become a resting and feeding area for more than 20 species of birds, 80 of which nest here. Fox, deer, muskrat, turtles, fish, frogs and a wide variety of wildflowers and plants callthe refuge home.

3458 Upper Delaware Scenic & Recreational River
274 River Road 570-729-7134
Beach Lake, PA 18405 *Fax:* 570-729-8565
www.nps.gov/upde
As a part of the National Wild and Scenic Rivers System, upper Delaware Scenic and Recreational River stretches 73.4 miles (118.3 km) along the New York/Pennsylvania border. The longest free flowing river in the Northeast, it includesriffles and Class I and II rapids between placid pools eddies. Public fishing and boating accesses are provided, although most land along the river is privately owned. Wintering bald eagles are among the wildlife that may be seen here.
Dave Forney, Superintendent
Michael Reubet, Chief Resource Management

Rhode Island: US Forests, Parks, Refuges

3459 Rhode Island National Wildlife Refuge Complex
3769 D Old Post Road 401-364-0170
PO Box 307 *Fax:* 401-364-0170
Charlestown, RI 02813 fw5rw_rinwr@fws.gov
www.fws.gov/northeast/ri.htm
Charles Vandemoer, Complex Refuge Manager
Gary M Andres, Deputy Refuge Manager

South Carolina: US Forests, Parks, Refuges

3460 Ace Basin National Wildlife Refuge
PO Box 848 843-889-3084
Hollywood, SC 29449 *Fax:* 843-889-3282
www.fws.gov/acebasin/
The Ace Basin National Wildlife Refuge was established in 1990 to assist in preserving the nationally significant wildlife and related habitats within the 350,000-acre Ashepoo, Combahee and South Edisto (ACE) rivers basin. The wetlandshabitat of the area has been preserved during the last several centuries through careful management by private landowners. An antebellum mansion that survived the Civil War now serves in part as office space for the refuge.
Jane Griess, Refuge Manager

3461 Cape Romain National Wildlife Refuge
5801 Highway 17 North 843-928-3264
Awendaw, SC 29429 *Fax:* 843-928-3803
caperomain@fws.gov
www.fws.gov/refuge/cape_romain
Refuge objectives are to: provide habitat for waterfowl, shorebirds, wading birds and resident species; provide habitat and management of endangered and threatened species; provide protection of Class I Wilderness Area; and provideenvironmental education and recreation for the public.
Sarah Dawsey, Refuge Manager
Raye Nilius, Project Leader

3462 Carolina Sandhills National Wildlife Refuge
23734 U.S. Highway 1 803-335-8350
McBee, SC 29101 *Fax:* 803-335-8406
carolinasandhills@fws.gov
www.fws.gov/refuge/Carolina_Sandhills/
Richard P Ingram, Manager

3463 Francis Marion-Sumter National Forest
4931 Broad River Road 803-561-4000
Columbia, SC 29212 *Fax:* 803-561-4004
www.fs.usda.gov/scnfs
Headquaters in the capital city of Columbia, both forests are managed for many uses; including timber and wood production, watershed protection and improvement, habitat for wildlife and fish species, wilderness area management,minerals leasing and outdoor recreation.
Paul Bradley, Forest Supervisor

3464 Santee National Wildlife Refuge
2125 Fort Watson Road 803-478-2217
Summerton, SC 29148 *Fax:* 803-478-2314
santee@fws.gov
www.fws.gov/santee
Wildlife viewing opportunities available at the refuge on hiking, biking, canoeing/kayaking, and driving trails. A refuge visitor center is open Tuesday thru Saturday from 8-4. Located off of I-95 at exit 102 in Summerton, SC, SanteeNational Wildlife offers something for everybody.

Marc Epstein, Refuge Manager
Christopher Spivey, Refuge Officer

South Dakota: US Forests, Parks, Refuges

3465 Badlands National Park
25216 Ben Reifel Road 605-433-5361
PO Box 6 *Fax:* 605-433-5404
Interior, SD 57750 www.nps.gov/badl/
Consists of acres of sharply eroded buttes, pinnacles and spires blended with the largest protected mixed grass prarie in the US. The Badlands Wilderness Area covers 64,000 acres and is the site of the reintroduction of theblack-footed ferret, the most endangered land mammal in North America. The Stronghold Unit is co-managed with the Oglala Sioux Tribe and includes site of 1890s Glost Dances. Over 11,000 years of human history pale to the ages old paleontologicalresources.

William R Supernaugh, Superintendent

3466 Black Hills National Forest
1019 N. 5th Street 605-673-9200
Custer, SD 57730 *Fax:* 605-673-9350
r2_blackhills_webinfo@fs.fed.us
www.fs.usda.gov/blackhills
Eleven reservoirs, 30 campgrounds, 2 scenic byways, 1300 miles of streams, 13,000 acres of wilderness, 353 miles of trails, and much more. The forest is managed for multiple use so don't be surprised to see mining, logging, cattlegrazing, and summer homes on your travel.

3467 Huron Wetland Management District
20721 392nd Ave 605-352-5894
Hwy 14 *Fax:* 605-352-6709
Wolsey, SD 57384 huronwetlands@fws.gov
www.fws.gov/refuge/huron_wmd
The public lands of the HWMD, called Waterfowl Production Areas, are part of the National Wildlife Refuge System. The refuges and WPAs are vitally important to wildlife and people. They provide food, water, cover and space for hundredsof species of birds, mammals, reptiles, amphibians, fish and plants. Managed to benefit endangered species, migratory birds and other wildlife and provide places to learn about and enjoy wildlife. HWMD's mission is to preserve wetlands and managehabitat.
harris Hoisted, Project Leader

3468 Jewel Cave National Monument
11149 U.S. Highway 16 605-673-8300
Building B12 *Fax:* 605-673-8301
Custer, SD 57730 www.nps.gov/jeca/
With more than 125 miles sureyed, jewel cave is recognized as the third longest cave in the world. Airflow within its passages indicates a vast area yet to be explored. Cave tours provide opportunities for viewing this pristine cavesystem and its wide varitey of speleothems including stalactites, stalagmites, draperies, frostwork, flowstone, boxwork and hydromagnesite balloons. The cave is an important hibernaculum for several species of bats.
Kate Cannon, Superintendent

3469 **Sand Lake National Wildlife Refuge**
39650 Sand Lake Drive 605-885-6320
Columbia, SD 57433 *Fax:* 605-885-6333
sandlake@fws.gov
www.fws.gov/sandlake/
Sand Lake Refuge is haven for wildlife and those who enjoy it. Home to more than 266 species of birds, 40 mammal species and a variety of fish, reptiles and amphibians, this 22,000 acre refuge is a mosaic of wildlife and the wildplaces they need. Sand Lake is also a very popular recreation spot. Wildlife observation, fishing, hunting, photography, interpretation and environmental education are all popular activities at the refuge.

3470 **Wind Cave National Park**
26611 US Highway 385 605-745-4600
Hot Springs, SD 57747-6027 *Fax:* 605-745-4207
www.nps.gov/wica
One of the world's longest and most complex caves lies beneath the 28,295 acres of rolling, mixed grass prairie ecosystems of Wind Cave National Park. The park is home to a large variety of prairie wildlife such as bison, pronghornantelope and prairie dogs. The cave is famous for the rare cave formation called boxwork.

Vidal Davila, Park Superintendent

Tennessee: US Forests, Parks, Refuges

3471 **Big South Fork National River Recreation Area**
4564 Leatherwood Road 423-569-9778
Onieda, TN 37841 *Fax:* 423-569-5505
www.nps.gov/biso/
The free-flowing Big South Fork of the Cumberland River and its tributaries pass through 90 miles of scenic gorges and valleys containing a wide range of natural and historic features. The area offers a broad range of recreationalopportunities including camping, whitewater rafting, kayaking, canoeing, hiking, horseback riding, mountain biking, hunting and fishing, The US Army Corps of Engineers, with its experience in managing river basins, was charged with land acquisition,planning and deve
William K Dickinson, Superintendent

3472 **Cherokee National Forest**
2800 N Ocoee Street NW 423-476-9700
Po Box 2010 *Fax:* 423-476-9721
Cleveland, TN 37312-5374 www.fs.usda.gov/cherokee
The Cherokee is steeped in colorful history and rich in the grandeur of the Appalachian Mountains. The forest is separated into two sections by Great Smoky Mountains Park and shares other boundaries with national forest in Georgia,North Carolina and Virginia.
Tom Speaks, Forest Supervisor

3473 **Chickasaw National Wildlife Refuge**
1505 Sand Bluff Road 731-635-7621
Ripley, TN 38063 *Fax:* 731-635-0178
www.fws.gov/refuge/chickasaw
Established to provide essentail habitat for migratory birds in the Lower Mississippi Valley. The refuge supports a variety of wildlife. Visitors can see large numbers of migratory wasterfowl in the winter. Neotropical migratory birdsand shorebirds are a common site yearround. The refuge is open to hunting and fishing-special regulations apply. Please contact the refuge manager for current regulations.
Bryan Woodward, Refuge Manager
Randy Cook, Refuge Complex Manager

3474 **Cross Creeks National Wildlife Refuge**
643 Wildlife Road 931-232-7477
Dover, TN 37058 *Fax:* 931-232-5958
crosscreeks@fws.gov
www.fws.gov/refuge/Cross_Creeks
Its primary purpose is to provide feeding and resting habitat for migratory birds with an emphasis placed on providing habitat for wintering waterfowl.
Vicki C Grafe, Manager

3475 **Great Smokey Mountains National Park**
107 Park Headquarters Road 865-436-1200
Gatlinburg, TN 37738 *Fax:* 865-436-1220
grsm_smokies_information@nps.gov
www.nps.gov/grsm
The national park, in the state of North Carolina is world renowned for the diversity of its plant and animal resources, the beauty of its ancient mountains, the quality of its remnants of Southern Appalachian mountain culture, and thedepth and integrity of the wilderness sanctuary within its boundaries, it is one the largest protected areas in the east.
Randall R Pope, Supt

3476 **Hatchie National Wildlife Refuge**
6772 Highway 76 South 731-772-0501
Stanton, TN 38069-8322 *Fax:* 731-772-7839
hatchie@fws.gov
www.fws.gov/refuge/hatchie
The dominant habitat type is 9,400 acres of seasonally flooded bottomland hardwoods. Other habitats include 400 acres of upland forest; 534 acres of open water, including 9 oxbow lakes; and 1,100 acres of agricultural areas managed ascropland, moist soil and old field habitats.
James B. Roberts, Manager

3477 **Lower Hatchie National Wildlife Refuge**
1505 Sand Bluff Road 901-635-7621
Ripley, TN 38063 *Fax:* 901-635-7621
r4rw_tn.rlf@fws.gov
www.fws.gov/refuge/Lower_Hatchie
The Refuge's primary purposes are to be a sanctuary for migratory birds and to preserve a representative portion of the fast vanishing bottomland hardwood forests as habitat for wintering waterfowl and other migratory birds.

3478 **Reelfoot National Wildlife Refuge**
4343 Highway 157 731-538-2481
Union City, TN 38261 *Fax:* 901-538-9760
r4rw_tn.rlf@fws.gov
www.fws.gov/refuge/reelfoot/
Reelfoot Lake is approximately 13,000 acres and provides numerous recreational opportunities including sport fishing and hunting.
Randy Cook, Manager

3479 **Tennessee National Wildlife Refuge**
1371 Wildlife Drive 901-642-2091
Springville, TN 38256 *Fax:* 901-644-3351
www.fws.gov/refuge/tennessee/
The refuge provides habitat for more than 226 species of birds, 47 species of mammals, 90 species of reptiles and amphibians and 109 species of fish.
John Taylor, Manager

Texas: US Forests, Parks, Refuges

3480 **Alibates Flint Quarries National Monument: Lake Meredith National Recreation Area**
PO Box 1460 806-857-3151
Fritch, TX 79036 *Fax:* 806-857-2319
www.nps.gov/alfl
ALIBATES: The only national monument in Texas. Preserves over 700 archeological sites. The monument can only be viewed by ranger-led guided tours. LAKE MEREDITH: A 45,000 acre recreation area that includes a 10,000 acre reservoirwhere visitors can enjoy water and land recreational activities such as hunting, fishing, boating, horseback riding, off-road vehicles, jetskies and the like.

Karren Brown, Supt

3481 Amistad National Recreation Area
4121 Veterans Blvd. 830-775-7491
Del Rio, TX 78840-9350 *Fax:* 830-778-9248
interpretation@nps.gov
www.nps.gov/amis

Situated on the United States-Mexico border, is know primarily for excellent year round, water-based recreation including: fishing , boating, swimming, suba diving. Also provides opportunities for picnicking, camping and hinting. Thereservoir, at the confluence of the Rio Grande, Devils and Pecos rivers, was created by Amistad Dam in 1969, This area is reach in technology and rock art, and contains a wide variety of plant and animal life.
Alan W. Cox, Supt

3482 Angelina National Forest
111 Walnut Ridge Road 936-897-1068
Zavalla, TX 75904 *Fax:* 936-639-8588
mailroom_r8_texas@fs.fed.us
www.fs.usda.gov/texas

The Angelina National Forest is located in the heart of Texas. The reservoir, a 114,500 acre lake on the Angelina River is noted for its fishing, boating and water skiing.

3483 Big Bend National Park
PO Box 129 915-477-2251
Big Bend National Park, TX 79834 *Fax:* 915-477-1175
www.nps.gov/bibe/

The Big Bend National Park is situated on the boundary with Mexico along the Rio Grande. It is a place where countries and cultures meet, also a place that merges natural environments, from desert to mountains. It's a place where southmeets north and east meets west, creating a great diversity of plants and animals. The park covers over 801,000 acres of west Texas in the place where the Rio Grande makes a sharp turn - the Big Bend.
Robert Arnberger, Supt

3484 Big Thicket National Preserve
6044 FM 420 409-951-6800
Kountze, TX 77625 *Fax:* 409-951-6714
BITH_Administration@nps.gov
www.nps.gov/bith

The Preserve consists of nine land units and six water corridors encompassing more than 97,000 acres. Big Thicket was the first Preserve in the National Park System and protects and area of rich biological diversity. A convergence ofecosystems occured here during the last Ice Age. It brought together, in one geographical location, the eastern hardwood forests, the Gulf coastal plains and the midwest praries.

Ronald Switzer, Supt

3485 Grulla National Wildlife Refuge
1531 County Road 1248 806-946-3341
P.O. Box 549 *Fax:* 806-946-3317
Muleshoe, TX 79347 jude_smith@fws.gov

Located in Roosevelt County, New Mexico, near the small town of Arch, approximately 25 miles northwest of Muleshoe National Wildlife Refuge. Grulla NWR, which is managed by the staff at Muleshoe NWR, has 3,236 acres, more than 2,000 ofwhich make up the saline lake bed of Salt Lake. The rest of the refuge is grassland. When the lake holds sufficient water, Grulla NWR is a wintering area for lesser sandhill cranes. Ring-necked pheasant, scaled quail and lesser prairie chickens maybe seen.

Jude Smith, Refuge Manager

3486 Guadalupe Mountains National Park
400 Pine Canyon Drive 915-828-3251
Salt Flat, TX 79847-9400 *Fax:* 915-828-3269
GUMO_Superintendent@nps.gov
www.nps.gov/gumo

This mountain mass contains portions of the world's most extensive and significant Permian limestone fossil reef, earth fault peaks, unusual flora and fauna. Guadalupe Peak, highest point in Texas at 8,749 feet.

John Lujan, Superintendent
Fred Armstrong, Chief of Resource Management

3487 Hagerman National Wildlife Refuge
6465 Refuge Road 903-786-2826
Sherman, TX 75092 *Fax:* 903-786-3327
gayle_ellis@fws.gov
www.fws.gov/refuge/hagerman/

Hagerman NWR lies on the Big Mineral Arm of Lake Texoma, on the Red River between Oklahoma and Texas. Established in 1946, the refuge includes 3,000 acres of marsh and water and 8,000 acres of upland and farmland. During fall, winterand spring, the marshes and waters are in constant use by migrating and wintering waterfowl.
Kathy Whaley, Manager

3488 Padre Island National Seashore
PO Box 181300 361-949-8068
Corpus Christi, TX 78480-1300 *Fax:* 361-949-8023
www.nps.gov/pais

Encompassing 130,434 acres, the longest remaining undeveloped stretch of barrier island in the world, and offers a wide variety of flora and fauna as well as recreation.

3489 Santa Ana National Wildlife Refuge
3325 Green Jay 956-784-7500
Box 202A *Fax:* 956-787-8338
Alamo, TX 78516 christine_donald@fws.gov
www.fws.gov/refuge/santa_ana/

The 2,088 acre refuge along the banks of the lower Rio Grande was established in 1943 for the protection of migratory birds. Considered the jewel of the refuge system, this essential island of thorn forest habitat is host or home tonearly 400 different types of birds and a myriad of other species, including the indigo snake, malachite butterfly and the endangered ocelot. Provides habitat for thousands of migrating birds and about one half of all butterfly species found in NorthAmerica.
Jeff Howland, Refuge Manager

Utah: US Forests, Parks, Refuges

3490 Arches National Park
PO Box 907 435-719-2299
Moab, UT 84532-0907 *Fax:* 435-719-2300
archinfo@nps.gov
www.nps.gov/arch/

Arches National Park preserves over two thousand natural sandstone arches and a variety of other unique geological resources. The extraordinary features of the park are highlighted by a striking environment of contrasting colors,landforms and textures. Administered by Canyonlands National Park
Laura Jess, Supt

3491 Ashley National Forest
355 North Vernal Avenue 435-789-1181
Vernal, UT 84078 *Fax:* 435-781-5295
www.fs.usda.gov/ashley

Remarkable features include Kings Peak (highest peak in Utah), Flaming Gorge National Recreation Area, Flaming Gorge-Uintas National Scenic Byway, The Green River Corridor
Rowdy Muir, District Ranger

3492 Bear River Migratory Bird Refuge
58 S 435-723-5887
Brigham City, UT 84302 *Fax:* 435-723-8873
bearriver@fws.gov
www.fws.gov/refuge/bear_river_migratory_bird_refuge/

To date, close to 1 million cubic yards of earth has been moved to restore and enhance the refuge. Forty-seven primary water control structures have been restored along with over forty-seven miles of dikes. Through volunteer efforts,debris has been removed from the old headquaters site and a new pavilion, restroom, demonstration pond, and kiosk have been built on the site. The 12-mile auto tour route has been reopened to the public.
Alan K Trout, Manager

3493 Bryce Canyon National Park
PO Box 640201 435-834-5322
Bryce Canyon, UT 84764-0201 *Fax:* 435-834-4102
www.nps.gov/brca
Consists of 37,277 acres of scenic colorful rock formations and desert wonderland. Bryce Canyon National Park is named for one of a series of horseshoe-shaped amphitheaters carved from the eastern edge of the Paunsaugunt Plateau insouthern Utah. Erosion has shaped colorful Claron limestones, sandstones and mudstones into thousands of spires, fins, pinnacles and mazes. Collectively called hoodoos, these unique formations are whimsically arranged and tinted with colors toonumerous to name.

Craig C Axtell

3494 Canyonlands National Park
2282 S West Resource Boulevard 435-719-2313
Moab, UT 84532 *Fax:* 435-719-2300
canyinfo@nps.gov
www.nps.gov/cany/index.htm
Canyonlands National Park preserves a stunning landscape of sedimentary sandstones eroded into countless canyons, mesas and buttes by the Colorado River and its tributaries. Largely undeveloped, the park is a popular backcountrydestination and scientific research site.

3495 Capitol Reef National Park
HC 70 Box 15 435-425-3791
Torrey, UT 84775-9602 *Fax:* 435-425-3026
care_administration@nps.gov
www.ehow.com/fashion
The Waterpocket Fold, a 100 mile long wrinkle in the earth's know as a monoclide, extends from nearby Thousand Lakes Mountain to the Colorado River. Capitol Reef National Park was established to protect this grand and colorful geologicfeature, as well as the unique historical and cultural history found in the area.

Albert J Hendricks, Supt

3496 Cedar Breaks National Monument
2390 W Highway 56 435-586-9451
Suite 11 *Fax:* 435-586-3813
Cedar City, UT 84720 www.nps.gov/cebr/
Millons of years of sedimentation, uplift and erosion continue to create a deep canyon of rock walls, fins, spires and columms, that spans some three miles, and over 2,000 feet deep. The rim of the canyon is over 10,000 feet above sealevel, and is forested with islands of Englemann spruce, subalpine fir and aspen: separated by broad meadows of brillant summertime wild flowers.
Denny Davies, Supt
Ateve Robinson, Chief Ranger

3497 Dixie National Forest
1789 N Wedgewood Ln 435-865-3700
Cedar City, UT 84721 *Fax:* 435-865-3791
www.fs.usda.gov/dixie
The Dixie is located adjacent to three National Parks, Bryce Canyon, Zion and Capitol Reef.The red sandstone formations of Red Canyon rival those of Bryce Canyon National park. From the top of Powell Point, it is possible to see farinto three different states. Boulder Mountain and the many different lakes provide opportunities for hiking, fishing and viewing outstanding scenery.
Mary Wagner, Forest Supervisor

3498 Fish Springs National Wildlife Refuge
PO Box 568 435-693-3122
Dugway, UT 84022 *Fax:* 435-693-9933
fishsprings@fws.gov
www.fws.gov/refuge/fish_springs
Located at the southern end of the Great Salt Lake Desert in western Utah, Fish Springs National Wildlife Refuge encompasses 17,992 acres between two small mountain ranges. Five major springs and several lesser springs and seeps flowfrom a faultline at the base of the eastern front of the Fish Springs Mountain Range, These warm, saline springs provide virtually all of the water for the Refuge's 10,000-acre marsh system.
Jerry Bana, Manager

3499 Fishlake National Forest
115 E 900 N 435-896-9233
Richfield, UT 84701 *Fax:* 435-896-9347
www.fs.usda.gov/fishlake
The Fishlake National Forest in central Utah features majestic stands of aspen encircling open mountain meadows that are lush with a diverse community of forbs and grasses. The mountains of the Fishlake are a source of water for manyof the neighboring communities and agricultural valleys in the region. Hunting, fishing and OHV use are among the most popular forms of recreation enjoyed by forest visitors.
Allen Rowley, Forest Supervisor

3500 Natural Bridges National Monument
HC 60 435-692-1234
Box 1 *Fax:* 435-692-1111
Lake Powell, UT 84533 nabrinfo@nps.gov
www.nps.gov/nabr
Natural Bridges protects some of the finest examples of ancient stone architecture in the southwest. The monument is located in the southeast Utah on a pinyon-juniper covered mesa bisected by deep canyons of Permian age Ceder MesaSandstone. Where meandering streams cut through the cayon walls, three natural bridges formed: Kachina, Owachomo and Sipapu.

Coralee S Hays, Superintendent

3501 Ouray National Wildlife Refuge
HC 69 Box 232 435-545-2522
Randlett, UT 84063 *Fax:* 435-545-2369
Ouray@fws.gov
www.fws.gov/refuge/ouray/
This organization is dedicated to the conservation of wildlife and endangered species. They provide and maintain safe habitats for these animals.

Dan Schaad, Refuge Manager
Sonja Jahrsdoerfer, Project Leader

3502 Timpanogos Cave National Monument
Rural Route 3 Box 200 801-756-5239
American Fork, UT 84003 *Fax:* 801-756-5661
www.nps.gov/tica
Timpanogos Cave Natioanl Monument sits high in the Wasatch Mountains. The cave system consists of three spectacularly decorated caverns. Each cavern has unique colors and formations. Helicitites and anthodites are just a few of themany dazzling formations to be found in the many chambers. As visitors climb to the cavern entrance, on a hike gaining over 1,000 feet in elevation, they are offered incredible views of American Fork Canyon.

Dennis Davis, Superintendent

3503 Uinta National Forest
857 West South Jordan 801-342-5100
South Jordan, UT 84095 *Fax:* 801-342-5144
uwc-info@fs.fed.us
www.fs.usda.gov/uwcnf
The Uinta National Forest ranges from high western desert at Vernon to lofty mountain peaks such as Mount Nebo (elevation 11,877 feet, the highest peak in the Wasatch Range) and Mount Timpanogos (elevation 11,750 feet). The forestcontains three wilderness areas: the Lone Peak, the Mount Timpanogos and the Mount Nebo Wildernesses. The Forest surrounds the Timpanogos Cave National Mounment.
Peter Karp, Forest Supervisor

3504 Wasatch-Cache National Forest
857 West South Jordan 801-466-6411
South Jordan, UT 84095 *Fax:* 801-524-3172
www.fs.usda.gov/uwcnf
Wasatch-Cache National Forest lands are located in three major areas: the northern and western slopes of the Uinta Mountains. The Wasatch Front from Lone Peak north to the Idaho border in-

cluding the Wasatch, Monte cristo, and BearRiver Ranges. The Stansbury Range, in the Great Basin.
Tom Tidwell, Forest Supervisor

3505 Zion National Park
Star Route 9 435-772-3256
Springdale, UT 84767-1099 *Fax:* 435-772-3426
zion_park_information@nps.gov
www.nps.gov/zion
Protected within Zion National Park's 229 square miles (593.1 km) is a spectacular cliff-and-cayon landscape and wilderness full of the unexpected including the world's largest arch -Kolob Arch- with a span that measures 310 feet(94.5m). Wildlife such as mule deer, golden eagles, and mountain lions also inhabit the park. Mukuntuweap National Monument proclaimed July 31, 1909; incorporated in Zion National Monument March 18, 1918; established as national park Nov. 19, 1919.
Ron Terry, Public Information Officer

Vermont: US Forests, Parks, Refuges

3506 Green Mountains & Finger Lakes National Forest
231 North Main Street 802-747-6700
Rutland, VT 05701 *Fax:* 802-747-6766
www.fs.usda.gov/greenmountain

3507 Missisquoi National Wildlife Refuge
29 Tabor Road 802-868-4781
Swanton, VT 05488 *Fax:* 802-868-2379
missisquoi@fws.gov
www.fws.gov/refuge/missisquoi
The 6,592-acre refuge includes most of the Missisquoi River delta where it flows into Missisquoi Bay. The refuge consists of quiet waters and wetlands which attract large flocks of migratory birds.
Mark Sweeny, Manager

Virginia: US Forests, Parks, Refuges

3508 George Washington National Forest
5162 Valleypointe Parkway 888-265-0019
PO Box 233 *Fax:* 540-265-5145
Roanoke, VA 24019 www.fs.usda.gov/gwj
Outstanding hiking trails, campsites, fishing and canoeing are the hallmarks of George Washington Forest in Virginia and West Virginia, part of the George Washington and Jefferson National Forest.

3509 Jefferson National Forest
5162 Valleypointe Parkway 888-265-0019
Roanoke, VA 24019 www.fs.usda.gov/gwj
The Jefferson National Forest is prize Appalachia country: tumbling waterfalls, rare wildflowers, vividly colored hills and Virginia's highest peak. Jefferson National Forest spreads 690,000 acres of hardwood and conifer forest acrosswest-central Virginia, West Virgina and Kentucky, including the ridge province of the Blue Ridge mountains.

3510 Mason Neck National Wildlife Refuge
12638 Darby Brooke Ct. 703-490-4979
Woodbridge, VA 22192 potomacriverrefuges@fws.gov
www.fws.gov/refuge/mason_neck/
The refuge, the Mason Neck State Park, the Northern Virginia Park Authority, the Gunston Hall Plantation and the Virginia Department of Game and Inland Fisheries are cooperating in the management of their combined 5,000+ acres on theMason Neck peninsula. This cooperation provides a wide variety of recreational activities while protecting natural resources. The primary objective of the refuge is to protect essential nesting, feeding and roosting habitat for bald eagles.
J Frederick Milton, Manager

3511 Shenandoah National Park
3655 US Highway 211 East 540-999-3500
Luray, VA 22835 *Fax:* 540-999-3601
www.nps.gov/shen/index.htm
Shenandoah National park lies astride a beautiful section of the blue rige mountains, which from the eastern rampart of the Appalachian Mountains between Pennsylvania and Georgia. The Shenandoah River flows through the valley to thewest, with Massanutten Mountain, 40 miles long, standing between the river's north and south forks. The rolling Piedmont country lies to the east of the park. Skyline Drive, a 105- mile road that winds along the crest of the mountainsthrough thelength of the park.
William Wade, Supt

Washington: US Forests, Parks, Refuges

3512 Colville National Forest
255 W. 11th Avenue Kettle Falls 509-684-7000
Coleville, WA 99114 *Fax:* 509-684-7280
www.fs.usda.gov/colville
The Colville National Forest encompasses over one million acres in northeastern Washington. The Sherman Pass National Scenic Byway leads through a portion of the Forest, with camping, fishing, hiking, picnicking, mountain biking,cross-country skiing, sonowmobiling and other recreational activities. 49 Degrees North, a full service ski resort, is located east of Chewelah, about one hour north of Spokane. The Salmo-Prist Wilderness Area sits in the northeast corner of theforest.

3513 Conboy Lake National Wildlife Refuge
PO Box 5 509-546-8300
Glenwood, WA 98619 *Fax:* 509-364-3667
mcriver@fws.gov
www.fws.gov/refuge/conboy_lake/
Located in the northwest corner of Klickitat County, Washington, the refuge was established primarily for waterfowl. The broad range of habitat diversity provides for a broad diversity of resident wildlife species.
Harold E Cole, Manager

3514 Gifford Pinchot National Forest
10600 N.E. 51st Circle 360-891-5000
Vancouver, WA 98682 *Fax:* 360-891-5045
www.fs.usda.gov/giffordpinchot/
The Gifford Pinchot National Forst is one of the oldest National Forests in the United States. Include as part of The Mount Rainier Forest Reserve in 1897, this area was set aside as the columbia National Forest in 1908, and renamedthe Gifford Pinchot National Forest in 1949. The Forest, located in southwest Washington State, now contains 1,312,000 acres and includes the 110,000- acre Mount St. Helens National Volcanic Mounument established by congress in 1982.

3515 Lewis & Clark National Wildlife Refuge
46 Steamboat Slough Rd 360-795-3915
PO Box 566 willapa@fws.gov
Cathlamet, WA 98612 www.fws.gov/refuges/profiles/

3516 McNary National Wildlife Refuge
64 Maple Road 509-546-8300
PO Box 544 *Fax:* 509-546-8303
Burbank, WA 99323 mcriver@fws.gov
www.fws.gov/mcnary/
A resting and feeding area for up to 100,000 migrating waterfowl. It includes 3,629 acres of water and marsh, croplands, grasslands, trees and shrubs.
Robyn Thorson, Regional Manager
Richard Hannon, Deputy Regional Manager

3517 Mount Baker-Snoqualmie National Forests
2930 Wetmore Avenue 425-783-6000
Suite 3A 800-627-0062
Everett, WA 98201 www.fs.usda.gov/mbs

An urban forest, extending over 140 miles along the western slopes of the Cascade Mountains from the Canadian border to Mount Rainier National Park.
Jennifer Eberlien, Forest Supervisor

3518 Mount Rainier National Park
55210 238th Avenue East 253-569-2211
Ashford, WA 98304 *Fax:* 360-569-2170
MORAInfo@nps.gov
www.nps.gov/mora/
Established in 1899. 235,625 acres (97% is designated Wilderness). Includes mount Rainier (14,410'), an active volcano encased in over 35 square miles of snow and ice. The park contains outstanding examples of old growth forests andsubalpine meadows. Designated a National Historic landmark District in 1997 as a showcase for the NPS Rustic style architecture of the 1920s and 1930s.
William Briggle, Supt

3519 North Cascades National Park Service Complex
810 State Route 20 360-854-7200
Sedro-Woolley, WA 98284 *Fax:* 360-856-1934
NOCA_Interpretation@nps.gov
www.nps.gov/noca

3520 Okanogan National Forest
1240 S 2nd Avenue 509-826-3275
PO Box 950 *Fax:* 509-826-3789
Okanogan, WA 98840 www.fs.usda.gov/okawen/
There is a variety of country from craggy peaks to rolling meadows, to rich old growth forest and classic groves of ponderosa pine. We're called the Sunny Okanogan and for good reason: summers here are hot and dry, and our winters arefamous for brilliant clear skies and plenty of snow.

3521 Okanogan and Wenatchee National Forests Headquarters
215 Melody Lane 509-664-9200
Wenatchee, WA 98801 *Fax:* 509-664-9280
www.fs.usda.gov/okawen
The 2.2 million acre Wenatchee National Forest extends about 135 miles along the east side of the crest of the Cascade Mountains in Washington State. This National Forest is most noted for its wide range of recreation opportunities.There truly is something for everyone who likes to have fun in the outdoors.
Rebecca Heath, Forest Supervisor

3522 Olympic National Forest
1835 Black Lake Boulevard SW 360-956-2402
Olympia, WA 98512 www.fs.fed.us/r6/olympic
The National Forests are part of America's great outdoors and are public lands. They are managed for the multiple uses of recreation, wildlife, timber, gazing, mining, oil and gas, watershed and wilderness. The Olympic National Forestis over 632,000 acres in size and is divided into two Ranger Districts: Hood Canal and Pacific.

3523 Olympic National Park
600 East Park Avenue 360-565-3000
Port Angeles, WA 98362 *Fax:* 360-565-3015
www.nps.gov/olym
Often referred to as three parks in one, Olympic National Park encompasses three distinctly different ecosystems-rugged glacier capped mountains, over 73 miles of wild Pacific coast and magnificent mountains are still largely pristinein character and are Olympic's gift to you.

Karen Gustin, Superintendent

3524 Ross Lake National Recreation Area North Cascades National Park
810 State Route 20 360-854-7200
Sedro Woolley, WA 98284 *Fax:* 360-856-1934
www.nps.gov/rola
The most accessible part of the North Cascades National Park Service Complex. Is also the corridor for scenic Washington State Route 20, the North Cascades Highway, and includes three reserviors.

3525 Toppenish National Wildlife Refuge
State Route 97 509-546-8300
Toppenish, WA 98948 800-344-9453
mcriver@fws.gov
www.fws.gov/refuge/toppenish/
An important migration and wintering area for waterfowl in the Yakima Valley of eastern Washington. Wetland impoundments along Toppenish Creek provide natural foods for wintering mallards and other ducks. Ducks and other water birdsbreed in the wetland impoundments during the summer. Native shrub-steppe communities and riparian areas along Toppenish and Snake creeks provide habitat for many other species of birds. The refuge has active hunting and wildlife-viewing programs.
George J Fenn, Manager

3526 Umatilla National Wildlife Refuge
Mid-Columbian River Refuges
64 Maple Street 509-546-8300
Burbank, WA 99323 *Fax:* 509-546-8303
mcriver@fws.gov
www.fws.gov/mcriver/
The refuge is a varied mix of open water, sloughs, shallow marsh, seasonal wetlands, cropland, islands, and shrub-steppe upland habitats
Morris C LeFever, Manager

3527 Willapa National Wildlife Refuge
3888 State Route 101 206-484-3482
Ilwaco, WA 98624 willapa@fws.gov
www.fws.gov/willapa/
Located on Willapa Bay in Pacific County, the southernmost coastal county in Washington. The upland forest varies in successional stages from recently logged areas to a unique remnant of virgin, coastal cedar-hemlock forest home todeer, bear, elk, grouse, beaver and numerous songbirds and small mammals.
James A Hidy, Manager

West Virginia: US Forests, Parks, Refuges

3528 Monongahela National Forest
200 Sycamore Street 304-636-1800
Elkins, WV 26241 *Fax:* 304-636-1875
www.fs.usda.gov/mnf
The Monongahela National Forest was established following passage of the 1911 Weeks Act. This act authorized the purchase of land for long-term watershed protection and natural resource management following massive cutting of theEastern forests in the late 1800's and at the turn of the century.

3529 Ohio River Islands National Wildlife Refuge
3982 Waverly Road 304-375-2923
Williamstown, WV 26187 *Fax:* 304-422-0754
OhioRiverIslands@fws.gov
www.fws.gov/refuge/ohio_river_islands/
The refuge extends 362 river miles from Shippingport, Pennsylvania to Manchester, Ohio along one of the nation's busiest waterways. The Ohio River Islands and their back channels have long been recognized for high quality fish andwildlife, recreation, scientific and natural heritage values.

Michael Schramm, Visitor Services Manager

Wisconsin: US Forests, Parks, Refuges

3530 Apostle Islands National Lakeshore
415 Washington Street 715-779-3397
Route 1, Box 4 *Fax:* 715-779-3049
Bayfield, WI 54814 APIS_Webmaster@nps.gov
www.nps.gov/apis/index.htm
The national lakeshore includes 21 islands and 12 miles of mainland Lake Superior shoreline, featuring pristine stretches of sand beach, spectacular sea caves, remnant old growth forests, resi-

dent bald eagles and black bears and thelargest collection of lighthouses anywhere in the National Park System.
Robert J Krumenaker, Superintendant

3531 Chequamegon National Forest
1170 4th Avenue S 715-762-2461
Park Falls, WI 54552 *Fax:* 715-762-5179
www.fs.usda.gov/cnnf
Shaped principally by glacial action some 10,000 years ago, the forest offers a variety of hiking, ATV, and cross-country ski trails at different levels of difficulty. These campgrounds are located on either a lake or a river and offerfishing and boating.

3532 Ice Age National Scientific Reserve
PO Box 7921 608-266-2183
Madison, WI 53707 *Fax:* 608-267-7474
info@iceagetrail.org
www.wildernet.com
This first national scientific reserve contains nationally significant features of continental glaciation. State parks in the area are open to the public.
Tom Gilbert, Supt

3533 Nicolet National Forest
500 Hanson Lake Road 715-362-1300
Rhinelander, WI 54501 *Fax:* 715-362-1359
www.fs.usda.gov/cnnf
Located in Wisconsin's Northwoods where towering pine and hardwood forests are interspersed with hundreds of crystal clear lakes and streams, the Nicolet offers you many opportunities to enjoy the outdoors. Within a day's drive of theChicago, Milwaukee, St. Paul and Minneapolis metropolitan areas, the forest is a place where urban dwellers can truly get away from it all in the scenic beauty of the northwoods.

3534 St Croix National Scenic Riverway
401 N Hamilton Street 715-483-3284
St Croix Falls, WI 54024 *Fax:* 715-483-3288
www.nps.gov/sacn/index.htm
The St. Croix National Scenic Riverway is home to the endangered Higgins Eye and Winged Mapleleaf mussels, bald eagles, gray wolves, and the prehistoric paddlefish. The 252 miles of Riverway provide numerous recreational opportunitiesfor boaters, canoeists, kayakers and others.

Tom Bradley, Superintendent
Ron Erickson, Education Team Manager

Wyoming: US Forests, Parks, Refuges

3535 Bighorn National Forest
2013 Eastside 2nd Street 307-674-2600
Sheridan, WY 82801 *Fax:* 307-674-2668
www.fs.usda.gov/bighorn
The forest has 32 campgrounds, 14 picnic areas, 2 visitor centers, 2 ski areas, 7 lodges, 2 recreation lakes, 3 scenic byways and over 1500 miles of trails. The Bighorn National Forest is 80 miles long and 30 miles wide. The mostcommon tree is the lodgepole pine. The Bighorn River, flowing along the west side of the forest was first named by American Indians due to the great herds of bighorn sheep at its mouth.
Bill Bass, Forest Supervisor

3536 Bridger-Teton National Forest
340 N Cache-Forest Service Bldg 307-739-5500
PO Box 1888 *Fax:* 307-739-5010
Jackson, WY 83001 r4_b-t_info@fs.fed.us
With it's 3.4 million acres, it is the second largest National Forest outside Alaska. Included are more than 1.2 million acres of wilderness in the Bridger, Gros Ventre, and Teton Wildernesses. The Bridger-Teton is a land of variedrecreational opportunities, beautiful vistas, and abundant wildlife. Its crystal blue skies are puctuated by awesome mountain ranges which include the Gros Ventre, Teton, Salt River, Wind River, and Wyoming Mountain Ranges.
Jacque Buchanan, Forest Supervisor
Pamela Bode, Resources Staff Officer

3537 Devils Tower National Monument
PO Box 10 307-467-5283
Devils Tower, WY 82714-0010 *Fax:* 307-467-5350
deto_interpretation@nps.gov
www.nps.gov
This unit of the National Park Service protects the nearly vertical monolith known as Devil's Tower. The rolling hills of this 1347 acre park are covered with pine forests, deciduous woodlands, and prairie grasslands. Known byseveral northern plains tribes as Bear Lodge, it is sacred to many American Indians. Devil's Tower was proclaimed in September, 1906 as the nation's first national monument by President Theodore Roosevelt.

Dorothy FireCloud, Superintendent

3538 Fossil Butte National Monument
PO Box 592 307-877-4455
Kemmerer, WY 83101 *Fax:* 307-877-4457
FOBU_Superintendent@nps.gov
www.nps.gov/fobu
Located in southwest Wyoming, Fossil Butte National Monument represents one of the richest fossil localities in the world. Fifty million-year-old fish, insects, birds, reptiles, and plants are nearly perfectly preserved in limestone.
David E McGinnis, Superintendent
Marcia Fagnant, Park Ranger

3539 Grand Teton National Park
PO Box 170 307-739-3300
Moose, WY 83012-0170 GRTE_info@nps.gov
www.nps.gov/grte
Grand Teton National Park seeks to protect the mountains and wildlife habitats in National Park Wyoming.

3540 Medicine Bow National Forest
2468 Jackson Street 307-745-2300
Laramie, WY 82070 *Fax:* 307-745-2398
www.fs.usda.gov/mbr
The Medicine Bow National Forest dates back to May 22, 1902, with the establishment of the Medicine Bow Forest Reserve by President Theodore Roosevelt. In 1929, the former Hayden National Forest along the Continental Divide wasformerly a War Department target and maneuver reservation under joint administration by the Forest Service and the War Department. In 1959, the area formerly used by the military was added to the Medicine Bow National Forest.

3541 National Elk Refuge
PO Box 510 307-733-9212
Jackson, WY 83001 *Fax:* 307-733-9729
nationalelkrefuge@fws.gov
www.fws.gov/refuge/national_elk_refuge
More than 7,500 elk make the winter range of National Elk Refuge their home from October until May. Adjacent to the north side of Jackson, Wyoming, the 25,000-acre refuge includes nearly 1600 acres of open water and marsh lands, 47different mammals and nearly 175 species of birds.
Mike Hedrick, Manager

3542 Seedskadee National Wildlife Refuge
37 miles north on Hwy 372 307-875-2187
PO Box 700 *Fax:* 307-875-4425
Green River, WY 82935 Seedskadee@fws.gov
www.fws.gov/refuge/seedskadee/
Fishery resource is managed cooperatively with the state G&F and includes a special regulations area to promote catch and release fishing for trophy trout (brown, Snake River cutthroat and rainbow trout). Refuge lands are rich inhistorical and cultural resources as the area was utilized by nomadic Indian tribes, fur trappers, early pioneers and travelers heading for the better life of

California and Oregon. Many of the old campsites, river crossings and early structuresstill exist.

3543 Shoshone National Forest
808 Meadow Lane 307-527-6241
Cody, WY 82414 *Fax:* 307-578-1212
www.fs.usda.gov/shoshone

The Shoshone consists of 2.4 million acres of varied terrain ranging from sagebrush flats to rugged mountain peaks and includes portions of the Absaroka, Wind River, and Beartooth Mountain Ranges. Elevations on the Shoshone range from4,600 feet at the mouth of the spectacular Clarks Fork Canyon to 13,804 feet on ganneett Peak, Wyoming's highest point. Geologists delightedly call the Shoshone's varied topography an open book.

Joe Alexander, Forest Supervisor

3544 Yellowstone National Park
PO Box 168 307-344-7381
Yellowstone National Park, WY 82190-0168 *Fax:* 307-344-2014
yell_visitor_services@nps.gov
www.nps.gov

Established on March 1, 1872, Yellowstone National Park is the first and oldest national park in the world. Preserved within Yellowstone are Old Faithful Geyser and some 10,000 hot springs and geysers, the majority of the plant'stotal. These geothermal wonders are evidence of one of the world's largest active volcanoes; its last eruption created a crater or caldera that spans almost half of the park.

Suzanne Lewis, Superintendent

Publications

Directories & Handbooks: Air & Climate

3545 **Acid Rain**
Watts, Franklin
1201 Constitution Avenue
Washington, DC 20004
202-343-9790
800-621-1115
Fax: 203-797-3657
www.epa.gov/acidrain

Lists over 4,000 citations, with abstracts, to the worldwide literature on the sources of acid rain and its effects on the environment.

3546 **Weather America**
Grey House Publishing
4919 Route 22
P.O. Box 56
Amenia, NY 12501
518-789-8700
800-562-2139
Fax: 518-789-0556
books@greyhouse.com
www.greyhouse.com

Provides extensive climatological data for over 2,000 national and cooperative weather stations throughout the US. Includes a new major storms section and a nationwide ranking section that provides rankings for maximum and minimumtemperatures, precipitation, snowfall, fog, humidity and wind speed. Each of 50 state sections contains a city index for locating the nearest weather station to the city/county being researched and a narrative description of the state's climaticconditions.
Publication Date: 2011 1,858 pages
ISBN: 1-592375-98-1
Leslie Mackenzie, Publisher
David Garoogian, Editor

Directories & Handbooks: Business

3547 **Associations Canada**
Grey House Publishing Canada
411 Queen Street West
3rd Floor
Toronto, Ontario M5V-2A5
416-644-6479
866-433-4739
Fax: 416-644-1904
info@greyhouse.ca
www.greyhouse.ca

Annual directory of Canadian associations and environmental groups including industry, commerical and professional organizations.
Publication Date: 2019 2,200 pages
ISBN: 1-642652-29-1
Bryon Moore, General Manager
Stuart Paterson, Managing Editor

3548 **Business and the Environment: A Resource Guide**
Island Press
2000 M Street NW
Suite 650
Washington, DC 20036
202-232-7933
800-828-1302
Fax: 202-234-1328
info@islandpress.org
www.islandpress.org

Includes more than 1,000 references to material from scholarly journals, government agencies, case clearing-houses, research organizations, trade magazines and the popular press. It was the most current (1992) listing of research onself-monitoring and compliance programs and environmental performance strategies for corporate competitiveness.
Publication Date: 1992 382 pages
ISBN: 1-559631-59-7
Katie Dolan, Chair
Pamela Murphy, Vice Chair

3549 **California Certified Organic Farmers: Membership Directory**
2155 Delaware Ave.
Suite 150
Santa Cruz, CA 95060
831-423-2263
Fax: 831-423-4528
ccof@ccof.org
www.ccof.org

Annual
Phil LaRocca, Chair
Malcolm Ricci, Vice Chair

3550 **Directory of Environmental Information Sources**
Government Institutes
4 Research Place
Suite 200A
Rockville, MD 20850
301-907-1000
Fax: 301-921-2362

Over 1,400 federal and state government agencies, professional and scientific organizations and trade associations are profiled.
322 pages

3551 **Directory of New York City Environmental Organizations**
Council on the Environment of New York City
100 Gold Street
Room 3035
New York, NY 10038
212-788-7900
Fax: 212-788-7913
conyc@cenyc.org
www.cenyc.org

Promotes environmental awareness and solutions to environmental problems.
Marcel Van Ooyen, Executive Director
Julie A. Walsh, Assistant Director

3552 **Directory of Professional Services**
Professional Services Institute
7918 Jones Branch Drive
Suite 300
McLean, VA 22102
703-556-7172
800-424-2869
Fax: 703-506-3266
www.resolve.org/resources

RESOLVE is dedicated to improving the lives of women and men living with the disease of infertility

3553 **Directory of Socially Responsible Investments**
Funding Exchange
4200 Connecticut Ave. NW
Suite 500
Washington, DC 20008
202-274-5000
Fax: 212-982-9272
alumni@udc.edu
www.udc.edu

Network of 15 community foundations around the country with a national office in New York City. Staff at the national office are responsible for three main program areas: grantmaking, donor programs and member fund services.

3554 **EPA Information Resources Directory**
National Technical Information Service
5301 Shawnee Road
Alexandria, VA 2231
703-605-6000
800-533-6847
helpdesk@ntis.gov
www.ntis.gov

Supports the nation's economic growth and job creation by providing access to information that stimulates innovation and discovery. NTIS accomplishes this mission through two major programs: information collection and dissemination tothe public and production and other services to federal agencies.

3555 **EnviroSafety Directory**
IEI Publishing Division
1635 W Alabama St
Houston, TX 77006
713-529-1616
800-654-1480
Fax: 281-529-0936

Approximately 6,000 environmental services, state agencies and EPA/Superfund sites within the EPA regions 4, 6 and 9.
Kelli Lauletta, Editor
Janis Johnson, Managing Editor

3556 **Environment: Books by Small Presses of the General Society of Mechanics & Tradesmen**
Small Press Center

P.O. Box 422460 212-764-7021
Palm Coast, FL 32142 Fax: 212-840-2046
smallpress@aol.com
www.pw.org/small_presses

Publication Date: 1992 250 pages
ISBN: 0-962276-93-6
Paula Matta, Author
Elliot Figman, Executive Director
Melissa Ford Gradel, Managing Director

3557 Environmental Address Book: The Environment's Greatest Champions and Worst Offenders
Perigee Books
200 Madison Avenue 212-951-8400
New York, NY 10016 www.penguin.com

3558 Fibre Market News: Paper Recycling Markets Directory
Recycling Media Group GIE Publishers
4012 Bridge Avenue 216-961-4130
Cleveland, OH 44113 800-456-0707
Fax: 216-961-0364

A list of over 2,000 dealers, brokers, packers and graders of paper stock in the US and Canada.
Dan Sandoval, Internet/Senior Editor
Jim Keefe, Group Publisher

3559 Greenpeace Guide to Anti-Environmental Organizations
Odonian Press
PO Box 776 510-486-0313
Berkeley, CA 94701 800-326-0959
Fax: 415-512-8699

Corporations, foundations and public relations firms determined to be anti-environmental despite their attempts to project the green image.
Publication Date: 1993 112 pages
ISBN: 1-878825-05-3
Carl Deal, Author

3560 Guide to Curriculum Planning in Environmental Education
125 S Webster Street 608-266-2188
PO Box 7841 800-441-4563
Madison, WI 53707-7841 Fax: 608-267-9110
sandi.mcnamer@dpi.state.wi.us
www.pubsales.dpi.wi.gov

Provides a direction in planning a comprehensive environmental education program based on perceptual awareness knowledge, environmental ethics, citizen action skills and citizen action experience.
Publication Date: 1994 167 pages Book
Sandi McNamer, Publications Director

3561 Harbinger File
Harbinger Communications, Inc
5 N Union Street 847-622-0905
Elgin, IL 60123 800-320-7206
Fax: 847-622-0830
www.harbingeronline.com

3562 National Environmental Data Referral Service
US National Environmental Data Referral Service
1825 Connecticut Avenue NW 202-606-4089
Washington, DC 20235

More than 22,200 data resources that have available data on climatology and meteorology, ecology and pollution, geography, geophysics and geology, hydrology and limnology, oceanography and transmissions from remote sensing satellites.

3563 National Environmental Organizations
US Environmental Directories
1201 New York Avenue
PO Box 65156
St Paul, MN 20005

3564 New Jersey Environmental Directory
Youth Environmental Society
PO Box 441 609-655-8030
Cranbury, NJ 00851 www.nj.gov/dep

Environmental education and leadership programs for high school students in New Jersey.

3565 Opportunities in Environmental Careers
VGM Career Books
601 N. Mechanic Street 847-679-5500
Suite 306 800-323-4900
Franklin, VA 23851 Fax: 847-679-2494
www.environmentalcareer.com/

Odom Fanning, Author

3566 State Environmental Agencies on the Internet
Government Institutes
16855 Northchase Drive 281-877-5800
Suite 200A Fax: 301-921-2362
Houston , TX 77060 www.govinst.com

Provides a concise profile of each state agency's requirements and resources-including hard-to-find online laws, rules, and regulations-in one quick-reference guide.

3567 Water Environment & Technology Buyer's Guide and Yearbook
Water Environment Federation
601 Wythe Street 800-666-0206
Alexandria, VA 22314 Fax: 703-684-2492
inquiry@wef.org
www.wef.org

Founded in 1928, the Water Environment Federation (WEF) is a not for profit technical and educational organization with members from varied disciplines who work toward the WEF vision of preservation and enhancement of the global waterenvironment. The WEF network includes water quality professionals from 76 Member Associations in 30 countries.
Ed Mc Comick, President
Paul Bowen, President-Elect

3568 World Directory of Environmental Organizations Online
California Institute of Public Affairs
PO Box 189040 916-442-2472
Sacramento, CA 95818 www.interenvironment.org

A guide to governmental and nongovernmental organizations and programs concerned with protecting the earth's resources. It also covers national and international organizations throughout the world. Only available online.

Directories & Handbooks: Design & Architecture

3569 Directory of International Periodicals and Newsletters on Built Environments
Van Nostrand Reinhold

More than 1,400 international periodicals and newsletters that cover architectural design and the building industry and the aspects of the environment that deal with the industry are covered.
Publication Date: 1992 175 pages
ISBN: 0-442230-03-6
Frances C Gretes, Author

Directories & Handbooks: Disaster Peparedness & Response

3570 Association of State Floodplain Managers
Association of State Floodplain Managers

575 D'Onofrio Drive 608-828-3000
Suite 200 *Fax:* 608-828-6319
Madison, WI 53719 asfpm@floods.org
www.floods.org

A complete name/address/phone listing for all key floodplain managers in the nation, comprehensive summary of ASFPM's activities of past year and planned future directions, key federal agency programs, much more. Free to currentmembers.

Ceil Strauss, Chair
Marica CoxLamm, Vice Chair

3571 El Environmental Services Directory Online
Environmental Information Limited
8525 Arjons Drive 858-695-0050
Suite H *Fax:* 952-831-6550
San Diego, CA 92126 www.envirobiz.com

The most comprehensive, largest directory of environmental services in the United States. Coverage includes asbestos & lead abatement, consulting, laboratories, transportation, industrial cleaning, municipal solid waste facilities,hazardous waste facilities, indsutrial waste facilities, well drilling, soil boring, drum reconditioning, spill response, and remediation services.

Cary Perket

3572 Floodplain Management: State & Local Programs
Association of State Floodplain Managers
575 D'Onofrio Drive 608-828-3000
Suite 200 *Fax:* 608-828-6319
Madison, WI 53719 asfpm@floods.org
www.floods.org

The most comprehensive source assembled to date, this report summarizes and analyzes various state and local programs and activities.

Publication Date: 2005
Ceil Strauss, Chair
Marica CoxLamm, Vice Chair

3573 Hazardous Materials Regulations Guide
JJ Keller
3003 West Breezewood Lane 877-564-2333
P.O. Box 368 *Fax:* 800-727-7516
Neenah, WI 54957 www.jjkeller.com

A complete reference guide of hazardous materials regulations.

May/November
ISBN: 0-934674-94-9
Tom Ziebell, Editor
Robert L. Keller, Publisher

3574 Institute of Chemical Waste Management Directory of Hazardous Waste Treatment
National Solid Wastes Management Assn.
4301 Connecticut Ave. 202-244-4700
Suite 1000 800-424-2869
Washington, DC 20008 *Fax:* 202-966-4824
www.nswma.org

3575 Pesticide Directory: A Guide to Producers and Products, Regulators, and Researchers
Thomson Publications
Box 9335 559-266-2964
Fresno, CA 93791 *Fax:* 559-266-0189
www.agbook.com

This directory is for the person who needs to know anything about the US pesticide industry. It includes basic manufacturers and formulators along with their products, key personnel, managers, district/regional offices and otherpertinent information. Other sections include Universities, State Extension Centers, USDA, EPA, National Organizations, US Forest Service, Poison Control Centers and much more.

Publication Date: 1987 153 pages Biannual
ISBN: 0-913702-45-5
WT Thomson, Author
Susan Heflin, President/Owner

3576 SEEK
520 Lafayette Rd N. 651-757-2700
St. Paul, MN 55155 800-657-3864

Minnesotas's interactive directory of environmetal education resources.

3577 The Grey House Guide to Homeland Security Resources
Grey House Publishing
4919 Route 22 518-789-8700
P.O. Box 56 800-562-2139
Amenia, NY 12510 *Fax:* 518-789-0556
books@greyhouse.com
www.greyhouse.com

A comprehensive, annual resource for national, state and local officials responsible for homeland security along with manufacturers of homeland security products and services.

Publication Date: 2018 1,208 pages
Leslie Mackenzie, Publisher
Laura Mars, Editorial Director

3578 Tracking Toxic Wastes in CA: A Guide to Federal and State Government Information Sources
INFORM
120 Wall Street 212-361-2400
14th Floor *Fax:* 212-361-2412
New York, NY 10005 www.dtsc.ca.gov/HazardousWaste/

Directories & Handbooks: Energy & Transportation

3579 Alternative Energy Network Online
Environmental Information Networks
119 South Fairfax Street 703-683-0774
Alexandria, VA 22314 *Fax:* 703-683-3893

Reports on news of all energy sources designed as alternatives to conventional fossil fuels, including wind, solar and alcohol fuels.

3580 Current Alternative Energy Research and Development in Illinois
Department of Energy & Natural Resources
325 W Adams 217-785-2800
Room 300 800-252-8955
Springfield, IL 62704 *Fax:* 217-785-2618

3581 Department of Energy Annual Procurement and Financial Assistance Report
US Department of Energy
Mail Stop 142 800-342-5303
Washington, DC 20585 *Fax:* 202-586-4403

Offers a list of universities, research centers and laboratories that represent the Department of Energy.

3582 Directory of Solar-Terrestrial Physics Monitoring Stations
Air Force Geophysics Laboratory
Department of Defense 781-377-3977
Hanscom Air Force Base, MA 00173 *Fax:* 781-377-4498

3583 Energy Science and Technology
US Department of Energy
1 Science Gov Way 865-576-1188
Oak Ridge, TN 37831 *Fax:* 865-576-2865
ISTIWebmaster@osti.gov
www.osti.gov

To collect, preserve, disseminate, and leverage the scientific and technical information (STI) resources of the Department of Energy to provide access to national and global STI for use by DOE, the scientific research community,academia, US industry, and the public to expand the knowledge base of science and technology.

3584 Energy Statistics Spreadsheets
Institute of Gas Technology
3424 S State St 312-842-4100
Chicago, IL 60616 *Fax:* 773-567-5209

The coverage of this database encompasses worldwide energy industry statistics, including production, consumption, reserves, imports and prices.

3585 **Women's Council on Energy and the Environment Membership Directory**
816 Connecticut Ave NW 202-997-4512
Suite 200 *Fax:* 202-478-2098
Washington, DC 20006 info@wcee.org
www.wcee.org
Offers valuable information on over 800 members representing consulting firms, private industry and the environmental community.
Publication Date: 1980
Robin Cantor, President
Mary Brosnan-Sell, Vice President

Directories & Handbooks: Environmental Engineering

3586 **Association of Conservation Engineers: Membership Directory**
Engineering Section Alabama Dept. of Conservation
573-522-2323
Fax: 573-522-2324
www.conservationengineers.org/

3587 **Energy Engineering: Directory of Software for Energy Managers and Engineers**
Fairmont Press
700 Indian Trail 770-925-9388
Liburn, GA 30047 *Fax:* 770-381-9865
linda@fairmontpress.com
www.fairmontpress.com
Directory of services and supplies to the industry.
Publication Date: 1904 80 pages Bimonthly
ISSN: 0199-8895
Wayne C Turner, Author
Wayne C Turner, Editor

3588 **IAEE Membership Directory**
International Association for Energy Economics
28790 Chagrin Boulevard 216-464-5365
Suite 350 *Fax:* 216-464-2737
Cleveland, OH 44122 iaee@iaee.org
www.iaee.org
Lists members contact information and affiliation and general association information. Also available online.
Annual
David L. Williams, Executive Director

3589 **NEPA Lessons Learned**
Office of NEPA Policy & Compliance
1000 Independence Avenue SW 202-586-4600
EH-42 800-472-2756
Washington, DC 20585 *Fax:* 202-586-7031
denise.freeman@eh.doe.gov
www.eh.doe.gov/nepa
Publication Date: 1994 Quarterly
Carol M Borgstrom, Director

3590 **Pollution Abstracts**
Cambridge Scientific Abstracts
7200 Wisconsin Avenue 301-961-6700
Suite 601 800-843-7751
Bethesda, MD 20814 *Fax:* 301-961-6720
sales@csa.com
www.csa.com
This database provides fast access to the environmental information necessary to resolve day to day problems, ensure ongoing compliance, and handle emergency situations more effectively.
James P McGinty, President
Ted Caris, Publisher

Directories & Handbooks: Environmental Health

3591 **Ecosystem Change and Public Health: A Global Perspective**
Johns Hopkins University Press
2715 N Charles Street 410-516-6900
Baltimore, MD 21218 800-537-5487
Fax: 410-516-6968
www.press.jhu.edu/books
The strength of the John Hopkins University Press' publications in medicine is in part a reflection of the university and medical institution's excellence and long term tradition of exceptional research and clinical care. Joan Aron'sEcosystem Change and Public Health is the first textbook devoted to this emerging field. The book covers such topics as global climate change, stratospheric ozone depletion, water resources management, ecology and infectious disease. Paperback
Publication Date: 2001 526 pages
ISBN: 0-801865-82-4
Joan Aron, Author
Joan Aron, Editor
Jonathan Pratz, Editor

3592 **Environmental Encyclopedia**
Thomson Gale
27500 Drake Road 248-699-4253
Farmington Hills, MI 48331 877-363-4253
Fax: 800-414-5043
www.cengage.com
Consisting of nearly 1,300 signed articles and term definitions. The encyclopedia provides in-depth, worldwide coverage of environmental issues. Each article written in a nontechnical style and provides current status, analysis andsuggests solutions whenever possible.
Publication Date: 2002 2000 pages
ISBN: 0-787654-86-8
Virginia Regish, Contact

3593 **Environmental Guidebook: A Selective Guide to Environmental Organizations and Related Entities**
Environmental Frontlines
PO Box 43 650-323-8452
Menlo Park, CA 94026 info@envirofront.org
www.envirofront.org
Designed to serve as an essential reference book profiling nearly 500 national organizations and other entities actively engaged in environmental issues in the US and beyond.
312 pages
ISBN: 0-972068-50-3
Jeff Staudinger, Author

3594 **Environmental Key Contacts and Information Sources**
Government Institutes
16855 Northchase Drive 281-877-5800
Suite 200A *Fax:* 301-921-2362
Houston, TX 77060 www.govinst.com
An updated and revised compilation of Government Institutes' two previous directories, this reference contains more than 400 pages of contact information for more than 2,700 federal, state, and local environmental agencies andorganizations. This directory also includes contacts for information concerning environmental protection, hazardous waste materials, clean water and air, environmental assessment and management, pesticides, pollution control, recycling, naturalresources and conservation.
Publication Date: 1998 424 pages
ISBN: 0-865876-39-8
Charlene Ikonomou and Diane Pacchione, Author

3595 **Pesticide Directory: A Guide to Producers and Products, Regulators, and Researchers**
Thomson Publications

Box 9335 559-266-2964
Fresno, CA 93791 *Fax:* 559-266-0189
This directory is for the person who needs to know anything about the US pesticide industry. It includes basic manufacturers and formulators along with their products, key personnel, managers, district/regional offices and otherpertinent information. Other sections include Universities, State Extension Centers, USDA, EPA, National Organizations, US Forest Service, Poison Control Centers and much more.
Publication Date: 1987 153 pages Biannual
ISBN: 0-913702-45-5
WT Thomson, Author
Susan Heflin, President/Owner

3596 The Environmental Debate
Grey House Publishing
4919 Route 22 518-789-8700
P.O. Box 56 800-562-2139
Amenia, NY 12501 *Fax:* 518-789-0556
books@greyhouse.com
www.greyhouse.com

A collection of primary documents examining the evolution of concern about environmental degradation, pollution, climate change, and resource conservation in America, from the Colonial period to the present day, and looking forwardtowards the future.
Publication Date: 2017 387 pages
ISBN: 1-682175-50-7
Leslie Mackenzie, Publisher
Laura Mars, Editorial Director

Directories & Handbooks: Habitat Preservation & Land Use

3597 Alliance for Wildlife Rehabilitation and Education Wildlife Care Directory
1441 Broadway 646-569-5860
5th Floor info@wildlifealliance.org
New York, NY 10018 www.wildlifealliance.org/

3598 Argia
editor@dragonflysocietyamericas.org
www.dragonflysocietyamericas.org

News journal of the Dragonfly Society of the Americas.
Quarterly
Celeste A. Searles Mazzacano, Editor-in-Chief

3599 Biodiversity Action Network
1630 Connecticut Avenue 202-547-8902
3rd Floor *Fax:* 202-265-0222
Washington, DC 20009
An information exchange network launched by the Center for International Environmental Law.

3600 Bulletin of American Odonatology (BAO)
editorBAO@dragonflysocietyamericas.org
www.dragonflysocietyamericas.org

Journal of the Dragonfly Society of the Americas featuring peer-reviewed articles.
Occasional
Steve Hummel, Editor

3601 County Conservation Board Outdoor Adventure Guide
Iowa Association of County Conservation Boards
405 SW 3rd Street 515-963-9582
Suite 1 *Fax:* 515-963-9582
Ankeny, IA 50021 www.dickinsoncountyconservationboard.com/
Includes a map of each county with the area to be shaded in or a pinpoint of the location, and has information on cabin rentals, camping, shelters, playgrounds, swimming, fishing, boating, boat rental, sports and fields, hunting,nature centers, praires, historic sites, wildlife exhibits and more.
184 pages
Don Brazelton, Contact

3602 DOCKET
US Environmental Protection Agency
US EPA Region 3 215-814-2993
1650 Arch Street (3PM52) *Fax:* 215-814-5102
Philadelphia, PA 19103 www.epa.gov
This database offers the complete text of summaries of all justice cases filed by the US Department of Justice on behalf of the US Environmental Protection Agency.
Gina McCarthy, Administrator
Stan Meiburg, Deputy Administrator

3603 Directory of Resource Recovery Projects and Services
Institute of Resource Recovery
1730 Rhode Island Avenue NW 202-659-4613
Suite 1000 *Fax:* 202-775-5917
Washington, DC 20036

3604 Ducks Unlimited Magazine
Ducks Unlimited
One Waterfowl Way 901-758-3825
Memphis, TN 38120 800-453-8257
www.ducks.org
DU's mission is to fulfill the annual life cycle needs of North American waterfowl by protecting, enhancing, restoring and managing important wetlands and associated uplands.
Rogers Hoyt, Jr., President
Dale Hall, CEO

3605 Ecology Abstracts
Cambridge Scientific Abstracts
7200 Wisconsin Avenue 301-961-6700
Suite 601 800-843-7751
Bethesda, MD 20814 *Fax:* 301-961-6720
sales@csa.com
www.csa.com
This large database updated continuously, offers over 150,000 citations, with abstracts, to the worldwide literature available on ecology and the environment.
James P McGinty, President
Theodore Caris, Publisher

3606 Environmental Bibliography
International Academy at Santa Barbara
5385 Hollister Avenue 805-683-8889
#210 *Fax:* 805-965-6071
Santa Barbara, CA 93111 info@iasb.org
www.ifrs.org
Over 615,000 citations are offered in this database, aimed at scientific, technical and popular periodical literature dealing with the environment.
ISSN: 1053-1440

3607 Environmental Concerns: Directory of the Environmental Industry in Colorado
Business Research Division-Univ. of Colorado
995 Regent Drive 303-492-8397
419 UCB *Fax:* 303-492-3620
Boulder, CO 80309-0419 leeds.colorado.edu/brd
Approximately 1,300 private businesses, government organizations and corporations in Colorado that contribute to environmental protection and rehabilitation.
ISBN: 1-883226-02-3
Gin Hayden, Editor
Sean Shepherd, Editor

3608 Environmental Guide to the Internet
Government Institutes
16855 Northchase Drive 281-877-5800
Suite 200A *Fax:* 301-921-2362
Houston , TX 77060 www.govinst.com
Provides information for the best sites in the internet dealing with the preservation and protection of the environment, ecology, and conservation and offers over 320 new listings and addresses. Writin for environmental consultants,industry professionals, researchers, lawyers, educators, and students, contains the top

1,200 environmental internet resources, including, newletters and journals, and world wide web sites
Publication Date: 1997 384 pages
ISBN: 0-865875-78-2
Carol Briggs-Erickson and Toni Murphy, Author

3609 Environmental Guidebook: A Selective Guide to Environmental Organizations and Related Entities
Environmental Frontlines
PO Box 43 650-323-8452
Menlo Park, CA 94026 www.envirofront.org
Designed to serve as an essential reference book profiling nearly 500 national organizations and other entities actively engaged in environmental issues in the US and beyond.
312 pages
ISBN: 0-972068-50-3
Jeff Staudinger, Author

3610 Helping Out in the Outdoors: A Directory of Volunteer Opportunities on Public Lands
American Hiking Society
1424 Fenwick Lane 301-565-6704
Silver Spring, MD 20910 *Fax:* 301-565-6714
info@americanhiking.org
www.americanhiking.org
Mary Margaret Sloan, President

3611 Hospitality Directory
Human Ecology Action League (HEAL)
PO Box 29629 404-248-1898
Atlanta, GA 30359 *Fax:* 404-248-0162
HEALNatnl@aol.com
Nonprofit organization founded in 1977 to serve those whose health has been adversely affected by environment exposures; to provide information to those who are concerned about the health effects of chemicals; and to alert the generalpublic about the potential dangers of chemicals.
Katherine P Collier, Contact

3612 Human Ecology Action League Directory
Human Ecology Action League
PO Box 29629 404-248-1898
Atlanta, GA 30359 *Fax:* 404-248-0162
HEALNatnl@aol.com
The Human Ecology Action League Inc (HEAL) is a nonprofit organization founded in 1977 to serve those whose health has been affected by environmental exposures; to provide information to those who are concerned about the health effectsof chemicals; and to alert the general public about the potential dangers of chemicals. Referrals to local HEAL chapters and other support groups are available from the League.
Katherine P Collier, Contact

3613 International Society of Tropical Foresters: Membership Directory
5400 Grosvenor Lane 301-897-8720
Bethesda, MD 20814 *Fax:* 301-897-3690
www.istf-bethesda.org/
The International Society of Tropical Foresters, Inc. (ISTF) is a nonprofit organization committed to the protection, wise management and rational use of the world's tropical forests. Established in 1950, ISTF was reactivated in 1979.It has about 1500 members in more than 100 countries. Financial support comes from membership dues, donations and grants. ISTF sponsors meetings, promotes chapters in other countries, maintains a web site and has chapters at universities.
Warren T Doolittle, President

3614 Journal of Wildlife Rehabilitation
International Wildlife Rehabilitation Council
PO Box 3197 866-871-1869
Eugene, OR 97403 *Fax:* 408-876-6153
info@theiwrc.org
theiwrc.org
A peer reviewed scientific journal that has served as a primary reference for wildlife rehabilitators and others involved in the care and conservation of wildlife. Features articles, columns and reviews, with topics ranging from allaspects of wildlife care to administration, fundraising, education programs, case studies, environmental issues, legalities, ethics and more. And is also a benefit of membership to IWRC.
Publication Date: 1978 Quarterly
Adam Grogan, President
Amanda Kamps, Vice President

3615 LEXIS Environmental Law Library
Lexis Nexis Group
PO Box 933 937-865-6800
Dayton, OH 45401 800-227-9597
Fax: 937-865-6909
www.lexis-nexis.com
This database contains decisions related to environmental law from the Supreme Court and other legislative bodies.

3616 Managed Area Basic Record
The Nature Conservancy
4245 N. Fairfax Drive 703-841-5300
Suite 100 *Fax:* 804-979-0370
Arlington, VA 22203-1606 cmullen@tnc.org
www.nature.org

3617 Morrison Environmental Directory
PO Box 2312 316-262-0100
Wichita, KS 67201
ISSN: 1060-488

3618 Natural Areas Journal
Natural Areas Association
PO Box 594 724-995-8466
Ligonier, PA 15658 info@naturalareas.org
naturalareas.org
Official peer-reviewed publication of the Natural Areas Association with content relating to natural area management and preservation.
Lisa Smith, Executive Director
Amy Willis, Operations Manager

3619 New York State Department of Environmental Conservation Personnel Directory: Internet Only
NYS Department of Environmental Conservation
625 Broadway 518-402-8013
Albany, NY 12233 *Fax:* 518-402-9036
dinnelson@gw.dec.state.ny.us
www.dec.ny.gov
Internet only, this directory includes DEC's executive management and division directors. Executive managers are appointed by the Governor to carry out the policies of the state. Division directors have direct management responsibilityfor the department's programs.
Mary A Kadlecek, Chief Internet Publications

3620 Nonprofit Sample and Core Repositories Open to the Public in the United States
Branch of Sedimentary Processes
MS 939 Federal Center 303-236-5760
Denver, CO 80225 *Fax:* 303-236-0459
Walter E Dean, Contact

3621 Puddler Magazine
Ducks Unlimited
One Waterfowl Way 901-758-3825
Memphis, TN 38120 800-453-8257
www.ducks.org
Kids magazine of Ducks Unlimited, whose mission is to fulfill the annual life cycle needs of North American waterfowl by protecting, enhancing, restoring and managing important wetlands and associated uplands.
Rogers Hoyt, Jr., President
Dale Hall, CEO

3622 Range and Land Management Handbook
Wyoming Association of Conservation Districts

517 E 19th Street 307-632-5716
Cheyenne, WY 82001 *Fax:* 307-638-4099
www.conservewy.com

This publication is intended for people from all walks of life who want to gain an appreciation of rangelands. This publication is also an introduction to the various fields of range management.
Annual

3623 Takings Litigation Handbook: Defending Takings Challenges to Land Use Regulations
American Legal Publishing Corporation
One West Fourth Street 800-445-5588
Ste. 300 *Fax:* 513-763-3562
Cincinnati, OH 45202 customerservice@amlegal.com
www.amlegal.com

No government attorney, land use planner or other local official can effectively protect their community from harmful land use without a working knowledge of takings law. Developers and other landowners increasingly are attempting touse takings litigation, or the mere threat of takings litigation, to convince government agencies to relax or abandon vital protections for our neighborhoods and natural environment.
Publication Date: 2000 404 pages
Kendall, Dowling and Schwartz, Author
Douglas Kendall, Executive Director

3624 The Bulletin
Garden Club of America
14 East 60th Street 212-753-8287
3rd Floor *Fax:* 212-753-0134
New York, NY 10022 gca@gcamerica.org
www.gcamerica.org

Print publication of the Garden Club of America.
Publication Date: 1913 Seasonal
Anne Neal Petri, President

3625 The Hummingbird Connection
6560 State Route 179 928-284-2251
Suite 124 800-529-3699
Sedona, AZ 86351 *Fax:* 928-284-2251
info@hummingbird.org
www.hummingbirdsociety.org

Published by the Hummingbird Society.
Publication Date: 1996 Quarterly
ISSN: 1097-3427
H. Ross Hawkins, Editor

3626 Turtle Help Network
New York Turtle and Tortoise Society
PO Box 878 212-459-4803
Orange, NJ 00705 www.turtle.net/

3627 Wilson Journal of Ornithology
Biological Sciences, Univ. of Missouri-Columbia
110 Tucker Hall 254-399-9636
Columbia, MO 65211-7400 wjo@missouri.edu
wilsonsociety.org

Scholarly journal consisting of articles on bird studies, orinthological news, reviews of new bird books and related subjects.
Quarterly
Mark Deutschlander, President
John Faaborg, Editor

3628 Wisconsin Department of Public Instruction
125 S Webster Street 800-441-4563
PO Box 7841 *Fax:* 608-267-9110
Madison, WI 53707-7841 sandi.mcnamer@dpi.state.wi.us
www.pubsales.dpi.wi.gov

State education department publisher of K-12 curriculum planning guides in 25 subject areas including environmental education and science.
Sandi McNamer, Publications Director

Directories & Handbooks: Recycling & Pollution Prevention

3629 American Recycling Market Directory: Reference Manual
Recycling Data Management Corp.
PO Box 577 315-471-0707
Ogdensburg, NY 13669 800-267-0707
Fax: 613-471-3258

Comprehensive directory/reference manual to materials recycling markets. Helps individuals locate buyers and sellers of recyclable materials on a regional basis throughout North America. Contains 20,000 cross-referenced company andagency listings. Sections include: scrap metals, waste paper, paper mills, auto dismantlers, demolition, glass, oil, rubber and textiles recyclers, recycling centers, MRF's composting, equipment and consulting services, industry references UBC specsand more.

3630 Analysis of the Stockholm Convention on Persistent Organic Pollutants
Oceana Publications, Inc
198 Madison Ave 800-334-4249
New York, NY 10016 *Fax:* 212-726-6476
oxfordonline@oup.com
www.oceanalaw.com

This book analyzes the Stockholm Convention on Persistent Organic Pollutants. Prepared under the auspices of the UN Environment Programme Chemical Division.
Publication Date: 2003 200 pages One Time
ISBN: 0-379215-06-3
Mario Antonio Olsen, Author

3631 Criteria Pollutant Point Source Directory
North American Water Office
3394 Lake Elmo Ave 651-770-3861
Lake Elmo, MN 55042 *Fax:* 651-770-3976
gwillc@mtn.org
www.nawo.org

3632 Directory of Municipal Solid Waste Management Facilities
The Institute of Solid Waste Disposal
1730 Rhode Island Avenue NW 202-659-4613
Suite 1000 *Fax:* 202-296-7915
Washington, DC 20036

3633 EI Environmental Services Directory
Environmental Information Networks
8525 Arjons Drive 858-695-0050
Suite H *Fax:* 952-831-6550
San Diego, CA 92126 www.envirobiz.com

Waste-handling facilities, transportation and spill response firms, laboratories and the broad scope of environmental services. Online versions are also available.
ISSN: 1053-475N
Cary Perket

3634 Environmental Encyclopedia
Thomson Gale
27500 Drake Road 248-699-4253
Farmington Hills, MI 48331 800-877-4253
Fax: 800-414-5043
www.galegroup.com

Consisting of nearly 1,300 signed articles and definitions. The encyclopedia provides in depth, worldwide coverage of environmental issues. Each article written in a non technical style and provides current status, analysis andsuggests solutions whenever possible.
Publication Date: 2002 2000 pages
ISBN: 0-787654-86-8
Virginia Regish, Contact

3635 Environmental Guide to the Internet
Government Institutes

16855 Northchase Drive 281-877-5800
Suite 200A *Fax:* 301-921-2362
Houston , TX 77060 www.govinst.com

Provides information for the best sites on the internet dealing with the preservation and protection of the environment, ecology, and conservation and offers over 320 new listings and addresses. Writin for environmental consultants,industry professionals, researchers, lawyers, educators, and students, contains the top 1,200 environmental internet resources, including, newletters and journals, and world wide web sites

Publication Date: 1997 384 pages
ISBN: 0-865875-78-2
Carol Briggs-Erickson and Toni Murphy, Author

3636 Environmental Guidebook: A Selective Guide to Environmental Organizations and Related Entities

Environmental Frontlines
PO Box 43 650-323-8452
Menlo Park, CA 94026 www.envirofront.org

Designed to serve as an essential reference book profiling nearly 500 national organizations and other entities actively engaged in environmental issues in the US and beyond.

312 pages
ISBN: 0-972068-50-3
Jeff Staudinger, Author

3637 Fibre Market News: Paper Recycling Markets Directory

Recycling Media Group GIE Publishers
4012 Bridge Avenue 216-961-4130
Cleveland, OH 44113 800-456-0707
Fax: 216-961-0364

A list of over 2,000 dealers, brokers, packers and graders of paper stock in the US and Canada.

Dan Sandoval, Editor

3638 Hazardous Materials Regulations Guide

JJ Keller
3003 West Breezewood Lane 877-564-2333
P.O. Box 368 *Fax:* 800-727-7516
Neenah, WI 54957 www.jjkeller.com

A complete reference guide of hazardous materials regulations.

May/November
ISBN: 0-934674-94-9
Tom Ziebell, Editor
Robert L. Keller, Publisher

3639 How-To: 1,400 Best Books on Doing Almost Everything

R.R. Bowker Company
630 Central Ave. 908-286-1090
New Providence, NJ 00797 888-269-5372
www.bowker.com

3640 Institute of Chemical Waste Management Directory of Hazardous Waste Treatment and Disposal

National Solid Wastes Management Assn.
4301 Connecticut Avenue NW 202-244-4700
Suite 300 *Fax:* 202-966-4824
Washington, DC 20008

3641 International Handbook of Pollution Control

Greenwood Publishing Group
P.O. Box 1911 203-226-3571
Santa Barbara, CA 93116-1911 webmaster@greenwood.com
www.abc-clio.com

Publication Date: 1989 482 pages
ISBN: 0-313240-17-5
Edward J Kormondy, Author

3642 List of Water Pollution Control Administrators

Assn. of State and Interstate Water Pollution Con.
1221 Connecticut Ave. NW 202-898-0905
2nd Floor *Fax:* 202-898-0929
Washington, DC 20036 www.asiwpca.org

Roberta Savage, Executive Director
Linda Eichmiller, Deputy Director

3643 Nebraska Recycling Resource Directory

Nebraska Dept of Environmental Quality
1200 N Street Suite 400 402-471-2186
PO Box 98922 877-253-2603
Lincoln, NE 68509 *Fax:* 402-471-2909
www.deq.state.ne.us

Publication Date: 1986 139 pages Bi-Annually
Steve Danahy, Unit Supervisor

3644 Pesticide Directory: A Guide to Producers and Products, Regulators, and Researchers

Thomson Publications
Box 9335 559-266-2964
Fresno, CA 93791 *Fax:* 559-266-0189

This directory is for the person who needs to know anything about the US pesticide industry. It includes basic manufacturers and formulators along with their products, key personnel, managers, district/regional offices and otherpertinent information. Other sections include Universities, State Extension Centers, USDA, EPA, National Organizations, US Forest Service, Poison Control Centers and much more.

Publication Date: 1987 153 pages Biannual
ISBN: 0-913702-45-5
WT Thomson, Author
Susan Heflin, President/Owner

3645 Pollution Abstracts

Cambridge Scientific Abstracts
7200 Wisconsin Avenue 301-961-6700
Suite 601 800-843-7751
Bethesda, MD 20814 *Fax:* 301-961-6720
www.csa.com

This database provides fast access to the environmental information necessary to resolve day to day problems, ensure ongoing compliance, and handle emergency situations more effectively.

James P McGinty, President
Ted Caris, Publisher

3646 Recycling Related Newsletters, Publications And Periodicals

Continnuus
PO Box 416 303-575-5676
Denver, CO 80201 *Fax:* 970-292-2136

3647 Recycling Today: Recycling Products & Services Buyers Guide

Recycling Today GIE Publishers
5811 Canal Road 216-961-4130
#201 800-456-0707
Valley View, OH 44125 *Fax:* 216-961-0364
jkeefe@gie.net
www.recyclingtoday.com

Directory of services and supplies to the industry.

Dan Sandoval, Internet/Senior Editor
James Keefe, Group Publisher

3648 Scholastic Environmental Atlas of the United States

Scholastic
4333 Brooklyn Avenue NE 206-543-4050
Seattle, NY 98195-9570 *Fax:* 206-543-3932
hfscustserv@press.jhu.edu
www.washington.edu/uwpress/

3649 Waste Age: Resource Recovery Acitivities Update Issue

National Solid Wastes Management Assn.
1730 Rhode Island Avenue NW 202-659-4613
Suite 1000
Washington, DC 20036

3650 Waste Age: Waste Industry Buyer Guide

National Solid Wastes Management

1730 Rhode Island Avenue NW 202-659-4613
Suite 1000 800-424-2869
Washington, DC 20036 *Fax:* 202-659-0925

3651 Wastes to Resources: Appropriate Technologies for Sewage Treatment and Conversion
National Center for Appropriate Techology
3040 Continental Drive 406-494-4572
Butte, MT 59701 800-275-6228
Fax: 406-494-2905
4info@ncat.org
www.ncat.org
Kathy Hadley, Executive Director

Directories & Handbooks: Sustainable Development

3652 Solar Energy Resource Guide/SERG
NorCal Solar
PO Box 3008 530-852-0354
Berkeley, CA 94703 info@norcalsolar.org
www.norcalsolar.org
Articles and resources on solar electric, solar thermal, financial analysis, etc. Also a guidebook for education on the workings and intstallation of solar technology.
96 pages
Claudia Wentworth, President
Liz Merry, Program Manager

Directories & Handbooks: Travel & Tourism

3653 Access America: An Atlas and Guide to the National Parks for Visitors with Disabilities
Northern Cartographic
4050 Williston Road 802-860-2886
South Burlington, VT 05403 *Fax:* 802-865-4912
info@ncarto.com
Publication Date: 1988
ISBN: 0-944187-00-5

3654 Audubon Society Field Guide to the Natural Places of the Northeast
National Audubon Society
700 Broadway 212-979-3000
New York, NY 10003 *Fax:* 212-979-3188
www.audubon.org

3655 Complete Guide to America's National Parks: The Official Visitor's Guide
National Park Foundation
11 Dupont Circle NW 202-238-4200
Suite 600 800-285-2448
Washington, DC 20036 *Fax:* 202-234-3103
ask-npf@nationalparks.org

3656 Field Guide to American Windmills
University of Oklahoma Press
2800 Venture Drive 405-325-2000
Norman, OK 73069 800-627-7377
Fax: 405-364-5798
This guide to America's windmills is both a complete general history of turbine wheel mills and an identification guide to the 112 most common models, which still dot landscapes today.
Publication Date: 1985 528 pages
T Lindsay Baker, Author

3657 Guide to the National Wildlife Refuges
Macmillan Publishing Company
National Wildlife Guide 212-832-2101
590 Madison Avenue
New York, NY 10022
More than 500 National Wildlife Refuges and satellite refuges are listed.
684 pages

3658 National Parks Visitor Facilities and Services
Conference of National Park Concessioners
PO Box 29041 480-967-6006
Phoenix, AZ 85038 www.nps.gov
Within the parks, private businesses provide accommodations and services for visitors under concession contracts.
Rex G Maughan, Chairman

3659 National Parks: National Park Campgrounds Issue
National Parks Conservation Association
777 6th Street, NW 800-628-7275
Suite 700 *Fax:* 202-659-0650
Washington, DC 20001-3723 npca@npca.org
www.npca.org
To safeguard the scenic beauty, wildlife, and historical and cultural treasures of the largest and most diverse park system in the world.
W.Clark Buntimg, President
Theresa Pierno, Chief Operating Officer

3660 National Wildlife Refuges: A Visitor's Guide
Fish and Wildlife Services, Interior Department
1849 C Street NW 703-358-2043
Washington, DC 20242 webteam@ios.doi.gov
www.fws.gov
Contains a map showing national wildlife refuges that provide recrational and educational opportunities. Provides tips for visiting national wildlife refuges. Also list refuges in all 50 States, Puerto Rico and the Virgin Islans, withthe best wildlife viewing season and the features of each refuge.
ISBN: 0-160617-00-6

3661 Nature Center Directory
Wisconsin Association for Environmental Education
2100 Main Street Stevens Point 715-346-0123
University of Wisconsin-Stevens Point *Fax:* 715-346-3835
Stevens Point, WI 54481-3897 webmaster@uwsp.edu
Annual

3662 Rails-to-Trails Magazine
2121 Ward Court, NW 202-331-9696
5th Floor *Fax:* 202-223-9257
Washington, DC 20037 www.railstotrails.org/magazine
Official magazine of the Rails-to-Trails Conservancy (RTC). The RTC is a national nonprofit organization dedicated to creating a nationwide network of trails from former rail lines and connecting corridors. It does not own or manageany rail trails.
Quarterly
Keith Laughlin, President
Elizabeth Thorstensen, VP Trail Development

3663 Recreation Sites in Southwestern National Forests
USDA Forest Service
Public Affairs Office 505-842-3292
333 Broadway Blvd SE *Fax:* 505-842-3106
Albuquerque, NM 87102 www.fs.usda.gov/r3
Listings for all recreation sites for Arizona and New Mexico.
72 pages
Corbin Newman, Regional Forester

3664 Sierra Club Guide to the Natural Areas of California
Sierra Club
2101 Webster Street 415-977-5500
Suite 1300 *Fax:* 510-208-3140
Oakland, CA 94612 information@sierraclub.org
www.sierraclub.org
Revised and updated, this comprehensive guide makes more than 200 wilderness areas in California, including many lesser known natural areas, accessible to the outdoor enthusiast.
Publication Date: 1997 352 pages
ISBN: 0-871568-50-0
John Perry and Jane Greverus Perry, Author
Michael Brune, Executive Director
Jennifer Trahan, Chief Operating Officer

3665 **Thermal Springs of Wyoming**
Wyoming State Geological Survey
PO Box 1347
Laramie, WY 82073
307-766-2286
Fax: 307-766-2605
wsgs-info@uwyo.edu
www.wsgs.uwyo.edu
Ronald C Surdam, Agency Director
Richard W Jones, Editor

3666 **Traveler's Guide to the Smoky Mountains Region**
Harvard Common Press
535 Albany Street
Boston, MA 00211
617-423-5803
Fax: 619-695-9794
info@harvardcommonpress.com
www.harvardcommonpress.com
Features museums, events of the South Appalachians of Tennessee, North Carolilna, Virginia and Georgia
Publication Date: 1985 288 pages
ISBN: 0-916782-64-6
Valerie Cimino, Executive Editor
Christine Alaimo, Associate Publisher

3667 **Wild Places & Open Spaces Map**
Division of Fish and Wildlife
PO Box 420
Trenton, NJ 00862
609-292-2965
Fax: 609-292-8207
www.njfishandwildlife.com
Designed similar to a road map, offers the outdoors person a welath of information on locating and exploring New Jersey's open spaces in compact and easy to read format. Showcasing a full color map of New Jersey, with more than 700,000acres of public open space.
David Chanda, Director
Larry Herrighty, Assis Dir of Operations

Directories & Handbooks: Water Resources

3668 **Coordination Directory of State and Federal Agency Water Resources Officials: Missouri Basin**
Department of Water Resources
5231 South 19th Street
Lincoln, NE 68512
402-328-4100
ne.water.usgs.gov
It operates the most extensive satellite network of stream-gaging stations in the state, many of which form the backbone of flood-warning systems.

3669 **Hydro Review: Industry Source Book Issue**
HCI Publications
410 Archibald Street
Kansas City, MO 64111
847-763-9540
Fax: 816-931-2015
hr@halldata.com
www.hydroworld.com
List of over 800 manufacturers and suppliers of products and services to the hydroelectric industry in the US and Canada.
January
David Appleyard, Editor-In-Chief
Elizabeth Ingram, Managing Editor

3670 **List of Water Pollution Control Administrators**
Assn. of State and Interstate Water Pollution Con.
1221 Connecticut Ave. NW
2nd Floor
Washington, DC 20036
202-898-0905
Fax: 202-898-0929
Roberta Savage, Executive Director
Linda Eichmiller, Deputy Director

3671 **Water Environment & Technology Buyer's Guide and Yearbook**
Water Environment Federation
601 Wythe Street
Alexandria, VA 22314
703-684-2400
800-666-0206
Fax: 703-684-2492
inquiry@wef.org
www.wef.org
Founded in 1928, the Water Environment Foundation (WEF) is a not for profit technical and educational organization with members from varied disiplines who work toward the WEF vision of preservation and enhancement of the globalwaterenvironment. The WEF network includes water quality professionals from 76 Member Associations in 30 countries.
Eileen O'Neill, Executive Director
Ed McCormick, President

Periodicals: Air & Climate

3672 **Air/Water Pollution Report**
Business Publishers
2222 Sedwick Drive
Durham, NC 27713
301-589-5103
800-223-8720
Fax: 800-508-2592
www.bpinews.com
Regulatory activities and governmental legislation and litigation are covered in this pulication.
Publication Date: 1963 Monthly
Leonard Eiserer, Publisher

3673 **Bulletin of the American Meteorological Society**
45 Beacon Street
Boston, MA 00210
617-227-2425
Fax: 617-742-8718
amsinfo@ametsoc.org
www.ametsoc.org
Professional organization disseminates information about the atmospheric, oceanic and hydrologic sciences.
Publication Date: 1919 Monthly
Keith L. Seitter, Executive Director
Gwendolyn Whittaker, Director, Publications

3674 **Climate Alert**
Climate Institute
1201 New York Avenue
Suite 400
Washington, DC 20005
202-552-0163
info@climate.org
climate.org
The Climate Institute seeks to implement innovative and practical solutions to climate change by supporting and collaborating with private, nonprofit and government organizations. Archived editions of Climate Alert are available on theInstitute's website.
Publication Date: 1988 8-12 pages
ISSN: 1071-3271
Mark Goldberg, Chief Executive Officer
Christopher Philipp, Director, E-Learning

3675 **EarthShare Georgia Newsletter**
715 Peachtree Street NE
Suite 100 & 200
Atlanta, GA 30308
404-873-3173
Fax: 404-873-3135
info@earthsharega.org
www.earthsharega.org
EarthShare Georgia works to protect, conserve, and enhance air, land, and water quality by connecting people to trusted nonprofit organizations dedicated to creating a healthy and sustainable environment.
Publication Date: 1992 Monthly
Madeline L. Reamy, Executive Director
Trecinia Wiggins, Development Manager

3676 **Environmental Policy Alert**
Inside Washington Publishers
1919 South Eads Street
Suite 201
Arlington, VA 22202
703-416-8500
800-424-9068
Fax: 703-416-8543
iwp@iwpnews.com
www.iwpnews.com
Addresses the legislative news and provides reports on the federal environmental policy process.
Publication Date: 1980
Paul Finger, Publisher

3677 **Journal of the Air and Waste Management Association**
Air and Waste Management Association

Koppers Building | 412-232-3444
436 Seventh Avenue, Suite 2100 | 800-270-3444
Pittsburgh, PA 15219 | *Fax:* 412-232-3450
info@awma.org
www.awma.org

Published for the working environmental professional and carries peer-reviewed technical papers on a variety of topics form control technology to science.

Publication Date: 1951 Monthly
ISSN: 1096-2247
Stephanie Glyptis, Executive Director
Lisa Bucher, Managing Editor

3678 Population Reference Bureau: Household Transportation Use and Urban Pollution

1875 Connecticut Avenue NW | 202-483-1100
Suite 520 | 800-877-9881
Washington, DC 20009 | *Fax:* 202-328-3937
popref@prb.org
www.prb.org

Publication Date: 1929
Jeffrey Jordan, President and CEO
James Scott, CFO, COO

3679 Population Reference Bureau: Population & Environment Dynamics

1875 Connecticut Avenue NW | 202-483-1100
Suite 520 | 800-877-9881
Washington, DC 20009 | *Fax:* 202-328-3937
popref@prb.org
www.prb.org

PRB publishes the quarterly Population Bulletin, the annual World Population Data Sheet, and PRB Reports on America, as well as specialized publications covering population and public policy issues in the U.S. and abroad, particularlyin developing countries.

Publication Date: 1929
Jeffrey Jordan, President and CEO
James Scott, CFO, COO

3680 Population Reference Bureau: Water

1875 Connecticut Avenue NW | 202-483-1100
Suite 520 | 800-877-9887
Washington, DC 20009 | *Fax:* 202-328-3937
popref@prb.org
www.prb.org

Publication Date: 1929
Jeffrey Jordan, President and CEO
James Scott, CFO, COO

3681 Trinity Consultants Air Issues Review

12770 Merit Drive | 972-661-8100
Suite 900 | 800-229-6655
Dallas, TX 75251 | *Fax:* 972-385-9203
information@trinityconsultants.com
www.trinityconsultants.com

An environmental consulting company that assists industrial facilities with issues related to regulatory compliance and environmental management. Founded in 1974, this nationwide firm has particular expertise in air quality issues.Trinity also sells environmental software and professional education. T3, a Trinity Consultants Company, provides EH&S management information systems (EMIS) implementation and integration services

Publication Date: 1990 8 pages Quarterly
John Hofmann, President and CEO
Dave Larsen, Chief Financial Officer

3682 Weather & Climate Report

Nautilus Press
1054 National Press Building | 202-347-6643
Washington, DC 20045

Reports on federal actions which impact weather, climate research and global changes in climate.

Monthly
ISSN: 0730-8256
John R Botzum, Editor

3683 World Resource Review

SUPCON International
PO Box 50303 | 630-910-1551
Palo Alto, CA 94303 | *Fax:* 630-910-1561
syshen@megsinet.net
www.globalwarming.net

For business and government readers, provides expert worldwide reviews of global warming and extreme events in relation to the management of natural, mineral and material resources. Subjects include global warming impacts onagriculture, energy, and infrastructure, monitoring of changes in resources using remote sensing, actions of national and international bodies, global carbon budget, greenhouse budget and more.

Publication Date: 1990 Quarterly
ISSN: 1042-8011
Dr. Sinya Shen, Production Manager

3684 World Watch

Worldwatch Institute
1400 16th Street NW | 202-745-8092
Suite 430 | *Fax:* 202-478-2534
Washington, DC 20036 | worldwatch@worldwatch.org
www.worldwatch.org

Magazine on global environmental issues.

Publication Date: 1975 40 pages
ISSN: 0896-0615
Ed Ayres, Author
Ed Groark, Chair/Acting Interim Pres
Robert Charles Friese, Vice Chair

Periodicals: Business

3685 AFE Journal

8200 Greensboro Drive | 571-395-8777
Suite 400 | *Fax:* 571-766-2142
McLean, VA 22102 | info@afe.org
www.afe.org

AFE Journal is a bimonthly publication from the Association for Facilities Engineering.

48 pages Bimonthly
ISSN: 1088-5900
Gabriella Jacobs, Author
Dennis M. Hydrick, President & Chairman
Wayne P. Saya, Executive Director

3686 ALBC News

American Livestock Breeds Conservancy
PO Box 477 | 919-542-5704
Pittsboro, NC 27312 | *Fax:* 919-545-0022
www.livestockconservancy.org

ALBC News is a bi-monthly newsletter published by the American Livestock Breeds Conservancy.

Publication Date: 1987 20 pages Bi-Monthly
ISSN: 1064-1599
Cindy Rubel, Author
Cindy Rubel, Editor

3687 Abstracts of Presentations

Wildlife Society
5410 Grosvenor Lane | 301-897-9770
Suite 200 | *Fax:* 301-530-2471
Bethesda, MD 20814 | tws@wildlife.org
www.wildlife.org

A yearly publication of the Wildlife Society.

Publication Date: 1994 300 pages Yearly
Rick Baydack, President
Bruce Thompson, Vice President

3688 Advisor

Great Lakes Commission
Eisenhower Corporate Park | 734-665-9135
2805 South Industrial Hwy, Suite 100 | *Fax:* 734-971-9150
Ann Arbor, MI 48104 | www.glc.org

Covers economic and environmental issues of the Great Lakes region with a special focus on activities of the Great Lakes Commission.
Publication Date: 1955 12 pages Bi-Monthly
Kelvin Burch, Chairman
Tim A. Eder, Executive Director

3689 Agribusiness Fieldman
Western Agricultural Publishing Company
4969 E Clinton Way 559-252-7000
Suite 104 *Fax:* 559-252-7387
Fresno, CA 93727
Aimed at keeping the professional agriculture consultant posted on changes in the agricultural-chemical industry. Provides news about pests and control measures for all segments of the agricultural-chemical industry.
Paul Baltimore, Publisher
Margi Katz, Editor

3690 American Environmental Laboratory
International Scientific Communications
PO Box 870 203-926-9300
Shelton, CT 00648 *Fax:* 203-926-9310
www.iscpubs.com
Laboratory activities, new equipment, and analysis and collection of samples are the main topics.
Bi-Monthly
Brian Howard, Publisher/Editor-in-Chief

3691 Business and the Environment
Cutter Information Corporation
37 Broadway 781-648-8700
Suite 1 800-888-8939
Arlington, MA 00247 *Fax:* 781-648-8707
service@cutter.com
www.cutter.com
Environmental investment trends, deals and market developments.
Karen Fine Coburn, President & CEO
Paul Bergeron, CFO & COO

3692 CAC Annual Reports
Citizens Advisory Council
13th Floor, RCSOB 717-787-4527
PO Box 8459 *Fax:* 717-787-2878
Harrisburg, PA 17105 mioff.stephanie@state.pa.us
www.cacdep.state.pa.us
Publisher by the Citizens Advisory Council.
Publication Date: 1977 20-40 pages Annual
Susan Wilson, Executive Director
Stephanie Mioff, Administrative Assistant

3693 Chemosphere
Pergamon Press
660 White Plains Road 914-524-9200
Tarrytown, NY 10591 *Fax:* 914-592-3625
Related to environmental affairs. Accepts advertising.
100 pages
T Stephen, Editor
Rosemarie Fazzolari, Advertising

3694 Connecticut Sea Grant
1080 Shennecossett Road 860-405-9128
Groton, CT 00634 *Fax:* 860-405-9109
peg.vanpatten@uconn.edu
www.seagrant.uconn.edu
Based at the University of Connecticut, CT Sea Grant is part of the National Sea Grant network, whose mission is the conservation and wise use of coastal and marine resources through research, education and outreach.
Jeffrey Seeman, Chair
Bonnie Burr, Advisory Board

3695 Earth First! Journal
PO Box 1112 541-244-1533
Grants Pass, OR 97528 collective@earthfirstjournal.org
earthfirstjournal.org
Earth First! was first created in response to a compromising and increasingly corporate environmental community. Earth First! publish Earth First! Journal. Earth First! Journal highlights radical environmental movements and causes.Earth First! pride themselves on being a grassroots organization fighting to saves lives and the environment, including tactics such as civil disobedience and monkeywrenching.
Publication Date: 1979 Quarterly
ISSN: 1055-8411

3696 Earth Island Journal
Earth Island Institute
2150 Allston Way 510-859-9100
Suite 460 *Fax:* 510-859-9091
Berkeley, CA 94704-1375 editor@earthisland.org
www.earthisland.org
Publication from the Earth Island Institute - cutting-edge news, analysis and commentary on vital international environmental news.
Publication Date: 1987 Quarterly
ISSN: 1041-0406
Zoe Loftus Farren, Managing Editor
Maureen Nandini Mitra, Editor

3697 Economic Opportunity Report
Business Publishers
2222 Sedwick Drive 301-589-5103
Durham, NC 27713 800-223-8720
Fax: 800-508-2592
www.bpinews.com
Regulatory activities and governmental legislation and litigation are covered in this pulication.
Publication Date: 1963
Leonard Eiserer, Publisher
Beth Early, Operations Director

3698 Environmental Business Journal
ZweigWhite
4452 Park Blvd. 508-651-1559
Suite 306 800-466-6275
San Diego, CA 92116 *Fax:* 800-842-1560
info@zweigwhite.com
EBJ is the leading business newsletter for the environmental industry, providing competive strategies, new business opportunities, and up-to-date market trends and data. Now published by ZweigWhite, the EBJ comes out every month.
Publication Date: 1988 16+ pages Monthly
Grant Ferrier, President and CEO
George Stubbs, Senior Editor

3699 Environmental Compliance Update
High Tech Publishing Company
PO Box 1275 413-534-4500
Amherst, MA 00100
Identifies and analyzes the issues and business and economic impact of environmental compliance laws and regulations. Monitors the relevant changes due to legislation, court decisions, private rulings and technology.
Lori Reilly, Editor

3700 Environmental News
CA Business Publications
PO Box 3359 817-924-5301
Fort Worth, TX 76113 *Fax:* 817-922-8893
txenv@aol.com
Follows the progress of public environmental stock companies, provides updates on environmental contract opportunities, news of international environmental opportunities, and profiles innovative new companies.
Carolyn Ashford, Publisher/Editor

3701 Environmental Packaging
Thompson Publishing Group
P.O. Box 41868 202-872-4000
Austin, TX 78704 800-677-3789
Fax: 800-999-5661
www.thompson.com

A newsletter aimed at the environmental regulatory specialist, product development managers, purchasing managers, legal counsel and package designers covering state-by-state regulations and the FCA guidelines and enforcement.
Publication Date: 1972
Daphne Musselwhite, Publisher

3702 Florida Forests Magazine
Florida Forestry Association
PO Box 1696 — 850-222-5646
Tallahassee, FL 32302 — *Fax:* 850-222-6179
info@forestfla.org
www.floridaforest.org

A publication of the Florida Forestry Association.
Publication Date: 1997 26-32 pages Quarterly
J Doran, Executive VP

3703 George Miksch Sutton Avian Research Center Sutton Newsletter
PO Box 2007 — 918-336-7778
Bartlesville, OK 74005 — *Fax:* 918-336-7783
info@suttoncenter.org
www.suttoncenter.org

Newsletter published by George Miksch Sutton Avian Research Center.
Publication Date: 1990 8-10 pages Semiannual
Steve Sherrod, Director of Conservation
Lena C. Larsson, Assistant Director

3704 Green Business Letter
Tilden Press
6 Hillwood Place — 202-332-1700
Oakland, CA 94610 — *Fax:* 202-332-3028
www.greenbiz.com

Hands-on journal for environmentally conscious companies, covering management strategies, facilities management, personnel policies and procurement with environmental consciousness. Emphasis on products, resources and how-toinformation.
8 pages
ISSN: 1056-490X
Joel Makower, Chairman & Executive Editor
Heather Clancy, Senior Writer

3705 In Business: The Magazine for Sustainable Enterprises and Communities
JG Press, Inc
419 State Avenue — 610-967-4135
Emmaus, PA 18049 — advert@jgpress.com
www.biocycle.net

It is the go-to magazine and website on composting, organics recycling, anaerobic digestion and renewable energy.
Jerome Goldstein, Editor

3706 International Environment Reporter
Bureau of National Affairs
1231 25th Street NW — 202-452-4200
Washington, DC 20037 — 800-372-1033
Fax: 202-822-8092
www.bna.com

A four-binder information and reference service covering international environmental law and developing policy in the major industrial nations.
William A Beltz, Publisher

3707 International Environmental Systems Update
BSI Management Systems
12110 Sunset Hills Road — 703-437-9000
Suite 200 — 800-862-4977
Reston, VA 20190 — *Fax:* 703-435-7979
Provides accurate, up-to-date and useful information for environmental professionals around the globe. Monthly publication brings current environmental events into the limelight, dissecting complex issues, helping hundreds oforganizations improve their environmental and business preformance.
Publication Date: 1994 24 pages Monthly
ISSN: 1079-0837
Marcus Darby, Publisher

3708 McCoy's RCRA Unraveled
McCoy & Associates
12596 West Bayaud Avenue — 303-526-2674
Suite 210 — *Fax:* 303-526-5471
Lakewood, CO 80228 — info@mccoyseminars.com
www.mccoyseminars.com

This book addresses the most troublesome areas in 40 CFR Parts 261 and 262 of the federal regulations. Our engineers have researched every scrap of guidance EPA has ever issued on these troublesome topics, studied the Federal Registerpreamble language, and talked to thousands of people who attented our RCRA seminars and shared their real-world experiences. It includes a keyword index with more than 1,300 entries, 200 probing examples from EPA's own guidance documents and ahelpful acronym list.
Publication Date: 2005 828 pages Yearly
Paul Gallagher, President
Nancy Pribble, Marketing Manager

3709 NFPA Journal
One Batterymarch Park — 617-770-3000
Quincy, MA 00216 — 800-344-3555
Fax: 617-770-0700
www.nfpa.org

A bi-monthly journal published by the National Fire Protection Association.
Bi-Monthly
Jim Pauley, President
Scott Sutherland, Editor

3710 NSS News
National Speleological Society
6001 Pulaski Pike — 256-852-1300
Huntsville, AL 35810 — nss@caves.org
www.caves.org

Published by the National Speleological Society.
Publication Date: 1942 Monthly
ISSN: 0027-7010
Geary Schindel, President
Scott Engel, Executive Vice President

3711 Newsleaf
4949 Tealtown Road — 513-831-1711
Milford, OH 45150 — *Fax:* 513-831-8052
cnc@cincynature.org
www.cincynature.org

Newsleaf is a quarterly publication for Cincinatti Nature Center members. This publication provides informative articles that teach readers about native flora and fauna.
Publication Date: 1965 20-24 pages Quarterly
Bill Hopple, Executive Director
Amy Johnson, Executive Assistant

3712 Proceedings of the Desert Fishes Council
Desert Fishes Council
1447 Edgecliff Drive — 760-872-8751
Sandy, UT 84092 — dfc-excomm@utlists.utexas.edu
www.desertfishes.org

Yearly publication from Desert Fishes Council. Archives back to 1969 are available online.
Publication Date: 1969 Yearly
ISSN: 1068-0381
Krissy Wilson, President
Phil Pister, Executive Secretary

3713 Proceedings of the Southeastern Association of Fish and Wildlife Agencies
27 Sylwood Place — 601-668-6916
Jackson, MS 39209 — *Fax:* 850-893-6204
crayhopkins@bellsouth.net
www.seafwa.org

Proceedings of the SEAFWA - an annual publication.
Publication Date: 1947 4-900 pages Yearly
Curtis R Hopkins, Executive Secretary

3714 Pumper
COLE Publishing

1720 Maple Lake Dam Road 715-546-3346
PO Box 220 800-257-7222
Three Lakes, WI 54562 *Fax:* 715-546-3786
info@pumper.com
www.pumper.com

Emphasis on companies, individuals and industry events while focusing on customer service, environmental issues and employment trends.

Publication Date: 1947
Ken Lowther, Editor

3715 Regulatory Update
Arkansas Environmental Federation
1400 W Markham Street 501-374-0263
Suite 302 *Fax:* 501-374-8752
Little Rock, AR 72201 cmiller@environmentark.org
www.environmentark.org

The AEF focuses on practical, common-sense laws and regulations based on sound science; a teamwork approach to compliance; waste minimization and pollution prevention. The AEF enables information to be exchanged on a daily basisbetween its members, government regulators, and policy makers.

Publication Date: 1967 Semi-Annual
Charles Miller, Executive Director
Marge Brookins, Office Manager

3716 Risk Policy Report
Inside Washington Publishers
1225 South Clark Street 703-416-8500
Suite 1400 800-424-9068
Arlington, VA 22202 iwp@iwpnews.com
www.iwnews.com

Contains analysis, great perspectives, industry news, policymaking profiles and a calendar of events.

Monthly
David P Clarke, Publisher/Editor

3717 Semillero
731 8th Street SE 202-547-3800
Washington, DC 20003 *Fax:* 202-546-4784

Our electronic publication has more than 2500 subscribers in the US and Latin America. It provides useful information and references to specifice resources regarding agro-forestry, rural development and grant information.

Publication Date: 1982
Erick Toledo and Catalina Serna, Author
Erick Toledo, Director

Periodicals: Design & Architecture

3718 AGC Environmental Observer
Associated General Contractors of America
2300 Wilson Boulevard 703-548-3118
Suite 300 800-242-1767
Arlington, VA 22201 *Fax:* 703-548-3119
info@agc.org
www.agc.org

Electronic newsletter of the Associated General Contractors of America with recent developments in in environmental regulations and green building.

10 issues/year
Stephen Sandherr, Chief Executive Officer
Jeff Shoaf, Chief Operating Officer

3719 MSW Management
Forester Communications
PO Box 3100 805-682-1300
Santa Barbara, CA 93130 *Fax:* 805-682-0200
www.mswmanagement.com

Provides general news on facility construction, financing, new equipment and revenue issues.

Publication Date: 1991 7 Times Yearly
Daniel Waldman, Publisher

Periodicals: Disaster Preparedness & Response

3720 Hazard Technology
EIS International
555 Herndon Parkway 703-478-9808
Herndon, VA 20170 *Fax:* 703-787-6720

Application of technology to the field of emergency and environmental management to save lives and protect property.

James W Morentz PhD, Publisher
Leslie Atkin, Managing Editor

3721 Hazardous Materials Newsletter
Hazardous Materials Publishing
243 West Main Street 610-683-6721
Kutztown, PA 19530 *Fax:* 610-683-3171
lfricker@hazmat-tsp.com
www.hazmatpublishing.com

Focuses on response to and control of hazardous materials emergencies. Particularly appropriate tools, equipment, materials, methods, procedures, strategies and lessons learned. Addresses leak, fore and spill control for incidentcommanders and experienced responders, including incident clauses, prevention and remedial actions; decisionmaking; scene management; control and containment; response teams; and product identification and hazards.

12 pages

3722 Natural Hazards Observer
Natural Hazards Center
University of Colorado 303-492-6818
482 UCB *Fax:* 303-492-2151
Boulder, CO 80309 hazctr@colorado.edu

A periodical of the Natural Hazards Center that covers current disaster issues; new international, national, and local disaster management, mitigation, and education programs; hazards research; political and policy developments; newinformation sources and Web sites; upcoming conference; and recent publications

Bi Monthly
Liesel Ritchie, Associate Director
Kathleen Tierney, Director

Periodicals: Energy & Transportation

3723 AERO SunTimes
Alternative Energy Resources Organization
432 N Last Chance Gulch 406-443-7272
Helena, MT 59601 *Fax:* 406-442-9120
aero@aeromt.org

The SunTimes is the newsletter for AERO. The organization is a statewide grassroots group whose members work together to strengthen communities through promoting sustainable agriculture, local food production and citizen-based SmartGrowth community planning.

Publication Date: 1978 4-24 pages Quarterly
ISSN: 1046-0993
Kiki Hubbard, Editor
Jean Duncan, Editor

3724 Alternative Energy and Distributed Generation Journal
Association of Energy Engineers
3168 Mercer University Drive 770-447-5083
Atlanta, GA 30341 *Fax:* 770-446-3969
info@aeecenter.org
www.aeecenter.org

Quarterly
Bill Kent, Executive Director
Jorge Wong, Editorial Contact

3725 Butane-Propane News
Butane-Propane News, Inc

PO Box 660698
Arcadia, CA 91066
626-357-2168
800-214-4386
Fax: 626-303-2854
arey@bpnews.com
www.bpnews.com

Offers information to professionals that are involved in the distribution, production, shipping and sales of butane and propane in the US and internationally. $32 for US one year subscription; $60 for international one yearsubscription.

Publication Date: 1939 48-96 pages Monthly
ISSN: 0007-7259
Natalie Peal, Publisher
John Needham, Editor

3726 Cars of Tomorrow
Northeast Sustainable Energy Association
50 Miles Street
Greenfield, MA 00130
413-774-6051
Fax: 413-774-6053
nesea@nesea.org
www.nesea.org

Offers a look at the energy options of vehicles of the future.

Curriculum
Jennifer Marrapese, Executive Director
Gina Sieber, Business Manager

3727 E&P Environment
Pasha Publications
1600 Wilson Boulevard
Suite 600
Arlington, VA 22209
703-528-1244
800-424-2908
Fax: 703-528-1253

Reports on environmental regulations, advances in technology and litigation aimed specifically at the exploration and production segments of the oil and gas industry.

Harry Baisden, Group Publisher
Michael Hopps, Editor

3728 Economics of Energy and Environmental Policy (EEEP)
International Association for Energy Economics
28790 Chagrin Boulevard
Suite 350
Cleveland, OH 44122
216-464-5365
iaee@iaee.org
www.iaee.org

Policy journal with accessible, yet authoritative information on energy and environmental economics.

Publication Date: 2012 Bi-annual
David L. Williams, Executive Director
Christian von Hirschhausen, Editor-in-Chief

3729 Energy Journal
International Association for Energy Economics
28790 Chagrin Boulevard
Suite 350
Cleveland, OH 44122
216-464-5365
iaee@iaee.org
www.iaee.org

Promotes the advancement and dissemination of new knowledge on energy matters and related topics. Topics include: transportation, electricity markets, environmental issues, natural gas topics, and carbon emissions reduction.

Publication Date: 1980 200 pages Bi-monthly
David L. Williams, Executive Director
Adonis Yatchew, Editor-in-Chief

3730 Getting Around Clean & Green
Northeast Sustainable Energy Association
50 Miles Street
Greenfield, MA 00130
413-774-6051
Fax: 413-774-6053
nesea@nesea.org
www.nesea.org

This interdisciplinary science/social studies curriculum allows students to explore the transportation and environmental issues in their own lives. Activities cover: transportation systems, health impacts, environmental andtransportation histories, carpooling, and mass transit.

90 pages Curriculum
Jennifer Marrapese, Executive Director
Gina Sieber, Business Manager

3731 Getting Around Without Gasoline
Northeast Sustainable Energy Association
50 Miles Street
Greenfield, MA 00130
413-774-6051
Fax: 413-774-6053
nesea@nesea.org
www.nesea.org

An interdisciplinary unit that explores the feasibility of getting around without using gasoline. Students can conduct various activities to compare powering vehicles with gasoline versus electricity.

60 pages S & H Only
Jennifer Marrapese, Executive Director
Gina Sieber, Business Manager

3732 Heliographs
Illinois Solar Energy Association
1281 E. Brummel Ave
Elk Grove Village, IL 60007
630-260-0424
contactisea@illinoissolar.org
www.illinoissolar.org

It is a non-profit organization that promotes the widespread application of solar and other forms of renewable energy through our mission of education and advocacy

Publication Date: 1975 12 pages Quarterly
Lesley McCain, Executive Director
Shannon Fulton, President

3733 IAEE Energy Forum
International Association for Energy Economics
28790 Chagrin Boulevard
Suite 350
Cleveland, OH 44122
216-464-5365
Fax: 216-464-2737
iaee@iaee.org
www.iaee.org

Association information including: upcoming events, conferences, special reports, affiliate activities, and chapter news.

Quarterly
David L. Williams, Executive Director
Kostas Andriosopoulos, VP, Publications

3734 International Journal of Energy Management
Association of Energy Engineers
3168 Mercer University Drive
Atlanta, GA 30341
770-447-5083
Fax: 770-446-3969
info@aeecenter.org
www.aeecenter.org

Presents engineering and analytical approaches to energy management.

Bi-monthly
Bill Kent, Executive Director
Steven Parker, Editorial Contact

3735 International Journal of Hydrogen Energy
5794 SW 40 Street
#303
Miami, FL 33155
305-284-4666
Fax: 305-284-4792
info@iahe.org
www.iahe.org

A monthly publication serving to inform scientists and the public of advances made in hydrogen energy research and development.

Publication Date: 1976 120 pages Monthly
ISSN: 0360-3199
T Nejat Veziroglu, Author
T Neja Veziroglu, President
Matthew M. Mench, Executive Vice President

3736 International Journal of Strategic Energy and Environmental Planning
Association of Energy Engineers
3168 Mercer University Drive
Atlanta, GA 30341
770-447-5083
Fax: 770-446-3969
info@aeecenter.org
www.aeecenter.org

Focuses on issues such as energy management, corporate sustainability initiatives, and energy policy.

Bi-monthly
Bill Kent, Executive Director
Stephen Roosa, Editorial Contact

3737 Midwest Renewable Energy Association Newsletter
7558 Deer Road
Custer, WI 54423
715-592-6595
Fax: 715-592-6596
www.midwestrenew.org

ReNews includes articles on energy issues, book reviews, case studies, and other general information about renewable energy.
Quarterly
Nick Hylla, Executive Director
Kaitlyn Kohl, Administrative Assistant

3738 Northeast Sun
Northeast Sustainable Energy Association
50 Miles Street 413-774-6051
Greenfield, MA 00130 *Fax:* 413-774-6053
nesea@nesea.org
www.nesea.org
Promotes responsible use of energy for a stronger economy and cleaner environment. Northeast Sun is a bi-annual Spring and Fall publication that includes articles by leading authorities on sustainable energy practices, energyefficiency and renewable energy, and each Fall issue includes the Sustainable Green Pages Directory of engery professionals in the Northeast. Subscription is free with membership.
Bi-Annual
Jennifer Marrapese, Executive Director
Gina Sieber, Business Manager

3739 Nuclear Waste News
Business Publishers
2222 Sedwick Drive 301-589-5103
Durham, NC 27713 800-223-8720
Fax: 800-508-2592
custserv@bpinews.com
www.bpinews.com
Worldwide coverage of the nuclear waste management industry, including waste generation, radiological environmental remediation, packaging, transport, processing and disposal.
Weekly
Leonard A Eiserer, Publisher
Beth Early, Associate Publisher

3740 Radwaste Magazine
American Nuclear Society
555 North Kensington Avenue 708-352-6611
LaGrange Park, IL 60526 800-323-3044
Fax: 708-352-0499
TMarc@ans.org
www.ans.org
Addresses issues in all fields of radioactive waste management, removal, handling, disposal, treatment, cleanup and environmental restoration.
6x per Year
Robert C. Fine, Executive Director
Patricia Schroeder, Manager

3741 ReNews
Midwest Renewable Energy Association
PO Box 249 715-592-6595
Amherst, WI 54406 *Fax:* 715-592-6596
www.midwestrenew.org
ReNews is a quarterly newsletter that includes articles on energy issues, book reviews, case studies, and other general information about renewable energy.
Quarterly
Nick Hylla, Executive Director
Kaitlyn Kohl, Administrative Assistant

3742 Solar Energy
Elsevier Science
360 Park Avenue South 212-989-5800
11th Floor *Fax:* 212-633-3990
New York, NY 10010 usinfo-f@elsevier.com
www.elsevier.com
It is a world-leading provider of information solutions that enhance the performance of science, health, and technology professionals, empowering them to make better decisions, deliver better care, and sometimes make groundbreakingdiscoveries that advance the boundaries of knowledge and human progress.
Ron Mobed, Chief Executive Officer
Stuart Whayman, Chief Financial Officer

3743 Solar Energy Report
1107 9th St. 949-837-7430
Suite 820 *Fax:* 949-709-8043
Sacramento, CA 95814 www.calseia.org
It advances the common interests of the California solar industry, helping make California's solar market the most robust in the United States
Bi-Monthly
Aaron Thurlow, Secretary
Cecilia Aguillon, Vice President

3744 Solar Reflector
Texas Solar Energy Society
PO Box 1447 512-326-3391
Austin, TX 78767 800-465-5049
Fax: 512-444-0333
info@txses.org
www.txses.org
A Texas Solar Energy Society publication. Promotes the wise use of sustainable and non-polluting resources.
Quarterly
Lucy Stolzenburg, Executive Director
Scot Arey, Chairman

3745 Solar Today
American Solar Energy Society
2525 Arapahoe Ave 303-443-3130
Ste E4-253 *Fax:* 303-443-3212
Boulder, CO 80302 info@ases.org
www.ases.org/solartoday
Provides information and case histories and reviews of a variety of renewable energy technologies, including solar, wind, biomass, and geothermal.
Publication Date: 1987 Quarterly
Carly Rixham, Executive Director
Carly Cipolla, Director, Operations

3746 Sustainable Green Pages Directory
Northeast Sustainable Energy Association
50 Miles Street 413-774-6051
Greenfield, MA 00130 *Fax:* 413-774-6053
nesea@nesea.org
www.nesea.org
The SPG Directory lists over 30 categories of sustainable energy professionals working throughout the Northeast, including architects, engineers, builders, energy auditors, consultants and renewable energy installers and manufacturers.It is the largest directory of its kind and the only one that targets the Northeastern USA. Published in the Northeast Sun magazine and onlines.
September Annual
Jennifer Marrapese, Executive Director
Gina Sieber, Business Manager

Periodicals: Environmental Engineering

3747 ASH at Work
American Coal Ash Association
38800 Country Club Drive 720-870-7897
Farmington Hills, MI 48331 *Fax:* 720-870-7889
info@acaa-usa.org
www.acaa-usa.org/publications/ashatwork.aspx
Magazine of the American Coal Ash Association, covering the coal combustion products industry.
Thomas Adams, Executive Director
Alyssa Barto, Member Liaison

3748 Asbestos & Lead Abatement Report
Business Publishers
2222 Sedwick Drive 301-589-5103
Durham, NC 27713 800-223-8720
Fax: 800-508-2592
custserv@bpinews.com
www.bpinews.com

Tracks the major legal, legislative, regulatory, business and technological developments in the asbestos and lead abatement industries.
Weekly
Leonard A Eiserer, Publisher
Beth Early, Associate Publisher

3749 **CEP Magazine**
American Institute of Chemical Engineers
120 Wall Street 203-702-7660
FL 23 800-242-4363
New York, NY 10005-4020 *Fax:* 203-775-5177
www.aiche.org
Environmental engineering magazine with articles on technical issues such as safety, environmental management, handling of fluids and solids, reactions and separations, IT, and more.
Monthly
Monty Alger, President

3750 **Defense Cleanup**
Business Publishers
2222 Sedwick Drive 301-589-5103
Durham, NC 27713 800-223-8720
Fax: 800-508-2592
custserv@bpinews.com
www.bpinews.com
Covers the latest news and analysis of defense cleanup activity. Including base remediation and closure, contract awards and site cleanups.
Weekly
Leonard A Eiserer, Publisher
Beth Early, Associate Publisher

3751 **EI Digest**
Environmental Information
8525 Arjons Drive 858-695-0050
Suite H *Fax:* 952-831-6550
San Diego, CA 92126 www.envirobiz.com
Contains market studies of commercial hazardous waste management companies with in-depth analysis of trends in policy, regulations, technology and business.
Publication Date: 1983
ISSN: 1042-251X
Cary Perket, Editor

3752 **EM Magazine**
Air and Waste Management Association
Koppers Building 412-232-3444
436 Seventh Avenue, Suite 2100 800-270-3444
Pittsburgh, PA 15219 *Fax:* 412-232-3450
info@awma.org
www.awma.org
A magazine for environmental managers that contains sections of Washington and Canadian reports, a calendar of events, government affairs, news focus, campus research, business briefs, district control news, porfessional developmentprograms, professional services and other issues facing environmental professionals.
Monthly
ISBN: 0-368750-43-4
ISSN: 1088-9981
Stephanie Glyptis, Executive Director
Lisa Bucher, Managing Editor

3753 **EM Plus**
Air and Waste Management Association
Koppers Building 412-232-3444
436 Seventh Avenue, Suite 2100 800-270-3444
Pittsburgh, PA 15219 *Fax:* 412-232-3450
info@awma.org
www.awma.org
Provides Air and Waste Management Association members with recent news, highlights from EM Magazine, and additional content.
Quarterly
Stephanie Glyptis, Executive Director
Lisa Bucher, Managing Editor

3754 **Environment**
Helen Dwight Reid Educational Foundation
325 Chestnut Street 215-625-8900
Suite 800 800-354-1420
Philadelphia, PA 19106 customer.service@taylorandfrancis.com
www.heldref.org
Provides environment professionals and concerned citizens with authoritative yet accessible articles that provide critical analysis of environmental science and policy issues, book recommendations, commentaries, news briefs and reviewson environmental websites and major governmental and institutional reports.
Publication Date: 1958 48 pages Monthly
ISSN: 0013-9157
Douglas Kirkpatrick, Executive Director
Barbara T Richman, Managing Editor

3755 **Environment 21**
Florida Environments Publishing
4010 Newberry Road 352-373-1401
#F *Fax:* 352-373-1405
Gainesville, FL 32607
Regulations, wildlife, hazard waste/materials, ground/surface/drinking water and other issues concerning Florida's environment are emphasized in this publication for the environmental management team.
Dave Newport, Publisher

3756 **Environmental Engineer & Scientist Magazine**
AAEES
147 Old Solomons Island Road 410-266-3311
Suite 303 *Fax:* 410-266-7653
Annapolis, MD 21401 www.aaees.org
Official magazine of the American Academy of Environmental Engineers & Scientists. It addresses issues and practice with: updates on legal developments affecting environmental engineering, documentation of the profession's heritage,articles on environmental policy, and profiles of leading environmental engineers.
Quarterly
Burk Kalweit, Executive Director

3757 **Environmental Engineering Science**
Mary Ann Liebert
140 Huguenot Street 914-740-2100
3rd Floor 800-MLI-EBER
New Rochelle, NY 10801 *Fax:* 914-740-2101
info@liebertpub.com
www.liebertpub.com
The focus is on pollution control of the suface, ground, and drinking water, and highlight research news and product developments that aid in the fight against pollution.
Bi-Monthly
ISSN: 1092-8758
Mary Ann Liebert, Publisher
Dumpnico Grosso PhD, Editor-in-Chief

3758 **Environmental Forensics**
Taylor & Francis Inc
150 Fearing Street 413-549-5170
Amherst, MA 01002 *Fax:* 413-549-0579
www.environmentalforensics.org
Journal of the International Society of Environmental Forensics and Association for Environmental Health and Sciences Foundation, peer-reviewed, with scientific studies exploring the source, fate, transport, and ecological effects ofenvironmental contamination.
Quarterly
Ioana G. Petrisor, Editor-in-Chief

3759 **Food Protection Trends**
International Association for Food Protection
6200 Aurora Avenue 515-276-3344
Suite 200W 800-369-6337
Des Moines, IA 50322 *Fax:* 515-276-8655
info@foodprotection.org
www.foodprotection.org
Published as the general membership publication by the International Association for Food Protection, each issue contains refer-

eed articles on applied research, applications of current technology and general interest subjects for foodsafety professionals. Regular features include industry and association news, an industry related product section and a calendar of meetings, seminars and workshops.Updates of government regulations and sanitary design is also featured. All membersreceive FPT.
Publication Date: 1981 80+ pages Monthly
ISSN: 1043-3546
David W Tharp, Executive Director
Lisa K Hovey, Assistant Director

3760 Hazardous Materials Intelligence Report
World Information Systems
129 Mount Auburn 617-491-5100
Cambridge, MA 00223 *Fax:* 617-492-3312
Provides news analysis on environmental business, hazardous materials, waste management, pollution prevention and control. Covers regulations, legislation and court decisions, new technology, contract opportunities and awards andconference notices.
Richard S Golob, Publisher
Roger B Wilson Jr, Editor

3761 Hazmat Transport News
Business Publishers
2222 Sedwick Drive 301-589-5103
Durham, NC 27713 800-223-8720
Fax: 800-508-2592
custserv@bpinews.com
www.bpinews.com
Reports on the regulatory, enforcement, legislative and litigation developments affecting hazardous materials transportation.
Monthly
Leonard A Eiserer, Publisher
Beth Early, Associate Publisher

3762 Human and Ecological Risk Assessment
Taylor & Francis Inc
150 Fearing Street 413-549-5170
Amherst, MA 00100 *Fax:* 413-549-0579
www.aehsfoundation.org
An official journal of the Association for Environmental Health and Sciences Foundation. Focuses on papers contributing to improvements in human and ecological health, including assessment, communication, and management.
8 issues/year
ISSN: 1080-7039
Ed Calabrese, Editor-in-Chief

3763 Integrated Waste Management
McGraw Hill
1221 Ave. of the Americas 212-904-2000
New YorK, NY 10020
Articles geared toward integration of solid waste management.
8 pages
Deirdre Borrego, VP and General Manager
Tina Morris, Operations Director

3764 International Journal of Phytoremediation
Taylor & Francis Inc
150 Fearing Street 413-549-5170
Amherst, MA 00100 *Fax:* 413-549-0579
www.aehsfoundation.org
An official journal of the Association for Environmental Health and Sciences Foundation. Dedicated to current laboratory and field research on how to use plant systems to remediate contaminated environments.
6 Issues Yr
ISSN: 1522-6514
Ed Calabrese, Editor-in-Chief

3765 Iowa Academy of Science Journal
Iowa Academy of Science
UNI - 175 Baker Hall 319-273-2021
2607 Campus Street *Fax:* 319-273-2807
Cedar Falls, IA 50614-0508 iascience@uni.edu
www.scienceiniowa.org
A non-profit organization whose mission is to further scientific research, science education, public understanding of science and to recognize excellence in these endeavors.
Quarterly
Craig Johnson, Executive Director

3766 Journal of Environmental Engineering
American Society of Civil Engineers
1801 Alexander Bell Drive 703-295-6300
Reston, VA 20191 *Fax:* 703-295-6211
onlinejls@asce.org
The journal of Environmental Engineering presents a collection of broad interdisciplinary information on the practice and status of research in environmental engineering science, systems engineering, and sanitation.
Publication Date: 1875
Raymond A Ferrara, Editor
Melissa Junior, Director, Journals

3767 Journal of Environmental Quality
American Society of Agronomy
5585 Guilford Road 608-273-8080
Madison, WI 53711 *Fax:* 608-273-2021
membership@agronomy.org
www.agronomy.org
Written for university, government and industry scientists interested in the impacts of environmental perturbations on the biological and physical sciences.
Bi-Monthly
Sylvie M. Brouder, President
Ellen G.M. Bergfeld, Chief Executive Officer

3768 Journal of Environmental and Engineering Geophysics: JEEG
Environmental and Engineering Geophysical Society
1720 South Bellaire Street 303-531-7517
Suite 110 *Fax:* 303-820-3844
Denver, CO 80222 staff@eegs.org
www.eegs.org
A peer reviewed journal of the EEGS made available to members and a variety of libraries.
Publication Date: 1992 Quarterly
ISSN: 1083-1363
Kathie Barstnar, Executive Director
Janet Simms, Editor

3769 Journal of IEST
Institute of Environmental Sciences & Technology
1827 Walden Office Square 847-981-0100
Suite 400 *Fax:* 847-981-4130
Schaumburg, IL 60173 www.iest.org/Journal
An annual journal published by the Institute of Environmental Sciences & Technology.
Publication Date: 1957 Annual
ISSN: 1098-4321
Shawn Windley, President
Wei Sun, President-elect

3770 Kennedy-Jenks Consultants: Alert Newsletter
303 Second Street 415-243-2150
Suite 300 S *Fax:* 415-896-0999
San Francisco, CA 94107 www.kennedyjenks.com
Environmental engineering consulting company.
Publication Date: 1990 6 pages 3 times/year
Gary Carlton, Chair
Keith London, President and CEO

3771 Kennedy-Jenks Consultants: Spotlights
303 Second Street 415-243-2150
Suite 300 S *Fax:* 415-896-0999
San Francisco, CA 94107 www.kennedyjenks.com
Environmental engineering consulting company.
Publication Date: 1981 12 pages 3 times/year
Gary Carlton, Chair
Keith London, President and CEO

3772 Lead Detection & Abatement Contractor
IAQ Publications

7920 Norfolk Avenue 301-913-0115
Suite 900 *Fax:* 301-913-0119
Bethesda, MD 20814 iaqpubs@aol.com
www.iaqpubs.com

Feature articles include new on legislation, operational and safety issues that affect the removal of lead and lead by-products from paint, water, soil, and air.
Susan Valenti, Editor

3773 Leading Edge
Society of Exploration Geophysicists
8801 South Yale Avenue 918-497-5500
Tulsa, OK 74137 *Fax:* 918-497-5557
jlawnick@seg.org
www.seg.org

Addresses a broad spectrum of topics related to applied geophysics. Material immediately accessible to a broad audience.
Publication Date: 1930 116 pages
ISSN: 1070-485X
Dean Clark, Editor
Linda Holeman, Associate Editor

3774 McCoy's CAA Unraveled
McCoy & Associates
12596 W Bayaud AvenueRoad 303-526-2674
Suite 210 *Fax:* 303-526-5471
Lakewood, CO 80228 info@mccoyseminars.com
www.mccoyseminars.com

It is an environmental engineering firm founded in 1982 by Drew McCoy. Our mission is to provide our customers current, accurate environmental compliance information in plain English
414 pages

3775 McCoy's RCRA Reference
McCoy & Associates
12596 W Bayaud AvenueRoad 303-526-2674
Suite 210 *Fax:* 303-526-5471
Lakewood, CO 80228 info@mccoyseminars.com
www.mccoyseminars.com

It is an environmental engineering firm founded in 1982 by Drew McCoy. Our mission is to provide our customers current, accurate environmental compliance information in plain English
1190 pages

3776 Medical Waste News
Business Publishers
2222 Sedwick Drive 301-589-5103
Durham, NC 27713 800-223-8720
Fax: 800-508-2592
custserv@bpinews.com
www.bpinews.com

Reports on the rapidly evolving legislative and regulatory actions in medical waste management. Includes coverage of incineration, laboratory wastes, infection control, liability and legal issues and waste transport.
Publication Date: 1963
Leonard A Eiserer, Publisher
Beth Early, Operations Director

3777 New York State Conservationist
NYS Department of Environmental Conservation
625 Broadway 518-402-8047
2nd Floor 800-678-6399
Albany, NY 12233 *Fax:* 518-402-9036
dinnelson@gw.dec.state.ny.us
www.dec.ny.gov

An informative and entertaining full-color bi-monthly magazine featuring New York State's natural resources and peoples' enjoyment of those resources.
Bi-Monthly
ISSN: 0010-650X
David Nelson, Editor

3778 Noise Control Engineering Journal
Institute of Noise Control Engineering
11130 Sunrise Valley Drive 703-234-4124
Suite 350 *Fax:* 703-435-4390
Reston, VA 20190 EditorNCEJ@inceusa.org
www.inceusa.org

The technical publication of the Institute of Noise Control Engineering, with assistance from the Korean Society of Noise and Vibration (KSNVE). It contains technical articles on all aspects of noise control engineering.
Bi-Monthly
ISSN: 0736-2501
Joseph M. Cuschieri, Executive Director
James K. Thompson, Editor

3779 Noise Regulation Report
Business Publishers
2222 Sedwick Drive 301-589-5103
Durham, NC 27713 800-223-8720
Fax: 800-508-2592
custserv@bpinews.com
www.bpinews.com

Exclusive coverage of airport, highway, occupational and open space noise, noise control and mitigation issues.
Publication Date: 1963
Leonard A Eiserer, Publisher
Beth Early, Operations Director

3780 Pollution Engineering
Cahners Business Information
2000 Clearwater Drive 630-320-7000
Oak Brook, IL 60523 *Fax:* 630-288-8282
www.pollutionengineering.com

Serves the field of pollution control in manufacturing industries, utilities, consulting engineers and constructors. Also serves government agencies including administration of federal, state and local environmental programs.
ISSN: 0032-3640
Barbara Olsen, Publisher
Roy Bigham, Managing Editor

3781 SPAC Newsletter
Soil and Plant Analysis Council
347 North Shores Circle 970-686-5702
Windsor, CO 80550 *Fax:* 402-476-0302

Quarterly newsletter.
Quarterly
Rao Mylavarapu, President
Robert Miller, Secretary/Treasurer

3782 Sludge
Business Publishers
2222 Sedwick Drive 301-589-5103
Durham, NC 27713 800-223-8720
Fax: 800-508-2592
custserv@bpinews.com
www.bpinews.com

Premier insider guide to the biosolids industry. Follows developments in and management of beneficial use and wastewater residuals, with practical information about industrial sludge, incineration, special wastes, permits andlandfills.
BiWeekly
Leonard A Eiserer, Publisher
Beth Early, Operations Director

3783 Soil & Sediment Contamination Journal
Taylor & Francis Inc
150 Fearing Street 413-549-5170
Amherst, MA 00100 *Fax:* 413-549-0579
www.aehsfoundation.org

An official journal of the Association for Environmental Health and Sciences Foundation. An internationally peer-reviewed publication that focuses on sediment and soil contamination.
Bi Monthly
ISSN: 1532-0383
Ed Calabrese, Editor-in-Chief

3784 Solid Waste Report
Business Publishers

2222 Sedwick Drive 301-589-5103
Durham, NC 27713 800-223-8720
Fax: 800-508-2592
custserv@bpinews.com
www.bpinews.com

Comprehensive news and analysis of legislation, regulation and litigation in solid waste management. Regularly features federal rules, congressional actions, state updates and business trends.
Weekly
Leonard A Eiserer, Publisher
Beth Early, Associate Publisher

3785 Waste News
Crain Communications
1725 Merriman Road 330-836-9180
#300 *Fax:* 330-836-1692
Akron, OH 44313

Editorial content focuses on waste management and recycling issues, primarily how businesses deal with the waste they generate. Covers waste management service providers, legistlative and regulatory environmental issues, emergingtechnologies, municipal recycling and waste issues, commodity market price, mergers, aquisitions and expansions.
Publication Date: 1995 Bi-Weekly
ISSN: 1091-699
Allan Gerlat, Editor
Brennan Lafferty, Managing Editor

3786 Widener University: International Conference on Solid Waste Proceedings
One University Place 610-499-4042
Chester, PA 19013 *Fax:* 610-499-4461
solid.waste@widener.edu
solid-waste.org

Publication of the annual conference on solid waste technology and management. Over 100 speakers from 35 countries present their work. Proceedings available.
Publication Date: 1983 Quarterly
ISSN: 1088-1697
James T. Harris III, Ed, President
Stephen C. Wilhite, Dphil, Provost of Academic Affairs

3787 Working Pressure
American Society of Sanitary Engineering
18927 Hickory Creek Drive 909-472-4208
Suite 220 info@workingpressuremag.com
Mokena, IL 60448 www.workingpressuremag.com

Magazine of the American Society of Sanitary Engineering with topics including codes and standards, health and safety, water quality, and association news.
Tom Palkon, Executive Director
Scott Hamilton, Senior Director

Periodicals: Environmental Health

3788 American College of Toxicology
1821 Michael Faraday Drive 703-547-0875
Suite 300 *Fax:* 703-438-3113
Reston, VA 20190 acthq@actox.org
www.actox.org

The American College of Toxicology is a 501-0-3 nonprofit organization. It is not a degree-granting organization. The American College of Toxicology is dedicated to providing an interactive forum for the advancement and exchange oftoxicologic information between industry, goverment, and academia. There is an annual meeting in November each year. The ACT publiches a journal, International Journal of Toxicology on a bi-monthly basis.
ISSN: 1091-5818
Mary Ellen Cosenza, President
Hanan Ghantous, President Elect

3789 American Journal of Public Health
American Public Health Association
800 I Street NW 202-777-2742
Washington, DC 20001 888-320-2742
Fax: 202-777-2533
www.apha.org

Peer-reviewed journal of the American Public Health Association (APHA) for public health workers and academics. Its emphasis is on research and practioners experiences.
12 Issues/Yr
Georges C. Benjamin, MD, Executive Director
James Carbo, Executive Office

3790 Applied and Environmental Microbiology
American Society for Microbiology
1752 N Street NW 202-737-3600
Washington, DC 20036 *Fax:* 202-942-9333
service@asmusa.org
www.asm.org

Contains current significant research in industrial microbiology, microbial ecology, biotechnology, public health microbiology and food microbiology.
Lynn Enquist, President
Joseph M. Campos, Secretary

3791 Asbestos & Lead Abatement Report
Business Publishers
2222 Sedwick Drive 301-589-5103
Durham, NC 27713 800-223-8720
Fax: 800-508-2592
custserv@bpinews.com
www.bpinews.com

Contains articles on regulation compliance, environmental trends and business opportunities.
Leonard A Eiserer, Publisher

3792 Aviation, Space and Environmental Medicine
Aerospace Medical Association
320 S Henry Street 703-739-2240
Alexandria, VA 22314 *Fax:* 703-739-9652
pday@asma.org
www.asma.org

Provides contact with physicians, life scientists, bioengineers, and medical specialists working in both basic medical research and in its clinical applications.
Publication Date: 1929 962 pages Monthly
ISSN: 0095-6562
Sarah A Nunneley MD, Author
Kris Belland, President
David Gradwell, President Elect

3793 Bio Integral Resource Center: Common Sense Pest Control
PO Box 7414 510-524-2567
Berkeley, CA 94707 *Fax:* 510-524-1758
birc@igc.org
www.birc.org

Features least toxic solutions to pest problems of the home and garden. Those who are chemically sensitive and looking for alternatives may find what they need in the Quarterly.
Publication Date: 1984 24 pages Quarterly
ISSN: 8756-7881
Dr. William Quarles, Executive Director

3794 Bio Integral Resource Center: IPM Practitioner
PO Box 7414 510-524-2567
Berkeley, CA 94707 *Fax:* 510-524-1758
birc@igc.org
www.birc.org

Focuses on management alternatives for pests such as insects, mites, ticks, vertebrates, weeds and plant pathogens.
Publication Date: 1979 24 pages 10 Times a Year
ISSN: 0738-969x
Dr. William Quarles, Executive Director

3795 Center for Statistical Ecology & Environmental Statistics: Environmental & Ecological Statistics
Kluwer Academic Publishers

Pennsylvania State University 814-865-9442
421 Thomas Building, Dept of Statistics *Fax:* 814-865-1278
University Park, PA 16802 gpp@stat.psu.edu
The Center is the first of its kind in the world and enjoys national and international reputation. They have an ongoing program of research that integrates statistics, ecology and the environment. The emphasis is on the environment andcollaborative research, training and exposition on improving the quantification and communication of man's impact on the environment. Major interest also lies in statistical investigations of the impact of the environment on man. Contact them forfull listings.
Publication Date: 1984 110 pages Quarterly
ISSN: 1352-8505
Ganapati P Patil, Editor-in-Chief

3796 EH&S Software News Online
Donley Technology
220 Garfield Avenue 804-224-9427
PO Box 152 *Fax:* 804-224-7958
Colonial Beach, VA 22443 donleytech@donleytech.com
www.donleytech.com
Reports on news and upgraded software products, database, and on-line systems from commercial developers and government resources.
Quarterly
John Donley, Editor
Elizabeth Donley, Managing Editor/Publisher

3797 Enterprise Software: Essential EH&S
Essential Technologies
1401 Rockville Pike 301-284-3000
#500 *Fax:* 301-284-3001
Rockville, MD 20852 www.essential-technologies.com
Integrated solutions for emissions management, hazard communication, compliance management, occupational health and safety and contingency management.
James Morentz, Publisher

3798 Environmental Connections
Connecticut College
270 Mohegan Avenue 860-439-5417
Box 5293 *Fax:* 860-439-2418
New London, CT 00632 ccbes@conncoll.edu
Publication Date: 1998 10 pages 2 times per year
Robert Askins, Director
Diane Whitelaw, Assistant Director

3799 Environmental Dimensions
Trine Publishers
C/O Blogar & Partners 919-653-2581
14600 Weston Parkway, Suite 300 866-541-3841
Cary, NC 27513 *Fax:* 919-678-8696
ehponline@niehs.nih.gov
ehp.niehs.nih.gov
Provides the environmental professionals with news and information on current environmental health issues, solution, and hazards, as well as examining governmental policies, legal news and Canada's environmental preformance.
22 times per year
Shaun R. Halloran, Operations Manager
Rita B. Hanson, Managing Editor

3800 Environmental Ethics
Center for Environmental Philosophy
University of North Texas 940-565-2727
1155 Union Circle #310980 *Fax:* 940-565-4439
Denton, TX 76203-5017 cep@unt.edu
www.cep.unt.edu
Published by the Center for Environmental Philosophy, the journal is devoted to the philisophical and ethical side to environmental issues.
ISSN: 0163-4275
Eugene C. Hargrove, President
Jan Dickson, Secretary-Treasurer

3801 Environmental Health Letter
Business Publishers
2222 Sedwick Drive 301-589-5103
Durham, NC 27713 800-223-8720
Fax: 800-508-2592
custserv@bpinews.com
www.bpinews.com
Comprehensive coverage of the latest policies and ground-breaking research that explores the potential links between environmental factors and human health.
8 pages
Leonard A Eiserer, Publisher
Beth Early, Operations Director

3802 Environmental Health perspectives
National Inst. of Environmental Health Sciences
C/O Blogar & Partners 919-653-2581
14600 Weston Parkway, Suite 300 866-541-3841
Cary, NC 27513 *Fax:* 919-678-8696
ehponline@niehs.nih.gov
ehp.niehs.nih.gov
Annual subscription.
224 pages Monthly
Shaun R. Halloran, Operations Manager
Rita B. Hanson, Managing Editor

3803 Florida Journal of Environmental Health
Florida Environmental Health Association
P.O. Box 350356 904-384-0838
Jacksonville, FL 32235 Contact_Us@feha.org
www.feha.org
Promotes public health by means of advanced environmental control.
Quarterly
ISSN: 0897-1823
Trisha Dall, President
Garry Schneider, President Elect

3804 Healthy Schools Network Newsletter
773 Madison Avenue 518-462-0632
Albany, NY 12208 *Fax:* 518-462-0433
info@healthyschools.org
www.healthyschools.org
HSN is a nationally recognized state-based advocate for the protection of children's environmental health in schools. Engages in research, education, outreach, technical assistance and coalition building to create schols that areenvironmentally responsible to children, and to their communities. Publishes a quarterly newsletter and maintains an Information Clearinghouse and Referral Service.
Quarterly
Claire L Barnett, Executive Director

3805 Human Ecology Action League Magazine
2250 N Druid Hills Road NE 404-248-1898
Atlanta, GA 30329 *Fax:* 404-248-0162
HEALNatnl@aol.com
lifestream.aol.com
The Human Ecology Action League Inc (HEAL) is a nonprofit organization founded in 1977 to serve those whose health has been adversely affected by environment exposures; to provide information to those who are concerned about the healtheffects of chemicals; and to alert the general public about the potential dangers of chemicals. Referrals to local HEAL chapters and other support groups are available from the League.
Publication Date: 1977 35 pages Quarterly
ISSN: 8755-7878
Diane Thomas, Editor

3806 Indoor Environment Review
IAQ Publications
7920 Norfolk Avenue 301-913-0115
Suite 900 *Fax:* 301-913-0119
Bethesda, MD 20814
New technology, research and legislation concerning all indoor air and water quality issues.
Robert Morrow, Editor

3807 Industrial Health and Hazards Update
InfoTeam

PO Box 15640 954-473-9560
Plantation, FL 33318 *Fax:* 954-473-0544
infoteamma@aol.com

Covers occupational safety, health hazards, and disease; mitigation and control of hazardous situations; waste recycling and treatment.
20 pages
Dr. David Allen, Associate Editor

3808 Journal of Environmental Health
National Environmental Health Association
720 S Colorado Boulevard 303-756-9090
Suite 1000-N 866-956-2258
Denver, CO 80246 *Fax:* 303-691-9490
staff@neha.org
www.neha.org

A practical journal containing information on a variety of environmental health issues.
Publication Date: 1937 70-76 pages 10 times a year
ISSN: 0022-0892
David T. Dyjack, Executive Director

3809 Journal of Medical Entomology
Journal of Entomology
3 Park Place 301-731-4535
Ste 307 *Fax:* 301-731-4538
Annapolis, MD 21401 esa@entsoc.org
www.entsoc.org

Contributions report on all phases of medical entomology and medical acarology, including the systematics and biology of insects, acarines, and other arthropods of public health and veterinary significance.
David Gammel, Executive Director
Neil Willoughby, Director of Finance

3810 Journal of Pesticide Reform
PO Box 1393 541-344-5044
Eugene, OR 97440 *Fax:* 541-344-6923
info@pesticide.org
www.pesticide.org

Pesticide factsheets, alternatives factsheets for common pest problems, and helpful information on how to take action for change are featured in this journal. Each issue also includes updates on NCAP's work, news on pesticide issues,and reviews of books and videos.
Publication Date: 1984 24 pages Quarterly
Jeremy Olsen, Assistant Director
Kim Leval, Executive Director

3811 Nation's Health, The
American Public Health Association
800 I Street NW 202-777-2742
Washington, DC 20001 888-320-2742
Fax: 202-777-2533
www.apha.org

Monthly newspaper of the American Public Health Association (APHA). It focuses on the latest public health news that public health professionals need to know such as food safety, racial and ethnic disparities, patients' rights,environmental issues, and health screening.
10 Issues/Yr
Georges C. Benjamin, MD, Executive Director
James Carbo, Executive Office

3812 National Institute of Environmental Health Sciences Journal
111 T.W. Alexander Drive 919-496-2433
Research Triangle Park, NC 27709 *Fax:* 919-496-8276
www.niehs.nih.gov

The National Institute of Environmental Health Sciences is the principal federal agency for basic biomedical research on the health effects of environmental agents. It is the headquarters for the National Toxicology Program whichcoordinates toxicology studies within the Department of Health and Human Services.
Publication Date: 1972 150 pages Monthly
ISSN: 0091-6765
Kenneth Olden PhD, Director

3813 Natural Resources Council of America: NEPA News
1616 P Street 202-232-6631
NW Suite 340 *Fax:* 240-465-0467
Washington, DC 20036
Publication Date: 1994 8 pages Quarterly
Andrea Yank, Executive Director

3814 Orion Magazine
Orion Society
187 Main Street 413-528-4422
Great Barrington, MA 01230 888-909-6568
orionmagazine.org

Features environmental and cultural writing, with the principle that humans are morally responsible for the world around them.
Publication Date: 1982 Bimonthly
H. Emerson Blake, Editor-in-Chief
Madeline Miller, Strategic Director

Periodicals: Gaming & Hunting

3815 American Bass e-Magazine
12340 Seal Beach Blvd. 310-376-1026
Suite B120 *Fax:* 310-376-5072
Seal Beach, CA 90277 www.americanbass.com

Tournament overviews and results.
Publication Date: 1989
David Plotnik, President & Founder

3816 American Trapper Magazine
PO Box 224 812-277-9670
Greenville, PA 16125 866-680-8727
Fax: 812-277-9672
at@zoominternet.net
www.nationaltrappers.com

A publication of the National Trappers Association, with content written by and intended for trappers.
Chris McAllister, President
Rich Faler, Editor

3817 Bison World
National Bison Association
8690 Wolff Ct. 303-292-2833
Suite 200 *Fax:* 303-845-9081
Westminster, CO 80031 info@bisoncentral.com
www.bisoncentral.com

Published by the NBA, an organization of bison producers dedicated to awareness of the healthy properties of bison meat and bison production.
Publication Date: 1975 100 pages Quarterly
Dave Carter, Executive Director
Jim Matheson, Assistant Director

3818 Fair Chase
Boone and Crockett Club
250 Station Drive 406-542-1888
Missoula, MT 59801 888-840-4868
Fax: 406-542-0784
bcclub@boone-crockett.org
www.boone-crockett.org

Full-color magazine of the Boone and Crockett Club, dedicated to hunting and conservation of big game in North America. Available only to members of the club.
Publication Date: 1986 Quarterly
Doug Painter, Editor-in-Chief
Julie Tripp, Director, Publications

3819 IPPL News
PO Box 776 843-871-2280
Summerville, SC 29484 *Fax:* 843-871-7988
info@ippl.org
www.ippl.org/gibbon

Educates readers in more than 50 countries about action that can be taken to protect primates.
Publication Date: 1974 32 pages 3 Times a Year
ISSN: 1040-3027
Dr Shirley McGreal, Chairperson
Barbara Allison, Office Manager

3820 International Game Fish Association Newsletter
300 Gulf Stream Way
Dania Beach, FL 33004
954-927-2628
Fax: 954-924-4299
hq@igfa.org
www.igfa.org
Founded as record-keeper and to maintain fishing rules. Today, emphasis is on conservation and education. Newsletters published are World Record Game Fish, annually and The International Angler, bi-monthly.
Bi-Monhtly
Rob Kramer, President
Michael J. Myatt, Chief Operating Officer

3821 JAKES Magazine
770 Augusta Road
PO Box 530
Edgefield, SC 29824
803-637-3106
800-THE-NWTF
Fax: 803-637-0034
nwtf@nwtf.net
www.nwtf.org
JAKES (Juniors Acquiring Knowledge, Ethics and Sportsmanship) is a magazine which provides fun and educational articles focusing on young hunters, outdoor activities, the environment and other items of interest to readers 17 years oldand younger. Free with membership.
Quarterly
Vern Ross, President
Marvin Hartley, Vice President

3822 Journal of Mammalogy
American Society of Mammalogists
PO Box 4973
Topeka, KS 66604
785-550-6904
cclassi@mammalsociety.org
www.mammalsociety.org
Official journal of the American Society of Mammalogists, promoting interest in mammals all over the world.
Publication Date: 1919 6 issues/year
Enrique P. Lessa, President
Paul T. Stapp, Publications Director

3823 Kind News
RedRover
PO Box 188890
Sacramento, CA 95818
202-452-1100
Fax: 916-378-5098
KindNews@RedRover.org
redrover.org/readers/kind-news-magazine
Classroom newspaper for kids in grades K-6. It features articles, puzzles and celebrity interviews that teach children the value of showing kindness and respect to animals, the environment, and one another. Formerly published by theHumane Society, it transferred to RedRover in 2017.
5 per year
Nicole Forsyth, President & CEO
Karly Noel, VP, Operations & Education

3824 Mammalian Species
American Society of Mammalogists
PO Box 4973
Topeka, KS 66604
785-550-6904
cclassi@mammalsociety.org
www.mammalsociety.org
Individual mammalian species accounts are released throughout the year.
5-14 pages 15-25 releases/year
Enrique P. Lessa, President
Paul T. Stapp, Publications Director

3825 Mid-Atlantic Fishery Management Council Newsletter
800 North State Street
Suite 201
Dover, DE 19901
302-674-2331
877-446-2362
Fax: 302-674-5399
contact@mafmc.org
www.mafmc.org
It is responsible for the conservation and management of fishery resources within the federal 200-mile limit of the Atlantic off the coasts of New York, New Jersey, Pennsylvania, Delaware, Maryland, Virginia and North Carolina.
Publication Date: 1998 8 pages Quarterly
Christopher M. Moore, Executive Director
Rich Seagraves, Senior Scientist

3826 Turkey Call
770 Augusta Road
PO Box 530
Edgefield, SC 29824
803-637-3106
800-THE-NWTF
Fax: 803-637-0034
nwtf@nwtf.net
www.nwtf.org
A magazine for turkey hunting enthusiasts, provides articles to help you improve your hunting skills and learn how to enhance your land for wildlife. Free with membership.
Bi-Monthly
Vern Ross, President
Marvin Hartley, Vice President

3827 Wheelin' Sportsmen
770 Augusta Road
PO Box 530
Edgefield, SC 29824
803-637-3106
800-THE-NWTF
Fax: 803-637-0034
nwtf@nwtf.net
www.nwtf.org
Magazine for all disabled people and their able-bodied partners who are interested in the outdoors, especially recreational shooting, hunting and fishing. Free with membership.
Quarterly
Vern Ross, President
Marvin Hartley, Vice President

3828 Women in the Outdoors
770 Augusta Road
PO Box 530
Edgefield, SC 29824
803-637-3106
800-THE-NWTF
Fax: 803-637-0034
www.nwtf.org
Magazine that delivers features on a variety of outdoor topics of interest to the novice and experienced outdoorswoman. Free with membership.
Quarterly
Vern Ross, President
Marvin Hartley, Vice President

Periodicals: Habitat Preservation & Land Use

3829 ANJEC Report
Association/New Jersey Environmental Commissions
PO Box 157
Mendham, NJ 00794
973-539-7547
Fax: 973-539-7713
info@anjec.org
www.anjec.org
Nonprofit organization promoting public interest in natural resource protection and supporting municipal environmental commissions throughout New Jersey.
Publication Date: 1970 32 pages Quarterly
Jennifer M. Coffey, Executive Director
Kerry Miller, Assistant Director

3830 Afield
4705 University Drive
Suite 290
Durham, NC 27707
919-403-8558
Fax: 919-403-0379
northcarolina@tnc.org
www.nature.org/northcarolina

Published by The Nature Conservancy, saving the last great places of North Carolina.
Quarterly Newsletter
Craig O. McCaw, Chairman
James E. Rogers, Vice Chair

3831 America's Wilderness
1615 M Street NW 202-833-2300
Washington, DC 20036 800-843-9453
action@tws.org
www.wilderness.org
Official newsletter of The Wilderness Society, featuring information on current campaigns, as well as profiles of interesting locations.
Jamie Williams, President
Melyssa Watson, Executive Director

3832 American Association for Advancement of Science: Animal Keeper's Forum
1200 New York Avenue Northwest 202-326-6400
Washington, DC 20005 *Fax:* 202-289-4985
webster@aaas.org
www.aaas.org
The American Association for the Advancement of Science is the world's largest general science and publisher of the peer-reviewed journal. With more than 138,000 members and 275, AAAS serves as an authoritative source for informationon the latest developments in science and bridges gaps among scientists, policy- makers and the public to advance science and science education.
Publication Date: 1947 54 pages Monthly
ISSN: 0164-9531
Gerald Fink, Chair
Geraldine Richmond, President

3833 American Currents
North American Native Fishes Association
info@nanfa.org
www.nanfa.org/ac.shtml
Journal of the North American Native Fishes Association, with articles on the biology and ecology of fishes and habitats, as well as science, legal, and other environmental information.
Quarterly
Fritz Rohde, President
Brian Zimmerman, Vice President

3834 American Entomologist
Journal of Entomology
3 Park Place 301-731-4535
Ste 307 *Fax:* 301-731-4538
Annapolis, MD 21401 esa@entsoc.org
www.entsoc.org
American Entomologist is a quarterly, general interest entomology magazine written for both scientists and nonscientists. It publishes colorful, illustrated feature articles, peer-reviewed scientific reports, provocative and humorouscolumns, letters, book reviews, and obituaries.
Publication Date: 1955 64 pages Quarterly
ISSN: 1046-2821
David Gammel, Executive Director
Neil Willoughby, Director of Finance

3835 American Forests Magazine
1220 L Street NW 202-737-1944
Suite 750 800-368-5748
Washington, DC 20005 *Fax:* 202-955-4588
info@amfor.org
www.americanforests.org/magazine
Published by American Forests, the oldest national citizens conservation organization in the US.
Publication Date: 1895 3 issues/year
Jad Daley, President & CEO
Peter Hutchins, Chief Operations Officer

3836 American Ground Water Trust Newsletter
American Ground Water Trust
50 Pleasant Street 603-228-5444
Suite 2 800-423-7748
Concord, NH 03301 *Fax:* 603-228-6557
trustinfo@agwt.org
www.agwt.org
4 pages Quarterly
David Kill, Chair
Andrew Stone, Executive Director

3837 Annals of the Entomological Society of America
Journal of Entomology
3 Park Place *Fax:* 301-731-4538
Ste 307 esa@entsoc.org
Annapolis, MD 21401 www.entsoc.org
Contributions report on the basic aspects of the biology of anthropods and are divided into categories by subject matter; systematics; ecology and population biology; arthropods in relation to plant disease; conservation biology andbiodiversity; physiology, biochemistry, and toxicology; morphology, history, and fine sructure; genetics and behavior.
Bi-Monthly
David Gammel, Executive Director
Neil Willoughby, Director of Finance

3838 Annual Review of Entomology
Annual Reviews
3 Park Place *Fax:* 301-731-4538
Ste 307 esa@entsoc.org
Annapolis, MD 21401 www.entsoc.org
This is published in Januray and made available through ESA on a regular subscription basis. The series occupies a special place within the field of entomology. Authoritative critical reviews by eminent scientists provide a valuableresource for students, teachers, and researchers: specialists and nonspecialists.
Yearly
David Gammel, Executive Director
Neil Willoughby, Director of Finance

3839 Appalachian Mountain Club
Appalachian Mountain Club Books
5 Joy Street 617-523-0636
Boston, MA 00210 800-262-4455
Fax: 617-523-0722
information@outdoors.org
www.outdoors.org
The AMC, founded in 1876, promotes the protection, enjoyment, and wise use of the mountains, rivers and trails of the Northeast. We encourage people to enjoy and protect the natural world because we believe that successful conservationdepends on this experience. The AMC publishes an award-winning magazine and more than 60 guide books to the Northeast.
Wayne Thornbrough, Chair
Rol Fessenden, Vice Chair

3840 Arthropod Management Tests
Journal of Entomology
3 Park Place *Fax:* 301-731-4538
Ste 307 esa@entsoc.org
Annapolis, MD 21401 www.entsoc.org
This is published in late spring. The purpose is to promote timely dissemination of information on preliminary and routine screening tests on management of arthropods, both beneficial and harmful. Pest management methods tested andreported may include the use of chemical pesticides as well as other materials or agents, such as insect growth regulators, pheromones, natural enemies for biological control, or pest-resistant plants/animals. Reports are based on tests conducted byreseachers.
Yearly
David Gammel, Executive Director
Neil Willoughby, Director of Finance

3841 Audubon
National Audubon Society
225 Varick Street 212-979-3196
7th Floor 844-428-3826
New York, NY 10014 *Fax:* 212-979-3188
audubon@emailcustomerservice.com
www.audubon.org

Print magazine of the National Audubon Society.
David Yarnold, President & CEO
Stephen Meyer, Chief Operations Officer

3842 BATS Magazine
500 North Capital of Texas Highway 512-327-9721
Building 1 800-538-2287
Austin, TX 78746 www.batcon.org
Official magazine of Bat Conservation International, with current research, news, and topics about bats and bat conservation.
Publication Date: 1982
Mike Daulton, Executive Director
Kevin Pierson, Chief Conservation Officer

3843 Biodiversity Institute Newsletter
University of Kansas
Dyche Hall 785-864-4540
Lawrence, KS 66045 *Fax:* 785-864-5335
A comprehensive research, graduate education and public service institution dedicated to biodiversity science and collections. Collections of more than 7 million plant and animal specimens, with particular strengths in neotropicalamphibians, great plains, flora, bees and antarctic plant fossils.
Publication Date: 1978 6 pages Quarterly
Dr Leonard Krishtalka, Director

3844 Birder's Guide
PO Box 744 302-838-3651
Delaware City, DE 19706 800-850-2473
Fax: 302-838-3651
info@aba.org
www.aba.org
Published by the American Birding Association, which represents the interests of birdwatchers in various arenas, and helps birders increase their knowledge, skills, and enjoyment of birding. ABA also contributes to bird conservation bylinking the skills of its members to on-the-ground projects. ABA promotes field-birding skills through meetings, workshops, equipment, and guided involvement in birding, promoting national and international birders networks and publications.
Irregular
Jeffrey A. Gordon, President & CEO
Michael Retter, Editor

3845 Birding Magazine
American Birding Association
PO Box 744 302-838-3660
Delaware City, DE 19706 800-850-2473
Fax: 302-838-3651
info@aba.org
www.aba.org
Published by the American Birding Association, which represents the interests of birdwatchers in various arenas, and helps birders increase their knowledge, skills, and enjoyment of birding. ABA also contributes to bird conservation bylinking the skills of its members to on-the-ground projects. ABA promotes field-birding skills through meetings, workshops, equipment, and guided involvement in birding, promoting national and international birders networks and publications.
Publication Date: 1972 Bi Monthly
Jeffrey A. Gordon, President & CEO
Ted Floyd, Editor

3846 Blowhole
3625 Brigantine Boulevard 609-266-0538
PO Box 773 *Fax:* 609-266-6300
Brigantine, NJ 00820 mmsc@verizon.net
mmsc.org
A quarterly newsletter published by the Marine Mammal Stranding Center.
Publication Date: 1978 8 pages Quarterly
Robert C Schoelkopf, President
Kenneth Schaffer, Chairman

3847 Carolina Bird Club
1809 Lakepark Drive 910-791-5726
Raleigh, NC 27612 *Fax:* 910-791-7228
hq@carolinabirdclub.org
www.carolinabirdclub.org
A nonprofit educational and scientific association, open to anyone interested in the study and conservation of wildlife, particularly birds. Meets each winter, spring and fall. Meeting sites are selected to give participants anopportunity to see many different kinds of birds. Guided field trips, informative programs and business sessions are combined for an exciting weekend of meeting with people who share an enthusiasm and concern for birds.
Publication Date: 1937 Quarterly
ISSN: 0009-1987
Irvin Pitts, President
Don Seriff, Editor

3848 Coalition for Education in the Outdoors
P.O. Box 2000 607-753-2011
Cortland, NY 13045 *Fax:* 607-753-5982
www.outdooredcoalition.org
A network of organizations, business, institutions, centers, agencies, and associations linked and communicating in support of the broad purpose of education in, for, and about the outdoors. Takes a board view of outdoor education andseeks not to duplicate or compete with the work of organizations, but to provide services not easily performed by other groups.
Publication Date: 1987 48-52 pages Bi-Annual
ISSN: 1065-5204
Erik J. Bitterbaum, President
Peter Perkins, VP Institutional Advancement

3849 College of Tropical Agriculture and Human Resources: Impact Report
University of Hawaii
3050 Maile Way 808-956-7056
Gilmore 119 *Fax:* 808-956-5966
Honolulu, HI 96822 ocs@ctahr.hawaii.edu
www.ctahr.hawaii.edu
The vision of the college is to be the premier resource for tropical agricultural systems and resource management in the Asia-Pacific region. Its mission outlines a commitment to the preparation of students and all citizens of Hawaiifor life in a global community through research and education programs supporting tropical agricultural systems that foster viable communities, a diversified economy and a healthy environment.
Annual
Maria Gallo, Dean/Director
Wimmie Wong Lui, Assistant to the Dean

3850 Connecticut Woodlands
Middlefield 860-346-2372
16 Meriden Road *Fax:* 860-347-7463
Rockfall, CT 00648 info@ctwoodlands.org
www.ctwoodlands.org
Quarterly publication of the Connecticut Forest and Park Association, an organization for forest and wildlife conservation. Develops outdoor recreation and natural resources. Provides forest management, construction of hiking trailsand consultation in the areas of forestry and environment.
Quarterly
Lori Paradis Brant, Education Director
Teresa Peters, Office Manager

3851 Conservancy of Southwest Florida
Eye On The Issues
1495 Smith Preserve Way 232-262-0304
Naples, FL 34102 *Fax:* 232-262-0672
info@conservancy.org
www.conservancy.org
It aims to protect the quality of life in the region
8 pages Quarterly
Rob Moher, President/CEO
Lynn Slabaugh, Board Chair

3852 **Conservation & Natural Resources: Water Resources Division, Nevada Wildlife Almanac**
901 S. Stewart Street 775-681-2800
Suite 2002 *Fax:* 775-684-2811
Carson City, NV 89701 ndwr.state.nv.us
The mission is to conserve, protect, manage and enhance the State's water resources for Nevada's citizens through the appropriation and reallocation of the public waters.
Publication Date: 1996 12 pages Twice/year
Hugh Ricci, State Engineer

3853 **Conservation Commission News**
New Hampshire Association of Conservation Comm.
54 Portsmouth Street 603-224-7867
Concord, NH 03301 info@nhacc.org
www.nhacc.org
Encourage conservation and appropriate use of New Hampshire's natural resources by providing assistance to New Hampshire's municipal conservation commissions and by facilitating communication among commissions and between commissionsand other public and private agencies involved in conservation.
8 pages
G. Wesley Robertson, President
Tom Duston, Secretary

3854 **Conservation Communique**
Wyoming Association of Conservation Districts
517 East 19th Street 307-632-5716
Cheyenne, WY 82001 *Fax:* 307-638-4099
www.conservewy.com
It provides leadership for the conservation of Wyoming's soil and water resources, promotes the control of soil erosion, promotes and protects the quality of Wyoming's waters, reduce siltation of stream channels and reservoirs, promotewise use of Wyoming's water, and all other natural resources, preserve and enhance wildlife habitat, protect the tax base and promote the health, safety and general welfare of the citizens of this state through a responsible conservation ethic.
Quarterly
Kelly Brown, Program Specialist
Bobbie Frank, Executive Director

3855 **Conservation Conversation**
Montana Association of Conservation Districts
3001 Coolidge Road 517-324-5274
Suite 250 *Fax:* 517-324-4435
East Lansing, MI 48823-6362 macd@macd.org
www.macd.org
It is Working to strengthen Michigan's Conservation Districts through leadership, information and representation at the state level.
Quarterly
Lori Phalen, Executive Director
Waynette Ginter, Bookkeeper

3856 **Conservation Leader**
Utah Association of Conservation Districts
1860 North 100 East 435-753-6029
Logan, UT 84341 *Fax:* 435-755-2117
Quarterly

3857 **Conservation Notes: New England Wildflower Society**
180 Hemenway Road 508-877-7630
Framingham, MA 00170 508-877-6553
Fax: 508-877-3658
information@newenglandwild.org
www.newenglandwild.org
The mission is to conserve and promote the region's native plants to ensure healthy, biologically diverse landscapes.
36 pages Yearly
Debbi Edelstein, Executive Director
Deirdre C. Menoyo, Chair, Board of Trustees

3858 **Conservation Partner**
Arkansas Association of Conservation Districts
101 E Capitol 501-682-2915
Suite 350 *Fax:* 501-682-3991
Little Rock, AR 72201 www.aracd.org
The purpose and mission is to assist the conservation districts of the state of Arkansas in their efforts to serve the soil and water conservation needs of the people of Arkansas.
Quarterly
Debbie Moreland, Program Administrator
Rocky Harrell, President

3859 **Conservation Visions**
Nebraska Association of Resources Districts
601 S 12th Street 402-471-7670
Suite 201 *Fax:* 402-471-7677
Lincoln, NE 68508 nard@nrdnet.org
www.nrdnet.org
The mission is to assist NRDs in a coordinated effort to accomplish collectively what may not be accomplished individually to conserve, sustain, and improve our natural resources and environment.
Bi-Monthly
Terry Martin, President
Jim Bendfeldt, Vice President

3860 **Conservogram**
Soil and Water Conservation Society
945 Southwest Ankeny Road 515-289-2331
Ankeny, IA 50023 *Fax:* 515-289-1227
pubs@swcs.org
www.swcs.org
Published for the professionals in the natural resource fields, and contains highlights on the news and ideas in the preservation of natural resources.
Monthly
Mark Berkland, President
Cheryl Simmons, Vice President

3861 **Consultant Magazine**
Association of Consutling Foresters
376 McLaws Circle 703-548-0990
Suite 1a *Fax:* 703-548-6395
Alexandria, VA 23185 membership@acf-foresters.org
www.theconsultant-digital.com
Publication from Association of Consulting Foresters of America, Inc.
Shannon M. McCabe, Executive Director
Lynn C. Wilson, Editor-in-Chief

3862 **Copeia**
ASIH
810 E 10th Street 785-865-9405
Lawrence, KA 66044 800-627-0326
asih@allenpress.com
www.asih.org
official journal of the American Society of Ichthyologists and Herpetologists (ASIH), publishing research papers on extant and extinct fishes, amphibians, and reptiles.
Publication Date: 1913
Chris Beachy, President
W. Leo Smith, Editor

3863 **Cornell Lab of Ornithology: Birdscope**
Birdscope
159 Sapsucker Woods Road 607-254-2451
Ithaca, NY 14850 *Fax:* 607-254-2415
cornellbirds@cornell.edu
www.birds.cornell.edu
It is a world leader in the study, appreciation, and conservation of birds.
Quarterly,Newsletter
Alex Chang, Communications Director
Gustave Axelson, Editorial Director

3864 **Cornell Lab of Ornithology: Living Bird**
Birdscope

159 Sapsucker Woods Road 607-254-2475
Ithaca, NY 14850 *Fax:* 607-254-2415
cornellbirds@cornell.edu
www.birds.cornell.edu

It is a world leader in the study, appreciation, and conservation of birds.

Quarterly, Magazine
Alex Chang, Communications Director
Gustave Axelson, Editorial Director

3865 Delta Wildlife Magazine
433 Stoneville Road 662-686-3370
PO Box 276 *Fax:* 662-686-3382
Stoneville, MS 38776 trey@deltawildlife.org
deltawildlife.org

Dedicated to the conservation, enhancement, and restoration of the wildlife and natural resources of the Delta and part-Delta counties of Northwest Mississippi.

Infrequent
Trey Cooke, Executive Director
Liz Brown, Director, Marketing

3866 Department of Natural Resources
301 Centennial Mall South 402-471-2363
PO Box 94676 *Fax:* 402-471-2900
Lincoln, NE 68509

Quarterly
Roger K Patterson, Director

3867 District Connection Newsletter
North Carolina Assoc. of Soil/Water Cons. Dist.
1614 Mail Service Center 919-733-2302
Raleigh, NC 27699 *Fax:* 919-715-3559

Monthly
David Williams, Acting Director

3868 E Magazine
Doug Moss
28 Knight St 203-854-5559
Norwalk, CT 00685 *Fax:* 203-866-0602
www.emagazine.com

A comprehensive magazine dealing with environmental issues and national conservation concerns.

Publication Date: 1990 64 pages Bimonthly
Doug Moss, Publisher/Executive Director
Roddy Scheer, Executive Director/Editor

3869 ESA Newsletter
Journal of Entomology
3 Park Place 301-731-4538
Ste 307 esa@entsoc.org
Annapolis, MD 21401 www.entsoc.org

Monthly
David Gammel, Executive Director
Neil Willoughby, Director of Finance

3870 Eagle Nature Foundation Ltd: Bald Eagle News
300 East Hickory Street 815-594-2306
Apple River, IL 61001 *Fax:* 815-594-2305
eaglenature.tni@juno.com
eaglenature.com

A quarterly publication from the Eagle Nature Foundation.

Publication Date: 1995 20 pages Quarterly
Terrence N. Ingram, Executive Director
Susan Ertmer, Vice President

3871 Earth Steward
Michigan Association of Conservation Districts
3001 Coolidge Road 517-324-5274
Suite 250 *Fax:* 517-324-4435
East Lansing, MI 48823-6362 macd@macd.org
www.macd.org

Quarterly membership newsletter

Quarterly
Waynette Ginter, Bookkeeper
Lori Phalen, Executive Director

3872 Ecosphere
Forum International
91 Gregory Lane 925-997-1864
Suite 21 800-252-4475
Pleasant Hill, CA 94523 *Fax:* 925-946-1500
www.foruminternational.com

Accepts advertising. The first ever environmental/ecological magazine. It is dedicated to the interrelations of man in nature and a balanced approach of its biological, economic, socio-political and spiritual components. Since 1965.

Publication Date: 1965 16-48 pages Bi Monthly
Dr. Nicolas Hetzer, Production Manager
J McCormack, Circulation Director

3873 Elm Leaves
Elm Research Institute
11 Kit Street 603-358-6198
Keene, NH 03431 800-367-3567
Fax: 603-358-6305

A semi annual publication published by the Elm Research Institute. Free with membership.

Publication Date: 1967 4-9 pages Semi-Annually
John Hansel, Editor/Executive Director
Yvonne Spalthoff, Assistant Director

3874 Environmental Concern: The Wonders of Wetlands, an Educators Guide
POW-The Planning of Wetlands
201 Boundary Lane 410-745-9620
PO Box P *Fax:* 410-745-3517
St Michaels, MD 21663 order@wetland.org
www.wetland.org

Since its founding in 1972, EC has been specializing in consulting, planning design, education services, construction services and research related to all aspects of wetlands. As wetlands and contiguous upland forests and meadows areinteracting ecosystems EC specializes in consulting, planning, design, and project supervision services for such upland ecosystem constructions and restorations for the purpose of wetland buffers, reforestation, wildlife habitat and critical areas ofpreservation.

Publication Date: 1995 Quarterly
ISSN: 1095-2063
Suzanne Pittengar Slear, President
Chuck Barbour, Nursery Manager

3875 Environmental Entomology
Journal of Entomology
3 Park Place 301-731-4535
Ste 307 *Fax:* 301-731-4538
Annapolis, MD 21401 esa@entsoc.org
www.entsoc.org

Contributions report on the interaction of insects with biological, chemical, and physiological and chemical ecology (abiotic effects, pheromonea, effects of miscellaneous pollutants), community/ecosystem ecology (trophic-levelsstudies, associations), population ecology (mating, reproduction, movement, behavior, parasitism, predation, microbial ecology, insect-plant relations), pest management and sampling (integrated pest management, sampling, distribution), and biologicalcontrol.

Bi-Monthly
David Gammel, Executive Director
Neil Willoughby, Director of Finance

3876 Environmental History
Forest History Society
2925 Academy Road 919-682-9319
Durham, NC 27705-9311 *Fax:* 919-682-2349
editor@environmentalhistory.net
environmentalhistory.net

Journal co-published by the American Society for Environmental History and the Forest History Society in association with Oxford University Press.

Publication Date: 1976
Mark Hersey, Co-Editor
Stephen Brain, Co-Editor

3877 Everglades Reporter
Friends of the Everglades

11767 South Dixie Highway 305-669-0858
#232 Fax: 305-669-0858
South Miami, FL 33156 www.everglades.org
Protecting the Everglades. A bi-annual publication from Friends of the Everglades.
Publication Date: 1971 8 pages Quarterly
Alan Farago, President
Connie Washburn, Vice-President

3878 Fisheries Focus: Atlantic
Atlantic States Marine Fisheries Commission
1050 N. Highland Street 703-842-0740
Suite 200 Fax: 703-842-0741
Arlington, VA 22201 info@asmfc.org
www.asmfc.org
12 pages Monthly
Robert E. Beal, Executive Director
Tina L Berger, Director of Communications

3879 Fisheries Magazine
American Fisheries Society
425 Barlow Place 301-897-8616
Suite 110 Fax: 307-897-8096
Bethesda, MD 20814-2144 main@fisheries.org
www.fisheries.org
Peer-reviewed articles that address contemporary issues and problems, techniques, philosophies and other areas of interest to the general fisheries profession. Monthly features include letters, meeting notices, book listings andreviews, environmental essays and organization profiles.
Douglas Austen, Executive Director
Laura Hendee, Manager, Journals

3880 Forest History Society Issues Series
2925 Academy Road 919-682-9319
Durham, NC 27705-9311 Fax: 919-682-2349
steven.anderson@foresthistory.org
www.foresthistory.org
Series of booklets bringing historical context to current issues in forestry and natural resource management.
Steven Anderson, President
Janet Askew, Assistant Director

3881 Forest History Today Magazine
Forest History Society
2925 Academy Road 919-682-9319
Durham, NC 27705-9311 Fax: 919-682-2349
james.lewis@foresthistory.org
www.foresthistory.org
Official magazine of the Forest History Society.
Publication Date: 1995
Steven Anderson, President
James G. Lewis, Editor and Historian

3882 Forest Timeline
Forest History Society
2925 Academy Road 919-682-9319
Durham, NC 27705-9311 Fax: 919-682-2349
steven.anderson@foresthistory.org
www.foresthistory.org
Newsletter of the Forest History Society.
Steven Anderson, President
Janet Askew, Assistant Director

3883 Forestry Source
Society of American Foresters
5400 Grosvernor Lane 301-897-8720
Bethesada, MD 20814 866-897-8720
Fax: 301-897-3690
www.safnet.org
Tabloid newsletter covering important information regarding critical issues in forestry research and technology, legislative updates and news about SAF programs and activities on a national and local level.
20 pages Monthly
Matt Walls, Editor

3884 Game & Fish Commission Wildlife Management Division Newsletter
2 Natural Resources Drive 501-223-6300
Little Rock, AR 72205 800-364-4263
Fax: 501-223-6452
askAGFC@agfc.state.ar.us
www.agfc.com
Dedicated to managing wildlife in the state of Arkansas.
Publication Date: 1920 33-35 pages 5x year
Mike Knoedl, Director
Andrew Bass, Assistant Deputy Director

3885 Golden Gate Audubon Society
2530 San Pablo Avenue 510-843-2222
Suite G Fax: 510-843-5351
Berkeley, CA 94702 ggas@goldengateaudubon.org
www.goldengateaudubon.org
Monthly publication from Golden Gate Audubon Society. Published 10 times yearly.
Publication Date: 1917 12 pages Monthly
ISSN: 0164-971x
Cindy Margulis, Executive Director
Ilana DeBare, Communications Director

3886 Good Day!
National Grange
1616 H Street NW 202-628-3507
Washington, DC 20006 888-447-2643
Fax: 202-347-1091
info@nationalgrange.org
www.nationalgrange.org
Magazine of the National Grange.
Betsy Huber, President
Amanda Leigh Brozana-Rios, Director, Communications

3887 Great Plains Native Plant Society Newsletter
P.O. Box 321 605-745-3397
Hermosa, SD 57744 Fax: 605-745-3397
info@gpnps.org
www.gpnps.org
The mission of the Society is to conduct scientific research regarding plants of the Great Plains of North America, and to disseminate this knowledge through the creation of one or more educational botanic gardens of plants of theGreat Plains. These gardens feature, but are not limited to, Barr's discoveries. The society also engages in educational activities that further public familiarity with plants of the Great Plains, their uses, and enjoyment.
Publication Date: 1984 4-8 pages Intermittent
Cindy Reed, President

3888 Green Space
New York Parks and Conservation Association
29 Elk Street 518-434-1583
Albany, NY 12207 Fax: 518-427-0067
ptny@ptny.org
www.nypca.org
Semi-Annual
Robin Dropkin, Executive Director

3889 Habitat Hotline
Atlantic States Marine Fisheries Commission
1050 N. Highland Street 703-842-0740
Suite 200 Fax: 703-842-0741
Arlington, VA 22201 info@asmfc.org
www.asmfc.org
6 pages Quarterly
Robert E. Beal, Executive Director
Tina L Berger, Director of Communications

3890 Illinois Audubon Society
PO Box 2547 217-544-BIRD
Springfield, IL 62708 Fax: 217-544-7433
ias@illinoisaudubon.org
www.illinoisaudubon.org
A membership organization dedicated to the preservation of Illinois Wildlife and the habitats which support them. Has sanctuar-

ies, conservation education and land acquisition programs and publishes quarterly magazines and newsletters.
Publication Date: 1916 28 pages Quarterly
ISSN: 1061-9801
Tom Clay, Executive Director
Jodie Owen, Accounts Manager

3891 Illinois Environmental Council: IEC Bulletin
230 Broadway
Suite 150
Springfield, IL 62701
217-544-5954
Fax: 217-544-5958
iec@ilenviro.org
www.ilenviro.org
The IEC is a coalition of over 70 environmental, conservation and health groups.
Bi-Monthly
Jonathan Goldman, Executive Director
Jennifer Sublett, Outreach Coordinator

3892 In Brief
50 California Street
Suite 500
San Francisco, CA 94111
800-584-6460
Fax: 415-217-2040
headquarters@earthjustice.org
www.earthjustice.org
Newsletter of Earthjustice, a nonprofit public interest law firm dedicated to protecting the magnificent places, natural resources and wildlife of this earth and to defending the right of all people to a healthy environment. We bringabout far-reaching change by enforcing and strengthening environmental laws on behalf of hundreds of organizations and communities.
Quarterly
Trip Van Noppen, President
DARRELL BYERS, Vice President, Development

3893 Iowa Cooperative Fish & Wildlife Research Unit: Annual Report
Iowa State University
Science Hall II
Ames, IA 50011
515-294-3056
Fax: 515-294-5468
Publication Date: 1932 50 pages Annual

3894 Iowa Native Plant Society Newsletter
Iowa State University
Botany Department
Ames, IA 50011
515-294-9499
Fax: 515-294-1337
dlewis@iastate.edu
An organization of amateur and professional botanists and native plant enthusiasts who are interested in the scientific, educational and cultural aspects, as well as the preservation and conservation of the native plants of Iowa. TheSociety was organized in 1995 to create a forum where plant enthusiasts, gardners and professional botanists could exchange ideas and coordinate activities such as field trips, work shops, and restoration of natural areas.
Publication Date: 1995 12 pages 3/4 times X year
Tom Rosburg, President
Deb Lewis, Contact Person

3895 Journal of Caves & Karst Studies
National Speleological Society
6001 Pulaski Pike
Huntsville, AL 35810
256-852-1300
nss@caves.org
www.caves.org
A quarterly journal published by the National Speleological Society.
Quarterly
ISSN: 1090-6924
Geary Schindel, President
Scott Engel, Executive Vice President

3896 Journal of Economic Entomology
Journal of Entomology
3 Park Place
Ste 307
Annapolis, MD 21401
301-731-4535
Fax: 301-731-4538
esa@entsoc.org
www.entsoc.org
Contributions report on the economic significance of insects and are divided into categories by subject matter: apiculture and social insects; arthropods in relation to plant disease; biological and microbial disease; ecology andbehavior; ecotoxicology; extension; field and forage crops; forest entomology; horticultural entomology; household and structural insects; insecticide resistance and resistance management; medical entomology; plant resistance; sampling andbiostatistics.
Bi-Monthly
David Gammel, Executive Director
Neil Willoughby, Director of Finance

3897 Land Use Law Report
Business Publishers
2222 Sedwick Drive
Durham, NC 27713
301-587-6300
800-223-8720
Fax: 800-508-2592
custserv@bpinews.com
www.bpinews.com
Provides timely news on court decisions, legislation and regulations that impact today's most pressing land-use policy planning and legal issues.
Biweekly
James D Lawlor, Author
Adam Goldstein, Publisher
James D Lawlor, Editor

3898 Land and Water Magazine
Land and Water
320 A Street
Fort Dodge, IA 50501
515-576-3191
Fax: 515-576-2606
landandwater@frontiernet.net
www.landandwater.com
Edited for contractors, engineers, architects, government officials and those working in the field of natural resource management and restoration from idea stage through project completion and maintenance.
Publication Date: 1974 72 pages Bimonthly
ISSN: 0192-9453
Amy Dencklau, Publisher/Editor

3899 Leaves Newsletter
Michigan Forest Association
6120 S. Clinton Trail
Eaton Rapids, MI 48827
517-663-3423
mfa@i-star.com
www.michiganforests.com
A monthly publication from the Michigan Forest Association.
Monthly
McClain B Smith Jr, Executive Director

3900 Leopold Outlook
E13701 Levee Road
PO Box 77
Baraboo, WI 53913
608-355-0279
Fax: 608-356-7309
mail@aldoleopold.org
www.aldoleopold.org
Official magazine of The Aldo Leopold Foundation, with content relating to environmental ethics and land care.
2 issues/year
Steve Swenson, Ecologist
Buddy Huffaker, Executive Director

3901 MACC Newsletter
Alba Press
10 Juniper Road
Belmont, MA 00247
617-489-3930
Fax: 617-489-3935
staff@maccweb.org
www.maccweb.org
Published six times a year, each issue features carefully chosen technical and interpreative articles, updates on government actions and policies, notices of workshops and meetings, publications, listings and a professional directory.
16 pages Bi-Monthly
Lindsay Martucci, Editor
Eugene Benson, Executive Director

3902 Michigan Forests Magazine
Michigan Forest Association
6120 S. Clinton Trail
Eaton Rapids, MI 48827
734-665-8279
Fax: 734-913-9167
www.michiganforests.com

A quarterly magazine published by the Michigan Forest Association.
Quarterly
McClain B Smith Jr, Executive Director

3903 Minnesota Plant Press
Minnesota Native Plant Society
P.O. Box 20401 president@mnnps.org
Bloomington, MN 55420 www.mnnps.org
A nonprofit organization dedicated to the conservation of the native plants of Minnesota through public education and advocacy. Offered are monthly meetings, field trips, symposia and a regular newsletter.
4 per year
Mike Lynch, President
Shirley Mah Kooyman, Vice President

3904 Monitor
Florida Defenders of the Environment
PO Box 357086 352-475-1119
Gainesville, FL 32635 *Fax:* 352-377-0869
floridadefenders@gmail.com
www.fladefenders.org
Newsletter of Florida Defenders of the Environment, one of the oldest and most accomplished conservation organizations in Florida with a network of scientists, economists and other professionals dedicated to preserving and protectingthe state's natural resources. FDE's top priority is currently the restoration of a 16-mile stretch of the Ocklawaha River and its 9,000-acre floodplain forest by removal of Rodman Dam- the last vestige of the Cross-Florida Barge Canal.
Publication Date: 1982 6-8 pages Bi-Annually
Thomas Hawkins, Executive Director
Tracy Marinello, Office Manager

3905 Montana Land Reliance Newsletter
324 Fuller Avenue 406-443-7027
PO Box 355 *Fax:* 406-443-7061
Helena, MT 59624 info@mtlandreliance.org
www.mtlandreliance.org
Montana's only private, statewide land trust, an apolitical, nonprofit corporation. Our mission is to provide permanent protection for private lands that are ecologically significant for agricultural production, fish and wildlifehabitat and scenic open space. We publish a newsletter twice per year.
8 pages Spring/Fall
George Olsen, President
Carol Bibler, Vice President

3906 National Gardener Magazine
National Garden Clubs
4401 Magnolia Avenue 314-776-7574
St Louis, MO 63110 800-550-6007
Fax: 314-776-5108
patricia.b.binder@gmail.com
www.gardenclub.org
Official magazine of National Garden Clubs, available in print and online.
Publication Date: 1970 Quarterly
ISSN: 0027-9331
Patricia Binder, Editor

3907 National Wildlife Magazine
National Wildlife Federation
11100 Wildlife Center Drive 800-822-9919
Reston, VA 20190 www.nwf.org/Magazines/National-Wildlife
The official member magazine of the National Wildlife Federation.
6 Issues/Yr
Collin O'Mara, President & CEO
Bob Harper, Executive Publisher

3908 National Woodlands Magazine
National Woodland Owners Association
374 Maple Avenue E 703-255-2700
Suite 310 800-476-8733
Vienna, VA 22180 *Fax:* 703-281-9200
argow@nwoa.net
www.nationalwoodlands.org
Provides timely information about forestry and forest practices with news from Washington, DC and state capitals. Written for non-industrial, private woodland owners. Includes state landowner association news.
28 pages Quarterly
Keith A Argow, President
Eric Johnson, Editor

3909 Natural Resources Department: Fish & Wildlife Newsletter
402 West Washington Street RMW273 317-232-4080
Indianapolis, IN 46204 *Fax:* 317-232-8150
www.state.in.us/dnr/fishwild/index.htm
Publication Date: 1985 12 pages Quarterly

3910 Nature Conservancy: Nebraska Chapter Newsletter
4245 North Fairfax Drive 703-841-5300
Suite 100 *Fax:* 402-342-0474
Arlington, VA 22203-1606 member@tnc.org
nature.org
The mission of the Nature Conservancy is to preserve the plants, animals and natural communities that represent the diversity of life on Earth by protecting the lands and waters they need to survive.
Publication Date: 1987 12 pages Quarterly
Thomas J. Tierney, Chairman
Mark R. Tercek, President and CEO

3911 Nature's Voice, The DNS Online Newsletter
Delaware Nature Society
PO Box 700 302-239-2334
Hockessin, DE 19707 *Fax:* 302-239-2473
dnsinfo@delawarenaturesociety.org
www.delawarenaturesociety.org
Now only available online, the newsletter offers trail information, nature center updates and programs, volunteer opportunities and more about what's happening in the outdoors of Delaware.
Brian Winslow, Executive Director
Christine Carlisle Odom, President

3912 New England WildFlower: New England Wildflower Society
180 Hemenway Road 508-877-7630
Framingham, MA 00170 *Fax:* 508-877-3658
information@newenglandwild.org
www.newenglandwild.org
36 pages Twice a Year
Debbi Edelstein, Executive Director
Christine Bennett, Office Manager

3913 New Jersey Environmental Lobby News
204 W State Street 609-396-3774
Trenton, NJ 00860 *Fax:* 609-396-4521
njel@earthlink.net
www.njenvironment.org
Quarterly publication from New Jersey Environmental Lobby.
Publication Date: 1971 8 pages Quarterly
ISSN: 1535-2021
Anne Poole, President
Noemi de la Puente, Executive Director

3914 North American Birds
American Birding Association
PO Box 744 302-838-3660
Delaware City, DE 19706 800-850-2473
Fax: 302-838-3651
info@aba.org
www.aba.org
Journal of the American Birding Association, previously published as part of Bird Lore, Audubon Field Notes, and later American Birds.
Jeffrey A. Gordon, President & CEO

3915 **North Dakota Association of Soil Conservation Districts Newsletter**
3310 University Drive 701-223-8518
Bismarck, ND 58504 *Fax:* 701-223-1291
kathy@lincolnoakes.com
www.ndascd.org

Quarterly
Roger Christenson, President
Brian Johnston, CEO

3916 **Outdoor America**
Izaak Walton League of America
707 Conservation Lane 301-548-0150
Gaithersburg, MD 20878 info@iwla.org
www.iwla.org

Magazine of the Izaak Walton League of America with information about the league's conservation efforts.
Quarterly
Scott Kovarovics, Executive Director
Jared Mott, Director, Conservation

3917 **Outdoors Unlimited**
615 Oak St. 406-728-7434
Ste. 201 *Fax:* 406-728-7445
Missoula, MT 59801 owaa@montana.com
www.owaa.org

Magazine of the Outdoor Writers Association of America. Membership fees are $175.00 (individual), $325.00 (supporting), $40.00 (student)
Publication Date: 1962 35 pages Monthly
Tom Sadler, Executive Director
Lisa Ballard, President/Board Chair:

3918 **Pacific Fishery Management Council Newsletter**
7700 NE Ambassador Place 503-820-2280
Suite 101 866-806-7204
Portland, OR 97220 *Fax:* 503-820-2299
pfmc.comments@noaa.gov
www.pcouncil.org

The Pacific Council has developed fishery management plans for salmon, groundfish and coastal species in the US Exclusive Economic Zone off the coast of Washington, Oregon and California.
24 pages 5x Year
Chuck Tracy, Executive Director
Mike Burner, Deputy Director

3919 **Parks & Recreation Magazine**
National Recreation and Park Association
22377 Belmont Ridge Road 800-626-6772
Ashburn, VA 20148 info@nrpa.org
www.nrpa.org

The NRPA, headquartered in Ashburn Virginia, is a national non-profit organization devoted to advancing park, recreation and conservation efforts that enhance the quality of life for all Americans. The Association works to extendsocial, health, cultural and economic benefits of parks and recreation, through its network of 60,000 recreation and park professionals and civic leaders. NRPA encourages recreation initiatives for youth in high-risk environments.
Monthly
ISSN: 0031-2215
Kristine Stratton, President & CEO
Gina Cohen, VP, Magazine & Marketing

3920 **Parks and Trails Council of Minnesota: Newsletter**
275 E 4th Street 651-726-2457
Suite 250 800-944-0707
Saint Paul, MN 55101 *Fax:* 651-726-2458
info@parksandtrails.org
www.parksandtrails.org

Parks and Trails Council of Minnesota seeks to aquire, protect and sustain long-term statewide land.
Quarterly
Julie Gugin, President
Bob Biersheid, Vice President

3921 **Powder River Basin Resource Council: Powder River Breaks Newsletter**
934 North Main 307-672-5809
Sheridan, WY 82801 *Fax:* 307-672-5800
info@powderriverbasin.org
www.powderriverbasin.org

Committed to the preservation and enrichment of Wyoming's agricultural heritage and rural lifestyle; the conservation of Wyomings unique land, mineral, water and clean air resources, consistent with responsible use of those resourcesto sustain the vitality of present and future generations; the education and empowerment of Wyoming's citizens to raise a coherent voice in decisions. They are the only group in Wyoming that addresses both agricultural and conservation issues.
Publication Date: 1973 8-12 pages 6x year
Stephanie Avey, Office Administrator
Kevin Lind, Director

3922 **Prairie Naturalist Magazine**
600 Park Street 785-628-4214
Department of Biological Sciences *Fax:* 316-341-5607
Hays, KS 67601 efinck@fhsu.edu
www.fhsu.edu

Published by the North Dakota Natural Science Society, a regional organization with interests in the natural history of grasslands and the Great Plains.
Publication Date: 1968 260 pages Quarterly
ISSN: 0091-0376
Elmer J Finck, Editor

3923 **Quail Call**
Tall Timbers Research Station
13093 Henry Beadel Drive 850-893-4153
Tallahassee, FL 32312 *Fax:* 850-668-7781
bpalmer@talltimbers.org
www.talltimbers.org

Newsletter from the Tall Timbers Research Station's Game Bird Program, featuring research on quail.
William E. Palmer, Ph.D., President & CEO
Crystal Davis, Director, Development

3924 **Reef Line**
Reef Relief Environmental Center
PO Box 430 305-294-3100
Key West, FL 33041 *Fax:* 305-293-9515
info@reefrelief.org
www.reefrelief.org

Reef Line is a quarterly publication from Reef Relief.
Publication Date: 1986 16 pages Quarterly
Bob Cardenas, President
Dave Kirwan, Vice President

3925 **SWOAM News**
Small Woodland Owners Association of Maine
153 Hospital Street 207-626-0005
PO Box 836 877-467-9626
Augusta, ME 00433 *Fax:* 207-626-7992
info@swoam.com
www.swoam.com

Monthly
Tom Doak, Executive Director
Bill S. Williams, Deputy Executive Director

3926 **Save San Francisco Bay Association: Watershed Newsletter**
1330 Broadway 510-463-6850
Suite 1800 *Fax:* 510-463-6851
Oakland, CA 94612 info@savesfbay.org
www.savesfbay.org

Save the Bay has worked for over 40 years to protect the San Francisco Bay-Delta from pollution, fill, shoreline destruction and fresh water diversion. We have launched a century of renewal to restore bay fish and wildlife, reclaimtidal wetlands and make the bay safe and accessible to all.
8-10 pages 3-4 times/year
David Lewis, Executive Director
Jackie Richardson, Development Coordinator

3927 Scenic America Newsletter
Scenic America
727 15th Street NW 202-792-1300
Suite 1100 max.ashburn@scenic.org
Washington, DC 20005-6029 scenic.org/resources/newsletter-archives
An archive of Scenic America's newsletter, from 2011-2017.
Mark Falzone, President
Max Ashburn, Director, Communications

3928 Shore and Beach
5460 Beaujolais Lane 239-489-2616
Fort Myers, FL 33919 *Fax:* 239-489-9917
derek.brockbank@asbpa.org
www.asbpa.org
Peer-reviewed publication from the American Shore and Beach Preservation Association.
Publication Date: 1933 Quarterly
ISSN: 0037-4237
Derek Brockbank, Executive Director
Beth Sciaudone, PhD, Managing Editor

3929 Sialia/Bluebird
North American Bluebird Society
PO Box 7844 513-300-8714
Bloomington, IN 47407 www.nabluebirdsociety.org
Archives of back editions of two publications of the North American Bluebird Society.
Bernie Daniel, President
Kevin Conway, 1st Vice President

3930 Sierra Club, NJ Chapter: The Jersey Sierran
85 Second Street 415-977-5500
2nd Floor *Fax:* 415-977-5797
San Francisco, CA 94105
The Sierra Club is our country's oldest and most effective grassroots environmental organization. Hikes and outings are scheduled throughout the year. We are dedicated to fighting sprawl and over-development.
Publication Date: 1992 14 pages Quarterly
Jeff Tittle, Director
Dennis Schvejda, Conservation Coordinator

3931 Sierra Club: Pennsylvania Chapter Newsletter
600 North 2nd Street 717-232-0101
Suite 300A *Fax:* 717-238-6330
Harrisburg, PA 17101 www.sierraclub.org
The Pennsylvania chapter includes 11 local Sierra Club groups. Emphasis is on state environmental policy advocacy, outings, education and local environmental protection efforts.
18 pages Quarterly
Jeff Schmidt, Sr. Chapter Director

3932 Southern Appalachian Botanical Society: Gastanea
Newberry College
2100 College Street 803-321-5257
Newberry, SC 29108 *Fax:* 803-321-5636
charles.horn@newberry.edu
www.sabs.us
This is a professional organization for those interested in botanical research, especially in the areas of ecology, floristics and systematics. To this end, they publish a journal, CASTANEA, and a newsletter, CHINQUAPIN.
Publication Date: 1936 350 pages Quarterly
ISSN: 0008-7475
Charles Horn, President
Kunsiri Grubbs, Treasurer

3933 Stages
Audrey.Geffen@uib.no
earlylifehistory.fisheries.org/elhs-newsletter
Newsletter of the Early Life History section of the American Fisheries Society.
3 issues/year
Audrey Geffen, Editor
Cindy van Damme, Editor

3934 TROUT Magazine
Trout Unlimited
PO Box 7400 703-522-0200
Woolly Bugger, WV 25438-7400 800-834-2419
Fax: 703-284-9400
trout@tu.org
www.tu.org
Official magazine of Trout Unlimited.
Quarterly
Chris Wood, President & CEO
Elizabeth Maclin, Executive Vice President

3935 Tall Timbers eJournal
Tall Timbers Research Station
13093 Henry Beadel Drive 850-893-4153
Tallahassee, FL 32312 *Fax:* 850-668-7781
bpalmer@talltimbers.org
www.talltimbers.org
Digital magazine of the Tall Timbers Research Station. Dedicated to protecting wildlands and preserving natural habitats. Promotes public education on the importance of natural disturbances to the environment and the subsequent needfor wildlife and land management.
Biannual
William E. Palmer, President & CEO
Crystal Davis, Director, Development

3936 Tall Timbers eNews
Tall Timbers Research Station
13093 Henry Beadel Drive 850-893-4153
Tallahassee, FL 32312 *Fax:* 850-668-7781
bpalmer@talltimbers.org
www.talltimbers.org
Ditigal newsletter of the Tall Timbers Research Station. Dedicated to protecting wildlands and preserving natural habitats. Promotes public education on the importance of natural disturbances to the environment and the subsequent needfor wildlife and land management.
William E. Palmer, President & CEO
Crystal Davis, Director, Development

3937 Tidbits Newsletter
Minnesota Association/Soil and Water Cons. Dist.
255 Kellogg Boulevard East 651-690-9028
Ste 101 *Fax:* 651-690-9065
St. Paul, MN 55101 leann.buck@maswcd.org
www.maswcd.org
Quarterly
Le Ann Buck, Executive Director
Ian Cunningham, President

3938 Tide
Coastal Conservation Association
4801 Woodway Drive 713-626-4234
Houston, TX 77056 800-201-FISH
ccantl@joincca.org
TIDE is the official bimonthly magazine of the Coastal Conservation Association. It has received local, state and national acclaim for writing, photography and layout and currently boasts a circulation of more than 70,000. TIDE isavailable only to members of the Coastal Conservation Association.

3939 Upper Mississippi River Conservation Committee Newsletter
9053 Route 148 618-997-6869
Marion, IL 62959 neal_jackson@fws.gov
www.umrcc.org
A bimonthly newsletter published by the Upper Mississippi River Conservation Committee.
10 pages Bi monthly
Neal Jackson, UMRCC Coordinator
Jeff Janvrin, Chair

3940 Urban Land Magazine
Urban Land Institute
1025 Thomas Jefferson Street NW 202-624-7000
Suite 500 W 800-321-5011
Washington, DC 20007 *Fax:* 202-624-7140
www.uli.org

Nonprofit research and education organization dedicated to improving land use policy and development practice. Publishes a monthly magazine, several quarterly publications and books. Topics relate to real estate development includinggovernment sensitive development, smart growth, sustainable development and city parks.
Monthly
Randall Rowe, Chairman
Patrick L. Phillips, Global CEO

3941 Utah Geological Survey: Survey Notes
1594 W N Temple Suite 3110 801-537-3300
PO Box 146100 *Fax:* 801-537-3400
Salt Lake City, UT 84114
The Utah Geological Survey is an applied scientific agency that creates, interprets and provides information about Utah's geologic environment, resources and hazards to promote safe, beneficial and wise use of land. This is theirpublication, which is issued three times yearly.
Publication Date: 1964 3 Times Yearly
ISSN: 1061-7930
Richard Allis, Director

3942 Virginia Forests Magazine
Virginia Forestry Association
3808 Augusta Avenue 804-278-8733
Richmond, VA 23255 *Fax:* 804-320-1447
www.vaforestry.org
Quarterly magazine published by the Virginia Forestry Association.
Quarterly
Paul Howe, VFA Executive Vice President

3943 WAEE Bulletin
Wisconsin Association for Environmental Education
8 Nelson Hall 715-346-2796
University of Wisconsin
Stevens Point, WI 54481
Quarterly
Carol Weston, Administrative Assistant

3944 Western Pennsylvania Conservancy Newsletter
800 Waterfront Drive 412-288-2777
Pittsburgh, PA 15222 866-JOI-NWPC
Fax: 412-231-1414
info@paconserve.org
waterlandlife.org
WPC, working together to save the places we care about, protects natural lands, promotes healthy and attractive communities, and preserves Fallingwater, Frank Lloyd Wright's masterwork in Mill Run, which was entrusted to theConservancy in 1963. Since its inception in 1932, the Conservancy has protected more than 280,000 acres of natural lands in Pennnsylvania. We continue to work to secure lands of ecological significance that frequently offer recreational and scenicvalues.
16 pages Quarterly
Susan Fitzsimmons, Chair
Stephen G. Robinson, Vice Chair

3945 Western Proceedings Newsletter
Western Association of Fish and Wildlife Agencies
5400 Bishop Boulevard 307-777-4580
Cheyenne, WY 82006 *Fax:* 307-777-4650
wildlife.org
Annual

3946 Western Society of Naturalists: Newsletter
San Diego State University Biology Department
P.O. Box 247 818-677-3256
Bodega Bay, CA 94923 *Fax:* 818-677-2034
secretariat@wsn-online.org
www.westsocnat.com
A scientific society with a strong focus on ecology, evolution, natural history and marine biology. Its memebers are predominantly from the west coast. The society organizes one or two meetings each year for its members.
Jenn Caselle, President
Brian Gaylord, Secretary

3947 Whalewatcher
PO Box 1391 310-548-6279
San Pedro, CA 90733 *Fax:* 310-548-6950
www.acsonline.org
A bi-annual publication from the American Cetacean Society. Cost included with membership fees.
Publication Date: 1967 30 pages Bi-Annual
Diane Alps, President
Kaye Reznick, Editorial Consultant

3948 Wilderness Education Association
2150 N 107th St 206-209-5275
Ste 205 *Fax:* 206-367-8777
Seattle, WA 98133 nationaloffice@weainfo.org
www.weainfo.org
Publication Date: 1976 4-6 pages 3 Times Per Year
Ricky Haro, President
Kelli McMahan, President-elect

3949 Wildfowl Trust of North America: Newsletter
Wildfowl Trust of North America
600 Discovery Lane 410-827-6694
PO Box 519 *Fax:* 410-827-6713
Grasonville, MD 21638 jwink@bayrestoration.org
www.bayrestoration.org
Published by the Wildfowl Trust of North America.
Publication Date: 1995 8 pages Qaurterly
Judy Wink, Executive Director
Katey Nelson, Education Manager

3950 Wildlife Law News Quarterly and Weekly Alerts
University of New Mexico School of Law
MSC 11 6060rd NE 505-277-5006
One University of New Mexico *Fax:* 505-277-7064
Albuquerque, NM 87131 musgrave@unm.edu
A quarterly publication from the New Mexico Center for Wildlife Law.
Publication Date: 1993 16 pages Quarterly
ISSN: 1085-7338
R Musgrave, Editor
D Macke, Editor

3951 Wildlife Society Bulletin
Wildlife Society
5410 Grosvenor Lane 301-897-9770
Suite 200 *Fax:* 301-530-2471
Bethesda, MD 20814 tws@wildlife.org
www.wildlife.org
A quarterly publication from the Wildlife Society.
Publication Date: 1973 Quarterly
ISSN: 0091-7648
Rick Baydack, President
Bruce Thompson, Vice President

3952 Woodland Management Newsletter
Wisconsin Woodland Owners Association
PO Box 285 715-346-4798
Stevens Point, WI 54481 *Fax:* 715-346-4821
wwoa@uwsp.edu
www.wisconsinwoodlands.org
Quarterly
Paul Kienitz, President
Marilyn Steele, VICE PRESIDENT

3953 Woodland Report
National Woodland Owners Association
374 Maple Avenue E 703-255-2700
Suite 310 800-476-8733
Vienna, VA 22180 *Fax:* 703-281-9200
argow@nwoa.net
www.nationalwoodlands.org
Provides timely information about forestry and forest practices with news from Washington, DC and state capitals. Written for non-industrial, private woodland owners. Includes state landowner association news.
2 pages
Keith A Argow, President
Eric Johnson, Editor

Periodicals: Recycling & Pollution Prevention

3954 **AARA Newsletter**
Arizona Automotive Recyclers Association
950 E. Baseline Rd. 480-609-3999
#104-1025 admin@aara.com
Tempe, AZ 85283 www.aara.com
Quarterly newsletter of the AARA, a select group of recyclers providing quality recycled parts for the benefit of our customers, communities and environment. There are 90 member companies. AARA is affiliated with the AutomotiveDismantlers and Recyclers Association.
Quarterly
Mike Pierson Jr, President
Leroy Liebermann, Secretary/Treasurer

3955 **Air/Water Pollution Report**
Business Publishers
2222 Sedwick Drive 301-589-5103
Durham, NC 27713 800-223-8720
Fax: 800-508-2592
custserv@bpinews.com
www.bpinews.com
Provides comprehensive coverage of economic, political, legislative, regulatory and domestic and international implications of air and water pollution.
Weekly
Leonard A Eiserer, Publisher
Beth Early, Associate Publisher

3956 **American Waste Digest**
Carasue Moody
226 King Street 610-326-9480
Pottstown, PA 19464 800-442-4215
Fax: 610-326-9752
awd@americanwastedigest.com
www.americanwastedigest.com
Provides reviews on new products, profiles on sucessful waste removal businesses, and provides discussion on legislation on municipal regulations on recycling.
100 pages Monthly
Carasue Moody, Publisher/Editor
Marlene Lowder, Sales Administrator

3957 **BNA's Environmental Compliance Bulletin**
Bureau of National Affairs
3 Bethesda Metro Center 202-452-4200
Suite 250 800-372-1033
Bethesda, MD 20814-5377 *Fax:* 800-253-0332
www.bna.com
Cover the water and air pollution, waste management and regulatory updates, as well as a summary of selected regulatory actions and a list of key environmental compliance dates.
Gregory C. McCaffery, President & CEO
Sue Martin, COO

3958 **Bio-Integral Resource Center: IPM Practitioner**
PO Box 7414 510-524-2567
Berkeley, CA 94707 *Fax:* 510-524-1758
birc@igc.org
www.birc.org
The goal of the Bio Integral Resources Center is to reduce pesticide use by educating the public about effective, least-toxic alternatives for pest problems.
Publication Date: 1979 6-12 pages
ISSN: 0738-968x
Dr. William Quarles, Executive Director

3959 **C&D Recycler**
Gie Publishing
5811 Canal Road 216-961-4130
Valley View, OH 44125 800-456-0707
Fax: 216-525-0515
btaylor@gie.net
www.cdrecycler.com
Brian Taylor, Editor

3960 **Common Sense Pest Control Quarterly**
PO Box 7414 510-524-2567
Berkeley, CA 94707 *Fax:* 510-524-1758
birc@igc.org
www.birc.org
A quarterly publication published by the Bio Integral Resource Center
Publication Date: 1984 24 pages Quarterly
ISSN: 8756-7881
Dr. William Quarles, Executive Director

3961 **Composting News**
McEntee Media Corporation
9815 Hazelwood Avenue 440-238-6603
Cleveland, OH 44149 *Fax:* 440-238-6712
ken@recycle.cc
www.recycle.cc
New composting projects, research, regulations and legislation, as well as the latest news in the composting industry.
Publication Date: 1992 Monthly
Ken McEntee, Publisher

3962 **Daily Environment Report**
Bureau of National Affairs
3 Bethesda Metro Center 202-452-4200
Suite 250 800-372-1033
Bethesda, MD 20814-5377 *Fax:* 800-253-0332
www.bna.com
A 40-page daily report providing comprehensive, in-depth coverage of national and international environmental news. Each issue contains summaries of the top news stories, articles, and in-brief items, and a journal of meetings, agencyactivities, hearings and legal proceedings. Coverage includes air and water pollution, hazardous substances, and hazardous waste, solid waste, oil spills, gas drilling, pollution prevention, impact statements and budget matters.
40 pages
ISSN: 1060-2976
Gregory C. McCaffery, President & CEO
Sue Martin, COO

3963 **E-Scrap News**
Resource Recycling
PO Box 42270 503-233-1305
Portland, OR 97242 *Fax:* 503-233-1356
info@resource-recycling.com
www.resource-recycling.com
64 pages
ISSN: 0744-4710
Jerry Powell, Executive Editor
Dylan de Thomas, Editorial Director

3964 **Earth Preservers**
PO Box 6 908-654-9293
Westfield, NJ 00709
Award winning monthly environmental newspaper for school children aged 7 to 15.
4 pages
Bill Paul, Publisher

3965 **Environment Reporter**
Bureau of National Affairs
3 Bethesda Metro Center 202-452-4200
Suite 250 800-372-1033
Bethesda, MD 20814-5377 *Fax:* 800-253-0332
www.bna.com
A weekly notification and reference service covering the full-spectrum of legislative, administrative, judicial, industrial and technological developments affecting pollution control and environmental protection.
ISSN: 0013-9211
Gregory C. McCaffery, President & CEO
Sue Martin, COO

3966 **Environmental Engineering Science**
Mary Ann Liebert

140 Huguenot Street 914-740-2100
3rd Floor 800-MLI-EBER
New Rochelle, NY 10801 *Fax:* 914-740-2101
info@liebertpub.com
www.liebertpub.com

The focus is on pollution control of the suface, ground, and drinking water, and highlight research news and product developments that aid in the fight against pollution.

Bi-Monthly
ISSN: 1092-8758
Mary Ann Liebert, Publisher
Dumpnico Grosso PhD, Editor-in-Chief

3967 Environmental Notice

75 Aupuni Street 808-974-6006
#201 *Fax:* 808-974-6000
Hilo, HI 96720 oeqc@doh.hawaii.gov
health.hawaii.gov

A bi-monthly publication from the Health Department Environmental Quality Control division.

Publication Date: 1978 24 pages Bi monthly
Keith Y. Yamamoto, Deputy Director
Virginia Pressler, Director of Health

3968 Environmental Regulation

State Capitals Newsletters
PO Box 7376 703-768-9600
Alexandria, VA 22307 *Fax:* 703-768-9690
www.statecapitals.com

Weekly news from the state capitals keeps you informed on state programs, recycling, wetlands, ground water protection, beach renourishment, land management, greenspace laws, brownfields, livestock regulation, wilderness preservation,urban sprawl and solid waste.

Publication Date: 1946 4-10 pages Newsletter 48x/Yr
ISSN: 1061-9682
Ellen Klein, Editor

3969 Environmental Science and Technology

American Chemical Society
1155 16th Street NW 614-447-3776
Washington, DC 20036 800-333-9511
eic@est.acs.org
pubs.acs.org/journal/esthag

Articles on pollution control, waste treatment, climate changes and various other environmental interests.

0 pages Semi-Monthly
David L. Sedlak, Editor-in-Chief

3970 Environmental Systems Corporation Newsletter

10801 N Mopac Bldg 1-200 865-688-7900
Austin, TX 78759 *Fax:* 512-258-5836
escsales@envirosys.com
www.envirosys.com

Data acquisition and reporting systems for electric power producers and industrial sources, ESC is the leading supplier of CEM and ambient data systems in the US Newsletter is free.

Publication Date: 1994 4 pages Quarterly
Jeff Rabensteine, President
Mmark Shell, Chief Engineer

3971 Environmental Times

Environmental Assessment Association
1224 N Nokomis NE 320-763-4320
Alexandria, MN 56308 *Fax:* 320-763-9290
eaa@iami.org
www.iami.org/eaa.cfm

This publication contains environmental conferences and expos, industry trends, federal regulations related to the environment and industry assessments.

Robert Johnson, Publisher/Editor

3972 From the Ground Up

Ecology Center
117 Division Street 734-761-3186
Ann Arbor, MI 48104 *Fax:* 734-663-2414

Progressive environmental news from southeast Michigan.

32 pages
Michael Garfield, Editor

3973 Full Circle

Northeast Resource Recovery Association
PO Box 721 603-798-5777
Concord, NH 03302 *Fax:* 603-798-5744

Bi-Monthly
Elizabeth Bedard, Executive Director

3974 Hauler

Hauler Magazine
166 South Main Street 215-997-3622
PO Box 508 800-220-6029
New Hope, PA 18938 *Fax:* 215-862-3455
mag@thehauler.com
www.thehauler.com

This magazine serves as an advertising guide to new products in the waste management, recycling, and environmental industries.

Publication Date: 1978 Monthly
Thomas N Smith, CEO
Leslie T. Smith, Publisher

3975 HazMat Management

Business Information Group
80 Valleybrook Drive 416-442-2223
Toronto, ON M3B2S 888-702-1111
Fax: 416-510-5133
amadden@bizinfogroup.ca

Solutions for the environment.

Publication Date: 1989 Bi-Annual
ISSN: 0843-9303
Brad O'Brien, Publisher
David Nesseth, Editor

3976 Hazardous Waste News

Business Publishers
2222 Sedwick Drive 301-589-5103
Durham, NC 27713 800-223-8720
Fax: 800-508-2592
custserv@bpinews.com
www.bpinews.com

Comprehensive federal, state and local coverage of legislation and regulation affecting all aspects of the hazardous waste industry including Superfund, Resource Conservation and Recovery Act, US EPA, incineration, land disposal andmore.

8 pages
Leonard A Eiserer, Publisher
Beth Early, Operations Director

3977 Hazardous Waste/Superfund Week

Business Publishers
2222 Sedwick Drive 301-589-5103
Durham, NC 27713 800-223-8720
Fax: 800-508-2592
custserv@bpinews.com
www.bpinews.com

Provides comprehensive coverage on hazardous waste disposal and cleanup, behind-the-scenes coverage of congressional action, EPA initiatives, Superfund sites, regulatory changes, court cases, enforcement news, contract opportunities,new technologies, research findings and business developments.

Weekly
Leonard A Eiserer, Publisher
Beth Early, Associate Publisher

3978 Hazmat Transportation News

Bureau of National Affairs
3 Bethesda Metro Center 800-372-1033
Suite 250 *Fax:* 800-253-0332
Bethesda, MD 20814-5377 www.bna.com

A two-binder service containing the full-text of rules and regulations governing shipment of hazardous material by rail, air, ship, highway and pipeline, including DOT's Hazardous Materials Tables and EPA's rules for its hazardouswaste tracking system.

Gregory C. McCaffery, President & CEO
Sue Martin, COO

3979 **Inside EPA**
Inside Washington Publishers
1919 South Eads Street 703-416-8500
Suite 201 800-424-9068
Arlington, VA 22202 *Fax:* 703-415-8543
custsvc@iwpnews.com
www.iwpnews.com
Gives timely information on all facets of waste, water, air, and other environmental regulatory programs.
Publication Date: 1980 Weekly
Al Sosenko, Publisher

3980 **JJ Keller and Associates**
3003 Breezewood Lane 877-564-2333
P.O. Box 368 *Fax:* 800-727-7516
Neenah, WI 54957 www.jjkeller.com
Offers services in regulatory compliance, best practices and training for environmental, safety, and transportation issues.
Publication Date: 1953
Rustin Keller, President & CEO
Dana Gilman, Chief Financial Officer

3981 **Journal of Environmental Education**
Heldref Publications
325 Chestnut Street 215-625-8900
Suite 800 *Fax:* 202-296-5149
Philadelphia, PA 19106 customer.service@taylorandfrancis.com
www.heldref.org
The issues featured are case studies, environmental philosophy and policy discussions, new research evaluations and information on environmental education.
Douglas Kirkpatrick, Publisher/Executive Director

3982 **Legislative Bulletin**
Arkansas Environmental Federation
1400 W Markham Street 501-374-0263
Suite 302 *Fax:* 501-374-8752
Little Rock, AR 72201 cmiller@environmentark.org
www.environmentark.org
Publication Date: 1967
Charles Miller, Executive Director
Rebecca Neely, Communications Director

3983 **Minnesota Pollution Control Agency Minnesota Environment Magazine**
520 Lafayette Road North 651-296-6300
St. Paul, MN 55155 800-657-3864
Fax: 651-296-7923
vicki.schindeldecker@pca.state.mn.us
www.pca.state.mn.us
Established in 1967 to protect Minnesota's environment through monitoring environmental quality and enforcing environmental regulations.
Publication Date: 2000 16-20 pages Quarterly
Paul Eger, Comm./Chair Citizens' Board

3984 **Northeast Recycling Council Bulletin**
139 Main Street 802-254-3636
Suite 401 info@nerc.org
Brattleboro, VT 05301 www.nerc.org
NERC's mission is to To advance an environmentally sustainable economy by promoting source and toxicity reduction, recycling, and the purchasing ofenvironmentally preferable products and services.
Monthly
Robert Isner, President
Lynn Rubinstein, Executive Director

3985 **Northeast Recycling Council News**
139 Main Street 802-254-3636
Suite 401 *Fax:* 802-254-5870
Brattleboro, VT 05301 info@nerc.org
www.nerc.org
NERC's mission is to To advance an environmentally sustainable economy by promoting source and toxicity reduction, recycling, and the purchasing of environmentally preferable products and services.
3x Year
Lynn Rubenstein, Executive Director
Mary Ann Remolador, Assistant Director

3986 **Oregon Refuse and Recycling Association Newsletter**
PO Box 2186 503-588-1837
Salem, OR 97308 800-527-7624
Fax: 503-399-7784
orrainfo@orra.net
www.orra.net
Monthly
Kristan Mitchell, Executive Director
Kimera Coady, Executive Assistant

3987 **Plastics Recycling Update**
Resource Recycling
PO Box 42270 503-233-1305
Portland, OR 97242 *Fax:* 503-233-1356
subscriptions@resource-recycling.com
www.resource-recycling.com
Monthly
Jerry Powell, Executive Editor
Dylan de Thomas, Editorial Director

3988 **Pollution Equipment News**
Rimbach Publishing
8650 Babcock Boulevard 412-364-5366
Pittsburgh, PA 15237 800-245-3182
Fax: 412-369-9720
info@rimbach.com
Provides information to those responsible for selecting products and services for air, water, wastewater and hazardous waste pollution control.
Publication Date: 1967 64 pages Bi-Monthly
ISSN: 0032-3659
Raquel Rimbach, Owner

3989 **Pollution Prevention News**
US EPA
1200 Pennsylvania Avenue, NW 202-272-0167
Washington, DC 20460 *Fax:* 202-260-2219
www.epa.gov
Articles include recent information on source reduction and sustainable technologies in industry, transportation, consumer, agriculture, energy, and the international sector.
Gina McCarthy, Administrator
Stan Meiburg, Acting Deputy Administrator

3990 **Recharger Magazine**
Recharger Magazine
15335 Don Julian Road 626-961-2688
Hacienda Heights, CA 91745 *Fax:* 626-961-2788
info@rechargermag.com
greenprojectinc.com
Information including articles that cover business and marketing, technical updates, association and industry news, and company profiles. On the remanufactured imaging supplies industry, related features focus on the importance ofrecycling, government legislation, and product comparisons. Annual trade event in Las Vegas.
Publication Date: 1989 300+ pages Monthly
ISSN: 1053-7503
Julie Kerrane, Author
Phyllis Gurgevich, Publisher
Amy Turner, Managing Editor

3991 **Recycled News**
Maryland Recyclers Coalition
PO Box 1046 888-496-3196
Laurel, MD 20725 *Fax:* 301-238-4579
info@marylandrecyclers.org
www.marylandrecyclers.org
2 pages Bi-Monthly
Jackie King, Executive Director

3992 Recycling Laws International
Raymond Communications
P.O. Box 4311 301-879-0628
Silver Spring, MD 20914-4311 *Fax:* 301-345-4768
circulation@raymond.com
www.raymond.com

Covers recycling, takeback and green labeling policy for business in 38 countries. Available online.
Publication Date: 1995 Bi-Monthly
Bruce Popka, Vice President

3993 Recycling Markets
NV Business Publishers Corporation
43 Main Street 732-502-0500
Avon by the Sea, NJ 00771 *Fax:* 732-502-9606
lprazych@nvpublications.com
www.nvpublications.com

Contains profiles on recycling mills, as well as large users and generators of recycled materials for the broker, dealers and processors of paper stock, scrap metal, plastics and glass.
Jim Curley, Editor
Anna Dutko Rowley, Managing Editor

3994 Recycling Product News
Baum Publications
124-2323 Boundary Rd 604-291-9900
Vancouver, Can, BC V5M *Fax:* 604-291-1906
webadmin@baumpub.com
www.baumpub.com

Published for the recycling center operators and other waste mangers, articles discuss technology and new products.
Engelbert J Baum, President
Keith Barker, Editor

3995 Recycling Today
GIE Media
5811 Canal Road 800-456-0707
Valley View, OH 44125 *Fax:* 216-525-0515
dtoto@gie.net
www.recyclingtoday.com

Published for the secondary commodity processing/recycling market.
James R Keefe, Group Publisher
Brian Taylor, Editor

3996 Resource Recovery Report
5313 38th Street NW 540-347-4500
PO Box 3356 800-627-8913
Warrenton, VA 20188 *Fax:* 540-348-4540
rwill@coordgrp.com

Covers all alternatives to landfills, i.e., recycling, energy recovery, composting in North America, Government, industry, associations, universities, etc. are included.
12 pages
Richard Will, Production Manager

3997 Resource Recycling Magazine
Resource Recycling
PO Box 42270 503-233-1305
Portland, OR 97242 *Fax:* 503-233-1356
info@resource-recycling.com
www.resource-recycling.com

Monthly
Jerry Powell, Executive Editor
Dylan de Thomas, Editorial Director

3998 Reuse/Recycle Newsletter
Technomic Publishing Company
PO Box 3535 717-291-5609
Lancaster, PA 17601 800-233-9936
Fax: 717-295-4538

Provides news and information on important developments in both industrial and municipal recycling, and focuses on large-scale post-consumer, post-commercial, and post-industrial waste recycling.
8 pages
ISSN: 0048-7457
Susan E Selke, Author
Amy Flannery, Marketing

3999 Scrap
Institute of Scrap Recycling Industries
1250 H Street 202-662-8500
Suite 400 *Fax:* 202-626-0900
Washington, DC 20005 isri@isri.org
www.isri.org

Magazine of the Institute of Scrap Recycling Industries, serving companies that process, broker, and consume scrap commodities.
Bob Ensigner, Publisher
Rachel H. Pollack, Editorial Director

4000 Scrap Specifications Circular
Institute of Scrap Recycling Industries
1250 H Street 202-662-8500
Suite 400 *Fax:* 202-626-0900
Washington, DC 20005 isri@isri.org
www.isri.org

Publication of the Institute of Scrap Recycling Industries with guidelines for buying and selling processed scrap commodities.
At least 1/year
ISSN: 0036-9527
Robin Wiener, President
David Wagger, Chief Scientist

4001 Solid Waste & Recycling
Southam Environment Group
80 Valleybrook Drive 416-442-5600
Toronto M3B2S 800-268-7742
Fax: 416-510-5130
www.solidwastemag.com

Published to emphasize on municipal and commercial aspects of collection, handling, transportation, hauling, disposal and treatment of solid waste , including incineration, recycling and landfill technology.
Brad O'Brien, Publisher
David Nesseth, Editor

4002 Solid Waste Report
Business Publishers
2222 Sedwick Drive 301-589-5103
Durham, NC 27713 800-223-8720
Fax: 800-508-2592
custserv@bpinews.com
www.bpinews.com

Comprehensive news and analysis of legislation, regulation and litigation in solid waste management including resource recovery, recycling, collection and disposal. Regularly features international news, state updates and businesstrends.
Bi-Weekly
Leonard A Eiserer, Publisher
Beth Early, Operations Director

4003 State Recycling Laws Update
Raymond Communications
P.O. Box 4311 301-879-0628
Silver Spring, MD 20914-4311 *Fax:* 301-345-4768
circulation@raymond.com
www.raymond.com

Provides coverage of recycling legislation affecting business, as well as the outlook on future legislation across the US and Canada.
Bruce Popka, Vice President

4004 Waste Age
Environmental Industry Associations
4301 Connecticut Avenue NW 202-244-4700
#300 800-424-2869
Washington, DC 20008 *Fax:* 202-966-4868
ptom@primediabusiness.com
www.wasteage.com

Contents focus on new system technologies, recycling, resource recovery and sanitary landfills with regular features on updates in the status of government regulations, new products, guides, company profiles, exclusive surveyinformation, legislative implications and news.
Warren Bimblick, Group President
David Bodamer, Executive Director

4005 Waste Age's Recycling Times
Environmental Industry Associations
4301 Connecticut Avenue NW 202-244-4700
#300 800-424-2869
Washington, DC 20008 *Fax:* 202-966-4868
Features municipalities, recycling goals and rates, program innovations, waste habits, and new materials being recycled.
Warren Bimblick, Group President
David Bodamer, Executive Director

4006 Waste Handling Equipment News
Lee Publications
6113 State Highway 5 518-673-3237
PO Box 121 800-218-5586
Palatine Bridge, NY 13428 *Fax:* 518-673-2381
mstanley@leepub.com
www.leepub.com
Dicusses the latest developments in woodwaste, C&D, scrapmetal, concrete, asphalt, recycling and composting with the emphasis on equipment.
Publication Date: 1993 50 pages Monthly
Coyle Rockwell, Author
Colleen Suo, Editor
Matt Stanley, Editor

4007 Waste Recovery Report
Icon/Information Concepts
211 S 45th Street 215-349-6500
Philadelphia, PA 19104 *Fax:* 215-349-6502
wasterec@aol.com
www.icodat.com
Contains information on waste-to-energy, recycling, composting and other technologies.
Publication Date: 1975 6 pages Monthly
ISSN: 0889-0072
Alan Krigman, Publisher/Editor

Periodicals: Sustainable Development

4008 AERO SunTimes
Alternative Energy Resources Organization
PO Box 1558 406-443-7272
Helena, MT 59621 aero@aeromt.org
aeromt.org
The SunTimes is the newsletter for the Alternative Energy Resources Organization. The organization is a statewide grassroots group whose members work together to strengthen communities through promoting sustainable agriculture, localfood production and citizen-based Smart Growth community planning.
Jenn Battles, Executive Director
Jackie Heinert, Coordinator, Food Systems

4009 California Association of Resource Conservation Districts- CCP News
801 K Street 916-457-7094
Suite 1415 *Fax:* 916-457-7934
Sacramento, CA 93101 www.carcd.org
Quarterly
Karen Buhr, Executive Director
Emily Sutherland, Office Manager

4010 Californians for Population Stabilization: CAPS News
1129 State Street 805-564-6626
Suite 3-D *Fax:* 805-564-6636
Santa Barbara, CA 93101 info@capsweb.org
www.capsweb.org
A nonprofit, public interest organization that works to protect California's environment and quality of life by turning the tide of population growth.
Publication Date: 1986 8 pages 3x year
Dick Schneider, Chairman
Ben Zuckerman PhD, Vice President

4011 Cultivar
Center for Agoecology
1156 High Street 831-459-2506
Santa Cruz, CA 95064 *Fax:* 831-459-2867
Publication Date: 1985 9-12 pages Bi-Yearly
Steven Gliessman, Professor Agroecology
Martha Brown, Editor

4012 Ecosphere
Forum International
91 Gregory Lane 800-252-4475
Suite 21 *Fax:* 925-946-1500
Pleasant Hill, CA 94523 www.foruminternational.com
Accepts advertising. The first ever environmental/ecological magazine. It is dedicated to the interrelations of man in nature and a balanced approach of its biological, economic, socio-political and spiritual components. Since 1965.
Publication Date: 1965 16-48 pages Bi-monthly
Dr. Nicolas Hetzer, Production Manager
J McCormack, Circulation Director

4013 EnviroNews
600 Forbes Avenue 412-396-6000
331 Fisher Hall 800-456-0590
Pittsburgh, PA 15282 *Fax:* 412-396-4092
bembic@duq.edu
Educating environmental professionals for the twenty-first century is the focus of the Duquesne University Environmental Science and Management (ESM) Masters Degree Program. The program grew out of the perceived need to combine depthof knowledge in environmental science with a comprehensive understanding of the business, legal and policy implications surrounding environmental issues.
4 pages Semester Newsletter
Charles Dougherty, President
Linda Drago, J.D., University Secretary

4014 Environmental News
Arkansas Environmental Federation
1400 W Markham Street 501-374-0263
Suite 302 *Fax:* 501-374-8752
Little Rock, AR 72201 cmiller@environmentark.org
www.environmentark.org
Charles Miller, Executive Director
Marge Brookins, Office Manager

4015 Environmental and Energy Study Institute (EESI)
1020 19th Street NW 202-628-1400
Suite 650 *Fax:* 202-204-5244
Washington, DC 20036 info@eesi.org
www.eesi.org
Nonprofit organization dedicated to promoting environmentally sustainable societies. EESI believes meeting this goal requires transitions to social and economic patterns that sustain people, the environment and the natural resourcesupon which present and future generations depend. Offers a variety of publications.
Publication Date: 1984
Carol Werner, Executive Director
Susan Williams, Director, Development

4016 Forest Magazine
Forest Service Employees for Environmental Ethics
PO Box 11615 541-484-2692
Eugene, OR 97440 *Fax:* 541-484-3004
fseee@fseee.org
www.fseee.org
FSEEE is the largest forest watchdog organization in the nation. Since 1989, FSEEE has defended the rights and responsibilities of brave scientists and resource professionals working to assure the long-term health and vitality of ournational forests. FSEEE

publishes Forest Magazine quarterly to educate the public on forest issues.
Publication Date: 1989 50 pages Bi-Monthly
ISSN: 1534-9284
Andy Stahl, Executive Director
Matt Rasmussen, Editor

4017 Forest Science
10100 Laureate Way 301-897-8720
Bethesda, MD 20814-2198 866-897-8720
Fax: 301-897-3690
membership@safnet.org
www.eforester.org

Peer-reviewed journal with research on function and management of forested ecosystems around the world.
Bimonthly
ISSN: 0015-749X
Terry Baker, Chief Executive Officer
W. Keith Moser, Editor

4018 Forest Service Employees for Environmental Ethics
PO Box 11615 541-484-2692
Eugene, OR 97440 *Fax:* 541-484-3004
fseee@fseee.org
www.fseee.org

FSEEE is the largest forest watchdog organization in the nation. Since 1989, FSEEE has defended the rights and responsibilities of brave scientists and resource professionals working to assure the long-term health and vitality of ournational forests. FSEEE publishes Forest Magazine quarterly to educate the public on forest issues.
Andy Stahl, Executive Director
Matt Rasmussen, Editor

4019 Greens/Green Party USA Green Politics Green Politics
PO Box 408316 978-682-4353
Chicago, IL 60640 866-GRE-ENS2
Fax: 978-682-4318

Is a national non-profit membership organization dedicated to advancing the Green Ten Key Values as a guiding force in American society and politics.
12 pages Quarterly
Don Fitz, Editor

4020 International Boreal Forest Newsletter
Institute for World Resource Research
PO Box 50303 630-910-1551
Palo Alto, CA 94303 *Fax:* 630-910-1561
www.globalwarming.net

Covers all phases of developments in forestry and reforestation of northern nations including the US, Canada, Russia, Sweden, Finland, Norway, China, Japan and others. Its goal is to increase the worldwide understanding of theecological and economic roles of the northern forest regions of the world.
Dr. Yuan Lee, Editor-in-Chief
BJ Jefferson, Advertising/Sales

4021 International Society of Tropical Foresters: ISTF Notices
5400 Grosvenor Lane 301-897-8720
Bethesda, MD 20814 *Fax:* 301-897-3690
istfi@igo.apc.org
www.istf-bethesda.org

The International Society of Tropical Foresters, Inc. (ISTF) is a nonprofit organization committed to the protection, wise management and rational use of the world's tropical forests. Established in 1950, ISTF was reactivated in 1979.It has about 1500 members in more than 100 countries. Financial support comes from membership dues, donations and grants. ISTF sponsors meetings, promotes chapters in other countries, maintains a web site and has chapters at universities.
Gary S. Harshorn, President
Roger R. B. Leakey, Vice President

4022 Jackson Hole Conservation Alliance: Alliance News
685 S. Cache St 307-733-9417
PO Box 2728 *Fax:* 307-733-9008
Jackson, WY 83001 info@jhalliance.org
www.jhalliance.org

An organization dedicated to responsible land stewardship in Jackson Hole, Wyoming to ensure that human activities are in harmony with the area's irreplaceable wildlife, scenery and other natural resources.
20 pages Quarterly
Craig M. Benjamin, Executive Director
David Hardie, Co-Chair

4023 Journal of Forestry
10100 Laureate Way 301-897-8720
Bethesda, MD 20814-2198 866-897-8720
Fax: 301-897-3690
membership@safnet.org
www.eforester.org

Seeks to advance the profession of forestry through the sharing of information on developments and new ideas in forestry.
Publication Date: 1902 Bimonthly
ISSN: 0022-1201
Terry Baker, Chief Executive Officer
Keith A. Blatner, Editor

4024 Leopold Letter
Iowa State University
209 Curtiss Hall 515-294-3711
513 Farm House Lane *Fax:* 515-294-9696
Ames, IA 50011-1054 leocenter@iastate.edu
www.leopold.iastate.edu

A newsletter informing diverse audiences about Leopold Center programs and activities, with the purpose of encouraging interest in and use of sustainable farming practices as well as stimulating public discussion on sustainableagriculture in Iowa.
Publication Date: 1987 12 pages Quarterly
ISSN: 1065-2116
Doug Gronau, Chair
Mark Rasmussen, Director

4025 Minnesota Department of Agriculture: MDA Quarterly
625 Robert St. N. 651-201-6000
St Paul, MN 55155 800-967-2474
Fax: 651-297-5522
webinfo@mda.state.mn.us
www.mda.state.mn.us

The MDA's mission is to work toward a diverse ag industry that is profitable as well as environmentally sound; to protect the public health safety regarding food and ag products; and to ensure orderly commerce in agricultural and foodproducts. We have two major branches of the department to accomplish this mission: regulatory divisions and non-regulatory divisions.
Publication Date: 2000
Dave Frederickson, Commissioner
Jim Boerboom, Deputy Commissioner

4026 Mountain Research and Development
810 E 10th Street mrd-journal@peertrack.net
Lawrence, KS 66044 www.mrd-journal.org

The leading journal specifically devoted to the world's mountains. It has been published since 1981 and has established itself as a renowned international publication containing well-researched, peer-reviewed scientific articles byauthors from around the world.
Thomas Breu, Editor-in-Chief
David Molden, Editor-in-Chief

4027 Northeast Sun
Northeast Sustainable Energy Association
50 Miles Street 413-774-6051
Greenfield, MA 00130 *Fax:* 413-774-6053
nesea@nesea.org
www.nesea.org

Promotes responsible use of energy for a stronger economy and cleaner environment. Northeast Sun is a bi-annual Spring and Fall publication that includes articles by leading authorities on

sustainable energy practices, energyefficiency and renewable energy, and each Fall issue includes the Sustainable Green Pages Directory of engery professionals in the Northeast. Subscription is free with membership.
Bi-Annual
Jennifer Marrapese, Executive Director
Gina Sieber, Business Manager

4028 Pinchot Letter
1400 16th Street NW 202-797-6580
Suite 350 *Fax:* 202-797-6583
Washington, DC 20036 pinchot@pinchot.org
www.pinchot.org
A tri-annual newsletter published by the Pinchot Institute for Conservation, an independent nonprofit organization that works collaboratively with all Americans-from federal and state policymakers to citizens in rural communities-tostrengthen forest conservation by advancing sustainable forest management, developing conservation leaders and providing science-based solutions to natural resource issues.
Publication Date: 1995 20 pages Tri-Annual
William C. Price, President
Alex Andrus, Director, External Affairs

4029 Population Connection Magazine
Population Connection
2120 L Street NW 202-332-2200
Suite 500 800-767-1956
Washington, DC 20037 *Fax:* 202-332-2302
info@populationconnection.org
www.populationconnection.org
Magazine of nonprofit organization Population Connection, working to slow population growth and achieve a sustainable balance between the Earth's people and its resources.
Publication Date: 1972 Quarterly
ISSN: 0199-0071
John Seager, President & CEO
Pamela Wasserman, Sr. VP, Education

4030 Population Reference Bureau: World Population Data Sheet
1875 Connecticut Avenue NW 202-483-1100
Suite 520 800-877-9881
Washington, DC 20009 *Fax:* 202-328-3937
popref@prb.org
www.prb.org
Up-to-date demographic data and estimates for all the countries and major regions of the world.
Jeffrey Jordan, President/CEO
Linda A. Jacobsen, VP, U.S. Programs

4031 Resource Development Newsletter
University of Tennessee
PO Box 1071 865-974-7448
Knoxville, TN 37901 *Fax:* 423-974-7448
Community development information.
4 pages
Dr Alan Barefield, Publisher

4032 Restoration Ecology Magazine
Blackwell Science
350 Main Street 781-388-8200
Commerce Place *Fax:* 781-388-8210
Malden, MA 00214 info@wiley.com
as.wiley.com
Provides the most recent developments in the ecological and biological restoration field for both the fundamental and practical implications of restorations.
Mark Mark Allin, President/CEO
Peter Booth Wiley, Chair

4033 Seed Listing
Native Seeds/SEARCH
3061 N Campbell Avenue 520-622-5561
Tucson, AZ 85719 info@nativeseeds.org
www.nativeseeds.org
Annual release cataloguing the seeds available from Native Seeds/SEARCH.
Joy Hought, Executive Director
Glenn Wagner, Manager, Operations

4034 Solar Energy Magazine
Elsevier Science
360 Park Avenue S 212-989-5800
11th Floor *Fax:* 212-633-3680
New York, NY 10010
Devoted exclusively to the science and technology of solar energy applications.
Publication Date: 1957
ISSN: 0380-92X
D Yogi Goswami, Editor-in-Chief

4035 Solar Energy Report
California Solar Energy Industries Association
1107 9th St. 916-747-6987
Ste 820 *Fax:* 707-374-4767
Sacramento, CA 95814 info@calseia.org
www.calseia.org
Bi-Monthly
Rick Reed, President
Cecilia Aguillon, Vice President

4036 Southface Journal of Sustainable Building
Southface Energy Institute
241 Pine Street NE 404-872-3549
Atlanta, GA 30308 *Fax:* 404-872-5009
info@southface.org
www.southface.org
Contains articles on numerous sustainable building topics. Free to members and available online.
Publication Date: 1978 24 pages Quarterly
Linda Bolan, Chair
Barry R. Goldman, Vice Chair

4037 Sustainable Green Pages Directory
Northeast Sustainable Energy Association
50 Miles Street 413-774-6051
Greenfield, MA 00130 *Fax:* 413-774-6053
nesea@nesea.org
www.nesea.org
The SPG Directory lists over 30 categories of sustainable energy professionals working throughout the Northeast, including architects, engineers, builders, energy auditors, consultants and renewable energy installers and manufacturers.It is the largest directory of its kind and the only one that targets the Northeastern USA. Published in the Northeast Sun magazine and online.
September Annual
Jennifer Marrapese, Executive Director
Gina Sieber, Business Manager

4038 Totally Tree-Mendous Activities
Northeast Sustainable Energy Association
50 Miles Street 413-774-6051
Greenfield, MA 00130 *Fax:* 413-774-6053
nesea@nesea.org
www.nesea.org
Resource for teachers and parents that offers creative and fun tree-based projects for students.
40 pages
Jennifer Marrapese, Executive Director
Gina Sieber, Business Manager

4039 Woodland Steward
Massachusetts Forestry Association
270 Jackson Street 413-323-7326
Belchertown, MA 00100 *Fax:* 413-323-9594
This publication is full of information about Massachusett's forest and ways that landowners can manage their woodlands to achieve their goals in an environmentally sustainable manner. Free with membership.
Bi-Monthly
Gregory Cox, Executive Director

4040 Worldwatch Institute: State of the World
1400 16th Street NW 202-745-8092
Suite 430 *Fax:* 202-478-2534
Washington, DC 20036 worldwatch@worldwatch.org
www.worldwatch.org

The most authorative go-to resource for those who understand the importance of nuturing a safe, sane and healthy global environment through both policy and action.
Annual
ISBN: 0-393326-66-7
Ed Groark, Chair/Acting Interim Pres
John Robbins, Treasurer

4041 Worldwatch Institute: Vital Signs
1400 16th Street NW 202-745-8092
Suite 430 *Fax:* 202-478-2534
Washington, DC 20036 worldwatch@worldwatch.org
www.worldwatch.org

Provides comprehensive, user-friendly information on key trends and includes tables and graphs that help readers access the developments that are changing their lives for better or for worse.
Annual
ISBN: 0-393326-89-6
Ed Groark, Chair/Acting Interim Pres
John Robbins, Treasurer

4042 Worldwatch Institute: World Watch
1400 16th Street NW 202-745-8092
Suite 430 *Fax:* 202-478-2534
Washington, DC 20036 worldwatch@worldwatch.org
www.worldwatch.org

The Worldwatch Institute is an independent, nonprofit environmental research organization in Washington DC. Its mission is to foster a sustainable society in which human needs are met in ways that do not threaten the health of thenatural environment or future generations. To this end, this Institute conducts interdisciplinary research on emerging global issues, the results of which are published and disseminated to decision-makers and the media.
Bi-Monthly
Ed Groark, Chair/Acting Interim Pres
John Robbins, Treasurer

4043 Worldwatch Institute: Worldwatch Papers
1400 16th Street NW 202-745-8092
Suite 430 *Fax:* 202-478-2534
Washington, DC 20036 worldwatch@worldwatch.org
www.worldwatch.org

Provides cutting-edge analysis on an environmental topic that is making - or is about to make - headlines worldwide.
50-70 pages 5x times year
Ed Groark, Chair/Acting Interim Pres
John Robbins, Treasurer

Periodicals: Travel & Tourism

4044 National Parks Magazine
National Parks Conservation Association
777 6th Street NW 202-223-6722
Suite 700 800-628-7275
Washington, DC 20001-3723 npca@npca.org
www.npca.org/articles/magazine

Online magazine articles released by the National Parks Conservation Association.
Theresa Pierno, President & CEO
Robin Martin McKenna, Executive Vice President

4045 New York State Parks, Recreation and Historic Preservation
Empire State Plaza 518-474-0456
Agency Building 1 *Fax:* 518-486-2924
Albany, NY 12238

Publishes New York State Boat Launching Guide, Camping/Cabin Reservation Info, Snowmobiling Guide and Preservation Magazine.
Bernadette Castro, Commissioner

4046 Potomac Appalachian
118 Park Street SE 703-242-0315
Vienna, VA 22180 *Fax:* 703-242-0968
info@patc.net
www.patc.net

Published by the Potomac Appalachian Trail Club, which through volunteer efforts, education and advocacy, acquires, maintains and protects the trail and lands of the Appalachian Trail, other trails and related facilities in theMid-Atlantic Region for the enjoyment of present and future hikers. PATC publishes hiking guides, maps and history books of the Appalachian Trail and other trails in our area of responsibility. The monthly newsletter is sent to members and uponrequest. Free to members.
16-20 pages Monthly
ISSN: 098 -8154
Richard Hostelley, President
Rachel Levin, Editor

4047 Sam D. Hamilton Noxubee National Wildlife Refuge
13723 Bluff Lake Road 662-323-5548
Brooksville, MS 39739 *Fax:* 662-323-6390
noxubee@fws.gov
www.fws.gov/refuge/noxubee

Noxubee National Wildlife Refuge was established to protect and enhance habitat for the conservation of migratory birds, endangered species and other wildlife. The recreational and educational opportunities provided on the refuge helpthe public experience nature and learn how sound management ensures that future generations continue to enjoy fish and wildlife and their habitats.
Publication Date: 1940 2 pages Bi-Annual

Periodicals: Water Resources

4048 Air Water Pollution Report's Environment Week
Business Publishers
2222 Sedwick Drive 301-589-5103
Durham, NC 27713 800-223-8720
Fax: 800-508-2592
custserv@bpinews.com
www.bpinews.com

Provides a balanced, insightful update on the week's most important environmental news from Washington, DC.
Leonard A Eiserer, Publisher
David Goeller, Editor

4049 Air/Water Pollution Report
Business Publishers
2222 Sedwick Drive 301-589-5103
Durham, NC 27713 800-223-8720
Fax: 800-508-2592
custserv@bpinews.com
www.bpinews.com

Regulatory activities and governmental legislation, in addition to litigation are covered in this pulication.
Leonard A Eiserer, Publisher
David Goeller, Editor

4050 American Fisheries Society: Water Quality Matters
324 25th Street 801-625-5358
Ogden, UT 84401 *Fax:* 801-625-5756
glampman@fs.fed.us

8 pages 1-2 per year
Georgina Lampman, President
Gregg Lominczy, Editor

4051 American Ground Water Trust Newsletter
American Ground Water Trust
50 Pleasant Street 603-228-5444
Suite 2 800-423-7748
Concord, NH 03301 *Fax:* 603-228-6557
trustinfo@agwt.org
www.agwt.org

4 pages Quarterly
David Kill, Chair
Andrew Stone, Executive Director

4052 **American Water Resources Association:Water Resources IMPACT Magazine**
P.O. Box 2663 540-687-8390
Woodbridge, VA 22195 *Fax:* 540-687-8395
info@awra.org
www.awra.org
AWRA advances water resources research, planning, development, management and education. AWRA takes a balanced, professional approach to solving water resources challenges by establishing discourse between physical, biological, andsocial scientists, engineers, and other persons concerned with water resources.
Publication Date: 1964 Bi-Monthly
Joe Berg, Chair

4053 **American Water Resources Association: Journal of the American Water Resources Association**
P.O. Box 2663 540-687-8390
Woodbridge, VA 22195 *Fax:* 540-687-8395
info@awra.org
www.awra.org
AWRA advances water resources research, planning, development, management and education. AWRA takes a balanced, professional approach to solving water resources challenges by establishing discourse between physical, biological, andsocial scientists, engineers, and other persons concerned with water resources.
Publication Date: 1964 Bi-Monthly
ISSN: 1752-1688
Venkatesh Uddameri, Editor-in-Chief

4054 **Bacteria and Water Wells**
American Ground Water Trust
50 Pleasant Street 603-228-5444
Suite 2 800-423-7748
Concord, NH 03301 *Fax:* 603-228-6557
trustinfo@agwt.org
www.agwt.org
David Kill, Chair
Andrew Stone, Executive Director

4055 **Blue Planet Magazine**
The Ocean Conservancy
1300 19th Street, NW 202-429-5609
8th Floor 800-519-1541
Washington, DC 20036 *Fax:* 202-429-0056
www.oceanconservancy.org
To educate peoeple about ocean issues; inspire readers with the beauty and wonder of oceans; encourage dedication to appreciating and protecting marine resources; and enlist new volunteers in the ocean community. Free with membershipfee of $25.00
46 pages Quarterly
Andreas Merkl, CEO
Janis Searles Jones, President

4056 **Clean Water Network: CWN Status Water Report**
Spills and Kills
1200 New York Avenue, NW 202-289-2421
Suite 400 *Fax:* 202-289-1060
Washington, DC 20005
A nonprofit network of over 1,000 organizations that deal with clean water issues covered by the Clean Water Act. Our member organizations consist of a variety of organizations representing environmentalists, family farmers, recreationanglers, commercial fishermen, surfers, boaters, faith communities, labor unions and civic associates. We publish a monthly newsletter and various reports.
8-12 pages Monthly
Katherine Smitherman, Executive Director

4057 **Clean Water Report Newsletter**
Business Publishers
2222 Sedwick Drive 301-589-5103
Durham, NC 27713 800-223-8720
Fax: 800-508-2592
Follows the latest news from the EPA, Congress, the states, the courts, and private industry. A key information source for environmental professionals, covering the important issues of ground and drinking water, wastewater treatment,wetlands, drought, coastal protection, non-point source pollution, agrichemical contamination and more.
8 pages Bi-Weekly
ISSN: 0009-8620
Leonard A Eiserer, Publisher
Louise Harris, Editor

4058 **Clearwaters Magazine**
New York Water Environment Association
525 Plum Street 315-422-7811
Suite 102 877-556-9932
Syracuse, NY 13204 *Fax:* 315-422-3851
pcr@nywea.org
www.nywea.org
Published by The New York Water Environment Association, a nonprofit educational association dedicated to the development and dissemination of information concerning water quality management and the nature, collection, treatment, anddisposal of wastewater. Founded in 1929, the Association has over 2,500 members. The NYWEA is a member association of the Water Environment Federation.
Quarterly
Patricia Cerro-Reehil, Executive Director
Maggie Hoose, Administrative Manager

4059 **Coastal Voice**
5460 Beaujolais Lane 239-489-2616
Fort Myers, FL 33919 *Fax:* 239-489-9917
managing@asbpa.org
www.asbpa.org
E-newsletter of the American Shore and Beach Preservation Association. The January issue serves as the association's annual report.
10 issues/year
Derek Brockbank, Executive Director
Beth Sciaudone, PhD, Managing Editor

4060 **Colorado Department of Natural Resources: Division of Water Resources: StreamLines**
1313 Sherman Street 303-866-3581
Room 818 *Fax:* 303-866-3589
Denver, CO 80203 www.water.state.co.us
The Colorado Division of Water Resources is an agency of the State of Colorado, Department of Natural Resources, operating under the direction of specific state stautes, court decrees, and interstate compacts. The DWR is empowered toadminister all surface and ground water rights throughout the state and ensure that the doctrine of prior appropiation is enforced.
Publication Date: 1988 4-8 pages Quearterly
Hal D Simpson, Director Water Resources
Russell George, Executive Director

4061 **Colorado Water Rights**
1580 Logan Street 303-837-0812
#700 *Fax:* 303-526-3864
Denver, CO 80203 cwc@cowatercongress.org
www.cowatercongress.org
This newsletter helps the Colorado Water Congress protect and conserve Colorado's water resouces by educating its readers.
Publication Date: 1982 4-16 pages Quarterly
Meg Meyer, Associate Director
Doug Kemper, Executive Director

4062 **Confluence**
Texas Water Conservation Association
221 E 9th Street 512-472-7216
Suite 206 *Fax:* 512-472-0537
Austin, TX 78701 drobbins@twca.org
The official newsletter of the Texas Water Conservation Association. For those interested in water issues from river authorities to industrial concerns.
Quarterly
Robert J. Brandes, President
John W. Grant, President-Elect

4063 **Domestic Water Treatment for Homeowners**
American Ground Water Trust

50 Pleasant Street 603-228-5444
Suite 2 800-423-7748
Concord, NH 03301 *Fax:* 603-228-6557
trustinfo@agwt.org
www.agwt.org

David Kill, Chair
Andrew Stone, Executive Director

4064 Environmental Policy Alert
Inside Washington Publishers
1919 South Eads Street 703-416-8500
Suite 201 800-424-9068
Arlington, VA 22202 *Fax:* 703-416-8543
custsvc@iwpnews.com
www.iwpnews.com
Is a reliable resource for all regulatory, congressional and litigation developments in air quality, waste cleanup, clean water and other environmental quality issues. Also provides a special focus on efforts to reinvent environmentalpolicies.
Publication Date: 1984 Bi-Weekly
Jeremy Bernstein, Editor

4065 Georgia Water and Pollution Control Association: Operator
2121 New Market Parkway 770-618-8690
Suite 144 *Fax:* 770-618-8695
Marietta, GA 30067 info@gwpca.org
The GW+PCA is dedicated to education, dissemination of technical and scientific information, increased public understanding and promotion of sound public laws and programs in the water resources and related environmental fields.Founded in 1932.
Publication Date: 1970 56-68 pages Quarterly
Jack C Dozier, PE, Executive Director

4066 Georgia Water and Pollution Control Association: News & Notes
2121 New Market Parkway 770-618-8690
Suite 144 *Fax:* 770-618-8695
Marietta, GA 30067
The GW+PCA is dedicated to education, dissemination of technical and scientific information, increased public understanding and promotion of sound public laws and programs in the water resources and related environmental fields.Founded in 1932.
Publication Date: 1970 20-28 pages Monthly
Jack C Dozier, PE, Executive Director

4067 Gulf of Mexico Science
Dauphin Island Sea Lab
101 Bienville Boulevard 251-861-2141
Dauphin Island, AL 36528 *Fax:* 251-861-4646
www.disl.org

Journal devoted to disemminating knowledge of the Gulf of Mexico and adjacent areas. Appropriate topics of consideration for publication include all areas of marine science.
2x Year
ISSN: 1087-688X
Lisa Young, Public Relations Consultant
Katy Blankenhorn, Scheduling Coordinator

4068 International Desalination and Water Reuse Quarterly
Lineal Publishing Company
306 Eagle Dr 561-451-9429
Jupiter, FL 33477 *Fax:* 561-451-9435
www.desalination.biz
Disseminates technical information, reviews and analyzes regional developments in the field, as well as new products and processes. The publication provides, on a continuing basis, a major vehicle in which to promote desalination andwater reuse technologies, equipment, and design to potential users.
Trevor Loveday, Editor
John Gould, Publisher

4069 Journal of Soil and Water Conservation
Soil & Water Conservation Society
945 SW Ankeny Road 515-289-2331
Ankeny, IA 50023 800-THE-SOIL
Fax: 515-289-1227
swcs@swcs.org
www.swcs.org
Publication includes a variety of conservation subjects, as well as international conservation issues.
Clare Lindahl, CEO
Jody Thompson, Editorial Assistant

4070 Journal of the New England Water Environment
New England Water Environment Association
10 Tower Office Park 781-939-0908
Suite 601 *Fax:* 781-939-0907
Woburn, MA 01801 mail@newea.org
www.newea.org
Quarterly publication from New England Water Environment Association.
Publication Date: 1929 150 pages Bi-Annual
ISSN: 1077-3002
Mary Barry, Executive Director
Janice Moran, Program Coordinator

4071 Journal of the North American Benthological Society
North American Benthological Society
PO Box 7065 www.benthos.org
Lawrence, KS 66044
The society is an international scientific organization that promotes better understanding of biotic communities of lake and stream bottoms and their role in aquatic ecosystems. The journal includes articles that promote the furtherunderstanding of benthic communities and helps members to keep current on interests.
Quarterly
ISSN: 0887-3593
N LeRoy Poff, President

4072 Mass Waters
Massachusetts Water Pollution Control Association
P.O. Box 60 774-276-9722
Rochdale, MA 00154 *Fax:* 774-670-9956
mwpca2011@yahoo.com
www.mwpca.org

Quarterly
Mike Foisy, President
Lynn Foisy, Executive Director

4073 Mono Lake Committee Newsletter
Corner of Hwy 395 & 3rd Street 760-647-6595
PO Box 29 *Fax:* 760-647-6377
Lee Vining, CA 93541 info@monolake.org
www.monolake.org
Nonprofit citizen's group dedicated to: protecting and restoring the Mono Basin ecosystem; educating the public about Mono Lake and the impacts on the environment of excessive water use; promoting cooperative solutions that protectMono Lake and meet real water needs without transferring environmental problems to other areas.
Publication Date: 1978 28 pages Quarterly
Geoffrey McQuilkin, Executive Director
Arya Degenhardt, Communications Director

4074 Montana Environmental Training Center Newsletter
Hagener Science Center
8336 Washington Place NE 505-884-1031
Albuquerque, NM 87113 *Fax:* 505-884-1032
www.nmrwa.org
METC is a cooperative effort between Montana State University-Northern and the Montana Department of Environmental Quality. Basic, advance training, and continuing education in the areas of water and wastewater operation, maintenance,safety, process control, cross connection and backflow prevention along with courses in basic water science and watershed awareness define the training activities of METC. A newsletter and Training Announcement are published quarterly.
Quarterly
David Kenneke, President
Jose E. Terrones, Vice-President

4075 **Montana Environmental Training Center Training Announcement**
Hagener Science Center
8336 Washington Place NE 505-884-1031
Albuquerque, NM 87113 *Fax:* 505-884-1032
www.nmrwa.org
METC is a cooperative effort between Montana State University-Northern and the Montana Department of Environmental Quality. Basic, advance training, and continuing education in the areas of water and wastewater operation, maintenance,safety, process control, cross connection and backflow prevention along with courses in basic water science and watershed awareness define the training activities of METC. A newsletter and Training Announcement are published quarterly.
Quarterly
David Kenneke, President
Jose E. Terrones, Vice-President

4076 **New Mexico Rural Water Association Newsletter**
8336 Washington Place NE 505-884-1031
Albuquerque, NM 87113 800-819-9893
Fax: 505-884-1032
www.nmrwa.org
To provide top quality, responsive technical assistance and training for rural water and wastewater systems in New Mexico.
Quarterly
David Kenneke, President
Jose E. Terrones, Vice-President

4077 **New York Water Environment Association Clearwaters**
525 Plum Street 315-422-7811
Suite 102 877-556-9932
Syracuse, NY 13204 *Fax:* 315-422-3851
pcr@nywea.org
www.nywea.org
Contains articles on environmental issues, regulatory changes, technological advances as well as, updates on members and activities.
50 pages Quarterly
Paul McGarvey, President
Geoffrey Baldwin, President Elect

4078 **Oregon Water Resources Congress Newsletter**
437 Union St. NE 503-363-0121
Salem, OR 97301 *Fax:* 503-371-4926
www.owrc.org
Is to promote the protection and use of water rights and the wise stewardship of water resources.
Quarterly
April Snell, Executive Director
Ken Crick, Office Manager

4079 **Ozark National Scenic Riverways**
Ozark National Scenic Riverways
PO Box 490 573-323-4236
Van Buren, MO 63965 *Fax:* 573-323-4140
ozar_superintendent@nps.gov
www.nps.gov/ozar
Missouri's largest National Park and America's first to preserve a free flowing river in its wild state. Covers some 80,000 acres along 134 miles of the Current and Jacks Fork Rivers. Staff provide elementary level environmentaleducation programs on natural history, with an emphasis on karst and water issues. Publishes More Than Skin Deep, a Teacher's Guide to Caves and Groundwater, a curriculum guide suitable for grades K-12.
Publication Date: 1964 Annual
Noel Poe, Superintendent

4080 **Pacific Rivers Council: Freeflow**
PO Box 10798 541-345-0119
Eugene, OR 97440 *Fax:* 541-345-0710
Promoting the protection and restoration of rivers, their watersheds, and native aquatic species.
Quarterly
David Bayles, Executive Director
Holly Spencer, Editor

4081 **Puerto Rico Water Resources and Environmental Research Institute Newsletter**
University of Puerto Rico
College of Engineering 787-833-0300
PO Box 9000 *Fax:* 787-833-3985
Mayaguez, PR 00681 PRWRERI@uprm.edu
www.ece.uprm.edu/rumhp/prwrri
Its objectives are to: conduct research aimed at resolving local and national water resources problems; train scientists and engineers through hands-on participation in research; and to facilitate the incorporation of research resultsin the knowledge base of water resources professionals.
Publication Date: 1990 4 pages Quarterly/thru Email
Walter Silva Araya, Associate Director
Jesenia Carrero, Administrative Assistant

4082 **Runoff Rundown**
Center for Watershed Protection
3290 North Ridge Road 410-461-8323
Suite 290 *Fax:* 410-461-8324
Ellicott City, MD 21043 center@cwp.org
www.cwp.org
Electronic newsletter published by the Center for Watershed Protection, a nonprofit 501(c)3 organization dedicated to finding new ways to protect and restore our nation's streams, lakes, rivers and estuaries. The center publishesnumerous technical publications on all aspects of watershed protection, including stormwater management, watershed planning and better site design.
Publication Date: 2000 Quarterly
Hye Yeong Kwon, Executive Director
Bill Stack, Deputy Director of Programs

4083 **Save San Francisco Bay Association: Watershed Newsletter**
1330 Broadway 510-463-6850
Suite 1800 *Fax:* 510-463-6851
Oakland, CA 94612 info@saveSFbay.org
www.savesfbay.org
Save the Bay has worked for over 40 years to protect the San Francisco Bay-Delta from pollution, fill, shoreline destruction and fresh water diversion. We have launched a century of renewal to restore bay fish and wildlife, reclaimtidal wetlands and make the bay safe and accessible to all.
8-10 pages 3-4 times/year
David Lewis, Executive Director
Jackie Richardson, Development Coordinator

4084 **Shore and Beach**
5460 Beaujolais Lane 239-489-2616
Fort Myers, FL 33919 *Fax:* 239-489-9917
derek.brockbank@asbpa.org
www.asbpa.org
Peer-reviewed publication from the American Shore and Beach Preservation Association.
Publication Date: 1933 Quarterly
ISSN: 0037-4237
Derek Brockbank, Executive Director
Beth Sciaudone, PhD, Managing Editor

4085 **South Carolina Sea Grant Consortium**
287 Meeting Street 843-727-2078
Charleston, SC 29401 *Fax:* 843-727-2080
www.scseagrant.org
A state agency that supports coastal and marine research, education, outreach, and one technical assistance program that fosters sustainable economic development and resource conservation. The consortium represents eight university andstate research organizations and induces a number of information products on coastal and marine resource topics.
Publication Date: 1982 16 pages
M Richard DeVoe, Executive Director

4086 **TCS Bulletin**
P. O. Box 3590 757-565-0999
Williamsburg, VA 23187 *Fax:* 757-565-0922
coastalsoc@aol.com
www.thecoastalsociety.org

Organization of private sector, academic, government professionals and students dedicated to actively addressing emerging coastal issues by fostering dialogue, forging partnerships and promoting communication and education. Thispublication covers issues of aquaculture-related law and coastal management research.

Publication Date: 1975 24 pages Yearly
Thomas Bigford, President
Susannah Sheldon, Secretary

4087 The American Well Owner
American Ground Water Trust
50 Pleasant Street 603-228-5444
Suite 2 800-423-7748
Concord, NH 03301 *Fax:* 603-228-6557
trustinfo@agwt.org
www.agwt.org

David Kill, Chair
Andrew Stone, Executive Director

4088 Tide
Coastal Conservation Association
6919 Portwest 713-626-4234
Suite 100 800-201-FISH
Houston, TX 77024 *Fax:* 713-626-5852
ccantl@joincca.org
www.joincca.org

TIDE is the official bimonthly magazine of the Coastal Conservation Association. It has received local, state and national acclaim for writing, photography and layout and currently boasts a circulation of more than 70,000. TIDE isavailable only to members of the Coastal Conservation Association.

Bi-Monthly
Degraaf Adams, Board Member
Bruce Arendale, Board Member

4089 Utah Watershed Review
Utah Association of Conservation Districts
40 West Cache Valley Blvd 435-374-4444
Building 8C *Fax:* 435-755-2117
Logan, UT 84341 www.uacd.org

Provides information about what's new in Utah and watershed volunteer work and management.

Bi-Monthly
Gordon Younker, EVP
Jack Wilbur, Editor

4090 Water & Wastes Digest
Scranton Gillette Communications
3030 W. Salt Creek Lane 847-391-1000
Suite 201 *Fax:* 847-390-0408
Arlington Heights, IL 60005 webmaster@sgcmail.com
www.scrantongillette.com

This serves readers in the water and/or wastewater industries. These people work for municipalities, in industry, or as engineers. They design, specify, buy, operate and maintain equipment, chemicals, software and wastewater treatmentservices.

128 pages
ISSN: 0043-1181
Dennis Martyka, Publisher
Tim Gregorski, Editorial Director

4091 Water Quality Products
Scranton Gillette Communications
3030 W. Salt Creek Lane 847-391-1000
Suite 201 *Fax:* 847-390-0408
Arlington Heights, IL 60005 webmaster@sgcmail.com
www.scrantongillette.com

Provides balanced editorial content including developments in water conditioning, filtration and disinfection for residential, commercial and industrial systems.

68 pages
ISSN: 1092-0978
Dennis Martyka, Publisher
Tracy Fabre, Editor

4092 Water Resource Center: Minnegram
University of Minnesota
173 McNeal 1985 Buford Avenue 612-624-9282
St Paul, MN 55108 *Fax:* 612-625-1263
Fax: ‘
ander045@umn.edu

Four University water programs, Extension Water Quality Program, Center for Hydrocultural Impacts on Water Quality, Water Resources Research Center and Water Resources Science Graduate Program make up the Water Resources Center. Thecenter sponsors and coordinates programs in research, graduate education, outreach and service to address water resource management issues.

Publication Date: 1986 Quarterly
Jim Anderson, Co-Director
Debra Swackhamer, Co-Director

4093 WaterMatters
Southwest Florida Water Management District
2379 Broad Street 352-796-7211
Brookville, FL 34604 *Fax:* 352-754-6885
www.swfwmd.state.fl.us

Newletter of the Southwest Florida Water Management District, which manages the water and water-related resources within its boundaries. Maintains balance between the water needs of current and future users while protecting andmaintaining the natural systems that provide the District with its existing and future water supply. The Conservation Projects Section, is reponsible for managing water conservation, reclaimed water, other alternative source projects, and estimatingfuture water demands.

2 pages Monthly
Michael A. Babb, Chair
Randall S. Maggard, Vice Chair

Books: Air & Climate

4094 Caring for Our Air
Enslow Publishers, Inc
101 West 23rd Street 908-771-9400
Suite #240 800-398-2504
New York, NY 10011 *Fax:* 877-980-4454
customerservice@enslow.com
www.enslow.com

Publication Date: 1976

4095 Center for Resource Economics
2000 M Street NW 202-232-7933
Suite 650 *Fax:* 202-234-1328
Wasington, DC 20036 info@islandpress.org
www.islandpress.org

Works to educate the public about global environmental issues. Methods include publishing literature on environmental concerns.

Charles C. Savitt, President
Shaina Lange, Executive Assistant

4096 Confronting Climate Change: Strategies for Energy Research and Development
National Academy Press
500 5th Street NW 202-334-3313
Lockbox 285 888-624-8373
Washington, DC 20055 *Fax:* 202-334-2451
www.nap.edu

Publication Date: 1990 144 pages
ISBN: 0-309043-47-6

4097 Fundamentals of Stack Gas Dispersion
Milton R. Beychok Consulting
1126 Colony Plaza 949-718-1360
Newport Beach, CA 92660 *Fax:* 949-718-1360
mbeychok@air-dispersion.com

The most comprehensive single-source reference book on dispertion modeling of continuous buoyant pollution plumes.

Milton R Beychok, Principal

4098 Healing the Planet: Strategies for Resolving the Environmental Crisis
Addison-Wesley Publishing Company

75 Arlington Street
Suite 300
Boston, MA 00211
617-848-7500
www.aw.com

4099 Indoor Air Quality: Design Guide Book
Fairmont Press
700 Indian Trail
Liburn, GA 30047
770-925-9388
Fax: 770-381-9865
www.fairmontpress.com

4100 Ozone Depletion and Climate Change: Constructing a Global Response
SUNY Press
22 Corporate Woods Boulevard
3rd Floor
Albany, NY 12211
518-472-5000
866-430-7869
Fax: 518-472-5038
info@sunypress.edu
www.sunypress.edu

Available in both soft and hardcover, this book offers solutions that address climate change from a global viewpoint.
Publication Date: 2005 276 pages
Matthew J Hoffman, Author
Tom Baker, Editorial Board
Sue Books, Editorial Board

4101 Politics of Air Pollution: Urban Growth, Ecological Modernization, and Symbolic Inclusion
SUNY Press
22 Corporate Woods Boulevard
3rd Floor
Albany, NY 12211
518-472-5000
866-430-7869
Fax: 518-472-5038
info@sunypress.edu
www.sunypress.edu

Available in both soft and hardcover, this title addresses the relationship between urban growth and pollution.
Publication Date: 2005 152 pages
George A Gonzalez, Author
Tom Baker, Editorial Board
Sue Books, Editorial Board

4102 To Breath Free: Eastern Europe's Environmental Crisis
John Hopkins University Press
3400 N Charles Street
Baltimore, MD 21218
410-516-6900
800-537-5487
Adam Glazer, Promotions Manager

Books: Business

4103 Environmental Career Guide: Job Opportunities with the Earth in Mind
J Wiley & Sons
111 River Street
Hoboken, NJ 00703-5774
212-850-6000
Fax: 212-850-6088
info@wiley.com
as.wiley.com

Publication Date: 1991 208 pages
ISBN: 0-471534-13-7
Nicholas Basta, Author
Mark Mark Allin, President/CEO
Peter Booth Wiley, Chair

4104 Environmental Disputes: Community Involvement in Conflict Resolution
Island Press
PO Box 7
Covelo, CA 95428
707-983-6432
800-828-1302
Fax: 707-983-6414

A book published by Island Press which helps citizen groups, business and government understand how Envionmental Dispute Settlement-a set of procedures for settling disputes over environmental policies without litigation-can work forthem.
Publication Date: 1990 295 pages
ISBN: 0-933280-74-2
James E Crowfoot, Julia Wondolleck, Author

4105 Globalization and the Environment: Greening Global Political Economy
SUNY Press
22 Corporate Woods Boulevard
3rd Floor
Albany, NY 12211
518-472-5000
866-430-7869
Fax: 518-472-5038
info@sunypress.edu
www.sunypress.edu

Also in hardcover, 40.00.
Publication Date: 2004 175 pages
Gabriela Kutting, Author
Tom Baker, Editorial Board
Sue Books, Editorial Board

4106 Shopping for a Better Environment: Brand Name Guide to Environmentally Responsible Shopping
Meadowbrook Press
6110 Blue Circle Drive
Suite 237
Minnetonka, MN 55343
800-338-2232
Fax: 952-930-1940
info@meadowbrookpress.com
www.meadowbrookpress.com

Books: Design & Architecture

4107 Designing Healthy Cities
Krieger Publishing Co.
1725 Krieger Drive
Malabar, FL 32950
321-724-9542
800-724-0025
Fax: 321-951-3671
info@krieger-publishing.com
www.krieger-publishing.com

Krieger Publishing Company produces quality books in various fields of interest. We have an extensive Natural Science listing.
Publication Date: 1998 158 pages
ISBN: 0-894649-27-2
Cheryl Stanton, Advertising

4108 Indoor Air Quality: Design Guide Book
Fairmont Press
700 Indian Trail
Liburn, GA 30047
770-925-9388
Fax: 770-381-9865
www.fairmontpress.com

Books: Disaster Preparedness & Response

4109 Acceptable Risk?: Making Decisions in a Toxic Environment
University of California Press
210 American Drive
Jackson, TN 38301
510-642-4247
800-343-4499
Fax: 800-351-5073
www.ucpress.edu

Alison Mudditt, Director

4110 Borrowed Earth, Borrowed Time: Healing America's Chemical Wounds
Plenum Publishers
233 Spring Street
New York, NY 10013
212-460-1500
Fax: 212-460-1575
support@apress.com
www.plenum.com

Publication Date: 1991
Derk Haank, CEO
Martin Mos, COO

Books: Energy & Transportation

4111 Coming Clean: Breaking America's Addiction to Oil And Coal
Sierra Club

2101 Webster Street
Suite 1300
Oakland, CA 94612
415-977-5500
Fax: 510-208-3140
information@sierraclub.org
www.sierraclub.org

This title provides the road map, showing how people can promote real solutions to oil and coal dependency, and collectively pressure government and corporations to change their energy priorities.
256 pages
Michael Brune, Author
Michael Brune, Executive Director
Jennifer Trahan, Chief Operating Officer

4112 Confronting Climate Change: Strategies for Energy Research and Development
National Academy Press
500 5th Street NW
Washington, DC 20055
202-334-3313
888-624-8373
Fax: 202-334-2451
www.nap.edu

Publication Date: 1990 144 pages
ISBN: 0-309043-47-6

4113 Energy & Environmental Strategies for the 1990's
Fairmont Press
700 Indian Tr.
Lilburn, GA 30047
770-925-9388
Fax: 770-381-9865
linda@fairmontpress.com
www.fairmontpress.com

4114 Getting Around Clean & Green
Northeast Sustainable Energy Association
50 Miles Street
Greenfield, MA 00130
413-774-6051
Fax: 413-774-6053
nesea@nesea.org
www.nesea.org

This interdisciplinary science/social studies curriculum allows students to explore the transportation and environmental issues in their own lives. Activities cover: transportation systems, health impacts, environmental andtransportation histories, carpooling, and mass transit.
90 pages Curriculum
Jennifer Marrapese, Executive Director
Gina Sieber, Business Manager

4115 Getting Around Without Gasoline
Northeast Sustainable Energy Association
50 Miles Street
Greenfield, MA 00130
413-774-6051
Fax: 413-774-6053
nesea@nesea.org
www.nesea.org

An interdisciplinary unit that explores the feasibility of getting around without using gasoline. Students can conduct various activities to compare powering vehicles with gasoline versus electricity.
60 pages S & H Only
Jennifer Marrapese, Executive Director
Gina Sieber, Business Manager

4116 Global Science: Energy, Resources, Environment
Kendall-Hunt Publishing Company
4050 Westmark Drive
PO Box 1840
Dubuque, IA 52004
563-589-1000
800-772-9165
Fax: 563-589-1046
orders@kendallhunt.com
www.kendallhunt.com

4117 Oil, Globalization, and the War for the Arctic Refuge
SUNY Press
22 Corporate Woods Boulevard
3rd Floor
Albany, NY 12211
518-472-5000
866-430-7869
Fax: 518-472-5038
info@sunypress.edu
www.sunypress.edu

Also in hardcover, 71.50.
Publication Date: 2006 227 pages
David M Stanlea, Author
Tom Baker, Editorial Board
Sue Books, Editorial Board

4118 Transporting Atlanta: The Mode of Mobility Under Construction
SUNY Press
22 Corporate Woods Boulevard
3rd Floor
Albany, NY 12211
518-472-5000
866-430-7869
Fax: 518-472-5038
info@sunypress.edu
www.sunypress.edu

Publication Date: 2009 220 pages
Miriam Konrad, Author
Tom Baker, Editorial Board
Sue Books, Editorial Board

Books: Environmental Engineering

4119 Principles of Environmental Science and Technology
Elsevier Science Publishers
360 Park Avenue South
New York, NY 10010
212-989-5800
Fax: 212-633-3990
www.elsevier.com

Ron Mobed, Chief Executive Officer
Youngsuk Chi, Chairman

Books: Environmental Health

4120 American Environmental Leaders: From Colonial Times to the Present
Grey House Publishing
4919 Route 22
P.O. Box 56
Amenia, NY 12501
518-789-8700
800-562-2139
Fax: 518-789-0556
books@greyhouse.com
www.greyhouse.com

A collection of biographies of important figures in American environmentalism, with coverage of 399 environmental men and women from the past 200 years, including scientists, advocates, businessmen, musicians, politicians, actors, andmore.
Publication Date: 2018 994 pages
ISBN: 1-682177-31-0
Leslie Mackenzie, Publisher
Laura Mars, Editorial Director

4121 Ecologue: The Environmental Catalogue and Consumer's Guide for a Safe Earth
Prentice Hall Press (Simon & Schuster Division)
1 Gulf & Western Plaza
New York, NY 10023
212-373-8500
800-223-1360
www.pearsonhighered.com

4122 Opinions Throughout History: The Environment
Grey House Publishing
4919 Route 22
P.O. Box 56
Amenia, NY 12501
518-789-8700
800-562-2139
Fax: 518-789-0556
books@greyhouse.com
www.greyhouse.com

This entry in the Opinions Throughout History series follows shifting public opinion on the environment, with each chapter providing commentary on a primary source drwn from the popular press, key court and legislative battles,scientific research, social activism and opinion polls.
Publication Date: 2018 994 pages
ISBN: 1-682177-31-0
Micah Issitt, Author
Leslie Mackenzie, Publisher
Laura Mars, Editorial Director

4123 **Wetlands: Development, Progress, and Environmental Protection Under The Changing Law**
American Law Institute
4025 Chestnut St 215-243-1600
Philadelphia, PA 19104 *Fax:* 215-243-1636
ali@ali.org
www.ali.org

A book about environmental law.
Stephanie Middleton, Deputy Director

Books: Gaming & Hunting

4124 **Better Trout Habitat: A Guide to Stream Restoration**
Island Press
2000 M Street NW 202-232-7933
Suite 650 *Fax:* 202-234-1328
Wasington, DC 20036 info@islandpress.org
www.islandpress.org

Charles C. Savitt, President
Shaina Lange, Executive Assistant

Books: Habitat Preservation & Land Use

4125 **50 Simple Things Kids Can Do to Save the Earth**
Andrews and McMeel
4520 Main Street 816-932-6700
Suite 700 *Fax:* 816-932-6706
Kansas City, MO 64111

4126 **Access EPA: Clearinghouses and Hotlines**
National Technical Information Service
5301 Shawnee Road 703-605-6000
Alexandria, VA 22312 800-553-6847
info@ntis.gov
www.ntis.gov

Publication Date: 1991 57 pages
John J. Regazzi, Board Member
Judith C. Russell, Board Member

4127 **Access EPA: Library and Information Services**
National Technical Information Service
5301 Shawnee Road 703-605-6000
Alexandria, VA 22312 800-553-6847
info@ntis.gov
www.ntis.gov

Publication Date: 1990 110 pages
John J. Regazzi, Board Member
Judith C. Russell, Board Member

4128 **After Earth Day: Continuing the Conservation Effort**
University of North Texas Press
1155 Union Circle 940-565-2142
#311336 800-826-8911
Denton, TX 76203 *Fax:* 940-565-4590
rchrisman@unt.edu
www.unt.edu/untpress

Publication Date: 1992 241 pages
ISBN: 1-574414-44-0
Karen DeVinney, Managing Editor
Ronald Chrisman, Director

4129 **Agatha's Feather Bed: Not Just Another Wild Goose Story**
Peachtree Publishers
1700 Chattahoochee Avenue 404-876-8761
Atlanta, GA 30318 *Fax:* 404-875-2578
hello@peachtree-online.com
www.peachtree-online.com

32 pages
ISBN: 1-561450-08-1

4130 **America in the 21st Century: Environmental Concerns**
Population Reference Bureau
1875 Connecticut Avenue, NW 202-530-5810
Suite 520 800-877-9881
Washington, DC 20009 *Fax:* 202-328-3937
popref@prb.org
www.prb.org

Jeffrey Jordan, President and CEO
Linda A. Jacobsen, VP U.S. Programs

4131 **Ancient Ones: The World of the Old-Growth Douglas Fir**
Sierra Club
2101 Webster Street 415-977-5500
Suite 1300 *Fax:* 510-208-3140
San Francisco, CA 94612 information@sierraclub.org
www.sierraclub.org

A children's book that offers insight on one of the oldest species of trees.
32 pages
ISBN: 0-871566-82-6
Barbara Bash, Author
Michael Brune, Executive Director
Jennifer Trahan, Chief Operating Officer

4132 **At Odds with Progress: Americans and Conservation**
University of Arizona Press
1510 E. University Blvd. 520-621-1441
P.O. Box 210055 800-621-2736
Tucson, AZ 85721 *Fax:* 520-621-1441
www.uapress.arizona.edu

Publication Date: 1991 255 pages
ISBN: 0-816509-17-4
Bret Wallach, Author
Kathryn Conrad, Director
Allyson Carter, Editor in Chief

4133 **Balancing on the Brink of Extinction**
Island Press
2000 M Street NW 202-232-7933
Suite 650 *Fax:* 202-232-1328
Wasington, DC 20036 info@islandpress.org
www.islandpress.org

Publication Date: 1991 329 pages
Kathryn A Kohm, Author
Charles C. Savitt, President
Shaina Lange, Executive Assistant

4134 **Beyond the Beauty Strip: Saving What's Left of Our Forests**
Tilbury House Publishers
12 Starr Street 207-582-1899
Thomaston, ME 00486 800-582-1899
Fax: 202-582-8227
tilbury@tilburyhouse.com
www.tilburyhouse.com

Joanne Parkin, Office Manager
Tristram Coburn, Co-Publisher

4135 **Biodiversity and Ecosystem Function**
Springer-Verlag
233 Spring Street 212-460-1500
New York, NY 10013 800-777-4643
Fax: 212-460-1575
service-ny@springer-sbm.com
www.springer.com

Publication Date: 1994 528 pages
Derk Haank, CEO
Martin Mos, COO

4136 **Bioemediation**
McGraw-Hill
1221 Avenue of the Americas 212-512-2000
New York, NY 10020 800-722-4726
www.magraw-hill.com

4137 **Butterflies of Delmarva**
Delware Nature Society and Tidewater Publishers

PO Box 700 301-239-2334
Hockessin, DE 19707 *Fax:* 302-239-2473
www.delawarenaturesociety.org

The result of the author's lifelong interest in the 61 adult butterfly species that naturally occur on the Delmarva Peninsula, this field guide clearly identifies the adult, larva and pulpa stages, discusses the differences in colorand wing patterns between sexes, as well as the habitat, range, and food sources of each species. 132 full-color photographs illustrate the text. Includes general butterfly information, and how to attrract them to your garden. Paperback

Publication Date: 1998 138 pages 2nd Edition
ISBN: 0-870334-53-0
Brian Winslow, Executive Director
Christine Carlisle Odom, President

4138 Connections: Linking Population and the Environment Teaching Kit
Population Reference Bureau
1875 Connecticut Avenue NW 202-483-1100
Suite 520 800-877-9881
Washington, DC 20009 *Fax:* 202-328-3937
popref@prb.org
www.prb.org

Jeffrey Jordan, President and CEO
Linda A. Jacobsen, VP U.S. Programs

4139 Conservation and Research Foundation Five Year Report
Conservation and Research Foundation
PO Box 909 913-268-0076
Shelburne, VT 00548 *Fax:* 913-268-0076

Publication from Conservation and Research Foundation which is published every five years and distributed to contributors. This publication is also available upon request.

Publication Date: 1998 43 pages
Dr Mary Wetzel, President

4140 Decade of Destruction: The Crusade to Save the Amazon Rain Forest
Henry Holt and Company
175 Fifth Avenue 646-307-5095
New York, NY 10010 *Fax:* 212-633-0748
publicity@hholt.com
www.henryholt.com

215 pages
Adrian Cowell, Author

4141 Discordant Harmonies: A New Ecology for the Twenty-first Century
Oxford University Press
198 Madison Avenue 212-679-7300
New York, NY 10016 *Fax:* 212-725-2972
global.oup.com

Publication Date: 1992 254 pages
ISBN: 0-195074-69-6
Daniel B Botkin, Author

4142 Earth Keeping
Zondervan Publishing House
5300 Patterson Avenue SE 616-698-6900
Grand Rapids, MI 49530 *Fax:* 616-698-3439
www.zondervan.com

4143 Earthright
Prima Publishing & Communications
PO Box 1260BK 916-786-0426
Rocklin, CA 95677 800-632-8676
Fax: 916-632-4405
www.primagames.com

4144 Ecology of Greenways: Design and Function of Linear Conservation
University of Minnesota Press
111 Third Avenue South 612-627-1970
Suite 290 800-388-3863
Minneapolis, MN 55401 *Fax:* 612-627-1980
www.upress.umn.edu

Publication Date: 1994 238 pages
ISBN: 0-816621-57-8
Daniel S Smith, Paul Cawood Hellmund, Author

4145 Eli's Songs
MacMillan Publishing Company
866 3rd Avenue 212-702-2000
New York, NY 10022 800-257-5755
www.macmillian.com

4146 Endangered Kingdom: The Struggle to Save America's Wildlife
John Wiley & Sons
605 3rd Avenue 212-850-6890
New York, NY 10158 800-825-7550
Fax: 212-850-8800
info@wiley.com
as.wiley.com

Publication Date: 1991 241 pages
ISBN: 0-471528-22-6
Roger L DiSilvestro, Author
Mark Mark Allin, President/CEO
Peter Booth Wiley, Chair

4147 Environment in Peril
Smithsonian Institution Press
SI Building, Room 153, MRC 010 202-633-1000
PO Box 37012 800-782-4612
Washington, DC 20013 *Fax:* 202-633-5285
info@si.edu
www.si.edu

Deron Burba, Chief Information Officer
Chandra P. Heilman, Ombudsman

4148 Environmental Concern in Florida and the Nation
University of Florida Press
15 NW 15th Street 352-392-1351
Gainesville, FL 32611 800-226-3822
Fax: 352-392-0590
press@upf.com
www.upf.com

Publication Date: 1997 144 pages
ISBN: 0-813010-56-X
Lance Dehaven-Smith, Author
Marthe Walters, Assistant Managing Editor
Judith Knight, Editor at Large

4149 Environmental Concern: A Comprehensive Review of Wetlands Assessment Producers
POW-The Planning of Wetlands
201 Boundary Lane 410-745-9620
PO Box P *Fax:* 410-745-3517
St Michaels, MD 21663 order@wetland.org
www.wetland.org

Since its founding in 1972, EC has been specializing in consulting, planning design, education services, construction services and research related to all aspects of wetlands. As wetlands and contiguous upland forests and meadows areinteracting ecosystems EC specializes in consulting, planning, design, and project supervision services for such upland ecosystem constructions and restorations for the purpose of wetland buffers, reforestation, wildlife habitat and critical areas ofpreservation.

Publication Date: 1999 Quarterly
ISBN: 1-883226-04-x
Suzanne Pitenger Slear, President
Katelin Frase, Education Director

4150 Environmental Concern: Evaluation for Planned Wetlands
POW-The Planning of Wetlands

201 Boundary Lane 410-745-9620
PO Box P *Fax:* 410-745-3517
St Michaels, MD 21663 order@wetland.org
www.wetland.org

Since its founding in 1972, EC has been specializing in consulting, planning design, education services, construction services and research related to all aspects of wetlands. As wetlands and contiguous upland forests and meadows areinteracting ecosystems EC specializes in consulting, planning, design, and project supervision services for such upland ecosystem constructions and restorations for the purpose of wetland buffers, reforestation, wildlife habitat and critical areas ofpreservation.

Publication Date: 1994 Quarterly
ISBN: 1-883226-03-1
Suzanne Pittenger Slear, President
Katelin Frase, Education Director

4151 Environmental Concern: The Wonders of Wetlands

POW-The Planning of Wetlands
201 Boundary Lane 410-745-9620
PO Box P *Fax:* 410-745-3517
St Michaels, MD 21663 order@wetland.org
www.wetland.org

Since its founding in 1972, EC has been specializing in consulting, planning design, education services, construction services and research related to all aspects of wetlands. As wetlands and contiguous upland forests and meadows areinteracting ecosystems EC specializes in consulting, planning, design, and project supervision services for such upland ecosystem constructions and restorations for the purpose of wetland buffers, reforestation, wildlife habitat and critical areas ofpreservation.

Publication Date: 1995
ISBN: 1-888631-00-7
Suzanne Pittenger Slear, President
Katelin Frase, Education Director

4152 Environmental Crisis: Opposing Viewpoints

Greenhaven Press
10650 Toebben Drive 858-485-9549
Independence, KY 41051 800-354-9706
Fax: 800-487-8488
solutions.cengage.com/greenhaven

4153 Environmental Profiles: A Global Guide to Projects and People

Garland Publishing
717 5th Avenue 212-751-7447
25th Floor *Fax:* 212-308-9399
New York, NY 10022 www.garlandpub.com
Publication Date: 1993 1112 pages
ISBN: 0-815300-63-8

4154 Friends of the Earth Foundation Annual Report

Friends of the Earth Found.
30 Sir Francis Drake Blvd 415-256-9604
P.O. Box 437 800-326-7491
Ross, CA 94957 *Fax:* 202-543-4710
www.oceanic-society.org

Roderic Mast, President and CEO
Brian Hutchinson, Director of Outreach

4155 Future Primitive

University of North Texas Press
1155 Union Circle 940-565-2142
#311336 800-826-8911
Denton, TX 76203 *Fax:* 940-565-4590
rchrisman@unt.edu
www.unt.edu/untpress

Publication Date: 1996 223 pages
ISBN: 1-574410-07-5
Ronald Chrisman, Director
Karen DeVinney, Managing Editor

4156 Going Green: A Kid's Handbook to Saving the Planet

Puffin Books
375 Hudson Street 212-366-2403
New York, NY 10014 www.puffin.co.uk

Out of print—limited availability.
Publication Date: 1990
ISBN: 0-140345-97-3

4157 Guide to Spring Wildflower Areas

Minnesota Native Plant Society
1520 St. Olaf Avenue 507-786-2222
Northfield, MN 55057 www.stolaf.edu

Updated its guide to over 40 wildflower sites in the Twin Cities area. The guide contains a description and location for each.

4 per year

4158 Guide to Urban Wildlife Management

National Institute for Urban Wildlife
10921 Trotting Ridge Way 301-596-3311
Columbia, MD 21044

4159 Information Please Environmental Almanac

Houghton Mifflin Company
222 Berkeley Street 617-725-5000
30th Floor www.hmco.com
Boston, MA 00211
Publication Date: 1992 704 pages
ISBN: 0-395637-67-8

4160 International Protection of the Environment

Oceana Publications, Inc
198 Madison Avenue 800-334-4249
New York, NY 10016 *Fax:* 212-726-6476

This set provides the documents which form the framework of softlaw administrative instruments for the implementation of international environment treaties under Agenda 21.

Publication Date: 1995 7 vol pages Bi-Monthly
ISBN: 0-379102-95-1
Nicholas A Robinson & Wolfgang Burhenne, Author

4161 International Society for Endangered Cats

3070 Riverside Drive Suite 160 614-487-8760
Columbus, OH 43221 *Fax:* 614-487-8769
Publication Date: 1990 237 pages
ISBN: 0-816019-44-4
Bill Simpson, President
Patricia Currie, Executive Director

4162 Just A Dream

Houghton Mifflin Company
Beacon Street 617-725-5000
30th Floor
Boston, MA 00210

4163 Krieger Publishing Company: Wildlife Habitat Management of Wetlands

Krieger Publishing Co.
1725 Krieger Drive 321-724-9542
Malabar, FL 32950 800-724-0025
Fax: 321-951-3671
info@krieger-publishing.com
www.krieger-publishing.com

Krieger Publishing Company produces quality books in various fields of interest. We have an extensive Natural Science listing.

Publication Date: 1992 572 pages
ISBN: 1-575240-89-0
Cheryl Stanton, Advertising

4164 Krieger Publishing Company: Wildlife Habitat Management of Forestlands/Rangelands/Farmlands

Krieger Publishing Co.
1725 Krieger Drive 321-724-9542
Malabar, FL 32950 800-724-0025
Fax: 321-951-3671
info@krieger-publishing.com
www.krieger-publishing.com

Krieger Publishing Company produces quality books in various fields of interest. We have an extensive Natural Science listing.

Publication Date: 1994 868 pages
ISBN: 1-575240-93-9
Cheryl Stanton, Advertising

4165 Last Extinction
MIT Press
5 Cambridge Center 617-253-5646
Cambridge, MA 00214 *Fax:* 617-258-6779
Today there is a new and more widespread awareness of what some consider to be the great tragedy of our time - organisms which took many thousands or even millions of years to evolve are being snuffed out permanently owing to humanactivity.
Publication Date: 1993
Les Kaufman, Kenneth Mallory, Author

4166 Look Who's Flying!
The International Osprey Foundation
PO Box 250 tiof@ospreys.com
Sanibel, FL 33957 www.ospreys.com
Downloadable coloring book produced by The International Osprey Foundation.
Susan Tucker, Acting President

4167 Nature and the American: Three Centuries of Changing Attitudes
Unviersity of Nebraska Press
1111 Lincoln Mall 402-472-3581
Lincoln, NE 68588 *Fax:* 402-472-6214
pressmail@unl.edu
www.nebraskapress.unl.edu
Kristen Elias Rowley, Editor
Donna Shear, Director

4168 Ozone Diplomacy: New Directions in Safeguarding the Planet
Harvard University Press
79 Garden Street 617-495-2600
Cambridge, MA 00213 *Fax:* 617-495-5898
botref@oeb.harvard.edu
www.hup.harvard.edu
Offers an insider's view of the politics, economics, science and diplomacy involved in creating the precedent-setting treaty to protect the Earth: the 1987 Montreal Protocol on Substances That Deplete the Ozone Layer.
Richard Elliot Benedick, Author

4169 Practical Guide to Environmental Management
1616 P Street NW 202-939-3800
Suite 200 *Fax:* 202-939-3868
Washington, DC 20036

4170 Preserving the World Ecology
H W Wilson Company
950 University Avenue 718-588-8400
Bronx, NY 10452 *Fax:* 718-588-6365
www.hwwilson.com

4171 Protecting Our Environment: Lessons from the European Union
SUNY Press
22 Corporate Woods Boulevard 518-472-5000
3rd Floor 866-430-7869
Albany, NY 12211 *Fax:* 518-472-5038
info@sunypress.edu
www.sunypress.edu
Available in both hard and soft cover, this title deals with the environment as a global issue.
Publication Date: 2005 204 pages
Janet R Hunter, Zachary A Smith, Author
Tom Baker, Editorial Board
Sue Books, Editorial Board

4172 Quill's Adventures in Grozzieland
John Muir Publications
PO Box 613 505-982-4078
Santa Fe, NM 87504 800-888-7504
Fax: 505-988-1680

4173 RARE Center for Tropical Conservation Annual Report
Rare Center for Tropical Conservation
1616 Walnut Street 215-735-3510
Suite 911 *Fax:* 215-735-3615
Philadelphia, PA 19103 www.rarecenter.org

4174 Resource Conservation and Management
Wadsworth Publishing Company
10 Davis Drive 415-595-2350
Belmont, CA 94002 *Fax:* 415-637-7544
www.wadsworth.com

4175 Revolution for Nature: From the Environment to the Connatural World
University of North Texas Press
1155 Union Circle 940-565-2142
#311336 800-826-8911
Denton, TX 76203 *Fax:* 940-565-4590
rchrisman@unt.edu
www.unt.edu/untpress
145 pages
ISBN: 1-574417-0X-
Ronald Chrisman, Director
Karen DeVinney, Managing Editor

4176 Saving Sterling Forest: The Epic Struggle to Preserve New York's Highlands
SUNY Press
22 Corporate Woods Boulevard 518-472-5000
3rd Floor 866-430-7869
Albany, NY 12211 *Fax:* 518-472-5038
info@sunypress.edu
www.sunypress.edu
Also in hardcover, 59.50.
Publication Date: 2007 216 pages
Ann Botshon, Author
Tom Baker, Editorial Board
Sue Books, Editorial Board

4177 Statement of Policy and Practices for Protection of Wetlands
National Wildlife Fed. Corporate Conservation Coun
1400 16th Street NW 202-797-6870
Washington, DC 20036 *Fax:* 202-797-6871

4178 Student Conservation Association Northwest: Lightly on the Land
1265 S Main Street 206-324-4649
Suite 210 *Fax:* 206-324-4998
Seattle, WA 98144 www.thesca.org
SCA is a national organization with regional offices in Seattle, Oakland, Pittsburg, Washington DC and headquartered in Charlestown NH. Our mission is to build the next generation of conservation leaders and inspire lifelongstewardship of the environment by engaging young people in hands-on environmental service. We offer a wide range of internships and crew based programs for ages 16 years and up.
Publication Date: 1996 267 pages
ISBN: 0-898869-91-7
Jaime Berman Matyas, President/CEO
Laura Herrin, SVP Programs

4179 Transactions of Annual North American Wildlife and Natural Resources Conference
Wildlife Management
1101 14th Street NW 202-371-1808
Suite 801 *Fax:* 202-408-5059
Washington, DC 20005

4180 Urban Wildlife Manager's Notebook
National Institute for Urban Wildlife
10921 Trotting Ridge Way 301-596-3311
Columbia, MD 21044

4181 Wetlands Protection: The Role of Economics
Environmental Law Institute

1616 P Street NW 202-939-3800
Suite 200 Fax: 202-939-3868
Washington, DC 20036

4182 **Whales**
Simon & Schuster Children's Publishing
1230 6th Ave 866-506-1949
New York, NY 10020 www.simonandschuster.com
A book studying the characteristics, behavior, and migration habits of the humpback whale.
Publication Date: 1993 24 pages
Cousteau Society, Author

4183 **Wildlife Conservation in Metropolitan Environments**
National Institute for Urban Wildlife
10921 Trotting Ridge Way 301-596-3311
Columbia, MD 21044

4184 **Wildlife Habitat Relationships in Forested Ecosystems**
Timber Press
133 SW 2nd Avenue 503-227-2878
Suite 450 800-327-5680
Portland, OR 97204 Fax: 503-227-3070
www.timber-press.com
Available by special order.
Publication Date: 1997
David R Patton, Author

4185 **Wildlife Research and Management in the National Parks**
University of Illinois Press
1325 S Oak Street 217-333-0950
Champaign, IL 61820 Fax: 217-244-8082
uipress@uillinois.edu
www.press.uillinois.edu
Publication Date: 1992 240 pages
ISBN: 0-252018-24-9
Gerald R Wright, Author
Willis G. Regier, Director
Laurie Matheson, Editor-in-Chief

4186 **Wildlife-Habitat Relationships: Concepts and Applications**
University of Wisconsin Press
114 N Murray Street 608-262-8782
Madison, WI 53715
Anyone working with wildlife must be concerned with its habitat identification, measurement and analysis. Wildlife-Habitat Relationships goes beyond introductory wildlife biology texts and specialized studies of single species toprovide a broad but advanced understanding of habitat relationships applicable to all terrestrial species.
Publication Date: 1998 416 pages
ISBN: 0-299156-40-0
Michael L Morrison, Bruce G Marcot, Author

Books: Recycling & Pollution Prevention

4187 **An Ontology of Trash: The Disposable and Its Problematic Nature**
SUNY Press
22 Corporate Woods Boulevard 518-472-5000
3rd Floor 866-430-7869
Albany, NY 12211 Fax: 518-472-5038
info@sunypress.edu
www.sunypress.edu
Also in hardcover, 65.00.
Publication Date: 2008 238 pages
Greg Kennedy, Author
Tom Baker, Editorial Board
Sue Books, Editorial Board

4188 **Aunt Ipp's Museum of Junk**
HarperCollins
195 Broadway 212-207-7000
New York, NY 10007 800-424-6234
Fax: 212-207-7433
orders@harpercollins.com
www.harpercollins.com
Brian Murray, President and CEO
Larry Nevins, EVP, Operations

4189 **Beyond 40 Percent: Record-Setting Recycling and Composting Programs**
Island Press
2000 M Street NW 202-232-7933
Suite 650 Fax: 202-234-1328
Wasington, DC 20036 info@islandpress.org
www.islandpress.org
Publication Date: 1991 280 pages
ISBN: 1-559630-73-6
Charles C. Savitt, President
Shaina Lange, Executive Assistant

4190 **Borrowed Earth, Borrowed Time: Healing America's Chemical Wounds**
Plenum Publishers
233 Spring Street 212-460-1500
New York, NY 10013 Fax: 212-460-1575
www.springer.com
Publication Date: 1991
Derk Haank, CEO
Martin Mos, COO

4191 **Caring for Our Air**
Enslow Publishers
101 West 23rd Street 908-771-9400
Suite #240 800-398-2504
New York, NY 10011 Fax: 877-980-4454
customerservice@enslow.com
www.enslow.com

4192 **Community Recycling: System Design to Management**
Prentice Hall
101 West 23rd Street 908-771-9400
Suite #240 800-398-2504
New York, NY 10011 Fax: 877-980-4454
customerservice@enslow.com
www.enslow.com
A guide for getting into the growing business of community recycling, for those with little or no previous experience with the technical details of recycling. Discusses marketing, management, equipment, profit comparisons of variousprocessing methods and legal considerations.
Publication Date: 1992 240 pages
ISBN: 0-131557-89-0
Nyles V Reinfeld, Carl M Layman, Author

4193 **Garbage and Recycling**
Kingfisher Publications
1 Gulf & Western Plaza 212-373-8500
New York, NY 10023 800-223-1360
home.pearsonhighered.com
Publication Date: 1995 32 pages
ISBN: 1-856976-15-7
Rosie Harlow, Sally Morgan, Author

4194 **Hey Mr. Green: Sierra Magazine's Answer Guy Tackles Your Toughest Green Living Questions**
Sierra Club
2101 Webster Street 415-977-5500
Suite 1300 Fax: 510-208-3140
Oakland, CA 94612 information@sierraclub.org
www.sierraclub.org
Bob Schildgen has been Mr. Green in Sierra Magazine for years, providing fact-backed replies to reader's questions. Well orga-

nized, funny, and supremely useful, this title offers green-living tips for everyday.
Publication Date: 2009 224 pages
ISBN: 1-578051-43-4
Bob Schildgen, Author
Michael Brune, Executive Director
Jennifer Trahan, Chief Operating Officer

4195 How On Earth Do We Recycle Glass?
Millbrook Press
2 Old New Milford Road 203-740-2220
PO Box 335 800-462-4703
Brookfield, CT 00680 *Fax:* 203-740-2526
www.millbrookpress.com

4196 Let's Talk Trash: The Kids' Book About Recycling
Waterfront Books
85 Crescent Road 802-658-7477
Burlington, VT 00540

4197 Plastic: America's Packaging Dilemma
Island Press
2000 M Street NW 202-232-7933
Suite 650 *Fax:* 202-234-1328
Wasington, DC 20036 info@islandpress.org
www.islandpress.org
Charles C. Savitt, President
Shaina Lange, Executive Assistant

4198 Pollution Knows No Frontiers
Paragon House of Publishers
3600 Labore Road 651-644-3087
Suite 1 *Fax:* 651-644-0997
St. Paul, MN 55110 info@paragonhouse.com
www.paragonhouse.com

4199 Recycle!: A Handbook for Kids
Little, Brown & Company
1271 Avenue of the Americas 800-759-0190
New York, NY 10020 *Fax:* 212-522-0885
Publication Date: 1996 32 pages
Gail Gibbons, Editor

4200 Recycling Paper: From Fiber to Finished Product
TAPPI Press
15 Technology Parkway South 770-446-1400
Norcross, GA 30092 *Fax:* 770-446-6947
memberconnection@tappi.org
www.tappi.org

4201 Reducing Toxics
Island Press
2000 M Street NW 202-232-7933
Suite 650 *Fax:* 202-234-1328
Wasington, DC 20036 info@islandpress.org
www.islandpress.org

Publication Date: 1995 460 pages
Charles C. Savitt, President
Shaina Lange, Executive Assistant

Books: Sustainable Development

4202 Biodiversity Prospecting: Using Genetic Resources for Sustainable Development
World Resources Institue
10 G Street NE 202-729-7600
Suite 800 *Fax:* 202-729-7610
Washington, DC 20002 www.wri.org
Andrew Steer, President/CEO
Lawrence MacDonald, VP, Communications

4203 Constructing Sustainable Development
SUNY Press
194 Washington Avenue 518-472-5000
Suite 305 800-666-2211
Albany, NY 12210 *Fax:* 518-472-5038
Publication Date: 2000 188 pages
Neil E Harrison, Author

4204 Ecological Literacy: Educating Our Children for a Sustainable World
Sierra Club
2101 Webster Street 415-977-5500
Suite 1300 *Fax:* 510-208-3140
Oakland, CA 94612 information@sierraclub.org
www.sierraclub.org

256 pages
ISBN: 1-578051-53-3
Michael K Stone and Zenobia Barlow, Author
Michael Brune, Executive Director
Jennifer Trahan, Chief Operating Officer

4205 Environmental Integration: Our Common Challenge
SUNY Press
22 Corporate Woods Boulevard 518-472-5000
3rd Floor 866-430-7869
Albany, NY 12211 *Fax:* 518-472-5038
info@sunypress.edu
www.sunypress.edu

Also in hardcover, 85.00.
Publication Date: 2009 290 pages
Ton Buhrs, Author
Tom Baker, Editorial Board
Sue Books, Editorial Board

4206 Environmental Policy Making: Assessing the Use of Alternative Policy Instruments
SUNY Press
22 Corporate Woods Boulevard 518-472-5000
3rd Floor 866-430-7869
Albany, NY 12211 *Fax:* 518-472-5038
info@sunypress.edu
www.sunypress.edu

Also in hardcover, 85.00.
Publication Date: 2005 276 pages
Michael T Hatch, Author
Tom Baker, Editorial Board
Sue Books, Editorial Board

4207 Environmental Profiles: A Global Guide to Projects and People
Garland Publishing
717 5th Avenue 212-751-7447
25th Floor *Fax:* 212-308-9399
New York, NY 10022 www.garlandpub.com
Publication Date: 1993 1112 pages
ISBN: 0-815300-63-8

4208 Global Environment
Jones and Bartlett Publishers
5 Wall Street 800-832-0034
Burlington, MA 00180 *Fax:* 978-443-8000
info@jblearning.com
www.jblearning.com

4209 Gnat is Older than Man: Global Environment and Human Agenda
Princeton University Press
41 William Street 609-258-4900
Princeton, NJ 00854 800-777-4726
Fax: 609-258-6305
press.princeton.edu

Peter Dougherty, Director
Patrick Carroll, Associate Director

4210 Implementation of Environmental Policies in Developing Countries
SUNY Press

22 Corporate Woods Boulevard
3rd Floor
Albany, NY 12211
518-472-5000
866-430-7869
Fax: 518-472-5038
info@sunypress.edu
www.sunypress.edu

A Case of Protected Areas and Tourism in Brazil. Also in hardcover, 50.00.
Publication Date: 2008 150 pages
Jose Antonio Puppim de Oliveira, Author
Tom Baker, Editorial Board
Sue Books, Editorial Board

4211 **Managing Sustainable Development**
Earthscan Publications
8-12 Camden High Street
London
207-387-8558
Fax: 207-387-8998
Publication Date: 2001 304 pages
Michael Carley, Editor

4212 **Practice of Sustainable Development**
Urban Land Institute
1025 Thomas Jefferson Street NW
Suite 500 W
Washington, DC 20007
202-624-7000
Fax: 202-624-7140
customerservice@uli.org
www.uli.org
Publication Date: 2000 160 pages
ISBN: 0-874208-31-9
Douglas R Porter, Author
Randall Rowe, Global Chair
Patrick L. Phillips, Global CEO

4213 **Sustainable Planning and Development**
WIT Press
25 Bridge Street,
Billerica, MA 01821
978-667-5841
Fax: 978-667-7582
salesUSA@witpress.com
www.witpress.com
Publication Date: 2003 1048 pages
ISBN: 1-853129-85-2
Simon Ibbotson, Marketing Co-ordinator
Dee Halzack, Marketing Manager

4214 **The Incompleat Eco-Philosopher:Essay from the Edges of Environmental Ethics**
SUNY Press
22 Corporate Woods Boulevard
3rd Floor
Albany, NY 12211
518-472-5000
866-430-7869
Fax: 518-472-5038
info@sunypress.edu
www.sunypress.edu
Also in hardcover for 65.50
Publication Date: 2009 210 pages
Anthony Weston, Author
Tom Baker, Editorial Board
Sue Books, Editorial Board

4215 **Urban Sprawl, Global Warming, and the Empire of Capital**
SUNY Press
22 Corporate Woods Boulevard
3rd Floor
Albany, NY 12211
518-472-5000
866-430-7869
Fax: 518-472-5038
info@sunypress.edu
www.sunypress.edu
Also in hardcover, 60.00.
Publication Date: 2009 170 pages
George A Gonzalez, Author
Tom Baker, Editorial Board
Sue Books, Editorial Board

4216 **Who Gets What? Domestic Influences on International Negotiations Allocating Shared Resources**
SUNY Press
22 Corporate Woods Boulevard
3rd Floor
Albany, NY 12211
518-472-5000
866-430-7869
Fax: 518-472-5038
info@sunypress.edu
www.sunypress.edu
Also in hardcover, 60.00.
Publication Date: 2008 192 pages
Aslaug Asgeirsdottir, Author
Tom Baker, Editorial Board
Sue Books, Editorial Board

4217 **Worldwatch Paper 101: Discarding the Throwaway Society**
Worldwatch Intitutes
1400 16th Street NW
Suite 430
Washington, DC 20036
202-745-8092
Fax: 202-478-2534
worldwatch@worldwatch.org
www.worldwatch.org
Ed Groark, Chair/Acting Interim Pres
John Robbins, Treasurer

Books: Travel & Tourism

4218 **Appalachian Mountain Club**
Appalachian Mountain Club Books
5 Joy Street
Boston, MA 00210
617-523-0636
800-262-4455
Fax: 617-523-0722
information@outdoors.org
www.outdoors.org
The AMC, founded in 1876, promotes the protection, enjoyment, and wise use of the mountains, rivers and trails of the Northeast. We encourage people to enjoy and protect the natural world because we believe that successful conservationdepends on this experience. The AMC publishes an award-winning magazine and more than 60 guide books to the Northeast.
Wayne Thornbrough, Chair
Rol Fessenden, Vice Chair

4219 **Prospect Park Handbook**
Greensward Found
Lenox Hill Station
PO Box 610
New York, NY 10021
212-473-6283
www.greenswardparks.org

Books: Water Resources

4220 **And Two if By Sea: Fighting the Attack on America's Coasts**
Coast Alliance
202-546-9609
This book is the benchmark in the effort to save the coasts.
Publication Date: 1986

4221 **Comparative Health Effects Assessment of Drinking Water Treatment Technologies**
Government Institutes Division
16855 Northchase Drive
Houston, TX 77060
281-673-2800
The report evaluates the public health impact of the most widespread drinking water treatment technologies, with particular emphasis on disinfection.
Publication Date: 1988 20 pages

4222 **Dying Oceans**
Gareth Stevens, Inc
111 East 14th Street
Suite #349
New York, NY 10003
414-332-3520
800-542-2595
Fax: 877-542-2596
www.garethstevens.com
Publication Date: 1991
ISBN: 0-836804-76-7

4223 Freshwater Resources and Interstate Cooperation: Strategies to Mitigate an Environmental Risk
SUNY Press
22 Corporate Woods Boulevard
3rd Floor
Albany, NY 12211
518-472-5000
866-430-7869
Fax: 518-472-5038
info@sunypress.edu
www.sunypress.edu

Also in hardcover, 60.00.
Publication Date: 2008 184 pages
Frederick D Gordon, Author

4224 Living Waters: Reading the Rivers of the Lower Great Lakes
SUNY Press
22 Corporate Woods Boulevard
3rd Floor
Albany, NY 12211
518-472-5000
866-430-7869
Fax: 518-472-5038
info@sunypress.edu
www.sunypress.edu

Also in hardcover for 45.00
Publication Date: 2009 213 pages
Margaret Wooster, Author

4225 Managing Troubled Water: The Role of Marine Environmental Monitoring
Duke University Press
905 W Main Street
Suite 18B
Durham, NC 27701
919-687-3600
Fax: 919-688-4574
Publication Date: 1990

4226 Turning the Tide: Saving the Chesapeake Bay
Island Press
2000 M Street NW
Suite 650
Wasington, DC 20036
707-983-6432
800-828-1302
info@islandpress.org
www.islandpress.org

The Chesapeake Bay is one of the most productive and important ecosystems on earth, and as such is a model for other estuaries facing the demands of commerce, tourism, transportation, recreation and other uses. Turning the Tidepresents a comprehensive look at two decades of efforts to save the bay, outlining which methods have worked and which have not.
Publication Date: 2003 352 pages
ISBN: 1-559635-48-7
Tom Horton, Author
Katie Dolan, Chair
Pamela Murphy, Vice Chair

4227 Using Common Sense to Protect the Coasts: The Need to Expand Coastal Barrier Resources
Coast Alliance
PO Box 505
Sandy Hook, NJ 00773
732-872-0111
coast@coastalliance.org
www.coastalliance.org

This report gives a common sense approach to protecting coastal areas from unwise development that would benefit American taxpayers.
Publication Date: 1990

Library Collections

4228 3M: 201 Technical Library
3M Center
St. Paul, MN 55133
651-575-1300
Fax: 651-736-3940
www.3M.com

High-tech library that manages its collection with 3M digital identification.

4229 ARCAT
173 Sherman Street
Fairfield, CT 06824
203-929-9444
www.arcat.com

Online resource of free building product information, including date specification and CAD detail libraries. Also available as an app.
Casey Jannott, Chief Executive Officer
Bill Jannott, President & CTO

4230 Acres International Library
100 Sylvan Parkway
Amherst, NY 14228
716-689-3737
Fax: 716-689-3749

Serves clients in the hydroelectric power, highways and bridges, mining, heavy industrial, civil/geotechnical and environmental and hazardous waste sectors.
Marion D'Amboise, Librarian

4231 Alaska Department of Fish and Game Habitat Library
333 Raspberry Road
Anchorage, AK 99518
907-267-2189
Fax: 907-349-1723
dfg.dwc.mcneil-info@alaska.gov
www.adfg.alaska.gov

Celia Rozen, Contact

4232 Alaska Resources Library and Information Services
ARLIS Suite 111 Library Building
3211 Providence Drive
Anchorage, AK 99508
907-272-7547
Fax: 907-786-7652
reference@arlis.org
www.arlis.org

ARLIS is the mother lode of Alaska resources information. ARLIS has served as the central library for rresource information supporting management of 235 million acres of federal and 100 million acres of state and water resourcesthroughout Alaska.
Publication Date: 1997
Carrie Holba, Reference Services Coord

4233 American Academy of Pediatrics
141 NW Point Boulevard
PO Box 747
Elk Grove Village, IL 60007
847-434-4000
800-433-9016
Fax: 847-434-8000
www.aap.org

Dedicated to the health of all children.

4234 American Water Works Association (AWWA)
6666 W Quincy Avenue
Denver, CO 80235
303-794-7711
800-926-7337
Fax: 303-347-0804
www.awwa.org

The AWWA is an international, nonprofit, scientific, and educational society that carries out the mission of assuring the effective management of water by providing water solutions. They offer education to water professionals, advocatefor safe and sustainable water, and educate the public on water resource management.
Publication Date: 1881
David B. LaFrance, CEO
Paula I. MacIlwaine, Deputy CEO

4235 Animal Welfare Institute (AWI)
900 Pennsylvania Ave SE
Washington, DC 20003
202-337-2332
Fax: 202-446-2131
awi@awionline.org
www.awionline.org

AWI works to alleviate the suffering inflicted on animals by humans including factory farming, experimentation, commercial whaling, as well as the impact on endangered species and their habitat. Their website features a library oftheir published books, reports, and brochures. They are available free of charge for libraries, research facilities, and others engaged in helping animals.
Publication Date: 1951
Nadia Adawi, Executive Director
Nancy Glaney, Director, Government Affairs

4236 Aquatic Research Institute: Aquatic Sciences and Technology Archive
2242 Davis Court
Hayward, CA 94545
510-782-4058
Fax: 510-784-0945

Library and data base in aquatic sciences and technologies also research faculty in aquatic sciences.
V Parker, Archv

4237 Arizona State Energy Office Information Center
3800 N Central 602-280-1402
Suite 1200 *Fax:* 602-280-1445
Phoenix, AZ 85012
Maxine Robertson, Assistant Director

4238 Arizona State University Architecture and Environmental Design Library
College of Architecture and Environmental Design
4300 480-965-6400
Tempe, AZ 85287 *Fax:* 480-727-6965
deborah.koshinsky@asu.edu
www.asu.edu
Deborah H Koshinsky, Director

4239 Arkansas Energy Office Library
1 State Capitol Mall 501-682-1370
Little Rock, AR 72201 *Fax:* 501-682-2703
cbenson@1800arkansas.com

4240 Atmospheric Sciences Model Division Library
US Environmental Protection Agency
1200 Pennsylvania Avenue N.W. 202-272-0167
Washington, DC 20004 www.epa.gov
Serves the NOAA Division assigned to support the EPA National Exposure Laboratory and Office of Air Quality Planning and Standards. The major field of interest is the meteorological aspects of air pollution, including numerical andphysical model development and application.
Evelyn M Poole-Kober, Tech. Pubns.

4241 Belle W Baruch Institute for Marine Biology and Coastal Research Library
607 EWS Building 803-777-5288
Columbia, SC 29208 *Fax:* 803-777-3935

4242 Bickelhaupt Arboretum Education Center
340 S 14th Street 319-242-4771
Clinton, IA 52742

4243 Brown University Center for Environmental Studies Library
85 Waterman Street 401-863-3449
Box 1951 *Fax:* 401-863-3839
Providence, RI 00291 envstudies@brown.edu
www.brown.edu
The Center for Environmental Studies at Brown University was established with the primary aim of educating individuals to solve challenging environmental problems both at the local and global levels. It also works directly to improvehuman well-being and environmental quality through community, city, and state partnerships in service and research.
J Timmons Roberts, Program Director

4244 Bureau of Land Management (BLM)
U.S. Department of the Interior
1849 C Street NW 202-208-3801
Room 5665 *Fax:* 202-208-5242
Washington, DC 20240 www.blm.gov
The mission of the Bureau of Land Management is to ensure the sustainability and diversity of the public lands for the use and enjoyment of present and future generations. The Bureau offers environmental education, news about theactivities of the Bureau, events, and regulations.
Publication Date: 1946
Michael Nedd, Deputy Director, Operations
Casey Hammond, Principal Deputy

4245 Burroughs Audubon Center and Library
Burroughs Audubon Society
21905 SW Woods Chapel Road 816-795-8177
Independence, MO 64050

4246 CH2M Hill
Corvallis Regional Office Library
9191 South Jamaica Street 720-286-2000
Englewood, CO 80112
The firm's solutions keep sustainability always in mind, along with government regulations, environmental concerns, maintenance requirements, and public perceptions. A team of experts brings the knowledge gained from a wide range ofprojects around the world, rigourous attention to detail, and a capability to create innovative solutions that are also models for the industry.
Shirley Fisher, COO

4247 California Energy Commission Library
1516 9th Street 916-654-4292
MS 10 *Fax:* 916-654-4046
Sacramento, CA 95814 library@energy.state.ca.us
www.energy.ca.gov
The state's central repository for information on all forms of energy. The collection consists of more than 22,000 titles on energy policy, energy conservation, energy consumption, electric utilities, environmental issues, petroleum,natural gas, solar, wind, biomass, nuclear power and related subjects. The Library serves Energy Commission staff, California state government agencies, the Legislature and its staff, and members of the public.
Robert Weisenmiller, Ph.D., Chair
Karen Douglas, J.D., Commissioner

4248 California State Resources Agency Library
1416 9th Street 916-653-2225
Room 117 *Fax:* 916-653-1856
Sacramento, CA 95814 www.water.ca.gov/about/contacts.cfm
Contains books, documents and subscriptions on topics including: flood control; natural resources (in California); endangered species (in California); soil conservation; water; water pollution; water quality; water resources;conservation and water supply.
Mark W. Cowin, Director
Laura King Moon, Chief Deputy Director

4249 Center for Coastal Fisheries and Habitat Research: Rice Library
101 Pivers Island Road 252-728-8713
Beaufort, NC 28516 *Fax:* 252-838-0809
patti.marraro@noaa.gov
Ensures the delivery of scientific, technical, and legistlative information to library users including NOAA staff, general public, academia, industry, and governmental agencies. Houses comprehensive coverage of marine fisheries,fisheries statistics, habitat restoration, mapping and remote sensing, marine chemistry, pollution and toxicology, living marine resources, protected species, and oceanography.
Patti M Marraro, Technical Info Specialist

4250 Clinton River Watershed Council Library
1115 W. Avon Road 248-601-0606
Rochester, MI 48309 *Fax:* 248-601-1280
contact@crwc.org
www.crwc.org
Susan Kelsey, President
Jeff Bednar, 1st Vice President

4251 Colorado River Board of California
770 Fairmont Avenue 818-500-1625
Suite 100 *Fax:* 818-543-4685
Glendale, CA 91203 crb@crb.ca.gov
www.crb.ca.gov
Tanya M. Trujillo, Executive Director

4252 Columbia River Inter-Tribal Fish Commission
StreamNet Library
700 NE Multnomah 503-238-0667
Ste 1200 *Fax:* 503-235-4228
Portland, OR 97232 oftl@critfc.org
www.streamnetlibrary.org
Serving the scientific and environmental community of the Pacific Northwest, The StreamNet Library works in cooperation with the region's fish and wildlife recovery efforts. The library provides access to technical information on theColumbia Basin fisheries, ecosystem and other relevant subjects for states in the

Pacfic Northwest. The library collections emphasize less commonly available grey literature, such as consultant's reports, state documents and nonprofit organizations'reports.
Lenora Oftedahl, Librarian
Todd Hannon, Assistant Librarian

4253 DER Research Library
Pennsylvania Department of Environmental Resources
Box 8458 717-787-9647
Harrisburg, PA 17105 *Fax:* 717-772-0288

4254 Dawes Arboretum Library
7770 Jacksontown Road SE 740-323-2355
Newark, OH 43056 800-44D-AWES
Fax: 740-323-4058
www.dawesarb.org
Luke Messinger, Executive Director
Laura Appleman, PR/Marketing Director

4255 Delaware River Basin Commission Library
25 State Police Drive 609-883-9500
Box 7360 *Fax:* 609-883-9522
West Trenton, NJ 00862 www.nj.gov/drbc
The Commission is a federal/interstate agency responsible for managing the water resources at the Delaware River Basin.
Steve Tambini, Executive Director
Paula Schmitt, Secretary

4256 Division of Water Resources Library
Kansas Department of Agriculture
109 SW 9th Street 785-296-3717
2nd Floor *Fax:* 785-296-1176
Topeka, KS 66612

4257 Duke University Biology: Forestry Library
Duke University
411 Chapel Drive 919-660-5880
Box 90193 *Fax:* 919-660-5923
Durham, NC 27708 asklib@duke.edu
www.lib.duke.edu
Shawn Miller, Director

4258 Earthworm Recycling Information Center
35 Medford Street 617-628-1844
Somerville, MA 00214 *Fax:* 617-628-2773
info@earthwormrecycling.org
www.earthwormrecycling.org
Jeff Coyne, Executive Director

4259 Eastern States Office Library
US Bureau of Land Management
7450 Boston Boulevard 703-440-1561
Springfield, VA 22153 *Fax:* 703-440-1599
Terry Lewis, Contact

4260 Eastern Technical Associates Library
PO Box 1009 919-878-3188
Garner, NC 27529 *Fax:* 919-872-5199
tomrose@eta-is-opacity.com
www.eta-is-opacity.com
Environmental consulting firm. Research results published in government reports.
Publication Date: 1979
Thomas H Rose, President

4261 Ecology Center Library
2530 San Pablo Avenue 510-548-2220
Berkeley, CA 94702 *Fax:* 510-548-2240
info@ecologycenter.org
www.ecologycenter.org
Provides educational materials with special focus on the environmental concerns of the California Bay Area. Some topics covered include renewable energy, permaculture, gardening, recycling, environmental education, sustainabledevelopment, climate action, and environmental justice.
Raquel Pinderhughes, President
Becca Prager, Secretary

4262 Environment and Natural Resources Branch Library
US Department of Justice
One Congress Street 617-918-1807
Suite 1100 *Fax:* 617-918-1810
Boston, MA 00211
Research library for Solid Wasteto conduct research and answer questions in the subject fields of nonhazarodus solid waste and recycling.
Leola Decker, Librarian

4263 Environmental Action Coalition Library: Resource Center
625 Broadway 212-677-1601
2nd Floor *Fax:* 212-505-8613
New York, NY 10012
Paul Berizzi, Executive Director

4264 Environmental Coalition on Nuclear Power Library
433 Orlando Avenue 814-237-3900
State College, PA 16803 *Fax:* 814-237-3900
Dr Judith Johnsrud, Executive Officer

4265 Environmental Contracting Center Library
ENSR Consulting and Engineering
Box 2105 970-493-8878
Fort Collins, CO 80522 800-722-2440
www.aecom.com
Michael Bruke, Chairman
Carla Christofferson, Executive Vice President

4266 Environmental Research Associates Library
PO Box 219 610-449-7400
Villanova, PA 19085 *Fax:* 610-449-7404
Research and consulting ecologists and testing firm. Research results published in professional journals. Research results for private clients.
Publication Date: 1970
M H Levin PhD, Director

4267 Federated Conservationists of Westchester County (FCWC) Office Resource Library
78 N Broadway 914-422-4053
White Plains, NY 10603 *Fax:* 914-289-0539
info@fcwc.org
www.fcwc.org
Jason Klien, Co-President
Sara Goddard, Vice President

4268 Fish and Wildlife Reference Service
5430 Grosvenor Lane 301-492-6403
Suite 110 800-582-3421
Bethesda, MD 20814 *Fax:* 301-564-4059
To provide policy guidance regarding the operation and use of the Fish and Wildlife Reference Service.
Paul E Wilson, Project Manager

4269 Florida Conservation Foundation
1191 Orange Avenue 407-644-5377
Winter Park, FL 32789

4270 Forest History Society Library and Archives
2925 Academy Road 919-682-9319
Durham, NC 27703-9311 *Fax:* 919-682-2349
eben.lehman@foresthistory.org
www.foresthistory.org
A nonprofit educational institution that links the past to the future by identifying, collecting, preserving, interpreting and disseminating information on the history of people, forests and their related resources. The society'slibrary and archives is its central activity, focusing on conservation, forestry, and the use of natural resources around the world.
Publication Date: 1946
Steven Anderson, President
Eben Lehman, Dir., Library and Archives

4271 Galveston District Library
US Army Corps of Engineers

Box 1229 409-766-3196
Galveston, TX 77553 *Fax:* 409-766-3905
clark.bartee@usace.army.mil
www.swg.usace.army.mil

Clark Bartee

4272 **Georgia State Forestry Commission Library**
PO Box 819 912-751-3480
Macon, GA 31202 *Fax:* 912-751-3465
Fred Allen, Director

4273 **Glen Helen Association Library**
405 Corry Street 937-767-7375
Yellow Springs, OH 45387 www.glenhelen.org

4274 **Great Lakes Environmental Research Laboratory**
2205 Commonwealth Boulevard 734-741-2235
Ann Arbor, MI 48105 *Fax:* 734-741-2055
Conducts integrated interdiciplinary environmental research in support of resource management and environmental services in costal and esturine water with special emphasis on the Great Lakes.

4275 **Huxley College of Environmental Studies**
516 High Street 360-650-3000
Bellingham, WA 98225 huxley.wwu.edu
One of the oldest environmental studies colleges in the nation. Innovative and indisciplinary academic programs reflect a broad view of the physical, biological, social and cultural world.
Hailey Outzs, Coordinater

4276 **Illinois State Water Survey Library**
208 Water Survey Research Center 217-244-5459
2204 Griffith Drive *Fax:* 217-333-6540
Champaign, IL 61820 info@isws.illinois.edu
The Illinois State Water Survey, a division of the office of Scientific Research and Analysis of the Illinois Department of Natural Resources and affiliated with the University of Illinois, is the primary agency in Illinois concernedwith water and atmosheric resources.
Patricia G Morse, Librarian
Dr. Misganaw Demissie, Director

4277 **Institute of Ecosystem Studies**
2801 Sharon Turnpike 845-677-5343
Millbrook, NY 12545 *Fax:* 845-677-5976
www.caryinstitute.org
Ecology research and education institution; independent; international.
Jill Cadwallader, Public Information Officer

4278 **International Academy at Santa Barbara Library**
800 Garden Street 805-965-5010
Suite D *Fax:* 805-965-6071
Santa Barbara, CA 93101
Susan J Shaffer, Office Manager

4279 **International Association for Disaster Preparedness and Response (DERA)**
PO Box 797 info@disasters.org
Longmont, CO 80502 www.disasters.org
Nonprofit association aiming to connect individuals and organizations involved in all aspects of emergency management. Website contains a reference library and archives.
Publication Date: 1962

4280 **International Game Fish Association**
300 Gulf Stream Way 954-927-2628
Dania Beach, FL 33004 *Fax:* 954-924-4299
hq@igfa.org
www.igfa.org
The International Game Fish Association is a nonprofit organization committed to the conservation of game fish and the promotion of responsible, ethical angling practices through science, education, rulemaking and record keeping.
Publication Date: 1939
Rob Kramer, President

4281 **Interstate Oil and Gas Compact Commission Library**
900 NE 23rd Street 405-525-3556
Box 53127 *Fax:* 405-525-3592
Oklahoma City, OK 73152
W Timothy Dowd, Executive Director

4282 **Knovel**
American Institute of Chemical Engineers
120 Wall Street 203-702-7660
FL 23 800-242-4363
New York, NY 10005-4020 *Fax:* 203-775-5177
www.aiche.org/resources/elibrary
Contains technical handbooks, materials, and databases on chemical engineering.
Monty Alger, President

4283 **Lake Michigan Federation**
150 N. Michigan Ave. 312-939-0838
Suite 700 *Fax:* 312-939-2708
Chicago, IL 60601 alliance@greatlakes.org
www.greatlakes.org
Works to restore fish and wildlife habitat, conserve land and water, and eliminate pollution in the watershed of America's largest lake. We achieve these through education, research, law, science, economics and strategic partnerships.
Lori Colman, Chair
Sanjiv Sinha , Ph.D., Vice Chairman

4284 **Lionael A Walford Library**
74 Magruder Road 732-872-3035
Highlands, NJ 00773 *Fax:* 732-872-3088
Claire L Steimle, Librarian

4285 **Los Angeles County Sanitation District Technical Library**
PO Box 4998 562-699-7411
Whittier, CA 90607 *Fax:* 562-699-5422
info@lacsd.org
www.lacsd.org

4286 **Louisiana Department of Environmental Quality Information Resource Center**
7290 Bluebonnet Boulevard 225-765-0169
2nd Floor *Fax:* 225-765-0222
Baton Rouge, LA 70810
To promote a healthy environment by providing a specialized environmental library to meet the informational and educational needs of the DEQ employees and the citizens of Louisiana.
Patty Birkett, Tech. Librarian

4287 **Marine Environmental Sciences Consortium**
Dauphin Island Sea Lab
101 Bienville Boulevard 251-861-2141
Dauphin Island, AL 36528 *Fax:* 251-861-4646
lpritchett@disl.org
www.disl.org

Carolyn Wood, Assistant Editor
Dr. Just Cebrian, Senior Marine Scientist III

4288 **Massachusetts Audubon Society's Berkshire Wildelife Sanctuaries**
Pleasant Valley Wildlife Sanctuary
472 W Mountain Road 413-637-0320
Lenox, MA 00124 *Fax:* 413-637-0499
berkshires@massaudubon.org
The Massachusetts Audubon Society is an environmental organization with emphases in conservation, advocacy and education. The advocacy effort is statewide and features a legislative team in Boston.
Publication Date: 1896
Rene Laubach, Sanctuary Director

4289 **Minneapolis Public Library and Information Center**
Technology and Science Department
300 Nicolet Mall 612-372-6570
Minneapolis, MN 55401 *Fax:* 312-372-6546
www.hclib.org/about/locations/minneapolis-central

The varied collection in the Technology/Science/Government Documents department runs from agriculture to zoology, computers to cooking, engineering to handicrafts, medicine to motorcycle repair to military science. Special resourcesinclude a complete US Patent and Trademark collection and the CASSIS Patent Trademark Databases, a collection of US industrial standards, including publications from ANSI (American National Standards Institutes).

4290 Minnesota Department of Natural Resources DNR Library
500 Lafayette Road 651-259-5506
Box 21 *Fax:* 651-297-4946
St. Paul, MN 55155 www.dnr.state.mn.us/library/index.html
15,000 titles on natural resource subjects available on interlibrary loan.
Jo Ann Musumeci, Librarian
Denise Legato, Administrator

4291 Minnesota Department of Trade and Economic Development Library
500 Metro Square 651-296-8902
121 7th Place E *Fax:* 651-296-1290
St. Paul, MN 55101
Pat Fenton, Sr. Librarian

4292 Minot State University Bottineau Library
105 Simrall Boulevard 701-228-5454
Bottineau, ND 58318 *Fax:* 701-228-5468
Jan Wysocki, Library Director

4293 Mississippi Department of Environmental Quality Library
P. O. Box 2261 601-961-5024
Jackson, MS 39225 *Fax:* 601-354-6965
ronnie_sanders@deq.state.ms.us
www.deq.state.ms.us
Geology and environmental reference library. Holdings in geosciences, hydrology, pollution control, paleontology, petroleum geology, land and water resources. Special collections; Topographic maps, United States, State andInternational Geoloical survey publications.
Ronnie Sanders, Librarian
Gray Rikard, Executive Director

4294 Missouri Department of Natural Resources Geological Survey & Resource Assessment Division
Box 250 573-368-2101
Rolla, MO 65401 *Fax:* 573-368-2111
Mimi Garstang, Director/State Geologist

4295 National Audubon Society: Aullwood Audubon Center and Farm Library
1000 Aullwood Road 937-890-7360
Dayton, OH 45414 *Fax:* 937-890-2382
aullwood@gemair.com
web4.audubon.org/local/sanctuary/aullwood
Known as the Miami Valley's first educational farm, here visitors will discover a variety of native grasses and flowers, 300 year old oak trees and threatened bird species.

4296 National Institute for Urban Wildlife Library
10921 Trotting Ridge Way 301-596-3311
Columbia, MD 21004 www.webdirectory.com/wildlife/
Louise E Dove, Wildlife Biology

4297 National Speleological Society Library
6001 Pulaski Pike 256-852-1300
Huntsville, AL 35810-1122 librarian@caves.org
caves.org
Contains literature about caves and caving, including NSS publications, as well as books, periodicals, and other literature.
Geary Schindel, President
Tricia Spiliotis, Library Chair

4298 Native Americans for a Clean Environment Resource Office
Box 1671 918-458-4322
Tahlequah, OK 74465 *Fax:* 918-458-0322
NACE is to raise the consciousness of Indian people and the general public about environment hazards, with an emphasis on the nuclear industry.
Lance Hughes, Executive Director

4299 Nature Conservancy Long Island Chapter
Uplands Farm Environmental Center
250 Lawrence Hill Road 516-367-3225
Cold Spring Harbor, NY 11724 *Fax:* 516-367-4715
To preserve the plants, animals and natural communities that represent the diversity of life on Earth by protecting the lands and waters they need to survive.
Mark R. Tercek, President/CEO
Thomas J. Tierney, Chairman

4300 Nebraska Natural Resources Commission Planning Library
301 Centennial Mall S 402-471-2081
Box 94876 *Fax:* 402-471-3132
Lincoln, NE 68509 www.nrc.state.ne.us/

4301 New England Coalition on Nuclear Pollution Library
PO Box 545 802-257-0336
Brattleboro, VT 00530 energy@necnp.org
www.necnp.org

4302 New England Governors' Conference Reference Library
76 Summer Street 617-423-6900
Boston, MA 00211 *Fax:* 617-423-7327
www.negc.org

4303 Occupational Safety and Health Library
1111 3rd Avenue 206-553-5930
Suite 715 *Fax:* 206-553-6499
Seattle, WA 98101

4304 Peninsula Conservation Foundation Library of the Environment
3921 E Bayshore Road 650-962-9876
Palo Alto, CA 94303 *Fax:* 650-962-8234

4305 People, Food and Land Foundation Library
PO Box 314 559-855-3710
Prather, CA 93651 mail@sunmt.org
www.sunmt.org

4306 Peregrine Fund Research Library
The Peregrine Fund
5668 W Flying Hawk Lane 208-362-3716
Boise, ID 83709 *Fax:* 208-362-2376
tpf@peregrinefund.org
www.peregrinefund.org
One of the world's largest collections of scientific literature on birds, containing more than 23,000 books and reports, 30,000 reprints, 1,500 journals, and numerous newsletters, magazines, and auvio-video content.
Publication Date: 1994
Rick Watson, PhD, President & CEO
Munir Virani, PhD, Vice President, Conservation

4307 Rainforest Action Network Library
221 Pine Street 415-398-4404
Suite 500 *Fax:* 415-398-2732
San Francisco, CA 94104
Rainforest Action Network works to protect the Earth's rainforests and support the rights of their inhabitants through education, grassroots organizing and non-violent direct action.
Michael Brune, Executive Director
Mrtha DiSario, Director

4308 Region 2 Library
US Environmental Protection Agency

1200 Pennsylvania Avenue N.W. 202-272-0167
Washington, DC 20004 www.epa.gov
Is a research and reference library for use by EPA staff, EPA contractors, other government agencies, and the public. The library contains or has access to scientific and technical materials in paper and electronic media related to awide variety of environmental issues, with and emphasis on EPA's Region 2.
Eveline M Goodman, Head Librarian

4309 Region 9 Library
US Environmental Protection Agency
1200 Pennsylvania Avenue N.W. 202-272-0167
Washington, DC 20004 www.epa.gov/region9/library
Deborra Samuels, Head Librarian & Coordinator

4310 Rob and Bessie Welder Wildlife Foundation Library
Walker Wildlife Foundation 361-364-2643
PO Box 1400 *Fax:* 361-364-2650
Sinton, TX 78387 www.members.aol.com/welderwf/welderhome
Private, nonprofit operation foundation which conducts research and education in wildlife management and related fields. Funds graduate fellowships and conducts its reserach and education program on its 7,800 acre wildlife refuge inthe surrounding South Texas region and throughout the United States.
Dr. D Lynn Drawe, Director
Vandra Davis, Librarian

4311 Schuylkill Center for Environmental Education
8480 Hagy's Mill Road 215-482-7300
Philadelphia, PA 19128 *Fax:* 215-482-8158
scee@schuylkillcenter.org
www.schuylkillcenter.org
Karin James, Resource Librarian
Barbara Baumgartner, Environmental Educator

4312 Sierra Club William E. Colby Library
Sierra Club
2101 Webster Street 415-977-5500
Suite 1300 *Fax:* 510-208-3140
Oakland, CA 94612 information@sierraclub.org
www.sierraclub.org
Library maintained by the Sierra Club for more than 125 years, orignally destroyed by San Francisco's 1906 earthquake, but rebuilt through club member donations. Contains 8,000 books, 100 periodical titles, photos and films, and theclub's history and archives.
Michael Brune, Executive Director
Jennifer Trahan, Chief Operating Officer

4313 Solartherm Library
1315 Apple Avenue 301-587-8686
Silver Spring, MD 20910 *Fax:* 301-587-8688
www.solartherm.com

4314 Southeast Fisheries Laboratory Library
75 Virginia Beach Drive 305-361-4229
Miami, FL 33149 *Fax:* 305-361-4499
www.sefsc.noaa.gov/library

4315 Southwest Research and Information Center
105 Stanford SE 505-262-1862
PO Box 4524 *Fax:* 505-262-1864
Albuquerque, NM 87106 Info@sric.org
www.sric.org
SRIC exists to provide timely, accurate information to the public on matters that affect the environment, human health, and communities in order to protect natural resources, promote citizen participation, and ensure environmental andsocial justice now and for future generations.
Dan Hancock, Administrator
Annette Aguayo, Information Specialist

4316 St Paul Plant Pathology Library
395 Borlaug Hall 612-625-9777
St Paul Campus
St Paul, MN 55108
Subject oriented library, specializing in plant diseases, plant virology, mycology, mycotoxicology and the effects of air pollution on vegetation. The collection contains approximately 8000 volumes of books, periodicals and PlantPathology theses. Over 50 current periodicals are recieved.

4317 St. Paul Forestry Library
University of Minnesota
499 Wilson Library 612-624-3321
309 19th Avenue South *Fax:* 612-624-3733
Minneapolis, MN 55455 heroL228@umn.edu
www.lib.umn.edu/naturalresources
Houses a general collection of books, journals, government documents, maps, and pamphlets relating to the subjects of forestry, forest products, outdoor recreation, range management, and remote sensing. There is also a small generalrefernce section. Also compiles and maintains four databases focused on aspects of forestry: Social Sciences in Forestry, Urban Forestry, Tropical Conservation and Development, Trails Planning Construction and Maintenance Planning.
Philip Herold, Librarian

4318 State University of New York
College of Environmental Science and Forestry
Environamental Science and Forestry 315-470-6715
Syracuse, NY 13210 *Fax:* 315-470-6512
www.esf.edu/moonlib
Moon Library supports the SUNY College of Environmental Science and Forestry where students major in Engineering, Chemistry, Biology, Landscape Architecture, Forest Resources Management and Environmental Studies.
Stephen Weiter, Director/College Libraries

4319 Staten Island Institute of Arts and Sciences
William T Davis Education Center
75 Stuyvesant Place 718-987-6233
State Island, NY 10301 *Fax:* 718-273-5683
www.statenislandmuseum.org
Ralph Branca, Chairperson
Doloerss Morris, Vice Chairperson

4320 Tall Timbers Research Station Parker-Williams Library
Tall Timbers Research Station
13093 Henry Beadel Drive 850-893-4153
Tallahassee, FL 32312 *Fax:* 850-668-7781
bpalmer@talltimbers.org
talltimbers.org
The library supports the work of the Tall Timbers Research Station & Land Conservancy. Collection specializes in forestry, fire ecology, plant and animal ecology, conservation biology, ornithology, mammalogy, herpetology, naturalhistory, and ecology, and features monographs, state documents and federal documents.
William E. Palmer, President & CEO
Crystal Davis, Director, Development

4321 Texas Water Commission Library
PO Box 13087 512-463-7834
Austin, TX 78711

4322 Turner, Collie and Braden Library
Box 130089 713-267-2826
Houston, TX 77219 *Fax:* 713-780-0838
rushbrookd@tcbhou.com
David Rushbrook, Librarian
Renee Miller, Library Assistant

4323 U.S. Geological Survey: Wetlands and Aquatic Research Center
700 Cajundome Boulevard 337-266-8500
Lafayette, LA 70506-3152 *Fax:* 337-266-8513
nwrcinfo@usgs.gov
www.nwrc.usgs.gov
The research center's mission is to develop and disseminate scientific information needed for understanding the ecology and values of the nation's wetlands and other aquatic and coastal eco-

systems, and to manage and restore wetland,coastal, and aquatic habitats and associated plant and animal communtities.
Publication Date: 2015
Thomas Doyle, Deputy Director
Kenneth Rice, Center Director

4324 US Bureau of Land Management Library
Denver Federal Center Building 50 303-236-6650
Box 25047 *Fax:* 303-236-4810
Denver, CO 80225 blm_library@blm.gov
www.blm.gov
The BLM Library serves the information and research needs of BLM personnel. The library also serves as the point of contract for bureau publications and information with other federal agencies and the public. The collection covers allaspects of land management and natural resources.
Barbara Campbell, Director

4325 US Department of Agriculture: National Agricultural Library, Water Quality Info Center
10301 Baltimore Boulevard 301-504-6077
Beltsville, MD 20705 *Fax:* 301-504-6409
Collects, organizes and communicates the scientific findings, educational methologies and public policy issues related to water and agriculture.
Joseph R Makuch, Coord. WQIC

4326 US Geological Survey: Great Lakes Science Center
1451 Green Road 734-994-3331
Ann Arbor, MI 48105 *Fax:* 734-994-8780
GS-B-GLSC-Webmaster@usgs.gov
www.glsc.usgs.gov
The USGS Great Lakes Science Center exists to meet the Nation's need for scientific information for restoring, enhancing, managing, and protecting living resources and their habitats in the Great Lakes. The center is headquartered inAnn Arbor, Michigan, and has biological research stations and vessels located throughout the Great Lakes basin.
Russell Strach, Center Director
Jacqueline F Savino, Deputy Center Director

4327 US Geological Survey: Upper Midwest Environmental Sciences Center Library
2630 Fanta Reed Road 608-783-6451
La Crosse, WI 54603 *Fax:* 608-783-6066
www.umesc.usgs.gov
A federal library with technical holdings mainly in aquatic sciences, bird and amphibean materials.
Kathy Mannstedt, Librarian

4328 US Geological Survey: Water Resources Division Library
375 S Euclid Avenue 520-670-6201
Tucson, AZ 85719

4329 Unexpected Wildlife Refuge Library
17314 McCourtney Ave 530-477-1757
Grass Valley, CA 95949 info@animalplace.org
www.animalplace.org
Kim Sturla, Executive Director
Marji Beach, Education Director

4330 University of California
1 Shields Avenue 530-752-1011
Davis, CA 95616 ucdavis.edu

4331 University of Florida Coastal Engineering Archives
209 Yon Hall 352-392-2710
Gainesville, FL 32611 *Fax:* 352-392-2710
Twedell@coastal.ufl.edu
Helen Twedell, Archivist
Kimberly Hunt, Sr. Library Technical Asst

4332 University of Hawaii at Manoa Water Resources Center
2540 Dole Street 808-956-7847
Homes Hall 283 *Fax:* 808-956-5044
Honolulu, HI 96822 morav@hawaii.edu
www.wrrc.hawaii.edu
Coordinates and conducts research to identify, characterize and quantify water/environmental related problems in the state of Hawaii. Based on the research WRRC makes recommendations to all agencies and organizations withresponsibilities to manage the water/ environmental resources in Hawaii.
Phillip Morakik, Technology Transfer Spec
James Moncur, Director

4333 University of Illinois at Chicago
Energy Resource Center
851 S Morgan Street 312-996-4490
12th Floor *Fax:* 312-996-5420
Chicago, IL 60607 uic.edu
The Energy Resources center is an interdiciplinary public service, research, and special projects organization dedicated to improving energy efficiency and the environment. Conducts studies in the fields of energy and environment andprovides industry, utilities, government agencies and the public with assistance, information, and advice on new technologies, public policy, and professional development training.
James Hartnett, Director

4334 University of Maryland: Center for Environmental Science Chesapeake Biological Lab
P.O. BOX 775 410-228-9250
Cambridge, MD 21613 *Fax:* 410-326-7302
boesch@umces.edu
www.umces.edu/cbl
Kathleen A Heil, Librarian
Thomas Miller, Director

4335 University of Montana Wilderness Institute Library
32 Campus Drive 406-243-5361
Missoula, MT 59812 *Fax:* 406-243-4845
wi@cfc.umt.edu
www.cfc.umt.edu/wi
Natalie Dawson, Director
Rachel James, Assistant Director

4336 Vermont Institute of Natural Sciences Library
27023 Church Hill Road 802-457-2779
Woodstock, VT 00509 *Fax:* 802-457-2779

4337 Voices from the Earth
105 Stanford SE 505-262-1862
PO Box 4524 *Fax:* 505-262-1864
Albuquerque, NM 87196 Info@sric.org
www.sric.org
SRIC exists to provide timely, accurate information to the public on matters that affect the environment, human health, and communities in order to protect natural resources, promote citizen participation, and ensure environmental andsocial justice now and for future generations.
Dan Hancock, Administrator
Annette Aguayo, Information Specialist

4338 Wasserman Public Affairs Library
University of Texas at Austin
General Libraries 512-495-4400
Sid Richardson Hall 3243 *Fax:* 512-495-4347
Austin, TX 78712 pal@lib.utexas.edu
Stephen Littrell, Head Librarian
Ester Bolmey, Library Technical Assistant

4339 Welder Wildlife Foundation Library
10429 Welder Wildlife 361-364-2643
PO Box 1400 *Fax:* 361-364-2650
Sinton, TX 78387 welderwildlife.org

Contains the collections of early conservationists, including serial journals and first issues from the 1800's, rare books from the 1600's, and totalling 24,000 books and journals.
Terry Blankenship, Director
Selma Glasscock, Assistant Director

4340 Western Ecology Division Library
US Environmental Protection Agency
1200 Pennsylvania Avenue N.W. 202-272-0167
Washington, DC 20004 www.epa.gov
Publication Date: 1966
Kathy Martin, Program Analyst
Mary O'Brien, Librarian

4341 Wisconsin Department of Natural Resources Library
Box 7921 608-266-8933
Madison, WI 53707 *Fax:* 608-266-5226
dnr.wi.gov
Contains books, journals, and EPA reports on air pollution, geology, hazardous waste, natural resources management, recycling, soil pollution, solid waste, toxic substances, waste minimization, wastewater, water pollution, andwetlands.
Erin Matiszik, Librarian

4342 Wisconsin's Water Library at UW Madison
University of Wisconsin
1975 Willow Drive, Floor 2 608-262-3069
Madison, WI 53706 *Fax:* 608-262-0591
AskWater@aqua.wisc.edu
Wisconsin's Water Library is a collection of materials that cover all major topics in water resources, but is particularly strong in Wisconsin and Great Lakes water issues, groundwater protection, wetlands issues, and the impacts ofagricultural chemicals. The collection consists of over 31,000 hard copy and microfiche documents, over 35 journals and 130 newsletters.
Anne K Moser, Special Librarian

4343 Yale University School of Forestry and Environmental Studies Library
205 Prospect Street 203-432-5132
New Haven, CT 00651 *Fax:* 203-432-5942
www.library.yale.edu/scilib/forestl.html
A part of the Yale University Library System, the library serves the resource needs of the graduate students and faculty of Yale's 100 year old school of Forestry and Environmental Studies.
Carla Heister, Librarian

Publishers

4344 Academic Press: New York
Academic Press
15 E 26th Street 212-592-1000
15th Floor
New York, NY 10010

4345 Adison Wesley Longman
Pearson
330 Hudson St 212-641-2400
New York, NY 10013 800-563-9196
Fax: 800-263-7733
pearson.com
One integrated and diverse company offering learning resources on an extraordinary level. Pearson has an estblished reputation for producing market-leading educational products and services as well as a comprehensive range ofbest-selling consumer, environmental technical and professional titles.
Glen Moreno, Chairman
John Fallon, Chief Executive

4346 Blackwell Publishers
Blackwell Publishers
350 Main Street 781-388-8200
Malden, MA 00214 *Fax:* 781-388-8210
as.wiley.com/WileyCDA/Section/id-301698.html
Blackwell Publishers are dedicated to serving the global academic community. We recognize that publishing is about making connections. Knowledge is not constrained by national or liguistic boundries. Many academics are engaged in bothteaching and research. Our readers are often our authors as well. We develop books for students which take account of the latest research and we aim to make the journals we publish as accessible as possible.

4347 Boxwood Press
183 Ocean View Boulevard 408-375-9110
Pacific Grove, CA 93950 *Fax:* 408-375-0430
boxwood@boxwoodpress.com
Publishes significant titles in the areas of Natural History, Area Studies, General Sciences and Local and Special Interest. Founded in 1952, it first published lab manuals, then expanded to include a variety of mainly biologicaltitles.

4348 CABI Publishing
CAB International 617-395-4056
875 Massachusetts Ave, 7th Floor 800-552-3083
Cambridge, MA 00213 *Fax:* 617-354-6875
cabi-nao@cabi.org
www.cabi.org
CABI publishing is a leading international, nonprofit publisher in applied life sciences, including animal science, nutrition, integrated crop management and forestry. Our products have a global reputation for quality, relevance andauthority, and are used in over 100 countries. Our long-established print publishing activities include a substantial book and reference work list, and an expanding primary and review journal program.

4349 CRC Press
CRC Press
2000 NW Corporate Boulevard 561-994-0555
Boca Raton, FL 33431 800-272-7737
Fax: 800-374-3401
www.crcpress.com
CRC Press LLC is recognized as a leader in scientific, medical, environmental science, engineering, business, technical, mathamatical, and statistics publishing. CRC Press LLC publishes books, journals, newsletters and databases.Customers have access to publications through individual purchases, bookstores, libraries and on-line acess at www.crcpress.com

4350 Chelsea Green Publishing Company
85 N Main Street 802-295-6300
PO Box 428 800-639-4099
White River Junction, VT 00500 *Fax:* 802-295-6444
publicity@chelseagreen.com
www.chelseagreen.com
Chelsea Green publishes information that helps us lead pleasurable lives on a planet where human activities are in harmony and balance with nature.Free catolog listing over 250 titles on sustainable living, innovative shelter andorganic gardening.
Alice Blackmer, Publicity Director

4351 DK Publishing
DK Publishing
95 Madison Avenue 212-213-4800
New York, NY 10016 *Fax:* 212-213-5240
Dorling Kindersley is an international publishing company specialising in the creation of high quality, illustrated information books, interactive software, TV programs and online resources for childern and adults. Founded in London1974, DK now has offices in the UK, USA, Australia, South Africa, India France, Germany and Russia.
Publication Date: 1974

4352 Elsevier Science
Elsevier Sciences
655 Avenue of the Americas 212-633-3730
New York, NY 10010 *Fax:* 212-633-3680
usinfo-f@elsevier.com
Our focus will be entirely on scientific, technical and medical publishing. Together we can offer customers choice across our portfolio, with outstanding platforms for the delivery of electronic services and a high level of investmentto ensure the development of leading electronic products.

4353 **Environmental Working Group**
1436 U Street 202-667-6982
Suite 100 www.ewg.org
Washington, DC 20009
The Environmental Working Group is a leading content provider for public interest groups and concerned citizens who are campaigning to protect the environment. Offers reports, articles, technical assistance and the development ofcomputer databases and Internet resources.
Ken Cook, President
Heather White, Executive Director

4354 **Global and Environmental Education Resources**
Global Change Research Information
Suite 250 1717 202-223-6262
Pennsylvania Ave NW *Fax:* 202-223-3065
Washington, DC 20006 information@gcrio.org
www.gcrio.org/edu.html
Multidisciplinary and international in scope, this collection of resources was selected for its relevance to global change and environmental education. Included is a wide range of resources in a variety of formats for educators andstudents at all levels (K-12 and higher education), librarians, citizens and community groups.

4355 **Grey House Publishing**
4919 Route 22 518-789-8700
P.O. Box 56 800-562-2139
Amenia, NY 12501 *Fax:* 518-789-0556
books@greyhouse.com
www.greyhouse.com
Resource guides, handbooks and reference works for public, high school and academic libraries and the business and health communities. Publishes environmental resources for the North American market.
Leslie Mackenzie, Publisher
Laura Mars, Editorial Director

4356 **Grey House Publishing Canada**
411 Queen Street West 416-644-6479
3rd Floor 866-433-4739
Toronto, Ontario M5V-2A5 *Fax:* 416-644-1904
info@greyhouse.ca
www.greyhouse.ca
Canada's largest developer, publisher and distributor of value-added reference information for the academic, library, government and corporate markets. Titles include the Canadian Almanac and Directory, Canadian Who's Who, andAssociations Canada.
Bryon Moore, General Manager
Stuart Paterson, Managing Editor

4357 **Institute for Food and Development Policy**
398 60th Street 510-654-4400
Oakland, CA 94618 *Fax:* 510-654-4551
foodfirst@foodfirst.org
www.foodfirst.org
Publishes books on poverty, agriculture and development, also backgrounders, policy briefs and development reports.
Publication Date: 1975
Eric Holt-GimèNez, Executive Director
Alexandra Toledo, Development Director

4358 **Island Press**
Distribution Center
PO Box 7 707-983-6432
Covelo, CA 95428 800-828-1302
Fax: 707-983-6414
service@islandpress.com
www.islandpress.com
Mission-oriented nonprofit publisher organized in 1984 to help meet the need for accessible, solutions-oriented information through a unique approach that addresses the multidisciplinary nature of environmental problems. Our program isdesigned to translate technical information from a range of disciplines into a book format that is accessible and informative to citizen activists, educators, students and professionals involved in the study or management of environmental problems.
Bernice Hiatt, Customer Service

4359 **It's Academic**
29 West 35th Street 212-216-7800
New York, NY 10001 *Fax:* 212-564-7854
A tool for teachers who use Routledge books in their classes. To aid in finding the books best suited for your needs, we offer: pages which highlight books designed specifically for your courses, a list of conferences at which wedisplay our books, journal information, a forum for instructors to send us their comments, supplements available on line and a subject search menu.

4360 **Kluwer Academic Publishers**
101 Philip Drive 781-871-6600
Assinippi Park *Fax:* 781-871-6528
Norwell, MA 00206
A sector of the Wolters Kluwer publishing group. Operates world-wide from offices in Dordrecht, Boston, New York and London. All over the world, scientists and professionals hold our publications in high esteem.

4361 **Krieger Publishing Company**
Krieger Publishing Co.
1725 Krieger Drive 321-724-9542
Malabar, FL 32950 800-724-0025
Fax: 321-951-3671
info@krieger-publishing.com
www.krieger-publishing.com
Krieger Publishing Company produces quality books in various fields of interest. We have an extensive Natural Science listing.
Cheryl Stanton, Advertising

4362 **MIT Press**
One Rogers Street 617-253-5646
Cambridge, MA 00214 *Fax:* 617-258-6779
mitpress.mit.edu
The only university press in the US whose list is based in science and technology. Our environment list is strong in policy and the social sciences. We are committed to the edges and frontiers of the world - to exploring new fields andnew modes of inquiry. We publish about 200 new books a year and over 40 journals including Global Environmental Politics. We have a long-term commitment to both design excellence and the efficient and creative use of new technologies.
Amy Brand, Director
Bill Trippe, Director of Technology

4363 **McGraw-Hill Education**
The McGraw-Hill Companies
P.O. Box 182605 212-512-2000
Columbus, OH 43218 800-338-3987
Fax: 609-308-4480
customer.service@mheducation.com
www.mheducation.com
A global leader in educational materials and professional information, with offices in more than 30 countries and publications in more than 40 languages, we develop products that influence people's lives from preschool through career.The scope of our operations, the quality of our editorial product and the pace at which we are developing new media to fulfill our customers' information requirements are increasing.
David Levin, President/ CEO
Angelo T. DeGenaro, Chief Information Officer

4364 **National Information Service Corporation**
NISC USA, Wyman Towers 410-243-0797
3100 St. Paul Street *Fax:* 410-243-0982
Baltimore, MD 21218 www.nisc.com
Publishes information products for access through BiblioLine, our Web search service, or on CD-ROM. Some of our abstract and index services are available in print. NISC's bibliographic and full-text databases cover a wide range oftopics in the natural and social sciences, arts and humanities. Some titles provide comprehensive coverage of particular geographic regions, such as Latin America, Africa, South-East Asia or the Arctic and Antarctic.

4365 O'Reilly & Associates
101 Morris Street 800-998-9938
Sebastopol, CA 95472 *Fax:* 707-829-0104
Premier information source for leading-edge computer technologies. We offer the knowledge of experts through our books, conferences and web sites. Our books, known for their animals on the covers, occupy a treasured place on theshelves of developers building the next generation of software. Conferences and summits bring innovators together to shape the ideas that spark new industries. From the Internet to the web, Linux, Open Source and peer-to-peer networking, we puttechnologies on the map.

4366 Random House
1540 Broadway 212-782-9000
New York, NY 10036 *Fax:* 212-302-7985
The world's largest English-language general trade book publisher. It is a division of the Bertelsmann Book Group of Bertelsmann AG, one of the foremost media companies in the world.

4367 Simon & Schuster
1230 Avenue of the Americas 212-698-7000
New York, NY 10020 *Fax:* 212-698-2359
www.simonandschuster.biz
Carolyn Reidy, President
Jon Anderson, Executive Vice President and

4368 Solano Press Books
Solano Press
PO Box 773 800-931-9373
Point Arena, CA 95468 *Fax:* 707-884-4109
spbooks@solano.com
www.solano.com
Solano Press Books is a California publishing house specializing in land use, planning law, urban affairs, and environmental subjects. Publications also offer readers detailed guidance on policy matters and instructions on implementingand complying with specific programs and procedures.
Publication Date: 1988
Ling-Yen Jones, Publisher

4369 Springer-Verlag New York
175 Fifth Avenue 212-460-1500
New York, NY 10010 *Fax:* 212-473-6272
Founded in 1964 and maintained its position last year as the Springer Group's largest foreign subsidiary. In 1999, 426 new titles were released. In addition, 50 journals were published, most of them available in electronic form as wellas via the Springer information system LINK. The number of license agreements in the North American market has increased fivefold due to the increasing demand for this leading Online Library.

4370 Virginia Museum of Natural History
1001 Douglas Avenue 540-666-8600
Martinsville, VA 24112 *Fax:* 540-632-6487
www.vmnh.org
Our publishing division specializes in works by natural scientists and environmental educators in the US and abroad. Writing, editorial, and design services available for books, reports, manuals, text books, presentations, fieldguides.
24 pages Quarterly
ISSN: 1085-5084
Susan Felker, Managing Editor\Outreach

4371 WW Norton & Company
500 5th Avenue 212-354-5500
New York, NY 10110 *Fax:* 212-869-0856
wwnorton.com
The oldest and largest publishing house owned wholly by its employees, strives to carry out the imperative of its founder to publish books of long-term value in the areas of fiction, nonfiction and poetry. The roots of the company dateback to 1923, when William Warder Norton and his wife, M.D. Herter Norton, began publishing lectures delivered at the People's Institute, the adult education division of New York City's Cooper Union.
Diane Ackerman, Author
Dalton Conley, Author

4372 Wiley North America
605 3rd Avenue 212-850-6000
New York, NY 10158 *Fax:* 212-850-6088
The company was founded in 1807, during the Jefferson presidency. In the early years, Wiley was best known for the works of Washington Irving, Edgar Allen Poe, Herman Melville and other 19th century American literary giants. By theturn of the century, Wiley was established as a leading publisher of scientific and technical information.

Research Centers

Corporate & Commercial Centers

4373 AAA & Associates
28 West Adams
Suite 1511
Detroit, MI 48226
313-961-4122
Fax: 313-588-6232

Katherine Banicki, President

4374 AB Gurda Company
6061 Whitnall Way
Hales Corners, WI 53130
414-529-3116
Environmental testing and analysis firm.

4375 ABC Research Corporation
3437 SW 24th Avenue
Gainesville, FL 32607
352-372-0436
866-233-5883
Fax: 352-378-6483
info@abcr.com

Research and analysis laboratory. Research results published in scientific journals.
Dr William L Brown, President
Dr Peter Bodnaruck, VP

4376 ACRES Research
6621 W Ridgeway Avenue
Cedar Falls, IA 50613
319-277-6661
Fax: 319-266-7569
Environmental research and testing.
Bert Schou PhD, President

4377 ACZ Laboratories, Inc
2773 Downhill Drive
Steamboat Springs, CO 80487
970-879-6590
800-334-5493
Fax: 815-301-3857
sales@acz.com
www.acz.com

A full service environmental analytical lab with inorganic, organic and radiochemical capabilities. We perform analysis on a wide variety of matrices including water, wastewater, waste, soil, plant and animal tissue as well as fishtissue.

Sue Webber, Project Manager
Tony Antalek, Project Manager

4378 ADA Technologies
8100 Shaffer Parkway
Suite 130
Littleton, CO 80127-4107
303-792-5615
800-232-0296
Fax: 303-792-5633
www.adatech.com
Product development and testing of environmental technologies.
James P. Budimlya, President & CEO
Russell Farmer, Executive Vice President

4379 AECOM
10 Iverness Center Parkway
Suite 120
Birmingham, AL 35242
205-980-0054
800-722-2440
Fax: 205-980-1509
askenvironment@aecom.com
www.aecom.com

AECOM is a global provider of environmental and energy development services to industry and government. As a full-service environmental firm, AECOM's professionals provide clients with consulting, engineering, remediation, and relatedservices from over 24 countries.

Michael S. Bruke, Chairman & CEO
Carla Christofferson, Executive Vice President

4380 AER
131 Hartwell Avenue
Lexington, MA 00242
781-761-2288
Fax: 781-761-2299
ross@aer.com
www.aer.com

Ron Isaacs, CEO
David B. Hogan, CTO/SVP

4381 AMA Analytical Services
4475 Forbes Boulevard
Lanham, MD 20706
301-459-2640
800-346-0961
Fax: 301-459-2643
info@amalab.com
www.amalab.com
Environmental research. Asbestos, lead and explosives analysis.
David P Hood, CEO

4382 ANA-Lab Corporation
2600 Dudley Road
PO Box 9000
Kilgore, TX 75663
903-984-0551
Fax: 903-984-5914
corp@ana-lab.com
www.ana-lab.com
Environmental laboratory specializing in the testing of wastewater, groundwater, and solid waste for pollutants, herbicides, pesticides, and PCBs.

Scott Moss, Vice President, Operations
Bill Peery, Executive Vice President

4383 APC Lab
13760 Manolia Avenue
Chino, CA 91710
909-590-1828
Fax: 909-590-1498
apcl@apclab.com
Environmental and industrial testing laboratory. Research results published in journals and conference reports.
Irene Huang, Public Relations

4384 APS Technology
7 Laser Lane
Wallingford, CT 00649
860-613-4450
Fax: 203-284-7428
contact@aps-tech.com
www.aps-tech.com
Product development, conceptual design, engineering, prototype manufacture and test analysis.
William E Turner, CEO
Denis Bigin, VP

4385 ARDL
400 Aviation Drive
Mount Vernon, IL 62864
618-244-3235
Fax: 618-244-1149
techserv@ardlinc.com
www.ardlinc.com
Environmental sampling and testing laboratory; Research Development Engineering. Alternate Name: Applied Research and Development Laboratories, Inc.
Larry Gibbons PhD, President
Don Gillespie, Marketing Manager

4386 ASW Environmental Consultants
20 N Plains Industrial Road
PO Box 495
Wallingford, CT 00649
203-265-0509
Fax: 203-265-1476
Jason J Sarojak, PE

4387 ATC Associates
5415 SW Westgate Drive
Suite 100
Portland, OR 97221
503-419-2500
Fax: 503-419-2600
www.cardno.com
Technical engineering research and environmental consulting firm.
John Marlay, Chairman
Richard Wankmuller, CEO & Mnanaging Director

4388 ATC Environmental
720 E Benson Road
Sioux Falls, SD 57103
605-338-0555
Donald Beck

4389 ATL
2921 N. 30th Avenue 602-241-1097
Phoenix, AZ 85017-5402 *Fax:* 602-277-1306
tatafcr@ATL-quality.com
Technical engineering evaluation firm. Research results published in test summaries and project reports.
Frank C Rivera, President
David P Hayes, VP

4390 AW Research Laboratories
16326 Airport Road 218-829-7974
Brainerd, MN 56401 *Fax:* 218-829-1316
awlab@awlab.com
www.awlab.com
A.W. Research Laboratories provides environmental consulting services and water quality analysis, specializing in the use of remote sensing techniques for lake analysis and management.
Sara Ahlers, CEO
Sarah Fogderud, Chief Financial Officer

4391 AZTEC Laboratories
6402 Stadium Drive 816-921-3922
PO Box 7953
Kansas City, MO 64129
Data collection and analysis, systems design and product development firm.

4392 Aaron Environmental
189 Atwater Street 860-276-1201
Plantsville, CT 00647 800-372-2766
Fax: 860-276-1233
info@aaronenvironmental.com
www.aaronenvironmental.com
Joyce Kogut, President
Mike Bolegh, Business Manager

4393 Accurate Engineering Laboratories
4831 S. Whipple Ave. 773-523-3100
Chicago, IL 60632 *Fax:* 773-384-8681
www.accu-labs.com
Environmental engineering laboratory.
Noel Buczkowski, President

4394 Accutest Laboratories
2235 Route 130 S 732-329-0200
Building B *Fax:* 732-329-3499
Dayton, NJ 00881 www.accutest.com
Environmental testing firm.
Phillip B. Rooney, Chairman & CEO
Gene Malloy, President & COO

4395 Acts Testing Labs
25 Anderson Rd 716-505-3300
Buffalo, NY 14228 *Fax:* 716-505-3301
Global consumer products testing organization providing quality assurance testing, inspections and consulting services.
Tom Fatta, Contact

4396 Adelaide Associates
7 Holland Avenue 914-949-3109
White Plains, NY 10603 *Fax:* 914-949-8103
Environmental health consulting and testing firm. Additional offices: White Plains, NY, Poughkeepsie, NY and Perth Amboy, NJ.
Ron Birlinski, CEO

4397 Adelaide Environmental Health Associates
1511 Route 22 845-278-7710
Suite C24 *Fax:* 845-278-7750
Brewster, NY 10509 www.adelaidellc.com
Stephanie A. Soter, President
John W. Soter, Vice President

4398 Adirondack Environmental Services
314 N Pearl Street 518-434-4546
Albany, NY 12207 800-848-4983
Fax: 518-434-0891
www.adirondackenvironmental.com
Analytical medical laboratory.

4399 Adirondack Lakes Survey Corporation
Route 86 518-897-1354
PO Box 296 *Fax:* 518-897-1364
Ray Brook, NY 12977 info@adirondacklakessurvey.org
www.adirondacklakessurvey.org
Determines the extent and magnitude of acidification of lakes and ponds in the Adironack region.

4400 Advance Pump and Filter Company
10 Calef Highway 603-868-3212
Lee, NH 00382 800-863-3212
Fax: 603-868-3230
info@advanceh2o.com
www.advancepumpandfilter.com
Services include water treatment, submersible pumps, jet pumps, water tanks, sewage and sump systems.
Cathleen Pleadwell, Business Manager

4401 Advanced Terra Testing
833 Parfet Street 303-232-8308
Unit A 888-859-8378
Lakewood, CO 80215 *Fax:* 303-232-1579
info@terratesting.com
www.terratesting.com
Geotechnical and geosynthetic testing firm.
Chris Wienecke, Co-Owner
Duke C. Wilson, Co-Owner

4402 AeroVironment
181 West Huntington Drive 626-357-9983
Suite 202 *Fax:* 626-359-9628
Monrovia, CA 91016 info@avinc.com
www.avinc.com
Research, service and consulting firm specializing in the environment, alternative energy and aerodynamic design. Research results published in project reports and technical journals.
Tim Conver, CEO
Raymond Cook, CFO

4403 Aerosol Monitoring & Analysis, Inc.
1331 Ashton Road 410-684-3327
Hanover, MD 21076 *Fax:* 410-684-3384
www.amatraining.com
AMA provides industrial hygiene, environmental, and health & safety services to government agencies, institutions, building owners, property managers, architects, and engineers.
Todd M. Woerner, President
Joseph A. Coco, Senior Vice President

4404 Agvise Laboratories
604 Highway 15 West 701-587-6010
PO Box 510 *Fax:* 701-587-6013
Northwood, ND 58267 www.agvise.com
Applied and product research in environmental applications.
Bob Deutsch, President
Bob Wallace, CEO/CFO

4405 Alan Plummer and Associates
1320 South University Drive 817-806-1700
Suite 300 *Fax:* 817-870-2536
Fort Worth, TX 76107-5737
Civil and environmental engineering consulting.
Alan H Plummer Jr, President

4406 Alar Engineering Corporation
9651 West 196th Street 708-479-6100
Mokena, IL 60448 *Fax:* 708-479-9059
www.alarcorp.com
Alex Doncer, President

4407 Alden Research Laboratory
30 Shrewsbury Street — 508-829-6000
Holden, MA 00152 — *Fax:* 508-829-5939
info@aldenlab.com
www.aldenlab.com
Hydraulic engineering firm solving air and water flow problems using physical and CFD models and field testing, for areas such as fish passage/protection systems, free surface and closed conduit flow, pump/turbine performance,hydraulic structures, environmental hydraulics, fluid equipment, 3D air flow, and flow meter calibration.
Stuart A. Cain, President
David K. Anderson, Vice President

4408 Allied Laboratories
716 North Iowa — 630-279-0390
Villa Park, IL 60181 — *Fax:* 630-279-3114
Irving I Domsky, Director

4409 Alloway Testing
1101 N Cole Street — 419-223-1362
Lima, OH 45805 — 800-436-1243
Fax: 419-227-3792
www.alloway.com
Environmental sampling and analysis laboratory.
John R Hoffman, President
Lana Jackson, Labrotary Manager

4410 Alpha Manufacturing Company
100 Old Barnwell Road — 803-739-4500
PO Box 2809 — *Fax:* 803-739-0517
West Columbia, SC 29170 — young@alphamfg.com
www.alphamfg.com
Physical testing of environmental testing and repair services, and instrument design.
Patricia O. Young, President & CEO
Dean Young, General Manager

4411 Alton Geoscience
650 Suffolk Street — 978-970-5600
Wannalancit Mills — *Fax:* 978-453-1995
Lowell, MA 01854 — www.trcsolutions.com
Environmental remediation and consulting firm.
Thomas W. Bennet, Jr., Chief Financial Officer
Larry Farrington, Contact

4412 Amalgamated Technologies
13901 N 73rd Street — 480-991-2901
Suite 208
Scottsdale, AZ 85260
Firm providing metals and materials development, processing and testing.
Roy E Beal, President

4413 American Environmental Network
9151 Rumsey Road — 410-730-8525
Suite 150 — *Fax:* 410-997-2586
Columbia, MD 21045
Paul Jackson, Marketing Manager

4414 American Testing Laboratory
11 Inductrial Road — 201-489-8573
Pequannock, NJ 00744 — 800-488-4951
Fax: 201-489-9365
info@mytestlab.com
www.americantestinglaboratory.com
Multidisciplinary testing laboratory offering a wide range of confidential testing services including environmental simulations (humidity, high/low temperature extremes).
Daniel Narbone, Manager

4415 American Waste Processing
2100 West Madison Street — 630-506-9977
Maywood, IL 60153 — *Fax:* 888-607-7441
www.americanrecyclingdisposal.com
Non-hazardous waste management, disposal/transfer, station/recycling, roll off containers.
William Vajdik, President

4416 Analab
One Omega Circle — 856-467-4555
Bridgeport, NJ 00801 — 800-262-5229
Fax: 856-467-1212
info@analab1.com
Compliance lab services for EMC/EMI, safety and ESD.
Jason Smith, Director/Manager

4417 Analyte Laboratories
2121 Cedar Circle Drive — 410-747-3844
Catonsville, MD 21228 — *Fax:* 410-747-4007

4418 Analytical Laboratories and Consulting
361 West 5th Avenue
Eugene, OR 97401 — 541-485-8404
Fax: 541-484-5995
Rory E White, Sr. Analyst

4419 Analytical Process Laboratories
8222 W Calumet Road — 414-355-3909
Milwaukee, WI 53223 — 800-236-3909
Fax: 414-355-3099
www.apl-inc.net
Materials analysis laboratory and environmental engineering.
Jitendra Shah, President
Rakesh Shah, Vice President

4420 Analytical Resources
4611 S 134th Place — 206-695-6200
Tukwila, WA 98168-3240 — *Fax:* 206-695-6201
www.arilabs.com
Environmental testing and analysis laboratory.
Mark Weidner, President
Stephanie Lucas, Project Manager

4421 Analytical Services
110 Technology Parkway — 770-734-4200
Nocross, GA 30092 — 800-ASI-7227
Fax: 770-734-4201
www.asi-lab.com
Environmental testing and analysis firm.
G Wyn Jones, President

4422 Anametrix
1961 Concourse Drive — 408-432-8192
Suite E — *Fax:* 408-432-8198
San Jose, CA 95131-1708
Doug Robbins, President

4423 AndCare
PO Box 14566 Parkway — 919-544-8220
Research Triangle Park, NC 27709 — *Fax:* 919-544-9808
Development and commercialization of low cost, simple to use diagnostic devices and tests for medical, environmental, and laboratory markets.
Dr. Steven Wagner, PhD, President

4424 Anderson Engineering Consultants
10205 W Rockwood Road — 501-455-4545
Little Rock, AR 72204 — *Fax:* 501-455-4552
aecigeo@comcast.net
www.aecigeo.com
Firm providing engineering, inspection, and testing services specializing in geotechnology and materials, and environmental sciences. Services include site studies, soil testing, engineering surveys, specification evaluation, andfailure investigation.

4425 Andrea Aromatics
PO Box 3091 609-695-7710
Princeton, NJ 00854 *Fax:* 609-392-8914
orders@andreaaromatics.com
www.andreaaromatics.com
Natural essential oils, fragrances, deodorants, odor neutralizers.

Michael D'Andrea, VP
Richard D'Andrea, President

4426 Anlab
1910 S Street 916-447-2946
Sacramento, CA 95814

4427 Anteon Corporation
3211 Jermantown Road 703-246-0200
Suite 200 *Fax:* 703-246-0797
Fairfax, VA 22030-2201
Joseph M. Kampf, CEO

4428 Applied Biomathematics
100 N Country Road 631-751-4350
Setauket, NY 11733 *Fax:* 631-751-3435
admin@ramas.com
www.ramas.com
Environmental and ecological software development firm.
Lev Ginzburg, President

4429 Applied Coastal Research & Engineering
766 Falmouth Road 508-539-3737
Suite A-1 *Fax:* 508-539-3739
Mashpee, MA 00264 info@appliedcoastal.com
www.appliedcoastal.com

Environmental analysis.
Mark Bynes PhD, President
John S. Ramsey, Senior Coastal Engineer

4430 Applied Technical Services
1049 Triad Court 770-423-1400
Marietta, GA 30066 888-287-5227
Fax: 770-514-3299
www.atslab.com
Environmental, chemical, and mechanical testing and consulting company.
Jim F Hill, President

4431 Aquatec Chemical International
408 Auburn Avenue 313-334-4747
Pontiac, MI 48342
Douglas Schwartz, President

4432 Ardaman & Associates
8008 S Orange Avenue 407-855-3860
Orlando, FL 32809 800-683-SOIL
Fax: 407-859-8121
mmongeau@ardaman.com
www.ardaman.com
Geotechnical, environmental and materials consultants.

Mark L Mongeau PE, Vice President

4433 Arete Associates
9301 Corbin Avenue 818-885-2201
Northridge, CA 91324 *Fax:* 818-885-2210
info@arete.com
www.arete.com

Environmental research.
John Mclean, President & CEO
David Kane, Vice President

4434 Aroostook Testing & Consulting Laboratory
160 Airport Drive 207-762-5771
Presque Isle, ME 00476 *Fax:* 207-764-8123
www.aroostooktesting.com
Toxiological and environmental laboratory.

G Noel Currie III, President

4435 Arro Laboratory
425 Caton Farm Road 815-727-5436
Crest Hill, IL 60431 www.arrolab.com
Provides environmental and chemical testing services for wastewater, drinking water, in addition to product quality control and process troubleshooting. They offer their services to manufacturers, municipalities, and design orengineering firms.

Joan Rolih, President

4436 Artesian Laboratories
630 Churchmans Road 302-266-9121
Newark, DE 19702 *Fax:* 302-454-8720
Environmental sampling and testing laboratory. Research results published in methods reports to clients.

4437 Association of Ecosystem Research Centers
730 11th Street NW 202-628-1500
Washington, DC 20001 *Fax:* 202-628-1509
aerc@culter.colorado.edu
www.ecosystemresearch.org
Brings together 39 US research programs in universities and private, state and federal laboratories that conduct research, provide training and analyze policy at the ecosystem level of environmental science and natural resourcesmanagement. Although AERC is an association of professional scientists rather than environmental activists, its goals and interest complement those of conservation organizations.
John A. Arnone III, President
Lucinda Johnson, Secretary

4438 Astro-Chem Services
4102 2nd Avenue W 701-572-7355
PO Box 972 800-568-6614
Williston, ND 58801 *Fax:* 701-774-3907
info@astrochemlab.com
www.astrochemlab.com
A modern analytical laboratory that specializes in the in the petroleum and agricultural industry

David Zander, President
Bruce Kyllo, Lab Manager

4439 Astro-Pure Water Purifiers
1441 SW 1st Way 954-422-8966
Deerfield Beach, FL 33441 *Fax:* 954-422-8966
Manufacturers complete line of water treatment equipment, purifiers, De Calcifiers, R.O., V.V., iron filters, chemical feed equipment. Sizes for portable, point of use, central commercial and industrial. Manufacturers and privatelabels counter top units.

RL Stefl, President

4440 Atlantic Testing Laboratories
6431 US Highway 11 315-386-4578
Canton, NY 13617 *Fax:* 315-386-1012
WBell@AtlanticTesting.com
www.atlantictesting.com
ATL is a full-service engineering support firm offering environmental services, subsurface investigations, water-based services, geotechnical engineering, construction materials testing and engineering, special inspections,nondestructive testing, and more.

William J. Bell, Assistant VP, Operations
James A. Trathen, Operations Manager

4441 Atlas Weathering Services Group
45601 N 47th Avenue 623-465-7356
Phoenix, AZ 85087 800-255-3738
Fax: 623-465-9409
atlas.info@ametek.com
atlas-mts.com
Technical research firm specializing in environmental testing. Research results published in reports to clients and in archival journals.
Jack Martin, President

4442 Atmospheric & Environmental Research
131 Hartwell Avenue 781-761-2288
Lexington, MA 00242 *Fax:* 781-761-2299
aer@aer.com
www.aer.com
Firm providing research, consulting, and assessment on atmospheric chemistry, meteorology, climate, and air quality.
Ron Isaacs, President & CEO
David B. Hogan, Executive Vice President

4443 Axiom Laboratories
24 Tobey Road 860-242-6291
Bloomfield, CT 00600 *Fax:* 860-286-0634
Environmental and materials analytical testing services.
William AG Macke, President

4444 B&P Laboratories
5635 Delridge Way SW 206-937-3644
Seattle, WA 98106 *Fax:* 206-937-1348
mail@bplabs.net
www.bplabs.net
Environmental testing and chemical laboratory water analyses (ICP);Mercury analyzer sulfates, fluorides, chlorides (DIONEX); cyandes (CONTES); storm waters; fats, oil & grease (FOG); Karl Fischer corrosion testing; process solutions
Victor Broto, President

4445 BC Analytical
4100 Atlas Court 661-327-4911
Bakersfield, CA 93308 *Fax:* 661-327-1918
www.bclabs.com
Lab capabilities include diversified sample matrices for drinkg waters, ground water monitoring and waste acceptance. Diversified analytical methods include general chemistry and field services including field analysis, sampling andcourier service.
Carolyn Jackson, President
Richard Eglin, Vice President

4446 BC Laboratories
4100 Atlas Court 661-327-4911
Bakersfield, CA 93308 *Fax:* 661-327-1918
www.bclabs.com
Chemical analysis and environmental monitoring of hazardous waste. Research results published in project reports.
Carolyn Jackson, President
Richard Eglin, Vice President

4447 BC Research
200 Granville Street 604-224-4331
Suite 1800 *Fax:* 604-224-0540
Vancouver, BC V6C1S info@bcri.ca
www.bcri.ca
Research results published in scientific journals and trade magazines.
Hassan Hamza, President
Kevin Dodds, CFO

4448 BCI Engineers & Scientists
2000 Edgewood Drive 863-667-2345
Suite 215 877-550-4224
Lakeland, FL 33807 *Fax:* 863-667-2262
www.bcieng.com
Environmental and civil engineering, geotechnical processes, and chemical research and development firm.
Rick Powers, President/CEO
Wendy Lee, Chief Financial Officer

4449 BCM Engineers
5415 SW Westgate Drive 503-419-2500
Suite 100 *Fax:* 503-419-2600
Portland, OR 97221 www.cardno.com
Services include environmental, geotechnical and materials, remedial design, industrial hygiene and hazardous management planning.
Richard Wankmuller, CEO & Managing Director
Trevor Johnson, General Manager

4450 Babcock & Wilcox Company
13024 Ballantyne Corporate Place 704-625-4900
Suite 700 *Fax:* 704-625-4910
Charlotte, NC 22827 www.babcock.com
Deliver innovative technologies and solutions to fulfill the needs of our customers
E.James Ferland, President
Jenny L. Apker, Vice President

4451 Badger Laboratories
501 West Bell Street 920-729-1100
Neenah, WI 54956 800-776-7196
Fax: 920-729-4945
www.badgerlabs.com
Badger Laboratories and Engineering provides customers with analytical, engineering and technical services focusing on the environmental field. The labs specialize in the testing and sampling of drinking water, groundwater, wastewater,solids and hazardous waste.
Richard Larson, President
Jeff Wagner, Lab Manager

4452 Baird Scientific
532 Oak Street 417-358-5567
Carthage, MO 64836
Gary Baird, President/Owner

4453 Baker Environmental
420 Rouser Road 412-269-6000
Coraopolis, PA 15108 *Fax:* 412-269-2534
Environmental engineering company.
Andrew P Paja, President

4454 Baker-Shiflett
5701 East Loop 820 South 817-478-8254
Fort Worth, TX 76119 *Fax:* 817-478-8874
Larry Gardner, Administrative Manager

4455 Barnebey & Sutcliffe Corporation
835 North Cassady Avenue 614-258-9501
PO Box 2526 *Fax:* 614-258-0222
Columbus, OH 43216 www.bscairfiltration.com
Unparalleled technical assistance in selection of the most cost-effective activated carbon for the application
Amanda L Fisher, Marketing Coordinator

4456 Barton & Loguidice
443 Electronics Parkway 315-457-5200
Liverpool, NY 13088 800-724-1070
Fax: 315-451-0052
info@BartonandLoguidice.com
www.BartonandLoguidice.com
B&L helps communities throughout the Northeast and Mid-Atlantic states meet their engineering, environmental science, planning, and landscape architecture needs. Provides planning, funding procurement, site design, engineering, andconstruction phase services for projects involving facilities, sustainable design, green infrastructure, recreational facilities, renewable energy, site utilities, water and wastewater, solid waste, transportation, community revitalization, andenvironmental issues.
John F. Brusa Jr., President/CEO
John A. Benson, Sr. Vice President

4457 Baxter and Woodman
8678 Ridgefield Road 815-459-1260
Crystal Lake, IL 60012 *Fax:* 815-455-0450
info@baxterwoodman.com
www.baxterwoodman.com
Provides services in the planning, design, and construction of public infrastructure. Focus is given to municipal technology,

water preservation, wastewater treatment, road and highway development, environmental design, and more.

Joanna MacCallum, Marketing Manager
John P. Mick II, Division Manager, Illinois

4458 Bell Evaluation Laboratory
17300 Mercury Drive 281-488-3701
Houston, TX 77058 *Fax:* 281-488-8543
www.bellabs.com
Coating testing and evaluation firm.
Bob Bell, Contact
Monte Middlebrooks, Contact

4459 Belle W Baruch Institute for Marine Biology and Coastal Research
607 EWS Building 803-777-5288
Columbia, SC 29208 *Fax:* 803-777-3935
Conducts basic and applied research in marine and coastal environments.
Jim Morris, Director
Margaret Bergin, Business Manager

4460 Beltran Associates
1133 East 35th Street 718-338-3311
Brooklyn, NY 11210 *Fax:* 718-253-9028
info@beltrantechnologies.com
www.beltrantechnologies.com
A leader in advanced gas cleaning and air pollution control for a broad spectrum of industrial processes and emission requirements. Our reputation is based on 50 years of successful research, development and problem solving leading tomore than 1000 installations worldwide.

Mike Beltran, President
Swapan Mitra, Sales Manager

4461 Benchmark Analytics
4777 Saucon Creek Road 610-974-8100
Center Valley, PA 18034-9004 *Fax:* 610-974-8104
f.adamsky@benchmarkanalyticslabs.com
Benchmark Analytics is an independent analytical testing laboratory. Benchmark analyzes many types of samples including drinking water, wastewater and soil in addition to testing food, mold, sludge, soot, air samples and industrialproducts.
Fiona Adamsky, General Manager

4462 Bhate Environmental Associates
1608 13th Avenue South 205-918-4000
Suite 300 *Fax:* 205-918-4050
Birmingham, AL 35205 www.bhate.com
Provides environmental, technical, and infrastructural services to the government and private industry. Services include environmental remediation and compliance, bulk fuels storage, construction services, demolition, and more.

Johnny Roberts, Chief Executive Officer
Sam Bhate, President

4463 Bio-Chem Analysts Inc
4940 North Memorial Pkwy 256-859-2161
PO Box 3270 *Fax:* 256-859-9222
Huntsville, AL 35810
Environmental testing of water, wastewater, air, soil, and hazardous waste.

Vijay Thakore, President

4464 Bio-Science Research Institute
4813 Cheyenne Way 909-628-3007
Chino, CA 91710 *Fax:* 909-590-8948
Independent environmental testing laboratory.

4465 Bio/West
1063 West 1400 North 435-752-4202
Logan, UT 84321-2291 *Fax:* 435-752-0507
www.bio-west.com
Using scientific principles, making sound resource decisions, and providing context-sensitive solutions for more than 35 years
Darren Oslen, President
Ed Oborny, Vice President

4466 Biomarine
16 E Main Street 978-281-0222
PO Box 1153 *Fax:* 978-283-6296
Gloucester, MA 00193 www.biomarinelab.com
Provides water and seafood analysis and consulting for the public, private companies and government.

Jim Groleau, Laboratory Director
John Marletta, Vice President

4467 Bionetics Corporation Analytical Laboratories
20 Research Drive 757-865-0880
Hampton, VA 23666 *Fax:* 757-865-8014
Joseph A Stern, President

4468 Bioscience
966 Postal Road 484-245-5232
Suite 200 800-627-3069
Allentown, PA 18109 *Fax:* 484-245-5236
bioscience@bioscienceinc.com
www.bioscienceinc.com
Specialized microbes for wastewater and hazardous waste, biological treatment. BOD and COD monitoring instruments and test kits for water and wastewater analysis.

Thomas G Zitrides, President
Richard Bleam, Director of Technical Svc.

4469 Biospherics
12051 Indian Creek Court 301-419-3900
Beltsville, MD 20705 *Fax:* 301-210-4909
Gilbert V Levin, PhD, President

4470 Black Rock Test Lab
5 Eastgate Plaza 304-296-8347
Morgantown, WV 26501

4471 BlazeTech Corporation
29B Montvale Ave 781-759-0700
Woburn, MA 00180 *Fax:* 781-759-0703
office@blazetech.com
www.blazetech.com
An engineering consulting firm specializing in fire, explosion, environmental safety and homeland defense. They have developed specialized software for the chemical, petroleum, aerospace and power industries: ADORA, BLAZETANK andothers.
Albert Moussa, President

4472 Bollyky Associates
31 Strawberry Hill Avenue 203-967-4223
Stamford, CT 06902 *Fax:* 203-967-4845
ljbbai@bai-ozone.com
www.bai-ozone.com
Engineering firm specializing in Ozone technology, water and wastewater treatment, treatability studies, and consulting services.
L Joseph Bollyky, President

4473 Braun Intertec Corporation
11001 Hampshire Avenue S 952-995-2000
Minneapolis, MN 55438 800-279-6100
Fax: 952-995-2020
bborth@braunintertec.com
braunintertec.com
An engineering firm providing consulting, management, and testing services to clients in the commercial, real estate, institutional, retail, financial, and government markets. Some services include environmental and geothermalconsulting, geospacial op-

erations, construction materials testing, structures evaluation and more.

Jon Carlson, Chief Executive Officer
Robert Janssen, President

4474 Briggs Associates
2300 Holcomb Bridge Road 770-993-4559
Suite 103, #366 *Fax:* 781-871-7982
Roswell, GA 30076 briggscentral@briggsassociates.org
www.briggsassociates.org
Environmental engineering and testing facility.
Meet David Kimmel, President/COO
Meet Al Blackwelder, COO

4475 Brighton Analytical
2105 Pless Drive 810-229-7575
Brighton, MI 48114 *Fax:* 810-229-8650
bai-brighton@sbcglobal.net
www.brightonanalytical.net
Specializes in the area of Environmental Laboratory Testing Services.
J Shawn Letwin, Laboratory Director

4476 Brooks Companies
3900 Essex Ln 713-337-2222
Suite 555 866-454-1900
Houston, TX 77027 *Fax:* 713-337-2239
www.brookecompanies.com
Margaret Y Brooks PhD, President

4477 Brotcke Engineering Company
750 Merus Court 636-343-3029
PO Box 1168 800-969-3029
Fenton, MO 63026-2028 *Fax:* 636-343-3773
www.brotcke.com
Professional engineering firm that provides well drilling and pump services.
Paul Brotcke, President

4478 Buchart-Horn
3700 Koppers Street 717-852-1400
Suite 540 800-274-2224
Baltimore, MD 21227 ckinney@bh-ba.com
www.bh-ba.com
This company provides environmental engineering, consulting, civil engineering, facility design and planning as well as laboratory and testing services.
Brian S. Funkhouser, President/CEO
Stephanie A. Schaefer, Regional Manager

4479 Burt Hill Kosar Rittelmann Associates
400 Morgan Center 724-285-4761
101 East Diamond Street *Fax:* 724-285-6815
Butler, PA 16001 www.burthill.com
John Brock, Chief Operating Office/Vice
Michael Carter, Principal

4480 Business Health Environmental Lab
33 E 7th Street 859-431-6224
300 Doctors Building *Fax:* 859-431-6228
Covington, KY 41011
Dan Moos, President

4481 C L Technology Division of Microbac Lab
101 Bellevue Road 412-459-1060
Suite 301 *Fax:* 866-515-4668
Pittsburgh, PA 15229-2132 microbac_info@microbac.com
www.microbac.com
Research and development laboratory specializing in analysis and testing. Services include: air quality; environmental testing, consulting and analysis; nutraceutical testing and analysis; consumer products testing; food producttesting; fuel and manufactured products testing.
J Trevor Boyce, Chairman/CEO
James Nokes, President

4482 CDS Laboratories
52 Biomedical Education Building
South Campus 716-829-2797
Buffalo, NY 14214 *Fax:* 716-829-3979
cdsdept@buffalo.edu
arts-sciences.buffalo.edu/cds/about.html
The department of Communicative Disorders and Sciences offers basic and clinical research from the molecular level to patient oriented diagnostic and rehabilitative research.
Carol M. Altman, Sr. Administrative Assistant
MaryAnn L. Doskocz, Department Administrator

4483 CENSOL
582 Hawthorne 416-219-6950
L9T-4N8 *Fax:* 905-878-8775
Milton, ON L9T4N contactme@censol.ca
www.laughton.ca
Environmental consulting and testing firm. Research results published in technical association papers.

4484 CET Environmental Services
7032 South Revere Parkway 720-875-9115
Englewood, CO 80112 *Fax:* 720-875-9114
Provides environmental consulting, engineering, remediation & construction servies. There are three primary segments: Industrial services, environmental remediation & government. programs.
Steven H Davis, President & CEO
Dale W Bleck, CFO

4485 CPAC
2364 Leicester Road 585-382-3223
PO Box 175 800-828-6011
Leicester, NY 14481 *Fax:* 585-382-3031
cpacinfo@cpac.com
www.cpac.com
CPAC, Inc. manages holdings in two industries: Cleaning and Personal Care and Imaging. The Fuller Brands segment develops, manufactures, and markets over 2799 branded and private lavel products for commercial cleaning, householdcleaning, and personal care. CPAC Imaging manufactures, packages, and distrubtes branded and private label chemicals for photographic, health care, and graphic arts markets as well as associated imaging equipment and silver refining services.
Thomas N Hendrickson, President

4486 Cardno ATC
10004 Park Meadows Drive 720-257-5800
Suite 300 *Fax:* 720-257-5801
Lone Tree, CO 80124 www.cardno.com
An infrastructure, environmental, and social development consulting firm offering services in environmental design, planning, software, construction management, material testing and more.
Ian Ball, Chief Executive Officer
Peter Barker, Chief Financial Officer

4487 Cascadia Research
218 1/2 W 4th Avenue 360-943-7325
Olympia, WA 98501 800-747-7329
calambokidis@cascadiaresearch.org
www.cascadiaresearch.org
Nonprofit tax-exempt scientific and educational organization founded to conduct research needed to manage and protect threatened marine mammals.

4488 Cedar Grove Environmental Laboratories
1401 Gallagherville Road 610-269-6977
Downingtown, PA 19335 *Fax:* 610-269-6965
www.cgelab.com
Environmental analysis firm serving agriculture and industry.

4489 Ceimic Corporation
10 Dean Knauss Drive 401-782-8900
Narragansett, RI 00288 *Fax:* 401-782-8905
www.ceimic.com

Environmental testing for water and soil.
Margaret Marple, Marketing
John McGarry, President

4490 Center for Solid & Hazardous Waste Management
1929 Stadium Road Nuclear Science 352-392-6264
Bldg 634, Room No. 528 *Fax:* 352-846-0183
Gainesville, FL 32611 rogersrd@ufl.edu
www.hinkleycenter.org
The center serves the citizens of Florida by providing leadership in the field of waste management research and by supporting the Florida Department of Environmental Protection in its mission to preserve and protect the state's naturalresources.
Nandra Weeks, Chairman
Sumpter H. Barker, President

4491 Center for Technology, Policy & Industrial Development
77 Massachusetts Avenue 617-324-7103
Building E38-600 *Fax:* 617-258-7845
Cambridge, MA 00213-4307 ssrcinfo@mit.edu
Environmental research.

Deborah Nightingale, Director
Nicolene Hengen, Assistant Director for Strat

4492 Central Virginia Laboratories and Consultants
3109 Odd Fellows Road 804-847-2852
PO Box 10938 *Fax:* 804-847-2830
Lynchburg, VA 24506
Adrian K Mood, President

4493 Century West Engineering Corporation
5331 SW Macadam Ave 503-419-2130
Suite 207 *Fax:* 503-639-2710
Portland, OR 97239 www.centurywest.com
Matt MacRostie, Project Manager
Ron Weigel, Project Manager

4494 Chas. T Main: Environmental Division
Prudential Center 617-262-3200
Boston, MA 00219 *Fax:* 781-401-2575
Environmental consulting firm specializing in site assessments, surveys, and tests and analysis.

4495 Chemical Resource Processing
2525 Battleground Road 281-930-2525
PO Box 1914 *Fax:* 281-930-2535
Deer Park, TX 77536
Environmental consulting and chemical processing firm.

4496 Chemical Waste Disposal Corporation
4214 19th Avenue 718-274-3339
Astoria, NY 11105 *Fax:* 718-726-7917
Environmental waste disposal and consulting company.

4497 Chemir Analytical Services
2672 Metro Boulevard 314-291-6620
Maryland Heights, MO 63043 800-659-7659
Fax: 314-291-6630
info@chemir.com
www.chemir.com
Provides a wide range of chemical analysis and chemical testing services. Experienced at solving difficult problems including product failure analysis, materials identification, plastic testing or reverse engineering. An independenttesting lab with scientists that can provide litigation support such as expert witness testimony in intellectual property or products liability cases.

Dr Shri Thanedar, President

4498 Chesner Engineering
38 West Park Avenue 516-431-4031
Suite 200 *Fax:* 516-717-2621
Long Beach, NY 11561 cemail@chesnerengineering.com
www.chesnerengineering.com
Civil, environmental, and waste management firm that provides professional services to industry and government. Specializes in the areas of waste and by-product material recycling and stabliization, marine and dredge environmentalmanagement, risk assessment and environmental modeling, environmental database program development, remedial site investigations and cleanup management, and water and wastewater treatment.
Warren Chesner, President

4499 Chihuahuan Desert Research Institute
43869 SH 118 432-364-2499
PO Box 905 *Fax:* 432-364-2686
Fort Davis, TX 79734 www.cdri.org
Conducts research on the Chihuahuan Desert.
Shirley Powell, President
Rick Herrman, Executive Director

4500 ChromatoChem
2837 Fort Missoula Road 406-728-5897
Missoula, MT 59801 *Fax:* 406-728-5924
Biotechnology firm. Research results published in proposals to the Environmental Protection Agency.
Bob Perciasepe, Administrator
Arthur A. Elkins, Jr. Inspector General

4501 Chyun Associates
267 Wall Street 609-924-5151
Princeton, NJ 00854

4502 Clark Engineering Corporation
621 Lilac Drive N 763-545-9196
Minneapolis, MN 55422-4609 877-246-9196
Fax: 763-541-0056
info@clark-eng.com
www.clark-eng.com
Offer structural engineering, civil engineering, and land surveying services throughout the world.
Dr. Abi Assadi, PE, President
Doug Fell, PE, Executive VP/CEO

4503 Clark's Industrial Hygiene and Environmental Laboratory
1801 Route 51 S 412-387-1001
Building 9 888-325-8517
Jefferson Hills, PA 15025 *Fax:* 412-387-1027
info@clarktesting.com
www.clarktesting.com
General industrial hygiene consulting and field services laboratory that provides support to the environmental efforts of industry, both light and heavy, refineries, power industry, aluminum, steel and environmental consulting firms.Maintains AIHA (American Industrial Hygiene Association) accreditation for asbestos (PLM and PCM), metals, organic solvents, diffusive samplers and silica.
Paul Heffernan, CEO
Lee Rogers, Quality Assurance Manager

4504 Clean Harbors
42 Longwater Drive 781-792-5000
PO Box 9149 800-282-7158
Norwell, MA 00206-9149 *Fax:* 781-282-0058
www.cleanharbors.com
Environmental consulting firm specializing in soil analysis, site assessments, and water sample testing.
Alan S. Mckim, Chairman & CEO
James M. Rutledge, Vice Chairman

4505 Clean Water Systems
2322 Marina Drive 541-882-9993
Klamath Falls, OR 97601-146 *Fax:* 541-882-9994
sales@cleanwatersysintl.com
www.cleanwatersysintl.com
Environmental research firm. Designs, develops and manufactures ultra-violet electronic water purification units and systems and electronic measuring systems. The Company has developed lines of proprietary electronic monitoring andcontrol systems and electronic ballast.
Charles Romary, President

4506 **CleanAir Engineering**
500 West Wood Street 847-991-3300
Palatine, IL 60067-4929 800-553-5511
info@cleanair.com
www.cleanair.com

Environmental consulting firm for air quality management, emissions measurement, and thermal performance and efficiency determination. CleanAir Engineering also offers permitting services, process engineering, emergency responsemonitoring, and measurement and analytical services.

Allen Kephart, President & CEO
Anthony Milianti, Project Engineer

4507 **Coastal Resources**
25 Old Solomons Island Road 410-956-9000
Annapolis, MD 24101 *Fax:* 410-956-0566
coastal@coastal-resources.net
www.coastal-resources.net

Environmental impact assessments and nontidal wetlands identification expert testimony. Also conducts field investigations for a broad range of natural resources including soils, wetlands, streams, water quality, forests, wildlife,habitats and rare, threatened and endangered species.

Betsy M Weinkam, President/Enviro Biologist
Chuck Weinkam, Sr Environmental Scientist

4508 **Colorado Analytical**
240 S Main Avenue 303-659-2313
PO Box 507 *Fax:* 303-659-2315
Brighton, CO 80601 info@coloradolab.com
www.coloradolab.com

Agricultural consulting and testing laboratory. Research results published in project reports and test summaries.

4509 **Colorado Research Associates**
4118 148th Ave NE 425-556-9055
Redmond, WA 98052-5164 *Fax:* 425-556-9099
info@nwra.com
www.nwra.com

Environmental research.
Debbi Bardsley, Manager Of HR
Marie Barrington, Accounts Receivable

4510 **Columbus Instruments International**
950 N Hague Avenue 614-276-0861
Columbus, OH 43204 800-669-5011
Fax: 614-276-0529
sales@colinst.com
www.colinst.com

Manufacturer of biomedical and environmental research equipment which includes respirometers and gas analysis monitoring systems.
Jan Czekdjewski, President
Ken Kober, Sales Manager

4511 **Columbus Water and Chemical Testing Laboratory**
4628 Indianola Avenue 614-262-4372
Columbus, OH 43214

4512 **Commonwealth Technology**
1263 E. New Circle Road 859-294-3911
Lexington, KY 40505 800-755-5672
Fax: 859-276-4374
www.commonwealthtechnology.com

Environmental engineering and analysis firm.
Troy W. Turner, President
Patricia Ulrich, Vice President

4513 **CompuChem Environmental Corporation**
501 Madison Avenue 919-379-4100
Cary, NC 27513 800-833-5097
Fax: 919-379-4050
markross@compuchemlabs.com

Environmental testing laboratory.
Kenneth Grzybowski, Vice President
Mark Ross, VP of Sales & Marketing

4514 **Conjun Laboratories**
9283 Highway 15 606-633-8027
Isom, KY 41824

4515 **Container Testing Laboratory**
P.O. Box 60508 805-683-5825
Santa Barbara, CA 93106 *Fax:* 805-683-5625
sales@containertechnology.com
www.containertechnology.com

Independent third party testing laboratory.
Anton Cotaj, Laboratory Director/Manager

4516 **Contaminated Site Clean-Up Information**
William Jefferson Clinton Federal B 703-603-8733
1200 Pennsylvania Avenue, N.W 800-527-3272
Washington, DC 20460-2298 *Fax:* 703-603-9135
www.clu-in.org

CLU-IN, a US Environmental Protection Agency forum, provides information about innovative treatment and site characterization technologies while acting as a forum for all waste remediation stakeholders.

Pamela Barr, Division Director
Jeff Heimerman, Associate Division Director

4517 **Conti Testing Laboratories**
3190 Industrial Blvd 412-833-7766
PO Box 174 *Fax:* 412-854-0373
Bethel Park, PA 15102 contilab@verizon.net
www.contitesting.com

Analytical commerical laboratory, fuel analysis (coal, coke, alternative fuels), metals, ore barge gauging, customize analysis.
Patricia A Otroba, President
Timothy Otrobe, CEO

4518 **Continental Systems**
7870 Deering Avenue 818-340-3217
Canoga Park, CA 91304 *Fax:* 818-340-2405
Environmental laboratory specializing in soil and water analysis.
Janis Butler, President

4519 **Controlled Environment Corporation**
Gorham Industrial Park 207-854-9126
29 Sanford Drive 800-569-5444
Gorham, ME 00403 *Fax:* 207-854-4357
ceec@ceecusa.com
www.ceecusa.com

Firm providing research, design, and development services relating to clean rooms and contamination control.
Matthew F Pec, President

4520 **Controls for Environmental Pollution**
1925 Rosina Street 505-982-9841
Box 5351 800-545-2188
Santa Fe, NM 87502 *Fax:* 505-982-9289

James J Mueller, President

4521 **Converse Consultants**
717 South Myrtle Avenue 626-930-1200
Monrovia, CA 91016 *Fax:* 626-930-1212
converse@converseconsultants.com
www.converseconsultants.com

Environmental consulting and engineering firm offering services in geotechnical engineering, materials testing, water resource management, environmental science, and laboratory services.

Hashmi S. Quazi, President & Chair
Ruben L. Romero, Chief Financial Officer

4522 **Copper State Analytical Lab**
1050 Spire Drive Suite I 928-443-5227
Prescott, AZ 86305 *Fax:* 928-443-5277
info@prescottlab.com
www.prescottlab.com

Hazardous waste characterization, organic and inorganic waste oil characterization, waste water analysis, potable water analysis, microbiology, general waters and soil chemistry.

D.A. Shah, President
Andrew Shah, Lab Manager

4523 Corning
1 Riverfront Plaza 607-974-9000
Corning, NY 14831 Inquiries@corning.com
www.corning.com

Corning is one of the world's leading innovators in materials science. For more than 160 years, Corning has applied its unparalleled expertise in speciality glass, ceramics, and optical physics to develop products that have created newindustries and transformed people's lives.
Wendell P. Weeks, Chairman/CEO
James B. Flaws, Vice Chair/CFO

4524 Corrosion Testing Laboratories
60 Blue Hen Drive 302-454-8200
Newark, DE 19713 *Fax:* 302-454-8204
web@corrosionlab.net
www.corrosionlab.com
Corrosion testing laboratory. Research results published in technical journals and conference proceedings.
Randy Nixon, President/Senior Consultant
Bradley D. Krantz, Vice President

4525 Coshocton Environmental Testing Service
709 Main Street 740-622-3328
Coshocton, OH 43812 800-870-6570
Fax: 740-622-3368
cets1@hotmail.com
www.cets1.com

Environmental testing service.

4526 Crane Environmental
2650 Eisenhower Avenue 610-631-7700
Bldg 100A 800-828-2447
Trooper, PA 19403 *Fax:* 610-631-6800
www.craneenv.com
Industrial water treatment equipment.

4527 Crosby & Overton
1610 W 17th Street 562-432-5445
Long Beach, CA 90813 800-827-6729
Fax: 562-436-7540
rangeles@crosbyoverton.com
www.crosbyoverton.com
Fully permitted RCRA Part B TSD facility located in Southern California. The Facility can process both bulk and drummed waste, including lab-packs. Crosby & Overton can process a wide variety of D,F,K,P and U listed RCRA waste.
Bob Ritter, Sales Manager
Raquel Angeles, Customer Service

4528 Curtis & Tompkins
2323 5th Street 510-486-0900
Berkeley, CA 94710 *Fax:* 510-486-0532
C Bruce Godfrey, President
Maggie Chan, CFO

4529 Cyberchron Corporation
33 Corporate Park Drive 845-765-8120
Suite 'A' *Fax:* 845-765-8119
Hopewell Junction, NY 12533 cybersales@cyberchron.com
www.cyberchron.com
Computer manufacturing firm specializing in the development of computers designed to withstand extreme travel, environmental, and work conditions.
Christopher R. Fadden, Vice President

4530 Cyrus Rice Consulting Group
1200 Fourth Avenue 412-269-2468
Coraopolis, PA 15108 *Fax:* 412-375-7507
support@cyrusrice.com
www.cyrusrice.com

Al Owens, VP

4531 DE3
2800 Woods Hollow Road 608-274-4330
Madison, WI 53711 800-356-9526
Fax: 608-277-2516
custserv@promega.com
Environmental engineering research and testing firm.
Harold N Danto, President

4532 DLZ
1425 Keystone Avenue 517-393-6800
PO Box 22127 800-336-5352
Lansing, MI 48911 *Fax:* 517-272-7390
www.dlzcorp.com
Consulting structural engineers.
Vikram (Raj) Rajadhyaksha, P.E., Chairman/CEO
Robert Kirkley, P.E., L.S., President

4533 DLZ Laboratories - Cleveland
614 W Superior Avenue 216-771-1090
Suite 1000 800-336-5352
Cleveland, OH 44113 *Fax:* 216-771-0334
dlzroundabouts.com
www.dlz.com
DLZ, a minority-owned business enterprise, is a full-service, multidisciplinary professional corporation that provides complete architectural, engineering, and environmental services to both the public and private sectors. Researchstudies are published in professional journals and project reports.
Vikram Rajadhyaksha, Chairman
Ram Rajyadhyaksha, Vice President

4534 DLZ Laboratories - Columbus/Corporate
6121 Huntley Road 614-888-0040
Columbus, OH 43229 800-336-5352
Fax: 614-436-0161
www.dlz.com
DLZ, a minority-owned business enterprise, is a full-service, multidisciplinary professional corporation that provides complete architectural, engineering, and environmental services to both the public and private sectors. Researchstudies are published in professional journals and project reports.
Vikram Rajadhyaksha, Chairman
Ram Rajyadhyaksha, Vice President

4535 DLZ Laboratories - Cuyahoga Falls
1 Canal Square Plaza 330-923-0401
Suite 1300 800-336-5352
Akron, OH 44308 *Fax:* 330-928-1029
dlz.com
DLZ, a minority-owned business enterprise, is a full-service, multidisciplinary professional corporation that provides complete architectural, engineering, and environmental services to both the public and private sectors. Researchstudies are published in professional journals and project reports.
Vikram Rajadhyaksha, P.E., Chairman
Ram Rajyadhyaksha, P.E., Vice President

4536 DOWL HKM
4041 B Street 907-562-2000
Anchorage, AK 99503 *Fax:* 800-865-9847
www.dowl.com
Serves clients' needs in the areas of environmental planning, National Environmental Policy Act (NEPA) documentation, permitting, engineering and public involvement. Environmental studies and analyses include wetland delineation andfunction and values assessment, vegetation mapping, GIS mapping and analysis, environmental site assessment, air and noise impact

analysis. Section 106 consultation, hydrology studies, and secondary and cumulative impact analysis.

Dayton H. Alsaker P.E., Wyoming Region Manager
Raymond L. Armstrong P.E., BCEE, Senior Project Manager

4537 DW Ryckman and Associates REACT Environmental Engineers
1120 S 6th Street 314-678-1398
St. Louis, MO 63104-3628 800-325-1398
Fax: 314-678-6610
stewart_ryckman@reactenvironmental.com
www.reactenvironmental.com
D.W. Ryckman & Associates, Inc., d.b.a. REACT Environmental Engineers, was founded in 1975 to provide rapid response and remediation services for environmental and hazardous contamination problems.

SE Ryckman, President

4538 Daily Analytical Laboratories
1621 West Candletree Drive 309-692-5252
Peoria, IL 61614 *Fax:* 309-692-0488
Kurt Stepping, Chief Chemist

4539 Dan Raviv Associates
57 E Willow Street 973-564-6006
Millburn, NJ 00704 *Fax:* 973-564-6442
www.danraviv.com
Environmental consulting firm specializing in environmental impact studies, waste management, site assessment and litigation support.
Dan D Raviv PhD, President
John J Trela PhD, Director/Manager

4540 Danaher Corporation
2200 Pennsylvania Avenue NW 202-828-0850
Suite 800 W *Fax:* 202-828-0860
Washington, DC 20037 www.danaher.com
Development of process and environmental controls, tools and components.
Thomas P. Joyce, President
Daniel L. Comas, Executive VP/CFO

4541 Datachem Laboratories
960 W Levoy Drive 801-266-7700
Salt Lake City, UT 84123 *Fax:* 801-268-9992
Brent.Stephens@alsglobal.com
www.alsglobal.com
Analytical laboratory provides lab analysis of soil, water, air and asbestos samples.
Greg Kilmister, Managing Director/CEO
Nerolie Withnall, BA, LLB, FAICD, Chairman

4542 Davis Research
23801 Calabasas Rd. 818-591-2408
Suite 1036 *Fax:* 818-591-2488
Calabasas, CA 91302-1595 info@davisresearch.com
www.davisresearch.com
Agricultural, food and environmental testing and research firm.
Bill Davis, CEO
Bob Davis, Chief Technical Officer

4543 Dellavalle Laboratory
1910 W McKinley Avenue 559-233-6129
Suite 110 800-228-9896
Fresno, CA 93728 *Fax:* 818-591-2488
www.dellavallelab.com
Agricultural laboatory analyzes plant, soil, manure and water (ag, domestic, wastewater). Certified Professional Soil Scientits/Agronomists/Crop Advisors and others provide consultation on nutrient and fertilizer management, cropfeasibility, regulatory compliance, troubleshooting and related areas.

Hugh A Rathbun, President
Bill Davis, CEO

4544 Department of Commerce: National Oceanic & Atmospheric Administration
1401 Constitution Avenue NW www.noaa.gov
Room 5128
Washington, DC 20230
The mission of the NOAA is to understand changes in climate, weather, oceans and coasts; to share that knowledge and information with the public; and to foster the conservation and management of coastal and marine ecosystems. Theagency studies the structure and behaviour of the ocean, atmosphere, and related ecosystems.

Neil Jacobs, Assistant Secretary
Craig McLean, Chief Scientist

4545 Douglass Environmental Services
8649 Bash Street 317-595-9108
Indianapolis, IN 46256 *Fax:* 317-822-8362
Environmental engineering and testing firm.

4546 Duke Solutions
1 Winthrop Square 617-482-8228
Boston, MA 00211 *Fax:* 617-482-3784

4547 Dynamac Corporation
CSS-Dynamac, 10301 Democracy Lane 703-691-4612
Suite 300 800-888-4612
Fairfax, VA 22030 *Fax:* 703-691-4615
ibaumel@dynamac.com
www.css-dynamac.com
A scientific research, engineering, and information technology company, conducting state of the art field and laboratory research, and providing scientific and technical support to federal and state environmental programs.
Jolanda Janczewski, Chairman
W. Dennis Lauchner, CEO

4548 E&A Environmental Consultants
11629 Central Street 781-344-6446
Stoughton, MA 00207 *Fax:* 781-575-8915
members.aol.com/eaenviron/index.html
An environmental consulting firm, E&A provides waste management solutions through the utilization of alternative and innovative management and treatment techniques. E&A has developed expertise in all aspects of composting and organicwaste utilization. Research results are published in presentations, journals, and newsletters.
Eliot Epstein PhD, Ch. Environmental Scientist
Charles M Alix PE, Senior Engineer

4549 E&S Environmental Chemistry
PO Box 609 541-758-5777
Corvallis, OR 97339-609 *Fax:* 541-758-4413
www.esenvironmental.com

Environmental research.
Tim Sullivan, President
Jayne Charles, Office Manager

4550 EA Engineering, Science, and Technology, Inc., PBC
225 Schilling Circle 410-584-7000
Suite 400 *Fax:* 410-771-1625
Hunt Valley, MD 21031 info@eaest.com
www.eaest.com
Provides environmental, compliance, natural resources, and infrastructure engineering and management solutions to a wide range of public and private sector clients.

Ian D. MacFarlane, President

4551 EADS Group
1126 8th Avenue 814-944-5035
Altoona, PA 16602 800-626-0904
Fax: 814-944-4862
ibelsel@eadsgroup.com
www.eadsgroup.com
The EADS Group has experienced personnel that provide environmental risk assessments and site investigations, wetlands delineation and mitigation, and all related permitting. The scope of

services covers terrestrial and aquaticecology, water resources, threatened and endangered species, vegetation and wetlands, soils and geology, air quality, noise, hazardous waste, socioeconomics and land use. The EADS Group has five offices in Pennsylvania and one in Maryland.
Dennis M Stidinger, President
David M. Yahner, P.E., Office Manager

4552 EAI Corporation
1308 Continental Drive 410-676-1449
Suite J *Fax:* 410-671-7241
Abingdon, MD 21009 www.eaicorp.com
Environmental engineering and scientific firm. Research results published in private reports to clients.
Charles Speranzella, President
Tom Albro, VP

4553 EMCO Testing & Engineering
PO Box 266 860-886-0697
Taftville, CT 00638 *Fax:* 860-886-0697
emco@99main.com
Water treatment and environmental research and consulting, including: storm water pollution prevention; well water contamination investigation; property contamination investigation; solar energy application to commercial andresidential buildings.
Dr Ernie Cohen, President/R&D

4554 EMCON Alaska
201 E 56th Avenue 907-562-3452
Suite 300 *Fax:* 907-563-2814
Anchorage, AK 99518
Environmental engineering firm.

4555 EMMES Corporation
401 North Washington Street 301-251-1161
Suite 700 *Fax:* 301-251-1355
Rockville, MD 20850 info@emmes.com
www.emmes.com
Firm providing medical data management and statistical support services. Research results published in scientific literature.
Brian Hochheimer, VP and CFO
Anne Laindblad, President

4556 EMS Laboratories, Inc.
117 W Bellevue Drive 626-568-4065
Pasadena, CA 91105-2503 800-675-5777
Fax: 626-796-5282
www.emslabs.com
Environmental testing lab services. Asbestos/Lead/,I.H. testing. Fully accreditted AIHA lab for metal waste characterization.
Bernadine Kolk, President
Anthony Kolk, CEO

4557 EN-CAS Analytical Laboratories
2359 Farrington Point Drive 336-785-3252
Winston-Salem, NC 27107 *Fax:* 336-785-3262
info@en-cas.com
www.en-cas.com
Chemical and environmental testing and analysis company.
Tim Ballard, President

4558 ENSR-Anchorage
700 G Street 907-562-3366
Suite 500 800-662-7232
Anchorage, AK 99501-3439 *Fax:* 907-562-1297
AECOMInvestorRelations@aecom.com
www.ensr.aecom.com
ENSR is a global provider of environmental and energy development services to industry and government. As a full-service environmental firm, ENSR's professionals provide clients with consulting, engineering, remediation, and relatedservices from over 15 countries.
Michael S. Burke, Chairman/CEO
Daniel R. Tishman, Director, Vice Chairman

4559 ENSR-Billings
207 North Broadway 406-652-7481
Suite 315 800-662-7232
Billings, MT 59101 *Fax:* 406-652-7485
AECOMInvestorRelations@aecom.com
www.ensr.aecom.com
ENSR is a global provider of environmental and energy development services to industry and government. As a full-service environmental firm, ENSR's professionals provide clients with consulting, engineering, remediation, and relatedservices from over 15 countries.
Michael S. Burke, Chairman/CEO
Daniel R. Tishman, Director, Vice Chairman

4560 ENSR-Carmel
4030 Vincennes Road 317-297-6200
Suite 250 800-662-7232
Indianapolis, IN 46268 *Fax:* 317-293-4295
AECOMInvestorRelations@aecom.com
www.ensr.aecom.com
ENSR is a global provider of environmental and energy development services to industry and government. As a full-service environmental firm, ENSR's professionals provide clients with consulting, engineering, remediation, and relatedservices from over 15 countries.
Michael S. Burke, Chairman/CEO
Daniel R. Tishman, Director, Vice Chairman

4561 ENSR-Chicago
303 East Wacker Drive 312-373-7700
Suite 1400 800-662-7232
Chicago, IL 60601 *Fax:* 312-373-6800
AECOMInvestorRelations@aecom.com
www.ensr.aecom.com
ENSR is a global provider of environmental and energy development services to industry and government. As a full-service environmental firm, ENSR's professionals provide clients with consulting, engineering, remediation, and relatedservices from over 15 countries.
Michael S. Burke, Chairman/CEO
Daniel R. Tishman, Director, Vice Chairman

4562 ENSR-Columbia (MD)
9755 Patuxent Woods Drive 410-423-2500
Suite 300 800-662-7232
Columbia, MD 21046 *Fax:* 410-423-2570
AECOMInvestorRelations@aecom.com
www.ensr.aecom.com
ENSR is a global provider of environmental and energy development services to industry and government. As a full-service environmental firm, ENSR's professionals provide clients with consulting, engineering, remediation, and relatedservices from over 15 countries.
Michael S. Burke, Chairman/CEO
Daniel R. Tishman, Director, Vice Chairman

4563 ENSR-Fort Collins
1601 Prospect Parkway 970-493-8878
Fort Collins, CO 80525-9769 800-662-7232
Fax: 970-493-0213
AECOMInvestorRelations@aecom.com
www.ensr.aecom.com
ENSR is a global provider of environmental and energy development services to industry and government. As a full-service environmental firm, ENSR's professionals provide clients with consulting, engineering, remediation, and relatedservices from over 15 countries.
Michael S. Burke, Chairman/CEO
Daniel R. Tishman, Director, Vice Chairman

4564 ENSR-Harvard
325 Ayer Road 978-772-2345
Harvard, MA 00145 800-662-7232
Fax: 978-772-4956
AECOMInvestorRelations@aecom.com
www.ensr.aecom.com
ENSR is a global provider of environmental and energy development services to industry and government. As a full-service envi-

ronmental firm, ENSR's professionals provide clients with consulting, engineering, remediation, and relatedservices from over 15 countries.
Michael S. Burke, Chairman/CEO
Daniel R. Tishman, Director, Vice Chairman

4565 ENSR-Kalamazoo
400 Monroe Street 313-961-9797
Suite 270 800-662-7232
Detroit, MI 48226-2977 *Fax:* 313-961-3480
AECOMInvestorRelations@aecom.com
www.ensr.aecom.com
ENSR is a global provider of environmental and energy development services to industry and government. As a full-service environmental firm, ENSR's professionals provide clients with consulting, engineering, remediation, and relatedservices from over 15 countries.
Michael S. Burke, Chairman/CEO
Daniel R. Tishman, Director, Vice Chairman

4566 ENSR-Minneapolis
800 LaSalle Avenue 612-376-2000
Suite 500 800-662-7232
Minneapolis, MN 55402 *Fax:* 612-376-2271
AECOMInvestorRelations@aecom.com
www.ensr.aecom.com
ENSR is a global provider of environmental and energy development services to industry and government. As a full-service environmental firm, ENSR's professionals provide clients with consulting, engineering, remediation, and relatedservices from over 15 countries.
Michael S. Burke, Chairman/CEO
Daniel R. Tishman, Director, Vice Chairman

4567 ENSR-New Orleans
1555 Poydras Street 504-586-8111
Suite 2700 800-662-7232
New Orleans, LA 70112 *Fax:* 504-582-0554
AECOMInvestorRelations@aecom.com
www.ensr.aecom.com
ENSR is a global provider of environmental and energy development services to industry and government. As a full-service environmental firm, ENSR's professionals provide clients with consulting, engineering, remediation, and relatedservices from over 15 countries.
Michael S. Burke, Chairman/CEO
Daniel R. Tishman, Director, Vice Chairman

4568 ENSR-Norcross
2 Sun Court at Technology Park 770-441-2364
Suite 200 800-662-7232
Norcross, GA 30092 *Fax:* 678-966-0751
AECOMInvestorRelations@aecom.com
www.ensr.aecom.com
ENSR is a global provider of environmental and energy development services to industry and government. As a full-service environmental firm, ENSR's professionals provide clients with consulting, engineering, remediation, and relatedservices from over 15 countries.
Michael S. Burke, Chairman/CEO
Daniel R. Tishman, Director, Vice Chairman

4569 ENSR-Portland (ME)
500 Southborough Drive 207-775-2800
South Portland, ME 00410-3209 800-662-7232
Fax: 207-775-4820
AECOMInvestorRelations@aecom.com
www.ensr.aecom.com
ENSR is a global provider of environmental and energy development services to industry and government. As a full-service environmental firm, ENSR's professionals provide clients with consulting, engineering, remediation, and relatedservices from over 15 countries.
Michael S. Burke, Chairman/CEO
Daniel R. Tishman, Director, Vice Chairman

4570 ENSR-Sacramento
2870 Gateway Oaks Drive 916-679-2000
Suite 150 800-662-7232
Sacramento, CA 95833-4308 *Fax:* 916-679-2900
AECOMInvestorRelations@aecom.com
www.ensr.aecom.com
ENSR is a global provider of environmental and energy development services to industry and government. As a full-service environmental firm, ENSR's professionals provide clients with consulting, engineering, remediation, and relatedservices from over 15 countries.
Michael S. Burke, Chairman/CEO
Daniel R. Tishman, Director, Vice Chairman

4571 ENSR-Shawnee Mission
6400 Glenwood Street 913-362-8444
Suite 105 800-662-7232
Shawnee Mission, KS 66202 *Fax:* 913-362-1044
AECOMInvestorRelations@aecom.com
www.ensr.aecom.com
ENSR is a global provider of environmental and energy development services to industry and government. As a full-service environmental firm, ENSR's professionals provide clients with consulting, engineering, remediation, and relatedservices from over 15 countries.
Michael S. Burke, Chairman/CEO
Daniel R. Tishman, Director, Vice Chairman

4572 ENSR-St Petersburg
10210 Highland Manor Drive 813-630-2500
Suite 350 800-662-7232
Tampa, FL 33610 *Fax:* 813-621-2300
AECOMInvestorRelations@aecom.com
www.ensr.aecom.com
ENSR is a global provider of environmental and energy development services to industry and government. As a full-service environmental firm, ENSR's professionals provide clients with consulting, engineering, remediation, and relatedservices from over 15 countries.
Michael S. Burke, Chairman/CEO
Daniel R. Tishman, Director, Vice Chairman

4573 ENSR-Stamford
500 Enterprise Drive 860-263-5800
Suite 1A 800-662-7232
Rocky Hill, CT 00606 *Fax:* 860-263-5777
AECOMInvestorRelations@aecom.com
www.ensr.aecom.com
ENSR is a global provider of environmental and energy development services to industry and government. As a full-service environmental firm, ENSR's professionals provide clients with consulting, engineering, remediation, and relatedservices from over 15 countries.
Michael S. Burke, Chairman/CEO
Daniel R. Tishman, Director, Vice Chairman

4574 ENVIRO Tech Services
910 54th Avenue 970-346-3900
Suite 230 800-369-3878
Greeley, CO 80634 *Fax:* 785-827-8765
www.envirotechservices.com
Developing superior road and surface solutions to manage all environments; both natural and man-made.
Roger Knoph, President/CEO
Kevin Whyrick, CFO

4575 ESA Laboratories
Laboratories, 22 Alpha Road 978-250-7150
Chelmsford, MA 00182 *Fax:* 978-250-7171
Environmental and biological testing laboratory.

4576 ESS Group
404 Wyman Street 781-419-7696
Suite 375 info@essgroup.com
Waltham, MA 02451 www.essgroup.com
ESS is a multi-disciplinary environmental consulting and engineering firm offering services in the areas of energy generation and transmission, coastal engineering and marine sciences, water

resources, natural resources, environmentalcompliance and more.

Charles Natale, President & CEO
Payson Whitney, VP, Chief Operating Officer

4577 ETTI Engineers and Consultants
1000 Rand Road 847-526-1606
Unit 210 *Fax:* 847-526-7443
Wauconda, IL 60084 solutions@ettinc.com
www.ettinc.com
Engineering research and testing laboratory specializing in construction services and environmental needs. Research results published in project reports and test summaries.
Wes Scott, President

4578 Eaglebrook Environmental Laboratories
1152 Junction Avenue 219-322-0450
Schererville, IN 46375 *Fax:* 219-322-0440
Environmental testing service.

4579 Earth Dimensions
1091 Jamison Road 716-655-1717
Elma, NY 14059 *Fax:* 716-655-2915
Geotechnical soil investigations and wetland delineations.

Don Owens, President
Brian Bartron, Geologist/Drilling Manager

4580 Earth Tech
4135 Technology Parkway 920-458-8711
PO Box 1067 *Fax:* 920-458-0537
Sheboygan, WI 53083 www.aecom.com
Specializes in the planning, design, and construction management and observation of environmental and infrastructure projects including water/wastewater; solid, hazardous and process waste facilities; environmental restoration;transportation; and architecture. The company's staff size, multiple office locations and comprehensive mix of expertise and experience combined iwht an in-depth knowledge of technical and regulatory issues, provide our clients with a valuableresource for solutions.
Diane Creel, President

4581 Earth Technology Corporation
300 Oceangate 562-951-2000
Suite 700 *Fax:* 562-951-2100
Long Beach, CA 90802 www.earthtech.com/
Alan P. Krusi, President

4582 Earthwatch International
114 Western Ave 978-461-0081
Boston, MA 00213 800-776-0188
Fax: 978-461-2332
info@earthwatch.org
earthwatch.org
Engages people worldwide in scientific research and education to promote the understanding and action necessary for a sustainable environment.
Larry Mason, CEO
Schott Kania, COO

4583 East Texas Testing Laboratory
1717 E Erwin Street 903-595-4421
Tyler, TX 75702 *Fax:* 903-595-6113
www.ettlinc.com
Engineering research and testing laboratory specializing in construction services and environmental needs. Research results published in project reports and test summaries.
Darrell Flatt, President
Thomas R. McLemore, CFO

4584 Eastern Technical Associates
PO Box 1009 919-878-3188
Garner, NC 27529 *Fax:* 919-872-5199
www.eta-is-opacity.com
Environmental consulting firm services of which include visible emissions training & certification. Research results published in government reports.

Jody Monk, General Manager
Sherri Sigworth, Office Manager

4585 Eberline Analytical, Lionville Laboratory
264 Welsh Pool Road 610-280-3060
Exton, PA 19341 800-841-5487
Fax: 610-280-3041
info@eberlineservices.com
www.eberlineservices.com
Analytical, consulting, and field services offer broad capabilities in: radiological characterization and analyses; environmental chemical analyses; hazardous, radioactive, and mixed waste management; and environmental, safety, andhealth management.

Carter Nulton, Laboratory Manager
William F Niemeyer, Business Development Manager

4586 Eberline Services - Albuquerque
10400 Academy NE 505-262-2694
Ste 300 877-477-8989
Albuquerque, NM 87111 *Fax:* 505-262-2698
info@eberlineservices.com
www.eberlineservices.com
Provides analytical, consulting and field services, offering broad capabilities in radiological characterizaion and analysis; hazaradous, radioactive, and mixed waste management; and environmental, safety, and health management. Inaddition, Eberline Services provides onsite staff and services for site characterization and remediation, decontamination and decommissioning, waste management, and facility operations.
Leva Jensen, Laboratory Manager
William F Niemeyer, Project Manager

4587 Eberline Services - Los Alamos
183 Central Park Square 505-262-2694
Los Almos, NM 87544 877-477-8989
Fax: 505-262-2698
info@eberlineservices.com
www.eberlineservices.com
Provides analytical, consulting and field services, offering broad capabilities in radiological characterizaion and analysis; hazaradous, radioactive, and mixed waste management; and environmental, safety, and health management. Inaddition, Eberline Services provides onsite staff and services for site characterization and remediation, decontamination and decommissioning, waste management, and facility operations.
Leva Jensen, Laboratory Manager
William F Niemeyer, Project Manager

4588 Eberline Services - Oak Ridge
601 Scarboro Road 865-481-0683
Oak Ridge, TN 37830-7371 877-477-8989
Fax: 865-483-4621
info@eberlineservices.com
www.eberlineservices.com
Provides analytical, consulting and field services, offering broad capabilities in radiological characterizaion and analysis; hazaradous, radioactive, and mixed waste management; and environmental, safety, and health management. Inaddition, Eberline Services provides onsite staff and services for site characterization and remediation, decontamination and decommissioning, waste management, and facility operations.
Leva Jensen, Laboratory Manager
William F Niemeyer, Project Manager

4589 Eberline Services - Richland
3200 George Washington Way 509-420-0841
Richland, WA 99352 877-477-8989
Fax: 505-262-2698
info@eberlineservices.com
www.eberlineservices.com
Provides analytical, consulting and field services, offering broad capabilities in radiological characterizaion and analysis; hazaradous, radioactive, and mixed waste management; and environmental, safety, and health management. Inaddition,

Eberline Services provides onsite staff and services for site characterization and remediation, decontamination and decommissioning, waste management, and facility operations.
Leva Jensen, Laboratory Manager
William F Niemeyer, Project Manager

4590 **Eberline Services - Richmond**
2030 Wright Avenue 510-235-2633
Richmond, CA 94804-3849 800-841-5487
Fax: 510-235-0438
info@eberlineservices.com
www.eberlineservices.com
Analytical, consulting, and field services offer broad capabilities in: radiological characterization and analysis; hazardous, radioactive, and mixed waste management; and environmental, safety, and health management.
Leva Jensen, Laboratory Manager
William F Niemeyer, Program Manager

4591 **Eco-Analysts**
1420 S. Blaine 208-882-2588
Suite 14 *Fax:* 208-883-4288
Moscow, ID 83843 eco@ecoanalysts.com
www.ecoanalysts.com
Specializes in Aquatic Taxonomy and Bioassessment. An independent environmental consulting firm located in Moscow, Idaho. Experienced in the identification of freshwater organisms; macroinvertebrates, periphyton, plankton, and fish.Offer aquatic bioassessment and biological monitoring services.
Gary Lester, President/CEO
Scott Lindstrom, CFO

4592 **EcoTest Laboratories**
575 Broadhollow Rd. 631-694-3040
Melville, NY 11747-5076 *Fax:* 631-422-5770
www.h2mlabs.com
Environmental testing laboratory.
John J. Molloy, President and CEO
Joann M. Slavin, SVP, Laboratory Manager

4593 **Ecological Engineering Associates**
508 Boston Post Road 978-369-9440
PO Box 415 *Fax:* 508-748-9740
Weston, MA 00249-0003 info@ecological-engineering.com
www.ecological-engineering.com
Ecological Engineering Group is a unique engineering and design practice combining conventional engineering, innovative ecological design, and permitting know-how.
Bruce Strong, Operations Manager

4594 **Ecology and Environment**
368 Pleasant View Drive 716-684-8060
Lancaster, NY 14086 info@ene.com
www.ene.com
Ecology and Environment is an environmental science and engineering company providing environmental consulting services and litigation support. Areas covered include engineering, restoration, water treatment, regulatory compliance,permitting, environmental impact assessments, air and noise studies, field studies, and more.
Mike Morgante, Contact

4595 **Economists**
2121 K Street, NW 202-223-4700
Suite 1100 *Fax:* 202-296-7138
Washington, DC 20037 info@ei.com
www.ei.com
Firm providing economic analysis and public policy evaluation, with emphasis on private antitrust litigation, communications regulation, and the Environment.
David Argue, President
Peter Greenhalgh, Director

4596 **Ecotope**
4056 9th Avenue NE 206-322-3753
Seattle, WA 98105 *Fax:* 206-325-7270
www.ecotope.com
Energy efficiency research, architecture, and engineering.
David Baylon, President
Jonathan Heller, Principal/Lead Mechanical En

4597 **Eder Associates**
480 Forest Avenue 516-671-8440
Locust Valley, NY 11560 *Fax:* 516-671-3349
Environmental engineering and consulting firm.
Leonard J Eden, President

4598 **Eichleay Corporation of Illinois**
11919 S Avenue O 773-731-7010
Chicago, IL 60617
Environmental consulting firm.

4599 **El Dorado Engineering**
2964 W 4700 South 801-966-8288
Suite 109 *Fax:* 801-966-8499
Salt Lake City, UT 84129 rfrandsen@eldoradoengineering.com
www.eldoradoengineering.com
Established in 1981, El Dorado Engineering (EDE) is a small business with the flexibility to meet the clients needs. In addition to the specialty work in Demilitarization, Environmental, Thermal Disposal, of energetics, EDE hasengineering experience that covers a wide variety of applications.
Bob Hayes, President/CEO
Ralph Hayes, Director, BD

4600 **Electron Microprobe Laboratory Bilby Research Center**
Northern Arizona University 928-523-9565
PO Box 6013 *Fax:* 928-523-7290
Flagstaff, AZ 86011 james.wittke@nau.edu
www4.nau.edu
The primary goal at the Bilby Research Center is to promote research across the Northern Arizona University campus. Research support services include professional editing; imaging services include illustration, photography, andvideography; and website design.
James H Wittke, Director
Marcelle Coder, Project Director

4601 **Element Houston**
222 Cavalcade Street 713-692-9151
PO Box 8768 888-786-7555
Houston, TX 77009 *Fax:* 713-696-6307
info.houston@element.com
www.element.com
Analysis and testing laboratory offering environmental control services including materials testing; nondestructive testing; polymer testing and polymeric materials testing; electrical and thermal testing; failure analysis;construction materials testing and engineering; product evaluation; surface testing, and air emissions.
Peter T Regan, Chairman
Charles Noall, President/CEO

4602 **Element Materials Technology**
1200 Westinghouse Boulevard 704-588-1131
Suite A 888-786-7555
Charlotte, NC 28273 *Fax:* 704-588-5412
info.charlotte@element.com
www.element.com
Analysis and testing laboratory offering environmental control services including mechanical, metallurgical, and chemical analysis in addition to materials testing, nondestructive testing, failure analysis and product evaluation.
Peter T Regan, Chairman
Charles Noall, President/CEO

4603 Elm Research Institute
11 Kit Street 603-358-6198
Keene, NH 00343 800-367-3567
Fax: 603-358-6305
libertytreesociety@gmail.com
www.libertytreesociety.org
A nonprofit organization dedicated to the restoration and preservation of the American Elm. Provides disease-resistant American Liberty Elms to municipalities, colleges and volunteer nonprofit groups for public planting. Distributionof Elm Fungicide for treatment of Dutch Elm Disease.

John Hansel, Executive Director
Yvonne Spalthoff, Assistant Director

4604 Emcon Baker-Shiflett
5701 E Loop S 817-478-8254
Fort Worth, TX 76119 *Fax:* 817-478-8874
Consulting engineers providing research services to the construction industry.
Larry Gardner, Contact

4605 Endyne Labs
160 James Brown Drive 802-879-4333
Williston, VT 00549 *Fax:* 802-879-7103
info@endynelabs.com
www.endynelabs.com
Endyne Labs is a full-service environmental testing laboratory that specializes in the analysis of organic, inorganic, metals and microbiological contaminants in a variety of matrices including drinking water, wastewater, soil,hazardous waste and air.

Harry B Locker PhD, President

4606 Energetics
7067 Columbia Gateway Drive 410-290-0370
Columbia, MD 21046 *Fax:* 410-290-0377
webmaster@energetics.com
www.energetics.com

Environmental engineering firm.
Nancy Margolis, President
Christopher Kelley, VP

4607 Energy & Environmental Technology
400 Perimeter Center Terrace NE 770-558-1205
Suite 105 *Fax:* 770-628-0459
Atlanta, GA 30346 Jaye@EandETech.com
www.eandetech.com

Environmental research.
Jack Locke, President
Russel Jones, VP

4608 Energy Conversion Devices
2956 Waterview Drive 248-293-0440
Rochester Hills, MI 48309 800-528-0617
Fax: 248-844-1214
www.ovonic.com
Maintained a strong core competence in materials research and advanced product development throughout its forty plus year history. The company protects the results of these efforts through an extensive patent collection.

Stanford Ovshinsky, President/CTO
Iris Ovshinsky, Vice President

4609 Energy Laboratories
400 West Boxelder Road 307-686-7175
Gillette, WY 82718 866-686-7175
Fax: 307-682-4625
casper@energylab.com
www.energylab.com
Environmental data collection, testing and analysis firm.
Tracey Archer, Project Manager
Alyson Degnan, Project Manager

4610 Energy and Environmental Analysis
9300 Lee Highway 703-934-3603
Fairfax, VA 22031-1207 800-532-4783
Fax: 703-934-3740
info@icfi.com
www.icfi.com
Consulting firm offering technical, analytical, and managerial services in the energy/environmental field.
Sudhakar Kesavan, Chairman/CEO
John Wasson, President/COO

4611 Engineering & Environmental Management Group
11251 Roger Bacon Drive 703-318-4522
Reston, VA 20910 *Fax:* 703-318-4729
Environmental applications.

4612 Engineering Analysis
715 Arcadia Circle 256-533-9391
Huntsville, AL 35801 *Fax:* 256-533-9325
eai@mindspring.com
www.mindspring.com/~eai/
Environmental and safety research and analysis organization. Research results published in client and technical reports and professional journals.
Frank B Tatom, President
Theodore (Ted) Sumrall, Consultant

4613 Entek Environmental & Technical Services
3 Agway Drive 518-269-3170
Rensselaer, NY 12144 800-888-9200
Fax: 518-283-4031
uhlig@entek-env.com
www.entek-env.com/
Environmental consulting and engineering firm.
Patrick J McDonough, Director/Manager

4614 Entropy
PO Box 90067 919-781-3550
Raleigh, NC 27675 800-486-3550
Fax: 919-787-8442
www.entropyinc.com

Provides air emission testing services.
Robert Drew, President

4615 Enviro Dynamics
1340 Old Chain Bridge Road 703-760-0023
Suite 300 *Fax:* 703-760-9382
Mc Lean, VA 22101
Occupational and environmental health analysis and consulting firm.
William J Keanet, President

4616 Enviro Systems
1 Lafayette Road 603-926-3345
PO Box 778 *Fax:* 603-926-3521
Hampton, NH 00384 pkarbe@envirosystems.com
www.envirosystems.com
Environmental compliance testing services, specializing in analytical chemistry and environmental toxicity testing with fresh and salt water, soil and sediment.

Petra Karbe, VP Marketing

4617 Enviro-Bio-Tech
4693 19th St. Court East 941-757-2591
Bradenton, FL 34203 800-314-6263
Fax: 941-757-2592
info@environmentalbiotech.com
www.environmentalbiotech.com

Chemical analysis firm.
Harpal Singh, President

4618 Enviro-Lab
45-10 Court Square 718-392-0185
Long Island City, NY 11101 *Fax:* 718-392-8654
www.envirolab.com
Environmental Toxicology Laboratory (ETL) is a research, development and testing laboratory; concentrating its efforts on

new approaches to toxicity testing. The mission of ETL is the further advancement of the Tetramitis Assay aswell as the promotion and commercialization of the test.

Dr. Robert L Jaffe, Ph.D, Director of Lab. Science

4619 Enviro-Sciences
781 Route 15 South 973-398-8183
Hopatcong, NJ 00784 *Fax:* 973-398-8037
info@enviro-sciences.com
www.enviro-sciences.com

Environmental sciences firm.
Irving D Cohen, CEO
Glenn Lechner, Marketing Manager

4620 EnviroAnalytical
286 Mask Island Drive 613-756-0101
Barry's Bay, ON K0J 1 800-427-8591
Fax: 613-756-0909
www.enviro-analytical.com
Environmental compliance analysis, R&D, personnel training and analytical method development.
Dr S Sethi, Job Director

4621 Envirodyne Engineers
303 E Wacker Drive 312-938-0300
Suite 600 *Fax:* 312-938-1109
Chicago, IL 60601
Environmental science research firm.

4622 Environ Laboratories
9725 Girard Avenue S 952-888-7795
Minneapolis, MN 55431 800-826-3710
Fax: 952-888-6345
Laboratory providing environmental and physical testing of products and materials to commercial and military specifications.
Alan G Thompson, President

4623 Environment Associates
9604 Variel Avenue 818-709-0568
Chatsworth, CA 91311 800-354-1522
Fax: 818-709-8914
Andrews@Eatest.com
www.eatest.com
Provides a full spectrum of environmental test services to Aerospace, Military and commercial manufacturers including temperature, humidity, altitude, thermal vacuum, shock, vibration, corrosive atmosphere, a DSCC approved connectortest lab, hydraulic and pneumatic test capabilities, flow testing firewall testing, EMMI/EMC testing and more. Services also include test procedure development formal test reports, certification and test fixture modifications and adaptations.

William Spaulding, President
Andrew Spaulding, Sales

4624 Environment/One Corporation
2773 Balltown Road 518-346-6161
Niskayuna, NY 12309-1090 *Fax:* 518-346-6188
eone@eone.com
www.eone.com
Environmental analysis and instrumentation firm. Research results published in technical journals.

George A. Vorsheim, Communications Director

4625 Environmental Acoustical Research
PO Box 18888 303-447-2619
Boulder, CO 80308 800-525-2690
Fax: 303-447-2637
info@earinc.com
Specialized hearing protection and enhancement systems.
Garry G. Gordon, President/Audiologist
Andrew Gordon, Lab/Marketing Director

4626 Environmental Analysis
3278 N Highway 67 314-921-4488
Florissant, MO 63033 *Fax:* 314-921-4494
Environmental analytical laboratory.
R M Ferris, President

4627 Environmental Analytical Laboratory
95 Beaver Street 781-893-8330
Waltham, MA 00245 *Fax:* 781-893-4414
Info@hubtesting.net
www.hubtesting.net
Environmental testing services company specializing in asbestos consulting and analysis, waste water, soils and surveys. Also mold remediation and screening.

Frederick Boyle, President

4628 Environmental Audits
11327 W. Lincoln Ave. 414-226-5563
West Allis, WI 53227 *Fax:* 414-231-9374
info@environmentalaudits.net
Consulting firm specializing in environmental science.

John R Ruetz, President

4629 Environmental Chemical
1240 Bayshore Highway 650-347-1555
Burlingame, CA 94010 *Fax:* 650-347-8789
www.ecc.net
Research and testing firm.

4630 Environmental Consultants
391 Newman Avenue 812-282-8481
Clarksville, IN 47129 *Fax:* 812-282-8554
Environmental consulting firm.
Robert E Fuchs, President

4631 Environmental Consulting Laboratories
1005 Boston Post Road 203-245-0568
Madison, CT 00644 800-246-9624
eclinc@aol.com
Environmental testing and consulting firm.

4632 Environmental Consulting Laboratories, Inc.
1005 Boston Post Road 203-245-0568
Madison, CT 00644 800-246-9624
Fax: 203-318-0830
eclinc@aol.com
Environmental testing and consulting firm. Specializing in Micro Biology and aquatic tixicity.

David Barris, President/Lab Director

4633 Environmental Control
6525 North Mineral Drive 208-772-8200
Coeur d'Alene *Fax:* 505-232-0942
Idaho, ID 83815-8788 www.environmentcontrol.com
Environmental consulting and analytical laboratory. Research results published in project reports and test summaries.
Reid Warner, Owner
James J Meuller, President

4634 Environmental Control Laboratories
38818 Talyor Industrial Parkway 440-353-3700
North Ridgeville, OH 44039 800-962-0118
Fax: 440-353-3773
E.C. Labs does environmental testing, such as: waste water, soil, asbestos, remediation and constrution projects.
Ron Schiedel, Marketing Manager
Phyllis Conley, Lab Manager

4635 Environmental Data Resources
6 Armstrong Road 203-783-0300
4th Floor 800-352-0050
Shelton, CT 00648 *Fax:* 800-231-6802
www.edrnet.com

Applied and product research in environmental applications.
Dan Gottlieb, CEO
Tom Flynn, CFO

4636 Environmental Elements Corporation
333 West Camden St. 410-333-1560
Suite 500 877-637-8234
Batlimore, MD 21201 *Fax:* 410-333-1888
www.EEC1.com
Environmental Elements Corporation, the leading supplier of air pollution control systems for over 50 years, designs, installs, and maintains electrostatic precipitators, fabric filters, gas, and particulate scrubbing andAmmonia-on-Demand (AOD) Systems. EEC technologies enable customers in a broad range of power and generation, pulp, and paper, waste-to-energy, rock products, metals and petrochemical industries to operate their facilities in compliance withparticulate and gaseous emissions.
Robert L. McKinney, Chairman
Alison L. Asti, Executive Director

4637 Environmental Health Sciences Research Laboratory
127 New Market Street 504-394-2233
PO Box 379 *Fax:* 504-394-7982
Belle Chasse, LA 70037

4638 Environmental Innovations
9600 West Flag Avenue 414-358-7760
Milwaukee, WI 53225 *Fax:* 414-358-7770
Environmental engineering and consulting firm.

4639 Environmental Laboratories
1 United Nations Plaza 212-963-6010
Room DC-1-1155 *Fax:* 917-367-4046
New York, NY 10017 iaeany@un.org
www.iaea.org
Yukiya Amano, Director General
Janice Dunn Lee, Head, Dept of Management

4640 Environmental Management: Guthrie
5200 N.E. Highway 33 405-282-8510
PO Box 700 800-510-8510
Guthrie, OK 73044 *Fax:* 405-282-8533
www.emiok.com
Full service environmental firm provides emergency response remediation routine waste management for hazardous and non hazardous materials and consulting. The firm owns the transportation and remediation equipment along with providinga full technical staff.
Terry Bobo, President
Keeton Hill, Health and Safety Officer

4641 Environmental Management: Waltham
95 Beaver Street 781-893-8330
Waltham, MA 00245 *Fax:* 781-893-4414
Info@hubtesting.net
www.hubtesting.net
Environmental testing services, consulting services, environmental abatement services, water quality/chemical testing, asbestos remediation monitoring and inspections, mold testing/mold remediation, industrial hygiene services.
Susan Boyle, Vice President

4642 Environmental Measurements
2660 California Street 415-567-8089
San Francisco, CA 94115 *Fax:* 415-398-7664
sales@langan.net

4643 Environmental Monitoring Laboratory
59 N Plains Industrial Road 203-284-0555
Suite A *Fax:* 203-284-2064
Wallingford, CT 00649
Laboratory providing environmental chemistry services including analysis, bioassays, product efficacy and research and development in the areas of water and wastewater, agricultural chemicals, protective coatings, petroleum products,metals and chemicals.
Jan D Dunn PhD, Director/Manager

4644 Environmental Quality Protection Systems Company
5150 Keele Street 601-961-5650
Jackson, MS 39206 *Fax:* 601-354-6612
Environmental engineering and science firm.

4645 Environmental Resource Associates
16341 Table Mountain Parkway 303-431-8454
Golden, CO 80403 800-372-0122
Fax: 303-421-0159
info@eraqc.com
www.eraqc.com
A division of Waters Corporation, ERA provides products and consultation services for laboratories in the areas of water pollution, chemistry, microbiology, soil testing and more.
Brian Murphy, PR, Waters Corporation

4646 Environmental Resources Management
3352 128th Avenue 616-399-3500
Holland, MI 49424 *Fax:* 616-399-3777
www.erm.com
Provides environmental, health, safety, risk, and social consulting services, including sustainability planning, health and safety, risk assessment, data management, asset management, and environmental compliance.
Keryn James, Chief Executive Officer
David McArthur, Chief Operating Officer

4647 Environmental Risk: Clifton Division
1373 Broad Street 973-773-8322
Suite 301 *Fax:* 973-243-9055
Clifton, NJ 00701
Environmental engineering and consulting services.

4648 Environmental Science & Engineering
1200 E. California Blvd 626-795-6070
MC 131-24 *Fax:* 626-795-6028
Pasadena, CA 91125 www.ese.caltech.edu
Comprehensive environmental and engineering consulting firm.
Nora Oshima, Grants Manager
Elizabeth Boyd, Academic Assistant

4649 Environmental Services International
6404 Maccorkle Avenue 304-768-2233
Saint Albans, WV 25177 *Fax:* 304-768-9988
esi@citynet.net
Consulting, engineering, and analytical firm. Research results published in reports to clients.

4650 Environmental Systems Corporation
10801 N Mopac Bldg 1-200 512-250-7900
Austin, TX 78759 *Fax:* 512-258-5836
support@envirosys.com
www.envirosys.com
Data acquisition and reporting systems for electric power producers and industrial sources, ESC is the leading supplier of CEM and ambient data systems in the US.
Rachael Morgan, VP
Jeff Rabenteine, President

4651 Environmental Technical Services
834 Castle Ridge Road 512-327-6672
Austin, TX 78746 *Fax:* 512-327-1974
www.wetlands.com/
Firm conducts sewer rehabilitation and tank testing.

4652 Environmental Testing Services
95 Beaver Street 781-893-8330
Waltham, MA 00245 *Fax:* 781-893-4414
Info@hubtesting.net
www.hubtesting.net
Environmental testing services company specializing in asbestos consulting and analysis, waste water, soils and surveys. Also mold remediation and screening.
Frederick Boyle, President

4653 Environmental Working Group
1436 U St. NW 202-667-6982
Suite 100 *Fax:* 202-232-2592
Washington, DC 20009 www.ewg.org

Cutting-edge research on health and the environment.
Carol Mcdonnell, Director, Chair
Ami Aronson, Director

4654 Enviropro
9765 Eton Avenue 818-998-7197
Chatsworth, CA 91311 *Fax:* 818-998-7258
Environmental engineering services. Spcialize in: Site investigation/remediation; Real Estate transfers: Phase I and II assessments; feasibility studies; clean-up of contaminated property, soil and groundwater; Methane gasinvestigations.
Zvia Uziel, President
Dr Michael Uziel, Director/Manager

4655 Enviroscan Inc
1051 Columbia Avenue 717-396-8922
Lancaster, PA 17603 *Fax:* 717-396-8746
email@enviroscan.com
www.enviroscan.com
Specializes in non-intrusive, non-deestructive land marine and borhole geophysics for engineers, environmental consultants, architects, industry, government and others. Geophysics is the earth science equivalent of medical radiology,and is used to locate subsurface objects such as utilities, underground storage tanks, drums, bedrock depths, sinkholes, contaminant plumes, fractures, graves, downed aircraft(in oceans, lakes) and submerged items.
Felicia Kegel Bechtel, President
Geoffrey T. Stankiewicz, Vice President

4656 Envisage Environmental
PO Box 152 440-526-0990
Richfield, OH 44286 *Fax:* 440-526-8555
Environmental engineering firm.

4657 Eppley Laboratory
12 Sheffield Avenue 401-847-1020
PO Box 419 *Fax:* 401-847-1031
Newport, RI 00284 info@eppleylab.com
www.eppleylab.com
Produces radiometer, pyranometers, pyrheliometers and pyrgeometers that measure solar and terrestrial radiation.
George L Kirk, President

4658 Era Laboratories
4730 Oneota Street 218-727-6380
Duluth, MN 55807-2719 800-727-6380
Fax: 218-727-3049
Environmental laboratory serving the agricultural industry through chemical analysis and sampling.
Robert D Manuson, President

4659 Ernaco
3740 Capulet Terr. 301-598-5025
Silver Spring, MD 20906
Firm offers biomedical, health and environmental research services.
Dr Muriel M Lippman, President

4660 Eureka Laboratories
4701 S. Whipple Street 773-847-9672
Chicago, IL 60632 *Fax:* 773-847-9675
Shao-Pin Yo, Laboratory Director

4661 Eurofins QC
1205 Industrial Highway 215-355-3900
P.O. Box 514 800-289-8378
Southampton, PA 18966-514 *Fax:* 215-355-7231
www.qclaboratories.com
Environmental testing lab.

4662 Eurofins SFA Laboratories
2345 South 170th Street 262-754-5300
New Berlin, WI 53151 800-300-6700
Fax: 262-754-5310
dkliber@sflabs.com
www.eurofinsus.com
Environmental and materials testing laboratory.
David L Kliber, President/CEO

4663 Eustis Engineering Services, LLC
3011 28th Street 504-834-0157
Metairie, LA 70002 800-966-0157
Fax: 504-834-0354
info@eustiseng.com
www.eustiseng.com
Geotechnical firm performing complete investigations, dynamic pile testing, cone penetrometer testing, CQC and materials testing and environmental services.
William W Gwyn, President
John R Eustis, Executive Vice President

4664 Evans Cooling Systems
1 Mountain Rd 860-668-1114
Suffield, CT 00607 *Fax:* 860-668-2757
tech@evanscooling.com
www.evanscooling.com
Environmental applications.
J. Thomas Light, President/CEO
Jeff Bye, VP/COO

4665 Everglades Laboratories
1602 Clare Avenue 561-833-4200
West Palm Beach, FL 33401 *Fax:* 561-833-7280
info@evergladeslabs.com
www.evergladeslabs.com/
EVERGLADES Laboratories, Inc. is a Florida state certified and NELAC accredited independent

environmental and analytical testing laboratory.

Dr. Ben Martin, Director

4666 Excel Environmental Resources
111 North Center Drive 732-545-9525
New Brunswick, NJ 00890 800-810-3923
Fax: 732-545-9425
info@excelenv.com
www.excelenv.com
Environmental research.
Laura J. Dodge, President
Ron Harwood, Executive VP

4667 First Coast Environmental Laboratory
8818 Arlington Expressway 904-725-4847
Jacksonville, FL 32211 *Fax:* 904-725-2215
Analytical laboratory.
Adolph W Wollitz, Director/Manager

4668 Fishbeck, Thompson, Carr & Huber, Inc.
1515 Arboretum Drive, SE 616-575-3824
Grand Rapids, MI 49546 *Fax:* 616-464-3993
info@ftch.com
www.ftch.com
Environmental consulting and engineering firm.
Ryan Eversole, Sr. Structural Engineer
Julia Smith, Sr. Mechanical Engineer

4669 Flowers Chemical Laboratories
481 Newburyport Avenue 407-339-5984
PO Box 150597 800-669-5227
Altamonte Springs, FL 32701 *Fax:* 407-260-6110
jeff@flowerslabs.com
www.flowerslabs.com
Analytical consulting firm. Research results published in reports to clients. Displays report in a pdf or html format.
Dr Jefferson Flowers, President

4670 Forensic Engineering
1439 Legion Road 905-632-3040
Burlington, ON L7S1T 800-263-6351
Fax: 905-632-2131
www.forensiceng.ca

Joe M Beard, President

4671 Fredericktowne Labs
3020 Ventrie Court 301-293-3340
PO Box 245 800-332-3340
Myersville, MD 21778 *Fax:* 301-293-2366
info@Fredericktownelabs.com
www.Fredericktownelabs.com
Environmental testing lab performing analyses on drinking water, waste water and natural waters for microbiological, inorganic, metal and organic contaminants. State certified laboratory. State certified sample collectors.Consulting services.
Mary Miller, PhD, Laboratory Director
Kathy Ryan, Special Projects Coordinator

4672 Free-Col Laboratories: A Division of Modern Industries
613 West 11th ST. 814-455-8061
Erie, PA 16501 *Fax:* 814-453-4382
johnp@modernind.com
www.modernind.com
Full service environmental laboratory - drinking water, waste water, solid waste, industrial hygiene testing; materials testing & engineering; non-destructive testing; mechanical testing; chemical analysis; failure analysis;consulting.
John Paraska, Director

4673 Froehling & Robertson
3015 Dumbarton Road 804-264-2701
Richmond, VA 23228 *Fax:* 804-264-1202
www.fandr.com
Environmental and construction materials testing lab.
Daniel K. Shaefer, VP
Scott Sutton, Business Development

4674 Froehling & Robertson, Inc.
3015 Dumbarton Road 804-264-2701
Richmond, VA 23228 *Fax:* 804-264-1202
jmingus@fandr.com
www.fandr.com
Independent testing laboratory whose mission is to provide excellent client service with its scope of both engineering and chemical services.
Bob Hill, PE, Branch Manager
Scott Sutton, Business Development

4675 FuelCell Energy
3 Great Pasture Road 203-825-6000
Danbury, CT 00681 www.fce.com
Developer and manufacturer of clean and efficient electric power generators. Products are designed for distributed generation users including schools, data centers, hospitals, buildings, waste water treatment plants and othercommercial and industrial applications.
Arthur Chipp Bottone, President/CEO
Michael Bishop, Sr. VP/CFO/Treasurer

4676 Fugro McClelland
6100 Hillcroft 713-369-5600
Houston, TX 77081 *Fax:* 512-444-3996
www.fugrogeoconsulting.com
Environmental, geotechnical, marine geoscience and environmental engineering firm.
Frank Marshall, President

4677 G&E Engineering
P.O. Box 3592 405-840-0301
Olympic Valley, CA 96146-3592 *Fax:* 405-840-4307
eidinger@earthlink.net
www.geengineeringsystems.com
Environmental impact assessment firm.
Richard Adams, President
John Eidinger

4678 GE Osmonics: GE Water Technologies
4636 Somerton Road 952-933-2277
Trevose, PA 19053 866-439-2837
Fax: 952-933-0141
Water and process technologies from GE Osmonics provide water, wastewater and process systems solutions.
Yuvbir Singh, General Manager
Heiner Markhoff, President/CEO

4679 GEO Plan Associates
30 Mann Street 781-740-1340
Hingham, MA 00204-1316 *Fax:* 781-740-1340
geoplanassoc@gmail.com
Scientific and technical consulting, environmental planning and analysis firm. Experienced in coastal and shallow marine geology, land-use planning, and transportation.
Peter S Rosen PhD, Partner
Michu Tcheng, Partner

4680 GEO-CENTERS
4805 Westway Park Blvd. 281-443-8150
Houston, TX 77041 *Fax:* 281-443-8010
mmohr@geocenter.com
Provider of WMD homeland security preparedness services and products with major strengths in chemical and biological research.
Sukhie Hyare, President
John Asma, VP of Marketing

4681 GKY and Associates
4229 Lafayette Ctr Dr 703-870-7000
Suite 1850 *Fax:* 703-870-7039
Chantilly, VA 21051 sstein@gky.com
www.gky.com
Civil and environmental systems engineering consulting organization. Research results published in project reports, government publications, and professional journals.
Stuart Stein, President
Brett Martin, VP

4682 GL Applied Research
142 Hawley Street 847-223-2220
PO Box 187 *Fax:* 847-223-2287
Grayslake, IL 60030 glapplied@glappliedresearch.com
www.glappliedresearch.com
Analytical and process control instrumentation development and manufacture; photometric analyzers.
Edgar Watson Jr, President

4683 GSEE
599 Waldron Road 615-793-7547
La Vergne, TN 37086 *Fax:* 615-793-5070
gsee@gseeinc.com
www.gseeinc.com
GSEE provides environmental engineering and technical services for municipal, industrial and governmental clientele as well as other engineering consultants and manufacturers throughout the United States and abroad. GSEE offersexisting plant evaluations, process engineering, detail engineering, and operations training.
Wendy Ingram, Lab Director

4684 GZA GeoEnvironmental
249 Vanderbilt Avenue 781-278-3700
Norwood, MA 02062 *Fax:* 781-278-5701
www.gza.com
GZA provides consulting services in the geotechnical, environmental, water, ecological, and construction fields. They work with a variety of organizations, including industrial, commercial, financial, public service, and governmententities.

Enda P. Fahey, Chief Financial Officer
Patrick F. Sheehan, President & CEO

4685 Gabriel Environmental Services
1421 North Elston 773-486-2123
Chicago, IL 60642 *Fax:* 773-486-0004
gabriel@gabrielenvironmental.com
www.gabrielenvironmental.com
Gabriel Environmental Services is a multi-disciplinary environmental consulting firm headquartered just northwest of downtown Chicago. They have been providing site assessment services, environmental testing and monitoring, andlaboratory analysis to a wide variety of clients since 1973.
William Gray, VP
Steve Sawyer, Evecutive VP

4686 Gas Technology Institute
1700 S Mount Prospect Road 847-768-0500
Des Plaines, IL 60018 *Fax:* 847-768-0501
info@gastechnology.org
www.gastechnology.org

Energy and environmental research.
David Carroll, President/CEO
Ronald Snedic, VP

4687 Gaynes Labs
9708 Industrial Drive 708-223-6655
Bridgeview, IL 60455 *Fax:* 708-233-6985
Gayneslabs@aol.com
www.gaynestesting.com
Research laboratories. Research results published in confidential test summaries and project reports. Services include environmental testing, atmospheric simulations, frequency vibration testing, temperature and humidity simulationtesting.
Philip Ross, Material Testing Manager

4688 General Engineering Labs
2040 Savage Road 843-556-8171
PO Box 30712 *Fax:* 843-766-1178
Charleston, SC 29417 grm@gel.com
www.gel.com

Environmental testing lab.
James M. Stelling, President/CEO
Kathleen S. Stelling, Chairman

4689 General Oil Company/GOC-Waste Compliance Services
35796 Veronica Street 734-266-6500
PO Box 1204 800-323-9905
Livonia, MI 48150 *Fax:* 734-266-6400
Waste Compliance Services (WCS) is an analytical laboratory, serving the industrial community. WCS services a broad client base that includes manufacturing industries, environmental consultants, independent contractors, andindividuals. Services include effluent management programs (permit negotiation and management, sampling, self monitoring reports and waste treatment assistance) and analytical testing services.
Timothy A Westerdale, President/CEO
Adam Westerdale, VP/Chief Operating Officer

4690 General Sciences Corporation
205 Schoolhouse Rd. 215-723-8588
Souderton, PA 18964 *Fax:* 215-723-8875
Consulting and research firm specializing in environmental sciences.
Jeffrey Chen, President

4691 General Systems Division
1025 West Nursery Road 410-636-8700
Suite 120 *Fax:* 410-636-8708
Linthicum Heights, MD 21090 www.nct-active.com
Environmental studies.
Michael Parella, President

4692 Geo Environmental Technologies
103 E. Lemon Ave. 626-305-0400
Suite 212 *Fax:* 401-751-8613
Monrovia, CA 91016 jcouture@geoenvironment-technologies.com
www.geoenvironment-technologies.com
Environmental testing and consulting company.
Jeff Couture, Contact Person

4693 Geo-Con
1250 Fifth Avenue 724-335-7273
New Kensington, PA 15068 *Fax:* 412-373-3357
www.geocon.net

Environmental services firm provides soil remediation by mixing soil with chemicals designed to eliminate the contaminants.
James Brannigan, VP of Opertaions
Loren Martin, Business Development Manager

4694 GeoPotential
22323 E Wild Fern Lane 503-622-0154
Brightwood, OR 97011 *Fax:* 503-492-4404
geopotential@aol.com
www.members.aol.com/resiii/geomain.htm
GeoPotential provides subsurface mapping surveys to locate underground objects such as underground storage tanks, utilities, geology, etc. They use geophysical methods consisting of ground penetrating radar, magnetics,electromagnetics and gravity.

Ralph Soule, President

4695 Geological Sciences & Laboratories
3133 N Main Street 606-439-3373
Hazard, KY 41701

4696 Geomatrix
210 East High Street 732-579-8283
Bound Brook, NJ 00880 *Fax:* 732-579-8305
info@geosoftinc.com
www.geosoftinc.com
Environmental engineering and consulting firm.

4697 Geophex
605 Mercury Street 919-839-8515
Raleigh, NC 27603 *Fax:* 919-839-8528
info@geophex.com
www.geophex.com

Environmental services firm.
IJ Won, President

4698 George Miksch Sutton Avian Research Center
PO Box 2007 918-336-7778
Bartlesville, OK 74005-2007 *Fax:* 918-336-7783
gmsarc@aol.com
www.suttoncenter.org
Finding cooperative conservation solutions for birds and the natural world through science and education.

George Kamp, Chairman
Lee Holcombe, President

4699 Geotechnical and Materials Testing
693 Plymouth Ave NE 616-456-5469
Grand Rapids, MI 49505 800-968-8378
Fax: 616-456-5784
www.mtc-test.com
Environmental engineering and consulting firm.
Ahmed N Elrefai, President

4700 Gerhart Laboratories
Route 219 814-634-0820
Garrett, PA 15542

Environmental testing laboratory.
Michael Gerhart, President

4701 Giblin Associates
PO Box 6172 707-528-3078
Santa Rosa, CA 95406 *Fax:* 707-528-2837
Environmental and geotechnical engineering firm.
Jere A Giblin, President

4702 Global Geochemistry Corporation
Station A 902-453-0061
PO Box 9469 *Fax:* 902-453-0061
Halifax, NS B3K5S
Consulting firm in the fields of geochemistry and environmental sciences. Research results published by the firm's scientists in journals.
Prasanta Mukhopadhyay, President

4703 Globetrotters Engineering Corporation
300 S Wacker Drive 312-922-6400
Suite 400 *Fax:* 312-922-2953
Chicago, IL 60606 marketing@gec-group.com
www.gec-group.com
Globetrotters helps its clients achieve their goals by understanding their needs and offering high quality, sustainable, and value added professional services that are specifically tailored to each project.
Niranjan S Shah, Chair/CEO/Co-founder
Michael J. McMurray, ESQ., President

4704 GoodKind & O'Dea
31 Saint James Avenue 617-695-3400
Suite 1601 *Fax:* 617-695-3310
Boston, MA 00211
Architectural and engineering consulting firm.
David K Blake, Contact

4705 Gordon & Associates
1 Gateway Center 617-227-2707
Suite 312 *Fax:* 617-916-9218
Newton, MA 00245 jsanders@gordonassociates.com
www.gordonassociates.com
Environmental consulting firm specializing in waste residuals.
Howard J. Gordon, President
Robert S. Kamanitz, Sr. VP

4706 Gordon Piatt Energy Group
7811 Baumgart Road 800-848-8197
Evansville, IN 47725 800-848-8197
Fax: 812-867-0760
sales@ciciboilers.com
www.gordonpiattparts.com
Jim Salomon, President

4707 Grand Junction Laboratories
435 North Avenue 970-242-7618
Grand Junction, CO 81501 *Fax:* 970-243-7235
Brian Bauer, Director

4708 Greeley-Polhemus Group
1310 Birmingham Road 610-793-9440
West Chester, PA 19382
Environmental consulting firm that has served clients in State and Federal agencies, as well as the private industry. Primary clients include the U.S. Army Corps of Engineers, as well as various Corps Districts throughout the U.S.
Maureen Polhemus, President & Owner

4709 Green Globe Laboratories
1860 Arthur Road 630-231-0680
West Chicago, IL 60185 *Fax:* 630-957-4394
rajan@therightstuff.com
www.therightstuff.com

Environmental testing and consulting firm.
Robert Fitzsimmons, President

4710 Ground Technology
14227 Fern Drive 281-597-8866
Houston, TX 77079 *Fax:* 281-597-8308
A multi-disciplinary engineering firm specializing in environmental services, geotechnical engineering, and construction materials and inspection services. GTI is a woman owned business enterprise as well as minority/disadvantagedenterprise certified by TxDOT, METRO, the State of Texas, and City of Houston, HISD, and the Houston Minority Business Council.
Ruma Acharya, President

4711 Groundwater Specialists
3806 Telluride Place 303-494-8122
Boulder, CO 80305 *Fax:* 303-494-5443
gws@qwest.net
Groundwater exploration; dewatering; waterwell design; mitigation of high groundwater problems.
William H Bellis, Hydrologist

4712 Gruen, Gruen & Associates
1160 Mission Street 415-433-7598
#2204 *Fax:* 415-989-4224
San Francisco, CA 94103 jlofton@ggassoc.com
www.ggassoc.com
The urban economists, sociologists, market and financial analysts, demographers and statisticians of Gruen Gruen + Associates (GG+A) are dedicated to helping make the best use of land, real property and urban and environmentalresources.
Nina J Gruen, Principle Sociologist
Claude Gruen, Ph.D., Principal Economist

4713 Guanterra Environmental Services
1721 S Grand Avenue 714-258-8610
Santa Ana, CA 92705 *Fax:* 714-258-0921
Chemical analysis technical and consulting research firm. Research results published in project reports and professional journals.

4714 Guardian Systems
1108 Ashville Road NE 205-699-6647
PO Box 190 866-729-7211
Leeds, AL 35094 *Fax:* 205-699-3882
awilliams@gsilab.com
www.gsilab.com
Laboratory division provides a full range of analysis for inorganic, organicand physical testing of drinking water, wastewater, groundwater sediments, sludge, waste materials and soils. Industrial Hygiene division provides equipmentand analysis to meet OSHA requirements. Bio-Assay division can accommodate Aquatic Toxicity monitoring requirement.
Linda Miller, President
Gerald Miller, CEO

4715 Gulf Coast Analytical Laboratories
7979 Innovation Park Drive 225-769-4900
Baton Rouge, LA 70820 *Fax:* 225-767-5717
edg@gcal.com
www.gcal.com
Environmental and industrial testing laboratory.
Randy K. Whittington, CEO
Mark Peterman, IT Director

4716 Gutierrez, Smouse, Wilmut and Associates
11117 Shady Trl 972-620-1255
Dallas, TX 75229 *Fax:* 972-620-8028
Environmental engineering consulting firm. Research results published in project reports and technical journals.
Charles G Wilmut, President

4717 H John Heinz III Center for Science
900 17th Street NW 202-737-6307
Suite 700 *Fax:* 202-737-6410
Washington, DC 20006 info@heinzctr.org
www.heinzctr.org
The Center is a nonpartisan, nonprofit institute dedicated to improving the scientific and economic foundation for environmental policy through nmultisectoral collaboration. The Heinz Center fosters collaboration among industry,environmental organizations, academia, and all levels of government in each of its program areas.

Conn Nugent, President
Matthew Grason, Fundraising Coordinator

4718 H2M Group: Holzmacherm McLendon & Murrell
575 Broad Hollow Road 631-694-3040
Melville, NY 11747-5076 *Fax:* 631-694-4122
www.h2mlabs.com
Engineers, hydrogeologists, geologists and scientists strive to balance society's dynamic industrial and commercial growth with appropriate development and conservation of natural and man-made resources.

John J Molloy, President
Joann M. Slavin, Sr. VP

4719 HDR
1917 67th Street S 402-399-1000
Omaha, NE 68106-2973 800-366-4411
Fax: 402-548-5015
www.hdrinc.com
Environmental engineering and consulting firm offering services such as site design, asset management, commissioning plans, funding, environmental remediation, impact analysis, compliance, natural resources management, permitting, andmore.

Eric L. Keen, Chair & CEO
Charles L. O'Reilly, Vice Chair & COO

4720 HTS
416 Pickering Street 713-692-8373
Houston, TX 77091
Ron Langston, President

4721 HWS Consulting Group
PO Box 80358 402-479-2200
Lincoln, NE 68501 *Fax:* 402-479-2276
James Linderholm, President

4722 Hach Company
PO Box 389 970-669-3050
Loveland, CO 80539-389 800-227-4224
Fax: 970-669-2932
techhelp@hach.com
www.hach.com
Offers water quality product for government buyers.

Bruce Hach, President

4723 Haley & Aldrich
70 Blanchard Road 617-886-7400
Suite 201 *Fax:* 619 285 7169
Burlington, MA 00180 info@haleyaldrich.com
www.haleyaldrich.com
Haley & Aldrich provides leading edge underground engineering and environmental consulting services, nationally and internationally. The staff encompass a wide range of disciplines, offering their clients integrated solutions.Environmental services include corrective action; environmental management, health and safety consulting; and environmental site assessment/due diligence.

Lawrence Smith, President/CEO
Ellie Haddad, Market Segment Leader

4724 Halliburton Company
3000 N. Sam Houston Pkwy E. 281-871-4000
Houston, TX 77032 *Fax:* 214-978-2611
www.halliburton.com
One of the world's largest providers of products and services to the oil and gas industries.

Milton Carroll, Chairman
David J. Lesar, Chairman of the Board

4725 Hamilton Research, Ltd.
80 Grove Street 914-631-9194
Tarrytown, NY 10591 *Fax:* 914-631-6134
Hamilton Research is a consulting firm specializing in environmental physiology. Our focus is mainly on exposure of people to pressures less and greater than atmospheric, and involves dealing with different breathing gases, especiallyhigh and low levels of oxygen, and the consequences of changes in pressure, especially decompression. Another important area of interest is hyperbaric oxygen therapy.

R W Hamilton, President

4726 Hampton Roads Testing Laboratories
611 Howmet Drive 757-826-5310
Hampton, VA 23661
Independent third party testing laboratory. Performs sampling and analysis in accordance with the required ASTM or ISO Standards.

4727 Handex Environmental Recovery
500 Campus Drive 732-536-8500
PO Box 451 *Fax:* 732-536-7751
Morganville, NJ 00775
Environmental management and analysis firm.
CL Smith, CEO

4728 Hart Crowser
3131 Elliott Avenue 206-324-9530
Suite 600 *Fax:* 206-328-5581
Seattle, WA 98121 www.hartcrowser.com
Hart Crowser provides a full range of services from initial site studies through regulatory permitting design and construction. Areas covered include environmental site assessments, biological surveys, regulatory strategy and support,geotechnical and environmental engineering, and oil and gas contamination support.

David Winter, President & CEO
Tony Bardana, Business Development

4729 Hatch Mott MacDonald
833 Rt 9 North 609-465-9377
Cape May, NJ 0 800-832-3272
Fax: 973-376-1072
www.hatchmott.com
Hatch Mott MacDonald is a client-focused consulting firm providing planning, investigation, design and management capabilities in engineering disciplines and environmental sciences. Areas of expertise include industrial wastewater,site utilities engineering, hazardous and solid waste management and environmental site assessments.

Nicholas DeNichilo, President/CEO
Albert Beninato, East Unit MD

4730 Hatcher-Sayre
905 Southlake Boulevard 804-794-0216
Richmond, VA 23236 *Fax:* 804-379-8934
Environmental consulting and engineering services firm.

4731 Havens & Emerson
700 Bond Court Building 216-621-2407
1300 E 9th Street *Fax:* 216-621-4972
Cleveland, OH 44114
Environmental engineering firm.
Gary Siegel, President/CEO

4732 **Hayden Environmental Group**
561 Congress Park Drive 937-438-3010
Dayton, OH 45459 *Fax:* 937-438-3020
www.heg.com
Testing, sampling, and analysis service.
Patrick Purvermuller, Group CEO
Andrear Palm, CEO Mass Hosting

4733 **Hayes, Seay, Mattern & Mattern**
PO Box 13446 540-857-3100
Roanoke, VA 24034 *Fax:* 540-857-3296
Troy S Kincer, PE, Principal Associate
Guy E Slagle, PE, LS, Vice President

4734 **HazMat Environmental Group**
60 Commerce Drive 716-827-7200
Buffalo, NY 14218-1040 www.hazmatinc.com
Offers transportation services for hazardous and non-hazardous materials via tank trailers, vacuum trailers, roll-offs, truckload, and less-than-truckload vans. Also offers OSHA certification training and other training courses forenvironmental consulting, logistics, and tank trailer repair.
John Stewart, President
Donna Crosta, Safety Manager

4735 **Henry Souther Laboratories**
24 Tobey Road 860-242-6291
Bloomfield, CT 00600 *Fax:* 860-286-0634
Richard J Lombardi, VP

4736 **Heritage Laboratories**
560 North Rogers Road 913-764-1045
Olathe, KS 66062 *Fax:* 913-764-3372
Environmental testing laboratory.

4737 **Heritage Remediation Engineering**
4925 Heller Street 502-473-0638
Louisville, KY 40218 *Fax:* 502-459-4988
Environemtal management and remediation company.

4738 **Hess Environmental Services**
6057 Executive Centre Drive 901-377-9139
Suite 6 *Fax:* 901-377-9150
Memphis, TN 38134
Hess Environmental Services, Inc. (HES) is an environmental consulting/engineering firm. Their primary activities are: Indoor air quality (IAQ) (Mold and Bacterial) Investigations; Title V Air and Other Permit Applications; Phase I,II, III Property Assessments; Remedial Investigations, Audits, Enviromental Health and Safety, Storm Water, Wastewater, Air Monitoring, Asbestos Inspection and Sampling.
Connie Hess, President
Gary Siebenschuh, VP

4739 **Hidell-Eyster Technical Services**
PO Box 325 781-749-8040
Accord, MA 00201 *Fax:* 781-749-2304
www.hidelleyster.com
Environmental and bottled water assessment and consulting company.
Henry R Hidell, Founder/Chairman
Carroll S. Keim, President/CEO

4740 **Hillmann Environmental Company**
1600 Route 22 East 908-377-5644
Suite 107 *Fax:* 908-686-2636
Union, NJ 00708 www.hillmannconsulting.com
Hillmann Consulting, LLC is a full-service Environmental and Engineering Consulting firm providing an array of customized Remediation Support, Environmental Health and Occupational Safety, Sustainability Consulting, Environmental DueDiligence, Geotechnical, and Laboratory Analysis services.
Christopher Hillmann, Founder
Joseph Hillmann, Executive VP

4741 **Honeywell Technology Center**
3660 Technology Drive 480-353-3020
Minneapolis, MN 55418 877-841-2840
Fax: 612-951-7438
www.honeywell.com
Parent holding company with numerous high-tech units involved in environmental, energy, computer hardware and industrial automation research and development.
David M. Cote, CEO/Chairman
Andreas Kramvis, Vice Chairman

4742 **Hoosier Microbiological Laboratory**
912 West McGalliard 765-288-1124
Muncie, IN 47303 *Fax:* 765-288-8378
Donald A Hendrickson, Owner

4743 **Horner & Shifrin**
401 S. 18th St. 314-531-4321
Ste. 400 *Fax:* 314-531-6966
Saint Louis, MO 63103 www.hornershifrin.com
Civil, structural, and environmental engineering firm.
Duane L. Siegfried, President
Gino E.B. Bernardez, VP

4744 **Houston Advanced Research Center**
4800 Research Forest Drive 281-364-6000
The Woodlands, TX 77381 *Fax:* 281-363-7914
www.harc.edu
Environmental studies
Lina Gonzalez, VP/COO
Jim Lester, President/CEO

4745 **Humphrey Energy Enterprises**
One Beacon Street 617-720-5222
Suite 2320 *Fax:* 617-720-5507
Boston, MA 00210 info@humphreyenterprises.com
www.humphreyenterprises.com
Humphrey Enterprises, LLC is a private equity investment firm focused on three primary industry sectors: automotive, healthcare, and training and education.
John W. Humphrey, Chairman/Principal
James Humphrey, CEO/Principal

4746 **Huntingdon Engineering & Environmental**
1940 Orange Tree Lane 909-793-2691
Redlands, CA 92374 800-285-1653
Fax: 909-793-1704
www.dell.com/outlet
Offers the following service(s): Environmental remediation, engineering services, environmental consultant, environmental research, petroleum, mining, and chemical engineers and sanitary engineers.
Michael S. Dell, Chairman/CEO
Jeffrey W. Clarke, President/VP Operations

4747 **Hydro Science Laboratories**
320 West Water Street 732-349-9692
Toms River, NJ 00875 800-624-3100
Fax: 732-349-9729
www.hydroscienceinc.com
Environmental testing and analysis laboratory.
Robert Salt, Director of Business Dvlpmt

4748 **Hydro-logic**
1927 North 1275 Road 785-550-6474
Eudora, KS 66025 *Fax:* 785-542-3971
info@hydro-logic.com
www.hydro-logic.com
Offers professional environmental services, specializing in hydraulic soil and groundwater sampling. Maintains a multidisiplinary team of geologists, hydrologists, chemists, and regulatory compliance specialists.
Thomas Barr, President

4749 Hydrocomp
13 Jenkins Court 603-868-3344
Suite 200 *Fax:* 603-868-3366
Durham, NH 00382 info@hydrocompinc.com
www.hydrocompinc.com
Responding to the growth in desktop computing during the mid-1980s, HydroComp introduced the first version of the NavCad® software in 1987. NavCad is still HydroComp's flagship product, with users in all corners of the world fromdesign to construction to academia.
Jill Aaron, Managing Director
Donald MacPherson, Technical Director

4750 Hydrologic Purification Systems
370 Encinal Street 888-426-5644
Suite 150 888-426-5644
Santa Cruz, CA 95060 *Fax:* 831-336-9840
marco@hydrologicsystems.com
www.hydrologicsystems.com
Manufactures water purification systems.
Richard Gellert, President
Jenifer Ringel, Accounting Manager

4751 IAS Laboratories Inter Ag Services
2515 E University Drive 602-273-7248
Phoenix, AZ 85034 *Fax:* 602-275-3836
www.iaslabs.com
IAS is an international agricultural laboratory and research facility serving that provides a variety of environmental services including: soil fertility and water suitability testing; ASTM, AASHTO, ADOT & CDOT testing; quality controltesting for the fertilizer industry; and plant tissue, petiole and soil analysis for agriculture and farmers.
Paul J Eberhardt PhD, President
Sheri K McLane, Laboratory Manager

4752 IC Laboratories
3253 Grapevine St. 951-681-4422
Mira Loma, CA 91752 *Fax:* 951-681-4404
iclabs@iclabs.net
www.iclabs.net
Firm providing qualitative and quantitative materials analysis through X-ray diffraction. Studies focus on powders, metals, fibers, and clays, including analysis of crystallinity, thin films, environmental dusts, geological materials,and fabrics. Also provides limited research and development and consulting.

4753 ICS Radiation Technologies
8416 Florence Avenue 562-923-1837
Suite 207 *Fax:* 562-923-3609
Downey, CA 90240
Testing, engineering and consulting firm specializing in radiation effects in semiconductor devices.
Dr Michael K Gauthier, President

4754 IHI Environmental
4685 S. Ash Ave. 480-897-8200
Suite H-4 *Fax:* 480-897-1133
Temple, AZ 85282 ihi@ihi-env.com
www.ihi-env.com/
William T. Hopkins, Chairman
Donald E. Marano, President

4755 Ike Yen Associates
867 Marymount Lane 714-621-2302
Claremont, CA 91711

4756 Image
4525 Kingston Street 303-371-3338
Denver, CO 80239 *Fax:* 303-371-3299
Biochemistry and environmental research firm. Research results published in professional journals.

4757 ImmuCell Corporation
56 Evergreen Drive 207-878-2770
Portland, ME 00410 800-466-8235
Fax: 207-878-2117
mail@immucell.com
www.immucell.com
Biotechnology testing kits, animal health products and environment water testing.
Michael F Brigham, President

4758 Industrial Laboratories
4046 Youngfield Street 303-287-9691
Wheat Ridge, CO 80033 800-456-5288
Fax: 303-287-0964
kinman@industriallabs.net
www.industriallabs.net
Provides quality laboratory analysis and consultation. ICP Mineral Analysis.
Petra Hartmann, Director
Lisle Goeldner, Controller

4759 Informatics Division of Bio-Rad
2000 Market Street 267-322-6931
Suite 1460 888-524-6723
Philadelphia, PA 19102-1737 *Fax:* 267-322-6932
informatics.usa@bio-rad.com
www.bio-rad.com
Richard Shaps, Division Manager

4760 Infrastructure and Energy Alternatives (IEA)
6325 Digital Way 800-688-3775
Suite 460 iea.net
Indianapolis, IN 46278
IEA is an infrastructure construction company that specializes in energy and provides civil expertise. Their mission is to provide quality engineering and construction services to meet clients' ongoing infrastructure requirements.
JP Roehm, Chief Executive Officer
Andrew Layman, Chief Financial Officer

4761 Innovative Biotechnologies International
335 Lang Boulevard 716-773-4232
Grand Island, NY 14702 *Fax:* 716-773-4257
www.ibi.cc
Manufacturing technology of biosensing technology.

4762 Inprimis
500 West Cypress Creek Road 954-556-4020
Suite 1 *Fax:* 954-556-4031
Fort Lauderdale, FL 33309 info@enerl.com
www.inprimis.com/
Provides hardware and software technology, communications solutions that enbale data transmission, connectivity of devices, and access to applications and information via the Internet, personal computers, and/or server-basedenvironments. Also designs, manufactures, markets, and supports quality, innovative products that have a cost, performance, and time-to-market advantage.
Kevin P. Fitzgerald, Chairman/CEO
Ronald N. Stewart, Executive VP

4763 Institute for Alternative Agriculture
9200 Edmonston Road 301-441-8777
Suite 117 *Fax:* 301-220-0164
Greenbelt, MD 20770
The Wallace Institute advances this goal by providing the leadership, and policy research and analysis necessary to influence national agriculturalpolicy. It is a contributing member of a growing national alternaative agriculturenetwork, and works directly with government agencies, educational and research institutions, producer groups, farmers, scientists, advocates, and other organizations that provide agricultural research, education, and information services.
Dr. I Garth Youngberg, Executive Director

4764 **Institute for Applied Research**
103 W. Lockwood 314-968-9625
Suite 200 contact@iarstl.org
St. Louis, MO 63119 www.iarstl.org
The Institute of Applied Research (IAR) is an independent research and consulting organization with offices in St. Louis, Missouri. Founded in 1978, the Institute has specialized in providing research and technical assistance servicesto state governments and agencies and other public service and community organizations.

4765 **Institute for Environmental Education**
16 Upton Drive 978-658-5272
Wilmington, MA 00188 800-823-6239
Fax: 978-658-5435
sales@ieetrains.com
www.ieetrains.com
IEE is New England's largest environmental training provider with over 57 classes in Asbestos, OSHA, Lead-paint and Environmental Health and Safety.

Martin Wood, President
Roy Teresky, VP Marketing

4766 **Integral System**
5200 Philadelphia Way 443-539-5330
Suite A *Fax:* 301-577-1982
Lanham, MD 20706 www.integ.com
Custom computer systems for satellite control; environmental monitoring.
John Byme, Director of Engineering

4767 **Inter-Mountain Laboratories**
1673 Terra Avenue 307-672-8945
Sheridan, WY 82801 *Fax:* 307-672-6053
ebrandjord@imlinc.com
www.intermountainlabs.com
Provides high-quality analytical, engineering and field services to industry and governmental agencies.

Kevin Chartier, President
Eric Brandjord, Business Development

4768 **International Asbestos Testing Laboratories**
9000 Commerce Parkway 856-231-9449
Suite B 877-428-4285
Mount Laurel, NJ 00805 *Fax:* 856-231-9818
info@iatl.com
www.iatl.com
An environmental laboratory specializing in asbestos, lead and mold analysis. Provides environmental laboratory services to environmental consultants, engineers, building owners and govt. agencies throughout the US, Canada and othercountries. Accredited by numerous agencies including the National Voluntary Laboratory Accreditation Program (NVLAP) and the American Industrial Hygiene Association (AIHA).

Eric M. Snyder, President
Christine Davis, Office Manager

4769 **International Maritime, Inc**
1250 24th Street N.W. 202-333-8501
Suite 350 *Fax:* 202-318-8114
Washington, DC 20037 imaassoc@msn.com
www.imastudies.com
International Maritime Associates (IMA) is a firm of business consultants specializing in market analysis and strategic planning for companies in the marine and offshore sectors.
Jim McCaul, Founder

4770 **International Science and Technology Institute**
1820 North Fort Myer Drive 703-807-2080
Suite 600 *Fax:* 703-807-1126
Arlington, VA 22209
Provides technical assistance in project design, implementation, and evaluation; database development and maintenance; institutional and human resource development; policy and economic analysis, methodological research and analysis;strategic planning; and workshop and conference design and organization.
BK Wesley Copeland, Vice Chair

4771 **International Society of Chemical Ecology**
University of California
Department of Entomology 909-787-5821
Riverside, CA 92521 *Fax:* 909-787-3086
jocelyn.millar@ucr.edu
www.isce.ucr.edu/Society/
ISCE is organized specifically to promote the understanding of interactions between organisms and their environment. Research areas include the chemistry, biochemistry and function of natural products, their importance at all levels ofecological organization, their evolutionary origin and their practical application.
John Hildebrand, President

4772 **Interpoll Laboratories**
4500 Ball Road NE 763-786-6020
Circle Pines, MN 55014 *Fax:* 763-786-7854
interpoll@interpoll-labs.com
www.interpoll-labs.com
Environmental laboratory offering stack testing, field services, pharmaceutical research, residential testing, and other laboratory services.

Dan Despen, President
Gregg Holman, VP & Laboratory Manager

4773 **Invensys Climate Controls**
191 East North Avneue 630-260-3400
Carol Stream, IL 60188 www.invensyscontrols.com
Formely the Robertshaw Controls Company. Founded after a successfully designing and manufacturing a line of top quality smoke alarms for the residential smoke alarm market.

Jean-Pascal Tricoire, Chairman/CEO
Jullo Rodriguez, Executive VP

4774 **J Dallon and Associates**
16 Fox Hollow Road 201-825-4574
Ramsey, NJ 00744
Research and consulting firm specializing in hortoculture.
Dr Joseph Dallon Jr, President

4775 **J Phillip Keathley: Agricultural Services Division**
25330 Ruess Avenue 209-599-2800
Ripon, CA 95366
Dr. J Phillip Keathley, President

4776 **JABA**
2766 North Country Club Road 520-327-7440
Tucson, AZ 85716 *Fax:* 520-327-7450
Mining exploration and environmental analysis firm.
James A Briscoe, President

4777 **JH Kleinfelder & Associates**
6700 Koll Center Parkway 925-484-1700
Suite 120 *Fax:* 925-484-5838
Pleasanton, CA 94566 www.kleinfelder.com
Geotechnical and environmental Engineering firm.
William C. Siegel, President
Michael P. Kesler, COO

4778 **JH Stuard Associates**
22 Tanglewood Drive 802-878-5171
Woodstock, VT 00509
Environmental Consulting firm.
Joe Shockcor, President

4779 **JK Research Associates**
86 Gold Hill Road 970-453-1760
Breckenridge, CO 80424

4780 **JL Rogers & Callcott Engineers**
PO Box 5655 864-232-1556
Greenville, SC 29606-5655 866-805-9596
Fax: 864-233-9058
rogers.callcott@rogersandcallcott.com
www.rogersandcallcott.com

Environmental engineering research firm.

4781 **JM Best**
119 S College Street 724-222-2102
Washington, PA 15301
Performs geologic, economic and engineering evaluations for oil and gas well drilling. Also provides completion operations, environmental studies, map preparations and investigative studies.

4782 **JR Henderson Labs**
123 Seaman Avenue 732-341-1211
Beachwood, NJ 00872 *Fax:* 732-505-1658
www.jrhendersonlabs.com

Environmental laboratory.
Elmer Hemphill, President

4783 **JWS Delavau Company**
10101 Roosevelt Blvd 215-671-1400
Philadelphia, PA 19154-2105 *Fax:* 215-671-1401
www.delavau.com

International environmental and technical company.
David L Sokol, President

4784 **James R Reed and Associates**
770 Pilot House Drive 757-873-4703
Newport News, VA 23606 800-873-4703
Fax: 757-873-1498
claiborne@jrreed.com
www.jrreed.com

Full service environmental testing facility offering quality analysis and reliable technical services to industry, local and federal government, engineers and private citizens. Areas of expertise include organic and inorganic chemicalanalyses, microbiological testing, and aquatic toxicity monitoring. Certificationto include NELAC Certification for the State of Virginia.

Han Ping Huang, President
Elaine Claiborne, Laboratory Director

4785 **James W Bunger and Associates**
PO Box 520037 801-975-1456
Salt Lake City, UT 84152-0037 *Fax:* 801-975-1530
jwba@jwba.com
www.jwba.com

Energy research and development firm specializing in environmental and oil remediation.
Christopher P. Russell, Director
Donald E. Cogswell, Process Development

4786 **Jane Goodall Institute**
1595 Spring Hill Road 703-682-9220
Suite 550 *Fax:* 703-682-9312
Vienna, VA 22182 www.janegoodall.org
A nonprofit corporation founded to concentrate on research, education and conservation of wildlife, pursuant to the life work of Jane Goodall. Offices are located across the world.
Jane Goodall, Ph.D., DBE, Founder
Tammy Palmer, Interim Executive Director

4787 **John D MacArthur Agro Ecology Research Center**
300 Buck Island Ranch Road 863-699-0242
Lake Placid, FL 33852 *Fax:* 863-699-2217
info@archbold-station.org
www.maerc.org
The MacArthur Agro Ecology Research Center at Buck Island Ranch is dedicated to a mission of long-term research, education and outreach related to the ecological and social value of subtropical grazing lands. The Center is at a 10,300acre cattle ranch on a long-term lease to Archbold Biological Station from the John D and Catherine T MacArthur Foundation. Provides researchers the opportunity to evaluate the relationship between economic and ecological factors and how these changeover time.
Elizabeth H. Boughton, Program Director
Gene Lollis, Ranch Manager

4788 **Johnson Company**
100 State Street 802-229-4600
Suite 600 *Fax:* 802-229-5876
Montpelier, VT 00560 info@jcomail.com
www.johnsonco.com
Environmental science and engineering consulting

Guy Wm. Vaillancourt, President
Glen A. Kirkpatrick, VP

4789 **Johnson Controls**
5757 N Green Bay Avenue 414-524-1200
P.O. Box 591 *Fax:* 414-228-2446
Milwaukee, WI 53201 www.johnsoncontrols.com
Research in environmental controls.
David Abney, CEO
Natalie A. Black, Sr. VP

4790 **Johnson Research Center**
University of Alabama at Huntsville 256-890-6343
Huntsville, AL 35899 *Fax:* 256-890-6848
Environmental research.
Dr. Michael Eley, CEO

4791 **Jones & Henry Laboratories**
2567 Tracy Road 419-666-0411
Northwood, OH 43619 *Fax:* 419-666-1657
jhlabs@glasscity.net
www.jhlaboratories.com
Environmental sampling and testing laboratory.
Fred W Doering, President
David Collins, Marketing Manager

4792 **Joyce Engineering, Inc.**
1604 Ownby Lane 804-355-4520
Richmond, VA 23220 *Fax:* 804-355-4282
info@joyceengineering.com
www.joyceengineering.com
Joyce Engineering, Inc. is a full-service consulting firm. They specialize in providing engineering and environmental solutions for clients throughout the southeastern United States. From siting to post-closure monitoring, managementplanning, construction services, landfill gas services, operator training and operations consulting, or environmental remediation, they provide expertise.

Connie Morrison, VP

4793 **KAI Technologies**
16 Marin Way 603-778-1888
Stratham, NH 00388 *Fax:* 603-778-0700
www.kaitechnologies.com

Applied and product research in the environment.
Bruce L. Cliff, Director

4794 **KCM**
3475 East Foothill Boulevard 626-470-2439
Pasadena, CA 91107-6024 *Fax:* 626-351-5291
info@tetratech.com
www.tetratech.com
Applied and product research in the environment.
Dan L. Batrack, Chairman/President/CEO
Steven M. Burdick, Executive VP

4795 **KE Sorrells Research Associates**
8100 National Drive 501-562-8139
Little Rock, AR 72209 800-331-8139
Fax: 501-562-7025
Analytical chemistry and applied research company providing consulting services in water technology and stream ecology.

KE Sorrells, President
Cecil Sorrells, CEO

4796 **KLM Engineering**
3394 Lake Elmo Avenue N 651-773-5111
PO Box 897 888-959-5111
Lake Elmo, MN 55042 *Fax:* 651-773-5222
www.klmengineering.com
Structural engineering and inspection firm specializing in the industry of steel and concrete plate structures.
Jack R Kollmer, President/Principal
Shawn A Mulhern, Vice President-Sales/Mktg.

4797 **Kag Laboratories International**
2323 Jackson Street 920-426-2222
Oshkosh, WI 54901 800-356-6045
Fax: 920-273-6128
akkhwaja@aol.com
www.kaglab.com/
An independent agricultural testing and consulting laboratory. Professional scientific services for agriculture, soil, feed, plant, water and other fields. Total farm management services including high value crops such as cranberry,stevia, blueberry, ginseng, strawberry, herbs, etc. Consultation and recommendation to increase net yield. Available for contractual applied research for all agribusiness industries in Wisconsin, North America and world-wide.
Dr. Akhtar Khwaja, President
Ruma Roy, Vice President/Chemist

4798 **Kansas City Testing Laboratory**
1308 Adams Street 913-321-8100
Kansas City, KS 66103 *Fax:* 913-321-8181
www.kctesting.com
Consulting engineering firm employed in geotechnical, materials, and environmental engineering. Research results published in Project reports.
Elisabeth DeCoursey, President/Co-Owner
Scott Martens, VP/Co-Owner

4799 **Kar Laboratories**
4425 Manchester Road 269-381-9666
Kalamazoo, MI 49001 *Fax:* 269-381-9698
info@karlabs.com
www.karlabs.com
Environmental testing laboratory, wastewater, drinking water, hay waste, soil and air.
William Rauch, President
Jayne Rauch, Marketing Manager

4800 **Kemper Research Foundation**
122 Main Street 513-249-2489
Milford, OH 45150
Richard Kemper, Director

4801 **Kemron Environmental Services**
2343-A State Route 821 740-373-4308
Marietta, OH 45750 *Fax:* 740-376-2536
mzumbro@kemron.com
Environmental testing and analysis firm.
Juan J. Gutierrez, President/CEO
John Dwyer, Executive VP

4802 **Kennedy-Jenks Consultants**
303 Second Street 415-243-2150
Suite 300 *Fax:* 415-896-0999
San Francisco, CA 94107 www.kennedyjenks.com
Environmental engineering consulting company.
Gary Carlton, Chair
Keith London, President/CEO

4803 **Kentucky Resource Laboratory**
Highway 421 606-598-2605
Manchester, KY 40962 *Fax:* 606-598-1544
Environmental testing firm.
Roy Rice, President

4804 **Kenvirons**
452 Versailles Road 502-695-4357
Frankfort, KY 40601 *Fax:* 502-695-4363
A multi-disciplined environmental and civil engineering firm. Offers engineering services in a range of areas to include water and wastewater related studies and system design, dam design, hydrological studies, environmentalassessments, air and water quality studies, urban and industrial planning, solid waste management, energy-environment interface, computer technology and laboratory services.
Randall Russell, President
Douglas Griffin, Chair

4805 **Keystone Labs**
600 East 17th Street South 800-858-5227
Suite B 800-858-5227
Newton, IA 50208 *Fax:* 641-792-7989
www.keystonelabs.com
Keystone Laboroatories, Inc. is a full service environmental laboratory committeed to providing the highest quality services at competitive prives.
Jodi King, President
Jerry Dawson, Manager

4806 **Kinnetic Laboratories**
307 Washington Street 831-457-3950
Santa Cruz, CA 95060 *Fax:* 831-426-0405
kkronsch@kinneticlabs.com
www.kineticlabs.com
Offers environmental consulting services in the areas of marine science, toxicology, water quality, biological research and more.
Patrick Kinney, President
Mark Savoie, Vice President

4807 **Kleinfelder**
981 Garcia Avenue 925-427-6477
Suite A *Fax:* 925-427-6478
Pittsburg, CA 94565 www.kleinfelder.com
Laboratories testing.
William C. Siegel, President
Michael P. Kesler, COO

4808 **Konheim & Ketcham**
175 Pacific Street 718-330-0550
Brooklyn, NY 11201 *Fax:* 718-330-0582
csk@konheimketcham.com
www.konheimketcham.com
Environmental and transportation planning.
Carolyn S Konheim, President
Brian T. Ketcham, Executive VP

4809 **Kraim Environmental Engineering Services**
11437 Etiwanda Avenue 818-363-0952
Northridge, CA 91326 *Fax:* 818-363-0492
luftmench@msn.com
Environmental engineering firm.
Jerry Kraim, President

4810 **Kramer & Associates**
20801 Biscayne Blvd 505-881-0243
Suite #403 800-281-1400
Miami, FL 33180 *Fax:* 505-881-7738
eservice@kramerandassociates.com
www.kramerandassociates.com
Environmental monitoring firm. Research results published in conference proceedings.
Lyn Kramer, MD/Partner
Gary Kramer, Contact

4811 **Ktech Corporation**
10800 Gibson S E 505-998-5830
Albuquerque, NM 87123 *Fax:* 505-998-5848
rswanson@ktech.com
Ktech Corporation, an employee-owned company based in Albuquerque, New Mexico, is dedicated to providing outstanding technical support services, sound scientific and engineering

work, and proven management expertise to a wide varietyof government and industry clients.

Steven E Downie, President
Robert E Swanson, VP/Chief Operations Officer

4812 LaBella Associates P.C.
300 State Street 872-626-6606
Suite 201 *Fax:* 585-454-3066
Rochester, NY 14614 labweb@labellapc.com
www.labellapc.com

Civil and environmental engineering firm.

Salvatore A. LaBella, Founder
Robert Healy, President

4813 LaQue Center for Corrosion Technology
521 Fort Fisher Blvd, North 910-256-2271
Kure Beach, NC 28449 *Fax:* 910-256-9816
www.laque.com

Corrosion technology firm. Research results published in trade journals and presented at technical association meetings.

W T Raines, President
D G Melton, VP

4814 Laboratory Corporation of America Holdings
1904 Alexander Drive 919-572-6900
Research Triangle Park, NC 27709 800-533-0567
www.labcorp.com

Whether the needs are large or small, routine or complex, physicians and patients can depend on them for access to a full range of the highest quality diagnostic testing.

Mark E. Breacher, CMO/SVP/Discipline Director
James K. Fleming, Div. Medical Director

4815 Laboratory Services Division of Consumers Energy
135 W Trail Street 517-788-2238
Jackson, MI 49201 *Fax:* 517-788-1104
naserafin@cmsenergy.com
www.laboratoryservices.com

Laboratory Services is a full-service testing laboratory. Services include: calibration, nondestructive testing, metallurgy, materials testing and chemistry. They are A2LA accredited (ISO/IEC 17025)-request scope-and 10CFR50 AppendixB authorized.

Nick Serafin, Marketing Manager

4816 Lancaster Laboratories
2425 New Holland Pike 717-656-2300
Lancaster, PA 17601 *Fax:* 717-656-2681
pha@lancasterlabs.com
www.lancasterlabs.com

Premier contract testing laboratory serving environmental, pharmaceutical and biophamaceutical clients worldwide. Offers a broad range of high quality analytical services in full compliance with EPA and FDA regulations and clientrequirements.

Gilles Martin, Chairman
Valerie Hanote, Board Member

4817 Lancy Environmental
181 Thorn Hill Road 724-772-0044
Warrendale, PA 15086 *Fax:* 724-772-1360
Gerald Rogers, President

4818 Land Management Decisions
3048 Research Drive 814-231-1248
State College, PA 16801 *Fax:* 814-231-1253
Dr. Dale E Baker, President

4819 Land Management Group Inc
3805 Wrightsville Avenue 910-452-0001
Suite 15 886-LMG-1078
Wilmington, NC 28403 *Fax:* 910-452-0060
rbrant@LMGroup.net
www.lmgroup.net

LMG provides environmental servicesin the following discplines: wetland delineations and permitting; soil mapping and waste water suitability studies; phase I & II environmental site assessments; EA and EIS land use and ecologicalstudies; wetland mitigations; and coastal management (CAMA) permitting assistance.

Robert L Moul, Founder/President
Craig Turner, VP

4820 Land Research Management
1300 N Congress Avenue 561-686-2481
Suite C *Fax:* 561-684-8709
West Palm Beach, FL 33409 lrmi@bellsouth.net

Land planning and zoning, environmental assessments and market analysis firm. Research results published in reports.

Kevin McGinley, President

4821 Lark Enterprises
2665 Ellwood Road 724-658-5676
New Castle, PA 16101 *Fax:* 508-943-8833
rjlark@aol.com
www.larkenterprises.org

Environmental research.

Justin Bruce, President
Roger Zallon, VP

4822 Laticrete International
1 Laticrete Park N 203-393-0010
91 Amity Road *Fax:* 203-393-1684
Bethany, CT 00652-3423 www.laticrete.com

Firm providing chemical, mechanical, and environmental simulation testing of concrete and aggregrate building materials.

Henry M. Rothberg, Chairman/Founder
David A. Rothberg, Chairman/CEO

4823 Law & Company of Wilmington
1711 Castle Street 910-762-7082
Wilmington, NC 28403 *Fax:* 910-762-8785

Richard W Spivey, President

4824 Lawrence Berkeley Laboratory: Structural Biology Division
1 Cyclotron Road 510-486-4311
Mail Stop 3-0226 *Fax:* 510-486-6059
Berkeley, CA 94720 www.lbl.gov
Paul Alivisatos, Director
Horst Simon, Deputy Director

4825 Lawrence G Spielvogel
21506 Valley Forge Circle 610-783-6350
King of Prussia, PA 19406 *Fax:* 610-783-6349

A consulting engineer who specializes in energy management and procurement and problem solving in buildings.

Lawrence G Spielvogel, President

4826 Ledoux and Company
359 Alfred Avenue 800-758-1201
Teaneck, NJ 00766-5755 *Fax:* 201-837-1235
info@ledoux.com

Ledoux & Company is an independent commercial metallurgical chemical laboratory, which has been family owned and operated since 1880.

A.R. Ledoux, Founder
LA Ledoux, President

4827 Lee Wilson and Associates
105 Cienega Street 505-988-9811
Santa Fe, NM 87501 *Fax:* 505-986-0092

Environmental consulting firm. Research results published in project reports.

Lee Wilson, President

4828 Leighton & Associates
17781 Cowan Street 949-250-1421
Irvine, CA 92614 *Fax:* 949-250-1114
www.leightongeo.com

Geotechnical and environmental engineering firm.
F. Beach Leighton, Founder
Bruce Clark, Contact

4829 Life Science Resources
Post Office Box 379 808-553-3211
Hoolehua, HI 96729 800-543-3211
Fax: 808-553-5033
Support@LifescienceResources.com
www.lifescienceresources.com
Biomedical and environmental sciences research firm.

4830 Life Systems
916-C Old Liverpool Road 315-378-4338
Liverpool, NY 13088 *Fax:* 315-299-5090
info@lifesysteminternational.com
www.lifesysteminternational.com
Environmental engineering research and consulting organization. Research results published In project reports and in technical journals.
R Wynveen, President

4831 Los Alamos Technical Associates
6501 Americas Parkway NE 505-884-3800
Suite 200 800-952-5282
Albuquerque, NM 87110 *Fax:* 505-880-3560
info@lata.com
www.lata.com
Environmental studies.
Dale Goralczyk, Contracts Manager
Bob Kingsbury, President/COO

4832 Louisville Testing Laboratory
1401 West Chestnut Street 502-584-5914
Louisville, KY 40203 *Fax:* 502-584-5914
Kenneth Smith Jr, President

4833 Lowry Systems
146 South Street 800-434-9080
Blue Hill, ME 00461 *Fax:* 207-374-3503
info@lowryh2o.com
www.lowryh2o.com
Environmental research.
Sylvia Lowry, President

4834 Lycott Environmental Inc
600 Charlton Street 508-765-0101
Southbridge, MA 00155 800-462-8211
Fax: 508-765-1352
lycottine@aol.com
www.lycott.com
Environmental science and ecological planning consultant and research firm. Research results published in project reports.
Lee D Lyman, President

4835 Lyle Environmental Management
1507 Chambers Road 614-488-1022
Columbus, OH 43212 *Fax:* 614-488-1198
Chemical research and consulting service.

4836 Lyle Laboratories
1507 Chambers Road 614-488-1022
Columbus, OH 43212 *Fax:* 614-867-5265
manager@lylelabs.com
www.lylelabs.com
They offer a wide range of testing and remediation services. They can test for biological contaminants, organic compounds, industrial pollutants, carcinogens, etc., and can do so in residential or commercial settings.
Dr. Thomas Eggers, Director

4837 Lynntech
2501 Earl Rudder Freeway South 979-764-2200
Suite 100 *Fax:* 979-764-2343
College Station, TX 77845 requests@lynntech.com
www.lynntech.com
Lynntech scientists and engineers develop world-class technology solutions for aerospace, defense and human health.
Oliver J Murphy, President
Jenifer Cross, Life Sciences Unit

4838 MBA Labs
340 South 66th Street 713-928-2701
Houston, TX 77261 800-472-1485
Fax: 281-292-7492
www.mbalabs.com
Independently owned and operated since 1968, mba Labs serves industry, government agencies and private citizens in Houston, the continental US and even across the globe. Conform to standards established by the EPA, the TNRCC and meetthe equivalent of ISO 9000 requirements for laboratories through their accreditation by NELAC.
Herman J Kresse

4839 MBA Polymers
500 West Ohio Avenue 510-231-9031
Richmond, CA 94804 *Fax:* 510-231-0302
info@mbapolymers.com
www.mbapolymers.com/
Environmental research.
Mike Biddle, Founder/President
Nigel Hunton, CEO

4840 MBC Applied Environmental Sciences
3000 Redhill Avenue 714-850-4830
Costa Mesa, CA 92626 *Fax:* 714-850-4840
info@mbcnet.net
www.mbcnet.net
Environmentatl consultants since 1969. Specializing in marine biology and ecology, oceanography, EIR, EIS, EA, toxicity testing, technical meetings, expert witnesses. MBE/DBE certified.
Shane Beck, President
Charles T. Mitchell, VP

4841 META Environmental
2200 West 25th Street 785-842-6382
Lawrence, KS 66047 800-444-6382
Fax: 785-842-6993
info@metaworldwide.com
www.metaenvironmental.net
Environmental testing lab offering site assessments.
Thomas Bradford Mayhew, Founder/Chairman
Fernando Ipanaque, CEO/General Manager

4842 MWH Global
380 Interlocken Crescent 303-533-1900
Suite 200 *Fax:* 303-533-1901
Broomfield, CO 80021 webinfo@mwhglobal.com
www.mwhglobal.com
MWH, globally driving the wet infrastructure sector, is leading the world in results-oriented management services, technical engineering, construction services and solutions to create a better world. The wet infrastructure sectorencompasses a full range of water related projects and programs from water supply, treatment and storage, dams, water management for the natural resources industry and coastal restoration to renewable power and environmental services.
Joseph D. Adams, President
Paul F. Boulos, President

4843 MWH Laboratories
750 Royal Oaks Drive 626-386-1100
Suite 100 800-566-5227
Monrovia, CA 91016 *Fax:* 626-386-1101
mwhlabs@mwhglobal.com
www.mwhlabs.com
Environmental testing laboratory that provides water and wastewater analyses including: drinking water synthetic organic and volatile organic tests; recycled water tests; organic disinfection byproduct and precursor analyses; inorganicdisinfection byproducts and precursors; inorganic tests including a complete

suite of metals to low-reporting levels; microbiological analyses ; and radiochemical analyses.

Andrew Eaton Ph.D, Technical Director
Ed Wilson, Laboratory Director

4844 Mabbett & Associates: Environmental Consultants and Engineers
5 Alfred Circle 888-748-6024
Bedford, MA 00173 800-877-6050
Fax: 781-275-5651
info@mabbett.com
www.mabbett.com

Mabbett & Associates (M&A) provides multi-disciplinary environmental, health and safety services to manufacturing and commercial industry, institutions and public agencies. M&A's services include pollution prevention and wasteminimization, site assessment and remediation, environmental pollution control, environmental management systems and auditing, training and occupational safety and health.

Arthur N Mabbett, Chairman/CEO
Paul D. Stelnberg, President

4845 Mack Laboratories
1163 Nicole Court 909-394-9007
Glendora, CA 91740 *Fax:* 909-394-9411
info@macklabs.com
www.macklabs.com

Mackenzie Laboratories, Inc. has been manufacturing and supplying American made products of the highest quality since 1954.

4846 Magma-Seal
10116 Aspen Street 512-836-4936
Austin, TX 78758 *Fax:* 512-836-4936

Develops materials (plastic and rubber) to withstand severe environmental conditions.
Earl Dumitro, President

4847 Malcolm Pirnie
630 Plaza Drive 720-344-3500
Suite 200 800-478-6870
Highlands Ranch, CO 80129 *Fax:* 720-344-3535
AUSInternet@arcadis-us.com

Provides environmental engineering, science and consulting services to over 3,000 public and private clients.
John Jastrem, CEO
Joachim Ebert, COO

4848 Maryland Spectral Services
1500 Caton Center Drive 410-247-7600
Suite G *Fax:* 410-247-7602
Baltimore, MD 21227 labman@mdspectral.com
www.mdspectral.com

Maryland Spectral Services, Inc. (MSS) is a privately owned, independent laboratory, which was incorporated in 1988, that provides environmental organic analytical services.
Samuel Hamner, VP

4849 Massachusetts Technological Lab
330 Pleasant Street 617-484-7314
Belmont, MA 00217

Applies research in the following areas: telecommunications and Internet.
Dr Ta-Ming Fang, President

4850 Mateson Chemical Corporation
1025 E Montgomery Avenue 215-423-3200
Philadelphia, PA 19125 *Fax:* 215-423-1164
www.matesonchemical.com

Environmental, toxic, materials, hazerdous waste research.

4851 McCoy & McCoy Laboratories
825 Industrial Road 270-821-7375
Madisonville, KY 42431 *Fax:* 270-444-6572
www.mccoylabs.com

Environmental assessment laboratory.
Bonnie Hewlett, Project Manager
Mike Baumgardner, Laboratory Operations

4852 McIlvaine Company
191 Waukegan Road 847-784-0012
Suite 208 *Fax:* 847-784-0061
Northfield, IL 60093 editor@mcilvainecompany.com
www.mcilvainecompany.com

Environmental research and consulting firm. Research results published in manuals updated by newsletters and abstracts.
Robert W McIlvaine, President
Marilyn McIlvaine, Marketing Manager

4853 McLaren-Hart
3039 Kilgore Road 916-638-3696
Rancho Cordova, CA 95670 *Fax:* 916-638-6840

Environmental research.

4854 McNamee Advanced Technology
3135 S State Street 734-665-5553
Suite 301 *Fax:* 734-665-2570
Ann Arbor, MI 48108

Environmental engineering firm, offering environmental consulting and environmental testing services.

4855 McVehil-Monnett Associates
9250 East Costilla Avenue 303-790-1332
Suite 630 *Fax:* 303-790-7820
Greenwood Village, CO 80112

Consulting firm providing services in air quality monitoring, permitting, litigation support, environmental management systems, compliance, and more. Industries served include the mining, oil and gas, electricity, and manufacturingindustries.

Bill Monnett, President
George McVehil, Principal

4856 McWhorter and Associates
33 Bull Street 912-234-8891
Suite 500 *Fax:* 912-234-8892
Savannah, GA 31401-9419 info@tankcarrobot.com
www.mcwhorterassoc.com

The company designs, builds, and installs robotic tools that clean residuals and strip linings from the interiors of rail tank cars and tanker trucks.

Thomas McWhorter, President

4857 Mega Engineering
10800 Lockwood Drive 301-681-4778
Silver Spring, MD 20901 *Fax:* 301-681-5683

Richard E Dame, PE

4858 Membrane Technology & Research Corporate Headquarters
39630 Eureka Drive 650-328-2228
Newark, CA 94560 *Fax:* 650-328-6580
sales@mtrinc.com
www.mtrinc.com

Supplier of membrane-based hydrocarbon recovery systems natural gas treatment systems and hydrogen recovery systems. Company capabilities include membrane and module manufacturing, process and system design, project engineering andcommissioning services.

Dr. Hans Wijmans, President
Nick Wynn, Commercial Operations

4859 Merck & Company
2000 Galloping Hill Road 908-740-4000
Kenilworth, NJ 00703 *Fax:* 732-594-3810
www.merck.com

The mission is to discover, develop and provide innovative products and services that save and improve lives around the world.

Kenneth C. Frazier, Chairman/President/CEO
Leslie A. Brun, Chairman/CEO

4860 Merrimack Engineering Services
66 Park Street 978-533-1659
Andover, MA 00181 *Fax:* 978-475-1448
merreng@aol.com
www.merrimackengineering.com
Research of all forms of environmental studies.
Stephen Stapinski, President

4861 Metro Services Laboratories
6309 Fern Valley Pass 502-964-0865
Louisville, KY 40228 *Fax:* 502-241-4347
Environmental testing laboratory offering air, water and soil testing services.

4862 Michael Baker International: Environmental Practice
500 Grant Street 813-466-6026
Suite 5400 800-553-1153
Pittsburgh, PA 15219www.mbakerintl.com/practices/environmental/
Michael Baker International provides engineering and consulting services for its clients' infrastructural challenges worldwide. The Environmental Practice is comprised of a team of engineers, geologists, planners, and environmentalscientists who help clients execute projects that balance ecological factors with other demands.
Mariben Andersen, Manager, Environmental

4863 Michael Baker International: Water Practice
500 Grant Street 213-372-1007
Suite 5400 800-553-1153
Pittsburgh, PA 15219 www.mbakerintl.com/practices/water
Michael Baker Corporation provides engineering and consulting services for its clients' infrastructural challenges worldwide. They offer solutions for the full spectrum of the water cycle, from the watershed level to the movement ofwater through urban and agricultural areas, reservoirs, water districution systems, and water/wastewater treatment plants.
Suad Cisic, Practice Lead, Water

4864 Mickle, Wagner & Coleman
3434 Country Club Avenue 479-649-8484
PO Box 1507 *Fax:* 479-649-8486
Fort Smith, AR 72903 info@mwc-engr.com
www.mwc-engr.com/
Provides civil and environmental engineering services, offering clients a broad range of plan designs and development capabilities from water, sewer, and drainage to streets, bridges, and dams, airports, recreational facilities, andresidential subdivisions.
Patrick J Mickle, PE, Chief Engineer

4865 Microseeps, Inc
220 William Pitt Way 412-826-5245
Pittsburgh, PA 15238 800-659-2887
Fax: 412-826-3433
www.microseeps.com
A full service, NELAP certified environmental laboratory which specializes in the evaluation of groundwater geochemistry for use in in-situ remediation processes.

Robert J Pirkle, President
Thomas W Hill, Sr. VP

4866 Microspec Analytical
3352 128th Avenue 616-399-6070
Holland, MI 49424 *Fax:* 616-399-6185
Environmental research and resting firm. Research results published in journals and client reports.
Tom Beamish, President

4867 Midwest Environmental Assistance Center
6561 N Seeley Avenue 773-973-4850
Chicago, IL 60645 *Fax:* 773-973-4851
meac2@aol.com
Noise pollution research firm.
Howard R Schechter, President

4868 Midwest Laboratories
13611 B Street 402-334-7770
Omaha, NE 68144 *Fax:* 402-334-9121
getinfo@midwestlabs.com
www.midwestlabs.com
Midwest Laboratories offers analytical services to agriculture, industry and municipal entities throughout the US and Canada. Using wet chemistry methods, the labs test soil, water, feed, food, plants, fertilizers and residues.

Brent Pohlman, President
Traci Grummert, Marketing Director

4869 Midwest Research Institute
425 Volker Boulevard 816-753-7600
Kansas City, MO 64110-2241 *Fax:* 816-753-8420
info@mriresearch.org
www.mriresearch.org
Midwest Research Institute is an independent, not-for-profit organization that performs contract research for clients in business, industry and government. MRI conducts programs in the areas of environment, health, engineering,technology development and energy research.
Dr. John Stanley, Business Development
Dr. Dan Kuchynka, Technical Enquires

4870 MikroPul Environmental Systems Division of Beacon Industrial Group
17 Wachung Avenue 704-908-2604
Chatham, NJ 00792 800-892-7278
Fax: 973-635-0678
info@mikropul.com
www.mikropul.com
Established in 1929, MikroPul is a manufacturer of dust control and product recovery products, from small unit collectors to complete engineered systems, for industrial applications worldwide.
Lacy Hayes, President/Beacon Ind Group
Richard Bearse, Chairman/Beacon Ind Group

4871 Miller Engineers
PO Box 422 315-682-0028
Manlius, NY 13104 *Fax:* 920-458-0369
DougMiller@MillerEngineers.com
www.millerengineers.com
Civil and environmental engineering firm.
Roger G Miller, President

4872 Minnesota Valley Testing Laboratories
1126 N Front Street 507-354-8517
New Ulm, MN 56073 800-782-3557
Fax: 507-359-1231
crc@mvtl.com
www.mvtl.com
Independent bacteriological and chemical analysis firm, with services in environmental, agricultural, and energy fields. Research results published in project reports.
Jerry Balbach, President
Thomas R. Berg, CEO

4873 Mirage Systems
PO Box 820 386-740-9222
DeLand, FL 32721 *Fax:* 386-740-9444
info@miragesys.com
www.miragesys.com
Environmental research.
Robert S Ziernicki, President

4874 Montgomery Watson Mining Group
380 Interlocken Crescent 303-533-1900
Suite 200 *Fax:* 303-533-1901
Broomfield, CO 80021 www.mwhglobal.com
Mine engineering and environmental services firm.
Joseph D. Adams, President
Alan J. Krause, CEO

4875 Mycotech
100 Commons Road 406-782-2386
Ste 7354 800-272-3716
Dripping Springs, TX 78620 *Fax:* 406-782-9912
mbi@mycotechbiological.com
www.mycotechbiological.com

Clifford Bradley, Director R&D

4876 Myra L Frank & Associates
811 W 7th Street 213-627-5376
Suite 800 *Fax:* 213-627-6853
Los Angeles, CA 90017
Environmental impact analysis firm. Architectural historic surveys.
Florence Williams

4877 Mystic Air Quality Consultants
1204 North Road 860-449-8903
Route 117 800-247-7746
Groton, CT 00634 *Fax:* 860-449-8860
maqc2@aol.com
www.mysticair.com
Indoor air quality and industrial hygiene services.

Chris Eident, CEO

4878 NET Pacific
3qb ODC International Plaza 632-893-9306
219 salcedo St. Legaspi Village *Fax:* 632-812-4852
Makati City, PH 01229 www.netpacific.net
Net Pacific is an award-winning, full-service telecommunications, data communications, and electrical systems provider.

4879 NORESCO United Technologies
1 Research Drive 508-614-1000
Suite 400C *Fax:* 508-836-9988
Westborough, MA 01581 www.noresco.com
Provides energy efficiency and sustainable design consulting services for building owners, architects and engineers. Services offered include energy auditing, commissioning and retro-commissioning, energy & daylighting modeling, LEED©certification consulting, and sustainability planning.
Neil Petchers, President & CEO
David G. Mannherz, Chief Financial Officer

4880 National Institute for Urban Wildlife
10921 Trotting Ridge Way 301-596-3311
Columbia, MD 21044
Promotes the preservation of wildlife in urban settings, providing support to individuals and organizations invloved in maintaining a place for wildlife in expanding American cities and suburbs. The Institute conducts researchexploring the relationship between humans and wildlife in these habitats, publicizes urban wildlife management methods, and raises public awareness of the value of wildlife in city settings. The Institute also provides consulting services.

4881 National Loss Control Service Corporation
1 Kemper Drive 847-320-2488
Long Grove, IL 60049 *Fax:* 847-320-4331
Environmental science laboratory.
Joan Wronski, Laboratory Manager

4882 National Renewable Energy Laboratory/NREL
15013 Denver West Parkway 303-275-3000
Golden, CO 80401 *Fax:* 303-275-4053
www.nrel.gov

The National Renewable Energy Laboratory/NREL began operating in 1977 as the Solar Energy Research Institute. It was designated a national laboratory of the U.S. Department of Energy (DOE) in September 1991 and its name changed toNREL. NREL develops renewable energy and energy efficiency technologies and practices, advances related science and engineering, and transfers knowledge and innovations to address the nation's energy and environmental goals.
Dan Arvizu, Director
Dana Christensen, Deputy Lab Director

4883 Neilson Research Corporation
245 South Grape Street 541-770-5678
Medford, OR 97501 800-600-5227
Fax: 541-770-2901
www.nrclabs.com
Provides analytical services to support environmental projects including testing of drinking water, wastewater, ground and surface water, foods soils, sediments, sludges, filters, air, and hazardous waste samples.
John WT Neils, CEO

4884 Neponset Valley Engineering Company
378 Page Street 781-297-7040
Suite 10 *Fax:* 781-297-7050
Stoughton, MA 00207
Environmental engineering analysis and consulting firm.

4885 New England Testing Laboratory
1254 Douglas Avenue 888-863-8522
North Providence, RI 00290 888-863-8522
Fax: 401-354-8951
rich.warila@newenglandtesting.com
www.newenglandtesting.com
New England Testing Laboratory provides environmental analytical services to the consulting engineering community, municipal utilities, private industry and commercial concerns, as well as state and federal agencies.
Richard Warila, VP
Mark Bishop, VP Operations

4886 New York Testing Laboratories
375 Rabro Drive 631-761-5555
Hauppage, NY 11788 800-281-3329
Fax: 718-657-3902
jhicks@mtllab.com
www.mtllab.net
Consulting on a range of disciplines including environmental.

Charles Realmuto, Director Marketing

4887 Newport Electronics
2229 South Yale Street 714-540-4914
Santa Ana, CA 92704-4401 800-639-7678
Fax: 203-968-7311
info@newportus.com
www.newportus.com
Manufacturer of industrial and environmental instrumentation including signal conditioners, digital panel meters, PID controllers and temperature sensors.

Milton Hollander, President

4888 Nobis Engineering
18 Chenell Drive 603-224-4182
Concord, NH 00330 *Fax:* 603-224-2507
www.nobisengineering.com
Environmental engineering consulting firm.

4889 Normandeau Associates
25 Nashua Road 603-472-5191
Bedford, NH 03110 *Fax:* 603-472-7052
www.normandeau.com
Normandeau Associates is an employee owned natural resources management consulting and testing services firm that provides: permit assistance, water quality studies, aquatic and terrestrial ecology, property transfer site assessments,wetlands services, contamination studies and biological laboratory services.

Pam Hall, CEO & Chair
Robert Varney, President

4890 North American Environmental Services
2848 Banwick Road 614-487-1109
Columbus, OH 43232 *Fax:* 614-291-8682
www.northamericanenviro.com
Environmental science research firm.
D Craig Kissock, President

4891 **Northeast Test Consultants**
587 Spring Street 207-854-3939
Westbrook, ME 00409-3918 *Fax:* 207-854-3658
info@netest.com
www.netest.com
Asbestos and lead testing/industrial hygiene.

Stephen Broadhead, Laboratory Manager

4892 **Northern Lights Institute**
210 N Higgins #326 406-721-7415
PO Box 8084 *Fax:* 406-721-7415
Missoula, MT 59807
Donald Snow, Program Director

4893 **Nuclear Consulting Services**
7000 Huntley Road 614-846-5710
Columbus, OH 43229 *Fax:* 614-431-0858
Joseph C Enneking, VP

4894 **O'Brien & Gere Engineers**
Box 4873 315-956-6100
Syracuse, NY 13221-4873 *Fax:* 315-463-7554
www.obg.com

R. Leland Davis, President
Timothy J. Barry, Sr. VP

4895 **OA Laboratories and Research, Inc.**
4717 North Shadeland Avenue 317-639-2626
Indianapolis, IN 46202-2628 *Fax:* 317-377-1924
oalabs@dajanigroup.com
OA Laboratories and Research, Inc. serves customers in Indiana and throughout the United States by meeting their Analytical needs.

Usama H. Dajani, President/CEO
Lisa K. Mesalam, Executive Secretary/Office M

4896 **Oak Ridge Institute for Science and Education**
1299 Bethel Valley Road 865-241-5947
Bldg SC-200 *Fax:* 865-576-5576
Oak Ridge, TN 37830 communications@orau.org
www.orau.org
As a consortium of major Ph.D.–granting academic institutions, ORAU cultivates collaborative partnerships that enhance the scientific research and education enterprise of our nation.
Andy Page, Director
Eric Abelquist, Executive VP

4897 **Occupational Health Conservation**
5118 N 56th Street 813-626-8156
Tampa, FL 33610 800-229-8156
Fax: 813-623-6702
Environmental impact assessment firm.
James F Rizk, President

4898 **Ogden Environment & Energy Services Company**
4455 Brookfield Corporate Drive 703-488-3700
Suite 100 *Fax:* 703-488-3701
Chantilly, VA 20151
Environmental engineering and consulting company.
J Mark Elliot, President

4899 **Ogden Environment & Energy Services Company**
5510 Morehouse Drive 858-458-9044
San Diego, CA 92121 *Fax:* 858-458-0943
Scientific and environmental engineering; analytical chemistry.
Mike Nienberg, Executive VP

4900 **Oil-Dri Corporation of America**
410 N Michigan Avenue 312-321-1515
Suite 400 800-645-3747
Chicago, IL 60611 *Fax:* 312-321-1271
info@oildri.com
www.oildri.com
Absorbents for consumers, industrial, agricultural, environmental and fluid purification.
Richard M. Jaffree, Chairman
Daniel S. Jafree, President/CEO

4901 **Olver**
1116 S Main Street 540-552-5548
Blacksburg, VA 24060 *Fax:* 540-552-5577
Engineering research and consulting firm specializing in environmental design and analysis. Research results published in project reports.

4902 **Omega Thermal Technologies**
21 Elbo Lane 610-572-2332
Mount Laurel, NJ 00805 *Fax:* 610-664-1258
contact@ottusa.com
www.ottusa.com
Technology consultants, designers and constructors offering technical expertise and hardware design for thermal processing and environmental studies.
Kenneth W Hladun, President
Peter V. Hewka, VP

4903 **Oneil M Banks**
336 S Main Street 410-879-4676
Suite 2D *Fax:* 410-836-8685
Bel Air, MD 21014
Industrial and environmental hygiene and toxicology consulting company.

4904 **Online Environs**
201 Broadway 617-577-0202
Suite 7 *Fax:* 617-577-0772
Cambridge, MA 00213
Telecommunications and Internet research.
Anrew Yu, President

4905 **Operational Technology Corporation**
4100 NW Loop 410 Street 210-731-0000
Suite 230 800-677-8072
San Antonio, TX 78229-4255 *Fax:* 210-731-0008
www.otcorp.com
Employment research firm providing information technologies, computer sales and service and environmental services.
John Fernandez, CEO

4906 **Orlando Laboratories**
820 Humphries Avenue 407-896-6645
Orlando, FL 32814 *Fax:* 407-898-6588
Independent environmental testing and analysis laboratory.

4907 **Ostergaard Acoustical Associates**
200 Executive Drive 973-731-7002
Suite 350 *Fax:* 973-731-6680
West Orange, NJ 00705 info@acousticalconsultant.com
www.acousticalconsultant.com
Environmental, acoustic and noise control testing and analysis firm. Research results published in project reports.

R Kring Herbert, Principal
Edward M. Clark, Principal

4908 **Ozark Environmental Laboratories**
PO Box 806 573-364-8900
Rolla, MO 65402 *Fax:* 573-341-2040
Firm providing construction materials testing on soils, aggregates, and asphaltic and portland cement concrete; water and wastewater physical and chemical analysis; and quality control studies encompassing physical measurements andchemical analysis.

4909 **P&P Laboratories**
2025 Woodlynne Avenue 856-962-6188
Oaklyn, NJ 00810
Environmental testing and chemical toxicology laboratory.

4910 PACE
100 Marshall Drive 724-772-0610
Warrendale, PA 15086 *Fax:* 724-772-1686
Environmental testing and analysis firm.

4911 PACE Analytical Services
1800 Elm Street SE 612-607-6400
Minneapolis, MN 55414 www.pacelabs.com
Sampling and analytical testing firm that offers inorganic, organic, and radiochemistry laboratory testing, as well as an Instrument Support Group to troubleshoot and repair laboratory equipment.

Steve A. Vanderboom, CEO
Michael R. Prasch, Executive VP & CFO

4912 PACE Environmental Products
5240 West Coplay Road 610-262-3818
Whitehall, PA 18052 800-303-4532
Fax: 610-262-4445
www.paceenvironmental.com
Manufacturer and Integrator of continuous emissions monitoring systems (EMS). Regulatory, process, and certification stack testing. In-shop analyzer repair, CEMS field service. Parts, sales, rentals, repairs and service.

Damian Gaiotti, Sales Manager

4913 PACE Resources, Incorporated
40 S Richland Avenue 717-852-1300
York, PA 17404 800-711-8075
Fax: 717-852-1301
pace40@aol.com
This company is the parent of units involved in environmental engineering and consulting, civil engineering, architectural planning, data processing, printing and other services.
Russell E Horn, Jr, President

4914 PAR Environmental Services
1906 21st Street 916-739-8356
Sacramento, CA 95811 mlmaniery@yahoo.com
www.parenvironmental.com
Provides clients with services in Cultural Resources Management and Environmental Planning. The planning department works on transportation and public works projects across California, while the cultural department provides historicpreservation, architectural history, and archaeological services to clients.

Mary L. Maniery, Chief Executive Officer
James G. Maniery, Chief Financial Officer

4915 PARS Environmental
500 Horizon Drive 609-890-7277
Suite 540 800-959-1119
Robbinsville, NJ 00869 *Fax:* 609-890-9116
info@parsenviro.com
www.parsenviro.com

Environmental consulting company.
HS Gill, President

4916 PCCI
300 North Lee Street 703-684-2060
Suite 201 *Fax:* 703-684-5343
Alexandria, VA 22314 thudon@pccii.com
www.pccii.com
Provides sensible solutions to difficult engineering and environmental problems in coastal, ocean and inland environments. Specialties include: environmental compliance; all hazards emergency response planning, trainings, drills andexercises; and marine engineering.

Robert Urban, President
Frank Marcinkowski, VP

4917 PDC and AREA Companies
4700 N Sterling Avenue 309-688-0760
Peoria, IL 61615 *Fax:* 309-692-9689
www.pdcarea.com
Environmental laboratory performs air sample analysis, soil analysis, and potential toxic waste analysis.

4918 PEI Associates
11499 Chester Road 513-782-4700
Suite 200 *Fax:* 513-782-4807
Cincinnati, OH 45246
Environmental consulting firm. Research results published in government publications.

4919 PELA GeoEnvironmental
P.O. Box 2310 205-752-5543
Tuscaloosa, AL 35403 *Fax:* 205-752-4043
mlee@pela.com
www.pela.com
PELA GeoEnvironmental is an environmental consulting company that engages in local and international projects revolving around geology, hydrogeology, and contamination remediation. These projects include wastewater treatment facilitydesign, regulatory compliance assessments, roadway design, and site development.
James LaMoreaux, Vice President & Chair
James Lee, President & CFO

4920 PRC Environmental Management
233 N Michigan Avenue 312-938-0300
Suite 1621 *Fax:* 312-931-1109
Chicago, IL 60601
Robert Banosten, VP

4921 PRD Tech
1776 Mentor Avenue 513-731-1800
Suite 400-A *Fax:* 513-984-5710
Cincinnati, OH 45212 prdbiofilter@aol.com
www.prdtechinc.com
Biological and chemical research and commercial technology development firm, serving primarily the baking, brewing, and other food industry segments with their environmental control needs - odor and volatile organic compound (VOC)control applications.
Ramesh Melarkode, President

4922 PSC Environmental Services
2337 N. Penn Road 215-822-2676
Hatfield, PA 19440 800-292-2510
Fax: 215-997-1315
www.pscnow.com

Environmental services
Bruce Roberson, President/CEO
Jeffrey Stocks, Sr. VP/CFO

4923 PSI
1901 South Meyers Road 630-691-1587
Suite 400 800-548-7901
Oakbrook Terrace, IL 60181 *Fax:* 630-691-1587
info@psiusa.com
www.psiusa.com
Distinguished as a leader in environmental consulting, geotechnical engineering, and construction testing services, PSI is nationally recognized in several disciplines, including: construction services, materials testing, roofconsulting and asbestos management.

4924 Pace
2400 Cumberland Drive 219-464-2389
Valparaiso, IN 46383 *Fax:* 219-462-2953
Environmental testing laboratory.
Les Arnold, President

4925 Pace Laboratory
9893 Brewers Court 301-490-9860
Laurel, MD 20723
Environmental testing laboratory.
Eric Holinger
Steve Marquez

4926 Pace New Jersey
284 Raritan Center Parkway 973-257-9300
Edison, NJ 00883 *Fax:* 973-257-0777
Environmental analytical laboratory and data management firm.

4927 Pacific Gamefish Research Foundation
47-381 Kealakehe Parkway 808-329-6105
PO Box 4800 *Fax:* 808-329-1148
Kailua Kona, HI 96740

4928 Pacific Northwest National Lab
902 Battelle Boulevard 509-375-2121
PO Box 999 888-375-7665
Richland, WA 99352 *Fax:* 509-375-2491
inquiry@pnl.gov
www.pnl.gov
Contract research and development for the government environmental restoration, energy, national security and health.
Mike Kluse, Lab Director
Steve Ashby, Deputy Director

4929 Pacific Northwest Research Institute
720 Broadway 206-726-1200
Seattle, WA 98122 800-745-1527
Fax: 206-726-1206
info@pndri.org
www.pnri.org
Established as Pacific Northwest Research Foundation in 1956 by Dr. William B Hutchinson, Sr. as the first private nonprofit biomedical and clinical research institute in the Northwest. As founder and first director, Dr. Hutchinson'sprimary objective was to provide a facility for basic and clinical research dedicated to the improvement of patient care. Sponsors basic science efforts in biochemistry, molecular biology and immunology as they pertain to the clinical areas of cancerand diabetes.
Erik Iverson, JD LLM, Chair
John Wecker, PH.D., President/CEO

4930 Pacific Nuclear
2525 West 10th St. 925-706-8300
Antioch, CA 94509-9111 800-706-3395
Fax: 925-706-8396
www.pacificnucleartechnology.com

4931 Package Research Laboratory
21 Pine Street 973-627-4405
Suite 105 *Fax:* 973-627-4407
Rockaway, NJ 00786 info@package-testing.com
www.package-testing.com
Packaged product testing facility. Research results published in reports, videos and pictures. Custom tests designed. DOT/UN certification on hazardous materials. Extreme environment testing. Pallet load and pallet merchandizingtesting. Design and packaging development, consulting, package analysis, project management, and vendor audits.
David Dixon, VP
Brian Berg, R&D

4932 PamLab
4099 Highway 190 East Service Rd 985-893-4097
Covington, LA 70433 844-639-9725
Fax: 985-893-6195
pamlab@pamlab.com
www.pamlab.com/
Pharmaceutical manufacturer.
Samuel Camp, Chairman
Kenny Ladner, President

4933 Pan Earth Designs
16525 103rd Street SE 360-458-9173
Suite A *Fax:* 360-458-9123
Yelm, WA 98597
Environmental research firm.

4934 Parsons Engineering Science
100 W Walnut Street 626-440-2000
Pasadena, CA 91124 *Fax:* 626-440-2630
erin.kuhlman@parsons.com
www.parsons.com
Environmental engineering testing and consulting company with expertise in advanced wastewater treatment.
Mark K. Holdsworth, Co-Founder
Kenneth C. Dahlberg, Chairman

4935 Peoria Disposal Company
2231 West Altorfer Drive 800-752-6651
Peoria, IL 61615 *Fax:* 309-688-0881
www.pdclab.com
Environmental services firm, especially hazardous waste testing.

4936 Pharmaco LSR
Mettlers Road 732-873-2550
Box 2360 *Fax:* 732-873-3992
East Millstone, NJ 00887
Dr. Geoffrey K Hogan, President

4937 Philip Environmental Services
210 W Sand Bank Road 618-281-7173
PO Box 230 *Fax:* 618-281-5120
Columbia, IL 62236 www.philipinc.com
Environmental research and analysis firm.
Jenny Penland, President

4938 Physical Sciences
20 New England Business Center 978-689-0003
Andover, MA 00181-1077 *Fax:* 978-689-3232
contact@psicorp.com
www.psicorp.com
PSI focuses on providing contract research and development services in a variety of technical areas to both government and commercial customers. Our interests range from basic research to technology development, with an emphasis onapplied research.
George.E Caledonia, Chairman
David Green, President/CEO

4939 Pittsburgh Mineral & Environmental Technology
700 5th Avenue 724-843-5000
New Brighton, PA 15066-1837 *Fax:* 724-843-5353
info@pmet-inc.com
www.pmet-inc.com
A full service company specializing in metals and mineral processing, coal ash utilization, waste stream management, and precision analysis. Also develops technologies dedicated to waste minimibation, treatment, and conversion tosafe,usable, profitable products.
Thomas E Weyand, President
William F Sutton, EVP

4940 Planning Concepts
1920 E. Northland Avenue 920-730-3333
Appleton, WI 54911 800-798-5722
Fax: 920-731-7401
cindy@planningconcepts.net
www.planningconcepts.net
Environmental impact assessment firm.
Richard Gasman, President
Randall Schmitz, VP

4941 Planning Design & Research Engineers
2000 Lindell Avenue 615-298-2065
Nashville, TN 37203-5509 *Fax:* 615-269-4119
pdre@pdre.net
www.PDRE.net
Environmental engineers, asbestos, lead paint design, testing underground tanks, hazardous waste projects, Phase I and II site assessments.
Teresa Tichenor, Office Manager

4942 Planning Resources
913 Parkview Boulevard — 630-668-3788
Lombard, IL 60148 — pri@planres.com
www.planres.com
A company that specializes in community planning, landscape architecture, park and recreation planning, and transportation planning. They aim to embrace the challenge of creating economically, socially, and environmentally impactfulsite solutions with intentional planning and design.
Darrell Garrison, Principal & Director
Mike Tait, Principal & CFO

4943 Plant Research Technologies
525 Del Rey Avenue Unit C — 408-245-4423
PO Box 6008 — *Fax:* 408-245-8043
Sunnyvale, CA 94086
Contact research organization which provides agricultural and analytical applied services.
Basil Burke PhD, President

4944 Plasma Science & Fusion Center
77 Massachusetts Avenue — 617-253-7232
North West 17 — *Fax:* 617-253-0570
Cambridge, MA 02139 — psfc-info@mit.edu
www.psfc.mit.edu
Center for plasma science and technology and plasma fusion energy research. The mission of the center is to invent alternative energy resources that are more environmentally friendly.
Dennis G Whyte, Director
Martin Greenwald, Deputy Director

4945 Polaroid Corporation
549 Technology Square — 617-577-2000
Cambridge, MA 00213 — *Fax:* 617-577-5618
www.polaroid.com

4946 Polyengineering
1935 Headland Avenue — 334-793-4700
PO Box 837 — 888-793-4700
Dothan, AL 36302 — *Fax:* 334-793-9015
info@polyengineering.com
www.polyengineering.com
Offers a broad range of professional engineering and architectural services as well as financial services and administrative support.
Max A. Mobley, Chairman
Bruce Bradley, P.E., President

4947 Polytechnic
3740 W Morse Avenue — 847-677-0450
Lincolnwood, IL 60712 — *Fax:* 847-677-0480

4948 Porter Consultants
4400 Old William Penn Highway — 412-380-7500
Suite 200 — *Fax:* 412-380-6899
Monroeville, PA 15146 — info@portercs.com
www.porter-consulting.com
Executive recruiting firm specializing in national and international placement of Sales, Marketing, Management, Executive-level, and Technical Support professionals within a wide rang of industries including High Tech, Exhibit.Telecommunications, Medical, and Pharmaceutical
William Porter, Founder/President
Art Floro, Sr.VP/Executive Recruiter

4949 Powell Labs Limited
1915 Aliceanna Street — 410-558-3540
Baltimore, MD 21231
Provides services in the specialty fields of metallurgical investigations, failure analysis, metal overheating and corrosion failures, remaining life assessments of high temperature components, identification of casting andmanufacturing defects, microbiological investigations, alloy identification, cycle water, cooling water, drinking water, high purity water, industrial process water, waste water, water and stream formed deposits, field examinations and training.

4950 Precision Environmental
2945 Townsgate Road — 805-500-3713
Suite 200 — 800-375-7786
Westlake Village, CA 91361 — *Fax:* 805-648-6999
info@precisionenv.com
www.precisionenv.com
Precision Environmental, Inc. was founded at Stanford University with the purpose of providing quality environmental contracting services to clients with asbestos contamination problems. State licensed and registered.

4951 Princeton Energy Resources International
2275 Research Blvd — 301-881-0650
Suite200 — *Fax:* 301-230-1232
Rockville, MD 20850 — www.perihq.com
Engineering and consulting firm: engineering and environmental technology, environmental management and global climate change issues, economic research, aviation economics, and human factors
Adolfo Menendez, Chairman/CEO
Nicholas P. Cheremisinoff, VP

4952 Priorities Institute
3233 Vallejo Street — 303-477-3792
#3B — *Fax:* 303-838-8105
Denver, CO 80211 — www.priorities.org
Nonprofit, educational research organization that explores issues of critical importance that are not adequately researched by existing educational, media, research, governmental or other organizations.
Logan Perkins, Director/Founder

4953 Professional Service Industries
1901 S. Meyers Road — 913-310-1600
Suite 400 — 800-548-7901
Oakbrook Terrace, IL 60181 — *Fax:* 913-310-1601
www.psiusa.com
Elizabeth Noakes, Department Manager

4954 Professional Service Industries Laboratory
4106 NW Riverside Drive — 816-741-9466
Riverside, MO 64150 — *Fax:* 816-587-2996
Engineering test laboratory.
Stephen Fitzer, President

4955 Professional Service Industries/Jammal & Associates Division
1675 Lee Road — 407-645-5560
Winter Park, FL 32789 — *Fax:* 407-645-1320
William N Phillips, Executive VP

4956 Q-Lab
1005 SW 18th Avenue — 305-245-5600
PO Box 349490 — *Fax:* 305-245-5656
Homestead, FL 33034-1725 — q-lab@q-lab.com
Firm providing environmental simulation testing.
George Grossman, Founder
Doug Grossman, President

4957 Quantum Environmental
167 Little Lake Drive — 734-930-2600
Ann Arbor, MI 48104 — *Fax:* 734-930-2798
info@quantumenvironmental.com
www.quantumenvironmental.com
Environmental remediation firm.

4958 RESPEC
3824 Jet Drive — 605-394-6400
Rapid City, SD 57703 — *Fax:* 605-394-6456
www.respec.com
RESPEC provides clients with technical and advisory services. They serve the mining and energy, water and environmental, and data and technology sectors, providing a range of products to meet their clients' needs.
Todd J. Kenner, President & CEO
Philip A. Welling, Treasurer & CFO

4959 RMC Corporation Laboratories
55 Charles St. East 416-633-4123
Suite 101 *Fax:* 416-633-9503
Toronto, ON 65775 info@reitter.com
www.reitter.com
Environmental waste studies. Research results published in journals.
Bert Reitter, President
Lianne Reitter, Vice Prsident/Director

4960 Radian Corporation
1601 Market Street 800-523-1988
Philadelphia, PA 19103 877-723-4261
Fax: 512-388-0966
Environmental science and industrial safety research and consulting firm. Research results published in project reports and in professional journals.
Teresa Bryce Bazemore, President
S.A. Ibrahim, CEO

4961 Ralph Stone and Company
10954 Santa Monica Boulevard 310-478-1501
Los Angeles, CA 90025 800-813-9613
Fax: 310-478-7359
rstoneco@aol.com
www.ralphstoneco.com
Environmental - Phase 1&2; Remediation; Geology
Richard Kahle, President
James Rowlands, VP

4962 Ramco
3150 Brunswick Pike 609-620-4800
Suite 130 800-472-6261
Lawrenceville, NJ 00864 *Fax:* 609-620-4860
www.ramco.com
P R Venketrama Raja, Vice Chairman
Virender Aggarwal, CEO

4963 RapidView
1828 W Olson Road 574-224-5426
Rochester, IN 46975 800-656-4225
Fax: 574-223-7953
info@rapidview.com
www.rapidview.com
Developing and providing unique inspection solutions to the nuclear, petrochemical, industrial and municipal sewer industries.
Rex Robinson, President/CEO
Matt Sutton, VP, Sales & Marketing

4964 Raytheon Company
870 Winter Street 781-522-3000
Waltham, MA 00245 *Fax:* 781-522-3001
cjkovalsky@raytheon.com
www.raytheon.com
An environmental testing firm, one of Raytheon's unique testing resources is the Andover Environmental Test Laboratory (ETL), a full-service, state-of-the-art facility. ETL specializes in performing static, dynamic (vibration, shock,and acceleration) and climatic test procedures, as well as comprehensive failure analysis studies.
Thomas A. Kennedy, Chairman/CEO
Daniel J. Crowley, Vice President

4965 Recon Environmental Corporation
1927 5th Avenue 619-308-9333
San Diego, CA 92101-2358 *Fax:* 619-308-9334
www.recon-us.com
Environmental engineering, consulting, and laboratory services. Research results published in project reports and government publications.
Robert MacAller, President
Bobbi Herdes, Private Team Leader

4966 Recon Systems
5815 Willowdale Ave. SE 330-484-8444
Waynesburg, OH 44688 *Fax:* 330-484-8555
www.reconsystems.com
Dr. Norman J Weinstein, President

4967 Reed and Associates
269 Germantown Bend Cove 847-718-0101
Memphis, TN 38018 *Fax:* 847-718-0202
www.myreedhome.com
Environmental testing laboratory.

4968 Reid, Quebe, Allison, Wilcox & Associates
4755 Kingsway Drive 317-255-6060
Suite 400 *Fax:* 317-255-8354
Indianapolis, IN 46205
Architectural and environmental engineering research firm.
J Edward Doyle, President

4969 Reliance Laboratories
2001 Young Court 304-842-5285
Racine, WI 53404 800-634-6155
Fax: 304-842-5351
neil_czarnecki@reliancelaboratories.com
www.reliancelaboratories.com
William F Kirk Jr, President

4970 Remtech
110 12th Street NW 205-682-7900
Suite E 106 *Fax:* 205-682-7953
Birmingham, AL 35203
Systems design and engineering firm specializing in energy and environmental control applications. Research results published in project reports and are presented in papers at conferences.
Gene Fuller, President

4971 Research Planning
1121 Park Street 803-256-7322
PO Box 328 *Fax:* 803-254-6445
Columbia, SC 29201 www.researchplanning.com
Scientific consulting firm specializing in the environment and natural resource assessment. Extensive experience in field surveys, EIS, spatial data analysis, and international work in Central America, West Africa and the Middle East.Research results published in professional journals, proceedings, and project reports. Woman-owned, small business concern.
Miles O. Hayes, Chairman
Jacqueline Michel, President

4972 Resource Technologies Corporation
204 East Calder Way 888-512-2721
Suite 205 *Fax:* 814-237-1769
State College, PA 16801 appraisals@resourcetec.com
www.resourcetec.com
RTC offers mineral appraisals for businesses or landowners who possess assets such as coal, oil and gas, aggregate, or specialty minerals. They provide GIS and digital mapping services, as well as industrial site appraisals, landappraisals, expert witness testimony, and more.
Jeffrey R. Kern, Senior Appraiser

4973 Resources for the Future
1616 P Street NW 202-328-5000
Suite 600 *Fax:* 202-939-3460
Washington, DC 20036 info@rff.org
www.rff.org
RFF is a nonprofit and nonpartisan think tank located in Washington DC that conducts independent research-rooted primarily in economics and other social sciences on environmental and natural resource issues. RFF was founded in 1952.
Richard L. Schmalensee, Chair
Philip R. Sharp, President

4974 Responsive Management
130 Fraklin Street 540-432-1888
Harrisonburg, VA 22801 *Fax:* 540-432-1892
mark@responsivemanagement.com
www.responsivemanagement.com

Responsive Management is a Virginia-based public opinion polling and survey research firm specializing in fisheries, wildlife, natural resource, outdoor recreation and environmental issues.
Mark Damian Duda, Executive Director
Steven J. Bissell, Qualitative Research Analyst

4975 Revet Environmental and Analytical Lab
181 Cedar Hill Street 508-460-7600
Marlborough, MA 00175 *Fax:* 508-460-7777
Environmental analysis and consulting laboratory.
V Taylor, President

4976 Ricerca Biosciences LLC
7528 Auburn Road 440-357-3300
Concord, OH 44077 888-742-3722
Fax: 440-354-6276
www.ricerca.com

Ricerca, a premier solution provider, offers expertise in both biology and chemistry to enable life sciences companies to fully leverage integrated, cost-effective, best practices approach to lead optimization and drug development.Services include in-vitro/in-vivo ADME, pharmacology, toxicology, medicinal, process, analytical chemistry, cGMP API scale-up production, regulatory support.

Dorothie L Okleson, Vice President
Clifford W . Croley, CEO

4977 Rich Technology
PO Box 4886 805-523-3415
Glen Allen, VA 23058 *Fax:* 815-229-1525
www.richtech.com

Environmental engineering research firm.
Robby Demeria, Executive Director
Tracy Dickerson, Financial & Ops Manager

4978 Riviana Foods: RVR Package Testing Center
1702 Taylor Street 713-861-8221
Houston, TX 77007 *Fax:* 713-861-9939
Lejo C Brana, Director Packaging

4979 Robert Bosch Corporation
32104 State Road 2 574-237-2100
New Carlisle, IN 46552 *Fax:* 219-654-8755
Controlled-road environmental testing of automotive components for passenger cars, trucks, buses, tractor-trailers and off-road vehicles; certification to federal brake commission and fuel economy requirements.

4980 Robert D Niehaus
140 E Carrillo Street 805-962-0611
Santa Barbara, CA 93101 *Fax:* 805-962-0097
Daniel@rdniehaus.com
www.rdniehaus.com

Socioeconomic and environmental planning organization. Research results published in reports.
Daniel Brown, Business Development Manager
Jessica Solis, Market Analyst

4981 Rocky Mountain Institute
Innovation Center
22830 Two Rivers Road 970-927-3851
Basalt, CO 81621 *Fax:* 970-927-3420
www.rmi.org

An independent, entrepreneurial, nonprofit think and do tank. Envisage a world thriving, verdant, and secure, for all.
Jules Kortenhorst, President & CEO
Amory Lovins, Chief Scientist

4982 Rone Engineers
8908 Ambassador Row 214-630-9745
Dallas, TX 75247 *Fax:* 214-630-9819
www.roneengineers.com

Provider of Geotechnical, Construction Materials Testing and Environmental Consulting services throughout Texas and the Southwest.
Richard Leigh, President
Mark D. Gray, VP

4983 Roux Associates
209 Shafter Street 631-232-2600
Islandia, NY 11749 800-322-ROUX
Fax: 631-232-9898
sales@rouxinc.com
www.rouxinc.com

Environmental Consulting and Management.

Paul Roux, Chairman
Doug Swanson, President/CEO

4984 Rummel, Klepper & Kahl
81 Mosher Street 410-728-2900
Baltimore, MD 21217 800-787-3755
Fax: 410-728-2992
www.rkk.com

Civil, site, transpotation, environmental, structural engineering services.
Ken Goon, AICP, Senior Director, Transportat
Bob Andryszak, PE, Director, Wastewater

4985 SGI International
1200 Prospect Street 858-551-1090
Suite 325 *Fax:* 858-551-0247
La Jolla, CA 92037
Environmental applications.
Michael L Rose, President

4986 SGS Environmental Services Inc
201 Route 17 North 201-508-3000
Rutherford, NJ 00707 *Fax:* 201-508-3183
julie.shumway@sgs.com
www.sgsgroup.us.com

Environmental laboratory services.

Olivier Coppey, Executive Vice President
Frankie NG, CEO

4987 SGS Galson
6601 Kirkville Road 315-671-3926
East Syracuse, NY 13057 888-432-5227
www.sgsgalson.com

Offers consulting services in industrial hygiene analysis with the aim of preventing hazardous exposures in the workplace. Services offered include sampling and analysis as well as equipment rentals.

Lisa Swab, Operations Manager
Ron McMahan, Development Director

4988 SHB AGRA
3232 W Virginia Avenue 602-995-3916
Phoenix, AZ 85009 *Fax:* 602-995-3921
Geotechnical and environmental research firm.

4989 SP Engineering
45 Congress Street, Building 4 978-745-4569
PO Box 848, Shetland Park *Fax:* 978-745-4881
Salem, MA 00197 brucepoolesp@aol.com
SP Engineering specializes in all areas of environmental compliance. Services include testing for chemical or bacterial contamination of well water and assessments for the presence of petroleum products or hazardous waste, in additionto performing environmental audits insuring owners that all the tenants in their industrial complexes are in compliance with government regulations relative to hazardous waste disposal.

Bruce Poole, Executive Director

4990 SPECTROGRAM Corporation
287 Boston Post Road 203-318-0535
Madison, CT 00644 *Fax:* 203-318-0535
spectrogram@msn.com
www.spectrogram.com
Research, development and manufacturing firm which produces analytical instrumentation and systems in the fields of analytical chemistry (environmental) and elastomeric physical testing (rubber and plastics). Also offers a line ofproducts, each of which is involved in on-line environmental monitoring for the detection of an accidental release of petroleum products (oil spills).
HR Gram, President/CEO

4991 STL Denver
4955 Yarrow Street 303-736-0100
Arvada, CO 80002 800-572-8958
Fax: 303-431-7171
Testing and analysis services.

4992 STS Consultants
750 Corporate Woods Parkway 847-279-2500
Vernon Hills, IL 60061 800-859-7871
Fax: 847-279-2510
stsltd.com
Consulting engineering firm offering an integrated package of services in geotechnical engineering, waste management, environmental management, and construction technology.
Thomas W Wolf, CEO

4993 STS Consultants
111 Pfingsten Road 630-272-6520
Northbrook, IL 60062 *Fax:* 847-498-2721
Mike Russell, President

4994 Saint Louis Testing Laboratories
2810 Clark Avenue 314-531-8080
Saint Louis, MO 63103 *Fax:* 314-531-8085
testlab@labinc.com
www.labinc.com/
Research and testing laboratory specializing in chemical, metallurgical, nondestructive and environmental testing and field services. Research results published in project reports.
W Trowbridge, President

4995 Samtest
3730 James Savage Road 989-496-3610
Midland, MI 48642 *Fax:* 989-496-3190
Geotechnical and environmental services firm.

4996 Sari Sommarstrom
PO Box 219 530-467-5783
Etna, CA 96027 *Fax:* 530-467-3623
sari@sisqtel.net

4997 Savannah Laboratories
PO Box 13548 912-354-7854
Savannah, GA 31416 *Fax:* 912-352-0165
Environmental and biological research and testing laboratory with expertise in fish farming technology.

4998 Scitest
1110 E. Collins Blvd. 972-479-1300
Suite 130 *Fax:* 972-479-1301
Richardson, TX 75081 info@scitest.com
www.scitest.com
Environmental testing and analysis laboratory.
Brandon Bailey, Vice President

4999 Separation Systems Technology
100 Nightingale Ln 850-932-1433
Gulf Breeze, FL 32561 *Fax:* 850-934-8642
office@separationsystems.com
www.separationsystems.com
Environmental research.
Robert L Riley, President

5000 Shannon & Wilson
400 N 34th Street 206-632-8020
PO Box 300303 *Fax:* 206-695-6777
Seattle, WA 98103 info-seattle@shanwil.com
www.shannonwilson.com
Environmental research.

5001 Sheladia Associates
15825 Shady Grove Road 301-590-3939
Suite 100 *Fax:* 301-948-7174
Rockville, MD 20850 www.sheladia.com
Consulting firm specializing in environmental studies. Research results published in research reports for the government.
A Moytayek, President

5002 Shell Engineering and Associates
2403 West Ash 573-445-0106
Columbia, MO 65203 *Fax:* 573-445-0137
charles@shellengr.com
www.shellengr.com
Harvey D Shell, Founder/Chairman
Charles Shell, President/CEO

5003 Sherry Laboratories
9301 Innovation Drive 765-378-4101
Suite 103 800-737-2378
Daleville, IN 47334-569 *Fax:* 765-378-4107
Analytical environmental laboratory.
Mel Burnell, President

5004 Shive-Hattery Engineers & Architects
316 2nd Street SE 319-364-0227
Suite 500 800-798-0227
Cedar Rapids, IA 52406-1803 *Fax:* 319-364-4251
shivecr@shive-hattery.com
www.shive-hattery.com
Jim Lee, President
Mark Anderson, Vice President/Office Direct

5005 Siebe Appliance Controls
2809 Emerywood Parkway 804-756-6500
Richmond, VA 23294 *Fax:* 804-756-6563
Automatic temperature, environmental, electronic appliance, heating, cooling and gas safety controls and valves; thermostats and oven burners.

5006 Siemens Water Technologies
10 Technology Drive 978-614-7156
Lowell, MA 00185 800-224-9474
Fax: 978-934-9499
Products and services includes: environmental devices and controls; system troubleshooting/diagnostics; system startup; instrumentation calibration and commissioning, and radio topographic path analysis.
Ursula Boehm, VP
Reudiger Knauf, VP

5007 Simpson Electric Company
520 Simpson Ave. 715-588-3311
PO Box 99 *Fax:* 715-588-3326
Lac Du Flambeau, WI 54538 www.simpsonelectric.com
Analog and digital panel meters, meter relays, controllers, volt-ohm-milliammeters, scopes and industrial and environmental test instruments.

5008 Skinner and Sherman Laboratories
1st Avenue 781-890-7200
Waltham, MA 00245 *Fax:* 781-890-7003

5009 Smith & Mahoney
540 Broadway
PO 22047
Albany, NY 12201
518-463-4107
Fax: 518-463-3823

Michael W McNarney, President

5010 Soil Engineering Testing/SET
2401 West 66th Street
Richfield, MN 55423
612-353-5770
Fax: 651-760-4312
labinfo@soilengineeringtesting.com
www.soilengineeringtesting.com/

A comprehensive soil mechanics laboratory facility for engineering disciplines, environmental and hydrological applications. Scope of services includes: water content; unit mass; liquid limit; sieve analysis; specific gravity; pH;organic content; unconfined compression; and expansion index.
Slade Olson, President
John Whelan, VP

5011 Solar Testing Laboratories
1125 Valley Belt Road
Cleveland, OH 44131
216-741-7007
Fax: 216-741-7011
www.stlohio.com

Geotechnical, environmental engineering, materials testing, and construction inspection laboratory. Services include environmental site assessments, assisting in the selection and coordination of the work of remediation contractors,asbestos inspection and abatement supervision, micro purgegroundwater sampling, sediment control inspection, landfill closure quality assurance, radiological assessments, U.S.T. closures and RCRA closures and facility investigation.
George J Ata PE, President

5012 Southeastern Engineering & Testing Laboratories
4761 SW 51st Street
Davie, FL 33314
954-584-4322
Fax: 954-584-4338
jack@seetl.com
www.seetl.com

Geotechnical and environmental engineering consulting firm and construction materials engineering laboratory.
Jack Krouskroup, Director

5013 Southern Petroleum Laboratory/SPL
8850 Interchange Drive
PO Box 20807
Houston, TX 77054
713-660-0901
877-775-5227
Fax: 713-660-8975
www.spl-inc.com

SPL provides technical and analytical services to the oil and gas industry including environmental and hydrocarbon analytical services as well as field (gas & liquid measurement) services.
Christopher F Brown, President
Steve Grenda, CEO

5014 Southern Research Institute COBRA Training Facility Center for Domestic Preparedness
2000 Ninth Avenue South
P.O. Box 55305
Birmingham, AL 35255-5305
205-581-2000
Fax: 800-967-6774
secrist@southernresearch.org
www.southernresearch.org

Southern Research Institute is an independent research corporation with established capabilities in pharmaceutical discovery and development, engineering, chemical and biological defense, environmental and energy-related sciences.Research is conducted through contracts and grants with government and commerical clients.
Ray L. Watts M.D, Chairman
Arthur J. Tipton, Ph.D., President/CEO

5015 Southern Research Institute Corporate Office: Life Sciences/Environment/Energy
757 Tom Martin Drive
PO Box 55305
Birmingham, AL 35211-5305
205-581-2000
800-967-6774
Fax: 800-967-6774
secrist@southernresearch.org
www.southernresearch.org

Southern Research Institute is an independent research corporation with established capabilities in pharmaceutical discovery and development, engineering, chemical and biological defense, environmental and energy-related sciences.Research is conducted through contracts and grants with government and commerical clients.
Ray L. Watts M.D, Chairman
Arthur J. Tipton, Ph.D., President/CEO

5016 Southern Research Institute: Carbon To Liquids Development Center
31972 Highway 25 North
Wilsonville, AL 35186
205-670-5068
800-967-6774
Fax: 205-670-5843
secrist@southernresearch.org
www.southernresearch.org

Southern Research Institute is an independent research corporation with established capabilities in pharmaceutical discovery and development, engineering, chemical and biological defense, environmental and energy-related sciences.Research is conducted through contracts and grants with government and commerical clients.
Ray L. Watts M.D, Chairman
Arthur J. Tipton, Ph.D., President/CEO

5017 Southern Research Institute: Chemical Defense Training Facility-Missouri
5201 International Drive
PO Box 55305
Durham, CA 27712-5305
919-282-1050
800-967-6774
Fax: 573-596-0722
secrist@southernresearch.org
www.southernresearch.org

Southern Research Institute is an independent research corporation with established capabilities in pharmaceutical discovery and development, engineering, chemical and biological defense, environmental and energy-related sciences.Research is conducted through contracts and grants with government and commerical clients.
Ray L. Watts M.D, Chairman
Arthur J. Tipton, Ph.D., President/CEO

5018 Southern Research Institute: Engineering Research Center
757 Tom Martin Drive
Birmingham, AL 35211
205-581-2000
800-967-6774
Fax: 205-581-2726
secrist@southernresearch.org
www.southernresearch.org

Southern Research Institute is an independent research corporation with established capabilities in pharmaceutical discovery and development, engineering, chemical and biological defense, environmental and energy-related sciences.Research is conducted through contracts and grants with government and commerical clients.
Ray L. Watts M.D, Chairman
Arthur J. Tipton, Ph.D., President/CEO

5019 Southern Research Institute: Environment & Energy Research
994 Ellington Field
Houston, AL 77034
256-726-9334
Fax: 256-726-9340
secrist@southernresearch.org
www.southernresearch.org

Southern Research Institute is an independent research corporation with established capabilities in pharmaceutical discovery and development, engineering, chemical and biological defense, environmental and energy-related sciences.Research is conducted through contracts and grants with government and commerical clients.
Ray L. Watts M.D, Chairman
Arthur J. Tipton, Ph.D., President/CEO

5020 Southern Research Institute: Infectious Disease Research Facility
431 Aviation Way
Frederick, MD 21701
301-694-3232
Fax: 301-694-7223
secrist@southernresearch.org
www.southernresearch.org

Southern Research Institute is an independent research corporation with established capabilities in pharmaceutical discovery

and development, engineering, chemical and biological defense, environmental and energy-related sciences.Research is conducted through contracts and grants with government and commerical clients.
Ray L. Watts M.D, Chairman
Arthur J. Tipton, Ph.D., President/CEO

5021 Southern Research Institute: Power Systems Development Facility
31972 Highway 25 North 205-670-5068
Wilsonville, AL 35186 *Fax:* 205-670-5843
secrist@southernresearch.org
www.southernresearch.org
Southern Research Institute is an independent research corporation with established capabilities in pharmaceutical discovery and development, engineering, chemical and biological defense, environmental and energy-related sciences.Research is conducted through contracts and grants with government and commerical clients.
Ray L. Watts M.D, Chairman
Arthur J. Tipton, Ph.D., President/CEO

5022 Southern Testing & Research Laboratories
317 Covered Bridge Road 252-237-4175
Catersville, GA 30120 *Fax:* 252-237-9341
www.southerntesting.com
Full-service laboratory with over 75 chemists, microbiologists and support personnel that provides personalized service to clients. Capabilities include pharmaceutical, foods and feeds, environmental, industrial hygiene, agriculturaland microbiological sciences. Laboratory is FDA-inspected GLP/cGMP laboratory utilizing AOAC, USP, EPA, USDA, AACC, AOCS, ISO, client and in-house validated methods.
Robert Dermer, Managing Director
Walter Hogg, Business Development

5023 Spears Professional Environmental & Archeological Research Services
13858 S Highway 170 479-839-3663
West Fork, AR 72774 *Fax:* 479-839-2575
SPEARSC@aol.com
Archeological research service. The company conducts cultural resources studies including background studies for Environmental Impact Studies, archeological surveys, significance testing, and data recovery/excavation. Large multi-yearprojects have included cultural resources surveys for timber sales and studies for proposed interstates and utilities.
Carol S Spears, President/Owner

5024 Spectrochem Laboratories
545 Commerce Street 201-337-4774
Franklin Lakes, NJ 00741 *Fax:* 201-337-1255
www.spectrochem.in
Research and development firm specializing in environmental sciences and inorganic chemistry. Research results published in proceedings at technical conferences.
Irene Van Dren, President

5025 Spectrum Sciences & Software
91 Hill Avenue NW 850-796-0909
Fort Walton Beach, FL 32548 *Fax:* 850-244-9560
www.specsci.com
An environmental research firm, Spectrum provides diversified capabilities of a large business in a number of advanced technologies. Services include all the disciplines and technologies relevant to operations and maintenance; computerand system sciences; manufacturing; comprehensive planning and environmental assessment technology; and system design testing and evaluation.
Jeremy Maines, Information Technology
Dwight Howard, VP Business Development

5026 Spotts, Stevens and McCoy
1047 North Park Road 610-621-2000
PO Box 6307 *Fax:* 610-621-2001
Reading, PA 19610-307 information@ssmgroup.com
www.ssmgroup.com
An engineering and consulting firm, serving business, industry, and government, SSM provides consulting services in the areas of environmental health and safety, regulatory compliance and training. In addition, SSM provides costeffective, well-engineered solutions to environmental health and safety issues facing facility owners in industry, education, healthcare and local government.
Eileen Kaley, Marketing Director

5027 Standard Testing and Engineering - Corporate
3400 N. Lincoln Boulevard 405-528-0541
Oklahoma City, OK 73105-5106 800-725-0541
Fax: 405-528-0559
bburris@stantest.com
www.stantest.com
Standard Testing and Engineering Company was founded in 1951 as a professional engineering firm specializing in materials testing and engineering for the construction and manufacturing industries. Standard Testing also providesenvironmental services such as groundwater studies. Standard Testing's capabilities include a wide variety of specialties such as environmental engineering, and industrial hygiene.
Thomas J Kelly, President
Richard W Mudd, Vice President

5028 Standard Testing and Engineering - Enid
902 Trails West Loop 580-725-3130
Enid, OK 73703-6336 800-725-3130
Fax: 580-237-3211
bburris@stantest.com
www.stantest.com
Standard Testing and Engineering Company was founded in 1951 as a professional engineering firm specializing in materials testing and engineering for the construction and manufacturing industries. Standard Testing also providesenvironmental services such as groundwater studies. Standard Testing's capabilities include a wide variety of specialties such as environmental engineering, and industrial hygiene.
Thomas J Kelly, President
Richard W Mudd, Vice President

5029 Standard Testing and Engineering - Lawton
202 S.E. 580-353-0872
J Ave. 800-725-0872
Lawton, OK 73501-2481 *Fax:* 580-353-1263
bburris@stantest.com
www.stantest.com
Standard Testing and Engineering Company was founded in 1951 as a professional engineering firm specializing in materials testing and engineering for the construction and manufacturing industries. Standard Testing also providesenvironmental services such as groundwater studies. Standard Testing's capabilities include a wide variety of specialties such as environmental engineering, and industrial hygiene.
Thomas J Kelly, President
Richard W Mudd, Vice President

5030 Standard Testing and Engineering - Oklahoma City Environmental Services Division
4300 N Lincoln Boulevard 405-424-8378
Oklahoma, OK 73105-5106 800-725-8378
Fax: 405-424-8129
tjkelly@stantest.com
www.stantest.com
Standard Testing and Engineering Company was founded in 1951 as a professional engineering firm specializing in materials testing and engineering for the construction and manufacturing industries. Standard Testing also providesenvironmental services such as groundwater studies. Standard Testing's capabilities include a wide variety of specialties such as environmental engineering, and industrial hygiene.
Thomas J Kelly, President
Richard W Mudd, Vice President

5031 Standard Testing and Engineering - Tulsa
10816 E. Newton St. 918-439-9539
Suite 110 800-725-4592
Tulsa, OK 74116 *Fax:* 918-437-0853
www.stantest.com

Standard Testing and Engineering Company was founded in 1951 as a professional engineering firm specializing in materials testing and engineering for the construction and manufacturing industries. Standard Testing also providesenvironmental services such as groundwater studies. Standard Testing's capabilities include a wide variety of specialties such as environmental engineering, and industrial hygiene.
Thomas J Kelly, President
Richard W Mudd, Vice President

5032 Stanford Technology Corporation
1010 N. Normandie 203-348-4080
Suite 301 866-717-7363
Spokane, WA 99201 *Fax:* 203-327-5225
stctestlab@aol.com
www.stanfordtechnology.com
High technology research firm. Research results published in confidential project reports.
Charles C Cullari, President
Gerald T Ciccone, VP

5033 Stantec Consulting Services
4875 Riverside Drive 780-917-7000
Macon, GA 31210 *Fax:* 478-474-8933
media@stantec.com
www.stantec.com
Stantec, founded in 1954, provides professional design and consulting services in planning, engineering, architecture, surveying, economics, and project management. Stantec supports public and private sector clients in a diverse rangeof markets in the infrastructure and facilities sector at every stage, from initial concept and financial feasibility to project completion and beyond.
Anton Germishuizen, VP/Business Leader
Bill Shelley, VP/Business Leader

5034 Steven Winter Associates - New York NY
307 7th Avenue 212-564-5800
Suite 1701 *Fax:* 212-741-8673
New York, NY 10001 swa@swinter.com
www.swinter.com
New York client base includes City, State, and Federal agencies, and owners of a wide array of buildings from small residential to well-known sustainable buildings, such as Battery Park City, 4 Times Square, AOL/Time Warner and HearstHeadquarters. SWA is working with many developers, architects, engineers, and building scientists to help deliver higher performance buildings throughout the NYC metropolitan area and in the surrounding region.
Steven Winter, President

5035 Steven Winter Associates - Norwalk CT
61 Washington Street 203-857-0200
Norwalk, CT 00685 *Fax:* 203-852-0741
swa@swinter.com
www.swinter.com
Founded in 1972, Steven Winter Associates, Inc. (SWA) provides a variety of services including: building system assessment, green materials and product specifications, LEED assessments and certification, green building commissioning,accessibility conformance, energy auditing capabilities, builder/operator training, preparation of green guidelines, HVAC troubleshooting, indoor air quality analysis and testing, solar and PV design engineering.
Steven Winter, President

5036 Steven Winter Associates - Washington DC
1001 G Street NW 202-628-6100
Suite 800 *Fax:* 202-393-5043
Washington, DC 20001 swadc@swinter.com
www.swinter.com
Located just a few blocks from the White House in the historic downtown section, SWA/DC focuses on technology transfer, buildings-related policy analysis, information dissemination, media outreach & publishing, association management,classroom and web-based training, and buildings research work on behalf of U.S. DOE, HUD, EPA, and the national energy laboratories. SWA/DC also provides logistical support to HUD's Office of Native American Programs (ONAP).
Steven Winter, President

5037 Stone Environmental
535 Stone Cutters Way 802-229-4541
Montpelier, VT 00560 603-273-9250
Fax: 802-229-5417
sei@stone-env.com
www.stone-env.com
Environmental consulting services and technologies that include: environmental planning and documentation; environmental compliance; waste management; environmental spatial analysis; remediation. Scientific disciplines include: civilengineering; environmental engineering and chemistry; forest biology; hydrogeology; geology; soil science; and geographic information systems.
Christopher Stone, President
David Healy, Vice President

5038 Suburban Laboratories
1950 S. Batavia Ave Ste 150 708-544-3260
Geneva, IL 60134 800-783-5227
Fax: 708-544-8587
Info@suburbanlabs.com
www.suburbanlabs.com
Environmental laboratory providing chemical, chromatographic, and spectrographic analysis of biological materials, including water and groundwater, soil, and hazardous materials for priority pollutants, metals, and pesticide residues.
Jarrett Thomas, President/CEO
Shane Clarke, Business Development Manager

5039 Sunsearch
PO Box 590 203-453-6591
393A Soundview Road 800-338-0258
Guilford, CT 00643 *Fax:* 203-458-9011
Designs, installs and services solar energy systems. Additional services includes: feasibility studies; inspections or assessments of existing systems; repair and redesign of existing systems; service agreements and evaluation ofcomplex systems.
Everett M Barber Jr, President

5040 Systech Environmental Corporation
3085 Woodman Drive 937-643-1240
Suite 300 800-888-8011
Dayton, OH 45420 *Fax:* 937-643-1203
www.go2systech.com
Provider of alternative fuels to cement kilns.
Erica Hawk, Corporate Mktg Specialist

5041 TAKA Asbestos Analytical Services
PO Box 208 631-261-2117
Greenlawn, NY 11740 *Fax:* 631-261-2120
TAKA provides environmental consultation, testing and analytical services for the assessment and detection of onsite asbestos materials. The president and owner of TAKA, Dr. Thomas A. Kubic, has extensive experience with forensicmicroscopy and advanced techniques in sampling and evaluation of airborne asbestos particles using Polarized Light Microscopy.
Thomas A Kubic PhD/MS/JD/FABC, President/Owner

5042 TRAC Laboratories
16969 North Texas Ave. 281-461-7886
Suite 300 *Fax:* 940-566-2698
Webster, TX 77598 info@traclabs.com
www.traclabs.com
Provide multi-disciplinary problem-solving approaches to environmental and public health issues.
David Kortenkamp, President/CEO
Bryn Wolfe, Director of Communication

5043 TRC Environmental Corporation-Alexandria
8550 United Plaza Blvd. 225-216-7483
Suite 502 *Fax:* 225-216-0732
Baton Rouge, LA 70809 cobrien@trcsolutions.com
www.trcsolutions.com

A provider of engineering, financial, risk management and construction services to large industrial and government customers throughout the United States, TRC provides customer focused solutions in three primary markets: environmental,energy and infrastructure. Environmental services include project development, resolving legacy environmental issues, ensuring compliance for continuing operations, and identifing and mitigating future environmental risks.

Christopher P Vincze, Chairman/CEO
John A. Carrig, President/COO

5044 **TRC Environmental Corporation-Atlanta**
4155 Shackleford Road. 770-270-1192
Norcross, GA 30093 *Fax:* 770-270-1392
cobrien@trcsolutions.com
www.trcsolutions.com
A provider of engineering, financial, risk management and construction services to large industrial and government customers throughout the United States, TRC provides customer focused solutions in three primary markets: environmental,energy and infrastructure. Environmental services include project development, resolving legacy environmental issues, ensuring compliance for continuing operations, and identifing and mitigating future environmental risks.

Christopher P Vincze, Chairman/CEO
John A. Carrig, President/COO

5045 **TRC Environmental Corporation-Augusta**
14 Gabriel Drive 207-621-7000
Augusta, ME 00433 *Fax:* 207-621-7001
cobrien@trcsolutions.com
www.trcsolutions.com
A provider of engineering, financial, risk management and construction services to large industrial and government customers throughout the United States, TRC provides customer focused solutions in three primary markets: environmental,energy and infrastructure. Environmental services include project development, resolving legacy environmental issues, ensuring compliance for continuing operations, and identifing and mitigating future environmental risks.

Christopher P Vincze, Chairman/CEO
John A. Carrig, President/COO

5046 **TRC Environmental Corporation-Boston**
2 Liberty Square 617-350-3444
6th Floor *Fax:* 617-350-3443
Boston, MA 00210 cobrien@trcsolutions.com
www.trcsolutions.com
A provider of engineering, financial, risk management and construction services to large industrial and government customers throughout the United States, TRC provides customer focused solutions in three primary markets: environmental,energy and infrastructure. Environmental services include project development, resolving legacy environmental issues, ensuring compliance for continuing operations, and identifing and mitigating future environmental risks.

Christopher P Vincze, Chairman/CEO
John A. Carrig, President/COO

5047 **TRC Environmental Corporation-Bridgeport**
10 Middle St 203-876-1453
Suite 600 *Fax:* 203-876-1486
Bridgeport, CT 00660 cobrien@trcsolutions.com
www.trcsolutions.com
A provider of engineering, financial, risk management and construction services to large industrial and government customers throughout the United States, TRC provides customer focused solutions in three primary markets: environmental,energy and infrastructure. Environmental services include project development, resolving legacy environmental issues, ensuring compliance for continuing operations, and identifing and mitigating future environmental risks.

Christopher P Vincze, Chairman/CEO
John A. Carrig, President/COO

5048 **TRC Environmental Corporation-Chicago**
230 West Monroe Street 312-269-5800
Suite 2370 *Fax:* 312-578-0877
Chicago, IL 60606 cobrien@trcsolutions.com
www.trcsolutions.com
A provider of engineering, financial, risk management and construction services to large industrial and government customers throughout the United States, TRC provides customer focused solutions in three primary markets: environmental,energy and infrastructure. Environmental services include project development, resolving legacy environmental issues, ensuring compliance for continuing operations, and identifing and mitigating future environmental risks.

Christopher P Vincze, Chairman/CEO
John A. Carrig, President/COO

5049 **TRC Environmental Corporation-Ellicott City**
4425 Forbes Blvd 301-306-6981
Lanham, MD 20706 *Fax:* 301-306-6986
cobrien@trcsolutions.com
www.trcsolutions.com
A provider of engineering, financial, risk management and construction services to large industrial and government customers throughout the United States, TRC provides customer focused solutions in three primary markets: environmental,energy and infrastructure. Environmental services include project development, resolving legacy environmental issues, ensuring compliance for continuing operations, and identifing and mitigating future environmental risks.

Christopher P Vincze, Chairman/CEO
John A. Carrig, President/COO

5050 **TRC Environmental Corporation-Henderson**
1009 Whitney Ranch Drive 702-248-6415
Henderson, NV 89014 *Fax:* 702-248-0626
cobrien@trcsolutions.com
www.trcsolutions.com
A provider of engineering, financial, risk management and construction services to large industrial and government customers throughout the United States, TRC provides customer focused solutions in three primary markets: environmental,energy and infrastructure. Environmental services include project development, resolving legacy environmental issues, ensuring compliance for continuing operations, and identifing and mitigating future environmental risks.

Christopher P Vincze, Chairman/CEO
John A. Carrig, President/COO

5051 **TRC Environmental Corporation-Honolulu**
1600 Kapiolani Blvd 808-728-4111
Suite 717 *Fax:* 808-638-5649
Honolulu Oahu, HI 96814 cobrien@trcsolutions.com
www.trcsolutions.com
A provider of engineering, financial, risk management and construction services to large industrial and government customers throughout the United States, TRC provides customer focused solutions in three primary markets: environmental,energy and infrastructure. Environmental services include project development, resolving legacy environmental issues, ensuring compliance for continuing operations, and identifing and mitigating future environmental risks.

Christopher P Vincze, Chairman/CEO
John A. Carrig, President/COO

5052 TRC Environmental Corporation-Indianapolis
10475 Crosspoint Blvd 317-517-2616
Suite 250 *Fax:* 651-686-4434
Indianapolis, IN 46256 cobrien@trcsolutions.com
www.trcsolutions.com

A provider of engineering, financial, risk management and construction services to large industrial and government customers throughout the United States, TRC provides customer focused solutions in three primary markets: environmental,energy and infrastructure. Environmental services include project development, resolving legacy environmental issues, ensuring compliance for continuing operations, and identifing and mitigating future environmental risks.

Christopher P Vincze, Chairman/CEO
John A. Carrig, President/COO

5053 TRC Environmental Corporation-Irvine
9685 Research Drive 949-727-9336
Irvine, CA 92618 *Fax:* 949-727-7311
dzarider@trcsolutions.com
www.trcsolutions.com

A provider of engineering, financial, risk management and construction services to large industrial and government customers throughout the United States, TRC provides customer focused solutions in three primary markets: environmental,energy and infrastructure. Environmental services include project development, resolving legacy environmental issues, ensuring compliance for continuing operations, and identifing and mitigating future environmental risks.

Christopher P Vincze, Chairman/CEO
John A. Carrig, President/COO

5054 TRC Environmental Corporation-Jackson
1540 Eisenhower Place 734-971-7080
Ann Arbor, MI 48108 *Fax:* 734-971-9022
cobrien@trcsolutions.com
www.trcsolutions.com

A provider of engineering, financial, risk management and construction services to large industrial and government customers throughout the United States, TRC provides customer focused solutions in three primary markets: environmental,energy and infrastructure. Environmental services include project development, resolving legacy environmental issues, ensuring compliance for continuing operations, and identifing and mitigating future environmental risks.

Christopher P Vincze, Chairman/CEO
John A. Carrig, President/COO

5055 TRC Environmental Corporation-Kansas City
Livestock Exchange Building 816-474-1500
1600 Genessee Street, Suite 416 *Fax:* 816-474-1853
Kansas City, MO 64102-1039 cobrien@trcsolutions.com
www.trcsolutions.com

A provider of engineering, financial, risk management and construction services to large industrial and government customers throughout the United States, TRC provides customer focused solutions in three primary markets: environmental,energy and infrastructure. Environmental services include project development, resolving legacy environmental issues, ensuring compliance for continuing operations, and identifing and mitigating future environmental risks.

Christopher P Vincze, Chairman/CEO
John A. Carrig, President/COO

5056 TRC Environmental Corporation-Lexington
670 Morrison Road 614-655-5360
Suite 220 *Fax:* 614-866-4359
Guhanna, OH 43230 cobrien@trcsolutions.com
www.trcsolutions.com

A provider of engineering, financial, risk management and construction services to large industrial and government customers throughout the United States, TRC provides customer focused solutions in three primary markets: environmental,energy and infrastructure. Environmental services include project development, resolving legacy environmental issues, ensuring compliance for continuing operations, and identifing and mitigating future environmental risks.

Christopher P Vincze, Chairman/CEO
John A. Carrig, President/COO

5057 TRC Environmental Corporation-Littleton
7761 Shaffer Parkway 970-419-4364
Suite 100 *Fax:* 303-792-0122
Littleton, CO 80127 cobrien@trcsolutions.com
www.trcsolutions.com

A provider of engineering, financial, risk management and construction services to large industrial and government customers throughout the United States, TRC provides customer focused solutions in three primary markets: environmental,energy and infrastructure. Environmental services include project development, resolving legacy environmental issues, ensuring compliance for continuing operations, and identifing and mitigating future environmental risks.

Christopher P Vincze, Chairman/CEO
John A. Carrig, President/COO

5058 TRC Environmental Corporation-Lowell
650 Suffolk Street 978-970-5600
Lowell, MA 00185 *Fax:* 978-453-1995
gharkness@trcsolutions.com
www.trcsolutions.com

A provider of engineering, financial, risk management and construction services to large industrial and government customers throughout the United States, TRC provides customer focused solutions in three primary markets: environmental,energy and infrastructure. Environmental services include project development, resolving legacy environmental issues, ensuring compliance for continuing operations, and identifing and mitigating future environmental risks.

Christopher P Vincze, Chairman/CEO
John A. Carrig, President/COO

5059 TRC Environmental Corporation-Phoenix
650 Suffolk Street 978-970-5600
Lowell, MA 00185 *Fax:* 978-453-1995
gharkness@trcsolutions.com
www.trcsolutions.com

A provider of engineering, financial, risk management and construction services to large industrial and government customers throughout the United States, TRC provides customer focused solutions in three primary markets: environmental,energy and infrastructure. Environmental services include project development, resolving legacy environmental issues, ensuring compliance for continuing operations, and identifing and mitigating future environmental risks.

Christopher P Vincze, Chairman/CEO
John A. Carrig, President/COO

5060 TRC Environmental Corporation-Princeton
Research Park 609-497-1379
322 Wall Street *Fax:* 609-497-1879
Princeton, NJ 00854 cobrien@trcsolutions.com
www.trcsolutions.com

A provider of engineering, financial, risk management and construction services to large industrial and government customers throughout the United States, TRC provides customer focused solutions in three primary markets: environmental,energy and infrastructure. Environmental services include project development, resolving legacy environmental issues, ensuring compliance for continuing operations, and identifing and mitigating future environmental risks.

Christopher P Vincze, Chairman/CEO
John A. Carrig, President/COO

5061 TRC Environmental Corporation-San Francisco
505 Sansome Street 415-434-2600
Suite 1600 *Fax:* 415-434-2321
San Francisco, CA 94111 cobrien@trcsolutions.com
www.trcsolutions.com
A provider of engineering, financial, risk management and construction services to large industrial and government customers throughout the United States, TRC provides customer focused solutions in three primary markets: environmental,energy and infrastructure. Environmental services include project development, resolving legacy environmental issues, ensuring compliance for continuing operations, and identifing and mitigating future environmental risks.

Christopher P Vincze, Chairman/CEO
John A. Carrig, President/COO

5062 TRC Environmental Corporation-West Palm Beach
1665 Palm Beach Lakes Boulevard 561-681-3494
Suite 720 *Fax:* 561-681-3496
West Palm Beach, FL 33401 cobrien@trcsolutions.com
www.trcsolutions.com
A provider of engineering, financial, risk management and construction services to large industrial and government customers throughout the United States, TRC provides customer focused solutions in three primary markets: environmental,energy and infrastructure. Environmental services include project development, resolving legacy environmental issues, ensuring compliance for continuing operations, and identifing and mitigating future environmental risks.

Christopher P Vincze, Chairman/CEO
John A. Carrig, President/COO

5063 TRC Environmental Corporation-Windsor
21 Griffin Road North 860-298-9692
Windsor, CT 00609 *Fax:* 860-298-6399
www.trcsolutions.com
A provider of engineering, financial, risk management and construction services to large industrial and government customers throughout the United States, TRC provides customer focused solutions in three primary markets: environmental,energy and infrastructure. Environmental services include project development, resolving legacy environmental issues, ensuring compliance for continuing operations, and identifing and mitigating future environmental risks.

Christopher P Vincze, Chairman/CEO
John A. Carrig, President/COO

5064 TRC Garrow Associates
3772 Pleasantdale Road 770-270-1192
Suite 200 *Fax:* 770-270-1392
Atlanta, GA 30340
TRC Garrow Associates provides business consulting services focusing on environmental analysis, planning and development.
Barbara Garrow, President

5065 Talos Technology Consulting
3336 Fern Hollow Place 703-715-3500
Suite 100 *Fax:* 703-715-0189
Herndon, VA 20171 information@talos.com
An environmental computer company, Talos works with businesses and government organizations to help them capitalize upon emerging technologies and achieve their organizational objectives. Talos professionals perform strategic planning;requirements analysis; design documentation; software trade surveying; system security planning; cost-benefit analysis; and surveys of technology markets.
Scott Little, Strategic Development
Rob Smith

5066 Taylor Engineering
10151 Deerwood Park Blvd. 904-731-7040
Bldg. 300, Suite 300 *Fax:* 904-731-9847
Jacksonville, FL 32256 www.taylorengineering.com
Services in coastal engineering consulting, dredging and dredged material management, hydrology and hydraulics, environmental services, and construction support services.

Terrence Hall P.E., President

5067 Tellus Institute
11 Arlington Street 617-266-5400
Boston, MA 00211-3411 *Fax:* 617-266-8303
www.tellus.org
Environmental research and strategic development firm. Services include: analyzing energy systems and environmental impacts; evaluating policies for transition to efficient and renewable energy technology; formulating strategies formitigating and adapting to climate change; evaluating long-term solutions that balance competing freshwater needs for basic services; and developing methods to support comprehensive river basin assessment.
Paul D Raskin PhD, President
David McAnulty, Administrative Director

5068 Terracon Consultants, Inc.
10841 South Ridgeview Road 800-593-7777
Olathe, KS 66061 www.terracon.com
Terracon is a geotechnical, environmental, facilities, and materials engineering firm. The company's aim is to provide private and public clients the services they expect at both small- and large-scale projects. Terracon has served adiverse range of markets, including the agricultural, financial, federal, oil and gas, and telecommunications sectors.

M. Gayle Packer, President

5069 TestAmerica-Austin
14050 Summit Drive 866-785-5227
Suite A100 *Fax:* 512-244-0160
Austin, TX 78728 webmaster@testamericainc.com
www.testamericainc.com
Environmental engineering research and consulting firm. Testing capabilities include chemical, physical and biological analyses of a variety of matrices, including aqueous, solid, drinking water, waste, tissue, air and saline/estuarinesamples. Specialty capabilities include air toxics testing, mixed waste testing, tissue preparation and analysis, aquatic toxicology, dioxin/furan testing and microscopy.
Rachel Brydon Jannetta, Chairman/CEO
James Miller, VP National Accounts & Progr

5070 TestAmerica-Buffalo
25 Kraft Ave. 866-785-5227
Albany, NY 12205 *Fax:* 518-438-8150
webmaster@testamericainc.com
www.testamericainc.com
Environmental engineering research and consulting firm. Testing capabilities include chemical, physical and biological analyses of a variety of matrices, including aqueous, solid, drinking water, waste, tissue, air and saline/estuarinesamples. Specialty capabilities include air toxics testing, mixed waste testing, tissue preparation and analysis, aquatic toxicology, dioxin/furan testing and microscopy.
Rachel Brydon Jannetta, Chairman/CEO
James Miller, VP National Accounts & Progr

5071 TestAmerica-Burlington
30 Community Drive 866-785-5227
Suite 11 *Fax:* 802-660-1919
South Burlington, VT 00540 webmaster@testamericainc.com
www.testamericainc.com
Environmental engineering research and consulting firm. Testing capabilities include chemical, physical and biological analyses of a variety of matrices, including aqueous, solid, drinking water, waste, tissue, air and saline/estuarinesamples. Specialty capabilities include air toxics testing, mixed waste testing, tissue preparation and analysis, aquatic toxicology, dioxin/furan testing and microscopy.
Rachel Brydon Jannetta, Chairman/CEO
James Miller, VP National Accounts & Progr

5072 TestAmerica-Chicago
2417 Bond Street 866-785-5227
University Park, IL 60484 *Fax:* 708-534-5211
webmaster@testamericainc.com
www.testamericainc.com
Environmental engineering research and consulting firm. Testing capabilities include chemical, physical and biological analyses of a variety of matrices, including aqueous, solid, drinking water, waste, tissue, air and saline/estuarinesamples. Specialty capabilities include air toxics testing, mixed waste testing, tissue preparation and analysis, aquatic toxicology, dioxin/furan testing and microscopy.
Rachel Brydon Jannetta, Chairman/CEO
James Miller, VP National Accounts & Progr

5073 TestAmerica-Connecticut
19 Old Kings Highway South 866-785-5227
Suite 100 *Fax:* 203-929-8142
Darien, CT 00682 webmaster@testamericainc.com
www.testamericainc.com
Environmental engineering research and consulting firm. Testing capabilities include chemical, physical and biological analyses of a variety of matrices, including aqueous, solid, drinking water, waste, tissue, air and saline/estuarinesamples. Specialty capabilities include air toxics testing, mixed waste testing, tissue preparation and analysis, aquatic toxicology, dioxin/furan testing and microscopy.
Rachel Brydon Jannetta, Chairman/CEO
James Miller, VP National Accounts & Progr

5074 TestAmerica-Corpus Christi
1733 N Padre Island Drive 866-785-5227
Corpus Christi, TX 78408 *Fax:* 361-289-2471
webmaster@testamericainc.com
www.testamericainc.com
Environmental engineering research and consulting firm. Testing capabilities include chemical, physical and biological analyses of a variety of matrices, including aqueous, solid, drinking water, waste, tissue, air and saline/estuarinesamples. Specialty capabilities include air toxics testing, mixed waste testing, tissue preparation and analysis, aquatic toxicology, dioxin/furan testing and microscopy.
Rachel Brydon Jannetta, Chairman/CEO
James Miller, VP National Accounts & Progr

5075 TestAmerica-Denver
4955 Yarrow Street 866-785-5227
Arvada, CO 80002 *Fax:* 303-431-7171
webmaster@testamericainc.com
www.testamericainc.com
Environmental engineering research and consulting firm. Testing capabilities include chemical, physical and biological analyses of a variety of matrices, including aqueous, solid, drinking water, waste, tissue, air and saline/estuarinesamples. Specialty capabilities include air toxics testing, mixed waste testing, tissue preparation and analysis, aquatic toxicology, dioxin/furan testing and microscopy.
Rachel Brydon Jannetta, Chairman/CEO
James Miller, VP National Accounts & Progr

5076 TestAmerica-Edison
3000 Lincoln Drive East 866-785-5227
Suite A *Fax:* 732-549-3679
Marlton, NJ 00805 webmaster@testamericainc.com
www.testamericainc.com
Environmental engineering research and consulting firm. Testing capabilities include chemical, physical and biological analyses of a variety of matrices, including aqueous, solid, drinking water, waste, tissue, air and saline/estuarinesamples. Specialty capabilities include air toxics testing, mixed waste testing, tissue preparation and analysis, aquatic toxicology, dioxin/furan testing and microscopy.
Rachel Brydon Jannetta, Chairman/CEO
James Miller, VP National Accounts & Progr

5077 TestAmerica-Houston
6310 Rothway Street 866-785-5227
Houston, TX 77040 *Fax:* 713-690-5646
webmaster@testamericainc.com
www.testamericainc.com
Environmental engineering research and consulting firm. Testing capabilities include chemical, physical and biological analyses of a variety of matrices, including aqueous, solid, drinking water, waste, tissue, air and saline/estuarinesamples. Specialty capabilities include air toxics testing, mixed waste testing, tissue preparation and analysis, aquatic toxicology, dioxin/furan testing and microscopy.
Rachel Brydon Jannetta, Chairman/CEO
James Miller, VP National Accounts & Progr

5078 TestAmerica-Knoxville
2960 Foster Creighton Drive 866-785-5227
Nashville, TN 37204 *Fax:* 615-726-3404
webmaster@testamericainc.com
www.testamericainc.com
Environmental engineering research and consulting firm. Testing capabilities include chemical, physical and biological analyses of a variety of matrices, including aqueous, solid, drinking water, waste, tissue, air and saline/estuarinesamples. Specialty capabilities include air toxics testing, mixed waste testing, tissue preparation and analysis, aquatic toxicology, dioxin/furan testing and microscopy.
Rachel Brydon Jannetta, Chairman/CEO
James Miller, VP National Accounts & Progr

5079 TestAmerica-Los Angeles
17461 Derian Ave. 866-785-5227
Suite 100 *Fax:* 949-260-3299
Irvine, CA 92614-5843 webmaster@testamericainc.com
www.testamericainc.com
Environmental engineering research and consulting firm. Testing capabilities include chemical, physical and biological analyses of a variety of matrices, including aqueous, solid, drinking water, waste, tissue, air and saline/estuarinesamples. Specialty capabilities include air toxics testing, mixed waste testing, tissue preparation and analysis, aquatic toxicology, dioxin/furan testing and microscopy.
Rachel Brydon Jannetta, Chairman/CEO
James Miller, VP National Accounts & Progr

5080 TestAmerica-Mobile
1870 W. Prince Road 866-785-5227
Suite 59 *Fax:* 251-666-6696
Tucson, AZ 85705 webmaster@testamericainc.com
www.testamericainc.com
Environmental engineering research and consulting firm. Testing capabilities include chemical, physical and biological analyses of a variety of matrices, including aqueous, solid, drinking water, waste, tissue, air and saline/estuarinesamples. Specialty capabilities include air toxics testing, mixed waste testing, tissue preparation and analysis, aquatic toxicology, dioxin/furan testing and microscopy.
Rachel Brydon Jannetta, Chairman/CEO
James Miller, VP National Accounts & Progr

5081 TestAmerica-New Orleans
6113 Benefit Dr 866-785-5227
Baton Rouge, LA 70809 *Fax:* 225-755-3080
webmaster@testamericainc.com
www.testamericainc.com
Environmental engineering research and consulting firm. Testing capabilities include chemical, physical and biological analyses of a variety of matrices, including aqueous, solid, drinking water, waste, tissue, air and saline/estuarinesamples. Specialty capabilities include air toxics testing, mixed waste testing, tissue preparation and analysis, aquatic toxicology, dioxin/furan testing and microscopy.
Rachel Brydon Jannetta, Chairman/CEO
James Miller, VP National Accounts & Progr

5082 TestAmerica-North Canton
4738 Gateway Circle 866-785-5227
Dayton, OH 45440 *Fax:* 937-499-1249
webmaster@testamericainc.com
www.testamericainc.com
Environmental engineering research and consulting firm. Testing capabilities include chemical, physical and biological analyses of a variety of matrices, including aqueous, solid, drinking water, waste, tissue, air and saline/estuarinesamples. Specialty capabilities include air toxics testing, mixed waste testing, tissue preparation and analysis, aquatic toxicology, dioxin/furan testing and microscopy.
Rachel Brydon Jannetta, Chairman/CEO
James Miller, VP National Accounts & Progr

5083 TestAmerica-Orlando
8010 Sunport Drive 866-785-5227
Suite 116 *Fax:* 407-856-0886
Orlando, FL 32809 webmaster@testamericainc.com
www.testamericainc.com
Environmental engineering research and consulting firm. Testing capabilities include chemical, physical and biological analyses of a variety of matrices, including aqueous, solid, drinking water, waste, tissue, air and saline/estuarinesamples. Specialty capabilities include air toxics testing, mixed waste testing, tissue preparation and analysis, aquatic toxicology, dioxin/furan testing and microscopy.
Rachel Brydon Jannetta, Chairman/CEO
James Miller, VP National Accounts & Progr

5084 TestAmerica-Pensacola
6301 NW 5th Way 866-785-5227
Suite 2850 *Fax:* 954-776-8485
Ft. Lauderdale, FL 33309 webmaster@testamericainc.com
www.testamericainc.com
Environmental engineering research and consulting firm. Testing capabilities include chemical, physical and biological analyses of a variety of matrices, including aqueous, solid, drinking water, waste, tissue, air and saline/estuarinesamples. Specialty capabilities include air toxics testing, mixed waste testing, tissue preparation and analysis, aquatic toxicology, dioxin/furan testing and microscopy.
Rachel Brydon Jannetta, Chairman/CEO
James Miller, VP National Accounts & Progr

5085 TestAmerica-Phoenix / Aerotech Environmental Laboratories
4645 East Cotton Center Blvd 866-785-5227
Building 3, Suite 189 *Fax:* 602-454-9303
Phoenix, AZ 85040 webmaster@testamericainc.com
www.testamericainc.com
Environmental engineering research and consulting firm. Testing capabilities include chemical, physical and biological analyses of a variety of matrices, including aqueous, solid, drinking water, waste, tissue, air and saline/estuarinesamples. Specialty capabilities include air toxics testing, mixed waste testing, tissue preparation and analysis, aquatic toxicology, dioxin/furan testing and microscopy.
Rachel Brydon Jannetta, Chairman/CEO
James Miller, VP National Accounts & Progr

5086 TestAmerica-Pittsburgh
301 Alpha Drive 866-785-5227
RIDC Park *Fax:* 412-963-2468
Pittsburgh, PA 15238 webmaster@testamericainc.com
www.testamericainc.com
Environmental engineering research and consulting firm. Testing capabilities include chemical, physical and biological analyses of a variety of matrices, including aqueous, solid, drinking water, waste, tissue, air and saline/estuarinesamples. Specialty capabilities include air toxics testing, mixed waste testing, tissue preparation and analysis, aquatic toxicology, dioxin/furan testing and microscopy.
Rachel Brydon Jannetta, Chairman/CEO
James Miller, VP National Accounts & Progr

5087 TestAmerica-Richland
2800 George Washington Way 866-785-5227
Richland, WA 99354 *Fax:* 509-375-5590
webmaster@testamericainc.com
www.testamericainc.com
Environmental engineering research and consulting firm. Testing capabilities include chemical, physical and biological analyses of a variety of matrices, including aqueous, solid, drinking water, waste, tissue, air and saline/estuarinesamples. Specialty capabilities include air toxics testing, mixed waste testing, tissue preparation and analysis, aquatic toxicology, dioxin/furan testing and microscopy.
Rachel Brydon Jannetta, Chairman/CEO
James Miller, VP National Accounts & Progr

5088 TestAmerica-San Francisco
1220 Quarry Lane 866-785-5227
Pleasanton, CA 94566 *Fax:* 925-600-3002
webmaster@testamericainc.com
www.testamericainc.com
Environmental engineering research and consulting firm. Testing capabilities include chemical, physical and biological analyses of a variety of matrices, including aqueous, solid, drinking water, waste, tissue, air and saline/estuarinesamples. Specialty capabilities include air toxics testing, mixed waste testing, tissue preparation and analysis, aquatic toxicology, dioxin/furan testing and microscopy.
Rachel Brydon Jannetta, Chairman/CEO
James Miller, VP National Accounts & Progr

5089 TestAmerica-Savannah
5102 LaRoche Avenue 866-785-5227
Savannah, GA 31404 *Fax:* 912-352-0165
webmaster@testamericainc.com
www.testamericainc.com
Environmental engineering research and consulting firm. Testing capabilities include chemical, physical and biological analyses of a variety of matrices, including aqueous, solid, drinking water, waste, tissue, air and saline/estuarinesamples. Specialty capabilities include air toxics testing, mixed waste testing, tissue preparation and analysis, aquatic toxicology, dioxin/furan testing and microscopy.
Rachel Brydon Jannetta, Chairman/CEO
James Miller, VP National Accounts & Progr

5090 TestAmerica-St Louis
13715 Rider Trail North 866-785-5227
Earth City, MO 63045 *Fax:* 314-298-8757
webmaster@testamericainc.com
www.testamericainc.com
Environmental engineering research and consulting firm. Testing capabilities include chemical, physical and biological analyses of a variety of matrices, including aqueous, solid, drinking water, waste, tissue, air and saline/estuarinesamples. Specialty capabilities include air toxics testing, mixed waste testing, tissue preparation and analysis, aquatic toxicology, dioxin/furan testing and microscopy.
Rachel Brydon Jannetta, Chairman/CEO
James Miller, VP National Accounts & Progr

5091 TestAmerica-Tacoma
5755 8th Street E 866-785-5227
Tacoma, WA 98424 *Fax:* 253-922-5047
webmaster@testamericainc.com
www.testamericainc.com
Environmental engineering research and consulting firm. Testing capabilities include chemical, physical and biological analyses of a variety of matrices, including aqueous, solid, drinking water, waste, tissue, air and saline/estuarinesamples. Specialty capabilities include air toxics testing, mixed waste testing, tissue preparation and analysis, aquatic toxicology, dioxin/furan testing and microscopy.
Rachel Brydon Jannetta, Chairman/CEO
James Miller, VP National Accounts & Progr

5092 TestAmerica-Tallahassee
2846 Industrial Plaza Drive 866-785-5227
Suite 100 *Fax:* 850-878-9504
Tallahassee, FL 32301 webmaster@testamericainc.com
www.testamericainc.com
Environmental engineering research and consulting firm. Testing capabilities include chemical, physical and biological analyses of a variety of matrices, including aqueous, solid, drinking water, waste, tissue, air and saline/estuarinesamples. Specialty capabilities include air toxics testing, mixed waste testing, tissue preparation and analysis, aquatic toxicology, dioxin/furan testing and microscopy.
Rachel Brydon Jannetta, Chairman/CEO
James Miller, VP National Accounts & Progr

5093 TestAmerica-Tampa
6712 Benjamin Road 866-785-5227
Suite 100 *Fax:* 813-885-7049
Tampa, FL 33634 webmaster@testamericainc.com
www.testamericainc.com
Environmental engineering research and consulting firm. Testing capabilities include chemical, physical and biological analyses of a variety of matrices, including aqueous, solid, drinking water, waste, tissue, air and saline/estuarinesamples. Specialty capabilities include air toxics testing, mixed waste testing, tissue preparation and analysis, aquatic toxicology, dioxin/furan testing and microscopy.
Rachel Brydon Jannetta, Chairman/CEO
James Miller, VP National Accounts & Progr

5094 TestAmerica-Valparaiso
2400 Cumberland Drive 866-785-5227
Valparaiso, IN 46383 *Fax:* 219-462-2953
webmaster@testamericainc.com
www.testamericainc.com
Environmental engineering research and consulting firm. Testing capabilities include chemical, physical and biological analyses of a variety of matrices, including aqueous, solid, drinking water, waste, tissue, air and saline/estuarinesamples. Specialty capabilities include air toxics testing, mixed waste testing, tissue preparation and analysis, aquatic toxicology, dioxin/furan testing and microscopy.
Rachel Brydon Jannetta, Chairman/CEO
James Miller, VP National Accounts & Progr

5095 TestAmerica-West Sacramento
880 Riverside Parkway 866-785-5227
West Sacramento, CA 95605 *Fax:* 916-372-1059
webmaster@testamericainc.com
www.testamericainc.com
Environmental engineering research and consulting firm. Testing capabilities include chemical, physical and biological analyses of a variety of matrices, including aqueous, solid, drinking water, waste, tissue, air and saline/estuarinesamples. Specialty capabilities include air toxics testing, mixed waste testing, tissue preparation and analysis, aquatic toxicology, dioxin/furan testing and microscopy.
Rachel Brydon Jannetta, Chairman/CEO
James Miller, VP National Accounts & Progr

5096 TestAmerica-Westfield
53 Southampton Road 866-785-5227
Westfield, MA 00108 *Fax:* 413-572-3707
webmaster@testamericainc.com
www.testamericainc.com
Environmental engineering research and consulting firm. Testing capabilities include chemical, physical and biological analyses of a variety of matrices, including aqueous, solid, drinking water, waste, tissue, air and saline/estuarinesamples. Specialty capabilities include air toxics testing, mixed waste testing, tissue preparation and analysis, aquatic toxicology, dioxin/furan testing and microscopy.
Rachel Brydon Jannetta, Chairman/CEO
James Miller, VP National Accounts & Progr

5097 Testing Engineers & Consultants (TEC) - Ann Arbor
3985 Varsity Drive 734-971-0030
Ann Arbor, MI 48108 *Fax:* 734-971-3721
tec@tectest.com
www.tectest.com
TEC specializes in environmental and geotechnical engineering, materials testing, roof systems management, facility asset management, and indoor air quality. Environmental services include: baseline assessments; contaminationassessments; expert testimony; feasibility studies; hazardous materials surveys; and hyrogeological/groundwater investigations.

John Banicki, Founder/Chairman
Katherine Banicki, President

5098 Testing Engineers & Consultants (TEC) - Detroit
601 W Fort Street 313-837-8464
Suite 440 800-835-2654
Detroit, MI 48226 *Fax:* 313-837-1305
tec@tectest.com
www.tectest.com
TEC specializes in environmental and geotechnical engineering, materials testing, roof systems management, facility asset management, and indoor air quality. Environmental services include: baseline assessments; contaminationassessments; expert testimony; feasibility studies; hazardous materials surveys; and hyrogeological/groundwater investigations.

John Banicki, Founder/Chairman
Katherine Banicki, President

5099 Testing Engineers & Consultants (TEC) - Troy
1343 Rochester Road 248-588-6200
Troy, MI 48083 *Fax:* 248-588-6232
tec@tectest.com
www.tectest.com
TEC specializes in environmental and geotechnical engineering, materials testing, roof systems management, facility asset management, and indoor air quality. Environmental services include: baseline assessments; contaminationassessments; expert testimony; feasibility studies; hazardous materials surveys; and hyrogeological/groundwater investigations.

John Banicki, Founder/Chairman
Katherine Banicki, President

5100 Testing Laboratories of Canada, Inc.
1840 Argentia Road 905-812-7783
Missssauga, ON L5N1P *Fax:* 905-812-3271
canada@consumertesting.com
www.consumertesting.com
Research in textiles, safety wear.
Stewart A. Satter, Chief Executive Officer

5101 Tetra Tech
3475 East Foothill Boulevard 802-658-3890
Pasadena, CA 91107 *Fax:* 802-658-4247
ard@ardinc.com
www.tetratech.com
Provides management consulting and technical services in resource management, infrastructure and communication. Tetra Tech's services include research and development, applied science and technology, engineering design, programmanagement, construction management, and operations and maintenance.
Dan L. Batrack, President & CEO
Steven M. Burdick, Chief Financial Officer

5102 Thermo Fisher Scientific
81 Wyman Street 781-622-1000
Waltham, MA 00245 800-678-5599
Fax: 781-622-1207
www.thermofisher.com
Provides a wide range of products, services and solutions for research, analysis, discovery and diagnostics using advanced technologies ranging from mass spectrometry and elemental analysis to chromatography, molecular spectroscopy,and microanalysis.

Additional services includes automated systems and technologies from standalone robots to complete liquid handling systems.

Marc N. Casper, President/CEO
Lori Gorski, Media Relations

5103 ThermoEnergy Corporation
10 New Bond Street 508-854-1628
Worcester, MA 00160 *Fax:* 508-854-1753
technology@thermoenergy.com
www.thermoenergy.com
ThermoEnergy Corporation is an integrated technologies company seeking to develop and commercialize patented water treatment and clean energy technologies. Products and services solutions include removing nitrogen from wastewaterstreams, converting sewage sludge to a renewable high-energy fuel, and enabling the conversion of coal and other hydrocarbon fuels into energy with zero air emissions.
James F. Wood, Chairman/President/CEO
Gregory M. Landegger, VP/COO/CFO

5104 Thermotron Industries
291 Kollen Park Drive 616-393-4580
Holland, MI 49423 800-409-3449
Fax: 616-392-5643
info@thermotron.com
www.thermotron.com
Manufacturers and suppliers of environmental testing, test system integration, screening, simulation equipment, and vibration equipment for transportation and screening test requirements. Additional services includes integrated testingsolutions with Research & Development and Total Quality Control to help insure product reliability and performance.
Mark Lamers, Technical Manager
Kevin Ewing, Marketing/Sales Manager

5105 Thompson Engineering
2970 Cottage Hill Road 251-666-2443
Suite 190 *Fax:* 251-666-6422
Mobile, AL 36606 info@thompsonengineering.com
www.thompsonengineering.com
A multi disciplined engineering design, environmental consulting, construction management, construction inspection and materials testing firm. The Environmental Division is comprised of a diverse team of professionals with significantknowledge and experience in environmental compliance and permitting, audits and assessments, engineering design, and monitoring and supervision of remedial activities.

Henry R. Seawell III, Chairman
John H. Baker III, President

5106 Thornton Laboratories Testing and Inspection Services, Inc.
Thornton Laboratories
1145 E Cass Street 813-223-9702
PO Box 2880 *Fax:* 813-223-9332
Tampa, FL 33602 steve.fickett@thorntonlab.com
www.thorntonlab.com
Environmental & fertilizer sampling and testing laboratory and general analytical testing lab.

Stephen B. Fickett, President
Hugh B. Rodriques, COO/VP lab Operations

5107 Tighe & Bond
4 Barlows Landing Road 508-564-7285
Unit 15 *Fax:* 413-562-5317
Pocasset, MA 00255 info@tighebond.com
www.tighebond.com
Tighe & Bond provides engineering and consulting services to a wide variety of clients, from some of the largest municipalities in the country to small, privately-held businesses. Areas of expertise includes water supply, wastewatermanagement, buildings, roadways, environmental permitting, remediation, health and safety training.
David E. Pinsky, President
Jeffrey P Bibeau, Environmental Manager

5108 Timber Products Inspection - Conyers
1641 Sigman Road 770-922-8000
Conyers, GA 30012 *Fax:* 770-922-1290
info@tpinspection.com
www.tpinspection.com
Timber Products Inspection, Inc. (TP) is an independent inspection, testing and consulting company with expertise in all phases of the wood products industry. TP provides quality auditing services in the areas of sawmilling, drying,component fabrication as well as value added processes such as pressure treating and gluing.
Donna Whitaker, Chairman
Bill Howard, Vice-Chairman

5109 Timber Products Inspection - Vancouver
1641 Sigman Road 770-922-8000
Conyers, GA 30012 *Fax:* 770-922-1290
info@tpinspection.com
www.tpinspection.com
Timber Products Inspection, Inc. (TP) is an independent inspection, testing and consulting company with expertise in all phases of the wood products industry. TP provides quality auditing services in the areas of sawmilling, drying,component fabrication as well as value added processes such as pressure treating and gluing.

Donna Whitaker, Chairman
Bill Howard, Vice-Chairman

5110 Tox Scan
42 Hangar Way 831-724-4522
Watsonville, CA 95076 *Fax:* 831-761-5449
Environmental bioassay and bioacoumulation testing.

David B. Lewis, Director

5111 Transviron
1624 York Road 410-321-6961
Lutherville, MD 21093 *Fax:* 410-949-9321
Transviron@comcast.net
www.transviron.com
Civil and environmental engineering firm. Technical consulting services includes: water supply and distribution; storm water management; highways and bridges; hazardous waste management; water and wastewater treatment plant operationsand construction management; wastewater collection and treatment.
Charles S. Bao, President
Michelle Ireland, Marketing Coordinator

5112 Tri-State Laboratories
2870 Salt Springs Road 330-797-8844
Youngstown, OH 44509 800-523-0347
Fax: 330-797-3264
www.tristatelabs.net
Environmental testing laboratory services of which include: asbestos testing; field services; forensic analysis and court testimony; hazardous waste analysis; inorganics/wet chemistry, metals, and organic analysis.

A Bari Lateef PhD, CEO
Wendy Hanna, COO

5113 Turner Laboratories
2445 North Coyote Drive 520-882-5880
Suite 104 *Fax:* 520-882-9788
Tucson, AZ 85745 sales@turnerlabs.com
www.turnerlabs.com
Turner Laboratories is an advanced, full-service environmental testing laboratory specializing in providing a wide range of analytical services including: inorganic, organic, wet chemistry and microbiological testing on soils/solids,drinking water, wastewater and groundwater.

Nancy D Turner, President
Michael McGovern, Executive VP

5114 URS
600 Montgomery Street 415-774-2700
26th Floor 888-877-7752
San Francisco, CA 94111-2728 *Fax:* 415-398-1905
www.urscorp.com
An environmental analysis and comprehensive engineering service firm, URS provides a full range of planning, design, program and construction management services to a wide variety of private and public sector clients. URS hasapproximately 30,000 employees in a network of more than 370 offices and contract-specific job sites in 20 countries.
Martin M Koffel, Chairman/CEO
Thomas W Biship, VP/Strategic Development

5115 US Public Interest Research Group
294 Washington St 617-747-4370
Suite 500 *Fax:* 617-292-8057
Boston, MA 00210 info@uspirg.org
www.uspirg.org
US PIRG is an advocate for the public interest. We uncover threats to public health and well-being and fight to end them, using the time-tested tools of investigative research, media exposes, grassroots organizing, advocacy andlitigation.
Douglas H Phelps, President/Chairman
Andre Delattre, Executive Director

5116 US Public Interest Research Group - Washington
218 D Street SE 202-546-9707
1st Floor *Fax:* 202-546-2461
Washington, DC 20003 www.uspirg.org
US PIRG is an advocate for the public interest. We uncover threats to public health and well-being and fight to end them, using the time-tested tools of investigative research, media exposes, grassroots organizing, advocacy andlitigation.
Douglas H Phelps, President/Chairman
Andre Delattre, Executive Director

5117 USDA Forest Service: Pacific Southwest Research Station
800 Buchanan Street 510-883-8830
West Annex Building *Fax:* 510-559-6440
Albany, CA 94710-11 psw_webmaster@fs.fed.us
www.fs.fed.us/psw/
A Governmental Research Organization specializing in research on forest ecosystems, including fire, watersheds, forest genetics and diversity, wildlife, forest diseases, and urban forestry.
Jim Baldwin, Project Manager
Marilyn Hartley, Communications Director

5118 Umpqua Research Company
125 Volunteer Way 541-863-7770
PO Box 609 *Fax:* 541-863-7775
Myrtle Creek, OR 97457 info@urcmail.net
www.urc.cc
UMPQUA Research Company (URC), founded in 1973 by David F. Putnam and Gerald V. Colombo, offers technical services in four primary areas: Drinking Water and Environmental Analysis; Air and Water Purification Related EngineeringServices (including NASA Flight Hardware); Research & Development; and Materials Testing. The staff includes chemical, electrical, and mechanical engineers, chemists, physicists, and biological scientists.
William F Michalek PE, President
James R. Akse, VP

5119 United Environmental Services
86 Hillside Drive 570-788-8180
Drums, PA 18222 *Fax:* 856-227-6578
www.unitedenvironmental.com
An environmental testing and analysis firm providing a full range of construction, remedial and maintenance services at landfills, commercial and industrial sites, including Brownfield re-development projects.
Rod Sterner, VP
Walter Meck, CEO

5120 Universal Environmental Technologies
87 Technology Way 603-883-9312
Nashua, NH 00306 *Fax:* 603-883-9314
An environmental research firm, Universal Environmental Technologies specializes in the design, fabrication and installation of integrated groundwater and soil remediation systems that are used on retail petroleum sites, industrialmanufacturing sites, EPA Superfund sites and U.S. military bases.
Sharon McMillin, VP/Remedial Services

5121 Upstate Laboratories
6034 Corporate Drive 315-437-0255
East Syracuse, NY 13057 *Fax:* 315-437-1209
enalyticsupport@enalytic.com
www.enalytic.com
Testing laboratory specializing in environmental and organic/synthetic analysis. Services include certification and air quality (mycology).
Anthony J Scala, President/CEO/Chemist
Corey Niland, Quality Assurance & Control

5122 Vara International: Division of Calgon Corporation
Calgon Carbon Corporation 412-787-6700
3000 GSK Drive 800-4CA-BON
Moon Township, PA 15108 *Fax:* 412-787-6676
www.calgoncarbon.com
An environmental and industrial process research firm, Vara International is a global manufacturer and supplier of granular activated carbon, innovative treatment systems, value added technologies and services for optimizing productionprocesses and safely purifying the environment.
Randall S. Dearth, President/CEO
Robert P. O'Brien, EVP/Chief Operating Officer

5123 Versar
6850 Versar Center 703-750-3000
PO Box 1549 800-283-7727
Springfield, VA 22151 *Fax:* 703-642-6825
info@versar.com
www.versar.com
Engineering and environmental research organization. Research results published in project reports, government publications, books, articles, and technical reports.
Jeffrey A. Wagonhurst, President/COO
Cynthia A. Downes, Executive VP/CFO

5124 Vista Leak Detection
755 N Mary Avenue 408-830-3300
Sunnyvale, CA 94085 *Fax:* 408-830-3399
info@VistaLD.com
Vista Research provides leak detection products and services to airport, oil industry and military clients for ensuring the integrity of underground/aboveground pipeline and tank systems.
William W Pickett, VP/Operations
Cody Freeman, Contracts Administrator

5125 Volumetric Techniques, Ltd. / VTEQE
317 Bernice Drive 631-472-4848
Bayport, NY 11705-1304 *Fax:* 631-472-4991
Sandy@vteqeltd.com
vteqeltd.com/137.html
Full service environmental engineering organization, VTEQE specializes in all aspects of the environmental services industry, including assessments (ESA Phase 1,2), site engineering, investigations/reports, remediation/cleanupstrategies, Phase 3, and bottled water facility licensing dealing with contaminated water, groundwater, soil, also engineering design, construction management, and full revitalization management.
Sander Sternig, President/CEO/Chairman
Benito San Pedro, Professional Engineer

5126 WERC: Consortium for Environmental Education & Technology Development
New Mexico State University

PO Box 30001 575-646-2038
Las Cruces, NM 88003-8001 800-523-5996
Fax: 505-646-5474
iee@nmsu.edu
www.ieenmsu.com

A consortium focusing on environmental education and technology development. The consortium's mission is to develop the human resources and technologies needed to address environmental issues. WERC's program aims to achieveenvironmental excellence through education, public outreach and technology development and deployment.
Abbas Ghassemi PhD, Executive Director
Patricia Pines, Administrative Asst.

5127 Waid & Associates - Austin/Corporate
10800 Pecan Park Blvd 512-255-9999
Suite 300 *Fax:* 512-255-8780
Austin, TX 78750 information@waid.com
www.waid.com

Waid & Associates is an engineering and environmental services firm that specializes in air quality services, particularly emissions control, permits, and compliance. Additional services include wastewater/waste management andenvironmental information management systems.
Jay R Hoover PE, President/Principal Engineer
Sara A. Hutson, Principal Engineer

5128 Waid & Associates - Houston
2600 South Shore Blvd. 281-333-9990
Suite 300 *Fax:* 512-255-8780
League City, TX 77573 information@waid.com
www.waid.com

Waid & Associates is an engineering and environmental services firm that specializes in air quality services, particularly emissions control, permits, and compliance. Additional services include wastewater/waste management andenvironmental information management systems.
Jay R Hoover PE, President/Principal Engineer
Sara A. Hutson, Principal Engineer

5129 Waid & Associates - Permian Basin
24 Smith Road 432-682-9999
Suite 304 *Fax:* 432-682-7774
Midland, TX 79705 information@waid.com
www.waid.com

Waid & Associates is an engineering and environmental services firm that specializes in air quality services, particularly emissions control, permits, and compliance. Additional services include wastewater/waste management andenvironmental information management systems.
Jay R Hoover PE, President/Principal Engineer
Sara A. Hutson, Principal Engineer

5130 Waste Water Engineers
210 Coy Court 248-236-9800
Oxford, MI 48371 *Fax:* 248-236-9870
www.wastewatereng.com

Environmental science research consultant. Research results published in project reports. Environmental civil engineering consultant.
Thomas H Patton Jr, President

5131 Water and Air Research
6821 SW Archer Road 352-372-1500
Gainesville, FL 32608 800-242-4927
Fax: 352-378-1500
lmosura-bliss@waterandair.com
www.waterandair.com

Environmental research and consulting firm. Research results published in client reports.
William C Zegel, President
Connie Bieber, Director/Manager

5132 Watkins Environmental Sciences
PO Box 6655 315-446-4763
Syracuse, NY 13217 *Fax:* 315-446-4764
awatkins3@gmail.com
www.watkinsenvironmental.com

Environmental assessments, septic system designs, residential water sampling and testing services, home inspections, radon, foundation designs & inspections.
Andrew A Watkins PE, President

5133 Waypoint Analytical
2790 Whitten Road 901-213-2400
Memphis, TN 38133 800-264-4522
Fax: 901-213-2440
supporttn@waypointanalytical.com
www.waypointanalytical.com

Environmental laboratory service specializing in soil testing.
Michael Sterling, Chief Financial Officer

5134 Weather Services Corporation
131A Great Road 781-275-8860
Bedford, MA 00173 *Fax:* 781-271-0178
Michael Leavitt, President

5135 West Coast Analytical Service
9240 Santa Fe Springs Road 562-948-2225
Santa Fe Springs, CA 90670 *Fax:* 562-948-5850
DJ Northington, PhD, President
Eric Lindsay, General Manager

5136 West Michigan Testing
815 E Ludington Avenue 231-843-3353
Ludington, MI 49431 *Fax:* 231-843-7676

We provide soil borings, geotechnical services, environmental assessments, construction materials testing and asbestos inspection.
James T Nordlund Jr, Vice President

5137 West More Mechanical Testing and Research
221 Westmoreland Drive 724-537-3131
PO Box 388 *Fax:* 724-537-3151
Youngstown, PA 15696-388 us.sales@wmtr.com
www.wmtr.com
Don Rossi, President
Mike Rossi, Vice President

5138 Western Environmental Services
913 N Foster Road 307-234-5511
Casper, WY 82601 800-545-5711
Fax: 307-234-8324
aroylance@testair.com
www.testair.com

Air emission testing.
James Meador, Founder/Project Manager
Alan Roylance, President

5139 Western Michigan Environmental Services
1007 Lake Drive 616-451-3051
Grand rapids, MI 49505 *Fax:* 616-451-3054
www.wmeac.org
Christine Helms, President
David Rein, VP

5140 Westinghouse Electric Company
1000 Westinghouse Drive 412-244-2000
Suite 572A 888-943-8442
Cranberry Township, PA 16066 *Fax:* 412-642-4985
www.westinghousenuclear.com
Danny Roderick, President/Chief Executive Of
Jim Brennan, Sr. VP

5141 Westinghouse Remediation Services
675 Park N Boulevard 404-298-7101
Suite F-100 *Fax:* 404-296-9752
Clarkston, GA 30021

Environmental remediation firm.

5142 Weston Solutions, Inc
1400 Weston Way 610-701-3000
Box 2653 800-7WE-STON
West Chester, PA 19380 *Fax:* 610-701-3186
info@westonsolutions.com
www.westonsolutions.com
Weston is a leading infrastructure redevelopment services firm delivering integrated environmental engineering solutions to industry and government worldwide. With an emphasis on creating lasting economic value for its clients, thecompany provides services in site remediation, redevelopment, infrastructure operations and knowledge management.
Alan J. Solow, President/Chief Executive Of
Vincent A. Laino, Sr. VP/CFO

5143 Whibco
87 East Commerce Street 856-455-9200
Bridgeton, NJ 00830 *Fax:* 856-455-9009
www.whibco.com
Andrew R Strelczyk, Director Quality Control

5144 Wik Associates
PO Box 230 302-322-2558
New Castle, DE 19720 *Fax:* 302-322-8921
Environmental testing and analysis firm.

5145 William T Lorenz & Company
3541 Norwegian Hollow Road 608-935-9285
Dodgeville, WI 53533 *Fax:* 608-935-2010
Environmental and water resources marketing, consulting, and product research firm.

5146 William W Walker Jr
1127 Lowell Road 978-369-8061
Concord, MA 00174-5522 *Fax:* 978-369-8061
bill@wwwalker.net
www.wwwalker.net
William W Walker, Jr, Environmental Engineer

5147 Woods End Research Laboratory
290 Belgrade Rd 207-293-2457
PO Box 297 800-451-0337
Mount Vernon, ME 00435 *Fax:* 207-293-2488
www.woodsend.org
Compost analysis; bioremediation design; solvita test kits for soil and compost. Quality Seal of Approval Program for Compost Products.
William Brinton, President

5148 World Resources Company
1600 Anderson Road 703-734-9800
Suite 200 *Fax:* 703-790-7245
Mc Lean, VA 22102 www.worldresourcescompany.com
World Resources Company (WRC) is a highly specialized environmental risk management company that designs, implements and manages recycling activities and provides environmental services for non-ferrous metal industries nationally andinternationally. This support includes regulatory, environmental, transportation, production, and all other aspects of business inherent to recycling services.
Peter T Halpin, CEO

5149 Yellowstone Environmental Science
65-1116 Hoku'ula Rd. 808-885-4194
PO Box 2709 *Fax:* 808-885-4114
Kamuela, HI 96743 yes@yestech.com
www.yestech.com
Mary M Hunter, President
Robert M. Hunter, Director

5150 Yes Technologies
65-1116 Hoku'ula Rd. 808-885-4194
PO Box 2709 *Fax:* 808-885-4114
Kamuela, HI 96743 yes@yestech.com
www.yestech.com
Environmental and public health research and development. Patent consulting.
Mary M Hunter, President
Robert M. Hunter, Director

5151 Zimpro Environmental
301 West Military Road 715-359-7211
Rothschild, WI 54474 *Fax:* 715-355-3219
William Copa, VP Technical Services

5152 Zurn Industries
1801 Pittsburgh Avenue 855-663-9876
Erie, PA 16502 800-997-3876
Fax: 919-775-3541
sean.martin@zurn.com
www.zurn.com
Environmental systems including air, land, thermal and water; energy systems including steam and heat; mechanical systems.
Sean Martin, VP Marketing & Sales
Michael Boone, General Manager

University Centers

5153 ASME
University of Florida
Two Park Avenue 973-882-1170
New York, NY 10016-5990 800-843-2763
Fax: 352-392-1071
CustomerCare@asme.org
www.asme.org
Has uniquely influenced the development of solar energy and renewable energy conversion systems all over the world through its research, education and training. Has pioneered research in many areas of solar energy, energy conversionand conservation. The lab has been designated as an ASME National Landmark.
Julio Guerrero, President
Thomas G. Loughlin, Executive Director

5154 Adirondack Ecological Center
SUNY College of Environmental Science & Forestry
1 Forestry Drive 315-470-6500
Syracuse, NY 13210 *Fax:* 518-582-2181
www.esf.edu
Provides the organizational framework for research, instructional, and public service activities thoughout the Adriondack region.
Vita DeMarchi, Chair
Matthew J. Marko, Vice Chair

5155 Agricultural Research and Development Center
University of Nebraska
1071 County Road G 402-624-8000
Ithaca, NE 68033 *Fax:* 402-624-8010
ardc@unl.edu
ardc.unl.edu
Serves as the primary site for field based reseach with 5,000 acres of row crops and 5,000 domestic farm animals used for teaching and research.
Mark Schroeder, Director
Ruby Urban, Asst. Director

5156 Akron Center for Environmental Studies
University of Akron
215 Crouse Hall 330-972-7111
Akron, OH 44325-4102 *Fax:* 330-972-7611
ids@uakron.edu
www.uakron.edu
Jonathan T. Pavloff, Chair
Jennifer E. Blickle, Vice Chair

5157 Albrook Hydraulics Laboratory
Washington State University

PO Box 641227 509-335-3564
Pullman, WA 99164 *Fax:* 509-335-7632
rhh@wsu.edu
www.wsu.edu
Research laboratory capable of performing projects with physically scaled hydraulic models. 15,000 square feet of floor space, discharge capacity up to 70 cubic feet per second, modern instrumentaion and shop facilities.
Elson S. Floyd, President
Daniel Bernardo, Vice President

5158 Alternative Energy Institute
Texas A&M University 806-656-2296
WTAMU Box 60248 *Fax:* 806-656-2733
Canyon, TX 79016 aeimail@wtamu.edu
Byungik Chang, Director
Ken Starcher, Associate Director

5159 American Petroleum Institute University
1220 L Street NW 202-682-8000
Washington, DC 20005-4070 *Fax:* 202-682-8232
training@api.org
www.api-u.org
API, through its university, provides training materials to help those in the oil and natural gas business meet regulatory requirements and industry standards. It works with the National Science Teachers Association and othereducational groups to impart scientific literacy and develop critical thinking skills in the classroom.
Jack N. Gerard, President/CEO
Kyle Isakower, Vice President

5160 American Society of Primatologists
University of Washington
PO Box 357330 206-543-0440
Seattle, WA 98195 *Fax:* 206-685-0305
www.asp.org
Conducts research on primates.
Marilyn A. Norconk, President
Justin McNulty, Executive Secretary

5161 Applied Energy Research Laboratory
North Carolina State University 919-515-5236
Raleigh, NC 27695 www.mae.ncsu.edu
Dr. John A Edwards, Director

5162 Aquatic Research Laboratory
Lake Superior State University
650 W Easterday Avenue 906-635-1949
Sault Sainte Marie, MI 49783 888-800-LSSU
Fax: 906-635-2266
Administered through the college of Arts and Sciences.
Prof Alex Litvinov, Director

5163 Architecture Research Laboratory
University of Arizona
College of Architecture 520-621-6751
Tucson, AZ 85721 *Fax:* 520-621-8700
www.architectureresearchlab.com
Provides assistance in the areas of education, applied research and public service.
Alexandra Fenton, Co-Founder
Michael S Bergin, Co-Founder

5164 Biological Reserve
Denison University 740-587-6261
Granville, OH 43023 stocker@denison.edu
Enhances the education of students in Biology and the Environmental Sciences by providing opportunities for field studies.
Dr. John E Fauth, Contact

5165 Caesar Kleberg Wildlife Research Institute
Texas A&M University
700 University Boulevard 361-595-3922
MSC 218 *Fax:* 361-593-3924
Kingsville, TX 78363 www.ckwri.tamuk.edu
Facilitates complex wildlife-related research studies. Includes modern high-tech facilities, specially designed wildlife pens, and rangeland tracts.
Henry R. Hamman, Chairman
Gus T. Canales, Co-Chairs

5166 California Sea Grant College Program
University of California
9500 Gilman Drive 858-534-4440
Deptartment 0232 *Fax:* 858-534-2231
La Jolla, CA 92093-0232 caseagrant@ucsd.edu
caseagrant.ucsd.edu
Offers products and services related to coastal and marine science, such as fellowship opportunities, grant administration services, library services and networking with Sea Grant experts and partners. The purpose of the programs is topromote conservation of coastal and marine resources.
James E. Eckman, Director
Caitlin Coomber, Marketing Communications

5167 Cedar Creek Natural History Area
University of Minnesota
2660 Fawn Lake Drive NE 763-434-5131
Bethel, MN 55005 *Fax:* 763-434-7361
Twenty-two hundred hectare experimental ecological reserve.

5168 Center for Applied Energy Research
University of Kentucky
2540 Research Park Drive 859-257-0200
Lexington, KY 40511-8479 *Fax:* 859-257-0220
rodney.andrews@uky.edu
www.caer.uky.edu
An applied research and development center with an international reputation, focusing on the optimal use of Kentucky's energy resources for the benefit of its people.
Jim Tracy, Vice President
Rodney Andrews, Director

5169 Center for Applied Environmental Research
University of Michigan
130 Mumford Hall 573-882-7458
Columbia, MO 65211 *Fax:* 573-884-2199
fulcherc@missouri.edu
Chris Barnett, Co-Director
Chris Fulcher, Co-Director

5170 Center for Aquatic Research and Resource Management
Florida State University
319 Stadium Drive 850-644-3700
Tallahassee, FL 32306-4295 *Fax:* 850-645-8447
livingston@bio.fsu.edu
Conducts research designed to answer aquatic resource-management questions posed by government agencies and private concerns. Research is conducted in lakes, rivers, and near-shore coastal systems throughout the southeastern UnitedStates with a multi-disciplinary approach to topics such as light, nutrients, primary productivity, fate and effects of storm water pollutants, sediment-water interactions, community assemblages of fish and invertebrates in various habitats andtrophic dynamics.
Dr. Robert J Livingston, Director

5171 Center for Cave and Karst Studies
Western Kentucky University
1906 College Heights Blvd. 270-745-0111
Bowling Green, KY 42101-3576 *Fax:* 270-745-3961
wku@wku.edu
www.wku.edu
Promotes research on all aspects of cave and karst studies with emphasis upon solving environmental problems associated with karst.
Gary A. Ransdell, President
Dr. Phillip W. Bale, Regent

5172 Center for Crops Utilization Research
Iowa State University of Science & Technology

1041 Food Sciences Building 515-294-0160
Iowa State University *Fax:* 515-294-6261
Ames, IA 50011 ccur@iastate.edu
www.ccur.iastate.edu

Incorporates various aspects of new product and product research, applications development, and technology transfer. Activities focus on developing technologies for producing food and industrial products from agricultural materials,developing agricultural substitutes for petrochemicals, and exploring and modifying the functional properties of crop-derived materials.

Dr. Lawrence A Johnson, Director
Peggy Best, Admin Specialist

5173 Center for Earth & Environmental Science
SUNY Plattsburgh
723 West Michigan Street 317-274-7154
SL 118 877-554-1041
Indianapolis, IN 46202 *Fax:* 317-274-7966
cees@iupui.edu
www.cees.iupui.edu

Undergraduate degree programs in environmental science, geology, planning and geography, with special emphasis on watershed science, remote sensing and geographic information systems, and aquatic and terrestrial ecology. The center isone of the oldest and largest environmental programs in the US, with 16 full-time interdisciplinary faculty and diverse field sites.
Dr. Pamela A. Martin, Director
Jessica Davis, Assistant Director

5174 Center for Environmental Communications (CEC)
Rutgers University
31 Pine Street 732-932-1966
New Brunswick, NJ 00890 *Fax:* 732-932-9544
cec@aesop.rutgers.edu

The CEC, located on the Cook College Campus, brings together university investigators to provide a social science perspective to environmental problem solving. CEC has gained international recognition for responding to environmentalcommunication dilemmas with research, training, and public service. Established in 1986, CEC is now jointly sponsored by the New Jersey Agricultural Experiment Station and the Edward J. Bloustein School of Planning and Public Policy.

Caron Chess, Director

5175 Center for Environmental Health Sciences
Massachusetts Institute of Technology
77 Massachusetts Avenue 617-253-1000
Building 16-743 *Fax:* 617-258-9344
Cambridge, MA 00213-4307 web.mit.edu
L. Rafael Reif, President
Israel Ruiz, Executive VP

5176 Center for Environmental Medicine Asthma & Lung Biology
University of North Carolina
554 Human Studies Facility 919-962-0126
CB# 7310, 104 Mason Farm Road 866-962-4457
Chapel Hill, NC 27599-7310 *Fax:* 919-966-9863
slshaw@med.unc.edu
www.med.unc.edu

The CEMALB are a group of investigators with diverse research interests that include cardiopulmonary medicine, immunology, lung physiology, cell biology, cell and molecular immunology, molecular toxicology and epidemiology. We conductresearch studies involving human volunteers that are aimed at understanding the negative health effects of air pollution on the lung and heart.
Philip A Bromberg, MD, Scientific Director
William L. Roper MD, MPH, Dean

5177 Center for Environmental Research Education
SUNY Buffalo
1300 Elmwood Avenue 716-878-4000
Upton Hall, Room 314 *Fax:* 716-878-6644
Buffalo, NY 14222 zolnowsa@buffalostate.edu
www.buffalostate.edu

Marsha D. Jackson, President
Father Robert J Pecoraro, VP

5178 Center for Environmental Studies
Williams College
Hopkins Hall, 880 Main Street 413-597-3131
Williamstown, MA 00126 *Fax:* 413-597-3489
www.williams.edu

Provides students with the opportunity to learn how environmental issues are interconnected with many traditional fields of study. Offered as a concentration, the program encourages students to become well grounded in a single field bypersuing a major in a traditional discipline or department, while focusing several of their elective courses on the interdisciplinary study of the environment.

Karen Merrill, Director
Sarah Gardner, Associate Director

5179 Center for Environmental Toxicology and Technology
Colorado State University 970-491-7051
1601 Campus Delivery *Fax:* 970-491-8304
Fort Collins, CO 80523-1601 dvmadmissions@colostate.edu
Mark Stetter, Dean
Chris Haase, Asst. to Dean

5180 Center for Field Biology
Austin Pay State University
PO Box 4718 931-221-7019
Clarksville, TN 37044 *Fax:* 931-221-6372
fieldbiology@apsu.edu

The Center of Excellence for Field Biology at Austin Peay State University brings together scholars and students from various biological disciplines to conduct research on topics in field biology and ecology, including toxicology,population and community ecology, and the ecology and biology of rare, threatened and endangered species. Major research efforts have focused on the ecology and biology of the flora and fauna of the Land Between the Lakes.
Dr. Steve Hamilton, Director
Michelle Rogers, Project Manager

5181 Center for Global & Regional Environmental Research
University of Iowa
The University of Iowa 319-335-3333
424 IATL *Fax:* 319-335-3337
Iowa City, IA 52242 www.cgrer.uiowa.edu
Greg Carmichael, Co-Director
Jerry Schnoor, Co-Director

5182 Center for Global Change Science (MIT)
Massachusetts Institute of Technology
77 Massachusetts Avenue 617-253-4902
Room 54-1312 *Fax:* 617-253-0354
Cambridge, MA 00213-4307 cgcs@mit.edu
cgcs.mit.edu

Addresses long-standing scientific problems whose solution is necessary for accurate prediction of changes in the global environment. The CGCS is interdisciplinary and interdepartmental, and builds on research and educational programsin earth sciences and engineering. The Center is also involved in substantial cooperative efforts focused on climate modeling, and on climate-policy research.

Ronald Prinn, Director
Anne Slinn, Executive Director

5183 Center for Groundwater Research (CGR)
Oregon Health & Science University
20000 NW Walker Road 503-748-1070
Beaverton, OR 97006-8921 *Fax:* 503-748-1273
cgr.ieh.ohsu.edu

The CGR coordinates a range of projects relating to the transport and fate of contaminants in soils and groundwater. The scope of the Center includes: the development of new sampling and site characterization techniques; thedevelopment of new analytical techniques; and other improved groundwater remediation techniques.
Richard L. Johnson, Director
Dr. James Pankow, Professor

5184 Center for Hazardous Substance Research
Kansas State University 785-532-6519
Ward Hall 104 *Fax:* 785-532-5985
Manhattan, KS 66506-2502 chsr@k-state.edu
www.engg.ksu.edu/CHSR

Dr. Larry E. Erickson, Director
Blase A. Leven, Associate Director

5185 Center for International Development Research
Duke University
PO Box 8500 613-236-6163
Ottawa, ON K1G3H *Fax:* 613-238-7230
info@idrc.ca
www.idrc.ca

Denis Desautels, Chairperson
Morton Solberg, Vice President

5186 Center for International Food and Agricultural Policy
University of Minnesota
University of Minnesota 612-625-8713
332 Classroom Office Bldg, 1994 Buford A *Fax:* 612-625-6245
St. Paul, MN 55108-6040 cifap@umn.edu
www.cifap.umn.edu
With its interdisciplinary approach, CIFAP uses its research and education activities to increase international understanding about food, agriculture, nutrition, natural and human resources, and the environment, and to positivelyaffect the policies of both developed and developing countries.

Terry Roe, Director
Marc Bellemare, Assistant Professor

5187 Center for Lake Superior Ecosystem Research
Michigan Technological University
1400 Townsend Drive 906-487-2769
Houghton, MI 49931 wkerfoot@mtu.edu
www.mtu.edu
An interdisiplinary center with goals to promote and strengthen ecological research and graduate programs at MTU through developing and applying technological advances to ecological problems, to advocate an ecosystem perspective forstudying aquatic and terrestrial portions of the Lake Superior watershed and to become a resource center for basic information on watershed and lake properties.

5188 Center for Marine Biology
University of New Hampshire
85 Adams Point Road 603-862-1234
The University of New Hampshire *Fax:* 603-862-1101
Durham, NH 00382 ray.grizzle@unh.edu
marine.unh.edu
The Center for Marine Biology (CMB) fosters excellence in marine biological research and education. Its primary goals are to strengthen and focus research and graduate education in modern marine biology and to encourage the developmentof high-quality undergraduate programs in all aspects of marine biology. The center helps faculty members compete for external grant funds and fosters coordination of marine research efforts, both with the life sciences and in other disciplines.
Larry Mayer, Director
Jonathan Pennock, Deputy Director

5189 Center for Population Biology
University of California
One Shields Avenue 530-752-1274
2320 Storer Hall *Fax:* 530-752-1449
Davis, CA 95616 cpb.ucdavis.edu
Founded in 1989, the Center for Population Biology unites UC Davis' population biologists. The center's membership comprises graduate students interested in population biology who are earning their degrees in graduate programs such as ecology or entomology, postdoctoral researchers, from nine academic departments and sections, 17 of whom have faculty appointments in the division.
John J. Stachowicz, Director
Theresa Garcia, Graduate Group Coordinator

5190 Center for Resource Policy Studies
University of Wisconsin
1450 Linden Drive 608-262-8254
Room 240
Madison, WI 53706
The Center for Resource Policy Studies and Programs uses interdisciplinary research, teaching and extension efforts to analyze resource policies and development programs. This center gives particular emphasis to the social scienceaspects of natural resource policy issues.

5191 Center for Statistical Ecology & Environmental Statistics
Pennsylvania State University
Dept of Statistics 814-865-9442
421 Thomas Building *Fax:* 814-865-1278
University Park, PA 16802 gpp@stat.psu.edu
www.stat.psu.edu/~gpp/aims_scope.htm
The Center is the first of its kind in the world and enjoys national and international reputation. They have an ongoing program of research that integrates statistics, ecology and the environment. The emphasis is on the environment andcollaborative research, training and exposition on improving the quantification and communication of man's impact on the environment. Major interest also lies in statistical investigations of the impact of the environment on man.
Ganapati P Patil, Director

5192 Center for Streamside Studies
University of Washington
Box 352100 206-543-6920
Seattle, WA 98195 *Fax:* 206-543-3254
www.washington.edu/cssuw/
The mission of the Center for Streamside Studies is to provide scientific information necessary for the resolution of management issues related to the production and protection of forest, fish, wildlife, and water resources associatedwith the streams and rivers in the Pacific Northwest.
Robert J Naiman, Director

5193 Center for Tropical Agriculture
University of Florida
Km 17, Recta Cali-Palmira 650-833-6625
Apartado Aéreo 6713 *Fax:* 650-833-6626
Cali, CO AA671 www.ciat.cgiar.org
Enhances research and education on tropical agriculture between University of Florida and tropical countries.
Wanda Collins, Board Chair
Geoffrey Hawtin, Vice Chair

5194 Center for Water Resources and Environmental Research (CWRER)
The City College of New York
160 Convent Avenue 212-650-7000
New York, NY 10031 www.ccny.cuny.edu
The Center investigates pollution movement, surface water and groundwater cleanup, wetland preservation, watershed management, hydraulics and hydrology of natural flow systems, ecology preservation and the technical and sociopoliticaloutcomes.
Dr. Lisa Staiano-Coico, President
Dr. Maurizio Trevisan, Provost

5195 Center for the Management, Utilization and Protection of Water Resources
Tennessee Technological University

P.O. Box 5033 931-372-3507
Cookeville, TN 38505 800-255-8881
Fax: 931-372-6346
sdodson@tntech.edu
www.tntech.edu/research/centers/wrc/

The Center for the Management, Utilization and Protection of Water Resources at Tennessee Technological University is dedicated to the vision of enhancing environmental education through research. Using interdisciplinary teams ofresearchers, the Center focuses its work in the core areas of environmental resource management and protection, environmental hazards, and environmental information.
Philip Oldham, President
Sandy Dodson, Academic Support Associate 3

5196 Clean Energy Research Institute
University of Miami
4202 East Fowler Avenue 813-974-7322
Mail Stop ENB118 *Fax:* 813-974-2050
Tampa, FL 33620 stefanak@eng.usf.edu
Acts as the focal point of energy and environmental related activities in the College of Engineering. Its goals are to conduct research and to generate research proposals to investigate energy and environmental problems; to organizeseminars, workshops and conferences using researchers within and without the University; to assemble, compile, publish and disseminate information on every aspect of energy and environmental problems; and to cooperate with other organs of theUniversity.
Elias (Lee) Stefanakos, Director
Yogi D. Goswami, Director

5197 Cobbs Creek Community Environment Educational Center (CCCEEC)
700 Cobbs Creek Parkway 215-685-1900
63rd & Catharine Streets *Fax:* 215-764-1586
Philadelphia, PA 19143 cobbscreekinfo@gmail.com
www.cobbscreekcenter.org

CCCEEC is designated to institutionalize the practice of Urban Environmental Education. Their mission is to preserve the quality for residents living in the Cobbs Creek area of Philadelphia through the establishment of a center foreducating and informing people about the issues affecting their environment.
Carole Williams-Green, Founder
Sharon Williams-Losier, President

5198 College of Forest Resources
University of Washington
College of Forest Resources 206-543-2730
PO Box 352100 *Fax:* 206-685-0790
Seattle, WA 98195-2100 www.cfr.washington.edu
The University of Washington College of Forest Resources is dedicated to generating and disseminating knowledge for the stewardship of natural and managed environments and the sustainable use of their products and services throughteaching, research and outreach.
Tom DeLuca, Director
Acker Steven, Associate Professor

5199 Colorado Cooperative Fish & Wildlife Research Unit
Colorado State University
1474 Campus Delivery 970-491-5396
Fort Collins, CO 80523-1474 *Fax:* 970-491-1413
www.warnercnr.colostate.edu
The Colorado Cooperative Wildlife Research Unit was founded in 1947, and the Colorado Cooperative Fishery Research Unit was established in 1963. The two Units were combined in 1984 into the Colorado Cooperative Fish and WildlifeResearch Unit. This unit is staffed, supported, and coordinated by the Colorado Division of Wildlife, Colorado State University, the United States Geological Survey , and the Wildlife Management Insisute.
David Anderson, Program Director/Chief Scien
Denise Culver, Research Associate

5200 Cooperative Fish & Wildlife Research Unit
University of Missouri
Colorado State University 970-491-5020
1474 Campus Delivery *Fax:* 970-491-5091
Fort Collins, CO 80523-1474 www.warnercnr.colostate.edu
David Anderson, Program Director
Carroll Bjork, Illustrator I

5201 Cornell Waste Management Institute
Department of Crop and Soil Science 607-255-1187
817 Bradfield Hall *Fax:* 607-255-8207
Ithaca, NY 14853 cwmi@cornell.edu
cwmi.css.cornell.edu
Conduct applied research and outreach focused on composting and land application of sewage sludges.

Jean Bonhotal, Director
Murray B. McBride, Professor

5202 ERI Earth Research Institute
University of California
6832 Ellison Hall 805-893-4885
University of California *Fax:* 805-893-2578
Santa Barbara, CA 93106-3060 webmaster@eri.ucsb.edu
www.eri.ucsb.edu
Purpose is to increase our understanding of the geological processes and evolution of the earth's crust and lithosphere, and the impact these processes have on society.
Susannah Porter, Director
David Siegel, Director

5203 Eagle Lake Biological Field Station
California State University
Department of Biology Sciences 530-898-4143
California State University *Fax:* 530-898-5060
Chico, CA 95929-0040 publicaffairs@csuchico.edu
www.csuchico.edu
The Eagle Lake Biological Field Station, located 26 miles northwest of Susanville in Lassen County, California is a ten building facility on the eastern shore of Eagle Lake. The field station is administered by California StateUniversity, Chico and the CSUC Foundation with support from the University of California Natural Reserve System and UC Davis. The ELBFS is open to any individual or group whose purpose is primarily academic and whose activities are consistent withthe isolation.
Raymond J Bogiatto, Director
Jeffrey Bell, Chair, Biology

5204 Earth Science & Observation Center
University of Colorado Boulder
University of Colorado at Boulder 303-492-8773
216 UCB *Fax:* 303-492-1149
Boulder, CO 80309-216 lornay.hansen@colorado.edu
www.cires.colorado.edu/esoc
We advance scientific and societal understanding of the Earth System based on innovative remote sensing research. Through our research, we provide fundamental insights into how the Earth system functions, how it is changing, and whatthose changes mean for life on earth, for the benefit of human kind.
Dr Waleed Abdalati, Director
Tom Chase, Associate Professor

5205 Ecology Center
2530 San Pablo Avenue 510-548-2220
Suite H *Fax:* 510-548-2240
Berkeley, CA 94702 info@ecologycenter.org
ecologycenter.org
The Utah State University Ecology Center supports and coordinates ecological research and graduate education in the science of ecology. Also offered by the center are services such as farmers' markets, produce stands, residentialcurbside recycling, classes and workshops, Youth Environmental Academy, help desk and hotline, book & DVD library and more.

Raquel Pinderhughes, President
Becca Prager, Secretary

5206 Energy Resources Center
University of Illinois at Chicago

The University of Illinois at Chica 312-996-4490
1309 South Halsted Street, 2nd Fl, Suit *Fax:* 312-996-5620
Chicago, IL 60607 uic.edu

The Center is a University of Illinois at Chicago interdisciplinary research and public service organization. It was established in 1973 by the University's Board of Trustees to conduct studies in the field of energy and to providelocal, state and federal governments and the public with current information on energy technology and policy.

Cliff Haefke, Acting Director
Henry C. Kurth, Associate Director

5207 Energy, Environment & Resource Center
University of Tennesse at Knoxville
University of Tennessee, Knoxville 865-974-8080
676 Dabney Hall *Fax:* 865-974-8086
Knoxville, TN 37996-1605 cebweb@utk.edu
www.ceb.utk.edu

Gary S Sayler, Founding Director
Sabine Nabenfuehr, Administrative Assistant

5208 Environmental & Water Resources Engineering
Texas A&M University
Civil Engineering Department 512-471-4921
301 E. Dean Keeton St. Stop C1700 *Fax:* 979-862-1542
Austin, TX 78712 www.ce.utexas.edu/ewre
Jessica Treptow, Graduate Coordinator
Dr. Desmond Lawler, Graduate Advisor

5209 Environmental Center
University of Hawaii
2500 Dole Street 808-956-7361
Krauss Annex 19 *Fax:* 808-956-3980
Honolulu, HI 96822

The Center's three areas of focus are education, research and service. The education function of the Center includes the administration of the Environmental Studies Major Equivalent and Certificate program. It fulfills its researchfunction by identifying and addressing environmentally related research needs, particularly those pertinent to Hawaii. The service function primarily involves the coordination and transfer of technical information from the University community togovernment agencies.

Chittaranjan Ray, Director
John Cusick, Assistant Specialist

5210 Environmental Chemistry and Technology Program
University of Wisconsin at Madison
1415 Engineering Drive 608-263-3264
Room 122 *Fax:* 608-262-0454
Madison, WI 53706-1481 mcpossin@wisc.edu
www.engr.wisc.edu

Marc A. Anderson, Professor and Chair
Anders W. Andren, Professor Research

5211 Environmental Exposure Laboratory
University of California
1000 Veterans Avenue 310-825-2739
Rehabilitation Center, Room A163
Los Angeles, CA 90024
Dr. Henry Gong Jr, Director

5212 Environmental Human Toxicology
University of Florida
Bldg 471 Mowry Road 352-294-4514
PO Box 110885 *Fax:* 352-392-4707
Gainesville, FL 32611

The Center serves as an interface between basic research and its applications for evaluation of human health and environmental risk. The research and teaching activities of the Center provide a resource to identify and reduce riskassociated with environmental pollution, food contamination, and workplace hazards. The center provides a forum for the discussion of specific and general problems concerning the potential adverse human health effects associated with chemicalexposure.

Dr. Stephen Roberts, Director
Dr. Steve Roberts, Director

5213 Environmental Institue and Water Resources Research Institute
Auburn University
1090 South Donahue Drive 334-844-4132
Auburn, AL 36849 *Fax:* 334-844-4462
info@alabamawaterwatch.org

Samuel Fowler, Director
Dr Upton Hatch, Director

5214 Environmental Institute of Houston
University ofg Houston
University of Houston-Clear Lake 281-283-3950
2700 Bay Area Blvd., MC 540, North Offic *Fax:* 281-283-3953
Houston, TX 77058-1002 eih@uhcl.edu
www.eih.uhcl.edu

The mission of EIH is to help people in the Houston region participate more effectively in environmental improvement. Information and technology will be obtained and disseminated from research supported by EIH in critical areasincluding pollution prevention, natural resource conservation, public policy and societal issues. EIH will seek to expand balanced environmental education based on objective scholarship to empower the community to make sound decisions onenvironmental issues.

Sheila Brown, Board Member
Alecya Gallaway, Board Member

5215 Environmental Remote Sensing Center
University of Wisconsin
1225 W Dayton Street 608-263-3251
Floor 12 *Fax:* 608-262-5964
Madison, WI 53706 sventura@wisc.edu

A university research center focused on application of remote sensing and attending geospatial technologies in government, business and science. Particular heritage in the application of remote sensing in natural resource managementand environmental monitoring. A NASA-sponsored Affiliated Research Center.

Prof Thomas Lillesand, Director

5216 Environmental Research Institute
University of Idaho
875 Perimeter Drive 208-885-6111
PO Box 444264 888-8UI-DAHO
Moscow, ID 83844-4264 *Fax:* 208-885-9119
info@uidaho.edu
www.uidaho.edu

The faculty, associated with the institute, perform multidisciplinary research in environmental molecular ecology, restoration of contaminated soils and waters, and microbial genomics related to environmental processes.

Chuck Staben, President
Brenda Helbling, Executive Assistant

5217 Environmental Resource Center
San Jose Southern University
101 Center Pointe Drive 919-469-1585
Cary, NC 27513-5706 800-537-2372
Fax: 919-342-0807
service@ercweb.com
www.ercweb.com

The Environmental Resource Center is a nonprofit information and outreach organization within the Environmental Studes department at San Jose Southern University, serving the San Jose community since 1971.

Annemarie Vallesteros, Executive Director

5218 Environmental Science & Engineering Program
Clarkson University
1200 E California Blvd. MC 131-24 626-395-6070
Pasadena, CA 91125 *Fax:* 626-795-6028
www.ese.caltech.edu

Elizabeth Boyd, Associate Academic Assistant
Nora Oshima, Grants Manager

5219 Environmental Science Institute
University of Pennsylvania

The University of Texas at Austin 512-471-5847
2275 Speedway, Mail Code C9000 *Fax:* 512-232-1913
Austin, TX 78712 esi@esi.utexas.edu
www.esi.utexas.edu

The Environmental Science Institute is dedicated to improving the understanding of key scientific, economic, and political issues that underlie environmental problems and their management. The mission of the Institute is to bringscholars together from across the University in order to promote collaborations in education and research endeavors in the area of environmental issues. These collaborative endeavors span basic and applied sciences, engineering and the social andhuman sciences.

Jay L. Banner, Director
Darrel Tremaine, Program Coordinator

5220 Environmental Systems Application Center
Indiana University
107 S Indiana Avenue 812-855-4848
Bloomington, IN 47405

The goals of the Center are to promote excellence in environmental science research and to foster increased interdisciplinary collaboration among environmental science faculty on the Indiana University-Bloomington campus. The Centerhas no degree programs. The Center can be listed as an affiliation of the associated faculty in publications and in correspondence.

5221 Environmental Systems Engineering Institute
University of Central Florida
University of Central Florida 407-823-2841
4000 Central Florida Boulevard *Fax:* 407-823-3315
Orlando, FL 32816-2450 www.cece.ucf.edu

Dr. Steven J. Duranceau, Associate Professor & Dir
Maria Pia Real-Robert, Laboratory Manager

5222 Environmental Toxicology Center
University of Wisconsin
1300 University Avenue 608-263-4580
1530 MSC *Fax:* 608-262-5245
Madison, WI 53706

Environmental Toxicology is the study of the adverse effects on individual life forms and ecosystems of environmental agents (chemical, physcial, biological) whether of natural origin or released through human activity, and origins andcontrol of these harmful agents.

Christopher A. Bradfield, Director
Prof. Colin R Jefcoate, Director

5223 Environmental and Occupational Health Science Institute
Rutgers University
170 Frelinghuysen Road 848-445-0202
PO Box 1179 *Fax:* 732-445-0131
Piscataway, NJ 00885 info@eohsi.rutgers.edu

The major objectives of the institute are to: improve understanding of the impact of environmental chemicals on human health; to find ways to quantify and prevent exposure to hazardous substances; and develop methods to identify andtreat people adversely affected by environmental agents. Devises approaches for educating the public about the relative risks from chemical exposure. Trains professionals to accomplish these tasks.

Kenneth Reuhl, Ph.D., Interim Director
Howard Kipen, M.D., M.P.H., Assoc Director

5224 Feed and Fertilizer Laboratory
Louisiana State University
Department Agriculture and Forestry 208-332-8500
PO Box 790 *Fax:* 208-334-2170
Boise, ID 83701-790 info@agri.idaho.gov
www.agri.idaho.gov

Celia R. Gould, Director
Brian J. Oakey, Deputy Director

5225 Field Station & Ecological Reserves
University of Kansas
c/o Kansas Biological Survey 785-864-1500
2101 Constant Ave. *Fax:* 785-864-5093
Lawrence, KS 66047-3759 biosurvey@ku.edu
biosurvey.ku.edu

The KSR is dedicated to field-based environmental reseach and education. KSR is located within the transition zone (ecotone) between the eastern deciduous forest and tallgrass prairie biomes. The 3,000 acres of diverse native andmanaged habitats, experimental systems, support facilities, and longterm databases are used to undertake an outstanding array of scholarly activities. Environmental stewardship is a stong emphasis as high-quality natural areas are preserved for thefuture.

Ed Martinko, Ph.D., Director
Jerry deNoyelles, Ph.D., Deputy Director

5226 Fitch Natural History Reservation
University of Kansas
Kansas Biological Survey 785-864-1500
2101 Constant Avenue *Fax:* 785-864-1534
Lawrence, KS 66047 biosurvey@ku.edu
biosurvey.ku.edu

Ed Martinko, Ph.D., Director
Jerry deNoyelles, Ph.D., Deputy Director

5227 Florida Cooperative Fish and Wildlife Research Unit
University of Florida
University of Florida 352-846-0643
110 Newins-Ziegler Hall, PO Box 110430 *Fax:* 352-846-0841
Gainesville, FL 32611-0430 mghale@ufl.edu
www.wec.ufl.edu

The Cooperative Research Unit has three facets to its mission: education—Cooperative Unit scientists teach university courses at the graduate level, provide academic guidence to graduate students, and serve on academic committees;research—Cooperative Unit scientists conduct research that is designed to meet the information needs expressed by unit cooperators; technical Assistance— unit provides technical assistance and training to State and federal personnel and othernatural resources.

James D Austin, Associate Professor
Benjamin Baiser, Assistant Professor

5228 Florida Museum of Natural History
University of Florida
Dickinson Hall, 1659 Museum Road 352-392-1721
PO Box 117800 *Fax:* 352-392-8783
Gainesville, FL 32611-7800 gdshaak@flmnh.ufl.edu
www.flmnh.ufl.edu

The Florida Museum of Natural History, on the University of Florida Campus, is one of the leading university natural history museums in the nation. With over 30 million specimens and artifacts in its permanent collections, it is thelargest collection-based museum in the southeastern US. The museum was established by the Legislature in 1917 at the University of Florida where it functions in a dual capacity as the official state museum of Florida and the University Museum.

Dr Douglas S Jones, Director
Dr Beverly Sensbach, Associate Director

5229 Formaldehyde Institute
1330 Connecticut Avenue NW 202-833-2131
Washington, DC 20036 *Fax:* 202-659-1699

John F Murray, Executive Director

5230 Gannett Energy Laboratory
Florida Institute of Technology
207 Senate Avenue 717-763-7211
Harrisburg, PA 17011-2316 800-233-1055
www.gannettfleming.com

Bill Stout, Chairman/CEO
Bob Scaer, President/COO

5231 Global Change & Environmental Quality Program
University of Colorado
University of Colorado at Boulder 303-492-1411
Campus Box 214 *Fax:* 303-492-1414
Boulder, CO 80309 bob.sievers@colorado.edu
www.colorado.edu

In addition to addressing CU's overall objectives, the Global Change and Environmental Quality Program is pursuing three main goals; studying environmental issues at the local level, including the cleanup and restoration of toxicsites, such as Rocky

Flats, the Rocky Mountain Arsenal, and mine tailing sites; waste treatment and water quality; and land use.
Bob Sievers, Director
Rosella Chavez, Admin Asst.

5232 **Graduate Program in Community and Regional Planning**
University of Texas
Main Building 512-471-0134
Austin, TX 78701 *Fax:* 512-471-0716
The CRP provides its graduates with the theoretical foundations, specific skills and practical experience to succeed in professional planning and related policy careers. They strive to create a diverse student body and program and arecommitted to building a professional planning community that rese,bles those where graduates will work. The program has a strong focus on sustainable development processes and practices. Finding paths that balance growth with improved environmentalperformance.
Jane Shaughness, Graduate Admissions Coor.

5233 **Great Lakes Coastal Research Laboratory**
Purdue University
School of Civil Engineering 765-494-4600
West Lafayette, IN 47907

5234 **Great Lakes/Mid-Atlantic Hazardous Substance Research Center**
University of Michigan
One Potomac Yard (South Building) 734-763-2274
2777 South Crystal Drive www.epa.gov
Arlington, VA 22202
The mission of the Great Lakes Mid- Atlantic Center for Hazardous Substances Research is to foster and support integrated, intersdisciplinary, and collaborative efforts that advance the science and technology of hazardous substancemanagement to benefit human and environmental health and well-being.
Gina McCarthy, Administrator
Stan Meiburg, Deputy Administrator

5235 **Great Plains: Rocky Mountain Hazardous Substance Research Center**
Kansas State University
Kansas State University 785-532-6519
104 Ward Hall 800-798-7796
Manhattan, KS 66506-2502 *Fax:* 785-532-5985
hsrc@ksu.edu
www.engg.ksu.edu/HSRC
Conducts research and transfers technology on hazardous substance management, and remediation of contaminated soil and water.
Dr. Larry Erickson, Center Director
Dr. Richard B. Hayter, Technology Transfer & Traini

5236 **Greenley Research Center**
University of Missouri
64399 Greenley Place 660-739-4410
Novelty, MO 63460 *Fax:* 660-739-4500
bradleytl@missouri.edu
greenley.cafnr.org
Located in the claypan soil region of northeast Missouri, this Center evaluates efficient and profitable crop production while emphasizing soil conservation, water quality and energy efficiency.
Jesse Schwanke, Chairman
Harold Beach, Vice-chairman

5237 **HT Peters Aquatic Biology Laboratory**
Sattgast 230 218-755-2001
1500 Birchmont Drive NE #27 800-475-2001
Bemidji, MN 56601-2699 *Fax:* 218-755-4107
www.bemidjistate.edu
Dr. Richard Hansen, President
Bill Maki, VP

5238 **Harry Reid Center for Environmental Studies**
University of Las Vegas
4505 Maryland Parkway 702-895-3382
Box 454009 *Fax:* 702-895-3094
Las Vegas, NV 89154-4009
The HRC was started in 1981 under UNLV's Marjorie Barrick Museum of Natural History. HRC currently includes 65 staff members and a 65,000 square foot building with four laboratories.
Dr. Oliver A. Hemmers, Executive Director
Leisa Baldwin-Rodriguez, Finance Director

5239 **Harvard NIEHS Center for Environmental Health**
Harvard University
665 Huntington Avenue 617-432-1271
Boston, MA 00211 ddockery@hsph.harvard.edu
www.hsph.harvard.edu
Serves as the focus for research and training activities in environmental health at the Harvard School of Public Health and elsewhere in the University. The Center was established in 1958 to promote interactions among biologicalscientists, physical scientists and engineers working on environmental problems of human health concern.
Douglas Dockery, Center Director
Julie Goodman, Center Coordinator

5240 **Hawaii Cooperative Fishery Research Unit**
University of Hawaii at Manoa
12201 Sunrise Valley Drive MS303 703-648-4260
Reston, VA 20192-2279 *Fax:* 703-648-4269
kkhardin@hawaii.edu
www.coopunits.org
John F. Organ, Chief
Suzanne Cartagirone, Admin Ops Assistant

5241 **Hawaii Undersea Research Laboratory**
University of Hawaii at Manoa
1 Sand Island Access Road 808-842-9813
Marine Science Building (MSB) 303 888-800-0460
Honolulu, HI 96819 *Fax:* 808-842-9833
www.soest.hawaii.edu
One of six research centers funded by NOAA's National Undersea Research Program. HURL operates two 2000-meter Pisces submersibles and a remotely operated vehicle. Research projects include fisheries research, geology and biology of thedeepsea around the Hawaiian Islands.
Diane Apau, Admin Officer
Karynne Chong Morgan, Admin Officer

5242 **Henry S Conrad Environmental Research Area**
1210 Grinnell College 641-269-4000
Grinnell, IA 50112-1690 *Fax:* 641-269-4984
bakermar@grinnell.edu
Paula V. Smith, Vp Academic Affairs
Retta Kelley, Administrative Asst. II

5243 **Highlands Biological Station**
University of North Carolina
265 N Sixth Street 828-526-2602
PO Box 580 *Fax:* 828-526-2797
Highlands, NC 28741 hbs@email.wcu.edu
www.highlandsbiological.org
The Highlands Biological Station is an interinstitutional center of the University of North Carolina administered by Western Carolina University. Through support of field biology research, immersive field courses, and an extensiveoutreach program, their mission is to foster understanding and appreciation of the natural heritage of the southern Appalachian region.
James T. Costa, Executive
Sarah W. Workman, Associate Director

5244 **Hudsonia**
30 Campus Rd 845-758-7053
PO Box 5000 *Fax:* 845-758-7033
Annandale, NY 12504-5000 kiviat@bard.edu
www.hudsonia.org
Since 1981 Hudsonia has conducted environmental research, education, training and technical assistance to protect the Hudson River Valley's natural heritage. Nonpartisan and non-ideologi-

cal, Hudsonia serves as a neutral voice in thechallenging process of land conservation.
Erik Kiviat PhD, Executive Director
Robert E. Schmidt PhD, Associate Director

5245 Huntsman Environmental Research Center
Utah State University
4105 Old Main Hill
Logan, UT 84322-1400
435-797-1000
Fax: 435-797-1248
herc@usu.edu
www.herc.usu.edu

The establishement of the Hunts man Environmental Research Center recognized the fundamental interdependence of the health of man and the health of the environment. The HERC's mission is to engage in research in the key areas ofrecycling, degradability, improvement of air and water quality and conservation of trees. The center purpose is to solve environmental problems and to provide realistic and comprehensive research solutions for our environment.

Stan L. Albrecht, President
Raymond T. Coward, Executive VP

5246 Idaho Cooperative Fish & Wildlife Research Unit
University of Idaho
875 Perimeter Drive
PO Box 444264
Moscow, ID 83844-4264
208-885-6111
888-8UI-DAHO
Fax: 208-885-9119
info@uidaho.edu
www.uidaho.edu

The faculty, associated with the institute, perform multidisciplinary research in environmental molecular ecology, restoration of contaminated soils and waters, and microbial genomics related to environmental processes.

Chuck Staben, President
John Wiencek, Provost/EVP

5247 Institute for Biopsychological Studies of Color, Light, Radiation, Health
San Jose State University
One Washington Square
Psychology Department
San Jose, CA 95192
408-924-1000
Fax: 408-924-1018
www.sjsu.edu
Dr Paul Lanning, VP
Dr Reginald Blaylock, VP for Student Affairs

5248 Institute for Ecological Infrastructure Engineering
Losuisiana State University
College of Engineering
102 ELAB
Baton Rouge, LA 70803
225-578-1399
Fax: 225-578-8662

Institute for Ecological Infrastructure Engineering integrates engineering with science (physical, chemical, life & social) for the co-development of society and nature (ecosystems).
Lily A Rusch, Director

5249 Institute for Lake Superior Research
University of Minnesota
University of Wisconsin-Superior
Belknap & Catlin, PO Box 2000
Superior, WI 54880
715-394-8101
relations@uwsuper.edu
www.uwsuper.edu
Janet Hanson, Vice Chancellor
Jeff Kahler, Budget & Policy Analyst

5250 Institute for Regional and Community Studies
Western Illinois University
Tillman Hall 413B
Macomb, IL 61455
309-298-1566

5251 Institute for Urban Ports and Harbors
School of Marine and Atmospheric Sciences
Stony Brook University
Endeavor Hall, Room 145
Stony Brook, NY 11794-5000
631-632-8700
Fax: 631-632-8820
somas@stonybrook.edu
www.somas.stonybrook.edu

Minghua Zhang, Dean/Director
R. Lawrence Swanson, Associate Dean

5252 Institute of Analytical and Environmental Chemistry
University of New Haven
300 Boston Post Road
West Haven, CT 00651
203-932-7171
800-342-5864
www.newhaven.edu

Steven H. Kaplan, President
Lourdes Alvarez, Dean

5253 Institute of Chemical Toxicology
Wayne State University
Wayne State University
42 W. Warren Ave.
Detroit, MI 48202
313-577-2424
Fax: 313-577-0082
www.wayne.edu
Gary S. Pollard, Chair
M. Roy Wilson, President

5254 Institute of Ecology
University of California
Davis 1 Shields Avenue Davis
Davis, CA 95616
530-752-1011
Fax: 530-752-3350
aking@ucdavis.edu
www.ucdavis.edu

Linda P.B. Katehi, Chancellor
Ralph Hexter, Provost/Executive Vice Chanc

5255 Interdisciplinary Center for Aeronomy & Other Atmospheric Sciences
University of Florida
317, Bryant Space Science Center
PO Box 112050
Gainesville, FL 32611-2050
352-392-2001
Fax: 352-392-2003
aesgreen@ufl.edu
Prof. Alex ES Green, Director

5256 Iowa Cooperative Fish & Wildlife Research Unit
Iowa State University
NREM-ICFWRU
339 Science II
Ames, IA 50011-3221
515-294-3056
Fax: 515-294-5468
coppunit@iastate.edu
www.cfwru.iastate.edu

The Iowa landscape and economy are dominated by production agriculture. Game and non-game wildlife species inhabinting the state are influenced by the destruction, degradation and frgamentation of wetland, prairie, and forest habitatscaused by intensified agricultural practices. This Unit is designed to identify, and emaphsize these effects through research and education programs.
Robert W Klaver, Unit Leader
Clay L Pierce, Assistant Unit leader

5257 Iowa Waste Reduction Center
University of Northern Iowa
113, BCS Building
University of Northern Iowa
Cedar Falls, IA 50614
319-273-8905
800-422-3109
Fax: 319-273-6582
www.iwrc.org

A service of the University of Northern Iowa, it provides free and confidential environmental regulatory assistance to Iowa small businesses. The IWRC has also developed two products available to the painting and coating industry:LaserPaint and VirtualPaint.
Diane Albertson, IT Specialist
Michael Bolick, Comm/PR Manager

5258 James H Barrow Field Station
Hiram College Biological Station
Garrettsville, OH 44231
330-527-2141
Fax: 330-527-3187

The James H Barrow Field Station was established in 1967 to provide Hiram College students the opportunity to supplement classroom activities with hands-on learning experiences. Over the Last 32 years the Station has grown anddeveloped into an active research and educational facility that not only echances the College's science and environmental studies programs, but also provides a means for the general public to increase their understanding and appreciation of Ohio'snatural history.

5259 John F Kennedy School of Government Environmental and Natural Resources Program
Harvard University

79 John F Kennedy Street 617-495-1351
Cambridge, MA 00213 *Fax:* 617-495-1635
enrp@ksg.harvard.edu
Henry Lee, Director

5260 Juneau Center School of Fisheries & Ocean Sciences
University of Alaska Fairbanks
17101 Point Lena Loop Rd 907-796-5441
UAF Fisheries Division *Fax:* 907-796-5447
Juneau, AK 99801-8344 www.sfos.uaf.edu
JCSFOS has the primary responsibility within the University for education, research and public service in support of fisheries related areas of oceanography, marine biology and limnology with emphasis on Alaskan waters and the Arctic.The school's goal is to maintain and develop the broad expertise among its faculty and students needed to contribute to the wise use of Alaska's natural resources.
Joan Braddock, Dean
Adkison Milo, Professor

5261 Laboratory for Energy and the Environment
Massachusetts Institute of Technology
Massachusetts Institute of Technolo 617-258-8891
77 Massachusetts Avenue, E19-307 *Fax:* 617-253-8013
Cambridge, MA 00213-4307 thill@mit.edu
The LFEE at the Massachusetts Institute of Technology brings together collaborating faculty and staff in 13 departments to address the complex interrelationships between energy and the environment, and other global environmentalchallenges.
Prof. Robert C. Armstrong, Director
Prof. Angela M. Belcher, Professor

5262 Leopold Center for Sustainable Agriculture
Iowa State University
209 Curtiss Hall 515-294-3711
513 Farm House Lane *Fax:* 515-294-9696
Ames, IA 50011-1054 leocenter@iastate.edu
www.leopold.iastate.edu
The center was created by the Iowa Groundwater Protection Act with the mission to identify and reduce adverse environmental impacts of farming practices while developing profitable farming systems that conserve natural resources.

Doug Gronau, Chair
Mark Rasmussen, Director

5263 Living Marine Resources Institute
Stony Brook University 631-632-6000
Stony Brook, NY 11794 *Fax:* 631-632-9441
www.stonybrook.edu
LIMRI is one of several specialized institutes subsumed within the Marine Sciences Research Center of Stony Brook University. LIMRI's program of research includes investigations on marine fisheries, harmful algal blooms, marine law &policy, and aquaculture. The Institute operates the Flax Pond Marine Laboratory, a seaside, seawater-equipped facility for experimental work, located 5 miles north of the main campus on a tidal pond adjacent to Long Island Sound.
Samuel L. Stanley, President
William Arens, Vice Provost

5264 Long-Term Ecological Research Project
University of Colorado
1 University of New Mexico 505-277-2649
Albuquerque, NM 87131 *Fax:* 303-492-0434
tech-support@lternet.edu
www.lternet.edu

Scott Collins, Chair
Bob Waide, Executive Director

5265 Louisiana Sea Grant College Program
Louisiana State University
Sea Grant Building 225-578-6564
Baton Rouge, LA 70803 *Fax:* 225-578-6331
www.laseagrant.org
Works to promote stewardship of the state's coastal resources through a combination of research, education and outreach programs critical to the cultural, economic, and environmental health of Louisiana's coastal zone. Part of theNational Sea Grant Program, it is one of 32 programs located in coastal, Great Lakes, and Puerto Rican coast areas.

Robert R. Twilley, Executive Director
Matthew Bethel Ph.D., Assistant Executive Director

5266 MIT Sea Grant College Program
Massachusetts Institute of Technology
77 Massachusettes Ave. 617-253-7131
E 38-300 *Fax:* 617-258-5730
Cambridge, MA 00213 chrys@mit.edu
Chrys Chryssostomidis, Director
Stefano Brizzolara, Asst Director

5267 Marine Science Institute
University of Texas
The University of Texas 361-749-6711
750 Channel View Drive *Fax:* 361-749-6777
Port Aransas, TX 78373 www.utmsi.utexas.edu
The Marine Institute is an organized research unit of The University of Texas at Austin. Institute scientists are engaged in both multi-investigator, multi-disciplinary studies and individual research projects in the local area andthroughout the world. Many of these projects are combinations of field and laboratory investigations. The Institute receives an operating budget annually that is based on a two-year advanced budget approval by the state legislature.

Perry R. Bass, Chair
Robert W. Dickey Ph.D., Director

5268 Massachusetts Cooperative Fish & Wildlife Unit
University of Massachusetts
12201 Sunrise Valley Drive MS303 703-648-4260
PO Box 34220 *Fax:* 703-648-4269
Reston, VA 20192-4220 sdestef@eco.umass.edu
www.coopunits.org

John F. Organ, Chief
Suzanne Cartagirone, Admin Ops Assistant

5269 Masschusetts Water Resources Research Center
University of Massachusetts
Blaisdell House 413-545-5531
113 Grinnell Way *Fax:* 413-253-1309
Amherst, MA 00100 wrrc@cns.umass.edu
The Center has three objectives: 1) to develop, through research, new technology and more efficient methods for resolving local, state and national water resources problems; 2) to train water scientists and engineers through on-the-jobparticipation in water resources research and outreach; 3) to facilitate water research coordination and the application of research results by means of information dissemination, technology transfer and outreach.
Paula Rees, Director
Marie-Françoise Hatte, Assoc. Director

5270 Millar Wilson Laboratory for Chemical Research
Jacksonville University
2800 University Boulevard N 904-744-3950
Jacksonville, FL 32211 *Fax:* 904-744-0101
Lsonnen@ju.edu

5271 Mining and Mineral Resources Research Center
205 Particle Science & Technology 352-846-1194
Gainesville, FL 32611 *Fax:* 352-846-1196
info@perc.ufl.edu
www.perc.ufl.edu/mrrc

Brij M. Moudgil, Director
B. Koopman, Affiliated Faculty

5272 Mississippi Cooperative Fish & Wildlife Research Unit
Mississippi State University
12201 Sunrise Valley Drive MS303 703-648-4260
Reston, VA 20192 *Fax:* 703-648-4269
www.coopunits.org

John F. Organ, Chief
Suzanne Cartagirone, Admin Ops Assistant

5273 **Mississippi State Chemical Laboratory**
Mississippi State University
262 Lee Boulevard 662-325-3742
PO Box BQ *Fax:* 662-325-4039
Mississippi State, MS 39762 www.msstate.edu
Mark E. Keenum, President
Jerome A. Gilbert, Provost/Executive Vice Presi

5274 **Montana Cooperative Fishery Research Unit**
Montana St University Dept Ecology 406-994-2672
100 Culbertson Hall, PO Box 172000 *Fax:* 406-994-7479
Bozeman, MT 59717-2000 www.montana.edu
Dr. Waded Cruzado, President
Wanda DeMay, Manager

5275 **Monterey Bay Watershed Project**
California State University
100 Campus Center 831-582-3689
Watershed Institute Building 42 *Fax:* 831-582-5114
Seaside, CA 93955-8001 laura_lienk@csumb.edu
The Watershed Institute is a direct action, community based coalition of researchers, restoration ecologists, educators, students, planners and area volunteers dedicated to restoring the watersheds of the Monterey Bay region throughrestoration, education and research. Their policy is to work with state and federal agencies, private landowners and local planners to gain access to critical lands. Institute staff are involved in local land and water planning.
Laura Lee Lienk, Co-Director
Doug Smith, Co-Director/Professor

5276 **Museum of Zoology**
University of Massachusetts
Zoology Department 413-545-2287
Amherst, MA 00100 web@admin.umass.edu
www.umass.edu
Kumble R. Subbaswamy, Chancellor
James V. Staros, Provost/Vice Chancellor

5277 **National Center for Ground Water Research**
University of Oklahoma
660 Parrington Oval 405-325-0311
Norman, OK 73019 *Fax:* 405-325-7596
canter@ou.edu
Dr Larry Canter, Director

5278 **National Center for Vehicle Emissions Control & Safety**
Colorado State University
1584 Campus Delivery 970-491-7240
Fort Collins, CO 80523 *Fax:* 970-491-7801
ncvecs@cahs.colostate.edu
www.colostate.edu
NCVECS is a nationally and internationally recognized university based research and training center devoted to motor vehicle emission issues. NCVECS primarily assists states with research and training related to their local vehicleinspection program. In addition, research is conducted on OBDII systems, alternative fuels and diesel vehicle issues.
Dr Lenora Bohren, Director
Joe Beebe, Automotive Emissions Testing

5279 **National Mine Land Reclamation Center: Eastern Region**
State University of Pennsylvania
106 Land & Water Resources Building 814-863-0291
University Park, PA 16802 *Fax:* 814-865-3378
www.wvmdtaskforce.com
Ben Greene, Chairman/President
Buddy Beach, VP

5280 **National Mine Land Reclamation Center: Midwest Region**
Southern Illinois University
1201 W Gregory 618-453-2496
Carbondale, IL 62901 *Fax:* 217-333-8816
www.wvmdtaskforce.com
Ben Greene, Chairman/President
Buddy Beach, VP

5281 **National Mine Land Reclamation Center: Western Region**
Highway 6 S 701-777-5217
Mandan, ND 58554 www.wvmdtaskforce.com
Ben Greene, Chairman/President
Buddy Beach, VP

5282 **National Park Service Cooperative Unit: Athens**
University of Georgia
Institute of Ecology 706-542-8301
Athens, GA 30602
Dr. Stephen Cover-Shabica, Contact

5283 **National Research Center for Coal and Energy (NRCCE)**
West Virginia University 304-293-4974
PO Box 6064 *Fax:* 304-293-3749
Morgantown, WV 26506 Paul.Ziemkiewicz@mail.wvu.edu
www.wvwri.org
A research and training center at West Virginia University, advances innovations for energy and the environment by working with research faculty across WVU and with other university, government, and private sector researchersnationwide. The center is organized into a variety of multidisciplinary programs, centers, and institutes focusing on topics such as clean energy production, energy distribution, energy efficiency, alternative fuels, watershed restorationandpreservation.
Paul F. Ziemkiewicz, PhD, Director
Tamara F. Vandivort, Associate Director

5284 **Natural Energy Laboratory of Hawaii Authority**
73-4460 Queen Kaahumanu Hwy. #101 808-327-9585
Kailua Kona, HI 96740-2637 *Fax:* 808-327-9586
nelha.hawaii.gov
The Natural Energy Laboratory of Hawaii Authority (NELHA) operates facilities at Keahole Point on Hawaii Island that pump ashore cold deep and warm surface seawater for commercial and research tenants from the private and publicsectors. Tenants utilize the seawater and NELHA's high sunlight and consistant temperatures in a wide range of aquaculture and energy projects.
Ron Baird, CEO

5285 **New Hampshire Sea Grant College Program**
University of New Hampshire
The University of New Hampshire 603-862-1234
Main Street 800-735-2964
Durham, NH 00382 *Fax:* 603-743-3997
www.seagrant.unh.edu
A component of the National Sea Grant College Program, NH Sea Grant works toward the conservation, wise use and development of marine resources in the state and region.
Mark W. Huddleston, President
John Aber, Provost

5286 **New York Cooperative Fish & Wildlife Research Unit**
Cornell University
211 Fernow Hall 607-255-2839
Ithaca, NY 14853-3001 *Fax:* 607-255-1895
meaton@usgs.gov
www.coopunits.org/New_York
Angela Fuller, Unit Leader
Mitchell Eaton, Asst. Unit Leader

5287 **New York State Water Resources Institute**
Cornell University

204A Rice Hall 607-255-5941
Ithaca, NY 14853 *Fax:* 607-255-5945
sjr4@cornell.edu

Susan J. Riha, Director
Brian G. Rahm, Post Doctoral Associate

5288 **Northwoods Field Station**
Hiram College
11715 Garfield Road 330-569-3211
Hiram, OH 44234 800-362-5280
www.hiram.edu
Lori E. Varlotta Ph.D, President
Gay Cull Addicott, President

5289 **Occupational & Environmental Health Laboratory**
University of North Alabama
2206 East Mall 604-822-2772
Vancouver, BC V6T1Z *Fax:* 604-822-4994
mha.program@ubc.ca
www.spph.ubc.ca
Dr. David Patrick, Director
Cecilia Gruber, Asst. Director

5290 **Ocean & Coastal Policy Center**
University of California
Woolley-5134 805-893-8393
Santa Barbara, CA 93106 *Fax:* 805-893-8062
Dr. Michael Vincent, Conratct

5291 **Ocean Engineering Center**
Massachusetts Institute of Technolo 617-253-9344
77 Massachusetts Avenue, Room 5-228 *Fax:* 603-862-0241
Cambridge, MA 00213 oe@mit.edu
Geoff Fox, Administrative Assistant II
Mary Mullowney, Administrative Assistant II

5292 **Oceanic Institute**
Makapuu Point 808-259-3102
41-202 Kalanianaole Highway *Fax:* 808-259-5971
Waimanalo, HI 96795 oi@oceanicinstitute.org
www.oceanicinstitute.org

Oceanic Institute is a not-for-profit organization dedicated to research, development and transfer of oceanographic, marine Environmental, and aquaculture technologies. Oceanic Institute is a world leader in conducting appliedresearch in aquaculture production and marine resource conservation. Its mission is to develop and transfer environmentally responsible technologies to increase aquatic food production while promoting the sustainable use of ocean resources.

Dr. Geoffrey Bannister, Chairman
James A. Ajello, Board Of Trustees

5293 **Oregon Cooperative Fishery Research Unit**
Oregon State University
Oregon State University 541-737-1000
104 Nash Hall *Fax:* 541-737-3590
Corvallis, OR 97330 OSU.Provost@oregonstate.edu
www.oregonstate.edu

Pat Reser, Chair
Darry Callahan, Vice Chair

5294 **Oregon Cooperative Park Studies Unit**
Oregon State University
3200 Jefferson Way 541-737-2056
Corvallis, OR 97331 www.cof.orst.edu/
Dr Edward E Starkey, Codirector

5295 **Oregon Sea Grant College Program**
Oregon State University
Oregon State University 541-737-1000
Suite 350 *Fax:* 541-737-7958
Corvallis, OR 97330 www.seagrant.oregonstate.edu
Pat Reser, Chair
Darry Callahan, Vice Chair

5296 **Pennsylvania Cooperative Fish & Wildlife Research Unit**
Pennsylvania State University
117 Forest Resources Bldg 814-865-7541
University Park, PA 16802 *Fax:* 814-865-3725
www.ecosystems.psu.edu

Michael G. Messina Ph.D., Head /Professor
Marc David Abrams Ph.D, Professor

5297 **Permaculture Gap Mountain**
9 Old County Road 603-532-6877
Jaffrey, NH 00345

5298 **Pesticide Research Center**
Michigan State University
Michigan State University 517-353-4647
426 Auditorium Rd, Board of Trustees Roo 800-500-1554
East Lansing, MI 48824-1046 *Fax:* 51- 35- 467
beekman@msu.edu
www.msu.edu
Joel I. Ferguson, Chairperson
Mitch Lyons, Vice Chairperson

5299 **Planning Institute**
University of Southern California
University of Southern California 213-740-2311
Los Angeles, CA 90089 *Fax:* 213-740-1801
sppd@usc.edu
www.usc.edu

Wallis Annenberg, Chairman
C.L. Max Nikias, President

5300 **Program for International Collaboration in Agroecology**
University of California Santa Cruz
MS: PICA 831-459-4051
1156 High Street *Fax:* 831-459-2867
Santa Cruz, CA 95064 gliess@ucsc.edu
Researches, develops, and advances sustainable food and agricultural systems that are environmentally sound, economically viable, socially responsible, nonexploitive, and that serve as a foundation for future generations. A specialfocus on promoting an international network of training programs in agroecology.
Stephen R. Gliessman, Professor of Agroecology
Vivan Vadakan, PICA Program Manager

5301 **Program in Freshwater Biology**
University of Mississippi
University of Mississippi 662-915-2787
P.O. Box 1848 *Fax:* 662-915-5144
University, MS 38677 biology@olemiss.edu
www.olemiss.edu

Dr. James Kushlan, Chairman
Daniel W. Jones, Chancellor

5302 **Randolph G Pack Environmental Institute**
1 Forestry Drive 315-470-6500
107 Marshall Hall *Fax:* 315-470-6915
Syracuse, NY 13210 envsty@esf.edu
www.esf.edu

The Institute seeks to advance scholoarly and popular knowledge of key contemporary issues related to environmental policy and regulartion. It focuses on how democratic public decisions affecting the natural environment are made,concentrating on such topics as public participation, environmental equity, and sustainable development.

Vita DeMarchi, Chair
Dr. Quentin Wheeler, President

5303 **Rare and/or Endangered Species Research Center**
215 Mitchell Street 256-760-4429
Florence, AL 35630

5304 Red Butte Garden and Arboretum
300 Wakara Way 801-585-0556
Salt Lake City, UT 84108 www.redbuttegarden.org
David Gee, Chair
Tom Ramsey, Vice Chair

5305 Remote Sensing/Geographic Information Systems Facility
Geography Building 517-353-7195
673 Auditorium Road *Fax:* 517-353-1821
East Lansing, MI 48824 boothj@msu.edu
www.rsgis.msu.edu
Dr Susan Berta, Interim Chairperson
Justin Booth, Director

5306 Research Triangle Institute
3040 Cornwallis Road 919-541-6000
PO Box 12194 *Fax:* 919-541-7155
Research Triangle Park, NC 27709-2194 listen@rti.org
www.rti.org
Clients around the world rely on RTI to conduct innovative, multidisciplinary research to meet their R and D challenges. RTI's staff of more then 1,850 people represents a diverse set of technical capabilities in health and medicine,environmental protection, technology commercialization, decision support systems and education and training.
William M. Moore, Chair
Richard H. Brodhead, President

5307 Resources for the Future
1616 P Street Northwest 202-328-5000
Suite 600 *Fax:* 202-939-3460
Washington, DC 20036 info@rff.org
www.rff.org
RFF is a nonprofit and nonpartisan think tank located in Washington DC that conducts independent research-rooted primarily in economics and other social sciences on environmental and natural resource issues. RFF was founded in 1952.
Richard L. Schmalensee, Chair
Philip R. Sharp, President

5308 Resources for the Future: Energy & Natural Resources Division
1616 P Street, Northwest 202-328-5000
Suite 600 *Fax:* 202-939-3460
Washington, DC 20036 info@rff.org
www.rff.org
Richard L. Schmalensee, Chair
Philip R. Sharp, President

5309 Resources for the Future: Quality of the Environment Division
1616 P Street, Northwest 202-328-5000
Suite 600 *Fax:* 202-939-3460
Washington, DC 20036 info@rff.org
www.rff.org
Richard L. Schmalensee, Chair
Philip R. Sharp, President

5310 River Studies Center
University of Wisconsin
University of Wisconsin-La Crosse 608-785-8000
1725 State Street *Fax:* 608-785-6460
La Crosse, WI 54601 www.uwlax.edu
Bob Hetzel, Vice Chancellor
Vickie Baer, University Exec Staff Assis

5311 Robert J Bernard Biological Field Station
1400 N Amherst Avenue 909-398-1751
Claremont, CA 91711 wallace.meyer@pomona.edu
www.bfs.claremont.edu/
Robert J. Bernard, Biological Field Station
Dr. Wallace Meyer III, Director

5312 Rocky Mountain Biological Laboratory
PO Box 519 970-349-7231
Crested Butte, CO 81224 *Fax:* 970-349-7481
admin@rmbl.org
www.rmbl.org
High-altitude field station whose principal purpose is to provide quality research and teaching facilities for biologists and biology students of all diciplines who can benefit personally and intellectually from studying at thislocation. An important further purpose of the Laboratory is to promote the understanding and protection of the high altitude ecosystems of Colorado and the watershed of the Gunnison River through through the professional activities of its members.
Scott Wissinger, President
Carol M. Johnson, VP

5313 Rocky Mountain Mineral Law Foundation
9191 Sheridan Boulevard #203 303-321-8100
Westminster, CO 80031 *Fax:* 303-321-7657
info@rmmlf.org
www.rmmlf.org
Phillip R. Clark, President
Jonathan A. Hunter, Vice President

5314 Romberg Tiburon Centers
San Francisco State University
3152 Paradise Drive 415-338-6063
PO Box 855 *Fax:* 415-435-7120
Tiburon, CA 94920 jviale@sfsu.edu
Karina Nielsen, Director
Sheldon Axler, Dean

5315 Roosevelt Wildlife Station
1 Forestry Drive 315-470-6764
405 Illick Hall *Fax:* 315-470-6934
Syracuse, NY 13210 jpgibbs@syr.edu
www.esf.edu
Dr. James P. Gibbs, Director
Jacqueline L Frair, Associate Director

5316 Salt Institute
700 N. Fairfax St 703-549-4648
Suite 600 *Fax:* 703-548-2194
Alexandria, VA 22314-2040 info@saltinstitute.org
www.saltinstitute.org
The Salt Institute is an international trade association of salt producers. It has information about the environmental impacts of salt production and use.
Lori Roman, President
Morton Satin, VP

5317 School for Field Studies
100 Cummings Center 978-741-3567
Suite 534-G 800-989-4435
Beverly, MA 00191 *Fax:* 978-922-3835
sfs@fieldstudies.org
www.fieldstudies.org
Students conduct hands-on, community-focused environmental field work around the world. Addresses critical environmental issues including preserving entire ecosystems or individual species, balancing economic development andconservation, and finding ways to manage and maintain wildlife, marine and agricultural resources.
James A. Cramer, President
Katlyn Osgood Armstrong, Vice President

5318 School of Marine Affairs (SMA)
University of Washington
University of Washington 206-543-7004
36 Gerberding Hall *Fax:* 206-543-1417
Seattle, WA 98195-6715 uwsmea@uw.edu
www.depts.washington.edu
SMA is a masters-level, professional school within the University of Washington specializing in the interdisciplinary teaching

and research on contemporary coastal and ocean resources, environmental and developmental problems.
Suanty Kaghan, Admin Specialist
Tiffany Dion, Program Advisor

5319 Science and Public Policy
Rockefeller University 212-327-8000
1230 York Avenue, Box 234 *Fax:* 212-327-7974
New York, NY 10065-6399 www.rockefeller.edu
David Rockefeller, Honorary Chair
Russel L. Carson, Chair

5320 Seatuck Foundation: Seatuck Research Program
Seatuck Environmental Association 631-581-6908
PO Box 31 staff@seatuck.org
Islip, NY 11751 www.seatuck.org
Anthony Graves, President
Lucinda Mullin, Co-VP

5321 Society for the Application of Free Energy
1315 Apple Avenue 301-587-8686
Silver Spring, MD 20910 *Fax:* 301-587-8688

5322 Soil and Water Research
4115 Gourrier Avenue 225-757-7726
Baton Rouge, LA 70808 *Fax:* 225-757-7728
mse.ars.usda.gov/la/btn/swr/
Mission is to characterize and quantify the transport and fate of agrochemicals in high water table soils, develop integrated soil, water, and agrochemical management systems that provide profitable yields and improve water table soilsin the humid, warm temperature areas of the US and develop improved soil and water management systems and operational procedures that enhance crop production conditions and increase the efficiency of conducting farming operationsin a timely manner.
Dr. James Fouss, Research Leader

5323 Solar Energy Group
University of Chicago
1835 E 6th Street 480-884-1603
Suite 24 *Fax:* 480-884-1888
Tempe, AZ 85281 solareg@gmail.com

5324 South Carolina Agromedicine Program
Medical University of South Carolin 843-792-2211
179 Ashley Avenue, Colcock Hall 800-922-5250
Charleston, SC 29425 *Fax:* 843-792-4702
Simpsowm@musc.edu
www.musc.edu
Information, consultation, referral service for professional and lay persons involved in or in contact with agriculture or agricultural products.

Raymond G. Greenberg, President
Dr. Mark Sothmann, VP for Academic Affairs/Prov

5325 South Carolina Sea Grant Consortium
287 Meeting Street 843-953-2078
Charleston, SC 29401 *Fax:* 843-953-2080
www.scseagrant.org
A state agency that supports coastal and marine research, education, outreach, one technical assistance program that foster sustainable economic development and resource conservation. The consortium represents eight university andstate research organizations and induces a number of information products on coastal and marine resource topics.
16 pages
Alvin A. Taylor, Board Chair/Director
David A DeCenzo, Ph.D., President

5326 Southern California Pacific Coastal Water Research Project
3535 Harbor Blvd 714-755-3200
Suite 110 *Fax:* 714-755-3299
Costa Mesa, CA 92626 www.sccwrp.org
SCCWRP is a joint powers agency focusing on marine environmental research. A joint powers agency is one that is formed when several government agencies have a common mission that can be better addressed by pooling resources andknowledge. In our case, the common mission is to gather the necessary scientific information so that our member agencies can effectively and cost-efficiently protect the Southern California marine environment.
Dr. Stephen Weisberg, Executive Director
Ken Schiff, Deputy Director

5327 Southwest Consortium on Plant Genetics & Water Resources
New Mexico State University 575-646-0111
Box 3GL 800-662-6678
Las Cruces, NM 88003 admissions@nmsu.edu
www.nmsu.edu

Dr. John D Kemp, Chairman
Garrey Carruthers, President

5328 Strom Thurmond Institute of Government & Public Affairs, Regional Development Group
Clemson University 864-656-4700
Clemson, SC 29634
Jeffrey S. Allen, Director
Carolyn Benson, Administrative Analyst

5329 Stroud Water Research Center
970 Spencer Road 610-268-2153
Avondale, PA 19311 *Fax:* 610-268-0490
webmaster@stroudcenter.org
www.stroudcenter.org
The Stroud Water Research Center seeks to understand streams and rivers and to use the knowledge gained from its research to promote environmental stewardship and resolve freshwater challenges throughout the world.
Bernard W. Sweeney, President/Director/Sr. Resea
David B. Arscott, VP

5330 Sustainable Agriculture Research & Education Program
ASI at UC Davis
One Shields Avenue 530-752-3915
Davis, CA 95616 *Fax:* 530-752-2829
asi@ucdavis.edu

Tom Tomich, Director
Raoul Adamchak, CSA Coordinator

5331 Tennessee Cooperative Fishery Research Unit
Tennessee Technological University
PO Box 5114 931-372-3094
Cookeville, TN 38505 *Fax:* 931-372-6257
jim_layzer@tntech.edu
www.tntech.edu

Betty Harris, Administrative Associate 3
Kendall Moles, Research Assistant 3

5332 Texas Center for Policy Studies
707 Rio Grande 512-474-0811
Suite 200 *Fax:* 512-474-7846
Austin, TX 78701 tcps@texascenter.org
www.texascenter.org

David Hall, Chair/Board Member
Cyrus Reed, Treasurer/Board Member

5333 Texas Water Resources Institute
500 Research Parkway A110 979-845-1851
2260 TAMU *Fax:* 979-845-0662
College Station, TX 77843-2260 twri@tamu.edu
Roel Lopez, Interim Director
Kevin Wagner, Assoc. Director

5334 The Natural History Museum & Biodiversity Research Center
University of Kansas
Dyche Hall 785-864-4540
1345 Jayhawk Boulevard *Fax:* 785-864-5335
Lawrence, KS 66045-7593 naturalhistory@ku.edu

At the UK Natural History Museum & Biodiversity Research Center, they study the life of the planet for the benefit of the earth and its inhabitants. They document the diverse life of the earth, uncover its patters and document theresearch in order to better understand the natural environments, enhance power to predict environmental phenomena, and provide knowledge for natural resource management. Their ability to discover, document and diesseminate their research leads thenation.

Dr. Leanord Krishtalka, Director-Admin
Linda Trueb, Assoc. Director

5335 Throckmorton-Purdue Agricultural Center
615 West State Street 765-494-8392
US 231 *Fax:* 765-538-3423
West Lafayette, IN 47907-2053 jayyoung@purdue.edu
www.ag.purdue.edu

Jay Akridge, Sample Dean of Agriculture
Marcos . Fernandez, Associate Dean

5336 Toxic Chemicals Laboratory
Cornell University
Cornell University, Tower Road 607-255-4538
New York State College of Agriculture
Ithaca, NY 14853

5337 US Forest Service: Wildlife Habitat & Silviculture Laboratory
USDA Forest Service, Southern Resea 870-367-3464
P.O. Box 3516 UAM *Fax:* 870-367-1164
Monticello, AR 71656 www.srs.fs.usda.gov

We assess impacts of forest management practices on wildlife populations and their habitats and provide guide lines to land managers for improving their management to accommodate wildlife.

Cory K. Adams, Wildlife Biologist
Gina Franke, Support Services Specialist

5338 USDA Forest Service: Northern Research Station
11 Campus Blvd. 610-557-4017
Suite 200 610-557-4132
Newtown Square, PA 19073 *Fax:* 517-355-5121
rhaack@fs.fed.us
www.nrs.fs.fed.us

Michael T Rains, Director
Deb Dietzman, Assistant Director

5339 USDA Forest Service: Rocky Mountain Research Station
240 West Prospect 970-498-1100
Fort Collins, CO 80526 *Fax:* 970-295-5927
www.fs.fed.us

We seek to be an unbiased source of scientific information; provide tools that consider the multidisciplinary nature of natural resource decisions and recognize that resource managers need scientific information that is integrated anddeveloped for application. Research results are made available through a variety of technical reports, seminars, demonstrations, exhibits and personal consultations. These help resource managers and planners balance economic and environmental demandsworldwide.

Cloetta Schroeder, AD Operations
Angela Baca, Director

5340 UVA Institute for Environmental Negotiation
University of Virginia
The Institute for Environmental Neg 434-924-1970
PO Box 400179 *Fax:* 434-924-0231
Charlottesville, VA 22904-4179 ed7k@virginia.edu
www.virginia.edu/ien

The Institute for Environmental Negotiation is committed to building a sustainable future for Virginia's communities and beyond by: bringing people together to develop sustainable solutions; providing people with learning opportunitiesto be creative and collaborative leaders; and building understanding of best collaborative practices.

Dr E Franklin Dukes PhD, Director
Tanya Denckla Cobb, Associate Director

5341 University Forest
University of Missouri
2600 Bay Area Boulevard 281-286-5959
Houston, TX 77058 *Fax:* 281-286-2095
info@universityforestUHCL.com
www.universityforestuhcl.com

Lawrance Samaranayake, Manager
Steven Fance, Maintenance Assistant

5342 VT Forest Resource Center and Arboretum
University of Tennessee
901 S Illinois Avenue 865-483-3571
Oak Ridge, TN 37830 *Fax:* 865-483-3572
utforest@utk.edu

The UT Forestry Experiment Station mission is to:(1) provide the land and supporting resources necessary for conducting modern and effective forestry, wildlife, and associated social, biological and ecological research programs;(2)demonstrate the application of optimal forest and wildlife management technologies; and (3) assist with transfer of new technology to forest land owners and industries.

Kevin P. Hoyt, Center Director
Lynne Lucas, Administrative Specialist I

5343 Vantuna Research Group
Moore Laboratory of Zoology
Occidental College 323-259-2500
1600 Campus Road *Fax:* 323-259-2958
Los Angeles, CA 90041 admission@oxy.edu
www.oxy.edu

John S Stephens, Director

5344 Virginia Center for Coal & Energy Research
Virginia Tech 540-231-5038
Mail Code 0411 *Fax:* 540-231-4078
Blacksburg, VA 24061 vccer@vt.edu
www.energy.vt.edu

Created by an Act of the VA General Assembly in 1977 as a study, research, information and resource facility for the commonwealth of VA, and is located at VA Tech. The mission involves four primary functions: research in energy andcoal related issues of interest to the Commonweatlth; coordination of coal and energy research at VA Tech; dissemination of coal and energy data to users in the Commonwealth; examination of socio-economic implications and environmental impacts ofcoal and energy.

K. Scott Keim, President
John R. Craynon, Director

5345 Washington Cooperative Fishery Research Unit
University of Washington
Box 355020 206-543-6475
Seattle, WA 98195-5020 www.depts.washington.edu
Dr. Christian Grue, Unit Leader
Dr. Glenn VanBlaricom, Asst. Unit Leader

5346 Waste Management Education & Research Consortium
New Mexico State University
Box 30001, MSC WERC 505-646-2038
Las Cruces, NM 88003 800-523-5996
Fax: 505-646-4149
iee@nmsu.edu
www.ieenmsu.com

A key component of WERC is higher education degree programs. To support this component, WERC administers a Fellowship Program at each academic partner institution. The primary objective for the WERC Fellowship program is to helpstudents develop a program which will lead to environmental related career opportunities upon graduation.

Barbara Valdez, Program Facilitator
Paul K. Anderson, Associate Professor

5347 Waste Management Research & Education Institute
University of Tennessee

The EERC & the University of Tennes
676 Dabney Hall
Knoxville, TN 37996
865-974-1000
Fax: 865-974-8086
ceb@utk.edu
Jack N. Barkenbus, Executive Director
Kim Davis, Asst. Director

5348 **Water Quality Laboratory**
Western Wyoming Community College
PO Box 428
Rock Springs, WY 82901
307-382-1662
www.wwcc.cc.wy.us/
Craig Thompson, Director

5349 **Water Resource Center**
University of Minnesota
173 McNeal Hall
1985 Buford Avenue
St Paul, MN 55108
612-624-9282
Fax: 612-625-1263
umwrc@umn.edu
www.wrc.umn.edu

The center coordinatoes research, education and extension programs on water resource issues. Administrative responsibility for Water Resource Sciences Graduate Program. Is the Water Resources Institute for Minnesota.

Faye Sleeper, Co-Director
Deborah L. Swackhamer, Co-Director

5350 **Water Resources Institute**
University of Wisconsin
1975 Willow Drive
Floor 2
Madison, WI 53706-1103
608-262-0905
Fax: 608-262-0591
hurley@aqua.wisc.edu
www.wri.wisc.edu

The University of Wisconsin Water Resources Institute's primary mission is to plan, develop and coordinate research programs that address present and emerging water-and land-related issues. It has developed a broadly based statewideprogram of basic and applied research that has effectively confronted a spectrum of societal concerns. It is one of 54 institutes or centers located at the Land Grant College in each state.

James Hurley, Director
Terri Liebmann, Assistant Director/Accountin

5351 **Water Resources Research Institute at Kent University**
Kent State University
800 E. Summit St.
PO Box 5190
Kent, OH 44240
330-672-3000
Fax: 330-672-4834
info@kent.edu
www.kent.edu

The institute fosters a broad-based approach to the evaluation and analysis of environmental problems related to water use. WRRI is a resouce for citizens, governmental agencies and policy makers, providing reliable scientificinformation on which to base decisions related to the wise use and management of water and land management, water policy decisions and environmental conservation.

Beverly Warren, President
Edward G. Mahon, Vice President

5352 **Water Resources Research of the University of North Carolina**
North Carolina State University
1575 Varsity Drive, Module 7
NCSU Campus Box 7912
Raleigh, NC 27695-7912
919-515-2815
Fax: 919-515-2839
www.ncsu.edu

One of 54 state water institutes authorized to administer and promote federal/state partnerships in research and information transfer on water-related issues. Identifies and supports research needed to help solve water quality andwater resources problems in NC. Publishes peer-reviewed reports on completed research projects. Sponsors educational seminars and conferences and provides public information on water issues through publication of a newsletter.

William R. Woodson, Chancellor
Kevin D. Howell, Assistant to the Chancellor

5353 **Water Testing Laboratory**
Morehead State University
150 University Blvd.
Morehead, KY 40351
606-783-2961
800-585-6781
Rita Wright, Contact

5354 **Weather Analysis Center**
University of Michigan
Space Research Building
2455 Hayward Street
Ann Arbor, MI 48109
734-936-0482
Fax: 734-763-0437
dbaker@umich.edu
Atmospheric, planetary and space science engineering.
Dr Dennis Baker, Director

5355 **West Virginia Water Research Institute**
West Virginia University
Room 202 NRCCE
Box 6064
Morgantown, WV 26506
304-293-4974
Fax: 304-293-7822
pziemkie@wvu.edu
www.wvwri.org

The West Virginia Water Research Institute (WVWRI) has served as a statewide vehicle for performing research related to water issues. WVWRI serves as the coordinating body for the following programs: the National Mine Land ReclamationCenter, Appalachian Clean Streams Initiatve, Acid Drainage Technology Initiative, Northern WV Brownfields Assistant Center, Hydrogeology Research Center, State Water Institutes, and more.

Paul F. Ziemkiewicz, PhD, Director
Tamara F. Vandivort, Assoc. Director

5356 **Western Research Farm**
36515 Highway 34 E
Castana, IA 51010
712-885-2802
Wayne B Roush, Ag Specialist

5357 **Wetland Biogeochemistry Institute**
University of Florida
106 Newell Hall, Box 110510
Gainesville, FL 32611
352-392-1803
Fax: 225-388-6423
William H Patrick Jr, Director
K. Ramesh Reddy

5358 **Wilderness Institute: University of Montana**
School of Forestry
32 Campus Drive
Missola, MT 59812
406-243-5361
800-462-8636
Fax: 406-243-4845
wi@cfc.umt.edu
www.cfc.umt.edu

Mission is to further understand wilderness and its stewardship through education, outreach, and scholarship. Activity is guided by the philosophy that wildlands are increasingly significant, ecologically and socially, and educateddialogue about the role of wild places in our nation's future should be promoted. Engaged in undergraduate education, graduate student research, the dissemination of wilderness information and the promotion of scholarship on wilderness issues.

Wayne Freimund, Director
Michael Patterson, Associate Dean

5359 **Wilderness Research Center**
University of Idaho
College of Natural Resources
Room 18a
Moscow, ID 83844-1139
208-885-7911
Fax: 208-885-6226
wrc@uidaho.edu

The mission of the WRC is to study the human dimensions of wilderness ecosystems. The WRC conducts research and teaches courses on the use of wilderness for personal growth, therapy, education, and leadership development.

Steve Hollenhorst, Ph.D, Director
Lilly Steinhorst, Administrative Assistant

5360 **Wisconsin Applied Water Pollution Research Consortium: University of Wisconsin-Madison**
University of Wisconsin

3232 Engineering Hall — 608-263-7773
1415 Engineering Drive — *Fax:* 608-262-5199
Madison, WI 53706-1691 — harringt@engr.wisc.edu
www.engr.wisc.edu

This consortium seeks effective and economical solutions to water supply problems and pollution control in Wisconsin. It conducts innovative practical research that cannot be carried out effectively by individual organizations.

Ian M. Robertson, Dean
James P. Blanchard, Executive Associate Dean

5361 Wisconsin Rural Development Center

USDA Rural Development-WI
P.O. Box 66889 — 715-345-7600
St. Louis, MO 63166 — 800-414-1226
Fax: 314-457-4431
RD.Webmaster@wi.usda.gov
www.rd.usda.gov/wi

Lisa Mensah, Under Secretary
Edna Primrose, Deputy Administrator

5362 Wisconsin Sea Grant Institute

University of Wisconsin
1975 Williw Drive — 608-262-0905
Floor 2 — *Fax:* 608-262-0591
Madison, WI 53706-1103 — hurley@aqua.wisc.edu
www.seagrant.wisc.edu

The University of Wisconsin Sea Grant Institute is a statewide program of basic and applied research, education, and technology transfer dedicated to the wise stewardship and sustainable use of Great Lakes and ocean resources. It ispart of a national network of 30 university-based programs.

James Hurley, Director
Terri Liebmann, Assistant Director/Accountin

5363 Yale Institute for Biospheric Studies (YIBS)

21 Sachem Street — 203-432-9856
PO Box 208105 — *Fax:* 203-432-9927
New Haven, CT 00652-8105 — roserita.riccitelli@yale.edu
www.yale.edu/yibs

Oswald J. Schmitz, Director
Toya Sealy Cotto, Sr. Administrative Assistant

Educational Resources & Programs

Universities

5364 Academy for Educational Development
Center for Environmental Strategies
1825 Connecticut Avenue NW 202-884-8000
Washington, DC 20009 *Fax:* 202-884-8400
web@aed.org
www.fhi360.org

Develops sustainable solutions to global environmental protection and natural resource management problems through individual and institutional behavior change, education, training and communication strategies. Efforts are driven by astrong commitment to improve or maintain environmental quality as well as the quality of life for diverse communities and groups through the provision of technical assistance, guided practice and capacity building support.
Patrick C. Fine, Chief Executive Officer
Robert S. Murphy, MBA, Chief Financial Officer

5365 Allegheny College
Environmental Science/Studies
520 North Main Street 814-332-3100
Meadville, PA 16335 info@allegheny.edu
www.allegheny.edu

Offers the study of interrelationships between human activities and the environment. Two major programs: 1) Environmental Science. Core courses include biology, chemistry, geology, and mathematics. Upper level courses synthesize,integrate and apply basic sciences toward solving real environmental problems; 2) Environmental Studies. Objective is to study the concept of sustainability in an integrated way.
Barbara D. Riess, Chairperson
Richard J Cook, President

5366 Antioch College
Glen Helen Outoor Education Center
1075 State Route 343 937-319-6082
1 Morgan Place *Fax:* 937-767-6655
Yellow Springs, OH 45387

Training in residential naturalist instruction for upper elementary aged students. Classes and field experience in outdoor education methods and natural history. Care for hawk or owl in Raptor Center.
Mark Roosevelt, President
Hassan Rahmanian, VP

5367 Antioch University/New England
Environmental Studies
40 Avon Street 800-553-8920
Keene, NH 00343-3516 *Fax:* 603-357-0718
admissions@antiochne.edu
www.antiochne.edu

For those committed to scholarly excellence and wish to design, implement and evaluate research regarding crucial environmental issues. The PhD program cultivates a dynamic learning community of environmental practioners who addresscomplex regional, national, and global issues responsibly, creatively, and compassionately.
Charlton MacVeagh, Chair
Stephen B. Jones, President

5368 Antioch University/Seattle
Center for Creative Change
2326 Sixth Avenue 206-441-5352
Seattle, WA 98121 www.antiochseattle.edu

Approches environmental concerns by emphasizing social science perspectives and natural science literacy. The program is part of the Center for Creative Change, an integrated professional studies center.
Dan Hocoy, President
Tsegereda Giorgis, Director of Finance

5369 Arkansas Tech University
Wildlife Conservation Program
1605 Coliseum Drive 479-968-0389
Suite 141 800-582-6953
Russellville, AR 72801 sdonnell@atu.edu
www.atu.edu

A two-year preparatory program in Wildlife Conservation with an outlined Wildlife Curriculum was developed at Arkansas Tech University in 1956. Two years later, plans were made to elevate this program to a four-year program. During the1959-1960 academic year, a full slate of courses was developed that provided the foudation for degree that specialized in fisheries and wildlife management.
Shauna Donnell, Vice President
Robin E. Bowen, President

5370 Auburn University
Environmental Institute
1090 South Donahue Drive 334-844-4132
Auburn, AL 36849 *Fax:* 334-844-4462
kochafr@auburn.edu
www.auburn.edu

Serves faculty, governments, and the general public in a coordinating role to bring together teams to develop acceptable and economically feasible means of enhancing the environmental quality of the state and nation.
Samuel Fowler, Director
M. Kay Stone, Program Administrator

5371 Ball State University
Natural Resources and Environmental Management
2000 West University 765-289-1241
Muncie, IN 47306 800-382-8540
Fax: 765-285-2606
nrem@bsu.edu
www.bsu.edu/nrem

The Natural Resources and Environmental Management Department enhances scientific competence and prepares students for a variety of environmental careers. Programs focus on air, energy, land, parks, recreation, soil, waste management,and water and emergency management.

Rick Hall, Chairperson
Paul W. Ferguson, President

5372 Bard College
Environmental and Urban Studies
PO Box 5000 845-758-6822
Annandale-on-Hudson, NY 12504-5000 admission@bard.edu
www.bard.edu

This program focuses on both the lived and built environments. Its goal is to involve students in empirically-based studies that bridge the divisions between natural and artificial, given and created. This approach is designed to buildon the transformations within a range of social and natual sciences, ranging from systems theory to enviornmental toxicology.
Sanjib Baruah, Director
Felicia Keesing, Professor

5373 Bemidji State University
Center for Environmental, Earth & Space Studies
1500 Birchmont Drive NE 218-755-2001
Bemidji, MN 56601-2699 800-475-2001
Fax: 218-755-4048
fchang@bemidjistate.edu
www.bemidjistate.edu/

The Center for Environmental, Earth and Space Studies (CEESS) offer a unique variety of interdisciplinary degree programs. Degrees in Environmental Studies include both B.S. and M.S., and a B.S. or B.A. with geology minor is alsoavailable. Students in the CEESS program are concerned with both the technological problems and social apects of enviromental issues.

Dr. Richard Hanson, President
Karen Snorek, VP Finance

5374 Bradley University
Geological Sciences Program
1501 West Bradley Avenue 309-676-1000
Peoria, IL 61625 800-447-6460
www.bradley.edu/admissions

Aims to develop an awareness of the Earth as a dynamic and unified system in time and space. Curriculum is preparatory for careers in geology, engineering geology, geophysics, hydrogeology, oceanography or secondary Earth scienceteaching.
Dr. Stan Liberty, Interim President
Dr. Joan Sattler, Interim Provost

5375 Brooklyn College
Environmental Studies
PO Box 8102 718-951-4159
Pittsburgh, PA 15217 *Fax:* 718-951-4546
yklein@brooklyn.cuny.edu
www.envirolink.org
Program is aimed at educating students to be fluent in social and physical sciences as related to the environment. In addition, the program draws from other courses in humanities, social sciences, mathematics, and sciences. Thisinterdisciplanary approach is designed to introduce the field of environmental studies and to apply this knowledge to various careers.
Yehuda Klein, Deputy Director

5376 Brown University
Center for Environmental Studies
135 Angel Street 401-863-1000
Box 1943 *Fax:* 401-863-3503
Providence, RI 00291 janet_blume@brown.edu
www.brown.edu
The Center for Environmental Studies at Brown University was established with the primary aim of educating individuals to solve challenging environmental problems both at the local and global levels. It also works directly to improvehuman well-being and environmental quality through community, city, and state partnerships in service and research.
Crystal Caesar, Financial Coordinator
Mariella DaSilva, Administrative Assistant

5377 California Polytechnic State University
Institute for City & Regional Planning
California Polytechnic State Univer 805-756-1111
San Luis Obispo, CA 93407-283 *Fax:* 805-756-1340
www.planning.calpoly.edu
Developed to coordinate interdisciplinary projects and research relating to the management of watersheds, urban areas, marine environments and related natural and human resources. The Institute offers specialists in various areas suchas biological science, business administation, city and regional planning, civil and environmental engineering, economics, geology, landscape architecture, natural resources management, political science and soil science.
Hemalata C. Dandekar, Department Head
Kathy Lehmkuhl, Administrative Support Coord

5378 California State University/Fullerton
Environmental Studies
PO Box 34080 714-278-2011
Fullerton, CA 92834-9480 arwebmaster@fullerton.edu
www.fullerton.edu
The Environmental Studies program is an interdisciplinary program that broadens environmental knowledge and awareness. It's designed to prepare students as professionals in the environmental field by providing an opportunity to learnapplicable skills and to develop an appropriate body of knowledge.
Mildred Garcia, President
Danny C. Kim, VP Finance/CFO

5379 California State University/Seaside
Capstone Project Program
100 Campus Center 831-582-3689
Building 42 laura_lienk@csumb.edu
Seaside, CA 93955-8001
Capstone Projects encompass a broad array of student interests, primarily within the programs of Earth Systems Science and Policy. A Capstone Project is similar to a senior thesis project at other universities, and showcases mastery ofESSP skills. They follow a set of outcome based, interdisciplinary criteria used to measure the competence of participants.
Laura Lee Lienk, Co-Director
Doug Smith, Co-Director

5380 California University of Pennsylvania
Biological & Environmental Sciences
250 University Avenue 724-938-4000
California, PA 15419 www.calu.edu
Department includes intensive scientific curricula that prepare students for graduate work in the biological and environmental sciences and career work in related areas.
Guido M. Pichini, Chairman
Geraldine M. Jones, Interim President

5381 Carnegie Mellon University
Civil and Environmental Engineering Program
5000 Forbes Avenue 412-268-2940
119 Porter Hall *Fax:* 412-268-7813
Pittsburgh, PA 15213 www.ce.cmu.edu
A major function of the Environmental Institute is to enable Carnegie Mellon to play a leadership role in developing educational programs on environmental issues. These include initiatives at both undergraduate and graduate levels.
Irving Oppenheim, Interim Department Head
Deborah Lange, Executive Director

5382 Clark University
Environmental Science & Policy
950 Main Street 508-793-7711
Worcester, MA 00161 idce@clarku.edu
www.clarku.edu/
An interdisciplinary approach that emphasizes policy questions involving the environment and use and misuse of science and technology. Its goal is to enable individuals to deal with technical and environmental issues in social andpolitical areas. Topics addresses deal with urgent and important issues, including assessment and management of environmental risks to humans and ecosystems, capacity for sustainable development in third world countriie, and integrated watershedmanagement.
David P. Angel, President
Davis Baird, Provost/VP for Academic Affa

5383 Clemson University
Environmental Engineering and Earth Sciences
Clemson University 864-656-3311
Clemson, SC 29634 www.clemson.edu
Programs in the environmental field focus on environmental process engineering, hydrogeology, environmental health physics and radiochemistry, environmental chemistry and sustainable systems.
Esin Gulari, Dean

5384 Colby-Sawyer College
Community & Environmental Studies
541 Main Street 603-526-3000
New London, NH 00325 www.colby-sawyer.edu
Bachelor of Science degree in Community and Environmental Studies. A minor in CES is also available.
Thomas C. Csatari, Chair
Thomas C. Galligan, President

5385 College of Natural Resources
Conservation Management Institute
1900 Kraft Drive 540-231-7348
Suite 250 *Fax:* 540-231-7019
Blacksburg, VA 24061 CMIinfo@vt.edu
www.cmi.vt.edu
Offers multi-disciplinary research that addresses conservation management effectiveness throughout the world. Faculty from far reaching research institutions work collaboratively on projects ranging from endangered species propagationto natural resource-based satellite imagery interpretation.
Scott D Klopfer, Director
Caitlin Carey, Research Fishery? Biologist

5386 College of William and Mary
Center for Conservation Biology
PO Box 1346 804-684-7000
1375 Greate Road *Fax:* 804-684-7097
Gloucester Point, VA 23062-1346 wmaster@vims.edu
www.vims.edu/

The Center for Conservation Biology is an organization dedicated to discovering innovative solutions to environmental problems that are both scientifically sound and practical within today's social context. It has been a leader inconservation issues throughout the mid-Atlantic region with a philosophy that uses a general systems approach to locate critical information needs and to plot a deliberate course of action to reach goals.

John T. Wells, Dean And Director
Jennifer Latour, CFO/CAO

5387 **Colorado Mountain College**
Natural Resource Management Program
802 Grand Avenue 970-945-8691
Glenwood Springs, CO 81601 800-621-8559
Fax: 970-947-8324
servicedesk@coloradomtn.edu
www.coloradomtn.edu

The Natural Resource Management program grew out of the Environmental Technology, which was one of the most well established programs of its kind in the country. It specializes in helping students graduate with entry-level skills in avariety of environmental fields, while combining aquatic and terrestrial resource management. Students are trained in career fields of environmental site assessment, hydrology, soil science, environmental law and others.

Ken Brenner, Treasurer
Glenn Davis, President

5388 **Colorado School of Mines**
Environmental Engineering & Applied Science
1500 Illinois Street 303-273-3000
Golden, CO 80401 800-446-9488
www.mines.edu

This public research university devoted to engineering and applied science, offers a curriculum and research program that is geared toward responsible stewardship of the earth and its resources. It has broad expertise in resourceexploration, extration, production and utilization. The programs at Mines are central to balancing resource availability with environmental protection.
James Spaanstra, Chairman
Richard Truly, Vice Chairman

5389 **Colorado State University**
College of Natural Resouses
101 Natural Resources Building 970-491-6675
Campus Delivery 1401 *Fax:* 970-491-0279
Fort Collins, CO 80523-1401 www.warnercnr.colostate.edu

The College of Natural Resources is one of the most comprehensive environment and natural resources programs in the nation. With four departments and eight undergraduate majors, 9 minors and 13 concentrations, students address the mostcurrent issues in environment and natural resources, including endangered species, water quality, biological diversity, parks forests and wildlife management, recreation and environmental and ecosystem sciences.
Joyce Berry, Dean
Scott Webb, Director of Development

5390 **Columbia University**
Public Admin in Environmental Science & Policy
116th and Broadway 212-854-1754
New York, NY 10027 www.columbia.edu

The program is designed to train sophisticated public managers and policymakers who apply innovative, system-based thinking to environmental issues. It emphasizes practical skills and is enriched by ecological and plantatary science.
Lee C. Bollinger, President
John H. Coatsworth, Provost

5391 **Connecticut College**
Goodwin Niering Center for Conservation Biology
270 Mohegan Avenue 860-447-1911
Box 5293 *Fax:* 860-439-5277
New London, CT 06320 info@conncoll.edu
www.conncoll.edu

A comprehensive, interdisciplinary program aimed at understanding contemporary ecological challenges. Its Certificate Program offers students the opportunity to blend thier interest in the environment with a non-science major and is ofparticular interest to those planning careers in environmental policy, law, economies or education.
Ulysses B. Hammond, VP for Administration
Glenn Dreyer, Executive Director

5392 **Conservation Leadership School**
117 Forest Resources Building 814-865-7541
University Park, PA 16802 877-778-2937
Fax: 814-865-3725
www.ecosystems.psu.edu

A one-week residential program for high school students to learn about the world around them through exploration and hands-on activities. The classroom includes over 700 acres of forest, fields, wetlands, and streams, and learningabout the environment includes having fun, meeting new friends and learning leadership skills.
Michael G. Messina, Head/Professor
Linda Spangler, Manager

5393 **Cornell University**
Center for the Environment
Day Hall Lobby 607-254-4636
Cornell University *Fax:* 607-254-6225
Ithaca, NY 14853 info@cornell.edu
www.cornell.edu

Offers opportunities for graduate study in the ecology, management, and policy of fishery, forest, wetland, wildlife, and other environmental resources. There also are opportunities to focus on conservation biology, agroforestry,environmetnal change, and conservation and sustainable development.
Elizabeth Garrett, President
Michael I. Kotlikoff, Provost

5394 **Dartmouth College**
Department of Earth Sciences
Dartmouth College 603-646-1110
Hanover, NH 00375 cantact@dartmouth.edu
www.dartmouth.edu/

Offers opportunities for learning and research in all major disciplines devoted to the study of the earth, including its structure and development, the oceans and atmosphere, weather and climate. Teaching and research at a moreadvanced level emphasize watershed processes, environmental biogeochemistry, geophysics and mechanics, sedimentology, paleontology, economic geology, end remote sensing of the earth from aircraft and satellites.
Philip J. Hanlon '77, President
Martin N. Wybourne, Interim Provost/Vice Provost

5395 **Delaware Valley College**
Agronomy & Environmental Science
700 East Butler Avenue 215-345-1500
Doylestown, PA 18901 800-233-5825
webmaster@delval.edu
www.delval.edu

The Department of Agronomy and Environmental Science offers courses designed to give a broad, workable background in the plant, soil, turf or environmental sciences. Focusing on the environmental issues facing society today, thesecourses provide the knowledge and training necessary to be successful in the field or to move on to the graduate level.
Dorothy Prisco, Vice President

5396 **Drake University**
Environmental Science & Policy Program
2507 University Avenue 515-271-2011
Olin Hall 800-443-7253
Des Moines, IA 50311-4505 *Fax:* 515-271-3702
thomas.rosburg@drake.edu
www.drake.edu

Environmental Science and Policy Program is an interdisciplinary program that awards BS and BA degrees in both Environmental Science and Environmental Policy.

Joe Lenz, Interim Provost
Deneese Jones, Immediate Past Provost

5397 Duke University/Marine Laboratory
Nicholas School of the Environment
Marine Laboratory 252-504-7502
135 Duke Marine Lab Road *Fax:* 252-504-7648
Beaufort, NC 28516-9721 webmanager@nicholas.duke.edu
www.nicholas.duke.edu/marinelab

The Laboratory is a campus of Duke University and a unit within the Nicholas School of the Environment. The mission is education, research, and service to understand marine systems, including the human component, and to developapproaches for marine conservation and restoration.

Belinda Williford, Administrator
Cindy Van Dover, Director

5398 Duquesne University
Environmental Science & Management Program
600 Forbes Avenue 412-396-6000
Pittsburgh, PA 15282 www.duq.edu

Educating environmental professionals for the twenty-first century is the focus of this program, which grew out of the need to combine depth of knowledge in environmental science with a comprehensive understanding of the business,legal and policy implications surrounding environmental issues.

Charles J. Dougherty, President
Madelyn A. Reilly, J.D., VP for Legal Affairs & Gener

5399 Eastern Illinois University
Aquatic and Fisheries Program
600 Lincoln Avenue 217-581-5000
Charleston, IL 61920 877-581-2348
admissions@eiu.edu
www.eiu.edu

Offers aquatic ecology, fisheries biology, and physiological ecology. Specific areas of concentration include community analysis of stream fishes, life history and demographics of fish, bioenergetics of development and life historyphenomena, and lipid storage and utilization patterns of fish.

William L. Perry, President
Blair M. Lord, Provost

5400 Eastern Michigan University
Kresge Environmental Education Center
202 Welch Hall 734-487-1849
Ypsilanti, MI 48197 800-468-6368
Fax: 734-487-6559
tkasper@emich.edu
www.emich.edu

The Kresge Environmental Education Center is located in Mayfield, about six miles north east of the city of Lapeer. The main buildings are located on Fish Lake Road in the middle of the center's 240 acres. These 240 acres sit next to7,000 acres of state land.

Mike Morris, Chair
Mary Treder, Vice Chair

5401 Eastern Nazarene College
Eastern Environmental Program
23 East Elm Avenue 617-745-3000
Quincy, MA 00217 800-88E-NC88
Fax: 617-745-3907
jonathan.e.twining@enc.edu
www.enc.edu

Cross-disciplinary program which provides for students strong pereparation in the several scientific disciplines involved in the study of environmental issues. The program is jointly sponsored by the Department of Biology andChemistry in order to provide the appropriate basis in all the sciences for students wishing to pursue environmental careers or graduate school.

Elizabeth Buckley, Chair
Dr. Corlis McGee, President

5402 Fairleigh Dickinson University
Environmental Studies/System Science
1000 River Road 973-443-8500
Teaneck, NJ 00766 800-338-8803
Fax: 973-443-8921
www.fdu.edu

This program offers students a wide variety of 18 concentrations, including environmental chemistry, environmental risk assessment, water treatment, environmental planning, groundwater hydrology, environmental remediation, soil science,land-use planning and air pollution.

Patrick J. Zenner, Chair
Sheldon Drucker, President

5403 Ferrum College
Environmental Science
PO Box 1000 540-365-2121
Ferrum, VA 24088 800-868-9797
Fax: 540-365-4203
webmaster@ferrum.edu
www.ferrum.edu

Offers programs in environmental science that includes informationon air pollutant deposition in the Great Lakes and the formulation of membrances for ion-selective electrodes. The program also includes participation in a water qualitymonitoring project on Smith Mountain Lake that uses a geographical information system to model soil loss in its watershed.

Samuel L. Lionberger, Chair
Jennifer L. Braaten, President

5404 Field Station & Ecological Reserves
University of Kansas
C/O Kansas Biological Survey 785-864-1500
2101 Constant Avenue *Fax:* 785-864-1534
Lawrence, KS 66047 biosurvey.ku.edu

The KSR is dedicated to field-based environmental reseach and education. KSR is located within the transition zone (ecotone) between the eastern deciduous forest and tallgrass prairie biomes. The 3,000 acres of diverse native andmanaged habitats, experimental systems, support facilities, and longterm databases are used to undertake an outstanding array of scholarly activities. Environmental stewardship is a stong emphasis as high-quality natural areas are preserved for thefuture.

LeeAnn Bennett, Senior Research
Kirsten Bosnak, Communications Director

5405 Florida State University
Environmental Studies
600 W. College Avenue 850-644-2525
Tallahassee, FL 32306 *Fax:* 850-644-9936
admissions@admin.fsu.edu
www.fsu.edu

Offers the study of environmental issues as they relate to geological phenomena, which include volcanic and earthquake hazards, resource and land- use planning, air and water pollution, waste disposal, glaciation and sea-level change,landslides, flooding, shoreline erosion, and global change issues.

Eric J. Barron, President
Dr. Garnett S. Stokes, Provost

5406 George Washington University
International Environmental Policy & Management
2121 1st Street NW 202-994-1000
Washington, DC 20052 www.gwu.edu/

Offers a program on International Environmental Policy and Management and Marketing Management, held in various locations around the world

Steven Knapp, President
Steven R. Lerman, Provost

5407 Georgetown University - Environmental Studies
Environmental Studies
37th O Streets NW 202-687-0100
Washington, DC 20057 webmaster@georgetown.edu
www.georgetown.edu

Environmental Studies is an interdisciplinary program designed to allow an undergraduate of the college majoring in any discipline to learn about environmental issues. Environmental Studies provides a framework for the study offundamental mechanisms of ecosystems and human interaction with the Earth, encompassing the humanities, social sciences and natural sciences as they relate to environmental questions.

John J DeGioia, Ph.D, President
Christopher Augostini, Sr. VP & COO

5408 **Hocking College**
Environmental Restoration Technology Program
3301 Hocking Parkway 740-753-3591
Nelsonville, OH 45764 877-462-5464
Fax: 740-753-7065
admissions@hocking.edu
www.hocking.edu

Growing concern for the environment has increased the need for technicians qualified in the restoration of environmentally unstable land, water, and air. Hocking College's Environmental Restoration technology prepares students for thatchallenge.
Tammy Andrews

5409 **Idaho State University**
Geochemistry & Hydrogeology Program
921 South Eighth Avenue 208-282-0211
Pocatello, ID 83209 webmaster@isu.edu
www.isu.edu/

Emphasizes environmental geochemistry and hydrogeology. This specialty is ideal in southern Idaho where problems of nuclear and toxic waste clean-up at the Idaho National Environmental Engineering Laboratory will require study andgenerate research monies for years to come.
Robert A. Wharton, Provost And Vice President

5410 **Indiana State University**
Department of Ecology & Organismal Biology
200 North Seventh Street 812-237-4000
Terre Haute, IN 47809-1902 800-468-6478
Fax: 812-237-8525
www.indstate.edu/

This department conducts research in the areas of ecology, evolution, and conservation. The M.S. and Ph.D degrees garnered in state-of-the-art laboratories and local field stations enable students to conduct innovative research andplay significant roles as well-trained evnironmentists.
Dr. Daniel J. Bradley, President
David Campbell, Secretary

5411 **International Erosion Control Association (IECA)**
3033 S Parker Road 303-640-7554
Suite 410 800-220-3153
Aurora, CO 80014 *Fax:* 866-308-3087
info@ieca.org
www.ieca.org

An organization dedicated to minimizing accelerated soil erosion. IECA offers an annual conference, chapter events, training courses as well as a variety of topic-specific publications and a quarterly newsletter.

Samantha Roe, Executive Director
Joanna Fetherolf, Director, Education

5412 **Iowa State University**
Environmental Studies Program
100 Enrollment Services Center 515-294-5836
Ames, IA 50011-2011 800-262-3810
Fax: 515-294-2592
contact@iastate.edu
www.iastate.edu

The Environmental Studies Program deals with the relationship between humans and nature, or between humans and natural systems. The curriculum is designed to give students an understanding of regional and global environmental issuesand an appreciation of different perspectives regarding these issues. Courses are provided for both students pursuing careers related to the environment and those with an interest in environmental issues.

5413 **Johns Hopkins University**
Department of Geography/Environmental Engineering
Wyman Park Building, 4th Floor 410-516-4050
3400 N Charles Street www.jhu.edu/
Baltimore, MD 21218

Concerned with understanding the nature and dynamics of ecosystems, engineered systems, and societies. Offers a broad range of graduate programs including the natural, social and engineering sciences.
Ronald J. Daniels, President
Jonathan A. Bagger, Interim Provost/Sr. VP for A

5414 **Kansas State University**
Department of Agricultural Economics
342 Waters Hall 785-532-6011
Manhattan, KS 66506 *Fax:* 785-532-6897
k-state@k-state.edu
www.k-state.edu

The Department of Agricultural Economics has a rich tradition of services to agriculture and related fields. The department has a history of succes in its land-grant mission, teaching, research, and extension outreach, maintaininglarge and diverse programs in undergraduate and graduate instruction, as well as research and extension outreach.
Kirk H Schulz, President
Dana Hastings, Administrative Assistant

5415 **Keene State College**
Environmental Studies
229 Main Street 800-572-1909
Keene, NH 00343 www.keene.edu

Environmental Studies is an interdisciplinary program comprised of courses in Biology, Chemistry, Economics, Geography, Geology, and Political Science. Two concentration options are Environmental Policy and Enviromental Science, bothof which will prepare students for a wide range of environment-related career opportunities.
Anne E. Huot, President
Barbara A. Hall, Administrative Assistant

5416 **Lake Erie College**
Environmental Management Program
391 West Washington Street 440-296-1856
Painesville, OH 44077 800-533-4996
Fax: 440-375-7005
webmaster@lec.edu

Interdisciplinary major, grounded in the sciences and liberal arts,designed for those who want to pursue career paths utilizing environmental science in decision making. Courses include environmental management, biology, chemistry,mathamatics and business. Program is designed to help students build a solid knolwledge base in regional and global environmental issues.
Elizabeth Abraham, Owner/CEO
Richard J. Kessler, Treasurer

5417 **Louisiana State University**
Environmental Sciences Program
1271 Energy, Coast and Environment 225-578-9421
Building *Fax:* 225-578-4286
Baton Rouge, LA 70803 cstrom4@lsu.edu
www.environmental.lsu.edu

Environmental Sciences program is designed to provide a broad-based graduate education to prepare students for careers in industrial, government, and academia. The program builds on a strong undergraduate background in the sciences.
Larry Rouse, Chair/Assoc. Professor
Edward Laws, Interim Chair

5418 **Louisiana Tech University**
Wildlife Conservation Program
305 Wisteria Street 318-257-4287
PO Box 10197 ANSmail@ans.latech.edu
Ruston, LA 71272 www.ans.latech.edu/

The Wildlife Conservation degree program meets the certification requirements of the Wildlife Society, and graduates may apply for certification as an Associate Wildlife Biologist.
Sally Strickland, Administrative Coordinator
Betty T. Jensen, Administrative Assistant

5419 **Miami University**
Institute of Environmental Sciences
501 E. High St. 513-529-2531
Oxford, OH 45056-3434 admission@muohio.edu
miamioh.edu

Offers a masters degree in Environmental Science. This interdisciplinary program stresses problem solving and community service, and provides practical experience in many potential areas of concentration, preparing students for avariety of practical careers in public and private sector jobs.

David C. Hodge, President
Phyllis Callahan, Provost

5420 Michigan Technological University
Applied Technology & Environmental Science
1400 Townsend Drive 906-487-1885
Houghton, MI 49931-1295 800-966-3764
Fax: 906-487-2915
forest@mtu.edu
www.mtu.edu

A degree in Applied Ecology and Environmental Sciences prepares students to address complex environmental problems posed by the use of natural resources. Students learn how to protect the integrity of ecosystems and help assure thatnatural resources will be managed wisely for generations of sustainable use.
Glenn Mroz, President
Max Seel, Professor, Physics

5421 Middlebury College
Environmental Studies
121a South Main Street 802-443-5000
Middlebury, VT 00575 *Fax:* 802-443-2060
admissions@middlebury.edu
www.middlebury.edu

Explores the relationship between humans and their environment. Students pursuing the ES major work in a variety of disciplines, including biology, chemistry, economics, geography, geology, literature, the performing arts, philosophy,political science, religion and sociology.
Gregory B. Buckles, Dean of Admissions
Susan Campbell, Provost

5422 Montana State University
Montana Environmental Training Center
2100 16th Avenue South 406-265-3730
Great Falls, MT 59405 800-662-6132
webmaster@msun.edu
www.msun.edu/

A cooperative effort between Montana State University/Northern and the Montana Department of Environmental Quality. Offers basic, advance training, and continuing education in the areas of water and wastewater operation, maintenance,safety, process control, cross connection and backflow prevention along with courses in basic water science and watershed awareness. A newsletter and Training Announcement are published quarterly.
Greg Kegel, Chancellor
Marianne Hamilton, Administrative Assistant

5423 Natural Resources and Environmental Science - Purdue University
Purdue University, College of Agriculture
Lilly Hall of Life Sciences 765-496-9024
915 West State Street 888-398-4636
West Lafayette, IN 47907-2054 *Fax:* 765-494-5876
nres@purdue.edu
www.ag.purdue.edu

An interdisciplinary program at the Purdue School of Agriculture designed to prepare students to work with environmental problems which impact our basic natural resources: specifically land, air and water. NRES is a flexible programthat allows students, working closely with an academic advisor, to develop their personal curriculum to meet individual career goals.

Linda Prokopy, Ph.D, Co-Director
Tami J Borror, Academic Advisor

5424 New Mexico State University
Department of Geological Sciences
Box 30001 575-646-2708
MSC 3AB *Fax:* 575-646-1056
Las Cruces, NM 88003 geology@nmsu.edu
www.nmsu.edu

Offers both undergraduate and graduate study leading to advanced degrees in geological science. Advanced training qualifies students for employment in such branches of geological science as mining, petroleum, environmental andengineering geology, government service or for further graduate study. The education experience may include sedimentology, geochemistry, volcanology, stratigraphy, geotectonics and paleontology.
Lee Hubbard, Administrative Department
Dr. Nancy S. McMillan, Department Head

5425 North Dakota State University
Department of Biological Sciences
PO Box 6050 701-231-8011
Fargo, ND 58108-6050 *Fax:* 701-231-7149
Department offers undergraduate and graduate degrees in biological disciplines, including environmental and conservation sciences.

Dean Bresciani, President
Barb Pederson, Executive Assistant

5426 Northeastern Illinois University
International Center for Tropical Ecology
5500 N St. Louis 773-583-4050
Chicago, IL 60625-4699 *Fax:* 773-442-4900
admrec@neiu.edu
www.neiu.edu

The International Center for Tropical Ecology provides a focal point for interdisciplinary research and graduate education in all aspects of the conservation of tropical ecosystems. The Center, formed in collaboration with the MissouriBotanical Garden, supports a network in the United States of students, scientists, and conservationists from tropical countries to study issues related to biodiversity conservation.

Sharon Hahs, President
Richard J. helldobler, Provost/VP for Academic Affa

5427 Northern Arizona University
Environmental Sciences
South San Francisco Street 928-523-9011
Flagstaff, AZ 86011 *Fax:* 928-523-6023
www.nau.edu/

Designed to offer students a technically rigorous foundation and broad exposure to the environmental science. The core courses in environmental sciences are interdisciplinary, and team taught by scientists with different backgroundsand specialties, providing multiple perspectives and rich learning experiences.
John D. Haeger, President
Tom Acker, Professor of Mechanical Engi

5428 Northern Michigan University
Environmental Studies
1401 Presque Isle Avenue 906-227-1000
Marquette, MI 49855-5301 *Fax:* 906-227-2249
www.nmu.edu

Research focuses on the Upper Peninsula environment, ethnic groups, economy, politics, folklore and literature.
L. Garnet Lewis, Chair
Richard M. Popp, Vice Chair

5429 Northland College
Environmental Studies
1411 Ellis Avenue S 715-682-1699
Ashland, WI 54806 800-753-1840
Fax: 715-682-1308
info@northland.edu
www.northland.edu

Offers a comprehensive range of environmental programs that integrate traditional study with a keen eye toward problem-solving and environmental impact.
Karen Halbersleben, President
Rick Fairbanks, Provost

5430 Ohio State University
School of Environment and Natural Resources

2021 Coffey Road 614-292-2265
210 Kottman Hall *Fax:* 614-292-7432
Columbus, OH 43210 geise.1@osu.edu
www.senr.osu.edu

Focuses on the science and management of natural resources and the environment. A variety of integrated undergraduate programs of study provide the foundation to a variety of career paths dealing with natural resources and theenvironment. Graduates are employed as environmental and ecosystem scientists; forest, wildlife and fisheries reserchers and biologists; environmental educators, communicators and naturalists; and park, forest, and wildlife managers.

Olivia Ameredes, Fiscal Manager
Laura Hughes, Office Associate

5431 Oregon State University

Environmental Sciences
Corvallis, OR 97331 541-737-1000
Fax: 541-737-3590
OSU.Provost@oregonstate.edu
www.oregonstate.edu

Offers programs that are central to the mission of the university, which includes wise use of natural resources. Recognized as a Land, Sea, and Space Grant institution, OSU has exceptional strength in many of the disciplines that arerequired to provide a high-quality interdisciplinary education for future environmental scientists.

Dr. Edward J. Ray, President
Sabah U. Randhawa, Provost

5432 Pennsylvania State University

Center for Statistical Ecology
323 Thomas Building 814-865-1348
University Park, PA 16802 *Fax:* 814-863-7114
www.stat.psu.edu

This ground-breaking program enjoys national and international recognition. With an ongoing program of research that integrates statistics, ecology and the environment, the emphasis is on the environment and collaborative research,training and exposition on improving the quantification and communication of human impact on the environment. Studies also include statistical investigations of the impact of the environment on man.

Bonnie Cain, Financial Secretary
Barbara Freed, Administrative Assistant

5433 Portland State University

Environmental Sciences & Resources Program
PO Box 751 503-725-3000
Portland, OR 97207 *Fax:* 503-725-4882
psuinfo@pdx.edu
www.pdx.edu

Environmental studies are central to the mission of Portland State University, which serves the state's major urban center. The Environmental Sciences and Resources program offers both undergraduate and graduate degrees.

Win Wiewel, President
John Reuter, Program Director

5434 Prescott College

Department of Environmental Studies
220 Grove Avenue 877-350-2100
Prescott, AZ 86301 *Fax:* 928-776-5242
admissions@prescott.edu
www.prescott.edu/

Prescott College is a private liberal arts collage offering a resident BA and limited residency BA, MA, and PhD. Small groups of students work actively on real-world projects with faculty who are leaders in the field of environmentalstudies. Offers dynamic and active laboratories for students and gives them the opportunity to be on the cutting edge of environmental and sustainabilty research.

Paul Burkhardt, President/Ececutive VP
Frank Cardamone, Provost

5435 Rensselaer Polytechnic Institute

Lally School of Management and Technology
110 8th Street 518-276-2812
Pittsburgh Building www.lallyschool.rpi.edu
Troy, NY 12180

Committed to integrating green business strategy throughout all management curriculum. An MBA with an Environmental Management and Policy Concentration is truly designed as an interdisciplinary degree, enabling graduates to work intraditional business settings with the knowledge and skill to help these businesses realize environmental, health and safety strategy.

Thomas Begley, Dean
Chaina Porter, Administrative Coordinator

5436 Rice University

Urban & Environmental Policy Program
6100 Main 713-348-7423
PO Box 1892 800-527-OWLS
Huston, TX 77251 www.rice.edu

This program is designed to introduce students to how environmental policies are developed and how science and engineering issues are included in effective policy.

David W. Leebron, President
David K. Vassar, Sr. Asst. to the President

5437 Roger Williams University

Center for Environmental Development
One Old Ferry Road 401-253-1040
Bristol, RI 00280 800-458-7144
Fax: 401-254-3310
www.rwu.edu/

Undergraduate program in marine biology combining chemistry, biology, physics, and mathmatics. Designed to keep and develop interest in the sciences by using field research and laboratory experimentation.

Rodney A. Butler, Chairman
Donald J. Farish, President

5438 SUNY/Cortland

Coalition for Education in the Outdoors
Park Center 607-753-4971
PO Box 2000 *Fax:* 607-753-5982
Cortland, NY 13045-900 outdoored@outdooredcoalition.org
www.outdooredcoalition.org

A nonprofit network of outdoor and environmental education centers, nature centers, conservation and recreation organizations, outdoor education and experimential education associations, public and private schools and fish and wildlifeagencies. All those involved in the coalition share the desire to support and encourage environmental and outdoor education and its goals.

Erik J. Bitterbaum, President
Mark Prus, Provost

5439 SUNY/Fredonia

Environmental Sciences
280 Central Avenue 716-673-3111
Fredonia, NY 14063 800-252-1212
Fax: 716-673-3249
admissions@fredonia.edu
www.fredonia.edu/

Rigorous, interdisciplinary program in environmental science with 68 semester hours of core courses in mathematics, biology, chemistry, environmental sciences, and geosciences. Students are prepared to pursue graduate studies,professional certifications, or employment in the private or public sector.

Ginny Horvath, President
Mrs. Denise Szalkowski, Assistant to the President

5440 SUNY/Plattsburgh

Environmental Science
101 Broad Street 518-564-2000
Plattsburgh, NY 12901

One of the largest and most established environmental science programs in the US, with 20 interdisciplinary faculty and nearly 300 majors among five degree programs. Opportunities for hands-on work and practical experience are providedby close proximity to the Adirondack Mountains State Forest Preserve, Plattsburgh's location on the banks of Lake Champlain, and affiliations with the Miner Agricultural Research Institute and more.

John Ettling, President
Dr. James Liszka, Provost

5441 SUNY/Syracuse
College of Environmental Science & Forestry
One Forestry Drive 315-470-6500
106 Bray Hall 800-777-7373
Syracuse, NY 13210 *Fax:* 315-470-6933
esfinfo@esf.edu
www.esf.edu

As part of its education mission, SUNY offers an accredited engineering undergraduate program in Forest Engineering and graduate programs at both the masters and doctoral levels. The Faculty also conducts research and public serviceprograms that study how a variety of events affect our environment.
Vita DeMarchi, Chair
Matthew J. Marko, Vice Chair

5442 School for Field Studies
Environmental Field Studies
100 Cummings Center 978-741-3567
Suite 534-G 800-989-4418
Beverly, MA 00191 *Fax:* 978-922-3835
sfs@fieldstudies.org
www.fieldstudies.org

Teaches students to address critical environmental problems using an interdisciplinary experimental approach to education.
Terry Andreas, Chairman
James A. Cramer, President

5443 Slippery Rock University
Environmental Geosciences
1 Morrow Way 724-738-2015
Slippery Rock, PA 16057 800-929-4778
Fax: 724-738-2913
asktherock@sru.edu
www.sru.edu/

Prepares students for ocupations with industrial laboratories concerned with air, water and soil pollution control, engineering firms that study industrial pollution and prepare environmental impact statements, and state and federalagencies charged with monitoring the environment.
James Hathaway, Chair
Michael May, Director of Admissions

5444 Sonoma State University
Environmental Studies & Planning Program
1801 E Cotati Avenue 707-664-2880
Rohnert Park, CA 94928-3609 *Fax:* 707-644-4060
www.sonoma.edu

Founded as an interdisciplinary program during a period of growing environmental concern. The department has evolved and matured, now stressing the development of a global prespective by synthesizing knowledge from a variety ofscientific and academic disciplines, the acquisition of specific professional skills through a focused course of study, and the application of knowledge and skills through effective strategies for environmental management.

Dr. Ruben Arminana, President
Lauren Furukawa-Schlereth, CFO and Vice President

5445 Southern Connecticut State University
Environmental Education Program
501 Crescent Avenue 203-392-7278
Jennings Hall, Room 342 888-500-SCSU
New Haven, CT 00651 *Fax:* 203-392-6614
information@southernct.edu
www.southernct.edu

This program focuses on practicality and application of theory bringing about environmental change through educational processes. The objective is to prepare well informed people who are dedicated to improving environmental conditions.
Cheryl J Norton, President
Susan Cusato, Chair Department of Science

5446 Southern Oregon University
Environmental Education Program
1250 Siskiyou Boulevard 541-552-6600
Siskiyou Environmental Center 855-470-3377
Ashland, OR 97520 *Fax:* 541-552-6614
presidentsoffice@sou.edu
www.sou.edu/

Designed to promote a better understanding of the environment and environmental issues, including an awarenesss and knowledge of biodiversity and ecosystem complexity. Seeks to prepare students for active roles in education and socialchange related to resolution of environmental problems and conflicts affecting present and future generations.
Mary Cullinan, President
James M. Klein, Provost/VP for Academic Affairs

5447 St. Lawrence University
Environmental Studies
23 Romoda Drive 315-229-5011
Canton, NY 13617 800-285-1856
icania@stlawu.edu
www.stlawu.edu

Programs offer ten options for combining environmental studies with traditional disciplines (eg. biology, economics) plus B.A. program in Environmental Studies.
Ms. Jacquelyn M Bouchard, President
Ms. Dayle B. Burgess, Assistant to the President

5448 Stanford University
Center for Environmental Studies
Building - MC 4205 650-736-8688
473 Via Ortega *Fax:* 650-725-3402
Stanford, CA 94305 environment@stanford.edu
woods.stanford.edu

Focuses on significant environmental problems and draws methods and analyses from multiple diciplines.
Luis Tam, Associate Director
Pam Sturner, ExecutiveDirector

5449 Sterling College
Center for Northern Studies
Sterling College Admissions 802-586-7711
PO Box 72 800-648-3591
Craftsbury Common, VT 00582 *Fax:* 802-586-2596
admissions@sterlingcollege.edu
www.sterlingcollege.edu

Center for Northern Studies is part of a small, undergraduate teaching and research institution located in Wolcott, Vermont. Its program is interdisciplinary in nature, integrating social and natural sciences, humanities and resourceissues in the Circumpolar North.

Matthew Allen Derr, President
Melissa Fisher '00, COO

5450 Tennessee Technological University
Bioenvironmental Sciences
1 William L Jones Dr 931-372-3101
Cookeville, TN 38505 800-255-8881
visit@tntech.edu
www.tntech.edu

Prepares graduates for high-level careers in various areas of biology and bioenvironmentl sciences.
Philip Oldham, President
Mark Stephens, Interim Provost/VP for Acade

5451 Texas A & M University
Center for Natural Resource Information Technology
113 Administration Building 979-845-1060
College Station, TX 77843 *Fax:* 409-845-6430
admissions@tamu.edu
www.tamu.edu

Serves as a point of contact for external organizations seeking cooperative efforts to assemble and disseminate information, create information technologies, and research critical natural resource concepts. The center strives tofacilitate technology transfer through training of end users and establishing necessary information infrastructures.
Michael K. Young, President
Dr. Karan L. Watson, Provost/Executive VP

5452 Texas Christian University
Environmental Science Program
PO Box 298830 817-257-7270
Fort Worth, TX 76129 *Fax:* 817-257-7789
m.slattery@tcu.edu
www.ensc.tcu.edu

A program helping students to understand the connection between science and the earth.
Michael C. Slattery, Director
John Breyer, Director

5453 Treasure Valley Community College
Biology Department
650 College Boulevard 541-881-8822
Ontario, OR 97914 888-987-8822
Fax: 541-881-2721
www.tvcc.cc

Offers several courses for those seeking careers in natural resource management including range management, wildland fire management, and forest management.
Dana M. Young, President
Randy Griffin, VP of Administrative Service

5454 Tulane University
Environmental Health & Sciences
6823 St. Charles Avenue 504-865-5000
New Orleans, LA 70118 800-873-9283
Fax: 504-862-8715
website@tulane.edu
www.tulane.edu

Environmental Health Sciences offers several graduate degree programs, including Public Health and Science. Graduates will be prepared to meet the needs of public health professionals such as environmental health and health officers,as well as undertake responsible positions in government, industrial facilities, research, or eduational institutions.
Scott S. Cowen, President
Yvette M. Jones, Executive VP

5455 UCLA - University of California/Los Angeles
Earth, Planetary, and Space Sciences
595 Charles Young Drive E 310-825-3880
PO Box 951567 *Fax:* 310-825-2779
Los Angeles, CA 90095 info@epss.ucla.edu
epss.ucla.edu

Offers programs in the study of soil mechanics and foundation engineering in light of geologic conditions, recognition, prediction, control or abatement of subsidence, landslides, earthquakes, and other geologic aspects of urbanplanning.
Vassilis Angelopoulos, Professor
Jonathan Aurnou, Professor

5456 University of Arizona
Soutywest Environmental Health Sciences Center
1501 Campbell Avenue 520-626-4555
PO Box 245018 *Fax:* 602-827-2074
Tucson, AZ 85721 admissions@arizona.edu
www.arizona.edu

This center serves as a platform to promote the study of health effects of environmental agents. The SWEHSC promotes interdisciplinary research collaborations driven by cutting-edge technologies. Research in the SWEHSC is focused onmechanisms of action of environmetnal agents in living systems.
Ann Weaver Hart, President
Keith A. Joiner, Vice Provost

5457 University of California/Berkeley
Environmental Management Program
1995 University Avenue 510-642-4111
Suite 110 extension-info@berkeley.edu
Berkeley, CA 94704-7000 extension.berkeley.edu/

The Environmental Management Program prepares students to take on significant leadership roles in the environmental community.
Diana Wu, Acting Dean
Scott Shireman, CFO

5458 University of California/Santa Barbara
Bren School of Environmental Studies
Bren Hall 805-893-2968
Room 4312 *Fax:* 805-893-8686
Santa Barbara, CA 93106-4160 esprogram@es.ucsb.edu
www.es.ucsb.edu

Program provides students with the scholarly background and intellectual skills necessary to understand complex environmental problems and formulate decisions that are environmentally sound. Academic process is interdisciplinary,drawing upon not only environmental science faculty, but also the resources of a variety of related departments and disciplines.

Dr. Carla D'Antonio, Chair
Cheryl Hutton, Financial Manager

5459 University of California/Santa Cruz
Environmental Studies
1156 Hight Street 831-459-2634
Santa Cruz, CA 95064 envs.ucsc.edu

Offers programs that prepare students to make significant contributions in the various fields of environmental study, whether pursing a career with private or non-profit institutions.
George Blumenthal, Chancellor
Alison Galloway, Provost/Executive Vice Chanc

5460 University of Colorado
Environmental Engineering Program
Regent Administrative Center 125 303-492-8908
552 UCB apply@colorado.edu
Boulder, CO 80309 www.colorado.edu

Environmental Engineering Progam in the Department of Civil, Environmental, and Architectural Engineering at the University of Colorado in Boulder welcomes students, alumni, and colleagues in environmental engineering with aninvitation to explore areas of environmental emphasis, B.S., M.S., and Ph.D programs, research, and facilities.
Philip P. DiStefano, Chancellor
Bob Sievers, Director

5461 University of Florida
College of Natural Resources & Environment
103 Black Hall 352-392-9230
PO Box 116455 *Fax:* 352-392-9748
Gainesville, FL 32611 kbray@ufl.edu
www.snre.ufl.edu

Science based, multidisciplinary and academically rigorous, the College of Natural Resources & Environment has students and a curriculum that includes 200 courses taught in 56 departments of other colleges. The 290 affiliate facultyhave their primary appointments in discipline-centered departments of other colleges.
Jack Payne, Chair
Joseph Glover, Provost/Sr. VP for Academic

5462 University of Florida/Gainesville
School of Forest Resources and Conservation
118 Newins-Ziegler Hall 352-392-3261
PO Box 110410 *Fax:* 352-392-1707
Gainesville, FL 32611 www.ufl.edu

Offers baccalaureate (BSFRC) and graduate (PhD, MS, MFRC, MFAS, incl. a joint JD with the College of Law and a co-major with Dept of Statistics) degree programs; conducts fundamental and applied research; and provides public servicethrough extension programs. Programs include forestry, geomatics, fisheries, and aquatic sciences, natural resource economics, management, and policy, as well as related programs in natural resource education, ecotourism, and agroforestry.
C. David Brown, II, Chair
Dr. W. Kent Fuchs, President

5463 University of Georgia
Savannah River Ecology Laboratory
P.O. Drawer E 803-725-2472
Aiken, SC 29802 *Fax:* 803-725-3309
srel.uga.edu

Our goal is to attract collaborating scientists from across the DOE complex and the nation for collaborative work at the interface of fundamental and applied environmental research. We strive to

improve the management of contaminatedstites. The staff and facilities of AACES are available to researchers in environmental science and engineering and to practitoneers from industry, government, academia and private foundations.
Olin E. Rhodes, Director
John Seaman, Assistant Director

5464 University of Hawaii/Manoa
Oceanography & Global Environmental Sciences
1000 Pope Road 808-956-9154
MSB 205 *Fax:* 808-956-9152
Honolulu, HI 96822 ocean@soest.hawaii.edu
www.soest.hawaii.edu

Bachelor of Science degree in Global Environmental Science offered through the Department of Oceanography, University of Hawaii at Manoa.

Brain Taylor, Dean
Chip Fletcher, Associate Dean

5465 University of Idaho
College of Natural Resources
875 Perimeter Drive 208-885-6111
Moscow, ID 83844 *Fax:* 208-885-5534
info@uidaho.edu
www.uidaho.edu

Consists of 5 departments which together form a comprehensive educational program on the study and management of natural resources. Each department has several degree options to provide students with a flexible curriculum for theirdegree. We educate resource professionals with truly integrated resource management skills using innovative instructional programs. Our education occurs in a residential setting and provides a balance between theoretical and pratical experiences.
Chuck Staben, President
Donald L. Burnett, Interim President

5466 University of Illinois/Springfield
Environmental Studies
One University Plaza 217-206-6600
MS UHB 1080 888-977-4847
Springfield, IL 62703 admissions@uis.edu
www.uis.edu/

Goal of the environmental studies program is to enhance society's ability to create an environmentally acceptable future. Program faculty with diverse backgrounds in social and natural sciences and humanities are committed todeveloping interdisciplinary approaches to environmental problem solving. The primary objective is to educate citizens and professionals who are aware of environmental issues and their origins, causes, effects, and resolutions.
Susan J. Koch, Chancellor
Patricia Sanchez, Executive Assistant

5467 University of Illinois/Urbana
Department of Natural Resources and Environment
1102 South Goodwin Avenue 217-333-2770
W-503 Turner Hall *Fax:* 217-244-3219
Urbana, IL 61801 nres@illinois.edu
nres.illinois.edu

Establishes and implements research and educational programs that enhance environmental stewardship in the management and use of natural, agricultural, and urban systems in a socially responsible manner.
Bruce Branham, Associate Prof/Interim Head
Jason Emmert, Assistant Dean

5468 University of Iowa
MacBride Raptor Project
309 S. Madison Street 319-335-9293
Iowa City, IA 52242 *Fax:* 319-335-6655
rec-services@uiowa.edu
www.recserv.uiowa.edu

Jointly sponsored by the University of Iowa and Kirkwood Community College, the project has two main facilities. Classes are held at the educational display facility and rehabilitation flight cage at the Macbride Nature RecreationalArea, and at the Raptor Clinic and educational display at KCC. The project is dedicated to the preservation of birds of prey and their habitats through rehabilitation of injured raptors, public education programs and raptor reseach.
Mark J. Braun, Interim VP for strategic Com
David Drake, Sr. Associate

5469 University of Maine
Environmental Studies
23 University Street 207-834-7500
Fort Kent, ME 00474 888-879-8635
Fax: 207-834-7466
umfkadm@maine.edu
www.umfk.maine.edu

Offers a broad knowledge of the natural and social sciences, with the ability to focus of an area of personal interest. Students learn to critically identify environmental problems, collect and interpret data, communicate complexenvironmental issues, and explore creative solutions, while working closely with an interdisciplinary group of faculty with expertise in biology, chemistry, forestry, the social sciences and the humanities.
Steven Selva, Professor

5470 University of Maryland
Environmental Policy Programs
2101 Van Munching Hall 301-405-1000
College Park, MD 20742 *Fax:* 301-403-4675
jbanders@umd.edu
www.umd.edu

This part-time degree program is intented for highly ambitious mid-career professionals who are ready to advance within the field, understand the importance and value of a professional degree and able to attend one or two classes perweek for two years. A minimum of 5 years of policy related work experience is required. For-profit, nonprofit and public sector work will be considered. A minimum udergraduate GPA of 3.0 is required.
Wallace D. Loh, President
Mary Ann Rankin, Provost

5471 University of Maryland/Baltimore
Environmental Science Studies
1000 Hilltop Circle 410-455-2274
Baltimore, MD 21250 800-UMB-C4US
Fax: 410-455-1094
www.umbc.edu

The goal of the MEES program is to train students with career interests in environmental science involving terrestrial, freshwater, marine, or estuarine systems. The program is university-wide and interdisciplinary, allowing studentsto use facilities and interact with all faculty in order to plan a program best suited to their particular interests.
Freeman A. Hrabowski, III, President
Philip Rous, Provost & SVP

5472 University of Maryland/College Park
Environmental Chemistry
0107 Chemistry Building 301-405-1788
College Park, MD 20742-4454 *Fax:* 301-314-9121
chem-web@umd.edu
www.chem.umd.edu

The combined Chemistry and Biochemistry Departments offers specialized training at the graduate level in environmental chemistry. In addition to course work in traditional chemistry subjects, students in this specialty take specificenvironmental courses and do research under the guidance of faculty members specializing in this area.

Michael Doyle, Professor & Chair
Herman Ammon, Associate Chair/Professor

5473 University of Miami
Rosenstiel School of Marine & Atmospheric Science
4600 Rickenbacker Causeway 305-421-4000
Miami, FL 33149-1098 *Fax:* 305-421-4711
dean@rsmas.miami.edu
www.rsmas.miami.edu/

Established as the Marine Laboratory of the University of Miami. It has grown from its modest beginnings in a boathouse to one of the nations leading institutions for oceanographic research and education.

Ron Avissar, Dean
Ramon Alfonso, Director

5474 University of Minnesota/St. Paul
College of Agriculatural & Environmental Sciences
3 Morrill Hall 612-625-2008
100 Church St. S.E. 800-752-1000
Minneapolis, MN 55455-213 *Fax:* 612-626-1693
spccc@umn.edu
www1.umn.edu

The programs offered through this college are designed to prepare students for work in a variety of environmental disciplines, specifically those that relate to the agriculture industry
Eric W. Kaler, President
Karen Hanson, Provost/Sr. VP for Academic

5475 University of Montana
Environmetal Studies
32 Campus Drive 406-243-0211
Missoula, MT 59812 david.micus@umontana.edu
www.umt.edu

Interdisciplinary graduate and undergraduate program in environmental studies.

Royce C. Engstrom, President
Perry J. Brown, Provost/Sr. VP for Academic

5476 University of Nebraska
Environmental Studies Program
1400 R Street 402-472-7211
Lincoln, NE 68588 hperlman1@unl.edu
www.unl.edu

The Environmental Studies Program is designed to serve a variety of students concerned about environmental issues and change. The program provides a thorough, holistic view of the environment and human-environmental interaction and thetechnical skills for active participation in an environmental career.
Harvey Perlman, Chancellor

5477 University of Nevada/Las Vegas
Department of Civil & Environmental Engineering
4505 S Maryland Parkway 702-895-3701
Box 454015 *Fax:* 702-895-3936
Las Vegas, NV 89154-4015 www.unlv.edu

Department of Civil and Environmental Engineering offers programs leading to a Master of Science in Engineering and Doctor of Philosophy, with concentration in six areas: environmental engineering; fluid mechanics and hydraulics;geotechnical engineering; structural engineering; construction engineering; and transportation systems.
Donald Hayes, Chair/Professor
Allen Sampson, Sr Development Tech

5478 University of Nevada/Reno
Civil & Environmental Engineering
1664 N. Virginia Street 775-784-1110
Reno, NV 89557-208 866-2NE-ADA
Fax: 775-784-4466
www.unr.edu

Offers an educational program in environmental engineering. Environmental engineers have taken an increasingly important role in the application on engineering and scientific principles to protect and preserve human health andenvironment. The curriculum is designed with the goal of providing each student with the necessary fundamentals and background in engineering science and design to address many different challenges.
Dr Manos Maragakis, Dean
Dr Indira Chatterjee, Professor/Assoc. Dean

5479 University of New Haven
Environmental Science
300 Boston Post Road 203-932-7319
Westhaven, CT 00651 800-342-5864
adminfo@newhaven.edu
www.newhaven.edu

The bachelor of science program in environmental science is designed to give students a strong foundation in the fudamental sciences, including biology, chemistry, physics, and geology, and how they relate to our environmentalconcerns.
Steven H. Kaplan, President
Lourdes Alvarez, Dean

5480 University of North Carolina/Chapel Hill
Environmental Science & Studies
153A Country Club Road 919-966-3621
Jackson Hall *Fax:* 919-962-3045
Chapel Hill, NC 27514 unchelp@admissions.unc.edu
www.admissions.unc.edu

The Environmental Science and Studies program leads to degrees in Environmental Science or Environmental Studies. Students investigate the relationship between the environment and society, focusing on environmental management, law andbusiness. The programs combines traditional classroom teaching with extensive use of interdisciplinary, team-based field projects, internships, study abroad and research.
Holden Thorp, Chancellor
Jim Dean, Provost

5481 University of Oregon
Environmental Studies
5223 University of Oregon 541-346-2549
Eugene, OR 97403-5223 *Fax:* 541-346-6056
adickman@uoregon.edu

Environmental Studies crosses the boundaries of traditional disciplines, challenging faculty and students to look at the relationship between humans and their environment from a new perspective. They are dedicated to gaining greaterunderstanding of the natural world from an ecological perspective; devising policy and behavior that address contemporary environmental problems; and promoting a rethinking of basic cultural premises, ways of structuring knowledge and the rootmetaphors of society.

Alan Dickman, Program Director
Monica Guy, Office Manager

5482 University of Pennsylvania
Natural Resource Conservation Program
3451 Walnut Street 215-898-5000
Philadelphia, PA 19104 webmaster@upenn.edu
www.upenn.edu

The mission of our department is to bring the time perspective of the Earth scientist/historian to bear on contemporary problems of natural resource conservation and environmental quality.
Dr. Amy Gutmann, President
Vincent Price, Provost

5483 University of Pittsburgh
Department of Geology & Planetary Science
4107 O'Hara Street 412-624-8780
200 SRCC Building *Fax:* 412-624-3914
Pittsburgh, PA 15260-3332 mookie@pitt.edu
www.geology.pitt.edu

Equips students with an understanding of earth systems and the impact of humans on the biosphere, atmosphere and hydrosphere. Courses in the natural and social sciences, humanities, and schools of law, business, and public healthprovide a comprehensive, interdisciplinary background in environmental issues and public policy.
Patricia DeMarco, Executive Director
Mark Ambott, Department Chair

5484 University of Redlands
Environmental Studies
1200 E Colton Avenue 909-793-2121
PO Box 3080 *Fax:* 909-793-2029
Redlands, CA 92373 kerry_robles@redlands.edu
www.redlands.edu

Designed to promote a new way of thinking and acting about our relationship to the world, including graduating students who are environmentally literate, sensitive to competing demands and

conflicting values of each issue and finally, and have the creativity, confidence and conviction to begin effecting change.
Dr. Ralph W. Kuncl, President
Bradley N. Adams '93, Managing Director

5485 University of South Carolina
Belle Baruch Institute of Marine Costalsciences
Petigru College 803-777-7161
Room 300 *Fax:* 803-777-4532
Columbia, SC 29208 artsandsciences.sc.edu
Environmental research and programs are focused on estuarine systems and their associated watersheds. More than 160 investigators representing 30 academic institutes and agencies are affiliated with over 100 projects. The lab providessupport for undergraduate classes, graduate students, and senior scientists. Long-term environmental monitoring, training programs and outreach activities are sponsored by the North-inlet-Winyah Bay National Estuarine research reserve.
Dr. Roger Sawyer, Executive Dean
Dr. Anne Bezuidenhout, Sr. Associate Dean

5486 University of Southern California
Environmental Sciences, Policy/Engineering Program
University Park Campus 213-740-2311
Hancock Building, Room 232 www.usc.edu
Los Angeles, CA 90089
This multidisciplinary doctoral training program is funded by the National Science Foundation, and prepares students to confront, analyze and resolve the challenges posed by problems of urban sustainablity. Engineering SustainableCities is high on the list of goals of the program, which allows students to transcend disciplines, and conduct policy-relevant research on major environmental problems.
Wallis Annenberg, Chairman
Wanda M. Austin, President & CEO

5487 University of Southern Mississippi
Environmental Science Program
118 College Drive 601-266-0001
Building #5018 *Fax:* 601-266-5797
Hattiesburg, MS 39406-0001 admissions@usm.edu
www.usm.edu
The Environmental Science concentration focuses on industrial problems related to the working environment, pollution control, and safety. Courses address major industrial issues, including environmental impact statements, industrialhygiene and environmental laws and regulations.
Frank Moore, Chair
Rodney D. Bennett, President

5488 University of Tennessee
Geoscience Program
554 University Street 731-881-7000
Martin, TN 38238 800-829-utm1
Fax: 901-587-7029
admitme@utm.edu
www.utm.edu
This program focuses on the application of geology to the interaction between man and the environment. Topics include geohazards, chemical and nuclear contamination of soils and water, remediation of environmental problems andgovernmental environmental agencies and laws.
Tom Rakes, Chancellor
Nancy Yarbrough, Interim Vice Chancellor

5489 University of Virginia
Department of Environmental Sciences
291 McCormick Road 434-924-7761
PO Box 400123 *Fax:* 434-982-2137
Charlottesville, VA 22904-4123 ralph@virginia.edu
www.evsc.virginia.edu
Offers instruction and research opportunities in Ecology, Geosciences, Hydrology, and Atmospheric Sciences. The research endeavors of both faculty and graduate students, whether disciplinary or interdisciplinary, deal largely withproblems of fundamental scientific interest and with applied sciences, management or policy making.
Allen Cindy, Asst to Dept/Chair/Clark
Sheila Riddle, Administrative Support Speci

5490 University of Washington
Environmental Science
18115 Campus Way NE 425-352-5000
Bothell, WA 98011-8246 *Fax:* 425-352-5455
info@uwb.edu
www.uwb.edu
Primary goal of this program is to train a new generation of interdisciplinary scientists who are able to work in both the public and private sectors to address some of the pressing environmental issues that face our society.
Bjong Wolf Yeigh, Chancellor
Marilyn Cox, Vice Chancellor

5491 University of West Florida
Environmental Studies
11000 University Parkway 850-474-2000
Pensacola, FL 32514 *Fax:* 850-474-3131
web@uwf.edu
www.uwf.edu
The program in Environmental Studies consists of a multi-disciplinary approach that combines natural science and resource management. Students learn to analyze physical and socioeconomic environments and to reach decisions concerningenvironmental use and protection. It offers a core curriculum that is designed to provide the student with a solid foundation in earth and life sciences, as well as in modern methods and techniques.
Lewis Bear, Chair
Judy A. Bense, President

5492 University of Wisconsin/Green Bay
Environmental Science
2420 Nicolet Drive 920-465-2000
Green Bay, WI 54311 uwgb@uwgb.edu
www.uwgb.edu
This program is interdisciplinary, emphasizing an integrated approach to knowledge in the field. Because the study of the environmental science major is grounded in the natural sciences and mathematics, the curriculum includes a socialscience component, enabling students to gain an understanding of environmental economic and policy issues. Field experiences, internships and practicums are emphasized.
Thomas K. Harden, Chancellor
Julia E. Wallace, Provost/Vice Chancellor for

5493 University of Wisconsin/Madison
Environmental Monitoring Program
212 Agricultural Hall 608-261-1432
1450 Linden Drive *Fax:* 608-265-9534
Madison, WI 53706 waes@cals.wisc.edu
www.cals.wisc.edu
Remote sensing and geographic information systems offer sophisticated and powerful tools for monitoring the environment on large geographic scales over time. Students in the Environmental Monitoring Program learn to employ thesetechnologies in fields of their choice, from forestry to urban planning to environmental engineering.
Kathryn VandenBosch, Dean/Director
Angela Seiler, Assistant Director

5494 University of Wisconsin/Stevens Point
Environmental Task Force Progeam
2100 Main Street 715-346-0123
Stevens Point, WI 54481-3897 *Fax:* 715-346-2561
webmaster@uwsp.edu
www.uwsp.edu/
This program involves two water chemistry labs which tests for organics and inorganics. This is staffed by five full time workers, plus a part time faculty director, and about 40 students are hired and/or trained each year. Samplingis performed with state-of-the-art field sampling and laboratory analytical equip-

ment nutrients, pesticides, polynuclear aromatic hydrocarbons, polychlorinated biphenyls, and volatile organic compounds.

Bernie L. Patterson, Chancellor
Greg Summers, Provost/Vice Chancellor

5495 University of the South
Environmental Studies
735 University Avenue 931-598-1000
Sewanee, TN 37383 800-522-2234
Fax: 931-598-1667
collegeadmission@sewanee.edu
www.sewanee.edu

Brings together students, faculty, and staff from thirteen academic departments to study, discuss, and research environmental issues at local, national, and international scales. The program's goal is to expose students to a variety ofviewpoints concerning environmental issues, and to offer the interdisciplinary tools they need to become environmental problem solvers before they graduate from Sewanee.

John McCardell, Vice Chancellor
John Swallow, Provost

5496 Utah State University
Berryman Institute
Wildland Resources Department 435-797-0242
5230 Old Main Hill *Fax:* 435-797-3796
Logan, UT 84322 www.berrymaninstitute.org

The Berryman Institute is a functional component of the Department of Wildland Resources and the College of Natural Resources. Its faculty members hold academics appointments in various departments throughout Utah State University andother universities. This multidisciplinary approach is calculated to speed the discovery and development of innovative methods to solve human wildlife conflict.

Dr. Terry A. Messmer, Director
Lana Barr, Assistant to the Director

5497 Vanderbilt University
Vanderbilt Center for Environmental Management
2301 Vanderbilt Place 615-322-7311
Nashville, TN 37240 *Fax:* 615-343-7177
mark.a.cohen@vanderbilt.edu
www.vanderbilt.edu

VCEMS provides guidance and support for the interdisciplinary study of environmental issues. The Center brings faculty and students together from various disciplines for collaborative study and research on topics such as environmentalrisk assessment, management and communication, policy analysis, civil and crim inal liability, environmentally conscious manufacturing and technology management, and global environmental studies.

Nicholas S. Zeppos, Chancellor
Dr. Mark Cohen, Co-Director

5498 Vermont Law School
Environmental Law Center
164 Chelsea Street 802-831-1000
PO Box 96 800-227-1395
South Royalton, VT 00506 www.vermontlaw.edu

The Environmental Law Center administers three different degrees in Environmental Law, each adaptable to career objectives in both public and private sectors. The school's mission is to educate for stewardship, to teach an awareness ofunderlining environmental issues and values, to provide a solid knowledge of environmental law and to develop skills to administer and improve policies.

J. Scott Cameron, Chair
Margaret Martin Barry, Professor of Law/Associate D

5499 Virginia Polytechnic Institute
Environmental Science
965 Prices Fork Road 540-231-6267
Blackburg, VA 24061 *Fax:* 540-231-3242
vtadmiss@vt.edu
www.vt.edu

This program deals with crop production, soil utilization, and environmental stewardship. Its professionals are concerned with helping to feed the world and protect the environment, and include women and men who work to grow crucialcommodities, improve water quality, develop environmentally acceptable methods for protecting crops from pests, and advise municipalities on use of the land resource.

Timothy D. Sands, President
Mark G. McNamee, Provost

5500 Virginia Tech
925 Prices Fork Road 540-231-6267
Blacksburg, VA 24061 *Fax:* 540-231-3242
admissions@vt.edu
www.vt.edu

Provides a B.S. degree for environmental professionals needed in the private and public sector and by nonprofit organizations. Virginia Tech offers a rigorous interdisciplinary curriculum that stresses the basic sciences, environmentaltechnologies, soils, and analytical skills. Graduates are in high demand in the environmental arena.

Timothy D. Sands, President
M. Dwight Shelton, Chief Financial Officer

5501 Warren Wilson College
Natural & Social Sciences
Warren Wilson College 828-298-3325
PO Box 9000 800-934-3536
Asheville, NC 28815-9000 *Fax:* 828-299-4841
admit@warren-wilson.edu
www.warren-wilson.edu

Combines rigorous courses in the natural and social sciences with abundant natural resources near the classrooom. Courses and work crews give students a balance of theory, first hand knowledge and field experience. Successful programsmost often result when students, with the help of an advisor, begin planning course work and indentifying goals during their first year.

Alice C. Buhl, Chair
Steven L. Solnick, President

5502 Washington State University
Environmental Science
PO Box 642812 509-335-3009
Pullman, WA 99164-2812 *Fax:* 509-335-3700
sees@wsu.edu
cahnrs.wsu.edu/soe/

The students in this diverse program are encouraged to specialize in their specific interest, including agricultural ecology, biological science, environmental education, environmental quality (air and water), natural resourcemanagement, systems, environmental/land use planning or hazardous waste management.

Elson Floyd, President
Stephen Bollens, Director

5503 West Virginia University
Environmental Geosciences Program
1168 Agricultural Sciences Building 304-293-2395
PO Box 6108 *Fax:* 304-293-3740
Morgantown, WV 26506-6108 www.davis.wvu.edu

The Environmental Geosciences program features an interdisciplinary approach to environmental issues. Graduates will be well prepared to face the environmental challenges, whether in government or in the corporate world.

Dan Robison, Dean
Dennis K. Smith, Assoc. Dean

5504 Western Montana College
Environmental Sciences Program
710 S Atlantic Street 406-683-7331
Dillon, MT 59725 877-683-7331
Fax: 406-683-7331
admissions@umwestern.edu
www.umwestern.edu

The mission of the environmental sciences programs is to provide students with an in-depth understanding of the natural processes which create and shape our environment. Students will become informed, critical thinkers capable of scientifically evaluating complex issues involving the environment. Student development

will occur through interdisciplinary, field-based research projects that have societal relevance.
Roxanne Engellant, Foundation Director
Kelly Allen, Administrative Assistant

5505 Williams College
Center for Environmental Studies
Hopkins Hall 413-597-3131
880 Main Street *Fax:* 412-597-3489
Williamstown, MA 00126 szepke@williams.edu
www.williams.edu

The Environmental Studies program provides students with tools, ideas, and opportunities to engage constructively with the environmental and social issues brought about by changes in population, economic activity, and values. Theenvironmental studies program is interdisciplinary and broad, including the coditions of inner-city poverty as well as the magnificent scenery of wildlands, encompassing the view of planet earth from near space as well as from culturalanthropologists.
Hank Art, Director

5506 Yale University
Office of Public Affairs
265 Church Street 203-432-1345
Suite 901 *Fax:* 203-432-1323
New Haven, CT 00651 undergraduate.admission@yale.edu
www.yale.edu

Our mission is to provide the leadership and knowledge needed to restore and sustain both the health of the biosphere and the well-being of its people. Believing that human enterprise can and must be conducted in harmony with theenvironment, we are committed to using natural resources in ways that sustain both resources and ourselves. Solving environmental problems must incorporate human values and motivations and a deep respect for both human and natural communities.
Richard Charles Levin, President

Workshops & Camps

5507 A Closer Look at Plant Life
Educational Images
PO Box 3456 607-732-1090
Westside Station 800-527-4264
Elmira, NY 14905-456 *Fax:* 607-732-1183
edimages@edimages.com
www.educationalimages.com

Access a wealth of information on every major group of vascular and nonvascular plants. Includes details on plant microanatomy; external and internal structures; life cycles; and processes such as growth transpiration andphotosynthesis.

Charles R Belinky, Ph.D, CEO

5508 A Closer Look at Pondlife - CD-ROM
Educational Images
PO Box 3456 607-732-1090
Westside Station 800-527-4264
Elmira, NY 14905-456 *Fax:* 607-732-1183
edimages@edimages.com
www.educationalimages.com

Through the wonders of close-up photography, this unique CD-ROM brings students face-to-face with the inner workings of a freshwater pond, the myriad creatures and plants that reside there, and the dynamic interactions that go onbeneath the surface. This disk features a library of reference information, images, illustrations, clip art, video clips and more!

Charles R Belinky, Ph.D, CEO

5509 Abbott's Mill Nature Center
Delaware Nature Society
3511 Barley Mill Road 302-239-2334
PO Box 700 *Fax:* 302-239-2473
Hockessin, DE 19707 dnsinfo@delawarenaturesociety.org
www.delawarenaturesociety.org

Abbott's Mill Nature Center features education programs for families, school classes and public groups, walking trails through fields, pine woods and streams, and a historic, fully-operating gristmill.
Peter H. Flint, President
Sharon Struthers, VP

5510 Air & Waste Management Association
Koppers Building 412-232-3444
436 Seventh Avenue, Suite 2100 800-270-3444
Pittsburgh, PA 15219 *Fax:* 412-232-3450
info@awma.org
www.awma.org

Professional development organization providing a forum for the exchange of information, networking, public education, and outreach to over 5,000 environmental professionals in 65 countries.

Stephanie Glyptis, Executive Director
Tracy Fedkoe, Director, Marketing

5511 American Academy of Clinical Toxicology
6728 Old McLean Village Drive 571-488-6000
McLean, VA 22101 admin@clintox.org
www.clintox.org

Offers programs such as the American Board of Medical Toxicology to provide physicians with certification in the field of clinical toxicology. The mission of the academy is to research and educate people about the prevention andtreatment of diseases caused by chemicals, drugs and toxins.

Robert Palmer, Ph.D, President
Mark Kostic, MD, President-Elect

5512 American Fisheries Society: Education Section
mhamel2@unl.edu
education.fisheries.org

Seeks to improve fisheries education and promote the exchange of information.
Trent Sutton, President
Marty Hamel, Secretary-Treasurer

5513 American Museum of Natural History
Center for Biodiversity and Conservation
Central Park West 212-769-5100
79th Street *Fax:* 212-769-5427
New York, NY 10024-5192 biodiversity@amnh.org
www.amnh.org

Conducts research and field projects based on information provided by Museum departments.
Lewis W. Bernard, Chairman
Ellen V. Futter, President

5514 American Society for Environmental History (ASEH)
UIC Department of History
601 S Morgan Street dspatz@aseh.net
MC 198 aseh.net
Chicago, IL 60607-7109

Promotes historical research and education on environmental matters, as a means of better understanding human interactions with the natural world. Affiliated with the Forest History Society, which co-publishes the Environmental Historyjournal. Offers courses on environmental history.
David Spatz, Executive Director

5515 Animal Tracks and Signs
Educational Images
PO Box 3456 607-732-1090
Westside Station 800-527-4264
Elmira, NY 14905-456 *Fax:* 607-732-1183
edimages@edimages.com
www.educationalimages.com

Presents various animal tracks and signs throughout the seasons, and provides useful information about the special characteristics and natural history of the animals that left the signs. Footprints, scratch marks, nesting places,wallows, scats and signs of food gathering are all detailed. Coverage includes deer, fox, porcu-

pine, rabbit, bear, mink, otter, owl, woodpecker, killdeer, wild turkey, sapsucker and grouse.
Charles R Belinky, Ph.D, CEO

5516 Annotated Invertebrate Clipart CD-ROM
Educational Images
PO Box 3456 607-732-1090
Westside Station 800-527-4264
Elmira, NY 14905-456 *Fax:* 607-732-1183
edimages@edimages.com
www.educationalimages.com
780 colorful graphics of invertebrates from protists through urochordates, supported by extensive written annotations in addition to traditional labels. Includes presentation graphics and page after page of supplemental information onclassification, anatomy, evolution, development, reproduction, etc.
Charles R Belinky, Ph.D, CEO

5517 Annotated Vertebrate Clipart CD-ROM
Educational Images
PO Box 3456 607-732-1090
Westside Station 800-527-4264
Elmira, NY 14905-456 *Fax:* 607-732-1183
edimages@edimages.com
www.educationalimages.com
792 colorful graphics of vertebrates from urochordates and tunicates through mammals, supported by extensive written annotations in addition to traditional labels. Includes presentation graphics and page after page of supplemental information on classification, organ systems, anatomy, evolution, development, reproduction, etc.
Charles R Belinky, Ph.D, CEO

5518 Argonne National Laboratory
9700 S Cass Avenue 630-252-2000
Lemont, IL 60439 www.anl.gov/
One of the US Department of Energy's largest research centers that develops and researches solutions in areas such as sustainable energy, environmental health, and national safety.
Tim Knewitz, Chief Financial Officer
Paul K Kearns, Laboratory Director

5519 Ashland Nature Center
Delaware Nature Society
3511 Barley Mill Road 302-239-2334
PO Box 700 *Fax:* 302-239-2473
Hockessin, DE 19707 dnsinfo@delawarenaturesociety.org
www.delawarenaturesociety.org
Open year round, seven days a week, Ashland is headquarters of the Delaware Nature Society. Ashland Nature Center offers self-guided nature trails traversing 81 acres of rolling terrain, through meadows, woodlands, and marshes.Programs for all ages are offered, including schools and groups.
Peter H. Flint, President
Sharon Struthers, VP

5520 Aspen Global Change Institute
104 Midland Ave 970-925-7376
Suite 205 *Fax:* 970-925-7097
Basalt, CO 81621 www.agci.org
A Colorado nonprofit dedicated to furthering the understanding of Earth systems through interdisciplinary science meetings, publications, and educational programs about global environmental change.
Dr. Martin Hoffert, Chairman
John Katzenberger, President

5521 Audubon Expedition Institute
29 Everett Street 617-868-9600
Cambridge, MA 00213 800-999-1959
info@lesley.edu
www.lesley.edu/
Students challenge themselves and their assumptions through experimental learning and direct contact with social, natural, historical and urban environments. Subjects are studied and integrated through real life experiences.
Deborah Schwartz Raizes, Chair
Hans D. Strauch, Vice Chair

5522 Bio-Integral Resource Center
PO Box 7414 510-524-2567
Berkeley, CA 94707 *Fax:* 510-524-1758
birc@igc.org
www.birc.org
The goal of the Bio Integral Resources Center is to reduce pesticide use by educating the public about effective, least-toxic alternatives for pest problems.
Dr. William Quarles, Executive Director

5523 Biosystems and Agricultural Engineering
University of Kentucky
128 C.E Barnhart Building 859-257-9000
University of Kentucky *Fax:* 859-257-5671
Lexington, KY 40546-276 gates@bae.uky.edu
www.uky.edu/bae/
Biosystems and Agricultural Engineering provides an essential link between the biological sciences and the engineering profession. The linkage is necessary for the development of food and fiber production and processing systems whichpreserves our natural resources base.
Dr. Sue E. Nokes, Chair
Dr. Czarena Crofcheck, Director of Undergraduate St

5524 Bishop Resource Area
3000 E. Line St. 760-873-4344
Bishop, CA 93514 *Fax:* 760-873-7830
wmrcinfo@ucla.edu
www.wmrc.edu
The Bishop Resource Area has facilitated aerial photo interpretation and remote sensing programs in local schools through corporate and public partnerships. The program incorporates aerial photo interpretation, its relationship tomapping and land use history.
Antony Orme, Director
Glen MacDonald, Director

5525 Bog Ecology
Educational Images Ltd
306 Academy Pl 607-732-1090
Elmira, NY 14901
A comprehensive program that explores the origin and formation of bogs, common plants and animals, and compares bogs to other types of wetlands. Bog succession is illustrated by use of diagrams and photographs. Includes 74 frames andguide.

5526 Camp Fire USA
1100 Walnut Street 816-285-2010
Suite 1900 800-669-6884
Kansas City, MO 64106-2197 *Fax:* 816-285-9444
info@campfireusa.org
www.campfireusa.org
Not-for-profit, youth development organization, Camp Fire USA provides fun, coeducational programs for approximately 650,000 youth from birth to age 21. Helps boys and girls learn and play side by side in comfortable, informalsettings.
Ms. Elizabeth Darling, President/CEO
Richard Goldfarb, Sr. VP

5527 Camp Habitat Northern Alaska Environmental Center
830 College Road 907-452-5021
Fairbanks, AK 99701-1535 *Fax:* 907-452-3100
info@northern.org
www.northern.org
Camp Habitat is a nature education program for young people ages 4-17 sponsored by the Northern Alaska Environmental Center, Friends of Creamer's Field, and Alaska Department of Fish & Game. The mission of Camp Habitat is to provideyoung people with guided explorations of their natural surroundings through interactive, hands-on activities. Skilled instructors and resource

specialists lead small groups through new outdoor activities focusing on the habitats of Interior Alaska.

Frank Williams, President
Carol Norton, Treasurer

5528 Center for Geography and Environmental Education
311 Conference Center Building 865-974-1000
University of Tennessee *Fax:* 865-974-1838
Knoxville, TN 37996 mckeowni@utk.edu
tennessee.edu
A research and outreach center at the University of Tennessee. The CGEE focuses on environmental and geography education contributions to education for sustainable development. CGEE is responsible for the Tennessee Solid WasteEducation Project.

Dr. Rosalyn McKeown-Ice, Director

5529 Center for Mathematical Services
4202 East Fowler Avenue 813-974-2011
Adm 147 *Fax:* 974-974-2700
Tampa, FL 33620 www.usf.edu
Mission is to help prepare students of all levels to effectively use mathematics as a tool to analyze situations and resolve problems. In the field of mathematical sciences it serves as an interface for the University with thesecondary schools in the area served by the University of South Florida. By means of this interface special programs in the mathematics, science, and engineering are offered at the University of South Florida for secondary students.
Ralph Wilcox, Provost/VP
Dr. Dwayne Smith, Sr. Vice Provost

5530 Chicago Botanic Garden
1000 Lake Cook Road 847-835-5440
Glencoe, IL 60022 www.chicagobotanic.org
The Chicago Horticultural Society has been promoting gardens and gardening since 1890. Generations of Chicagoans have been touched by the Society's flower shows, victory gardens, horticultural lectures and more. The mission encompassesthree important components: collections, programs and research. A living museum, the Chicago Botanic Garden serves both a public and a scientific community.
Robert F. Finke, Chair
John L. Howard, Vice Chair/Secretary

5531 Cleaner and Greener Environment
PO Box 5425 608-280-0255
Madison, WI 53705-425 877-977-9277
Fax: 608-255-7202
info@cleanerandgreener.org
www.cleanerandgreener.org
Cleaner and Greener Environment is a program of Leonardo Academy, a 501 environmental nonprofit organization. Leonardo Academy reports reductions in emissions, and promotes the development of markets for the emission reductions thatresult from energy efficiency, renewable energy, and other emission reduction action.

5532 Climate Change Program
Dade County Dept. of Env. Res. Mgm. 305-372-6825
701 NW 1st Court *Fax:* 305-372-6954
Miami, FL 33136
Receives monies from sources such as fees from pollution prevention events, grants, allocations, appropriations and workshop fees. These funds are then used in developing, promoting and conducting environmental workshops, expositions,symposia, conferences and other forms of public information for the purpose of educating industry, government and the public about pollution prevention.
Nichole Hefty, Coordinator

5533 Coastal Resources Center
University of Rhode Island
220 South Ferry Road 401-874-6224
Narragansett, RI 00288 *Fax:* 401-874-6920
info@crc.uri.edu
www.crc.uri.edu
Mobilizes governments, business and communities around the world to work together as stewards of coastal ecosystems. With partners we strive to define and achieve the health, equitable allocation of wealth, and sustainable intensitiesof human activity at the transition between the land and sea.
Brian Crawford, Director
Lesley Squillante, Asst. Director

5534 Columbia Environmental Research Center
1200 Amsterdam Avenue 212-854-8179
New York, NY 10027-5557 *Fax:* 212-854-8188
eices@columbia.edu
www.cerc.columbia.edu
CERC, a consortium of five education and research institutions, was created in response to critical environmental concerns facing the Earth. Within the next fifty years human influence will affect every place on the planet. That impactwill almost certainly result in species extinctions, ecosystem degradation and a loss of the benefits those species and ecosystems provide to people.
Shahid Naeem, Director
Alexandra Varga, Deputy Director

5535 Comet Halley: Once in a Lifetime!
Educational Images
PO Box 3456 607-732-1090
Westside Station 800-527-4264
Elmira, NY 14905-456 *Fax:* 607-732-1183
edimages@edimages.com
www.educationalimages.com
Particularly relevant because of the recent appearance of Hale-Bopp, this program presents the reactions to comets in ancient, historic and relatively modern times, press coverage of the 1910 Halley return, superstitions and beliefs,current scientific knowledge and research, and much more.

Charles R Belinky, Ph.D, CEO

5536 Cooch-Dayett Mills
Delaware Nature Society
3511 Barley Mill Road 302-239-2334
PO Box 700 *Fax:* 302-239-2473
Hockessin, DE 19707 dnsinfo@delawarenaturesociety.org
www.delawarenaturesociety.org
Programming provided by the delaware nature society features environmental education and natural history for families, classes, groups and the public. The historic roller mills, along with natural features of the site, become theclassroom.
Peter H. Flint, President
Sharon Struthers, VP

5537 Cooperative Institute for Research in Environmental Sciences: K-12 and Public Outreach
University of Colorado
449 UCB 303-492-5670
PO Box 700 *Fax:* 303-492-1149
Boulder, CO 80309-449 info@cires.colorado.edu
www.cires.colorado.edu/education/outreach
We educate people about Earth and environmental science issues that are relevant to our everyday lives, through outreach to the public and to the K-12 education community.
Waleed Abdalati, Director
William M. Lewis, Jr., Assoc. Director

5538 Coverdale Farm
Delaware Nature Society
3511 Barley Mill Road 302-239-2334
PO Box 700 *Fax:* 302-239-2473
Hockessin, DE 19707 dnsinfo@delawarenaturesociety.org
www.delawarenaturesociety.org

School students and guests of all ages participate in seasonal programs, learning about the farm cycle of life and humans' dependence on soil, water, plants and animals for survival.
Peter H. Flint, President
Sharon Struthers, VP

5539 Deep Portage Conservation Reserve
2197 Nature Center Drive NW 218-682-2325
Hackensack, MN 56452 888-280-9908
Fax: 218-682-3121
portage@uslink.net
www.deep-portage.org

Deep Portage serves schools, groups, organizations, research teams, area residents and visitor with resident environmental education programs, weekly classes, interpretive programs, wildflower garden displays, land use demonstrations,summer youth camps and recreation opportunities of birding, hiking, hunting and skiing.
Dale Yerger, Executive Director
Molly Malecek, Assistant Director

5540 Department of Energy and Geo-Environmental Engineering
116 Deike Building 814-865-6546
University Park, PA 16802 *Fax:* 814-863-7708
contact@ems.psu.edu
www.ems.psu.edu

Through education, research and service, EGEE aspires to insure that socisty is provided with an affordable supply of energy and minerals, concomitant with protecting the environment.
William E. Easterling, Dean
John Hellmann, Associate Dean

5541 DuPont Environmental Education Center
Delaware Nature Society
3511 Barley Mill Road 302-239-2334
PO Box 700 *Fax:* 302-239-2473
Hockessin, DE 19707 dnsinfo@delawarenaturesociety.org
www.delawarenaturesociety.org

Programming provided by the delaware nature society features environmental education and natural history for families, classes, groups and the public. The historic roller mills, along with natural features of the site, become theclassroom.
Peter H. Flint, President
Sharon Struthers, VP

5542 Earth Day Network
1616 P Street NW 202-518-0044
Suite 340 *Fax:* 202-518-8794
Washington, DC 20036 buchanan@earthday.org
www.earthday.net

This nonprofit network was created to be a vehicle for increased awareness & responsibility through the promotion of Earth Day. Offers workshops.
Denis Hayes, Board Chair/President/CEO
Gerald Torres, Vice Chair

5543 Earth Force
2555 W 34th Avenue 303-433-0016
PO Box 1228 *Fax:* 888-899-5324
Denver, CO 80211 earthforce@earthforce.org
www.earthforce.org

Earth Force offers educators innovatove programs and resources. The young graduates of these programs create lasting solutions to environmental problems in their communities. Earth Force's goal is to help youth become environmentalproblem solvers.

James Macgregor, Chairman
Chris Chopyak, President

5544 Ecological & Environmental Learning Services
46 Back Bone Hill Road 732-577-5599
Clarksburg, NJ 00851 800-206-6672
Fax: 732-577-5598

Ecological & Environmental Learning Services provides K-12 education consulting for teacher professional development, curriculum development and education programs and assemblies. EELS has the expertise and experience to providesolutions for enhancing the academic excellence of students in the following areas: Science (particularly in science research); Ecology; Environmental Science; and Environmental Education.

5545 Ecology and Environmental Sciences
5703 Alumni Hall 207-581-1512
Suite 200 877-486-2364
Orono, ME 00446 *Fax:* 207-581-1517
president@umaine.edu
www.umaine.edu

Faculty from five different academic departments, covering biological, physical and social sciences, work together to offer a broad educational experience for our students. Since these faculty have active research programs, studentsnot only get access to the most up-to-date information, but also get employment opportunities in their fields of study during the academic year and the summer months.
Susan J. Hunter, President

5546 Economic Development/Marketing California Environmental Business Council
UC Extention 408-748-2170
3120 De La Cruz *Fax:* 408-748-2189
Santa Clara, CA 95054 br1027@aol.com

The CEBC is a nonprofit trade and business assoication that promotes and assists California's environmental technology and services industry at the state, national, and international levels. Founded in 1994, the CEBC currently has morethan 100 member compines and other organizations throughout the state that represent all segments of the environmental industry.

5547 Energy Thinking for Massachusetts
Northeast Sustainable Energy Association
50 Miles Street 413-774-6051
Greenfield, MA 00130 *Fax:* 413-774-6053
nesea@nesea.org
www.nesea.org

CD
Jennifer Marrapese, Executive Director
Mary Biddle, Deputy Executive Director

5548 Energy Thinking for Pennsylvania
Northeast Sustainable Energy Association
50 Miles Street 413-774-6051
Greenfield, MA 00130 *Fax:* 413-774-6053
nesea@nesea.org
www.nesea.org

CD
Jennifer Marrapese, Executive Director
Mary Biddle, Deputy Executive Director

5549 Environmental Data Resources
6 Armstrong Road 203-783-0300
4th Floor 800-352-0050
Shelton, CT 00648 *Fax:* 800-231-6802
resinfo@edrnet.com
www.edrnet.com

Applied and product research in environmental applications.
Guy Tassinari, Managing Director
Tom Flynn, Chief Financial Officer

5550 Environmental Education Council of Ohio
PO Box 1004 740-653-2649
Lancaster, OH 43130-1004 800-992-6682
Fax: 330-823-8531
director@eeco-online.org
www.eeco.wildapricot.org

EECO believes that: we are all learners interacting with others in lifelong process, education is vital for individuals to reach their full potential as members of our global community, a healthy and sustainable environment isessential to the survival of the planet. It is the mission of EECO to lead in facilitating and promoting environmental education which nurtures knowledge, attitudes and behaviors that foster global stewardship.
Denise Natoli Brooks, President
Brenda Metcalf, Executive Director

5551 Environmental Education K-12
Archbold Biological Station 863-465-2571
123 Main Dr. *Fax:* 863-699-1927
Venus, FL 33960 archbold@archbold-station.org

Archbold Biological Station provides environmental education programs to help people af all ages discover and understand the unique and endangered Florida scrib. Several programs for children Grades K-12 are offered each year. Theprogram goals are; promote a sound foundation in ecological principles, nurture a sense of stewardship for Florida scrub habitat, demostrate the value of scientific research, and develop a deeper understanding of the importance of natural habitatsfor investigation.
Dr. Hilary Swain, Executive Director
Frances C. James, Advisor

5552 Environmental Forum of Marin
PO Box 151546 415-484-8336
San Rafael, CA 94915 board@MarinEFM.org
www.marinefm.org
Dedicated to protecting and enhancing the environment by educating its members and the Marin citizenry on environmental issues. In futherance of this goal, the Environmental Forum of Marin conducts annual training programs onenvironmental matters, provides continuing education for its members and public, and supports citizen action to influence environmental decision-making and public policy.
Vicki Rupp, President
Kathryn Olson, Vice President

5553 Environmental Law Institute
1730 M Street, NW 202-939-3800
Suite 700 *Fax:* 202-939-3868
Washington, DC 20036 law@eli.org
www.eli.org
Jose R Allen, Partner
Paul J Allen, Senior Vice President

5554 Environmental Protection Agency: Great Lakes National Program Office
77 West Jackson Boulevard 312-353-2117
Chicago, IL 60604-3590 *Fax:* 312-886-6869
www.epa.gov/greatlakes
EPA's Great Lakes National Program Office (GLNPO) works under the Great Lakes Water Quality Agreement (GLWQA) with Canada to restore and maintain the integrity of the Great Lakes ecosystem. The office works with partners at thefederal, state, tribal, local, and industrial levels to accomplish the objectives of their action plan.
Cathy Stepp, Program Manager
Chris Korleski, Director

5555 Environmental Resources Management
3352 128th Avenue 616-399-3500
Holland, MI 49424 *Fax:* 616-399-3777
www.erm.com
Provides environmental, health, safety, risk, and social consulting services, including sustainability planning, health and safety, risk assessment, data management, asset management, and environmental compliance.
Keryn James, Chief Executive Officer
David McArthur, Chief Operating Officer

5556 Environmental Sciences
900 University Ave. 951-827-1012
Riverside, CA 92521 *Fax:* 951-827-3993
enviro@eas.slu.edu
www.envisci.ucr.edu
Environmental Sciences is concerned with the near-surface realm of Earth and the way humans interact with that environment. Environmental scientist are concerned with water availability and equal, waste disposal, the use of Earth'slimited resources, and natural hazards such as earthquakes, landslides, and floods. Environmental scientists use the principles of geology, physics, chemistry, and biology to understand these phenomena and solve environmental problems.
Janice Border, Finance Officer
RC Sutton, Financial Operations Manager

5557 Exploring Animal Life - CD-ROM
Educational Images
PO Box 3456 607-732-1090
Westside Station 800-527-4264
Elmira, NY 14905-456 *Fax:* 607-732-1183
edimages@edimages.com
www.educationalimages.com
A curriculum oriented presentation and an instant encyclopedia, filled with superb photographs, informative text, exciting video clips, printable diagrams and illustrations, and lab activities. Provides a fascinating survey of themajor divisions of animal life and their characteristics: sponges, molluscs, insects, arthropods, fish, reptiles, birds and mammals are fully presented in the order in which you teach them.
Charles R Belinky, Ph.D, CEO

5558 Exploring Environmental Science Topics
Educational Images
PO Box 3456 607-732-1090
Westside Station 800-527-4264
Elmira, NY 14905-456 *Fax:* 607-732-1183
edimages@edimages.com
www.educationalimages.com
Provides a curriculum oriented presentation, an instant encyclopedia, superb photographs, video clips, informative text, printable diagrams & illustrations, & lab activities. This program offers a fascinating survey of environmentaltopics & concerns such as the environmental costs of energy; acid rain; energy flow and the greenhouse effect; oil spills; tundra, chaparral, desert, grassland and forest biomes; the hydrological cycle and water pollution; and the recycling elementsin the biosphere.
CD-Rom
Charles R Belinky, Ph.D, CEO

5559 Exploring Freshwater Communities
Educational Images
PO Box 3456 607-732-1090
Westside Station 800-527-4264
Elmira, NY 14905-456 *Fax:* 607-732-1183
edimages@edimages.com
www.educationalimages.com
A complete resource for studying freshwater biomes. It provides a fascinating survey of the ecology of swamps, bogs, marshes, wetlands, streams, ponds, lakes and the Everglades. There is even an introduction to fish restoration andwater pollution.
CD-Rom
Charles R Belinky, Ph.D, CEO

5560 Five Winds International
Hauptstraße 111-113 711-341- 170
Echterdingen, ON 70771 *Fax:* 711-341- 172
www.thinkstep.com
Five Winds helps companies and organizations understand sustainability to improve their performance and succeed in the marketplace.
Christoph Wilfert, CEO
Thomas Dollhoph, CFO

5561 Fossil Rim Wildlife Center
2155 County Road 2008 254-897-2960
PO Box 2189 888-775-6742
Glen Rose, TX 76043 *Fax:* 254-897-3785
www.fossilrim.org
Fossil Rim Wildlife Center is dedicated to conservation of species in peril, scientific research, training of professionals, creative management of natural resources, and impactful public education. Through these activities we providea diversity of compelling learning experiences which invoke positive change in the way people think, feel and act environmentally. Also provides scenic drives and lodgings for visitors, and is open all seasons.
Billie Kinnard, Marketing/PR Director
Lisa Roberts, Membership Director

5562 GLOBE Program
Mailstop T28H
Moffett Field, CA 94035
800-858-9947
Fax: 650-604-1913
help@globe.gov
www.globe.gov

GLOBE is a worldwide hands-on, primary and secondary school based science and education program.

5563 Glacier Institute
137 Main Street
PO Box 1887
Kalispell, MT 59903
406-755-1211
Fax: 406-755-7154
register@glacierinstitute.org
www.glacierinstitute.org

The Glacier Institute serves adults and children as an educational leader in the Crown of the Continent ecosystem with Glacier National Park at its center. Emphasizing field based learning experiences, the Institute provides anobjective and science based understanding of the area's ecology and its interaction with people. Through this non advocacy approach to outdoor education, participants can be better prepared to make informed and constructive decisions which impactthis & other ecosystems.

Joyce H Baltz, Executive Director
Dawn Glynn, Office Administrator

5564 Global Nest
Michigan State University
281 State Route 79
Suite 208
Morganville, NJ 00775
732-333-5848
Fax: 732-333-5946
info@globalnest.com
www.globalnest.com

The Global Nest constitutes an international association of scientists, technologists, engineers and other interested groups involved in all scientific and technological aspects of the environment as well as in application techniquesaiming at the development of sustainable solutions. Its main target is to support and assist the dissemination of information regarding the most contemporary methods for improving quality of life through the development and application oftechnologies.

5565 Gore Range Natural Science School
318 Walking Mountains Lane
PO Box 9469
Avon, CO 81620
970-827-9725
Fax: 970-827-9730
info@walkingmountains.org
www.walkingmountains.org

Offers summer day and overnight programs for students in 3rd grade up. During the academic school year GRNSS provides integrated field science education to local and visiting schools. Its mission is to raise environmental awareness andinspire stewardship of the Eagle River watershed.
Alix Berglund, Director
Hans Berglund, Advisory Director

5566 Groundwater Foundation
The Groundwater Foundation
3201 Pioneers Blvd
Suite 105
Lincoln, NE 68502
402-434-2740
800-858-4844
Fax: 402-434-2742
info@groundwater.org
www.groundwater.org

the groundwater foundation is a non profit organization, that is dedicated to informing the public about one of our greatest hidden resources, groundwater since 1985 our program and publications presents the benefits everyone recievesfrom groundwater,and the risks that threaten groundwater quality. we make learning about ground water fun and understandable for kids and adults alike.
Cathy Lotzer, Chair
Andy Belanger, Vice Chair

5567 Hazardous Chemicals: Handle With Care
Educational Images
PO Box 3456
Westside Station
Elmira, NY 14905-456
607-732-1090
800-527-4264
Fax: 607-732-1183
edimages@edimages.com
www.educationalimages.com

Shows the importance of hazardous chemicals in our daily lives and problems caused by ignorance, mistakes, accidents and occasionally, recklessness in their use. Four case studies show how toxic chemicals were introduced into theenvironment causing serious health and environmental effects. Video, 56 page guide with lesson plans, projects, reproducible handouts.

Charles R Belinky, CEO

5568 Hidden Villa
26870 Moody Road
Los Altos Hills, CA 94022
650-949-8650
Fax: 650-948-4159
info@hiddenvilla.org
www.hiddenvilla.org

Hidden Villa is a nonprofit educational organization that uses its organic farm, wilderness, and community to provide learning opportunities about the environment and social justice.
Chris Overington, Executive Director
Ken Ebbitt, Chair

5569 ISPTR-PARD
72902 Raymond Way
Twentynine Palms, CA 92277
310-303-9050
pard_expeditions@yahoo.com

ISPTR-PARD is a partnership between The International Society for the Preservation of the Tropical Rainforest and Pink Amazon River Dolphin Expedition. The organization is focused on conserving the Peruvian Amazon Rainforest and theAmazon pink river dolphin. Educational resources are also offered on their website for those that want to learn more.
Roxanne Kremer, Executive Director

5570 Ice Age Relicts: Living Glaciers and Signs of Ancient Ice Sheets
Educational Images
PO Box 3456
Westside Station
Elmira, NY 14905-456
607-732-1090
800-527-4264
Fax: 607-732-1183
edimages@edimages.com
www.educationalimages.com

Glaciers, living relicts of the ice age, are still important today. They hold much of the earth's fresh water, sculpted much of North America, and promise an early return to finish their work. Provides a coherent picture of howglaciers work, and what they did. 26 page guide. Video or filmstrips.

Charles R Belinky, Ph.D, CEO

5571 International Center for Earth Concerns
Centennial Valley, MT
805-649-3535
Fax: 805-649-1757

Dedicated to providing for public use, a world class botanic garden, outdoor learning-ecology center and a 50-passenger all-electric floating classroom on Lake Casitas. These facilities are used to promote a better understanding ofman's place in the environment, as well as to help develop a sense of respect, responsibility and compassion for animals and nature.
John Hoyt, Founding President
John Taft, Chairman

5572 International Hunter Education Association (IHEA-USA)
800 East 73rd Avenue
Unit 3
Denver, CO 80229
303-430-7233
Fax: 303-430-7236
www.ihea-usa.org

Operates programs across the U.S. teaching hunting and shooting safety and responsibility. Courses cover firearm safety, bowhunting, wildlife management, field care, responsible hunting, landowner relations, wildlife identification,and more. Affiliated with the Association of Fish and Wildlife Agencies and local state fish and hunter education programs.

Marisa Lee Futral, President
David Allen, Executive Director

5573 International Society of Environmental Forensics
150 Fearing Street
Suite 21
Amherst, MA 01002
413-549-5170
Fax: 413-549-0579
www.environmentalforensics.org

The society aims to provide training via workshops on environmental contamination of areas of air, water, soil, and biota. Also publishes the journal Environmental Forensics.

5574 Invertebrate Animal Videos
Educational Images
PO Box 3456 607-732-1090
Westside Station 800-527-4264
Elmira, NY 14905-456 *Fax:* 607-732-1183
edimages@edimages.com
www.educationalimages.com

Four part series. Each a 40-minute multimedia presentation with easy going narration and hundreds of interactive links. Part I: sponges, anemones, corals and flatworms. Part II: molluscs, segmented worms and minor phyla. Part III:the insects. Part IV: noninsect arthropods and echinoderms.

Charles R Belinky, Ph.D, CEO

5575 Jane Goodall's Roots & Shoots
1595 Spring Hill Road 703-682-9220
Suite 550 *Fax:* 703-682-9312
Vienna, VA 22182 rootsandshoots@janegoodall.org
www.rootsandshoots.org

Youth service program aiming to teach young people respect and compassion for all living things.
Jane Goodall, Ph.D., DBE, Founder

5576 Jones & Stokes
11820 Northup Way 425-822-1077
Suite E300 *Fax:* 425-822-1079
Bellevue, WA 98005

An employee-owned company, Jones & Stokes is the best consulting source for integrated environmental planning and natural resources management services in the western United States.
Grant Bailey

5577 Killer Whales: Lords of the Sea
Educational Images
PO Boc 3456 607-732-1090
Westside Station 800-527-4264
Elmira, NY 14905-456 *Fax:* 607-732-1183
edimages@edimages.com
www.educationalimages.com

Separates facts from myth about these majestic, maligned and usually misrepresented scagoing mammals: both wild and captive killer whales, their mental and physical powers, their feeding and reproductive behavior, physiology,sociology and echolocation. Information on other cetaceans is presented for comparison and better understanding. Provides scientific information and reports on ongoing research.

Charles R Belinky, Ph.D, CEO

5578 Legacy International
1020 Legacy Drive 540-297-5982
Bedford, VA 24523 *Fax:* 540-297-1860
mail@legacyintl.org
www.legacyintl.org

Creates environments where people can address personal, community, and global needs while developing skills and effective responses to change.Whether working with youths, corporate leaders, educational professionals, entrepreneurs, orindividuals on opposing sides of a conflict, our goal is the same. Programs provide experiences, skills, and strategies that enable people to build better lives for themselves and others around them.
JE Rash, President/Founder
Shanti Thompson, VP

5579 Lesley/Audubon Environmental Education Programs
Lesley University
29 Everett Street 617-868-9600
Cambridge, MA 00213 info@lesley.edu
www.lesley.edu

In partership with Audubon Expedition Institute in Belfast, Lesley University offers a Bachelor of Science degree in Environmental Studies, a Master of Science degree in Environmental Education and a Master of Science in EcologicalTeaching and Learning. Students travel throughout the US earning academic credit and gaining first-hand experience of environmental issues.
Donald Perrin, Chair

5580 Let's Grow Houseplants
Educational Images
Po Box 3456 607-732-1090
Westside Station 800-527-4264
Elmira, NY 14905-456 *Fax:* 607-732-1183
edimages@edimages.com
www.educationalimages.com

Details different kinds of plants and their needs, when to water, selection, how to start from seeds and cuttings, how to make inexpensive pots, etc. Perfect to initiate an elementary classroom gardening project. 74 frames and guide.For elementary and preschool.

Charles R Belinky, Ph.D, CEO

5581 Lost Valley Educational Center
81868 Lost Valley Lane 541-937-3351
Dexter, OR 97431 info@lostvalley.org
www.lostvalley.org

Offers a wide variety of programs, including residential interships, educational workshops that emphasize hands on, experiential learning and personal/spiritual growth workshops. The Center also provides a supportive and nourishingplace to hold individuals and organizations who share our vision for an environmentally sound, pollution free world to hold conferences, retreats and workshops.
Dianne Brause, Co-Founder
Justin Michelson, Executive Director

5582 MacKenzie Environmental Education Center
Wisconsin Department of Natural Resources
W7303 County Road CS & Q 608-635-8105
Poynette, WI 53955 *Fax:* 608-635-2743
info@naturenet.com
www.mackenziecenter.com

Located only 20 miles north of Madison, the MacKenzie Center offers a wide array of outdoor experiences. Five themed nature trails, prairie restorations, picnic area, nature study, three museums and a wildlife exhibit containing liveanimals that are native to Wisconsin, are here to help you gain a better understanding of our natural resources.

Ruth Ann Lee, Director
Derek A. Duane, Maintenance

5583 Marine Biological Laboratory
7 Mbl Street 508-548-3705
Woods Hole, MA 00254 *Fax:* 508-457-1924
www.mbl.edu

For more than a century, scientists from around the world have been gathering in Woods Hole. The best students from the best universities, the brightest young faculty, the most succesful scientists working at the pinnacle of theprofession, an unmatched collection of researchers and educators congregates every year in the seaside village whose name has become synonimous with science.
John W. Rowe, Chairman
Huntington F. Willard, Director

5584 Microscopic Pond
Educational Images
PO Box 3456 607-732-1090
Westside Station 800-527-4264
Elmira, NY 14905-456 *Fax:* 607-732-1183
edimages@edimages.com
www.educationalimages.com

Introduces students to both the micrscopic plant and animal life of a pond. Various groups of algae are discussed and illustrated, including desmids, Pediastrum, Pithophora, Spyrogyra, Volvox, Nostac, calothrix, Bacillariophyseae,Dinophyseae, and amoebas (includeing Amoeba proteus), Arcella, the testaceans, and many others. With only a few exceptions, all of the organisms in this program were photographed live.

Charles R Belinky, Ph.D, CEO

5585 Mote Environmental Services
1600 Ken Thompson Parkway 941-388-4441
Sarasota, FL 34236 800-691-6683
www.mote.org
Mote Environmental Services offers consulting services focused on marine and coastal issues, where our expertise is strongest. We provide superior, results-oriented investigations and management planning service within our areas oftechnical and policy specialty. MESI is a wholly owned subsidiary of Mote Marine Laboratory, an independent, nonprofit research and public education institution dedicated to excellence in marine and environmental sciences.
Eugene Beckstein, Chairman
Dr. Michael P. Crosby, President & CEO

5586 National Environmental Health Association (NEHA)
720 S Colorado Boulevard 303-756-9090
Suite 1000-N *Fax:* 303-691-9490
Denver, CO 80246-1926 staff@neha.org
www.neha.org
Represents all of environmental health and protection from terrorism and all-hazards preparedness, to food safety and protection and on site wastewater systems. Over 4,500 members and the profession are served by the associationthrough its Journal of Environmental Health, Annual Education Conference and Exhibition credentialing programs, research and development activities and other services.

David T. Dyjack, Executive Director

5587 National Institute of Environmental Health Sciences
NIEHS Central Receiving
105 T.W. Alexander Drive 919-541-3345
Building 110 *Fax:* 301-480-2978
Research Triangle Park, NC 27709 webcenter@niehs.nih.gov
www.niehs.nih.gov
NIEHS' mission is to research how the environment affects people in order to promote healthier lives, and to provide global leadership for research that improves public health. NIEHS accomplishes this mission by translating theirfindings into comprehensible information that can inform real-life individual and public health outcomes.

Linda S. Birnbaum, Director
Richard Woychik, Deputy Director

5588 Natural Resources Conservation and Management
Lexindton Convention And Visitors Bureau
301 East Vine Street 859-244-7706
Lexington, KY 40507 800-845-3959
lexadmin@visitlex.com
As a trained professional, you will have a variety of challenging employment opportunities in public agencies and industry to contribute to sustained productivity and equality of all of our natural resources. In addition, some studentsfind that the Natural Resource Conservation and Management program satisfies their desire for a career in environmental education or environmental journalism.
David Lord, President

5589 Nicodemus Wilderness Project
PO Box 40712 mail@wildernessproject.org
Albuquerque, NM 87196-0712 www.wildernessproject.org
The Nicodemus Wilderness Project was founded because of the need for environmental restoration, stewardship, and projection of neglected public lands. Offers wilderness education for children.
Robert K. Dudley, PhD, President/Executive Director
Yih Ming Hsu, VP, Program Manager

5590 Nielsen Environmental Field School
9600 Achenbach Canyon Road 575-532-5535
Las Cruces, NM 88011 *Fax:* 575-532-5978
info@envirofieldschool.com
www.envirofieldschool.com
In 1990, the Nielsen Environmental Field School was created in reponse to a demand from the environmental industry for practically oriented, hands-on environmental field training.
David M. Nielsen, Co-Founder
Gillian L. Nielsen, Co-Founder

5591 Northwest Environmental Education Council
Northwest Environmental Education Council
650 S. Orcas Street 206-762-1976
Suite 220 *Fax:* 206-762-1979
Seattle, WA 98108
The Northwest Environmental Education Council increases environmental awareness, appreciation and stewardship by providing environmental education and science training opportunities for youth and adults.
Tasya Gray, President
Lief Horwitz, Vice President

5592 Northwest Interpretive Association
Northwest Interpretive Association
164 South Jackson Street 206-220-4140
Seattle, WA 98104 877-874-6775
www.discovernw.org
Works with public and management agencies to operate educational bookstores. Our mission is to provide visitors with information they need to learn about the nature and natural history of public lands so they can make wise choicesabout the lands use, preservation and protection. We accomplish our mission by selling educational and interpretive materials directly to visitors as well as returning net proceeds to the site where they were guaranteed to help fund other programs.
Lori Brockman, Chair
Jim Caplan, Vice Chair

5593 Office of Energy and Environmental Industries
1401 Constitution Ave, NW 202-482-5225
Washington, DC 20230 800-usa-trad
Fax: 202-482-5665
www.ita.doc.gov
The Office of Energy and Environmental Industries (OEEI) is the principal resource and key contact point within the US Department of Commerce for American environmental technology companies. OEEI's goal is to facilitate and increaseexports of environmental technologuies-goods and services-by providing support and guidance to US exporters.
Adam O'Malley, Office Director
Man Cho, Team Leader, Energy

5594 PAWS Wildlife Rehabilitation Center & Hospital
15305 44th Avenue West 425-787-2500
PO Box 1037 *Fax:* 425-742-5711
Lynnwood, WA 98087 www.paws.org/wildlife
Rehabilitating injured and orphaned wildlife, provides shelter and adoption for animals. PAWS educates people to recognize the intrinsic value of animals and make choices that demonstrate compassion and respect. Offers a three-monthwildlife rehabilitation internship, a two-to four-week veterinary technician externship, and a four-week veterinary externship.

Annette Laico, Chief Executive Officer
James J. Marshall-Ward, Chief Operating Officer

5595 Perkiomen Watershed Conservancy
1 Skippack Pike 610-287-9383
Schwenksville, PA 19473 *Fax:* 610-287-9237
pwc@perkiomenwatershed.org
www.perkiomenwatershed.org/
A nonprofit organization founded in 1964 by local citizens that works to protect the watershed of the Perkiomen Creek and its tributaries. This is accomplished through environmental educa-

tion, conservation programs and watershedstewardship activities.

Michael Stokes, Chairman
Andrew Meadows, Vice Chairman

5596 Primary Ecological Succession
Educational Images
PO Box 3456 607-732-1090
Westside Station 800-527-4264
Elmira, NY 14905-456 *Fax:* 607-732-1183
edimages@edimages.com
www.educationalimages.com

An illustrated explanation of basic concepts of primary succession: the pioneer community; tolerant vs. intolerant species; stabilization; stratification and the climax community. Concise overview followed by classic, specificexamples of succession - on bare rock, on the sand dunes of Lake Michigan, on the outer banks of North Carolina - all explored in detail. 72 frames and guide.

Charles R Belinky, Ph.D, CEO

5597 Project Oceanology
University Of Connecticut
Avery Point Campus 860-445-9007
1084 Shennecossett Road 800-364-8472
Groton, CT 00634 *Fax:* 860-449-8008
projecto@oceanology.org
www.oceanology.org

Project Oceanology is owned and operated by Interdistrict Committee for Project Oceanology and association of 25 educational institutions in Massachusetts, Rodhe Island, Connecticut and New York. Members of this associations includepublic school districts, private schools, states university, public and private colleges, a maritime museum and an aquarium. The project is governed by an assembly of delegates representing the member institutions.

Thaxter Tewksbury, Director
Lauren Rader, Chief Instructor

5598 Project WILD
5555 Morningside Drive 713-520-1936
Suite 212 *Fax:* 713-520-8008
Houston, TX 77005 info@councilforee.org
www.projectwild.org

Project WILD is one of the most widely-used conservation and environmental education programs among educators of students in kindergarten through high school. Project WILD is based on the premise that young people and educators have avital interest in learning about natural world.

Mark LeFebre, Senior Program Manager
Josetta Hawthorne, Executive Director

5599 Resource-Use Education Council
The Virginia Natural Resources Education Guide
PO Box 11104 804-698-4442
Richmond, VA 23230 *Fax:* 804-698-4522

In the mid 1950s, representatives from Virginia and federal natural resource agencies, along with professors in the colleges of education and resource management, came together as the Virginia Resource Use Education Council. For 35years, the VRUEC sponsored a summer conservation course for teachers at four of Virginia's colleges.

Ann Regn, Chairman

5600 Risk Management Internet Services
Managerial Technologies Corporation
2400 East Main Street 630-221-9116
Suite 103- 319 *Fax:* 312-602-4935
St Charles, IL 60174 info@rmis.com
rmis.com

Dedicated to bringing risk management related professions together with the consultants, developers and providers who service them.

5601 Ross & Associates Environmental Consulting,Ltd
1218 Third Avenue 206-447-1805
Suite 1207 *Fax:* 206-447-0956
Seattle, WA 98101

Ross and Associates environmental consulting, is a small group of highly motivated professionals committed to helping environmental and natural resources agencies improve management programs and achieve better environmental results.

Rob Greenwood, Principal
Tim Larson, Principal

5602 SEEK
520 Lafayette Rd. N. 651-757-2700
St. Paul, MN 55155-4194 800-857-3864
seek.pca@state.mn.us

The SEEK directory works as a clearinghouse for all types of environmental education resources, from articles to lesson plans, from performances to displays, and many more. These resources come a variety of organizations throughoutMinnesota, including schools and colleges, government agencies, libraries and businesses.

Lee Ann Landstrom, Chair
Karen Balmer, Board of Teaching

5603 Sacramento River Discovery Center
1000 Sale Lane 530-527-1196
Red Bluff, CA 96080 *Fax:* 530-527-1312

The mission of the Sacramento River Discovery Center is to educate the public's school programs. Teacher professional development, camping, rafting and tourist events are available.

Lupe Green, Executive Director
Anna Draper, Program Manager

5604 Schlitz Audubon Nature Center
1111 E Brown Deer Road 414-352-2880
Milwaukee, WI 53217 *Fax:* 414-352-6091
smanning@sanc.org
www.schlitzauduboncenter.com

A unique urban area of green just 15 minutes north of downtown Milwaukee, we are located along the shore of Lake Michigan. Escape from the world of concrete to hike seven miles of trails, walk along the beach and feel far away from thecity or view forests and wildlife from the 60-foot observation tower. Remember to bring your binoculars, you never know what you may want to take a closer look at while visiting the Center.

Margarete R. Harvey, President
Stuart D. Findlay, Treasurer

5605 School of Public & Environmental Affairs
Indiana University
1315 East Tenth Street 812-855-4848
Bloomington, IN 47405 800-765-7755
www.spea.indiana.edu

The School of Public Environmental Affairs offer environmental science summer programs to high school students and middle/high school teachers who want answers to environmental questions.

Michael McRobbie, President
Mary Anna Weber, VP

5606 Science House
909 Capability Drive 919-515-6118
Suite 1200 *Fax:* 919-515-7545
Raleigh, NC 27606 science_house@ncsu.edu
www.thesciencehouse.org

The activities of The Science House is itself a partership of facultu and stuff from science and education departments across the NC State campus, and collaborates with many other k-12 support organization in North Carolina.

5607 Seacamp Association, Inc
Newfound Harbor Marine Institute
1300 Big Pine Avenue 305-872-2331
Big Pine Key, FL 33043 877-SEA-AMP
Fax: 305-872-2555
info@seacamp.org
www.seacamp.org

To create awareness of the complex and fragile marine world and to foster critical thinking and informed decision making about man's use of natural resources. One of the few organizations in the US providing experiential education inmarine studies to students aged 8 to 21 years.

Irene Hooper, President
Betty Rein, VP

5608 Setting Up a Small Aquarium
Educational Images
PO Box 3456 607-732-1090
Westside Station 800-527-4264
Elmira, NY 14905-456 *Fax:* 607-732-1183
Details the exact procedure to be followed in setting up either a marine or freshwater aquarium successfully. Methods are scientifically sound, well documented, and up-to-date.

Charles R Belinky, Ph.D, CEO

5609 Sierra Club
2101 Webster Street 415-977-5500
Suite 1300 *Fax:* 510-208-3140
Oakland, CA 94612 information@sierraclub.org
www.sierraclub.org
Seeks to advance the preservation and protection of the natural environment by empowering the citizenry with charitable resources to further the cause of environmental protection.

Michael Brune, Executive Director
Jennifer Trahan, Chief Operating Officer

5610 Smithsonian Environmental Research Center
647 Contees Wharf Road 443-482-2200
Edgewater, MD 21037-0028 *Fax:* 443-482-2380
www.serc.si.edu
The Smithsonian Environmental Research Center advances stewardship of the biosphere through interdisciplinary research and educational outreach. SERC's scientists study a variety of interconnected ecosystems at the Center's primaryresearch site in Maryland, and at affiliated sites around the world.
Robert Gallagher, Executive Officer
Brian Magness, Director, Development

5611 Society of Environmental Toxicology and Chemistry
SETAC N America Office
229 South Baylen Street 850-469-1500
2nd Floor *Fax:* 850-469-9778
Pensacola, FL 32502 setac@setac.org
www.setac.org
The Society of Environmental Toxicology and Chemistry provides a forum for the examination of environmental issues by environmental professionals from industry, academia, government, and public-interest groups.
Patrick D. Guiney, President
Kurt J. Maier, VP

5612 Southwest Environmental Health Sciences: Community Outreach and Education Program
University Of Arizona College Of Pharmacy
Room 244 520-626-5594
Po Box 210207 *Fax:* 520-626-6944
Tucson, AZ 85721-207
The COEP goals are to review, develop, and disseminate quality environmental health science curricula. Develop and host K-12 teacher training workshops, communicate with the general public about local and common environmental healthscience concerns, share research results from SWEHSC investigators with the COEP target audiences.
Marti Lindsey, Director
Stephanie Nardei, Information Specialist

5613 Spiders in Perspective: Their Webs, Ways and Worth
Educational Images
PO Box 3456 607-732-1090
Elmira, NY 14905 800-527-4264
Fax: 607-732-1183
Comprehensive coverage of the nature of spiders, their diversity of structures, and their remarkable behavior patterns. Presents the unique world of creatures you may have ignored before, but probably never will again. Coverslocomotion, the various perceptual senses, silk production, camouflage and mimicry, webs, hunting, predation by wasps, kleptoparasitism, courtship and reproduction, population densities, impact on humans, etc. 2 parts, 76 & 78 frames. Video, slidesor filmstrip.

Charles R Belinky, Ph.D., CEO

5614 Student Conservation Association
Po Box 550 603-543-1700
689 River Road *Fax:* 603-543-1828
Charlestown, NH 00360 internships@thesca.org
www.thesca.org
America's largest and oldest provider of conservation service opportunities, outdoor education and career training for youth. SCA is building the next generation of conservation leaders and inspire lifelong stewardship of ourenvironment and communities.
Dale Penny, President/CEO
Valrie Bailey, Executive VP/Chaief of Staff

5615 The Groundwater Foundation
5561 S 48th Street 402-434-2740
Suite 215 800-858-4844
Lincoln, NE 68516 *Fax:* 402-434-2742
info@groundwater.org
www.groundwater.org
The Groundwater Foundation is a nonprofit organization that is dedicated to informing the public about one of our greatest hidden resources, groundwater. Since 1985, our programs and publications present the benefits everyone receivesfrom groundwater and the risks that threaten groundwater quality. We make learning about groundwater fun and understandable for kids and adults alike.

James Burks, Chair
Jay Beaumont, Vice Chair

5616 The Nelson Institute for Environmental Studies
UW Madison, 550 N Park Street 608-262-7996
70 Science Hall *Fax:* 608-262-2273
Madison, WI 53706-1491 nelson@mailplus.wisc.edu
www.nelson.wisc.edu
Few institutions can match the University of Wisconsin-Madison's expertise in environmental studies. Literally hundreds of professors teach and conduct research in environmentally related subjects ranging from agriculture to zoology.Their scholarship and achievement are widely recognized. In dozens of academic fields, the university is consistently rated the nation's best and most prolific.
Janet Silbernagel, Program Chairs, Conservation
Jess Gilbert, Program Chairs, Culture, His

5617 Thorne Ecological Institute
1466 N 63rd Street 303-499-3647
PO Box 19107 *Fax:* 720-565-3873
Boulder, CO 80308 info@thornenature.org
www.thornenature.org
Offers hands-on environmental education for young people along the Front Range of Colorado.
Melissa Amold, Chair
Mike Moelter, Vice Chair

5618 Trees for Tomorrow
519 Sheridan Street 715-479-6456
PO Box 609 800-838-9472
Eagle River, WI 54521 *Fax:* 715-479-2318
www.treesfortomorrow.com
Private, nonprofit natural resource education school that uses a combination of field studies and classroom presentations to teach conservation values, as well as demonstrate the benefits of modern resource management.

Maggie Bishop, Executive Director
Sheri Buller, Assistant Director

5619 Treetures Environmental Education Program
18 Channing Place treeture@aol.com
Eastchester, NY 10709 www.treetures.com
The program focuses on teaching children ages 3-10 the importance of trees to the environment, through whimsical cartoon characters known as Treetures.
Judith Hope Blau, Founder

5620 Triumvirate Environmental
200 Inner Belt Road 800-966-9282
Somerville, MA 00214 *Fax:* 617-628-8099
contactus@triumvirate.com
www.triumvirate.com
Triumvirate Environmental is a full-service environmental management firm headquartered in eastern Massachusetts. Serving the environmental and hazardous waste needs of clients throughout the northeast in the areas of biotechnology andpharmaceuticals, education, health care, metal platers and finishers, manufacturing, and utilities, Triumvirate Environmental is the industry leader in personalized service.

5621 Tropical Forest Foundation
2121 Eisenhower Avenue 703-518-8834
Suite 200 *Fax:* 703-518-8974
Alexandria, VA 22314 www.tropicalforestfoundation.org
A non-profit educational institution dedicated to the conservation of tropical forests through sustainable forestry. Its Board of Directors includes representatives from industry, government, science, academia and conservation.
Shawn Draper, Chairman
Steve Tourek, President

5622 UL Environment Greenguard Certification Program
2211 Newmarket Parkway 888-485-4733
Suite 110 *Fax:* 770-980-0072
Marietta, GA 30067 environment@ul.com
www.greenguard.org
Certification program for products that have low chemical emissions.
Henning Bloech, Executive Director

5623 Water Resources Management
550 N Park Street 608-265-5296
122 Science Hall *Fax:* 608-262-0014
Madison, WI 53706-1491 nelsongrad@mailplus.wisc.edu
www.nelson.wisc.edu
The program addresses the complex, interdisciplinary aspects of managing resources by helping students integrate the biological and phisical sciences with engineering and law and the social sciences. The workshop provides anopportunity for students to work outside of the textbook environment and tackle a rea-world problem.
Eileen Hanneman, Sr. Administrative Program S
Carol Enseki, Department Administrator

5624 Western Forestry and Conservation Association
4033 SW Canyon Road 503-226-4562
Portland, OR 97221 *Fax:* 503-226-2515
richard@westernforestry.org
westernforestry.org
Offers continuing education workshops and seminars for professional foresters. The association awards medals for distinguished service to forestry at their annual conference.
Richard Zabel, Executive Director

5625 Wilderness Education Association
2150 N 107th Street 206-367-8704
Suite 205 800-572-3015
Seattle, WA 98133 *Fax:* 206-367-8777
nationaloffice@weainfo.org
www.weainfo.org
Mike McGowan, President
Ricky Haro, VP

5626 Windows on the Wild
World Wildlife Fund
1250 24th Street Northwest 202-293-4800
Po Box 97180 800-225-5993
Washington, DC 20037 *Fax:* 202-293-9211
www.windowsonthewild.com
Provides educators with interdisciplinary curriculum materials and training programs. By using biodiversity as its organizing theme, WOW provides students with a unique window for exploring a range of topics including science,economics, social studies, language arts, geography and civics.
Jennifer A Zadwick, Program Information Coord.

5627 World Resources Institute
10 G Street, NE 202-729-7600
Suite 800 *Fax:* 202-729-7610
Washington, DC 20002 www.wri.org
WRI provides information, ideas, and solutions to global environmental problems. Our mission is to move human society to live in ways that protect the environment for current and future generations, with programs that meet globalchallenges by using knowledge to catalyze public and private action. Goals include safeguarding earth's climate from further harm, protecting the ecosystems, and reducing the use of materials and generation of wastes in the production of goods andservices.
James Gustave Speth, Founder/Trustee
James A. Harmon, Chairman

5628 Young Entomologists Society
6907 West Grand River Avenue 517-886-0630
Lansing, MI 48906 *Fax:* 517-886-0630
www.members.@aol.com/YESbugs/mainmenu.html
To provide young people with a combination of programs, publications, and educational materials that enrich their insect and spider studies through dynamic, innovative, and enjoyable learning experience.
Gary Dunn, Director Of Education

Industry Web Sites

Environmental

5629 ABS Group Training
www.abs-group.com/Training
ABS Group offers training programs that deliver information on safety, risk and compliance services. Provide advanced engineering support and certify management systems for the marine; offshore oil, gas & chemical; and power sectors.

5630 ARCAT
www.arcat.com
Online resource of free building product information, including date specification and CAD detail libraries, and a specwriting tool. Also available as an app.

5631 ASSE International Webstore
American Society of Sanitary Engineering
18927 Hickory Creek Drive
Suite 220
Mokena, IL 60448
909-472-4208
info@asse-plumbing.org
www.assewebstore.com
Product and professional standards and other publications for the plumbing industry.
Tom Palkon, Executive Director
Scott Hamilton, Senior Director

5632 Academy of Natural Sciences of Drexel University
www.ansp.org
The Academy of Natural Sciences of Drexel University is a natural history museum dedicated to advancing research, education and public engagement in biodiversity and environmental science, while aiming to promote positive human impactsthrough the communication and application of rigorous science.
George Gephart, President & CEO
Robert Peck, Curator of Art & Artifacts

5633 ActiveSet.org
www.activeset.org
ActiveSet.org allows professionals involved in all aspects of environmental air quality testing, monitoring and management to easily research and contact emissions testing firms, services and products either by state, region, or usingthe site's built-in search engine.

5634 Adirondack Council
www.adirondackcouncil.org
The Adirondack Council is a non-profit environmental group working to protect the open space resources of New York's six million acre Adirondack Park and to help sustain the natural and human communities of the region. It monitorsdevelopment on private lands and ensures the mandated constitutional protection of public lands.

5635 Advanced Buildings
www.advancedbuildings.org
A community resource pertaining to green residential and commerical construction information. The organization aims to provide insights on individual green consturction methods that improve energy efficiency, conserve natural resourcesand preserve the environment.

5636 Advanced Recovery, Inc
Advanced Recovery, based in New Jersey, concentrates on the proper disposal and recycling of all scrap, but are particularly interested in the disposal of electronic equipment, such as computer monitors containing lead.

5637 Advanced Technology Environmental Education Center
www.ateec.org
The Advanced Technology Environmental Education Center (ATEEC) aims to advance environmental technology education through curriculum development, professional development and program improvement in the nation's community colleges andhigh schools. ATEEC is funded by the National Science Foundation and is a partnership of the Hazardous Materials Training and Research Institute, the National Partnership for Environmental Technology Education and the University of Northern Iowa.

5638 African Environmental Research and Consulting Group
www.africanenviro.org
The African Environmental Research and Consulting Group (AERCG) is a non-profit organization headquartered in Kansas City with regional offices in Africa. The group, consisting of native African expatriates who are professionals in theenvironmental industry, focuses on improving the quality of life, mitigating environmental hazards and protecting human health in Africa. They are also involved in promoting sustainable development in African communities.

5639 Agency for Toxic Substances and Disease Registry
Centers for Disease Control and Prevention
4770 Buford Highway NE
Atlanta, GA 30341-3717
770-488-0706
800-232-4636
Fax: 770-488-1544
www.atsdr.cdc.gov
This agency provides leadership and direction to programs and activities designed to protect both the public and workers from exposure or adverse health effects of hazardous substances in storage sites or released in fires, explosions,or transportation accidents. The agency also collects, maintains, analyzes and disseminates information relating to serious diseases, mortality and human exposure to toxic or hazardous substances.

Patrick Breysse, Director
Christopher M Reh, Associate Director

5640 Agriculture Network Information Collaborative
www.agnic.org
AgNIC is a voluntary alliance of the National Agricultural Library, land-grant universities and other agricultural organizations in cooperation with citizen groups and government agencies. They focus on providing agriculturalinformation in electronic format via the Internet.

5641 Air Force Center for Environmental Excellence
www.usaf.com/orgs/environmental.htm
The Center for Environmental Excellence provides Air Force leaders with the comprehensive expertise they need to protect, preserve, restore, develop and sustain America's environmental and installation resources.

5642 Air and Waste Management Association
www.awma.org
Professional development organization providing a forum for the exchange of information, networking, public education, and outreach to over 5,000 environmental professionals in 65 countries.

5643 Alabama Department of Environmental Management
www.adem.state.al.us
The Alabama Department of Environmental Management (ADEM) provides environmental stewardship through the implementation of authorized environmental statutes, advocating statutory change as needed.

5644 Alaska Chilkat Bald Eagle Preserve
dnr.alaska.gov/parks/units/eagleprv.htm
The Alaska Chilkat Bald Eagle Preserve was created by the State of Alaska in June 1982 to protect and perpetuate the world's largest concentration of bald eagles and their critical habitat. It also sustains and protects the naturalsalmon runs.

5645 Alfred Wegener Institute for Polar and Marine Research
www.awi.de/en.html
The Alfred Wegener Institute conducts research in the Arctic, the Antarctic and at temperate latitudes. It coordinates Polar research in Germany and provides both the necessary equipment and the essential logistic back up for polarexpeditions.

5646 **Alliance for Environmental Technology**

The Alliance for Environmental Technology is an international association of chemical manufacturers dedicated to improving the environmental performance of the pulp and paper industry. AET was established to gather and distributeeducational and technical resources relating to Chlorine Dioxide and its use in papermaking.

5647 **American Academy of Environmental Engineers & Scientists (AAEES)**

www.aaees.org

The American Academy of Environmental Engineers & Scientists is dedicated to excellence in the practice of environmental engineering to ensure public health, safety and welfare and enable humankind to co-exist in harmony with nature.

5648 **American Chemical Society**

www.acs.org

The American Chemical Society aims to promote a positive public perception and understanding of chemistry and the chemical sciences through public outreach programs and public awareness campaigns; involve the Society's 150,000+ membersin improving the public's perception of chemistry.

5649 **American Conference of Governmental Industrial Hygienists**

www.acgih.org

ACGIH is a charitable scientific organization that aims to advance occupational and environmental health through education and the development and dissemination of scientific and technical knowledge.

5650 **American Council for an Energy-Efficient Economy (ACEEE)**

www.aceee.org

The American Council for an Energy-Efficient Economy is a non-profit organization dedicated to advancing energy efficiency as a means of promoting both economic prosperity and environmental protection.

5651 **American Eagle Foundation**

www.eagles.org

Not-for-profit organization of concerned citizens and professionals who develop and conduct bald eagle and environmental recovery programs in the United States and assist private, state and federal projects that do the same. Websitefeatures nest cams, information on eagles and raptors, and more.

5652 **American Farmland Trust**

1150 Connecticut Ave NW — 202-331-7300
Suite 600 — 800-431-1499
Washington, DC 20036 — www.farmland.org

American Farmland Trust aims to stop the loss of productive farmland, and to promote sound farming practices that lead to a healthy environment and keeps farmers on the land.

John Piotti, President
Ashley Bovino, Chief Financial Officer

5653 **American Fisheries Society: Estuaries Section**

estuaries.fisheries.org

Dedicated to to advancing conservation development, disseminating information, influence public policy, evaluating research, and supporting students and professionals involved in estuarine research and management.

5654 **American Fisheries Society: Fish Culture Section**

fishculture.fisheries.org

Represents fish culturists, as well as related fields such as nutrition, physiology, toxicology, drug development, genetics and breeding, bioengineering, economics, fish ecology, and more. Dedicated to advancing cultivation technology.

5655 **American Fisheries Society: Fish Health Section**

units.fisheries.org/fhs

Established in 1972, the section focuses on aquatic animal health problems and disseminates information to the public, including research and other educational information.

5656 **American Fisheries Society: Fisheries Management Section**

fms.fisheries.org

A section of the American Fisheries Society, Fisheries Management is composed of people dedicated to developing, applying, and evaluating effective fishery management concepts or techniques. The section sponsors workshops andsymposiums in promotion of the exchange of information among fishery professionals, students, and individuals or groups interested in fish.

5657 **American Fisheries Society: Habitat Section**

habitat.fisheries.org

Supports fish habitat programs and research.

5658 **American Fisheries Society: Introduced Fish Section**

fish.fisheries.org

Founded in 1990, the section is dedicated to aquatic organisms that are regulated by fisheries legislation, or affecting the well-being of fisheries resources.

5659 **American Fisheries Society: Water Quality Section**

waterquality.fisheries.org

Serves professionals engaged in protecting watersheds, water quality, and aquatic habitats.

5660 **American Forests**

www.americanforests.org

American Forests aims to inspire and advance the conservation of forests, which they do through protecting and restoring threatened forest ecosystems; promoting and expanding urban forests; and increasing public understanding of theimportance of forests.

5661 **American Geophysical Union**

sites.agu.org

The American Geophysical Union is dedicated to the furtherance of Earth and space sciences, and to communicating science's ability to benefit humanity. They promote cooperation among scientific organizations involved in geophysics andrelated disciplines, and initiate and participate in geophysical research programs.

5662 **American Hydrogen Association**

www.clean-air.org

The American Hydrogen Association aims to close the information gap between researchers, industries and the public concerning solar hydrogen technologies that will eliminate economic, environmental and energy hardships caused byburning fossil fuels.

5663 **American Rivers**

www.americanrivers.org

American Rivers is an organization that uses advocacy and field work to accomplish their mission of protecting and restoring the nation's rivers. They work with local river advocates, business and agricultural interests, recreationgroups, and others to accomplish their goals.

5664 **American Society for Environmental History (ASEH)**

aseh.net

Promotes historical research and education on environmental matters, as a means of better understanding human interactions with the natural world. Affiliated with the Forest History Society, which co-publishes the Environmental Historyjournal. The website provides access to a membership directory, publications, awards, education, and other resources.

5665 **American Solar Energy Society (ASES)**

www.ases.org

National organization dedicated to advancing the use of solar energy for the benefit of US citizens and the global environment. ASES promotes the widespread near-term and long-term use of solar energy.

5666 **Ames Laboratory: Environmental & Protection Sciences Program**
www.ameslab.gov/epsci/epsci-home
The Ames Laboratory's Environmental & Protection Sciences Program aims to exploit expertise and developing sciences for the benefit of problems associated with environmental characterization and monitoring.

5667 **Antarctic and Southern Ocean Coalition (ASCO)**
www.asoc.org
ASOC is a collaborative effort by conservation organizations from around the world to defend the integrity of Antarctic and Southern Ocean ecosystems from encroaching human activities. Responsible for national and inernationalcampaigns to protect the biological diversity and pristine wilderness of Antarctica, including its oceans and marine life.

5668 **Argonne National Laboratory**
9700 S Cass Avenue 630-252-2000
Lemont, IL 60439 www.anl.gov/
One of the US Department of Energy's largest research centers that develops and researches solutions in areas such as sustainable energy, environmental health, and national safety.

Tim Knewitz, Chief Financial Officer
Paul K Kearns, Laboratory Director

5669 **Arizona Geological Survey**
www.azgs.state.az.us
The Arizona Geological Survey aims to inform and advise the public about the geologic character of Arizona in order to foster understanding and prudent development of the State's land, water, mineral and energy resources.

5670 **Arkansas Natural Heritage Commission**
www.naturalheritage.org
The Arkansas Natural Heritage Commission (ANHC) is responsible for maintaining the most up-to-date and comprehensive source of information concerning the rare plant and animal species, and high-quality natural communities of Arkansas.

5671 **Asia Pacific Centre for Environmental Law**
law.nus.edu.sg/apcel
The Asia acific Centre for Environmental Law (APCEL) was established in response to the need for capacity-building in environmental legal education and the need for promotion of awareness in environmental issues. It is currentlyworking closely with the International Union for Conservation of Nature's Commission on Environmental Law.

5672 **Associated General Contractors of America (AGC)**
www.agc.org/industry-priorities/energy-environment
Advocates for and on behalf of the construction industry. Priorities include health and safety, and energy and the environment, with dedicated environmental resources available to members. Website features an Environmental Forum, aswell as resources on environmental regulations and green building.

5673 **Association of Energy Engineers (AEE)**
www.aeecenter.org
Nonprofit professional society that promotes the scientific and educational interests of those engaged in the energy industry, while fostering action for sustainable development.

5674 **Association of State Floodplain Managers (ASFPM)**
www.floods.org
ASFPM is an organization of professionals involved in floodplain management, flood hazard mitigation, the National Flood Insurance Program, and flood preparedness, warning and recovery.

5675 **Associations of University Leaders for a Sustainable Future**
ulsf.org
The mission of the Association of University Leaders for a Sustainable Future is to make sustainability a major focus of teaching, research, operations and outreach at colleges and universities worldwide. ULSF pursues this missionthrough advocacy, education, research, assessment, membership support and international partnerships to advance education for sustainability.

5676 **Atlantic Salmon Federation**
www.asf.ca
The Atlantic Salmon Federation is an international non-profit organization that promotes the conservation and wise management of wild Atlantic salmon and their habitat.

5677 **Audubon Society of Missouri**
mobirds.org
The Audubon Society of Missouri is dedicated to the preservation and protection of birds and other wildlife; to education and appreciation of the natural world; and to effective wildlife and habitat conservation practices.

5678 **Australian Ocean Data Network**
portal.aodn.org.au
The Australian Ocean Data Network provides access to all available Australian marine and climate science data and provides primary access to IMOS data, including access to IMOS metadata.

5679 **Bat Conservation International**
www.batcon.org
Bat Conservation International is dedicated to the preservation and restoration of bat populations and their habitats around the world. The website features information on the organization's work, education about bats, and programssuch as Adopt-a-Bat.

5680 **Battelle Memorial Institute**
www.battelle.org
Battelle Memorial Institute is a multidimensional organization providing research and development across a number of fields. Their Environmental Services division handles air quality & regulatory compliance; analytical chemistry;contaminated sites; ecological sampling & analysis; and sediment assessment & management. Their Environmental & Analytical Services division deals with reducing risk, increasing sustainability and mitigating environmental impacts in sensative anddeepwater environments.

5681 **Bellona Foundation**
www.bellona.org
The Bellona Foundation is an independent non-profit organization that aims to meet and fight climate challenges through identifying and implementing sustainable environmental solutions. Although they are headquarted in Norway, withoffices in Belgium and Russia, they are engaged in a broad spectrum of current national and international environmental questions that have a global impact.

5682 **Bioelectromagnetics Society**
www.bems.org
The Bioeletromagnetics Society is an independent organization of biological and physical scientists, physicians and engineers interested in the interactions of non-ionizing radiation within biological systems.

5683 **Birdingonthe.Net**
www.birdingonthe.net
Birdingonthe.net serves as a resource for birdwatchers who may be interested in joining mailing lists including comprehensive archive indexes of birds and rare bird alerts. Also provides information about birdwatching worldwide.

5684 **Blue Frontier**
Blue Frontier
PO Box 19367 202-387-8030
Washington, DC 20036 *Fax:* 202-234-5176
bluefront.org
The Blue Frontier is a nonprofit organization working towards preserving oceans and marine wildlife by providing resources to other organizations and communities. The website contains information on their projects, as well as links tobooks written by executive director David Helvarg.
David Helvarg, Executive Director
Eleanor Kewlow, Sr. Communications Advisor

5685 BlueVoice.org
bluevoice.org
BlueVoice.org is an ocean conservation organization seeking to protect dolphins, save the whales, and other marine mammals and to raise popular awareness about toxic chemicals in the oceans. The website features web films, as well asinformation about dolphins, whales, and sharks.

5686 Brookhaven National Laboratory
www.bnl.gov/world
Brookhaven National Laboratory is a multipurpose research institution funded primarily by the US Department of Energy's Office of Science. Brookhaven conducts research in physical, biomedical and environmental sciences, as well as inenergy technologies; it also builds and operates major facilities available to university, industrial and government scientists.

5687 Brown is Green
www.brown.edu/initiatives/brown-is-green/
The Brown is Green website (BIG) is the Energy & Environmental Initiatives office's primary communication medium to report progress on Brown University's sustainability programs and related goals. It is not, however,a reliable sourceof information for students, faculty and staff working on campus environmental programs.

5688 Bureau of International Recycling
www.bir.org
The Bureau of International Recycling (BIR) is an international trade federation representing the world's recycling industry, specifically focusing on ferrous and non-ferrous metals, paper and textiles. Plastics, rubber, tires andglass are also studied and traded by some BIR members.

5689 Bureau of Transportation Statistics
www.bts.gov
The Bureau of Transportation Statistics focuses on data collection, analysis and reporting and aims to ensure the most cost-effective use of transportation-monitoring resources. They strive to increase public awareness of the nation'stransportation system and its implications.

5690 California Conservation Corps
www.ccc.ca.gov
The California Conservation Corps is a state agency that puts young people and the environment together to help improve California's natural resources; they also assist with emergency responses, including fighting fires, floods,earthquakes and pest infestations.

5691 California Energy Commission
www.energy.ca.gov
The California Energy Commission is the state's primary energy policy and planning agency. It was created by the Legislature in 1974 and located in Sacramento.

5692 California Environmental Protection Agency
1001 I Street 916-323-2514
P.O. Box 2815 calepa.ca.gov
Sacramento, CA 95812-2815
The CalEPA's goals are to protect the environment, public health, and economic vitality. They accomplish these goals by implementing regulatory laws that focus on air, water, and soil quality as well as pesticide use and wastereduction.

Jared Blumenfeld, Secretary
Serena McIlwain, Undersecretary

5693 California League of Conservation Voters
www.ecovote.org
The California League of Conservation Voters mobilizes California voters to support environmentally responsible candidates and issues and serves as a watchdog to hold elected officials accountable for their environmental votes.

5694 California Resources Agency
resources.ca.gov
The California Resources Agency is responsible for the conservation, enhancement and management of California's natural and cultural resources, including land, water, wildlife, parks, minerals and historic sites. The CaliforniaEnvironmental Resources Evaluation System is an initative within the agency.

5695 California/Nevada Amphibian Populations Task Force
www.canvamphibs.com
The California/Nevada Working Group seeks to understand and reverse amphibian population declines in California and Nevada, and to provide for the continued existance of both declining and non-declining species.

5696 Canadian Chlorine Chemistry Council
www.cfour.org
The Canadian Chlorine Chemistry Council aims to facilitate dialogue and promote coordinated action in Canada among key stakeholders in order to bring about a balanced view of chlorine chemistry to enable society to make informed,science based decisions on issues involving chlorine.

5697 Canadian Council of Ministers of the Environment
www.ccme.ca
The Canadian Coucil of Ministers of the Environment (CCME) works to promote cooperation on and coordination of interjurisdictional issues such as waste management, air pollution and toxic chemicals. CCME members proposenationally-consistent environmental standards and objectives to help achieve a high level of environmental quality across the country.

5698 Canadian Environmental Assessment Agency
www.ceaa.gc.ca
The Canadian Environmenal Assessment Agency provides Canadians with high quality environmental assessments that contribute to informed decision-making in support of sustainable development.

5699 Canadian Institute for Environmental Law and Policy
www.cielap.org
The Canadian Institute for Environmental Law and Policy (CIELAP) provides leadership in the research and development of environmental law and policy that promotes public interest and principles of sustainability.

5700 Carnegie Mellon University: Department of Civil & Environmental Engineering
www.cmu.edu/cee
Carnegie Mellon's Department of Civil and Environmental Engineering is a part of the engineering college, Carnegie Institute of Technology. The department maintains a commitment to excellence and innovation in education and research.

5701 Center for Environmental Biotechnology
www.ceb.utk.edu
The Center for Environmental Biotechnology at the University of Tennessee, Knoxville was established to foster a multidisciplinary approach for training the next generation of environmental scientists and solving environmental problems through biotechnology.

5702 Center for Environmental Design Research
www.cedr.berkeley.edu
The Center for Environmental Design Research is an Organized Research Unit of the University of California at Berkeley. The Center encourages research in environmental planning and design, in order to increase the factual content ofdesign decisions and to promote systematic approaches to design decision making.

5703 Center for Environmental Philosophy
www.cep.unt.edu
The Center for Environmental Philosophy, a non-profit organization affiliated with the University of North Texas, is responsible for the publication of the Environmental Ethics journal, as well as the training and promotion of researchin environmental ethics through workshops and conferences. The website maintains its original look from 1995.

5704 **Center for Environmental and Regulatory Information Systems**

ceris.purdue.edu/ceris

The Center for Environmental and Regulatory Information Systems (CERIS) is a center within the Entomology Department at Purdue University and is home to a collection of databases concerning pesticides, plant export/import requirementsand exotic pest tracking. Some of the databases include the National Pesticide Information Retrieval System (NPIRS), the National Agricultural Pest Information System (NAPIS) and the National Plant Diagnostic Network (NPDN).

5705 **Center for Health Effects of Environmental Contamination**

www.cheec.uiowa.edu

The University of Iowa's Center for Health Effects of Environmental Contamination supports and conducts research to identify, measure and prevent adverse health outcomes related to exposure to environmental toxins. CHEEC organizes andparticipates in educational and outreach programs; provides environmental health expertise to local, state and federal entities and serves as a resource to Iowans in the field of environmental health.

5706 **Center for International Earth Science Information Network**

www.ciesin.org

The Center for International Earth Science Informatio nNetwork (CIESIN) works at the intersection of the social, natural and information services, specializing in online data and information management; spatial data integration andtraining and interdisciplinary research related to human interactions in the environment.

5707 **Center for International Environmental Law**

www.ciel.org

The Center for International Environmental Law is a public interest non-profit environmental law firm founded in 1989 to strengthen international and comparative environmental law and policy around the world. CIEL provides a full rangeof environmental legal services in both international and comparative national law.

5708 **Center for Plant Conservation**

www.saveplants.org

The Center for Plant Conservation is dedicated solely to preventing the extinction of native US plant species. The CPC is a network of more than 50 leading botanic institutions that are involved in plant conservation, research andeducation.

5709 **Center for Renewable Energy and Sustainable Technology**

thecrestproject.com

The Center for Renewable Energy and Sustainable Technology (CREST) aims to accelerate the use of renewable energy by providing credible information, insightful analysis and innovative strategies amid changing energy markets andmounting environmental needs. The combined CREST organization boasts a strong platform for research, publication and dissemination of timely information regarding sustainable energy.

5710 **Center for Wildlife Information**

www.centerforwildlifeinformation.org

A resource that provides information on ways to interact and enjoy wildlife safely and responsibly. The objective is to reduce conflcits between humans and wildlife, in particular with bears, alligators and cougars. The websitefeatures tips, wildlife information, and access to educational kits.

5711 **Center for the Study of Carbon Dioxide and Global Change**

www.co2science.org

Also known as CO2 Science, the Center reviews articles, books and other educational materials, attempting to separate reality from rhetoric in the debate that surrounding the subject of carbon dioxide and global change. The Centermaintains on-line intructions on how to conduct CO2 enrichment and depletion experiments in its Global Change Laboratory.

5712 **Centers for Disease Control and Prevention**

1600 Clifton Road 800-232-4636
Atlanta, GA www.cdc.gov

To promote health and quality of life by preventing and controlling disease, injury and disability. The CDC seeks to accomplish its mission by working with partners throughout the nation and world to monitor health; detect andinvestigate health problems; conduct research to enhance prevention; develop and advocate sound public health policies; implement prevention strategies; promote healthy behaviors; foster safe and healthful environments and provide leadership andtraining.

Brenda Fitzgerald, Director
Anne Schuchat, Deputy Director

5713 **Central European Environmental Data Request Facility**

www.cedar.at/sitemap.htm

The Cebntral European Environmental Data Request Facility (CEDAR) was created to provide computing and Internetworking facilities to support international data exchange with the Central and Eastern European environmental community.Focusing at first on mainly Central and Eastern European countries, CEDAR's activities expanded quickly to an audience all over the world.

5714 **Centre for Environmental Data Analysis**

www.ceda.ac.uk

The Centre for Environmental Data Analysis serves the environmental sciences community through four data centres, data anaylsis environments and participation in a host of relevant research projects.

5715 **Cetacean Society International**

csiwhalesalive.org

All-volunteer, nonprofit conservation, educational and research organization to benefit whales, dolphins, porpoises and the marine environment. Promotes education and conservation programs, including whale and dolphin watching, andnoninvasive, benign research. Website gives access to a newsletter archive, and a whale adoption program.

5716 **Charles Darwin Foundation**

www.darwinfoundation.org/en

The Charles Darwin Foundation conducts scientific research and provides environmental education about conservation and natural resource management in the Galapagos archipelago and its surrounding Marine Reserve.

5717 **Chicago Wilderness**

www.chicagowilderness.org

Chicago Wilderness is a regional organization that aims to preserve, improve and expand nature and quality of life in parts of Illinois, Indiana, Wisconsin and Michigan. The alliance covers projects that tackle invasive speciesremoval, land regeneration, childhood education and volunteer initiatives.

5718 **China Council for International Cooperation on Environment and Development**

www.cciced.net/cciceden

The main goals of the China Council for International Cooperation on Environment & Development include exchanging and disseminating international successful experience; studying key environment and development issues of China;providing forward-looking, strategic and early warning policies; facilitating the implementation of sustainable development strategies and the development of a resource-saving and environment-friendly society in China.

5719 **Chlorine Chemistry Council**

c3.org

The Chlorine Chemistry Council, a business council of the American Chemistry Council, represents the manufacturers and users of chlorine and chlorine-related products. Chlorine is widely used as a disease-fighting disinfection agent,as a basic component in pharmaceuticals and a myriad other products that are essential to modern life.

5720 **City Farmer News**
www.cityfarmer.info
City Farmer News is a non-profit society that promotes urban food production and environmental conservation by teaching people how to grow food in the city, compost their waste and take care of their home landscape in anenvironmentally responsible way.

5721 **Climate Institute**
climate.org
The Climate Institute seeks to implement innovative and practical solutions to climate change by supporting and collaborating with private, nonprofit and government organizations. Its website hosts a number of essays and ongoingpublications.

5722 **Coastal Conservation Association**
www.joincca.org
The Coastal Conservation Association conserves, promotes and enhances the present and future available resources for the benefit of the general public.

5723 **Colorado Department of Natural Resources**
cdnr.us
The Colorado Department of Natural Resources was created to develop, protect and enhance Colorado's natural resources for the use and enjoyment of the state's present and future residents, as well as for visitors to the state.

5724 **Colorado School of Mines**
www.mines.edu
The Colorado School of Mines is a public research university devoted to engineering and applied sciences with a curriculum and research program geared towards responsible stewardship of the earth and its resources.

5725 **Commission for Environmental Cooperation**
www.cec.org
The Commission for Environmental Cooperation (CEC) is an international organization created by Canada, Mexico and the US under the North American Agreement on Environmental Cooperation. The CEC was established to address regionalenvironmental concerns, help prevent potential trade and environmental conflicts and to promote the effective enforcement of environmental law.

5726 **Connecticut Department of Energy and Environmental Protection**
www.ct.gov/deep/site/default.asp
Connecticut's Department of Energy and Environmental Protection aims to conserve, improve and protect the natural resources and environment of the State of Connecticut while preserving the natural environment and the life forms itsupports in a delicate, interrelated and complex balance, to the end that the state may fulfill its responsibility as trustee of the environment for present and future generations.

5727 **Conservation International**
www.conservation.org
CI promotes sustainable development and the conservation of earth's ecosystems as keys to solving climate change.

5728 **Consortium on Green Design and Manufacturing**
cgdm.berkeley.edu
The Consortium on Green Design and Manfacturing is an interdisciplinary research initiative at the University of California, Berkeley. The CGDM is an industry/government/university partnership that develops linkages betweenmanufacturing and design and their environmental effects while integrating engineering information, management practices and government policy-making.

5729 **Consultative Group on International Agricultural Research**
www.cgiar.org
The Consultative Group on International Agricultural Research aims to contribute to food security and poverty eradication in developing countries through research, partnerships, capacity building and policy support. CGIAR promotessustainable agricultural development based on the environmentally sound management of natural resources.

5730 **Contaminated Site Clean-Up Information**
www.clu-in.org
CLU-IN, a US Environmental Protection Agency forum, provides information about innovative treatment and site characterization technologies while acting as a forum for all waste remediation stakeholders.

5731 **Coral Health and Monitoring Program**
www.coral.noaa.gov
The goal of the Coral Health and Monitoring Program is to provide services to help improve and sustain coral reef health throughout the world.

5732 **Coral Reef Alliance**
coral.org
The Coral Reef Alliance is a member supported, non-profit organization dedicated to keeping coral reefs alive around the world. The Alliance works with marine park managers, businesses and communities to help increase their capacity toprotect their local coral reefs.

5733 **Council for Agricultural Science & Technology**
www.cast-science.org
The Council for Agricultural Science & Technology is a non-profit organization composed of scientific societies and many individual, student, company, nonprofit and associate society members. CAST assembles, interprets and communicatesscience based information regionally, nationally and internationally on food, fiber, agricultural, natural resources and related environmental issues to stakeholders.

5734 **Council on Environmental Quality**
730 Jackson Place NW 202-395-5750
Washington, DC 20503 www.whitehouse.gov/ceq/
The Council on Environmental Quality coordinates federal environmental efforts and works closely with agencies and other White House offices in the development of environmental policies and initiatives.
Mary B Neumayr, Chair

5735 **Coweeta Long Term Ecological Research**
coweeta.uga.edu
The Coweeta LTER Program was developed to support research of ecological phenomena that occur on time scales of decades or centuries.

5736 **CropLife Canada**
croplife.ca
CropLife Canada aims to support sustainable agriculture in Canada, in cooperation with others, by building trust and appreciation for plant life science technologies.

5737 **David R. Atkinson Center for a Sustainable Future**
www.atkinson.cornell.edu
Cornell University's David R. Atkinson Center for a Sustainable Future is committed to research, teaching and outreach focused on environmental issues, with the goals of enhancing the quality of life, encouraging economic vitality andpromoting the conservation of natural resources for sustainable future.

5738 **Defenders of Wildlife**
www.defenders.org
Defenders of Wildlife is dedicated to the protection of all native wild animals and plants and their natural communities. Their focus is placed on the accelerating rate of extinction of species and the associated loss of biologicaldiversity, and habitat alteration and destruction.

5739 **Delaware Department of Natural Resources and Environmental Control**
dnrec.alpha.delaware.gov
Delaware's Department of Natural Resources and Environmental Control aims to protect and manage the state's vital natural resources, protect public health and safety, provide quality outdoor recreation and to serve and educate thecitizens of the state about

the wise use, conservation and enhancement of Delaware's environment.

5740 **Department of Commerce: National Oceanic & Atmospheric Administration**
1401 Constitution Avenue NW www.noaa.gov
Room 5128
Washington, DC 20230
The mission of the NOAA is to understand changes in climate, weather, oceans and coasts; to share that knowledge and information with the public; and to foster the conservation and management of coastal and marine ecosystems. Theagency studies the structure and behaviour of the ocean, atmosphere, and related ecosystems.

Neil Jacobs, Assistant Secretary
Craig McLean, Chief Scientist

5741 **Department of the Interior**
1849 C Street NW 202-208-3100
Washington, DC 20240 feedback@ios.doi.gov
www.doi.gov
The Department of the Interior protects and manages the Nation's natural resources and cultural heritage, honoring its trust responsibilities to American Indians, Alaska Natives, and affiliated island communities. It also providesinformation about natural resources and hazards.

David Bernhardt, Secretary
Susan Combs, Assistant Secretary

5742 **Ducks Unlimited (DU)**
www.ducks.org
The mission is to fulfill the annual life cycle needs of North American waterfowl by protecting, enhancing, restoring and managing important wetlands and associated uplands. The website features conservation information, a web store,hunting tips, and media such as quizzes, films, and other video content.

5743 **EAWAG Biocatalysis/Biodegradation Database**
eawag-bbd.ethz.ch
This database contains information on microbial biocatalytic reations and biodegradation pathways for primarily xenobiotic, chemical compounds. The goal of the EAWAG-BBD is to provide information on microbial enzyme catalyzed reactionsthat are important for biotechnology.

5744 **ECOLOGIA**
www.ecologia.org
ECOLOGIA, or ECOlogists Linked for Organizing Grassroots Initiatives and Action, is a private non-profit organization providing information, training and technical support for grassroots environmental groups. ECOLOGIA offers technicaland humanitarian assistance to individuals and organizations working to solve ecological problems at the local, regional, national and global levels.

5745 **Earth Day Network**
www.earthday.org
Earth Day Network is a non-profit coordinating body of worldwide Earth Day activities that aims to promote environmental awareness by providing educational materials and publications and by organizing events, activities and annualcampaigns. The network includes more than 5,000 organizations in 184 countries.

5746 **Earth First!**
earthfirstjournal.org
Earth First! was first created in response to a compromising and increasingly corporate environmental community. Earth First! publish Earth First! Journal. Earth First! Journal highlights radical environmental movements and causes.Earth First! pride themselves on being a grassroots organization fighting to saves lives and the evironment, including tactics such as civil disobedience and monkeywrenching. The website features activist guides both for purchase and for free.

5747 **Earth Resources Laboratory at MIT**
erlweb.mit.edu
MIT's Earth Resources Laboratory, brings together faculty, staff and students dedicated to research in applied geophysics that will further understanding of the Earth, its resources and the environment.

5748 **EarthVote**
www.earthvote.org
EarthVote is the purveyor of the idea of Common Planet, a plan to end global poverty, homelessness, Masters, war & nuclear Weapons.

5749 **EarthWatch Institute**
earthwatch.org
The EarthWatch Institute aims to engage people worldwide in scientific field research and education to promote the understanding and action necesary for a sustainable environment.

5750 **Earthworks**
earthworks.org
Earthworks carries out research and publishes reports on the environmental impacts of mining, as well as promoting sustainable solutions.

5751 **EcoInternet**
ecointernet.org
EcoInternet provides people, families and businesses with tools, services and information pertaining to green living and the environmental sustainability movement.

5752 **Ecology Action Centre**
ecologyaction.ca
The Ecology Action Centre has been working at the local, regional, national and more recently, international level to build a healthier and more sustainable world while working closely with communities, social and natural scientists.

5753 **Edison Electric Institute**
www.eei.org
The Edison Electric Institute is the association that represents all US investor-owned electric companies; providing electricity for over 220 million Americans.

5754 **Edwards Aquifer Research and Data Center**
www.eardc.txstate.edu
The Edwards Aquifer Research and Data Center was established in 1979 by the Southwest Texas State University to provide a public service in the study, understanding and use of the Edwards Aquifer System.

5755 **Electric Power Research Institute**
www.epri.com
The Electric Power Research Institute (EPRI) is a non-profit organization committed to providing science and technology-based energy solutions of indispensable value to global energy customers.

5756 **Elsevier**
www.elsevier.com
Elsevier provides information and analytics that help institutions and professionals progress science, advance healthcare and improve performance.

5757 **Endangered Species Recovery Program**
esrp.csustan.edu
California State University, Stanislaus' Endangered Species Recovery Program aims to facilitate endangered species recovery and resolve conservation conflicts through scientifically based recovery planning and implementation.

5758 **Energy & Environmental Research Center**
www.eerc.und.nodak.edu
The Energy & Environmental Research Center (EERC) is dedicated to moving promising technologies out of the laboratory and into the marketplace to produce energy cleanly and efficiently, minimizing enviromental impacts and conservingprecious natural resources.

5759 **Energy Technology Data Exchange**
www.etde.org
The Energy Technology Data Exchange (ETDE) was a multilateral energy information exchange initiative under the International Energy Agency from 1987-2014. ETDE's World Energy Base's content remains freely available online.

5760 **EnergyHog.org**
energyhog.org
Dual websites for adults and kids, with tips on how to improve energy efficiency at home. Created by the Alliance to Save Energy.

5761 **EnergyIdeas Clearinghouse**
www.energyideas.org/products.aspx
EnergyIdeas Clearinghouse is a database comprised of a series of publications that addressed the energy saving claims of products and technologies of interest to electric utility staff in the Pacific Northwest. Although the WSUExtension Energy Program, from which these publications resulted, became inactive in 2008, the publications are still accesible online.

5762 **Enviro-access: GHG Experts**
www.enviroaccess.ca
Enviro-access is an investor in the development of environmental technologies by supplying companies in the environemtal sector with the professional services required during the various steps of bringing their products and services tothe marketplace.

5763 **Enviro.BLR.com**
enviro.blr.com
The environment division of Buisness & Legal Resources aims to provide the public with the most comprehensive state and federal environmental compliance information available.

5764 **EnviroCitizen.org**
www.envirocitizen.org
EnviroCitizen.org encourages college students to be environmental citizens and is dedicated to educating, training and organizing a diverse national network of young leaders to protect the environment.

5765 **EnviroLink**
www.envirolink.org
EnviroLink is an online community that is dedicated to providing comprehensive, up-to-date environmental information and news.

5766 **EnviroOne**
www.enviroone.org
EnviroOne is a non-profit company that promotes sustainable environmental and agricultural activities in the US and around the world.

5767 **Environmental Alliance for Senior Involvement**
www.easi.org
The Environmental Alliance for Senior Involvement aims to build, promote and utilize the environmental ethic, expertise and commitment of older persons to expand citizen involvement in protecting and caring for the environment forpresent and future generations.

5768 **Environmental Assessment Association**
www.eaa-assoc.org
The Environmental Assessment Association is an international organization dedicated to providing members with information and education in the environmental industry in respect to environmental inspections and testing.

5769 **Environmental Contaminants Encyclopedia**
www.nature.nps.gov/hazardssafety/toxic/index.cfm
The Environmental Contaminants Encyclopedia summarizes information about 118 environmental contaminants and serves as a quick reference for determining whether or not concentrations of potential contaminants are above levels that mightaffect living things. Important to note: last update was in 1998.

5770 **Environmental Defense Fund**
www.edf.org
Environmental Defense Fund is dedicated to protecting the environmental rights of all people, including future generations. Among these rights are clean and water, healthy, nourishing food and flourishing ecosystem.

5771 **Environmental News Network**
www.enn.com
The Environmental News Network works to inform, educate, enable and create a platform for global environmental action. Aims to be provide a collection of resources, teachers, experts and tools to provide onjective information andknowledge about the increasingly complex field of environmental science.

5772 **Environmental Protection**
www.eponline.com
Environmental Protection provides online content pertaining to pollution and waste treatment solutions for environmental professionals.

5773 **Environmental Protection Agency (EPA)**
1200 Pennsylvania Ave NW 202-564-4700
Washington, DC 20460 www.epa.gov
EPA's mission is to protect human health and to safeguard the natural environment - air, water and land - upon which life depends. This agency also ensures that communities, individuals, businesses, and governments have access toaccurate information about human health and environmental risks.

Andrew Wheeler, Administrator
Ryan Jackson, Chief of Staff

5774 **Environmental Protection Agency: Environmental Compliance Assistance Centers**
Environmental Protection Agency
1200 Pennsylvania Avenue NW 202-564-2395
Mail Code 2227A www.epa.gov/compliance
Washington, DC 20460
In partnership with state governments, tribal governments and other federal agencies, the EPA's Compliance Centers aim to assure compliance with the nation's environmental laws to help protect public health and the environment.
Tracy Back, Contact

5775 **Environmental Protection Agency: National Estuary Program**
Environmental Protection Agency
1200 Pennsylvania Avenue NW www.epa.gov/nep
Mail Code 4204M
Washington 20460
The National Estuary Program (NEP) was established to identify, restore, and protect nationally significant estuaries of the United States. NEP targets a broad range of issues and engages local communities in the process. The programfocuses not just on improving water quality in estuaries, but on maintaining the integrity of entire systems, including chemical, physical and biological properties, as well as economic, recreational and aesthetic values.

5776 **Environmental Resource Center**
www.ercweb.com/home
Environmental Resource Center is a full-service environmental consulting firm that has been serving the needs of industry, academia and federal and state government agencies with the goal of helping its clients effectively comply withenvironmental, safety and health regulations.

5777 **Environmental Resources Management**
www.erm.com
Provides environmental, health, safety, risk, and social consulting services, including sustainability planning, health and safety, risk assessment, data management, asset management, and environmental compliance.

5778 **Environmental Simulations, Inc.**
www.groundwatermodels.com
Environmental Simulations, Inc. (ESI) specializes in software, consulting and training for groundwater modeling.

5779 **Environmental Treaties and Resource Indicators**
sedac.ciesin.columbia.edu/entri/
Environmental Treaties and Resource Indicators (ENTRI), a database of searchable treaties and resource indicators, is provided by the Center for International Earth Science Information Network of the Earth Institute of ColumbiaUniversity.

5780 **Environmental Working Group**
www.ewg.org
The Environmental Working Group is a leading content provider for public interest groups and concerned citizens who are campaigning to protect the environment.

5781 **European Centre for Nature Conservation**
The European Centre for Nature Conservation (ECNC) is an independent European expertise centre for biodiversity and sustainable development that promotes an integrated approach that actively stimulates the internation between science,society and policy.

5782 **European Forest Institute**
www.efi.int
The European Forest Institute (EFI) aims to promote, conduct and co-operate in research of forests, forestry and forest products at the pan-European level; and to make the results of the research known to all interested parties,notably in the areas of policy formulation and implementation, in order to promote the conservation and sustainable management of forests in Europe.

5783 **Everglades Digital Library**
everglades.fiu.edu
The Everglades Information Network & Digital Library at Florida International University Libraries is a program of library and information services in support of research, restoration, and resource management of the south Floridaenvironment. The EIN serves researchers, resource managers, educators, students, researchers, decision makers, and concerned citizens both within south Florida and around the world.

5784 **Federal Emergency Management Agency**
www.fema.gov
The Federal Emergency Management Agency (FEMA) supports citizens and first responders to ensure that the nation works together to build, sustain and improve capabilities to prepare for, protect against, respond to, recover from andmitigate all hazards.

5785 **Federal Geographic Data Committee**
www.fgdc.gov
The Federal Geographic Data Committee is an interagency committee composed of representatives from the Executive Office of the President, Cabinet-level and independent agencies. The FGDC is developing the National Spatial DataInfrasturcture (NSDI) in cooperation with organizations from state, local and tribal governments, the academic community and the private sector.

5786 **Florida Center for Environmental Studies**
www.ces.fau.edu
The Florida Center for Environmental Studies at Florida Atlantic University is dedicated to advancing Florida's sustainability by promoting collaborative research, education and community engagaement activities.

5787 **Florida Department of Environmental Protection**
www.dep.state.fl.us
The Florida Department of Environmental Protection promotes the idea of: More Protection, Less Process, which is accomplishes by providing stewardship of Florida's ecosystems so that the state's unique quality of life may be preservedfor present and future generations.

5788 **Florida Wildlife Extension**
www.wec.ufl.edu/extension
The Florida Wildlife Extenstion serves, advises and develops educational programs for Florida citizens in conjunction with county extension agents and other state, county and local organizations interested in wildlife issues.

5789 **Forest History Society**
www.foresthistory.org
The Forest History Society is a non-profit educational institution that links the past to the future by identifying, collecting, preserving, interpreting, and disseminating information on the history of people, forests, and theirrelated resources. The website features access to a database, library and archives, educational material, and a range of publications.

5790 **Forest Service Employees for Environmental Ethics**
www.fseee.org
Forest Service Employess for Environmental Ethics is a non-profit organization whose goal is to forge a socially responsible value system for the Forest Service based on a land ethic that ensures ecologically and economicallysustainable resource management.

5791 **Fresh Energy**
fresh-energy.org
Fresh Energy is working to shape and drive realistic, visionary energy policies by promoting energy efficiency and the sound use of renewable energy resources. Through program research, public education and intervention in the decisionmaking process, Fresh Energy seeks to develop and build a consensus for energy vision that will ensure the well being of future generations.

5792 **Friends of the Earth International**
www.foei.org
Friends of the Earth International is a worldwide federation of national environmental organizations that aims to protect the earth against futher deterioration and repair damage inflicted upon the environment by human activities andnegligence; preserve the earth's ecological, cultural and ethic diversity.

5793 **GLOBE Program**
www.globe.gov
GLOBE, or Global Learning and Observations to Benefit the Environment, is an international science and education program that provides students and the public with the opportunity to participate in data collection and contributemeaningfully to the understanding of the Earth system and global environment.

5794 **GRID-Arendal**
www.grida.no
GRID-Arendal provides environmental information, communications and capacity buildings services for information management and assessment. Established to strengthen the United Nations through its Environmental Program, its focus is tomake credible, science-based knowledge understandable to the public and to decision makeing personnel for sustainable development.

5795 **GeoHydrodynamics and Environment Research**
modb.oce.ulg.ac.be
GeoHydrodynamics and Environment Research (GHER) is a research group based out of the University of LiŠge (Belgium) devoted to marine and environmental study and modelling in sites such as the North Sea, the Black Sea, the Aral Sea,the South China Sea, the Bering Sea, the PeErsian Gulf and the Mediterranean Sea.

5796 **Georgia Department of Natural Resources**
www.gadnr.org
The Georgia Department of Natural Resources aims to sustain, enhance, protect and conserve Georgia's natural, historic and cultural resources for present and future generations, while recognizing the importance of promoting thedevelopment of commerce and industry that utilize sound environmental practices.

5797 **Geotechnical & Geoenvironmental Software Directory**
www.ggsd.com
The Geotechnical & Geoenvironmental Software Directory (GGSD) catalogues over 1750 programs in the fields of Geotechnical Engineering, Soil Mechanics, Rock Mechanics, Engineering Geology, Foundation Engineering, Hydogeology,Geoenvironmental Engineering, Environmental Engineering, Data Alaysis and Data Visualization.

5798 Global Change Master Directory
gcmd.gsfc.nasa.gov
The Global Change Master Directory (GCMD) aims to assist the scientific community in the discovery of and linkage to Earth science data, as well as to provide data holders a means to advertise their data to the Earth Science Community.

5799 Global Ecovillage Network
ecovillage.org
The Global Ecovillage Network (GEN) builds bridges between policy-makers, governments, NGOs, academics, entrepreneurs, activists, community networks and ecologically-minded individuals across the globe in order to develop strategiesfor a global transition to sustainable communities and cultures.

5800 Global Energy and Water Cycle Exchanges
www.gewex.org
The Global Energy and Water Cycle Exhcnages (GEWEX) Project is dedicated to understanding Earth's water cycle and energy fluxes at the surface and in the atmosphere.

5801 Global Network on Environmental Science and Technology
www.gnest.org
The Global Network on Environmental Science and Technology (NEST) constitutes an international association of scientists, technologists, engineers and other interested groups involved in all scientific and technological aspects of theenvironment as well as in application techniques aimed at the development of sustainable solutions.

5802 Great Lakes Fishery Commission
www.glfc.org
The Great Lakes Fishery Commission facilitates successful cross-border cooperation that ensures Canada and the United States work together to improve and perpetuate the Greak Lakes fishery.

5803 Great Lakes Information Network
The Great Lakes Information Network (GLIN) is a partnership that provides information relating to the binational Great Lakes-St. Lawrence region of North America. GLIN offers a wealth of data and information about the region'senvironment, economy, tourism, education and more.

5804 Green Mountain Institute for Environmental Democracy
www.gmied.org
The Green Mountain Institute for Environmental Democracy (GMI) works to reinvigorate the essential connections among the public, government and information necessary for effective improvements in environmental quality and the long-termvitality of communities and regions.

5805 Green Seal
www.greenseal.org
An independent nonprofit organization dedicated to safeguarding the environment and transforming the marketplace by promoting the manufacture, purchase, and use of environmentally responsible products and services.

5806 Greenbelt Alliance
www.greenbelt.org
The Greenbelt Alliance's goal is to make the San Francisco Bay Area a better place to live by protecting the region's greenbelts and improving the livability of its cities and towns. They work in partnership with diverse coalitions onpublic policy development, advocacy and education.

5807 Greenpeace USA
www.greenpeace.org
Greenpeace is an independent, international organization dedicated to using peaceful protest and communication to draw attention to environmental issues, and to promote solutions. The website features stories, news, and research.

5808 Groundwater Remediation Technologies Analysis Center
www.gwrtac.org
The Groundwater Remediation Technologies Analysis Center (GWRTAC) compiles, analyzes and disseminates information on innovative groundwater remediation technologies. GWRTAC prepares reports by technical teams selectively chosen fromConcurrent Technologies Corporation, the University of Pittsburgh and other supporting institutions, while also maintaining an active outreach program.

5809 Harbor Branch Oceanographic Institute
The Harbor Branch Oceanographic Institute of Florida Atlantic University is dedicated to exploring the world's oceans and integrating the science and technology of the sea with the needs of humankind.

5810 Harvard Forest
harvardforest.fas.harvard.edu
Harvard Forest is a department of the Faculty of Arts and Sciences of Harvard University where scientists, students and collaborators explore topics ranging from conservation and environmental change to land-use history and the ways inwhich physical, biological and human systems interact to impact the earth.

5811 Hawaii Biological Survey
hbs.bishopmuseum.org
The Hawaii Biological Survey is an ongoing natural history inventory of the Hawaiian archipelago created to locate, identify and evaluate all native and non-native species of flora and fauna within the state, and maintain the referencecollections of that flora and fauna for a wide range of uses.

5812 Hawaiian Ecosystems at Risk Project
www.hear.org
The mission of the Hawaiian Ecosystem at Risk (HEAR) Project is to promote technology, methods and information to decision-makers, resource managers and the general public to aid in the fight against harmful alien species in Hawaii andthe Pacific Basin.

5813 HawkWatch International
hawkwatch.org
HawkWatch International is a non-profit organization that works to protect raptors and their environment through scientific research and public education.

5814 Hazardous Substance Research Centers
The Hazardous Substance Research Center is a national organization that carries out an active program of basic and applied research, technology transfer and training. Their activities are conducted regionally by five multi-universitycenters, which focus on different aspects of hazardous substance management.

5815 Headwaters Science Center
www.hscbemidji.org
The Headwaters Science Center is dedicated to science education and environmental awareness. It features hands-on exhibits, a live animal collection, special events and science-related programs and demonstrations.

5816 Heartwood
heartwood.org
Heartwood is a regional network that protects forests and supports community activism in the eastern United States through education, advocacy and citizen empowerment.

5817 Horned Lizard Conservation Society
www.hornedlizards.org
The Horned Lizard Conservation Society (HLCS) is a non-profit organization devoted to protecting horned lizards throughout North America.

5818 Illinois Recycling Association
www.illinoisrecycles.org

The Illinois Recycling Association's mission is to encourage the responsible use of resources by promoting waste reduction, re-use and recycling.

5819 **Indiana Department of Natural Resources**
www.in.gov/dnr
The Indianan Department of Natural Resources aims to protect, enhance, preserve and wisely use natural, cultural and recreational resources for the benefit of Indiana's citizens through professional leadership, management andeducation.

5820 **Inform, Inc.**
www.informinc.org
Seeks to educate the public about the environmental effects of consumer products.

5821 **Information Center for the Environment**
ice.ucdavis.edu
The Information Center for the Environment (ICE) at the University of California, Davis aims to participate actively in all activities and efforts of protection, preservation and exploitation of mangrove ecosystems.

5822 **Inland Seas Education Association**
schoolship.org
The Inland Seas Education Association is a non-profit organization whose that provides a 'floating classroom' where people of all ages can gain first-hand training and experience in the Great Lakes ecosystem. The knowledge gainedthrough these experiences provides the leadership, understanding and commitment needed for the long-term stewardship of the Great Lakes.

5823 **Institute for Earth Education (IEE)**
www.ieetree.org/iee
The IEE develops and disseminates instructional programs aimed at helping people live more lightly, harmoniously, and joyously with the natural world, through three pillars: interpretation, education, and contemplation. The websitefeatures a history of the Institute, plus an archive of their Talking Leaves journal.

5824 **Institute for Energy and Environmental Research (IEER)**
www.ieer.org
IEER's aim is to provide scientific information about environmental issues in an easy to understand format for use by activists, policy-makers, journalists and the public. The educational material covers emissions-free energy systems,energy equity, energy democracy, nuclear weapons security and more. Website features resources for classrooms, plus fact sheets, newsletters, audio/video content, and an archive, among other information.

5825 **Institute for the Study of Society and Environment**

The Institute for the Study of Society and Environment (ISSE) aims to improve societal welfare in the context of natural and changing climate and weater by conducting interdisciplinary research on societal activities related toclimate, the consequence of those activities on the atmosphere and the environment and providing effective communication of this information to decision-makers associated with weather and climate risks.

5826 **Institute of Environmental Sciences and Technology (IEST)**
www.iest.org
An international professional society that serves the environmental sciences in the areas of contamination control in electronics manufacturing and pharmaceutical processes, design, test and evaluation of commercial and militaryequipment and product reliability issues. The website features an extensive bookstore with documents in areas such as contamination control, environmental testing, nanotechnology, and more.

5827 **International Association for Disaster Preparedness and Response (DERA)**
www.disasters.org
Nonprofit association aiming to connect individuals and organizations involved in all aspects of emergency management. Website contains a reference library and archives.

5828 **International Association for Energy Economics (IAEE)**
www.iaee.org
Provides a forum for the exchange of ideas, experience and issues among professionals interested in energy economics. IAEE's scope is worldwide, as are its members who come from diverse corporate, academic, scientific and governmentbackgrounds. Website features podcasts, access to publications, educational resources, and more.

5829 **International Association for Environmental Hydrology**
www.hydroweb.com
The International Association for Environmental Hydrology (IAEH) is a worldwide association of environmental hydrologists dedicated to the protection and cleanup of fresh water resources.

5830 **International Canopy Network**
internationalcanopynetwork.org
The International Canopy Network (ICAN) is devoted to facilitating the continuing interaction of people concerned with forest canopies and forest ecosystems around the world. ICAN is a non-profit organization supported by a globalcommunity of scientists, conservation advocates, canopy educators and environmental professionals.

5831 **International Council for the Exploration of the Sea**
www.ices.dk
The International Council for the Exploration of the Seas (ICES) is a scientific organization concerning marine ecosystems that provides the knowledge to secure the sustainable use of the seas.

5832 **International Crane Foundation**
www.savingcranes.org
The International Crane Foundation (ICF) works worldwide to conserve cranes and the wetland and grasslands communities on which they depend. ICF is dedicated to providing experience, knowledge, and inspiration to involve people inresolving threats to these ecosystems.

5833 **International Energy Agency: Solar Heating & Cooling Programme**
www.iea-shc.org
The Solar Heating and Cooling Programme was one of the frist IEA Implementing Agreements to be established. Since 1977, its 21 members have collaborated to advance active solar, passive solar and photovoltaic technologies and theirapplication in buildings

5834 **International Fund for Animal Welfare (IFAW)**
www.ifaw.org
Aims to improve the welfare of wild and domestic animals throughout the world by reducing commercial exploitation of animals in distress, primarily by motivating the public to prevent cruelty to animals and promoting animal welfare andconservation policies that advance the well-being of both animals and people.

5835 **International Geosphere-Biosphere Programme**
www.igbp.net
The International Geosphere-Biosphere Programme (IGBP) aimed to coordinate international research on global-scale and regional-scale interactions between Earth's biological, chemical and physical processes and their interactions withhuman systems. The programme ended in 2015, however information still remains accessible on their website.

5836 **International Ground Source Heat Pump Association**
www.igshpa.org
The International Ground Source Heat Pump Association (IGSHPA) supports GHP industry research and development; promotes GHP-related current events internationally; develops and distributes internationally recognized training materials.

5837 **International Hunter Education Association (IHEA-USA)**
www.ihea-usa.org

Operates programs across the U.S. teaching hunting and shooting safety and responsibility. Courses cover firearm safety, bowhunting, wildlife management, field care, responsible hunting, landowner relations, wildlife identification,and more. Affiliated with the Association of Fish and Wildlife Agencies and local state fish and hunter education programs. The website features online courses and resources.

5838 International Institute for Industrial Environmental Economics
www.iiiee.lu.se
The International Institute for Industrial Environmental Economics (IIIEE) aims to advance knowledge on how to catalyse the transition to low-carbon and resource efficient economies and to promote sustainable solutions pursued bypublic authorities and businesses.

5839 International Institute for Sustainable Development
www.iisd.org
The International Institute for Sustainable Development (IISD) aims to champion innovation, enabling societies to live sustainably.

5840 International Otter Survival Fund
www.otter.org/Public
The International Otter Survival Fund (IOSF) is a global organization working to conserve all 13 species of otter by helping to support scientists and other workers in practical conservation, education, research, rescue andrehabilitation practices.

5841 International Primate Protection League
www.ippl.org/gibbon
The International Primate Protection League (IPPL) is dedicated to the preservation of the world's primates and maintaining a gibbon sanctuary in South Carolina.

5842 International Research Institute for Climateand Society
iri.columbia.edu
The International Research Institute for Climate and Society (IRI) aims to enhance society's capability to understand, anticipate and manage the impacts of climate in order to improve human welfare and the environment, especially indeveloping countries. This goal is conducted through strategic and applied research and education.

5843 International Rivers
www.internationalrivers.org
International Rivers works with an international network of dam-affected people, grassroots organizations, environmentalists, human rights advocates and others who are committed to stopping destructive river projects and promotingbetter options.

5844 International Society for Ecological Modelling
www.isemna.org
The International Society for Ecological Modelling (ISEM) promotes the international exchange of ideas, scientific results and general knowledge in the area of the application of systems analysis and simulation in ecology and naturalresource management.

5845 International Society of Arboriculture (ISA)

Through research, technology, and education ISA is able to promote the professional practice of arboriculture and foster a greater public awareness of the benefits of trees.

5846 International Solar Energy Society
www.ises.org
The International Solar Energy Society aims to encourage the use and acceptance of Renewable Energy technologies; to realise a global community of industry, individuals and institutions in support of renewable energy and to create astructure to faciliate cooperation and exchange.

5847 International Union of Forestry Research Organizations
www.iufro.org
The International Union of Forestry Research Organizations (IUFRO) is a non-profit, non-governmental international network of forest scientists. Its objective is to promote international cooperation in forestry and forest productsresearch. IUFRO's activities are organized primarily through its 268 specialized Units in 8 technical Divisions.

5848 International Wolf Center
www.wolf.org
The mission of the International Wolf Center is to support the survival of wolf populations around the world by teaching about their lives, associations with other species and dynamic relationships to humans.

5849 Iowa Department of Natural Resources
www.iowadnr.gov
The Iowa Department of Natural Resources aims to conserve and enhance natural resources in cooperation with individuals and organizations in the state to improve quality of life and ensure a legacy for future generations.

5850 Island Wildlife Natural Care Centre
www.sealrescue.org
The Island Wildlife Natural Care Centre aims to rehabilitate North American wildlife, including marine mammals, with emphasis on alternative, non-toxic, non-invasive treatments; and furthering knowledge of treatments available toprofessionals in the field while educationg the public on both rehabilitation and the interaction of humans and wild animals.

5851 Izaak Walton League of America (IWLA)
www.iwla.org
The Izaak Walton League of America aims to conserve, maintain, protect and restore the soil, forest, water and other natural resources of the United States and other lands; to promote means and opportunities for education of the publicwith respect to such resources and their enjoyment and wholesome utilization.

5852 Jane Goodall Institute
www.janegoodall.org
A nonprofit corporation founded to concentrate on research, education and conservation of wildlife, pursuant to the life work of Jane Goodall. Offices are located across the world. The website has information on Institute projects andresearch.

5853 Jefferson Land Trust
www.saveland.org
Jefferson Land Trust is a private, non-profit, grass-roots organization with a mission to conserve property and natural resources. Landowners may work with a Land Trust when they wish to permanently protect the ecological, scenic,historic or recreational qualities of land they own from inappropriate development.

5854 Journey North
www.learner.org/jnorth/index.html
Journey North: A Global Study of Wildlife Migration and Seasonal Change engages students in a global study of wildlife migration and seasonal change by allowing K-12 students to share their own field observations with classmates acrossNorth America.

5855 Kentucky Department of Fish and Wildlife Resources
fw.ky.gov
The Kentucky Department of Fish and Wildlife Resources aims to conserve and enhance fish and wildlife resources and provide opportunities for hunting, fishing, trapping, boating and other wildlife related activities.

5856 Kentucky Water Resources Research Institute
www.uky.edu/WaterResources/
The Kentucky Water Resources Research Institute aims to assist and stimulate academic units in the conduct of undergraduate and graduate education in water resources and water-related environmental issues.

5857 LaVidaLocal
www.holisticmanagement.org/blog

Blog of Holistic Management International, with articles about healthy land and enriching the community.

5858 Lake Pontchartrain Basin Foundation
saveourlake.org
The Lake Pontchartrain Basin Foundation (LPBF) aims to restore and preserve the Lake Pontchartrain Basin for the benefit of present and future generations.

5859 Land Conservancy of San Luis Obispo County
lcslo.org
The Land Conservancy of San Luis Obispo County (LCSLO) pursues the protection of open space through land aquisition, conservation easements, restoration and stewardship.

5860 Land Improvement Contractors of America
www.licanational.com
Organization composed primarily of small contractors whose activities related to the conservation, use and improvement of land and water resources ranging from grading, excavating, paving, landscaping, wetland development, drainage,and site preparation. Strives to improve the climate within which members conduct their businesses by working for better legislation and regulations. Website features archives of official publications The LICA Contractor and The LICA News.

5861 Land Trust Alliance
www.landtrustalliance.org
The Land Trust Alliance is a national conservation organization that works to influence the conservation movement, by promoting voluntary land conservation across the country and providing resources, leadership and training to thenation's 1,200+ non-profit, grassroots land trusts, helping them to protect important open spaces.

5862 League of Conservation Voters
www.lcv.org
The League of Conservation Voters (LCV) works to turn environmental values into national, state and local priorities. LCV advocates for sound environmental laws and policies; holds elected officials accountable for their votes andactions and elects pro-environment candidates who will champion priority issues.

5863 Leave No Trace: Canada
www.leavenotrace.com
The mission of the Leave No Trace (LNT) program is to promote and inspire responsible outdoor recreation through education, research and partnerships. LNT builds awareness, appreciation and respect for our wildlands.

5864 Living on Earth
www.loe.org
Living on Earth with Steve Curwood is a weekly environmental radio program distributed by National Public Radio that includes news, features, interviews and commentary on a broad range of ecological issues.

5865 Lloyd Center for the Environment
lloydcenter.org
The Lloyd Center for the Environment is a non-profit organization that provides education programs and conducts research to develop a scientific and public understanding of coastal, estaurine and watershed environments in southeasternNew England.

5866 Long Term Ecological Research Network
lternet.edu
The Long Term Ecological Research Network (LTER Network) aims to facilitate and conduct ecological research through the understanding of ecological pheonmena over long temporal and large spatial scales. LTER creates a legacy ofwell-designed and documented long-term experiments and observations for future generations.

5867 Louisiana Department of Agriculture & Forestry
www.ldaf.state.la.us
The Louisiana Department of Agriculture & Forestry is responsible for administering many of the programs and enforcing the regulations that impact every aspect of the state's agriculture and forestry industries.

5868 Louisiana Energy & Environmental Resources & Information Center
www.leeric.lsu.edu
The Louisiana Energy & Environmental Resource & Information Center (LEERIC) was a cooperative program that aimed to serve the information needs of Luisiana State University's faculty, staff and researchers. LEERIC also provided energyand environmental educational programs for consumers and non-college educators and students. The program is currently inactive, however their website has been archived and remains accessible.

5869 Luke: Natural Resources Institute Finland
www.luke.fi
Researchers and specialists working at Luke provide new solutions towards the sustainable development of the Finnish bioeconomy and the promotion of new biobased businesses.

5870 Maine Department of Agriculture, Conservationand Forestry
www.maine.gov/dacf
The Maine Department of Agriculture, Conservation and Forestry balances for and develops the state's various land-based, natural resources including agriculture, forests, outdoor recreation and public-access.

5871 Maine Department of Inland Fisheries & Wildlife
www.state.me.us/ifw
The Maine Department of Inland Fisheries & Wildlife conserves, protects and enhances the inland fisheries and wildlife resources of Maine while promoting efficiency in program management through employee involvement, intitiative,innovation and teamwork.

5872 Mangrove.org
mangrove.org
Mangrove.org began as a local project along the central east coast of Florida; however, now it contributes to a wide range of habitat creation and restoration programs that are international in scope.

5873 Manomet
www.manomet.org
Manomet aims to conserve natural resources for the benefit of wildlife and human populations. Through research and collaboration, Manomet builds science-based, cooperative solutions to environmental problems.

5874 Marine & Environmental Research Institute
www.meriresearch.org
The Marine & Environmental Research Institute is a non-profit scientific organization dedicated to protecting wildlife and people from the harmful impacts of toxic and chemical exposure.

5875 Marine Technology Society
www.mtsociety.org/home.aspx
The Marine Technology Society (MTS) aims to disseminate marine science and technical knowledge; to promote and support education for marine scientists, engineers and technicians; to advance the development of tools and proceduresrequired to explore, study and further the responsible and sustainable use of the oceans; and provide services that create a broader understanding of the relevance of marine sciences to other technologies, arts and human affairs.

5876 Maryland Department of Natural Resources
dnr.maryland.gov
The Maryland Department of Natural Resources hopes to help secure a sustainable future for the environment, society and economy by preserving, protecting, restoring and enhancing the state's natural resources.

5877 Maryland Forests Association, Inc.
www.mdforests.org
The Maryland Forest Association, Inc. (MFA) is a non-profit organization that acts as a voice for the forest, wildlife and natural resource management throughout Maryland and the tri-state area.

The website acts as a tool to learnabout Maryland's issues concerning forest resources, forest land ownership, forest management and the forest products industry.

5878 Massachusetts Department of Energy And Environmental Affairs
www.mass.gov/eea
Massachusetts Department of Energy and Environmental Affairs aims to preserve open spaces, species habitat and working landscapes; enforce pollution laws to protect public health and natural resources; enhance the state's role inenergy conservation and production; manage fish and wildlife and provide opportunities for outdoor recreation.

5879 Medomak Valley Land Trust
www.medomakvalley.org
The Medomak Valley Land Trust is a local, private non-profit oragnization edstablished that aims to preserve the natural, recreational, scenic and productive values of the Medomak River watershed. The Trust's goals are to foster aregional perspective of the watershed and to encourage valley residents to work together to ensure that the resources they value will remain for future generations.

5880 Messinger Woods Wildlife Care & Education Center, Inc.
www.messingerwoods.org
The Messinger Woods Wildlife Care & Education Center is a non-profit organization that promotes community awareness, education and instruction; involvement and understanding; and appreciation and acceptance of wildlife in an attempt toconserve it.

5881 Michigan Department of Environmental Quality
www.michigan.gov/deq
The Michigan Department of Environmental Quality drives improvements in environmental quality for the protection of public health and natural resources to benefit current and future generations. This is attempted through effectiveadministration of agency programs and by providing for the use of innovative strategies, all while helping to foster a strong and sustainable economy.

5882 Michigan Department of Natural Resources
www.michigan.gov/dnr
The Michigan Department of Natural Resources is responsible for the stewardship of Michigan's natural resources and for the provision of outdoor recreational opportunities.

5883 Michigan Forest Association
www.michiganforests.com
The mission of the Michigan Forest Association is to promote good management on all forest land, to educate its members about good forest practices and stewardship of the land and to inform the general public about forestry issues andthe benefits of good forest management.

5884 Michigan United Conservation Clubs
www.mucc.org
Michigan United Conservation Clubs (MUCC) aims to unite citizens to conserve Michigan's natural resources and protect its outdoor heritage. MUCC works to conserve Michigan's wildlife, fisheries, waters, forest, air and soils byproviding information, education and advocacy.

5885 Midwest Renewable Energy Association
www.midwestrenew.org
The Midwest Renewable Energy Association (MREA) is a non-profit network for sharing ideas, resources and information with individuals, businesses and communities to promote a sustainable future through renewable energy and energyefficiency.

5886 Minnesota Department of Natural Resources
www.dnr.state.mn.us
The Minnesota Department of Natural Resources aims to protect and restore the state's natural environment while enhancing economic opportunities and community well-being. The DNR endorsed ecosystem-based management as its method toachieve sustainability, and uses the concept of ecosystem integrity as a benchmark to measure progress toward sustainability goals.

5887 Minnesota Pollution Control Agency
www.pca.state.mn.us
The Minnesota Pollution Control Agency (MPCA) collects data on air, water, and waste pollution in Minnesota, as well as data on regulations and permits, clean-up techniques, prevention, publications, and programs to protect Minnesota'senvironment.

5888 Missouri Department of Conservation
mdc.mo.gov
The mission of the Missouri Department of Conservation is to protect and manage the fish, forest, and wildlife resources of the state, to serve the public and facilitate their participation in resources management activities, toprovide opportunity fos all citizens to use, enjoy, and learn about fish, forest and wildlife resources.

5889 Missouri Prairie Foundation
www.moprairie.org
The Missouri Praire Foundation's mission is to preserve the Greater Praire Chicken while also restoring the vegetative and faunal balance of Missouri's grassland ecosystem.

5890 Monarch Watch
www.monarchwatch.org
Monarch Watch aims to further science education, particularly in primary and secondary school systems; to promote the conservation of Monarch butterflies; and to invlove thousands of students and adults in a cooperative study of theMonarch's spectacular fall migration.

5891 Mountain Lion Foundation
www.mountainlion.org
The Mountain Lion Foundation is a non-profit conservation and education organization dedicated to protecting the mountain lion, its wild habitat and the other wildlife that shares that habitat.

5892 NEMO: Oceanographic Data Server
archive.li/ILKXH
NEMO is a collection of data sets useful for physical oceanographers based out of Scripps Institution of Oceanography.

5893 Napa County Resource Conservation District
naparcd.org
Napa County Resource Conservation District aims to encourage and assist acceptance of individual responsibility for watershed management, including goals of enhacement of wildlife habitat; reduction of soil erosion; protection andenhacement of water quality; and promotion of land stewardship and sustainable agriculture.

5894 Nation Centers for Environmental Information
www.ngdc.noaa.gov
The National Centers for Environmental Information (NOAA) provide stewardship, products and services for geophysical data from the Sun to the Earth's sea floor; offer sceientist around the world access to global databases throughinternational exchange. Formerly known as the National Geophysical Data Center (NGDC).

5895 National Arborists
www.natlarb.com
National Arborists is a trade association of commercial tree care firms that develops safety and educational programs, standards of tree care practice and management information for arboriculture firms around the world.

5896 National Association for Environmental Management
www.naem.org
The National Association for Environmental Management (NAEM) aims to empower corporate leaders to advance environmental stewardship, create safe and healthy workplaces and promote global sustainability through Environmental Health andSafety (EHS) practices.

5897 **National Association for PET Container Resources (NAPCOR)**
www.napcor.com
Trade association for the PET plastic industry in the United States and Canada. Its mission is to facilitate PET plastic recycling and to promote the usage of PET packaging.

5898 **National Association of Conservation Districts (NACD)**
www.nacdnet.org
The National Association of Conservation Districts (NACD) aims to serve conservation districts by providing national leadership and a unified voice for natural resource conservation. The association works with landowners, organizationsand agency partners in a district to help protect the soil, water, forests, wildlife and other resources.

5899 **National Association of Environmental Professionals (NAEP)**
2150 N 107th Street
Suite 205
Seattle, WA 98133
206-209-5286
Fax: 206-367-8777
office@naep.org
www.naep.org
NAEP is a multidisciplinary association dedicated to the advancement of environmental professionals in the US and abroad, and a forum for current information on environmental planning, research, and management.
Krystina Toscas, Executive Director
Makenna Wallingford, Marketing & Communications

5900 **National Association of State Foresters**
444 N Capitol Street NW
Suite 540
Washington, DC 20001
202-624-5415
Fax: 202-624-5407
info@stateforesters.org
www.stateforesters.org/
The National Association of State Foresters provides management assistance and protection services for more than two thirds of America's forests. It is a non-profit organization comprised of forestry agency directors.

Jay Farrell, Executive Director
Robyn Whitney, Policy Director

5901 **National Audubon Society (NAS)**
www.audubon.org
The mission of the National Audubon Society is to conserve and restor natural ecosystems, focusing on birds and other wildlife for the benefit of humanity and the earth's biological diversity.

5902 **National Center for Atmospheric Research**
ncar.ucar.edu
The National Center for Atmospheric Research (NCAR) aims to plan, organize and conduct atmospheric and related research programs in collaboration with universities and other institutions; to provide state of the art research tools andfacilities to the atmospheric sciences community; to support and enhance university atmospheric science education and to facilitate the transfer of technology to both the public and private sectors.

5903 **National Center for Ecological Analysis and Synthesis**
www.nceas.ucsb.edu
The National Center for Ecological Analysis and Synthesis (NCEAS) aims to advance the state of ecological knowledge through the search for general patterns and principles, and to organize and synthesize ecological information in amanner useful to researchers, resource managers, and policy makers addressing important environmental issues.

5904 **National Energy Foundation (NEF)**
nef1.org
A non-profit educational organization dedicated to the development, dissemination and implementation of supplemental educational materials and programs primarily related to the environment, conservation, science, energy, water andnatural resources.

5905 **National Energy Technology Laboratory**
www.netl.doe.gov
The National Energy Technology Laboratory (NETL) is a part of the US Department of Energy national laboratory system and helps to implement a broad spectrum of energy and environmental research and development programs that intend tobenefit future generations.

5906 **National Environmental Health Association**
www.neha.org
The National Environmental Health Association (NEHA) aims to advance the environmental health professional for the purpose of providing a healthful environment for all.

5907 **National Gap Analysis Program**
gapanalysis.usgs.gov
The US Geological Survey Gap Analysis Program (GAP) works to ensure that common species - those that are not officially endangered - remain that way by idetifying the species and plant communities that are not adequately represented inexisting conservation lands. GAP works with a wide range of government, academic, non-profit and private partners, providing them with essential data and analyses that they can use to protect the habitats that the survival of common species dependsupon.

5908 **National Geographic Kids**
kids.nationalgeographic.com
Site features videos, games, animal information, and more, seeking to connect children with nature.

5909 **National Geographic Society**
www.nationalgeographic.com
Seeks to inspire people to care about the planet. Programs support scientific fieldwork and expeditions; encourage geography education for students; and promote natural and cultural conservation. Website features access to TV shows,podcasts, articles, travel assistance, and more.

5910 **National Ground Water Association**
www.ngwa.org
Works to provide and protect the world's ground water resources; enhance the skills and credibility of all ground water professionals; develop and exchange industry knowledge and promote the ground water industry and understanding ofground water resources.

5911 **National Institute of Environmental Health Sciences**
NIEHS Central Receiving
105 T.W. Alexander Drive
Building 110
Research Triangle Park, NC 27709
919-541-3345
Fax: 301-480-2978
webcenter@niehs.nih.gov
www.niehs.nih.gov
NIEHS' mission is to research how the environment affects people in order to promote healthier lives, and to provide global leadership for research that improves public health. NIEHS accomplishes this mission by translating theirfindings into comprehensible information that can inform real-life individual and public health outcomes.

Linda S. Birnbaum, Director
Richard Woychik, Deputy Director

5912 **National Outdoor Leadership School**
www.nols.edu
The National Outdoor Leadership School (NOLS) is an institution that focuses on wilderness education, offering courses in Leadership, Wilderness Skills, Risk Management, Environmental Studies and Wilderness Medicine.

5913 **National Park Conservation Association (NPCA)**
www.npca.org
The National Parks Conservation Association (NPCA) aims to protect and enhance America's national parks.

5914 **National Renewable Energy Laboratory**
www.nrel.gov
The National Renewable Energy Laboratory (NREL) advances the science and engineering of energy efficiency, sustainable transportation and renewable power technologies, and provides the knowledge to integrate and optimize energysystems.

5915 National Sea Grant Library
nsgd.gso.uri.edu
The National Sea Grant Library (NSGL) was established as an archive and lending library for Sea Grant funded documents. These documents cover a wide variety of subjects, including oceanography, marine education, aquaculture, fisheries,limonology, coastal zone management, marine recreation and law. NSGL staff lends documents all over the world to aid scientists, teachers, students, fishermen and many other individuals in their reseacrh and studies.

5916 National Wildlife Health Center
The National Wildlife Health Center is a science center of the US Geological Survey dedicated to assessing the impact of disease on wildlife and to identify the role of various pathogens in contributing to wildlife losses.

5917 National Wildlife Rehabilitators Association (NWRA)
www.nwrawildlife.org
Nonprofit international membership organization committed to promoting and improving the integrity and professionalism of wildlife rehabilitation and contributing to the preservation of natural ecosystems.

5918 National Woodland Owners Association
woodlandowners.org
The National Woodland Owners Association (NWOA) is an independent landowners group with the purpose of developing policy, legislation and representation at the national level, and providing educational and networking opportunities tolandowners throughout the country.

5919 Natural Energy Laboratory of Hawaii Authority: Hawaii Ocean Science & Technology Park
nelha.hawaii.gov
The Natural Energy Laboratory of Hawaii Authority (NELHA) operates facilities at Keahole Point on Hawaii Island that pump ashore cold deep and warm surface seawater for commercial and research tenants from the private and publicsectors. Tenants utilize the seawater and NELHA's high sunlight and consistant temperatures in a wide range of aquaculture and energy projects.

5920 Natural Environment Research Council
www.nerc.ac.uk
The Natural Environment Research Council (NERC) is an independent UK charity which brings together people from all sectors of business, non-governmental organizations, government and the community to develop long term solutions toenvironmental issues.

5921 Natural Environmental Research Council
www.nerc.ac.uk
The Natural Environmental Research Council (NERC) aims to promote and support high-quality strategic and applied research, survey, long-term environmental monitoring and related post-graduate training in environmental and relatedsciences; and to generate public awareness, communicate research outcomes, encourage public engagement and dialogue, disseminate knowledge and proivide advice in relation to those activities.

5922 Natural Resources Canada
www.nrcan.gc.ca/home
Natural Resources Canada aims to be on the frontlines: fighting climate change, developing clean enery practices for the future, driving economic growth and creating job opportunities for Canadians.

5923 Natural Resources Defense Council (NRDC)
www.nrdc.org
Seeks to create solutions for lasting environmental change, protecting natural resources in the United States and around the world.

5924 Nature Conservancy
www.nature.org
The Nature Conservancy aims to preserve the plants, animals and natural communities that represent the diversity of life on Earth by protecting the lands and waters they need to survive.

5925 Nature Saskatchewan
www.naturesask.ca
Nature Saskatcgewan aims to promote appreciation and understanding of nature and the environment through education, conservation and research, and to protect and preserve natural ecosystems and their biodiversity.

5926 Naturenet
naturenet.net/index.php
Naturenet is a voluntary enterprise that aims to provide resources for practical nature conservation and countryside management. Based in the UK, most of the information available on Naturenet relates to the UK, particulary England.

5927 New England Wild Flower Society
www.newfs.org
The New England Wild Flower Society (NEWFS) promotes the conservation of New England's native plants to ensure healthy, biologically diverse landscapes.

5928 New England Wildlife Center
www.newildlife.com
The New England Wildlife Center is an informal hands-on science education organization that uses the practices of veterinary medical care and wildlife rehabilitation as a teaching resource for students of all ages.

5929 New Forests Project
1001 North Carolina Avenue SE 202-285-4328
Washington, DC 20003 info-newforests@theintlcenter.org
www.newforestsproject.org/
The New Forests Project strives to protect, conserve, and enhance the health of the Earth's ecosystems along with the people depending on them, by supporting integrated grassroots efforts in agroforestry, reforestation, protection ofwatersheds, water and sanitation, and renewable energy initiatives.

Catalina Serna-Valencia, Executive Director
Lysette House, Program Officer

5930 New Hampshire Department of Environmental Services
The New Hampshire Department of Environmental Services aims to protect, maintain and enhance environmental quality and public health in New Hampshire.

5931 New Hampshire Fish and Game Department
www.wildlife.state.nh.us
New Hampshire's Fish and Game Department aims to conserve, manage and protect the state's fish and game populations and their respective habitats, as well as inform and educate the public about these resources and provide the publicwith opportunities to use and appreciate them.

5932 New Jersey Department of Environmental Protection
www.state.nj.us/dep/
The New Jersey Department of Environmental Protection aims to assist the residents of New Jersey in preserving, restoring, sustaining, protecting and enhancing the environment to ensure the integration of high environmental quality,public health and economic vitality.

5933 New Jersey Division of Fish & Wildlife
www.state.nj.us/dep/fgw
The New Jersey Division of Fish & Wildlife aims to protect and manage the state's fish and wildlife resources to maximize their long term economic, recreational and biological values for the citizens of New Jersey.

5934 New Mexico Wilderness Alliance
www.nmwild.org
The New Mexico Wilderness Allince is dedicated to the protection, restoration, and rewilding of New Mexico's Wilderness ar-

eas by focusing on forward-looking measures to develop an active and educational wilderness constituencythroughout the state.

5935 New York Association for Reduction, Reuse and Recycling

www.nysar3.org

The New York Association for Reduction, Reuse and Recycling (NYSAR3) aims to provide statewide leadership on waste reduction, reuse and recycling issues and practices to improve the environment.

5936 New York State Department of Environmental Conservation

www.dec.ny.gov

The New York State Department of Environmental Conservation aims to conserve, imrpove and protect New York's natural resources and environment and to prevent, abate and control water, land and air pollution.

5937 North American Association for Environmental Education (NAAEE)

www.naaee.org

The North American Association for Environmental Education is a professional association that promotes excellence in environmental education and serves environmental educators for the purpose of achieveing environmental literacy toallow present and future generationas to benefit from a safe and healthy environment.

5938 North American Lake Management Society

www.nalms.org

The North American Lake Management Society (NALMS) works to forge partnerships among citizens, scientists and professionals to foster the management and protection of lakes and reservoirs.

5939 North Carolina Coastal Federation

www.nccoast.org

The North Carolina Coastal Federation (NNCF) is a non-profit organization that seeks to protect and restore the states's coastal environment, culture and economy through citizen involvement in the management of coastal resources.

5940 North Carolina Department of Environment Quality

deq.nc.gov

The North Carolina Department of Environmental Quality aims to leadthe preservation and protection of North Carolina's natural resources by administering regulatory programs designed to protect air quality, water quality and thepublic's health.

5941 North Cascades Conservation Council

www.northcascades.org/wordpress

The North Cascades Conservation Council (NCCC) keeps government officials, environmental organizations and the general public informed about issues affecting the Greater North Cascade Ecosystem. Action is pursued through legislative,legal and public participation channels to protect the lands, waters, plants and wildlife.

5942 Northeast Sustainable Energy Association

www.nesea.org

The Northeast Sustainable Energy Association (NESEA) is a regional membership organization comprised of engineers, educators, builders, students, energy experts, environmental activists, transportation planners, architects, and othercitizens interested in responsible energy use. The goal is to bring clean electricity, green transportation, and healthy, efficient buildings into everyday use in order to strengthen the economy and improve the environment.

5943 Northern Prairie Wildlife Research Center

www.npwrc.usgs.gov

The Northern Prairie Wildlife Research Center (NPWRC) conducts integrated research to fulfill the Department of the Interior's responsibilities to the Nation's natureal resources. The NPWRC develops and disseminates scientificinformation needed to understand, conserve and manage the Nation's biological resources through focus on mid-continental plant and animal species and ecosystems of the United States.

5944 Oceania Project

www.oceania.org.au

The Oceania Project is a non-profit research and information organization dedicated to raising awareness about whales, dolphins, porpoises and the ocean environment.

5945 Office of Protected Resources

www.nmfs.noaa.gov/pr/

The Office of Protected Resources (OPR) is a program office of NOAA's NAtional Marine Fisheries Service. The program provides oversight, national policy direction and guidance on the conservation of marine mammals and endangeredspecies, and their habitats, under the jurisdiction of the Secretary of Commerce.

5946 Ohio Environmental Protection Agency

50 W Town Street — 614-644-3020
Suite 700 — www.epa.state.oh.us
Columbus, OH 43215

The mission of the Ohio EPA is to protect the environment and public health by ensuring compliance with environmental laws and demonstrating leadership in environmental stewardship. They work to enforce standards for air, water, andwaste management, and help businesses minimize their waste at the source.

Laurie A. Stevenson, Director
Laura Factor, Assistant Director

5947 Ohio Wildlife Center

www.ohiowildlifecenter.org

The Ohio Wildlife Center (OWC) is a non-profit educational organization that promotes increased appreciation and understanding of the natural environment, with particular emphasis on wildlife. OWC is supported by individuals who wishto improve their own understanding of native wild species and local wildlife issues.

5948 Oklahoma Department of Wildlife Conservation

www.wildlifedepartment.com

The Oklahoma Department of Wildlife Conservation aims to manage Oklahoma's wildlife resources and habitat in order to provide scientific, educational, aesthetic, economic and recreational benefits for present and future generations ofhunters, anglers and others who appreciate wildlife related activities.

5949 Ontario Environment Network

www.oen.ca

The Ontario Environment Network (OEN) is a non-profit, non-governmental network serving Ontario's environmental environmental community that seeks to increase awareness of these organizations and encourage discussions about means toprotect the environment.

5950 Organization of American States: Environment

www.oas.org/en/topics/environment.asp

The OAS supports member states in the design and implementation of policies and projects to integrate environmental priorities into poverty alleviation and socio-economic development goals.

5951 Organization of Fish and Wildlife Information Managers

www.ofwim.org

The Organization of Fish and Wildlife Information Managers (OFWIM) is an international non-profit organization that promotes the management and convervation of natural resources by facilitating technology and information exchange amongmanagers of fish and wildlife information.

5952 Population Institute

www.populationinstitute.org

The Population Institute is the World's largest independent non-profit, educational organization dedicated exclusively to achieving a more equitable balance between the worlds population, environment, and resources. The Institute uses avariety of resources and programs to bring its concerns about the consequences of rapid poulation growth to the forefront of the national agenda. The website includes a podcast, videos, news, op-eds, and more.

5953 Population and Environment Linkages Service
popenvironment.org
Provides links and resources to information on the relationship between population and the environment.

5954 Rachel Carson Council
rachelcarsoncouncil.org
The Rachel Carson Council (RCC) is a clearinghouse and library with information at both scientific and layperson levels on pesticide related issues. The RCC collections contain literature searches and conservation information byexperts to educate the public. The council also produces various publications clarifying pesticide dangers and bringing alternative pest controls to the public's attention.

5955 Renewable Fuels Association (RFA)
www.ethanolrfa.org
Comprised of companies and individuals involved in the production and use of ethanol. Ethanol is sold nationwide as a high-octane fuel that delivers improved vehicle performance while reducing emissions and improving air quality.

5956 Renewable Natural Resources Foundation
www.rnrf.org
The Renewable Natural Resources Foundation (RNRF) aims to advance the application of science and related disciplines in decision-making while promoting interdisciplinary collaboration to educate policymakers and the public on managingand conserving renewable natural resources.

5957 River Systems Research Group
boto.ocean.washington.edu
The River Systems Research Group is a project of NASA's Earth Observing System Interdisciplinary Investigation with the purpose of trying to understand the biogeochemistry, hydrology and sedimentation of the Amazon River and itsdrainage basin. Other research sites are located in Southeast Asia, Zambezi, Bhutan and Puget Sound.

5958 Scenic America
www.scenic.org
A national nonprofit organization dedicated solely to protecting natural beauty and distinctive community character. The website features issues of concern, particularly information relating to billboards and sign control, as well asresources including videos, studies, speeches, and a newsletter archive.

5959 Snow Leopard Trust
www.snowleopard.org
The Snow Leopard Trust is dedicated to the conservation of the endangered snow leopard and its mountain ecosystem through a community-based conservation approach that is based on improved scientific understanding of snow leopardbehavior, needs, habitats and threats.

5960 Society for Conservation Biology (SCB)
conbio.org
International professional organization dedicated to promoting the scientific study of the phenomena that affect the maintenance, loss and restoration of biological diversity.

5961 Society of Chemical Manufacturers and Affiliates (SOCMA)
www.socma.com
International trade association serving small and mid-sized batch chemical manufacturers, striving for safe, sustainable and environmentally sound operations.

5962 Steel Recycling Institute (SRI)
www.steelsustainability.org
The Steel Recycling Institute, a unit of the American Iron and Steel Institute, is an industry association that promotes and sustains the recycling of all steel products. The SRI educates the solid waste industry, government, bussinesand ultimately the consumer about the benefit of steel's infinite recycling cycle.

5963 Student Conservation Association
www.thesca.org
The Student Conservation Association (SCA) aims to build the next generation of conservation leaders and inspire lifelong stewardship of the environment by engaging young people in hands on environmental service.

5964 Sustainable Communities Online
www.sustainable.org
Run by CONCERN, and formerly known as Sustainable Communities Network, this website offers a variety of resources to help communities become more sustainable.

5965 The Conservation Fund
www.conservationfund.org
The Conservation Fund works with private and public agencies and organizations to protect wildlife habitats, historic sites and parks.

5966 The Earth Institute: Columbia University
www.earthinstitute.columbia.edu
The Earth Institute at Columbia University blends research in the physical and social sciences, education and practical solutions to help guide its students on a path towards sustainability. Offers initiatives including water, climate,energy, urbanization, hazards & risk reduction, global health, agriculture and ecosystems.

5967 The Marine Mammal Center
www.marinemammalcenter.org
The Marine Mammal Center is working towards advancing global ocean conservation through marine mammal rescue and rehabilitation, scientific research and education.

5968 The Web Directory
www.webdirectory.com
The Web Directory is a database directory for environmental and other resources. It includes topics such as: agriculture, animals, arts, business, databases, design, disasters, education, employment, energy, forestry, generalenvironmental interest, government, health, land conservation, parks and recreation, pollution, products and services, publications, recycling, science, social science, sustainable development, transportation, vegetarianism, water resources, weatherand wildlife.

5969 Treetures Environmental Education Program
www.treetures.com
The program focuses on teaching children ages 3-10 the importance of trees to the environment, through whimsical cartoon characters known as Treetures. The website features interactive content for children, as well as information onthe Treetures series of books.

5970 U.S. Department of Energy
1000 Independence Ave SW 202-586-5000
Washington, DC 20585 www.energy.gov
The Department of Energy's goal is to foster a secure and reliable energy system that is environmentally and economically sustainable, to be a responsible steward of the nation's nuclear weapons and to support continued US leadershipin science and technology.

Rick Perry, Secretary of Energy
Dan Brouillette, Deputy Secretary of Energy

5971 UK Environmental Change Network
www.ecn.ac.uk
The Environmental Change Network aims to establish and maintain a selected network of sites within the UK from which to obtain comparable long-term datasets through the monitoring of a range of variables identified as being of majorenvironmental importance.

5972 US Government Accountability Office
www.gao.gov

The Government Accountability Office (GAO) supports the Congress in meeting its constitutional responsibilities and to help improve the performance and ensure the accountability of the federal government. GAO examines the use of publicfunds; evaluates federal programs and activities and provides analysis, options, recommendations and other assistance to help the Congress make effective oversight, policy and funding decisions.

5973 United States Geological Survey: Earthquake Hazards Program

earthquake.usgs.gov

The USGS Earthquake Hazards Program aims to provide and apply relevant scientific information and knowledge to reduce deaths, inhuries and property damage from earthquakes.

5974 Wisconsin Sea Grant Program

www.seagrant.wisc.edu

The Wisconsin Sea Grant Program is a statewide program of basic and applied research, education, outreach and technology dedicated to the stewardship and sustainable use of the nation's Great Lakes and ocean resources.

5975 WorldFish

www.worldfishcenter.org

WorldFish's goal is to reduce poverty and hunger by improving fisheries and aquaculture.

5976 edie.net

www.edie.net

EDIE is a free, personalized, interactive news, information and communications service for water, waste and environmental professionals around the world. With comprehensive independent coverage, powerful search facilities, e-mailalerts and discussion forums, EDIE enables the easy exchange of specialized information.

Online Databases & Clearinghouses

Environmental

5977 **AAR Bureau of Explosives**
50 F Street NW
Washington, DC 20001
BOE@aar.org
www.aar.org/boe

5978 **AIChE Graduate School Directory**
American Institute of Chemical Engineers
120 Wall Street
FL 23
New York, NY 10005-4020
203-702-7660
800-242-4363
Fax: 203-775-5177
www.aiche.org/community/students/graduate-school-directory
Provides prospective chemical engineering students with the ability to compare programs across the U.S.
Monty Alger, President

5979 **ARCAT**
173 Sherman Street
Fairfield, CT 06824
203-929-9444
www.arcat.com
Online resource of free building product information, including date specification and CAD detail libraries, and a specwriting tool. Also available as an app.
Casey Jannott, Chief Executive Officer
Bill Jannott, President & CTO

5980 **American Society for Environmental History Membership Directory**
UIC Department of History
601 S Morgan Street
MC 198
Chicago, IL 60607-7109
dspatz@aseh.net
aseh.net
Online access to the members of ASEH.
David Spatz, Executive Director

5981 **Asbestos Ombudsman**
401 M Street SW
A-149 C
Washington, DC 20460
800-368-5888
Answers questions about asbestos in schools.

5982 **Blue Movement Directory**
Blue Frontier
PO Box 19367
Washington, DC 20036
202-387-8030
Fax: 202-234-5176
bluefront.org
Run by Blue Frontier, the directory houses over 1,400 ocean groups.
David Helvarg, Executive Director
Eleanor Kewlow, Sr. Communications Advisor

5983 **CHEMTREC**
American Chemistry Council
703-741-5500
800-262-8200
chemtrec@chemtrec.com
www.chemtrec.com
Critical response information for incidents involving hazardous materials.

5984 **Carbon Dioxide Information Analysis Center**
Oak Ridge National Laboratory
PO Box 2008, MS6290
Oak Ridge, TN 37831-6290
Fax: 865-241-4064
cdiac.ornl.gov
Operations to cease Sept. 30, 2017. Plans to preserve data beyond 2017 are in development.
Tom Boden, Director

5985 **Center for Environmental and Regulatory Information Systems**
Purdue University
1231 Cumberland Ave
Suite A
West Layfayette, IN 47906
317-494-7309
Fax: 317-494-9727
www.ceris.purdue.edu/ceris
Eileen Luke, Director

5986 **Center for Health, Environment & Justice**
7139 Shreve Road
Falls Church, VA 22046-6806
703-237-2249
info@chej.org
chej.org
Provides tools for communities to fight toxic threats.
Sharon Franklin, Chief of Operations

5987 **Center for Sustainable Systems**
University of Michigan
3012 Dana Building
440 Church St
Ann Arbor, MI 48109-1041
734-764-1412
css.info@umich.edu
css.umich.edu
Leads interdisciplinary research into systems that will support society's needs in a more sustainable manner.
Gregory A. Keoleian, Director

5988 **Clean Ocean Action**
18 Hartshorne Dr
Suite 2
Highlands, NJ 07732
732-872-0111
Fax: 732-872-8041
info@cleanoceanaction.org
www.cleanoceanaction.org
Clean Ocean Action is a broad-based coalition of over 150 conservation, community, diving, fishing, environmental, surfing, women's and business groups that works to improve and protect the waters off the New York and New Jersey coast.
Cindy Zipf, Executive Director

5989 **Compressed Gas Association (CGA)**
www.cganet.com
Mission is to promote the safe manufacture, transportation, storage, transfilling, and disposal of industrial and medical gases and their containers. Strategies employed by the CGA include developing standards and practices, workingwith other organizations, providing safety training and more. Website features access to a database of technical publications.

5990 **DIPPR Database**
American Institute of Chemical Engineers
120 Wall Street
FL 23
New York, NY 10005-4020
203-702-7660
800-242-4363
Fax: 203-775-5177
www.aiche.org/dippr
Data and estimation methods developed by the Design Institute for Physical Properties.
Monty Alger, President

5991 **EPA Indoor Air Quality Information**
U.S. EPA Office of Radiation and Indoor Air
Indoor Environments Division
1200 Pennsylvania Ave NW
Washington, DC 20460
www.epa.gov/indoor-air-quality-iaq
Scott Pruitt, EPA Administrator

5992 **EPA Ozone Layer Protection**
U.S. EPA
Stratospheric Protection Division
1200 Pennsylvania Ave NW
Washington, DC 20460
www.epa.gov/ozone-layer-protection
Scott Pruitt, EPA Administrator

5993 **EPA Public Information Center**
US EPA
401 M Street
PM- 211B
Washington, DC 20460
202-260-7751

5994 **EPCRA (SARA Title III) Hotline**
US EPA

401 M Street SW 202-479-2449
OS120 800-535-0202
Washington, DC 20460 *Fax:* 703-412-3333

5995 Electronic Bulletin Board System
US EPA
26 West Martin Luther King Drive 513-569-7358
Cincinnati, OH 800-258-9605
Fax: 513-569-7585
Charles W Guion

5996 Emergency Planning and Community Right-to-Know Information Hotline
Booz, Allen & Hamilton
1725 Jefferson Davis Highway 703-920-8977
Arlington, VA 22202 800-535-0202
Fax: 703-486-3333
Dan Kovacs, Contractor

5997 Emission Factor Clearinghouse
US EPA
MD-14 919-541-1000
Research Triangle Park, NC 27709 *Fax:* 919-541-0684
Dennis Shipman

5998 Energy Economics Education Database
International Association for Energy Economics
28790 Chagrin Boulevard 216-464-5365
Suite 350 iaee@iaee.org
Cleveland, OH 44122 www.iaee.org
Listings of energy economics courses taught in universities around the world, for use by students and faculty.
David L. Williams, Executive Director
Jean-Michael Glachant, VP, Communications

5999 Environmental Financing Information Network
US EPA
EFN, WH-547 202-564-4994
401 M Street, East Tower, Room 1117 *Fax:* 202-565-2694
Washington, DC 20460
June Lobit

6000 Forest History Society
2925 Academy Road 919-682-9319
Durham, NC 27705-9311 *Fax:* 919-682-2349
steven.anderson@foresthistory.org
www.foresthistory.org
A nonprofit educational institution that links the past to the future by identifying, collecting, preserving, interpreting and disseminating information on the history of people, forests and their related resources. The websitefeatures a searchable database and a digital library and archives.
Steven Anderson, President
Janet Askew, Assistant Director

6001 Global Change Information System
U.S. Global Change Research Program
1800 G St NW 202-223-6262
Suite 9100 *Fax:* 202-223-3065
Washington, DC 20006 data.globalchange.gov
Open-source, web-based resource for global change data, information and products for use by scientists, decision makers and the public.
Dr. Michael Kuperberg, Executive Director

6002 Green Committees of Correspondence Clearinghouse
PO Box 30208 816-931-9366
Kansas City, MO 64112
Amy Belanger, Coordinator

6003 Green Lights Program
Bruce Company
1850 K Street 290 202-775-6650
Washington, DC 20006 *Fax:* 202-775-6680
Maria Theesen

6004 Inspector General Hotline
US EPA
1200 Pennsylvania Avenue NW 800-424-4000
Washington, DC 20460 *Fax:* 202-260-6976
Ed Maddox

6005 International Ground Water Modeling Center
Colorado School of Mines 303-273-3103
Golden, CO 80401 *Fax:* 303-273-3278
Paul van der Hijde, Director

6006 Kentucky Partners State Waste Reduction Center
University of Louisville
Ernst Hall 502-588-7260
Room 312
Louisville, KY 40292
Joyce St. Clair, Executive Director

6007 Minority Energy Information Clearinghouse
Office of Minority Economic Impact/US Energy Dept.
100 Independence Ave SW 202-586-8698
Forrestal Building, Room 5B-110 800-543-2325
Washington, DC 20585
Effie A Young, Officer

6008 Montana Natural Resource Information System
Montana State Library
1515 East 6th Avenue 406-444-3115
Helena, MT 59620 *Fax:* 406-444-5612
Alan Cox

6009 NYS Department of Environmental Conservation Publications, Forms, Maps
NYS Office of Communication Services
625 Broadway 518-402-8013
Albany, NY 12233-4500 *Fax:* 518-402-9036
www.dec.ny.gov/64.html
List of New York State Department of Environmental Conservation publications, online newsletters, bulletins, forms, maps and grant applications.

6010 National Air Toxics Information Clearinghouse
US EPA
Mail Drop 13 919-541-3586
Office of Air Quality and Standards *Fax:* 919-541-7674
Research Triangle Park, NC 27709
Vasu Kilaru, Database Administrator

6011 National Capital Poison Center
Georgetown Univertisy Hospital
3201 New Mexico Avenue 202-362-3867
Suite 310
Washington, DC 20016

6012 National Center for Biotechnology Information
U.S. National Library of Medicine www.ncbi.nlm.nih.gov
8600 Rockville Pike
Bethesda, MD 20894
NCBI's mission is to develop new information technologies for biomedical research.
Valerie De Crecy-Lagard, Chair

6013 National Center for Environmental Research
EPA's Office of Research and Development
1200 Pennsylvania Ave NW
MC 8722F
Washington, DC 20460
Funds research that forms scientific basis for policy decisions on environmental issues.
James H. Johnson Jr., Director

6014 National Ground Water Information Center
601 Dempsey Road 800-551-7379
Westerville, OH 43081 800-242-4965
Fax: 614-898-7786
Kevin McCray, Assistant Executive Director

6015 National Pesticide Information Retrieval System
1231 Cumberland Avenue 317-494-7309
Suite A *Fax:* 317-494-9727
West Lafayette, IN 4706
Virginia Walters

6016 National Pesticide Telecommunications Network
Preventive Medicine & Community Health
Texas Tech University 806-858-7378
Sciences Center 800-858-PEST
Lubbock, TX 79430 *Fax:* 806-743-3094
Frank L Davido

6017 National Renewable Energy Laboratory
Technical Inquiry Service
1617 Cole Boulevard 303-275-4099
Golden, CO 80401
Steve Rubin, Manager

6018 National Response Center
US Coast Guard
2100 2nd Street SW 202-267-2675
Room 2611 800-424-8802
Washington, DC 20593 *Fax:* 202-267-2181
Commander David Beach

6019 New York State Department of Environmental Conservation
625 Broadway 518-402-8013
Pollution Prevention Unit
Albany, NY 12233
John E Iannotti, PE

6020 Noise Pollution Clearinghouse
PO Box 1137 888-200-8332
Montpelier, VT 05601-1137 npc@nonoise.org
www.nonoise.org
National nonprofit organization with extensive online noise related resources. Creates more civil cities and more natural rural and wilderness areas by reducing noise pollution at the source.

6021 Northeast Multi-Media Pollution Prevention
Northeast Waste Management Officials Association
85 Merrimac Street 617-367-8558
Boston, MA 00211
Terri Goldberg, Program Manager

6022 Nuclear Information and Resource Service
6930 Carroll Ave 301-270-6477
Suite 340 *Fax:* 301-270-4291
Takoma Park, MD 20912 nirs@nirs.org
www.nirs.org
Non-profit organization working for a nuclear-free, sustainable energy future.
Tim Judson, Executive Director

6023 OTS Chemical Assessment Desk
401 M Street SW 202-260-3583
(TS-778)
Washington, DC 20460
Terry O'Bryan, Executive Officer

6024 Pesticide Action Network North America
49 Powell Street 415-981-1771
Suite 500 *Fax:* 415-981-1991
San Francisco, CA 94102
Kathryn Gilje, Executive Director

6025 Powder River Basin Resource Council
Energy Conservation Education Committee
23 North Scott 307-672-5809
Sheridan, WY 82801
Jill Morrision, Organizer

6026 Public Information Center
US EPA
401 M Street SW 202-260-7751
PM-211B
Washington, DC 20460
Alison Cook, Director

6027 RACT/BACT/LAER Clearinghouse
Office of Air Quality Planning
Emissions Standards Division 919-541-0800
MD-13 *Fax:* 919-541-0072
Research Triangle Park, NC 27709
Bob Blaszczak, ESD

6028 RAPID Directory
American Institute of Chemical Engineers
120 Wall Street 203-702-7660
FL 23 800-242-4363
New York, NY 10005-4020 *Fax:* 203-775-5177
www.aiche.org/rapid/membership/directory
Listings of companies, projects, and individuals involved in efficient processes and distributed industrial modularization.
Monty Alger, President

6029 Rachel Carson Council
rachelcarsoncouncil.org
Contains a collection of literature on the dangers of pesticides.

6030 Radon Hotline
785-532-6026
800-557-2366
Fax: 785-532-6952
radon@ksu.edu
www.epa.gov/home/epa-hotlines

6031 Records of Decision System Hotline
Computer Sciences Corporation
401 M Street SW 202-260-3770
Room L101
Washington, DC 20460
Thomas Batts

6032 Risk Communication Hotline
US EPA
401 M Street SW 202-260-5606
W Tower, Room 425 *Fax:* 202-260-9757
Washington, DC 20460
Ernestine Thomas

6033 Spot UL
UL Environment
2211 Newmarket Parkway 888-485-4733
Suite 106 *Fax:* 770-980-0072
Marietta, GA 30067 environment@ul.com
www.greenguard.org
Allows purchasers to find product information across an array of categories. Targeted to architects and designers, manufacturers, professional purchasers, and retailers.

6034 Sustainable Buildings Industry Council
National Institute of Building Sciences
1090 Vermont Ave NW 202-289-7800
Suite 700 *Fax:* 202-289-1092
Washington, DC 20005 nibs@nibs.org
www.nibs.org
Council of the National Institute of Building Sciences advocates for improving the performance and value of buildings through the use of sustainable design and construction strategies.
Ryan Colker, Director

6035 TNN Bulletin Board System
Office of Air Quality Planning
Standards Tech Transfer Network 919-541-5616
Research Triangle Park, NC 27709 *Fax:* 919-541-0824
Hersch Rorex, System Manager

6036 TOXNET
U.S. Dept. of Health & Human Services

Specialized Information Services 301-496-3147
6707 Democracy Blvd, MSC 5467 888-346-3656
Bethesda, MD 20892-5467 *Fax:* 301-480-3537
toxnet.nlm.nih.gov

Data network for toxicology, hazardous chemicals, environmental health and toxic releases.

6037 TSCA Assistance Information Service Hotline
Environmental Assistance Division
1200 Pennsylvania Avenue NW 202-554-1404
Mail Code 74080 *Fax:* 202-554-5603
Washington, DC 20460 tsca-hotline@epamail.epa.gov

The information service furnishes TSCA regulation information to the chemical industry, labor and trade organization, environmental groups and the general public. Technical as well as general information is available.

John Alter, Primary EPA

6038 Waste Exchange Clearinghouse
University of Michigan
400 Ann Street NW 616-363-3262
Number 201-A
Grand Rapids, MI 49504
Jeffery L Duphin

6039 Wastewater Treatment Information Exhange
National Small Flows Clearinghouse
West Virginia University 800-624-8301
PO Box 6064 *Fax:* 304-293-3161
Morgantown, WV 56506
Loukis Kissonergis

6040 Wetlands Protection Hotline
Geological Resource Consultants
1555 Wilson Boulevard 703-527-5190
Suite 500 800-832-7828
Arlington, VA 22209
John Ruffing

6041 White Lung Association
PO Box 1483 410-243-5864
Baltimore, MD 21203 *Fax:* 410-243-5892
James Fite, Executive Director

6042 Wisconsin Home Energy Plus Program
Home Energy +
PO Box 7970 866-432-8947
Madison, WI 53707-7970 *Fax:* 608-267-6931
www.homeenergyplus.wi.gov

Provides energy assistance to qualified residents.

6043 Wisconsin State Energy Office
610 North Whitney Way 608-261-6609
2nd Floor *Fax:* 608-266-3957
Madison, WI 53707 oei@wisconsin.gov
www.stateenergyoffice.wi.gov

Promotes and invests in clean energy projects and assists businesses, local governments and citizens with energy-related issues.

Maria Redmond, Dir., Off. of Energy Innov.

Videos

Environmental

6044 Acid Rain: A North American Challenge
National Film Board of Canada
1123 Broadway
Suite 307
New York, NY 10010
212-629-8890
Fax: 212-629-8502
www.nfb.ca
Summarizes what we know today about the causes and effect of the menace of acid rain.

6045 Adventures of the Little Koala & Friends: Laura and the Mystery Egg
Family Home Entertaiment
15400 Sherman Way
PO Box 10124
Van Nuys, CA 91410
A cartoon exploring the topic of conservation and the protection of animals. The English dub release contains four episodes: "Laura Finds an Egg", "Conquering Mt. Breadknife", "Saving the Eucalyptus" and "Mommy Can Fly".
Noel Bloom, Founder

6046 Air Pollution: A First Film
Phoenix Learning Group
2349 Chaffee Dr.
St. Louis, MO 63146
314-569-0211
800-221-1274
Fax: 314-569-2834
phoenixlearninggroup.com
Program exploring the subject of air pollution such as acid rain and the solutions to this issue.
Bryan Sullivan, Executive Vice President

6047 Basic Ecology
Coast Community College District
1370 Adams Ave
Costa Mesa, CA 92626-5429
714-438-4600
www.cccd.edu
A film about ecology and the abiotic factors that contribute to the creation of an ecosystem.

Lori Adrian, Contact

6048 Battle for the Trees
National Film Board of Canada
Norman McLaren Building
3155 C"te de Liesse Rd
Montreal, QC H4N-2N4
800-542-2164
webmaster@onf.ca
www.nfb.ca
A documentary about those fighting to preserve their forests, including commentary by citizens, scientists, loggers, environmentalists and First Nations people.

Mireille Potvin, Rights Acquisitions
James Roberts, Director of Distribution

6049 Beyond Pollution
National Film Board of Canada
Norman McLaren Building
3155 C"te de Liesse Rd
Montreal, QC H4N-2N4
800-542-2164
webmaster@onf.ca
www.nfb.ca
A film examining the effects of the Gulf of Mexico oil spill, with interviews by environmental experts, government officials, fisherman & distributors, scientists, drilling engineers and others.

Mireille Potvin, Rights Acquisitions

6050 Captain Planet & the Planeteers: Toxic Terror
Turner Home Entertainment Company
1 CNN Center
Atlanta, GA 30303
404-827-1700
turner.info@turner.com
www.turner.com
Educational adventures of the Planeteers and Captain Planet exploring environmental issues such as damage to the ozone layer.
John Martin, CEO
David Levy, President

6051 Chelyabinsk: The Most Contaminated Spot on the Planet
Filmakers Library
3212 Duke St
Alexandria, VA 22314
703-212-8520
800-889-5937
alexanderstreet.com
The story of the Chelyabinsk atomic weapons complex, including a 1957 explosion, 1967 storm that spread radioactive dust, and the dumping of radioactive waste into a water-supply river.

Linda Gottesman, Co-President
Sue Oscar, Co-President

6052 Children of Chernobyl
Filmakers Library
3212 Duke St
Alexandria, VA 22314
703-212-8520
800-889-5937
alexanderstreet.com
Reveals the tragedy at Chernobyl through exclusive archival film and eyewitness accounts.

Linda Gottesman, Co-President
Sue Oscar, Co-President

6053 Coral Cities of the Caribbean
Nancy Sefton/Triton Productions
Earthwise Media
PO Box 2593
Silverdale, WA 98383
360-271-1584
Fax: 360-394-2168
info@earthwisevideos.com
www.earthwisevideos.com
A film taking us on a journey to the coral reefs of the Caribbean, where fish and invertebrates reside in their coral cities.

Nancy Sefton, Creative Director
Wes Nicholson, Technical Director

6054 Cousteau - Alaska: Outrage at Valdez
The Cousteau Society
Cousteau Society
P.O.Box 506
Etna, NH 03750-0506
212-532-2588
communication@cousteau.org
www.cousteau.org
About the impact of U.S.'s oil spill in Alaska.

6055 Dolphins
Freeman Films
P.O. Box 205
Laguna Beach, CA 92652
949-494-1055
Fax: 949-494-2079
contact@macfreefilms.com
macgillivrayfreeman.com
This film takes you on an underwater journey to observe the habitats and behaviors of dolphins.

Greg Macgillivray, Chairman & Film Director
Shaun Macgillivray, President & Producer

6056 E - Is For Elephant
TMW Media Group
#103, 2321 Abbot Kinney Blvd
Venice, CA 90291
310-577-8581
800-262-8862
general@tmwmedia.com
www.tmwmedia.com
This film explores the interdependence of all living creatures, with the focus on an elephants' life cycle, appearance and habitat.

6057 Earth Revealed
Annenberg Learner
PO Box 26983
St. Louis, MO 63118
202-783-0500
800-532-7637
Fax: 202-783-0333
order@learner.org
www.learner.org

A video series about the processes that shape Earth. Some topics explored are earthquakes, volcanoes, the creation of sea-floor crusts and shifting river courses.

6058 Earth's Physical Resources
The Open University
openlearn@open.ac.uk
www.open.edu
Series exploring the effectiveness of sustainable energy in the face of environmental issues. Some of the strategies discussed include wind power, biomass, hydro power, wave and tidal power, solar and geothermal power.

6059 Earthwise Media Educational Videos
Earthwise Media
PO Box 2593 360-271-1584
Silverdale, WA 98383 *Fax:* 360-394-2168
info@earthwisevideos.com
earthwisevideos.com
Production company specializing in environmental educational videos, multi-media presentations and computer aided learning tools.
Wes Nicholson, Technical Coordinator

6060 Ecological Realities: Natural Laws at Work
University of California
Berkeley, CA 94720 510-642-6000
webmaster@berkeley.edu
abt.ucpress.edu
A short film about a food pyramid in a marsh.

6061 Ecology: Succession
Coronet/MTI Film & Video
#212, 1990 E Lohman Ave 800-221-1274
Las Cruces, NM 88001 orders@phoenixlearninggroup.com
phoenixlearninggroup.com
A film exploring population density and its connection to the ecosystem. The focus is on the different factors that can limit population growth: climate, food shortages, predation and more.

6062 Ecology: Tree Top Insects
Kanopy Streaming
#410, 781 Beach St 415-513-1026
San Francisco, CA 94109 www.kanopystreaming.com
In this film, students explore the forest to learn about the organisms that dwell in the tree tops, most of which are insects.

6063 Ecosystems: The Florida Everglades
TMW Media Group
#103, 2321 Abbot Kinney Blvd 310-577-8581
Venice, CA 90291 800-262-8862
general@tmwmedia.com
www.tmwmedia.com
A film about the diverse ecosystems within the Florida Everglades, how they formed and how they were affected by the increase in human population. The film also looks at the measures being taken to monitor and protect the health of theEverglades.

6064 Effluents of Affluence
University of Michigan
Film Video Library 734-764-1817
500 S State St *Fax:* 734-764-6849
Ann Arbor, MI 48109 mirlyn.lib.umich.edu
A film examining waste disposal methods, land fills, and metal reclamation.
Pamela Mackintosh, Coordinator

6065 Elephant Boy
London Film Productions
Ilford House londonfilmproductions@gmail.com
133 - 135 Oxford St www.londonfilmproduction.com
London W1D-2HY
British adventure film about a young Indian boy and his elephant.

6066 Empire of the Red Bear
Discovery Communications
1 Discovery Pl 240-662-2000
Silver Spring, MD 20910 corporate.discovery.com
Series about Russian wildlife, with a focus on the brown bears of the Kamchatka Peninsula.

6067 Energetics of Life
John Wiley & Sons
111 River St 201-748-6000
Hoboken, NJ 07030-5774 *Fax:* 201-748-6088
info@wiley.com
ca.wiley.com
Film exploring different kinds of energy such as kinetic energy, potential energy, thermodynamics and more.
Matthew Kissner, Chairman & CEO
John Kritzmacher, Chief Financial Officer

6068 Energy NOW
Energy Now
#203, 621 - 4th Ave SW energynow.ca
Calgary, AB T2P-0K2
A magazine style TV show exploring topics of sustainable energy.

6069 Energy, The Alternatives
Media Guild
www.worldcat.org
Film about energy alternatives to fossil fuels. Some methods mentioned include harnessing the ocean's tidal cycles, harvesting the wind and developming methanol fuels.

6070 Environmental Science: Our Ozone Blanket
TMW Media Group
#103, 2321 Abbot Kinney Blvd 310-577-8581
Venice, CA 90291 800-262-8862
general@tmwmedia.com
www.tmwmedia.com
A program on the subject of science and Earth's atmosphere, exploring solutions to the damages caused to the ozone layer by CFCs.

6071 Everglades Region: An Ecological Study
John Wiley & Sons
111 River St 201-748-6000
Hoboken, NJ 07030-5774 *Fax:* 201-748-6088
info@wiley.com
ca.wiley.com
Film showing the ecology of the Atlantic Coastal Ridge, the Everglades, Big Cypress Swamp, and Coastal Mangrove Swamps of South Florida.

6072 Extinction in Progress
Kanopy Streaming
#410, 781 Beach St 415-513-1026
San Francisco, CA 94109 www.kanopystreaming.com
A film about the future of Haiti's natural resources, with a focus on the potential extinction of its biodiversity.
Lisa Landi, Licensing Director

6073 Forever Wild
Kanopy Streaming
#410, 781 Beach St 415-513-1026
San Francisco, CA 94109 www.kanopystreaming.com
A film about America's wilderness preservation efforts. The film follows those who have dedicated their time to protecting mountains, forests, deserts, prairies, and rivers from the hazzards brought on by development.
Lisa Landi, Licensing Director

6074 Forms of Energy
Films Media Group

132 West 31st St, 16th Fl 800-322-8755
New York, NY 10001 *Fax:* 800-678-3633
custserv@films.com
www.films.com
Film about different kinds of energy and their effects on objects.

6075 Fragile Earth: Enemies of the Oak
Oxford Scientific Films
21 Berners St, 4th fl www.oxfordscientificfilms.tv
London W1T-3LP
Film examining the economic balance within an English Oak tree, and the insect species that inhabit the tree.

6076 From Flint: Voices of a Poisoned City
Kanopy Streaming
#410, 781 Beach St 415-513-1026
San Francisco, CA 94109 www.kanopystreaming.com
Film about the water contamination crisis in Flint, Michigan and its detrimental affects on the health of the local people.

Lisa Landi, Licensing Director

6077 GPN Educational Media
Destination Education
4910 S 75th St 402-435-0110
Lincoln, NE 68516 slenzen@shopdei.com
shopgpn.com
Produces educational media - video, CD-ROM, DVD, Internet-for-16. Free previews available on line and on video. GPN offers over 1000 educational DVDs, including titles such as Animal Behavior, Bugs and Butterflies.

6078 Glaciers: Clues to Future Climate
TMW Media Group
#103, 2321 Abbot Kinney Blvd 310-577-8581
Venice, CA 90291 800-262-8862
general@tmwmedia.com
www.tmwmedia.com
This film presents a study of glaciers and their relevance to the irrigation of crops, hydroelectric power and underground water reservoirs. Settings discussed include Antarctica, Greenland and Iceland.

6079 Great American Woodlots: Minnesota
University of Maine Extension Service
420 Johnston Hall 612-625-3394
101 Pleasant St. S.E. www.extension.umn.edu
Minneapolis, MN 55455
Film about the ruffed grouse, its habitat and behaviours.

6080 Green TV
1125 Hayes St 415-255-4797
San Francisco, CA 94117 www.greentv.org
Video production company that combines environmental journalism with dramatic wildlife and natural history footage. Some of their titles include Counting Sheep, The Forest Through The Trees, Ocean Parables, Spotted in the Woodsandmore.
Frank Green, Owner & President

6081 Guardians of the Cliff
Nature Episodes
www.worldcat.org
Film about Cornell University's reintroduction of the Peregrine falcon into Northeastern U.S.

6082 Happy Campers with Miss Shirley & Friends
Kids Express

A guide to exploring nature, made for young children.

6083 How to Boil a Frog
Kanopy Streaming
#410, 781 Beach St 415-513-1026
San Francisco, CA 94109 www.kanopystreaming.com
An alternative documentary about environmental problems faced by the world today. A story told through characters, this film mixes comedy with facts to make the subject more engaging. The film covers the topics of overpopulation, thewar on nature, income inequality, oil and global warming.

Lisa Landi, Licensing Director

6084 I Walk in the Desert
Educational Images
www.worldcat.org
Film exploring the landscape of the Southwest deserts, and the specialized plants and animals which live there.

6085 In the Mind of Plants
XiveTV
#21, West 14th North St www.xivetv.com
New York, NY
A film exploring plants as sentient beings, with the ability to feel and perceive their environments in unique ways.

6086 Joe Albert's Fox Hunt
Education Development Center
43 Foundry Ave 617-969-7100
Waltham, MA 02453-8313 *Fax:* 617-969-5979
www@edc.org
www.edc.org
A series about "The Pine Barrens" of New Jersey.

6087 Kanopy Streaming
Kanopy Streaming
#410, 781 Beach St 415-513-1026
San Francisco, CA 94109 www.kanopystreaming.com
Kanopy Streaming is a video streaming company offering many environmental science videos as part of their collection. Topics covered include pollution, climate change, environmental activism, sustainability, environment & health,nuclear power, conservation, endangered species, Marine ecosystems and more.
Lisa Landi, Licensing Director
Lauren Silagyi, Publishing Director

6088 Last Call: Are There Limits to Growth?
Kanopy Streaming
#410, 781 Beach St 415-513-1026
San Francisco, CA 94109 www.kanopystreaming.com
A film exploring the limits of human development in a world of finite natural resources. The scientists and authors of the book 'The Limits to Growth' send out their final message about the measures we must take to sustain ourecosytems.

Lisa Landi, Licensing Director

6089 Legacy of an Oil Spill: Tens Years After Exxon
The Alaska Department of Fish and Game
1255 W. 8th St 907-465-4100
P.O. Box 115526 dfg.webmaster@alaska.gov
Juneau, AK 99811-5526 www.adfg.alaska.gov
Film documenting the Exxon Valdez Oil Spill 10 years after the event, with a focus on the recovery of affected wildlife and people of the area.
Sam Cotton, Commissioner

6090 Life Off Grid
Kanopy Streaming
#410, 781 Beach St 415-513-1026
San Francisco, CA 94109 www.kanopystreaming.com
A film about the Canadians who have made the decision to live away from the cities and build their lives around renewable energy.

Lisa Landi, Licensing Director

6091 Life on a Rocky Shore
Earthwise Media

PO Box 2593 360-271-1584
Silverdale, WA 98383-2593 *Fax:* 360-394-2168
info@earthwisevideos.com
www.earthwisevideos.com
Film giving an introduction to the plants and animals of the Pacific Northwest's rich Intertidal Zone. The self-paced presentation uses 100 photos, video clips and graphics to illustrate the story of life in the Zone. Learn about thetides, changing bands of life, and adaptation of life in the Zone. Film covers marine biology and comes with printable teacher's guide for grades 6-12.

Wes Nicholson, Technical Coordinator

6092 Man: The Polluter
National Film Board of Canada
Norman McLaren Building 800-542-2164
3155 C"te de Liesse Rd webmaster@onf.ca
Montreal, QC H4N-2N4 www.nfb.ca
An animated film investigating the consequences of man-made pollution, including commentary by Dr. Fred H. Knelman, Professor of Science and Human Affairs at Montreal's Concordia University.

Mireille Potvin, Rights Acquisitions

6093 Manatees, A Living Resource
Educational Images
www.worldcat.org
Film exploring manatees and the preservation efforts being made to prevent them from extinction.

6094 Microbial Ecology
Annenberg Learner
PO Box 26983 202-783-0500
St. Louis, MO 63118 800-532-7637
Fax: 202-783-0333
order@learner.org
www.learner.org
A film revealing the role microorganisms play in supporting all life forms; microorganisms are presented as being processors of oxygen, mineral nutrients for plant growth and waste materials.

Kristine Inchausti, Operations Analyst
Michele McLeod, Senior Program Officer

6095 Mitzi a Da Si
Nature Episodes
www.worldcat.org
A film examining the thermal features of Yellowstone National Park . Also covered is the subject of the Park's wildlife and their habitats.

6096 Oceans: The Mystery of the Missing Plastic
Kanopy Streaming
#410, 781 Beach St 415-513-1026
San Francisco, CA 94109 www.kanopystreaming.com
This film investigates the affects of plastics on the environment, as well as the mystery of plastic materials that have gone missing.

Lisa Landi, Licensing Director

6097 Origins
Vital Origins Productions

A film examining the affects of civilization and technology on the Earth's environment.

6098 Our Endangered Wildlife: The Massasauga Rattler
Nature Episodes
www.worldcat.org
Film examining the survival challenges faced by the Massasauga rattler as its natural habitats shrink. The focus is on a colony in a central New York wetland.

6099 Paradise Lost
National Film Board of Canada
Norman McLaren Building 800-542-2164
3155 C"te de Liesse Rd webmaster@onf.ca
Montreal, QC H4N-2N4 www.nfb.ca
A short animation film by Evelyn Lambart capturing the need for a clean environment for all living things. The film centers on the affects of air pollution on birds, butterflies and other wild animals.

Mireille Potvin, Rights Acquisitions

6100 Queen of the Sun
Kanopy Streaming
#410, 781 Beach St 415-513-1026
San Francisco, CA 94109 www.kanopystreaming.com
A film about the challenges faced by the bee population as a result of environmental change. The film includes commentary by Beekeepers, scientists and philosophers from around the world (such as Michael Pollan, Gunther Hauk andVandana Shiva).

Lisa Landi, Licensing Director

6101 Rainbows in the Sea: A Guide to Earth's Coral Reefs
Earthwise Media
PO Box 2593 360-271-1584
Silverdale, WA 98383-2593 *Fax:* 360-394-2168
info@earthwisevideos.com
www.earthwisevideos.com
Showcases the wide variety of colorful fish and invertebrates living in coral reefs, how they form and what they need to blossom. The guide also includes a teacher's guide for elementary and highschool students.
28 minutes
Wes Nicholson, Technical Coordinator

6102 Return of the Dragons
Nature Episodes
www.worldcat.org
A film about alligators and alligator farming.

6103 Salt Marshes: A Special Resource
Educational Images

Video examining the ecology of salt marshes, with a focus on marsh plants, marine vegetation, animals, migrating birds, insects, fish and shellfish.

6104 Sand Dune Ecology and Formation
Educational Images
www.worldcat.org
A film exploring the formation of sand dunes and vegetation in Oregon.

6105 Science & Environment: Pollution
TMW Media Group
#103, 2321 Abbot Kinney Blvd 310-577-8581
Venice, CA 90291 800-262-8862
general@tmwmedia.com
www.tmwmedia.com
A film about the different types of pollution created by both nature as well as humans; also discussed are ways by which we may reduce waste to protect the environment.

6106 Science in Focus: Energy
Annenberg Learner
PO Box 26983 202-783-0500
St. Louis, MO 63118 800-532-7637
Fax: 202-783-0333
order@learner.org
www.learner.org
A video series of 8 one-hour programs exploring the subject of energy and its role in motion, machines, food, the human body and the universe.

6107 Seals
Media Guild
www.worldcat.org

Film discussing the management of British Isles seal population.

6108 Song of the Salish Sea: A Natural History of Northwest Waters
Earthwise Media
PO Box 2593 360-271-1584
Silverdale, WA 98383-2593 *Fax:* 360-394-2168
info@earthwisevideos.com
www.earthwisevideos.com
Examines the fragile habitats that make up the Strait of Georgia, Strait of Juan de Fuca and Puget Sound. DVD includes a teacher's guide, Puget Sound Beach Guide, Kids for Puget Sound Passport, and curriculums for grades 6-12.
45 minutes
Wes Nicholson, Technical Coordinator

6109 Survey of the Animal Kingdom: The Vertebrates
Educational Images
www.worldcat.org
Video exploring creatures of aquatic environments: tunicates, lamprey, hagfish, sharks, rays, coelacanth, lungfish, ray-finned fish, sturgeon and more.

6110 The Changing Forest
A film examining the ecology of a forest near the Laurentian Shield, Quebec. We learn why the maple tree is

6111 The Chemical Kids
Filmakers Library
3212 Duke St 703-212-8520
Alexandria, VA 22314 800-889-5937
alexanderstreet.com
Alarming facts about man-made chemicals in food and water, especially how children are the most affected.

Linda Gottesman, Co-President
Sue Oscar, Co-President

6112 The Cost of Oil
Kanopy Streaming
#410, 781 Beach St 415-513-1026
San Francisco, CA 94109 www.kanopystreaming.com
A film about oil drilling in the Arctic and how it is affecting the Alaskan Inupiat people in their struggle to perserve their lifestyles and cultures.

Lisa Landi, Licensing Director

6113 The Earth at Risk Environmental Video Series
Schlessinger Video Productions
Cerebellum Corporation 415-541-9901
#406, 145 Corte Madera Town Center 866-386-0253
Corte Madera, CA 94925 *Fax:* 805-426-8136
customerservice@cerebellum.com
www.libraryvideocompany.com
Follows Kevin Seal in an educational series involving environmental projects, nature footage, and interviews with leading experts.

6114 The Habitable Planet: A Systems Approach to Environmental Science
Annenberg Learner
PO Box 26983 202-783-0500
St. Louis, MO 63118 800-532-7637
Fax: 202-783-0333
order@learner.org
www.learner.org
A video series containing 13 half-hour video programs about various sciences for teachers of biology, chemistry, and Earth science. The series begins with an examination of Earth's systems (geophysical, atmospheric, oceanic, andecosystems) and goes on to reveal how human activities have impacted these systems.

Kristine Inchausti, Operations Analyst
Michele McLeod, Senior Program Officer

6115 The Unnatural History of the Kakapo
Kanopy Streaming
#410, 781 Beach St 415-513-1026
San Francisco, CA 94109 www.kanopystreaming.com
Film about the endangered species of the Kakapo and scientists' efforts to save the Kakapo population from extinction.

Lisa Landi, Licensing Director

6116 The Windrifters
Nature Episodes
www.worldcat.org
Film about the re-introduction of bald eagles to the Montezuma Wildlife Refuge.

6117 The World Between the Tides: A Guide to Pacific Rocky Shores
Earthwise Media
PO Box 2593 360-271-1584
Silverdale, WA 98383-2593 *Fax:* 360-394-2168
info@earthwisevideos.com
www.earthwisevideos.com
A narrated journey along the intertidal area that examines harsh conditions, and how animals and plants have adapted. DVD includes teacher's guide.
23 minutes
Wes Nicholson, Technical Coordinator

6118 Tropical Rainforest
Media Guild
www.worldcat.org
Film exploring animal ecology in a rainforest environment. Also covered is a scientific research project carried out in the Los Tuxtlas Reserve (Veracruz, Mexico).

6119 Tropical Rainforests Under Fire
Educational Images
www.worldcat.org
Film about the ecology and exploitation of tropical rain forests.

6120 Unseen Life on Earth: An Introduction to Microbiology
Annenberg Learner
PO Box 26983 202-783-0500
St. Louis, MO 63118 800-532-7637
Fax: 202-783-0333
order@learner.org
www.learner.org
An educational video series on the subject of microbial functions. The series discusses the affects of microorganisms on various aspects of our lives.

6121 Walking On Oil: Alberta's Oil Sands
TMW Media Group
#103, 2321 Abbot Kinney Blvd 310-577-8581
Venice, CA 90291 800-262-8862
general@tmwmedia.com
www.tmwmedia.com
A film that examines oil deposits throughout the world, including the possibilities offered by "oil sands" as well as the dangers to the environment posed by invasive extraction processes.

6122 Warm Blooded Sea: Mammals of the Deep
Warner Home Video
Cousteau Society 212-532-2588
P.O. Box 506 communication@cousteau.org
Etna, NH 03750-0506 www.cousteau.org
A film exploring the evolution and behavior of Marine mammals such as dolphins, whales and seals. Regions explored include the South Pacific, Florida Keys, South Carolina and Argentina.

6123 Warming Warning
Media Guild
www.worldcat.org
Film covering theories about future global warming.

6124 Waters Of The World
TMW Media Group
#103, 2321 Abbot Kinney Blvd 310-577-8581
Venice, CA 90291 800-262-8862
general@tmwmedia.com
www.tmwmedia.com

Film revealing the distribution and placement of water bodies throughout the world, with a focus on the Hydrologic Cycle and major river systems of the world.

6125 Watershed: Canada's Threatened Rainforest
Media Guild
www.worldcat.org

Chronicles the expedition to Canada's Pacific Coast rainforests, covering environmental issues, complex ecosystems, and the work of conservationists.

6126 Weather Systems
TMW Media Group
#103, 2321 Abbot Kinney Blvd 310-577-8581
Venice, CA 90291 800-262-8862
general@tmwmedia.com
www.tmwmedia.com

This video series presents scientific contents in a simplified format, exploring weather and its many forms (atmosphere, air density, winds, clouds and storms) and how weather affects our lives.

6127 Wilderness Video
Wilderness Video
888 Beswick Way 541-488-9363
Ashland, OR 97520 *Fax:* 541-488-9363
bob@wildernessvideo.com
wildernessvideo.com

A production company offering footage and videos of nature scenes such as sunrises and sunsets, rainbows, waterfalls, storms, cities and wildlife.

Bob Glusic, Owner

Green Products & Services

General

6128 **18 Rabbits Organics**
31 Water St 415-922-6006
San Francisco, CA 94133 customerservice@18rabbits.com
www.18rabbits.com
Manufacturer of organic bars and granola.
Alison Seibert, Founder

6129 **A.V. Olsson Trading Co., Inc.**
2001 West Main St 203-969-2090
Suite 215 customerservice@avolsson.com
Stamford, CT 06902 www.avolsson.com
A.V. Olsson Trading Co. is a family-owned business focusing on the importation of fine dairy products, quality herring, and environmentally-friendly cooking and baking products.

6130 **AIYA America**
386 Beech Ave Unit B3 310-212-1395
Torrance, CA 90501 *Fax:* 310-212-1386
info@aiya-america.com
www.aiya-america.com
AIYA is Japan's leading Matcha tea producer. Matcha is the most exciting discovery of the 21st century's modern tea world. Created over 800 years ago by Buddhist monks as a meditational drink, Matcha is known today as the healthiest,rarest and most premium of all tea varieties of Japan.
Fumi Sugita, Executive General Manager

6131 **Acorn Designs**
5066 Mott Evans Road 607-387-3424
Trumansburg, NY 14886 800-299-3997
Fax: 607-387-5609
info@acorndesigns.org
www.acorndesigns.org
Totes and other items with wildlife and nature themes; high post-consumer recycled paper; 100% post-consumer recycled paper journals and cards. Images from nature artwork from over 30 artists.

Steve Sierigk, Owner

6132 **Adventure Coffee Roasting**
633 N Jasmine Place 520-247-2651
Tucson, AZ 85710 Info@AdventureCoffeeRoasting.com
www.adventurecoffeeroasting.com
Adventure Coffee Roasting encourages sustainable pesticide-free farming. They roast only certified organically grown coffee in small batches, assuring product freshness and consistency.

6133 **Ak-mak Bakeries**
89 Academy Avenue 559-875-5511
Sanger, CA 93657-2104 www.akmakbakeries.com
Their goal is to consistently produce and market the best Armenian flat breads, selecting only the purest and highest quality ingredients, from hand-picked reliable sources, and to leverage our family recipes handed down throughgenerations of Armenian bread baking traditions for the benefit of our customers.

6134 **Alexandra Avery Purely Natural Body Care**
4717 SE Belmont Street 503-236-5926
Portland, OR 97215 800-669-1863
Fax: 503-234-7272
100% natural and cruelty free aromatherapy products for face and body care.
Alexandra Avery, President

6135 **All Terrain**
20 North Main St, Unit 1 603-763-8800
Newport, NH 03773 800-246-7328
info@allterrainco.com
www.allterrainco.com
All Terrain sells natural products to help people live more active, healthier lives. Safe and highly effective, All Terrain's products disprove the myth that if it's natural, it can't work as well as chemical-based products. Theproducts are developed by and for outdoor enthusiasts for use whether trekking in the backcountry or relaxing with family in your backyard.

6136 **Allen's Naturally**
PO Box 1779 800-352-8971
Birmingham, Mi 48012 www.allensnaturally.com
Making Laundry Detergents Free of Perfumes, Fragrances and Dyes for Cloth Diapering and those with MCS (Multiple Chemical Sensitivities) since 1979

6137 **Allsop Home & Garden**
660 North Main Street, Ste #220 866-425-5767
PO Box 4921 www.allsopgarden.com
Ketchum, Id 83340
Allsop Home & Garden is known for combining creative materials with solar power for efficient, beautiful and sustainable outdoor lighting.

6138 **Alter Eco**
2339 Third Street 415-701-1212
Suite 70 *Fax:* 415-701-1213
San Francisco, CA 94107 sales@alterecofoods.com
www.alterecofoods.com
Alter Eco is based on the premise that food is fundamental to life – and whole, healthy, delicious food can make life better for people all over the world. By working directly with the small-scale farmers who grow our quinoa, rice,sugar and cacao, helping them institute Fair Trade and Organic practices and assisting them in improving both quality of food and quality of life, they are creating a system that benefits everyone involved.
Mathieu Senard, Co-Founder/Co-CEO
Edouard Rollet, Co-Founder/Co-CEO

6139 **Amy's Kitchen**
PO Box 449 707-781-7535
Petaluma, CA 94953 www.amys.com
Since its inception in 1987 Amy's has created over 250 frozen meals, including pizzas, pocket sandwiches, pot pies, entrées, snacks and whole meals. In 1999, they introduced a grocery line that now includes canned soups, beans andchili as well as jarred pasta sauces and salsas.
Jack Chipman, VP of Sales
Dennis Bee, Planning Manager

6140 **Ancient Harvest**
1722 14th Street 310-217-8125
Suite 212 ancientharvest.com
Boulder, CO 80302
They serve up great tasting, non-GMO and organic, gluten-free foods for all, including gluten-free pasta, ancient grain blends, mac and cheese, quinoa flour, quinoa flakes and ready-to-eat polenta in a variety of inspired culinaryflavors.

6141 **Andalou Naturals**
7250 Redwood Blvd. 415-446-9470
Suite 208 888-898-6955
Novato, CA 94945 *Fax:* 415-446-9479
support@andalou.com
andalou.com
Offers skin care, hair care and body care products which are made thoughtfully and beautifully, blending advanced Fruit Stem Cell Science with natural and fair-trade ingredients, with a minimum 70% certified organic content, forvisible and healthy results.
Stacey Kelly Egide, CEO
Mark A. Egide, President

6142 **Annie's**
1610 5th Street 510-558-7500
Berkeley, CA 94710 800-288-1089
www.annies.com
Annie's Homegrown is a Berkeley, California-based maker of natural and organic pastas, meals and snacks.
John Foraker, CEO
Zahir Ibrahim, EVP, CFO

6143 Ark Naturals
6166 Taylor Road
Suite 103
Naples, FL 34109
239-592-9388
800-926-5100
Fax: 239-592-9338
info@arknaturals.com
www.arknaturals.com
Ark Naturals is the leading manufacturer of health, remedy and lifestyle solutions for pets from head to tail. For over 16 years, Ark Naturals has provided the most complete line of wellness and remedy products of the highest quality.
Susan D. Weiss, President

6144 Arora Creations
254 Dekalb Ave.
Suite #4
Brooklyn, NY 11205
347-294-4815
www.aroracreations.com
Arora Creations, Inc. launched the first-ever USDA-certified Organic Indian Grocery product line in the US market.
Dhiraj C. Arora, Founder/CEO/President

6145 Artisana Organics
810 81st Avenue
Suite B
Oakland, CA 94621
510-632-8612
866-237-8688
Fax: 510-380-6942
www.artisanaorganics.com
There passion is creating unique, delicious, healthy, gourmet food. Handmade with care, there organic foods are crafted using a temperature controlled process that preserves the life-essential fatty acids, proteins, vitamins, andenzymes.

6146 Artistic Video
87 Tyler Avenue
Sound Beach, NY 11789
631-744-5999
888-982-4244
Fax: 631-744-5993
bobklien@movementsofmagic.com
www.movementsofmagic.com
Instructional videos and DVDs on health and fitness, alternative healing, children's programs about animals, free interactive section with articles, discussion forums, video clips, classes, instructions, Tai-Chi and other natureoriented cultures and practices.

Bob Klein, President

6147 Associated Building Maintenance Co., Inc.
2140 Priest Bridge Court
Suite 3
Crofton, Ma 21114
410-721-1818
800-721-9068
info@abmcoinc.com
www.abmcoinc.com
Associated Building Maintenance Co., Inc. is a woman-owned, contract cleaning company headquartered in Crofton, Maryland. Over 1,000 employees clean over 14 million square feet daily in the Maryland, Virginia, and Washington DC area.
Deborah Zagami, President
Harry Zagami, General Manager

6148 Aura Cacia
5398 31st Avenue
Urbana, I 52345
319-227-7996
800-437-3301
Fax: 800-717-4372
customercare@auracacia.com
www.auracacia.com
Aura Cacia makes aromatherapy accessible with innovative ready-to-use products that let even beginners realize the full benefits of our high-quality essential oils in a variety of ways that can easily be a part of any lifestyle.

6149 AusPen
99 Madison Avenue
Suite 405
New York, NY 10016
Fax: 929-214-4112
kerrie@auspen.us
www.auspen.us
Auspen supplies quality, eco-friendly refillable whiteboard markers to the general public and the education community.

Kerrie Sharpley, Founder & General Manager

6150 Aztec Secret
P.O. Box 841
Pahrump, NV 89041
775-727-8351
Fax: 775-727-1882
www.aztec-secret.com
Aztec Secret Indian Healing Clay, Jojoba Oil, Kukui Nut Oil, Tee Tree Oil and other beauty products available online and at local health food stores.

6151 BDM Holdings
7915 Jones Branch Drive
McLean, VA 22102
703-848-5000
Bennie Dibona, VP Engineering/Environment

6152 Balance of Nature
Unviersity of Chicago Press
1427 East 60th Street
Chicago, IL 60637
773-702-7700
Fax: 773-702-9756

6153 Bamboo Studio
31878 Del Obispo St.
Building 118 – 336
San Juan Capistrano, CA 92675
949-951-2064
Fax: 949-951-4726
sales@ecobambooware.com
www.ecobambooware.com
Bamboo Studio is a all-occasion dinnerware that is both disposable and reusable.

6154 Bare
38 Keyes Avenue
Suite 210
San Francisco, CA 94129
509-554-5540
Fax: 509-554-5510
info@baresnacks.com
www.baresnacks.com

6155 Barlean's
3660 Slater Road
Ferndale, WA 98248
360-384-0485
800-445-3529
questions@barleans.com
www.barleans.com
Offers flax and borage oil products.
Bruce Barlean, Owner

6156 Bee's Wrap
394 Rockydale Road
Bristol, VT 05443
802-643-2132
info@beeswrap.com
www.beeswrap.com
Offers sustainable food storage products.

6157 Begley's
3627 Briggeman Drive
Los Alamitos, CA 90720
714-689-0063
Fax: 714-242-0551
begleysbest.com
Offers earth responsible household product.
Ed Begley, Jr., Owner

6158 Bellino Fine Linens
471 South Dean Street
Englewood, NJ 07631
201-568-5255
Fax: 201-568-0155
info@bellinofinelinens.com
www.bellinofinelinens.com
BELLINO has been providing exqui- site luxury linens for the bed, bath and table for 25 years.

6159 Betty Lou's
750 SE Booth Bend Rd
McMinnville, OR 97128
503-434-5205
800-242-5205
www.bettylousinc.com
Healthy, all natural snack products; low carb, all natural, dairy, gluten, and wheat free.
Betty Lou, Owner

6160 Big Dipper Wax Works
700 South Orchard St.
Seattle, WA 98108
206-767-7322
888-826-7770
Fax: 206-938-5444
info@bigdipperwaxworks.com
www.bigdipperwaxworks.com
Hand crafted pure natural beeswax candles available in many unique styles.

6161 Big Green Cleaning Company
4860 Calle Real
Santa Barbara, CA 93110
805-692-1000
Fax: 805-967-3915
biggreen@biggreenclean.com
biggreenclean.com

Offers cleaning services.
Allen Williams, President

6162 Bio-Sun Systems
RR 2 Box 134A
Millerton, PA 16936
570-527-2200
800-847-8840
Fax: 570-537-6200
biosun@npacc.net
www.bio-sun.com

Composting toilets and modular restrooms.
Donna White, President
Al White, VP

6163 BioBag Americas, Inc.
1059 Broadway
Suite F
Dunedin, FL 34698
727-789-1646
Fax: 727-614-9746
info@biobagusa.com
biobagusa.com

BioBag provides bags and films for the collection of organic waste for the purpose of composting.

6164 Biokleen
PO Box 820689
Vancouver, WA 98682
800-477-0188
biokleenhome.com

Biokleen laundry products are triple concentrated to reduce packaging, waste and energy.
Cindy Rimer
Barry Firth

6165 Bionaturae
PO Box 98
North Franklin, CT 06254
860-642-6996
Fax: 860-642-6990
info@bionaturae.com
www.bionaturae.com

Organic Italian food.

6166 Biotta
484 East Carmel Drive
#137
Carmel, IN 46032
866-595-8917
888-524-6882
Fax: 888-816-9725
info@biottajuices.com
www.biottajuices.com

Non-GMO. Vegan. 100% pure juice.

6167 Bob's Red Mill
13521 SE Pheasant Ct
Milwaukie, OR 97222
800-349-2173
www.bobsredmill.com

Whole grain store and bakery.

6168 Bolana Enterprises, Inc.
10739 Tucker Street
Suite 270
Beltsville, MD 20705
301-595-2577
Fax: 888-750-0179
www.bolanainc.com

Bolona offer comprehensive janitorial services tailored to your organization's unique needs.

6169 Bonga Foods
21955 Paicifie Coast Hwy
Suite B201
Malibu, CA 90265
310-456-1526

Through trading, Bonga-Baobab enables local harvesters to support themselves.

6170 Botanical Interests
660 Compton Street
Broomfield, CO 80020
303-464-6464
800-486-2647
www.botanicalinterests.com

Supplies gardeners with the highest quality seed in informative seed packets on the market.

6171 Bottled Up Designs
202 Glenrose
East Fallowfield, PA 19320
484-885-7171
www.bottledupdesigns.com

Designs recycled from reclaimed antique glass and bottles.

6172 Bragg Live Foods
Box 7
Santa Barbara, CA 93102
805-968-1020
800-446-1990
Fax: 805-968-1001
info@bragg.com
bragg.com

Paul C. Bragg, originator of Health Food Stores in America, founded the company, now run by his daughter Patricia Bragg, N.D., Ph.D., who continues to provide natural healthy products, and a library of self-help books.
Paul C. Bragg, Founder

6173 Building Maintenance Services
11 Penn Plaza
New York, NY 10001
212-714-0004
bmsbuildingservices.com

BMS provides building maintinance service, provides an environment that is clean, safe, and an enhancement to the work day.
Michael Doherty, President & CEO
Carol Gambardella, Vice President & CFO

6174 Cangles
PO Box 74
Vassar, MI 48768
877-491-5655
Service@Cangles.com
www.cangles.com

Makes jewelry out of recycled can.

6175 Celtic Sea Salt
4 Celtic Dr.
Arden, NC 28704
800-867-7258
Fax: 828-654-0529
info@selinanaturally.com
www.celticseasalt.com

Celtic Sea Salt® Brand Sea Salt is authentic, unprocessed whole salt from pristine coastal regions of the world.

6176 Cheri's Desert Harvest
1840 E. Winsett
Tucson, AZ 85719
800-743-1141
Fax: 520-623-7741
www.cherisdesertharvest.com

Cheri's all-natural products are made from fresh fruits and vegetables indigenous to the Sonoran Desert.

6177 Chia Burst
9461 Charleville Blvd.
#123
Beverly Hills, CA 90212
310-500-5119
chiabursts@yahoo.com

Supplies organic Chia seed.

6178 Chicago Vegan Foods
905 N. Ridge Ave.
Suite 7
Lombard, IL 60148
630-629-9667
info@chicagoveganfoods.com
chicagoveganfoods.com

Teese Vegan Cheese is created with the goal of mimicking cheesy-based comfort foods, minus the dairy.

6179 ChicoBag
13434 Browns Valley Drive
Chico, CA 95973
530-342-4426
888-496-6166
Fax: 530-267-5434
info@chicobag.com
www.chicobag.com

Designs long lasting reusable bags.

6180 ChildLife Essentials
8690 Hayden Place
Culver City, CA 90232
310-305-4640
800-993-0332
Fax: 310-305-4680
mailroom@childlife.net
www.childlife.net

ChildLife Essentials® provides a complete line of nutritional supplements designed specifically for infants and children.

6181 Choice Organic Tea
600 South Brandon Street 206-525-0051
Seattle, WA 98108 866-972-6879
Fax: 206-523-9750
choiceorganicteas@worldpantry.com
www.choiceorganicteas.com
A firm belief in organics, with a dedication to ensure the ethical treatment of workers who cultivate tea, and a team of dedicated employees at Choice Organic Teas, has made the company a modern day tea pioneer.

6182 Christi's Green Cleaning
Christi's Green Cleaning 831-406-0145
Santa Cruz, CA 95060 christisgreencleaning@gmail.com
www.christisgreencleaning.com
Christi's Green Cleaning uses cleaning products such as Envirox, Bon Ami, Biokleen, and Howard's Naturals which are non-toxic and environmentally friendly.

6183 Clean Conscience
4715 Broadway Street 303-495-2444
Suite C-6 www.cleanconscience.com
Boulder, CO 80304
Provides healthy home cleaning services.

6184 CleanNet USA
2010 Corporate Ridge 800-735-8838
Suite 700 *Fax:* 703-749-7719
McLean, VA 22102 www.cleannetusa.com
CleanNet USA® was created in response to an increasing demand for a go-to company with access to commercial cleaning service companies nationwide.

6185 Clenz Cleaning
1215 Crease St. 215-545-0066
Philadelphia, PA 19125 info@clenzphilly.com
www.clenzphilly.com
Provides cleaning service in the Greater Philadelphia area.

6186 Clif Bar & Company
1451 66th Street 800-254-3227
Emeryville, CA 94608-1004 www.clifbar.com

6187 Coconut Secret
298 Miller Ave. 415-383-9800
Mill Valley, CA 94941 888-369-3393
Fax: 415-383-9804
info@coconutsecret.com
www.coconutsecret.com
Create a low glycemic, gluten-free snack line that is safe for diabetics, using the purest, most organic, least processed ingredients.

6188 Cole's
11 Broadcommon Rd. 401-396-5966
Bristol, RI 02809 info@colestrout.com
www.colestrout.com
Cole's is the earth-friendly company dedicated to bringing you the finest, freshest foods from around the globe while preserving the delicate balance between nature and our own nutritional needs.

6189 Color Garden
1300 N Hancock 714-572-0444
Anaheim, CA 92807 *Fax:* 714-572-0999
inquire@colormaker.com
www.colorgarden.net
Color Garden™ pure natural food colors are 100% plant based.

6190 Colorado Mountain Jam
3573 G Rd. 970-464-0745
Palisade, CO 81526 www.plumdaisy.com
Colorado Mountain Fine Jams & Jellies mission is to offer a diverse gourmet line of jams and jellies that are as nutritious and healthy as they are delicious and pleasurable to eat.

6191 Coombs Family Farms
PO Box 117 888-266-6271
Brattleboro, VT 05302 www.coombsfamilyfarms.com
Provides maple products nad supports small family farms.

6192 Cotton Clouds
5176 S 14th Avenue 520-428-7000
Safford, AZ 85546 *Fax:* 520-428-6630
Yarn, patterns, books, video's, kit for weaving crochet, knitting and spinning.

6193 CureAll Cleaning Services
48B Paine Ave 973-251-9968
Suite#2 *Fax:* 973-251-9801
Irvington, NJ 07111 info@cureallcleaning.com
www.cureallcleaning.com
CureAll Cleaning Services, LLC is a family owned and operated company located in the northern New Jersey area.

6194 Curry Love
PO Box 25397 888-635-8886
Los Angeles, CA 90025 www.mycurrylove.com
Organic Curries

6195 DCD Cleaning Service
18895 S. Highlite 586-343-3457
Clinton Township, MI 48035 www.dcdcleaningservice.com
DCD cleaning services uses commercial products, many of which are all natural and Green Sealed certified.

6196 Dastony
PO Box 328 800-518-0727
Glenview, IL 60025 dastony.com
Dastony uses an ancient method known as stone-grinding in the production of its products.

6197 DeVita
1616 West Williams Drive 877-2DE-VITA
Phoenix, AZ 85027 devitastyle.com
DeVita Natural Skin Care and Color Cosmetics is wholly owned and operated by Cherylanne DeVita, Ph.D., President/CEO, and is a certified woman-owned business by the Women's Business Enterprise National Council (WBENC).
Cherylanne DeVita, Ph.D.,, President/CEO

6198 Delallo
6390 Route 30 877-DEL-LLO
Jeannette, PA 15644 info@DeLallo.com
www.delallo.com
Italian foods company.

6199 Denver Concierge
1450 Grove Street 303-975-2808
Denver, CO 80204 www.denverconcierge.com
Denver House Cleaning serives.
John Kitts, President
Maria Herrera, General Manager

6200 Desert Essence
PO Box 14007 800-645-5768
Hauppauge, NY 11788 CustomerCare@DesertEssence.com
www.desertessence.com
Desert Essence was founded in 1978 around a simple concept: beauty is natural, and nature is beautiful.

6201 Doctor Kracker
1100 Klein Road 972-633-1100
Suite 200 *Fax:* 972-633-1130
Plano, TX 75074
Dr. Kracker was founded in 2003 in Dallas, Texas by a group of European and American bakers with a unique love for Artisan breads.

6202 Dr. Bronner's
1335 Park Center Drive 844-937-2551
Vista, CA 92081 *Fax:* 760-745-6675
info@drbronner.com
www.drbronner.com

Family-Owned and Run, Natural Product Pioneers provides high quality liquid and bar soaps

6203 DrTung's
PO Box 667 — 808-239-5799
Kaneohe, HI 96744 — *Fax:* 808-239-5299
drtungs.com

Innovative Oral care products

6204 Drew's
926 Vermont Rt. 103 South — 802-875-1184
Chester, VT 05143 — 800-228-2980
Fax: 802-875-5126
info@chefdrew.com
www.chefdrew.com

Drew's unique dressings and salsas are produced in small batches infused with authentic regional and ethnic flavors

6205 ECOBAGS
23-25 Spring Street — 914-944-4556
Suite 302 — 800-720-2247
Ossining, NY 10562 — *Fax:* 914-944-4609
info@ecobags.com
www.ecobags.com

Eco-Bags Products, Inc. opened for business in 1989 makes reusable bags

6206 EO Products
90 Windward Way — 415-945-1900
San Rafael, CA 94901 — 800-570-3775
customerservice@eoproducts.com
www.eoproducts.com

Organic essential products
Max Geiser, Creative Director
Rosa Prado, Production Supervisor

6207 Earth Mama Angel Baby
9866 SE Empire Court — 503-607-0607
Clackamas, OR 97015 — *Fax:* 503-607-0667
earthmamaangelbaby.com

Provide safe, herbal alternatives for pregnant, postpartum and breastfeeding women, and babies of all ages, and to help educate people about traditional plant medicine and safe personal care.

6208 Earth Options
Solar Electric Engineering
117 Morris Street — 707-824-4150
Sebastopol, CA 95472 — 882-198-1986
Fax: 707-542-4358

Environmental retail products.

6209 Earth Science
PO Box 1925 — 909-371-7565
Corona, CA 91718 — 800-222-6720
Fax: 909-371-0509

All-natural, environmentally sound skin and hair care products.
Kristine Schoenauer, President

6210 Earth Therapeutics
163 E. Bethpage Rd. — 800-789-3579
Plainview, NY 11803 — *Fax:* 516-454-6599
service@earththerapeutics.us
www.earththerapeutics.com

6211 Eco Touch
One Washington St. — 888-375-7970
Suite 200 — *Fax:* 603-319-1257
Dover, NH 03820 — www.ecotouch.net
Rangeof car care products

6212 Eco-Dent Premium Natural Oral Care Products
PO Box 325 — 262-889-8561
Twin Lakes, WI 53181 — *Fax:* 262-889-2461
ecodent@lotuspress.com
www.eco-dent.com

Natural oral care products

6213 Eco-Store
2441 Edgewater Drive — 407-426-9949
Orlando, FL 32804 — 800-556-9949
Fax: 407-649-3148
beth@eco-store.com

Environmental home products, gifts, etc.

6214 EcoPaper
1884 Eastman Ave — 805-644-4462
Suite 107 — www.ecopaper.com
Ventura, CA 93003

EcoPaper makes, distributes, and sell finest environmental papers.

6215 Ecology Store
6928 Queens Boulevard — 718-446-4444
Flushing, NY 11377 — 800-548-9660
Fax: 718-446-9860

Range of environmental products.

6216 Eden Foods
701 Tecumseh Road — 517-456-7424
Clinton, MI 49236 — 888-424-3336
Fax: 517-456-6075
info@edenfoods.com
www.edenfoods.com

Eden Foods began in Ann Arbor in the late 1960s with friends sourcing natural food.

6217 Edison Grainery
Oakland, CA 94621 — 510-382-0202
Fax: 510-263-5778
service@edisongrainery.com
www.edisongrainery.com

Organic Food Ingredients and Pantry Staples.

6218 Edward & Sons
PO Box 1326 — 805-684-8500
Carpinteria, CA 93014 — *Fax:* 805-684-8220
www.edwardandsons.com

Edward & Sons Trading Company, Inc. supplies innovative natural and organic vegetarian foods to stores and consumers throughout the world

6219 Effi Foods
11620 Wilshire Boulevard — 310-582-5938
Suite 900 — *Fax:* 310-388-8798
Los Angeles, CA 90025 — info@effifoods.com
www.effifoods.com

EFFi Foods is a company for producing organic, holistic foods and nutraceuticals with its main focus on delivering nutritionally unprecedented snacking options with exceptional taste for people on-the-go.
Carina Ayden, Founder, Executive Director
Liz Rodriguez, Branding / Public Relations

6220 Ener-G Foods
5960 1st AVE S — 206-767-3928
Seattle, WA 98108 — 800-331-5222
Fax: 206-764-3398
customerservice@ener-g.com
www.ener-g.com

Provide a wide range of ready-made foods and mixes that are wholesome, nutritious, risk-free and great tasting.

6221 Energy Efficient Environments
2119 Inverness Lane — 847-475-3005
Glen View, IL 60025 — 800-336-3749
Efficient and earth-friendly devices for energy, water and light use.

6222 Environment Friendly Papers
Cherry Paper
13520 Liberty Avenue — 718-297-3000
Jamaica, NY 11419 — *Fax:* 718-297-2986
cherryop@AOL.com

100% recycled gift stationary, with original designs depicting flora and fauna of South Africa and environmental themes.

6223 **Equal Exchange**
50 United Drive 774-776-7333
West Bridgewater, MA 02379 *Fax:* 508-587-3833
orders@equalexchange.coop
equalexchange.coop
Equal Exchange's mission is to build long-term trade partnerships that are economically just and environmentally sound, to foster mutually beneficial relationships between farmers and consumers and to demonstrate, through our success,the contribution of worker co-operatives and Fair Trade to a more equitable, democratic and sustainable world.

6224 **Erlander's Natural Products**
Nature's Department Store
2279 Lake Avenue 626-797-7004
Altadena, CA 91001 800-562-8873
Fax: 626-798-2663
Natural olive oil-wine soap; bar and liquid roach killer from herbs, organic red zinfandel wine, 100% organic cotton pillows and mattresses, jewelry - semi-precious and costume, washing compound/non-detergent, sodium sesquicarbonate.
Leatrice Erlander, Co-Owner
Stig Erlander, Co-Owner

6225 **Eton**
1015 Corporation Way 650-903-3866
Palo Alto, CA 94303 800-872-2228
Fax: 650-903-3867
Info@etoncorp.com
www.etoncorp.com
Etón's vision is to harness nature's energy to power consumer products that keep people prepared, informed, entertained, and on-the-go.

6226 **Executive Building Maintenance**
7910 Woodmont Ave. 301-657-4211
Suite 1310 *Fax:* 301-657-3066
Bethesda, MD 20814 ebm@exebm.com
www.exebm.com
EBM, Inc., is a full service company offering superior cleaning and general janitorial maintenance to commercial & residential building owners, managers and construction companies.
David N. Kydd, President
Steve Chamberlain, Vice President Operations

6227 **Extreme Green Cleaning**
1825 North Oxnard Blvd 805-252-9435
Suite 23 extremegreencleanings.com
Oxnard, CA 93030
Cleaning services in Ventura County

6228 **Fig Food Co.**
PO Box 265 855-FIG-FOOD
New York, NY 10014 figfood.com
Organic food supplies

6229 **Flavorganics**
268 Doremus Avenue 973-344-8014
Newark, NJ 07105 *Fax:* 973-344-1948
flavorganics@worldpantry.com
www.flavorganics.com
Offers Organic Vanilla Extract.

6230 **Florida Crystals**
One North Clematis Street 561-366-5100
Suite 200 877-835-2828
West Palm Beach, FL 33401 *Fax:* 561-366-5158
retailproducts@floridacrystals.com
www.floridacrystals.com
Florida Crystals Corporation is a privately owned and diversified agriculture, consumer products, real estate and energy company which produces sugar.

6231 **Foods Alive**
4840 County Road 4 260-488-4497
Waterloo, IN 46793 www.foodsalive.com
Foods Alive is a family owned company dedicated to creating the healthiest foods.

6232 **Frieling**
398 York Southern Road 803-548-2000
Fort Mill, SC 29715 800-827-2582
Fax: 803-548-2060
frieling.com

6233 **From The Fields**
1945 East Francisco Boulevard 415-578-2990
Suite #47 / L info@fromthefields.net
San Rafael, CA 94901 www.fromthefields.net
Makes Oragnic food like granola, porridge, oatmeal and muesli that is fresh, delicious and nourishing.

6234 **From War to Peace**
PO Box 4358 805-545-0383
San Luis Obispo, CA 93403 *Fax:* 805-888-2878
info@fromwartopeace.com
www.fromwartopeace.com
Accessories mande from recycled weapon

6235 **Fruit Bliss**
220 42nd Street 646-225-6565
Brooklyn, NY 11232 *Fax:* 718-398-2005
info@fruitbliss.com
fruitbliss.com
Deliciously juicy, organic whole fruit, sun sweetened and infused with water.

6236 **FungusAmongUs**
PO Box 352 360-568-3403
Snohomish, WA 98291 www.fungusamongus.com
SuppliesOrganic Mushrooms

6237 **Futurebiotics**
70 Commerce Drive 631-273-6300
Hauppauge, NY 11788 800-645-1721
customerservice@futurebiotics.com
www.futurebiotics.com

6238 **GAIA Clean Earth Products**
PO Box 1906 717-840-1638
York, PA 17405 800-726-5496
Fax: 800-726-5496
gaia@blazenet.net
Environmentally-compatible products.
Brian N Hartman, President

6239 **GarbageMan**
13895 Industrial Park Blvd. 763-269-8182
Suite 100 866-808-8777
Plymouth, MN 55441 *Fax:* 763-269-8183
email@garbagemanco.com
www.garbagemanco.com
GarbageMan, A Green Company started operations with one small truck during the spring of 2008 in Maple Grove, MN.

6240 **Giusto's**
344 Littlefield Avenue 650-873-6566
South San Francisco, CA 94080 888-884-1940
Fax: 650-873-2826
homebaking@giustos.com
giustos.com/landing
For three generations, the Giusto's family has been committed to providing the freshest, highest quality natural and organic products available. They offer flours, as well as an entire selection of ingredients for the home baker!

6241 **GladRags**
215 SE Morrison 503-282-0436
#2000-E 800-799-4523
Portland, OR 97214 hello@gladrags.com
gladrags.com
Period essential supplies

6242 **GlassDharma**
17900 Ocean Drive 707-964-9350
Suite 48 *Fax:* 707-964-9320
Fort Bragg, CA 95437 info@glassdharma.com
glassdharma.com
Manufactures glass drinking straws and accessories.

David Leonhardt, Founder

6243 **Glenny's**
1081 East 48th Street 516-377-1400
Brooklyn, NY 11234 *Fax:* 516-377-9046
Gluten-free Snacks

6244 **GloryBee**
120 N. Seneca Rd. 800-456-7923
Eugene, OR 97402 glorybee.com
GloryBee started in the family garage of Dick and Pat Turanski in 1975 with a dream of providing natural, healthy ingredients for the people of their town

6245 **Go Green World Products, LLC**
11460 N Cave Creek Road 602-944-4442
Suite 7 866-995-4442
Phoenix, AZ 85020 *Fax:* 602-944-4956
info@greenplanetpaints.com
www.greenplanetpaints.com
Go Green World Products offer a complete line of architectural plant and clay based paints, plant based stains and sealers/varnishes for home improvement projects.

Ted Sosnicki, President/CEO

6246 **Goddess Garden**
6525 Gunpark Drive 303-651-3678
Ste. 370-415 855-723-3786
Boulder, CO 80301 *Fax:* 888-370-2878
customerservice@goddessgarden.com
www.goddessgarden.com
Oragnic product suppliers

6247 **Good Boy Organics**
320 Canisteo Street 607-324-2200
Hornell, NY 14843 *Fax:* 607-324-2388
info@goodboyorganics.com
www.goodboyorganics.com
Good Boy Organics and a growing family of delicious certified organic, non-GMO snacks and sauces

6248 **Gorilly Goods**
N173 W21170 Northwest Psge. 262-423-8000
Jackson, WI 53037 www.gorillygoods.com
Gorilly Goods deliver a crunchy mix of fruits and nuts, or seeds and greens, all organically grown and dehydrated raw by folks who care.

6249 **Grain Millers**
10400 Viking Drive 952-829-8821
Suite 301 800-232-6287
Eden Prairie, MN 55344 *Fax:* 952-829-8819
www.grainmillers.com
Grain Millers, Inc. sells a variety of specialized ingredients such as organic industrial alcohol, molasses, soy beans, flax and tapioca.

6250 **Green Clean**
PO Box 7921 208-345-2109
Boise, ID 83707 greenclean@cableone.net
www.greencleanidaho.com
Commercial & Residential Cleaning Services Using Environmentally Sensitive Products

6251 **Green Clean Maine**
179 Sheridan St. 207-221-6600
Ste 200 info@greencleanmaine.com
Portland, ME 00410 www.greencleanmaine.com
Green Clean for your home or small office.

6252 **Green Clean, LLC**
PO Box 1180 301-486-7334
Greenbelt, MD 20768 www.greencleanusa.org
Provide a clean, non-toxic environment for its family, friends, and employees.

6253 **Green Cleaning Seattle**
4615 Aurora Ave N. 206-307-2270
Seattle, WA 98103 customerservice@greencleaningseattle.com
www.greencleaningseattle.com
Seattle's 100% locally-owned & operated green home & office cleaning company.

6254 **Green Foods**
2220 Camino Del Sol 805-983-7470
Oxnard, CA 93030 800-777-4430
Fax: 805-983-8843
info@greenfoods.com
www.greenfoods.com
Green Foods Corporation, founded by pharmacological researcher Yoshihide Hagiwara, M.D. in 1979 is an industry leader who is dedicated to improving human health and well-being.

6255 **Green Goods for the Home**
333 East Grand 515-309-2196
Suite 102 info@greengoodsforthehome.com
Des Moines, IA greengoodsforthehome.com
Green goods for home

6256 **Green Guru Gear**
2500 47th St 303-258-1611
Unit 12 info@greengurugear.com
Boulder, CO 80301 www.greengurugear.com
Upcycle materials into great products, provide recycling source for adventure sports, and create tangible environmental awareness.

6257 **Green Home and Office**
4300 Montgomery Avenue 301-565-7888
102B *Fax:* 301-565-5055
Bethesda, MD 20814 info@greenhomeandoffice.net
greenhomeandoffice.net
Home and office cleaning
Merced Bermudez, Founder

6258 **Green Products**
221 E. Rocbaar Drive 815-407-0900
Romeoville, IL 60446 www.greenproducts.net/#
Green Products brings biobased product innovations from the fields of the farm, to the lab and ultimately to the buildings.

6259 **Green Ray**
115 E Putnam Avenue 203-485-1435
Greenwich, CT 00683 info@greenrayled.com
test.crmgreenrayled.com
Green Ray LED is a leading manufacturer and turn-key provider of high-quality LED lighting solutions for commercial, industrial and municipal markets.

6260 **Green Roof Technology**
3646 Roland Avenue 443-345-1578
Baltimore, MD 21211 *Fax:* 443-345-1533
info@greenroofservice.com
www.greenrooftechnology.com
Green Roof Technology are professional consultants, architects, and engineers who are specialized in the specification and design of any type of living technology especially when in ground remote locations.
Jörg Breuning, President/Founder

6261 **Green Toys**
4000 Bridgeway 415-839-9971
Suite 100 *Fax:* 415-651-9147
Sausalito, CA 94965 kelley@southardinc.com
www.greentoys.com
Recycled and oragnic toys

6262 GreenClean Colorado
6820 North Franklin Avenue 970-663-0018
Suite 100 info@greencleaningcolorado.com
Loveland, CO 80538 greencleaningcolorado.com
Green Cleaning Services from Green Clean Colorado adheres to the Reduce, Re-use and Recycle business practices.

6263 GreenIT
414 1st St. East 707-938-9300
Suite 7 info@greenit.net
Sonoma, CA 95476 www.greenit.net
Mr. Hodges established GreenIT as the first consultancy to combine those elements into a systemic and strategic approach to sustainability for Information and Communications Technology Systems.
Richard Hodges, CEO

6264 GreenShield Organic
8305 Falls of the Neuse Road 877-473-3650
Suite 206 info@greenologyproducts.com
Raleigh, NC 27615 www.greenshieldorganic.com
Greenshield Organic, a division of Greenology Products, Inc. was created by a dad on a mission to protect families from the harmful chemicals found in most cleaning products.

6265 Greenerways Organic
668 Stony Hill Road 800-777-1603
Suite 143 alan@greenerdays.net
Yardley, PA 19067 www.greenerways.com
Greener Days, is to provide affordable organic products with the belief that everyone deserves the ability to enjoy the benefits of an organic lifestyle.
Alan Neiburg, President
Jayme Bella, VP of Sales

6266 Greenpeace
564 Mission Street Box 416 510-538-7842
San Francisco, CA 94105 800-326-0959
Fax: 202-462-4517
greenpeace@npgear.com
Environmentally and socially responsible apparel, accessories and gifts.

6267 Groceries Apparel
5510 Soto St. 213-488-1002
Unit A *Fax:* 213-488-1102
Vernon, CA 90058 hello@groceriesapparel.com
www.groceriesapparel.com
Apparel made from 100% organic and recyciled fabrics and dyes.

Robert W. Lohman, President/Co-Founder

6268 Guayaki
6782 Sebastopol Ave. 888-482-9254
Suite 100 guayaki.com
Sebastopol, CA 95472
The mission is to steward and restore 200,000 acres of South American Atlantic rainforest and create over 1,000 living wage jobs by 2020 by leveraging the Market Driven Restoration business model.

6269 Halo, Purely for Pets
12400 Race Track Road 800-426-4256
Tampa, FL 33626 customers@halopets.com
halopets.com
Natural pet care products are made with the finest natural ingredients available, designed to enhance your pet's well-being

6270 Handy Pantry
175 W 2700 S 800-735-0630
Salt Lake City, UT 84115 support@handypantry.com
www.handypantry.com
Handy Pantry Sprouting has been providing wholesale Certified Organic sprouting seed and sprouting supplies to natural foods retailers for over 20 years. We are proud to have tens of thousands of satisfied customers.

6271 Happy Family
40 Fulton St. 855-64 -APPY
17th FL parents@happyfamilybrands.com
New York, NY 10038 happyfamilybrands.com
Shazi Visram, Founder & CEO
Jessica Rolph, Founding Partner & COO

6272 Heavenly Organics
106 S Green 866-923-2184
PO Box 7 *Fax:* 866-243-7096
Keota, IA 52248 info@heavenlyorganics.com
www.heavenlyorganics.com
Heavenly Organics is a grower, producer and worldwide distributor of premium organic food ingredients and products.
Amit Hooda, CEO
Alok Sharma, Webmaster

6273 Honey Bee Cleaners
One Waterfront Tower 808-383-9983
419 South Street, Suite 101 *Fax:* 808-383-9983
Honolulu, HI 96813 info@honeybeecleaners.com
www.honeybeecleaners.com
The only green commercial cleaning company accredited by Green Cleaning Institute in Hawaii.
Shota Mkheidze, President/CEO

6274 Horizon Fuel Cells Technologies
18 S. Michigan Avenue 312-757-5909
12th floor *Fax:* 312-757-5905
Chicago, IL 60603 sales@horizonfuelcell.com
www.horizonfuelcell.com
Its mission is to change the game in fuel cells, by working globally on immediate commercialization, dropping technology costs, and removing the age-old hydrogen supply barriers.
George Gu, CEO
Jack Zhang, CFO

6275 Howard Products
560 Linne Road 805-227-1000
Paso Robles, CA 93446 custserv@howardproducts.com
www.howardproducts.com
Restor-A-Finish, Howard's first in an entire line of wood care products

6276 HybridLight
566 N. Dixie Dr. 800-365-0350
Saint George, UT 84770 info@hybridlight.com
hybridlight.com
Terry Peterson, Owner
Mack Peterson, Electrical Engineer

6277 Ice Chips Candy
PO Box 2401 360-232-1106
Yelm, WA 98597 866-202-6623
support@icechipscandy.com
www.icechipscandy.com
Sweet candy for diabetics

6278 Indosole
1122 Howard Street 415-570-2102
San Francisco, CA 94103 indo@indosole.com
indosole.com
Indosole's mission to salvage tires and other waste materials to give them new life as fashionable and functional goods. The soles of their shoes are derived from old tires salvaged directly from landfills, sanitized, and transformedinto brand new products manufactured in an organic process without the use of fuel powered machines.

Kyle Parsons, CEO/Founder
Kai Stober-Paul, Production Manager

6279 InterNatural Foods
1455 Broad Street 973-338-1499
4th Floor *Fax:* 973-338-1485
Bloomfield, NJ 07003 www.internaturalfoods.com
Represents a variety of natural and organic food products in the U.S. marketplace.

6280 JanCore
610 16th St
Oakland, CA 94612
888-998-0511
Admin@JanCoreLLC.com
www.jancorellc.com
JanCore's corporate structure consists of corporate and regional management, support personnel, and an extensive service provider network that services locations throughout the state and across the country.

6281 JaniTek Cleaning Solutions
2735 Teepee Drive
Suite D
Stockton, CA 95205
888-833-7705
admin@janitek.net
janitek.net
JaniTek delivers a technology enhanced, superior cleaning and customer service experience.

6282 Jason Natural Cosmetics
8468 Warern Drive
Culver City, CA 90232
Fax: 310-838-9274
All natural cosmetics.
Jeffrey Light, President

6283 Jovial Foods, Inc.
PO Box 98
North Franklin, CT 06254
877-642-0644
info@jovialfoods.com
jovialfoods.com
Jovial Foods, Inc. was founded by a husband and wife team who has always been passionate about food, farming and traditions. They offer fluten free food products.
Carla , Co-Owner
Rodolfo , Co-Owner

6284 Julian Bakery
624 Garrison St
Suite 102
Oceanside, CA 92054
760-721-5200
www.julianbakery.com

6285 Kettle Foods
3125 Kettle Court SE
Salem, OR 97301
503-364-0399
Fax: 503-371-1447
www.kettlebrand.com
Vision: great taste with real, less processed foods

6286 King's Green Cleaning
1802 N. Shartel
Oklahoma City, OK 73103
405-549-6862
amy@kingsgreencleaning.com
kingsgreencleaning.com
Offers commercial and residential cleaning services that are safe.

6287 Kiss My Face
144 Main St.
Gardiner, NY 12525
845-255-0884
sales@kissmyface.com
www.kissmyface.com

6288 Kombucha Wonder Drink
PO Box 4244
Portland, OR 97208
503-224-7331
Fax: 503-224-2295
wonderdrink.com
Pasturised drinks

6289 Kopali Organics
2103 Coral Way
2nd Floor
Miami, FL 33145
305-204-7873
kopali@kopali.com
kopali.net
Organic, natural chocolates

6290 LTC Cleaning Services
18 Anacostia Rd. NE
Washington, DC 20019
202-642-6067
lipscomb@ltccleaningservices.com
www.ltccleaningservices.com
Certified Green Cleaning Company, uses only environmental friendly cleaning products to reduce sick leave and promote a healthy work environment.

6291 La Preferida
3400 W. 35th Street
Chicago, IL 60632
800-621-5422
info@lapreferida.com
www.lapreferida.com
David Brand, Quality Assurance
Juan Badillo, Sales

6292 La Tourangelle
125 University Avenue
Berkeley, CA 94710
510-970-9960
Fax: 510-970-9964
latourangelle.com
La Tourangelle, are an authentic & traditional family producer of specialty oils handcrafting a wide range of delicious artisan nut oils both in France and California.

6293 Lafes Natural BodyCare
8204 N. Lamar B-12
Austin, TX 78753
512-926-9662
800-926-5233
lafes.com
Natural personal care products

6294 Late July Snacks
15 Channel Center Street
#105
Boston, MA 02210
508-362-5859
www.latejuly.com

6295 Lifefactory
3 Harbor Drive
Suite 200
Sausalito, CA 94965
415-729-9820
Fax: 415-520-4444
info@lifefactory.com
www.lifefactory.com

6296 Light Mountain
P O Box 325
Twin Lakes, WI 53181
262-889-8561
800-824-6396
lightmountain@lotuspress.com
www.light-mountain-hair-color.com
A natural hair color and conditioner product line.

6297 Lily of the Desert
1887 Geesling Rd.
Denton, TX 76208
940-566-9914
800-229-5459
Fax: 940-566-9925
www.lilyofthedesert.com
Founded in 1971, Lily of the Desert Organic Aloeceuticals is a family-owned vertically integrated grower, processor, and manufacturer of leading aloe vera based products.

6298 Little Me Tea
930 New Hope Road
Suite 11-189
Lawrenceville, GA 30045
404-375-3754
littlemetea.com
Sweetented tea with fruits and veggies

6299 Living Intentions
250 S Garrard Blvd
Richmond, CA 94801
415-824-5483
www.livingintentions.com
Pure food ingredients

6300 Look Alive!
Rice Lake Products
100 27th Street NE
Minot, ND 58703
701-857-6357
800-998-7450
Fax: 701-857-6300
Environmentally safe movement devices for hunting decoys, as well as bird and pest deterring owls for home garden, boats and businesses.
Virgil Farstad, President

6301 Love Child
202B -1002 Lynham Road
Whistler, BC VON 1
604-962-5683
Fax: 604-962-5684
hello@lovechildorganics.com
lovechildorganics.com
Leah Garrad-Cole, President
John Garrad-Cole, CEO

6302 Lundberg Family Farms
5311 Midway
PO Box 369
Richvale, CA 95974
530-538-3500
www.lundberg.com
Finest qulaity of rice and rice products

6303 Made in Nature
1708 13th Street
Boulder, CO 80302
800-906-7426
www.madeinnature.com
Best-tasting, healthy organic foods.

6304 Maine Coast Sea Vegetables
3 George's Pond Road
Franklin, ME 04634
207-565-2907
Fax: 207-565-2144
info@seaveg.com
www.seaveg.com/shop/
Offer eight organically certified North Atlantic varieties of marine vegetables

6305 Manitoba Harvest
69 Eagle Drive
Winnipeg, MB R2R 1
800-665-4367
manitobaharvest.com
Manitoba Harvest Hemp Foods products are all non-gmo project verified

6306 Mass Probiotics
139 Charles Street
Boston, MA 02114
617-479-5900
golivebewell.com
Mass Probiotics, Inc. researches, develops, produces and markets a family of probiotic and prebiotic bottled beverage and supplement products under the brand name GoLive

6307 Meyenberg
PO Box 934
Turlock, CA 95381
800-891-GOAT
Fax: 209-668-4977
info@meyenberg.com
meyenberg.com
Goat milk products.

6308 Mountain Green
731 W. Fairmont Dr.
Tempe, AZ 85282
480-272-9621
info@ahealthierclean.com
Mountain Green products have cleaned family and baby laundry, kitchens and homes with concentrated formulas that are non-toxic and biodegradable

6309 Mr. Ellie Pooh
350 Wiconisco Street
Millersburg, PA 17061
347-662-6581
mrelliepooh.com
100% recycled paper products.

6310 Mrs. Leepers
1455 Broad Street
4th Floor
Bloomfield, NJ 07003
973-338-0300
winfo@worldfiner.com
mrsleepers.com
Mrs. Leepers offers a variety of Organic, Gluten Free Corn Pasta and Rice Pasta, imported from Italy for authentic taste and texture

6311 My Cleaning Service
2701 Cresmont Avenue
Baltimore, MD 21211
410-889-0505
Fax: 410-889-0553
general@mycleaningservice.com
www.mycleaningservice.com
My Cleaning Service, Inc., is women-owned businesses in Baltimore with more than 300 employees.
Kathleen Bands, Director, Marketing

6312 Nasoya Foods USA
One New England Way
Ayer, MA 01432
800-328-8638
info@nasoya-usa.com
www.nasoya.com
Produces premium vegetarian foods such as all-natural organic and all-natural tofu, Asian style wraps, shirataki noodles, Asian style noodles and Nayonaise vegan sandwich spread. The organization is dedicated to environmentallysustainable practices.
Ross Gatta, CEO

6313 Natural Value Inc.
14 Waterthrush Ct
Sacramento, CA 95831
916-836-3561
Fax: 916-914-2446
Info@NaturalValue.com
www.naturalvalue.com
To make atural and organic foods and environmentally friendly nonfood products more affordable.
Stephanie Harrison, Sales Manager
Anna Ishizaki, Sales & Marketing

6314 Natural Vitality
8500 Shoal Creek Blvd.
Building 4, Suite 208
Austin, TX 78757
866-416-9216
naturalvitality.com
To provide premium and efficacious products that have a valid and unique reason for being.

6315 Naturally Green
2710 S. Denison Ave.
San Pedro, CA 90731
800-731-5769
bryan@naturallygreencleaning.com
www.naturallygreencleaning.com
Naturally Green provides excellent organic carpet cleaning in Los Angeles with safe, natural products, using no chemicals while keeping prices affordable.

6316 Naturally It's Clean
Post Office Box 292
Westmont, IL 60559
800-375-5059
Fax: 800-809-4319
Sales@NaturallyItsClean.com
naturallyitsclean.com
Naturally It's Clean delivers the ultimate promise of natural cleaners clean and safe by using nature's most powerful cleaner, enzymes.
Mike Wallrich, Co-Founder/President
Ed Mac, SVP, Operations

6317 Nature's Baby Organics
1560-1 Newbury Rd.
#284
Newbury Park, CA 91320
818-999-2229
888-902-2229
Fax: 818-702-0110
nicole@naturesbaby.com
naturesbaby.com
Offers baby care products which contain 70% organic ingredients.

6318 Nature's Way
3051 West Maple Loop Dr.
Suite 125
Lehi, UT 84043
800-962-8873
Fax: 800-688-3303
www.naturesway.com
Manufacturer of complete vitamin, mineral, herbal products line.

6319 Naturepedic
16925 Park Circle Drive
Chagrin Falls, OH 44023
800-917-3342
cs@naturepedic.com
www.naturepedic.com
Naturepedic specializes in the design and manufacturing of quality organic mattresses for infants, toddlers, children and adults that promote natural and organic materials, a non-toxic design, fire-safety, and overall health & safety.

6320 Navitas Organics
936 B Seventh St.
Box # 141
Novato, CA 94945
415-883-8116
888-645-4282
info@navitasnaturals.com
www.navitasorganics.com
Navitas Organics is a family-owned green business headquartered in Marin County, California. They specialize in organic superfoods from around the world, and strive to be the industry leader in this fast-growing category.

6321 New Leaf Paper
510 16th Street
Suite 520
Oakland, CA 94612
888-989-5323
Fax: 415-291-9353
info@newleafpaper.com
www.newleafpaper.com

New Leaf Paper has gathered an eclectic group of people as passionate about the print and graphic design process as they are about sustainability and environmental responsibility.
Joe Fanelli, Chief Executive Officer
Leila Gilbert, Vice President, Finance

6322 NibMor
P.O. Box 6 844-Nib-Morl
Kennebunk, ME 04043 info@nibmor.com
nibmor.com
Produces organic and natural dark chocolate bars as well as vegan drinking chocolate mixes.
Ralph Chauvin, CEO

6323 Nourish Organic Food for Healthy Skin
3740 W. 4th Avenue 888-385-0786
Beaver Falls, PA 15010 nourishorganic.com
100% USDA organic skincare and bodycare that is clinically proven to moisturize skin. Nourish is gluten-free, vegan & 100% chemical-free.

6324 Numi Organic Tea
P.O. Box 20420 888-404-6864
Oakland, CA 94620 *Fax:* 510-536-6864
info@numitea.com
www.numitea.com
Numi Organic Tea is a premium, Fair Trade sustainable company; specializing in unique and innovative blends of green, black, white, oolong teas.

6325 NurturMe
Freed Foods LLC 512-326-2223
PO Box 163302 info@nurturme.com
Austin, TX 78716 nurturme.com
Offers quinoa products.

6326 Nutiva
213 West Cutting Blvd 800-993-4367
Richmond, CA 94804 help@nutiva.com
nutiva.com
Nutiva offers the best Extra Virgin Organic Coconut Oil, Hemp Protein, Hemp Seed Oil and Chia Seed.
John Roulac, Founder & CEO
Neil Blomquist, Senior Advisor

6327 Old Fashioned Milk Paint
436 Main Street 978-448-6336
Groton, MA 00145 866-350-6455
Fax: 978-448-2754
anne@milkpaint.com
www.milkpaint.com
In 1974, after much experimentation, the company recreated an old Milk Paint formula to provide an authentic finish for there primary business of building reproduction furniture. Since then they have sold our paint to professionals whoare either restoring original Colonial or Shaker furniture, making reproductions, or striving for an interior design look that is both authentic and beautiful.
Anne Thibeau, President
Terri Senecal, Sales

6328 Once Again Nut Butter Collective
12 S. State St. 585-468-2535
P.O. Box 429 888-800-8075
Nunda, NY 14517 *Fax:* 585-468-5995
customerservice@oanb.com
www.onceagainnutbutter.com
Organic and Natural Nut Butter Manufacturer and Nut Ingredient Supplier.
Scott Owens, Employee-Owner
Robert Collins, Employee-Owner

6329 Oregon's Wild Harvest
1601 NE Hemlock Ave. 541-548-9400
Redmond, OR 97756 800-316-6869
Fax: 541-923-7235
webmaster@owharvest.com
www.oregonswildharvest.com
Oregon's Wild Harvest is an independently owned and operated herb farm in Sandy, Oregon.
Randy Buresh R.N., Co-founder, President, CVO
Pamela Martin-Buresh, Co-founder/CFO

6330 Orgain
P.O. Box 4918 info@drinkorgain.com
Irvine, CA 92616 orgain.com

6331 Organic Essence
629 Bertsch Avenue 707-465-8955
Crescent City, CA 95531 *Fax:* 707-465-8959
www.organic-essence.com
Organic Essence was founded in 2006 after the USDA National Organic Program allowed non-food agriculturally derived products to certify to their existing organic food standard.

6332 Organic Excellence
4727 E. Bell Road 800-611-8331
#45-125 *Fax:* 602-493-7917
Phoenix, AZ 85032-231 CustomerService@OrganicExcellence.com
shop.organicexcellence.com
Organic Excellence began as a home based business in 1999. They have since grown to a worldwide company featuring high quality, chemical, fragrance, gluten and GMO free health and personal care products with the added benefits ofcertified organic herbs.

6333 Organic Gourmet
14431 Ventura Blvd. 800-400-7772
#192 *Fax:* 818-906-7417
Sherman Oaks, CA 91423 scenar@earthlink.net
www.organic-gourmet.com
Offers natural and organic Products for wellbeing.
Elke Heitmeyer, Founder

6334 Oriental Building Services
2526 Manana Dr. 469-522-0001
Suite 208 *Fax:* 469-522-0003
Dallas, TX 75220
Oriental Building Services, Inc. has always believed and supported for a cleaner and safer environment. They believe that making eco-friendly change can help make a difference to your building, office, your family and the world. Notonly does it change by using eco-friendly products and techniques but uses attention to detail, care and love.

6335 PINES International, Inc.
1992 East 1400 Road 785-841-6016
Lawrence, KS 66044 800-697-4637
Fax: 785-841-1252
www.wheatgrass.com
Supply high-quality cereal grasses, grown in the soils of northeastern Kansas.

6336 Pacific Foods of Oregon
19480 SW 97th Ave. 503-692-9666
Tualatin, OR 97062 *Fax:* 503-692-9610
www.pacificfoods.com
Pacific food has goal- to make tasty, healthy foods with integrity.

6337 Pamela's Products
1 Carousel Lane 707-462-6605
Ukiah, CA 95482 *Fax:* 707-462-6642
info@pamelasproducts.com
www.pamelasproducts.com
Pamela's Products, started in 1988, is known for delicious, gluten free foods with a full line of baking mixes, cookies and snack bars.

6338 Pangea Organics
3195 Sterling Circle 303-413-8493
Suite 200 877-679-5854
Boulder, CO 80301 support@pangeaorganics.com
www.pangeaorganics.com
The skincare products are designed to be used as a platform that inspires people to lead, live, and make a living in a purposeful way.

6339 Peeled Snacks
65 15th Street
Fl 1
Brooklyn, NY 11215
212-706-2001
Fax: 646-478-9518
sales@peeledsnacks.com
peeledsnacks.com
Supplies best tasting organic, non-GMO and gluten-free ingredients and turn them into delicious snacks.
Noha Waibsnaider, Founder and CEO
Beth Kennedy, Director, Marketing

6340 Plum Organics
1485 Park Avenue
Emeryville, CA 94608
877-914-7586
info@plumorganics.com
www.plumorganics.com
Plum Organics boasts of healthful and trendy ingredients such as kale, quinoa.
Neil Grimmer, Co-Founder, CEO

6341 Polywood
1001 W. Brooklyn St.
Syracuse, IN 46567
574-457-3284
877-457-3284
Fax: 574-457-4723
corp@polywoodinc.com
www.polywoodinc.com
Low-maintenance, recyclable lumber Plywood

6342 Premier Green Cleaning Services
110 Redmond
Jackson, WY 83001
307-690-3605
www.premiergreencleaningservices.com
Green cleaning service providers

6343 Purity Organic
1625 Bush Street
Suite 3
San Francisco, CA 94109
415-440-7777
info@purityorganic.com
purityorganic.com
Supplies organic juice, coconut water and produce to market.

6344 RMC Medical Inc
7940 A State Rd
Philadephia, PA 19136
215-824-4100
800-332-0672
Fax: 215-824-1371
dan@rmcmedical.com
www.rmcmedical.com
Manufacturer of decontamination emergency response equipment.

6345 Rainbow Light Nutritional Systems
100 Avenue Tea
Santa Cruz, CA 95060
800-635-1233
Fax: 831-429-0189
www.rainbowlight.com
Rainbow Light began in 1981 by offering consumers a nutritious spirulina supplement and went on to become the first-ever food-based supplement brand.
Linda Kahler, President
Sharon Minski, VP Operation/Administration

6346 Raw Revolution
PO Box 359
Hawthorne, NY 10532
914-326-4095
www.rawrev.com
Provides irresistible, affordable, convenient superfoods using certified organic, mostly raw ingredients.

6347 Rawmio
PO Box 328
Glenview, IL 60025
800-518-0727
800-518-0727
rawmio.com
Rawmio produces handcrafted raw vegan chocolate treats

6348 Real Goods
Real Goods Solar
833 West South Boulder Road
Louisville, CO 80027
800-919-2400
www.realgoods.com
Source for simple living products designed to balance with a conscious lifestyle. Offers products that reduce energy consumption, from solar panels and wind turbines to complete solar power systems.

6349 Real Goods Trading Company
PO Box 8507
Ukiah, CA 95482
707-744-2100
800-347-0070
Fax: 707-468-9394
Recycled papers, environmental gifts and household goods.

6350 Redmond Trading Company
475 West 910 South
Heber City, UT 84032
800-367-7258
www.redmondtrading.com
Provides natural Sea-salt.

6351 Reserveage Nutrition
2255 Glades Road
Suite 342W
Boca Raton, FL 33431
800-553-1896
sales@reserveage.com
reserveage.com
ertified organic grapes direct from our Southern France vineyards.
Naomi Whittel, Founder and CEO

6352 Rustic Crust
5 Main Street
Pittsfield, NH 03263
603-435-5119
888-519-5119
info@rusticcrust.com
www.rusticcrust.com
Forzen flatbread crust

6353 Sambazon
1160 Calle Cordillera
San Clemente, CA 92673
877-726-2296
info@sambazon.com
www.sambazon.com
Make juices, smoothies, and sorbets from the finest organic ingredients. Wild harvested directly from the Amazon.

6354 Santa Barbara Olive Company
3070 Skyway Dr.
Suite 401
Santa Maria, CA 93455
805-562-1456
800-624-4896
Fax: 805-562-1464
info@sbolive.com
www.sbolive.com
Provides Gourmet olives, extra virgin olive oils, sauces and vegetable, a Santa Barbara Family Tradition since 1850.

6355 Sappo Hill Soapworks
654 Tolman Creek Road
Ashland, OR 97520
800-863-7627
www.sappohill.com
Sappo Hill makes all natural vegetable oil soaps according to traditional methods

6356 Second Renaissance Books
17 George Washington Plaza
Gaylordsville, CT 00675
800-729-6149
Fax: 860-355-7160
Editorially selected books and audio tapes. Complete selection of writing and letters by Ayn Rand.

6357 Seventh Generation
60 Lake Street
Burlington, VT 05401
800-211-4279
Fax: 802-658-1771
www.seventhgeneration.com
Formulating plant-based products that are safe and that work.

6358 Similasan
1805 Shea Center Drive
Suite 270
Highlands Ranch, CO 80129
800-240-9780
www.similasanusa.com
Similasan homeopathic products are formulated using traditional guidelines and produced according to strict Good Manufacturing Practices (GMP) by Similasan AG.

6359 Simple Squares
501 North Clinton Street
Suite 705
Chicago, IL 60654
888-966-7622
joinus@simplesquares.com
simplesquares.com
Organic nutrition bars

6360 Singing Dog Vanilla
PO Box 50042
Eugene, OR 97405
541-343-2746
888-343-0002
Fax: 541-610-1868
info@singingdogvanilla.com
www.singingdogvanilla.com
Organic vanilla lip balm, organic vanilla coffee, organic vanilla tea, organic vanilla chai, vanilla bean paste, alcohol free pure vanilla flavor and vanilla salt.

6361 Solar Service
7312 N. Milwaukee Ave.
Niles, IL 60714
847-647-9312
Fax: 847-647-9360
info@solarserviceinc.com
www.solarserviceinc.com
Solar Service is the premier solar installation company in the Midwest and among the most experienced solar providers in the United States.
Brandon Leavitt, Owner & President
Kevin Bart, System Manager

6362 Sparky Boy Enterprises
1512 Gold Avenue
Bozeman, MT 59715
406-587-5891
800-289-6656
Fax: 406-587-0223
Natural products for the home, lawn and garden.
Wayne Vinje, President

6363 St. Peter Woolen Mills
101 W. Broadway
St. Peter, MN 56082
507-934-3734
800-208-9821
spwoolen@hickorytech.net
www.woolenmill.com
Makes luxurious wool-filled comforters, mattress toppers and pillows

6364 SunRidge Farms
423 Salinas Road
Royal Oaks, CA 95076
831-786-7000
Fax: 831-786-8618
www.sunridgefarms.com
SunRidge farms are producing foods without highly processed or refined ingredients.

6365 Sunbiotics
PO Box 328
Glenview, IL 60025
800-925-0577
www.sunbiotics.com
Sunbiotics Gourmet Probiotic Snacks are delicious take on combining healthy snacks and probiotics.

6366 Sunrise Lane Products
780 Greenwich Street
New York, NY 10014
212-243-4745
Environmentally safe and cruelty-free products for home and personal care.
Rossella Mocerino, President

6367 Sunshine Solar Services
2805 Oakland Park Blvd
Suite 422
Fort Lauderdale, FL 33306
954-568-4876
info@sunshinesolarservices.com
www.sunshinesolarservices.com/index.html
Sunshine Solar Services specializes in generating solar energy in the hurricane zones of Florida and the Caribbean.

6368 Sweet Green Fields
11 Bellwether Way
Suite 305
Bellingham, WA 98225
360-483-4555
Fax: 360-483-4554
info@sweetgreenfields.com
sweetgreenfields.com
SGF produces and markets Reb-A, a great tasting, high purity, natural sweetener that is 200-350 times the sweetness of sugar.

6369 TaterPiks
1459 Depot Road
Malin, OR 97632
541-723-3200
TaterPiks - Gourmet Pickled Potatoes

6370 Teeccino Caffé, Inc.
PO Box 40829
Santa Barbara, CA 93140
805-966-0999
800-498-3434
Fax: 805-966-0522
info@teeccino.com
teeccino.com
Teeccino, America's #1 Coffee Alternative, is roasted and ground to brew and taste just like coffee

6371 Tera's whey
222 West Washington Ave
Suite #250
Madison, WI 53703
888-292-7408
info@teraswhey.com
Teras use minimal processing and organic ingredients that taste great and contribute to health.

6372 The Ginger People
215 Reindollar Avenue
Marina, CA 93933
800-551-5284
Fax: 831-582-2495
info@gingerpeople.com
gingerpeople.com
Established in 1984, The Ginger People began its mission to produce the world's finest range of ginger products and ingredients

6373 The Green Catalog
Advertising Specialty Institute
www.asicentral.com
Features products that are friendly to the enviroment, designed to inspire social responsibility.

6374 The Green Life
The Green Life Store
2409 Main Street
Santa Monica, CA 90405
310-392-4702
www.thegreenlifecostore.com
Green products that are the most ecologically friendly available, for home & garden, bed & bath, children, cleaning, office, and pets.
Scott O'Brien, Owner

6375 The Hain Celestial Group
4600 Sleepytime Dr.
Boulder, CO 80301
800-434-4246
www.hain-celestial.com
The Hain Celestial Group is natural and organic food and personal care products company in North America and Europe.

6376 Thoughtful Food, Inc.
3939 West Capitol Ave.
Unit F West
Sacramento, CA 95691
916-372-1040
It's Dairy Free, Vegan and certified USDA Organic! Uses only 100% organic agave nectar which also makes it a safe choice for diabetics.
Jennifer Bielawski, CEO/Founder

6377 To-Go Ware
747 Fortress Street
Chico, CA 95973
530-342-4426
888-496-6166
info@to-goware.com
to-goware.com
To-Go Ware is committed to inspiring healthy lifestyle through food, community, and planet by providing products that are innovative safe, environmentally responsible, affordable and convenient.
Andy Keller, President/CEO
Sierra Brodleit, Marketing Manager

6378 Torie & Howard
143 West Street
Suite 121-C
New Milford, CT 06776
888-826-9554
www.torieandhoward.com
Suplly products which are delicious, tasty treats that are made in a way that is as health-friendly, eco-friendly and socially conscious as possible.

6379 Traditional Medicinals
4515 Ross Road
Sebastopol, CA 95472
800-543-4372
www.traditionalmedicinals.com

Offers a quality difference in wellness teas not found anywhere else.
Drake Sadler, Co-Founder, Chairman
Blair Kellison, CEO

6380 TreeHouse
4477 S Lamar Blvd 512-861-0712
Ste 600 888-799-5779
Austin, TX 78745 *Fax:* 512-900-2084
treehouse.co
The construction, repair, and upgrading of homes

6381 Triangle Green Cleaning
5878 Faringdon Place 919-801-8588
#100 trianglegreencleaning@yahoo.com
Raleigh, NC 27609 www.trianglegreencleaning.com
Uses house cleaning products that are free of ammonia, phosphates, chlorine and synthetic fragrances.

6382 Tropical Valley Foods
50 Clinton Street 877-756-6831
Plattsburgh, NY 12901 *Fax:* 518-478-8838
chelsea@tropical-valley-foods.com
www.tropical-valley-foods.com
Tropical Valley Foods is a producer-distributor of organic and natural food products, supplying health food stores throughout the US.
Eric Bertheau, President/Owner
Jeremy , Logistics/Ops Manager

6383 TruRoots
6999 Southfront Road 800-288-3637
Livemore, CA 94551 truroots.com
All TruRoots products are a fusion of the world's wise traditions and modern convenience.
Esha Ray, Founder
Nimesh Ray, Founder

6384 TruSweets
648 Wheeling Road 334-676-1070
Wheeling, IL 60090 info@trusweets.com
www.trusweets.com
Produces flavorful sweet treats using organic ingredients.

6385 Trujoy Sweets
648 Wheeling Road 224-676-1070
Wheeling, IL 60090 info@trusweets.com
www.trujoysweets.com
Sweets that are made with organic ingredients, corn syrup free, no artificial colors or flavors, gluten free, vegan and kosher.

6386 Two Bettys Green Cleaning Service
3702 E 34th St. 612-720-8768
Minneapolis, MN 55406 info@twobettysclean.com
www.twobettysclean.com
Two Bettys Green Cleaning Company provides high quality eco-friendly green cleaning services.

6387 USA Green Clean
6522 Frietchie Row 301-661-6765
Columbia, MD 21045 Usagreenclean@gmail.com
usacleangreen.com
100% Green Nationwide Janitorial Cleaning Services

6388 Valley Fresh
1 Hormel Place 800-523-4635
Austin, MN 55912 www.valleyfresh.com
They are committed to all-natural protein that you can feel good about.

6389 Veggie Go's
2825 Wilderness Place 888-297-9426
Suite 900 info@nakededgesnacks.com
Boulder, CO 80301 nakededgesnacks.com
Lisa , Founder & President
John , Founder & CEO

6390 VitalityGOODS
5325 Gravenstein Hwy North 707-861-0386
Sebastopol, CA 95472 anne@vitalitygoods.com
www.vitalitygoods.com
Glasswares made of miron glass

6391 Voltaic Systems
155 Water Street 212-401-1192
Suite 410 info@voltaicsystems.com
Brooklyn, NY 11201 www.voltaicsystems.com
Voltaic Systems is a portable power company based in Brooklyn, New York.

6392 Williams Distributors
1801 S Cardinal Lane 262-597-9865
New Berlin, WI 53151
All natural products; nutrition, health, home care and personal care, plus water purification systems.
GL Williams, President

6393 Wisdom Natural Brands
1203 West San Pedro Street 800-899-9908
Gilbert, AZ 85233 info@wisdomnaturalbrands.com
www.wisdomnaturalbrands.com
Wisdom Natural Brands is the parent company of two highly respected consumer brands: SweetLeaf Sweetener and Wisdom of the Ancients herbal teas.

6394 World Centric
101 H Street 707-241-9190
Suite M *Fax:* 866-850-9732
Petaluma, CA 94952 worldcentric.org
Provides compostable food service disposables and food packaging products.

6395 Yummy Earth
79 N Franklin Tpke 201-857-8489
Suite 200 *Fax:* 201-606-8215
Ramsey, NJ 00744 support@yumearth.com
yummyearth.com
Rob Wunder, Co-Founder

6396 Zambeezi Organic Beeswax Lip Balm
Sambah Naturals 720-323-5975
777 Broadway info@sambahnaturals.com
Boulder, CO 80302 www.zambeezi.com
Produces lip balm with organic ingredients.
Bruce Hale, Contact

SECTION TWO:

STATISTICS & RANKINGS

Table 1. Historical Highlights: 2017 and Earlier Census Years

[For meaning of abbreviations and symbols, see introductory text.]

All farms	2017	2012	2007	2002	1997	Not adjusted for coverage		
						1997	1992	1987
Farms ....number	2,042,220	2,109,303	2,204,792	2,128,982	2,215,876	1,911,859	1,925,300	2,087,759
Land in farms ....acres	900,217,576	914,527,657	922,095,840	938,279,056	954,752,502	931,795,255	945,531,506	964,470,625
Average size of farm ....acres	441	434	418	441	431	487	491	462
Estimated market value of land and buildings [1]:								
Average per farm ....dollars	1,311,808	1,075,491	791,138	537,833	416,007	449,748	357,056	289,387
Average per acre ....dollars	2,976	2,481	1,892	1,213	967	933	727	627
Estimated market value of all machinery and equipment [1] $1,000	272,297,744	243,966,688	194,783,471	136,624,880	119,302,923	110,256,802	93,316,496	85,801,360
Average per farm ....dollars	133,363	115,706	88,357	66,570	53,861	57,678	48,605	41,227
Farms by size:								
1 to 9 acres	273,325	223,634	232,849	179,346	205,390	153,515	166,496	183,257
10 to 49 acres	583,001	589,549	620,283	563,772	530,902	410,833	387,711	412,437
50 to 179 acres	564,763	634,047	660,530	658,705	694,489	592,972	584,146	644,849
180 to 499 acres	315,017	346,038	368,368	388,617	428,215	402,769	427,648	478,294
500 to 999 acres	133,321	142,555	149,713	161,552	179,447	175,690	186,387	200,058
1,000 to 1,999 acres	87,666	91,273	92,656	99,020	103,007	101,468	101,923	102,078
2,000 acres or more	85,127	82,207	80,393	77,970	74,426	74,612	70,989	66,786
Total cropland ....farms	1,475,627	1,551,654	1,685,339	1,751,450	1,857,239	1,661,395	1,697,137	1,848,574
acres	396,433,817	389,690,414	406,424,909	434,164,946	445,324,765	431,144,896	435,365,878	443,318,233
Harvested cropland....farms	1,245,548	1,288,875	1,328,004	1,362,608	1,545,681	1,410,606	1,491,786	1,643,633
acres	320,041,858	314,964,600	309,607,601	302,697,252	318,937,401	309,395,475	295,936,976	282,223,880
Irrigated land ....farms	294,235	296,303	301,028	299,583	308,818	279,442	279,357	291,628
acres	58,013,907	55,822,231	56,599,305	55,311,236	56,289,172	55,058,128	49,404,030	46,386,201
Market value of agricultural products sold (see text) $1,000	388,522,695	394,644,481	297,220,491	200,646,355	201,379,812	196,864,649	162,608,334	136,048,516
Average per farm ....dollars	190,245	187,097	134,807	94,245	90,880	102,970	84,459	65,165
Crops, including nursery and greenhouse crops $1,000	193,546,699	212,397,074	143,657,928	95,151,954	100,668,794	98,055,656	75,228,256	58,931,085
Livestock, poultry, and their products $1,000	194,975,996	182,247,407	153,562,563	105,494,401	100,711,018	98,808,993	87,380,078	77,117,431
Farms by value of sales:								
Less than $2,500	791,701	788,310	900,327	826,558	693,026	496,514	422,767	490,296
$2,500 to $4,999	185,341	191,422	200,302	213,326	265,667	228,477	231,867	262,918
$5,000 to $9,999	208,074	214,245	218,531	223,168	267,575	237,975	251,883	274,972
$10,000 to $24,999	228,218	244,954	248,285	256,157	293,639	274,040	301,804	326,166
$25,000 to $49,999	144,113	152,873	154,732	157,906	179,629	170,705	195,354	219,636
$50,000 to $99,999	119,434	129,366	125,456	140,479	163,510	158,160	187,760	218,050
$100,000 to $499,999	218,771	232,955	240,873	240,746	282,422	277,194	286,951	263,698
$500,000 or more	146,568	155,178	116,286	70,642	70,408	68,794	46,914	32,023
Farms by legal status for tax purposes:								
Family or individual	1,751,126	1,828,946	1,906,335	1,909,598	1,922,590	1,643,424	1,653,491	1,809,324
Partnership	130,173	137,987	174,247	129,593	185,607	169,462	186,806	199,559
Corporation	116,840	106,716	96,074	73,752	90,432	84,002	72,567	66,969
Other - estate or trust, prison farm, grazing association, American Indian Reservation, etc.	44,081	35,654	28,136	16,039	17,247	14,971	12,436	11,907
Total farm production expenses [1] $1,000	326,390,640	328,939,354	241,113,666	173,199,216	157,752,357	150,590,993	130,779,261	108,138,053
Selected farm production expenses [1]:								
Livestock and poultry purchased or leased $1,000	44,934,482	41,586,018	38,003,682	27,420,965	22,213,229	21,614,559	23,043,431	19,344,645
Feed purchased $1,000	62,625,223	75,706,467	49,095,106	31,694,850	34,749,048	32,759,966	24,084,507	19,163,364
Fertilizer, lime, and soil conditioners purchased [2] $1,000	23,543,177	28,532,713	18,107,194	9,751,460	9,999,752	9,597,128	8,204,324	6,684,944
Gasoline, fuels, and oils purchased $1,000	13,474,121	16,573,188	12,912,179	6,675,419	6,715,936	6,371,515	6,120,452	5,277,227
Hired farm labor $1,000	31,635,981	26,986,669	21,877,661	18,568,446	15,457,896	14,841,036	12,961,639	10,866,236
Interest expense $1,000	12,396,094	12,123,573	10,880,731	9,571,577	9,392,431	8,928,107	8,111,337	8,158,268
Chemicals purchased $1,000	17,585,163	16,459,840	10,074,914	7,608,921	7,934,936	7,581,424	6,133,705	4,690,243
Livestock and poultry:								
Cattle and calves inventory ....farms	882,692	913,246	963,669	1,018,359	1,188,659	1,046,863	1,074,349	1,176,346
number	93,648,041	89,994,614	96,347,858	95,497,994	99,907,017	98,989,244	96,135,825	95,847,299
Beef cows ....farms	729,046	727,906	764,984	796,436	899,756	804,595	803,241	841,778
number	31,722,039	28,956,553	32,834,801	33,398,271	34,193,965	34,066,615	32,545,976	31,652,593
Milk cows ....farms	54,599	64,098	69,890	91,989	125,041	116,874	155,339	202,068
number	9,539,631	9,252,272	9,266,574	9,103,959	9,139,812	9,095,439	9,491,818	10,084,697
Cattle and calves sold ....farms	711,827	740,978	798,290	851,971	1,121,003	1,011,809	1,034,189	1,150,523
number	69,812,061	69,759,776	74,071,936	73,509,165	75,005,184	74,089,046	70,562,908	72,603,841
Hogs and pigs inventory ....farms	66,439	63,246	75,442	78,895	124,889	109,754	191,347	243,398
number	72,381,007	66,026,785	67,786,318	60,405,103	61,188,149	61,206,236	57,563,118	52,271,120
Hogs and pigs sold ....farms	64,871	55,882	74,789	82,028	112,377	102,106	188,167	238,819
number	235,282,860	199,115,305	206,807,181	184,997,686	142,956,569	142,611,882	111,326,807	96,569,359
Layers inventory (see text) ....farms	232,500	198,272	145,615	98,315	(NA)	(NA)	(NA)	(NA)
number	368,241,393	350,715,978	349,772,508	334,435,155	(NA)	(NA)	(NA)	(NA)
Broilers and other meat-type chickens sold ....farms	32,751	32,935	27,091	32,006	27,737	23,937	23,949	27,645
number	8,889,759,283	8,463,194,794	8,914,828,122	8,500,313,357	7,366,526,456	6,741,927,110	5,428,589,485	4,361,975,630
Selected crops harvested:								
Corn for grain ....farms	304,801	348,530	347,760	348,590	450,520	430,711	503,935	627,602
acres	84,738,562	87,413,045	86,248,542	68,230,523	71,088,454	69,796,716	69,339,869	58,701,505
bushels	14,773,403,430	10,333,410,157	12,738,519,330	8,613,061,814	8,732,478,098	8,578,634,770	8,697,362,804	6,725,001,837
Corn for silage or greenchop ....farms	59,500	86,365	84,317	103,621	123,325	119,308	(NA)	(NA)
acres	6,109,414	7,196,628	5,979,661	6,683,995	5,771,666	5,727,594	(NA)	(NA)
tons	120,443,839	113,153,064	104,224,795	97,132,738	89,219,954	88,380,934	(NA)	(NA)
Wheat for grain, all ....farms	104,792	147,632	160,810	169,528	252,922	243,568	292,464	352,237
acres	38,811,620	49,040,226	50,932,969	45,519,976	62,084,743	58,836,344	59,089,470	53,224,174
bushels	1,788,456,593	2,185,108,114	1,993,648,378	1,577,005,140	2,329,807,815	2,204,026,684	2,206,729,476	1,887,103,964
Durum wheat for grain ....farms	3,093	3,515	3,723	5,325	7,070	6,887	(NA)	(NA)
acres	2,206,169	2,139,150	2,138,734	2,717,841	3,202,949	3,099,732	(NA)	(NA)
bushels	63,273,647	86,110,218	73,201,303	81,170,077	88,251,199	85,802,466	(NA)	(NA)
Other spring wheat for grain (see text) ....farms	20,076	25,794	28,733	30,333	47,193	46,268	(NA)	(NA)
acres	10,419,033	12,177,715	13,008,266	13,498,842	18,024,687	17,488,113	(NA)	(NA)
bushels	440,770,319	521,904,259	475,906,637	391,500,672	537,892,213	519,176,940	(NA)	(NA)

See footnote(s) at end of table.

--continued

Table 1. **Historical Highlights: 2017 and Earlier Census Years** (continued)

[For meaning of abbreviations and symbols, see introductory text.]

All farms		2017	2012	2007	2002	1997	Not adjusted for coverage		
							1997	1992	1987
Selected crops harvested: - Con.									
Wheat for grain, all - Con.									
Winter wheat for grain	farms	86,596	126,085	136,103	141,062	(NA)	(NA)	(NA)	(NA)
	acres	26,186,417	34,723,361	35,785,969	29,303,293	(NA)	(NA)	(NA)	(NA)
	bushels	1,284,412,628	1,577,093,637	1,444,540,438	1,104,334,391	(NA)	(NA)	(NA)	(NA)
Oats for grain	farms	19,842	35,038	42,558	63,763	94,811	89,606	(NA)	(NA)
	acres	814,140	1,078,698	1,509,149	1,996,916	2,739,810	2,680,958	(NA)	(NA)
	bushels	50,406,624	65,646,178	89,508,669	109,840,449	154,654,269	151,327,329	(NA)	(NA)
Barley for grain	farms	11,188	18,667	19,848	24,747	43,269	41,930	(NA)	(NA)
	acres	2,206,808	3,283,905	3,521,957	4,015,654	6,108,682	5,944,951	(NA)	(NA)
	bushels	161,624,924	215,059,358	207,089,232	214,800,035	346,413,080	336,435,009	(NA)	(NA)
Sorghum for grain	farms	15,339	20,037	26,242	33,172	50,860	49,397	(NA)	(NA)
	acres	5,070,159	5,142,099	6,769,834	6,755,326	8,647,643	8,470,353	(NA)	(NA)
	bushels	354,737,072	264,337,547	482,452,865	333,485,523	569,984,239	559,070,136	(NA)	(NA)
Sorghum for silage or greenchop	farms	3,064	5,288	5,625	7,042	7,962	7,918	(NA)	(NA)
	acres	335,647	466,645	450,041	406,031	384,320	382,024	(NA)	(NA)
	tons	4,434,915	5,639,863	5,763,450	3,904,834	4,669,985	4,640,291	(NA)	(NA)
Soybeans for beans	farms	303,191	302,963	279,110	317,611	367,300	354,692	381,000	441,899
	acres	90,149,480	76,104,780	63,915,821	72,399,844	67,773,274	66,147,726	56,351,304	55,291,205
	bushels	4,356,024,186	2,926,822,777	2,582,423,697	2,707,719,216	2,560,330,804	2,504,307,294	2,053,163,265	1,838,053,979
Dry edible beans, excluding chickpeas and limas (see text)	farms	5,408	6,896	6,236	8,647	11,348	10,911	(NA)	(NA)
	acres	1,470,136	1,642,797	1,455,549	1,691,775	1,731,898	1,691,899	(NA)	(NA)
	cwt	30,625,986	31,424,290	25,353,900	29,687,475	27,888,555	27,223,851	(NA)	(NA)
Cotton, all	farms	16,149	18,155	18,605	24,805	33,640	31,493	34,812	43,046
	acres	11,401,965	9,384,080	10,493,238	12,456,162	13,897,404	13,235,236	10,961,720	9,826,081
	bales	20,413,180	16,534,302	18,898,128	17,145,345	18,706,703	17,878,743	15,370,310	13,280,143
Tobacco	farms	6,237	10,014	16,234	56,977	93,530	89,706	124,270	136,682
	acres	331,552	342,932	359,846	428,631	837,363	838,530	831,231	633,310
	pounds	715,446,022	766,609,252	778,301,825	873,350,412	1,744,192,909	1,747,702,321	1,697,831,562	1,215,221,360
Forage - land used for all hay and haylage, grass silage, and greenchop (see text)	farms	799,627	813,583	869,534	884,831	(NA)	(NA)	(NA)	(NA)
	acres	56,858,622	55,775,162	61,455,483	64,041,337	(NA)	(NA)	(NA)	(NA)
	tons, dry equivalent	140,229,237	127,345,016	155,393,762	154,976,932	(NA)	(NA)	(NA)	(NA)
Rice	farms	4,637	5,591	6,084	8,046	9,627	9,291	(NA)	(NA)
	acres	2,395,054	2,693,759	2,758,792	3,197,641	3,161,576	3,122,120	(NA)	(NA)
	cwt	176,274,671	200,239,288	198,538,690	210,358,014	184,412,536	182,231,457	(NA)	(NA)
Sunflower seed, all	farms	3,389	4,953	6,403	7,506	11,176	11,067	(NA)	(NA)
	acres	1,324,030	1,877,145	2,000,153	1,833,435	(D)	2,534,708	(NA)	(NA)
	pounds	2,086,855,236	2,728,794,260	2,820,962,445	2,042,510,240	(D)	3,198,790,249	(NA)	(NA)
Sugarbeets for sugar	farms	3,496	3,913	4,022	5,027	7,057	7,102	(NA)	(NA)
	acres	1,150,682	1,249,481	1,253,817	1,365,769	1,449,819	1,453,824	(NA)	(NA)
	tons	35,488,911	35,417,494	31,937,325	27,793,126	29,740,760	29,775,479	(NA)	(NA)
Sugarcane for sugar	farms	627	666	692	953	1,079	973	(NA)	(NA)
	acres	843,454	(D)	846,666	978,393	890,193	875,180	(NA)	(NA)
	tons	30,949,944	30,269,684	31,127,405	35,319,767	31,986,258	31,549,377	(NA)	(NA)
Peanuts for nuts	farms	6,379	6,561	6,182	8,640	12,788	12,221	(NA)	(NA)
	acres	1,786,767	1,621,631	1,200,564	1,223,093	1,377,097	1,352,155	(NA)	(NA)
	pounds	7,114,985,199	6,660,492,899	3,703,138,887	3,137,586,781	3,434,648,039	3,377,142,874	(NA)	(NA)
Vegetables harvested for sale [3] (see text)	farms	74,276	72,045	69,172	54,391	60,631	53,727	61,969	60,819
	acres	4,365,149	4,492,086	4,682,588	3,698,744	3,906,983	3,773,219	3,782,358	3,467,563
Potatoes	farms	16,554	21,079	15,014	9,408	11,649	10,523	(NA)	(NA)
	acres	1,133,128	1,168,199	1,131,963	1,266,087	1,372,458	1,355,241	(NA)	(NA)
Sweet potatoes	farms	4,798	2,202	1,910	2,366	1,976	1,770	(NA)	(NA)
	acres	172,983	125,726	105,284	92,310	80,953	77,384	(NA)	(NA)
Land in orchards [4]	farms	111,955	106,488	115,935	113,649	123,420	106,069	116,207	120,434
	acres	5,665,600	5,199,729	5,039,476	5,330,439	5,349,292	5,158,064	4,770,778	4,560,163

[1] Data for 2002 and prior years are based on a sample of farms.
[2] Data for 1997 and prior years exclude cost of lime and manure.
[3] Data for 2002 and prior years exclude potatoes, sweet potatoes, and ginseng.
[4] Data for 2012 and prior years exclude pineapples.

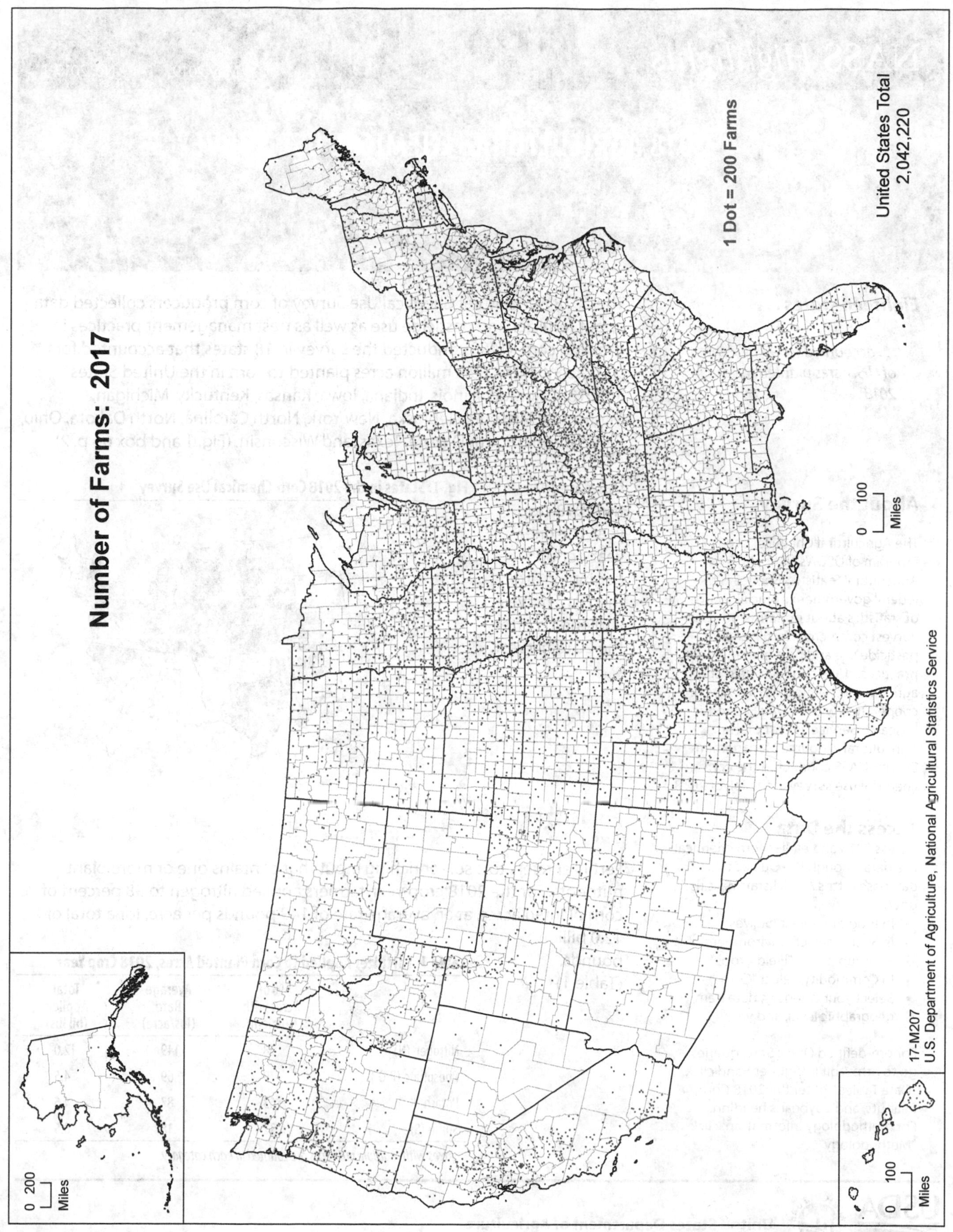

2017 Census of Agriculture

NASS *Highlights*

May 2019 • No. 2019-1

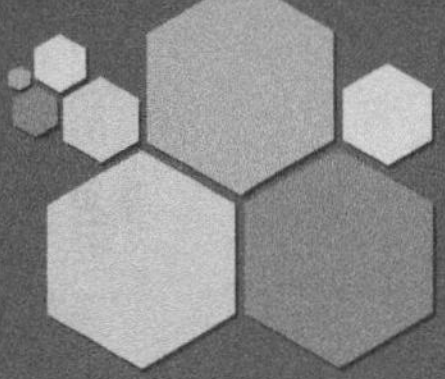

2018 AGRICULTURAL CHEMICAL USE SURVEY

Corn

Eighteen states . . .

. . . accounted for 93 percent of U.S. acres planted to corn in 2018.

The 2018 Agricultural Chemical Use Survey of corn producers collected data about fertilizer and pesticide use as well as pest management practices in growing corn. NASS conducted the survey in 18 states that accounted for 93 percent of the 89.1 million acres planted to corn in the United States in 2018: Colorado, Illinois, Indiana, Iowa, Kansas, Kentucky, Michigan, Minnesota, Missouri, Nebraska, New York, North Carolina, North Dakota, Ohio, Pennsylvania, South Dakota, Texas, and Wisconsin. (Fig. 1 and box on p. 2)

Data are for the 2018 crop year, the one-year period beginning after the 2017 harvest and ending after the 2018 harvest.

Fig. 1. States in the 2018 Corn Chemical Use Survey

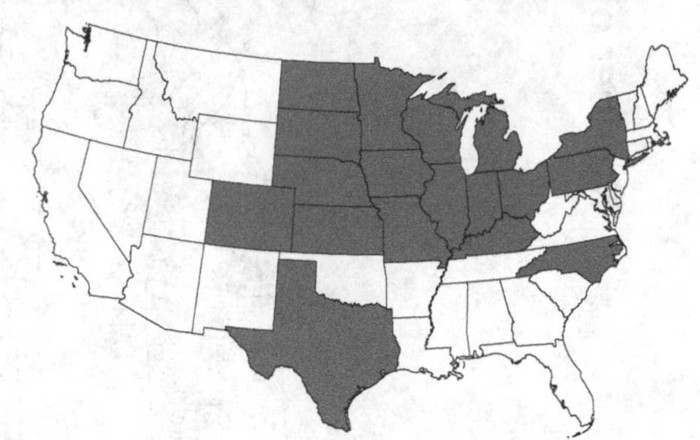

About the Survey

The Agricultural Chemical Use Program of USDA's National Agricultural Statistics Service is the federal government's official source of statistics about on-farm and post-harvest commercial fertilizer and pesticide use and pest management practices. NASS conducts field crop agricultural chemical use surveys in cooperation with USDA's Economic Research Service as part of the Agricultural Resource Management Survey. NASS conducted the corn chemical use survey in the fall of 2018.

Access the Data

Access 2018 and earlier corn chemical use data through the Quick Stats database (https://quickstats.nass.usda.gov/).

- In Program, select "Survey"
- In Sector, select "Environmental"
- In Group, select "Field Crops"
- In Commodity, select "Corn"
- Select your category, data item, geographic level, and year

For pre-defined Quick Stats queries, go to http://bit.ly/AgChem and click "Data Tables" under the 2018 Corn, Peanuts, and Soybeans heading. For methodology information, click "Methodology."

Fertilizer Use

Fertilizer refers to a soil-enriching input that contains one or more plant nutrients. For the 2018 crop year, farmers applied nitrogen to 98 percent of corn planted acres, at an average rate of 149 pounds per acre, for a total of 12.0 billion pounds. (Table 1)

Table 1. Fertilizer Applied to Corn Planted Acres, 2018 Crop Year

	% of Acres with Nutrient[a]	Average Rate (lbs/acre)	Total Applied (bil lbs)
Nitrogen (N)	98	149	12.0
Phosphate (P_2O_5)	79	69	4.5
Potash (K_2O)	63	87	4.5
Sulfur (S)	32	18	0.5

[a]*Acres with multiple nutrients are counted in each category.*

United States Department of Agriculture
National Agricultural Statistics Service

www.nass.usda.gov

Pesticide Use

The pesticide active ingredients used on corn are classified as herbicides (targeting weeds), insecticides (targeting insects), fungicides (targeting fungal disease), or other chemicals (targeting all other pests and other materials, including extraneous crop foliage). Herbicides were used most extensively, applied to 97 percent of planted acres. Fungicides and insecticides were applied to 17 and 13 percent of planted acres, respectively. (Fig. 2)

Among herbicides, atrazine was the most widely used active ingredient (applied to 65 percent of planted acres), followed by mesotrione (42 percent) and glyphosate isopropylamine salt (34 percent). (Table 2) Atrazine was also the most widely applied ingredient in the 2014 and 2016 surveys of corn producers.

Fig. 2. Pesticides Applied to Corn Planted Acres, 2018 Crop Year
(% of planted acres)

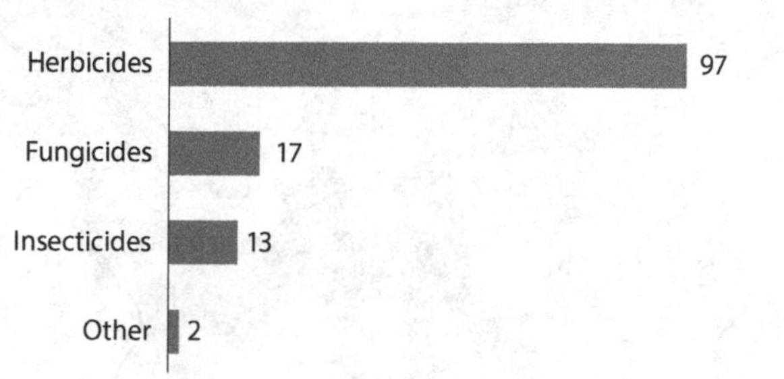

Table 2. Top Herbicides Applied to Corn Planted Acres, 2018 Crop Year

Active Ingredient	% of Acres with Ingredient[a]	Average Rate (lbs/acre)	Total Applied (mil lbs)
Atrazine	65	1.037	55.9
Mesotrione	42	0.121	4.2
Glyphosate isopropylamine salt	34	0.993[b]	27.7[b]
Acetochlor	33	1.433	38.8
S-metolachlor	29	1.198	28.3

[a]*Acres with multiple ingredients are counted in each category.*
[b]*Expressed in acid equivalent.*

Pest Management Practices

The survey asked growers to report on the practices they used to manage pests, defined as weeds, insects, or diseases. Corn growers reported practices in four categories: prevention, avoidance, monitoring, and suppression (PAMS).

- *Prevention* practices involve actions to keep a pest population from infesting a crop or field.
- *Avoidance* practices use cultural measures to mitigate or eliminate the detrimental effects of pests.
- *Monitoring* practices involve observing or detecting pests through systematic sampling, counting, or other forms of scouting.
- *Suppression* practices involve controlling or reducing existing pest populations to mitigate crop damage.

Table 3 shows the top practice in each category. In all categories, the top practice in 2018 was also the top practice in the 2014 and 2016 surveys.

Table 3. Top Practice in Pest Management Category, 2018
(% of corn planted acres)

Prevention: No till or minimum till	65
Avoidance: Rotated crops during past three years	84
Monitoring: Scouted for weeds (deliberately, or by general observations while performing tasks)	94
Suppression: Maintained ground covers, mulches, or other physical barriers	45

Surveyed States: Acres of Corn Planted, 2018

U.S. Total	millions of acres 89.1	% of U.S. 100
Iowa	13.2	14.8
Illinois	11.0	12.3
Nebraska	9.6	10.8
Minnesota	7.9	8.9
Kansas	5.5	6.1
Indiana	5.4	6.0
South Dakota	5.3	5.9
Wisconsin	3.9	4.4
Ohio	3.5	3.9
Missouri	3.5	3.9
North Dakota	3.2	3.5
Michigan	2.3	2.6
Texas	2.2	2.5
Colorado	1.5	1.6
Pennsylvania	1.4	1.5
Kentucky	1.3	1.5
New York	1.1	1.2
North Carolina	0.9	1.0
Total, Surveyed States	**82.5**	**92.6**

Numbers may not add due to rounding.

USDA is an equal opportunity provider, employer, and lender.
www.nass.usda.gov

NASS *Highlights*

May 2018 • No. 2018-3

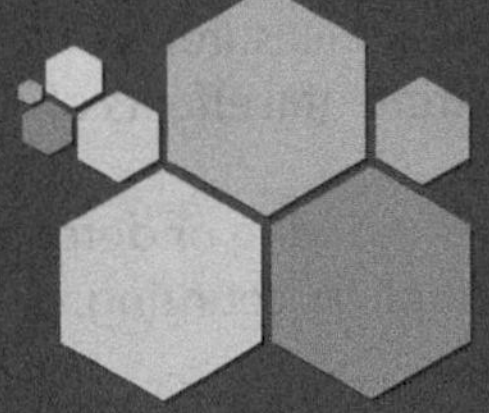

2017 AGRICULTURAL CHEMICAL USE SURVEY

Cotton

Nine states . . .

. . . accounted for 89 percent of U.S. acres planted to cotton in 2017.

About the Survey

The Agricultural Chemical Use Program of USDA's National Agricultural Statistics Service (NASS) is the federal government's official source of statistics about on-farm and post-harvest commercial fertilizer and pesticide use and pest management practices. NASS conducts field crop agricultural chemical use surveys as part of the Agricultural Resource Management Survey. NASS conducted the cotton chemical use survey in the fall of 2017.

Access the Data

Access 2017 cotton chemical use data, as well as results from prior surveys of cotton chemical use, through the Quick Stats 2.0 database (http://quickstats.nass.usda.gov).

- In Program, select "Survey"
- In Sector, select "Environmental"
- In Group, select "Field Crops"
- In Commodity, select "Cotton"
- Select your category, data item, geographic level, and year

For pre-defined Quick Stats queries, go to http://bit.ly/AgChem and click "Data Tables" under the 2017 Cotton, Soybeans, and Wheat heading. For methodology information, click "Methodology."

The 2017 Agricultural Chemical Use Survey of cotton producers collected data about fertilizer and pesticide use as well as pest management practices in growing cotton. NASS conducted the survey in nine states that together accounted for 89 percent of the 12.6 million acres planted to cotton in the United States in 2017: Alabama, Arkansas, Georgia, Mississippi, Missouri, North Carolina, Oklahoma, Tennessee, and Texas. (Fig. 1 and box on p. 2)

Data are for the 2017 crop year, the one-year period beginning after the 2016 harvest and ending after the 2017 harvest.

Fig. 1. States in the 2017 Cotton Chemical Use Survey

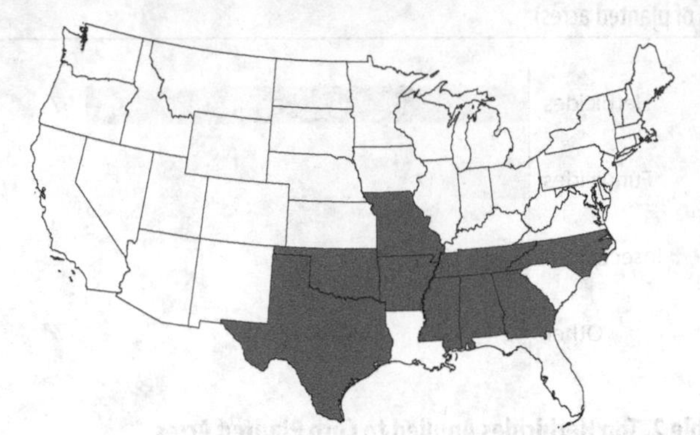

Fertilizer Use

Fertilizer refers to a soil-enriching input that contains one or more plant nutrients. For the 2017 crop year, farmers applied nitrogen to 78 percent of planted acres, at an average rate of 94 pounds per acre, for a total of 821.5 million pounds. They applied phosphate to 59 percent of cotton planted acres and potash to 45 percent of acres. (Table 1)

Table 1. Fertilizer Applied to Cotton Planted Acres, 2017 Crop Year

	% of Planted Acres	Avg. Rate for Year (lbs/acre)	Total Applied (mil lbs)
Nitrogen (N)	78	94	821.5
Phosphate (P_2O_5)	59	45	298.4
Potash (K_2O)	45	64	325.3

United States Department of Agriculture
National Agricultural Statistics Service

www.nass.usda.gov

Pesticide Use

The pesticide active ingredients used on cotton are classified in this report as herbicides (targeting weeds), insecticides (targeting insects), fungicides (targeting fungal disease), and other chemicals (targeting all other pests and other materials, including extraneous crop foliage). Herbicides were used most extensively, applied to 91 percent of cotton planted acres. Other chemicals such as desiccants were applied to 69 percent of the acres, insecticides and fungicides to fewer. (Fig. 2)

Among herbicides, glyphosate isopropylamine salt was the most widely applied active ingredients (on 59 percent of planted acres), followed by trifluralin and diuron (each with 23 percent). (Table 2)

Fig. 2. Pesticides Applied to Cotton Planted Acres, 2017 Crop Year
(% of planted acres)

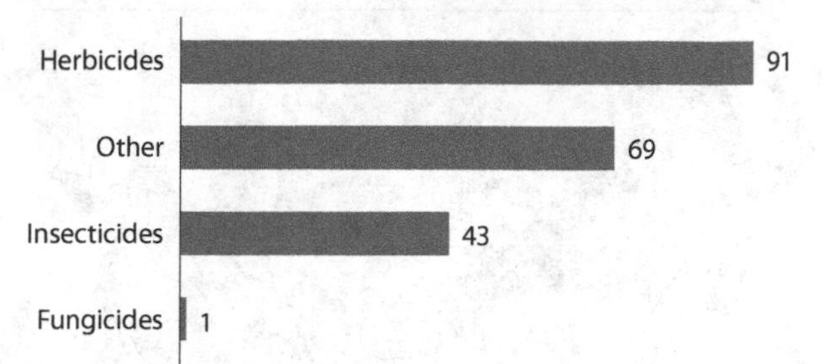

Table 2. Top Herbicides Applied to Cotton Planted Acres, 2017 Crop Year

Active Ingredient	% of Planted Acres	Avg. Rate for Year (lbs/acre)	Total Applied (mil lbs)
Glyphosate isopropylamine salt	59	1.494[a]	10.0[a]
Trifluralin	23	0.885	2.3
Diuron	23	0.417	1.1
Glyphosate potassium salt	18	2.068[a]	4.1[a]
Glufosinate-ammonium	17	0.592	1.2

[a] *Expressed in acid equivalent.*

Pest Management Practices

The survey asked growers to report on the practices they used to manage pests, defined as weeds, insects, or diseases. Cotton growers reported practices in four categories: prevention, avoidance, monitoring, and suppression (PAMS).

- *Prevention* practices involve actions to keep a pest population from infesting a crop or field.
- *Avoidance* practices use cultural measures to mitigate or eliminate the detrimental effects of pests.
- *Monitoring* practices observe or detect pests by systematic sampling, counting, or other forms of scouting.
- *Suppression* practices involve controlling or reducing existing pest populations to mitigate crop damage.

The most widely used prevention practice in growing cotton was cleaning equipment and implements after field work, used on 64 percent of planted acres. The top avoidance practice was rotating crops (64 percent). Scouting for weeds was the most widely used monitoring practice (92 percent), and maintaining ground cover, mulching, or using other physical barriers was the top suppression practice (38 percent). (Table 3)

Table 3. Top Practice in Pest Management Category, 2017
(% of cotton planted acres)

Practice	%
Prevention: Cleaned equipment and implements after field work	64
Avoidance: Rotated crops during past three years	64
Monitoring: Scouted for weeds (deliberately, or by general observations while performing other tasks)	92
Suppression: Maintained ground covers, mulches, or other physical barriers	38

Surveyed States: Acres of Cotton Planted, 2017

U.S. Total	millions of acres 12.6	% of U.S. 100
Texas	6.9	54.8
Georgia	1.3	10.1
Mississippi	0.6	4.9
Oklahoma	0.6	4.6
Arkansas	0.4	3.5
Alabama	0.4	3.4
North Carolina	0.4	2.9
Tennessee	0.3	2.7
Missouri	0.3	2.4
Total, Surveyed States	11.2	89.3

Numbers may not add due to rounding.

NASS *Highlights*

May 2017 • No. 2017-3

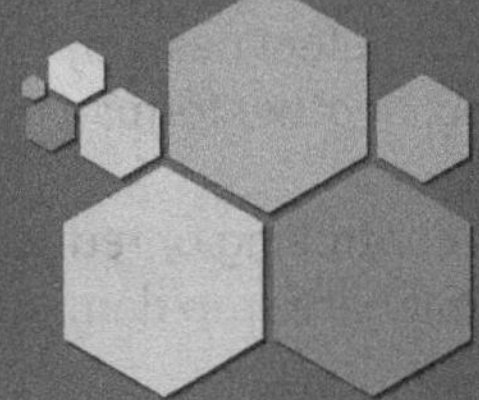

2016 AGRICULTURAL CHEMICAL USE SURVEY

Fall Potatoes

Eight states . . .

. . . accounted for 90 percent of U.S. acres planted to fall potatoes in 2016.

The 2016 Agricultural Chemical Use Survey of potato producers collected data about fertilizer and pesticide use as well as pest management practices in growing fall potatoes. NASS conducted the survey in eight states that together accounted for 90 percent of the 920,800 acres planted to fall potatoes in the United States in 2016: Colorado, Idaho, Maine, Michigan, Minnesota, North Dakota, Washington, and Wisconsin (Fig. 1).

Data are for the 2016 crop year, the one-year period beginning after the 2015 harvest and ending after the 2016 harvest.

Fig. 1. States in the 2016 Fall Potato Chemical Use Survey

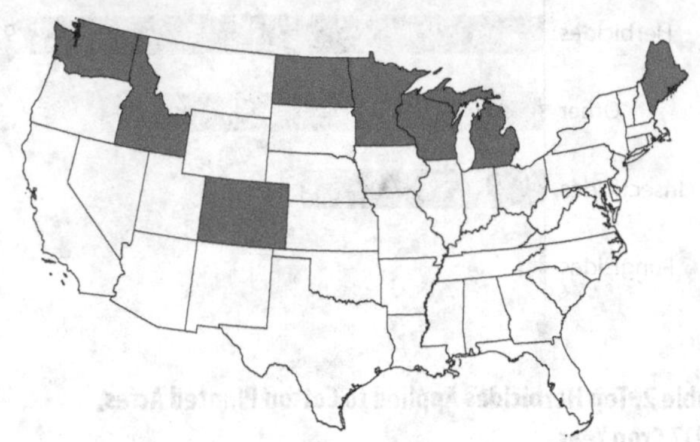

About the Survey

The Agricultural Chemical Use Program of USDA's National Agricultural Statistics Service (NASS) is the federal government's official source of statistics about on-farm and post-harvest commercial fertilizer and pesticide use and pest management practices. NASS conducts field crop agricultural chemical use surveys as part of the Agricultural Resource Management Survey. NASS conducted the fall potato chemical use survey in fall 2016.

Access the Data

Access fall potato chemical use data through the Quick Stats 2.0 database (quickstats.nass.usda.gov).

- In Program, select "Survey"
- In Sector, select "Environmental"
- In Group, select "Vegetables"
- In Commodity, select "Potatoes"
- Select your category, data item, geographic level, and year

For pre-defined Quick Stats queries, go to bit.ly/AgChem and click "Data Tables" under the 2016 Corn and Potatoes heading. For methodology information, click "Methodology."

Fertilizer Use

Fertilizer refers to a soil-enriching input that contains one or more plant nutrients. Farmers applied nitrogen to 98 percent of planted acres, at an average rate of 233 pounds per acre, for a total of 182 million pounds in the 2016 crop year. They applied phosphate to 92 percent of fall potato planted acres, potash to 90 percent, and sulfur to 76 percent. (Table 1)

Table 1. Fertilizer Applied to Fall Potato Planted Acres, 2016 Crop Year

	% of Planted Acres	Avg. Rate for Year (lbs/acre)	Total Applied (mil lbs)
Nitrogen (N)	98	233	182.1
Phosphate (P_2O_5)	92	155	118.1
Potash (K_2O)	90	172	128.5
Sulfur (S)	76	78	49.4

United States Department of Agriculture
National Agricultural Statistics Service

www.nass.usda.gov

Pesticide Use

The pesticide active ingredients used on fall potatoes are classified as herbicides (targeting weeds), insecticides (targeting insects), fungicides (targeting fungal disease), or other chemicals (targeting all other pests and other materials, including extraneous crop foliage). Fungicides were used most extensively, applied to 97 percent of planted acres. Herbicides and insecticides were applied to 94 and 82 percent of planted acres, respectively. (Fig. 2)

Among fungicides, chlorothalonil and mancozeb were the most widely applied active ingredients (used on 79 and 56 percent of planted acres, respectively). The most widely used herbicide was metribuzin (68 percent of planted acres). (Table 2)

Fig. 2. Pesticides Applied to Fall Potato Planted Acres, 2016 Crop Year
(% of planted acres)

Table 2. Top Pesticides Applied to Fall Potato Planted Acres, 2016 Crop Year

Active Ingredient	% of Planted Acres	Avg. Rate for Year (lbs/acre)	Total Applied (mil lbs)
Chlorothalonil (fungicide)	79	3.598	2.4
Metribuzin (herbicide)	68	0.447	0.3
Mancozeb (fungicide)	56	4.232	2.0

Pest Management Practices

The survey asked growers to report on the practices they used to manage pests, which the survey identifies as weeds, insects, and diseases. Fall potato growers reported practices in four categories:

- *Prevention* practices involve actions to keep a pest population from infesting a crop or field.
- *Avoidance* practices use cultural measures to mitigate or eliminate detrimental effects of pests.
- *Monitoring* practices observe or detect pests by sampling, counting, or other forms of scouting.
- *Suppression* practices involve controlling or reducing existing pest populations to mitigate crop damage.

The most widely reported monitoring practice was scouting for diseases, used on 98 percent of fall potato planted acres. Among avoidance practices, crop rotation was practiced on 97 percent of planted acres. The most widely used prevention practice was cleaning equipment and implements after field work to reduce the spread of pests (86 percent). Using pesticides with different mechanisms of action to keep pests from becoming resistant to pesticides was the most reported suppression practice (70 percent). (Table 3)

These practices were also the top practice in each category in 2014, when NASS last conducted the fall potato chemical use survey.

Table 3. Top Practice in Pest Management Category, 2016 Crop Year
(% of planted acres, fall potatoes)

Monitoring: Scouted for diseases (deliberately, or by general observations while performing other tasks)	98
Avoidance: Rotated crops during last three years	97
Prevention: Cleaned equipment and implements after field work	86
Suppression: Used pesticides with different mechanisms of action	70

Surveyed States: Acres Planted to Fall Potatoes, 2016

	thousands of acres	% of U.S.
U.S. Total	920.8	100
Idaho	325.0	35.3
Washington	170.0	18.5
North Dakota	80.0	8.7
Wisconsin	65.0	7.1
Colorado	57.1	6.2
Maine	47.0	5.1
Michigan	47.0	5.1
Minnesota	40.0	4.3
Total, Surveyed States	**831.1**	**90.3**

Numbers may not add due to rounding.

USDA is an equal opportunity provider, employer, and lender.
www.nass.usda.gov

NASS *Highlights*

July 2018 • No. 2018-6

2017 AGRICULTURAL CHEMICAL USE

Fruit Crops

The 2017 Agricultural Chemical Use Survey of fruit producers collected data about pesticide use and pest management practices on acres planted to 22 different fruit crops. NASS conducted the survey among producers in 12 states, focusing on the states that are major producers for the surveyed crops. (Fig. 1)

Data are for the 2017 crop year, the one-year period beginning after the 2016 harvest and ending after the 2017 harvest. Data are available online for all 22 fruit crops (see sidebar for how to access data for each fruit). This document highlights three fruits – apples, blueberries, and peaches, each produced in at least six geographically diverse states.

Fig. 1. States Included in the 2017 Fruit Chemical Use Survey
(number of crops surveyed in state)

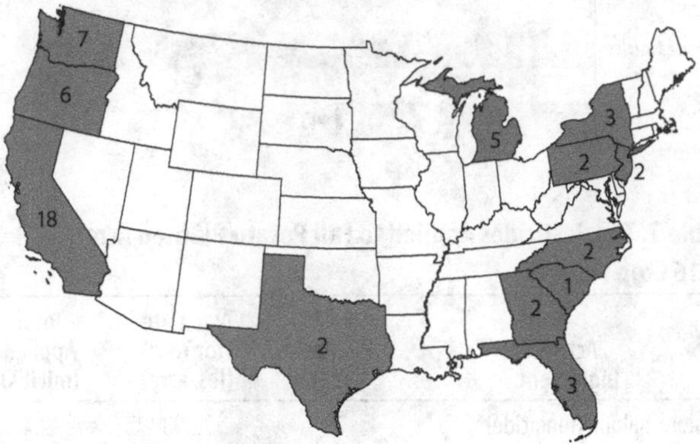

About the Survey

The Agricultural Chemical Use Program of USDA's National Agricultural Statistics Service (NASS) is the federal government's official source of statistics about on-farm and post-harvest commercial fertilizer and pesticide use and pest management practices. NASS conducts agricultural chemical use surveys as part of the Agricultural Resource Management Survey. NASS conducted the fruit chemical use survey in fall 2017.

Access the Data

For detailed data on the pesticides applied to each of the 22 fruits surveyed in 2017, go to http://bit.ly/AgChem. Under "2017 Fruits – released July 25, 2018," click "Data Tables," then select the fruit for which you want data. For survey methodology information, click "Methodology."

To access fruit chemical use data from this survey and previous years, go to the Quick Stats 2.0 database (http://quickstats.nass.usda.gov).

- In Program, select "Survey"
- In Sector, select "Environmental"
- In Group, select "Fruit"
- In Commodity, select the fruit(s) you want data for
- Select your category, data item, geographic level, and year

Pesticide Use

The pesticide active ingredients used on fruit are classified as herbicides (targeting weeds), insecticides (targeting insects), fungicides (targeting fungal disease), and other chemicals (targeting all other pests and other materials, including extraneous crop foliage).

Blueberry and peach growers applied fungicides most widely (to 90 and 84 percent of acres, respectively) followed by insecticides (87 and 82 percent). Apple growers applied fungicides, insecticides, and other chemicals nearly equally (88, 87, and 88 percent, respectively). (Fig. 2) The box on page 2 shows the top pesticides in each category applied to the featured fruits.

United States Department of Agriculture
National Agricultural Statistics Service

www.nass.usda.gov

Fig. 2. Pesticides Applied to Selected Fruits, 2017 Crop Year
(% of planted acres)

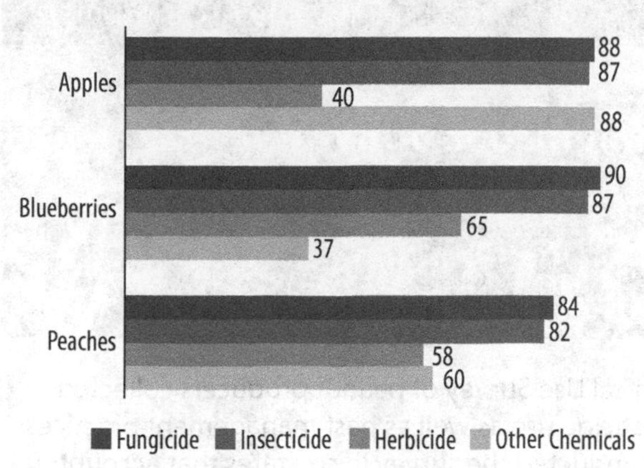

Pest Management Practices

The survey asked growers to report on practices they used to manage pests, including weeds, insects, and diseases. Fruit growers reported practices in three categories. Table 1 shows the most widely applied practices in each category.

- *Prevention* practices involve actions to keep a pest population from infesting a crop or field.
- *Monitoring* practices involve observing or detecting pests through systematic sampling, counting, or other forms of scouting.
- *Suppression* practices involve controlling or reducing existing pest populations to mitigate crop damage.

Table 1. Top Practices in Pest Management Category, 2017 Crop Year
(% of planted acres, 22 fruits)

Prevention	
Irrigated the fruit acres	89
Cleaned equipment and implements after field work	79
Monitoring	
Scouted for insects and mites	99
Monitored weather to assist in decision making	89
Scouted for diseases	89
Suppression	
Used pesticides with different mechanisms of action to keep pest from becoming resistant to pesticide	72
Compared scouting data to published information to assist in decision making	63

Top Pesticides, by percent of planted acres, Selected Fruits, 2017 Crop Year

	% of Planted Acres	Avg. Rate for Year (lbs/acre)	Total Applied (lbs)
Fungicides			
Apples			
Sulfur	42	10.012	1,173,000
Trifloxystrobin	39	0.109	11,900
Blueberries			
Fenbuconazole	56	0.159	6,300
Captan	51	4.998	178,200
Peaches			
Propiconazole	58	0.219	9,600
Captan	38	11.291	327,800
Insecticides			
Apples			
Chlorantranilprole	52	0.130	19,100
Spinetoram	44	0.150	18,500
Blueberries			
Phosmet	49	1.808	62,700
Zeta-cypermethrin	47	0.055	1,800
Peaches			
Lambda-sypermethrin	32	0.099	2,400
Chlorpyrifos	25	1.810	36,300
Herbicides			
Apples			
Glyphosate isopropylamine salt	25	2.059[a]	145,200[a]
2,4-D, dimethylamine salt	15	1.297[a]	52,600[a]
Blueberries			
Flumioxazin	21	0.254	3,800
Glufosinate-ammonium	21	1.408	20,700
Peaches			
Glyphosate isopropylamine salt	30	2.302[a]	50,400[a]
2,4-D, dimethylamine salt	26	1.378[a]	27,400[a]
Other Chemicals			
Apples			
Mineral oil	67	31.960	5,977,500
Gibberellins A4A7	34	0.024	2,300
Blueberries			
Cuprammonium acetate	10	0.377	2,500
Hydrogen peroxide	7	1.760	8,900
Peaches			
Mineral oil	51	37.874	1,303,600
Z-8-Dodecen acetate	11	0.113	1,000

[a] *Expressed in acid equivalent.*

USDA is an equal opportunity provider, employer, and lender.
www.nass.usda.gov

NASS *Highlights*

May 2019 • No. 2019-2

2018 AGRICULTURAL CHEMICAL USE SURVEY

Peanuts

Six states . . .

. . . accounted for 93 percent of U.S. acres planted to peanuts in 2018.

The 2018 Agricultural Chemical Use Survey of peanut producers collected data about fertilizer and pesticide use as well as pest management practices in growing peanuts. NASS conducted the survey in six states that accounted for 93 percent of the 1.4 million acres planted to peanuts in the United States in 2018: Alabama, Florida, Georgia, North Carolina, South Carolina, and Texas (Fig. 1 and box on p. 2).

Data are for the 2018 crop year, the one-year period beginning after the 2017 harvest and ending after the 2018 harvest.

Fig. 1. States in the 2018 Peanut Chemical Use Survey

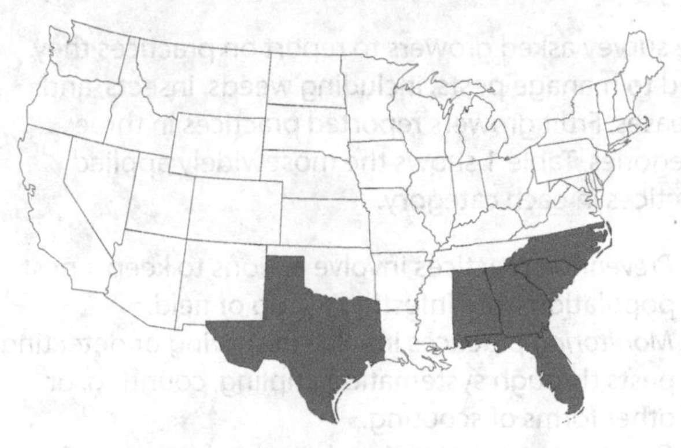

About the Survey

The Agricultural Chemical Use Program of USDA's National Agricultural Statistics Service (NASS) is the federal government's official source of statistics about on-farm and post-harvest commercial fertilizer and pesticide use and pest management practices. NASS conducts field crop agricultural chemical use surveys in cooperation with USDA's Economic Research Service as part of the Agricultural Resource Management Survey. NASS conducted the peanut chemical use survey in the fall of 2018.

Access the Data

Access 2018 and earlier peanut chemical use data through the Quick Stats database (https://quickstats.nass.usda.gov/).

- In Program, select "Survey"
- In Sector, select "Environmental"
- In Group, select "Field Crops"
- In Commodity, select "Peanuts"
- Select your category, data item, geographic level, and year

For pre-defined Quick Stats queries, go to http://bit.ly/AgChem and click "Data Tables" under the 2018 Corn, Peanut, and Soybean heading. For methodology information, click "Methodology."

Fertilizer Use

Fertilizer refers to a soil-enriching input that contains one or more plant nutrients. For the 2018 crop year, farmers applied nitrogen and phosphate to 32 percent of acres planted to peanuts, at an average rate of 32 and 38 pounds per acre, respectively. They applied potash and sulfur to 33 and 12 percent of peanut planted acres, at an average rate of 68 and14 pounds per acre, respectively. (Table 1)

Table 1. Fertilizer Applied to Peanut Planted Acres, 2018 Crop Year

	% of Acres with Nutrient[a]	Average Rate (lbs/acre)	Total Applied (mil lbs)
Nitrogen (N)	32	32	13.5
Phosphate (P_2O_5)	32	38	16.1
Potash (K_2O)	33	68	30.2
Sulfur (S)	12	14	2.1

[a]*Acres with multiple nutrients are counted in each category.*

United States Department of Agriculture
National Agricultural Statistics Service

www.nass.usda.gov

Pesticide Use

The pesticide active ingredients used on peanuts are classified as herbicides (targeting weeds), insecticides (targeting insects), fungicides (targeting fungal disease), and other chemicals (targeting all other pests and other materials, including extraneous crop foliage). Herbicides were used most extensively, applied to 94 percent of planted acres. Fungicides and insecticides were applied to 88 and 37 percent of planted acres, respectively. (Fig. 2)

Among herbicides, flumioxazin was the most widely used active ingredient (applied to 65 percent of planted acres), followed by pendimethalin and s-metolachlor (each applied to 34 percent). (Table 2)

Fig. 2. Pesticides Applied to Peanut Planted Acres, 2018 Crop Year
(% of planted acres)

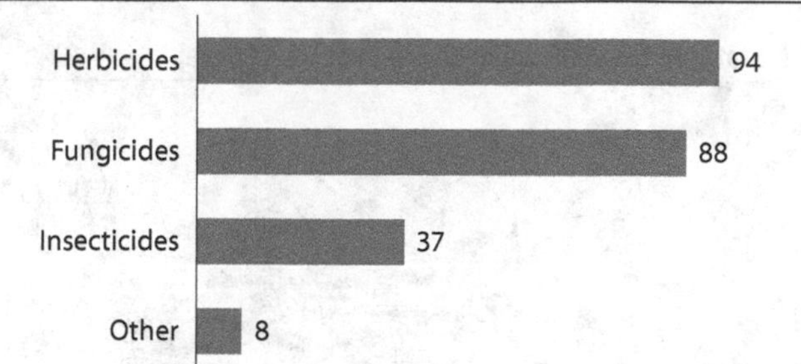

Table 2. Top Herbicides Applied to Peanut Planted Acres, 2018 Crop Year

Active Ingredient	% of Acres with Ingredient[a]	Average Rate (lbs/acre)	Total Applied (lbs)
Flumioxazin	65	0.104	90,000
Pendimethalin	34	0.831	376,000
S-metolachlor	34	1.336	598,000
2;4-D; dimethylamine salt	31	0.354[b]	146,000[b]
Imazapic-ammonium	31	0.070	29,000

[a] *Acres with multiple ingredients are counted in each category.*
[b] *Expressed in acid equivalent.*

Pest Management Practices

The survey asked growers to report on the practices they used to manage pests, defined as weeds, insects, or diseases. Peanut growers reported practices in four categories: prevention, avoidance, monitoring, and suppression (PAMS).

- *Prevention* practices involve actions to keep a pest population from infesting a crop or field.
- *Avoidance* practices use cultural measures to mitigate or eliminate the detrimental effects of pests.
- *Monitoring* practices involve observing or detecting pests through systematic sampling, counting, or other forms of scouting.
- *Suppression* practices involve controlling or reducing existing pest populations to mitigate crop damage.

The most widely used pest prevention practice in growing peanuts was cleaning equipment and implements after field work to reduce the spread of pests, used on 67 percent of planted acres. The top avoidance practice was rotating crops (84 percent). Scouting for weeds was the most widely used monitoring practice (96 percent). Maintaining ground covers, mulches or other physical barriers and using pesticides with different mechanisms of action were the top suppression practices (each with 42 percent). (Table 3)

Table 3. Top Practice in Pest Management Category, 2018
(% of peanut planted acres)

Prevention: Cleaned equipment and implements after field work	67
Avoidance: Rotated crops during past three years	84
Monitoring: Scouted for weeds (deliberately, or by general observations while performing tasks)	96
Suppression:	
Maintained ground covers, mulches, or other physical barriers	42[a]
Used pesticides with different mechanisms of action	42[a]

[a] *The same acres may have both practices.*

Surveyed States: Acres of Peanuts Planted, 2018

U.S. Total	thousands of acres 1,425.5	% of U.S. 100
Georgia	665.0	46.7
Alabama	165.0	11.6
Florida	155.0	10.9
Texas	155.0	10.9
North Carolina	102.0	7.2
South Carolina	87.0	6.1
Total, Surveyed States	**1,329.0**	**93.2**

Numbers may not add due to rounding.

NASS *Highlights*

May 2019 • No. 2019-3

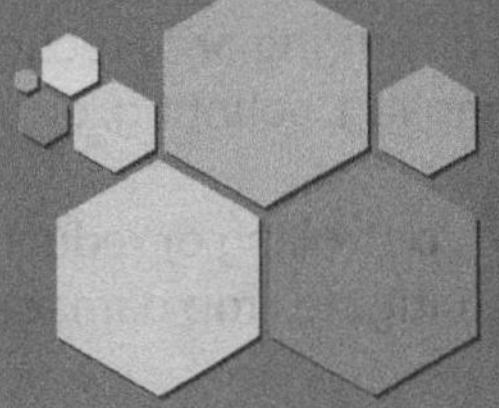

2018 AGRICULTURAL CHEMICAL USE SURVEY

Soybeans

Nineteen states . . .

. . . accounted for 96 percent of U.S. acres planted to soybeans in 2018.

About the Survey

The Agricultural Chemical Use Program of USDA's National Agricultural Statistics Service (NASS) is the federal government's official source of statistics about on-farm and post-harvest commercial fertilizer and pesticide use and pest management practices. NASS conducts field crop agricultural chemical use surveys in cooperation with USDA's Economic Research Service as part of the Agricultural Resource Management Survey. NASS conducted the soybean chemical use survey in the fall of 2018.

Access the Data

Access 2018 and earlier soybean chemical use data through the Quick Stats database (https://quickstats.nass.usda.gov/).

- In Program, select "Survey"
- In Sector, select "Environmental"
- In Group, select "Field Crops"
- In Commodity, select "Soybeans"
- Select your category, data item, geographic level, and year

For pre-defined Quick Stats queries, go to http://bit.ly/AgChem and click "Data Tables" under the 2018 Corn, Peanut, and Soybean heading. For methodology information, click "Methodology."

The 2018 Agricultural Chemical Use Survey of soybean producers collected data about fertilizer and pesticide use as well as pest management practices in growing soybeans. NASS conducted the survey in 19 states that accounted for 96 percent of the 89.2 million acres planted to soybeans in the United States in 2018: Arkansas, Illinois, Indiana, Iowa, Kansas, Kentucky, Louisiana, Michigan, Minnesota, Mississippi, Missouri, Nebraska, North Carolina, North Dakota, Ohio, South Dakota, Tennessee, Virginia, and Wisconsin. (Fig. 1 and box on p. 2)

Data are for the 2018 crop year, the one-year period beginning after the 2017 harvest and ending after the 2018 harvest.

Fig. 1. States in the 2018 Soybean Chemical Use Survey

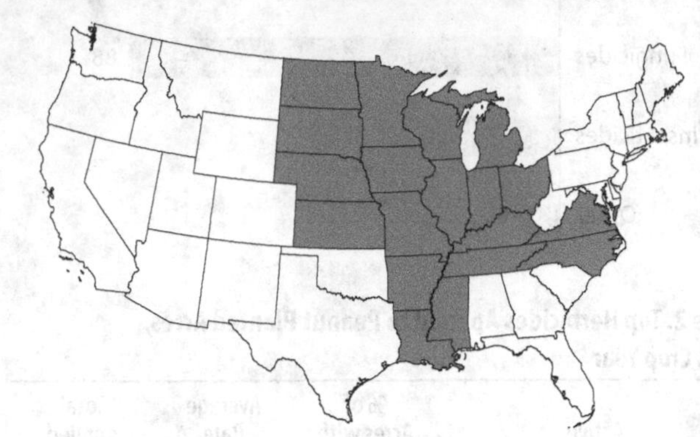

Fertilizer Use

Fertilizer refers to a soil-enriching input that contains one or more plant nutrients. For the 2018 crop year, farmers applied nitrogen to 29 percent of soybean planted acres, at an average rate of 17 pounds per acre, for a total of 416.4 million pounds. (Table 1)

Table 1. Fertilizer Applied to Soybean Planted Acres, 2018 Crop Year

	% of Acres with Nutrient[a]	Average Rate (lbs/acre)	Total Applied (mil lbs)
Nitrogen (N)	29	17	416.4
Phosphate (P_2O_5)	42	55	1,974.3
Potash (K_2O)	43	87	3,221.4
Sulfur (S)	10	13	111.5

[a]*Acres with multiple nutrients are counted in each category.*

Pesticide Use

The pesticide active ingredients used on soybeans are classified in this report as herbicides (targeting weeds), insecticides (targeting insects), fungicides (targeting fungal disease), and other chemicals (targeting all other pests and other materials, including extraneous crop foliage). Herbicides were used most extensively, applied to 99 percent of planted acres. Insecticides were applied to 16 percent of planted acres, fungicides to 15 percent. (Fig. 2)

Among herbicides, glyphosate isopropylamine salt was the most widely used active ingredient (applied to 47 percent of planted acres), followed by glyphosate potassium salt (28 percent) (Table 2). These were also the most widely applied active ingredients in the 2015 and 2017 surveys of soybean producers.

Fig. 2. Pesticides Applied to Soybean Planted Acres, 2018 Crop Year
(% of planted acres)

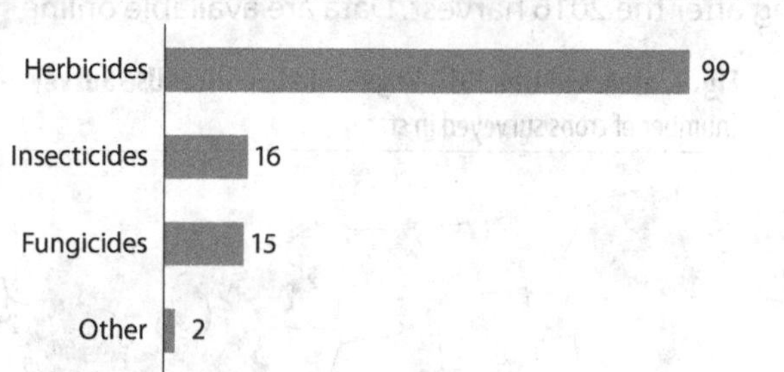

Table 2. Top Herbicides Applied to Soybean Planted Acres, 2018 Crop Year

Active Ingredient	% of Acres with Ingredient[a]	Average Rate (lbs/acre)	Total Applied (mil lbs)
Glyphosate isopropylamine salt	47	1.202[b]	48.3[b]
Glyphosate potassium salt	28	1.527[b]	36.7[b]
Sulfentrazone	20	0.195	3.3
Metribuzin	19	0.270	4.4
Fomesafen sodium	18	0.234	3.6

[a]*Acres with multiple ingredients are counted in each category.*
[b]*Expressed in acid equivalent.*

Pest Management Practices

The survey asked growers to report on the practices they used to manage pests, defined as weeds, insects, or diseases. Soybean growers reported practices in four categories: prevention, avoidance, monitoring, and suppression (PAMS).

- *Prevention* practices involve actions to keep a pest population from infesting a crop or field.
- *Avoidance* practices use cultural measures to mitigate or eliminate the detrimental effects of pests.
- *Monitoring* practices observe or detect pests by systematic sampling, counting, or other forms of scouting.
- *Suppression* practices involve controlling or reducing existing pest populations to mitigate crop damage.

Table 3 shows the top practice in each category. For example, the most widely used prevention practice in growing soybeans in 2018 was no till or minimum till.

Table 3. Top Practice in Pest Management Category, 2018
(% of soybean planted acres)

Prevention: Used no till or minimum till	64
Avoidance: Rotated crops during past three years	77
Monitoring: Scouted for weeds (deliberately, or by general observations while performing tasks)	94
Suppression: Used pesticides with different mechanisms of action	40

Surveyed States: Acres of Soybeans Planted, 2018

	millions of acres	% of U.S.
U.S. Total	89.2	100
Illinois	10.8	12.1
Iowa	10.0	11.2
Minnesota	7.8	8.7
North Dakota	6.9	7.7
Indiana	6.0	6.7
Missouri	5.9	6.6
Nebraska	5.7	6.4
South Dakota	5.7	6.3
Ohio	5.0	5.6
Kansas	4.8	5.3
Arkansas	3.3	3.7
Michigan	2.3	2.6
Mississippi	2.2	2.5
Wisconsin	2.2	2.5
Kentucky	2.0	2.2
Tennessee	1.7	1.9
North Carolina	1.7	1.8
Louisiana	1.3	1.5
Virginia	0.6	0.7
Total, Surveyed States	85.7	96.1

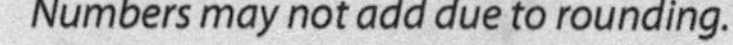

Numbers may not add due to rounding.

NASS *Highlights*

July 2017 • No. 2017-4

2016 AGRICULTURAL CHEMICAL USE SURVEY

Vegetable Crops

99 percent . . .

. . . of vegetable acres were monitored for pests by scouting for insects, mites, and diseases.

About the Survey

The Agricultural Chemical Use Program of USDA's National Agricultural Statistics Service (NASS) is the federal government's official source of statistics about on-farm and post-harvest commercial fertilizer and pesticide use and pest management practices. NASS conducts agricultural chemical use surveys as part of the Agricultural Resource Management Survey. NASS collected data on vegetable chemical use in fall 2016.

Access the Data

Access vegetable chemical use data through the Quick Stats 2.0 database (http://quickstats.nass.usda.gov).

- In Program, select "Survey"
- In Sector, select "Environmental"
- In Group, select "Vegetables"
- In Commodity, select the vegetable(s) you want data for
- Select your category, data item, geographic level, and year

For pre-defined Quick Stats queries that take you to data for a particular vegetable, go to http://bit.ly/AgChem and click "Data Tables" under the 2016 Vegetables heading. For survey methodology information, click "Methodology."

The 2016 Agricultural Chemical Use Survey collected data about pesticide use and pest management practices on acres planted to 28 different vegetable crops. NASS conducted the survey among producers in 19 states, focusing on the states that were major producers for the surveyed crops. (Fig. 1) In most cases, the combination of states surveyed represented a significant percentage of the acres planted in 2015. (See the matrix on page 4 for the specific crops surveyed in each state.)

Data are for the 2016 crop year, the one-year period beginning after the 2015 harvest and ending after the 2016 harvest. Data are available online for all 28 vegetables (see sidebar for how to access). This document highlights five selected vegetables: bell peppers, onions, pumpkins, squash, and watermelons.

Fig. 1. States in the 2016 Vegetable Chemical Use Survey
(number of crops surveyed in state)

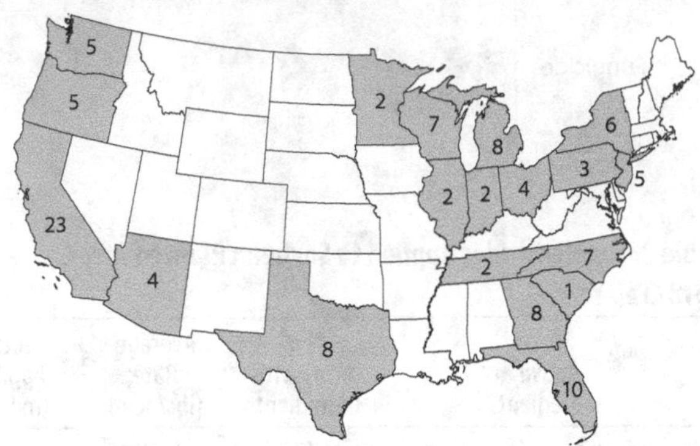

Pesticide Use

The pesticide active ingredients used on vegetables are classified as herbicides (targeting weeds), insecticides (targeting insects), fungicides (targeting fungal disease), and other chemicals (targeting all other pests and other materials, including extraneous crop foliage).

Bell pepper growers applied fungicides to more acres (84 percent of planted acres) than insecticides or herbicides (81 and 44 percent of planted acres, respectively). Watermelon and squash growers similarly applied fungicides to more acres than other pesticides. Pumpkin growers, on the other hand,

United States Department of Agriculture
National Agricultural Statistics Service

www.nass.usda.gov

Who Uses Agricultural Chemical Use Data?

Producers, consumers, suppliers, policymakers, USDA and other federal and state agencies rely on chemical use and other pest management data to make decisions about health, environment, safety, and trade issues. Some examples of how the data are used:

- To evaluate the quality and safety of U.S. food products, providing assurances to both domestic and international customers.
- To establish industry trends and determine the impact of on-farm chemical use and pest management.
- To assess the quality of streams, rivers, and groundwater; the impact of human activities; the benefits of conservation practices; and the effectiveness of integrated pest management.
- To identify which chemicals farmers count on, making it more likely regulators will re-register the product.

applied herbicides to 76 percent of planted acres, but fungicides and insecticides to fewer acres. Onion growers applied the various kinds of pesticides more equally. (Fig. 2)

Tables 1 through 3 show the top herbicides, insecticides, and fungicides applied to each featured vegetable.

Fig. 2. Pesticides Applied to Selected Vegetables, 2016 (% of planted acres)

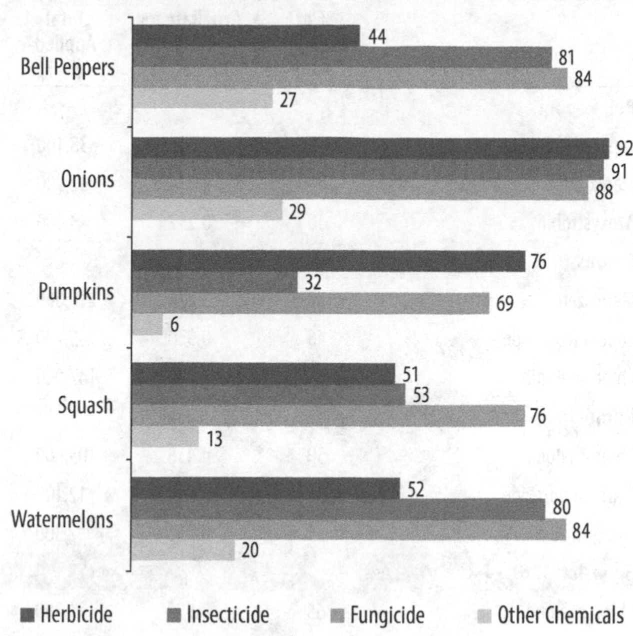

Table 1. Top Herbicides, by percent of planted acres, Selected Vegetables, 2016 Crop Year

	% of Planted Acres	Avg. Rate for Year (lbs/acre)	Total Applied (lbs)
Bell Peppers			
Napropamide	13	1.825	9,800
S-Metolachlor	11	1.373	6,500
Pendimethalin	8	1.047	3,700
Onions			
Oxyfluorfen	83	0.316	28,300
Bromoxynil octanoate	72	0.250	19,500
Pendimethalin	71	1.187	93,500
Pumpkins			
Clomazone	57	0.527	12,100
S-Metolachlor	41	1.244	20,600
Ethalfluralin	15	0.704	4,100
Squash			
Clomazone	35	0.294	3,300
Ethalfluralin	15	0.621	3,000
S-Metolachlor	9	1.060	3,200
Watermelons			
Clethodim	26	0.129	3,600
Trifluralin	17	0.979	17,400
Ethalfluralin	13	0.560	7,900

Table 2. Top Insecticides, by percent of planted acres, Selected Vegetables, 2016 Crop Year

	% of Planted Acres	Avg. Rate for Year (lbs/acre)	Total Applied (lbs)
Bell Peppers			
Chlorantraniliprole	49	0.103	2,100
Zeta-cypermethrin	38	0.095	1,500
Imidacloprid	29	0.367	4,400
Onions			
Methomyl	47	1.508	76,100
Spirotetramat	43	0.116	5,400
Spinetoram	41	0.103	4,500
Pumpkins			
Lambda-cyhalothrin	9	0.080	300
Bifenthrin	7	0.122	400
Permethrin	7	0.369	1,100
Squash			
Bifenthrin	23	0.241	1,700
Zeta-cypermethrin	17	0.063	300
Acetamiprid	7	0.332	700
Watermelons			
Flubendiamide	38	0.084	3,400
Imidacloprid	30	0.151	4,700
Chlorantraniliprole	22	0.083	1,900

Table 3. Top Fungicides, by percent of planted acres, Selected Vegetables, 2016 Crop Year

	% of Planted Acres	Avg. Rate for Year (lbs/acre)	Total Applied (lbs)
Bell Peppers			
Copper hydroxide	50	1.818	38,100
Mancozeb	36	2.914	42,300
Azoxystrobin	36	0.237	3,500
Onions			
Mancozeb	57	3.276	219,000
Copper hydroxide	46	0.930	45,700
Chlorothalonil	44	3.080	147,000
Pumpkins			
Chlorothalonil	59	4.438	105,600
Copper hydroxide	34	0.893	12,100
Azoxystrobin	25	0.226	2,300
Squash			
Chlorothalonil	65	3.550	74,300
Copper hydroxide	26	1.466	12,200
Sulfur	17	10.219	56,100
Watermelons			
Mancozeb	56	3.046	176,700
Chlorothalonil	55	4.257	244,300
Copper hydroxide	48	0.534	26,700

Pest Management Practices

The survey asked growers to report on the practices they used to manage pests, including weeds, insects, and diseases. Vegetable growers reported practices in four categories of pest management strategy, widely referred to as PAMS – prevention, avoidance, monitoring, and suppression.

- *Prevention* practices involve actions to keep a pest population from infesting a crop or field.
- *Avoidance* practices use cultural measures to mitigate or eliminate the detrimental effects of pests.
- *Monitoring* practices observe or detect pests by sampling, counting, or other forms of scouting.
- *Suppression* practices involve controlling or reducing existing pest populations to mitigate crop damage.

Scouting for insects, mites, and diseases were the most widely reported monitoring practices, used on 99 percent of vegetable planted acres. The most widely used avoidance practice was crop rotation, used on 82 percent of planted acres.

The prevention practice of chopping, spraying, mowing, plowing, or burning field edges, ditches, and fence lines was used on 78 percent of planted acres, and the suppression practice of applying various pesticides to keep pests from becoming resistant was used on 73 percent of acres. (Table 4)

Table 4. Top Practices in Pest Management Category, 2016 Crop Year
(% of planted acres, 28 vegetables)

Prevention	
Chopped, sprayed, mowed, plowed, or burned field edges, ditches or fence lines	78
Cleaned equipment and implements after field work to reduce spread of pests	75
Removed or burned crop residues	68
Cultivated crop acres for weed control	67
Used water management practices	62
Avoidance	
Rotated crops during past three years	82
Chose crop or plan variety for specific pest resistance	45
Planned planting locations to avoid cross infestation of pests	35
Adjusted planting or harvesting dates	31
Adjusted row spacing, plant density, or row directions	24
Monitoring	
Scouted for insects and mites (deliberately or by general observations while performing other tasks)	99
Scouted for diseases (deliberately or by general observations while performing other tasks)	99
Scouted for weeds (deliberately or by general observations while performing other tasks)	96
Scouted for pests (deliberately)	92
Used weather data in decision making	75
Suppression	
Used pesticides with different mechanisms of action to keep pest from becoming resistant to pesticides	73
Maintained ground covers, mulches, or other physical barriers	48
Compared scoutinq data to published information to assist in decision making	45
Applied biological pesticides	28
Used floral lures, attractants, repellents, pheromone traps, or biological pest controls	17

States and Crops in the 2016 Agricultural Chemical Use Survey

	Arizona	California	Florida	Georgia	Illinois	Indiana	Michigan	Minnesota	New Jersey	New York	North Carolina	Ohio	Oregon	Pennsylvania	South Carolina	Tennessee	Texas	Washington	Wisconsin
Asparagus		X					X											X	
Beans, snap (FM)		X	X	X						X	X					X			
Beans, snap (PR)							X			X			X	X					X
Broccoli		X																	
Cabbage (FM)		X	X	X						X	X						X		X
Cantaloupes	X	X															X		
Carrots (FM)		X					X										X		
Carrots (PR)																			X
Cauliflower		X																	
Celery		X																	
Corn, sweet (FM)		X	X	X	X	X	X		X	X		X	X	X			X		X
Corn, sweet (PR)								X										X	X
Cucumbers (FM)		X	X	X			X		X		X								
Cucumbers (PR)			X				X					X					X		X
Garlic		X																	
Honeydews		X																	
Lettuce, head	X	X																	
Lettuce, other	X	X																	
Onions		X		X						X			X				X	X	
Peas, green (PR)								X					X					X	X
Peppers, bell		X	X	X					X		X								
Pumpkins		X			X		X					X		X					
Spinach (FM)	X	X															X		
Squash		X	X	X			X		X	X	X								
Strawberries		X	X										X					X	
Tomatoes (FM)		X	X						X		X	X				X			
Tomatoes (PR)		X																	
Watermelons		X	X	X		X					X				X		X		
No. of Crops	**4**	**23**	**10**	**8**	**2**	**2**	**8**	**2**	**5**	**6**	**7**	**4**	**5**	**3**	**1**	**2**	**8**	**5**	**7**

FM = fresh market. PR = processing.

USDA is an equal opportunity provider, employer, and lender.
www.nass.usda.gov

NASS Highlights
May 2018 • No. 2018-5

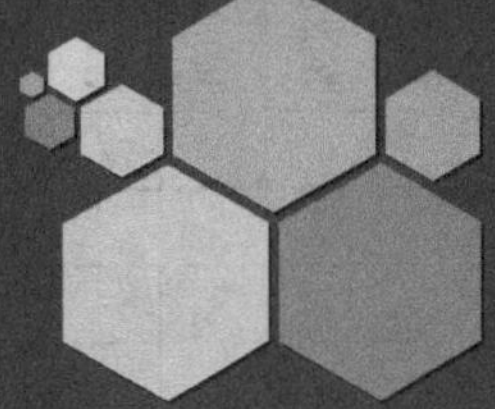

2017 AGRICULTURAL CHEMICAL USE SURVEY

Wheat

Eighteen states . . .

. . . accounted for 90 percent of U.S. acres planted to wheat in 2017.

About the Survey

The Agricultural Chemical Use Program of the National Agricultural Statistics Service (NASS) is the U.S. Department of Agriculture's official source of statistics about on-farm and post-harvest commercial fertilizer and pesticide use and pest management practices. NASS conducts field crop agricultural chemical use surveys as part of the Agricultural Resource Management Survey. NASS conducted the wheat chemical use survey in the fall of 2017.

Access the Data

Access wheat chemical use data through the Quick Stats 2.0 database (http://quickstats.nass.usda.gov).

- In Program, select "Survey"
- In Sector, select "Environmental"
- In Group, select "Field Crops"
- In Commodity, select "Wheat"
- Select your category, data item, geographic level, and year

For methodology information, go to http://bit.ly/AgChem and click "Methodology."

The 2017 Agricultural Chemical Use Survey of wheat producers collected data about fertilizer and pesticide use as well as pest management practices in growing wheat. NASS conducted the survey in 18 states that together accounted for 90 percent of the 46.0 million acres planted to wheat in the United States in 2017, including 85 percent of winter wheat acres and 99 percent of spring and durum wheat acres. (Fig. 1 and box on p. 2)

Fig. 1. States in the 2017 Wheat Chemical Use Survey

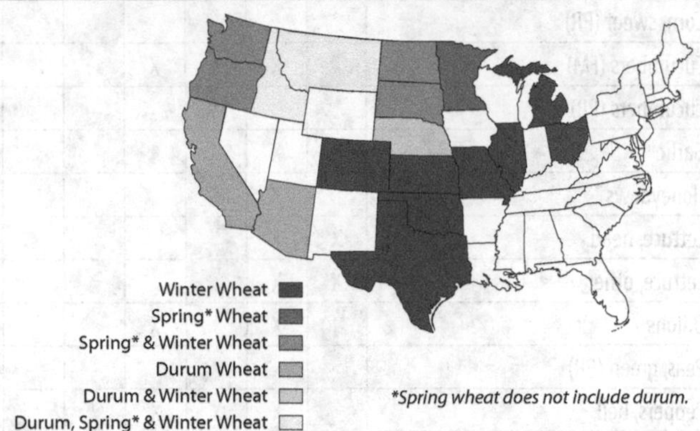

Data are for the 2017 crop year, the one-year period beginning after the 2016 harvest and ending after the 2017 harvest.

Fertilizer Use

Fertilizer refers to a soil-enriching input that contains one or more plant nutrients, primarily nitrogen (N), phosphate (P_2O_5), and potash (K_2O). For the 2017 crop year, farmers applied nitrogen to nearly all acres planted to spring and durum wheat. (Table 1)

Table 1. Fertilizer Applied to Wheat Planted Acres, 2017 Crop Year

	% of Planted Acres	Avg. Rate for Year (lbs/acre)	Total Applied (mil lbs)
Winter			
Nitrogen	83	72	1,690.0
Phosphate	58	31	506.3
Potash	15	40	172.5
Spring (excl durum)			
Nitrogen	96	98	984.5
Phosphate	89	40	367.7
Potash	34	21	73.9
Durum			
Nitrogen	98	88	196.8
Phosphate	91	31	64.7
Potash	28	13	8.2

United States Department of Agriculture
National Agricultural Statistics Service

www.nass.usda.gov

Pesticide Use

In the surveyed states, farmers used 96 different pesticide active ingredients on winter wheat acres, 82 different ingredients on spring (excl durum) wheat acres, and 63 on durum wheat acres. These pesticide active ingredients are classified as herbicides (targeting weeds), insecticides (targeting insects), fungicides (targeting fungal disease), and other. Herbicides were used most extensively, applied to 61 percent of winter wheat planted acres, 96 percent of spring (excl durum) wheat acres, and 93 percent of durum wheat acres (Fig. 2). Table 2 shows the most widely applied herbicides for each wheat type.

Fig. 2. Pesticides Applied to Wheat Planted Acres, 2017 Crop Year
(% of planted acres)

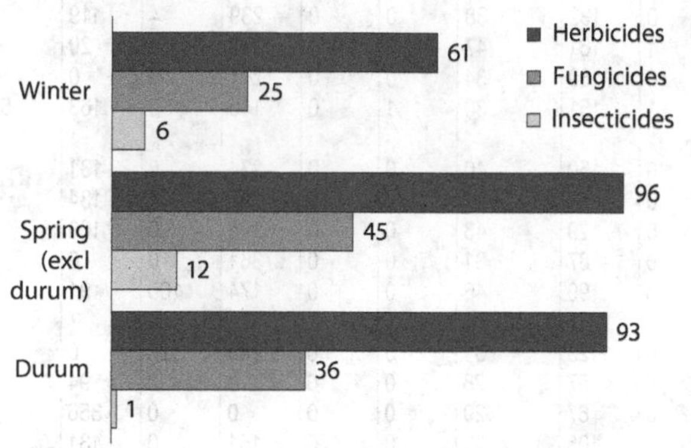

Table 2. Top Herbicides Applied to Wheat Planted Acres, 2017 Crop Year

Active Ingredient	% of Planted Acres	Avg. Rate for Year (lbs/acre)	Total Applied (mil lbs)
Winter			
Glyphosate isopropylamine salt	22	1.299[a]	8.2[a]
2;4-D; 2-EHE	18	0.529	2.6
Spring (excl durum)			
Fluroxypyr 1-MHE	46	0.083	0.4
Glyphosate isopropylamine salt	37	0.845[a]	3.2[a]
Durum			
Glyphosate isopropylamine salt	58	0.772[a]	1.0[a]
Fluroxypyr 1-MHE	39	0.094	0.1

[a] *Expressed in acid equivalent.*

Pest Management Practices

The survey asked growers to report on the practices they used to manage pests, defined as weeds, insects, or diseases. Wheat growers reported practices in four categories. Table 3 shows the most widely used practice in each category.

- *Prevention* practices involve actions to keep a pest population from infesting a crop or field.
- *Avoidance* practices use cultural measures to mitigate or eliminate the detrimental effects of pests.
- *Monitoring* practices observe or detect pests by systematic sampling, counting, or other forms of scouting.
- *Suppression* practices involve controlling or reducing existing pest populations to mitigate crop damage.

Table 3. Top Practice in Pest Management Category, 2017
(% of wheat planted acres)

	Winter	Spring*	Durum
Prevention: Used no-till or minimum till	64	80	90
Avoidance: Rotated crops during past three years	53	87	84
Monitoring: Scouted for weeds (deliberately, or by general observations while performing tasks)	87	98	97
Suppression: Maintained ground covers, mulches, or other physical barriers	36	51	55

**Excluding durum.*

Surveyed States: Acres of Wheat Planted, 2017

	Winter	Spring*	Durum
U.S. Total (thousands of acres)	**32,696.0**	**11,009.0**	**2,307.0**
	(percent of total)		
Arizona			3.9
California			1.5
Colorado	6.8		
Idaho	2.2	3.8	1.0
Illinois	1.5		
Kansas	23.2		
Michigan	1.4		
Minnesota		10.5	
Missouri	1.9		
Montana	5.3	22.7	38.5
Nebraska	3.4		
North Dakota	0.2	48.5	54.6
Ohio	1.4		
Oklahoma	13.7		
Oregon	2.1	0.6	
South Dakota	2.7	8.8	
Texas	14.3		
Washington	5.1	4.4	
Total, Surveyed States (percent of U.S. Total)	**85.2** (15 states)	**99.3** (7 states)	**99.5** (5 states)

Numbers may not add due to rounding. **Excluding durum.*

USDA is an equal opportunity provider, employer, and lender.
www.nass.usda.gov

Air Quality Index Report, 2018

Metropolitan Statistical Area	Days with AQI Data	Number of Days when Air Quality was...				AQI Statistics		Number of Days when AQI Pollutant was...					
		Good	Moderate	Unhealthy for Sensitive Groups	Unhealthy, Very Unhealthy, or Hazardous	Max	Median	CO	NO_2	O_3	SO_2	$PM_{2.5}$	PM_{10}
Aberdeen, SD	121	114	5	1	1	429	24	0	0	0	0	109	12
Aberdeen, WA	365	344	17	1	3	163	22	0	0	0	0	365	0
Adjuntas, PR	27	27	0	0	0	32	14	0	0	0	0	27	0
Adrian, MI	322	263	55	4	0	115	38	0	0	221	0	101	0
Akron, OH	365	256	108	1	0	105	42	0	0	171	0	194	0
Albany, GA	356	292	63	1	0	137	30	0	0	0	0	356	0
Albany, OR	273	243	24	6	0	133	24	0	0	0	0	273	0
Albany-Schenectady-Troy, NY	365	288	74	3	0	119	38	0	0	233	0	132	0
Albuquerque, NM	365	151	190	23	1	165	54	0	1	259	0	51	54
Alexandria, LA	119	102	17	0	0	91	31	0	0	0	0	119	0
Allentown-Bethlehem-Easton, PA-NJ	365	246	114	5	0	136	42	0	6	180	0	179	0
Altoona, PA	362	296	65	1	0	132	38	0	0	239	4	119	0
Amarillo, TX	365	224	112	28	1	161	47	0	0	277	68	20	0
Americus, GA	241	219	22	0	0	80	34	0	0	241	0	0	0
Anchorage, AK	365	293	68	3	1	151	30	1	0	145	0	163	56
Ann Arbor, MI	365	281	78	6	0	150	40	0	0	234	0	131	0
Appleton, WI	365	271	85	9	0	132	41	0	0	187	44	134	0
Ardmore, OK	365	253	103	9	0	129	43	0	0	196	0	169	0
Arkadelphia, AR	361	342	19	0	0	87	31	0	0	361	0	0	0
Asheville, NC	365	234	101	24	6	199	46	0	0	174	100	91	0
Ashtabula, OH	365	329	33	3	0	129	31	0	0	243	122	0	0
Athens, OH	94	88	6	0	0	57	28	0	0	0	0	94	0
Athens, TN	356	316	40	0	0	67	29	0	0	0	0	356	0
Athens-Clarke County, GA	332	262	68	2	0	105	39	0	0	151	0	181	0
Atlanta-Sandy Springs-Roswell, GA	365	209	146	10	0	133	48	0	11	157	0	197	0
Atlantic City-Hammonton, NJ	365	327	37	1	0	112	37	0	0	250	0	115	0
Augusta-Richmond County, GA-SC	365	252	107	6	0	150	41	0	0	166	23	176	0
Augusta-Waterville, ME	360	344	16	0	0	90	30	0	114	217	1	25	3
Austin-Round Rock, TX	365	239	117	9	0	115	44	0	15	156	0	193	1
Bakersfield, CA	365	65	170	103	27	190	84	0	0	246	0	106	13
Baltimore-Columbia-Towson, MD	365	208	141	16	0	150	47	0	10	167	6	182	0
Bangor, ME	364	336	28	0	0	97	32	0	0	197	0	163	4
Baraboo, WI	365	301	63	1	0	122	39	0	0	209	0	153	3
Barnstable Town, MA	360	338	18	4	0	133	36	0	0	356	0	4	0
Bartlesville, OK	8	5	3	0	0	60	43	0	0	2	0	6	0
Baton Rouge, LA	365	224	122	18	1	153	45	0	3	186	6	170	0
Bay City, MI	356	321	35	0	0	83	28	0	0	0	0	356	0
Beaumont-Port Arthur, TX	365	195	152	17	1	154	49	0	0	137	37	191	0
Beaver Dam, WI	365	278	84	3	0	133	41	0	0	251	0	114	0
Bellingham, WA	365	249	98	15	3	182	38	0	0	56	195	114	0
Bemidji, MN	352	327	24	1	0	106	23	0	0	0	0	352	0
Bend-Redmond, OR	271	223	31	10	7	189	18	0	0	0	0	271	0
Bennington, VT	365	333	31	1	0	101	35	0	0	278	0	87	0
Berlin, NH-VT	243	195	45	3	0	115	44	0	0	227	0	16	0
Big Spring, TX	362	314	39	8	1	200	7	0	0	0	362	0	0
Billings, MT	364	317	44	2	1	154	27	0	0	0	26	338	0
Birmingham-Hoover, AL	365	166	190	8	1	156	52	0	1	103	43	215	3
Bishop, CA	365	198	130	26	11	624	48	0	0	311	0	20	34
Bismarck, ND	363	282	76	3	2	153	40	2	1	232	0	125	3
Blacksburg-Christiansburg-Radford, VA	362	313	46	3	0	139	37	0	0	326	36	0	0
Bloomington, IL	365	248	116	1	0	108	44	0	0	167	0	198	0
Bloomington, IN	364	256	105	3	0	129	43	0	0	184	0	180	0

Metropolitan Statistical Area	Days with AQI Data	Number of Days when Air Quality was...				AQI Statistics		Number of Days when AQI Pollutant was...					
		Good	Moderate	Unhealthy for Sensitive Groups	Unhealthy, Very Unhealthy, or Hazardous	Max	Median	CO	NO_2	O_3	SO_2	$PM_{2.5}$	PM_{10}
Boise City, ID	365	200	154	11	0	134	49	0	0	151	0	203	11
Borger, TX	358	222	50	78	8	168	20	0	0	0	358	0	0
Boston-Cambridge-Newton, MA-NH	365	225	135	5	0	126	45	0	9	121	0	235	0
Boulder, CO	362	219	114	28	1	159	46	0	0	285	0	77	0
Bowling Green, KY	365	280	85	0	0	100	40	0	0	169	0	196	0
Bozeman, MT	365	323	36	5	1	153	25	0	8	0	0	357	0
Brainerd, MN	364	316	47	1	0	107	30	0	0	149	0	215	0
Branson, MO	81	72	9	0	0	75	25	0	0	0	0	81	0
Bremerton-Silverdale, WA	349	333	11	2	3	172	12	0	0	0	0	349	0
Bridgeport-Stamford-Norwalk, CT	365	258	86	14	7	185	41	0	21	196	0	148	0
Brookings, SD	365	317	47	1	0	101	36	0	0	292	0	51	22
Brownsville-Harlingen, TX	365	246	119	0	0	99	41	0	0	127	0	238	0
Brunswick, GA	272	255	17	0	0	74	34	0	0	225	0	47	0
Buffalo-Cheektowaga-Niagara Falls, NY	365	273	89	3	0	112	40	0	15	211	0	139	0
Burlington-South Burlington, VT	365	322	43	0	0	89	38	0	0	280	0	85	0
Butte-Silver Bow, MT	363	308	54	1	0	120	20	0	0	0	0	200	163
Cadillac, MI	365	324	39	2	0	122	37	0	1	341	0	23	0
Cambridge, MD	365	305	58	1	1	151	38	0	0	314	0	51	0
Canton-Massillon, OH	365	237	125	3	0	108	45	1	0	167	0	197	0
Cape Coral-Fort Myers, FL	365	316	48	1	0	106	35	0	0	294	0	71	0
Carlsbad-Artesia, NM	365	214	131	17	3	185	47	0	8	355	0	2	0
Carson City, NV	365	269	88	5	3	160	44	0	0	311	0	54	0
Casper, WY	365	289	76	0	0	90	42	0	12	345	1	7	0
CaAon City, CO	20	20	0	0	0	36	15	0	0	0	0	0	20
Cedar City, UT	365	259	106	0	0	90	43	0	0	320	0	45	0
Cedar Rapids, IA	365	249	112	4	0	129	44	0	0	150	3	211	1
Centralia, WA	365	324	35	3	3	167	21	0	0	0	0	365	0
Chambersburg-Waynesboro, PA	353	343	10	0	0	74	32	0	0	353	0	0	0
Champaign-Urbana, IL	365	283	78	4	0	112	42	0	0	222	0	143	0
Charleston, WV	365	303	61	1	0	105	39	2	0	168	1	194	0
Charleston-North Charleston, SC	356	323	33	0	0	97	36	0	3	211	0	141	1
Charlotte-Concord-Gastonia, NC-SC	364	229	125	10	0	122	45	0	2	221	0	140	1
Charlottesville, VA	310	275	35	0	0	93	36	0	0	213	0	97	0
Chattanooga, TN-GA	365	252	112	1	0	101	44	0	0	159	0	206	0
Cheyenne, WY	365	295	69	1	0	109	43	0	7	332	0	22	4
Chicago-Naperville-Elgin, IL-IN-WI	365	117	222	20	6	177	57	0	29	112	6	205	13
Chico, CA	365	152	173	22	18	445	54	0	0	203	0	161	1
Cincinnati, OH-KY-IN	365	163	189	11	2	159	52	0	11	141	5	204	4
Claremont-Lebanon, NH-VT	365	336	29	0	0	90	36	0	0	259	0	106	0
Clarksburg, WV	117	104	13	0	0	61	27	0	0	0	0	117	0
Clarksville, TN-KY	365	289	76	0	0	90	40	0	0	229	0	136	0
Clearlake, CA	357	346	7	1	3	267	33	0	0	344	0	11	2
Cleveland, MS	312	237	73	2	0	129	41	0	0	163	0	149	0
Cleveland-Elyria, OH	365	202	148	15	0	138	48	0	6	177	8	165	9
Clinton, IA	365	244	121	0	0	100	43	0	0	145	2	218	0
Coeur d'Alene, ID	331	272	49	5	5	204	25	0	0	0	0	331	0
College Station-Bryan, TX	332	332	0	0	0	26	0	0	0	0	332	0	0
Colorado Springs, CO	365	233	124	8	0	119	46	0	0	329	0	36	0
Columbia, MO	245	208	36	1	0	105	40	0	0	245	0	0	0
Columbia, SC	365	279	85	1	0	101	40	0	0	210	0	155	0
Columbus, GA-AL	365	271	94	0	0	99	40	0	0	132	0	233	0
Columbus, IN	365	290	71	4	0	108	40	0	0	242	0	123	0
Columbus, OH	365	254	108	3	0	122	44	0	20	193	0	151	1
Concord, NH	365	355	10	0	0	87	27	0	0	213	152	0	0
Cookeville, TN	352	319	33	0	0	64	27	0	0	0	0	352	0

Metropolitan Statistical Area	Days with AQI Data	Number of Days when Air Quality was... Good	Moderate	Unhealthy for Sensitive Groups	Unhealthy, Very Unhealthy, or Hazardous	AQI Statistics Max	Median	Number of Days when AQI Pollutant was... CO	NO_2	O_3	SO_2	$PM_{2.5}$	PM_{10}
Corning, NY	361	326	35	0	0	87	32	1	0	295	0	65	0
Corpus Christi, TX	365	284	81	0	0	99	38	0	0	170	0	195	0
Corsicana, TX	365	254	98	11	2	200	40	0	4	213	66	82	0
Corvallis, OR	269	261	6	2	0	124	14	0	0	0	0	269	0
Craig, CO	331	262	68	1	0	108	42	0	0	331	0	0	0
Crescent City, CA	146	130	16	0	0	77	26	0	0	0	0	146	0
Crestview-Fort Walton Beach-Destin, FL	353	325	28	0	0	80	33	0	0	345	0	0	8
Cullowhee, NC	125	116	9	0	0	66	26	0	0	0	0	125	0
Cumberland, MD-WV	365	261	59	33	12	200	17	0	0	0	365	0	0
Dallas-Fort Worth-Arlington, TX	365	186	143	27	9	166	50	0	9	189	0	167	0
Dalton, GA	253	223	30	0	0	100	38	0	0	222	0	31	0
Daphne-Fairhope-Foley, AL	270	245	25	0	0	97	35	0	0	214	0	56	0
Davenport-Moline-Rock Island, IA-IL	365	172	189	4	0	108	52	0	1	82	0	193	89
Dayton, OH	365	218	142	5	0	140	46	0	0	179	0	186	0
Decatur, AL	364	304	60	0	0	100	37	0	0	176	0	188	0
Decatur, IL	365	172	179	14	0	126	51	0	0	98	103	164	0
Deltona-Daytona Beach-Ormond Beach, FL	365	329	36	0	0	80	36	0	0	279	0	86	0
Deming, NM	357	343	11	3	0	137	16	0	0	0	0	0	357
Denver-Aurora-Lakewood, CO	365	93	225	41	6	159	61	0	64	218	0	59	24
Des Moines-West Des Moines, IA	365	284	79	2	0	112	40	0	5	225	0	135	0
Detroit-Warren-Dearborn, MI	365	138	204	21	2	151	54	0	5	80	66	194	20
Dickinson, ND	361	321	40	0	0	90	38	0	0	304	0	57	0
Dodge City, KS	354	325	28	1	0	129	17	0	0	0	0	0	354
Dothan, AL	277	249	28	0	0	80	35	0	0	211	0	66	0
Douglas, GA	116	112	4	0	0	65	22	0	0	0	0	116	0
Dover, DE	365	309	54	2	0	133	38	0	0	276	0	89	0
DuBois, PA	343	320	22	1	0	101	33	0	0	343	0	0	0
Duluth, MN-WI	365	305	58	2	0	109	35	0	0	283	0	74	8
Durango, CO	365	240	105	10	10	218	45	0	0	330	0	32	3
Durant, OK	301	257	41	3	0	119	38	0	0	301	0	0	0
Durham-Chapel Hill, NC	359	268	91	0	0	100	43	0	0	169	2	187	1
Dyersburg, TN	356	325	31	0	0	80	29	0	0	0	0	356	0
Eagle Pass, TX	342	292	50	0	0	100	28	0	0	0	0	342	0
East Stroudsburg, PA	355	319	34	2	0	108	35	0	0	331	0	24	0
Eau Claire, WI	365	282	82	1	0	129	41	0	0	190	0	175	0
Effingham, IL	245	214	30	1	0	112	39	0	0	245	0	0	0
El Centro, CA	365	95	221	40	9	286	62	0	7	129	0	100	129
El Dorado, AR	365	276	86	3	0	122	37	0	0	0	0	365	0
El Paso, TX	365	133	215	15	2	164	55	0	26	190	0	147	2
Elizabethtown-Fort Knox, KY	361	269	92	0	0	100	40	0	0	121	0	240	0
Elkhart-Goshen, IN	363	285	75	3	0	105	38	0	0	194	0	169	0
Elko, NV	339	323	15	1	0	123	16	0	0	0	0	16	323
Ellensburg, WA	358	310	36	5	7	197	19	0	0	0	0	358	0
Emporia, KS	78	72	6	0	0	63	26	0	0	0	0	78	0
Enid, OK	357	349	8	0	0	70	0	0	0	0	357	0	0
Erie, PA	365	280	85	0	0	84	38	0	7	198	0	159	1
EspaAola, NM	360	244	113	3	0	126	46	0	0	360	0	0	0
Eugene, OR	365	266	91	7	1	154	36	0	0	102	0	259	4
Eureka-Arcata-Fortuna, CA	365	324	35	5	1	163	34	0	2	251	0	94	18
Evanston, WY	365	287	77	1	0	108	44	0	2	354	0	0	9
Evansville, IN-KY	365	204	146	15	0	143	47	0	0	159	56	150	0
Fairbanks, AK	365	258	77	25	5	155	34	0	35	114	5	206	5
Fairmont, WV	117	105	12	0	0	63	28	0	0	0	0	117	0
Fallon, NV	332	256	71	5	0	129	44	0	0	332	0	0	0
Fargo, ND-MN	360	315	44	1	0	121	35	0	9	239	0	103	9

Metropolitan Statistical Area	Days with AQI Data	Number of Days when Air Quality was...				AQI Statistics		Number of Days when AQI Pollutant was...					
		Good	Moderate	Unhealthy for Sensitive Groups	Unhealthy, Very Unhealthy, or Hazardous	Max	Median	CO	NO_2	O_3	SO_2	$PM_{2.5}$	PM_{10}
Farmington, NM	365	213	136	16	0	129	47	0	2	363	0	0	0
Fayetteville, NC	349	284	65	0	0	100	38	0	0	194	0	145	10
Fayetteville-Springdale-Rogers, AR-MO	365	266	99	0	0	87	42	0	0	216	0	149	0
Fernley, NV	362	304	50	8	0	133	40	0	0	362	0	0	0
Flagstaff, AZ	365	243	119	3	0	126	45	0	0	363	0	2	0
Flint, MI	362	291	68	3	0	122	38	0	0	214	0	148	0
Florence, SC	363	321	42	0	0	87	36	0	0	153	0	210	0
Florence-Muscle Shoals, AL	277	251	26	0	0	93	35	0	0	209	0	68	0
Fond du Lac, WI	244	213	30	1	0	101	39	0	0	244	0	0	0
Fort Collins, CO	365	201	137	24	3	169	49	0	0	320	0	44	1
Fort Madison-Keokuk, IA-IL-MO	121	99	22	0	0	76	34	0	0	0	0	121	0
Fort Payne, AL	350	316	34	0	0	84	35	0	0	317	0	33	0
Fort Smith, AR-OK	363	308	55	0	0	90	35	0	6	206	0	151	0
Fort Wayne, IN	365	243	116	6	0	122	44	0	0	191	0	174	0
Fresno, CA	365	84	183	79	19	185	74	0	3	231	0	121	10
Gadsden, AL	324	231	92	0	1	153	41	0	0	179	0	145	0
Gainesville, FL	364	335	29	0	0	90	33	0	0	293	0	71	0
Gainesville, GA	322	282	40	0	0	68	30	0	0	0	0	322	0
Gardnerville Ranchos, NV	362	315	37	6	4	205	15	0	0	0	0	362	0
Georgetown, SC	326	326	0	0	0	44	15	0	0	0	0	0	326
Gettysburg, PA	365	294	69	2	0	105	40	0	0	258	0	107	0
Gillette, WY	365	266	95	2	2	169	42	0	1	231	0	17	116
Glenwood Springs, CO	365	261	102	1	1	151	44	0	3	342	0	15	5
Grand Island, NE	111	104	7	0	0	68	23	0	0	0	0	111	0
Grand Junction, CO	365	256	106	3	0	126	44	1	0	293	0	70	1
Grand Rapids-Wyoming, MI	365	290	71	4	0	115	40	0	0	233	0	132	0
Grants Pass, OR	286	194	56	5	31	228	30	0	0	0	0	286	0
Great Falls, MT	360	329	25	5	1	162	25	0	0	0	0	360	0
Greeley, CO	365	200	155	10	0	133	48	0	0	236	0	128	1
Green Bay, WI	365	288	71	5	1	151	41	0	0	223	7	135	0
Greenfield Town, MA	365	325	40	0	0	100	36	0	0	280	0	85	0
Greensboro-High Point, NC	357	277	79	1	0	105	41	0	0	224	0	117	16
Greenville, NC	345	306	39	0	0	87	35	0	0	189	0	156	0
Greenville-Anderson-Mauldin, SC	365	291	74	0	0	87	40	0	13	232	0	120	0
Grenada, MS	105	97	8	0	0	80	27	0	0	0	0	105	0
Guayama, PR	342	342	0	0	0	40	3	0	0	0	342	0	0
Gulfport-Biloxi-Pascagoula, MS	364	278	82	4	0	115	40	0	1	163	0	200	0
Hagerstown-Martinsburg, MD-WV	359	285	74	0	0	93	39	0	0	198	0	161	0
Hailey, ID	363	327	33	3	0	143	13	0	0	0	0	363	0
Hammond, LA	125	110	15	0	0	78	28	0	0	0	0	125	0
Hanford-Corcoran, CA	365	86	221	49	9	180	70	0	0	184	0	122	59
Harrisburg-Carlisle, PA	365	251	113	1	0	108	42	0	0	159	0	206	0
Harrison, AR	364	337	27	0	0	84	35	0	0	354	0	10	0
Harrisonburg, VA	365	339	26	0	0	80	32	0	96	229	0	40	0
Hartford-West Hartford-East Hartford, CT	365	286	69	10	0	143	39	0	21	216	0	125	3
Hattiesburg, MS	359	284	74	1	0	119	37	0	0	0	0	359	0
Helena, MT	365	284	71	7	3	164	43	0	0	253	0	112	0
Hermiston-Pendleton, OR	254	221	25	3	5	295	33	0	0	94	0	160	0
Hickory-Lenoir-Morganton, NC	365	278	87	0	0	100	40	0	0	182	0	183	0
Hilo, HI	365	127	68	66	104	249	87	0	0	0	221	144	0
Hobbs, NM	365	227	132	6	0	143	45	0	3	302	0	60	0
Holland, MI	286	232	46	8	0	150	40	0	0	229	0	57	0
Homosassa Springs, FL	356	318	38	0	0	71	32	0	0	0	20	336	0
Hot Springs, AR	121	99	22	0	0	86	31	0	0	0	0	121	0
Houghton, MI	78	77	1	0	0	61	11	0	0	0	0	78	0

Metropolitan Statistical Area	Days with AQI Data	Number of Days when Air Quality was...				AQI Statistics		Number of Days when AQI Pollutant was...					
		Good	Moderate	Unhealthy for Sensitive Groups	Unhealthy, Very Unhealthy, or Hazardous	Max	Median	CO	NO_2	O_3	SO_2	$PM_{2.5}$	PM_{10}
Houma-Thibodaux, LA	363	314	49	0	0	90	36	0	0	240	0	123	0
Houston-The Woodlands-Sugar Land, TX	365	166	164	26	9	204	51	0	27	153	3	179	3
Huntington, IN	358	337	21	0	0	97	31	0	0	358	0	0	0
Huntington-Ashland, WV-KY-OH	365	291	72	2	0	119	40	0	2	167	2	194	0
Huntsville, AL	365	275	89	1	0	115	41	0	0	130	0	234	1
Idaho Falls, ID	365	287	73	4	1	154	43	0	0	266	0	99	0
Indiana, PA	356	322	33	1	0	105	35	0	0	349	7	0	0
Indianapolis-Carmel-Anderson, IN	365	187	162	15	1	156	50	0	1	145	11	208	0
Iowa City, IA	362	287	75	0	0	92	38	0	0	0	0	362	0
Ithaca, NY	364	330	32	2	0	101	33	0	0	353	11	0	0
Jackson, MS	365	255	109	1	0	112	44	0	1	146	0	218	0
Jackson, TN	351	321	30	0	0	78	26	0	0	0	0	351	0
Jackson, WY-ID	365	286	78	1	0	106	44	0	0	340	0	24	1
Jacksonville, FL	365	267	91	6	1	155	41	0	1	145	6	198	15
Jamestown-Dunkirk-Fredonia, NY	362	311	47	4	0	126	36	0	0	336	4	22	0
Janesville-Beloit, WI	246	217	28	1	0	133	39	0	0	246	0	0	0
Jasper, IN	361	338	23	0	0	87	3	0	0	0	242	116	3
Jefferson City, MO	245	210	35	0	0	90	40	0	0	245	0	0	0
Johnstown, PA	363	297	66	0	0	93	38	0	4	189	1	168	1
Jonesboro, AR	90	71	19	0	0	72	35	0	0	0	0	90	0
Joplin, MO	365	304	61	0	0	95	36	0	0	226	0	0	139
Juneau, AK	352	306	46	0	0	83	23	0	0	0	0	348	4
Kahului-Wailuku-Lahaina, HI	361	357	4	0	0	73	19	0	0	0	0	361	0
Kalamazoo-Portage, MI	356	282	70	4	0	115	40	0	0	170	0	186	0
Kalispell, MT	365	268	81	11	5	182	41	0	0	186	0	160	19
Kansas City, MO-KS	365	211	141	12	1	172	47	0	13	186	0	159	7
Kapaa, HI	355	355	0	0	0	48	15	0	166	0	0	189	0
Keene, NH	365	334	31	0	0	84	35	0	0	272	0	93	0
Kennewick-Richland, WA	365	289	62	12	2	178	34	0	0	126	0	203	36
Killeen-Temple, TX	365	320	40	5	0	136	36	0	0	365	0	0	0
Kingsport-Bristol-Bristol, TN-VA	365	239	112	14	0	114	44	0	0	156	121	88	0
Kingsville, TX	342	243	95	3	1	160	35	0	0	0	0	342	0
Kinston, NC	278	249	28	1	0	108	36	0	0	222	0	0	56
Klamath Falls, OR	298	184	70	9	35	310	32	0	0	0	0	298	0
Knoxville, TN	365	240	123	2	0	133	45	0	0	225	0	140	0
Kokomo, IN	365	293	67	5	0	108	39	0	0	214	0	151	0
La Crosse-Onalaska, WI-MN	365	300	65	0	0	97	39	0	0	186	0	179	0
La Grande, OR	286	259	19	6	2	208	21	0	0	0	0	266	20
Laconia, NH	283	269	14	0	0	80	32	0	0	206	0	77	0
Lafayette, LA	365	266	99	0	0	97	41	0	0	203	0	162	0
Lafayette-West Lafayette, IN	365	286	76	3	0	115	40	0	0	199	0	166	0
Lake Charles, LA	365	236	123	6	0	108	44	0	4	111	7	243	0
Lake City, FL	359	315	43	1	0	111	34	0	0	218	0	141	0
Lake Havasu City-Kingman, AZ	363	350	12	1	0	105	18	0	0	0	0	18	345
Lakeland-Winter Haven, FL	365	324	39	2	0	112	35	0	0	275	1	89	0
Lancaster, PA	365	246	114	5	0	126	44	0	0	183	0	182	0
Lansing-East Lansing, MI	365	296	65	4	0	147	39	0	0	230	0	135	0
Laramie, WY	365	223	139	3	0	115	48	0	1	296	0	8	60
Laredo, TX	313	237	74	2	0	107	39	0	0	150	0	161	2
Las Cruces, NM	365	144	189	28	4	187	57	0	3	258	0	50	54
Las Vegas-Henderson-Paradise, NV	365	122	194	48	1	154	61	0	50	226	0	76	13
Lawrenceburg, TN	352	328	24	0	0	66	27	0	0	0	0	352	0
Lawton, OK	365	275	86	4	0	122	40	0	0	298	0	67	0
Lebanon, PA	365	260	103	2	0	101	39	0	0	187	0	178	0
Lewiston, ID-WA	365	290	67	6	2	187	26	0	0	0	0	365	0

Metropolitan Statistical Area	Days with AQI Data	Number of Days when Air Quality was... Good	Moderate	Unhealthy for Sensitive Groups	Unhealthy, Very Unhealthy, or Hazardous	AQI Statistics Max	Median	Number of Days when AQI Pollutant was... CO	NO_2	O_3	SO_2	$PM_{2.5}$	PM_{10}
Lewiston-Auburn, ME	361	336	25	0	0	84	31	0	0	190	0	169	2
Lexington-Fayette, KY	365	266	99	0	0	90	40	0	13	124	1	226	1
Lima, OH	365	304	56	5	0	119	39	0	0	215	9	141	0
Lincoln, NE	365	330	35	0	0	78	31	0	0	229	77	59	0
Little Rock-North Little Rock-Conway, AR	365	257	106	2	0	122	43	0	1	146	0	218	0
Logan, UT-ID	365	235	122	8	0	133	46	0	0	263	0	102	0
Longview, TX	365	290	63	12	0	140	37	0	2	275	88	0	0
Longview, WA	365	338	23	2	2	152	20	0	0	0	0	365	0
Los Alamos, NM	81	81	0	0	0	33	12	0	0	0	0	81	0
Los Angeles-Long Beach-Anaheim, CA	365	35	220	90	20	201	77	0	31	178	0	153	3
Louisville/Jefferson County, KY-IN	365	205	149	9	2	166	48	0	16	154	0	195	0
Lubbock, TX	303	275	27	1	0	134	25	0	0	0	0	303	0
Ludington, MI	252	226	25	1	0	133	37	0	0	252	0	0	0
Lynchburg, VA	112	106	6	0	0	55	26	0	0	0	0	112	0
Macon, GA	365	312	52	1	0	106	35	0	0	168	10	187	0
Madera, CA	365	152	178	30	5	165	56	0	0	210	0	120	35
Madison, WI	365	271	92	2	0	122	42	0	0	182	0	182	1
Malone, NY	341	341	0	0	0	24	0	0	0	0	341	0	0
Manchester-Nashua, NH	365	338	27	0	0	97	36	1	0	350	0	14	0
Manitowoc, WI	239	202	30	5	2	169	40	0	0	239	0	0	0
Marietta, OH	245	216	26	3	0	105	39	0	0	245	0	0	0
Marshall, MN	365	332	33	0	0	84	32	0	0	166	0	199	0
Marshall, TX	365	301	63	1	0	111	36	0	1	196	22	146	0
Mason City, IA	115	115	0	0	0	46	16	0	0	0	0	0	115
McAlester, OK	364	285	78	1	0	108	40	0	0	213	0	151	0
McAllen-Edinburg-Mission, TX	363	238	121	4	0	115	41	0	0	114	0	249	0
Medford, OR	302	208	48	11	35	294	39	0	0	85	0	217	0
Memphis, TN-MS-AR	365	242	112	10	1	159	44	0	8	188	0	169	0
Merced, CA	365	173	151	32	9	171	51	0	1	196	0	167	1
Meridian, MS	237	206	31	0	0	87	37	0	0	237	0	0	0
Miami, OK	365	252	112	1	0	107	44	0	0	139	0	224	2
Miami-Fort Lauderdale-W. Palm Beach, FL	365	264	97	4	0	126	43	0	15	122	0	218	10
Michigan City-La Porte, IN	363	305	51	6	1	161	36	0	0	335	0	28	0
Middlesborough, KY	256	231	25	0	0	84	39	0	0	226	0	30	0
Milwaukee-Waukesha-West Allis, WI	365	236	120	7	2	169	44	0	12	190	0	163	0
Minneapolis-St. Paul-Bloomington, MN-WI	365	173	187	5	0	122	51	4	7	103	1	149	101
Minot, ND	360	328	29	3	0	112	31	0	0	224	0	124	12
Missoula, MT	365	198	163	3	1	153	48	0	0	111	0	252	2
Mobile, AL	365	290	74	1	0	105	38	0	0	150	13	202	0
Modesto, CA	365	157	161	32	15	240	54	0	2	203	0	151	9
Monroe, LA	363	338	25	0	0	100	32	0	0	313	0	50	0
Monroe, MI	365	364	1	0	0	59	1	0	0	0	304	0	61
Montgomery, AL	326	150	176	0	0	93	52	0	0	49	0	277	0
Montrose, CO	326	257	68	1	0	122	42	0	0	326	0	0	0
Morehead City, NC	222	202	20	0	0	77	38	0	0	222	0	0	0
Morgantown, WV	341	311	30	0	0	93	34	0	0	224	66	51	0
Morristown, TN	244	202	42	0	0	100	42	0	0	244	0	0	0
Moscow, ID	365	339	20	5	1	176	10	0	0	0	0	365	0
Moses Lake, WA	365	307	47	4	7	248	20	0	30	0	0	335	0
Mount Pleasant, TX	353	353	0	0	0	50	0	0	0	0	353	0	0
Mount Vernon, IL	362	284	75	3	0	105	40	0	0	170	0	192	0
Mount Vernon, OH	245	208	36	1	0	115	40	0	0	245	0	0	0
Mount Vernon-Anacortes, WA	365	341	16	5	3	180	29	0	6	195	0	164	0
Muncie, IN	361	320	37	4	0	129	35	0	0	317	0	44	0
Muscatine, IA	365	249	116	0	0	95	41	0	0	0	3	361	1

Metropolitan Statistical Area	Days with AQI Data	Number of Days when Air Quality was...				AQI Statistics		Number of Days when AQI Pollutant was...					
		Good	Moderate	Unhealthy for Sensitive Groups	Unhealthy, Very Unhealthy, or Hazardous	Max	Median	CO	NO_2	O_3	SO_2	$PM_{2.5}$	PM_{10}
Muskegon, MI	240	203	31	3	3	174	40	0	0	240	0	0	0
Muskogee, OK	365	332	30	2	1	196	19	0	0	0	32	0	333
Myrtle Bch-Conway-N. Myrtle Bch, SC-NC	354	314	39	1	0	116	34	0	0	264	90	0	0
Napa, CA	364	273	79	4	8	183	39	1	1	165	0	196	1
Naples-Immokalee-Marco Island, FL	365	320	45	0	0	80	36	0	0	246	0	119	0
Nashville-Davidson—Murfreesboro—Franklin, TN	365	247	111	6	1	151	43	0	17	148	0	200	0
New Castle, IN	116	100	15	1	0	111	31	0	0	0	0	116	0
New Castle, PA	358	329	29	0	0	97	32	0	0	358	0	0	0
New Haven-Milford, CT	365	276	75	12	2	156	40	0	29	205	0	131	0
New Orleans-Metairie, LA	365	219	140	6	0	112	46	0	4	141	29	191	0
New York-Newark-Jersey City, NY-NJ-PA	365	156	182	24	3	210	53	0	43	130	1	191	0
Niles-Benton Harbor, MI	245	208	29	8	0	126	40	0	0	245	0	0	0
Nogales, AZ	365	294	69	1	1	183	31	0	0	0	0	215	150
North Port-Sarasota-Bradenton, FL	365	300	63	2	0	119	38	0	0	242	0	123	0
Norwich-New London, CT	315	284	25	6	0	140	35	0	0	189	0	126	0
Ocala, FL	365	325	40	0	0	90	35	0	0	229	0	136	0
Odessa, TX	337	296	41	0	0	91	30	0	0	0	0	337	0
Ogden-Clearfield, UT	365	184	157	21	3	157	50	0	36	245	0	76	8
Ogdensburg-Massena, NY	359	282	66	11	0	110	14	0	0	0	359	0	0
Oklahoma City, OK	365	212	141	12	0	150	47	0	6	182	0	173	4
Olympia-Tumwater, WA	343	305	32	1	5	173	26	0	0	133	0	210	0
Omaha-Council Bluffs, NE-IA	365	229	131	5	0	108	46	0	0	143	11	197	14
Orlando-Kissimmee-Sanford, FL	365	309	53	2	1	151	38	0	0	297	0	68	0
Othello, WA	350	313	29	4	4	183	13	0	0	0	0	350	0
Ottawa-Peru, IL	362	360	2	0	0	62	1	0	0	0	362	0	0
Owensboro, KY	357	270	86	1	0	112	40	0	17	156	4	180	0
Oxford, NC	233	193	40	0	0	93	42	0	0	233	0	0	0
Oxnard-Thousand Oaks-Ventura, CA	365	174	174	16	1	166	52	0	2	213	0	138	12
Paducah, KY-IL	365	244	121	0	0	100	43	0	1	151	0	213	0
Pahrump, NV	365	350	15	0	0	99	18	0	0	0	0	0	365
Palatka, FL	345	344	1	0	0	51	14	0	0	0	49	0	296
Palm Bay-Melbourne-Titusville, FL	365	330	34	1	0	129	37	0	0	284	0	81	0
Panama City, FL	324	273	50	1	0	126	37	0	0	190	0	134	0
Parkersburg-Vienna, WV	363	341	22	0	0	77	33	0	0	220	80	63	0
Payson, AZ	365	107	170	80	8	184	71	0	0	161	188	0	16
Pensacola-Ferry Pass-Brent, FL	365	295	70	0	0	93	39	0	0	252	0	113	0
Peoria, IL	365	255	107	3	0	101	43	0	0	192	0	173	0
Philadelphia-Camden-Wilmington, PA-NJ-DE-MD	365	132	214	16	3	164	55	0	3	103	0	259	0
Phoenix-Mesa-Scottsdale, AZ	365	42	238	66	19	996	77	0	10	144	0	58	153
Pierre, SD	354	339	14	1	0	108	13	0	0	0	0	354	0
Pittsburgh, PA	365	136	204	24	1	154	55	0	0	98	25	242	0
Pittsfield, MA	365	284	80	1	0	122	33	0	0	80	0	285	0
Platteville, WI	351	296	55	0	0	81	31	0	0	0	0	351	0
Pocatello, ID	365	305	56	2	2	174	30	0	0	0	143	162	60
Point Pleasant, WV-OH	365	347	16	2	0	124	7	0	0	0	365	0	0
Ponca City, OK	365	275	88	2	0	114	41	0	0	123	8	234	0
Ponce, PR	357	179	173	5	0	118	50	8	0	0	0	302	47
Port Angeles, WA	365	297	60	3	5	205	38	0	0	182	0	183	0
Port St. Lucie, FL	365	328	36	1	0	112	37	0	0	251	0	114	0
Portland-South Portland, ME	365	311	52	2	0	119	39	0	13	256	0	94	2
Portland-Vancouver-Hillsboro, OR-WA	365	280	75	5	5	163	37	0	16	205	0	144	0
Portsmouth, OH	365	353	12	0	0	82	14	0	0	0	57	109	199
Prescott, AZ	365	292	72	1	0	101	43	0	0	363	0	2	0

Metropolitan Statistical Area	Days with AQI Data	Number of Days when Air Quality was...				AQI Statistics		Number of Days when AQI Pollutant was...					
		Good	Moderate	Unhealthy for Sensitive Groups	Unhealthy, Very Unhealthy, or Hazardous	Max	Median	CO	NO_2	O_3	SO_2	$PM_{2.5}$	PM_{10}
Price, UT	364	231	128	5	0	115	46	0	3	361	0	0	0
Prineville, OR	302	246	49	4	3	177	24	0	0	0	0	302	0
Providence-Warwick, RI-MA	365	265	87	13	0	147	44	0	10	211	0	143	1
Provo-Orem, UT	365	218	115	25	7	162	46	0	33	252	0	75	5
Pueblo, CO	123	117	5	1	0	101	23	0	0	0	0	84	39
Pullman, WA	365	325	33	5	2	177	17	0	0	0	0	365	0
Quincy, IL-MO	245	228	17	0	0	87	35	0	0	245	0	0	0
Racine, WI	236	187	38	9	2	161	42	0	0	236	0	0	0
Raleigh, NC	361	239	121	0	1	155	45	1	0	149	0	211	0
Rapid City, SD	365	258	105	2	0	118	44	0	0	258	0	39	68
Reading, PA	365	270	90	5	0	117	40	0	0	239	0	126	0
Red Bluff, CA	365	226	110	16	13	190	45	0	0	239	0	126	0
Red Wing, MN	231	206	24	1	0	133	38	0	0	231	0	0	0
Redding, CA	365	282	63	14	6	190	43	0	0	349	0	15	1
Reno, NV	365	213	133	19	0	146	48	0	8	281	0	59	17
Richmond, VA	365	280	83	2	0	147	41	0	8	219	0	138	0
Riverside-San Bernardino-Ontario, CA	365	25	167	108	65	296	97	0	14	210	0	108	33
Riverton, WY	365	252	111	2	0	120	46	0	0	325	7	33	0
Roanoke, VA	365	318	47	0	0	87	37	0	15	184	7	159	0
Rochester, MN	361	292	69	0	0	98	38	0	0	148	0	213	0
Rochester, NY	365	296	65	4	0	115	38	0	1	229	0	135	0
Rock Springs, WY	365	207	149	8	1	163	48	0	3	287	8	5	62
Rockford, IL	362	316	43	2	1	151	35	0	0	346	0	16	0
Rockland, ME	219	209	9	1	0	112	36	0	0	219	0	0	0
Rocky Mount, NC	354	321	33	0	0	80	33	0	0	187	0	167	0
Rome, GA	365	247	118	0	0	80	41	0	0	0	3	362	0
Roseburg, OR	234	221	10	2	1	160	19	0	0	0	0	234	0
Roswell, NM	79	76	3	0	0	57	24	0	0	0	0	79	0
Ruidoso, NM	77	76	1	0	0	52	13	0	0	0	0	77	0
Rutland, VT	365	306	59	0	0	90	37	1	1	238	0	125	0
Sacramento—Roseville—Arden-Arcade, CA	365	124	172	45	24	314	61	0	0	246	0	117	2
Salem, OH	303	302	1	0	0	52	1	0	0	0	240	0	63
Salem, OR	271	244	21	5	1	153	31	0	0	139	0	132	0
Salinas, CA	365	319	39	5	2	155	38	0	1	212	0	93	59
Salisbury, MD-DE	365	295	66	4	0	140	40	0	0	295	0	70	0
Salt Lake City, UT	365	169	160	34	2	169	54	0	48	228	0	86	3
San Antonio-New Braunfels, TX	365	251	103	10	1	162	43	0	6	199	2	157	1
San Diego-Carlsbad, CA	365	73	257	35	0	143	64	0	1	202	0	162	0
San Francisco-Oakland-Hayward, CA	365	147	199	7	12	245	53	0	14	62	0	289	0
San Jose-Sunnyvale-Santa Clara, CA	365	216	131	7	11	194	47	0	1	193	0	171	0
San Juan-Carolina-Caguas, PR	364	206	144	7	7	169	48	12	1	19	1	330	1
San Luis Obispo-Paso Robles-Arroyo Grande, CA	365	202	154	9	0	133	49	0	0	234	0	92	39
Sandpoint, ID	363	308	39	11	5	245	29	0	0	0	0	318	45
Sanford, NC	210	145	65	0	0	83	45	0	0	127	0	83	0
Santa Cruz-Watsonville, CA	365	331	24	5	5	170	36	0	0	221	0	144	0
Santa Fe, NM	365	279	83	3	0	122	44	0	0	353	0	12	0
Santa Maria-Santa Barbara, CA	365	244	119	2	0	114	47	0	0	266	0	86	13
Santa Rosa, CA	365	325	27	3	10	226	36	0	2	280	0	82	1
Sault Ste. Marie, MI	271	229	42	0	0	70	34	0	0	111	0	160	0
Savannah, GA	365	303	62	0	0	82	38	0	0	99	37	229	0
Sayre, PA	356	310	46	0	0	97	35	0	2	246	0	108	0
Scottsbluff, NE	116	108	8	0	0	71	22	0	0	0	0	116	0
Scranton—Wilkes-Barre—Hazleton, PA	365	300	64	1	0	101	38	0	15	220	0	130	0
Seattle-Tacoma-Bellevue, WA	365	239	110	9	7	192	44	0	37	193	0	135	0
Sebastian-Vero Beach, FL	356	325	30	1	0	101	36	0	0	356	0	0	0

Metropolitan Statistical Area	Days with AQI Data	Number of Days when Air Quality was...				AQI Statistics		Number of Days when AQI Pollutant was...					
		Good	Moderate	Unhealthy for Sensitive Groups	Unhealthy, Very Unhealthy, or Hazardous	Max	Median	CO	NO_2	O_3	SO_2	$PM_{2.5}$	PM_{10}
Sebring, FL	351	337	13	1	0	108	31	0	0	351	0	0	0
Seneca Falls, NY	364	364	0	0	0	17	0	0	0	0	364	0	0
Seneca, SC	364	323	41	0	0	97	37	0	0	311	0	53	0
Sevierville, TN	364	306	54	4	0	115	43	0	0	364	0	0	0
Seymour, IN	341	321	20	0	0	90	32	0	0	341	0	0	0
Sheboygan, WI	239	186	42	9	2	185	43	0	0	239	0	0	0
Shelton, WA	365	331	28	4	2	164	21	0	0	0	0	365	0
Sheridan, WY	365	260	102	3	0	123	45	0	0	303	0	57	5
Show Low, AZ	363	261	100	2	0	115	44	0	0	353	0	2	8
Shreveport-Bossier City, LA	365	279	84	2	0	128	40	0	0	262	0	103	0
Sierra Vista-Douglas, AZ	365	276	89	0	0	90	44	0	0	313	0	18	34
Sioux City, IA-NE-SD	365	284	78	3	0	112	41	0	0	227	0	105	33
Sioux Falls, SD	365	309	53	3	0	115	37	0	11	269	0	82	3
Somerset, KY	282	243	39	0	0	74	38	0	0	218	0	64	0
Somerset, PA	357	330	27	0	0	90	33	0	0	357	0	0	0
Sonora, CA	348	254	73	20	1	154	43	0	0	348	0	0	0
South Bend-Mishawaka, IN-MI	365	244	113	8	0	133	43	0	3	185	0	177	0
Spartanburg, SC	365	296	69	0	0	77	40	0	0	154	0	211	0
Spokane-Spokane Valley, WA	365	224	121	9	11	257	44	0	0	106	0	218	41
Springfield, IL	363	253	109	1	0	122	43	0	0	197	0	166	0
Springfield, MA	365	277	85	3	0	126	40	0	2	235	0	128	0
Springfield, MO	365	294	71	0	0	93	39	0	0	198	0	161	6
Springfield, OH	365	240	121	4	0	140	44	0	0	160	3	202	0
St. Cloud, MN	365	309	55	1	0	101	34	0	0	186	0	179	0
St. George, UT	365	228	136	1	0	108	44	0	1	332	0	32	0
St. Joseph, MO-KS	365	251	113	1	0	112	43	0	0	167	0	173	25
St. Louis, MO-IL	365	157	189	17	2	182	54	0	9	129	5	210	12
St. Marys, PA	351	325	26	0	0	97	34	0	0	351	0	0	0
State College, PA	365	286	77	2	0	122	40	0	1	225	0	139	0
Steamboat Springs, CO	355	354	1	0	0	51	15	0	0	0	0	0	355
Stockton-Lodi, CA	365	152	180	20	13	308	54	0	1	154	0	204	6
Summerville, GA	245	224	21	0	0	87	35	0	0	245	0	0	0
Syracuse, NY	365	318	45	2	0	115	36	0	0	322	0	43	0
Tallahassee, FL	358	272	86	0	0	98	38	1	0	149	0	208	0
Tampa-St. Petersburg-Clearwater, FL	365	242	118	5	0	129	43	0	0	183	13	165	4
Taos, NM	365	346	19	0	0	66	23	0	0	0	0	365	0
Terre Haute, IN	365	242	120	3	0	115	43	0	0	191	0	174	0
Texarkana, TX-AR	297	246	50	1	0	106	35	0	0	0	0	297	0
The Dalles, OR	267	242	20	4	1	154	30	0	0	76	0	186	5
Toledo, OH	365	272	83	9	1	151	41	0	0	195	22	148	0
Topeka, KS	365	272	93	0	0	99	42	0	0	181	0	184	0
Torrington, CT	363	319	40	4	0	133	36	2	0	327	0	34	0
Traverse City, MI	250	218	30	1	1	154	38	0	0	250	0	0	0
Trenton, NJ	365	283	75	6	1	187	40	0	0	234	0	131	0
Truckee-Grass Valley, CA	363	245	90	19	9	196	44	0	0	327	0	36	0
Tucson, AZ	365	196	158	11	0	129	49	0	0	255	0	31	79
Tulsa, OK	365	184	170	10	1	192	50	0	0	156	0	208	1
Tupelo, MS	243	226	17	0	0	80	36	0	0	243	0	0	0
Tuscaloosa, AL	320	265	54	1	0	115	37	0	0	195	0	125	0
Twin Falls, ID	365	319	41	3	2	151	29	0	0	0	0	365	0
Tyler, TX	364	324	38	2	0	112	33	0	3	361	0	0	0
Ukiah, CA	364	289	54	13	8	314	37	0	0	151	0	209	4
Urban Honolulu, HI	365	358	7	0	0	75	30	0	2	240	41	74	8
Utica-Rome, NY	364	337	27	0	0	93	34	0	0	196	1	167	0
Valdosta, GA	315	264	51	0	0	93	37	0	0	0	0	315	0

Metropolitan Statistical Area	Days with AQI Data	Number of Days when Air Quality was...				AQI Statistics		Number of Days when AQI Pollutant was...					
		Good	Moderate	Unhealthy for Sensitive Groups	Unhealthy, Very Unhealthy, or Hazardous	Max	Median	CO	NO_2	O_3	SO_2	$PM_{2.5}$	PM_{10}
Vallejo-Fairfield, CA	365	263	87	3	12	247	42	0	3	184	0	178	0
Vernal, UT	365	218	143	4	0	136	47	0	0	341	0	24	0
Victoria, TX	279	270	7	2	0	112	28	0	0	279	0	0	0
Vincennes, IN	357	311	42	4	0	122	35	0	0	357	0	0	0
Vineland-Bridgeton, NJ	365	305	60	0	0	93	38	0	15	173	0	177	0
Vineyard Haven, MA	359	331	25	3	0	108	37	0	0	354	0	5	0
Virginia Beach-Norfolk-Newport News, VA-NC	365	321	44	0	0	97	36	0	37	218	2	108	0
Visalia-Porterville, CA	365	73	171	96	25	174	77	0	0	233	0	123	9
Wabash, IN	362	315	42	5	0	129	35	0	0	362	0	0	0
Waco, TX	312	268	44	0	0	98	35	1	0	267	0	44	0
Walla Walla, WA	365	311	46	5	3	217	20	0	0	0	0	306	59
Walterboro, SC	364	339	25	0	0	77	31	0	0	234	0	130	0
Warner Robins, GA	322	259	61	2	0	108	34	0	0	0	0	322	0
Warren, PA	365	363	1	1	0	146	7	0	0	0	365	0	0
Washington Court House, OH	364	337	27	0	0	80	35	0	0	364	0	0	0
Washington, IN	325	325	0	0	0	21	0	0	0	0	325	0	0
Washington, NC	299	299	0	0	0	30	0	0	0	0	299	0	0
Washington-Arlington-Alexandria, DC-VA-MD-WV	365	194	161	9	1	166	49	0	9	169	0	187	0
Waterloo-Cedar Falls, IA	365	230	133	2	0	112	45	0	0	114	0	251	0
Watertown, SD	365	322	42	1	0	103	31	0	0	0	0	275	90
Watertown-Fort Atkinson, WI	243	209	32	2	0	126	39	0	0	243	0	0	0
Watertown-Fort Drum, NY	329	307	20	2	0	105	33	0	0	329	0	0	0
Wausau, WI	232	205	27	0	0	97	39	0	0	232	0	0	0
Weatherford, OK	364	355	8	1	0	104	16	0	0	0	0	0	364
Weirton-Steubenville, WV-OH	365	207	153	5	0	110	48	0	0	94	31	234	6
Wenatchee, WA	365	290	50	8	17	426	27	0	0	0	0	365	0
Wheeling, WV-OH	365	271	93	1	0	105	41	1	41	193	0	129	1
Whitewater-Elkhorn, WI	237	202	33	2	0	126	40	0	0	237	0	0	0
Wichita, KS	365	261	104	0	0	100	41	0	17	227	0	59	62
Williamsport, PA	345	327	18	0	0	97	31	0	0	344	0	0	1
Williston, ND	365	287	77	1	0	119	38	0	0	207	60	95	3
Wilmington, NC	329	308	21	0	0	77	30	0	0	201	0	128	0
Wilmington, OH	245	202	42	1	0	112	41	0	0	245	0	0	0
Winchester, VA-WV	352	309	43	0	0	85	35	0	0	198	0	154	0
Winona, MN	76	70	6	0	0	71	23	0	0	0	0	76	0
Winston-Salem, NC	365	233	130	2	0	101	44	0	4	175	0	186	0
Worcester, MA-CT	365	302	56	7	0	129	38	0	8	282	0	75	0
Yakima, WA	365	239	110	7	9	214	40	0	0	0	0	359	6
York-Hanover, PA	365	268	96	1	0	101	40	0	9	214	0	142	0
Youngstown-Warren-Boardman, OH-PA	365	245	115	5	0	115	44	0	0	215	0	150	0
Yuba City, CA	365	153	177	22	13	335	54	0	0	166	0	198	1
Yuma, AZ	365	239	110	15	1	169	45	0	0	235	0	33	97

Notes: *Dashes indicates data was not available; The Air Quality Index (AQI) is an index for reporting daily air quality. It tells you how clean or polluted your air is, and what associated health concerns you should be aware of. The AQI focuses on health effects that can happen within a few hours or days after breathing polluted air. EPA uses the AQI for six major air pollutants regulated by the Clean Air Act: CO (carbon monoxide), NO_2 (nitrogen dioxide), O_3 (ground-level ozone), SO_2 (sulfur dioxide), PM_{10} (particulate matter 10 - particles with diameters of 10 micrometers or less), $PM_{2.5}$ (particulate matter 2.5 - particles with diameters of 2.5 micrometers or less). For each of these pollutants, EPA has established national air quality standards to protect against harmful health effects.*

The AQI runs from 0 to 500. The higher the AQI value, the greater the level of air pollution and the greater the health danger. For example, an AQI value of 50 represents good air quality and little potential to affect public health, while an AQI value over 300 represents hazardous air quality. An AQI value of 100 generally corresponds to the national air quality standard for the pollutant, which is the level EPA has set to protect public health. So, AQI values below 100 are generally thought of as satisfactory. When AQI values are above 100, air quality is considered to be unhealthy-at first for certain sensitive groups of people, then for everyone as AQI values get higher. Each category corresponds to a different level of health concern. For example, when the AQI for a pollutant is between 51 and 100, the health concern is "Moderate." Here are the six levels of health concern and what they mean:

"Good" The AQI value for your community is between 0 and 50. Air quality is considered satisfactory and air pollution poses little or no risk.

"Moderate" The AQI for your community is between 51 and 100. Air quality is acceptable; however, for some pollutants there may be a moderate health concern for a very small number of individuals. For example, people who are unusually sensitive to ozone may experience respiratory symptoms.

"Unhealthy for Sensitive Groups" Certain groups of people are particularly sensitive to the harmful effects of certain air pollutants. This means they are likely to be affected at lower levels than the general public. For example, children and adults who are active outdoors and people with respiratory disease are at greater risk from exposure to ozone, while people with heart disease are at greater risk from carbon monoxide. Some people may be sensitive to more than one pollutant. When AQI values are between 101 and 150, members of sensitive groups may experience health effects. The general public is not likely to be affected when the AQI is in this range.

"Unhealthy" AQI values are between 151 and 200. Everyone may begin to experience health effects. Members of sensitive groups may experience more serious health effects.

"Very Unhealthy" AQI values between 201 and 300 trigger a health alert, meaning everyone may experience more serious health effects.

"Hazardous" AQI values over 300 trigger health warnings of emergency conditions. The entire population is more likely to be affected.

***Source:** U.S. Environmental Protection Agency, Office of Air and Radiation, Air Quality Index Report, 2018*

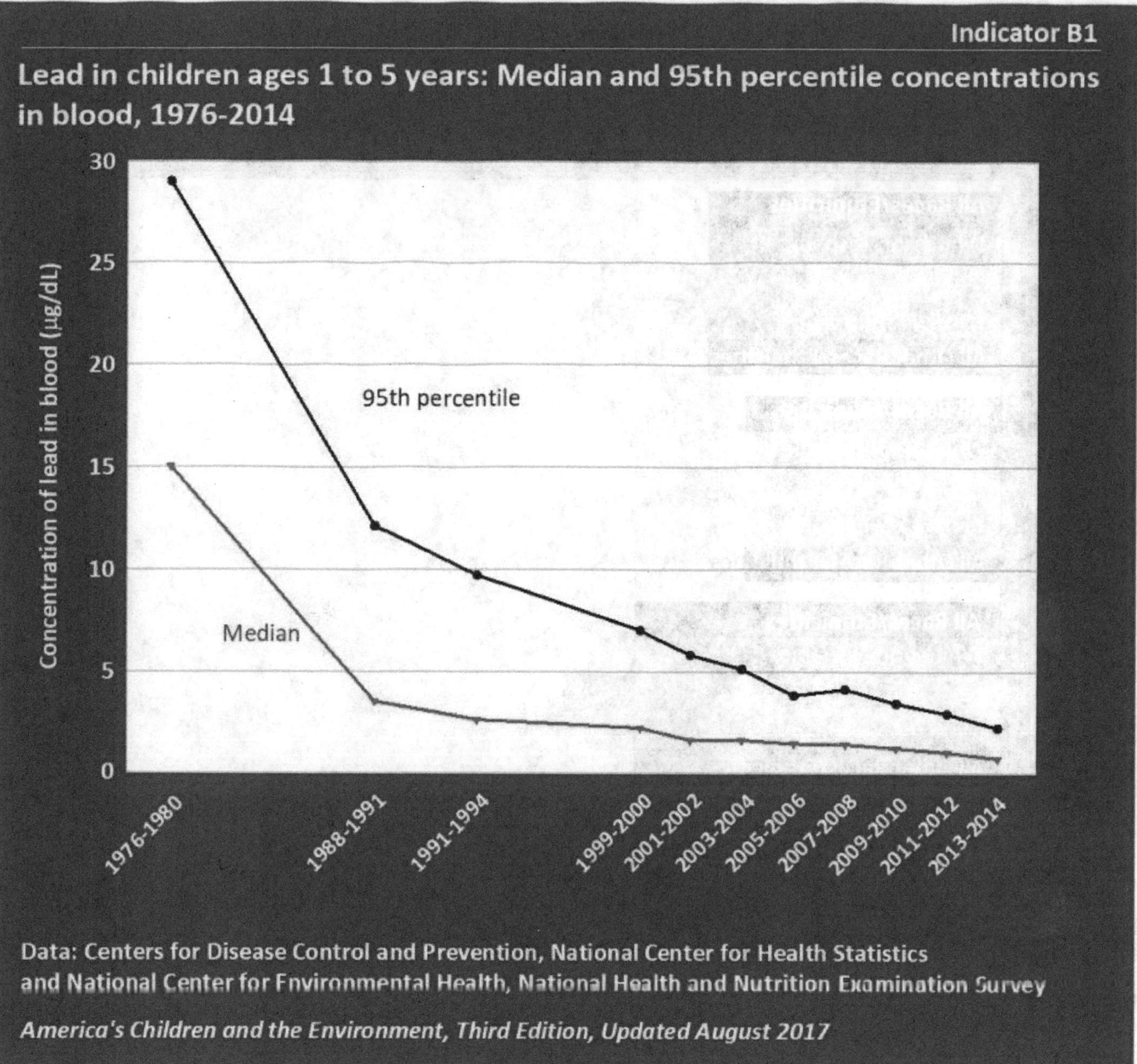
Indicator B1
Lead in children ages 1 to 5 years: Median and 95th percentile concentrations in blood, 1976-2014
Concentration of lead in blood (µg/dL)
30
25
20
15
10
5
0
95th percentile
Median
1976-1980
1988-1991
1991-1994
1999-2000
2001-2002
2003-2004
2005-2006
2007-2008
2009-2010
2011-2012
2013-2014
Data: Centers for Disease Control and Prevention, National Center for Health Statistics and National Center for Environmental Health, National Health and Nutrition Examination Survey
America's Children and the Environment, Third Edition, Updated August 2017

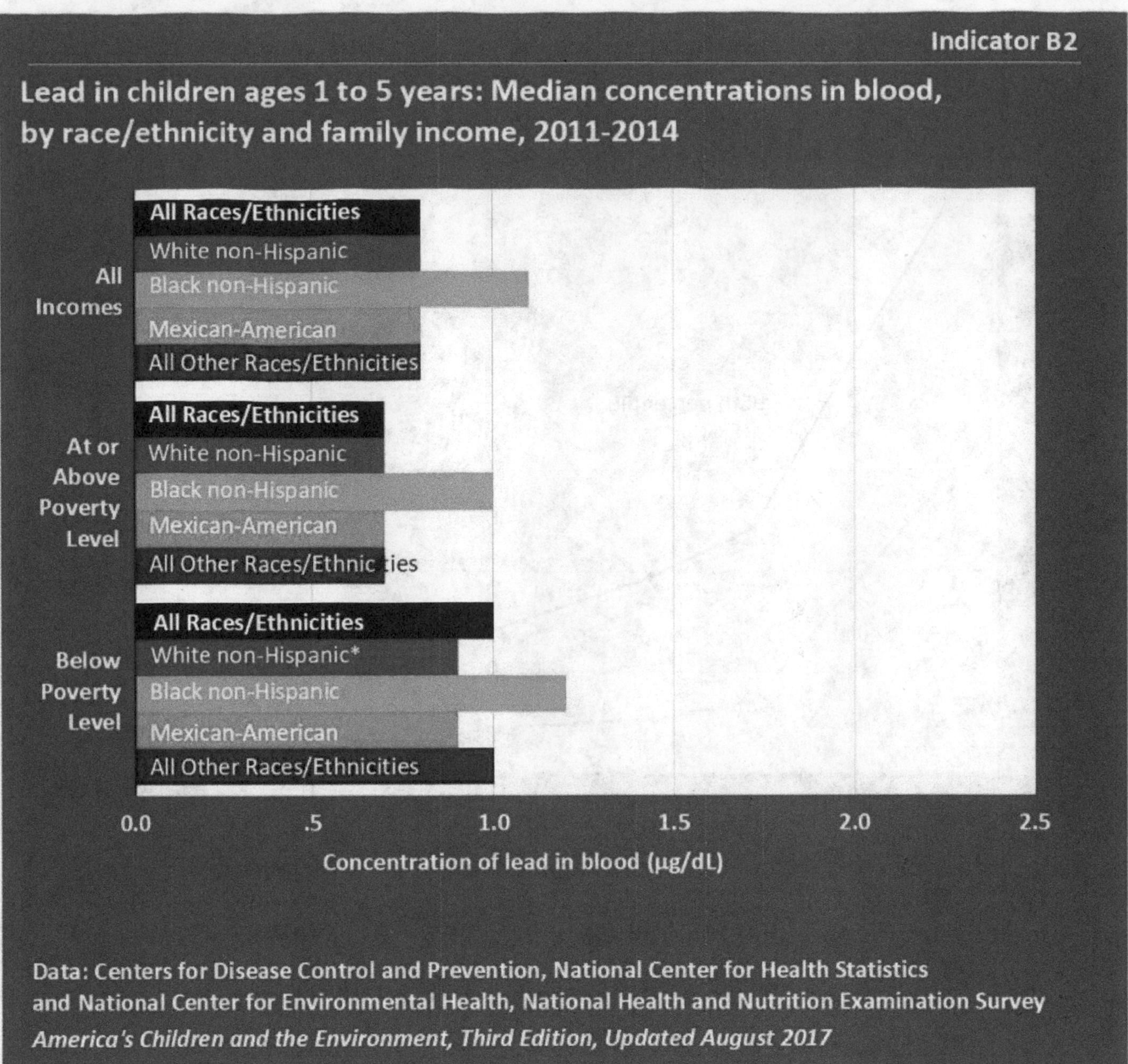
Indicator B2
Lead in children ages 1 to 5 years: Median concentrations in blood, by race/ethnicity and family income, 2011-2014
All Incomes
All Races/Ethnicities
White non-Hispanic
Black non-Hispanic
Mexican-American
All Other Races/Ethnicities
At or Above Poverty Level
All Races/Ethnicities
White non-Hispanic
Black non-Hispanic
Mexican-American
All Other Races/Ethnicities
Below Poverty Level
All Races/Ethnicities
White non-Hispanic*
Black non-Hispanic
Mexican-American
All Other Races/Ethnicities
0.0
.5
1.0
1.5
2.0
2.5
Concentration of lead in blood (µg/dL)
Data: Centers for Disease Control and Prevention, National Center for Health Statistics and National Center for Environmental Health, National Health and Nutrition Examination Survey
America's Children and the Environment, Third Edition, Updated August 2017

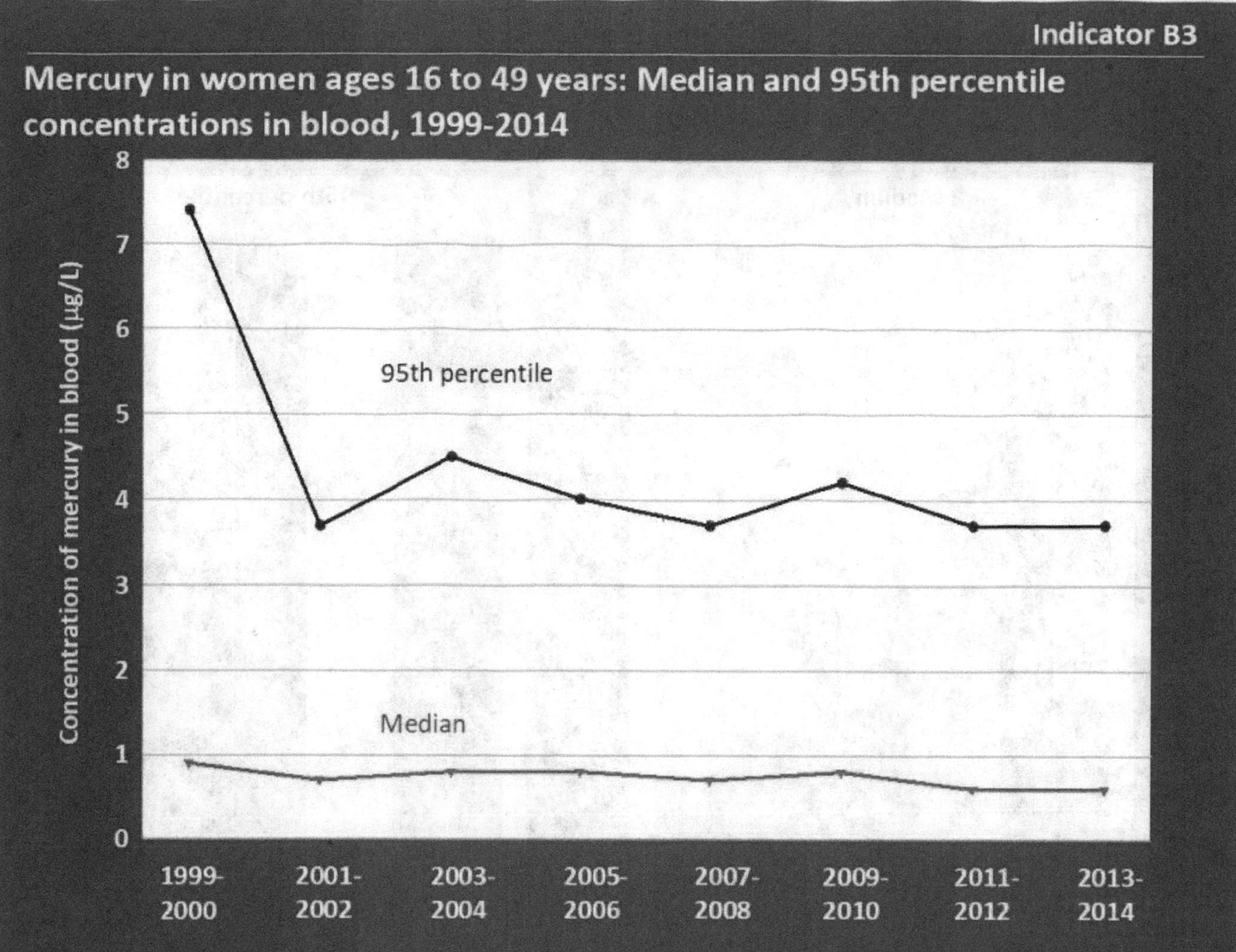
Indicator B3
Mercury in women ages 16 to 49 years: Median and 95th percentile concentrations in blood, 1999-2014
Concentration of mercury in blood (µg/L)
0
1
2
3
4
5
6
7
8
95th percentile
Median
1999-2000
2001-2002
2003-2004
2005-2006
2007-2008
2009-2010
2011-2012
2013-2014
Data: Centers for Disease Control and Prevention, National Center for Health Statistics and National Center for Environmental Health, National Health and Nutrition Examination Survey
Note: To reflect exposures to women who are pregnant or may become pregnant, the estimates are adjusted for the probability (by age and race/ethnicity) that a woman gives birth.
America's Children and the Environment, Third Edition, Updated August 2017

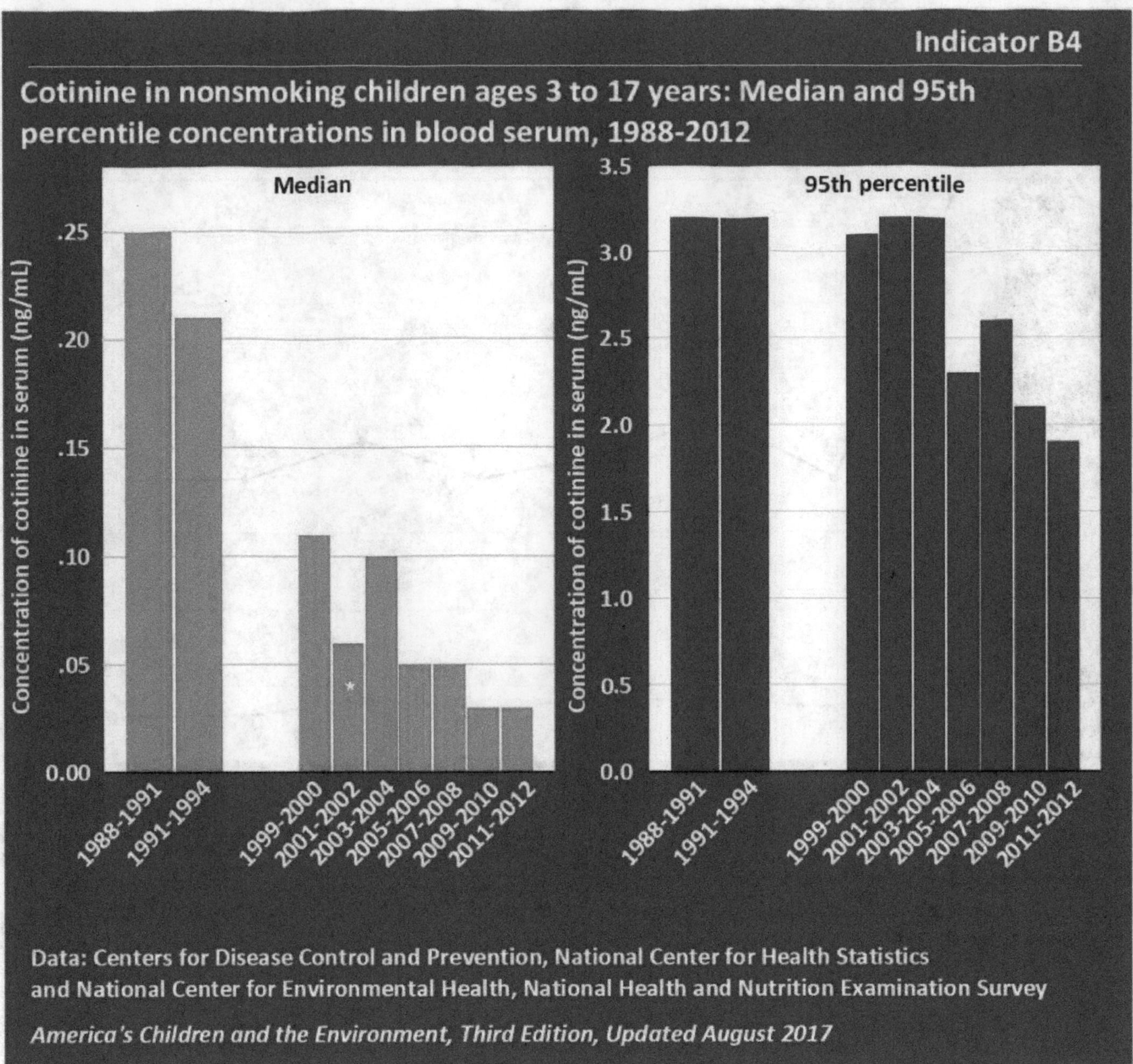
Indicator B4
Cotinine in nonsmoking children ages 3 to 17 years: Median and 95th percentile concentrations in blood serum, 1988-2012
Median
95th percentile
Concentration of cotinine in serum (ng/mL)
0.00
.05
.10
.15
.20
.25
0.0
0.5
1.0
1.5
2.0
2.5
3.0
3.5
1988-1991
1991-1994
1999-2000
2001-2002
2003-2004
2005-2006
2007-2008
2009-2010
2011-2012
Data: Centers for Disease Control and Prevention, National Center for Health Statistics and National Center for Environmental Health, National Health and Nutrition Examination Survey
America's Children and the Environment, Third Edition, Updated August 2017

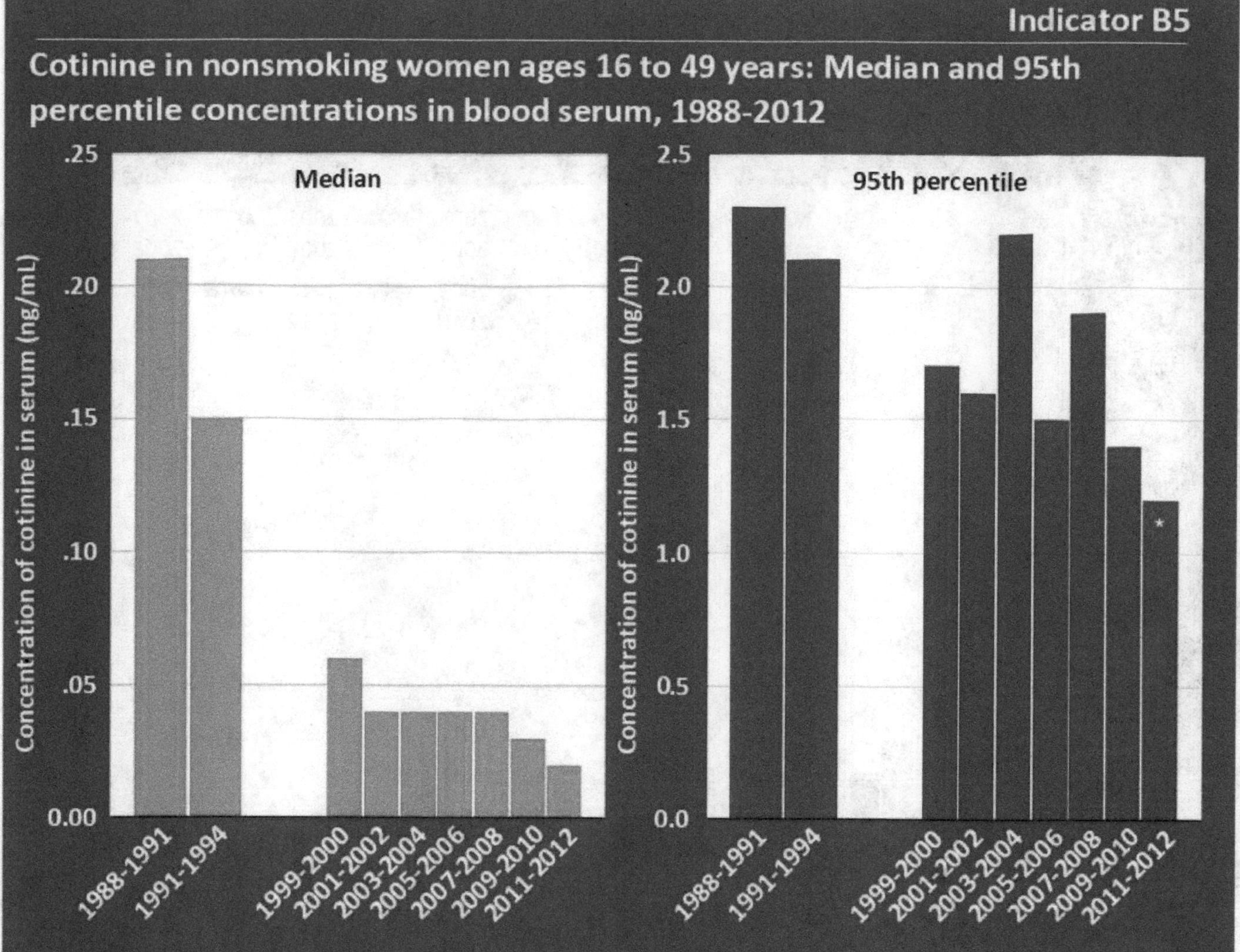
Indicator B5
Cotinine in nonsmoking women ages 16 to 49 years: Median and 95th percentile concentrations in blood serum, 1988-2012
Median
95th percentile
Concentration of cotinine in serum (ng/mL)
.25
.20
.15
.10
.05
0.00
2.5
2.0
1.5
1.0
0.5
0.0
1988-1991
1991-1994
1999-2000
2001-2002
2003-2004
2005-2006
2007-2008
2009-2010
2011-2012
Data: Centers for Disease Control and Prevention, National Center for Health Statistics and National Center for Environmental Health, National Health and Nutrition Examination Survey
Note: To reflect exposures to women who are pregnant or may become pregnant, the estimates are adjusted for the probability (by age and race/ethnicity) that a woman gives birth.
America's Children and the Environment, Third Edition, Updated August 2017

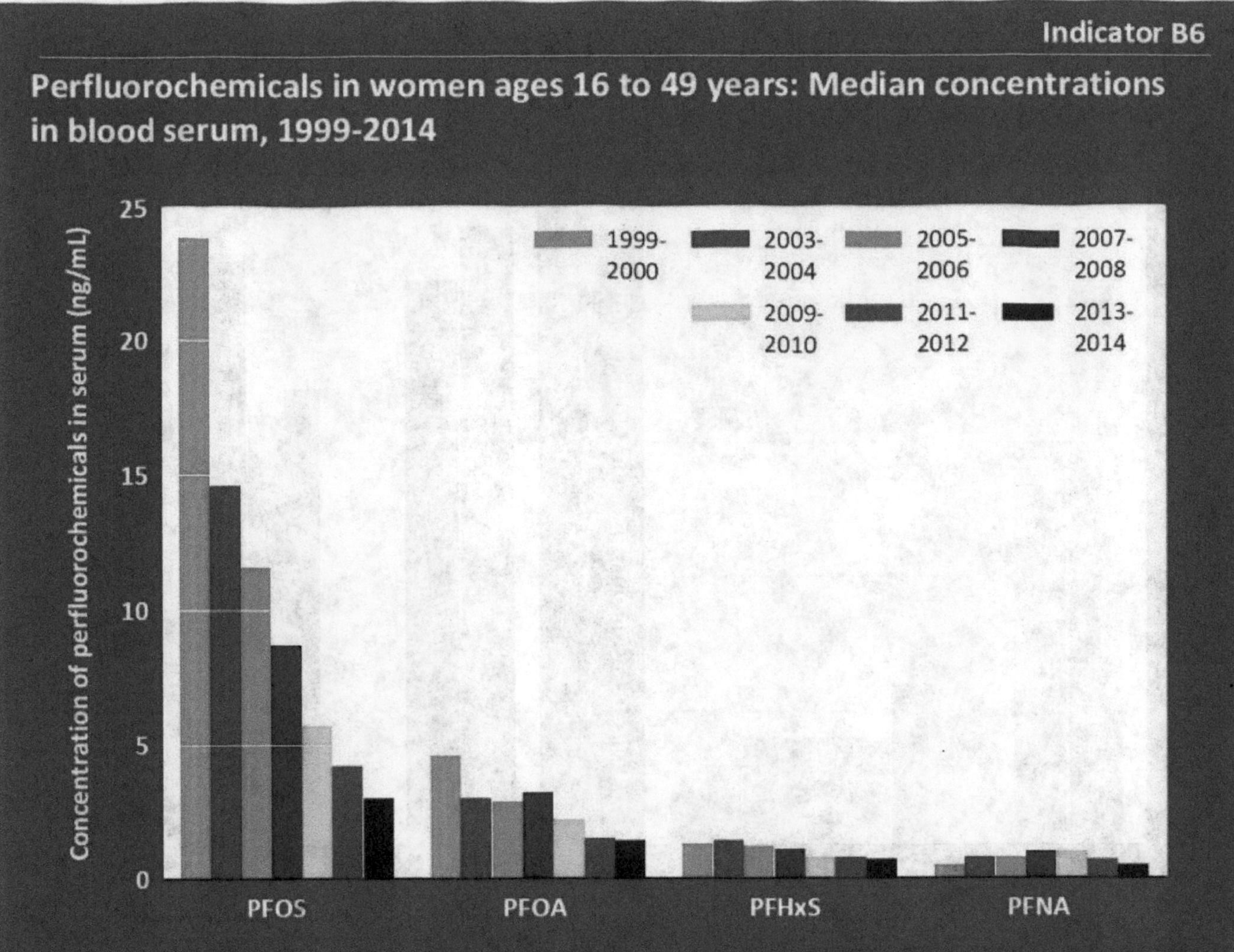
Indicator B6
Perfluorochemicals in women ages 16 to 49 years: Median concentrations in blood serum, 1999-2014
Concentration of perfluorochemicals in serum (ng/mL)
25
20
15
10
5
0
1999-2000
2003-2004
2005-2006
2007-2008
2009-2010
2011-2012
2013-2014
PFOS
PFOA
PFHxS
PFNA
Data: Centers for Disease Control and Prevention, National Center for Health Statistics and National Center for Environmental Health, National Health and Nutrition Examination Survey
Note: To reflect exposures to women who are pregnant or may become pregnant, the estimates are adjusted for the probability (by age and race/ethnicity) that a woman gives birth.
America's Children and the Environment, Third Edition, Updated August 2017

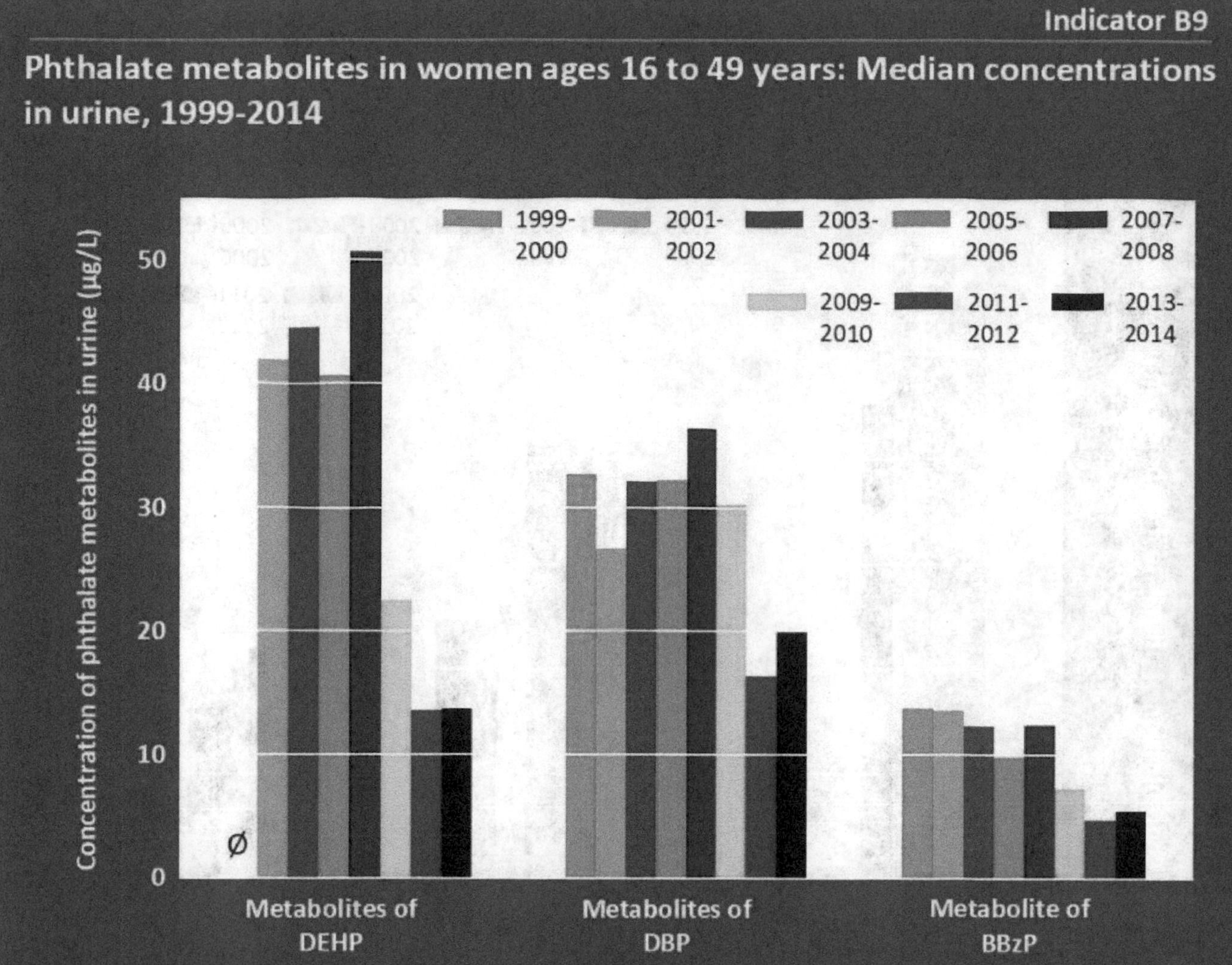

Data: Centers for Disease Control and Prevention, National Center for Health Statistics and National Center for Environmental Health, National Health and Nutrition Examination Survey

Note: To reflect exposures to women who are pregnant or may become pregnant, the estimates are adjusted for the probability (by age and race/ethnicity) that a woman gives birth.

America's Children and the Environment, Third Edition, Updated August 2017

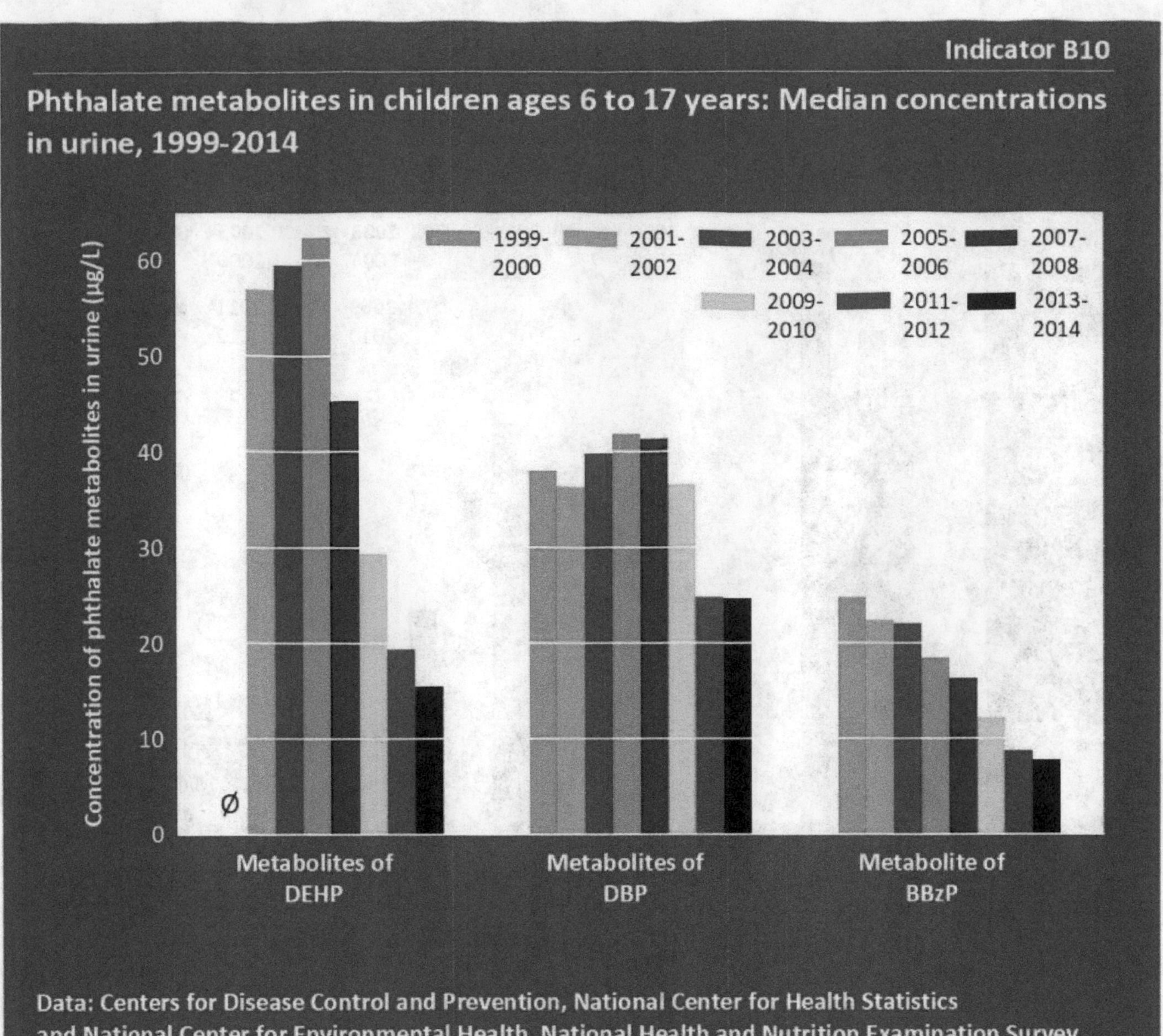
Indicator B10
Phthalate metabolites in children ages 6 to 17 years: Median concentrations in urine, 1999-2014
Concentration of phthalate metabolites in urine (µg/L)
0
10
20
30
40
50
60
1999-2000
2001-2002
2003-2004
2005-2006
2007-2008
2009-2010
2011-2012
2013-2014
Ø
Metabolites of DEHP
Metabolites of DBP
Metabolite of BBzP
Data: Centers for Disease Control and Prevention, National Center for Health Statistics and National Center for Environmental Health, National Health and Nutrition Examination Survey
America's Children and the Environment, Third Edition, Updated August 2017

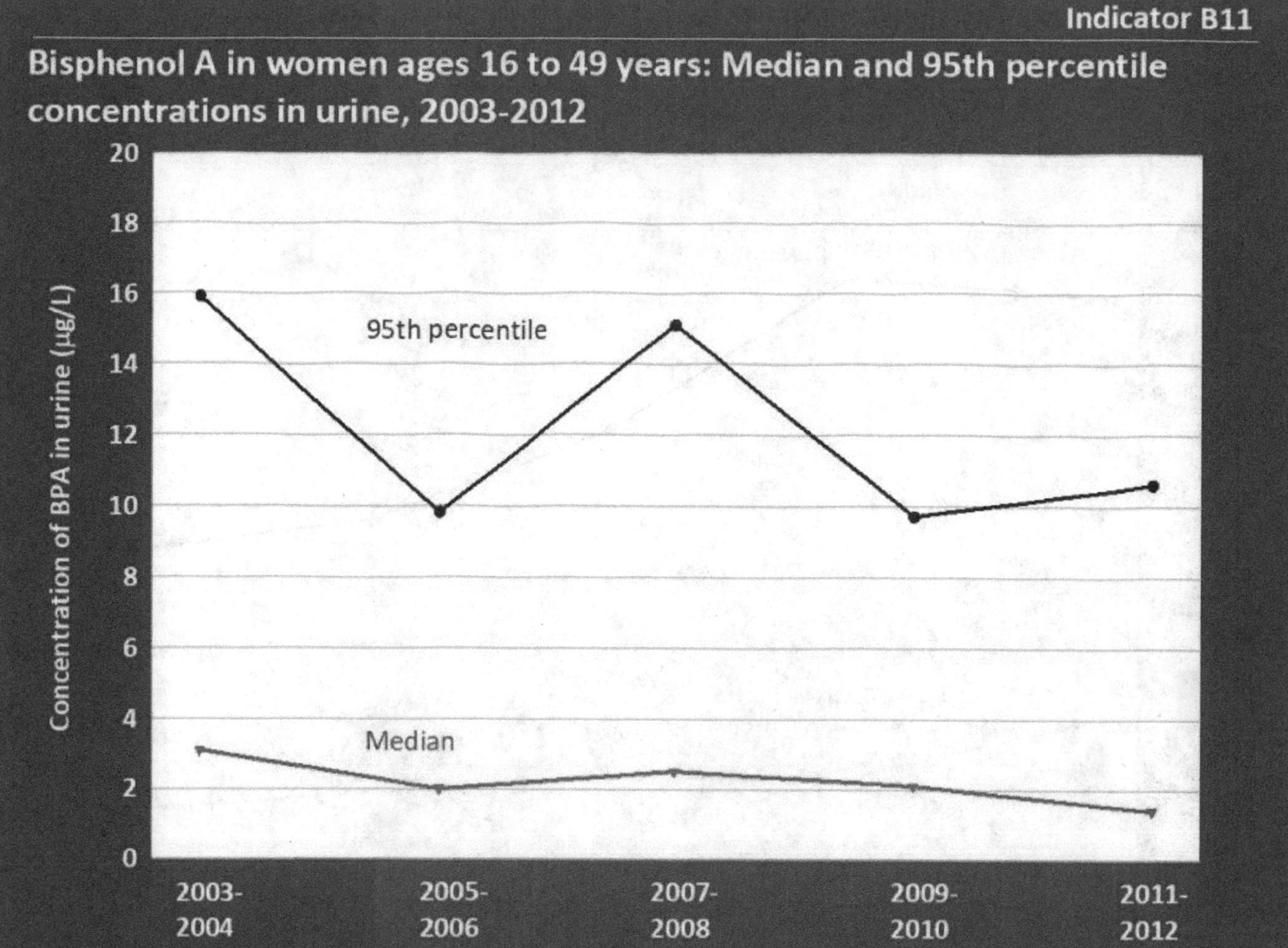

Data: Centers for Disease Control and Prevention, National Center for Health Statistics and National Center for Environmental Health, National Health and Nutrition Examination Survey

Note: To reflect exposures to women who are pregnant or may become pregnant, the estimates are adjusted for the probability (by age and race/ethnicity) that a woman gives birth.

America's Children and the Environment, Third Edition, Updated August 2017

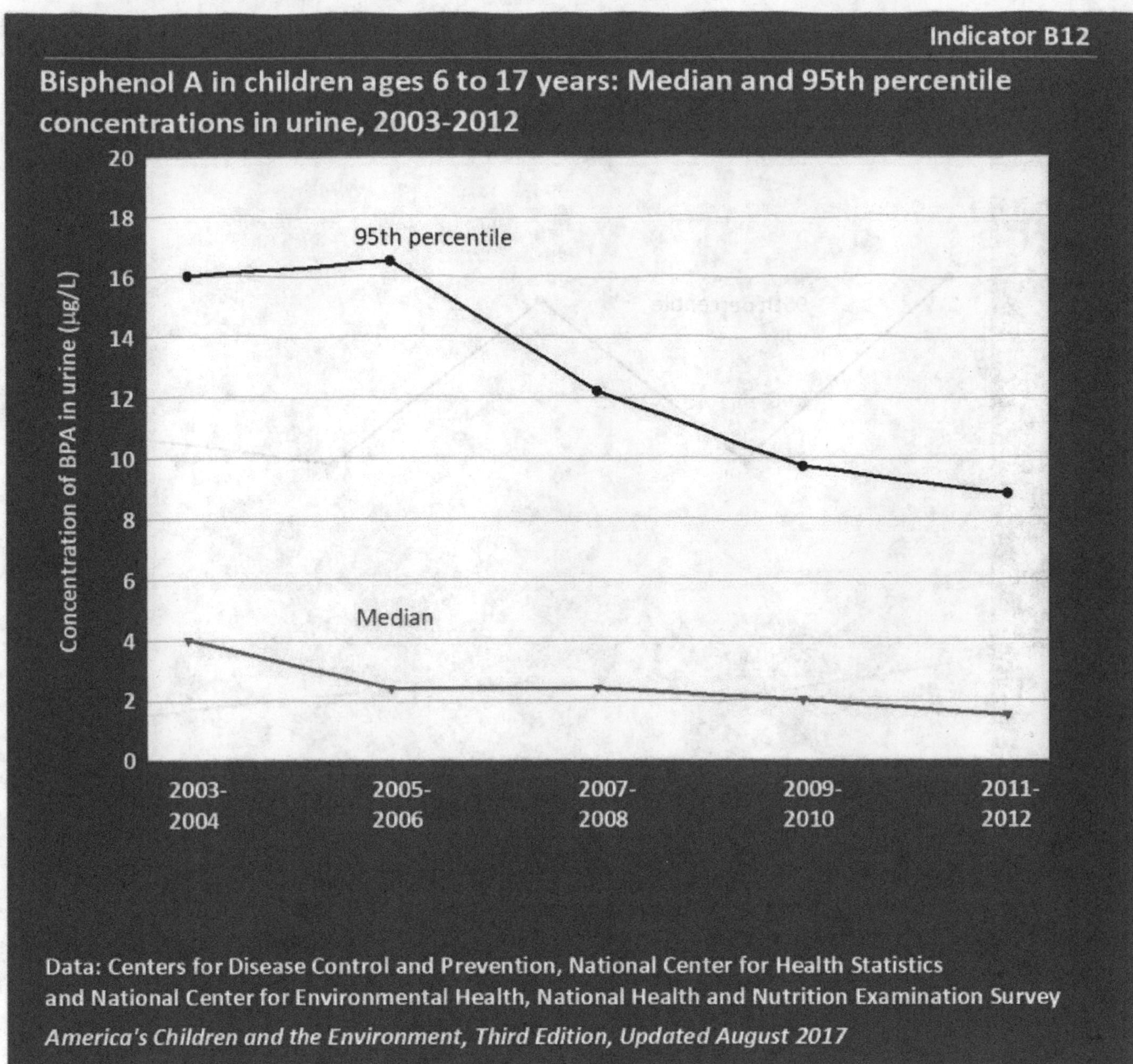
Indicator B12
Bisphenol A in children ages 6 to 17 years: Median and 95th percentile concentrations in urine, 2003-2012
Concentration of BPA in urine (µg/L)
20
18
16
14
12
10
8
6
4
2
0
95th percentile
Median
2003-2004
2005-2006
2007-2008
2009-2010
2011-2012
Data: Centers for Disease Control and Prevention, National Center for Health Statistics and National Center for Environmental Health, National Health and Nutrition Examination Survey
America's Children and the Environment, Third Edition, Updated August 2017

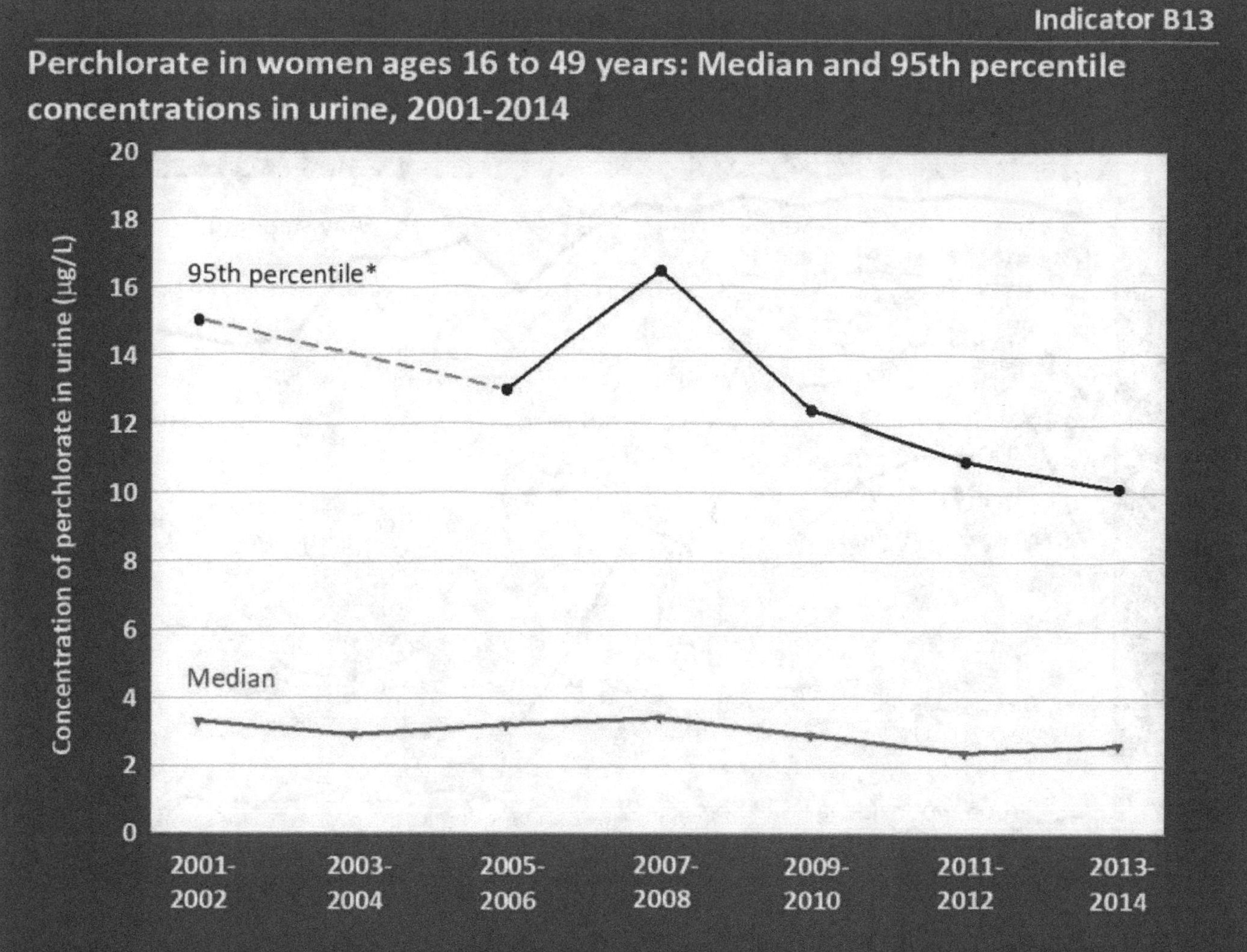

Data: Centers for Disease Control and Prevention, National Center for Health Statistics and National Center for Environmental Health, National Health and Nutrition Examination Survey
Note: To reflect exposures to women who are pregnant or may become pregnant, the estimates are adjusted for the probability (by age and race/ethnicity) that a woman gives birth.
America's Children and the Environment, Third Edition, Updated August 2017

Percentage of children ages 0 to 17 years living in counties with pollutant concentrations above the levels of the current air quality standards, 1999-2016

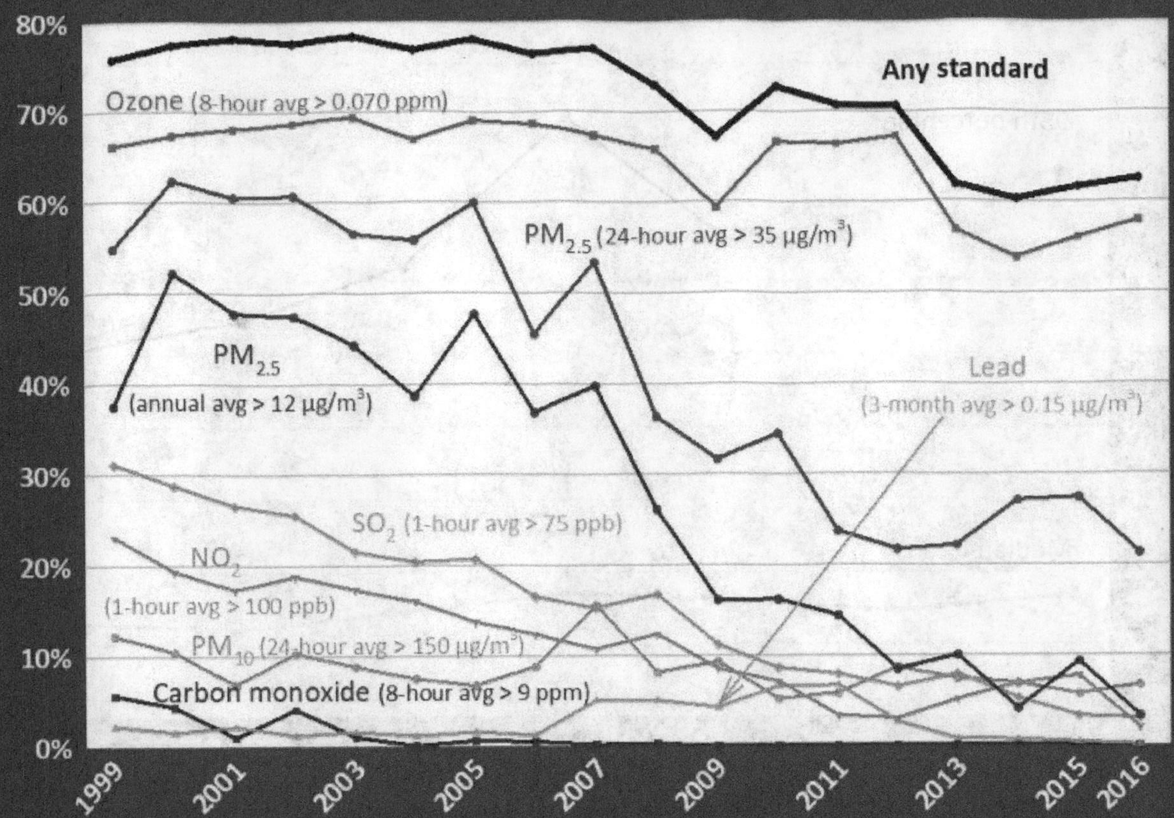

Data: U.S. Environmental Protection Agency, Office of Air and Radiation, Air Quality System

Note: EPA periodically reviews air quality standards and may change them based on updated scientific findings. Measuring concentrations above the level of a standard is not equivalent to violating the standard. The level of a standard may be exceeded on multiple days before the exceedance is considered a violation of the standard. See text for additional discussion.

America's Children and the Environment, Third Edition, Updated January 2018

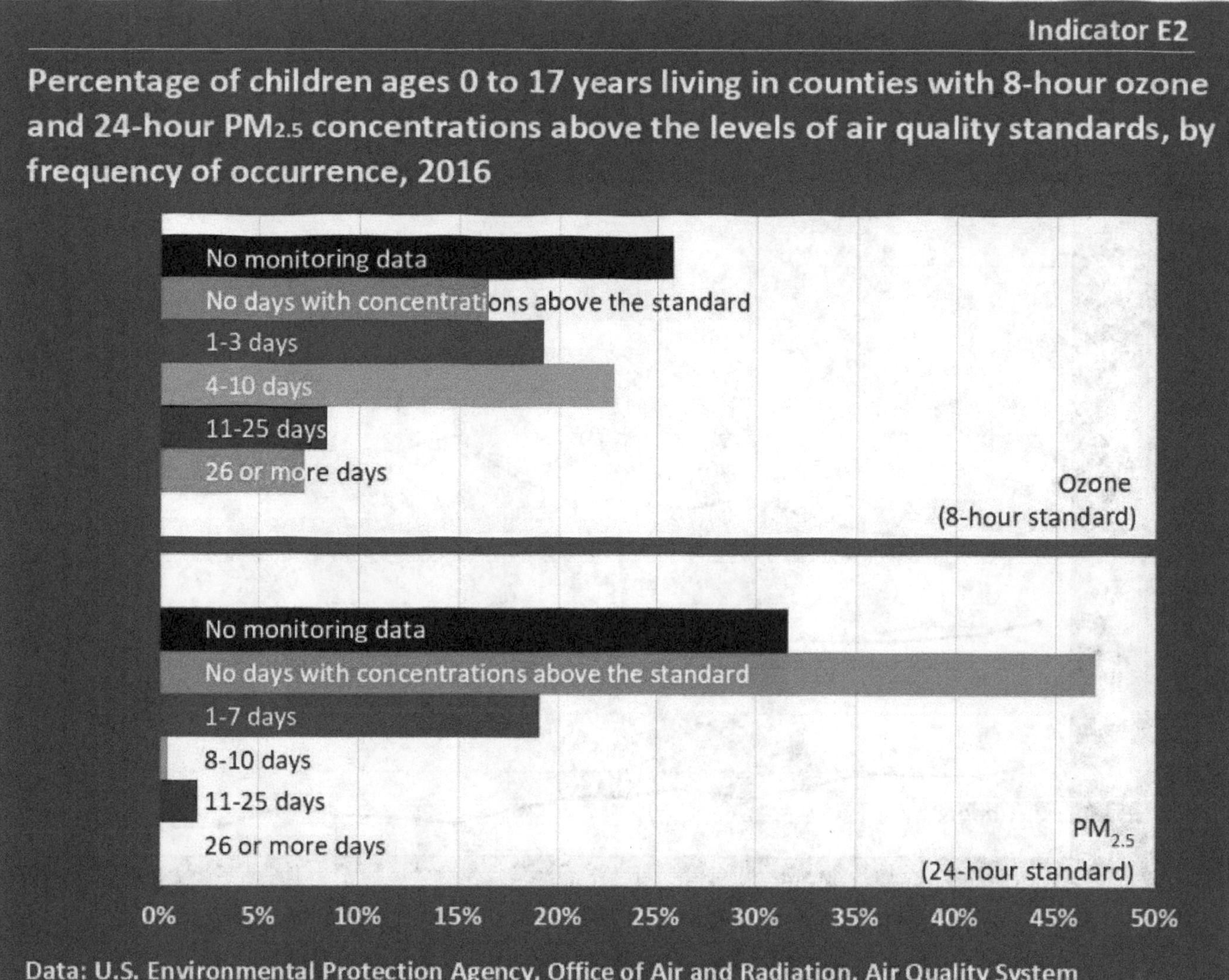

Data: U.S. Environmental Protection Agency, Office of Air and Radiation, Air Quality System

Note: EPA periodically reviews air quality standards and may change them based on updated scientific findings. Measuring concentrations above the level of a standard is not equivalent to violating the standard. The level of a standard may be exceeded on multiple days before the exceedance is considered a violation of the standard. See text for additional discussion.

America's Children and the Environment, Third Edition, Updated January 2018

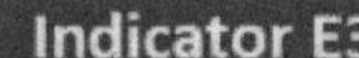

Percentage of days with good, moderate, or unhealthy air quality for children ages 0 to 17 years, 1999-2015

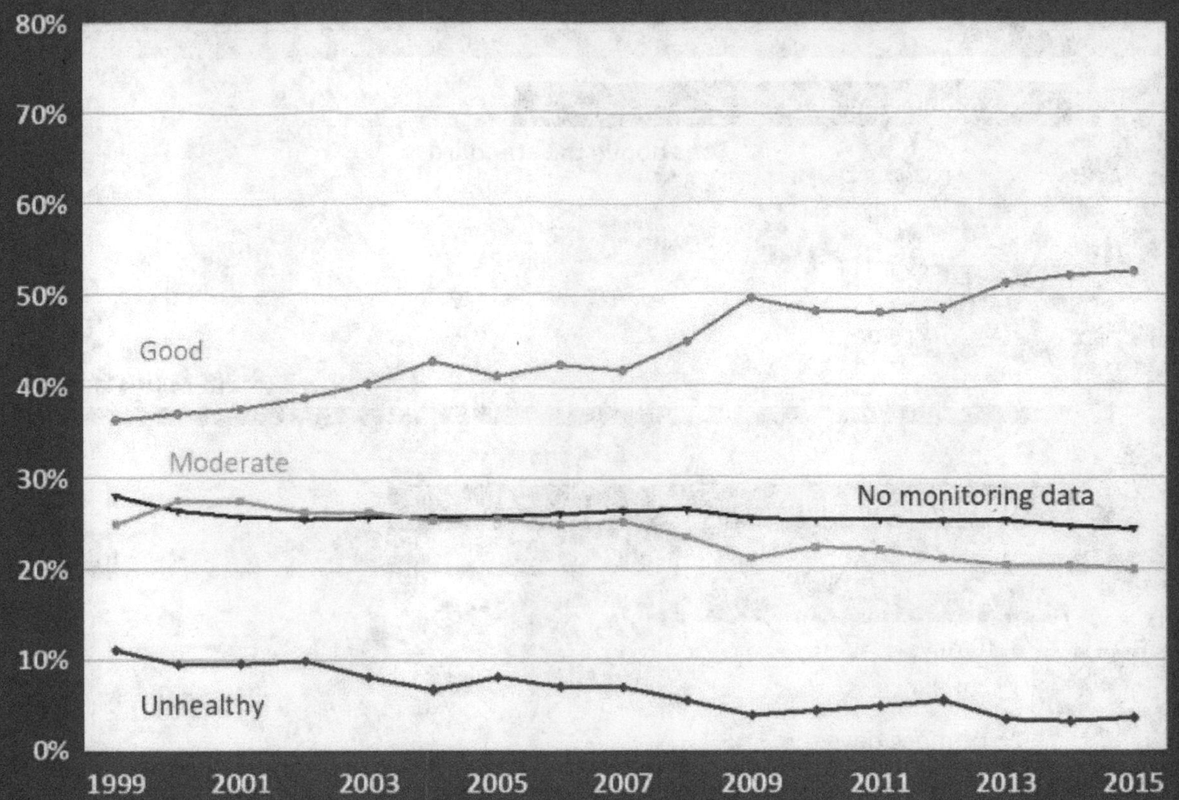

Data: U.S. Environmental Protection Agency, Office of Air and Radiation, Air Quality System

Note: Good, moderate, and unhealthy air quality are defined using EPA's Air Quality Index (AQI). The health information that supports EPA's periodic reviews of the air quality standards informs decisions on the AQI breakpoints and may change based on updated scientific findings. See text for additional discussion.

America's Children and the Environment, Third Edition, Updated August 2017

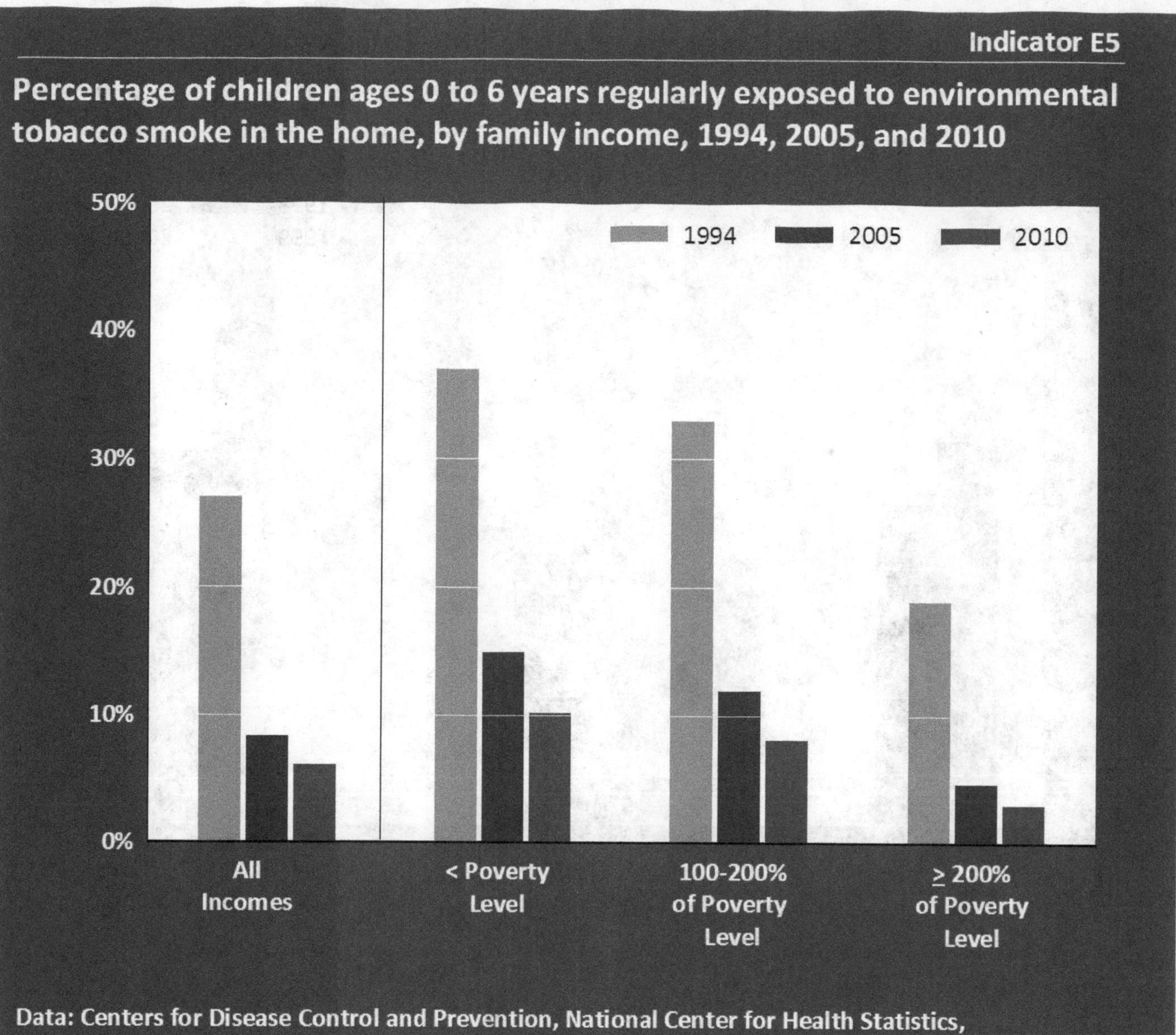
Indicator E5
Percentage of children ages 0 to 6 years regularly exposed to environmental tobacco smoke in the home, by family income, 1994, 2005, and 2010
50%
40%
30%
20%
10%
0%
1994
2005
2010
All Incomes
< Poverty Level
100-200% of Poverty Level
≥ 200% of Poverty Level
Data: Centers for Disease Control and Prevention, National Center for Health Statistics, National Health Interview Survey
America's Children and the Environment, Third Edition

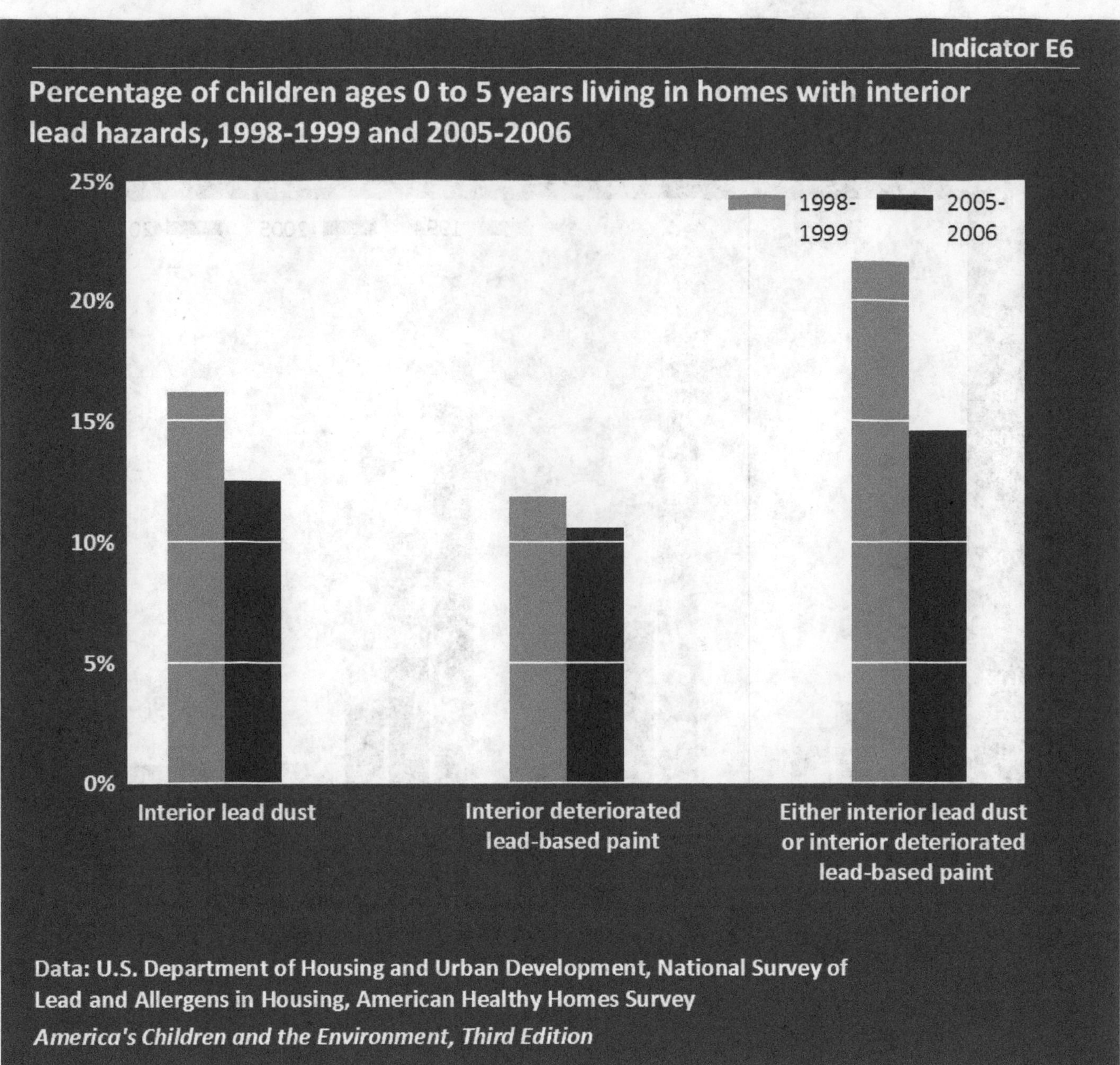
Indicator E6
Percentage of children ages 0 to 5 years living in homes with interior lead hazards, 1998-1999 and 2005-2006
25%
20%
15%
10%
5%
0%
1998-1999
2005-2006
Interior lead dust
Interior deteriorated lead-based paint
Either interior lead dust or interior deteriorated lead-based paint
Data: U.S. Department of Housing and Urban Development, National Survey of Lead and Allergens in Housing, American Healthy Homes Survey
America's Children and the Environment, Third Edition

Indicator E7

Estimated percentage of children ages 0 to 17 years served by community water systems that did not meet all applicable health-based drinking water standards, 1993-2015

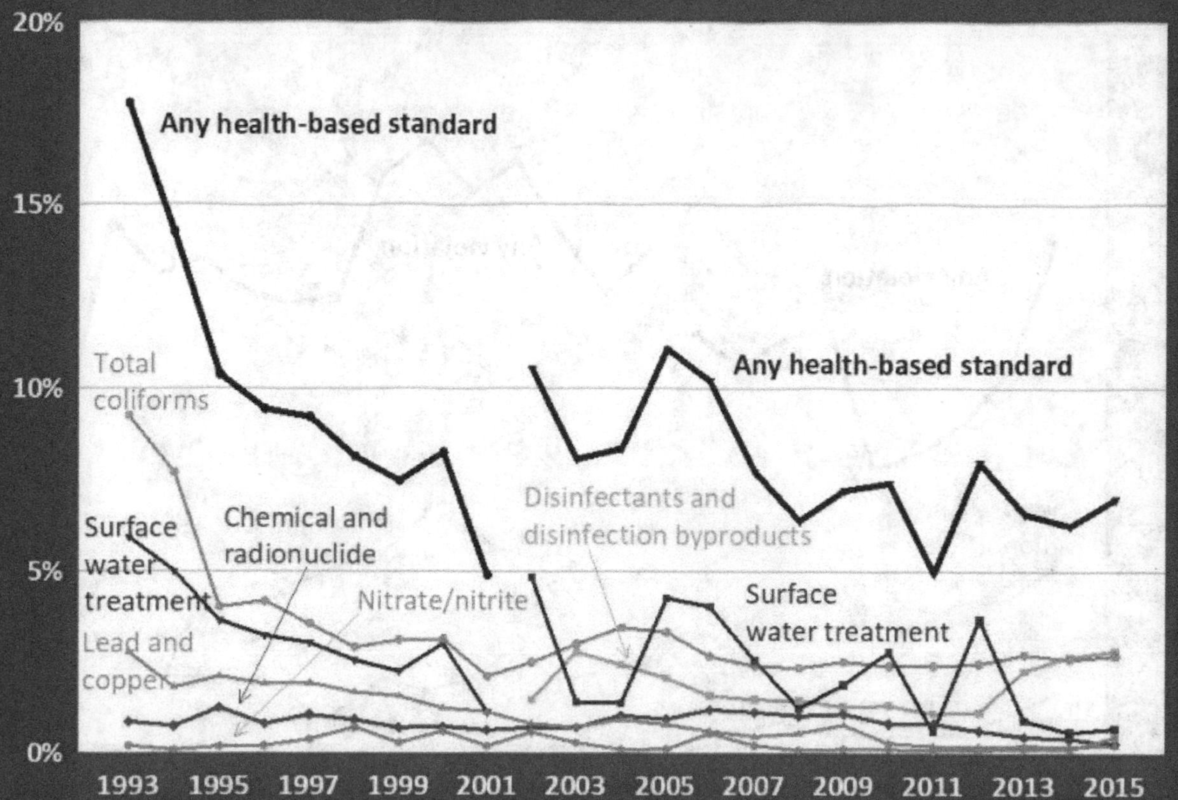

Data: U.S. Environmental Protection Agency, Office of Water, Safe Drinking Water Information System, Federal Version

Note: Breaks in lines for "Any health-based standard" and "Surface water treatment" reflect substantial regulatory changes implemented in 2002.

America's Children and the Environment, Third Edition, Updated August 2017

Estimated percentage of children ages 0 to 17 years served by community water systems with violations of drinking water monitoring and reporting requirements, 1993-2015

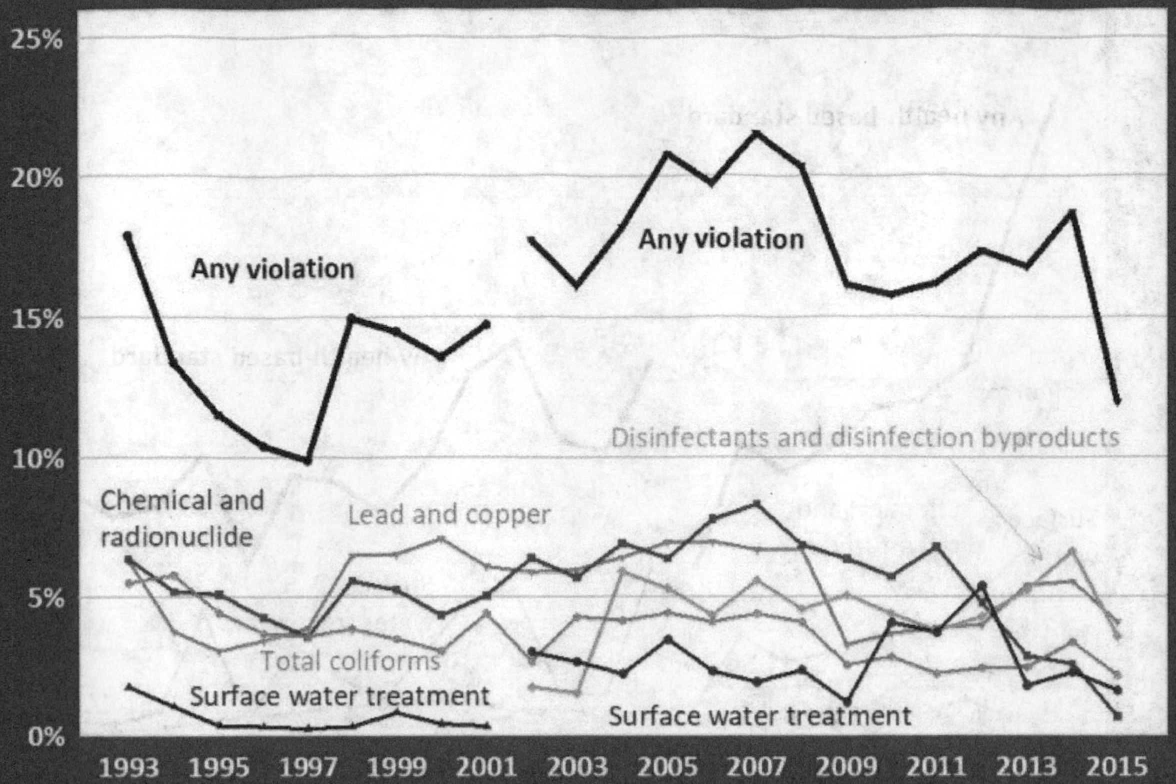

Data: U.S. Environmental Protection Agency, Office of Water, Safe Drinking Water Information System, Federal Version

Note: Breaks in lines for "Any violation" and "Surface water treatment" reflect substantial regulatory changes implemented in 2002.

America's Children and the Environment, Third Edition, Updated August 2017

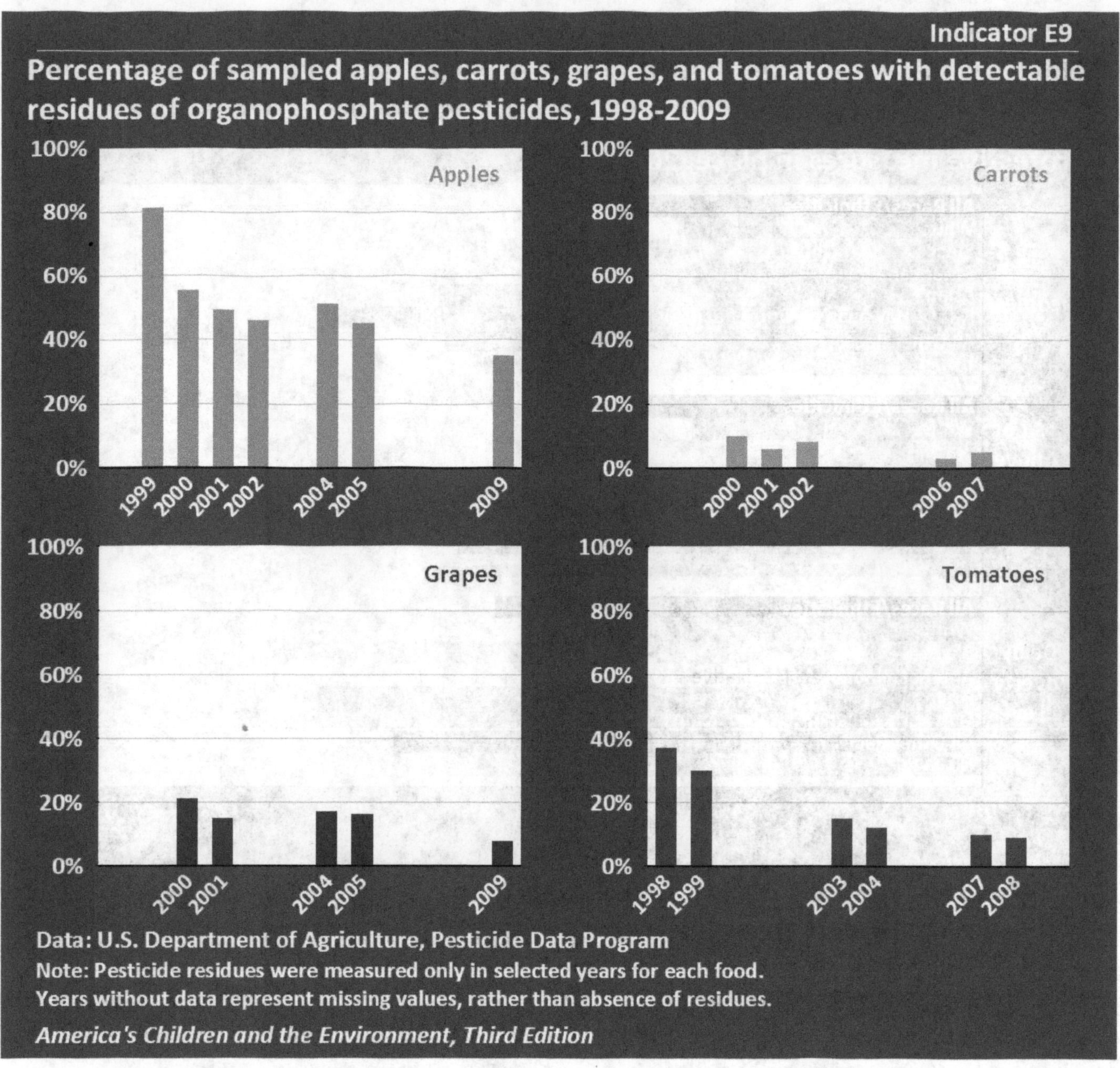
Indicator E9
Percentage of sampled apples, carrots, grapes, and tomatoes with detectable residues of organophosphate pesticides, 1998-2009
Apples
Carrots
Grapes
Tomatoes
100%
80%
60%
40%
20%
0%
1999
2000
2001
2002
2004
2005
2009
2006
2007
1998
2003
2008
Data: U.S. Department of Agriculture, Pesticide Data Program
Note: Pesticide residues were measured only in selected years for each food.
Years without data represent missing values, rather than absence of residues.
America's Children and the Environment, Third Edition

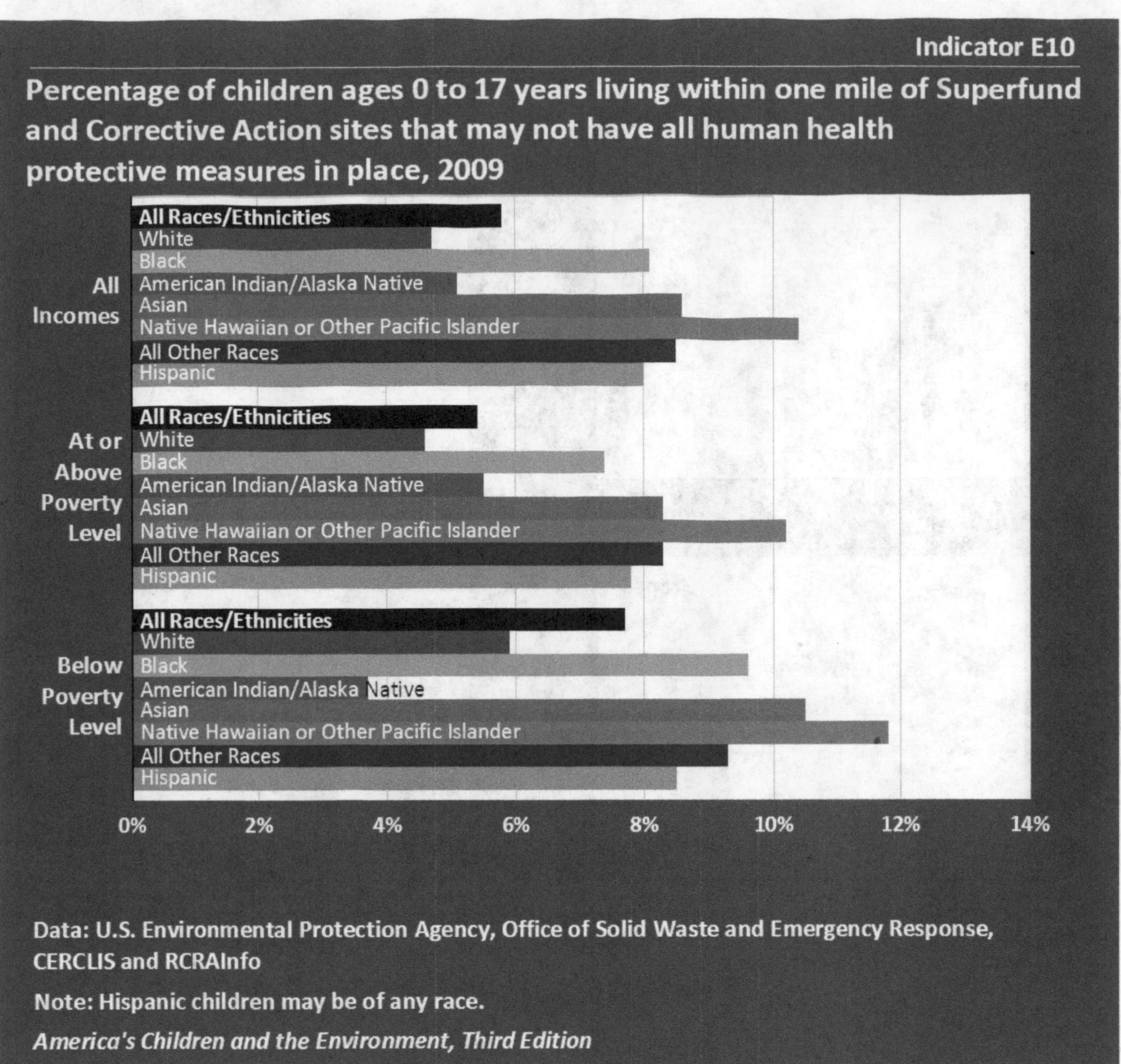
Indicator E10
Percentage of children ages 0 to 17 years living within one mile of Superfund and Corrective Action sites that may not have all human health protective measures in place, 2009
All Incomes
All Races/Ethnicities
White
Black
American Indian/Alaska Native
Asian
Native Hawaiian or Other Pacific Islander
All Other Races
Hispanic
At or Above Poverty Level
All Races/Ethnicities
White
Black
American Indian/Alaska Native
Asian
Native Hawaiian or Other Pacific Islander
All Other Races
Hispanic
Below Poverty Level
All Races/Ethnicities
White
Black
American Indian/Alaska Native
Asian
Native Hawaiian or Other Pacific Islander
All Other Races
Hispanic
0%
2%
4%
6%
8%
10%
12%
14%
Data: U.S. Environmental Protection Agency, Office of Solid Waste and Emergency Response, CERCLIS and RCRAInfo
Note: Hispanic children may be of any race.
America's Children and the Environment, Third Edition

Indicator E11

Distribution by race/ethnicity and family income of children living near selected contaminated lands* in 2009, compared with the distribution by race/ethnicity and income of children in the general U.S. population

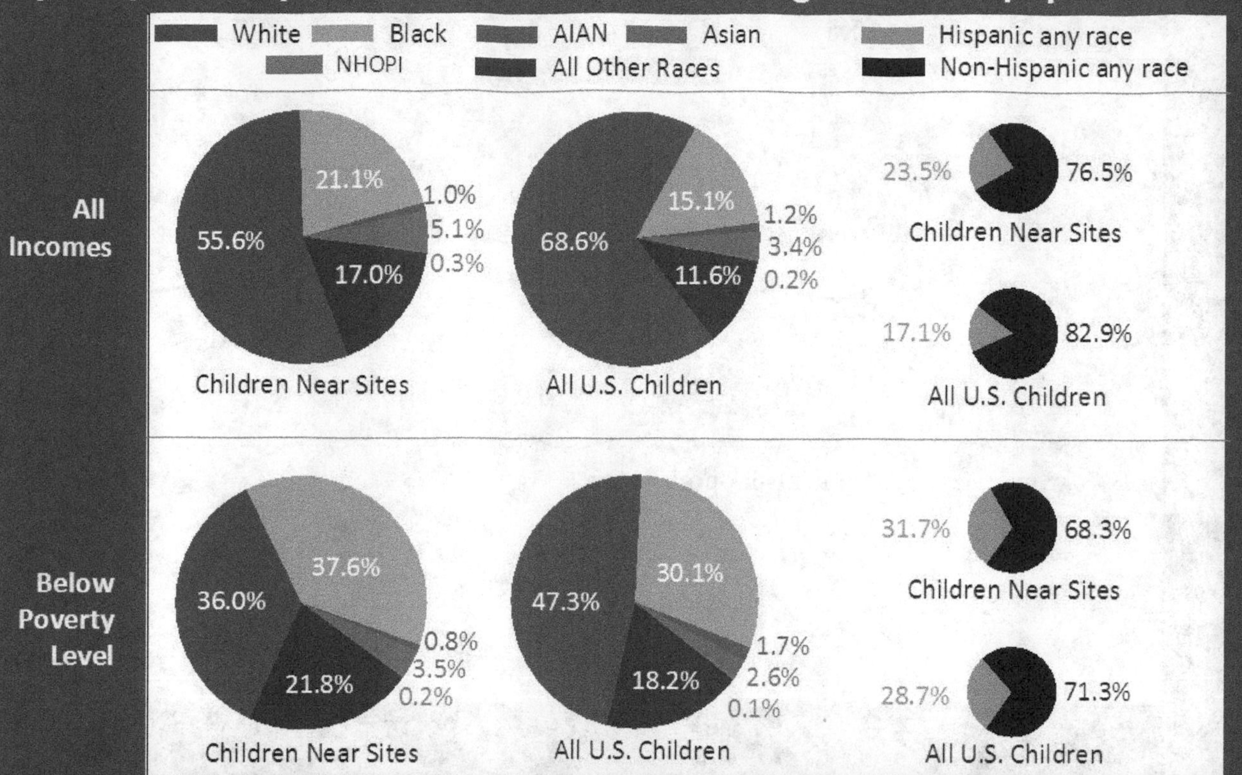

Data: U.S. EPA, Office of Solid Waste and Emergency Response, CERCLIS and RCRAInfo

Note: AIAN = American Indian/Alaska Native. NHOPI = Native Hawaiian or Other Pacific Islander. Hispanic children may be of any race.

* Within one mile of Superfund and Corrective Action sites that may not have all human health protective measures in place.

America's Children and the Environment, Third Edition

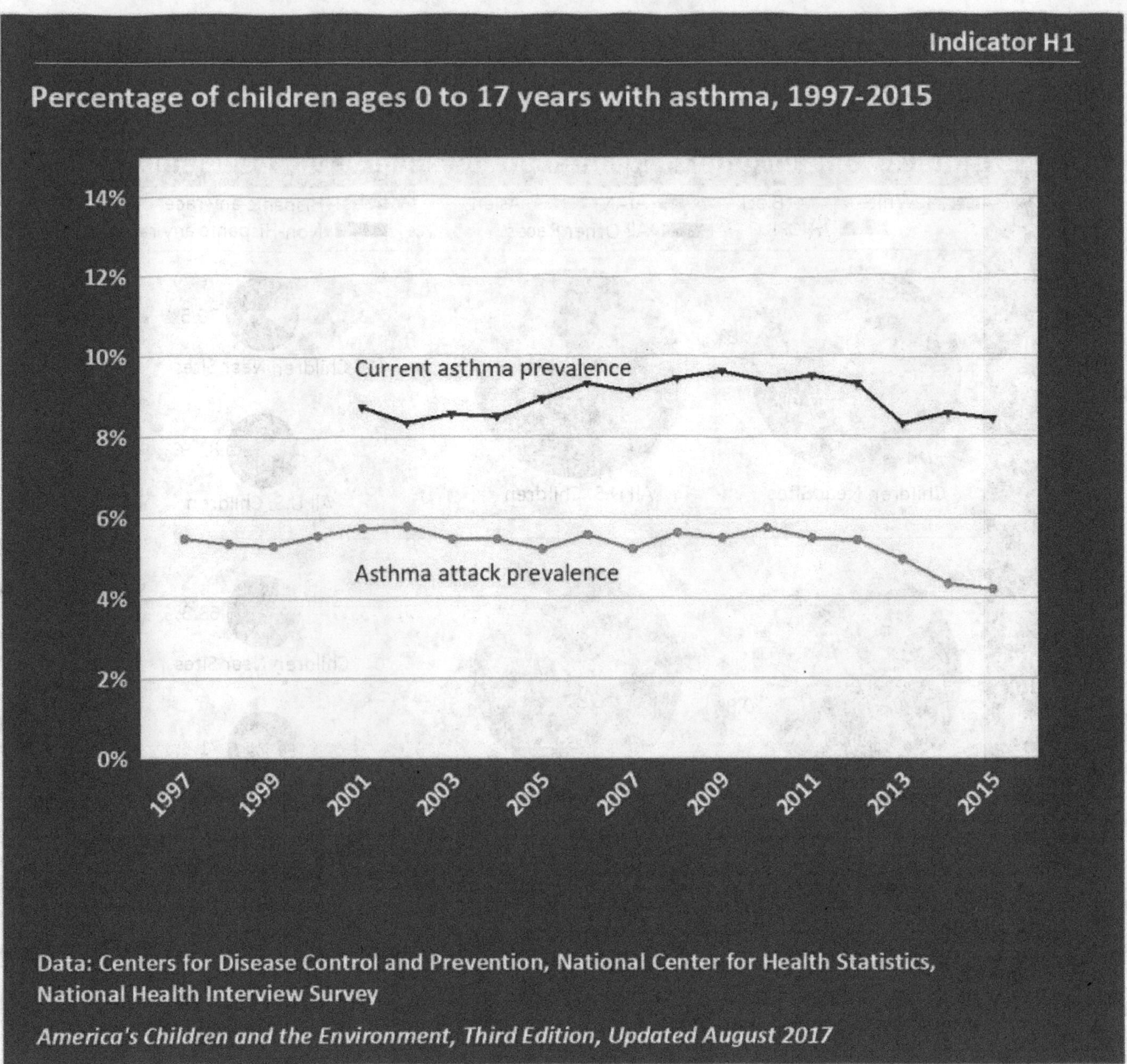
Indicator H1
Percentage of children ages 0 to 17 years with asthma, 1997-2015
14%
12%
10%
8%
6%
4%
2%
0%
Current asthma prevalence
Asthma attack prevalence
1997
1999
2001
2003
2005
2007
2009
2011
2013
2015
Data: Centers for Disease Control and Prevention, National Center for Health Statistics, National Health Interview Survey
America's Children and the Environment, Third Edition, Updated August 2017

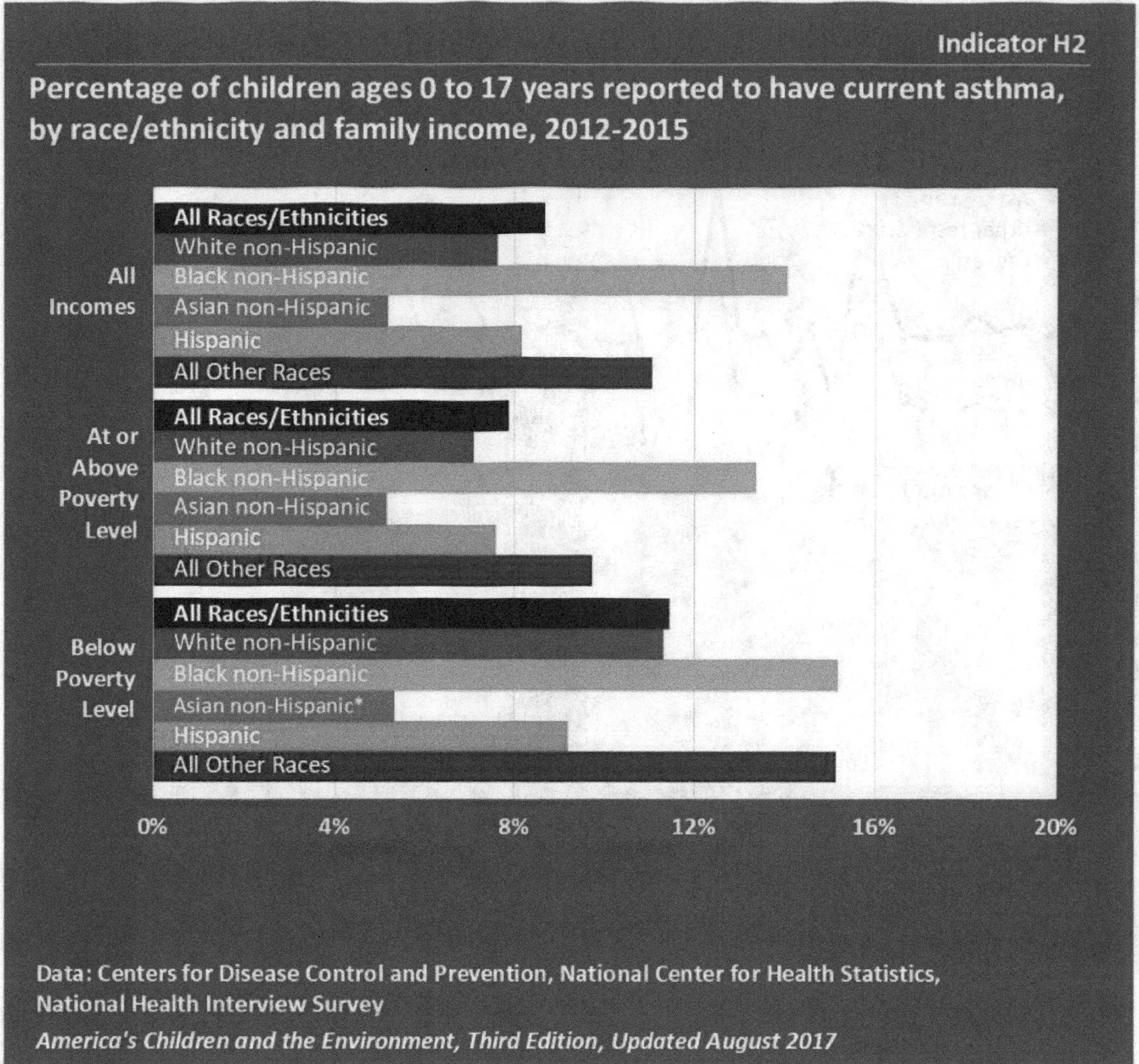
Indicator H2
Percentage of children ages 0 to 17 years reported to have current asthma, by race/ethnicity and family income, 2012-2015
All Incomes
At or Above Poverty Level
Below Poverty Level
All Races/Ethnicities
White non-Hispanic
Black non-Hispanic
Asian non-Hispanic
Hispanic
All Other Races
All Races/Ethnicities
White non-Hispanic
Black non-Hispanic
Asian non-Hispanic
Hispanic
All Other Races
All Races/Ethnicities
White non-Hispanic
Black non-Hispanic
Asian non-Hispanic*
Hispanic
All Other Races
0%
4%
8%
12%
16%
20%
Data: Centers for Disease Control and Prevention, National Center for Health Statistics, National Health Interview Survey
America's Children and the Environment, Third Edition, Updated August 2017

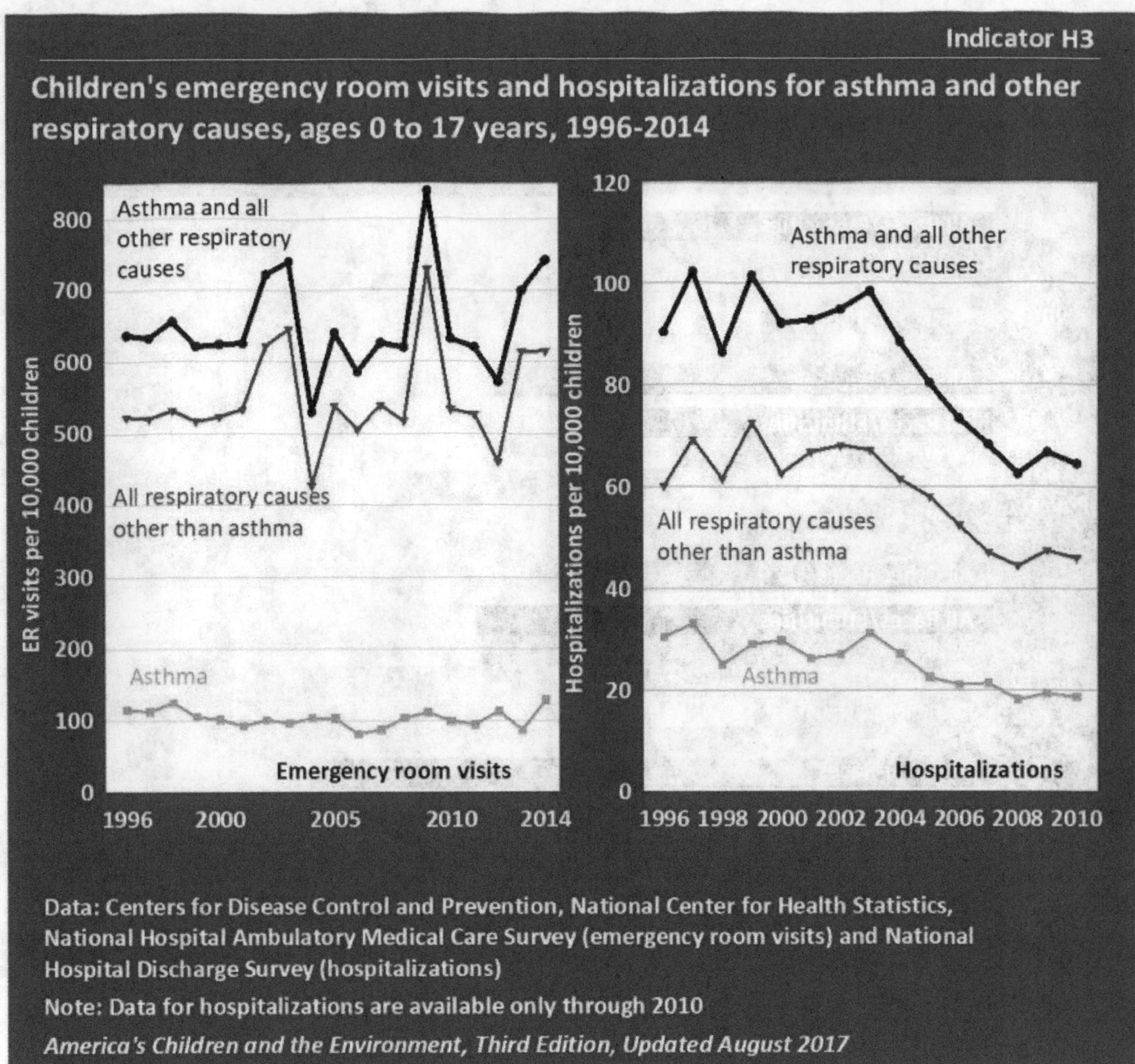
Indicator H3
Children's emergency room visits and hospitalizations for asthma and other respiratory causes, ages 0 to 17 years, 1996-2014
Asthma and all other respiratory causes
All respiratory causes other than asthma
Asthma
ER visits per 10,000 children
0
100
200
300
400
500
600
700
800
1996
2000
2005
2010
2014
Emergency room visits
Hospitalizations per 10,000 children
0
20
40
60
80
100
120
1996 1998 2000 2002 2004 2006 2008 2010
Hospitalizations
Asthma and all other respiratory causes
All respiratory causes other than asthma
Asthma
Data: Centers for Disease Control and Prevention, National Center for Health Statistics, National Hospital Ambulatory Medical Care Survey (emergency room visits) and National Hospital Discharge Survey (hospitalizations)
Note: Data for hospitalizations are available only through 2010
America's Children and the Environment, Third Edition, Updated August 2017

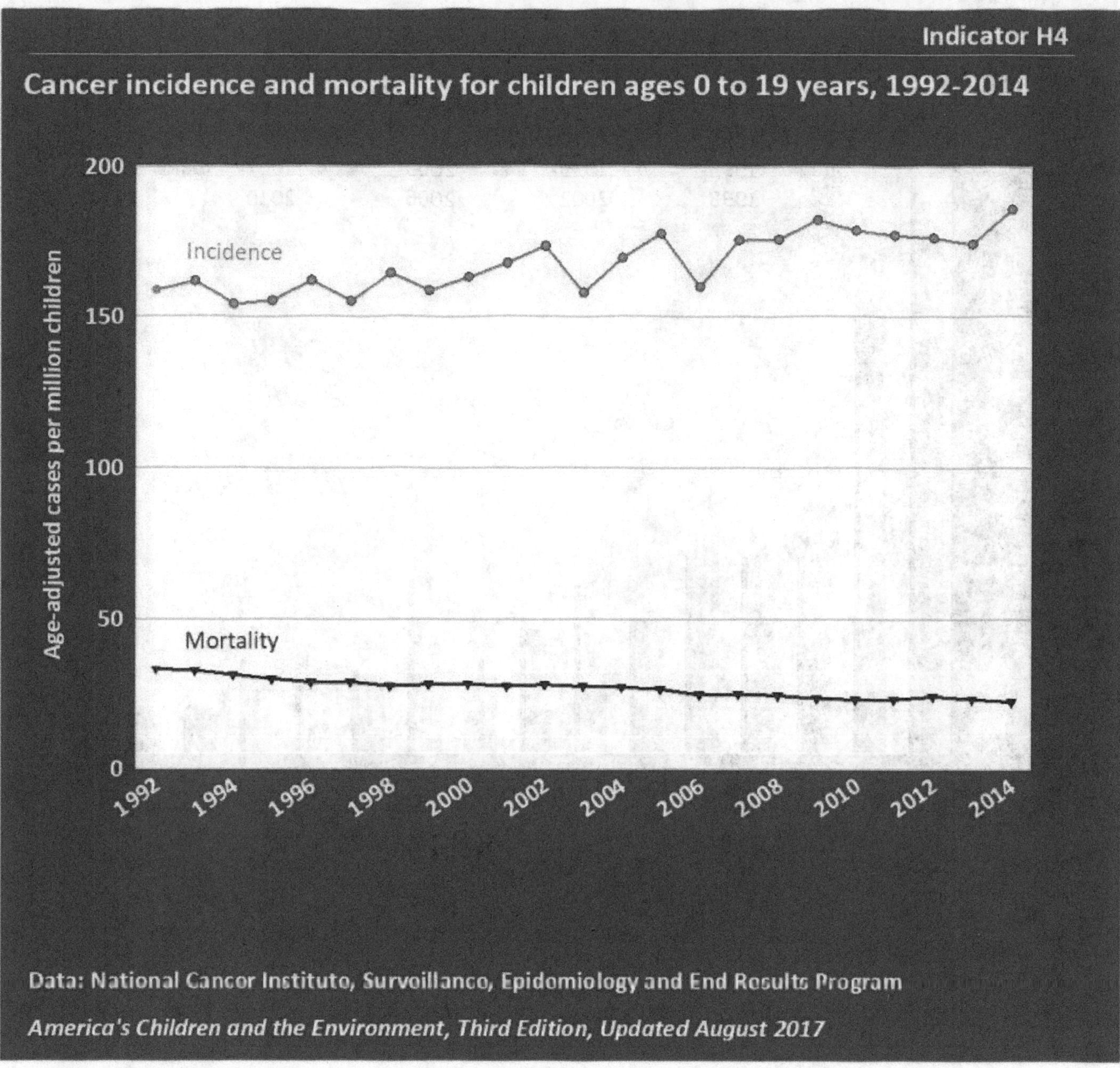
Indicator H4
Cancer incidence and mortality for children ages 0 to 19 years, 1992-2014
Age-adjusted cases per million children
200
150
100
50
0
Incidence
Mortality
1992
1994
1996
1998
2000
2002
2004
2006
2008
2010
2012
2014
Data: National Cancer Institute, Surveillance, Epidemiology and End Results Program
America's Children and the Environment, Third Edition, Updated August 2017

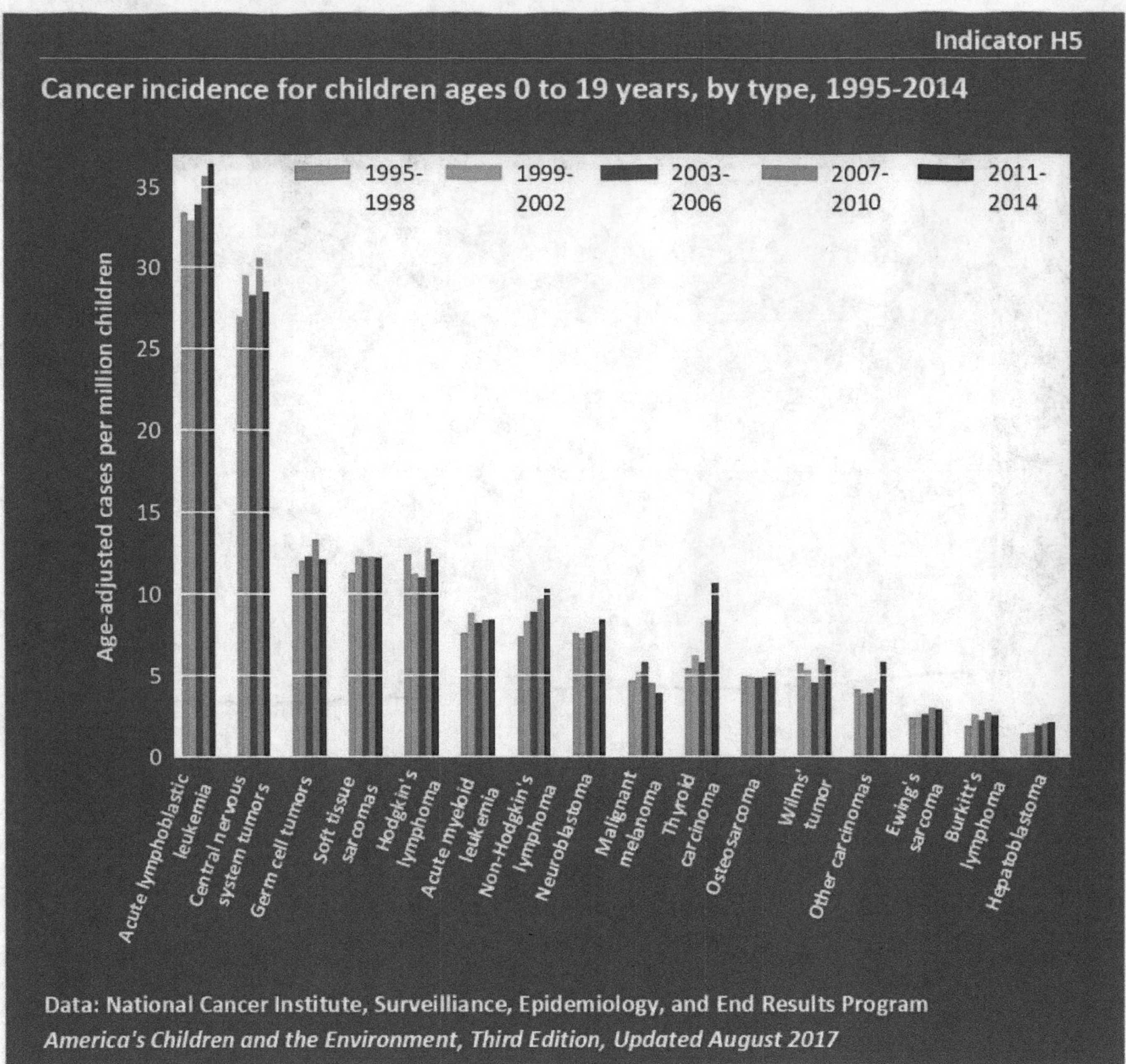
Indicator H5
Cancer incidence for children ages 0 to 19 years, by type, 1995-2014
1995-1998
1999-2002
2003-2006
2007-2010
2011-2014
Age-adjusted cases per million children
0
5
10
15
20
25
30
35
Acute lymphoblastic leukemia
Central nervous system tumors
Germ cell tumors
Soft tissue sarcomas
Hodgkin's lymphoma
Acute myeloid leukemia
Non-Hodgkin's lymphoma
Neuroblastoma
Malignant melanoma
Thyroid carcinoma
Osteosarcoma
Wilms' tumor
Other carcinomas
Ewing's sarcoma
Burkitt's lymphoma
Hepatoblastoma
Data: National Cancer Institute, Surveilliance, Epidemiology, and End Results Program
America's Children and the Environment, Third Edition, Updated August 2017

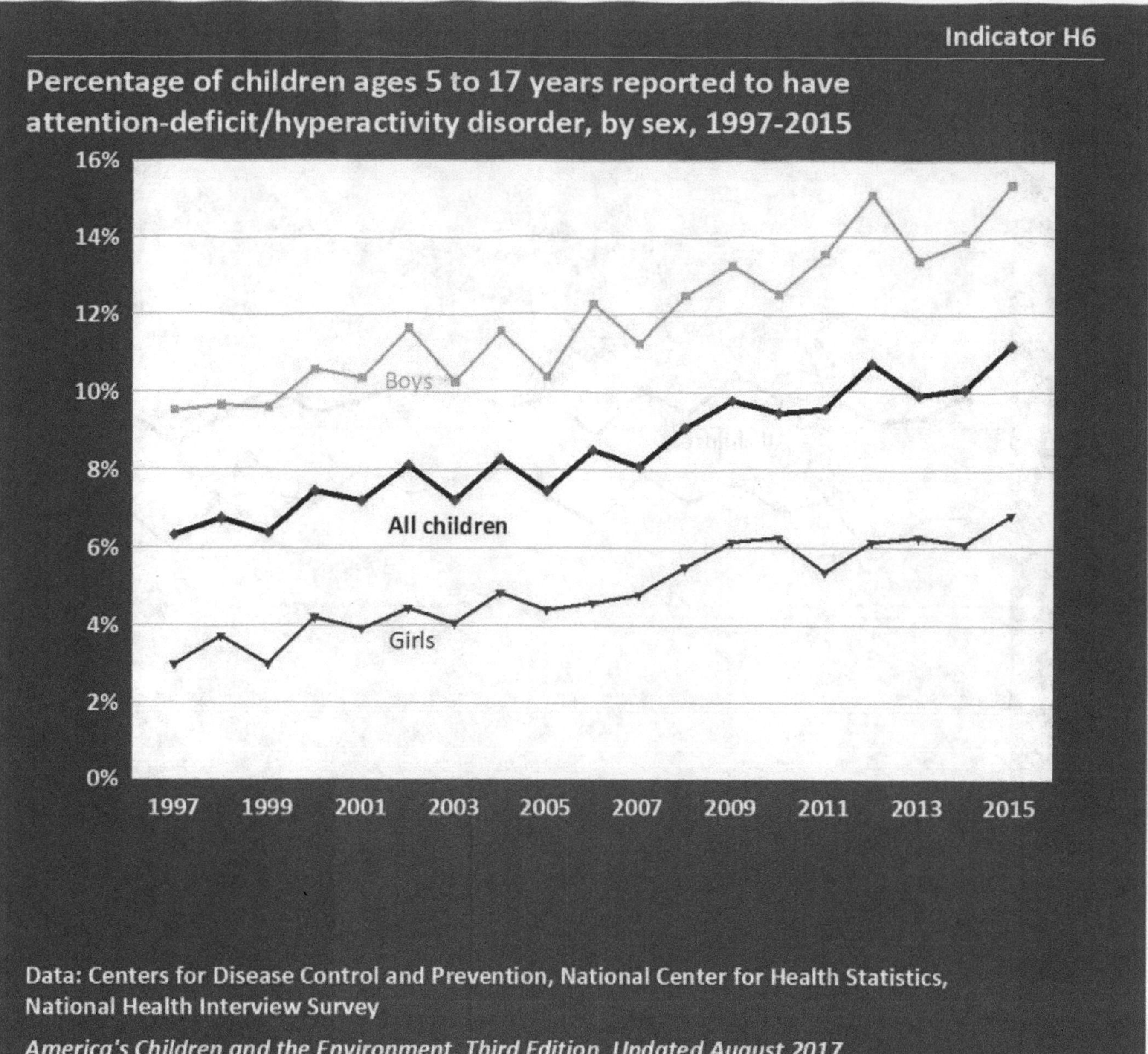

Indicator H6
Percentage of children ages 5 to 17 years reported to have attention-deficit/hyperactivity disorder, by sex, 1997-2015
16%
14%
12%
10%
8%
6%
4%
2%
0%
Boys
All children
Girls
1997
1999
2001
2003
2005
2007
2009
2011
2013
2015
Data: Centers for Disease Control and Prevention, National Center for Health Statistics, National Health Interview Survey
America's Children and the Environment, Third Edition, Updated August 2017

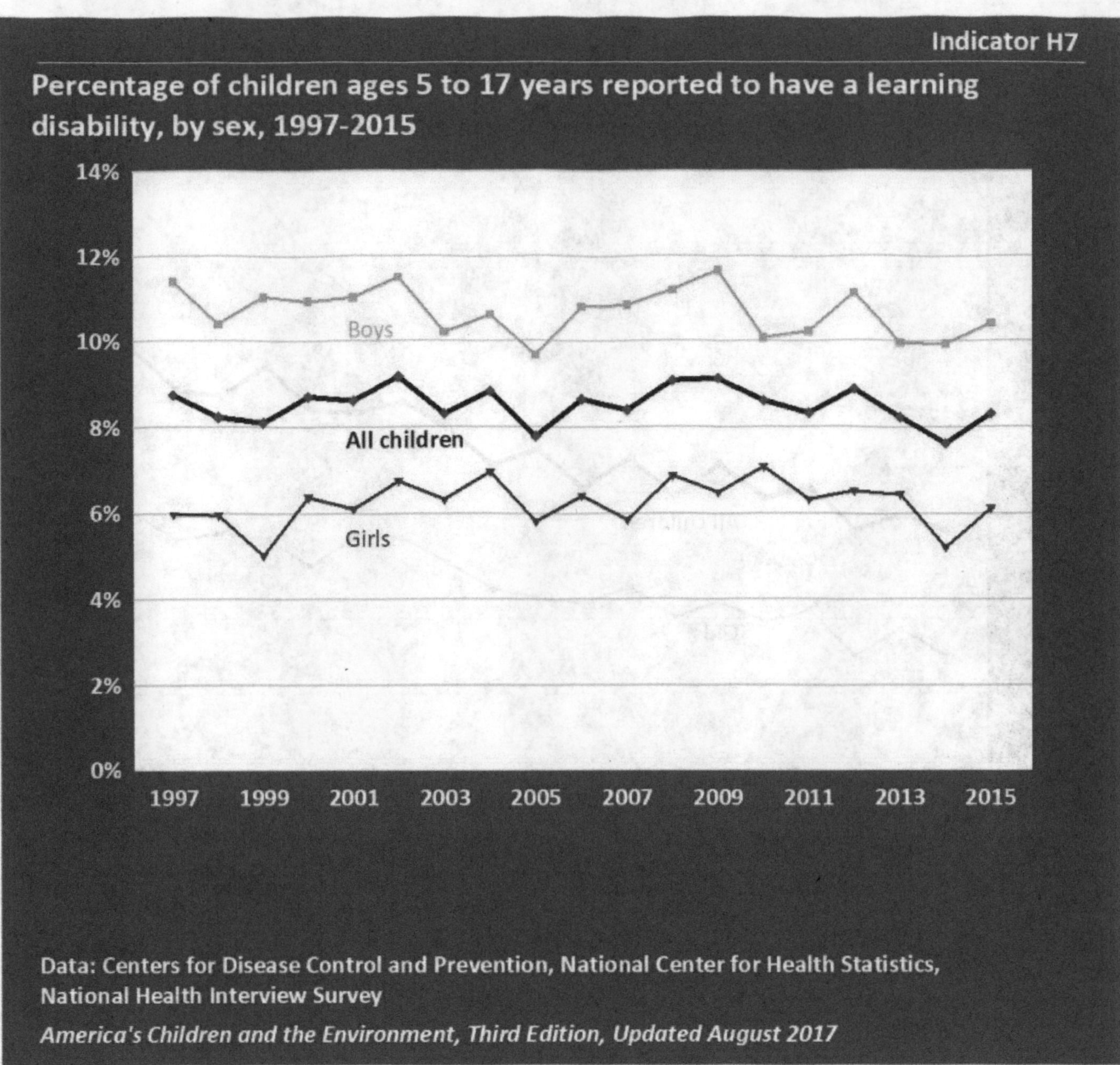
Indicator H7
Percentage of children ages 5 to 17 years reported to have a learning disability, by sex, 1997-2015
14%
12%
10%
8%
6%
4%
2%
0%
Boys
All children
Girls
1997
1999
2001
2003
2005
2007
2009
2011
2013
2015
Data: Centers for Disease Control and Prevention, National Center for Health Statistics, National Health Interview Survey
America's Children and the Environment, Third Edition, Updated August 2017

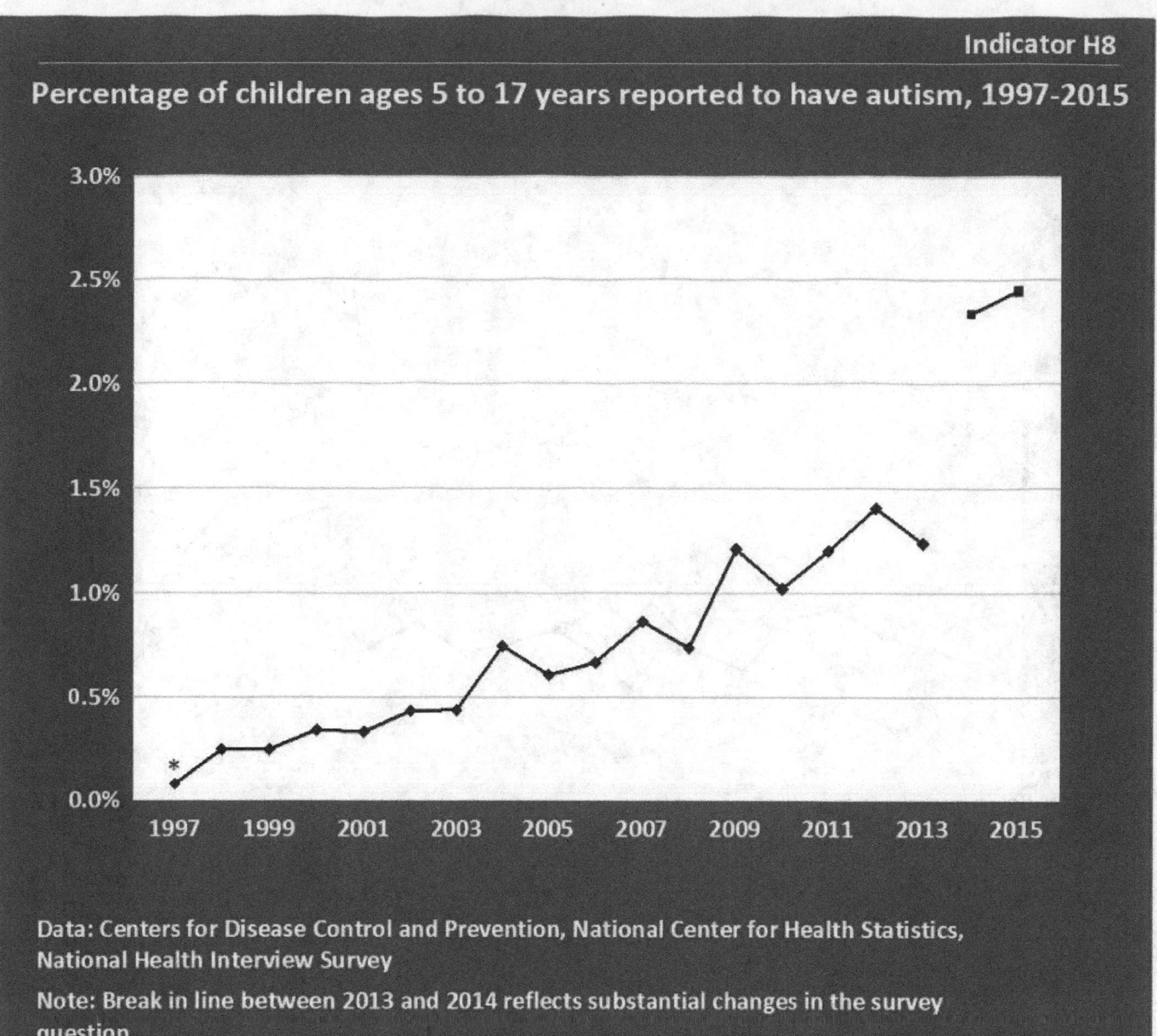
Indicator H8
Percentage of children ages 5 to 17 years reported to have autism, 1997-2015
3.0%
2.5%
2.0%
1.5%
1.0%
0.5%
0.0%
*
1997
1999
2001
2003
2005
2007
2009
2011
2013
2015
Data: Centers for Disease Control and Prevention, National Center for Health Statistics, National Health Interview Survey
Note: Break in line between 2013 and 2014 reflects substantial changes in the survey question.
America's Children and the Environment, Third Edition, Updated August 2017

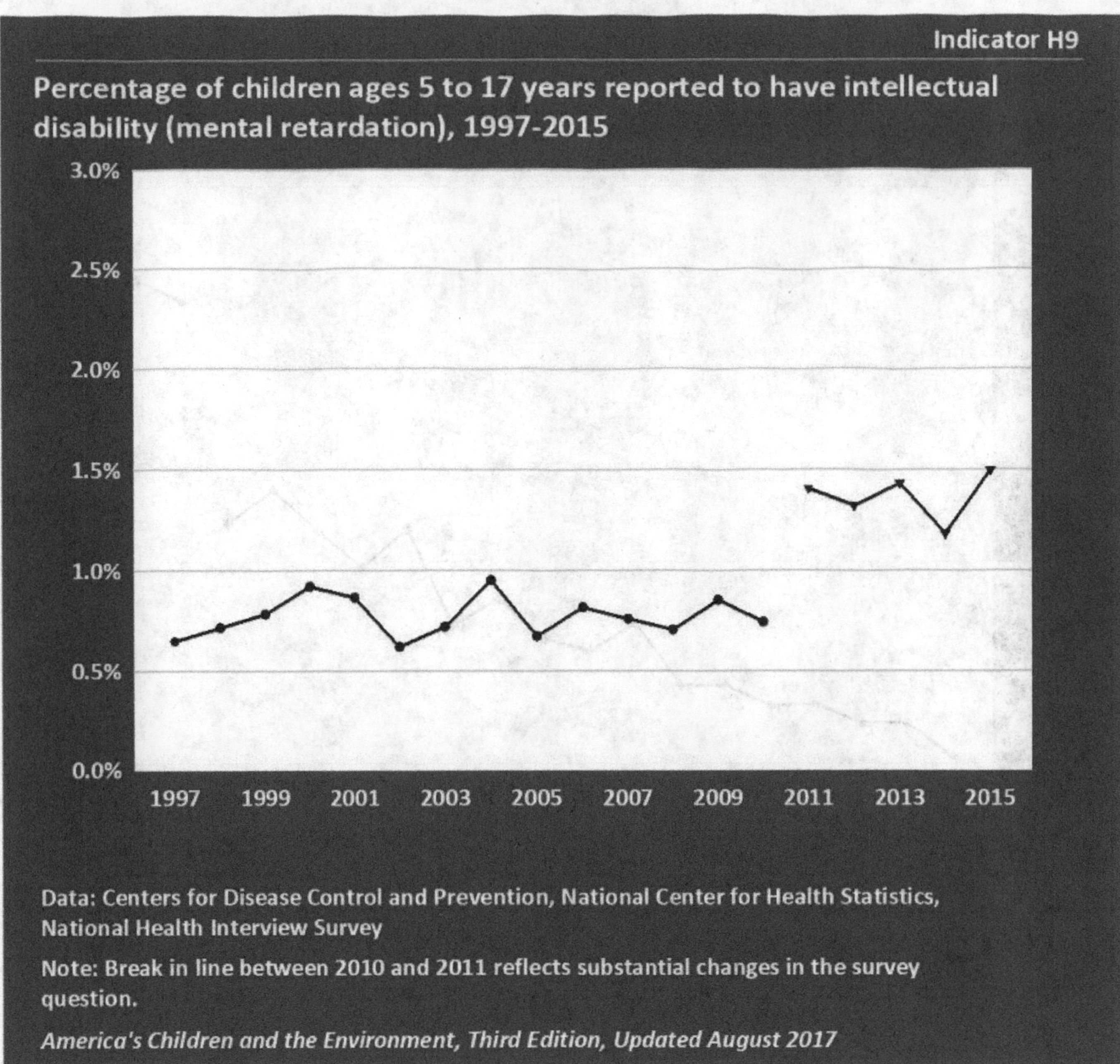
Indicator H9
Percentage of children ages 5 to 17 years reported to have intellectual disability (mental retardation), 1997-2015
3.0%
2.5%
2.0%
1.5%
1.0%
0.5%
0.0%
1997
1999
2001
2003
2005
2007
2009
2011
2013
2015
Data: Centers for Disease Control and Prevention, National Center for Health Statistics, National Health Interview Survey
Note: Break in line between 2010 and 2011 reflects substantial changes in the survey question.
America's Children and the Environment, Third Edition, Updated August 2017

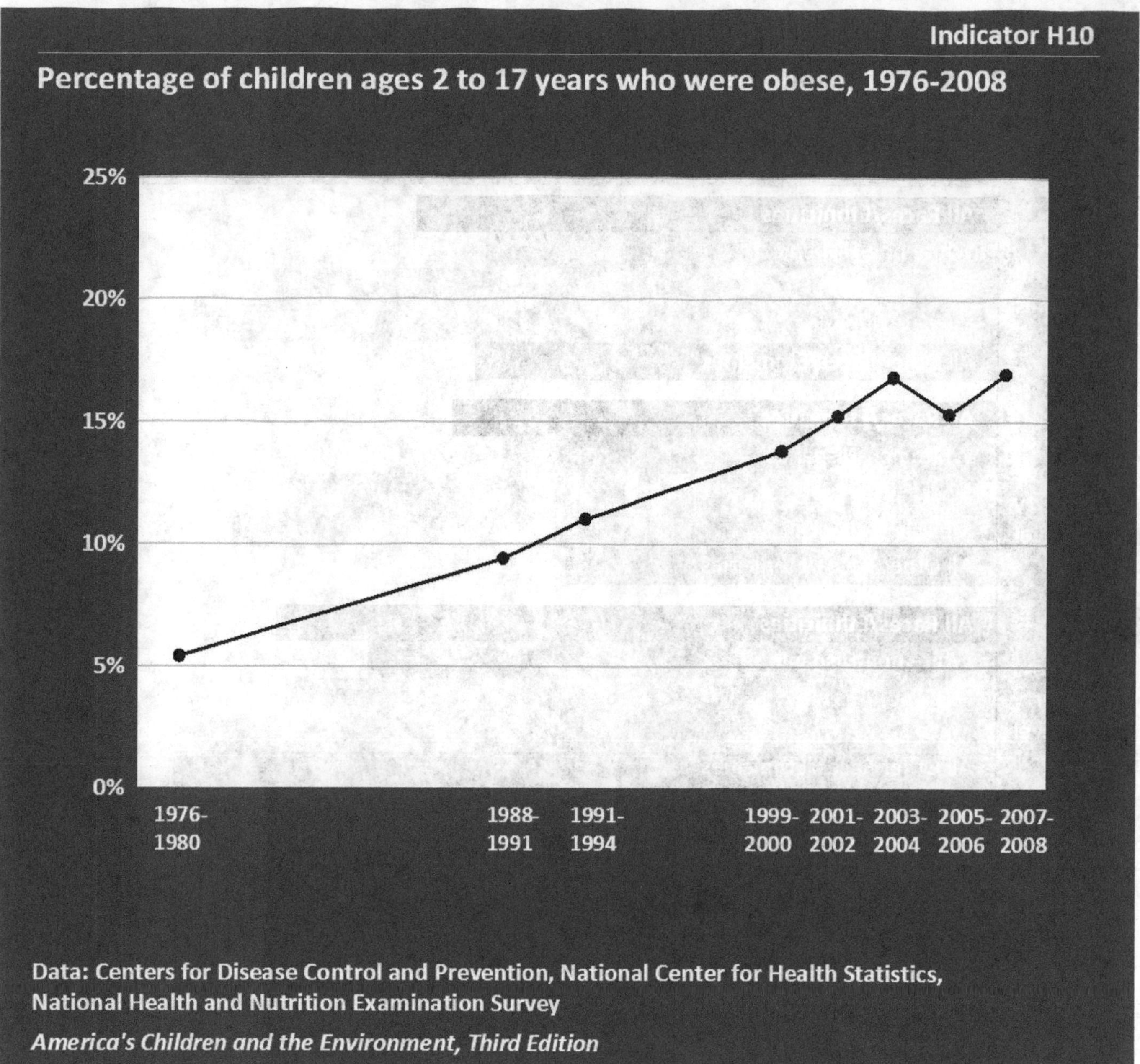
Indicator H10
Percentage of children ages 2 to 17 years who were obese, 1976-2008
25%
20%
15%
10%
5%
0%
1976-1980
1988-1991
1991-1994
1999-2000
2001-2002
2003-2004
2005-2006
2007-2008
Data: Centers for Disease Control and Prevention, National Center for Health Statistics, National Health and Nutrition Examination Survey
America's Children and the Environment, Third Edition

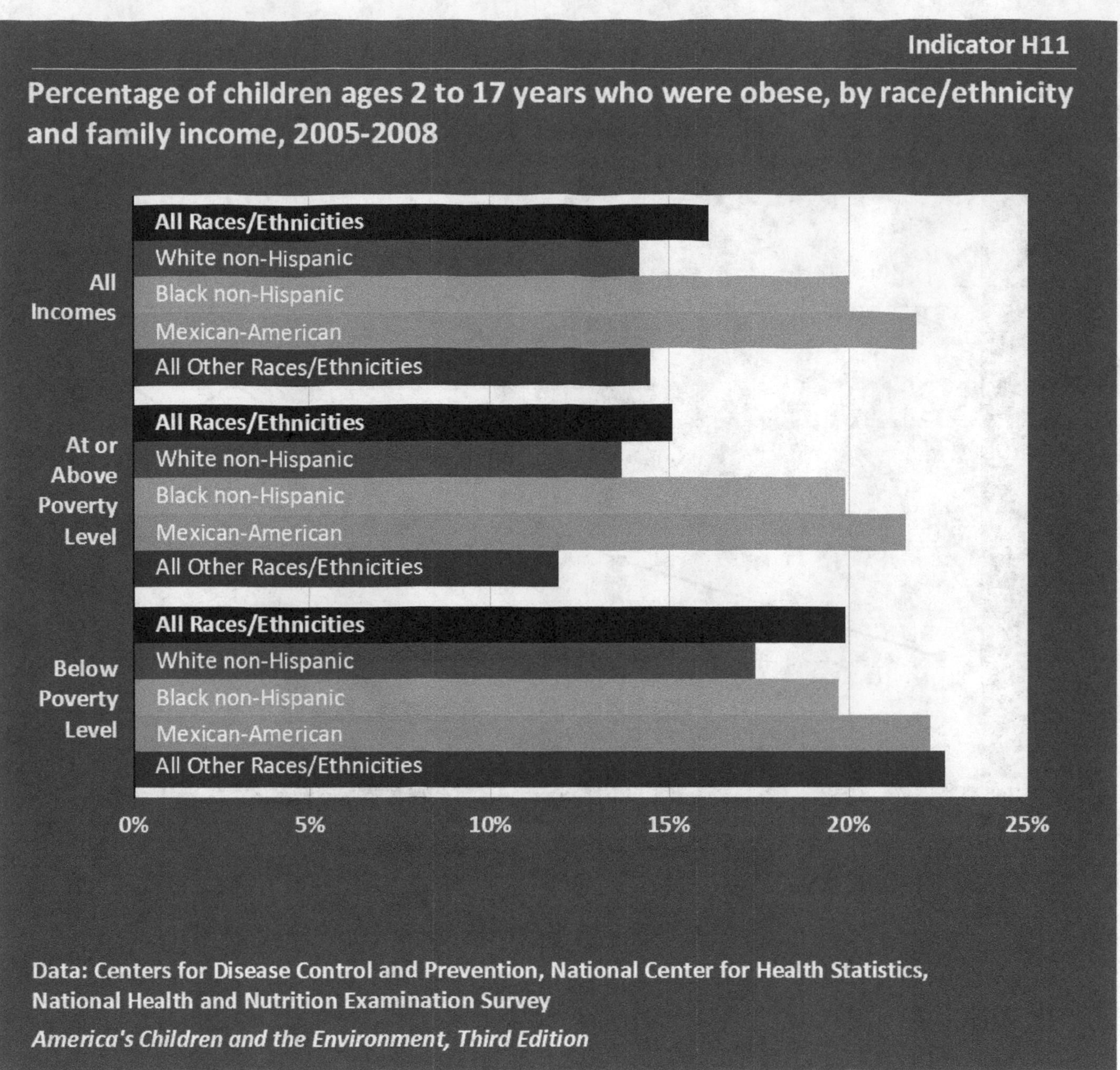
Indicator H11
Percentage of children ages 2 to 17 years who were obese, by race/ethnicity and family income, 2005-2008
All Incomes
At or Above Poverty Level
Below Poverty Level
All Races/Ethnicities
White non-Hispanic
Black non-Hispanic
Mexican-American
All Other Races/Ethnicities
0%
5%
10%
15%
20%
25%
Data: Centers for Disease Control and Prevention, National Center for Health Statistics, National Health and Nutrition Examination Survey
America's Children and the Environment, Third Edition

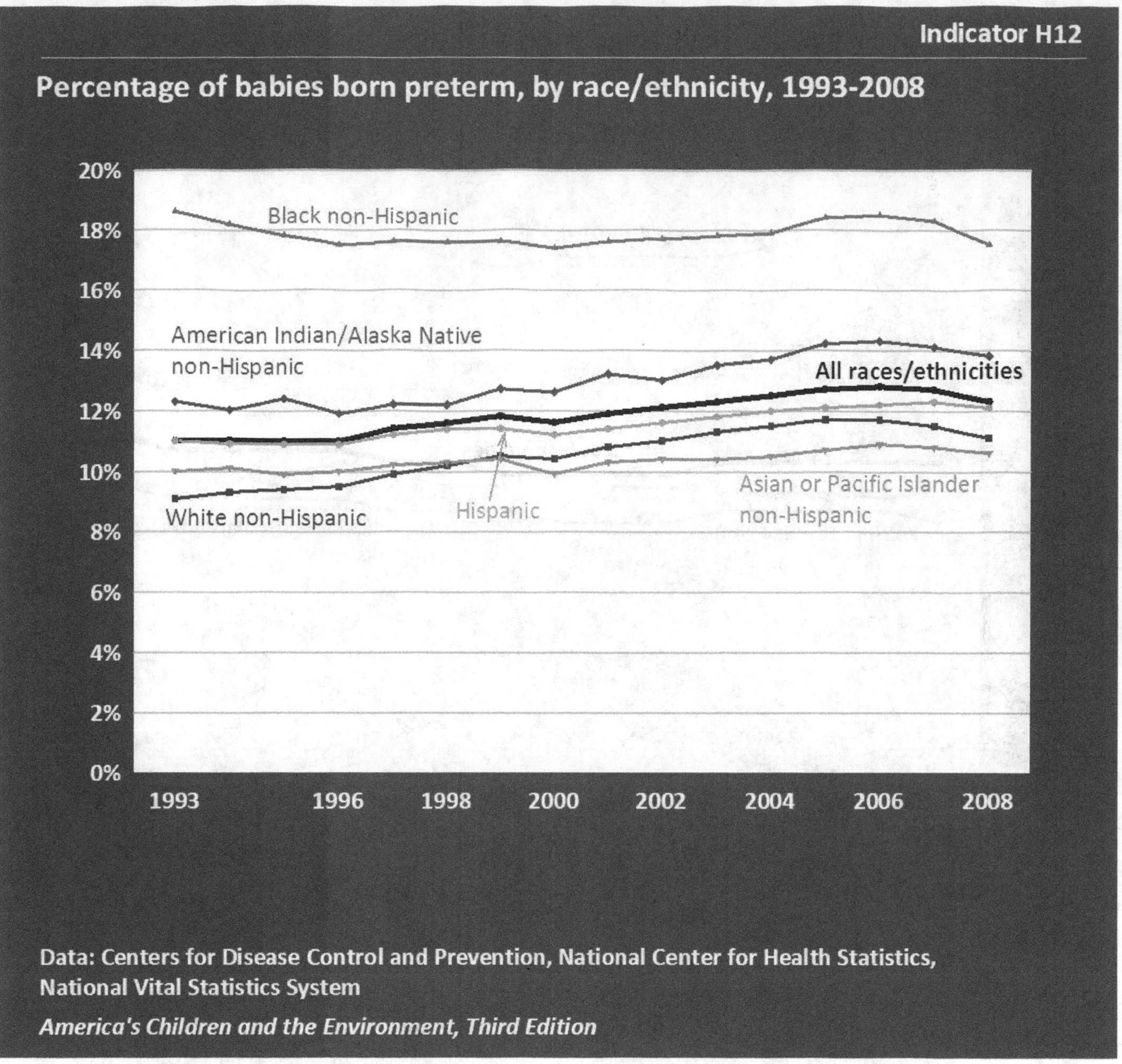
Indicator H12
Percentage of babies born preterm, by race/ethnicity, 1993-2008
20%
18%
16%
14%
12%
10%
8%
6%
4%
2%
0%
Black non-Hispanic
American Indian/Alaska Native
non-Hispanic
All races/ethnicities
White non-Hispanic
Hispanic
Asian or Pacific Islander
non-Hispanic
1993
1996
1998
2000
2002
2004
2006
2008
Data: Centers for Disease Control and Prevention, National Center for Health Statistics,
National Vital Statistics System
America's Children and the Environment, Third Edition

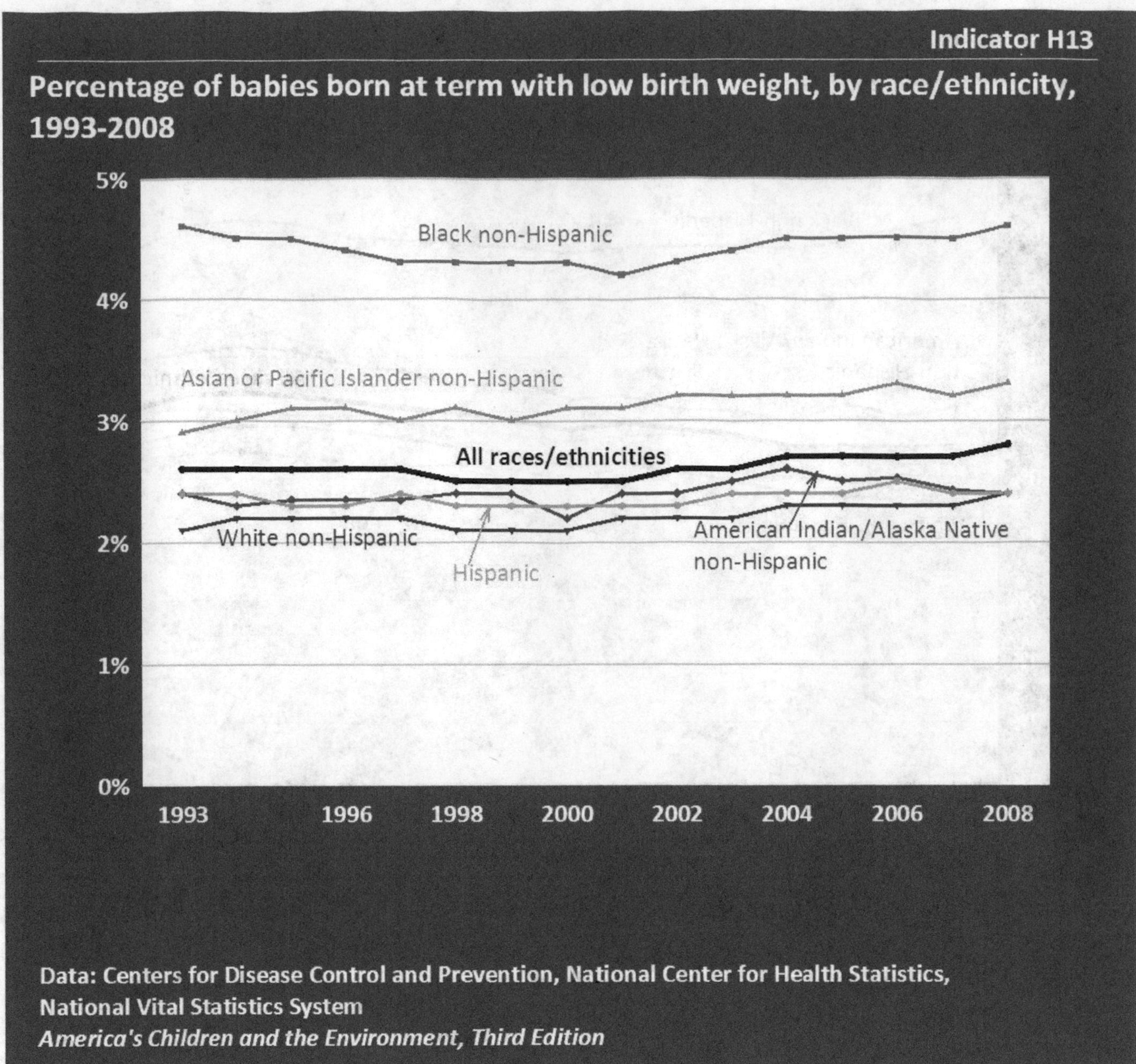
Indicator H13
Percentage of babies born at term with low birth weight, by race/ethnicity, 1993-2008
5%
4%
3%
2%
1%
0%
Black non-Hispanic
Asian or Pacific Islander non-Hispanic
All races/ethnicities
White non-Hispanic
Hispanic
American Indian/Alaska Native non-Hispanic
1993
1996
1998
2000
2002
2004
2006
2008
Data: Centers for Disease Control and Prevention, National Center for Health Statistics, National Vital Statistics System
America's Children and the Environment, Third Edition

Report on the Environment https://www.epa.gov/roe/

Drinking Water

Community water systems (CWS) are public water systems that supply water to the same population year-round. In fiscal year (FY) 2017, more than 300 million Americans (U.S. EPA, 2018a)—roughly 94 percent of the U.S. population (U.S. Census Bureau, 2018)—got at least some of their drinking water from a CWS. This indicator presents the percentage of Americans served by CWS for which states reported no violations of EPA health-based standards for more than 90 contaminants (U.S. EPA, 2018a).

Health-based standards include Maximum Contaminant Levels (MCLs), Maximum Residual Disinfection Levels (MRDLs), and Treatment Techniques (TTs). An MCL is the highest level of a contaminant that is allowed in drinking water. An MRDL is the level of a disinfectant added for water treatment that may not be exceeded at the consumer's tap without an unacceptable possibility of adverse health effects. A TT is a required treatment process (such as filtration) intended to reduce the level of a contaminant in drinking water (U.S. EPA, 2018b). TTs are adopted where it is not economically or technologically feasible to ascertain the level of a contaminant, such as microbes, where even single organisms that occur unpredictably or episodically can cause adverse health effects. Compliance with TTs may require finished water sampling, along with quantitative or descriptive measurements of process performance to gauge the efficacy of the treatment process. In general, MCL-regulated contaminants tend to have long-term rather than acute health effects, and concentrations may vary seasonally. Thus, compliance is based on averages of seasonal, quarterly, annual, or less frequent sampling.

This indicator tracks the population served by CWS for which no violations were reported to EPA annually for the period from FY 1993 to FY 2017, the latest year for which data are available. Results are reported as a percentage of the overall population served by CWS, both nationally and by EPA Region. This indicator also reports the number of persons served by systems with reported violations of standards covering surface water treatment, microbial contaminants (microorganisms that can cause disease), disinfection byproducts (chemicals that may form when disinfectants, such as chlorine, react with naturally occurring materials in water and may pose health risks), and other contaminants. The indicator is based on violations reported quarterly by states, EPA, and the Navajo Nation, who each review monitoring results for the CWS that they oversee.

What the Data Show

Of the population served by CWS nationally, the percentage served by systems for which no health-based violations were reported for the entire year increased overall from 79 percent in 1993 to 93 percent in FY 2017 (Exhibit 1). Drinking water regulations have changed in recent years. This indicator is based on reported violations of the standards in effect in any given year.

When results are broken down by EPA Region, some variability over time is evident (Exhibit 2). Between FY 1998 and FY 2017, most Regions were consistently above the national percentage. Only Region 2 remained consistently below the national percentage over the entire period of record, largely because of a small number of public water systems serving large populations.

In FY 2017, reported violations involving surface water treatment rules were responsible for exceeding health-based standards for 12 million people (4 percent of the population served by CWS nationally). Reported violations of the health-based disinfection byproducts rules (Stage 2) affected 8 million people (3 percent of the CWS-served population) (Exhibit 3).

Limitations

- Non-community water systems (typically small systems) that serve only transient populations such as restaurants or campgrounds, or serving those in a non-domestic setting for only part of their day (e.g., a school, hospital, or office building), are not included in population served figures.
- Domestic (home) use of drinking water supplied by private wells is not included. More than 13 million households get at least some of their drinking water from private wells (U.S. EPA, 2018c).
- Bottled water, which is regulated by standards set by the Food and Drug Administration, is not included.
- National statistics based on population served can be volatile, because a single very large system can sway the results by up to 2 to 3 percent. This effect becomes more pronounced when statistics are broken down at the regional level, and still more so for a single rule.
- Some factors may lead to overstating the extent of population served by systems that violate standards. For example, the entire population served by each system in violation is reported, even though only part of the total population served may actually receive water that is out of compliance. SDWIS data does not indicate whether any, part, or all of the population served by a system receives water in violation. Therefore, there is no way to know how many, if any, people are actually drinking water in violation. In addition, violations stated on an annual basis may suggest a longer duration of violation than may be the case, as some violations may be as brief as an hour or a day.
- Other factors may lead to understating the population served by systems that violate standards. For instance, CWS that

purchase water from other CWS are not always required to sample for all contaminants themselves.

- Under-reporting and late reporting of violations by states to EPA affect the ability to accurately report the national violations total.
- Data reviews and other quality assurance analyses indicate that the most widespread data quality problem is under-reporting of monitoring violations. Even though these violations are separate from the health-based violations covered by this indicator, failures to monitor could mask violations of TTs, MRDLs, and MCLs.

Data Sources

Data for this indicator were obtained from EPA's Safe Drinking Water Information System (U.S. EPA, 2018a) (https://obipublic11.epa.gov/analytics/saw.dll?PortalPages&PortalPath=/shared/SFDW/_portal/Public&Page=Summary). This database provides information about violations in the public water system. Users can filter the data to see inventory or violation summaries.

References

U.S. Census Bureau. 2018. Monthly population estimates for the United States: April 1, 2010 to December 1, 2017. Accessed May 2018. https://www.census.gov/data/tables/2016/demo/popest/nation-total.html.

U.S. EPA (United States Environmental Protection Agency). 2018a. Government Performance and Results Act (GPRA) tool. Accessed June 2018. https://obipublic11.epa.gov/analytics/saw.dll?PortalPages&PortalPath=/shared/SFDW/_portal/Public&Page=Summary.

U.S. EPA. 2018b. National primary drinking water regulations. Accessed May 2018. https://www.epa.gov/ground-water-and-drinking-water/national-primary-drinking-water-regulations.

U.S. EPA. 2018c. Private drinking water wells. Accessed May 2018. https://www.epa.gov/privatewells.

U.S. EPA. 2008. 2006 drinking water data reliability analysis and action plan: For state reported public water system data in the EPA Safe Drinking Water Information System/Federal Version (SDWIS/FED). March 2008. https://nepis.epa.gov/.

Exhibit 1. U.S. population served by community water systems with no reported violations of EPA health-based standards, fiscal years 1993–2017

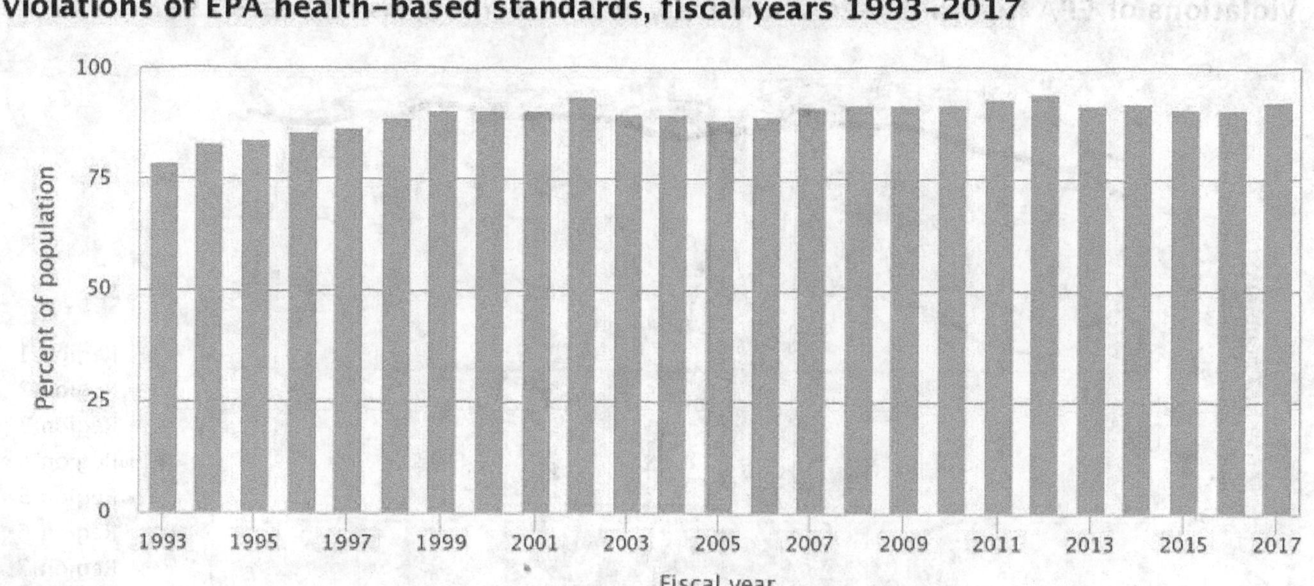

Coverage: U.S. residents served by community water systems (CWS) (approximately 94% of the total U.S. population).

Several new standards went into effect during the time period shown.

Information on the statistical significance of the trend in this exhibit is not currently available. For more information about uncertainty, variability, and statistical analysis, view the technical documentation for this indicator.

Data source: U.S. EPA, 2018a

Exhibit 2. U.S. population served by community water systems with no reported violations of EPA health-based standards, by EPA Region, fiscal years 1993-2017

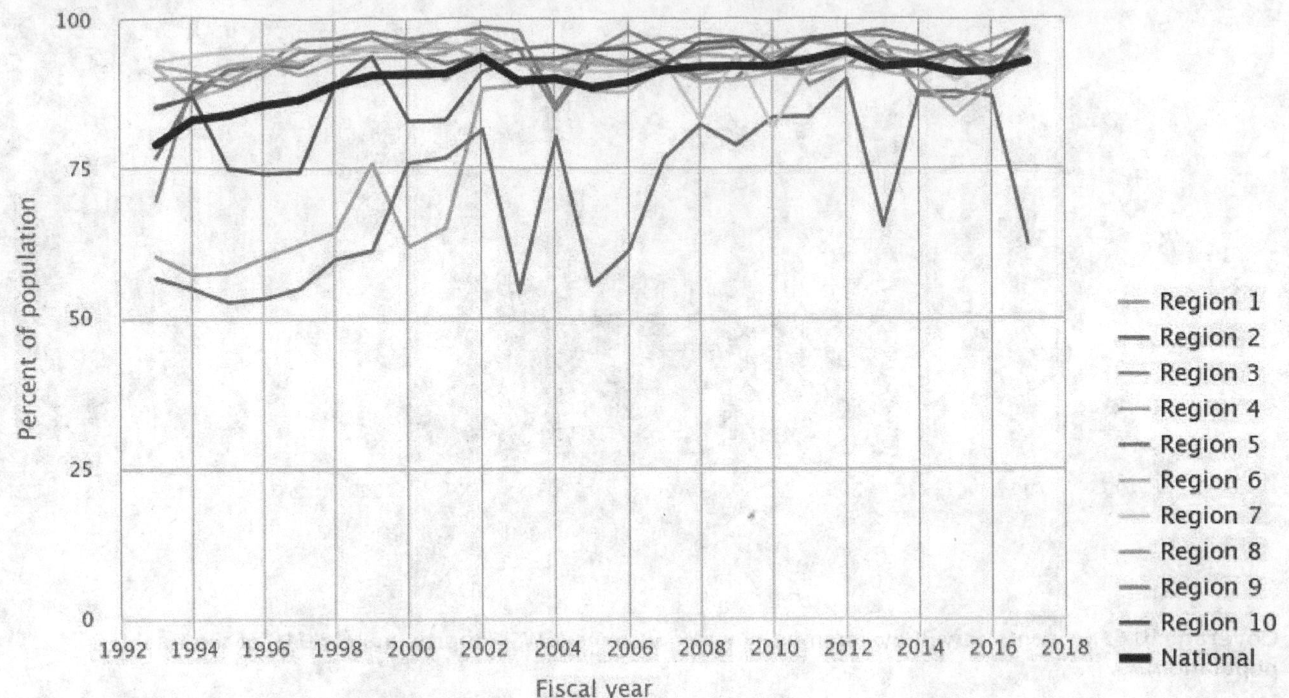

Coverage: U.S. residents served by community water systems (CWS) (approximately 94% of the total U.S. population).

Based on reported violations of the standards in effect in any given year.

Information on the statistical significance of the trends in this exhibit is not currently available. For more information about uncertainty, variability, and statistical analysis, view the technical documentation for this indicator.

Data source: U.S. EPA, 2018a

Exhibit 3. U.S. population served by community water systems with reported violations of EPA health-based standards, by type of violation, fiscal year 2017

	Population served	Percent of CWS customers
Any violation	22,119,687	7.2
Selected violations		
Stage 2 Disinfectants and Disinfection Byproducts Rules	8,347,188	2.7
Surface Water Treatment Rules	12,179,795	4
Total Coliform Rule	7,192	0.002
Arsenic	466,652	0.2
Nitrate	378,843	0.1

Coverage: U.S. residents served by community water systems (CWS) (approximately 94% of the total U.S. population).

Some CWS violated more than one of the selected rules.

Trend analysis has not been conducted because these data represent a single snapshot in time. For more information about uncertainty, variability, and statistical analysis, view the technical documentation for this indicator.

Data source: U.S. EPA, 2018a

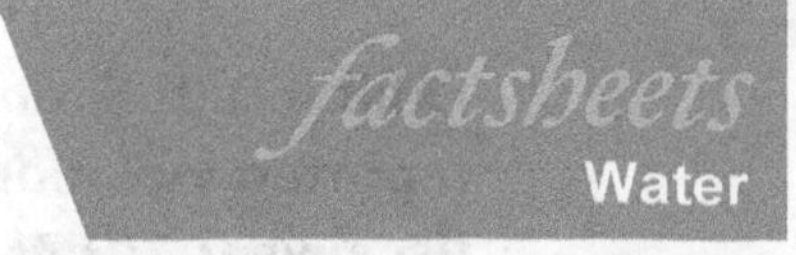

U.S. Water Supply and Distribution

Patterns of Use

All life on Earth depends on water. Human uses include drinking, bathing, crop irrigation, electricity generation, and industrial activity. For some of these uses, the available water requires treatment prior to use. Over the last century, the primary goals of water treatment have remained the same—to produce water that is biologically and chemically safe, appealing to consumers, and non-corrosive and non-scaling.

Water Uses

- In 2015, total U.S. water use was approximately 322 billion gallons per day (Bgal/d). Thermoelectric power (133 Bgal/d) and irrigation (118 Bgal/d) accounted for the largest withdrawals.[1]
- Per capita use was roughly 48% higher in western states than in eastern states in 2015, primarily due to the volume of water used for crop irrigation in the west.[1]
- In 2015, California and Texas accounted for 16% of U.S. total water withdrawals, even after reducing public-supply withdrawal by 18% and 28%, respectively, from 2010 levels.[1,2] Florida, New York and Maryland accounted for half of saline water withdrawals.[1]

Estimated Uses of Water, 2015[1]

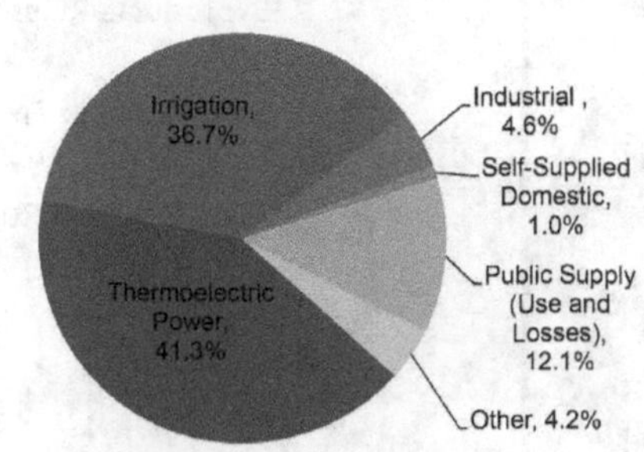

Sources of Water

- Approximately 87% of the U.S. population relied on public water supply in 2015; the remainder relies on water from domestic wells.[1]
- Surface sources account for 74% of all water withdrawals.[1]
- About 153,000 publicly owned water systems provide piped water for human consumption, of which roughly 51,000 (34%) are community water systems (CWSs).[3] 8% of all CWSs provide water to 82% of the population served.[4]
- In 2006, CWSs delivered an average of 96,000 gallons per year to each residential connection and 797,000 gallons per year to non-residential connections.[5]

Sources of Water Withdrawals, 2015[1]

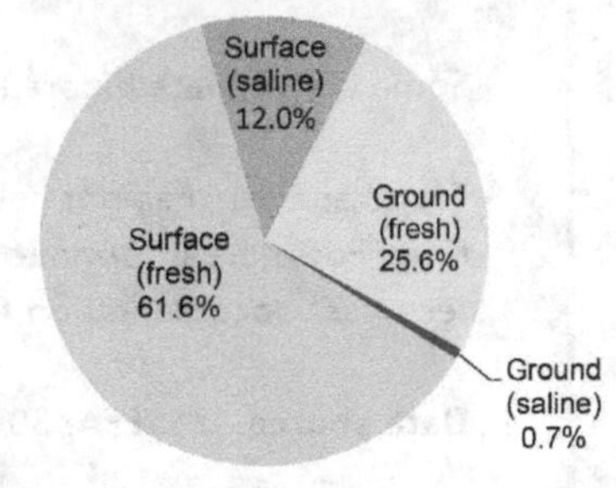

Energy Consumption

- 2% of total U.S. electricity use goes towards moving and treating water and wastewater, a 52% increase in electricity use since 1996.[4] Electricity use accounts for around 80% of municipal water processing and distribution costs.[6]
- Groundwater supply from public sources requires 2,100 kilowatt-hours per million gallons—about 31% more electricity than surface water supply, mainly due to higher raw water pumping requirements for groundwater systems.[4]
- The California State Water Project is the largest single user of energy in California, consuming 5 billion kWh per year, on average—more than 25% of the total electricity consumption for the entire state of New Mexico. In the process of delivering water from the San Francisco Bay-Delta to Southern California, the project uses 2%-3% of all electricity consumed in the state.[7]

Water Treatment

- The Safe Drinking Water Act (SDWA), enacted in 1974 and amended in 1986 and 1996, regulates contaminants in public water supplies, provides funding for infrastructure projects, protects sources of drinking water, and promotes the capacity of water systems to comply with SDWA regulations.[8]
- Typical parameters that the U.S. Environmental Protection Agency monitors for violations of drinking water standards include: microorganism, disinfectants, radionuclides, organics (e.g., volatile organic compounds and synthetic organic chemicals), and inorganics (e.g., nitrates, arsenic, radionuclides, lead, and copper).[9]
- Of all CWSs, 91% are designed to disinfect water, 23% are designed to remove or sequester iron, 13% are designed to remove or sequester manganese, and 21% are designed for corrosion control.[5]

Size Categories of Community Water Systems[3]

System Size (population served)	Number of CWSs	Population Served (millions)	% of CWSs	% of U.S. Population Served by CWSs
Very Small (25-500)	28,462	4.8	55%	2%
Small (501-3,300)	13,737	19.7	27%	7%
Medium (3,301-10,000)	4,936	28.7	10%	10%
Large (10,001-100,000)	3,802	108.8	7%	36%
Very Large (>100,000)	419	137.3	1%	46%
Total	**51,356**	**299.2**	**100%**	**100%**

For Complete Set of Factsheets visit **css.umich.edu**

Life Cycle Impacts

Total 20-Year Need, by Project Type[10]

Treatment 17.6%
Storage 10.1%
Source 4.6%
Other 1.6%
Transmission and Distribution 66.2%

Infrastructure Requirements

- The 2015 Drinking Water Infrastructure Needs Survey and Assessment found that U.S. water systems need to invest $472.6 billion over the next 20 years to continue providing clean safe drinking water.[10]
- 66% ($312.6 billion) of the total national investment need is for transmission and distribution. The remaining 34% of need is for treatment ($83.0 billion), storage ($47.6 billion), source development ($21.8 billion), and other systems ($7.5 billion).[10]
- Water systems maintain more than 2 million miles of distribution mains.[11] In 2000, nearly 80% of systems were less than 40 years old, while 4% were more than 80 years old.[12] From 2001 to 2006, over 56,000 miles of distribution mains were replaced and 225,000 miles were newly added.[5]

Electricity Requirements

- Supplying fresh water to public agencies required about 31 billion kWh of electricity in 2000.[6]
- One study projects electricity consumption to exceed 36 billion kWh by 2020 and 46 billion kWh by 2050. This increased production of electricity may result in environmental burdens, whose magnitude will depend directly on the fuel mix at generating facilities—fossil, nuclear, hydropower, solar, wind, and biomass.[6]
- Household appliances contribute greatly to the energy burden. Dishwashers, showers, and faucets require 0.312 kWh/gallon, 0.143 kWh/gallon, and 0.139 kWh/gallon, respectively.[13]

Projected Electricity Consumption, Public Water Supply[3,6]

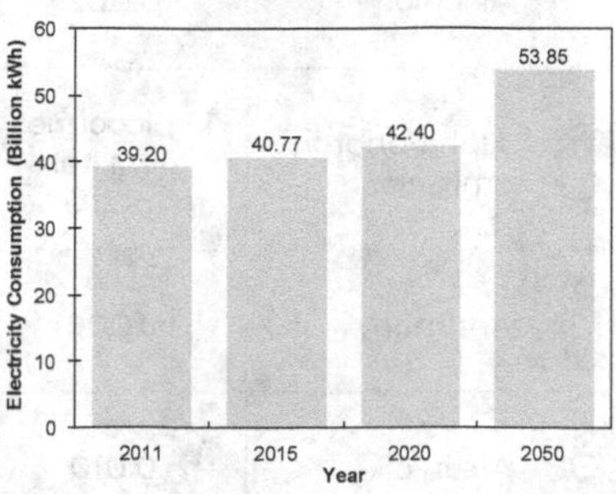

Consumptive Use

- Consumptive use is an activity that draws water from a source within a basin and returns only a portion or none of the withdrawn water to the basin. The water might have been lost to evaporation, incorporated into a product such as a beverage and shipped out of the basin, or transpired into the atmosphere through the natural action of plants and leaves.[1]
- Agriculture accounts for the largest loss of water (80-90% of total U.S. consumptive water use).[14] Of the 118 Bgal/d freshwater withdrawn for irrigation, over half is lost as a consequence of consumptive use.[1] Of the 133 Bgal/d of water withdrawn for thermoelectric power in the U.S., 3% is consumed (4.31 Bgal/d).[1]

Solutions and Sustainable Alternatives

Supply Side

- Major components that offer significant energy efficiency improvement opportunities include pumping systems, pumps, and motors.[15]
- Periodic rehabilitation, repair, and replacement of water distribution infrastructure would help improve water quality and avoid leaks.[10]
- Achieve on-site energy and chemical usage efficiency to minimize the life cycle environmental impacts related to the production and distribution of energy and chemicals used in the treatment and distribution process.
- Reduce chemical usage for treatment and sludge disposal by efficient process design, recycling of sludge, and recovery and reuse of chemicals.
- On-site energy generation from renewable sources such as solar and wind.[16]
- Effective watershed management plans to protect source water are often more cost-effective and environmentally sound than treating contaminated water. For example, NYC chose to invest between $1-1.5 billion in a watershed protection project to improve the water quality in the Catskill/Delaware watershed rather than construct a new filtration plant at a capital cost of $6-8 billion.[17]
- Less than 4% of U.S. freshwater comes from brackish or saltwater, though this segment is growing. Desalination technology, such as reverse osmosis membrane filtering, unlocks large resources, but more research is needed to lower costs, energy use, and environmental impacts.[4]

Demand Side

- Better engineering practices:
  - Plumbing fixtures to reduce water consumption, e.g., high-efficiency toilets, low-flow showerheads, and faucet aerators.[18]
  - Water reuse and recycling, e.g., graywater systems and rain barrels.[18]
  - Efficient landscape irrigation practices.[18]
- Better planning and management practices:
  - Pricing and retrofit programs.[18]
  - Proper leak detection and metering.[18]
  - Residential water audit programs and public education programs.[18]

Center Pivot Irrigation System[19]

1. Dieter, C., et al. (2018) Estimated use of water in the United States in 2015. U.S. Geological Survey Circular 1441.
2. Dieter, C. and M. Maupin. (2017) Public supply and domestic water use in the United States, 2015: U.S. Geological Survey Open-File Report.
3. U.S. Environmental Protection Agency (EPA) (2013) Fiscal Year 2011 Drinking Water and Ground Water Statistics Report.
4. Electric Power Research Institute (2013) Electricity Use and Management in the Municipal Water Supply and Wastewater Industries.
5. U.S. EPA (2009) 2006 Community Water System Survey.
6. Electric Power Research Institute, Inc. (2002) Water & Sustainability (Volume 4): U.S. Electricity Consumption for Water Supply & Treatment – The Next Half Century. Technical Report.
7. Natural Resources Defense Council (2004) Energy Down the Drain: The Hidden Costs of California's Water Supply.
8. Tiemann, M. (2017) Safe Drinking Water Act: A Summary of the Act and Its Major Requirements. Congressional Research Service.
9. U.S. EPA (2017) "Table of Regulated Drinking Water Contaminants."
10. U.S. EPA (2018) Drinking Water Infrastructure Needs Survey and Assessment – Sixth Report.
11. American Water Works Association (2017) "Disinfection and Distribution."
12. U.S. EPA (2002) Community Water System Survey 2000.
13. Abdallah, A. and D. Rosenberg (2014) Heterogeneous Residential Water and Energy Linkages and Implications for Conservation and Management. Journal of Water Resources Planning and Management, 140(3): 288-297.
14. U.S. Department of Agriculture Economic Research Service (2015) "Irrigation & Water Use Background."
15. Water Research Foundation (2011) Energy Efficiency Best Practices for North American Drinking Water Utilities.
16. U.S. EPA (2017) "Energy Efficiency for Water Utilities."
17. Chichilnisky, G. and G. Heal (1998) Economic returns from the biosphere. Nature, 391: 629-630.
18. U.S. EPA (2012) "How to conserve water and use it efficiently."
19. Photo courtesy of U.S. Department of Agriculture, Natural Resources Conservation Service.

Cite as: Center for Sustainable Systems, University of Michigan. 2018. "U.S. Water Supply and Distribution Factsheet." Pub. No. CSS05-17. **August 2018**

National Primary Drinking Water Regulations

Contaminant	MCL or TT[1] (mg/L)[2]	Potential health effects from long-term[3] exposure above the MCL	Common sources of contaminant in drinking water	Public Health Goal (mg/L)[2]
Acrylamide	TT[4]	Nervous system or blood problems; increased risk of cancer	Added to water during sewage/ wastewater treatment	zero
Alachlor	0.002	Eye, liver, kidney, or spleen problems; anemia; increased risk of cancer	Runoff from herbicide used on row crops	zero
Alpha/photon emitters	15 picocuries per Liter (pCi/L)	Increased risk of cancer	Erosion of natural deposits of certain minerals that are radioactive and may emit a form of radiation known as alpha radiation	zero
Antimony	0.006	Increase in blood cholesterol; decrease in blood sugar	Discharge from petroleum refineries; fire retardants; ceramics; electronics; solder	0.006
Arsenic	0.010	Skin damage or problems with circulatory systems, and may have increased risk of getting cancer	Erosion of natural deposits; runoff from orchards; runoff from glass & electronics production wastes	0
Asbestos (fibers >10 micrometers)	7 million fibers per Liter (MFL)	Increased risk of developing benign intestinal polyps	Decay of asbestos cement in water mains; erosion of natural deposits	7 MFL
Atrazine	0.003	Cardiovascular system or reproductive problems	Runoff from herbicide used on row crops	0.003
Barium	2	Increase in blood pressure	Discharge of drilling wastes; discharge from metal refineries; erosion of natural deposits	2
Benzene	0.005	Anemia; decrease in blood platelets; increased risk of cancer	Discharge from factories; leaching from gas storage tanks and landfills	zero
Benzo(a)pyrene (PAHs)	0.0002	Reproductive difficulties; increased risk of cancer	Leaching from linings of water storage tanks and distribution lines	zero
Beryllium	0.004	Intestinal lesions	Discharge from metal refineries and coal-burning factories; discharge from electrical, aerospace, and defense industries	0.004
Beta photon emitters	4 millirems per year	Increased risk of cancer	Decay of natural and man-made deposits of certain minerals that are radioactive and may emit forms of radiation known as photons and beta radiation	zero
Bromate	0.010	Increased risk of cancer	Byproduct of drinking water disinfection	zero
Cadmium	0.005	Kidney damage	Corrosion of galvanized pipes; erosion of natural deposits; discharge from metal refineries; runoff from waste batteries and paints	0.005
Carbofuran	0.04	Problems with blood, nervous system, or reproductive system	Leaching of soil fumigant used on rice and alfalfa	0.04

LEGEND

DISINFECTANT

DISINFECTION BYPRODUCT

INORGANIC CHEMICAL

MICROORGANISM

ORGANIC CHEMICAL

RADIONUCLIDES

National Primary Drinking Water Regulations

EPA 816-F-09-004 | MAY 2009

Contaminant	MCL or TT[1] (mg/L)[2]	Potential health effects from long-term[3] exposure above the MCL	Common sources of contaminant in drinking water	Public Health Goal (mg/L)[2]
Carbon tetrachloride	0.005	Liver problems; increased risk of cancer	Discharge from chemical plants and other industrial activities	zero
Chloramines (as Cl_2)	MRDL=4.0[1]	Eye/nose irritation; stomach discomfort; anemia	Water additive used to control microbes	MRDLG=4[1]
Chlordane	0.002	Liver or nervous system problems; increased risk of cancer	Residue of banned termiticide	zero
Chlorine (as Cl_2)	MRDL=4.0[1]	Eye/nose irritation; stomach discomfort	Water additive used to control microbes	MRDLG=4[1]
Chlorine dioxide (as ClO_2)	MRDL=0.8[1]	Anemia; infants, young children, and fetuses of pregnant women: nervous system effects	Water additive used to control microbes	MRDLG=0.8[1]
Chlorite	1.0	Anemia; infants, young children, and fetuses of pregnant women: nervous system effects	Byproduct of drinking water disinfection	0.8
Chlorobenzene	0.1	Liver or kidney problems	Discharge from chemical and agricultural chemical factories	0.1
Chromium (total)	0.1	Allergic dermatitis	Discharge from steel and pulp mills; erosion of natural deposits	0.1
Copper	TT[5]; Action Level=1.3	Short-term exposure: Gastrointestinal distress. Long-term exposure: Liver or kidney damage. People with Wilson's Disease should consult their personal doctor if the amount of copper in their water exceeds the action level	Corrosion of household plumbing systems; erosion of natural deposits	1.3
Cryptosporidium	TT[7]	Short-term exposure: Gastrointestinal illness (e.g., diarrhea, vomiting, cramps)	Human and animal fecal waste	zero
Cyanide (as free cyanide)	0.2	Nerve damage or thyroid problems	Discharge from steel/metal factories; discharge from plastic and fertilizer factories	0.2
2,4-D	0.07	Kidney, liver, or adrenal gland problems	Runoff from herbicide used on row crops	0.07
Dalapon	0.2	Minor kidney changes	Runoff from herbicide used on rights of way	0.2
1,2-Dibromo-3-chloropropane (DBCP)	0.0002	Reproductive difficulties; increased risk of cancer	Runoff/leaching from soil fumigant used on soybeans, cotton, pineapples, and orchards	zero
o-Dichlorobenzene	0.6	Liver, kidney, or circulatory system problems	Discharge from industrial chemical factories	0.6
p-Dichlorobenzene	0.075	Anemia; liver, kidney, or spleen damage; changes in blood	Discharge from industrial chemical factories	0.075
1,2-Dichloroethane	0.005	Increased risk of cancer	Discharge from industrial chemical factories	zero

LEGEND

DISINFECTANT

DISINFECTION BYPRODUCT

INORGANIC CHEMICAL

MICROORGANISM

ORGANIC CHEMICAL

RADIONUCLIDES

National Primary Drinking Water Regulations

EPA 816-F-09-004 | MAY 2009

Contaminant	MCL or TT[1] (mg/L)[2]	Potential health effects from long-term[3] exposure above the MCL	Common sources of contaminant in drinking water	Public Health Goal (mg/L)[2]
1,1-Dichloroethylene	0.007	Liver problems	Discharge from industrial chemical factories	**0.007**
cis-1,2-Dichloroethylene	0.07	Liver problems	Discharge from industrial chemical factories	**0.07**
trans-1,2, Dichloroethylene	0.1	Liver problems	Discharge from industrial chemical factories	**0.1**
Dichloromethane	0.005	Liver problems; increased risk of cancer	Discharge from industrial chemical factories	**zero**
1,2-Dichloropropane	0.005	Increased risk of cancer	Discharge from industrial chemical factories	**zero**
Di(2-ethylhexyl) adipate	0.4	Weight loss, liver problems, or possible reproductive difficulties	Discharge from chemical factories	**0.4**
Di(2-ethylhexyl) phthalate	0.006	Reproductive difficulties; liver problems; increased risk of cancer	Discharge from rubber and chemical factories	**zero**
Dinoseb	0.007	Reproductive difficulties	Runoff from herbicide used on soybeans and vegetables	**0.007**
Dioxin (2,3,7,8-TCDD)	0.00000003	Reproductive difficulties; increased risk of cancer	Emissions from waste incineration and other combustion; discharge from chemical factories	**zero**
Diquat	0.02	Cataracts	Runoff from herbicide use	**0.02**
Endothall	0.1	Stomach and intestinal problems	Runoff from herbicide use	**0.1**
Endrin	0.002	Liver problems	Residue of banned insecticide	**0.002**
Epichlorohydrin	TT[4]	Increased cancer risk; stomach problems	Discharge from industrial chemical factories; an impurity of some water treatment chemicals	**zero**
Ethylbenzene	0.7	Liver or kidney problems	Discharge from petroleum refineries	**0.7**
Ethylene dibromide	0.00005	Problems with liver, stomach, reproductive system, or kidneys; increased risk of cancer	Discharge from petroleum refineries	**zero**
Fecal coliform and *E. coli*	MCL[6]	Fecal coliforms and *E. coli* are bacteria whose presence indicates that the water may be contaminated with human or animal wastes. Microbes in these wastes may cause short term effects, such as diarrhea, cramps, nausea, headaches, or other symptoms. They may pose a special health risk for infants, young children, and people with severely compromised immune systems.	Human and animal fecal waste	**zero[6]**

LEGEND

DISINFECTANT

DISINFECTION BYPRODUCT

INORGANIC CHEMICAL

MICROORGANISM

ORGANIC CHEMICAL

RADIONUCLIDES

National Primary Drinking Water Regulations

EPA 816-F-09-004 | MAY 2009

Contaminant	MCL or TT[1] (mg/L)[2]	Potential health effects from long-term[3] exposure above the MCL	Common sources of contaminant in drinking water	Public Health Goal (mg/L)[2]
Fluoride	4.0	Bone disease (pain and tenderness of the bones); children may get mottled teeth	Water additive which promotes strong teeth; erosion of natural deposits; discharge from fertilizer and aluminum factories	**4.0**
Giardia lamblia	TT[7]	Short-term exposure: Gastrointestinal illness (e.g., diarrhea, vomiting, cramps)	Human and animal fecal waste	**zero**
Glyphosate	0.7	Kidney problems; reproductive difficulties	Runoff from herbicide use	**0.7**
Haloacetic acids (HAA5)	0.060	Increased risk of cancer	Byproduct of drinking water disinfection	**n/a[9]**
Heptachlor	0.0004	Liver damage; increased risk of cancer	Residue of banned termiticide	**zero**
Heptachlor epoxide	0.0002	Liver damage; increased risk of cancer	Breakdown of heptachlor	**zero**
Heterotrophic plate count (HPC)	TT[7]	HPC has no health effects; it is an analytic method used to measure the variety of bacteria that are common in water. The lower the concentration of bacteria in drinking water, the better maintained the water system is.	HPC measures a range of bacteria that are naturally present in the environment	**n/a**
Hexachlorobenzene	0.001	Liver or kidney problems; reproductive difficulties; increased risk of cancer	Discharge from metal refineries and agricultural chemical factories	**zero**
Hexachloro-cyclopentadiene	0.05	Kidney or stomach problems	Discharge from chemical factories	**0.05**
Lead	TT[5]; Action Level=0.015	Infants and children: Delays in physical or mental development; children could show slight deficits in attention span and learning abilities; Adults: Kidney problems; high blood pressure	Corrosion of household plumbing systems; erosion of natural deposits	**zero**
Legionella	TT[7]	Legionnaire's Disease, a type of pneumonia	Found naturally in water; multiplies in heating systems	**zero**
Lindane	0.0002	Liver or kidney problems	Runoff/leaching from insecticide used on cattle, lumber, and gardens	**0.0002**
Mercury (inorganic)	0.002	Kidney damage	Erosion of natural deposits; discharge from refineries and factories; runoff from landfills and croplands	**0.002**
Methoxychlor	0.04	Reproductive difficulties	Runoff/leaching from insecticide used on fruits, vegetables, alfalfa, and livestock	**0.04**
Nitrate (measured as Nitrogen)	10	Infants below the age of six months who drink water containing nitrate in excess of the MCL could become seriously ill and, if untreated, may die. Symptoms include shortness of breath and blue-baby syndrome.	Runoff from fertilizer use; leaching from septic tanks, sewage; erosion of natural deposits	**10**

LEGEND

DISINFECTANT

DISINFECTION BYPRODUCT

INORGANIC CHEMICAL

MICROORGANISM

ORGANIC CHEMICAL

RADIONUCLIDES

National Primary Drinking Water Regulations

EPA 816-F-09-004 | MAY 2009

Contaminant	MCL or TT[1] (mg/L)[2]	Potential health effects from long-term[3] exposure above the MCL	Common sources of contaminant in drinking water	Public Health Goal (mg/L)[2]
Nitrite (measured as Nitrogen)	1	Infants below the age of six months who drink water containing nitrite in excess of the MCL could become seriously ill and, if untreated, may die. Symptoms include shortness of breath and blue-baby syndrome.	Runoff from fertilizer use; leaching from septic tanks, sewage; erosion of natural deposits	1
Oxamyl (Vydate)	0.2	Slight nervous system effects	Runoff/leaching from insecticide used on apples, potatoes, and tomatoes	0.2
Pentachlorophenol	0.001	Liver or kidney problems; increased cancer risk	Discharge from wood-preserving factories	zero
Picloram	0.5	Liver problems	Herbicide runoff	0.5
Polychlorinated biphenyls (PCBs)	0.0005	Skin changes; thymus gland problems; immune deficiencies; reproductive or nervous system difficulties; increased risk of cancer	Runoff from landfills; discharge of waste chemicals	zero
Radium 226 and Radium 228 (combined)	5 pCi/L	Increased risk of cancer	Erosion of natural deposits	zero
Selenium	0.05	Hair or fingernail loss; numbness in fingers or toes; circulatory problems	Discharge from petroleum and metal refineries; erosion of natural deposits; discharge from mines	0.05
Simazine	0.004	Problems with blood	Herbicide runoff	0.004
Styrene	0.1	Liver, kidney, or circulatory system problems	Discharge from rubber and plastic factories; leaching from landfills	0.1
Tetrachloroethylene	0.005	Liver problems; increased risk of cancer	Discharge from factories and dry cleaners	zero
Thallium	0.002	Hair loss; changes in blood; kidney, intestine, or liver problems	Leaching from ore-processing sites; discharge from electronics, glass, and drug factories	0.0005
Toluene	1	Nervous system, kidney, or liver problems	Discharge from petroleum factories	1
Total Coliforms	5.0 percent[8]	Coliforms are bacteria that indicate that other, potentially harmful bacteria may be present. See fecal coliforms and *E. coli*	Naturally present in the environment	zero
Total Trihalomethanes (TTHMs)	0.080	Liver, kidney, or central nervous system problems; increased risk of cancer	Byproduct of drinking water disinfection	n/a[9]
Toxaphene	0.003	Kidney, liver, or thyroid problems; increased risk of cancer	Runoff/leaching from insecticide used on cotton and cattle	zero
2,4,5-TP (Silvex)	0.05	Liver problems	Residue of banned herbicide	0.05
1,2,4-Trichlorobenzene	0.07	Changes in adrenal glands	Discharge from textile finishing factories	0.07

LEGEND

DISINFECTANT

DISINFECTION BYPRODUCT

INORGANIC CHEMICAL

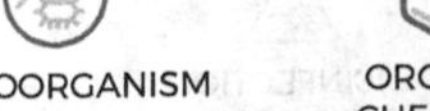
MICROORGANISM

ORGANIC CHEMICAL

RADIONUCLIDES

National Primary Drinking Water Regulations — EPA 816-F-09-004 | MAY 2009

Contaminant	MCL or TT[1] (mg/L)[2]	Potential health effects from long-term[3] exposure above the MCL	Common sources of contaminant in drinking water	Public Health Goal (mg/L)[2]
1,1,1-Trichloroethane	0.2	Liver, nervous system, or circulatory problems	Discharge from metal degreasing sites and other factories	**0.2**
1,1,2-Trichloroethane	0.005	Liver, kidney, or immune system problems	Discharge from industrial chemical factories	**0.003**
Trichloroethylene	0.005	Liver problems; increased risk of cancer	Discharge from metal degreasing sites and other factories	**zero**
Turbidity	TT[7]	Turbidity is a measure of the cloudiness of water. It is used to indicate water quality and filtration effectiveness (e.g., whether disease-causing organisms are present). Higher turbidity levels are often associated with higher levels of disease-causing microorganisms such as viruses, parasites, and some bacteria. These organisms can cause short term symptoms such as nausea, cramps, diarrhea, and associated headaches.	Soil runoff	**n/a**
Uranium	30µg/L	Increased risk of cancer, kidney toxicity	Erosion of natural deposits	**zero**
Vinyl chloride	0.002	Increased risk of cancer	Leaching from PVC pipes; discharge from plastic factories	**zero**
Viruses (enteric)	TT[7]	Short-term exposure: Gastrointestinal illness (e.g., diarrhea, vomiting, cramps)	Human and animal fecal waste	**zero**
Xylenes (total)	10	Nervous system damage	Discharge from petroleum factories; discharge from chemical factories	**10**

LEGEND

DISINFECTANT

DISINFECTION BYPRODUCT

INORGANIC CHEMICAL

MICROORGANISM

ORGANIC CHEMICAL

RADIONUCLIDES

NOTES

1 Definitions

- **Maximum Contaminant Level Goal (MCLG):** The level of a contaminant in drinking water below which there is no known or expected risk to health. MCLGs allow for a margin of safety and are non-enforceable public health goals.
- **Maximum Contaminant Level (MCL):** The highest level of a contaminant that is allowed in drinking water. MCLs are set as close to MCLGs as feasible using the best available treatment technology and taking cost into consideration. MCLs are enforceable standards.
- **Maximum Residual Disinfectant Level Goal (MRDLG):** The level of a drinking water disinfectant below which there is no known or expected risk to health. MRDLGs do not reflect the benefits of the use of disinfectants to control microbial contaminants.
- **Maximum Residual Disinfectant Level (MRDL):** The highest level of a disinfectant allowed in drinking water. There is convincing evidence that addition of a disinfectant is necessary for control of microbial contaminants.
- **Treatment Technique (TT):** A required process intended to reduce the level of a contaminant in drinking water.

2 Units are in milligrams per liter (mg/L) unless otherwise noted. Milligrams per liter are equivalent to parts per million (ppm).

3 Health effects are from long-term exposure unless specified as short-term exposure.

4 Each water system must certify annually, in writing, to the state (using third-party or manufacturers certification) that when it uses acrylamide and/or epichlorohydrin to treat water, the combination (or product) of dose and monomer level does not exceed the levels specified, as follows: Acrylamide = 0.05 percent dosed at 1 mg/L (or equivalent); Epichlorohydrin = 0.01 percent dosed at 20 mg/L (or equivalent).

5 Lead and copper are regulated by a Treatment Technique that requires systems to control the corrosiveness of their water. If more than 10 percent of tap water samples exceed the action level, water systems must take additional steps. For copper, the action level is 1.3 mg/L, and for lead is 0.015 mg/L.

6 A routine sample that is fecal coliform-positive or E. coli-positive triggers repeat samples--if any repeat sample is total coliform-positive, the system has an acute MCL violation. A routine sample that is total coliform-positive and fecal coliform-negative or E. coli-negative triggers repeat samples--if any repeat sample is fecal coliform-positive or E. coli-positive, the system has an acute MCL violation. See also Total Coliforms.

7 EPA's surface water treatment rules require systems using surface water or ground water under the direct influence of surface water to (1) disinfect their water, and (2) filter their water or meet criteria for avoiding filtration so that the following contaminants are controlled at the following levels:

- ***Cryptosporidium*:** 99 percent removal for systems that filter. Unfiltered systems are required to include Cryptosporidium in their existing watershed control provisions.
- **Giardia lamblia:** 99.9 percent removal/inactivation
- **Viruses:** 99.9 percent removal/inactivation
- ***Legionella*:** No limit, but EPA believes that if *Giardia* and viruses are removed/inactivated, according to the treatment techniques in the surface water treatment rule, *Legionella* will also be controlled.
- **Turbidity:** For systems that use conventional or direct filtration, at no time can turbidity (cloudiness of water) go higher than 1 nephelometric turbidity unit (NTU), and samples for turbidity must be less than or equal to 0.3 NTU in at least 95 percent of the samples in any month. Systems that use filtration other than the conventional or direct filtration must follow state limits, which must include turbidity at no time exceeding 5 NTU.
- **HPC:** No more than 500 bacterial colonies per milliliter
- **Long Term 1 Enhanced Surface Water Treatment:** Surface water systems or ground water systems under the direct influence of surface water serving fewer than 10,000 people must comply with the applicable Long Term 1 Enhanced Surface Water Treatment Rule provisions (e.g. turbidity standards, individual filter monitoring, *Cryptosporidium* removal requirements, updated watershed control requirements for unfiltered systems).
- **Long Term 2 Enhanced Surface Water Treatment:** This rule applies to all surface water systems or ground water systems under the direct influence of surface water. The rule targets additional *Cryptosporidium* treatment requirements for higher risk systems and includes provisions to reduce risks from uncovered finished water storages facilities and to ensure that the systems maintain microbial protection as they take steps to reduce the formation of disinfection byproducts. (Monitoring start dates are staggered by system size. The largest systems (serving at least 100,000 people) will begin monitoring in October 2006 and the smallest systems (serving fewer than 10,000 people) will not begin monitoring until October 2008. After completing monitoring and determining their treatment bin, systems generally have three years to comply with any additional treatment requirements.)
- **Filter Backwash Recycling:** The Filter Backwash Recycling Rule requires systems that recycle to return specific recycle flows through all processes of the system's existing conventional or direct filtration system or at an alternate location approved by the state.

8 No more than 5.0 percent samples total coliform-positive in a month. (For water systems that collect fewer than 40 routine samples per month, no more than one sample can be total coliform-positive per month.) Every sample that has total coliform must be analyzed for either fecal coliforms or E. coli. If two consecutive TC-positive samples, and one is also positive for E. coli or fecal coliforms, system has an acute MCL violation.

9 Although there is no collective MCLG for this contaminant group, there are individual MCLGs for some of the individual contaminants:

- **Haloacetic acids:** dichloroacetic acid (zero); trichloroacetic acid (0.3 mg/L)
- **Trihalomethanes:** bromodichloromethane (zero); bromoform (zero); dibromochloromethane (0.06 mg/L)

NATIONAL SECONDARY DRINKING WATER REGULATION

National Secondary Drinking Water Regulations are non-enforceable guidelines regarding contaminants that may cause cosmetic effects (such as skin or tooth discoloration) or aesthetic effects (such as taste, odor, or color) in drinking water. EPA recommends secondary standards to water systems but does not require systems to comply. However, some states may choose to adopt them as enforceable standards.

Contaminant	Secondary Maximum Contaminant Level
Aluminum	0.05 to 0.2 mg/L
Chloride	250 mg/L
Color	15 (color units)
Copper	1.0 mg/L
Corrosivity	Noncorrosive
Fluoride	2.0 mg/L
Foaming Agents	0.5 mg/L
Iron	0.3 mg/L
Manganese	0.05 mg/L
Odor	3 threshold odor number
pH	6.5-8.5
Silver	0.10 mg/L
Sulfate	250 mg/L
Total Dissolved Solids	500 mg/L
Zinc	5 mg/L

FOR MORE INFORMATION ON EPA'S SAFE DRINKING WATER:

visit: **epa.gov/safewater**

call: **(800) 426-4791**

ADDITIONAL INFORMATION:

To order additional posters or other ground water and drinking water publications, please contact the National Service Center for Environmental Publications at: **(800) 490-9198**, or email: **nscep@bps-lmit.com**.

OFFICE OF GROUND WATER AND DRINKING WATER

2014 Water Fluoridation Statistics

These statistics were prepared using water system data reported by states to the CDC Water Fluoridation Reporting System as of December 31, 2014, and the US Census Bureau state population estimates for 2014.

National Water Fluoridation Statistics

Total US population, persons[a]	318,857,056
US population on community water systems (CWS), persons[b]	286,756,186
Total US population on fluoridated drinking water systems, persons[b]	214,213,860
Percentage of US population receiving fluoridated water[c]	67.2%
Percentage of US population on CWS receiving fluoridated water[d]	74.7%
Number of CWS providing fluoridated water[b]	19,089
Number of CWS adjusting fluoride[b]	5,956
Number of CWS consecutive to systems with optimal fluoride levels[b]	6,930
Number of CWS with naturally occurring fluoride at or above optimal levels[b,e]	6,151
Population served by CWS with naturally occurring fluoride at or above optimal levels[b,e]	11,914,156

State Fluoridation Percentage Calculations and States Ranked by Fluoridation Percentage

State	Persons receiving fluoridated water	Persons served by CWS	%	Rank
United States	214,213,860	286,756,186	74.7%	
Alabama[f]	3,812,180	4,849,377	78.6%	23
Alaska	339,415	685,165	49.5%	43
Arizona[f]	3,199,068	5,536,324	57.8%	38
Arkansas	1,986,099	2,809,741	70.7%	31
California[f]	24,699,693	38,802,500	63.7%	35
Colorado	3,963,053	5,355,866	74.0%	28

Connecticut[f]	2,409,333	2,691,768	89.5%	14
Delaware	712,420	818,110	87.1%	19
District of Columbia[f]	595,000	595,000	100.0%	
Florida	13,309,950	17,161,354	77.6%	24
Georgia[f]	9,721,504	10,097,343	96.3%	6
Hawaii	166,650	1,419,516	11.7%	50
Idaho[f]	390,344	1,220,794	32.0%	47
Illinois	12,687,788	12,880,580	98.5%	3
Indiana[f]	4,388,330	4,582,546	94.7%	8
Iowa	2,577,587	2,780,685	92.7%	11
Kansas[f]	1,716,415	2,693,999	63.7%	34
Kentucky	4,388,383	4,393,871	99.9%	1
Louisiana[f]	2,021,233	4,649,676	43.5%	45
Maine	527,163	666,228	79.1%	21
Maryland[f]	5,029,321	5,214,672	96.4%	5
Massachusetts	4,750,952	6,745,408	70.4%	32
Michigan[f]	7,579,494	8,264,474	91.7%	13
Minnesota	4,165,301	4,215,391	98.8%	2
Mississippi[f]	1,795,154	2,994,079	60.0%	37
Missouri	4,013,047	5,236,187	76.6%	26
Montana[f]	265,783	788,805	33.7%	46
Nebraska	1,020,358	1,425,930	71.6%	30
Nevada[f]	1,873,848	2,544,079	73.7%	29
New Hampshire	406,336	872,864	46.6%	44
New Jersey[f]	1,222,597	8,311,417	14.7%	49
New Mexico	1,210,877	1,571,600	77.0%	25
New York[f]	15,006,168	19,746,227	76.0%	27
North Carolina	6,190,022	7,077,809	87.5%	18
North Dakota[f]	617,110	638,166	96.7%	4
Ohio	9,806,835	10,587,923	92.6%	12
Oklahoma[f]	2,235,367	3,576,005	62.5%	36

Oregon	833,557	3,688,540	22.6%	48
Pennsylvania[f]	5,943,890	10,869,278	54.7%	41
Rhode Island	902,170	1,055,173	85.5%	20
South Carolina[f]	3,488,316	3,737,053	93.3%	10
South Dakota	647,954	692,042	93.6%	9
Tennessee[f]	5,133,626	5,829,529	88.1%	17
Texas	19,924,236	25,230,638	79.0%	22
Utah[f]	1,384,638	2,676,475	51.7%	42
Vermont	254,700	453,736	56.1%	40
Virginia[f]	6,213,102	6,486,523	95.8%	7
Washington	3,530,835	5,525,840	63.9%	33
West Virginia[f]	1,369,124	1,532,138	89.4%	15
Wisconsin	3,581,184	4,028,474	88.9%	16
Wyoming[f]	256,350	449,223	57.1%	39

Footnotes

a. Census Population Count 2014. Annual Estimates of the Population for the United States, Regions, States, and Puerto Rico: April 1, 2010, to July 1, 2014, (NST-EST2012-01). Source: US Census Bureau, Population Division. Release Date: December 2014. Available at http://www.census.gov/popest/data/state/totals/2014/index.html.

b. Reported in CDC Water Fluoridation Reporting System (WFRS). For purposes of this report, a water system is considered a community water system if so designated by the state drinking water administrator in accordance with the regulatory requirements of the US Environmental Protection Agency. In general, public water systems provide water for human consumption through pipes or other constructed conveyances to at least 15 service connections, or serve an average of at least 25 people for at least 60 days a year. A community water system is a public water system that supplies water to the same population year-round. Available at http://water.epa.gov/infrastructure/drinkingwater/pws/factoids.cfm.

c. Fluoridated population divided by total population.

d. Fluoridated population divided by population served by community water systems.

e. The increase from 2012 to 2014 in the population served by CWS with naturally occurring fluoride at or above optimal levels likely resulted from inclusion, for the first time, of the number of persons served by these systems in California as reported in WFRS. The total number of persons receiving fluoridated water in California was based on state data and may not fully reflect this increase derived from WFRS data.

f. Population served by CWS exceeded the US Census state population estimate; number of people was reduced by the ratio of the population estimate to the CWS population estimate.

g. Complete data were not available from WFRS; state provided additional information.

Delisted Species

Common name	Scientific name	Description	Date species first listed	Date species delisted	Reason delisted
Aleutian Canada goose	Branta canadensis leucopareia	Wherever found	3/11/1967	3/20/2001	Recovery
American alligator	Alligator mississippiensis	Wherever found	3/11/1967	6/4/1987	Recovery
American peregrine falcon	Falco peregrinus anatum	Wherever found	6/2/1970	8/25/1999	Recovery
Amistad gambusia	Gambusia amistadensis	Wherever found	4/30/1980	12/4/1987	Extinction
Arctic peregrine falcon	Falco peregrinus tundrius	Wherever found	6/2/1970	10/5/1994	Recovery
Arizona agave	Agave arizonica	-	5/18/1984	6/19/2006	Not a listable entity
Bahama swallowtail butterfly	Heraclides andraemon bonhotei	Wherever found	4/28/1976	8/31/1984	Act amendment
Bald eagle	Haliaeetus leucocephalus	Lower 48 states	3/11/1967	8/8/2007	Recovery
Black-capped Vireo	Vireo atricapilla	Wherever found	10/6/1987	5/16/2018	Recovery
Blue pike	Stizostedion vitreum glaucum	Wherever found	3/11/1967	9/2/1983	Extinction
Brown pelican	Pelecanus occidentalis	Ex. U.S. Atlantic coast, FL, AL	6/2/1970	12/17/2009	Recovery
Brown pelican	Pelecanus occidentalis	U.S. Atlantic coast, FL, AL	6/2/1970	2/4/1985	Recovery
Cactus ferruginous pygmy-owl	Glaucidium brasilianum cactorum	AZ pop.	3/10/1997	4/14/2006	Not a listable entity
Caribbean monk seal	Monachus tropicalis	Wherever found	4/10/1979	10/28/2008	Extinction
Coastal cutthroat trout	Oncorhynchus clarkii clarkii	Umpqua R.	9/13/1996	4/26/2000	Taxonomic revision
Columbian white-tailed deer	Odocoileus virginianus leucurus	Douglas County DPS	3/11/1967	7/24/2003	Recovery
Concho water snake	Nerodia paucimaculata	Wherever found	9/3/1986	11/28/2011	Recovery
Cuneate bidens	Bidens cuneata	Wherever found	2/17/1984	2/6/1996	Taxonomic revision
Delmarva Peninsula fox squirrel	Sciurus niger cinereus	Wherever found, except where listed as an experimental pop.	3/11/1967	12/16/2015	Recovery
Deseret milkvetch	Astragalus desereticus	Wherever found	10/20/1999	11/19/2018	Recovery
Dismal Swamp southeastern shrew	Sorex longirostris fisheri	Wherever found	9/26/1986	2/28/2000	New info. discovered
Dusky seaside sparrow	Ammodramus maritimus nigrescens	Wherever found	3/11/1967	12/12/1990	Extinction
Eastern gray kangaroo	Macropus giganteus	Wherever found	12/30/1974	3/9/1995	Recovery
Eastern puma (=cougar)	Puma (=Felis) concolor couguar	Wherever found	6/4/1973	1/23/2018	Extinction
Eggert's sunflower	Helianthus eggertii	Wherever found	5/22/1997	8/18/2005	Recovery
Eureka Valley evening-primrose	Oenothera avita ssp. eurekensis	-	5/27/1978	3/29/2018	Recovery
Gray whale	Eschrichtius robustus	Except where listed	6/16/1994	6/16/1994	Recovery
Gray wolf	Canis lupus	Northern Rocky Mountain DPS	3/9/1978	5/1/2017	Recovery
Guam broadbill	Myiagra freycineti	Wherever found	8/27/1984	2/23/2004	Extinction
Hidden Lake bluecurls	Trichostema austromontanum ssp. compactum	Wherever found	10/14/1998	7/2/2018	Recovery
Hoover's woolly-star	Eriastrum hooveri	-	7/19/1990	10/7/2003	Recovery, new info.
Hualapai Mexican vole	Microtus mexicanus hualpaiensis	Wherever found	10/1/1987	6/23/2017	Not a listable entity
Humpback whale	Megaptera novaeangliae	Southeastern Pacific DPS	6/2/1970	10/11/2016	Recovery
Humpback whale	Megaptera novaeangliae	West Indies DPS	6/2/1970	10/11/2016	Recovery
Humpback whale	Megaptera novaeangliae	Hawaii DPS	6/2/1970	10/11/2016	Recovery
Humpback whale	Megaptera novaeangliae	Brazil DPS	6/2/1970	10/11/2016	Recovery
Humpback whale	Megaptera novaeangliae	Gabon/SW Africa DPS	6/2/1970	10/11/2016	Recovery
Humpback whale	Megaptera novaeangliae	SE Africa/Madagascar DPS	6/2/1970	10/11/2016	Recovery
Humpback whale	Megaptera novaeangliae	West Australia DPS	6/2/1970	10/11/2016	Recovery
Humpback whale	Megaptera novaeangliae	East Australia DPS	6/2/1970	10/11/2016	Recovery
Humpback whale	Megaptera novaeangliae	Oceania DPS	6/2/1970	10/11/2016	Recovery
Idaho springsnail	Pyrgulopsis idahoensis	Wherever found	12/14/1992	9/5/2007	Taxonomic revision
Indian flap-shelled turtle	Lissemys punctata punctata	Wherever found	6/14/1970	2/29/1984	Erroneous data
Island night lizard	Xantusia riversiana	Wherever found	9/12/1977	4/1/2014	Recovery
Johnston's frankenia	Frankenia johnstonii	Wherever found	8/7/1984	2/11/2016	Recovery
Lake Erie water snake	Nerodia sipedon insularum	Subspecies range clarified	8/30/1999	9/15/2011	Recovery
Lesser long-nosed bat	Leptonycteris curasoae yerbabuenae	Wherever found	9/30/1988	5/18/2018	Recovery
Lloyd's hedgehog cactus	Echinocereus lloydii	Wherever found	11/28/1979	6/24/1999	Not a listable entity
Longjaw cisco	Coregonus alpenae	Wherever found	3/11/1967	9/2/1983	Extinction
Louisiana black bear	Ursus americanus luteolus	Wherever found	1/7/1992	3/11/2016	Recovery
Magazine Mountain shagreen	Inflectarius magazinensis	Wherever found	4/17/1989	6/14/2013	Recovery
Maguire daisy	Erigeron maguirei	Wherever found	9/5/1985	2/18/2011	Recovery
Mariana mallard	Anas oustaleti	Wherever found	12/8/1977	2/23/2004	Extinction
Mckittrick pennyroyal	Hedeoma apiculatum	Wherever found	7/13/1982	9/22/1993	New info. discovered
Mexican duck	Anas diazi	U.S.A. only	3/11/1967	7/25/1978	Taxonomic revision

Common name	Scientific name	Description	Date species first listed	Date species delisted	Reason delisted
Modoc Sucker	Catostomus microps	Wherever found	6/11/1985	1/7/2016	Recovery
Morelet's crocodile	Crocodylus moreletii	Wherever found	6/2/1970	5/23/2012	Recovery
No common name	Gahnia lanaiensis	Wherever found	9/20/1991	5/28/2013	Taxonomic revision
Oregon chub	Oregonichthys crameri	Wherever found	10/18/1993	3/23/2015	Recovery
Palau Owl	Pyrroglaux podargina	Wherever found	6/2/1970	9/12/1985	Recovery
Palau fantail flycatcher	Rhipidura lepida	Wherever found	6/2/1970	9/12/1985	Recovery
Palau ground dove	Gallicolumba canifrons	Wherever found	6/2/1970	9/12/1985	Recovery
Pine barrens treefrog	Hyla andersonii	FL pop.	12/18/1977	11/22/1983	New info. discovered
Purple-spined Hedgehog cactus	Echinocereus engelmannii var. purpureus	-	10/11/1979	11/27/1989	Taxonomic revision
Red kangaroo	Macropus rufus	Wherever found	12/30/1974	3/9/1995	Recovery
Robbins' cinquefoil	Potentilla robbinsiana	Wherever found	9/17/1980	8/27/2002	Recovery
Rydberg milk-vetch	Astragalus perianus	-	5/27/1978	9/14/1989	New info. discovered
Sampson's pearlymussel	Epioblasma sampsoni	Wherever found	6/14/1976	1/9/1984	Extinction
San Miguel Island fox	Urocyon littoralis littoralis	Wherever found	3/5/2004	9/12/2016	Recovery
Santa Barbara song sparrow	Melospiza melodia graminea	Wherever found	6/4/1973	10/12/1983	Extinction
Santa Cruz Island fox	Urocyon littoralis santacruzae	Wherever found	3/5/2004	9/12/2016	Recovery
Santa Rosa Island fox	Urocyon littoralis santarosae	Wherever found	3/5/2004	9/12/2016	Recovery
Scarlet-chested parakeet	Neophema splendida	Wherever found	12/2/1970	5/5/2017	Recovery
Spineless hedgehog cactus	Echinocereus triglochidiatus var. inermis	-	12/7/1979	9/22/1993	Not a listable entity
Steller sea lion	Eumetopias jubatus	Eastern DPS	4/5/1990	12/4/2013	Recovery
Tecopa pupfish	Cyprinodon nevadensis calidae	Wherever found	10/13/1970	1/15/1982	Extinction
Tennessee purple coneflower	Echinacea tennesseensis	Wherever found	7/5/1979	9/2/2011	Recovery
Tinian Monarch (old world flycatcher)	Monarcha takatsukasae	Wherever found	6/2/1970	9/21/2004	Recovery
Truckee Barberry	Berberis (=Mahonia) sonnei	-	12/6/1979	10/1/2003	Taxonomic revision
Tumamoc globeberry	Tumamoca macdougalii	Wherever found	4/29/1986	6/18/1993	New info. discovered
Turquoise parakeet	Neophema pulchella	Wherever found	6/2/1970	5/5/2017	Recovery
Utah valvata snail	Valvata utahensis	Wherever found	12/14/1992	9/24/2010	New info. discovered
Virginia northern flying squirrel	Glaucomys sabrinus fuscus	Wherever found	7/31/1985	3/4/2013	Recovery
Western gray kangaroo	Macropus fuliginosus	Wherever found	12/30/1974	3/9/1995	Recovery
White-haired goldenrod	Solidago albopilosa	Wherever found	4/7/1988	10/11/2016	Recovery

Notes: *Data as of July 2, 2019*
Source: *U.S. Fish & Wildlife Service, Threatened and Endangered Species System (TESS)*

Summary of Listed Species, Listed Populations[1] and Recovery Plans[2]

Group	United States[3]		Foreign		Total listings (U.S. and foreign)	U.S. listings with active recovery plans[2]
	Endangered	Threatened	Endangered	Threatened		
Animals						
Amphibians	21	15	8	1	45	23
Annelid Worms	0	0	0	0	0	0
Arachnids	12	0	5	0	17	12
Birds	80	21	218	20	339	85
Clams	76	15	2	0	93	72
Corals	0	7	3	15	25	0
Crustaceans	24	4	0	0	28	19
Fishes	93	74	22	6	195	107
Flatworms and Roundworms	0	0	0	0	0	0
Hydroids	0	0	0	0	0	0
Insects	74	11	4	0	89	42
Mammals	66	28	260	23	377	57
Millipedes	0	0	0	0	0	0
Reptiles	17	29	71	24	141	40
Snails	40	12	1	0	53	33
Sponges	0	0	0	0	0	0
Animal Subtotal	503	216	594	89	1,402	490
Plants						
Conifers and Cycads	1	3	0	2	6	3
Ferns and Allies	36	2	0	0	38	26
Flowering Plants	733	167	1	0	901	648
Lichens	2	0	0	0	2	2
Plant Subtotal	772	172	1	2	947	679
Grand Total	1,275	388	595	91	2,349	1,169

Notes: *Data as of July 2, 2019; (1) A listing has an E or a T in the "status" column of the tables in 50 CFR 17.11(h) or 50 CFR 17.12(h) (the "List of Endangered and Threatened Wildlife and Plants"). 22 animal species (14 in the U.S.[3] and 8 Foreign) are counted more than once in the above table, primarily because these animals have distinct population segments (each with its own individual listing status).*

The U.S. species counted more than once are:

- *Frog, mountain yellow-legged (Rana muscosa)*
- *Plover, piping (Charadrius melodus)*
- *Salamander, California tiger (Ambystoma californiense)*
- *Salmon, chinook (Oncorhynchus (=Salmo) tshawytscha)*
- *Salmon, chum (Oncorhynchus (=Salmo) keta)*
- *Salmon, coho (Oncorhynchus (=Salmo) kisutch)*
- *Salmon, sockeye (Oncorhynchus (=Salmo) nerka)*
- *Seal, bearded (Erignathus barbatus nauticus)*
- *Sea turtle, green (Chelonia mydas)*
- *Sea turtle, loggerhead (Caretta caretta)*
- *Steelhead (Oncorhynchus (=Salmo) mykiss)*
- *Sturgeon, Atlantic (Acipenser oxyrinchus oxyrinchus)*
- *Tern, roseate (Sterna dougallii dougallii)*
- *Wolf, gray (Canis lupus)*

The foreign species counted more than once are:

- *Argali (Ovis ammon)*
- *Caiman, broad-snouted (Caiman latirostris)*
- *Leopard (Panthera pardus)*
- *Sea turtle, green (Chelonia mydas)*
- *Sea turtle, loggerhead (Caretta caretta)*
- *Shark, Scalloped Hammerhead (Sphyrna lewini)*
- *Vicuna (Vicugna vicugna)*
- *Whale, humpback (Megaptera novaeangliae)*

(2) There are a total of 609 distinct active (Draft and Final) recovery plans. Some recovery plans cover more than one species, and a few species have separate plans covering different parts of their ranges. This count includes only plans generated by the USFWS (or jointly by the USFWS and NMFS), and only listed species that occur in the United States; (3) United States listings include those populations in which the United States shares jurisdiction with another nation.

Source: *U.S. Fish & Wildlife Service, Threatened and Endangered Species System (TESS)*

Figure 1.1 Primary Energy Overview

(Quadrillion Btu)

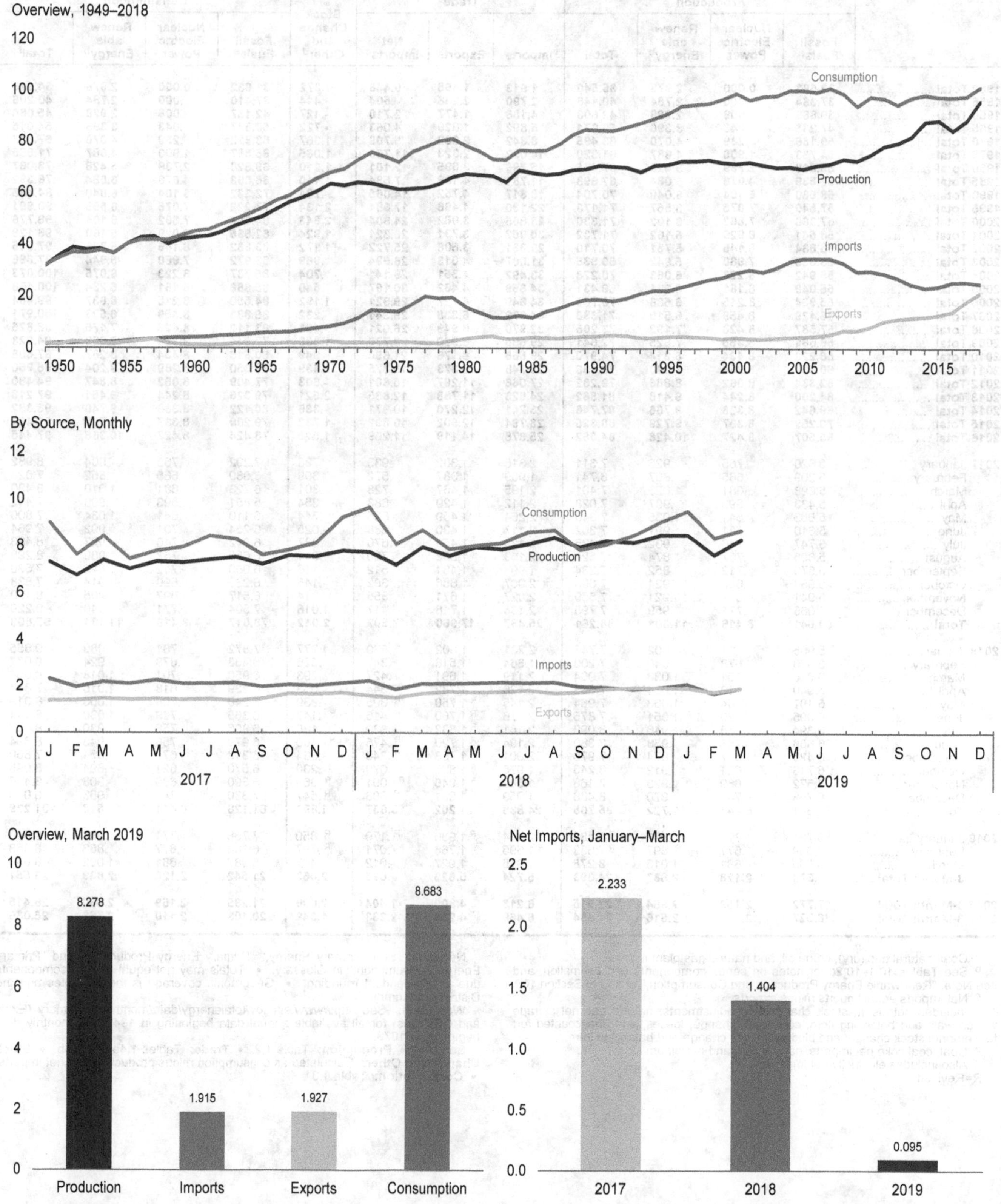

Web Page: http://www.eia.gov/totalenergy/data/monthly/#summary.
Source: Table 1.1.

Source: *U.S. Energy Information Administration, Monthly Energy Review, June 2019*

Table 1.1 Primary Energy Overview

(Quadrillion Btu)

	Production				Trade			Stock Change and Other[d]	Consumption			
	Fossil Fuels[a]	Nuclear Electric Power	Renewable Energy[b]	Total	Imports	Exports	Net Imports[c]		Fossil Fuels[e]	Nuclear Electric Power	Renewable Energy[b]	Total[f]
1950 Total	**32.563**	**0.000**	**2.978**	**35.540**	**1.913**	**1.465**	**0.448**	**-1.372**	**31.632**	**0.000**	**2.978**	**34.616**
1955 Total	**37.364**	**.000**	**2.784**	**40.148**	**2.790**	**2.286**	**.504**	**-.444**	**37.410**	**.000**	**2.784**	**40.208**
1960 Total	**39.869**	**.006**	**2.928**	**42.803**	**4.188**	**1.477**	**2.710**	**-.427**	**42.137**	**.006**	**2.928**	**45.086**
1965 Total	**47.235**	**.043**	**3.396**	**50.674**	**5.892**	**1.829**	**4.063**	**-.722**	**50.577**	**.043**	**3.396**	**54.015**
1970 Total	**59.186**	**.239**	**4.070**	**63.495**	**8.342**	**2.632**	**5.709**	**-1.367**	**63.522**	**.239**	**4.070**	**67.838**
1975 Total	**54.733**	**1.900**	**4.687**	**61.320**	**14.032**	**2.323**	**11.709**	**-1.065**	**65.357**	**1.900**	**4.687**	**71.965**
1980 Total	**59.008**	**2.739**	**5.428**	**67.175**	**15.796**	**3.695**	**12.101**	**-1.210**	**69.828**	**2.739**	**5.428**	**78.067**
1985 Total	**57.539**	**4.076**	**6.084**	**67.698**	**11.781**	**4.196**	**7.584**	**1.110**	**66.093**	**4.076**	**6.084**	**76.392**
1990 Total	**58.560**	**6.104**	**6.040**	**70.704**	**18.817**	**4.752**	**14.065**	**-.284**	**72.332**	**6.104**	**6.040**	**84.485**
1995 Total	**57.540**	**7.075**	**6.557**	**71.173**	**22.180**	**4.496**	**17.684**	**2.134**	**77.222**	**7.075**	**6.559**	**90.991**
2000 Total	**57.366**	**7.862**	**6.102**	**71.330**	**28.865**	**3.962**	**24.904**	**2.543**	**84.694**	**7.862**	**6.104**	**98.776**
2001 Total	**58.541**	**8.029**	**5.162**	**71.732**	**30.052**	**3.731**	**26.321**	**-1.924**	**82.865**	**8.029**	**5.160**	**96.129**
2002 Total	**56.834**	**8.145**	**5.731**	**70.710**	**29.331**	**3.608**	**25.722**	**1.172**	**83.662**	**8.145**	**5.726**	**97.605**
2003 Total	**56.033**	**7.960**	**5.942**	**69.935**	**31.007**	**4.013**	**26.994**	**.969**	**83.972**	**7.960**	**5.944**	**97.898**
2004 Total	**55.942**	**8.223**	**6.063**	**70.228**	**33.492**	**4.351**	**29.141**	**.704**	**85.737**	**8.223**	**6.075**	**100.073**
2005 Total	**55.049**	**8.161**	**6.221**	**69.431**	**34.659**	**4.462**	**30.197**	**.540**	**85.689**	**8.161**	**6.234**	**100.168**
2006 Total	**55.934**	**8.215**	**6.586**	**70.735**	**34.649**	**4.727**	**29.921**	**-1.192**	**84.550**	**8.215**	**6.637**	**99.464**
2007 Total	**56.429**	**8.459**	**6.510**	**71.398**	**34.679**	**5.338**	**29.341**	**.232**	**85.883**	**8.459**	**6.523**	**100.971**
2008 Total	**57.587**	**8.426**	**7.192**	**73.205**	**32.970**	**6.949**	**26.021**	**-.401**	**83.112**	**8.426**	**7.175**	**98.825**
2009 Total	**56.661**	**8.355**	**7.625**	**72.641**	**29.690**	**6.920**	**22.770**	**-1.388**	**77.944**	**8.355**	**7.608**	**94.023**
2010 Total	**58.222**	**8.434**	**8.314**	**74.970**	**29.866**	**8.176**	**21.690**	**.949**	**80.818**	**8.434**	**8.267**	**97.608**
2011 Total	**60.567**	**8.269**	**9.300**	**78.136**	**28.748**	**10.373**	**18.375**	**.439**	**79.350**	**8.269**	**9.204**	**96.950**
2012 Total	**62.334**	**8.062**	**8.886**	**79.282**	**27.068**	**11.267**	**15.801**	**-.603**	**77.409**	**8.062**	**8.847**	**94.480**
2013 Total	**64.200**	**8.244**	**9.418**	**81.862**	**24.623**	**11.788**	**12.835**	**2.521**	**79.326**	**8.244**	**9.451**	**97.218**
2014 Total	**69.642**	**8.338**	**9.766**	**87.746**	**23.241**	**12.270**	**10.971**	**-.336**	**80.122**	**8.338**	**9.740**	**98.382**
2015 Total	**70.259**	**8.337**	**9.729**	**88.325**	**23.794**	**12.902**	**10.892**	**-1.732**	**79.200**	**8.337**	**9.720**	**97.484**
2016 Total	**65.507**	**8.427**	**10.428**	**84.362**	**25.378**	**14.119**	**11.259**	**1.824**	**78.424**	**8.427**	**10.368**	**97.445**
2017 January	5.620	.765	.926	7.311	2.315	1.382	.933	.738	7.292	.765	.904	8.982
February	5.209	.665	.867	6.741	1.959	1.387	.572	.309	6.089	.665	.852	7.623
March	5.698	.681	1.023	7.401	2.195	1.467	.728	.301	6.723	.681	1.010	8.430
April	5.433	.593	.997	7.023	2.112	1.429	.683	-.254	5.851	.593	.993	7.452
May	5.663	.641	1.035	7.340	2.264	1.459	.805	-.344	6.110	.641	1.034	7.800
June	5.610	.701	.991	7.302	2.117	1.430	.688	-.025	6.254	.701	.992	7.964
July	5.747	.746	.932	7.425	2.129	1.459	.670	.337	6.742	.746	.927	8.433
August	5.895	.757	.874	7.526	2.153	1.392	.760	.011	6.652	.757	.869	8.298
September	5.670	.712	.852	7.234	1.993	1.481	.512	-.116	6.060	.712	.842	7.630
October	5.988	.690	.924	7.603	2.067	1.686	.382	-.146	6.223	.690	.914	7.838
November	5.941	.697	.921	7.559	2.027	1.671	.356	.214	6.517	.697	.905	8.130
December	6.066	.771	.959	7.795	2.136	1.718	.417	1.016	7.504	.771	.940	9.229
Total	**68.541**	**8.419**	**11.301**	**88.261**	**25.467**	**17.960**	**7.507**	**2.042**	**78.017**	**8.419**	**11.181**	**97.809**
2018 January	5.965	.781	1.002	7.748	2.231	1.602	R .630	1.277	7.872	.781	.989	9.655
February	5.576	.678	.949	7.203	1.864	1.516	.347	.526	6.463	.678	.924	8.077
March	6.230	.701	1.033	7.964	2.119	1.691	.427	.293	6.950	.701	1.018	8.684
April	5.940	.618	1.034	7.593	2.126	1.782	R .344	R -.053	6.239	.618	1.016	7.884
May	6.197	.704	1.063	7.964	2.145	R 1.750	R .395	-.339	6.248	.704	1.053	8.019
June	6.095	.729	1.051	7.875	2.176	R 1.760	R .416	R -.147	6.365	.729	1.036	8.144
July	6.394	.758	.946	8.098	2.161	R 1.832	R .330	R .180	6.905	.758	.930	8.607
August	6.666	.756	.958	8.380	2.194	R 1.720	R .475	R -.160	6.979	.756	.943	8.694
September	6.425	.677	.874	7.976	2.001	R 1.753	R .248	R -.364	6.318	.677	.854	7.860
October	6.713	.621	.912	8.246	1.976	R 1.897	R .079	R -.230	6.570	.621	.894	8.095
November	6.572	.669	.928	8.168	1.887	R 1.948	R -.061	R .369	6.890	.669	.908	8.476
December	6.768	.749	.970	8.488	1.959	R 1.951	R .008	R .547	7.330	.749	.953	9.043
Total	**75.541**	**8.441**	**11.722**	**95.705**	**24.838**	R **21.202**	R **3.637**	R **1.898**	**81.128**	**8.441**	**11.518**	**101.239**
2019 January	R 6.734	.771	.978	R 8.482	R 2.114	R 1.936	R .179	R .850	7.768	.771	.954	9.510
February	R 6.059	.677	R .897	R 7.632	R 1.695	R 1.766	R -.071	R .797	6.786	.677	.883	8.358
March	6.585	.681	1.013	8.278	1.915	1.927	-.012	.417	6.987	.681	1.002	8.683
3-Month Total	**19.378**	**2.128**	**2.887**	**24.393**	**5.724**	**5.629**	**.095**	**2.063**	**21.542**	**2.128**	**2.839**	**26.551**
2018 3-Month Total	**17.772**	**2.159**	**2.984**	**22.915**	**6.213**	**4.809**	**1.404**	**2.096**	**21.285**	**2.159**	**2.930**	**26.415**
2017 3-Month Total	**16.527**	**2.110**	**2.816**	**21.454**	**6.469**	**4.236**	**2.233**	**1.349**	**20.103**	**2.110**	**2.766**	**25.036**

[a] Coal, natural gas (dry), crude oil, and natural gas plant liquids.
[b] See Tables 10.1–10.2c for notes on series components and estimation; and see Note, "Renewable Energy Production and Consumption," at end of Section 10.
[c] Net imports equal imports minus exports.
[d] Includes petroleum stock change and adjustments; natural gas net storage withdrawals and balancing item; coal stock change, losses, and unaccounted for; fuel ethanol stock change; and biodiesel stock change and balancing item.
[e] Coal, coal coke net imports, natural gas, and petroleum.
[f] Also includes electricity net imports.
R=Revised.

Notes: • See "Primary Energy," "Primary Energy Production," and "Primary Energy Consumption," in Glossary. • Totals may not equal sum of components due to independent rounding. • Geographic coverage is the 50 states and the District of Columbia.

Web Page: See http://www.eia.gov/totalenergy/data/monthly/#summary (Excel and CSV files) for all available annual data beginning in 1949 and monthly data beginning in 1973.

Sources: • **Production:** Table 1.2. • **Trade:** Tables 1.4a and 1.4b. • **Stock Change and Other:** Calculated as consumption minus production and net imports. • **Consumption:** Table 1.3.

Source: *U.S. Energy Information Administration, Monthly Energy Review, June 2019*

Figure 1.2 Primary Energy Production
(Quadrillion Btu)

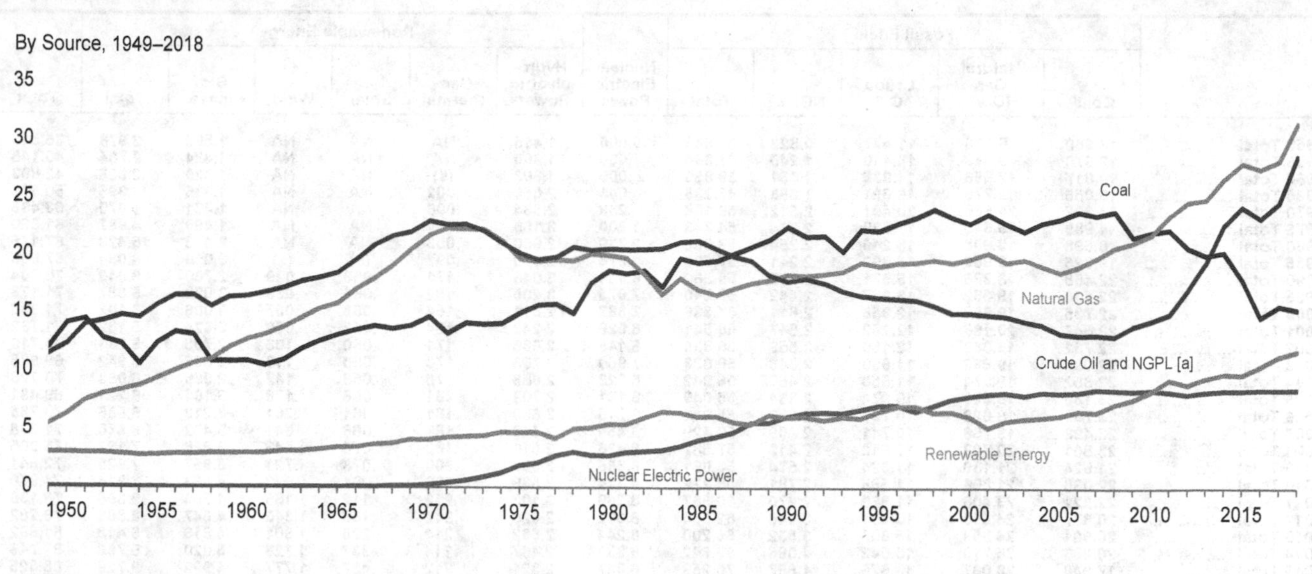

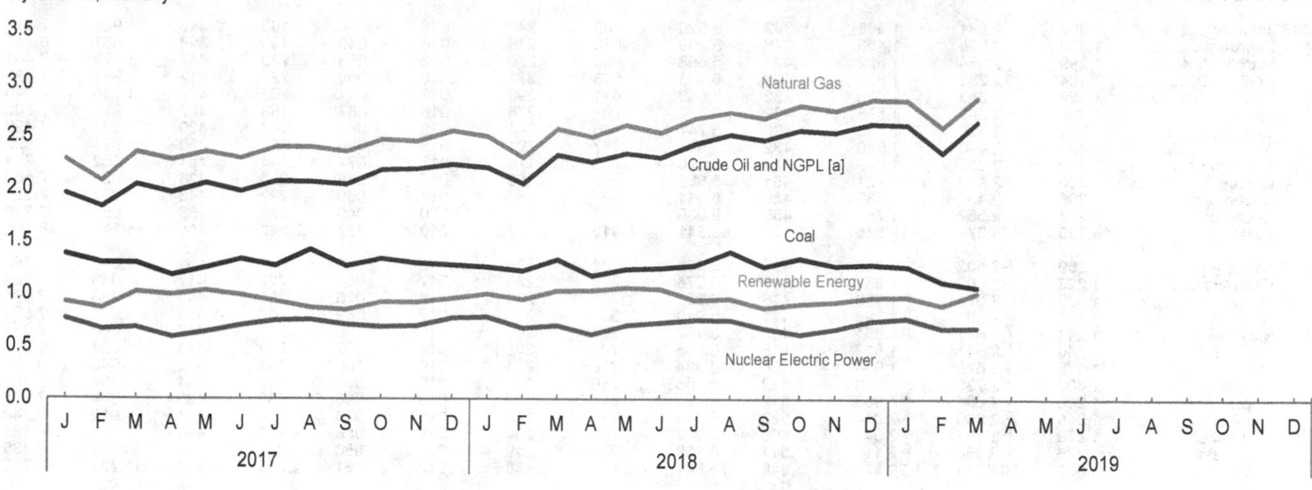

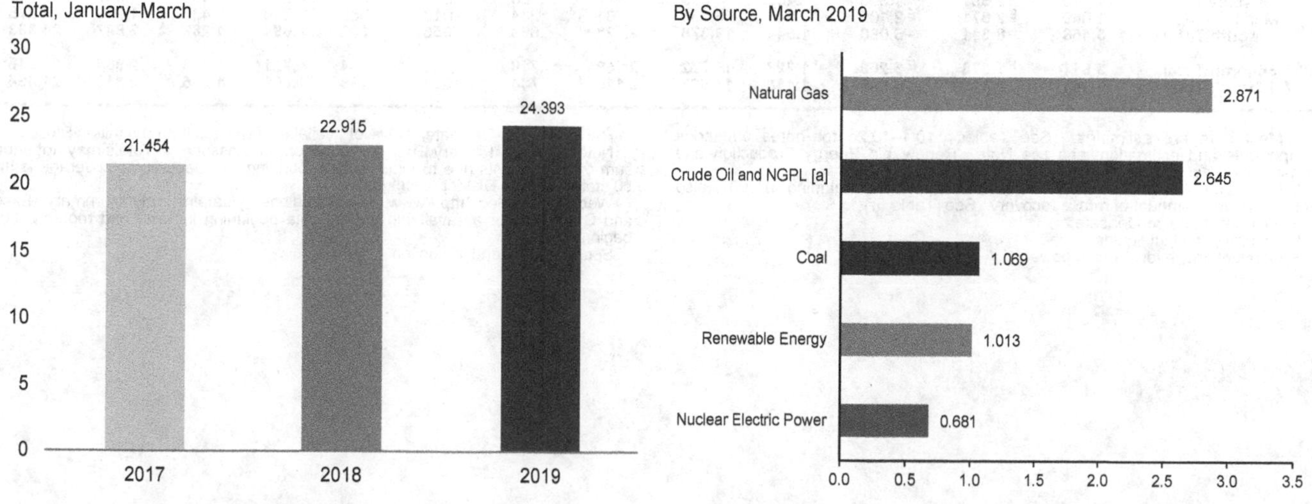

[a] National gas plant liquids.
Web Page: http://www.eia.gov/totalenergy/data/monthly/#summary.
Source: Table 1.2.

Source: *U.S. Energy Information Administration, Monthly Energy Review, June 2019*

Table 1.2 Primary Energy Production by Source
(Quadrillion Btu)

	Fossil Fuels						Renewable Energy[a]						
	Coal[b]	Natural Gas (Dry)	Crude Oil[c]	NGPL[d]	Total	Nuclear Electric Power	Hydro-electric Power[e]	Geo-thermal	Solar	Wind	Bio-mass	Total	Total
1950 Total	**14.060**	**6.233**	**11.447**	**0.823**	**32.563**	**0.000**	**1.415**	**NA**	**NA**	**NA**	**1.562**	**2.978**	**35.540**
1955 Total	**12.370**	**9.345**	**14.410**	**1.240**	**37.364**	**.000**	**1.360**	**NA**	**NA**	**NA**	**1.424**	**2.784**	**40.148**
1960 Total	**10.817**	**12.656**	**14.935**	**1.461**	**39.869**	**.006**	**1.608**	**(s)**	**NA**	**NA**	**1.320**	**2.928**	**42.803**
1965 Total	**13.055**	**15.775**	**16.521**	**1.883**	**47.235**	**.043**	**2.059**	**.002**	**NA**	**NA**	**1.335**	**3.396**	**50.674**
1970 Total	**14.607**	**21.666**	**20.401**	**2.512**	**59.186**	**.239**	**2.634**	**.006**	**NA**	**NA**	**1.431**	**4.070**	**63.495**
1975 Total	**14.989**	**19.640**	**17.729**	**2.374**	**54.733**	**1.900**	**3.155**	**.034**	**NA**	**NA**	**1.499**	**4.687**	**61.320**
1980 Total	**18.598**	**19.908**	**18.249**	**2.254**	**59.008**	**2.739**	**2.900**	**.053**	**NA**	**NA**	**2.475**	**5.428**	**67.175**
1985 Total	**19.325**	**16.980**	**18.992**	**2.241**	**57.539**	**4.076**	**2.970**	**.097**	**(s)**	**(s)**	**3.016**	**6.084**	**67.698**
1990 Total	**22.488**	**18.326**	**15.571**	**2.175**	**58.560**	**6.104**	**3.046**	**.171**	**.059**	**.029**	**2.735**	**6.040**	**70.704**
1995 Total	**22.130**	**19.082**	**13.887**	**2.442**	**57.540**	**7.075**	**3.205**	**.152**	**.068**	**.033**	**3.099**	**6.557**	**71.173**
2000 Total	**22.735**	**19.662**	**12.358**	**2.611**	**57.366**	**7.862**	**2.811**	**.164**	**.063**	**.057**	**3.006**	**6.102**	**71.330**
2001 Total	**23.547**	**20.166**	**12.282**	**2.547**	**58.541**	**8.029**	**2.242**	**.164**	**.062**	**.070**	**2.624**	**5.162**	**71.732**
2002 Total	**22.732**	**19.382**	**12.160**	**2.559**	**56.834**	**8.145**	**2.689**	**.171**	**.060**	**.105**	**2.705**	**5.731**	**70.710**
2003 Total	**22.094**	**19.633**	**11.960**	**2.346**	**56.033**	**7.960**	**2.793**	**.173**	**.058**	**.113**	**2.805**	**5.942**	**69.935**
2004 Total	**22.852**	**19.074**	**11.550**	**2.466**	**55.942**	**8.223**	**2.688**	**.178**	**.058**	**.142**	**2.996**	**6.063**	**70.228**
2005 Total	**23.185**	**18.556**	**10.974**	**2.334**	**55.049**	**8.161**	**2.703**	**.181**	**.058**	**.178**	**3.101**	**6.221**	**69.431**
2006 Total	**23.790**	**19.022**	**10.767**	**2.356**	**55.934**	**8.215**	**2.869**	**.181**	**.061**	**.264**	**3.212**	**6.586**	**70.735**
2007 Total	**23.493**	**19.786**	**10.741**	**2.409**	**56.429**	**8.459**	**2.446**	**.186**	**.066**	**.341**	**3.472**	**6.510**	**71.398**
2008 Total	**23.851**	**20.703**	**10.613**	**2.419**	**57.587**	**8.426**	**2.511**	**.192**	**.074**	**.546**	**3.868**	**7.192**	**73.205**
2009 Total	**21.624**	**21.139**	**11.324**	**2.574**	**56.661**	**8.355**	**2.669**	**.200**	**.078**	**.721**	**3.957**	**7.625**	**72.641**
2010 Total	**22.038**	**21.806**	**11.596**	**2.781**	**58.222**	**8.434**	**2.539**	**.208**	**.091**	**.923**	**4.553**	**8.314**	**74.970**
2011 Total	**22.221**	**23.406**	**11.970**	**2.970**	**60.567**	**8.269**	**3.103**	**.212**	**.112**	**1.168**	**4.704**	**9.300**	**78.136**
2012 Total	**20.677**	**24.610**	**13.801**	**3.246**	**62.334**	**8.062**	**2.629**	**.212**	**.159**	**1.340**	**4.547**	**8.886**	**79.282**
2013 Total	**20.001**	**24.859**	**15.807**	**3.532**	**64.200**	**8.244**	**2.562**	**.214**	**.225**	**1.601**	**4.816**	**9.418**	**81.862**
2014 Total	**20.286**	**26.718**	**18.542**	**4.096**	**69.642**	**8.338**	**2.467**	**.214**	**.337**	**1.728**	**5.020**	**9.766**	**87.746**
2015 Total	**17.946**	**28.067**	**19.679**	**4.567**	**70.259**	**8.337**	**2.321**	**.212**	**.427**	**1.777**	**4.992**	**9.729**	**88.325**
2016 Total	**14.667**	**27.576**	**18.494**	**4.770**	**65.507**	**8.427**	**2.472**	**.210**	**.570**	**2.096**	**5.081**	**10.428**	**84.362**
2017 January	1.382	2.281	1.568	.389	5.620	.765	.247	.018	.034	.183	.445	.926	7.311
February	1.300	2.078	1.456	.376	5.209	.665	.218	.016	.040	.195	.398	.867	6.741
March	1.299	2.354	1.622	.423	5.698	.681	.270	.018	.063	.230	.442	1.023	7.401
April	1.184	2.281	1.560	.409	5.433	.593	.271	.018	.069	.227	.412	.997	7.023
May	1.252	2.353	1.626	.432	5.663	.641	.298	.017	.081	.207	.432	1.035	7.340
June	1.335	2.295	1.558	.422	5.610	.701	.278	.016	.087	.183	.427	.991	7.302
July	1.271	2.400	1.638	.438	5.747	.746	.244	.018	.083	.147	.439	.932	7.425
August	1.424	2.400	1.640	.432	5.895	.757	.201	.018	.080	.125	.450	.874	7.526
September	1.269	2.357	1.630	.414	5.670	.712	.176	.017	.074	.164	.421	.852	7.234
October	1.336	2.470	1.721	.461	5.988	.690	.168	.017	.068	.233	.438	.924	7.603
November	1.296	2.455	1.735	.456	5.941	.697	.189	.017	.050	.222	.443	.921	7.559
December	1.277	2.552	1.781	.455	6.066	.771	.206	.020	.049	.226	.458	.959	7.795
Total	**15.625**	**28.274**	**19.535**	**5.107**	**68.541**	**8.419**	**2.767**	**.210**	**.777**	**2.343**	**5.204**	**11.301**	**88.261**
2018 January	1.259	E 2.502	E 1.768	.437	5.965	.781	.236	.018	.050	.247	.451	1.002	7.748
February	1.223	E 2.302	E 1.637	.415	5.576	.678	.235	.017	.058	.222	.417	.949	7.203
March	1.329	E 2.574	E 1.850	.476	6.230	.701	.239	.018	.076	.251	.448	1.033	7.964
April	1.177	E 2.500	E 1.793	.471	5.940	.618	.253	.017	.089	.247	.429	1.034	7.593
May	1.241	E 2.611	E 1.851	.493	6.197	.704	.280	.019	.100	.217	.447	1.063	7.964
June	1.249	E 2.541	E 1.827	.478	6.095	.729	.258	.018	.107	.225	.445	1.051	7.875
July	1.278	E 2.678	E 1.934	.504	6.394	.758	.221	.019	.100	.148	.459	.946	8.098
August	1.406	E 2.735	E 2.003	.522	6.666	.756	.197	.019	.099	.180	.464	.958	8.380
September	1.266	E 2.684	E 1.963	.512	6.425	.677	.172	.018	.090	.166	.428	.874	7.976
October	1.345	E 2.800	E 2.044	.523	6.713	.621	.173	.018	.076	.195	.451	.912	8.246
November	1.273	E 2.752	E 2.041	.505	6.572	.669	.204	.018	.058	.207	.440	.928	8.168
December	1.286	E 2.856	E 2.116	.511	6.768	.749	.219	.020	.050	.229	.454	.970	8.488
Total	**15.333**	**E 31.536**	**E 22.826**	**5.846**	**75.541**	**8.441**	**2.688**	**.218**	**.951**	**2.533**	**5.332**	**11.722**	**95.705**
2019 January	1.267	RE 2.850	RE 2.098	.519	R 6.734	.771	.226	.019	.055	.232	.446	.978	R 8.482
February	1.119	RE 2.591	RE 1.863	.485	R 6.059	.677	.203	.017	.059	.212	R .405	R .897	R 7.632
March	1.069	E 2.871	E 2.105	.540	6.585	.681	.234	.019	.088	.240	.431	1.013	8.278
3-Month Total	**3.456**	**E 8.311**	**E 6.066**	**1.544**	**19.378**	**2.128**	**.663**	**.055**	**.202**	**.684**	**1.282**	**2.887**	**24.393**
2018 3-Month Total	**3.811**	**E 7.378**	**E 5.255**	**1.328**	**17.772**	**2.159**	**.710**	**.054**	**.184**	**.721**	**1.316**	**2.984**	**22.915**
2017 3-Month Total	**3.981**	**6.713**	**4.646**	**1.188**	**16.527**	**2.110**	**.734**	**.053**	**.136**	**.608**	**1.285**	**2.816**	**21.454**

[a] Most data are estimates. See Tables 10.1–10.2c for notes on series components and estimation; and see Note, "Renewable Energy Production and Consumption," at end of Section 10.
[b] Beginning in 1989, includes waste coal supplied. Beginning in 2001, also includes a small amount of refuse recovery. See Table 6.1.
[c] Includes lease condensate.
[d] Natural gas plant liquids.
[e] Conventional hydroelectric power.

R=Revised. E=Estimate. NA=Not available. (s)=Less than 0.5 trillion Btu.
Notes: • See "Primary Energy Production" in Glossary. • Totals may not equal sum of components due to independent rounding. • Geographic coverage is the 50 states and the District of Columbia.
Web Page: See http://www.eia.gov/totalenergy/data/monthly/#summary (Excel and CSV files) for all available annual data beginning in 1949 and monthly data beginning in 1973.
Sources: See end of section.

***Source:** U.S. Energy Information Administration, Monthly Energy Review, June 2019*

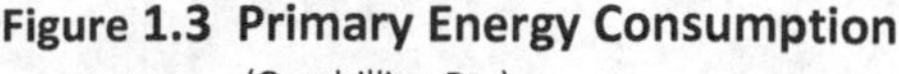

Figure 1.3 Primary Energy Consumption
(Quadrillion Btu)

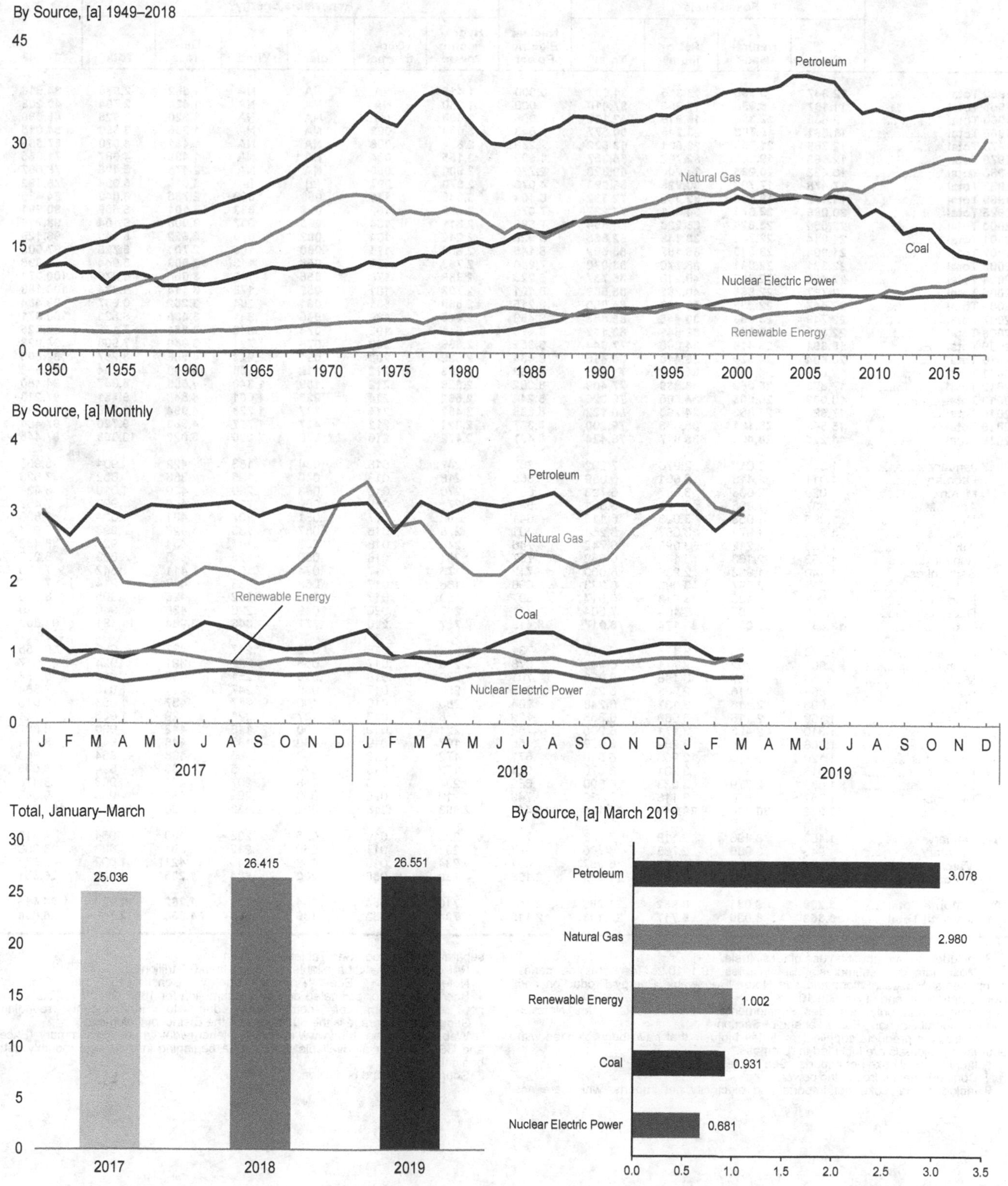

By Source, [a] 1949–2018

Petroleum
Natural Gas
Coal
Nuclear Electric Power
Renewable Energy

By Source, [a] Monthly

Petroleum
Natural Gas
Renewable Energy
Coal
Nuclear Electric Power

Total, January–March

Year	Total
2017	25.036
2018	26.415
2019	26.551

By Source, [a] March 2019

Petroleum	3.078
Natural Gas	2.980
Renewable Energy	1.002
Coal	0.931
Nuclear Electric Power	0.681

[a] Small quantities of net imports of coal coke and electricity are not shown.
Web Page: http://www.eia.gov/totalenergy/data/monthly/#summary.
Source: Table 1.3.

Source: *U.S. Energy Information Administration, Monthly Energy Review, June 2019*

Table 1.3 Primary Energy Consumption by Source

(Quadrillion Btu)

	Fossil Fuels[a]					Renewable Energy[b]						
	Coal	Natural Gas[c]	Petroleum[d]	Total[e]	Nuclear Electric Power	Hydroelectric Power[f]	Geothermal	Solar	Wind	Biomass	Total	Total[g]
1950 Total	12.347	5.968	13.315	31.632	0.000	1.415	NA	NA	NA	1.562	2.978	34.616
1955 Total	11.167	8.998	17.255	37.410	.000	1.360	NA	NA	NA	1.424	2.784	40.208
1960 Total	9.838	12.385	19.919	42.137	.006	1.608	(s)	NA	NA	1.320	2.928	45.086
1965 Total	11.581	15.769	23.246	50.577	.043	2.059	.002	NA	NA	1.335	3.396	54.015
1970 Total	12.265	21.795	29.521	63.522	.239	2.634	.006	NA	NA	1.431	4.070	67.838
1975 Total	12.663	19.948	32.732	65.357	1.900	3.155	.034	NA	NA	1.499	4.687	71.965
1980 Total	15.423	20.235	34.205	69.828	2.739	2.900	.053	NA	NA	2.475	5.428	78.067
1985 Total	17.478	17.703	30.925	66.093	4.076	2.970	.097	(s)	(s)	3.016	6.084	76.392
1990 Total	19.173	19.603	33.552	72.332	6.104	3.046	.171	.059	.029	2.735	6.040	84.485
1995 Total	20.089	22.671	34.401	77.222	7.075	3.205	.152	.068	.033	3.101	6.559	90.991
2000 Total	22.580	23.824	38.226	84.694	7.862	2.811	.164	.063	.057	3.008	6.104	98.776
2001 Total	21.914	22.773	38.149	82.865	8.029	2.242	.164	.062	.070	2.622	5.160	96.129
2002 Total	21.904	23.510	38.187	83.662	8.145	2.689	.171	.060	.105	2.701	5.726	97.605
2003 Total	22.321	22.831	38.770	83.972	7.960	2.793	.173	.058	.113	2.806	5.944	97.898
2004 Total	22.466	22.923	40.210	85.737	8.223	2.688	.178	.058	.142	3.008	6.075	100.073
2005 Total	22.797	22.565	40.283	85.689	8.161	2.703	.181	.058	.178	3.114	6.234	100.168
2006 Total	22.447	22.239	39.803	84.550	8.215	2.869	.181	.061	.264	3.262	6.637	99.464
2007 Total	22.749	23.663	39.445	85.883	8.459	2.446	.186	.066	.341	3.485	6.523	100.971
2008 Total	22.387	23.843	36.841	83.112	8.426	2.511	.192	.074	.546	3.851	7.175	98.825
2009 Total	19.691	23.416	34.860	77.944	8.355	2.669	.200	.078	.721	3.940	7.608	94.023
2010 Total	20.834	24.575	35.416	80.818	8.434	2.539	.208	.091	.923	4.506	8.267	97.608
2011 Total	19.658	24.955	34.727	79.350	8.269	3.103	.212	.112	1.168	4.609	9.204	96.950
2012 Total	17.378	26.089	33.939	77.409	8.062	2.629	.212	.159	1.340	4.508	8.847	94.480
2013 Total	18.039	26.805	34.500	79.326	8.244	2.562	.214	.225	1.601	4.848	9.451	97.218
2014 Total	17.998	27.383	34.763	80.122	8.338	2.467	.214	.337	1.728	4.994	9.740	98.382
2015 Total	15.549	28.191	35.478	79.200	8.337	2.321	.212	.427	1.777	4.983	9.720	97.484
2016 Total	14.226	28.400	35.817	78.424	8.427	2.472	.210	.570	2.096	5.020	10.368	97.445
2017 January	1.313	3.012	2.970	7.292	.765	.247	.018	.034	.183	.422	.904	8.982
February	1.011	2.418	2.661	6.089	.665	.218	.016	.040	.195	.383	.852	7.623
March	1.029	2.608	3.087	6.723	.681	.270	.018	.063	.230	.429	1.010	8.430
April	.937	1.995	2.920	5.851	.593	.271	.018	.069	.227	.408	.993	7.452
May	1.066	1.953	3.093	6.110	.641	.298	.017	.081	.207	.431	1.034	7.800
June	1.218	1.972	3.067	6.254	.701	.278	.016	.087	.183	.428	.992	7.964
July	1.433	2.212	3.099	6.742	.746	.244	.018	.083	.147	.434	.927	8.433
August	1.356	2.163	3.137	6.652	.757	.201	.018	.080	.125	.445	.869	8.298
September	1.140	1.983	2.939	6.060	.712	.176	.017	.074	.164	.411	.842	7.630
October	1.051	2.097	3.080	6.223	.690	.168	.017	.068	.233	.427	.914	7.838
November	1.069	2.433	3.018	6.517	.697	.189	.017	.050	.222	.426	.905	8.130
December	1.216	3.187	3.104	7.504	.771	.206	.020	.049	.226	.439	.940	9.229
Total	**13.837**	**28.034**	**36.174**	**78.017**	**8.419**	**2.767**	**.210**	**.777**	**2.343**	**5.084**	**11.181**	**97.809**
2018 January	1.328	3.423	3.125	7.872	.781	.236	.018	.050	.247	.437	.989	9.655
February	.961	2.792	2.711	6.463	.678	.235	.017	.058	.222	.391	.924	8.077
March	.939	2.867	3.146	6.950	.701	.239	.018	.076	.251	.433	1.018	8.684
April	.863	2.416	2.963	6.239	.618	.253	.017	.089	.247	.411	1.016	7.884
May	.996	2.116	3.137	6.248	.704	.280	.019	.100	.217	.437	1.053	8.019
June	1.159	2.118	3.089	6.365	.729	.258	.018	.107	.225	.429	1.036	8.144
July	1.310	2.425	3.171	6.905	.758	.221	.019	.100	.148	.442	.930	8.607
August	1.308	2.388	3.284	6.979	.756	.197	.019	.099	.180	.448	.943	8.694
September	1.120	2.230	2.968	6.318	.677	.172	.018	.090	.166	.408	.854	7.860
October	1.018	2.352	3.201	6.570	.621	.173	.018	.076	.195	.433	.894	8.095
November	1.082	2.779	3.033	6.890	.669	.204	.018	.058	.207	.421	.908	8.476
December	1.157	3.060	3.116	7.330	.749	.219	.020	.050	.229	.436	.953	9.043
Total	**13.242**	**30.966**	**36.945**	**81.128**	**8.441**	**2.688**	**.218**	**.951**	**2.533**	**5.128**	**11.518**	**101.239**
2019 January	1.157	R3.496	3.118	7.768	.771	.226	.019	.055	.232	.423	.954	9.510
February	.943	3.086	2.758	6.786	.677	.203	.017	.059	.212	.391	.883	8.358
March	.931	2.980	3.078	6.987	.681	.234	.019	.088	.240	.421	1.002	8.683
3-Month Total	**3.031**	**9.561**	**8.954**	**21.542**	**2.128**	**.663**	**.055**	**.202**	**.684**	**1.235**	**2.839**	**26.551**
2018 3-Month Total	**3.228**	**9.081**	**8.982**	**21.285**	**2.159**	**.710**	**.054**	**.184**	**.721**	**1.262**	**2.930**	**26.415**
2017 3-Month Total	**3.353**	**8.039**	**8.717**	**20.103**	**2.110**	**.734**	**.053**	**.136**	**.608**	**1.234**	**2.766**	**25.036**

[a] Includes non-combustion use of fossil fuels.

[b] Most data are estimates. See Tables 10.1–10.2c for notes on series components and estimation; and see Note, "Renewable Energy Production and Consumption," at end of Section 10.

[c] Natural gas only; excludes supplemental gaseous fuels. See Note 3, "Supplemental Gaseous Fuels," at end of Section 4.

[d] Petroleum products supplied; excludes biofuels that have been blended with petroleum biofuels are included in "Biomass."

[e] Includes coal coke net imports. See Tables 1.4a and 1.4b.

[f] Conventional hydroelectric power.

[g] Includes coal coke net imports and electricity net imports, which are not separately displayed. See Tables 1.4a and 1.4b.

R=Revised. NA=Not available. (s)=Less than 0.5 trillion Btu.

Notes: • See "Primary Energy Consumption" in Glossary. • See Table D1 for estimated energy consumption for 1635–1945. • Totals may not equal sum of components due to independent rounding. • Geographic coverage is the 50 states and the District of Columbia.

Web Page: See http://www.eia.gov/totalenergy/data/monthly/#summary (Excel and CSV files) for all available annual data beginning in 1949 and monthly data beginning in 1973.

Sources: See end of section.

Source: *U.S. Energy Information Administration, Monthly Energy Review, June 2019*

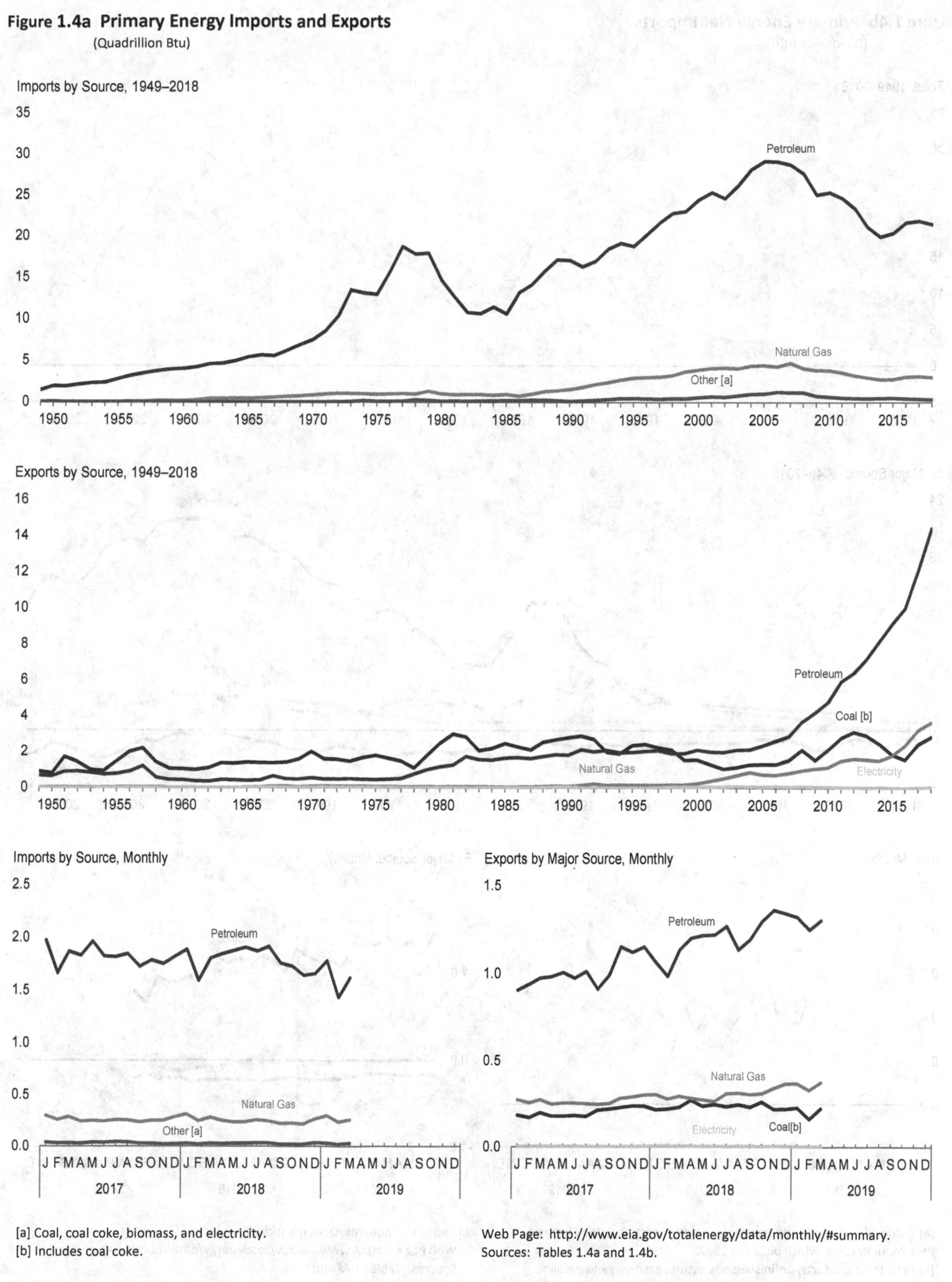

[a] Coal, coal coke, biomass, and electricity.
[b] Includes coal coke.

Web Page: http://www.eia.gov/totalenergy/data/monthly/#summary.
Sources: Tables 1.4a and 1.4b.

Source: *U.S. Energy Information Administration, Monthly Energy Review, June 2019*

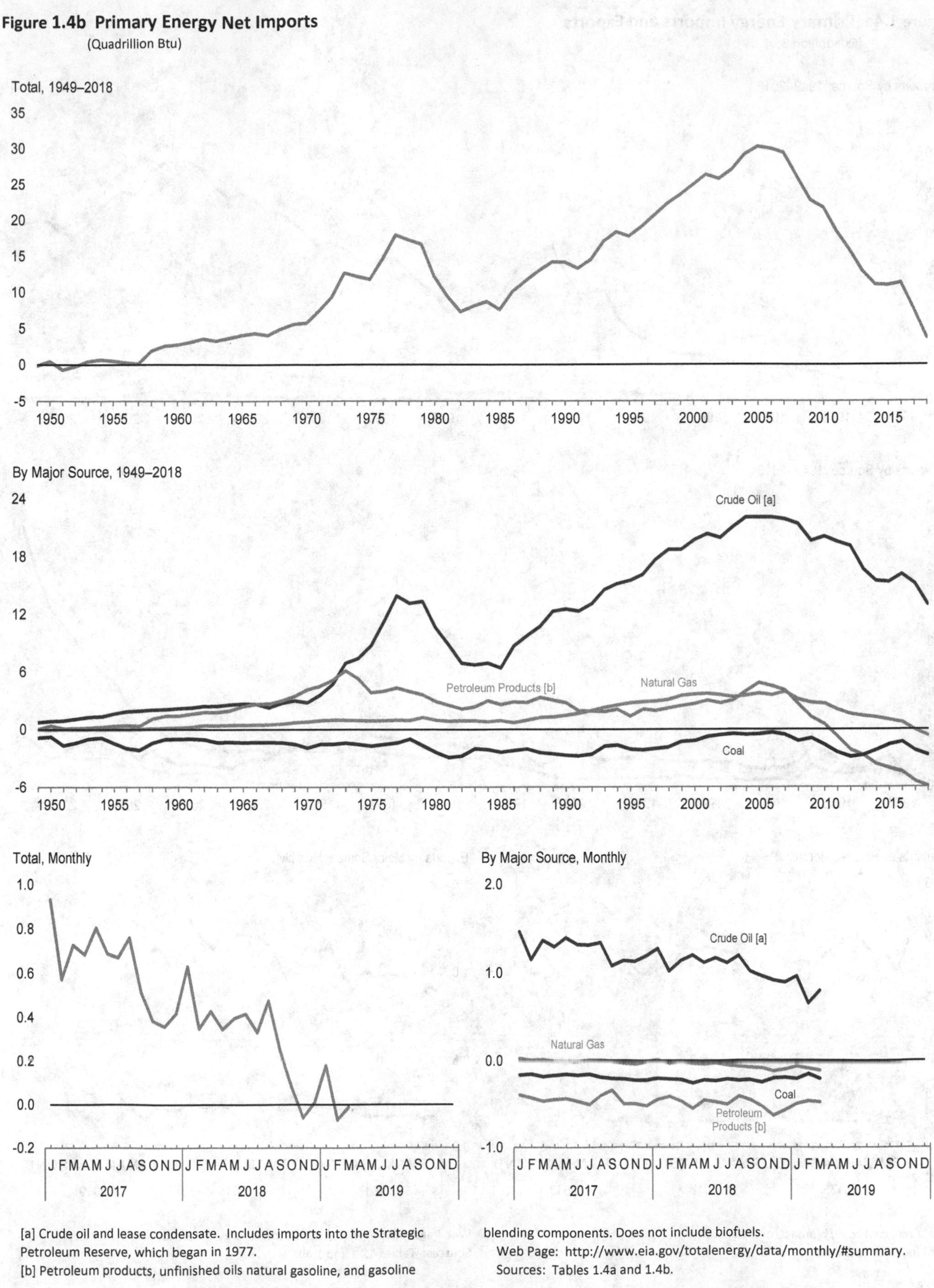

[a] Crude oil and lease condensate. Includes imports into the Strategic Petroleum Reserve, which began in 1977.

[b] Petroleum products, unfinished oils natural gasoline, and gasoline blending components. Does not include biofuels.

Web Page: http://www.eia.gov/totalenergy/data/monthly/#summary.

Sources: Tables 1.4a and 1.4b.

Source: *U.S. Energy Information Administration, Monthly Energy Review, June 2019*

Table 1.4a Primary Energy Imports by Source
(Quadrillion Btu)

	Imports								
				Petroleum					
	Coal	Coal Coke	Natural Gas	Crude Oil[a]	Petroleum Products[b]	Total	Biomass[c]	Electricity	Total
1950 Total	**0.009**	**0.011**	**0.000**	**1.056**	**0.830**	**1.886**	**NA**	**0.007**	**1.913**
1955 Total	**.008**	**.003**	**.011**	**1.691**	**1.061**	**2.752**	**NA**	**.016**	**2.790**
1960 Total	**.007**	**.003**	**.161**	**2.196**	**1.802**	**3.999**	**NA**	**.018**	**4.188**
1965 Total	**.005**	**.002**	**.471**	**2.654**	**2.748**	**5.402**	**NA**	**.012**	**5.892**
1970 Total	**.001**	**.004**	**.846**	**2.814**	**4.656**	**7.470**	**NA**	**.021**	**8.342**
1975 Total	**.024**	**.045**	**.978**	**8.721**	**4.227**	**12.948**	**NA**	**.038**	**14.032**
1980 Total	**.030**	**.016**	**1.006**	**11.195**	**3.463**	**14.658**	**NA**	**.085**	**15.796**
1985 Total	**.049**	**.014**	**.952**	**6.814**	**3.796**	**10.609**	**NA**	**.157**	**11.781**
1990 Total	**.067**	**.019**	**1.551**	**12.766**	**4.351**	**17.117**	**NA**	**.063**	**18.817**
1995 Total	**.237**	**.095**	**2.901**	**15.669**	**3.131**	**18.800**	**.001**	**.146**	**22.180**
2000 Total	**.313**	**.094**	**3.869**	**19.783**	**4.641**	**24.424**	**(s)**	**.166**	**28.865**
2001 Total	**.495**	**.063**	**4.068**	**20.348**	**4.946**	**25.294**	**.002**	**.131**	**30.052**
2002 Total	**.422**	**.080**	**4.104**	**19.920**	**4.677**	**24.597**	**.002**	**.125**	**29.331**
2003 Total	**.626**	**.068**	**4.042**	**21.060**	**5.105**	**26.165**	**.002**	**.104**	**31.007**
2004 Total	**.682**	**.170**	**4.365**	**22.082**	**6.063**	**28.145**	**.013**	**.117**	**33.492**
2005 Total	**.762**	**.088**	**4.450**	**22.091**	**7.108**	**29.198**	**.012**	**.150**	**34.659**
2006 Total	**.906**	**.101**	**4.291**	**22.085**	**7.054**	**29.139**	**.066**	**.146**	**34.649**
2007 Total	**.909**	**.061**	**4.723**	**21.914**	**6.842**	**28.756**	**.055**	**.175**	**34.679**
2008 Total	**.855**	**.089**	**4.084**	**21.448**	**6.214**	**27.662**	**.085**	**.195**	**32.970**
2009 Total	**.566**	**.009**	**3.845**	**19.699**	**5.367**	**25.066**	**.027**	**.178**	**29.690**
2010 Total	**.484**	**.030**	**3.834**	**20.140**	**5.219**	**25.359**	**.004**	**.154**	**29.866**
2011 Total	**.327**	**.035**	**3.555**	**19.595**	**5.038**	**24.633**	**.019**	**.178**	**28.748**
2012 Total	**.212**	**.028**	**3.216**	**19.239**	**4.122**	**23.361**	**.049**	**.202**	**27.068**
2013 Total	**.199**	**.003**	**2.955**	**16.957**	**4.169**	**21.126**	**.102**	**.236**	**24.623**
2014 Total	**.252**	**.002**	**2.763**	**16.178**	**3.773**	**19.951**	**.046**	**.227**	**23.241**
2015 Total	**.256**	**.003**	**2.786**	**16.299**	**4.111**	**20.410**	**.079**	**.259**	**23.794**
2016 Total	**.220**	**.006**	**3.082**	**17.392**	**4.309**	**21.700**	**.123**	**.248**	**25.378**
2017 January	.016	(s)	.299	1.590	.383	1.973	.003	.024	2.315
February	.013	(s)	.261	1.334	.327	1.661	.004	.019	1.959
March	.012	(s)	.288	1.531	.337	1.869	.006	.021	2.195
April	.011	(s)	.244	1.489	.342	1.831	.006	.019	2.112
May	.023	(s)	.250	1.592	.374	1.965	.008	.017	2.264
June	.014	.001	.246	1.468	.355	1.824	.013	.020	2.117
July	.021	(s)	.257	1.484	.335	1.819	.012	.020	2.129
August	.018	(s)	.254	1.486	.361	1.847	.011	.022	2.153
September	.011	(s)	.235	1.329	.396	1.725	.004	.018	1.993
October	.012	(s)	.250	1.441	.346	1.787	.004	.013	2.067
November	.008	(s)	.250	1.393	.358	1.751	.005	.013	2.027
December	.009	(s)	.285	1.460	.362	1.822	.004	.016	2.136
Total	**.167**	**.001**	**3.118**	**17.597**	**4.277**	**21.874**	**.081**	**.224**	**25.467**
2018 January	.010	(s)	.311	1.507	.381	1.888	.004	.018	2.231
February	.007	(s)	.247	1.273	.318	1.591	.003	.016	1.864
March	.011	(s)	.281	1.432	.371	1.804	.004	.019	2.119
April	.010	.001	.250	1.501	.345	1.846	.004	.015	2.126
May	.011	.001	.235	1.472	.405	1.877	.004	.018	2.145
June	.010	(s)	.236	1.543	.363	1.906	.004	.019	2.176
July	.014	(s)	.255	1.490	.381	1.871	.002	.018	2.161
August	.010	(s)	.245	1.505	.409	1.914	.005	.021	2.194
September	.005	(s)	.221	1.381	.375	1.756	.003	.015	2.001
October	.006	.001	.223	1.276	.352	1.707	.000	.013	1.970
November	.008	(s)	.218	1.363	.279	1.642	.005	.013	1.887
December	.018	(s)	.264	1.335	.323	1.658	.004	.014	1.959
Total	**.122**	**.003**	**2.987**	**17.177**	**4.303**	**21.480**	**.048**	**.199**	**24.838**
2019 January	.013	(s)	R .298	1.414	.365	1.779	.005	.019	R 2.114
February	.007	(s)	R .239	1.130	.301	1.431	.003	.015	R 1.695
March	.014	(s)	.259	1.271	.348	1.619	.006	.016	1.915
3-Month Total	**.034**	**(s)**	**.797**	**3.816**	**1.013**	**4.829**	**.014**	**.050**	**5.724**
2018 3-Month Total	**.028**	**(s)**	**.839**	**4.212**	**1.070**	**5.283**	**.011**	**.053**	**6.213**
2017 3-Month Total	**.041**	**(s)**	**.847**	**4.456**	**1.048**	**5.503**	**.013**	**.064**	**6.469**

[a] Crude oil and lease condensate. Includes imports into the Strategic Petroleum Reserve, which began in 1977.
[b] Petroleum products, unfinished oils, natural gasoline, and gasoline blending components. Does not include biofuels.
[c] Fuel ethanol (minus denaturant) and biodiesel.
R=Revised. NA=Not available. (s)=Less than 0.5 trillion Btu.
Notes: • See "Primary Energy" in Glossary. • Totals may not equal sum of components due to independent rounding. • Geographic coverage is the 50 states and the District of Columbia.
Web Page: See http://www.eia.gov/totalenergy/data/monthly/#summary (Excel and CSV files) for all available annual data beginning in 1949 and monthly data beginning in 1973.
Sources: See end of section.

Source: *U.S. Energy Information Administration, Monthly Energy Review, June 2019*

Table 1.4b Primary Energy Exports by Source and Total Net Imports

(Quadrillion Btu)

	Exports									Net Imports[a]
				Petroleum						
	Coal	Coal Coke	Natural Gas	Crude Oil[b]	Petroleum Products[c]	Total	Biomass[d]	Electricity	Total	Total
1950 Total	0.786	0.010	0.027	0.202	0.440	0.642	NA	0.001	1.465	0.448
1955 Total	1.465	.013	.032	.067	.707	.774	NA	.002	2.286	.504
1960 Total	1.023	.009	.012	.018	.413	.431	NA	.003	1.477	2.710
1965 Total	1.376	.021	.027	.006	.386	.392	NA	.013	1.829	4.063
1970 Total	1.936	.061	.072	.029	.520	.549	NA	.014	2.632	5.709
1975 Total	1.761	.032	.074	.012	.427	.439	NA	.017	2.323	11.709
1980 Total	2.421	.051	.049	.609	.551	1.160	NA	.014	3.695	12.101
1985 Total	2.438	.028	.056	.432	1.225	1.657	NA	.017	4.196	7.584
1990 Total	2.772	.014	.087	.230	1.594	1.824	NA	.055	4.752	14.065
1995 Total	2.318	.034	.156	.200	1.776	1.976	NA	.012	4.496	17.684
2000 Total	1.528	.028	.245	.106	2.003	2.110	NA	.051	3.962	24.904
2001 Total	1.265	.033	.377	.043	1.956	1.999	(s)	.056	3.731	26.321
2002 Total	1.032	.020	.520	.019	1.963	1.982	(s)	.054	3.608	25.722
2003 Total	1.117	.018	.686	.026	2.083	2.110	.001	.082	4.013	26.994
2004 Total	1.253	.033	.862	.057	2.068	2.125	.001	.078	4.351	29.141
2005 Total	1.273	.043	.735	.067	2.276	2.344	.001	.065	4.462	30.197
2006 Total	1.264	.040	.730	.052	2.554	2.606	.005	.083	4.727	29.921
2007 Total	1.507	.036	.830	.058	2.803	2.861	.036	.069	5.338	29.341
2008 Total	2.071	.049	.972	.061	3.626	3.686	.089	.083	6.949	26.021
2009 Total	1.515	.032	1.082	.093	4.101	4.194	.035	.062	6.920	22.770
2010 Total	2.101	.036	1.147	.088	4.691	4.780	.047	.065	8.176	21.690
2011 Total	2.751	.024	1.519	.100	5.820	5.919	.108	.051	10.373	18.375
2012 Total	3.087	.024	1.633	.143	6.261	6.404	.078	.041	11.267	15.801
2013 Total	2.895	.021	1.587	.284	6.886	7.170	.076	.039	11.788	12.835
2014 Total	2.435	.023	1.528	.744	7.414	8.158	.081	.045	12.270	10.971
2015 Total	1.852	.021	1.800	.964	8.153	9.118	.080	.031	12.902	10.892
2016 Total	1.546	.025	2.356	1.238	8.752	9.990	.181	.021	14.119	11.259
2017 January	.182	.003	.274	.126	.778	.904	.017	.002	1.382	.933
February	.170	.001	.257	.184	.754	.938	.018	.002	1.387	.572
March	.197	.002	.274	.165	.807	.972	.018	.003	1.467	.728
April	.178	.001	.249	.194	.787	.981	.015	.004	1.429	.683
May	.178	.001	.256	.195	.808	1.004	.017	.003	1.459	.805
June	.180	.003	.256	.149	.823	.972	.016	.003	1.430	.688
July	.177	.001	.251	.170	.840	1.010	.018	.002	1.459	.670
August	.211	.004	.249	.145	.764	.910	.017	.003	1.392	.760
September	.219	.002	.253	.252	.738	.990	.015	.002	1.481	.512
October	.226	.005	.284	.306	.847	1.153	.016	.002	1.686	.382
November	.235	.003	.291	.266	.856	1.122	.016	.003	1.671	.356
December	.234	.003	.302	.271	.882	1.152	.024	.003	1.718	.417
Total	**2.388**	**.030**	**3.196**	**2.424**	**9.684**	**12.108**	**.206**	**.032**	**17.960**	**7.507**
2018 January	.213	.004	.304	.238	.826	1.064	.013	.004	1.602	R .630
February	.219	.001	.279	.257	.729	.986	.027	.004	1.516	.347
March	.229	.002	.295	.296	.840	1.136	.025	.004	1.691	.427
April	.269	.003	.282	.301	.899	1.201	.022	.006	1.782	R .344
May	.234	.002	R .275	.356	.861	1.217	.018	.004	R 1.750	R .395
June	.246	.002	R .265	.378	.843	1.220	.023	.004	R 1.760	R .416
July	.232	.002	R .309	.379	.889	1.268	.017	.003	R 1.832	R .330
August	.244	.001	R .315	.310	.825	1.135	.020	.004	R 1.720	R .475
September	.230	.001	R .305	.363	.832	1.195	.017	.004	R 1.753	R .248
October	.259	.002	R .310	.412	.884	1.297	.025	.003	R 1.897	R .079
November	.216	.003	R .341	.448	.913	1.361	.022	.004	R 1.948	R -.061
December	.217	.003	R .367	.445	.895	1.341	.021	.003	R 1.951	R .008
Total	**2.809**	**.029**	**R 3.646**	**4.184**	**10.237**	**14.421**	**.250**	**.047**	**R 21.202**	**R 3.637**
2019 January	.226	.003	R .368	.457	.863	1.320	.017	.002	R 1.936	R .179
February	.163	.001	R .332	.479	.770	1.249	.018	.003	R 1.766	R -.071
March	.224	.001	.376	.476	.827	1.303	.021	.003	1.927	-.012
3-Month Total	**.612**	**.005**	**1.076**	**1.412**	**2.460**	**3.871**	**.056**	**.008**	**5.629**	**.095**
2018 3-Month Total	**.661**	**.008**	**.877**	**.791**	**2.394**	**3.186**	**.065**	**.012**	**4.809**	**1.404**
2017 3-Month Total	**.549**	**.006**	**.806**	**.476**	**2.338**	**2.814**	**.053**	**.007**	**4.236**	**2.233**

[a] Net imports equal imports minus exports.
[b] Crude oil and lease condensate.
[c] Petroleum products, unfinished oils, natural gasoline, and gasoline blending components. Does not include biofuels.
[d] Beginning in 2001, includes biodiesel. Beginning in 2010, also includes fuel ethanol (minus denaturant). Beginning in 2016, also includes wood and wood-derived fuels.

R=Revised. NA=Not available. (s)=Less than 0.5 trillion Btu.

Notes: • See "Primary Energy" in Glossary. • Totals may not equal sum of components due to independent rounding. • Geographic coverage is the 50 states and the District of Columbia.

Web Page: See http://www.eia.gov/totalenergy/data/monthly/#summary (Excel and CSV files) for all available annual data beginning in 1949 and monthly data beginning in 1973.

Sources: See end of section.

Source: *U.S. Energy Information Administration, Monthly Energy Review, June 2019*

Figure 1.5 Merchandise Trade Value

(Billion Dollars[a])

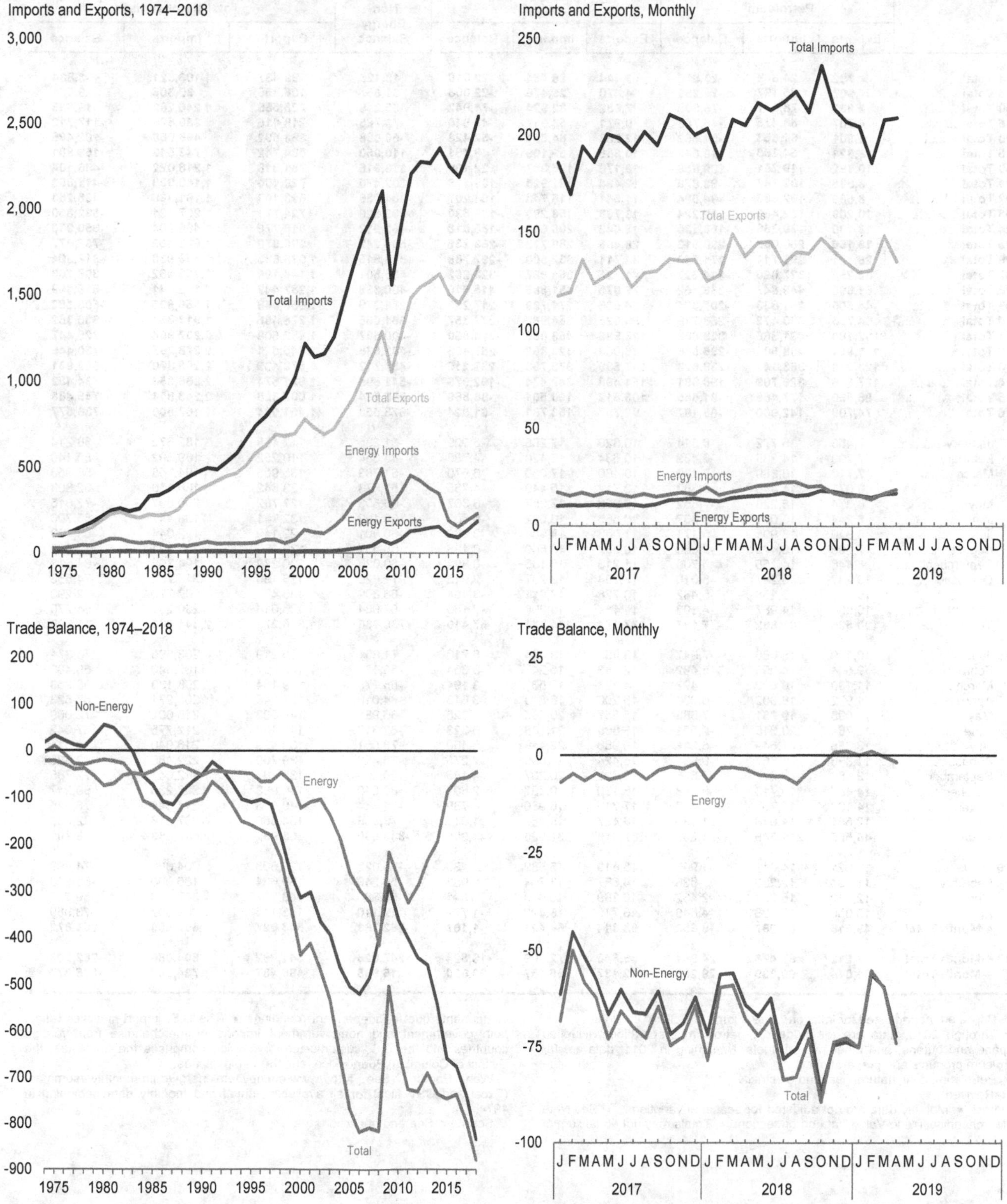

[a] Prices are not adjusted for inflation. See "Nominal Dollars" in Glossary.
Web Page: http://www.eia.gov/totalenergy/data/monthly/#summary.
Source: Table 1.5.

Source: *U.S. Energy Information Administration, Monthly Energy Review, June 2019*

Table 1.5 Merchandise Trade Value

(Million Dollars[a])

	Petroleum[b]			Energy[c]			Non-Energy Balance	Total Merchandise		
	Exports	Imports	Balance	Exports	Imports	Balance		Exports	Imports	Balance
1974 Total	**792**	**24,668**	**-23,876**	**3,444**	**25,454**	**-22,010**	**18,126**	**99,437**	**103,321**	**-3,884**
1975 Total	**907**	**25,197**	**-24,289**	**4,470**	**26,476**	**-22,006**	**31,557**	**108,856**	**99,305**	**9,551**
1980 Total	**2,833**	**78,637**	**-75,803**	**7,982**	**82,924**	**-74,942**	**55,246**	**225,566**	**245,262**	**-19,696**
1985 Total	**4,707**	**50,475**	**-45,768**	**9,971**	**53,917**	**-43,946**	**-73,765**	**218,815**	**336,526**	**-117,712**
1990 Total	**6,901**	**61,583**	**-54,682**	**12,233**	**64,661**	**-52,428**	**-50,068**	**393,592**	**496,088**	**-102,496**
1995 Total	**6,321**	**54,368**	**-48,047**	**10,358**	**59,109**	**-48,751**	**-110,050**	**584,742**	**743,543**	**-158,801**
2000 Total	**10,192**	**119,251**	**-109,059**	**13,179**	**135,367**	**-122,188**	**-313,916**	**781,918**	**1,218,022**	**-436,104**
2001 Total	**8,868**	**102,747**	**-93,879**	**12,494**	**121,923**	**-109,429**	**-302,470**	**729,100**	**1,140,999**	**-411,899**
2002 Total	**8,569**	**102,663**	**-94,094**	**11,541**	**115,748**	**-104,207**	**-364,056**	**693,103**	**1,161,366**	**-468,263**
2003 Total	**10,209**	**132,433**	**-122,224**	**13,768**	**153,298**	**-139,530**	**-392,820**	**724,771**	**1,257,121**	**-532,350**
2004 Total	**13,130**	**179,266**	**-166,136**	**18,642**	**206,660**	**-188,018**	**-462,912**	**818,775**	**1,469,704**	**-650,930**
2005 Total	**19,155**	**250,068**	**-230,913**	**26,488**	**289,723**	**-263,235**	**-504,242**	**905,978**	**1,673,455**	**-767,477**
2006 Total	**28,171**	**299,714**	**-271,543**	**34,711**	**332,500**	**-297,789**	**-519,515**	**1,036,635**	**1,853,938**	**-817,304**
2007 Total	**33,293**	**327,620**	**-294,327**	**41,725**	**364,987**	**-323,262**	**-485,501**	**1,148,199**	**1,956,962**	**-808,763**
2008 Total	**61,695**	**449,847**	**-388,152**	**76,075**	**491,885**	**-415,810**	**-400,389**	**1,287,442**	**2,103,641**	**-816,199**
2009 Total	**44,509**	**251,833**	**-207,324**	**54,536**	**271,739**	**-217,203**	**-286,379**	**1,056,043**	**1,559,625**	**-503,582**
2010 Total	**64,753**	**333,472**	**-268,719**	**80,625**	**354,982**	**-274,357**	**-361,005**	**1,278,495**	**1,913,857**	**-635,362**
2011 Total	[b]**102,180**	[b]**431,866**	[b]**-329,686**	**128,989**	**453,839**	**-324,850**	**-400,597**	**1,482,508**	**2,207,954**	**-725,447**
2012 Total	**111,951**	**408,509**	**-296,558**	**136,054**	**423,862**	**-287,808**	**-442,638**	**1,545,821**	**2,276,267**	**-730,446**
2013 Total	**123,218**	**363,141**	**-239,923**	**147,539**	**379,758**	**-232,219**	**-457,712**	**1,578,439**	**2,268,370**	**-689,931**
2014 Total	**127,818**	**326,709**	**-198,891**	**154,498**	**347,474**	**-192,976**	**-541,506**	**1,621,874**	**2,356,356**	**-734,482**
2015 Total	**85,890**	**177,455**	**-91,565**	**103,612**	**190,501**	**-86,889**	**-658,594**	**1,503,328**	**2,248,811**	**-745,483**
2016 Total	**74,703**	**142,900**	**-68,197**	**92,757**	**153,781**	**-61,024**	**-675,553**	**1,451,024**	**2,187,600**	**-736,577**
2017 January	7,458	15,772	-8,314	10,329	17,258	-6,929	-61,285	117,458	185,672	-68,214
February	7,799	14,238	-6,439	10,634	15,420	-4,786	-45,354	119,252	169,392	-50,140
March	7,710	15,889	-8,179	10,460	17,030	-6,570	-51,783	135,905	194,258	-58,353
April	8,077	14,440	-6,363	10,714	15,449	-4,735	-57,573	123,842	186,150	-62,308
May	8,374	16,226	-7,852	10,950	17,257	-6,307	-66,508	127,782	200,597	-72,815
June	8,244	15,081	-6,837	10,555	16,062	-5,507	-60,199	132,741	198,447	-65,706
July	8,820	13,991	-5,171	11,083	14,985	-3,902	-66,001	122,140	192,044	-69,903
August	7,799	15,479	-7,680	10,302	16,500	-6,198	-66,437	129,186	201,821	-72,635
September	8,446	14,155	-5,709	11,213	15,105	-3,892	-60,626	130,278	194,796	-64,518
October	10,237	15,247	-5,010	13,294	16,207	-2,913	-71,620	136,199	210,732	-74,533
November	10,676	16,158	-5,482	13,728	17,212	-3,484	-68,809	135,477	207,770	-72,293
December	10,884	14,987	-4,103	14,112	16,298	-2,186	-62,084	136,014	200,285	-64,270
Total	**104,525**	**181,662**	**-77,137**	**137,374**	**194,784**	**-57,410**	**-738,280**	**1,546,273**	**2,341,963**	**-795,690**
2018 January	10,139	18,086	-7,947	13,231	19,944	-6,713	-71,661	125,219	203,593	-78,374
February	9,504	14,996	-5,492	12,643	15,947	-3,304	-56,179	128,057	187,540	-59,483
March	11,130	16,622	-5,492	14,373	17,567	-3,194	-55,775	149,164	208,133	-58,969
April	11,972	18,002	-6,030	15,200	18,813	-3,613	-64,010	137,648	205,271	-67,623
May	12,098	19,781	-7,683	15,557	20,585	-5,028	-66,981	144,593	216,602	-72,009
June	12,764	20,315	-7,551	15,865	21,188	-5,323	-62,319	145,134	212,775	-67,642
July	13,338	21,549	-8,211	16,988	22,448	-5,460	-78,051	133,429	216,940	-83,511
August	11,836	21,667	-9,831	15,424	22,699	-7,275	-75,450	139,760	222,485	-82,725
September	12,651	19,277	-6,626	16,022	20,207	-4,185	-68,600	139,262	212,047	-72,785
October	14,465	19,713	-5,248	18,130	20,737	-2,607	-86,640	146,983	236,230	-89,247
November	14,107	15,797	-1,690	17,719	16,930	789	-74,464	140,373	214,048	-73,675
December	12,551	14,040	-1,489	16,467	15,456	1,011	R-73,668	134,360	207,018	-72,657
Total	**146,555**	**219,845**	**-73,290**	**187,619**	**232,520**	**-44,901**	R**-833,800**	**1,663,982**	**2,542,683**	**-878,701**
2019 January	12,021	14,017	-1,996	15,619	15,589	30	-75,022	129,608	204,600	-74,992
February	11,734	12,260	-526	14,687	13,704	983	-56,249	130,634	185,900	-55,266
March	12,812	15,294	-2,482	16,289	16,630	-341	R-59,385	R148,267	R207,993	R-59,726
April	13,050	17,696	-4,646	16,719	18,498	-1,779	-72,110	135,118	209,007	-73,889
4-Month Total	**49,618**	**59,267**	**-9,650**	**63,314**	**64,421**	**-1,107**	**-262,766**	**543,627**	**807,500**	**-263,872**
2018 4-Month Total	**44,212**	**67,478**	**-24,961**	**56,848**	**72,309**	**-16,824**	**-247,625**	**541,092**	**804,086**	**-262,993**
2017 4-Month Total	**31,044**	**60,339**	**-29,295**	**42,137**	**65,157**	**-23,020**	**-215,995**	**496,487**	**734,864**	**-238,377**

[a] Prices are not adjusted for inflation. See "Nominal Dollars" in Glossary.

[b] Through 2010, data are for crude oil, petroleum preparations, liquefied propane and butane, and other mineral fuels. Beginning in 2011, data are for petroleum products and preparations.

[c] Petroleum, coal, natural gas, and electricity.

R=Revised.

Notes: • Monthly data are not adjusted for seasonal variations. • See Note 1, "Merchandise Trade Value," at end of section. • Totals may not equal sum of components due to independent rounding. • The U.S. import statistics reflect both government and nongovernment imports of merchandise from foreign countries into the U.S. customs territory, which comprises the 50 states, the District of Columbia, Puerto Rico, and the Virgin Islands.

Web Page: See http://www.eia.gov/totalenergy/data/monthly/#summary (Excel and CSV files) for all available annual and monthly data beginning in 1974.

Sources: See end of section.

Source: *U.S. Energy Information Administration, Monthly Energy Review, June 2019*

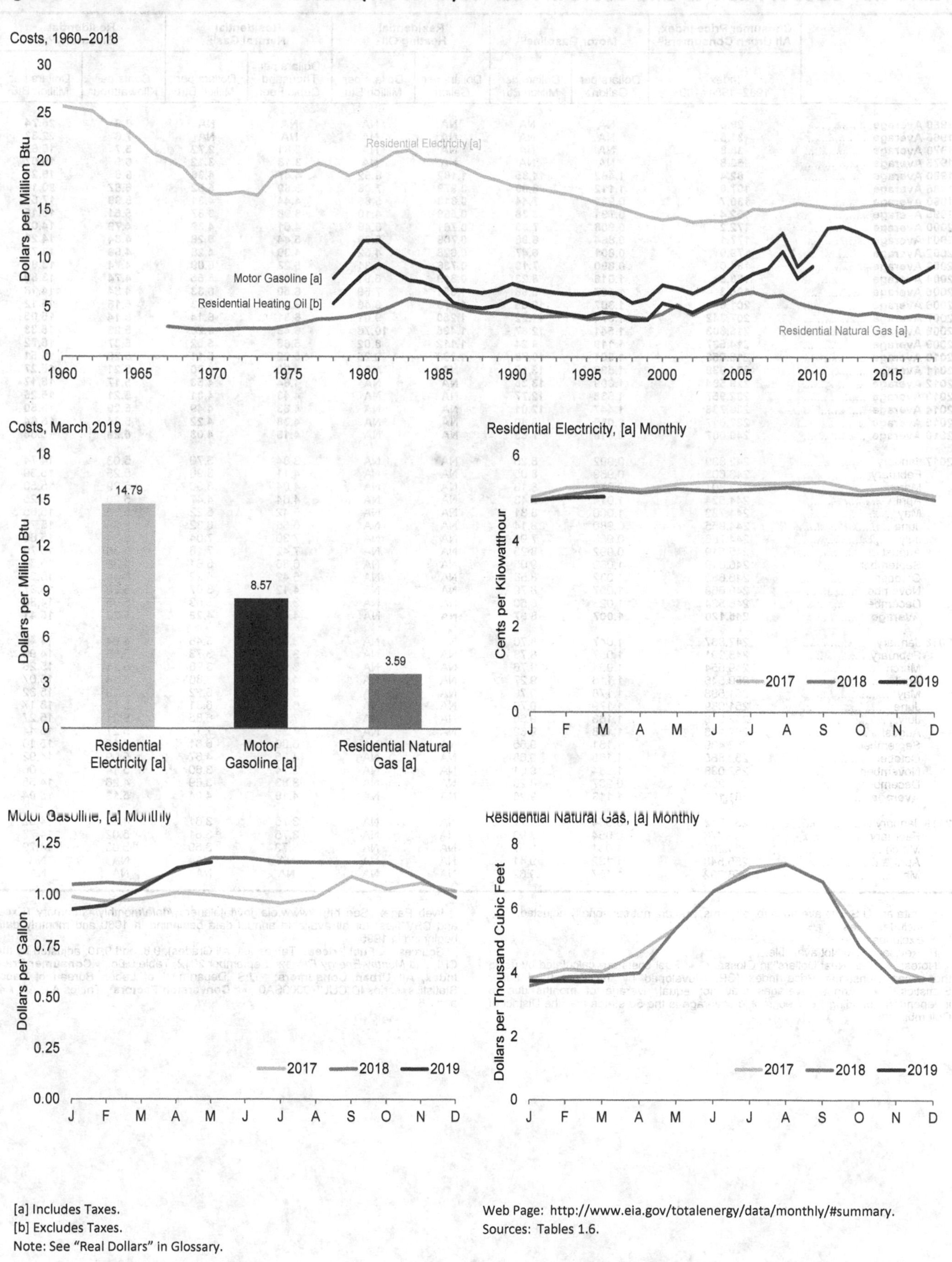

[a] Includes Taxes.
[b] Excludes Taxes.
Note: See "Real Dollars" in Glossary.

Web Page: http://www.eia.gov/totalenergy/data/monthly/#summary.
Sources: Tables 1.6.

Source: *U.S. Energy Information Administration, Monthly Energy Review, June 2019*

Table 1.6 Cost of Fuels to End Users in Real (1982–1984) Dollars

	Consumer Price Index, All Urban Consumers[a]	Motor Gasoline[b]		Residential Heating Oil[c]		Residential Natural Gas[b]		Residential Electricity[b]	
	Index 1982–1984=100	Dollars per Gallon	Dollars per Million Btu	Dollars per Gallon	Dollars per Million Btu	Dollars per Thousand Cubic Feet	Dollars per Million Btu	Cents per Kilowatthour	Dollars per Million Btu
1960 Average	**29.6**	**NA**	**NA**	**NA**	**NA**	**NA**	**NA**	**8.8**	**25.74**
1965 Average	**31.5**	**NA**	**NA**	**NA**	**NA**	**NA**	**NA**	**7.6**	**22.33**
1970 Average	**38.8**	**NA**	**NA**	**NA**	**NA**	**2.81**	**2.72**	**5.7**	**16.62**
1975 Average	**53.8**	**NA**	**NA**	**NA**	**NA**	**3.18**	**3.12**	**6.5**	**19.07**
1980 Average	**82.4**	**1.482**	**11.85**	**1.182**	**8.52**	**4.47**	**4.36**	**6.6**	**19.21**
1985 Average	**107.6**	**1.112**	**8.89**	**0.979**	**7.06**	**5.69**	**5.52**	**6.87**	**20.13**
1990 Average	**130.7**	**0.931**	**7.44**	**0.813**	**5.86**	**4.44**	**4.31**	**5.99**	**17.56**
1995 Average	**152.4**	**0.791**	**6.38**	**0.569**	**4.10**	**3.98**	**3.87**	**5.51**	**16.15**
2000 Average	**172.2**	**0.908**	**7.33**	**0.761**	**5.49**	**4.51**	**4.39**	**4.79**	**14.02**
2001 Average	**177.1**	**0.864**	**6.98**	**0.706**	**5.09**	**5.44**	**5.28**	**4.84**	**14.20**
2002 Average	**179.9**	**0.801**	**6.47**	**0.628**	**4.52**	**4.39**	**4.28**	**4.69**	**13.75**
2003 Average	**184.0**	**0.890**	**7.19**	**0.736**	**5.31**	**5.23**	**5.09**	**4.74**	**13.89**
2004 Average	**188.9**	**1.018**	**8.23**	**0.819**	**5.91**	**5.69**	**5.55**	**4.74**	**13.89**
2005 Average	**195.3**	**1.197**	**9.68**	**1.051**	**7.58**	**6.50**	**6.33**	**4.84**	**14.18**
2006 Average	**201.6**	**1.307**	**10.59**	**1.173**	**8.46**	**6.81**	**6.63**	**5.16**	**15.12**
2007 Average	**207.342**	**1.374**	**11.22**	**1.250**	**9.01**	**6.31**	**6.14**	**5.14**	**15.05**
2008 Average	**215.303**	**1.541**	**12.67**	**1.495**	**10.78**	**6.45**	**6.28**	**5.23**	**15.33**
2009 Average	**214.537**	**1.119**	**9.24**	**1.112**	**8.02**	**5.66**	**5.52**	**5.37**	**15.72**
2010 Average	**218.056**	**1.301**	**10.78**	**1.283**	**9.25**	**5.22**	**5.11**	**5.29**	**15.51**
2011 Average	**224.939**	**1.590**	**13.19**	**NA**	**NA**	**4.90**	**4.80**	**5.21**	**15.27**
2012 Average	**229.594**	**1.609**	**13.35**	**NA**	**NA**	**4.64**	**4.53**	**5.17**	**15.17**
2013 Average	**232.957**	**1.538**	**12.77**	**NA**	**NA**	**4.43**	**4.31**	**5.21**	**15.26**
2014 Average	**236.736**	**1.447**	**12.01**	**NA**	**NA**	**4.63**	**4.49**	**5.29**	**15.50**
2015 Average	**237.017**	**1.059**	**8.80**	**NA**	**NA**	**4.38**	**4.22**	**5.34**	**15.64**
2016 Average	**240.007**	**0.918**	**7.63**	**NA**	**NA**	**4.19**	**4.03**	**5.23**	**15.33**
2017 January	242.839	0.992	8.25	NA	NA	3.84	3.70	5.03	14.74
February	243.603	0.969	8.05	NA	NA	4.11	3.96	5.25	15.39
March	243.801	0.979	8.13	NA	NA	4.04	3.90	5.29	15.50
April	244.524	1.014	8.43	NA	NA	4.64	4.47	5.20	15.25
May	244.733	1.000	8.31	NA	NA	5.42	5.22	5.34	15.65
June	244.955	0.980	8.14	NA	NA	6.56	6.32	5.39	15.79
July	244.786	0.958	7.96	NA	NA	7.30	7.04	5.34	15.66
August	245.519	0.992	8.25	NA	NA	7.42	7.16	5.36	15.70
September	246.819	1.089	9.05	NA	NA	6.86	6.61	5.38	15.77
October	246.663	1.032	8.58	NA	NA	5.42	5.22	5.19	15.21
November	246.669	1.057	8.79	NA	NA	4.12	3.97	5.25	15.37
December	246.524	1.023	8.50	NA	NA	3.77	3.63	5.05	14.80
Average	**245.120**	**1.007**	**8.37**	**NA**	**NA**	**4.45**	**4.29**	**5.26**	**15.41**
2018 January	247.867	1.047	8.70	NA	NA	3.60	3.46	4.94	14.48
February	248.991	1.057	8.78	NA	NA	3.87	3.73	5.08	14.90
March	249.554	1.054	8.76	NA	NA	3.92	3.78	5.21	15.26
April	250.546	1.116	9.27	NA	NA	4.01	3.86	5.14	15.07
May	251.588	1.178	9.79	NA	NA	5.42	5.22	5.23	15.32
June	251.989	1.179	9.79	NA	NA	6.55	6.31	5.17	15.17
July	252.006	1.163	9.66	NA	NA	7.11	6.85	5.21	15.27
August	252.146	1.158	9.62	NA	NA	7.39	7.12	5.27	15.44
September	252.439	1.161	9.65	NA	NA	6.86	6.61	5.15	15.10
October	252.885	1.165	9.68	NA	NA	4.85	4.67	5.09	14.92
November	252.038	1.084	9.01	NA	NA	3.74	3.60	5.14	15.06
December	251.233	0.987	8.20	NA	NA	3.83	3.69	4.96	14.55
Average	**251.107**	**1.113**	**9.25**	**NA**	**NA**	**4.19**	**4.04**	**5.13**	**15.04**
2019 January	251.712	0.934	7.77	NA	NA	3.75	3.61	4.95	14.52
February	252.776	0.954	7.93	NA	NA	3.75	R 3.61	5.02	14.73
March	254.202	1.031	8.57	NA	NA	R 3.73	R 3.59	R 5.05	R 14.79
April	255.548	1.132	9.41	NA	NA	NA	NA	NA	NA
May	256.092	1.157	9.62	NA	NA	NA	NA	NA	NA

[a] Data are U.S. city averages for all items, and are not seasonally adjusted.
[b] Includes taxes.
[c] Excludes taxes.
R=Revised. NA=Not available.
Notes: • See "Real Dollars" in Glossary. • Fuel costs are calculated by using the Urban Consumer Price Index (CPI) developed by the Bureau of Labor Statistics. • Annual averages may not equal average of months due to independent rounding. • Geographic coverage is the 50 states and the District of Columbia.

Web Page: See http://www.eia.gov/totalenergy/data/monthly/#summary (Excel and CSV files) for all available annual data beginning in 1960 and monthly data beginning in 1995.

Sources: • **Fuel Prices:** Tables 9.4 (All Grades), 9.8, and 9.10, adjusted by the CPI; and *Monthy Energy Review*, September 2012, Table 9.8c. • **Consumer Price Index, All Urban Consumers:** U.S. Department of Labor, Bureau of Labor Statistics, series ID CUUR0000SA0. • **Conversion Factors:** Tables A1, A3, A4, and A6.

Source: *U.S. Energy Information Administration, Monthly Energy Review, June 2019*

Figure 1.7 Primary Energy Consumption and Energy Expenditures Indicators

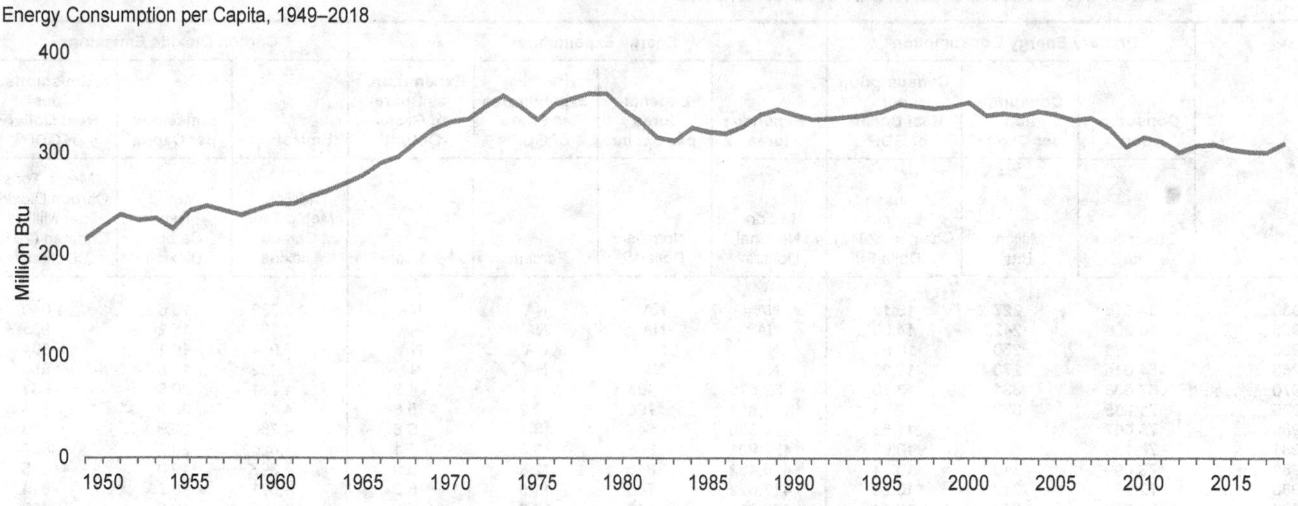

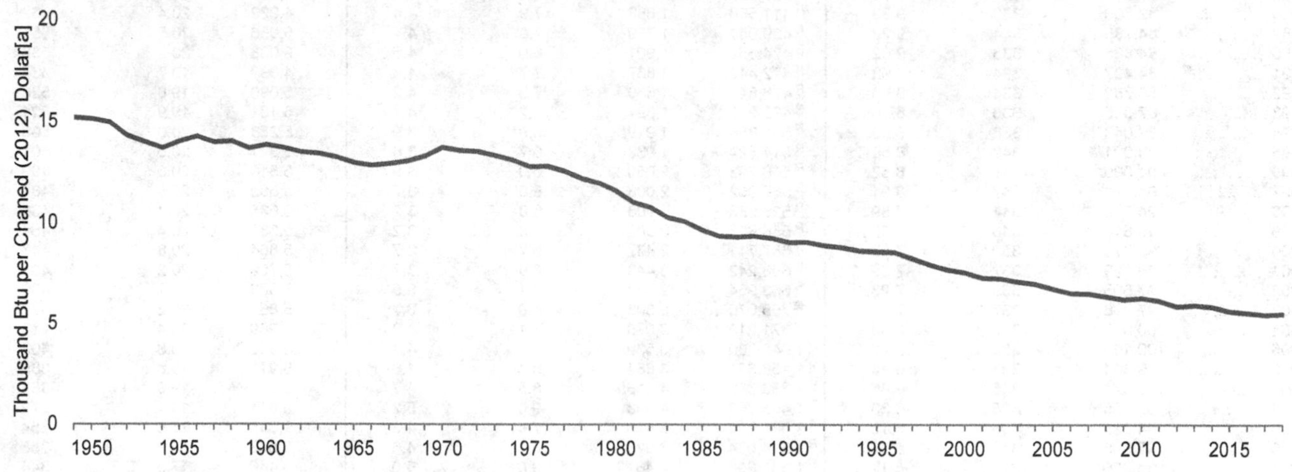

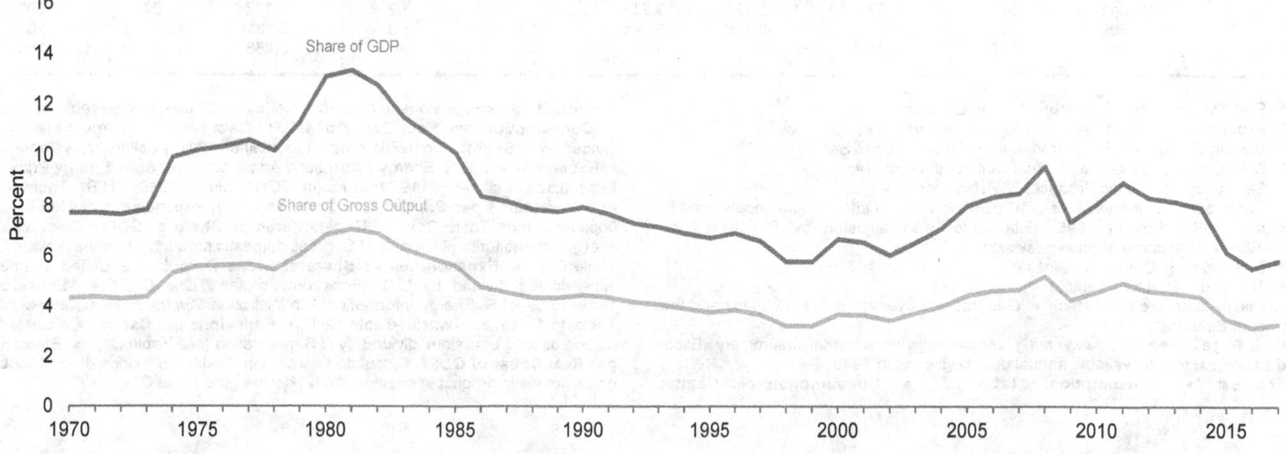

[a] See "Chained Dollars" and "Real Dollars" in Glossary.

[b] Gross output is the value of gross domestic product (GDP) plus the value of intermediate inputs used to produce GDP. Through 1996, data have been adjusted by EIA based on BEA's 2012 comprehensive revision.

Web Page: http://www.eia.gov/totalenergy/data/monthly/#summary.

Source: Table 1.7.

Source: *U.S. Energy Information Administration, Monthly Energy Review, June 2019*

Table 1.7 Primary Energy Consumption, Energy Expenditures, and Carbon Dioxide Emissions Indicators

	Primary Energy Consumption[a]			Energy Expenditures[b]				Carbon Dioxide Emissions[c]		
	Consumption	Consumption per Capita	Consumption per Real Dollar[d] of GDP[e]	Expenditures	Expenditures per Capita	Expenditures as Share of GDP[e]	Expenditures as Share of Gross Output[f]	Emissions	Emissions per Capita	Emissions per Real Dollar[d] of GDP[e]
	Quadrillion Btu	Million Btu	Thousand Btu per Chained (2012) Dollar[d]	Million Nominal Dollars[g]	Nominal Dollars[g]	Percent	Percent	Million Metric Tons Carbon Dioxide	Metric Tons Carbon Dioxide	Metric Tons Carbon Dioxide per Million Chained (2012) Dollars[d]
1950	34.616	227	15.12	NA	NA	NA	NA	2,382	15.6	1,040
1955	40.208	242	14.00	NA	NA	NA	NA	2,685	16.2	935
1960	45.086	250	13.83	NA	NA	NA	NA	2,914	16.1	894
1965	54.015	278	12.95	NA	NA	NA	NA	3,462	17.8	830
1970	67.838	331	13.70	82,875	404	7.7	4.3	4,261	20.8	861
1975	71.965	333	12.75	[R]171,854	796	10.2	5.6	4,421	20.5	783
1980	78.067	344	11.55	[R]374,350	1,647	13.1	6.8	4,750	20.9	703
1981	76.106	332	10.98	[R]427,901	1,865	13.3	7.1	4,625	20.2	667
1982	73.099	316	10.74	[R]426,482	1,841	12.8	6.9	4,393	19.0	645
1983	72.971	312	10.25	[R]417,622	1,786	11.5	6.3	4,371	18.7	614
1984	76.632	325	10.04	[R]435,313	1,846	10.8	5.9	4,600	19.5	603
1985	76.392	321	9.61	[R]438,343	1,842	10.1	5.6	4,593	19.3	578
1986	76.647	319	9.32	[R]384,091	1,599	8.4	4.8	4,598	19.1	559
1987	79.054	326	9.29	[R]397,627	1,641	8.2	4.6	4,757	19.6	559
1988	82.709	338	9.33	[R]411,568	1,683	7.9	4.4	4,982	20.4	562
1989	84.785	344	9.22	[R]439,051	1,779	7.8	4.4	5,066	20.5	551
1990	84.485	338	9.02	[R]474,652	1,901	8.0	4.5	5,038	20.2	538
1991	84.437	334	9.03	[R]472,440	1,867	7.7	4.4	4,993	19.7	534
1992	85.782	334	8.86	[R]476,845	1,859	7.3	4.2	5,090	19.8	526
1993	87.325	336	8.78	[R]492,275	1,894	7.2	4.1	5,181	19.9	521
1994	89.040	338	8.60	[R]504,856	1,919	6.9	3.9	5,258	20.0	508
1995	90.991	342	8.56	[R]514,624	1,933	6.7	3.8	5,321	20.0	501
1996	94.000	349	8.52	[R]560,293	2,080	6.9	3.9	5,510	20.5	499
1997	94.571	347	8.21	[R]567,962	2,083	6.6	3.7	5,582	20.5	484
1998	94.982	344	7.89	[R]526,283	1,908	5.8	3.2	5,635	20.4	468
1999	96.615	346	7.66	[R]558,627	2,002	5.8	3.2	5,687	20.4	451
2000	98.776	350	7.52	[R]687,711	2,437	6.7	3.7	5,864	20.8	447
2001	96.129	337	7.25	[R]696,242	2,443	6.6	3.7	5,759	20.2	434
2002	97.605	339	7.23	[R]663,964	2,308	6.1	3.5	5,803	20.2	430
2003	97.898	337	7.05	[R]755,070	2,603	6.6	3.7	5,854	20.2	422
2004	100.073	342	6.95	[R]871,210	2,975	7.1	4.0	5,969	20.4	414
2005	100.168	339	6.72	[R]1,045,730	3,539	8.0	4.4	5,990	20.3	402
2006	99.464	333	6.48	[R]1,158,821	3,884	8.4	4.6	5,911	19.8	385
2007	100.971	335	6.46	[R]1,233,869	4,096	8.5	4.7	6,002	19.9	384
2008	98.825	325	6.33	[R]1,408,759	4,633	9.6	5.2	5,811	19.1	372
2009	94.023	306	6.18	[R]1,066,293	3,476	7.4	4.3	5,388	17.6	354
2010	97.608	316	6.26	[R]1,214,034	[R]3,925	8.1	4.6	5,586	18.1	358
2011	96.950	311	6.12	[R]1,391,696	[R]4,467	9.0	5.0	5,446	17.5	344
2012	94.480	301	5.83	[R]1,355,024	4,317	8.4	4.6	5,237	16.7	323
2013	97.218	308	5.89	[R]1,376,134	4,354	8.2	4.5	5,363	17.0	325
2014	98.382	309	5.82	[R]1,394,918	4,381	8.0	4.4	5,411	17.0	320
2015	97.484	304	5.61	[R]1,128,062	[R]3,517	6.2	3.5	5,265	16.4	303
2016	97.445	302	5.52	[R]1,038,120	[R]3,213	[R]5.5	3.2	5,172	16.0	293
2017	97.809	301	5.42	[R]1,136,496	[R]3,495	[R]5.8	[R]3.3	5,131	15.8	284
2018	101.239	309	5.45	NA	NA	NA	NA	5,268	16.1	284

[a] See "Primary Energy Consumption" in Glossary.
[b] Expenditures include taxes where data are available.
[c] Carbon dioxide emissions from energy consumption. See Table 12.1.
[d] See "Chained Dollars" and "Real Dollars" in Glossary.
[e] See "Gross Domestic Product (GDP)" in Glossary.
[f] Gross output is the value of GDP plus the value of intermediate inputs used to produce GDP. Through 1996, data have been adjusted by EIA based on DOC/BEA's 2012 comprehensive revision.
[g] See "Nominal Dollars" in Glossary.

R=Revised. NA=Not available.

Notes: • Data are estimates. • Geographic coverage is the 50 states and the District of Columbia.

Web Page: See http://www.eia.gov/totalenergy/data/monthly/#summary (Excel and CSV files) for all available annual data beginning in 1949.

Sources: • **Consumption:** Table 1.3. • **Consumption per Capita:** Calculated as energy consumption divided by U.S. population (see Table C1). • **Consumption per Real Dollar of GDP:** Calculated as energy consumption divided by U.S. gross domestic product in chained (2012) dollars (see Table C1). • **Expenditures:** U.S. Energy Information Administration, "State Energy Price and Expenditure Estimates, 1970 Through 2017" (June 2019), U.S. Table ET1. • **Expenditures per Capita:** Calculated as energy expenditures divided by U.S. population (see Table C1). • **Expenditures as Share of GDP:** Calculated as energy expenditures divided by U.S. gross domestic product in nominal dollars (see Table C1). • **Expenditures as Share of Gross Output:** Calculated as energy expenditures divided by U.S. gross output (see Table C1). • **Emissions: 1949–1972**—U.S. Energy Information Administration, *Annual Energy Review 2011*, Table 11.1. **1973 forward**—Table 12.1. • **Emissions per Capita:** Calculated as carbon dioxide emissions divided by U.S. population (see Table C1). • **Emissions per Real Dollar of GDP:** Calculated as carbon dioxide emissions divided by U.S. gross domestic product in chained (2012) dollars (see Table C1).

Source: *U.S. Energy Information Administration, Monthly Energy Review, June 2019*

Figure 1.8 Motor Vehicle Mileage, Fuel Consumption, and Fuel Economy, 1949-2016

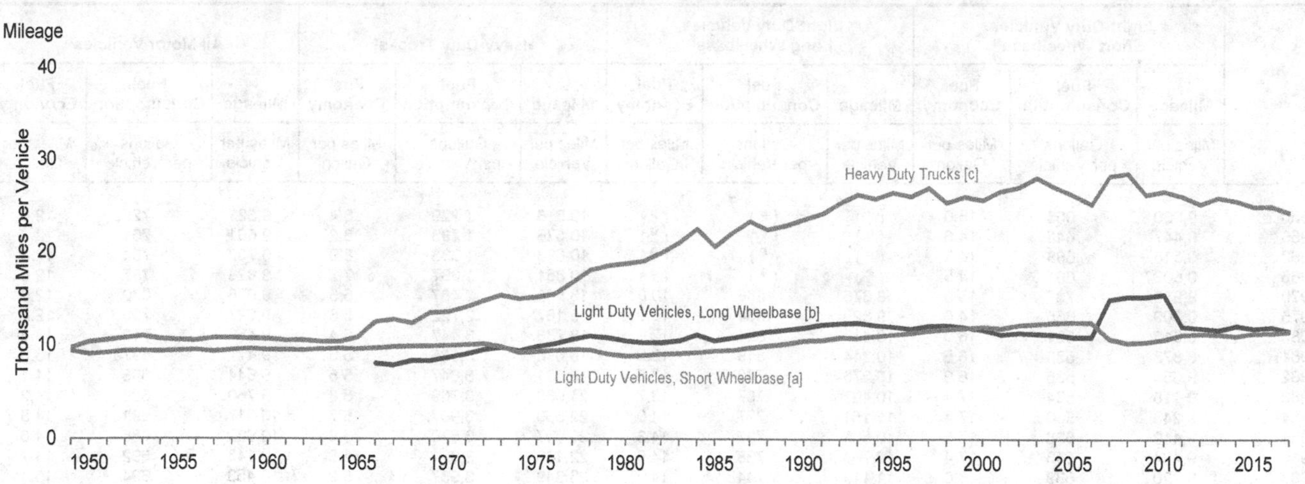

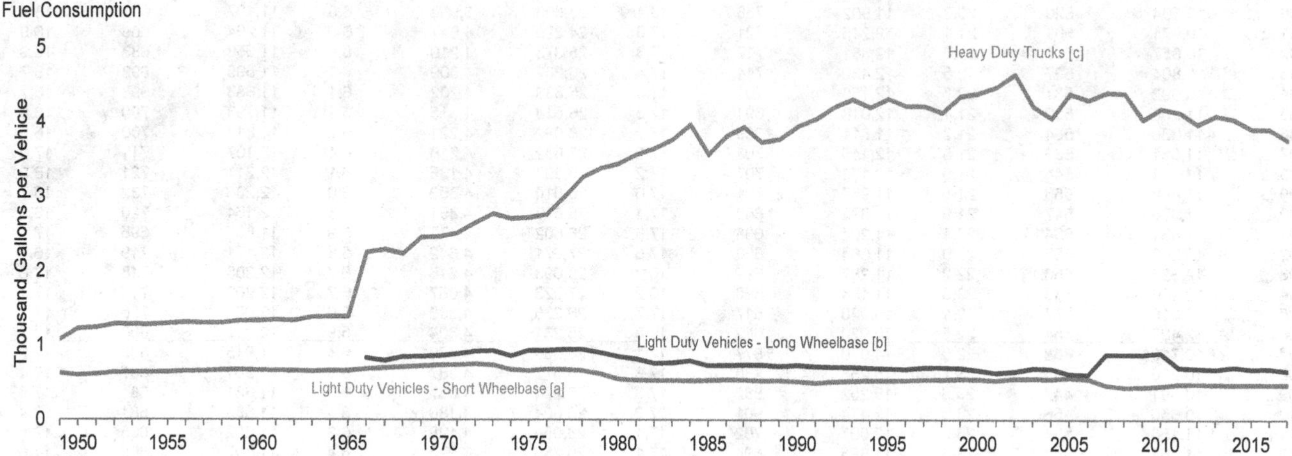

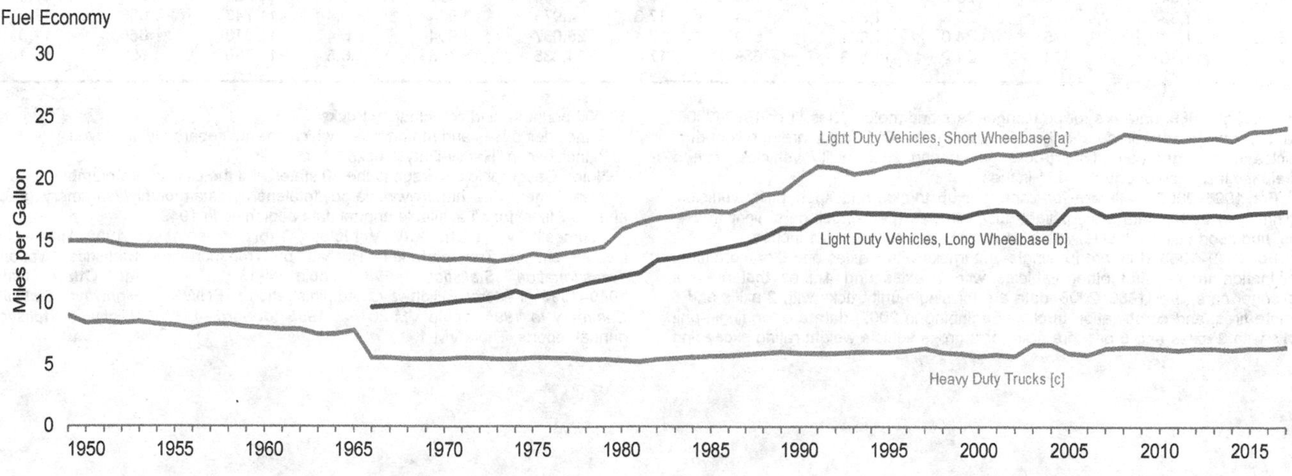

[a] Through 1989, data are for passenger cars and motorcycles. For 1990–2006, data are for passenger cars only. Beginning in 2007, data are for light-duty vehicles (passenger cars, light trucks, vans, and sport utility vehicles) with a wheelbase less than or equal to 121 inches.

[b] For 1966–2000, data are for vans, pickup trucks, and sport utility vehicles. Beginning in 2007, data are for light-duty vehicles (passenger cars, light trucks, vans, and sport utility vehicles) with a wheelbase greater than 121 inches.

[c] For 1949–1965, data are for single-unit trucks with 2 axles and 6 or more tires, combination trucks, and other vehicles with 2 axles and 4 tires that are not passenger cars. For 1966–2006 data are for single-unit truck with 2 axles and 6 or more tires, and combination trucks. Beginning in 2007, data are for single-unit trucks with 2 axles and 6 or more tires (or a gross vehicle weight rating exceeding 10,000 pounds), and combination trucks.

Note: Through 1965, "Light-Duty Vehicles, Long Wheelbase" data are included in "Heavy-Duty Trucks."

Web Page: http://www.eia.gov/totalenergy/data/monthly/#summary.

Source: Table 1.8.

Source: *U.S. Energy Information Administration, Monthly Energy Review, June 2019*

Table 1.8 Motor Vehicle Mileage, Fuel Consumption, and Fuel Economy

	Light-Duty Vehicles, Short Wheelbase[a]			Light-Duty Vehicles, Long Wheelbase[b]			Heavy-Duty Trucks[c]			All Motor Vehicles[d]		
	Mileage	Fuel Consumption	Fuel Economy	Mileage	Fuel Consumption	Fuel Economy	Mileage	Fuel Consumption	Fuel Economy	Mileage	Fuel Consumption	Fuel Economy
	Miles per Vehicle	Gallons per Vehicle	Miles per Gallon	Miles per Vehicle	Gallons per Vehicle	Miles per Gallon	Miles per Vehicle	Gallons per Vehicle	Miles per Gallon	Miles per Vehicle	Gallons per Vehicle	Miles per Gallon
1950	9,060	603	15.0	([e])	([e])	([e])	10,316	1,229	8.4	9,321	725	12.8
1955	9,447	645	14.6	([e])	([e])	([e])	10,576	1,293	8.2	9,661	761	12.7
1960	9,518	668	14.3	([e])	([e])	([e])	10,693	1,333	8.0	9,732	784	12.4
1965	9,603	661	14.5	([e])	([e])	([e])	10,851	1,387	7.8	9,826	787	12.5
1970	9,989	737	13.5	8,676	866	10.0	13,565	2,467	5.5	9,976	830	12.0
1975	9,309	665	14.0	9,829	934	10.5	15,167	2,722	5.6	9,627	790	12.2
1980	8,813	551	16.0	10,437	854	12.2	18,736	3,447	5.4	9,458	712	13.3
1981	8,873	538	16.5	10,244	819	12.5	19,016	3,565	5.3	9,477	697	13.6
1982	9,050	535	16.9	10,276	762	13.5	19,931	3,647	5.5	9,644	686	14.1
1983	9,118	534	17.1	10,497	767	13.7	21,083	3,769	5.6	9,760	686	14.2
1984	9,248	530	17.4	11,151	797	14.0	22,550	3,967	5.7	10,017	691	14.5
1985	9,419	538	17.5	10,506	735	14.3	20,597	3,570	5.8	10,020	685	14.6
1986	9,464	543	17.4	10,764	738	14.6	22,143	3,821	5.8	10,143	692	14.7
1987	9,720	539	18.0	11,114	744	14.9	23,349	3,937	5.9	10,453	694	15.1
1988	9,972	531	18.8	11,465	745	15.4	22,485	3,736	6.0	10,721	688	15.6
1989	10,157	533	19.0	11,676	724	16.1	22,926	3,776	6.1	10,932	688	15.9
1990	10,504	520	20.2	11,902	738	16.1	23,603	3,953	6.0	11,107	677	16.4
1991	10,571	501	21.1	12,245	721	17.0	24,229	4,047	6.0	11,294	669	16.9
1992	10,857	517	21.0	12,381	717	17.3	25,373	4,210	6.0	11,558	683	16.9
1993	10,804	527	20.5	12,430	714	17.4	26,262	4,309	6.1	11,595	693	16.7
1994	10,992	531	20.7	12,156	701	17.3	25,838	4,202	6.1	11,683	698	16.7
1995	11,203	530	21.1	12,018	694	17.3	26,514	4,315	6.1	11,793	700	16.8
1996	11,330	534	21.2	11,811	685	17.2	26,092	4,221	6.2	11,813	700	16.9
1997	11,581	539	21.5	12,115	703	17.2	27,032	4,218	6.4	12,107	711	17.0
1998	11,754	544	21.6	12,173	707	17.2	25,397	4,135	6.1	12,211	721	16.9
1999	11,848	553	21.4	11,957	701	17.0	26,014	4,352	6.0	12,206	732	16.7
2000	11,976	547	21.9	11,672	669	17.4	25,617	4,391	5.8	12,164	720	16.9
2001	11,831	534	22.1	11,204	636	17.6	26,602	4,477	5.9	11,887	695	17.1
2002	12,202	555	22.0	11,364	650	17.5	27,071	4,642	5.8	12,171	719	16.9
2003	12,325	556	22.2	11,287	697	16.2	28,093	4,215	6.7	12,208	718	17.0
2004	12,460	553	22.5	11,184	690	16.2	27,023	4,057	6.7	12,200	714	17.1
2005	12,510	567	22.1	10,920	617	17.7	26,235	4,385	6.0	12,082	706	17.1
2006	12,485	554	22.5	10,920	612	17.8	25,231	4,304	5.9	12,017	698	17.2
2007	[a] 10,710	[a] 468	[a] 22.9	[b] 14,970	[b] 877	[b] 17.1	[c] 28,290	[c] 4,398	6.4	11,915	693	17.2
2008	10,290	435	23.7	15,256	880	17.3	28,573	4,387	6.5	11,631	667	17.4
2009	10,391	442	23.5	15,252	882	17.3	26,274	4,037	6.5	11,631	661	17.6
2010	10,650	456	23.3	15,474	901	17.2	26,604	4,180	6.4	11,866	681	17.4
2011	11,150	481	23.2	12,007	702	17.1	26,054	4,128	6.3	11,652	665	17.5
2012	11,262	484	23.3	11,885	694	17.1	25,255	3,973	6.4	11,707	665	17.6
2013	11,244	480	23.4	11,712	683	17.2	25,951	4,086	6.4	11,679	663	17.6
2014	11,048	476	23.2	12,138	710	17.1	25,594	4,036	6.3	11,621	666	17.5
2015	11,327	475	23.9	11,855	684	17.3	24,979	3,904	6.4	11,742	656	17.9
2016	11,370	475	24.0	11,991	689	17.4	25,037	3,904	6.4	11,810	658	17.9
2017	11,467	474	24.2	11,543	659	17.5	24,335	3,758	6.5	11,789	653	18.1

[a] Through 1989, data are for passenger cars and motorcycles. For 1990–2006, data are for passenger cars only. Beginning in 2007, data are for light-duty vehicles (passenger cars, light trucks, vans, and sport utility vehicles) with a wheelbase less than or equal to 121 inches.

[b] For 1966–2006, data are for vans, pickup trucks, and sport utility vehicles. Beginning in 2007, data are for light-duty vehicles (passenger cars, light trucks, vans, and sport utility vehicles) with a wheelbase greater than 121 inches.

[c] For 1949–1965, data are for single-unit trucks with 2 axles and 6 or more tires, combination trucks, and other vehicles with 2 axles and 4 tires that are not passenger cars. For 1966–2006, data are for single-unit trucks with 2 axles and 6 or more tires, and combination trucks. Beginning in 2007, data are for single-unit trucks with 2 axles and 6 or more tires (or a gross vehicle weight rating exceeding 10,000 pounds), and combination trucks.

[d] Includes buses and motorcycles, which are not separately displayed.

[e] Included in "Heavy-Duty Trucks."

Note: Geographic coverage is the 50 states and the District of Columbia.

Web Page: See http://www.eia.gov/totalenergy/data/monthly/#summary (Excel and CSV files) for all available annual data beginning in 1949.

Sources: • **Light-Duty Vehicles, Short Wheelbase: 1990–1994**—U.S. Department of Transportation, Bureau of Transportation Statistics, *National Transportation Statistics 1998,* Table 4-13. • **All Other Data: 1949–1994**—Federal Highway Administration (FHWA), *Highway Statistics Summary to 1995,* Table VM-201A. **1995 forward**—FHWA, *Highway Statistics,* annual reports, Table VM-1.

Source: *U.S. Energy Information Administration, Monthly Energy Review, June 2019*

Table 1.9 Heating Degree Days by Census Division

	New England[a]	Middle Atlantic[b]	East North Central[c]	West North Central[d]	South Atlantic[e]	East South Central[f]	West South Central[g]	Mountain[h]	Pacific[i]	United States
1950 Total	**6,794**	**6,324**	**7,027**	**7,455**	**3,521**	**3,547**	**2,277**	**6,341**	**3,906**	**5,367**
1955 Total	**6,872**	**6,231**	**6,486**	**6,912**	**3,508**	**3,513**	**2,294**	**6,704**	**4,320**	**5,246**
1960 Total	**6,828**	**6,391**	**6,908**	**7,184**	**3,780**	**4,134**	**2,767**	**6,281**	**3,799**	**5,404**
1965 Total	**7,029**	**6,393**	**6,587**	**6,932**	**3,372**	**3,501**	**2,237**	**6,086**	**3,819**	**5,146**
1970 Total	**7,022**	**6,388**	**6,721**	**7,090**	**3,452**	**3,823**	**2,558**	**6,119**	**3,726**	**5,218**
1975 Total	**6,547**	**5,892**	**6,406**	**6,880**	**2,970**	**3,437**	**2,312**	**6,260**	**4,117**	**4,905**
1980 Total	**7,071**	**6,477**	**6,975**	**6,836**	**3,378**	**3,964**	**2,494**	**5,554**	**3,539**	**5,080**
1985 Total	**6,749**	**5,971**	**6,668**	**7,262**	**2,899**	**3,660**	**2,535**	**6,059**	**3,935**	**4,889**
1990 Total	**5,987**	**5,252**	**5,780**	**6,137**	**2,307**	**2,942**	**1,968**	**5,391**	**3,603**	**4,180**
1995 Total	**6,684**	**6,093**	**6,740**	**6,911**	**2,988**	**3,648**	**2,147**	**5,101**	**3,269**	**4,640**
2000 Total	**6,625**	**5,999**	**6,315**	**6,500**	**2,905**	**3,551**	**2,153**	**4,971**	**3,460**	**4,494**
2001 Total	**6,202**	**5,541**	**5,844**	**6,221**	**2,604**	**3,327**	**2,162**	**5,004**	**3,545**	**4,257**
2002 Total	**6,234**	**5,550**	**6,128**	**6,485**	**2,664**	**3,443**	**2,292**	**5,197**	**3,510**	**4,356**
2003 Total	**6,975**	**6,258**	**6,536**	**6,593**	**2,884**	**3,559**	**2,205**	**4,817**	**3,355**	**4,544**
2004 Total	**6,709**	**5,892**	**6,178**	**6,329**	**2,715**	**3,291**	**2,041**	**5,010**	**3,346**	**4,344**
2005 Total	**6,644**	**5,950**	**6,222**	**6,213**	**2,775**	**3,380**	**1,985**	**4,896**	**3,377**	**4,348**
2006 Total	**5,885**	**5,211**	**5,703**	**5,821**	**2,475**	**3,211**	**1,802**	**4,915**	**3,557**	**4,040**
2007 Total	**6,537**	**5,756**	**6,074**	**6,384**	**2,525**	**3,187**	**2,105**	**4,939**	**3,506**	**4,268**
2008 Total	**6,434**	**5,782**	**6,677**	**7,118**	**2,712**	**3,600**	**2,125**	**5,233**	**3,566**	**4,494**
2009 Total	**6,644**	**5,922**	**6,512**	**6,841**	**2,812**	**3,536**	**2,152**	**5,139**	**3,538**	**4,481**
2010 Total	**5,934**	**5,553**	**6,185**	**6,565**	**3,167**	**3,948**	**2,449**	**5,082**	**3,624**	**4,463**
2011 Total	**6,114**	**5,483**	**6,172**	**6,565**	**2,565**	**3,343**	**2,114**	**5,322**	**3,818**	**4,312**
2012 Total	**5,561**	**4,970**	**5,356**	**5,515**	**2,306**	**2,876**	**1,650**	**4,574**	**3,411**	**3,769**
2013 Total	**6,426**	**5,838**	**6,621**	**7,135**	**2,736**	**3,648**	**2,326**	**5,273**	**3,362**	**4,465**
2014 Total	**6,675**	**6,203**	**7,194**	**7,304**	**2,951**	**3,932**	**2,422**	**4,744**	**2,774**	**4,550**
2015 Total	**6,521**	**5,777**	**6,165**	**6,088**	**2,487**	**3,222**	**2,087**	**4,602**	**2,898**	**4,087**
2016 Total	**5,929**	**5,353**	**5,701**	**5,786**	**2,456**	**3,094**	**1,752**	**4,619**	**3,031**	**3,878**
2017 January	1,038	971	1,082	1,212	476	579	417	962	666	766
February	906	780	776	818	323	409	208	627	496	547
March	1,037	908	834	783	346	387	147	467	392	543
April	451	341	349	401	76	94	52	404	309	248
May	303	233	249	224	47	57	14	235	171	154
June	45	25	27	37	2	3	0	59	50	25
July	9	3	6	10	0	0	0	6	14	5
August	26	18	34	50	1	1	0	27	8	15
September	57	53	64	78	14	24	3	120	45	45
October	237	215	291	363	89	146	59	358	178	193
November	743	699	773	805	322	407	180	489	351	490
December	1,186	1,087	1,197	1,218	535	729	501	815	507	798
Total	**6,038**	**5,332**	**5,684**	**5,997**	**2,231**	**2,835**	**1,582**	**4,568**	**3,187**	**3,828**
2018 January	R 1,258	1,213	1,309	1,374	700	R 929	R 661	771	459	896
February	R 869	R 808	981	R 1,178	307	411	R 347	R 749	R 495	624
March	R 927	913	922	869	R 435	R 474	R 184	R 604	R 485	R 608
April	R 676	R 616	703	715	206	312	R 142	380	R 298	410
May	R 168	R 107	99	89	12	13	0	R 164	R 177	R 86
June	62	29	24	23	1	0	0	57	65	26
July	2	1	4	11	0	0	0	9	8	3
August	3	2	8	20	0	0	0	25	14	7
September	R 65	34	48	90	2	2	3	90	62	38
October	R 458	355	420	R 495	99	137	R 69	R 383	R 186	253
November	R 819	765	913	1,003	R 379	565	372	R 678	R 352	593
December	R 1,029	R 929	1,004	1,103	R 489	R 636	R 469	R 897	R 562	731
Total	**R 6,337**	**R 5,773**	**R 6,435**	**R 6,969**	**2,630**	**R 3,480**	**R 2,246**	**R 4,806**	**R 3,162**	**4,276**
2019 January	1,222	R 1,154	R 1,304	R 1,360	R 581	749	546	R 895	R 543	859
February	R 1,030	R 941	1,064	1,284	377	R 461	R 357	868	R 654	R 719
March	977	892	963	1,001	375	505	305	669	489	632
3-Month Total	**3,230**	**2,987**	**3,331**	**3,644**	**1,334**	**1,716**	**1,208**	**2,432**	**1,686**	**2,211**
2018 3-Month Total	**3,055**	**2,935**	**3,212**	**3,421**	**1,442**	**1,815**	**1,192**	**2,124**	**1,438**	**2,129**
2017 3-Month Total	**2,980**	**2,659**	**2,691**	**2,812**	**1,145**	**1,375**	**773**	**2,056**	**1,554**	**1,856**

[a] Connecticut, Maine, Massachusetts, New Hampshire, Rhode Island, and Vermont.
[b] New Jersey, New York, and Pennsylvania.
[c] Illinois, Indiana, Michigan, Ohio, and Wisconsin.
[d] Iowa, Kansas, Minnesota, Missouri, Nebraska, North Dakota, and South Dakota.
[e] Delaware, Florida, Georgia, Maryland (and the District of Columbia), North Carolina, South Carolina, Virginia, and West Virginia.
[f] Alabama, Kentucky, Mississippi, and Tennessee.
[g] Arkansas, Louisiana, Oklahoma, and Texas.
[h] Arizona, Colorado, Idaho, Montana, Nevada, New Mexico, Utah, and Wyoming.
[i] Alaska, California, Hawaii, Oregon, and Washington.
R=Revised.

Notes: • Degree days are relative measurements of outdoor air temperature used as an index for heating and cooling energy requirements. Heating degree days are the number of degrees that the daily average temperature falls below 65 degrees Fahrenheit (°F). Cooling degree days are the number of degrees that the daily average temperature rises above 65°F. The daily average temperature is the mean of the maximum and minimum temperatures in a 24-hour period. For example, a weather station recording an average daily temperature of 40°F would report 25 heating degree days for that day (and 0 cooling degree days). If a weather station recorded an average daily temperature of 78°F, cooling degree days for that station would be 13 (and 0 heating degree days). • Totals may not equal sum of components due to independent rounding. • Geographic coverage is the 50 states and the District of Columbia.

Web Page: See http://www.eia.gov/totalenergy/data/monthly/#summary (Excel and CSV files) for all available annual data beginning in 1949 and monthly data beginning in 1973.

Source: State-level degree day data are from U.S. Department of Commerce, National Oceanic and Atmospheric Administration, National Centers for Environmental Information. Using these state-level data, the U.S. Energy Information Administration calculates population-weighted census-division and U.S. degree day averages using state populations from the same year the degree days are measured. See methodology at http://www.eia.gov/forecasts/steo/special/pdf/2012_sp_04.pdf.

Source: *U.S. Energy Information Administration, Monthly Energy Review, June 2019*

Table 1.10 Cooling Degree Days by Census Division

	New England[a]	Middle Atlantic[b]	East North Central[c]	West North Central[d]	South Atlantic[e]	East South Central[f]	West South Central[g]	Mountain[h]	Pacific[i]	United States
1950 Total	295	401	505	647	1,414	1,420	2,282	682	629	871
1955 Total	532	761	922	1,139	1,636	1,674	2,508	780	558	1,144
1960 Total	318	487	626	871	1,583	1,532	2,367	974	796	1,000
1965 Total	310	498	618	832	1,613	1,552	2,461	780	577	979
1970 Total	423	615	747	980	1,744	1,571	2,282	971	734	1,079
1975 Total	422	584	721	937	1,791	1,440	2,162	903	597	1,049
1980 Total	438	680	769	1,158	1,911	1,754	2,651	1,071	653	1,214
1985 Total	324	509	602	780	1,878	1,522	2,519	1,095	761	1,121
1990 Total	429	562	602	913	2,054	1,563	2,526	1,212	838	1,200
1995 Total	471	704	877	928	2,028	1,613	2,398	1,213	794	1,261
2000 Total	279	458	632	983	1,925	1,674	2,775	1,480	772	1,232
2001 Total	464	623	722	994	1,897	1,478	2,543	1,508	861	1,255
2002 Total	508	772	899	1,045	2,182	1,757	2,515	1,467	783	1,363
2003 Total	475	615	619	907	1,980	1,452	2,496	1,553	978	1,268
2004 Total	368	591	585	722	2,038	1,517	2,482	1,290	828	1,217
2005 Total	598	892	944	1,063	2,098	1,676	2,647	1,372	777	1,388
2006 Total	485	693	734	1,034	2,053	1,648	2,786	1,466	922	1,360
2007 Total	447	694	881	1,102	2,219	1,892	2,475	1,564	828	1,392
2008 Total	462	667	683	818	1,993	1,537	2,501	1,385	918	1,282
2009 Total	350	524	534	698	2,029	1,479	2,590	1,393	894	1,241
2010 Total	635	908	964	1,096	2,269	1,977	2,757	1,358	674	1,456
2011 Total	554	836	859	1,074	2,259	1,727	3,112	1,450	736	1,470
2012 Total	565	815	974	1,221	2,162	1,762	2,915	1,573	917	1,495
2013 Total	540	683	690	892	2,000	1,441	2,536	1,462	892	1,306
2014 Total	420	596	610	814	2,009	1,493	2,474	1,431	1,068	1,299
2015 Total	555	804	729	942	2,405	1,718	2,741	1,478	1,068	1,488
2016 Total	626	888	958	1,073	2,412	1,957	2,882	1,497	928	1,559
2017 January	0	0	0	0	50	20	36	0	7	17
February	0	0	0	3	55	18	67	5	7	22
March	0	0	1	6	56	28	111	32	17	32
April	0	2	7	9	124	74	141	51	25	56
May	3	14	37	51	213	135	240	109	46	106
June	72	123	167	206	337	272	445	308	150	241
July	170	251	242	331	469	430	582	414	283	363
August	128	162	148	166	406	341	508	329	281	292
September	66	87	92	127	282	194	368	178	139	184
October	11	22	16	14	159	66	145	92	68	78
November	0	0	0	0	66	6	67	29	21	27
December	0	0	0	0	38	1	6	1	10	10
Total	**450**	**661**	**709**	**911**	**2,254**	**1,585**	**2,718**	**1,548**	**1,053**	**1,428**
2018 January	0	0	0	0	21	1	4	R 4	15	R 7
February	0	0	0	0	82	21	33	3	8	23
March	0	0	0	2	34	15	R 89	14	9	21
April	0	0	0	0	R 79	7	R 57	72	25	33
May	25	R 66	140	168	R 265	268	R 396	138	39	175
June	56	R 112	192	272	R 385	375	R 551	R 299	117	270
July	R 251	R 288	257	304	R 441	431	R 608	R 416	321	376
August	R 264	R 299	257	257	R 438	R 392	566	R 346	256	351
September	64	122	122	124	R 391	339	R 391	R 239	R 145	232
October	0	4	4	6	176	78	R 143	46	R 47	70
November	0	0	0	0	66	1	13	5	R 17	18
December	0	0	0	0	R 39	R 2	10	0	9	11
Total	**R 659**	**R 889**	**973**	**R 1,134**	**R 2,416**	**R 1,931**	**R 2,860**	**R 1,581**	**R 1,007**	**1,587**
2019 January	0	0	0	0	30	5	12	0	8	9
February	0	0	0	0	R 68	13	R 24	0	5	18
March	0	0	0	0	57	10	36	10	8	19
3-Month Total	**0**	**0**	**0**	**0**	**155**	**28**	**72**	**10**	**22**	**46**
2018 3-Month Total	**0**	**0**	**0**	**2**	**137**	**37**	**127**	**21**	**31**	**52**
2017 3-Month Total	**0**	**0**	**1**	**9**	**161**	**65**	**214**	**37**	**30**	**70**

[a] Connecticut, Maine, Massachusetts, New Hampshire, Rhode Island, and Vermont.
[b] New Jersey, New York, and Pennsylvania.
[c] Illinois, Indiana, Michigan, Ohio, and Wisconsin.
[d] Iowa, Kansas, Minnesota, Missouri, Nebraska, North Dakota, and South Dakota.
[e] Delaware, Florida, Georgia, Maryland (and the District of Columbia), North Carolina, South Carolina, Virginia, and West Virginia.
[f] Alabama, Kentucky, Mississippi, and Tennessee.
[g] Arkansas, Louisiana, Oklahoma, and Texas.
[h] Arizona, Colorado, Idaho, Montana, Nevada, New Mexico, Utah, and Wyoming.
[i] Alaska, California, Hawaii, Oregon, and Washington.

R=Revised.

Notes: • Degree days are relative measurements of outdoor air temperature used as an index for heating and cooling energy requirements. Cooling degree days are the number of degrees that the daily average temperature rises above 65 degrees Fahrenheit (°F). Heating degree days are the number of degrees that the daily average temperature falls below 65°F. The daily average temperature is the mean of the maximum and minimum temperatures in a 24-hour period. For example, if a weather station recorded an average daily temperature of 78°F, cooling degree days for that station would be 13 (and 0 heating degree days). A weather station recording an average daily temperature of 40°F would report 25 heating degree days for that day (and 0 cooling degree days). • Totals may not equal sum of components due to independent rounding. • Geographic coverage is the 50 states and the District of Columbia.

Web Page: See http://www.eia.gov/totalenergy/data/monthly/#summary (Excel and CSV files) for all available annual data beginning in 1949 and monthly data beginning in 1973.

Source: State-level degree day data are from U.S. Department of Commerce, National Oceanic and Atmospheric Administration, National Centers for Environmental Information. Using these state-level data, the U.S. Energy Information Administration calculates population-weighted census-division and U.S. degree day averages using state populations from the same year the degree days are measured. See methodology at http://www.eia.gov/forecasts/steo/special/pdf/2012_sp_04.pdf.

Source: *U.S. Energy Information Administration, Monthly Energy Review, June 2019*

Figure 2.1 Energy Consumption by Sector
(Quadrillion Btu)

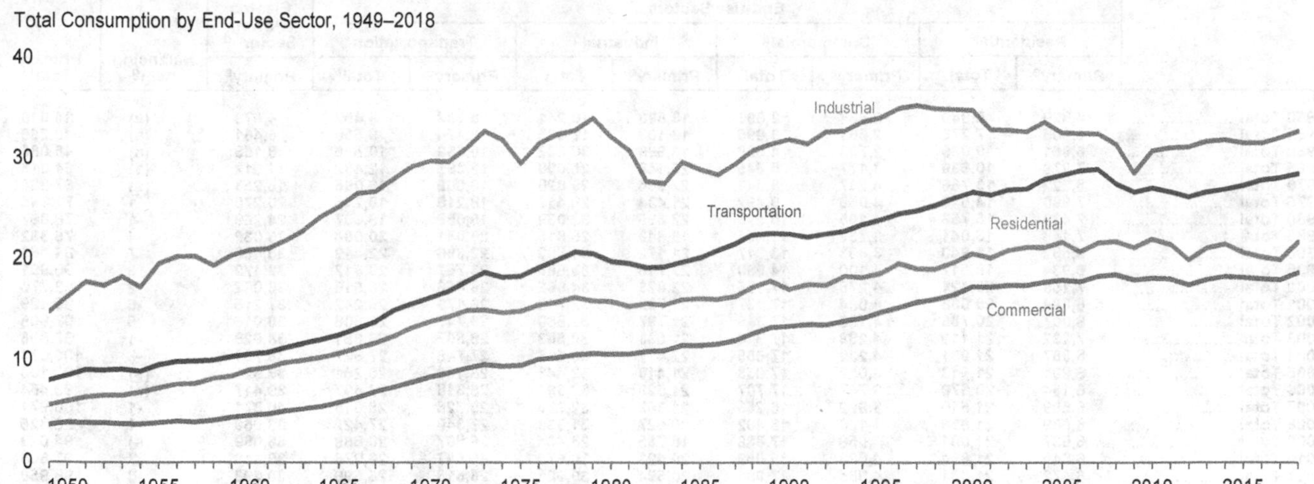

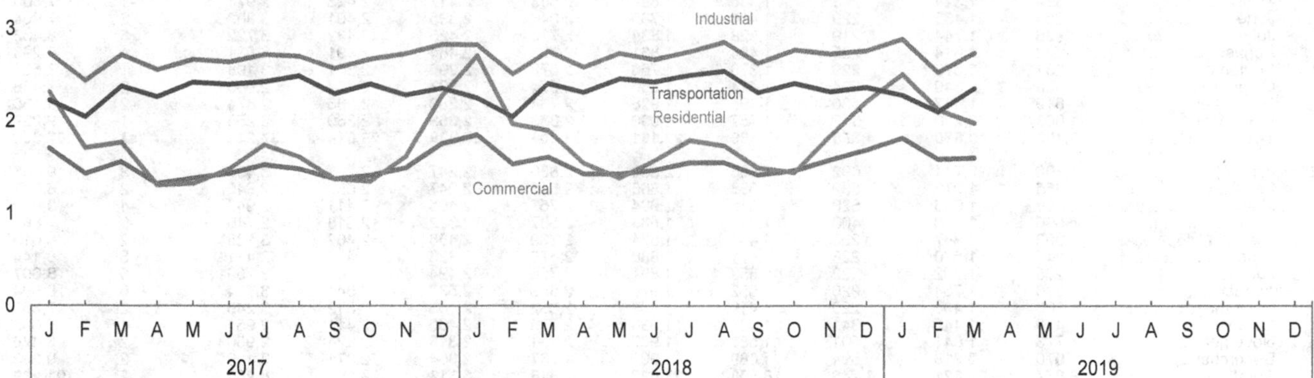

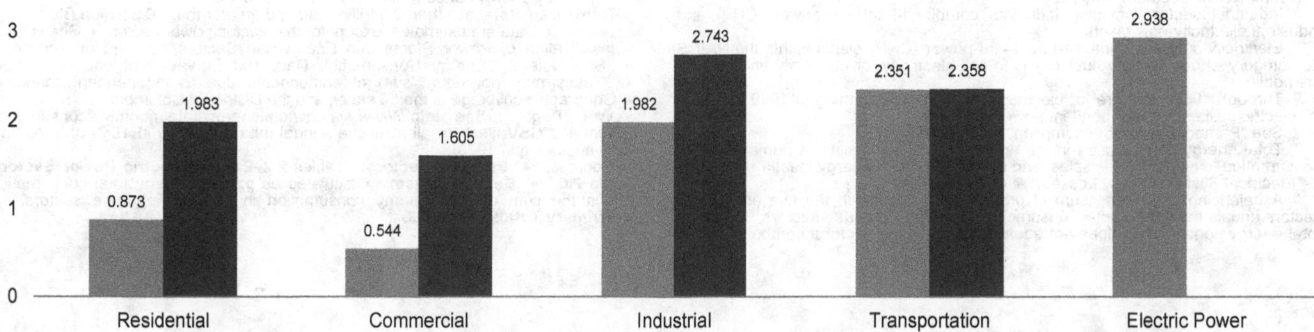

Web Page: http://www.eia.gov/totalenergy/data/monthly/#consumption.
Source: Table 2.1.

***Source:** U.S. Energy Information Administration, Monthly Energy Review, June 2019*

Table 2.1 Energy Consumption by Sector
(Trillion Btu)

	End-Use Sectors								Electric Power Sector[c,d]	Balancing Item[g]	Primary Total[h]
	Residential		Commercial[a]		Industrial[b]		Transportation				
	Primary[e]	Total[f]	Primary[e]	Total[f]	Primary[e]	Total[f]	Primary[e]	Total[f]	Primary[e]		
1950 Total	**4,829**	**5,989**	**2,834**	**3,893**	**13,890**	**16,241**	**8,383**	**8,492**	**4,679**	**(s)**	**34,616**
1955 Total	**5,608**	**7,278**	**2,561**	**3,895**	**16,103**	**19,485**	**9,474**	**9,550**	**6,461**	**(s)**	**40,208**
1960 Total	**6,651**	**9,039**	**2,723**	**4,609**	**16,996**	**20,842**	**10,560**	**10,596**	**8,158**	**(s)**	**45,086**
1965 Total	**7,279**	**10,639**	**3,177**	**5,845**	**20,148**	**25,098**	**12,399**	**12,432**	**11,012**	**(s)**	**54,015**
1970 Total	**8,322**	**13,766**	**4,237**	**8,346**	**22,964**	**29,628**	**16,062**	**16,098**	**16,253**	**(s)**	**67,838**
1975 Total	**7,990**	**14,813**	**4,059**	**9,492**	**21,434**	**29,413**	**18,210**	**18,245**	**20,270**	**1**	**71,965**
1980 Total	**7,439**	**15,753**	**4,105**	**10,578**	**22,595**	**32,039**	**19,659**	**19,697**	**24,269**	**-1**	**78,067**
1985 Total	**7,148**	**16,041**	**3,732**	**11,451**	**19,443**	**28,816**	**20,041**	**20,088**	**26,032**	**-4**	**76,392**
1990 Total	**6,552**	**16,940**	**3,893**	**13,317**	**21,172**	**31,802**	**22,366**	**22,419**	[d] **30,495**	**7**	**84,485**
1995 Total	**6,934**	**18,517**	**4,100**	**14,690**	**22,718**	**33,969**	**23,757**	**23,812**	**33,479**	**3**	**90,991**
2000 Total	**7,156**	**20,421**	**4,278**	**17,175**	**22,823**	**34,662**	**26,456**	**26,516**	**38,062**	**2**	**98,776**
2001 Total	**6,864**	**20,038**	**4,084**	**17,137**	**21,792**	**32,718**	**26,179**	**26,242**	**37,215**	**-6**	**96,129**
2002 Total	**6,907**	**20,786**	**4,132**	**17,346**	**21,797**	**32,660**	**26,747**	**26,808**	**38,016**	**5**	**97,605**
2003 Total	**7,232**	**21,119**	**4,298**	**17,346**	**21,533**	**32,553**	**26,807**	**26,881**	**38,028**	**-1**	**97,898**
2004 Total	**6,987**	**21,081**	**4,232**	**17,655**	**22,411**	**33,515**	**27,748**	**27,827**	**38,701**	**-6**	**100,073**
2005 Total	**6,901**	**21,613**	**4,052**	**17,853**	**21,410**	**32,441**	**28,180**	**28,261**	**39,626**	**(s)**	**100,168**
2006 Total	**6,154**	**20,670**	**3,747**	**17,707**	**21,529**	**32,390**	**28,618**	**28,697**	**39,417**	**(s)**	**99,464**
2007 Total	**6,589**	**21,519**	**3,922**	**18,253**	**21,362**	**32,385**	**28,728**	**28,815**	**40,371**	**-1**	**100,971**
2008 Total	**6,889**	**21,668**	**4,100**	**18,402**	**20,527**	**31,333**	**27,340**	**27,422**	**39,969**	**1**	**98,825**
2009 Total	**6,637**	**21,081**	**4,056**	**17,888**	**18,755**	**28,465**	**26,507**	**26,589**	**38,069**	**(s)**	**94,023**
2010 Total	**6,640**	**21,894**	**4,023**	**18,059**	**20,423**	**30,670**	**26,897**	**26,978**	**39,619**	**7**	**97,608**
2011 Total	**6,472**	**21,381**	**4,065**	**17,981**	**20,594**	**30,981**	**26,518**	**26,599**	**39,293**	**8**	**96,950**
2012 Total	**5,684**	**19,870**	**3,725**	**17,421**	**20,888**	**31,061**	**26,050**	**26,126**	**38,131**	**2**	**94,480**
2013 Total	**6,688**	**21,051**	**4,161**	**17,929**	**21,481**	**31,627**	**26,533**	**26,612**	**38,357**	**-1**	**97,218**
2014 Total	**7,006**	**21,445**	**4,390**	**18,264**	**21,562**	**31,798**	**26,789**	**26,869**	**38,629**	**6**	**98,382**
2015 Total	**6,464**	**20,617**	**4,441**	**18,157**	**21,528**	**31,472**	**27,161**	**27,238**	**37,890**	**1**	**97,484**
2016 Total	**6,032**	**20,181**	**4,321**	**18,030**	**21,659**	**31,453**	**27,710**	**27,786**	**37,727**	**-4**	**97,445**
2017 January	1,015	2,315	605	1,707	1,940	2,733	2,219	2,226	3,201	2	8,982
February	725	1,708	463	1,433	1,713	2,438	2,041	2,047	2,684	-2	7,623
March	735	1,772	482	1,560	1,911	2,721	2,373	2,379	2,932	-2	8,430
April	412	1,310	307	1,322	1,777	2,558	2,260	2,265	2,700	-3	7,452
May	324	1,324	268	1,386	1,822	2,668	2,417	2,423	2,971	-1	7,800
June	250	1,482	229	1,436	1,785	2,643	2,395	2,401	3,303	2	7,964
July	226	1,744	219	1,528	1,834	2,723	2,425	2,432	3,722	5	8,433
August	222	1,614	225	1,484	1,831	2,705	2,484	2,491	3,531	4	8,298
September	231	1,379	229	1,376	1,766	2,573	2,295	2,301	3,108	(s)	7,630
October	333	1,349	294	1,414	1,856	2,674	2,397	2,403	2,960	-2	7,838
November	619	1,617	430	1,495	1,928	2,734	2,280	2,286	2,874	-2	8,130
December	1,008	2,280	617	1,757	1,996	2,833	2,353	2,360	3,255	-1	9,229
Total	**6,100**	**19,890**	**4,368**	**17,899**	**22,161**	**32,006**	**27,939**	**28,014**	**37,241**	**(s)**	**97,809**
2018 January	1,198	2,711	692	1,856	2,058	2,830	2,247	2,255	3,457	3	9,655
February	855	1,973	532	1,538	1,805	2,515	2,047	2,053	2,840	-2	8,077
March	828	1,905	528	1,615	1,984	2,757	2,405	2,411	2,943	-4	8,684
April	596	1,550	403	1,434	1,833	2,587	2,312	2,318	2,746	-5	7,884
May	303	1,387	253	1,433	1,884	2,739	2,456	2,462	3,125	-2	8,019
June	245	1,570	226	1,471	1,836	2,670	2,423	2,430	3,411	3	8,144
July	235	1,792	222	1,553	1,891	2,756	2,494	2,501	3,759	6	8,607
August	226	1,734	226	1,552	1,976	2,859	2,537	2,544	3,724	6	8,694
September	238	1,496	229	1,419	1,837	2,632	2,305	2,312	3,249	2	7,860
October	410	1,445	341	1,465	1,988	2,775	2,405	2,411	2,951	-1	8,095
November	773	1,841	501	1,581	1,937	2,731	2,318	2,324	2,950	-2	8,476
December	970	2,218	594	1,689	1,991	2,767	2,364	2,371	3,126	-2	9,043
Total	**6,877**	**21,621**	**4,746**	**18,608**	**23,022**	**32,618**	**28,313**	**28,391**	**38,280**	**2**	**101,239**
2019 January	1,165	2,511	691	1,820	R 2,104	2,893	2,279	2,285	3,271	1	9,510
February	995	R 2,129	593	1,594	R 1,827	2,532	2,097	R 2,103	2,848	-1	8,358
March	873	1,983	544	1,605	1,982	2,743	2,351	2,358	2,938	-5	8,683
3-Month Total	**3,034**	**6,623**	**1,827**	**5,019**	**5,912**	**8,168**	**6,726**	**6,746**	**9,058**	**-6**	**26,551**
2018 3-Month Total	**2,881**	**6,589**	**1,752**	**5,008**	**5,848**	**8,103**	**6,699**	**6,719**	**9,239**	**-3**	**26,415**
2017 3-Month Total	**2,476**	**5,795**	**1,550**	**4,699**	**5,565**	**7,893**	**6,632**	**6,652**	**8,817**	**-3**	**25,036**

[a] Commercial sector, including commercial combined-heat-and-power (CHP) and commercial electricity-only plants.

[b] Industrial sector, including industrial combined-heat-and-power (CHP) and industrial electricity-only plants.

[c] Electricity-only and combined-heat-and-power (CHP) plants within the NAICS 22 category whose primary business is to sell electricity, or electricity and heat, to the public.

[d] Through 1988, data are for electric utilities only. Beginning in 1989, data are for electric utilities and independent power producers.

[e] See "Primary Energy Consumption" in Glossary.

[f] Total energy consumption in the end-use sectors consists of primary energy consumption, electricity retail sales, and electrical system energy losses. See Note 1, "Electrical System Energy Losses," at end of section.

[g] A balancing item. The sum of primary consumption in the five energy-use sectors equals the sum of total consumption in the four end-use sectors. However, total energy consumption does not equal the sum of the sectoral components due to the use of sector-specific conversion factors for coal and natural gas.

[h] Primary energy consumption total. See Table 1.3.

R=Revised. (s)=Less than 0.5 trillion Btu and greater than -0.5 trillion Btu.

Notes: • Data are estimates, except for the electric power sector. • See Note 2, "Classification of Power Plants Into Energy-Use Sectors," at end of Section 7. • See Note 2, "Energy Consumption Data and Surveys," at end of section. • Totals may not equal sum of components due to independent rounding. • Geographic coverage is the 50 states and the District of Columbia.

Web Page: See http://www.eia.gov/totalenergy/data/monthly/#consumption (Excel and CSV files) for all available annual data beginning in 1949 and monthly data beginning in 1973.

Sources: • **End-Use Sectors:** Tables 2.2–2.5. • **Electric Power Sector:** Table 2.6. • **Balancing Item:** Calculated as primary energy total consumption minus the sum of total energy consumption in the four end-use sectors. • **Primary Total:** Table 1.3.

Source: *U.S. Energy Information Administration, Monthly Energy Review, June 2019*

Figure 2.2 Residential Sector Energy Consumption
(Quadrillion Btu)

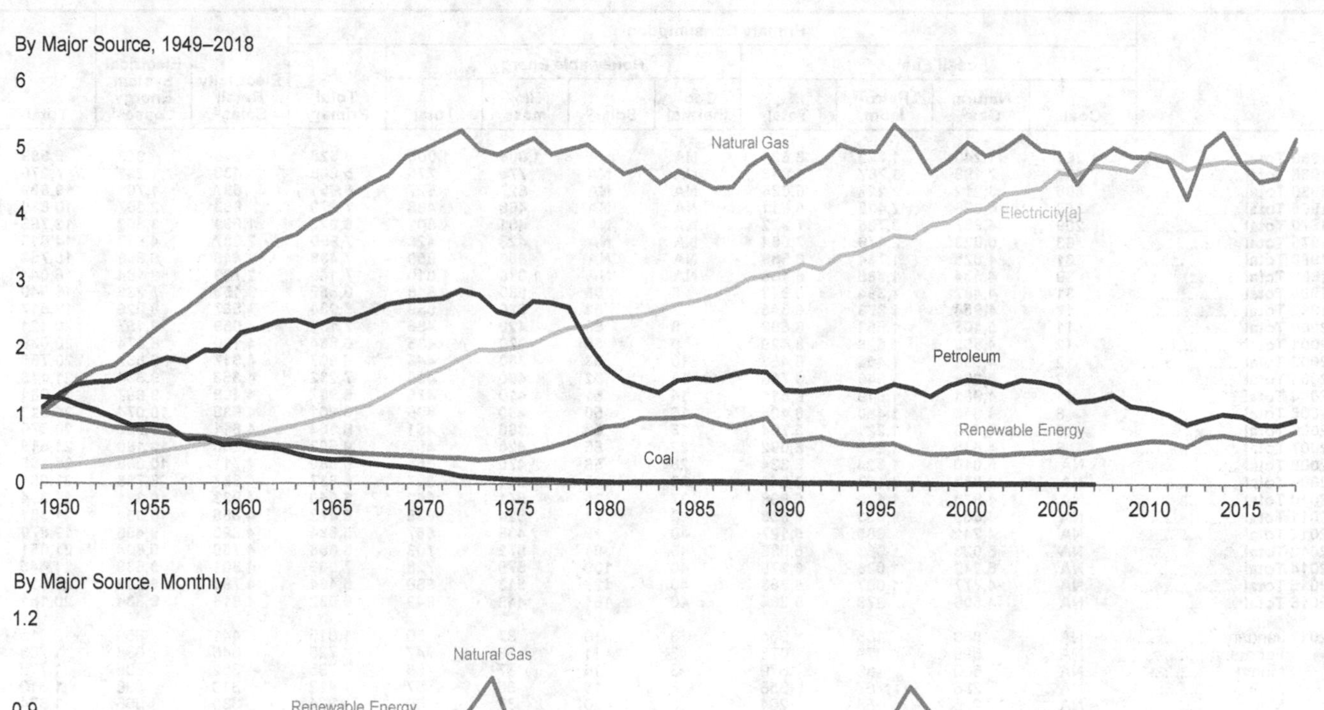

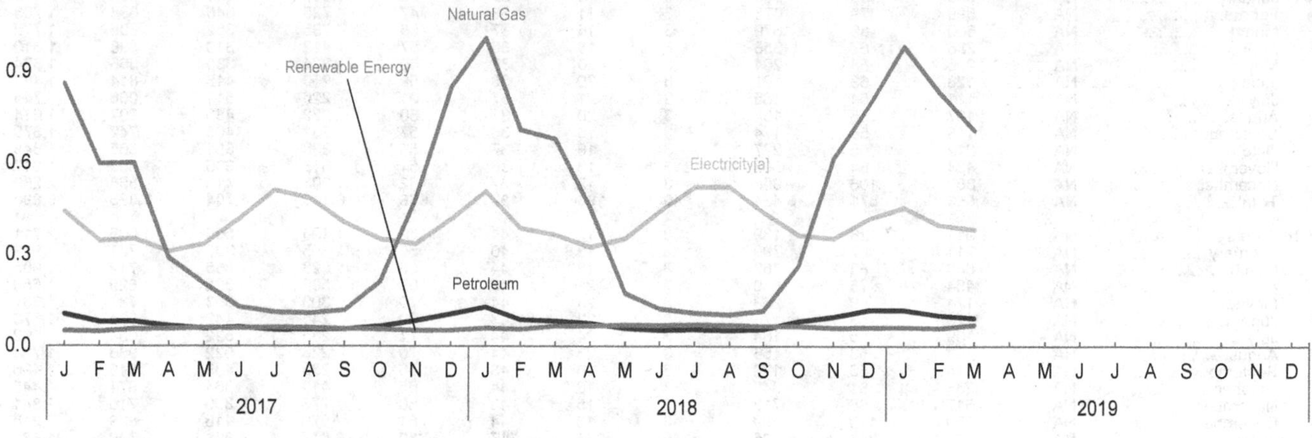

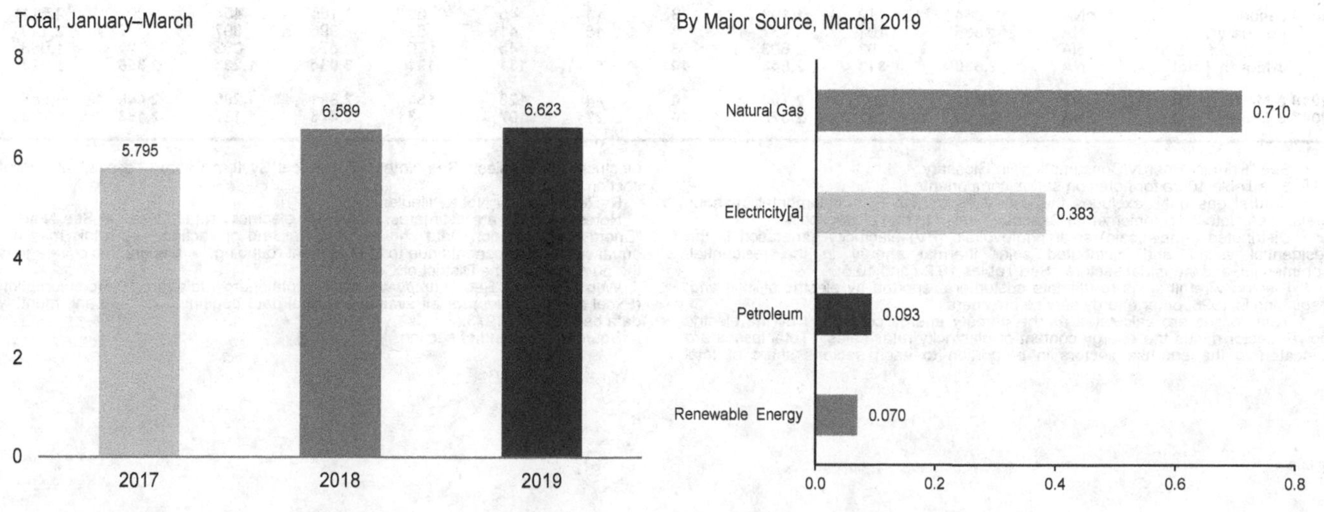

[a] Electricity retail sales.
Web Page: http://www.eia.gov/totalenergy/data/monthly/#consumption.
Source: Table 2.2.

Source: *U.S. Energy Information Administration, Monthly Energy Review, June 2019*

Table 2.2 Residential Sector Energy Consumption
(Trillion Btu)

	Primary Consumption[a]											
	Fossil Fuels				Renewable Energy[b]							
	Coal	Natural Gas[c]	Petro-leum	Total	Geo-thermal	Solar[d]	Bio-mass	Total	Total Primary	Electricity Retail Sales[e]	Electrical System Energy Losses[f]	Total
1950 Total	**1,261**	**1,240**	**1,322**	**3,824**	**NA**	**NA**	**1,006**	**1,006**	**4,829**	**246**	**913**	**5,989**
1955 Total	**867**	**2,198**	**1,767**	**4,833**	**NA**	**NA**	**775**	**775**	**5,608**	**438**	**1,232**	**7,278**
1960 Total	**585**	**3,212**	**2,227**	**6,024**	**NA**	**NA**	**627**	**627**	**6,651**	**687**	**1,701**	**9,039**
1965 Total	**352**	**4,028**	**2,432**	**6,811**	**NA**	**NA**	**468**	**468**	**7,279**	**993**	**2,367**	**10,639**
1970 Total	**209**	**4,987**	**2,725**	**7,922**	**NA**	**NA**	**401**	**401**	**8,322**	**1,591**	**3,852**	**13,766**
1975 Total	**63**	**5,023**	**2,479**	**7,564**	**NA**	**NA**	**425**	**425**	**7,990**	**2,007**	**4,817**	**14,813**
1980 Total	**31**	**4,825**	**1,734**	**6,589**	**NA**	**NA**	**850**	**850**	**7,439**	**2,448**	**5,866**	**15,753**
1985 Total	**39**	**4,534**	**1,565**	**6,138**	**NA**	**NA**	**1,010**	**1,010**	**7,148**	**2,709**	**6,184**	**16,041**
1990 Total	**31**	**4,487**	**1,394**	**5,912**	**6**	**55**	**580**	**640**	**6,552**	**3,153**	**7,235**	**16,940**
1995 Total	**17**	**4,954**	**1,373**	**6,345**	**7**	**63**	**520**	**589**	**6,934**	**3,557**	**8,026**	**18,517**
2000 Total	**11**	**5,105**	**1,553**	**6,669**	**9**	**58**	**420**	**486**	**7,156**	**4,069**	**9,197**	**20,421**
2001 Total	**12**	**4,889**	**1,528**	**6,429**	**9**	**55**	**370**	**435**	**6,864**	**4,100**	**9,074**	**20,038**
2002 Total	**12**	**4,995**	**1,456**	**6,463**	**10**	**53**	**380**	**443**	**6,907**	**4,317**	**9,562**	**20,786**
2003 Total	**12**	**5,209**	**1,546**	**6,768**	**13**	**52**	**400**	**465**	**7,232**	**4,353**	**9,534**	**21,119**
2004 Total	**11**	**4,981**	**1,519**	**6,511**	**14**	**51**	**410**	**475**	**6,987**	**4,408**	**9,687**	**21,081**
2005 Total	**8**	**4,946**	**1,450**	**6,405**	**16**	**50**	**430**	**496**	**6,901**	**4,638**	**10,074**	**21,613**
2006 Total	**6**	**4,476**	**1,221**	**5,704**	**18**	**53**	**380**	**451**	**6,154**	**4,611**	**9,905**	**20,670**
2007 Total	**8**	**4,835**	**1,249**	**6,092**	**22**	**55**	**420**	**497**	**6,589**	**4,750**	**10,180**	**21,519**
2008 Total	**NA**	**5,010**	**1,324**	**6,334**	**26**	**58**	**470**	**555**	**6,889**	**4,711**	**10,068**	**21,668**
2009 Total	**NA**	**4,883**	**1,157**	**6,040**	**33**	**60**	**504**	**597**	**6,637**	**4,657**	**9,788**	**21,081**
2010 Total	**NA**	**4,878**	**1,120**	**5,998**	**37**	**65**	**541**	**642**	**6,640**	**4,933**	**10,321**	**21,894**
2011 Total	**NA**	**4,805**	**1,033**	**5,838**	**40**	**71**	**524**	**635**	**6,472**	**4,855**	**10,054**	**21,381**
2012 Total	**NA**	**4,242**	**885**	**5,127**	**40**	**79**	**438**	**557**	**5,684**	**4,690**	**9,496**	**19,870**
2013 Total	**NA**	**5,023**	**963**	**5,986**	**40**	**91**	**572**	**703**	**6,688**	**4,759**	**9,604**	**21,051**
2014 Total	**NA**	**5,242**	**1,036**	**6,278**	**40**	**109**	**579**	**728**	**7,006**	**4,801**	**9,638**	**21,445**
2015 Total	**NA**	**4,777**	**1,007**	**5,783**	**40**	**128**	**513**	**680**	**6,464**	**4,791**	**9,362**	**20,617**
2016 Total	**NA**	**4,506**	**878**	**5,384**	**40**	**161**	**448**	**649**	**6,032**	**4,815**	**9,334**	**20,181**
2017 January	NA	860	105	965	3	10	37	50	1,015	441	859	2,315
February	NA	599	79	678	3	11	33	47	725	345	638	1,708
March	NA	600	80	679	3	16	37	56	735	352	685	1,772
April	NA	288	67	356	3	18	36	57	412	310	588	1,310
May	NA	206	58	264	3	20	37	60	324	335	665	1,324
June	NA	128	63	191	3	20	36	59	250	418	814	1,482
July	NA	111	54	165	3	21	37	61	226	511	1,006	1,744
August	NA	107	55	162	3	20	37	60	222	485	907	1,614
September	NA	118	56	174	3	18	36	57	231	405	742	1,379
October	NA	212	65	277	3	16	37	56	333	351	665	1,349
November	NA	484	84	568	3	13	36	51	619	335	662	1,617
December	NA	850	106	956	3	12	37	52	1,008	416	856	2,280
Total	**NA**	**4,563**	**871**	**5,434**	**40**	**193**	**433**	**666**	**6,100**	**4,704**	**9,085**	**19,890**
2018 January	NA	1,011	128	1,139	3	12	44	59	1,198	508	1,005	2,711
February	NA	711	87	799	3	13	40	56	855	387	731	1,973
March	NA	680	83	762	3	18	44	66	828	365	712	1,905
April	NA	454	75	530	3	21	43	67	596	325	629	1,550
May	NA	174	59	233	3	23	44	70	303	353	731	1,387
June	NA	123	53	176	3	23	43	69	245	442	884	1,570
July	NA	109	55	164	3	24	44	71	235	522	1,034	1,792
August	NA	103	53	156	3	23	44	70	226	522	986	1,734
September	NA	116	56	172	3	20	43	66	238	438	819	1,496
October	NA	264	81	345	3	18	44	65	410	364	671	1,445
November	NA	617	96	713	3	15	43	60	773	353	715	1,841
December	NA	790	119	909	3	13	44	61	970	418	829	2,218
Total	**NA**	**5,151**	**945**	**6,096**	**40**	**224**	**517**	**780**	**6,877**	**4,996**	**9,748**	**21,621**
2019 January	NA	984	119	1,103	3	14	45	62	1,165	454	892	2,511
February	NA	R 835	101	937	3	15	41	59	995	397	737	R 2,129
March	NA	710	93	803	3	22	45	70	873	383	727	1,983
3-Month Total	**NA**	**2,530**	**313**	**2,843**	**10**	**51**	**131**	**191**	**3,034**	**1,234**	**2,356**	**6,623**
2018 3-Month Total	**NA**	**2,402**	**298**	**2,700**	**10**	**44**	**128**	**181**	**2,881**	**1,260**	**2,448**	**6,589**
2017 3-Month Total	**NA**	**2,059**	**263**	**2,322**	**10**	**37**	**107**	**153**	**2,476**	**1,137**	**2,183**	**5,795**

[a] See "Primary Energy Consumption" in Glossary.
[b] See Table 10.2a for notes on series components.
[c] Natural gas only; excludes the estimated portion of supplemental gaseous fuels. See Note 3, "Supplemental Gaseous Fuels," at end of Section 4.
[d] Distributed (small-scale) solar photovoltaic (PV) electricity generation in the residential sector and distributed solar thermal energy in the residential, commercial, and industrial sectors. See Tables 10.2a and 10.5.
[e] Electricity retail sales to ultimate customers reported by electric utilities and, beginning in 1996, other energy service providers.
[f] Total losses are calculated as the primary energy consumed by the electric power sector minus the energy content of electricity retail sales. Total losses are allocated to the end-use sectors in proportion to each sector's share of total electricity retail sales. See Note 1, "Electrical System Energy Losses," at end of section.

R=Revised. NA=Not available.

Notes: • Data are estimates, except for electricity retail sales. • See Note 2, "Energy Consumption Data and Surveys," at end of section. • Totals may not equal sum of components due to independent rounding. • Geographic coverage is the 50 states and the District of Columbia.

Web Page: See http://www.eia.gov/totalenergy/data/monthly/#consumption (Excel and CSV files) for all available annual data beginning in 1949 and monthly data beginning in 1973.

Sources: See end of section.

Source: *U.S. Energy Information Administration, Monthly Energy Review, June 2019*

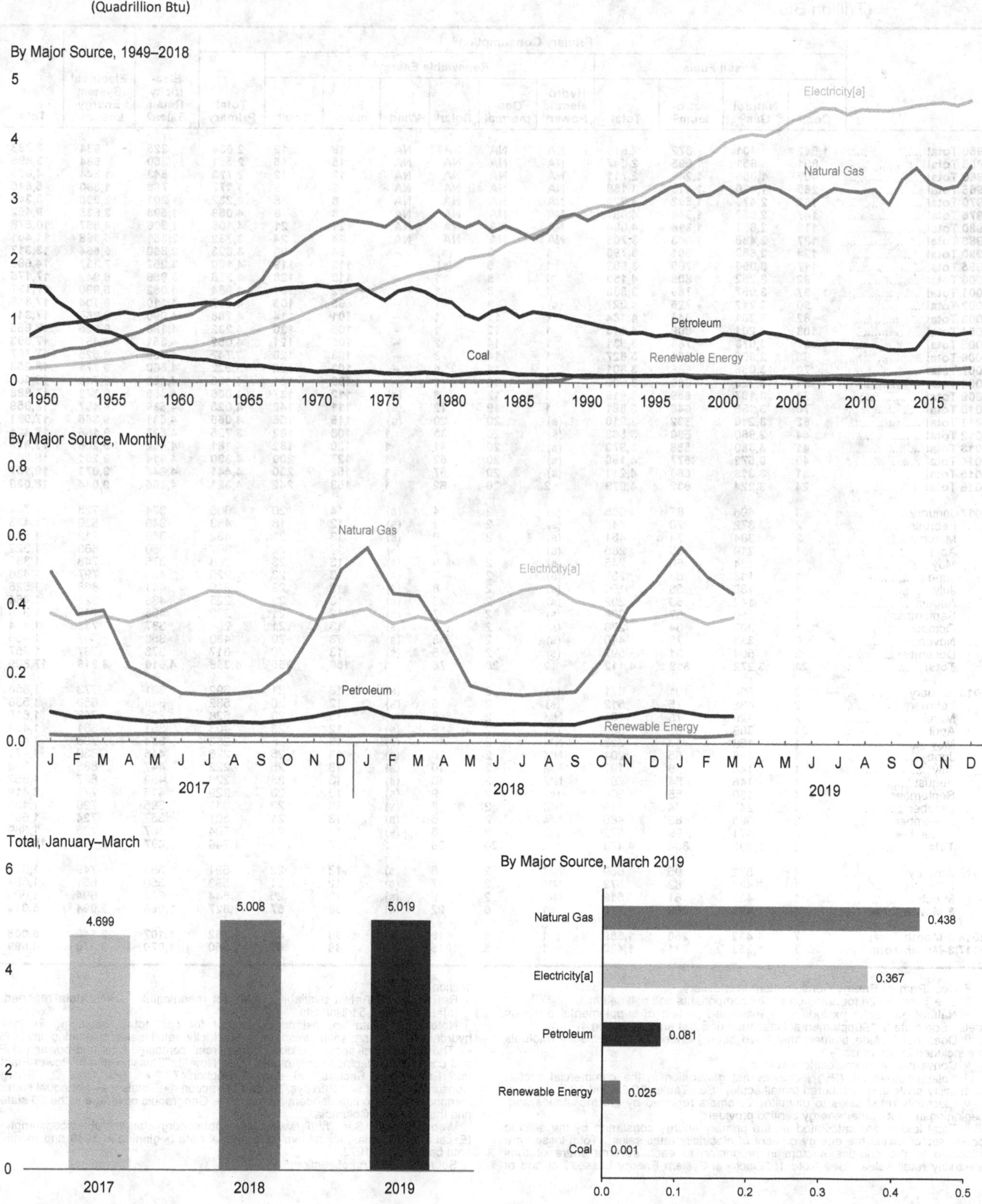

[a] Electricity retail sales.
Web Page: http://www.eia.gov/totalenergy/data/monthly/#consumption.
Source: Table 2.3.

Source: *U.S. Energy Information Administration, Monthly Energy Review, June 2019*

Table 2.3 Commercial Sector Energy Consumption

(Trillion Btu)

	Primary Consumption[a]													
	Fossil Fuels				Renewable Energy[b]									
	Coal	Natural Gas[c]	Petroleum[d]	Total	Hydroelectric Power[e]	Geothermal	Solar[f]	Wind	Biomass	Total	Total Primary	Electricity Retail Sales[g]	Electrical System Energy Losses[h]	Total
1950 Total	**1,542**	**401**	**872**	**2,815**	**NA**	**NA**	**NA**	**NA**	**19**	**19**	**2,834**	**225**	**834**	**3,893**
1955 Total	**801**	**651**	**1,095**	**2,547**	**NA**	**NA**	**NA**	**NA**	**15**	**15**	**2,561**	**350**	**984**	**3,895**
1960 Total	**407**	**1,056**	**1,248**	**2,711**	**NA**	**NA**	**NA**	**NA**	**12**	**12**	**2,723**	**543**	**1,344**	**4,609**
1965 Total	**265**	**1,490**	**1,413**	**3,168**	**NA**	**NA**	**NA**	**NA**	**9**	**9**	**3,177**	**789**	**1,880**	**5,845**
1970 Total	**165**	**2,473**	**1,592**	**4,229**	**NA**	**NA**	**NA**	**NA**	**8**	**8**	**4,237**	**1,201**	**2,908**	**8,346**
1975 Total	**147**	**2,558**	**1,346**	**4,051**	**NA**	**NA**	**NA**	**NA**	**8**	**8**	**4,059**	**1,598**	**3,835**	**9,492**
1980 Total	**115**	**2,651**	**1,318**	**4,084**	**NA**	**NA**	**NA**	**NA**	**21**	**21**	**4,105**	**1,906**	**4,567**	**10,578**
1985 Total	**137**	**2,488**	**1,083**	**3,708**	**NA**	**NA**	**NA**	**NA**	**24**	**24**	**3,732**	**2,351**	**5,368**	**11,451**
1990 Total	**124**	**2,680**	**991**	**3,795**	**1**	**3**	**(s)**	**–**	**94**	**98**	**3,893**	**2,860**	**6,564**	**13,317**
1995 Total	**117**	**3,096**	**769**	**3,982**	**1**	**5**	**(s)**	**–**	**113**	**119**	**4,100**	**3,252**	**7,337**	**14,690**
2000 Total	**92**	**3,252**	**806**	**4,150**	**1**	**8**	**1**	**–**	**119**	**128**	**4,278**	**3,956**	**8,942**	**17,175**
2001 Total	**97**	**3,097**	**789**	**3,983**	**1**	**8**	**1**	**–**	**92**	**101**	**4,084**	**4,062**	**8,990**	**17,137**
2002 Total	**90**	**3,212**	**725**	**4,027**	**(s)**	**9**	**1**	**–**	**95**	**105**	**4,132**	**4,110**	**9,104**	**17,346**
2003 Total	**82**	**3,261**	**841**	**4,184**	**1**	**11**	**1**	**–**	**101**	**114**	**4,298**	**4,090**	**8,958**	**17,346**
2004 Total	**103**	**3,201**	**809**	**4,113**	**1**	**12**	**1**	**–**	**105**	**120**	**4,232**	**4,198**	**9,225**	**17,655**
2005 Total	**97**	**3,073**	**761**	**3,931**	**1**	**14**	**2**	**–**	**105**	**121**	**4,052**	**4,351**	**9,451**	**17,853**
2006 Total	**65**	**2,902**	**661**	**3,627**	**1**	**14**	**3**	**–**	**103**	**120**	**3,747**	**4,435**	**9,525**	**17,707**
2007 Total	**70**	**3,085**	**646**	**3,801**	**1**	**14**	**4**	**–**	**103**	**122**	**3,922**	**4,560**	**9,771**	**18,253**
2008 Total	**81**	**3,228**	**660**	**3,969**	**1**	**15**	**6**	**–**	**109**	**131**	**4,100**	**4,559**	**9,743**	**18,402**
2009 Total	**73**	**3,187**	**659**	**3,919**	**1**	**17**	**8**	**(s)**	**112**	**137**	**4,056**	**4,459**	**9,373**	**17,888**
2010 Total	**70**	**3,165**	**646**	**3,881**	**1**	**19**	**12**	**(s)**	**111**	**142**	**4,023**	**4,539**	**9,497**	**18,059**
2011 Total	**62**	**3,216**	**632**	**3,910**	**(s)**	**20**	**20**	**(s)**	**115**	**155**	**4,065**	**4,531**	**9,385**	**17,981**
2012 Total	**44**	**2,960**	**560**	**3,563**	**(s)**	**20**	**33**	**1**	**108**	**162**	**3,725**	**4,528**	**9,168**	**17,421**
2013 Total	**41**	**3,380**	**558**	**3,979**	**(s)**	**20**	**41**	**1**	**120**	**182**	**4,161**	**4,562**	**9,206**	**17,929**
2014 Total	**40**	**3,572**	**577**	**4,190**	**(s)**	**20**	**52**	**1**	**127**	**200**	**4,390**	**4,614**	**9,261**	**18,264**
2015 Total	**31**	**3,316**	**864**	**4,211**	**(s)**	**20**	**57**	**1**	**152**	**230**	**4,441**	**4,643**	**9,073**	**18,157**
2016 Total	**24**	**3,224**	**832**	**4,079**	**2**	**20**	**62**	**1**	**158**	**242**	**4,321**	**4,665**	**9,044**	**18,030**
2017 January	3	496	87	585	(s)	2	4	(s)	14	20	605	374	728	1,707
February	2	372	70	445	(s)	2	4	(s)	12	18	463	340	630	1,433
March	2	384	74	461	(s)	2	6	(s)	13	21	482	366	712	1,560
April	1	219	65	285	(s)	2	7	(s)	13	22	307	350	665	1,322
May	1	184	59	245	(s)	2	8	(s)	13	23	268	375	743	1,386
June	1	143	63	207	(s)	2	8	(s)	13	23	229	409	797	1,436
July	1	138	56	196	(s)	2	8	(s)	13	23	219	441	868	1,528
August	1	142	59	202	(s)	2	8	(s)	13	23	225	438	821	1,484
September	1	150	57	208	(s)	2	7	(s)	12	21	229	405	742	1,376
October	1	207	64	273	(s)	2	6	(s)	13	21	294	387	733	1,414
November	2	333	75	410	(s)	2	5	(s)	13	20	430	358	707	1,495
December	2	504	91	597	(s)	2	5	(s)	13	20	617	373	767	1,757
Total	**21**	**3,272**	**819**	**4,112**	**2**	**20**	**76**	**1**	**156**	**255**	**4,368**	**4,616**	**8,916**	**17,899**
2018 January	3	568	101	671	(s)	2	5	(s)	13	21	692	391	773	1,856
February	2	435	75	512	(s)	2	6	(s)	12	20	532	348	658	1,538
March	2	429	75	505	NM	2	8	(s)	13	23	528	368	718	1,615
April	1	309	69	380	(s)	2	9	(s)	12	23	403	351	681	1,434
May	1	168	59	228	NM	2	10	(s)	13	25	253	384	796	1,433
June	1	145	55	201	NM	2	10	(s)	13	25	226	415	830	1,471
July	1	140	56	197	NM	2	10	(s)	13	25	222	447	885	1,553
August	1	146	54	202	NM	2	10	(s)	13	25	226	459	867	1,552
September	1	150	55	206	(s)	2	9	(s)	12	23	229	415	775	1,419
October	1	243	74	319	NM	2	8	(s)	13	23	341	395	729	1,465
November	2	395	83	480	NM	2	6	(s)	13	21	501	357	724	1,581
December	2	471	99	572	(s)	2	6	(s)	13	21	594	367	728	1,689
Total	**19**	**3,600**	**854**	**4,473**	**2**	**20**	**96**	**2**	**153**	**273**	**4,746**	**4,697**	**9,165**	**18,608**
2019 January	1	572	95	669	NM	2	6	(s)	13	22	691	381	749	1,820
February	1	R488	82	572	NM	2	7	(s)	12	21	593	350	651	1,594
March	1	438	81	519	NM	2	9	(s)	13	25	544	367	694	1,605
3-Month Total	**4**	**1,499**	**258**	**1,760**	**1**	**6**	**22**	**(s)**	**38**	**67**	**1,827**	**1,098**	**2,094**	**5,019**
2018 3-Month Total	**7**	**1,432**	**250**	**1,689**	**1**	**5**	**19**	**(s)**	**38**	**63**	**1,752**	**1,107**	**2,149**	**5,008**
2017 3-Month Total	**7**	**1,252**	**231**	**1,490**	**1**	**5**	**15**	**(s)**	**39**	**59**	**1,550**	**1,079**	**2,070**	**4,699**

[a] See "Primary Energy Consumption" in Glossary.
[b] See Table 10.2a for notes on series components and estimation.
[c] Natural gas only; excludes the estimated portion of supplemental gaseous fuels. See Note 3, "Supplemental Gaseous Fuels," at end of Section 4.
[d] Does not include biofuels that have been blended with petroleum—biofuels are included in "Biomass."
[e] Conventional hydroelectric power.
[f] Solar photovoltaic (PV) electricity net generation in the commercial sector, both utility-scale and distributed (small-scale). See Tables 10.2a and 10.5.
[g] Electricity retail sales to ultimate customers reported by electric utilities and, beginning in 1996, other energy service providers.
[h] Total losses are calculated as the primary energy consumed by the electric power sector minus the energy content of electricity retail sales. Total losses are allocated to the end-use sectors in proportion to each sector's share of total electricity retail sales. See Note 1, "Electrical System Energy Losses," at end of section.

R=Revised. NA=Not available. NM=Not meaningful. – =No data reported. (s)=Less than 0.5 trillion Btu.

Notes: • Data are estimates, except for coal totals beginning in 2008; hydroelectric power; solar; wind; and electricity retail sales beginning in 1979. • The commercial sector includes commercial combined-heat-and-power (CHP) and commercial electricity-only plants. See Note 2, "Classification of Power Plants Into Energy-Use Sectors," at end of Section 7. • See Note 2, "Energy Consumption Data and Surveys," at end of section. • Totals may not equal sum of components due to independent rounding. • Geographic coverage is the 50 states and the District of Columbia.

Web Page: See http://www.eia.gov/totalenergy/data/monthly/#consumption (Excel and CSV files) for all available annual data beginning in 1949 and monthly data beginning in 1973.

Sources: See end of section.

Source: *U.S. Energy Information Administration, Monthly Energy Review, June 2019*

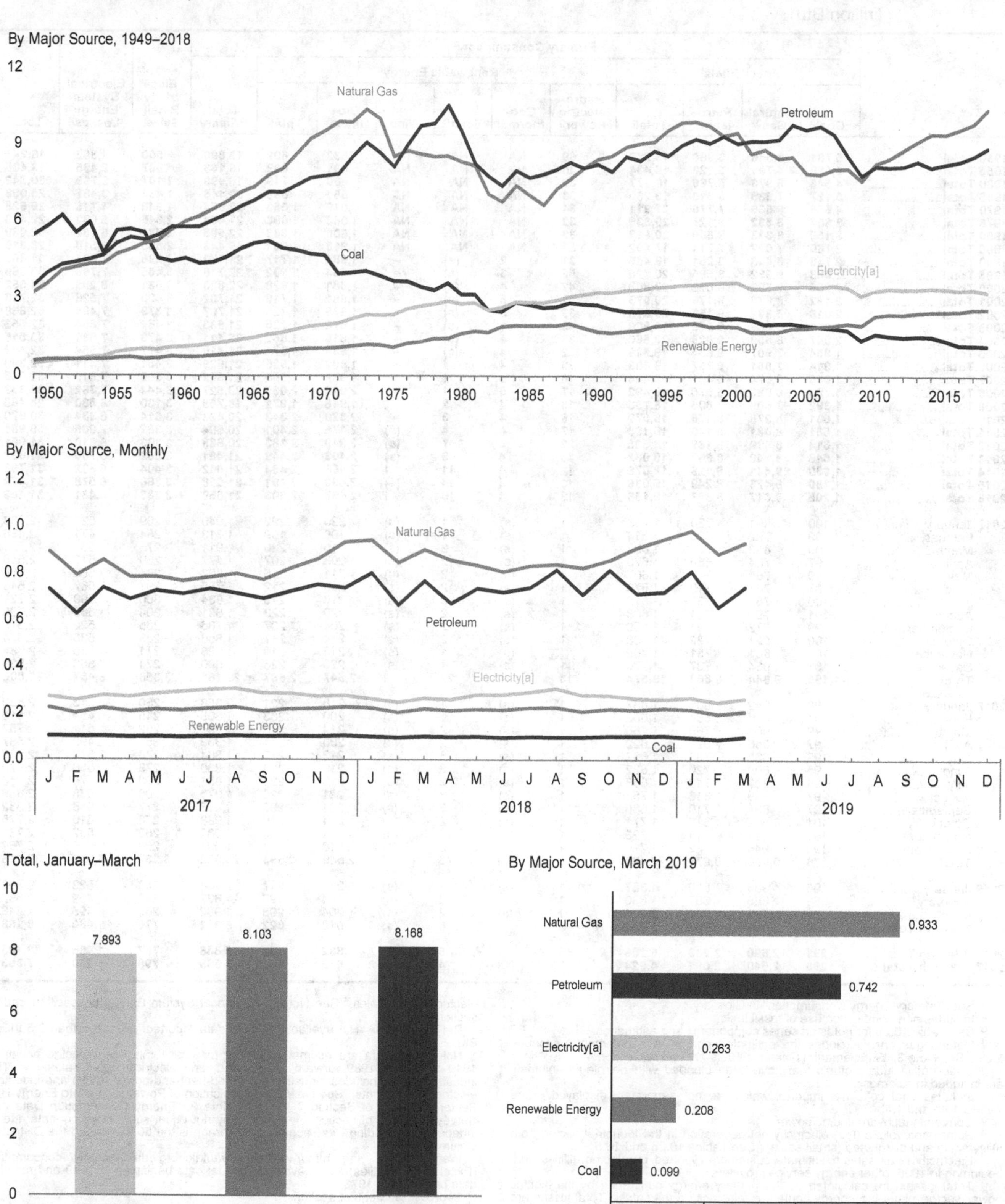

[a] Electricity retail sales.
Web Page: http://www.eia.gov/totalenergy/data/monthly/#consumption.
Source: Table 2.4.

Source: *U.S. Energy Information Administration, Monthly Energy Review, June 2019*

Table 2.4 Industrial Sector Energy Consumption
(Trillion Btu)

	Primary Consumption[a]													
	Fossil Fuels[b]				Renewable Energy[c]									
	Coal	Natural Gas[d]	Petroleum[e]	Total[f]	Hydroelectric Power[g]	Geothermal	Solar[h]	Wind	Biomass	Total	Total Primary	Electricity Retail Sales[i]	Electrical System Energy Losses[j]	Total[f]
1950 Total	5,781	3,546	3,960	13,288	69	NA	NA	NA	532	602	13,890	500	1,852	16,241
1955 Total	5,620	4,701	5,123	15,434	38	NA	NA	NA	631	669	16,103	887	2,495	19,485
1960 Total	4,543	5,973	5,766	16,277	39	NA	NA	NA	680	719	16,996	1,107	2,739	20,842
1965 Total	5,127	7,339	6,813	19,260	33	NA	NA	NA	855	888	20,148	1,463	3,487	25,098
1970 Total	4,656	9,536	7,776	21,911	34	NA	NA	NA	1,019	1,053	22,964	1,948	4,716	29,628
1975 Total	3,667	8,532	8,127	20,339	32	NA	NA	NA	1,063	1,096	21,434	2,346	5,632	29,413
1980 Total	3,155	8,333	9,509	20,962	33	NA	NA	NA	1,600	1,633	22,595	2,781	6,664	32,039
1985 Total	2,760	7,032	7,714	17,492	33	NA	NA	NA	1,918	1,951	19,443	2,855	6,518	28,816
1990 Total	2,756	8,443	8,251	19,455	31	2	(s)	–	1,684	1,717	21,172	3,226	7,404	31,802
1995 Total	2,488	9,592	8,585	20,726	55	3	(s)	–	1,934	1,992	22,718	3,455	7,796	33,969
2000 Total	2,256	9,500	9,073	20,895	42	4	(s)	–	1,881	1,928	22,823	3,631	8,208	34,662
2001 Total	2,192	8,676	9,176	20,073	33	5	(s)	–	1,681	1,719	21,792	3,400	7,526	32,718
2002 Total	2,019	8,832	9,166	20,078	39	5	(s)	–	1,676	1,720	21,797	3,379	7,484	32,660
2003 Total	2,041	8,488	9,228	19,809	43	3	(s)	–	1,678	1,725	21,533	3,454	7,565	32,553
2004 Total	2,047	8,550	9,825	20,560	33	4	(s)	–	1,815	1,852	22,411	3,473	7,631	33,515
2005 Total	1,954	7,907	9,634	19,539	32	4	(s)	–	1,834	1,871	21,410	3,477	7,554	32,441
2006 Total	1,914	7,861	9,767	19,603	29	4	1	–	1,892	1,926	21,529	3,451	7,411	32,390
2007 Total	1,865	8,074	9,441	19,404	16	5	1	–	1,937	1,958	21,362	3,507	7,515	32,385
2008 Total	1,793	8,083	8,575	18,492	17	5	1	–	2,012	2,035	20,527	3,444	7,362	31,333
2009 Total	1,392	7,609	7,805	16,783	18	4	2	–	1,948	1,972	18,755	3,130	6,580	28,465
2010 Total	1,631	8,278	8,176	18,079	16	4	3	–	2,320	2,343	20,423	3,314	6,934	30,670
2011 Total	1,561	8,481	8,140	18,193	17	4	4	(s)	2,375	2,401	20,594	3,382	7,005	30,981
2012 Total	1,513	8,819	8,169	18,505	22	4	7	(s)	2,349	2,383	20,888	3,363	6,810	31,061
2013 Total	1,546	9,140	8,362	19,032	33	4	9	(s)	2,403	2,449	21,481	3,362	6,785	31,627
2014 Total	1,530	9,441	8,128	19,078	12	4	11	1	2,456	2,484	21,562	3,404	6,832	31,798
2015 Total	1,380	9,426	8,249	19,036	13	4	14	(s)	2,460	2,491	21,528	3,366	6,578	31,472
2016 Total	1,205	9,617	8,353	19,156	12	4	19	1	2,467	2,503	21,659	3,333	6,461	31,453
2017 January	100	891	730	1,718	1	(s)	1	(s)	220	222	1,940	269	524	2,733
February	99	792	625	1,514	1	(s)	1	(s)	196	199	1,713	254	471	2,438
March	100	856	737	1,692	1	(s)	2	(s)	216	220	1,911	275	535	2,721
April	97	784	689	1,570	1	(s)	2	(s)	203	207	1,777	269	512	2,558
May	99	785	725	1,607	1	(s)	2	(s)	211	215	1,822	284	562	2,668
June	97	767	712	1,573	1	(s)	2	(s)	208	212	1,785	291	567	2,643
July	100	783	733	1,615	1	(s)	2	(s)	216	219	1,834	300	590	2,723
August	101	797	714	1,608	1	(s)	2	(s)	220	223	1,831	304	569	2,705
September	99	772	691	1,559	1	(s)	2	(s)	204	207	1,766	285	522	2,573
October	100	821	722	1,638	1	(s)	2	(s)	214	217	1,856	283	536	2,674
November	100	861	751	1,709	1	(s)	1	(s)	216	219	1,928	271	535	2,734
December	103	934	737	1,770	1	(s)	1	(s)	223	226	1,996	274	563	2,833
Total	1,195	9,844	8,564	19,574	13	4	22	1	2,547	2,587	22,161	3,358	6,487	32,006
2018 January	98	942	801	1,837	1	(s)	1	(s)	218	221	2,058	260	513	2,830
February	94	846	664	1,602	1	(s)	1	(s)	200	203	1,805	245	464	2,515
March	99	901	768	1,766	1	(s)	2	(s)	214	218	1,984	262	511	2,757
April	97	856	671	1,622	1	(s)	2	(s)	208	211	1,833	257	498	2,587
May	99	835	736	1,667	1	(s)	3	(s)	213	217	1,884	278	576	2,739
June	95	808	720	1,622	1	(s)	3	(s)	210	214	1,836	278	556	2,670
July	98	833	740	1,668	1	(s)	3	(s)	219	223	1,891	290	575	2,756
August	97	839	816	1,751	1	(s)	3	(s)	221	225	1,976	306	578	2,859
September	97	824	710	1,630	1	(s)	2	(s)	204	207	1,837	277	518	2,632
October	101	857	815	1,771	1	(s)	2	(s)	214	218	1,988	276	510	2,775
November	101	911	714	1,723	1	(s)	2	(s)	211	214	1,937	262	532	2,731
December	103	948	722	1,770	1	(s)	2	(s)	218	221	1,991	260	515	2,767
Total	1,178	10,400	8,876	20,429	13	4	25	1	2,549	2,593	23,022	3,252	6,344	32,618
2019 January	96	984	810	1,887	1	(s)	2	(s)	214	217	R 2,104	266	523	2,893
February	89	R 885	657	R 1,630	1	(s)	2	(s)	194	197	R 1,827	247	459	2,532
March	99	933	742	1,774	1	(s)	2	(s)	204	208	1,982	263	498	2,743
3-Month Total	284	2,802	2,209	5,291	2	1	6	(s)	612	622	5,912	776	1,480	8,168
2018 3-Month Total	291	2,690	2,233	5,206	3	1	5	(s)	632	642	5,848	767	1,488	8,103
2017 3-Month Total	299	2,540	2,091	4,924	3	1	4	(s)	632	641	5,565	798	1,530	7,893

[a] See "Primary Energy Consumption" in Glossary.
[b] Includes non-combustion use of fossil fuels.
[c] See Table 10.2b for notes on series components and estimation.
[d] Natural gas only; excludes the estimated portion of supplemental gaseous fuels. See Note 3, "Supplemental Gaseous Fuels," at end of Section 4.
[e] Does not include biofuels that have been blended with petroleum—biofuels are included in "Biomass."
[f] Includes coal coke net imports, which are not separately displayed. See Tables 1.4a and 1.4b.
[g] Conventional hydroelectric power.
[h] Solar photovoltaic (PV) electricity net generation in the industrial sector, both utility-scale and distributed (small-scale). See Tables 10.2b and 10.5.
[i] Electricity retail sales to ultimate customers reported by electric utilities and, beginning in 1996, other energy service providers.
[j] Total losses are calculated as the primary energy consumed by the electric power sector minus the energy content of electricity retail sales. Total losses are allocated to the end-use sectors in proportion to each sector's share of total electricity retail sales. See Note 1, "Electrical System Energy Losses," at end of section.

R=Revised. NA=Not available. – =No data reported. (s)=Less than 0.5 trillion Btu.

Notes: • Data are estimates, except for coal totals; hydroelectric power in 1949–1978 and 1989 forward; solar; wind; and electricity retail sales. • The industrial sector includes industrial combined-heat-and-power (CHP) and industrial electricity-only plants. See Note 2, "Classification of Power Plants Into Energy-Use Sectors," at end of Section 7. • See Note 2, "Energy Consumption Data and Surveys," at end of section. • Totals may not equal sum of components due to independent rounding. • Geographic coverage is the 50 states and the District of Columbia.

Web Page: See http://www.eia.gov/totalenergy/data/monthly/#consumption (Excel and CSV files) for all available annual data beginning in 1949 and monthly data beginning in 1973.

Sources: See end of section.

Source: *U.S. Energy Information Administration, Monthly Energy Review, June 2019*

Figure 2.5 Transportation Sector Energy Consumption
(Quadrillion Btu)

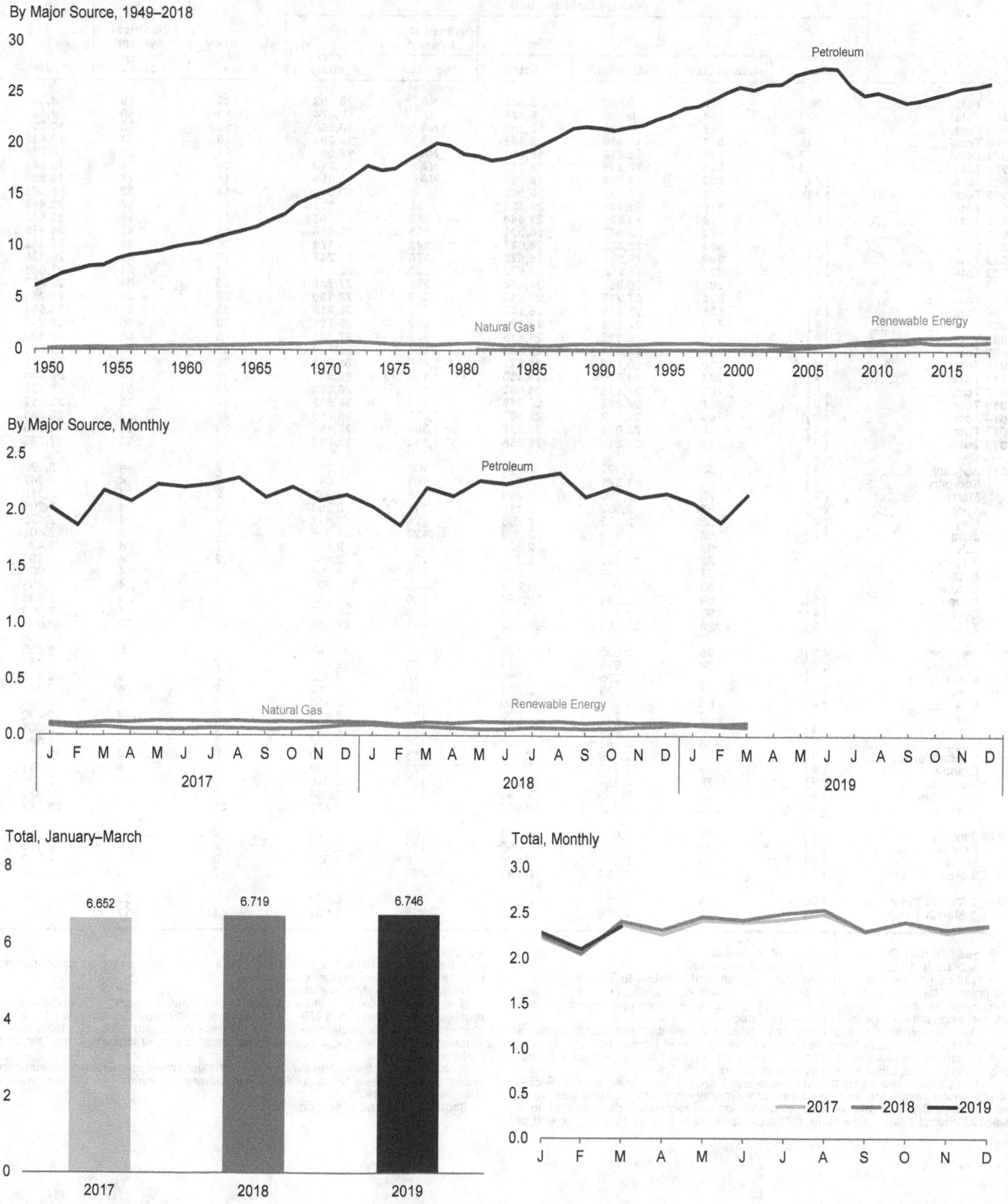

By Major Source, 1949–2018
30
25
20
15
10
5
0
Petroleum
Natural Gas
Renewable Energy
1950
1955
1960
1965
1970
1975
1980
1985
1990
1995
2000
2005
2010
2015
By Major Source, Monthly
2.5
2.0
1.5
1.0
0.5
0.0
Petroleum
Natural Gas
Renewable Energy
J F M A M J J A S O N D J F M A M J J A S O N D J F M A M J J A S O N D
2017
2018
2019
Total, January–March
8
6
4
2
0
6.652
6.719
6.746
2017
2018
2019
Total, Monthly
3.0
2.5
2.0
1.5
1.0
0.5
0.0
2017
2018
2019
J F M A M J J A S O N D

Web Page: http://www.eia.gov/totalenergy/data/monthly/#consumption.
Source: Table 2.5.

Source: *U.S. Energy Information Administration, Monthly Energy Review, June 2019*

Table 2.5 Transportation Sector Energy Consumption
(Trillion Btu)

	Primary Consumption[a]								
	Fossil Fuels				Renewable Energy[b]	Total Primary	Electricity Retail Sales[e]	Electrical System Energy Losses[f]	Total
	Coal	Natural Gas[c]	Petroleum[d]	Total	Biomass				
1950 Total	1,564	130	6,690	8,383	NA	8,383	23	86	8,492
1955 Total	421	254	8,799	9,474	NA	9,474	20	56	9,550
1960 Total	75	359	10,125	10,560	NA	10,560	10	26	10,596
1965 Total	16	517	11,866	12,399	NA	12,399	10	24	12,432
1970 Total	7	745	15,310	16,062	NA	16,062	11	26	16,098
1975 Total	1	595	17,615	18,210	NA	18,210	10	24	18,245
1980 Total	(g)	650	19,009	19,659	NA	19,659	11	27	19,697
1985 Total	(g)	519	19,472	19,992	50	20,041	14	32	20,088
1990 Total	(g)	679	21,626	22,305	60	22,366	16	37	22,419
1995 Total	(g)	724	22,920	23,644	112	23,757	17	38	23,812
2000 Total	(g)	672	25,649	26,321	135	26,456	18	42	26,516
2001 Total	(g)	658	25,379	26,037	142	26,179	20	43	26,242
2002 Total	(g)	699	25,879	26,578	170	26,747	19	42	26,808
2003 Total	(g)	627	25,950	26,577	230	26,807	23	51	26,881
2004 Total	(g)	602	26,856	27,458	290	27,748	25	54	27,827
2005 Total	(g)	624	27,217	27,840	339	28,180	26	56	28,261
2006 Total	(g)	625	27,518	28,143	475	28,618	25	54	28,697
2007 Total	(g)	663	27,462	28,126	602	28,728	28	60	28,815
2008 Total	(g)	692	25,823	26,515	825	27,340	26	56	27,422
2009 Total	(g)	715	24,857	25,572	935	26,507	27	56	26,589
2010 Total	(g)	719	25,103	25,822	1,075	26,897	26	55	26,978
2011 Total	(g)	734	24,626	25,360	1,159	26,518	26	54	26,599
2012 Total	(g)	780	24,111	24,890	1,160	26,050	25	51	26,126
2013 Total	(g)	887	24,362	25,249	1,284	26,533	26	53	26,612
2014 Total	(g)	760	24,727	25,487	1,302	26,789	26	53	26,869
2015 Total	(g)	745	25,082	25,827	1,334	27,161	26	51	27,238
2016 Total	(g)	757	25,510	26,268	1,443	27,710	26	50	27,786
2017 January	(g)	86	2,027	2,113	107	2,219	2	4	2,226
February	(g)	69	1,871	1,939	101	2,041	2	4	2,047
March	(g)	75	2,180	2,255	118	2,373	2	4	2,379
April	(g)	57	2,085	2,142	117	2,260	2	4	2,265
May	(g)	56	2,232	2,288	129	2,417	2	4	2,423
June	(g)	56	2,209	2,266	129	2,395	2	4	2,401
July	(g)	63	2,238	2,301	125	2,425	2	4	2,432
August	(g)	62	2,292	2,354	131	2,484	2	4	2,491
September	(g)	57	2,119	2,175	120	2,295	2	4	2,301
October	(g)	60	2,214	2,274	123	2,397	2	4	2,403
November	(g)	69	2,091	2,160	120	2,280	2	4	2,286
December	(g)	90	2,143	2,233	120	2,353	2	5	2,360
Total	(g)	**799**	**25,702**	**26,500**	**1,439**	**27,939**	**26**	**50**	**28,014**
2018 January	(g)	95	2,035	2,130	117	2,247	3	5	2,255
February	(g)	78	1,870	1,949	98	2,047	2	4	2,053
March	(g)	80	2,206	2,286	119	2,405	2	4	2,411
April	(g)	68	2,133	2,201	110	2,312	2	4	2,318
May	(g)	60	2,270	2,330	126	2,456	2	4	2,462
June	(g)	60	2,242	2,302	121	2,423	2	4	2,430
July	(g)	69	2,302	2,371	124	2,494	2	4	2,501
August	(g)	68	2,341	2,409	128	2,537	2	4	2,544
September	(g)	63	2,129	2,192	113	2,305	2	4	2,312
October	(g)	67	2,216	2,283	122	2,405	2	4	2,411
November	(g)	78	2,124	2,202	116	2,318	2	4	2,324
December	(g)	86	2,159	2,245	119	2,364	2	4	2,371
Total	(g)	**873**	**26,027**	**26,900**	**1,413**	**28,313**	**26**	**52**	**28,391**
2019 January	(g)	98	2,073	2,171	108	2,279	2	4	2,285
February	(g)	86	1,903	1,990	107	2,097	2	4	R 2,103
March	(g)	84	2,148	2,232	119	2,351	2	4	2,358
3-Month Total	(g)	**268**	**6,124**	**6,392**	**334**	**6,726**	**7**	**13**	**6,746**
2018 3-Month Total	(g)	**254**	**6,111**	**6,365**	**334**	**6,699**	**7**	**13**	**6,719**
2017 3-Month Total	(g)	**229**	**6,078**	**6,307**	**325**	**6,632**	**7**	**13**	**6,652**

[a] See "Primary Energy Consumption" in Glossary.
[b] See Table 10.2b for notes on series components.
[c] Natural gas only; does not include supplemental gaseous fuels—see Note 3, "Supplemental Gaseous Fuels," at end of Section 4. Data are for natural gas consumed in the operation of pipelines (primarily in compressors) and small amounts consumed as vehicle fuel—see Table 4.3.
[d] Does not include biofuels that have been blended with petroleum—biofuels are included in "Biomass." Includes non-combustion use of lubricants.
[e] Electricity retail sales to ultimate customers reported by electric utilities and, beginning in 1996, other energy service providers.
[f] Total losses are calculated as the primary energy consumed by the electric power sector minus the energy content of electricity retail sales. Total losses are allocated to the end-use sectors in proportion to each sector's share of total electricity retail sales. See Note 1, "Electrical System Energy Losses," at end of section.
[g] Beginning in 1978, the small amounts of coal consumed for transportation are reported as industrial sector consumption.

R=Revised. NA=Not available.

Notes: • Data are estimates, except for coal totals through 1977; and electricity retail sales beginning in 1979. • See Note 2, "Energy Consumption Data and Surveys," at end of section. • Totals may not equal sum of components due to independent rounding. • Geographic coverage is the 50 states and the District of Columbia.

Web Page: See http://www.eia.gov/totalenergy/data/monthly/#consumption (Excel and CSV files) for all available annual data beginning in 1949 and monthly data beginning in 1973.

Sources: See end of section.

Source: *U.S. Energy Information Administration, Monthly Energy Review, June 2019*

Figure 2.6 Electric Power Sector Energy Consumption

(Quadrillion Btu)

By Major Source, 1949–2018

Coal
Nuclear Electric Power
Natural Gas
Renewable Energy
Petroleum

0 4 8 12 16 20 24

1950 1955 1960 1965 1970 1975 1980 1985 1990 1995 2000 2005 2010 2015

By Major Source, Monthly

Coal
Natural Gas
Nuclear Electric Power
Renewable Energy
Petroleum

0.0 0.6 1.2 1.8

J F M A M J J A S O N D J F M A M J J A S O N D J F M A M J J A S O N D

2017 2018 2019

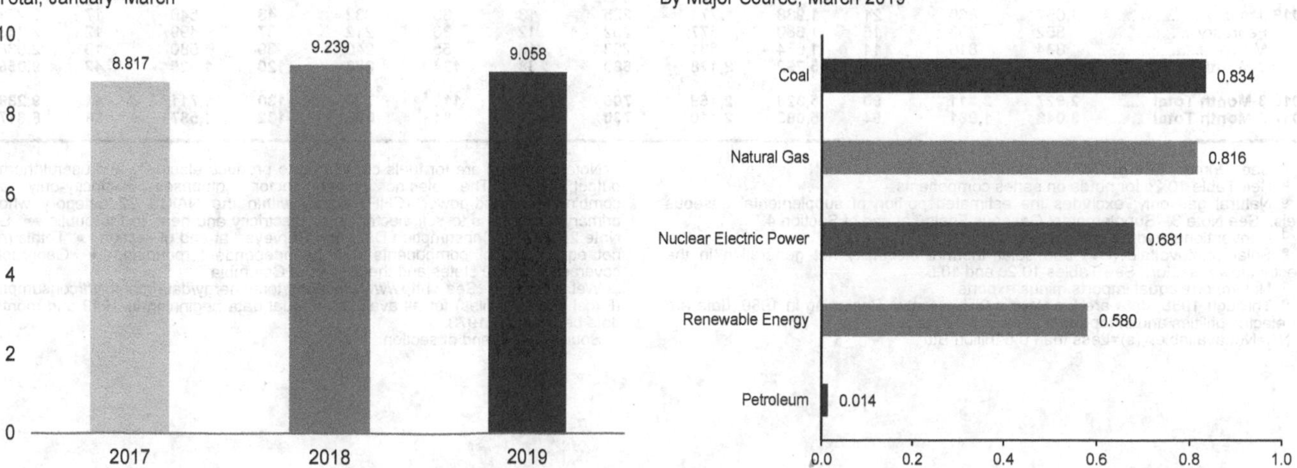

Web Page: http://www.eia.gov/totalenergy/data/monthly/#consumption.
Source: Table 2.6.

Source: *U.S. Energy Information Administration, Monthly Energy Review, June 2019*

Table 2.6 Electric Power Sector Energy Consumption
(Trillion Btu)

	Primary Consumption[a]													
	Fossil Fuels					Renewable Energy[b]								
	Coal	Natural Gas[c]	Petro-leum	Total	Nuclear Electric Power	Hydro-electric Power[d]	Geo-thermal	Solar[e]	Wind	Bio-mass	Total	Elec-tricity Net Imports[f]	Total Primary
1950 Total	**2,199**	**651**	**472**	**3,322**	**0**	**1,346**	**NA**	**NA**	**NA**	**5**	**1,351**	**6**	**4,679**
1955 Total	**3,458**	**1,194**	**471**	**5,123**	**0**	**1,322**	**NA**	**NA**	**NA**	**3**	**1,325**	**14**	**6,461**
1960 Total	**4,228**	**1,785**	**553**	**6,565**	**6**	**1,569**	**(s)**	**NA**	**NA**	**2**	**1,571**	**15**	**8,158**
1965 Total	**5,821**	**2,395**	**722**	**8,938**	**43**	**2,026**	**2**	**NA**	**NA**	**3**	**2,031**	**(s)**	**11,012**
1970 Total	**7,227**	**4,054**	**2,117**	**13,399**	**239**	**2,600**	**6**	**NA**	**NA**	**4**	**2,609**	**7**	**16,253**
1975 Total	**8,786**	**3,240**	**3,166**	**15,191**	**1,900**	**3,122**	**34**	**NA**	**NA**	**2**	**3,158**	**21**	**20,270**
1980 Total	**12,123**	**3,778**	**2,634**	**18,534**	**2,739**	**2,867**	**53**	**NA**	**NA**	**4**	**2,925**	**71**	**24,269**
1985 Total	**14,542**	**3,135**	**1,090**	**18,767**	**4,076**	**2,937**	**97**	**(s)**	**(s)**	**14**	**3,049**	**140**	**26,032**
1990 Total	**16,261**	**3,309**	**1,289**	**20,859**	**6,104**	**3,014**	**161**	**4**	**29**	**317**	**3,524**	**8**	[g]**30,495**
1995 Total	**17,466**	**4,302**	**755**	**22,523**	**7,075**	**3,149**	**138**	**5**	**33**	**422**	**3,747**	**134**	**33,479**
2000 Total	**20,220**	**5,293**	**1,144**	**26,658**	**7,862**	**2,768**	**144**	**5**	**57**	**453**	**3,427**	**115**	**38,062**
2001 Total	**19,614**	**5,458**	**1,276**	**26,348**	**8,029**	**2,209**	**142**	**6**	**70**	**337**	**2,763**	**75**	**37,215**
2002 Total	**19,783**	**5,767**	**961**	**26,511**	**8,145**	**2,650**	**147**	**6**	**105**	**380**	**3,288**	**72**	**38,016**
2003 Total	**20,185**	**5,246**	**1,205**	**26,636**	**7,960**	**2,749**	**146**	**5**	**113**	**397**	**3,411**	**22**	**38,028**
2004 Total	**20,305**	**5,595**	**1,201**	**27,101**	**8,223**	**2,655**	**148**	**6**	**142**	**388**	**3,339**	**39**	**38,701**
2005 Total	**20,737**	**6,015**	**1,222**	**27,974**	**8,161**	**2,670**	**147**	**6**	**178**	**406**	**3,406**	**85**	**39,626**
2006 Total	**20,462**	**6,375**	**637**	**27,474**	**8,215**	**2,839**	**145**	**5**	**264**	**412**	**3,665**	**63**	**39,417**
2007 Total	**20,808**	**7,005**	**648**	**28,461**	**8,459**	**2,430**	**145**	**6**	**341**	**423**	**3,345**	**107**	**40,371**
2008 Total	**20,513**	**6,829**	**459**	**27,801**	**8,426**	**2,494**	**146**	**9**	**546**	**435**	**3,630**	**112**	**39,969**
2009 Total	**18,225**	**7,022**	**382**	**25,630**	**8,355**	**2,650**	**146**	**9**	**721**	**441**	**3,967**	**116**	**38,069**
2010 Total	**19,133**	**7,528**	**370**	**27,031**	**8,434**	**2,521**	**148**	**12**	**923**	**459**	**4,064**	**89**	**39,619**
2011 Total	**18,035**	**7,712**	**295**	**26,042**	**8,269**	**3,085**	**149**	**17**	**1,167**	**437**	**4,855**	**127**	**39,293**
2012 Total	**15,821**	**9,287**	**214**	**25,322**	**8,062**	**2,606**	**148**	**40**	**1,339**	**453**	**4,586**	**161**	**38,131**
2013 Total	**16,451**	**8,376**	**255**	**25,082**	**8,244**	**2,529**	**151**	**83**	**1,600**	**470**	**4,833**	**197**	**38,357**
2014 Total	**16,427**	**8,362**	**295**	**25,085**	**8,338**	**2,454**	**151**	**165**	**1,726**	**530**	**5,026**	**182**	**38,629**
2015 Total	**14,138**	**9,926**	**276**	**24,341**	**8,337**	**2,308**	**148**	**228**	**1,776**	**525**	**4,985**	**227**	**37,890**
2016 Total	**12,996**	**10,301**	**244**	**23,542**	**8,427**	**2,459**	**146**	**328**	**2,094**	**505**	**5,531**	**227**	**37,727**
2017 January	1,207	681	21	1,909	765	245	13	19	183	46	505	22	3,201
February	912	587	16	1,515	665	217	11	23	195	41	487	17	2,684
March	929	693	17	1,639	681	268	13	39	230	45	595	17	2,932
April	842	646	13	1,501	593	269	12	43	227	39	590	15	2,700
May	967	722	19	1,708	641	297	12	52	207	40	607	15	2,971
June	1,118	877	19	2,015	701	277	11	56	182	42	569	18	3,303
July	1,326	1,115	18	2,460	746	243	12	52	147	44	498	18	3,722
August	1,251	1,054	18	2,322	757	200	12	50	125	45	432	20	3,531
September	1,040	886	17	1,942	712	175	12	47	164	40	438	15	3,108
October	951	796	16	1,763	690	167	11	44	233	40	496	11	2,960
November	968	687	17	1,672	697	188	12	31	222	42	495	11	2,874
December	1,111	810	27	1,948	771	205	14	31	226	45	522	14	3,255
Total	**12,622**	**9,555**	**218**	**22,395**	**8,419**	**2,752**	**147**	**486**	**2,341**	**510**	**6,235**	**192**	**37,241**
2018 January	1,222	809	60	2,091	781	235	13	31	247	45	571	14	3,457
February	865	723	15	1,603	678	234	12	38	222	41	547	12	2,840
March	840	779	15	1,634	701	238	13	47	251	44	593	15	2,943
April	768	729	15	1,512	618	252	11	57	246	38	605	10	2,746
May	898	879	14	1,791	704	279	13	64	217	42	615	14	3,125
June	1,061	981	19	2,060	729	256	13	71	224	43	607	15	3,411
July	1,207	1,273	19	2,500	758	220	13	63	147	43	487	15	3,759
August	1,206	1,231	19	2,456	756	196	13	64	180	42	495	17	3,724
September	1,021	1,076	19	2,115	677	171	13	59	165	37	445	11	3,249
October	918	922	15	1,854	621	172	12	48	195	40	466	10	2,951
November	979	779	16	1,775	669	203	13	36	207	39	498	9	2,950
December	1,052	767	17	1,835	749	217	14	29	228	41	530	11	3,126
Total	**12,037**	**10,949**	**243**	**23,229**	**8,441**	**2,673**	**154**	**607**	**2,530**	**495**	**6,459**	**152**	**38,280**
2019 January	1,057	860	21	1,938	771	225	13	33	232	43	546	17	3,271
February	852	793	15	1,660	677	202	12	36	212	37	499	12	2,848
March	834	816	14	1,664	681	233	13	55	240	39	580	13	2,938
3-Month Total	**2,742**	**2,470**	**50**	**5,262**	**2,128**	**660**	**38**	**124**	**683**	**120**	**1,625**	**42**	**9,058**
2018 3-Month Total	**2,927**	**2,311**	**90**	**5,328**	**2,159**	**706**	**38**	**116**	**720**	**130**	**1,711**	**41**	**9,239**
2017 3-Month Total	**3,048**	**1,961**	**54**	**5,063**	**2,110**	**730**	**37**	**81**	**608**	**132**	**1,587**	**56**	**8,817**

[a] See "Primary Energy Consumption" in Glossary.
[b] See Table 10.2c for notes on series components.
[c] Natural gas only; excludes the estimated portion of supplemental gaseous fuels. See Note 3, "Supplemental Gaseous Fuels," at end of Section 4.
[d] Conventional hydroelectric power.
[e] Solar photovoltaic (PV) and solar thermal electricity net generation in the electric power sector. See Tables 10.2c and 10.5.
[f] Net imports equal imports minus exports.
[g] Through 1988, data are for electric utilities only. Beginning in 1989, data are for electric utilities and independent power producers.
NA=Not available. (s)=Less than 0.5 trillion Btu.

Notes: • Data are for fuels consumed to produce electricity and useful thermal output. • The electric power sector comprises electricity-only and combined-heat-and-power (CHP) plants within the NAICS 22 category whose primary business is to sell electricity, or electricity and heat, to the public. • See Note 2, "Energy Consumption Data and Surveys," at end of section. • Totals may not equal sum of components due to independent rounding. • Geographic coverage is the 50 states and the District of Columbia.

Web Page: See http://www.eia.gov/totalenergy/data/monthly/#consumption (Excel and CSV files) for all available annual data beginning in 1949 and monthly data beginning in 1973.

Sources: See end of section.

***Source:** U.S. Energy Information Administration, Monthly Energy Review, June 2019*

Table 2.7 U.S. Government Energy Consumption by Agency, Fiscal Years
(Trillion Btu)

Fiscal Year[a]	Agri- culture	Defense	DHS[b]	Energy	GSA[c]	HHS[d]	Interior	Justice	NASA[e]	Postal Service	Trans- portation	Veterans Affairs	Other[f]	Total
1975	9.5	1,360.2	– –	50.4	22.3	6.5	9.4	5.9	13.4	30.5	19.3	27.1	10.5	1,565.0
1976	9.3	1,183.3	– –	50.3	20.6	6.7	9.4	5.7	12.4	30.0	19.5	25.0	11.2	1,383.4
1977	8.9	1,192.3	– –	51.6	20.4	6.9	9.5	5.9	12.0	32.7	20.4	25.9	11.9	1,398.5
1978	9.1	1,157.8	– –	50.1	20.4	6.5	9.2	5.9	11.2	30.9	20.6	26.8	12.4	1,360.9
1979	9.2	1,175.8	– –	49.6	19.6	6.4	10.4	6.4	11.1	29.3	19.6	25.7	12.3	1,375.4
1980	8.6	1,183.1	– –	47.4	18.1	6.0	8.5	5.7	10.4	27.2	19.2	24.8	12.3	1,371.2
1981	7.9	1,239.5	– –	47.3	18.0	6.7	7.6	5.4	10.0	27.9	18.8	24.0	11.1	1,424.2
1982	7.6	1,264.5	– –	49.0	18.1	6.4	7.4	5.8	10.1	27.5	19.1	24.2	11.6	1,451.4
1983	7.4	1,248.3	– –	49.5	16.1	6.2	7.7	5.5	10.3	26.5	19.4	24.1	10.8	1,431.8
1984	7.9	1,292.1	– –	51.6	16.2	6.4	8.4	6.4	10.6	27.7	19.8	24.6	10.7	1,482.5
1985	8.4	1,250.6	– –	52.2	20.7	6.0	7.8	8.2	10.9	27.8	19.6	25.1	13.1	1,450.3
1986	6.8	1,222.8	– –	46.9	14.0	6.2	6.9	8.6	11.2	28.0	19.4	25.0	10.8	1,406.7
1987	7.3	1,280.5	– –	48.5	13.1	6.6	6.6	8.1	11.3	28.5	19.0	24.9	11.9	1,466.3
1988	7.8	1,165.8	– –	49.9	12.4	6.4	7.0	9.4	11.3	29.6	18.7	26.3	15.8	1,360.3
1989	8.7	1,274.4	– –	44.2	12.7	6.7	7.1	7.7	12.4	30.3	18.5	26.2	15.6	1,464.7
1990	9.6	1,241.7	– –	43.5	17.5	7.1	7.4	7.0	12.4	30.6	19.0	24.9	17.5	1,438.0
1991	9.6	1,269.3	– –	42.1	14.0	6.2	7.1	8.0	12.5	30.8	19.0	25.1	18.1	1,461.7
1992	9.1	1,104.0	– –	44.3	13.8	6.8	7.0	7.5	12.6	31.7	17.0	25.3	15.7	1,294.8
1993	9.3	1,048.8	– –	43.4	14.1	7.2	7.5	9.1	12.4	33.7	19.4	25.7	16.2	1,246.8
1994	9.4	977.0	– –	42.1	14.0	7.5	7.9	10.3	12.6	35.0	19.8	25.6	17.1	1,178.2
1995	9.0	926.0	– –	47.3	13.7	6.1	6.4	10.2	12.4	36.2	18.7	25.4	17.1	1,128.5
1996	9.1	904.5	– –	44.6	14.5	6.6	4.3	12.1	11.5	36.4	19.6	26.8	17.7	1,107.7
1997	7.4	880.0	– –	43.1	14.4	7.9	6.6	12.0	12.0	40.8	19.1	27.3	20.8	1,091.2
1998	7.9	837.1	– –	31.5	14.1	7.4	6.4	15.8	11.7	39.5	18.5	27.6	19.5	1,037.1
1999	7.8	810.7	– –	27.0	14.4	7.1	7.5	15.4	11.4	39.8	22.6	27.5	19.8	1,010.9
2000	7.4	779.1	– –	30.5	17.6	8.0	7.8	19.7	11.1	43.3	21.2	27.0	20.3	993.1
2001	7.4	787.2	– –	31.1	18.4	8.5	9.5	19.7	10.9	43.4	17.8	27.7	20.7	1,002.3
2002	7.2	837.5	– –	30.7	17.5	8.0	8.2	17.7	10.7	41.6	18.3	27.7	18.4	1,043.4
2003	7.7	895.1	18.3	31.9	18.5	10.1	7.3	22.7	10.8	50.9	5.5	30.6	22.7	1,132.3
2004	7.0	960.7	23.5	31.4	18.3	8.8	8.7	17.5	9.9	50.5	5.2	29.9	20.4	1,191.7
2005	7.5	933.2	18.9	29.6	18.4	9.6	8.6	18.8	10.3	53.5	5.0	30.0	23.2	1,166.4
2006	6.8	843.7	17.1	32.9	18.2	9.3	8.1	23.5	10.2	51.8	4.6	29.3	20.9	1,076.4
2007	6.8	864.6	17.1	31.5	19.1	9.9	7.5	20.7	10.6	45.8	5.6	30.0	21.0	1,090.2
2008	6.5	910.8	21.7	32.1	18.8	10.3	7.1	19.0	10.8	47.1	7.7	29.0	22.4	1,143.2
2009	6.6	874.3	18.6	31.1	18.6	10.8	7.9	16.5	10.2	44.2	4.3	29.9	21.8	1,094.8
2010	6.8	889.9	21.2	31.7	18.8	10.4	7.3	15.7	10.1	43.3	5.7	30.2	21.8	1,112.7
2011	8.3	890.3	20.3	33.1	18.5	10.5	7.3	13.9	10.1	43.0	6.7	30.6	21.4	1,114.1
2012	6.7	828.5	20.1	30.3	16.3	10.0	6.7	15.1	8.9	40.8	5.6	29.7	20.5	1,039.3
2013	7.3	749.5	18.9	28.9	16.4	10.5	6.2	15.3	8.7	41.9	5.3	29.9	20.4	959.3
2014	6.3	730.6	18.5	29.4	17.0	9.5	6.2	15.6	8.3	43.0	5.2	31.4	20.6	941.5
2015	6.2	734.5	17.9	30.1	16.3	9.0	6.8	16.2	8.4	44.0	6.0	30.7	19.8	945.8
2016	6.2	709.2	18.1	28.9	15.8	8.7	6.4	15.6	8.5	43.9	6.0	30.3	19.5	917.2
2017	6.3	707.9	19.2	28.8	14.9	8.8	5.9	15.5	8.6	43.7	6.7	29.1	19.7	915.1

[a] For 1975 and 1976, the U.S. Government's fiscal year was July 1 through June 30. Beginning in 1977, the U.S. Government's fiscal year is October 1 through September 30 (for example, fiscal year 2014 is October 2013 through September 2014).

[b] U.S. Department of Homeland Security.

[c] General Services Administration.

[d] U.S. Department of Health and Human Services.

[e] National Aeronautics and Space Administration.

[f] Includes all U.S. government agencies not separately displayed. See http://ctsedwweb.ee.doe.gov/Annual/Report/AgencyReference.aspx for agency list.

– – =Not applicable.

Notes: • Data in this table are developed using conversion factors that often differ from those in Tables A1–A6. • Data include energy consumed at foreign installations and in foreign operations, including aviation and ocean bunkering, primarily by the U.S. Department of Defense. U.S. Government energy use for electricity generation and uranium enrichment is excluded. • Totals may not equal sum of components due to independent rounding.

Web Page: See http://www.eia.gov/totalenergy/data/monthly/#consumption (Excel and CSV files) for all annual data beginning in 1975.

Source: U.S. Department of Energy, Office of Energy Efficiency and Renewable Energy, Federal Energy Management Program. See http://ctsedwweb.ee.doe.gov/Annual/Report/Report.aspx, "A-1 Total Site-Delivered Energy Use in All End-Use Sectors, by Federal Agency (Billion Btu)".

Source: *U.S. Energy Information Administration, Monthly Energy Review, June 2019*

Table 2.8 U.S. Government Energy Consumption by Source, Fiscal Years

(Trillion Btu)

Fiscal Year[a]	Coal	Natural Gas[b]	Petroleum: Aviation Gasoline	Petroleum: Fuel Oil[c]	Petroleum: Jet Fuel	Petroleum: LPG[d]	Petroleum: Motor Gasoline[e]	Petroleum: Total	Other Mobility Fuels[f]	Elec-tricity	Purchased Steam and Other[g]	Total
1975	77.9	166.2	22.0	376.0	707.4	5.6	63.2	1,174.2	0.0	141.5	5.1	1,565.0
1976	71.3	151.8	11.6	329.7	610.0	4.7	60.4	1,016.4	.0	139.3	4.6	1,383.4
1977	68.4	141.2	8.8	348.5	619.2	4.1	61.4	1,042.1	.0	141.1	5.7	1,398.5
1978	66.0	144.7	6.2	332.3	601.1	3.0	60.1	1,002.9	.0	141.0	6.4	1,360.9
1979	65.1	148.9	4.7	327.1	618.6	3.7	59.1	1,013.1	.0	141.2	7.1	1,375.4
1980	63.5	147.3	4.9	307.7	638.7	3.8	56.5	1,011.6	.2	141.9	6.8	1,371.2
1981	65.1	142.2	4.6	351.3	653.3	3.5	53.2	1,066.0	.2	144.5	6.2	1,424.2
1982	68.6	146.2	3.6	349.4	672.7	3.7	53.1	1,082.5	.2	147.5	6.2	1,451.4
1983	62.4	147.8	2.6	329.5	673.4	3.8	51.6	1,060.8	.2	151.5	9.0	1,431.8
1984	65.3	157.4	1.9	342.9	693.7	3.9	51.2	1,093.6	.2	155.9	10.1	1,482.5
1985	64.8	149.9	1.9	292.6	705.7	3.8	50.4	1,054.3	.2	167.2	13.9	1,450.3
1986	63.8	140.9	1.4	271.6	710.2	3.6	45.3	1,032.1	.3	155.8	13.7	1,406.7
1987	67.0	145.6	1.0	319.5	702.3	3.6	43.1	1,069.5	.4	169.9	13.9	1,466.3
1988	60.2	144.6	6.0	284.8	617.2	2.7	41.2	951.9	.4	171.2	32.0	1,360.3
1989	48.7	152.4	.8	245.3	761.7	3.5	41.1	1,052.4	2.2	188.6	20.6	1,464.7
1990	44.3	159.4	.5	245.2	732.4	3.8	37.2	1,019.1	2.6	193.6	19.1	1,438.0
1991	45.9	154.1	.4	232.6	774.5	3.0	34.1	1,044.7	6.0	192.7	18.3	1,461.7
1992	51.7	151.2	1.0	200.6	628.2	3.0	35.6	868.4	8.4	192.5	22.5	1,294.8
1993	38.3	152.9	.7	187.0	612.4	3.5	34.5	838.1	5.8	193.1	18.6	1,246.8
1994	35.0	143.9	.6	198.5	550.7	3.2	29.5	782.6	7.7	190.9	18.2	1,178.2
1995	31.7	149.4	.3	178.4	522.3	3.0	31.9	735.9	8.4	184.8	18.2	1,128.5
1996	23.3	147.3	.2	170.5	513.0	3.1	27.6	714.4	18.7	184.0	20.1	1,107.7
1997	22.5	153.8	.3	180.0	475.7	2.6	39.0	697.6	14.5	183.6	19.2	1,091.2
1998	23.9	140.4	.2	174.5	445.5	3.5	43.0	666.8	5.9	181.4	18.8	1,037.1
1999	21.2	137.4	.1	162.1	444.7	2.4	41.1	650.4	.4	180.0	21.5	1,010.9
2000	22.7	133.8	.2	171.3	403.1	2.5	43.9	621.0	1.8	193.6	20.2	993.1
2001	18.8	133.7	.2	176.9	415.2	3.1	42.5	638.0	4.8	188.4	18.6	1,002.3
2002	16.9	133.7	.2	165.6	472.9	2.8	41.3	682.8	3.2	188.3	18.5	1,043.4
2003	18.1	135.5	.3	190.8	517.9	3.2	46.3	758.4	3.3	193.8	23.2	1,132.3
2004	17.4	135.3	.2	261.4	508.2	2.9	44.1	816.9	3.1	197.1	22.0	1,191.7
2005	17.1	135.7	.4	241.4	492.2	3.4	48.8	786.1	5.6	197.6	24.3	1,166.4
2006	23.5	132.6	.6	209.3	442.6	2.7	48.3	703.6	2.1	196.7	18.2	1,076.4
2007	20.4	131.5	.4	212.9	461.1	2.7	46.5	723.7	2.9	194.9	16.7	1,090.2
2008	20.8	129.6	.4	198.4	525.4	2.3	49.0	775.4	3.6	196.1	17.7	1,143.2
2009	20.3	131.7	.3	166.4	505.7	3.2	48.3	723.9	10.1	191.3	17.7	1,094.8
2010	20.0	130.1	.4	157.8	535.8	2.5	51.3	747.7	3.0	193.7	18.2	1,112.7
2011	18.5	124.7	.9	166.5	533.6	2.0	52.7	755.8	2.7	193.2	19.1	1,114.1
2012	15.9	116.2	.4	148.6	493.5	1.7	50.1	694.4	3.1	187.2	22.5	1,039.3
2013	14.3	122.5	.7	140.0	424.0	1.9	46.6	613.2	2.8	184.7	21.8	959.3
2014	13.5	125.6	.3	133.5	414.3	1.8	44.9	594.8	3.6	182.1	21.9	941.5
2015	12.6	122.2	.3	134.4	418.9	1.8	46.8	602.2	3.7	184.3	20.9	945.8
2016	10.2	115.4	.3	129.7	403.9	1.7	46.5	582.2	3.6	184.5	21.4	917.2
2017	9.1	115.1	.3	133.9	400.1	1.5	46.4	582.3	3.9	181.7	23.0	915.1

[a] For 1975 and 1976, the U.S. Government's fiscal year was July 1 through June 30. Beginning in 1977, the U.S. Government's fiscal year is October 1 through September 30 (for example, fiscal year 2014 is October 2013 through September 2014).

[b] Natural gas, plus a small amount of supplemental gaseous fuels.

[c] Distillate fuel oil, including diesel fuel; and residual fuel oil, including Navy Special.

[d] Liquefied petroleum gases, primarily propane.

[e] Includes E10 (a mixture of 10% ethanol and 90% motor gasoline) and E15 (a mixture of 15% ethanol and 85% motor gasoline).

[f] Other types of fuel used in vehicles and equipment. Primarily includes alternative fuels such as compressed natural gas (CNG); liquefied natural gas (LNG); E85 (a mixture of 85% ethanol and 15% motor gasoline); B20 (a mixture of 20% biodiesel and 80% diesel fuel); B100 (100% biodiesel); hydrogen; and methanol.

[g] Other types of energy used in facilities. Primarily includes chilled water, but also includes small amounts of renewable energy such as wood and solar thermal.

Notes: • Data in this table are developed using conversion factors that often differ from those in Tables A1–A6. • Data include energy consumed at foreign installations and in foreign operations, including aviation and ocean bunkering, primarily by the U.S. Department of Defense. U.S. Government energy use for electricity generation and uranium enrichment is excluded. • Totals may not equal sum of components due to independent rounding.

Web Page: See http://www.eia.gov/totalenergy/data/monthly/#consumption (Excel and CSV files) for all annual data beginning in 1975.

Source: U.S. Department of Energy, Office of Energy Efficiency and Renewable Energy, Federal Energy Management Program. See http://ctsedwweb.ee.doe.gov/Annual/Report/Report.aspx, "A-5 Historical Federal Energy Consumption and Cost Data by Agency and Energy Type (FY 1975 to Present)".

Source: *U.S. Energy Information Administration, Monthly Energy Review, June 2019*

Figure 3.1 Petroleum Overview

(Million Barrels Per Day)

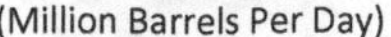

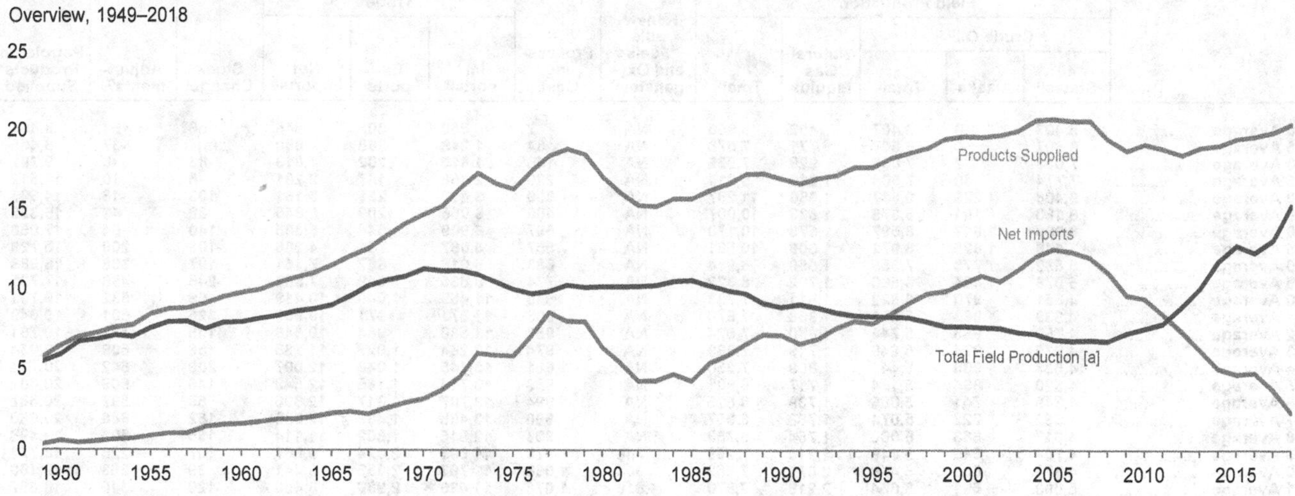

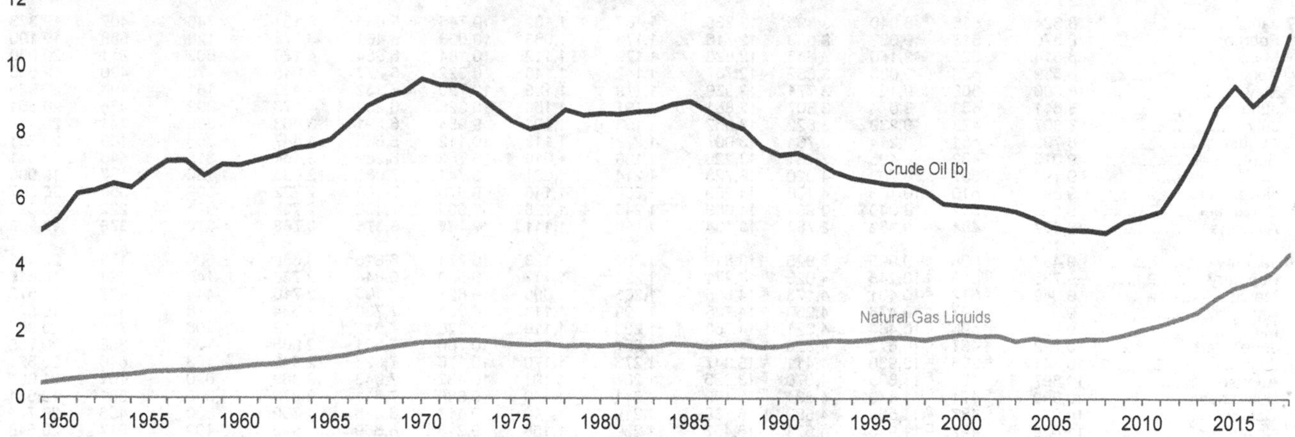

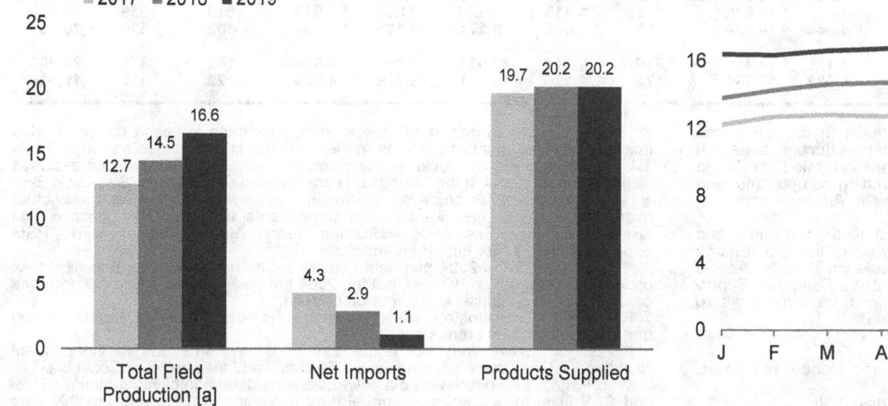

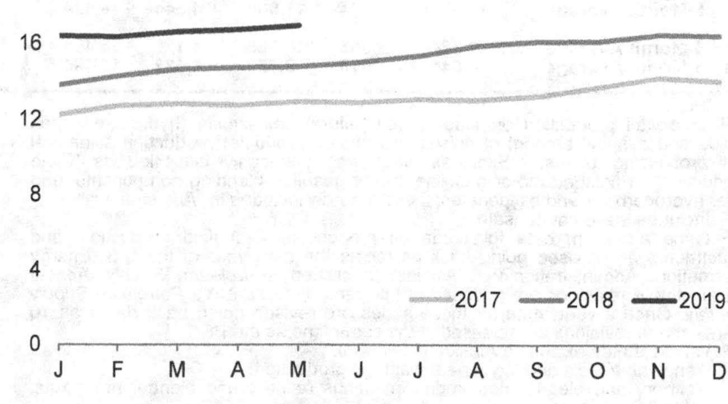

[a] Crude oil, including lease condensate, and natural gas liquids field production.

[b] Includes lease condensate.

Web Page: http://www.eia.gov/totalenergy/data/monthly/#petroleum.

Source: Table 3.1.

Source: *U.S. Energy Information Administration, Monthly Energy Review, June 2019*

Table 3.1 Petroleum Overview
(Thousand Barrels per Day)

	Field Production[a]					Renewable Fuels and Oxygenates[e]	Processing Gain[f]	Trade			Stock Change[i]	Adjustments[c,j]	Petroleum Products Supplied
	Crude Oil[b,c]			Natural Gas Liquids	Total[c]			Imports[g]	Exports	Net Imports[h]			
	48 States[d]	Alaska	Total										
1950 Average	**5,407**	**0**	**5,407**	**499**	**5,906**	**NA**	**2**	**850**	**305**	**545**	**-56**	**-51**	**6,458**
1955 Average	**6,807**	**0**	**6,807**	**771**	**7,578**	**NA**	**34**	**1,248**	**368**	**880**	**(s)**	**-37**	**8,455**
1960 Average	**7,034**	**2**	**7,035**	**929**	**7,965**	**NA**	**146**	**1,815**	**202**	**1,613**	**-83**	**-8**	**9,797**
1965 Average	**7,774**	**30**	**7,804**	**1,210**	**9,014**	**NA**	**220**	**2,468**	**187**	**2,281**	**-8**	**-10**	**11,512**
1970 Average	**9,408**	**229**	**9,637**	**1,660**	**11,297**	**NA**	**359**	**3,419**	**259**	**3,161**	**103**	**-16**	**14,697**
1975 Average	**8,183**	**191**	**8,375**	**1,633**	**10,007**	**NA**	**460**	**6,056**	**209**	**5,846**	**32**	**41**	**16,322**
1980 Average	**6,980**	**1,617**	**8,597**	**1,573**	**10,170**	**NA**	**597**	**6,909**	**544**	**6,365**	**140**	**64**	**17,056**
1985 Average	**7,146**	**1,825**	**8,971**	**1,609**	**10,581**	**NA**	**557**	**5,067**	**781**	**4,286**	**-103**	**200**	**15,726**
1990 Average	**5,582**	**1,773**	**7,355**	**1,559**	**8,914**	**NA**	**683**	**8,018**	**857**	**7,161**	**107**	**338**	**16,988**
1995 Average	**5,076**	**1,484**	**6,560**	**1,762**	**8,322**	**NA**	**774**	**8,835**	**949**	**7,886**	**-246**	**496**	**17,725**
2000 Average	**4,851**	**970**	**5,822**	**1,911**	**7,733**	**NA**	**948**	**11,459**	**1,040**	**10,419**	**-69**	**532**	**19,701**
2001 Average	**4,839**	**963**	**5,801**	**1,868**	**7,670**	**NA**	**903**	**11,871**	**971**	**10,900**	**325**	**501**	**19,649**
2002 Average	**4,759**	**985**	**5,744**	**1,880**	**7,624**	**NA**	**957**	**11,530**	**984**	**10,546**	**-105**	**529**	**19,761**
2003 Average	**4,675**	**974**	**5,649**	**1,719**	**7,369**	**NA**	**974**	**12,264**	**1,027**	**11,238**	**56**	**509**	**20,034**
2004 Average	**4,533**	**908**	**5,441**	**1,809**	**7,250**	**NA**	**1,051**	**13,145**	**1,048**	**12,097**	**209**	**542**	**20,731**
2005 Average	**4,320**	**864**	**5,184**	**1,717**	**6,901**	**NA**	**989**	**13,714**	**1,165**	**12,549**	**[k]146**	**509**	**20,802**
2006 Average	**4,345**	**741**	**5,086**	**1,739**	**6,825**	**NA**	**994**	**13,707**	**1,317**	**12,390**	**59**	**537**	**20,687**
2007 Average	**4,352**	**722**	**5,074**	**1,783**	**6,857**	**NA**	**996**	**13,468**	**1,433**	**12,036**	**-152**	**640**	**20,680**
2008 Average	**4,317**	**683**	**5,000**	**1,784**	**6,783**	**NA**	**993**	**12,915**	**1,802**	**11,114**	**195**	**803**	**19,498**
2009 Average	**4,704**	**645**	**5,349**	**1,910**	**7,259**	**746**	**979**	**11,691**	**2,024**	**9,667**	**107**	**228**	**18,771**
2010 Average	**4,878**	**600**	**5,478**	**2,074**	**7,552**	**907**	**1,068**	**11,793**	**2,353**	**9,441**	**39**	**253**	**19,180**
2011 Average	**5,093**	**561**	**5,654**	**2,216**	**7,870**	**1,016**	**1,076**	**11,436**	**2,986**	**8,450**	**-129**	**345**	**18,887**
2012 Average	**5,976**	**526**	**6,502**	**2,408**	**8,909**	**964**	**1,059**	**10,598**	**3,205**	**7,393**	**147**	**308**	**18,487**
2013 Average	**6,952**	**515**	**7,467**	**2,606**	**10,073**	**1,002**	**1,087**	**9,859**	**3,621**	**6,237**	**-139**	**429**	**18,967**
2014 Average	**8,262**	**496**	**8,759**	**3,015**	**11,773**	**1,055**	**1,081**	**9,241**	**4,176**	**5,065**	**267**	**394**	**19,100**
2015 Average	**8,948**	**483**	**9,431**	**3,342**	**12,773**	**1,095**	**1,062**	**9,449**	**4,738**	**4,711**	**429**	**322**	**19,534**
2016 Average	**8,341**	**490**	**8,831**	**3,509**	**12,340**	**1,158**	**1,118**	**10,055**	**5,261**	**4,795**	**130**	**406**	**19,687**
2017 January	8,324	516	8,840	3,395	12,235	1,187	1,139	10,745	5,645	5,101	746	407	19,323
February	8,570	513	9,083	3,633	12,716	1,173	1,063	10,033	6,461	3,573	-128	538	19,190
March	8,614	526	9,140	3,685	12,826	1,179	1,112	10,184	6,054	4,130	-602	211	20,060
April	8,559	525	9,085	3,682	12,767	1,142	1,146	10,322	6,277	4,045	-70	426	19,595
May	8,660	508	9,168	3,771	12,939	1,179	1,135	10,729	6,232	4,498	181	496	20,066
June	8,611	463	9,074	3,807	12,881	1,191	1,159	10,325	6,252	4,073	-802	454	20,561
July	8,807	423	9,230	3,822	13,052	1,193	1,101	9,954	6,291	3,663	-369	741	20,119
August	8,793	451	9,244	3,764	13,007	1,222	1,113	10,112	5,665	4,447	-363	100	20,251
September	9,013	482	9,495	3,731	13,226	1,180	1,010	9,752	6,289	3,464	-315	446	19,641
October	9,196	507	9,703	4,020	13,723	1,214	1,081	9,741	7,086	2,655	-1,180	137	19,990
November	9,593	510	10,103	4,106	14,209	1,268	1,146	9,876	7,144	2,732	-596	356	20,307
December	9,528	512	10,040	3,969	14,009	1,240	1,126	9,935	7,136	2,799	-927	222	20,323
Average	**8,857**	**494**	**9,352**	**3,783**	**13,134**	**1,198**	**1,111**	**10,144**	**6,376**	**3,768**	**-370**	**376**	**19,958**
2018 January	[E]9,487	[E]508	[E]9,995	3,825	[E]13,819	1,204	1,123	10,274	6,615	3,659	-500	155	20,461
February	[E]9,735	[E]513	[E]10,248	4,023	[E]14,271	1,221	1,117	9,580	6,844	2,736	-140	134	19,619
March	[E]9,949	[E]512	[E]10,461	4,173	[E]14,635	1,206	1,096	9,821	7,105	2,716	-444	477	20,573
April	[E]9,978	[E]497	[E]10,475	4,260	[E]14,735	1,199	1,114	10,364	7,730	2,634	78	337	19,941
May	[E]9,968	[E]496	[E]10,464	4,321	[E]14,785	1,223	1,119	10,228	7,517	2,712	206	723	20,357
June	[E]10,222	[E]451	[E]10,672	4,326	[E]14,998	1,257	1,129	10,706	7,801	2,905	-108	308	20,705
July	[E]10,541	[E]395	[E]10,936	4,411	[E]15,347	1,273	1,170	10,176	7,827	2,349	163	646	20,621
August	[E]10,897	[E]428	[E]11,325	4,570	[E]15,895	1,287	1,191	10,432	7,043	3,389	620	161	21,302
September	[E]10,999	[E]471	[E]11,470	4,631	[E]16,102	1,211	1,140	9,885	7,611	2,273	1,336	561	19,951
October	[E]11,072	[E]487	[E]11,559	4,580	[E]16,139	1,219	1,110	9,417	8,018	1,399	-500	406	20,774
November	[E]11,429	[E]497	[E]11,926	4,571	[E]16,497	1,239	1,158	9,213	8,669	545	-192	917	20,548
December	[E]11,467	[E]496	[E]11,963	4,479	[E]16,442	1,222	1,210	9,022	8,250	772	39	872	20,479
Average	**[E]10,483**	**[E]479**	**[E]10,962**	**4,349**	**[E]15,311**	**1,230**	**1,140**	**9,928**	**7,588**	**2,340**	**45**	**477**	**20,453**
2019 January	[RE]11,364	[E]496	[RE]11,860	4,545	[RE]16,405	1,190	1,110	9,693	8,104	1,589	260	[R]419	20,452
February	[RE]11,177	[E]488	[RE]11,664	4,706	[RE]16,370	1,198	1,020	8,628	8,453	176	-616	[R]814	20,194
March	[RE]11,424	[RE]481	[RE]11,905	[R]4,728	[RE]16,633	[R]1,163	[R]1,042	[R]8,837	[R]7,996	[R]842	[R]-136	[R]389	[R]20,204
April	[E]11,722	[E]478	[E]12,200	[E]4,545	[E]16,745	[E]1,139	[E]1,097	[E]9,310	[E]7,797	[E]1,513	[E]802	[E]533	[E]20,225
May	[E]11,771	[E]477	[E]12,248	[E]4,696	[E]16,945	[E]1,151	[E]1,118	[E]9,826	[E]8,313	[E]1,513	[E]1,613	[E]959	[E]20,073
5-Month Average	**[E]11,496**	**[E]484**	**[E]11,980**	**[E]4,644**	**[E]16,624**	**[E]1,168**	**[E]1,078**	**[E]9,271**	**[E]8,128**	**[E]1,143**	**[E]402**	**[E]620**	**[E]20,230**
2018 5-Month Average	**[E]9,824**	**[E]505**	**[E]10,329**	**4,121**	**[E]14,451**	**1,210**	**1,114**	**10,061**	**7,165**	**2,896**	**-162**	**370**	**20,203**
2017 5-Month Average	**8,545**	**518**	**9,063**	**3,633**	**12,696**	**1,172**	**1,120**	**10,411**	**6,126**	**4,284**	**29**	**413**	**19,656**

[a] Crude oil production on leases, and natural gas liquids (hydrocarbon gas liquids and a small amount of finished petroleum products) production at natural gas processing plants. Excludes what was previously classified as "Field Production" of finished motor gasoline, motor gasoline blending components, and other hydrocarbons and oxygenates; these are now included in "Adjustments."

[b] Includes lease condensate.

[c] Once a month, data for crude oil production, total field production, and adjustments are revised going back as far as the data year of the U.S. Energy Information Administration's (EIA) last published *Petroleum Supply Annual (PSA)*—these revisions are released at the same time as EIA's *Petroleum Supply Monthly*. Once a year, data for these series are revised going back as far as 10 years—these revisions are released at the same time as the PSA.

[d] United States excluding Alaska and Hawaii.

[e] Renewable fuels and oxygenate plant net production.

[f] Refinery and blender net production minus refinery and blender net inputs. See Table 3.2.

[g] Includes Strategic Petroleum Reserve imports. See Table 3.3b.

[h] Net imports equal imports minus exports.

[i] A negative value indicates a decrease in stocks and a positive value indicates an increase. The current month stock change estimate is based on the change from the previous month's estimate, rather than the stocks values shown in Table 3.4. Includes crude oil stocks in the Strategic Petroleum Reserve, but excludes distillate fuel oil stocks in the Northeast Home Heating Oil Reserve. See Table 3.4.

[j] An adjustment for crude oil, hydrogen, oxygenates, renewable fuels, other hydrocarbons, motor gasoline blending components, finished motor gasoline, and distillate fuel oil. See EIA's *Petroleum Supply Monthly*, Appendix B, "PSM Explanatory Notes," for further information.

[k] Derived from the 2004 petroleum stocks value that excludes crude oil stocks on leases (1,628 million barrels), not the 2004 petroleum stocks value that includes crude oil stocks on leases (1,645 million barrels).

R=Revised. E=Estimate. NA=Not available. (s)=Less than 500 barrels per day and greater than -500 barrels per day.

Notes: • Totals may not equal sum of components due to independent rounding. • Geographic coverage is the 50 states and the District of Columbia.

Web Page: See http://www.eia.gov/totalenergy/data/monthly/#petroleum (Excel and CSV files) for all available annual data beginning in 1949 and monthly data beginning in 1973.

Sources: See end of section.

Source: *U.S. Energy Information Administration, Monthly Energy Review, June 2019*

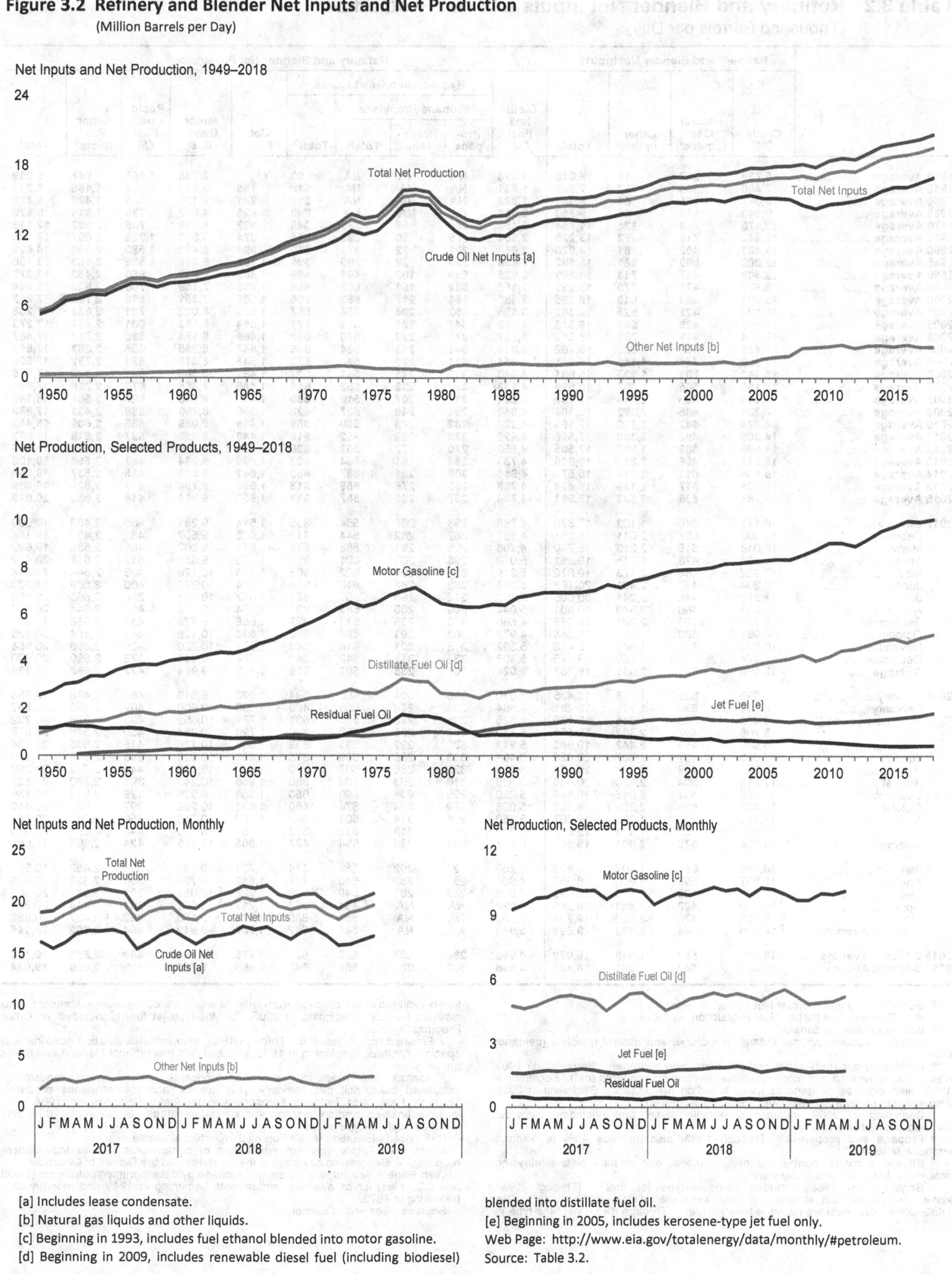

[a] Includes lease condensate.
[b] Natural gas liquids and other liquids.
[c] Beginning in 1993, includes fuel ethanol blended into motor gasoline.
[d] Beginning in 2009, includes renewable diesel fuel (including biodiesel) blended into distillate fuel oil.
[e] Beginning in 2005, includes kerosene-type jet fuel only.
Web Page: http://www.eia.gov/totalenergy/data/monthly/#petroleum.
Source: Table 3.2.

Source: *U.S. Energy Information Administration, Monthly Energy Review, June 2019*

Table 3.2 Refinery and Blender Net Inputs and Net Production
(Thousand Barrels per Day)

	Refinery and Blender Net Inputs[a]				Refinery and Blender Net Production[b]									
						Hydrocarbon Gas Liquids								
						Propane/Propylene								
	Crude Oil[c]	Natural Gas Liquids[d]	Other Liquids[e]	Total	Distillate Fuel Oil[f]	Propane	Propylene	Total[g]	Total[h]	Jet Fuel[i]	Motor Gasoline[j]	Residual Fuel Oil	Other Products[k]	Total
1950 Average	**5,739**	**259**	**19**	**6,018**	**1,093**	**NA**	**NA**	**NA**	**80**	([i])	**2,735**	**1,165**	**947**	**6,019**
1955 Average	**7,480**	**345**	**32**	**7,857**	**1,651**	**NA**	**NA**	**NA**	**119**	**155**	**3,648**	**1,152**	**1,166**	**7,891**
1960 Average	**8,067**	**455**	**61**	**8,583**	**1,823**	**NA**	**NA**	**NA**	**212**	**241**	**4,126**	**908**	**1,420**	**8,729**
1965 Average	**9,043**	**618**	**88**	**9,750**	**2,096**	**NA**	**NA**	**NA**	**293**	**523**	**4,507**	**736**	**1,814**	**9,970**
1970 Average	**10,870**	**763**	**121**	**11,754**	**2,454**	E **184**	E **55**	**239**	**345**	**827**	**5,699**	**706**	**2,082**	**12,113**
1975 Average	**12,442**	**710**	**72**	**13,225**	**2,653**	E **179**	E **60**	**238**	**311**	**871**	**6,518**	**1,235**	**2,097**	**13,685**
1980 Average	**13,481**	**462**	**81**	**14,025**	**2,661**	E **202**	E **72**	**273**	**330**	**999**	**6,492**	**1,580**	**2,559**	**14,622**
1985 Average	**12,002**	**509**	**681**	**13,192**	**2,686**	E **223**	E **72**	**295**	**391**	**1,189**	**6,419**	**882**	**2,183**	**13,750**
1990 Average	**13,409**	**467**	**713**	**14,589**	**2,925**	**299**	**105**	**404**	**499**	**1,488**	**6,959**	**950**	**2,452**	**15,272**
1995 Average	**13,973**	**471**	**775**	**15,220**	**3,155**	**352**	**151**	**503**	**654**	**1,416**	**7,459**	**788**	**2,522**	**15,994**
2000 Average	**15,067**	**380**	**849**	**16,295**	**3,580**	**366**	**217**	**583**	**705**	**1,606**	**7,951**	**696**	**2,705**	**17,243**
2001 Average	**15,128**	**429**	**825**	**16,382**	**3,695**	**352**	**204**	**556**	**667**	**1,530**	**8,022**	**721**	**2,651**	**17,285**
2002 Average	**14,947**	**429**	**941**	**16,316**	**3,592**	**347**	**225**	**572**	**671**	**1,514**	**8,183**	**601**	**2,712**	**17,273**
2003 Average	**15,304**	**419**	**791**	**16,513**	**3,707**	**341**	**229**	**570**	**658**	**1,488**	**8,194**	**660**	**2,780**	**17,487**
2004 Average	**15,475**	**422**	**866**	**16,762**	**3,814**	**341**	**243**	**584**	**645**	**1,547**	**8,265**	**655**	**2,887**	**17,814**
2005 Average	**15,220**	**441**	**1,149**	**16,811**	**3,954**	**311**	**229**	**540**	**573**	**1,546**	**8,318**	**628**	**2,782**	**17,800**
2006 Average	**15,242**	**501**	**1,238**	**16,981**	**4,040**	**302**	**241**	**543**	**627**	**1,481**	**8,364**	**635**	**2,827**	**17,975**
2007 Average	**15,156**	**505**	**1,337**	**16,999**	**4,133**	**330**	**232**	**562**	**655**	**1,448**	**8,358**	**673**	**2,728**	**17,994**
2008 Average	**14,648**	**485**	**2,019**	**17,153**	**4,294**	**312**	**207**	**519**	**630**	**1,493**	**8,548**	**620**	**2,561**	**18,146**
2009 Average	**14,336**	**485**	**2,082**	**16,904**	**4,048**	**291**	**246**	**537**	**623**	**1,396**	**8,786**	**598**	**2,431**	**17,882**
2010 Average	**14,724**	**442**	**2,219**	**17,385**	**4,223**	**282**	**278**	**560**	**659**	**1,418**	**9,059**	**585**	**2,509**	**18,452**
2011 Average	**14,806**	**490**	**2,300**	**17,596**	**4,492**	**270**	**282**	**552**	**619**	**1,449**	**9,058**	**537**	**2,518**	**18,673**
2012 Average	**14,999**	**509**	**1,997**	**17,505**	**4,550**	**276**	**277**	**553**	**630**	**1,471**	**8,926**	**501**	**2,487**	**18,564**
2013 Average	**15,312**	**496**	**2,211**	**18,019**	**4,733**	**284**	**281**	**564**	**623**	**1,499**	**9,234**	**467**	**2,550**	**19,106**
2014 Average	**15,848**	**511**	**2,214**	**18,574**	**4,916**	**306**	**281**	**587**	**653**	**1,541**	**9,570**	**435**	**2,537**	**19,654**
2015 Average	**16,188**	**517**	**2,119**	**18,824**	**4,983**	**283**	**276**	**559**	**615**	**1,590**	**9,754**	**417**	**2,527**	**19,886**
2016 Average	**16,187**	**536**	**2,238**	**18,961**	**4,834**	**307**	**280**	**587**	**632**	**1,650**	**9,995**	**418**	**2,550**	**20,079**
2017 January	16,118	649	1,102	17,870	4,785	298	266	564	355	1,614	9,281	485	2,488	19,009
February	15,493	587	2,011	18,091	4,657	282	262	544	413	1,603	9,507	482	2,492	19,154
March	16,048	519	2,213	18,780	4,793	295	291	586	678	1,674	9,802	406	2,539	19,892
April	16,954	478	1,918	19,351	5,019	298	303	601	857	1,735	9,855	417	2,614	20,497
May	17,222	484	2,173	19,879	5,216	324	298	622	908	1,713	10,126	408	2,644	21,014
June	17,204	473	2,491	20,168	5,284	333	282	615	915	1,764	10,270	406	2,689	21,328
July	17,317	446	2,241	20,005	5,162	312	295	607	877	1,817	10,164	390	2,695	21,106
August	16,981	480	2,340	19,801	5,044	309	280	589	834	1,764	10,176	453	2,644	20,914
September	15,460	606	2,201	18,267	4,560	278	235	513	477	1,665	9,778	459	2,338	19,277
October	16,061	593	2,391	19,045	4,972	303	291	594	520	1,611	10,129	442	2,454	20,126
November	16,840	731	1,848	19,418	5,362	315	301	616	348	1,671	10,220	408	2,556	20,564
December	17,274	750	1,450	19,475	5,408	332	311	642	341	1,784	10,104	373	2,590	20,600
Average	**16,590**	**566**	**2,031**	**19,187**	**5,024**	**307**	**285**	**592**	**628**	**1,702**	**9,954**	**427**	**2,563**	**20,298**
2018 January	16,599	629	1,206	18,435	5,010	296	304	600	394	1,690	9,519	467	2,478	19,558
February	15,932	634	1,715	18,281	4,584	295	274	568	409	1,690	9,800	462	2,453	19,397
March	16,665	556	1,915	19,136	4,825	295	276	571	631	1,784	10,052	403	2,538	20,232
April	16,766	497	2,302	19,564	5,119	307	286	593	800	1,798	9,964	450	2,546	20,678
May	16,989	454	2,442	19,885	5,213	300	292	591	853	1,808	10,130	415	2,585	21,004
June	17,666	457	2,307	20,430	5,406	323	286	609	875	1,893	10,326	348	2,712	21,559
July	17,355	442	2,396	20,194	5,256	320	286	607	870	1,894	10,166	444	2,732	21,363
August	17,612	504	2,320	20,436	5,369	310	293	604	880	1,955	10,243	391	2,790	21,627
September	16,986	565	2,045	19,596	5,230	296	294	590	650	1,856	9,926	429	2,644	20,736
October	16,409	686	2,205	19,300	5,036	279	294	574	460	1,691	10,299	397	2,527	20,410
November	17,152	746	1,709	19,607	5,350	294	314	608	395	1,769	10,240	450	2,563	20,766
December	17,409	732	1,474	19,615	5,576	303	313	615	372	1,856	10,020	440	2,561	20,825
Average	**16,968**	**575**	**2,005**	**19,547**	**5,168**	**301**	**293**	**594**	**634**	**1,808**	**10,059**	**424**	**2,595**	**20,687**
2019 January	16,785	681	1,407	18,873	5,252	297	292	589	374	1,771	9,735	398	2,452	19,983
February	15,837	590	1,930	18,357	4,902	257	289	545	427	1,689	9,730	306	2,321	19,376
March	R 15,939	R 509	R 2,575	R 19,023	R 4,968	R 288	R 261	R 549	R 629	R 1,728	R 10,051	R 357	R 2,331	R 20,065
April	E 16,339	F 492	RE 2,453	RF 19,285	E 5,023	NA	NA	RE 491	F 827	E 1,717	E 10,007	E 394	RE 2,414	RE 20,382
May	E 16,729	F 476	E 2,529	F 19,734	E 5,252	NA	NA	E 563	F 886	E 1,748	E 10,166	E 362	E 2,437	E 20,852
5-Month Average	E **16,335**	E **549**	E **2,182**	E **19,066**	E **5,083**	**NA**	**NA**	E **548**	E **632**	E **1,732**	E **9,942**	E **364**	E **2,392**	E **20,145**
2018 5-Month Average	**16,602**	**553**	**1,918**	**19,072**	**4,956**	**298**	**287**	**585**	**621**	**1,755**	**9,894**	**439**	**2,521**	**20,186**
2017 5-Month Average	**16,381**	**543**	**1,881**	**18,804**	**4,898**	**300**	**284**	**584**	**645**	**1,669**	**9,717**	**439**	**2,556**	**19,924**

[a] See "Refinery and Blender Net Inputs" in Glossary.
[b] See "Refinery and Blender Net Production" in Glossary.
[c] Includes lease condensate.
[d] Ethane, propane, normal butane, isobutane, and natural gasoline (pentanes plus).
[e] Unfinished oils (net), other hydrocarbons, and hydrogen. Beginning in 1981, also includes aviation and motor gasoline blending components (net). Beginning in 1993, also includes oxygenates (net), including fuel ethanol. Beginning in 2009, also includes renewable diesel fuel (including biodiesel).
[f] Beginning in 2009, includes renewable diesel fuel (including biodiesel) blended into distillate fuel oil.
[g] Propane and propylene. Through 1983, also includes 40% of "Butane-Propane Mixtures."
[h] Ethane, propane, normal butane, isobutane, and refinery olefins (ethylene, propylene, butylene, and isobutylene).
[i] Beginning in 1965, includes kerosene-type jet fuel. (Through 1964, kerosene-type jet fuel is included with kerosene in "Other Products.") For 1952–2004, also includes naphtha-type jet fuel. (Through 1951, naphtha-type jet fuel is included in the products from which it was blended—gasoline, kerosene, and distillate fuel oil. Beginning in 2005, naphtha-type jet fuel is included in "Other Products.")
[j] Finished motor gasoline. Through 1963, also includes aviation gasoline and special naphthas. Beginning in 1993, also includes fuel ethanol blended into motor gasoline.
[k] Asphalt and road oil, kerosene, lubricants, petrochemical feedstocks, petroleum coke, still gas (refinery gas), waxes, and miscellaneous products. Through 1964, also includes kerosene-type jet fuel. Beginning in 1964, also includes finished aviation gasoline and special naphthas. Beginning in 2005, also includes naphtha-type jet fuel.

R=Revised. E=Estimate. F=Forecast. NA=Not available.

Notes: • Totals may not equal sum of components due to independent rounding. • Geographic coverage is the 50 states and the District of Columbia.

Web Page: See http://www.eia.gov/totalenergy/data/monthly/#petroleum (Excel and CSV files) for all available annual data beginning in 1949 and monthly data beginning in 1973.

Sources: See end of section.

Source: *U.S. Energy Information Administration, Monthly Energy Review, June 2019*

Figure 3.3a Petroleum Trade: Overview

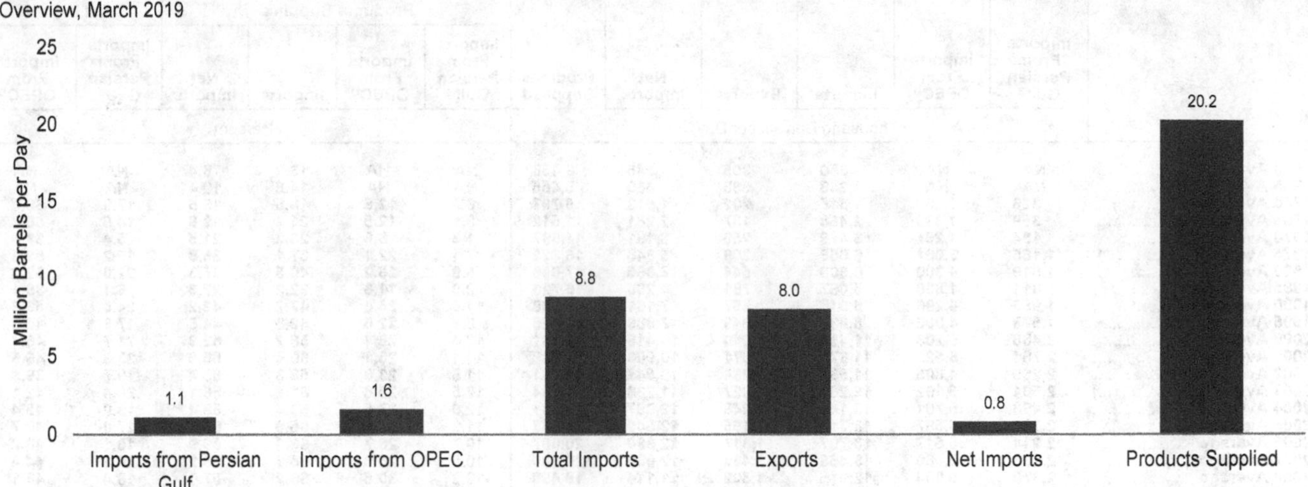

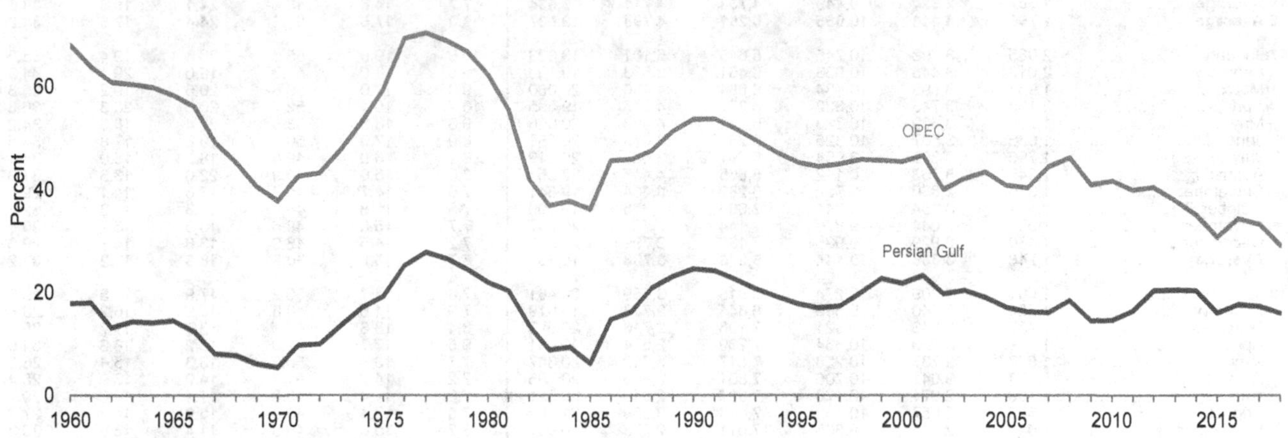

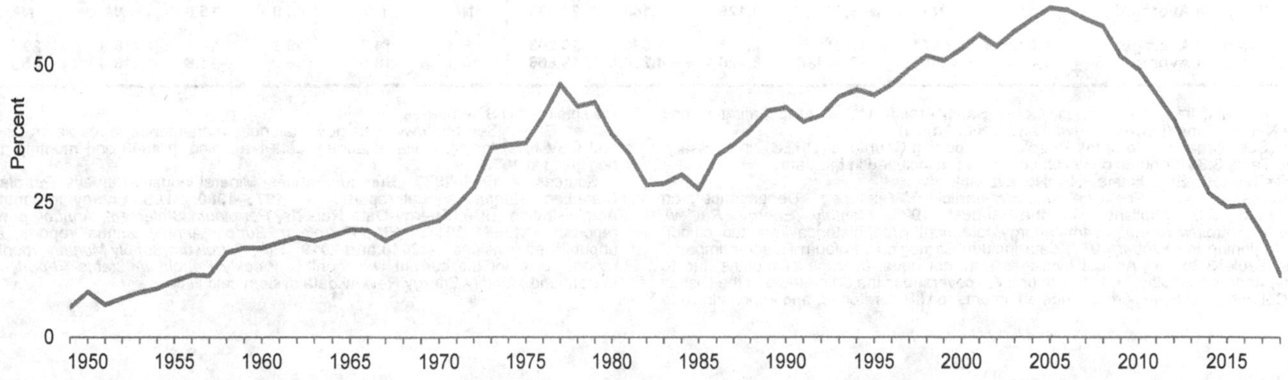

Note: OPEC=Organization of the Petroleum Exporting Countries.
Web Page: http://www.eia.gov/totalenergy/data/monthly/#petroleum.
Source: Table 3.3a.

Source: *U.S. Energy Information Administration, Monthly Energy Review, June 2019*

Table 3.3a Petroleum Trade: Overview

	Imports From Persian Gulf[a]	Imports From OPEC[b]	Imports	Exports	Net Imports	Products Supplied	As Share of Products Supplied: Imports From Persian Gulf[a]	As Share of Products Supplied: Imports From OPEC[b]	As Share of Products Supplied: Imports	As Share of Products Supplied: Net Imports	As Share of Total Imports: Imports From Persian Gulf[a]	As Share of Total Imports: Imports From OPEC[b]
	Thousand Barrels per Day						Percent					
1950 Average	**NA**	**NA**	**850**	**305**	**545**	**6,458**	**NA**	**NA**	**13.2**	**8.4**	**NA**	**NA**
1955 Average	**NA**	**NA**	**1,248**	**368**	**880**	**8,455**	**NA**	**NA**	**14.8**	**10.4**	**NA**	**NA**
1960 Average	**326**	**1,233**	**1,815**	**202**	**1,613**	**9,797**	**3.3**	**12.6**	**18.5**	**16.5**	**17.9**	**68.0**
1965 Average	**359**	**1,439**	**2,468**	**187**	**2,281**	**11,512**	**3.1**	**12.5**	**21.4**	**19.8**	**14.5**	**58.3**
1970 Average	**184**	**1,294**	**3,419**	**259**	**3,161**	**14,697**	**1.3**	**8.8**	**23.3**	**21.5**	**5.4**	**37.8**
1975 Average	**1,165**	**3,601**	**6,056**	**209**	**5,846**	**16,322**	**7.1**	**22.1**	**37.1**	**35.8**	**19.2**	**59.5**
1980 Average	**1,519**	**4,300**	**6,909**	**544**	**6,365**	**17,056**	**8.9**	**25.2**	**40.5**	**37.3**	**22.0**	**62.2**
1985 Average	**311**	**1,830**	**5,067**	**781**	**4,286**	**15,726**	**2.0**	**11.6**	**32.2**	**27.3**	**6.1**	**36.1**
1990 Average	**1,966**	**4,296**	**8,018**	**857**	**7,161**	**16,988**	**11.6**	**25.3**	**47.2**	**42.2**	**24.5**	**53.6**
1995 Average	**1,573**	**4,002**	**8,835**	**949**	**7,886**	**17,725**	**8.9**	**22.6**	**49.8**	**44.5**	**17.8**	**45.3**
2000 Average	**2,488**	**5,203**	**11,459**	**1,040**	**10,419**	**19,701**	**12.6**	**26.4**	**58.2**	**52.9**	**21.7**	**45.4**
2001 Average	**2,761**	**5,528**	**11,871**	**971**	**10,900**	**19,649**	**14.1**	**28.1**	**60.4**	**55.5**	**23.3**	**46.6**
2002 Average	**2,269**	**4,605**	**11,530**	**984**	**10,546**	**19,761**	**11.5**	**23.3**	**58.3**	**53.4**	**19.7**	**39.9**
2003 Average	**2,501**	**5,162**	**12,264**	**1,027**	**11,238**	**20,034**	**12.5**	**25.8**	**61.2**	**56.1**	**20.4**	**42.1**
2004 Average	**2,493**	**5,701**	**13,145**	**1,048**	**12,097**	**20,731**	**12.0**	**27.5**	**63.4**	**58.4**	**19.0**	**43.4**
2005 Average	**2,334**	**5,587**	**13,714**	**1,165**	**12,549**	**20,802**	**11.2**	**26.9**	**65.9**	**60.3**	**17.0**	**40.7**
2006 Average	**2,211**	**5,517**	**13,707**	**1,317**	**12,390**	**20,687**	**10.7**	**26.7**	**66.3**	**59.9**	**16.1**	**40.2**
2007 Average	**2,163**	**5,980**	**13,468**	**1,433**	**12,036**	**20,680**	**10.5**	**28.9**	**65.1**	**58.2**	**16.1**	**44.4**
2008 Average	**2,370**	**5,954**	**12,915**	**1,802**	**11,114**	**19,498**	**12.2**	**30.5**	**66.2**	**57.0**	**18.4**	**46.1**
2009 Average	**1,689**	**4,776**	**11,691**	**2,024**	**9,667**	**18,771**	**9.0**	**25.4**	**62.3**	**51.5**	**14.4**	**40.9**
2010 Average	**1,711**	**4,906**	**11,793**	**2,353**	**9,441**	**19,180**	**8.9**	**25.6**	**61.5**	**49.2**	**14.5**	**41.6**
2011 Average	**1,861**	**4,555**	**11,436**	**2,986**	**8,450**	**18,887**	**9.9**	**24.1**	**60.6**	**44.7**	**16.3**	**39.8**
2012 Average	**2,156**	**4,271**	**10,598**	**3,205**	**7,393**	**18,487**	**11.7**	**23.1**	**57.3**	**40.0**	**20.3**	**40.3**
2013 Average	**2,009**	**3,720**	**9,859**	**3,621**	**6,237**	**18,967**	**10.6**	**19.6**	**52.0**	**32.9**	**20.4**	**37.7**
2014 Average	**1,875**	**3,237**	**9,241**	**4,176**	**5,065**	**19,100**	**9.8**	**16.9**	**48.4**	**26.5**	**20.3**	**35.0**
2015 Average	**1,507**	**2,894**	**9,449**	**4,738**	**4,711**	**19,534**	**7.7**	**14.8**	**48.4**	**24.1**	**15.9**	**30.6**
2016 Average	**1,766**	**3,446**	**10,055**	**5,261**	**4,795**	**19,687**	**9.0**	**17.5**	**51.1**	**24.4**	**17.6**	**34.3**
2017 January	2,085	3,793	10,745	5,645	5,101	19,323	10.8	19.6	55.6	26.4	19.4	35.3
February	2,013	3,445	10,033	6,461	3,573	19,190	10.5	18.0	52.3	18.6	20.1	34.3
March	1,956	3,593	10,184	6,054	4,130	20,060	9.8	17.9	50.8	20.6	19.2	35.3
April	2,100	3,743	10,322	6,277	4,045	19,595	10.7	19.1	52.7	20.6	20.3	36.3
May	1,968	3,669	10,729	6,232	4,498	20,066	9.8	18.3	53.5	22.4	18.3	34.2
June	1,836	3,567	10,325	6,252	4,073	20,561	8.9	17.3	50.2	19.8	17.8	34.5
July	1,796	3,399	9,954	6,291	3,663	20,119	8.9	16.9	49.5	18.2	18.0	34.1
August	1,345	3,163	10,112	5,665	4,447	20,251	6.6	15.6	49.9	22.0	13.3	31.3
September	1,370	2,880	9,752	6,289	3,464	19,641	7.0	14.7	49.7	17.6	14.1	29.5
October	1,491	3,154	9,741	7,086	2,655	19,990	7.5	15.8	48.7	13.3	15.3	32.4
November	1,555	3,044	9,876	7,144	2,732	20,307	7.7	15.0	48.6	13.5	15.7	30.8
December	1,460	2,939	9,935	7,136	2,799	20,323	7.2	14.5	48.9	13.8	14.7	29.6
Average	**1,746**	**3,366**	**10,144**	**6,376**	**3,768**	**19,958**	**8.7**	**16.9**	**50.8**	**18.9**	**17.2**	**33.2**
2018 January	1,591	3,009	10,274	6,615	3,659	20,461	7.8	14.7	50.2	17.9	15.5	29.3
February	1,554	2,740	9,580	6,844	2,736	19,619	7.9	14.0	48.8	13.9	16.2	28.6
March	1,738	2,843	9,821	7,105	2,716	20,573	8.4	13.8	47.7	13.2	17.7	29.0
April	1,899	3,523	10,364	7,730	2,634	19,941	9.5	17.7	52.0	13.2	18.3	34.0
May	1,573	2,737	10,228	7,517	2,712	20,357	7.7	13.4	50.2	13.3	15.4	26.8
June	1,487	3,041	10,706	7,801	2,905	20,705	7.2	14.7	51.7	14.0	13.9	28.4
July	1,489	2,971	10,176	7,827	2,349	20,621	7.2	14.4	49.3	11.4	14.6	29.2
August	1,599	2,857	10,432	7,043	3,389	21,302	7.5	13.4	49.0	15.9	15.3	27.4
September	1,645	2,996	9,885	7,611	2,273	19,951	8.2	15.0	49.5	11.4	16.6	30.3
October	1,563	2,729	9,417	8,018	1,399	20,774	7.5	13.1	45.3	6.7	16.6	29.0
November	1,567	2,703	9,213	8,669	545	20,548	7.6	13.2	44.8	2.6	17.0	29.3
December	1,237	2,516	9,022	8,250	772	20,479	6.0	12.3	44.1	3.8	13.7	27.9
Average	**1,578**	**2,888**	**9,928**	**7,588**	**2,340**	**20,453**	**7.7**	**14.1**	**48.5**	**11.4**	**15.9**	**29.1**
2019 January	1,298	2,542	9,693	8,104	1,589	20,452	6.3	12.4	47.4	7.8	13.4	26.2
February	1,272	1,803	8,628	8,453	176	20,194	6.3	8.9	42.7	0.9	14.7	20.9
March	R 1,096	R 1,643	R 8,837	R 7,996	R 842	R 20,204	R 5.4	R 8.1	R 43.7	R 4.2	R 12.4	R 18.6
April	NA	NA	E 9,310	E 7,797	E 1,513	E 20,225	NA	NA	E 46.0	E 7.5	NA	NA
May	NA	NA	E 9,826	E 8,313	E 1,513	E 20,073	NA	NA	E 49.0	E 7.5	NA	NA
5-Month Average	**NA**	**NA**	**E 9,271**	**E 8,128**	**E 1,143**	**E 20,230**	**NA**	**NA**	**E 45.8**	**E 5.6**	**NA**	**NA**
2018 5-Month Average	**1,672**	**2,971**	**10,061**	**7,165**	**2,896**	**20,203**	**8.3**	**14.7**	**49.8**	**14.3**	**16.6**	**29.5**
2017 5-Month Average	**2,024**	**3,652**	**10,411**	**6,126**	**4,284**	**19,656**	**10.3**	**18.6**	**53.0**	**21.8**	**19.4**	**35.1**

[a] Bahrain, Iran, Iraq, Kuwait, Qatar, Saudi Arabia, United Arab Emirates, and the Neutral Zone (between Kuwait and Saudi Arabia).

[b] See "Organization of the Petroleum Exporting Countries (OPEC)" in Glossary. See Table 3.3c for notes on which countries are included in the data.

R=Revised. E=Estimate. NA=Not available.

Notes: • For the feature article "Measuring Dependence on Imported Oil," published in the August 1995 *Monthly Energy Review*, see http://www.eia.gov/totalenergy/data/monthly/pdf/historical/imported_oil.pdf. • Beginning in October 1977, data include Strategic Petroleum Reserve imports. See Table 3.3b. • Annual averages may not equal average of months due to independent rounding. • U.S. geographic coverage is the 50 states and the District of Columbia. U.S. exports include shipments to U.S. territories, and imports include receipts from U.S. territories.

Web Page: See http://www.eia.gov/totalenergy/data/monthly/#petroleum (Excel and CSV files) for all available annual data beginning in 1949 and monthly data beginning in 1973.

Sources: • **1949–1975:** Bureau of Mines, Mineral Industry Surveys, *Petroleum Statement, Annual*, annual reports. • **1976–1980:** U.S. Energy Information Administration (EIA), Energy Data Reports, *Petroleum Statement, Annual*, annual reports. • **1981–2017:** EIA, *Petroleum Supply Annual*, annual reports, and unpublished revisions. • **2018 and 2019:** EIA, *Petroleum Supply Monthly*, monthly reports; and, for the current two months, *Weekly Petroleum Status Report* data system and *Monthly Energy Review* data system calculations.

Source: *U.S. Energy Information Administration, Monthly Energy Review, June 2019*

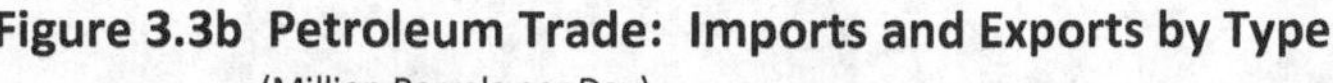

Figure 3.3b Petroleum Trade: Imports and Exports by Type

(Million Barrels per Day)

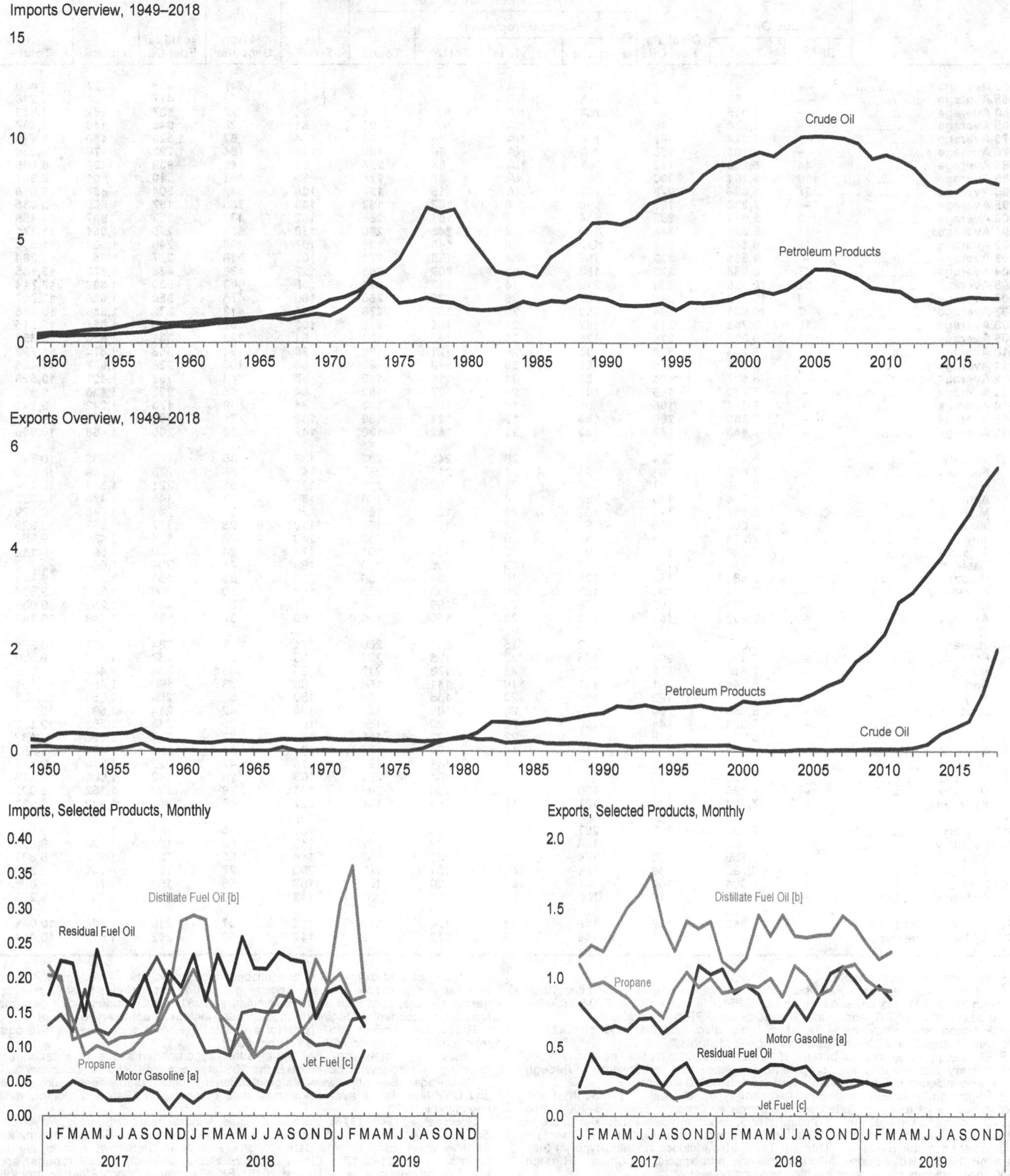

Imports Overview, 1949–2018

15 10 5 0

Crude Oil

Petroleum Products

1950 1955 1960 1965 1970 1975 1980 1985 1990 1995 2000 2005 2010 2015

Exports Overview, 1949–2018

6 4 2 0

Petroleum Products

Crude Oil

1950 1955 1960 1965 1970 1975 1980 1985 1990 1995 2000 2005 2010 2015

Imports, Selected Products, Monthly

0.40 0.35 0.30 0.25 0.20 0.15 0.10 0.05 0.00

Distillate Fuel Oil [b]

Residual Fuel Oil

Propane

Motor Gasoline [a]

Jet Fuel [c]

J F M A M J J A S O N D J F M A M J J A S O N D J F M A M J J A S O N D

2017 2018 2019

Exports, Selected Products, Monthly

2.0 1.5 1.0 0.5 0.0

Distillate Fuel Oil [b]

Propane

Motor Gasoline [a]

Residual Fuel Oil

Jet Fuel [c]

J F M A M J J A S O N D J F M A M J J A S O N D J F M A M J J A S O N D

2017 2018 2019

[a] Includes fuel ethanol blended into motor gasoline.

[b] Includes renewable diesel fuel (including biodiesel) blended into distillate fuel oil.

[c] Includes kerosene-type jet fuel only.

Web Page: http://www.eia.gov/totalenergy/data/monthly/#petroleum.

Sources: Tables 3.3b and 3.3e.

Source: *U.S. Energy Information Administration, Monthly Energy Review, June 2019*

Table 3.3b Petroleum Trade: Imports by Type
(Thousand Barrels per Day)

	Crude Oil[a]		Distillate Fuel Oil	Hydrocarbon Gas Liquids				Jet Fuel[e]	Motor Gasoline[f]	Residual Fuel Oil	Other[g]	Total
				Propane/Propylene								
	SPR[b]	Total		Propane	Propylene	Total[c]	Total[d]					
1950 Average	--	**487**	**7**	**NA**	**NA**	**–**	**–**	**(e)**	**(s)**	**329**	**27**	**850**
1955 Average	--	**782**	**12**	**NA**	**NA**	**–**	**–**	**(e)**	**13**	**417**	**24**	**1,248**
1960 Average	--	**1,015**	**35**	**NA**	**NA**	**NA**	**4**	**34**	**27**	**637**	**62**	**1,815**
1965 Average	--	**1,238**	**36**	**NA**	**NA**	**NA**	**21**	**81**	**28**	**946**	**119**	**2,468**
1970 Average	--	**1,324**	**147**	**NA**	**NA**	**26**	**58**	**144**	**67**	**1,528**	**150**	**3,419**
1975 Average	--	**4,105**	**155**	**NA**	**NA**	**60**	**185**	**133**	**184**	**1,223**	**70**	**6,056**
1980 Average	**44**	**5,263**	**142**	**NA**	**NA**	**84**	**226**	**80**	**140**	**939**	**120**	**6,909**
1985 Average	**118**	**3,201**	**200**	**NA**	**NA**	**67**	**235**	**39**	**381**	**510**	**501**	**5,067**
1990 Average	**27**	**5,894**	**278**	**NA**	**NA**	**115**	**197**	**108**	**342**	**504**	**695**	**8,018**
1995 Average	**–**	**7,230**	**193**	**95**	**6**	**102**	**192**	**106**	**265**	**187**	**662**	**8,835**
2000 Average	**8**	**9,071**	**295**	**154**	**7**	**161**	**256**	**162**	**427**	**352**	**897**	**11,459**
2001 Average	**11**	**9,328**	**344**	**140**	**6**	**145**	**250**	**148**	**454**	**295**	**1,051**	**11,871**
2002 Average	**16**	**9,140**	**267**	**137**	**8**	**145**	**199**	**107**	**498**	**249**	**1,069**	**11,530**
2003 Average	**–**	**9,665**	**333**	**159**	**9**	**168**	**271**	**109**	**518**	**327**	**1,041**	**12,264**
2004 Average	**77**	**10,088**	**325**	**198**	**11**	**209**	**305**	**127**	**496**	**426**	**1,377**	**13,145**
2005 Average	**52**	**10,126**	**329**	**219**	**14**	**233**	**374**	**190**	**603**	**530**	**1,562**	**13,714**
2006 Average	**8**	**10,118**	**365**	**201**	**26**	**228**	**360**	**186**	**475**	**350**	**1,854**	**13,707**
2007 Average	**7**	**10,031**	**304**	**162**	**20**	**182**	**276**	**217**	**413**	**372**	**1,856**	**13,468**
2008 Average	**19**	**9,783**	**213**	**162**	**23**	**185**	**275**	**103**	**302**	**349**	**1,891**	**12,915**
2009 Average	**56**	**9,013**	**225**	**126**	**21**	**147**	**194**	**81**	**223**	**331**	**1,623**	**11,691**
2010 Average	**–**	**9,213**	**228**	**93**	**29**	**121**	**179**	**98**	**134**	**366**	**1,574**	**11,793**
2011 Average	**–**	**8,935**	**179**	**82**	**28**	**110**	**183**	**69**	**105**	**328**	**1,637**	**11,436**
2012 Average	**–**	**8,527**	**126**	**85**	**31**	**116**	**170**	**55**	**44**	**256**	**1,421**	**10,598**
2013 Average	**–**	**7,730**	**155**	**103**	**24**	**127**	**182**	**84**	**45**	**225**	**1,438**	**9,859**
2014 Average	**–**	**7,344**	**195**	**89**	**19**	**108**	**143**	**94**	**49**	**173**	**1,242**	**9,241**
2015 Average	**–**	**7,363**	**200**	**104**	**19**	**124**	**156**	**132**	**71**	**192**	**1,335**	**9,449**
2016 Average	**–**	**7,850**	**147**	**120**	**22**	**142**	**180**	**147**	**59**	**205**	**1,468**	**10,055**
2017 January	–	8,478	204	217	28	245	287	132	35	176	1,433	10,745
February	–	7,877	202	194	24	218	257	147	36	225	1,289	10,033
March	–	8,165	111	140	29	169	198	123	51	221	1,314	10,184
April	–	8,204	118	89	24	113	154	183	42	146	1,475	10,322
May	–	8,487	125	102	21	123	169	126	37	241	1,545	10,729
June	–	8,089	105	95	23	119	155	119	23	177	1,657	10,325
July	–	7,915	114	87	26	113	152	140	23	174	1,436	9,954
August	–	7,923	115	97	25	122	161	173	24	159	1,558	10,112
September	–	7,324	120	117	19	136	170	199	41	204	1,694	9,752
October	–	7,681	134	125	15	139	186	230	33	151	1,327	9,741
November	–	7,674	180	163	20	183	223	194	10	209	1,385	9,876
December	–	7,782	282	176	23	198	240	151	32	187	1,261	9,935
Average	**–**	**7,969**	**151**	**133**	**23**	**156**	**196**	**160**	**32**	**189**	**1,448**	**10,144**
2018 January	–	8,012	290	212	15	227	260	131	19	234	1,327	10,274
February	–	7,493	284	175	23	198	231	93	33	167	1,280	9,580
March	–	7,616	157	150	23	173	217	95	38	234	1,463	9,821
April	–	8,244	91	131	10	141	168	88	33	190	1,550	10,364
May	–	7,825	122	114	20	135	158	150	62	259	1,654	10,228
June	–	8,480	90	85	20	105	135	154	42	214	1,591	10,706
July	–	7,923	144	100	20	120	156	151	35	213	1,553	10,176
August	–	8,000	175	99	22	121	159	152	82	237	1,626	10,432
September	–	7,589	172	110	14	124	172	181	94	227	1,451	9,885
October	–	7,312	161	127	15	141	192	116	42	223	1,370	9,417
November	–	7,490	227	151	13	164	222	103	29	142	1,001	9,213
December	–	7,099	190	190	15	206	268	105	29	180	1,152	9,022
Average	**–**	**7,757**	**175**	**137**	**17**	**154**	**195**	**127**	**45**	**211**	**1,420**	**9,928**
2019 January	–	7,520	308	207	15	223	290	100	45	187	1,241	9,693
February	–	6,652	361	169	13	182	242	140	52	162	1,020	8,628
March	–	R 6,759	R 180	R 174	R 10	R 185	R 252	R 144	R 95	R 131	R 1,274	R 8,837
April	–	E 6,792	E 136	NA	NA	E 131	NA	E 200	E 127	E 163	NA	E 9,310
May	–	E 7,304	E 109	NA	NA	E 120	NA	E 163	E 158	E 153	NA	E 9,826
5-Month Average	**–**	**E 7,014**	**E 217**	**NA**	**NA**	**E 168**	**NA**	**E 149**	**E 96**	**E 159**	**NA**	**E 9,271**
2018 5-Month Average	**–**	**7,842**	**188**	**156**	**18**	**174**	**206**	**112**	**37**	**218**	**1,458**	**10,061**
2017 5-Month Average	**–**	**8,250**	**151**	**148**	**25**	**173**	**212**	**142**	**40**	**202**	**1,413**	**10,411**

[a] Includes lease condensate.

[b] "SPR" is the Strategic Petroleum Reserve, which began in October 1977. Through 2003, includes crude oil imports by SPR only; beginning in 2004, includes crude oil imports by SPR, and crude oil imports into SPR by others.

[c] Propane and propylene. Through 1983, also includes 40% of "Butane-Propane Mixtures" and 30% of "Ethane-Propane Mixtures."

[d] Ethane, propane, normal butane, isobutane, natural gasoline (pentanes plus), and refinery olefins (ethylene, propylene, butylene, and isobutylene). Through 1983, also includes plant condensate and unfractionated stream.

[e] Beginning in 1965, includes kerosene-type jet fuel. (Through 1964, kerosene-type jet fuel is included with kerosene in "Other.") For 1956–2004, also includes naphtha-type jet fuel. (Through 1955, naphtha-type jet fuel is included in "Motor Gasoline." Beginning in 2005, naphtha-type jet fuel is included in "Other.")

[f] Finished motor gasoline. Through 1955, also includes naphtha-type jet fuel. Through 1963, also includes aviation gasoline and special naphthas. Through 1980, also includes motor gasoline blending components.

[g] Asphalt and road oil, aviation gasoline blending components, kerosene, lubricants, petrochemical feedstocks, petroleum coke, unfinished oils, waxes, other hydrocarbons and oxygenates, and miscellaneous products. Through 1964, also includes kerosene-type jet fuel. Beginning in 1964, also includes finished aviation gasoline and special naphthas. Beginning in 1981, also includes motor gasoline blending components. Beginning in 2005, also includes naphtha-type jet fuel.

R=Revised. E=Estimate. NA=Not available. – – =Not applicable. – =No data reported. (s)=Less than 500 barrels per day.

Notes: • Totals may not equal sum of components due to independent rounding. • Geographic coverage is the 50 states and the District of Columbia.

Web Page: See http://www.eia.gov/totalenergy/data/monthly/#petroleum (Excel and CSV files) for all available annual data beginning in 1949 and monthly data beginning in 1973.

Sources: • **1949–1975:** Bureau of Mines, Mineral Industry Surveys, *Petroleum Statement, Annual,* annual reports. • **1976–1980:** U.S. Energy Information Administration (EIA), Energy Data Reports, *Petroleum Statement, Annual,* annual reports. • **1981–2017:** EIA, *Petroleum Supply Annual,* annual reports, and unpublished revisions. • **2018 and 2019:** EIA, *Petroleum Supply Monthly,* monthly reports; and, for the current two months, *Weekly Petroleum Status Report* data system and *Monthly Energy Review* data system calculations.

Source: *U.S. Energy Information Administration, Monthly Energy Review, June 2019*

Table 3.3c Petroleum Trade: Imports From OPEC Countries

(Thousand Barrels per Day)

	Algeria[a]	Angola[b]	Ecuador[c]	Iraq	Kuwait[d]	Libya[e]	Nigeria[f]	Saudi Arabia[d]	Vene-zuela	Other[g]	Total OPEC
1960 Average	(a)	(b)	(c)	**22**	**182**	(e)	(f)	**84**	**911**	**34**	**1,233**
1965 Average	(a)	(b)	(c)	**16**	**74**	**42**	(f)	**158**	**994**	**155**	**1,439**
1970 Average	**8**	(b)	(c)	**–**	**48**	**47**	(f)	**30**	**989**	**172**	**1,294**
1975 Average	**282**	(b)	**57**	**2**	**16**	**232**	**762**	**715**	**702**	**832**	**3,601**
1980 Average	**488**	(b)	**27**	**28**	**27**	**554**	**857**	**1,261**	**481**	**577**	**4,300**
1985 Average	**187**	(b)	**67**	**46**	**21**	**4**	**293**	**168**	**605**	**439**	**1,830**
1990 Average	**280**	(b)	**49**	**518**	**86**	**–**	**800**	**1,339**	**1,025**	**199**	**4,296**
1995 Average	**234**	(b)	(c)	**–**	**218**	**–**	**627**	**1,344**	**1,480**	**98**	**4,002**
2000 Average	**225**	(b)	(c)	**620**	**272**	**–**	**896**	**1,572**	**1,546**	**72**	**5,203**
2001 Average	**278**	(b)	(c)	**795**	**250**	**–**	**885**	**1,662**	**1,553**	**105**	**5,528**
2002 Average	**264**	(b)	(c)	**459**	**228**	**–**	**621**	**1,552**	**1,398**	**83**	**4,605**
2003 Average	**382**	(b)	(c)	**481**	**220**	**–**	**867**	**1,774**	**1,376**	**61**	**5,162**
2004 Average	**452**	(b)	(c)	**656**	**250**	**20**	**1,140**	**1,558**	**1,554**	**70**	**5,701**
2005 Average	**478**	(b)	(c)	**531**	**243**	**56**	**1,166**	**1,537**	**1,529**	**47**	**5,587**
2006 Average	**657**	(b)	(c)	**553**	**185**	**87**	**1,114**	**1,463**	**1,419**	**38**	**5,517**
2007 Average	**670**	**508**	(c)	**484**	**181**	**117**	**1,134**	**1,485**	**1,361**	**39**	**5,980**
2008 Average	**548**	**513**	**221**	**627**	**210**	**103**	**988**	**1,529**	**1,189**	**26**	**5,954**
2009 Average	**493**	**460**	**185**	**450**	**182**	**79**	**809**	**1,004**	**1,063**	**50**	**4,776**
2010 Average	**510**	**393**	**212**	**415**	**197**	**70**	**1,023**	**1,096**	**988**	**3**	**4,906**
2011 Average	**358**	**346**	**206**	**459**	**191**	**15**	**818**	**1,195**	**951**	**16**	**4,555**
2012 Average	**242**	**233**	**180**	**476**	**305**	**61**	**441**	**1,365**	**960**	**9**	**4,271**
2013 Average	**115**	**216**	**236**	**341**	**328**	**59**	**281**	**1,329**	**806**	**10**	**3,720**
2014 Average	**110**	**154**	**215**	**369**	**311**	**6**	**92**	**1,166**	**789**	**23**	**3,237**
2015 Average	**108**	**136**	**231**	**229**	**204**	**7**	**81**	**1,059**	**827**	**12**	**2,894**
2016 Average	**182**	**168**	**239**	**424**	**210**	**16**	**235**	**1,106**	**796**	**69**	**3,446**
2017 January	232	118	247	622	105	31	332	1,345	749	10	3,793
February	234	64	141	413	251	22	223	1,338	751	9	3,445
March	193	30	278	544	219	30	342	1,173	764	21	3,593
April	153	84	180	811	101	45	332	1,160	857	21	3,743
May	196	105	230	619	174	87	294	1,132	767	66	3,669
June	254	178	212	587	162	38	320	1,045	663	108	3,567
July	215	189	166	756	206	108	241	795	686	37	3,399
August	229	296	193	456	87	35	397	739	606	125	3,163
September	145	171	223	502	127	59	292	676	620	65	2,880
October	144	124	163	708	119	176	441	591	562	127	3,154
November	120	77	193	611	117	72	470	780	558	47	3,044
December	149	172	253	605	78	73	323	719	513	55	2,939
Average	**189**	**135**	**207**	**604**	**145**	**65**	**334**	**955**	**674**	**58**	**3,366**
2018 January	234	71	161	699	100	76	349	744	528	46	3,009
February	119	34	123	617	177	38	386	667	472	107	2,740
March	107	10	136	721	131	79	153	760	559	187	2,843
April	208	169	225	834	107	87	275	904	632	84	3,523
May	134	118	162	588	49	40	102	872	559	112	2,737
June	147	193	173	421	92	75	267	847	643	182	3,041
July	243	188	288	485	63	44	43	876	625	117	2,971
August	198	146	183	421	83	19	66	1,039	592	109	2,857
September	200	73	172	485	36	61	113	1,043	708	106	2,996
October	178	94	111	377	–	32	182	1,108	570	76	2,729
November	162	28	196	392	101	(s)	180	1,001	563	81	2,703
December	183	–	192	226	16	121	177	930	576	95	2,516
Average	**176**	**94**	**177**	**521**	**79**	**56**	**189**	**901**	**586**	**108**	**2,888**
2019 January	98	8	238	429	21	60	181	770	631	106	2,542
February	51	–	154	422	106	36	33	663	289	49	1,803
March	136	10	124	275	129	25	142	666	69	65	1,643
3-Month Average	**97**	**6**	**173**	**374**	**85**	**40**	**122**	**701**	**331**	**74**	**2,003**
2018 3-Month Average	**155**	**39**	**141**	**681**	**135**	**65**	**293**	**726**	**521**	**113**	**2,868**
2017 3-Month Average	**219**	**71**	**225**	**530**	**190**	**28**	**301**	**1,284**	**755**	**13**	**3,616**

[a] Algeria joined OPEC in 1969. For 1960–1968, Algeria is included in "Total Non-OPEC" on Table 3.3d.

[b] Angola joined OPEC in January 2007. For 1960–2006, Angola is included in "Total Non-OPEC" on Table 3.3d.

[c] Ecuador was a member of OPEC from 1973–1992, and rejoined OPEC in November 2007. For 1960–1972 and 1993–2007, Ecuador is included in "Total Non-OPEC" on Table 3.3d.

[d] Through 1970, includes half the imports from the Neutral Zone between Kuwait and Saudi Arabia. Beginning in 1971, imports from the Neutral Zone are reported as originating in either Kuwait or Saudi Arabia depending on the country reported to U.S. Customs.

[e] Libya joined OPEC in 1962. For 1960 and 1961, Libya is included in "Total Non-OPEC" on Table 3.3d.

[f] Nigeria joined OPEC in 1971. For 1960–1970, Nigeria is included in "Total Non-OPEC" on Table 3.3d.

[g] Includes these countries for the dates indicated: Congo-Brazzaville (June 2018 forward), Equatorial Guinea (May 2017 forward), Gabon (1975–1994 and July 2016 forward), Indonesia (1962–2008 and January–November 2016), Iran (1960 forward), Qatar (1961–2018), and United Arab Emirates (1967 forward).

– =No data reported. (s)=Less than 500 barrels per day.

Notes: • See "Organization of the Petroleum Exporting Countries (OPEC)" in Glossary. Petroleum imports not classified as "OPEC" on this table are included on Table 3.3d. • The country of origin for petroleum products may not be the country of origin for the crude oil from which the products were produced. For example, refined products imported from West European refining areas may have been produced from Middle East crude oil. • Includes imports for the Strategic Petroleum Reserve, which began in October 1977. • Totals may not equal sum of components due to independent rounding. • U.S. geographic coverage is the 50 states and the District of Columbia.

Web Page: See http://www.eia.gov/totalenergy/data/monthly/#petroleum (Excel and CSV files) for all available annual data beginning in 1960 and monthly data beginning in 1973.

Sources: • **1960–1972:** Bureau of Mines, *Minerals Yearbook*, annual reports. • **1973–1975:** Bureau of Mines, Mineral Industry Surveys, *Petroleum Statement, Annual*, annual reports. • **1976–1980:** U.S. Energy Information Administration (EIA), Energy Data Reports, *Petroleum Statement, Annual*, annual reports. • **1981–2017:** EIA, *Petroleum Supply Annual*, annual reports. • **2018 and 2019:** EIA, *Petroleum Supply Monthly*, monthly reports.

Source: *U.S. Energy Information Administration, Monthly Energy Review, June 2019*

Table 3.3d Petroleum Trade: Imports From Non-OPEC Countries

(Thousand Barrels per Day)

	Brazil	Canada	Colombia	Mexico	Nether-lands	Norway	Russia[a]	United Kingdom	U.S. Virgin Islands	Other	Total Non-OPEC
1960 Average	**1**	**120**	**42**	**16**	**NA**	**NA**	**–**	**(s)**	**NA**	**NA**	**581**
1965 Average	**–**	**323**	**51**	**48**	**1**	**–**	**–**	**(s)**	**–**	**606**	**1,029**
1970 Average	**2**	**766**	**46**	**42**	**39**	**–**	**3**	**11**	**189**	**1,027**	**2,126**
1975 Average	**5**	**846**	**9**	**71**	**19**	**17**	**14**	**14**	**406**	**1,052**	**2,454**
1980 Average	**3**	**455**	**4**	**533**	**2**	**144**	**1**	**176**	**388**	**903**	**2,609**
1985 Average	**61**	**770**	**23**	**816**	**58**	**32**	**8**	**310**	**247**	**913**	**3,237**
1990 Average	**49**	**934**	**182**	**755**	**55**	**102**	**45**	**189**	**282**	**1,128**	**3,721**
1995 Average	**8**	**1,332**	**219**	**1,068**	**15**	**273**	**25**	**383**	**278**	**1,233**	**4,833**
2000 Average	**51**	**1,807**	**342**	**1,373**	**30**	**343**	**72**	**366**	**291**	**1,581**	**6,257**
2001 Average	**82**	**1,828**	**296**	**1,440**	**43**	**341**	**90**	**324**	**268**	**1,631**	**6,343**
2002 Average	**116**	**1,971**	**260**	**1,547**	**66**	**393**	**210**	**478**	**236**	**1,649**	**6,925**
2003 Average	**108**	**2,072**	**195**	**1,623**	**87**	**270**	**254**	**440**	**288**	**1,766**	**7,103**
2004 Average	**104**	**2,138**	**176**	**1,665**	**101**	**244**	**298**	**380**	**330**	**2,008**	**7,444**
2005 Average	**156**	**2,181**	**196**	**1,662**	**151**	**233**	**410**	**396**	**328**	**2,413**	**8,127**
2006 Average	**193**	**2,353**	**155**	**1,705**	**174**	**196**	**369**	**272**	**328**	**2,446**	**8,190**
2007 Average	**200**	**2,455**	**155**	**1,532**	**128**	**142**	**414**	**277**	**346**	**1,839**	**7,489**
2008 Average	**258**	**2,493**	**200**	**1,302**	**168**	**102**	**465**	**236**	**320**	**1,416**	**6,961**
2009 Average	**309**	**2,479**	**276**	**1,210**	**140**	**108**	**563**	**245**	**277**	**1,307**	**6,915**
2010 Average	**272**	**2,535**	**365**	**1,284**	**108**	**89**	**612**	**256**	**253**	**1,112**	**6,887**
2011 Average	**253**	**2,729**	**433**	**1,206**	**100**	**113**	**624**	**159**	**186**	**1,077**	**6,881**
2012 Average	**226**	**2,946**	**433**	**1,035**	**99**	**75**	**477**	**149**	**12**	**874**	**6,327**
2013 Average	**151**	**3,142**	**389**	**919**	**89**	**54**	**460**	**147**	**–**	**786**	**6,138**
2014 Average	**160**	**3,388**	**318**	**842**	**85**	**45**	**330**	**117**	**–**	**720**	**6,004**
2015 Average	**215**	**3,765**	**395**	**758**	**57**	**61**	**371**	**123**	**–**	**811**	**6,554**
2016 Average	**167**	**3,780**	**483**	**669**	**60**	**76**	**441**	**122**	**(s)**	**812**	**6,610**
2017 January	206	4,285	345	730	75	134	361	143	–	673	6,952
February	240	4,098	401	607	80	34	331	96	–	700	6,588
March	229	4,147	338	630	48	12	379	120	–	689	6,590
April	168	3,892	417	680	62	86	308	123	–	844	6,579
May	132	4,159	424	810	49	73	401	167	–	847	7,061
June	202	3,837	334	784	72	122	503	126	–	779	6,759
July	376	3,824	357	668	45	64	358	113	–	752	6,555
August	258	4,023	388	581	74	186	448	67	–	924	6,950
September	250	3,984	374	430	93	118	450	149	–	1,024	6,872
October	230	3,976	270	654	51	71	355	83	–	897	6,587
November	228	4,046	337	841	43	38	384	61	–	854	6,832
December	166	4,373	363	767	59	7	389	88	–	784	6,995
Average	**224**	**4,054**	**362**	**682**	**62**	**79**	**389**	**111**	**–**	**814**	**6,778**
2018 January	272	4,424	512	669	69	57	386	80	–	797	7,265
February	187	4,259	477	713	51	56	297	110	–	692	6,840
March	84	4,191	364	784	91	90	356	94	–	925	6,978
April	184	4,269	282	632	64	122	243	205	–	840	6,841
May	123	4,452	437	608	80	72	491	180	–	1,049	7,492
June	283	4,545	240	876	53	85	439	151	–	994	7,665
July	179	4,157	319	681	43	166	454	164	–	1,041	7,205
August	248	4,233	334	935	67	39	515	175	–	1,028	7,575
September	77	4,034	229	771	44	74	519	207	–	935	6,889
October	230	4,144	229	718	89	138	271	106	–	763	6,688
November	93	4,327	259	601	49	136	254	155	–	638	6,510
December	92	4,279	333	635	49	94	271	132	–	620	6,506
Average	**171**	**4,276**	**334**	**719**	**63**	**94**	**375**	**146**	**–**	**862**	**7,040**
2019 January	142	4,628	380	569	100	88	321	122	–	800	7,150
February	91	4,298	420	720	97	69	221	47	–	861	6,825
March	162	4,404	412	712	60	80	361	118	–	884	7,194
3-Month Average	**133**	**4,448**	**403**	**665**	**85**	**80**	**304**	**97**	**–**	**848**	**7,064**
2018 3-Month Average	**181**	**4,292**	**450**	**722**	**71**	**68**	**348**	**94**	**–**	**808**	**7,034**
2017 3-Month Average	**225**	**4,179**	**360**	**657**	**68**	**61**	**358**	**120**	**–**	**687**	**6,714**

[a] Through 1992, may include imports from republics other than Russia in the former U.S.S.R. See "Union of Soviet Socialist Republics (U.S.S.R.)" in Glossary.

NA=Not available. – =No data reported. (s)=Less than 500 barrels per day.

Notes: • See "Organization of the Petroleum Exporting Countries (OPEC)" in Glossary. Petroleum imports not classified as "OPEC" on Table 3.3c are included on this table. • The country of origin for petroleum products may not be the country of origin for the crude oil from which the products were produced. For example, refined products imported from West European refining areas may have been produced from Middle East crude oil. • Includes imports for the Strategic Petroleum Reserve, which began in October 1977. • Totals may not equal sum of components due to independent rounding. • U.S. geographic coverage is the 50 states and the District of Columbia.

Web Page: See http://www.eia.gov/totalenergy/data/monthly/#petroleum (Excel and CSV files) for all available annual data beginning in 1960 and monthly data beginning in 1973.

Sources: • **1960–1972:** Bureau of Mines, *Minerals Yearbook*, annual reports. • **1973–1975:** Bureau of Mines, Mineral Industry Surveys, *Petroleum Statement, Annual*, annual reports. • **1976–1980:** U.S. Energy Information Administration (EIA), Energy Data Reports, *Petroleum Statement, Annual*, annual reports. • **1981–2017:** EIA, *Petroleum Supply Annual*, annual reports. • **2018 and 2019:** EIA, *Petroleum Supply Monthly*, monthly reports.

Source: *U.S. Energy Information Administration, Monthly Energy Review, June 2019*

Table 3.3e Petroleum Trade: Exports by Type
(Thousand Barrels per Day)

	Crude Oil[a]	Distillate Fuel Oil	Hydrocarbon Gas Liquids		Jet Fuel[d]	Motor Gasoline[e]	Residual Fuel Oil	Other[f]	Total
			Propane[b]	Total[c]					
1950 Average	**95**	**34**	**NA**	**4**	**(d)**	**68**	**44**	**58**	**305**
1955 Average	**32**	**67**	**NA**	**12**	**(s)**	**95**	**93**	**69**	**368**
1960 Average	**8**	**27**	**NA**	**8**	**(s)**	**37**	**51**	**71**	**202**
1965 Average	**3**	**10**	**NA**	**21**	**3**	**2**	**41**	**108**	**187**
1970 Average	**14**	**2**	**13**	**27**	**6**	**1**	**54**	**154**	**259**
1975 Average	**6**	**1**	**13**	**26**	**2**	**2**	**15**	**158**	**209**
1980 Average	**287**	**3**	**10**	**21**	**1**	**1**	**33**	**197**	**544**
1985 Average	**204**	**67**	**48**	**64**	**13**	**10**	**197**	**225**	**781**
1990 Average	**109**	**109**	**28**	**41**	**43**	**55**	**211**	**287**	**857**
1995 Average	**95**	**183**	**38**	**59**	**26**	**104**	**136**	**12**	**949**
2000 Average	**50**	**173**	**53**	**78**	**32**	**144**	**139**	**46**	**1,040**
2001 Average	**20**	**119**	**31**	**45**	**29**	**133**	**191**	**433**	**971**
2002 Average	**9**	**112**	**55**	**67**	**15**	**124**	**177**	**479**	**984**
2003 Average	**12**	**107**	**37**	**59**	**20**	**125**	**197**	**506**	**1,027**
2004 Average	**27**	**110**	**28**	**45**	**40**	**124**	**205**	**497**	**1,048**
2005 Average	**32**	**138**	**37**	**60**	**53**	**136**	**251**	**496**	**1,165**
2006 Average	**25**	**215**	**45**	**68**	**41**	**142**	**283**	**544**	**1,317**
2007 Average	**27**	**268**	**42**	**70**	**41**	**127**	**330**	**569**	**1,433**
2008 Average	**29**	**528**	**53**	**101**	**61**	**172**	**355**	**555**	**1,802**
2009 Average	**44**	**587**	**85**	**139**	**69**	**195**	**415**	**574**	**2,024**
2010 Average	**42**	**656**	**109**	**164**	**84**	**296**	**405**	**706**	**2,353**
2011 Average	**47**	**854**	**124**	**249**	**97**	**479**	**424**	**835**	**2,986**
2012 Average	**67**	**1,007**	**171**	**314**	**132**	**409**	**388**	**886**	**3,205**
2013 Average	**134**	**1,134**	**302**	**468**	**156**	**373**	**362**	**994**	**3,621**
2014 Average	**351**	**1,101**	**423**	**703**	**163**	**442**	**364**	**1,052**	**4,176**
2015 Average	**465**	**1,176**	**615**	**966**	**168**	**476**	**326**	**1,161**	**4,738**
2016 Average	**591**	**1,179**	**799**	**1,211**	**175**	**635**	**298**	**1,171**	**5,261**
2017 January	711	1,156	1,100	1,456	174	820	217	1,111	5,645
February	1,146	1,237	947	1,441	178	718	453	1,288	6,461
March	930	1,192	973	1,486	175	630	317	1,323	6,054
April	1,128	1,355	916	1,478	203	657	313	1,144	6,277
May	1,098	1,510	859	1,347	172	622	276	1,206	6,232
June	865	1,604	756	1,249	235	707	363	1,229	6,252
July	956	1,750	795	1,282	220	712	342	1,029	6,291
August	817	1,380	716	1,232	198	605	218	1,215	5,665
September	1,463	1,196	923	1,442	129	671	330	1,057	6,289
October	1,720	1,413	1,044	1,431	148	734	388	1,251	7,086
November	1,544	1,358	936	1,495	201	1,090	228	1,227	7,144
December	1,522	1,408	1,002	1,515	175	1,027	259	1,230	7,136
Average	**1,158**	**1,381**	**914**	**1,404**	**184**	**749**	**308**	**1,192**	**6,376**
2018 January	1,342	1,119	894	1,481	187	1,066	264	1,156	6,615
February	1,605	1,053	913	1,430	175	894	332	1,355	6,844
March	1,671	1,150	951	1,452	244	951	340	1,296	7,105
April	1,756	1,457	939	1,678	235	886	321	1,397	7,730
May	2,005	1,306	1,002	1,749	235	685	376	1,160	7,517
June	2,200	1,458	868	1,628	215	686	375	1,239	7,801
July	2,139	1,308	1,093	1,677	267	825	343	1,270	7,827
August	1,749	1,295	1,015	1,641	223	699	366	1,070	7,043
September	2,116	1,310	878	1,640	167	857	267	1,255	7,611
October	2,326	1,316	920	1,586	295	1,037	295	1,163	8,018
November	2,609	1,450	1,077	1,654	200	1,085	253	1,417	8,669
December	2,511	1,377	1,103	1,597	220	987	264	1,294	8,250
Average	**2,004**	**1,301**	**972**	**1,602**	**222**	**888**	**316**	**1,254**	**7,588**
2019 January	2,575	1,249	988	1,572	254	866	247	1,340	8,104
February	2,990	1,139	925	1,560	197	949	223	1,394	8,453
March	R 2,684	R 1,192	R 911	R 1,628	R 179	R 852	R 243	R 1,219	R 7,996
April	E 2,495	NA	NA	NA	NA	NA	NA	NA	E 7,797
May	E 3,160	NA	NA	NA	NA	NA	NA	NA	E 8,313
5-Month Average	**E 2,778**	**NA**	**NA**	**NA**	**NA**	**NA**	**NA**	**NA**	**E 8,128**
2018 5-Month Average	**1,677**	**1,219**	**940**	**1,560**	**216**	**897**	**327**	**1,270**	**7,165**
2017 5-Month Average	**999**	**1,291**	**959**	**1,441**	**180**	**689**	**313**	**1,214**	**6,126**

[a] Includes lease condensate.

[b] Through 1983, also includes 40% of "Butane-Propane Mixtures." Through 2012, also includes propylene.

[c] Ethane, propane, normal butane, isobutane, and natural gasoline (pentanes plus). Through 2012, also includes refinery olefins (ethylene, propylene, butylene, and isobutylene).

[d] Beginning in 1965, includes kerosene-type jet fuel. (Through 1964, kerosene-type jet fuel is included with kerosene in "Other.") For 1953–2004, also includes naphtha-type jet fuel. (Through 1952, naphtha-type jet fuel is included in the products from which it was blended: motor gasoline, kerosene, and distillate fuel oil. Beginning in 2005, naphtha-type jet fuel is included in "Other.")

[e] Finished motor gasoline. Through 1952, also includes naphtha-type jet fuel. Through 1963, also includes aviation gasoline and special naphthas. Through 1980, also includes motor gasoline blending components.

[f] Asphalt and road oil, kerosene, lubricants, petrochemical feedstocks, petroleum coke, unfinished oils, waxes, other hydrocarbons and oxygenates, and miscellaneous products. Through 1964, also includes kerosene-type jet fuel. Beginning in 1964, also includes finished aviation gasoline and special naphthas. Beginning in 1981, also includes motor gasoline blending components. Beginning in 2005, also includes naphtha-type jet fuel.

R=Revised. E=Estimate. NA=Not available. (s)=Less than 500 barrels per day.

Notes: • Totals may not equal sum of components due to independent rounding. • Geographic coverage is the 50 states and the District of Columbia.

Web Page: See http://www.eia.gov/totalenergy/data/monthly/#petroleum (Excel and CSV files) for all available annual data beginning in 1949 and monthly data beginning in 1973.

Sources: • **1949–1975:** Bureau of Mines, Mineral Industry Surveys, *Petroleum Statement, Annual,* annual reports. • **1976–1980:** U.S. Energy Information Administration (EIA), Energy Data Reports, *Petroleum Statement, Annual,* annual reports. • **1981–2017:** EIA, *Petroleum Supply Annual,* annual reports, and unpublished revisions. • **2018 and 2019:** EIA, *Petroleum Supply Monthly,* monthly reports; and, for the current two months, *Weekly Petroleum Status Report* data system and *Monthly Energy Review* data system calculations.

Source: *U.S. Energy Information Administration, Monthly Energy Review, June 2019*

Table 3.3f Petroleum Trade: Exports by Country of Destination
(Thousand Barrels per Day)

	Brazil	Canada	China	India	Japan	Mexico	Netherlands	Singapore	South Korea	United Kingdom	Other	Total
1960 Average	**4**	**34**	**NA**	**NA**	**62**	**18**	**6**	**NA**	**NA**	**12**	**NA**	**202**
1965 Average	**3**	**26**	**NA**	**NA**	**40**	**27**	**10**	**NA**	**NA**	**12**	**NA**	**187**
1970 Average	**7**	**31**	**NA**	**NA**	**69**	**33**	**15**	**NA**	**NA**	**12**	**NA**	**259**
1975 Average	**6**	**22**	**NA**	**1**	**27**	**42**	**23**	**NA**	**NA**	**7**	**NA**	**209**
1980 Average	**4**	**108**	**–**	**1**	**32**	**28**	**23**	**6**	**2**	**7**	**335**	**544**
1985 Average	**3**	**74**	**–**	**2**	**108**	**61**	**44**	**24**	**27**	**14**	**424**	**781**
1990 Average	**2**	**91**	**–**	**6**	**92**	**89**	**54**	**15**	**60**	**11**	**438**	**857**
1995 Average	**16**	**73**	**2**	**3**	**76**	**125**	**33**	**46**	**57**	**14**	**505**	**949**
2000 Average	**28**	**110**	**3**	**3**	**90**	**358**	**42**	**36**	**20**	**10**	**342**	**1,040**
2001 Average	**23**	**112**	**6**	**3**	**62**	**274**	**45**	**67**	**14**	**13**	**352**	**971**
2002 Average	**26**	**106**	**14**	**3**	**74**	**254**	**23**	**81**	**11**	**12**	**380**	**984**
2003 Average	**27**	**141**	**24**	**7**	**69**	**228**	**15**	**51**	**10**	**6**	**447**	**1,027**
2004 Average	**27**	**158**	**13**	**11**	**63**	**209**	**36**	**41**	**12**	**14**	**464**	**1,048**
2005 Average	**39**	**181**	**12**	**11**	**56**	**268**	**25**	**43**	**16**	**21**	**492**	**1,165**
2006 Average	**42**	**159**	**11**	**8**	**58**	**255**	**83**	**45**	**21**	**28**	**607**	**1,317**
2007 Average	**46**	**189**	**14**	**14**	**54**	**279**	**81**	**71**	**16**	**9**	**660**	**1,433**
2008 Average	**54**	**264**	**13**	**10**	**54**	**333**	**131**	**77**	**18**	**17**	**830**	**1,802**
2009 Average	**55**	**223**	**44**	**30**	**58**	**322**	**192**	**115**	**23**	**33**	**928**	**2,024**
2010 Average	**123**	**233**	**52**	**10**	**88**	**448**	**165**	**128**	**13**	**19**	**1,073**	**2,353**
2011 Average	**157**	**351**	**73**	**17**	**79**	**570**	**248**	**121**	**15**	**35**	**1,320**	**2,986**
2012 Average	**166**	**416**	**85**	**36**	**89**	**565**	**239**	**115**	**16**	**41**	**1,435**	**3,205**
2013 Average	**179**	**549**	**129**	**41**	**117**	**532**	**274**	**136**	**13**	**36**	**1,616**	**3,621**
2014 Average	**217**	**809**	**89**	**70**	**150**	**559**	**241**	**124**	**46**	**53**	**1,817**	**4,176**
2015 Average	**188**	**955**	**191**	**78**	**166**	**690**	**226**	**122**	**65**	**89**	**1,968**	**4,738**
2016 Average	**260**	**935**	**203**	**140**	**250**	**880**	**265**	**147**	**108**	**92**	**1,980**	**5,261**
2017 January	270	809	333	102	323	1,120	155	252	124	89	2,067	5,645
February	317	827	611	249	379	980	306	306	159	93	2,233	6,461
March	312	794	387	193	323	883	268	291	128	187	2,288	6,054
April	405	885	452	191	377	909	152	192	251	167	2,297	6,277
May	393	957	384	166	249	887	320	125	197	170	2,383	6,232
June	414	936	272	211	256	1,087	292	237	175	184	2,188	6,252
July	410	980	208	140	316	1,125	269	188	137	195	2,324	6,291
August	415	824	354	239	264	1,022	167	162	179	152	1,889	5,665
September	476	872	531	235	463	1,074	261	174	240	175	1,789	6,289
October	492	655	773	264	393	1,133	312	278	150	211	2,426	7,086
November	444	999	499	217	390	1,377	194	143	257	316	2,308	7,144
December	391	918	576	200	468	1,365	322	182	116	288	2,309	7,136
Average	**395**	**871**	**447**	**200**	**350**	**1,081**	**251**	**210**	**176**	**186**	**2,209**	**6,376**
2018 January	357	923	508	161	354	1,364	289	206	74	145	2,235	6,615
February	394	1,008	608	190	301	1,097	269	233	144	179	2,421	6,844
March	420	864	594	212	321	1,275	208	135	246	282	2,548	7,105
April	355	1,028	426	214	338	1,252	377	200	236	336	2,967	7,730
May	292	1,030	568	264	291	977	340	303	348	279	2,825	7,517
June	411	907	679	413	289	1,020	409	243	499	303	2,629	7,801
July	353	959	545	217	503	1,336	312	121	433	231	2,816	7,827
August	362	841	130	301	433	1,104	289	182	457	273	2,671	7,043
September	376	944	72	276	585	1,176	429	191	406	304	2,852	7,611
October	584	1,016	102	418	497	1,386	465	201	598	267	2,483	8,018
November	387	1,067	71	287	785	1,442	531	333	422	255	3,089	8,669
December	460	931	205	360	728	1,094	425	162	718	372	2,794	8,250
Average	**396**	**959**	**375**	**277**	**453**	**1,211**	**362**	**209**	**384**	**269**	**2,694**	**7,588**
2019 January	465	871	147	446	645	1,187	619	48	309	365	3,001	8,104
February	339	1,143	171	458	333	1,251	455	208	604	345	3,147	8,453
March	567	925	150	694	523	1,294	349	140	515	284	2,556	7,996
3-Month Average	**461**	**974**	**156**	**535**	**506**	**1,244**	**475**	**129**	**472**	**331**	**2,893**	**8,175**
2018 3-Month Average	**390**	**929**	**569**	**188**	**326**	**1,250**	**255**	**190**	**155**	**203**	**2,401**	**6,855**
2017 3-Month Average	**299**	**809**	**438**	**179**	**341**	**995**	**241**	**282**	**136**	**124**	**2,195**	**6,039**

NA=Not available. – =No data reported.

Notes: • Totals may not equal sum of components due to independent rounding. • U.S. geographic coverage is the 50 states and the District of Columbia.

Web Page: See http://www.eia.gov/totalenergy/data/monthly/#petroleum (Excel and CSV files) for all available annual data beginning in 1960 and monthly data beginning in 1981.

Sources: • **1960–1972:** Bureau of Mines, *Minerals Yearbook,* annual reports. • **1973–1975:** Bureau of Mines, Mineral Industry Surveys, *Petroleum Statement, Annual,* annual reports. • **1976–1980:** U.S. Energy Information Administration (EIA), Energy Data Reports, *Petroleum Statement, Annual,* annual reports. • **1981–2017:** EIA, *Petroleum Supply Annual,* annual reports. • **2018 and 2019:** EIA, *Petroleum Supply Monthly,* monthly reports.

Source: *U.S. Energy Information Administration, Monthly Energy Review, June 2019*

Figure 3.4 Petroleum Stocks

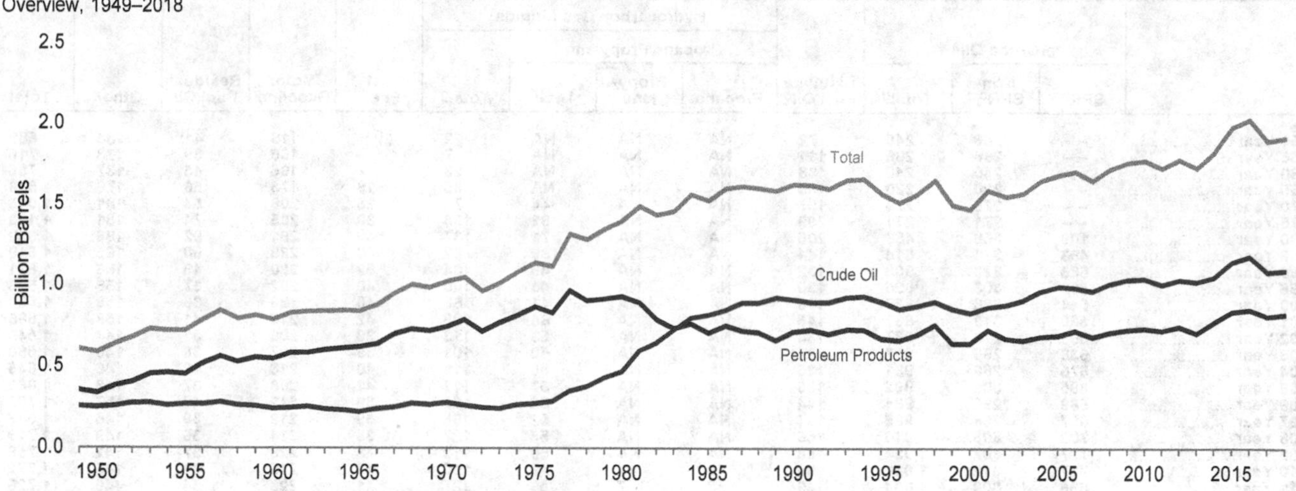

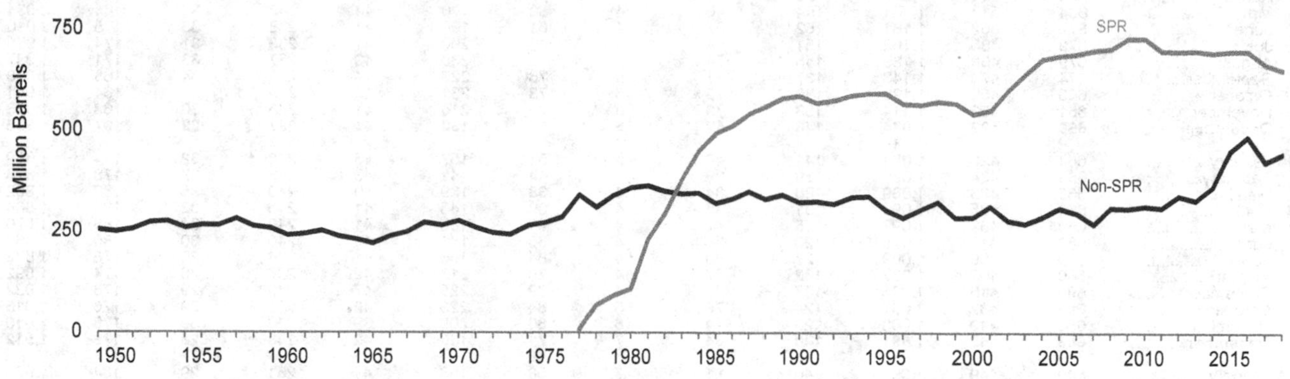

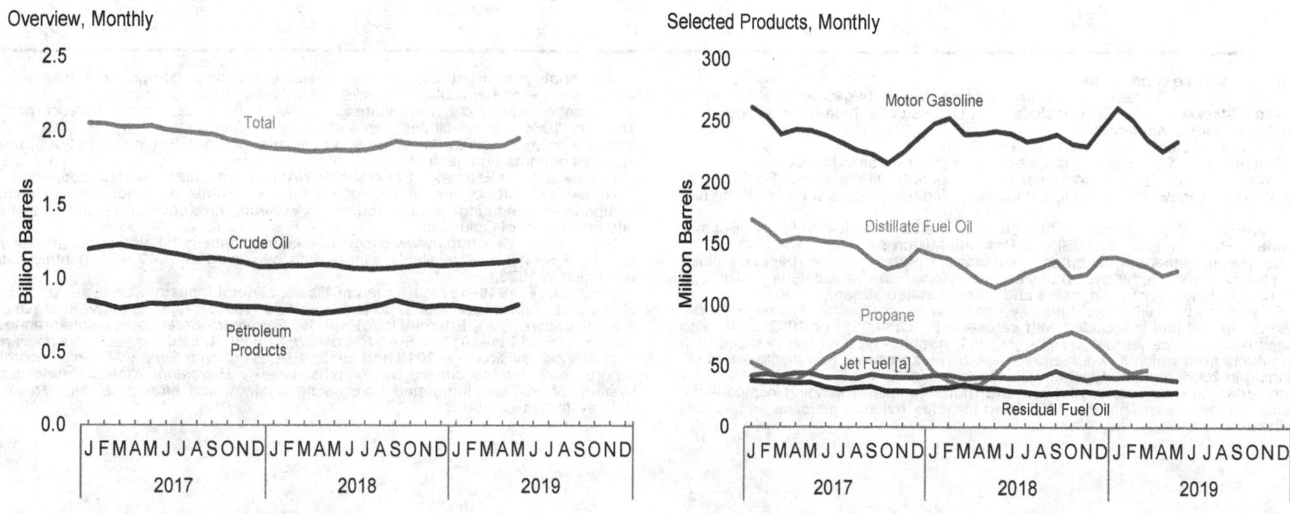

[a] Includes kerosene-type jet fuel only.

Notes: • SPR=Strategic Petroleum Reserve. • Stocks are at end of period.

Web Page: http://www.eia.gov/totalenergy/data/monthly/#petroleum.

Source: Table 3.4.

Source: *U.S. Energy Information Administration, Monthly Energy Review, June 2019*

Table 3.4 Petroleum Stocks
(Million Barrels)

	Crude Oil[a]			Distillate Fuel Oil[e]	Hydrocarbon Gas Liquids				Jet Fuel[h]	Motor Gasoline[i]	Residual Fuel Oil	Other[j]	Total
					Propane/Propylene								
	SPR[b]	Non-SPR[c,d]	Total[d]		Propane	Propylene	Total[f]	Total[g]					
1950 Year	**– –**	**248**	**248**	**72**	**NA**	**NA**	**NA**	**2**	**(h)**	**116**	**41**	**104**	**583**
1955 Year	**– –**	**266**	**266**	**111**	**NA**	**NA**	**NA**	**7**	**3**	**165**	**39**	**123**	**715**
1960 Year	**– –**	**240**	**240**	**138**	**NA**	**NA**	**NA**	**23**	**7**	**195**	**45**	**137**	**785**
1965 Year	**– –**	**220**	**220**	**155**	**NA**	**NA**	**NA**	**35**	**19**	**175**	**56**	**176**	**836**
1970 Year	**– –**	**276**	**276**	**195**	**NA**	**NA**	**44**	**74**	**28**	**209**	**54**	**181**	**1,018**
1975 Year	**– –**	**271**	**271**	**209**	**NA**	**NA**	**82**	**133**	**30**	**235**	**74**	**181**	**1,133**
1980 Year	**108**	**358**	**466**	**205**	**NA**	**NA**	**71**	**137**	**42**	**261**	**92**	**189**	**1,392**
1985 Year	**493**	**321**	**814**	**144**	**NA**	**NA**	**39**	**82**	**40**	**223**	**50**	**165**	**1,519**
1990 Year	**586**	**323**	**908**	**132**	**NA**	**NA**	**49**	**104**	**52**	**220**	**49**	**156**	**1,621**
1995 Year	**592**	**303**	**895**	**130**	**NA**	**NA**	**43**	**100**	**40**	**202**	**37**	**158**	**1,563**
2000 Year	**541**	**286**	**826**	**118**	**NA**	**NA**	**41**	**88**	**45**	**196**	**36**	**159**	**1,468**
2001 Year	**550**	**312**	**862**	**145**	**NA**	**NA**	**66**	**128**	**42**	**210**	**41**	**158**	**1,586**
2002 Year	**599**	**278**	**877**	**134**	**NA**	**NA**	**53**	**113**	**39**	**209**	**31**	**144**	**1,548**
2003 Year	**638**	**269**	**907**	**137**	**NA**	**NA**	**50**	**101**	**39**	**207**	**38**	**140**	**1,568**
2004 Year	**676**	**286**	**961**	**126**	**NA**	**NA**	**55**	**111**	**40**	**218**	**42**	**146**	**1,645**
2005 Year	**685**	**308**	**992**	**136**	**NA**	**NA**	**57**	**117**	**42**	**208**	**37**	**148**	**1,682**
2006 Year	**689**	**296**	**984**	**144**	**NA**	**NA**	**62**	**125**	**39**	**212**	**42**	**157**	**1,703**
2007 Year	**697**	**268**	**965**	**134**	**NA**	**NA**	**52**	**106**	**39**	**218**	**39**	**146**	**1,648**
2008 Year	**702**	**308**	**1,010**	**146**	**NA**	**NA**	**55**	**127**	**38**	**214**	**36**	**149**	**1,719**
2009 Year	**727**	**307**	**1,034**	**166**	**NA**	**NA**	**50**	**113**	**43**	**223**	**37**	**142**	**1,758**
2010 Year	**727**	**312**	**1,039**	**164**	**46**	**4**	**49**	**120**	**43**	**219**	**41**	**145**	**1,772**
2011 Year	**696**	**308**	**1,004**	**149**	**48**	**7**	**55**	**127**	**41**	**223**	**34**	**146**	**1,725**
2012 Year	**695**	**338**	**1,033**	**135**	**63**	**5**	**68**	**152**	**40**	**231**	**34**	**154**	**1,779**
2013 Year	**696**	**327**	**1,023**	**128**	**40**	**5**	**45**	**125**	**37**	**228**	**38**	**149**	**1,728**
2014 Year	**691**	**361**	**1,052**	**136**	**72**	**6**	**78**	**174**	**38**	**240**	**34**	**151**	**1,825**
2015 Year	**695**	**449**	**1,144**	**161**	**91**	**5**	**96**	**194**	**40**	**235**	**42**	**164**	**1,982**
2016 Year	**695**	**485**	**1,180**	**166**	**77**	**7**	**84**	**200**	**43**	**239**	**41**	**161**	**2,030**
2017 January	695	507	1,202	170	53	6	59	165	43	261	39	174	2,053
February	695	525	1,220	163	47	3	51	154	44	254	38	177	2,049
March	692	539	1,230	152	40	4	44	148	42	240	38	181	2,030
April	689	524	1,213	155	38	4	43	153	45	244	37	182	2,028
May	684	517	1,201	154	46	4	50	170	44	242	37	184	2,034
June	679	502	1,181	152	57	4	61	190	41	238	33	175	2,010
July	679	483	1,162	151	64	5	68	206	41	233	31	174	1,998
August	679	460	1,139	148	74	5	79	230	40	227	33	171	1,987
September	674	470	1,143	137	71	5	76	229	44	223	34	168	1,978
October	669	460	1,129	130	73	5	78	231	42	216	30	164	1,941
November	661	453	1,114	133	70	5	75	216	41	225	30	163	1,923
December	**663**	**422**	**1,084**	**146**	**62**	**5**	**67**	**190**	**41**	**237**	**29**	**167**	**1,895**
2018 January	664	420	1,084	141	46	5	51	157	43	248	32	174	1,879
February	665	424	1,089	139	39	5	44	142	43	253	33	178	1,876
March	665	423	1,089	130	34	4	38	139	40	240	35	188	1,862
April	664	435	1,099	121	35	4	39	145	41	240	32	186	1,864
May	660	433	1,093	115	44	4	48	163	41	242	32	183	1,870
June	660	415	1,075	120	56	4	60	181	41	240	30	180	1,867
July	660	409	1,069	127	60	4	64	196	41	234	29	176	1,872
August	660	407	1,067	132	67	4	70	213	42	236	28	174	1,892
September	660	416	1,076	137	75	4	79	225	47	240	29	178	1,932
October	655	432	1,087	124	79	5	84	225	42	232	29	176	1,916
November	650	449	1,098	126	74	6	80	209	39	230	30	178	1,910
December	**649**	**442**	**1,091**	**140**	**64**	**7**	**71**	**189**	**42**	**246**	**28**	**176**	**1,912**
2019 January	649	449	1,098	140	51	7	58	166	41	261	29	184	1,920
February	649	452	1,101	136	45	8	53	155	42	251	28	189	1,902
March	649	R 459	R 1,108	R 132	R 48	R 8	R 56	R 163	R 42	R 236	29	R 188	R 1,898
April	E 648	E 468	E 1,116	E 126	NA	NA	E 60	RF 177	E 40	E 226	E 28	RE 191	E 1,904
May	E 645	E 484	E 1,128	E 129	NA	NA	E 69	F 197	E 39	E 234	E 29	E 198	E 1,954

[a] Includes lease condensate.
[b] "SPR" is the Strategic Petroleum Reserve, which began in October 1977. Crude oil stocks in the SPR include non-U.S. stocks held under foreign or commercial storage agreements.
[c] All crude oil stocks other than those in "SPR."
[d] Beginning in 1981, includes stocks of Alaskan crude oil in transit.
[e] Excludes stocks in the Northeast Home Heating Oil Reserve. Beginning in 2009, includes renewable diesel fuel (including biodiesel) blended into distillate fuel oil.
[f] Propane and propylene. Through 1983, also includes 40% of "Butane-Propane Mixtures" and 30% of "Ethane-Propane Mixtures."
[g] Ethane, propane, normal butane, isobutane, natural gasoline (pentanes plus), and refinery olefins (ethylene, propylene, butylene, and isobutylene). Through 1983, also includes plant condensate and unfractionated stream.
[h] Beginning in 1965, includes kerosene-type jet fuel. (Through 1964, kerosene-type jet fuel is included with kerosene in "Other.") For 1952–2004, also includes naphtha-type jet fuel. (Through 1951, naphtha-type jet fuel is included in the products from which it was blended—gasoline, kerosene, and distillate fuel oil. Beginning in 2005, naphtha-type jet fuel is included in "Other.")
[i] Includes finished motor gasoline and motor gasoline blending components; excludes oxygenates. Through 1963, also includes aviation gasoline and special naphthas.
[j] Asphalt and road oil, aviation gasoline blending components, kerosene, lubricants, petrochemical feedstocks, petroleum coke, unfinished oils, waxes, miscellaneous products, oxygenates, renewable fuels, and other hydrocarbons. Through 1964, also includes kerosene-type jet fuel. Beginning in 1964, also includes finished aviation gasoline and special naphthas. Beginning in 2005, also includes naphtha-type jet fuel.

R=Revised. E=Estimate. F=Forecast. NA=Not available. – – =Not applicable.

Notes: • Stocks are at end of period. • Totals may not equal sum of components due to independent rounding. • Geographic coverage is the 50 states and the District of Columbia.

Web Page: See http://www.eia.gov/totalenergy/data/monthly/#petroleum (Excel and CSV files) for all available annual data beginning in 1949 and monthly data beginning in 1973.

Sources: • **1949–1975:** Bureau of Mines, Mineral Industry Surveys, *Petroleum Statement, Annual,* annual reports. • **1976–1980:** U.S. Energy Information Administration (EIA), Energy Data Reports, *Petroleum Statement, Annual,* annual reports. • **1981–2017:** EIA, *Petroleum Supply Annual,* annual reports, and unpublished revisions. • **2018 and 2019:** EIA, *Petroleum Supply Monthly,* monthly reports; and, for the current two months, *Weekly Petroleum Status Report* data system, Short-Term Integrated Forecasting System, and *Monthly Energy Review* data system calculations.

Source: *U.S. Energy Information Administration, Monthly Energy Review, June 2019*

Figure 3.5 Petroleum Products Supplied by Type
(Million Barrels per Day)

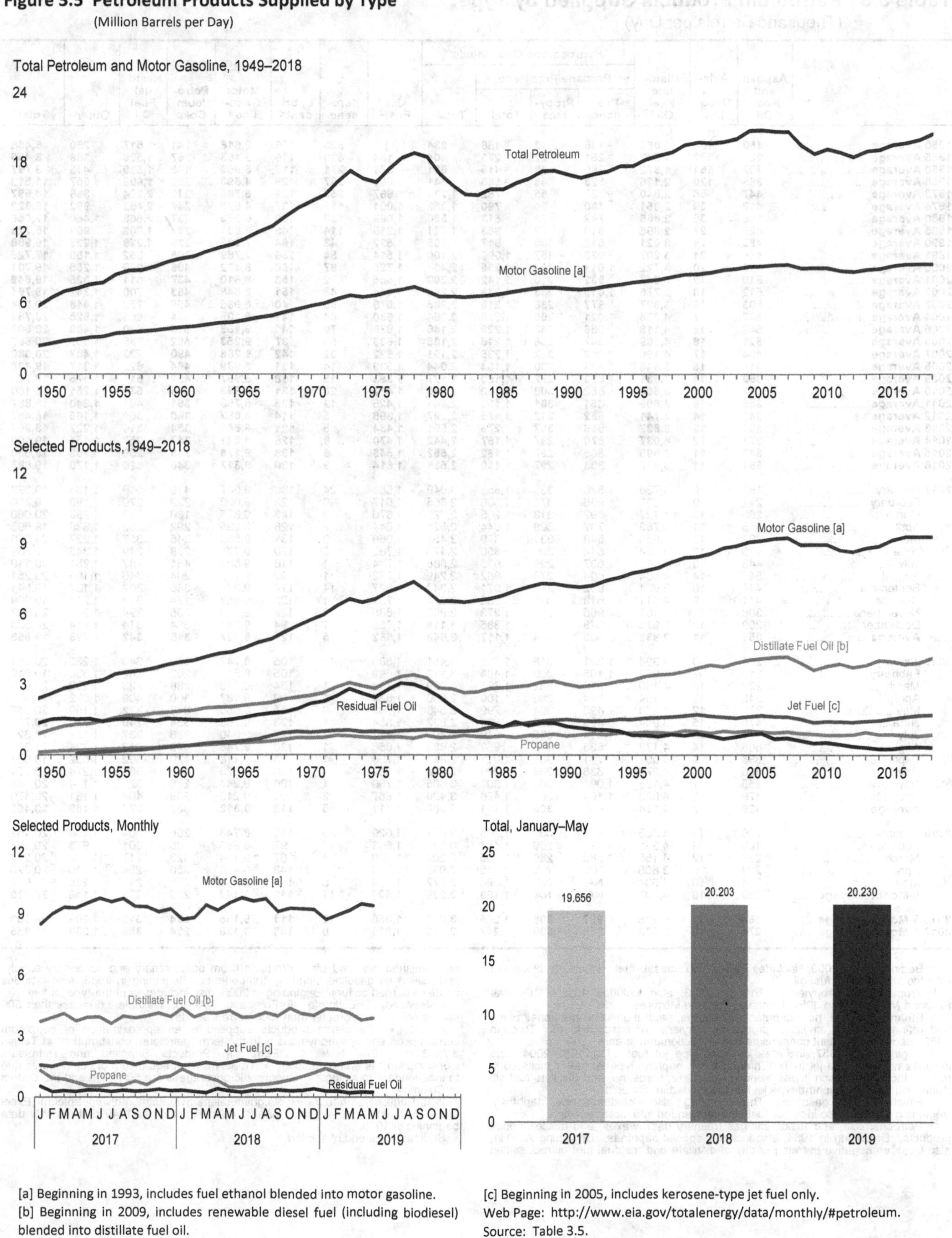

[a] Beginning in 1993, includes fuel ethanol blended into motor gasoline.
[b] Beginning in 2009, includes renewable diesel fuel (including biodiesel) blended into distillate fuel oil.
[c] Beginning in 2005, includes kerosene-type jet fuel only.
Web Page: http://www.eia.gov/totalenergy/data/monthly/#petroleum.
Source: Table 3.5.

Source: *U.S. Energy Information Administration, Monthly Energy Review, June 2019*

Table 3.5 Petroleum Products Supplied by Type
(Thousand Barrels per Day)

	Asphalt and Road Oil	Aviation Gasoline	Distillate Fuel Oil[a]	Hydrocarbon Gas Liquids: Propane/Propylene: Propane	Propylene	Total[b]	Hydrocarbon Gas Liquids Total[c]	Jet Fuel[d]	Kerosene	Lubricants	Motor Gasoline[e]	Petroleum Coke	Residual Fuel Oil	Other[f]	Total
1950 Average	180	108	1,082	E 146	E 13	E 158	234	(d)	323	106	2,616	41	1,517	250	6,458
1955 Average	254	192	1,592	E 251	E 22	E 273	404	154	320	116	3,463	67	1,526	366	8,455
1960 Average	302	161	1,872	E 386	E 33	E 419	621	371	271	117	3,969	149	1,529	435	9,797
1965 Average	368	120	2,126	E 523	E 45	E 568	841	602	267	129	4,593	202	1,608	657	11,512
1970 Average	447	55	2,540	E 727	E 55	782	1,224	967	263	136	5,785	212	2,204	866	14,697
1975 Average	419	39	2,851	E 730	E 60	790	1,352	1,001	159	137	6,675	247	2,462	982	16,322
1980 Average	396	35	2,866	E 742	E 72	813	1,590	1,068	158	159	6,579	237	2,508	1,460	17,056
1985 Average	425	27	2,868	E 810	E 72	883	1,721	1,218	114	145	6,831	264	1,202	909	15,726
1990 Average	483	24	3,021	E 812	E 105	917	1,705	1,522	43	164	7,235	339	1,229	1,225	16,988
1995 Average	486	21	3,207	E 938	E 157	1,096	2,100	1,514	54	156	7,789	365	852	1,180	17,725
2000 Average	525	20	3,722	E 1,011	E 224	1,235	2,434	1,725	67	166	8,472	406	909	1,255	19,701
2001 Average	519	19	3,847	E 932	E 210	1,142	2,200	1,655	72	153	8,610	437	811	1,325	19,649
2002 Average	512	18	3,776	E 1,015	E 233	1,248	2,295	1,614	43	151	8,848	463	700	1,342	19,761
2003 Average	503	16	3,927	E 977	E 238	1,215	2,205	1,578	55	140	8,935	455	772	1,448	20,034
2004 Average	537	17	4,058	E 1,021	E 255	1,276	2,264	1,630	64	141	9,105	524	865	1,525	20,731
2005 Average	546	19	4,118	E 986	E 243	1,229	2,146	1,679	70	141	9,159	515	920	1,489	20,802
2006 Average	521	18	4,169	E 947	E 268	1,215	2,135	1,633	54	137	9,253	522	689	1,557	20,687
2007 Average	494	17	4,196	E 983	E 252	1,235	2,191	1,622	32	142	9,286	490	723	1,487	20,680
2008 Average	417	15	3,945	E 924	E 230	1,154	2,044	1,539	14	131	8,989	464	622	1,317	19,498
2009 Average	360	14	3,631	E 893	E 267	1,160	2,127	1,393	18	118	8,997	427	511	1,176	18,771
2010 Average	362	15	3,800	852	308	1,160	2,265	1,432	20	131	8,993	376	535	1,251	19,180
2011 Average	355	15	3,899	851	301	1,153	2,241	1,425	12	125	8,753	361	461	1,240	18,887
2012 Average	340	14	3,741	862	312	1,175	2,297	1,398	5	114	8,682	360	369	1,165	18,487
2013 Average	323	12	3,827	969	307	1,275	2,501	1,434	5	121	8,843	354	319	1,227	18,967
2014 Average	327	12	4,037	870	297	1,167	2,442	1,470	9	126	8,921	347	257	1,151	19,100
2015 Average	343	11	3,995	865	297	1,162	2,552	1,548	6	138	9,178	349	259	1,153	19,534
2016 Average	351	11	3,877	833	297	1,130	2,536	1,614	9	130	9,317	345	326	1,170	19,687
2017 January	183	9	3,736	1,320	333	1,653	3,049	1,588	24	136	8,507	419	540	1,133	19,323
February	242	9	3,935	935	371	1,306	2,655	1,517	9	128	9,008	229	279	1,180	19,190
March	260	10	4,127	892	313	1,205	2,729	1,676	2	143	9,325	180	319	1,288	20,060
April	316	11	3,763	737	308	1,044	2,524	1,644	2	128	9,295	292	283	1,338	19,595
May	367	12	3,955	548	331	879	2,451	1,669	3	131	9,550	345	357	1,227	20,066
June	475	17	3,964	544	306	850	2,479	1,762	2	120	9,772	278	349	1,345	20,561
July	443	13	3,642	637	298	935	2,588	1,734	1	116	9,595	451	287	1,251	20,119
August	543	14	4,004	604	278	882	2,249	1,762	1	92	9,752	294	346	1,195	20,251
September	444	10	3,921	802	269	1,071	2,347	1,627	14	114	9,378	346	302	1,137	19,641
October	411	9	4,011	618	315	933	2,614	1,751	1	123	9,357	174	323	1,214	19,990
November	308	11	4,157	956	317	1,273	2,902	1,685	3	122	9,110	395	394	1,219	20,307
December	209	12	3,975	1,048	338	1,385	3,118	1,756	1	94	9,247	384	314	1,214	20,323
Average	**351**	**11**	**3,932**	**803**	**314**	**1,117**	**2,643**	**1,682**	**5**	**121**	**9,327**	**316**	**342**	**1,228**	**19,958**
2018 January	204	10	4,394	1,391	315	1,706	3,451	1,586	40	105	8,742	359	340	1,232	20,461
February	219	7	3,962	1,105	300	1,404	3,119	1,599	1	105	8,817	202	282	1,306	19,619
March	233	13	4,169	989	332	1,321	3,069	1,718	1	134	9,446	288	223	1,280	20,573
April	242	13	4,154	814	286	1,100	2,830	1,634	1	99	9,187	300	409	1,072	19,941
May	370	12	4,273	495	304	799	2,543	1,707	8	111	9,550	312	312	1,159	20,357
June	475	15	3,954	499	330	830	2,632	1,854	1	133	9,798	354	249	1,240	20,705
July	471	16	3,958	614	305	919	2,806	1,772	1	127	9,640	336	337	1,157	20,621
August	508	14	4,173	636	316	952	2,889	1,856	1	120	9,748	449	312	1,234	21,302
September	388	9	4,007	711	301	1,011	2,841	1,700	(s)	73	9,118	420	362	1,032	19,951
October	396	16	4,378	836	263	1,099	2,935	1,662	4	110	9,273	420	305	1,274	20,774
November	255	7	4,128	1,007	300	1,307	3,306	1,769	1	136	9,247	275	320	1,104	20,548
December	179	12	4,028	1,194	301	1,496	3,426	1,667	2	92	9,219	269	404	1,181	20,479
Average	**329**	**12**	**4,134**	**857**	**305**	**1,161**	**2,987**	**1,711**	**5**	**112**	**9,319**	**333**	**322**	**1,189**	**20,453**
2019 January	206	11	4,355	1,405	300	1,705	3,671	1,629	26	113	8,743	286	304	1,109	20,452
February	193	9	4,331	1,215	269	1,484	3,582	1,603	16	97	8,963	126	301	973	20,194
March	R 238	R 12	R 4,155	R 985	R 280	R 1,265	R 3,202	R 1,709	R 4	R 67	R 9,174	R 323	R 217	R 1,103	R 20,204
April	RF 263	F 9	E 3,805	NA	NA	E 715	RF 2,939	E 1,746	RF 2	RF 143	E 9,499	F 250	E 254	RE 1,316	E 20,225
May	F 344	F 10	E 3,904	NA	NA	E 694	F 2,772	E 1,782	F 5	F 141	E 9,403	F 255	E 241	E 1,216	E 20,073
5-Month Average	**E 250**	**E 10**	**E 4,107**	**NA**	**NA**	**E 1,169**	**E 3,228**	**E 1,695**	**E 11**	**E 112**	**E 9,158**	**E 250**	**E 263**	**E 1,146**	**E 20,230**
2018 5-Month Average	**254**	**11**	**4,195**	**957**	**308**	**1,265**	**3,001**	**1,650**	**10**	**111**	**9,155**	**294**	**313**	**1,209**	**20,203**
2017 5-Month Average	**274**	**10**	**3,903**	**886**	**330**	**1,217**	**2,683**	**1,621**	**8**	**133**	**9,138**	**294**	**358**	**1,233**	**19,656**

[a] Beginning in 2009, includes renewable diesel fuel (including biodiesel) blended into distillate fuel oil.

[b] Propane and propylene. Through 1983, also includes 40% of "Butane-Propane Mixtures" and 30% of "Ethane-Propane Mixtures."

[c] Ethane, propane, normal butane, isobutane, natural gasoline (pentanes plus), and refinery olefins (ethylene, propylene, butylene, and isobutylene). Through 1983, also includes plant condensate and unfractionated stream.

[d] Beginning in 1957, includes kerosene-type jet fuel. For 1952–2004, also includes naphtha-type jet fuel. (Through 1951, naphtha-type jet fuel is included in the products from which it was blended—gasoline, kerosene, and distillate fuel oil. Beginning in 2005, naphtha-type jet fuel is included in "Other.")

[e] Finished motor gasoline. Through 1963, also includes special naphthas. Beginning in 1993, also includes fuel ethanol blended into motor gasoline.

[f] Petrochemical feedstocks, still gas (refinery gas), waxes, and miscellaneous products. Beginning in 1964, also includes special naphthas. Beginning in 1981, also includes negative barrels per day of distillate and residual fuel oil reclassified as unfinished oils, and other products (from both primary and secondary supply) reclassified as gasoline blending components. Beginning in 1983, also includes crude oil burned as fuel. Beginning in 2005, also includes naphtha-type jet fuel.

R=Revised. E=Estimate. F=Forecast. NA=Not available. (s)=Less than 500 barrels per day and greater than -500 barrels per day.

Notes: • Petroleum products supplied is an approximation of petroleum consumption and is synonymous with the term "petroleum consumption" in Tables 3.7a–3.8c. See Note 1, "Petroleum Products Supplied and Petroleum Consumption," at end of section. • Totals may not equal sum of components due to independent rounding. • Geographic coverage is the 50 states and the District of Columbia.

Web Page: See http://www.eia.gov/totalenergy/data/monthly/#petroleum (Excel and CSV files) for all available annual data beginning in 1949 and monthly data beginning in 1973.

Sources: See end of section.

Source: *U.S. Energy Information Administration, Monthly Energy Review, June 2019*

Figure 3.6 Heat Content of Petroleum Products Supplied by Type

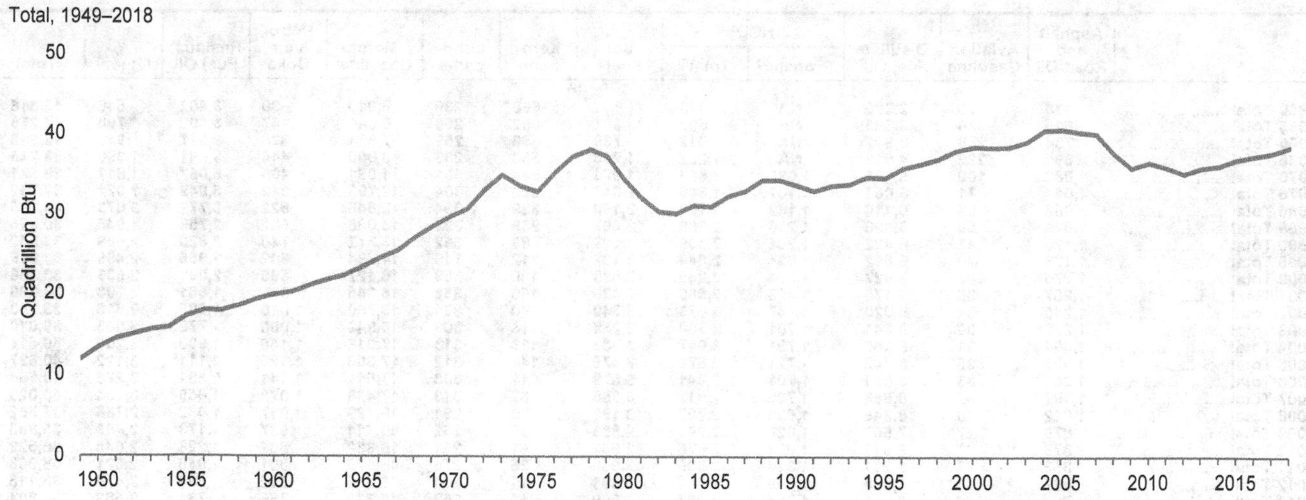

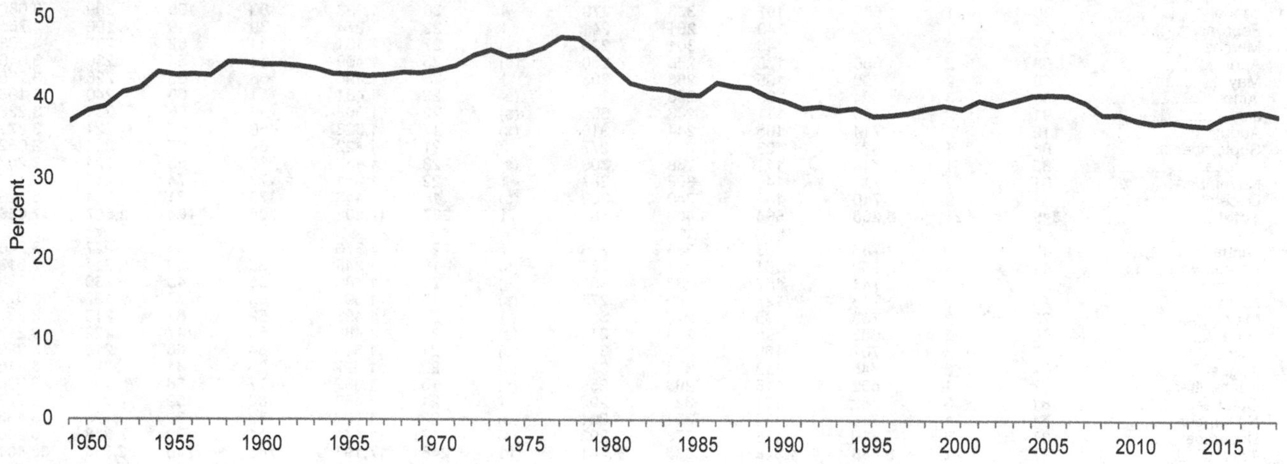

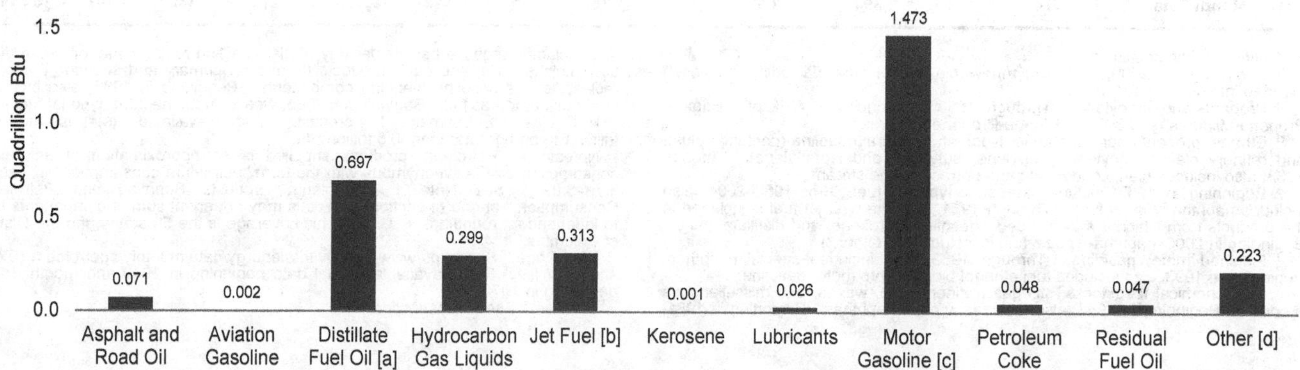

[a] Includes renewable diesel fuel (including biodiesel) blended into distillate fuel oil.
[b] Includes kerosene-type jet fuel only.
[c] Includes fuel ethanol blended into motor gasoline.
[d] All petroleum products not separately displayed.
Web Page: http://www.eia.gov/totalenergy/data/monthly/#petroleum
Sources: Tables 1.1 and 3.6.

Source: *U.S. Energy Information Administration, Monthly Energy Review, June 2019*

Table 3.6 Heat Content of Petroleum Products Supplied by Type
(Trillion Btu)

	Asphalt and Road Oil	Aviation Gasoline	Distillate Fuel Oil[b]	HGL[a] Propane[c]	HGL[a] Total[d]	Jet Fuel[e]	Kero-sene	Lubri-cants	Motor Gasoline[f]	Petro-leum Coke	Residual Fuel Oil	Other[g]	Total
1950 Total	**435**	**199**	**2,300**	**NA**	**343**	**(e)**	**668**	**236**	**5,015**	**90**	**3,482**	**546**	**13,315**
1955 Total	**615**	**354**	**3,385**	**NA**	**592**	**301**	**662**	**258**	**6,640**	**147**	**3,502**	**798**	**17,255**
1960 Total	**734**	**298**	**3,992**	**NA**	**912**	**739**	**563**	**259**	**7,631**	**328**	**3,517**	**947**	**19,919**
1965 Total	**890**	**222**	**4,519**	**NA**	**1,232**	**1,215**	**553**	**286**	**8,806**	**444**	**3,691**	**1,390**	**23,246**
1970 Total	**1,082**	**100**	**5,401**	**1,095**	**1,689**	**1,973**	**544**	**301**	**11,091**	**465**	**5,057**	**1,817**	**29,521**
1975 Total	**1,014**	**71**	**6,061**	**1,107**	**1,845**	**2,047**	**329**	**304**	**12,798**	**542**	**5,649**	**2,071**	**32,732**
1980 Total	**962**	**64**	**6,110**	**1,142**	**2,180**	**2,190**	**329**	**354**	**12,648**	**522**	**5,772**	**3,073**	**34,205**
1985 Total	**1,029**	**50**	**6,098**	**1,236**	**2,309**	**2,497**	**236**	**322**	**13,098**	**582**	**2,759**	**1,945**	**30,925**
1990 Total	**1,170**	**45**	**6,422**	**1,284**	**2,309**	**3,129**	**88**	**362**	**13,872**	**745**	**2,820**	**2,589**	**33,552**
1995 Total	**1,178**	**40**	**6,812**	**1,534**	**2,849**	**3,132**	**112**	**346**	**14,794**	**802**	**1,955**	**2,499**	**34,519**
2000 Total	**1,276**	**36**	**7,927**	**1,734**	**3,288**	**3,580**	**140**	**369**	**16,127**	**895**	**2,091**	**2,636**	**38,366**
2001 Total	**1,257**	**35**	**8,170**	**1,598**	**2,960**	**3,426**	**150**	**338**	**16,345**	**961**	**1,861**	**2,793**	**38,296**
2002 Total	**1,240**	**34**	**8,020**	**1,747**	**3,076**	**3,340**	**90**	**334**	**16,790**	**1,018**	**1,605**	**2,816**	**38,363**
2003 Total	**1,220**	**30**	**8,341**	**1,701**	**2,968**	**3,265**	**113**	**309**	**16,949**	**1,000**	**1,772**	**3,043**	**39,010**
2004 Total	**1,304**	**31**	**8,642**	**1,791**	**3,047**	**3,383**	**133**	**313**	**17,316**	**1,148**	**1,990**	**3,205**	**40,511**
2005 Total	**1,323**	**35**	**8,745**	**1,721**	**2,878**	**3,475**	**144**	**312**	**17,358**	**1,125**	**2,111**	**3,122**	**40,627**
2006 Total	**1,261**	**33**	**8,831**	**1,701**	**2,841**	**3,379**	**111**	**303**	**17,511**	**1,141**	**1,581**	**3,276**	**40,268**
2007 Total	**1,197**	**32**	**8,858**	**1,729**	**2,912**	**3,358**	**67**	**313**	**17,428**	**1,072**	**1,659**	**3,134**	**40,029**
2008 Total	**1,012**	**28**	**8,346**	**1,620**	**2,727**	**3,193**	**30**	**291**	**16,799**	**1,017**	**1,432**	**2,788**	**37,662**
2009 Total	**873**	**27**	**7,657**	**1,624**	**2,791**	**2,883**	**36**	**262**	**16,711**	**937**	**1,173**	**2,483**	**35,833**
2010 Total	**878**	**27**	**8,011**	**1,624**	**2,976**	**2,963**	**41**	**291**	**16,632**	**831**	**1,228**	**2,645**	**36,522**
2011 Total	**859**	**27**	**8,211**	**1,614**	**2,899**	**2,950**	**25**	**276**	**16,175**	**801**	**1,058**	**2,621**	**35,903**
2012 Total	**827**	**25**	**7,898**	**1,649**	**2,992**	**2,901**	**11**	**254**	**16,085**	**802**	**849**	**2,474**	**35,118**
2013 Total	**783**	**22**	**8,051**	**1,785**	**3,267**	**2,969**	**11**	**268**	**16,332**	**786**	**731**	**2,583**	**35,804**
2014 Total	**793**	**22**	**8,492**	**1,634**	**3,172**	**3,042**	**19**	**280**	**16,473**	**772**	**590**	**2,430**	**36,084**
2015 Total	**832**	**21**	**8,402**	**1,627**	**3,331**	**3,204**	**13**	**305**	**16,941**	**776**	**595**	**2,435**	**36,855**
2016 Total	**853**	**20**	**8,170**	**1,586**	**3,289**	**3,350**	**18**	**289**	**17,238**	**771**	**751**	**2,553**	**37,303**
2017 January	38	1	667	197	338	279	4	26	1,333	80	105	209	3,080
February	45	1	635	140	261	241	1	22	1,274	39	49	196	2,765
March	53	2	737	143	301	295	(s)	27	1,461	34	62	237	3,208
April	63	2	650	120	268	280	(s)	23	1,409	54	53	239	3,040
May	75	2	706	105	266	293	1	25	1,496	66	69	226	3,225
June	95	3	684	98	258	300	(s)	22	1,481	51	66	240	3,199
July	91	2	650	111	283	305	(s)	22	1,503	86	56	231	3,228
August	112	2	714	105	244	310	(s)	17	1,528	56	67	221	3,271
September	88	1	677	123	250	277	2	21	1,422	64	57	204	3,062
October	85	1	716	111	288	308	(s)	23	1,466	33	63	224	3,207
November	61	2	718	146	306	287	1	22	1,381	73	74	217	3,142
December	43	2	710	165	340	309	(s)	18	1,448	73	61	224	3,228
Total	**849**	**21**	**8,263**	**1,564**	**3,403**	**3,481**	**11**	**267**	**17,201**	**708**	**784**	**2,667**	**37,656**
2018 January	42	1	785	203	381	279	7	20	1,370	68	66	227	3,246
February	41	1	639	151	311	254	(s)	18	1,248	35	50	217	2,813
March	48	2	744	157	332	302	(s)	25	1,480	55	43	236	3,268
April	48	2	718	127	296	278	(s)	18	1,393	55	77	192	3,077
May	76	2	763	95	273	300	1	21	1,496	59	61	215	3,267
June	95	2	683	95	274	315	(s)	24	1,486	65	47	222	3,213
July	97	3	707	109	303	312	(s)	24	1,510	64	66	215	3,299
August	104	2	745	113	314	326	(s)	22	1,527	85	61	228	3,416
September	77	1	692	116	298	289	(s)	13	1,382	77	68	185	3,085
October	81	3	782	131	322	292	1	21	1,453	80	59	234	3,327
November	51	1	713	150	351	301	(s)	25	1,402	50	60	198	3,153
December	37	2	719	178	378	293	(s)	17	1,444	51	79	218	3,240
Total	**797**	**22**	**8,689**	**1,626**	**3,833**	**3,541**	**11**	**248**	**17,191**	**743**	**738**	**2,588**	**38,401**
2019 January	42	2	778	203	407	286	5	21	1,370	54	59	205	3,229
February	36	1	699	159	354	255	3	16	1,268	22	53	163	2,869
March	R 49	R 2	R 742	R 150	R 350	R 300	R 1	R 13	R 1,437	R 61	R 42	R 204	R 3,201
April	RF 52	F 1	E 657	E 82	RF 308	E 297	F (s)	RF 26	E 1,440	F 46	E 48	RE 245	E 3,121
May	F 71	F 2	E 697	E 83	F 299	E 313	F 1	F 26	E 1,473	F 48	E 47	E 223	E 3,201
5-Month Total	**E 250**	**E 8**	**E 3,572**	**E 677**	**E 1,717**	**E 1,451**	**E 9**	**E 103**	**E 6,989**	**E 231**	**E 249**	**E 1,040**	**E 15,621**
2018 5-Month Total	**255**	**8**	**3,649**	**732**	**1,593**	**1,412**	**9**	**102**	**6,986**	**272**	**297**	**1,087**	**15,670**
2017 5-Month Total	**274**	**8**	**3,394**	**705**	**1,434**	**1,388**	**7**	**122**	**6,973**	**273**	**339**	**1,107**	**15,319**

[a] Hydrocarbon gas liquids.

[b] Beginning in 2009, includes renewable diesel fuel (including biodiesel) blended into distillate fuel oil.

[c] Propane and propylene. Through 1983, also includes 40% of "Butane-Propane Mixtures" and 30% of "Ethane-Propane Mixtures."

[d] Ethane, propane, normal butane, isobutane, natural gasoline (pentanes plus), and refinery olefins (ethylene, propylene, butylene, and isobutylene). Through 1983, also includes plant condensate and unfractionated stream.

[e] Beginning in 1957, includes kerosene-type jet fuel. For 1952–2004, also includes naphtha-type jet fuel. (Through 1951, naphtha-type jet fuel is included in the products from which it was blended—gasoline, kerosene, and distillate fuel oil. Beginning in 2005, naphtha-type jet fuel is included in "Other.")

[f] Finished motor gasoline. Through 1963, also includes special naphthas. Beginning in 1993, also includes fuel ethanol blended into motor gasoline.

[g] Petrochemical feedstocks, still gas (refinery gas), waxes, and miscellaneous products. Beginning in 1964, also includes special naphthas. Beginning in 1981, also includes negative barrels per day of distillate and residual fuel oil reclassified as unfinished oils, and other products (from both primary and secondary supply) reclassified as gasoline blending components. Beginning in 1983, also includes crude oil burned as fuel. Beginning in 2005, also includes naphtha-type jet fuel.

R=Revised. E=Estimate. F=Forecast. NA=Not available. (s)=Less than 0.5 trillion Btu and greater than -0.5 trillion Btu.

Notes: • Petroleum products supplied is an approximation of petroleum consumption and is synonymous with the term "petroleum consumption" in Tables 3.7a–3.8c. See Note 1, "Petroleum Products Supplied and Petroleum Consumption," at end of section. • Totals may not equal sum of components due to independent rounding. • Geographic coverage is the 50 states and the District of Columbia.

Web Page: See http://www.eia.gov/totalenergy/data/monthly/#petroleum (Excel and CSV files) for all available annual data beginning in 1949 and monthly data beginning in 1973.

Sources: See end of section.

Source: *U.S. Energy Information Administration, Monthly Energy Review, June 2019*

Figure 3.7 Petroleum Consumption by Sector

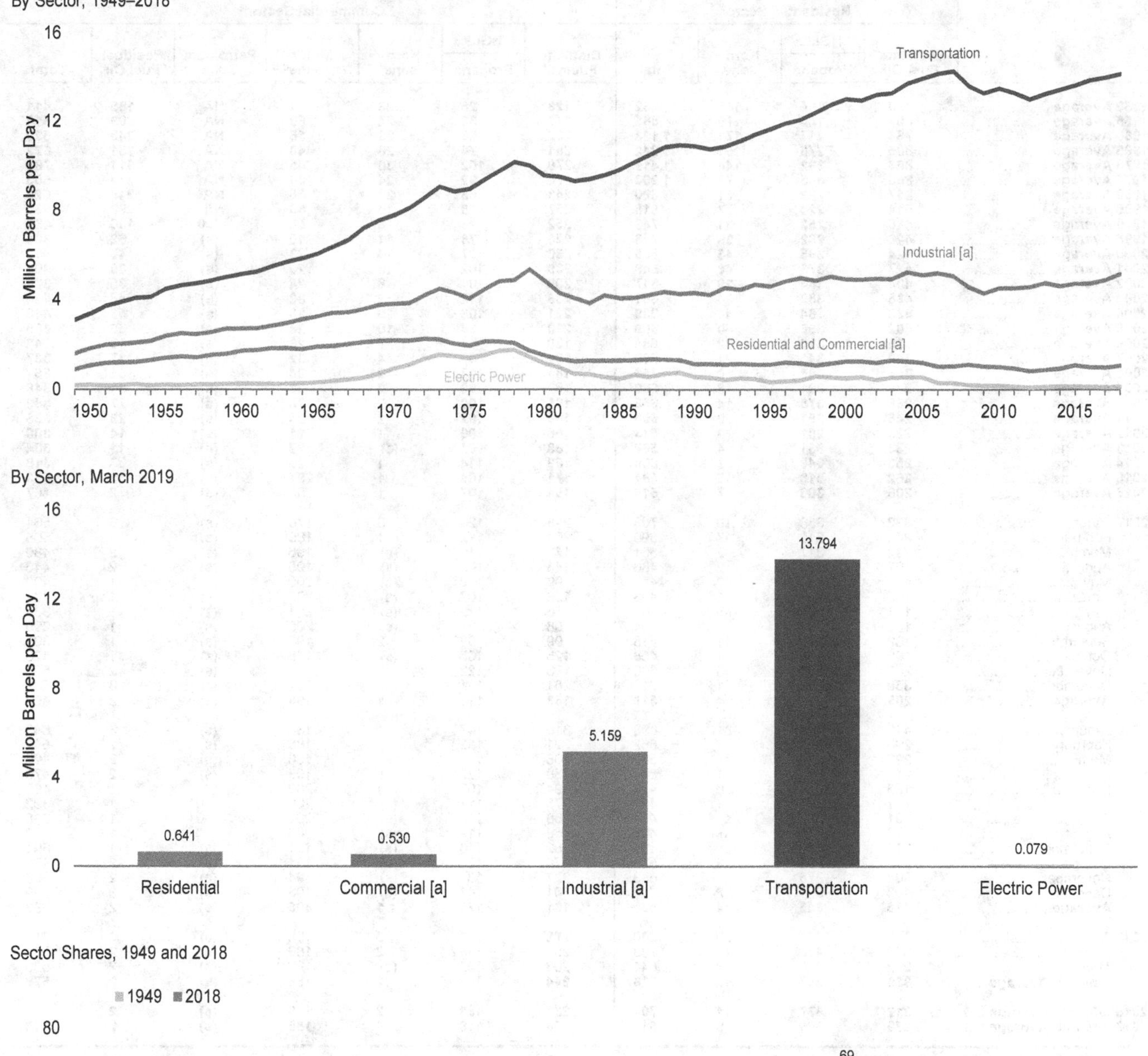

[a] Includes combined-heat-and-power plants and a small number of electricity-only plants.

Web Page: http://www.eia.gov/totalenergy/data/monthly/#petrol
Sources: Tables 3.7a–3.7c.

Source: *U.S. Energy Information Administration, Monthly Energy Review, June 2019*

Table 3.7a Petroleum Consumption: Residential and Commercial Sectors
(Thousand Barrels per Day)

	Residential Sector				Commercial Sector[a]						
	Distillate Fuel Oil	HGL[b] Propane	Kero-sene	Total	Distillate Fuel Oil	HGL[b] Propane	Kero-sene	Motor Gasoline[c,d]	Petroleum Coke	Residual Fuel Oil	Total
1950 Average	**390**	**104**	**168**	**662**	**123**	**28**	**23**	**52**	**NA**	**185**	**411**
1955 Average	**562**	**144**	**179**	**885**	**177**	**38**	**24**	**69**	**NA**	**209**	**519**
1960 Average	**736**	**217**	**171**	**1,123**	**232**	**58**	**23**	**35**	**NA**	**243**	**590**
1965 Average	**805**	**275**	**161**	**1,242**	**251**	**74**	**26**	**40**	**NA**	**281**	**672**
1970 Average	**883**	**392**	**144**	**1,419**	**276**	**102**	**30**	**45**	**NA**	**311**	**764**
1975 Average	**850**	**365**	**78**	**1,293**	**276**	**92**	**24**	**46**	**NA**	**214**	**653**
1980 Average	**617**	**222**	**51**	**890**	**243**	**63**	**20**	**56**	**NA**	**245**	**626**
1985 Average	**514**	**224**	**77**	**815**	**297**	**68**	**16**	**50**	**NA**	**99**	**530**
1990 Average	**460**	**252**	**31**	**742**	**252**	**73**	**6**	**58**	**0**	**100**	**489**
1995 Average	**426**	**282**	**36**	**743**	**225**	**78**	**11**	**10**	**(s)**	**62**	**385**
2000 Average	**424**	**395**	**46**	**865**	**230**	**107**	**14**	**23**	**(s)**	**40**	**415**
2001 Average	**427**	**375**	**46**	**849**	**239**	**102**	**15**	**20**	**(s)**	**30**	**406**
2002 Average	**404**	**384**	**29**	**817**	**209**	**101**	**8**	**24**	**(s)**	**35**	**376**
2003 Average	**438**	**389**	**34**	**861**	**233**	**112**	**9**	**32**	**(s)**	**48**	**434**
2004 Average	**433**	**364**	**41**	**839**	**221**	**108**	**10**	**23**	**(s)**	**53**	**416**
2005 Average	**402**	**366**	**40**	**809**	**210**	**94**	**10**	**24**	**(s)**	**50**	**389**
2006 Average	**335**	**318**	**32**	**685**	**189**	**88**	**7**	**26**	**(s)**	**33**	**343**
2007 Average	**342**	**345**	**21**	**708**	**181**	**87**	**4**	**32**	**(s)**	**33**	**337**
2008 Average	**354**	**394**	**10**	**758**	**181**	**113**	**2**	**24**	**(s)**	**31**	**351**
2009 Average	**276**	**391**	**13**	**680**	**187**	**99**	**2**	**28**	**(s)**	**31**	**348**
2010 Average	**266**	**378**	**14**	**658**	**185**	**100**	**2**	**28**	**(s)**	**27**	**343**
2011 Average	**248**	**351**	**9**	**608**	**186**	**102**	**2**	**24**	**(s)**	**23**	**336**
2012 Average	**228**	**281**	**4**	**513**	**168**	**96**	**1**	**21**	**(s)**	**14**	**300**
2013 Average	**233**	**331**	**4**	**568**	**163**	**108**	**(s)**	**22**	**(s)**	**11**	**304**
2014 Average	**253**	**349**	**7**	**609**	**169**	**114**	**1**	**29**	**(s)**	**3**	**318**
2015 Average	**262**	**318**	**5**	**584**	**171**	**106**	**1**	[d] **204**	**(s)**	**2**	**483**
2016 Average	**206**	**306**	**7**	**518**	**154**	**107**	**1**	**203**	**(s)**	**2**	**467**
2017 January	332	358	19	708	248	129	3	178	(s)	3	561
February	273	310	7	590	204	112	1	189	(s)	2	508
March	232	317	2	551	173	115	(s)	196	(s)	2	486
April	192	293	2	486	143	106	(s)	195	(s)	2	446
May	133	283	2	418	99	102	(s)	200	(s)	1	403
June	165	297	1	463	123	107	(s)	205	(s)	1	437
July	101	304	(s)	406	76	110	(s)	201	(s)	1	388
August	132	262	1	394	98	95	(s)	205	(s)	1	399
September	132	272	11	415	99	98	2	197	(s)	1	397
October	168	290	1	458	125	105	(s)	196	(s)	1	428
November	259	338	3	600	193	122	(s)	191	(s)	2	509
December	350	362	1	712	261	131	(s)	194	(s)	3	589
Average	**205**	**307**	**4**	**517**	**153**	**111**	**1**	**196**	**(s)**	**2**	**462**
2018 January	416	406	31	853	310	147	4	183	(s)	3	648
February	296	365	1	662	221	132	(s)	185	(s)	2	541
March	222	360	(s)	583	166	130	(s)	198	(s)	2	496
April	212	332	1	546	158	120	(s)	193	(s)	2	473
May	126	295	6	427	94	107	1	200	0	1	403
June	101	307	1	408	75	111	(s)	206	0	1	392
July	91	322	(s)	414	68	116	(s)	202	0	1	388
August	77	329	(s)	406	58	119	(s)	204	0	1	382
September	110	322	(s)	433	82	116	(s)	191	(s)	1	391
October	228	336	3	568	170	121	(s)	194	(s)	2	489
November	304	378	1	683	227	137	(s)	194	(s)	2	560
December	403	391	2	795	301	141	(s)	193	(s)	3	639
Average	**215**	**345**	**4**	**565**	**161**	**125**	**1**	**195**	**(s)**	**2**	**483**
2019 January	369	417	20	806	275	151	3	183	(s)	3	615
February	R 340	410	13	R 763	R 254	148	2	188	(s)	2	R 594
March	272	366	3	641	203	132	(s)	192	(s)	2	530
3-Month Average	**326**	**397**	**12**	**736**	**244**	**144**	**2**	**188**	**(s)**	**2**	**579**
2018 3-Month Average	**312**	**377**	**11**	**701**	**233**	**136**	**2**	**189**	**(s)**	**2**	**562**
2017 3-Month Average	**279**	**329**	**9**	**617**	**208**	**119**	**1**	**188**	**(s)**	**2**	**519**

[a] Commercial sector fuel use, including that at commercial combined-heat-and-power (CHP) and commercial electricity-only plants.
[b] Hydrocarbon gas liquids.
[c] Finished motor gasoline. Through 1963, also includes special naphthas. Beginning in 1993, also includes fuel ethanol blended into motor gasoline.
[d] There is a discontinuity in this time series between 2014 and 2015 due to a change in the method for allocating motor gasoline consumption to the end-use sectors. Beginning in 2015, the commercial and industrial sector shares of motor gasoline consumption are larger than in 2014, while the transportation sector share is smaller.
R=Revised. NA=Not available. (s)=Less than 500 barrels per day and greater than -500 barrels per day.

Notes: • Data are estimates. • For total petroleum consumption by all sectors, see petroleum products supplied data in Table 3.5. Petroleum products supplied is an approximation of petroleum consumption and is synonymous with the term "petroleum consumption" in Tables 3.7a–3.8c. See Note 1, "Petroleum Products Supplied and Petroleum Consumption," at end of section. • Totals may not equal sum of components due to independent rounding. • Geographic coverage is the 50 states and the District of Columbia.
Web Page: See http://www.eia.gov/totalenergy/data/monthly/#petroleum (Excel and CSV files) for all available annual data beginning in 1949 and monthly data beginning in 1973.
Sources: See end of section.

Source: U.S. Energy Information Administration, Monthly Energy Review, June 2019

Table 3.7b Petroleum Consumption: Industrial Sector
(Thousand Barrels per Day)

	Industrial Sector[a]										
	Asphalt and Road Oil	Distillate Fuel Oil	HGL[b]		Kerosene	Lubricants	Motor Gasoline[e,f]	Petroleum Coke	Residual Fuel Oil	Other[g]	Total
			Propane[c]	Total[d]							
1950 Average	180	328	NA	100	132	43	131	41	617	250	1,822
1955 Average	254	466	NA	212	116	47	173	67	686	366	2,387
1960 Average	302	476	NA	333	78	48	198	149	689	435	2,708
1965 Average	368	541	NA	470	80	62	179	202	689	657	3,247
1970 Average	447	577	256	699	89	70	150	203	708	866	3,808
1975 Average	419	630	302	863	58	68	116	246	658	982	4,038
1980 Average	396	621	516	1,293	87	82	82	234	586	1,460	4,842
1985 Average	425	526	569	1,408	21	75	114	261	326	909	4,065
1990 Average	483	541	576	1,364	6	84	97	325	179	1,225	4,304
1995 Average	486	532	723	1,727	7	80	105	328	147	1,180	4,594
2000 Average	525	563	724	1,923	8	86	79	361	105	1,255	4,903
2001 Average	519	611	654	1,713	11	79	155	390	89	1,325	4,892
2002 Average	512	566	754	1,801	7	78	163	383	83	1,342	4,934
2003 Average	503	551	701	1,691	12	72	171	375	96	1,448	4,918
2004 Average	537	570	790	1,778	14	73	195	423	108	1,525	5,222
2005 Average	546	594	749	1,666	19	72	187	404	123	1,489	5,100
2006 Average	521	594	789	1,710	14	71	198	425	104	1,557	5,193
2007 Average	494	595	787	1,744	6	73	161	412	84	1,487	5,056
2008 Average	417	637	619	1,510	2	67	131	394	84	1,317	4,559
2009 Average	360	509	650	1,617	2	61	128	363	57	1,175	4,272
2010 Average	362	547	677	1,782	4	61	140	310	52	1,251	4,510
2011 Average	355	586	694	1,783	2	58	138	295	59	1,240	4,515
2012 Average	340	602	792	1,915	1	53	136	319	30	1,165	4,562
2013 Average	323	601	831	2,058	1	57	142	295	21	1,227	4,724
2014 Average	327	648	698	1,974	1	59	114	290	18	1,151	4,582
2015 Average	343	555	734	2,124	1	64	[f]140	295	15	1,153	4,689
2016 Average	351	548	712	2,119	1	61	142	289	23	1,170	4,702
2017 January	183	539	1,159	2,555	2	64	131	360	34	1,133	5,001
February	242	652	879	2,228	1	60	138	180	17	1,180	4,698
March	260	748	768	2,292	(s)	67	143	139	21	1,288	4,957
April	316	477	641	2,121	(s)	60	143	265	18	1,338	4,738
May	367	610	490	2,061	(s)	61	147	293	22	1,227	4,789
June	475	519	441	2,069	(s)	56	150	221	22	1,345	4,858
July	443	370	516	2,168	(s)	54	147	397	18	1,251	4,848
August	543	547	522	1,889	(s)	43	150	247	21	1,195	4,635
September	444	590	697	1,973	1	54	144	301	19	1,137	4,663
October	411	616	533	2,215	(s)	58	144	138	20	1,214	4,817
November	308	695	807	2,436	(s)	57	140	347	28	1,219	5,231
December	209	509	887	2,619	(s)	44	142	337	21	1,214	5,095
Average	**351**	**572**	**694**	**2,220**	**1**	**56**	**143**	**269**	**22**	**1,228**	**4,862**
2018 January	204	701	1,147	2,891	4	49	134	303	22	1,232	5,540
February	219	575	902	2,617	(s)	49	135	153	17	1,306	5,072
March	233	712	825	2,573	(s)	63	145	249	14	1,280	5,269
April	242	614	642	2,372	(s)	47	141	260	25	1,072	4,772
May	370	730	392	2,136	1	52	147	287	19	1,159	4,900
June	475	495	407	2,209	(s)	62	151	305	17	1,240	4,954
July	471	488	475	2,362	(s)	60	148	282	20	1,157	4,988
August	508	622	500	2,436	(s)	56	150	397	19	1,234	5,421
September	388	585	568	2,397	(s)	34	140	369	22	1,032	4,969
October	396	696	636	2,472	(s)	52	142	390	19	1,274	5,441
November	255	552	787	2,785	(s)	63	142	234	20	1,104	5,157
December	179	425	957	2,888	(s)	43	142	221	25	1,181	5,105
Average	**329**	**600**	**686**	**2,511**	**1**	**53**	**143**	**289**	**20**	**1,189**	**5,135**
2019 January	206	809	1,131	3,097	3	53	134	236	19	1,109	5,664
February	193	R 753	919	3,017	2	45	138	78	18	973	R 5,218
March	238	651	760	2,697	(s)	32	141	283	14	1,103	5,159
3-Month Average	**213**	**737**	**937**	**2,934**	**2**	**43**	**138**	**203**	**17**	**1,064**	**5,352**
2018 3-Month Average	**218**	**666**	**960**	**2,696**	**1**	**54**	**138**	**238**	**18**	**1,271**	**5,301**
2017 3-Month Average	**228**	**646**	**937**	**2,363**	**1**	**64**	**137**	**228**	**24**	**1,201**	**4,892**

[a] Industrial sector fuel use, including that at industrial combined-heat-and-power (CHP) and industrial electricity-only plants.
[b] Hydrocarbon gas liquids.
[c] Propane and propylene. Through 1983, also includes 40% of "Butane-Propane Mixtures" and 30% of "Ethane-Propane Mixtures."
[d] Ethane, propane, normal butane, isobutane, natural gasoline (pentanes plus), and refinery olefins (ethylene, propylene, butylene, and isobutylene). Through 1983, also includes plant condensate and unfractionated stream.
[e] Finished motor gasoline. Through 1963, also includes special naphthas. Beginning in 1993, also includes fuel ethanol blended into motor gasoline.
[f] There is a discontinuity in this time series between 2014 and 2015 due to a change in the method for allocating motor gasoline consumption to the end-use sectors. Beginning in 2015, the commercial and industrial sector shares of motor gasoline consumption are larger than in 2014, while the transportation sector share is smaller.
[g] Petrochemical feedstocks, still gas (refinery gas), waxes, and miscellaneous products. Beginning in 1964, also includes special naphthas. Beginning in 1981, also includes negative barrels per day of distillate and residual fuel oil reclassified as unfinished oils, and other products (from both primary and secondary supply) reclassified as gasoline blending components. Beginning in 1983, also includes crude oil burned as fuel. Beginning in 2005, also includes naphtha-type jet fuel.

R=Revised. NA=Not available. (s)=Less than 500 barrels per day and greater than -500 barrels per day.

Notes: • Data are estimates. • For total petroleum consumption by all sectors, see petroleum products supplied data in Table 3.5. Petroleum products supplied is an approximation of petroleum consumption and is synonymous with the term "petroleum consumption" in Tables 3.7a–3.8c. See Note 1, "Petroleum Products Supplied and Petroleum Consumption," at end of section. • Totals may not equal sum of components due to independent rounding. • Geographic coverage is the 50 states and the District of Columbia.

Web Page: See http://www.eia.gov/totalenergy/data/monthly/#petroleum (Excel and CSV files) for all available annual data beginning in 1949 and monthly data beginning in 1973.

Sources: See end of section.

Source: *U.S. Energy Information Administration, Monthly Energy Review, June 2019*

Table 3.7c Petroleum Consumption: Transportation and Electric Power Sectors

(Thousand Barrels per Day)

	Transportation Sector								Electric Power Sector[a]			
			HGL[b]									
	Aviation Gasoline	Distillate Fuel Oil[c]	Propane[d]	Jet Fuel[e]	Lubricants	Motor Gasoline[f,g]	Residual Fuel Oil	Total	Distillate Fuel Oil[h]	Petroleum Coke	Residual Fuel Oil[i]	Total
1950 Average	**108**	**226**	**2**	**(e)**	**64**	**2,433**	**524**	**3,356**	**15**	**NA**	**192**	**207**
1955 Average	**192**	**372**	**9**	**154**	**70**	**3,221**	**440**	**4,458**	**15**	**NA**	**191**	**206**
1960 Average	**161**	**418**	**13**	**371**	**68**	**3,736**	**367**	**5,135**	**10**	**NA**	**231**	**241**
1965 Average	**120**	**514**	**23**	**602**	**67**	**4,374**	**336**	**6,036**	**14**	**NA**	**302**	**316**
1970 Average	**55**	**738**	**32**	**967**	**66**	**5,589**	**332**	**7,778**	**66**	**9**	**853**	**928**
1975 Average	**39**	**998**	**31**	**992**	**70**	**6,512**	**310**	**8,951**	**107**	**1**	**1,280**	**1,388**
1980 Average	**35**	**1,311**	**13**	**1,062**	**77**	**6,441**	**608**	**9,546**	**79**	**2**	**1,069**	**1,151**
1985 Average	**27**	**1,491**	**21**	**1,218**	**71**	**6,667**	**342**	**9,838**	**40**	**3**	**435**	**478**
1990 Average	**24**	**1,722**	**16**	**1,522**	**80**	**7,080**	**443**	**10,888**	**45**	**14**	**507**	**566**
1995 Average	**21**	**1,973**	**13**	**1,514**	**76**	**7,674**	**397**	**11,668**	**51**	**37**	**247**	**334**
2000 Average	**20**	**2,422**	**8**	**1,725**	**81**	**8,370**	**386**	**13,012**	**82**	**45**	**378**	**505**
2001 Average	**19**	**2,489**	**10**	**1,655**	**74**	**8,435**	**255**	**12,938**	**80**	**47**	**437**	**564**
2002 Average	**18**	**2,536**	**10**	**1,614**	**73**	**8,662**	**295**	**13,208**	**60**	**80**	**287**	**427**
2003 Average	**16**	**2,629**	**13**	**1,578**	**68**	**8,733**	**249**	**13,286**	**76**	**79**	**379**	**534**
2004 Average	**17**	**2,783**	**14**	**1,630**	**69**	**8,887**	**321**	**13,720**	**52**	**101**	**382**	**535**
2005 Average	**19**	**2,858**	**20**	**1,679**	**68**	**8,948**	**365**	**13,957**	**54**	**111**	**382**	**547**
2006 Average	**18**	**3,017**	**20**	**1,633**	**67**	**9,029**	**395**	**14,178**	**35**	**97**	**157**	**289**
2007 Average	**17**	**3,037**	**16**	**1,622**	**69**	**9,093**	**433**	**14,287**	**42**	**78**	**173**	**293**
2008 Average	**15**	**2,738**	**29**	**1,539**	**64**	**8,834**	**402**	**13,621**	**34**	**70**	**104**	**209**
2009 Average	**14**	**2,626**	**20**	**1,393**	**57**	**8,841**	**344**	**13,297**	**33**	**63**	**79**	**175**
2010 Average	**15**	**2,764**	[d] **5**	**1,432**	**70**	**8,824**	**389**	**13,499**	**38**	**65**	**67**	**170**
2011 Average	**15**	**2,849**	**5**	**1,425**	**67**	**8,591**	**338**	**13,291**	**30**	**66**	**41**	**137**
2012 Average	**14**	**2,719**	**5**	**1,398**	**61**	**8,525**	**291**	**13,013**	**25**	**41**	**33**	**99**
2013 Average	**12**	**2,804**	**5**	**1,434**	**65**	**8,679**	**253**	**13,253**	**26**	**59**	**34**	**119**
2014 Average	**12**	**2,928**	**5**	**1,470**	**67**	**8,778**	**195**	**13,455**	**39**	**57**	**41**	**137**
2015 Average	**11**	**2,974**	**5**	**1,548**	**74**	[g] **8,835**	**202**	**13,649**	**33**	**54**	**41**	**128**
2016 Average	**11**	**2,944**	**5**	**1,614**	**70**	**8,973**	**271**	**13,887**	**26**	**57**	**31**	**113**
2017 January	9	2,588	6	1,588	72	8,198	476	12,937	30	58	28	116
February	9	2,781	5	1,517	68	8,680	234	13,295	25	49	26	99
March	10	2,948	5	1,676	76	8,986	273	13,975	26	41	24	91
April	11	2,930	5	1,644	68	8,957	239	13,853	21	27	24	72
May	12	3,088	5	1,669	70	9,203	307	14,353	25	52	26	104
June	17	3,134	5	1,762	64	9,417	296	14,694	23	57	30	110
July	13	3,074	5	1,734	62	9,247	242	14,375	22	54	26	101
August	14	3,206	4	1,762	49	9,397	294	14,726	20	47	30	97
September	10	3,078	4	1,627	61	9,037	254	14,071	22	45	27	95
October	9	3,079	5	1,751	65	9,017	274	14,201	23	36	27	86
November	11	2,985	5	1,685	65	8,779	341	13,872	24	47	24	96
December	12	2,806	6	1,756	50	8,911	239	13,780	50	46	51	147
Average	**11**	**2,976**	**5**	**1,682**	**64**	**8,988**	**290**	**14,016**	**26**	**47**	**29**	**101**
2018 January	10	2,801	7	1,586	56	8,424	209	13,092	166	56	106	328
February	7	2,849	6	1,599	56	8,497	239	13,252	20	49	24	93
March	13	3,048	6	1,718	71	9,103	186	14,145	20	39	21	80
April	13	3,146	5	1,634	53	8,853	359	14,063	23	40	24	87
May	12	3,298	5	1,707	59	9,203	266	14,549	26	25	26	78
June	15	3,257	5	1,854	71	9,442	202	14,845	26	49	30	105
July	16	3,289	5	1,772	68	9,289	288	14,728	21	54	28	103
August	14	3,394	5	1,856	64	9,393	262	14,988	22	52	31	105
September	9	3,208	5	1,700	39	8,786	306	14,054	20	51	33	105
October	16	3,262	5	1,662	59	8,936	256	14,196	22	29	29	80
November	7	3,020	6	1,769	72	8,911	273	14,058	24	40	26	90
December	12	2,875	6	1,667	49	8,884	354	13,848	23	47	22	93
Average	**12**	**3,122**	**6**	**1,711**	**60**	**8,981**	**266**	**14,158**	**35**	**44**	**34**	**113**
2019 January	11	2,870	7	1,629	60	8,425	250	13,251	33	49	33	115
February	9	R 2,962	7	1,603	51	8,637	259	R 13,528	22	48	21	91
March	12	3,009	6	1,709	36	8,841	181	13,794	20	39	20	79
3-Month Average	**11**	**2,946**	**6**	**1,649**	**49**	**8,635**	**229**	**13,524**	**25**	**45**	**25**	**95**
2018 3-Month Average	**10**	**2,901**	**6**	**1,635**	**61**	**8,681**	**210**	**13,505**	**70**	**48**	**51**	**169**
2017 3-Month Average	**10**	**2,772**	**5**	**1,596**	**72**	**8,619**	**331**	**13,406**	**27**	**49**	**26**	**102**

[a] Electricity-only and combined-heat-and-power (CHP) plants within the NAICS 22 category whose primary business is to sell electricity, or electricity and heat, to the public. Through 1988, data are for electric utilities only; beginning in 1989, data are for electric utilities and independent power producers.

[b] Hydrocarbon gas liquids.

[c] Beginning in 2009, includes renewable diesel fuel (including biodiesel) blended into distillate fuel oil.

[d] There is a discontinuity in this time series between 2009 and 2010 due to a change in data sources.

[e] Beginning in 1957, includes kerosene-type jet fuel. For 1952–2004, also includes naphtha-type jet fuel. (Through 1951, naphtha-type jet fuel is included in the products from which it was blended—gasoline, kerosene, and distillate fuel oil. Beginning in 2005, naphtha-type jet fuel is included in "Other" on Table 3.7b.)

[f] Finished motor gasoline. Through 1963, also includes special naphthas. Beginning in 1993, also includes fuel ethanol blended into motor gasoline.

[g] There is a discontinuity in this time series between 2014 and 2015 due to a change in the method for allocating motor gasoline consumption to the end-use sectors. Beginning in 2015, the commercial and industrial sector shares of motor gasoline consumption are larger than in 2014, while the transportation sector share is smaller.

[h] Fuel oil nos. 1, 2, and 4. Through 1979, data are for gas turbine and internal combustion plant use of petroleum. Through 2000, electric utility data also include small amounts of kerosene and jet fuel.

[i] Fuel oil nos. 5 and 6. Through 1979, data are for steam plant use of petroleum. Through 2000, electric utility data also include a small amount of fuel oil no. 4.

R=Revised. NA=Not available.

Notes: • Transportation sector data are estimates. • For total petroleum consumption by all sectors, see petroleum products supplied data in Table 3.5. Petroleum products supplied is an approximation of petroleum consumption and is synonymous with the term "petroleum consumption" in Tables 3.7a–3.8c. Other measurements of consumption by fuel type or sector may differ. For example, jet fuel product supplied may not equal jet fuel consumed by U.S-flagged aircraft. See Note 1, "Petroleum Products Supplied and Petroleum Consumption," at end of section. • Totals may not equal sum of components due to independent rounding. • Geographic coverage is the 50 states and the District of Columbia.

Web Page: See http://www.eia.gov/totalenergy/data/monthly/#petroleum (Excel and CSV files) for all available annual data beginning in 1949 and monthly data beginning in 1973.

Sources: See end of section.

Source: *U.S. Energy Information Administration, Monthly Energy Review, June 2019*

Figure 3.8a Heat Content of Petroleum Consumption by End-Use Sector, 1949-2018
(Quadrillion Btu)

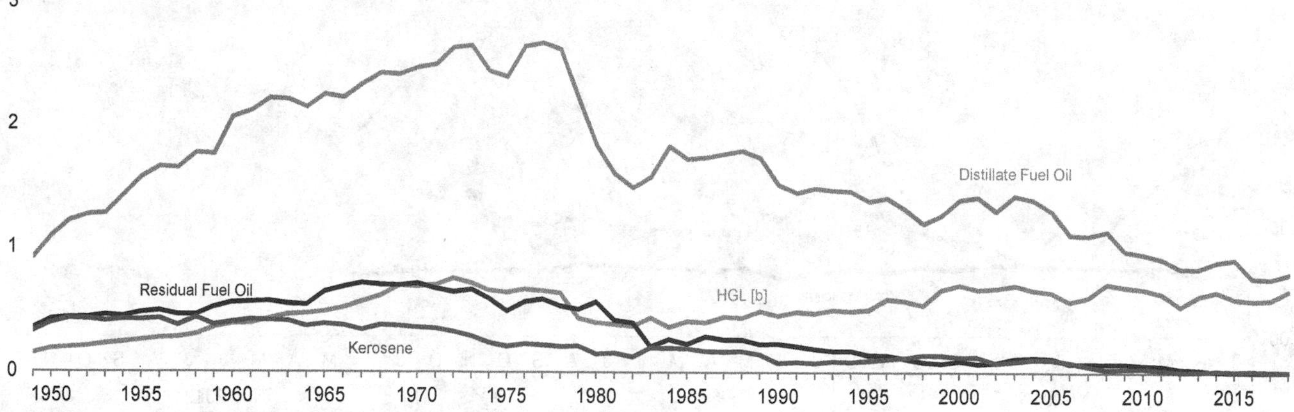

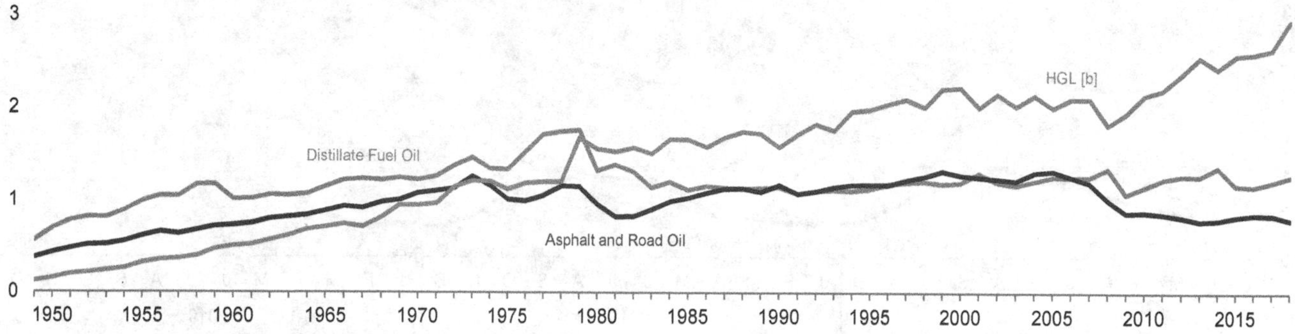

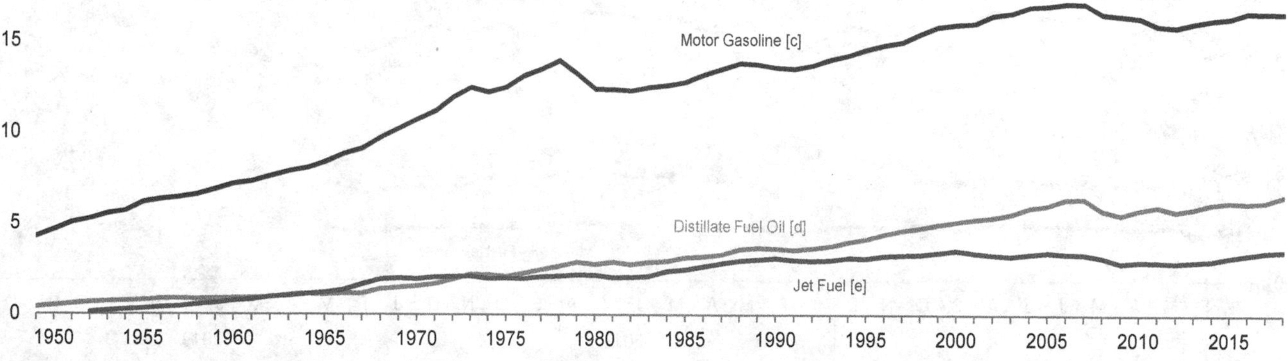

[a] Includes combined-heat-and-power plants and a small number of electricity-only plants.
[b] Hydrocarbon gas liquids.
[c] Beginning in 1993, includes fuel ethanol blended into motor gasoline.
[d] Beginning in 2009, includes renewable diesel fuel (including biodiesel) blended into distillate fuel oil.
[e] Beginning in 2005, includes kerosene-type jet fuel only.

Note: Petroleum products supplied is an approximation of petroleum consumption and is synonymous with the term "petroleum consumption" in Tables 3.7a–3.8c. Other measurements of consumption by fuel type or sector may differ. For example, jet fuel product supplied may not equal jet fuel consumed by U.S.-flagged aircraft.
Web Page: http://www.eia.gov/totalenergy/data/monthly/#petroleum.
Sources: Tables 3.8a–3.8c.

Source: *U.S. Energy Information Administration, Monthly Energy Review, June 2019*

Figure 3.8b Heat Content of Petroleum Consumption by End-Use Sector, Monthly
(Quadrillion Btu)

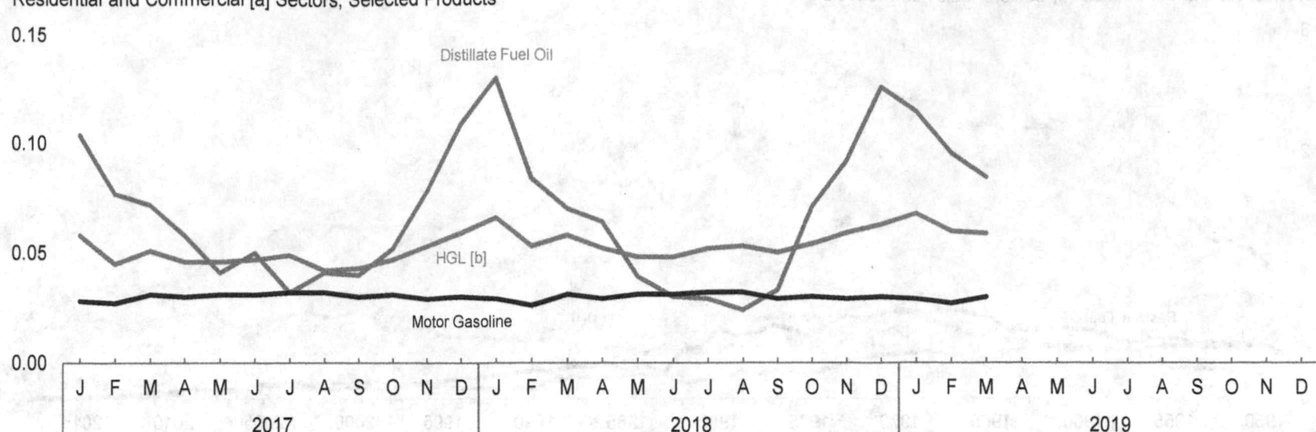

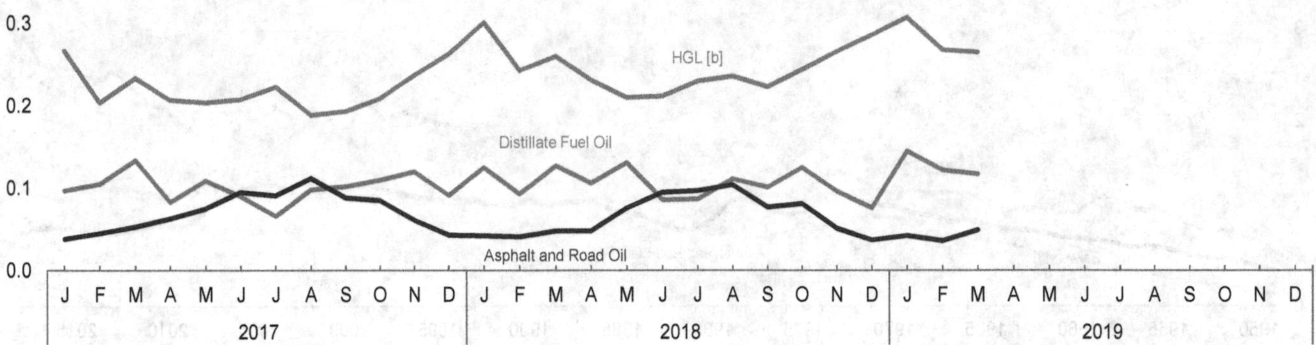

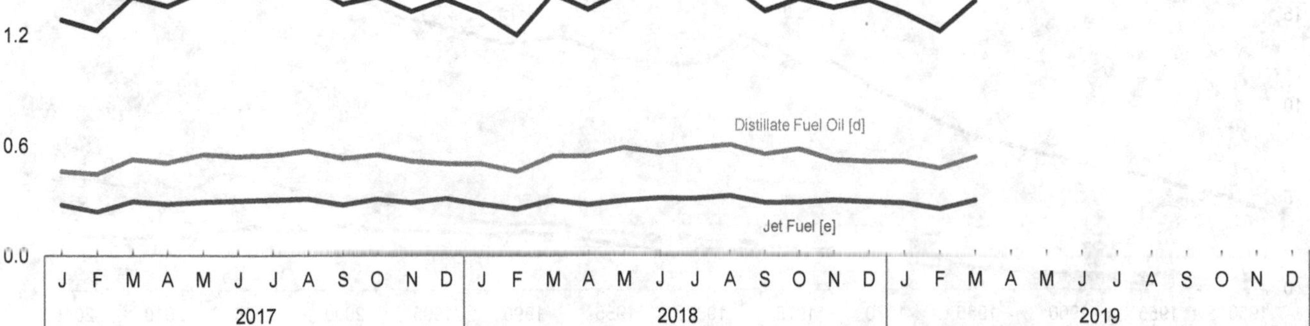

[a] Includes combined-heat-and-power plants and a small number of electricity-only plants.
[b] Hydrocarbon gas liquids.
[c] Includes fuel ethanol blended into motor gasoline.
[d] Includes renewable diesel fuel (including biodiesel) blended into distillate fuel oil.
[e] Includes kerosene-type jet fuel only.

Note: Petroleum products supplied is an approximation of petroleum consumption and is synonymous with the term "petroleum consumption" in Tables 3.7a–3.8c. Other measurements of consumption by fuel type or sector may differ. For example, jet fuel product supplied may not equal jet fuel consumed by U.S.-flagged aircraft.
Web Page: http://www.eia.gov/totalenergy/data/monthly/#petroleum.
Sources: Tables 3.8a–3.8c.

Source: *U.S. Energy Information Administration, Monthly Energy Review, June 2019*

Table 3.8a Heat Content of Petroleum Consumption: Residential and Commercial Sectors
(Trillion Btu)

	Residential Sector				Commercial Sector[a]						
		HGL[b]				HGL[b]					
	Distillate Fuel Oil	Propane	Kero-sene	Total	Distillate Fuel Oil	Propane	Kero-sene	Motor Gasoline[c,d]	Petroleum Coke	Residual Fuel Oil	Total
1950 Total	**829**	**146**	**347**	**1,322**	**262**	**39**	**47**	**100**	**NA**	**424**	**872**
1955 Total	**1,194**	**202**	**371**	**1,767**	**377**	**54**	**51**	**133**	**NA**	**480**	**1,095**
1960 Total	**1,568**	**305**	**354**	**2,227**	**494**	**81**	**48**	**67**	**NA**	**559**	**1,248**
1965 Total	**1,713**	**385**	**334**	**2,432**	**534**	**103**	**54**	**77**	**NA**	**645**	**1,413**
1970 Total	**1,878**	**549**	**298**	**2,725**	**587**	**143**	**61**	**86**	**NA**	**714**	**1,592**
1975 Total	**1,807**	**512**	**161**	**2,479**	**587**	**129**	**49**	**89**	**NA**	**492**	**1,346**
1980 Total	**1,316**	**311**	**107**	**1,734**	**518**	**88**	**41**	**107**	**NA**	**565**	**1,318**
1985 Total	**1,092**	**314**	**159**	**1,565**	**631**	**95**	**33**	**96**	**NA**	**228**	**1,083**
1990 Total	**978**	**352**	**64**	**1,394**	**536**	**102**	**12**	**111**	**0**	**230**	**991**
1995 Total	**904**	**395**	**74**	**1,373**	**478**	**109**	**22**	**18**	**(s)**	**141**	**769**
2000 Total	**904**	**555**	**95**	**1,553**	**490**	**150**	**30**	**44**	**(s)**	**92**	**807**
2001 Total	**907**	**526**	**95**	**1,528**	**508**	**143**	**31**	**37**	**(s)**	**70**	**789**
2002 Total	**859**	**537**	**60**	**1,456**	**444**	**141**	**16**	**45**	**(s)**	**80**	**725**
2003 Total	**931**	**544**	**70**	**1,546**	**496**	**157**	**19**	**60**	**(s)**	**111**	**842**
2004 Total	**923**	**512**	**85**	**1,519**	**470**	**152**	**20**	**45**	**(s)**	**122**	**810**
2005 Total	**853**	**513**	**84**	**1,450**	**447**	**131**	**22**	**46**	**(s)**	**116**	**762**
2006 Total	**709**	**446**	**66**	**1,221**	**400**	**123**	**15**	**48**	**(s)**	**75**	**662**
2007 Total	**721**	**484**	**44**	**1,249**	**381**	**121**	**9**	**60**	**(s)**	**75**	**648**
2008 Total	**750**	**553**	**21**	**1,324**	**384**	**158**	**4**	**45**	**(s)**	**71**	**662**
2009 Total	**582**	**547**	**28**	**1,157**	**395**	**139**	**4**	**52**	**(s)**	**71**	**662**
2010 Total	**562**	**529**	**29**	**1,120**	**391**	**140**	**5**	**52**	**(s)**	**62**	**650**
2011 Total	**523**	**492**	**19**	**1,033**	**391**	**142**	**3**	**44**	**(s)**	**54**	**635**
2012 Total	**482**	**395**	**8**	**885**	**355**	**135**	**1**	**39**	**(s)**	**31**	**562**
2013 Total	**491**	**463**	**8**	**963**	**344**	**151**	**1**	**40**	**(s)**	**24**	**561**
2014 Total	**533**	**489**	**14**	**1,036**	**357**	**160**	**2**	**54**	**1**	**8**	**581**
2015 Total	**551**	**445**	**10**	**1,007**	**360**	**148**	**1**	**[d] 376**	**1**	**4**	**890**
2016 Total	**435**	**429**	**14**	**878**	**326**	**150**	**2**	**375**	**(s)**	**4**	**857**
2017 January	59	43	3	105	44	15	(s)	28	(s)	1	89
February	44	33	1	79	33	12	(s)	27	(s)	(s)	72
March	41	38	(s)	80	31	14	(s)	31	(s)	(s)	76
April	33	34	(s)	67	25	12	(s)	30	(s)	(s)	67
May	24	34	(s)	58	18	12	(s)	31	(s)	(s)	62
June	29	34	(s)	63	21	12	(s)	31	(s)	(s)	65
July	18	36	(s)	54	14	13	(s)	32	(s)	(s)	58
August	24	31	(s)	55	18	11	(s)	32	(s)	(s)	61
September	23	31	2	56	17	11	(s)	30	(s)	(s)	59
October	30	34	(s)	65	22	12	(s)	31	(s)	(s)	66
November	45	39	(s)	84	33	14	(s)	29	(s)	(s)	77
December	63	43	(s)	106	47	16	(s)	30	(s)	1	93
Total	**432**	**430**	**8**	**871**	**323**	**155**	**1**	**361**	**(s)**	**4**	**844**
2018 January	74	48	6	128	56	17	1	29	(s)	1	103
February	48	39	(s)	87	36	14	(s)	26	(s)	(s)	77
March	40	43	(s)	83	30	15	(s)	31	(s)	(s)	77
April	37	38	(s)	75	27	14	(s)	29	(s)	(s)	71
May	22	35	1	59	17	13	(s)	31	0	(s)	61
June	17	35	(s)	53	13	13	(s)	31	0	(s)	57
July	16	38	(s)	55	12	14	(s)	32	0	(s)	58
August	14	39	(s)	53	10	14	(s)	32	0	(s)	57
September	19	37	(s)	56	14	13	(s)	29	(s)	(s)	57
October	41	40	1	81	30	14	(s)	30	(s)	(s)	76
November	53	43	(s)	96	39	16	(s)	29	(s)	(s)	85
December	72	46	(s)	119	54	17	(s)	30	(s)	1	102
Total	**454**	**483**	**8**	**945**	**339**	**175**	**1**	**361**	**(s)**	**4**	**879**
2019 January	66	50	4	119	49	18	1	29	(s)	1	97
February	55	44	2	101	41	16	(s)	27	(s)	(s)	84
March	49	44	1	93	36	16	(s)	30	(s)	(s)	83
3-Month Total	**170**	**137**	**6**	**313**	**127**	**50**	**1**	**85**	**(s)**	**1**	**264**
2018 3-Month Total	**162**	**130**	**6**	**298**	**121**	**47**	**1**	**86**	**(s)**	**1**	**256**
2017 3-Month Total	**145**	**114**	**5**	**263**	**108**	**41**	**1**	**85**	**(s)**	**1**	**237**

[a] Commercial sector fuel use, including that at commercial combined-heat-and-power (CHP) and commercial electricity-only plants.
[b] Hydrocarbon gas liquids.
[c] Finished motor gasoline. Through 1963, also includes special naphthas. Beginning in 1993, also includes fuel ethanol blended into motor gasoline.
[d] There is a discontinuity in this time series between 2014 and 2015 due to a change in the method for allocating motor gasoline consumption to the end-use sectors. Beginning in 2015, the commercial and industrial sector shares of motor gasoline consumption are larger than in 2014, while the transportation sector share is smaller.
NA=Not available. (s)=Less than 0.5 trillion Btu and greater than -0.5 trillion Btu.

Notes: • Data are estimates. • For total heat content of petroleum consumption by all sectors, see data for heat content of petroleum products supplied in Table 3.6. Petroleum products supplied is an approximation of petroleum consumption and is synonymous with the term "petroleum consumption" in Tables 3.7a–3.8c. See Note 1, "Petroleum Products Supplied and Petroleum Consumption," at end of section. • Totals may not equal sum of components due to independent rounding. • Geographic coverage is the 50 states and the District of Columbia.

Web Page: See http://www.eia.gov/totalenergy/data/monthly/#petroleum (Excel and CSV files) for all available annual data beginning in 1949 and monthly data beginning in 1973.

Sources: See end of section.

Source: *U.S. Energy Information Administration, Monthly Energy Review, June 2019*

Table 3.8b Heat Content of Petroleum Consumption: Industrial Sector
(Trillion Btu)

	Industrial Sector[a]										
	Asphalt and Road Oil	Distillate Fuel Oil	HGL[b]		Kerosene	Lubricants	Motor Gasoline[e,f]	Petroleum Coke	Residual Fuel Oil	Other[g]	Total
			Propane[c]	Total[d]							
1950 Total	435	698	NA	156	274	94	251	90	1,416	546	3,960
1955 Total	615	991	NA	323	241	103	332	147	1,573	798	5,123
1960 Total	734	1,016	NA	507	161	107	381	328	1,584	947	5,766
1965 Total	890	1,150	NA	712	165	137	342	444	1,582	1,390	6,813
1970 Total	1,082	1,226	359	953	185	155	288	446	1,624	1,817	7,776
1975 Total	1,014	1,339	422	1,161	119	149	223	540	1,509	2,071	8,127
1980 Total	962	1,324	725	1,763	181	182	158	516	1,349	3,073	9,509
1985 Total	1,029	1,119	797	1,871	44	166	218	575	748	1,945	7,714
1990 Total	1,170	1,150	807	1,832	12	186	185	714	411	2,589	8,251
1995 Total	1,178	1,130	1,013	2,328	15	178	200	721	337	2,499	8,586
2000 Total	1,276	1,199	1,016	2,571	16	190	150	796	241	2,636	9,074
2001 Total	1,257	1,299	916	2,278	23	174	295	858	203	2,793	9,179
2002 Total	1,240	1,203	1,055	2,383	14	172	308	842	190	2,816	9,169
2003 Total	1,220	1,169	981	2,249	24	159	323	825	220	3,043	9,233
2004 Total	1,304	1,213	1,109	2,364	28	161	371	937	249	3,205	9,832
2005 Total	1,323	1,262	1,049	2,205	39	160	354	894	281	3,122	9,641
2006 Total	1,261	1,258	1,105	2,244	30	156	374	938	239	3,276	9,776
2007 Total	1,197	1,256	1,102	2,285	13	161	302	910	193	3,134	9,451
2008 Total	1,012	1,348	870	1,976	4	150	245	870	194	2,788	8,587
2009 Total	873	1,073	910	2,077	4	135	238	805	130	2,483	7,818
2010 Total	878	1,153	947	2,300	7	136	260	694	120	2,645	8,193
2011 Total	859	1,236	972	2,257	4	127	254	663	135	2,621	8,157
2012 Total	827	1,271	1,112	2,455	2	118	252	717	70	2,474	8,186
2013 Total	783	1,266	1,164	2,646	1	125	263	663	48	2,583	8,380
2014 Total	793	1,366	977	2,516	3	131	210	653	41	2,430	8,142
2015 Total	832	1,170	1,027	2,731	2	142	258	663	34	2,435	8,266
2016 Total	853	1,157	1,000	2,703	2	135	262	653	52	2,553	8,371
2017 January	38	97	138	279	(s)	12	20	69	7	209	731
February	45	105	94	215	(s)	10	20	32	3	196	626
March	53	134	91	249	(s)	13	22	27	4	237	739
April	63	83	74	222	(s)	11	22	49	3	239	691
May	75	109	58	220	(s)	12	23	56	4	226	726
June	95	90	51	211	(s)	10	23	41	4	240	714
July	91	66	61	233	(s)	10	23	76	3	231	734
August	112	98	62	201	(s)	8	23	48	4	221	715
September	88	102	80	207	(s)	10	22	56	4	204	692
October	85	110	63	241	(s)	11	23	27	4	224	723
November	61	120	93	252	(s)	10	21	64	5	217	753
December	43	91	105	281	(s)	8	22	65	4	224	738
Total	849	1,205	972	2,810	1	125	264	610	50	2,667	8,582
2018 January	42	125	136	314	1	9	21	58	4	227	802
February	41	93	97	257	(s)	8	19	27	3	217	665
March	48	127	98	273	(s)	12	23	48	3	236	770
April	48	106	74	243	(s)	8	21	48	5	192	672
May	76	131	47	225	(s)	10	23	55	4	215	737
June	95	86	47	225	(s)	11	23	57	3	222	722
July	97	87	56	250	(s)	11	23	54	4	215	742
August	104	111	59	260	(s)	11	23	76	4	228	818
September	77	101	65	247	(s)	6	21	68	4	185	711
October	81	125	76	267	(s)	10	22	74	4	234	817
November	51	96	91	291	(s)	12	22	43	4	198	716
December	37	76	114	315	(s)	8	22	43	5	218	724
Total	797	1,265	960	3,167	1	116	264	650	46	2,588	8,895
2019 January	42	145	134	338	(s)	10	21	45	4	205	811
February	36	122	99	293	(s)	8	19	14	3	163	658
March	49	117	90	290	(s)	6	22	54	3	204	744
3-Month Total	127	383	324	921	1	24	63	114	10	572	2,213
2018 3-Month Total	130	346	331	845	1	29	63	133	10	680	2,237
2017 3-Month Total	136	336	324	743	1	35	63	128	14	642	2,096

[a] Industrial sector fuel use, including that at industrial combined-heat-and-power (CHP) and industrial electricity-only plants.

[b] Hydrocarbon gas liquids.

[c] Propane and propylene. Through 1983, also includes 40% of "Butane-Propane Mixtures" and 30% of "Ethane-Propane Mixtures."

[d] Ethane, propane, normal butane, isobutane, natural gasoline (pentanes plus), and refinery olefins (ethylene, propylene, butylene, and isobutylene). Through 1983, also includes plant condensate and unfractionated stream.

[e] Finished motor gasoline. Through 1963, also includes special naphthas. Beginning in 1993, also includes fuel ethanol blended into motor gasoline.

[f] There is a discontinuity in this time series between 2014 and 2015 due to a change in the method for allocating motor gasoline consumption to the end-use sectors. Beginning in 2015, the commercial and industrial sector shares of motor gasoline consumption are larger than in 2014, while the transportation sector share is smaller.

[g] Petrochemical feedstocks, still gas (refinery gas), waxes, and miscellaneous products. Beginning in 1964, also includes special naphthas. Beginning in 1981, also includes negative barrels per day of distillate and residual fuel oil reclassified as unfinished oils, and other products (from both primary and secondary supply) reclassified as gasoline blending components. Beginning in 1983, also includes crude oil burned as fuel. Beginning in 2005, also includes naphtha-type jet fuel.

NA=Not available. (s)=Less than 0.5 trillion Btu and greater than -0.5 trillion Btu.

Notes: • Data are estimates. • For total heat content of petroleum consumption by all sectors, see data for heat content of petroleum products supplied in Table 3.6. Petroleum products supplied is an approximation of petroleum consumption and is synonymous with the term "petroleum consumption" in Tables 3.7a–3.8c. See Note 1, "Petroleum Products Supplied and Petroleum Consumption," at end of section. • Totals may not equal sum of components due to independent rounding. • Geographic coverage is the 50 states and the District of Columbia.

Web Page: See http://www.eia.gov/totalenergy/data/monthly/#petroleum (Excel and CSV files) for all available annual data beginning in 1949 and monthly data beginning in 1973.

Sources: See end of section.

Source: *U.S. Energy Information Administration, Monthly Energy Review, June 2019*

Table 3.8c Heat Content of Petroleum Consumption: Transportation and Electric Power Sectors (Trillion Btu)

	Transportation Sector								Electric Power Sector[a]			
			HGL[b]									
	Aviation Gasoline	Distillate Fuel Oil[c]	Propane[d]	Jet Fuel[e]	Lubri-cants	Motor Gasoline[f,g]	Residual Fuel Oil	Total	Distillate Fuel Oil[h]	Petroleum Coke	Residual Fuel Oil[i]	Total
1950 Total	**199**	**480**	**3**	**(e)**	**141**	**4,664**	**1,201**	**6,690**	**32**	**NA**	**440**	**472**
1955 Total	**354**	**791**	**13**	**301**	**155**	**6,175**	**1,009**	**8,799**	**32**	**NA**	**439**	**471**
1960 Total	**298**	**892**	**19**	**739**	**152**	**7,183**	**844**	**10,125**	**22**	**NA**	**530**	**553**
1965 Total	**222**	**1,093**	**32**	**1,215**	**149**	**8,386**	**770**	**11,866**	**29**	**NA**	**693**	**722**
1970 Total	**100**	**1,569**	**44**	**1,973**	**147**	**10,716**	**761**	**15,310**	**141**	**19**	**1,958**	**2,117**
1975 Total	**71**	**2,121**	**43**	**2,029**	**155**	**12,485**	**711**	**17,615**	**226**	**2**	**2,937**	**3,166**
1980 Total	**64**	**2,795**	**18**	**2,179**	**172**	**12,383**	**1,398**	**19,009**	**169**	**5**	**2,459**	**2,634**
1985 Total	**50**	**3,170**	**30**	**2,497**	**156**	**12,784**	**786**	**19,472**	**85**	**7**	**998**	**1,090**
1990 Total	**45**	**3,661**	**23**	**3,129**	**176**	**13,575**	**1,016**	**21,626**	**97**	**30**	**1,163**	**1,289**
1995 Total	**40**	**4,191**	**18**	**3,132**	**168**	**14,576**	**911**	**23,036**	**108**	**81**	**566**	**755**
2000 Total	**36**	**5,159**	**12**	**3,580**	**179**	**15,933**	**888**	**25,787**	**175**	**99**	**871**	**1,144**
2001 Total	**35**	**5,286**	**14**	**3,426**	**164**	**16,013**	**586**	**25,524**	**170**	**103**	**1,003**	**1,276**
2002 Total	**34**	**5,387**	**14**	**3,340**	**162**	**16,437**	**677**	**26,051**	**127**	**175**	**659**	**961**
2003 Total	**30**	**5,584**	**18**	**3,265**	**150**	**16,565**	**571**	**26,184**	**161**	**175**	**869**	**1,205**
2004 Total	**31**	**5,925**	**19**	**3,383**	**152**	**16,901**	**740**	**27,150**	**111**	**211**	**879**	**1,201**
2005 Total	**35**	**6,068**	**28**	**3,475**	**151**	**16,958**	**837**	**27,553**	**114**	**231**	**876**	**1,222**
2006 Total	**33**	**6,390**	**27**	**3,379**	**147**	**17,088**	**906**	**27,972**	**73**	**203**	**361**	**637**
2007 Total	**32**	**6,411**	**22**	**3,358**	**152**	**17,066**	**994**	**28,034**	**89**	**163**	**397**	**648**
2008 Total	**28**	**5,792**	**40**	**3,193**	**141**	**16,510**	**926**	**26,630**	**73**	**146**	**240**	**459**
2009 Total	**27**	**5,537**	**28**	**2,883**	**127**	**16,422**	**791**	**25,814**	**70**	**132**	**181**	**382**
2010 Total	**27**	**5,826**	[d] **7**	**2,963**	**155**	**16,320**	**892**	**26,190**	**80**	**137**	**154**	**370**
2011 Total	**27**	**5,997**	**7**	**2,950**	**148**	**15,877**	**776**	**25,783**	**64**	**138**	**93**	**295**
2012 Total	**25**	**5,736**	**7**	**2,901**	**135**	**15,795**	**671**	**25,270**	**52**	**85**	**77**	**214**
2013 Total	**22**	**5,894**	**7**	**2,969**	**143**	**16,030**	**581**	**25,646**	**55**	**123**	**77**	**255**
2014 Total	**22**	**6,154**	**7**	**3,042**	**149**	**16,209**	**447**	**26,030**	**82**	**118**	**95**	**295**
2015 Total	**21**	**6,251**	**7**	**3,204**	**163**	[g] **16,308**	**463**	**26,416**	**70**	**112**	**94**	**276**
2016 Total	**20**	**6,197**	**7**	**3,350**	**154**	**16,601**	**623**	**26,953**	**55**	**118**	**71**	**244**
2017 January	1	462	1	279	14	1,284	93	2,134	5	10	5	21
February	1	448	1	241	12	1,228	41	1,972	4	8	5	16
March	2	526	1	295	14	1,408	53	2,298	5	7	5	17
April	2	506	1	280	12	1,358	45	2,203	4	5	4	13
May	2	550	1	293	13	1,442	60	2,361	5	9	5	19
June	3	541	1	300	12	1,428	56	2,338	4	10	6	19
July	2	548	1	305	12	1,448	47	2,362	4	10	5	18
August	2	572	1	310	9	1,472	57	2,422	4	8	6	18
September	1	531	1	277	11	1,370	48	2,239	4	8	5	17
October	1	549	1	308	12	1,412	53	2,337	4	6	5	16
November	2	515	1	287	12	1,331	64	2,211	4	8	4	17
December	2	500	1	309	9	1,396	47	2,263	9	8	10	27
Total	**21**	**6,248**	**7**	**3,481**	**142**	**16,576**	**665**	**27,140**	**55**	**97**	**66**	**218**
2018 January	1	500	1	279	10	1,320	41	2,152	30	10	21	60
February	1	459	1	254	10	1,202	42	1,969	3	8	4	15
March	2	544	1	302	13	1,426	36	2,324	4	7	4	15
April	2	543	1	278	10	1,342	68	2,243	4	7	4	15
May	2	588	1	300	11	1,442	52	2,396	5	4	5	14
June	2	562	1	315	13	1,432	38	2,363	5	8	6	19
July	3	587	1	312	13	1,455	56	2,426	4	10	6	19
August	2	605	1	326	12	1,472	51	2,469	4	9	6	19
September	1	554	1	289	7	1,332	58	2,242	4	9	6	19
October	3	582	1	292	11	1,400	50	2,338	4	5	6	15
November	1	521	1	301	13	1,351	51	2,240	4	7	5	16
December	2	513	1	293	9	1,392	69	2,279	4	8	4	17
Total	**22**	**6,559**	**8**	**3,541**	**132**	**16,567**	**612**	**27,440**	**70**	**92**	**77**	**243**
2019 January	2	512	1	286	11	1,320	49	2,181	6	9	6	21
February	1	R 477	1	255	9	1,222	46	R 2,010	4	8	4	15
March	2	537	1	300	7	1,385	35	2,267	4	7	4	14
3-Month Total	**5**	**1,526**	**2**	**841**	**27**	**3,928**	**130**	**6,458**	**13**	**23**	**14**	**50**
2018 3-Month Total	**5**	**1,503**	**2**	**835**	**33**	**3,948**	**119**	**6,445**	**36**	**25**	**29**	**90**
2017 3-Month Total	**4**	**1,436**	**2**	**815**	**39**	**3,920**	**187**	**6,403**	**14**	**25**	**15**	**54**

[a] Electricity-only and combined-heat-and-power (CHP) plants within the NAICS 22 category whose primary business is to sell electricity, or electricity and heat, to the public. Through 1988, data are for electric utilities only; beginning in 1989, data are for electric utilities and independent power producers.

[b] Hydrocarbon gas liquids.

[c] Beginning in 2009, includes renewable diesel fuel (including biodiesel) blended into distillate fuel oil.

[d] There is a discontinuity in this time series between 2009 and 2010 due to a change in data sources.

[e] Beginning in 1957, includes kerosene-type jet fuel. For 1952–2004, also includes naphtha-type jet fuel. (Through 1951, naphtha-type jet fuel is included in the products from which it was blended—gasoline, kerosene, and distillate fuel oil. Beginning in 2005, naphtha-type jet fuel is included in "Other" on Table 3.8b.)

[f] Finished motor gasoline. Through 1963, also includes special naphthas. Beginning in 1993, also includes fuel ethanol blended into motor gasoline.

[g] There is a discontinuity in this time series between 2014 and 2015 due to a change in the method for allocating motor gasoline consumption to the end-use sectors. Beginning in 2015, the commercial and industrial sector shares of motor gasoline consumption are larger than in 2014, while the transportation sector share is smaller.

[h] Fuel oil nos. 1, 2, and 4. Through 1979, data are for gas turbine and internal combustion plant use of petroleum. Through 2000, electric utility data also include small amounts of kerosene and jet fuel.

[i] Fuel oil nos. 5 and 6. Through 1979, data are for steam plant use of petroleum. Through 2000, electric utility data also include a small amount of fuel oil no. 4.

R=Revised. NA=Not available.

Notes: • Transportation sector data are estimates. • For total heat content of petroleum consumption by all sectors, see data for heat content of petroleum products supplied in Table 3.6. Petroleum products supplied is an approximation of petroleum consumption and is synonymous with the term "petroleum consumption" in Tables 3.7a–3.8c. Other measurements of consumption by fuel type or sector may differ. For example, jet fuel product supplied may not equal jet fuel consumed by U.S.-flagged aircraft. See Note 1, "Petroleum Products Supplied and Petroleum Consumption," at end of section. • Totals may not equal sum of components due to independent rounding. • Geographic coverage is the 50 states and the District of Columbia.

Web Page: See http://www.eia.gov/totalenergy/data/monthly/#petroleum (Excel and CSV files) for all available annual data beginning in 1949 and monthly data beginning in 1973.

Sources: See end of section.

Source: *U.S. Energy Information Administration, Monthly Energy Review, June 2019*

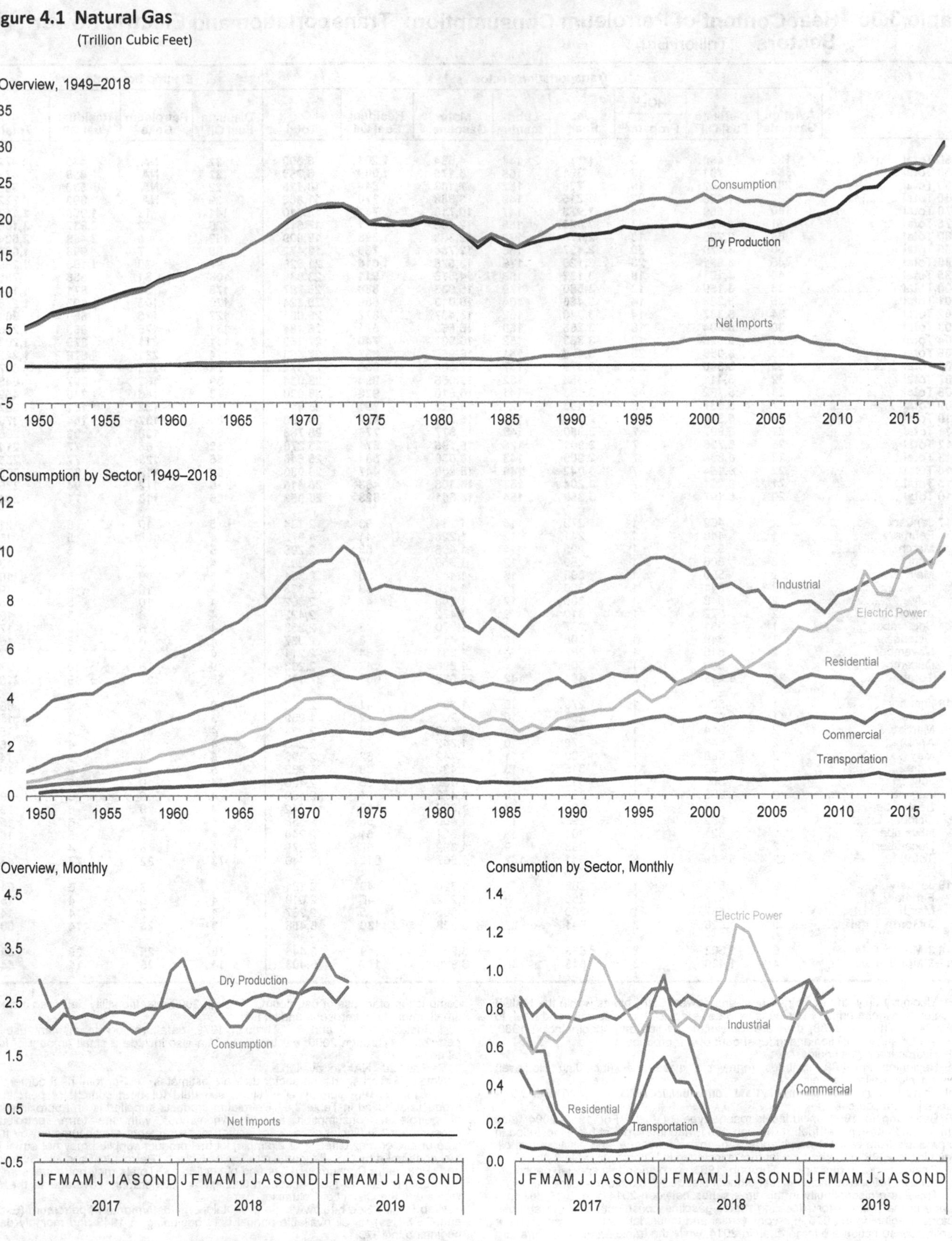

Web Page: http://www.eia.gov/totalenergy/data/monthly/#naturalgas.
Sources: Tables 4.1 and 4.3.

Source: *U.S. Energy Information Administration, Monthly Energy Review, June 2019*

Table 4.1 Natural Gas Overview

(Billion Cubic Feet)

	Gross With-drawals[a]	Marketed Production (Wet)[b]	NGPL Production[c]	Dry Gas Production[d]	Supple-mental Gaseous Fuels[e]	Trade			Net Storage With-drawals[f]	Balancing Item[g]	Consump-tion[h]
						Imports	Exports	Net Imports			
1950 Total	**8,480**	**[i]6,282**	**260**	**[i]6,022**	**NA**	**0**	**26**	**-26**	**-54**	**-175**	**5,767**
1955 Total	**11,720**	**[i]9,405**	**377**	**[i]9,029**	**NA**	**11**	**31**	**-20**	**-68**	**-247**	**8,694**
1960 Total	**15,088**	**[i]12,771**	**543**	**[i]12,228**	**NA**	**156**	**11**	**144**	**-132**	**-274**	**11,967**
1965 Total	**17,963**	**[i]16,040**	**753**	**[i]15,286**	**NA**	**456**	**26**	**430**	**-118**	**-319**	**15,280**
1970 Total	**23,786**	**[i]21,921**	**906**	**[i]21,014**	**NA**	**821**	**70**	**751**	**-398**	**-228**	**21,139**
1975 Total	**21,104**	**[i]20,109**	**872**	**[i]19,236**	**NA**	**953**	**73**	**880**	**-344**	**-235**	**19,538**
1980 Total	**21,870**	**20,180**	**777**	**19,403**	**155**	**985**	**49**	**936**	**23**	**-640**	**19,877**
1985 Total	**19,607**	**17,270**	**816**	**16,454**	**126**	**950**	**55**	**894**	**235**	**-428**	**17,281**
1990 Total	**21,523**	**18,594**	**784**	**17,810**	**123**	**1,532**	**86**	**1,447**	**-513**	**307**	**[j]19,174**
1995 Total	**23,744**	**19,506**	**908**	**18,599**	**110**	**2,841**	**154**	**2,687**	**415**	**396**	**22,207**
2000 Total	**24,174**	**20,198**	**1,016**	**19,182**	**90**	**3,782**	**244**	**3,538**	**829**	**-306**	**23,333**
2001 Total	**24,501**	**20,570**	**954**	**19,616**	**86**	**3,977**	**373**	**3,604**	**-1,166**	**99**	**22,239**
2002 Total	**23,941**	**19,885**	**957**	**18,928**	**68**	**4,015**	**516**	**3,499**	**467**	**65**	**23,027**
2003 Total	**24,119**	**19,974**	**876**	**19,099**	**68**	**3,944**	**680**	**3,264**	**-197**	**44**	**22,277**
2004 Total	**23,970**	**19,517**	**927**	**18,591**	**60**	**4,259**	**854**	**3,404**	**-114**	**461**	**22,403**
2005 Total	**23,457**	**18,927**	**876**	**18,051**	**64**	**4,341**	**729**	**3,612**	**52**	**236**	**22,014**
2006 Total	**23,535**	**19,410**	**906**	**18,504**	**66**	**4,186**	**724**	**3,462**	**-436**	**103**	**21,699**
2007 Total	**24,664**	**20,196**	**930**	**19,266**	**63**	**4,608**	**822**	**3,785**	**192**	**-203**	**23,104**
2008 Total	**25,636**	**21,112**	**953**	**20,159**	**61**	**3,984**	**963**	**3,021**	**34**	**2**	**23,277**
2009 Total	**26,057**	**21,648**	**1,024**	**20,624**	**65**	**3,751**	**1,072**	**2,679**	**-355**	**-103**	**22,910**
2010 Total	**26,816**	**22,382**	**1,066**	**21,316**	**65**	**3,741**	**1,137**	**2,604**	**-13**	**115**	**24,087**
2011 Total	**28,479**	**24,036**	**1,134**	**22,902**	**60**	**3,469**	**1,506**	**1,963**	**-354**	**-94**	**24,477**
2012 Total	**29,542**	**25,283**	**1,250**	**24,033**	**61**	**3,138**	**1,619**	**1,519**	**-9**	**-66**	**25,538**
2013 Total	**29,523**	**25,562**	**1,357**	**24,206**	**55**	**2,883**	**1,572**	**1,311**	**546**	**38**	**26,155**
2014 Total	**31,405**	**27,498**	**1,608**	**25,890**	**60**	**2,695**	**1,514**	**1,181**	**-254**	**-283**	**26,593**
2015 Total	**32,915**	**28,772**	**1,707**	**27,065**	**59**	**2,718**	**1,784**	**935**	**-547**	**-268**	**27,244**
2016 Total	**32,592**	**28,400**	**1,808**	**26,592**	**57**	**3,006**	**2,335**	**671**	**340**	**-216**	**27,444**
2017 January	2,749	2,355	154	2,202	5	292	272	20	687	-1	2,913
February	2,505	2,146	140	2,005	5	255	255	(s)	292	38	2,339
March	2,812	2,431	159	2,272	5	281	272	9	281	-45	2,523
April	2,703	2,355	154	2,201	5	238	247	-9	-236	-31	1,931
May	2,787	2,430	159	2,271	5	244	254	-10	-348	-28	1,891
June	2,693	2,370	155	2,215	5	240	253	-14	-287	-11	1,909
July	2,764	2,479	162	2,317	6	251	248	2	-155	-29	2,140
August	2,781	2,478	162	2,316	6	248	247	1	-201	-28	2,093
September	2,767	2,434	159	2,275	5	229	250	-21	-323	-17	1,920
October	2,907	2,550	166	2,384	6	244	281	-37	-254	-69	2,030
November	2,884	2,535	165	2,370	6	244	288	-45	90	-66	2,355
December	3,006	2,635	172	2,463	6	278	299	-22	707	-72	3,083
Total	**33,357**	**29,197**	**1,906**	**27,291**	**66**	**3,042**	**3,168**	**-125**	**254**	**-360**	**27,126**
2018 January	[E]2,959	[E]2,586	171	[E]2,415	6	304	301	3	896	-10	3,310
February	[E]2,724	[E]2,385	163	[E]2,222	6	241	276	-36	467	42	2,701
March	[E]3,048	[E]2,673	188	[E]2,485	6	274	292	-18	285	15	2,773
April	[E]2,960	[E]2,598	185	[E]2,413	5	244	279	-35	-32	-14	2,337
May	[E]3,082	[E]2,713	193	[E]2,521	5	229	273	-44	-423	-11	2,047
June	[E]2,955	[E]2,641	188	[E]2,453	6	230	[R]263	[R]-32	-349	[R]-28	2,050
July	[E]3,108	[E]2,784	198	[E]2,585	5	249	[R]307	[R]-58	-186	[R](s)	2,346
August	[E]3,180	[E]2,845	205	[E]2,640	6	239	[R]312	[R]-73	-235	[R]-26	2,311
September	[E]3,135	[E]2,790	199	[E]2,591	6	216	[R]302	[R]-86	-334	[R]-17	2,159
October	[E]3,272	[E]2,909	206	[E]2,703	6	217	[R]307	[R]-90	-291	[R]-52	2,276
November	[E]3,233	[E]2,855	198	[E]2,657	6	213	[R]338	[R]-125	205	[R]-55	2,688
December	[E]3,353	[E]2,957	200	[E]2,756	5	257	[R]363	[R]-106	320	[R]-17	2,959
Total	**[E]37,009**	**[E]32,735**	**2,295**	**[E]30,440**	**68**	**2,914**	**[R]3,614**	**[R]-700**	**323**	**[R]-173**	**29,958**
2019 January	[RE]3,356	[RE]2,955	204	[RE]2,751	5	[R]291	[R]365	[R]-74	709	[R]-11	3,379
February	[RE]3,044	[RE]2,691	191	[RE]2,501	6	[R]233	[R]329	[R]-96	568	[R]6	2,985
March	[E]3,364	[E]2,984	213	[E]2,771	6	253	372	-119	245	-20	2,882
3-Month Total	**[E]9,764**	**[E]8,630**	**608**	**[E]8,022**	**17**	**777**	**1,067**	**-289**	**1,522**	**-25**	**9,246**
2018 3-Month Total	**[E]8,731**	**[E]7,644**	**522**	**[E]7,122**	**19**	**819**	**869**	**-51**	**1,647**	**47**	**8,784**
2017 3-Month Total	**8,065**	**6,932**	**452**	**6,479**	**16**	**827**	**799**	**28**	**1,260**	**-9**	**7,775**

[a] Gases withdrawn from natural gas, crude oil, coalbed, and shale gas wells. Includes natural gas, natural gas plant liquids, and nonhydrocarbon gases; but excludes lease condensate.

[b] Gross withdrawals minus repressuring, nonhydrocarbon gases removed, and vented and flared. See Note 1, "Natural Gas Production," at end of section.

[c] Natural gas plant liquids (NGPL) production, gaseous equivalent. This data series was previously called "Extraction Loss." See Note 2, "Natural Gas Plant Liquids Production," at end of section.

[d] Marketed production (wet) minus NGPL production.

[e] See Note 3, "Supplemental Gaseous Fuels," at end of section.

[f] Net withdrawals from underground storage. For 1980–2017, also includes net withdrawals of liquefied natural gas in above-ground tanks. See Note 4, "Natural Gas Storage," at end of section.

[g] See Note 5, "Natural Gas Balancing Item," at end of section. Beginning in 1980, excludes transit shipments that cross the U.S.-Canada border (i.e., natural gas delivered to its destination via the other country).

[h] See Note 6, "Natural Gas Consumption," at end of section.

[i] Through 1979, may include unknown quantities of nonhydrocarbon gases.

[j] For 1989–1992, a small amount of consumption at independent power producers may be counted in both "Other Industrial" and "Electric Power Sector" on Table 4.3. See Note 7, "Natural Gas Consumption, 1989–1992," at end of section.

R=Revised. E=Estimate. (s)=Less than 0.5 billion cubic feet and greater than -0.5 billion cubic feet. NA=Not available.

Notes: • See Note 8, "Natural Gas Data Adjustments, 1993–2000," at end of section. • Through 1964, all volumes are shown on a pressure base of 14.65 psia (pounds per square inch absolute) at 60° Fahrenheit; beginning in 1965, the pressure base is 14.73 psia at 60° Fahrenheit. • Totals may not equal sum of components due to independent rounding. • Geographic coverage is the 50 states and the District of Columbia (except Alaska, for which underground storage is excluded from "Net Storage Withdrawals" through 2012).

Web Page: See http://www.eia.gov/totalenergy/data/monthly/#naturalgas (Excel and CSV files) for all available annual data beginning in 1949 and monthly data beginning in 1973.

Sources: • **Imports and Exports:** Table 4.2. • **Consumption:** Table 4.3. • **Balancing Item:** Calculated as consumption minus dry gas production, supplemental gaseous fuels, net imports, and net storage withdrawals. • **All Other Data: 1949–2017—**U.S. Energy Information Administration (EIA), *Natural Gas Annual,* annual reports. **2018 forward—**EIA, *Natural Gas Monthly,* May 2019, Table 1.

Source: *U.S. Energy Information Administration, Monthly Energy Review, June 2019*

Table 4.2 Natural Gas Trade by Country
(Billion Cubic Feet)

	Imports									Exports[a]				
	Algeria[b]	Canada[c]	Egypt[b]	Mexico[c]	Nigeria[b]	Qatar[b]	Trinidad and Tobago[b]	Other[b,d]	Total	Canada[c]	Japan[b]	Mexico[c]	Other[b,e]	Total
1950 Total	0	0	0	0	0	0	0	0	0	3	0	23	0	26
1955 Total	0	11	0	(s)	0	0	0	0	11	11	0	20	0	31
1960 Total	0	109	0	47	0	0	0	0	156	6	0	6	0	11
1965 Total	0	405	0	52	0	0	0	0	456	18	0	8	0	26
1970 Total	1	779	0	(s)	0	0	0	0	821	11	44	15	0	70
1975 Total	5	948	0	0	0	0	0	0	953	10	53	9	0	73
1980 Total	86	797	0	102	0	0	0	0	985	(s)	45	4	0	49
1985 Total	24	926	0	0	0	0	0	0	950	(s)	53	2	0	55
1990 Total	84	1,448	0	0	0	0	0	0	1,532	17	53	16	0	86
1995 Total	18	2,816	0	7	0	0	0	0	2,841	28	65	61	0	154
2000 Total	47	3,544	0	12	13	46	99	21	3,782	73	66	106	0	244
2001 Total	65	3,729	0	10	38	23	98	14	3,977	167	66	141	0	373
2002 Total	27	3,785	0	2	8	35	151	8	4,015	189	63	263	0	516
2003 Total	53	3,437	0	0	50	14	378	11	3,944	271	66	343	0	680
2004 Total	120	3,607	0	0	12	12	462	46	4,259	395	62	397	0	854
2005 Total	97	3,700	73	9	8	3	439	11	4,341	358	65	305	0	729
2006 Total	17	3,590	120	13	57	0	389	0	4,186	341	61	322	0	724
2007 Total	77	3,783	115	54	95	18	448	18	4,608	482	47	292	2	822
2008 Total	0	3,589	55	43	12	3	267	15	3,984	559	39	365	0	963
2009 Total	0	3,271	160	28	13	13	236	29	3,751	701	31	338	3	1,072
2010 Total	0	3,280	73	30	42	46	190	81	3,741	739	33	333	32	1,137
2011 Total	0	3,117	35	3	2	91	129	92	3,469	937	18	499	52	1,506
2012 Total	0	2,963	3	(s)	0	34	112	26	3,138	971	14	620	14	1,619
2013 Total	0	2,786	0	1	3	7	70	17	2,883	911	0	661	0	1,572
2014 Total	0	2,635	0	1	0	0	43	16	2,695	770	13	729	3	1,514
2015 Total	0	2,626	0	1	0	0	71	20	2,718	701	8	1,054	20	1,784
2016 Total	0	2,918	0	1	0	0	84	3	3,006	771	11	1,405	148	2,335
2017 January	0	279	0	(s)	3	0	10	0	292	99	11	136	27	272
February	0	246	0	(s)	0	0	8	0	255	88	4	130	34	255
March	0	276	0	(s)	0	0	5	0	281	100	0	140	33	272
April	0	233	0	(s)	0	0	5	0	238	81	7	130	29	247
May	0	239	0	(s)	0	0	5	0	244	64	4	139	47	254
June	0	234	0	(s)	0	0	5	0	240	67	4	159	24	253
July	0	245	0	(s)	0	0	5	0	251	60	0	150	39	248
August	0	240	0	(s)	0	0	8	0	248	66	4	142	35	247
September	0	227	0	(s)	0	0	2	0	229	70	0	136	44	250
October	0	242	0	(s)	0	0	2	0	244	68	7	140	66	281
November	0	237	0	(s)	0	0	6	0	244	74	0	145	69	288
December	0	266	0	1	3	0	8	0	278	81	14	139	65	299
Total	0	2,965	0	1	6	0	70	0	3,042	917	53	1,684	513	3,168
2018 January	0	287	0	(s)	0	0	14	3	304	92	4	147	58	301
February	0	233	0	1	0	0	7	0	241	77	7	R 140	52	276
March	0	268	0	(s)	0	0	4	3	274	68	0	161	63	292
April	0	241	0	(s)	0	0	3	0	244	63	11	142	64	279
May	0	227	0	(s)	0	0	2	0	229	40	13	R 151	68	273
June	0	228	0	(s)	0	0	3	0	230	52	10	R 164	37	R 263
July	0	243	0	1	0	0	5	0	249	58	13	R 172	64	R 307
August	0	233	0	1	0	0	5	0	239	66	10	R 175	60	R 312
September	0	213	0	(s)	0	0	3	0	216	71	17	R 161	54	R 302
October	0	212	0	(s)	0	0	6	0	217	65	3	R 159	80	R 307
November	0	210	0	(s)	0	0	3	0	213	90	R 24	R 147	R 77	R 338
December	0	243	0	(s)	3	0	12	0	257	100	14	R 151	98	R 363
Total	0	2,836	0	3	3	0	66	6	2,914	843	R 126	R 1,871	R 775	R 3,614
2019 January	0	R 276	0	(s)	0	0	12	3	R 291	87	14	R 165	99	R 365
February	0	R 226	0	(s)	0	0	7	0	R 233	92	10	R 142	86	R 329
March	0	249	0	(s)	0	0	3	0	253	93	7	156	117	372
3-Month Total	0	752	0	(s)	0	0	23	3	777	272	31	463	301	1,067
2018 3-Month Total	0	788	0	1	0	0	24	6	819	237	11	449	173	869
2017 3-Month Total	0	800	0	(s)	3	0	24	0	827	286	14	405	93	799

[a] Includes re-exports.

[b] As liquefied natural gas.

[c] By pipeline, except for small amounts of: liquefied natural gas (LNG) imported from Canada in 1973, 1977, 1981, and 2013 forward; LNG exported to Canada in 2007 and 2012 forward; compressed natural gas (CNG) imported from Canada in 2014 forward; CNG exported to Canada in 2013 forward; and LNG exported to Mexico beginning in 1998. See Note 9, "Natural Gas Imports and Exports," at end of section.

[d] Australia in 1997–2001 and 2004; Brunei in 2002; Equatorial Guinea in 2007; Indonesia in 1986 and 2000; Malaysia in 1999 and 2002–2005; Norway in 2008–2016; Oman in 2000–2005; Peru in 2010 and 2011; United Arab Emirates in 1996–2000; United Kingdom in 2018; Yemen in 2010–2015; and Other (unassigned) in 2004–2015.

[e] Argentina in 2016–2018; Bahamas in 2017 and 2018; Barbados in 2016–2018; Brazil in 2010–2012, and 2014–2018; Chile in 2011, 2016–2018; China in 2011, 2016–2018; Colombia in 2018, Dominican Republic in 2016–2018; Egypt in 2015–2018; France in 2018; Greece in 2018; India in 2010–2012, 2016–2018; Israel 2018; Italy in 2016–2018; Jamaica 2018; Jordan in 2016–2018; Kuwait in 2016–2018; Lithuania in 2017; Malta in 2017 and 2018; Netherlands in 2017 and 2018; Pakistan in 2017 and 2018; Panama in 2018; Poland in 2017 and 2018; Portugal in 2012, 2016, 2017–2018; Russia in 2007; Singapore in 2018; South Korea in 2009–2011, 2016–2018; Spain in 2010–2011, 2016–2018; Taiwan in 2015, 2017 and 2018; Thailand in 2017; Turkey in 2015–2018; United Arab Emirates in 2016–2018; and United Kingdom in 2010, 2011, 2017 and 2018.

R=Revised. (s)=Less than 500 million cubic feet.

Notes: • See Note 9, "Natural Gas Imports and Exports," at end of section. • Through 1964, all volumes are shown on a pressure base of 14.65 psia (pounds per square inch absolute) at 60° Fahrenheit; beginning in 1965, the pressure base is 14.73 psia at 60° Fahrenheit. • Totals may not equal sum of components due to independent rounding. • U.S. geographic coverage is the 50 states and the District of Columbia.

Web Page: See http://www.eia.gov/totalenergy/data/monthly/#naturalgas (Excel and CSV files) for all available annual data beginning in 1949 and monthly data beginning in 1973.

Sources: • **1949–1954:** U.S. Energy Information Administration (EIA) estimates based on Bureau of Mines, Minerals Yearbook, "Natural Gas" chapter. • **1955–1971:** Federal Power Commission data. • **1972–1987:** EIA, Form FPC-14, "Annual Report for Importers and Exporters of Natural Gas." • **1988–2017:** EIA, *Natural Gas Annual,* annual reports. • **2018 forward:** EIA, *Natural Gas Monthly,* May 2019, Tables 4 and 5; and U.S. Department of Energy, Office of Fossil Energy, "Natural Gas Imports and Exports."

Source: *U.S. Energy Information Administration, Monthly Energy Review, June 2019*

Table 4.3 Natural Gas Consumption by Sector

(Billion Cubic Feet)

	End-Use Sectors											
			Industrial					Transportation				
				Other Industrial								
	Residential	Commercial[a]	Lease and Plant Fuel	CHP[b]	Non-CHP[c]	Total	Total	Pipelines[d] and Distribution[e]	Vehicle Fuel	Total	Electric Power Sector[f,g]	Total
1950 Total	1,198	388	928	(h)	2,498	2,498	3,426	126	NA	126	629	5,767
1955 Total	2,124	629	1,131	(h)	3,411	3,411	4,542	245	NA	245	1,153	8,694
1960 Total	3,103	1,020	1,237	(h)	4,535	4,535	5,771	347	NA	347	1,725	11,967
1965 Total	3,903	1,444	1,156	(h)	5,955	5,955	7,112	501	NA	501	2,321	15,280
1970 Total	4,837	2,399	1,399	(h)	7,851	7,851	9,249	722	NA	722	3,932	21,139
1975 Total	4,924	2,508	1,396	(h)	6,968	6,968	8,365	583	NA	583	3,158	19,538
1980 Total	4,752	2,611	1,026	(h)	7,172	7,172	8,198	635	NA	635	3,682	19,877
1985 Total	4,433	2,432	966	(h)	5,901	5,901	6,867	504	NA	504	3,044	17,281
1990 Total	4,391	2,623	1,236	1,055	[i]5,963	[i]7,018	8,255	660	(s)	660	[i]3,245	[i]19,174
1995 Total	4,850	3,031	1,220	1,258	6,906	8,164	9,384	700	5	705	4,237	22,207
2000 Total	4,996	3,182	1,151	1,386	6,757	8,142	9,293	642	13	655	5,206	23,333
2001 Total	4,771	3,023	1,119	1,310	6,035	7,344	8,463	625	15	640	5,342	22,239
2002 Total	4,889	3,144	1,113	1,240	6,287	7,527	8,640	667	15	682	5,672	23,027
2003 Total	5,079	3,179	1,122	1,144	6,007	7,150	8,273	591	18	610	5,135	22,277
2004 Total	4,869	3,129	1,098	1,191	6,066	7,256	8,354	566	21	587	5,464	22,403
2005 Total	4,827	2,999	1,112	1,084	5,518	6,601	7,713	584	23	607	5,869	22,014
2006 Total	4,368	2,832	1,142	1,115	5,412	6,527	7,669	584	24	608	6,222	21,699
2007 Total	4,722	3,013	1,226	1,050	5,604	6,655	7,881	621	25	646	6,841	23,104
2008 Total	4,892	3,153	1,220	955	5,715	6,670	7,890	648	26	674	6,668	23,277
2009 Total	4,779	3,119	1,275	990	5,178	6,167	7,443	670	27	697	6,873	22,910
2010 Total	4,782	3,103	1,286	1,029	5,797	6,826	8,112	674	29	703	7,387	24,087
2011 Total	4,714	3,155	1,323	1,063	5,931	6,994	8,317	688	30	718	7,574	24,477
2012 Total	4,150	2,895	1,396	1,149	6,077	7,226	8,622	731	30	761	9,111	25,538
2013 Total	4,897	3,295	1,483	1,170	6,255	7,425	8,909	833	30	863	8,191	26,155
2014 Total	5,087	3,466	1,512	1,145	6,501	7,646	9,158	700	35	735	8,146	26,593
2015 Total	4,613	3,202	1,576	1,222	6,300	7,522	9,098	678	39	718	9,613	27,244
2016 Total	4,347	3,110	1,545	1,209	6,519	7,729	9,274	687	42	729	9,985	27,444
2017 January	831	479	126	107	628	735	861	78	4	83	660	2,913
February	579	359	115	97	554	650	765	63	4	66	569	2,339
March	580	372	130	103	594	697	827	68	4	72	672	2,523
April	279	212	126	99	533	632	758	51	4	55	627	1,931
May	199	178	130	102	527	629	759	50	4	54	700	1,891
June	124	138	127	104	510	615	741	50	4	54	851	1,909
July	107	134	133	112	512	624	757	56	4	61	1,082	2,140
August	104	137	133	108	529	638	770	56	4	60	1,022	2,093
September	115	145	130	103	513	616	747	51	4	55	859	1,920
October	205	201	137	104	553	657	794	54	4	58	773	2,030
November	468	322	136	104	593	696	832	63	4	67	666	2,355
December	822	487	141	115	647	761	903	83	4	87	785	3,083
Total	**4,412**	**3,164**	**1,564**	**1,257**	**6,693**	**7,949**	**9,514**	**722**	**49**	**770**	**9,266**	**27,126**
2018 January	976	548	E 139	115	656	771	910	E 88	E 4	E 92	785	3,310
February	687	420	E 128	101	588	689	817	E 72	E 3	E 75	701	2,701
March	656	414	E 143	107	620	727	870	E 74	E 4	E 77	755	2,773
April	439	299	E 139	104	582	687	826	E 62	E 4	E 66	707	2,337
May	168	162	E 145	104	556	660	806	E 54	E 4	E 58	853	2,047
June	119	140	E 142	107	532	639	780	E 55	E 4	E 58	952	2,050
July	105	135	E 149	112	543	655	804	E 62	E 4	E 66	1,236	2,346
August	99	141	E 152	113	545	658	810	E 62	E 4	E 65	1,195	2,311
September	112	145	E 149	108	538	647	796	E 57	E 4	E 61	1,045	2,159
October	255	235	E 156	107	564	671	827	E 61	E 4	E 64	895	2,276
November	595	382	E 153	114	612	726	879	E 72	E 4	E 75	756	2,688
December	763	455	E 158	117	639	756	914	E 79	E 4	E 82	744	2,959
Total	**4,975**	**3,477**	**E 1,754**	**1,310**	**6,976**	**8,286**	**10,040**	**E 797**	**E 43**	**E 841**	**10,626**	**29,958**
2019 January	949	552	E 158	120	671	791	949	E 90	E 4	E 94	834	3,379
February	807	472	E 144	107	R 603	710	854	E 79	E 4	E 83	769	2,985
March	686	423	E 160	111	630	741	901	E 77	E 4	E 81	792	2,882
3-Month Total	**2,442**	**1,447**	**E 462**	**339**	**1,903**	**2,242**	**2,704**	**E 246**	**E 12**	**E 258**	**2,396**	**9,246**
2018 3-Month Total	**2,319**	**1,382**	**E 410**	**323**	**1,864**	**2,187**	**2,597**	**E 234**	**E 11**	**E 244**	**2,242**	**8,784**
2017 3-Month Total	**1,990**	**1,210**	**371**	**307**	**1,775**	**2,082**	**2,453**	**209**	**12**	**221**	**1,901**	**7,775**

[a] All commercial sector fuel use, including that at commercial combined-heat-and-power (CHP) and commercial electricity-only plants. See Table 7.4c for CHP fuel use.

[b] Industrial combined-heat-and-power (CHP) and a small number of industrial electricity-only plants.

[c] All industrial sector fuel use other than that in "Lease and Plant Fuel" and "CHP."

[d] Natural gas consumed in the operation of pipelines, primarily in compressors. Beginning in 2009, includes line loss, which is known volumes of natural gas that are the result of leaks, damage, accidents, migration, and/or blow down.

[e] Natural gas used as fuel in the delivery of natural gas to consumers. Beginning in 2009, includes line loss, which is known volumes of natural gas that are the result of leaks, damage, accidents, migration, and/or blow down.

[f] The electric power sector comprises electricity-only and combined-heat-and-power (CHP) plants within the NAICS 22 category whose primary business is to sell electricity, or electricity and heat, to the public.

[g] Through 1988, data are for electric utilities only. Beginning in 1989, data are for electric utilities and independent power producers.

[h] Included in "Non-CHP."

[i] For 1989–1992, a small amount of consumption at independent power producers may be counted in both "Other Industrial" and "Electric Power Sector." See Note 7, "Natural Gas Consumption, 1989–1992," at end of section.

R=Revised. E=Estimate. NA=Not available. (s)=Less than 500 million cubic feet.

Notes: • Data are for natural gas, plus a small amount of supplemental gaseous fuels. See Note 3, "Supplemental Gaseous Fuels," at end of section. • See Note 8, "Natural Gas Data Adjustments, 1993–2000," at end of section. • See Note 2, "Classification of Power Plants Into Energy-Use Sectors," at end of Section 7. • Through 1964, all volumes are shown on a pressure base of 14.65 psia (pounds per square inch absolute) at 60° Fahrenheit; beginning in 1965, the pressure base is 14.73 psia at 60° Fahrenheit. • Totals may not equal sum of components due to independent rounding. • Geographic coverage is the 50 states and the District of Columbia.

Web Page: See http://www.eia.gov/totalenergy/data/monthly/#naturalgas (Excel and CSV files) for all available annual data beginning in 1949 and monthly data beginning in 1973.

Sources: • **Residential, Commercial, Lease and Plant Fuel, Other Industrial Total** and **Pipelines and Distribution: 1949–2017**—U.S. Energy Information Administration (EIA), *Natural Gas Annual (NGA),* annual reports and unpublished revisions. **2018 forward**—EIA, *Natural Gas Monthly (NGM),* May 2019, Table 2. • **Other Industrial CHP:** Table 7.4c. • **Other Industrial Non-CHP:** Calculated as other industrial total minus other industrial CHP. • **Industrial Total:** Calculated as lease and plant fuel plus other industrial total. • **Vehicle Fuel: 1990 and 1991**—EIA, NGA 2000, (November 2001), Table 95. **1992–1998**—EIA, "Alternatives to Traditional Transportation Fuels 1999" (October 1999), Table 10, and "Alternatives to Traditional Transportation Fuels 2003" (February 2004), Table 10. Data for compressed natural gas and liquefied natural gas in gasoline-equivalent gallons were converted to cubic feet by multiplying by the motor gasoline conversion factor (see Table A3) and dividing by the natural gas end-use sectors conversion factor (see Table A4). **1999–2017**—EIA, NGA, annual reports. **2018 forward**—EIA, NGM, May 2019, Table 2. • **Transportation Total:** Calculated as pipelines and distribution plus vehicle fuel. • **Electric Power Sector:** Table 7.4b. • **Total Consumption:** Calculated as the sum of residential, commercial, industrial total, transportation total, and electric power sector.

Source: *U.S. Energy Information Administration, Monthly Energy Review, June 2019*

Table 4.4 Natural Gas in Underground Storage
(Volumes in Billion Cubic Feet)

	Natural Gas in Underground Storage, End of Period			Change in Working Gas From Same Period Previous Year		Storage Activity		
	Base Gas	Working Gas	Total[a]	Volume	Percent	Withdrawals	Injections	Net[b,c]
1950 Total	**NA**	**NA**	**NA**	**NA**	**NA**	**175**	**230**	**-54**
1955 Total	**863**	**505**	**1,368**	**40**	**8.7**	**437**	**505**	**-68**
1960 Total	**NA**	**NA**	**2,184**	**NA**	**NA**	**713**	**844**	**-132**
1965 Total	**1,848**	**1,242**	**3,090**	**83**	**7.2**	**960**	**1,078**	**-118**
1970 Total	**2,326**	**1,678**	**4,004**	**257**	**18.1**	**1,459**	**1,857**	**-398**
1975 Total	**3,162**	**2,212**	**5,374**	**162**	**7.9**	**1,760**	**2,104**	**-344**
1980 Total	**3,642**	**2,655**	**6,297**	**-99**	**-3.6**	**1,910**	**1,896**	**14**
1985 Total	**3,842**	**2,607**	**6,448**	**-270**	**-9.4**	**2,359**	**2,128**	**231**
1990 Total	**3,868**	**3,068**	**6,936**	**555**	**22.1**	**1,934**	**2,433**	**-499**
1995 Total	**4,349**	**2,153**	**6,503**	**-453**	**-17.4**	**2,974**	**2,566**	**408**
2000 Total	**4,352**	**1,719**	**6,071**	**-806**	**-31.9**	**3,498**	**2,684**	**814**
2001 Total	**4,301**	**2,904**	**7,204**	**1,185**	**68.9**	**2,309**	**3,464**	**-1,156**
2002 Total	**4,340**	**2,375**	**6,715**	**-528**	**-18.2**	**3,138**	**2,670**	**468**
2003 Total	**4,303**	**2,563**	**6,866**	**187**	**7.9**	**3,099**	**3,292**	**-193**
2004 Total	**4,201**	**2,696**	**6,897**	**133**	**5.2**	**3,037**	**3,150**	**-113**
2005 Total	**4,200**	**2,635**	**6,835**	**-61**	**-2.3**	**3,057**	**3,002**	**55**
2006 Total	**4,211**	**3,070**	**7,281**	**435**	**16.5**	**2,493**	**2,924**	**-431**
2007 Total	**4,234**	**2,879**	**7,113**	**-191**	**-6.2**	**3,325**	**3,133**	**192**
2008 Total	**4,232**	**2,840**	**7,073**	**-39**	**-1.4**	**3,374**	**3,340**	**34**
2009 Total	**4,277**	**3,130**	**7,407**	**290**	**10.2**	**2,966**	**3,315**	**-349**
2010 Total	**4,301**	**3,111**	**7,412**	**-19**	**-.6**	**3,274**	**3,291**	**-17**
2011 Total	**4,302**	**3,462**	**7,764**	**351**	**11.3**	**3,074**	**3,422**	**-348**
2012 Total	**4,372**	**3,413**	**7,785**	**-49**	**-1.4**	**2,818**	**2,825**	**-7**
2013 Total	**4,365**	**2,890**	**7,255**	**-523**	**-15.3**	**3,702**	**3,156**	**546**
2014 Total	**4,365**	**3,141**	**7,506**	**251**	**8.7**	**3,586**	**3,839**	**-253**
2015 Total	**4,372**	**3,667**	**8,038**	**525**	**16.7**	**3,100**	**3,638**	**-539**
2016 Total	**4,380**	**3,297**	**7,677**	**-370**	**-10.1**	**3,325**	**2,977**	**348**
2017 January	4,378	2,622	7,000	-316	-10.8	787	113	675
February	4,377	2,337	6,715	-197	-7.8	422	137	285
March	4,378	2,063	6,440	-424	-17.0	449	175	274
April	4,379	2,291	6,670	-354	-13.4	122	352	-230
May	4,385	2,627	7,011	-340	-11.5	90	430	-341
June	4,354	2,907	7,261	-279	-8.8	105	386	-281
July	4,356	3,054	7,410	-264	-8.0	154	303	-150
August	4,355	3,250	7,605	-191	-5.6	158	353	-196
September	4,355	3,567	7,923	-138	-3.7	103	419	-317
October	4,354	3,816	8,170	-196	-4.9	131	378	-247
November	4,353	3,709	8,062	-267	-6.7	285	199	86
December	4,360	3,033	7,392	-264	-8.0	785	91	695
Total	**4,360**	**3,033**	**7,392**	**-264**	**-8.0**	**3,590**	**3,337**	**254**
2018 January	4,357	2,141	6,498	-481	-18.4	1,037	141	896
February	4,357	1,673	6,030	-664	-28.4	599	133	467
March	4,353	1,391	5,744	-672	-32.6	449	164	285
April	4,350	1,427	5,778	-864	-37.7	224	256	-32
May	4,352	1,848	6,200	-778	-29.6	66	489	-423
June	4,354	2,196	6,550	-711	-24.5	88	436	-349
July	4,354	2,382	6,736	-672	-22.0	175	362	-186
August	4,355	2,618	6,973	-632	-19.5	172	407	-235
September	4,356	2,951	7,307	-616	-17.3	130	464	-334
October	4,357	3,237	7,594	-580	-15.2	131	422	-291
November	4,356	3,031	7,387	-678	-18.3	418	213	205
December	4,361	2,709	7,070	-324	-10.7	511	191	320
Total	**4,361**	**2,709**	**7,070**	**-324**	**-10.7**	**3,999**	**3,676**	**323**
2019 January	4,366	1,994	6,360	-147	-6.9	804	95	709
February	4,366	1,426	5,792	-247	-14.8	672	104	568
March	4,360	1,185	5,545	-206	-14.8	435	190	245
3-Month Total	**– –**	**– –**	**– –**	**– –**	**– –**	**1,911**	**389**	**1,522**
2018 3-Month Total	**– –**	**– –**	**– –**	**– –**	**– –**	**2,085**	**437**	**1,647**
2017 3-Month Total	**– –**	**– –**	**– –**	**– –**	**– –**	**1,659**	**424**	**1,234**

[a] For total underground storage capacity at the end of each calendar year, see Note 4, "Natural Gas Storage," at end of section.

[b] For 1980–2017, data differ from those shown on Table 4.1, which includes liquefied natural gas storage for that period.

[c] Positive numbers indicate that withdrawals are greater than injections. Negative numbers indicate that injections are greater than withdrawals. Net withdrawals or injections may not equal the difference between applicable ending stocks. See Note 4, "Natural Gas Storage," at end of section.

– – =Not applicable. NA=Not available.

Notes: • Through 1964, all volumes are shown on a pressure base of 14.65 psia (pounds per square inch absolute) at 60° Fahrenheit; beginning in 1965, the pressure base is 14.73 psia at 60° Fahrenheit. • Totals may not equal sum of components due to independent rounding. • Geographic coverage is the 50 states and the District of Columbia (except Alaska, which is excluded through 2012).

Web Page: See http://www.eia.gov/totalenergy/data/monthly/#naturalgas (Excel and CSV files) for all available annual data beginning in 1949 and monthly data beginning in 1973.

Sources: • **Storage Activity: 1949–1975**—U.S. Energy Information Administration (EIA), *Natural Gas Annual 1994, Volume 2*, Table 9. **1976–1979**—EIA, *Natural Gas Production and Consumption 1979*, Table 1. **1980–1995**—EIA, *Historical Natural Gas Annual 1930 Through 2000*, Table 11. **1996–2014**—EIA, *Natural Gas Monthly (NGM)*, monthly issues. **2015 forward**—EIA, NGM, May 2019, Table 8. • **All Other Data: 1954–1974**—American Gas Association, *Gas Facts*, annual issues. **1975 and 1976**—Federal Energy Administration (FEA), Form FEA-G318-M-0, "Underground Gas Storage Report," and Federal Power Commission (FPC), Form FPC-8, "Underground Gas Storage Report." **1977 and 1978**—EIA, Form FEA-G318-M-0, "Underground Gas Storage Report," and Federal Energy Regulatory Commission (FERC), Form FERC-8, "Underground Gas Storage Report." **1979–1995**—EIA, Form EIA-191, "Underground Gas Storage Report," and FERC, Form FERC-8, "Underground Gas Storage Report." **1996–2017**—EIA, NGA, annual reports. **2018 forward**—EIA, NGM, May 2019, Table 8.

Source: *U.S. Energy Information Administration, Monthly Energy Review, June 2019*

Figure 5.1 Crude Oil and Natural Gas Resource Development Indicators

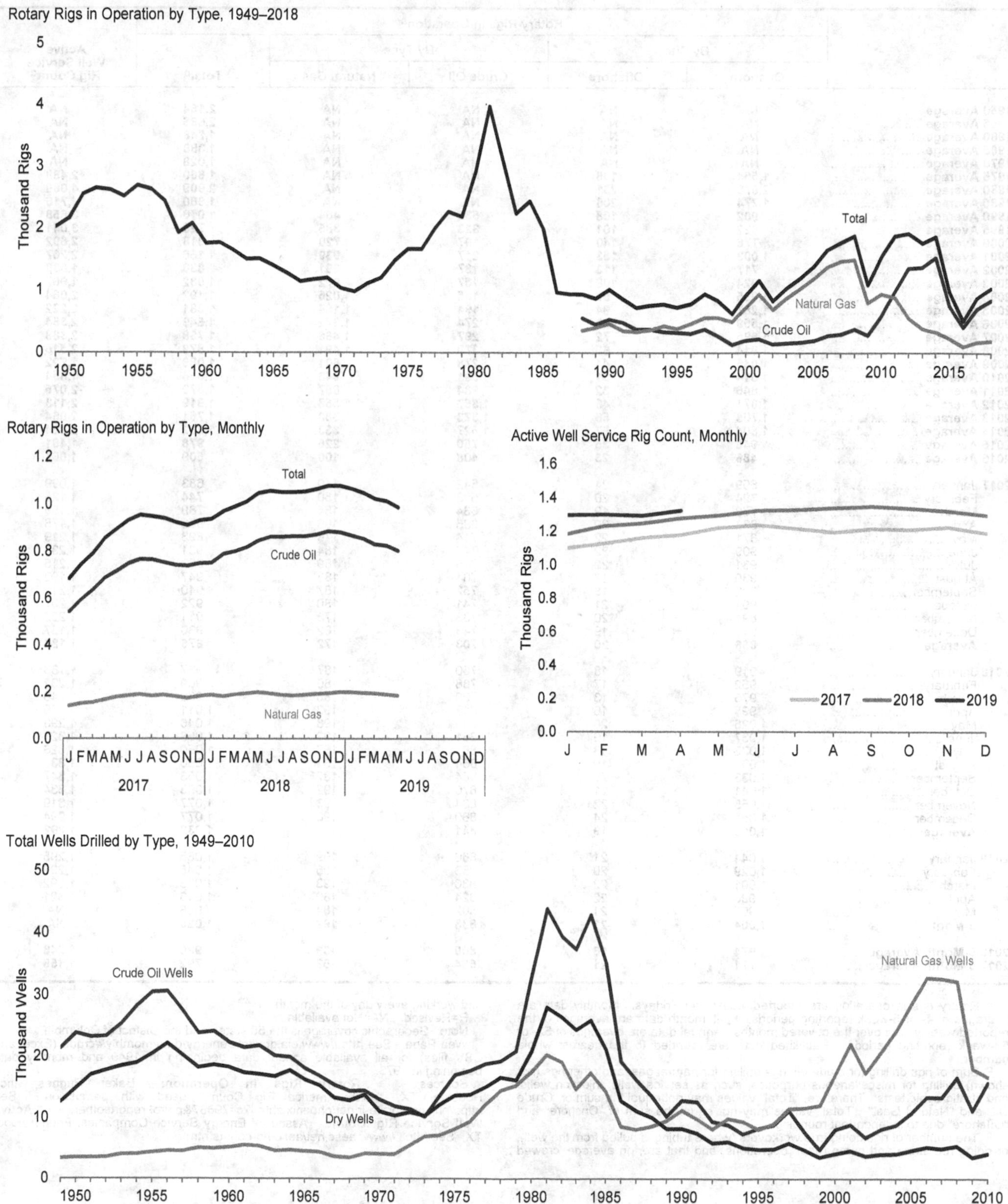

Web Page: http://www.eia.gov/totalenergy/data/monthly/#crude.
Sources: Tables 5.1 and 5.2.

Source: *U.S. Energy Information Administration, Monthly Energy Review, June 2019*

Table 5.1 Crude Oil and Natural Gas Drilling Activity Measurements
(Number of Rigs)

	Rotary Rigs in Operation[a]					Active Well Service Rig Count[c]
	By Site		By Type			
	Onshore	Offshore	Crude Oil	Natural Gas	Total[b]	
1950 Average	**NA**	**NA**	**NA**	**NA**	**2,154**	**NA**
1955 Average	**NA**	**NA**	**NA**	**NA**	**2,686**	**NA**
1960 Average	**NA**	**NA**	**NA**	**NA**	**1,748**	**NA**
1965 Average	**NA**	**NA**	**NA**	**NA**	**1,388**	**NA**
1970 Average	**NA**	**NA**	**NA**	**NA**	**1,028**	**NA**
1975 Average	**1,554**	**106**	**NA**	**NA**	**1,660**	**2,486**
1980 Average	**2,678**	**231**	**NA**	**NA**	**2,909**	**4,089**
1985 Average	**1,774**	**206**	**NA**	**NA**	**1,980**	**4,716**
1990 Average	**902**	**108**	**532**	**464**	**1,010**	**3,658**
1995 Average	**622**	**101**	**323**	**385**	**723**	**3,041**
2000 Average	**778**	**140**	**197**	**720**	**918**	**2,692**
2001 Average	**1,003**	**153**	**217**	**939**	**1,156**	**2,267**
2002 Average	**717**	**113**	**137**	**691**	**830**	**1,830**
2003 Average	**924**	**108**	**157**	**872**	**1,032**	**1,967**
2004 Average	**1,095**	**97**	**165**	**1,025**	**1,192**	**2,064**
2005 Average	**1,287**	**94**	**194**	**1,184**	**1,381**	**2,222**
2006 Average	**1,559**	**90**	**274**	**1,372**	**1,649**	**2,364**
2007 Average	**1,695**	**72**	**297**	**1,466**	**1,768**	**2,388**
2008 Average	**1,814**	**65**	**379**	**1,491**	**1,879**	**2,515**
2009 Average	**1,046**	**44**	**278**	**801**	**1,089**	**1,722**
2010 Average	**1,514**	**31**	**591**	**943**	**1,546**	**1,854**
2011 Average	**1,846**	**32**	**984**	**887**	**1,879**	**2,075**
2012 Average	**1,871**	**48**	**1,357**	**558**	**1,919**	**2,113**
2013 Average	**1,705**	**56**	**1,373**	**383**	**1,761**	**2,064**
2014 Average	**1,804**	**57**	**1,527**	**333**	**1,862**	**2,024**
2015 Average	**943**	**35**	**750**	**226**	**978**	**1,481**
2016 Average	**486**	**23**	**408**	**100**	**509**	**1,061**
2017 January	659	24	542	140	683	1,099
February	724	20	593	150	744	1,125
March	770	19	634	154	789	1,159
April	833	20	685	166	853	1,176
May	871	22	714	178	893	1,219
June	909	22	747	184	931	1,235
July	931	22	765	189	953	1,215
August	930	17	764	183	947	1,192
September	922	18	752	187	940	1,212
October	901	21	741	180	922	1,207
November	891	20	738	173	911	1,222
December	911	19	748	182	930	1,187
Average	**856**	**20**	**703**	**172**	**876**	**1,187**
2018 January	919	18	750	187	937	1,183
February	952	17	788	180	969	1,232
March	976	13	799	188	989	1,246
April	995	16	817	193	1,011	1,276
May	1,026	20	845	198	1,046	1,293
June	1,037	19	861	193	1,056	1,321
July	1,032	18	861	187	1,050	1,326
August	1,031	19	864	184	1,050	1,338
September	1,033	20	864	187	1,053	1,347
October	1,041	21	870	192	1,063	1,334
November	1,055	22	884	193	1,077	1,319
December	1,054	24	880	198	1,077	1,294
Average	**1,013**	**19**	**841**	**190**	**1,032**	**1,292**
2019 January	1,044	21	866	199	1,065	1,295
February	1,029	20	853	195	1,048	1,299
March	1,001	22	830	193	1,023	1,292
April	990	22	824	189	1,013	R 1,321
May	965	21	802	184	986	NA
5-Month Average	**1,004**	**21**	**833**	**192**	**1,025**	**NA**
2018 5-Month Average	**974**	**16**	**800**	**189**	**990**	**1,246**
2017 5-Month Average	**771**	**21**	**634**	**157**	**792**	**1,156**

[a] Rotary rigs in operation are reported weekly on Fridays. Monthly data are averages of 4- or 5-week reporting periods. Multi-month data are averages of the reported weekly data over the covered months. Annual data are averages of 52- or 53-week reporting periods. Published data are rounded to the nearest whole number.

[b] Sum of rigs drilling for crude oil, rigs drilling for natural gas, and other rigs (not shown) drilling for miscellaneous purposes, such as service wells, injection wells, and stratigraphic tests. Therefore, "Total" values may not equal the sum of "Crude Oil" and "Natural Gas." "Total" values may not equal the sum of "Onshore" and "Offshore" due to independent rounding.

[c] The number of rigs doing true workovers (where tubing is pulled from the well), or doing rod string and pump repair operations, and that are, on average, crewed and working every day of the month.

R=Revised. NA=Not available.

Note: Geographic coverage is the 50 states and the District of Columbia.

Web Page: See http://www.eia.gov/totalenergy/data/monthly/#crude (Excel and CSV files) for all available annual data beginning in 1949 and monthly data beginning in 1973.

Sources: • **Rotary Rigs in Operation:** Baker Hughes, Inc., Houston, TX, "North America Rig Count," used with permission. See http://phx.corporate-ir.net/phoenix.zhtml?c=79687&p=irol-reportsother. • **Active Well Service Rig Count:** Assoc. of Energy Service Companies, Friendswood, TX. See https://www.aesc.net/aesc-rig-counts.html.

Source: *U.S. Energy Information Administration, Monthly Energy Review, June 2019*

Table 5.2 Crude Oil and Natural Gas Exploratory and Development Wells

	Wells Drilled												Total Footage Drilled
	Exploratory				Development				Total				
	Crude Oil	Natural Gas	Dry	Total	Crude Oil	Natural Gas	Dry	Total	Crude Oil	Natural Gas	Dry	Total	
	Number												Thousand Feet
1950 Total	**1,583**	**431**	**8,292**	**10,306**	**22,229**	**3,008**	**6,507**	**31,744**	**23,812**	**3,439**	**14,799**	**42,050**	**157,358**
1955 Total	**2,236**	**874**	**11,832**	**14,942**	**28,196**	**3,392**	**8,620**	**40,208**	**30,432**	**4,266**	**20,452**	**55,150**	**226,182**
1960 Total	**1,321**	**868**	**9,515**	**11,704**	**20,937**	**4,281**	**8,697**	**33,915**	**22,258**	**5,149**	**18,212**	**45,619**	**192,176**
1965 Total	**946**	**515**	**8,005**	**9,466**	**17,119**	**3,967**	**8,221**	**29,307**	**18,065**	**4,482**	**16,226**	**38,773**	**174,882**
1970 Total	**757**	**477**	**6,162**	**7,396**	**12,211**	**3,534**	**4,869**	**20,614**	**12,968**	**4,011**	**11,031**	**28,010**	**138,556**
1975 Total	**982**	**1,248**	**7,129**	**9,359**	**15,966**	**6,879**	**6,517**	**29,362**	**16,948**	**8,127**	**13,646**	**38,721**	**180,494**
1980 Total	**1,777**	**2,099**	**9,081**	**12,957**	**31,182**	**15,362**	**11,704**	**58,248**	**32,959**	**17,461**	**20,785**	**71,205**	**316,943**
1985 Total	**1,680**	**1,200**	**8,954**	**11,834**	**33,581**	**13,124**	**12,257**	**58,962**	**35,261**	**14,324**	**21,211**	**70,796**	**314,409**
1990 Total	**778**	**811**	**3,652**	**5,241**	**12,061**	**10,435**	**4,593**	**27,089**	**12,839**	**11,246**	**8,245**	**32,330**	**156,044**
1995 Total	**570**	**558**	**2,024**	**3,152**	**7,678**	**7,524**	**2,790**	**17,992**	**8,248**	**8,082**	**4,814**	**21,144**	**117,156**
2000 Total	**288**	**657**	**1,341**	**2,286**	**7,802**	**16,394**	**2,805**	**27,001**	**8,090**	**17,051**	**4,146**	**29,287**	**144,425**
2001 Total	**357**	**1,052**	**1,733**	**3,142**	**8,531**	**21,020**	**2,865**	**32,416**	**8,888**	**22,072**	**4,598**	**35,558**	**180,141**
2002 Total	**258**	**844**	**1,282**	**2,384**	**6,517**	**16,498**	**2,472**	**25,487**	**6,775**	**17,342**	**3,754**	**27,871**	**145,159**
2003 Total	**350**	**997**	**1,297**	**2,644**	**7,779**	**19,725**	**2,685**	**30,189**	**8,129**	**20,722**	**3,982**	**32,833**	**177,239**
2004 Total	**383**	**1,671**	**1,350**	**3,404**	**8,406**	**22,515**	**2,732**	**33,653**	**8,789**	**24,186**	**4,082**	**37,057**	**204,279**
2005 Total	**539**	**2,141**	**1,462**	**4,142**	**10,240**	**26,449**	**3,191**	**39,880**	**10,779**	**28,590**	**4,653**	**44,022**	**240,307**
2006 Total	**646**	**2,456**	**1,547**	**4,649**	**12,739**	**30,382**	**3,659**	**46,780**	**13,385**	**32,838**	**5,206**	**51,429**	**282,675**
2007 Total	**808**	**2,794**	**1,582**	**5,184**	**12,563**	**29,925**	**3,399**	**45,887**	**13,371**	**32,719**	**4,981**	**51,071**	**301,515**
2008 January	88	208	144	440	1,111	2,321	272	3,704	1,199	2,529	416	4,144	25,306
February	82	230	107	419	1,080	2,261	247	3,588	1,162	2,491	354	4,007	24,958
March	66	216	127	409	1,132	2,363	271	3,766	1,198	2,579	398	4,175	26,226
April	68	189	130	387	1,177	2,415	281	3,873	1,245	2,604	411	4,260	26,920
May	88	206	124	418	1,317	2,449	240	4,006	1,405	2,655	364	4,424	27,947
June	63	195	139	397	1,428	2,540	299	4,267	1,491	2,735	438	4,664	28,739
July	79	163	171	413	1,439	2,695	344	4,478	1,518	2,858	515	4,891	29,140
August	67	165	144	376	1,448	2,735	379	4,562	1,515	2,900	523	4,938	28,942
September	52	166	164	382	1,488	2,667	355	4,510	1,540	2,833	519	4,892	28,960
October	80	243	173	496	1,549	2,841	373	4,763	1,629	3,084	546	5,259	31,505
November	97	192	160	449	1,361	2,418	334	4,113	1,458	2,610	494	4,562	29,276
December	67	172	132	371	1,206	2,196	313	3,715	1,273	2,368	445	4,086	26,222
Total	**897**	**2,345**	**1,715**	**4,957**	**15,736**	**29,901**	**3,708**	**49,345**	**16,633**	**32,246**	**5,423**	**54,302**	**334,141**
2009 January	80	171	99	350	1,192	2,253	250	3,695	1,272	2,424	349	4,045	28,077
February	62	125	88	275	991	1,925	195	3,111	1,053	2,050	283	3,386	25,440
March	59	146	88	293	867	1,771	210	2,848	926	1,917	298	3,141	25,304
April	36	68	93	197	755	1,396	205	2,356	791	1,464	298	2,553	21,406
May	47	90	80	217	584	1,136	156	1,876	631	1,226	236	2,093	20,055
June	44	91	75	210	804	1,297	189	2,290	848	1,388	264	2,500	16,301
July	40	100	101	241	789	1,188	217	2,194	829	1,288	318	2,435	13,543
August	49	84	88	221	867	1,372	207	2,446	916	1,456	295	2,667	15,970
September	61	71	96	228	945	1,170	207	2,322	1,006	1,241	303	2,550	15,547
October	55	79	78	212	966	1,167	222	2,355	1,021	1,246	300	2,567	17,261
November	38	83	85	206	931	1,133	199	2,263	969	1,216	284	2,469	16,236
December	34	98	84	216	894	1,074	213	2,181	928	1,172	297	2,397	16,424
Total	**605**	**1,206**	**1,055**	**2,866**	**10,585**	**16,882**	**2,470**	**29,937**	**11,190**	**18,088**	**3,525**	**32,803**	**231,562**
2010 January	55	91	81	227	898	1,264	169	2,331	953	1,355	250	2,558	15,304
February	44	71	67	182	871	1,096	144	2,111	915	1,167	211	2,293	16,862
March	59	85	88	232	1,062	1,224	216	2,502	1,121	1,309	304	2,734	15,102
April	49	78	77	204	1,173	1,152	249	2,574	1,222	1,230	326	2,778	17,904
May	48	107	86	241	1,282	1,208	255	2,745	1,330	1,315	341	2,986	17,987
June	61	100	90	251	1,385	1,250	302	2,937	1,446	1,350	392	3,188	19,408
July	46	103	105	254	1,386	1,443	390	3,219	1,432	1,546	495	3,473	20,847
August	56	104	94	254	1,434	1,402	314	3,150	1,490	1,506	408	3,404	22,923
September	57	73	88	218	1,374	1,358	268	3,000	1,431	1,431	356	3,218	23,037
October	75	87	117	279	1,502	1,463	283	3,248	1,577	1,550	400	3,527	22,123
November	62	114	103	279	1,400	1,352	263	3,015	1,462	1,466	366	3,294	24,561
December	57	92	70	219	1,317	1,379	243	2,939	1,374	1,471	313	3,158	23,189
Total	**669**	**1,105**	**1,066**	**2,840**	**15,084**	**15,591**	**3,096**	**33,771**	**15,753**	**16,696**	**4,162**	**36,611**	**239,247**

Notes: • Data are estimates. • For 1960–1969, data are for well completion reports received by the American Petroleum Institute during the reporting year; for all other years, data are for well completions in a given year. • Through 1989, these well counts include only the original drilling of a hole intended to discover or further develop already discovered crude oil or natural gas resources. Other drilling activities, such as drilling an old well deeper, drilling of laterals from the original well, drilling of service and injection wells, and drilling for resources other than crude oil or natural gas are excluded. Beginning in 1990, a new well is defined as the first hole in the ground whether it is lateral or not. Due to the methodology used to estimate ultimate well counts from the available partially reported data, the counts shown on this page are frequently revised. See Note, "Crude Oil and Natural Gas Exploratory and Development Wells," at end of section. • Geographic coverage is the 50 states and the District of Columbia.

Web Page: See http://www.eia.gov/totalenergy/data/monthly/#crude (Excel and CSV files) for all available annual data beginning in 1949 and monthly data beginning in 1973.

Sources: • **1949–1965:** Gulf Publishing Company, *World Oil*, "Forecast-Review" issue. • **1966–1969:** American Petroleum Institute (API), *Quarterly Review of Drilling Statistics for the United States*, annual summaries and monthly reports. • **1970–1989:** U.S. Energy Information Administration (EIA) computations based on well reports submitted to the API. • **1990 forward:** EIA computations based on well reports submitted to IHS, Inc., Denver, CO.

Data for 2011 forward in this table have been removed while EIA evaluates the quality of the data and the estimation methodology.

Source: *U.S. Energy Information Administration, Monthly Energy Review, June 2019*

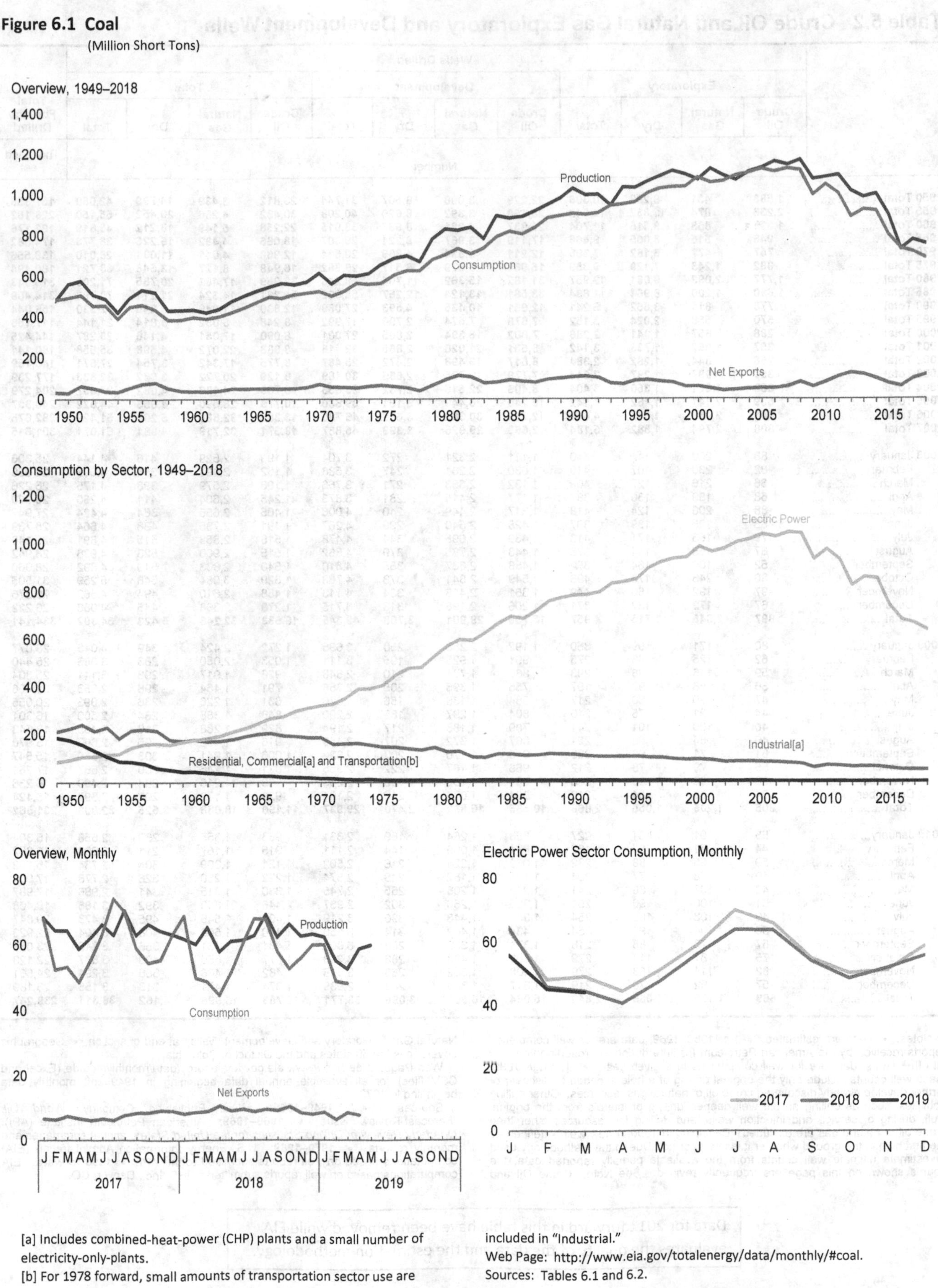

[a] Includes combined-heat-power (CHP) plants and a small number of electricity-only-plants.

[b] For 1978 forward, small amounts of transportation sector use are included in "Industrial."

Web Page: http://www.eia.gov/totalenergy/data/monthly/#coal.

Sources: Tables 6.1 and 6.2.

Source: *U.S. Energy Information Administration, Monthly Energy Review, June 2019*

Table 6.1 Coal Overview
(Thousand Short Tons)

	Production[a]	Waste Coal Supplied[b]	Trade			Stock Change[d,e]	Losses and Unaccounted for[e,f]	Consumption
			Imports	Exports	Net Imports[c]			
1950 Total	**560,388**	**NA**	**365**	**29,360**	**-28,995**	**27,829**	**9,462**	**494,102**
1955 Total	**490,838**	**NA**	**337**	**54,429**	**-54,092**	**-3,974**	**-6,292**	**447,012**
1960 Total	**434,329**	**NA**	**262**	**37,981**	**-37,719**	**-3,194**	**1,722**	**398,081**
1965 Total	**526,954**	**NA**	**184**	**51,032**	**-50,848**	**1,897**	**2,244**	**471,965**
1970 Total	**612,661**	**NA**	**36**	**71,733**	**-71,697**	**11,100**	**6,633**	**523,231**
1975 Total	**654,641**	**NA**	**940**	**66,309**	**-65,369**	**32,154**	**-5,522**	**562,640**
1980 Total	**829,700**	**NA**	**1,194**	**91,742**	**-90,548**	**25,595**	**10,827**	**702,730**
1985 Total	**883,638**	**NA**	**1,952**	**92,680**	**-90,727**	**-27,934**	**2,796**	**818,049**
1990 Total	**1,029,076**	**3,339**	**2,699**	**105,804**	**-103,104**	**26,542**	**-1,730**	**904,498**
1995 Total	**1,032,974**	**8,561**	**9,473**	**88,547**	**-79,074**	**-275**	**632**	**962,104**
2000 Total	**1,073,612**	**9,089**	**12,513**	**58,489**	**-45,976**	**-48,309**	**938**	**1,084,095**
2001 Total	**1,127,689**	**10,085**	**19,787**	**48,666**	**-28,879**	**41,630**	**7,120**	**1,060,146**
2002 Total	**1,094,283**	**9,052**	**16,875**	**39,601**	**-22,726**	**10,215**	**4,040**	**1,066,355**
2003 Total	**1,071,753**	**10,016**	**25,044**	**43,014**	**-17,970**	**-26,659**	**-4,403**	**1,094,861**
2004 Total	**1,112,099**	**11,299**	**27,280**	**47,998**	**-20,718**	**-11,462**	**6,887**	**1,107,255**
2005 Total	**1,131,498**	**13,352**	**30,460**	**49,942**	**-19,482**	**-9,702**	**9,092**	**1,125,978**
2006 Total	**1,162,750**	**14,409**	**36,246**	**49,647**	**-13,401**	**42,642**	**8,824**	**1,112,292**
2007 Total	**1,146,635**	**14,076**	**36,347**	**59,163**	**-22,816**	**5,812**	**4,085**	**1,127,998**
2008 Total	**1,171,809**	**14,146**	**34,208**	**81,519**	**-47,311**	**12,354**	**5,740**	**1,120,548**
2009 Total	**1,074,923**	**13,666**	**22,639**	**59,097**	**-36,458**	**39,668**	**14,985**	**997,478**
2010 Total	**1,084,368**	**13,651**	**19,353**	**81,716**	**-62,363**	**-13,039**	**182**	**1,048,514**
2011 Total	**1,095,628**	**13,209**	**13,088**	**107,259**	**-94,171**	**211**	**11,506**	**1,002,948**
2012 Total	**1,016,458**	**11,196**	**9,159**	**125,746**	**-116,586**	**6,902**	**14,980**	**889,185**
2013 Total	**984,842**	**11,279**	**8,906**	**117,659**	**-108,753**	**-38,525**	**1,451**	**924,442**
2014 Total	**1,000,049**	**12,090**	**11,350**	**97,257**	**-85,907**	**-2,601**	**11,101**	**917,731**
2015 Total	**896,941**	**9,969**	**11,318**	**73,958**	**-62,640**	**40,704**	**5,452**	**798,115**
2016 Total	**728,364**	**10,138**	**9,850**	**60,271**	**-50,421**	**-45,441**	**2,452**	**731,071**
2017 January	68,414	1,027	743	7,385	-6,642	-6,368	1,161	68,006
February	64,389	916	612	6,908	-6,296	4,246	2,383	52,381
March	64,335	975	560	8,013	-7,453	1,096	3,436	53,325
April	58,754	651	493	7,236	-6,744	2,198	1,898	48,565
May	62,115	696	1,053	7,243	-6,190	-2,116	3,536	55,202
June	66,229	777	651	7,317	-6,666	-5,351	2,592	63,099
July	62,966	907	956	7,177	-6,221	-10,088	-6,473	74,214
August	70,582	901	839	8,573	-7,734	-5,767	-713	70,229
September	62,891	801	513	8,894	-8,381	-2,349	-1,378	59,039
October	66,368	630	582	9,159	-8,577	1,847	2,137	54,436
November	64,345	668	368	9,552	-9,185	2,135	-1,663	55,357
December	63,220	1,003	408	9,495	-9,087	-5,516	-2,352	63,003
Total	**774,609**	**9,951**	**7,777**	**96,953**	**-89,176**	**-26,033**	**4,562**	**716,856**
2018 January	61,937	1,013	500	8,772	-8,273	-13,394	-842	68,913
February	60,235	834	349	9,022	-8,673	-1,077	3,576	49,897
March	65,467	909	518	9,426	-8,908	5,496	3,213	48,759
April	58,032	714	494	11,092	-10,598	2,350	1,020	44,777
May	61,196	771	544	9,645	-9,102	-2,004	3,174	51,695
June	61,557	789	509	10,138	-9,629	-7,514	59	60,173
July	62,945	878	692	9,532	-8,840	-10,463	-2,572	68,018
August	69,301	907	484	10,052	-9,569	-8,632	1,376	67,895
September	62,417	807	263	9,483	-9,220	-2,446	-1,695	58,145
October	66,384	719	304	10,681	-10,377	5,306	-1,438	52,858
November	62,718	887	400	8,872	-8,472	-1,515	494	56,154
December	63,333	871	898	8,916	-8,018	-973	-2,886	60,044
Total	**755,523**	**10,098**	**5,954**	**115,632**	**-109,678**	**-34,865**	**3,479**	**687,328**
2019 January	62,479	[F]778	625	9,285	-8,661	-6,128	659	60,066
February	55,140	[F]778	358	6,707	-6,349	735	-114	48,947
March	52,657	[RF]778	706	9,217	-8,512	[R]-1,275	[R]-2,101	[R]48,299
April	58,765	NA	[R]537	[R]8,285	[R]-7,749	NA	NA	NA
May	59,867	NA	NA	NA	NA	NA	NA	NA
5-Month Total	**288,907**	**NA**	**NA**	**NA**	**NA**	**NA**	**NA**	**NA**
2018 5-Month Total	**306,867**	**4,241**	**2,405**	**47,958**	**-45,554**	**-8,629**	**10,142**	**264,040**
2017 5-Month Total	**318,008**	**4,265**	**3,461**	**36,786**	**-33,325**	**-944**	**12,413**	**277,479**

[a] Beginning in 2001, includes a small amount of refuse recovery (coal recaptured from a refuse mine and cleaned to reduce the concentration of noncombustible materials).

[b] Waste coal (including fine coal, coal obtained from a refuse bank or slurry dam, anthracite culm, bituminous gob, and lignite waste) consumed by the electric power and industrial sectors. Beginning in 1989, waste coal supplied is counted as a supply-side item to balance the same amount of waste coal included in "Consumption."

[c] Net imports equal imports minus exports. A minus sign indicates exports are greater than imports.

[d] A negative value indicates a decrease in stocks and a positive value indicates an increase. See Table 6.3 for stocks data coverage.

[e] In 1949, stock change is included in "Losses and Unaccounted for."

[f] The difference between calculated coal supply and disposition, due to coal quantities lost or to data reporting problems.

R=Revised. NA=Not available. F=Forecast.

Notes: • For methodology used to calculate production, consumption, and stocks, see Note 1, "Coal Production," Note 2, "Coal Consumption," and Note 3, "Coal Stocks," at end of section. • Data values preceded by "F" are derived from the U.S. Energy Information Administration's Short-Term Integrated Forecasting System. See Note 4, "Coal Forecast Values," at end of section. • Totals may not equal sum of components due to independent rounding. • Geographic coverage is the 50 states and the District of Columbia.

Web Page: See http://www.eia.gov/totalenergy/data/monthly/#coal (Excel and CSV files) for all available annual data beginning in 1949 and monthly data beginning in 1973.

Sources: See end of section.

***Source:** U.S. Energy Information Administration, Monthly Energy Review, June 2019*

Table 6.2 Coal Consumption by Sector

(Thousand Short Tons)

	End-Use Sectors											
		Commercial			Industrial							
						Other Industrial						
	Residential	CHP[a]	Other[b]	Total	Coke Plants	CHP[c]	Non-CHP[d]	Total	Total	Transportation	Electric Power Sector[e,f]	Total
1950 Total	51,562	([g])	63,021	63,021	104,014	([h])	120,623	120,623	224,637	63,011	91,871	494,102
1955 Total	35,590	([g])	32,852	32,852	107,743	([h])	110,096	110,096	217,839	16,972	143,759	447,012
1960 Total	24,159	([g])	16,789	16,789	81,385	([h])	96,017	96,017	177,402	3,046	176,685	398,081
1965 Total	14,635	([g])	11,041	11,041	95,286	([h])	105,560	105,560	200,846	655	244,788	471,965
1970 Total	9,024	([g])	7,090	7,090	96,481	([h])	90,156	90,156	186,637	298	320,182	523,231
1975 Total	2,823	([g])	6,587	6,587	83,598	([h])	63,646	63,646	147,244	24	405,962	562,640
1980 Total	1,355	([g])	5,097	5,097	66,657	([h])	60,347	60,347	127,004	([h])	569,274	702,730
1985 Total	1,711	([g])	6,068	6,068	41,056	([h])	75,372	75,372	116,429	([h])	693,841	818,049
1990 Total	1,345	1,191	4,189	5,379	38,877	27,781	48,549	76,330	115,207	([h])	[f]782,567	904,498
1995 Total	755	1,419	3,633	5,052	33,011	29,363	43,693	73,055	106,067	([h])	850,230	962,104
2000 Total	454	1,547	2,126	3,673	28,939	28,031	37,177	65,208	94,147	([h])	985,821	1,084,095
2001 Total	481	1,448	2,441	3,888	26,075	25,755	39,514	65,268	91,344	([h])	964,433	1,060,146
2002 Total	533	1,405	2,506	3,912	23,656	26,232	34,515	60,747	84,403	([h])	977,507	1,066,355
2003 Total	551	1,816	1,869	3,685	24,248	24,846	36,415	61,261	85,509	([h])	1,005,116	1,094,861
2004 Total	512	1,917	2,693	4,610	23,670	26,613	35,582	62,195	85,865	([h])	1,016,268	1,107,255
2005 Total	378	1,922	2,420	4,342	23,434	25,875	34,465	60,340	83,774	([h])	1,037,485	1,125,978
2006 Total	290	1,886	1,050	2,936	22,957	25,262	34,210	59,472	82,429	([h])	1,026,636	1,112,292
2007 Total	353	1,927	1,247	3,173	22,715	22,537	34,078	56,615	79,331	([h])	1,045,141	1,127,998
2008 Total	([i])	2,021	1,485	3,506	22,070	21,902	32,491	54,393	76,463	([h])	1,040,580	1,120,548
2009 Total	([i])	1,798	1,412	3,210	15,326	19,766	25,549	45,314	60,641	([h])	933,627	997,478
2010 Total	([i])	1,720	1,361	3,081	21,092	24,638	24,650	49,289	70,381	([h])	975,052	1,048,514
2011 Total	([i])	1,668	1,125	2,793	21,434	22,319	23,919	46,238	67,671	([h])	932,484	1,002,948
2012 Total	([i])	1,450	595	2,045	20,751	20,065	22,773	42,838	63,589	([h])	823,551	889,185
2013 Total	([i])	1,356	595	1,951	21,474	19,761	23,294	43,055	64,529	([h])	857,962	924,442
2014 Total	([i])	1,063	824	1,887	21,297	19,076	23,870	42,946	64,243	([h])	851,602	917,731
2015 Total	([i])	798	706	1,503	19,708	16,984	21,475	38,459	58,167	([h])	738,444	798,115
2016 Total	([i])	683	500	1,183	16,485	14,720	20,129	34,849	51,333	([h])	678,554	731,071
2017 January	([i])	71	65	136	1,431	1,264	1,579	2,844	4,274	([h])	63,595	68,006
February	([i])	58	53	111	1,368	1,077	1,778	2,854	4,222	([h])	48,048	52,381
March	([i])	66	61	126	1,438	1,141	1,695	2,836	4,274	([h])	48,925	53,325
April	([i])	42	29	71	1,441	1,008	1,688	2,696	4,137	([h])	44,358	48,565
May	([i])	39	27	66	1,482	1,043	1,658	2,702	4,184	([h])	50,952	55,202
June	([i])	40	27	67	1,402	1,045	1,665	2,710	4,111	([h])	58,920	63,099
July	([i])	47	21	68	1,494	1,042	1,728	2,769	4,264	([h])	69,882	74,214
August	([i])	43	19	62	1,528	1,050	1,707	2,757	4,285	([h])	65,883	70,229
September	([i])	45	20	65	1,469	991	1,734	2,725	4,194	([h])	54,780	59,039
October	([i])	42	34	76	1,470	1,098	1,694	2,791	4,261	([h])	50,099	54,436
November	([i])	52	43	95	1,457	1,077	1,716	2,793	4,250	([h])	51,013	55,357
December	([i])	66	54	119	1,559	1,139	1,647	2,787	4,346	([h])	58,538	63,003
Total	([i])	**610**	**451**	**1,061**	**17,538**	**12,975**	**20,289**	**33,264**	**50,801**	([h])	**664,993**	**716,856**
2018 January	([i])	70	71	141	1,458	1,245	1,463	2,708	4,166	([h])	64,606	68,913
February	([i])	54	55	109	1,288	1,111	1,632	2,742	4,031	([h])	45,757	49,897
March	([i])	51	53	104	1,482	1,140	1,594	2,734	4,216	([h])	44,439	48,759
April	([i])	45	23	69	1,549	1,016	1,543	2,558	4,107	([h])	40,601	44,777
May	([i])	41	21	61	1,596	1,041	1,511	2,552	4,148	([h])	47,485	51,695
June	([i])	42	21	63	1,465	989	1,567	2,556	4,021	([h])	56,089	60,173
July	([i])	47	8	55	1,592	978	1,542	2,520	4,112	([h])	63,851	68,018
August	([i])	49	9	58	1,569	942	1,575	2,517	4,086	([h])	63,751	67,895
September	([i])	51	9	59	1,577	977	1,534	2,511	4,088	([h])	53,998	58,145
October	([i])	42	34	76	1,549	933	1,780	2,713	4,262	([h])	48,520	52,858
November	([i])	48	39	87	1,558	1,018	1,701	2,720	4,278	([h])	51,789	56,154
December	([i])	47	38	85	1,630	1,078	1,642	2,720	4,350	([h])	55,610	60,044
Total	([i])	**587**	**380**	**967**	**18,312**	**12,468**	**19,083**	**31,551**	**49,863**	([h])	**636,498**	**687,328**
2019 January	([i])	58	[F]15	[F]73	[F]1,352	1,099	[F]1,656	[F]2,755	[F]4,107	([h])	55,885	60,066
February	([i])	53	[F]7	[F]61	[F]1,181	999	[F]1,655	[F]2,654	[F]3,836	([h])	45,051	48,947
March	([i])	55	[F]7	[F]62	[F]1,679	942	[F]1,539	[F]2,481	[F]4,160	([h])	44,078	48,299
3-Month Total	([i])	**166**	[E]**30**	[E]**196**	[E]**4,213**	**3,040**	[E]**4,850**	[E]**7,890**	[E]**12,102**	([h])	**145,014**	**157,313**
2018 3-Month Total	([i])	**175**	**179**	**354**	**4,228**	**3,496**	**4,688**	**8,184**	**12,412**	([h])	**154,803**	**167,569**
2017 3-Month Total	([i])	**194**	**179**	**373**	**4,236**	**3,482**	**5,052**	**8,534**	**12,770**	([h])	**160,569**	**173,712**

[a] Commercial combined-heat-and-power (CHP) and a small number of commercial electricity-only plants, such as those at hospitals and universities. See Note 2, "Classification of Power Plants Into Energy-Use Sectors," at end of Section 7.

[b] All commercial sector fuel use other than that in "Commercial CHP."

[c] Industrial combined-heat-and-power (CHP) and a small number of industrial electricity-only plants. See Note 2, "Classification of Power Plants Into Energy-Use Sectors," at end of Section 7.

[d] All industrial sector fuel use other than that in "Coke Plants" and "Industrial CHP."

[e] The electric power sector comprises electricity-only and combined-heat-and-power (CHP) plants within the NAICS 22 category whose primary business is to sell electricity, or electricity and heat, to the public.

[f] Through 1988, data are for electric utilities only. Beginning in 1989, data are for electric utilities and independent power producers.

[g] Included in "Commercial Other."

[h] Included in "Industrial Non-CHP."

[i] Beginning in 2008, residential coal consumption data are no longer collected by the U.S. Energy Information Administration (EIA).

E=Estimate. F=Forecast.

Notes: • CHP monthly values are from Table 7.4c; electric power sector monthly values are from Table 7.4b; all other monthly values are estimates derived from collected quarterly and annual data. See Note 2, "Coal Consumption," at end of section. • Data values preceded by "F" are derived from EIA's Short-Term Integrated Forecasting System. See Note 4, "Coal Forecast Values," at end of section. • Totals may not equal sum of components due to independent rounding. • Geographic coverage is the 50 states and the District of Columbia.

Web Page: See http://www.eia.gov/totalenergy/data/monthly/#coal (Excel and CSV files) for all available annual data beginning in 1949 and monthly data beginning in 1973.

Sources: See end of section.

Source: *U.S. Energy Information Administration, Monthly Energy Review, June 2019*

Table 6.3 Coal Stocks by Sector
(Thousand Short Tons)

	Producers and Distributors	End-Use Sectors					Electric Power Sector[c,d]	Total
		Residential[a] and Commercial	Industrial			Total		
			Coke Plants	Other[b]	Total			
1950 Year	NA	2,462	16,809	26,182	42,991	45,453	31,842	77,295
1955 Year	NA	998	13,422	15,880	29,302	30,300	41,391	71,691
1960 Year	NA	666	11,122	11,637	22,759	23,425	51,735	75,160
1965 Year	NA	353	10,640	13,122	23,762	24,115	54,525	78,640
1970 Year	NA	300	9,045	11,781	20,826	21,126	71,908	93,034
1975 Year	12,108	233	8,797	8,529	17,326	17,559	110,724	140,391
1980 Year	24,379	NA	9,067	11,951	21,018	21,018	183,010	228,407
1985 Year	33,133	NA	3,420	10,438	13,857	13,857	156,376	203,367
1990 Year	33,418	NA	3,329	8,716	12,044	12,044	156,166	201,629
1995 Year	34,444	NA	2,632	5,702	8,334	8,334	126,304	169,083
2000 Year	31,905	NA	1,494	4,587	6,081	6,081	102,296	140,282
2001 Year	35,900	NA	1,510	6,006	7,516	7,516	138,496	181,912
2002 Year	43,257	NA	1,364	5,792	7,156	7,156	141,714	192,127
2003 Year	38,277	NA	905	4,718	5,623	5,623	121,567	165,468
2004 Year	41,151	NA	1,344	4,842	6,186	6,186	106,669	154,006
2005 Year	34,971	NA	2,615	5,582	8,196	8,196	101,137	144,304
2006 Year	36,548	NA	2,928	6,506	9,434	9,434	140,964	186,946
2007 Year	33,977	NA	1,936	5,624	7,560	7,560	151,221	192,758
2008 Year	34,688	498	2,331	6,007	8,338	8,836	161,589	205,112
2009 Year	47,718	529	1,957	5,109	7,066	7,595	189,467	244,780
2010 Year	49,820	552	1,925	4,525	6,451	7,003	174,917	231,740
2011 Year	51,897	603	2,610	4,455	7,065	7,668	172,387	231,951
2012 Year	46,157	583	2,522	4,475	6,997	7,581	185,116	238,853
2013 Year	45,652	495	2,200	4,097	6,297	6,792	147,884	200,328
2014 Year	38,894	449	2,640	4,196	6,836	7,285	151,548	197,727
2015 Year	35,871	394	2,236	4,382	6,618	7,012	195,548	238,431
2016 Year	25,309	360	1,675	3,637	5,312	5,672	162,009	192,990
2017 January	24,974	352	1,579	3,503	5,082	5,434	156,214	186,622
February	25,170	343	1,483	3,370	4,853	5,196	160,502	190,868
March	25,190	335	1,388	3,236	4,624	4,959	161,815	191,964
April	25,169	333	1,467	3,256	4,723	5,056	163,937	194,162
May	24,350	331	1,547	3,275	4,822	5,153	162,542	192,045
June	23,430	329	1,626	3,295	4,921	5,250	158,014	186,694
July	25,465	332	1,641	3,357	4,998	5,330	145,811	176,606
August	24,226	335	1,655	3,419	5,075	5,409	141,204	170,839
September	23,430	337	1,670	3,482	5,152	5,489	139,571	168,490
October	23,459	328	1,686	3,402	5,088	5,416	141,463	170,338
November	23,705	319	1,702	3,322	5,024	5,343	143,424	172,472
December	**23,999**	**310**	**1,718**	**3,242**	**4,960**	**5,270**	**137,687**	**166,956**
2018 January	F 24,769	298	1,648	3,124	4,772	5,070	123,723	153,562
February	F 26,594	287	1,578	3,008	4,586	4,873	121,019	152,485
March	F 26,775	275	1,508	2,892	4,400	4,675	126,532	157,982
April	F 26,558	269	1,544	2,890	4,434	4,703	129,071	160,332
May	F 25,142	263	1,580	2,889	4,469	4,732	128,454	158,328
June	F 24,524	257	1,616	2,888	4,504	4,761	121,529	150,814
July	F 24,691	259	1,681	2,926	4,606	4,866	110,794	140,351
August	F 22,574	261	1,746	2,966	4,711	4,972	104,172	131,719
September	F 23,413	263	1,811	3,005	4,816	5,079	100,781	129,273
October	F 24,198	259	1,809	3,105	4,914	5,173	105,209	134,580
November	F 23,490	255	1,808	3,188	4,996	5,250	104,324	133,064
December	**F 23,978**	**250**	**1,807**	**3,270**	**5,077**	**5,328**	**102,786**	**132,092**
2019 January	F 21,391	F 240	F 1,741	F 3,390	F 5,132	F 5,372	99,201	125,963
February	F 23,051	F 223	F 1,536	F 3,144	F 4,680	F 4,903	98,744	126,698
March	F 23,158	F 225	F 1,354	F 3,558	F 4,912	F 5,137	97,127	125,423

[a] Through 1979, data are for the residential and commercial sectors. Beginning in 2008, data are for the commercial sector only.
[b] Through 1979, data are for manufacturing plants and the transportation sector. For 1980–2007, data are for manufacturing plants only. Beginning in 2008, data are for manufacturing plants and coal transformation/processing plants.
[c] The electric power sector comprises electricity-only and combined-heat-and-power (CHP) plants within the NAICS 22 category whose primary business is to sell electricity, or electricity and heat, to the public.
[d] Excludes waste coal. Through 1998, data are for electric utilities only. Beginning in 1999, data are for electric utilities and independent power producers.

NA=Not available. F=Forecast.

Notes: • Stocks are at end of period. • Electric power sector monthly values are from Table 7.5; producers and distributors monthly values are estimates derived from collected annual data; all other monthly values are estimates derived from collected quarterly values. • Data values preceded by "F" are derived from the U.S. Energy Information Administration's Short-Term Integrated Forecasting System. See Note 4, "Coal Forecast Values," at end of section. • Totals may not equal sum of components due to independent rounding. • Geographic coverage is the 50 states and the District of Columbia.

Web Page: See http://www.eia.gov/totalenergy/data/monthly/#coal (Excel and CSV files) for all available annual data beginning in 1949 and monthly data beginning in 1973.

Sources: See end of section.

Source: *U.S. Energy Information Administration, Monthly Energy Review, June 2019*

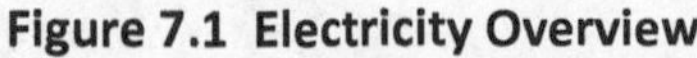

Figure 7.1 Electricity Overview

(Billion Kilowatthours)

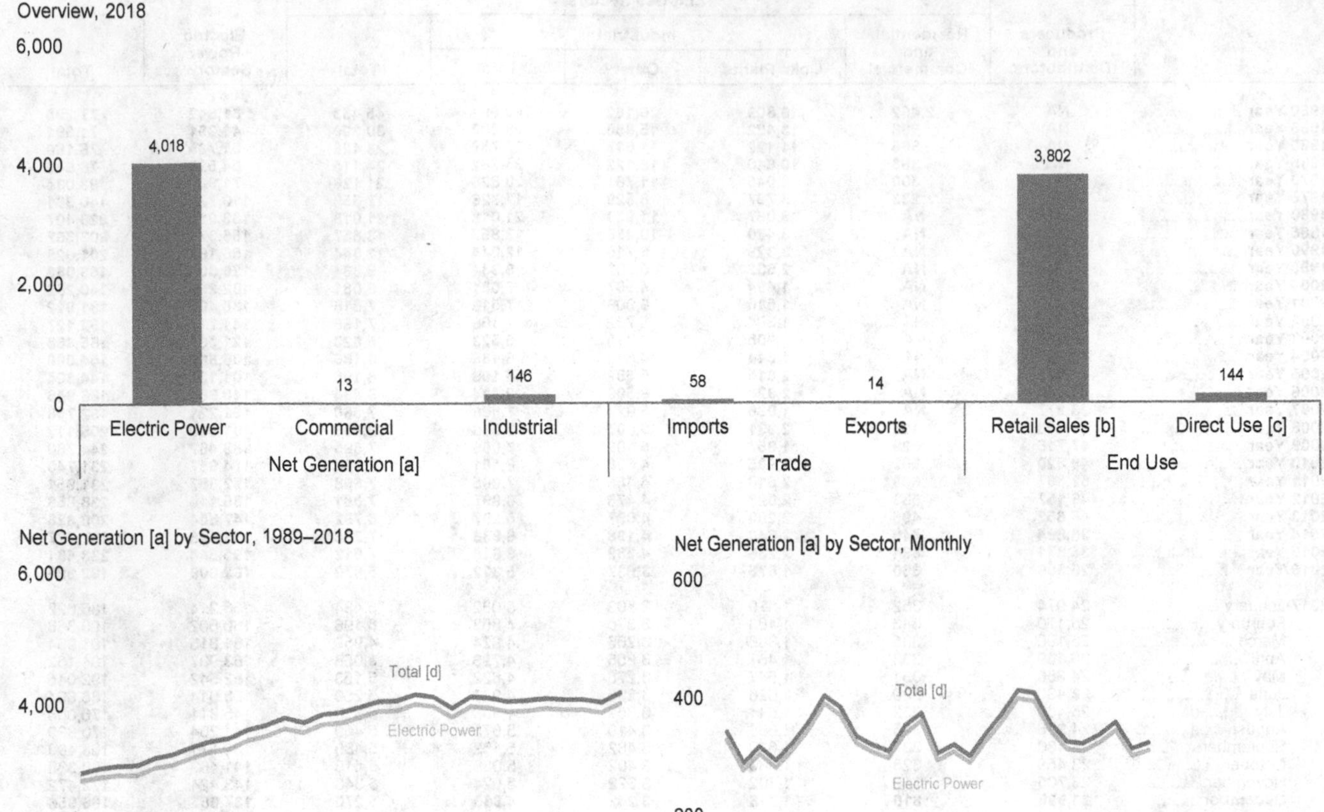

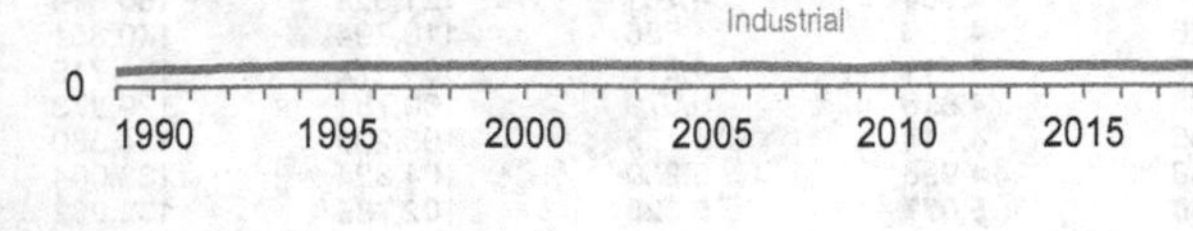

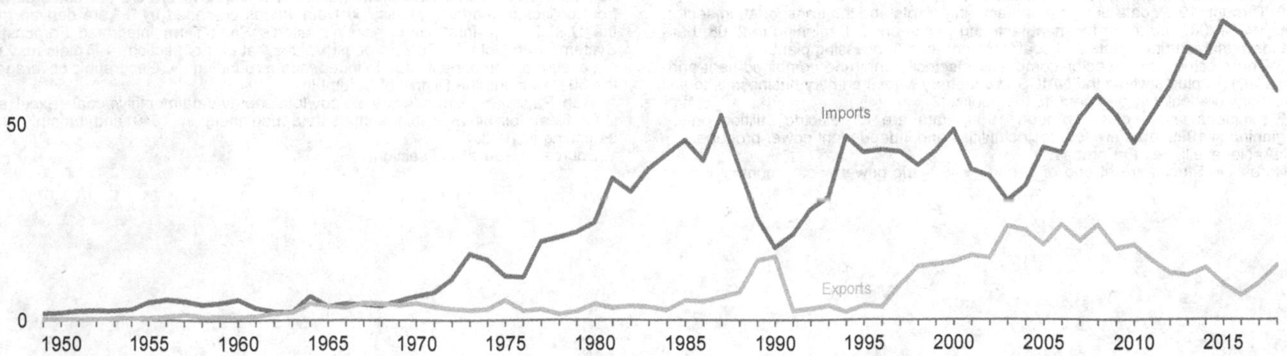

[a] Data are for utility-scale facilities.

[b] Electricity retail sales to ultimate customers reported by electric utilities and other energy service providers.

[c] See "Direct Use" in Glossary.

[d] Includes commercial sector.

Web Page: http://www.eia.gov/totalenergy/data/monthly/#electricity.

Source: Table 7.1.

***Source:** U.S. Energy Information Administration, Monthly Energy Review, June 2019*

Table 7.1 Electricity Overview

(Billion Kilowatthours)

	Net Generation[a]				Trade			T&D Losses[f] and Unaccounted for[g]	End Use		
	Electric Power Sector[b]	Commercial Sector[c]	Industrial Sector[d]	Total	Imports[e]	Exports[e]	Net Imports[e]		Retail Sales[h]	Direct Use[i]	Total
1950 Total	**329**	**NA**	**5**	**334**	**2**	**(s)**	**2**	**44**	**291**	**NA**	**291**
1955 Total	**547**	**NA**	**3**	**550**	**5**	**(s)**	**4**	**58**	**497**	**NA**	**497**
1960 Total	**756**	**NA**	**4**	**759**	**5**	**1**	**5**	**76**	**688**	**NA**	**688**
1965 Total	**1,055**	**NA**	**3**	**1,058**	**4**	**4**	**(s)**	**104**	**954**	**NA**	**954**
1970 Total	**1,532**	**NA**	**3**	**1,535**	**6**	**4**	**2**	**145**	**1,392**	**NA**	**1,392**
1975 Total	**1,918**	**NA**	**3**	**1,921**	**11**	**5**	**6**	**180**	**1,747**	**NA**	**1,747**
1980 Total	**2,286**	**NA**	**3**	**2,290**	**25**	**4**	**21**	**216**	**2,094**	**NA**	**2,094**
1985 Total	**2,470**	**NA**	**3**	**2,473**	**46**	**5**	**41**	**190**	**2,324**	**NA**	**2,324**
1990 Total	**2,901**	**6**	[d] **131**	**3,038**	**18**	**16**	**2**	**203**	**2,713**	**125**	**2,837**
1995 Total	**3,194**	**8**	**151**	**3,353**	**43**	**4**	**39**	**229**	**3,013**	**151**	**3,164**
2000 Total	**3,638**	**8**	**157**	**3,802**	**49**	**15**	**34**	**244**	**3,421**	**171**	**3,592**
2001 Total	**3,580**	**7**	**149**	**3,737**	**39**	**16**	**22**	**202**	**3,394**	**163**	**3,557**
2002 Total	**3,698**	**7**	**153**	**3,858**	**37**	**16**	**21**	**248**	**3,465**	**166**	**3,632**
2003 Total	**3,721**	**7**	**155**	**3,883**	**30**	**24**	**6**	**228**	**3,494**	**168**	**3,662**
2004 Total	**3,808**	**8**	**154**	**3,971**	**34**	**23**	**11**	**266**	**3,547**	**168**	**3,716**
2005 Total	**3,902**	**8**	**145**	**4,055**	**44**	**19**	**25**	**269**	**3,661**	**150**	**3,811**
2006 Total	**3,908**	**8**	**148**	**4,065**	**43**	**24**	**18**	**266**	**3,670**	**147**	**3,817**
2007 Total	**4,005**	**8**	**143**	**4,157**	**51**	**20**	**31**	**298**	**3,765**	**126**	**3,890**
2008 Total	**3,974**	**8**	**137**	**4,119**	**57**	**24**	**33**	**286**	**3,734**	**132**	**3,866**
2009 Total	**3,810**	**8**	**132**	**3,950**	**52**	**18**	**34**	**261**	**3,597**	**127**	**3,724**
2010 Total	**3,972**	**9**	**144**	**4,125**	**45**	**19**	**26**	**264**	**3,755**	**132**	**3,887**
2011 Total	**3,948**	**10**	**142**	**4,100**	**52**	**15**	**37**	**255**	**3,750**	**133**	**3,883**
2012 Total	**3,890**	**11**	**146**	**4,048**	**59**	**12**	**47**	**263**	**3,695**	**138**	**3,832**
2013 Total	**3,904**	**12**	**150**	**4,066**	**69**	**11**	**58**	**256**	**3,725**	**143**	**3,868**
2014 Total	**3,937**	**13**	**144**	**4,094**	**67**	**13**	**53**	**244**	**3,765**	**139**	**3,903**
2015 Total	**3,919**	**13**	**146**	**4,078**	**76**	**9**	**67**	**244**	**3,759**	**141**	**3,900**
2016 Total	**3,918**	**13**	**146**	**4,077**	**73**	**6**	**67**	**241**	**3,762**	**140**	**3,902**
2017 January	330	1	12	343	7	(s)	7	19	318	E 12	330
February	278	1	11	290	6	1	5	8	276	E 11	287
March	305	1	12	318	6	1	5	20	291	E 12	303
April	282	1	11	294	6	1	4	15	273	E 11	284
May	310	1	12	323	5	1	4	23	292	E 11	303
June	345	1	12	358	6	1	5	23	329	E 12	341
July	390	1	13	404	6	1	5	29	368	E 13	380
August	370	1	13	384	7	1	6	17	360	E 13	373
September	323	1	11	336	5	1	5	7	322	E 11	333
October	308	1	12	320	4	1	3	13	300	E 11	311
November	298	1	12	310	4	1	3	19	283	E 11	295
December	340	1	13	353	5	1	4	33	312	E 13	325
Total	**3,877**	**13**	**144**	**4,034**	**66**	**9**	**56**	**226**	**3,723**	**141**	**3,864**
2018 January	360	1	13	374	5	1	4	26	340	E 12	353
February	294	1	11	306	5	1	4	11	288	E 11	299
March	308	1	12	321	6	1	4	22	292	E 12	304
April	289	1	11	302	5	2	3	19	274	E 11	285
May	327	1	12	340	5	1	4	34	298	E 12	310
June	359	1	12	372	5	1	4	32	333	E 12	345
July	398	1	13	413	5	1	4	35	370	E 13	382
August	394	1	13	408	6	1	5	22	378	E 13	391
September	344	1	12	357	4	1	3	16	332	E 12	344
October	313	1	12	326	4	1	3	13	304	E 12	316
November	309	1	12	322	4	1	3	27	286	E 12	298
December	323	1	13	337	4	1	3	21	307	E 12	320
Total	**4,018**	**13**	**146**	**4,178**	**58**	**14**	**44**	**277**	**3,802**	E **144**	**3,946**
2019 January	344	1	13	358	F 6	F 1	F 5	27	323	E 13	336
February	301	1	11	313	F 4	F 1	F 4	14	292	E 11	303
March	310	1	12	323	F 5	F 1	F 4	18	297	E 12	309
3-Month Total	**955**	**3**	**36**	**994**	F **15**	F **2**	F **12**	**58**	**913**	E **36**	**948**
2018 3-Month Total	**962**	**3**	**36**	**1,001**	**16**	**4**	**12**	**58**	**921**	E **35**	**956**
2017 3-Month Total	**912**	**3**	**35**	**951**	**19**	**2**	**17**	**47**	**885**	E **35**	**920**

[a] Electricity net generation at utility-scale facilities. Does not include distributed (small-scale) solar photovoltaic (PV) generation shown on Table 10.6. See Note 1, "Coverage of Electricity Statistics," at end of section.

[b] Electricity-only and combined-heat-and-power (CHP) plants within the NAICS 22 category whose primary business is to sell electricity, or electricity and heat, to the public. Through 1988, data are for electric utilities only; beginning in 1989, data are for electric utilities and independent power producers.

[c] Commercial combined-heat-and-power (CHP) and commercial electricity-only plants.

[d] Industrial combined-heat-and-power (CHP) and industrial electricity-only plants. Through 1988, data are for industrial hydroelectric power only.

[e] Electricity transmitted across U.S. borders. Net imports equal imports minus exports.

[f] Transmission and distribution losses (electricity losses that occur between the point of generation and delivery to the customer). See Note 1, "Electrical System Energy Losses," at end of Section 2.

[g] Data collection frame differences and nonsampling error.

[h] Electricity retail sales to ultimate customers by electric utilities and, beginning in 1996, other energy service providers.

[i] Use of electricity that is 1) self-generated, 2) produced by either the same entity that consumes the power or an affiliate, and 3) used in direct support of a service or industrial process located within the same facility or group of facilities that house the generating equipment. Direct use is exclusive of station use.

E=Estimate. NA=Not available. F=Forecast. (s)=Less than 0.5 billion kilowatthours.

Notes: • See Note 1, "Coverage of Electricity Statistics," and Note 2, "Classification of Power Plants Into Energy-Use Sectors," at end of section. • Data values preceded by "F" are derived from the U.S. Energy Information Administration's Short-Term Integrated Forecasting System. See Note 3, "Electricity Forecast Values," at end of section. • Totals may not equal sum of components due to independent rounding. • Geographic coverage is the 50 states and the District of Columbia.

Web Page: See http://www.eia.gov/totalenergy/data/monthly/#electricity (Excel and CSV files) for all available annual data beginning in 1949 and monthly data beginning in 1973.

Sources: See end of section.

Source: *U.S. Energy Information Administration, Monthly Energy Review, June 2019*

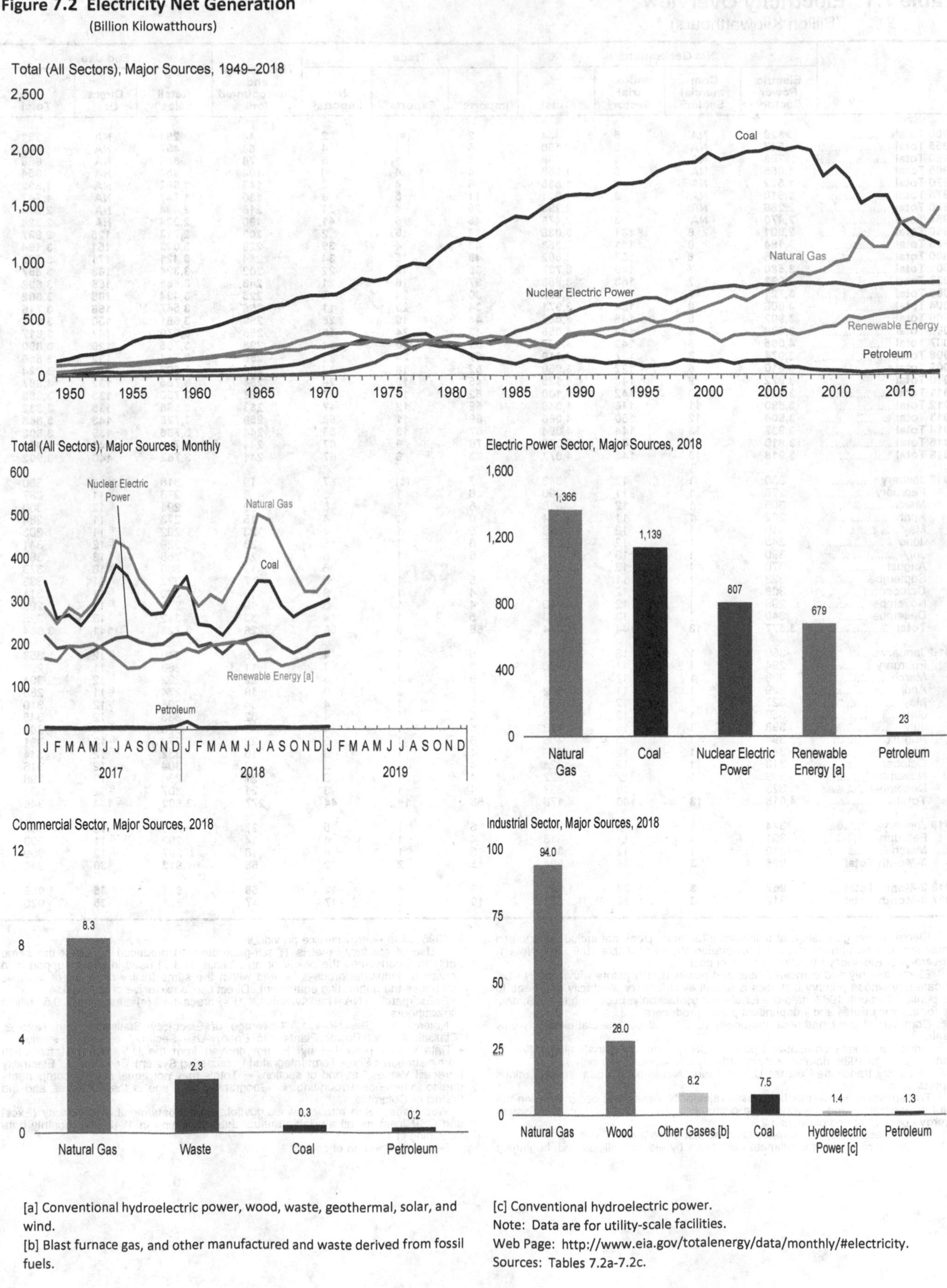

[a] Conventional hydroelectric power, wood, waste, geothermal, solar, and wind.

[b] Blast furnace gas, and other manufactured and waste derived from fossil fuels.

[c] Conventional hydroelectric power.

Note: Data are for utility-scale facilities.

Web Page: http://www.eia.gov/totalenergy/data/monthly/#electricity.

Sources: Tables 7.2a-7.2c.

Source: *U.S. Energy Information Administration, Monthly Energy Review, June 2019*

Table 7.2a Electricity Net Generation: Total (All Sectors)

(Sum of Tables 7.2b and 7.2c; Million Kilowatthours)

	Fossil Fuels						Renewable Energy						
								Biomass					
	Coal[a]	Petroleum[b]	Natural Gas[c]	Other Gases[d]	Nuclear Electric Power	Hydroelectric Pumped Storage[e]	Conventional Hydroelectric Power[f]	Wood[g]	Waste[h]	Geothermal	Solar[i]	Wind	Total[j]
1950 Total	154,520	33,734	44,559	NA	0	(f)	100,885	390	NA	NA	NA	NA	334,088
1955 Total	301,363	37,138	95,285	NA	0	(f)	116,236	276	NA	NA	NA	NA	550,299
1960 Total	403,067	47,987	157,970	NA	518	(f)	149,440	140	NA	33	NA	NA	759,156
1965 Total	570,926	64,801	221,559	NA	3,657	(f)	196,984	269	NA	189	NA	NA	1,058,386
1970 Total	704,394	184,183	372,890	NA	21,804	(f)	250,957	136	220	525	NA	NA	1,535,111
1975 Total	852,786	289,095	299,778	NA	172,505	(f)	303,153	18	174	3,246	NA	NA	1,920,755
1980 Total	1,161,562	245,994	346,240	NA	251,116	(f)	279,182	275	158	5,073	NA	NA	2,289,600
1985 Total	1,402,128	100,202	291,946	NA	383,691	(f)	284,311	743	640	9,325	11	6	2,473,002
1990 Total[k]	1,594,011	126,460	372,765	10,383	576,862	-3,508	292,866	32,522	13,260	15,434	367	2,789	3,037,827
1995 Total	1,709,426	74,554	496,058	13,870	673,402	-2,725	310,833	36,521	20,405	13,378	497	3,164	3,353,487
2000 Total	1,966,265	111,221	601,038	13,955	753,893	-5,539	275,573	37,595	23,131	14,093	493	5,593	3,802,105
2001 Total	1,903,956	124,880	639,129	9,039	768,826	-8,823	216,961	35,200	14,548	13,741	543	6,737	3,736,644
2002 Total	1,933,130	94,567	691,006	11,463	780,064	-8,743	264,329	38,665	15,044	14,491	555	10,354	3,858,452
2003 Total	1,973,737	119,406	649,908	15,600	763,733	-8,535	275,806	37,529	15,812	14,424	534	11,187	3,883,185
2004 Total	1,978,301	121,145	710,100	15,252	788,528	-8,488	268,417	38,117	15,421	14,811	575	14,144	3,970,555
2005 Total	2,012,873	122,225	760,960	13,464	781,986	-6,558	270,321	38,856	15,420	14,692	550	17,811	4,055,423
2006 Total	1,990,511	64,166	816,441	14,177	787,219	-6,558	289,246	38,762	16,099	14,568	508	26,589	4,064,702
2007 Total	2,016,456	65,739	896,590	13,453	806,425	-6,896	247,510	39,014	16,525	14,637	612	34,450	4,156,745
2008 Total	1,985,801	46,243	882,981	11,707	806,208	-6,288	254,831	37,300	17,734	14,840	864	55,363	4,119,388
2009 Total	1,755,904	38,937	920,979	10,632	798,855	-4,627	273,445	36,050	18,443	15,009	891	73,886	3,950,331
2010 Total	1,847,290	37,061	987,697	11,313	806,968	-5,501	260,203	37,172	18,917	15,219	1,212	94,652	4,125,060
2011 Total	1,733,430	30,182	1,013,689	11,566	790,204	-6,421	319,355	37,449	19,222	15,316	1,818	120,177	4,100,141
2012 Total	1,514,043	23,190	1,225,894	11,898	769,331	-4,950	276,240	37,799	19,823	15,562	4,327	140,822	4,047,765
2013 Total	1,581,115	27,164	1,124,836	12,853	789,016	-4,681	268,565	40,028	20,830	15,775	9,036	167,840	4,065,964
2014 Total	1,581,710	30,232	1,126,609	12,022	797,166	-6,174	259,367	42,340	21,650	15,877	17,691	181,655	4,093,606
2015 Total	1,352,398	28,249	1,333,482	13,117	797,178	-5,091	249,080	41,929	21,703	15,918	24,893	190,719	4,077,601
2016 Total	1,239,149	24,205	1,378,307	12,807	805,694	-6,686	267,812	40,947	21,813	15,826	36,054	226,993	4,076,675
2017 January	115,333	2,065	95,473	1,046	73,121	-435	26,788	3,505	1,948	1,383	2,030	19,840	343,190
February	86,822	1,597	82,694	977	63,560	-508	23,643	3,186	1,694	1,239	2,555	21,198	289,652
March	89,365	1,649	95,022	1,060	65,093	-521	29,272	3,457	1,854	1,385	4,245	24,993	317,935
April	81,335	1,277	88,418	1,001	56,743	-439	29,390	3,149	1,755	1,337	4,696	24,613	294,325
May	92,777	1,818	98,067	1,055	61,313	-423	32,384	3,189	1,859	1,283	5,663	22,450	322,518
June	107,508	1,902	117,317	992	67,011	-568	30,222	3,439	1,795	1,214	6,175	19,809	357,916
July	127,697	1,806	146,994	1,048	71,314	-759	26,491	3,703	1,813	1,355	5,753	15,960	404,386
August	119,488	1,734	141,209	1,134	72,384	-638	21,851	3,753	1,808	1,345	5,434	13,621	384,342
September	98,203	1,637	118,112	1,060	68,098	-606	19,067	3,294	1,696	1,297	5,115	17,855	335,861
October	89,775	1,528	106,852	999	65,995	-463	18,284	3,306	1,717	1,229	4,821	25,306	320,376
November	90,986	1,658	94,883	1,001	66,618	-478	20,565	3,430	1,795	1,289	3,409	24,082	310,315
December	106,546	2,719	111,373	1,096	73,700	-656	22,377	3,738	1,877	1,571	3,389	24,575	353,452
Total	**1,205,835**	**21,390**	**1,296,415**	**12,469**	**804,950**	**-6,495**	**300,333**	**41,152**	**21,610**	**15,927**	**53,286**	**254,303**	**4,034,268**
2018 January	118,939	6,243	110,046	994	74,649	-547	25,596	3,759	1,854	1,407	3,407	26,862	374,324
February	81,922	1,518	96,002	990	64,790	-315	25,533	3,379	1,761	1,326	4,113	24,096	306,115
March	80,612	1,459	104,933	1,064	67,033	-490	25,951	3,535	1,870	1,414	5,203	27,283	320,982
April	73,383	1,546	99,446	940	59,133	-377	27,490	3,096	1,766	1,246	6,249	26,783	301,739
May	85,311	1,437	116,107	1,000	67,320	-390	30,434	3,550	1,744	1,434	7,070	23,603	339,694
June	101,509	1,827	130,823	1,010	69,688	-433	27,955	3,573	1,787	1,369	7,804	24,376	372,398
July	115,477	1,892	167,250	1,105	72,456	-644	24,014	3,690	1,798	1,436	6,938	16,014	412,542
August	115,216	1,914	162,377	1,225	72,282	-747	21,400	3,570	1,797	1,429	6,981	19,530	407,981
September	96,742	1,874	142,772	1,001	64,725	-603	18,665	3,284	1,635	1,388	6,469	17,977	356,728
October	87,452	1,473	124,171	930	59,397	-492	18,781	3,277	1,766	1,347	5,223	21,147	325,563
November	93,005	1,652	107,109	933	63,948	-343	22,176	3,284	1,752	1,397	3,958	22,457	322,409
December	96,825	1,737	106,978	998	71,657	-522	23,728	3,414	1,825	1,535	3,188	24,825	337,334
Total	**1,146,393**	**24,572**	**1,468,013**	**12,191**	**807,078**	**-5,905**	**291,724**	**41,411**	**21,354**	**16,728**	**66,604**	**274,952**	**4,177,810**
2019 January	101,019	2,136	118,935	994	73,701	-323	24,544	3,529	1,755	1,456	3,652	25,165	357,690
February	80,008	1,512	110,428	1,015	64,715	-389	22,031	3,165	1,570	1,339	3,913	23,047	313,278
March	78,454	1,439	112,574	1,143	65,080	-409	25,400	3,241	1,713	1,480	6,020	26,036	323,187
3-Month Total	**259,481**	**5,086**	**341,936**	**3,151**	**203,495**	**-1,121**	**71,974**	**9,935**	**5,038**	**4,274**	**13,585**	**74,247**	**994,155**
2018 3-Month Total	**281,473**	**9,220**	**310,981**	**3,049**	**206,472**	**-1,352**	**77,081**	**10,673**	**5,484**	**4,147**	**12,723**	**78,241**	**1,001,421**
2017 3-Month Total	**291,520**	**5,311**	**273,190**	**3,082**	**201,774**	**-1,464**	**79,703**	**10,149**	**5,495**	**4,006**	**8,831**	**66,031**	**950,777**

[a] Anthracite, bituminous coal, subbituminous coal, lignite, waste coal, and coal synfuel.
[b] Distillate fuel oil, residual fuel oil, petroleum coke, jet fuel, kerosene, other petroleum, waste oil, and, beginning in 2011, propane.
[c] Natural gas, plus a small amount of supplemental gaseous fuels.
[d] Blast furnace gas, and other manufactured and waste gases derived from fossil fuels. Through 2010, also includes propane gas.
[e] Pumped storage facility production minus energy used for pumping.
[f] Through 1989, hydroelectric pumped storage is included in "Conventional Hydroelectric Power."
[g] Wood and wood-derived fuels.
[h] Municipal solid waste from biogenic sources, landfill gas, sludge waste, agricultural byproducts, and other biomass. Through 2000, also includes non-renewable waste (municipal solid waste from non-biogenic sources, and tire-derived fuels).
[i] Electricity net generation from solar thermal and photovoltaic (PV) energy at utility-scale facilities. Does not include distributed (small-scale) solar photovoltaic generation. See Table 10.6.
[j] Includes batteries, chemicals, hydrogen, pitch, purchased steam, sulfur, miscellaneous technologies, and, beginning in 2001, non-renewable waste (municipal solid waste from non-biogenic sources, and tire-derived fuels).
[k] Through 1988, all data except hydroelectric are for electric utilities only; hydroelectric data through 1988 include industrial plants as well as electric utilities. Beginning in 1989, data are for electric utilities, independent power producers, commercial plants, and industrial plants.

NA=Not available.

Notes: • Data are for utility-scale facilities. See Note 1, "Coverage of Electricity Statistics," at end of section. • Totals may not equal sum of components due to independent rounding. • Geographic coverage is the 50 states and the District of Columbia.

Web Page: See http://www.eia.gov/totalenergy/data/monthly/#electricity (Excel and CSV files) for all available annual data beginning in 1949 and monthly data beginning in 1973.

Sources: See end of section, "Table 7.2b Sources" and "Table 7.2c Sources."

Source: *U.S. Energy Information Administration, Monthly Energy Review, June 2019*

Table 7.2b Electricity Net Generation: Electric Power Sector
(Subset of Table 7.2a; Million Kilowatthours)

	Fossil Fuels						Renewable Energy						
							Conventional Hydroelectric Power[f]	Biomass					
	Coal[a]	Petroleum[b]	Natural Gas[c]	Other Gases[d]	Nuclear Electric Power	Hydroelectric Pumped Storage[e]		Wood[g]	Waste[h]	Geothermal	Solar[i]	Wind	Total[j]
1950 Total	**154,520**	**33,734**	**44,559**	**NA**	**0**	**(f)**	**95,938**	**390**	**NA**	**NA**	**NA**	**NA**	**329,141**
1955 Total	**301,363**	**37,138**	**95,285**	**NA**	**0**	**(f)**	**112,975**	**276**	**NA**	**NA**	**NA**	**NA**	**547,038**
1960 Total	**403,067**	**47,987**	**157,970**	**NA**	**518**	**(f)**	**145,833**	**140**	**NA**	**33**	**NA**	**NA**	**755,549**
1965 Total	**570,926**	**64,801**	**221,559**	**NA**	**3,657**	**(f)**	**193,851**	**269**	**NA**	**189**	**NA**	**NA**	**1,055,252**
1970 Total	**704,394**	**184,183**	**372,890**	**NA**	**21,804**	**(f)**	**247,714**	**136**	**220**	**525**	**NA**	**NA**	**1,531,868**
1975 Total	**852,786**	**289,095**	**299,778**	**NA**	**172,505**	**(f)**	**300,047**	**18**	**174**	**3,246**	**NA**	**NA**	**1,917,649**
1980 Total	**1,161,562**	**245,994**	**346,240**	**NA**	**251,116**	**(f)**	**276,021**	**275**	**158**	**5,073**	**NA**	**NA**	**2,286,439**
1985 Total	**1,402,128**	**100,202**	**291,946**	**NA**	**383,691**	**(f)**	**281,149**	**743**	**640**	**9,325**	**11**	**6**	**2,469,841**
1990 Total[k]	**1,572,109**	**118,864**	**309,486**	**621**	**576,862**	**-3,508**	**289,753**	**7,032**	**11,500**	**15,434**	**367**	**2,789**	**2,901,322**
1995 Total	**1,686,056**	**68,146**	**419,179**	**1,927**	**673,402**	**-2,725**	**305,410**	**7,597**	**17,986**	**13,378**	**497**	**3,164**	**3,194,230**
2000 Total	**1,943,111**	**105,192**	**517,978**	**2,028**	**753,893**	**-5,539**	**271,338**	**8,916**	**20,307**	**14,093**	**493**	**5,593**	**3,637,529**
2001 Total	**1,882,826**	**119,149**	**554,940**	**586**	**768,826**	**-8,823**	**213,749**	**8,294**	**12,944**	**13,741**	**543**	**6,737**	**3,580,053**
2002 Total	**1,910,613**	**89,733**	**607,683**	**1,970**	**780,064**	**-8,743**	**260,491**	**9,009**	**13,145**	**14,491**	**555**	**10,354**	**3,698,458**
2003 Total	**1,952,714**	**113,697**	**567,303**	**2,647**	**763,733**	**-8,535**	**271,512**	**9,528**	**13,808**	**14,424**	**534**	**11,187**	**3,721,159**
2004 Total	**1,957,188**	**114,678**	**627,172**	**3,568**	**788,528**	**-8,488**	**265,064**	**9,736**	**13,062**	**14,811**	**575**	**14,144**	**3,808,360**
2005 Total	**1,992,054**	**116,482**	**683,829**	**3,777**	**781,986**	**-6,558**	**267,040**	**10,570**	**13,031**	**14,692**	**550**	**17,811**	**3,902,192**
2006 Total	**1,969,737**	**59,708**	**734,417**	**4,254**	**787,219**	**-6,558**	**286,254**	**10,341**	**13,927**	**14,568**	**508**	**26,589**	**3,908,077**
2007 Total	**1,998,390**	**61,306**	**814,752**	**4,042**	**806,425**	**-6,896**	**245,843**	**10,711**	**14,294**	**14,637**	**612**	**34,450**	**4,005,343**
2008 Total	**1,968,838**	**42,881**	**802,372**	**3,200**	**806,208**	**-6,288**	**253,096**	**10,638**	**15,379**	**14,840**	**864**	**55,363**	**3,974,349**
2009 Total	**1,741,123**	**35,811**	**841,006**	**3,058**	**798,855**	**-4,627**	**271,506**	**10,738**	**15,954**	**15,009**	**891**	**73,886**	**3,809,837**
2010 Total	**1,827,738**	**34,679**	**901,389**	**2,967**	**806,968**	**-5,501**	**258,455**	**11,446**	**16,376**	**15,219**	**1,206**	**94,636**	**3,972,386**
2011 Total	**1,717,891**	**28,202**	**926,290**	**2,939**	**790,204**	**-6,421**	**317,531**	**10,733**	**15,989**	**15,316**	**1,727**	**120,121**	**3,948,186**
2012 Total	**1,500,557**	**20,072**	**1,132,791**	**2,984**	**769,331**	**-4,950**	**273,859**	**11,050**	**16,555**	**15,562**	**4,164**	**140,749**	**3,890,358**
2013 Total	**1,567,722**	**24,510**	**1,028,949**	**4,322**	**789,016**	**-4,681**	**265,058**	**12,302**	**16,918**	**15,775**	**8,724**	**167,742**	**3,903,715**
2014 Total	**1,568,774**	**28,043**	**1,033,172**	**3,358**	**797,166**	**-6,174**	**258,046**	**15,027**	**17,602**	**15,877**	**17,304**	**181,496**	**3,937,003**
2015 Total	**1,340,993**	**26,505**	**1,237,656**	**3,715**	**797,178**	**-5,091**	**247,636**	**14,563**	**17,823**	**15,918**	**24,456**	**190,547**	**3,919,294**
2016 Total	**1,229,663**	**22,710**	**1,279,380**	**3,912**	**805,694**	**-6,686**	**266,326**	**13,420**	**18,183**	**15,826**	**35,497**	**226,790**	**3,918,078**
2017 January	114,572	1,947	86,885	349	73,121	-435	26,635	1,189	1,646	1,383	2,011	19,822	329,751
February	86,158	1,491	75,045	308	63,560	-508	23,513	1,061	1,423	1,239	2,526	21,179	277,548
March	88,688	1,519	86,855	358	65,093	-521	29,126	1,216	1,544	1,385	4,200	24,968	304,996
April	80,743	1,179	80,578	300	56,743	-439	29,221	975	1,465	1,337	4,646	24,591	281,892
May	92,141	1,720	90,021	350	61,313	-423	32,205	977	1,554	1,283	5,605	22,429	309,762
June	106,825	1,793	108,833	324	67,011	-568	30,083	1,093	1,515	1,214	6,109	19,791	344,617
July	127,019	1,687	137,841	369	71,314	-759	26,363	1,239	1,513	1,355	5,690	15,948	390,204
August	118,810	1,610	132,376	360	72,384	-638	21,741	1,271	1,508	1,345	5,374	13,611	370,387
September	97,560	1,543	110,219	346	68,098	-606	18,978	1,088	1,422	1,297	5,059	17,840	323,400
October	89,114	1,427	98,826	326	65,995	-463	18,171	1,083	1,436	1,229	4,771	25,283	307,760
November	90,347	1,543	86,819	352	66,618	-478	20,421	1,163	1,496	1,289	3,372	24,059	297,585
December	105,860	2,582	102,457	383	73,700	-656	22,255	1,286	1,564	1,571	3,358	24,552	339,547
Total	**1,197,838**	**20,039**	**1,196,754**	**4,126**	**804,950**	**-6,495**	**298,711**	**13,641**	**18,084**	**15,927**	**52,723**	**254,074**	**3,877,450**
2018 January	118,151	6,050	101,254	329	74,649	-547	25,462	1,316	1,567	1,407	3,375	26,834	360,468
February	81,226	1,413	88,169	326	64,790	-315	25,399	1,155	1,500	1,326	4,072	24,070	293,720
March	79,910	1,352	96,975	346	67,033	-490	25,806	1,172	1,582	1,414	5,151	27,253	308,123
April	72,769	1,442	91,456	334	59,133	-377	27,346	872	1,492	1,246	6,183	26,755	289,228
May	84,660	1,333	107,960	360	67,320	-390	30,283	1,125	1,471	1,434	6,995	23,578	326,710
June	100,873	1,699	122,324	330	69,688	-433	27,818	1,206	1,526	1,369	7,712	24,353	359,105
July	114,811	1,760	158,158	363	72,456	-644	23,882	1,216	1,530	1,436	6,861	15,995	398,473
August	114,554	1,803	153,127	393	72,282	-747	21,277	1,169	1,527	1,429	6,900	19,510	393,724
September	96,121	1,757	134,147	319	64,725	-603	18,547	1,047	1,390	1,388	6,393	17,957	343,548
October	86,881	1,366	115,791	259	59,397	-492	18,652	1,032	1,489	1,347	5,165	21,122	312,618
November	92,407	1,555	98,296	298	63,948	-343	22,032	1,002	1,485	1,397	3,918	22,431	309,038
December	96,172	1,619	98,001	342	71,657	-522	23,576	1,020	1,542	1,502	3,156	24,799	323,498
Total	**1,138,535**	**23,148**	**1,365,658**	**3,998**	**807,078**	**-5,905**	**290,080**	**13,333**	**18,102**	**16,695**	**65,882**	**274,656**	**4,018,253**
2019 January	100,364	2,021	109,631	377	73,701	-323	24,428	1,225	1,472	1,414	3,616	25,137	343,679
February	79,425	1,416	102,335	373	64,715	-389	21,932	1,074	1,322	1,298	3,875	23,021	300,928
March	77,883	1,345	104,092	377	65,080	-409	25,287	981	1,433	1,435	5,959	26,008	310,030
3-Month Total	**257,672**	**4,782**	**316,057**	**1,127**	**203,495**	**-1,121**	**71,648**	**3,280**	**4,227**	**4,148**	**13,450**	**74,166**	**954,638**
2018 3-Month Total	**279,288**	**8,814**	**286,398**	**1,001**	**206,472**	**-1,352**	**76,666**	**3,643**	**4,649**	**4,147**	**12,598**	**78,157**	**962,311**
2017 3-Month Total	**289,417**	**4,957**	**248,785**	**1,016**	**201,774**	**-1,464**	**79,274**	**3,466**	**4,612**	**4,006**	**8,738**	**65,968**	**912,295**

[a] Anthracite, bituminous coal, subbituminous coal, lignite, waste coal, and coal synfuel.
[b] Distillate fuel oil, residual fuel oil, petroleum coke, jet fuel, kerosene, other petroleum, waste oil, and, beginning in 2011, propane.
[c] Natural gas, plus a small amount of supplemental gaseous fuels.
[d] Blast furnace gas, and other manufactured and waste gases derived from fossil fuels. Through 2010, also includes propane gas.
[e] Pumped storage facility production minus energy used for pumping.
[f] Through 1989, hydroelectric pumped storage is included in "Conventional Hydroelectric Power."
[g] Wood and wood-derived fuels.
[h] Municipal solid waste from biogenic sources, landfill gas, sludge waste, agricultural byproducts, and other biomass. Through 2000, also includes non-renewable waste (municipal solid waste from non-biogenic sources, and tire-derived fuels).
[i] Electricity net generation from solar thermal and photovoltaic (PV) energy at utility-scale facilities. Does not include distributed (small-scale) solar photovoltaic generation. See Table 10.6.
[j] Includes batteries, chemicals, hydrogen, pitch, purchased steam, sulfur, miscellaneous technologies, and, beginning in 2001, non-renewable waste (municipal solid waste from non-biogenic sources, and tire-derived fuels).
[k] Through 1988, data are for electric utilities only. Beginning in 1989, data are for electric utilities and independent power producers.

NA=Not available.

Notes: • Data are for utility-scale facilities. See Note 1, "Coverage of Electricity Statistics," at end of section. • The electric power sector comprises electricity-only and combined-heat-and-power (CHP) plants within the NAICS 22 category whose primary business is to sell electricity, or electricity and heat, to the public. • Totals may not equal sum of components due to independent rounding. • Geographic coverage is the 50 states and the District of Columbia.

Web Page: See http://www.eia.gov/totalenergy/data/monthly/#electricity (Excel and CSV files) for all available annual data beginning in 1949 and monthly data beginning in 1973.

Sources: See end of section.

Source: *U.S. Energy Information Administration, Monthly Energy Review, June 2019*

Table 7.2c Electricity Net Generation: Commercial and Industrial Sectors

(Subset of Table 7.2a; Million Kilowatthours)

	Commercial Sector[a]					Industrial Sector[b]							
	Coal[c]	Petroleum[d]	Natural Gas[e]	Biomass: Waste[f]	Total[g]	Coal[c]	Petroleum[d]	Natural Gas[e]	Other Gases[h]	Hydroelectric Power[i]	Biomass: Wood[j]	Biomass: Waste[f]	Total[k]
1950 Total	NA	NA	NA	NA	NA	NA	NA	NA	NA	4,946	NA	NA	4,946
1955 Total	NA	NA	NA	NA	NA	NA	NA	NA	NA	3,261	NA	NA	3,261
1960 Total	NA	NA	NA	NA	NA	NA	NA	NA	NA	3,607	NA	NA	3,607
1965 Total	NA	NA	NA	NA	NA	NA	NA	NA	NA	3,134	NA	NA	3,134
1970 Total	NA	NA	NA	NA	NA	NA	NA	NA	NA	3,244	NA	NA	3,244
1975 Total	NA	NA	NA	NA	NA	NA	NA	NA	NA	3,106	NA	NA	3,106
1980 Total	NA	NA	NA	NA	NA	NA	NA	NA	NA	3,161	NA	NA	3,161
1985 Total	NA	NA	NA	NA	NA	NA	NA	NA	NA	3,161	NA	NA	3,161
1990 Total	796	589	3,272	812	5,837	21,107	7,008	60,007	9,641	2,975	25,379	949	130,830
1995 Total	998	379	5,162	1,519	8,232	22,372	6,030	71,717	11,943	5,304	28,868	900	151,025
2000 Total	1,097	432	4,262	1,985	7,903	22,056	5,597	78,798	11,927	4,135	28,652	839	156,673
2001 Total	995	438	4,434	1,007	7,416	20,135	5,293	79,755	8,454	3,145	26,888	596	149,175
2002 Total	992	431	4,310	1,053	7,415	21,525	4,403	79,013	9,493	3,825	29,643	846	152,580
2003 Total	1,206	423	3,899	1,289	7,496	19,817	5,285	78,705	12,953	4,222	27,988	715	154,530
2004 Total	1,340	499	3,969	1,562	8,270	19,773	5,967	78,959	11,684	3,248	28,367	797	153,925
2005 Total	1,353	375	4,249	1,657	8,492	19,466	5,368	72,882	9,687	3,195	28,271	733	144,739
2006 Total	1,310	235	4,355	1,599	8,371	19,464	4,223	77,669	9,923	2,899	28,400	572	148,254
2007 Total	1,371	189	4,257	1,599	8,273	16,694	4,243	77,580	9,411	1,590	28,287	631	143,128
2008 Total	1,261	142	4,188	1,534	7,926	15,703	3,219	76,421	8,507	1,676	26,641	821	137,113
2009 Total	1,096	163	4,225	1,748	8,165	13,686	2,963	75,748	7,574	1,868	25,292	740	132,329
2010 Total	1,111	124	4,725	1,672	8,592	18,441	2,258	81,583	8,343	1,668	25,706	869	144,082
2011 Total	1,049	89	5,487	2,315	10,080	14,490	1,891	81,911	8,624	1,799	26,691	917	141,875
2012 Total	883	196	6,603	2,319	11,301	12,603	2,922	86,500	8,913	2,353	26,725	948	146,107
2013 Total	839	124	7,154	2,567	12,234	12,554	2,531	88,733	8,531	3,463	27,691	1,346	150,015
2014 Total	595	255	7,227	2,681	12,520	12,341	1,934	86,209	8,664	1,282	27,239	1,367	144,083
2015 Total	509	191	7,471	2,637	12,595	10,896	1,552	88,355	9,401	1,410	27,318	1,243	145,712
2016 Total	383	82	7,730	2,496	12,706	9,103	1,412	91,197	8,895	1,269	27,458	1,134	145,890
2017 January	41	14	681	213	1,098	720	104	7,907	696	126	2,308	89	12,341
February	32	8	597	188	963	632	98	7,052	668	115	2,118	83	11,142
March	33	10	652	214	1,071	644	120	7,515	702	131	2,239	95	11,868
April	20	5	574	202	976	573	93	7,266	701	146	2,169	88	11,457
May	19	7	619	225	1,069	616	91	7,428	704	155	2,205	80	11,686
June	21	6	718	207	1,135	662	104	7,765	668	124	2,340	73	12,164
July	25	7	786	222	1,227	653	112	8,367	679	115	2,457	79	12,956
August	23	9	766	218	1,202	655	116	8,067	774	93	2,475	82	12,754
September	27	7	701	202	1,107	615	86	7,191	715	75	2,204	72	11,354
October	24	6	661	197	1,079	637	94	7,366	673	84	2,217	85	11,537
November	29	8	611	207	1,020	610	108	7,453	649	121	2,261	91	11,710
December	35	24	674	218	1,114	651	113	8,242	713	99	2,446	95	12,790
Total	329	112	8,042	2,515	13,060	7,669	1,239	91,619	8,343	1,383	27,440	1,012	143,758
2018 January	44	NM	673	199	1,124	744	148	8,119	665	112	2,435	87	12,732
February	32	9	635	179	1,008	664	96	7,197	665	112	2,218	82	11,387
March	26	9	651	199	1,063	676	97	7,307	718	122	2,358	89	11,796
April	22	9	634	190	1,040	591	94	7,356	607	119	2,222	85	11,471
May	19	9	644	195	1,070	632	96	7,503	640	125	2,420	78	11,915
June	21	8	706	193	1,148	615	120	7,793	680	114	2,359	68	12,144
July	25	12	821	194	1,251	641	121	8,271	742	113	2,465	73	12,819
August	30	10	831	196	1,269	633	100	8,419	832	106	2,391	74	12,989
September	29	9	749	179	1,148	592	108	7,876	682	103	2,229	65	12,031
October	24	8	673	197	1,070	547	99	7,707	671	115	2,241	80	11,876
November	27	13	641	184	1,014	572	84	8,172	634	127	2,279	82	12,357
December	29	11	685	197	1,114	623	106	8,292	656	135	2,386	85	12,723
Total	327	154	8,343	2,304	13,318	7,531	1,270	94,012	8,193	1,403	28,002	948	146,239
2019 January	35	15	717	198	1,169	620	100	8,587	617	95	2,296	84	12,842
February	29	10	661	171	1,060	554	86	7,432	641	81	2,082	78	11,290
March	33	10	689	190	1,148	538	84	7,794	766	92	2,249	90	12,008
3-Month Total	97	34	2,067	559	3,377	1,712	270	23,812	2,024	268	6,628	251	36,140
2018 3-Month Total	101	63	1,960	578	3,195	2,085	342	22,623	2,048	346	7,010	258	35,915
2017 3-Month Total	105	33	1,931	616	3,131	1,997	322	22,474	2,067	371	6,665	267	35,351

[a] Commercial combined-heat-and-power (CHP) and commercial electricity-only plants.
[b] Industrial combined-heat-and-power (CHP) and industrial electricity-only plants.
[c] Anthracite, bituminous coal, subbituminous coal, lignite, waste coal, and coal synfuel.
[d] Distillate fuel oil, residual fuel oil, petroleum coke, jet fuel, kerosene, other petroleum, waste oil, and, beginning in 2011, propane.
[e] Natural gas, plus a small amount of supplemental gaseous fuels.
[f] Municipal solid waste from biogenic sources, landfill gas, sludge waste, agricultural byproducts, and other biomass. Through 2000, also includes non-renewable waste (municipal solid waste from non-biogenic sources, and tire-derived fuels).
[g] Includes a small amount of conventional hydroelectric power, geothermal, other gases, solar photovoltaic (PV) energy, wind, wood, and other, which are not separately displayed. Does not include distributed (small-scale) solar photovoltaic generation. shown on Table 10.6.
[h] Blast furnace gas, and other manufactured and waste gases derived from fossil fuels. Through 2010, also includes propane gas.
[i] Conventional hydroelectric power.
[j] Wood and wood-derived fuels.
[k] Includes photovoltaic (PV) energy, wind, batteries, chemicals, hydrogen, pitch, purchased steam, sulfur, miscellaneous technologies, and, beginning in 2001, non-renewable waste (municipal solid waste from non-biogenic sources, and tire-derived fuels). Does not include distributed (small-scale) solar photovoltaic generation shown on Table 10.6.

NA=Not available. NM=Not meaningful.

Notes: • Data are for utility-scale facilities. See Note 1, "Coverage of Electricity Statistics," at end of section. • See Note 2, "Classification of Power Plants Into Energy-Use Sectors," at end of section. • Totals may not equal sum of components due to independent rounding. • Geographic coverage is the 50 states and the District of Columbia.

Web Page: See http://www.eia.gov/totalenergy/data/monthly/#electricity (Excel and CSV files) for all available annual data beginning in 1949 and monthly data beginning in 1973.

Sources: See end of section.

Source: *U.S. Energy Information Administration, Monthly Energy Review, June 2019*

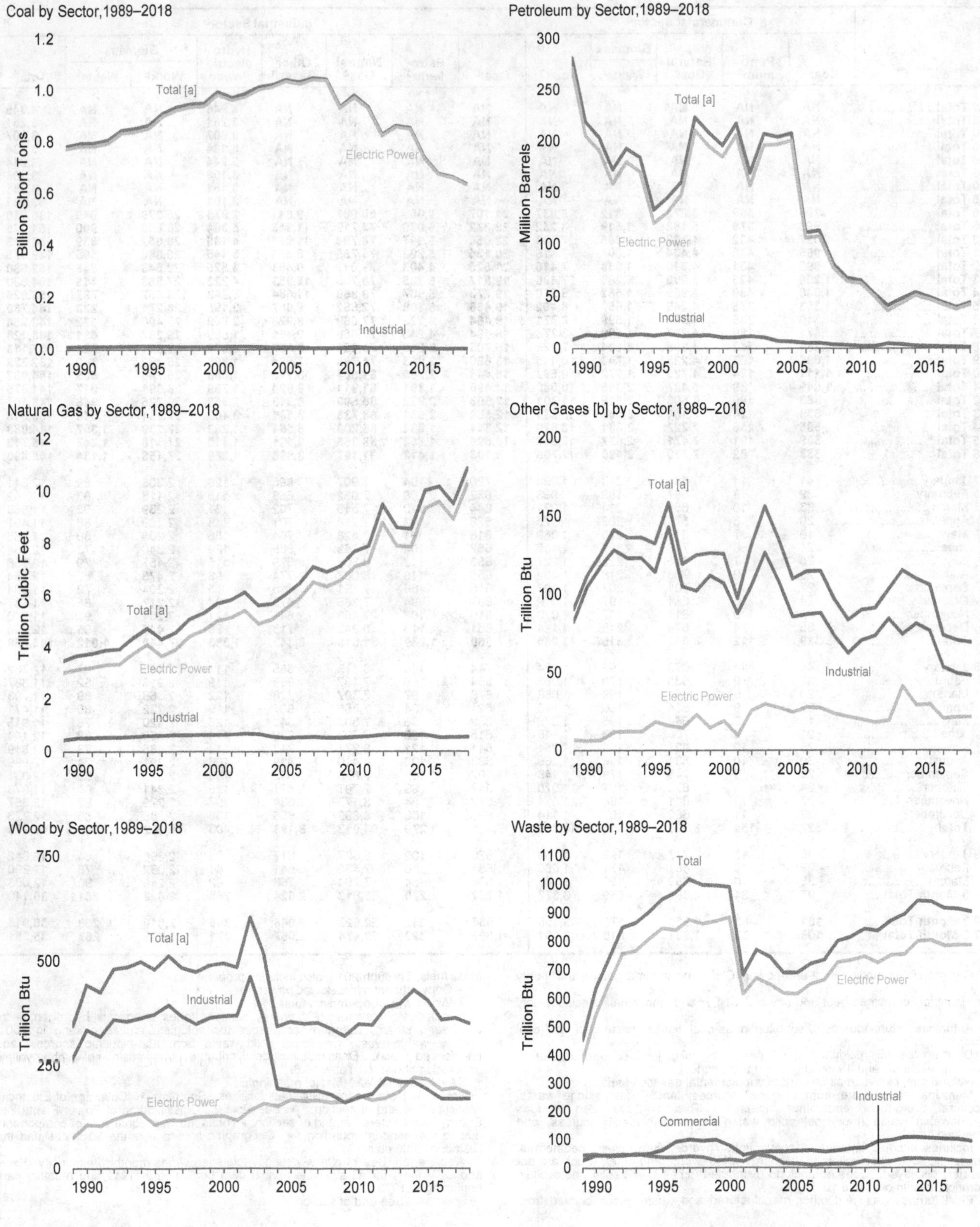

[a] Includes commercial sector.

[b] Blast furnace gas, and other manufactured and waste gases derived from fossil fuels. Through 2010, also includes propane gas.

Note: Data are for utility-scale facilities.

Web Page: http://www.eia.gov/totalenergy/data/monthly/#electricity.

Sources: Tables 7.3a-7.3c.

***Source:** U.S. Energy Information Administration, Monthly Energy Review, June 2019*

Table 7.3a Consumption of Combustible Fuels for Electricity Generation: Total (All Sectors) (Sum of Tables 7.3b and 7.3c)

	Coal[a]	Petroleum: Distillate Fuel Oil[b]	Petroleum: Residual Fuel Oil[c]	Petroleum: Other Liquids[d]	Petroleum: Petroleum Coke[e]	Petroleum: Total[e]	Natural Gas[f]	Other Gases[g]	Biomass: Wood[h]	Biomass: Waste[i]	Other[j]
	Thousand Short Tons	Thousand Barrels			Thousand Short Tons	Thousand Barrels	Billion Cubic Feet	Trillion Btu			
1950 Total	91,871	5,423	69,998	NA	NA	75,421	629	NA	5	NA	NA
1955 Total	143,759	5,412	69,862	NA	NA	75,274	1,153	NA	3	NA	NA
1960 Total	176,685	3,824	84,371	NA	NA	88,195	1,725	NA	2	NA	NA
1965 Total	244,788	4,928	110,274	NA	NA	115,203	2,321	NA	3	NA	NA
1970 Total	320,182	24,123	311,381	NA	636	338,686	3,932	NA	1	2	NA
1975 Total	405,962	38,907	467,221	NA	70	506,479	3,158	NA	(s)	2	NA
1980 Total	569,274	29,051	391,163	NA	179	421,110	3,682	NA	3	2	NA
1985 Total	693,841	14,635	158,779	NA	231	174,571	3,044	NA	8	7	NA
1990 Total[k]	792,457	18,143	190,652	437	1,914	218,800	3,692	112	442	211	36
1995 Total	860,594	19,615	95,507	680	3,355	132,578	4,738	133	480	316	42
2000 Total	994,933	31,675	143,381	1,450	3,744	195,228	5,691	126	496	330	46
2001 Total	972,691	31,150	165,312	855	3,871	216,672	5,832	97	486	228	160
2002 Total	987,583	23,286	109,235	1,894	6,836	168,597	6,126	131	605	257	191
2003 Total	1,014,058	29,672	142,518	2,947	6,303	206,653	5,616	156	519	249	193
2004 Total	1,020,523	20,163	142,088	2,856	7,677	203,494	5,675	135	344	230	183
2005 Total	1,041,448	20,651	141,518	2,968	8,330	206,785	6,036	110	355	230	173
2006 Total	1,030,556	13,174	58,473	2,174	7,363	110,634	6,462	115	350	241	172
2007 Total	1,046,795	15,683	63,833	2,917	6,036	112,615	7,089	115	353	245	168
2008 Total	1,042,335	12,832	38,191	2,822	5,417	80,932	6,896	97	339	267	172
2009 Total	934,683	12,658	28,576	2,328	4,821	67,668	7,121	84	320	272	170
2010 Total	979,684	14,050	23,997	2,056	4,994	65,071	7,680	90	350	281	184
2011 Total	934,938	11,231	14,251	1,844	5,012	52,387	7,884	91	348	279	205
2012 Total	825,734	9,285	11,755	1,565	3,675	40,977	9,485	103	390	290	204
2013 Total	860,729	9,784	11,766	1,681	4,852	47,492	8,596	115	398	298	200
2014 Total	853,634	14,465	14,704	2,363	4,412	53,593	8,544	110	431	314	200
2015 Total	739,594	12,438	14,124	2,363	4,044	49,145	10,017	106	407	313	204
2016 Total	677,371	9,662	11,195	1,548	4,253	43,671	10,170	74	360	305	199
2017 January	63,460	940	846	151	368	3,775	679	6	31	27	16
February	47,985	714	724	104	277	2,928	587	6	28	24	14
March	48,840	814	738	105	265	2,984	690	6	31	26	16
April	44,279	658	718	103	168	2,317	647	6	27	25	15
May	50,898	808	811	94	329	3,357	720	6	28	26	16
June	58,852	707	908	148	350	3,512	873	6	30	26	16
July	69,769	689	811	93	344	3,312	1,105	6	33	26	17
August	65,761	655	930	124	300	3,211	1,043	6	33	26	17
September	54,713	692	820	110	276	3,004	878	6	29	24	15
October	50,015	731	844	100	228	2,816	792	6	29	24	15
November	50,882	751	711	129	293	3,054	686	6	30	25	15
December	58,457	1,548	1,581	285	292	4,875	806	6	33	26	16
Total	**663,911**	**9,707**	**10,442**	**1,547**	**3,490**	**39,144**	**9,508**	**71**	**364**	**304**	**190**
2018 January	64,517	5,155	3,273	619	349	10,790	804	6	32	26	16
February	45,655	578	676	114	275	2,743	717	6	29	25	14
March	44,388	629	666	114	245	2,636	771	6	30	27	16
April	40,554	711	716	102	246	2,757	727	6	26	25	15
May	47,470	839	810	131	161	2,587	872	6	31	25	16
June	56,031	815	898	114	312	3,388	972	6	31	26	16
July	63,805	686	874	131	344	3,408	1,255	6	32	25	16
August	63,710	724	948	145	327	3,454	1,216	7	30	26	16
September	53,945	641	992	142	316	3,356	1,064	6	28	23	14
October	48,488	695	895	141	190	2,680	914	5	28	24	15
November	51,720	759	766	129	247	2,888	777	5	27	24	15
December	55,549	745	691	183	299	3,116	764	6	29	25	16
Total	**635,833**	**12,977**	**12,205**	**2,063**	**3,311**	**43,802**	**10,855**	**69**	**351**	**301**	**184**
2019 January	55,769	1,031	1,008	255	312	3,854	854	5	31	24	16
February	44,982	622	586	155	269	2,709	787	6	27	22	13
March	43,971	646	611	141	247	2,632	810	7	28	24	14
3-Month Total	**144,722**	**2,299**	**2,205**	**550**	**828**	**9,194**	**2,451**	**18**	**86**	**70**	**43**
2018 3-Month Total	**154,560**	**6,362**	**4,616**	**847**	**869**	**16,170**	**2,293**	**17**	**91**	**78**	**45**
2017 3-Month Total	**160,285**	**2,468**	**2,309**	**360**	**910**	**9,686**	**1,957**	**17**	**91**	**77**	**46**

[a] Anthracite, bituminous coal, subbituminous coal, lignite, waste coal, and coal synfuel.
[b] Fuel oil nos. 1, 2, and 4. For 1949–1979, data are for gas turbine and internal combustion plant use of petroleum. For 1980–2000, electric utility data also include small amounts of kerosene and jet fuel.
[c] Fuel oil nos. 5 and 6. For 1949–1979, data are for steam plant use of petroleum. For 1980–2000, electric utility data also include a small amount of fuel oil no. 4.
[d] Jet fuel, kerosene, other petroleum liquids, waste oil, and, beginning in 2011, propane.
[e] Petroleum coke is converted from short tons to barrels by multiplying by 5.
[f] Natural gas, plus a small amount of supplemental gaseous fuels.
[g] Blast furnace gas, and other manufactured and waste gases derived from fossil fuels. Through 2010, also includes propane gas.
[h] Wood and wood-derived fuels.
[i] Municipal solid waste from biogenic sources, landfill gas, sludge waste, agricultural byproducts, and other biomass. Through 2000, also includes non-renewable waste (municipal solid waste from non-biogenic sources, and tire-derived fuels).
[j] Batteries, chemicals, hydrogen, pitch, purchased steam, sulfur, miscellaneous technologies, and, beginning in 2001, non-renewable waste (municipal solid waste from non-biogenic sources, and tire-derived fuels).
[k] Through 1988, data are for electric utilities only. Beginning in 1989, data are for electric utilities, independent power producers, commercial plants, and industrial plants.

NA=Not available. (s)=Less than 0.5 trillion Btu.

Notes: • Data are for utility-scale facilities. See Note 1, "Coverage of Electricity Statistics," at end of section. • Data are for fuels consumed to produce electricity. Data also include fuels consumed to produce useful thermal output at a small number of electric utility combined-heat-and-power (CHP) plants. • Totals may not equal sum of components due to independent rounding. • Geographic coverage is the 50 states and the District of Columbia.

Web Page: See http://www.eia.gov/totalenergy/data/monthly/#electricity (Excel and CSV files) for all available annual data beginning in 1949 and monthly data beginning in 1973.

Sources: See "Table 7.3b Sources" at end of section and sources for Table 7.3c.

Source: *U.S. Energy Information Administration, Monthly Energy Review, June 2019*

Table 7.3b Consumption of Combustible Fuels for Electricity Generation: Electric Power Sector (Subset of Table 7.3a)

		Petroleum								Biomass		
	Coal[a]	Distillate Fuel Oil[b]	Residual Fuel Oil[c]	Other Liquids[d]	Petroleum Coke[e]	Total[e]	Natural Gas[f]	Other Gases[g]	Wood[h]	Waste[i]	Other[j]
	Thousand Short Tons	Thousand Barrels			Thousand Short Tons	Thousand Barrels	Billion Cubic Feet	Trillion Btu			
1950 Total	**91,871**	**5,423**	**69,998**	**NA**	**NA**	**75,421**	**629**	**NA**	**5**	**NA**	**NA**
1955 Total	**143,759**	**5,412**	**69,862**	**NA**	**NA**	**75,274**	**1,153**	**NA**	**3**	**NA**	**NA**
1960 Total	**176,685**	**3,824**	**84,371**	**NA**	**NA**	**88,195**	**1,725**	**NA**	**2**	**NA**	**NA**
1965 Total	**244,788**	**4,928**	**110,274**	**NA**	**NA**	**115,203**	**2,321**	**NA**	**3**	**NA**	**NA**
1970 Total	**320,182**	**24,123**	**311,381**	**NA**	**636**	**338,686**	**3,932**	**NA**	**1**	**2**	**NA**
1975 Total	**405,962**	**38,907**	**467,221**	**NA**	**70**	**506,479**	**3,158**	**NA**	**(s)**	**2**	**NA**
1980 Total	**569,274**	**29,051**	**391,163**	**NA**	**179**	**421,110**	**3,682**	**NA**	**3**	**2**	**NA**
1985 Total	**693,841**	**14,635**	**158,779**	**NA**	**231**	**174,571**	**3,044**	**NA**	**8**	**7**	**NA**
1990 Total[k]	**781,301**	**16,394**	**183,285**	**25**	**1,008**	**204,745**	**3,147**	**6**	**106**	**180**	**(s)**
1995 Total	**847,854**	**18,066**	**88,895**	**441**	**2,452**	**119,663**	**4,094**	**18**	**106**	**282**	**2**
2000 Total	**982,713**	**29,722**	**138,047**	**403**	**3,155**	**183,946**	**5,014**	**19**	**126**	**294**	**1**
2001 Total	**961,523**	**29,056**	**159,150**	**374**	**3,308**	**205,119**	**5,142**	**9**	**116**	**205**	**109**
2002 Total	**975,251**	**21,810**	**104,577**	**1,243**	**5,705**	**156,154**	**5,408**	**25**	**141**	**224**	**137**
2003 Total	**1,003,036**	**27,441**	**137,361**	**1,937**	**5,719**	**195,336**	**4,909**	**30**	**156**	**216**	**136**
2004 Total	**1,012,459**	**18,793**	**138,831**	**2,511**	**7,135**	**195,809**	**5,075**	**27**	**150**	**206**	**131**
2005 Total	**1,033,567**	**19,450**	**138,337**	**2,591**	**7,877**	**199,760**	**5,485**	**24**	**166**	**205**	**116**
2006 Total	**1,022,802**	**12,578**	**56,347**	**1,783**	**6,905**	**105,235**	**5,891**	**28**	**163**	**216**	**117**
2007 Total	**1,041,346**	**15,135**	**62,072**	**2,496**	**5,523**	**107,316**	**6,502**	**27**	**165**	**221**	**117**
2008 Total	**1,036,891**	**12,318**	**37,222**	**2,608**	**5,000**	**77,149**	**6,342**	**23**	**159**	**242**	**122**
2009 Total	**929,692**	**11,848**	**27,768**	**2,110**	**4,485**	**64,151**	**6,567**	**21**	**160**	**244**	**115**
2010 Total	**971,245**	**13,677**	**23,560**	**1,848**	**4,679**	**62,477**	**7,085**	**20**	**177**	**249**	**116**
2011 Total	**928,857**	**10,961**	**13,861**	**1,655**	**4,726**	**50,105**	**7,265**	**18**	**166**	**241**	**133**
2012 Total	**820,762**	**9,000**	**11,292**	**1,339**	**2,861**	**35,937**	**8,788**	**19**	**171**	**250**	**132**
2013 Total	**855,546**	**9,511**	**11,322**	**1,488**	**4,189**	**43,265**	**7,888**	**41**	**187**	**251**	**130**
2014 Total	**848,803**	**14,052**	**14,132**	**2,157**	**4,039**	**50,537**	**7,849**	**29**	**220**	**266**	**127**
2015 Total	**735,433**	**12,056**	**13,893**	**2,086**	**3,789**	**46,978**	**9,322**	**29**	**215**	**268**	**127**
2016 Total	**674,239**	**9,421**	**11,056**	**1,284**	**4,018**	**41,853**	**9,590**	**20**	**191**	**261**	**126**
2017 January	63,179	907	832	131	352	3,629	629	2	17	24	11
February	47,731	693	714	81	262	2,797	542	2	16	21	9
March	48,581	789	726	89	245	2,830	642	2	18	22	10
April	44,059	637	707	90	152	2,192	600	2	14	21	9
May	50,667	784	802	77	313	3,227	673	2	14	22	10
June	58,625	686	899	131	330	3,366	823	2	16	22	10
July	69,531	663	804	76	322	3,151	1,051	2	17	22	11
August	65,528	627	922	107	278	3,047	991	2	18	22	11
September	54,487	665	812	94	260	2,870	831	2	15	21	10
October	49,781	709	833	81	210	2,675	744	2	15	21	10
November	50,652	729	691	112	274	2,904	638	2	16	21	10
December	58,212	1,509	1,557	265	275	4,707	754	2	18	22	11
Total	**661,033**	**9,398**	**10,299**	**1,332**	**3,273**	**37,394**	**8,917**	**21**	**195**	**262**	**121**
2018 January	64,230	5,070	3,237	594	334	10,571	753	2	17	23	10
February	45,403	557	664	89	264	2,631	672	2	15	22	10
March	44,138	606	654	96	233	2,518	724	2	16	23	10
April	40,338	686	706	84	231	2,629	679	2	12	22	10
May	47,235	809	801	108	148	2,459	824	2	16	22	10
June	55,806	785	883	96	293	3,231	922	2	17	23	11
July	63,568	648	866	92	326	3,234	1,201	2	17	22	11
August	63,479	685	937	131	312	3,312	1,162	2	16	22	11
September	53,725	605	981	133	299	3,211	1,014	2	14	20	10
October	48,289	669	884	124	173	2,544	865	1	14	21	10
November	51,496	724	754	113	234	2,761	726	1	14	21	10
December	55,309	710	676	169	282	2,966	711	2	15	22	10
Total	**633,016**	**12,553**	**12,044**	**1,828**	**3,128**	**42,067**	**10,252**	**21**	**181**	**262**	**124**
2019 January	55,533	995	993	237	298	3,713	799	2	17	21	10
February	44,766	600	576	132	257	2,594	739	2	14	19	9
March	43,785	620	600	123	233	2,509	760	2	14	21	10
3-Month Total	**144,084**	**2,215**	**2,169**	**492**	**788**	**8,816**	**2,299**	**6**	**45**	**60**	**29**
2018 3-Month Total	**153,771**	**6,233**	**4,555**	**779**	**831**	**15,720**	**2,148**	**5**	**48**	**67**	**31**
2017 3-Month Total	**159,491**	**2,389**	**2,272**	**300**	**859**	**9,256**	**1,812**	**5**	**50**	**67**	**30**

[a] Anthracite, bituminous coal, subbituminous coal, lignite, waste coal, and coal synfuel.

[b] Fuel oil nos. 1, 2, and 4. For 1949–1979, data are for gas turbine and internal combustion plant use of petroleum. For 1980–2000, electric utility data also include small amounts of kerosene and jet fuel.

[c] Fuel oil nos. 5 and 6. For 1949–1979, data are for steam plant use of petroleum. For 1980–2000, electric utility data also include a small amount of fuel oil no. 4.

[d] Jet fuel, kerosene, other petroleum liquids, waste oil, and, beginning in 2011, propane.

[e] Petroleum coke is converted from short tons to barrels by multiplying by 5.

[f] Natural gas, plus a small amount of supplemental gaseous fuels.

[g] Blast furnace gas, and other manufactured and waste gases derived from fossil fuels. Through 2010, also includes propane gas.

[h] Wood and wood-derived fuels.

[i] Municipal solid waste from biogenic sources, landfill gas, sludge waste, agricultural byproducts, and other biomass. Through 2000, also includes non-renewable waste (municipal solid waste from non-biogenic sources, and tire-derived fuels).

[j] Batteries, chemicals, hydrogen, pitch, purchased steam, sulfur, miscellaneous technologies, and, beginning in 2001, non-renewable waste (municipal solid waste from non-biogenic sources, and tire-derived fuels).

[k] Through 1988, data are for electric utilities only. Beginning in 1989, data are for electric utilities and independent power producers.

NA=Not available. (s)=Less than 0.5 trillion Btu.

Notes: • Data are for utility-scale facilities. See Note 1, "Coverage of Electricity Statistics," at end of section. • Data are for fuels consumed to produce electricity. Data also include fuels consumed to produce useful thermal output at a small number of electric utility combined-heat-and-power (CHP) plants. • The electric power sector comprises electricity-only and combined-heat-and-power (CHP) plants within the NAICS 22 category whose primary business is to sell electricity, or electricity and heat, to the public. • Totals may not equal sum of components due to independent rounding. • Geographic coverage is the 50 states and the District of Columbia.

Web Page: See http://www.eia.gov/totalenergy/data/monthly/#electricity (Excel and CSV files) for all available annual data beginning in 1949 and monthly data beginning in 1973.

Sources: See end of section.

Source: *U.S. Energy Information Administration, Monthly Energy Review, June 2019*

Table 7.3c Consumption of Selected Combustible Fuels for Electricity Generation: Commercial and Industrial Sectors (Subset of Table 7.3a)

	Commercial Sector[a]				Industrial Sector[b]						
				Biomass					Biomass		
	Coal[c]	Petroleum[d]	Natural Gas[e]	Waste[f]	Coal[c]	Petroleum[d]	Natural Gas[e]	Other Gases[g]	Wood[h]	Waste[f]	Other[i]
	Thousand Short Tons	Thousand Barrels	Billion Cubic Feet	Trillion Btu	Thousand Short Tons	Thousand Barrels	Billion Cubic Feet	Trillion Btu			
1990 Total	**417**	**953**	**28**	**15**	**10,740**	**13,103**	**517**	**104**	**335**	**16**	**36**
1995 Total	**569**	**649**	**43**	**21**	**12,171**	**12,265**	**601**	**114**	**373**	**13**	**40**
2000 Total	**514**	**823**	**37**	**26**	**11,706**	**10,459**	**640**	**107**	**369**	**10**	**45**
2001 Total	**532**	**1,023**	**36**	**15**	**10,636**	**10,530**	**654**	**88**	**370**	**7**	**44**
2002 Total	**477**	**834**	**33**	**18**	**11,855**	**11,608**	**685**	**106**	**464**	**15**	**43**
2003 Total	**582**	**894**	**38**	**19**	**10,440**	**10,424**	**668**	**127**	**362**	**13**	**46**
2004 Total	**377**	**766**	**33**	**19**	**7,687**	**6,919**	**566**	**108**	**194**	**5**	**41**
2005 Total	**377**	**585**	**34**	**20**	**7,504**	**6,440**	**518**	**85**	**189**	**5**	**46**
2006 Total	**347**	**333**	**35**	**21**	**7,408**	**5,066**	**536**	**87**	**187**	**3**	**45**
2007 Total	**361**	**258**	**34**	**19**	**5,089**	**5,041**	**554**	**88**	**188**	**4**	**41**
2008 Total	**369**	**166**	**33**	**20**	**5,075**	**3,617**	**520**	**73**	**179**	**5**	**39**
2009 Total	**317**	**190**	**34**	**23**	**4,674**	**3,328**	**520**	**62**	**160**	**4**	**42**
2010 Total	**314**	**172**	**39**	**24**	**8,125**	**2,422**	**555**	**70**	**172**	**8**	**55**
2011 Total	**347**	**137**	**47**	**31**	**5,735**	**2,145**	**572**	**74**	**182**	**7**	**57**
2012 Total	**307**	**279**	**63**	**33**	**4,665**	**4,761**	**633**	**84**	**219**	**8**	**54**
2013 Total	**513**	**335**	**67**	**36**	**4,670**	**3,892**	**642**	**74**	**210**	**11**	**50**
2014 Total	**202**	**462**	**72**	**36**	**4,629**	**2,594**	**623**	**81**	**210**	**11**	**54**
2015 Total	**163**	**260**	**70**	**35**	**3,999**	**1,907**	**625**	**77**	**191**	**10**	**58**
2016 Total	**111**	**116**	**46**	**34**	**3,021**	**1,701**	**534**	**53**	**169**	**10**	**53**
2017 January	11	22	4	3	270	124	47	4	14	1	4
February	9	14	4	3	245	117	42	4	13	1	4
March	9	16	4	3	250	139	45	4	14	1	4
April	6	10	4	3	214	115	43	4	13	1	4
May	6	16	4	3	224	114	44	4	14	1	4
June	6	14	4	3	221	132	46	4	14	1	4
July	7	16	5	3	230	145	49	4	15	1	5
August	7	20	5	3	227	143	47	5	15	1	5
September	8	15	4	3	218	119	42	4	13	1	4
October	7	14	4	3	227	127	43	4	14	1	4
November	8	16	4	3	222	135	44	4	14	1	4
December	9	33	4	3	236	134	49	4	15	1	4
Total	**95**	**204**	**50**	**34**	**2,783**	**1,545**	**541**	**49**	**169**	**8**	**49**
2018 January	12	68	4	3	274	152	48	4	15	1	4
February	9	16	4	3	243	96	42	4	13	1	3
March	8	14	4	3	243	104	43	4	14	1	4
April	6	16	4	3	210	111	44	4	14	1	3
May	6	20	4	3	230	108	44	4	15	1	4
June	6	19	4	3	219	138	46	4	14	1	3
July	7	28	5	3	230	146	48	4	15	1	3
August	9	25	5	3	223	116	49	5	14	1	4
September	8	21	5	2	212	125	46	4	13	(s)	3
October	7	18	4	3	191	118	45	4	13	1	4
November	7	24	4	3	216	102	48	4	14	1	4
December	8	22	4	3	232	127	49	4	14	1	4
Total	**94**	**292**	**52**	**32**	**2,723**	**1,444**	**552**	**48**	**170**	**8**	**42**
2019 January	10	25	4	3	226	115	50	4	14	1	4
February	8	15	4	2	207	100	44	4	13	1	3
March	9	18	4	3	177	106	46	4	14	1	3
3-Month Total	**27**	**58**	**13**	**8**	**610**	**321**	**139**	**12**	**41**	**2**	**10**
2018 3-Month Total	**29**	**98**	**12**	**8**	**760**	**352**	**132**	**12**	**43**	**2**	**10**
2017 3-Month Total	**30**	**51**	**12**	**8**	**764**	**380**	**133**	**12**	**40**	**2**	**12**

[a] Commercial combined-heat-and-power (CHP) and commercial electricity-only plants.
[b] Industrial combined-heat-and-power (CHP) and industrial electricity-only plants.
[c] Anthracite, bituminous coal, subbituminous coal, lignite, waste coal, and coal synfuel.
[d] Distillate fuel oil, residual fuel oil, petroleum coke, jet fuel, kerosene, other petroleum, waste oil, and, beginning in 2011, propane.
[e] Natural gas, plus a small amount of supplemental gaseous fuels.
[f] Municipal solid waste from biogenic sources, landfill gas, sludge waste, agricultural byproducts, and other biomass. Through 2000, also includes non-renewable waste (municipal solid waste from non-biogenic sources, and tire-derived fuels).
[g] Blast furnace gas, and other manufactured and waste gases derived from fossil fuels. Through 2010, also includes propane gas.
[h] Wood and wood-derived fuels.
[i] Batteries, chemicals, hydrogen, pitch, purchased steam, sulfur, miscellaneous technologies, and, beginning in 2001, non-renewable waste (municipal solid waste from non-biogenic sources, and tire-derived fuels).

(s)=Less than 0.5 trillion Btu.

Notes: • Data are for utility-scale facilities. See Note 1, "Coverage of Electricity Statistics," at end of section. • See Note 2, "Classification of Power Plants Into Energy-Use Sectors," at end of section. • Data are for fuels consumed to produce electricity. Through 1988, data are not available. • Totals may not equal sum of components due to independent rounding. • Geographic coverage is the 50 states and the District of Columbia.

Web Page: See http://www.eia.gov/totalenergy/data/monthly/#electricity (Excel and CSV files) for all available annual and monthly data beginning in 1989.

Sources: • **1989–1997:** U.S. Energy Information Administration (EIA), Form EIA-867, "Annual Nonutility Power Producer Report." • **1998–2000:** EIA, Form EIA-860B, "Annual Electric Generator Report—Nonutility." • **2001–2003:** EIA, Form EIA-906, "Power Plant Report." • **2004–2007:** EIA, Form EIA-906, "Power Plant Report," and Form EIA-920, "Combined Heat and Power Plant Report." • **2008 forward:** EIA, Form EIA-923, "Power Plant Operations Report."

Source: *U.S. Energy Information Administration, Monthly Energy Review, June 2019*

Figure 7.4 Consumption of Selected Combustible Fuels for Electricity Generation and Useful Thermal Output

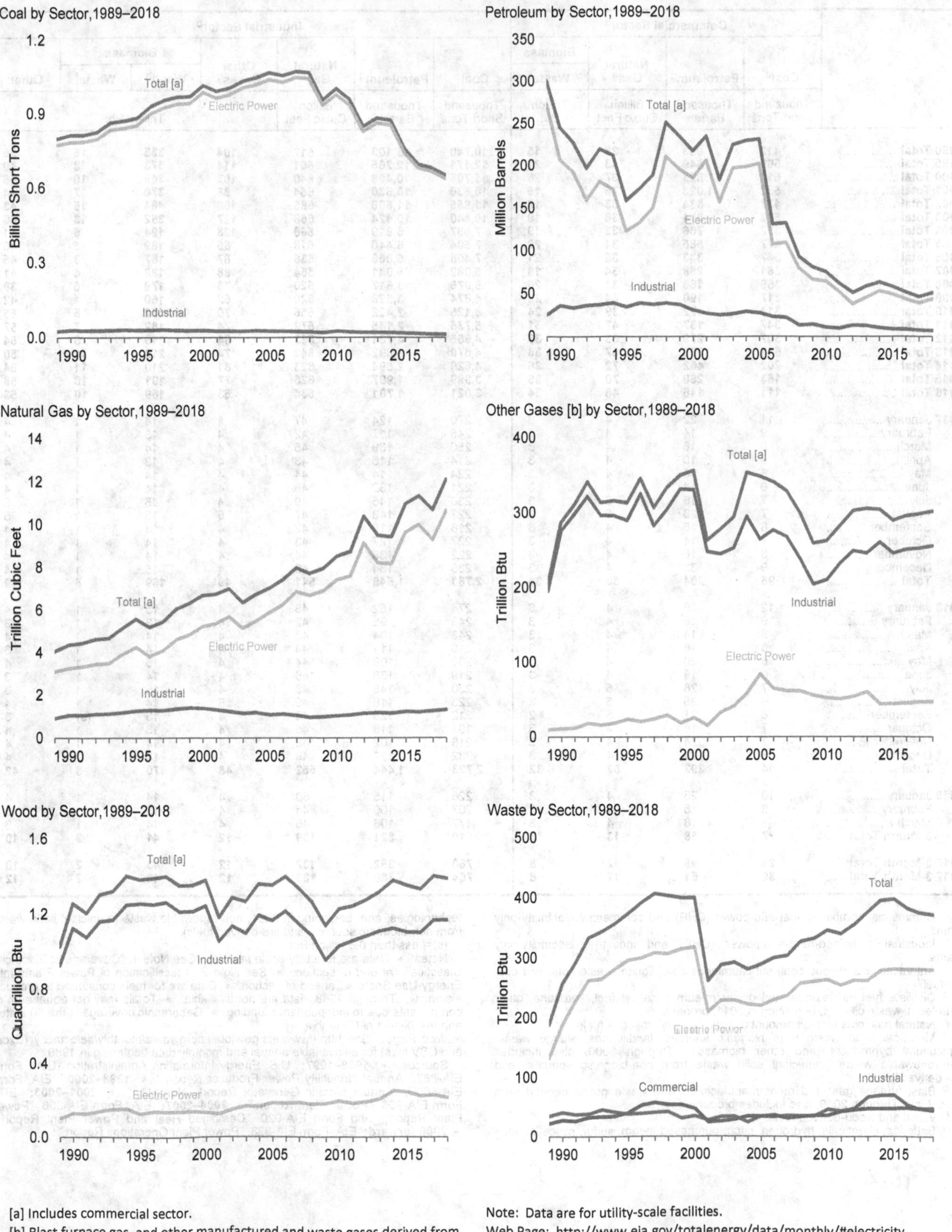

[a] Includes commercial sector.

[b] Blast furnace gas, and other manufactured and waste gases derived from fossil fuels. Through 2010, also includes propane gas.

Note: Data are for utility-scale facilities.

Web Page: http://www.eia.gov/totalenergy/data/monthly/#electricity.

Sources: Tables 7.4a-7.4c.

Source: *U.S. Energy Information Administration, Monthly Energy Review, June 2019*

Table 7.4a Consumption of Combustible Fuels for Electricity Generation and Useful Thermal Output: Total (All Sectors) (Sum of Tables 7.4b and 7.4c)

	Coal[a]	Petroleum					Natural Gas[f]	Other Gases[g]	Biomass		Other[j]
		Distillate Fuel Oil[b]	Residual Fuel Oil[c]	Other Liquids[d]	Petroleum Coke[e]	Total[e]			Wood[h]	Waste[i]	
	Thousand Short Tons	Thousand Barrels			Thousand Short Tons	Thousand Barrels	Billion Cubic Feet	Trillion Btu			
1950 Total	**91,871**	**5,423**	**69,998**	**NA**	**NA**	**75,421**	**629**	**NA**	**5**	**NA**	**NA**
1955 Total	**143,759**	**5,412**	**69,862**	**NA**	**NA**	**75,274**	**1,153**	**NA**	**3**	**NA**	**NA**
1960 Total	**176,685**	**3,824**	**84,371**	**NA**	**NA**	**88,195**	**1,725**	**NA**	**2**	**NA**	**NA**
1965 Total	**244,788**	**4,928**	**110,274**	**NA**	**NA**	**115,203**	**2,321**	**NA**	**3**	**NA**	**NA**
1970 Total	**320,182**	**24,123**	**311,381**	**NA**	**636**	**338,686**	**3,932**	**NA**	**1**	**2**	**NA**
1975 Total	**405,962**	**38,907**	**467,221**	**NA**	**70**	**506,479**	**3,158**	**NA**	**(s)**	**2**	**NA**
1980 Total	**569,274**	**29,051**	**391,163**	**NA**	**179**	**421,110**	**3,682**	**NA**	**3**	**2**	**NA**
1985 Total	**693,841**	**14,635**	**158,779**	**NA**	**231**	**174,571**	**3,044**	**NA**	**8**	**7**	**NA**
1990 Total[k]	**811,538**	**20,194**	**209,081**	**1,332**	**2,832**	**244,765**	**4,346**	**288**	**1,256**	**257**	**86**
1995 Total	**881,012**	**21,697**	**112,168**	**1,322**	**4,590**	**158,140**	**5,572**	**313**	**1,382**	**374**	**97**
2000 Total	**1,015,398**	**34,572**	**156,673**	**2,904**	**4,669**	**217,494**	**6,677**	**356**	**1,380**	**401**	**109**
2001 Total	**991,635**	**33,724**	**177,137**	**1,418**	**4,532**	**234,940**	**6,731**	**263**	**1,182**	**263**	**229**
2002 Total	**1,005,144**	**24,749**	**118,637**	**3,257**	**7,353**	**183,409**	**6,986**	**278**	**1,287**	**289**	**252**
2003 Total	**1,031,778**	**31,825**	**152,859**	**4,576**	**7,067**	**224,593**	**6,337**	**294**	**1,266**	**293**	**262**
2004 Total	**1,044,798**	**23,520**	**157,478**	**4,764**	**8,721**	**229,364**	**6,727**	**353**	**1,360**	**282**	**254**
2005 Total	**1,065,281**	**24,446**	**156,915**	**4,270**	**9,113**	**231,193**	**7,021**	**348**	**1,353**	**289**	**237**
2006 Total	**1,053,783**	**14,655**	**69,846**	**3,396**	**8,622**	**131,005**	**7,404**	**341**	**1,399**	**300**	**247**
2007 Total	**1,069,606**	**17,042**	**74,616**	**4,237**	**7,299**	**132,389**	**7,962**	**329**	**1,336**	**304**	**239**
2008 Total	**1,064,503**	**14,137**	**43,477**	**3,765**	**6,314**	**92,948**	**7,689**	**300**	**1,263**	**328**	**212**
2009 Total	**955,190**	**14,800**	**33,672**	**3,218**	**5,828**	**80,830**	**7,938**	**259**	**1,137**	**333**	**228**
2010 Total	**1,001,411**	**15,247**	**26,944**	**2,777**	**6,053**	**75,231**	**8,502**	**262**	**1,226**	**346**	**237**
2011 Total	**956,470**	**11,735**	**16,877**	**2,540**	**6,092**	**61,610**	**8,724**	**282**	**1,241**	**340**	**261**
2012 Total	**845,066**	**9,945**	**13,571**	**2,185**	**5,021**	**50,805**	**10,371**	**302**	**1,273**	**355**	**252**
2013 Total	**879,078**	**10,277**	**14,199**	**2,212**	**6,338**	**58,378**	**9,479**	**305**	**1,318**	**376**	**236**
2014 Total	**871,741**	**15,107**	**16,615**	**2,908**	**5,695**	**63,106**	**9,410**	**304**	**1,378**	**395**	**236**
2015 Total	**756,226**	**12,924**	**16,136**	**3,008**	**5,188**	**58,009**	**10,952**	**290**	**1,351**	**398**	**237**
2016 Total	**693,958**	**10,278**	**12,231**	**2,173**	**5,352**	**51,441**	**11,322**	**296**	**1,330**	**383**	**238**
2017 January	64,930	987	943	207	449	4,381	781	26	121	35	19
February	49,183	741	790	148	347	3,412	678	23	108	30	17
March	50,132	846	825	139	355	3,584	787	25	119	33	19
April	45,408	687	787	146	242	2,829	736	24	110	31	18
May	52,034	836	878	136	406	3,881	813	26	112	31	19
June	60,005	726	973	183	441	4,087	968	24	116	30	19
July	70,971	710	870	129	430	3,861	1,209	25	122	31	21
August	66,975	678	988	163	390	3,780	1,145	25	124	31	21
September	55,817	723	894	139	352	3,517	975	24	111	28	18
October	51,238	758	919	139	314	3,386	889	25	115	30	18
November	52,142	797	873	164	373	3,696	782	25	118	32	18
December	59,743	1,678	1,769	340	368	5,629	913	26	125	33	19
Total	**678,578**	**10,168**	**11,508**	**2,033**	**4,467**	**46,043**	**10,677**	**299**	**1,400**	**375**	**226**
2018 January	65,921	5,475	3,578	711	421	11,870	914	26	120	34	18
February	46,922	608	747	161	338	3,206	815	24	112	31	17
March	45,631	673	748	153	307	3,110	875	26	116	34	18
April	41,662	742	790	144	323	3,293	824	24	111	31	17
May	48,567	876	894	174	225	3,069	969	24	115	31	18
June	57,119	852	1,037	158	378	3,937	1,072	25	116	30	19
July	64,876	734	940	191	416	3,944	1,362	26	120	30	19
August	64,743	767	1,036	180	395	3,960	1,323	27	121	30	19
September	55,025	683	1,091	171	389	3,887	1,166	24	110	27	17
October	49,496	729	991	180	264	3,221	1,015	25	114	31	18
November	52,856	816	854	165	312	3,396	883	24	113	31	18
December	56,735	810	801	278	376	3,766	874	26	120	32	19
Total	**649,554**	**13,766**	**13,507**	**2,666**	**4,144**	**50,660**	**12,091**	**302**	**1,388**	**372**	**217**
2019 January	57,043	1,230	1,132	308	380	4,568	969	26	120	31	18
February	46,104	679	667	204	329	3,196	889	25	107	28	16
March	45,074	691	703	181	317	3,159	917	27	108	31	17
3-Month Total	**148,221**	**2,600**	**2,501**	**693**	**1,026**	**10,922**	**2,774**	**78**	**335**	**90**	**51**
2018 3-Month Total	**158,473**	**6,756**	**5,073**	**1,025**	**1,066**	**18,186**	**2,604**	**76**	**348**	**99**	**54**
2017 3-Month Total	**164,245**	**2,574**	**2,557**	**494**	**1,150**	**11,377**	**2,246**	**75**	**348**	**98**	**55**

[a] Anthracite, bituminous coal, subbituminous coal, lignite, waste coal, and coal synfuel.
[b] Fuel oil nos. 1, 2, and 4. For 1949–1979, data are for gas turbine and internal combustion plant use of petroleum. For 1980–2000, electric utility data also include small amounts of kerosene and jet fuel.
[c] Fuel oil nos. 5 and 6. For 1949–1979, data are for steam plant use of petroleum. For 1980–2000, electric utility data also include a small amount of fuel oil no. 4.
[d] Jet fuel, kerosene, other petroleum liquids, waste oil, and, beginning in 2011, propane.
[e] Petroleum coke is converted from short tons to barrels by multiplying by 5.
[f] Natural gas, plus a small amount of supplemental gaseous fuels.
[g] Blast furnace gas, and other manufactured and waste gases derived from fossil fuels. Through 2010, also includes propane gas.
[h] Wood and wood-derived fuels.
[i] Municipal solid waste from biogenic sources, landfill gas, sludge waste, agricultural byproducts, and other biomass. Through 2000, also includes non-renewable waste (municipal solid waste from non-biogenic sources, and tire-derived fuels).
[j] Batteries, chemicals, hydrogen, pitch, purchased steam, sulfur, miscellaneous technologies, and, beginning in 2001, non-renewable waste (municipal solid waste from non-biogenic sources, and tire-derived fuels).
[k] Through 1988, data are for electric utilities only. Beginning in 1989, data are for electric utilities, independent power producers, commercial plants, and industrial plants.

NA=Not available. (s)=Less than 0.5 trillion Btu.

Notes: • Data are for utility-scale facilities. See Note 1, "Coverage of Electricity Statistics," at end of section. • Totals may not equal sum of components due to independent rounding. • Geographic coverage is the 50 states and the District of Columbia.

Web Page: See http://www.eia.gov/totalenergy/data/monthly/#electricity (Excel and CSV files) for all available annual data beginning in 1949 and monthly data beginning in 1973.

Sources: See "Table 7.4b Sources" at end of section and sources for Table 7.4c.

Source: *U.S. Energy Information Administration, Monthly Energy Review, June 2019*

Table 7.4b Consumption of Combustible Fuels for Electricity Generation and Useful Thermal Output: Electric Power Sector (Subset of Table 7.4a)

		Petroleum							Biomass		
	Coal[a]	Distillate Fuel Oil[b]	Residual Fuel Oil[c]	Other Liquids[d]	Petroleum Coke[e]	Total[e]	Natural Gas[f]	Other Gases[g]	Wood[h]	Waste[i]	Other[j]
	Thousand Short Tons	Thousand Barrels			Thousand Short Tons	Thousand Barrels	Billion Cubic Feet	Trillion Btu			
1950 Total	**91,871**	**5,423**	**69,998**	**NA**	**NA**	**75,421**	**629**	**NA**	**5**	**NA**	**NA**
1955 Total	**143,759**	**5,412**	**69,862**	**NA**	**NA**	**75,274**	**1,153**	**NA**	**3**	**NA**	**NA**
1960 Total	**176,685**	**3,824**	**84,371**	**NA**	**NA**	**88,195**	**1,725**	**NA**	**2**	**NA**	**NA**
1965 Total	**244,788**	**4,928**	**110,274**	**NA**	**NA**	**115,203**	**2,321**	**NA**	**3**	**NA**	**NA**
1970 Total	**320,182**	**24,123**	**311,381**	**NA**	**636**	**338,686**	**3,932**	**NA**	**1**	**2**	**NA**
1975 Total	**405,962**	**38,907**	**467,221**	**NA**	**70**	**506,479**	**3,158**	**NA**	**(s)**	**2**	**NA**
1980 Total	**569,274**	**29,051**	**391,163**	**NA**	**179**	**421,110**	**3,682**	**NA**	**3**	**2**	**NA**
1985 Total	**693,841**	**14,635**	**158,779**	**NA**	**231**	**174,571**	**3,044**	**NA**	**8**	**7**	**NA**
1990 Total[k]	**782,567**	**16,567**	**184,915**	**26**	**1,008**	**206,550**	**3,245**	**11**	**129**	**188**	**(s)**
1995 Total	**850,230**	**18,553**	**90,023**	**499**	**2,674**	**122,447**	**4,237**	**24**	**125**	**296**	**2**
2000 Total	**985,821**	**30,016**	**138,513**	**454**	**3,275**	**185,358**	**5,206**	**25**	**134**	**318**	**1**
2001 Total	**964,433**	**29,274**	**159,504**	**377**	**3,427**	**206,291**	**5,342**	**15**	**126**	**211**	**113**
2002 Total	**977,507**	**21,876**	**104,773**	**1,267**	**5,816**	**156,996**	**5,672**	**33**	**150**	**230**	**143**
2003 Total	**1,005,116**	**27,632**	**138,279**	**2,026**	**5,799**	**196,932**	**5,135**	**41**	**167**	**230**	**140**
2004 Total	**1,016,268**	**19,107**	**139,816**	**2,713**	**7,372**	**198,498**	**5,464**	**58**	**165**	**223**	**138**
2005 Total	**1,037,485**	**19,675**	**139,409**	**2,685**	**8,083**	**202,184**	**5,869**	**84**	**185**	**221**	**123**
2006 Total	**1,026,636**	**12,646**	**57,345**	**1,870**	**7,101**	**107,365**	**6,222**	**65**	**182**	**231**	**125**
2007 Total	**1,045,141**	**15,327**	**63,086**	**2,594**	**5,685**	**109,431**	**6,841**	**61**	**186**	**237**	**124**
2008 Total	**1,040,580**	**12,547**	**38,241**	**2,670**	**5,119**	**79,056**	**6,668**	**61**	**177**	**258**	**131**
2009 Total	**933,627**	**12,035**	**28,782**	**2,210**	**4,611**	**66,081**	**6,873**	**55**	**180**	**261**	**124**
2010 Total	**975,052**	**13,790**	**24,503**	**1,877**	**4,777**	**64,055**	**7,387**	**52**	**196**	**264**	**124**
2011 Total	**932,484**	**11,021**	**14,803**	**1,658**	**4,837**	**51,667**	**7,574**	**50**	**182**	**255**	**143**
2012 Total	**823,551**	**9,080**	**12,203**	**1,339**	**2,974**	**37,495**	**9,111**	**54**	**190**	**262**	**143**
2013 Total	**857,962**	**9,598**	**12,283**	**1,489**	**4,285**	**44,794**	**8,191**	**60**	**207**	**262**	**139**
2014 Total	**851,602**	**14,235**	**15,132**	**2,208**	**4,132**	**52,235**	**8,146**	**44**	**251**	**279**	**137**
2015 Total	**738,444**	**12,193**	**14,929**	**2,131**	**3,907**	**48,787**	**9,613**	**44**	**244**	**281**	**136**
2016 Total	**678,554**	**9,510**	**11,242**	**1,322**	**4,138**	**42,763**	**9,985**	**45**	**224**	**281**	**139**
2017 January	63,595	916	856	147	362	3,728	660	4	20	26	12
February	48,048	697	730	87	272	2,872	569	3	18	22	10
March	48,925	794	733	90	256	2,898	672	4	21	24	11
April	44,358	640	716	90	162	2,255	627	4	17	22	10
May	50,952	789	812	78	324	3,297	700	4	17	24	11
June	58,920	690	910	133	340	3,435	851	4	18	24	11
July	69,882	667	815	77	332	3,220	1,082	4	20	24	12
August	65,883	630	932	109	289	3,118	1,022	4	21	23	12
September	54,780	675	822	95	270	2,942	859	4	18	22	11
October	50,099	713	847	82	221	2,746	773	4	18	22	10
November	51,013	734	707	113	285	2,979	666	4	19	23	11
December	58,538	1,536	1,585	276	286	4,828	785	4	21	24	12
Total	**664,993**	**9,481**	**10,464**	**1,375**	**3,399**	**38,318**	**9,266**	**46**	**229**	**280**	**132**
2018 January	64,606	5,141	3,294	623	344	10,780	785	4	20	25	11
February	45,757	561	674	90	273	2,690	701	4	18	23	11
March	44,439	611	664	97	242	2,584	755	4	19	25	11
April	40,601	691	715	86	242	2,700	707	4	15	23	11
May	47,485	817	813	108	155	2,512	853	4	18	23	11
June	56,089	791	895	97	296	3,261	952	4	19	24	12
July	63,851	652	876	93	335	3,298	1,236	4	20	23	12
August	63,751	690	947	132	322	3,379	1,195	4	19	24	12
September	53,998	609	994	133	307	3,270	1,045	4	17	21	10
October	48,520	674	898	126	183	2,612	895	4	17	23	11
November	51,789	728	767	114	243	2,823	756	3	16	23	11
December	55,610	714	696	228	292	3,095	744	4	18	24	11
Total	**636,498**	**12,680**	**12,231**	**1,927**	**3,233**	**43,005**	**10,626**	**46**	**215**	**280**	**136**
2019 January	55,885	1,014	1,021	249	307	3,816	834	4	20	23	11
February	45,051	609	592	133	267	2,667	769	4	17	20	10
March	44,078	627	616	123	243	2,579	792	5	17	23	11
3-Month Total	**145,014**	**2,250**	**2,228**	**505**	**816**	**9,063**	**2,396**	**13**	**54**	**66**	**31**
2018 3-Month Total	**154,803**	**6,313**	**4,631**	**810**	**860**	**16,054**	**2,242**	**11**	**57**	**73**	**34**
2017 3-Month Total	**160,569**	**2,408**	**2,319**	**324**	**890**	**9,498**	**1,901**	**11**	**60**	**72**	**33**

[a] Anthracite, bituminous coal, subbituminous coal, lignite, waste coal, and coal synfuel.
[b] Fuel oil nos. 1, 2, and 4. For 1949–1979, data are for gas turbine and internal combustion plant use of petroleum. For 1980–2000, electric utility data also include small amounts of kerosene and jet fuel.
[c] Fuel oil nos. 5 and 6. For 1949–1979, data are for steam plant use of petroleum. For 1980–2000, electric utility data also include a small amount of fuel oil no. 4.
[d] Jet fuel, kerosene, other petroleum liquids, waste oil, and, beginning in 2011, propane.
[e] Petroleum coke is converted from short tons to barrels by multiplying by 5.
[f] Natural gas, plus a small amount of supplemental gaseous fuels.
[g] Blast furnace gas, and other manufactured and waste gases derived from fossil fuels. Through 2010, also includes propane gas.
[h] Wood and wood-derived fuels.
[i] Municipal solid waste from biogenic sources, landfill gas, sludge waste, agricultural byproducts, and other biomass. Through 2000, also includes non-renewable waste (municipal solid waste from non-biogenic sources, and tire-derived fuels).
[j] Batteries, chemicals, hydrogen, pitch, purchased steam, sulfur, miscellaneous technologies, and, beginning in 2001, non-renewable waste (municipal solid waste from non-biogenic sources, and tire-derived fuels).
[k] Through 1988, data are for electric utilities only. Beginning in 1989, data are for electric utilities and independent power producers.

NA=Not available. (s)=Less than 0.5 trillion Btu.

Notes: • Data are for utility-scale facilities. See Note 1, "Coverage of Electricity Statistics," at end of section. • The electric power sector comprises electricity-only and combined-heat-and-power (CHP) plants within the NAICS 22 category whose primary business is to sell electricity, or electricity and heat, to the public. • Totals may not equal sum of components due to independent rounding. • Geographic coverage is the 50 states and the District of Columbia.

Web Page: See http://www.eia.gov/totalenergy/data/monthly/#electricity (Excel and CSV files) for all available annual data beginning in 1949 and monthly data beginning in 1973.

Sources: See end of section.

Source: U.S. Energy Information Administration, Monthly Energy Review, June 2019

Table 7.4c Consumption of Selected Combustible Fuels for Electricity Generation and Useful Thermal Output: Commercial and Industrial Sectors (Subset of Table 7.4a)

	Commercial Sector[a]				Industrial Sector[b]						
				Biomass					Biomass		
	Coal[c]	Petroleum[d]	Natural Gas[e]	Waste[f]	Coal[c]	Petroleum[d]	Natural Gas[e]	Other Gases[g]	Wood[h]	Waste[f]	Other[i]
	Thousand Short Tons	Thousand Barrels	Billion Cubic Feet	Trillion Btu	Thousand Short Tons	Thousand Barrels	Billion Cubic Feet	Trillion Btu			
1990 Total	**1,191**	**2,056**	**46**	**28**	**27,781**	**36,159**	**1,055**	**275**	**1,125**	**41**	**86**
1995 Total	**1,419**	**1,245**	**78**	**40**	**29,363**	**34,448**	**1,258**	**290**	**1,255**	**38**	**95**
2000 Total	**1,547**	**1,615**	**85**	**47**	**28,031**	**30,520**	**1,386**	**331**	**1,244**	**35**	**108**
2001 Total	**1,448**	**1,832**	**79**	**25**	**25,755**	**26,817**	**1,310**	**248**	**1,054**	**27**	**101**
2002 Total	**1,405**	**1,250**	**74**	**26**	**26,232**	**25,163**	**1,240**	**245**	**1,136**	**34**	**92**
2003 Total	**1,816**	**1,449**	**58**	**29**	**24,846**	**26,212**	**1,144**	**253**	**1,097**	**34**	**103**
2004 Total	**1,917**	**2,009**	**72**	**34**	**26,613**	**28,857**	**1,191**	**295**	**1,193**	**24**	**94**
2005 Total	**1,922**	**1,630**	**68**	**34**	**25,875**	**27,380**	**1,084**	**264**	**1,166**	**34**	**94**
2006 Total	**1,886**	**935**	**68**	**36**	**25,262**	**22,706**	**1,115**	**277**	**1,216**	**33**	**102**
2007 Total	**1,927**	**752**	**70**	**31**	**22,537**	**22,207**	**1,050**	**268**	**1,148**	**36**	**98**
2008 Total	**2,021**	**671**	**66**	**34**	**21,902**	**13,222**	**955**	**239**	**1,084**	**35**	**60**
2009 Total	**1,798**	**521**	**76**	**36**	**19,766**	**14,228**	**990**	**204**	**955**	**35**	**82**
2010 Total	**1,720**	**437**	**86**	**36**	**24,638**	**10,740**	**1,029**	**210**	**1,029**	**47**	**91**
2011 Total	**1,668**	**333**	**87**	**43**	**22,319**	**9,610**	**1,063**	**232**	**1,057**	**43**	**94**
2012 Total	**1,450**	**457**	**111**	**45**	**20,065**	**12,853**	**1,149**	**249**	**1,082**	**47**	**81**
2013 Total	**1,356**	**887**	**118**	**47**	**19,761**	**12,697**	**1,170**	**246**	**1,109**	**67**	**69**
2014 Total	**1,063**	**758**	**119**	**47**	**19,076**	**10,112**	**1,145**	**260**	**1,122**	**70**	**72**
2015 Total	**798**	**622**	**116**	**47**	**16,984**	**8,600**	**1,222**	**246**	**1,103**	**70**	**73**
2016 Total	**683**	**404**	**127**	**48**	**14,720**	**8,273**	**1,209**	**251**	**1,100**	**54**	**70**
2017 January	71	68	14	4	1,264	584	107	22	100	5	5
February	58	43	12	4	1,077	496	97	20	89	4	5
March	66	50	12	4	1,141	637	103	21	98	5	5
April	42	24	10	4	1,008	550	99	20	93	4	5
May	39	34	11	4	1,043	550	102	22	95	3	5
June	40	27	13	4	1,045	625	104	20	97	3	6
July	47	30	15	4	1,042	611	112	21	101	3	6
August	43	45	15	4	1,050	618	108	22	102	3	6
September	45	35	13	4	991	539	103	20	92	3	5
October	42	33	13	4	1,098	607	104	21	97	4	5
November	52	38	12	4	1,077	679	104	21	98	5	5
December	66	88	14	4	1,139	713	115	22	103	5	5
Total	**610**	**516**	**154**	**48**	**12,975**	**7,209**	**1,257**	**253**	**1,166**	**47**	**65**
2018 January	70	186	14	4	1,245	904	115	22	100	5	5
February	54	50	13	4	1,111	466	101	20	93	4	4
March	51	44	13	4	1,140	482	107	22	97	5	5
April	45	38	12	4	1,016	555	104	20	95	5	4
May	41	37	12	4	1,041	520	104	20	97	4	5
June	42	36	13	4	989	640	107	21	97	3	5
July	47	58	14	4	978	588	112	22	100	3	4
August	49	50	14	4	942	531	113	23	102	3	5
September	51	42	13	3	977	576	108	21	93	3	4
October	42	39	13	4	933	570	107	21	96	4	5
November	48	62	12	4	1,018	511	114	21	96	5	5
December	47	67	13	4	1,078	604	117	22	101	5	5
Total	**587**	**706**	**155**	**44**	**12,468**	**6,949**	**1,310**	**255**	**1,167**	**47**	**55**
2019 January	58	80	14	4	1,099	672	120	21	99	5	5
February	53	48	13	3	999	481	107	20	90	4	4
March	55	54	13	4	942	525	111	22	91	4	5
3-Month Total	**166**	**181**	**40**	**11**	**3,040**	**1,678**	**339**	**64**	**279**	**13**	**13**
2018 3-Month Total	**175**	**279**	**39**	**11**	**3,496**	**1,853**	**323**	**64**	**290**	**14**	**14**
2017 3-Month Total	**194**	**161**	**38**	**12**	**3,482**	**1,717**	**307**	**63**	**287**	**14**	**15**

[a] Commercial combined-heat-and-power (CHP) and commercial electricity-only plants.
[b] Industrial combined-heat-and-power (CHP) and industrial electricity-only plants.
[c] Anthracite, bituminous coal, subbituminous coal, lignite, waste coal, and coal synfuel.
[d] Distillate fuel oil, residual fuel oil, petroleum coke, jet fuel, kerosene, other petroleum, waste oil, and, beginning in 2011, propane.
[e] Natural gas, plus a small amount of supplemental gaseous fuels.
[f] Municipal solid waste from biogenic sources, landfill gas, sludge waste, agricultural byproducts, and other biomass. Through 2000, also includes non-renewable waste (municipal solid waste from non-biogenic sources, and tire-derived fuels).
[g] Blast furnace gas, and other manufactured and waste gases derived from fossil fuels. Through 2010, also includes propane gas.
[h] Wood and wood-derived fuels.
[i] Batteries, chemicals, hydrogen, pitch, purchased steam, sulfur, miscellaneous technologies, and, beginning in 2001, non-renewable waste (municipal solid waste from non-biogenic sources, and tire-derived fuels).

Notes: • Data are for utility-scale facilities. See Note 1, "Coverage of Electricity Statistics," at end of section. • See Note 2, "Classification of Power Plants Into Energy-Use Sectors," at end of section. • Totals may not equal sum of components due to independent rounding. • Geographic coverage is the 50 states and the District of Columbia.

Web Page: See http://www.eia.gov/totalenergy/data/monthly/#electricity (Excel and CSV files) for all available annual and monthly data beginning in 1989.

Sources: • **1989–1997:** U.S. Energy Information Administration (EIA), Form EIA-867, "Annual Nonutility Power Producer Report." • **1998–2000:** EIA, Form EIA-860B, "Annual Electric Generator Report—Nonutility." • **2001–2003:** EIA, Form EIA-906, "Power Plant Report." • **2004–2007:** EIA, Form EIA-906, "Power Plant Report," and Form EIA-920, "Combined Heat and Power Plant Report." • **2008 forward:** EIA, Form EIA-923, "Power Plant Operations Report."

Source: *U.S. Energy Information Administration, Monthly Energy Review, June 2019*

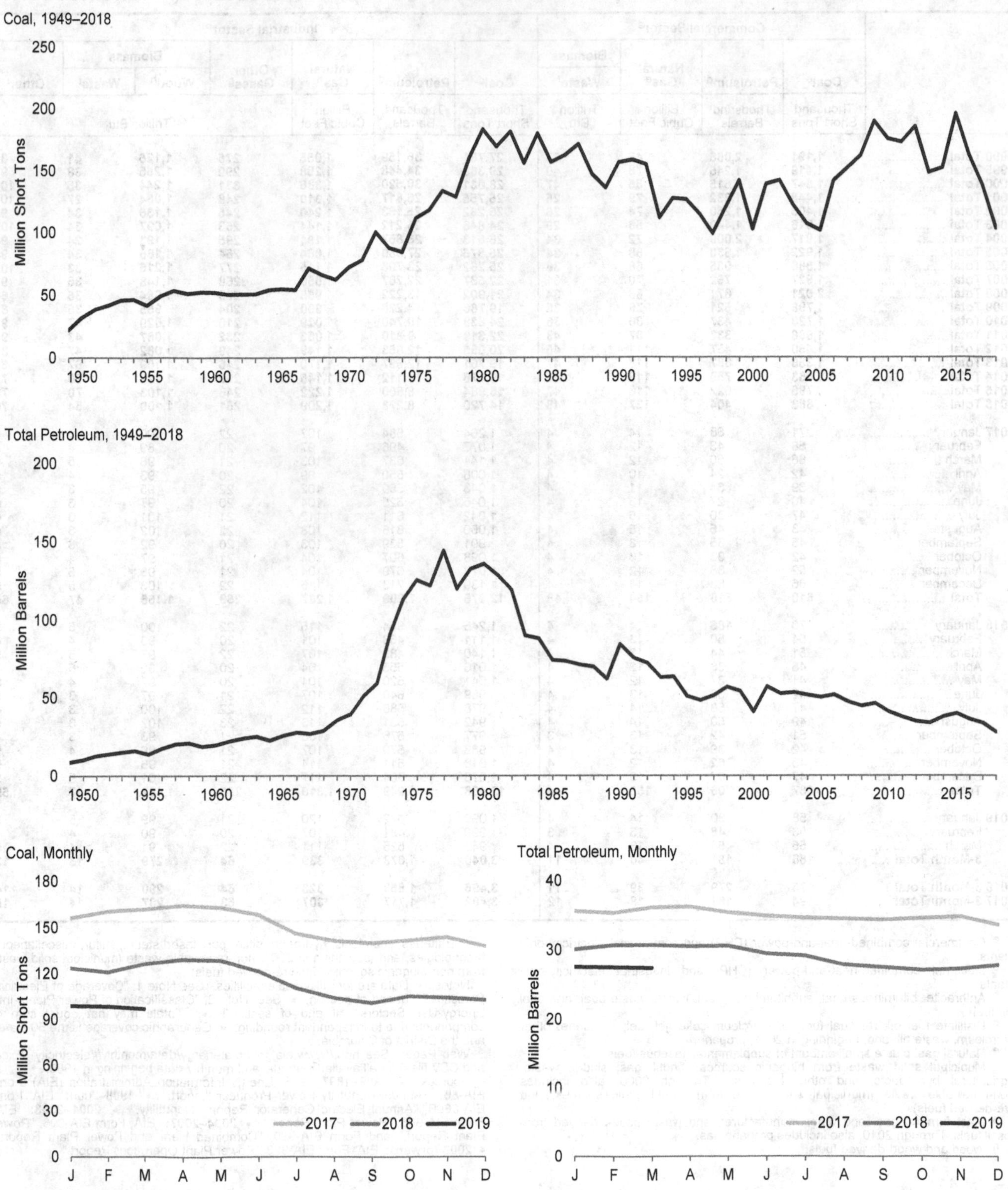

Note: Data are for utility-sale facilities.
Web Page: http://www.eia.gov/totalenergy/data/monthly/#electricity.
Source: Table 7.5.

Source: *U.S. Energy Information Administration, Monthly Energy Review, June 2019*

Table 7.5 Stocks of Coal and Petroleum: Electric Power Sector

	Coal[a]	Petroleum				
		Distillate Fuel Oil[b]	Residual Fuel Oil[c]	Other Liquids[d]	Petroleum Coke[e]	Total[e,f]
	Thousand Short Tons	Thousand Barrels			Thousand Short Tons	Thousand Barrels
1950 Year	31,842	NA	NA	NA	NA	10,201
1955 Year	41,391	NA	NA	NA	NA	13,671
1960 Year	51,735	NA	NA	NA	NA	19,572
1965 Year	54,525	NA	NA	NA	NA	25,647
1970 Year	71,908	NA	NA	NA	239	39,151
1975 Year	110,724	16,432	108,825	NA	31	125,413
1980 Year	183,010	30,023	105,351	NA	52	135,635
1985 Year	156,376	16,386	57,304	NA	49	73,933
1990 Year	156,166	16,471	67,030	NA	94	83,970
1995 Year	126,304	15,392	35,102	NA	65	50,821
2000 Year[g]	102,296	15,127	24,748	NA	211	40,932
2001 Year	138,496	20,486	34,594	NA	390	57,031
2002 Year	141,714	17,413	25,723	800	1,711	52,490
2003 Year	121,567	19,153	25,820	779	1,484	53,170
2004 Year	106,669	19,275	26,596	879	937	51,434
2005 Year	101,137	18,778	27,624	1,012	530	50,062
2006 Year	140,964	18,013	28,823	1,380	674	51,583
2007 Year	151,221	18,395	24,136	1,902	554	47,203
2008 Year	161,589	17,761	21,088	1,955	739	44,498
2009 Year	189,467	17,886	19,068	2,257	1,394	46,181
2010 Year	174,917	16,758	16,629	2,319	1,019	40,800
2011 Year	172,387	16,649	15,491	2,707	508	37,387
2012 Year	185,116	16,433	12,999	2,792	495	34,698
2013 Year	147,884	16,068	12,926	2,679	390	33,622
2014 Year	151,548	18,309	12,764	2,432	827	37,643
2015 Year	195,548	17,955	12,566	2,363	1,340	39,586
2016 Year	162,009	17,855	11,789	2,195	845	36,064
2017 January	156,214	17,718	11,858	2,186	768	35,601
February	160,502	17,588	11,744	2,168	756	35,277
March	161,815	17,336	12,681	2,157	785	36,099
April	163,937	17,362	12,439	2,168	844	36,187
May	162,542	17,265	12,170	2,143	772	35,439
June	158,014	17,082	11,993	2,133	742	34,916
July	145,811	17,150	11,740	2,143	724	34,655
August	141,204	17,091	11,531	2,129	749	34,497
September	139,571	16,844	11,382	2,120	798	34,334
October	141,463	16,806	11,292	2,128	862	34,537
November	143,424	16,980	11,381	2,140	859	34,796
December	**137,687**	**16,356**	**10,930**	**2,008**	**864**	**33,612**
2018 January	123,723	14,989	9,676	1,842	721	30,109
February	121,019	15,223	10,137	1,878	689	30,685
March	126,532	15,143	10,102	1,881	717	30,710
April	129,071	15,064	10,032	1,884	710	30,527
May	128,454	15,176	9,927	1,950	715	30,628
June	121,529	14,860	9,871	1,846	583	29,491
July	110,794	14,800	9,356	1,806	643	29,178
August	104,172	14,396	8,694	1,737	607	27,863
September	100,781	14,430	8,434	1,729	576	27,476
October	105,209	14,468	8,404	1,630	517	27,088
November	104,324	14,706	8,206	1,625	546	27,269
December	**102,786**	**14,906**	**8,557**	**1,619**	**541**	**27,787**
2019 January	99,201	14,912	8,399	1,624	529	27,579
February	98,744	14,758	8,656	1,544	507	27,495
March	97,127	14,675	8,688	1,557	500	27,419

[a] Anthracite, bituminous coal, subbituminous coal, and lignite; excludes waste coal.
[b] Fuel oil nos. 1, 2 and 4. For 1973–1979, data are for gas turbine and internal combustion plant stocks of petroleum. For 1980–2000, electric utility data also include small amounts of kerosene and jet fuel.
[c] Fuel oil nos. 5 and 6. For 1973–1979, data are for steam plant stocks of petroleum. For 1980–2000, electric utility data also include a small amount of fuel oil no. 4.
[d] Jet fuel and kerosene. Through 2003, data also include a small amount of waste oil.
[e] Petroleum coke is converted from short tons to barrels by multiplying by 5.
[f] Distillate fuel oil and residual fuel oil. Beginning in 1970, also includes petroleum coke. Beginning in 2002, also includes other liquids.
[g] Through 1998, data are for electric utilities only. Beginning in 1999, data are for electric utilities and independent power producers.
NA=Not available.
Notes: • Data are for utility-scale facilities. See Note 1, "Coverage of Electricity Statistics," at end of section. • The electric power sector comprises electricity-only and combined-heat-and-power (CHP) plants within the NAICS 22 category whose primary business is to sell electricity, or electricity and heat, to the public. • Stocks are at end of period. • Totals may not equal sum of components due to independent rounding. • Geographic coverage is the 50 states and the District of Columbia.

Web Page: See http://www.eia.gov/totalenergy/data/monthly/#electricity (Excel and CSV files) for all available annual data beginning in 1949 and monthly data beginning in 1973.

Sources: • **1949–September 1977:** Federal Power Commission, Form FPC-4, "Monthly Power Plant Report." • **October 1977–1981:** Federal Energy Regulatory Commission, Form FPC-4, "Monthly Power Plant Report." • **1982–1988:** U.S. Energy Information Administration (EIA), Form EIA-759, "Monthly Power Plant Report." • **1989–1997:** EIA, Form EIA-759, "Monthly Power Plant Report," and Form EIA-867, "Annual Nonutility Power Producer Report." • **1998–2000:** EIA, Form EIA-759, "Monthly Power Plant Report," and Form EIA-860B, "Annual Electric Generator Report—Nonutility." • **2001–2003:** EIA, Form EIA-906, "Power Plant Report." • **2004–2007:** EIA, Form EIA-906, "Power Plant Report," and Form EIA-920, "Combined Heat and Power Plant Report." • **2008 forward:** EIA, Form EIA-923, "Power Plant Operations Report."

Source: *U.S. Energy Information Administration, Monthly Energy Review, June 2019*

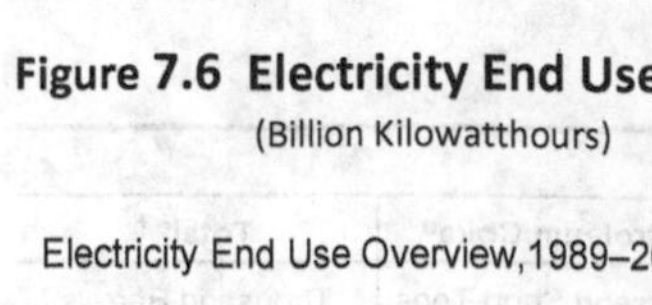
Figure 7.6 Electricity End Use
(Billion Kilowatthours)

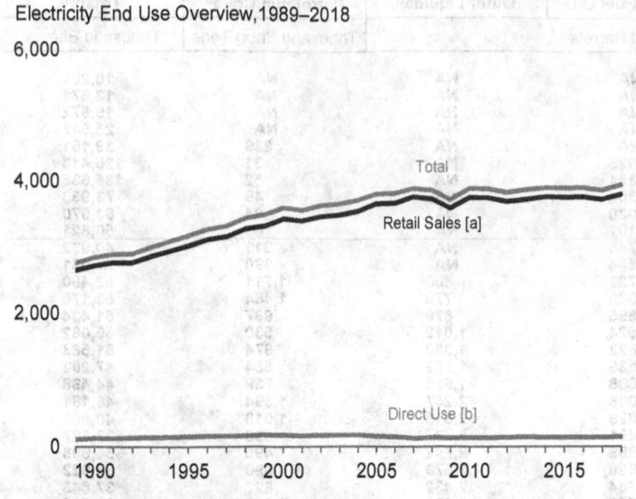

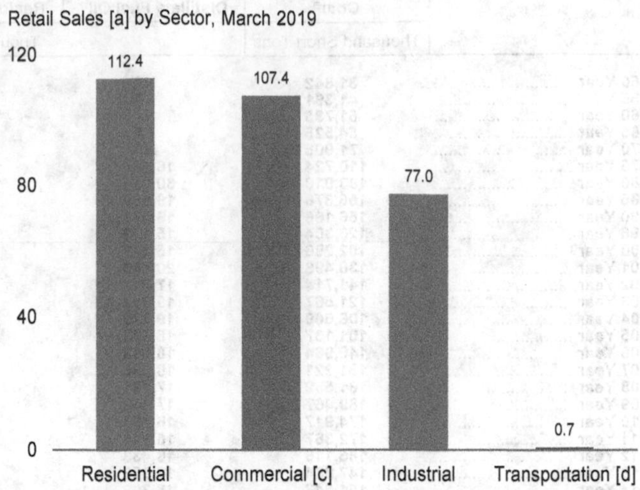

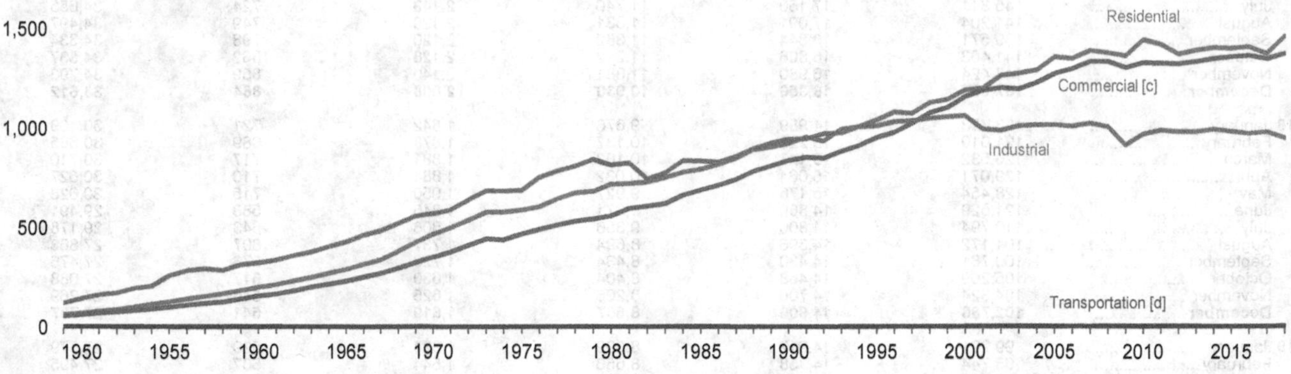

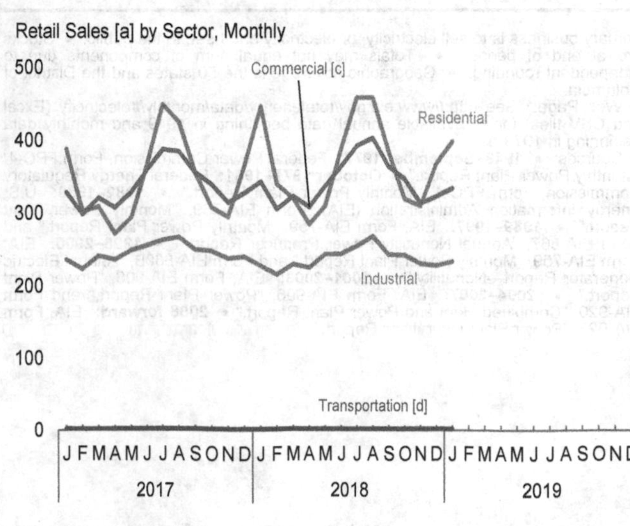

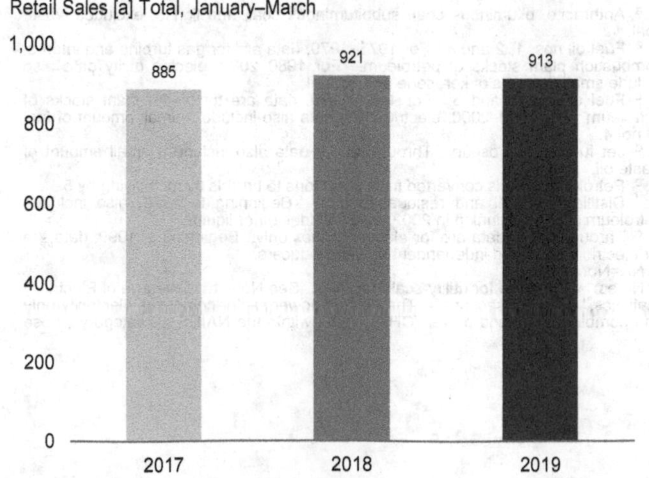

[a] Electricity retail sales to ultimate customers reported by utilities and other energy service providers.

[b] See "Direct Use" in Glossary.

[c] Commercial sector, including public street and highway lighting, interdepartmental sales, and other sales to public authorities.

[d] Transportation sector, including sales to railroads and railways.

Web Page: http://www.eia.gov/totalenergy/data/monthly/#electricity.

Source: Table 7.6.

***Source:** U.S. Energy Information Administration, Monthly Energy Review, June 2019*

Table 7.6 Electricity End Use
(Million Kilowatthours)

	Retail Sales[a]					Direct Use[f]	Total End Use[g]
	Residential	Commercial[b]	Industrial[c]	Transportation[d]	Total Retail Sales[e]		
1950 Total	**72,200**	**[E]65,971**	**146,479**	**[E]6,793**	**291,443**	**NA**	**291,443**
1955 Total	**128,401**	**[E]102,547**	**259,974**	**[E]5,826**	**496,748**	**NA**	**496,748**
1960 Total	**201,463**	**[E]159,144**	**324,402**	**[E]3,066**	**688,075**	**NA**	**688,075**
1965 Total	**291,013**	**[E]231,126**	**428,727**	**[E]2,923**	**953,789**	**NA**	**953,789**
1970 Total	**466,291**	**[E]352,041**	**570,854**	**[E]3,115**	**1,392,300**	**NA**	**1,392,300**
1975 Total	**588,140**	**[E]468,296**	**687,680**	**[E]2,974**	**1,747,091**	**NA**	**1,747,091**
1980 Total	**717,495**	**558,643**	**815,067**	**3,244**	**2,094,449**	**NA**	**2,094,449**
1985 Total	**793,934**	**689,121**	**836,772**	**4,147**	**2,323,974**	**NA**	**2,323,974**
1990 Total	**924,019**	**838,263**	**945,522**	**4,751**	**2,712,555**	**124,529**	**2,837,084**
1995 Total	**1,042,501**	**953,117**	**1,012,693**	**4,975**	**3,013,287**	**150,677**	**3,163,963**
2000 Total	**1,192,446**	**1,159,347**	**1,064,239**	**5,382**	**3,421,414**	**170,943**	**3,592,357**
2001 Total	**1,201,607**	**1,190,518**	**996,609**	**5,724**	**3,394,458**	**162,649**	**3,557,107**
2002 Total	**1,265,180**	**1,204,531**	**990,238**	**5,517**	**3,465,466**	**166,184**	**3,631,650**
2003 Total	**1,275,824**	**1,198,728**	**1,012,373**	**6,810**	**3,493,734**	**168,295**	**3,662,029**
2004 Total	**1,291,982**	**1,230,425**	**1,017,850**	**7,224**	**3,547,479**	**168,470**	**3,715,949**
2005 Total	**1,359,227**	**1,275,079**	**1,019,156**	**7,506**	**3,660,969**	**150,016**	**3,810,984**
2006 Total	**1,351,520**	**1,299,744**	**1,011,298**	**7,358**	**3,669,919**	**146,927**	**3,816,845**
2007 Total	**1,392,241**	**1,336,315**	**1,027,832**	**8,173**	**3,764,561**	**125,670**	**3,890,231**
2008 Total	**1,380,662**	**1,336,133**	**1,009,516**	**7,653**	**3,733,965**	**132,197**	**3,866,161**
2009 Total	**1,364,758**	**1,306,853**	**917,416**	**7,768**	**3,596,795**	**126,938**	**3,723,733**
2010 Total	**1,445,708**	**1,330,199**	**971,221**	**7,712**	**3,754,841**	**131,910**	**3,886,752**
2011 Total	**1,422,801**	**1,328,057**	**991,316**	**7,672**	**3,749,846**	**132,754**	**3,882,600**
2012 Total	**1,374,515**	**1,327,101**	**985,714**	**7,320**	**3,694,650**	**137,657**	**3,832,306**
2013 Total	**1,394,812**	**1,337,079**	**985,352**	**7,625**	**3,724,868**	**143,462**	**3,868,330**
2014 Total	**1,407,208**	**1,352,158**	**997,576**	**7,758**	**3,764,700**	**138,574**	**3,903,274**
2015 Total	**1,404,096**	**1,360,752**	**986,508**	**7,637**	**3,758,992**	**141,168**	**3,900,160**
2016 Total	**1,411,058**	**1,367,191**	**976,715**	**7,497**	**3,762,462**	**139,844**	**3,902,306**
2017 January	129,212	109,488	78,809	667	318,177	[E]12,093	330,270
February	100,968	99,640	74,534	635	275,777	[E]10,892	286,669
March	103,096	107,173	80,530	645	291,444	[E]11,643	303,087
April	90,725	102,589	78,899	589	272,801	[E]11,188	283,989
May	98,281	109,872	83,134	583	291,871	[E]11,478	303,348
June	122,543	120,013	85,399	628	328,583	[E]11,967	340,550
July	149,900	129,277	87,806	630	367,613	[E]12,763	380,376
August	142,007	128,481	89,134	640	360,263	[E]12,558	372,820
September	118,779	118,789	83,540	618	321,726	[E]11,213	332,939
October	102,811	113,287	82,815	626	299,539	[E]11,353	310,892
November	98,321	104,973	79,456	598	283,347	[E]11,455	294,802
December	122,005	109,306	80,242	664	312,216	[E]12,512	324,728
Total	**1,378,648**	**1,352,888**	**984,298**	**7,523**	**3,723,356**	**141,114**	**3,864,470**
2018 January	148,978	114,618	76,061	751	340,408	[E]12,468	352,876
February	113,383	102,001	71,948	643	287,975	[E]11,154	299,129
March	106,939	107,886	76,811	625	292,262	[E]11,572	303,833
April	95,128	102,922	75,241	608	273,898	[E]11,258	285,156
May	103,395	112,597	81,461	591	298,044	[E]11,684	309,728
June	129,478	121,578	81,527	628	333,212	[E]11,961	345,173
July	153,031	130,916	85,041	640	369,629	[E]12,661	382,289
August	152,951	134,479	89,632	686	377,748	[E]12,830	390,578
September	128,459	121,581	81,192	648	331,881	[E]11,859	343,741
October	106,638	115,861	81,023	636	304,157	[E]11,649	315,807
November	103,372	104,622	76,927	622	285,543	[E]12,032	297,574
December	122,620	107,678	76,213	660	307,171	[E]12,451	319,622
Total	**1,464,373**	**1,376,741**	**953,076**	**7,738**	**3,801,928**	[E]143,579	**3,945,507**
2019 January	132,989	111,613	78,033	664	323,300	[E]12,608	335,908
February	116,311	102,690	72,371	677	292,049	[E]11,113	303,161
March	112,384	107,422	77,007	685	297,498	[E]11,839	309,337
3-Month Total	**361,684**	**321,725**	**227,411**	**2,026**	**912,846**	**[E]35,560**	**948,406**
2018 3-Month Total	**369,301**	**324,506**	**224,819**	**2,019**	**920,645**	**[E]35,194**	**955,839**
2017 3-Month Total	**333,276**	**316,301**	**233,873**	**1,947**	**885,398**	**[E]34,629**	**920,026**

[a] Electricity retail sales to ultimate customers reported by electric utilities and, beginning in 1996, other energy service providers.
[b] Commercial sector, including public street and highway lighting, interdepartmental sales, and other sales to public authorities.
[c] Industrial sector. Through 2002, excludes agriculture and irrigation; beginning in 2003, includes agriculture and irrigation.
[d] Transportation sector, including sales to railroads and railways.
[e] The sum of "Residential," "Commercial," "Industrial," and "Transportation."
[f] Use of electricity that is 1) self-generated, 2) produced by either the same entity that consumes the power or an affiliate, and 3) used in direct support of a service or industrial process located within the same facility or group of facilities that house the generating equipment. Direct use is exclusive of station use.
[g] The sum of "Total Retail Sales" and "Direct Use."
E=Estimate. NA=Not available.
Notes: • See Note 1, "Coverage of Electricity Statistics," at end of section. • Totals may not equal sum of components due to independent rounding. • Geographic coverage is the 50 states and the District of Columbia.
Web Page: See http://www.eia.gov/totalenergy/data/monthly/#electricity (Excel and CSV files) for all available annual data beginning in 1949 and monthly data beginning in 1973.
Sources: See end of section.

Source: *U.S. Energy Information Administration, Monthly Energy Review, June 2019*

Figure 8.1 Nuclear Energy Overview

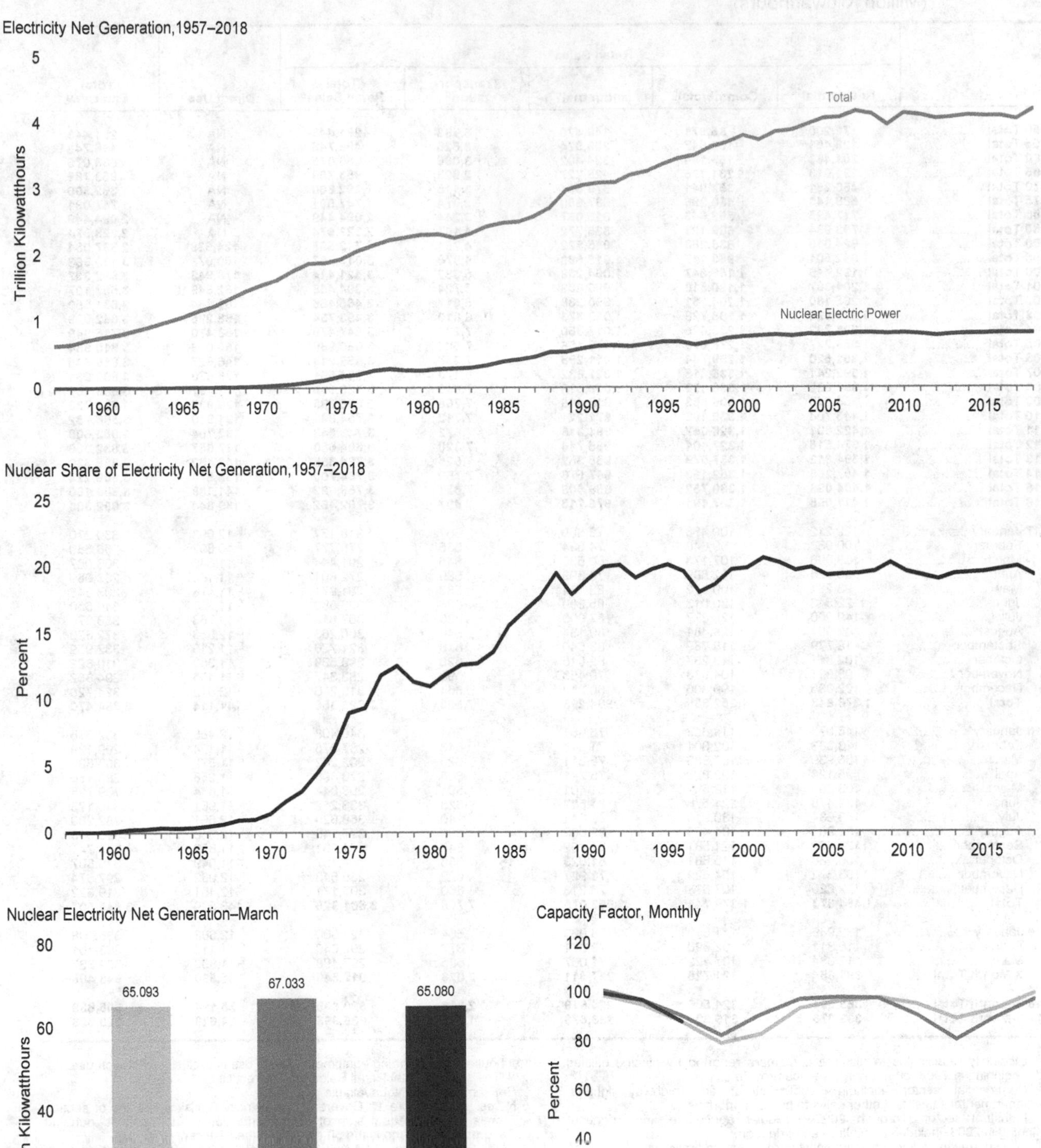

Web Page: http://www.eia.gov/totalenergy/data/monthly/#nuclear.
Sources: Tables 7.2a and 8.1.

Source: *U.S. Energy Information Administration, Monthly Energy Review, June 2019*

Table 8.1 Nuclear Energy Overview

	Total Operable Units[a,b]	Net Summer Capacity of Operable Units[b,c]	Nuclear Electricity Net Generation	Nuclear Share of Electricity Net Generation	Capacity Factor[d]
	Number	Million Kilowatts	Million Kilowatthours	Percent	
1957 Total	1	0.055	10	(s)	NA
1960 Total	3	.411	518	.1	NA
1965 Total	13	.793	3,657	.3	NA
1970 Total	20	7.004	21,804	1.4	NA
1975 Total	57	37.267	172,505	9.0	55.9
1980 Total	71	51.810	251,116	11.0	56.3
1985 Total	96	79.397	383,691	15.5	58.0
1990 Total	112	99.624	576,862	19.0	66.0
1995 Total	109	99.515	673,402	20.1	77.4
2000 Total	104	97.860	753,893	19.8	88.1
2001 Total	104	98.159	768,826	20.6	89.4
2002 Total	104	98.657	780,064	20.2	90.3
2003 Total	104	99.209	763,733	19.7	87.9
2004 Total	104	99.628	788,528	19.9	90.1
2005 Total	104	99.988	781,986	19.3	89.3
2006 Total	104	100.334	787,219	19.4	89.6
2007 Total	104	100.266	806,425	19.4	91.8
2008 Total	104	100.755	806,208	19.6	[d] 91.1
2009 Total	104	101.004	798,855	20.2	90.3
2010 Total	104	101.167	806,968	19.6	91.1
2011 Total	104	[c] 101.419	790,204	19.3	89.1
2012 Total	104	101.885	769,331	19.0	86.1
2013 Total	100	99.240	789,016	19.4	89.9
2014 Total	99	98.569	797,166	19.5	91.7
2015 Total	99	98.672	797,178	19.6	92.3
2016 Total	99	99.565	805,694	19.8	92.3
2017 January	99	99.610	73,121	21.3	98.7
February	99	99.610	63,560	21.9	94.9
March	99	99.610	65,093	20.5	87.8
April	99	99.610	56,743	19.3	79.1
May	99	99.610	61,313	19.0	82.7
June	99	99.610	67,011	18.7	93.4
July	99	99.629	71,314	17.6	96.2
August	99	99.629	72,384	18.8	97.6
September	99	99.629	68,098	20.3	94.9
October	99	99.629	65,995	20.6	89.0
November	99	99.629	66,618	21.5	92.9
December	99	99.629	73,700	20.9	99.4
Total	**99**	**99.629**	**804,950**	**20.0**	**92.2**
2018 January	99	E 99.653	74,649	19.9	E 100.7
February	99	E 99.653	64,790	21.2	E 96.7
March	99	E 99.653	67,033	20.9	E 90.4
April	99	E 99.653	59,133	19.6	E 82.4
May	99	E 99.653	67,320	19.8	E 90.8
June	99	E 99.653	69,688	18.7	E 97.1
July	99	E 99.653	72,456	17.6	E 97.7
August	99	E 99.653	72,282	17.7	E 97.5
September	98	E 99.200	64,725	18.1	E 90.4
October	98	E 99.200	59,397	18.2	E 80.5
November	98	E 99.355	63,948	19.8	E 89.4
December	98	E 99.355	71,657	21.2	E 96.9
Total	**98**	E **99.355**	**807,078**	**19.3**	E **92.6**
2019 January	98	E 99.360	73,701	20.6	E 99.7
February	98	E 99.446	64,715	20.7	RE 96.8
March	98	E 99.377	65,080	20.1	E 88.0
3-Month Total	**98**	E **99.377**	**203,495**	**20.5**	E **94.8**
2018 3-Month Total	**99**	E **99.653**	**206,472**	**20.6**	E **95.9**
2017 3-Month Total	**99**	**99.610**	**201,774**	**21.2**	**93.8**

[a] Total of nuclear generating units holding full-power licenses, or equivalent permission to operate, at end of period. See Note 1, "Operable Nuclear Reactors," at end of section.

[b] At end of period.

[c] For the definition of "Net Summer Capacity," see Note 2, "Nuclear Capacity," at end of section. Beginning in 2011, monthly capacity values are estimated in two steps: 1) uprates and derates reported on Form EIA-860M are added to specific months; and 2) the difference between the resulting year-end capacity (from data reported on Form EIA-860M) and final capacity (reported on Form EIA-860) is allocated to the month of January.

[d] Beginning in 2008, capacity factor data are calculated using a new methodology. For an explanation of the method of calculating the capacity factor, see Note 2, "Nuclear Capacity," at end of section.

R=Revised. E=Estimate. NA=Not available. (s)=Less than 0.05%.

Notes: • For a discussion of nuclear reactor unit coverage, see Note 1, "Operable Nuclear Reactors," at end of section. • Nuclear electricity net generation totals may not equal sum of components due to independent rounding. • Geographic coverage is the 50 states and the District of Columbia.

Web Page: See http://www.eia.gov/totalenergy/data/monthly/#nuclear (Excel and CSV files) for all available annual data beginning in 1957 and monthly data beginning in 1973.

Sources: See end of section.

Source: *U.S. Energy Information Administration, Monthly Energy Review, June 2019*

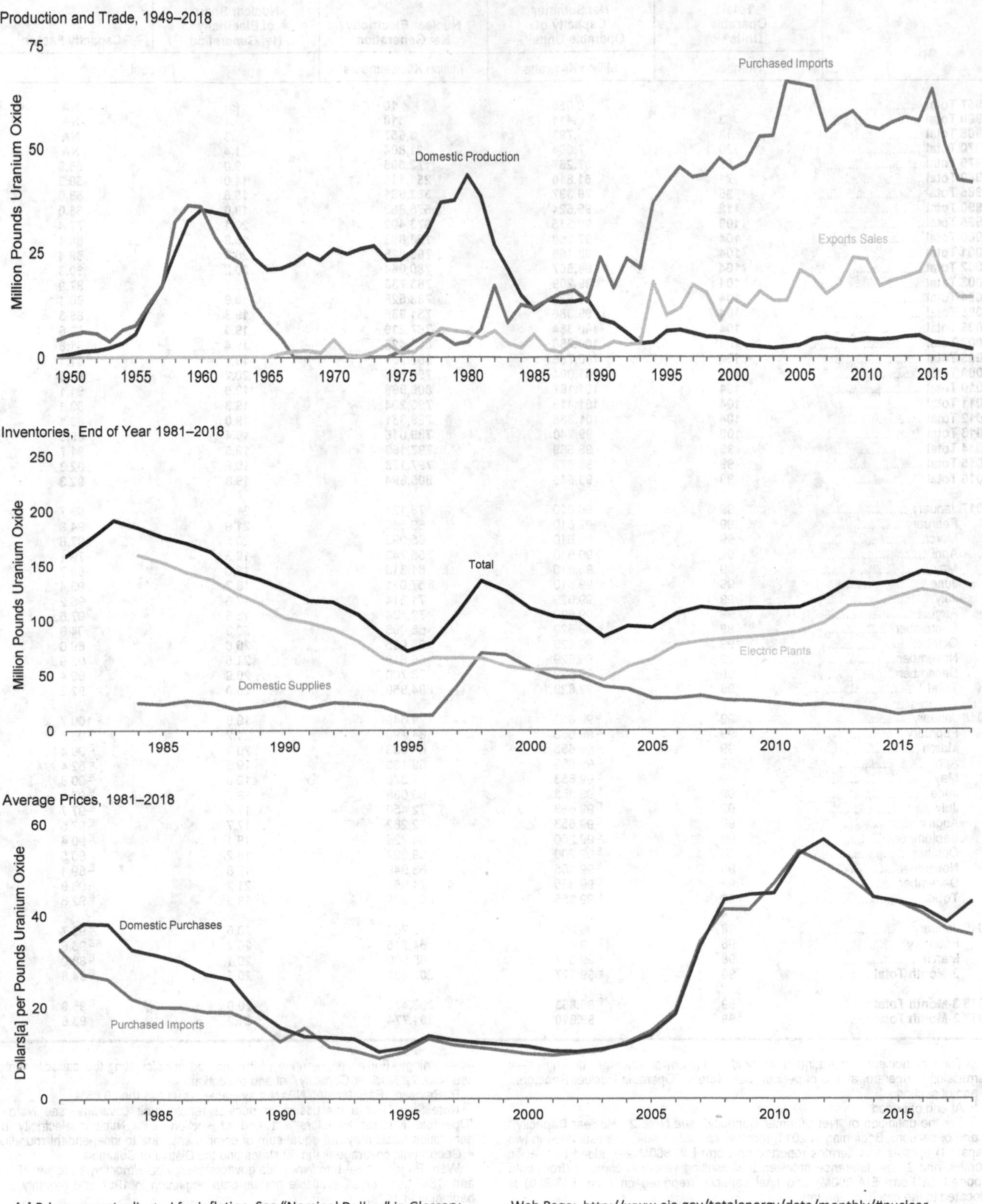

[a] Prices are not adjusted for inflation. See "Nominal Dollars" in Glossary.
Note: See "Uranium Oxide" in Glossary.

Web Page: http://www.eia.gov/totalenergy/data/monthly/#nuclear.
Source: Table 8.2.

Source: *U.S. Energy Information Administration, Monthly Energy Review, June 2019*

Table 8.2 Uranium Overview

	Domestic Concentrate Production[a]	Purchased Imports[b]	Export[b] Sales	Electric Plant Purchases From Domestic Suppliers	Loaded Into U.S. Nuclear Reactors[c]	Inventories			Average Price	
						Domestic Suppliers	Electric Plants	Total	Purchased Imports	Domestic Purchases
	Million Pounds Uranium Oxide								Dollars[d] per Pound Uranium Oxide	
1950	0.92	5.5	0.0	NA	NA	NA	NA	NA	NA	NA
1955	5.56	7.6	.0	NA	NA	NA	NA	NA	NA	NA
1960	35.28	36.0	.0	NA	NA	NA	NA	NA	NA	NA
1965	20.88	8.0	.0	NA	NA	NA	NA	NA	NA	NA
1970	25.81	.0	4.2	NA	NA	NA	NA	NA	– –	NA
1975	23.20	1.4	1.0	NA	NA	NA	NA	NA	NA	NA
1980	43.70	3.6	5.8	NA	NA	NA	NA	NA	NA	NA
1981	38.47	6.6	4.4	32.6	NA	NA	NA	159.2	32.90	34.65
1982	26.87	17.1	6.2	27.1	NA	NA	NA	174.8	27.23	38.37
1983	21.16	8.2	3.3	24.2	NA	NA	NA	191.8	26.16	38.21
1984	14.88	12.5	2.2	22.5	NA	25.0	160.2	185.2	21.86	32.65
1985	11.31	11.7	5.3	21.7	NA	23.7	153.2	176.9	20.08	31.43
1986	13.51	13.5	1.6	18.9	NA	27.0	144.1	171.1	20.07	30.01
1987	12.99	15.1	1.0	20.8	NA	25.4	137.8	163.2	19.14	27.37
1988	13.13	15.8	3.3	17.6	NA	19.3	125.5	144.8	19.03	26.15
1989	13.84	13.1	2.1	18.4	NA	22.2	115.8	138.1	16.75	19.56
1990	8.89	23.7	2.0	20.5	NA	26.4	102.7	129.1	12.55	15.70
1991	7.95	16.3	3.5	26.8	34.6	20.7	98.0	118.7	15.55	13.66
1992	5.65	23.3	2.8	23.4	43.0	25.2	92.1	117.3	11.34	13.45
1993	3.06	21.0	3.0	15.5	45.1	24.5	81.2	105.7	10.53	13.14
1994	3.35	36.6	17.7	22.7	40.4	21.5	65.4	86.9	8.95	10.30
1995	6.04	41.3	9.8	22.3	51.1	13.7	58.7	72.5	10.20	11.11
1996	6.32	45.4	11.5	23.7	46.2	13.9	66.1	80.0	13.15	13.81
1997	5.64	43.0	17.0	19.4	48.2	40.4	65.9	106.2	11.81	12.87
1998	4.70	43.7	15.1	21.6	38.2	70.7	65.8	136.5	11.19	12.31
1999	4.61	47.6	8.5	21.4	58.8	68.8	58.3	127.1	10.55	11.88
2000	3.98	44.9	13.6	24.3	51.5	56.5	54.8	111.3	9.84	11.45
2001	2.64	46.7	11.7	27.5	52.7	48.1	55.6	103.8	9.51	10.45
2002	[e,E]2.34	52.7	15.4	22.7	57.2	48.7	53.5	102.1	10.05	10.35
2003	[e,E]2.00	53.0	13.2	21.7	62.3	39.9	45.6	85.5	10.59	10.84
2004	2.28	66.1	13.2	28.2	50.1	37.5	57.7	95.2	12.25	11.91
2005	2.69	65.5	20.5	27.3	58.3	29.1	64.7	93.8	14.83	13.98
2006	4.11	64.8	18.7	27.9	51.7	29.1	77.5	106.6	19.31	18.54
2007	4.53	54.1	14.8	18.5	45.5	31.2	81.2	112.4	34.18	33.13
2008	3.90	57.1	17.2	20.4	51.3	27.0	83.0	110.0	41.30	43.43
2009	3.71	58.9	23.5	17.6	49.4	26.8	84.8	111.5	41.23	44.53
2010	4.23	55.3	23.1	16.2	44.3	24.7	86.5	111.3	47.01	44.88
2011	3.99	54.4	16.7	19.8	50.9	22.3	89.8	112.1	54.00	53.41
2012	4.15	56.2	18.0	21.5	49.5	23.3	97.6	120.9	51.44	56.51
2013	4.66	57.4	18.9	23.3	42.6	21.3	113.1	134.4	48.27	52.51
2014	4.89	56.5	20.0	20.5	50.5	18.7	114.0	132.7	44.03	43.99
2015	3.34	64.2	25.7	19.6	47.4	14.3	121.1	135.5	42.95	43.03
2016	2.92	50.7	17.2	18.8	41.7	16.7	128.0	144.6	40.45	41.64
2017	2.44	42.1	14.0	14.0	45.5	17.8	123.9	141.7	37.09	38.57
2018	1.65	41.5	13.9	11.1	[P]50.2	[P]19.9	[P]111.6	[P]131.5	35.73	42.98

[a] See "Uranium Concentrate" in Glossary.
[b] Import quantities through 1970 are reported for fiscal years. Prior to 1968, the Atomic Energy Commission was the sole purchaser of all imported uranium oxide. Trade data prior to 1982 were for transactions conducted by uranium suppliers only. For 1982 forward, transactions by uranium buyers (consumers) have been included. Buyer imports and exports prior to 1982 are believed to be small.
[c] Does not include any fuel rods removed from reactors and later reloaded.
[d] Prices are not adjusted for inflation. See "Nominal Dollars" in Glossary.
[e] Value has been rounded to avoid disclosure of individual company data.
P=Preliminary. E=Estimate. NA=Not available. – – =Not applicable.
Note: See "Uranium Oxide" in Glossary.

Web Page: See http://www.eia.gov/totalenergy/data/monthly#nuclear (Excel and CSV files) for all available annual data beginning in 1949.
Sources: • **1949–1966:** U.S. Department of Energy, Grand Junction Office, *Statistical Data of the Uranium Industry,* Report No. GJO-100, annual reports. • **1967–2002:** U.S. Energy Information Administration (EIA), *Uranium Industry Annual,* annual reports. • **2003–2015:** EIA, "Domestic Uranium Production Report," annual reports; and EIA, "Uranium Marketing Annual Report," annual reports. • **2016 forward:** EIA, "2018 Domestic Uranium Production Report" (May 2019), Table 3; and EIA, "2018 Uranium Marketing Annual Report" (May 2019), Tables 5, 18, 19, 21, and 22.

Source: *U.S. Energy Information Administration, Monthly Energy Review, June 2019*

Figure 9.1 Petroleum Prices

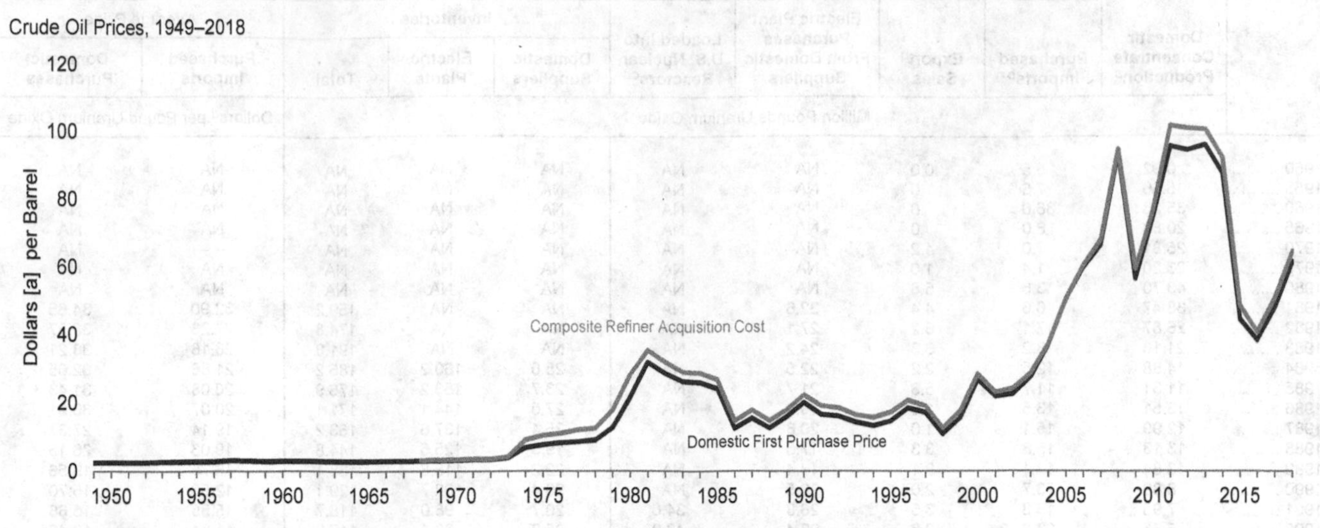

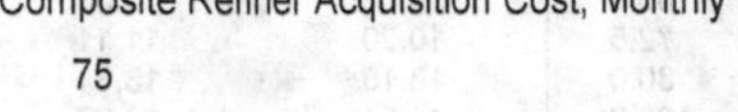

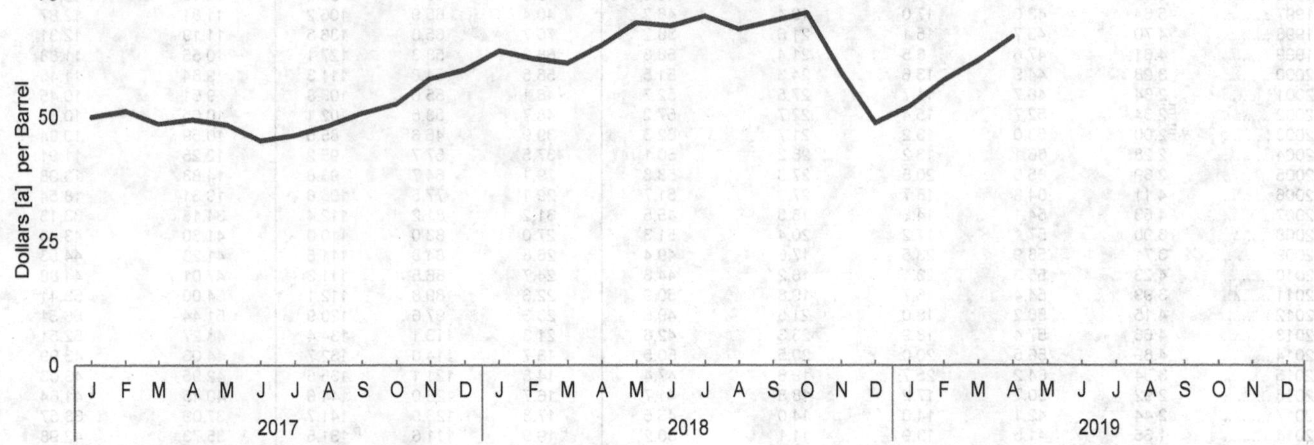

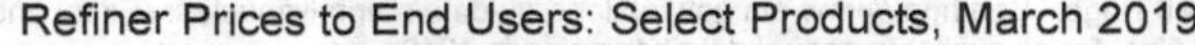

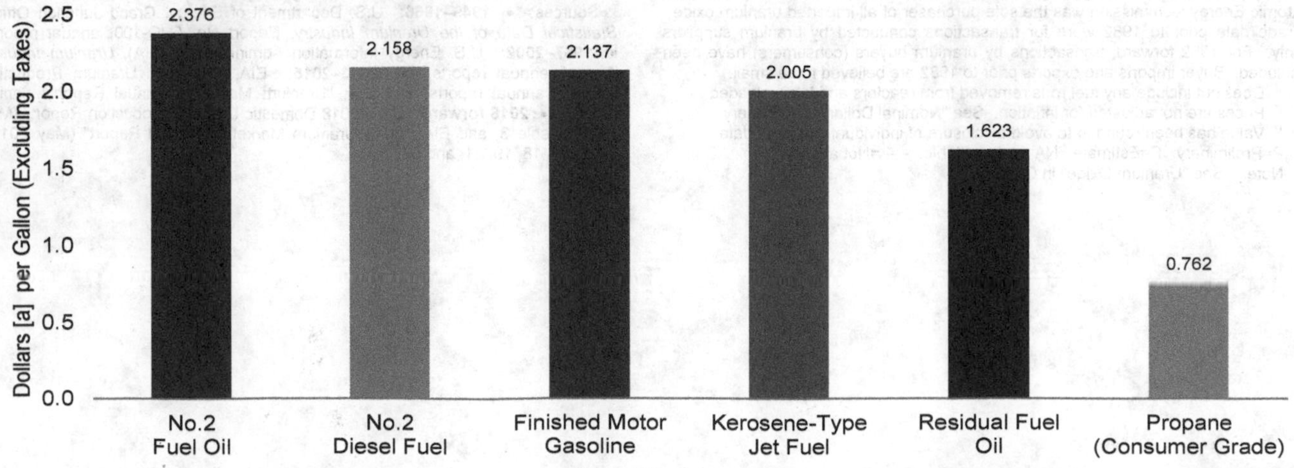

[a] Prices are not adjusted for inflation. See "Nominal Dollars" in Glossary.

Web Page: http://www.eia.gov/totalenergy/data/monthly/#prices.
Sources: Tables 9.1, 9.5 and 9.7.

Source: *U.S. Energy Information Administration, Monthly Energy Review, June 2019*

Table 9.1 Crude Oil Price Summary

(Dollars[a] per Barrel)

	Domestic First Purchase Price[c]	F.O.B. Cost of Imports[d]	Landed Cost of Imports[e]	Refiner Acquisition Cost[b]		
				Domestic	Imported	Composite
1950 Average	**2.51**	**NA**	**NA**	**NA**	**NA**	**NA**
1955 Average	**2.77**	**NA**	**NA**	**NA**	**NA**	**NA**
1960 Average	**2.88**	**NA**	**NA**	**NA**	**NA**	**NA**
1965 Average	**2.86**	**NA**	**NA**	**NA**	**NA**	**NA**
1970 Average	**3.18**	**NA**	**NA**	E **3.46**	E **2.96**	E **3.40**
1975 Average	**7.67**	**11.18**	**12.70**	**8.39**	**13.93**	**10.38**
1980 Average	**21.59**	**32.37**	**33.67**	**24.23**	**33.89**	**28.07**
1985 Average	**24.09**	**25.84**	**26.67**	**26.66**	**26.99**	**26.75**
1990 Average	**20.03**	**20.37**	**21.13**	**22.59**	**21.76**	**22.22**
1995 Average	**14.62**	**15.69**	**16.78**	**17.33**	**17.14**	**17.23**
2000 Average	**26.72**	**26.27**	**27.53**	**29.11**	**27.70**	**28.26**
2001 Average	**21.84**	**20.46**	**21.82**	**24.33**	**22.00**	**22.95**
2002 Average	**22.51**	**22.63**	**23.91**	**24.65**	**23.71**	**24.10**
2003 Average	**27.56**	**25.86**	**27.69**	**29.82**	**27.71**	**28.53**
2004 Average	**36.77**	**33.75**	**36.07**	**38.97**	**35.90**	**36.98**
2005 Average	**50.28**	**47.60**	**49.29**	**52.94**	**48.86**	**50.24**
2006 Average	**59.69**	**57.03**	**59.11**	**62.62**	**59.02**	**60.24**
2007 Average	**66.52**	**66.36**	**67.97**	**69.65**	**67.04**	**67.94**
2008 Average	**94.04**	**90.32**	**93.33**	**98.47**	**92.77**	**94.74**
2009 Average	**56.35**	**57.78**	**60.23**	**59.49**	**59.17**	**59.29**
2010 Average	**74.71**	**74.19**	**76.50**	**78.01**	**75.86**	**76.69**
2011 Average	**95.73**	**101.66**	**102.92**	**100.71**	**102.63**	**101.87**
2012 Average	**94.52**	**99.78**	**101.00**	**100.72**	**101.09**	**100.93**
2013 Average	**95.99**	**96.56**	**96.99**	**102.91**	**98.11**	**100.49**
2014 Average	**87.39**	**85.65**	**88.16**	**94.05**	**89.56**	**92.02**
2015 Average	**44.39**	**41.91**	**45.38**	**49.94**	**46.38**	**48.39**
2016 Average	**38.29**	**36.37**	**38.56**	**42.41**	**38.75**	**40.66**
2017 January	48.19	44.62	47.05	51.81	48.12	49.99
February	49.41	45.91	48.08	53.15	49.38	51.24
March	46.39	44.09	46.26	50.60	46.53	48.65
April	47.23	43.60	46.00	51.34	47.47	49.47
May	45.19	43.92	46.15	49.58	47.21	48.47
June	42.17	41.34	43.85	46.26	44.03	45.25
July	43.42	42.09	44.82	47.59	44.76	46.27
August	44.96	44.18	46.93	48.76	47.62	48.22
September	47.17	46.50	49.80	51.07	50.46	50.78
October	49.12	47.22	51.11	53.71	51.40	52.67
November	55.19	52.11	56.10	58.92	56.30	57.75
December	56.98	53.68	56.96	61.10	57.44	59.53
Average	**48.05**	**45.58**	**48.50**	**52.05**	**49.12**	**50.68**
2018 January	62.25	55.73	R 58.25	66.08	R 59.71	R 63.25
February	R 61.18	53.42	R 56.76	64.68	R 58.03	R 61.74
March	60.68	53.35	56.32	64.03	R 56.82	R 60.81
April	63.50	R 58.56	R 60.62	67.14	R 61.24	R 64.41
May	66.16	62.95	65.15	R 71.29	R 65.89	R 68.91
June	62.80	63.09	65.48	R 69.63	R 66.82	R 68.35
July	67.00	62.35	R 65.44	R 73.33	R 66.62	R 70.29
August	62.64	R 61.41	R 64.16	69.45	65.48	67.68
September	R 63.54	61.56	63.69	R 71.09	R 66.70	R 69.29
October	65.18	R 60.23	R 61.78	R 73.07	R 67.79	R 70.99
November	55.65	R 44.66	R 47.16	62.47	54.40	59.01
December	R 47.63	36.91	R 39.14	53.25	42.80	48.83
Average	R **61.40**	R **56.31**	R **58.89**	R **67.05**	**60.95**	R **64.38**
2019 January	47.85	R 48.72	R 49.25	53.86	49.57	52.11
February	R 52.51	R 53.67	R 55.40	R 57.89	R 56.50	R 57.35
March	R 57.47	R 56.48	R 58.24	R 61.41	R 61.20	R 61.33
April	NA	NA	NA	E 66.52	E 65.71	E 66.15

[a] Prices are not adjusted for inflation. See "Nominal Dollars" in Glossary.
[b] See Note 1, "Crude Oil Refinery Acquisition Costs," at end of section.
[c] See Note 2, "Crude Oil Domestic First Purchase Prices," at end of section.
[d] See Note 3, "Crude Oil F.O.B. Costs," at end of section.
[e] See Note 4, "Crude Oil Landed Costs," at end of section.
R=Revised. NA=Not available. E=Estimate.

Notes: • Domestic first purchase prices and refinery acquisition costs for the current two months are preliminary. F.O.B. and landed costs for the current three months are preliminary. • Through 1980, F.O.B. and landed costs reflect the period of reporting; beginning in 1981, they reflect the period of loading. • Annual averages are the averages of the monthly prices, weighted by volume. • Geographic coverage is the 50 states, the District of Columbia, Puerto Rico, the Virgin Islands, and all U.S. Territories and Possessions.

Web Page: See http://www.eia.gov/totalenergy/data/monthly/#prices (Excel and CSV files) for all available annual data beginning in 1949 and monthly data beginning in 1973.

Sources: See end of section.

Source: *U.S. Energy Information Administration, Monthly Energy Review, June 2019*

Table 9.2 F.O.B. Costs of Crude Oil Imports From Selected Countries

(Dollars[a] per Barrel)

	Selected Countries							Persian Gulf Nations[b]	Total OPEC[c]	Total Non-OPEC[c]
	Angola	Colombia	Mexico	Nigeria	Saudi Arabia	United Kingdom	Venezuela			
1973 Average[d]	W	W	–	7.81	3.25	–	5.39	3.68	5.43	4.80
1975 Average	10.97	–	11.44	11.82	10.87	–	11.04	10.88	11.34	10.62
1980 Average	33.45	W	31.06	35.93	28.17	34.36	24.81	28.92	32.21	32.85
1985 Average	26.30	–	25.33	28.04	22.04	27.64	23.64	23.31	25.67	25.96
1990 Average	20.23	20.75	19.26	22.46	20.36	23.43	19.55	18.54	20.40	20.32
1995 Average	16.58	16.73	15.64	17.40	W	16.94	13.86	W	15.36	16.02
2000 Average	27.90	29.04	25.39	28.70	24.62	27.21	24.45	24.72	25.56	26.77
2001 Average	23.25	24.25	18.89	24.85	18.98	23.30	18.01	18.89	19.73	21.04
2002 Average	24.09	24.64	21.60	25.38	23.92	24.50	20.13	23.38	22.18	22.93
2003 Average	28.22	28.89	24.83	29.40	25.03	28.76	23.81	25.17	25.36	26.21
2004 Average	37.26	37.73	31.55	38.71	34.08	37.30	31.78	33.08	33.95	33.58
2005 Average	52.48	51.89	43.00	55.95	47.96	54.48	46.39	47.21	49.60	45.79
2006 Average	62.23	59.77	52.91	65.69	56.09	66.03	55.80	56.02	59.18	55.35
2007 Average	67.80	67.93	61.35	76.64	W	69.96	64.10	69.93	69.58	62.69
2008 Average	95.66	91.17	84.61	102.06	93.03	96.33	88.06	91.44	93.15	87.15
2009 Average	57.07	57.90	56.47	64.61	57.87	65.63	55.58	59.53	58.53	57.16
2010 Average	78.18	72.56	72.46	80.83	76.44	W	70.30	75.65	75.23	73.24
2011 Average	111.82	100.21	100.90	115.35	107.08	–	97.23	106.47	105.34	98.49
2012 Average	111.23	106.43	101.84	114.51	106.65	–	100.15	105.45	104.39	95.71
2013 Average	107.71	101.24	98.40	110.06	101.16	W	97.52	100.62	100.57	93.67
2014 Average	W	80.75	86.55	W	95.60	–	84.51	94.03	89.76	82.95
2015 Average	W	47.52	44.90	W	47.53	–	40.73	46.95	43.25	41.19
2016 Average	42.68	35.28	36.22	46.20	39.30	W	34.71	38.76	38.51	34.81
2017 January	–	47.92	45.50	W	W	–	45.94	47.61	47.30	43.25
February	W	46.97	45.91	W	51.03	–	45.69	50.01	49.11	43.63
March	W	46.05	42.10	W	48.54	–	42.47	47.78	46.83	41.73
April	W	46.76	44.32	W	50.00	W	43.71	48.93	47.16	41.46
May	W	44.70	44.85	W	47.95	–	42.27	47.14	46.08	42.66
June	W	41.30	41.86	48.88	45.41	–	39.16	44.45	43.52	40.28
July	W	44.44	44.33	50.26	46.94	–	41.72	45.95	45.40	40.39
August	W	47.16	46.33	52.18	49.33	–	45.41	48.06	48.32	41.38
September	–	W	48.06	W	53.41	–	49.22	51.74	52.36	43.26
October	–	52.69	49.01	58.58	55.44	–	52.51	50.92	53.93	44.21
November	–	W	54.66	W	60.22	W	55.88	59.12	58.89	48.57
December	–	W	55.32	W	62.09	–	58.27	60.36	61.52	49.87
Average	W	48.34	46.66	54.77	51.30	W	45.60	50.16	49.55	43.30
2018 January	W	61.24	58.75	W	65.03	W	62.07	63.50	64.12	51.34
February	W	59.66	56.74	W	63.19	W	55.72	61.90	61.07	49.79
March	–	W	56.73	W	65.04	W	56.84	61.90	60.90	49.09
April	W	65.95	57.68	W	68.33	W	R63.28	66.05	66.09	53.73
May	–	W	63.32	W	70.57	W	66.56	69.66	70.07	58.99
June	W	W	64.46	W	71.32	W	64.82	70.18	69.44	59.81
July	W	68.32	66.21	–	70.62	–	62.93	70.30	67.64	R59.85
August	W	67.29	63.08	W	R71.08	W	63.09	R70.11	R68.40	57.46
September	W	W	68.15	W	72.90	W	68.94	72.05	71.80	56.39
October	W	W	R73.91	W	74.73	W	68.44	74.61	73.26	R54.18
November	–	64.87	63.76	W	R62.34	W	53.25	R63.44	R60.58	36.18
December	–	50.04	52.70	W	57.79	–	46.46	55.74	53.04	28.95
Average	74.44	62.51	R62.75	71.41	R68.23	71.65	R61.25	R66.55	R65.61	R51.41
2019 January	–	53.27	R54.81	W	W	W	R48.38	R58.54	R55.22	R46.13
February	–	56.59	R58.52	W	W	W	RW	61.20	R62.51	R51.44
March	–	61.28	60.61	W	W	W	–	64.23	64.48	55.01

[a] Prices are not adjusted for inflation. See "Nominal Dollars" in Glossary.

[b] Bahrain, Iran, Iraq, Kuwait, Qatar, Saudi Arabia, United Arab Emirates, and the Neutral Zone (between Kuwait and Saudi Arabia).

[c] See "Organization of the Petroleum Exporting Countries (OPEC)" in Glossary for exact years of each country's membership. On this table, "Total OPEC" for all years includes Algeria, Iran, Iraq, Kuwait, Libya, Nigeria, Qatar, Saudi Arabia, United Arab Emirates, and Venezuela; Angola is included in "Total OPEC" 2007 forward; Gabon is included in "Total OPEC" 1974–1995 and July 2016 forward; Ecuador is included in "Total OPEC" 1973–1992 and 2008 forward; Indonesia is included in "Total OPEC" 1973–2008 and 2016.

[d] Based on October, November, and December data only.

R=Revised. – =No data reported. W=Value withheld to avoid disclosure of individual company data.

Notes: • The Free on Board (F.O.B.) cost at the country of origin excludes all costs related to insurance and transportation. See "F.O.B. (Free on Board)" in Glossary, and Note 3, "Crude Oil F.O.B. Costs," at end of section. • Values for the current two months are preliminary. • Through 1980, prices reflect the period of reporting; beginning in 1981, prices reflect the period of loading. • Annual averages are averages of the monthly prices, including prices not published, weighted by volume. • Cargoes that are purchased on a "netback" basis, or under similar contractual arrangements whereby the actual purchase price is not established at the time the crude oil is acquired for importation into the United States, are not included in the published data until the actual prices have been determined and reported. • U.S. geographic coverage is the 50 states and the District of Columbia.

Web Page: See http://www.eia.gov/totalenergy/data/monthly/#prices (Excel and CSV files) for all available annual and monthly data beginning in 1973.

Sources: See end of section.

Source: *U.S. Energy Information Administration, Monthly Energy Review, June 2019*

Table 9.3 Landed Costs of Crude Oil Imports From Selected Countries

(Dollars[a] per Barrel)

	Selected Countries								Persian Gulf Nations[b]	Total OPEC[c]	Total Non-OPEC[c]
	Angola	Canada	Colombia	Mexico	Nigeria	Saudi Arabia	United Kingdom	Venezuela			
1973 Average[d]	**W**	**5.33**	**W**	**–**	**9.08**	**5.37**	**–**	**5.99**	**5.91**	**6.85**	**5.64**
1975 Average	**11.81**	**12.84**	**–**	**12.61**	**12.70**	**12.50**	**–**	**12.36**	**12.64**	**12.70**	**12.70**
1980 Average	**34.76**	**30.11**	**W**	**31.77**	**37.15**	**29.80**	**35.68**	**25.92**	**30.59**	**33.56**	**33.99**
1985 Average	**27.39**	**25.71**	**–**	**25.63**	**28.96**	**24.72**	**28.36**	**24.43**	**25.50**	**26.86**	**26.53**
1990 Average	**21.51**	**20.48**	**22.34**	**19.64**	**23.33**	**21.82**	**22.65**	**20.31**	**20.55**	**21.23**	**20.98**
1995 Average	**17.66**	**16.65**	**17.45**	**16.19**	**18.25**	**16.84**	**17.91**	**14.81**	**16.78**	**16.61**	**16.95**
2000 Average	**29.57**	**26.69**	**29.68**	**26.03**	**30.04**	**26.58**	**29.26**	**26.05**	**26.77**	**27.29**	**27.80**
2001 Average	**25.13**	**20.72**	**25.88**	**19.37**	**26.55**	**20.98**	**25.32**	**19.81**	**20.73**	**21.52**	**22.17**
2002 Average	**25.43**	**22.98**	**25.28**	**22.09**	**26.45**	**24.77**	**26.35**	**21.93**	**24.13**	**23.83**	**23.97**
2003 Average	**30.14**	**26.76**	**30.55**	**25.48**	**31.07**	**27.50**	**30.62**	**25.70**	**27.54**	**27.70**	**27.68**
2004 Average	**39.62**	**34.51**	**39.03**	**32.25**	**40.95**	**37.11**	**39.28**	**33.79**	**36.53**	**36.84**	**35.29**
2005 Average	**54.31**	**44.73**	**53.42**	**43.47**	**57.55**	**50.31**	**55.28**	**47.87**	**49.68**	**51.36**	**47.31**
2006 Average	**64.85**	**53.90**	**62.13**	**53.76**	**68.26**	**59.19**	**67.44**	**57.37**	**58.92**	**61.21**	**57.14**
2007 Average	**71.27**	**60.38**	**70.91**	**62.31**	**78.01**	**70.78**	**72.47**	**66.13**	**69.83**	**71.14**	**63.96**
2008 Average	**98.18**	**90.00**	**93.43**	**85.97**	**104.83**	**94.75**	**96.95**	**90.76**	**93.59**	**95.49**	**90.59**
2009 Average	**61.32**	**57.60**	**58.50**	**57.35**	**68.01**	**62.14**	**63.87**	**57.78**	**62.15**	**61.90**	**58.58**
2010 Average	**80.61**	**72.80**	**74.25**	**72.86**	**83.14**	**79.29**	**80.29**	**72.43**	**78.60**	**78.28**	**74.68**
2011 Average	**114.05**	**89.92**	**102.57**	**101.21**	**116.43**	**108.83**	**118.45**	**100.14**	**108.01**	**107.84**	**98.64**
2012 Average	**114.95**	**84.24**	**107.07**	**102.45**	**116.88**	**108.15**	**W**	**101.58**	**107.74**	**107.56**	**95.05**
2013 Average	**110.81**	**84.41**	**103.00**	**99.06**	**112.87**	**102.60**	**111.23**	**99.34**	**102.53**	**102.98**	**91.99**
2014 Average	**99.25**	**81.30**	**88.29**	**87.48**	**102.16**	**94.91**	**W**	**86.88**	**95.30**	**93.10**	**84.67**
2015 Average	**51.73**	**41.99**	**49.53**	**45.51**	**54.70**	**49.78**	**W**	**42.87**	**49.43**	**47.44**	**44.09**
2016 Average	**44.65**	**36.27**	**38.86**	**36.64**	**48.11**	**42.14**	**W**	**35.50**	**41.20**	**40.54**	**37.09**
2017 January	–	44.70	49.17	46.35	54.74	50.40	W	47.53	49.35	49.22	45.76
February	W	44.97	49.66	46.57	54.42	52.27	–	46.28	50.92	50.48	46.26
March	W	43.00	48.29	42.97	W	50.36	W	43.91	49.58	48.91	44.03
April	W	43.05	48.38	44.65	W	50.18	W	44.53	49.03	48.47	44.31
May	W	44.24	45.92	45.51	51.83	49.17	W	43.50	47.37	47.36	45.23
June	50.74	41.76	44.89	42.36	50.36	47.97	W	40.88	46.86	45.77	42.67
July	50.20	41.60	46.72	45.17	50.89	48.22	–	42.25	47.48	46.91	43.36
August	52.23	43.18	48.56	46.86	53.18	51.43	W	46.16	49.71	49.55	45.41
September	56.59	45.14	52.43	49.63	57.99	55.03	W	50.98	52.93	53.53	47.42
October	W	45.68	53.95	50.28	59.35	58.34	W	53.05	55.14	55.71	48.21
November	61.03	51.16	59.52	55.47	64.27	61.66	62.24	57.19	59.63	59.83	53.67
December	W	51.15	61.58	56.01	67.20	63.52	–	58.80	61.48	62.13	53.90
Average	**54.17**	**44.93**	**50.60**	**47.73**	**56.48**	**52.56**	**56.11**	**47.02**	**51.42**	**51.26**	**46.67**
2018 January	66.55	R 51.17	63.25	R 59.86	69.15	64.81	W	62.79	R 63.83	R 64.78	R 54.69
February	W	R 48.27	62.55	57.37	69.60	65.30	68.19	55.98	63.21	62.93	R 53.05
March	70.27	47.01	63.59	56.99	70.59	66.77	W	57.72	63.72	R 63.53	51.07
April	W	52.22	66.34	58.62	W	69.44	73.82	R 63.62	67.09	R 66.95	R 56.32
May	W	58.19	70.63	64.03	79.38	71.28	W	67.45	70.85	71.50	61.72
June	76.28	58.57	70.64	65.38	W	72.17	72.88	65.81	71.49	70.65	62.95
July	75.55	R 59.00	71.20	66.82	W	72.56	–	63.67	71.62	70.54	62.54
August	75.45	56.78	68.79	64.18	W	R 72.85	72.41	64.12	R 71.64	R 70.48	60.79
September	75.83	52.35	73.88	69.79	W	72.56	W	70.73	72.26	72.45	58.76
October	W	R 47.96	R 74.22	R 74.76	W	73.75	W	69.31	72.24	72.19	R 57.15
November	–	28.06	66.20	64.52	68.03	R 65.87	W	55.70	R 64.99	R 63.30	38.56
December	–	21.62	54.71	53.89	62.21	60.39	W	48.93	58.67	57.11	R 30.89
Average	**73.42**	**R 48.34**	**R 66.75**	**R 63.48**	**71.93**	**R 69.40**	**73.28**	**R 62.46**	**R 67.55**	**R 67.22**	**54.27**
2019 January	–	R 40.33	56.26	R 56.12	W	R 61.69	W	R 51.82	R 59.80	R 57.46	R 45.44
February	–	R 49.84	R 59.69	R 59.72	W	R 63.53	W	R 52.72	R 61.99	R 61.32	R 53.53
March	–	53.81	64.14	61.71	W	65.01	W	W	65.56	63.70	56.66

[a] Prices are not adjusted for inflation. See "Nominal Dollars" in Glossary.

[b] Bahrain, Iran, Iraq, Kuwait, Qatar, Saudi Arabia, United Arab Emirates, and the Neutral Zone (between Kuwait and Saudi Arabia).

[c] See "Organization of the Petroleum Exporting Countries (OPEC)" in Glossary for exact years of each country's membership. On this table, "Total OPEC" for all years includes Algeria, Iran, Iraq, Kuwait, Libya, Nigeria, Qatar, Saudi Arabia, United Arab Emirates, and Venezuela; Angola is included in "Total OPEC" 2007 forward; Gabon is included in "Total OPEC" 1974–1995 and July 2016 forward; Ecuador is included in "Total OPEC" 1973–1992 and 2008 forward; Indonesia is included in "Total OPEC" 1973–2008 and 2016.

[d] Based on October, November, and December data only.

R=Revised. – =No data reported. W=Value withheld to avoid disclosure of individual company data.

Notes: • See "Landed Costs" in Glossary, and Note 4, "Crude Oil Landed Costs," at end of section. • Values for the current two months are preliminary. • Through 1980, prices reflect the period of reporting; beginning in 1981, prices reflect the period of loading. • Annual averages are averages of the monthly prices, including prices not published, weighted by volume. • Cargoes that are purchased on a "netback" basis, or under similar contractual arrangements whereby the actual purchase price is not established at the time the crude oil is acquired for importation into the United States, are not included in the published data until the actual prices have been determined and reported. • U.S. geographic coverage is the 50 states and the District of Columbia.

Web Page: See http://www.eia.gov/totalenergy/data/monthly/#prices (Excel and CSV files) for all available annual and monthly data beginning in 1973.

Sources: • **October 1973–September 1977:** Federal Energy Administration, Form FEA-F701-M-0, "Transfer Pricing Report." • **October 1977–December 1977:** U.S. Energy Information Administration (EIA), Form FEA-F701-M-0, "Transfer Pricing Report." • **1978–2007:** EIA, *Petroleum Marketing Annual 2008*, Table 22. • **2008 forward:** EIA, *Petroleum Marketing Monthly,* June 2019, Table 22.

Source: *U.S. Energy Information Administration, Monthly Energy Review, June 2019*

Table 9.4 Retail Motor Gasoline and On-Highway Diesel Fuel Prices

(Dollars[a] per Gallon, Including Taxes)

	Platt's / Bureau of Labor Statistics Data				U.S. Energy Information Administration Data			
		Motor Gasoline by Grade			Regular Motor Gasoline by Area Type			
	Leaded Regular	Unleaded Regular	Unleaded Premium[b]	All Grades[c]	Conventional Gasoline Areas[d]	Reformulated Gasoline Areas[e]	All Areas	On-Highway Diesel Fuel
1950 Average	0.268	NA	NA	NA	--	--	--	--
1955 Average	.291	NA	NA	NA	--	--	--	--
1960 Average	.311	NA	NA	NA	--	--	--	--
1965 Average	.312	NA	NA	NA	--	--	--	--
1970 Average	.357	NA	NA	NA	--	--	--	--
1975 Average	.567	NA	NA	NA	--	--	--	--
1980 Average	1.191	1.245	NA	1.221	--	--	--	--
1985 Average	1.115	1.202	1.340	1.196	--	--	--	--
1990 Average	1.149	1.164	1.349	1.217	NA	NA	NA	NA
1995 Average	--	1.147	1.336	1.205	1.103	1.163	1.111	1.109
2000 Average	--	1.510	1.693	1.563	1.462	1.543	1.484	1.491
2001 Average	--	1.461	1.657	1.531	1.384	1.498	1.420	1.401
2002 Average	--	1.358	1.556	1.441	1.313	1.408	1.345	1.319
2003 Average	--	1.591	1.777	1.638	1.516	1.655	1.561	1.509
2004 Average	--	1.880	2.068	1.923	1.812	1.937	1.852	1.810
2005 Average	--	2.295	2.491	2.338	2.240	2.335	2.270	2.402
2006 Average	--	2.589	2.805	2.635	2.533	2.654	2.572	2.705
2007 Average	--	2.801	3.033	2.849	2.767	2.857	2.796	2.885
2008 Average	--	3.266	3.519	3.317	3.213	3.314	3.246	3.803
2009 Average	--	2.350	2.607	2.401	2.315	2.433	2.353	2.467
2010 Average	--	2.788	3.047	2.836	2.742	2.864	2.782	2.992
2011 Average	--	3.527	3.792	3.577	3.476	3.616	3.521	3.840
2012 Average	--	3.644	3.922	3.695	3.552	3.757	3.618	3.968
2013 Average	--	3.526	3.843	3.584	3.443	3.635	3.505	3.922
2014 Average	--	3.367	3.713	3.425	3.299	3.481	3.358	3.825
2015 Average	--	2.448	2.866	2.510	2.334	2.629	2.429	2.707
2016 Average	--	2.142	2.610	2.204	2.070	2.296	2.143	2.304
2017 January	--	2.351	2.815	2.409	2.285	2.482	2.349	2.580
February	--	2.299	2.793	2.360	2.227	2.467	2.304	2.568
March	--	2.323	2.827	2.386	2.243	2.498	2.325	2.554
April	--	2.418	2.909	2.479	2.340	2.579	2.417	2.583
May	--	2.386	2.894	2.448	2.303	2.577	2.391	2.560
June	--	2.337	2.859	2.400	2.257	2.536	2.347	2.511
July	--	2.281	2.800	2.344	2.211	2.486	2.300	2.496
August	--	2.374	2.883	2.436	2.297	2.557	2.380	2.595
September	--	2.630	3.120	2.688	2.570	2.802	2.645	2.785
October	--	2.484	2.996	2.545	2.430	2.663	2.505	2.794
November	--	2.548	3.056	2.608	2.474	2.751	2.564	2.909
December	--	2.459	2.985	2.521	2.388	2.663	2.477	2.909
Average	--	**2.408**	**2.911**	**2.469**	**2.333**	**2.586**	**2.415**	**2.650**
2018 January	--	2.539	3.042	2.596	2.467	2.738	2.555	3.018
February	--	2.575	3.091	2.632	2.488	2.795	2.587	3.046
March	--	2.572	3.101	2.631	2.488	2.808	2.591	2.988
April	--	2.737	3.258	2.795	2.652	2.978	2.757	3.096
May	--	2.907	3.423	2.963	2.808	3.096	2.901	3.244
June	--	2.914	3.440	2.970	2.802	3.078	2.891	3.253
July	--	2.873	3.399	2.930	2.770	3.015	2.849	3.233
August	--	2.862	3.384	2.919	2.768	2.983	2.836	3.218
September	--	2.873	3.400	2.930	2.769	2.979	2.836	3.262
October	--	2.887	3.431	2.945	2.785	3.017	2.860	3.365
November	--	2.671	3.251	2.733	2.561	2.829	2.647	3.300
December	--	2.414	3.015	2.479	2.263	2.581	2.366	3.123
Average	--	**2.735**	**3.270**	**2.794**	**2.631**	**2.904**	**2.719**	**3.178**
2019 January	--	2.289	2.874	2.352	2.145	2.464	2.248	2.980
February	--	2.353	2.901	2.412	2.223	2.495	2.309	2.997
March	--	2.564	3.079	2.620	2.443	2.673	2.516	3.076
April	--	2.835	3.382	2.894	2.694	3.023	2.798	3.121
May	--	2.901	3.471	2.963	2.731	3.136	2.859	3.161

[a] Prices are not adjusted for inflation. See "Nominal Dollars" in Glossary.
[b] The 1981 average (available in Web file) is based on September through December data only.
[c] Also includes grades of motor gasoline not shown separately.
[d] Any area that does not require the sale of reformulated gasoline.
[e] "Reformulated Gasoline Areas" are ozone nonattainment areas designated by the U.S. Environmental Protection Agency that require the use of reformulated gasoline (RFG). Areas are reclassified each time a shift in or out of an RFG program occurs due to federal or state regulations.

NA=Not available. – – =Not applicable.

Notes: • See Note 5, "Motor Gasoline Prices," at end of section. • See "Motor Gasoline Grades," "Motor Gasoline, Conventional," "Motor Gasoline, Oxygenated," and "Motor Gasoline, Reformulated" in Glossary. • Geographic coverage: for columns 1–4, current coverage is 85 urban areas; for columns 5–7, coverage is the 50 states and the District of Columbia; for column 8, coverage is the 48 contiguous states and the District of Columbia.

Web Page: See http://www.eia.gov/totalenergy/data/monthly/#prices (Excel and CSV files) for all available annual data beginning in 1949 and monthly data beginning in 1973.

Sources: • **Motor Gasoline by Grade, Monthly Data: October 1973 forward**—U.S. Department of Labor, Bureau of Labor Statistics (BLS), *U.S. City Average Gasoline Prices.* • **Motor Gasoline by Grade, Annual Data: 1949–1973**—*Platt's Oil Price Handbook and Oilmanac, 1974,* 51st Edition. **1974 forward**—calculated by the U.S. Energy Information Administration (EIA) as simple averages of the BLS monthly data. • **Regular Motor Gasoline by Area Type.** EIA, calculated as simple averages of weighted weekly estimates from "Weekly U.S. Retail Gasoline Prices, Regular Grade." • **On-Highway Diesel Fuel:** EIA, calculated as simple averages of weighted weekly estimates from "Weekly Retail On-Highway Diesel Prices."

Source: *U.S. Energy Information Administration, Monthly Energy Review, June 2019*

Table 9.5 Refiner Prices of Residual Fuel Oil

(Dollars[a] per Gallon, Excluding Taxes)

	Residual Fuel Oil Sulfur Content Less Than or Equal to 1%		Residual Fuel Oil Sulfur Content Greater Than 1%		Average	
	Sales for Resale	Sales to End Users	Sales for Resale	Sales to End Users	Sales for Resale	Sales to End Users
1978 Average	**0.293**	**0.314**	**0.245**	**0.275**	**0.263**	**0.298**
1980 Average	**.608**	**.675**	**.479**	**.523**	**.528**	**.607**
1985 Average	**.610**	**.644**	**.560**	**.582**	**.577**	**.610**
1990 Average	**.472**	**.505**	**.372**	**.400**	**.413**	**.444**
1995 Average	**.383**	**.436**	**.338**	**.377**	**.363**	**.392**
2000 Average	**.627**	**.708**	**.512**	**.566**	**.566**	**.602**
2001 Average	**.523**	**.642**	**.428**	**.492**	**.476**	**.531**
2002 Average	**.546**	**.640**	**.508**	**.544**	**.530**	**.569**
2003 Average	**.728**	**.804**	**.588**	**.651**	**.661**	**.698**
2004 Average	**.764**	**.835**	**.601**	**.692**	**.681**	**.739**
2005 Average	**1.115**	**1.168**	**.842**	**.974**	**.971**	**1.048**
2006 Average	**1.202**	**1.342**	**1.085**	**1.173**	**1.136**	**1.218**
2007 Average	**1.406**	**1.436**	**1.314**	**1.350**	**1.350**	**1.374**
2008 Average	**1.918**	**2.144**	**1.843**	**1.889**	**1.866**	**1.964**
2009 Average	**1.337**	**1.413**	**1.344**	**1.306**	**1.342**	**1.341**
2010 Average	**1.756**	**1.920**	**1.679**	**1.619**	**1.697**	**1.713**
2011 Average	**2.389**	**2.736**	**2.316**	**2.257**	**2.336**	**2.401**
2012 Average	**2.548**	**3.025**	**2.429**	**2.433**	**2.457**	**2.592**
2013 Average	**2.363**	**2.883**	**2.249**	**2.353**	**2.278**	**2.482**
2014 Average	**2.153**	**2.694**	**1.996**	**2.221**	**2.044**	**2.325**
2015 Average	**.971**	**1.529**	**.999**	**1.227**	**.996**	**1.285**
2016 Average	**.736**	**1.138**	**.746**	**.897**	**.745**	**.945**
2017 January	1.099	W	1.121	1.249	1.119	1.309
February	1.174	W	1.115	1.243	1.121	1.291
March	1.103	W	1.075	1.186	1.077	1.239
April	1.038	W	1.039	1.147	1.039	1.201
May	.986	W	1.047	1.153	1.043	1.213
June	.937	W	.995	1.129	.991	1.195
July	1.026	W	1.040	1.154	1.039	1.211
August	1.042	W	1.081	1.142	1.079	1.204
September	1.150	W	1.137	1.295	1.138	1.314
October	1.153	W	1.178	1.249	1.176	1.304
November	1.302	W	1.277	1.384	1.279	1.413
December	1.254	W	1.249	1.447	1.249	1.484
Average	**1.112**	**W**	**1.117**	**1.237**	**1.116**	**1.287**
2018 January	1.301	W	1.311	1.476	1.310	1.507
February	1.221	W	1.325	1.415	1.319	1.490
March	1.227	W	1.306	1.386	1.302	1.452
April	1.311	W	1.349	1.438	1.348	1.504
May	1.462	W	1.501	1.615	1.500	1.667
June	1.487	W	1.558	1.643	1.553	1.731
July	1.543	W	1.583	1.709	1.581	1.767
August	1.499	W	1.552	1.680	1.549	1.764
September	1.520	W	1.561	1.696	1.560	1.761
October	1.620	W	1.703	1.816	1.700	1.875
November	1.360	W	1.562	1.731	1.556	1.827
December	1.252	W	1.295	1.467	1.293	1.608
Average	**1.397**	**W**	**1.466**	**1.587**	**1.463**	**1.662**
2019 January	1.626	W	1.326	1.417	1.357	1.425
February	1.808	W	1.458	1.553	1.508	1.568
March	W	W	1.542	1.607	1.572	1.623

[a] Prices are not adjusted for inflation. See "Nominal Dollars" in Glossary.
W=Value withheld to avoid disclosure of individual company data.

Notes: • Sales for resale are those made to purchasers other than ultimate consumers. Sales to end users are those made directly to ultimate consumers, including bulk consumers (such as agriculture, industry, and electric utilities) and commercial consumers. • Values for the current month are preliminary. • Through 1982, prices are U.S. Energy Information Administration (EIA) estimates. See Note 6, "Historical Petroleum Prices," at end of section. • Geographic coverage is the 50 states and the District of Columbia.

Web Page: See http://www.eia.gov/totalenergy/data/monthly/#prices (Excel and CSV files) for all available annual data beginning in 1978 and monthly data beginning in 1982.

Sources: • **1978–2007:** EIA, *Petroleum Marketing Annual 2007,* Table 17. • **2008 forward:** EIA, *Petroleum Marketing Monthly,* June 2019, Table 16.

Source: *U.S. Energy Information Administration, Monthly Energy Review, June 2019*

Table 9.6 Refiner Prices of Petroleum Products for Resale

(Dollars[a] per Gallon, Excluding Taxes)

	Finished Motor Gasoline[b]	Finished Aviation Gasoline	Kerosene-Type Jet Fuel	Kerosene	No. 2 Fuel Oil	No. 2 Diesel Fuel	Propane (Consumer Grade)
1978 Average	0.434	0.537	0.386	0.404	0.369	0.365	0.237
1980 Average	.941	1.128	.868	.864	.803	.801	.415
1985 Average	.835	1.130	.794	.874	.776	.772	.398
1990 Average	.786	1.063	.773	.839	.697	.694	.386
1995 Average	.626	.975	.539	.580	.511	.538	.344
2000 Average	.963	1.330	.880	.969	.886	.898	.595
2001 Average	.886	1.256	.763	.821	.756	.784	.540
2002 Average	.828	1.146	.716	.752	.694	.724	.431
2003 Average	1.002	1.288	.871	.955	.881	.883	.607
2004 Average	1.288	1.627	1.208	1.271	1.125	1.187	.751
2005 Average	1.670	2.076	1.723	1.757	1.623	1.737	.933
2006 Average	1.969	2.490	1.961	2.007	1.834	2.012	1.031
2007 Average	2.182	2.758	2.171	2.249	2.072	2.203	1.194
2008 Average	2.586	3.342	3.020	2.851	2.745	2.994	1.437
2009 Average	1.767	2.480	1.719	1.844	1.657	1.713	.921
2010 Average	2.165	2.874	2.185	2.299	2.147	2.214	1.212
2011 Average	2.867	3.739	3.014	3.065	2.907	3.034	1.467
2012 Average	2.929	3.919	3.080	3.163	3.031	3.109	1.033
2013 Average	2.812	3.869	2.953	3.084	2.966	3.028	1.048
2014 Average	2.618	3.687	2.763	2.882	2.741	2.812	1.165
2015 Average	1.726	2.764	1.592	1.735	1.565	1.667	.555
2016 Average	1.454	2.404	1.295	1.383	1.239	1.378	.523
2017 January	1.627	2.614	1.561	1.761	1.560	1.636	.788
February	1.625	2.592	1.592	1.657	1.553	1.641	.792
March	1.634	2.618	1.520	1.580	1.495	1.581	.671
April	1.723	2.724	1.545	1.572	1.499	1.627	.641
May	1.668	2.620	1.459	1.481	1.447	1.552	.631
June	1.574	2.552	1.378	1.360	1.375	1.465	.585
July	1.621	2.608	1.436	1.468	1.392	1.533	.634
August	1.711	2.710	1.587	1.630	1.522	1.681	.742
September	1.826	2.893	1.771	1.809	1.668	1.847	.864
October	1.730	2.716	1.704	1.805	1.695	1.852	.942
November	1.806	2.841	1.795	1.961	1.781	1.936	.997
December	1.720	2.691	1.846	2.034	1.841	1.918	.991
Average	**1.689**	**2.682**	**1.603**	**1.730**	**1.600**	**1.691**	**.800**
2018 January	1.849	2.900	1.969	2.209	1.990	2.042	.990
February	1.823	2.893	1.911	2.088	1.889	1.972	.889
March	1.889	2.904	1.893	1.969	1.848	1.952	.827
April	2.054	3.085	2.032	2.075	1.982	2.099	.792
May	2.205	3.181	2.175	2.205	2.143	2.258	.867
June	2.135	3.138	2.152	2.145	2.089	2.203	.807
July	2.148	3.111	2.140	2.133	2.079	2.192	.854
August	2.118	3.085	2.148	2.169	2.114	2.203	.907
September	2.136	3.124	2.214	2.246	2.214	2.282	.951
October	2.090	3.099	2.296	2.437	2.281	2.379	.948
November	1.732	2.762	2.100	2.206	2.098	2.130	.826
December	1.514	2.463	1.811	1.954	1.796	1.794	.798
Average	**1.980**	**3.006**	**2.073**	**2.160**	**2.002**	**2.130**	**.877**
2019 January	1.483	2.394	1.822	2.021	1.813	1.789	.775
February	1.624	2.527	1.925	2.111	1.907	1.950	.772
March	1.881	2.874	1.960	2.087	1.958	2.020	.754

[a] Prices are not adjusted for inflation. See "Nominal Dollars" in Glossary.
[b] See Note 5, "Motor Gasoline Prices," at end of section.

Notes: • Sales for resale are those made to purchasers other than ultimate consumers. Sales to end users are shown in Table 9.7; they are sales made directly to ultimate consumers, including bulk consumers (such as agriculture, industry, and electric utilities) and residential and commercial consumers. • Values for the current month are preliminary. • Through 1982, prices are U.S. Energy Information Administration (EIA) estimates. See Note 6, "Historical Petroleum Prices," at end of section. • Geographic coverage is the 50 states and the District of Columbia.

Web Page: See http://www.eia.gov/totalenergy/data/monthly/#prices (Excel and CSV files) for all available annual data beginning in 1978 and monthly data beginning in 1982.

Sources: • **1978–2007:** EIA, *Petroleum Marketing Annual 2007,* Table 4. • **2008 forward:** EIA, *Petroleum Marketing Monthly,* June 2019, Table 4.

Source: *U.S. Energy Information Administration, Monthly Energy Review, June 2019*

Table 9.7 Refiner Prices of Petroleum Products to End Users

(Dollars[a] per Gallon, Excluding Taxes)

	Finished Motor Gasoline[b]	Finished Aviation Gasoline	Kerosene-Type Jet Fuel	Kerosene	No. 2 Fuel Oil	No. 2 Diesel Fuel	Propane (Consumer Grade)
1978 Average	**0.484**	**0.516**	**0.387**	**0.421**	**0.400**	**0.377**	**0.335**
1980 Average	**1.035**	**1.084**	**.868**	**.902**	**.788**	**.818**	**.482**
1985 Average	**.912**	**1.201**	**.796**	**1.030**	**.849**	**.789**	**.717**
1990 Average	**.883**	**1.120**	**.766**	**.923**	**.734**	**.725**	**.745**
1995 Average	**.765**	**1.005**	**.540**	**.589**	**.562**	**.560**	**.492**
2000 Average	**1.106**	**1.306**	**.899**	**1.123**	**.927**	**.935**	**.603**
2001 Average	**1.032**	**1.323**	**.775**	**1.045**	**.829**	**.842**	**.506**
2002 Average	**.947**	**1.288**	**.721**	**.990**	**.737**	**.762**	**.419**
2003 Average	**1.156**	**1.493**	**.872**	**1.224**	**.933**	**.944**	**.577**
2004 Average	**1.435**	**1.819**	**1.207**	**1.160**	**1.173**	**1.243**	**.839**
2005 Average	**1.829**	**2.231**	**1.735**	**1.957**	**1.705**	**1.786**	**1.089**
2006 Average	**2.128**	**2.682**	**1.998**	**2.244**	**1.982**	**2.096**	**1.358**
2007 Average	**2.345**	**2.849**	**2.165**	**2.263**	**2.241**	**2.267**	**1.489**
2008 Average	**2.775**	**3.273**	**3.052**	**3.283**	**2.986**	**3.150**	**1.892**
2009 Average	**1.888**	**2.442**	**1.704**	**2.675**	**1.962**	**1.834**	**1.220**
2010 Average	**2.301**	**3.028**	**2.201**	**3.063**	**2.462**	**2.314**	**1.481**
2011 Average	**3.050**	**3.803**	**3.054**	**3.616**	**3.193**	**3.117**	**1.709**
2012 Average	**3.154**	**3.971**	**3.104**	**3.843**	**3.358**	**3.202**	**1.139**
2013 Average	**3.049**	**3.932**	**2.979**	**3.842**	**3.335**	**3.122**	**1.028**
2014 Average	**2.855**	**3.986**	**2.772**	**W**	**3.329**	**2.923**	**1.097**
2015 Average	**2.003**	**W**	**1.629**	**W**	**2.016**	**1.819**	**.481**
2016 Average	**1.730**	**W**	**1.319**	**W**	**1.716**	**1.511**	**.498**
2017 January	1.900	W	1.584	W	NA	1.747	.774
February	1.862	W	1.615	W	2.033	1.755	.814
March	1.904	W	1.554	W	1.909	1.699	.657
April	1.997	W	1.595	W	2.081	1.747	.652
May	1.963	W	1.492	2.637	NA	1.693	.650
June	1.906	W	1.434	2.600	1.739	1.618	.611
July	1.871	W	1.478	2.621	1.728	1.665	.667
August	1.952	W	1.613	2.579	1.904	1.792	.768
September	2.154	W	1.795	2.703	2.044	1.959	.895
October	2.042	W	1.743	W	2.048	1.982	.972
November	2.122	W	1.831	W	2.134	2.047	1.011
December	2.034	W	1.869	W	2.263	2.037	1.028
Average	**1.976**	**W**	**1.629**	**W**	**2.010**	**1.811**	**.772**
2018 January	2.108	W	2.012	W	2.206	2.144	.971
February	2.127	W	1.970	W	2.365	2.107	.948
March	2.160	W	1.924	W	2.484	2.076	.842
April	2.315	W	2.080	W	2.486	2.201	.839
May	2.494	W	2.221	3.219	2.478	2.368	.916
June	2.469	W	2.196	3.292	2.413	2.340	.883
July	2.442	W	2.176	W	2.436	2.316	.956
August	2.421	W	2.183	3.272	2.499	2.327	.989
September	2.428	W	2.257	3.189	2.612	2.388	1.062
October	2.441	W	2.349	W	2.696	2.500	.988
November	2.205	W	2.162	W	2.431	2.282	.876
December	1.973	W	1.852	W	2.222	1.981	.794
Average	**2.303**	**W**	**2.119**	**3.113**	**2.380**	**2.256**	**.925**
2019 January	1.854	W	1.827	W	2.195	1.960	.756
February	R 1.949	W	1.956	W	2.367	R 2.080	.784
March	2.137	W	2.005	W	2.376	2.158	.762

[a] Prices are not adjusted for inflation. See "Nominal Dollars" in Glossary.

[b] See Note 5, "Motor Gasoline Prices," at end of section.

R=Revised. NA=Not available. W=Value withheld to avoid disclosure of individual company data.

Notes: • Sales to end users are those made directly to ultimate consumers, including bulk consumers (such as agriculture, industry, and electric utilities) and residential and commercial consumers. Sales for resale are shown in Table 9.6; they are sales made to purchasers other than ultimate consumers. • Values for the current month are preliminary. • Through 1982, prices are U.S. Energy Information Administration (EIA) estimates. See Note 6, "Historical Petroleum Prices," at end of section. • Geographic coverage is the 50 states and the District of Columbia.

Web Page: See http://www.eia.gov/totalenergy/data/monthly/#prices (Excel and CSV files) for all available annual data beginning in 1978 and monthly data beginning in 1982.

Sources: • **1978–2007:** EIA, *Petroleum Marketing Annual 2007,* Table 2. • **2008 forward:** EIA, *Petroleum Marketing Monthly,* June 2019, Table 2.

Source: *U.S. Energy Information Administration, Monthly Energy Review, June 2019*

Figure 9.2 Average Retail Prices of Electricity
(Cents [a] per Kilowatthour)

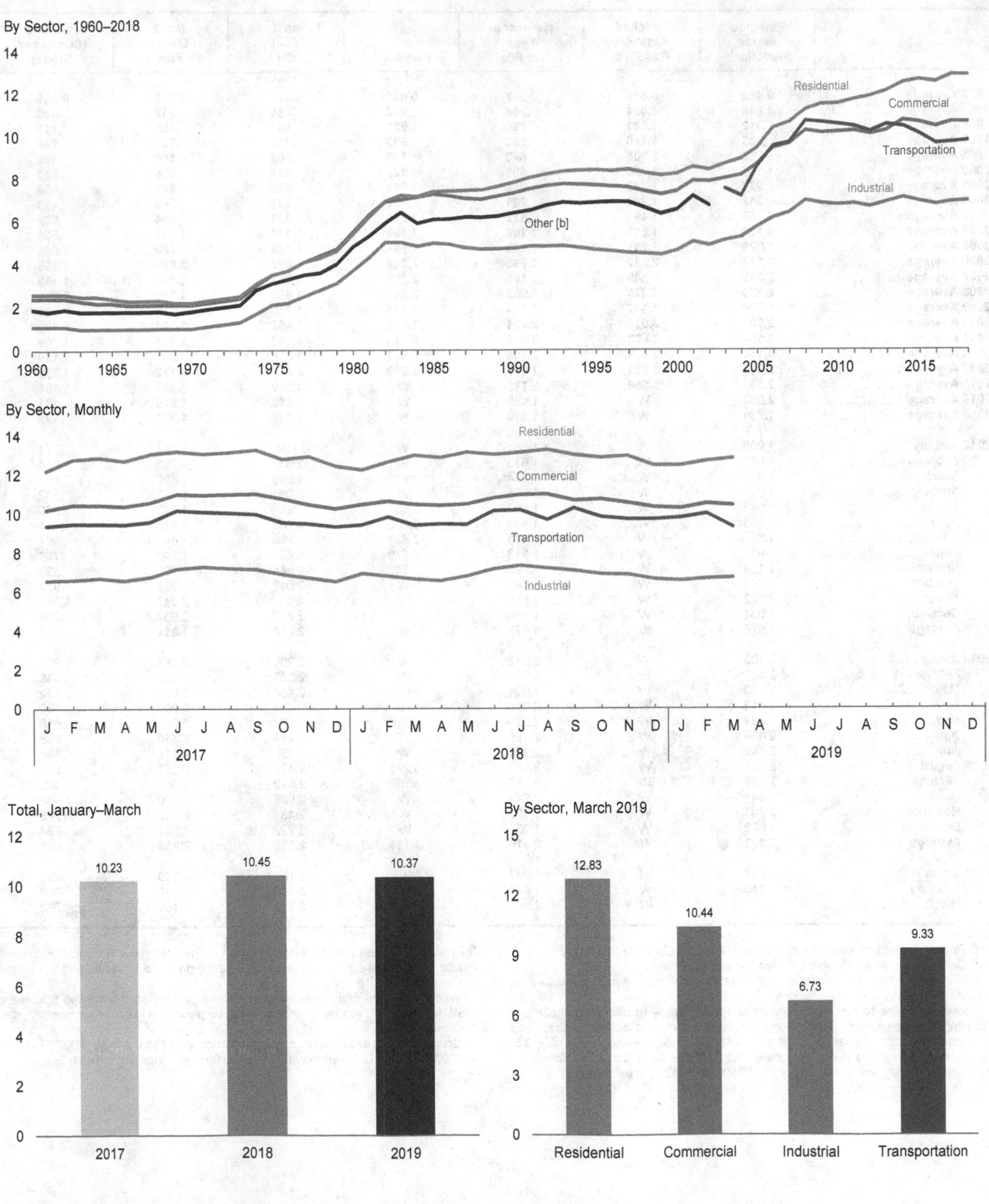

[a] Prices are not adjusted for inflation. See "Nominal Dollars" in Glossary.
[b] Public street and highway lighting, interdepartmental sales, other sales to public authorities, agricultural and irrigation, and transportation including railroads and railways.

Note: Includes taxes.
Web Page: http://www.eia.gov/totalenergy/data/monthly/#prices.
Source: Table 9.8.

Source: *U.S. Energy Information Administration, Monthly Energy Review, June 2019*

Table 9.8 Average Retail Prices of Electricity

(Cents[a] per Kilowatthour, Including Taxes)

	Residential	Commercial[b]	Industrial[c]	Transportation[d]	Other[e]	Total
1960 Average	**2.60**	**2.40**	**1.10**	**NA**	**1.90**	**1.80**
1965 Average	**2.40**	**2.20**	**1.00**	**NA**	**1.80**	**1.70**
1970 Average	**2.20**	**2.10**	**1.00**	**NA**	**1.80**	**1.70**
1975 Average	**3.50**	**3.50**	**2.10**	**NA**	**3.10**	**2.90**
1980 Average	**5.40**	**5.50**	**3.70**	**NA**	**4.80**	**4.70**
1985 Average	**7.39**	**7.27**	**4.97**	**NA**	**6.09**	**6.44**
1990 Average	**7.83**	**7.34**	**4.74**	**NA**	**6.40**	**6.57**
1995 Average	**8.40**	**7.69**	**4.66**	**NA**	**6.88**	**6.89**
2000 Average	**8.24**	**7.43**	**4.64**	**NA**	**6.56**	**6.81**
2001 Average	**8.58**	**7.92**	**5.05**	**NA**	**7.20**	**7.29**
2002 Average	**8.44**	**7.89**	**4.88**	**NA**	**6.75**	**7.20**
2003 Average	**8.72**	**8.03**	**5.11**	**7.54**	**– –**	**7.44**
2004 Average	**8.95**	**8.17**	**5.25**	**7.18**	**– –**	**7.61**
2005 Average	**9.45**	**8.67**	**5.73**	**8.57**	**– –**	**8.14**
2006 Average	**10.40**	**9.46**	**6.16**	**9.54**	**– –**	**8.90**
2007 Average	**10.65**	**9.65**	**6.39**	**9.70**	**– –**	**9.13**
2008 Average	**11.26**	**10.26**	**6.96**	**10.71**	**– –**	**9.74**
2009 Average	**11.51**	**10.16**	**6.83**	**10.66**	**– –**	**9.82**
2010 Average	**11.54**	**10.19**	**6.77**	**10.56**	**– –**	**9.83**
2011 Average	**11.72**	**10.24**	**6.82**	**10.46**	**– –**	**9.90**
2012 Average	**11.88**	**10.09**	**6.67**	**10.21**	**– –**	**9.84**
2013 Average	**12.13**	**10.26**	**6.89**	**10.55**	**– –**	**10.07**
2014 Average	**12.52**	**10.74**	**7.10**	**10.45**	**– –**	**10.44**
2015 Average	**12.65**	**10.64**	**6.91**	**10.09**	**– –**	**10.41**
2016 Average	**12.55**	**10.43**	**6.76**	**9.63**	**– –**	**10.27**
2017 January	12.21	10.21	6.59	9.39	– –	10.13
February	12.79	10.48	6.63	9.50	– –	10.28
March	12.89	10.46	6.71	9.49	– –	10.28
April	12.72	10.40	6.60	9.46	– –	10.07
May	13.07	10.59	6.78	9.61	– –	10.34
June	13.20	11.01	7.19	10.18	– –	10.83
July	13.08	10.97	7.31	10.12	– –	10.95
August	13.15	11.01	7.22	10.06	– –	10.91
September	13.28	11.03	7.17	9.99	– –	10.86
October	12.80	10.78	6.91	9.57	– –	10.40
November	12.94	10.49	6.73	9.50	– –	10.28
December	12.45	10.28	6.54	9.35	– –	10.17
Average	**12.89**	**10.66**	**6.88**	**9.68**	**– –**	**10.48**
2018 January	12.25	10.49	6.96	9.44	– –	10.47
February	12.66	10.65	6.81	9.84	– –	10.48
March	12.99	10.49	6.66	9.43	– –	10.40
April	12.88	10.44	6.58	9.48	– –	10.23
May	13.15	10.50	6.82	9.46	– –	10.41
June	13.04	10.82	7.18	10.16	– –	10.79
July	13.13	10.98	7.34	10.19	– –	11.03
August	13.28	11.00	7.21	9.69	– –	11.02
September	13.01	10.68	7.09	10.30	– –	10.70
October	12.87	10.75	6.91	9.84	– –	10.46
November	12.95	10.56	6.88	9.72	– –	10.43
December	12.47	10.33	6.65	9.72	– –	10.27
Average	**12.89**	**10.66**	**6.93**	**9.77**	**– –**	**10.58**
2019 January	12.47	10.29	6.58	9.80	– –	10.29
February	12.70	10.52	6.68	10.01	– –	10.43
March	12.83	10.44	6.73	9.33	– –	10.38
3-Month Average	**12.65**	**10.41**	**6.67**	**9.71**	**– –**	**10.37**
2018 3-Month Average	**12.59**	**10.54**	**6.81**	**9.56**	**– –**	**10.45**
2017 3-Month Average	**12.60**	**10.38**	**6.64**	**9.46**	**– –**	**10.23**

[a] Prices are not adjusted for inflation. See "Nominal Price" in Glossary.
[b] Commercial sector. For 1960–2002, prices exclude public street and highway lighting, interdepartmental sales, and other sales to public authorities.
[c] Industrial sector. For 1960–2002, prices exclude agriculture and irrigation.
[d] Transportation sector, including railroads and railways.
[e] Public street and highway lighting, interdepartmental sales, other sales to public authorities, agriculture and irrigation, and transportation including railroads and railways.

NA=Not available. – – =Not applicable.

Notes: • Beginning in 2003, the category "Other" has been replaced by "Transportation," and the categories "Commercial" and "Industrial" have been redefined. • Prices are calculated by dividing revenue by sales. Revenue may not correspond to sales for a particular month because of energy service provider billing and accounting procedures. That lack of correspondence could result in uncharacteristic increases or decreases in the monthly prices. • Prices include state and local taxes, energy or demand charges, customer service charges, environmental surcharges, franchise fees, fuel adjustments, and other miscellaneous charges applied to end-use customers during normal billing operations. Prices do not include deferred charges, credits, or other adjustments, such as fuel or revenue from purchased power, from previous reporting periods. • Through 1979, data are for Classes A and B privately owned electric utilities only. (Class A utilities are those with operating revenues of $2.5 million or more; Class B utilities are those with operating revenues between $1 million and $2.5 million.) For 1980–1982, data are for selected Class A utilities whose electric operating revenues were $100 million or more during the previous year. For 1983, data are for a selected sample of electric utilities. Beginning in 1984, data are for a census of electric utilities. Beginning in 1996, data also include energy service providers selling to retail customers. • See Note 7, "Electricity Retail Prices," at end of section for plant coverage, and for information on preliminary and final values. • Geographic coverage is the 50 states and the District of Columbia.

Web Page: See http://www.eia.gov/totalenergy/data/monthly/#prices (Excel and CSV files) for all available annual data beginning in 1960 and monthly data beginning in 1976.

Sources: • **1960–September 1977:** Federal Power Commission, Form FPC-5, "Monthly Statement of Electric Operating Revenues and Income." • **October 1977–February 1980:** Federal Energy Regulatory Commission (FERC), Form FPC-5, "Monthly Statement of Electric Operating Revenues and Income." • **March 1980–1982:** FERC, Form FERC-5, "Electric Utility Company Monthly Statement." • **1983:** U.S. Energy Information Administration (EIA), Form EIA-826, "Electric Utility Company Monthly Statement." • **1984–2010:** EIA, Form EIA-861, "Annual Electric Power Industry Report." • **2011 forward:** EIA, *Electric Power Monthly*, May 2019, Table 5.3.

Source: *U.S. Energy Information Administration, Monthly Energy Review, June 2019*

Figure 9.3 Cost of Fossil-Fuel Receipts at Electric Generating Plants
(Dollars [a] per Million Btu, Including Taxes)

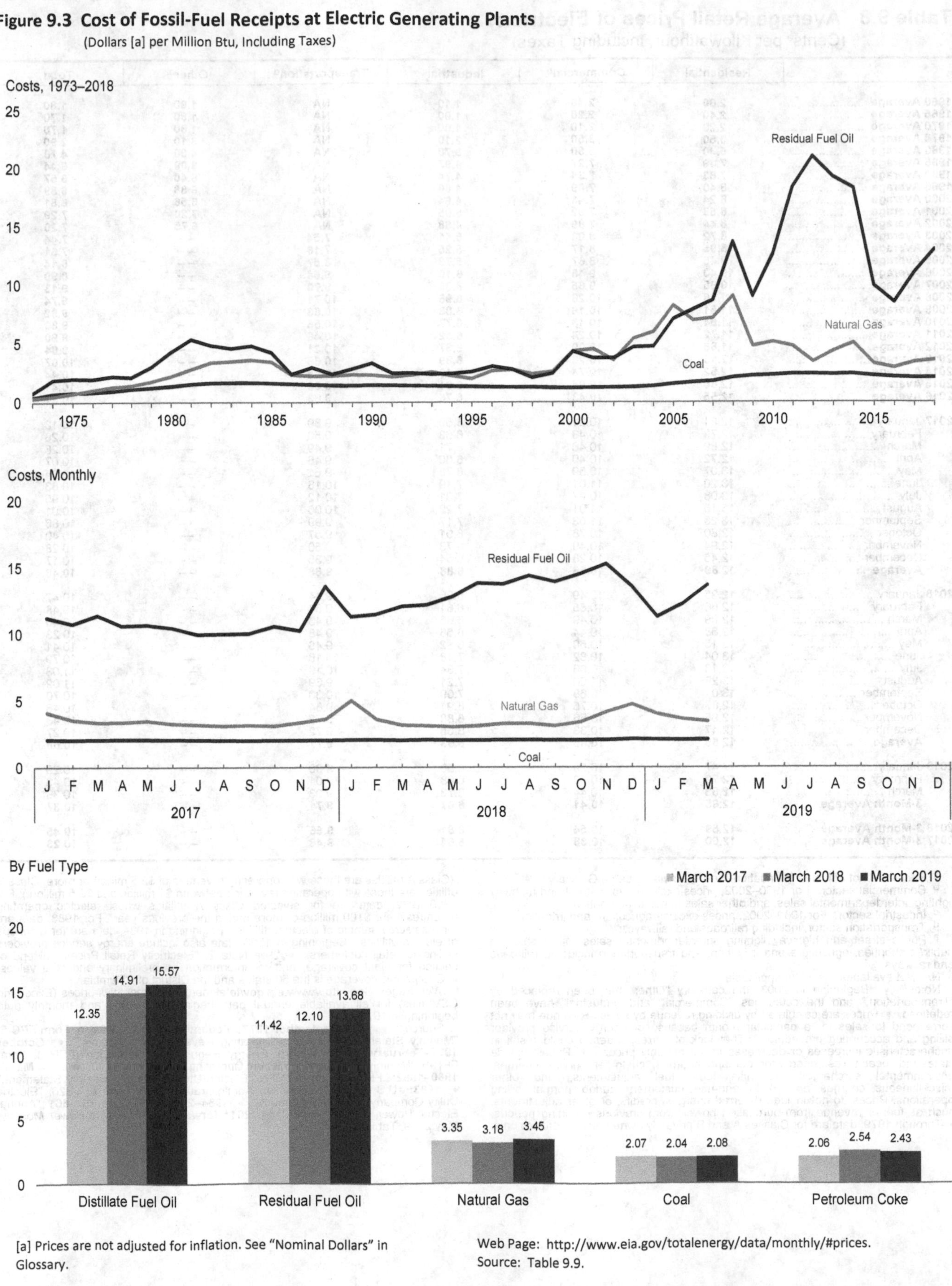

[a] Prices are not adjusted for inflation. See "Nominal Dollars" in Glossary.

Web Page: http://www.eia.gov/totalenergy/data/monthly/#prices.
Source: Table 9.9.

Source: *U.S. Energy Information Administration, Monthly Energy Review, June 2019*

Table 9.9 Cost of Fossil-Fuel Receipts at Electric Generating Plants

(Dollars[a] per Million Btu, Including Taxes)

	Coal	Petroleum				Natural Gas[e]	All Fossil Fuels[f]
		Residual Fuel Oil[b]	Distillate Fuel Oil[c]	Petroleum Coke	Total[d]		
1973 Average	**0.41**	**0.79**	**NA**	**NA**	**0.80**	**0.34**	**0.48**
1975 Average	**.81**	**2.01**	**NA**	**NA**	**2.02**	**.75**	**1.04**
1980 Average	**1.35**	**4.27**	**NA**	**NA**	**4.35**	**2.20**	**1.93**
1985 Average	**1.65**	**4.24**	**NA**	**NA**	**4.32**	**3.44**	**2.09**
1990 Average	**1.45**	**3.32**	**5.38**	**.80**	**3.35**	**2.32**	**1.69**
1995 Average	**1.32**	**2.59**	**3.99**	**.65**	**2.57**	**1.98**	**1.45**
2000 Average	**1.20**	**4.29**	**6.65**	**.58**	**4.18**	**4.30**	**1.74**
2001 Average	**1.23**	**3.73**	**6.30**	**.78**	**3.69**	**4.49**	**1.73**
2002 Average[g]	**1.25**	**3.73**	**5.34**	**.78**	**3.34**	**3.56**	**1.86**
2003 Average	**1.28**	**4.66**	**6.82**	**.72**	**4.33**	**5.39**	**2.28**
2004 Average	**1.36**	**4.73**	**8.02**	**.83**	**4.29**	**5.96**	**2.48**
2005 Average	**1.54**	**7.06**	**11.72**	**1.11**	**6.44**	**8.21**	**3.25**
2006 Average	**1.69**	**7.85**	**13.28**	**1.33**	**6.23**	**6.94**	**3.02**
2007 Average	**1.77**	**8.64**	**14.85**	**1.51**	**7.17**	**7.11**	**3.23**
2008 Average	**2.07**	**13.62**	**21.46**	**2.11**	**10.87**	**9.01**	**4.12**
2009 Average	**2.21**	**8.98**	**13.22**	**1.61**	**7.02**	**4.74**	**3.04**
2010 Average	**2.27**	**12.57**	**16.61**	**2.28**	**9.54**	**5.09**	**3.26**
2011 Average	**2.39**	**18.35**	**22.46**	**3.03**	**12.48**	**4.72**	**3.29**
2012 Average	**2.38**	**21.03**	**23.49**	**2.24**	**12.48**	**3.42**	**2.83**
2013 Average	**2.34**	**19.26**	**23.03**	**2.18**	**11.57**	**4.33**	**3.09**
2014 Average	**2.37**	**18.30**	**21.88**	**1.98**	**11.60**	**5.00**	**3.31**
2015 Average	**2.22**	**9.89**	**14.06**	**1.84**	**6.74**	**3.23**	**2.65**
2016 Average	**2.11**	**8.45**	**10.90**	**1.65**	**5.24**	**2.87**	**2.47**
2017 January	2.09	11.25	13.02	2.14	7.80	4.11	2.88
February	2.06	10.77	12.98	2.00	6.37	3.56	2.63
March	2.07	11.42	12.35	2.06	7.66	3.35	2.66
April	2.08	10.64	13.00	2.00	7.01	3.38	2.65
May	2.09	10.69	12.22	2.05	6.69	3.48	2.70
June	2.07	10.48	11.56	2.11	6.18	3.29	2.64
July	2.06	9.99	11.82	2.09	5.97	3.21	2.64
August	2.05	10.03	12.95	2.08	6.31	3.13	2.56
September	2.02	10.06	14.52	2.10	6.42	3.16	2.56
October	2.03	10.61	14.11	2.31	6.88	3.13	2.54
November	2.04	10.28	14.61	2.49	8.04	3.35	2.62
December	2.04	13.60	14.63	2.17	8.90	3.63	2.80
Average	**2.06**	**11.00**	**13.22**	**2.13**	**7.10**	**3.37**	**2.65**
2018 January	2.07	11.33	15.96	2.38	11.32	5.02	3.50
February	2.07	11.51	15.00	2.43	8.26	3.61	2.79
March	2.04	12.10	14.91	2.54	7.69	3.18	2.57
April	2.07	12.21	16.07	2.56	8.08	3.13	2.58
May	2.05	12.82	16.78	2.41	10.31	3.04	2.56
June	2.05	13.85	16.91	2.73	9.14	3.11	2.61
July	2.06	13.76	16.40	2.71	8.12	3.29	2.73
August	2.06	14.38	16.76	2.79	8.22	3.28	2.69
September	2.05	13.92	17.35	2.94	8.85	3.11	2.62
October	2.05	14.52	17.66	2.48	10.29	3.39	2.71
November	2.06	15.27	16.20	2.21	9.47	4.16	3.01
December	2.12	13.58	14.27	2.03	9.17	4.73	3.25
Average	**2.06**	**12.98**	**16.09**	**2.54**	**9.27**	**3.55**	**2.80**
2019 January	2.10	11.31	14.12	2.08	8.41	4.01	2.98
February	2.07	12.27	15.31	2.27	9.37	3.64	2.85
March	2.08	13.68	15.57	2.43	10.14	3.45	2.78
3-Month Average	**2.09**	**12.37**	**14.88**	**2.24**	**9.23**	**3.70**	**2.88**
2018 3-Month Average	**2.06**	**11.51**	**15.63**	**2.45**	**9.67**	**3.97**	**2.97**
2017 3-Month Average	**2.07**	**11.24**	**12.82**	**2.06**	**7.36**	**3.67**	**2.73**

[a] Prices are not adjusted for inflation. See "Nominal Dollars" in Glossary.

[b] For 1973–2001, electric utility data are for heavy oil (fuel oil nos. 5 and 6, and small amounts of fuel oil no. 4).

[c] For 1973–2001, electric utility data are for light oil (fuel oil nos. 1 and 2).

[d] For all years, includes residual fuel oil and distillate fuel oil. For 1990 forward, also includes petroleum coke. For 1973–2012, also includes jet fuel, kerosene, and waste oil. For 1983–2012, also includes other petroleum, such as propane and refined motor oil.

[e] Natural gas, plus a small amount of supplemental gaseous fuels. For 1973–2000, data also include a small amount of blast furnace gas and other gases derived from fossil fuels.

[f] Weighted average of costs shown under "Coal," "Petroleum," and "Natural Gas."

[g] Through 2001, data are for electric utilities only. Beginning in 2002, data also include independent power producers, and electric generating plants in the commercial and industrial sectors.

NA=Not available.

Notes: • Receipts are purchases of fuel. • Yearly costs are averages of monthly values, weighted by quantities in Btu. • For this table, there are several breaks in the data series related to what plants and fuels are covered. Beginning in 2013, data cover all regulated generating plants; plus unregulated plants whose total fossil-fueled nameplate generating capacity is 50 megawatts or more for coal, and 200 megawatts or more for natural gas, residual fuel oil, distillate fuel oil, and petroleum coke. For data coverage before 2013, see EIA, *Electric Power Monthly,* Appendix C, Form EIA-923 notes, "Receipts and cost and quality of fossil fuels" section. • Geographic coverage is the 50 states and the District of Columbia.

Web Page: See http://www.eia.gov/totalenergy/data/monthly/#prices (Excel and CSV files) for all available annual and monthly data beginning in 1973.

Sources: See end of section.

Source: *U.S. Energy Information Administration, Monthly Energy Review, June 2019*

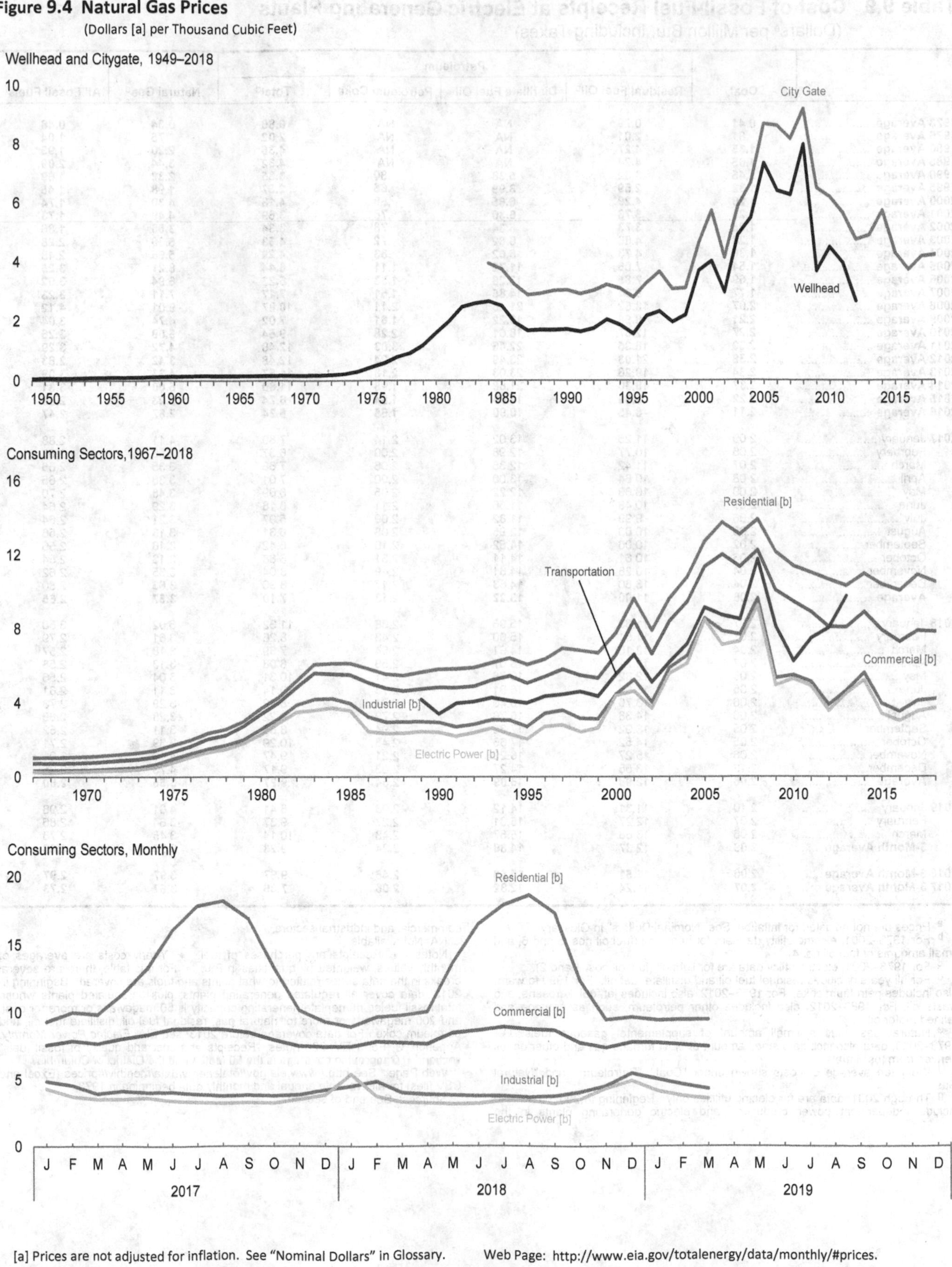

[a] Prices are not adjusted for inflation. See "Nominal Dollars" in Glossary.
[b] Includes taxes.

Web Page: http://www.eia.gov/totalenergy/data/monthly/#prices.
Source: Table 9.10.

***Source:** U.S. Energy Information Administration, Monthly Energy Review, June 2019*

Table 9.10 Natural Gas Prices

(Dollars[a] per Thousand Cubic Feet)

	Wellhead Price[f]	City-gate Price[g]	Consuming Sectors[b]								
			Residential		Commercial[c]		Industrial[d]		Transportation	Electric Power[e]	
			Price[h]	Percentage of Sector[i]	Price[h]	Percentage of Sector[i]	Price[h]	Percentage of Sector[i]	Vehicle Fuel[j] Price[h]	Price[h]	Percentage of Sector[i,k]
1950 Average	**0.07**	**NA**	**NA**	**NA**	**NA**	**NA**	**NA**	**NA**	**NA**	**NA**	**NA**
1955 Average	**.10**	**NA**	**NA**	**NA**	**NA**	**NA**	**NA**	**NA**	**NA**	**NA**	**NA**
1960 Average	**.14**	**NA**	**NA**	**NA**	**NA**	**NA**	**NA**	**NA**	**NA**	**NA**	**NA**
1965 Average	**.16**	**NA**	**NA**	**NA**	**NA**	**NA**	**NA**	**NA**	**NA**	**NA**	**NA**
1970 Average	**.17**	**NA**	**1.09**	**NA**	**.77**	**NA**	**.37**	**NA**	**NA**	**.29**	**NA**
1975 Average	**.44**	**NA**	**1.71**	**NA**	**1.35**	**NA**	**.96**	**NA**	**NA**	**.77**	**96.1**
1980 Average	**1.59**	**NA**	**3.68**	**NA**	**3.39**	**NA**	**2.56**	**NA**	**NA**	**2.27**	**96.9**
1985 Average	**2.51**	**3.75**	**6.12**	**NA**	**5.50**	**NA**	**3.95**	**68.8**	**NA**	**3.55**	**94.0**
1990 Average	**1.71**	**3.03**	**5.80**	**99.2**	**4.83**	**86.6**	**2.93**	**35.2**	**3.39**	**2.38**	**76.8**
1995 Average	**1.55**	**2.78**	**6.06**	**99.0**	**5.05**	**76.7**	**2.71**	**24.5**	**3.98**	**2.02**	**71.4**
2000 Average	**3.68**	**4.62**	**7.76**	**92.6**	**6.59**	**63.9**	**4.45**	**19.8**	**5.54**	**4.38**	**50.5**
2001 Average	**4.00**	**5.72**	**9.63**	**92.4**	**8.43**	**66.0**	**5.24**	**20.8**	**6.60**	**4.61**	**40.2**
2002 Average	**2.95**	**4.12**	**7.89**	**97.9**	**6.63**	**77.4**	**4.02**	**22.7**	**5.10**	[e] **3.68**	**83.9**
2003 Average	**4.88**	**5.85**	**9.63**	**97.5**	**8.40**	**78.2**	**5.89**	**22.1**	**6.19**	**5.57**	**91.2**
2004 Average	**5.46**	**6.65**	**10.75**	**97.7**	**9.43**	**78.0**	**6.53**	**23.6**	**7.16**	**6.11**	**89.8**
2005 Average	**7.33**	**8.67**	**12.70**	**98.1**	**11.34**	**82.1**	**8.56**	**24.0**	**9.14**	**8.47**	**91.3**
2006 Average	**6.39**	**8.61**	**13.73**	**98.1**	**12.00**	**80.8**	**7.87**	**23.4**	**8.72**	**7.11**	**93.4**
2007 Average	**6.25**	**8.16**	**13.08**	**98.0**	**11.34**	**80.4**	**7.68**	**22.2**	**8.50**	**7.31**	**92.2**
2008 Average	**7.97**	**9.18**	**13.89**	**97.5**	**12.23**	**79.7**	**9.65**	**20.4**	**11.75**	**9.26**	**101.1**
2009 Average	**3.67**	**6.48**	**12.14**	**97.4**	**10.06**	**77.8**	**5.33**	**18.8**	**8.13**	**4.93**	**101.1**
2010 Average	**4.48**	**6.18**	**11.39**	**97.4**	**9.47**	**77.5**	**5.49**	**18.0**	**6.25**	**5.27**	**100.8**
2011 Average	**3.95**	**5.63**	**11.03**	**96.3**	**8.91**	**67.3**	**5.13**	**16.3**	**7.48**	**4.89**	**101.2**
2012 Average	E **2.66**	**4.73**	**10.65**	**95.8**	**8.10**	**65.2**	**3.88**	**16.2**	**8.04**	**3.54**	**95.5**
2013 Average	**NA**	**4.88**	**10.32**	**95.7**	**8.08**	**65.8**	**4.64**	**16.6**	**9.76**	**4.49**	**94.9**
2014 Average	**NA**	**5.71**	**10.97**	**95.5**	**8.90**	**65.8**	**5.62**	**15.9**	**NA**	**5.19**	**94.6**
2015 Average	**NA**	**4.26**	**10.38**	**95.6**	**7.91**	**65.7**	**3.93**	**14.8**	**NA**	**3.38**	**94.6**
2016 Average	**NA**	**3.71**	**10.05**	**95.8**	**7.28**	**64.8**	**3.51**	**14.9**	**NA**	**2.99**	**95.6**
2017 January	NA	4.21	9.32	95.9	7.58	70.5	4.87	15.0	NA	4.31	94.6
February	NA	4.13	10.01	95.8	7.89	69.0	4.56	14.9	NA	3.72	95.5
March	NA	3.84	9.86	95.7	7.68	67.7	3.94	14.9	NA	3.51	95.6
April	NA	4.20	11.34	95.2	8.04	65.0	4.13	14.5	NA	3.50	96.0
May	NA	4.42	13.26	95.5	8.31	60.8	4.03	13.9	NA	3.61	96.8
June	NA	4.82	16.06	94.4	8.75	58.2	4.06	14.5	NA	3.40	96.0
July	NA	4.73	17.86	95.8	8.81	57.2	3.93	14.6	NA	3.32	95.1
August	NA	4.61	18.22	95.6	8.76	55.9	3.79	14.2	NA	3.24	95.6
September	NA	4.52	16.92	96.1	8.52	56.2	3.84	13.7	NA	3.27	95.1
October	NA	4.03	13.36	96.4	7.97	61.5	3.79	14.2	NA	3.24	95.2
November	NA	3.97	10.15	96.0	7.51	65.8	3.85	14.5	NA	3.50	94.9
December	NA	4.00	9.29	96.5	7.42	69.1	4.21	15.0	NA	3.81	94.8
Average	**NA**	**4.16**	**10.91**	**95.9**	**7.88**	**65.4**	**4.10**	**14.5**	**NA**	**3.51**	**95.4**
2018 January	NA	4.29	8.91	96.1	7.43	71.2	4.48	14.9	NA	5.35	87.6
February	NA	3.99	9.64	96.0	7.82	69.1	4.86	14.6	NA	3.74	86.8
March	NA	3.71	9.78	95.9	7.74	68.4	4.02	15.0	NA	3.32	88.2
April	NA	3.64	10.04	95.6	7.66	65.3	3.90	14.7	NA	3.25	88.5
May	NA	4.13	13.64	94.8	8.46	59.7	3.81	13.8	NA	3.15	85.4
June	NA	4.46	16.51	95.7	8.65	57.4	3.78	13.7	NA	3.21	87.7
July	NA	4.71	17.92	95.8	8.93	56.0	3.76	13.7	NA	3.41	84.9
August	NA	4.84	18.63	95.6	8.74	54.8	3.67	13.9	NA	3.39	86.1
September	NA	4.70	17.31	96.2	8.64	56.5	3.75	13.7	NA	3.21	86.7
October	NA	4.07	12.26	96.5	7.71	61.0	4.04	13.7	NA	3.50	88.4
November	NA	4.29	9.43	96.4	7.35	66.5	4.51	14.2	NA	4.32	88.8
December	NA	4.75	9.63	96.2	7.77	68.8	5.46	14.3	NA	4.89	91.6
Average	**NA**	**4.21**	**10.52**	**96.0**	**7.83**	**65.6**	**4.20**	**14.2**	**NA**	**3.68**	**87.3**
2019 January	NA	4.09	9.43	96.3	7.75	70.2	5.04	13.6	NA	4.16	91.1
February	NA	3.89	R 9.47	96.1	R 7.61	69.4	4.65	14.0	NA	3.79	90.5
March	NA	4.06	9.48	96.0	7.47	69.1	4.33	13.6	NA	3.59	89.9
3-Month Average	**NA**	**4.02**	**9.46**	**96.2**	**7.62**	**69.6**	**4.68**	**13.7**	**NA**	**3.86**	**90.5**
2018 3-Month Average	**NA**	**4.03**	**9.38**	**96.0**	**7.64**	**69.7**	**4.45**	**14.9**	**NA**	**4.17**	**87.5**
2017 3-Month Average	**NA**	**4.08**	**9.69**	**95.8**	**7.71**	**69.2**	**4.46**	**14.9**	**NA**	**3.85**	**95.2**

[a] Prices are not adjusted for inflation. See "Nominal Dollars" in Glossary.
[b] See Note 8, "Natural Gas Prices," at end of section.
[c] Commercial sector, including commercial combined-heat-and-power (CHP) and commercial electricity-only plants. See Note 2, "Classification of Power Plants Into Energy-Use Sectors," at end of Section 7.
[d] Industrial sector, including industrial combined-heat-and-power (CHP) and industrial electricity-only plants. See Note 2, "Classification of Power Plants Into Energy-Use Sectors," at end of Section 7.
[e] The electric power sector comprises electricity-only and combined-heat-and-power (CHP) plants within the NAICS 22 category whose primary business is to sell electricity, or electricity and heat, to the public. Through 2001, data are for electric utilities only; beginning in 2002, data also include independent power producers.
[f] See "Natural Gas Wellhead Price" in Glossary.
[g] See "Citygate" in Glossary.
[h] Includes taxes.
[i] The percentage of the sector's consumption in Table 4.3 for which price data are available. For details on how the percentages are derived, see Table 9.10 sources at end of section.
[j] Much of the natural gas delivered for vehicle fuel represents deliveries to fueling stations that are used primarily or exclusively by fleet vehicles. Thus, the prices are often those associated with the cost of gas in the operation of fleet vehicles.
[k] Percentages exceed 100% when reported natural gas receipts are greater than reported natural gas consumption—this can occur when combined-heat-and-power plants report fuel receipts related to non-electric generating activities.

R=Revised. NA=Not available. E=Estimate.

Notes: • Prices are for natural gas, plus a small amount of supplemental gaseous fuels. • Prices are intended to include all taxes. See Note 8, "Natural Gas Prices," at end of section. • Wellhead annual and year-to-date prices are simple averages of the monthly prices; all other annual and year-to-date prices are volume-weighted averages of the monthly prices. • Geographic coverage is the 50 states and the District of Columbia.

Web Page: See http://www.eia.gov/totalenergy/data/monthly/#prices (Excel and CSV files) for all available annual data beginning in 1949 and monthly data beginning in 1976.

Sources: See end of section.

Source: *U.S. Energy Information Administration, Monthly Energy Review, June 2019*

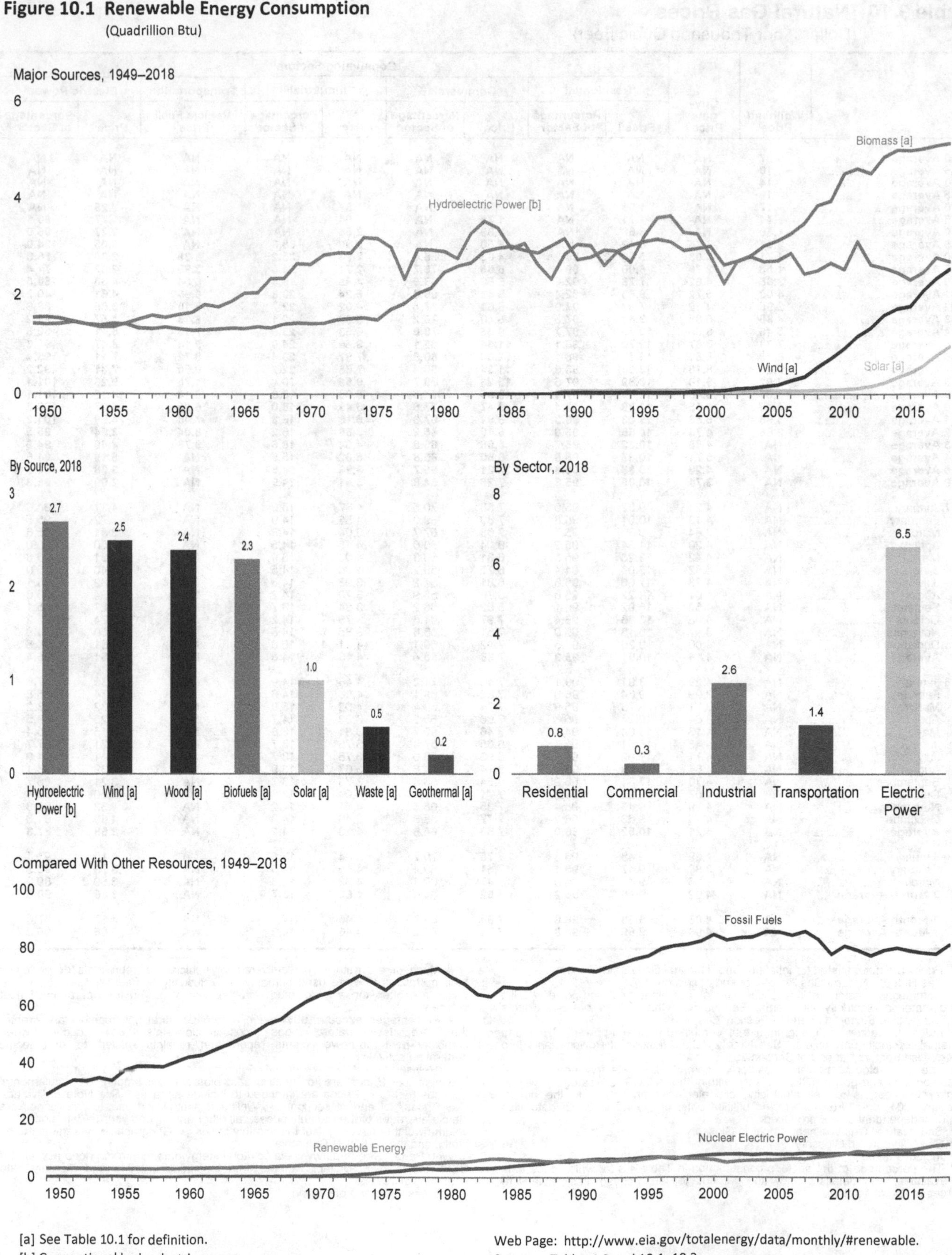

[a] See Table 10.1 for definition.
[b] Conventional hydroelectric power.

Web Page: http://www.eia.gov/totalenergy/data/monthly/#renewable.
Sources: Tables 1.3 and 10.1–10.2c.

Source: *U.S. Energy Information Administration, Monthly Energy Review, June 2019*

Table 10.1 Renewable Energy Production and Consumption by Source

(Trillion Btu)

	Production[a]			Consumption								
	Biomass		Total Renew-able Energy[d]	Hydro-electric Power[e]	Geo-thermal[f]	Solar[g]	Wind[h]	Biomass				Total Renew-able Energy
	Bio-fuels[b]	Total[c]						Wood[i]	Waste[j]	Bio-fuels[k]	Total	
1950 Total	NA	1,562	2,978	1,415	NA	NA	NA	1,562	NA	NA	1,562	2,978
1955 Total	NA	1,424	2,784	1,360	NA	NA	NA	1,424	NA	NA	1,424	2,784
1960 Total	NA	1,320	2,928	1,608	(s)	NA	NA	1,320	NA	NA	1,320	2,928
1965 Total	NA	1,335	3,396	2,059	2	NA	NA	1,335	NA	NA	1,335	3,396
1970 Total	NA	1,431	4,070	2,634	6	NA	NA	1,429	2	NA	1,431	4,070
1975 Total	NA	1,499	4,687	3,155	34	NA	NA	1,497	2	NA	1,499	4,687
1980 Total	NA	2,475	5,428	2,900	53	NA	NA	2,474	2	NA	2,475	5,428
1985 Total	93	3,016	6,084	2,970	97	(s)	(s)	2,687	236	93	3,016	6,084
1990 Total	111	2,735	6,040	3,046	171	59	29	2,216	408	111	2,735	6,040
1995 Total	198	3,099	6,557	3,205	152	68	33	2,370	531	200	3,101	6,559
2000 Total	233	3,006	6,102	2,811	164	63	57	2,262	511	236	3,008	6,104
2001 Total	254	2,624	5,162	2,242	164	62	70	2,006	364	253	2,622	5,160
2002 Total	308	2,705	5,731	2,689	171	60	105	1,995	402	303	2,701	5,726
2003 Total	401	2,805	5,942	2,793	173	58	113	2,002	401	403	2,806	5,944
2004 Total	486	2,996	6,063	2,688	178	58	142	2,121	389	498	3,008	6,075
2005 Total	561	3,101	6,221	2,703	181	58	178	2,137	403	574	3,114	6,234
2006 Total	716	3,212	6,586	2,869	181	61	264	2,099	397	766	3,262	6,637
2007 Total	970	3,472	6,510	2,446	186	66	341	2,089	413	983	3,485	6,523
2008 Total	1,374	3,868	7,192	2,511	192	74	546	2,059	435	1,357	3,851	7,175
2009 Total	1,570	3,957	7,625	2,669	200	78	721	1,935	452	1,553	3,940	7,608
2010 Total	1,868	4,553	8,314	2,539	208	91	923	2,217	468	1,821	4,506	8,267
2011 Total	2,029	4,704	9,300	3,103	212	112	1,168	2,213	462	1,934	4,609	9,204
2012 Total	1,929	4,547	8,886	2,629	212	159	1,340	2,151	467	1,890	4,508	8,847
2013 Total	1,981	4,816	9,418	2,562	214	225	1,601	2,338	496	2,014	4,848	9,451
2014 Total	2,103	5,020	9,766	2,467	214	337	1,728	2,401	516	2,077	4,994	9,740
2015 Total	2,161	4,992	9,729	2,321	212	427	1,777	2,312	518	2,153	4,983	9,720
2016 Total	2,275	5,081	10,428	2,472	210	570	2,096	2,230	503	2,287	5,020	10,368
2017 January	197	445	926	247	18	34	183	196	45	181	422	904
February	177	398	867	218	16	40	195	176	40	168	383	852
March	197	442	1,023	270	18	63	230	194	43	191	429	1,010
April	183	412	997	271	18	69	227	183	41	185	408	993
May	197	432	1,035	298	17	81	207	188	41	202	431	1,034
June	192	427	991	278	16	87	183	188	40	199	428	992
July	196	439	932	244	18	83	147	197	41	196	434	927
August	203	450	874	201	18	80	125	199	41	205	445	869
September	192	421	852	176	17	74	164	183	38	190	411	842
October	201	438	924	168	17	68	233	190	40	196	427	914
November	203	443	921	189	17	50	222	191	42	194	426	905
December	205	458	959	206	20	49	226	200	43	195	439	940
Total	**2,344**	**5,204**	**11,301**	**2,767**	**210**	**777**	**2,343**	**2,285**	**495**	**2,304**	**5,084**	**11,181**
2018 January	198	451	1,002	236	18	50	247	203	44	191	437	989
February	182	417	949	235	17	58	222	186	41	165	391	924
March	200	448	1,033	239	18	76	251	198	44	191	433	1,018
April	190	429	1,034	253	17	89	247	190	41	179	411	1,016
May	201	447	1,063	280	19	100	217	198	41	199	437	1,053
June	200	445	1,051	258	18	107	225	196	40	193	429	1,036
July	210	459	946	221	19	100	148	203	40	200	442	930
August	212	464	958	197	19	99	180	203	40	205	448	943
September	193	428	874	172	18	90	166	190	36	182	408	854
October	204	451	912	173	18	76	195	196	41	196	433	894
November	198	440	928	204	18	58	207	192	41	187	421	908
December	200	454	970	219	20	50	229	202	43	191	436	953
Total	**2,389**	**5,332**	**11,722**	**2,688**	**218**	**951**	**2,533**	**2,357**	**492**	**2,279**	**5,128**	**11,518**
2019 January	195	446	978	226	19	55	232	203	41	178	423	954
February	177	R405	R897	203	17	59	212	182	37	171	391	883
March	191	431	1,013	234	19	88	240	192	41	189	421	1,002
3-Month Total	**563**	**1,282**	**2,887**	**663**	**55**	**202**	**684**	**577**	**120**	**538**	**1,235**	**2,839**
2018 3-Month Total	**581**	**1,316**	**2,984**	**710**	**54**	**184**	**721**	**587**	**128**	**547**	**1,262**	**2,930**
2017 3-Month Total	**572**	**1,285**	**2,816**	**734**	**53**	**136**	**608**	**566**	**128**	**540**	**1,234**	**2,766**

[a] For hydroelectric power, geothermal, solar, wind, and biomass waste, production equals consumption. For biofuels, production equals total biomass inputs to the production of fuel ethanol and biodiesel. For wood, through 2015, production equals consumption; beginning in 2016, production equals consumption plus densified biomass exports.

[b] Total biomass inputs to the production of fuel ethanol and biodiesel.

[c] Wood and wood-derived fuels, biomass waste, and total biomass inputs to the production of fuel ethanol and biodiesel.

[d] Hydroelectric power, geothermal, solar, wind, and biomass.

[e] Conventional hydroelectricity net generation (converted to Btu by multiplying by the total fossil fuels heat rate factors in Table A6).

[f] Geothermal electricity net generation (converted to Btu by multiplying by the total fossil fuels heat rate factors in Table A6), and geothermal heat pump and direct use energy.

[g] Solar photovoltaic (PV) and solar thermal electricity net generation (converted to Btu by multiplying by the total fossil fuels heat rate factors in Table A6), and solar thermal direct use energy.

[h] Wind electricity net generation (converted to Btu by multiplying by the total fossil fuels heat rate factors in Table A6).

[i] Wood and wood-derived fuels.

[j] Municipal solid waste from biogenic sources, landfill gas, sludge waste, agricultural byproducts, and other biomass. Through 2000, also includes non-renewable waste (municipal solid waste from non-biogenic sources, and tire-derived fuels).

[k] Fuel ethanol (minus denaturant), biodiesel, other renewable diesel fuel, and other renewable fuels consumption; plus losses and co-products from the production of fuel ethanol and biodiesel.

R=Revised. NA=Not available. (s)=Less than 0.5 trillion Btu.

Notes: • Production data are estimates. Consumption data are estimates, except for hydroelectric power in 1949–1978 and 1989 forward, and wind. • See Note, "Renewable Energy Production and Consumption," at end of section. • Totals may not equal sum of components due to independent rounding. • Geographic coverage is the 50 states and the District of Columbia.

Web Page: See http://www.eia.gov/totalenergy/data/monthly/#renewable (Excel and CSV files) for all available annual data beginning in 1949 and monthly data beginning in 1973.

Sources: • **Production:** Tables 10.2a–10.4 and U.S. Energy Information Administration, Form EIA-63C, "Densified Biomass Fuel Report." • **Consumption:** Tables 10.2a–10.2c.

Source: *U.S. Energy Information Administration, Monthly Energy Review, June 2019*

Table 10.2a Renewable Energy Consumption: Residential and Commercial Sectors

(Trillion Btu)

	Residential Sector				Commercial Sector[a]								
			Biomass						Biomass				
	Geo-thermal[b]	Solar[c]	Wood[d]	Total	Hydro-electric Power[e]	Geo-thermal[f]	Solar[g]	Wind[h]	Wood[d]	Waste[i]	Fuel Ethanol[j,k]	Total	Total
1950 Total	NA	NA	1,006	1,006	NA	NA	NA	NA	19	NA	NA	19	19
1955 Total	NA	NA	775	775	NA	NA	NA	NA	15	NA	NA	15	15
1960 Total	NA	NA	627	627	NA	NA	NA	NA	12	NA	NA	12	12
1965 Total	NA	NA	468	468	NA	NA	NA	NA	9	NA	NA	9	9
1970 Total	NA	NA	401	401	NA	NA	NA	NA	8	NA	NA	8	8
1975 Total	NA	NA	425	425	NA	NA	NA	NA	8	NA	NA	8	8
1980 Total	NA	NA	850	850	NA	NA	NA	NA	21	NA	NA	21	21
1985 Total	NA	NA	1,010	1,010	NA	NA	NA	NA	24	NA	(s)	24	24
1990 Total	6	55	580	640	1	3	(s)	–	66	28	(s)	94	98
1995 Total	7	63	520	589	1	5	(s)	–	72	40	(s)	113	119
2000 Total	9	58	420	486	1	8	1	–	71	47	(s)	119	128
2001 Total	9	55	370	435	1	8	1	–	67	25	(s)	92	101
2002 Total	10	53	380	443	(s)	9	1	–	69	26	(s)	95	105
2003 Total	13	52	400	465	1	11	1	–	71	29	1	101	114
2004 Total	14	51	410	475	1	12	1	–	70	34	1	105	120
2005 Total	16	50	430	496	1	14	2	–	70	34	1	105	121
2006 Total	18	53	380	451	1	14	3	–	65	36	1	103	120
2007 Total	22	55	420	497	1	14	4	–	70	31	2	103	122
2008 Total	26	58	470	555	1	15	6	–	73	34	2	109	131
2009 Total	33	60	504	597	1	17	8	(s)	73	36	3	112	137
2010 Total	37	65	541	642	1	19	12	(s)	72	36	3	111	142
2011 Total	40	71	524	635	(s)	20	20	(s)	69	43	3	115	155
2012 Total	40	79	438	557	(s)	20	33	1	61	45	3	108	162
2013 Total	40	91	572	703	(s)	20	41	1	70	47	3	120	182
2014 Total	40	109	579	728	(s)	20	52	1	76	47	4	127	200
2015 Total	40	128	513	680	(s)	20	57	1	79	47	[j]26	152	230
2016 Total	40	161	448	649	2	20	62	1	84	48	26	158	242
2017 January	3	10	37	50	(s)	2	4	(s)	7	4	2	14	20
February	3	11	33	47	(s)	2	4	(s)	7	4	2	12	18
March	3	16	37	56	(s)	2	6	(s)	7	4	2	13	21
April	3	18	36	57	(s)	2	7	(s)	7	4	2	13	22
May	3	20	37	60	(s)	2	8	(s)	7	4	2	13	23
June	3	20	36	59	(s)	2	8	(s)	7	4	2	13	23
July	3	21	37	61	(s)	2	8	(s)	7	4	2	13	23
August	3	20	37	60	(s)	2	8	(s)	7	4	2	13	23
September	3	18	36	57	(s)	2	7	(s)	7	4	2	12	21
October	3	16	37	56	(s)	2	6	(s)	7	4	2	13	21
November	3	13	36	51	(s)	2	5	(s)	7	4	2	13	20
December	3	12	37	52	(s)	2	5	(s)	7	4	2	13	20
Total	40	193	433	666	2	20	76	1	84	48	25	156	255
2018 January	3	12	44	59	(s)	2	5	(s)	7	4	2	13	21
February	3	13	40	56	(s)	2	6	(s)	7	4	2	12	20
March	3	18	44	66	NM	2	8	(s)	7	4	2	13	23
April	3	21	43	67	(s)	2	9	(s)	7	4	2	12	23
May	3	23	44	70	NM	2	10	(s)	7	4	2	13	25
June	3	23	43	69	NM	2	10	(s)	7	4	2	13	25
July	3	24	44	71	NM	2	10	(s)	7	4	2	13	25
August	3	23	44	70	NM	2	10	(s)	7	4	2	13	25
September	3	20	43	66	(s)	2	9	(s)	7	3	2	12	23
October	3	18	44	65	NM	2	8	(s)	7	4	2	13	23
November	3	15	43	60	NM	2	6	(s)	7	4	2	13	21
December	3	13	44	61	(s)	2	6	(s)	7	4	2	13	21
Total	40	224	517	780	2	20	96	2	84	44	25	153	273
2019 January	3	14	45	62	NM	2	6	(s)	7	4	2	13	22
February	3	15	41	59	NM	2	7	(s)	7	3	2	12	21
March	3	22	45	70	NM	2	9	(s)	7	4	2	13	25
3-Month Total	10	51	131	191	1	6	22	(s)	21	11	6	38	67
2018 3-Month Total	10	44	128	181	1	5	19	(s)	21	11	6	38	63
2017 3-Month Total	10	37	107	153	1	5	15	(s)	21	12	6	39	59

[a] Commercial sector, including commercial combined-heat-and-power (CHP) and commercial electricity-only plants. See Note 2, "Classification of Power Plants Into Energy-Use Sectors," at end of Section 7.

[b] Geothermal heat pump and direct use energy.

[c] Distributed (small-scale) solar photovoltaic (PV) electricity generation in the residential sector (converted to Btu by multiplying by the total fossil fuels heat rate factors in Table A6) and distributed solar thermal energy in the residential, commercial, and industrial sectors. See Table 10.5.

[d] Wood and wood-derived fuels.

[e] Conventional hydroelectricity net generation (converted to Btu by multiplying by the total fossil fuels heat rate factors in Table A6).

[f] Geothermal heat pump and direct use energy. Beginning in December 2018, also includes geothermal electricity net generation (converted to Btu by multiplying by the total fossil fuels heat rate factors in Table A6).

[g] Solar photovoltaic (PV) electricity net generation in the commercial sector (converted to Btu by multiplying by the total fossil fuels heat rate factors in Table A6), both utility-scale and distributed (small-scale). See Table 10.5.

[h] Wind electricity net generation (converted to Btu by multiplying by the total fossil fuels heat rate factors in Table A6).

[i] Municipal solid waste from biogenic sources, landfill gas, sludge waste, agricultural byproducts, and other biomass. Through 2000, also includes non-renewable waste (municipal solid waste from non-biogenic sources, and tire-derived fuels).

[j] The fuel ethanol (minus denaturant) portion of motor fuels, such as E10, consumed by the commercial sector.

[k] There is a discontinuity in this time series between 2014 and 2015 due to a change in the method for allocating motor gasoline consumption to the end-use sectors. Beginning in 2015 the commercial and industrial sector shares of fuel ethanol consumption are larger than in 2014, while the transportation sector share is smaller.

NA=Not available. NM=Not meaningful. – =No data reported. (s)=Less than 0.5 trillion Btu.

Notes: • Residential sector data are estimates. Commercial sector data are estimates, except for hydroelectric power, wind, and biomass waste. • Totals may not equal sum of components due to independent rounding. • Geographic coverage is the 50 states and the District of Columbia.

Web Page: See http://www.eia.gov/totalenergy/data/monthly/#renewable (Excel and CSV files) for all available annual data beginning in 1949 and monthly data beginning in 1973.

Sources: See end of section.

Source: *U.S. Energy Information Administration, Monthly Energy Review, June 2019*

Table 10.2b Renewable Energy Consumption: Industrial and Transportation Sectors

(Trillion Btu)

	Industrial Sector[a]										Transportation Sector			
					Biomass						Biomass			
	Hydro-electric Power[b]	Geo-thermal[c]	Solar[d]	Wind[e]	Wood[f]	Waste[g]	Fuel Ethanol[h,i]	Losses and Co-products[j]	Total	Total	Fuel Ethanol[i,k]	Bio-diesel[l]	Other[m]	Total
1950 Total	69	NA	NA	NA	532	NA	NA	NA	532	602	NA	NA	NA	NA
1955 Total	38	NA	NA	NA	631	NA	NA	NA	631	669	NA	NA	NA	NA
1960 Total	39	NA	NA	NA	680	NA	NA	NA	680	719	NA	NA	NA	NA
1965 Total	33	NA	NA	NA	855	NA	NA	NA	855	888	NA	NA	NA	NA
1970 Total	34	NA	NA	NA	1,019	NA	NA	NA	1,019	1,053	NA	NA	NA	NA
1975 Total	32	NA	NA	NA	1,063	NA	NA	NA	1,063	1,096	NA	NA	NA	NA
1980 Total	33	NA	NA	NA	1,600	NA	NA	NA	1,600	1,633	NA	NA	NA	NA
1985 Total	33	NA	NA	NA	1,645	230	1	42	1,918	1,951	50	NA	NA	50
1990 Total	31	2	(s)	–	1,442	192	1	49	1,684	1,717	60	NA	NA	60
1995 Total	55	3	(s)	–	1,652	195	2	86	1,934	1,992	112	NA	NA	112
2000 Total	42	4	(s)	–	1,636	145	1	99	1,881	1,928	135	NA	NA	135
2001 Total	33	5	(s)	–	1,443	129	3	108	1,681	1,719	141	1	NA	142
2002 Total	39	5	(s)	–	1,396	146	3	130	1,676	1,720	168	2	NA	170
2003 Total	43	3	(s)	–	1,363	142	4	168	1,678	1,725	228	2	NA	230
2004 Total	33	4	(s)	–	1,476	132	6	201	1,815	1,852	286	3	NA	290
2005 Total	32	4	(s)	–	1,452	148	7	227	1,834	1,871	327	12	NA	339
2006 Total	29	4	1	–	1,472	130	10	280	1,892	1,926	442	33	NA	475
2007 Total	16	5	1	–	1,413	145	10	369	1,937	1,958	557	45	NA	602
2008 Total	17	5	1	–	1,339	143	12	519	2,012	2,035	786	39	NA	825
2009 Total	18	4	2	–	1,178	154	13	603	1,948	1,972	894	41	–	935
2010 Total	16	4	3	–	1,409	168	17	727	2,320	2,343	1,041	33	(s)	1,075
2011 Total	17	4	4	(s)	1,438	165	17	756	2,375	2,401	1,045	113	1	1,159
2012 Total	22	4	7	(s)	1,462	159	17	711	2,349	2,383	1,045	115	1	1,160
2013 Total	33	4	9	(s)	1,489	187	18	709	2,403	2,449	1,072	182	30	1,284
2014 Total	12	4	11	1	1,495	190	14	757	2,456	2,484	1,093	181	28	1,302
2015 Total	13	4	14	(s)	1,476	190	[i]18	776	2,460	2,491	[i]1,110	191	33	1,334
2016 Total	12	4	19	1	1,474	174	18	801	2,467	2,503	1,143	266	34	1,443
2017 January	1	(s)	1	(s)	132	15	1	71	220	222	91	13	3	107
February	1	(s)	1	(s)	118	14	1	63	196	199	84	14	3	101
March	1	(s)	2	(s)	129	15	2	70	216	220	96	19	3	118
April	1	(s)	2	(s)	123	14	1	64	203	207	94	21	3	117
May	1	(s)	2	(s)	127	14	2	69	211	215	100	25	3	129
June	1	(s)	2	(s)	128	12	2	67	208	212	100	25	4	129
July	1	(s)	2	(s)	133	13	2	68	216	219	99	24	2	125
August	1	(s)	2	(s)	134	13	2	71	220	223	103	26	2	131
September	1	(s)	2	(s)	123	13	2	67	204	207	96	22	2	120
October	1	(s)	2	(s)	128	14	2	70	214	217	99	22	2	123
November	1	(s)	1	(s)	129	15	2	71	216	219	97	21	1	120
December	1	(s)	1	(s)	135	15	2	71	223	226	97	21	2	120
Total	**13**	**4**	**22**	**1**	**1,539**	**168**	**18**	**821**	**2,547**	**2,587**	**1,156**	**253**	**30**	**1,439**
2018 January	1	(s)	1	(s)	131	15	2	70	218	221	98	18	2	117
February	1	(s)	1	(s)	122	14	1	63	200	203	81	14	3	98
March	1	(s)	2	(s)	128	15	2	69	214	218	96	20	3	119
April	1	(s)	2	(s)	126	14	1	66	208	211	88	20	2	110
May	1	(s)	3	(s)	128	14	2	69	213	217	103	21	2	126
June	1	(s)	3	(s)	127	12	2	69	210	214	98	22	1	121
July	1	(s)	3	(s)	132	13	2	72	219	223	101	22	1	124
August	1	(s)	3	(s)	134	13	2	73	221	225	104	23	1	128
September	1	(s)	2	(s)	124	13	1	66	204	207	91	21	1	113
October	1	(s)	2	(s)	128	15	2	70	214	218	99	22	1	122
November	1	(s)	2	(s)	127	14	2	68	211	214	94	19	2	116
December	1	(s)	2	(s)	133	15	2	68	218	221	97	21	2	119
Total	**13**	**4**	**25**	**1**	**1,540**	**168**	**18**	**823**	**2,549**	**2,593**	**1,150**	**242**	**21**	**1,413**
2019 January	1	(s)	2	(s)	131	15	1	67	214	217	90	16	2	108
February	1	(s)	2	(s)	118	14	1	61	194	197	89	17	2	107
March	1	(s)	2	(s)	123	14	2	66	204	208	97	20	2	119
3-Month Total	**2**	**1**	**6**	**(s)**	**371**	**43**	**4**	**194**	**612**	**622**	**276**	**53**	**5**	**334**
2018 3-Month Total	**3**	**1**	**5**	**(s)**	**382**	**44**	**4**	**202**	**632**	**642**	**275**	**52**	**7**	**334**
2017 3-Month Total	**3**	**1**	**4**	**(s)**	**379**	**44**	**4**	**204**	**632**	**641**	**271**	**46**	**8**	**325**

[a] Industrial sector, including industrial combined-heat-and-power (CHP) and industrial electricity-only plants. See Note 2, "Classification of Power Plants Into Energy-Use Sectors," at end of Section 7.

[b] Conventional hydroelectricity net generation (converted to Btu by multiplying by the total fossil fuels heat rate factors in Table A6).

[c] Geothermal heat pump and direct use energy.

[d] Solar photovoltaic (PV) electricity net generation in the industrial sector (converted to Btu by multiplying by the total fossil fuels heat rate factors in Table A6), both utility-scale and distributed (small-scale). See Table 10.5.

[e] Wind electricity net generation (converted to Btu by multiplying by the total fossil fuels heat rate factors in Table A6).

[f] Wood and wood-derived fuels.

[g] Municipal solid waste from biogenic sources, landfill gas, sludge waste, agricultural byproducts, and other biomass. Through 2000, also includes non-renewable waste (municipal solid waste from non-biogenic sources, and tire-derived fuels).

[h] The fuel ethanol (minus denaturant) portion of motor fuels, such as E10, consumed by the industrial sector.

[i] There is a discontinuity in this time series between 2014 and 2015 due to a change in the method for allocating motor gasoline consumption to the end-use sectors. Beginning in 2015, the commercial and industrial sector shares of fuel ethanol consumption are larger than in 2014, while the transportation sector share is smaller.

[j] Losses and co-products from the production of fuel ethanol and biodiesel. Does not include natural gas, electricity, and other non-biomass energy used in the production of fuel ethanol and biodiesel—these are included in the industrial sector consumption statistics for the appropriate energy source.

[k] The fuel ethanol (minus denaturant) portion of motor fuels, such as E10 and E85, consumed by the transportation sector.

[l] Although there is biodiesel use in other sectors, all biodiesel consumption is assigned to the transportation sector.

[m] Other renewable diesel fuel and other renewable fuels consumption. See "Renewable Diesel Fuel (Other)" and "Renewable Fuels (Other)" in Glossary.

NA=Not available. – =No data reported. (s)=Less than 0.5 trillion Btu.

Notes: • Industrial sector data are estimates, except for hydroelectric power in 1949–1978 and 1989 forward, and wind. Transportation sector data are estimates, except for biodiesel beginning in 2012. • Totals may not equal sum of components due to independent rounding. • Geographic coverage is the 50 states and the District of Columbia.

Web Page: See http://www.eia.gov/totalenergy/data/monthly/#renewable (Excel and CSV files) for all available annual data beginning in 1949 and monthly data beginning in 1973.

Sources: See end of section.

Source: *U.S. Energy Information Administration, Monthly Energy Review, June 2019*

Table 10.2c Renewable Energy Consumption: Electric Power Sector

(Trillion Btu)

	Hydro-electric Power[a]	Geo-thermal[b]	Solar[c]	Wind[d]	Biomass			Total
					Wood[e]	Waste[f]	Total	
1950 Total	1,346	NA	NA	NA	5	NA	5	1,351
1955 Total	1,322	NA	NA	NA	3	NA	3	1,325
1960 Total	1,569	(s)	NA	NA	2	NA	2	1,571
1965 Total	2,026	2	NA	NA	3	NA	3	2,031
1970 Total	2,600	6	NA	NA	1	2	4	2,609
1975 Total	3,122	34	NA	NA	(s)	2	2	3,158
1980 Total	2,867	53	NA	NA	3	2	4	2,925
1985 Total	2,937	97	(s)	(s)	8	7	14	3,049
1990 Total[g]	3,014	161	4	29	129	188	317	3,524
1995 Total	3,149	138	5	33	125	296	422	3,747
2000 Total	2,768	144	5	57	134	318	453	3,427
2001 Total	2,209	142	6	70	126	211	337	2,763
2002 Total	2,650	147	6	105	150	230	380	3,288
2003 Total	2,749	146	5	113	167	230	397	3,411
2004 Total	2,655	148	6	142	165	223	388	3,339
2005 Total	2,670	147	6	178	185	221	406	3,406
2006 Total	2,839	145	5	264	182	231	412	3,665
2007 Total	2,430	145	6	341	186	237	423	3,345
2008 Total	2,494	146	9	546	177	258	435	3,630
2009 Total	2,650	146	9	721	180	261	441	3,967
2010 Total	2,521	148	12	923	196	264	459	4,064
2011 Total	3,085	149	17	1,167	182	255	437	4,855
2012 Total	2,606	148	40	1,339	190	262	453	4,586
2013 Total	2,529	151	83	1,600	207	262	470	4,833
2014 Total	2,454	151	165	1,726	251	279	530	5,026
2015 Total	2,308	148	228	1,776	244	281	525	4,985
2016 Total	2,459	146	328	2,094	224	281	505	5,531
2017 January	245	13	19	183	20	26	46	505
February	217	11	23	195	18	22	41	487
March	268	13	39	230	21	24	45	595
April	269	12	43	227	17	22	39	590
May	297	12	52	207	17	24	40	607
June	277	11	56	182	18	24	42	569
July	243	12	52	147	20	24	44	498
August	200	12	50	125	21	23	45	432
September	175	12	47	164	18	22	40	438
October	167	11	44	233	18	22	40	496
November	188	12	31	222	19	23	42	495
December	205	14	31	226	21	24	45	522
Total	2,752	147	486	2,341	229	280	510	6,235
2018 January	235	13	31	247	20	25	45	571
February	234	12	38	222	18	23	41	547
March	238	13	47	251	19	25	44	593
April	252	11	57	246	15	23	38	605
May	279	13	64	217	18	23	42	615
June	256	13	71	224	19	24	43	607
July	220	13	63	147	20	23	43	487
August	196	13	64	180	19	24	42	495
September	171	13	59	165	17	21	37	445
October	172	12	48	195	17	23	40	466
November	203	13	36	207	16	23	39	498
December	217	14	29	228	18	24	41	530
Total	2,673	154	607	2,530	215	280	495	6,459
2019 January	225	13	33	232	20	23	43	546
February	202	12	36	212	17	20	37	499
March	233	13	55	240	17	23	39	580
3-Month Total	660	38	124	683	54	66	120	1,625
2018 3-Month Total	706	38	116	720	57	73	130	1,711
2017 3-Month Total	730	37	81	608	60	72	132	1,587

[a] Conventional hydroelectricity net generation (converted to Btu by multiplying by the total fossil fuels heat rate factors in Table A6).

[b] Geothermal electricity net generation (converted to Btu by multiplying by the total fossil fuels heat rate factors in Table A6).

[c] Solar photovoltaic (PV) and solar thermal electricity net generation in the electric power sector (converted to Btu by multiplying by the total fossil fuels heat rate factors in Table A6). See Table 10.5.

[d] Wind electricity net generation (converted to Btu by multiplying by the total fossil fuels heat rate factors in Table A6).

[e] Wood and wood-derived fuels.

[f] Municipal solid waste from biogenic sources, landfill gas, sludge waste, agricultural byproducts, and other biomass. Through 2000, also includes non-renewable waste (municipal solid waste from non-biogenic sources, and tire-derived fuels).

[g] Through 1988, data are for electric utilities only. Beginning in 1989, data are for electric utilities and independent power producers.

NA=Not available. (s)=Less than 0.5 trillion Btu.

Notes: • The electric power sector comprises electricity-only and combined-heat-and-power (CHP) plants within the NAICS 22 category whose primary business is to sell electricity, or electricity and heat, to the public. • Totals may not equal sum of components due to independent rounding. • Geographic coverage is the 50 states and the District of Columbia.

Web Page: See http://www.eia.gov/totalenergy/data/monthly/#renewable (Excel and CSV files) for all available annual data beginning in 1949 and monthly data beginning in 1973.

Sources: Tables 7.2b, 7.4b, and A6.

Source: U.S. Energy Information Administration, Monthly Energy Review, June 2019

Table 10.3 Fuel Ethanol Overview

	Feed-stock[a]	Losses and Co-products[b]	Dena-turant[c]	Production[d]			Trade[d] Net Imports[e]	Stocks[d,f]	Stock Change[d,g]	Consumption[d]			Consump-tion Minus Denaturant[h]
	TBtu	TBtu	Mbbl	Mbbl	MMgal	TBtu	Mbbl	Mbbl	Mbbl	Mbbl	MMgal	TBtu	*TBtu*
1981 Total	**13**	**6**	**40**	**1,978**	**83**	**7**	**NA**	**NA**	**NA**	**1,978**	**83**	**7**	***7***
1985 Total	**93**	**42**	**294**	**14,693**	**617**	**52**	**NA**	**NA**	**NA**	**14,693**	**617**	**52**	***51***
1990 Total	**111**	**49**	**356**	**17,802**	**748**	**63**	**NA**	**NA**	**NA**	**17,802**	**748**	**63**	***62***
1995 Total	**198**	**86**	**647**	**32,325**	**1,358**	**115**	**387**	**2,186**	**-207**	**32,919**	**1,383**	**117**	***114***
2000 Total	**233**	**99**	**773**	**38,627**	**1,622**	**138**	**116**	**3,400**	**-624**	**39,367**	**1,653**	**140**	***137***
2001 Total	**253**	**108**	**841**	**42,028**	**1,765**	**150**	**315**	**4,298**	**898**	**41,445**	**1,741**	**148**	***144***
2002 Total	**307**	**130**	**1,019**	**50,956**	**2,140**	**182**	**306**	**6,200**	**1,902**	**49,360**	**2,073**	**176**	***171***
2003 Total	**400**	**168**	**1,335**	**66,772**	**2,804**	**238**	**292**	**5,978**	**-222**	**67,286**	**2,826**	**240**	***233***
2004 Total	**482**	**201**	**1,621**	**81,058**	**3,404**	**289**	**3,542**	**6,002**	**24**	**84,576**	**3,552**	**301**	***293***
2005 Total	**550**	**227**	**1,859**	**92,961**	**3,904**	**331**	**3,234**	**5,563**	**-439**	**96,634**	**4,059**	**344**	***335***
2006 Total	**683**	**280**	**2,326**	**116,294**	**4,884**	**414**	**17,408**	**8,760**	**3,197**	**130,505**	**5,481**	**465**	***453***
2007 Total	**907**	**368**	**3,105**	**155,263**	**6,521**	**553**	**10,457**	**10,535**	**1,775**	**163,945**	**6,886**	**584**	***569***
2008 Total	**1,286**	**518**	**4,433**	**221,637**	**9,309**	**790**	**12,610**	**14,226**	**3,691**	**230,556**	**9,683**	**821**	***800***
2009 Total	**1,503**	**602**	**5,688**	**260,424**	**10,938**	**928**	**4,720**	**16,594**	**2,368**	**262,776**	**11,037**	**936**	***910***
2010 Total	**1,823**	**726**	**6,506**	**316,617**	**13,298**	**1,127**	**-9,115**	**17,941**	**1,347**	**306,155**	**12,858**	**1,090**	***1,061***
2011 Total	**1,904**	**754**	**6,649**	**331,646**	**13,929**	**1,181**	**-24,365**	**18,238**	**297**	**306,984**	**12,893**	**1,093**	***1,065***
2012 Total	**1,801**	**709**	**6,264**	**314,714**	**13,218**	**1,120**	**-5,891**	**20,350**	**2,112**	**306,711**	**12,882**	**1,092**	***1,064***
2013 Total	**1,805**	**707**	**6,181**	**316,493**	**13,293**	**1,126**	**-5,761**	**16,424**	**-3,926**	**314,658**	**13,216**	**1,120**	***1,092***
2014 Total	**1,938**	**755**	**6,476**	**340,781**	**14,313**	**1,212**	**-18,371**	**18,739**	**2,315**	**320,095**	**13,444**	**1,139**	***1,111***
2015 Total	**1,998**	**774**	**6,636**	**352,553**	**14,807**	**1,254**	**-17,632**	**21,596**	**2,857**	**332,064**	**13,947**	**1,181**	***1,153***
2016 Total	**2,072**	**798**	**6,920**	**366,981**	**15,413**	**1,306**	**-27,002**	**19,758**	**-1,838**	**341,817**	**14,356**	**1,216**	***1,187***
2017 January	185	71	600	32,887	1,381	117	-2,844	22,679	2,921	27,122	1,139	96	*94*
February	165	63	545	29,307	1,231	104	-3,605	23,195	516	25,186	1,058	90	*87*
March	182	70	603	32,393	1,361	115	-3,023	23,981	786	28,584	1,201	102	*99*
April	167	64	545	29,639	1,245	105	-1,918	23,671	-310	28,031	1,177	100	*97*
May	180	69	562	31,863	1,338	113	-2,831	22,855	-816	29,848	1,254	106	*104*
June	173	66	543	30,794	1,293	110	-2,045	21,770	-1,085	29,834	1,253	106	*104*
July	177	68	559	31,384	1,318	112	-2,553	21,167	-603	29,434	1,236	105	*102*
August	184	70	577	32,672	1,372	116	-2,029	21,186	19	30,624	1,286	109	*106*
September	173	66	535	30,701	1,289	109	-1,757	21,507	321	28,623	1,202	102	*100*
October	182	70	536	32,212	1,353	115	-2,419	21,663	156	29,637	1,245	105	*103*
November	184	71	523	32,631	1,371	116	-2,069	23,203	1,540	29,022	1,219	103	*101*
December	186	71	529	32,952	1,384	117	-4,175	23,043	-160	28,937	1,215	103	*101*
Total	**2,138**	**819**	**6,657**	**379,435**	**15,936**	**1,349**	**-31,268**	**23,043**	**3,285**	**344,882**	**14,485**	**1,226**	***1,199***
2018 January	182	69	504	32,428	1,362	115	-2,104	24,229	[i]1,181	29,143	1,224	104	*102*
February	166	63	441	29,519	1,240	105	-5,298	24,335	106	24,115	1,013	86	*84*
March	181	69	484	32,216	1,353	114	-5,122	22,883	-1,452	28,546	1,199	101	*100*
April	172	65	462	30,532	1,282	108	-3,866	23,256	373	26,293	1,104	93	*92*
May	181	69	487	32,215	1,353	114	-2,280	22,636	-620	30,555	1,283	109	*106*
June	180	68	473	31,924	1,341	113	-3,609	21,880	-756	29,071	1,221	103	*101*
July	188	72	519	33,496	1,407	119	-2,487	22,802	922	30,087	1,264	107	*105*
August	190	72	527	33,773	1,418	120	-2,638	22,833	31	31,104	1,306	111	*108*
September	173	66	471	30,667	1,288	109	-2,106	24,422	1,589	26,972	1,133	96	*94*
October	182	69	450	32,380	1,360	115	-3,714	23,675	-747	29,413	1,235	105	*103*
November	177	68	470	31,514	1,324	112	-3,384	23,679	4	28,126	1,181	100	*98*
December	178	68	518	31,736	1,333	113	-3,075	23,338	-341	29,002	1,218	103	*101*
Total	**2,152**	**819**	**5,806**	**382,400**	**16,061**	**1,359**	**-39,682**	**23,338**	**[i]290**	**342,428**	**14,382**	**1,217**	***1,193***
2019 January	177	67	548	31,601	1,327	112	-3,048	25,026	1,688	26,866	1,128	95	*93*
February	160	61	499	28,576	1,200	102	-2,715	24,448	-578	26,439	1,110	94	*92*
March	173	65	504	30,895	1,298	110	-3,084	23,311	-1,137	28,948	1,216	103	*101*
3-Month Total	**510**	**193**	**1,551**	**91,072**	**3,825**	**324**	**-8,847**	**23,311**	**-27**	**82,252**	**3,455**	**292**	***286***
2018 3-Month Total	**530**	**202**	**1,429**	**94,163**	**3,955**	**335**	**-12,523**	**22,883**	**-165**	**81,805**	**3,436**	**291**	***285***
2017 3-Month Total	**532**	**204**	**1,748**	**94,587**	**3,973**	**336**	**-9,472**	**23,981**	**4,223**	**80,892**	**3,397**	**288**	***281***

[a] Total corn and other biomass inputs to the production of undenatured ethanol used for fuel ethanol.

[b] Losses and co-products from the production of fuel ethanol. Does not include natural gas, electricity, and other non-biomass energy used in the production of fuel ethanol—these are included in the industrial sector consumption statistics for the appropriate energy source.

[c] The amount of denaturant in fuel ethanol produced.

[d] Includes denaturant.

[e] Through 2009, data are for fuel ethanol imports only; data for fuel ethanol exports are not available. Beginning in 2010, data are for fuel ethanol imports minus fuel ethanol (including industrial alcohol) exports.

[f] Stocks are at end of period.

[g] A negative value indicates a decrease in stocks and a positive value indicates an increase.

[h] Consumption of fuel ethanol minus denaturant. Data for fuel ethanol minus denaturant are used to develop data for "Renewable Energy/Biomass" in Tables 10.1–10.2b, as well as in Sections 1 and 2.

[i] Derived from the preliminary 2017 stocks value (23,048 thousand barrels), not the final 2017 value (23,043 thousand barrels) that is shown under "Stocks."

NA=Not available.

Notes: • Mbbl = thousand barrels. MMgal = million U.S. gallons. TBtu = trillion Btu. • Fuel ethanol data in thousand barrels are converted to million gallons by multiplying by 0.042, and are converted to Btu by multiplying by the approximate heat content of fuel ethanol—see Table A3. • Through 1980, data are not available. For 1981–1992, data are estimates. For 1993–2008, only data for feedstock, losses and co-products, and denaturant are estimates. Beginning in 2009, only data for feedstock, and losses and co-products, are estimates. • See "Denaturant," "Ethanol," "Fuel Ethanol," and "Fuel Ethanol Minus Denaturant" in Glossary. • Totals may not equal sum of components due to independent rounding. • Geographic coverage is the 50 states and the District of Columbia.

Web Page: See http://www.eia.gov/totalenergy/data/monthly/#renewable (Excel and CSV files) for all available annual and monthly data beginning in 1981.

Sources: See end of section.

Source: *U.S. Energy Information Administration, Monthly Energy Review, June 2019*

Table 10.4 Biodiesel and Other Renewable Fuels Overview

	Biodiesel													Other Renewable Fuels[f]
	Feedstock[a]	Losses and Coproducts[b]	Production			Trade			Stocks[d]	Stock Change[e]	Consumption			
						Imports	Exports	Net Imports[c]						
	TBtu	TBtu	Mbbl	MMgal	TBtu	Mbbl	Mbbl	Mbbl	Mbbl	Mbbl	Mbbl	MMgal	TBtu	TBtu
2001 Total	**1**	**(s)**	**204**	**9**	**1**	**81**	**41**	**40**	**NA**	**NA**	**244**	**10**	**1**	**NA**
2002 Total	**1**	**(s)**	**250**	**10**	**1**	**197**	**57**	**140**	**NA**	**NA**	**390**	**16**	**2**	**NA**
2003 Total	**2**	**(s)**	**338**	**14**	**2**	**97**	**113**	**-17**	**NA**	**NA**	**322**	**14**	**2**	**NA**
2004 Total	**4**	**(s)**	**666**	**28**	**4**	**101**	**128**	**-27**	**NA**	**NA**	**639**	**27**	**3**	**NA**
2005 Total	**12**	**(s)**	**2,162**	**91**	**12**	**214**	**213**	**1**	**NA**	**NA**	**2,163**	**91**	**12**	**NA**
2006 Total	**32**	**(s)**	**5,963**	**250**	**32**	**1,105**	**856**	**250**	**NA**	**NA**	**6,213**	**261**	**33**	**NA**
2007 Total	**63**	**1**	**11,662**	**490**	**62**	**3,455**	**6,696**	**-3,241**	**NA**	**NA**	**8,422**	**354**	**45**	**NA**
2008 Total	**88**	**1**	**16,145**	**678**	**87**	**7,755**	**16,673**	**-8,918**	**NA**	**NA**	**7,228**	**304**	**39**	**NA**
2009 Total	**67**	**1**	**12,281**	**516**	**66**	**1,906**	**6,546**	**-4,640**	**711**	**711**	**[g]7,663**	**322**	**41**	**–**
2010 Total	**44**	**1**	**8,177**	**343**	**44**	**564**	**2,588**	**-2,024**	**672**	**-39**	**6,192**	**260**	**33**	**(s)**
2011 Total	**125**	**2**	**23,035**	**967**	**123**	**890**	**1,799**	**-908**	**2,005**	**[h]1,028**	**21,099**	**886**	**113**	**1**
2012 Total	**128**	**2**	**23,588**	**991**	**126**	**853**	**3,056**	**-2,203**	**1,984**	**-20**	**21,406**	**899**	**115**	**1**
2013 Total	**176**	**2**	**32,368**	**1,359**	**173**	**8,152**	**4,675**	**3,477**	**3,810**	**1,825**	**34,020**	**1,429**	**182**	**30**
2014 Total	**165**	**2**	**30,452**	**1,279**	**163**	**4,578**	**1,974**	**2,604**	**3,131**	**-679**	**33,735**	**1,417**	**181**	**28**
2015 Total	**163**	**2**	**30,080**	**1,263**	**161**	**8,399**	**2,091**	**6,308**	**3,943**	**813**	**35,575**	**1,494**	**191**	**33**
2016 Total	**203**	**3**	**37,327**	**1,568**	**200**	**16,879**	**2,098**	**14,781**	**6,398**	**2,455**	**49,653**	**2,085**	**266**	**34**
2017 January	12	(s)	2,208	93	12	241	42	199	6,397	(s)	2,407	101	13	3
February	12	(s)	2,238	94	12	549	59	490	6,475	78	2,650	111	14	3
March	15	(s)	2,761	116	15	650	136	514	6,189	-286	3,561	150	19	3
April	16	(s)	3,020	127	16	681	283	398	5,706	-484	3,901	164	21	3
May	18	(s)	3,242	136	17	948	239	709	4,909	-797	4,748	199	25	3
June	18	(s)	3,344	140	18	1,736	226	1,510	5,052	144	4,711	198	25	4
July	19	(s)	3,560	150	19	1,670	453	1,217	5,405	353	4,424	186	24	2
August	19	(s)	3,559	149	19	1,582	387	1,195	5,356	-49	4,803	202	26	2
September	19	(s)	3,507	147	19	205	100	105	4,849	-507	4,119	173	22	2
October	19	(s)	3,515	148	19	386	217	169	4,485	-364	4,047	170	22	2
November	19	(s)	3,523	148	19	222	49	173	4,233	-252	3,948	166	21	1
December	19	(s)	3,515	148	19	504	35	469	4,268	35	3,949	166	21	2
Total	**206**	**3**	**37,993**	**1,596**	**204**	**9,374**	**2,228**	**7,146**	**4,268**	**-2,130**	**47,269**	**1,985**	**253**	**30**
2018 January	16	(s)	2,945	124	16	246	102	144	4,557	[i]-193	3,282	138	18	2
February	16	(s)	2,996	126	16	146	103	43	4,924	367	2,672	112	14	3
March	19	(s)	3,493	147	19	457	255	202	4,916	-8	3,702	155	20	3
April	18	(s)	3,344	140	18	308	217	91	4,681	-235	3,670	154	20	2
May	19	(s)	3,538	149	19	325	382	-57	4,257	-424	3,905	164	21	2
June	20	(s)	3,718	156	20	296	275	21	3,845	-412	4,150	174	22	1
July	21	(s)	3,892	163	21	157	259	-102	3,583	-262	4,052	170	22	1
August	22	(s)	4,028	169	22	281	263	18	3,412	-172	4,217	177	23	1
September	21	(s)	3,850	162	21	277	190	87	3,360	-52	3,989	168	21	1
October	22	(s)	4,039	170	22	468	188	280	3,647	287	4,032	169	22	1
November	21	(s)	3,783	159	20	416	156	260	4,056	409	3,633	153	19	2
December	22	(s)	3,991	168	21	536	61	475	4,684	628	3,838	161	21	2
Total	**237**	**3**	**43,616**	**1,832**	**234**	**3,913**	**2,453**	**1,460**	**4,684**	**[i]-65**	**45,141**	**1,896**	**242**	**21**
2019 January	19	(s)	3,427	144	18	308	72	236	5,377	692	2,971	125	16	2
February	17	(s)	3,108	131	17	267	92	175	5,509	133	3,150	132	17	2
March	18	(s)	3,353	141	18	509	240	269	5,371	-138	3,760	158	20	2
3-Month Total	**54**	**1**	**9,888**	**415**	**53**	**1,084**	**404**	**680**	**5,371**	**687**	**9,881**	**415**	**53**	**5**
2018 3-Month Total	**51**	**1**	**9,434**	**396**	**51**	**849**	**460**	**389**	**4,916**	**166**	**9,656**	**406**	**52**	**7**
2017 3-Month Total	**39**	**1**	**7,207**	**303**	**39**	**1,440**	**238**	**1,202**	**6,189**	**-208**	**8,618**	**362**	**46**	**8**

[a] Total vegetable oil and other biomass inputs to the production of biodiesel—calculated by multiplying biodiesel production by 5.433 million Btu per barrel. See "Biodiesel Feedstock" entry in the "Thermal Conversion Factor Source Documentation" at the end of Appendix A.

[b] Losses and co-products from the production of biodiesel. Does not include natural gas, electricity, and other non-biomass energy used in the production of biodiesel—these are included in the industrial sector consumption statistics for the appropriate energy source.

[c] Net imports equal imports minus exports.

[d] Stocks are at end of period. Includes biodiesel stocks at (or in) refineries, pipelines, and bulk terminals. Beginning in 2011, also includes stocks at biodiesel production plants.

[e] A negative value indicates a decrease in stocks and a positive value indicates an increase.

[f] Other renewable diesel fuel and other renewable fuels consumption. See "Renewable Diesel Fuel (Other)" and "Renewable Fuels (Other)" in Glossary.

[g] In 2009, because of incomplete data coverage and differing data sources, a "Balancing Item" amount of 733 thousand barrels (653 thousand barrels in January 2009; 80 thousand barrels in February 2009) is used to balance biodiesel supply and disposition.

[h] Derived from the final 2010 stocks value for bulk terminals and biodiesel production plants (977 thousand barrels), not the final 2010 value for bulk terminals only (672 thousand barrels) that is shown under "Stocks."

[i] Derived from the preliminary 2017 stocks value (4,750 thousand barrels), not the final 2017 value (4,268 thousand barrels) that is shown under "Stocks."

NA=Not available. – =No data reported. (s)=Less than 0.5 trillion Btu and greater than -0.5 trillion Btu, or less than 500 barrels and greater than -500 barrels.

Notes: • Mbbl = thousand barrels. MMgal = million U.S. gallons. TBtu = trillion Btu. • Biodiesel data in thousand barrels are converted to million gallons by multiplying by 0.042, and are converted to Btu by multiplying by 5.359 million Btu per barrel (the approximate heat content of biodiesel—see Table A1). • Through 2000, data are not available. Beginning in 2001, data not from U.S. Energy Information Administration (EIA) surveys are estimates. • Totals may not equal sum of components due to independent rounding. • Geographic coverage is the 50 states and the District of Columbia.

Web Page: See http://www.eia.gov/totalenergy/data/monthly/#renewable (Excel and CSV files) for all available annual and monthly data beginning in 2001.

Sources: See end of section.

Source: *U.S. Energy Information Administration, Monthly Energy Review, June 2019*

Table 10.5 Solar Energy Consumption

(Trillion Btu)

	Distributed[a] Solar Energy[b]						Utility-Scale[c] Solar Energy[b]				
		Electricity[d]					Electricity[e]				
	Heat[f]	Residential Sector	Commercial Sector	Industrial Sector	Total	Total[g]	Commercial Sector[h]	Industrial Sector[i]	Electric Power Sector[j]	Total	Total[k]
1985 Total	**NA**	**NA**	**NA**	**NA**	**NA**	**NA**	**NA**	**NA**	**(s)**	**(s)**	**(s)**
1990 Total	**55**	**(s)**	**(s)**	**(s)**	**(s)**	**55**	**–**	**–**	**4**	**4**	**59**
1995 Total	**63**	**(s)**	**(s)**	**(s)**	**1**	**63**	**–**	**–**	**5**	**5**	**68**
2000 Total	**57**	**(s)**	**1**	**(s)**	**1**	**58**	**–**	**–**	**5**	**5**	**63**
2001 Total	**55**	**(s)**	**1**	**(s)**	**1**	**56**	**–**	**–**	**6**	**6**	**62**
2002 Total	**53**	**1**	**1**	**(s)**	**2**	**54**	**–**	**–**	**6**	**6**	**60**
2003 Total	**51**	**1**	**1**	**(s)**	**2**	**53**	**–**	**–**	**5**	**5**	**58**
2004 Total	**50**	**1**	**1**	**(s)**	**2**	**53**	**–**	**–**	**6**	**6**	**58**
2005 Total	**49**	**1**	**2**	**(s)**	**3**	**52**	**–**	**–**	**6**	**6**	**58**
2006 Total	**51**	**2**	**3**	**1**	**5**	**56**	**–**	**–**	**5**	**5**	**61**
2007 Total	**53**	**2**	**4**	**1**	**7**	**60**	**–**	**–**	**6**	**6**	**66**
2008 Total	**54**	**4**	**6**	**1**	**11**	**66**	**(s)**	**–**	**9**	**9**	**74**
2009 Total	**55**	**5**	**8**	**2**	**15**	**69**	**(s)**	**–**	**9**	**9**	**78**
2010 Total	**56**	**9**	**12**	**3**	**24**	**79**	**(s)**	**(s)**	**12**	**12**	**91**
2011 Total	**58**	**13**	**20**	**4**	**37**	**95**	**1**	**(s)**	**17**	**18**	**112**
2012 Total	**59**	**20**	**32**	**7**	**59**	**118**	**1**	**(s)**	**40**	**41**	**159**
2013 Total	**61**	**31**	**38**	**9**	**78**	**138**	**3**	**(s)**	**83**	**86**	**225**
2014 Total	**62**	**47**	**49**	**11**	**107**	**169**	**4**	**(s)**	**165**	**168**	**337**
2015 Total	**63**	**65**	**53**	**14**	**132**	**195**	**4**	**(s)**	**228**	**232**	**427**
2016 Total	**63**	**98**	**57**	**19**	**174**	**237**	**5**	**(s)**	**328**	**333**	**570**
2017 January	3	6	4	1	11	15	(s)	(s)	19	19	34
February	4	7	4	1	13	16	(s)	(s)	23	24	40
March	5	11	6	2	18	24	(s)	(s)	39	39	63
April	6	12	6	2	20	26	(s)	(s)	43	43	69
May	7	13	7	2	22	29	(s)	(s)	52	52	81
June	7	14	7	2	23	30	1	(s)	56	57	87
July	7	14	7	2	24	30	1	(s)	52	53	83
August	7	13	7	2	23	30	1	(s)	50	50	80
September	6	12	7	2	21	27	(s)	(s)	47	47	74
October	5	11	6	2	18	24	(s)	(s)	44	44	68
November	4	8	5	1	14	19	(s)	(s)	31	31	50
December	4	8	5	1	14	18	(s)	(s)	31	31	49
Total	**65**	**128**	**71**	**22**	**221**	**286**	**5**	**(s)**	**486**	**491**	**777**
2018 January	4	8	5	1	15	18	(s)	(s)	31	31	50
February	4	9	6	1	16	20	(s)	(s)	38	38	58
March	5	13	7	2	22	28	(s)	(s)	47	48	76
April	6	15	8	2	25	31	1	(s)	57	58	89
May	7	16	9	2	28	34	1	(s)	64	65	100
June	7	17	9	2	28	35	1	(s)	71	72	107
July	7	17	10	3	29	36	1	(s)	63	64	100
August	7	16	9	2	28	35	1	(s)	64	64	99
September	6	14	8	2	25	31	1	(s)	59	60	90
October	5	13	7	2	22	27	(s)	(s)	48	48	76
November	4	10	6	2	18	22	(s)	(s)	36	36	58
December	4	9	5	1	16	20	(s)	(s)	29	29	50
Total	**66**	**158**	**90**	**24**	**272**	**338**	**6**	**1**	**607**	**614**	**951**
2019 January	4	10	6	2	18	21	(s)	(s)	33	34	55
February	4	11	6	2	19	23	(s)	(s)	36	36	59
March	5	16	9	2	27	33	(s)	(s)	55	55	88
3-Month Total	**13**	**38**	**21**	**6**	**64**	**77**	**1**	**(s)**	**124**	**125**	**202**
2018 3-Month Total	**13**	**31**	**18**	**5**	**53**	**66**	**1**	**(s)**	**116**	**117**	**184**
2017 3-Month Total	**12**	**24**	**14**	**4**	**42**	**55**	**1**	**(s)**	**81**	**81**	**136**

[a] Data are estimates for distributed (small-scale) facilities (combined generator nameplate capacity less than 1 megawatt).
[b] See "Photovoltaic Energy" and "Solar Thermal Energy" in Glossary.
[c] Data are for utility-scale facilities (combined generator nameplate capacity of 1 megawatt or more).
[d] Solar photovoltaic (PV) electricity generation at distributed (small-scale) facilities connected to the electric power grid (converted to Btu by multiplying by the fossil fuels heat rate factors in Table A6).
[e] Solar photovoltaic (PV) and solar thermal electricity net generation at utility-scale facilities (converted to Btu by multiplying by the fossil fuels heat rate factors in Table A6).
[f] Solar thermal direct use energy in the residential, commercial, and industrial sectors for all end uses, such as pool heating, hot water heating, and space heating.
[g] Data are the sum of "Distributed Solar Energy Heat" and "Distributed Solar Energy Electricity."
[h] Commercial combined-heat-and-power (CHP) and commercial electricity-only plants. See Note 2, "Classification of Power Plants Into Energy-Use Sectors," at end of Section 7.
[i] Industrial combined-heat-and-power (CHP) and industrial electricity-only plants. See Note 2, "Classification of Power Plants Into Energy-Use Sectors," at end of Section 7.
[j] Electricity-only and combined-heat-and-power (CHP) plants within the NAICS 22 category whose primary business is to sell electricity, or electricity and heat, to the public. Through 1988, data are for electric utilities only; beginning in 1989, data are for electric utilities and independent power producers.
[k] Data are the sum of "Distributed Solar Energy Total" and "Utility-Scale Solar Energy Total."

NA=Not available. – =No data reported. (s)=Less than 0.5 trillion Btu.

Notes: • Distributed (small-scale) solar energy data for all years, and utility-scale solar energy data for the current two years, are estimates. • Totals may not equal sum of components due to independent rounding. • Geographic coverage is the 50 states and the District of Columbia.

Web Page: See http://www.eia.gov/totalenergy/data/monthly/#renewable (Excel and CSV files) for all available annual and monthly data beginning in 1984.

Sources: See end of section.

Source: *U.S. Energy Information Administration, Monthly Energy Review, June 2019*

Table 10.6 Solar Electricity Net Generation

(Million Kilowatthours)

	Distributed[a] Solar Generation[b]				Utility-Scale[c] Solar Generation[b]				
	Residential Sector	Commercial Sector	Industrial Sector	Total	Commercial Sector[d]	Industrial Sector[e]	Electric Power Sector[f]	Total	Total
1985 Total	**NA**	**NA**	**NA**	**NA**	**NA**	**NA**	**11**	**11**	**11**
1990 Total	**12**	**18**	**4**	**33**	**–**	**–**	**367**	**367**	**400**
1995 Total	**20**	**30**	**7**	**58**	**–**	**–**	**497**	**497**	**554**
2000 Total	**39**	**59**	**13**	**110**	**–**	**–**	**493**	**493**	**604**
2001 Total	**47**	**71**	**16**	**134**	**–**	**–**	**543**	**543**	**676**
2002 Total	**56**	**84**	**19**	**158**	**–**	**–**	**555**	**555**	**713**
2003 Total	**65**	**98**	**22**	**185**	**–**	**–**	**534**	**534**	**719**
2004 Total	**81**	**121**	**27**	**229**	**–**	**–**	**575**	**575**	**804**
2005 Total	**121**	**182**	**40**	**344**	**–**	**–**	**550**	**550**	**894**
2006 Total	**177**	**266**	**59**	**501**	**–**	**–**	**508**	**508**	**1,009**
2007 Total	**250**	**375**	**83**	**708**	**–**	**–**	**612**	**612**	**1,319**
2008 Total	**401**	**603**	**133**	**1,137**	**(s)**	**–**	**864**	**864**	**2,002**
2009 Total	**539**	**810**	**179**	**1,529**	**(s)**	**–**	**891**	**891**	**2,420**
2010 Total	**900**	**1,237**	**274**	**2,411**	**5**	**2**	**1,206**	**1,212**	**3,623**
2011 Total	**1,358**	**2,020**	**447**	**3,825**	**84**	**7**	**1,727**	**1,818**	**5,643**
2012 Total	**2,058**	**3,351**	**742**	**6,151**	**148**	**14**	**4,164**	**4,327**	**10,478**
2013 Total	**3,217**	**4,024**	**891**	**8,132**	**294**	**17**	**8,724**	**9,036**	**17,167**
2014 Total	**4,947**	**5,146**	**1,139**	**11,233**	**371**	**16**	**17,304**	**17,691**	**28,924**
2015 Total	**6,999**	**5,689**	**1,451**	**14,139**	**416**	**21**	**24,456**	**24,893**	**39,032**
2016 Total	**10,595**	**6,158**	**2,060**	**18,812**	**529**	**27**	**35,497**	**36,054**	**54,866**
2017 January	703	420	123	1,246	17	1	2,011	2,030	3,276
February	789	458	137	1,384	27	2	2,526	2,555	3,939
March	1,147	629	197	1,972	42	3	4,200	4,245	6,218
April	1,283	699	213	2,195	46	4	4,646	4,696	6,891
May	1,415	770	239	2,423	53	4	5,605	5,663	8,086
June	1,469	777	241	2,487	61	5	6,109	6,175	8,662
July	1,495	808	252	2,555	58	5	5,690	5,753	8,308
August	1,446	788	246	2,480	55	5	5,374	5,434	7,914
September	1,293	709	223	2,225	52	4	5,059	5,115	7,340
October	1,157	632	201	1,990	47	4	4,771	4,821	6,811
November	904	502	156	1,561	34	3	3,372	3,409	4,970
December	841	492	138	1,472	29	3	3,358	3,389	4,861
Total	**13,942**	**7,685**	**2,364**	**23,990**	**521**	**42**	**52,723**	**53,286**	**77,276**
2018 January	922	547	146	1,615	28	4	3,375	3,407	5,022
February	1,008	599	154	1,762	35	5	4,072	4,113	5,875
March	1,394	813	220	2,427	45	7	5,151	5,203	7,630
April	1,596	900	240	2,736	57	8	6,183	6,249	8,984
May	1,758	986	266	3,010	65	9	6,995	7,070	10,080
June	1,793	999	267	3,060	81	11	7,712	7,804	10,863
July	1,839	1,032	276	3,147	68	9	6,861	6,938	10,085
August	1,762	989	268	3,018	70	11	6,900	6,981	9,999
September	1,545	890	245	2,681	66	10	6,393	6,469	9,150
October	1,391	786	223	2,400	50	8	5,165	5,223	7,624
November	1,114	624	176	1,914	34	6	3,918	3,958	5,873
December	1,025	591	159	1,774	28	4	3,156	3,188	4,962
Total	**17,146**	**9,756**	**2,641**	**29,543**	**629**	**92**	**65,882**	**66,604**	**96,147**
2019 January	1,122	647	168	1,938	31	5	3,616	3,652	5,590
February	1,219	688	178	2,085	33	5	3,875	3,913	5,999
March	1,754	959	255	2,968	53	8	5,959	6,020	8,988
3-Month Total	**4,096**	**2,294**	**601**	**6,991**	**117**	**18**	**13,450**	**13,585**	**20,576**
2018 3-Month Total	**3,325**	**1,959**	**520**	**5,804**	**109**	**17**	**12,598**	**12,723**	**18,528**
2017 3-Month Total	**2,639**	**1,507**	**456**	**4,603**	**86**	**6**	**8,738**	**8,831**	**13,433**

[a] Data are estimates for solar photovoltaic (PV) electricity generation at small-scale facilities (combined generator nameplate capacity less than 1 megawatt) connected to the electric power grid.

[b] See "Photovoltaic Energy" and "Solar Thermal Energy" in Glossary.

[c] Solar photovoltaic (PV) and solar thermal electricity net generation at utility-scale facilities (combined generator nameplate capacity of 1 megawatt or more).

[d] Commercial combined-heat-and-power (CHP) and commercial electricity-only plants. See Note 2, "Classification of Power Plants Into Energy-Use Sectors," at end of Section 7.

[e] Industrial combined-heat-and-power (CHP) and industrial electricity-only plants. See Note 2, "Classification of Power Plants Into Energy-Use Sectors," at end of Section 7.

[f] Electricity-only and combined-heat-and-power (CHP) plants within the NAICS 22 category whose primary business is to sell electricity, or electricity and heat, to the public. Through 1988, data are for electric utilities only; beginning in 1989, data are for electric utilities and independent power producers.

NA=Not available. – =No data reported. (s)=Less than 0.5 million kilowatthours.

Notes: • Distributed (small-scale) solar generation data for all years, and utility-scale solar energy data for the current two years, are estimates. • Totals may not equal sum of components due to independent rounding. • Geographic coverage is the 50 states and the District of Columbia.

Web Page: See http://www.eia.gov/totalenergy/data/monthly/#renewable (Excel and CSV files) for all available annual and monthly data beginning in 1984.

Sources: • **Distributed Solar Generation: 1989–2013—**Calculated as distributed solar energy consumption (see Table 10.5) divided by the total fossil fuels heat rate factors (see Table A6). **2014 forward—**U.S. Energy Information Administration (EIA), *Electric Power Monthly,* monthly reports, Tables 1.1, 1.2.C, 1.2.D, and 1.2.E. • **Utility-Scale Solar Generation: 1984–1988—**EIA, Form EIA-759, "Monthly Power Plant Report." **1989–1997:** EIA, Form EIA-759, "Monthly Power Plant Report," and Form EIA-867, "Annual Nonutility Power Producer Report." **1998–2000:** EIA, Form EIA-759, "Monthly Power Plant Report," and Form EIA-860B, "Annual Electric Generator Report—Nonutility." **2001–2003:** EIA, Form EIA-906, "Power Plant Report." **2004–2007:** EIA, Form EIA-906, "Power Plant Report," and Form EIA-920, "Combined Heat and Power Plant Report." **2008 forward:** EIA, Form EIA-923, "Power Plant Operations Report." • **Total:** Calculated as distributed solar generation plus utility-scale solar generation.

Source: *U.S. Energy Information Administration, Monthly Energy Review, June 2019*

Figure 11.1a World Crude Oil Production Overview
(Million Barrels per Day)

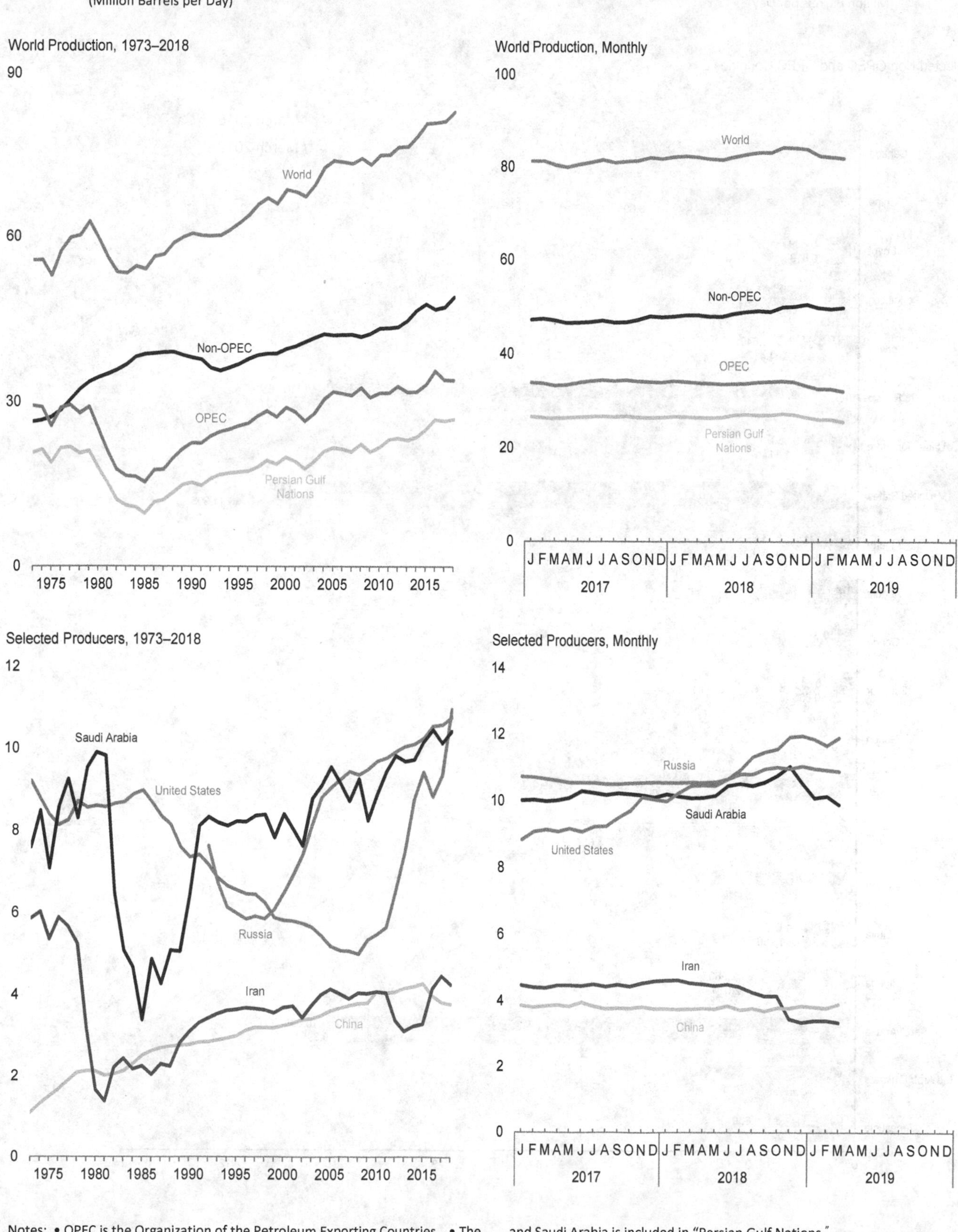

Notes: • OPEC is the Organization of the Petroleum Exporting Countries. • The Persian Gulf Nations are Bahrain, Iran, Iraq, Kuwait, Qatar, Saudi Arabia, and the United Arab Emirates. Production from the Neutral Zone between Kuwait and Saudi Arabia is included in "Persian Gulf Nations."
Web Page: http://www.eia.gov/totalenergy/data/monthly/#international.
Sources: Tables 11.1a and 11.1b.

Source: *U.S. Energy Information Administration, Monthly Energy Review, June 2019*

Figure 11.1b World Crude Oil Production by Selected Countries
(Million Barrels per Day)

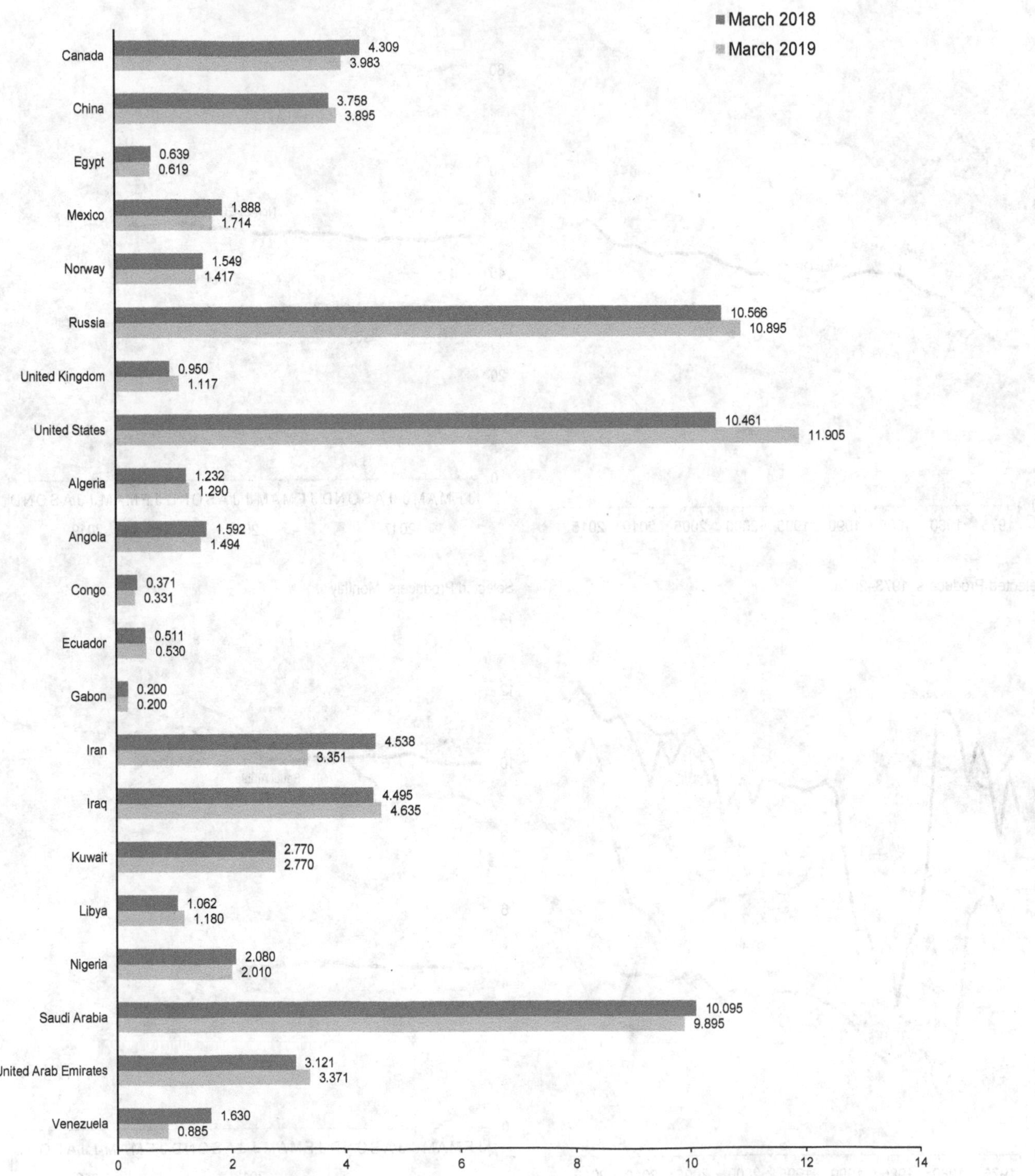

Note: OPEC is the Organization of the Petroleum Exporting Countries.
Web Page: http://www.eia.gov/totalenergy/data/monthly/#international.
Sources: Tables 11.1a and 11.1b.

Source: *U.S. Energy Information Administration, Monthly Energy Review, June 2019*

Table 11.1a World Crude Oil Production: Selected OPEC Members
(Thousand Barrels per Day)

	Algeria	Angola	Congo (Brazzaville)	Ecuador	Gabon	Iran	Iraq	Kuwait[a]	Libya	Nigeria	Saudi Arabia[a]	United Arab Emirates	Venezuela	Total OPEC[b]
1973 Average	1,097	162	35	209	150	5,861	2,018	3,020	2,175	2,054	7,596	1,533	3,366	29,276
1975 Average	983	165	37	161	223	5,350	2,262	2,084	1,480	1,783	7,075	1,664	2,346	25,612
1980 Average	1,106	150	65	204	175	1,662	2,514	1,656	1,787	2,055	9,900	1,709	2,168	25,151
1985 Average	1,036	231	120	281	172	2,250	1,433	1,023	1,059	1,495	3,388	1,193	1,677	15,358
1990 Average	1,180	475	165	285	270	3,088	2,040	1,175	1,375	1,810	6,410	2,117	2,137	22,527
1995 Average	1,162	646	188	392	365	3,643	560	2,057	1,390	1,993	8,231	2,233	2,750	25,616
1996 Average	1,227	709	201	396	368	3,686	579	2,062	1,401	2,001	8,218	2,278	2,938	26,079
1997 Average	1,259	714	253	388	370	3,664	1,155	2,007	1,446	2,132	8,362	2,316	3,280	27,399
1998 Average	1,226	735	265	375	352	3,634	2,150	2,085	1,390	2,153	8,389	2,345	3,167	28,351
1999 Average	1,177	745	270	373	331	3,557	2,508	1,898	1,319	2,130	7,833	2,169	2,826	27,237
2000 Average	1,214	746	280	395	315	3,696	2,571	2,079	1,410	2,165	8,404	2,368	3,155	28,965
2001 Average	1,265	742	255	412	270	3,724	2,390	1,998	1,367	2,256	8,031	2,205	3,010	28,106
2002 Average	1,349	896	249	393	251	3,444	2,023	1,894	1,319	2,118	7,634	2,082	2,604	26,469
2003 Average	1,516	903	247	411	241	3,743	1,308	2,136	1,421	2,275	8,775	2,348	2,335	27,865
2004 Average	1,582	1,052	235	528	239	4,001	2,011	2,376	1,515	2,329	9,101	2,478	2,557	30,371
2005 Average	1,692	1,239	229	532	266	4,139	1,878	2,529	1,651	2,627	9,550	2,535	2,565	31,795
2006 Average	1,699	1,398	242	536	237	4,028	1,996	2,535	1,736	2,440	9,152	2,636	2,511	31,488
2007 Average	1,708	1,724	207	511	244	3,912	2,086	2,464	1,787	2,350	8,722	2,603	2,490	31,153
2008 Average	1,705	1,951	233	505	248	4,050	2,375	2,586	1,803	2,165	9,261	2,821	2,510	32,550
2009 Average	1,585	1,877	268	486	242	4,037	2,391	2,350	1,696	2,208	8,250	2,560	2,520	30,791
2010 Average	1,540	1,909	340	486	246	4,080	2,399	2,300	1,710	2,408	8,900	2,570	2,410	31,596
2011 Average	1,540	1,756	288	500	241	4,054	2,626	2,530	485	2,474	9,458	2,849	2,500	31,579
2012 Average	1,532	1,787	260	504	230	3,387	2,983	2,635	1,432	2,457	9,832	2,994	2,500	32,822
2013 Average	1,462	1,803	239	526	220	3,113	3,054	2,650	978	2,307	9,693	2,938	2,500	31,754
2014 Average	1,420	1,742	233	556	220	3,239	3,368	2,642	530	2,347	9,735	3,010	2,500	31,803
2015 Average	1,429	1,802	238	543	213	3,293	4,045	2,784	484	2,171	10,168	3,149	2,500	33,070
2016 Average	1,348	1,770	198	548	211	4,151	4,444	2,905	466	1,871	10,461	3,243	2,277	34,119
2017 January	1,340	1,658	190	536	200	4,467	4,553	2,812	759	1,849	10,020	3,205	2,100	33,891
February	1,340	1,688	198	535	185	4,405	4,433	2,752	769	1,869	10,040	3,185	2,090	33,691
March	1,316	1,630	160	531	190	4,392	4,418	2,742	669	1,730	9,992	3,165	2,090	33,227
April	1,306	1,700	171	528	210	4,464	4,413	2,742	614	1,780	10,022	3,145	2,080	33,361
May	1,306	1,660	200	533	200	4,464	4,463	2,742	859	1,900	10,093	3,165	2,080	33,851
June	1,306	1,690	257	540	200	4,445	4,478	2,752	929	1,945	10,293	3,185	2,030	34,236
July	1,306	1,670	278	541	210	4,495	4,488	2,742	1,084	2,022	10,243	3,185	2,030	34,480
August	1,306	1,690	270	536	200	4,431	4,513	2,742	969	2,027	10,183	3,185	2,025	34,258
September	1,306	1,670	273	529	200	4,490	4,553	2,762	1,004	2,038	10,233	3,185	2,010	34,434
October	1,256	1,695	299	526	200	4,439	4,403	2,772	1,039	2,021	10,204	3,175	1,960	34,175
November	1,276	1,600	310	521	190	4,532	4,333	2,742	1,059	2,065	10,174	3,145	1,890	34,018
December	1,306	1,640	321	520	200	4,596	4,393	2,732	999	2,099	10,105	3,165	1,710	33,967
Average	1,306	1,666	244	531	199	4,469	4,454	2,753	897	1,946	10,134	3,174	2,007	33,967
2018 January	1,282	1,632	322	513	200	4,617	4,445	2,760	1,092	2,140	10,205	3,181	1,710	34,275
February	1,272	1,622	333	513	200	4,624	4,485	2,760	1,067	2,110	10,145	3,141	1,670	34,118
March	1,232	1,592	371	511	200	4,538	4,495	2,770	1,062	2,080	10,095	3,121	1,630	33,873
April	1,232	1,587	370	517	190	4,515	4,455	2,760	1,082	2,060	10,105	3,131	1,600	33,780
May	1,262	1,592	365	516	200	4,462	4,505	2,760	1,067	1,880	10,165	3,111	1,545	33,606
June	1,282	1,562	342	517	200	4,508	4,589	2,770	827	1,810	10,465	3,151	1,485	33,679
July	1,292	1,572	332	523	180	4,428	4,619	2,850	732	1,860	10,525	3,181	1,450	33,720
August	1,282	1,582	347	530	200	4,271	4,690	2,850	1,067	1,930	10,465	3,221	1,405	34,016
September	1,242	1,602	342	519	200	4,151	4,715	2,850	1,157	2,030	10,565	3,221	1,371	34,141
October	1,242	1,572	337	514	200	4,151	4,745	2,850	1,157	1,990	10,765	3,271	1,341	34,311
November	1,242	1,612	307	515	180	3,451	4,785	2,850	1,207	R 1,980	11,045	3,411	1,321	R 34,067
December	1,242	1,592	317	519	200	3,351	4,815	2,850	957	2,010	10,545	3,451	1,291	33,291
Average	1,259	1,593	340	517	196	4,254	4,613	2,807	1,039	R 1,989	10,425	3,216	1,484	R 33,905
2019 January	1,190	1,594	326	524	200	3,401	4,865	2,800	R 920	1,950	10,095	3,371	1,261	R 32,643
February	1,280	1,484	341	533	200	3,401	4,795	2,800	R 950	1,980	10,145	3,421	1,131	R 32,597
March	1,290	1,494	331	530	200	3,351	4,635	2,770	1,180	2,010	9,895	3,371	885	32,098
3-Month Average	1,252	1,525	332	529	200	3,384	4,764	2,790	1,019	1,980	10,042	3,387	1,091	32,441
2018 3-Month Average	1,262	1,615	342	512	200	4,592	4,475	2,763	1,074	2,110	10,148	3,148	1,670	34,088
2017 3-Month Average	1,332	1,658	182	534	192	4,422	4,469	2,769	731	1,814	10,017	3,185	2,093	33,600

[a] Except for the period from August 1990 through May 1991, includes about one-half of the production in the Kuwait-Saudi Arabia Neutral Zone. Kuwaiti Neutral Zone output was discontinued following Iraq's invasion of Kuwait on August 2, 1990, but was resumed in June 1991. As of July 2015 all Neutral Zone production is offline. Data for Saudi Arabia include approximately 150 thousand barrels per day from the Abu Safah field produced on behalf of Bahrain.

[b] See "Organization of the Petroleum Exporting Countries (OPEC)" in Glossary. On Tables 11.1a and 11.1b, countries are classified as "OPEC" or "Non-OPEC" in all years based on their status in the most current year. For example, Equatorial Guinea joined OPEC in May 2017 and is thus included in "Total OPEC" for all years.

R=Revised.

Notes: • Data are for crude oil and lease condensate; they exclude natural gas plant liquids. • Monthly data are often preliminary figures and may not average to the annual totals because of rounding or because updates to the preliminary monthly data are not available.

Web Page: See http://www.eia.gov/totalenergy/data/monthly/#international (Excel and CSV files) for all available annual and monthly data beginning in 1973.

Sources: See end of section.

Source: *U.S. Energy Information Administration, Monthly Energy Review, June 2019*

Table 11.1b World Crude Oil Production: Persian Gulf Nations, Non-OPEC, and World
(Thousand Barrels per Day)

	Persian Gulf Nations[b]	Selected Non-OPEC[a] Producers									Total Non-OPEC[a]	World
		Canada	China	Egypt	Mexico	Norway	Former U.S.S.R.	Russia	United Kingdom	United States		
1973 Average	**20,668**	**1,798**	**1,090**	**165**	**465**	**32**	**8,324**	**– –**	**2**	**9,208**	**26,403**	**55,679**
1975 Average	**18,934**	**1,430**	**1,490**	**235**	**705**	**189**	**9,523**	**– –**	**12**	**8,375**	**27,216**	**52,828**
1980 Average	**17,961**	**1,435**	**2,114**	**595**	**1,936**	**486**	**11,706**	**– –**	**1,622**	**8,597**	**34,406**	**59,558**
1985 Average	**9,630**	**1,471**	**2,505**	**887**	**2,745**	**773**	**11,585**	**– –**	**2,530**	**8,971**	**38,608**	**53,966**
1990 Average	**15,278**	**1,553**	**2,774**	**873**	**2,553**	**1,630**	**10,975**	**– –**	**1,820**	**7,355**	**37,970**	**60,498**
1995 Average	**17,208**	**1,805**	**2,990**	**920**	**2,711**	**2,766**	**– –**	**5,995**	**2,489**	**6,560**	**36,818**	**62,434**
1996 Average	**17,367**	**1,837**	**3,131**	**922**	**2,944**	**3,091**	**– –**	**5,850**	**2,568**	**6,465**	**37,739**	**63,818**
1997 Average	**18,095**	**1,922**	**3,200**	**856**	**3,104**	**3,142**	**– –**	**5,920**	**2,518**	**6,452**	**38,406**	**65,806**
1998 Average	**19,337**	**1,981**	**3,198**	**834**	**3,160**	**3,011**	**– –**	**5,854**	**2,616**	**6,252**	**38,681**	**67,032**
1999 Average	**18,667**	**1,907**	**3,195**	**852**	**2,998**	**3,019**	**– –**	**6,079**	**2,684**	**5,881**	**38,730**	**65,967**
2000 Average	**19,897**	**1,977**	**3,249**	**768**	**3,104**	**3,222**	**– –**	**6,479**	**2,275**	**5,822**	**39,562**	**68,527**
2001 Average	**19,114**	**2,029**	**3,300**	**720**	**3,218**	**3,226**	**– –**	**6,917**	**2,282**	**5,801**	**40,026**	**68,132**
2002 Average	**17,824**	**2,171**	**3,390**	**715**	**3,263**	**3,131**	**– –**	**7,408**	**2,292**	**5,744**	**40,821**	**67,290**
2003 Average	**19,154**	**2,306**	**3,409**	**713**	**3,459**	**3,042**	**– –**	**8,132**	**2,093**	**5,649**	**41,595**	**69,460**
2004 Average	**20,906**	**2,398**	**3,485**	**673**	**3,476**	**2,954**	**– –**	**8,805**	**1,845**	**5,441**	**42,225**	**72,595**
2005 Average	**21,644**	**2,369**	**3,609**	**623**	**3,423**	**2,698**	**– –**	**9,043**	**1,649**	**5,184**	**42,074**	**73,869**
2006 Average	**21,377**	**2,525**	**3,673**	**616**	**3,345**	**2,491**	**– –**	**9,247**	**1,490**	**5,086**	**42,134**	**73,621**
2007 Average	**20,904**	**2,628**	**3,736**	**608**	**3,143**	**2,270**	**– –**	**9,437**	**1,498**	**5,074**	**42,178**	**73,331**
2008 Average	**22,301**	**2,579**	**3,790**	**633**	**2,839**	**2,182**	**– –**	**9,357**	**1,391**	**5,000**	**41,751**	**74,301**
2009 Average	**20,898**	**2,579**	**3,796**	**649**	**2,646**	**2,067**	**– –**	**9,495**	**1,328**	**5,349**	**42,329**	**73,121**
2010 Average	**21,736**	**2,741**	**4,078**	**636**	**2,621**	**1,871**	**– –**	**9,694**	**1,233**	**5,478**	**43,291**	**74,887**
2011 Average	**23,102**	**2,901**	**4,052**	**637**	**2,600**	**1,760**	**– –**	**9,774**	**1,026**	**5,654**	**43,329**	**74,908**
2012 Average	**23,394**	**3,138**	**4,074**	**642**	**2,593**	**1,612**	**– –**	**9,922**	**888**	**6,502**	**43,561**	**76,382**
2013 Average	**23,037**	**3,325**	**4,164**	**645**	**2,562**	**1,533**	**– –**	**10,054**	**801**	**7,467**	**44,695**	**76,449**
2014 Average	**23,582**	**3,613**	**4,208**	**645**	**2,469**	**1,562**	**– –**	**10,107**	**787**	**8,759**	**46,559**	**78,362**
2015 Average	**24,989**	**3,677**	**4,278**	**686**	**2,302**	**1,610**	**– –**	**10,253**	**893**	**9,431**	**47,685**	**80,755**
2016 Average	**26,748**	**3,679**	**3,983**	**654**	**2,187**	**1,648**	**– –**	**10,551**	**933**	**8,831**	**46,723**	**80,842**
2017 January	26,622	4,097	3,855	630	2,054	1,653	– –	10,733	970	8,840	47,277	81,168
February	26,360	4,137	3,803	622	2,051	1,693	– –	10,713	945	9,083	47,471	81,162
March	26,254	3,917	3,843	613	2,053	1,745	– –	10,654	943	9,140	47,127	80,354
April	26,331	3,577	3,863	622	2,046	1,738	– –	10,603	915	9,085	46,564	79,925
May	26,472	3,690	3,822	630	2,053	1,636	– –	10,543	930	9,168	46,658	80,509
June	26,698	3,793	3,947	631	2,042	1,576	– –	10,543	937	9,074	46,803	81,039
July	26,698	3,990	3,832	628	2,020	1,653	– –	10,546	912	9,230	47,105	81,585
August	26,599	4,154	3,760	636	1,962	1,584	– –	10,507	831	9,244	46,716	80,974
September	26,768	3,950	3,779	644	1,761	1,473	– –	10,503	885	9,495	46,738	81,172
October	26,528	3,902	3,769	638	1,933	1,576	– –	10,530	944	9,703	47,218	81,393
November	26,461	4,230	3,820	634	1,896	1,520	– –	10,543	979	10,103	48,027	82,045
December	26,536	4,287	3,764	635	1,903	1,567	– –	10,553	741	10,040	47,834	81,801
Average	**26,528**	**3,977**	**3,821**	**630**	**1,981**	**1,618**	**– –**	**10,580**	**911**	**9,352**	**47,126**	**81,094**
2018 January	26,708	4,131	3,763	634	1,953	1,650	– –	10,550	1,020	E 9,995	47,975	82,250
February	26,655	4,284	3,753	639	1,919	1,598	– –	10,552	1,007	E 10,248	R 48,305	R 82,423
March	26,529	4,309	3,758	639	1,888	1,549	– –	10,566	950	E 10,461	R 48,292	R 82,165
April	26,466	3,996	3,774	645	1,911	1,544	– –	10,562	1,077	E 10,475	48,027	81,807
May	26,503	4,206	3,761	647	1,891	1,348	– –	10,569	992	E 10,464	47,996	81,602
June	26,993	4,188	3,857	614	1,871	1,517	– –	10,663	953	E 10,672	48,570	82,249
July	27,113	4,311	3,732	637	1,865	1,556	– –	10,814	1,003	E 10,936	48,995	82,715
August	27,017	4,520	3,768	645	1,841	1,535	– –	10,811	927	E 11,325	49,169	83,185
September	27,002	4,174	3,694	643	1,849	1,335	– –	10,964	902	E 11,470	49,059	83,200
October	27,282	4,450	3,789	636	1,785	1,511	– –	11,014	1,043	E 11,559	49,994	84,305
November	27,042	4,223	3,779	641	1,720	1,525	– –	10,972	1,037	E 11,926	R 50,154	R 84,221
December	26,512	4,362	3,845	646	1,733	1,535	– –	11,051	1,086	E 11,963	50,654	83,945
Average	**26,819**	**4,264**	**3,773**	**639**	**1,852**	**1,517**	**– –**	**10,759**	**1,000**	**E 10,962**	**48,938**	**R 82,842**
2019 January	26,082	4,021	3,812	R 638	1,647	1,487	– –	10,973	R 1,054	RE 11,860	R 49,888	R 82,531
February	26,112	R 4,081	3,780	R 632	R 1,724	1,420	– –	10,931	R 1,135	RE 11,664	R 49,655	R 82,252
March	25,572	3,983	3,895	619	1,714	1,417	– –	10,895	1,117	E 11,905	49,872	81,970
3-Month Average	**25,916**	**4,027**	**3,831**	**630**	**1,694**	**1,442**	**– –**	**10,933**	**1,101**	**E 11,815**	**49,810**	**82,251**
2018 3-Month Average	**26,630**	**4,240**	**3,758**	**637**	**1,920**	**1,599**	**– –**	**10,556**	**992**	**E 10,234**	**48,187**	**82,275**
2017 3-Month Average	**26,414**	**4,047**	**3,835**	**622**	**2,053**	**1,697**	**– –**	**10,700**	**953**	**9,019**	**47,286**	**80,886**

[a] See "Organization of the Petroleum Exporting Countries (OPEC)" in Glossary. On Tables 11.1a and 11.1b, countries are classified as "OPEC" or "Non-OPEC" in all years based on their status in the most current year. For example, Equatorial Guinea joined OPEC in May 2017 and is thus included in "Total OPEC" for all years.

[b] Bahrain, Iran, Iraq, Kuwait, Qatar, Saudi Arabia, United Arab Emirates, and the Neutral Zone (between Kuwait and Saudi Arabia).

R=Revised. – – =Not applicable. E=Estimate.

Notes: • Data are for crude oil and lease condensate; they exclude natural gas plant liquids. • Monthly data are often preliminary figures and may not average to the annual totals because of rounding or because updates to the preliminary monthly data are not available. • Data for countries may not sum to World totals due to independent rounding. • U.S. geographic coverage is the 50 states and the District of Columbia.

Web Page: See http://www.eia.gov/totalenergy/data/monthly/#international (Excel and CSV files) for all available annual and monthly data beginning in 1973.

Sources: See end of section.

Source: *U.S. Energy Information Administration, Monthly Energy Review, June 2019*

Figure 11.2 Petroleum Consumption in OECD Countries
(Million Barrels per Day)

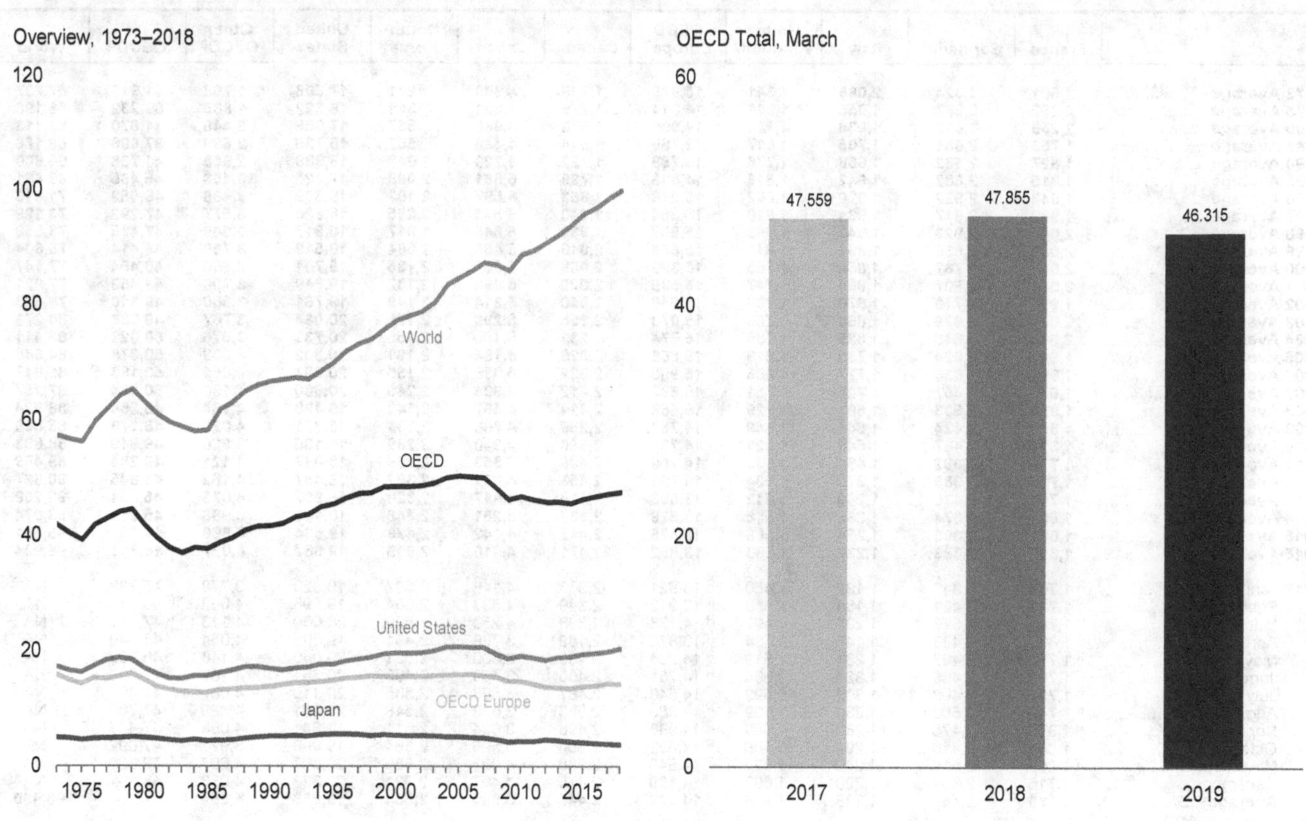

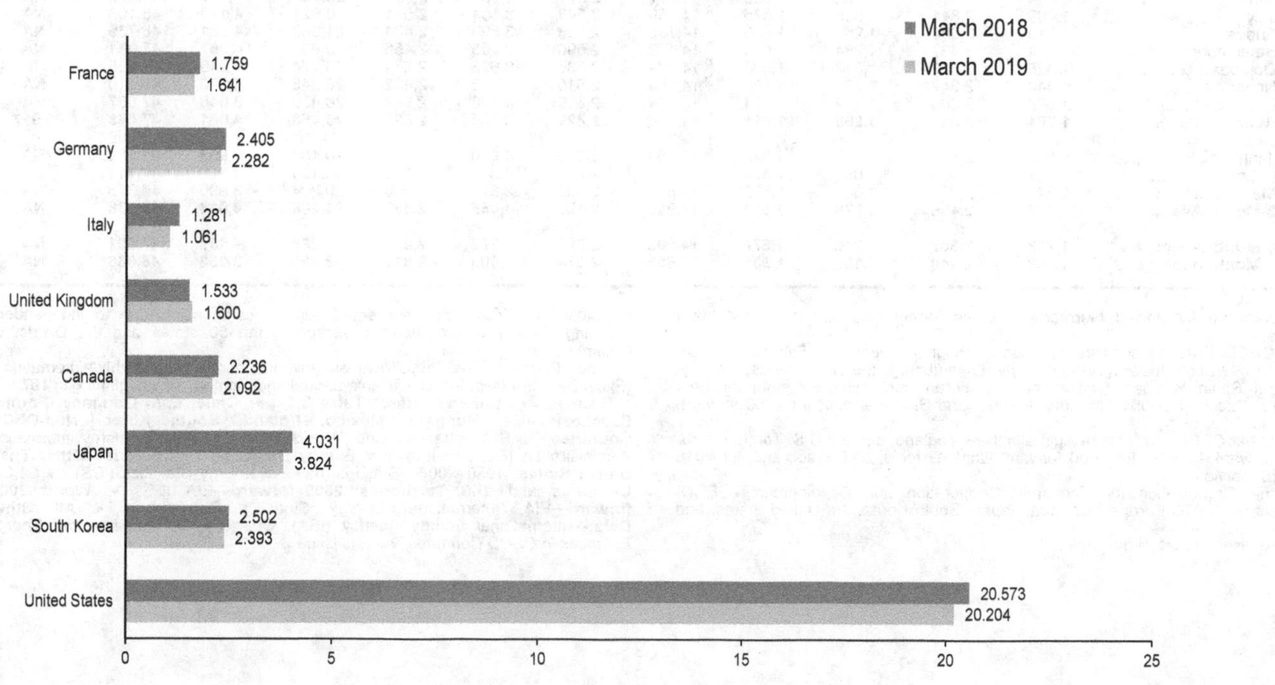

Note: OECD is the Organization for Economic Cooperation and Development.

Web Page: http://www.eia.gov/totalenergy/data/monthly/#international.
Source: Table 11.2.

Source: *U.S. Energy Information Administration, Monthly Energy Review, June 2019*

Table 11.2 Petroleum Consumption in OECD Countries

(Thousand Barrels per Day)

	France	Germany[a]	Italy	United Kingdom	OECD Europe[b]	Canada	Japan	South Korea	United States	Other OECD[c]	OECD[d]	World
1973 Average	**2,601**	**3,324**	**2,068**	**2,341**	**15,879**	**1,729**	**4,949**	**281**	**17,308**	**1,768**	**41,913**	**57,237**
1975 Average	**2,252**	**2,957**	**1,855**	**1,911**	**14,314**	**1,779**	**4,621**	**311**	**16,322**	**1,885**	**39,232**	**56,198**
1980 Average	**2,256**	**3,082**	**1,934**	**1,725**	**14,995**	**1,873**	**4,960**	**537**	**17,056**	**2,449**	**41,870**	**63,113**
1985 Average	**1,753**	**2,651**	**1,705**	**1,617**	**12,769**	**1,514**	**4,436**	**552**	**15,726**	**2,699**	**37,696**	**58,176**
1990 Average	**1,827**	**2,682**	**1,868**	**1,776**	**13,789**	**1,722**	**5,223**	**1,048**	**16,988**	**2,968**	**41,738**	**66,660**
1995 Average	**1,915**	**2,882**	**1,942**	**1,816**	**14,899**	**1,799**	**5,581**	**2,008**	**17,725**	**3,453**	**45,465**	**69,861**
1996 Average	**1,943**	**2,922**	**1,920**	**1,852**	**15,216**	**1,853**	**5,587**	**2,101**	**18,309**	**3,486**	**46,552**	**71,913**
1997 Average	**1,962**	**2,917**	**1,934**	**1,810**	**15,354**	**1,940**	**5,545**	**2,255**	**18,620**	**3,577**	**47,292**	**73,129**
1998 Average	**2,040**	**2,923**	**1,943**	**1,792**	**15,653**	**1,931**	**5,348**	**1,917**	**18,917**	**3,649**	**47,415**	**73,950**
1999 Average	**2,034**	**2,836**	**1,891**	**1,811**	**15,558**	**2,016**	**5,486**	**2,084**	**19,519**	**3,750**	**48,414**	**75,604**
2000 Average	**2,001**	**2,767**	**1,854**	**1,765**	**15,399**	**2,008**	**5,361**	**2,135**	**19,701**	**3,850**	**48,454**	**77,147**
2001 Average	**2,054**	**2,807**	**1,835**	**1,747**	**15,585**	**2,029**	**5,269**	**2,132**	**19,649**	**3,796**	**48,459**	**77,921**
2002 Average	**1,991**	**2,710**	**1,870**	**1,739**	**15,546**	**2,040**	**5,314**	**2,149**	**19,761**	**3,800**	**48,610**	**78,648**
2003 Average	**2,001**	**2,679**	**1,860**	**1,759**	**15,670**	**2,155**	**5,296**	**2,175**	**20,034**	**3,767**	**49,096**	**80,273**
2004 Average	**2,008**	**2,648**	**1,829**	**1,789**	**15,774**	**2,233**	**5,159**	**2,155**	**20,731**	**3,976**	**50,029**	**83,411**
2005 Average	**1,990**	**2,624**	**1,781**	**1,819**	**15,856**	**2,326**	**5,164**	**2,191**	**20,802**	**4,039**	**50,378**	**84,645**
2006 Average	**1,991**	**2,636**	**1,777**	**1,805**	**15,905**	**2,322**	**5,038**	**2,180**	**20,687**	**4,051**	**50,183**	**85,847**
2007 Average	**1,975**	**2,407**	**1,729**	**1,751**	**15,637**	**2,412**	**4,904**	**2,240**	**20,680**	**4,190**	**50,064**	**87,257**
2008 Average	**1,935**	**2,533**	**1,667**	**1,729**	**15,489**	**2,324**	**4,667**	**2,142**	**19,498**	**4,134**	**48,254**	**86,824**
2009 Average	**1,859**	**2,434**	**1,544**	**1,649**	**14,763**	**2,269**	**4,266**	**2,188**	**18,771**	**4,020**	**46,278**	**85,860**
2010 Average	**1,818**	**2,467**	**1,544**	**1,624**	**14,731**	**2,380**	**4,340**	**2,269**	**19,180**	**3,920**	**46,819**	**88,693**
2011 Average	**1,778**	**2,392**	**1,494**	**1,582**	**14,256**	**2,408**	**4,353**	**2,259**	**18,887**	**4,121**	**46,284**	**89,489**
2012 Average	**1,736**	**2,389**	**1,370**	**1,534**	**13,791**	**2,453**	**4,631**	**2,322**	**18,487**	**4,162**	**45,845**	**90,827**
2013 Average	**1,714**	**2,435**	**1,260**	**1,512**	**13,606**	**2,429**	**4,487**	**2,328**	**18,967**	**4,073**	**45,891**	**92,259**
2014 Average	**1,691**	**2,374**	**1,266**	**1,518**	**13,529**	**2,387**	**4,261**	**2,348**	**19,100**	**3,988**	**45,613**	**93,874**
2015 Average	**1,691**	**2,368**	**1,274**	**1,556**	**13,828**	**2,417**	**4,142**	**2,473**	**19,534**	**3,966**	**46,359**	**95,861**
2016 Average	**1,652**	**2,383**	**1,237**	**1,583**	**13,992**	**2,471**	**4,010**	**2,605**	**19,687**	**4,027**	**46,793**	**96,934**
2017 January	[R]1,767	2,342	1,132	1,450	[R]13,521	2,373	4,148	2,597	19,323	3,778	[R]45,738	NA
February	[R]1,731	2,421	1,184	1,658	[R]13,912	2,349	4,533	2,664	19,190	4,062	[R]46,710	NA
March	[R]1,744	2,577	1,235	1,497	[R]14,138	2,398	4,250	2,599	20,060	4,113	[R]47,559	NA
April	[R]1,661	2,438	1,149	1,634	[R]13,870	2,182	3,786	2,451	19,595	4,064	[R]45,949	NA
May	[R]1,718	2,492	1,234	1,519	[R]14,264	2,435	3,500	2,521	20,066	4,148	[R]46,933	NA
June	[R]1,784	2,495	1,324	1,634	[R]14,751	2,460	3,469	2,492	20,561	4,166	[R]47,899	NA
July	[R]1,763	2,498	1,302	1,592	[R]14,646	2,487	3,583	2,565	20,119	4,009	[R]47,409	NA
August	[R]1,749	2,500	1,233	1,589	[R]14,585	2,583	3,693	2,548	20,251	4,129	[R]47,789	NA
September	[R]1,870	2,475	1,283	1,650	[R]14,988	2,498	3,624	2,611	19,641	4,085	[R]47,447	NA
October	[R]1,656	2,416	1,294	1,569	[R]14,522	2,504	3,596	2,564	19,990	3,922	[R]47,097	NA
November	[R]1,669	2,556	1,240	1,632	[R]14,546	2,586	4,093	2,680	20,307	4,097	[R]48,309	NA
December	[R]1,716	2,309	1,220	1,603	[R]14,189	2,475	4,497	2,721	20,323	4,086	[R]48,291	NA
Average	[R]**1,736**	**2,460**	**1,236**	**1,584**	[R]**14,329**	**2,445**	**3,894**	**2,584**	**19,958**	**4,054**	[R]**47,264**	[R]**98,490**
2018 January	1,590	[R]2,206	1,163	[R]1,505	[R]13,389	2,360	4,257	2,704	20,461	4,041	[R]47,213	NA
February	1,784	[R]2,502	1,301	[R]1,704	[R]14,633	2,377	4,556	2,686	19,619	4,167	[R]48,037	NA
March	1,759	[R]2,405	1,281	[R]1,533	[R]14,307	2,236	4,031	2,502	20,573	4,206	[R]47,855	NA
April	1,699	[R]2,403	1,270	[R]1,689	[R]14,282	2,253	3,604	2,544	19,941	4,051	[R]46,674	NA
May	1,657	[R]2,300	1,261	[R]1,573	[R]14,060	2,408	3,437	2,559	20,357	4,137	[R]46,957	NA
June	1,714	[R]2,316	1,292	[R]1,660	[R]14,477	2,371	3,238	2,537	20,705	4,157	[R]47,485	NA
July	1,789	[R]2,341	1,339	[R]1,575	[R]14,859	2,548	3,504	2,511	20,621	4,120	[R]48,163	NA
August	1,713	[R]2,382	1,262	[R]1,640	[R]14,735	2,538	3,599	2,484	21,302	4,081	[R]48,739	NA
September	1,704	[R]2,337	1,284	[R]1,683	[R]14,482	2,590	3,496	2,455	19,951	4,057	[R]47,031	NA
October	1,825	[R]2,362	1,317	1,536	[R]14,589	2,636	3,623	2,274	20,774	4,040	[R]47,935	NA
November	1,643	[R]2,347	1,251	[R]1,656	[R]14,184	2,515	3,862	2,432	20,548	4,070	[R]47,610	NA
December	1,578	[R]2,204	1,202	[R]1,594	[R]13,624	2,309	4,198	2,599	20,479	3,848	[R]47,057	NA
Average	**1,704**	[R]**2,341**	**1,268**	[R]**1,611**	[R]**14,298**	**2,429**	**3,780**	**2,523**	**20,453**	**4,081**	[R]**47,563**	[R]**99,917**
2019 January	[R]1,695	[R]2,437	1,096	[R]1,522	[R]13,803	[R]2,205	4,060	2,678	20,452	[R]3,953	[R]47,151	NA
February	[R]1,727	[R]2,509	[R]1,081	[R]1,676	[R]14,213	[R]2,310	[R]4,305	2,518	20,194	[R]4,172	[R]47,713	NA
March	1,641	2,282	1,061	1,600	13,812	2,092	3,824	2,393	20,204	3,990	46,315	NA
3-Month Average	**1,686**	**2,406**	**1,079**	**1,597**	**13,933**	**2,199**	**4,055**	**2,530**	**20,286**	**4,034**	**47,038**	**NA**
2018 3-Month Average	**1,708**	**2,367**	**1,246**	**1,577**	**14,092**	**2,322**	**4,272**	**2,629**	**20,238**	**4,137**	**47,691**	**NA**
2017 3-Month Average	**1,748**	**2,448**	**1,183**	**1,531**	**13,855**	**2,374**	**4,303**	**2,618**	**19,536**	**3,982**	**46,668**	**NA**

[a] Data are for unified Germany, i.e., the former East Germany and West Germany.

[b] "OECD Europe" consists of Austria, Belgium, Denmark, Finland, France, Germany, Greece, Iceland, Ireland, Italy, Luxembourg, the Netherlands, Norway, Portugal, Spain, Sweden, Switzerland, Turkey, and the United Kingdom; for 1984 forward, Czech Republic, Hungary, Poland, and Slovakia; and, for 2000 forward, Slovenia.

[c] "Other OECD" consists of Australia, New Zealand, and the U.S. Territories; for 1984 forward, Mexico; for 2000 forward, Chile, Estonia, and Israel; and, for 2016 forward, Latvia.

[d] The Organization for Economic Cooperation and Development (OECD) consists of "OECD Europe," Canada, Japan, South Korea, the United States, and "Other OECD."

R=Revised. NA=Not available.

Notes: • Totals may not equal sum of components due to independent rounding. • U.S. geographic coverage is the 50 states and the District of Columbia.

Web Page: See http://www.eia.gov/totalenergy/data/monthly/#international (Excel and CSV files) for all available annual and monthly data beginning in 1973.

Sources: • **United States:** Table 3.1. • **Chile, East Germany, Former Czechoslovakia, Hungary, Mexico, Poland, South Korea, Non-OECD Countries, U.S. Territories,** and **World: 1973–1979**—U.S. Energy Information Administration (EIA), International Energy Database. • **Countries Other Than United States: 1980–2008**—EIA, International Energy Statistics (IES). • **OECD Countries,** and **U.S. Territories: 2009 forward**—EIA, IES. • **World: 2008 forward**—EIA, International Energy Statistics Database. • **All Other Data:**—International Energy Agency (IEA), *Quarterly Oil Statistics and Energy Balances in OECD Countries,* various issues.

Source: *U.S. Energy Information Administration, Monthly Energy Review, June 2019*

Figure 11.3 Petroleum Stocks in OECD Countries
(Billion Barrels)

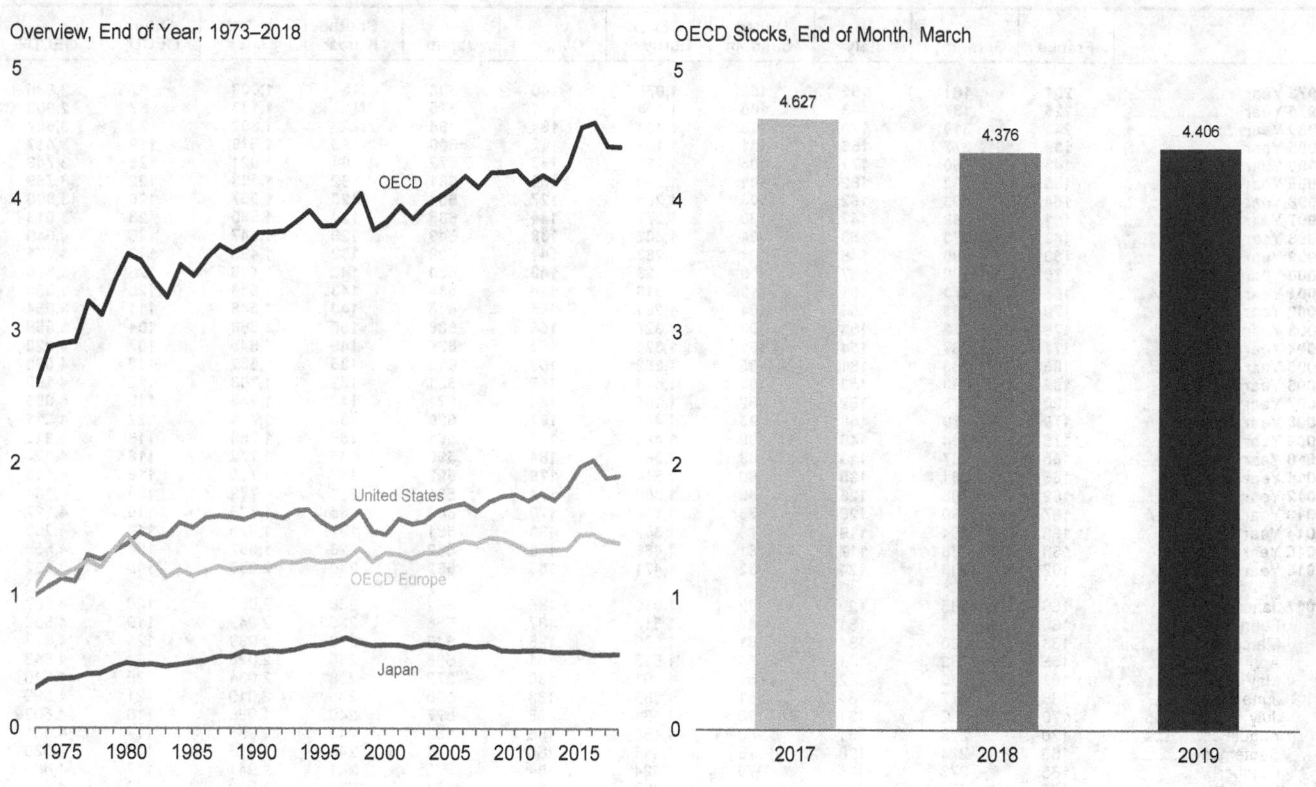

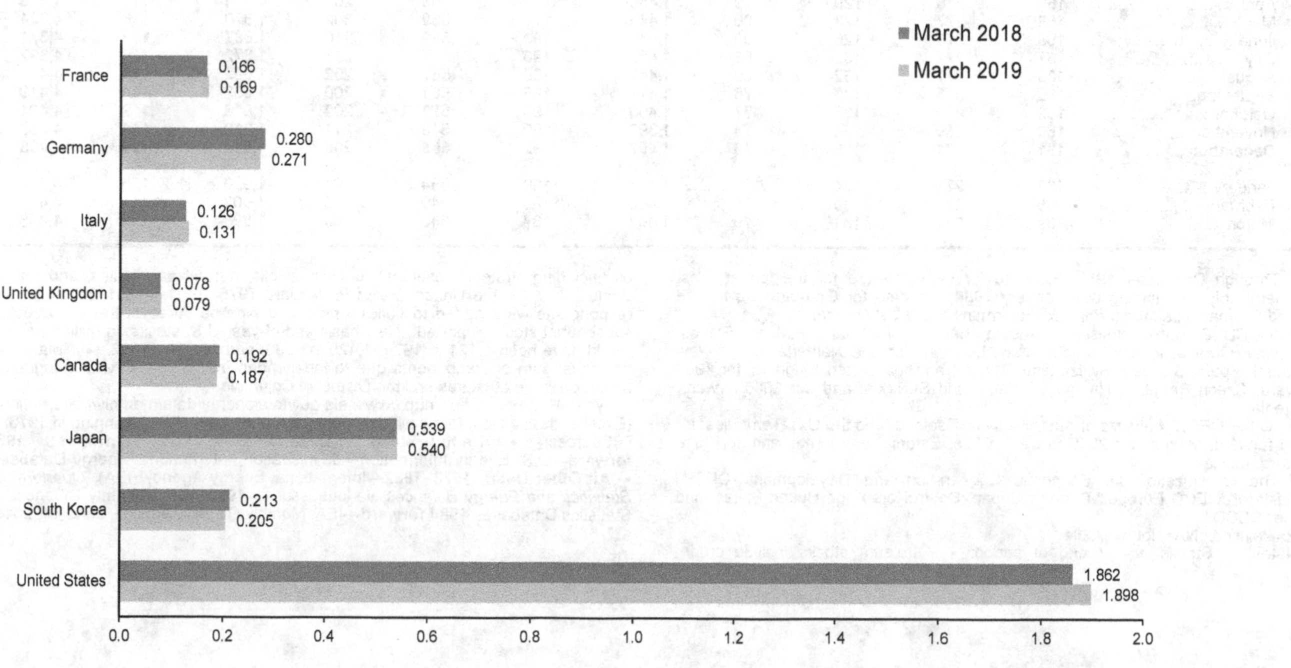

Note: OECD is the Organization for Economic Cooperation and Development.
Web Page: http://www.eia.gov/totalenergy/data/monthly/#international.
Source: Table 11.3.

Source: *U.S. Energy Information Administration, Monthly Energy Review, June 2019*

Table 11.3 Petroleum Stocks in OECD Countries

(Million Barrels)

	France	Germany[a]	Italy	United Kingdom	OECD Europe[b]	Canada	Japan	South Korea	United States	Other OECD[c]	OECD[d]
1973 Year	**201**	**181**	**152**	**156**	**1,070**	**140**	**303**	**NA**	**1,008**	**67**	**2,588**
1975 Year	**225**	**187**	**143**	**165**	**1,154**	**174**	**375**	**NA**	**1,133**	**67**	**2,903**
1980 Year	**243**	**319**	**170**	**168**	**1,464**	**164**	**495**	**NA**	**1,392**	**72**	**3,587**
1985 Year	**139**	**277**	**156**	**131**	**1,154**	**112**	**500**	**13**	**1,519**	**119**	**3,417**
1990 Year	**143**	**280**	**171**	**103**	**1,221**	**143**	**572**	**64**	**1,621**	**126**	**3,748**
1995 Year	**155**	**302**	**162**	**101**	**1,260**	**132**	**631**	**92**	**1,563**	**122**	**3,799**
1996 Year	**154**	**303**	**152**	**103**	**1,265**	**127**	**651**	**123**	**1,507**	**126**	**3,800**
1997 Year	**161**	**299**	**147**	**100**	**1,277**	**144**	**685**	**124**	**1,560**	**123**	**3,913**
1998 Year	**169**	**323**	**153**	**104**	**1,362**	**139**	**649**	**129**	**1,647**	**120**	**4,045**
1999 Year	**160**	**290**	**148**	**101**	**1,263**	**141**	**629**	**132**	**1,493**	**113**	**3,771**
2000 Year	**170**	**272**	**157**	**100**	**1,326**	**143**	**634**	**140**	**1,468**	**126**	**3,836**
2001 Year	**165**	**273**	**151**	**113**	**1,316**	**154**	**634**	**143**	**1,586**	**120**	**3,954**
2002 Year	**170**	**253**	**156**	**104**	**1,284**	**155**	**615**	**140**	**1,548**	**111**	**3,854**
2003 Year	**179**	**273**	**153**	**100**	**1,327**	**165**	**636**	**155**	**1,568**	**104**	**3,956**
2004 Year	**177**	**267**	**154**	**101**	**1,329**	**154**	**635**	**149**	**1,645**	**107**	**4,020**
2005 Year	**185**	**283**	**151**	**95**	**1,382**	**168**	**612**	**135**	**1,682**	**112**	**4,090**
2006 Year	**182**	**283**	**153**	**103**	**1,416**	**169**	**631**	**152**	**1,703**	**112**	**4,182**
2007 Year	**180**	**275**	**152**	**92**	**1,401**	**163**	**621**	**143**	**1,648**	**119**	**4,096**
2008 Year	**179**	**279**	**148**	**93**	**1,443**	**162**	**629**	**135**	**1,719**	**122**	**4,211**
2009 Year	**175**	**284**	**146**	**89**	**1,435**	**157**	**591**	**155**	**1,758**	**116**	**4,213**
2010 Year	**168**	**287**	**143**	**83**	**1,395**	**184**	**590**	**165**	**1,772**	**118**	**4,224**
2011 Year	**165**	**281**	**135**	**80**	**1,341**	**178**	**592**	**167**	**1,725**	**116**	**4,119**
2012 Year	**162**	**288**	**126**	**80**	**1,350**	**174**	**594**	**181**	**1,779**	**106**	**4,184**
2013 Year	**167**	**290**	**125**	**78**	**1,356**	**170**	**580**	**185**	**1,728**	**110**	**4,127**
2014 Year	**168**	**284**	**119**	**78**	**1,359**	**193**	**581**	**197**	**1,825**	**113**	**4,268**
2015 Year	**168**	**285**	**117**	**81**	**1,468**	**188**	**582**	**228**	**1,982**	**108**	**4,556**
2016 Year	**162**	**285**	**124**	**82**	**1,471**	**183**	**562**	**230**	**2,030**	**115**	**4,592**
2017 January	166	285	129	82	1,510	185	562	238	2,053	120	4,667
February	166	285	131	82	1,513	187	556	236	2,049	119	4,659
March	168	280	134	81	1,506	185	546	238	2,030	121	4,627
April	165	283	131	84	1,513	181	558	240	2,028	121	4,643
May	167	280	132	81	1,491	180	572	238	2,034	125	4,640
June	165	277	134	81	1,483	183	566	236	2,010	121	4,599
July	170	279	131	80	1,481	188	577	240	1,998	118	4,602
August	170	278	131	80	1,468	186	582	240	1,987	117	4,581
September	165	274	128	78	1,444	186	571	244	1,978	114	4,536
October	165	273	125	79	1,424	184	575	241	1,941	117	4,483
November	164	271	125	82	1,430	185	574	235	1,923	110	4,457
December	**166**	**279**	**125**	**80**	**1,423**	**189**	**563**	**231**	**1,895**	**109**	**4,409**
2018 January	167	283	125	83	1,467	186	560	225	1,879	116	4,434
February	165	278	130	79	1,463	184	545	230	1,876	117	4,415
March	166	280	126	78	1,454	192	539	213	1,862	117	4,376
April	168	R 278	129	79	R 1,456	186	553	207	1,864	115	4,380
May	168	277	128	80	1,446	190	559	202	1,870	116	R 4,384
June	168	278	125	82	1,442	190	549	210	1,867	113	4,371
July	167	R 277	133	83	1,450	190	557	207	1,872	116	R 4,392
August	165	277	132	80	1,442	200	567	202	1,892	115	4,417
September	165	273	125	78	1,417	195	561	200	1,932	114	R 4,419
October	162	R 270	125	77	R 1,400	194	573	202	1,916	119	4,404
November	160	269	124	74	1,393	190	578	211	1,910	111	4,393
December	**161**	**271**	**125**	**76**	**1,407**	**192**	**565**	**206**	**1,912**	**124**	**4,406**
2019 January	162	276	124	R 79	R 1,433	R 189	554	201	1,920	125	R 4,422
February	165	271	130	78	1,453	R 185	549	213	1,902	R 111	4,415
March	169	271	131	79	1,462	187	540	205	1,898	115	4,406

[a] Through December 1983, the data for Germany are for the former West Germany only. Beginning with January 1984, the data for Germany are for the unified Germany, i.e., the former East Germany and West Germany.

[b] "OECD Europe" consists of Austria, Belgium, Denmark, Finland, France, Germany, Greece, Iceland, Ireland, Italy, Luxembourg, the Netherlands, Norway, Portugal, Spain, Sweden, Switzerland, Turkey, and the United Kingdom; for 1984 forward, Czech Republic, Hungary, Poland, and Slovakia; and, for 2000 forward, Slovenia.

[c] "Other OECD" consists of Australia, New Zealand, and the U.S. Territories; for 1984 forward, Mexico; for 2000 forward, Chile, Estonia, and Israel; and, for 2016 forward, Latvia.

[d] The Organization for Economic Cooperation and Development (OECD) consists of "OECD Europe," Canada, Japan, South Korea, the United States, and "Other OECD."

R=Revised. NA=Not available.

Notes: • Stocks are at end of period. • Petroleum stocks include crude oil (including strategic reserves), unfinished oils, natural gas liquids, and refined products. • In the United States in January 1975, 1981, and 1983, numerous respondents were added to bulk terminal and pipeline surveys, thereby affecting subsequent stocks reported. New-basis end-of-year U.S. stocks, in million barrels, would have been 1,121 in 1974, 1,425 in 1980, and 1,461 in 1982. • Totals may not equal sum of components due to independent rounding. • U.S. geographic coverage is the 50 states and the District of Columbia.

Web Page: See http://www.eia.gov/totalenergy/data/monthly/#international (Excel and CSV files) for all available annual and monthly data beginning in 1973.

Sources: • **United States:** Table 3.4. • **U.S. Territories: 1983 forward**—U.S. Energy Information Administration, International Energy Database. • **All Other Data: 1973–1982**—International Energy Agency (IEA), *Quarterly Oil Statistics and Energy Balances*, various issues. **1983**—IEA, Monthly Oil and Gas Statistics Database. **1984 forward**—IEA, Monthly Oil Data Service, June 14, 2019.

Source: *U.S. Energy Information Administration, Monthly Energy Review, June 2019*

Figure 12.1 Carbon Dioxide Emissions From Energy Consumption by Source
(Million Metric Tons of Carbon Dioxide)

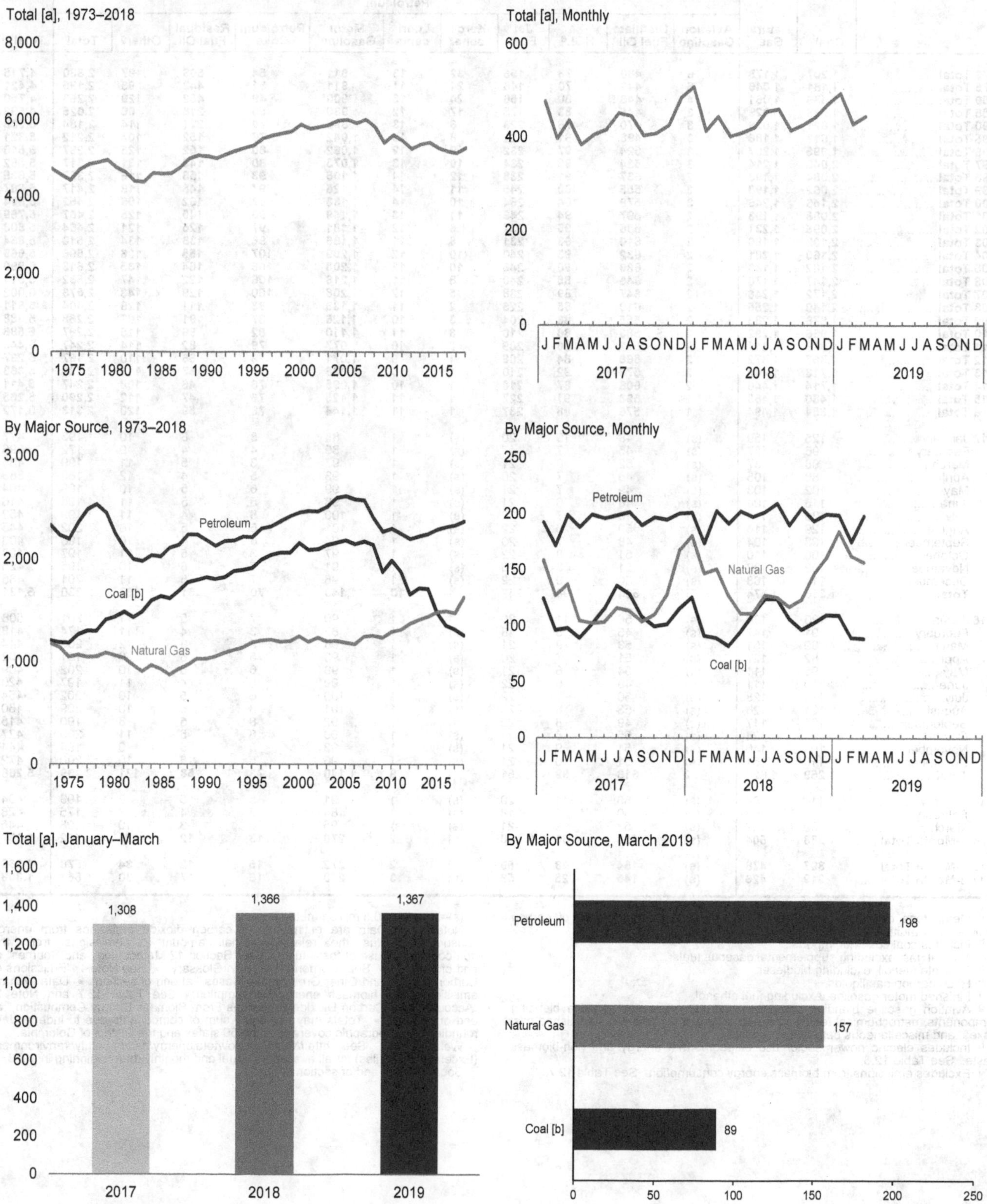

[a] Excludes emissions from biomass energy consumption.
[b] Includes coal coke net imports.

Web Page: http://www.eia.gov/totalenergy/data/monthly/#environment.
Source: Table 12.1.

Source: *U.S. Energy Information Administration, Monthly Energy Review, June 2019*

Table 12.1 Carbon Dioxide Emissions From Energy Consumption by Source

(Million Metric Tons of Carbon Dioxide[a])

			Petroleum											
	Coal[b]	Natural Gas[c]	Aviation Gasoline	Distillate Fuel Oil[d]	HGL[e]	Jet Fuel	Kero-sene	Lubri-cants	Motor Gasoline[f]	Petroleum Coke	Residual Fuel Oil	Other[g]	Total	Total[h,i]
1973 Total	**1,207**	**1,179**	**6**	**480**	**76**	**155**	**32**	**13**	**911**	**54**	**506**	**97**	**2,330**	**4,715**
1975 Total	**1,181**	**1,046**	**5**	**442**	**70**	**146**	**24**	**11**	**911**	**51**	**442**	**93**	**2,195**	**4,421**
1980 Total	**1,436**	**1,061**	**4**	**446**	**80**	**156**	**24**	**13**	**900**	**49**	**452**	**129**	**2,253**	**4,750**
1985 Total	**1,638**	**929**	**3**	**445**	**83**	**178**	**17**	**12**	**930**	**55**	**216**	**86**	**2,025**	**4,593**
1990 Total	**1,821**	**1,026**	**3**	**470**	**76**	**223**	**6**	**13**	**988**	**70**	**221**	**114**	**2,184**	**5,038**
1995 Total	**1,913**	**1,186**	**3**	**498**	**91**	**222**	**8**	**13**	**1,042**	**76**	**152**	**107**	**2,212**	**5,321**
1996 Total	**1,995**	**1,207**	**3**	**524**	**97**	**232**	**9**	**12**	**1,062**	**80**	**152**	**125**	**2,297**	**5,510**
1997 Total	**2,040**	**1,214**	**3**	**534**	**95**	**234**	**10**	**13**	**1,073**	**80**	**143**	**131**	**2,317**	**5,582**
1998 Total	**2,064**	**1,193**	**2**	**537**	**91**	**238**	**12**	**14**	**1,105**	**93**	**158**	**116**	**2,367**	**5,635**
1999 Total	**2,062**	**1,198**	**3**	**555**	**100**	**245**	**11**	**14**	**1,125**	**97**	**148**	**119**	**2,417**	**5,687**
2000 Total	**2,156**	**1,246**	**3**	**579**	**104**	**254**	**10**	**14**	**1,133**	**87**	**162**	**106**	**2,452**	**5,864**
2001 Total	**2,088**	**1,193**	**2**	**597**	**94**	**243**	**11**	**13**	**1,149**	**90**	**145**	**125**	**2,467**	**5,759**
2002 Total	**2,095**	**1,231**	**2**	**586**	**96**	**237**	**6**	**12**	**1,181**	**97**	**125**	**121**	**2,464**	**5,803**
2003 Total	**2,136**	**1,196**	**2**	**610**	**93**	**231**	**8**	**11**	**1,186**	**96**	**138**	**134**	**2,510**	**5,854**
2004 Total	**2,160**	**1,201**	**2**	**632**	**95**	**240**	**10**	**12**	**1,209**	**107**	**155**	**136**	**2,596**	**5,969**
2005 Total	**2,182**	**1,183**	**2**	**639**	**90**	**246**	**10**	**12**	**1,208**	**106**	**164**	**135**	**2,613**	**5,990**
2006 Total	**2,147**	**1,170**	**2**	**645**	**85**	**240**	**8**	**11**	**1,216**	**106**	**122**	**147**	**2,582**	**5,911**
2007 Total	**2,172**	**1,246**	**2**	**647**	**89**	**238**	**5**	**12**	**1,208**	**100**	**129**	**143**	**2,573**	**6,002**
2008 Total	**2,140**	**1,255**	**2**	**610**	**85**	**226**	**2**	**11**	**1,139**	**93**	**111**	**126**	**2,404**	**5,811**
2009 Total	**1,876**	**1,233**	**2**	**555**	**83**	**204**	**3**	**10**	**1,126**	**87**	**91**	**107**	**2,268**	**5,388**
2010 Total	**1,986**	**1,292**	**2**	**583**	**86**	**210**	**3**	**11**	**1,110**	**82**	**96**	**115**	**2,297**	**5,586**
2011 Total	**1,876**	**1,311**	**2**	**592**	**80**	**209**	**2**	**10**	**1,077**	**79**	**82**	**114**	**2,247**	**5,446**
2012 Total	**1,657**	**1,372**	**2**	**569**	**84**	**206**	**1**	**9**	**1,071**	**79**	**66**	**110**	**2,197**	**5,237**
2013 Total	**1,718**	**1,409**	**2**	**573**	**92**	**210**	**1**	**10**	**1,086**	**77**	**57**	**116**	**2,224**	**5,363**
2014 Total	**1,714**	**1,440**	**2**	**606**	**87**	**216**	**1**	**10**	**1,095**	**76**	**46**	**108**	**2,247**	**5,411**
2015 Total	**1,480**	**1,483**	**1**	**598**	**91**	**227**	**1**	**11**	**1,125**	**76**	**47**	**112**	**2,290**	**5,265**
2016 Total	**1,354**	**1,494**	**1**	**576**	**88**	**237**	**1**	**11**	**1,144**	**76**	**59**	**120**	**2,313**	**5,172**
2017 January	125	159	(s)	48	10	20	(s)	1	88	8	8	10	193	477
February	96	127	(s)	45	7	17	(s)	1	85	4	4	9	172	396
March	98	137	(s)	52	8	21	(s)	1	97	3	5	11	199	435
April	89	105	(s)	46	7	20	(s)	1	93	5	4	12	188	383
May	102	103	(s)	49	7	21	(s)	1	99	6	5	10	199	404
June	116	104	(s)	48	6	21	(s)	1	98	5	5	11	196	416
July	136	116	(s)	46	7	22	(s)	1	100	8	4	11	199	452
August	129	114	(s)	50	6	22	(s)	1	101	5	5	10	202	445
September	108	104	(s)	48	7	20	(s)	1	94	6	4	10	190	403
October	100	110	(s)	51	8	22	(s)	1	97	3	5	11	197	408
November	102	128	(s)	51	8	20	(s)	1	91	7	6	10	195	425
December	116	168	(s)	50	9	22	(s)	1	96	7	5	11	201	485
Total	**1,316**	**1,474**	**1**	**584**	**90**	**247**	**1**	**10**	**1,140**	**70**	**61**	**126**	**2,330**	**5,131**
2018 January	126	180	(s)	56	11	20	1	1	90	7	5	11	201	508
February	91	147	(s)	45	8	18	(s)	1	83	3	4	11	174	413
March	89	151	(s)	53	9	21	(s)	1	98	5	3	12	203	444
April	82	127	(s)	51	7	20	(s)	1	93	5	6	8	191	402
May	95	111	(s)	54	6	21	(s)	1	99	6	5	10	202	409
June	110	111	(s)	48	6	22	(s)	1	99	6	4	11	197	420
July	124	128	(s)	50	7	22	(s)	1	100	6	5	10	202	454
August	124	126	(s)	53	8	23	(s)	1	101	8	5	10	209	460
September	107	117	(s)	49	8	20	(s)	(s)	92	8	5	8	190	415
October	97	124	(s)	55	8	21	(s)	1	96	8	5	11	205	427
November	103	146	(s)	51	9	21	(s)	1	93	5	5	9	194	444
December	110	161	(s)	51	10	21	(s)	1	96	5	6	10	200	472
Total	**1,259**	**1,629**	**2**	**616**	**99**	**251**	**1**	**9**	**1,140**	**73**	**58**	**121**	**2,369**	**5,268**
2019 January	110	184	(s)	56	11	20	(s)	1	91	5	5	9	199	494
February	90	163	(s)	50	9	18	(s)	1	84	2	4	7	175	428
March	89	157	(s)	53	9	21	(s)	(s)	95	6	3	10	198	445
3-Month Total	**288**	**504**	**(s)**	**158**	**30**	**60**	**1**	**2**	**270**	**13**	**12**	**26**	**572**	**1,367**
2018 3-Month Total	**307**	**478**	**(s)**	**154**	**28**	**59**	**1**	**2**	**272**	**15**	**12**	**34**	**578**	**1,366**
2017 3-Month Total	**319**	**423**	**(s)**	**145**	**25**	**58**	**(s)**	**3**	**270**	**15**	**17**	**30**	**563**	**1,308**

[a] Metric tons of carbon dioxide can be converted to metric tons of carbon equivalent by multiplying by 12/44.
[b] Includes coal coke net imports.
[c] Natural gas, excluding supplemental gaseous fuels.
[d] Distillate fuel oil, excluding biodiesel.
[e] Hydrocarbon gas liquids.
[f] Finished motor gasoline, excluding fuel ethanol.
[g] Aviation gasoline blending components, crude oil, motor gasoline blending components, petrochemical feedstocks, special naphthas, still gas, unfinished oils, waxes, and miscellaneous petroleum products.
[h] Includes electric power sector use of geothermal energy and non-biomass waste. See Table 12.6.
[i] Excludes emissions from biomass energy consumption. See Table 12.7.

(s)=Less than 0.5 million metric tons.

Notes: • Data are estimates for carbon dioxide emissions from energy consumption, plus the relatively small amount of emissions from the non-combustion use of fossil fuels. See "Section 12 Methodology and Sources" at end of section. • See "Carbon Dioxide" in Glossary. • See Note 1, "Emissions of Carbon Dioxide and Other Greenhouse Gases," at end of section. • Data exclude emissions from biomass energy consumption. See Table 12.7 and Note 2, "Accounting for Carbon Dioxide Emissions From Biomass Energy Combustion," at end of section. • Totals may not equal sum of components due to independent rounding. • Geographic coverage is the 50 states and the District of Columbia.

Web Page: See http://www.eia.gov/totalenergy/data/monthly/#environment (Excel and CSV files) for all available annual and monthly data beginning in 1970.

Sources: See end of section.

Source: *U.S. Energy Information Administration, Monthly Energy Review, June 2019*

Figure 12.2 Carbon Dioxide Emissions From Energy Consumption by Sector
(Million Metric Tons of Carbon Dioxide)

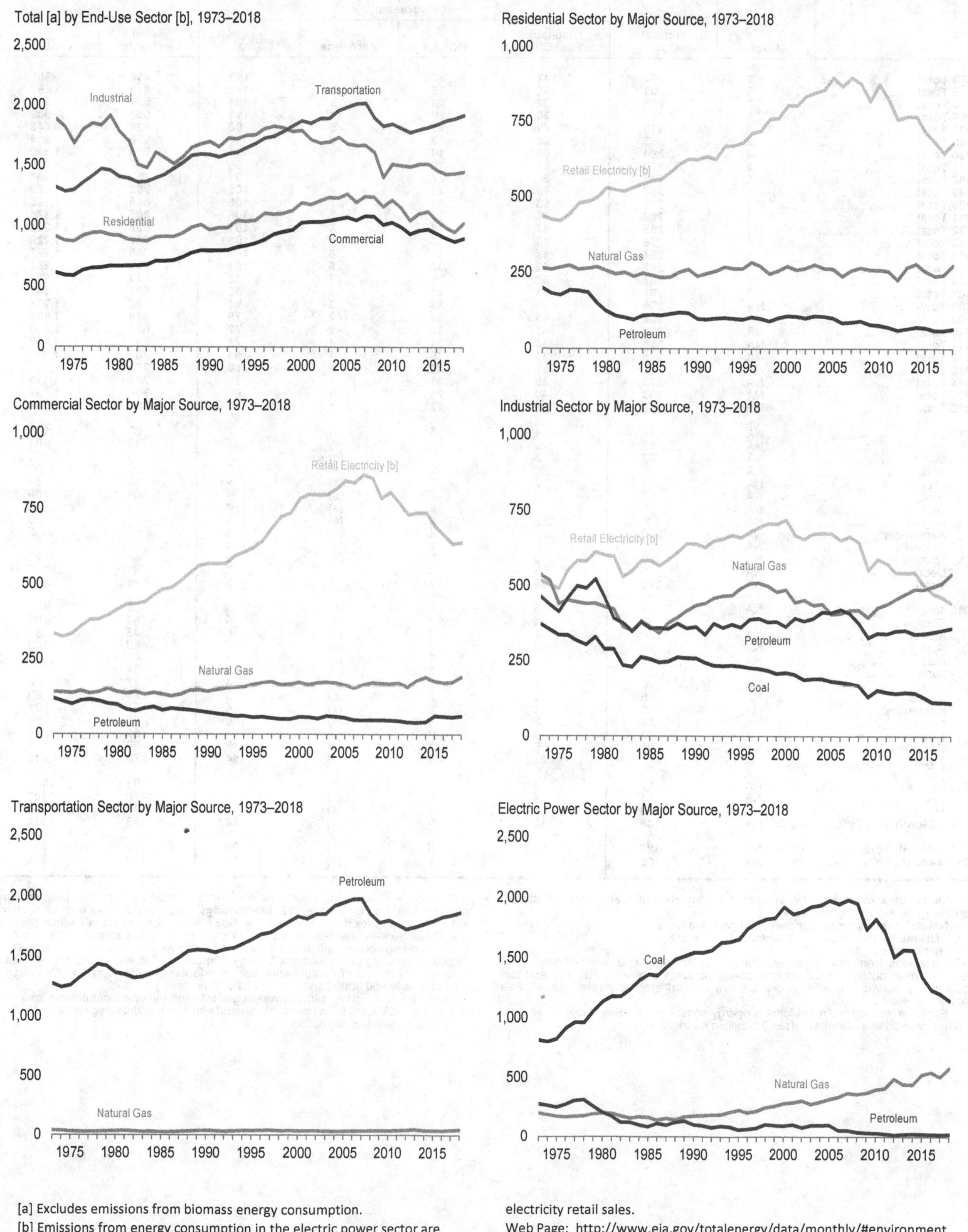

[a] Excludes emissions from biomass energy consumption.
[b] Emissions from energy consumption in the electric power sector are allocated to the end-use sectors in proportion to each sector's share of total electricity retail sales.
Web Page: http://www.eia.gov/totalenergy/data/monthly/#environment.
Sources: Tables 12.2–12.6.

***Source:** U.S. Energy Information Administration, Monthly Energy Review, June 2019*

Table 12.2 Carbon Dioxide Emissions From Energy Consumption: Residential Sector

(Million Metric Tons of Carbon Dioxide[a])

	Coal	Natural Gas[b]	Petroleum				Retail Electricity[e]	Total[f]
			Distillate Fuel Oil[c]	HGL[d]	Kerosene	Total		
1973 Total	**9**	**264**	**147**	**36**	**16**	**199**	**435**	**907**
1975 Total	**6**	**266**	**132**	**32**	**12**	**176**	**419**	**867**
1980 Total	**3**	**256**	**96**	**20**	**8**	**124**	**529**	**911**
1985 Total	**4**	**241**	**80**	**20**	**11**	**111**	**553**	**909**
1990 Total	**3**	**238**	**72**	**22**	**5**	**98**	**624**	**963**
1995 Total	**2**	**263**	**66**	**25**	**5**	**96**	**678**	**1,039**
1996 Total	**2**	**284**	**68**	**30**	**6**	**104**	**710**	**1,099**
1997 Total	**2**	**270**	**64**	**29**	**7**	**99**	**719**	**1,090**
1998 Total	**1**	**247**	**56**	**27**	**8**	**91**	**759**	**1,097**
1999 Total	**1**	**257**	**60**	**33**	**8**	**102**	**762**	**1,122**
2000 Total	**1**	**271**	**66**	**35**	**7**	**108**	**805**	**1,185**
2001 Total	**1**	**259**	**66**	**33**	**7**	**106**	**805**	**1,171**
2002 Total	**1**	**265**	**63**	**34**	**4**	**101**	**835**	**1,203**
2003 Total	**1**	**276**	**68**	**34**	**5**	**108**	**847**	**1,232**
2004 Total	**1**	**264**	**67**	**32**	**6**	**106**	**856**	**1,227**
2005 Total	**1**	**262**	**62**	**32**	**6**	**101**	**897**	**1,261**
2006 Total	**1**	**237**	**52**	**28**	**5**	**85**	**869**	**1,191**
2007 Total	**1**	**257**	**53**	**31**	**3**	**86**	**897**	**1,241**
2008 Total	**NA**	**266**	**55**	**35**	**2**	**91**	**877**	**1,234**
2009 Total	**NA**	**259**	**43**	**35**	**2**	**79**	**819**	**1,157**
2010 Total	**NA**	**259**	**41**	**33**	**2**	**77**	**874**	**1,210**
2011 Total	**NA**	**255**	**38**	**31**	**1**	**71**	**823**	**1,149**
2012 Total	**NA**	**225**	**35**	**25**	**1**	**61**	**757**	**1,043**
2013 Total	**NA**	**267**	**36**	**29**	**1**	**66**	**768**	**1,100**
2014 Total	**NA**	**278**	**39**	**31**	**1**	**71**	**766**	**1,115**
2015 Total	**NA**	**253**	**40**	**28**	**1**	**69**	**714**	**1,037**
2016 Total	**NA**	**239**	**32**	**27**	**1**	**60**	**683**	**982**
2017 January	NA	46	4	3	(s)	7	63	116
February	NA	32	3	2	(s)	5	44	81
March	NA	32	3	2	(s)	5	45	82
April	NA	15	2	2	(s)	5	39	59
May	NA	11	2	2	(s)	4	45	60
June	NA	7	2	2	(s)	4	58	69
July	NA	6	1	2	(s)	4	77	86
August	NA	6	2	2	(s)	4	70	80
September	NA	6	2	2	(s)	4	55	65
October	NA	11	2	2	(s)	4	46	62
November	NA	26	3	2	(s)	6	46	77
December	NA	45	5	3	(s)	7	60	112
Total	**NA**	**242**	**32**	**27**	**1**	**59**	**645**	**947**
2018 January	NA	54	5	3	(s)	9	72	135
February	NA	38	4	2	(s)	6	49	92
March	NA	36	3	3	(s)	6	45	87
April	NA	24	3	2	(s)	5	40	69
May	NA	9	2	2	(s)	4	47	60
June	NA	7	1	2	(s)	4	61	71
July	NA	6	1	2	(s)	4	77	86
August	NA	5	1	2	(s)	3	74	83
September	NA	6	1	2	(s)	4	61	71
October	NA	14	3	3	(s)	6	49	68
November	NA	33	4	3	(s)	7	50	89
December	NA	42	5	3	(s)	8	57	107
Total	**NA**	**273**	**33**	**30**	**1**	**64**	**679**	**1,016**
2019 January	NA	52	5	3	(s)	8	61	122
February	NA	44	4	3	(s)	7	50	101
March	NA	38	4	3	(s)	6	47	91
3-Month Total	**NA**	**134**	**12**	**9**	**(s)**	**22**	**159**	**314**
2018 3-Month Total	**NA**	**127**	**12**	**8**	**(s)**	**20**	**166**	**314**
2017 3-Month Total	**NA**	**109**	**11**	**7**	**(s)**	**18**	**152**	**279**

[a] Metric tons of carbon dioxide can be converted to metric tons of carbon equivalent by multiplying by 12/44.
[b] Natural gas, excluding supplemental gaseous fuels.
[c] Distillate fuel oil, excluding biodiesel.
[d] Hydrocarbon gas liquids.
[e] Emissions from energy consumption (for electricity and a small amount of useful thermal output) in the electric power sector are allocated to the end-use sectors in proportion to each sector's share of total electricity retail sales. See Tables 7.6 and 12.6.
[f] Excludes emissions from biomass energy consumption. See Table 12.7.
NA=Not available. (s)=Less than 0.5 million metric tons.

Notes: • Data are estimates for carbon dioxide emissions from energy consumption. See "Section 12 Methodology and Sources" at end of section. • See "Carbon Dioxide" in Glossary. • See Note 1, "Emissions of Carbon Dioxide and Other Greenhouse Gases," at end of section. • Data exclude emissions from biomass energy consumption. See Table 12.7 and Note 2, "Accounting for Carbon Dioxide Emissions From Biomass Energy Combustion," at end of section. • Totals may not equal sum of components due to independent rounding. • Geographic coverage is the 50 states and the District of Columbia.

Web Page: See http://www.eia.gov/totalenergy/data/monthly/#environment (Excel and CSV files) for all available annual and monthly data beginning in 1973.

Sources: See end of section.

Source: *U.S. Energy Information Administration, Monthly Energy Review, June 2019*

Table 12.3 Carbon Dioxide Emissions From Energy Consumption: Commercial Sector

(Million Metric Tons of Carbon Dioxide[a])

			Petroleum								
	Coal	Natural Gas[b]	Distillate Fuel Oil[c]	HGL[d]	Kerosene	Motor Gasoline[e]	Petroleum Coke	Residual Fuel Oil	Total	Retail Electricity[f]	Total[g]
1973 Total	**15**	**141**	**47**	**9**	**5**	**6**	**NA**	**52**	**120**	**334**	**609**
1975 Total	**14**	**136**	**43**	**8**	**4**	**6**	**NA**	**39**	**100**	**333**	**583**
1980 Total	**11**	**141**	**38**	**6**	**3**	**8**	**NA**	**44**	**98**	**412**	**662**
1985 Total	**13**	**132**	**46**	**6**	**2**	**7**	**NA**	**18**	**79**	**480**	**704**
1990 Total	**12**	**142**	**39**	**6**	**1**	**8**	**0**	**18**	**73**	**566**	**793**
1995 Total	**11**	**164**	**35**	**7**	**2**	**1**	**(s)**	**11**	**56**	**620**	**851**
1996 Total	**12**	**171**	**35**	**8**	**2**	**2**	**(s)**	**11**	**57**	**643**	**883**
1997 Total	**12**	**174**	**32**	**8**	**2**	**3**	**(s)**	**9**	**54**	**686**	**926**
1998 Total	**9**	**164**	**31**	**7**	**2**	**3**	**(s)**	**7**	**50**	**724**	**947**
1999 Total	**10**	**165**	**32**	**9**	**2**	**2**	**(s)**	**6**	**51**	**735**	**960**
2000 Total	**9**	**173**	**36**	**9**	**2**	**3**	**(s)**	**7**	**58**	**783**	**1,022**
2001 Total	**9**	**164**	**37**	**9**	**2**	**3**	**(s)**	**6**	**57**	**797**	**1,027**
2002 Total	**9**	**170**	**32**	**9**	**1**	**3**	**(s)**	**6**	**52**	**795**	**1,026**
2003 Total	**8**	**173**	**36**	**10**	**1**	**4**	**(s)**	**9**	**60**	**796**	**1,037**
2004 Total	**10**	**170**	**34**	**10**	**1**	**3**	**(s)**	**10**	**58**	**815**	**1,053**
2005 Total	**9**	**163**	**33**	**8**	**2**	**3**	**(s)**	**9**	**55**	**841**	**1,069**
2006 Total	**6**	**154**	**29**	**8**	**1**	**3**	**(s)**	**6**	**47**	**835**	**1,043**
2007 Total	**7**	**164**	**28**	**8**	**1**	**4**	**(s)**	**6**	**46**	**861**	**1,078**
2008 Total	**8**	**171**	**28**	**10**	**(s)**	**3**	**(s)**	**6**	**47**	**849**	**1,075**
2009 Total	**7**	**169**	**29**	**9**	**(s)**	**3**	**(s)**	**6**	**47**	**784**	**1,007**
2010 Total	**7**	**168**	**29**	**9**	**(s)**	**3**	**(s)**	**5**	**46**	**804**	**1,025**
2011 Total	**6**	**171**	**29**	**9**	**(s)**	**3**	**(s)**	**4**	**45**	**768**	**990**
2012 Total	**4**	**157**	**26**	**9**	**(s)**	**3**	**(s)**	**2**	**40**	**731**	**932**
2013 Total	**4**	**179**	**25**	**10**	**(s)**	**3**	**(s)**	**2**	**39**	**736**	**958**
2014 Total	**4**	**190**	**26**	**10**	**(s)**	**4**	**(s)**	**1**	**41**	**736**	**970**
2015 Total	**3**	**176**	**26**	**9**	**(s)**	**25**	**(s)**	**(s)**	**61**	**692**	**932**
2016 Total	**2**	**171**	**24**	**9**	**(s)**	**25**	**(s)**	**(s)**	**59**	**662**	**894**
2017 January	(s)	26	3	1	(s)	2	(s)	(s)	6	53	86
February	(s)	20	2	1	(s)	2	(s)	(s)	5	44	68
March	(s)	20	2	1	(s)	2	(s)	(s)	5	47	73
April	(s)	12	2	1	(s)	2	(s)	(s)	5	44	60
May	(s)	10	1	1	(s)	2	(s)	(s)	4	50	64
June	(s)	8	2	1	(s)	2	(s)	(s)	4	57	69
July	(s)	7	1	1	(s)	2	(s)	(s)	4	66	78
August	(s)	8	1	1	(s)	2	(s)	(s)	4	63	75
September	(s)	8	1	1	(s)	2	(s)	(s)	4	55	67
October	(s)	11	2	1	(s)	2	(s)	(s)	4	51	67
November	(s)	18	2	1	(s)	2	(s)	(s)	5	49	72
December	(s)	27	3	1	(s)	2	(s)	(s)	6	53	87
Total	**2**	**174**	**24**	**10**	**(s)**	**24**	**(s)**	**(s)**	**58**	**633**	**867**
2018 January	(s)	30	4	1	(s)	2	(s)	(s)	7	56	93
February	(s)	23	3	1	(s)	2	(s)	(s)	5	44	72
March	(s)	23	2	1	(s)	2	(s)	(s)	5	46	74
April	(s)	16	2	1	(s)	2	(s)	(s)	5	43	64
May	(s)	9	1	1	(s)	2	0	(s)	4	51	64
June	(s)	8	1	1	(s)	2	0	(s)	4	57	69
July	(s)	7	1	1	(s)	2	0	(s)	4	66	77
August	(s)	8	1	1	(s)	2	0	(s)	4	65	77
September	(s)	8	1	1	(s)	2	(s)	(s)	4	58	69
October	(s)	13	2	1	(s)	2	(s)	(s)	5	53	71
November	(s)	21	3	1	(s)	2	(s)	(s)	6	50	77
December	(s)	25	4	1	(s)	2	(s)	(s)	7	50	83
Total	**2**	**191**	**25**	**11**	**(s)**	**24**	**(s)**	**(s)**	**60**	**638**	**891**
2019 January	(s)	30	4	1	(s)	2	(s)	(s)	7	52	89
February	(s)	26	3	1	(s)	2	(s)	(s)	6	44	76
March	(s)	23	3	1	(s)	2	(s)	(s)	6	45	74
3-Month Total	**(s)**	**80**	**9**	**3**	**(s)**	**6**	**(s)**	**(s)**	**18**	**141**	**239**
2018 3-Month Total	**1**	**76**	**9**	**3**	**(s)**	**6**	**(s)**	**(s)**	**18**	**145**	**239**
2017 3-Month Total	**1**	**66**	**8**	**3**	**(s)**	**6**	**(s)**	**(s)**	**16**	**144**	**227**

[a] Metric tons of carbon dioxide can be converted to metric tons of carbon equivalent by multiplying by 12/44.
[b] Natural gas, excluding supplemental gaseous fuels.
[c] Distillate fuel oil, excluding biodiesel.
[d] Hydrocarbon gas liquids.
[e] Finished motor gasoline, excluding fuel ethanol.
[f] Emissions from energy consumption (for electricity and a small amount of useful thermal output) in the electric power sector are allocated to the end-use sectors in proportion to each sector's share of total electricity retail sales. See Tables 7.6 and 12.6.
[g] Excludes emissions from biomass energy consumption. See Table 12.7.
NA=Not available. (s)=Less than 0.5 million metric tons.

Notes: • Data are estimates for carbon dioxide emissions from energy consumption. See "Section 12 Methodology and Sources" at end of section. • See "Carbon Dioxide" in Glossary. • See Note 1, "Emissions of Carbon Dioxide and Other Greenhouse Gases," at end of section. • Data exclude emissions from biomass energy consumption. See Table 12.7 and Note 2, "Accounting for Carbon Dioxide Emissions From Biomass Energy Combustion," at end of section. • Totals may not equal sum of components due to independent rounding. • Geographic coverage is the 50 states and the District of Columbia.

Web Page: See http://www.eia.gov/totalenergy/data/monthly/#environment (Excel and CSV files) for all available annual and monthly data beginning in 1973.

Sources: See end of section.

Source: *U.S. Energy Information Administration, Monthly Energy Review, June 2019*

Table 12.4 Carbon Dioxide Emissions From Energy Consumption: Industrial Sector
(Million Metric Tons of Carbon Dioxide[a])

	Coal	Coal Coke Net Imports	Natural Gas[b]	Petroleum: Distillate Fuel Oil[c]	HGL[d]	Kero-sene	Lubri-cants	Motor Gasoline[e]	Petroleum Coke	Residual Fuel Oil	Other[f]	Total	Retail Elec-tricity[g]	Total[h]
1973 Total	**371**	**-1**	**536**	**106**	**28**	**11**	**7**	**18**	**53**	**142**	**97**	**463**	**515**	**1,884**
1975 Total	**336**	**2**	**440**	**97**	**27**	**9**	**6**	**16**	**51**	**115**	**93**	**413**	**490**	**1,680**
1980 Total	**289**	**-4**	**430**	**96**	**54**	**13**	**7**	**11**	**49**	**103**	**129**	**461**	**601**	**1,776**
1985 Total	**256**	**-2**	**363**	**81**	**55**	**3**	**6**	**15**	**54**	**57**	**86**	**358**	**583**	**1,558**
1990 Total	**258**	**1**	**435**	**84**	**46**	**1**	**7**	**13**	**67**	**32**	**114**	**363**	**638**	**1,695**
1995 Total	**233**	**7**	**492**	**82**	**58**	**1**	**7**	**14**	**68**	**25**	**107**	**362**	**659**	**1,752**
1996 Total	**227**	**3**	**508**	**86**	**59**	**1**	**6**	**14**	**72**	**25**	**125**	**389**	**678**	**1,804**
1997 Total	**224**	**5**	**509**	**88**	**58**	**1**	**7**	**15**	**70**	**22**	**131**	**392**	**694**	**1,824**
1998 Total	**219**	**8**	**500**	**88**	**56**	**2**	**7**	**14**	**80**	**16**	**116**	**379**	**706**	**1,811**
1999 Total	**208**	**7**	**480**	**86**	**57**	**1**	**7**	**11**	**85**	**14**	**119**	**381**	**704**	**1,780**
2000 Total	**211**	**7**	**486**	**87**	**58**	**1**	**7**	**11**	**77**	**17**	**106**	**364**	**719**	**1,787**
2001 Total	**204**	**3**	**444**	**94**	**51**	**2**	**6**	**21**	**79**	**14**	**125**	**392**	**667**	**1,712**
2002 Total	**188**	**7**	**453**	**88**	**52**	**1**	**6**	**22**	**79**	**13**	**121**	**382**	**654**	**1,684**
2003 Total	**190**	**6**	**435**	**85**	**48**	**2**	**6**	**23**	**78**	**15**	**134**	**391**	**672**	**1,694**
2004 Total	**190**	**16**	**438**	**88**	**52**	**2**	**6**	**26**	**85**	**17**	**136**	**413**	**674**	**1,732**
2005 Total	**183**	**5**	**406**	**92**	**48**	**3**	**6**	**25**	**82**	**20**	**135**	**410**	**672**	**1,677**
2006 Total	**179**	**7**	**408**	**91**	**47**	**2**	**6**	**26**	**85**	**16**	**147**	**421**	**650**	**1,664**
2007 Total	**175**	**3**	**418**	**91**	**50**	**1**	**6**	**21**	**83**	**13**	**143**	**408**	**662**	**1,666**
2008 Total	**168**	**5**	**419**	**98**	**38**	**(s)**	**6**	**17**	**78**	**13**	**126**	**375**	**642**	**1,608**
2009 Total	**131**	**-3**	**395**	**78**	**38**	**(s)**	**5**	**16**	**73**	**9**	**107**	**327**	**550**	**1,400**
2010 Total	**153**	**-1**	**427**	**84**	**43**	**1**	**5**	**17**	**68**	**8**	**115**	**342**	**587**	**1,508**
2011 Total	**146**	**1**	**438**	**90**	**40**	**(s)**	**5**	**17**	**65**	**9**	**114**	**340**	**574**	**1,498**
2012 Total	**141**	**(s)**	**455**	**93**	**50**	**(s)**	**4**	**17**	**70**	**5**	**110**	**350**	**543**	**1,490**
2013 Total	**145**	**-2**	**472**	**92**	**53**	**(s)**	**5**	**17**	**65**	**3**	**116**	**352**	**542**	**1,508**
2014 Total	**143**	**-2**	**488**	**100**	**46**	**(s)**	**5**	**14**	**64**	**3**	**108**	**339**	**543**	**1,511**
2015 Total	**129**	**-2**	**487**	**85**	**53**	**(s)**	**5**	**17**	**65**	**2**	**112**	**340**	**502**	**1,457**
2016 Total	**113**	**-2**	**497**	**84**	**51**	**(s)**	**5**	**17**	**64**	**4**	**120**	**345**	**473**	**1,426**
2017 January	9	(s)	46	7	6	(s)	(s)	1	7	(s)	10	32	38	125
February	9	(s)	41	8	4	(s)	(s)	1	3	(s)	9	26	33	109
March	9	(s)	44	10	5	(s)	(s)	1	3	(s)	11	31	35	119
April	9	(s)	41	6	4	(s)	(s)	1	5	(s)	12	29	34	112
May	9	(s)	41	8	4	(s)	(s)	2	6	(s)	10	30	38	117
June	9	(s)	40	7	3	(s)	(s)	2	4	(s)	11	27	41	116
July	9	(s)	41	5	4	(s)	(s)	2	7	(s)	11	29	45	124
August	9	(s)	41	7	4	(s)	(s)	2	5	(s)	10	28	44	122
September	9	(s)	40	7	4	(s)	(s)	1	5	(s)	10	29	39	116
October	9	(s)	42	8	5	(s)	(s)	1	3	(s)	11	28	37	117
November	9	(s)	44	9	5	(s)	(s)	1	6	(s)	10	32	37	123
December	10	(s)	48	7	5	(s)	(s)	1	6	(s)	11	31	39	128
Total	**112**	**-3**	**509**	**88**	**53**	**(s)**	**5**	**18**	**60**	**3**	**126**	**352**	**461**	**1,430**
2018 January	9	(s)	49	9	6	(s)	(s)	1	6	(s)	11	35	37	129
February	9	(s)	44	7	5	(s)	(s)	1	3	(s)	11	27	31	110
March	9	(s)	47	9	5	(s)	(s)	2	5	(s)	12	33	33	121
April	9	(s)	44	8	4	(s)	(s)	1	5	(s)	8	27	31	112
May	9	(s)	43	10	3	(s)	(s)	2	5	(s)	10	30	37	119
June	9	(s)	42	6	3	(s)	(s)	2	6	(s)	11	28	38	117
July	9	(s)	43	6	4	(s)	(s)	2	5	(s)	10	28	43	122
August	9	(s)	43	8	4	(s)	(s)	2	7	(s)	10	33	43	128
September	9	(s)	43	7	4	(s)	(s)	1	7	(s)	8	28	38	118
October	9	(s)	44	9	5	(s)	(s)	1	7	(s)	11	34	37	125
November	9	(s)	47	7	5	(s)	(s)	1	4	(s)	9	28	37	121
December	10	(s)	49	6	6	(s)	(s)	1	4	(s)	10	28	36	122
Total	**110**	**-3**	**538**	**92**	**57**	**(s)**	**4**	**18**	**63**	**3**	**121**	**358**	**442**	**1,445**
2019 January	9	(s)	51	11	7	(s)	(s)	1	4	(s)	9	34	36	129
February	8	(s)	46	9	6	(s)	(s)	1	1	(s)	7	25	31	110
March	9	(s)	48	9	5	(s)	(s)	1	5	(s)	10	31	32	121
3-Month Total	**27**	**-1**	**145**	**28**	**18**	**(s)**	**1**	**4**	**11**	**1**	**26**	**89**	**100**	**360**
2018 3-Month Total	**27**	**-1**	**139**	**25**	**16**	**(s)**	**1**	**4**	**13**	**1**	**34**	**95**	**100**	**360**
2017 3-Month Total	**28**	**-1**	**131**	**24**	**15**	**(s)**	**1**	**4**	**12**	**1**	**30**	**88**	**106**	**353**

[a] Metric tons of carbon dioxide can be converted to metric tons of carbon equivalent by multiplying by 12/44.
[b] Natural gas, excluding supplemental gaseous fuels.
[c] Distillate fuel oil, excluding biodiesel.
[d] Hydrocarbon gas liquids.
[e] Finished motor gasoline, excluding fuel ethanol.
[f] Aviation gasoline blending components, crude oil, motor gasoline blending components, petrochemical feedstocks, special naphthas, still gas, unfinished oils, waxes, and miscellaneous petroleum products.
[g] Emissions from energy consumption (for electricity and a small amount of useful thermal output) in the electric power sector are allocated to the end-use sectors in proportion to each sector's share of total electricity retail sales. See Tables 7.6 and 12.6.
[h] Excludes emissions from biomass energy consumption. See Table 12.7.

(s)=Less than 0.5 million metric tons and greater than -0.5 million metric tons.

Notes: • Data are estimates for carbon dioxide emissions from energy consumption, plus the relatively small amount of emissions from the non-combustion use of fossil fuels. See "Section 12 Methodology and Sources" at end of section. • See "Carbon Dioxide" in Glossary. • See Note 1, "Emissions of Carbon Dioxide and Other Greenhouse Gases," at end of section. • Data exclude emissions from biomass energy consumption. See Table 12.7 and Note 2, "Accounting for Carbon Dioxide Emissions From Biomass Energy Combustion," at end of section. • Totals may not equal sum of components due to independent rounding. • Geographic coverage is the 50 states and the District of Columbia.

Web Page: See http://www.eia.gov/totalenergy/data/monthly/#environment (Excel and CSV files) for all available annual and monthly data beginning in 1973.

Sources: See end of section.

Source: *U.S. Energy Information Administration, Monthly Energy Review, June 2019*

Table 12.5 Carbon Dioxide Emissions From Energy Consumption: Transportation Sector
(Million Metric Tons of Carbon Dioxide[a])

	Coal	Natural Gas[b]	Petroleum								Retail Elec- tricity[f]	Total[g]
			Aviation Gasoline	Distillate Fuel Oil[c]	HGL[d]	Jet Fuel	Lubri- cants	Motor Gasoline[e]	Residual Fuel Oil	Total		
1973 Total	**(s)**	**39**	**6**	**163**	**3**	**152**	**6**	**886**	**57**	**1,273**	**2**	**1,315**
1975 Total	**(s)**	**32**	**5**	**155**	**3**	**145**	**6**	**889**	**56**	**1,258**	**2**	**1,292**
1980 Total	(h)	**34**	**4**	**204**	**1**	**155**	**6**	**881**	**110**	**1,363**	**2**	**1,400**
1985 Total	(h)	**28**	**3**	**232**	**2**	**178**	**6**	**908**	**62**	**1,391**	**3**	**1,421**
1990 Total	(h)	**36**	**3**	**268**	**1**	**223**	**7**	**967**	**80**	**1,548**	**3**	**1,588**
1995 Total	(h)	**38**	**3**	**307**	**1**	**222**	**6**	**1,026**	**72**	**1,637**	**3**	**1,679**
1996 Total	(h)	**39**	**3**	**327**	**1**	**232**	**6**	**1,046**	**67**	**1,681**	**3**	**1,724**
1997 Total	(h)	**41**	**3**	**341**	**1**	**234**	**6**	**1,055**	**56**	**1,698**	**3**	**1,742**
1998 Total	(h)	**35**	**2**	**352**	**1**	**238**	**7**	**1,088**	**53**	**1,741**	**3**	**1,779**
1999 Total	(h)	**36**	**3**	**365**	**1**	**245**	**7**	**1,113**	**52**	**1,786**	**3**	**1,826**
2000 Total	(h)	**36**	**3**	**377**	**1**	**254**	**7**	**1,119**	**70**	**1,830**	**4**	**1,870**
2001 Total	(h)	**35**	**2**	**387**	**1**	**243**	**6**	**1,125**	**46**	**1,810**	**4**	**1,849**
2002 Total	(h)	**37**	**2**	**394**	**1**	**237**	**6**	**1,156**	**53**	**1,849**	**4**	**1,890**
2003 Total	(h)	**33**	**2**	**408**	**1**	**231**	**6**	**1,159**	**45**	**1,853**	**5**	**1,891**
2004 Total	(h)	**32**	**2**	**433**	**1**	**240**	**6**	**1,180**	**58**	**1,921**	**5**	**1,957**
2005 Total	(h)	**33**	**2**	**444**	**2**	**246**	**6**	**1,180**	**66**	**1,946**	**5**	**1,984**
2006 Total	(h)	**33**	**2**	**467**	**2**	**240**	**5**	**1,187**	**71**	**1,974**	**5**	**2,012**
2007 Total	(h)	**35**	**2**	**469**	**1**	**238**	**6**	**1,183**	**78**	**1,977**	**5**	**2,018**
2008 Total	(h)	**37**	**2**	**424**	**3**	**226**	**5**	**1,119**	**73**	**1,852**	**5**	**1,893**
2009 Total	(h)	**38**	**2**	**400**	**2**	**204**	**5**	**1,107**	**62**	**1,782**	**5**	**1,825**
2010 Total	(h)	**38**	**2**	**423**	**(s)**	**210**	**6**	**1,089**	**70**	**1,800**	**5**	**1,843**
2011 Total	(h)	**39**	**2**	**431**	**(s)**	**209**	**6**	**1,057**	**61**	**1,766**	**4**	**1,809**
2012 Total	(h)	**41**	**2**	**411**	**(s)**	**206**	**5**	**1,051**	**53**	**1,728**	**4**	**1,773**
2013 Total	(h)	**47**	**2**	**416**	**(s)**	**210**	**5**	**1,066**	**46**	**1,745**	**4**	**1,796**
2014 Total	(h)	**40**	**2**	**435**	**(s)**	**216**	**6**	**1,077**	**35**	**1,770**	**4**	**1,815**
2015 Total	(h)	**40**	**1**	**441**	**(s)**	**227**	**6**	**1,083**	**37**	**1,795**	**4**	**1,839**
2016 Total	(h)	**40**	**1**	**431**	**(s)**	**237**	**6**	**1,102**	**49**	**1,827**	**4**	**1,871**
2017 January	(h)	5	(s)	33	(s)	20	1	85	7	145	(s)	150
February	(h)	4	(s)	32	(s)	17	(s)	82	3	134	(s)	138
March	(h)	4	(s)	37	(s)	21	1	93	4	156	(s)	160
April	(h)	3	(s)	35	(s)	20	(s)	90	4	149	(s)	153
May	(h)	3	(s)	38	(s)	21	(s)	96	5	160	(s)	163
June	(h)	3	(s)	37	(s)	21	(s)	95	4	158	(s)	162
July	(h)	3	(s)	38	(s)	22	(s)	96	4	160	(s)	164
August	(h)	3	(s)	40	(s)	22	(s)	98	5	164	(s)	168
September	(h)	3	(s)	37	(s)	20	(s)	91	4	152	(s)	155
October	(h)	3	(s)	38	(s)	22	(s)	94	4	159	(s)	162
November	(h)	4	(s)	36	(s)	20	(s)	88	5	150	(s)	154
December	(h)	5	(s)	35	(s)	22	(s)	93	4	154	(s)	159
Total	(h)	**42**	**1**	**436**	**(s)**	**247**	**5**	**1,099**	**52**	**1,842**	**4**	**1,888**
2018 January	(h)	5	(s)	35	(s)	20	(s)	87	3	146	(s)	151
February	(h)	4	(s)	32	(s)	18	(s)	80	3	134	(s)	138
March	(h)	4	(s)	38	(s)	21	(s)	95	3	158	(s)	162
April	(h)	4	(s)	38	(s)	20	(s)	89	5	153	(s)	157
May	(h)	3	(s)	41	(s)	21	(s)	95	4	163	(s)	166
June	(h)	3	(s)	39	(s)	22	(s)	95	3	161	(s)	164
July	(h)	4	(s)	41	(s)	22	(s)	97	4	165	(s)	169
August	(h)	4	(s)	43	(s)	23	(s)	97	4	168	(s)	172
September	(h)	3	(s)	39	(s)	20	(s)	88	5	153	(s)	156
October	(h)	4	(s)	41	(s)	21	(s)	93	4	159	(s)	163
November	(h)	4	(s)	37	(s)	21	(s)	90	4	152	(s)	157
December	(h)	5	(s)	36	(s)	21	(s)	92	5	155	(s)	160
Total	(h)	**46**	**2**	**461**	**(s)**	**251**	**5**	**1,099**	**48**	**1,865**	**4**	**1,915**
2019 January	(h)	5	(s)	36	(s)	20	(s)	88	4	149	(s)	154
February	(h)	5	(s)	34	(s)	18	(s)	81	4	136	(s)	141
March	(h)	4	(s)	38	(s)	21	(s)	92	3	154	(s)	159
3-Month Total	(h)	**14**	**(s)**	**107**	**(s)**	**60**	**1**	**260**	**10**	**439**	**1**	**454**
2018 3-Month Total	(h)	**13**	**(s)**	**106**	**(s)**	**59**	**1**	**262**	**9**	**438**	**1**	**452**
2017 3-Month Total	(h)	**12**	**(s)**	**101**	**(s)**	**58**	**1**	**260**	**15**	**435**	**1**	**449**

[a] Metric tons of carbon dioxide can be converted to metric tons of carbon equivalent by multiplying by 12/44.
[b] Natural gas, excluding supplemental gaseous fuels.
[c] Distillate fuel oil, excluding biodiesel.
[d] Hydrocarbon gas liquids.
[e] Finished motor gasoline, excluding fuel ethanol.
[f] Emissions from energy consumption (for electricity and a small amount of useful thermal output) in the electric power sector are allocated to the end-use sectors in proportion to each sector's share of total electricity retail sales. See Tables 7.6 and 12.6.
[g] Excludes emissions from biomass energy consumption. See Table 12.7.
[h] Beginning in 1978, the small amounts of coal consumed for transportation are reported as industrial sector consumption.

(s)=Less than 0.5 million metric tons.

Notes: • Data are estimates for carbon dioxide emissions from energy consumption, plus the relatively small amount of emissions from the non-combustion use of fossil fuels. See "Section 12 Methodology and Sources" at end of section. • See "Carbon Dioxide" in Glossary. • See Note 1, "Emissions of Carbon Dioxide and Other Greenhouse Gases," at end of section. • Data exclude emissions from biomass energy consumption. See Table 12.7 and Note 2, "Accounting for Carbon Dioxide Emissions From Biomass Energy Combustion," at end of section. • Totals may not equal sum of components due to independent rounding. • Geographic coverage is the 50 states and the District of Columbia.

Web Page: See http://www.eia.gov/totalenergy/data/monthly/#environment (Excel and CSV files) for all available annual and monthly data beginning in 1973.

Sources: See end of section.

Source: *U.S. Energy Information Administration, Monthly Energy Review, June 2019*

Table 12.6 Carbon Dioxide Emissions From Energy Consumption: Electric Power Sector
(Million Metric Tons of Carbon Dioxide[a])

	Coal	Natural Gas[b]	Petroleum				Geo-thermal	Non-Biomass Waste[d]	Total[e]
			Distillate Fuel Oil[c]	Petroleum Coke	Residual Fuel Oil	Total			
1973 Total	812	199	20	2	254	276	NA	NA	1,286
1975 Total	824	172	17	(s)	231	248	NA	NA	1,244
1980 Total	1,137	200	12	1	194	207	NA	NA	1,544
1985 Total	1,367	166	6	1	79	86	NA	NA	1,619
1990 Total	1,548	176	7	3	92	102	(s)	6	1,831
1995 Total	1,661	228	8	8	45	61	(s)	10	1,960
1996 Total	1,752	205	8	8	50	66	(s)	10	2,033
1997 Total	1,797	219	8	10	56	75	(s)	10	2,101
1998 Total	1,828	248	10	13	82	105	(s)	10	2,192
1999 Total	1,836	260	10	11	76	97	(s)	10	2,204
2000 Total	1,927	281	13	10	69	91	(s)	10	2,310
2001 Total	1,870	290	12	11	79	102	(s)	11	2,273
2002 Total	1,890	306	9	18	52	79	(s)	13	2,288
2003 Total	1,931	278	12	18	69	98	(s)	11	2,319
2004 Total	1,943	297	8	22	69	99	(s)	11	2,350
2005 Total	1,984	319	8	24	69	101	(s)	11	2,416
2006 Total	1,954	338	5	21	28	55	(s)	12	2,358
2007 Total	1,987	372	6	17	31	54	(s)	11	2,425
2008 Total	1,959	362	5	15	19	39	(s)	12	2,373
2009 Total	1,741	373	5	13	14	33	(s)	11	2,158
2010 Total	1,828	399	6	14	12	32	(s)	11	2,270
2011 Total	1,723	409	5	14	7	26	(s)	11	2,170
2012 Total	1,511	493	4	9	6	19	(s)	11	2,034
2013 Total	1,571	444	4	13	6	23	(s)	11	2,050
2014 Total	1,569	444	6	12	7	26	(s)	11	2,050
2015 Total	1,350	527	5	11	7	24	(s)	11	1,913
2016 Total	1,241	547	4	12	6	22	(s)	11	1,821
2017 January	115	36	(s)	1	(s)	2	(s)	1	154
February	87	31	(s)	1	(s)	1	(s)	1	121
March	89	37	(s)	1	(s)	1	(s)	1	128
April	80	34	(s)	(s)	(s)	1	(s)	1	117
May	92	38	(s)	1	(s)	2	(s)	1	133
June	107	47	(s)	1	(s)	2	(s)	1	156
July	127	59	(s)	1	(s)	2	(s)	1	188
August	119	56	(s)	1	(s)	2	(s)	1	178
September	99	47	(s)	1	(s)	1	(s)	1	149
October	91	42	(s)	1	(s)	1	(s)	1	135
November	92	36	(s)	1	(s)	1	(s)	1	131
December	106	43	1	1	1	2	(s)	1	152
Total	**1,206**	**507**	**4**	**10**	**5**	**19**	**(s)**	**11**	**1,743**
2018 January	117	43	2	1	2	5	(s)	1	165
February	83	38	(s)	1	(s)	1	(s)	1	123
March	80	41	(s)	1	(s)	1	(s)	1	124
April	73	39	(s)	1	(s)	1	(s)	1	114
May	86	47	(s)	(s)	(s)	1	(s)	1	135
June	101	52	(s)	1	(s)	2	(s)	1	156
July	115	68	(s)	1	(s)	2	(s)	1	186
August	115	65	(s)	1	(s)	2	(s)	1	183
September	98	57	(s)	1	(s)	2	(s)	1	157
October	88	49	(s)	1	(s)	1	(s)	1	139
November	94	41	(s)	1	(s)	1	(s)	1	137
December	100	41	(s)	1	(s)	1	(s)	1	144
Total	**1,150**	**581**	**5**	**9**	**6**	**21**	**(s)**	**11**	**1,763**
2019 January	101	46	(s)	1	1	2	(s)	1	149
February	81	42	(s)	1	(s)	1	(s)	1	126
March	80	43	(s)	1	(s)	1	(s)	1	125
3-Month Total	**262**	**131**	**1**	**2**	**1**	**4**	**(s)**	**3**	**400**
2018 3-Month Total	**280**	**123**	**3**	**3**	**2**	**7**	**(s)**	**3**	**412**
2017 3-Month Total	**291**	**104**	**1**	**3**	**1**	**5**	**(s)**	**3**	**403**

[a] Metric tons of carbon dioxide can be converted to metric tons of carbon equivalent by multiplying by 12/44.
[b] Natural gas, excluding supplemental gaseous fuels.
[c] Distillate fuel oil, excluding biodiesel.
[d] Municipal solid waste from non-biogenic sources, and tire-derived fuels. Through 1994, also includes blast furnace gas, and other manufactured and waste gases derived from fossil fuels.
[e] Excludes emissions from biomass energy consumption. See Table 12.7.
NA=Not available. (s)=Less than 0.5 million metric tons.
Notes: • Data are estimates for carbon dioxide emissions from energy consumption. See "Section 12 Methodology and Sources" at end of section. • See "Carbon Dioxide" in Glossary. • See Note 1, "Emissions of Carbon Dioxide and Other Greenhouse Gases," at end of section. • Data exclude emissions from biomass energy consumption. See Table 12.7 and Note 2, "Accounting for Carbon Dioxide Emissions From Biomass Energy Combustion," at end of section. • Totals may not equal sum of components due to independent rounding. • Geographic coverage is the 50 states and the District of Columbia.
Web Page: See http://www.eia.gov/totalenergy/data/monthly/#environment (Excel and CSV files) for all available annual and monthly data beginning in 1973.
Sources: See end of section.

Source: *U.S. Energy Information Administration, Monthly Energy Review, June 2019*

Table 12.7 Carbon Dioxide Emissions From Biomass Energy Consumption

(Million Metric Tons of Carbon Dioxide[a])

	By Source					By Sector					
	Wood[b]	Biomass Waste[c]	Fuel Ethanol[d]	Bio-diesel	Total	Resi-dential	Com-mercial[e]	Indus-trial[f]	Trans-portation	Electric Power[g]	Total
1973 Total	**143**	**(s)**	**NA**	**NA**	**143**	**33**	**1**	**109**	**NA**	**(s)**	**143**
1975 Total	**140**	**(s)**	**NA**	**NA**	**141**	**40**	**1**	**100**	**NA**	**(s)**	**141**
1980 Total	**232**	**(s)**	**NA**	**NA**	**232**	**80**	**2**	**150**	**NA**	**(s)**	**232**
1985 Total	**252**	**14**	**3**	**NA**	**270**	**95**	**2**	**168**	**3**	**1**	**270**
1990 Total	**208**	**24**	**4**	**NA**	**237**	**54**	**8**	**147**	**4**	**23**	**237**
1995 Total	**222**	**30**	**8**	**NA**	**260**	**49**	**9**	**166**	**8**	**28**	**260**
1996 Total	**229**	**32**	**6**	**NA**	**266**	**51**	**10**	**170**	**6**	**30**	**266**
1997 Total	**222**	**30**	**7**	**NA**	**259**	**40**	**10**	**172**	**7**	**30**	**259**
1998 Total	**205**	**30**	**8**	**NA**	**242**	**36**	**9**	**160**	**8**	**30**	**242**
1999 Total	**208**	**29**	**8**	**NA**	**245**	**37**	**9**	**161**	**8**	**30**	**245**
2000 Total	**212**	**27**	**9**	**NA**	**248**	**39**	**9**	**161**	**9**	**29**	**248**
2001 Total	**188**	**33**	**10**	**(s)**	**231**	**35**	**9**	**147**	**10**	**31**	**231**
2002 Total	**187**	**36**	**12**	**(s)**	**235**	**36**	**9**	**144**	**12**	**35**	**235**
2003 Total	**188**	**36**	**16**	**(s)**	**240**	**38**	**9**	**141**	**16**	**37**	**240**
2004 Total	**199**	**35**	**20**	**(s)**	**255**	**38**	**10**	**151**	**20**	**36**	**255**
2005 Total	**200**	**37**	**23**	**1**	**261**	**40**	**10**	**150**	**23**	**37**	**261**
2006 Total	**197**	**36**	**31**	**2**	**266**	**36**	**9**	**151**	**33**	**38**	**266**
2007 Total	**196**	**37**	**39**	**3**	**276**	**39**	**9**	**146**	**41**	**39**	**276**
2008 Total	**193**	**39**	**55**	**3**	**290**	**44**	**10**	**139**	**57**	**40**	**290**
2009 Total	**182**	**41**	**62**	**3**	**288**	**47**	**10**	**125**	**64**	**41**	**288**
2010 Total	**208**	**42**	**73**	**2**	**325**	**51**	**10**	**149**	**74**	**42**	**325**
2011 Total	**208**	**42**	**73**	**8**	**331**	**49**	**11**	**151**	**80**	**40**	**331**
2012 Total	**202**	**42**	**73**	**8**	**325**	**41**	**10**	**153**	**80**	**42**	**325**
2013 Total	**219**	**45**	**75**	**13**	**353**	**54**	**11**	**158**	**87**	**43**	**353**
2014 Total	**225**	**47**	**76**	**13**	**361**	**54**	**12**	**158**	**88**	**49**	**361**
2015 Total	**217**	**47**	**79**	**14**	**357**	**48**	**13**	**157**	**90**	**48**	**357**
2016 Total	**209**	**46**	**81**	**20**	**356**	**42**	**14**	**155**	**98**	**47**	**356**
2017 January	18	4	6	1	30	3	1	14	7	4	30
February	16	4	6	1	27	3	1	12	7	4	27
March	18	4	7	1	30	3	1	14	8	4	30
April	17	4	7	2	29	3	1	13	8	4	29
May	18	4	7	2	30	3	1	13	9	4	30
June	18	4	7	2	30	3	1	13	9	4	30
July	18	4	7	2	31	3	1	14	8	4	31
August	19	4	7	2	32	3	1	14	9	4	32
September	17	3	7	2	29	3	1	13	8	4	29
October	18	4	7	2	30	3	1	13	8	4	30
November	18	4	7	2	30	3	1	14	8	4	30
December	19	4	7	2	31	3	1	14	8	4	31
Total	**214**	**45**	**82**	**19**	**360**	**41**	**14**	**161**	**98**	**47**	**360**
2018 January	19	4	7	1	31	4	1	14	8	4	31
February	17	4	6	1	28	4	1	13	7	4	28
March	19	4	7	1	31	4	1	13	8	4	31
April	18	4	6	1	29	4	1	13	7	3	29
May	19	4	7	2	31	4	1	13	9	4	31
June	18	4	7	2	31	4	1	13	8	4	31
July	19	4	7	2	31	4	1	14	9	4	31
August	19	4	7	2	32	4	1	14	9	4	32
September	18	3	6	2	29	4	1	13	8	3	29
October	18	4	7	2	31	4	1	13	8	4	31
November	18	4	7	1	30	4	1	13	8	4	30
December	19	4	7	2	31	4	1	14	8	4	31
Total	**221**	**45**	**82**	**18**	**365**	**49**	**14**	**161**	**97**	**46**	**365**
2019 January	19	4	6	1	30	4	1	14	7	4	30
February	17	3	6	1	28	4	1	12	7	3	28
March	18	4	7	1	30	4	1	13	8	4	30
3-Month Total	**54**	**11**	**20**	**4**	**88**	**12**	**3**	**39**	**23**	**11**	**88**
2018 3-Month Total	**55**	**12**	**20**	**4**	**90**	**12**	**3**	**40**	**23**	**12**	**90**
2017 3-Month Total	**53**	**12**	**19**	**3**	**87**	**10**	**3**	**40**	**22**	**12**	**87**

[a] Metric tons of carbon dioxide can be converted to metric tons of carbon equivalent by multiplying by 12/44.
[b] Wood and wood-derived fuels.
[c] Municipal solid waste from biogenic sources, landfill gas, sludge waste, agricultural byproducts, and other biomass.
[d] Fuel ethanol minus denaturant.
[e] Commercial sector, including commercial combined-heat-and-power (CHP) and commercial electricity-only plants.
[f] Industrial sector, including industrial combined-heat-and-power (CHP) and industrial electricity-only plants.
[g] The electric power sector comprises electricity-only and combined-heat-and-power (CHP) plants within the NAICS 22 category whose primary business is to sell electricity, or electricity and heat, to the public.

NA=Not available. (s)=Less than 0.5 million metric tons.

Notes: • Carbon dioxide emissions from biomass energy consumption are excluded from the energy-related carbon dioxide emissions reported in Tables 12.1–12.6. See Note 2, "Accounting for Carbon Dioxide Emissions From Biomass Energy Combustion," at end of section. • Data are estimates. See "Section 12 Methodology and Sources" at end of section. • See "Carbon Dioxide" in Glossary. • See Note 1, "Emissions of Carbon Dioxide and Other Greenhouse Gases," at end of section. • Totals may not equal sum of components due to independent rounding. • Geographic coverage is the 50 states and the District of Columbia.

Web Page: See http://www.eia.gov/totalenergy/data/monthly/#environment (Excel and CSV files) for all available annual and monthly data beginning in 1973.

Sources: See end of section.

Source: *U.S. Energy Information Administration, Monthly Energy Review, June 2019*

Environmental Revenue and Expenditures, by State

State	Revenue[1] ($/per capita)				Current Operational Expenses ($/per capita)			
	Natural Resources, Other	Park & Recreation	Sewerage	Solid Waste Management	Natural Resources, Other	Parks & Recreation	Sewerage	Solid Waste Management
Alabama	1.25	0.31	0.00	1.31	38.56	2.60	0.00	0.00
Alaska	58.28	5.09	0.00	0.00	528.34	18.75	0.00	0.00
Arizona	4.91	6.83	0.00	0.16	33.89	10.96	0.00	0.16
Arkansas	8.92	11.65	0.00	0.00	94.92	22.80	0.08	3.13
California	28.31	2.79	0.00	0.00	102.18	12.04	12.36	14.32
Colorado	5.23	0.82	0.00	0.62	60.28	13.95	0.53	3.02
Connecticut	1.31	4.71	0.00	23.21	42.43	9.03	0.00	23.43
Delaware	2.33	14.12	0.00	73.51	91.24	46.58	0.00	40.49
Florida	3.67	2.76	0.00	1.50	46.50	6.19	0.00	6.71
Georgia	5.24	12.49	0.00	0.00	32.14	20.02	0.84	0.15
Hawaii	13.67	7.90	0.00	0.00	75.96	25.08	0.00	0.00
Idaho	40.12	5.76	0.00	0.00	131.98	15.39	0.00	0.00
Illinois	1.56	0.48	0.00	0.00	12.79	4.69	0.85	1.73
Indiana	7.43	4.67	0.00	0.00	44.48	8.67	0.20	0.89
Iowa	16.74	1.63	0.00	1.33	66.37	7.00	0.25	1.01
Kansas	12.84	2.65	0.00	0.00	71.62	10.81	0.00	0.00
Kentucky	12.70	14.51	0.00	0.24	83.75	27.68	0.00	6.44
Louisiana	3.82	18.58	0.00	0.00	79.67	44.09	0.00	0.00
Maine	14.46	1.08	0.00	0.00	135.00	5.93	0.00	0.00
Maryland	2.38	5.37	24.20	0.00	59.64	13.42	26.66	4.21
Massachusetts	6.20	12.38	66.68	0.00	37.27	25.47	24.11	1.40
Michigan	4.32	0.48	0.00	0.00	30.65	10.30	0.00	0.49
Minnesota	13.12	7.46	46.31	0.00	101.38	35.94	27.40	2.71
Mississippi	4.01	9.13	0.00	0.00	63.80	14.34	0.00	0.00
Missouri	1.50	0.79	0.00	0.26	42.45	7.89	0.00	0.37
Montana	16.14	1.51	0.00	0.00	200.67	16.40	0.00	0.00
Nebraska	18.48	4.89	0.00	0.00	78.87	20.06	2.24	5.60
Nevada	3.02	2.44	0.00	0.04	31.05	5.97	0.00	1.67
New Hampshire	3.16	16.13	1.47	0.00	40.05	17.66	12.75	22.01
New Jersey	0.60	5.90	2.48	4.16	36.98	20.78	0.29	0.55
New Mexico	6.91	0.57	0.00	0.00	85.58	25.52	0.00	0.05
New York	8.96	21.31	0.00	0.01	16.10	23.63	0.00	2.06
North Carolina	4.04	2.11	0.00	0.04	43.45	13.98	0.06	1.05
North Dakota	32.93	7.51	0.00	0.00	118.12	43.02	0.00	4.04
Ohio	2.52	1.58	0.00	0.00	26.39	9.03	0.00	2.48
Oklahoma	4.43	6.30	0.00	0.42	26.43	16.25	0.00	0.12
Oregon	40.22	6.48	0.00	0.04	137.58	15.34	0.41	1.71
Pennsylvania	4.20	3.50	0.00	0.00	43.62	18.88	1.34	3.30
Rhode Island	2.93	32.75	93.73	9.52	45.02	41.86	49.42	43.48
South Carolina	4.66	6.41	0.00	0.00	37.51	22.06	0.00	0.00
South Dakota	16.26	21.20	0.00	0.00	157.24	33.02	0.00	0.00
Tennessee	3.31	5.56	0.00	1.03	42.24	13.64	0.09	0.99
Texas	1.47	2.17	0.01	2.63	25.05	6.52	0.74	2.32
Utah	5.04	6.42	0.00	1.30	59.87	13.81	0.00	0.03
Vermont	3.28	16.63	0.00	0.00	155.95	22.58	3.13	8.22
Virginia	0.35	2.33	0.00	0.00	24.53	13.87	4.94	0.15
Washington	22.69	0.36	0.17	1.61	101.99	11.27	0.00	1.37
West Virginia	20.50	8.21	5.56	0.70	97.53	25.08	0.00	5.08
Wisconsin	9.50	11.47	0.01	0.16	69.16	9.61	1.44	0.98
Wyoming	9.54	1.51	0.00	0.00	455.40	40.53	0.00	7.62

Note: *(1) Includes revenue raised through current charges only. Does not include intergovernmental revenue.*
Source: *U.S. Census Bureau, State and Local Government Finances, 2016*

Environmental Revenue and Expenditures for U.S Counties with Populations of 50,000+

County/Parish	State	Revenue[1] ($/per capita)				Current Operational Expenses ($/per capita)			
		Natural Resources, Other	Park & Recreation	Sewerage	Solid Waste Management	Natural Resources, Other	Parks & Recreation	Sewerage	Solid Waste Management
Acadia Parish	LA	0.18	1.36	0.00	0.00	23.40	3.72	0.00	76.64
Ada County	ID	11.31	0.29	0.00	42.80	10.84	1.62	0.00	34.31
Adams County	CO	0.00	7.46	0.00	0.80	23.13	7.90	0.00	0.92
Adams County	IL	0.00	0.00	0.00	0.00	0.00	0.00	0.00	0.00
Adams County	PA	0.00	0.00	0.00	0.00	15.91	20.19	0.00	0.00
Aiken County	SC	0.00	0.19	0.00	11.15	2.01	4.56	0.00	36.83
Alachua County	FL	1.41	0.00	0.00	33.12	16.75	6.49	0.00	71.44
Alamance County	NC	0.00	0.27	0.00	23.89	0.00	10.73	0.00	17.80
Alameda County	CA	0.08	0.00	0.00	0.00	22.06	0.40	0.00	0.00
Albany County	NY	0.00	18.53	5.54	0.00	7.73	15.95	58.19	0.00
Albemarle County	VA	0.00	0.00	0.28	0.00	2.79	31.68	0.00	3.86
Allegan County	MI	0.00	0.89	0.00	0.00	5.85	2.33	0.00	0.00
Allegany County	MD	0.00	0.00	126.75	0.00	3.38	12.42	188.20	12.52
Allegheny County	PA	0.00	3.98	0.00	0.00	1.27	12.52	0.00	0.00
Allen County	IN	0.00	14.95	0.23	0.00	1.18	29.04	0.25	0.00
Anderson County	SC	0.00	5.05	32.84	32.44	0.24	12.21	16.53	28.00
Anderson County	TN	0.00	1.70	0.00	6.47	3.09	5.02	0.00	20.70
Androscoggin County	ME	0.00	0.00	0.00	0.00	0.00	0.00	0.00	0.00
Anne Arundel County	MD	0.00	18.42	102.20	92.98	6.36	57.49	113.97	80.40
Anoka County	MN	0.34	11.55	0.00	13.01	0.63	22.07	0.00	7.89
Apache County	AZ	0.00	0.00	0.00	0.00	0.00	0.29	0.00	0.00
Arapahoe County	CO	0.69	0.17	0.00	0.00	0.68	30.04	0.00	0.00
Arlington County	VA	0.00	0.00	317.79	0.00	9.12	165.95	173.40	64.67
Armstrong County	PA	0.00	0.00	0.00	0.00	5.46	11.13	0.00	0.00
Aroostook County	ME	0.00	0.00	0.00	0.00	1.43	0.17	0.06	1.78
Ascension Parish	LA	0.00	2.50	0.00	0.00	82.68	38.14	30.30	0.00
Ashtabula County	OH	0.00	0.00	25.75	2.34	2.61	13.40	19.18	1.73
Atlantic County	NJ	0.00	0.14	100.36	111.11	1.99	4.55	74.30	99.29
Baldwin County	AL	0.00	0.09	0.00	64.35	0.00	6.06	0.00	48.86
Baltimore County	MD	0.00	4.95	188.83	8.10	13.55	35.24	179.77	83.06
Bannock County	ID	0.00	0.00	0.00	50.49	0.00	0.98	0.00	33.91
Barnstable County	MA	3.21	0.00	0.00	0.00	12.10	0.00	0.00	0.00
Barrow County	GA	0.00	3.38	28.65	10.35	0.07	13.75	37.51	0.00
Bartholomew County	IN	0.00	0.41	0.00	0.00	3.75	1.74	0.00	0.00
Bartow County	GA	0.00	4.24	58.15	38.74	1.24	24.03	50.73	42.75
Bastrop County	TX	0.00	0.00	0.00	1.23	1.09	0.35	0.00	2.41
Bay County	FL	0.00	4.15	47.46	74.21	7.79	10.59	57.21	84.46
Beaufort County	SC	0.00	3.28	0.00	0.04	0.00	43.58	0.00	29.59
Beaver County	PA	0.00	0.00	0.00	0.00	0.00	9.94	0.00	2.41
Bedford County	VA	0.00	0.15	0.00	35.92	4.71	17.47	0.00	65.78
Belknap County	NH	0.00	185.70	0.00	0.00	0.00	168.78	0.00	0.00
Bell County	TX	0.00	7.52	0.00	0.00	2.04	16.68	0.00	0.01
Belmont County	OH	0.00	0.00	32.46	0.00	0.00	0.00	55.83	0.00
Benton County	AR	0.00	0.00	0.00	0.00	0.00	0.00	0.00	1.57
Benton County	OR	8.35	0.00	1.27	0.00	12.60	17.56	1.16	0.00
Benton County	WA	0.11	0.01	0.00	0.81	3.45	3.87	0.00	2.74
Bergen County	NJ	0.00	10.61	78.15	8.31	0.00	11.74	52.93	8.95
Berkeley County	SC	0.00	0.00	115.43	54.03	3.72	4.67	54.70	36.78
Berkeley County	WV	0.00	0.00	0.00	0.00	0.00	10.78	0.00	0.00
Berks County	PA	0.00	0.00	0.00	0.00	5.72	7.25	0.00	2.39
Bernalillo County	NM	0.00	1.40	0.00	7.98	1.48	15.70	0.00	10.57
Bexar County	TX	0.00	0.19	1.07	0.00	1.55	1.74	0.87	0.00
Black Hawk County	IA	0.00	4.21	1.33	0.00	0.12	13.43	0.53	0.00
Blair County	PA	0.00	0.00	0.00	0.65	1.11	7.23	0.00	0.00

County/Parish	State	Revenue[1] ($/per capita)				Current Operational Expenses ($/per capita)			
		Natural Resources, Other	Park & Recreation	Sewerage	Solid Waste Management	Natural Resources, Other	Parks & Recreation	Sewerage	Solid Waste Management
Blount County	AL	0.00	0.00	0.00	0.00	0.00	8.36	0.00	4.21
Blount County	TN	0.00	0.00	0.00	0.08	2.17	0.92	0.00	0.63
Blue Earth County	MN	0.00	2.40	0.00	0.00	41.00	8.00	0.00	24.59
Bonneville County	ID	0.00	1.20	0.00	41.95	0.20	0.00	0.00	25.15
Boone County	IL	0.00	0.00	0.00	0.00	0.00	0.00	0.00	0.00
Boone County	IN	0.00	0.00	0.00	0.00	5.00	0.00	0.05	0.00
Boone County	KY	0.00	5.48	0.00	2.13	0.00	16.92	0.00	2.72
Boone County	MO	0.00	0.00	0.00	0.00	0.00	0.30	1.82	0.47
Bossier Parish	LA	0.00	0.00	0.00	0.00	17.33	2.36	11.44	0.08
Boulder County	CO	0.00	0.00	0.00	17.30	25.81	51.06	0.00	15.70
Bowie County	TX	0.00	0.00	0.00	0.00	0.00	0.00	0.00	0.00
Box Elder County	UT	0.00	0.00	0.00	0.00	1.04	11.48	0.00	14.24
Bradford County	PA	0.00	0.00	0.00	0.00	0.00	0.00	0.00	0.00
Bradley County	TN	0.00	0.00	0.00	1.47	5.76	9.66	2.24	5.62
Brazoria County	TX	0.00	0.00	0.00	0.00	2.59	9.23	0.00	0.00
Brazos County	TX	0.00	0.00	0.00	0.18	1.61	6.13	0.00	0.30
Brevard County	FL	0.62	12.57	0.00	65.24	15.96	48.52	0.00	62.68
Bristol County	MA	0.00	0.00	0.00	0.00	0.00	0.00	0.00	0.00
Broome County	NY	0.00	9.95	0.00	46.50	5.66	25.58	0.00	35.01
Broward County	FL	1.14	11.64	40.16	5.05	8.90	39.98	22.55	7.47
Brown County	WI	0.37	14.49	0.00	38.91	10.13	41.51	0.00	39.17
Brunswick County	NC	0.00	2.39	198.05	17.61	3.27	20.62	71.09	113.75
Bucks County	PA	0.00	0.00	0.00	0.00	0.59	6.85	0.00	0.26
Bullitt County	KY	0.00	0.00	0.00	0.00	1.17	2.92	0.00	3.81
Bulloch County	GA	0.00	22.67	0.00	9.19	2.99	58.02	0.00	56.28
Buncombe County	NC	1.31	0.51	0.00	30.65	0.00	9.52	0.00	19.86
Burke County	NC	0.70	0.46	6.26	47.05	7.05	5.28	0.00	47.70
Burleigh County	ND	0.00	0.00	0.00	0.00	16.44	5.71	0.00	0.00
Burlington County	NJ	0.00	0.00	0.00	59.82	0.10	0.00	0.00	33.34
Butler County	KS	0.81	0.00	0.00	27.60	7.31	0.25	1.81	14.91
Butler County	OH	0.00	0.09	48.68	0.00	1.04	0.14	32.93	0.04
Butler County	PA	1.47	0.74	0.00	0.58	1.79	3.38	0.00	1.11
Butte County	CA	0.00	0.00	0.00	37.42	14.76	0.00	0.00	32.73
Cabarrus County	NC	0.04	6.40	0.00	3.44	1.83	16.93	0.00	5.11
Cabell County	WV	0.00	0.00	0.00	0.00	4.27	9.60	0.00	0.58
Cache County	UT	0.00	0.00	0.00	0.00	3.78	22.15	0.51	0.24
Caddo Parish	LA	0.00	0.10	4.29	0.00	0.00	24.04	3.17	9.71
Calcasieu Parish	LA	0.00	18.23	1.50	0.00	12.35	70.93	3.30	37.01
Caldwell County	NC	0.75	0.00	0.00	10.65	9.83	1.19	0.00	0.00
Calhoun County	AL	0.00	0.00	0.00	21.59	0.00	3.73	0.00	21.99
Calhoun County	MI	0.00	0.00	0.00	1.91	6.51	9.76	0.00	3.56
Calvert County	MD	0.00	38.67	51.57	112.14	29.92	213.06	49.72	121.42
Cambria County	PA	0.00	0.18	0.00	1.17	8.50	4.30	0.00	0.00
Camden County	GA	0.00	23.97	0.00	90.38	1.61	63.28	0.00	56.56
Camden County	NJ	0.00	0.50	0.00	11.45	0.01	5.50	0.00	9.99
Cameron County	TX	0.00	17.83	0.00	0.50	0.58	16.44	0.00	0.05
Campbell County	KY	0.00	10.51	0.00	0.08	0.01	12.46	0.00	1.92
Campbell County	VA	0.00	3.10	0.00	0.00	2.47	11.76	0.00	35.64
Canadian County	OK	0.00	0.00	0.00	43.61	2.26	1.93	0.00	44.05
Canyon County	ID	0.00	0.00	0.00	16.27	0.00	9.61	0.00	15.33
Cape Girardeau County	MO	0.00	0.00	0.00	0.00	0.00	4.84	0.00	0.00
Cape May County	NJ	0.00	3.16	0.00	88.45	2.83	20.11	171.70	111.92
Carbon County	PA	0.00	6.88	0.00	0.09	2.60	17.65	0.00	0.00
Carroll County	GA	0.00	7.24	0.00	23.52	1.75	20.06	0.00	41.40
Carroll County	MD	0.00	9.13	41.55	37.74	75.92	32.26	40.16	59.31
Carteret County	NC	4.73	4.63	0.00	47.91	11.69	31.91	0.00	39.93

County/Parish	State	Revenue[1] ($/per capita) Natural Resources, Other	Park & Recreation	Sewerage	Solid Waste Management	Current Operational Expenses ($/per capita) Natural Resources, Other	Parks & Recreation	Sewerage	Solid Waste Management
Carver County	MN	0.00	2.77	0.00	12.25	15.22	16.55	0.00	20.38
Cascade County	MT	0.96	27.61	0.00	0.05	4.35	37.41	0.00	13.64
Cass County	MI	0.00	0.91	0.00	0.00	5.25	3.23	0.00	0.00
Cass County	MO	0.00	0.00	0.00	0.00	0.00	0.00	0.00	0.00
Cass County	ND	0.00	0.09	0.00	0.00	201.41	6.74	0.00	0.00
Catawba County	NC	6.68	0.05	0.00	34.41	3.70	6.24	0.00	29.56
Cattaraugus County	NY	0.00	7.58	0.00	15.68	26.89	31.21	0.00	22.07
Cayuga County	NY	0.00	3.24	0.00	0.00	78.89	13.67	0.00	0.00
Cecil County	MD	0.00	1.66	60.94	70.80	8.20	47.97	62.41	62.49
Centre County	PA	0.00	0.00	0.00	0.00	7.83	0.32	0.00	1.00
Champaign County	IL	4.91	0.00	0.00	0.00	19.70	0.00	0.00	0.04
Charles County	MD	11.59	18.12	115.68	43.26	51.69	56.28	1.11	24.96
Charleston County	SC	0.00	46.41	0.00	72.83	0.00	92.40	0.00	68.75
Charlotte County	FL	0.00	13.81	145.59	100.77	47.36	210.98	190.46	104.55
Chatham County	GA	0.00	3.14	3.39	7.24	0.04	22.52	5.61	15.44
Chatham County	NC	5.65	1.10	0.00	41.79	11.60	13.77	0.00	35.83
Chautauqua County	NY	0.00	0.00	29.69	68.31	25.23	3.49	29.23	51.05
Chaves County	NM	0.00	0.00	0.00	0.00	10.90	0.00	0.00	2.37
Chelan County	WA	2.27	3.50	5.66	23.28	20.73	7.87	2.12	25.24
Chemung County	NY	0.00	2.15	31.55	16.73	26.83	30.57	47.19	16.29
Cherokee County	GA	0.00	10.06	0.00	8.83	0.61	17.96	0.00	1.28
Cherokee County	SC	0.11	0.00	0.00	4.72	0.00	0.00	0.00	40.11
Cheshire County	NH	0.00	0.00	0.00	0.00	0.88	0.00	0.00	0.00
Chester County	PA	0.00	0.00	0.00	0.00	23.00	10.82	0.00	0.00
Chesterfield County	VA	0.00	1.60	130.11	10.70	14.22	28.57	59.35	3.92
Chippewa County	WI	8.88	2.72	0.00	0.44	51.23	7.19	0.00	4.41
Chisago County	MN	0.00	0.52	0.00	0.66	22.45	5.12	0.00	7.51
Chittenden County	VT	0.00	0.00	0.00	0.00	0.00	0.00	0.00	0.00
Christian County	KY	0.00	0.00	0.00	0.00	0.04	1.53	0.00	0.38
Christian County	MO	0.00	0.00	0.00	0.00	0.00	0.00	0.00	0.00
Citrus County	FL	10.44	2.37	54.35	33.81	25.44	6.78	91.96	22.64
Clackamas County	OR	2.71	12.74	83.38	0.44	9.28	41.29	53.45	5.90
Clallam County	WA	0.59	2.87	3.74	0.41	22.18	26.15	4.16	0.97
Clark County	IN	0.00	0.00	0.00	3.32	2.30	9.77	0.23	0.90
Clark County	NV	0.00	33.80	68.52	0.00	13.04	111.96	36.30	0.00
Clark County	OH	0.00	0.00	25.88	6.20	0.00	3.22	19.29	6.51
Clark County	WA	3.38	11.12	26.11	4.75	8.98	33.31	11.06	8.02
Clay County	FL	0.00	0.00	0.00	25.01	6.36	8.87	0.00	85.99
Clay County	MN	0.00	0.00	0.00	40.06	11.39	3.26	0.00	42.54
Clay County	MO	0.00	11.39	0.00	0.00	0.00	26.97	0.00	0.00
Clayton County	GA	0.00	0.00	0.00	21.13	1.13	31.79	0.00	43.65
Clearfield County	PA	0.00	0.00	0.00	0.00	1.72	2.96	0.00	0.00
Clermont County	OH	0.00	0.00	79.97	1.84	0.00	0.00	36.99	4.08
Cleveland County	NC	0.00	0.00	0.00	59.32	3.00	1.09	0.00	45.63
Cleveland County	OK	0.00	0.00	0.00	0.00	0.00	0.00	0.00	0.00
Cobb County	GA	0.00	30.65	107.99	0.63	0.00	53.41	90.69	0.96
Cochise County	AZ	0.02	0.00	0.00	32.78	30.35	0.00	0.00	32.25
Coconino County	AZ	0.00	2.89	8.45	0.96	19.92	14.27	10.25	4.59
Coffee County	TN	0.00	0.00	0.00	2.12	5.47	0.00	0.00	29.11
Colbert County	AL	0.00	4.67	0.00	39.04	0.00	5.92	0.00	38.91
Cole County	MO	0.00	0.00	0.00	0.00	0.00	0.23	0.00	0.00
Coles County	IL	0.00	0.00	0.00	0.00	0.00	0.00	0.00	0.00
Collier County	FL	7.88	21.79	163.23	109.00	44.54	90.59	117.81	98.55
Collin County	TX	0.00	0.00	0.00	0.00	0.29	0.76	0.00	0.00
Columbia County	FL	0.00	0.91	0.61	42.20	11.60	17.37	3.51	84.32

County/Parish	State	Revenue[1] ($/per capita)				Current Operational Expenses ($/per capita)			
		Natural Resources, Other	Park & Recreation	Sewerage	Solid Waste Management	Natural Resources, Other	Parks & Recreation	Sewerage	Solid Waste Management
Columbia County	GA	0.00	7.68	180.99	0.38	1.28	16.06	56.05	16.06
Columbia County	NY	0.00	2.68	2.15	31.08	37.30	28.83	3.12	43.91
Columbia County	PA	0.00	0.00	0.00	0.00	0.00	1.21	0.00	0.00
Columbiana County	OH	0.00	0.00	15.69	0.00	0.00	0.24	14.57	0.00
Columbus County	NC	0.00	0.51	0.28	92.09	13.00	7.81	0.00	75.72
Comanche County	OK	0.00	2.12	0.00	0.00	1.19	2.62	0.00	0.00
Contra Costa County	CA	0.00	0.00	30.90	1.38	29.93	0.00	20.48	0.00
Cook County	IL	0.00	10.47	0.00	0.00	41.60	23.18	0.00	0.00
Coos County	OR	84.25	13.78	0.00	28.34	16.89	17.70	0.00	19.20
Coweta County	GA	0.00	2.93	0.00	12.43	1.54	21.97	3.03	20.87
Cowlitz County	WA	1.22	8.41	90.72	149.33	7.97	28.49	39.21	70.07
Craighead County	AR	0.00	0.00	0.00	0.00	0.00	0.00	0.00	0.00
Craven County	NC	0.00	0.64	0.00	22.53	14.92	21.01	0.00	33.75
Crawford County	AR	0.00	0.00	7.89	0.00	0.00	0.16	5.79	0.00
Crawford County	PA	0.00	2.12	0.00	0.00	5.58	5.10	0.00	2.37
Creek County	OK	0.00	0.00	0.00	0.00	1.55	3.40	0.00	0.00
Crow Wing County	MN	0.00	0.00	0.00	36.67	49.30	2.43	19.53	42.41
Cullman County	AL	0.00	0.00	0.00	60.02	0.00	5.22	0.00	55.61
Cumberland County	ME	0.00	0.00	0.00	0.00	0.69	0.08	0.00	0.00
Cumberland County	NJ	0.00	0.00	0.00	104.16	2.39	0.46	0.00	45.36
Cumberland County	NC	0.00	5.69	1.64	12.16	0.38	26.49	1.07	26.68
Cumberland County	PA	0.00	0.00	0.00	0.54	3.88	0.00	0.00	0.86
Cumberland County	TN	0.00	0.00	0.00	0.07	2.83	3.57	0.00	36.10
Curry County	NM	0.00	0.00	0.00	0.00	0.00	0.00	0.00	0.00
Cuyahoga County	OH	0.00	0.00	18.46	1.68	0.28	0.56	17.98	1.61
Dakota County	MN	0.00	1.52	0.00	18.77	13.08	32.78	0.00	10.37
Dallas County	IA	0.00	0.00	0.00	0.00	11.82	0.00	0.00	1.57
Dallas County	TX	0.00	1.50	0.00	0.00	0.12	0.62	0.00	0.00
Dane County	WI	0.13	19.00	0.00	25.44	7.83	32.69	0.00	18.81
Darke County	OH	0.00	0.00	0.00	0.00	0.00	0.00	0.00	0.00
Darlington County	SC	0.00	0.65	0.00	31.87	0.00	7.68	0.00	40.10
Dauphin County	PA	1.46	0.00	0.00	3.61	16.98	46.07	0.00	5.57
Davidson County	NC	0.00	1.07	3.30	26.11	1.23	5.91	2.70	17.36
Daviess County	KY	0.00	0.66	0.00	70.69	0.41	17.44	0.00	54.82
Davis County	UT	0.00	8.03	0.00	53.18	0.00	5.55	0.00	36.84
De Kalb County	AL	0.00	0.00	0.00	3.64	0.00	0.42	0.00	0.00
Dekalb County	GA	0.00	2.14	147.13	83.67	0.00	22.31	99.18	63.58
Dekalb County	IL	0.00	0.00	0.00	0.00	18.74	0.00	0.00	0.00
Delaware County	IN	0.00	0.00	0.00	0.00	0.00	17.50	0.00	0.00
Delaware County	OH	0.00	0.00	1.90	80.21	0.00	0.00	1.52	47.14
Delaware County	PA	0.00	0.00	0.00	0.00	0.62	3.01	0.00	15.96
Denton County	TX	0.00	0.00	0.00	0.00	0.53	0.64	0.00	0.00
Deschutes County	OR	0.00	11.60	0.00	49.75	2.32	17.85	0.00	29.31
Desoto County	MS	0.00	35.15	0.00	7.34	1.98	46.87	0.00	12.28
Dickson County	TN	0.00	0.00	0.00	44.54	3.11	0.00	0.00	60.17
Dodge County	WI	0.44	1.88	0.00	0.00	14.97	7.71	0.00	0.67
Dona Ana County	NM	0.00	0.00	3.38	0.00	3.91	0.00	6.99	0.00
Dorchester County	SC	0.00	0.00	135.19	42.81	0.00	2.05	11.89	41.82
Dougherty County	GA	0.00	1.22	0.00	42.36	1.05	5.65	0.00	33.69
Douglas County	CO	0.00	3.61	0.00	0.16	7.26	13.27	0.00	0.28
Douglas County	GA	0.00	3.42	0.00	12.56	0.00	24.93	0.00	12.22
Douglas County	KS	4.56	0.00	0.00	0.00	8.55	3.17	0.00	0.00
Douglas County	NE	0.00	0.00	0.00	0.00	26.92	6.00	0.00	0.66
Douglas County	OR	0.00	39.59	0.00	53.24	28.03	49.58	0.00	18.67
Dubuque County	IA	0.00	4.89	0.00	0.00	12.01	2.12	0.00	0.00
Dupage County	IL	0.00	0.00	12.01	0.00	0.00	0.00	7.27	0.00

County/Parish	State	Revenue[1] ($/per capita)				Current Operational Expenses ($/per capita)			
		Natural Resources, Other	Park & Recreation	Sewerage	Solid Waste Management	Natural Resources, Other	Parks & Recreation	Sewerage	Solid Waste Management
Durham County	NC	0.33	0.00	27.63	7.11	18.09	6.00	13.01	6.64
Dutchess County	NY	0.00	0.79	0.00	0.00	14.11	6.43	0.00	0.78
Eagle County	CO	0.06	0.00	0.00	65.12	45.63	15.86	0.00	45.37
Eaton County	MI	0.00	0.67	0.00	2.67	8.80	4.12	0.00	3.09
Eau Claire County	WI	13.42	3.33	0.00	9.62	24.87	10.53	0.00	12.27
Ector County	TX	0.00	5.48	0.00	0.00	0.83	10.91	0.00	0.00
Eddy County	NM	0.00	0.00	0.00	0.00	0.89	0.26	0.00	35.46
Edgecombe County	NC	0.00	0.00	8.42	37.06	0.00	1.16	5.17	55.20
El Dorado County	CA	0.00	0.60	0.00	1.12	21.32	6.74	0.00	0.00
El Paso County	CO	0.00	0.00	0.00	1.65	3.07	2.98	0.00	1.49
El Paso County	TX	0.00	2.87	0.08	0.82	0.28	9.10	0.12	0.81
Elkhart County	IN	0.00	0.48	12.94	16.58	0.00	7.11	9.25	10.01
Elko County	NV	0.00	0.31	5.16	0.00	3.20	10.11	2.20	0.00
Erie County	NY	0.00	1.47	8.25	0.00	2.91	19.07	39.35	0.00
Erie County	PA	0.00	0.00	0.00	0.00	0.00	0.00	0.00	0.00
Escambia County	FL	0.06	15.41	0.22	43.36	6.03	29.80	0.00	32.39
Essex County	NJ	0.00	17.38	0.00	46.99	0.00	17.03	0.00	34.25
Etowah County	AL	0.00	0.00	0.00	0.00	0.00	0.25	0.00	0.00
Fairbanks North Star Borough	AK	0.00	11.67	0.00	100.92	0.00	95.87	0.00	174.50
Fairfax County	VA	0.00	51.05	228.83	69.60	0.00	87.73	103.90	64.58
Fairfield County	OH	0.00	0.00	22.63	0.00	2.60	0.00	12.15	0.00
Faulkner County	AR	0.00	0.00	1.14	0.00	0.03	0.58	0.90	0.00
Fauquier County	VA	0.00	7.91	0.00	48.81	18.51	55.36	1.45	121.81
Fayette County	GA	0.00	2.24	59.12	0.63	1.20	10.17	4.86	1.88
Fayette County	PA	0.00	0.00	0.00	0.00	37.12	0.57	0.00	0.00
Flagler County	FL	0.12	1.27	1.39	12.69	4.50	19.39	0.00	15.71
Flathead County	MT	7.32	1.97	0.00	68.33	10.75	5.53	0.00	39.42
Florence County	SC	0.00	4.34	0.00	27.52	0.06	25.54	0.00	29.82
Floyd County	GA	0.00	16.63	29.13	5.50	1.55	33.74	20.56	15.90
Floyd County	IN	0.00	2.16	10.68	0.00	3.15	4.21	7.83	1.77
Fond Du Lac County	WI	0.25	11.51	0.00	0.00	13.35	21.19	0.00	1.25
Forrest County	MS	0.00	0.00	0.00	0.00	1.66	26.69	0.00	0.00
Forsyth County	GA	0.00	12.13	74.85	9.82	0.90	35.61	65.14	4.13
Forsyth County	NC	0.00	11.07	0.00	0.00	7.55	19.99	0.00	0.00
Fort Bend County	TX	0.14	0.28	0.00	0.00	13.85	2.43	0.00	0.45
Franklin County	KY	0.00	3.06	0.00	7.68	0.00	10.74	0.00	30.37
Franklin County	MO	0.00	0.00	0.00	0.00	1.89	0.00	4.08	0.00
Franklin County	NC	0.00	0.00	28.22	0.00	0.00	0.93	17.06	0.00
Franklin County	OH	0.00	11.90	3.10	0.00	0.00	40.97	2.78	0.00
Franklin County	PA	0.00	0.00	0.00	0.00	0.62	0.16	0.00	0.00
Franklin County	WA	0.02	13.90	0.00	0.64	18.84	33.06	0.00	0.50
Frederick County	MD	0.00	5.71	57.21	101.47	47.22	39.94	72.22	79.31
Frederick County	VA	0.00	26.19	0.00	80.85	0.00	62.78	0.00	19.19
Fresno County	CA	0.00	0.24	8.61	18.36	9.84	2.75	6.29	17.85
Fulton County	GA	0.00	1.26	48.24	0.00	0.10	3.71	26.10	0.70
Gallatin County	MT	0.00	0.00	0.00	51.76	11.23	0.68	0.00	35.26
Galveston County	TX	0.42	1.42	0.00	0.00	6.46	6.51	0.00	0.00
Garfield County	CO	0.00	10.95	0.00	26.20	0.00	22.98	0.00	16.77
Garfield County	OK	0.00	0.00	0.00	0.00	4.74	4.04	0.00	0.00
Garland County	AR	0.00	0.00	0.00	82.54	0.00	0.81	0.00	83.05
Gaston County	NC	0.00	0.71	0.00	33.14	0.30	6.75	0.00	23.82
Genesee County	MI	0.00	6.00	82.92	0.00	3.07	20.97	49.48	0.00
Genesee County	NY	0.00	0.36	0.00	0.00	25.45	15.80	0.00	0.00
Georgetown County	SC	0.00	3.85	27.85	55.53	0.13	42.11	9.80	73.97
Gila County	AZ	0.00	0.00	0.36	28.24	2.71	3.82	0.09	11.81
Gloucester County	NJ	0.00	6.35	0.00	55.42	2.00	5.54	0.00	63.94

County/Parish	State	Revenue[1] ($/per capita)				Current Operational Expenses ($/per capita)			
		Natural Resources, Other	Park & Recreation	Sewerage	Solid Waste Management	Natural Resources, Other	Parks & Recreation	Sewerage	Solid Waste Management
Glynn County	GA	0.00	11.93	0.00	39.24	2.72	61.89	0.00	42.32
Gordon County	GA	0.00	2.76	0.00	5.20	3.41	26.02	0.00	22.55
Grady County	OK	0.00	0.00	0.00	0.00	0.00	0.00	0.00	0.00
Grafton County	NH	0.00	0.00	0.00	0.00	10.57	0.00	0.00	0.00
Grand Forks County	ND	0.00	0.00	0.00	0.00	11.66	0.00	0.00	0.00
Grand Traverse County	MI	0.00	3.69	14.23	3.23	6.05	8.29	69.67	4.17
Grant County	IN	0.00	0.00	0.00	1.32	2.66	5.99	0.40	1.38
Grant County	WA	1.07	4.00	0.00	32.75	26.79	3.84	3.14	23.10
Granville County	NC	0.00	4.58	5.18	46.97	5.04	8.57	5.44	46.82
Grays Harbor County	WA	0.22	18.10	8.14	14.68	15.59	26.35	8.35	30.57
Grayson County	TX	0.00	0.00	0.00	0.00	1.58	1.00	0.00	0.00
Greene County	MO	0.00	0.00	0.00	0.00	0.09	0.00	0.47	0.00
Greene County	OH	0.00	0.00	124.91	0.00	6.33	12.70	39.67	0.00
Greene County	TN	0.00	0.00	0.00	1.66	2.96	0.00	0.00	28.22
Greenville County	SC	0.00	10.76	0.00	13.62	0.00	30.96	13.09	18.65
Greenwood County	SC	0.00	3.41	0.00	46.81	0.00	24.46	0.00	43.26
Gregg County	TX	0.00	0.00	0.00	0.00	0.89	0.00	0.00	0.00
Grundy County	IL	0.00	0.00	0.00	0.00	0.00	0.00	0.00	0.00
Guadalupe County	TX	0.00	0.00	0.00	0.00	2.84	0.00	0.00	3.29
Guilford County	NC	0.00	1.87	0.00	0.02	0.75	7.12	0.00	2.32
Gwinnett County	GA	0.00	4.27	137.26	48.02	0.00	35.83	82.60	45.28
Hall County	GA	0.00	6.57	10.72	36.65	0.53	21.73	8.60	35.35
Hall County	NE	0.97	0.65	0.00	0.00	7.07	31.94	0.00	0.00
Hamblen County	TN	0.00	1.97	0.00	0.00	0.00	4.72	0.00	34.04
Hamilton County	IN	0.00	1.31	0.00	0.02	7.37	10.50	0.00	2.83
Hamilton County	OH	0.00	17.44	337.43	0.00	3.08	63.39	0.00	0.00
Hamilton County	TN	0.00	1.86	0.00	0.00	1.00	20.71	0.00	2.14
Hancock County	IN	0.00	0.00	0.00	0.66	0.00	0.00	0.00	0.07
Hancock County	ME	0.00	0.00	0.00	0.00	0.00	0.00	0.00	0.00
Hancock County	OH	3.28	0.00	0.00	65.76	31.12	0.00	0.00	53.27
Hanover County	VA	0.00	4.63	152.05	4.07	1.55	31.58	80.14	54.56
Hardin County	KY	0.00	0.00	0.00	41.31	0.03	0.10	0.00	32.07
Harford County	MD	0.00	0.23	64.16	49.27	8.10	68.70	54.53	95.98
Harnett County	NC	0.00	0.97	134.47	41.44	1.43	4.59	71.32	32.84
Harris County	TX	0.10	0.18	0.00	0.00	12.57	0.00	0.00	0.00
Harrison County	MS	0.00	0.00	0.00	0.00	1.01	14.27	0.00	0.00
Harrison County	WV	0.00	0.26	0.00	0.00	0.00	10.52	0.00	0.00
Hawaii County	HI	0.00	6.62	37.88	47.69	0.00	98.68	39.08	123.17
Hawkins County	TN	0.00	0.07	0.00	0.04	2.57	1.66	0.00	23.75
Hays County	TX	0.00	0.00	0.00	0.00	1.15	1.48	0.00	2.08
Haywood County	NC	0.00	0.28	0.00	98.97	6.65	3.37	0.00	58.38
Henderson County	NC	2.68	2.04	13.10	49.44	4.76	14.14	8.45	44.00
Henderson County	TX	4.34	0.00	0.00	0.00	7.63	0.00	0.00	0.00
Hendricks County	IN	0.00	0.18	2.91	0.37	2.43	0.00	0.36	0.00
Hennepin County	MN	0.00	0.79	0.00	44.19	0.00	1.87	0.00	37.88
Henrico County	VA	0.00	4.71	164.34	77.81	1.02	54.10	89.20	39.77
Henry County	GA	0.00	4.34	15.65	0.00	1.53	20.21	0.00	0.97
Hernando County	FL	1.32	3.54	78.19	15.38	7.79	13.12	91.86	18.76
Hidalgo County	TX	0.06	0.05	0.00	0.12	14.85	4.92	0.00	0.03
Highlands County	FL	21.57	0.73	0.00	33.78	30.12	14.65	0.02	78.93
Hillsborough County	FL	3.49	3.05	0.00	74.84	22.32	31.70	0.00	68.45
Hillsborough County	NH	0.00	0.00	0.00	0.00	2.42	0.00	0.00	0.00
Hinds County	MS	0.00	0.00	0.00	0.00	1.19	0.36	0.00	9.93
Horry County	SC	0.00	0.37	0.00	0.00	15.22	17.31	0.00	0.00
Houston County	AL	0.00	0.17	0.00	20.53	1.18	0.58	0.00	19.05
Houston County	GA	0.00	0.00	18.57	42.83	0.71	0.07	0.00	46.59

County/Parish	State	Revenue[1] ($/per capita) Natural Resources, Other	Park & Recreation	Sewerage	Solid Waste Management	Current Operational Expenses ($/per capita) Natural Resources, Other	Parks & Recreation	Sewerage	Solid Waste Management
Howard County	IN	0.00	0.00	0.00	0.00	3.27	0.00	2.54	3.91
Howard County	MD	0.00	67.37	107.91	67.62	24.92	206.88	66.99	54.67
Hudson County	NJ	0.00	0.23	0.00	68.64	0.00	10.49	0.00	53.25
Humboldt County	CA	0.00	2.91	0.00	5.10	10.24	7.46	0.00	4.97
Hunterdon County	NJ	0.00	12.22	0.00	0.68	2.61	19.05	0.00	0.14
Iberia Parish	LA	0.00	15.34	29.58	0.00	30.93	53.59	32.91	39.38
Imperial County	CA	0.00	0.36	0.00	12.09	21.73	4.37	0.09	23.15
Indian River County	FL	0.00	28.75	96.54	13.96	5.23	64.91	59.52	80.39
Indiana County	PA	0.00	0.67	0.00	0.00	3.22	15.16	0.00	0.39
Ingham County	MI	2.86	5.96	0.00	0.00	14.04	36.92	0.00	0.00
Iredell County	NC	0.00	2.18	0.00	52.44	0.00	8.19	0.00	28.11
Isabella County	MI	0.00	0.00	0.00	0.00	0.00	12.48	0.00	13.85
Island County	WA	3.93	0.32	6.17	75.83	10.12	16.63	7.77	71.41
Jackson County	GA	0.00	7.20	0.00	20.38	23.26	21.61	0.00	22.51
Jackson County	IL	0.00	0.00	0.00	0.00	0.00	0.00	0.00	0.00
Jackson County	MI	7.86	5.35	0.00	0.00	10.90	19.64	0.00	1.79
Jackson County	MS	0.00	4.84	0.00	0.00	2.24	35.94	0.00	8.87
Jackson County	MO	0.00	16.66	0.05	0.00	0.00	44.90	0.05	0.00
Jackson County	OR	0.00	13.49	0.00	5.10	5.60	24.02	0.00	0.18
James City County	VA	0.00	48.72	81.47	4.24	14.61	73.33	0.00	38.40
Jasper County	MO	0.00	0.00	0.00	0.00	0.00	0.00	0.00	0.00
Jefferson County	AL	0.00	0.00	282.90	1.84	0.00	0.00	78.77	0.92
Jefferson County	AR	0.00	0.00	0.00	25.77	0.00	0.18	0.00	27.15
Jefferson County	CO	0.00	0.98	0.00	0.00	1.36	20.03	0.00	0.57
Jefferson County	MO	0.00	8.27	45.31	0.00	2.14	24.92	24.12	0.00
Jefferson County	NY	0.00	0.00	0.00	17.77	17.29	1.42	0.00	22.25
Jefferson County	TN	0.00	0.00	0.00	14.78	2.59	0.00	0.00	56.14
Jefferson County	TX	0.00	13.55	0.00	0.00	1.50	42.37	0.00	0.00
Jefferson County	WV	0.00	0.00	0.00	0.00	0.00	20.17	0.00	0.00
Jefferson County	WI	0.46	13.12	0.00	0.84	12.91	22.86	0.00	1.95
Jefferson Parish	LA	0.00	10.34	54.41	50.48	69.31	64.77	69.41	67.99
Jessamine County	KY	0.00	0.00	0.00	6.50	0.79	15.01	0.00	16.09
Johnson County	IN	0.00	2.33	0.41	0.00	2.12	0.82	0.12	0.00
Johnson County	IA	0.03	0.84	0.00	0.00	3.05	12.40	0.00	0.00
Johnson County	KS	0.00	28.31	167.96	0.00	1.66	50.52	82.39	0.00
Johnson County	MO	0.00	0.00	0.00	0.00	0.00	0.00	0.00	0.00
Johnston County	NC	1.91	0.00	51.25	29.84	0.00	1.00	24.42	32.27
Jones County	MS	0.00	0.00	0.00	31.33	3.33	13.12	0.00	29.74
Josephine County	OR	8.67	8.94	0.00	1.16	22.17	10.81	0.00	1.14
Kalamazoo County	MI	0.00	0.00	0.00	0.00	0.00	14.99	0.00	0.00
Kanawha County	WV	0.00	11.47	0.00	0.00	0.31	12.09	0.00	0.00
Kane County	IL	7.64	0.00	0.00	0.10	14.85	0.00	0.00	1.31
Kankakee County	IL	0.00	0.00	0.00	0.00	0.82	0.00	0.00	0.00
Kauai County	HI	0.00	16.57	133.07	123.04	0.33	196.84	139.42	205.60
Kenai Peninsula Borough	AK	0.98	3.48	0.00	12.35	4.01	30.30	0.00	104.43
Kendall County	IL	0.78	0.00	0.00	0.00	9.09	0.00	0.00	0.00
Kennebec County	ME	0.00	0.00	0.00	0.00	0.00	0.00	0.00	0.00
Kenosha County	WI	0.08	18.70	0.00	0.72	7.23	28.31	0.00	0.00
Kent County	DE	0.00	2.05	105.85	19.57	0.58	15.56	59.38	17.46
Kent County	MI	0.00	3.42	0.00	49.40	4.34	11.33	0.00	40.16
Kenton County	KY	0.00	11.84	572.29	0.01	0.64	15.04	244.28	0.00
Kern County	CA	0.00	1.90	5.37	61.80	7.22	12.60	4.57	53.43
Kerr County	TX	0.00	0.00	0.00	0.00	0.00	3.49	0.00	0.00
Kershaw County	SC	0.00	4.87	30.49	2.31	0.00	21.12	21.46	33.72
King County	WA	5.09	4.48	216.29	58.45	30.54	22.61	79.17	43.00
Kings County	CA	0.00	0.28	0.00	9.05	16.20	12.90	0.00	0.00

County/Parish	State	Revenue[1] ($/per capita) Natural Resources, Other	Park & Recreation	Sewerage	Solid Waste Management	Current Operational Expenses ($/per capita) Natural Resources, Other	Parks & Recreation	Sewerage	Solid Waste Management
Kitsap County	WA	0.23	3.47	119.94	56.82	9.30	14.98	64.53	58.23
Klamath County	OR	10.79	0.33	0.00	68.44	26.24	7.71	0.00	59.06
Knox County	OH	0.00	0.00	32.23	0.00	6.86	0.00	24.39	1.16
Knox County	TN	0.00	1.75	0.00	0.00	1.97	28.98	0.00	9.69
Kootenai County	ID	9.06	2.97	0.00	79.96	15.78	6.10	0.00	43.54
La Crosse County	WI	0.71	5.02	0.00	100.72	20.57	10.18	0.00	94.70
La Plata County	CO	0.00	1.28	0.00	0.00	5.08	13.04	0.00	3.15
La Porte County	IN	0.00	1.06	0.01	0.08	6.86	4.60	0.79	0.00
Lackawanna County	PA	0.00	0.00	0.00	0.00	0.00	11.41	0.00	0.00
Lafayette County	MS	0.00	0.00	0.00	31.61	1.86	5.17	0.00	41.22
Lafourche Parish	LA	1.30	0.50	4.51	0.02	83.16	16.61	3.15	83.06
Lake County	CA	0.00	0.19	102.58	262.00	35.33	25.73	80.57	43.06
Lake County	FL	0.33	0.79	0.00	40.02	6.94	13.98	0.00	46.30
Lake County	IL	6.48	5.45	33.98	0.00	41.42	5.46	29.61	0.00
Lake County	IN	0.00	5.25	0.61	0.00	1.40	23.95	1.30	0.00
Lake County	OH	0.00	0.00	78.78	29.69	0.00	0.00	51.07	18.50
Lamar County	MS	0.00	0.00	0.00	0.00	2.06	19.30	0.00	23.52
Lancaster County	NE	0.00	0.00	0.00	0.00	0.00	0.00	0.00	0.00
Lancaster County	PA	0.00	0.81	0.00	0.00	6.19	1.82	0.00	0.00
Lancaster County	SC	0.00	13.29	0.00	1.20	0.00	28.21	0.00	28.48
Lane County	OR	7.72	3.54	0.00	48.51	10.56	7.45	0.00	44.00
Lapeer County	MI	0.00	1.93	0.00	0.00	4.73	3.99	0.00	0.00
Laramie County	WY	0.00	0.00	0.00	0.00	2.01	4.81	0.00	0.00
Larimer County	CO	2.63	18.51	0.00	22.58	14.97	31.00	1.08	13.38
Lasalle County	IL	0.00	0.00	0.00	0.00	0.00	1.23	0.00	0.00
Lauderdale County	AL	0.00	0.26	0.00	51.18	0.38	0.50	0.00	33.85
Lauderdale County	MS	0.00	0.00	0.00	0.00	1.32	7.23	0.00	22.24
Laurel County	KY	0.00	0.00	0.00	0.00	0.05	9.83	0.00	2.71
Laurens County	SC	0.00	0.00	0.00	29.73	0.56	2.69	0.00	31.06
Lawrence County	OH	0.00	0.00	52.58	0.00	0.00	0.00	27.10	0.00
Lawrence County	PA	0.00	0.00	0.00	0.00	8.62	2.55	0.00	3.22
Lea County	NM	0.00	0.15	0.00	2.53	2.16	39.45	0.00	24.29
Leavenworth County	KS	0.00	0.00	0.00	13.14	8.75	0.06	0.00	14.21
Lebanon County	PA	0.00	0.00	0.00	0.00	0.00	0.00	0.00	0.00
Lee County	FL	4.68	8.74	80.86	75.62	17.32	55.19	22.98	92.67
Lee County	MS	0.00	0.00	0.00	30.18	2.63	8.99	0.00	20.62
Lee County	NC	0.00	5.87	0.00	20.40	1.84	20.28	0.00	21.32
Lehigh County	PA	0.03	0.00	0.00	0.00	2.17	4.57	0.00	0.00
Lenoir County	NC	0.00	0.00	0.00	41.67	0.00	15.73	0.00	62.63
Leon County	FL	0.50	0.17	0.01	24.88	30.18	18.42	1.02	28.84
Lewis And Clark County	MT	0.00	0.00	0.00	52.43	0.00	21.67	0.00	17.09
Lewis County	WA	0.57	8.38	0.00	99.65	30.75	8.12	0.03	102.20
Lexington County	SC	0.00	0.01	0.00	9.50	6.02	0.79	0.00	36.78
Liberty County	GA	0.00	7.00	0.67	56.78	1.62	26.85	0.64	87.44
Licking County	OH	0.00	0.00	13.92	0.00	0.00	3.24	9.67	0.00
Limestone County	AL	0.00	1.08	0.00	0.00	0.00	6.05	0.00	2.09
Lincoln County	NC	0.95	0.57	41.51	46.35	3.11	15.67	15.55	43.41
Lincoln County	SD	0.00	0.00	0.00	0.00	25.70	0.40	0.00	7.08
Linn County	IA	0.00	2.59	0.00	0.00	2.45	23.06	0.00	0.13
Linn County	OR	0.00	22.56	0.00	0.00	4.15	21.74	0.00	0.00
Livingston County	MI	0.00	0.00	0.00	0.00	0.00	0.00	0.00	0.00
Livingston Parish	LA	0.00	11.52	4.41	0.00	11.82	16.89	3.35	0.00
Lonoke County	AR	0.00	0.00	0.00	0.00	0.00	0.00	0.00	9.56
Lorain County	OH	0.00	0.00	8.57	0.00	0.00	0.00	0.61	0.00
Los Angeles County	CA	0.00	0.43	7.48	5.01	21.31	31.21	5.52	2.06
Loudon County	TN	0.00	0.00	0.00	0.00	0.47	0.00	0.00	13.69

County/Parish	State	Revenue[1] ($/per capita)				Current Operational Expenses ($/per capita)			
		Natural Resources, Other	Park & Recreation	Sewerage	Solid Waste Management	Natural Resources, Other	Parks & Recreation	Sewerage	Solid Waste Management
Loudoun County	VA	0.00	45.53	0.00	14.93	2.98	94.25	4.49	13.44
Lowndes County	GA	0.00	10.36	32.35	3.26	1.36	52.07	16.68	0.00
Lowndes County	MS	0.00	0.00	0.00	0.00	3.33	18.86	0.00	0.00
Lubbock County	TX	0.00	0.00	0.00	0.00	0.96	1.51	0.00	0.00
Lucas County	OH	0.00	70.16	26.18	18.68	0.00	107.00	12.32	7.52
Luzerne County	PA	0.00	0.00	0.00	1.79	4.59	8.78	0.00	0.00
Lycoming County	PA	0.00	0.00	0.00	105.62	5.06	2.77	1.71	113.39
Lyon County	NV	0.00	1.86	73.18	0.00	0.00	15.08	29.69	0.00
Macomb County	MI	0.00	0.32	0.00	0.00	5.66	0.67	7.25	0.00
Macon County	IL	0.00	0.00	0.00	0.00	0.00	0.00	0.00	0.00
Madera County	CA	5.03	0.00	0.00	29.72	13.38	0.39	0.00	35.63
Madison County	AL	0.00	0.61	0.00	28.94	0.00	4.70	0.00	22.95
Madison County	IL	0.00	0.00	12.62	1.81	12.85	5.50	9.56	0.94
Madison County	IN	0.00	0.00	0.00	0.11	2.47	0.00	0.93	1.29
Madison County	KY	0.00	0.00	0.00	0.00	0.15	7.25	0.23	0.00
Madison County	MS	0.00	0.00	0.00	0.00	3.26	1.07	0.00	19.19
Madison County	NY	0.00	0.00	6.53	57.68	39.25	7.11	7.35	66.17
Madison County	TN	0.00	0.11	0.00	1.79	3.78	11.94	0.00	8.87
Mahoning County	OH	0.00	0.00	101.65	0.00	0.00	0.00	86.99	10.43
Manatee County	FL	0.65	11.03	179.35	108.66	33.16	39.04	110.92	95.50
Marathon County	WI	1.35	6.33	0.00	33.93	4.04	27.67	0.00	28.52
Maricopa County	AZ	0.01	1.88	0.00	0.11	6.53	3.72	0.00	1.59
Marin County	CA	0.00	18.41	59.28	0.00	35.67	113.18	39.44	7.71
Marion County	FL	0.02	4.65	42.37	7.07	9.33	13.50	11.71	26.49
Marion County	OH	0.00	0.00	16.92	0.00	2.02	0.31	15.82	0.00
Marion County	OR	0.00	0.70	6.22	50.59	4.04	0.58	2.21	55.55
Marion County	WV	0.00	4.81	0.00	0.00	0.00	36.03	0.00	0.51
Martin County	FL	0.00	20.01	98.92	131.43	39.06	77.76	54.09	122.34
Mason County	WA	0.84	0.46	32.55	50.18	59.09	7.85	41.87	44.39
Matanuska-susitna Borough	AK	0.00	12.59	1.15	71.28	0.00	44.58	1.40	59.85
Maui County	HI	0.00	2.76	300.95	101.02	0.00	172.16	161.04	148.45
Maury County	TN	0.00	0.35	0.00	21.33	1.24	3.56	0.00	29.32
Maverick County	TX	0.00	0.00	0.00	40.00	0.00	17.24	0.00	50.60
Mccracken County	KY	0.00	6.15	0.00	0.12	1.23	10.57	0.00	5.88
Mchenry County	IL	0.00	3.88	0.00	0.00	0.00	26.94	0.00	0.00
Mckinley County	NM	0.00	0.00	0.00	0.00	0.63	2.26	0.00	4.98
Mclean County	IL	0.00	0.00	0.00	0.00	0.00	6.18	0.00	0.00
Mecklenburg County	NC	0.00	4.96	15.82	15.11	10.49	37.31	8.92	15.04
Medina County	OH	0.00	0.00	108.28	48.66	0.00	0.00	73.42	46.20
Mendocino County	CA	0.00	0.22	62.80	16.09	19.67	6.29	63.82	6.15
Merced County	CA	0.00	1.07	0.00	6.06	13.01	7.10	0.00	0.00
Mercer County	NJ	0.00	19.60	0.00	106.31	0.87	33.93	0.00	82.64
Mercer County	PA	0.00	0.00	0.00	0.00	0.00	0.13	0.00	1.32
Mercer County	WV	0.00	0.00	0.00	0.00	0.00	14.26	0.00	1.78
Merrimack County	NH	0.00	0.00	0.00	0.00	2.71	0.00	0.00	0.00
Miami County	OH	0.00	0.00	20.32	48.68	0.00	9.38	21.24	49.06
Miami-dade County	FL	0.00	20.97	124.03	99.28	33.62	101.16	75.53	87.90
Middlesex County	NJ	0.00	3.37	104.80	57.18	1.16	3.10	61.06	42.94
Milwaukee County	WI	0.00	48.90	0.00	0.00	0.00	115.41	0.00	0.00
Minnehaha County	SD	0.00	0.00	0.00	0.00	0.63	7.46	0.00	0.00
Missoula County	MT	5.92	6.93	0.00	2.69	20.68	23.02	0.00	2.33
Mobile County	AL	0.00	0.81	0.00	0.10	0.00	7.01	0.00	7.47
Mohave County	AZ	8.89	9.41	0.00	6.25	15.81	22.93	0.00	4.03
Monmouth County	NJ	0.00	11.99	0.00	41.72	2.70	28.38	0.00	34.03
Monongalia County	WV	0.00	0.00	0.00	0.00	0.00	19.03	0.00	6.42

County/Parish	State	Revenue[1] ($/per capita) Natural Resources, Other	Park & Recreation	Sewerage	Solid Waste Management	Current Operational Expenses ($/per capita) Natural Resources, Other	Parks & Recreation	Sewerage	Solid Waste Management
Monroe County	FL	0.00	10.09	0.00	229.87	34.07	23.59	173.58	223.77
Monroe County	IN	0.00	1.92	7.93	0.00	2.42	10.64	3.34	0.00
Monroe County	MI	0.00	0.07	0.00	0.00	4.66	4.89	0.00	0.00
Monroe County	NY	0.00	4.90	28.11	8.38	1.86	16.20	77.13	18.01
Monroe County	PA	0.00	0.03	0.00	0.00	12.81	15.94	0.00	0.00
Montcalm County	MI	0.00	0.51	0.00	2.84	4.69	0.43	0.00	2.94
Monterey County	CA	0.00	12.36	5.43	0.00	66.09	23.51	5.28	0.41
Montgomery County	AL	0.00	0.00	0.00	0.00	0.05	1.61	0.60	0.00
Montgomery County	MD	0.00	59.70	343.20	98.54	36.24	389.44	180.45	95.37
Montgomery County	OH	0.00	0.00	79.28	44.12	0.00	27.20	58.54	32.21
Montgomery County	PA	0.00	0.29	0.00	0.00	0.00	5.84	0.00	0.46
Montgomery County	TN	0.00	0.65	0.00	0.00	0.01	9.87	0.00	0.69
Montgomery County	TX	0.00	0.91	0.00	0.00	1.20	2.74	0.00	0.00
Montgomery County	VA	0.00	6.32	16.24	0.00	0.00	10.62	20.05	30.55
Moore County	NC	0.22	1.89	92.09	16.26	5.11	6.04	63.53	22.35
Morgan County	AL	0.00	0.00	0.00	23.54	0.00	5.26	0.00	30.49
Morgan County	IN	0.00	0.00	0.00	0.00	3.37	0.17	0.00	0.00
Morris County	NJ	0.00	27.80	0.00	78.11	1.81	50.14	0.00	70.69
Multnomah County	OR	0.00	0.00	1.14	0.00	0.06	0.07	0.67	0.00
Muskegon County	MI	0.00	4.38	98.26	17.03	0.00	4.22	50.84	31.26
Muskingum County	OH	0.00	0.00	52.79	0.00	2.51	0.00	44.07	0.00
Muskogee County	OK	0.00	0.00	0.00	0.00	0.86	0.00	0.00	0.00
Nacogdoches County	TX	0.00	1.90	0.00	0.00	1.32	16.28	0.00	0.00
Napa County	CA	0.00	0.00	180.96	0.00	139.56	3.77	123.83	0.00
Nash County	NC	1.15	0.00	3.58	27.10	3.72	6.02	5.38	27.81
Nassau County	FL	0.00	0.00	28.64	0.05	75.31	5.14	25.16	7.05
Nassau County	NY	0.00	14.28	0.98	0.00	5.99	27.35	79.48	0.00
Natrona County	WY	0.00	12.07	0.00	0.00	5.59	9.46	0.00	0.00
Navajo County	AZ	0.00	0.00	0.00	0.00	15.80	1.45	0.00	0.00
Nevada County	CA	0.00	0.05	47.58	17.26	7.09	0.00	39.84	11.75
New Castle County	DE	0.00	1.71	130.48	0.00	1.51	7.93	83.57	0.00
New Hanover County	NC	0.00	6.75	0.00	60.48	0.00	38.16	0.00	20.44
Newton County	GA	0.00	0.06	34.37	30.34	0.90	20.13	0.00	58.88
Niagara County	NY	0.00	2.59	1.83	0.00	5.35	20.95	17.53	4.46
Norfolk County	MA	0.00	1.52	0.00	0.00	0.00	1.22	0.00	0.00
Northampton County	PA	0.00	0.03	0.00	0.00	13.17	4.07	0.00	1.38
Northumberland County	PA	0.00	0.00	0.00	0.00	2.69	20.82	0.00	0.00
Nueces County	TX	0.00	3.27	0.00	0.00	0.75	13.44	0.00	0.00
Oakland County	MI	0.00	7.43	89.23	0.00	0.59	14.02	197.82	0.00
Ocean County	NJ	0.00	2.30	0.00	0.01	0.87	9.73	0.00	5.45
Oconee County	SC	0.00	5.68	0.00	16.83	1.02	25.50	0.00	50.02
Ogle County	IL	0.00	0.00	85.52	0.00	0.00	0.00	0.00	0.00
Okaloosa County	FL	2.11	4.02	10.81	39.84	5.37	27.83	53.99	36.02
Oklahoma County	OK	0.00	0.00	0.00	0.00	0.00	0.00	0.00	0.00
Oldham County	KY	0.00	4.07	0.00	0.40	13.76	15.82	0.00	3.64
Olmsted County	MN	0.00	0.00	0.60	152.49	1.60	33.05	0.00	0.00
Oneida County	NY	0.00	0.00	59.16	0.00	4.40	3.42	35.29	0.00
Onondaga County	NY	0.00	5.45	163.68	67.31	10.93	54.54	111.67	72.68
Onslow County	NC	0.00	0.93	0.00	29.87	2.87	11.07	0.00	25.88
Ontario County	NY	0.00	0.38	29.23	0.00	17.48	4.00	26.20	0.01
Orange County	CA	5.53	15.10	0.00	46.71	21.46	33.31	0.00	27.81
Orange County	FL	1.07	43.83	86.06	61.34	19.39	28.61	144.18	58.92
Orange County	NY	0.00	4.49	16.57	30.91	10.59	17.73	20.48	32.22
Orange County	NC	5.33	23.41	1.50	55.70	7.55	43.97	2.43	74.82
Orangeburg County	SC	0.00	0.00	1.36	16.38	0.00	0.00	0.00	59.49
Osceola County	FL	0.00	10.55	0.00	13.15	7.26	46.95	0.00	39.17

County/Parish	State	Revenue[1] ($/per capita)				Current Operational Expenses ($/per capita)			
		Natural Resources, Other	Park & Recreation	Sewerage	Solid Waste Management	Natural Resources, Other	Parks & Recreation	Sewerage	Solid Waste Management
Oswego County	NY	0.00	0.07	0.00	59.04	42.96	8.81	0.00	49.57
Otero County	NM	0.00	0.00	0.00	1.24	0.00	0.00	0.00	13.11
Ottawa County	MI	0.00	2.29	40.20	1.26	0.00	10.49	24.18	2.38
Otter Tail County	MN	0.00	0.00	0.00	211.69	27.15	3.52	0.00	239.71
Ouachita Parish	LA	0.07	0.00	0.00	0.00	0.08	0.00	25.64	0.00
Outagamie County	WI	0.00	0.40	0.00	90.03	15.35	6.01	0.00	122.40
Oxford County	ME	0.00	0.00	0.00	0.00	3.48	0.00	0.00	0.00
Palm Beach County	FL	3.31	13.64	46.99	187.83	24.82	43.32	48.50	143.60
Pasco County	FL	2.77	3.17	123.47	56.33	3.73	17.20	98.19	53.78
Passaic County	NJ	0.00	3.58	0.00	0.00	0.28	6.23	0.00	2.39
Paulding County	GA	0.00	3.94	95.63	7.57	0.41	14.40	34.11	9.45
Payne County	OK	0.00	0.00	0.00	0.00	3.77	9.55	0.00	0.00
Pearl River County	MS	0.00	0.00	0.00	0.00	4.89	6.11	0.00	3.99
Pender County	NC	0.00	0.42	3.82	83.20	2.01	7.81	23.76	85.24
Pennington County	SD	1.21	0.00	0.00	0.00	5.48	1.67	0.00	0.00
Penobscot County	ME	0.00	0.00	0.00	0.00	0.00	0.00	0.00	0.00
Peoria County	IL	0.00	0.00	0.00	1.39	0.00	0.00	0.00	1.25
Pickens County	SC	0.00	5.03	11.26	0.00	0.53	12.63	12.82	29.07
Pierce County	WA	0.61	13.08	90.79	5.84	8.77	23.28	43.69	6.69
Pike County	KY	0.13	0.08	0.00	18.00	11.57	11.62	0.44	27.16
Pike County	PA	0.00	0.00	0.00	0.00	33.12	19.54	0.00	0.00
Pima County	AZ	6.36	0.98	166.80	0.00	20.82	22.55	80.94	2.21
Pinal County	AZ	0.03	0.86	0.00	0.06	8.81	0.24	0.00	0.07
Pinellas County	FL	1.14	6.30	77.24	97.32	25.59	18.98	61.48	97.90
Pitt County	NC	0.00	0.00	0.00	43.70	1.48	3.78	0.00	44.92
Pittsylvania County	VA	0.00	0.80	0.00	18.20	0.55	25.29	0.00	38.97
Placer County	CA	0.00	6.49	0.00	10.35	8.02	15.54	0.00	6.77
Platte County	MO	0.00	5.22	0.00	0.00	0.00	37.12	0.00	0.00
Plymouth County	MA	0.00	0.00	0.00	0.00	0.65	0.00	0.00	0.00
Polk County	FL	0.50	0.78	0.00	100.05	11.48	12.94	0.00	44.94
Polk County	IA	0.00	37.52	1.99	0.00	10.80	34.19	0.88	0.70
Polk County	OR	1.07	0.00	0.00	0.00	9.59	0.91	0.00	0.00
Pope County	AR	0.00	0.00	0.00	0.00	0.00	0.43	0.00	0.00
Portage County	OH	0.35	0.00	77.91	18.18	2.96	0.00	49.24	17.59
Porter County	IN	0.00	2.62	0.00	0.00	1.88	10.47	0.00	0.00
Pottawatomie County	OK	0.00	0.00	0.00	0.00	0.82	0.00	0.00	0.00
Pottawattamie County	IA	0.00	0.00	0.00	0.00	12.81	12.59	0.00	2.57
Prince Georges County	MD	0.00	23.67	4.18	103.66	1.45	222.26	60.71	89.64
Prince William County	VA	0.00	30.08	144.05	43.52	0.00	94.35	95.53	27.99
Pueblo County	CO	0.00	0.00	0.00	0.00	0.00	9.09	0.00	0.00
Pulaski County	AR	0.00	0.00	0.00	10.65	0.05	0.00	0.00	9.87
Pulaski County	KY	0.00	1.80	0.00	0.00	1.47	8.61	0.00	14.44
Pulaski County	MO	0.00	0.13	0.00	0.00	0.53	13.21	0.00	0.00
Putnam County	FL	0.00	0.78	3.07	15.04	5.46	14.87	1.57	128.70
Putnam County	NY	0.00	24.06	0.00	0.25	7.12	40.31	0.00	1.23
Putnam County	TN	2.76	0.56	0.00	7.58	3.38	12.55	0.00	50.46
Putnam County	WV	0.00	15.48	0.00	0.00	0.00	9.24	0.00	0.00
Racine County	WI	0.12	2.94	0.00	0.60	6.11	10.30	0.00	0.00
Raleigh County	WV	0.00	0.00	0.00	0.00	0.00	22.58	0.00	0.00
Ramsey County	MN	0.00	9.99	0.00	0.00	1.27	29.86	0.00	37.73
Randolph County	NC	1.24	0.00	0.00	15.67	0.00	0.21	0.00	19.91
Rankin County	MS	0.00	0.00	0.00	30.80	1.95	0.24	0.00	30.30
Rapides Parish	LA	0.00	0.00	0.00	0.00	0.00	2.07	0.00	0.00
Reno County	KS	0.00	0.00	0.11	61.60	2.65	2.70	2.24	41.10
Rensselaer County	NY	0.00	0.00	55.88	0.00	0.71	3.43	27.84	0.00
Rice County	MN	0.00	0.38	1.38	36.09	14.27	3.21	1.96	34.24

County/Parish	State	Revenue[1] ($/per capita)				Current Operational Expenses ($/per capita)			
		Natural Resources, Other	Park & Recreation	Sewerage	Solid Waste Management	Natural Resources, Other	Parks & Recreation	Sewerage	Solid Waste Management
Richland County	OH	0.00	0.00	20.05	0.00	0.00	1.04	19.95	0.00
Richland County	SC	0.00	7.61	8.49	55.08	1.92	48.02	14.09	71.15
Riverside County	CA	0.00	10.88	1.44	33.91	46.42	18.78	1.37	29.67
Roane County	TN	0.00	1.73	11.22	2.14	2.48	4.19	5.59	30.77
Robertson County	TN	0.00	0.00	0.00	13.11	2.03	0.00	0.00	32.80
Robeson County	NC	0.00	0.18	0.00	53.42	4.25	7.85	0.00	52.56
Rock County	WI	0.74	0.92	0.00	0.00	14.02	4.39	0.00	0.00
Rock Island County	IL	0.00	14.04	0.00	0.00	0.00	28.72	0.00	0.00
Rockdale County	GA	0.00	6.72	310.11	0.81	2.27	25.30	129.69	3.64
Rockingham County	NH	0.00	0.00	0.00	0.00	1.30	0.00	0.00	0.00
Rockingham County	NC	0.49	0.00	4.68	41.67	5.01	0.00	7.44	67.15
Rockingham County	VA	0.00	9.99	0.00	69.84	0.00	28.18	0.00	44.38
Rockland County	NY	0.00	0.07	2.53	0.00	2.47	6.28	114.03	0.00
Rogers County	OK	0.00	0.00	0.00	0.00	2.10	2.44	0.00	0.00
Ross County	OH	0.00	0.00	0.76	0.00	7.97	0.00	1.05	1.62
Rowan County	NC	0.07	10.46	0.00	36.49	0.38	16.73	0.00	29.52
Rutherford County	NC	0.00	0.26	0.00	57.03	2.05	0.00	0.09	52.75
Rutherford County	TN	0.00	0.00	0.00	5.96	3.35	1.74	0.00	10.94
Rutland County	VT	0.00	0.00	0.00	0.00	0.00	0.00	0.00	0.00
Sacramento County	CA	0.00	12.15	14.37	48.23	21.43	31.58	15.08	38.58
Saginaw County	MI	0.00	0.29	0.00	1.81	2.81	29.82	0.00	2.06
Salem County	NJ	0.00	0.00	0.00	0.00	1.00	0.00	0.00	0.00
Saline County	AR	0.00	0.00	2.47	0.00	0.58	0.00	1.79	0.00
Saline County	KS	3.97	0.00	0.20	0.04	15.10	0.77	0.00	0.04
Salt Lake County	UT	0.00	6.32	0.00	9.71	4.60	77.74	1.08	21.33
San Benito County	CA	0.00	10.48	0.00	21.40	19.32	2.28	0.00	12.37
San Bernardino County	CA	0.00	4.03	4.80	37.54	16.03	7.83	0.99	28.02
San Diego County	CA	0.00	1.41	5.97	3.26	5.17	6.93	5.77	3.35
San Joaquin County	CA	0.00	2.47	5.75	35.80	20.58	7.94	4.68	27.50
San Juan County	NM	0.00	5.20	0.00	3.45	17.11	39.33	0.00	23.84
San Luis Obispo County	CA	0.00	32.16	15.95	9.72	42.87	43.81	5.22	1.87
San Mateo County	CA	0.00	2.73	15.67	5.31	7.94	17.51	19.01	1.31
Sandoval County	NM	0.00	0.00	0.00	19.33	0.00	0.00	0.00	13.72
Sangamon County	IL	0.00	0.00	0.00	0.00	0.00	0.00	0.00	0.00
Santa Barbara County	CA	0.00	13.65	28.21	57.40	29.88	29.94	9.18	51.08
Santa Clara County	CA	0.81	3.05	6.45	0.02	2.79	22.51	6.24	0.91
Santa Cruz County	CA	0.00	6.35	143.39	0.00	19.84	26.17	128.34	0.00
Santa Fe County	NM	0.00	0.00	4.41	2.00	0.00	0.00	0.00	0.00
Santa Rosa County	FL	4.97	2.28	0.00	34.78	10.66	6.83	11.05	27.87
Sarasota County	FL	1.00	6.33	143.37	46.67	65.70	73.60	50.82	94.55
Saratoga County	NY	0.00	0.00	81.32	0.00	12.90	4.89	68.15	0.00
Sarpy County	NE	0.00	4.38	12.04	28.41	1.22	12.33	4.53	15.92
Sauk County	WI	3.79	1.71	0.00	0.02	26.30	11.01	0.00	1.76
Schenectady County	NY	0.00	2.68	0.00	1.17	11.16	7.22	0.00	2.35
Schuylkill County	PA	0.00	0.00	0.00	0.00	13.55	2.39	0.00	0.00
Scott County	IA	0.00	13.86	0.00	0.00	15.00	7.15	0.00	4.76
Scott County	KY	0.00	0.00	0.00	0.48	2.98	15.57	0.00	3.64
Scott County	MN	1.54	4.98	0.00	0.00	25.07	33.57	4.72	0.00
Sebastian County	AR	0.00	3.98	0.00	0.00	0.00	10.24	0.00	0.00
Sedgwick County	KS	0.23	0.23	0.00	3.34	5.74	9.95	0.00	3.75
Seminole County	FL	1.31	2.83	67.12	27.45	3.53	15.56	47.45	55.19
Seneca County	OH	0.00	0.00	9.15	0.00	0.00	0.00	6.35	0.00
Sevier County	TN	0.00	0.00	0.00	0.25	3.13	0.94	0.00	29.64
Shasta County	CA	0.00	0.00	0.87	19.68	8.30	0.79	1.38	13.54
Shawnee County	KS	0.00	25.84	7.15	67.20	0.00	87.32	3.56	59.01
Sheboygan County	WI	3.35	0.00	0.00	0.00	20.29	2.46	0.00	1.20

County/Parish	State	Revenue[1] ($/per capita) Natural Resources, Other	Park & Recreation	Sewerage	Solid Waste Management	Current Operational Expenses ($/per capita) Natural Resources, Other	Parks & Recreation	Sewerage	Solid Waste Management
Shelby County	AL	0.00	0.00	0.00	22.98	0.60	11.95	0.00	14.73
Shelby County	TN	4.74	0.30	0.32	0.72	4.13	4.18	0.35	1.36
Sherburne County	MN	0.00	0.00	0.00	36.12	10.78	2.10	0.00	12.05
Skagit County	WA	1.86	5.17	9.35	75.41	47.44	7.37	16.61	65.63
Smith County	TX	0.00	0.00	0.00	0.00	0.87	0.00	0.00	0.65
Snohomish County	WA	0.54	4.09	1.10	70.85	3.72	11.58	23.59	61.51
Solano County	CA	0.00	1.29	0.00	13.26	6.25	3.02	0.00	0.00
Somerset County	ME	0.00	0.25	0.00	0.00	0.00	0.37	0.00	0.00
Somerset County	NJ	0.00	0.00	0.00	0.00	2.92	28.03	0.00	5.88
Somerset County	PA	0.00	0.00	0.00	0.00	20.15	7.08	0.00	0.00
Sonoma County	CA	0.00	9.53	47.46	14.74	9.58	45.23	33.17	10.94
Spalding County	GA	0.00	2.92	48.66	0.00	2.44	33.29	0.00	13.58
Spartanburg County	SC	0.00	3.85	0.00	29.59	0.00	23.18	0.00	17.17
Spokane County	WA	3.05	10.16	68.52	20.37	10.65	12.98	43.44	23.75
Spotsylvania County	VA	0.00	2.74	101.65	17.05	0.00	21.18	43.88	31.16
St Charles County	MO	0.00	14.93	0.00	0.00	0.30	30.15	0.00	0.00
St Charles Parish	LA	0.00	0.00	0.00	0.00	0.00	0.00	0.00	0.00
St Clair County	AL	0.00	0.00	0.00	0.00	0.38	0.00	0.00	0.00
St Clair County	IL	0.00	0.00	0.00	2.20	0.00	0.00	0.00	10.38
St Clair County	MI	14.59	0.68	4.26	44.10	19.08	22.42	6.14	30.83
St Croix County	WI	0.18	2.30	0.00	0.08	34.91	8.39	0.00	2.95
St Johns County	FL	19.42	48.15	68.51	88.74	4.02	90.07	36.04	81.23
St Joseph County	IN	0.03	1.21	0.00	2.05	2.56	19.02	0.00	0.00
St Landry Parish	LA	0.00	0.00	0.49	0.00	23.52	5.12	0.38	0.00
St Louis County	MN	41.30	0.00	0.00	31.43	50.37	11.95	0.00	0.00
St Louis County	MO	0.00	1.26	2.95	1.14	9.94	31.62	2.43	0.89
St Lucie County	FL	0.00	9.69	16.00	35.96	17.53	43.29	7.74	58.47
St Martin Parish	LA	0.06	1.43	3.66	0.00	15.60	4.16	3.99	0.00
St Mary Parish	LA	0.00	27.72	32.72	100.17	57.09	105.17	64.68	110.30
St Marys County	MD	0.00	33.58	148.49	3.58	15.36	96.57	116.27	40.65
St Tammany Parish	LA	1.80	2.56	24.66	2.23	28.19	24.24	15.75	0.94
Stafford County	VA	0.00	0.00	149.86	12.96	1.19	50.74	11.06	0.00
Stanislaus County	CA	0.00	5.24	0.00	17.27	8.51	22.65	0.00	14.12
Stark County	OH	0.00	0.00	66.87	0.00	0.00	0.00	39.41	0.00
Stearns County	MN	0.00	0.75	0.00	4.34	60.07	0.00	0.00	3.24
Story County	IA	0.00	0.00	0.00	0.00	18.58	9.00	0.00	3.76
Strafford County	NH	0.00	0.00	0.00	0.00	0.00	0.00	0.00	0.00
Suffolk County	NY	0.00	8.08	20.77	0.00	2.50	15.04	31.71	0.00
Sullivan County	TN	0.00	2.21	0.00	2.14	1.09	2.19	0.00	8.90
Summit County	OH	0.00	0.00	82.27	0.00	0.00	0.00	82.43	0.00
Sumner County	TN	0.00	0.00	0.00	0.01	2.63	2.41	0.00	1.21
Sumter County	FL	0.00	0.00	0.00	1.46	12.11	6.33	0.47	2.63
Sumter County	SC	0.00	0.00	0.00	0.00	0.33	25.55	0.00	0.00
Surry County	NC	0.00	0.48	0.22	38.38	2.21	8.55	0.01	29.16
Sussex County	DE	0.00	0.00	99.95	0.00	0.00	0.00	80.05	0.00
Sussex County	NJ	0.00	0.00	43.79	76.08	2.22	0.08	26.22	40.10
Sutter County	CA	0.00	0.00	0.00	0.00	25.83	6.27	0.00	0.00
Talladega County	AL	0.00	0.00	0.00	0.00	0.00	0.00	0.00	4.27
Taney County	MO	0.00	0.00	27.53	0.00	0.00	0.00	79.28	0.00
Tangipahoa Parish	LA	0.00	0.43	18.33	28.41	33.69	20.52	11.50	40.82
Tarrant County	TX	0.00	0.00	0.00	0.00	0.36	0.00	0.00	0.13
Tazewell County	IL	0.00	0.00	0.00	0.00	0.00	0.00	0.00	0.00
Tehama County	CA	0.00	0.35	1.72	0.00	23.61	4.49	1.64	0.36
Thurston County	WA	0.75	1.29	4.57	80.99	5.31	5.16	11.53	69.73
Tippecanoe County	IN	0.00	1.19	0.00	0.09	6.03	5.32	0.29	2.16
Tipton County	TN	0.00	0.00	0.00	3.05	2.83	0.27	0.00	16.24

County/Parish	State	Revenue[1] ($/per capita)				Current Operational Expenses ($/per capita)			
		Natural Resources, Other	Park & Recreation	Sewerage	Solid Waste Management	Natural Resources, Other	Parks & Recreation	Sewerage	Solid Waste Management
Tom Green County	TX	0.00	0.06	0.00	0.00	1.81	0.96	0.00	0.00
Tompkins County	NY	0.00	0.00	0.00	48.30	28.37	16.67	0.00	45.87
Tooele County	UT	0.00	4.75	0.00	52.85	3.40	16.17	0.00	38.24
Travis County	TX	0.19	0.55	0.00	0.00	4.59	9.04	0.00	0.50
Troup County	GA	0.00	7.20	0.00	8.80	10.99	83.41	0.00	17.17
Trumbull County	OH	0.00	0.00	59.21	0.00	0.00	0.00	52.12	0.00
Tulare County	CA	0.00	0.55	1.31	30.89	14.52	3.19	1.51	19.60
Tulsa County	OK	0.00	3.30	0.00	0.00	1.60	14.01	0.00	0.00
Tuolumne County	CA	0.00	4.41	0.00	25.27	11.12	19.05	0.00	18.64
Tuscaloosa County	AL	0.00	0.00	0.00	0.00	0.00	14.45	0.00	2.34
Tuscarawas County	OH	0.00	0.00	22.81	0.00	6.76	0.00	16.85	0.00
Twin Falls County	ID	13.05	0.00	0.00	29.71	13.31	6.60	0.00	36.42
Ulster County	NY	0.00	0.62	0.00	0.00	10.06	3.94	0.00	0.00
Umatilla County	OR	0.00	0.00	0.00	0.59	10.00	3.88	0.00	0.10
Union County	NJ	0.00	11.54	0.00	0.00	0.60	19.10	0.00	0.11
Union County	NC	0.00	2.36	82.14	21.19	0.00	8.47	39.13	18.91
Union County	OH	0.99	0.41	9.29	0.00	4.83	1.31	6.80	0.00
Utah County	UT	0.00	0.27	39.02	18.01	0.00	2.37	13.54	13.21
Valencia County	NM	0.00	0.00	0.00	0.00	0.00	0.00	0.00	0.00
Van Buren County	MI	0.00	0.00	0.00	0.00	0.00	0.00	0.00	0.00
Vanderburgh County	IN	0.00	3.91	0.49	0.00	1.45	14.14	0.02	0.00
Venango County	PA	0.00	0.00	0.00	0.00	12.16	5.35	0.00	0.00
Ventura County	CA	0.00	4.89	36.74	3.37	38.56	4.49	33.05	0.00
Vermilion County	IL	0.00	0.00	0.00	0.00	0.00	0.00	0.00	2.27
Vermilion Parish	LA	0.00	0.00	0.00	14.13	68.33	0.08	0.00	106.94
Vernon Parish	LA	2.34	0.00	0.00	0.00	1.83	3.96	0.00	34.94
Victoria County	TX	0.00	0.00	0.00	0.00	2.76	0.56	0.00	0.00
Vigo County	IN	0.00	0.00	0.22	1.22	5.69	13.73	0.02	1.07
Volusia County	FL	1.87	15.55	9.65	27.99	11.34	47.08	21.76	39.94
Wagoner County	OK	0.00	0.00	0.00	0.00	0.54	0.00	0.33	0.00
Wake County	NC	0.00	0.13	0.01	25.77	7.21	2.71	0.05	28.53
Walla Walla County	WA	0.51	16.03	3.89	0.00	37.27	0.31	1.33	1.09
Walton County	FL	0.00	1.02	0.00	16.42	7.51	8.88	0.00	148.26
Walton County	GA	0.00	6.07	47.35	6.32	2.93	30.40	0.17	12.85
Walworth County	WI	1.17	0.46	0.00	0.90	19.33	1.78	0.00	2.22
Ward County	ND	0.46	0.08	0.00	0.00	8.38	8.25	0.00	0.00
Warren County	KY	0.00	1.12	0.00	0.00	7.85	37.39	0.00	1.39
Warren County	NJ	0.00	0.00	0.00	55.41	4.78	0.73	0.00	48.36
Warren County	NY	0.00	1.45	0.20	0.00	33.05	18.58	0.20	0.00
Warren County	OH	0.00	0.00	39.89	0.00	0.00	0.00	29.02	0.00
Warrick County	IN	0.00	3.76	2.63	0.00	2.88	9.27	8.87	0.29
Washington County	AR	0.00	0.00	0.00	2.32	0.45	0.00	0.00	1.80
Washington County	MD	0.00	8.96	62.99	36.47	23.67	29.03	45.50	47.85
Washington County	MN	0.00	0.00	0.00	0.00	0.97	10.74	0.00	28.14
Washington County	NY	0.00	0.37	27.51	1.03	34.85	10.54	23.59	1.02
Washington County	OK	0.00	0.00	0.00	0.00	0.19	0.00	0.00	0.00
Washington County	OR	0.71	0.03	216.31	0.00	3.89	1.79	120.41	0.00
Washington County	PA	0.00	0.00	0.00	0.00	1.74	1.02	0.00	0.00
Washington County	TN	0.00	0.00	0.00	0.63	3.02	0.00	0.51	12.70
Washington County	UT	0.00	2.76	24.46	64.61	28.23	5.87	9.95	58.38
Washington County	VT	0.00	0.00	0.00	0.00	0.00	0.00	0.00	0.00
Washington County	VA	0.00	0.90	0.00	5.50	2.51	8.21	0.00	35.94
Washington County	WI	0.28	12.66	0.00	0.06	12.70	24.54	0.00	0.77
Washoe County	NV	0.00	25.45	25.46	0.00	16.32	73.77	17.06	0.00
Washtenaw County	MI	0.29	11.02	0.00	0.00	8.56	40.08	0.00	2.31
Waukesha County	WI	0.38	15.01	0.00	4.12	5.58	29.83	0.00	12.73

County/Parish	State	Revenue[1] ($/per capita) Natural Resources, Other	Park & Recreation	Sewerage	Solid Waste Management	Current Operational Expenses ($/per capita) Natural Resources, Other	Parks & Recreation	Sewerage	Solid Waste Management
Waupaca County	WI	0.17	1.96	0.00	8.49	26.07	12.26	0.00	17.33
Wayne County	IN	0.00	0.00	0.00	0.00	8.66	16.22	2.21	0.18
Wayne County	MI	1.24	1.19	61.88	0.00	0.95	6.05	59.82	0.00
Wayne County	NY	0.00	3.37	0.00	0.00	26.80	8.97	0.00	0.00
Wayne County	NC	0.00	0.00	3.71	31.27	0.00	0.78	4.63	28.52
Wayne County	OH	0.00	0.00	6.28	0.00	4.73	0.00	4.60	0.66
Wayne County	PA	0.00	0.00	0.00	0.00	9.36	1.02	0.00	1.09
Webb County	TX	0.19	0.69	0.00	0.00	0.60	1.73	1.74	0.00
Weber County	UT	0.00	14.38	0.70	26.38	0.00	20.17	1.09	27.49
Weld County	CO	0.00	0.00	0.00	3.70	5.81	1.42	0.00	0.30
Westchester County	NY	0.00	34.26	4.55	19.56	0.01	47.91	145.21	61.75
Westmoreland County	PA	0.00	0.85	0.00	0.00	3.27	7.39	0.00	0.00
Whatcom County	WA	0.44	1.26	0.00	3.35	21.52	12.68	0.00	4.89
White County	AR	0.00	0.00	0.00	0.00	0.28	0.08	0.00	0.00
Whiteside County	IL	0.00	0.00	0.00	14.00	0.00	0.00	0.00	6.13
Whitfield County	GA	0.00	1.44	0.00	54.00	1.02	8.33	0.00	53.99
Wicomico County	MD	0.00	54.91	0.00	69.24	0.97	112.08	0.00	55.03
Wilkes County	NC	0.00	1.28	0.00	33.50	7.62	11.68	0.00	29.33
Will County	IL	2.03	0.00	0.00	2.46	18.05	0.00	0.00	2.17
Williamson County	TN	0.00	21.70	0.00	3.81	1.74	53.97	0.00	25.56
Williamson County	TX	0.00	0.54	0.00	0.00	1.27	3.41	0.00	0.06
Wilson County	NC	0.00	0.00	0.00	21.31	3.26	1.21	0.00	29.95
Wilson County	TN	2.57	0.02	0.00	5.29	10.57	0.40	0.00	19.74
Winnebago County	IL	0.00	0.00	0.00	0.00	0.00	0.00	0.00	0.00
Winnebago County	WI	0.05	1.36	0.00	51.17	8.83	9.62	0.00	52.67
Wood County	OH	0.00	0.00	0.00	22.69	0.00	1.19	0.00	0.00
Wood County	WV	0.00	0.00	0.00	0.00	0.00	9.29	0.00	0.00
Wood County	WI	9.36	6.48	0.00	0.00	21.56	27.21	0.00	0.00
Woodbury County	IA	3.76	0.00	0.00	0.00	15.48	3.51	0.00	2.05
Worcester County	MD	0.00	4.83	176.95	77.69	21.25	61.45	194.76	92.12
Wright County	MN	0.59	2.19	0.00	0.37	5.19	11.74	0.00	3.34
Yakima County	WA	1.39	0.00	0.62	35.70	11.12	0.25	4.44	35.96
Yamhill County	OR	0.00	4.25	0.00	11.59	0.00	5.80	0.00	4.05
Yavapai County	AZ	0.00	0.00	0.11	0.11	23.50	1.46	0.04	8.32
Yellowstone County	MT	0.00	34.20	0.00	1.37	2.59	3.61	0.00	0.00
Yolo County	CA	0.00	1.06	0.00	58.90	11.26	4.10	0.00	40.86
York County	ME	0.00	0.00	0.00	0.00	0.78	0.00	0.00	0.00
York County	PA	0.00	2.62	0.00	0.00	3.72	8.91	0.00	0.00
York County	SC	0.00	0.00	28.54	25.38	0.34	28.21	19.10	40.23
York County	VA	0.00	7.67	159.09	68.19	0.00	28.26	112.11	60.98
Yuba County	CA	0.00	1.01	0.00	10.56	16.95	2.56	0.00	0.00
Yuma County	AZ	0.03	0.00	0.00	0.30	5.52	0.03	0.00	4.10

Note: *(1) Includes revenue raised through current charges only. Does not include intergovernmental revenue.*
Source: *U.S. Census Bureau, State and Local Government Finances, 2016*

Environmental Revenue and Expenditures for U.S. Cities/Townships with Populations of 50,000+

City	State	Revenue[1] ($/per capita)				Current Operational Expenses ($/per capita)			
		Natural Resources, Other	Park & Recreation	Sewerage	Solid Waste Management	Natural Resources, Other	Parks & Recreation	Sewerage	Solid Waste Management
Abilene (city)	TX	0.00	5.49	100.26	106.49	0.00	66.12	78.38	86.31
Abington (township)	PA	0.00	16.78	162.62	97.72	0.00	74.71	157.71	105.95
Akron (city)	OH	0.29	11.01	449.63	70.17	0.00	44.18	342.73	64.20
Albany (city)	GA	0.00	1.82	132.53	132.09	0.00	68.80	108.21	234.02
Albany (city)	NY	0.00	11.08	0.00	121.21	0.00	32.90	0.00	78.96
Albany (city)	OR	0.00	15.98	318.10	0.00	0.00	105.64	168.84	0.00
Albuquerque (city)	NM	0.00	26.61	121.92	127.47	0.00	126.83	71.76	115.77
Alexandria (city)	VA	0.00	31.09	316.92	42.41	0.00	203.79	193.27	0.00
Allen (city)	TX	0.00	103.95	138.49	65.96	15.49	218.02	36.50	56.65
Allentown (city)	PA	0.00	12.25	3.93	119.90	0.00	54.55	0.00	250.04
Alpharetta (city)	GA	0.00	35.22	0.00	49.93	2.14	127.13	0.00	48.31
Ames (city)	IA	0.00	23.32	145.68	50.60	0.00	58.84	80.42	61.31
Amherst (town)	NY	0.00	36.26	2.12	2.43	26.97	70.39	102.97	44.40
Anaheim (city)	CA	0.00	116.50	0.00	173.93	0.00	161.10	0.00	149.70
Anchorage (municipality)	AK	0.00	8.81	171.99	112.49	0.00	89.15	98.18	71.73
Anderson (city)	IN	0.00	6.51	401.05	43.81	0.00	32.69	226.24	52.36
Ankeny (city)	IA	0.00	47.32	288.55	11.89	0.00	77.58	167.55	11.13
Ann Arbor (city)	MI	0.00	9.38	263.44	25.33	0.00	103.12	147.48	162.58
Apple Valley (city)	MN	0.00	77.90	145.27	0.00	0.00	141.58	66.81	0.12
Appleton (city)	WI	0.09	19.77	146.08	18.59	12.68	55.94	135.29	43.35
Arlington (city)	TX	0.00	32.99	177.97	5.88	0.00	67.13	122.97	0.87
Arlington Heights (village)	IL	0.00	0.50	0.00	23.79	0.00	12.84	0.00	17.52
Arvada (city)	CO	0.00	0.00	0.00	0.00	0.00	0.00	0.00	0.00
Asheville (city)	NC	0.00	32.53	60.87	44.43	0.00	126.65	38.48	51.87
Athens-Clarke County (unified govt)	GA	0.00	69.65	294.81	58.51	1.28	63.70	110.05	59.24
Atlanta (city)	GA	0.00	7.01	429.24	100.30	0.00	106.53	193.98	133.98
Auburn (city)	AL	0.00	11.25	185.77	72.24	0.00	80.18	68.43	58.91
Auburn (city)	WA	0.00	30.23	436.47	178.83	0.00	144.04	158.36	162.40
Augusta-Richmond Co. (consol. govt)	GA	0.00	25.50	189.13	164.81	1.15	97.73	81.41	119.91
Aurora (city)	CO	0.00	22.67	160.44	0.00	0.00	110.06	58.73	0.00
Aurora (city)	IL	0.00	8.53	16.94	10.19	0.00	28.76	13.48	9.94
Austin (city)	TX	83.70	45.05	279.07	103.69	60.67	139.86	109.45	96.68
Avondale (city)	AZ	0.00	4.45	105.98	66.96	0.00	49.35	77.56	54.05
Babylon (town)	NY	0.00	11.46	0.00	115.61	1.63	45.01	0.00	208.41
Bakersfield (city)	CA	0.00	2.67	102.78	122.75	0.00	69.57	40.11	118.87
Baltimore (city)	MD	0.00	0.26	412.72	17.53	0.00	59.65	226.78	114.57
East Baton Rouge City-Baton Rouge Parish (city/parish)	LA	0.00	28.34	344.17	170.74	0.00	54.84	191.19	168.86
Battle Creek (city)	MI	0.00	48.71	354.30	62.28	0.00	106.32	220.98	58.52
Bayonne (city)	NJ	0.00	0.00	3.97	0.00	0.00	66.29	7.57	72.16
Baytown (city)	TX	0.00	48.54	211.37	62.04	9.04	97.48	51.50	60.12
Beaumont (city)	TX	0.00	11.86	153.82	87.33	0.00	71.92	66.43	59.63
Beaverton (city)	OR	0.00	0.00	117.43	0.00	0.00	2.59	76.62	0.00
Bellevue (city)	NE	0.00	10.07	92.45	43.51	0.00	30.64	80.87	40.80
Bellevue (city)	WA	0.00	98.84	555.76	5.02	4.36	260.96	403.86	13.08
Bellingham (city)	WA	0.00	21.30	329.41	1.30	0.00	85.18	196.76	8.54
Bend (city)	OR	0.00	0.00	275.36	0.00	0.00	0.00	101.68	0.00
Bensalem (township)	PA	0.00	51.05	0.00	0.00	0.00	79.07	0.00	0.00
Berkeley (city)	CA	0.00	17.09	128.24	335.03	0.00	194.20	76.84	265.95
Berwyn (city)	IL	0.00	8.69	112.48	1.54	0.00	31.86	71.30	89.39
Bethlehem (city)	PA	0.00	27.85	192.76	27.41	0.00	51.63	154.10	71.02
Billings (city)	MT	0.00	4.32	172.13	126.64	0.00	52.68	74.76	90.03
Birmingham (city)	AL	0.00	7.85	0.00	0.00	0.00	109.66	0.00	0.00
Bismarck (city)	ND	0.00	94.58	119.68	115.33	0.00	139.10	123.02	82.19

City	State	Revenue[1] ($/per capita) Natural Resources, Other	Park & Recreation	Sewerage	Solid Waste Management	Current Operational Expenses ($/per capita) Natural Resources, Other	Parks & Recreation	Sewerage	Solid Waste Management
Blaine (city)	MN	0.00	8.53	117.25	56.45	0.00	20.15	86.97	55.61
Bloomington (city)	IL	0.00	72.60	99.64	76.79	0.00	204.27	40.39	72.71
Bloomington (city)	IN	0.00	37.89	241.31	11.18	0.00	100.10	233.59	24.21
Bloomington (city)	MN	0.00	86.09	193.54	13.11	0.00	174.50	83.32	15.69
Blue Springs (city)	MO	0.00	30.45	135.46	0.00	0.00	97.55	100.59	0.00
Boca Raton (city)	FL	27.45	83.86	211.03	84.75	229.46	367.76	187.97	76.12
Boise (city)	ID	0.16	34.88	201.41	116.29	0.31	107.15	114.65	139.66
Bolingbrook (village)	IL	0.00	112.59	50.01	0.00	0.00	166.27	33.07	73.37
Bossier City (city)	LA	0.00	3.39	239.07	94.81	0.00	48.20	78.45	77.44
Boston (city)	MA	0.00	0.00	280.98	0.00	2.84	32.47	55.12	90.35
Boulder (city)	CO	0.00	68.12	135.07	0.00	36.63	379.48	156.35	0.00
Bowie (city)	MD	0.00	21.09	57.01	0.00	0.00	129.12	55.49	98.47
Bowling Green (city)	KY	0.00	37.16	197.72	0.00	0.00	105.02	113.48	1.89
Boynton Beach (city)	FL	0.00	55.54	295.22	146.49	3.07	109.82	156.95	94.08
Bradenton (city)	FL	0.00	22.96	189.08	130.37	19.56	50.35	157.76	115.88
Brick (township)	NJ	0.00	5.53	236.68	1.07	0.03	28.00	26.97	101.52
Bridgeport (city)	CT	0.00	13.34	247.91	1.50	0.00	48.75	194.48	50.17
Bristol (city)	CT	0.28	4.98	100.72	6.72	3.97	48.90	71.51	67.77
Bristol (township)	PA	0.00	1.31	96.33	96.59	0.00	7.03	78.54	78.02
Brockton (city)	MA	0.00	9.43	223.43	79.85	0.51	17.11	93.29	74.30
Broken Arrow (city)	OK	0.00	19.75	137.56	58.75	0.00	46.28	78.70	48.66
Brookhaven (city)	GA	0.00	0.00	217.13	214.97	0.00	78.79	147.35	170.22
Brookhaven (town)	NY	0.00	10.09	0.00	119.35	0.16	42.46	0.76	113.21
Brookline (town)	MA	0.00	21.56	241.49	45.17	2.18	62.78	11.49	47.10
Brooklyn Park (city)	MN	0.00	70.13	95.09	18.07	0.00	142.02	85.03	11.71
Broomfield (city/county)	CO	0.00	83.78	156.46	0.00	1.03	283.72	110.00	4.41
Brownsville (city)	TX	0.00	6.30	119.02	74.03	0.00	47.29	80.31	28.24
Bryan (city)	TX	0.00	51.83	156.88	93.35	0.00	51.83	120.98	75.92
Buckeye (town)	AZ	0.00	10.88	142.81	66.85	0.00	33.28	96.00	76.67
Buffalo (city)	NY	0.00	0.79	0.00	75.36	0.00	33.44	0.00	154.84
Burbank (city)	CA	0.00	40.86	165.43	158.57	0.47	98.33	95.20	127.76
Burlington (city)	NC	0.00	37.05	0.00	26.45	0.00	128.56	0.00	42.23
Burnsville (city)	MN	0.00	48.19	155.64	0.00	13.26	104.28	129.28	3.56
Caldwell (city)	ID	23.04	19.08	159.00	67.14	17.61	33.92	69.48	74.28
Calumet (township)	IN	0.00	0.03	0.00	0.00	0.00	2.97	0.00	0.00
Cambridge (city)	MA	0.00	11.06	442.19	0.00	0.00	167.27	18.87	57.27
Camden (city)	NJ	0.00	0.00	105.40	0.00	0.00	38.12	93.93	64.40
Canton (charter township)	MI	0.00	68.60	178.41	42.32	0.00	132.07	92.55	39.55
Canton (city)	OH	0.00	0.00	197.18	84.26	48.66	37.38	150.74	86.19
Cape Coral (city)	FL	0.00	47.97	233.61	0.00	19.95	99.22	138.30	0.00
Carlsbad (city)	CA	0.00	88.49	147.36	29.64	0.36	187.48	83.67	27.12
Carmel (city)	IN	0.00	117.50	180.20	0.00	0.00	140.46	60.09	0.00
Carrollton (city)	TX	0.00	15.87	90.07	61.86	7.63	101.16	13.19	56.51
Carson City (city)	NV	0.00	26.16	209.59	68.73	3.28	137.87	99.96	30.52
Cary (town)	NC	0.00	45.18	263.44	56.23	0.00	89.80	0.00	53.06
Casa Grande (city)	AZ	0.00	22.44	167.49	133.23	0.00	173.26	84.20	99.18
Casper (city)	WY	0.00	83.74	157.24	211.68	0.00	169.03	121.12	142.08
Castle Rock (town)	CO	0.00	123.37	232.48	0.00	0.00	201.85	179.85	0.00
Cedar Park (city)	TX	0.00	18.74	184.78	53.12	0.00	47.92	80.26	50.39
Cedar Rapids (city)	IA	0.00	132.82	357.82	80.90	0.00	77.11	197.22	73.87
Center (township)	IN	0.00	0.00	0.00	0.00	0.00	0.16	0.00	0.00
Champaign (city)	IL	0.00	1.57	24.81	6.53	0.00	0.00	17.05	6.05
Chandler (city)	AZ	0.00	0.00	196.76	57.28	0.00	0.00	88.39	53.32
Chapel Hill (town)	NC	0.00	0.00	0.00	0.00	0.00	0.00	0.00	0.00
Charleston (city)	SC	0.00	44.08	54.57	0.00	0.00	121.92	23.37	43.83
Charlotte (city)	NC	2.12	38.25	339.89	10.26	6.55	108.00	75.52	60.73

City	State	Revenue[1] ($/per capita)				Current Operational Expenses ($/per capita)			
		Natural Resources, Other	Park & Recreation	Sewerage	Solid Waste Management	Natural Resources, Other	Parks & Recreation	Sewerage	Solid Waste Management
Chattanooga (city)	TN	0.00	3.74	511.07	38.71	5.35	108.13	329.84	112.18
Cheektowaga (town)	NY	0.00	11.19	2.97	1.73	4.60	55.74	111.67	65.99
Cherry Hill (township)	NJ	0.00	0.00	65.66	0.00	0.00	11.45	27.56	73.90
Chesapeake (city)	VA	0.12	5.63	182.61	0.00	1.67	58.75	71.41	33.70
Cheyenne (city)	WY	0.00	38.51	230.95	218.32	0.00	123.14	98.70	141.86
Chicago (city)	IL	0.00	3.98	138.16	0.00	0.01	11.32	30.54	61.86
Chicopee (city)	MA	0.00	15.65	232.16	19.77	0.00	28.85	88.33	26.35
Chula Vista (city)	CA	0.00	5.29	137.30	7.57	0.00	97.68	77.65	10.03
Cicero (town)	IL	0.00	0.00	60.44	45.49	0.00	5.13	69.00	20.49
Cincinnati (city)	OH	0.00	68.88	39.04	1.40	11.94	126.12	448.71	0.00
Clarkstown (town)	NY	0.00	20.79	0.00	0.05	17.41	72.34	10.86	105.81
Clarksville (city)	TN	0.00	11.13	231.12	0.00	0.00	50.70	131.40	0.00
Clay (town)	NY	0.00	5.34	0.00	0.00	33.37	17.50	12.51	48.57
Clay (township)	IN	0.00	0.00	0.00	0.00	0.00	0.91	0.00	0.00
Clearwater (city)	FL	157.77	64.11	365.63	195.73	144.24	238.16	186.97	214.52
Cleveland (city)	OH	0.00	7.08	58.68	11.89	0.00	89.91	45.04	63.73
Clifton (city)	NJ	0.00	1.68	121.32	3.42	9.41	13.78	90.12	56.76
Clinton (charter township)	MI	0.00	6.14	225.23	36.57	0.00	24.91	47.89	34.89
Colerain (township)	OH	0.00	0.00	0.00	0.00	0.00	18.54	0.00	0.00
College Station (city)	TX	19.89	15.31	137.56	80.46	11.65	71.99	51.65	62.01
Colonie (town)	NY	0.00	20.38	1.91	0.22	0.17	45.48	71.90	1.45
Colorado Springs (city)	CO	0.00	5.15	157.16	0.00	0.00	37.75	74.13	0.00
Columbia (city)	MO	0.00	34.81	172.94	151.31	0.00	111.76	67.46	116.66
Columbia (city)	SC	0.00	7.59	395.07	1.44	15.28	88.91	264.04	78.16
Columbus (city)	OH	0.00	10.92	328.83	0.02	0.00	130.12	135.22	46.54
Columbus (consol. govt)	GA	0.00	17.60	156.64	55.54	0.62	54.71	49.50	66.38
Commerce (city)	CO	0.00	0.00	0.00	0.00	0.00	183.37	0.00	0.00
Concord (city)	NC	0.00	22.35	246.50	1.36	5.92	69.27	159.24	62.99
Conway (city)	AR	0.00	14.20	208.02	148.08	0.00	38.44	71.93	107.06
Coon Rapids (city)	MN	0.00	50.64	128.79	0.00	0.00	78.08	108.95	0.00
Coral Gables (city)	FL	0.67	85.63	245.98	192.95	185.05	166.05	123.23	184.81
Coral Springs (city)	FL	0.86	34.89	94.70	0.00	0.00	115.00	61.81	32.78
Corona (city)	CA	0.00	11.80	199.51	43.25	0.00	40.35	108.20	43.08
Corpus Christi (city)	TX	0.00	31.19	209.45	115.64	0.32	99.90	105.28	60.44
Corvallis (city)	OR	0.00	27.00	232.68	0.00	7.98	113.16	141.75	5.49
Council Bluffs (city)	IA	0.00	18.42	94.43	80.82	3.96	159.58	90.61	84.62
Cranston (city)	RI	0.00	0.00	266.99	0.00	0.00	30.60	218.64	0.00
Dallas (city)	TX	0.00	42.92	214.46	69.85	3.59	114.56	110.35	51.59
Daly City (city)	CA	0.00	19.65	185.84	3.53	0.00	82.07	165.68	0.08
Danbury (city)	CT	0.00	32.04	153.96	0.00	3.44	66.43	78.93	2.76
Davenport (city)	IA	0.00	67.76	216.88	52.45	0.00	69.08	148.37	47.03
Davie (town)	FL	1.30	8.15	0.00	0.00	19.83	41.90	0.00	0.00
Dayton (city)	OH	0.00	20.84	286.42	0.00	0.00	64.61	204.86	0.00
Daytona Beach (city)	FL	155.11	112.63	419.55	214.19	130.34	241.67	102.22	144.23
Dearborn (city)	MI	0.00	52.64	321.83	0.00	0.00	17.70	130.27	07.21
Dearborn Heights (city)	MI	0.00	0.00	208.05	0.00	0.00	12.57	90.53	68.88
Decatur (city)	AL	0.00	9.92	294.10	110.29	0.00	134.10	118.82	143.68
Decatur (city)	IL	0.00	0.00	64.91	9.54	0.00	9.42	36.33	0.00
Delray Beach (city)	FL	32.30	88.42	0.00	70.83	29.49	255.78	0.00	95.48
Denton (city)	TX	0.00	29.91	229.88	220.14	0.00	91.27	132.04	148.39
Denver (city/county)	CO	0.00	59.48	125.57	23.14	0.22	216.88	136.64	14.60
Des Moines (city)	IA	0.00	6.94	295.10	57.96	2.97	62.83	190.60	54.41
Des Plaines (city)	IL	0.00	0.00	56.24	49.88	0.00	0.00	60.31	3.99
Detroit (city)	MI	0.00	4.95	598.85	74.52	2.93	40.34	301.22	60.36
Dothan (city)	AL	0.00	40.30	208.31	68.85	0.00	146.86	129.87	108.32
Dubuque (city)	IA	0.00	31.21	269.21	65.31	2.26	130.87	101.74	55.63

City	State	Revenue[1] ($/per capita)				Current Operational Expenses ($/per capita)			
		Natural Resources, Other	Park & Recreation	Sewerage	Solid Waste Management	Natural Resources, Other	Parks & Recreation	Sewerage	Solid Waste Management
Duluth (city)	MN	0.00	171.19	244.52	0.00	0.00	67.44	265.51	47.56
Dupage (township)	IL	0.00	0.10	0.00	0.00	0.00	5.72	0.00	0.00
Durham (city)	NC	0.00	17.87	239.43	25.13	4.31	52.57	129.79	70.23
Eagan (city)	MN	0.00	41.28	142.29	0.00	0.00	86.01	131.45	0.00
East Hartford (town)	CT	0.00	1.06	0.00	2.26	0.10	63.54	0.00	45.89
East Orange (city)	NJ	0.00	4.39	110.63	0.00	0.00	43.45	90.06	65.70
Eau Claire (city)	WI	0.00	26.37	138.45	1.56	10.37	108.88	112.68	1.56
Eden Prairie (city)	MN	0.00	97.90	105.50	0.00	0.00	182.97	117.46	64.07
Edina (city)	MN	0.00	190.08	61.93	8.32	0.00	235.49	30.04	10.49
Edison (township)	NJ	0.00	0.00	174.72	0.00	0.00	26.00	52.02	12.63
Edmond (city)	OK	0.00	30.64	169.34	101.31	0.00	96.31	65.08	81.21
El Paso (city)	TX	0.00	20.90	115.61	97.90	0.00	54.40	49.42	53.98
Elgin (city)	IL	0.00	56.37	48.50	41.00	0.00	142.83	0.00	49.23
Elizabeth (city)	NJ	0.00	0.63	193.49	1.29	0.00	81.84	83.72	74.48
Elkhart (city)	IN	0.00	13.30	981.39	0.00	3.84	39.35	114.50	3.94
Elyria (city)	OH	0.00	5.21	214.41	78.36	0.00	35.52	154.61	68.68
Enid (city)	OK	0.00	7.84	0.00	0.00	0.00	35.36	59.12	59.89
Erie (city)	PA	0.00	3.96	196.56	84.61	0.00	30.38	117.58	47.24
Escondido (city)	CA	0.00	16.57	225.81	0.00	0.00	63.50	153.36	0.00
Eugene (city)	OR	0.00	38.45	245.90	0.03	1.13	164.28	186.88	12.11
Evanston (city)	IL	0.00	77.80	165.38	53.01	0.00	146.70	21.41	68.16
Everett (city)	WA	0.00	46.92	335.60	20.28	0.00	135.18	238.35	5.09
Fairfield (town)	CT	0.07	25.91	96.27	0.00	16.32	72.98	83.85	55.20
Fall River (city)	MA	0.00	0.00	203.68	68.73	0.00	14.46	136.18	108.01
Fargo (city)	ND	18.06	51.21	100.91	99.99	17.68	67.46	55.05	71.78
Farmington Hills (city)	MI	0.00	57.03	136.55	0.00	0.00	95.78	35.07	46.18
Fayetteville (city)	AR	0.00	11.52	220.16	128.37	0.00	46.58	154.68	130.46
Fayetteville (city)	NC	0.00	6.74	33.63	0.00	0.69	65.53	50.84	43.53
Federal Way (city)	WA	0.00	25.66	0.00	3.16	7.81	71.81	0.00	5.03
Fishers (town)	IN	0.00	1.44	129.25	0.00	0.00	15.38	112.97	0.00
Flagstaff (city)	AZ	0.00	0.00	149.42	181.95	0.00	100.77	90.49	157.91
Flint (city)	MI	0.00	0.00	295.40	0.00	0.00	4.57	224.31	45.70
Florissant (city)	MO	0.00	28.60	0.00	0.00	0.00	81.43	3.73	0.00
Flower Mound (city)	TX	0.00	31.21	147.90	0.00	0.00	86.02	119.67	0.00
Fort Collins (city)	CO	0.00	57.90	230.18	0.00	83.20	182.62	76.33	0.00
Fort Lauderdale (city)	FL	64.78	41.19	0.00	85.32	64.62	167.22	0.00	87.58
Fort Myers (city)	FL	52.36	106.49	526.34	196.51	118.11	206.26	458.74	130.10
Fort Smith (city)	AR	0.00	11.29	195.32	155.97	0.00	42.26	89.10	122.99
Fort Wayne (city)	IN	0.00	18.30	266.72	39.73	0.00	63.92	112.19	35.51
Fort Worth (city)	TX	0.00	9.75	230.20	69.86	0.00	95.98	152.11	59.03
Framingham (town)	MA	0.00	6.59	362.75	3.44	2.44	43.76	55.71	49.32
Franklin (city)	TN	0.00	0.94	257.48	114.90	0.00	60.11	171.74	104.30
Franklin (township)	NJ	0.00	0.00	189.41	0.00	0.00	7.44	166.37	10.90
Frederick (city)	MD	0.00	42.19	147.17	1.77	0.00	244.03	108.52	50.76
Fremont (city)	CA	0.00	31.21	0.00	31.27	0.00	35.82	0.00	26.92
Fresno (city)	CA	0.00	18.94	150.34	80.20	4.30	25.39	69.10	64.41
Frisco (city)	TX	0.00	53.09	174.62	82.55	0.00	90.60	164.55	78.96
Fullerton (city)	CA	0.00	26.06	41.50	75.04	0.00	63.46	17.89	72.30
Gainesville (city)	FL	4.13	16.31	337.36	62.22	142.51	80.08	174.58	65.11
Gaithersburg (city)	MD	0.00	54.61	0.00	16.99	0.00	159.27	0.00	39.55
Galveston (city)	TX	0.00	78.82	237.31	112.81	0.00	478.54	169.23	90.31
Garden Grove (city)	CA	0.00	13.21	42.74	0.00	0.00	26.59	22.13	0.00
Garland (city)	TX	0.00	21.30	199.26	81.23	0.00	55.84	101.72	70.62
Gary (city)	IN	0.00	8.06	375.12	62.76	0.00	19.70	413.18	65.56
Gastonia (city)	NC	0.00	10.54	272.74	18.45	0.00	73.34	205.14	63.06

City	State	Revenue[1] ($/per capita) Natural Resources, Other	Park & Recreation	Sewerage	Solid Waste Management	Current Operational Expenses ($/per capita) Natural Resources, Other	Parks & Recreation	Sewerage	Solid Waste Management
Georgetown (charter township)	MI	0.00	0.00	0.00	0.00	0.00	80.69	170.74	0.00
Georgetown (city)	TX	0.00	33.76	185.57	96.46	0.00	127.86	25.44	83.42
Gilbert (town)	AZ	0.00	12.85	102.31	75.63	0.00	65.07	53.46	65.88
Glendale (city)	AZ	0.00	19.74	138.36	104.27	0.00	89.74	70.58	93.64
Glendale (city)	CA	0.00	15.57	72.36	108.35	0.00	75.18	49.02	84.82
Gloucester (township)	NJ	0.00	4.75	92.31	1.22	0.00	30.64	81.95	80.65
Goodyear (city)	AZ	0.00	5.89	151.48	90.25	0.00	71.45	50.92	77.09
Grand Forks (city)	ND	0.00	88.04	212.96	181.65	0.00	39.06	89.49	104.61
Grand Island (city)	NE	0.00	19.98	207.54	30.75	0.00	90.80	124.28	41.00
Grand Junction (city)	CO	0.00	86.60	179.76	59.00	0.00	225.69	182.86	63.62
Grand Prairie (city)	TX	0.00	45.73	173.18	61.40	0.00	95.68	105.84	58.18
Grand Rapids (city)	MI	0.00	4.04	277.40	30.04	0.00	57.23	119.56	50.57
Grapevine (city)	TX	0.00	127.17	164.33	0.00	0.00	235.95	93.65	0.00
Great Falls (city)	MT	0.00	44.18	212.06	57.92	0.00	62.58	147.88	56.21
Greece (town)	NY	0.00	3.26	1.38	0.00	7.75	18.82	11.35	7.05
Greeley (city)	CO	0.00	78.73	197.83	0.00	7.51	148.62	62.48	2.10
Green Bay (city)	WI	0.35	34.37	173.26	2.59	28.12	79.39	167.59	82.69
Green (township)	OH	0.00	3.20	0.00	0.00	0.00	16.00	0.00	0.00
Greenburgh (town)	NY	0.00	20.10	0.00	0.24	0.00	85.73	5.04	39.25
Greensboro (city)	NC	0.00	10.22	204.99	66.51	3.50	145.79	122.30	112.60
Greenville (city)	NC	0.00	11.20	523.89	81.39	0.00	84.88	275.55	67.22
Greenville (city)	SC	0.00	150.25	158.84	43.50	2.28	121.40	94.04	77.78
Greenwich (town)	CT	5.36	52.32	3.53	5.49	37.99	153.52	74.38	95.21
Greenwood (city)	IN	0.00	25.69	232.99	54.40	0.00	34.40	131.17	42.46
Gresham (city)	OR	0.00	0.52	214.67	5.28	0.00	17.14	153.34	6.19
Gulfport (city)	MS	0.00	12.15	271.24	81.72	0.00	102.13	49.81	56.49
Hamden (town)	CT	0.00	3.95	0.00	0.00	0.00	14.02	0.00	0.00
Hamilton (city)	OH	0.00	52.27	230.49	60.01	0.00	56.00	148.22	59.78
Hamilton (township)	NJ	0.00	1.31	179.28	0.09	0.01	45.25	148.34	45.87
Hammond (city)	IN	0.00	57.62	234.73	74.64	0.52	127.86	265.43	81.35
Hampton (city)	VA	0.00	118.57	128.26	156.46	0.00	221.21	79.72	113.51
Harlingen (city)	TX	0.00	31.35	170.90	147.35	0.00	89.12	106.62	105.53
Harrisonburg (city)	VA	0.00	22.48	205.18	215.33	0.00	103.68	161.50	178.00
Hartford (city)	CT	0.00	0.00	0.00	0.76	0.00	10.35	0.00	21.52
Haverhill (city)	MA	0.00	0.00	142.55	0.00	1.02	52.32	110.67	58.33
Hempstead (town)	NY	0.00	7.56	0.05	14.71	12.47	82.56	18.13	107.38
Hempstead (village)	NY	0.00	0.36	0.00	72.10	0.00	44.90	0.67	50.19
Henderson (city)	NV	0.00	37.70	157.97	0.00	0.00	152.57	104.60	0.00
Hendersonville (city)	TN	0.00	18.15	0.00	73.85	0.00	48.45	0.00	90.24
Hialeah (city)	FL	20.39	0.00	147.91	63.75	24.79	53.25	154.80	56.14
High Point (city)	NC	0.00	32.34	300.80	103.96	0.00	127.02	119.12	127.27
Hillsboro (city)	OR	0.00	35.46	321.56	0.00	0.00	193.80	82.27	0.00
Hoboken (city)	NJ	0.00	0.00	0.00	0.00	2.91	19.76	0.00	87.85
Hoffman Estates (village)	IL	0.00	0.00	220.57	0.00	0.00	222.81	41.43	0.00
Hollywood (city)	FL	23.69	23.38	414.55	88.74	31.76	99.08	182.52	76.97
Honolulu (city/county)	HI	0.00	29.18	421.56	123.15	0.98	107.24	110.66	141.43
Hoover (city)	AL	0.00	17.83	48.79	0.08	0.00	96.97	22.49	76.89
Houston (city)	TX	0.00	10.50	212.67	1.00	0.00	28.29	109.66	26.00
Howell (township)	NJ	0.00	0.00	123.10	0.00	0.00	0.00	110.53	9.67
Huntersville (town)	NC	0.00	65.54	15.52	23.91	0.00	121.89	4.10	0.00
Huntington (town)	NY	0.00	35.06	7.96	105.42	4.25	62.30	23.38	185.81
Huntsville (city)	AL	0.00	58.26	197.71	63.41	3.44	112.97	78.72	0.00
Idaho Falls (city)	ID	0.00	73.43	171.55	68.08	0.00	134.06	82.18	42.53
Independence (city)	MO	0.00	93.86	208.54	0.00	0.00	97.10	141.09	0.00
Indianapolis (city)	IN	0.00	41.35	279.71	10.64	0.00	109.12	25.86	111.99
Inglewood (city)	CA	0.00	2.34	30.04	125.34	0.00	99.68	27.64	128.29

City	State	Revenue[1] ($/per capita)				Current Operational Expenses ($/per capita)			
		Natural Resources, Other	Park & Recreation	Sewerage	Solid Waste Management	Natural Resources, Other	Parks & Recreation	Sewerage	Solid Waste Management
Iowa City (city)	IA	0.00	10.33	181.00	121.05	0.00	86.30	83.10	101.10
Irvine (city)	CA	0.00	37.76	0.00	0.00	0.00	218.29	0.00	0.00
Irving (city)	TX	22.15	2.37	119.52	53.02	22.73	115.10	128.88	47.04
Irvington (township)	NJ	0.00	0.00	104.75	0.00	0.00	15.48	80.91	59.99
Islip (town)	NY	0.00	21.85	0.00	0.00	0.06	37.76	0.00	134.79
Jackson (city)	MS	0.00	15.63	179.62	67.02	0.00	95.58	79.24	62.02
Jackson (city)	TN	0.00	30.44	0.00	199.27	0.00	83.76	0.00	186.77
Jacksonville (city)	FL	44.70	11.06	262.52	74.45	70.64	112.18	101.82	77.72
Jacksonville (city)	NC	0.00	10.54	175.75	69.55	0.00	84.70	139.01	70.33
Janesville (city)	WI	0.00	32.64	139.11	92.93	7.78	63.58	123.65	86.07
Jersey City (city)	NJ	0.00	2.82	237.13	2.17	0.00	25.51	52.34	2.37
Johns Creek (city)	GA	0.00	1.84	0.00	0.00	0.00	26.64	0.00	0.00
Johnson City (city)	TN	0.00	67.09	260.06	183.08	0.00	145.62	131.48	169.23
Joliet (city)	IL	0.00	24.53	167.29	83.15	0.00	44.22	67.60	84.28
Jonesboro (city)	AR	0.00	7.36	96.63	0.66	0.00	42.46	61.08	29.94
Joplin (city)	MO	0.00	22.48	213.40	49.92	0.00	86.17	85.49	60.09
Kalamazoo (city)	MI	0.00	26.37	260.79	0.00	4.84	49.67	213.86	34.21
Kansas City (city)	MO	0.00	17.85	407.27	0.00	0.00	94.93	198.65	47.12
Kenner (city)	LA	0.00	4.72	121.42	47.23	0.00	106.11	86.76	64.00
Kennewick (city)	WA	0.00	22.99	111.36	0.00	16.76	86.63	57.91	0.00
Kenosha (city)	WI	0.00	10.50	98.70	3.03	1.21	71.99	82.71	46.48
Kent (city)	WA	0.00	29.38	364.83	4.65	36.81	78.75	277.82	0.10
Kentwood (city)	MI	0.00	0.00	0.00	0.00	0.00	37.46	58.96	3.33
Kettering (city)	OH	0.00	139.85	0.00	0.00	0.00	257.60	0.00	0.00
Killeen (city)	TX	29.08	22.35	124.57	115.49	17.00	56.45	64.49	84.36
Kingsport (city)	TN	0.00	75.34	259.37	16.45	24.90	150.02	100.84	85.83
Kirkland (city)	WA	0.00	16.90	278.04	183.76	23.50	78.56	102.78	152.63
Kissimmee (city)	FL	74.26	23.74	67.32	51.67	55.15	75.02	46.25	51.51
Knoxville (city)	TN	0.00	43.02	449.23	6.27	0.00	128.88	202.73	51.48
Kokomo (city)	IN	0.00	6.05	222.31	0.00	0.00	53.30	136.06	60.83
La Crosse (city)	WI	0.00	115.84	119.72	0.00	8.20	192.44	117.14	44.35
La Habra (city)	CA	0.00	15.47	52.42	64.32	0.00	151.45	53.31	54.56
Lafayette (city)	IN	0.00	4.32	458.47	0.00	0.00	73.80	124.06	26.82
Lafayette City (city/parish)	LA	0.00	101.47	225.53	114.78	0.00	201.47	137.61	106.00
Lake Charles (city)	LA	0.00	28.61	176.40	0.00	0.00	113.51	108.70	0.00
Lake Havasu City (city)	AZ	0.00	18.39	472.60	119.43	0.00	60.93	138.82	117.83
Lakeland (city)	FL	44.47	81.09	261.77	135.97	14.11	252.33	212.03	118.45
Lakeville (city)	MN	0.00	54.26	89.49	0.00	0.00	58.25	22.96	0.00
Lakewood (city)	CO	0.44	68.38	40.49	0.00	21.16	144.52	24.61	0.00
Lakewood (city)	OH	0.00	0.00	164.72	0.00	0.00	53.58	113.87	58.93
Lakewood (city)	WA	0.00	4.46	60.86	0.00	0.00	28.61	29.13	0.00
Lakewood (township)	NJ	0.00	0.00	40.04	0.42	0.01	13.27	38.21	76.06
Lancaster (city)	PA	0.00	4.04	240.31	64.24	0.00	25.04	121.89	111.63
Lansing (city)	MI	0.00	55.53	281.33	47.79	0.00	131.68	126.26	50.84
Laredo (city)	TX	0.00	4.03	109.58	83.55	0.00	51.26	64.67	67.40
Las Cruces (city)	NM	0.00	12.37	114.16	132.13	12.91	57.86	97.23	102.64
Las Vegas (city)	NV	0.00	13.17	159.04	0.00	8.43	92.17	92.78	8.56
Lawrence (city)	KS	0.00	21.85	201.78	124.76	2.31	98.53	120.55	135.63
Lawrence (city)	MA	0.00	0.00	0.00	0.00	0.00	6.41	0.00	49.54
Lawton (city)	OK	0.00	17.38	144.70	95.33	0.00	82.88	60.57	43.90
Layton (city)	UT	0.00	26.57	109.88	40.13	13.58	51.02	85.16	36.02
League City (city)	TX	0.00	7.10	124.06	44.93	0.00	42.35	50.71	42.27
Lees Summit (city)	MO	0.00	37.54	173.83	21.47	0.00	74.74	138.68	27.52
Leesburg (town)	VA	0.00	97.46	186.16	0.00	0.00	152.20	135.37	46.91
Lehi (city)	UT	0.00	58.75	189.00	0.17	29.46	108.97	110.01	35.55
Lenexa (city)	KS	0.00	23.93	100.63	0.00	0.00	107.30	127.34	0.00

City	State	Revenue[1] ($/per capita)				Current Operational Expenses ($/per capita)			
		Natural Resources, Other	Park & Recreation	Sewerage	Solid Waste Management	Natural Resources, Other	Parks & Recreation	Sewerage	Solid Waste Management
Lewisville (city)	TX	0.00	15.32	103.58	29.49	0.00	76.01	52.52	0.00
Lexington-Fayette County (urban county govt)	KY	0.00	53.23	222.82	27.88	0.00	131.88	114.66	122.07
Lincoln (city)	NE	0.00	7.98	86.16	23.25	0.00	36.26	51.59	31.00
Little Rock (city)	AR	0.00	72.36	258.48	90.20	0.00	164.36	126.32	64.82
Livermore (city)	CA	0.00	95.06	256.89	14.79	0.00	38.47	221.52	6.34
Livonia (city)	MI	0.00	64.66	189.93	1.49	0.00	94.82	178.39	119.12
Logan (city)	UT	0.00	17.17	242.54	239.42	0.00	172.54	31.96	115.19
Long Beach (city)	CA	0.00	13.08	38.71	176.62	0.00	225.72	29.38	164.30
Longmont (city)	CO	0.00	75.25	142.09	66.99	35.47	164.64	87.97	60.49
Longview (city)	TX	0.00	15.02	163.63	67.39	27.90	112.03	85.81	59.44
Lorain (city)	OH	0.00	0.00	264.05	0.00	0.00	10.46	131.84	0.00
Los Angeles (city)	CA	0.00	48.17	156.89	89.17	0.98	105.52	89.14	96.67
Louisville-Jefferson Co. (metro govt)	KY	0.00	20.84	0.00	2.96	5.38	64.10	0.00	33.19
Loveland (city)	CO	0.00	56.02	169.62	90.17	0.00	198.93	118.01	71.84
Lowell (city)	MA	0.00	24.99	171.70	28.01	0.00	50.44	97.49	46.25
Lower Merion (township)	PA	0.00	6.02	134.90	116.01	0.00	92.44	120.67	125.62
Lubbock (city)	TX	0.00	10.09	233.22	82.97	0.00	56.81	78.93	53.87
Lynchburg (city)	VA	0.00	6.15	310.09	12.47	0.00	97.43	155.44	33.04
Lynn (city)	MA	0.00	3.52	0.00	0.00	0.03	3.06	0.00	53.88
Macomb (township)	MI	0.00	24.02	150.02	0.00	0.00	32.93	119.09	0.00
Macon (city)	GA	0.00	0.18	0.00	60.60	0.00	10.56	2.72	55.36
Madison (city)	WI	4.40	33.46	131.93	3.17	18.84	146.21	115.05	63.89
Malden (city)	MA	0.00	0.00	312.75	21.86	0.07	15.11	50.58	45.41
Manchester (city)	NH	0.00	13.74	186.42	0.00	0.00	90.70	77.39	21.84
Manchester (town)	CT	0.00	4.91	148.22	183.98	0.00	109.16	72.78	110.06
Manhattan (city)	KS	0.00	9.23	171.31	0.00	0.00	121.12	33.96	0.00
Mansfield (city)	TX	23.70	8.85	146.65	36.81	8.76	71.85	77.28	31.23
Maple Grove (city)	MN	0.00	94.03	108.37	21.31	10.21	144.78	80.22	19.21
Marietta (city)	GA	0.00	29.93	417.76	63.50	0.00	27.29	239.46	0.00
Marysville (city)	WA	0.00	15.72	266.16	105.48	12.73	43.95	62.70	53.85
Mcallen (city)	TX	0.00	38.25	110.30	124.03	8.62	116.40	55.32	119.63
Mckinney (city)	TX	0.00	4.58	146.48	48.17	0.00	62.48	109.73	41.88
Medford (city)	MA	0.00	0.00	232.20	0.00	0.12	12.82	23.81	94.51
Medford (city)	OR	0.00	14.70	144.18	0.00	0.00	59.83	96.03	0.00
Melbourne (city)	FL	40.52	35.88	256.18	4.88	16.44	100.43	329.74	0.00
Memphis (city)	TN	0.00	12.66	186.18	85.67	0.00	65.06	118.53	74.59
Menifee (city)	CA	0.00	2.70	0.00	0.00	0.00	9.62	0.00	0.00
Meriden (city)	CT	0.00	1.58	139.38	0.95	0.00	36.41	183.75	24.75
Meridian (city)	ID	0.00	9.54	216.68	0.00	0.00	39.31	70.94	0.00
Mesa (city)	AZ	0.00	9.98	151.98	116.30	0.00	72.91	66.37	71.43
Mesquite (city)	TX	16.23	14.37	145.84	73.88	4.79	76.04	45.42	53.44
Miami Beach (city)	FL	0.00	184.17	142.32	103.19	97.17	720.12	358.02	180.01
Miami (city)	FL	0.31	49.56	0.00	56.04	35.22	122.80	0.00	77.59
Miami (township)	OH	0.00	0.00	0.00	0.00	0.00	0.50	0.00	5.43
Middletown (township)	NJ	0.00	3.14	145.40	0.00	0.00	23.48	134.50	66.69
Midland (city)	TX	0.00	28.25	85.05	97.31	0.00	76.15	58.62	85.32
Midwest City (city)	OK	0.00	25.26	123.86	100.23	0.00	45.56	94.03	0.00
Milford (city)	CT	1.02	7.49	1.90	15.99	1.27	25.27	0.00	89.87
Millcreek (township)	PA	0.00	3.24	186.79	0.00	0.00	19.63	143.95	12.11
Milwaukee (city)	WI	5.23	8.37	73.74	69.03	11.95	0.00	78.06	70.55
Minneapolis (city)	MN	0.00	51.08	238.13	86.37	0.00	306.30	208.10	83.14
Minnetonka (city)	MN	17.03	76.60	187.44	0.00	21.83	145.87	113.09	0.00
Miramar (city)	FL	1.84	16.26	146.19	1.01	42.44	105.93	57.65	3.64
Mission (city)	TX	0.00	13.93	72.43	77.17	0.00	39.14	33.60	51.05
Mission Viejo (city)	CA	0.00	15.21	0.00	0.00	0.00	136.94	0.00	0.00
Missoula (city)	MT	0.00	23.46	116.92	0.00	19.97	77.06	79.43	0.00

City	State	Revenue[1] ($/per capita)				Current Operational Expenses ($/per capita)			
		Natural Resources, Other	Park & Recreation	Sewerage	Solid Waste Management	Natural Resources, Other	Parks & Recreation	Sewerage	Solid Waste Management
Mobile (city)	AL	0.00	23.55	303.25	0.00	7.61	139.28	209.62	40.13
Modesto (city)	CA	0.00	18.49	234.23	36.21	0.00	64.16	119.40	58.24
Montgomery (city)	AL	0.00	31.55	0.00	89.76	0.00	135.22	0.00	79.98
Moore (city)	OK	0.00	4.43	123.89	76.08	0.00	40.35	78.06	21.27
Mount Pleasant (town)	SC	0.00	36.72	269.24	0.01	2.80	65.42	13.59	80.38
Mount Prospect (village)	IL	0.00	0.00	48.37	72.42	0.00	8.55	37.15	81.10
Mount Vernon (city)	NY	0.00	1.22	0.31	0.00	0.00	83.04	11.18	78.66
Muncie (city)	IN	0.00	3.94	221.31	0.00	0.00	22.91	315.75	84.31
Murfreesboro (city)	TN	0.00	30.86	0.00	0.02	0.00	98.81	0.00	32.41
Nampa (city)	ID	0.00	107.06	138.51	100.36	0.00	142.04	55.20	78.62
Naperville (city)	IL	0.00	2.92	100.88	6.86	0.00	51.41	49.10	47.67
Nashua (city)	NH	0.00	0.00	132.23	38.82	0.00	43.92	73.87	95.06
Nashville-Davidson Co. (metro govt)	TN	6.25	19.95	265.89	8.51	7.81	133.39	85.74	34.41
New Bedford (city)	MA	0.00	0.53	216.26	0.01	3.05	30.00	132.01	56.29
New Braunfels (city)	TX	0.00	34.40	166.04	113.07	0.00	88.71	82.98	81.84
New Britain (city)	CT	0.00	0.00	126.04	0.00	0.00	93.05	104.48	44.49
New Brunswick (city)	NJ	0.00	0.00	213.06	0.00	0.00	26.56	42.29	42.69
New Haven (city)	CT	0.00	9.44	0.00	53.64	0.00	37.08	0.00	51.18
New Orleans (city)	LA	0.00	118.12	245.46	91.39	0.00	184.31	217.38	104.93
New Rochelle (city)	NY	0.00	36.40	0.00	78.58	4.87	48.54	24.01	61.12
New York (city)	NY	0.00	9.34	266.13	1.16	0.00	79.18	53.40	149.20
Newark (city)	NJ	0.00	0.00	179.89	0.00	0.00	31.56	21.97	94.08
Newport News (city)	VA	0.00	40.22	219.25	79.23	0.00	119.57	148.24	68.29
Newton (city)	MA	0.00	1.45	355.71	0.00	0.73	63.77	51.51	86.22
Noblesville (city)	IN	0.00	23.66	232.29	1.62	0.00	45.40	67.67	0.00
Norfolk (city)	VA	0.00	8.54	176.69	87.97	0.00	145.98	86.59	79.50
Normal (town)	IL	0.00	73.18	42.37	45.67	0.00	165.84	35.86	37.08
Norman (city)	OK	0.00	22.88	132.38	237.97	0.00	10.37	86.75	174.53
North Bergen (township)	NJ	0.00	5.29	257.19	3.76	0.00	35.46	151.79	110.68
North Charleston (city)	SC	0.00	4.42	0.00	0.00	0.00	66.58	0.00	70.06
North Hempstead (town)	NY	0.00	62.56	12.54	66.57	0.66	120.44	49.13	121.53
North Las Vegas (city)	NV	0.00	17.89	184.68	0.00	0.59	100.46	63.83	0.00
North Little Rock (city)	AR	0.00	19.16	221.75	12.10	0.00	83.53	152.80	65.44
Norwalk (city)	CT	0.00	11.89	181.34	0.00	0.00	54.45	104.73	0.00
Novi (city)	MI	0.00	24.56	198.25	0.00	0.00	81.40	187.01	0.00
O'fallon (city)	MO	0.00	37.05	89.30	53.34	8.07	83.23	38.43	37.12
Oak Lawn (village)	IL	0.00	0.00	57.52	60.90	0.00	4.16	30.42	60.04
Oak Park (village)	IL	0.00	0.00	78.83	65.04	0.00	0.00	50.62	59.40
Oakland (city)	CA	0.00	11.61	140.01	0.00	2.03	112.95	76.97	0.00
Ocala (city)	FL	134.15	27.72	382.39	174.91	113.37	129.44	338.61	142.46
Oceanside (city)	CA	0.00	5.07	263.93	144.16	0.00	72.49	125.39	109.51
Odessa (city)	TX	0.00	14.08	120.65	111.35	0.00	48.59	46.96	96.18
Ogden (city)	UT	0.00	10.40	0.00	61.64	0.00	15.89	0.00	35.04
Oklahoma City (city)	OK	0.00	59.41	144.09	80.66	0.00	155.08	43.50	71.98
Olathe (city)	KS	0.00	22.02	29.02	96.53	0.00	95.82	17.09	89.59
Old Bridge (township)	NJ	0.00	8.93	248.07	0.00	0.00	35.54	91.96	8.33
Olympia (city)	WA	0.00	15.03	482.51	199.42	0.00	110.83	162.76	178.46
Omaha (city)	NE	0.00	18.79	283.10	0.00	0.00	68.81	82.04	47.29
Ontario (city)	CA	0.00	3.41	135.18	192.92	6.04	66.59	86.55	148.44
Orangetown (town)	NY	0.00	78.29	30.73	0.00	0.00	114.44	149.59	15.73
Orem (city)	UT	0.00	16.67	110.46	37.27	0.00	52.83	55.47	11.44
Orland Park (village)	IL	0.00	63.61	124.12	87.77	0.00	168.07	104.13	92.19
Orlando (city)	FL	84.65	133.15	331.73	113.19	172.73	368.23	279.45	99.31
Oshkosh (city)	WI	0.00	20.51	169.50	9.57	5.06	97.21	135.80	30.50
Overland Park (city)	KS	0.00	105.05	33.82	0.00	0.00	50.77	17.19	0.00
Owensboro (city)	KY	0.00	34.40	345.40	124.83	0.00	106.75	309.95	65.19

City	State	Revenue[1] ($/per capita)				Current Operational Expenses ($/per capita)			
		Natural Resources, Other	Park & Recreation	Sewerage	Solid Waste Management	Natural Resources, Other	Parks & Recreation	Sewerage	Solid Waste Management
Oxnard (city)	CA	0.00	11.16	147.76	200.23	0.00	79.86	105.12	175.77
Oyster Bay (town)	NY	0.00	20.67	1.66	27.67	6.37	111.82	12.49	197.47
Palatine (village)	IL	0.00	0.00	50.47	65.46	0.00	0.00	29.72	65.71
Palm Coast (city)	FL	85.03	19.80	0.00	89.30	90.61	50.57	247.32	87.33
Palo Alto (city)	CA	0.00	87.46	608.51	478.20	0.00	426.62	483.85	440.59
Parma (city)	OH	0.00	10.02	0.00	0.00	0.00	52.93	0.00	0.00
Parsippany-Troy Hills (township)	NJ	0.00	74.53	290.79	29.16	0.00	101.99	167.33	73.38
Pasadena (city)	CA	0.00	241.94	50.14	83.51	0.00	271.92	30.62	90.66
Pasadena (city)	TX	0.00	11.77	91.98	45.77	0.00	54.20	67.58	62.72
Pasco (city)	WA	0.00	18.11	151.92	0.00	27.49	74.07	114.40	0.00
Passaic (city)	NJ	0.00	0.84	79.95	2.19	0.00	21.47	75.12	71.83
Paterson (city)	NJ	0.00	0.00	77.48	2.38	0.00	31.83	6.71	66.89
Pawtucket (city)	RI	0.00	0.17	0.00	3.45	0.00	25.56	7.57	51.38
Peabody (city)	MA	0.00	42.53	176.86	0.00	0.00	64.93	184.23	59.14
Pearland (city)	TX	0.00	19.87	121.92	68.98	0.00	59.15	82.32	67.39
Pembroke Pines (city)	FL	0.17	60.73	135.56	0.00	46.48	44.96	232.13	0.00
Pensacola (city)	FL	48.75	44.84	0.00	132.76	105.22	185.89	0.00	118.08
Peoria (city)	AZ	0.00	55.07	125.43	69.25	0.00	133.02	67.35	61.58
Peoria (city)	IL	0.00	0.00	38.19	55.63	0.00	0.00	9.67	62.48
Perth Amboy (city)	NJ	0.00	4.78	181.33	0.00	0.00	26.29	92.31	52.60
Pflugerville (city)	TX	0.00	12.10	107.70	72.11	0.00	48.77	71.86	72.21
Pharr (city)	TX	0.00	10.87	77.69	36.56	0.00	55.45	47.52	33.57
Philadelphia (city)	PA	0.00	0.23	198.64	0.86	0.00	54.83	156.08	96.00
Phoenix (city)	AZ	0.01	23.00	125.08	93.78	0.36	92.96	87.82	65.70
Pike (township)	IN	0.00	0.00	0.00	0.00	0.00	0.00	0.00	0.00
Piscataway (township)	NJ	0.00	0.00	179.03	0.10	0.00	24.92	70.54	14.41
Pittsburgh (city)	PA	0.00	21.77	0.00	0.00	0.00	38.07	0.00	56.33
Plainfield (city)	NJ	0.00	0.51	185.41	235.16	0.64	15.50	165.84	254.23
Plano (city)	TX	20.68	43.81	203.78	62.95	11.91	113.13	48.81	60.21
Plantation (city)	FL	5.53	62.64	170.96	43.89	71.89	151.94	128.90	23.68
Plymouth (city)	MN	37.08	18.90	105.02	6.55	32.01	121.77	98.04	13.90
Plymouth (town)	MA	0.00	2.89	82.56	41.38	0.90	6.15	40.75	37.94
Pocatello (city)	ID	0.00	23.90	184.81	131.02	6.43	75.90	111.50	92.01
Pompano Beach (city)	FL	0.00	40.48	172.01	54.77	133.38	112.82	157.88	39.19
Pontiac (city)	MI	0.00	0.00	0.00	0.00	0.00	11.30	0.00	59.38
Port Arthur (city)	TX	0.00	13.95	252.15	123.40	0.00	80.72	90.89	133.07
Port St Lucie (city)	FL	116.81	20.99	185.05	97.87	3.10	65.16	31.69	95.51
Portland (city)	ME	0.00	34.14	349.23	49.30	0.00	122.98	231.01	31.46
Portland (city)	OR	0.00	88.85	541.95	8.79	0.00	159.41	235.63	8.43
Portsmouth (city)	VA	0.00	34.27	191.65	130.18	0.00	99.58	57.12	96.65
Providence (city)	RI	0.12	5.81	0.06	0.00	59.51	63.66	4.32	56.97
Provo (city)	UT	32.09	42.76	108.61	39.27	23.25	104.06	99.45	5.64
Pueblo (city)	CO	0.00	20.03	176.54	0.00	0.00	61.03	124.04	0.00
Quincy (city)	MA	0.23	4.51	289.61	0.00	0.00	33.43	61.01	63.57
Racine (city)	WI	0.00	14.18	198.01	12.35	0.04	102.00	170.49	62.41
Raleigh (city)	NC	0.00	57.64	319.50	56.67	3.63	149.12	113.56	71.35
Ramapo (town)	NY	0.00	31.35	0.50	9.00	0.00	78.30	21.39	24.08
Rapid City (city)	SD	1.81	123.98	151.30	126.55	0.00	209.65	83.73	93.08
Reading (city)	PA	0.00	9.21	475.34	75.50	0.00	15.93	196.83	88.20
Redding (city)	CA	0.00	10.60	277.91	231.33	0.00	66.33	158.09	201.21
Redlands (city)	CA	0.00	4.46	134.55	190.10	0.01	46.93	103.03	146.94
Redmond (city)	WA	0.00	44.77	557.11	0.00	19.36	176.92	138.42	3.47
Reno (city)	NV	0.00	15.88	275.95	0.00	0.00	41.98	152.46	0.00
Renton (city)	WA	0.00	36.42	354.04	170.14	0.00	98.87	234.73	168.76
Revere (city)	MA	0.00	0.00	15.63	0.00	0.13	10.50	20.61	61.98
Richardson (city)	TX	0.00	63.72	201.15	112.23	23.57	197.57	156.66	90.36

City	State	Revenue[1] ($/per capita)				Current Operational Expenses ($/per capita)			
		Natural Resources, Other	Park & Recreation	Sewerage	Solid Waste Management	Natural Resources, Other	Parks & Recreation	Sewerage	Solid Waste Management
Richland (city)	WA	0.00	27.78	201.92	156.61	0.00	149.15	110.05	120.61
Richmond (city)	VA	0.00	6.26	408.98	62.57	0.00	90.03	224.55	156.66
Rio Rancho (city)	NM	0.00	14.48	201.05	0.00	0.00	0.00	110.21	0.00
Riverside (city)	CA	0.00	47.40	165.20	68.51	0.00	91.77	56.41	52.73
Roanoke (city)	VA	0.00	6.51	0.00	22.15	0.00	75.60	29.11	71.06
Rochester (city)	MN	0.00	64.55	284.42	0.00	4.23	147.51	112.09	0.00
Rochester (city)	NY	0.00	8.37	0.00	124.86	0.00	73.53	2.31	196.67
Rochester Hills (city)	MI	0.00	36.88	189.73	0.00	0.00	154.66	36.91	0.00
Rock Hill (city)	SC	0.00	30.78	301.63	98.83	16.95	156.15	84.07	48.89
Rockford (city)	IL	0.00	0.00	0.00	83.48	0.00	0.00	0.00	83.34
Rockville (city)	MD	0.00	83.01	164.86	86.59	0.00	325.44	178.58	87.25
Rocky Mount (city)	NC	0.00	16.68	303.14	110.78	11.18	140.36	238.13	96.50
Rogers (city)	AR	0.00	26.03	186.53	2.34	0.00	64.52	65.31	4.81
Roseville (city)	CA	0.00	52.38	317.62	171.97	0.00	182.65	150.14	134.58
Roswell (city)	GA	0.00	55.35	48.12	86.20	0.75	0.00	13.70	81.87
Round Rock (city)	TX	0.00	26.06	174.10	11.78	0.00	92.36	66.28	1.09
Rowlett (city)	TX	0.00	15.24	190.38	81.43	0.00	58.07	43.33	62.69
Royal Oak (city)	MI	0.00	40.21	312.64	0.03	0.00	73.80	222.78	107.15
Sacramento (city)	CA	0.00	13.57	64.26	122.79	0.00	150.43	49.89	102.80
Salem (city)	OR	0.00	0.00	331.23	0.00	0.00	43.55	213.16	0.00
Salt Lake City (city)	UT	0.00	15.23	113.36	64.17	11.48	49.22	78.68	0.98
San Antonio (city)	TX	0.87	18.81	173.55	72.65	1.39	93.29	100.61	73.76
San Bernardino (city)	CA	0.00	1.64	117.65	90.71	0.00	32.90	80.51	65.97
San Diego (city)	CA	0.00	57.03	248.72	58.52	11.03	165.17	255.51	43.43
San Francisco (city/county)	CA	0.00	43.88	312.22	0.00	0.00	284.47	169.73	0.00
San Jose (city)	CA	0.00	39.68	203.58	127.76	0.00	126.99	125.13	107.39
San Marcos (city)	TX	0.00	9.36	303.01	42.66	0.00	61.75	105.23	38.79
San Mateo (city)	CA	0.00	60.71	302.78	12.53	0.00	139.81	224.22	11.85
Sandy (city)	UT	0.00	57.52	44.71	48.37	0.00	94.87	14.83	11.17
Sandy Springs (city)	GA	0.00	6.52	0.00	0.00	0.00	27.58	0.00	0.00
Sanford (city)	FL	81.26	30.42	228.01	87.01	14.04	100.03	164.91	94.27
Santa Ana (city)	CA	0.00	19.47	20.01	54.35	0.00	60.49	12.41	49.08
Santa Barbara (city)	CA	0.00	76.40	203.74	228.41	0.00	218.08	148.73	221.45
Santa Clara (city)	CA	0.00	1	163.16	310.02	173.03	0.00	1	081.56
Santa Fe (city)	NM	0.38	44.32	185.20	233.58	5.04	274.49	138.25	204.93
Santa Monica (city)	CA	0.00	89.87	207.17	293.10	0.00	453.73	102.69	266.99
Sarasota (city)	FL	1.56	235.33	420.95	190.03	138.12	291.94	227.62	177.64
Savannah (city)	GA	0.00	5.93	187.76	184.92	0.00	141.10	196.85	156.02
Schaumburg (village)	IL	0.00	6.47	40.55	0.00	0.00	36.90	36.71	56.58
Schenectady (city)	NY	0.00	18.38	175.19	85.06	0.00	26.08	115.67	66.49
Scottsdale (city)	AZ	0.00	43.10	215.29	84.95	0.00	151.63	81.46	81.66
Scranton (city)	PA	0.00	0.64	294.28	93.90	0.00	7.11	196.22	47.39
Seattle (city)	WA	0.00	78.40	537.46	259.93	12.20	277.12	127.48	207.97
Shawnee (city)	KS	0.00	19.92	26.60	0.00	0.00	64.26	24.91	0.00
Shelby (charter township)	MI	0.00	0.00	122.75	0.00	0.00	33.45	21.52	0.00
Shoreline (city)	WA	0.00	27.94	65.26	0.00	39.07	54.98	45.85	0.00
Shreveport (city)	LA	0.00	88.03	171.06	54.60	0.00	161.43	109.94	93.14
Sioux City (city)	IA	0.00	14.27	244.14	56.07	0.00	159.78	136.15	80.86
Sioux Falls (city)	SD	0.00	5.79	148.50	62.26	0.00	108.12	55.10	38.98
Skokie (village)	IL	0.00	19.07	0.00	2.47	0.00	34.19	0.00	76.75
Smithtown (town)	NY	0.00	15.35	0.00	154.89	11.35	52.04	0.00	139.56
Smyrna (city)	GA	0.00	20.82	237.77	112.88	0.00	56.69	196.54	4.45
Somerville (city)	MA	0.00	10.78	232.68	1.38	5.08	22.81	11.31	91.24
South Bend (city)	IN	0.00	57.69	360.89	52.85	0.00	130.70	148.08	47.07
South Jordan (city)	UT	0.00	0.00	0.00	36.36	0.00	5.90	0.00	0.00

City	State	Revenue[1] ($/per capita) Natural Resources, Other	Park & Recreation	Sewerage	Solid Waste Management	Current Operational Expenses ($/per capita) Natural Resources, Other	Parks & Recreation	Sewerage	Solid Waste Management
Southampton (town)	NY	0.00	42.78	0.00	33.80	2.03	172.18	1.48	39.00
Southaven (city)	MS	0.00	49.90	39.82	38.47	0.00	87.62	46.30	48.77
Southfield (city)	MI	0.00	29.94	0.00	43.47	0.00	103.53	0.00	42.21
Sparks (city)	NV	0.00	30.84	266.88	0.00	0.00	66.22	176.95	0.00
Spokane (city)	WA	0.00	33.00	403.95	303.84	0.21	93.22	215.37	330.73
Spokane Valley (city)	WA	0.00	3.14	19.61	1.32	2.50	26.87	17.95	0.99
Springdale (city)	AR	0.00	8.36	135.04	39.34	0.00	40.64	84.56	28.89
Springfield (city)	IL	0.00	0.00	52.99	0.00	0.00	0.00	69.18	0.00
Springfield (city)	MA	0.00	16.39	0.00	27.72	0.00	54.11	0.00	64.84
Springfield (city)	MO	0.00	66.21	239.70	43.99	0.00	190.68	107.10	28.68
Springfield (city)	OH	0.00	0.00	188.86	0.00	11.03	0.00	118.41	0.00
Springfield (city)	OR	0.00	0.00	810.78	0.00	0.00	0.00	384.87	0.00
St Charles (city)	MO	0.00	32.63	148.22	0.00	0.00	70.47	139.76	0.00
St Clair Shores (city)	MI	0.00	56.22	285.29	0.00	0.00	83.80	252.09	51.83
St Cloud (city)	MN	0.00	51.89	130.59	50.34	0.00	145.02	65.24	50.38
St George (city)	UT	0.00	86.74	149.44	55.87	0.81	211.00	97.40	52.27
St Joseph (city)	MO	0.00	10.97	339.93	48.49	0.00	92.65	163.57	23.94
St Louis (city)	MO	0.00	1.02	8.39	0.00	0.00	61.12	8.73	47.74
St Paul (city)	MN	0.00	54.62	178.22	33.53	0.00	216.16	137.96	20.00
St Peters (city)	MO	0.00	124.27	88.01	170.72	0.00	236.89	67.35	149.08
St Petersburg (city)	FL	0.00	72.13	227.20	152.07	57.01	219.35	168.18	174.71
Stamford (city)	CT	0.00	0.00	211.75	0.00	2.37	28.91	114.38	100.09
Sterling Heights (city)	MI	0.00	0.00	177.01	0.00	0.00	14.20	34.85	36.10
Stockton (city)	CA	0.00	20.14	225.54	4.34	0.00	69.61	144.61	4.51
Stratford (town)	CT	0.00	12.03	234.24	7.13	0.00	31.44	216.58	71.51
Suffolk (city)	VA	0.00	11.33	200.55	67.32	0.75	91.93	41.88	57.33
Sugar Land (city)	TX	0.00	7.20	246.81	63.01	0.00	59.70	85.09	64.14
Sunrise (city)	FL	81.78	30.72	557.80	103.53	55.86	131.17	313.86	112.98
Surprise (city)	AZ	0.00	8.21	138.20	55.29	0.00	136.88	85.62	55.54
Syracuse (city)	NY	0.00	4.95	39.01	0.99	0.00	49.74	63.19	47.28
Tacoma (city)	WA	0.00	15.33	463.25	282.02	0.00	76.22	294.25	234.64
Tallahassee (city)	FL	93.01	24.97	279.56	124.00	94.03	116.66	171.34	107.99
Tampa (city)	FL	0.12	49.20	301.91	217.95	4.12	137.52	245.13	174.96
Taunton (city)	MA	0.49	0.26	190.09	49.38	4.86	22.47	78.92	36.70
Taylor (city)	MI	0.00	104.96	127.68	7.57	0.00	82.09	45.28	69.71
Taylorsville (city)	UT	0.00	0.00	0.00	0.00	9.42	0.00	0.00	0.00
Tempe (city)	AZ	0.00	18.97	228.75	87.14	0.00	109.16	110.76	76.54
Temple (city)	TX	16.20	44.58	176.03	160.41	10.40	132.08	120.95	70.45
Terre Haute (city)	IN	0.00	20.09	454.24	0.00	0.00	45.77	3.42	0.00
Thornton (city)	CO	0.00	10.64	101.85	37.98	0.00	157.36	92.84	34.39
Tigard (city)	OR	0.00	0.00	99.92	0.00	0.00	32.86	68.04	0.00
Tinley Park (village)	IL	0.00	0.49	0.00	0.00	0.00	0.00	0.00	0.00
Toledo (city)	OH	0.00	1.49	293.85	0.00	2.92	37.74	159.61	13.54
Toms River (township)	NJ	0.00	31.16	201.45	0.45	0.00	31.64	250.94	93.59
Tonawanda (town)	NY	0.00	58.08	127.97	0.59	4.98	114.66	143.77	63.52
Topeka (city)	KS	0.00	0.17	247.59	0.00	0.00	22.85	191.92	0.00
Torrance (city)	CA	0.00	35.62	16.28	77.98	0.00	119.54	28.67	67.98
Trenton (city)	NJ	0.00	0.00	144.38	0.00	0.00	14.47	113.84	102.97
Troy (city)	MI	0.00	69.99	149.75	0.11	0.00	114.84	16.68	54.25
Tucson (city)	AZ	0.00	25.18	0.00	93.40	0.00	100.33	0.00	73.89
Tulsa (city)	OK	0.00	48.92	238.66	65.92	0.00	95.49	119.00	52.67
Tuscaloosa (city)	AL	0.00	0.00	327.78	49.63	0.00	74.94	63.79	49.32
Tustin (city)	CA	0.00	9.95	0.00	0.00	0.00	41.49	0.00	0.00
Union City (city)	NJ	0.00	0.00	0.00	0.00	0.00	29.63	0.00	149.17
Union (town)	NY	0.00	3.95	6.66	0.00	25.09	17.22	14.38	24.91
Union (township)	NJ	0.00	0.00	96.03	0.00	12.46	8.09	19.59	76.25

City	State	Revenue[1] ($/per capita)				Current Operational Expenses ($/per capita)			
		Natural Resources, Other	Park & Recreation	Sewerage	Solid Waste Management	Natural Resources, Other	Parks & Recreation	Sewerage	Solid Waste Management
Upper Darby (township)	PA	0.00	8.77	111.18	55.29	0.00	32.99	91.71	53.42
Utica (city)	NY	0.00	6.81	41.65	0.00	0.00	43.06	16.79	26.25
Vancouver (city)	WA	0.00	29.89	303.10	9.88	0.00	55.50	118.43	13.71
Victoria (city)	TX	0.00	7.13	189.53	75.38	0.00	73.96	57.37	38.27
Vineland (city)	NJ	0.00	0.00	166.04	60.97	0.00	10.93	136.36	53.31
Virginia Beach (city)	VA	0.06	52.46	187.69	87.80	13.78	241.14	107.81	86.27
Waco (city)	TX	0.00	44.84	170.77	134.95	0.00	157.31	71.65	96.57
Waltham (city)	MA	0.00	9.77	316.53	0.00	0.71	32.28	221.86	62.62
Warner Robins (city)	GA	0.00	7.48	182.19	115.38	0.00	24.03	101.77	113.91
Warren (city)	MI	0.00	14.83	135.55	0.00	0.00	50.81	108.71	53.88
Warwick (city)	RI	0.00	11.52	231.53	0.00	0.00	27.83	79.72	25.20
Washington Dc (city)	DC	0.00	45.57	445.78	6.97	90.42	280.73	247.91	172.64
Waterbury (city)	CT	0.00	15.85	162.21	1.65	0.00	41.55	155.25	51.48
Waterford (charter township)	MI	0.00	9.13	222.78	0.00	0.00	20.26	177.52	0.00
Waterloo (city)	IA	0.00	52.48	207.64	52.15	0.00	113.51	128.43	49.90
Waukegan (city)	IL	0.00	0.00	32.04	0.00	0.00	0.00	27.24	49.31
Waukesha (city)	WI	0.00	24.15	161.78	0.00	63.44	74.61	122.90	39.91
Wayne (township)	IN	0.00	0.13	0.00	0.00	0.00	0.00	0.00	0.00
Wayne (township)	NJ	0.00	12.90	160.21	0.00	0.00	60.93	149.28	77.98
West Allis (city)	WI	0.00	0.00	124.98	32.32	34.54	9.01	87.30	65.95
West Bloomfield (charter township)	MI	0.00	7.39	168.76	0.00	0.00	0.76	146.38	0.00
West Chester (township)	OH	0.00	1.59	0.00	0.00	0.00	7.78	0.00	0.00
West Des Moines (city)	IA	0.00	20.54	204.11	28.81	0.73	84.21	80.75	29.26
West Hartford (town)	CT	0.00	54.02	0.00	0.00	0.00	111.59	0.00	0.00
West Haven (city)	CT	0.00	17.64	204.94	0.42	4.02	36.18	141.88	53.71
West Jordan (city)	UT	0.00	0.00	83.51	30.72	0.00	0.00	31.75	16.54
West New York (town)	NJ	0.00	2.75	0.00	0.00	0.00	35.66	0.00	63.00
West Palm Beach (city)	FL	106.53	30.91	298.81	132.96	26.91	168.58	566.50	84.30
West Valley City (city)	UT	0.00	41.72	0.35	35.42	0.98	106.02	7.59	27.78
Westland (city)	MI	0.00	7.50	200.28	0.00	0.00	29.94	175.10	36.21
Westminster (city)	CO	0.00	103.46	190.81	0.00	3.79	148.65	62.72	2.03
Weymouth Town (city)	MA	0.00	0.00	282.13	0.00	2.14	11.96	23.09	97.66
Wheaton (city)	IL	0.00	0.00	68.14	0.00	0.00	12.86	71.79	0.00
White Plains (city)	NY	0.00	19.36	43.98	0.00	0.00	141.09	37.15	128.09
Wichita (city)	KS	0.00	11.88	160.50	2.78	5.18	66.31	85.70	2.96
Wichita Falls (city)	TX	0.00	23.30	26.39	122.15	0.00	67.35	41.81	82.48
Wilmington (city)	DE	0.00	0.00	261.81	0.00	0.00	97.07	146.37	108.18
Wilmington (city)	NC	0.00	18.39	85.64	77.61	19.59	72.56	46.15	75.81
Winston-Salem (city)	NC	0.00	25.60	240.11	53.13	0.61	62.89	93.03	102.12
Woodbridge (township)	NJ	0.00	49.18	228.91	5.44	0.00	82.20	180.95	78.36
Woodbury (city)	MN	0.00	80.67	143.85	0.00	4.92	107.13	84.22	0.00
Worcester (city)	MA	0.00	6.90	218.25	17.73	0.00	31.18	165.67	29.42
Kansas City-Wyandotte County (unified govt)	KS	0.00	8.93	180.10	7.03	0.00	42.69	132.11	47.42
Wyoming (city)	MI	0.00	4.33	233.84	0.00	0.00	70.41	172.30	10.69
Yakima (city)	WA	32.53	13.08	247.98	60.47	25.31	50.80	164.13	60.11
Yonkers (city)	NY	0.00	12.27	30.11	0.00	0.00	43.20	8.46	98.71
Youngstown (city)	OH	0.00	3.51	328.29	73.42	0.00	40.86	313.33	45.09
Ypsilanti (charter township)	MI	0.00	0.00	0.00	0.00	0.00	41.77	0.00	45.59
Yuma (city)	AZ	0.00	29.36	161.46	35.34	0.00	141.51	98.33	34.95

Note: *(1) Includes revenue raised through current charges only. Does not include intergovernmental revenue.*
Source: *U.S. Census Bureau, State and Local Government Finances, 2016*

2. Trends in Greenhouse Gas Emissions

2.1 Recent Trends in U.S. Greenhouse Gas Emissions and Sinks

In 2017, total gross U.S. greenhouse gas emissions were 6,456.7 MMT, or million metric tons, carbon dioxide (CO_2) Eq.[1] Total U.S. emissions have increased by 1.3 percent from 1990 to 2017, and emissions decreased from 2016 to 2017 by 0.5 percent (35.5 MMT CO_2 Eq.). The decrease in total greenhouse gas emissions between 2016 and 2017 was driven in part by a decrease in CO_2 emissions from fossil fuel combustion. The decrease in CO_2 emissions from fossil fuel combustion was a result of multiple factors, including a continued shift from coal to natural gas and increased use of renewable energy in the electric power sector, and milder weather that contributed to less overall electricity use.

Since 1990, U.S. emissions have increased at an average annual rate of 0.1 percent. Figure 2-1 through Figure 2-3 illustrate the overall trend in total U.S. emissions by gas, annual changes, and absolute changes since 1990. Overall, net emissions in 2017 were 13.0 percent below 2005 levels as shown in Table 2-1.

Figure 2-1: Gross U.S. Greenhouse Gas Emissions by Gas (MMT CO_2 Eq.)

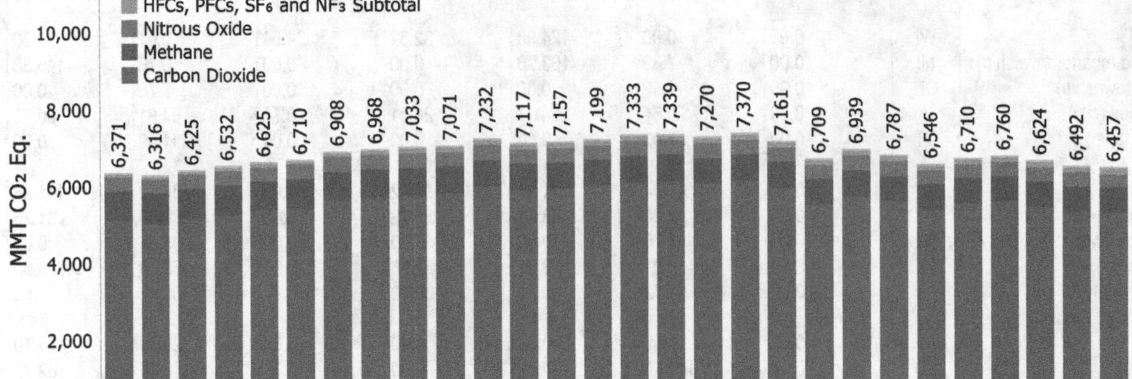

[1] The gross emissions total presented in this report for the United States excludes emissions and removals from Land Use, Land-Use Change, and Forestry (LULUCF). The net emissions total presented in this report for the United States includes emissions and removals from LULUCF.

Source: *U.S. EPA, Inventory of U.S. Greenhouse Gas Emissions and Sinks: 1990–2017*

Figure 2-2: Annual Percent Change in Gross U.S. Greenhouse Gas Emissions Relative to the Previous Year

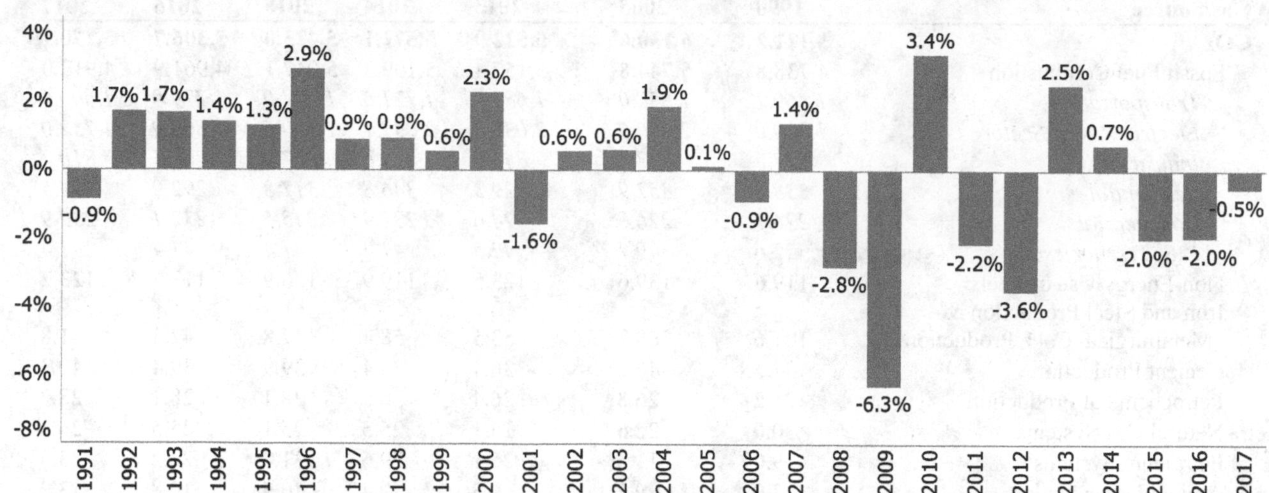

Figure 2-3: Cumulative Change in Annual Gross U.S. Greenhouse Gas Emissions Relative to 1990 (1990=0, MMT CO_2 Eq.)

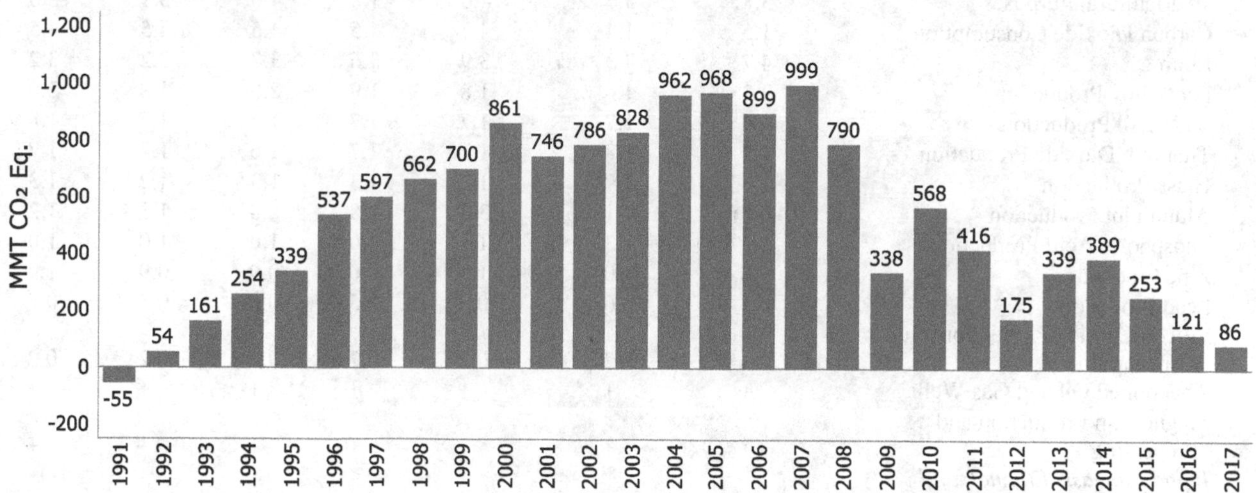

Overall, from 1990 to 2017, total emissions of CO_2 increased by 149.6 MMT CO_2 Eq. (2.9 percent), while total emissions of methane (CH_4) decreased by 123.5 MMT CO_2 Eq. (15.8 percent), and total emissions of nitrous oxide (N_2O) decreased by 9.8 MMT CO_2 Eq. (2.6 percent). During the same period, aggregate weighted emissions of hydrofluorocarbons (HFCs), perfluorocarbons (PFCs), sulfur hexafluoride (SF_6), and nitrogen trifluoride (NF_3) rose by 69.5 MMT CO_2 Eq. (69.7 percent). Despite being emitted in smaller quantities relative to the other principal greenhouse gases, emissions of HFCs, PFCs, SF_6, and NF_3 are significant because many of them have extremely high global warming potentials (GWPs), and, in the cases of PFCs, SF_6, and NF_3, long atmospheric lifetimes. Conversely, U.S. greenhouse gas emissions were partly offset by carbon (C) sequestration in managed forests, trees in urban areas, agricultural soils, landfilled yard trimmings, and coastal wetlands. These were estimated to offset 11.3 percent of total emissions in 2017.

Table 2-1 summarizes emissions and sinks from all U.S. anthropogenic sources in weighted units of MMT CO_2 Eq., while unweighted gas emissions and sinks in kilotons (kt) are provided in Table 2-2.

***Source:** U.S. EPA, Inventory of U.S. Greenhouse Gas Emissions and Sinks: 1990–2017*

Table 2-1: Recent Trends in U.S. Greenhouse Gas Emissions and Sinks (MMT CO_2 Eq.)

Gas/Source	1990	2005	2013	2014	2015	2016	2017
CO_2	**5,121.2**	**6,130.6**	**5,522.9**	**5,572.1**	**5,423.0**	**5,306.7**	**5,270.7**
Fossil Fuel Combustion	4,738.8	5,744.8	5,157.4	5,199.3	5,047.1	4,961.9	4,912.0
Transportation	*1,469.1*	*1,857.0*	*1,682.7*	*1,721.6*	*1,734.0*	*1,779.0*	*1,800.6*
Electric Power Sector	*1,820.0*	*2,400.0*	*2,038.3*	*2,037.1*	*1,900.6*	*1,808.9*	*1,732.0*
Industrial	*857.5*	*853.4*	*840.0*	*819.6*	*807.9*	*807.6*	*810.7*
Residential	*338.2*	*357.9*	*329.3*	*346.8*	*317.8*	*292.9*	*294.5*
Commercial	*226.5*	*226.8*	*224.6*	*232.9*	*245.5*	*232.1*	*232.9*
U.S. Territories	*27.6*	*49.7*	*42.5*	*41.4*	*41.4*	*41.4*	*41.4*
Non-Energy Use of Fuels	119.6	139.6	123.5	119.9	126.9	113.7	123.2
Iron and Steel Production & Metallurgical Coke Production	101.6	68.2	53.5	58.4	47.8	42.3	41.8
Cement Production	33.5	46.2	36.4	39.4	39.9	39.4	40.3
Petrochemical Production	21.2	26.8	26.4	26.5	28.1	28.1	28.2
Natural Gas Systems	30.0	22.6	25.1	25.5	25.1	25.5	26.3
Petroleum Systems	9.0	11.6	25.1	29.6	31.7	22.2	23.3
Ammonia Production	13.0	9.2	9.5	9.4	10.6	10.8	13.2
Lime Production	11.7	14.6	14.0	14.2	13.3	12.9	13.1
Incineration of Waste	8.0	12.5	10.3	10.4	10.7	10.8	10.8
Other Process Uses of Carbonates	6.3	7.6	11.5	13.0	12.2	11.0	10.1
Urea Fertilization	2.4	3.5	4.4	4.5	4.7	4.9	5.1
Urea Consumption for Non-Agricultural Purposes	3.8	3.7	4.6	1.8	4.6	5.1	5.0
Carbon Dioxide Consumption	1.5	1.4	4.2	4.5	4.5	4.5	4.5
Liming	4.7	4.3	3.9	3.6	3.7	3.2	3.2
Ferroalloy Production	2.2	1.4	1.8	1.9	2.0	1.8	2.0
Soda Ash Production	1.4	1.7	1.7	1.7	1.7	1.7	1.8
Titanium Dioxide Production	1.2	1.8	1.7	1.7	1.6	1.7	1.7
Glass Production	1.5	1.9	1.3	1.3	1.3	1.2	1.3
Aluminum Production	6.8	4.1	3.3	2.8	2.8	1.3	1.2
Phosphoric Acid Production	1.5	1.3	1.1	1.0	1.0	1.0	1.0
Zinc Production	0.6	1.0	1.4	1.0	0.9	0.9	1.0
Lead Production	0.5	0.6	0.5	0.5	0.5	0.5	0.5
Silicon Carbide Production and Consumption	0.4	0.2	0.2	0.2	0.2	0.2	0.2
Abandoned Oil and Gas Wells	+	+	+	+	+	+	+
Magnesium Production and Processing	+	+	+	+	+	+	+
Wood Biomass, Ethanol, and Biodiesel Consumption[a]	*219.4*	*230.7*	*315.5*	*323.2*	*317.7*	*317.2*	*322.2*
International Bunker Fuels[b]	*103.5*	*113.1*	*99.8*	*103.4*	*110.9*	*116.6*	*120.1*
CH_4[c]	**779.8**	**691.4**	**663.0**	**662.1**	**661.4**	**654.9**	**656.3**
Enteric Fermentation	164.2	168.9	165.5	164.2	166.5	171.9	175.4
Natural Gas Systems	193.1	171.4	165.6	165.1	167.2	165.7	165.6
Landfills	179.6	131.4	112.9	112.5	111.2	108.0	107.7
Manure Management	37.1	53.7	58.1	57.8	60.9	61.5	61.7
Coal Mining	96.5	64.1	64.6	64.6	61.2	53.8	55.7
Petroleum Systems	42.1	36.7	41.6	42.1	39.5	38.2	37.7
Wastewater Treatment	15.3	15.4	14.3	14.3	14.5	14.2	14.2
Rice Cultivation	16.0	16.7	11.5	12.7	12.3	13.7	11.3
Stationary Combustion	8.6	7.8	8.7	8.9	8.5	7.9	7.8
Abandoned Oil and Gas Wells	6.6	6.9	7.0	7.1	7.1	7.2	6.9
Abandoned Underground Coal Mines	7.2	6.6	6.2	6.3	6.4	6.7	6.4
Mobile Combustion	12.9	9.6	4.5	4.1	3.6	3.4	3.2
Composting	0.4	1.9	2.0	2.1	2.1	2.1	2.2
Petrochemical Production	0.2	0.1	0.1	0.1	0.2	0.2	0.3

Source: *U.S. EPA, Inventory of U.S. Greenhouse Gas Emissions and Sinks: 1990–2017*

Field Burning of Agricultural Residues	0.1	0.2	0.2	0.2	0.2	0.2	0.2
Ferroalloy Production	+	+	+	+	+	+	+
Silicon Carbide Production and Consumption	+	+	+	+	+	+	+
Iron and Steel Production & Metallurgical Coke Production	+	+	+	+	+	+	+
Incineration of Waste	+	+	+	+	+	+	+
International Bunker Fuels[b]	*0.2*	*0.1*	*0.1*	*0.1*	*0.1*	*0.1*	*0.1*
N_2O[c]	**370.3**	**375.8**	**365.4**	**362.7**	**374.1**	**364.5**	**360.5**
Agricultural Soil Management	251.7	254.5	265.2	262.3	277.8	267.6	266.4
Stationary Combustion	25.1	34.3	32.7	33.0	30.6	30.1	28.6
Manure Management	14.0	16.5	17.4	17.4	17.6	18.2	18.7
Mobile Combustion	42.0	39.0	22.1	20.2	18.8	17.9	16.9
Nitric Acid Production	12.1	11.3	10.7	10.9	11.6	10.1	9.3
Adipic Acid Production	15.2	7.1	3.9	5.4	4.3	7.0	7.4
Wastewater Treatment	3.4	4.4	4.7	4.8	4.8	4.9	5.0
N_2O from Product Uses	4.2	4.2	4.2	4.2	4.2	4.2	4.2
Composting	0.3	1.7	1.8	1.9	1.9	1.9	1.9
Caprolactam, Glyoxal, and Glyoxylic Acid Production	1.7	2.1	2.0	2.0	2.0	2.0	1.4
Incineration of Waste	0.5	0.4	0.3	0.3	0.3	0.3	0.3
Semiconductor Manufacture	+	0.1	0.2	0.2	0.2	0.2	0.2
Field Burning of Agricultural Residues	+	0.1	0.1	0.1	0.1	0.1	0.1
Petroleum Systems	+	+	+	+	+	+	+
Natural Gas Systems	+	+	+	+	+	+	+
International Bunker Fuels[b]	*0.9*	*1.0*	*0.9*	*0.9*	*0.9*	*1.0*	*1.0*
HFCs	**46.6**	**122.3**	**146.1**	**150.7**	**153.8**	**155.0**	**158.3**
Substitution of Ozone Depleting Substances[d]	0.3	102.1	141.7	145.2	149.2	151.7	152.7
HCFC-22 Production	46.1	20.0	4.1	5.0	4.3	2.8	5.2
Semiconductor Manufacture	0.2	0.2	0.3	0.3	0.3	0.3	0.4
Magnesium Production and Processing	0.0	0.0	0.1	0.1	0.1	0.1	0.1
PFCs	**24.3**	**6.7**	**5.9**	**5.6**	**5.1**	**4.4**	**4.1**
Semiconductor Manufacture	2.8	3.2	2.9	3.1	3.1	3.0	3.0
Aluminum Production	21.5	3.4	3.0	2.5	2.0	1.4	1.1
Substitution of Ozone Depleting Substances	0.0	+	+	+	+	+	+
SF_6	**28.8**	**11.8**	**6.3**	**6.3**	**5.8**	**6.3**	**6.1**
Electrical Transmission and Distribution	23.1	8.3	4.4	4.6	4.1	4.4	4.3
Magnesium Production and Processing	5.2	2.7	1.3	0.9	1.0	1.1	1.1
Semiconductor Manufacture	0.5	0.7	0.7	0.7	0.7	0.9	0.7
NF_3	+	**0.5**	**0.5**	**0.5**	**0.6**	**0.6**	**0.6**
Semiconductor Manufacture	+	0.5	0.5	0.5	0.6	0.6	0.6
Total Emissions	**6,371.0**	**7,339.0**	**6,710.2**	**6,760.0**	**6,623.8**	**6,492.3**	**6,456.7**
LULUCF Emissions[c]	**7.8**	**16.0**	**17.5**	**17.7**	**28.3**	**15.5**	**15.5**
LULUCF CH_4 Emissions	5.0	9.0	9.9	10.1	16.5	8.8	8.8
LULUCF N_2O Emissions	2.8	7.0	7.6	7.7	11.8	6.7	6.7
LULUCF Carbon Stock Change[e]	**(814.8)**	**(756.1)**	**(731.0)**	**(687.8)**	**(739.4)**	**(738.1)**	**(729.6)**
LULUCF Sector Net Total[f]	**(807.0)**	**(740.0)**	**(713.5)**	**(670.0)**	**(711.1)**	**(722.6)**	**(714.1)**
Net Emissions (Sources and Sinks)	**5,564.0**	**6,599.0**	**5,996.8**	**6,090.0**	**5,912.7**	**5,769.7**	**5,742.6**

Notes: Total emissions presented without LULUCF. Net emissions presented with LULUCF. Totals may not sum due to independent rounding. Parentheses indicate negative values or sequestration.

\+ Does not exceed 0.05 MMT CO_2 Eq.

Source: *U.S. EPA, Inventory of U.S. Greenhouse Gas Emissions and Sinks: 1990–2017*

[a] Emissions from Wood Biomass, Ethanol, and Biodiesel Consumption are not included specifically in summing Energy sector totals. Net carbon fluxes from changes in biogenic carbon reservoirs are accounted for in the estimates for LULUCF.
[b] Emissions from International Bunker Fuels are not included in totals.
[c] LULUCF emissions of CH_4 and N_2O are reported separately from gross emissions totals. LULUCF emissions include the CH_4 and N_2O emissions reported for *Peatlands Remaining Peatlands*, Forest Fires, Drained Organic Soils, Grassland Fires, and *Coastal Wetlands Remaining Coastal Wetlands*; CH_4 emissions from *Land Converted to Coastal Wetlands*; and N_2O emissions from Forest Soils and Settlement Soils. Refer to Table 2-8 for a breakout of emissions and removals for LULUCF by gas and source category.
[d] Small amounts of PFC emissions also result from this source.
[e] LULUCF Carbon Stock Change is the net C stock change from the following categories: *Forest Land Remaining Forest Land, Land Converted to Forest Land, Cropland Remaining Cropland, Land Converted to Cropland, Grassland Remaining Grassland, Land Converted to Grassland, Wetlands Remaining Wetlands, Land Converted to Wetlands, Settlements Remaining Settlements*, and *Land Converted to Settlements*. Refer to Table 2-8 for a breakout of emissions and removals for LULUCF by gas and source category.
[f] The LULUCF Sector Net Total is the net sum of all CH_4 and N_2O emissions to the atmosphere plus net carbon stock changes.

Table 2-2: Recent Trends in U.S. Greenhouse Gas Emissions and Sinks (kt)

Gas/Source	1990	2005	2013	2014	2015	2016	201[illegible]
CO_2	**5,121,179**	**6,130,552**	**5,522,908**	**5,572,106**	**5,422,966**	**5,306,662**	**5,270,74[illegible]**
Fossil Fuel Combustion	4,738,756	5,744,754	5,157,391	5,199,345	5,047,107	4,961,876	4,911,96[illegible]
Transportation	*1,469,090*	*1,856,999*	*1,682,675*	*1,721,581*	*1,733,961*	*1,779,031*	*1,800,56[illegible]*
Electric Power Sector	*1,819,951*	*2,399,974*	*2,038,258*	*2,037,148*	*1,900,624*	*1,808,863*	*1,732,02[illegible]*
Industrial	*857,463*	*853,423*	*840,023*	*819,556*	*807,876*	*807,599*	*810,65[illegible]*
Residential	*338,170*	*357,893*	*329,328*	*346,835*	*317,816*	*292,885*	*294,46[illegible]*
Commercial	*226,528*	*226,755*	*224,643*	*232,864*	*245,462*	*232,137*	*232,89[illegible]*
U.S. Territories	*27,555*	*49,710*	*42,463*	*41,361*	*41,367*	*41,362*	*41,36[illegible]*
Non-Energy Use of Fuels	119,551	139,625	123,476	119,895	126,939	113,719	123,22[illegible]
Iron and Steel Production & Metallurgical Coke Production	101,630	68,210	53,471	58,353	47,825	42,309	41,78[illegible]
Cement Production	33,484	46,194	36,369	39,439	39,907	39,439	40,32[illegible]
Petrochemical Production	21,222	26,810	26,395	26,496	28,062	28,110	28,22[illegible]
Natural Gas Systems	30,048	22,638	25,148	25,518	25,071	25,488	26,32[illegible]
Petroleum Systems	8,950	11,552	25,130	29,597	31,672	22,200	23,33[illegible]
Ammonia Production	13,047	9,196	9,480	9,377	10,634	10,838	13,21[illegible]
Lime Production	11,700	14,552	14,028	14,210	13,342	12,942	13,14[illegible]
Incineration of Waste	7,950	12,469	10,333	10,429	10,742	10,765	10,79[illegible]
Other Process Uses of Carbonates	6,297	7,644	11,524	12,954	12,182	10,969	10,13[illegible]
Urea Fertilization	2,417	3,504	4,443	4,515	4,728	4,877	5,05[illegible]
Urea Consumption for Non-Agricultural Purposes	3,784	3,653	4,556	1,807	4,578	5,132	4,95[illegible]
Carbon Dioxide Consumption	1,472	1,375	4,188	4,471	4,471	4,471	4,47[illegible]
Liming	4,667	4,349	3,907	3,609	3,737	3,206	3,18[illegible]
Ferroalloy Production	2,152	1,392	1,785	1,914	1,960	1,796	1,97[illegible]
Soda Ash Production	1,431	1,655	1,694	1,685	1,714	1,723	1,75[illegible]
Titanium Dioxide Production	1,195	1,755	1,715	1,688	1,635	1,662	1,68[illegible]
Glass Production	1,535	1,928	1,317	1,336	1,299	1,249	1,31[illegible]
Aluminum Production	6,831	4,142	3,255	2,833	2,767	1,334	1,20[illegible]
Phosphoric Acid Production	1,529	1,342	1,149	1,038	999	998	1,02[illegible]
Zinc Production	632	1,030	1,429	956	933	925	1,00[illegible]
Lead Production	516	553	546	459	473	450	45[illegible]
Silicon Carbide Production and Consumption	375	219	169	173	180	174	18[illegible]
Abandoned Oil and Gas Wells	6	7	7	7	7	7	[illegible]

Source: *U.S. EPA, Inventory of U.S. Greenhouse Gas Emissions and Sinks: 1990–2017*

Magnesium Production and Processing	1	3	2	2	3	3	3
Wood Biomass, Ethanol, and Biodiesel Consumption[a]	*219,413*	*230,700*	*315,545*	*323,187*	*317,742*	*317,191*	*322,223*
International Bunker Fuels[b]	*103,463*	*113,139*	*99,763*	*103,400*	*110,887*	*116,594*	*120,107*
CH_4[c]	**31,194**	**27,657**	**26,522**	**26,483**	**26,456**	**26,196**	**26,253**
Enteric Fermentation	6,566	6,755	6,620	6,568	6,661	6,875	7,018
Natural Gas Systems	7,723	6,856	6,624	6,603	6,686	6,629	6,624
Landfills	7,182	5,256	4,517	4,502	4,448	4,319	4,309
Manure Management	1,486	2,150	2,322	2,311	2,435	2,461	2,467
Coal Mining	3,860	2,565	2,584	2,583	2,449	2,154	2,227
Petroleum Systems	1,682	1,469	1,665	1,682	1,579	1,528	1,506
Wastewater Treatment	611	616	572	572	579	568	568
Rice Cultivation	641	667	462	510	493	549	454
Stationary Combustion	344	313	350	355	340	318	312
Abandoned Oil and Gas Wells	262	277	282	283	285	289	277
Abandoned Underground Coal Mines	288	264	249	253	256	268	257
Mobile Combustion	518	384	181	163	143	135	128
Composting	15	75	81	84	85	85	86
Petrochemical Production	9	3	3	5	7	10	10
Field Burning of Agricultural Residues	4	7	8	8	8	8	8
Ferroalloy Production	1	+	1	1	1	1	1
Silicon Carbide Production and Consumption	1	+	+	+	+	+	+
Iron and Steel Production & Metallurgical Coke Production	1	1	+	+	+	+	+
Incineration of Waste	+	+	+	+	+	+	+
International Bunker Fuels[b]	*7*	*5*	*3*	*3*	*3*	*4*	*4*
N_2O[c]	**1,243**	**1,261**	**1,226**	**1,217**	**1,255**	**1,223**	**1,210**
Agricultural Soil Management	845	854	890	880	932	898	894
Stationary Combustion	84	115	110	111	103	101	96
Manure Management	47	55	58	58	59	61	63
Mobile Combustion	141	131	74	68	63	60	57
Nitric Acid Production	41	38	36	37	39	34	31
Adipic Acid Production	51	24	13	18	14	23	25
Wastewater Treatment	11	15	16	16	16	16	17
N_2O from Product Uses	14	14	14	14	14	14	14
Composting	1	6	6	6	6	6	6
Caprolactam, Glyoxal, and Glyoxylic Acid Production	6	7	7	7	7	7	5
Incineration of Waste	2	1	1	1	1	1	1
Semiconductor Manufacture	+	+	1	1	1	1	1
Field Burning of Agricultural Residues	+	+	+	+	+	+	+
Petroleum Systems	+	+	+	+	+	+	+
Natural Gas Systems	+	+	+	+	+	+	+
International Bunker Fuels[b]	*3*	*3*	*3*	*3*	*3*	*3*	*3*
HFCs	**M**	**M**	**M**	**M**	**M**	**M**	**M**
Substitution of Ozone Depleting Substances[d]	M	M	M	M	M	M	M
HCFC-22 Production	3	1	+	+	+	+	+
Semiconductor Manufacture	M	M	M	M	M	M	M
Magnesium Production and Processing	0	0	+	+	+	+	+
PFCs	**M**	**M**	**M**	**M**	**M**	**M**	**M**

Source: *U.S. EPA, Inventory of U.S. Greenhouse Gas Emissions and Sinks: 1990–2017*

Semiconductor Manufacture	M	M	M	M	M	M	M
Aluminum Production	M	M	M	M	M	M	M
Substitution of Ozone Depleting Substances[d]	0	+	+	+	+	+	+
SF_6	**1**	**1**	+	+	+	+	+
Electrical Transmission and Distribution	1	+	+	+	+	+	+
Magnesium Production and Processing	+	+	+	+	+	+	+
Semiconductor Manufacture	+	+	+	+	+	+	+
NF_3	+	+	+	+	+	+	+
Semiconductor Manufacture	+	+	+	+	+	+	+

+ Does not exceed 0.5 kt.
M - Mixture of multiple gases
[a] Emissions from Wood Biomass, Ethanol, and Biodiesel Consumption are not included specifically in summing Energy sector totals. Net carbon fluxes from changes in biogenic carbon reservoirs are accounted for in the estimates for LULUCF.
[b] Emissions from International Bunker Fuels are not included in totals.
[c] LULUCF emissions of CH_4 and N_2O are reported separately from gross emissions totals. Refer to Table 2-8 for a breakout of emissions and removals for LULUCF by gas and source category.
[d] Small amounts of PFC emissions also result from this source.
Notes: Totals may not sum due to independent rounding. Parentheses indicate negative values or sequestration.

Emissions of all gases can be summed from each source category into a set of five sectors defined by the Intergovernmental Panel on Climate Change (IPCC). Figure 2-4 and Table 2-3 illustrate that over the twenty-eight-year period of 1990 to 2017, total emissions from the Energy, Industrial Processes and Product Use, and Agriculture sectors grew by 85.1 MMT CO_2 Eq. (1.6 percent), 16.8 MMT CO_2 Eq. (4.9 percent), and 51.8 MMT CO_2 Eq. (10.6 percent), respectively. Emissions from the Waste sector decreased by 68.0 MMT CO_2 Eq. (34.2 percent). Over the same period, total C sequestration in the Land Use, Land-Use Change, and Forestry (LULUCF) sector decreased by 85.2 MMT CO_2 (10.5 percent decrease in total C sequestration), and emissions from the LULUCF sector increased by 7.7 MMT CO_2 Eq. (99.1 percent).

Figure 2-4: U.S. Greenhouse Gas Emissions and Sinks by Chapter/IPCC Sector (MMT CO_2 Eq.)

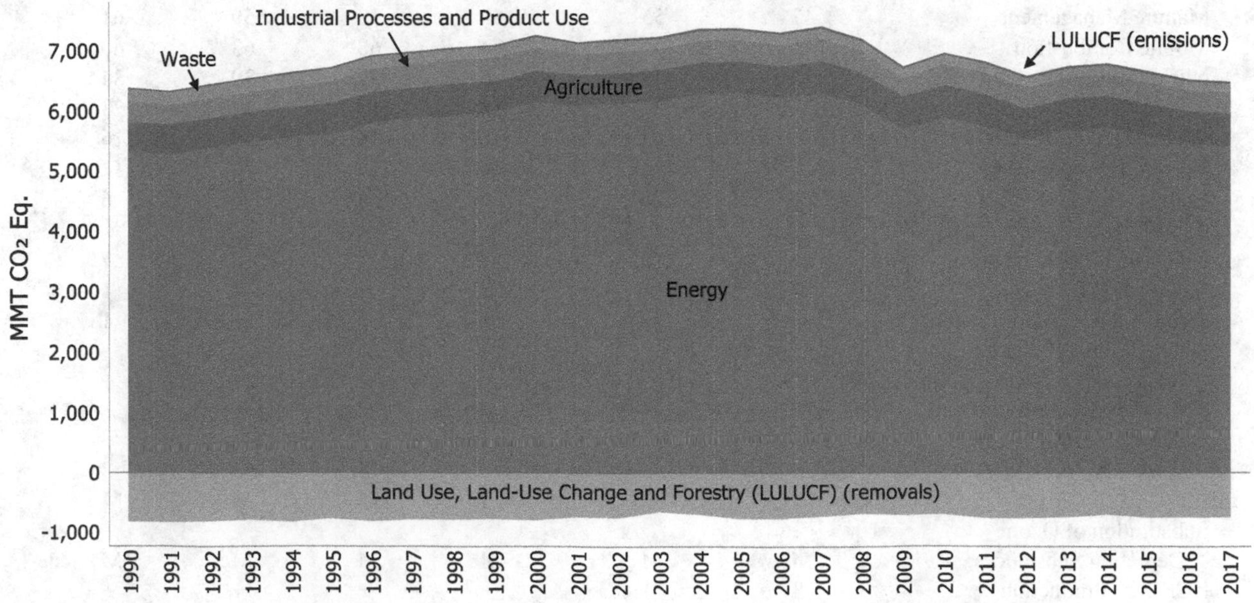

Source: *U.S. EPA, Inventory of U.S. Greenhouse Gas Emissions and Sinks: 1990–2017*

Table 2-3: Recent Trends in U.S. Greenhouse Gas Emissions and Sinks by Chapter/IPCC Sector (MMT CO_2 Eq.)

Chapter/IPCC Sector	1990	2005	2013	2014	2015	2016	2017
Energy	**5,339.8**	**6,308.0**	**5,695.0**	**5,736.4**	**5,584.7**	**5,465.3**	**5,424.8**
Fossil Fuel Combustion	4,738.8	5,744.8	5,157.4	5,199.3	5,047.1	4,961.9	4,912.0
Natural Gas Systems	223.1	194.0	190.8	190.6	192.2	191.2	191.9
Non-Energy Use of Fuels	119.6	139.6	123.5	119.9	126.9	113.7	123.2
Petroleum Systems	51.0	48.3	66.8	71.7	71.2	60.4	61.0
Coal Mining	96.5	64.1	64.6	64.6	61.2	53.8	55.7
Stationary Combustion	33.7	42.2	41.5	41.9	39.0	38.0	36.4
Mobile Combustion	55.0	48.6	26.6	24.3	22.4	21.2	20.1
Incineration of Waste	8.4	12.9	10.6	10.7	11.1	11.1	11.1
Abandoned Oil and Gas Wells	6.6	6.9	7.0	7.1	7.1	7.2	6.9
Abandoned Underground Coal Mines	7.2	6.6	6.2	6.3	6.4	6.7	6.4
Industrial Processes and Product Use	**342.1**	**358.0**	**353.1**	**365.2**	**360.8**	**354.6**	**358.9**
Substitution of Ozone Depleting Substances	0.3	102.1	141.7	145.3	149.2	151.8	152.7
Iron and Steel Production & Metallurgical Coke Production	101.7	68.2	53.5	58.4	47.8	42.3	41.8
Cement Production	33.5	46.2	36.4	39.4	39.9	39.4	40.3
Petrochemical Production	21.4	26.9	26.5	26.6	28.2	28.4	28.5
Ammonia Production	13.0	9.2	9.5	9.4	10.6	10.8	13.2
Lime Production	11.7	14.6	14.0	14.2	13.3	12.9	13.1
Other Process Uses of Carbonates	6.3	7.6	11.5	13.0	12.2	11.0	10.1
Nitric Acid Production	12.1	11.3	10.7	10.9	11.6	10.1	9.3
Adipic Acid Production	15.2	7.1	3.9	5.4	4.3	7.0	7.4
HCFC-22 Production	46.1	20.0	4.1	5.0	4.3	2.8	5.2
Urea Consumption for Non-Agricultural Purposes	3.8	3.7	4.6	1.8	4.6	5.1	5.0
Semiconductor Manufacture	3.6	4.7	4.6	4.8	4.9	5.0	5.0
Carbon Dioxide Consumption	1.5	1.4	4.2	4.5	4.5	4.5	4.5
Electrical Transmission and Distribution	23.1	8.3	4.4	4.6	4.1	4.4	4.3
N_2O from Product Uses	4.2	4.2	4.2	4.2	4.2	4.2	4.2
Aluminum Production	28.3	7.6	6.2	5.4	4.8	2.7	2.3
Ferroalloy Production	2.2	1.4	1.8	1.9	2.0	1.8	2.0
Soda Ash Production	1.4	1.7	1.7	1.7	1.7	1.7	1.8
Titanium Dioxide Production	1.2	1.8	1.7	1.7	1.6	1.7	1.7
Caprolactam, Glyoxal, and Glyoxylic Acid Production	1.7	2.1	2.0	2.0	2.0	2.0	1.4
Glass Production	1.5	1.9	1.3	1.3	1.3	1.2	1.3
Magnesium Production and Processing	5.2	2.7	1.4	1.0	1.1	1.2	1.2
Phosphoric Acid Production	1.5	1.3	1.1	1.0	1.0	1.0	1.0
Zinc Production	0.6	1.0	1.4	1.0	0.9	0.9	1.0
Lead Production	0.5	0.6	0.5	0.5	0.5	0.5	0.5
Silicon Carbide Production and Consumption	0.4	0.2	0.2	0.2	0.2	0.2	0.2
Agriculture	**490.2**	**518.4**	**526.3**	**522.8**	**543.8**	**541.2**	**542.1**
Agricultural Soil Management	251.7	254.5	265.2	262.3	277.8	267.6	266.4
Enteric Fermentation	164.2	168.9	165.5	164.2	166.5	171.9	175.4
Manure Management	51.1	70.2	75.5	75.2	78.5	79.7	80.4
Rice Cultivation	16.0	16.7	11.5	12.7	12.3	13.7	11.3
Urea Fertilization	2.4	3.5	4.4	4.5	4.7	4.9	5.1
Liming	4.7	4.3	3.9	3.6	3.7	3.2	3.2
Field Burning of Agricultural Residues	0.2	0.3	0.3	0.3	0.3	0.3	0.3

Source: *U.S. EPA, Inventory of U.S. Greenhouse Gas Emissions and Sinks: 1990–2017*

Waste	**198.9**	**154.7**	**135.8**	**135.6**	**134.5**	**131.1**	**131.0**
Landfills	179.6	131.4	112.9	112.5	111.2	108.0	107.7
Wastewater Treatment	18.7	19.8	19.0	19.1	19.3	19.1	19.2
Composting	0.7	3.5	3.9	4.0	4.0	4.0	4.1
Total Emissions[a]	**6,371.0**	**7,339.0**	**6,710.2**	**6,760.0**	**6,623.8**	**6,492.3**	**6,456.7**
Land Use, Land-Use Change, and Forestry	**(807.0)**	**(740.0)**	**(713.5)**	**(670.0)**	**(711.1)**	**(722.6)**	**(714.1)**
Forest land	(788.0)	(750.2)	(726.4)	(678.6)	(744.4)	(741.0)	(733.1)
Cropland	34.6	40.1	55.6	54.7	60.4	57.4	56.6
Grassland	4.7	11.3	4.9	1.2	20.0	7.5	8.9
Wetlands	(0.5)	(2.0)	(0.7)	(0.6)	(0.7)	(0.7)	(0.7)
Settlements	(57.8)	(39.2)	(46.9)	(46.7)	(46.4)	(45.8)	(45.9)
Net Emission (Sources and Sinks)[b]	**5,564.0**	**6,599.0**	**5,996.8**	**6,090.0**	**5,912.7**	**5,769.7**	**5,742.6**

Notes: Total emissions presented without LULUCF. Net emissions presented with LULUCF. Totals may not sum due to independent rounding. Parentheses indicate negative values or sequestration.

[a] Total emissions without LULUCF.

[b] Net emissions with LULUCF.

Energy

Energy-related activities, primarily fossil fuel combustion, accounted for the vast majority of U.S. CO_2 emissions for the period of 1990 through 2017. Fossil fuel combustion is the largest source of energy-related emissions, with CO_2 being the primary gas emitted (see Figure 2-5). Due to their relative importance, fossil fuel combustion-related CO_2 emissions are considered in detail in the Energy chapter (see Figure 2-6).

In 2017, approximately 80 percent of the energy consumed in the United States (on a Btu basis) was produced through the combustion of fossil fuels. The remaining 20 percent came from other energy sources such as hydropower, biomass, nuclear, wind, and solar energy. A discussion of specific trends related to CO_2 as well as other greenhouse gas emissions from energy use is presented in the Energy chapter. Energy-related activities are also responsible for CH_4 and N_2O emissions (43 percent and 13 percent of total U.S. emissions of each gas, respectively). Table 2-4 presents greenhouse gas emissions from the Energy chapter, by source and gas.

Figure 2-5: 2017 Energy Chapter Greenhouse Gas Sources (MMT CO_2 Eq.)

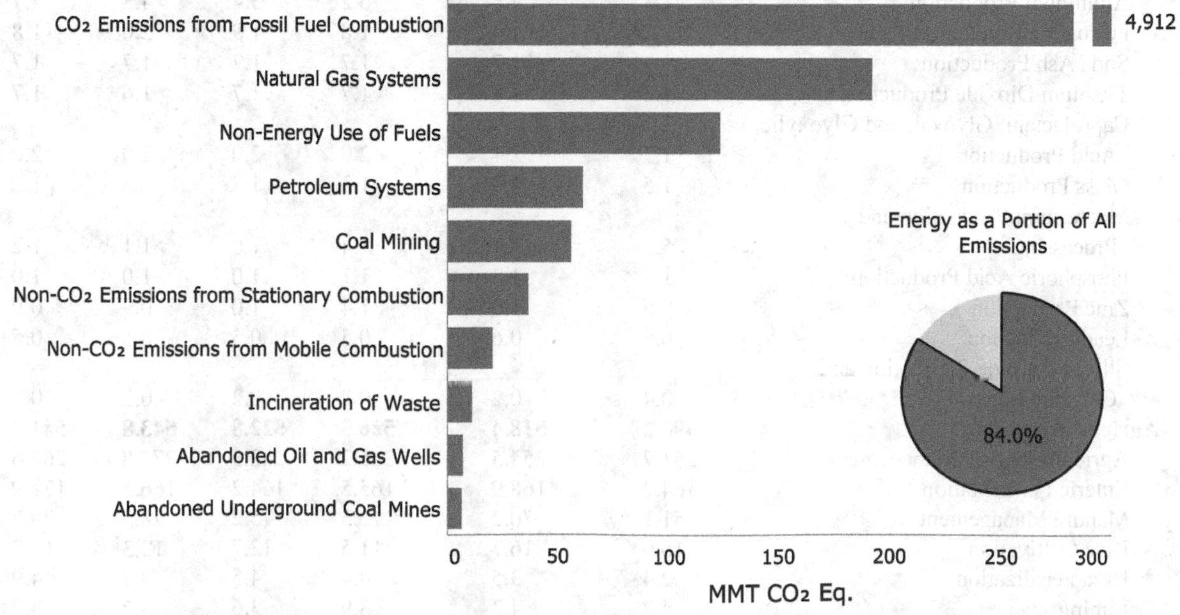

Source: *U.S. EPA, Inventory of U.S. Greenhouse Gas Emissions and Sinks: 1990–2017*

Figure 2-6: 2017 U.S. Fossil Carbon Flows (MMT CO_2 Eq.)

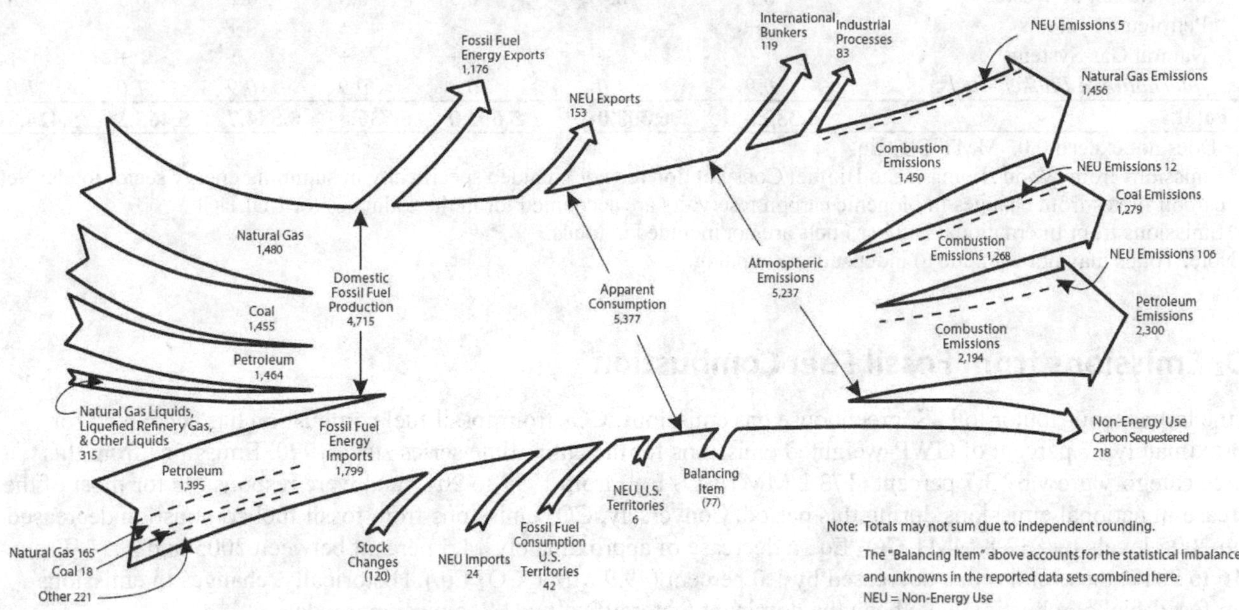

Table 2-4: Emissions from Energy (MMT CO_2 Eq.)

Gas/Source	1990	2005	2013	2014	2015	2016	2017
CO_2	**4,905.3**	**5,931.0**	**5,341.5**	**5,384.8**	**5,241.5**	**5,134.1**	**5,095.6**
Fossil Fuel Combustion	4,738.8	5,744.8	5,157.4	5,199.3	5,047.1	4,961.9	4,912.0
Transportation	*1,469.1*	*1,857.0*	*1,682.7*	*1,721.6*	*1,734.0*	*1,779.0*	*1,800.6*
Electricity Generation	*1,820.0*	*2,400.0*	*2,038.3*	*2,037.1*	*1,900.6*	*1,808.9*	*1,732.0*
Industrial	*857.5*	*853.4*	*840.0*	*819.6*	*807.9*	*807.6*	*810.7*
Residential	*338.2*	*357.9*	*329.3*	*346.8*	*317.8*	*292.9*	*294.5*
Commercial	*226.5*	*226.8*	*224.6*	*232.9*	*245.5*	*232.1*	*232.9*
U.S. Territories	*27.6*	*49.7*	*42.5*	*41.4*	*41.4*	*41.4*	*41.4*
Non-Energy Use of Fuels	119.6	139.6	123.5	119.9	126.9	113.7	123.2
Natural Gas Systems	30.0	22.6	25.1	25.5	25.1	25.5	26.3
Petroleum Systems	9.0	11.6	25.1	29.6	31.7	22.2	23.3
Incineration of Waste	8.0	12.5	10.3	10.4	10.7	10.8	10.8
Abandoned Oil and Gas Wells	+	+	+	+	+	+	+
Biomass-Wood[a]	*215.2*	*206.9*	*227.3*	*233.8*	*224.7*	*216.3*	*221.4*
International Bunker Fuels[b]	*103.5*	*113.1*	*99.8*	*103.4*	*110.9*	*116.6*	*120.1*
Biofuels-Ethanol[a]	*4.2*	*22.9*	*74.7*	*76.1*	*78.9*	*81.2*	*82.1*
Biofuels-Biodiesel[a]	*0.0*	*0.9*	*13.5*	*13.3*	*14.1*	*19.6*	*18.7*
CH_4	**366.9**	**303.2**	**298.4**	**298.1**	**293.5**	**283.0**	**283.3**
Natural Gas Systems	193.1	171.4	165.6	165.1	167.2	165.7	165.6
Coal Mining	96.5	64.1	64.6	64.6	61.2	53.8	55.7
Petroleum Systems	42.1	36.7	41.6	42.1	39.5	38.2	37.7
Stationary Combustion	8.6	7.8	8.7	8.9	8.5	7.9	7.8
Abandoned Oil and Gas Wells	6.6	6.9	7.0	7.1	7.1	7.2	6.9
Abandoned Underground Coal Mines	7.2	6.6	6.2	6.3	6.4	6.7	6.4
Mobile Combustion	12.9	9.6	4.5	4.1	3.6	3.4	3.2
Incineration of Waste	+	+	+	+	+	+	+
International Bunker Fuels[b]	*0.2*	*0.1*	*0.1*	*0.1*	*0.1*	*0.1*	*0.1*
N_2O	**67.6**	**73.7**	**55.2**	**53.5**	**49.7**	**48.3**	**45.9**
Stationary Combustion	25.1	34.3	32.7	33.0	30.6	30.1	28.6

Source: *U.S. EPA, Inventory of U.S. Greenhouse Gas Emissions and Sinks: 1990–2017*

Mobile Combustion	42.0	39.0	22.1	20.2	18.8	17.9	16.9
Incineration of Waste	0.5	0.4	0.3	0.3	0.3	0.3	0.3
Petroleum Systems	+	+	+	+	+	+	+
Natural Gas Systems	+	+	+	+	+	+	+
International Bunker Fuels[b]	*0.9*	*1.0*	*0.9*	*0.9*	*0.9*	*1.0*	*1.0*
Total	**5,339.8**	**6,308.0**	**5,695.0**	**5,736.4**	**5,584.7**	**5,465.3**	**5,424.8**

+ Does not exceed 0.05 MMT CO_2 Eq.

[a] Emissions from Wood Biomass and Biofuel Consumption are not included specifically in summing energy sector totals. Net carbon fluxes from changes in biogenic carbon reservoirs are accounted for in the estimates for LULUCF.

[b] Emissions from International Bunker Fuels are not included in totals.

Note: Totals may not sum due to independent rounding.

CO_2 Emissions from Fossil Fuel Combustion

As the largest contributor to U.S. greenhouse gas emissions, CO_2 from fossil fuel combustion has accounted for approximately 77 percent of GWP-weighted emissions for the entire time series since 1990. Emissions from this source category grew by 3.7 percent (173.2 MMT CO_2 Eq.) from 1990 to 2017 and were responsible for most of the increase in national emissions during this period. Conversely, CO_2 emissions from fossil fuel combustion decreased from 2005 levels by 832.8 MMT CO_2 Eq., a decrease of approximately 14.5 percent between 2005 and 2017. From 2016 to 2017, these emissions decreased by 1.0 percent (49.9 MMT CO_2 Eq.). Historically, changes in emissions from fossil fuel combustion have been the dominant factor affecting U.S. emission trends.

Changes in CO_2 emissions from fossil fuel combustion are influenced by many long-term and short-term factors, including population and economic growth, energy price fluctuations and market trends, technological changes, energy fuel choices, and seasonal temperatures. On an annual basis, the overall consumption and mix of fossil fuels in the United States fluctuates primarily in response to changes in general economic conditions, overall energy prices, the relative price of different fuels, weather, and the availability of non-fossil alternatives. For example, coal consumption for electric power is influenced by a number of factors including the relative price of coal and alternative sources, the ability to switch fuels, and longer-term trends in coal markets. Likewise, warmer winters lead to a decrease in heating degree days and result in a decreased demand for heating fuel and electricity for heat in the residential and commercial sector, which leads to a decrease in emissions from reduced fuel consumption.

Energy-related CO_2 emissions also depend on the type of fuel consumed or energy used and its C intensity. Producing a unit of heat or electricity using natural gas instead of coal, for example, reduces CO_2 emissions because of the lower C content of natural gas (see Table A-41 in Annex 2.1 for more detail on the C Content Coefficient of different fossil fuels).

Trends in CO_2 emissions from fossil fuel combustion over the past five years have been strongly influenced by the electric power sector, which historically has accounted for the largest share of emissions from this source (see Figure 2-7). In recent years, the types of fuel consumed to produce electricity have changed. Total electric power generation remained relatively flat over the past five years, but emissions have decreased due to a decreasing reliance on coal used to generate electricity and increased generation from natural gas and renewable energy sources. Carbon dioxide emissions from coal consumption for electric power generation decreased by 23.2 percent since 2013, which can be largely attributed to a shift to the use of less-CO_2-intensive natural gas to generate electricity and a rapid increase in the use of renewable energy in the electric power sector in recent years. Electricity generation from renewable sources increased by 35.9 percent from 2013 to 2017 and natural gas generation increased by 16.3 percent over the same time period (see Table 3-12 for more detail on electricity generation by source). The decrease in coal powered electricity generation and increase in natural gas and renewable energy electricity generation have contributed to a 15.0 percent decrease in overall CO_2 emissions from electric power generation from 2013 to 2017 (see Figure 2-9).

The trends in CO_2 emissions from fossil fuel combustion over the past five years also follow changes in heating degree days. Carbon dioxide emissions from natural gas consumption in the residential and commercial sectors decreased by 9.3 percent and 3.4 percent from 2013 to 2017, respectively. This trend can be largely attributed to a 14 percent decrease in heating degree days, which led to a decreased demand for heating fuel and electricity for heat in these sectors. In addition, an increase in energy efficiency standards and the use of energy-efficient products in residential and commercial buildings has resulted in an overall reduction in energy use, contributing to a decrease in

Source: *U.S. EPA, Inventory of U.S. Greenhouse Gas Emissions and Sinks: 1990–2017*

CO_2 emissions in both of these sectors (EIA 2018). Combined residential and commercial sector CO_2 emissions decreased by 4.8 percent from 2013 to 2017.

Petroleum use is another major driver of CO_2 emissions from fossil fuel combustion, particularly in the transportation sector, which represents the largest source of CO_2 emissions from fossil fuel combustion in 2017. Despite the overall decreasing trend in CO_2 emissions from fossil fuel combustion over the past five years, emissions from petroleum consumption for transportation (including bunkers) have increased by 7.5 percent since 2013; this trend can be primarily attributed to a 7.5 percent increase in vehicle miles traveled (VMT) over the same time period. Fuel economy of light-duty vehicles is another important factor. The decline in new light-duty vehicle fuel economy between 1990 and 2004 reflected the increasing market share of light-duty trucks, which grew from about 30 percent of new vehicle sales in 1990 to 48 percent in 2004. Starting in 2005, average new vehicle fuel economy began to increase while light-duty VMT grew only modestly for much of the period.

Although CO_2 emissions from the transportation sector have increased over the past five years, CO_2 emissions from all other sectors and U.S. Territories have decreased in recent years, contributing to a 1.0 percent decrease in total CO_2 emissions from fossil fuel combustion from 2016 to 2017 and a 4.8 percent reduction since 2013.

Carbon dioxide emissions from fossil fuel combustion are presented in Table 2-5 based on the underlying U.S. energy consumer data collected by the U.S. Energy Information Administration (EIA). Estimates of CO_2 emissions from fossil fuel combustion are calculated from these EIA "end-use sectors" based on total fuel consumption and appropriate fuel properties described below. (Any additional analysis and refinement of the EIA data is further explained in the Energy chapter of this report.)

- *Transportation.* EIA's fuel consumption data for the transportation sector consists of all vehicles whose primary purpose is transporting people and/or goods from one physical location to another.
- *Industry.* EIA statistics for the industrial sector include fossil fuel consumption that occurs in the fields of manufacturing, agriculture, mining, and construction. EIA's fuel consumption data for the industrial sector consist of all facilities and equipment used for producing, processing, or assembling goods. (EIA includes generators that produce electricity and/or useful thermal output primarily to support on-site industrial activities in this sector.)
- *Electric Power.* EIA's fuel consumption data for the electric power sector are comprised of electricity-only and combined-heat-and-power (CHP) plants within the North American Industry Classification System (NAICS) 22 category whose primary business is to sell electricity, or electricity and heat, to the public. (Non-utility power producers are included in this sector as long as they meet the electric power sector definition.)
- *Residential.* EIA's fuel consumption data for the residential sector consist of living quarters for private households.
- *Commercial.* EIA's fuel consumption data for the commercial sector consist of service-providing facilities and equipment from private and public organizations and businesses. (EIA includes generators that produce electricity and/or useful thermal output primarily to support the activities at commercial establishments in this sector.)

Table 2-5 and Figure 2-7 summarize CO_2 emissions from fossil fuel combustion by end-use sector.

Figure 2-8 further describes direct and indirect CO_2 emissions from fossil fuel combustion, separated by end-use sector.

Table 2-5: CO_2 Emissions from Fossil Fuel Combustion by End-Use Sector (MMT CO_2 Eq.)

End-Use Sector	1990	2005	2013	2014	2015	2016	2017
Transportation	**1,472.1**	**1,861.7**	**1,686.9**	**1,726.0**	**1,738.2**	**1,783.2**	**1,804.9**
Combustion	1,469.1	1,857.0	1,682.7	1,721.6	1,734.0	1,779.0	1,800.6
Electricity	3.0	4.7	4.3	4.5	4.3	4.2	4.3
Industrial	**1,543.9**	**1,589.7**	**1,434.8**	**1,412.5**	**1,357.4**	**1,325.2**	**1,315.1**
Combustion	857.5	853.4	840.0	819.6	807.9	807.6	810.7
Electricity	686.4	736.3	594.8	593.0	549.5	517.6	504.4
Residential	**930.9**	**1,213.9**	**1,064.1**	**1,080.9**	**1,001.6**	**946.3**	**911.5**

Source: *U.S. EPA, Inventory of U.S. Greenhouse Gas Emissions and Sinks: 1990–2017*

Combustion	338.2	357.9	329.3	346.8	317.8	292.9	294.5
Electricity	592.7	856.0	734.7	734.1	683.8	653.5	617.1
Commercial	**764.3**	**1,029.7**	**929.1**	**938.5**	**908.5**	**865.8**	**839.1**
Combustion	226.5	226.8	224.6	232.9	245.5	232.1	232.9
Electricity	537.7	803.0	704.5	705.6	663.0	633.6	606.2
U.S. Territories[a]	**27.6**	**49.7**	**42.5**	**41.4**	**41.4**	**41.4**	**41.4**
Total	**4,738.8**	**5,744.8**	**5,157.4**	**5,199.3**	**5,047.1**	**4,961.9**	**4,912.0**
Electric Power	**1,820.0**	**2,400.0**	**2,038.3**	**2,037.1**	**1,900.6**	**1,808.9**	**1,732.0**

[a] Fuel consumption by U.S. Territories (i.e., American Samoa, Guam, Puerto Rico, U.S. Virgin Islands, Wake Island, and other U.S. Pacific Islands) is included in this report.

Notes: Combustion-related emissions from electric power are allocated based on aggregate national electricity use by each end-use sector. Totals may not sum due to independent rounding.

Figure 2-7: 2017 CO_2 Emissions from Fossil Fuel Combustion by Sector and Fuel Type (MMT CO_2 Eq.)

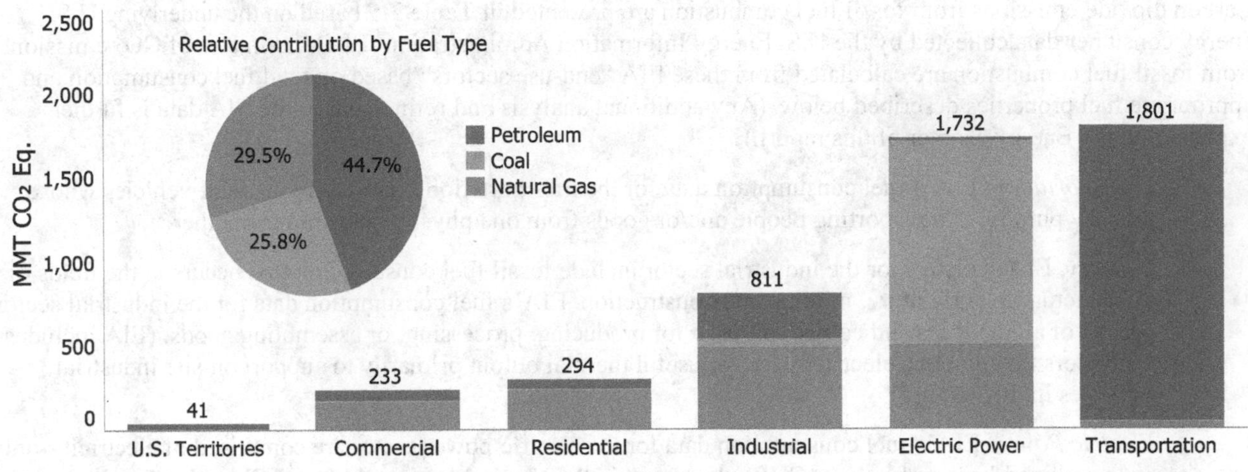

Note on Figure 2-7: Fossil Fuel Combustion for electric power also includes emissions of less than 0.5 MMT CO_2 Eq. from geothermal-based generation.

Figure 2-8: 2017 End-Use Sector Emissions of CO_2 from Fossil Fuel Combustion (MMT CO_2 Eq.)

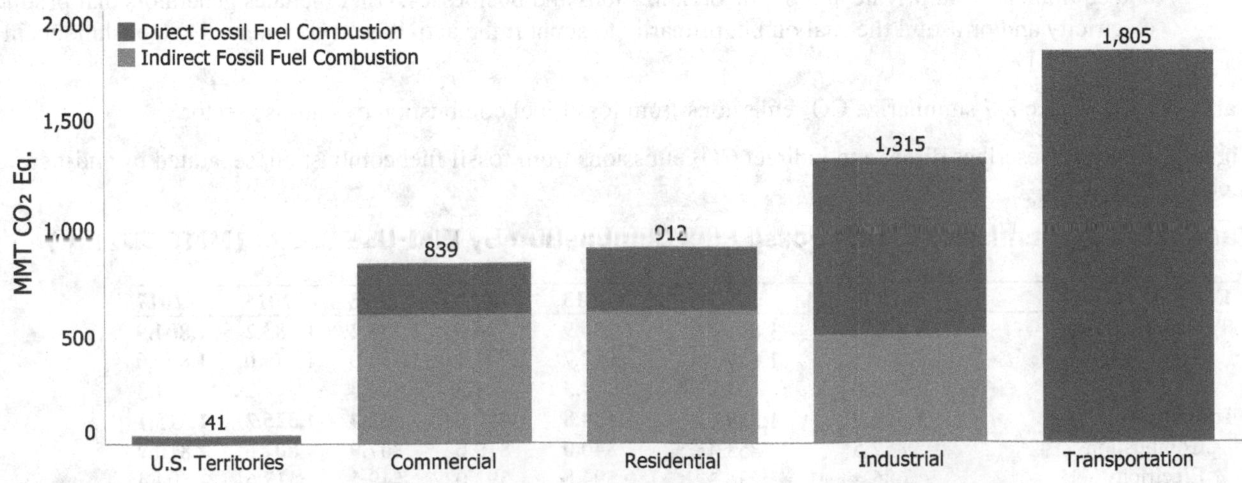

Source: *U.S. EPA, Inventory of U.S. Greenhouse Gas Emissions and Sinks: 1990–2017*

Electric power was the second largest emitter of CO_2 in 2017 (surpassed by transportation); electricity generators used 32 percent of U.S. energy from fossil fuels and emitted 35 percent of the CO_2 from fossil fuel combustion in 2017. Changes in electricity demand and the carbon intensity of fuels used for electric power generation have a significant impact on CO_2 emissions. Carbon dioxide emissions from the electric power sector have decreased by approximately 4.8 percent since 1990, and the carbon intensity of the electric power sector, in terms of CO_2 Eq. per QBtu input, has significantly decreased by 11 percent during that same timeframe. This decoupling of the level of electric power generation and the resulting CO_2 emissions is shown below in Figure 2-9.

Figure 2-9: Electric Power Generation (Billion kWh) and Emissions (MMT CO_2 Eq.)

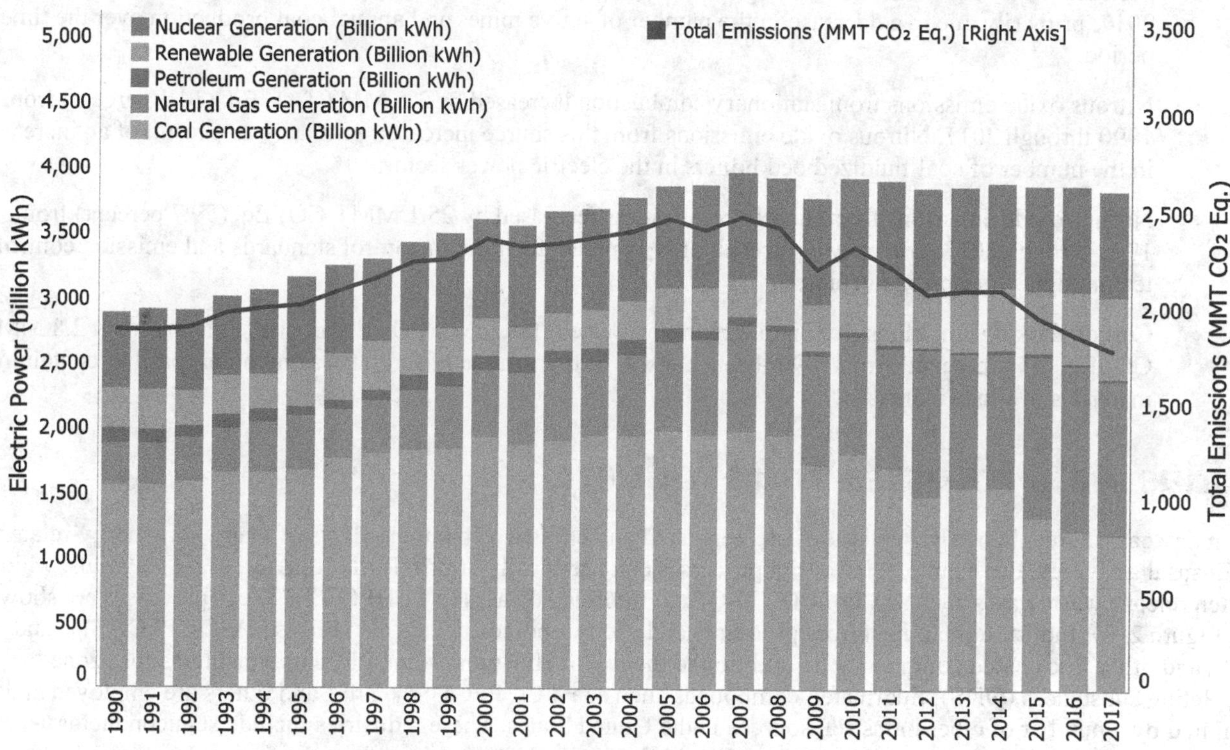

Electric power CO_2 emissions can also be allocated to the end-use sectors that use electricity, as presented in Table 2-5. With electricity CO_2 emissions allocated to end-use sectors, the transportation end-use sector accounted for 1,804.9 MMT CO_2 Eq. in 2017 or approximately 37 percent of total CO_2 emissions from fossil fuel combustion. The industrial end-use sector accounted for 27 percent of CO_2 emissions from fossil fuel combustion when including allocated electricity emissions. The residential and commercial end-use sectors accounted for 19 and 17 percent, respectively, of CO_2 emissions from fossil fuel combustion when including allocated electricity emissions. Both of these end-use sectors were heavily reliant on electricity for meeting energy needs, with electricity use for lighting, heating, air conditioning, and operating appliances contributing 68 and 72 percent of emissions from the residential and commercial end-use sectors, respectively.

Other Significant Trends in Energy

Other significant trends in emissions from energy source categories over the twenty-eight-year period from 1990 through 2017 included the following:

- Methane emissions from natural gas systems and petroleum systems (combined here) decreased from 235.1 MMT CO_2 Eq. in 1990 to 203.3 MMT CO_2 Eq. in 2017 (31.9 MMT CO_2 Eq. or 13.6 percent decrease from 1990 to 2017). Natural gas systems CH_4 emissions decreased by 27.5 MMT CO_2 Eq. (14.2 percent) since 1990, largely due to a decrease in emissions from distribution, transmission and storage, processing, and exploration. The decrease in distribution is largely due to decreased emissions from pipelines and distribution station leaks, and the decrease in transmission and storage emissions is largely due to reduced compressor station emissions (including emissions from compressors and leaks). Petroleum systems CH_4

Source: *U.S. EPA, Inventory of U.S. Greenhouse Gas Emissions and Sinks: 1990–2017*

emissions decreased by 4.4 MMT CO_2 Eq. (or 10.5 percent) since 1990. This decrease is due primarily to decreases in tank emissions and associated gas venting. Carbon dioxide emissions from natural gas and petroleum systems increased by 27 percent from 1990 to 2017, due to increases in flaring emissions.

- Carbon dioxide emissions from non-energy uses of fossil fuels increased by 3.7 MMT CO_2 Eq. (3.1 percent) from 1990 through 2017. Emissions from non-energy uses of fossil fuels were 123.2MMT CO_2 Eq. in 2017, which constituted 2.3 percent of total national CO_2 emissions, approximately the same proportion as in 1990.
- Methane emissions from coal mining decreased by 40.8 MMT CO_2 Eq. (42.3 percent) from 1990 through 2017, primarily due to a decrease in the number of active mines and annual coal production over the time period.
- Nitrous oxide emissions from stationary combustion increased by 3.5 MMT CO_2 Eq. (14.1 percent) from 1990 through 2017. Nitrous oxide emissions from this source increased primarily as a result of an increase in the number of coal fluidized bed boilers in the electric power sector.
- Nitrous oxide emissions from mobile combustion decreased by 25.1 MMT CO_2 Eq. (59.7 percent) from 1990 through 2017, primarily as a result of N_2O national emission control standards and emission control technologies for on-road vehicles.
- Carbon dioxide emissions from incineration of waste (10.8 MMT CO_2 Eq. in 2017) increased by 2.8 MMT CO_2 Eq. (35.7 percent) from 1990 through 2017, as the volume of scrap tires and other fossil C-containing materials in waste increased.

Industrial Processes and Product Use

In many cases, greenhouse gas emissions are generated and emitted as the byproducts of many non-energy-related industrial activities. For example, industrial processes can chemically or physically transform raw materials, which often release waste gases such as CO_2, CH_4, N_2O, and fluorinated gases (e.g., HFC-23). These processes are shown in Figure 2-10. Industrial manufacturing processes and use by end-consumers also release HFCs, PFCs, SF_6, and NF_3 and other fluorinated compounds. In addition to the use of HFCs and some PFCs as substitutes for ozone depleting substances (ODS), fluorinated compounds such as HFCs, PFCs, SF_6, NF_3, and others are employed and emitted by a number of other industrial sources in the United States. These industries include semiconductor manufacture, electric power transmission and distribution, and magnesium metal production and processing. In addition, N_2O is used in and emitted by semiconductor manufacturing and anesthetic and aerosol applications. Table 2-6 presents greenhouse gas emissions from industrial processes by source category. Overall, emission sources in the Industrial Processes and Product Use (IPPU) chapter account for 5.6 percent of U.S. greenhouse gas emissions in 2017.

Source: *U.S. EPA, Inventory of U.S. Greenhouse Gas Emissions and Sinks: 1990–2017*

Figure 2-10: 2017 Industrial Processes and Product Use Chapter Greenhouse Gas Sources (MMT CO_2 Eq.)

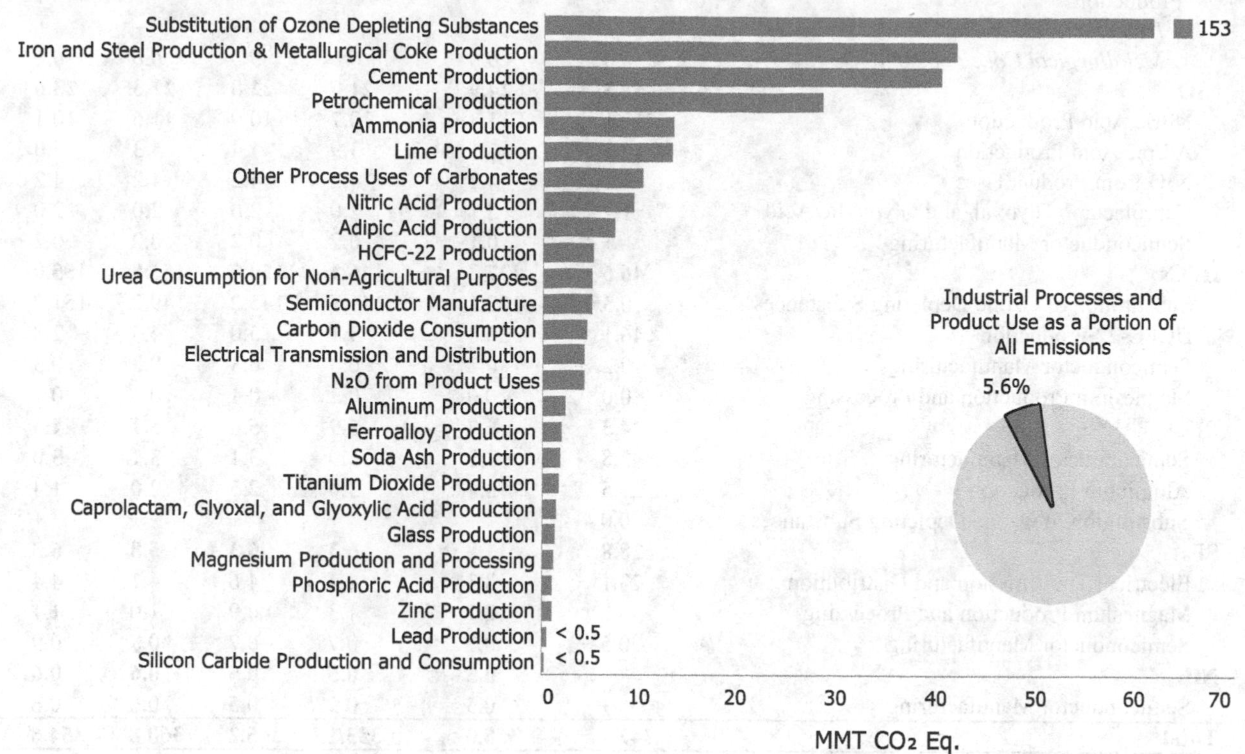

Table 2-6: Emissions from Industrial Processes and Product Use (MMT CO_2 Eq.)

Gas/Source	1990	2005	2013	2014	2015	2016	20
CO_2	**208.8**	**191.7**	**173.1**	**179.2**	**173.0**	**164.5**	**16(**
Iron and Steel Production & Metallurgical Coke Production	101.6	68.2	53.5	58.4	47.8	42.3	4]
Iron and Steel Production	*99.1*	*66.2*	*51.6*	*56.3*	*45.0*	*41.0*	*4.*
Metallurgical Coke Production	*2.5*	*2.1*	*1.8*	*2.0*	*2.8*	*1.3*	*(*
Cement Production	33.5	46.2	36.4	39.4	39.9	39.4	4(
Petrochemical Production	21.2	26.8	26.4	26.5	28.1	28.1	2ε
Ammonia Production	13.0	9.2	9.5	9.4	10.6	10.8	1:
Lime Production	11.7	14.6	14.0	14.2	13.3	12.9	1:
Other Process Uses of Carbonates	6.3	7.6	11.5	13.0	12.2	11.0	1(
Urea Consumption for Non-Agricultural Purposes	3.8	3.7	4.6	1.8	4.6	5.1	:
Carbon Dioxide Consumption	1.5	1.4	4.2	4.5	4.5	4.5	4
Ferroalloy Production	2.2	1.4	1.8	1.9	2.0	1.8	2
Soda Ash Production	1.4	1.7	1.7	1.7	1.7	1.7	1
Titanium Dioxide Production	1.2	1.8	1.7	1.7	1.6	1.7	1
Glass Production	1.5	1.9	1.3	1.3	1.3	1.2	1
Aluminum Production	6.8	4.1	3.3	2.8	2.8	1.3	1
Phosphoric Acid Production	1.5	1.3	1.1	1.0	1.0	1.0	1
Zinc Production	0.6	1.0	1.4	1.0	0.9	0.9	1
Lead Production	0.5	0.6	0.5	0.5	0.5	0.5	(
Silicon Carbide Production and Consumption	0.4	0.2	0.2	0.2	0.2	0.2	(
Magnesium Production and Processing	+	+	+	+	+	+	
CH_4	**0.3**	**0.1**	**0.1**	**0.2**	**0.2**	**0.3**	**(**
Petrochemical Production	0.2	0.1	0.1	0.1	0.2	0.2	(
Ferroalloy Production	+	+	+	+	+	+	

Source: *U.S. EPA, Inventory of U.S. Greenhouse Gas Emissions and Sinks: 1990–2017*

Silicon Carbide Production and Consumption	+	+	+	+	+	+	
Iron and Steel Production & Metallurgical Coke Production	+	+	+	+	+	+	
Iron and Steel Production	+	+	+	+	+	+	
Metallurgical Coke Production	*0.0*	*0.0*	*0.0*	*0.0*	*0.0*	*0.0*	(
N_2O	**33.3**	**24.9**	**21.0**	**22.8**	**22.3**	**23.6**	**2:**
Nitric Acid Production	12.1	11.3	10.7	10.9	11.6	10.1	9
Adipic Acid Production	15.2	7.1	3.9	5.4	4.3	7.0	7
N_2O from Product Uses	4.2	4.2	4.2	4.2	4.2	4.2	4
Caprolactam, Glyoxal, and Glyoxylic Acid	1.7	2.1	2.0	2.0	2.0	2.0	1
Semiconductor Manufacturing	+	0.1	0.2	0.2	0.2	0.2	(
HFCs	**46.6**	**122.3**	**146.1**	**150.7**	**153.8**	**155.0**	**15**
Substitution of Ozone Depleting Substances[a]	0.3	102.1	141.7	145.2	149.2	151.7	15
HCFC-22 Production	46.1	20.0	4.1	5.0	4.3	2.8	5
Semiconductor Manufacturing	0.2	0.2	0.3	0.3	0.3	0.3	(
Magnesium Production and Processing	0.0	0.0	0.1	0.1	0.1	0.1	(
PFCs	**24.3**	**6.7**	**5.9**	**5.6**	**5.1**	**4.4**	**4**
Semiconductor Manufacturing	2.8	3.2	2.9	3.1	3.1	3.0	3
Aluminum Production	21.5	3.4	3.0	2.5	2.0	1.4	1
Substitution of Ozone Depleting Substances	0.0	+	+	+	+	+	
SF_6	**28.8**	**11.8**	**6.3**	**6.3**	**5.8**	**6.3**	**(**
Electrical Transmission and Distribution	23.1	8.3	4.4	4.6	4.1	4.4	4
Magnesium Production and Processing	5.2	2.7	1.3	0.9	1.0	1.1	1
Semiconductor Manufacturing	0.5	0.7	0.7	0.7	0.7	0.9	(
NF_3	**+**	**0.5**	**0.5**	**0.5**	**0.6**	**0.6**	**(**
Semiconductor Manufacturing	+	0.5	0.5	0.5	0.6	0.6	(
Total	**342.1**	**358.0**	**353.1**	**365.2**	**360.8**	**354.6**	**35**

+ Does not exceed 0.05 MMT CO_2 Eq.
[a] Small amounts of PFC emissions also result from this source.
Note: Totals may not sum due to independent rounding.

Overall, emissions from the IPPU sector increased by 4.9 percent from 1990 to 2017. Significant trends in emissions from IPPU source categories over the twenty-eight-year period from 1990 through 2017 included the following:

- Hydrofluorocarbon and perfluorocarbon emissions resulting from the substitution of ODS (e.g., chlorofluorocarbons [CFCs]) have been increasing from small amounts in 1990 to 152.7 MMT CO_2 Eq. in 2017. This increase was in large part the result of efforts to phase out CFCs and other ODS in the United States. In the short term, this trend is expected to continue, and will likely continue over the next decade as hydrochlorofluorocarbons (HCFCs), which are interim substitutes in many applications, are themselves phased-out under the provisions of the Copenhagen Amendments to the Montreal Protocol.

- Combined CO_2 and CH_4 emissions from iron and steel production and metallurgical coke production decreased by 1.2 percent to 41.8 MMT CO_2 Eq. from 2016 to 2017, and have declined overall by 59.9 MMT CO_2 Eq. (58.9 percent) from 1990 through 2017, due to restructuring of the industry, technological improvements, and increased scrap steel utilization.

- Carbon dioxide emissions from cement production increased by 20.4 percent (6.8 MMT CO_2 Eq.) from 1990 through 2017. They rose from 1990 through 2006 (with the exception of a slight decrease in 1997) and then fell until 2009 due to a decrease in demand for construction materials during the economic recession. Since 2010, CO_2 emissions from cement production have risen 28.2 percent (8.9 MMT CO_2 Eq.).

- Carbon dioxide emissions from ammonia production (13.2 MMT CO_2 Eq. in 2017) decreased by 1.3 percent (0.2 MMT CO_2 Eq.) since 1990. Ammonia production relies on natural gas as both a feedstock and a fuel, and as such, market fluctuations and volatility in natural gas prices affect the production of ammonia.

- Nitrous oxide emissions from adipic acid production were 7.4 MMT CO_2 Eq. in 2017, and have decreased significantly since 1990 due to both the widespread installation of pollution control measures in the late

Source: *U.S. EPA, Inventory of U.S. Greenhouse Gas Emissions and Sinks: 1990–2017*

1990s and plant idling in the late 2000s. Emissions from adipic acid production have decreased by 51.5 percent since 1990 and by 56.3 percent since a peak in 1995.

- PFC emissions from aluminum production decreased by 94.8 percent (20.3 MMT CO_2 Eq.) from 1990 to 2017, due to both industry emission reduction efforts and lower domestic aluminum production.

Agriculture

Agricultural activities contribute directly to emissions of greenhouse gases through a variety of processes, including the following source categories: enteric fermentation in domestic livestock, livestock manure management, rice cultivation, agricultural soil management, liming, urea fertilization, and field burning of agricultural residues. Methane, N_2O, and CO_2 were the primary greenhouse gases emitted by agricultural activities.

In 2017, agricultural activities were responsible for emissions of 542.1 MMT CO_2 Eq., or 8.4 percent of total U.S. greenhouse gas emissions. Methane emissions from enteric fermentation and manure management represented approximately 26.7 percent and 9.4 percent of total CH_4 emissions from anthropogenic activities, respectively, in 2017. Agricultural soil management activities, such as application of synthetic and organic fertilizers, deposition of livestock manure, and growing N-fixing plants, were the largest source of U.S. N_2O emissions in 2017, accounting for 73.9 percent. Carbon dioxide emissions from the application of crushed limestone and dolomite (i.e., soil liming) and urea fertilization represented 0.2 percent of total CO_2 emissions from anthropogenic activities. Figure 2-11 and Table 2-7 illustrate agricultural greenhouse gas emissions by source.

Figure 2-11: 2017 Agriculture Chapter Greenhouse Gas Sources (MMT CO_2 Eq.)

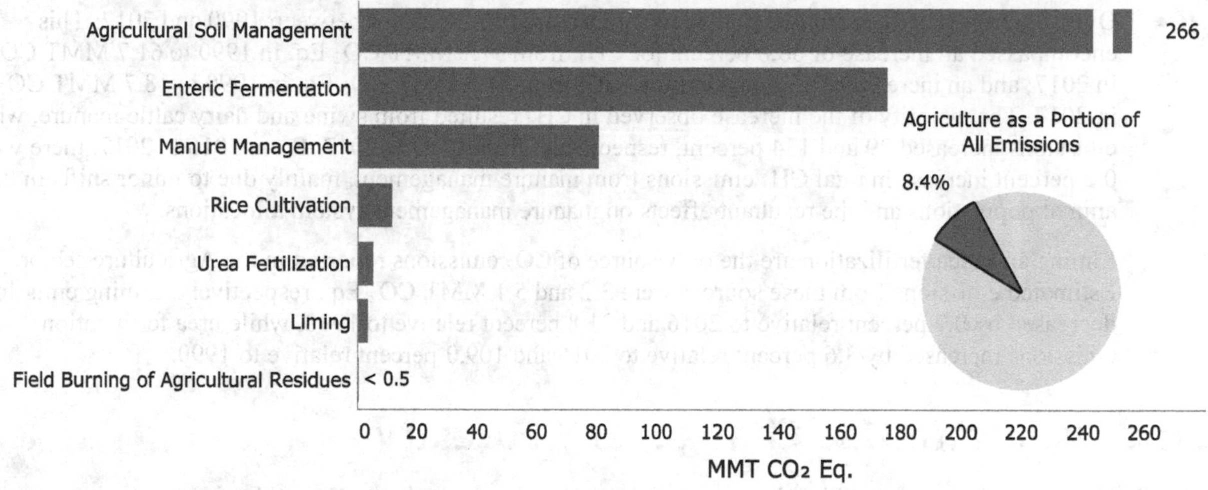

Table 2-7: Emissions from Agriculture (MMT CO_2 Eq.)

Gas/Source	1990	2005	2013	2014	2015	2016	2017
CO_2	**7.1**	**7.9**	**8.4**	**8.1**	**8.5**	**8.1**	**8.2**
Urea Fertilization	2.4	3.5	4.4	4.5	4.7	4.9	5.1
Liming	4.7	4.3	3.9	3.6	3.7	3.2	3.2
CH_4	**217.4**	**239.5**	**235.3**	**234.9**	**239.9**	**247.3**	**248.7**
Enteric Fermentation	164.2	168.9	165.5	164.2	166.5	171.9	175.4
Manure Management	37.1	53.7	58.1	57.8	60.9	61.5	61.7
Rice Cultivation	16.0	16.7	11.5	12.7	12.3	13.7	11.3
Field Burning of Agricultural Residues	0.1	0.2	0.2	0.2	0.2	0.2	0.2
N_2O	**265.7**	**271.1**	**282.7**	**279.7**	**295.4**	**285.8**	**285.2**
Agricultural Soil Management	251.7	254.5	265.2	262.3	277.8	267.6	266.4
Manure Management	14.0	16.5	17.4	17.4	17.6	18.2	18.7
Field Burning of Agricultural Residues	+	0.1	0.1	0.1	0.1	0.1	0.1

Source: *U.S. EPA, Inventory of U.S. Greenhouse Gas Emissions and Sinks: 1990–2017*

Total	490.2	518.4	526.3	522.8	543.8	541.2	542.1

+ Does not exceed 0.05 MMT CO_2 Eq.
Note: Totals may not sum due to independent rounding.

Some significant trends in U.S. emissions from Agriculture source categories include the following:

- Agricultural soils are the largest anthropogenic source of N_2O emissions in the United States, accounting for approximately 73.9 percent of N_2O emissions in 2017 and 4.1 percent of total emissions in the United States in 2017. Estimated emissions from this source in 2017 were 266.4 MMT CO_2 Eq. Annual N_2O emissions from agricultural soils fluctuated between 1990 and 2017, although overall emissions were 5.8 percent higher in 2017 than in 1990. Year-to-year fluctuations are largely a reflection of annual variation in weather patterns, synthetic fertilizer use, and crop production.
- Enteric fermentation is the largest anthropogenic source of CH_4 emissions in the United States. In 2017, enteric fermentation CH_4 emissions were 26.7 percent of total CH_4 emissions (175.4 MMT CO_2 Eq.), which represents an increase of 11.3 MMT CO_2 Eq. (6.9 percent) since 1990. This increase in emissions from 1990 to 2017 in enteric fermentation generally follows the increasing trends in cattle populations. From 1990 to 1995, emissions increased and then generally decreased from 1996 to 2004, mainly due to fluctuations in beef cattle populations and increased digestibility of feed for feedlot cattle. Emissions increased from 2005 to 2007, as both dairy and beef populations increased. Research indicates that the feed digestibility of dairy cow diets decreased during this period. Emissions decreased again from 2008 to 2014 as beef cattle populations again decreased. Emissions increased from 2014 to 2017, consistent with an increase in beef cattle population over those same years.
- Overall, emissions from manure management increased 57.1 percent between 1990 and 2017. This encompassed an increase of 66.0 percent for CH_4, from 37.1 MMT CO_2 Eq. in 1990 to 61.7 MMT CO_2 Eq. in 2017; and an increase of 33.6 percent for N_2O, from 14.0 MMT CO_2 Eq. in 1990 to 18.7 MMT CO_2 Eq. in 2017. The majority of the increase observed in CH_4 resulted from swine and dairy cattle manure, where emissions increased 29 and 134 percent, respectively, from 1990 to 2017. From 2016 to 2017, there was a 0.2 percent increase in total CH_4 emissions from manure management, mainly due to minor shifts in the animal populations and the resultant effects on manure management system allocations.
- Liming and urea fertilization are the only source of CO_2 emissions reported in the Agriculture sector. Estimated emissions from these sources were 3.2 and 5.1 MMT CO_2 Eq., respectively. Liming emissions decreased by 0.7 percent relative to 2016 and 31.8 percent relative to 1990, while urea fertilization emissions increased by 3.6 percent relative to 2016 and 109.0 percent relative to 1990.

Land Use, Land-Use Change, and Forestry

When humans alter the terrestrial biosphere through land use, changes in land use, and land management practices, they also influence the carbon (C) stock fluxes on these lands and cause emissions of CH_4 and N_2O. Overall, managed land is a net sink for CO_2 (C sequestration) in the United States. The primary drivers of fluxes on managed lands include, for example, forest management practices, tree planting in urban areas, the management of agricultural soils, the landfilling of yard trimmings and food scraps, and activities that cause changes in C stocks in coastal wetlands. The main drivers for net forest sequestration include net forest growth, increasing forest area, and a net accumulation of C stocks in harvested wood pools. The net sequestration in *Settlements Remaining Settlements,* is driven primarily by C stock gains in urban forests through net tree growth and increased urban area, as well as long-term accumulation of C in landfills from additions of yard trimmings and food scraps.

The LULUCF sector in 2017 resulted in a net increase in C stocks (i.e., net CO_2 removals) of 729.6 MMT CO_2 Eq. (Table 2-8).[2] This represents an offset of approximately 11.3 percent of total (i.e., gross) greenhouse gas emissions

[2] LULUCF Carbon Stock Change is the net C stock change from the following categories: *Forest Land Remaining Forest Land, Land Converted to Forest Land, Cropland Remaining Cropland, Land Converted to Cropland, Grassland Remaining Grassland,*

Source: *U.S. EPA, Inventory of U.S. Greenhouse Gas Emissions and Sinks: 1990–2017*

in 2017. Emissions of CH_4 and N_2O from LULUCF activities in 2017 were 15.5 MMT CO_2 Eq. and represent 0.2 percent of total greenhouse gas emissions.[3] Between 1990 and 2017, total C sequestration in the LULUCF sector decreased by 10.5 percent, primarily due to a decrease in the rate of net C accumulation in forests and *Cropland Remaining Cropland*, as well as an increase in CO_2 emissions from *Land Converted to Settlements*.

Forest fires were the largest source of CH_4 emissions from LULUCF in 2017, totaling 4.9 MMT CO_2 Eq. (194 kt of CH_4). *Coastal Wetlands Remaining Coastal Wetlands* resulted in CH_4 emissions of 3.6 MMT CO_2 Eq. (144 kt of CH_4). Grassland fires resulted in CH_4 emissions of 0.3 MMT CO_2 Eq. (12 kt of CH_4). *Peatlands Remaining Peatlands*, *Land Converted to Wetlands*, and *Drained Organic Soils* resulted in CH_4 emissions of less than 0.05 MMT CO_2 Eq. each.

Forest fires were also the largest source of N_2O emissions from LULUCF in 2017, totaling 3.2 MMT CO_2 Eq. (11 kt of N_2O). Nitrous oxide emissions from fertilizer application to settlement soils in 2017 totaled to 2.5 MMT CO_2 Eq. (8 kt of N_2O). Additionally, the application of synthetic fertilizers to forest soils in 2017 resulted in N_2O emissions of 0.5 MMT CO_2 Eq. (2 kt of N_2O). Grassland fires resulted in N_2O emissions of 0.3 MMT CO_2 Eq. (1 kt of N_2O). *Coastal Wetlands Remaining Coastal Wetlands* and *Drained Organic Soils* resulted in N_2O emissions of 0.1 MMT CO_2 Eq. each (less than 0.5 kt of N_2O). *Peatlands Remaining Peatlands* resulted in N_2O emissions of less than 0.05 MMT CO_2 Eq.

Carbon dioxide removals from C stock changes are presented in Figure 2-12 and Table 2-8 along with CH_4 and N_2O emissions for LULUCF source categories.

Figure 2-12: 2017 LULUCF Chapter Greenhouse Gas Sources and Sinks (MMT CO_2 Eq.)

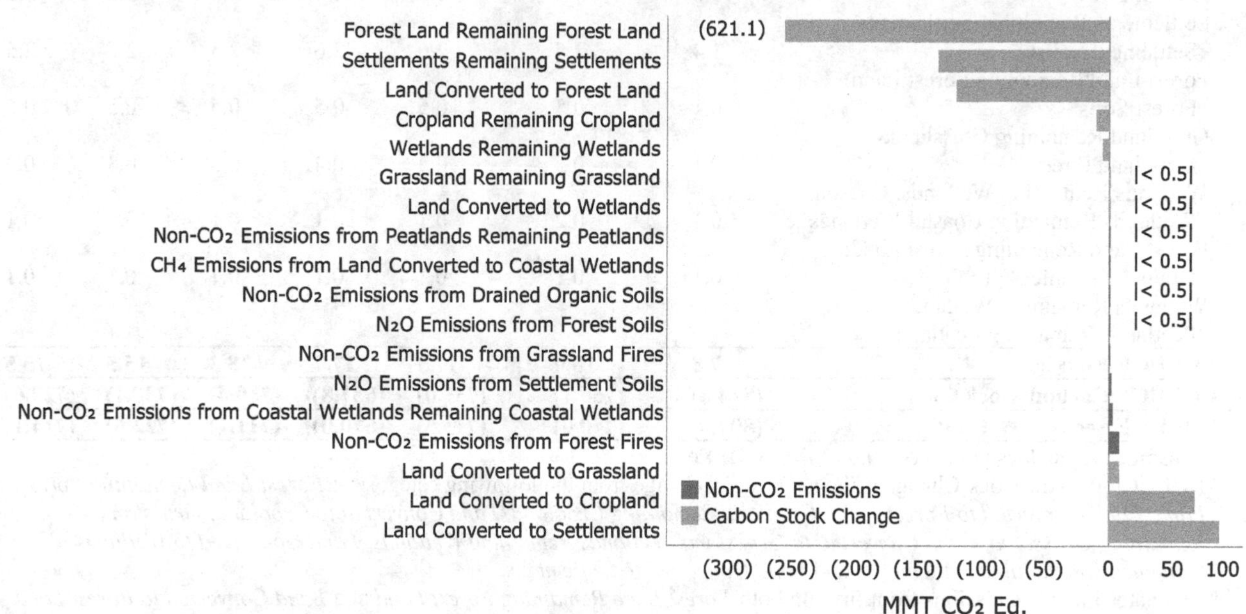

Table 2-8: U.S. Greenhouse Gas Emissions and Removals (Net Flux) from Land Use, Land-Use Change, and Forestry (MMT CO_2 Eq.)

Gas/Land-Use Category	1990	2005	2013	2014	2015	2016	2017
Carbon Stock Change[a]	**(814.8)**	**(756.1)**	**(731.0)**	**(687.8)**	**(739.4)**	**(738.1)**	**(729.6)**
Forest Land Remaining Forest Land	(671.6)	(639.4)	(616.7)	(568.8)	(645.2)	(628.9)	(621.1)
Land Converted to Forest Land	(119.1)	(120.0)	(120.5)	(120.5)	(120.6)	(120.6)	(120.6)

Land Converted to Grassland, Wetlands Remaining Wetlands, Land Converted to Wetlands, Settlements Remaining Settlements, and *Land Converted to Settlements.*

[3] LULUCF emissions include the CH_4 and N_2O emissions reported for *Peatlands Remaining Peatlands*, Forest Fires, Drained Organic Soils, Grassland Fires, and *Coastal Wetlands Remaining Coastal Wetlands*; CH_4 emissions from *Land Converted to Coastal Wetlands*; and N_2O emissions from Forest Soils and Settlement Soils.

Source: *U.S. EPA, Inventory of U.S. Greenhouse Gas Emissions and Sinks: 1990–2017*

Cropland Remaining Cropland	(40.9)	(26.5)	(11.4)	(12.0)	(6.3)	(9.9)	(10.3)
Land Converted to Cropland	75.6	66.7	66.9	66.7	66.7	67.3	66.9
Grassland Remaining Grassland	(4.2)	5.5	(3.7)	(7.5)	9.6	(1.6)	(0.1)
Land Converted to Grassland	8.7	5.1	8.3	7.9	9.8	8.5	8.3
Wetlands Remaining Wetlands	(4.0)	(5.7)	(4.3)	(4.3)	(4.4)	(4.4)	(4.4)
Land Converted to Wetlands	(+)	(+)	(+)	(+)	(+)	(+)	(+)
Settlements Remaining Settlements	(122.1)	(127.8)	(135.9)	(135.8)	(135.4)	(134.7)	(134.5)
Land Converted to Settlements	62.9	86.0	86.4	86.5	86.5	86.4	86.2
CH_4	**5.0**	**9.0**	**9.9**	**10.1**	**16.5**	**8.8**	**8.8**
Forest Land Remaining Forest Land: Forest Fires[b]	1.5	5.2	6.1	6.1	12.6	4.9	4.9
Wetlands Remaining Wetlands: Coastal Wetlands Remaining Coastal Wetlands	3.4	3.5	3.6	3.6	3.6	3.6	3.6
Grassland Remaining Grassland: Grassland Fires[c]	0.1	0.3	0.2	0.4	0.3	0.3	0.3
Land Converted to Wetlands: Land Converted to Coastal Wetlands	+	+	+	+	+	+	+
Forest Land Remaining Forest Land: Drained Organic Soils[d]	+	+	+	+	+	+	+
Wetlands Remaining Wetlands: Peatlands Remaining Peatlands	+	+	+	+	+	+	+
N_2O	**2.8**	**7.0**	**7.6**	**7.7**	**11.8**	**6.7**	**6.7**
Forest Land Remaining Forest Land: Forest Fires[b]	1.0	3.4	4.0	4.0	8.3	3.2	3.2
Settlements Remaining Settlements: Settlement Soils[e]	1.4	2.5	2.6	2.6	2.5	2.5	2.5
Forest Land Remaining Forest Land: Forest Soils[f]	0.1	0.5	0.5	0.5	0.5	0.5	0.5
Grassland Remaining Grassland: Grassland Fires[c]	0.1	0.3	0.2	0.4	0.3	0.3	0.3
Wetlands Remaining Wetlands: Coastal Wetlands Remaining Coastal Wetlands	0.1	0.2	0.1	0.1	0.1	0.1	0.1
Forest Land Remaining Forest Land: Drained Organic Soils[d]	0.1	0.1	0.1	0.1	0.1	0.1	0.1
Wetlands Remaining Wetlands: Peatlands Remaining Peatlands	+	+	+	+	+	+	+
LULUCF Emissions[g]	**7.8**	**16.0**	**17.5**	**17.7**	**28.3**	**15.5**	**15.5**
LULUCF Carbon Stock Change[a]	**(814.8)**	**(756.1)**	**(731.0)**	**(687.8)**	**(739.4)**	**(738.1)**	**(729.6)**
LULUCF Sector Net Total[h]	**(807.0)**	**(740.0)**	**(713.5)**	**(670.0)**	**(711.1)**	**(722.6)**	**(714.1)**

\+ Absolute value does not exceed 0.05 MMT CO_2 Eq.

[a] LULUCF Carbon Stock Change is the net C stock change from the following categories: *Forest Land Remaining Forest Land, Land Converted to Forest Land, Cropland Remaining Cropland, Land Converted to Cropland, Grassland Remaining Grassland, Land Converted to Grassland, Wetlands Remaining Wetlands, Land Converted to Wetlands, Settlements Remaining Settlements,* and *Land Converted to Settlements.*

[b] Estimates include emissions from fires on both *Forest Land Remaining Forest Land* and *Land Converted to Forest Land.*

[c] Estimates include emissions from fires on both *Grassland Remaining Grassland* and *Land Converted to Grassland.*

[d] Estimates include emissions from drained organic soils on both *Forest Land Remaining Forest Land* and *Land Converted to Forest Land.*

[e] Estimates include emissions from N fertilizer additions on both *Settlements Remaining Settlements* and *Land Converted to Settlements.*

[f] Estimates include emissions from N fertilizer additions on both *Forest Land Remaining Forest Land* and *Land Converted to Forest Land.*

[g] LULUCF emissions include the CH_4 and N_2O emissions reported for *Peatlands Remaining Peatlands*, Forest Fires, Drained Organic Soils, Grassland Fires, and *Coastal Wetlands Remaining Coastal Wetlands*; CH_4 emissions from *Land Converted to Coastal Wetlands*; and N_2O emissions from Forest Soils and Settlement Soils.

[h] The LULUCF Sector Net Total is the net sum of all CH_4 and N_2O emissions to the atmosphere plus net carbon stock changes.

Notes: Totals may not sum due to independent rounding. Parentheses indicate net sequestration.

Source: *U.S. EPA, Inventory of U.S. Greenhouse Gas Emissions and Sinks: 1990–2017*

Other significant trends from 1990 to 2017 in emissions from LULUCF categories include:

- Annual C sequestration by forest land (i.e., annual C stock accumulation in the five C pools and harvested wood products for *Forest Land Remaining Forest Land* and *Land Converted to Forest Land*) has decreased by approximately 6.2 percent since 1990. This is primarily due to decreased C stock gains in *Land Converted to Forest Land* and the harvested wood products pools within *Forest Land Remaining Forest Land*.
- Annual C sequestration from *Settlements Remaining Settlements* (which includes organic soils, settlement trees, and landfilled yard trimmings and food scraps) has increased by 10.2 percent over the period from 1990 to 2017. This is primarily due to an increase in urbanized land area in the United States.
- Annual emissions from *Land Converted to Settlements* increased by approximately 37.0 percent from 1990 to 2017 due to losses in aboveground biomass C stocks from *Forest Land Converted to Settlements* and mineral soils C stocks from *Grassland Converted to Settlements*.
- Nitrous oxide emissions from fertilizer application to settlement soils in 2017 totaled to 2.5 MMT CO_2 Eq. (8 kt of N_2O). This represents an increase of 72.0 percent since 1990. Additionally, the application of synthetic fertilizers to forest soils in 2017 resulted in N_2O emissions of 0.5 MMT CO_2 Eq. (2 kt of N_2O). Nitrous oxide emissions from fertilizer application to forest soils have increased by 455 percent since 1990, but still account for a relatively small portion of overall emissions.

Waste

Waste management and treatment activities are sources of greenhouse gas emissions (see Figure 2-13). In 2017, landfills were the third-largest source of U.S. anthropogenic CH_4 emissions, accounting for 16.4 percent of total U.S. CH_4 emissions.[4] Additionally, wastewater treatment accounts for 14.6 percent of waste emissions, 2.2 percent of U.S. CH_4 emissions, and 1.4 percent of N_2O emissions. Emissions of CH_4 and N_2O from composting are also accounted for in this chapter, generating emissions of 2.2 MMT CO_2 Eq. and 1.9 MMT CO_2 Eq., respectively. A summary of greenhouse gas emissions from the Waste chapter is presented in Table 2-9.

Figure 2-13: 2017 Waste Chapter Greenhouse Gas Sources (MMT CO_2 Eq.)

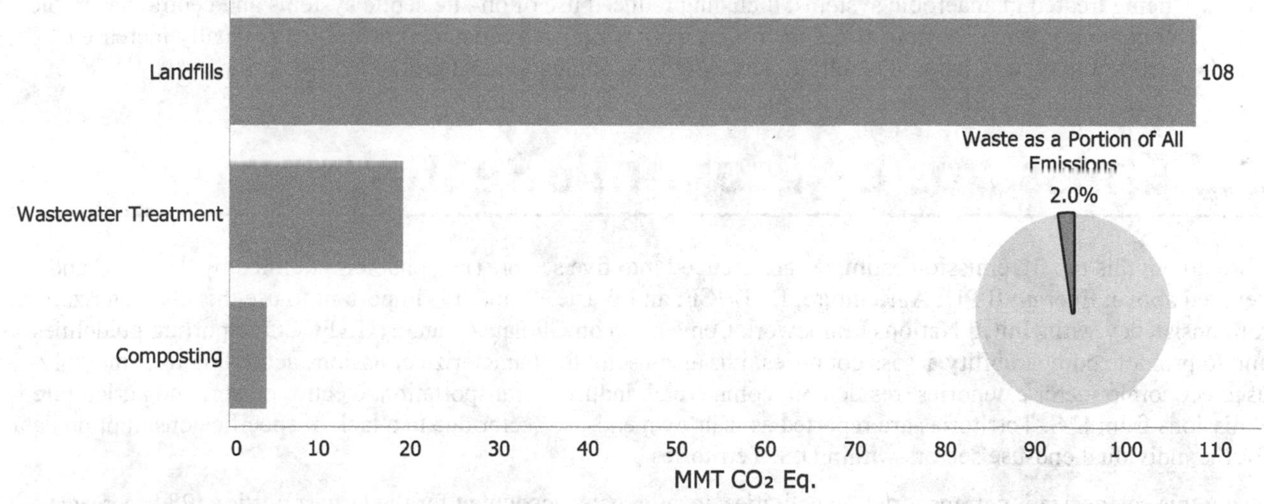

Overall, in 2017, waste activities generated emissions of 131.0 MMT CO_2 Eq., or 2.0 percent of total U.S. greenhouse gas emissions.

[4] Landfills also store carbon, due to incomplete degradation of organic materials such as wood products and yard trimmings, as described in the Land Use, Land-Use Change, and Forestry chapter.

Source: *U.S. EPA, Inventory of U.S. Greenhouse Gas Emissions and Sinks: 1990–2017*

Table 2-9: Emissions from Waste (MMT CO_2 Eq.)

Gas/Source	1990	2005	2013	2014	2015	2016	2017
CH_4	**195.2**	**148.7**	**129.3**	**128.9**	**127.8**	**124.3**	**124.1**
Landfills	179.6	131.4	112.9	112.5	111.2	108.0	107.7
Wastewater Treatment	15.3	15.4	14.3	14.3	14.5	14.2	14.2
Composting	0.4	1.9	2.0	2.1	2.1	2.1	2.2
N_2O	**3.7**	**6.1**	**6.5**	**6.6**	**6.7**	**6.8**	**6.9**
Wastewater Treatment	3.4	4.4	4.7	4.8	4.8	4.9	5.0
Composting	0.3	1.7	1.8	1.9	1.9	1.9	1.9
Total	**198.9**	**154.7**	**135.8**	**135.6**	**134.5**	**131.1**	**131.0**

Note: Totals may not sum due to independent rounding.

Some significant trends in U.S. emissions from waste source categories include the following:

- From 1990 to 2017, net CH_4 emissions from landfills decreased by 71.8 MMT CO_2 Eq. (40.0 percent), with small increases occurring in interim years. This downward trend in emissions coincided with increased landfill gas collection and control systems, and a reduction of decomposable materials (i.e., paper and paperboard, food scraps, and yard trimmings) discarded in municipal solid waste (MSW) landfills over the time series.
- Combined CH_4 and N_2O emissions from composting have generally increased since 1990, from 0.7 MMT CO_2 Eq. to 4.1 MMT CO_2 Eq. in 2017, which represents slightly less than a five-fold increase over the time series. The growth in composting since the 1990s is attributable to primarily four factors: (1) the enactment of legislation by state and local governments that discouraged the disposal of yard trimmings and food waste in landfills; (2) yard trimming collection and yard trimming drop off sites provided by local solid waste management districts; (3) an increased awareness of the environmental benefits of composting; and (4) loans or grant programs to establish or expand composting infrastructure.
- From 1990 to 2017, CH_4 and N_2O emissions from wastewater treatment decreased by 1.1 MMT CO_2 Eq. (7.0 percent) and increased by 1.6 MMT CO_2 Eq. (46.4 percent), respectively. Methane emissions from domestic wastewater treatment have decreased since 1999 due to decreasing percentages of wastewater being treated in anaerobic systems, including reduced use of on-site septic systems and central anaerobic treatment systems. Nitrous oxide emissions from wastewater treatment processes gradually increased across the time series as a result of increasing U.S. population and protein consumption.

2.2 Emissions by Economic Sector

Throughout this report, emission estimates are grouped into five sectors (i.e., chapters) defined by the IPCC and detailed above: Energy; IPPU; Agriculture; LULUCF; and Waste. While it is important to use this characterization for consistency with United Nations Framework Convention on Climate Change (UNFCCC) reporting guidelines and to promote comparability across countries, it is also useful to characterize emissions according to commonly used economic sector categories: residential, commercial, industry, transportation, electric power, and agriculture. Emissions from U.S. Territories are reported as their own end-use sector due to a lack of specific consumption data for the individual end-use sectors within U.S. Territories.

Using this categorization, transportation activities, in aggregate, accounted for the largest portion (28.9 percent) of total U.S. greenhouse gas emissions in 2017. Emissions from electric power accounted for the second largest portion (27.5 percent), while emissions from industry accounted for the third largest portion (22.2 percent) of total U.S. greenhouse gas emissions in 2017. Emissions from industry have in general declined over the past decade due to a number of factors, including structural changes in the U.S. economy (i.e., shifts from a manufacturing-based to a service-based economy), fuel switching, and efficiency improvements.

The remaining 21.3 percent of U.S. greenhouse gas emissions were contributed by, in order of magnitude, the agriculture, commercial, and residential sectors, plus emissions from U.S. Territories. Activities related to agriculture accounted for roughly 9.0 percent of emissions; unlike other economic sectors, agricultural sector

***Source:** U.S. EPA, Inventory of U.S. Greenhouse Gas Emissions and Sinks: 1990–2017*

emissions were dominated by N_2O emissions from agricultural soil management and CH_4 emissions from enteric fermentation, rather than CO_2 from fossil fuel combustion. The commercial and residential sectors accounted for roughly 6.4 percent and 5.1 percent of emissions, respectively, and U.S. Territories accounted for 0.7 percent of emissions; emissions from these sectors primarily consisted of CO_2 emissions from fossil fuel combustion. Carbon dioxide was also emitted and sequestered (in the form of C) by a variety of activities related to forest management practices, tree planting in urban areas, the management of agricultural soils, landfilling of yard trimmings, and changes in C stocks in coastal wetlands.

Table 2-10 presents a detailed breakdown of emissions from each of these economic sectors by source category, as they are defined in this report. Figure 2-14 shows the trend in emissions by sector from 1990 to 2017.

Figure 2-14: U.S. Greenhouse Gas Emissions Allocated to Economic Sectors (MMT CO_2 Eq.)

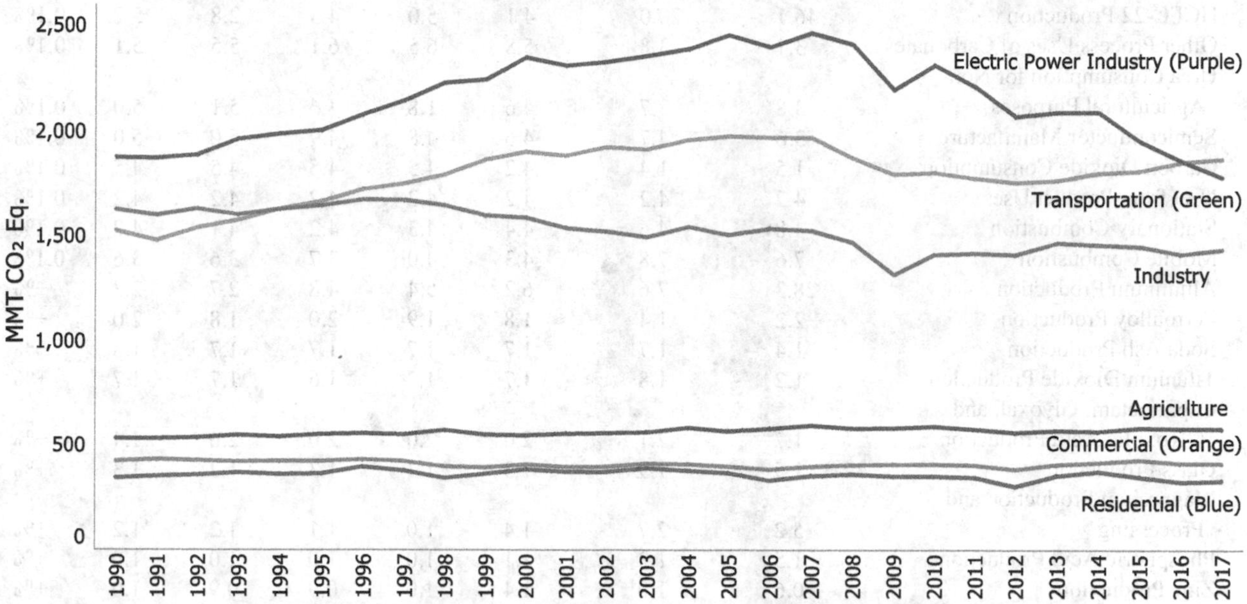

Table 2-10: U.S. Greenhouse Gas Emissions Allocated to Economic Sectors (MMT CO_2 Eq. and Percent of Total in 2017)

Sector/Source	1990	2005	2013	2014	2015	2016	2017[a]	Percent[a]
Transportation	**1,527.1**	**1,976.0**	**1,765.4**	**1,799.9**	**1,809.3**	**1,849.7**	**1,866.2**	**28.9%**
CO_2 from Fossil Fuel Combustion	1,469.1	1,857.0	1,682.7	1,721.6	1,734.0	1,779.0	1,800.6	27.9%
Substitution of Ozone Depleting Substances	+	69.3	51.6	48.8	46.3	43.3	40.1	0.6%
Mobile Combustion	46.1	39.5	21.5	19.5	18.1	17.0	15.9	0.2%
Non-Energy Use of Fuels	11.8	10.2	9.6	10.0	11.0	10.4	9.6	0.1%
Electric Power Industry	**1,875.5**	**2,455.9**	**2,088.7**	**2,088.9**	**1,949.5**	**1,857.2**	**1,778.3**	**27.5%**
CO_2 from Fossil Fuel Combustion	1,820.0	2,400.0	2,038.3	2,037.1	1,900.6	1,808.9	1,732.0	26.8%
Stationary Combustion	20.9	30.9	29.7	29.9	27.7	27.4	25.9	0.4%
Incineration of Waste	8.4	12.9	10.6	10.7	11.1	11.1	11.1	0.2%
Other Process Uses of Carbonates	3.1	3.8	5.8	6.5	6.1	5.5	5.1	0.1%
Electrical Transmission and Distribution	23.1	8.3	4.4	4.6	4.1	4.4	4.3	0.1%
Industry	**1,628.6**	**1,508.4**	**1,469.5**	**1,459.3**	**1,451.2**	**1,414.1**	**1,436.5**	**22.2%**
CO_2 from Fossil Fuel Combustion	814.1	803.0	794.7	774.0	767.2	767.9	771.2	11.9%
Natural Gas Systems	223.1	194.0	190.8	190.6	192.2	191.2	191.9	3.0%
Non-Energy Use of Fuels	102.1	121.3	108.4	104.7	110.9	98.2	108.5	1.7%

Source: *U.S. EPA, Inventory of U.S. Greenhouse Gas Emissions and Sinks: 1990–2017*

Petroleum Systems	51.0	48.3	66.8	71.7	71.2	60.4	61.0	0.9%
Coal Mining	96.5	64.1	64.6	64.6	61.2	53.8	55.7	0.9%
Iron and Steel Production	101.7	68.2	53.5	58.4	47.8	42.3	41.8	0.6%
Cement Production	33.5	46.2	36.4	39.4	39.9	39.4	40.3	0.6%
Substitution of Ozone Depleting Substances	+	7.8	21.2	23.1	25.6	27.9	30.1	0.5%
Petrochemical Production	21.4	26.9	26.5	26.6	28.2	28.4	28.5	0.4%
Ammonia Production	13.0	9.2	9.5	9.4	10.6	10.8	13.2	0.2%
Lime Production	11.7	14.6	14.0	14.2	13.3	12.9	13.1	0.2%
Nitric Acid Production	12.1	11.3	10.7	10.9	11.6	10.1	9.3	0.1%
Adipic Acid Production	15.2	7.1	3.9	5.4	4.3	7.0	7.4	0.1%
Abandoned Oil and Gas Wells	6.6	6.9	7.0	7.1	7.1	7.2	6.9	0.1%
Abandoned Underground Coal Mines	7.2	6.6	6.2	6.3	6.4	6.7	6.4	0.1%
HCFC-22 Production	46.1	20.0	4.1	5.0	4.3	2.8	5.2	0.1%
Other Process Uses of Carbonates	3.1	3.8	5.8	6.5	6.1	5.5	5.1	0.1%
Urea Consumption for Non-Agricultural Purposes	3.8	3.7	4.6	1.8	4.6	5.1	5.0	0.1%
Semiconductor Manufacture	3.6	4.7	4.6	4.8	4.9	5.0	5.0	0.1%
Carbon Dioxide Consumption	1.5	1.4	4.2	4.5	4.5	4.5	4.5	0.1%
N_2O from Product Uses	4.2	4.2	4.2	4.2	4.2	4.2	4.2	0.1%
Stationary Combustion	4.8	4.6	4.4	4.3	4.2	4.1	4.2	0.1%
Mobile Combustion	7.6	7.8	4.3	4.0	3.7	3.6	3.6	0.1%
Aluminum Production	28.3	7.6	6.2	5.4	4.8	2.7	2.3	+%
Ferroalloy Production	2.2	1.4	1.8	1.9	2.0	1.8	2.0	+%
Soda Ash Production	1.4	1.7	1.7	1.7	1.7	1.7	1.8	+%
Titanium Dioxide Production	1.2	1.8	1.7	1.7	1.6	1.7	1.7	+%
Caprolactam, Glyoxal, and Glyoxylic Acid Production	1.7	2.1	2.0	2.0	2.0	2.0	1.4	+%
Glass Production	1.5	1.9	1.3	1.3	1.3	1.2	1.3	+%
Magnesium Production and Processing	5.2	2.7	1.4	1.0	1.1	1.2	1.2	+%
Phosphoric Acid Production	1.5	1.3	1.1	1.0	1.0	1.0	1.0	+%
Zinc Production	0.6	1.0	1.4	1.0	0.9	0.9	1.0	+%
Lead Production	0.5	0.6	0.5	0.5	0.5	0.5	0.5	+%
Silicon Carbide Production and Consumption	0.4	0.2	0.2	0.2	0.2	0.2	0.2	+%
Agriculture	**534.9**	**570.0**	**572.6**	**569.2**	**585.2**	**581.7**	**582.2**	**9.0%**
N_2O from Agricultural Soil Management	251.7	254.5	265.2	262.3	277.8	267.6	266.4	4.1%
Enteric Fermentation	164.2	168.9	165.5	164.2	166.5	171.9	175.4	2.7%
Manure Management	51.1	70.2	75.5	75.2	78.5	79.7	80.4	1.2%
CO_2 from Fossil Fuel Combustion	43.4	50.4	45.4	45.5	40.7	39.7	39.4	0.6%
Rice Cultivation	16.0	16.7	11.5	12.7	12.3	13.7	11.3	0.2%
Urea Fertilization	2.4	3.5	4.4	4.5	4.7	4.9	5.1	0.1%
Liming	4.7	4.3	3.9	3.6	3.7	3.2	3.2	+%
Mobile Combustion	1.2	1.2	0.8	0.8	0.6	0.6	0.6	+%
Field Burning of Agricultural Residues	0.2	0.3	0.3	0.3	0.3	0.3	0.3	+%
Stationary Combustion	0.1	+	0.1	0.1	0.1	0.1	0.1	+%
Commercial	**426.9**	**400.7**	**409.6**	**419.5**	**432.2**	**416.1**	**416.0**	**6.4%**
CO_2 from Fossil Fuel Combustion	226.5	226.8	224.6	232.9	245.5	232.1	232.9	3.6%
Landfills	179.6	131.4	112.9	112.5	111.2	108.0	107.7	1.7%
Substitution of Ozone Depleting Substances	+	17.8	47.8	49.6	50.7	51.3	50.6	0.8%
Wastewater Treatment	15.3	15.4	14.3	14.3	14.5	14.2	14.2	0.2%
Human Sewage	3.4	4.4	4.7	4.8	4.8	4.9	5.0	0.1%
Composting	0.7	3.5	3.9	4.0	4.0	4.0	4.1	0.1%

Source: *U.S. EPA, Inventory of U.S. Greenhouse Gas Emissions and Sinks: 1990–2017*

Stationary Combustion	1.5	1.4	1.4	1.4	1.6	1.5	1.5	+%
Residential	**344.7**	**370.0**	**356.3**	**376.6**	**349.7**	**326.9**	**330.9**	**5.1%**
CO_2 from Fossil Fuel Combustion	338.2	357.9	329.3	346.8	317.8	292.9	294.5	4.6%
Substitution of Ozone Depleting Substances	0.3	7.2	21.1	23.8	26.5	29.3	31.9	0.5%
Stationary Combustion	6.3	4.9	5.9	6.0	5.3	4.7	4.6	0.1%
U.S. Territories	**33.3**	**58.1**	**48.1**	**46.6**	**46.6**	**46.6**	**46.6**	**0.7%**
CO_2 from Fossil Fuel Combustion	27.6	49.7	42.5	41.4	41.4	41.4	41.4	0.6%
Non-Energy Use of Fuels	5.7	8.1	5.4	5.1	5.1	5.1	5.1	0.1%
Stationary Combustion	0.1	0.2	0.2	0.2	0.2	0.2	0.2	+%
Total Emissions	**6,371.0**	**7,339.0**	**6,710.2**	**6,760.0**	**6,623.8**	**6,492.3**	**6,456.7**	**100.0%**
LULUCF Sector Net Total[b]	**(807.0)**	**(740.0)**	**(713.5)**	**(670.0)**	**(711.1)**	**(722.6)**	**(714.1)**	**(11.1%)**
Net Emissions (Sources and Sinks)	**5,564.0**	**6,599.0**	**5,996.8**	**6,090.0**	**5,912.7**	**5,769.7**	**5,742.6**	**88.9%**

Notes: Total emissions presented without LULUCF. Total net emissions presented with LULUCF. Totals may not sum due to independent rounding. Parentheses indicate negative values or sequestration.

\+ Does not exceed 0.05 MMT CO_2 Eq. or 0.05 percent.

[a] Percent of total (gross) emissions excluding emissions from LULUCF for 2017.

[b] The LULUCF Sector Net Total is the net sum of all CH_4 and N_2O emissions to the atmosphere plus net carbon stock changes.

Emissions with Electricity Distributed to Economic Sectors

It is also useful to view greenhouse gas emissions from economic sectors with emissions related to electric power distributed into end-use categories (i.e., emissions from electric power are allocated to the economic sectors in which the electricity is used). The generation, transmission, and distribution of electricity, accounted for 28 percent of total U.S. greenhouse gas emissions in 2017. Electric power-related emissions decreased by 5.2 percent since 1990 and by 4.2 percent from 2016 to 2017, primarily due to decreased CO_2 emissions from fossil fuel combustion and increased use of renewable energy. Between 2016 to 2017, the consumption of coal, natural gas, and petroleum for electric power generation decreased by 2.9, 7.2, and 10.7 percent, respectively, while the amount of electricity generated (in kWh) decreased by 1.1 percent.

From 2016 to 2017, electricity sales to the residential and commercial end-use sectors decreased by 2.3 percent and 1.0 percent, respectively. Electricity sales to the industrial sector increased by approximately 0.8 percent. Overall, from 2016 to 2017, the amount of electricity retail sales (in kWh) decreased by 1.0 percent. The sales trend in the residential and commercial sectors can largely be attributed to milder weather conditions (i.e., warmer winter months and cooler summer months). A decrease in both heating and cooling degree days from 2016 to 2017 resulted in less demand for electricity to power heating and cooling equipment (EIA 2018). Table 2-11 provides a detailed summary of emissions from electric power-related activities.

Table 2-11: Electric Power-Related Greenhouse Gas Emissions (MMT CO_2 Eq.)

Gas/Fuel Type or Source	1990	2005	2013	2014	2015	2016	2017
CO_2	**1,831.0**	**2,416.3**	**2,054.4**	**2,054.1**	**1,917.5**	**1,825.1**	**1,747.9**
Fossil Fuel Combustion	1,820.0	2,400.0	2,038.3	2,037.1	1,900.6	1,808.9	1,732.0
Coal	*1,546.5*	*1,982.8*	*1,571.3*	*1,568.6*	*1,351.4*	*1,242.0*	*1,207.1*
Natural Gas	*175.4*	*318.9*	*444.2*	*442.9*	*525.2*	*545.0*	*505.6*
Petroleum	*97.5*	*97.9*	*22.4*	*25.3*	*23.7*	*21.4*	*18.9*
Geothermal	*0.5*	*0.5*	*0.4*	*0.4*	*0.4*	*0.4*	*0.4*
Incineration of Waste	8.0	12.5	10.3	10.4	10.7	10.8	10.8
Other Process Uses of Carbonates	3.1	3.8	5.8	6.5	6.1	5.5	5.1
CH_4	**0.4**	**0.9**	**1.0**	**1.1**	**1.2**	**1.2**	**1.1**
Stationary Sources[a]	0.4	0.9	1.0	1.1	1.2	1.2	1.1
Incineration of Waste	+	+	+	+	+	+	+
N_2O	**21.0**	**30.4**	**28.9**	**29.2**	**26.8**	**26.5**	**25.1**
Stationary Sources[a]	20.5	30.1	28.6	28.9	26.5	26.2	24.8
Incineration of Waste	0.5	0.4	0.3	0.3	0.3	0.3	0.3

Source: *U.S. EPA, Inventory of U.S. Greenhouse Gas Emissions and Sinks: 1990–2017*

SF_6	**23.1**	**8.3**	**4.4**	**4.6**	**4.1**	**4.4**	**4.3**
Electrical Transmission and Distribution	23.1	8.3	4.4	4.6	4.1	4.4	4.3
Total	**1,875.5**	**2,455.9**	**2,088.7**	**2,088.9**	**1,949.5**	**1,857.2**	**1,778.3**

+ Does not exceed 0.05 MMT CO_2 Eq.

[a] Includes only stationary combustion emissions related to the generation of electricity.

Note: Totals may not sum due to independent rounding.

To distribute electricity emissions among economic end-use sectors, emissions from the source categories assigned to the electric power sector were allocated to the residential, commercial, industry, transportation, and agriculture economic sectors according to each economic sector's share of retail sales of electricity (EIA 2019a; Duffield 2006). These source categories include CO_2 from Fossil Fuel Combustion, CH_4 and N_2O from Stationary Combustion, Incineration of Waste, Other Process Uses of Carbonates, and SF_6 from Electrical Transmission and Distribution Systems. Note that only 50 percent of the Other Process Uses of Carbonates emissions were associated with electric power and distributed as described; the remainder of Other Process Uses of Carbonates emissions were attributed to the industrial processes economic end-use sector.[5]

When emissions from electricity use are distributed among these economic end-use sectors, industrial activities account for the largest share of total U.S. greenhouse gas emissions (29.7 percent), followed closely by emissions from transportation (29.0 percent). Emissions from the commercial and residential sectors also increase substantially when emissions from electricity are included (16.1 and 14.9 percent, respectively). In all economic end-use sectors except agriculture, CO_2 accounts for more than 81.3 percent of greenhouse gas emissions, primarily from the combustion of fossil fuels.

Table 2-12 presents a detailed breakdown of emissions from each of these economic sectors, with emissions from electric power distributed to them. Figure 2-12 shows the trend in these emissions by sector from 1990 to 2017.

Figure 2-15: U.S. Greenhouse Gas Emissions with Electricity-Related Emissions Distributed to Economic Sectors (MMT CO_2 Eq.)

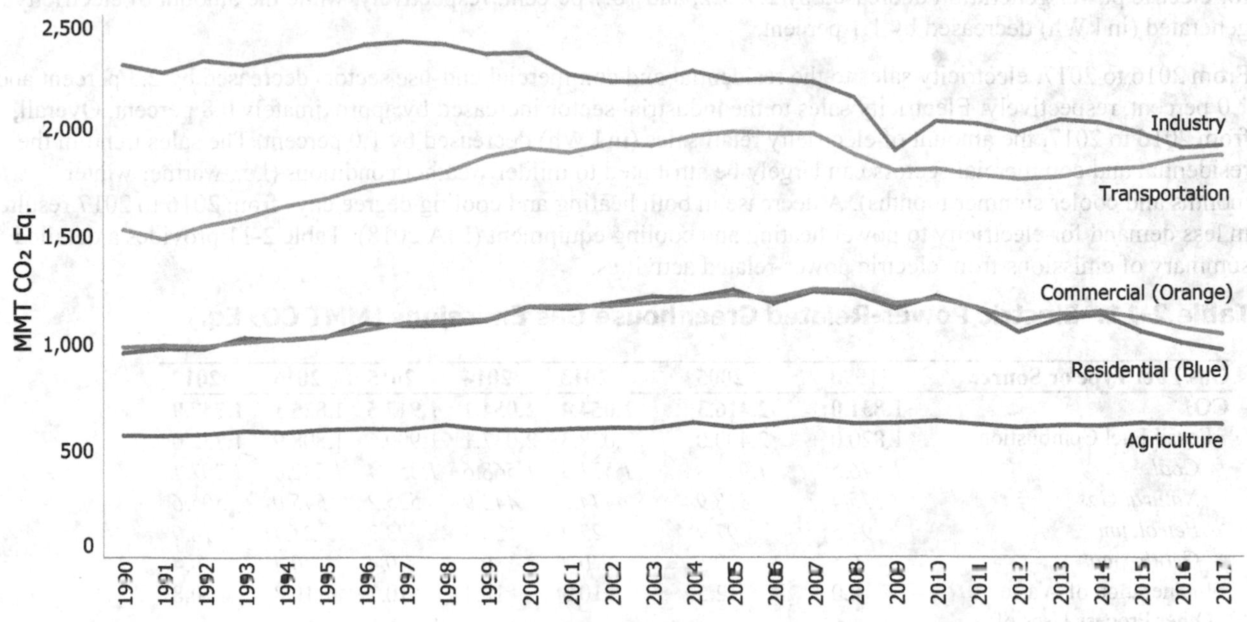

[5] Emissions were not distributed to U.S. Territories, since the electric power sector only includes emissions related to the generation of electricity in the 50 states and the District of Columbia.

Source: U.S. EPA, Inventory of U.S. Greenhouse Gas Emissions and Sinks: 1990–2017

Table 2-12: U.S. Greenhouse Gas Emissions by Economic Sector and Gas with Electricity-Related Emissions Distributed (MMT CO_2 Eq.) and Percent of Total in 2017

Sector/Gas	1990	2005	2013	2014	2015	2016	2017	Percent[a]
Industry	**2,300.9**	**2,223.5**	**2,036.7**	**2,023.0**	**1,973.6**	**1,906.4**	**1,915.6**	**29.7%**
Direct Emissions	**1,628.6**	**1,508.4**	**1,469.5**	**1,459.3**	**1,451.2**	**1,414.1**	**1,436.5**	**22.2%**
CO_2	1,160.8	1,146.4	1,120.6	1,106.6	1,101.7	1,072.8	1,091.3	16.9%
CH_4	353.8	293.6	289.3	289.1	285.1	275.3	275.9	4.3%
N_2O	37.6	29.7	25.6	27.3	26.7	28.0	27.1	0.4%
HFCs, PFCs, SF_6, and NF_3	76.3	38.7	34.0	36.3	37.7	38.0	42.2	0.7%
Electricity-Related	**672.3**	**715.2**	**567.2**	**563.7**	**522.4**	**492.3**	**479.2**	**7.4%**
CO_2	656.4	703.6	557.9	554.3	513.8	483.8	470.9	7.3%
CH_4	0.2	0.3	0.3	0.3	0.3	0.3	0.3	+%
N_2O	7.5	8.9	7.9	7.9	7.2	7.0	6.8	0.1%
SF_6	8.3	2.4	1.2	1.2	1.1	1.2	1.2	+%
Transportation	**1,530.2**	**1,980.8**	**1,769.8**	**1,804.5**	**1,813.7**	**1,854.1**	**1,870.6**	**29.0%**
Direct Emissions	**1,527.1**	**1,976.0**	**1,765.4**	**1,799.9**	**1,809.3**	**1,849.7**	**1,866.2**	**28.9%**
CO_2	1,480.9	1,867.2	1,692.3	1,731.6	1,744.9	1,789.4	1,810.1	28.0%
CH_4	5.9	3.0	1.8	1.7	1.6	1.5	1.4	+%
N_2O	40.2	36.5	19.7	17.8	16.5	15.5	14.5	0.2%
HFCs[b]	+	69.3	51.6	48.8	46.3	43.3	40.1	0.6%
Electricity-Related	**3.1**	**4.8**	**4.4**	**4.6**	**4.4**	**4.3**	**4.4**	**0.1%**
CO_2	3.1	4.8	4.3	4.5	4.3	4.2	4.4	0.1%
CH_4	+	+	+	+	+	+	+	+%
N_2O	+	0.1	0.1	0.1	0.1	0.1	0.1	+%
SF_6	+	+	+	+	+	+	+	+%
Commercial	**981.1**	**1,222.4**	**1,131.5**	**1,143.1**	**1,112.3**	**1,066.6**	**1,038.4**	**16.1%**
Direct Emissions	**426.9**	**400.7**	**409.6**	**419.5**	**432.2**	**416.1**	**416.0**	**6.4%**
CO_2	226.5	226.8	224.6	232.9	245.5	232.1	232.9	3.6%
CH_4	196.3	149.7	130.3	130.0	129.0	125.5	125.3	1.9%
N_2O	4.1	6.4	6.8	7.0	7.0	7.1	7.2	0.1%
HFCs	+	17.8	47.8	49.6	50.7	51.3	50.6	0.8%
Electricity-Related	**554.2**	**821.7**	**721.9**	**723.6**	**680.1**	**650.5**	**622.4**	**9.6%**
CO_2	541.0	808.4	710.0	711.5	668.9	639.3	611.8	9.5%
CH_4	0.1	0.3	0.4	0.4	0.4	0.4	0.4	+%
N_2O	6.2	10.2	10.0	10.1	9.4	9.3	8.8	0.1%
SF_6	6.8	2.8	1.5	1.6	1.4	1.5	1.5	+%
Residential	**955.6**	**1,246.0**	**1,109.2**	**1,129.3**	**1,051.1**	**997.8**	**964.5**	**14.9%**
Direct Emissions	**344.7**	**370.0**	**356.3**	**376.6**	**349.7**	**326.9**	**330.9**	**5.1%**
CO_2	338.2	357.9	329.3	346.8	317.8	292.9	294.5	4.6%
CH_4	5.2	4.1	4.9	5.0	4.5	3.9	3.8	0.1%
N_2O	1.0	0.9	1.0	1.0	0.9	0.8	0.8	+%
HFCs	0.3	7.2	21.1	23.8	26.5	29.3	31.9	0.5%
Electricity-Related	**610.8**	**875.9**	**752.9**	**752.7**	**701.4**	**670.9**	**633.6**	**9.8%**
CO_2	596.4	861.8	740.5	740.2	689.8	659.3	622.7	9.6%
CH_4	0.1	0.3	0.4	0.4	0.4	0.4	0.4	+%
N_2O	6.8	10.9	10.4	10.5	9.7	9.6	8.9	0.1%
SF_6	7.5	3.0	1.6	1.7	1.5	1.6	1.5	+%
Agriculture	**569.9**	**608.3**	**614.9**	**613.5**	**626.5**	**620.8**	**620.9**	**9.6%**
Direct Emissions	**534.9**	**570.0**	**572.6**	**569.2**	**585.2**	**581.7**	**582.2**	**9.0%**
CO_2	50.5	58.2	53.7	53.6	49.2	47.8	47.6	0.7%
CH_4	218.1	240.1	235.5	235.2	240.0	247.4	248.8	3.9%
N_2O	266.3	271.7	283.3	280.4	296.0	286.4	285.8	4.4%
Electricity-Related	**35.1**	**38.3**	**42.3**	**44.3**	**41.2**	**39.1**	**38.7**	**0.6%**
CO_2	34.2	37.7	41.6	43.6	40.6	38.4	38.1	0.6%
CH_4	+	+	+	+	+	+	+	+%
N_2O	0.4	0.5	0.6	0.6	0.6	0.6	0.5	+%
SF_6	0.4	0.1	0.1	0.1	0.1	0.1	0.1	+%
U.S. Territories	**33.3**	**58.1**	**48.1**	**46.6**	**46.6**	**46.6**	**46.6**	**0.7%**

Source: *U.S. EPA, Inventory of U.S. Greenhouse Gas Emissions and Sinks: 1990–2017*

Total Emissions	**6,371.0**	**7,339.0**	**6,710.2**	**6,760.0**	**6,623.8**	**6,492.3**	**6,456.7**	**100.0%**
LULUCF Sector Net Total[c]	**(807.0)**	**(740.0)**	**(713.5)**	**(670.0)**	**(711.1)**	**(722.6)**	**(714.1)**	**-11.1%**
Net Emissions (Sources and Sinks)	**5,564.0**	**6,599.0**	**5,996.8**	**6,090.0**	**5,912.7**	**5,769.7**	**5,742.6**	**88.9%**

Notes: Total emissions presented without LULUCF. Net emissions presented with LULUCF. Emissions from electric power a allocated based on aggregate electricity use in each end-use sector. Totals may not sum due to independent rounding.
+ Does not exceed 0.05 MMT CO_2 Eq. or 0.05 percent.
[a] Percent of total (gross) emissions excluding emissions from LULUCF for year 2017.
[b] Includes primarily HFC-134a.
[c] The LULUCF Sector Net Total is the net sum of all CH_4 and N_2O emissions to the atmosphere plus net carbon stock changes

Industry

The industry end-use sector includes CO_2 emissions from fossil fuel combustion from all manufacturing facilities, in aggregate, and with the distribution of electricity-related emissions, accounts for 29.7 percent of U.S. greenhouse gas emissions in 2017. This end-use sector also includes emissions that are produced as a byproduct of the non-energy-related industrial process activities. The variety of activities producing these non-energy-related emissions includes CH_4 emissions from petroleum and natural gas systems, fugitive CH_4 emissions from coal mining, byproduct CO_2 emissions from cement manufacture, and HFC, PFC, SF_6, and NF_3 byproduct emissions from semiconductor manufacture, to name a few.

Since 1990, industrial sector emissions have declined by 14.8 percent. The decline has occurred both in direct emissions and indirect emissions associated with electricity use. Structural changes within the U.S. economy that led to shifts in industrial output away from energy-intensive manufacturing products to less energy-intensive products (e.g., from steel to computer equipment) have had a significant effect on industrial emissions.

Transportation

When electricity-related emissions are distributed to economic end-use sectors, transportation activities accounted for 29.0 percent of U.S. greenhouse gas emissions in 2017. The largest sources of transportation greenhouse gas emissions in 2017 were passenger cars (41.2 percent); freight trucks (23.3 percent); light-duty trucks, which include sport utility vehicles, pickup trucks, and minivans (17.5 percent); commercial aircraft (6.9 percent); other aircraft (2.4 percent); ships and boats (2.4 percent); rail (2.2 percent); and pipelines (2.2 percent). These figures include direct CO_2, CH_4, and N_2O emissions from fossil fuel combustion used in transportation and emissions from non-energy use (i.e., lubricants) used in transportation, as well as HFC emissions from mobile air conditioners and refrigerated transport allocated to these vehicle types.

In terms of the overall trend, from 1990 to 2017, total transportation emissions increased due, in large part, to increased demand for travel. The number of VMT by light-duty motor vehicles (passenger cars and light-duty trucks) increased 45.1 percent from 1990 to 2017, as a result of a confluence of factors including population growth, economic growth, urban sprawl, and periods of low fuel prices.

The decline in new light-duty vehicle fuel economy between 1990 and 2004 reflected the increasing market share of light-duty trucks, which grew from about 30 percent of new vehicle sales in 1990 to 48 percent in 2004. Starting in 2005, average new vehicle fuel economy began to increase while light-duty VMT grew only modestly for much of the period. Light-duty VMT grew by less than one percent or declined each year between 2005 and 2013[6] and has since grown at a faster rate (2.5 percent from 2015 to 2016, and 1.0 percent from 2016 to 2017). Average new vehicle fuel economy has increased almost every year since 2005, while light-duty truck market share decreased to

---

[6] VMT estimates are based on data from FHWA Highway Statistics Table VM-1 (FHWA 1996 through 2017). In 2007 and 2008 light-duty VMT decreased 3.0 percent and 2.3 percent, respectively. Note that the decline in light-duty VMT from 2006 to 2007 is due at least in part to a change in FHWA's methods for estimating VMT. In 2011, FHWA changed its methods for estimating VMT by vehicle class, which led to a shift in VMT and emissions among on-road vehicle classes in the 2007 to 2017 time period. In absence of these method changes, light-duty VMT growth between 2006 and 2007 would likely have been higher.

Source: *U.S. EPA, Inventory of U.S. Greenhouse Gas Emissions and Sinks: 1990–2017*

about 33 percent in 2009 and has since varied from year to year between 36 and 45 percent. Light-duty truck market share was about 42 percent of new vehicles in model year 2017 (EPA 2019).

Table 2-13 provides a detailed summary of greenhouse gas emissions from transportation-related activities with electricity-related emissions included in the totals.

Almost all of the energy used for transportation was supplied by petroleum-based products, with more than half being related to gasoline consumption in automobiles and other highway vehicles. Other fuel uses, especially diesel fuel for freight trucks and jet fuel for aircraft, accounted for the remainder. The primary driver of transportation-related emissions was CO_2 from fossil fuel combustion, which increased by 23 percent from 1990 to 2017.[7] This rise in CO_2 emissions, combined with an increase in HFCs from close to zero emissions in 1990 to 40.1 MMT CO_2 Eq. in 2017, led to an increase in overall greenhouse gas emissions from transportation activities of 22 percent.[8]

Table 2-13: Transportation-Related Greenhouse Gas Emissions (MMT CO_2 Eq.)

Gas/Vehicle	1990	2005	2013	2014	2015	2016	2017
Passenger Cars	**639.6**	**693.8**	**747.0**	**761.8**	**762.0**	**772.6**	**770.7**
CO_2	612.2	643.3	717.2	734.8	736.9	749.9	750.6
CH_4	3.2	1.3	0.8	0.7	0.6	0.6	0.5
N_2O	24.1	17.6	11.8	10.5	9.7	8.9	8.2
HFCs	0.0	31.7	17.2	15.8	14.7	13.2	11.4
Light-Duty Trucks	**326.7**	**540.2**	**315.1**	**335.5**	**324.5**	**333.8**	**327.3**
CO_2	312.2	491.1	283.6	306.2	297.5	309.1	304.8
CH_4	1.7	0.8	0.3	0.2	0.2	0.2	0.2
N_2O	12.8	15.0	4.7	4.4	3.8	3.5	3.1
HFCs	0.0	33.3	26.5	24.7	23.0	21.1	19.2
Medium- and Heavy-Duty Trucks	**230.3**	**400.1**	**395.2**	**407.6**	**415.5**	**423.6**	**436.5**
CO_2	229.3	395.4	389.0	401.4	409.1	417.2	430.0
CH_4	0.3	0.1	0.1	0.1	0.1	0.1	0.1
N_2O	0.7	1.2	0.9	0.9	0.8	0.8	0.8
HFCs	0.0	3.4	5.2	5.3	5.5	5.5	5.7
Buses	**8.5**	**12.2**	**17.9**	**19.3**	**19.8**	**19.5**	**20.4**
CO_2	8.4	11.6	17.2	18.6	19.1	18.8	19.7
CH_4	+	0.2	0.2	0.2	0.2	0.2	0.2
N_2O	+	+	+	+	+	+	+
HFCs	0.0	0.3	0.4	0.4	0.4	0.4	0.4
Motorcycles	**1.7**	**1.6**	**3.9**	**3.8**	**3.7**	**3.9**	**3.8**
CO_2	1.7	1.6	3.8	3.8	3.7	3.8	3.7
CH_4	+	+	+	+	+	+	+
N_2O	+	+	+	+	+	+	+
Commercial Aircraft[a]	**110.9**	**134.0**	**115.4**	**116.3**	**120.1**	**121.5**	**129.2**
CO_2	109.9	132.7	114.3	115.2	119.0	120.4	128.0
CH_4	0.0	0.0	0.0	0.0	0.0	0.0	0.0
N_2O	1.0	1.2	1.1	1.1	1.1	1.1	1.2
Other Aircraft[b]	**78.3**	**59.7**	**34.7**	**35.0**	**40.4**	**47.5**	**45.6**
CO_2	77.5	59.1	34.4	34.7	40.0	47.0	45.2
CH_4	0.1	0.1	+	+	+	+	+
N_2O	0.7	0.5	0.3	0.3	0.4	0.4	0.4
Ships and Boats[c]	**47.4**	**45.7**	**40.1**	**29.4**	**34.1**	**41.3**	**44.4**
CO_2	46.3	44.2	37.2	26.4	30.8	37.5	40.3
CH_4	0.6	0.5	0.3	0.3	0.3	0.3	0.3
N_2O	0.6	0.6	0.5	0.3	0.4	0.5	0.5
HFCs	0.0	0.5	2.0	2.3	2.6	2.9	3.3

[7] See previous footnote.

[8] See previous footnote.

Source: *U.S. EPA, Inventory of U.S. Greenhouse Gas Emissions and Sinks: 1990–2017*

Rail	**39.0**	**50.9**	**44.8**	**46.3**	**44.2**	**40.8**	**41.9**
CO_2	38.5	50.3	44.2	45.7	43.6	40.2	41.2
CH_4	0.1	0.1	0.1	0.1	0.1	0.1	0.1
N_2O	0.3	0.4	0.4	0.4	0.4	0.3	0.3
HFCs	0.0	0.1	0.1	0.1	0.1	0.1	0.1
Other Emissions from Electric Power[d]	0.1	+	+	+	+	+	0.1
Pipelines[e]	**36.0**	**32.4**	**46.2**	**39.4**	**38.5**	**39.2**	**41.4**
CO_2	36.0	32.4	46.2	39.4	38.5	39.2	41.4
Lubricants	**11.8**	**10.2**	**9.6**	**10.0**	**11.0**	**10.4**	**9.6**
CO_2	11.8	10.2	9.6	10.0	11.0	10.4	9.6
Total Transportation	**1,530.2**	**1,980.8**	**1,769.8**	**1,804.5**	**1,813.7**	**1,854.1**	**1,870.6**
International Bunker Fuels[f]	*54.8*	*44.7*	*29.5*	*28.7*	*31.6*	*34.9*	*34.6*
Ethanol CO_2[g]	*4.1*	*21.6*	*70.5*	*74.0*	*74.2*	*76.9*	*77.7*
Biodiesel CO_2[g]	*0.0*	*0.9*	*13.5*	*13.3*	*14.1*	*19.6*	*18.7*

+ Does not exceed 0.05 MMT CO_2 Eq.

[a] Consists of emissions from jet fuel consumed by domestic operations of commercial aircraft (no bunkers).

[b] Consists of emissions from jet fuel and aviation gasoline consumption by general aviation and military aircraft.

[c] Fluctuations in emission estimates are associated with fluctuations in reported fuel consumption, and may reflect issues with data sources.

[d] Other emissions from electric power are a result of waste incineration (as the majority of municipal solid waste is combusted in "trash-to-steam" electric power plants), electrical transmission and distribution, and a portion of Other Process Uses of Carbonates (from pollution control equipment installed in electric power plants).

[e] CO_2 estimates reflect natural gas used to power pipelines, but not electricity. While the operation of pipelines produces CH_4 and N_2O, these emissions are not directly attributed to pipelines in the Inventory.

[f] Emissions from International Bunker Fuels include emissions from both civilian and military activities; these emissions are not included in the transportation totals.

[g] Ethanol and biodiesel CO_2 estimates are presented for informational purposes only. See Section 3.11 and the estimates in Land Use, Land-Use Change, and Forestry (see Chapter 6), in line with IPCC methodological guidance and UNFCCC reporting obligations, for more information on ethanol and biodiesel.

Notes: Passenger cars and light-duty trucks include vehicles typically used for personal travel and less than 8,500 lbs; medium- and heavy-duty trucks include vehicles larger than 8,500 lbs. HFC emissions primarily reflect HFC-134a. Totals may not sum due to independent rounding.

Commercial

The commercial end-use sector, with electricity-related emissions distributed, accounts for 16.1 percent of U.S. greenhouse gas emissions in 2017 and is heavily reliant on electricity for meeting energy needs, with electricity use for lighting, heating, air conditioning, and operating appliances. The remaining emissions were largely due to the direct consumption of natural gas and petroleum products, primarily for heating and cooking needs. Energy-related emissions from the commercial sector have generally been increasing since 1990, and annual variations are often correlated with short-term fluctuations in energy use caused by weather conditions, rather than prevailing economic conditions. Decreases in energy-related emissions in the commercial sector in recent years can be largely attributed to an overall reduction in energy use driven by a reduction in heating degree days, and increases in energy efficiency.

Landfills and wastewater treatment are included in the commercial sector, with landfill emissions decreasing since 1990 and wastewater treatment emissions decreasing slightly.

Residential

The residential end-use sector, with electricity-related emissions distributed, accounts for 14.9 percent of U.S. greenhouse gas emissions in 2017 and similarly, is heavily reliant on electricity for meeting energy needs, with electricity use for lighting, heating, air conditioning, and operating appliances. The remaining emissions were largely due to the direct consumption of natural gas and petroleum products, primarily for heating and cooking needs. Emissions from the residential sector have generally been increasing since 1990, and annual variations are often correlated with short-term fluctuations in energy use caused by weather conditions, rather than prevailing

***Source:** U.S. EPA, Inventory of U.S. Greenhouse Gas Emissions and Sinks: 1990–2017*

economic conditions. In the long term, the residential sector is also affected by population growth, migration trends toward warmer areas, and changes in housing and building attributes (e.g., larger sizes and improved insulation). A shift toward energy-efficient products and more stringent energy efficiency standards for household equipment has also contributed to recent trends in energy demand in households (EIA 2018).

Agriculture

The agriculture end-use sector accounts for 9.6 percent of U.S. greenhouse gas emissions in 2017 when electricity-related emissions are distributed, and includes a variety of processes, including enteric fermentation in domestic livestock, livestock manure management, and agricultural soil management. In 2017, agricultural soil management was the largest source of N_2O emissions, and enteric fermentation was the largest source of CH_4 emissions in the United States. This sector also includes small amounts of CO_2 emissions from fossil fuel combustion by motorized farm equipment such as tractors.

Box 2-1: Methodology for Aggregating Emissions by Economic Sector

In presenting the Economic Sectors in the annual *Inventory of U.S. Greenhouse Gas Emissions and Sinks*, the Inventory expands upon the standard IPCC sectors common for UNFCCC reporting. Discussing greenhouse gas emissions relevant to U.S.-specific economic sectors improves communication of the report's findings.

The *Electric Power* economic sector includes CO_2 emissions from the combustion of fossil fuels that are included in the EIA electric power sector. Stationary combustion emissions of CH_4 and N_2O are also based on the EIA electric power sector. Additional sources include CO_2, CH_4, and N_2O from waste incineration, as the majority of municipal solid waste is combusted in plants that produce electricity. The Electric Power economic sector also includes SF_6 from Electrical Transmission and Distribution, and a portion of CO_2 from Other Process Uses of Carbonates (from pollution control equipment installed in electric power plants).

The *Transportation* economic sector includes CO_2 emissions from the combustion of fossil fuels that are included in the EIA transportation fuel-consuming sector. (Additional analyses and refinement of the EIA data are further explained in the Energy chapter of this report.) Emissions of CH_4 and N_2O from mobile combustion are also apportioned to the Transportation economic sector based on the EIA transportation fuel-consuming sector. Substitution of Ozone Depleting Substances emissions are apportioned to the Transportation economic sector based on emissions from refrigerated transport and motor vehicle air-conditioning systems. Finally, CO_2 emissions from Non-Energy Uses of Fossil Fuels identified as lubricants for transportation vehicles are included in the Transportation economic sector.

The *Industry* economic sector includes CO_2 emissions from the combustion of fossil fuels that are included in the EIA industrial fuel-consuming sector, minus the agricultural use of fuel explained below. The CH_4 and N_2O emissions from stationary and mobile combustion are also apportioned to the Industry economic sector based on the EIA industrial fuel-consuming sector, minus emissions apportioned to the Agriculture economic sector. Substitution of Ozone Depleting Substances emissions are apportioned based on their specific end-uses within the source category, with most emissions falling within the Industry economic sector.

Additionally, all process-related emissions from sources with methods considered within the IPCC IPPU sector are apportioned to the Industry economic sector. This includes the process-related emissions (i.e., emissions from the actual process to make the material, not from fuels to power the plant) from activities such as Cement Production, Iron and Steel Production and Metallurgical Coke Production, and Ammonia Production. Additionally, fugitive emissions from energy production sources, such as Natural Gas Systems, Coal Mining, and Petroleum Systems are included in the Industry economic sector. A portion of CO_2 from Other Process Uses of Carbonates (from pollution control equipment installed in large industrial facilities) is also included in the Industry economic sector. Finally, all remaining CO_2 emissions from Non-Energy Uses of Fossil Fuels are assumed to be industrial in nature (besides the lubricants for transportation vehicles specified above) and are attributed to the Industry economic sector.

The *Agriculture* economic sector includes CO_2 emissions from the combustion of fossil fuels that are based on supplementary sources of agriculture fuel use data, because EIA does not include an agriculture fuel-consuming sector. Agriculture equipment is included in the EIA industrial fuel-consuming sector. Agriculture fuel use estimates are obtained from U.S. Department of Agriculture survey data, in combination with separate EIA fuel sales reports (USDA 2018; EIA 2019b). These supplementary data are subtracted from the industrial fuel use reported by EIA to

Source: *U.S. EPA, Inventory of U.S. Greenhouse Gas Emissions and Sinks: 1990–2017*

obtain agriculture fuel use. CO_2 emissions from fossil fuel combustion, and CH_4 and N_2O emissions from stationary and mobile combustion, are then apportioned to the Agriculture economic sector based on agricultural fuel use.

The other IPCC Agriculture emission source categories apportioned to the Agriculture economic sector include N_2O emissions from Agricultural Soils, CH_4 from Enteric Fermentation, CH_4 and N_2O from Manure Management, CH_4 from Rice Cultivation, CO_2 emissions from Liming and Urea Application, and CH_4 and N_2O from Field Burning of Agricultural Residues.

The *Residential* economic sector includes CO_2 emissions from the combustion of fossil fuels that are included in the EIA residential fuel-consuming sector. Stationary combustion emissions of CH_4 and N_2O are also based on the EIA residential fuel-consuming sector. Substitution of Ozone Depleting Substances are apportioned to the Residential economic sector based on emissions from residential air-conditioning systems. Nitrous oxide emissions from the application of fertilizers to developed land (termed "settlements" by the IPCC) are also included in the Residential economic sector.

The *Commercial* economic sector includes CO_2 emissions from the combustion of fossil fuels that are included in the EIA commercial fuel-consuming sector. Emissions of CH_4 and N_2O from Mobile Combustion are also apportioned to the Commercial economic sector based on the EIA commercial fuel-consuming sector. Substitution of Ozone Depleting Substances emissions are apportioned to the Commercial economic sector based on emissions from commercial refrigeration/air-conditioning systems. Public works sources, including direct CH_4 from Landfills, CH_4 and N_2O from Wastewater Treatment, and Composting, are also included in the Commercial economic sector.

Box 2-2: Recent Trends in Various U.S. Greenhouse Gas Emissions-Related Data

Total greenhouse gas emissions can be compared to other economic and social indices to highlight changes over time. These comparisons include: (1) emissions per unit of aggregate energy use, because energy-related activities are the largest sources of emissions; (2) emissions per unit of fossil fuel consumption, because almost all energy-related emissions involve the combustion of fossil fuels; (3) emissions per unit of electricity use, because the electric power industry—utilities and non-utilities combined—was the second largest source of emissions in 2017; (4) emissions per unit of total gross domestic product as a measure of national economic activity; and (5) emissions per capita.

Table 2-14 provides data on various statistics related to U.S. greenhouse gas emissions normalized to 1990 as a baseline year. These values represent the relative change in each statistic since 1990. Greenhouse gas emissions in the United States have grown at an average annual rate of 0.1 percent since 1990. This growth rate is slightly slower than that for total energy use and fossil fuel consumption, and much slower than that for electricity use, overall gross domestic product (GDP) and national population (see Table 2-14 and Figure 2-16). These trends vary after 2005, when greenhouse gas emissions, total energy use and fossil fuel consumption began to peak. Greenhouse gas emissions in the United States have decreased at an average annual rate of 1.0 percent since 2005. Total energy use and fossil fuel consumption have also decreased at slower rates than emissions since 2005, while electricity use, GDP, and national population continued to increase.

Table 2-14: Recent Trends in Various U.S. Data (Index 1990 = 100)

Variable	1990	2005	2013	2014	2015	2016	2017	Avg. Annual Change Since 1990[a]	Avg. Annual Change Since 2005[a]
Greenhouse Gas Emissions[b]	100	115	105	106	104	102	101	0.1%	-1.0%
Energy Use[c]	100	118	115	117	116	116	116	0.6%	-0.1%
Fossil Fuel Consumption[c]	100	119	110	111	110	109	108	0.3%	-0.7%
Electricity Use[c]	100	134	136	138	137	138	136	1.2%	0.1%
GDP[d]	100	159	176	180	186	189	193	2.5%	1.6%
Population[e]	100	118	126	127	128	129	130	1.0%	0.8%

\+ Does not exceed 0.05 percent.
[a] Average annual growth rate
[b] GWP-weighted values
[c] Energy-content-weighted values (EIA 2019a)

Source: *U.S. EPA, Inventory of U.S. Greenhouse Gas Emissions and Sinks: 1990–2017*

[d] GDP in chained 2009 dollars (BEA 2019)
[e] U.S. Census Bureau (2018)

Figure 2-16: U.S. Greenhouse Gas Emissions Per Capita and Per Dollar of Gross Domestic Product

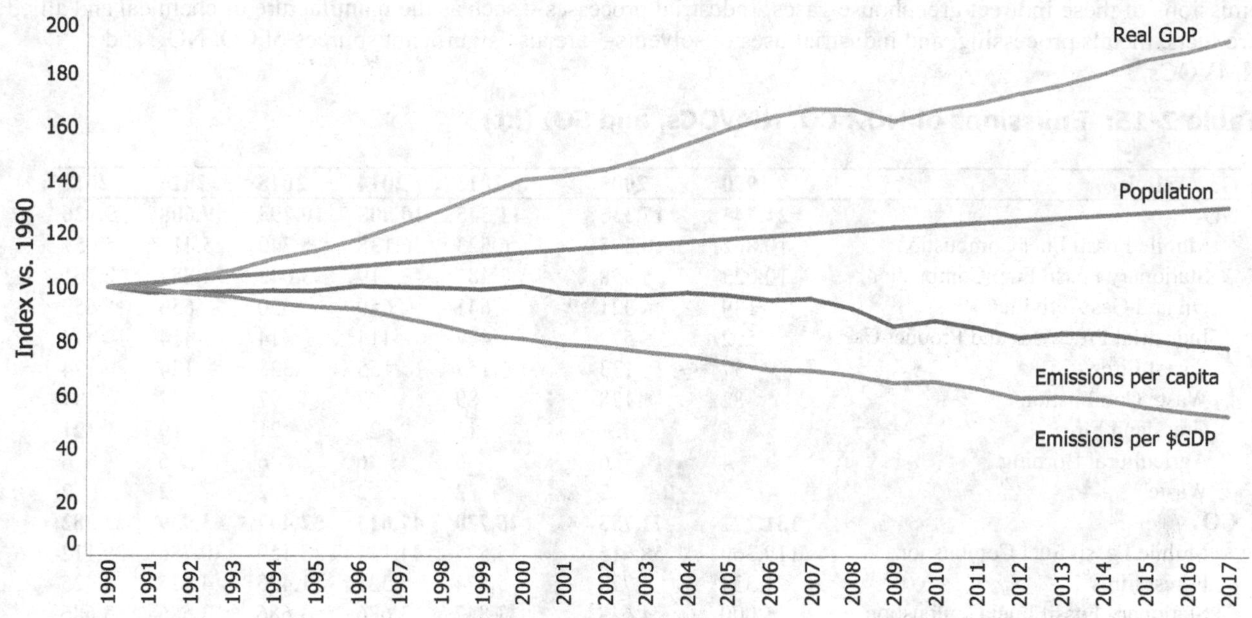

Source: BEA (2018), U.S. Census Bureau (2018), and emission estimates in this report.

2.3 Precursor Greenhouse Gas Emissions (CO, NO_x, NMVOCs, and SO_2)

The reporting requirements of the UNFCCC[9] request that information be provided on indirect greenhouse gases, which include CO, NO_x, NMVOCs, and SO_2. These gases are not direct greenhouse gases, but indirectly affect terrestrial radiation absorption by influencing the formation and destruction of tropospheric and stratospheric ozone, or, in the case of SO_2, by affecting the absorptive characteristics of the atmosphere. Additionally, some of these gases may react with other chemical compounds in the atmosphere to form compounds that are greenhouse gases. Carbon monoxide is produced when carbon-containing fuels are combusted incompletely. Nitrogen oxides (i.e., NO and NO_2) are created by lightning, fires, fossil fuel combustion, and in the stratosphere from N_2O. Non-methane volatile organic compounds—which include hundreds of organic compounds that participate in atmospheric chemical reactions (i.e., propane, butane, xylene, toluene, ethane, and many others)—are emitted primarily from transportation, industrial processes, and non-industrial consumption of organic solvents. In the United States, SO_2 is primarily emitted from coal combustion for electric power generation and the metals industry. Sulfur-containing compounds emitted into the atmosphere tend to exert a negative radiative forcing (i.e., cooling) and therefore are discussed separately.

One important indirect climate change effect of NMVOCs and NO_x is their role as precursors for tropospheric ozone formation. They can also alter the atmospheric lifetimes of other greenhouse gases. Another example of indirect

[9] See <http://unfccc.int/resource/docs/2013/cop19/eng/10a03.pdf>.

***Source:** U.S. EPA, Inventory of U.S. Greenhouse Gas Emissions and Sinks: 1990–2017*

greenhouse gas formation into greenhouse gases is the interaction of CO with the hydroxyl radical—the major atmospheric sink for CH_4 emissions—to form CO_2. Therefore, increased atmospheric concentrations of CO limit the number of hydroxyl molecules (OH) available to destroy CH_4.

Since 1970, the United States has published estimates of emissions of CO, NO_x, NMVOCs, and SO_2 (EPA 2018),[10] which are regulated under the Clean Air Act. Table 2-15 shows that fuel combustion accounts for the majority of emissions of these indirect greenhouse gases. Industrial processes—such as the manufacture of chemical and allied products, metals processing, and industrial uses of solvents—are also significant sources of CO, NO_x, and NMVOCs.

Table 2-15: Emissions of NO_x, CO, NMVOCs, and SO_2 (kt)

Gas/Activity	1990	2005	2013	2014	2015	2016	2017
NO_x	**21,745**	**17,336**	**11,345**	**10,808**	**10,293**	**9,608**	**9,126**
Mobile Fossil Fuel Combustion	10,862	10,295	6,523	6,138	5,740	5,413	5,051
Stationary Fossil Fuel Combustion	10,023	5,858	3,487	3,319	3,042	2,882	2,761
Oil and Gas Activities	139	321	641	650	650	650	650
Industrial Processes and Product Use	592	572	427	414	414	414	414
Forest Fires	37	133	157	155	321	124	124
Waste Combustion	82	128	89	97	97	97	97
Grassland Fires	5	21	13	27	21	19	21
Agricultural Burning	4	6	6	6	6	6	6
Waste	+	2	2	2	2	2	2
CO	**131,277**	**71,783**	**48,720**	**47,613**	**52,447**	**43,039**	**41,382**
Mobile Fossil Fuel Combustion	119,360	58,615	35,525	34,135	33,159	30,786	29,112
Forest Fires	1,334	4,723	5,574	5,525	11,425	4,425	4,425
Stationary Fossil Fuel Combustion	5,000	4,648	3,847	3,686	3,686	3,686	3,686
Waste Combustion	978	1,403	1,518	1,776	1,776	1,776	1,776
Industrial Processes and Product Use	4,129	1,557	1,247	1,251	1,251	1,251	1,251
Oil and Gas Activities	302	318	628	637	637	637	637
Grassland Fires	84	358	217	442	356	324	345
Agricultural Burning	89	154	157	152	148	144	141
Waste	1	7	7	8	8	8	8
NMVOCs	**20,930**	**13,154**	**11,332**	**11,130**	**10,965**	**10,719**	**10,513**
Industrial Processes and Product Use	7,638	5,849	3,855	3,816	3,816	3,816	3,816
Mobile Fossil Fuel Combustion	10,932	5,724	4,023	3,754	3,589	3,342	3,137
Oil and Gas Activities	554	510	2,741	2,853	2,853	2,853	2,853
Stationary Fossil Fuel Combustion	912	716	532	497	497	497	497
Waste Combustion	222	241	122	143	143	143	143
Waste	673	114	58	68	68	68	68
Agricultural Burning	NA	NA	NA	NA	NA	NA	NA
SO_2	**20,935**	**13,196**	**4,421**	**4,241**	**3,343**	**2,686**	**2,553**
Stationary Fossil Fuel Combustion	18,407	11,541	3,644	3,532	2,635	1,978	1,846
Industrial Processes and Product Use	1,307	831	548	498	498	498	498
Mobile Fossil Fuel Combustion	390	180	99	94	94	94	94
Oil and Gas Activities	793	619	106	88	87	87	87
Waste Combustion	38	25	23	27	27	27	27
Waste	+	1	1	1	1	1	1
Agricultural Burning	NA	NA	NA	NA	NA	NA	NA

\+ Does not exceed 0.5 kt.
NA (Not Available)
Note: Totals may not sum due to independent rounding.
Source: (EPA 2018) except for estimates from Forest Fires, Grassland Fires, and Field Burning of Agricultural Residues.

[10] NO_x and CO emission estimates from Field Burning of Agricultural Residues were estimated separately, and therefore not taken from EPA (2018).

Source: *U.S. EPA, Inventory of U.S. Greenhouse Gas Emissions and Sinks: 1990–2017*

Box 2-3: Sources and Effects of Sulfur Dioxide

Sulfur dioxide (SO_2) emitted into the atmosphere through natural and anthropogenic processes affects the earth's radiative budget through its photochemical transformation into sulfate aerosols that can:

(1) scatter radiation from the sun back to space, thereby reducing the radiation reaching the earth's surface;
(2) affect cloud formation; and
(3) affect atmospheric chemical composition (e.g., by providing surfaces for heterogeneous chemical reactions).

The indirect effect of sulfur-derived aerosols on radiative forcing can be considered in two parts. The first indirect effect is the aerosols' tendency to decrease water droplet size and increase water droplet concentration in the atmosphere. The second indirect effect is the tendency of the reduction in cloud droplet size to affect precipitation by increasing cloud lifetime and thickness. Although still highly uncertain, the radiative forcing estimates from both the first and the second indirect effect are believed to be negative, as is the combined radiative forcing of the two (IPCC 2013).

Sulfur dioxide is also a major contributor to the formation of regional haze, which can cause significant increases in acute and chronic respiratory diseases. Once SO_2 is emitted, it is chemically transformed in the atmosphere and returns to the earth as the primary source of acid rain. Because of these harmful effects, the United States has regulated SO_2 emissions in the Clean Air Act.

Electric power is the largest anthropogenic source of SO_2 emissions in the United States, accounting for 49.2 percent in 2017. Coal combustion contributes nearly all of those emissions (approximately 92 percent). Sulfur dioxide emissions have decreased in recent years, primarily as a result of electric power generators switching from high-sulfur to low-sulfur coal and installing flue gas desulfurization equipment.

Source: *U.S. EPA, Inventory of U.S. Greenhouse Gas Emissions and Sinks: 1990–2017*

Green Metro Area Rankings by Category

Metro Area	State	Air Quality[1]	Toxic Releases[2]	Superfund Sites[3]	Energy Use[4]	Motor Vehicle Use[5]	Mass Transit Use[6]	Overall Score[7]	Overall Rank[8]
Akron	OH	21	13	39	61	52	44	230	38
Albany	NY	9	29	65	72	58	21	254	53
Albuquerque	NM	60	6	47	40	17	41	211	31
Allentown	PA	25	44	70	53	16	59	267	57
Atlanta	GA	43	23	6	24	63	28	187	18
Austin	TX	31	15	3	23	21	22	115	1
Bakersfield	CA	72	57	25	12	1	62	229	37
Baltimore	MD	44	18	40	45	42	7	196	22
Baton Rouge	LA	37	74	52	13	54	69	299	64
Birmingham	AL	55	69	34	25	73	72	328	73
Boston	MA	36	8	66	49	35	10	204	28
Buffalo	NY	15	26	35	66	31	50	223	33
Charleston	SC	2	68	33	14	20	64	201	27
Charlotte	NC	34	41	60	28	55	23	241	46
Chicago	IL	68	65	31	68	12	8	252	52
Cincinnati	OH	57	51	36	48	59	55	306	66
Cleveland	OH	46	59	4	60	34	33	236	40
Columbus	OH	22	40	2	52	40	45	201	24
Dallas-Ft. Worth	TX	50	17	7	32	48	47	201	25
Dayton	OH	39	35	75	56	57	36	298	63
Denver	CO	69	45	45	57	18	9	243	47
Detroit	MI	62	72	41	64	45	58	342	74
El Paso	TX	64	31	10	27	5	43	180	15
Fresno	CA	70	7	61	15	8	63	224	35
Grand Rapids	MI	8	49	69	73	56	32	287	61
Greensboro	NC	11	33	14	33	72	15	178	14
Greenville	SC	7	36	57	26	36	75	237	41
Hartford	CT	10	19	48	62	43	57	239	43
Honolulu	HI	1	46	42	22	3	6	120	4
Houston	TX	55	71	43	16	29	29	243	49
Indianapolis	IN	49	62	51	54	69	68	353	75
Jacksonville	FL	17	53	49	8	67	37	231	39
Kansas City	MO	42	48	38	58	65	60	311	69
Knoxville	TN	30	67	50	31	66	65	309	67
Las Vegas	NV	67	52	54	38	6	26	243	48
Little Rock	AR	20	34	13	34	71	67	239	44
Los Angeles	CA	74	20	15	2	33	14	158	11
Louisville	KY	45	61	27	44	60	35	272	58
Memphis	TN	27	60	62	35	51	70	305	65
Miami	FL	19	5	21	18	38	20	121	5
Milwaukee	WI	33	43	53	74	13	24	240	45
Minneapolis-St. Paul	MN	53	50	56	75	47	11	292	62
Nashville	TN	24	55	5	36	74	49	243	50
New Orleans	LA	38	73	29	11	4	51	206	29
New York-Northern NJ	NY	59	16	63	46	2	1	187	17
Oklahoma City	OK	41	3	24	41	75	74	258	56
Omaha	NE	35	54	46	70	9	71	285	60
Orlando	FL	5	22	30	9	61	19	146	10
Oxnard	CA	52	1	28	3	19	38	141	9
Philadelphia	PA	65	39	74	47	7	16	248	51
Phoenix	AZ	73	14	9	39	23	34	192	21
Pittsburgh	PA	63	66	12	55	11	13	220	32
Portland	OR	12	30	32	20	10	12	116	2
Providence	RI	18	12	71	51	24	48	224	34
Raleigh	NC	29	9	26	30	64	52	210	30

Metro Area	State	Air Quality[1]	Toxic Releases[2]	Superfund Sites[3]	Energy Use[4]	Motor Vehicle Use[5]	Mass Transit Use[6]	Overall Score[7]	Overall Rank[8]
Richmond	VA	12	58	44	37	62	42	255	55
Riverside	CA	75	11	19	6	39	40	190	19
Rochester	NY	6	37	37	67	30	61	238	42
Sacramento	CA	66	27	23	7	14	46	183	16
Saint Louis	MO	58	56	64	50	68	25	321	70
Salt Lake City	UT	54	75	68	59	25	4	285	59
San Antonio	TX	23	32	17	21	28	17	138	7
San Diego	CA	71	10	1	1	32	18	133	6
San Francisco	CA	61	25	11	4	15	2	118	3
San Jose	CA	40	2	73	5	26	31	177	13
Seattle	WA	31	21	55	17	41	5	170	12
Springfield	MA	14	24	16	71	37	39	201	23
Syracuse	NY	4	47	59	69	46	30	255	54
Tampa-St. Petersburg	FL	27	28	58	10	50	53	226	36
Toledo	OH	16	70	72	65	44	54	321	71
Tucson	AZ	47	64	8	19	27	27	192	20
Tulsa	OK	51	63	22	42	70	73	321	72
Virginia Beach	VA	3	42	18	29	53	56	201	26
Washington	DC	48	4	20	43	22	3	140	8
Youngstown	OH	26	38	67	63	49	66	309	68

Note: *The Green Metro Index compares 75 major metropolitan areas in the U.S. on measures of environmental quality and performance appropriate to metro areas as a whole. The index is based on federal and private data for six environmental measures including: air quality, toxic releases, superfund sites, energy use, mass transit use and motor vehicle use; The figures above rank how each metro area fared in each category. Lower numbers are better; (1) Based on the percent of days the Air Quality Index (AQI) was in the "Good" range in 2018; (2) Calculated by adding the total toxic releases for each metro area and dividing by the metro area population. Data is from the Environmental Protection Agency's Toxic Release Inventory for 2017; (3) Based on the per capita number of final and proposed Superfund Sites located within each metro area. Data is from the Environmental Protection Agency's Superfund National Priorities list (data extracted 7/2/2019); (4) Based on total heating and cooling degree days per year. Data is from Weather America, A Thirty-Year Summary of Statistical Weather Data and Rankings, 2011; (5) Based on the DVMT (daily vehicle-miles of travel) per capita for each urbanized area. Data is from the Department of Transportation's Urbanized Areas: 2011 Selected Characteristics report; (6) Calculated by dividing the total vehicle revenue miles by the population of the urbanized area. Data is from the Federal Transit Administration's 2017 National Transit Summaries and Trends report; (7) The overall score was calculated by combining the rankings of all six environmental indicators, giving equal weight to each indicator; (8) 1=best, 75=worst*

Sources: *U.S Environmental Protection Agency; U.S. Department of Transportation; Federal Transit Administration; Grey House Publishing, Weather America, A Thirty-Year Summary of Statistical Weather Data and Rankings, 2011*

Green Metro Area Overall Rankings

Metro Area	State	Overall Rank[1]	Overall Score[2]
Austin	TX	1	115
Portland	OR	2	116
San Francisco	CA	3	118
Honolulu	HI	4	120
Miami	FL	5	121
San Diego	CA	6	133
San Antonio	TX	7	138
Washington	DC	8	140
Oxnard	CA	9	141
Orlando	FL	10	146
Los Angeles	CA	11	158
Seattle	WA	12	170
San Jose	CA	13	177
Greensboro	NC	14	178
El Paso	TX	15	180
Sacramento	CA	16	183
New York-Northern NJ	NY	17	187
Atlanta	GA	18	187
Riverside	CA	19	190
Tucson	AZ	20	192
Phoenix	AZ	21	192
Baltimore	MD	22	196
Springfield	MA	23	201
Columbus	OH	24	201
Dallas-Ft. Worth	TX	25	201
Virginia Beach	VA	26	201
Charleston	SC	27	201
Boston	MA	28	204
New Orleans	LA	29	206
Raleigh	NC	30	210
Albuquerque	NM	31	211
Pittsburgh	PA	32	220
Buffalo	NY	33	223
Providence	RI	34	224
Fresno	CA	35	224
Tampa-St. Petersburg	FL	36	226
Bakersfield	CA	37	229
Akron	OH	38	230
Jacksonville	FL	39	231
Cleveland	OH	40	236
Greenville	SC	41	237
Rochester	NY	42	238
Hartford	CT	43	239
Little Rock	AR	44	239
Milwaukee	WI	45	240
Charlotte	NC	46	241
Denver	CO	47	243
Las Vegas	NV	48	243
Houston	TX	49	243
Nashville	TN	50	243
Philadelphia	PA	51	248
Chicago	IL	52	252
Albany	NY	53	254
Syracuse	NY	54	255
Richmond	VA	55	255
Oklahoma City	OK	56	258

Metro Area	State	Overall Rank[1]	Overall Score[2]
Allentown	PA	57	267
Louisville	KY	58	272
Salt Lake City	UT	59	285
Omaha	NE	60	285
Grand Rapids	MI	61	287
Minneapolis-St. Paul	MN	62	292
Dayton	OH	63	298
Baton Rouge	LA	64	299
Memphis	TN	65	305
Cincinnati	OH	66	306
Knoxville	TN	67	309
Youngstown	OH	68	309
Kansas City	MO	69	311
Saint Louis	MO	70	321
Toledo	OH	71	321
Tulsa	OK	72	321
Birmingham	AL	73	328
Detroit	MI	74	342
Indianapolis	IN	75	353

***Note:** The Green Metro Index compares 75 major metropolitan areas in the U.S. on measures of environmental quality and performance appropriate to metro areas as a whole. The index is based on federal data for six environmental measures including: air quality, toxic releases, superfund sites, energy use, mass transit use and motor vehicle use; (1) A lower number indicates better environmental quality or performance; (2) The overall score was calculated by combining the rankings of all six environmental indicators, giving equal weight to each indicator.*

***Sources:** U.S Environmental Protection Agency; U.S. Department of Transportation; Federal Transit Administration; Grey House Publishing, Weather America, A Thirty-Year Summary of Statistical Weather Data and Rankings, 2011*

Broad Land Cover/Use

The contiguous 48 states, Hawaii, Puerto Rico, and the U.S. Virgin Islands cover over 1.94 billion acres of land and water; about 71 percent of this area is non-Federal rural land – nearly 1.4 billion acres.

Non-Federal rural lands are predominantly forest land (416 million acres), rangeland (404 million acres), and cropland (367 million acres).

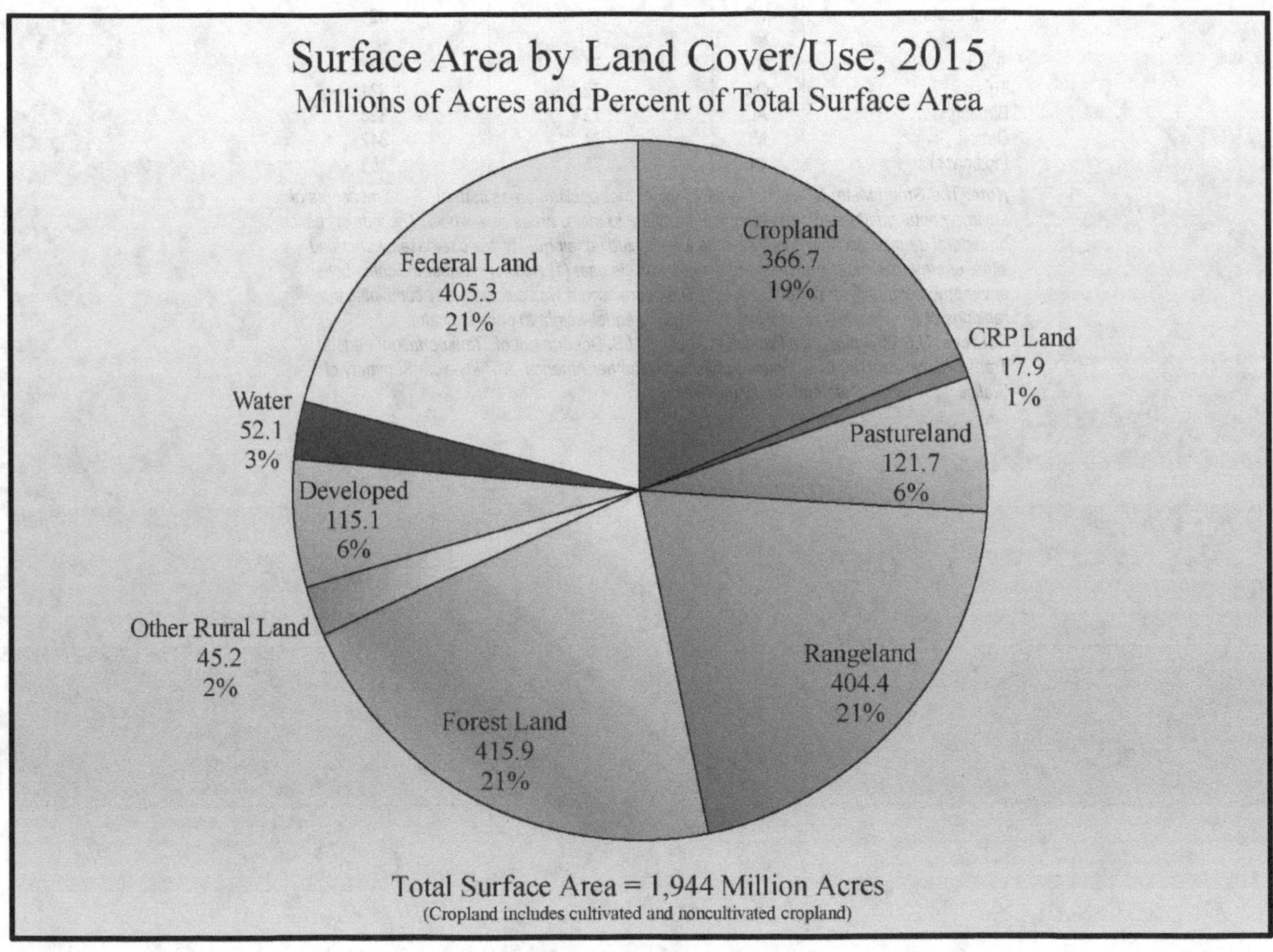

Source: *U.S. Department of Agriculture, 2015 National Resources Inventory, Summary Report, September 2018*

Rural Land Distribution

Below is a depiction of the distribution of the four primary rural land types (forest, rangeland, cropland, and pasture) across the 48 contiguous States, Hawaii, and the Caribbean territories.

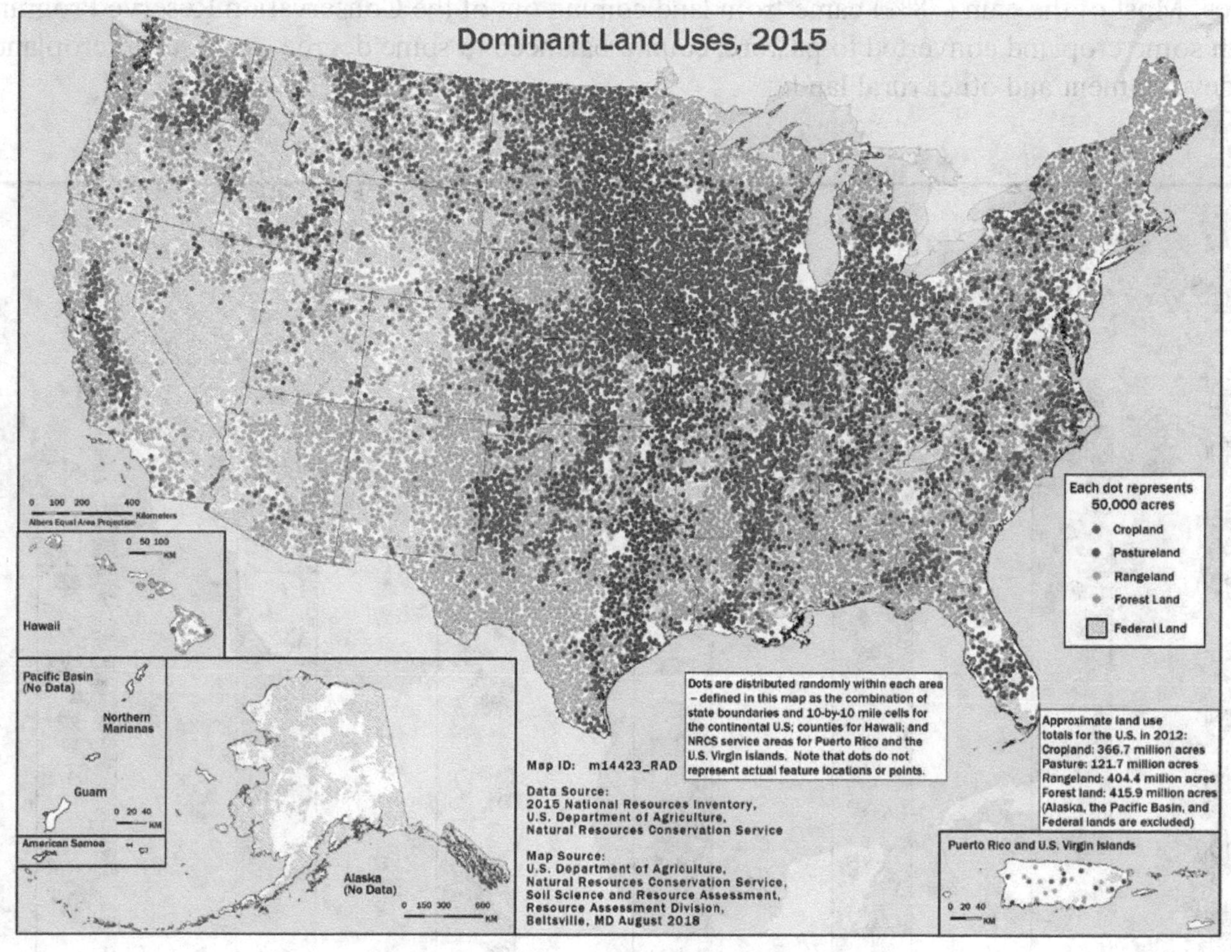

Source: *U.S. Department of Agriculture, 2015 National Resources Inventory, Summary Report, September 2018*

Cropland

Cropland acreage increased by about 4.6 million acres from 2012 to 2015. It had steadily declined since the NRI began in 1982 up until 2007 (25 years). Since 2007, it has increased every year. The increase since 2012 was a little less than 1.3 percent from 362 to 367 million acres. Most of the gain (78%) came from land coming out of the Conservation Reserve Program with some cropland converted to pasture, counterbalanced to some degree by losses of cropland to development and other rural land.

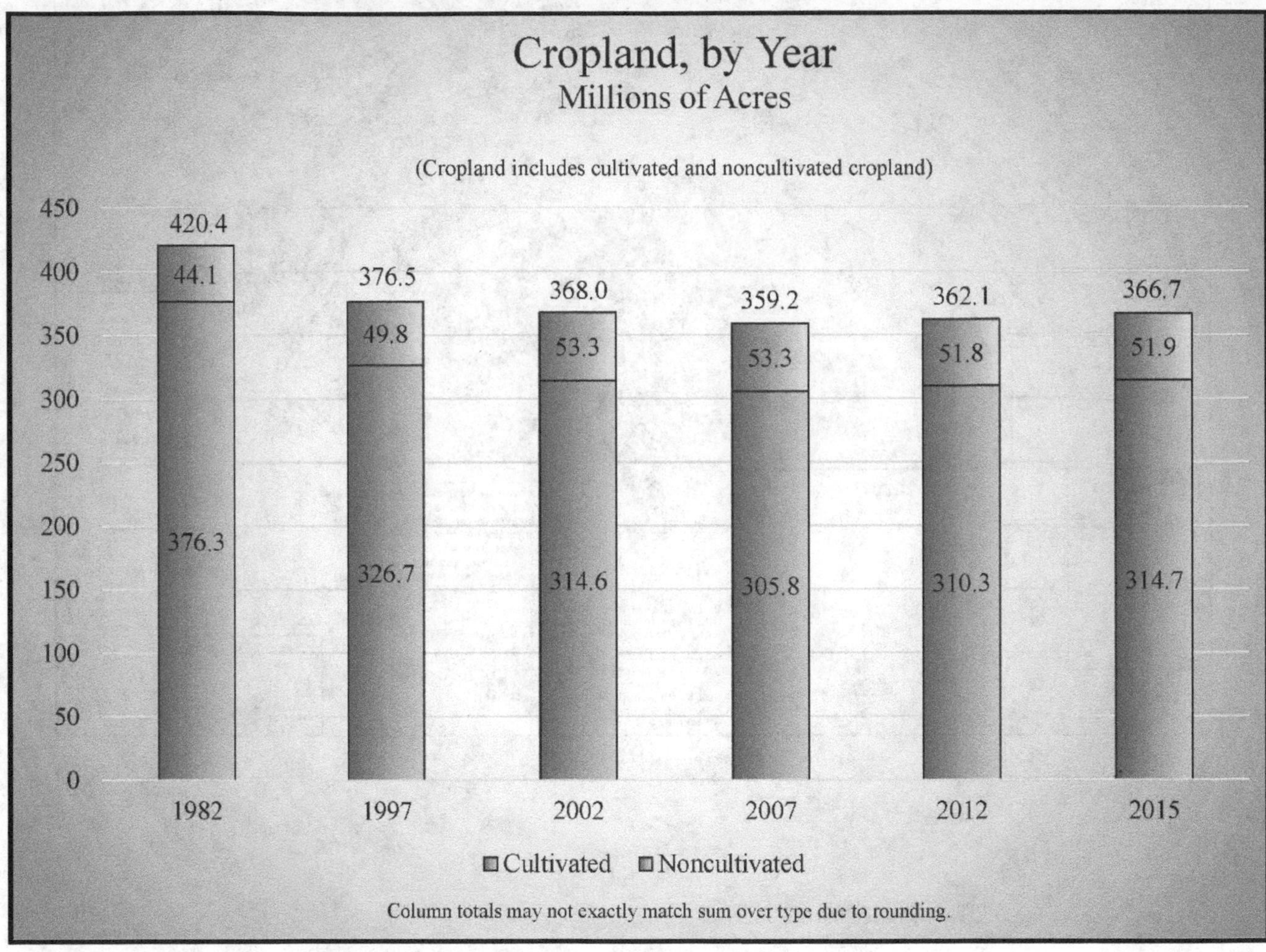

Source: *U.S. Department of Agriculture, 2015 National Resources Inventory, Summary Report, September 2018*

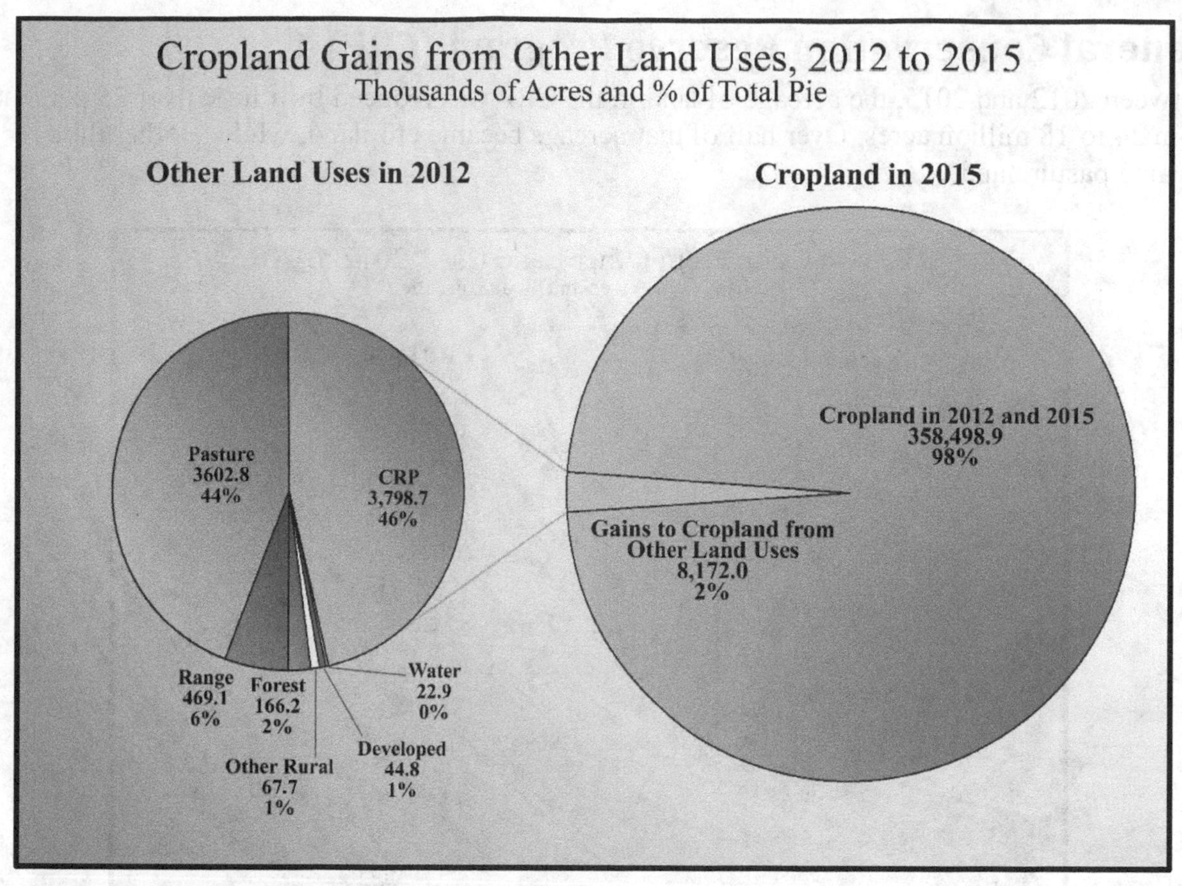

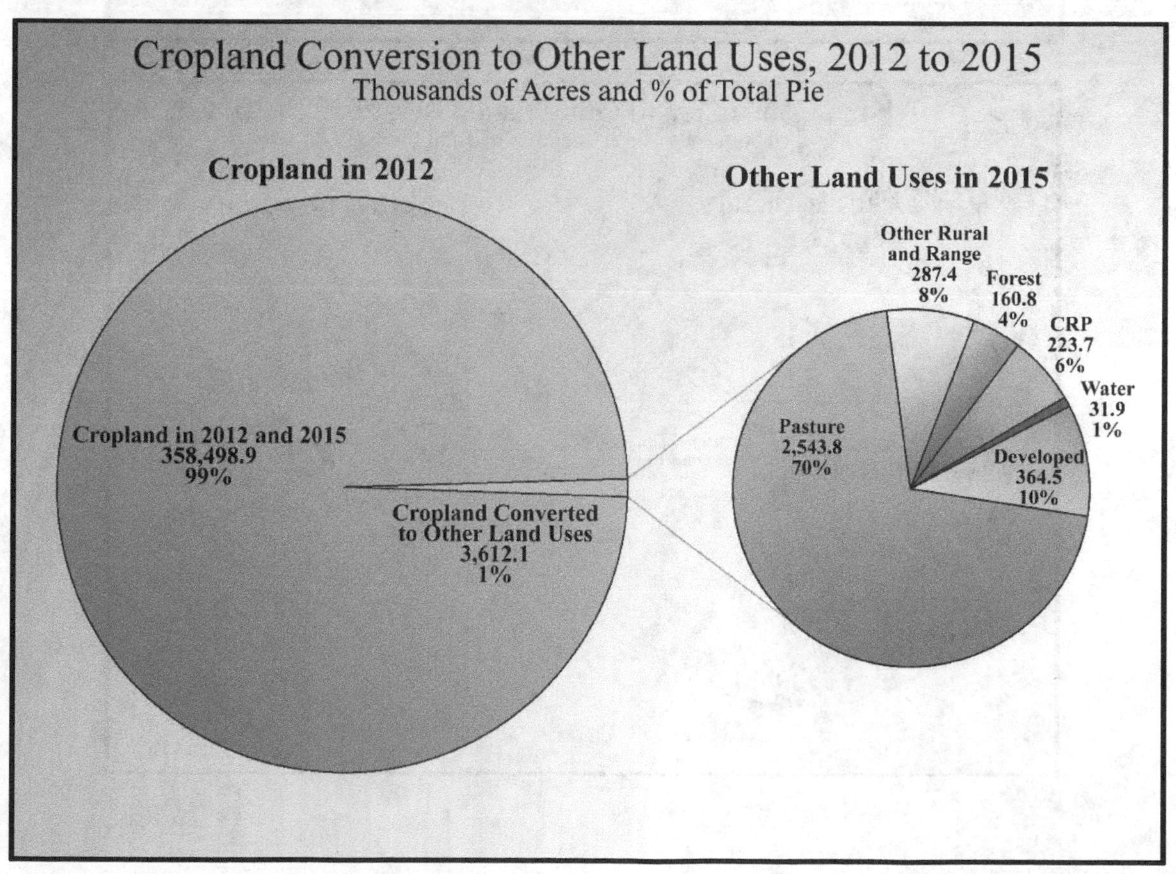

Source: *U.S. Department of Agriculture, 2015 National Resources Inventory, Summary Report, September 2018*

General Conservation Reserve Program (CRP)

Between 2012 and 2015, the acreage of land in the CRP was reduced by a little over 25 percent, from 24 to 18 million acres. Over half of that acreage became cropland, while another third became pastureland.

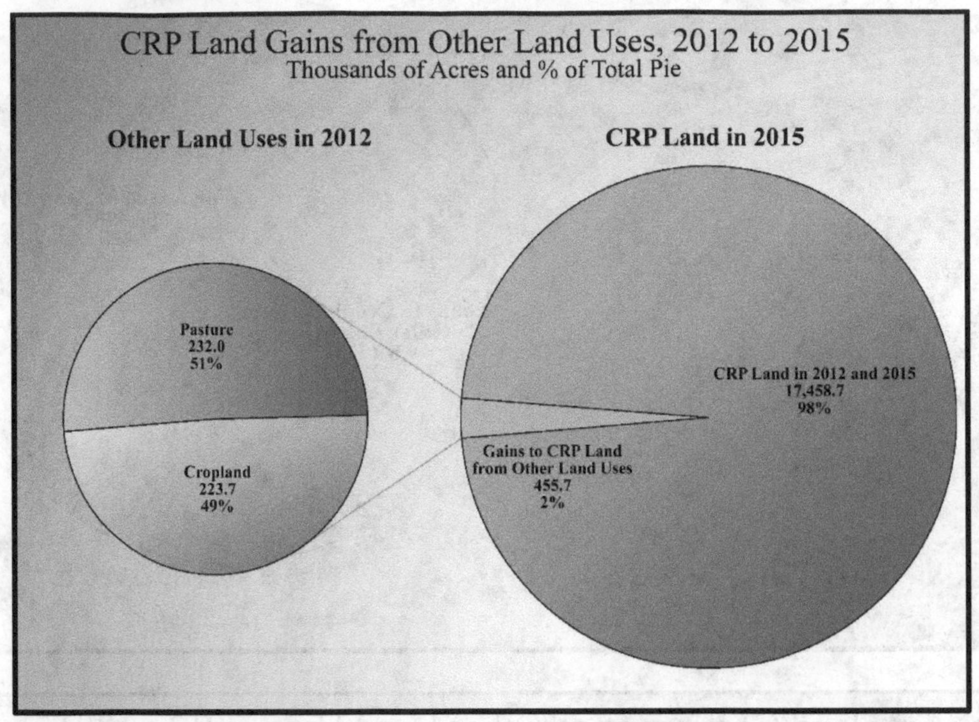

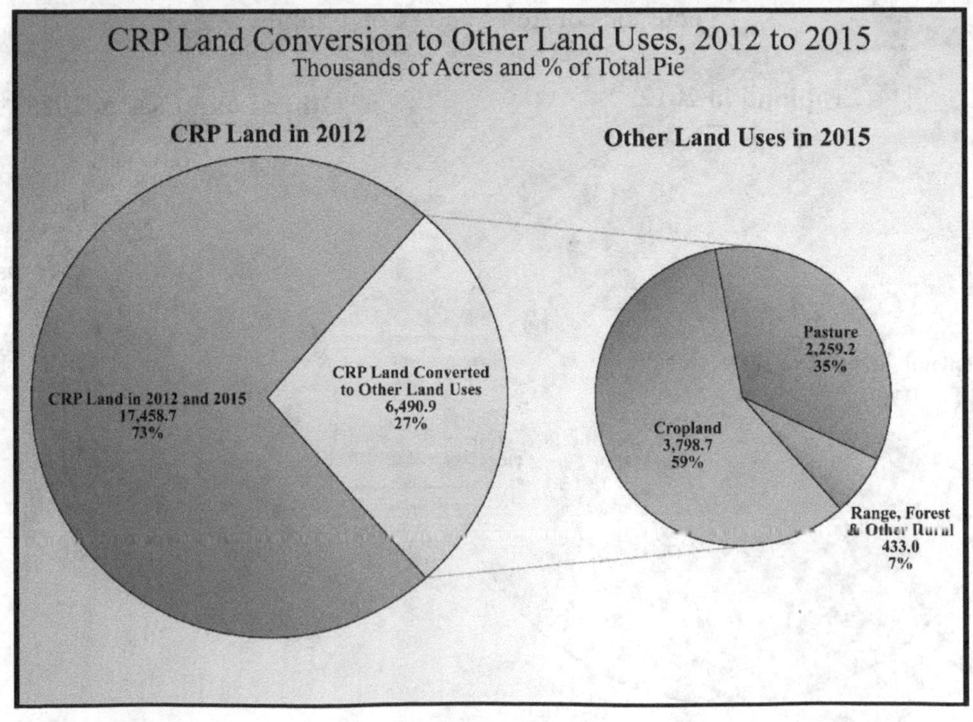

Source: *U.S. Department of Agriculture, 2015 National Resources Inventory, Summary Report, September 2018*

Development

About 43 million acres of land was newly developed between 1982 and 2015, bringing the total to about 115 million acres; that represents a 60 percent increase. Thus, more than 37 percent of developed land in the 48 conterminous states, Hawaii, Puerto Rico and the Virgin Islands was developed during the last 33 years.

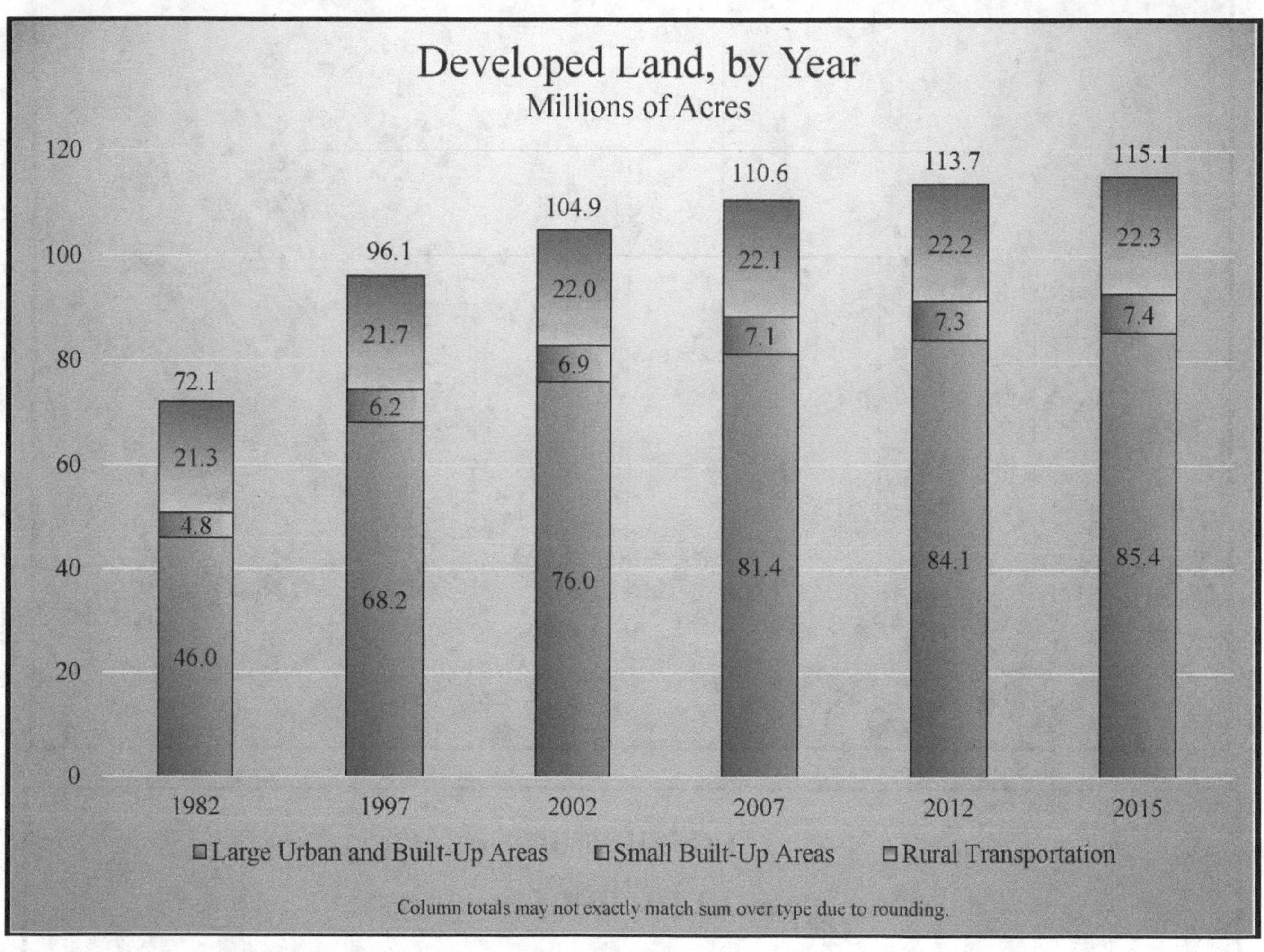

Source: *U.S. Department of Agriculture, 2015 National Resources Inventory, Summary Report, September 2018*

Newly Developed Land Continues to Slow

As the population has increased, the acres developed per person has dropped off.

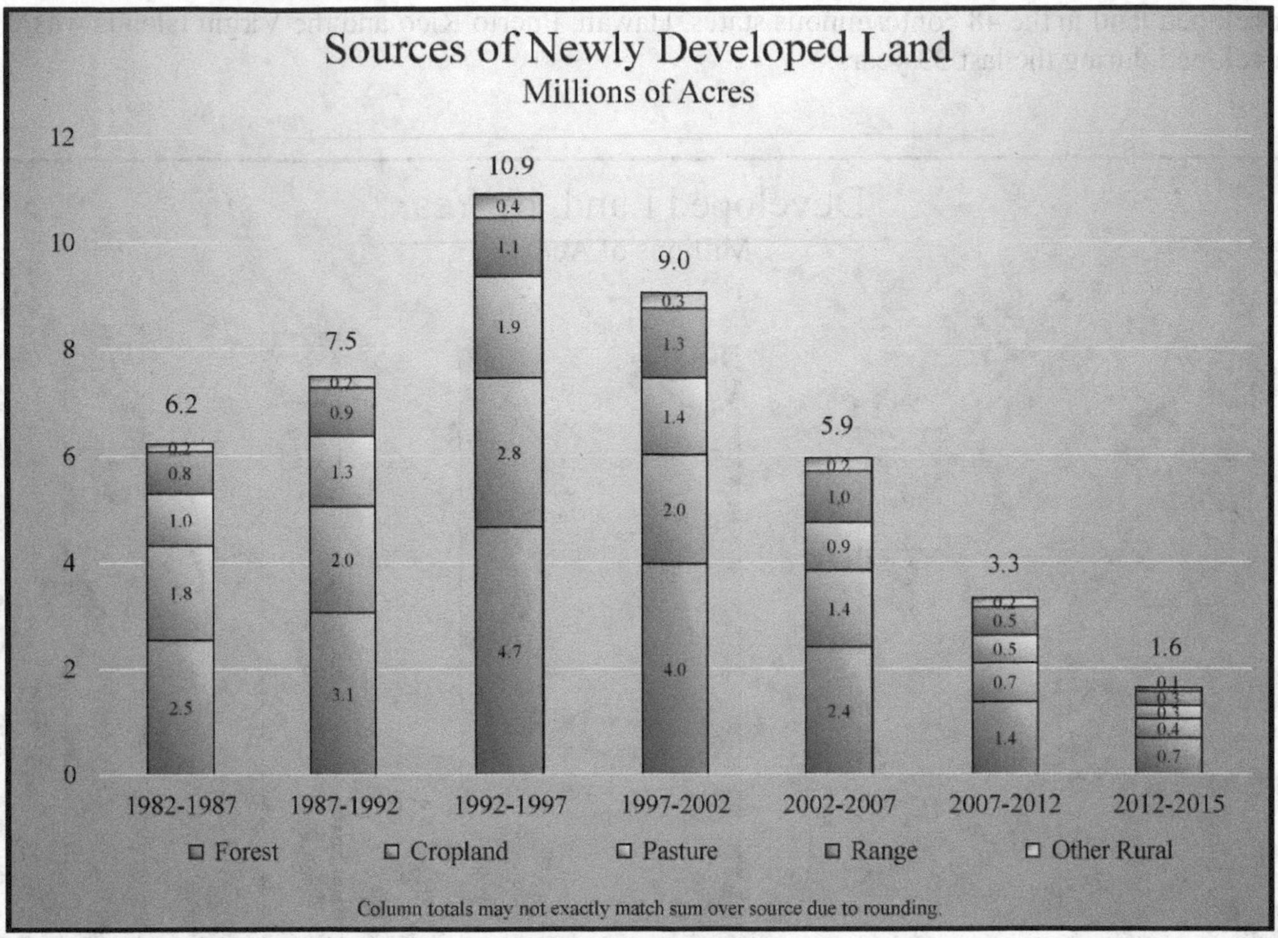

Sources of Newly Developed Land

Millions of Acres

	1982-1987	1987-1992	1992-1997	1997-2002	2002-2007	2007-2012	2012-2015
Total	6.2	7.5	10.9	9.0	5.9	3.3	1.6
Forest	2.5	3.1	4.7	4.0	2.4	1.4	0.7
Cropland	1.8	2.0	2.8	2.0	1.4	0.7	0.4
Pasture	1.0	1.3	1.9	1.4	0.9	0.5	[illegible]
Range	0.8	0.9	1.1	1.3	1.0	0.5	[illegible]
Other Rural	0.2	0.2	0.4	0.3	0.2	0.2	0.1

Column totals may not exactly match sum over source due to rounding.

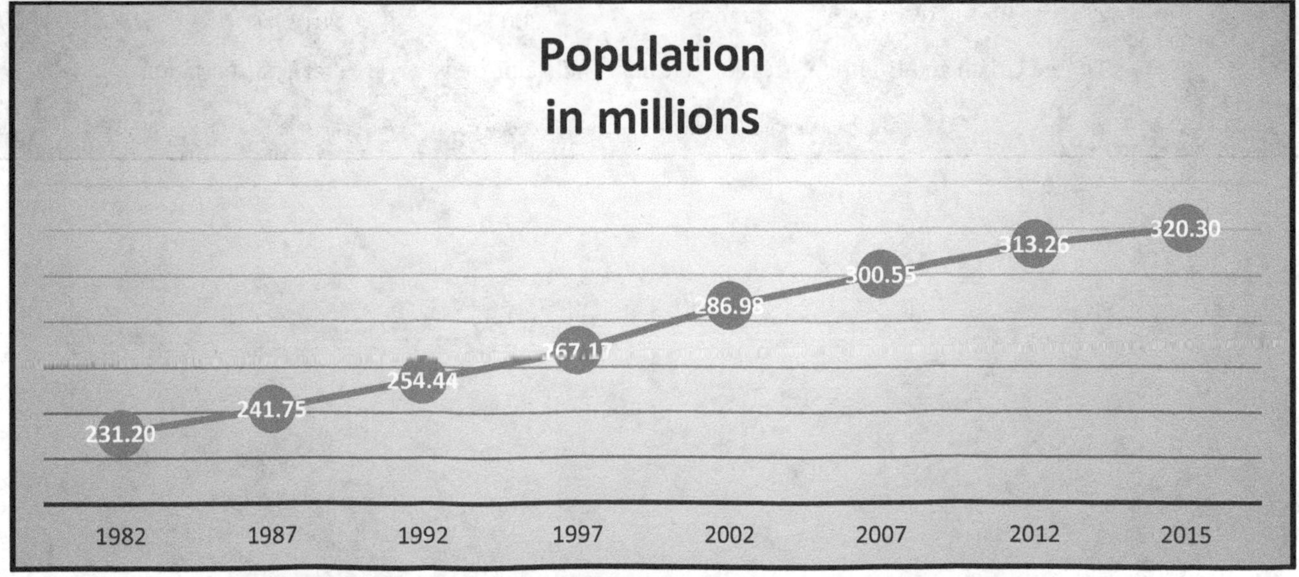

Source: *U.S. Department of Agriculture, 2015 National Resources Inventory, Summary Report, September 2018*

Erosion

Soil erosion rates on cropland decreased 34 percent between 1982 and 2015. The water (sheet and rill) erosion rate declined from 3.82 tons per acre per year to 2.71 tons per acre per year, and the erosion rate due to wind decreased from 3.21 tons per acre per year to 1.91 tons per acre per year. (See charts below and maps on the next page).

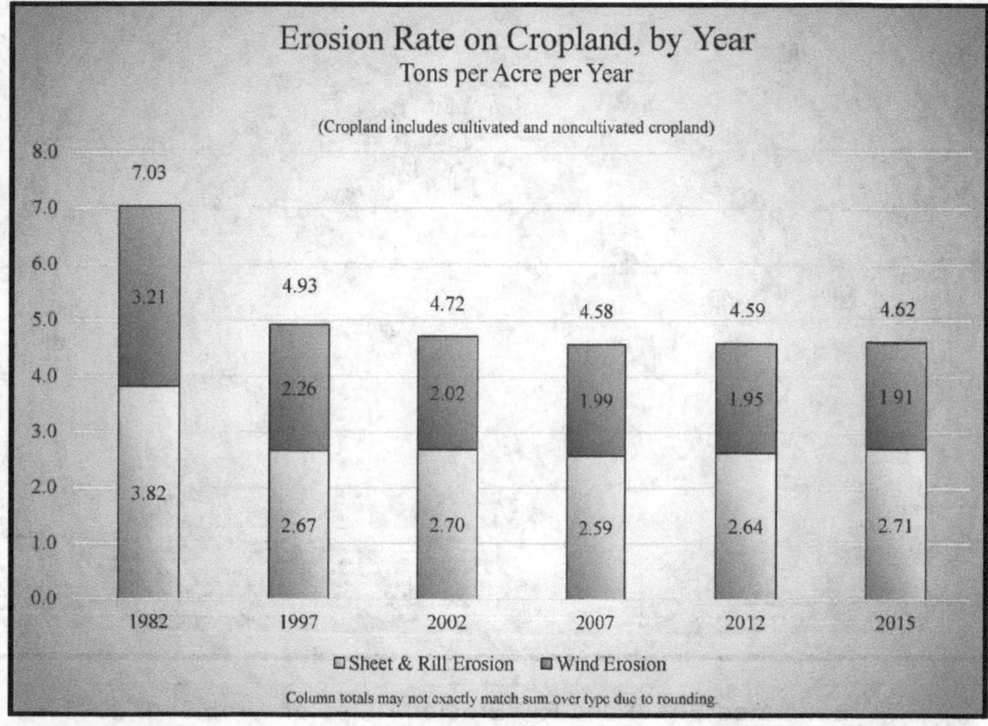

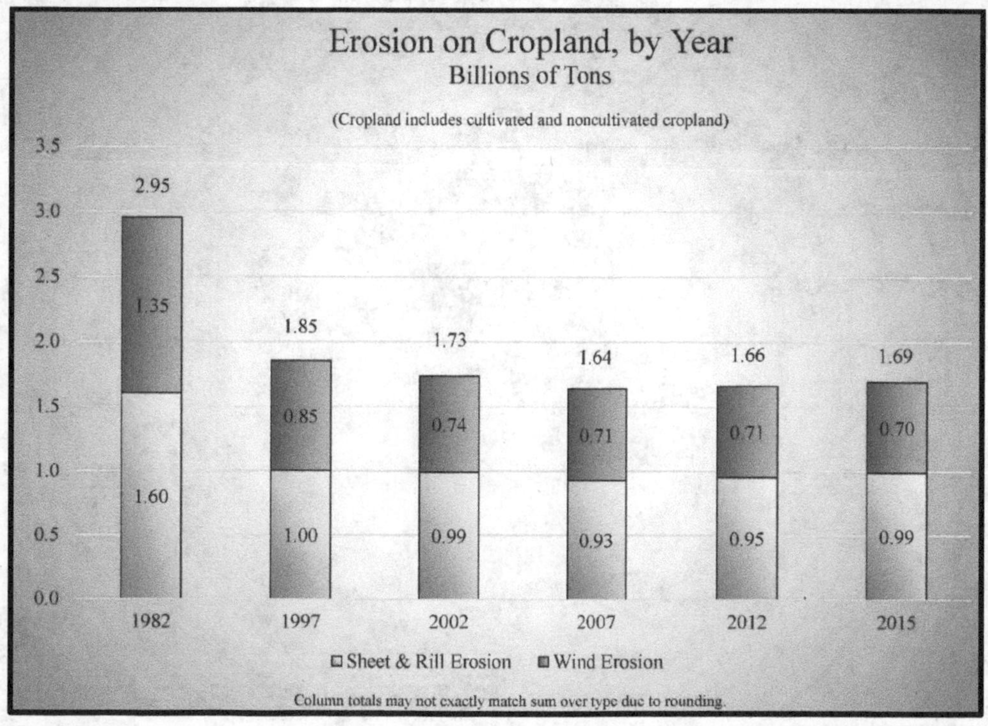

Source: *U.S. Department of Agriculture, 2015 National Resources Inventory, Summary Report, September 2018*

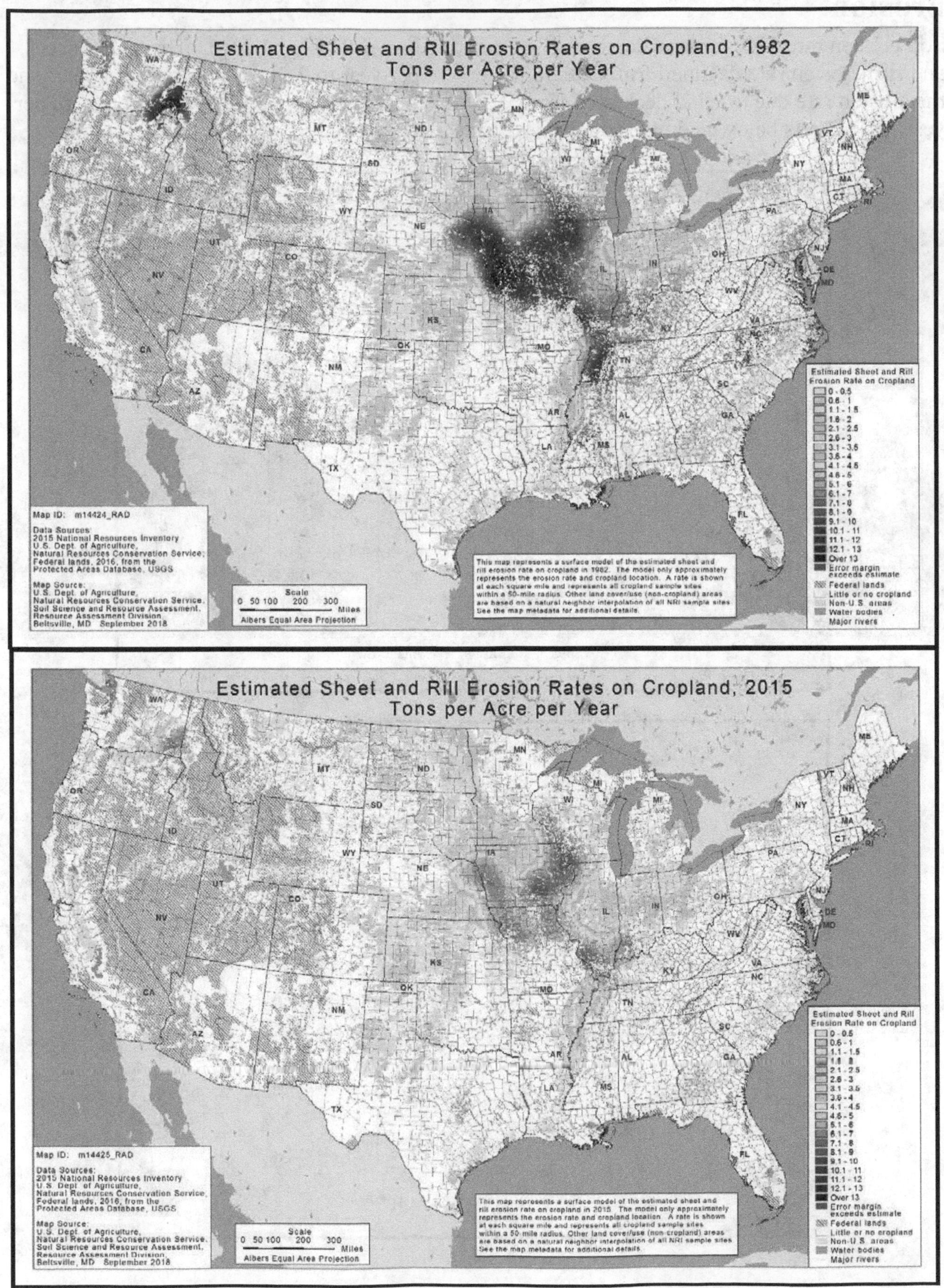

Source: *U.S. Department of Agriculture, 2015 National Resources Inventory, Summary Report, September 2018*

Wetlands

Palustrine and Estuarine wetlands covered 7.2 percent of the water and non-federal lands in the 48 conterminous states, Hawaii, Puerto Rico, and the Virgin Islands, with over half being in forest lands.

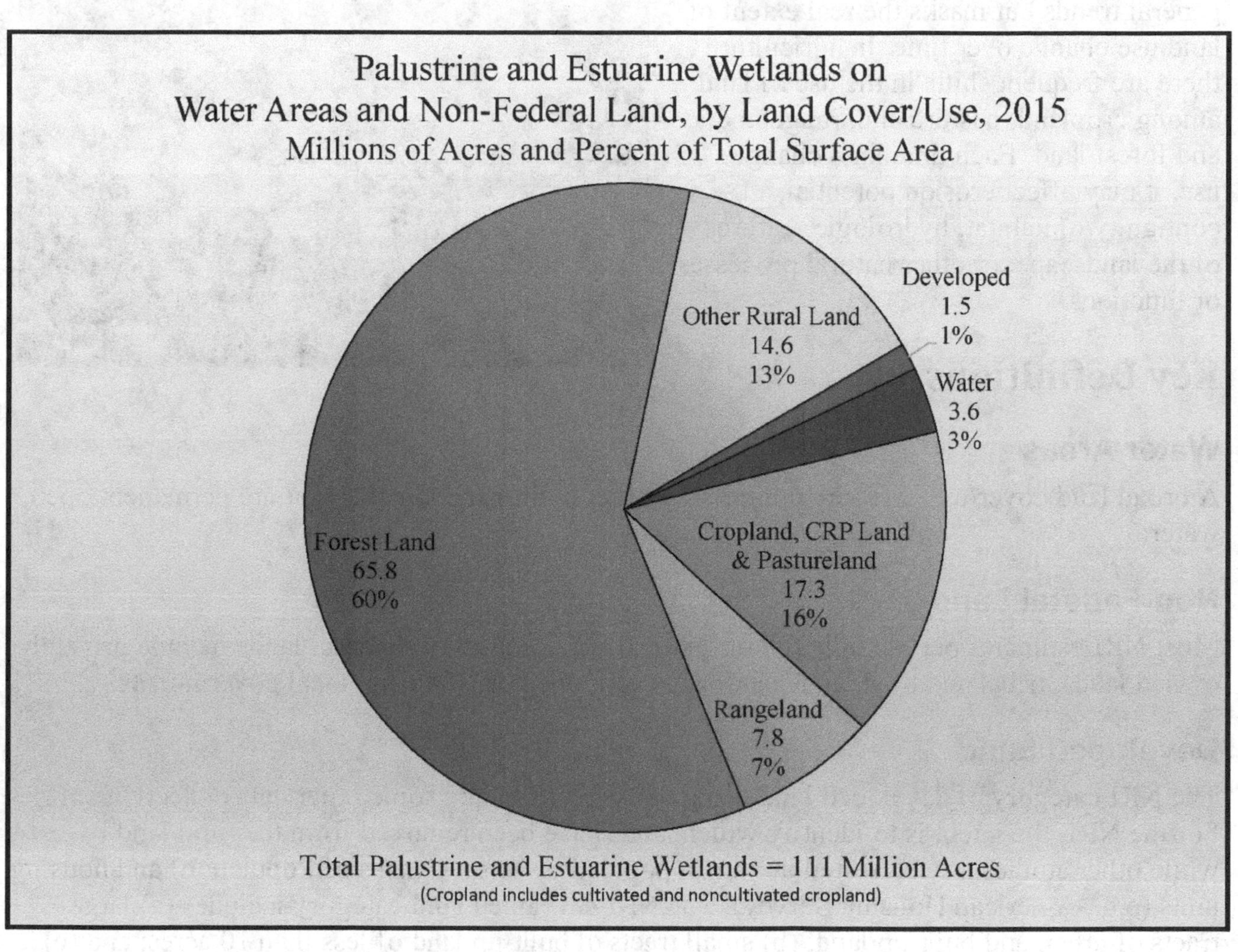

Source: *U.S. Department of Agriculture, 2015 National Resources Inventory, Summary Report, September 2018*

Broad Land Cover/Use

Land use is surprisingly dynamic, with annual shifts in and out of different uses. Examining net change in land use reveals general trends but masks the real extent of land use change over time. In agriculture there are frequent shifts in the use of land among cropland, pastureland, rangeland, and forest land. Each time land changes use, it may affect erosion potential, contiguity of habitat, hydrologic features of the landscape, or other natural processes or functions.

Key Definitions

Water Areas

A broad land cover/use category comprising water bodies and streams that are permanent open water.

Non-Federal Land

Most NRI estimates pertain only to non-Federal rural lands; non-Federal lands include privately owned lands, tribal and trust lands, and lands controlled by State and local governments.

Developed Land

The NRI category of developed land differs from that used by some other data collection entities. For the NRI, the intent is to identify which lands have been removed from the rural land base, while other studies are interested in human populations (e.g., Census of Population) and housing units (e.g., American Housing Survey). The NRI developed land category includes (a) large tracts of urban and built-up land; (b) small tracts of built-up land of less than 10 acres; and (c) land outside of these built-up areas that is in a rural transportation corridor (roads, railroads, and associated rights-of-way).

Cropland and Pastureland

These definitions are provided in Chapter 4.

Conservation Reserve Program (CRP) Land

This definition is provided in chapter 4.

Source: *U.S. Department of Agriculture, 2015 National Resources Inventory, Summary Report, September 2018*

Rangeland

A broad land cover/use category on which the climax or potential plant cover is composed principally of native grasses, grass-like plants, forbs or shrubs suitable for grazing and browsing, and introduced forage species that are managed like rangeland. This would include areas where introduced hardy and persistent grasses, such as crested wheatgrass, are planted and such practices as deferred grazing, burning, chaining, and rotational grazing are used, with little or no chemicals or fertilizer being applied. Grasslands, savannas, many wetlands, some deserts, and tundra are considered to be rangeland. Certain communities of low forbs and shrubs, such as mesquite, chaparral, mountain shrub, and pinyon-juniper, are also included as rangeland.

Forest Land

A broad land cover/use category that is at least 10 percent stocked by single-stemmed woody species of any size that will be at least 4 meters (13 feet) tall at maturity. Also included is land bearing evidence of natural regeneration of tree cover (cut over forest or abandoned farmland) and not currently developed for non-forest use. Ten percent stocked, when viewed from a vertical direction, equates to an areal canopy cover of leaves and branches of 25 percent or greater. The minimum area for classification as forest land is 1 acre, and the area must be at least 100 feet wide.

Other Rural Land

A broad land cover/use category that includes farmsteads and other land in farms, barren land, marshland, and permanent snow-ice.

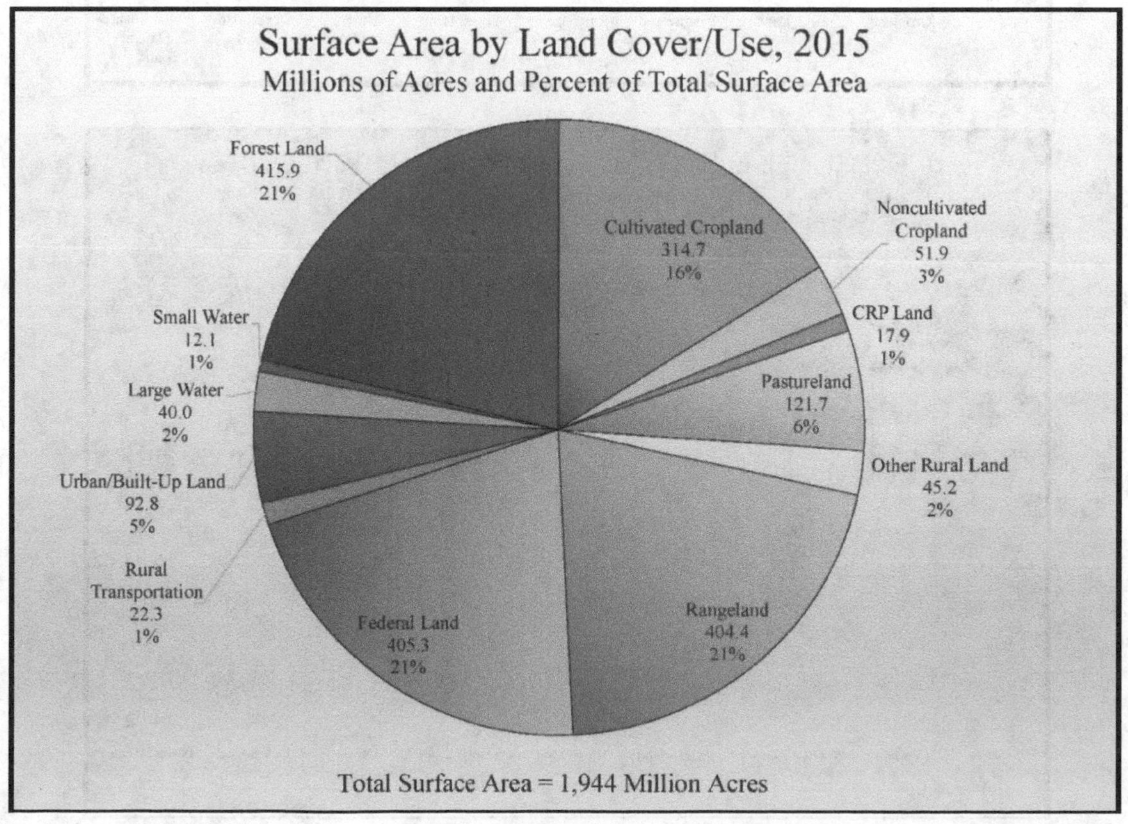

Source: *U.S. Department of Agriculture, 2015 National Resources Inventory, Summary Report, September 2018*

Change in Broad Land Cover/Use

The land cover/use change tables (3 – 8) show estimates of both gross change from one category to another between the two specific years, as well as net change from the initial year to the subsequent year along the bottom. Along the diagonal of each of these tables is an estimate of the acreage that was in the same land cover/use category in both years. Under each estimate is the margin of error, as discussed further in chapter 7. Note: there was no CRP in 1982.

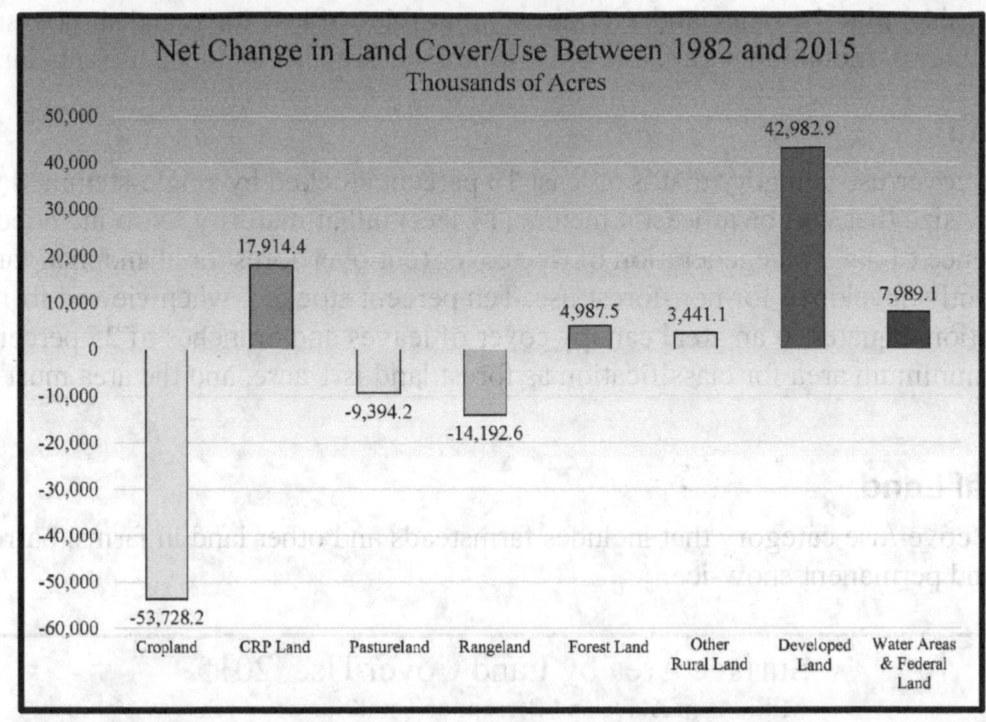

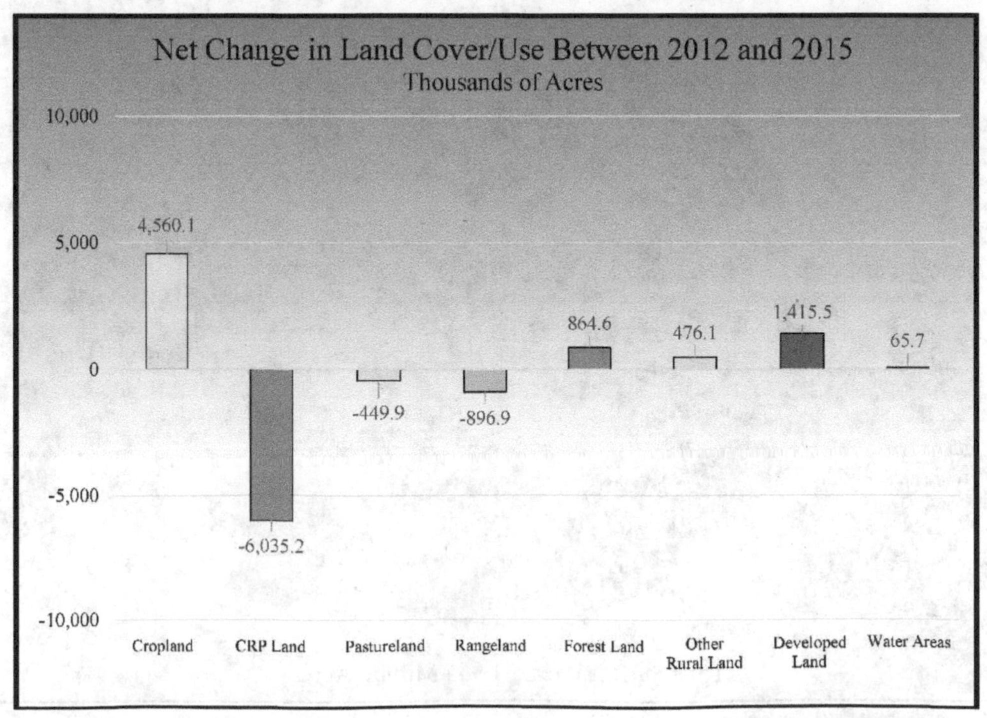

Source: *U.S. Department of Agriculture, 2015 National Resources Inventory, Summary Report, September 2018*

Table 1 - Surface area of non-Federal and Federal land and water areas, by State and year
In thousands of acres, with margins of error

State	Year	Federal land	Water areas	Non-Federal Land			Total surface area
				Developed	Rural	Total	
Alabama	1982	885.1 --	1,182.3 --	1,643.8 ±114.9	29,712.6 ±112.8	31,356.4 ±29.1	33,423.8 --
	1987	885.9 --	1,199.3 --	1,837.7 ±120.0	29,500.9 ±116.9	31,338.6 ±28.3	33,423.8 --
	1992	905.8 --	1,214.8 --	1,973.4 ±129.6	29,329.8 ±124.5	31,303.2 ±28.1	33,423.8 --
	1997	933.8 --	1,236.9 --	2,286.8 ±141.9	28,966.3 ±139.8	31,253.1 ±28.4	33,423.8 --
	2002	937.0 --	1,283.9 --	2,630.7 ±147.4	28,572.2 ±151.7	31,202.9 ±35.9	33,423.8 --
	2007	942.8 --	1,297.0 --	2,815.3 ±157.7	28,368.7 ±164.9	31,184.0 ±38.8	33,423.8 --
	2012	945.6 --	1,306.2 --	2,892.8 ±160.7	28,279.2 ±168.1	31,172.0 ±40.3	33,423.8 --
	2015	945.6 --	1,304.7 --	2,923.1 ±160.2	28,250.4 ±168.1	31,173.5 ±40.5	33,423.8 --
Arizona	1982	30,797.3 --	190.4 --	989.3 ±270.2	40,987.4 ±270.6	41,976.7 ±7.9	72,964.4 --
	1987	30,582.3 --	192.1 --	1,144.9 ±286.6	41,045.1 ±286.7	42,190.0 ±7.9	72,964.4 --
	1992	30,218.1 --	194.4 --	1,236.2 ±294.9	41,315.7 ±295.4	42,551.9 ±8.6	72,964.4 --
	1997	30,218.1 --	196.3 --	1,335.5 ±308.8	41,214.5 ±309.4	42,550.0 ±9.2	72,964.4 --
	2002	30,235.5 --	197.5 --	1,761.3 ±347.0	40,770.1 ±346.8	42,531.4 ±10.6	72,964.4 --
	2007	30,239.3 --	196.7 --	1,974.1 ±385.6	40,554.3 ±385.1	42,528.4 ±9.9	72,964.4 --
	2012	30,248.5 --	196.7 --	2,083.4 ±411.7	40,435.8 ±411.0	42,519.2 ±10.0	72,964.4 --
	2015	30,248.5 --	196.8 --	2,108.6 ±418.1	40,410.5 ±417.3	42,519.1 ±10.0	72,964.4 --
Arkansas	1982	3,182.7 --	809.2 --	1,219.7 ±95.1	28,825.3 ±100.1	30,045.0 ±26.1	34,036.9 --
	1987	3,190.1 --	843.1 --	1,259.9 ±99.5	28,743.8 ±104.7	30,003.7 ±25.9	34,036.9 --
	1992	3,243.9 --	848.9 --	1,326.3 ±103.9	28,617.8 ±108.5	29,944.1 ±26.2	34,036.9 --
	1997	3,243.9 --	875.7 --	1,512.4 ±109.2	28,404.9 ±113.3	29,917.3 ±30.0	34,036.9 --
	2002	3,263.6 --	889.3 --	1,667.6 ±116.4	28,216.4 ±119.8	29,884.0 ±30.0	34,036.9 --
	2007	3,246.2 --	892.4 --	1,782.0 ±122.3	28,116.3 ±125.4	29,898.3 ±30.8	34,036.9 --
	2012	3,250.9 --	897.1 --	1,849.9 ±126.9	28,039.0 ±128.6	29,888.9 ±30.6	34,036.9 --
	2015	3,250.9 --	888.6 --	1,870.2 ±125.7	28,027.2 ±126.2	29,897.4 ±22.8	34,036.9 --

Source: *U.S. Department of Agriculture, 2015 National Resources Inventory, Summary Report, September 2018*

Table 1 - Surface area of non-Federal and Federal land and water areas, by State and year
In thousands of acres, with margins of error

State	Year	Federal land	Water areas	Non-Federal Land			Total surface area
				Developed	Rural	Total	
California	1982	45,913.3 --	1,794.7 --	4,093.3 ±351.0	49,708.9 ±349.6	53,802.2 ±28.6	101,510.2 --
	1987	45,937.5 --	1,800.9 --	4,354.7 ±365.9	49,417.1 ±363.4	53,771.8 ±28.9	101,510.2 --
	1992	46,542.0 --	1,803.3 --	4,850.5 ±376.5	48,314.4 ±372.7	53,164.9 ±28.2	101,510.2 --
	1997	46,542.0 --	1,792.1 --	5,377.0 ±376.6	47,799.1 ±375.0	53,176.1 ±26.9	101,510.2 --
	2002	47,088.1 --	1,804.7 --	5,754.4 ±369.7	46,863.0 ±369.1	52,617.4 ±27.8	101,510.2 --
	2007	47,295.1 --	1,810.6 --	6,054.8 ±360.6	46,349.7 ±362.1	52,404.5 ±28.7	101,510.2 --
	2012	47,384.0 --	1,811.7 --	6,185.8 ±360.1	46,128.7 ±362.4	52,314.5 ±28.9	101,510.2 --
	2015	47,384.0 --	1,811.5 --	6,250.7 ±356.5	46,064.0 ±359.0	52,314.7 ±28.8	101,510.2 --
Caribbean	1982	88.2 --	46.0 --	279.7 ±27.4	1,893.2 ±27.0	2,172.9 ±2.7	2,307.1 --
	1987	80.9 --	46.6 --	325.7 ±28.0	1,853.9 ±27.8	2,179.6 ±2.9	2,307.1 --
	1992	83.4 --	46.9 --	401.2 ±29.9	1,775.6 ±30.1	2,176.8 ±3.0	2,307.1 --
	1997	83.4 --	46.7 --	513.7 ±30.6	1,663.3 ±30.5	2,177.0 ±3.1	2,307.1 --
	2002	84.4 --	46.5 --	544.1 ±32.4	1,632.1 ±32.6	2,176.2 ±3.1	2,307.1 --
	2007	84.4 --	46.4 --	563.7 ±34.6	1,612.6 ±34.8	2,176.3 ±3.1	2,307.1 --
	2012	84.9 --	47.8 --	579.6 ±34.9	1,594.8 ±35.1	2,174.4 ±3.3	2,307.1 --
	2015	84.9 --	48.0 --	581.1 ±34.9	1,593.1 ±35.1	2,174.2 ±3.2	2,307.1 --
Colorado	1982	23,673.1 --	322.1 --	1,210.3 ±110.5	41,419.0 ±108.2	42,629.3 ±17.5	66,624.5 --
	1987	23,805.8 --	323.4 --	1,358.4 ±142.2	41,136.9 ±139.7	42,495.3 ±17.3	66,624.5 --
	1992	23,882.9 --	322.5 --	1,499.3 ±152.0	40,919.8 ±150.0	42,419.1 ±18.2	66,624.5 --
	1997	23,884.6 --	324.5 --	1,605.9 ±166.8	40,809.5 ±165.5	42,415.4 ±18.5	66,624.5 --
	2002	23,964.7 --	317.7 --	1,779.8 ±193.6	40,562.3 ±192.6	42,342.1 ±18.3	66,624.5 --
	2007	24,027.7 --	318.7 --	1,886.0 ±201.2	40,392.1 ±200.3	42,278.1 ±18.4	66,624.5 --
	2012	24,075.9 --	322.9 --	1,938.3 ±202.8	40,287.4 ±201.2	42,225.7 ±18.3	66,624.5 --
	2015	24,075.9 --	323.4 --	1,970.6 ±204.4	40,254.6 ±202.8	42,225.2 ±18.3	66,624.5 --

Source: *U.S. Department of Agriculture, 2015 National Resources Inventory, Summary Report, September 2018*

Table 1 - Surface area of non-Federal and Federal land and water areas, by State and year
In thousands of acres, with margins of error

State	Year	Federal land	Water areas	Non-Federal Land			Total surface area
				Developed	Rural	Total	
Connecticut	1982	9.7 --	125.2 --	845.8 ±33.2	2,214.0 ±35.3	3,059.8 ±5.4	3,194.7 --
	1987	14.3 --	125.1 --	897.8 ±35.0	2,157.5 ±36.8	3,055.3 ±5.4	3,194.7 --
	1992	14.5 --	126.0 --	942.1 ±35.1	2,112.1 ±36.9	3,054.2 ±5.2	3,194.7 --
	1997	14.5 --	126.3 --	987.4 ±32.9	2,066.5 ±34.5	3,053.9 ±5.1	3,194.7 --
	2002	14.9 --	126.3 --	1,042.2 ±35.8	2,011.3 ±37.3	3,053.5 ±5.1	3,194.7 --
	2007	14.9 --	126.5 --	1,074.8 ±36.9	1,978.5 ±38.5	3,053.3 ±5.1	3,194.7 --
	2012	15.3 --	127.0 --	1,084.8 ±36.9	1,967.6 ±38.4	3,052.4 ±5.0	3,194.7 --
	2015	15.3 --	127.0 --	1,090.1 ±37.6	1,962.3 ±39.0	3,052.4 ±5.0	3,194.7 --
Delaware	1982	23.7 --	301.1 --	160.5 ±26.2	1,048.2 ±25.9	1,208.7 ±2.7	1,533.5 --
	1987	23.6 --	301.3 --	177.4 ±28.8	1,031.2 ±28.5	1,208.6 ±2.7	1,533.5 --
	1992	23.6 --	301.4 --	194.2 ±29.9	1,014.3 ±29.2	1,208.5 ±2.7	1,533.5 --
	1997	23.6 --	301.7 --	214.9 ±31.7	993.3 ±30.9	1,208.2 ±2.9	1,533.5 --
	2002	23.9 --	302.3 --	249.2 ±33.6	958.1 ±32.8	1,207.3 ±3.0	1,533.5 --
	2007	24.0 --	303.4 --	276.3 ±36.2	929.8 ±35.5	1,206.1 ±3.1	1,533.5 --
	2012	24.3 --	303.4 --	289.8 ±37.5	916.0 ±37.0	1,205.8 ±3.1	1,533.5 --
	2015	24.3 --	303.4 --	297.3 ±38.8	908.5 ±38.3	1,205.8 ±3.1	1,533.5 --
Florida	1982	3,630.7 --	3,088.2 --	2,815.4 ±245.5	27,999.4 ±243.4	30,814.8 ±25.6	37,533.7 --
	1987	3,662.7 --	3,091.6 --	3,133.6 ±251.6	27,645.8 ±249.7	30,779.4 ±26.1	37,533.7 --
	1992	3,825.0 --	3,120.4 --	3,728.5 ±273.1	26,859.8 ±271.4	30,588.3 ±26.5	37,533.7 --
	1997	3,838.9 --	3,120.7 --	4,395.7 ±289.2	26,178.4 ±295.2	30,574.1 ±30.0	37,533.7 --
	2002	3,849.0 --	3,141.9 --	4,923.2 ±304.4	25,619.6 ±314.9	30,542.8 ±31.0	37,533.7 --
	2007	3,875.9 --	3,165.5 --	5,322.7 ±318.9	25,169.6 ±328.6	30,492.3 ±32.5	37,533.7 --
	2012	3,880.0 --	3,165.7 --	5,479.9 ±320.2	25,008.1 ±330.9	30,488.0 ±30.6	37,533.7 --
	2015	3,880.0 --	3,169.2 --	5,528.3 ±322.9	24,956.2 ±333.8	30,484.5 ±30.8	37,533.7 --

Source: *U.S. Department of Agriculture, 2015 National Resources Inventory, Summary Report, September 2018*

Table 1 - Surface area of non-Federal and Federal land and water areas, by State and year
In thousands of acres, with margins of error

State	Year	Federal land	Water areas	Non-Federal Land			Total surface area
				Developed	Rural	Total	
Georgia	1982	2,050.5	937.9	2,232.8	32,519.3	34,752.1	37,740.5
		--	--	±117.4	±116.3	±23.2	--
	1987	2,057.6	944.1	2,477.2	32,261.6	34,738.8	37,740.5
		--	--	±131.4	±129.9	±23.5	--
	1992	2,076.2	976.1	2,917.3	31,770.9	34,688.2	37,740.5
		--	--	±141.3	±141.9	±24.3	--
	1997	2,074.6	1,001.8	3,692.5	30,971.6	34,664.1	37,740.5
		--	--	±155.4	±156.9	±26.7	--
	2002	2,072.9	1,035.5	4,198.8	30,433.3	34,632.1	37,740.5
		--	--	±188.6	±190.4	±30.0	--
	2007	2,081.8	1,055.8	4,480.3	30,122.6	34,602.9	37,740.5
		--	--	±203.8	±205.1	±32.8	--
	2012	2,084.0	1,074.4	4,599.5	29,982.6	34,582.1	37,740.5
		--	--	±208.2	±209.7	±36.1	--
	2015	2,084.0	1,080.4	4,645.8	29,930.3	34,576.1	37,740.5
		--	--	±209.4	±210.6	±36.6	--
Hawaii	1982	407.2	22.7	164.3	3,528.8	3,693.1	4,123.0
		--	--	±32.7	±32.6	±4.2	--
	1987	473.7	22.8	168.8	3,457.7	3,626.5	4,123.0
		--	--	±33.2	±33.0	±4.2	--
	1992	475.4	22.6	190.4	3,434.6	3,625.0	4,123.0
		--	--	±36.0	±35.9	±4.2	--
	1997	446.9	22.6	197.8	3,455.7	3,653.5	4,123.0
		--	--	±35.7	±35.5	±4.1	--
	2002	453.4	22.5	213.2	3,433.9	3,647.1	4,123.0
		--	--	±38.3	±38.1	±4.1	--
	2007	605.7	22.7	219.3	3,275.3	3,494.6	4,123.0
		--	--	±39.6	±39.3	±4.1	--
	2012	610.7	22.7	242.8	3,246.8	3,489.6	4,123.0
		--	--	±40.2	±39.6	±4.1	--
	2015	610.7	22.8	248.5	3,241.0	3,489.5	4,123.0
		--	--	±41.3	±40.7	±4.1	--
Idaho	1982	33,469.0	544.0	558.6	18,915.9	19,474.5	53,487.5
		--	--	±49.8	±52.0	±10.5	--
	1987	33,262.3	546.8	620.2	19,058.2	19,678.4	53,487.5
		--	--	±51.7	±54.4	±10.5	--
	1992	33,363.6	549.5	678.6	18,895.8	19,574.4	53,487.5
		--	--	±57.7	±59.9	±10.1	--
	1997	33,415.9	551.4	772.9	18,747.3	19,520.2	53,487.5
		--	--	±65.2	±66.7	±9.8	--
	2002	33,440.4	552.8	821.7	18,672.6	19,494.3	53,487.5
		--	--	±68.5	±69.8	±9.9	--
	2007	33,445.6	555.0	880.9	18,606.0	19,486.9	53,487.5
		--	--	±75.8	±77.1	±10.2	--
	2012	33,448.8	555.7	903.7	18,579.3	19,483.0	53,487.5
		--	--	±76.7	±78.3	±10.3	--
	2015	33,448.8	555.7	915.0	18,568.0	19,483.0	53,487.5
		--	--	±79.7	±81.3	±10.3	--

Source: *U.S. Department of Agriculture, 2015 National Resources Inventory, Summary Report, September 2018*

Table 1 - Surface area of non-Federal and Federal land and water areas, by State and year
In thousands of acres, with margins of error

State	Year	Federal land	Water areas	Non-Federal Land			Total surface area
				Developed	Rural	Total	
Illinois	1982	476.5 --	733.4 --	2,620.7 ±120.3	32,228.1 ±125.5	34,848.8 ±23.4	36,058.7 --
	1987	477.2 --	729.7 --	2,755.1 ±125.0	32,096.7 ±130.2	34,851.8 ±21.6	36,058.7 --
	1992	492.6 --	725.7 --	2,852.1 ±128.2	31,988.3 ±130.6	34,840.4 ±20.4	36,058.7 --
	1997	490.8 --	722.9 --	3,090.3 ±126.4	31,754.7 ±126.9	34,845.0 ±20.7	36,058.7 --
	2002	493.0 --	735.7 --	3,226.0 ±136.3	31,604.0 ±135.4	34,830.0 ±22.1	36,058.7 --
	2007	499.6 --	744.2 --	3,353.8 ±145.0	31,461.1 ±142.8	34,814.9 ±23.0	36,058.7 --
	2012	502.1 --	750.1 --	3,413.5 ±150.0	31,393.0 ±146.5	34,806.5 ±23.3	36,058.7 --
	2015	502.1 --	753.4 --	3,448.8 ±151.1	31,354.4 ±146.3	34,803.2 ±23.4	36,058.7 --
Indiana	1982	469.9 --	352.1 --	1,789.2 ±88.4	20,547.2 ±91.9	22,336.4 ±18.5	23,158.4 --
	1987	468.9 --	361.1 --	1,903.5 ±89.6	20,424.9 ±94.0	22,328.4 ±18.3	23,158.4 --
	1992	470.1 --	364.8 --	2,009.3 ±98.6	20,314.2 ±102.5	22,323.5 ±18.0	23,158.4 --
	1997	468.8 --	363.1 --	2,199.1 ±109.6	20,127.4 ±114.3	22,326.5 ±17.9	23,158.4 --
	2002	475.1 --	371.5 --	2,339.6 ±117.0	19,972.2 ±121.3	22,311.8 ±17.2	23,158.4 --
	2007	476.9 --	380.0 --	2,455.5 ±121.7	19,846.0 ±126.4	22,301.5 ±17.9	23,158.4 --
	2012	479.3 --	385.5 --	2,511.0 ±124.0	19,782.6 ±129.3	22,293.6 ±18.4	23,158.4 --
	2015	479.3 --	386.0 --	2,541.1 ±124.5	19,752.0 ±129.8	22,293.1 ±18.4	23,158.4 --
Iowa	1982	178.0 --	457.5 --	1,639.6 ±97.6	33,741.4 ±95.5	35,381.0 ±14.9	36,016.5 --
	1987	179.1 --	461.1 --	1,666.3 ±102.1	33,710.0 ±101.4	35,376.3 ±15.3	36,016.5 --
	1992	177.7 --	472.8 --	1,695.4 ±102.9	33,670.6 ±101.9	35,366.0 ±15.6	36,016.5 --
	1997	199.1 --	479.7 --	1,770.8 ±105.4	33,566.9 ±104.4	35,337.7 ±16.2	36,016.5 --
	2002	208.2 --	488.6 --	1,843.5 ±108.2	33,476.2 ±108.9	35,319.7 ±17.4	36,016.5 --
	2007	211.9 --	495.7 --	1,905.2 ±115.4	33,403.7 ±115.1	35,308.9 ±17.6	36,016.5 --
	2012	214.2 --	501.5 --	1,941.0 ±120.0	33,359.8 ±119.6	35,300.8 ±17.7	36,016.5 --
	2015	214.2 --	503.6 --	1,961.5 ±121.6	33,337.2 ±121.2	35,298.7 ±17.5	36,016.5 --

Source: *U.S. Department of Agriculture, 2015 National Resources Inventory, Summary Report, September 2018*

Table 1 - Surface area of non-Federal and Federal land and water areas, by State and year
In thousands of acres, with margins of error

State	Year	Federal land	Water areas	Non-Federal Land			Total surface area
				Developed	Rural	Total	
Kansas	1982	475.1 --	516.1 --	1,737.1 ±68.2	49,932.5 ±72.3	51,669.6 ±18.1	52,660.8 --
	1987	475.8 --	516.6 --	1,764.6 ±67.8	49,903.8 ±72.7	51,668.4 ±18.1	52,660.8 --
	1992	485.0 --	516.3 --	1,865.7 ±72.8	49,793.8 ±76.4	51,659.5 ±18.7	52,660.8 --
	1997	491.8 --	526.5 --	1,964.0 ±71.2	49,678.5 ±76.7	51,642.5 ±19.9	52,660.8 --
	2002	492.2 --	535.3 --	2,035.5 ±75.1	49,597.8 ±78.5	51,633.3 ±19.5	52,660.8 --
	2007	483.3 --	547.5 --	2,088.1 ±83.9	49,541.9 ±87.7	51,630.0 ±20.9	52,660.8 --
	2012	469.4 --	552.2 --	2,117.8 ±88.9	49,521.4 ±92.0	51,639.2 ±20.8	52,660.8 --
	2015	469.4 --	555.3 --	2,132.6 ±91.4	49,503.5 ±94.3	51,636.1 ±21.1	52,660.8 --
Kentucky	1982	1,043.4 --	600.6 --	1,134.0 ±67.6	23,085.4 ±70.8	24,219.4 ±14.7	25,863.4 --
	1987	1,089.2 --	603.0 --	1,326.4 ±77.4	22,844.8 ±82.4	24,171.2 ±14.8	25,863.4 --
	1992	1,132.8 --	618.6 --	1,484.9 ±80.4	22,627.1 ±85.4	24,112.0 ±15.7	25,863.4 --
	1997	1,142.1 --	626.3 --	1,714.8 ±92.7	22,380.2 ±95.6	24,095.0 ±15.4	25,863.4 --
	2002	1,261.9 --	637.7 --	1,952.4 ±91.4	22,011.4 ±95.1	23,963.8 ±15.6	25,863.4 --
	2007	1,271.2 --	644.6 --	2,049.5 ±94.5	21,898.1 ±98.0	23,947.6 ±16.3	25,863.4 --
	2012	1,273.5 --	649.1 --	2,100.4 ±94.7	21,840.4 ±98.5	23,940.8 ±16.5	25,863.4 --
	2015	1,273.5 --	650.5 --	2,121.6 ±96.2	21,817.8 ±99.8	23,939.4 ±16.7	25,863.4 --
Louisiana	1982	1,036.9 --	4,304.3 --	1,236.9 ±53.0	24,798.7 ±63.8	26,035.6 ±32.9	31,376.8 --
	1987	1,098.5 --	4,351.6 --	1,389.7 ±52.6	24,537.0 ±59.6	25,926.7 ±31.0	31,376.8 --
	1992	1,171.3 --	4,413.3 --	1,496.1 ±57.8	24,296.1 ±63.7	25,792.2 ±32.2	31,376.8 --
	1997	1,177.8 --	4,421.5 --	1,631.7 ±62.2	24,145.8 ±64.5	25,777.5 ±35.1	31,376.8 --
	2002	1,229.1 --	4,446.3 --	1,766.8 ±61.7	23,934.6 ±64.1	25,701.4 ±41.2	31,376.8 --
	2007	1,228.2 --	4,535.6 --	1,852.7 ±65.4	23,760.3 ±66.6	25,613.0 ±44.7	31,376.8 --
	2012	1,244.4 --	4,549.0 --	1,923.7 ±67.3	23,659.7 ±69.1	25,583.4 ±46.9	31,376.8 --
	2015	1,244.4 --	4,555.0 --	1,969.2 ±70.5	23,608.2 ±69.8	25,577.4 ±47.9	31,376.8 --

Source: *U.S. Department of Agriculture, 2015 National Resources Inventory, Summary Report, September 2018*

Table 1 - Surface area of non-Federal and Federal land and water areas, by State and year In thousands of acres, with margins of error

State	Year	Federal land	Water areas	Non-Federal Land			Total surface area
				Developed	Rural	Total	
Maine	1982	153.2 –	1,299.3 –	503.1 ±68.6	19,010.6 ±77.7	19,513.7 ±32.6	20,966.2 –
	1987	178.8 –	1,300.3 –	548.5 ±73.4	18,938.6 ±83.1	19,487.1 ±32.7	20,966.2 –
	1992	183.1 –	1,300.9 –	591.3 ±76.8	18,890.9 ±85.8	19,482.2 ±32.9	20,966.2 –
	1997	192.5 –	1,300.4 –	698.0 ±85.8	18,775.3 ±93.7	19,473.3 ±33.1	20,966.2 –
	2002	201.4 –	1,299.8 –	786.4 ±85.7	18,678.6 ±93.5	19,465.0 ±33.1	20,966.2 –
	2007	206.3 –	1,299.8 –	837.3 ±88.8	18,622.8 ±97.2	19,460.1 ±33.1	20,966.2 –
	2012	206.5 –	1,300.1 –	859.2 ±92.6	18,600.4 ±101.4	19,459.6 ±33.2	20,966.2 –
	2015	206.5 –	1,300.1 –	866.3 ±92.6	18,593.3 ±101.8	19,459.6 ±33.2	20,966.2 –
Maryland	1982	154.7 –	1,668.8 –	974.6 ±114.8	5,071.8 ±113.8	6,046.4 ±7.8	7,869.9 –
	1987	155.1 –	1,671.3 –	1,060.0 ±118.5	4,983.5 ±117.6	6,043.5 ±7.6	7,869.9 –
	1992	162.1 –	1,673.0 –	1,134.9 ±122.0	4,899.9 ±121.0	6,034.8 ±7.9	7,869.9 –
	1997	162.1 –	1,675.4 –	1,322.6 ±127.6	4,709.8 ±126.7	6,032.4 ±7.9	7,869.9 –
	2002	164.9 –	1,677.1 –	1,412.2 ±125.9	4,615.7 ±125.4	6,027.9 ±8.0	7,869.9 –
	2007	165.5 –	1,678.3 –	1,477.7 ±126.0	4,548.4 ±125.3	6,026.1 ±8.1	7,869.9 –
	2012	168.2 –	1,679.1 –	1,509.7 ±124.8	4,512.9 ±124.0	6,022.6 ±8.0	7,869.9 –
	2015	168.2 –	1,680.1 –	1,524.1 ±126.2	4,497.5 ±126.4	6,021.6 ±8.0	7,869.9 –
Massachusetts	1982	88.5 –	369.0 –	1,115.9 ±65.7	3,765.6 ±66.6	4,881.5 ±13.4	5,339.0 –
	1987	89.7 –	369.6 –	1,229.3 ±68.7	3,650.4 ±69.6	4,879.7 ±13.3	5,339.0 –
	1992	89.8 –	371.6 –	1,368.5 ±69.0	3,509.1 ±69.9	4,877.6 ±13.1	5,339.0 –
	1997	89.8 –	370.5 –	1,588.5 ±69.5	3,290.2 ±71.1	4,878.7 ±12.2	5,339.0 –
	2002	91.1 –	371.3 –	1,673.1 ±68.1	3,203.5 ±69.2	4,876.6 ±12.2	5,339.0 –
	2007	91.3 –	371.5 –	1,727.5 ±66.7	3,148.7 ±68.0	4,876.2 ±12.3	5,339.0 –
	2012	73.6 –	370.5 –	1,753.6 ±67.9	3,141.3 ±70.6	4,894.9 ±11.9	5,339.0 –
	2015	73.6 –	370.5 –	1,763.6 ±68.7	3,131.3 ±71.3	4,894.9 ±11.9	5,339.0 –

Source: *U.S. Department of Agriculture, 2015 National Resources Inventory, Summary Report, September 2018*

Table 1 - Surface area of non-Federal and Federal land and water areas, by State and year
In thousands of acres, with margins of error

State	Year	Federal land	Water areas	Non-Federal Land			Total surface area
				Developed	Rural	Total	
Michigan	1982	3,099.4 --	1,146.1 --	2,819.4 ±129.3	30,284.3 ±135.0	33,103.7 ±22.5	37,349.2 --
	1987	3,137.6 --	1,143.3 --	3,023.6 ±140.0	30,044.7 ±145.8	33,068.3 ±22.5	37,349.2 --
	1992	3,179.7 --	1,148.0 --	3,290.5 ±147.8	29,731.0 ±151.9	33,021.5 ±22.3	37,349.2 --
	1997	3,179.7 --	1,147.8 --	3,661.7 ±162.1	29,360.0 ±169.1	33,021.7 ±23.1	37,349.2 --
	2002	3,188.4 --	1,157.9 --	3,959.3 ±159.8	29,043.6 ±167.6	33,002.9 ±23.3	37,349.2 --
	2007	3,198.0 --	1,165.3 --	4,107.9 ±163.4	28,878.0 ±170.5	32,985.9 ±24.3	37,349.2 --
	2012	3,202.8 --	1,171.1 --	4,160.4 ±165.7	28,814.9 ±173.8	32,975.3 ±25.3	37,349.2 --
	2015	3,202.8 --	1,174.3 --	4,193.0 ±163.9	28,779.1 ±172.0	32,972.1 ±25.5	37,349.2 --
Minnesota	1982	3,402.0 --	3,169.1 --	1,724.8 ±79.5	45,714.0 ±89.0	47,438.8 ±29.1	54,009.9 --
	1987	3,417.9 --	3,176.9 --	1,848.3 ±82.3	45,566.8 ±91.2	47,415.1 ±28.8	54,009.9 --
	1992	3,412.0 --	3,179.7 --	1,957.2 ±87.4	45,461.0 ±95.9	47,418.2 ±29.0	54,009.9 --
	1997	3,412.0 --	3,177.9 --	2,174.4 ±95.8	45,245.6 ±105.0	47,420.0 ±31.2	54,009.9 --
	2002	3,427.1 --	3,185.1 --	2,290.8 ±102.2	45,106.9 ±111.3	47,397.7 ±32.2	54,009.9 --
	2007	3,407.6 --	3,187.9 --	2,370.8 ±106.7	45,043.6 ±114.1	47,414.4 ±32.2	54,009.9 --
	2012	3,434.4 --	3,193.8 --	2,416.4 ±110.3	44,965.3 ±117.3	47,381.7 ±34.8	54,009.9 --
	2015	3,434.4 --	3,194.7 --	2,436.3 ±114.2	44,944.5 ±120.4	47,380.8 ±35.3	54,009.9 --
Mississippi	1982	1,518.2 --	718.8 --	1,175.1 ±94.8	27,115.2 ±96.0	28,290.3 ±27.0	30,527.3 --
	1987	1,557.1 --	789.4 --	1,253.4 ±95.7	26,927.4 ±102.7	28,180.8 ±32.9	30,527.3 --
	1992	1,635.6 --	828.7 --	1,334.3 ±97.2	26,728.7 ±105.7	28,063.0 ±32.7	30,527.3 --
	1997	1,653.4 --	857.3 --	1,548.2 ±108.9	26,468.4 ±121.1	28,016.6 ±35.0	30,527.3 --
	2002	1,677.6 --	880.5 --	1,707.0 ±118.6	26,262.2 ±132.7	27,969.2 ±37.5	30,527.3 --
	2007	1,685.0 --	868.6 --	1,811.6 ±130.6	26,162.1 ±148.4	27,973.7 ±42.8	30,527.3 --
	2012	1,685.3 --	831.5 --	1,887.1 ±138.8	26,123.4 ±155.1	28,010.5 ±43.4	30,527.3 --
	2015	1,685.3 --	820.5 --	1,919.6 ±141.6	26,101.9 ±156.9	28,021.5 ±42.3	30,527.3 --

Source: *U.S. Department of Agriculture, 2015 National Resources Inventory, Summary Report, September 2018*

Table 1 - Surface area of non-Federal and Federal land and water areas, by State and year In thousands of acres, with margins of error

State	Year	Federal land	Water areas	Non-Federal Land			Total surface area
				Developed	Rural	Total	
Missouri	1982	2,002.8 --	767.5 --	2,172.8 ±97.2	39,670.8 ±99.0	41,843.6 ±17.1	44,613.9 --
	1987	1,974.0 --	799.4 --	2,279.4 ±101.1	39,561.1 ±101.4	41,840.5 ±17.9	44,613.9 --
	1992	1,988.9 --	814.4 --	2,398.2 ±105.7	39,412.4 ±107.6	41,810.6 ±18.2	44,613.9 --
	1997	2,000.5 --	828.3 --	2,637.6 ±118.5	39,147.5 ±118.7	41,785.1 ±18.1	44,613.9 --
	2002	2,009.8 --	849.9 --	2,794.6 ±120.2	38,959.6 ±117.2	41,754.2 ±19.6	44,613.9 --
	2007	2,016.3 --	866.5 --	2,914.8 ±125.3	38,816.3 ±122.4	41,731.1 ±20.0	44,613.9 --
	2012	2,018.7 --	875.1 --	2,984.1 ±131.0	38,736.0 ±128.9	41,720.1 ±20.2	44,613.9 --
	2015	2,018.7 --	878.7 --	3,009.4 ±133.7	38,707.1 ±131.8	41,716.5 ±20.5	44,613.9 --
Montana	1982	26,940.9 --	1,049.3 --	857.2 ±94.9	65,262.6 ±99.9	66,119.8 ±37.1	94,110.0 --
	1987	26,851.0 --	1,048.0 --	869.4 ±94.0	65,341.6 ±99.8	66,211.0 ±37.5	94,110.0 --
	1992	26,757.2 --	1,038.9 --	927.6 ±99.9	65,386.3 ±107.5	66,313.9 ±33.7	94,110.0 --
	1997	26,756.5 --	1,028.2 --	994.2 ±104.1	65,331.1 ±111.9	66,325.3 ±31.0	94,110.0 --
	2002	26,779.9 --	1,030.3 --	1,028.4 ±106.2	65,271.4 ±115.9	66,299.8 ±31.3	94,110.0 --
	2007	26,843.3 --	1,029.9 --	1,079.7 ±112.9	65,157.1 ±121.6	66,236.8 ±31.7	94,110.0 --
	2012	26,983.6 --	1,034.6 --	1,105.7 ±115.4	64,986.1 ±124.1	66,091.8 ±31.4	94,110.0 --
	2015	26,983.6 --	1,034.9 --	1,117.8 ±118.1	64,973.7 ±126.7	66,091.5 ±31.5	94,110.0 --
Nebraska	1982	515.3 --	472.3 --	1,096.9 ±101.9	47,425.1 ±107.6	48,522.0 ±19.7	49,509.6 --
	1987	522.8 --	480.8 --	1,112.5 ±104.9	47,393.5 ±110.6	48,506.0 ±19.5	49,509.6 --
	1992	589.2 --	482.8 --	1,134.1 ±109.7	47,303.5 ±115.4	48,437.6 ±19.5	49,509.6 --
	1997	587.3 --	487.0 --	1,188.8 ±111.8	47,246.5 ±117.3	48,435.3 ±18.8	49,509.6 --
	2002	586.9 --	491.5 --	1,208.8 ±111.0	47,222.4 ±116.7	48,431.2 ±20.4	49,509.6 --
	2007	582.8 --	494.1 --	1,237.9 ±112.3	47,194.8 ±117.9	48,432.7 ±20.8	49,509.6 --
	2012	581.2 --	498.1 --	1,252.3 ±112.1	47,178.0 ±117.4	48,430.3 ±21.6	49,509.6 --
	2015	581.2 --	503.0 --	1,264.6 ±113.0	47,160.8 ±118.6	48,425.4 ±22.6	49,509.6 --

Source: *U.S. Department of Agriculture, 2015 National Resources Inventory, Summary Report, September 2018*

Table 1 - Surface area of non-Federal and Federal land and water areas, by State and year
In thousands of acres, with margins of error

State	Year	Federal land	Water areas	Non-Federal Land			Total surface area
				Developed	Rural	Total	
Nevada	1982	59,500.7 --	393.3 --	225.2 ±55.3	10,643.9 ±56.4	10,869.1 ±5.1	70,763.1 --
	1987	59,409.4 --	399.8 --	262.1 ±61.9	10,691.8 ±63.1	10,953.9 ±5.4	70,763.1 --
	1992	59,500.4 --	400.8 --	289.8 ±62.4	10,572.1 ±63.5	10,861.9 ±5.3	70,763.1 --
	1997	59,500.4 --	401.1 --	311.0 ±64.0	10,550.6 ±65.1	10,861.6 ±5.1	70,763.1 --
	2002	59,520.5 --	400.3 --	440.1 ±77.7	10,402.2 ±77.6	10,842.3 ±5.0	70,763.1 --
	2007	59,469.8 --	401.0 --	501.0 ±89.3	10,391.3 ±89.7	10,892.3 ±5.3	70,763.1 --
	2012	59,478.6 --	401.2 --	525.6 ±92.6	10,357.7 ±93.0	10,883.3 ±5.4	70,763.1 --
	2015	59,478.6 --	401.0 --	531.0 ±93.3	10,352.5 ±93.8	10,883.5 ±5.5	70,763.1 --
New Hampshire	1982	736.1 --	230.6 --	402.4 ±43.6	4,571.9 ±47.7	4,974.3 ±9.8	5,941.0 --
	1987	736.4 --	230.8 --	498.9 ±56.8	4,474.9 ±60.5	4,973.8 ±9.8	5,941.0 --
	1992	758.5 --	231.6 --	560.6 ±58.4	4,390.3 ±62.4	4,950.9 ±9.9	5,941.0 --
	1997	763.7 --	232.8 --	629.0 ±62.7	4,315.5 ±66.7	4,944.5 ±10.1	5,941.0 --
	2002	779.2 --	232.9 --	671.4 ±62.8	4,257.5 ±67.3	4,928.9 ±10.2	5,941.0 --
	2007	788.2 --	233.3 --	712.4 ±65.1	4,207.1 ±69.6	4,919.5 ±10.0	5,941.0 --
	2012	801.8 --	233.5 --	727.2 ±64.3	4,178.5 ±68.6	4,905.7 ±9.9	5,941.0 --
	2015	801.8 --	233.5 --	732.8 ±63.7	4,172.9 ±68.0	4,905.7 ±9.9	5,941.0 --
New Jersey	1982	156.3 --	553.4 --	1,179.2 ±65.4	3,326.7 ±67.9	4,505.9 ±9.3	5,215.6 --
	1987	159.1 --	555.2 --	1,387.0 ±70.9	3,114.3 ±74.6	4,501.3 ±9.1	5,215.6 --
	1992	169.4 --	558.4 --	1,456.6 ±71.0	3,031.2 ±74.5	4,487.8 ±9.0	5,215.6 --
	1997	169.4 --	561.7 --	1,653.6 ±75.1	2,830.9 +77.7	4,484.5 ±9.1	5,215.6 --
	2002	175.0 --	563.1 --	1,769.8 ±72.1	2,707.7 ±75.1	4,477.5 ±8.7	5,215.6 --
	2007	176.7 --	563.0 --	1,827.3 ±72.0	2,648.6 ±74.3	4,475.9 ±8.4	5,215.6 --
	2012	177.6 --	563.3 --	1,853.0 ±72.5	2,621.7 ±74.6	4,474.7 ±8.6	5,215.6 --
	2015	177.6 --	563.6 --	1,863.7 ±72.5	2,610.7 ±74.5	4,474.4 ±8.4	5,215.6 --

Source: *U.S. Department of Agriculture, 2015 National Resources Inventory, Summary Report, September 2018*

Table 1 - Surface area of non-Federal and Federal land and water areas, by State and year
In thousands of acres, with margins of error

State	Year	Federal land	Water areas	Non-Federal Land			Total surface area
				Developed	Rural	Total	
New Mexico	1982	25,458.9 --	161.9 --	712.7 ±97.3	51,489.8 ±99.1	52,202.5 ±16.3	77,823.3 --
	1987	26,000.0 --	162.7 --	776.1 ±103.9	50,884.5 ±107.3	51,660.6 ±16.5	77,823.3 --
	1992	26,262.3 --	158.9 --	832.4 ±112.4	50,569.7 ±115.5	51,402.1 ±16.7	77,823.3 --
	1997	26,262.3 --	162.4 --	1,002.6 ±121.8	50,396.0 ±124.5	51,398.6 ±16.1	77,823.3 --
	2002	26,344.2 --	164.9 --	1,209.2 ±157.4	50,105.0 ±159.0	51,314.2 ±15.8	77,823.3 --
	2007	26,349.0 --	165.2 --	1,268.5 ±163.9	50,040.6 ±165.7	51,309.1 ±15.9	77,823.3 --
	2012	26,355.1 --	165.2 --	1,307.0 ±163.7	49,996.0 ±165.8	51,303.0 ±15.9	77,823.3 --
	2015	26,355.1 --	165.2 --	1,320.2 ±161.6	49,982.8 ±163.7	51,303.0 ±15.9	77,823.3 --
New York	1982	235.6 --	1,394.8 --	2,831.4 ±120.9	26,947.3 ±125.7	29,778.7 ±21.1	31,409.1 --
	1987	235.0 --	1,396.2 --	2,939.3 ±128.1	26,838.6 ±133.0	29,777.9 ±21.1	31,409.1 --
	1992	225.2 --	1,402.3 --	3,085.6 ±133.2	26,696.0 ±137.6	29,781.6 ±21.7	31,409.1 --
	1997	232.5 --	1,407.0 --	3,430.8 ±144.0	26,338.8 ±147.9	29,769.6 ±23.6	31,409.1 --
	2002	214.0 --	1,417.7 --	3,668.5 ±147.3	26,108.9 ±151.3	29,777.4 ±24.2	31,409.1 --
	2007	212.0 --	1,422.6 --	3,774.8 ±145.6	25,999.7 ±148.6	29,774.5 ±24.3	31,409.1 --
	2012	212.5 --	1,429.6 --	3,835.5 ±145.8	25,931.5 ±148.6	29,767.0 ±24.9	31,409.1 --
	2015	212.5 --	1,431.7 --	3,860.7 ±148.1	25,904.2 ±151.0	29,764.9 ±25.1	31,409.1 --
North Carolina	1982	2,037.0 --	2,733.6 --	2,361.5 ±108.5	26,577.2 ±102.0	28,938.7 ±17.3	33,709.3 --
	1987	2,190.8 --	2,750.3 --	2,786.8 ±119.1	25,981.4 ±112.0	28,768.2 ±17.8	33,709.3 --
	1992	2,362.6 --	2,757.5 --	3,258.3 ±145.0	25,330.9 ±140.1	28,589.2 ±18.4	33,709.3 --
	1997	2,363.5 --	2,765.8 --	3,739.0 ±167.8	24,841.0 ±166.5	28,580.0 ±21.0	33,709.3 --
	2002	2,371.0 --	2,780.1 --	4,390.0 ±201.7	24,168.2 ±201.2	28,558.2 ±22.3	33,709.3 --
	2007	2,377.9 --	2,788.8 --	4,644.0 ±213.2	23,898.6 ±215.6	28,542.6 ±22.7	33,709.3 --
	2012	2,380.8 --	2,796.5 --	4,786.8 ±220.8	23,745.2 ±224.1	28,532.0 ±22.9	33,709.3 --
	2015	2,380.8 --	2,797.6 --	4,870.4 ±219.0	23,660.5 ±222.5	28,530.9 ±22.7	33,709.3 --

Source: *U.S. Department of Agriculture, 2015 National Resources Inventory, Summary Report, September 2018*

Table 1 - Surface area of non-Federal and Federal land and water areas, by State and year
In thousands of acres, with margins of error

State	Year	Federal land	Water areas	Non-Federal Land			Total surface area
				Developed	Rural	Total	
North Dakota	1982	1,706.1 --	1,088.2 --	893.3 ±70.8	41,563.1 ±72.8	42,456.4 ±16.6	45,250.7 --
	1987	1,722.2 --	1,085.5 --	901.6 ±71.2	41,541.4 ±73.4	42,443.0 ±16.4	45,250.7 --
	1992	1,764.0 --	1,084.6 --	915.1 ±70.9	41,487.0 ±73.5	42,402.1 ±16.7	45,250.7 --
	1997	1,763.9 --	1,159.4 --	942.8 ±71.4	41,384.6 ±75.4	42,327.4 ±17.7	45,250.7 --
	2002	1,765.3 --	1,201.9 --	954.8 ±73.0	41,328.7 ±76.6	42,283.5 ±17.7	45,250.7 --
	2007	1,771.7 --	1,204.3 --	970.7 ±75.3	41,304.0 ±79.4	42,274.7 ±18.2	45,250.7 --
	2012	1,766.0 --	1,255.4 --	1,006.0 ±77.3	41,223.3 ±81.7	42,229.3 ±18.6	45,250.7 --
	2015	1,766.0 --	1,257.5 --	1,033.8 ±79.1	41,193.4 ±83.7	42,227.2 ±18.8	45,250.7 --
Ohio	1982	301.7 --	391.6 --	2,859.6 ±117.8	22,891.9 ±119.8	25,751.5 ±12.5	26,444.8 --
	1987	298.7 --	396.1 --	3,063.6 ±123.0	22,686.4 ±125.7	25,750.0 ±12.2	26,444.8 --
	1992	323.1 --	400.3 --	3,331.9 ±134.8	22,389.5 ±137.7	25,721.4 ±12.5	26,444.8 --
	1997	323.2 --	400.4 --	3,697.5 ±147.3	22,023.7 ±150.6	25,721.2 ±13.3	26,444.8 --
	2002	330.9 --	410.7 --	3,917.5 ±139.6	21,785.7 ±143.7	25,703.2 ±14.3	26,444.8 --
	2007	336.6 --	418.1 --	4,091.1 ±142.6	21,599.0 ±147.6	25,690.1 ±15.7	26,444.8 --
	2012	359.1 --	421.6 --	4,169.5 ±144.3	21,494.6 ±148.8	25,664.1 ±15.6	26,444.8 --
	2015	359.1 --	424.5 --	4,207.4 ±144.2	21,453.8 ±148.8	25,661.2 ±15.7	26,444.8 --
Oklahoma	1982	1,071.2 --	1,002.5 --	1,488.3 ±89.1	41,176.1 ±97.3	42,664.4 ±24.5	44,738.1 --
	1987	1,058.3 --	1,020.3 --	1,564.3 ±88.5	41,095.2 ±96.7	42,659.5 ±22.7	44,738.1 --
	1992	1,057.9 --	1,041.2 --	1,628.8 ±94.8	41,010.2 ±100.7	42,639.0 ±26.6	44,738.1 --
	1997	1,175.8 --	1,050.7 --	1,778.1 ±106.3	40,733.5 ±111.0	42,511.6 ±20.0	44,738.1 --
	2002	1,183.0 --	1,071.2 --	1,937.2 ±113.8	40,546.7 ±120.4	42,483.9 ±33.7	44,738.1 --
	2007	1,185.0 --	1,083.7 --	2,053.4 ±114.1	40,416.0 ±120.2	42,469.4 ±32.0	44,738.1 --
	2012	1,186.0 --	1,089.2 --	2,140.0 ±116.3	40,322.9 ±122.9	42,462.9 ±31.9	44,738.1 --
	2015	1,186.0 --	1,095.9 --	2,188.0 ±121.5	40,268.2 ±127.4	42,456.2 ±32.0	44,738.1 --

Source: *U.S. Department of Agriculture, 2015 National Resources Inventory, Summary Report, September 2018*

Table 1 - Surface area of non-Federal and Federal land and water areas, by State and year
In thousands of acres, with margins of error

State	Year	Federal land	Water areas	Non-Federal Land			Total surface area
				Developed	Rural	Total	
Oregon	1982	31,949.4 --	843.4 --	974.0 ±98.7	28,394.2 ±98.2	29,368.2 ±19.0	62,161.0 --
	1987	32,020.7 --	844.7 --	1,062.2 ±109.7	28,233.4 ±110.3	29,295.6 ±19.2	62,161.0 --
	1992	32,127.1 --	845.1 --	1,140.1 ±114.2	28,048.7 ±114.2	29,188.8 ±19.2	62,161.0 --
	1997	32,153.6 --	844.3 --	1,249.0 ±121.1	27,914.1 ±124.0	29,163.1 ±18.6	62,161.0 --
	2002	32,087.1 --	847.2 --	1,316.2 ±131.7	27,910.5 ±135.2	29,226.7 ±19.2	62,161.0 --
	2007	32,094.6 --	847.9 --	1,365.0 ±139.0	27,853.5 ±142.9	29,218.5 ±19.2	62,161.0 --
	2012	32,108.5 --	849.9 --	1,383.8 ±139.6	27,818.8 ±143.6	29,202.6 ±19.4	62,161.0 --
	2015	32,108.5 --	850.9 --	1,393.8 ±140.9	27,807.8 ±145.0	29,201.6 ±19.7	62,161.0 --
Pennsylvania	1982	672.8 --	467.0 --	2,773.3 ±103.1	25,082.1 ±109.5	27,855.4 ±19.0	28,995.2 --
	1987	674.1 --	468.3 --	2,954.5 ±112.5	24,898.3 ±120.1	27,852.8 ±19.3	28,995.2 --
	1992	676.8 --	471.2 --	3,385.6 ±129.9	24,461.6 ±135.3	27,847.2 ±19.0	28,995.2 --
	1997	676.8 --	472.6 --	3,921.9 ±145.0	23,923.9 ±149.2	27,845.8 ±18.2	28,995.2 --
	2002	677.0 --	476.9 --	4,174.5 ±156.5	23,666.8 ±160.0	27,841.3 ±18.5	28,995.2 --
	2007	677.3 --	480.8 --	4,339.6 ±165.3	23,497.5 ±168.6	27,837.1 ±18.4	28,995.2 --
	2012	679.9 --	481.8 --	4,428.2 ±167.4	23,405.3 ±170.4	27,833.5 ±17.9	28,995.2 --
	2015	679.9 --	482.6 --	4,476.7 ±171.9	23,356.0 ±174.9	27,832.7 ±17.7	28,995.2 --
Rhode Island	1982	8.6 --	151.9 --	171.1 ±12.3	481.7 ±12.5	652.8 ±2.3	813.3 --
	1987	8.8 --	151.7 --	181.0 ±13.6	471.8 ±13.8	652.8 ±2.2	813.3 --
	1992	9.4 --	152.0 --	198.1 ±13.7	453.8 ±13.8	651.9 ±2.2	813.3 --
	1997	6.1 --	151.9 --	204.9 ±14.1	450.4 ±14.3	655.3 ±2.3	813.3 --
	2002	3.9 --	152.0 --	219.8 ±14.4	437.6 ±14.6	657.4 ±2.3	813.3 --
	2007	4.0 --	152.1 --	228.3 ±14.9	428.9 ±15.1	657.2 ±2.3	813.3 --
	2012	4.0 --	152.0 --	231.0 ±15.0	426.3 ±15.2	657.3 ±2.3	813.3 --
	2015	4.0 --	152.0 --	233.2 ±14.4	424.1 ±14.6	657.3 ±2.3	813.3 --

Source: *U.S. Department of Agriculture, 2015 National Resources Inventory, Summary Report, September 2018*

Table 1 - Surface area of non-Federal and Federal land and water areas, by State and year
In thousands of acres, with margins of error

State	Year	Federal land	Water areas	Non-Federal Land			Total surface area
				Developed	Rural	Total	
South Carolina	1982	1,009.8 --	780.6 --	1,361.2 ±78.3	16,787.7 ±78.1	18,148.9 ±14.6	19,939.3 --
	1987	1,006.7 --	789.2 --	1,527.8 ±92.8	16,615.6 ±92.1	18,143.4 ±14.4	19,939.3 --
	1992	1,013.7 --	792.2 --	1,753.8 ±101.1	16,379.6 ±100.3	18,133.4 ±14.9	19,939.3 --
	1997	1,013.7 --	794.4 --	2,114.5 ±108.8	16,016.7 ±109.6	18,131.2 ±16.3	19,939.3 --
	2002	1,028.2 --	806.0 --	2,411.9 ±105.2	15,693.2 ±105.9	18,105.1 ±17.3	19,939.3 --
	2007	1,046.8 --	814.8 --	2,571.4 ±107.9	15,506.3 ±109.7	18,077.7 ±18.0	19,939.3 --
	2012	1,050.9 --	820.6 --	2,661.5 ±110.7	15,406.3 ±112.4	18,067.8 ±18.1	19,939.3 --
	2015	1,050.9 --	822.2 --	2,693.2 ±114.9	15,373.0 ±115.7	18,066.2 ±18.2	19,939.3 --
South Dakota	1982	2,696.2 --	875.7 --	812.2 ±65.9	44,973.9 ±67.4	45,786.1 ±14.3	49,358.0 --
	1987	2,732.0 --	883.0 --	817.9 ±68.4	44,925.1 ±69.7	45,743.0 ±14.4	49,358.0 --
	1992	2,771.2 --	885.3 --	870.3 ±95.2	44,831.2 ±96.4	45,701.5 ±14.8	49,358.0 --
	1997	2,771.2 --	890.5 --	921.2 ±103.6	44,775.1 ±105.0	45,696.3 ±13.8	49,358.0 --
	2002	2,773.8 --	889.2 --	938.6 ±106.5	44,756.4 ±108.5	45,695.0 ±14.3	49,358.0 --
	2007	2,776.1 --	891.8 --	956.9 ±110.1	44,733.2 ±112.7	45,690.1 ±15.1	49,358.0 --
	2012	2,782.6 --	892.6 --	964.7 ±112.2	44,718.1 ±115.3	45,682.8 ±15.5	49,358.0 --
	2015	2,782.6 --	893.7 --	969.0 ±113.1	44,712.7 ±116.3	45,681.7 ±15.3	49,358.0 --
Tennessee	1982	1,289.6 --	751.2 --	1,653.2 ±97.7	23,279.6 ±96.4	24,932.8 ±11.2	26,973.6 --
	1987	1,311.3 --	753.1 --	1,887.7 ±105.3	23,021.5 ±104.8	24,909.2 ±10.7	26,973.6 --
	1992	1,309.6 --	761.2 --	2,181.6 ±109.3	22,721.2 ±108.3	24,902.8 ±10.4	26,973.6 --
	1997	1,309.6 --	767.1 --	2,627.4 ±120.0	22,269.5 ±100.0	24,896.9 ±10.7	26,973.6 --
	2002	1,384.4 --	775.4 --	2,826.9 ±134.4	21,986.9 ±134.5	24,813.8 ±11.6	26,973.6 --
	2007	1,391.0 --	781.5 --	3,001.1 ±144.2	21,800.0 ±145.9	24,801.1 ±11.1	26,973.6 --
	2012	1,406.3 --	785.0 --	3,087.5 ±144.0	21,694.8 ±145.5	24,782.3 ±11.2	26,973.6 --
	2015	1,406.3 --	786.5 --	3,123.1 ±142.1	21,657.7 ±142.6	24,780.8 ±11.0	26,973.6 --

Source: *U.S. Department of Agriculture, 2015 National Resources Inventory, Summary Report, September 2018*

Table 1 - Surface area of non-Federal and Federal land and water areas, by State and year
In thousands of acres, with margins of error

State	Year	Federal land	Water areas	Non-Federal Land			Total surface area
				Developed	Rural	Total	
Texas	1982	2,830.1 --	3,776.7 --	5,252.2 ±182.2	159,192.9 ±188.7	164,445.1 ±40.6	171,051.9 --
	1987	2,876.4 --	3,919.8 --	5,773.8 ±198.7	158,481.9 ±202.6	164,255.7 ±44.6	171,051.9 --
	1992	2,966.4 --	4,042.6 --	6,333.1 ±242.9	157,709.8 ±245.5	164,042.9 ±46.3	171,051.9 --
	1997	2,966.6 --	4,122.6 --	7,015.0 ±259.4	156,947.7 ±265.3	163,962.7 ±44.4	171,051.9 --
	2002	3,021.2 --	4,160.4 --	7,827.6 ±274.5	156,042.7 ±281.5	163,870.3 ±46.4	171,051.9 --
	2007	3,053.8 --	4,206.2 --	8,517.9 ±289.3	155,274.0 ±301.8	163,791.9 ±50.4	171,051.9 --
	2012	3,086.7 --	4,238.4 --	8,962.6 ±305.0	154,764.2 ±318.6	163,726.8 ±52.8	171,051.9 --
	2015	3,086.7 --	4,261.0 --	9,214.2 ±315.2	154,490.0 ±330.4	163,704.2 ±55.5	171,051.9 --
Utah	1982	34,837.8 --	1,506.4 --	455.4 ±88.1	17,539.3 ±105.0	17,994.7 ±21.4	54,338.9 --
	1987	34,483.0 --	2,043.2 --	498.2 ±96.9	17,314.5 ±113.5	17,812.7 ±21.4	54,338.9 --
	1992	34,607.8 --	1,525.4 --	557.5 ±108.1	17,648.2 ±123.7	18,205.7 ±21.5	54,338.9 --
	1997	34,607.8 --	1,539.3 --	636.0 ±118.5	17,555.8 ±132.6	18,191.8 ±21.4	54,338.9 --
	2002	34,824.1 --	1,539.2 --	733.8 ±124.5	17,241.8 ±138.0	17,975.6 ±21.4	54,338.9 --
	2007	34,835.8 --	1,539.3 --	815.3 ±127.6	17,148.5 ±140.3	17,963.8 ±21.6	54,338.9 --
	2012	34,842.0 --	1,539.9 --	865.7 ±132.9	17,091.3 ±145.1	17,957.0 ±21.7	54,338.9 --
	2015	34,842.0 --	1,539.9 --	892.8 ±135.8	17,064.2 ±147.5	17,957.0 ±21.7	54,338.9 --
Vermont	1982	317.1 --	267.3 --	264.0 ±23.2	5,305.2 ±24.8	5,569.2 ±5.6	6,153.6 --
	1987	349.8 --	267.8 --	305.6 ±24.9	5,230.4 ±26.1	5,536.0 ±5.5	6,153.6 --
	1992	368.5 --	268.2 --	334.2 ±25.8	5,182.7 ±26.6	5,516.9 ±5.5	6,153.6 --
	1997	395.1 --	267.4 --	347.0 ±26.7	5,144.1 ±28.0	5,491.1 ±5.5	6,153.6 --
	2002	440.1 --	267.4 --	370.2 ±28.3	5,075.9 ±29.9	5,446.1 ±5.3	6,153.6 --
	2007	452.6 --	267.8 --	386.8 ±29.6	5,046.4 ±31.2	5,433.2 ±5.3	6,153.6 --
	2012	455.6 --	268.3 --	396.3 ±30.6	5,033.4 ±32.1	5,429.7 ±5.3	6,153.6 --
	2015	455.6 --	268.4 --	402.4 ±31.1	5,027.2 ±32.6	5,429.6 ±5.3	6,153.6 --

Source: *U.S. Department of Agriculture, 2015 National Resources Inventory, Summary Report, September 2018*

Table 1 - Surface area of non-Federal and Federal land and water areas, by State and year
In thousands of acres, with margins of error

State	Year	Federal land	Water areas	Non-Federal Land			Total surface area
				Developed	Rural	Total	
Virginia	1982	2,292.6 --	1,882.4 --	1,839.9 ±107.7	21,072.2 ±107.9	22,912.1 ±13.1	27,087.1 --
	1987	2,310.5 --	1,884.1 --	2,080.3 ±108.1	20,812.2 ±108.1	22,892.5 ±13.3	27,087.1 --
	1992	2,330.8 --	1,892.8 --	2,281.1 ±115.8	20,582.4 ±116.1	22,863.5 ±13.7	27,087.1 --
	1997	2,330.8 --	1,893.6 --	2,623.7 ±109.9	20,239.0 ±111.0	22,862.7 ±14.6	27,087.1 --
	2002	2,347.7 --	1,898.6 --	2,880.2 ±107.4	19,960.6 ±108.5	22,840.8 ±15.2	27,087.1 --
	2007	2,353.8 --	1,905.3 --	3,060.4 ±112.3	19,767.6 ±113.5	22,828.0 ±15.6	27,087.1 --
	2012	2,354.4 --	1,908.7 --	3,163.0 ±116.8	19,661.0 ±117.7	22,824.0 ±15.2	27,087.1 --
	2015	2,354.4 --	1,910.1 --	3,212.4 ±118.2	19,610.2 ±119.4	22,822.6 ±15.0	27,087.1 --
Washington	1982	12,400.4 --	1,569.4 --	1,612.4 ±147.5	28,453.1 ±155.1	30,065.5 ±20.7	44,035.3 --
	1987	12,420.6 --	1,570.2 --	1,694.2 ±148.9	28,350.3 ±156.3	30,044.5 ±20.5	44,035.3 --
	1992	12,424.6 --	1,569.7 --	1,919.9 ±162.7	28,121.1 ±169.2	30,041.0 ±20.9	44,035.3 --
	1997	12,426.2 --	1,570.4 --	2,172.7 ±179.3	27,866.0 ±185.2	30,038.7 ±19.1	44,035.3 --
	2002	12,512.0 --	1,575.1 --	2,352.0 ±185.4	27,596.2 ±191.0	29,948.2 ±21.5	44,035.3 --
	2007	12,536.7 --	1,575.9 --	2,450.8 ±186.2	27,471.9 ±191.1	29,922.7 ±19.9	44,035.3 --
	2012	12,546.2 --	1,578.6 --	2,496.0 ±184.1	27,414.5 ±188.0	29,910.5 ±20.5	44,035.3 --
	2015	12,546.2 --	1,577.8 --	2,512.5 ±184.6	27,398.8 ±188.6	29,911.3 ±20.8	44,035.3 --
West Virginia	1982	1,137.0 --	160.2 --	639.1 ±44.5	13,571.9 ±47.5	14,211.0 ±8.6	15,508.2 --
	1987	1,150.5 --	160.9 --	682.5 ±46.4	13,514.3 ±49.5	14,196.8 ±8.6	15,508.2 --
	1992	1,240.8 --	164.6 --	769.2 ±52.0	13,333.6 ±54.3	14,102.8 ±8.2	15,508.2 --
	1997	1,241.5 --	167.8 --	971.3 ±60.7	13,127.6 ±6[illegible]	14,098.9 ±[illegible]	15,508.2 --
	2002	1,257.2 --	174.9 --	1,088.7 ±60.5	12,987.4 ±61.6	14,076.1 ±10.7	15,508.2 --
	2007	1,267.5 --	176.2 --	1,137.8 ±63.2	12,926.7 ±64.0	14,064.5 ±10.7	15,508.2 --
	2012	1,270.2 --	176.6 --	1,159.8 ±62.5	12,901.6 ±63.5	14,061.4 ±10.9	15,508.2 --
	2015	1,270.2 --	177.0 --	1,163.7 ±62.9	12,897.3 ±64.1	14,061.0 ±10.9	15,508.2 --

Source: *U.S. Department of Agriculture, 2015 National Resources Inventory, Summary Report, September 2018*

Table 1 - Surface area of non-Federal and Federal land and water areas, by State and year
In thousands of acres, with margins of error

State	Year	Federal land	Water areas	Non-Federal Land			Total surface area
				Developed	Rural	Total	
Wisconsin	1982	1,776.4 --	1,286.1 --	1,984.3 ±102.6	30,873.2 ±110.2	32,857.5 ±25.3	35,920.0 --
	1987	1,783.3 --	1,288.0 --	2,098.1 ±108.0	30,750.6 ±115.8	32,848.7 ±27.1	35,920.0 --
	1992	1,811.5 --	1,286.7 --	2,222.6 ±112.7	30,599.2 ±119.8	32,821.8 ±25.7	35,920.0 --
	1997	1,811.5 --	1,283.0 --	2,406.4 ±122.3	30,419.1 ±128.2	32,825.5 ±26.5	35,920.0 --
	2002	1,812.1 --	1,287.2 --	2,557.9 ±139.3	30,262.8 ±144.2	32,820.7 ±26.7	35,920.0 --
	2007	1,819.0 --	1,290.6 --	2,685.8 ±146.0	30,124.6 ±150.5	32,810.4 ±26.4	35,920.0 --
	2012	1,824.5 --	1,295.2 --	2,759.1 ±147.9	30,041.2 ±151.6	32,800.3 ±26.6	35,920.0 --
	2015	1,824.5 --	1,296.6 --	2,785.8 ±148.6	30,013.1 ±152.4	32,798.9 ±26.6	35,920.0 --
Wyoming	1982	29,517.2 --	464.6 --	537.1 ±67.9	32,083.9 ±66.0	32,621.0 ±15.0	62,602.8 --
	1987	29,516.9 --	466.5 --	578.7 ±68.9	32,040.7 ±70.0	32,619.4 ±15.8	62,602.8 --
	1992	29,566.3 --	467.5 --	590.3 ±71.1	31,978.7 ±72.9	32,569.0 ±16.1	62,602.8 --
	1997	29,566.3 --	467.7 --	624.7 ±73.5	31,944.1 ±76.4	32,568.8 ±16.1	62,602.8 --
	2002	29,546.4 --	469.6 --	644.4 ±75.2	31,942.4 ±78.5	32,586.8 ±16.3	62,602.8 --
	2007	29,559.8 --	472.0 --	666.6 ±75.8	31,904.4 ±80.7	32,571.0 ±17.7	62,602.8 --
	2012	29,558.8 --	474.2 --	685.2 ±77.5	31,884.6 ±83.0	32,569.8 ±18.9	62,602.8 --
	2015	29,558.8 --	474.3 --	697.1 ±78.7	31,872.6 ±84.4	32,569.7 ±19.0	62,602.8 --
Total	1982	399,623.9 --	49,720.8 --	72,093.8 ±775.7	1,422,704.1 ±831.5	1,494,797.9 ±135.2	1,944,142.6 --
	1987	400,103.9 --	50,726.6 --	78,108.5 ±844.6	1,415,203.6 ±898.0	1,493,312.1 ±137.6	1,944,142.6 --
	1992	402,229.4 --	50,636.4 --	85,374.6 ±960.3	1,405,902.2 ±996.0	1,491,276.8 ±133.4	1,944,142.6 --
	1997	402,555.9 --	50,983.4 --	96,097.3 ±1,010.3	1,394,506.0 ±1,052.9	1,490,603.3 ±146.8	1,944,142.6 --
	2002	404,112.7 --	51,441.3 --	104,911.8 ±1,172.8	1,383,676.8 ±1,207.2	1,488,588.6 ±141.7	1,944,142.6 --
	2007	404,786.3 --	51,782.4 --	110,627.1 ±1,249.5	1,376,946.8 ±1,284.1	1,487,573.9 ±139.8	1,944,142.6 --
	2012	405,278.2 --	51,989.9 --	113,661.2 ±1,282.4	1,373,213.3 ±1,312.3	1,486,874.5 ±136.4	1,944,142.6 --
	2015	405,278.2 --	52,055.6 --	115,076.7 ±1,308.4	1,371,732.1 ±1,340.8	1,486,808.8 ±132.7	1,944,142.6 --

Source: *U.S. Department of Agriculture, 2015 National Resources Inventory, Summary Report, September 2018*

Table 1 - Surface area of non-Federal and Federal land and water areas, by State and year
In thousands of acres, with margins of error

State	Year	Federal land	Water areas	Non-Federal Land			Total surface area
				Developed	Rural	Total	

Notes:
• Acreages for Federal land, water areas, and total surface area are established through geospatial processes and administrative records; therefore, statistical margins of error are not applicable and shown as a dashed line (--).

Source: *U.S. Department of Agriculture, 2015 National Resources Inventory, Summary Report, September 2018*

Table 2 - Land Cover/use of non-Federal rural land, by State and year
In thousands of acres, with margins of error

State	Year	Cropland	CRP land	Pastureland	Rangeland	Forest land	Other rural land	Total rural land
Alabama	1982	4,464.7 ±176.9	--	3,793.9 ±186.4	53.7 ±47.3	20,876.8 ±184.4	523.5 ±73.2	29,712.6 ±112.8
	1987	3,944.7 ±187.9	207.5 --	3,643.8 ±157.9	52.8 ±45.6	21,160.9 ±181.1	491.2 ±74.0	29,500.9 ±116.9
	1992	3,126.2 ±192.4	535.2 --	3,753.3 ±147.5	52.7 ±45.6	21,250.7 ±189.7	611.7 ±84.8	29,329.8 ±124.5
	1997	2,915.5 ±209.9	522.2 --	3,558.0 ±134.4	53.8 ±46.7	21,325.9 ±200.6	590.9 ±78.9	28,966.3 ±139.8
	2002	2,508.5 ±183.0	504.6 --	3,452.2 ±194.7	50.7 ±108.9	21,550.4 ±250.2	505.8 ±83.3	28,572.2 ±151.7
	2007	2,200.2 ±180.6	459.8 --	3,434.9 ±177.3	50.7 ±108.9	21,668.5 ±262.4	554.6 ±90.2	28,368.7 ±164.9
	2012	2,217.0 ±189.0	329.2 --	3,302.9 ±175.9	50.7 ±108.9	21,787.8 ±264.1	591.6 ±85.8	28,279.2 ±168.1
	2015	2,274.9 ±194.2	225.6 --	3,220.2 ±187.2	50.7 ±108.9	21,887.4 ±263.4	591.6 ±85.2	28,250.4 ±168.1
Arizona	1982	1,253.0 ±146.6	--	83.6 ±50.4	33,366.4 ±1,026.6	4,572.6 ±862.1	1,711.8 ±577.2	40,987.4 ±270.6
	1987	1,234.6 ±145.5	0.0 --	76.6 ±40.2	33,395.7 ±1,046.3	4,553.8 ±860.8	1,784.4 ±594.7	41,045.1 ±286.7
	1992	1,199.9 ±148.8	0.0 --	83.3 ±36.0	33,796.0 ±1,069.5	4,434.9 ±881.6	1,801.6 ±569.8	41,315.7 ±295.4
	1997	1,199.8 ±142.6	0.0 --	74.6 ±34.5	33,630.1 ±1,093.6	4,358.6 ±892.0	1,951.4 ±555.0	41,214.5 ±309.4
	2002	945.7 ±127.6	0.0 --	66.5 ±53.0	33,634.0 ±1,141.4	4,230.9 ±877.8	1,893.0 ±546.1	40,770.1 ±346.8
	2007	916.0 ±131.8	0.0 --	58.1 ±57.8	33,479.5 ±1,115.6	4,190.4 ±880.7	1,910.3 ±530.7	40,554.3 ±385.1
	2012	900.5 ±119.4	0.0 --	46.7 ±44.2	33,398.3 ±1,133.3	4,179.4 ±875.3	1,910.9 ±538.1	40,435.8 ±411.0
	2015	898.2 ±121.6	0.0 --	44.4 ±44.1	33,341.4 ±1,122.6	4,179.1 ±875.4	1,947.4 ±531.5	40,410.5 ±417.3
Arkansas	1982	8,043.3 ±437.9	--	5,575.1 ±323.6	17.1 ±57.2	14,874.2 ±452.7	315.6 ±44.7	28,825.3 ±100.1
	1987	7,917.7 ±431.7	91.5 --	5,556.6 ±320.7	17.1 ±57.2	14,833.1 ±455.0	327.8 ±42.2	28,743.8 ±104.7
	1992	7,667.2 ±435.0	232.8 --	5,493.3 ±322.2	11.4 ±51.9	14,872.7 ±455.0	340.4 ±41.4	28,617.8 ±108.5
	1997	7,582.4 ±427.1	230.4 --	5,275.3 ±292.9	11.4 ±51.9	14,940.9 ±459.2	364.5 ±49.7	28,404.9 ±113.3
	2002	7,500.1 ±477.1	146.8 --	5,252.1 ±306.4	17.3 ±50.3	14,920.3 ±472.2	379.8 ±60.0	28,216.4 ±119.8
	2007	7,282.2 ±430.8	160.5 --	5,263.2 ±324.6	17.3 ±50.3	14,997.1 ±496.0	396.0 ±56.9	28,116.3 ±125.4
	2012	7,160.5 ±440.2	124.7 --	5,304.2 ±333.6	20.5 ±49.9	15,044.9 ±497.8	384.2 ±59.8	28,039.0 ±128.6
	2015	7,133.5 ±440.1	79.7 --	5,298.0 ±344.9	20.5 ±49.9	15,074.8 ±503.3	420.7 ±69.5	28,027.2 ±126.2

Source: *U.S. Department of Agriculture, 2015 National Resources Inventory, Summary Report, September 2018*

Table 2 - Land Cover/use of non-Federal rural land, by State and year
In thousands of acres, with margins of error

State	Year	Cropland	CRP land	Pastureland	Rangeland	Forest land	Other rural land	Total rural land
California	1982	10,525.0 ±586.4	--	1,278.0 ±222.5	21,110.7 ±1,003.2	14,812.4 ±672.3	1,982.8 ±548.6	49,708.9 ±349.6
	1987	10,232.6 ±622.4	97.3 --	1,379.5 ±263.7	20,851.0 ±1,061.6	14,841.6 ±703.5	2,015.1 ±569.5	49,417.1 ±363.4
	1992	10,070.1 ±607.4	164.3 --	1,082.5 ±238.3	20,278.6 ±1,018.6	14,633.8 ±718.2	2,085.1 ±575.7	48,314.4 ±372.7
	1997	9,719.4 ±627.8	173.0 --	1,030.3 ±218.4	20,252.5 ±1,085.0	14,446.1 ±694.6	2,177.8 ±561.4	47,799.1 ±375.0
	2002	9,499.7 ±609.7	210.0 --	1,174.2 ±216.6	19,480.2 ±1,020.2	14,262.0 ±673.4	2,236.9 ±563.4	46,863.0 ±369.1
	2007	9,253.0 ±626.1	130.6 --	1,218.0 ±216.6	19,357.1 ±996.8	14,124.5 ±671.6	2,266.5 ±522.2	46,349.7 ±362.1
	2012	9,200.1 ±636.2	21.3 --	1,295.3 ±200.9	19,192.8 ±1,012.6	14,070.5 ±666.7	2,348.7 ±540.8	46,128.7 ±362.4
	2015	9,315.7 ±637.4	21.3 --	1,277.0 ±220.1	19,010.6 ±1,003.8	14,060.8 ±666.2	2,378.6 ±560.1	46,064.0 ±359.0
Caribbean	1982	399.9 ±28.1	--	761.7 ±42.7	151.5 ±18.3	534.7 ±39.5	45.4 ±12.3	1,893.2 ±27.0
	1987	372.0 ±27.9	0.0 --	747.0 ±40.0	147.2 ±18.6	536.0 ±39.7	51.7 ±11.8	1,853.9 ±27.8
	1992	357.8 ±31.0	0.0 --	689.2 ±34.5	135.4 ±16.9	535.0 ±35.9	58.2 ±11.6	1,775.6 ±30.1
	1997	357.7 ±30.4	0.0 --	455.4 ±28.7	134.5 ±18.6	654.9 ±39.5	60.8 ±13.4	1,663.3 ±30.5
	2002	343.4 ±37.9	0.0 --	422.1 ±33.7	128.2 ±22.6	671.1 ±41.2	67.3 ±16.1	1,632.1 ±32.6
	2007	262.0 ±42.3	0.0 --	449.4 ±51.3	122.0 ±22.9	716.7 ±49.0	62.5 ±13.7	1,612.6 ±34.8
	2012	256.7 ±47.0	0.0 --	360.0 ±50.6	118.6 ±22.7	810.4 ±52.3	49.1 ±16.2	1,594.8 ±35.1
	2015	252.3 ±49.3	0.0 --	349.7 ±45.1	118.5 ±22.8	824.9 ±55.8	47.7 ±16.8	1,593.1 ±35.1
Colorado	1982	10,548.1 ±628.6	--	1,112.8 ±144.0	25,255.2 ±751.0	3,850.8 ±429.1	652.1 ±156.1	41,419.0 ±108.2
	1987	9,633.9 ±666.3	1,113.7 --	1,114.9 ±142.5	24,767.8 ±756.9	3,811.7 ±424.3	694.9 ±172.7	41,136.9 ±139.7
	1992	8,817.6 ±614.5	1,912.7 --	1,134.6 ±150.9	24,683.3 ±764.1	3,653.7 ±441.8	717.9 ±161.5	40,919.8 ±150.0
	1997	8,739.4 ±598.9	1,890.1 --	1,153.8 ±147.9	24,694.9 ±752.5	3,620.3 ±439.7	711.0 ±166.2	40,809.5 ±165.5
	2002	8,202.9 ±584.5	2,201.2 --	1,017.9 ±125.1	24,858.2 ±711.7	3,537.1 ±426.1	745.0 ±162.7	40,562.3 ±192.6
	2007	7,745.5 ±548.2	2,446.6 --	1,144.7 ±156.7	24,760.7 ±714.0	3,519.8 ±426.4	774.8 ±162.7	40,392.1 ±200.3
	2012	7,887.4 ±533.3	2,125.6 --	1,387.2 ±162.7	24,594.4 ±682.5	3,503.9 ±425.8	788.9 ±161.2	40,287.4 ±201.2
	2015	8,055.6 ±537.8	1,843.4 --	1,488.8 ±208.6	24,511.4 ±672.3	3,498.5 ±423.1	856.9 ±178.8	40,254.6 ±202.8

Source: *U.S. Department of Agriculture, 2015 National Resources Inventory, Summary Report, September 2018*

Table 2 - Land Cover/use of non-Federal rural land, by State and year
In thousands of acres, with margins of error

State	Year	Cropland	CRP land	Pastureland	Rangeland	Forest land	Other rural land	Total rural land
Connecticut	1982	232.7 ±38.1	--	116.7 ±23.8	0.0 --	1,754.1 ±57.8	110.5 ±23.6	2,214.0 ±35.3
	1987	218.0 ±34.3	0.0 --	117.3 ±26.1	0.0 --	1,713.1 ±55.6	109.1 ±23.4	2,157.5 ±36.8
	1992	213.4 ±34.6	0.0 --	108.2 ±22.1	0.0 --	1,686.0 ±54.3	104.5 ±20.9	2,112.1 ±36.9
	1997	196.0 ±33.7	0.0 --	103.1 ±20.9	0.0 --	1,668.0 ±52.4	99.4 ±18.4	2,066.5 ±34.5
	2002	174.3 ±31.6	0.0 --	108.6 ±21.0	0.0 --	1,625.4 ±52.6	103.0 ±19.7	2,011.3 ±37.3
	2007	173.3 ±29.4	0.0 --	96.9 ±20.7	0.0 --	1,604.2 ±54.5	104.1 ±20.0	1,978.5 ±38.5
	2012	172.9 ±34.1	0.0 --	97.3 ±20.8	0.0 --	1,597.1 ±55.2	100.3 ±21.9	1,967.6 ±38.4
	2015	165.0 ±29.8	0.0 --	103.0 ±22.4	0.0 --	1,592.7 ±55.5	101.6 ±22.1	1,962.3 ±39.0
Delaware	1982	523.3 ±36.4	--	36.3 ±10.9	0.0 --	373.7 ±43.2	114.9 ±26.1	1,048.2 ±25.9
	1987	512.1 ±36.7	0.0 --	34.7 ±10.5	0.0 --	370.1 ±44.7	114.3 ±25.8	1,031.2 ±28.5
	1992	499.4 ±36.8	0.8 --	32.8 ±9.3	0.0 --	364.1 ±42.7	117.2 ±25.4	1,014.3 ±29.2
	1997	485.8 ±34.2	0.8 --	25.9 ±7.7	0.0 --	359.8 ±39.9	121.0 ±25.7	993.3 ±30.9
	2002	459.2 ±35.4	0.9 --	27.2 ±9.3	0.0 --	350.0 ±37.2	120.8 ±27.9	958.1 ±32.8
	2007	418.8 ±33.8	1.3 --	37.0 ±10.3	0.0 --	343.2 ±35.2	129.5 ±29.9	929.8 ±35.5
	2012	408.2 ±38.9	0.4 --	39.2 ±12.2	0.0 --	344.9 ±38.5	123.3 ±27.8	916.0 ±37.0
	2015	398.9 ±39.0	0.4 --	39.5 ±12.6	0.0 --	346.7 ±39.0	123.0 ±27.8	908.5 ±38.3
Florida	1982	3,572.7 ±234.2	--	4,320.3 ±248.2	4,274.8 ±331.2	13,424.1 ±361.6	2,407.5 ±305.8	27,999.4 ±243.4
	1987	3,218.6 ±245.3	93.1 --	4,599.2 ±278.5	3,931.4 ±347.4	13,367.1 ±373.0	2,436.4 ±309.5	27,645.8 ±249.7
	1992	3,085.5 ±262.2	119.5 --	4,509.8 ±293.2	3,373.9 ±318.5	13,326.3 ±367.1	2,444.8 ±325.5	26,859.8 ±271.4
	1997	2,792.9 ±276.3	120.0 --	4,445.8 ±336.3	3,073.9 ±355.6	13,245.1 ±385.6	2,500.7 ±326.6	26,178.4 ±295.2
	2002	2,873.8 ±289.6	97.2 --	4,032.8 ±335.5	2,766.7 ±331.4	13,313.0 ±375.3	2,536.1 ±324.1	25,619.6 ±314.9
	2007	2,782.7 ±313.5	78.1 --	3,848.6 ±348.2	2,560.3 ±328.9	13,206.6 ±338.8	2,693.3 ±319.4	25,169.6 ±328.6
	2012	2,822.2 ±294.3	45.4 --	3,771.3 ±333.6	2,515.6 ±330.4	13,190.4 ±333.3	2,663.2 ±326.1	25,008.1 ±330.9
	2015	2,819.9 ±311.7	34.2 --	3,720.9 ±345.7	2,465.0 ±331.2	13,224.5 ±334.2	2,691.7 ±331.2	24,956.2 ±333.8

Source: *U.S. Department of Agriculture, 2015 National Resources Inventory, Summary Report, September 2018*

Table 2 - Land Cover/use of non-Federal rural land, by State and year
In thousands of acres, with margins of error

State	Year	Cropland	CRP land	Pastureland	Rangeland	Forest land	Other rural land	Total rural land
Georgia	1982	6,599.1 ±208.8	--	2,952.2 ±168.6	0.0 --	22,056.7 ±386.9	911.3 ±115.9	32,519.3 ±116.3
	1987	5,956.4 ±207.9	299.8 --	2,938.5 ±146.1	0.0 --	22,181.0 ±365.5	885.9 ±112.1	32,261.6 ±129.9
	1992	5,174.8 ±256.5	613.1 --	3,048.0 ±152.2	0.0 --	22,056.9 ±390.3	878.1 ±108.2	31,770.9 ±141.9
	1997	4,748.2 ±188.3	595.3 --	2,907.2 ±167.8	0.0 --	21,857.5 ±377.6	863.4 ±122.8	30,971.6 ±156.9
	2002	4,457.8 ±207.2	264.4 --	2,833.5 ±174.9	0.0 --	22,014.6 ±369.5	863.0 ±121.9	30,433.3 ±190.4
	2007	4,251.9 ±257.2	237.3 --	2,800.4 ±198.0	0.0 --	21,922.8 ±362.3	910.2 ±127.1	30,122.6 ±205.1
	2012	4,266.8 ±275.7	155.0 --	2,722.1 ±201.3	0.0 --	21,870.0 ±400.5	968.7 ±133.8	29,982.6 ±209.7
	2015	4,403.6 ±267.2	139.7 --	2,604.2 ±201.6	0.0 --	21,796.7 ±397.0	986.1 ±141.5	29,930.3 ±210.6
Hawaii	1982	287.7 ±73.2	--	65.3 ±22.7	1,135.5 ±139.2	1,578.1 ±169.5	462.2 ±185.8	3,528.8 ±32.6
	1987	282.2 ±71.5	0.0 --	57.4 ±22.5	1,121.9 ±140.6	1,549.8 ±170.0	446.4 ±185.5	3,457.7 ±33.0
	1992	263.4 ±69.6	0.0 --	57.7 ±21.0	1,131.4 ±139.1	1,541.7 ±171.2	440.4 ±188.9	3,434.6 ±35.9
	1997	231.7 ±59.1	0.0 --	59.7 ±21.1	1,125.7 ±140.6	1,560.8 ±163.6	477.8 ±182.3	3,455.7 ±35.5
	2002	150.0 ±49.0	0.0 --	89.6 ±22.3	1,156.1 ±137.8	1,557.2 ±167.4	481.0 ±180.3	3,433.9 ±38.1
	2007	105.0 ±60.9	0.0 --	92.8 ±21.6	1,124.1 ±132.3	1,492.3 ±163.0	461.1 ±181.6	3,275.3 ±39.3
	2012	89.3 ±59.6	0.0 --	94.5 ±24.1	1,116.6 ±133.4	1,489.5 ±166.5	456.9 ±186.1	3,246.8 ±39.6
	2015	84.7 ±58.9	0.0 --	98.1 ±25.6	1,115.9 ±132.4	1,487.2 ±166.7	455.1 ±186.5	3,241.0 ±40.7
Idaho	1982	6,442.4 ±318.3	--	1,231.7 ±165.2	6,825.5 ±344.7	4,036.4 ±350.7	379.9 ±106.6	18,915.9 ±52.0
	1987	6,111.9 ±310.7	444.9 --	1,228.0 ±149.2	6,744.0 ±334.4	4,126.9 ±348.7	402.5 ±105.0	19,058.2 ±54.4
	1992	5,658.5 ±314.3	819.0 --	1,243.8 ±161.8	6,711.5 ±338.8	4,048.7 ±351.4	414.3 ±108.7	18,895.8 ±59.9
	1997	5,537.2 ±312.9	784.2 --	1,270.5 ±159.2	6,698.4 ±345.7	4,027.0 ±344.0	430.0 ±110.9	18,747.3 ±66.7
	2002	5,401.7 ±317.8	753.5 --	1,287.2 ±160.5	6,712.3 ±355.1	4,050.1 ±324.4	437.8 ±104.1	18,672.6 ±69.8
	2007	5,274.6 ±353.0	778.0 --	1,318.1 ±188.1	6,724.4 ±374.9	4,047.9 ±326.2	463.0 ±110.5	18,606.0 ±77.1
	2012	5,344.7 ±338.4	528.4 --	1,434.7 ±183.6	6,766.7 ±377.9	4,036.7 ±326.9	468.1 ±109.2	18,579.3 ±78.3
	2015	5,390.5 ±342.4	440.7 --	1,415.5 ±186.9	6,807.0 ±375.3	4,035.0 ±326.6	479.3 ±107.8	18,568.0 ±81.3

Source: *U.S. Department of Agriculture, 2015 National Resources Inventory, Summary Report, September 2018*

Table 2 - Land Cover/use of non-Federal rural land, by State and year
In thousands of acres, with margins of error

State	Year	Cropland	CRP land	Pastureland	Rangeland	Forest land	Other rural land	Total rural land
Illinois	1982	24,754.4 ±262.7	--	3,183.2 ±221.1	0.0 --	3,635.8 ±167.5	654.7 ±34.7	32,228.1 ±125.5
	1987	24,721.5 ±253.0	120.8 --	2,935.8 ±207.9	0.0 --	3,662.2 ±164.6	656.4 ±36.1	32,096.7 ±130.2
	1992	24,130.7 ±247.3	710.5 --	2,768.4 ±203.6	0.0 --	3,722.7 ±165.6	656.0 ±37.1	31,988.3 ±130.6
	1997	24,051.9 ±212.8	725.6 --	2,519.6 ±188.5	0.0 --	3,814.4 ±159.5	643.2 ±46.1	31,754.7 ±126.9
	2002	24,119.8 ±240.5	609.5 --	2,271.0 ±171.4	0.0 --	3,944.4 ±168.4	659.3 ±48.8	31,604.0 ±135.4
	2007	23,870.4 ±251.6	665.5 --	2,264.2 ±168.3	0.0 --	3,978.9 ±168.0	682.1 ±55.3	31,461.1 ±142.8
	2012	23,887.3 ±264.0	554.1 --	2,230.7 ±169.3	0.0 --	4,031.5 ±167.5	689.4 ±58.0	31,393.0 ±146.5
	2015	23,952.4 ±253.4	402.0 --	2,220.8 ±173.0	0.0 --	4,072.9 ±173.8	706.3 ±56.5	31,354.4 ±146.3
Indiana	1982	13,806.7 ±189.5	--	2,198.3 ±123.0	0.0 --	3,811.2 ±143.5	731.0 ±74.3	20,547.2 ±91.9
	1987	13,891.8 ±198.8	140.6 --	1,892.7 ±114.3	0.0 --	3,823.9 ±142.2	675.9 ±72.6	20,424.9 ±94.0
	1992	13,556.9 ±204.7	413.2 --	1,834.4 ±115.5	0.0 --	3,824.6 ±144.2	685.1 ±78.6	20,314.2 ±102.5
	1997	13,441.7 ±225.5	377.9 --	1,842.0 ±110.8	0.0 --	3,816.4 ±145.6	649.4 ±67.0	20,127.4 ±114.3
	2002	13,361.8 ±219.7	213.3 --	1,913.1 ±125.0	0.0 --	3,849.3 ±150.8	634.7 ±71.0	19,972.2 ±121.3
	2007	13,237.2 ±233.7	178.5 --	1,894.0 ±132.2	0.0 --	3,887.2 ±153.3	649.1 ±84.4	19,846.0 ±126.4
	2012	13,281.8 ±233.0	109.1 --	1,825.7 ±132.3	0.0 --	3,918.2 ±156.7	647.8 ±87.9	19,782.6 ±129.3
	2015	13,325.0 ±235.5	93.6 --	1,756.7 ±133.6	0.0 --	3,913.3 ±157.3	663.4 ±87.8	19,752.0 ±129.8
Iowa	1982	26,377.2 ±251.7	--	4,522.3 ±185.3	0.0 --	1,916.0 ±140.6	925.9 ±60.2	33,741.4 ±95.5
	1987	25,640.2 ±240.0	1,244.1 --	3,954.8 ±188.8	0.0 --	1,985.4 ±140.5	885.5 ±60.4	33,710.0 ±101.4
	1992	24,888.3 ±231.3	2,091.4 --	3,704.2 ±196.2	0.0 --	2,124.6 ±148.5	862.1 ±60.0	33,670.6 ±101.9
	1997	25,201.2 ±237.5	1,739.0 --	3,539.7 ±188.2	0.0 --	2,216.5 ±149.0	870.5 ±60.5	33,566.9 ±104.4
	2002	25,347.0 ±216.9	1,512.4 --	3,429.9 ±165.6	0.0 --	2,330.0 ±152.3	856.9 ±77.5	33,476.2 ±108.9
	2007	25,435.3 ±209.9	1,429.1 --	3,292.1 ±152.2	0.0 --	2,364.8 ±140.7	882.4 ±78.2	33,403.7 ±115.1
	2012	25,807.3 ±215.6	1,030.0 --	3,228.1 ±172.9	0.0 --	2,395.7 ±145.7	898.7 ±83.4	33,359.8 ±119.6
	2015	26,023.7 ±221.1	776.0 --	3,251.5 ±164.9	0.0 --	2,393.6 ±145.1	892.4 ±85.8	33,337.2 ±121.2

Source: *U.S. Department of Agriculture, 2015 National Resources Inventory, Summary Report, September 2018*

Table 2 - Land Cover/use of non-Federal rural land, by State and year
In thousands of acres, with margins of error

State	Year	Cropland	CRP land	Pastureland	Rangeland	Forest land	Other rural land	Total rural land
Kansas	**1982**	29,090.0 ±389.8	--	2,128.7 ±139.9	16,442.6 ±340.6	1,587.0 ±102.7	684.2 ±67.8	49,932.5 ±72.3
	1987	28,463.2 ±387.9	646.6 --	2,179.0 ±135.3	16,346.5 ±338.2	1,590.4 ±104.4	678.1 ±68.2	49,903.8 ±72.7
	1992	26,538.1 ±395.2	2,864.1 --	2,285.1 ±137.1	15,741.7 ±334.6	1,677.6 ±108.6	687.2 ±63.8	49,793.8 ±76.4
	1997	26,488.2 ±401.9	2,848.8 --	2,318.8 ±138.8	15,643.1 ±344.5	1,685.5 ±104.2	694.1 ±62.2	49,678.5 ±76.7
	2002	26,445.6 ±396.6	2,634.3 --	2,367.2 ±180.6	15,731.7 ±334.1	1,713.4 ±105.0	705.6 ±67.8	49,597.8 ±78.5
	2007	25,614.1 ±433.0	3,166.1 --	2,545.8 ±195.9	15,720.7 ±347.8	1,751.6 ±116.4	743.6 ±79.7	49,541.9 ±87.7
	2012	25,808.1 ±445.3	2,351.8 --	3,083.9 ±233.7	15,723.8 ±345.3	1,791.2 ±117.4	762.6 ±81.0	49,521.4 ±92.0
	2015	26,218.0 ±433.8	1,981.8 --	3,054.8 ±233.2	15,667.3 ±336.7	1,805.2 ±121.1	776.4 ±89.2	49,503.5 ±94.3
Kentucky	**1982**	5,933.1 ±152.4	--	5,920.8 ±164.3	0.0 --	10,541.4 ±180.1	690.1 ±62.6	23,085.4 ±70.8
	1987	5,485.5 ±175.9	204.4 --	5,858.8 ±167.1	0.0 --	10,588.8 ±194.2	707.3 ±66.5	22,844.8 ±82.4
	1992	5,146.2 ±158.8	421.9 --	5,818.6 ±138.7	0.0 --	10,680.2 ±200.2	560.2 ±53.7	22,627.1 ±85.4
	1997	5,194.8 ±143.8	332.2 --	5,675.0 ±114.6	0.0 --	10,720.3 ±201.7	457.9 ±42.7	22,380.2 ±95.6
	2002	5,316.1 ±261.8	282.1 --	5,235.3 ±228.6	0.0 --	10,645.5 ±199.3	532.4 ±53.1	22,011.4 ±95.1
	2007	5,246.9 ±257.1	283.9 --	5,190.4 ±242.7	0.0 --	10,648.3 ±195.6	528.6 ±68.1	21,898.1 ±98.0
	2012	5,504.1 ±263.7	169.7 --	4,924.7 ±250.4	0.0 --	10,715.3 ±199.7	526.6 ±70.5	21,840.4 ±98.5
	2015	5,661.5 ±266.0	104.3 --	4,691.5 ±224.1	0.0 --	10,809.7 ±208.2	550.8 ±76.4	21,817.8 ±99.8
Louisiana	**1982**	6,394.8 ±200.3	--	2,330.3 ±132.1	219.5 ±37.1	13,172.0 ±204.7	2,682.1 ±157.5	24,798.7 ±63.8
	1987	6,250.4 ±176.7	42.2 --	2,336.6 ±146.1	213.6 ±36.6	12,974.2 ±213.8	2,720.0 ±152.9	24,537.0 ±59.6
	1992	5,962.2 ±179.4	146.6 --	2,338.2 ±137.9	213.4 ±33.6	12,893.9 ±213.7	2,741.8 ±150.4	24,296.1 ±63.7
	1997	5,650.7 ±166.3	140.4 --	2,460.4 ±139.3	206.7 ±29.9	12,934.0 ±200.4	2,753.6 ±160.2	24,145.8 ±64.5
	2002	5,426.0 ±163.0	161.3 --	2,481.7 ±142.2	104.4 ±36.3	12,919.1 ±227.6	2,752.1 ±164.5	23,934.6 ±64.1
	2007	5,093.1 ±197.5	230.9 --	2,603.0 ±139.2	203.9 ±31.4	12,881.5 ±220.0	2,747.9 ±153.9	23,760.3 ±66.6
	2012	4,923.4 ±203.4	199.9 --	2,607.7 ±174.9	196.6 ±33.6	12,954.2 ±225.3	2,777.9 ±158.8	23,659.7 ±69.1
	2015	4,915.8 ±215.5	99.0 --	2,560.8 ±179.3	193.2 ±32.5	13,062.5 ±234.5	2,776.9 ±160.7	23,608.2 ±69.8

Source: *U.S. Department of Agriculture, 2015 National Resources Inventory, Summary Report, September 2018*

Table 2 - Land Cover/use of non-Federal rural land, by State and year
In thousands of acres, with margins of error

State	Year	Cropland	CRP land	Pastureland	Rangeland	Forest land	Other rural land	Total rural land
Maine	1982	520.7 ±112.1	--	308.9 ±76.1	0.0 –	17,596.0 ±245.2	585.0 ±169.1	19,010.6 ±77.7
	1987	509.5 ±104.6	0.0 –	263.3 ±69.9	0.0 –	17,597.6 ±239.0	568.2 ±165.6	18,938.6 ±83.1
	1992	474.7 ±86.8	35.6 –	193.1 ±55.2	0.0 –	17,611.0 ±240.9	576.5 ±150.4	18,890.9 ±85.8
	1997	447.6 ±83.3	29.7 –	163.0 ±40.6	0.0 –	17,614.6 ±252.9	520.4 ±151.1	18,775.3 ±93.7
	2002	409.7 ±90.8	29.7 –	168.8 ±43.1	0.0 –	17,565.2 ±258.2	505.2 ±149.9	18,678.6 ±93.5
	2007	387.7 ±89.7	29.7 –	169.5 ±48.4	0.0 –	17,528.7 ±265.5	507.2 ±166.0	18,622.8 ±97.2
	2012	377.6 ±82.6	29.7 –	164.1 ±46.9	0.0 –	17,522.0 ±265.6	507.0 ±166.2	18,600.4 ±101.4
	2015	368.3 ±82.5	29.7 –	171.3 ±48.8	0.0 –	17,514.4 ±264.9	509.6 ±165.9	18,593.3 ±101.8
Maryland	1982	1,769.7 ±87.3	--	546.2 ±44.4	0.0 –	2,425.9 ±111.7	330.0 ±32.0	5,071.8 ±113.8
	1987	1,707.8 ±82.6	1.2 –	569.0 ±37.6	0.0 –	2,396.6 ±108.1	308.9 ±33.0	4,983.5 ±117.6
	1992	1,639.8 ±81.8	19.2 –	565.8 ±39.4	0.0 –	2,368.6 ±110.1	306.5 ±32.5	4,899.9 ±121.0
	1997	1,581.2 ±83.1	19.1 –	472.4 ±36.2	0.0 –	2,331.3 ±107.1	305.8 ±32.7	4,709.8 ±126.7
	2002	1,484.9 ±88.8	9.9 –	450.2 ±44.5	0.0 –	2,346.9 ±107.6	323.8 ±29.7	4,615.7 ±125.4
	2007	1,427.8 ±81.8	10.7 –	451.2 ±52.7	0.0 –	2,320.8 ±103.3	337.9 ±28.7	4,548.4 ±125.3
	2012	1,413.6 ±82.0	5.8 –	431.9 ±47.4	0.0 –	2,314.5 ±101.0	347.1 ±29.6	4,512.9 ±124.0
	2015	1,422.4 ±79.5	4.6 –	407.2 ±49.3	0.0 –	2,313.4 ±102.3	349.9 ±31.3	4,497.5 ±126.4
Massachusetts	1982	289.9 ±52.4	--	184.4 ±31.9	0.0 –	3,044.9 ±109.3	246.4 ±34.9	3,765.6 ±66.6
	1987	280.0 ±53.0	0.0 –	160.0 ±28.9	0.0 –	2,961.1 ±108.3	249.3 ±35.9	3,650.4 ±69.6
	1992	263.4 ±55.0	0.0 –	155.1 ±29.1	0.0 –	2,850.8 ±107.5	239.8 ±34.3	3,509.1 ±69.9
	1997	265.6 ±55.2	0.0 –	123.0 ±23.9	0.0 –	2,678.5 ±106.8	223.1 ±31.3	3,290.2 ±71.1
	2002	246.9 ±52.5	0.0 –	129.3 ±28.5	0.0 –	2,607.0 ±103.4	220.3 ±32.0	3,203.5 ±69.2
	2007	226.7 ±48.7	0.0 –	138.5 ±27.1	0.0 –	2,565.4 ±101.6	218.1 ±33.3	3,148.7 ±68.0
	2012	224.7 ±50.3	0.0 –	139.4 ±29.3	0.0 –	2,557.2 ±101.8	220.0 ±33.0	3,141.3 ±70.6
	2015	220.9 ±50.4	0.0 –	141.2 ±33.1	0.0 –	2,548.4 ±100.4	220.8 ±33.3	3,131.3 ±71.3

Source: *U.S. Department of Agriculture, 2015 National Resources Inventory, Summary Report, September 2018*

Table 2 - Land Cover/use of non-Federal rural land, by State and year
In thousands of acres, with margins of error

State	Year	Cropland	CRP land	Pastureland	Rangeland	Forest land	Other rural land	Total rural land
Michigan	1982	9,387.9 ±280.9	--	2,930.7 ±177.1	0.0 --	15,921.1 ±276.1	2,044.6 ±134.4	30,284.3 ±135.0
	1987	9,250.5 ±255.1	54.9 --	2,605.7 ±186.6	0.0 --	16,116.6 ±262.0	2,017.0 ±137.6	30,044.7 ±145.8
	1992	8,919.9 ±249.8	259.5 --	2,421.8 ±169.8	0.0 --	16,131.8 ±254.1	1,998.0 ±136.7	29,731.0 ±151.9
	1997	8,487.5 ±265.3	321.3 --	2,131.9 ±143.3	0.0 --	16,398.7 ±249.6	2,020.6 ±134.0	29,360.0 ±169.1
	2002	8,158.6 ±235.7	202.5 --	2,211.8 ±146.0	0.0 --	16,662.9 ±260.4	1,807.8 ±138.6	29,043.6 ±167.6
	2007	7,949.0 ±270.0	179.9 --	2,251.1 ±178.2	0.0 --	16,656.5 ±231.0	1,841.5 ±124.6	28,878.0 ±170.5
	2012	7,982.9 ±267.3	108.0 --	2,217.6 ±186.2	0.0 --	16,651.6 ±235.1	1,854.8 ±125.8	28,814.9 ±173.8
	2015	7,990.9 ±260.1	69.9 --	2,187.6 ±176.7	0.0 --	16,673.7 ±237.2	1,857.0 ±127.6	28,779.1 ±172.0
Minnesota	1982	22,946.4 ±481.7	--	3,801.2 ±265.8	0.0 --	16,254.0 ±591.4	2,712.4 ±201.3	45,714.0 ±89.0
	1987	22,340.9 ±481.2	779.9 --	3,553.6 ±267.7	0.0 --	16,148.3 ±609.7	2,744.1 ±198.1	45,566.8 ±91.2
	1992	21,321.7 ±469.4	1,810.0 --	3,389.9 ±239.2	0.0 --	16,194.0 ±608.2	2,745.4 ±189.5	45,461.0 ±95.9
	1997	21,343.1 ±495.7	1,543.7 --	3,413.3 ±215.3	0.0 --	16,270.9 ±585.8	2,674.6 ±182.8	45,245.6 ±105.0
	2002	21,104.2 ±514.3	1,423.6 --	3,547.2 ±258.1	0.0 --	16,326.3 ±565.8	2,705.6 ±192.8	45,106.9 ±111.3
	2007	20,837.4 ±514.3	1,441.8 --	3,664.5 ±273.9	0.0 --	16,370.1 ±579.9	2,729.8 ±199.4	45,043.6 ±114.1
	2012	21,035.3 ±468.2	1,079.4 --	3,693.6 ±295.8	0.0 --	16,407.3 ±580.2	2,749.7 ±199.5	44,965.3 ±117.3
	2015	21,330.7 ±486.3	597.3 --	3,821.3 ±317.9	0.0 --	16,432.3 ±584.3	2,762.9 ±198.7	44,944.5 ±120.4
Mississippi	1982	7,384.8 ±261.1	--	3,997.9 ±223.1	0.0 --	15,402.0 ±324.2	330.5 ±39.2	27,115.2 ±96.0
	1987	6,628.8 ±250.5	293.6 --	3,900.3 ±215.4	0.0 --	15,783.6 ±330.0	321.1 ±39.6	26,927.4 ±102.7
	1992	5,721.4 ±237.7	776.2 --	3,928.1 ±214.4	0.0 --	15,983.4 ±333.1	319.6 ±39.1	26,728.7 ±105.7
	1997	5,345.1 ±227.3	797.6 --	3,686.6 ±179.1	0.0 --	16,268.4 ±317.8	370.7 ±48.4	26,468.4 ±121.1
	2002	4,901.1 ±244.9	731.0 --	3,416.6 ±207.9	0.0 --	10,002.0 ±304.5	410.8 ±54.4	26,262.2 ±132.7
	2007	4,684.6 ±253.1	743.5 --	3,287.3 ±218.5	0.0 --	16,983.5 ±305.8	463.2 ±69.5	26,162.1 ±148.4
	2012	4,701.0 ±263.9	609.1 --	3,128.9 ±210.9	0.0 --	17,202.4 ±305.9	482.0 ±75.4	26,123.4 ±155.1
	2015	4,755.4 ±247.9	482.8 --	3,014.5 ±205.5	0.0 --	17,354.5 ±312.0	494.7 ±74.1	26,101.9 ±156.9

Source: *U.S. Department of Agriculture, 2015 National Resources Inventory, Summary Report, September 2018*

Table 2 - Land Cover/use of non-Federal rural land, by State and year
In thousands of acres, with margins of error

State	Year	Cropland	CRP land	Pastureland	Rangeland	Forest land	Other rural land	Total rural land
Missouri	1982	14,927.9 ±261.9	--	12,431.8 ±329.6	125.4 ±49.3	11,509.9 ±300.9	675.8 ±48.7	39,670.8 ±99.0
	1987	14,366.1 ±261.4	570.6 –	12,002.4 ±329.2	90.5 ±39.5	11,862.4 ±309.8	669.1 ±44.6	39,561.1 ±101.4
	1992	13,315.8 ±291.8	1,603.0 –	11,662.9 ±297.0	85.8 ±40.1	12,091.7 ±312.8	653.2 ±48.0	39,412.4 ±107.6
	1997	13,547.2 ±250.8	1,606.6 –	10,860.8 ±282.7	72.7 ±39.4	12,424.0 ±312.9	636.2 ±48.6	39,147.5 ±118.7
	2002	13,561.2 ±313.2	1,488.0 –	10,693.1 ±309.2	64.9 ±120.0	12,513.2 ±327.4	639.2 ±52.8	38,959.6 ±117.2
	2007	13,560.5 ±300.2	1,464.7 –	10,531.1 ±311.1	66.5 ±84.1	12,514.8 ±315.6	678.7 ±66.6	38,816.3 ±122.4
	2012	14,131.6 ±338.0	1,107.9 –	10,124.3 ±272.7	65.2 ±111.5	12,602.6 ±316.0	704.4 ±66.6	38,736.0 ±128.9
	2015	14,816.4 ±340.4	788.8 –	9,689.1 ±283.3	65.2 ±111.5	12,635.6 ±306.7	712.0 ±68.7	38,707.1 ±131.8
Montana	1982	17,109.7 ±886.5	--	3,119.0 ±343.4	38,115.2 ±1,076.5	5,916.3 ±540.3	1,002.4 ±208.4	65,262.6 ±99.9
	1987	16,161.4 ±847.5	1,485.5 –	3,226.3 ±268.5	37,549.1 ±1,098.0	5,920.2 ±536.9	999.1 ±205.0	65,341.6 ±99.8
	1992	15,017.5 ±868.0	2,780.3 –	3,428.2 ±310.7	37,262.4 ±1,070.3	5,919.1 ±537.2	978.8 ±206.2	65,386.3 ±107.5
	1997	15,152.5 ±861.1	2,720.9 –	3,530.5 ±332.5	36,954.0 ±1,040.3	5,975.7 ±513.9	997.5 ±206.7	65,331.1 ±111.9
	2002	14,414.8 ±896.5	3,261.6 –	3,746.5 ±357.5	36,924.4 ±1,031.1	5,959.4 ±515.3	964.7 ±206.4	65,271.4 ±115.9
	2007	14,127.8 ±893.4	3,315.9 –	3,846.3 ±430.3	36,922.7 ±1,036.8	5,943.0 ±516.6	1,001.4 ±205.4	65,157.1 ±121.6
	2012	14,732.5 ±938.2	2,360.6 –	4,162.9 ±497.6	36,876.6 ±1,037.8	5,845.5 ±539.8	1,008.0 ±195.9	64,986.1 ±124.1
	2015	15,427.1 ±1,018.0	1,344.3 –	4,485.4 ±554.1	36,856.9 ±1,025.4	5,850.1 ±538.5	1,009.9 ±198.0	64,973.7 ±126.7
Nebraska	1982	20,287.9 ±451.3	--	1,949.0 ±127.7	23,598.7 ±499.8	861.6 ±100.5	727.9 ±47.9	47,425.1 ±107.6
	1987	19,963.7 ±408.5	590.4 –	1,890.2 ±139.3	23,329.7 ±472.5	874.4 ±101.6	745.1 ±52.0	47,393.5 ±110.6
	1992	19,270.5 ±403.4	1,363.9 –	1,866.7 ±135.4	23,175.9 ±470.7	874.8 ±102.1	751.7 ±54.0	47,303.5 ±115.4
	1997	19,487.8 ±408.5	1,244.8 –	1,776.3 ±120.1	23,099.6 ±464.0	887.3 ±102.0	750.7 ±59.4	47,246.5 ±117.3
	2002	19,561.1 ±395.8	1,100.4 –	1,830.4 ±143.6	23,066.5 ±443.2	875.0 ±96.1	789.0 ±65.7	47,222.4 ±116.7
	2007	19,530.3 ±409.3	1,195.7 –	1,842.8 ±150.0	22,969.1 ±464.4	861.0 ±96.0	795.9 ±82.0	47,194.8 ±117.9
	2012	19,929.3 ±398.0	815.5 –	1,895.5 ±169.4	22,886.0 ±476.9	841.7 ±98.4	810.0 ±85.9	47,178.0 ±117.4
	2015	20,164.0 ±424.5	581.5 –	1,925.7 ±185.3	22,842.9 ±483.2	834.1 ±104.2	812.6 ±86.8	47,160.8 ±118.6

Source: *U.S. Department of Agriculture, 2015 National Resources Inventory, Summary Report, September 2018*

Table 2 - Land Cover/use of non-Federal rural land, by State and year
In thousands of acres, with margins of error

State	Year	Cropland	CRP land	Pastureland	Rangeland	Forest land	Other rural land	Total rural land
Nevada	1982	856.2 ±176.5	--	287.4 ±72.5	8,764.5 ±230.5	387.5 ±145.9	348.3 ±94.0	10,643.9 ±56.4
	1987	833.9 ±181.4	0.0 --	296.7 ±73.5	8,819.5 ±236.7	390.0 ±145.9	351.7 ±101.0	10,691.8 ±63.1
	1992	769.2 ±179.1	1.4 --	288.2 ±71.3	8,795.4 ±220.7	391.0 ±146.3	326.9 ±103.7	10,572.1 ±63.5
	1997	703.7 ±169.2	2.4 --	287.7 ±78.3	8,886.0 ±213.2	333.3 ±128.8	337.5 ±97.1	10,550.6 ±65.1
	2002	671.9 ±155.1	0.0 --	270.4 ±74.8	8,779.0 ±232.8	341.3 ±134.0	339.6 ±103.6	10,402.2 ±77.6
	2007	642.8 ±149.7	0.0 --	243.2 ±70.9	8,809.5 ±239.1	338.8 ±143.0	357.0 ±99.2	10,391.3 ±89.7
	2012	600.2 ±153.2	0.0 --	275.8 ±78.0	8,779.9 ±240.3	338.5 ±145.5	363.3 ±99.6	10,357.7 ±93.0
	2015	597.7 ±148.8	0.0 --	272.4 ±78.1	8,779.9 ±238.0	338.5 ±145.5	364.0 ±99.1	10,352.5 ±93.8
New Hampshire	1982	159.3 ±27.5	--	125.5 ±27.4	0.0 --	4,112.8 ±70.3	174.3 ±32.8	4,571.9 ±47.7
	1987	146.6 ±28.3	0.0 --	111.6 ±26.6	0.0 --	4,035.8 ±70.4	180.9 ±30.8	4,474.9 ±60.5
	1992	140.6 ±27.5	0.0 --	103.5 ±25.9	0.0 --	3,957.7 ±75.3	188.5 ±33.6	4,390.3 ±62.4
	1997	130.1 ±26.1	0.0 --	101.1 ±27.0	0.0 --	3,910.6 ±79.8	173.7 ±31.3	4,315.5 ±66.7
	2002	121.0 ±27.0	0.0 --	100.7 ±27.4	0.0 --	3,858.5 ±82.7	177.3 ±31.9	4,257.5 ±67.3
	2007	117.4 ±27.7	0.0 --	98.5 ±26.3	0.0 --	3,818.0 ±83.2	173.2 ±29.5	4,207.1 ±69.6
	2012	114.4 ±27.9	0.0 --	99.8 ±25.2	0.0 --	3,787.4 ±81.5	176.9 ±30.1	4,178.5 ±68.6
	2015	112.8 ±28.3	0.0 --	97.1 ±24.6	0.0 --	3,787.1 ±80.1	175.9 ±30.7	4,172.9 ±68.0
New Jersey	1982	803.1 ±59.2	--	224.5 ±36.6	0.0 --	1,916.6 ±62.2	382.5 ±42.4	3,326.7 ±67.9
	1987	688.3 ±54.8	0.0 --	178.3 ±24.6	0.0 --	1,871.3 ±68.7	376.4 ±41.3	3,114.3 ±74.6
	1992	652.8 ±51.8	0.5 --	159.6 ±24.5	0.0 --	1,847.9 ±71.0	370.4 ±42.2	3,031.2 ±74.5
	1997	593.3 ±50.3	0.5 --	125.9 ±19.1	0.0 --	1,747.7 ±69.5	363.5 ±43.6	2,830.9 ±77.7
	2002	535.0 ±53.8	0.0 --	125.2 ±23.6	0.0 --	1,675.6 ±71.2	371.9 ±46.1	2,707.7 ±75.1
	2007	495.0 ±51.9	0.0 --	141.7 ±27.6	0.0 --	1,644.7 ±73.4	367.2 ±45.0	2,648.6 ±74.3
	2012	480.2 ±49.9	0.0 --	147.0 ±28.4	0.0 --	1,629.8 ±75.7	364.7 ±44.3	2,621.7 ±74.6
	2015	480.2 ±51.1	0.0 --	141.4 ±28.6	0.0 --	1,621.6 ±75.0	367.5 ±44.6	2,610.7 ±74.5

Source: *U.S. Department of Agriculture, 2015 National Resources Inventory, Summary Report, September 2018*

Table 2 - Land Cover/use of non-Federal rural land, by State and year
In thousands of acres, with margins of error

State	Year	Cropland	CRP land	Pastureland	Rangeland	Forest land	Other rural land	Total rural land
New Mexico	1982	2,413.2 ±168.6	--	186.5 ±172.7	42,502.2 ±951.8	5,536.9 ±811.1	851.0 ±383.2	51,489.8 ±99.1
	1987	1,964.1 ±181.7	425.7 --	220.3 ±174.3	41,925.6 ±971.4	5,382.6 ±797.6	966.2 ±414.0	50,884.5 ±107.3
	1992	1,895.4 ±184.0	480.0 --	228.3 ±173.4	41,435.7 ±879.2	5,538.4 ±785.4	991.9 ±416.1	50,569.7 ±115.5
	1997	1,864.0 ±173.0	467.2 --	236.1 ±179.8	41,094.9 ±973.3	5,747.2 ±839.9	986.6 ±411.3	50,396.0 ±124.5
	2002	1,548.7 ±183.5	626.2 --	268.5 ±169.0	41,096.3 ±967.1	5,600.0 ±836.9	965.3 ±387.8	50,105.0 ±159.0
	2007	1,490.9 ±196.0	582.3 --	294.7 ±186.5	41,099.9 ±952.9	5,573.2 ±836.1	999.6 ±395.8	50,040.6 ±165.7
	2012	1,498.4 ±186.7	409.1 --	464.8 ±195.8	40,944.1 ±937.8	5,595.8 ±857.9	1,083.8 ±428.7	49,996.0 ±165.8
	2015	1,425.6 ±195.2	396.8 --	558.7 ±206.3	40,982.4 ±973.9	5,593.8 ±858.0	1,025.5 ±401.6	49,982.8 ±163.7
New York	1982	5,855.3 ±229.5	--	3,850.5 ±166.1	0.0 --	16,584.9 ±221.2	656.6 ±70.4	26,947.3 ±125.7
	1987	5,680.7 ±220.2	18.4 --	3,423.1 ±170.2	0.0 --	16,913.5 ±231.8	802.9 ±72.2	26,838.6 ±133.0
	1992	5,567.5 ±206.4	57.8 --	3,056.2 ±153.5	0.0 --	17,246.9 ±251.0	767.6 ±72.4	26,696.0 ±137.6
	1997	5,341.5 ±217.0	53.8 --	2,727.1 ±136.0	0.0 --	17,478.7 ±253.0	737.7 ±70.6	26,338.8 ±147.9
	2002	5,224.6 ±199.9	49.9 --	2,641.9 ±159.3	0.0 --	17,434.8 ±248.0	757.7 ±63.1	26,108.9 ±151.3
	2007	5,003.4 ±221.7	49.4 --	2,684.5 ±189.5	0.0 --	17,489.0 ±245.0	773.4 ±68.8	25,999.7 ±148.6
	2012	5,013.2 ±227.6	30.1 --	2,575.5 ±203.7	0.0 --	17,526.0 ±232.9	786.7 ±65.9	25,931.5 ±148.6
	2015	4,982.5 ±237.0	20.2 --	2,535.5 ±199.2	0.0 --	17,579.2 ±241.2	786.8 ±65.7	25,904.2 ±151.0
North Carolina	1982	6,703.8 ±252.7	--	1,964.9 ±128.1	0.0 --	17,150.5 ±287.5	758.0 ±100.7	26,577.2 ±102.0
	1987	6,380.0 ±269.8	31.3 --	1,988.9 ±139.9	0.0 --	16,807.8 ±262.9	773.4 ±102.5	25,981.4 ±112.0
	1992	5,970.3 ±247.8	139.3 --	2,009.6 ±127.2	0.0 --	16,434.8 ±275.6	776.9 ±102.1	25,330.9 ±140.1
	1997	5,682.9 ±244.5	131.2 --	2,048.7 ±136.5	0.0 --	16,172.1 ±270.9	806.1 ±97.6	24,841.0 ±166.5
	2002	5,464.3 ±223.5	55.6 --	1,976.3 ±163.8	0.0 --	15,834.2 ±285.6	837.8 ±101.4	24,168.2 ±201.2
	2007	5,274.8 ±229.2	64.4 --	1,946.1 ±172.0	0.0 --	15,722.7 ±286.8	890.6 ±107.4	23,898.6 ±215.6
	2012	5,105.4 ±255.1	41.3 --	2,012.5 ±200.3	0.0 --	15,697.5 ±298.1	888.5 ±104.6	23,745.2 ±224.1
	2015	5,079.4 ±260.3	42.0 --	1,972.5 ±203.3	0.0 --	15,672.9 ±296.7	893.7 ±103.9	23,660.5 ±222.5

Source: *U.S. Department of Agriculture, 2015 National Resources Inventory, Summary Report, September 2018*

Table 2 - Land Cover/use of non-Federal rural land, by State and year
In thousands of acres, with margins of error

State	Year	Cropland	CRP land	Pastureland	Rangeland	Forest land	Other rural land	Total rural land
North Dakota	1982	27,044.8 ±399.6	--	1,190.4 ±151.5	11,508.2 ±352.0	466.5 ±85.3	1,353.2 ±122.6	41,563.1 ±72.8
	1987	27,106.6 ±382.1	526.1 --	1,135.4 ±118.1	10,961.3 ±356.6	465.2 ±85.5	1,346.8 ±112.4	41,541.4 ±73.4
	1992	24,760.3 ±395.7	2,897.6 --	1,106.5 ±133.3	10,909.8 ±375.2	461.2 ±84.9	1,351.6 ±114.2	41,487.0 ±73.5
	1997	24,974.9 ±359.7	2,801.9 --	1,015.5 ±129.2	10,754.7 ±378.5	459.9 ±82.6	1,377.7 ±120.0	41,384.6 ±75.4
	2002	24,301.8 ±366.6	3,196.7 --	1,080.5 ±161.6	10,923.6 ±398.9	457.4 ±81.3	1,368.7 ±114.4	41,328.7 ±76.6
	2007	24,068.9 ±410.1	3,212.5 --	1,329.0 ±185.2	10,829.1 ±414.5	456.9 ±81.0	1,407.6 ±125.0	41,304.0 ±79.4
	2012	24,605.7 ±448.2	2,038.7 --	2,002.3 ±271.2	10,705.7 ±415.4	454.3 ±81.2	1,416.6 ±115.6	41,223.3 ±81.7
	2015	25,231.9 ±409.2	990.9 --	2,424.1 ±298.3	10,659.1 ±406.2	446.0 ±77.5	1,441.4 ±116.5	41,193.4 ±83.7
Ohio	1982	12,388.1 ±165.5	--	2,768.0 ±132.4	0.0 --	6,725.3 ±180.4	1,010.5 ±66.1	22,891.9 ±119.8
	1987	12,266.4 ±176.1	57.7 --	2,474.7 ±123.6	0.0 --	6,945.3 ±202.6	942.3 ±71.0	22,686.4 ±125.7
	1992	11,857.3 ±160.9	312.9 --	2,347.0 ±125.0	0.0 --	6,966.5 ±218.5	905.8 ±60.3	22,389.5 ±137.7
	1997	11,613.5 ±198.5	323.3 --	2,054.3 ±143.3	0.0 --	7,070.5 ±203.9	962.1 ±60.2	22,023.7 ±150.6
	2002	11,314.7 ±205.6	198.9 --	2,243.9 ±148.4	0.0 --	7,163.7 ±211.5	864.5 ±77.4	21,785.7 ±143.7
	2007	11,099.4 ±222.2	201.4 --	2,262.4 ±163.6	0.0 --	7,124.0 ±202.3	911.8 ±89.4	21,599.0 ±147.6
	2012	11,096.4 ±238.0	154.6 --	2,196.2 ±177.3	0.0 --	7,138.6 ±202.0	908.8 ±99.4	21,494.6 ±148.8
	2015	11,172.1 ±234.2	86.3 --	2,116.9 ±168.0	0.0 --	7,155.8 ±197.1	922.7 ±99.9	21,453.8 ±148.8
Oklahoma	1982	11,606.5 ±326.6	--	7,208.2 ±216.3	14,670.5 ±415.0	7,289.8 ±261.4	401.1 ±53.3	41,176.1 ±97.3
	1987	10,947.3 ±347.9	595.0 --	7,582.3 ±195.8	14,103.9 ±414.7	7,438.8 ±271.3	427.9 ±52.9	41,095.2 ±96.7
	1992	10,133.9 ±346.9	1,161.6 --	7,818.9 ±209.8	13,833.6 ±417.7	7,608.3 ±281.3	453.9 ±51.2	41,010.2 ±100.7
	1997	9,740.2 ±353.6	1,137.1 --	7,989.4 ±207.4	13,762.7 ±421.3	7,667.8 ±273.8	436.3 ±48.1	40,733.5 ±111.9
	2002	9,118.0 ±390.3	1,005.2 --	8,409.2 ±281.0	13,789.1 ±432.2	7,779.6 ±250.1	445.6 ±54.2	40,546.7 ±120.4
	2007	8,836.1 ±379.9	1,058.9 --	8,503.5 ±224.0	13,691.9 ±397.1	7,856.0 ±244.0	469.6 ±58.5	40,416.0 ±120.2
	2012	8,774.8 ±381.6	804.7 --	8,767.3 ±250.5	13,553.4 ±431.2	7,934.0 ±259.5	488.7 ±66.3	40,322.9 ±122.9
	2015	8,715.7 ±382.5	720.4 --	8,803.8 ±259.8	13,510.2 ±437.9	8,015.3 ±257.0	502.8 ±73.2	40,268.2 ±127.4

Source: *U.S. Department of Agriculture, 2015 National Resources Inventory, Summary Report, September 2018*

Table 2 - Land Cover/use of non-Federal rural land, by State and year
In thousands of acres, with margins of error

State	Year	Cropland	CRP land	Pastureland	Rangeland	Forest land	Other rural land	Total rural land
Oregon	1982	4,289.8 ±310.4	--	1,997.7 ±265.5	9,179.8 ±575.1	12,395.8 ±446.8	531.1 ±132.1	28,394.2 ±98.2
	1987	3,902.6 ±330.3	392.5 --	1,972.3 ±267.3	9,086.6 ±577.0	12,344.8 ±454.6	534.6 ±136.1	28,233.4 ±110.3
	1992	3,707.2 ±329.3	521.1 --	1,947.3 ±244.1	9,041.2 ±587.6	12,309.7 ±485.9	522.2 ±122.5	28,048.7 ±114.2
	1997	3,697.5 ±312.4	482.7 --	1,902.2 ±232.3	8,970.3 ±596.6	12,298.3 ±484.9	563.1 ±123.6	27,914.1 ±124.0
	2002	3,630.9 ±327.0	448.7 --	1,786.7 ±238.1	9,050.2 ±601.8	12,385.3 ±500.1	608.7 ±116.5	27,910.5 ±135.2
	2007	3,525.9 ±309.9	511.6 --	1,773.7 ±220.0	9,025.0 ±592.0	12,386.4 ±498.2	630.9 ±116.1	27,853.5 ±142.9
	2012	3,521.6 ±291.1	471.2 --	1,806.6 ±235.2	9,002.4 ±594.2	12,376.5 ±489.0	640.5 ±110.7	27,818.8 ±143.6
	2015	3,604.0 ±350.5	485.9 --	1,737.1 ±217.8	8,979.0 ±597.4	12,365.1 ±480.3	636.7 ±111.3	27,807.8 ±145.0
Pennsylvania	1982	5,889.3 ±250.9	--	2,635.9 ±152.8	0.0 --	15,613.2 ±285.2	943.7 ±104.4	25,082.1 ±109.5
	1987	5,740.6 ±248.3	15.9 --	2,494.1 ±172.3	0.0 --	15,687.4 ±296.9	960.3 ±101.9	24,898.3 ±120.1
	1992	5,583.6 ±249.2	91.5 --	2,324.5 ±155.1	0.0 --	15,552.3 ±289.6	909.7 ±93.1	24,461.6 ±135.3
	1997	5,456.3 ±258.6	90.3 --	1,899.5 ±146.9	0.0 --	15,604.4 ±297.0	873.4 ±103.7	23,923.9 ±149.2
	2002	5,140.7 ±271.8	29.3 --	2,042.2 ±145.7	0.0 --	15,693.7 ±315.1	760.9 ±93.8	23,666.8 ±160.0
	2007	4,964.7 ±274.5	30.8 --	2,024.9 ±160.8	0.0 --	15,679.9 ±312.4	797.2 ±109.9	23,497.5 ±168.6
	2012	4,944.0 ±272.3	18.2 --	1,962.8 ±154.8	0.0 --	15,673.1 ±319.2	807.2 ±109.1	23,405.3 ±170.4
	2015	4,928.2 ±262.0	13.8 --	1,894.5 ±149.5	0.0 --	15,710.9 ±315.2	808.6 ±110.3	23,356.0 ±174.9
Rhode Island	1982	26.2 ±7.3	--	34.8 ±11.2	0.0 --	395.9 ±19.2	24.8 ±8.8	481.7 ±12.5
	1987	26.2 ±7.5	0.0 --	31.9 ±10.5	0.0 --	391.7 ±20.1	22.0 ±8.4	471.8 ±13.8
	1992	22.2 ±7.2	0.0 --	24.9 ±8.6	0.0 --	383.0 ±19.7	23.7 ±8.5	453.8 ±13.8
	1997	18.5 ±6.5	0.0 --	26.6 ±7.4	0.0 --	381.7 ±19.3	23.6 ±8.6	450.4 ±14.3
	2002	17.3 ±7.1	0.0 --	25.1 ±6.4	0.0 --	373.0 ±20.6	22.2 ±7.5	437.6 ±14.6
	2007	15.9 ±6.4	0.0 --	25.6 ±7.8	0.0 --	364.5 ±21.5	22.9 ±7.2	428.9 ±15.1
	2012	15.7 ±7.2	0.0 --	25.3 ±7.9	0.0 --	361.2 ±21.8	24.1 ±7.5	426.3 ±15.2
	2015	17.4 ±9.0	0.0 --	23.1 ±6.3	0.0 --	358.8 ±21.3	24.8 ±7.8	424.1 ±14.6

Source: *U.S. Department of Agriculture, 2015 National Resources Inventory, Summary Report, September 2018*

Table 2 - Land Cover/use of non-Federal rural land, by State and year
In thousands of acres, with margins of error

State	Year	Cropland	CRP land	Pastureland	Rangeland	Forest land	Other rural land	Total rural land
South Carolina	1982	3,526.7 ±121.6	--	1,195.8 ±120.7	0.0 --	11,361.4 ±170.1	703.8 ±71.8	16,787.7 ±78.1
	1987	3,280.6 ±121.2	94.9 --	1,161.2 ±113.3	0.0 --	11,367.8 ±163.2	711.1 ±78.4	16,615.6 ±92.1
	1992	2,929.7 ±104.7	261.2 --	1,165.6 ±109.2	0.0 --	11,311.6 ±165.1	711.5 ±81.5	16,379.6 ±100.3
	1997	2,559.5 ±93.7	262.5 --	1,166.0 ±105.9	0.0 --	11,277.3 ±174.5	751.4 ±82.3	16,016.7 ±109.6
	2002	2,403.7 ±101.8	204.3 --	1,083.2 ±130.0	0.0 --	11,250.8 ±184.7	751.2 ±79.9	15,693.2 ±105.9
	2007	2,210.4 ±131.6	170.4 --	1,137.3 ±181.1	0.0 --	11,190.7 ±220.7	797.5 ±74.3	15,506.3 ±109.7
	2012	2,157.6 ±146.1	98.0 --	1,138.3 ±179.3	0.0 --	11,203.6 ±220.5	808.8 ±69.4	15,406.3 ±112.4
	2015	2,133.8 ±167.7	60.2 --	1,113.2 ±171.3	0.0 --	11,248.9 ±232.3	816.9 ±71.5	15,373.0 ±115.7
South Dakota	1982	17,103.1 ±305.6	--	2,676.3 ±243.7	23,202.5 ±427.6	571.3 ±111.5	1,420.7 ±141.6	44,973.9 ±67.4
	1987	17,656.4 ±368.3	359.5 --	2,253.4 ±219.3	22,661.1 ±439.6	572.5 ±109.3	1,422.2 ±139.7	44,925.1 ±69.7
	1992	16,574.2 ±363.6	1,758.1 --	2,148.1 ±204.7	22,357.3 ±443.6	567.5 ±107.1	1,426.0 ±138.9	44,831.2 ±96.4
	1997	16,866.5 ±363.2	1,685.9 --	2,051.4 ±170.8	22,162.9 ±454.8	557.6 ±107.6	1,450.8 ±142.9	44,775.1 ±105.0
	2002	17,205.3 ±421.2	1,304.2 --	2,001.6 ±236.2	22,232.4 ±464.8	565.0 ±107.0	1,447.9 ±151.5	44,756.4 ±108.5
	2007	17,127.8 ±369.4	1,346.3 --	1,981.0 ±264.0	22,257.4 ±458.4	563.3 ±109.5	1,457.4 ±150.4	44,733.2 ±112.7
	2012	17,651.1 ±388.8	671.5 --	2,130.7 ±308.2	22,216.3 ±467.0	565.9 ±109.3	1,482.6 ±147.6	44,718.1 ±115.3
	2015	18,008.2 ±422.1	338.4 --	2,181.6 ±323.8	22,141.6 ±472.5	553.5 ±106.9	1,489.4 ±148.4	44,712.7 ±116.3
Tennessee	1982	5,523.3 ±159.9	--	5,239.2 ±207.4	0.0 --	12,022.0 ±283.0	495.1 ±56.5	23,279.6 ±96.4
	1987	5,292.4 ±151.1	172.7 --	5,044.5 ±205.9	0.0 --	12,037.9 ±280.1	474.0 ±53.1	23,021.5 ±104.8
	1992	4,757.5 ±152.0	439.0 --	5,061.0 ±194.2	0.0 --	12,016.7 ±267.7	447.0 ±48.1	22,721.2 ±108.3
	1997	4,549.5 ±176.9	374.8 --	4,892.0 ±215.0	0.0 --	11,933.3 ±263.5	519.9 ±53.5	22,269.5 ±130.3
	2002	4,535.3 ±191.0	214.3 --	4,804.7 ±244.2	0.0 --	11,904.8 ±257.5	527.8 ±62.8	21,986.9 ±134.5
	2007	4,404.3 ±221.5	236.4 --	4,691.2 ±254.0	0.0 --	11,882.8 ±271.2	585.3 ±73.5	21,800.0 ±145.9
	2012	4,571.3 ±213.6	159.9 --	4,467.6 ±257.1	0.0 --	11,903.3 ±278.4	592.7 ±80.0	21,694.8 ±145.5
	2015	4,567.5 ±213.2	112.9 --	4,406.0 ±248.6	0.0 --	11,943.7 ±269.9	627.6 ±100.6	21,657.7 ±142.6

Source: *U.S. Department of Agriculture, 2015 National Resources Inventory, Summary Report, September 2018*

Table 2 - Land Cover/use of non-Federal rural land, by State and year
In thousands of acres, with margins of error

State	Year	Cropland	CRP land	Pastureland	Rangeland	Forest land	Other rural land	Total rural land
Texas	1982	33,502.2 ±696.5	--	16,901.6 ±440.9	93,615.9 ±902.3	13,372.4 ±241.2	1,800.8 ±178.4	159,192.9 ±188.7
	1987	31,441.1 ±710.2	1,588.3 --	16,600.1 ±472.8	93,033.2 ±964.1	13,929.3 ±297.0	1,889.9 ±180.5	158,481.9 ±202.6
	1992	28,500.4 ±702.0	3,983.8 --	16,576.8 ±496.3	92,469.0 ±997.1	14,180.2 ±304.4	1,999.6 ±178.4	157,709.8 ±245.5
	1997	27,174.2 ±691.4	3,905.2 --	15,996.3 ±464.2	92,968.9 ±923.8	14,784.4 ±340.4	2,118.7 ±177.2	156,947.7 ±265.3
	2002	25,759.8 ±716.0	4,024.9 --	16,263.3 ±499.4	93,048.4 ±964.2	14,777.9 ±355.4	2,168.4 ±175.3	156,042.7 ±281.5
	2007	24,211.0 ±780.6	4,021.1 --	16,798.3 ±450.2	93,001.6 ±985.5	14,914.8 ±374.2	2,327.2 ±169.8	155,274.0 ±301.8
	2012	23,612.8 ±818.8	3,222.9 --	17,961.7 ±447.4	92,666.3 ±983.9	14,922.8 ±373.4	2,377.7 ±201.0	154,764.2 ±318.6
	2015	23,678.1 ±792.9	2,857.8 --	18,162.5 ±413.3	92,416.0 ±989.5	14,960.1 ±437.4	2,415.5 ±185.8	154,490.0 ±330.4
Utah	1982	2,003.5 ±284.8	--	531.3 ±90.1	11,073.8 ±679.0	2,221.0 ±444.0	1,709.7 ±517.8	17,539.3 ±105.0
	1987	1,905.2 ±311.5	150.4 --	569.2 ±91.0	10,876.3 ±669.8	2,207.3 ±446.5	1,606.1 ±519.0	17,314.5 ±113.5
	1992	1,796.7 ±318.1	224.9 --	628.5 ±98.1	11,110.3 ±670.5	2,173.5 ±441.7	1,714.3 ±516.5	17,648.2 ±123.7
	1997	1,649.6 ±311.8	216.4 --	680.5 ±103.9	10,990.3 ±703.6	2,286.2 ±506.9	1,732.8 ±511.9	17,555.8 ±132.6
	2002	1,569.9 ±263.7	209.9 --	657.7 ±123.1	10,848.6 ±700.5	2,252.1 ±547.9	1,703.6 ±535.5	17,241.8 ±138.0
	2007	1,524.9 ±285.3	212.7 --	619.4 ±111.9	10,829.8 ±700.1	2,244.9 ±547.6	1,716.8 ±526.5	17,148.5 ±140.3
	2012	1,529.6 ±284.7	179.8 --	650.0 ±110.6	10,757.6 ±697.3	2,255.1 ±551.9	1,719.2 ±532.5	17,091.3 ±145.1
	2015	1,561.5 ±278.5	176.0 --	611.0 ±126.1	10,742.3 ±694.0	2,254.4 ±551.8	1,719.0 ±532.4	17,064.2 ±147.5
Vermont	1982	644.1 ±56.3	--	441.6 ±46.7	0.0 --	4,140.0 ±72.1	79.5 ±17.1	5,305.2 ±24.8
	1987	633.6 ±64.7	0.0 --	385.6 ±48.0	0.0 --	4,133.5 ±72.3	77.7 ±15.8	5,230.4 ±26.1
	1992	620.0 ±65.0	0.0 --	352.6 ±36.7	0.0 --	4,129.2 ±71.5	80.9 ±18.8	5,182.7 ±26.6
	1997	593.5 ±62.0	0.0 --	339.4 ±33.0	0.0 --	4,124.9 ±71.9	86.3 ±20.1	5,144.1 ±28.0
	2002	560.1 ±61.4	0.0 --	322.2 ±35.6	0.0 --	4,102.9 ±72.4	90.7 ±21.2	5,075.9 ±29.9
	2007	542.6 ±57.9	0.0 --	322.4 ±41.8	0.0 --	4,075.8 ±73.9	105.6 ±26.4	5,046.4 ±31.2
	2012	529.4 ±54.4	0.0 --	331.0 ±41.4	0.0 --	4,059.1 ±76.9	113.9 ±32.7	5,033.4 ±32.1
	2015	525.7 ±56.4	0.0 --	330.5 ±44.5	0.0 --	4,057.2 ±78.4	113.8 ±32.7	5,027.2 ±32.6

Source: *U.S. Department of Agriculture, 2015 National Resources Inventory, Summary Report, September 2018*

Table 2 - Land Cover/use of non-Federal rural land, by State and year
In thousands of acres, with margins of error

State	Year	Cropland	CRP land	Pastureland	Rangeland	Forest land	Other rural land	Total rural land
Virginia	1982	3,459.3 ±172.5	--	3,297.9 ±157.3	0.0 –	13,706.3 ±230.6	608.7 ±57.5	21,072.2 ±107.9
	1987	3,167.1 ±180.4	22.7 –	3,268.9 ±156.8	0.0 –	13,767.6 ±226.8	585.9 ±58.8	20,812.2 ±108.1
	1992	2,952.4 ±174.3	72.6 –	3,263.4 ±153.7	0.0 –	13,720.4 ±216.9	573.6 ±52.7	20,582.4 ±116.1
	1997	2,933.5 ±175.8	70.3 –	3,047.3 ±164.7	0.0 –	13,609.5 ±212.1	578.4 ±53.5	20,239.0 ±111.0
	2002	2,866.3 ±184.7	26.5 –	3,030.9 ±185.5	0.0 –	13,475.9 ±200.6	561.0 ±57.2	19,960.6 ±108.5
	2007	2,790.7 ±182.1	25.1 –	2,979.2 ±182.2	0.0 –	13,350.6 ±188.5	622.0 ±60.5	19,767.6 ±113.5
	2012	2,805.0 ±196.5	22.2 –	2,915.6 ±189.4	0.0 –	13,284.3 ±202.9	633.9 ±66.1	19,661.0 ±117.7
	2015	2,829.4 ±174.2	22.2 –	2,843.5 ±183.9	0.0 –	13,255.4 ±204.5	659.7 ±74.6	19,610.2 ±119.4
Washington	1982	7,636.0 ±393.4	--	1,308.6 ±140.0	6,030.5 ±381.0	12,840.5 ±391.2	637.5 ±143.0	28,453.1 ±155.1
	1987	7,161.3 ±397.4	455.1 –	1,335.5 ±166.8	5,998.7 ±371.3	12,764.4 ±385.7	635.3 ±138.8	28,350.3 ±156.3
	1992	6,601.5 ±389.4	1,014.9 –	1,309.6 ±169.4	5,906.4 ±363.4	12,647.8 ±378.4	640.9 ±135.8	28,121.1 ±169.2
	1997	6,535.7 ±390.6	1,016.9 –	1,163.3 ±131.9	5,908.2 ±369.3	12,555.4 ±378.3	686.5 ±130.4	27,866.0 ±185.2
	2002	6,311.4 ±403.9	1,185.8 –	1,047.6 ±118.4	5,919.9 ±376.0	12,426.8 ±382.4	704.7 ±119.9	27,596.2 ±191.0
	2007	5,918.3 ±372.6	1,427.9 –	1,059.5 ±118.4	5,967.6 ±395.4	12,364.6 ±383.6	734.0 ±124.9	27,471.9 ±191.1
	2012	5,921.8 ±373.2	1,299.8 –	1,135.9 ±133.2	5,971.9 ±400.8	12,331.5 ±384.5	753.6 ±133.7	27,414.5 ±188.0
	2015	6,093.5 ±379.8	1,109.0 –	1,138.7 ±139.3	5,972.0 ±401.7	12,318.3 ±385.7	767.3 ±135.7	27,398.8 ±188.6
West Virginia	1982	1,080.7 ±87.0	--	1,878.0 ±118.9	0.0 –	10,370.5 ±161.9	242.7 ±39.7	13,571.9 ±47.5
	1987	980.5 ±81.2	0.6 –	1,735.7 ±114.9	0.0 –	10,544.8 ±160.6	252.7 ±41.7	13,514.3 ±49.5
	1992	906.7 ±78.2	0.6 –	1,612.8 ±112.3	0.0 –	10,530.5 ±154.7	283.0 ±52.1	13,333.6 ±54.3
	1997	850.4 ±79.6	0.0 –	1,517.7 ±106.7	0.0 –	10,502.4 ±149.8	257.1 ±42.2	13,127.6 ±63.2
	2002	780.0 ±91.3	1.0 –	1,492.4 ±104.7	0.0 –	10,450.2 ±128.3	254.5 ±63.9	12,987.4 ±61.6
	2007	725.6 ±102.4	1.0 –	1,459.9 ±120.7	0.0 –	10,463.2 ±120.3	277.0 ±74.1	12,926.7 ±64.0
	2012	655.7 ±100.6	0.0 –	1,454.5 ±130.1	0.0 –	10,491.4 ±132.8	300.0 ±73.9	12,901.6 ±63.5
	2015	644.9 ±96.0	0.0 –	1,431.5 ±144.2	0.0 –	10,513.6 ±140.6	307.3 ±80.2	12,897.3 ±64.1

Source: *U.S. Department of Agriculture, 2015 National Resources Inventory, Summary Report, September 2018*

Table 2 - Land Cover/use of non-Federal rural land, by State and year
In thousands of acres, with margins of error

State	Year	Cropland	CRP land	Pastureland	Rangeland	Forest land	Other rural land	Total rural land
Wisconsin	1982	11,477.1 ±284.2	--	3,523.8 ±178.1	0.0 --	14,278.9 ±246.1	1,593.4 ±144.0	30,873.2 ±110.2
	1987	11,353.2 ±307.2	218.2 --	3,190.1 ±195.3	0.0 --	14,367.5 ±251.0	1,621.6 ±143.4	30,750.6 ±115.8
	1992	10,853.8 ±287.3	665.8 --	3,069.8 ±209.4	0.0 --	14,383.7 ±249.5	1,626.1 ±140.1	30,599.2 ±119.8
	1997	10,606.1 ±303.2	661.9 --	3,021.8 ±214.9	0.0 --	14,488.8 ±272.2	1,640.5 ±137.5	30,419.1 ±128.2
	2002	10,276.9 ±311.6	577.0 --	3,085.8 ±236.3	0.0 --	14,610.5 ±272.6	1,712.6 ±146.7	30,262.8 ±144.2
	2007	10,127.6 ±301.2	524.0 --	3,074.7 ±237.4	0.0 --	14,687.7 ±273.1	1,710.6 ±146.4	30,124.6 ±150.5
	2012	10,298.2 ±278.0	279.6 --	3,031.1 ±231.5	0.0 --	14,717.2 ±282.7	1,715.1 ±147.9	30,041.2 ±151.6
	2015	10,338.4 ±288.0	165.1 --	2,985.9 ±240.6	0.0 --	14,815.9 ±297.8	1,707.8 ±148.7	30,013.1 ±152.4
Wyoming	1982	2,534.7 ±283.3	--	743.2 ±345.3	27,335.8 ±429.8	1,082.9 ±254.5	387.3 ±337.6	32,083.9 ±66.0
	1987	2,387.1 ±310.6	129.2 --	832.0 ±350.4	27,217.4 ±449.1	1,086.5 ±251.8	388.5 ±336.4	32,040.7 ±70.0
	1992	2,217.4 ±316.8	251.5 --	918.5 ±363.8	27,076.3 ±460.5	1,088.6 ±251.9	426.4 ±326.3	31,978.7 ±72.9
	1997	2,126.4 ±312.2	246.9 --	1,065.1 ±415.4	27,031.4 ±450.9	1,086.0 ±245.4	388.3 ±194.4	31,944.1 ±76.4
	2002	2,191.1 ±301.0	282.7 --	818.5 ±343.0	27,189.7 ±444.6	1,085.5 ±246.3	374.9 ±184.9	31,942.4 ±78.5
	2007	2,140.6 ±278.2	274.5 --	791.4 ±337.6	27,223.7 ±435.4	1,088.8 ±236.0	385.4 ±192.3	31,904.4 ±80.7
	2012	2,141.7 ±282.6	187.4 --	880.9 ±339.6	27,159.8 ±430.9	1,082.2 ±227.1	432.6 ±202.0	31,884.6 ±83.0
	2015	2,157.3 ±283.2	175.9 --	877.5 ±336.0	27,133.9 ±422.8	1,082.1 ±226.9	445.9 ±211.0	31,872.6 ±84.4
Total	1982	420,399.3 ±2,079.8	--	131,091.9 ±1,339.3	418,575.5 ±3,269.9	410,882.6 ±2,393.4	41,754.8 ±1,340.0	1,422,704.1 ±831.5
	1987	406,237.8 ±1,989.9	13,776.8 --	127,107.8 ±1,365.8	413,241.9 ±3,304.1	412,784.1 ±2,564.6	42,055.2 ±1,398.0	1,415,203.6 ±898.0
	1992	382,071.5 ±1,991.1	34,028.9 --	125,118.2 ±1,227.4	409,588.4 ±3,152.3	412,800.7 ±2,581.8	42,294.5 ±1,342.7	1,405,902.2 ±996.0
	1997	376,453.4 ±2,032.0	32,694.8 --	120,227.8 ±1,228.0	408,181.6 ±3,237.5	414,179.4 ±2,604.0	42,769.0 ±1,264.8	1,394,506.0 ±1,052.9
	2002	367,963.9 ±2,011.7	31,479.3 --	119,234.4 ±1,461.9	407,662.8 ±3,287.2	414,642.0 ±2,498.5	42,694.4 ±1,244.9	1,383,676.8 ±1,207.2
	2007	359,153.0 ±2,157.5	32,578.8 --	119,976.0 ±1,320.3	406,814.5 ±3,407.4	414,371.4 ±2,466.3	44,053.1 ±1,278.6	1,376,946.8 ±1,284.1
	2012	362,111.0 ±2,100.3	23,949.6 --	122,147.6 ±1,257.6	405,279.8 ±3,382.1	415,005.5 ±2,550.6	44,719.8 ±1,310.3	1,373,213.3 ±1,312.3
	2015	366,671.1 ±2,318.9	17,914.4 --	121,697.7 ±1,504.7	404,382.9 ±3,322.5	415,870.1 ±2,643.4	45,195.9 ±1,309.3	1,371,732.1 ±1,340.8

Source: *U.S. Department of Agriculture, 2015 National Resources Inventory, Summary Report, September 2018*

Table 2 - Land Cover/use of non-Federal rural land, by State and year In thousands of acres, with margins of error

State	Year	Cropland	CRP land	Pastureland	Rangeland	Forest land	Other rural land	Total rural land

Notes:
• Acreages for Conservation Reserve Program (CRP) land are established through geospatial processes and administrative records; therefore, statistical margins of error are not applicable and shown as a dashed line (--). CRP was not implemented until 1985.
• Cropland includes cultivated and non-cultivated cropland.
• When the estimate is 0.0, margins of error are not applicable and shown as a dashed line (--).
• Estimates in red have a large margin of error in relation to the estimate. They are usually based on very few observations. The lower bound of the confidence interval may also be inappropriately negative.

Source: U.S. Department of Agriculture, 2015 National Resources Inventory, Summary Report, September 2018

Superfund Sites

St.	City/Area	Site Name	NPL[1] Status	SA Approach[2]	HEUC[3]	HRS Score[4]
AK	Adak	Adak Naval Air Station	Final	No	No	51.37
AK	Anchorage	Alaska Railroad Anchorage Yard	Not NPL	Yes	No	-
AK	Anchorage	Elmendorf Air Force Base	Final	No	No	45.91
AK	Anchorage	Fort Richardson (USARMY)	Final	No	No	50
AK	Anchorage	Standard Steel & Metal Salvage Yard (USDOT)	Deleted	No	No	-
AK	Fairbanks	Alaska Battery Enterprises	Deleted	No	No	-
AK	Fairbanks	Arctic Surplus	Deleted	No	No	-
AK	Fairbanks	Eielson Air Force Base	Final	No	No	48.14
AK	Fort Wainwright	Fort Wainwright	Final	No	No	42.4
AK	Thorne Bay	Salt Chuck Mine	Final	No	No	50
AL	Anniston	Anniston Army Depot (Southeast Industrial Area)	Final	No	No	51.91
AL	Anniston	Anniston PCB Site (Monsanto Co)	Not NPL	Yes	No	-
AL	Axis	Stauffer Chemical Co. (LeMoyne Plant)	Final	No	No	32.34
AL	Birmingham	35th Avenue	Proposed	No	-	50
AL	Bucks	Stauffer Chemical Co. (Cold Creek Plant)	Final	No	No	46.77
AL	Childersburg	Alabama Army Ammunition Plant	Final	No	No	36.83
AL	Greenville	Mowbray Engineering Co.	Deleted	No	No	-
AL	Headland	American Brass	Final	No	No	55.61
AL	Huntsville	Redstone Arsenal (USARMY/NASA)	Final	No	No	50
AL	Leeds	Interstate Lead Co. (ILCO)	Final	No	No	42.86
AL	Limestone/Morgan	Triana/Tennessee River	Final	No	No	61.42
AL	Mcintosh	Ciba-Geigy Corp. (McIntosh Plant)	Final	No	Yes	53.42
AL	Mcintosh	Olin Corp. (McIntosh Plant)	Final	No	No	39.71
AL	Montgomery	Capitol City Plume	Proposed	No	No	50
AL	Montgomery	T.H. Agriculture & Nutrition Co. (Montgomery Plant)	Final	No	No	44.46
AL	Perdido	Perdido Ground Water Contamination	Deleted	No	No	-
AL	Saraland	Redwing Carriers, Inc. (Saraland)	Deleted	No	No	-
AL	Vincent	Alabama Plating Company, Inc.	Final	No	No	30.2
AR	Edmondsen	Gurley Pit	Deleted	No	No	
AR	El Dorado	Popile, Inc.	Final	No	No	50.03
AR	Fort Smith	Industrial Waste Control	Deleted	No	No	-
AR	Jacksonville	Jacksonville Municipal Landfill	Deleted	No	No	-
AR	Jacksonville	Rogers Road Municipal Landfill	Deleted	No	No	-
AR	Jacksonville	Vertac, Inc.	Final	No	No	65.46
AR	Mena	Mid-South Wood Products	Final	No	No	45.87
AR	Newport	Cecil Lindsey	Deleted	No	No	-
AR	Norphlet	MacMillan Ring Free Oil	Final	No	No	50
AR	Ola/Birta	Midland Products	Final	No	No	30.77
AR	Omaha	Arkwood, Inc.	Final	No	No	28.95
AR	Paragould	Monroe Auto Equipment Co. (Paragould Pit)	Deleted	No	No	-
AR	Plainview	Mountain Pine Pressure Treating	Final	No	No	41.93
AR	Reader	Ouachita Nevada Wood Treater	Final	No	No	50
AR	Walnut Ridge	Frit Industries	Deleted	No	No	-
AR	West Helena	Cedar Chemical Corporation	Final	No	No	-
AR	West Memphis	South 8th Street Landfill	Deleted	No	No	-
AS	Pago Pago	Taputimu Farm	Deleted	No	No	-
AZ	Casa Grande	Cyprus Tohono Mine	Not NPL	Yes	No	-
AZ	Chandler	Williams Air Force Base	Final	No	No	37.93
AZ	Dewey-humboldt	Iron King Mine - Humboldt Smelter	Final	No	No	52.69
AZ	Glendale	Luke Air Force Base	Deleted	No	No	-
AZ	Globe	Mountain View Mobile Home Estates	Deleted	No	No	-
AZ	Goodyear	Phoenix-Goodyear Airport Area	Final	No	No	45.91
AZ	Hassayampa	Hassayampa Landfill	Final	No	No	42.79
AZ	Hayden	Asarco Hayden Plant	Not NPL	Yes	No	-
AZ	Phoenix	Motorola, Inc. (52nd Street Plant)	Final	No	No	40.83

St.	City/Area	Site Name	NPL[1] Status	SA Approach[2]	HEUC[3]	HRS Score[4]
AZ	Phoenix	Nineteenth Avenue Landfill	Deleted	No	No	-
AZ	Saint David	Apache Powder Co.	Final	No	No	39.09
AZ	Scottsdale	Indian Bend Wash Area	Final	No	No	-
AZ	Tucson	Tucson International Airport Area	Final	No	No	57.8
AZ	Yuma	Yuma Marine Corps Air Station	Final	No	No	32.24
CA	Alameda	Alameda Naval Air Station	Final	No	No	50
CA	Alhambra	San Gabriel Valley (Area 3)	Final	No	No	28.9
CA	Alviso	South Bay Asbestos Area	Final	No	No	44.68
CA	Arvin	Brown & Bryant, Inc. (Arvin Plant)	Final	No	No	53.36
CA	Baldwin Park	San Gabriel Valley (Area 2)	Final	No	No	42.24
CA	Barstow	Barstow Marine Corps Logistics Base	Final	No	No	37.93
CA	Camp Pendleton	Camp Pendleton Marine Corps Base	Final	No	No	33.79
CA	Casmalia	Casmalia Resources	Final	No	No	30
CA	Clearlake Oaks	Sulphur Bank Mercury Mine	Final	No	No	44.42
CA	Cloverdale	MGM Brakes	Final	No	No	34.7
CA	Coalinga	Atlas Asbestos Mine	Final	No	No	45.55
CA	Coalinga	Coalinga Asbestos Mine	Deleted	No	No	-
CA	Concord	Concord Naval Weapons Station	Final	No	No	50
CA	Crescent City	Del Norte Pesticide Storage	Deleted	No	No	-
CA	Cupertino	Intersil Inc./Siemens Components	Final	No	No	28.9
CA	Davis	Frontier Fertilizer	Final	No	No	35.04
CA	Davis	Lab for Energy-Related Health Res./Old Campus Landfill (USDOE)	Final	No	No	50
CA	Edwards Afb	Edwards Air Force Base	Final	No	No	33.62
CA	El Monte	San Gabriel Valley (Area 1)	Final	No	No	42.24
CA	El Toro	El Toro Marine Corps Air Station	Final	No	No	-
CA	Fillmore	Pacific Coast Pipe Lines	Final	No	No	-
CA	Fresno	Fresno Municipal Sanitary Landfill	Final	No	No	35.57
CA	Fresno	Industrial Waste Processing	Final	No	No	51.13
CA	Fresno	T.H. Agriculture & Nutrition Co.	Deleted	No	No	-
CA	Fullerton	McColl	Final	No	No	41.77
CA	Fullerton And Anaheim	Orange County North Basin	Proposed	No	No	50
CA	Glendale	San Fernando Valley (Area 2)	Final	No	No	42.24
CA	Glendale	San Fernando Valley (Area 3)	Deleted	No	No	-
CA	Hoopa	Celtor Chemical Works	Deleted	No	No	-
CA	Hoopa	Copper Bluff Mine	Final	No	-	50
CA	Idria	New Idria Mercury Mine	Final	No	No	31.66
CA	Imperial	Stoker Company	Proposed	No	No	70.94
CA	Jackson	Argonaut Mine	Final	No	No	58.31
CA	La Puente	San Gabriel Valley (Area 4)	Final	No	No	28.9
CA	Lathrop	Sharpe Army Depot	Final	No	No	42.24
CA	Livermore	Lawrence Livermore Laboratory (USDOE)	Final	No	No	42.24
CA	Los Angeles	Del Amo	Final	No	No	47.12
CA	Los Angeles	San Fernando Valley (Area 4)	Final	No	No	35.57
CA	Malaga	Purity Oil Sales, Inc.	Final	No	No	43.27
CA	Marina	Fort Ord	Final	No	No	42.24
CA	Markleeville	Leviathan Mine	Final	No	No	50
CA	Mather	Mather Air Force Base	Final	No	No	28.9
CA	Maywood	Pemaco Maywood	Final	No	No	45.23
CA	Mcclellan Afb	McClellan Air Force Base (Ground Water Contamination)	Final	No	No	57.93
CA	Merced	Castle Air Force Base (6 Areas)	Final	No	No	37.93
CA	Mira Loma	Stringfellow	Final	No	No	-
CA	Modesto	Modesto Ground Water Contamination	Final	No	No	28.9
CA	Moffett Field	Moffett Naval Air Station	Final	No	No	29.49
CA	Monterey Park	Operating Industries, Inc., Landfill	Final	No	No	57.22
CA	Mountain View	CTS Printex, Inc.	Final	No	No	33.62
CA	Mountain View	Fairchild Semiconductor Corp. (Mountain View Plant)	Final	No	No	31.94
CA	Mountain View	Intel Corp. (Mountain View Plant)	Final	No	No	29.76
CA	Mountain View	Jasco Chemical Corp.	Final	No	No	35.36
CA	Mountain View	Raytheon Corp.	Final	No	No	29.76

St.	City/Area	Site Name	NPL[1] Status	SA Approach[2]	HEUC[3]	HRS Score[4]
CA	Mountain View	Spectra-Physics, Inc.	Final	No	No	37.2
CA	Mountain View	Teledyne Semiconductor	Final	No	No	35.35
CA	Nevada City	Lava Cap Mine	Final	No	No	33.66
CA	North Hollywood	San Fernando Valley (Area 1)	Final	No	No	42.24
CA	Oakland	AMCO Chemical	Final	No	No	50
CA	Oroville	Koppers Co., Inc. (Oroville Plant)	Final	No	No	33.73
CA	Oroville	Louisiana-Pacific Corp.	Deleted	No	No	-
CA	Oroville	Western Pacific Railroad Co.	Deleted	No	No	-
CA	Oxnard	Halaco Engineering Company	Final	No	No	51.94
CA	Palo Alto	Hewlett-Packard (620-640 Page Mill Road)	Final	No	No	29.76
CA	Pasadena	Jet Propulsion Laboratory (NASA)	Final	No	No	50
CA	Paso Robles	Klau/Buena Vista Mine	Final	No	No	50
CA	Petaluma	Sola Optical USA, Inc.	Deleted	No	No	-
CA	Porterville	Beckman Instruments (Porterville Plant)	Final	No	No	-
CA	Rancho Cordova	Aerojet General Corp.	Final	No	No	54.63
CA	Redding	Iron Mountain Mine	Final	No	No	56.16
CA	Rialto	Rockets, Fireworks, and Flares (RFF)	Final	No	No	50
CA	Richmond	Liquid Gold Oil Corp.	Deleted	No	No	-
CA	Richmond	United Heckathorn Co.	Final	No	No	38.49
CA	Riverbank	Riverbank Army Ammunition Plant	Final	No	No	63.94
CA	Riverside	Alark Hard Chrome	Final	No	No	50.5
CA	Riverside	March Air Force Base	Final	No	No	31.94
CA	Rogue River-Siskiyou NF	Blue Ledge Mine	Final	No	No	50.28
CA	Sacramento	Jibboom Junkyard	Deleted	No	No	-
CA	Sacramento	Sacramento Army Depot	Final	No	No	44.46
CA	Salinas	Crazy Horse Sanitary Landfill	Final	No	No	37.93
CA	Salinas	Firestone Tire & Rubber Co. (Salinas Plant)	Deleted	No	No	-
CA	San Bernardino	Newmark Ground Water Contamination	Final	No	No	35.57
CA	San Bernardino	Norton Air Force Base	Final	No	No	39.65
CA	San Francisco	Treasure Island Naval Air Station - Hunters Point Annex	Final	No	No	-
CA	San Jose	Fairchild Semiconductor Corp. (South San Jose Plant)	Final	No	No	44.46
CA	San Jose	Lorentz Barrel & Drum Co.	Final	No	No	33.94
CA	Santa Clara	Applied Materials	Final	No	No	31.94
CA	Santa Clara	Intel Corp. (Santa Clara III)	Final	No	No	31.94
CA	Santa Clara	Intel Magnetics	Final	No	No	31.94
CA	Santa Clara	National Semiconductor Corp.	Final	No	No	35.57
CA	Santa Clara	Synertek, Inc. (Building 1)	Final	No	No	31.94
CA	Santa Fe Springs	Waste Disposal, Inc.	Final	No	No	34.6
CA	Scotts Valley	Watkins-Johnson Co. (Stewart Dvision Plant)	Final	No	No	28.9
CA	Selma	Selma Treating Co.	Final	No	No	48.83
CA	South Gate	Cooper Drum Company	Final	No	No	50
CA	South Gate	Jervis B. Webb Co.	Final	No	No	45.76
CA	South Gate	Southern Avenue Industrial Area	Final	No	No	50
CA	Stockton	McCormick & Baxter Creosoting Co.	Final	No	No	74.86
CA	Sunnyvale	Advanced Micro Devices, Inc.	Final	No	No	37.93
CA	Sunnyvale	Advanced Micro Devices, Inc. (Building 915)	Final	No	No	31.94
CA	Sunnyvale	Monolithic Memories	Final	No	No	35.57
CA	Sunnyvale	TRW Microwave, Inc. (Building 825)	Final	No	No	31.94
CA	Sunnyvale	Westinghouse Electric Corp. (Sunnyvale Plant)	Final	No	No	39.93
CA	Torrance	Montrose Chemical Corp.	Final	No	No	32.1
CA	Tracy	Lawrence Livermore National Laboratory (Site 300) (USDOE)	Final	No	No	31.58
CA	Tracy	Tracy Defense Depot (USARMY)	Final	No	No	37.16
CA	Travis Afb	Travis Air Force Base	Final	No	No	29.49
CA	Turlock	Valley Wood Preserving, Inc.	Final	No	No	32.01
CA	Ukiah	Coast Wood Preserving	Final	No	No	44.73
CA	Victorville	George Air Force Base	Final	No	No	33.62
CA	Visalia	Southern California Edison Co. (Visalia Poleyard)	Deleted	No	No	-
CA	Weed	J.H. Baxter & Co.	Final	No	No	34.78

St.	City/Area	Site Name	NPL[1] Status	SA Approach[2]	HEUC[3]	HRS Score[4]
CA	Westminster	Ralph Gray Trucking Co.	Deleted	No	No	-
CA	Whittier	Omega Chemical Corporation	Final	No	No	30.94
CO	Adams County	Rocky Mountain Arsenal (USARMY)	Final	No	No	-
CO	Aspen	Smuggler Mountain	Deleted	No	No	-
CO	Boulder	Marshall Landfill	Final	No	No	-
CO	Canon City	Lincoln Park	Final	No	No	31.31
CO	Commerce City	Sand Creek Industrial	Deleted	No	No	-
CO	Commerce City	Woodbury Chemical Co.	Deleted	No	No	-
CO	Creede	Nelson Tunnel/Commodore Waste Rock	Final	No	No	48.03
CO	Denver	Broderick Wood Products	Final	No	No	35.13
CO	Denver	Chemical Sales Co.	Final	No	No	37.93
CO	Denver	Denver Radium Site	Final	No	No	-
CO	Denver	Vasquez Boulevard and I-70	Final	No	No	50
CO	Golden	Rocky Flats Plant (USDOE)	Final	No	No	-
CO	Gunnison NF	Standard Mine	Final	No	No	50
CO	Idaho Springs	Central City, Clear Creek	Final	No	No	51.39
CO	Leadville	California Gulch	Final	No	No	-
CO	Littleton	Air Force Plant PJKS	Final	No	No	42.93
CO	Minturn	Eagle Mine	Final	No	No	47.19
CO	Pueblo	Colorado Smelter	Final	No	No	50
CO	Rio Grande County	Summitville Mine	Final	No	No	50
CO	Salida	Smeltertown Site	Proposed	No	No	58.56
CO	Unincorp. Arapahoe Co.	Lowry Landfill	Final	No	No	48.36
CO	Unincorporated	Bonita Peak Mining District	Final	No	No	50
CO	Uravan	Uravan Uranium Project (Union Carbide Corp.)	Final	No	No	-
CO	Ward	Captain Jack Mill	Final	No	Yes	50.56
CT	Barkhamsted	Barkhamsted-New Hartford Landfill	Final	No	No	38.05
CT	Beacon Falls	Beacon Heights Landfill	Final	No	No	46.77
CT	Canterbury	Yaworski Waste Lagoon	Final	No	No	36.72
CT	Cheshire	Cheshire Ground Water Contamination	Deleted	No	No	-
CT	Durham	Durham Meadows	Final	No	No	33.94
CT	East Windsor	Broad Brook Mill	Proposed	No	No	54.35
CT	Naugatuck Borough	Laurel Park, Inc.	Final	No	No	-
CT	New London	New London Submarine Base	Final	No	No	36.53
CT	Norwalk	Kellogg-Deering Well Field	Final	No	No	39.92
CT	Plainfield	Gallup's Quarry	Final	No	No	46.29
CT	Southington	Old Southington Landfill	Deleted	No	No	-
CT	Southington	Solvents Recovery Service of New England	Final	No	No	44.93
CT	Sterling	Revere Textile Prints Corp.	Deleted	No	No	-
CT	Stratford	Raymark Industries, Inc.	Final	No	No	-
CT	Vernon	Precision Plating Corp.	Final	No	No	49.1
CT	Waterbury	Scovill Industrial Landfill	Final	No	No	50
CT	Wolcott	Nutmeg Valley Road	Deleted	No	No	-
CT	Woodstock	Linemaster Switch Corp.	Final	No	No	33.71
DC	Washington	Washington Navy Yard	Final	No	No	48.57
DE	Cheswold	Coker's Sanitation Service Landfills	Deleted	No	No	-
DE	Dover	Chem-Solv, Inc.	Final	No	No	37.93
DE	Dover	Dover Air Force Base	Final	No	No	35.89
DE	Dover	Dover Gas Light Co.	Final	No	No	35.57
DE	Dover	Wildcat Landfill	Deleted	No	No	-
DE	Hockessin	Hockessin Groundwater	Final	No	No	50
DE	Kirkwood	Harvey & Knott Drum, Inc.	Final	No	No	30.77
DE	Laurel	Sussex County Landfill No. 5	Deleted	No	No	-
DE	Middletown	Sealand Limited	Deleted	No	No	-
DE	Millsboro	Millsboro TCE	Proposed	No	No	50
DE	Millsboro	NCR Corp. (Millsboro Plant)	Final	No	No	38.21
DE	New Castle	Army Creek Landfill	Final	No	No	69.92
DE	New Castle	Delaware City PVC Plant	Final	No	No	30.55

St.	City/Area	Site Name	NPL[1] Status	SA Approach[2]	HEUC[3]	HRS Score[4]
DE	New Castle	Delaware Sand & Gravel Landfill	Final	No	No	46.6
DE	New Castle	Halby Chemical Co.	Final	No	No	30.9
DE	New Castle	New Castle Spill	Deleted	No	No	-
DE	New Castle	New Castle Steel	Deleted	No	No	-
DE	New Castle	Standard Chlorine of Delaware, Inc.	Final	No	No	35.42
DE	New Castle	Tybouts Corner Landfill	Final	No	No	-
DE	Newark	Newark South Ground Water Plume	Final	No	No	50
DE	Newport	E.I. du Pont de Nemours & Co. (Newport Pigment Plant Landfill)	Final	No	No	51.91
DE	Newport	Koppers Co., Inc. (Newport Plant)	Final	No	No	33.56
DE	Smyrna	Tyler Refrigeration Pit	Deleted	No	No	-
FL	Baldwin	Yellow Water Road Dump	Deleted	No	No	-
FL	Brandon	Sydney Mine Sludge Ponds	Final	No	No	38.93
FL	Cantonment	Dubose Oil Products Co.	Deleted	No	No	-
FL	Clermont	Tower Chemical Co.	Final	No	No	44.03
FL	Cottondale	Sapp Battery Salvage	Final	No	No	47.7
FL	Davie	Davie Landfill	Deleted	No	No	-
FL	Deland	Sherwood Medical Industries	Final	No	No	39.83
FL	Duval County	Hipps Road Landfill	Deleted	No	No	-
FL	Fort Lauderdale	Florida Petroleum Reprocessors	Final	No	No	50
FL	Fort Lauderdale	Hollingsworth Solderless Terminal	Final	No	Yes	44.53
FL	Fort Lauderdale	Wingate Road Municipal Incinerator Dump	Final	No	No	31.72
FL	Gainesville	Cabot/Koppers	Final	No	No	36.69
FL	Hialeah	B&B Chemical Co., Inc.	Deleted	No	No	-
FL	Hialeah	Northwest 58th Street Landfill	Deleted	No	No	-
FL	Hialeah	Standard Auto Bumper Corp.	Deleted	No	No	-
FL	Homestead AFB	Homestead Air Force Base	Final	No	No	42.4
FL	Indiantown	Florida Steel Corp.	Final	No	No	45.92
FL	Jacksonville	Brown's Dump	Not NPL	Yes	No	-
FL	Jacksonville	Fairfax St. Wood Treaters	Final	No	No	50
FL	Jacksonville	Jacksonville Ash Site	Not NPL	Yes	No	-
FL	Jacksonville	Jacksonville Naval Air Station	Final	No	No	32.08
FL	Jacksonville	Kerr-McGee Chemical Corp - Jacksonville	Final	No	No	70.71
FL	Jacksonville	Pickettville Road Landfill	Final	No	No	42.94
FL	Jacksonville	Cecil Field Naval Air Station	Final	No	No	-
FL	Lake Alfred	Callaway & Son Drum Service	Deleted	No	No	-
FL	Lake Park	BMI-Textron	Deleted	No	No	-
FL	Lake Park	Trans Circuits, Inc.	Final	No	No	50
FL	Lakeland	Alpha Chemical Corp.	Deleted	No	No	-
FL	Lakeland	Landia Chemical Company	Final	No	No	50
FL	Live Oak	Brown Wood Preserving	Deleted	No	No	-
FL	Longwood	General Dynamics Longwood	Final	No	No	50
FL	Longwood	Sprague Electric Company	Not NPL	Yes	No	-
FL	Madison	ITT-Thompson Industries, Inc	Not NPL	Yes	No	-
FL	Madison	Madison County Sanitary Landfill	Final	No	No	37.93
FL	Marianna	United Metals, Inc.	Final	No	No	33.73
FL	Medley	Pepper Steel & Alloys, Inc.	Final	No	No	31.92
FL	Miami	Airco Plating Co.	Final	No	No	42.47
FL	Miami	Anaconda Aluminum Co./Milgo Electronics Corp.	Deleted	No	No	-
FL	Miami	Continental Cleaners	Final	No	No	50
FL	Miami	Gold Coast Oil Corp.	Deleted	No	No	-
FL	Miami	Miami Drum Services	Final	No	No	53.56
FL	Miami	Varsol Spill	Deleted	No	No	-
FL	Milton	Whiting Field Naval Air Station	Final	No	No	50
FL	Mount Pleasant	Parramore Surplus	Deleted	No	Yes	-
FL	Nocatee	Nocatee Hull Creosote	Not NPL	Yes	No	-
FL	North Miami	Munisport Landfill	Deleted	No	No	-
FL	North Miami Beach	Anodyne, Inc.	Final	No	No	31.03
FL	Orlando	Chevron Chemical Co. (Ortho Division)	Final	No	No	50
FL	Orlando	City Industries, Inc.	Final	No	No	32

St.	City/Area	Site Name	NPL[1] Status	SA Approach[2]	HEUC[3]	HRS Score[4]
FL	Orlando	Orlando Gasification Plant	Not NPL	Yes	No	-
FL	Palm Bay	Harris Corp. (Palm Bay Plant)	Final	No	No	35.57
FL	Panama City	Tyndall Air Force Base	Final	No	No	50
FL	Pembroke Park	Petroleum Products Corp.	Final	No	No	40.11
FL	Pensacola	Agrico Chemical Co.	Final	No	No	44.98
FL	Pensacola	American Creosote Works (Pensacola Plant)	Final	No	No	58.41
FL	Pensacola	Beulah Landfill	Deleted	No	No	-
FL	Pensacola	Escambia Wood - Pensacola	Final	No	No	50
FL	Pensacola	Pensacola Naval Air Station	Final	No	No	42.4
FL	Pensacola	Pioneer Sand Co.	Deleted	No	No	-
FL	Plant City	Coronet Industries	Not NPL	Yes	No	-
FL	Plant City	Schuylkill Metals Corp.	Deleted	No	No	-
FL	Pompano Beach	Chemform, Inc.	Deleted	No	No	-
FL	Pompano Beach	Flash Cleaners	Final	No	No	50
FL	Pompano Beach	Wilson Concepts of Florida, Inc.	Deleted	No	No	-
FL	Princeton	Woodbury Chemical Co. (Princeton Plant)	Deleted	No	No	-
FL	Quincy	Post and Lumber Preserving Co. Inc.	Final	No	No	36.33
FL	Ruskin	JJ Seifert Machine	Final	No	No	50
FL	Sanford	Sanford Dry Cleaners	Final	No	No	50
FL	Sanford	Sanford Gasification Plant	Not NPL	Yes	No	-
FL	Seffner	Taylor Road Landfill	Final	No	No	51.37
FL	Stuart	Solitron Microwave	Final	No	No	50
FL	Tallahassee	Cascade Landfill	Not NPL	Yes	No	-
FL	Tallahassee	Cascade Park Gasification Plant	Not NPL	Yes	No	-
FL	Tampa	Alaric Area Ground Water Plume	Final	No	No	41.91
FL	Tampa	Helena Chemical Co. (Tampa Plant)	Final	No	No	30.19
FL	Tampa	Kassauf-Kimerling Battery Disposal	Deleted	No	No	-
FL	Tampa	MRI Corp (Tampa)	Final	No	No	37.62
FL	Tampa	Peak Oil Co./Bay Drum Co.	Final	No	No	58.15
FL	Tampa	Raleigh Street Dump	Final	No	No	50
FL	Tampa	Reeves Southeastern Galvanizing Corp.	Final	No	No	58.75
FL	Tampa	Sixty-Second Street Dump	Deleted	No	No	-
FL	Tampa	Southern Solvents, Inc.	Final	No	No	50
FL	Tampa	Stauffer Chemical Co (Tampa)	Final	No	No	59.81
FL	Tampa	Tri-City Oil Conservationist, Inc.	Deleted	No	No	-
FL	Tarpon Springs	Stauffer Chemical Co. (Tarpon Springs)	Final	No	No	50
FL	Temple Terrace	Normandy Park Apartments	Proposed	No	No	49.98
FL	Thonotosassa	Arkla Terra Property	Final	No	No	50
FL	Vero Beach	Piper Aircraft Corp./Vero Beach Water & Sewer Department	Final	No	No	31.13
FL	West Palm Beach	Solitron Devices Inc	Not NPL	Yes	No	-
FL	Whitehouse	Coleman-Evans Wood Preserving Co.	Deleted	No	No	-
FL	Whitehouse	Whitehouse Oil Pits	Deleted	No	No	-
FL	Zellwood	Zellwood Ground Water Contamination	Final	No	No	51.91
FM	Palau	PCB Wastes	Deleted	No	No	-
GA	Albany	Firestone Tire & Rubber Co. (Albany Plant)	Final	No	No	30.08
GA	Albany	Marine Corps Logistics Base	Final	No	No	44.65
GA	Albany	T.H. Agriculture & Nutrition Co. (Albany Plant)	Final	No	No	40.93
GA	Athens	Luminous Processes, Inc.	Deleted	No	Yes	-
GA	Augusta	Alternate Energy Resources	Final	No	No	50
GA	Augusta	Monsanto Corp. (Augusta Plant)	Deleted	No	No	-
GA	Augusta	Peach Orchard Road PCE Ground Water Plume	Final	No	No	50
GA	Brunswick	Brunswick Wood Preserving	Final	No	No	54.49
GA	Brunswick	Hercules 009 Landfill	Final	No	No	52.58
GA	Brunswick	LCP Chemicals Georgia	Final	No	No	-
GA	Brunswick	Terry Creek Dredge Spoil Areas/Hercules Outfall	Proposed	Yes	No	50.18
GA	Byron	Powersville Site	Deleted	No	No	-
GA	Camilla	Camilla Wood Preserving Company	Final	No	No	50
GA	Cedartown	Cedartown Industries, Inc.	Deleted	No	No	-

St.	City/Area	Site Name	NPL[1] Status	SA Approach[2]	HEUC[3]	HRS Score[4]
GA	Cedartown	Cedartown Municipal Landfill	Deleted	No	No	-
GA	Cedartown	Diamond Shamrock Corp. Landfill	Final	No	No	35.6
GA	Fort Valley	Woolfolk Chemical Works, Inc.	Final	No	No	42.24
GA	Houston County	Robins Air Force Base (Landfill #4/Sludge Lagoon)	Final	No	No	51.66
GA	Kensington	Mathis Brothers Landfill (South Marble Top Road)	Final	No	No	30.78
GA	Macon	Armstrong World Industries	Final	No	No	50
GA	Macon	Macon Naval Ordnance Plant	Final	No	No	48.97
GA	Tifton	Marzone Inc./Chevron Chemical Co.	Final	No	No	30.26
GU	Agana	Ordot Landfill	Final	No	No	-
GU	Yigo	Andersen Air Force Base	Final	No	No	50
HI	Kunia	Del Monte Corp. (Oahu Plantation)	Final	No	No	-
HI	Pearl Harbor	Pearl Harbor Naval Complex	Final	No	No	70.82
HI	Schofield	Schofield Barracks (USARMY)	Deleted	No	No	-
HI	Wahiawa	Naval Computer and Telecom Area Master Station Eastern Pacific	Final	No	No	50
IA	Atlantic	PCE Former Dry Cleaner	Final	No	No	50
IA	Camanche	Lawrence Todtz Farm	Final	No	No	52.11
IA	Cedar Rapids	Electro-Coatings, Inc.	Final	No	No	42.24
IA	Charles City	LaBounty Site	Deleted	No	No	-
IA	Charles City	Shaw Avenue Dump	Final	No	No	30.01
IA	Charles City	White Farm Equipment Co. Dump	Deleted	No	No	-
IA	Des Moines	Des Moines TCE	Final	No	No	42.28
IA	Dubuque	Peoples Natural Gas Co.	Final	No	No	46.24
IA	Fairfield	Fairfield Coal Gasification Plant	Final	No	No	38.05
IA	Hospers	Farmers' Mutual Cooperative	Deleted	No	No	-
IA	Iowa City	Iowa City Fmgp	Not NPL	Yes	No	-
IA	Kellogg	Midwest Manufacturing/North Farm	Final	No	No	32.04
IA	Keokuk	Sheller-Globe Corp. Disposal	Deleted	No	No	-
IA	Mason City	Mason City Coal Gasification Plant	Final	No	No	69.33
IA	Mason City	Northwestern States Portland Cement Co.	Deleted	No	No	-
IA	Maurice	Vogel Paint & Wax Co.	Final	No	No	31.45
IA	Middletown	Iowa Army Ammunition Plant	Final	No	No	29.73
IA	Mineola	Aidex Corp.	Deleted	No	No	-
IA	Ottumwa	John Deere (Ottumwa Works Landfills)	Deleted	No	No	-
IA	Red Oak	Red Oak City Landfill	Deleted	No	No	-
IA	Sergeant Bluff	Mid-America Tanning Co.	Deleted	No	No	-
IA	Waterloo	Waterloo Coal Gasification Plant	Proposed	No	No	50
IA	West Des Moines	Railroad Avenue Groundwater Contamination	Final	No	No	50
IA	West Point	E.I. du Pont de Nemours & Co., Inc. (County Road X23)	Deleted	No	No	-
ID	Idaho Falls	Idaho National Engineering Laboratory (USDOE)	Final	No	No	51.91
ID	Lemhi County	Blackbird Mine	Proposed	No	No	50
ID	Mountain Home	Mountain Home Air Force Base	Final	No	No	57.8
ID	Pocatello	Eastern Michaud Flats Contamination	Final	No	No	57.8
ID	Pocatello	Pacific Hide & Fur Recycling Co.	Deleted	No	No	-
ID	Pocatello	Union Pacific Railroad Co.	Deleted	No	No	-
ID	Rathdrum	Arrcom (Drexler Enterprises)	Deleted	No	No	-
ID	Smelterville	Bunker Hill Mining & Metallurgical Complex	Final	No	No	54.76
ID	Soda Springs	Kerr-McGee Chemical Corp. (Soda Springs Plant)	Final	No	No	51.91
ID	Soda Springs	Monsanto Chemical Co. (Soda Springs Plant)	Final	No	No	54.77
ID	St. Maries	St. Maries Creosote	Proposed	No	No	50
ID	Stibnite	Stibnite/Yellow Pine Mining Area	Proposed	No	No	50
IL	Antioch	H.O.D. Landfill	Final	No	No	34.68
IL	Beckemeyer	Circle Smelting Corp	Proposed	No	No	70.71
IL	Belvidere	Belvidere Municipal Landfill	Deleted	No	No	-
IL	Belvidere	MIG/Dewane Landfill	Final	No	No	49.91
IL	Belvidere	Parsons Casket Hardware Co.	Final	No	No	55.58
IL	Byron	Byron Salvage Yard	Final	No	No	33.93
IL	Calumet City	Estech General Chemical Company	Final	No	No	30
IL	Carterville	Sangamo Electric Dump/Crab Orchard NWR (USDOI)	Final	No	No	43.7

St.	City/Area	Site Name	NPL[1] Status	SA Approach[2]	HEUC[3]	HRS Score[4]
IL	Chicago	Lake Calumet Cluster	Final	No	No	30
IL	Chicago	Peoples Gas Crawford Station Former MGP	Not NPL	Yes	No	-
IL	Chicago	Peoples Gas Light & Coke - 22nd St	Not NPL	Yes	No	-
IL	Chicago	Peoples Gas Light & Coke - Division St	Not NPL	Yes	No	-
IL	Chicago	Peoples Gas Light & Coke North Sta	Not NPL	Yes	No	-
IL	Chicago	Peoples Gas Light & Coke Willow St Station	Not NPL	Yes	No	-
IL	Chicago	Peoples Gas North Shore Avenue Station Former MGP	Not NPL	Yes	No	-
IL	Chicago	Peoples Gas South Station Former MGP	Not NPL	Yes	No	-
IL	Chicago	Peoples Gas Throop Street Former MGP	Not NPL	Yes	No	-
IL	Chicago	Schroud Property	Proposed	No	-	50
IL	Danville	Hegeler Zinc	Final	No	No	50
IL	Depue	DePue/New Jersey Zinc/Mobil Chemical Corp.	Final	No	No	70.71
IL	Downers Grove	Ellsworth Industrial Park	Not NPL	Yes	No	-
IL	Dupage County	Kerr-McGee (Kress Creek/West Branch of DuPage River)	Final	No	No	39.05
IL	East Cape Girardeau	Ilada Energy Co.	Deleted	No	No	-
IL	East St. Louis	Alcoa Properties	Not NPL	Yes	No	-
IL	Elgin	Tri-County Landfill Co./Waste Management of Illinois, Inc.	Final	No	No	42.76
IL	Fairmont City	Old American Zinc Plant	Final	No	No	30
IL	Galena	Bautsch-Gray Mine	Final	No	No	48.97
IL	Galesburg	Galesburg/Koppers Co.	Final	No	No	34.78
IL	Granite City	Jennison-Wright Corporation	Final	No	No	40.3
IL	Granite City	NL Industries/Taracorp Lead Smelter	Final	No	No	38.11
IL	Greenup	A & F Materials Reclaiming, Inc.	Deleted	No	No	-
IL	Hartford	Chemetco	Final	No	No	30
IL	Hillsboro	Eagle Zinc Co Div T L Diamond	Final	No	No	50
IL	Joliet	Amoco Chemicals (Joliet Landfill)	Final	No	No	39.44
IL	Joliet	Joliet Army Ammunition Plant (Load-Assembly-Packing Area)	Final	No	No	35.23
IL	Joliet	Joliet Army Ammunition Plant (Manufacturing Area)	Final	No	No	32.08
IL	La Salle	LaSalle Electric Utilities	Final	No	No	42.06
IL	La Salle	Matthiessen and Hegeler Zinc Company	Final	No	No	50
IL	Lawrenceville	Indian Refinery-Texaco Lawrenceville	Final	No	No	56.67
IL	Lemont	Lenz Oil Service, Inc.	Final	No	No	42.33
IL	Libertyville	Petersen Sand & Gravel	Deleted	No	No	-
IL	Marshall	Velsicol Chemical Corp. (Marshall Plant)	Final	No	No	48.78
IL	Morristown	Acme Solvents Reclaiming, Inc. (Morristown Plant)	Final	No	No	31.98
IL	Naplate	Ottawa Township Flat Glass Site	Not NPL	Yes	No	-
IL	Ottawa	Ottawa Radiation Areas	Final	No	No	50
IL	Pembroke Township	Cross Brothers Pail Recycling (Pembroke)	Final	No	No	42.04
IL	Quincy	Adams County Quincy Landfills 2&3	Final	No	No	34.21
IL	Rantoul	Chanute Air Force Base	Proposed	No	No	48.3
IL	Rockford	Interstate Pollution Control, Inc.	Final	No	No	46.01
IL	Rockford	Pagel's Pit	Final	No	No	45.91
IL	Rockford	Southeast Rockford Ground Water Contamination	Final	No	No	42.24
IL	Rockton	Beloit Corp.	Final	No	No	-
IL	Sandoval	Sandoval Zinc Company	Final	No	No	30
IL	Sauget	Sauget Area 1	Proposed	No	No	50
IL	Sauget	Sauget Area 2	Proposed	No	No	50
IL	Savanna	Savanna Army Depot Activity	Final	No	No	-
IL	Taylor Springs	ASARCO Taylor Springs	Final	No	No	30
IL	Taylorville	Central Illinois Public Service Co.	Final	No	No	28.95
IL	Warrenville	DuPage County Landfill/Blackwell Forest	Final	No	No	35.57
IL	Wauconda	Wauconda Sand & Gravel	Final	No	No	53.42
IL	Waukegan	Johns-Manville Corp.	Final	No	No	38.2
IL	Waukegan	North Shore Gas (NSG) North Plant	Not NPL	Yes	No	-
IL	Waukegan	North Shore Gas South Plant	Not NPL	Yes	No	-
IL	Waukegan	Outboard Marine Corp.	Final	No	No	-
IL	Waukegan	Yeoman Creek Landfill	Final	No	No	33.23
IL	West Chicago	Kerr-McGee (Reed-Keppler Park)	Deleted	No	No	-
IL	West Chicago	Kerr-McGee (Residential Areas)	Final	No	No	38.15

St.	City/Area	Site Name	NPL[1] Status	SA Approach[2]	HEUC[3]	HRS Score[4]
IL	West Chicago	Kerr-McGee (Sewage Treatment Plant)	Deleted	No	No	-
IL	Winnebago County	Evergreen Manor Ground Water Contamination	Removed	Yes	No	-
IL	Woodstock	Woodstock Municipal Landfill	Final	No	No	50.1
IN	Anderson	Broadway Street Corridor Groundwater Contamination	Final	No	-	50
IN	Bloomington	Bennett Stone Quarry	Final	No	No	32.55
IN	Bloomington	Lemon Lane Landfill	Final	No	No	29.31
IN	Bloomington	Neal's Landfill (Bloomington)	Final	No	No	42.93
IN	Claypool	Lakeland Disposal Service, Inc.	Final	No	No	34.1
IN	Columbia City	Wayne Waste Oil	Final	No	No	42.33
IN	Columbus	Columbus Old Municipal Landfill #1	Deleted	No	No	-
IN	Columbus	Tri-State Plating	Deleted	No	No	-
IN	East Chicago	U.S. Smelter and Lead Refinery, Inc.	Final	No	No	58.31
IN	Elkhart	Conrail Rail Yard (Elkhart)	Final	No	No	42.24
IN	Elkhart	Himco Dump	Final	No	No	42.31
IN	Elkhart	Lane Street Ground Water Contamination	Final	No	No	40.53
IN	Elkhart	Lusher Street Ground Water Contamination	Final	No	No	50
IN	Elkhart	Main Street Well Field	Final	No	No	42.49
IN	Elkhart	North Shore Drive	Final	No	No	50
IN	Evansville	Jacobsville Neighborhood Soil Contamination	Final	No	No	35.52
IN	Fort Wayne	Fort Wayne Reduction Dump	Final	No	No	42.47
IN	Garden City	Garden City Ground Water Plume	Final	No	No	50
IN	Gary	Gary Development Landfill	Final	No	No	30
IN	Gary	Lake Sandy Jo (M&M Landfill)	Final	No	No	38.21
IN	Gary	MIDCO I	Final	No	No	46.44
IN	Gary	MIDCO II	Final	No	No	30.16
IN	Gary	Ninth Avenue Dump	Final	No	No	40.32
IN	Griffith	American Chemical Service, Inc.	Final	No	No	34.98
IN	Hancock County	Poer Farm	Deleted	No	No	-
IN	Indianapolis	Carter Lee Lumber Co.	Deleted	No	No	-
IN	Indianapolis	Keystone Corridor Ground Water Contamination	Final	No	No	50
IN	Indianapolis	Reilly Tar & Chemical Corp. (Indianapolis Plant)	Final	No	No	34.03
IN	Indianapolis	Riverside Ground Water Contamination	Proposed	No	No	50
IN	Indianapolis	Southside Sanitary Landfill	Deleted	No	No	-
IN	Kokomo	Continental Steel Corp.	Final	No	No	31.85
IN	Kokomo	Kokomo Contaminated Ground Water Plume	Final	No	No	50
IN	La Porte	Fisher-Calo	Final	No	No	52.05
IN	Lafayette	Tippecanoe Sanitary Landfill, Inc	Final	No	No	42.24
IN	Lebanon	Wedzeb Enterprises, Inc.	Deleted	No	No	-
IN	Logansport	Cliff Drive Groundwater Contamination	Final	No	-	50
IN	Marion	Marion (Bragg) Dump	Final	No	No	35.25
IN	Martinsville	Pike and Mulberry Streets PCE Plume	Final	No	No	50
IN	Michigan City	Waste, Inc., Landfill	Deleted	No	No	-
IN	Mishawaka	Douglass Road/Uniroyal, Inc., Landfill	Final	No	No	36.61
IN	Osceola	Galen Myers Dump/Drum Salvage	Final	No	No	42.24
IN	Seymour	Seymour Recycling Corp.	Final	No	No	-
IN	South Bend	Beck's Lake	Final	No	No	50
IN	South Bend	Whiteford Sales & Service Inc./Nationalease	Deleted	No	No	-
IN	Spencer	Franklin Street Groundwater Contamination	Final	No	No	50
IN	Spencer	Neal's Dump (Spencer)	Deleted	No	No	-
IN	Terre Haute	Elm Street Ground Water Contamination	Final	No	No	50
IN	Terre Haute	International Minerals & Chemicals Corp. (Terre Haute East Plant)	Deleted	No	No	-
IN	Town Of Pines	Town Of Pines Groundwater Plume	Not NPL	Yes	No	-
IN	Vincennes	Prestolite Battery Division	Final	No	No	40.63
IN	Westville	Cam-Or Inc.	Final	No	No	58.91
IN	Zionsville	Envirochem Corp.	Final	No	No	46.44
IN	Zionsville	Northside Sanitary Landfill, Inc.	Final	No	No	46.04
KS	Arkansas City	Arkansas City Dump	Deleted	No	No	-
KS	Colby	Ace Services	Final	No	No	50

St.	City/Area	Site Name	NPL[1] Status	SA Approach[2]	HEUC[3]	HRS Score[4]
KS	Delavan	Tri-County Public Airport	Proposed	No	No	50
KS	El Dorado	Pester Refinery Co.	Final	No	No	30.16
KS	Galena	Cherokee County	Final	No	No	58.15
KS	Great Bend	Plating, Inc.	Final	No	No	50
KS	Hutchinson	Obee Road	Final	No	No	33.62
KS	Iola	Former United Zinc & Associated Smelters	Final	No	No	50
KS	Junction City	Fort Riley	Final	No	No	33.79
KS	Olathe	Chemical Commodities, Inc.	Final	No	No	50
KS	Shawnee Mission	Doepke Disposal (Holliday)	Final	No	No	47.46
KS	Topeka	Hydro-Flex Inc.	Deleted	No	No	-
KS	Wichita	29th & Mead Ground Water Contamination	Deleted	No	No	-
KS	Wichita	57th and North Broadway Streets Site	Final	No	No	50
KS	Wichita	Big River Sand Co.	Deleted	No	No	-
KS	Wichita	Johns' Sludge Pond	Deleted	No	No	-
KS	Winfield	Strother Field Industrial Park	Final	No	No	33.62
KS	Wright	Wright Ground Water Contamination	Final	No	No	50
KY	Auburn	Caldwell Lace Leather Co., Inc.	Final	No	No	34.21
KY	Brooks	A.L. Taylor (Valley of Drums)	Deleted	No	Yes	-
KY	Brooks	Smith's Farm	Final	No	No	32.69
KY	Calvert City	Airco	Final	No	No	33.29
KY	Calvert City	B.F. Goodrich	Final	No	No	33.01
KY	Dayhoit	National Electric Coil Co./Cooper Industries	Final	No	No	50
KY	Hawesville	National Southwire Aluminum Co.	Deleted	No	No	-
KY	Hillsboro	Maxey Flats Nuclear Disposal	Final	No	No	31.71
KY	Howe Valley	Howe Valley Landfill	Deleted	No	No	-
KY	Island	Brantley Landfill	Final	No	No	52.73
KY	Jefferson County	Distler Farm	Final	No	No	34.62
KY	Louisville	Lee's Lane Landfill	Deleted	No	No	-
KY	Maceo	Green River Disposal, Inc.	Final	No	No	29.12
KY	Mayfield	General Tire & Rubber Co. (Mayfield Landfill)	Deleted	No	No	-
KY	Newport	Newport Dump	Deleted	No	No	-
KY	Olaton	Fort Hartford Coal Co. Stone Quarry	Final	No	No	43.84
KY	Paducah	Paducah Gaseous Diffusion Plant (USDOE)	Final	No	No	56.95
KY	Peewee Valley	Red Penn Sanitation Co. Landfill	Deleted	No	No	-
KY	Shepherdsville	Tri-City Disposal Co.	Final	No	No	33.82
KY	West Point	Distler Brickyard	Final	No	No	44.77
LA	Abbeville	D.L. Mud, Inc.	Deleted	No	No	-
LA	Abbeville	Gulf Coast Vacuum Services	Deleted	No	No	-
LA	Abbeville	PAB Oil & Chemical Service, Inc.	Deleted	No	No	-
LA	Alexandria	Ruston Foundry	Deleted	No	No	-
LA	Ascension Parish	Dutchtown Treatment Plant	Deleted	No	No	-
LA	Bayou Sorrel	Bayou Sorrel	Deleted	No	No	-
LA	Bogalusa	Colonial Creosote	Final	No	No	50
LA	Bossier City	Highway 71/72 Refinery	Proposed	Yes	No	50
LA	Darrow	Old Inger Oil Refinery	Deleted	No	No	-
LA	Denham Springs	Combustion, Inc.	Final	No	No	33.79
LA	Deridder	American Creosote Deridder	Final	No	No	50
LA	Doyline	Louisiana Army Ammunition Plant	Final	No	No	30.26
LA	Evangeline	EVR-Wood Treating/Evangeline Refining Company	Final	No	No	48.2
LA	Grand Cheniere	Mallard Bay Landing Bulk Plant	Deleted	No	No	-
LA	Houma	Delta Shipyard	Final	No	No	48.05
LA	Jennings	SBA Shipyard	Final	No	No	50
LA	Lake Charles	Gulf State Utilities-North Ryan Street	Proposed	No	No	50.43
LA	Madisonville	Madisonville Creosote Works	Final	No	No	48.01
LA	Marion	Marion Pressure Treating	Final	No	No	50
LA	New Orleans	Agriculture Street Landfill	Final	No	No	-
LA	Ponchatoula	Delatte Metals	Deleted	No	No	-
LA	Scotlandville	Devil's Swamp Lake	Proposed	No	No	50

St.	City/Area	Site Name	NPL[1] Status	SA Approach[2]	HEUC[3]	HRS Score[4]
LA	Scotlandville	Petro-Processors of Louisiana, Inc.	Final	No	No	41.44
LA	Slaughter	Central Wood Preserving Co.	Deleted	No	No	-
LA	Slidell	Bayou Bonfouca	Final	No	No	29.78
LA	Slidell	Southern Shipbuilding	Deleted	No	No	-
LA	Sorrento	Cleve Reber	Deleted	No	No	-
LA	Winnfield	American Creosote Works, Inc. (Winnfield Plant)	Final	No	No	50.7
MA	Acton	W.R. Grace & Co., Inc. (Acton Plant)	Final	No	No	59.31
MA	Amesbury	Microfab Inc (Former)	Final	No	No	50
MA	Ashland	Nyanza Chemical Waste Dump	Final	No	No	69.22
MA	Attleboro	Walton & Lonsbury Inc.	Final	No	No	58.3
MA	Bedford	Hanscom Field/Hanscom Air Force Base	Final	No	No	50
MA	Bedford	Naval Weapons Industrial Reserve Plant	Final	No	No	50
MA	Billerica	Iron Horse Park	Final	No	No	42.93
MA	Bridgewater	Cannon Engineering Corp. (CEC)	Deleted	No	No	-
MA	Concord	Nuclear Metals, Inc.	Final	No	No	58.31
MA	Danvers	Creese & Cook Tannery (Former)	Final	No	No	60.57
MA	Dartmouth	Re-Solve, Inc.	Final	No	No	47.71
MA	Fairhaven	Atlas Tack Corp.	Final	No	No	42.6
MA	Falmouth	Otis Air National Guard Base/Camp Edwards	Final	No	No	-
MA	Fort Devens	Fort Devens	Final	No	No	42.24
MA	Franklin	BJAT LLC	Final	No	No	41.91
MA	Groveland	Groveland Wells	Final	No	No	40.74
MA	Haverhill	Haverhill Municipal Landfill	Final	No	No	30.29
MA	Holbrook	Baird & McGuire	Final	No	No	66.35
MA	Lanesboro	Rose Disposal Pit	Final	No	No	33.03
MA	Lowell	Silresim Chemical Corp.	Final	No	No	42.72
MA	Mansfield	Hatheway and Patterson Company	Deleted	No	No	-
MA	Natick	Natick Lab Army Research, Development, and Engineering Ctr	Final	No	No	50
MA	New Bedford	New Bedford Site	Final	No	No	-
MA	New Bedford	Sullivan's Ledge	Final	No	No	32.77
MA	Norton/Attleboro	Shpack Landfill	Deleted	No	No	-
MA	Norwood	Norwood PCBs	Deleted	No	No	-
MA	Palmer	PSC Resources	Final	No	No	38.66
MA	Pittsfield	GE - Housatonic River	Proposed	No	No	70.71
MA	Plymouth	Plymouth Harbor/Cannon Engineering Corp.	Deleted	No	No	-
MA	Salem	Salem Acres	Deleted	No	No	-
MA	Sudbury	Fort Devens-Sudbury Training Annex	Deleted	No	No	-
MA	Tewksbury	Sutton Brook Disposal Area	Final	No	No	57.12
MA	Tyngsborough	Charles-George Reclamation Trust Landfill	Final	No	No	47.2
MA	Walpole	Blackburn and Union Privileges	Final	No	No	50
MA	Watertown	Materials Technology Laboratory (USARMY)	Deleted	No	No	-
MA	Westborough	Hocomonco Pond	Final	No	No	44.8
MA	Weymouth	South Weymouth Naval Air Station	Final	No	No	50
MA	Wilmington	Olin Chemical	Final	No	No	50
MA	Woburn	Industri-Plex	Final	No	No	72.42
MA	Woburn	Wells G&H	Final	No	No	42.71
MD	Aberdeen	Aberdeen Proving Ground (Michaelsville Landfill)	Final	No	No	31.09
MD	Abingdon	Bush Valley Landfill	Final	No	No	40.3
MD	Andrews AFB	Andrews Air Force Base	Final	No	No	50
MD	Annapolis	Middletown Road Dump	Deleted	No	No	-
MD	Baltimore	Chemical Metals Industries, Inc.	Deleted	No	No	-
MD	Baltimore	Curtis Bay Coast Guard Yard	Final	No	No	50
MD	Baltimore	Kane & Lombard Street Drums	Final	No	No	30.15
MD	Beltsville	Beltsville Agricultural Research Center (USDA)	Final	No	No	50
MD	Brandywine	Brandywine DRMO	Final	No	No	50.15
MD	Colora	Woodlawn County Landfill	Final	No	No	48.13
MD	Cumberland	Limestone Road	Final	No	No	30.54
MD	Dundalk	Sauer Dump	Final	No	No	50
MD	Edgewood	Aberdeen Proving Ground (Edgewood Area)	Final	No	No	53.57

St.	City/Area	Site Name	NPL[1] Status	SA Approach[2]	HEUC[3]	HRS Score[4]
MD	Elkton	Dwyer Property Ground Water Plume	Final	No	No	50
MD	Elkton	Sand, Gravel and Stone	Final	No	No	41.08
MD	Elkton	Spectron, Inc.	Final	No	No	51.42
MD	Fort Detrick	Fort Detrick Area B Ground Water	Final	No	No	49.52
MD	Hagerstown	Central Chemical (Hagerstown)	Final	No	No	50
MD	Harmans	Mid-Atlantic Wood Preservers, Inc.	Deleted	No	No	-
MD	Hollywood	Southern Maryland Wood Treating	Deleted	No	No	-
MD	Indian Head	Indian Head Naval Surface Warfare Center	Final	No	No	50
MD	North East	Ordnance Products, Inc.	Final	No	No	32.15
MD	Odenton	Fort George G. Meade	Final	No	No	-
MD	Patuxent River	Patuxent River Naval Air Station	Final	No	No	50
MD	Rosedale	68th Street Dump	Proposed	Yes	No	50
ME	Augusta	O'Connor	Deleted	No	No	-
ME	Brooksville (Cape Rosier)	Callahan Mine	Final	No	No	50
ME	Brunswick	Brunswick Naval Air Station	Final	No	No	43.38
ME	Corinna	Eastland Woolen Mill	Final	No	No	-
ME	Gray	McKin Co.	Final	No	No	60.97
ME	Kittery	Portsmouth Naval Shipyard	Final	No	No	50
ME	Leeds	Leeds Metal	Final	No	No	32.25
ME	Limestone	Loring Air Force Base	Final	No	No	34.49
ME	Meddybemps	Eastern Surplus	Final	No	No	50
ME	Plymouth	West Site/Hows Corners	Final	No	No	50
ME	Saco	Saco Municipal Landfill	Final	No	No	29.49
ME	Saco	Saco Tannery Waste Pits	Deleted	No	No	-
ME	South Hope	Union Chemical Co., Inc.	Deleted	No	No	-
ME	Washburn	Pinette's Salvage Yard	Deleted	No	No	-
ME	Windham	Keddy Mill	Final	No	No	50
ME	Winthrop	Winthrop Landfill	Final	No	No	35.62
MI	Adrian	Anderson Development Co.	Deleted	No	No	-
MI	Albion	Albion-Sheridan Township Landfill	Final	No	No	33.79
MI	Albion	McGraw Edison Corp.	Final	No	No	33.42
MI	Allegan	Rockwell International Corp. (Allegan Plant)	Final	No	No	52.15
MI	Battle Creek	Verona Well Field	Final	No	No	46.86
MI	Bay City	Bay City Middlegrounds	Proposed	No	No	50
MI	Belding	H & K Sales	Deleted	No	No	-
MI	Benton Harbor	Aircraft Components (D & L Sales)	Final	No	No	-
MI	Brighton	Rasmussen's Dump	Final	No	No	31.8
MI	Bronson	North Bronson Industrial Area	Final	No	No	33.93
MI	Buchanan	Electrovoice	Final	No	No	35.36
MI	Cadillac	Kysor Industrial Corp.	Final	No	No	33.94
MI	Cadillac	Northernaire Plating	Final	No	No	57.93
MI	Charlevoix	Charlevoix Municipal Well	Deleted	No	No	-
MI	Clare	Clare Water Supply	Final	No	No	38.43
MI	Dalton Township	Duell & Gardner Landfill	Final	No	No	34.68
MI	Dalton Township	Ott/Story/Cordova Chemical Co.	Final	No	No	53.41
MI	Davisburg	Springfield Township Dump	Final	No	No	51.97
MI	Detroit	Carter Industrials, Inc.	Deleted	No	No	-
MI	Filer City	Packaging Corp. of America	Final	No	No	51.91
MI	Gibraltar	DSC McLouth Steel Gibraltar Plant	Final	No	No	50
MI	Grand Ledge	Parsons Chemical Works, Inc.	Final	No	No	31.32
MI	Grand Rapids	Butterworth #2 Landfill	Final	No	No	50.31
MI	Grand Rapids	Folkertsma Refuse	Deleted	No	No	-
MI	Grand Rapids	H. Brown Co., Inc.	Final	No	No	39.88
MI	Grand Rapids	State Disposal Landfill, Inc.	Final	No	No	42.24
MI	Grandville	Organic Chemicals, Inc.	Final	No	No	32.93
MI	Green Oak Township	Spiegelberg Landfill	Deleted	No	No	-
MI	Greilickville	Grand Traverse Overall Supply Co.	Final	No	No	35.53
MI	Hartford	Burrows Sanitation	Deleted	No	No	-

St.	City/Area	Site Name	NPL[1] Status	SA Approach[2]	HEUC[3]	HRS Score[4]
MI	Highland	Hi-Mill Manufacturing Co.	Final	No	No	49.54
MI	Holland	Waste Management of Michigan (Holland Lagoons)	Deleted	No	No	
MI	Houghton County	Torch Lake	Final	No	No	-
MI	Howard Township	U.S. Aviex	Final	No	No	33.66
MI	Howell	Shiawassee River	Final	No	No	31.01
MI	Ionia	American Anodco, Inc.	Final	No	No	57.99
MI	Ionia	Ionia City Landfill	Final	No	No	31.31
MI	Kalamazoo	Allied Paper, Inc./Portage Creek/Kalamazoo River	Final	No	No	36.41
MI	Kalamazoo	Auto Ion Chemicals, Inc.	Final	No	No	32.07
MI	Kalamazoo	Michigan Disposal Service (Cork Street Landfill)	Final	No	No	37.93
MI	Kalamazoo	Roto-Finish Co., Inc.	Final	No	No	40.7
MI	Kent City	Kent City Mobile Home Park	Deleted	No	No	-
MI	Kentwood	Kentwood Landfill	Final	No	No	35.39
MI	Lake Ann	Metal Working Shop	Deleted	No	No	-
MI	Lansing	Adam's Plating	Final	No	No	29.64
MI	Lansing	Barrels, Inc.	Final	No	No	42.24
MI	Lansing Township	Motor Wheel, Inc.	Final	No	No	-
MI	Macomb Township	South Macomb Disposal Authority (Landfills #9 and #9A)	Final	No	No	33.67
MI	Mancelona Township	Tar Lake	Final	No	No	-
MI	Marquette	Cliff/Dow Dump	Deleted	No	No	-
MI	Metamora	Metamora Landfill	Final	No	No	35.51
MI	Midland	Tittabawassee River, Saginaw River & Bay	Not NPL	Yes	No	-
MI	Muskegon	Bofors Nobel, Inc.	Final	No	No	53.42
MI	Muskegon	Kaydon Corp.	Final	No	No	34.21
MI	Muskegon	Peerless Plating Co.	Final	No	No	43.94
MI	Muskegon	Thermo-Chem, Inc.	Final	No	No	53.36
MI	Muskegon Heights	SCA Independent Landfill	Final	No	No	34.75
MI	Oscoda	Hedblum Industries	Final	No	No	37.29
MI	Oscoda	Wurtsmith Air Force Base	Proposed	No	No	50
MI	Oshtemo Township	K&L Avenue Landfill	Final	No	No	38.1
MI	Ossineke	Ossineke Ground Water Contamination	Deleted	No	No	-
MI	Otisville	Forest Waste Products	Final	No	No	38.64
MI	Park Township	Southwest Ottawa County Landfill	Final	No	No	39.66
MI	Pere Marquette Twp	Mason County Landfill	Deleted	No	No	-
MI	Petoskey	Petoskey Municipal Well Field	Final	No	No	42.68
MI	Pleasant Plains Twp	Wash King Laundry	Final	No	No	40.03
MI	Rochester Hills	J & L Landfill	Final	No	No	31.65
MI	Rose Center	Cemetery Dump	Deleted	No	No	-
MI	Rose Township	Rose Township Dump	Final	No	No	50.92
MI	Sault Ste Marie	Cannelton Industries, Inc.	Final	No	No	30.16
MI	Sparta Township	Sparta Landfill	Final	No	No	32
MI	St. Clair Shores	Ten-Mile Drain	Final	No	No	48.88
MI	St. Joseph	Bendix Corp./Allied Automotive	Final	No	No	37.27
MI	St. Louis	Gratiot County Golf Course	Deleted	No	No	-
MI	St. Louis	Gratiot County Landfill	Final	No	No	-
MI	St. Louis	Gratiot County Golf Course	Final	No	No	29.54
MI	St. Louis	Velsicol Chemical Corp.(Michigan)	Final	No	No	52.29
MI	Sturgis	Sturgis Municipal Wells	Final	No	No	42.24
MI	Swartz Creek	Berlin & Farro	Deleted	No	No	-
MI	Temperance	Novaco Industries	Deleted	No	No	-
MI	Traverse City	Avenue E Ground Water Contamination	Deleted	No	No	-
MI	Trenton	Mclouth Steel Corp	Final	No	-	50
MI	Utica	G&H Landfill	Final	No	No	49.09
MI	Utica	Liquid Disposal, Inc.	Final	No	No	63.28
MI	Whitehall	Muskegon Chemical Co.	Final	No	No	34.19
MI	Whitehall	Whitehall Municipal Wells	Deleted	No	No	-
MI	Wyandotte	Lower Ecorse Creek Dump	Deleted	No	No	-
MI	Wyoming	Spartan Chemical Co.	Final	No	No	41.05

St.	City/Area	Site Name	NPL[1] Status	SA Approach[2]	HEUC[3]	HRS Score[4]
MI	Wyoming Township	Chem Central	Final	No	No	38.2
MN	Adrian	Adrian Municipal Well Field	Deleted	No	No	-
MN	Andover	South Andover Site	Final	No	No	-
MN	Andover	Waste Disposal Engineering	Deleted	No	No	-
MN	Baytown Township	Baytown Township Ground Water Plume	Final	No	No	35.62
MN	Bemidji	Kummer Sanitary Landfill	Deleted	No	No	-
MN	Brainerd/Baxter	Burlington Northern (Brainerd/Baxter Plant)	Final	No	No	46.77
MN	Brooklyn Center	Joslyn Manufacturing & Supply Co.	Final	No	No	-
MN	Burnsville	Freeway Sanitary Landfill	Final	No	No	45.91
MN	Cannon Falls	Dakhue Sanitary Landfill	Deleted	No	No	-
MN	Cass Lake	St. Regis Paper Co.	Final	No	No	52.88
MN	Dakota County	Pine Bend Sanitary Landfill	Deleted	No	No	-
MN	East Bethel Township	East Bethel Demolition Landfill	Deleted	No	No	-
MN	Fairview Township	Agate Lake Scrapyard	Deleted	No	No	-
MN	Faribault	Nutting Truck & Caster Co.	Deleted	No	No	-
MN	Fridley	Boise Cascade/Onan Corp./Medtronics, Inc.	Deleted	No	No	-
MN	Fridley	FMC Corp. (Fridley Plant)	Final	No	No	65.5
MN	Fridley	Fridley Commons Park Well Field	Final	No	No	50
MN	Fridley	Kurt Manufacturing Co.	Final	No	No	31.41
MN	Fridley	Naval Industrial Reserve Ordnance Plant	Final	No	No	-
MN	Hermantown	Arrowhead Refinery Co.	Final	No	No	43.75
MN	Lagrand Township	LaGrand Sanitary Landfill	Deleted	No	No	-
MN	Lake Elmo	Washington County Landfill	Deleted	No	No	-
MN	Lehillier	Lehillier/Mankato Site	Final	No	No	42.49
MN	Long Prairie	Long Prairie Ground Water Contamination	Final	No	No	31.94
MN	Minneapolis	General Mills/Henkel Corp.	Final	No	No	36.28
MN	Minneapolis	South Minneapolis Residential Soil Contamination	Final	No	No	44.58
MN	Minneapolis	Twin Cities Air Force Reserve Base (Small Arms Range Landfill)	Deleted	No	No	-
MN	Minneapolis	Union Scrap Iron & Metal Co.	Deleted	No	No	-
MN	Minneapolis	Whittaker Corp.	Deleted	No	No	-
MN	Morris	Morris Arsenic Dump	Deleted	No	No	-
MN	New Brighton	MacGillis & Gibbs/Bell Lumber & Pole Co.	Final	No	No	48.33
MN	New Brighton	New Brighton/Arden Hills/TCAAP (USARMY)	Final	No	No	59.16
MN	Oak Grove Township	Oak Grove Sanitary Landfill	Deleted	No	No	-
MN	Oakdale	Oakdale Dump	Final	No	No	55.71
MN	Oronoco	Olmsted County Sanitary Landfill	Deleted	No	No	-
MN	Perham	Perham Arsenic Site	Final	No	No	37.98
MN	Rosemount	Koch Refining Co./N-Ren Corp.	Deleted	No	No	-
MN	Rosemount	University of Minnesota (Rosemount Research Center)	Deleted	No	No	-
MN	Sebeka	Ritari Post & Pole	Final	No	No	29.81
MN	Spring Park	Spring Park Municipal Well Field	Final	No	No	50
MN	St. Augusta Township	St. Augusta Sanitary Landfill/Engen Dump	Deleted	No	No	-
MN	St. Louis County	St. Louis River Site	Final	No	No	32.08
MN	St. Louis Park	NL Industries/Taracorp/Golden Auto	Deleted	No	No	-
MN	St. Louis Park	Reilly Tar & Chemical Corp. (St. Louis Park Plant)	Final	No	No	-
MN	St. Paul	Koppers Coke	Final	No	No	55.05
MN	Waite Park	Waite Park Wells	Final	No	No	31.94
MN	Windom	Windom Dump	Deleted	No	No	-
MO	Amazonia	Wheeling Disposal Service Co., Inc., Landfill	Deleted	No	No	-
MO	Annapolis	Annapolis Lead Mine	Final	No	No	56.67
MO	Bridgeton	Westlake Landfill	Final	No	No	29.85
MO	Caledonia	Washington County Lead District - Furnace Creek	Final	No	No	50
MO	Cape Girardeau	Kem-Pest Laboratories	Deleted	No	No	-
MO	Cape Girardeau	Missouri Electric Works	Final	No	No	31.2
MO	Desloge	Big River Mine Tailings/St. Joe Minerals Corp.	Final	No	No	84.91
MO	Ellisville	Ellisville Site	Final	No	No	-
MO	Fredericktown	Madison County Mines	Final	No	No	58.41
MO	Granby	Newton County Mine Tailings	Final	No	No	50
MO	Imperial	Minker/Stout/Romaine Creek	Final	No	No	36.78

St.	City/Area	Site Name	NPL[1] Status	SA Approach[2]	HEUC[3]	HRS Score[4]
MO	Independence	Lake City Army Ammunition Plant (Northwest Lagoon)	Final	No	No	33.62
MO	Jefferson County	Southwest Jefferson County Mining	Final	No	No	70.71
MO	Joplin	Newton County Wells	Final	No	No	50
MO	Joplin	Oronogo-Duenweg Mining Belt	Final	No	No	46.2
MO	Kansas City	Conservation Chemical Co.	Final	No	No	29.85
MO	Liberty	Lee Chemical	Final	No	No	46.81
MO	Malden	Bee Cee Manufacturing Co.	Final	No	No	28.59
MO	Moscow Mills	Shenandoah Stables	Deleted	No	No	-
MO	Neosho	Pools Prairie	Final	No	Yes	50
MO	New Haven	Riverfront	Final	No	Yes	50
MO	North Kansas City	Armour Road	Final	No	No	50
MO	Old Mines	Washington County Lead District - Old Mines	Final	No	No	76.81
MO	Potosi	Washington County Lead District - Potosi	Final	No	No	50
MO	Republic	Solid State Circuits, Inc.	Final	No	No	37.93
MO	Richwoods	Washington County Lead District - Richwoods	Final	No	No	76.81
MO	Rogersville	Compass Plaza Well TCE	Final	No	No	50
MO	Sikeston	Quality Plating	Final	No	No	40.7
MO	Springfield	Fulbright Landfill	Final	No	No	40.6
MO	Springfield	North-U Drive Well Contamination	Deleted	No	No	-
MO	St. Charles	Weldon Spring Former Army Ordnance Works	Final	No	Yes	30.26
MO	St. Charles	Weldon Spring Quarry/Plant/Pits (USDOE/Army)	Final	No	No	58.6
MO	St. Louis	St. Louis Airport/Hazelwood Interim Storage/Futura Coatings Co.	Final	No	No	38.31
MO	Sullivan	Oak Grove Village Well	Final	No	No	50
MO	Times Beach	Times Beach	Deleted	No	No	-
MO	Valley Park	Valley Park TCE	Final	No	No	35.57
MO	Verona	Syntex Facility	Final	No	No	43.78
MO	Vienna	Vienna Wells	Final	No	Yes	50
MO	Washington	Sporlan Valve Plant #1	Final	No	-	35.15
MP	Garapan	PCB Warehouse	Deleted	No	No	-
MS	Canton	Southeastern Wood Preserving	Final	No	No	48.03
MS	Clarksdale	Red Panther Chemical Company	Final	No	No	39.43
MS	Columbia	Newsom Brothers/Old Reichhold Chemicals, Inc.	Deleted	No	No	-
MS	Columbus	Kerr-McGee Chemical Corp - Columbus	Final	No	No	52.47
MS	Flowood	Flowood Site	Deleted	No	No	-
MS	Flowood	Sonford Products	Final	No	No	31.66
MS	Greenville	Walcotte Chemical Co. Warehouses	Deleted	No	No	-
MS	Grenada	Rockwell International Wheel & Trim	Final	No	No	50
MS	Gulfport	Chemfax, Inc.	Final	No	No	38.4
MS	Hattiesburg	Davis Timber Company	Deleted	No	No	-
MS	Louisville	American Creosote Works, Inc.	Final	No	No	62.2
MS	Pascagoula	Mississippi Phosphates Corporation	Final	No	No	50
MS	Picayune	Picayune Wood Treating	Final	No	No	51.03
MS	Wesson	Potter Co.	Proposed	No	No	50
MT	Anaconda	Anaconda Co. Smelter	Final	No	No	58.71
MT	Basin	Basin Mining Area	Final	No	Yes	61.15
MT	Billings	Lockwood Solvent Ground Water Plume	Final	No	No	45.69
MT	Black Eagle	ACM Smelter and Refinery	Final	No	No	54.26
MT	Bozeman	Idaho Pole Co.	Final	No	No	38.29
MT	Butte	Montana Pole and Treating	Final	No	No	33.03
MT	Butte	Silver Bow Creek/Butte Area	Final	No	No	63.76
MT	Columbia Falls	Anaconda Aluminum Co Columbia Falls Reduction Plant	Final	No	No	68.39
MT	Columbus	Mouat Industries	Final	No	No	-
MT	East Helena	East Helena Site	Final	No	No	61.65
MT	Helena	Upper Tenmile Creek Mining Area	Final	No	No	50
MT	Libby	Libby Asbestos	Final	No	No	-
MT	Libby	Libby Ground Water Contamination	Final	No	No	37.67
MT	Milltown	Milltown Reservoir Sediments	Final	No	Yes	43.78
MT	Missoula	Smurfit-Stone Mill	Proposed	No	No	50

St.	City/Area	Site Name	NPL[1] Status	SA Approach[2]	HEUC[3]	HRS Score[4]
MT	Monarch	Barker Hughesville Mining District	Final	No	No	50
MT	Neihart	Carpenter Snow Creek Mining District	Final	No	No	50
MT	Superior	Flat Creek IMM	Final	No	No	51.33
NC	210 Miles Of Roads	PCB Spills	Deleted	No	No	-
NC	Aberdeen	Aberdeen Contaminated Ground Water	Final	No	No	50
NC	Aberdeen	Aberdeen Pesticide Dumps	Final	No	No	52.7
NC	Aberdeen	Geigy Chemical Corp. (Aberdeen Plant)	Final	No	No	33.02
NC	Arden	Blue Ridge Plating Company	Final	No	No	38.67
NC	Ashe County	Ore Knob Mine	Final	No	No	50
NC	Asheville	CTS of Asheville, Inc.	Final	No	No	38.4
NC	Belmont	Jadco-Hughes Facility	Final	No	No	42
NC	Castle Hayne	Reasor Chemical Company	Deleted	No	No	-
NC	Charlotte	Martin-Marietta, Sodyeco, Inc.	Deleted	No	No	-
NC	Charlotte	Ram Leather Care	Final	No	No	40.43
NC	Concord	Bypass 601 Ground Water Contamination	Final	No	No	-
NC	Cordova	Charles Macon Lagoon & Drum Storage	Final	No	No	47.1
NC	East Flat Rock	General Electric Co/Shepherd Farm	Final	No	No	-
NC	Fayetteville	Cape Fear Wood Preserving	Final	No	No	34.09
NC	Fayetteville	Carolina Transformer Co.	Final	No	No	33.76
NC	Gastonia	Davis Park Road TCE	Final	No	No	33.5
NC	Gastonia	Hemphill Road TCE	Final	No	No	50
NC	Havelock	Cherry Point Marine Corps Air Station	Final	No	No	70.71
NC	Hazelwood	Benfield Industries, Inc.	Final	No	No	31.67
NC	Jacksonville	ABC One Hour Cleaners	Final	No	No	29.11
NC	Maco	Potter's Septic Tank Service Pits	Final	No	No	29.14
NC	Morrisville	Koppers Co., Inc. (Morrisville Plant)	Final	No	No	-
NC	Navassa	Kerr-McGee Chemical Corp - Navassa	Final	No	No	50
NC	North Belmont	North Belmont PCE	Final	No	No	50
NC	Onslow County	Camp Lejeune Military Reservation	Final	No	No	33.13
NC	Oxford	Cristex Drum	Final	No	No	48
NC	Oxford	JFD Electronics/Channel Master	Final	No	No	39.03
NC	Plymouth	Weyerhaeuser Co Plymouth Wood Treating Plant	Not NPL	Yes	No	-
NC	Raleigh	North Carolina State University (Lot 86, Farm Unit #1)	Final	No	No	48.36
NC	Raleigh	Ward Transformer	Final	No	No	50
NC	Riegelwood	Holtra Chem/Honeywell Inc.	Not NPL	Yes	No	-
NC	Riegelwood	Wright Chemical Corporation	Final	No	No	48.03
NC	Roxboro	GMH Electronics	Final	No	Yes	50
NC	Salisbury	National Starch & Chemical Corp.	Final	No	No	46.51
NC	Selma	Gurley Pesticide Burial	Not NPL	Yes	No	-
NC	Shelby	Celanese Corp. (Shelby Fiber Operations)	Final	No	No	-
NC	Statesville	FCX, Inc. (Statesville Plant)	Final	No	No	37.93
NC	Statesville	Sigmon's Septic Tank Service	Final	No	No	30.03
NC	Swannanoa	Chemtronics, Inc.	Final	No	No	30.16
NC	Washington	FCX, Inc. (Washington Plant)	Final	No	No	40.39
NC	Waynesville	Barber Orchard	Final	No	No	70.71
NC	Wilmington	Horton Iron and Metal	Final	No	No	48.03
NC	Wilmington	New Hanover County Airport Burn Pit	Deleted	No	No	
NC	Yadkinville	Holcomb Creosote Co	Final	No	No	48
ND	Minot	Minot Landfill	Deleted	No	No	-
ND	Southeast	Arsenic Trioxide Site	Deleted	No	No	-
NE	Bruno	Bruno Co-op Association/Associated Properties	Final	No	No	50
NE	Columbus	10th Street Site	Final	No	No	28.9
NE	Grand Island	Cleburn Street Well	Final	No	No	50
NE	Grand Island	Cornhusker Army Ammunition Plant	Final	No	No	51.13
NE	Grand Island	Parkview Well	Final	No	No	50
NE	Hastings	Garvey Elevator	Final	No	Yes	50
NE	Hastings	Hastings Ground Water Contamination	Final	No	No	42.24
NE	Hastings	West Highway 6 & Highway 281	Final	No	Yes	50

St.	City/Area	Site Name	NPL[1] Status	SA Approach[2]	HEUC[3]	HRS Score[4]
NE	Lindsay	Lindsay Manufacturing Co.	Final	No	No	47.91
NE	Mead	Nebraska Ordnance Plant (Former)	Final	No	No	31.94
NE	Norfolk	Iowa-Nebraska Light & Power Co	Final	No	No	40.8
NE	Norfolk	Sherwood Medical Co.	Final	No	No	50
NE	Ogallala	Ogallala Ground Water Contamination	Final	No	No	50
NE	Omaha	Omaha Lead	Final	No	No	-
NE	Valley	Old HWY 275 and N 288th Street	Final	No	No	50
NE	Waverly	Waverly Ground Water Contamination	Deleted	No	No	-
NE	York	PCE Southeast Contamination	Final	No	No	43.33
NE	York	PCE/TCE Northeast Contamination	Final	No	No	50
NH	Barrington	Tibbetts Road	Final	No	No	41.09
NH	Berlin	Chlor-Alkali Facility (Former)	Final	No	No	30.54
NH	Conway	Kearsarge Metallurgical Corp.	Final	No	No	38.45
NH	Dover	Dover Municipal Landfill	Final	No	No	36.98
NH	Epping	Keefe Environmental Services	Final	No	No	65.19
NH	Farmington	Collins & Aikman Plant (Former)	Final	No	No	50
NH	Kingston	Ottati & Goss/Kingston Steel Drum	Final	No	No	53.41
NH	Londonderry	Auburn Road Landfill	Final	No	No	36.3
NH	Londonderry	Tinkham Garage	Final	No	No	43.24
NH	Londonderry	Town Garage/Radio Beacon	Deleted	No	No	-
NH	Merrimack	New Hampshire Plating Co.	Final	No	No	50
NH	Milford	Fletcher's Paint Works & Storage	Final	No	No	35.39
NH	Milford	Savage Municipal Water Supply	Final	No	No	37.52
NH	Nashua	Mohawk Tannery	Proposed	No	No	52.4
NH	Nashua	Sylvester	Final	No	No	-
NH	North Hampton	Coakley Landfill	Final	No	No	29.16
NH	Peterborough	South Municipal Water Supply Well	Final	No	No	35.64
NH	Plaistow	Beede Waste Oil	Final	No	No	70.71
NH	Portsmouth/Newington	Pease Air Force Base	Final	No	No	39.42
NH	Raymond	Mottolo Pig Farm	Final	No	Yes	40.7
NH	Somersworth	Somersworth Sanitary Landfill	Final	No	No	65.56
NH	Troy	Troy Mills Landfill	Final	No	No	50
NJ	Alexandria Township	Crown Vantage Landfill	Deleted	No	No	-
NJ	Asbury Park	M&T Delisa Landfill	Deleted	No	No	-
NJ	Atlantic County	Federal Aviation Administration Technical Center	Final	No	No	39.65
NJ	Bayville	Denzer & Schafer X-Ray Co.	Deleted	No	No	-
NJ	Berkeley Township	Beachwood/Berkley Wells	Deleted	No	No	-
NJ	Beverly	Cosden Chemical Coatings Corp.	Final	No	No	33.86
NJ	Boonton	Pepe Field	Deleted	No	No	-
NJ	Bound Brook	Brook Industrial Park	Final	No	No	58.12
NJ	Brick Township	Brick Township Landfill	Final	No	No	58.13
NJ	Bridgeport	Bridgeport Rental & Oil Services	Final	No	No	60.73
NJ	Bridgeport	Chemical Leaman Tank Lines, Inc.	Final	No	No	47.53
NJ	Bridgewater	American Cyanamid Co.	Final	No	No	-
NJ	Byram	Mansfield Trail Dump	Final	No	No	50
NJ	Camden	Martin Aaron, Inc.	Final	No	No	50
NJ	Camden and Gloucester	Welsbach & General Gas Mantle (Camden Radiation)	Final	No	No	41.46
NJ	Carlstadt	Scientific Chemical Processing	Final	No	No	55.97
NJ	Chester Township	Combe Fill South Landfill	Final	No	No	45.22
NJ	Cinnaminson Township	Cinnaminson Township (Block 702) Ground Water Contamination	Final	No	No	37.93
NJ	Colts Neck	Naval Weapons Station Earle (Site A)	Final	No	No	29.65
NJ	Dover	Dover Municipal Well 4	Final	No	No	28.9
NJ	E. Brunswick Township	Fried Industries	Final	No	No	33.61
NJ	East Rutherford	Universal Oil Products (Chemical Division)	Final	No	No	54.63
NJ	Edgewater	Quanta Resources	Final	No	No	50
NJ	Edison Township	Chemical Insecticide Corp.	Final	No	No	37.93
NJ	Edison Township	Kin-Buc Landfill	Final	No	No	50.64
NJ	Edison Township	Renora, Inc.	Deleted	No	No	-
NJ	Egg Harbor Township	Delilah Road	Deleted	No	No	-

St.	City/Area	Site Name	NPL[1] Status	SA Approach[2]	HEUC[3]	HRS Score[4]
NJ	Elizabeth	Chemical Control	Final	No	No	47.13
NJ	Evesham Township	Ellis Property	Final	No	No	34.62
NJ	Fair Lawn	Fair Lawn Well Field	Final	No	No	42.49
NJ	Fairfield	Caldwell Trucking Co.	Final	No	No	58.3
NJ	Fairfield	Unimatic Manufacturing Corporation	Final	No	No	50
NJ	Florence	Roebling Steel Co.	Final	No	No	41.02
NJ	Florence Township	Florence Land Recontouring, Inc., Landfill	Deleted	No	No	-
NJ	Franklin Borough	Metaltec/Aerosystems	Final	No	No	48.95
NJ	Franklin Township	Franklin Burn	Final	No	No	40.67
NJ	Franklin Township	Higgins Farm	Final	No	No	30.47
NJ	Franklin Township	Myers Property	Final	No	No	33.83
NJ	Freehold Township	Lone Pine Landfill	Final	No	No	66.33
NJ	Galloway Township	Emmell's Septic Landfill	Final	No	No	50
NJ	Galloway Township	Mannheim Avenue Dump	Deleted	No	No	-
NJ	Galloway Township	Pomona Oaks Residential Wells	Deleted	No	No	-
NJ	Garfield	Garfield Ground Water Contamination	Final	No	No	0
NJ	Gibbsboro	Route 561 Dump	Proposed	No	No	50
NJ	Gibbsboro	Sherwin-Williams/Hilliards Creek	Final	No	No	50
NJ	Gibbsboro	United States Avenue Burn	Final	No	No	50
NJ	Gibbstown	Hercules, Inc. (Gibbstown Plant)	Final	No	No	40.36
NJ	Glen Ridge	Glen Ridge Radium Site	Deleted	No	No	-
NJ	Gloucester Township	GEMS Landfill	Final	No	No	68.53
NJ	Green Village	Rolling Knolls Landfill	Final	No	No	58.31
NJ	Hamilton Township	D'Imperio Property	Final	No	No	55.79
NJ	Hillsborough Township	Krysowaty Farm	Deleted	No	No	-
NJ	Hoboken	Grand Street Mercury	Deleted	No	No	-
NJ	Howell Township	Bog Creek Farm	Final	No	No	43.23
NJ	Howell Township	Zschiegner Refining	Final	No	No	50
NJ	Jackson Township	Jackson Township Landfill	Deleted	No	No	-
NJ	Jersey City	PJP Landfill	Final	No	No	28.73
NJ	Kearny	Diamond Head Oil Refinery Div.	Final	No	No	30
NJ	Kearny	Standard Chlorine	Final	No	No	50
NJ	Kingston	Higgins Disposal	Final	No	No	30.87
NJ	Kingwood Township	De Rewal Chemical Co.	Final	No	No	35.72
NJ	Lakehurst	Naval Air Engineering Center	Final	No	No	50.53
NJ	Linden	LCP Chemicals Inc.	Final	No	No	50
NJ	Lodi	Lodi Municipal Well	Deleted	No	No	-
NJ	Mantua Township	Helen Kramer Landfill	Final	No	No	72.66
NJ	Manville	Federal Creosote	Deleted	No	No	-
NJ	Marlboro Township	Burnt Fly Bog	Final	No	No	59.16
NJ	Maywood/Rochelle Pk	Maywood Chemical Co.	Final	No	No	51.19
NJ	Middlesex	Middlesex Sampling Plant (USDOE)	Final	No	No	50
NJ	Milford	Curtis Specialty Papers, Inc.	Final	No	No	50
NJ	Millington	Asbestos Dump	Deleted	No	No	-
NJ	Millville	Nascolite Corp.	Final	No	No	51.13
NJ	Minotola	Garden State Cleaners Co.	Final	No	No	28.9
NJ	Minotola	South Jersey Clothing Co.	Final	No	No	42.24
NJ	Monroe Township	Monroe Township Landfill	Deleted	No	No	-
NJ	Montclair/West Orange	Montclair/West Orange Radium Site	Deleted	No	No	-
NJ	Montgomery Township	Montgomery Township Housing Development	Final	No	No	37.93
NJ	Morganville	Imperial Oil Co., Inc./Champion Chemicals	Final	No	No	33.87
NJ	Mount Holly	Landfill & Development Co.	Final	No	No	33.62
NJ	Mount Olive Township	Combe Fill North Landfill	Deleted	No	No	-
NJ	Newark	Diamond Alkali Co.	Final	No	No	35.4
NJ	Newark	Pierson's Creek	Final	No	No	50
NJ	Newark	Riverside Industrial Park	Final	No	No	50
NJ	Newark	White Chemical Corp.	Final	No	No	-
NJ	Newfield Borough	Shieldalloy Corp.	Final	No	No	58.75

St.	City/Area	Site Name	NPL[1] Status	SA Approach[2]	HEUC[3]	HRS Score[4]
NJ	Oakland	Witco Chemical Corp. (Oakland Plant)	Deleted	No	No	-
NJ	Old Bridge Township	CPS/Madison Industries	Final	No	No	69.73
NJ	Old Bridge Township	Evor Phillips Leasing	Final	No	No	36.64
NJ	Old Bridge Township	Global Sanitary Landfill	Final	No	No	45.92
NJ	Old Bridge Twp/Sayreville	Raritan Bay Slag	Final	No	No	50
NJ	Orange	U.S. Radium Corp.	Final	No	Yes	
NJ	Parsippany, Troy Hills	Sharkey Landfill	Final	No	No	48.85
NJ	Pedricktown	NL Industries	Final	No	No	52.96
NJ	Pemberton Township	Fort Dix (Landfill Site)	Deleted	No	No	-
NJ	Pemberton Township	Lang Property	Final	No	No	48.89
NJ	Pennsauken Township	Puchack Well Field	Final	No	No	50
NJ	Pennsauken Township	Swope Oil & Chemical Co.	Final	No	No	35.68
NJ	Piscataway	Chemsol, Inc.	Final	No	No	42.69
NJ	Pitman	Lipari Landfill	Final	No	No	75.6
NJ	Pleasant Plains	Reich Farms	Final	No	No	53.48
NJ	Pleasantville	Price Landfill	Final	No	No	-
NJ	Plumstead Township	Goose Farm	Final	No	No	47.71
NJ	Plumstead Township	Hopkins Farm	Deleted	No	No	-
NJ	Plumstead Township	Pijak Farm	Deleted	No	No	-
NJ	Plumstead Township	Spence Farm	Deleted	No	No	-
NJ	Plumstead Township	Wilson Farm	Deleted	No	No	-
NJ	Ringwood Borough	Ringwood Mines/Landfill	Final	No	No	52.58
NJ	Rockaway Township	Picatinny Arsenal (USARMY)	Final	No	No	42.92
NJ	Rockaway Township	Radiation Technology, Inc.	Final	No	No	42.56
NJ	Rockaway Township	Rockaway Borough Well Field	Final	No	No	42.34
NJ	Rockaway Township	Rockaway Township Wells	Final	No	No	28.9
NJ	Rocky Hill Borough	Rocky Hill Municipal Well	Final	No	No	37.93
NJ	Saddle Brook Twp	Curcio Scrap Metal, Inc.	Final	No	No	34.37
NJ	Sayreville	Atlantic Resources Corporation	Final	No	No	50
NJ	Sayreville	Horseshoe Road	Final	No	No	51.37
NJ	Sayreville	Sayreville Landfill	Deleted	No	No	-
NJ	Shamong Township	Ewan Property	Final	No	No	50.19
NJ	South Brunswick	JIS Landfill	Final	No	No	45.14
NJ	South Brunswick	South Brunswick Landfill	Deleted	No	No	-
NJ	South Kearny	Syncon Resins	Final	No	No	43.43
NJ	South Plainfield	Cornell Dubilier Electronics, Inc.	Final	No	No	50.27
NJ	South Plainfield	Woodbrook Road Dump	Final	No	No	50
NJ	Sparta Township	A. O. Polymer	Final	No	No	-
NJ	Springfield Twp	Kauffman & Minteer, Inc.	Final	No	No	28.51
NJ	Swainton Middle	Williams Property	Final	No	No	40.45
NJ	Tabernacle Township	Tabernacle Drum Dump	Deleted	No	No	-
NJ	Thorofare	Matteo & Sons, Inc.	Final	No	No	50
NJ	Toms River	Ciba-Geigy Corp.	Final	No	No	50.33
NJ	Upper Deerfield Twp	Upper Deerfield Township Sanitary Landfill	Deleted	No	No	-
NJ	Upper Freehold Twp	Friedman Property	Deleted	No	No	-
NJ	Vineland	Former Kil-Tone Company	Final	No	No	65.29
NJ	Vineland	Iceland Coin Laundry Area Ground Water Plume	Final	No	No	30.3
NJ	Vineland	Vineland Chemical Co., Inc.	Final	No	No	59.16
NJ	Vineland	Vineland State School	Deleted	No	No	-
NJ	Voorhees Township	Cooper Road	Deleted	No	No	-
NJ	Wall Township	Monitor Devices, Inc./Intercircuits, Inc.	Final	No	No	41.93
NJ	Wall Township	Waldick Aerospace Devices, Inc.	Final	No	No	44.86
NJ	Wall Twp	White Swan Cleaners/Sun Cleaners Area Ground Water Contam.	Final	No	No	41.63
NJ	Wallington Borough	Industrial Latex Corp.	Deleted	No	No	-
NJ	Warren County	Pohatcong Valley Ground Water Contamination	Final	No	No	28.9
NJ	Wayne Township	W.R. Grace & Co., Inc./Wayne Interim Storage Site (USDOE)	Deleted	No	No	-
NJ	West Orange/Orange	Orange Valley Regional Ground Water Contamination	Final	No	No	50
NJ	Wharton Borough	Dayco Corp./L.E. Carpenter Co.	Final	No	No	46.13

St.	City/Area	Site Name	NPL[1] Status	SA Approach[2]	HEUC[3]	HRS Score[4]
NJ	Winslow Township	King of Prussia	Final	No	No	47.19
NJ	Winslow Township	Lightman Drum Company	Final	No	No	42.03
NJ	Wood Ridge Borough	Ventron/Velsicol	Final	No	No	51.38
NJ	Woodland Township	Woodland Route 532 Dump	Final	No	No	34.98
NJ	Woodland Township	Woodland Route 72 Dump	Final	No	No	31.17
NJ	Woolwich Township	Matlack, Inc.	Final	No	No	45.54
NJ	Wrightstown	McGuire Air Force Base #1	Final	No	No	47.2
NM	Albuquerque	AT&SF (Albuquerque)	Final	No	No	-
NM	Albuquerque	Fruit Avenue Plume	Final	No	No	50
NM	Albuquerque	South Valley	Final	No	No	-
NM	Carrizozo	Cimarron Mining Corp.	Final	No	No	
NM	Church Rock	United Nuclear Corp.	Final	No	No	30.36
NM	Clovis	AT & SF (Clovis)	Deleted	No	No	-
NM	Espanola	North Railroad Avenue Plume	Final	No	No	50
NM	Farmington	Lee Acres Landfill (USDOI)	Final	No	No	39.37
NM	Grants	Grants Chlorinated Solvents Plume	Final	No	No	50
NM	Laguna Pueblo	Jackpile-Paguate Uranium Mine	Final	No	No	50
NM	Las Cruces	Griggs & Walnut Ground Water Plume	Final	No	No	50
NM	Lemitar	Cal West Metals (USSBA)	Deleted	No	No	-
NM	Los Lunas	Pagano Salvage	Deleted	No	No	-
NM	Milan	Homestake Mining Co.	Final	No	No	34.21
NM	Prewitt	Prewitt Abandoned Refinery	Final	No	No	-
NM	Questa	Chevron Questa Mine	Final	No	No	50
NM	Roswell	Lea and West Second Street	Final	No	No	50
NM	Roswell	McGaffey and Main Groundwater Plume	Final	No	No	50
NM	Silver City	Cleveland Mill	Deleted	No	No	-
NM	Socorro	Eagle Picher Carefree Battery	Final	No	No	50
NV	Dayton	Carson River Mercury Site	Final	No	No	39.07
NV	Mountain City	Rio Tinto Copper Mine	Not NPL	Yes	No	-
NV	Yerington	Anaconda Copper Mine	Proposed	No	No	50
NY	Amenia	Sarney Farm	Final	No	No	33.2
NY	Batavia	Batavia Landfill	Deleted	No	No	-
NY	Bohemia	BioClinical Laboratories, Inc.	Deleted	No	No	-
NY	Brant	Wide Beach Development	Deleted	No	No	-
NY	Brooklyn	Gowanus Canal	Final	No	No	50
NY	Brooklyn, Queens	Newtown Creek	Final	No	No	50
NY	Byron Township	Byron Barrel & Drum	Final	No	Yes	37.27
NY	Caledonia	Jones Chemicals, Inc.	Final	No	No	33.62
NY	Carthage	Crown Cleaners of Watertown, Inc.	Final	No	No	49
NY	Central Islip	MacKenzie Chemical Works, Inc.	Final	No	No	50
NY	Cheektowaga	Pfohl Brothers Landfill	Deleted	No	No	-
NY	Clayville	Ludlow Sand & Gravel	Deleted	No	No	-
NY	Cold Springs	Marathon Battery Corp.	Deleted	No	No	-
NY	Colonie	Mercury Refining, Inc.	Final	No	No	44.58
NY	Conklin	Conklin Dumps	Deleted	No	No	-
NY	Copiague	Action Anodizing, Plating, & Polishing Corp.	Deleted	No	No	-
NY	Cortland	Rosen Brothers Scrap Yard/Dump	Final	No	No	51.35
NY	Cortlandt Manor	Magna Metals	Final	No	-	50
NY	Dayton	Peter Cooper Corporation (Markhams)	Deleted	No	No	-
NY	Deer Park	SMS Instruments, Inc.	Deleted	No	No	-
NY	East Farmingdale	Circuitron Corp.	Final	No	No	54.27
NY	East Fishkill	Shenandoah Road Ground Water Contamination	Final	No	No	50
NY	Ellenville	Ellenville Scrap Iron and Metal	Final	No	No	50.27
NY	Elmira	Facet Enterprises, Inc.	Final	No	No	46.67
NY	Farmingdale	Kenmark Textile Corp.	Deleted	No	No	-
NY	Farmingdale	Liberty Industrial Finishing	Final	No	No	50.65
NY	Farmingdale	Preferred Plating Corp.	Final	No	No	35.06
NY	Farmingdale	Tronic Plating Co., Inc.	Deleted	No	No	-
NY	Franklin Square	Genzale Plating Co.	Final	No	No	33.79

St.	City/Area	Site Name	NPL[1] Status	SA Approach[2]	HEUC[3]	HRS Score[4]
NY	Fulton	Fulton Terminals	Deleted	No	No	-
NY	Garden City	Old Roosevelt Field Contaminated Ground Water Area	Final	No	No	50
NY	Garden City Park	Fulton Avenue	Final	No	No	33.08
NY	Glen Cove	Li Tungsten Corp.	Final	No	No	50
NY	Glen Cove	Mattiace Petrochemical Co., Inc.	Final	No	No	31.9
NY	Glenwood Landing	Applied Environmental Services	Final	No	No	41.15
NY	Gowanda	Peter Cooper	Final	No	No	50
NY	Great Neck	Stanton Cleaners Area Ground Water Contamination	Final	No	No	35.76
NY	Hamilton	C & J Disposal Leasing Co. Dump	Deleted	No	No	-
NY	Hauppauge	Computer Circuits	Final	No	No	50
NY	Hempstead	Pasley Solvents & Chemicals, Inc.	Deleted	No	No	-
NY	Hewlett	Peninsula Boulevard Ground Water Plume	Final	No	No	50
NY	Hicksville	Anchor Chemicals	Deleted	No	No	-
NY	Hicksville	Hooker Chemical & Plastics Corp./Ruco Polymer Corp.	Final	No	No	41.6
NY	High Falls	Mohonk Road Industrial Plant	Final	No	No	50
NY	Hillburn	Hudson Technologies, Inc.	Proposed	No	No	50
NY	Holbrook	Goldisc Recordings, Inc.	Final	No	No	33.39
NY	Holley	Diaz Chemical Corporation	Final	No	No	50
NY	Hoosick Falls Village	Saint-Gobain Performance Plastics	Final	No	No	50
NY	Hopewell Junction	Hopewell Precision Area Contamination	Final	No	No	50
NY	Horseheads	Kentucky Avenue Well Field	Final	No	No	39.65
NY	Hudson River	Hudson River PCBs	Final	No	No	54.66
NY	Hyde Park	Jones Sanitation	Deleted	No	No	-
NY	Islip	Islip Municipal Sanitary Landfill	Final	No	No	33.39
NY	Kent	Arsenic Mine	Proposed	No	-	0
NY	Le Roy	Lehigh Valley Railroad	Final	No	No	50
NY	Lincklaen	Solvent Savers	Final	No	No	34.78
NY	Lisbon	Sealand Restoration, Inc.	Final	No	No	29.36
NY	Little Valley	Little Valley	Final	No	No	-
NY	Lockport	Eighteenmile Creek	Final	No	No	50
NY	Malta	Malta Rocket Fuel Area	Final	No	No	33.62
NY	Massena	General Motors (Central Foundry Division)	Final	No	No	40.71
NY	Maybrook	Nepera Chemical Co., Inc.	Final	No	No	39.87
NY	Mineola/N. Hempstead	Jackson Steel	Deleted	No	No	-
NY	Moira	York Oil Co.	Final	No	No	47.7
NY	Nassau	Dewey Loeffel Landfill	Final	No	No	50
NY	New Cassel/Hicksville	New Cassel/Hicksville Ground Water Contamination	Final	No	No	50
NY	Newburgh	Consolidated Iron and Metal	Deleted	No	No	-
NY	Niagara Falls	Forest Glen Mobile Home Subdivision	Final	No	No	-
NY	Niagara Falls	Hooker (102nd Street)	Deleted	No	No	-
NY	Niagara Falls	Hooker (Hyde Park)	Deleted	No	No	-
NY	Niagara Falls	Hooker (S Area)	Final	No	No	51.62
NY	Niagara Falls	Love Canal	Deleted	No	No	-
NY	North Sea	North Sea Municipal Landfill	Deleted	No	No	-
NY	Noyack/Sag Harbor	Rowe Industries Ground Water Contamination	Final	No	No	31.94
NY	Old Bethpage	Claremont Polychemical	Final	No	No	31.62
NY	Olean	Olean Well Field	Final	No	No	44.46
NY	Oswego	Pollution Abatement Services	Final	No	No	-
NY	Oyster Bay	Old Bethpage Landfill	Final	No	No	58.83
NY	Oyster Bay	Syosset Landfill	Deleted	No	No	-
NY	Plattekill	Hertel Landfill	Final	No	No	33.62
NY	Plattsburgh	Plattsburgh Air Force Base	Final	No	No	30.34
NY	Port Crane	Tri-Cities Barrel Co., Inc.	Final	No	No	44.06
NY	Port Jefferson Station	Lawrence Aviation Industries, Inc.	Final	No	No	50
NY	Port Jervis	Carroll & Dubies Sewage Disposal	Final	No	No	33.74
NY	Port Washington	Port Washington Landfill	Final	No	No	45.46
NY	Putnam County	Brewster Well Field	Final	No	No	37.93
NY	Queens	Radium Chemical Co., Inc.	Deleted	No	No	-

St.	City/Area	Site Name	NPL[1] Status	SA Approach[2]	HEUC[3]	HRS Score[4]
NY	Ramapo	Ramapo Landfill	Final	No	No	44.73
NY	Ridgewood	Wolff-Alport Chemical Company	Final	No	No	50
NY	Rome	Griffiss Air Force Base	Final	No	No	
NY	Romulus	Seneca Army Depot	Final	No	No	-
NY	Saratoga Springs	Niagara Mohawk Power Corp. (Saratoga Spings Plant)	Final	No	No	35.48
NY	Sidney	Sidney Landfill	Final	No	No	29.36
NY	Sidney Center	Richardson Hill Road Landfill/Pond	Final	No	No	34.86
NY	Smithtown	Smithtown Ground Water Contamination	Final	No	No	50
NY	South Cairo	American Thermostat Co.	Final	No	No	33.61
NY	South Glens Falls	GE Moreau	Final	No	No	58.21
NY	Syracuse	Onondaga Lake	Final	No	No	50
NY	Town Of Bedford	Katonah Municipal Well	Deleted	No	No	-
NY	Town Of Champion	Black River PCBs	Final	No	No	48.03
NY	Town Of Colesville	Colesville Municipal Landfill	Final	No	No	30.26
NY	Town Of Granby	Clothier Disposal	Deleted	No	No	-
NY	Town Of Hyde Park	Haviland Complex	Final	No	No	33.62
NY	Town Of Johnstown	Johnstown City Landfill	Final	No	No	48.36
NY	Town Of Shelby	FMC Corp. (Dublin Road Landfill)	Final	No	No	32.9
NY	Town Of Vestal	Robintech, Inc./National Pipe Co.	Final	No	No	-
NY	Town Of Volney	Volney Municipal Landfill	Final	No	No	32.89
NY	Union Springs	Cayuga County Ground Water Contamination	Final	No	No	50
NY	Upton	Brookhaven National Laboratory (USDOE)	Final	No	No	39.92
NY	Vestal	BEC Trucking	Deleted	No	No	-
NY	Vestal	Vestal Water Supply Well 1-1	Final	No	No	37.93
NY	Vestal	Vestal Water Supply Well 4-2	Deleted	No	No	-
NY	Vil Of Narrowsburg	Cortese Landfill	Final	No	No	32.11
NY	Village Of Endicott	Endicott Village Well Field	Final	No	No	35.57
NY	Village Of Sidney	GCL Tie and Treating Inc.	Final	No	No	48.54
NY	Village Of Suffern	Suffern Village Well Field	Deleted	No	No	-
NY	Wappinger Falls	Wappinger Creek	Final	No	No	50
NY	Warwick	Warwick Landfill	Deleted	No	No	-
NY	Wellsville	Sinclair Refinery	Final	No	No	53.9
NY	West Winfield	Hiteman Leather	Deleted	No	No	-
NY	Wheatfield	Niagara County Refuse	Deleted	No	No	-
OH	Ashtabula	Fields Brook	Final	No	No	44.95
OH	Beavercreek	Lammers Barrel	Final	No	No	69.33
OH	Circleville	Bowers Landfill	Deleted	No	No	-
OH	Cleveland	Chemical & Minerals Reclamation	Deleted	No	No	-
OH	Columbus	Air Force Plant 85	Proposed	No	No	50
OH	Copley	Copley Square Plaza	Final	No	No	50
OH	Darke County	Arcanum Iron & Metal	Deleted	No	No	-
OH	Dayton	Behr Dayton Thermal System VOC Plume	Final	No	No	50
OH	Dayton	North Sanitary Landfill	Final	No	No	50
OH	Dayton	Powell Road Landfill	Final	No	No	31.62
OH	Dayton	Wright-Patterson Air Force Base	Final	No	No	57.85
OH	Deerfield Township	Summit National	Final	No	No	52.28
OH	Donnelsville	Donnelsville Contaminated Aquifer	Final	No	-	35.06
OH	Dover	Dover Chemical Corp.	Proposed	No	No	50
OH	Dover	Reilly Tar & Chemical Corp. (Dover Plant)	Final	No	No	31.38
OH	Elyria	Chemical Recovery	Not NPL	Yes	No	-
OH	Elyria	Ford Rd Ind Landfill	Not NPL	Yes	No	-
OH	Elyria	Republic Steel Corp. Quarry	Deleted	No	No	-
OH	Fernald	Feed Materials Production Center (USDOE)	Final	No	No	57.56
OH	Franklin Township	Coshocton Landfill	Deleted	No	No	-
OH	German Township	Tremont City Barrel Fill	Not NPL	Yes	No	-
OH	Gnadenhutten	Alsco Anaconda	Deleted	No	No	-
OH	Hamilton	Armco Inc., Hamilton Plant	Proposed	No	No	69.34
OH	Hamilton	Chem-Dyne	Final	No	No	-

St.	City/Area	Site Name	NPL[1] Status	SA Approach[2]	HEUC[3]	HRS Score[4]
OH	Hamilton Township	E.H. Schilling Landfill	Final	No	No	34.56
OH	Hannibal	Ormet Corp.	Final	No	No	46.44
OH	Ironton	Allied Chemical & Ironton Coke	Final	No	No	47.05
OH	Jackson Township	Fultz Landfill	Final	No	No	39.42
OH	Jefferson Township	Laskin/Poplar Oil Co.	Deleted	No	No	
OH	Kings Mills	Peters Cartridge Factory	Final	No	No	-
OH	Kingsville	Big D Campground	Final	No	No	30.77
OH	Marietta	Van Dale Junkyard	Final	No	No	33.03
OH	Marion County	Little Scioto River	Final	No	No	48.03
OH	Miamisburg	Mound Plant (USDOE)	Final	No	No	
OH	Milford	Milford Contaminated Aquifer	Final	No	No	50
OH	Minerva	TRW, Inc. (Minerva Plant)	Final	No	No	38.08
OH	Moraine	Sanitary Landfill Co. (Industrial Waste Disposal Co., Inc.)	Final	No	No	35.57
OH	Moraine	South Dayton Dump & Landfill	Proposed	Yes	No	48.63
OH	New Carlisle	New Carlisle Landfill	Final	No	No	46.4
OH	New Lyme	New Lyme Landfill	Final	No	No	31.19
OH	Painesville	Diamond Shamrock Corp. (Painesville Works)	Proposed	No	No	50
OH	Reading	Pristine, Inc.	Final	No	No	35.25
OH	Riverside	Valley Pike VOCs	Final	No	No	50
OH	Rock Creek	Old Mill	Final	No	No	35.95
OH	Salem	Nease Chemical	Final	No	No	47.19
OH	South Point	South Point Plant	Final	No	No	46.33
OH	St. Clairsville	Buckeye Reclamation	Final	No	No	35.1
OH	Troy	East Troy Contaminated Aquifer	Final	No	No	50
OH	Troy	Miami County Incinerator	Final	No	No	57.84
OH	Troy	United Scrap Lead Co., Inc.	Final	No	No	58.15
OH	Troy	West Troy Contaminated Aquifer	Final	No	No	50
OH	Uniontown	Industrial Excess Landfill	Final	No	No	51.13
OH	West Chester	Skinner Landfill	Final	No	No	30.23
OH	Zanesville	Zanesville Well Field	Final	No	No	35.59
OK	Ardmore	Imperial Refining Company	Deleted	No	No	-
OK	Bartlesville	National Zinc Corp.	Proposed	No	No	50
OK	Collinsville	Tulsa Fuel and Manufacturing	Final	No	No	50
OK	Creek County	Wilcox Oil Company	Final	No	No	50
OK	Criner	Hardage/Criner	Final	No	No	51.01
OK	Cushing	Hudson Refinery	Final	No	No	29.34
OK	Cyril	Oklahoma Refining Co.	Final	No	No	46.01
OK	Midwest City	Eagle Industries	Final	No	No	50
OK	Oklahoma City	Double Eagle Refinery Co.	Deleted	No	No	-
OK	Oklahoma City	Fourth Street Abandoned Refinery	Deleted	No	No	-
OK	Oklahoma City	Mosley Road Sanitary Landfill	Deleted	No	No	-
OK	Oklahoma City	Tenth Street Dump/Junkyard	Deleted	No	No	-
OK	Oklahoma City	Tinker Air Force Base (Soldier Creek/Building 3001)	Final	No	No	42.24
OK	Ottawa County	Tar Creek (Ottawa County)	Final	No	No	58.15
OK	Sand Springs	Sand Springs Petrochemical Complex	Deleted	No	No	-
OK	Tulsa	Compass Industries (Avery Drive)	Deleted	No	No	-
OR	Albany	Teledyne Wah Chang	Final	No	No	54.27
OR	Astoria	Astoria Marine Construction Company	Proposed	No	No	50
OR	Clackamas	Northwest Pipe & Casing/Hall Process Co	Final	No	No	51.09
OR	Corvallis	United Chrome Products, Inc.	Final	No	No	31.07
OR	Cottage Grove	Black Butte Mine	Final	No	No	50
OR	Hermiston	Umatilla Army Depot (Lagoons)	Final	No	No	31.31
OR	Joseph	Joseph Forest Products	Deleted	No	No	-
OR	Klamath Falls	North Ridge Estates	Final	No	No	0
OR	Lakeview	Fremont Ntl Forest/White King/Lucky Lass Uranium Mines (USDA)	Final	No	No	50
OR	Portland	Allied Plating, Inc.	Deleted	No	No	-
OR	Portland	Gould, Inc.	Deleted	No	No	-
OR	Portland	Harbor Oil	Deleted	No	No	-
OR	Portland	McCormick & Baxter Creosoting Co. (Portland Plant)	Final	No	No	50

St.	City/Area	Site Name	NPL[1] Status	SA Approach[2]	HEUC[3]	HRS Score[4]
OR	Portland	Portland Harbor	Final	No	No	50
OR	Riddle	Formosa Mine	Final	No	No	50
OR	Sheridan	Taylor Lumber and Treating	Final	No	No	71.78
OR	The Dalles	Martin-Marietta Aluminum Co.	Deleted	No	No	-
OR	The Dalles	Union Pacific Railroad Co. Tie-Treating Plant	Final	No	No	37.93
OR	Troutdale	Reynolds Metals Company	Final	No	No	70.71
PA	Ambler	Ambler Asbestos Piles	Deleted	No	No	-
PA	Ambler	BoRit Asbestos	Final	No	No	50
PA	Antis/Logan Twps	Delta Quarries & Disposal, Inc./Stotler Landfill	Final	No	No	41.08
PA	Bally	Bally Ground Water Contamination	Final	No	No	37.93
PA	Bloomsburg	Safety Light Corporation	Final	No	Yes	70.71
PA	Bridgeton Township	Boarhead Farms	Final	No	No	39.92
PA	Bruin Borough	Bruin Lagoon	Deleted	No	No	-
PA	Buffalo Township	Hranica Landfill	Deleted	No	No	-
PA	Chambersburg	Letterkenny Army Depot (SE Area)	Final	No	No	-
PA	Chester	Wade (ABM)	Deleted	No	No	-
PA	Columbia	UGI Columbia Gas Plant	Final	No	No	50.78
PA	Coraopolis	Breslube-Penn, Inc	Final	No	No	50
PA	Croydon Township	Croydon TCE	Final	No	No	31.6
PA	Darby Twp	Lower Darby Creek Area	Final	No	No	50
PA	Delaware County	Austin Avenue Radiation Site	Deleted	No	No	-
PA	Denver	Berkley Products Co. Dump	Deleted	No	No	-
PA	Douglassville	Douglassville Disposal	Final	No	No	55.18
PA	Doylestown	Chem-Fab	Final	No	No	50
PA	Dublin Borough	Dublin TCE Site	Final	No	No	28.9
PA	E Coventry Twp	Recticon/Allied Steel Corp.	Deleted	No	No	-
PA	E. Whiteland Township	Foote Mineral Co.	Final	No	No	50
PA	Eagleville	Moyers Landfill	Deleted	No	No	-
PA	East Pikeland Twp	Kimberton	Final	No	No	29.44
PA	Elizabethtown	Elizabethtown Landfill	Final	No	No	28.98
PA	Emmaus Borough	Rodale Manufacturing Co., Inc.	Final	No	No	50
PA	Erie	Mill Creek Dump	Final	No	No	49.31
PA	Erie	Presque Isle	Deleted	No	No	-
PA	Exton	A.I.W. Frank/Mid-County Mustang	Final	No	No	42.4
PA	Falls Creek	Jackson Ceramix	Final	No	No	30.22
PA	Foster Township	C & D Recycling	Deleted	No	No	-
PA	Frackville	Metropolitan Mirror and Glass Co., Inc.	Deleted	No	No	-
PA	Franklin County	Letterkenny Army Depot (PDO Area)	Final	No	No	-
PA	Gettysburg	Westinghouse Elevator Co. Plant	Final	No	No	36.37
PA	Girard Township	Lord-Shope Landfill	Final	No	No	38.89
PA	Glen Rock	AMP, Inc. (Glen Rock Facility)	Deleted	No	No	-
PA	Grove City	Osborne Landfill	Final	No	No	54.6
PA	Hamburg	Brown's Battery Breaking	Final	No	No	37.34
PA	Hamburg	Price Battery	Final	No	No	37.86
PA	Harleysville	Baghurst Drive	Final	No	No	50
PA	Harrison Township	Lindane Dump	Final	No	No	51.62
PA	Hatboro	Raymark	Final	No	No	53.42
PA	Hatfield	North Penn - Area 2	Final	No	No	35.57
PA	Haverford	Havertown PCP	Final	No	No	38.34
PA	Heidelberg Twp	Ryeland Road Arsenic	Final	No	No	60.3
PA	Hellertown	Hellertown Manufacturing Co.	Final	No	No	51.91
PA	Hereford Township	Crossley Farm	Final	No	No	29.66
PA	Hermitage	River Road Landfill (Waste Management, Inc.)	Deleted	No	No	-
PA	Hermitage	Sharon Steel Corp (Farrell Works Disposal Area)	Final	No	No	50
PA	Hometown	Eastern Diversified Metals	Final	No	No	31.02
PA	Honeybrook Township	Walsh Landfill	Final	No	No	33.64
PA	Hopewell Township	York County Solid Waste and Refuse Authority Landfill	Deleted	No	No	-
PA	Horsham	Willow Grove Naval Air and Air Reserve Station	Final	No	No	50

St.	City/Area	Site Name	NPL[1] Status	SA Approach[2]	HEUC[3]	HRS Score[4]
PA	Jackson Township	Whitmoyer Laboratories	Final	No	No	46.25
PA	Jefferson Borough	Resin Disposal	Deleted	No	No	-
PA	King Of Prussia	Stanley Kessler	Final	No	No	33.89
PA	Lansdale	North Penn - Area 6	Final	No	No	-
PA	Lansdowne	Lansdowne Radiation Site	Deleted	No	No	-
PA	Lock Haven	Drake Chemical	Final	No	No	38.52
PA	Longswamp Township	Berks Sand Pit	Final	No	No	32.02
PA	Lower Pottsgrove Twp	Occidental Chemical Corp./Firestone Tire & Rubber Co.	Final	No	No	45.91
PA	Lower Providence Twp	Commodore Semiconductor Group	Final	No	No	42.35
PA	Lower Salford Twp	Salford Quarry	Final	No	No	50
PA	Lower Windsor Twp	Modern Sanitation Landfill	Final	No	No	33.93
PA	Maitland	Jacks Creek/Sitkin Smelting & Refining, Inc.	Final	No	No	40.37
PA	Malvern	Malvern TCE	Final	No	No	46.69
PA	Marcus Hook	East Tenth Street	Proposed	No	No	67.68
PA	Mcadoo Borough	McAdoo Associates	Deleted	No	No	-
PA	Mechanicsburg	Navy Ships Parts Control Center	Final	No	No	50
PA	Middletown	Middletown Air Field	Deleted	No	No	-
PA	Montgomery Township	North Penn - Area 5	Final	No	No	35.57
PA	Mountain Top	Foster Wheeler Energy Corporation/Church Road TCE	Proposed	Yes	No	50
PA	Nesquehoning	Tonolli Corp.	Final	No	No	46.58
PA	Neville Island	Ohio River Park	Final	No	No	42.24
PA	Newlin Township	Strasburg Landfill	Final	No	No	30.71
PA	Nockamixon Township	Revere Chemical Co.	Final	No	No	31.31
PA	North Wales	North Penn - Area 7	Final	No	No	35.57
PA	North Whitehall Twp	Heleva Landfill	Final	No	No	50.23
PA	Old Forge	Lackawanna Refuse	Deleted	No	No	-
PA	Old Forge	Lehigh Electric & Engineering Co.	Deleted	No	No	-
PA	Palmerton	Palmerton Zinc Pile	Final	No	No	42.93
PA	Paoli	Paoli Rail Yard	Final	No	No	32.18
PA	Parker	Craig Farm Drum	Deleted	No	No	-
PA	Philadelphia	Enterprise Avenue	Deleted	No	No	-
PA	Philadelphia	Franklin Slag Pile (MDC)	Final	No	No	50.2
PA	Philadelphia	Metal Banks	Final	No	No	33.23
PA	Philadelphia	Publicker Industries Inc.	Deleted	No	No	-
PA	Pittston Township	Butler Mine Tunnel	Final	No	No	49.51
PA	Pocono Summit	Route 940 Drum Dump	Deleted	No	No	-
PA	Richland Township	Watson Johnson Landfill	Final	No	No	70.71
PA	Sadsburyville	Old Wilmington Road Ground Water Contamination	Final	No	No	50
PA	Saegertown	Saegertown Industrial Area	Final	No	No	-
PA	Scott Township	Aladdin Plating	Deleted	No	No	-
PA	Seven Valleys	Old City of York Landfill	Final	No	No	33.93
PA	Sharon	Westinghouse Electric Corp. (Sharon Plant)	Final	No	No	41.33
PA	Souderton	North Penn - Area 1	Final	No	No	35.57
PA	South Montrose	Bendix Flight Systems Division	Final	No	No	33.74
PA	South Whitehall Twp	Novak Sanitary Landfill	Final	No	No	42.31
PA	Spring Township	Berks Landfill	Deleted	No	No	-
PA	Springettsbury Twp	East Mount Zion	Final	No	No	41.01
PA	State College	Centre County Kepone	Final	No	No	-
PA	Straban Township	Hunterstown Road	Final	No	No	48.27
PA	Straban Township	Shriver's Corner	Final	No	No	46.13
PA	Stroudsburg	Brodhead Creek	Deleted	No	No	-
PA	Stroudsburg	Butz Landfill	Final	No	No	32
PA	Taylor Borough	Taylor Borough Dump	Deleted	No	No	-
PA	Terry Township	Bell Landfill	Final	No	No	34.79
PA	Tobyhanna	Tobyhanna Army Depot	Final	No	No	-
PA	Trainer	Metro Container Corporation	Final	No	No	50
PA	Union Township	Keystone Sanitation Landfill	Final	No	No	33.76
PA	Upper Macungie Twp	Dorney Road Landfill	Deleted	No	No	-

St.	City/Area	Site Name	NPL[1] Status	SA Approach[2]	HEUC[3]	HRS Score[4]
PA	Upper Macungie Twp	Reeser's Landfill	Deleted	No	No	-
PA	Upper Merion Township	Crater Resources, Inc./Keystone Coke Co./Alan Wood Steel Co.	Final	No	No	50
PA	Upper Merion Township	Henderson Road	Final	No	No	41.69
PA	Upper Merion Twp	Tysons Dump	Final	No	No	63.1
PA	Upper Saucon Twp	Voortman Farm	Deleted	No	No	-
PA	Valley Township	MW Manufacturing	Final	No	No	46.44
PA	Warminster	Fischer & Porter Co.	Final	No	No	29.07
PA	Warminster Township	Naval Air Development Center (8 Waste Areas)	Final	No	No	57.93
PA	Weisenberg Township	Hebelka Auto Salvage Yard	Deleted	No	No	-
PA	West Caln Township	Blosenski Landfill	Final	No	No	30.57
PA	West Caln Township	William Dick Lagoons	Final	No	No	36.64
PA	West Hazleton	Valmont TCE	Final	No	No	43.16
PA	Westline	Westline Site	Deleted	No	No	-
PA	Williams Township	Industrial Lane	Final	No	No	42.47
PA	Williamsport	Avco Lycoming (Williamsport Division)	Final	No	No	42.24
PA	Worcester	North Penn - Area 12	Final	No	No	28.9
PA	Worman Township	CryoChem, Inc.	Final	No	No	28.58
PR	Almirante Norte Ward	V&M/Albaladejo	Deleted	No	No	-
PR	Arecibo	Pesticide Warehouse I	Final	No	No	50
PR	Arecibo	The Battery Recycling Company	Final	No	No	56.66
PR	Barceloneta	RCA Del Caribe	Deleted	No	No	-
PR	Barceloneta	Upjohn Facility	Final	No	No	41.92
PR	Cabo Rojo	Cabo Rojo Ground Water Contamination	Final	No	No	50
PR	Caguas	Hormigas Ground Water Plume	Final	No	No	50
PR	Candeleria Ward	Scorpio Recycling, Inc.	Final	No	No	50
PR	Cidra	Cidra Ground Water Contamination	Final	No	No	50
PR	Corozal	Corozal Well	Final	No	No	50
PR	Dorado	Dorado Ground Water Contamination	Final	No	No	50
PR	Florida Afuera	Barceloneta Landfill	Deleted	No	No	-
PR	Jobos	Fibers Public Supply Wells	Final	No	No	35.34
PR	Juana Diaz	GE Wiring Devices	Deleted	No	No	-
PR	Juncos	Juncos Landfill	Final	No	No	32.57
PR	Manati	Pesticide Warehouse III	Final	No	No	50
PR	Maunabo	Maunabo Area Ground Water Contamination	Final	No	No	50
PR	Penuelas	Proteco	Final	No	-	36.33
PR	Rio Abajo	Frontera Creek	Deleted	No	No	-
PR	Rio Abajo Ward	Vega Baja Solid Waste Disposal	Final	No	No	50.37
PR	Sabana Seca	Naval Security Group Activity	Deleted	No	No	-
PR	San German	San German Ground Water Contamination	Final	No	No	50
PR	Utuado	Papelera Puertorriquena, Inc.	Final	No	No	34.69
PR	Vega Alta	Vega Alta Public Supply Wells	Final	No	No	42.24
PR	Vieques	Atlantic Fleet Weapons Training Area - Vieques	Final	No	No	-
RI	Burrillville	Western Sand & Gravel	Final	No	No	51.35
RI	Coventry	Picillo Farm	Final	No	No	-
RI	Glocester	Davis (GSR) Landfill	Deleted	No	No	-
RI	Johnston	Central Landfill	Final	No	No	46.71
RI	Lincoln/Cumberland	Peterson/Puritan, Inc.	Final	No	No	-
RI	Newport	Newport Naval Education/Training Center	Final	No	No	32.25
RI	North Kingstown	Davisville Naval Construction Battalion Center	Final	No	No	34.52
RI	North Providence	Centredale Manor Restoration Project	Final	No	No	70.71
RI	North Smithfield	Landfill & Resource Recovery, Inc. (L&RR)	Final	No	No	49.58
RI	North Smithfield	Stamina Mills, Inc.	Final	No	No	34.07
RI	Smithfield	Davis Liquid Waste	Final	No	No	47.25
RI	South Kingstown	Rose Hill Regional Landfill	Final	No	No	38.11
RI	South Kingstown	West Kingston Town Dump/URI Disposal Area	Final	No	No	50
SC	Aiken	Savannah River Site (USDOE)	Final	No	No	47.7
SC	Barnwell	Shuron Inc.	Final	No	No	68.26
SC	Beaufort	Independent Nail Co.	Deleted	No	No	-
SC	Beaufort	Kalama Specialty Chemicals	Final	No	No	57.9

St.	City/Area	Site Name	NPL[1] Status	SA Approach[2]	HEUC[3]	HRS Score[4]
SC	Burton	Wamchem, Inc.	Final	No	No	47.7
SC	Cayce	Lexington County Landfill Area	Final	No	No	37.93
SC	Cayce	SCRDI Dixiana	Final	No	No	40.7
SC	Charleston	Koppers Co., Inc. (Charleston Plant)	Final	No	No	50
SC	Cheraw	Burlington Industries Cheraw	Final	No	-	48
SC	Clover	Henry's Knob	Not NPL	Yes	No	-
SC	Columbia	Palmetto Recycling, Inc.	Deleted	No	No	-
SC	Columbia	SCRDI Bluff Road	Final	No	No	-
SC	Dixiana	Palmetto Wood Preserving	Final	No	No	38.43
SC	Fairfax	Helena Chemical Co. Landfill	Final	No	No	33.89
SC	Florence	Koppers Co., Inc. (Florence Plant)	Deleted	No	No	-
SC	Fort Lawn	Carolawn, Inc.	Final	No	No	32.04
SC	Fountain Inn	Beaunit Corp. (Circular Knit & Dye)	Final	No	No	32.44
SC	Gaffney	Medley Farm Drum Dump	Final	No	No	31.58
SC	Greenville	US Finishing/Cone Mills	Final	No	No	50
SC	Greer	Aqua-Tech Environmental Inc. (Groce Laboratories)	Final	No	No	50
SC	Greer	Elmore Waste Disposal	Final	No	No	31.45
SC	Hollywood	Geiger (C & M Oil)	Deleted	No	No	-
SC	Jefferson	Brewer Gold Mine	Final	No	No	50
SC	Lyman	Lyman Dyeing And Finishing	Not NPL	Yes	No	-
SC	Mccormick	Barite Hill/Nevada Goldfields	Final	No	No	50
SC	North Charleston	Macalloy Corporation	Final	No	No	50
SC	Parris Island	Parris Island Marine Corps Recruit Depot	Final	No	No	50
SC	Pickens	Sangamo Weston/Twelve-Mile Creek/Lake Hartwell PCB Contam.	Final	No	No	-
SC	Pontiac	Townsend Saw Chain Co.	Final	No	No	35.94
SC	Rock Hill	Leonard Chemical Co., Inc.	Final	No	No	47.1
SC	Rock Hill	Rock Hill Chemical Co.	Final	No	No	40.29
SC	Simpsonville	Golden Strip Septic Tank Service	Deleted	No	No	-
SC	Simpsonville	Para-Chem Southern, Inc.	Final	No	No	-
SC	Spartanburg	International Minerals and Chemicals (IMC)	Not NPL	Yes	No	-
SC	Travelers Rest	Rochester Property	Deleted	No	No	-
SC	Williston	Admiral Home Appliances	Not NPL	Yes	No	-
SD	Ellsworth Afb	Ellsworth Air Force Base	Final	No	No	-
SD	Lead	Gilt Edge Mine	Final	No	No	50
SD	Sioux Falls	Williams Pipe Line Co. Disposal Pit	Deleted	No	No	-
SD	Whitewood	Whitewood Creek	Deleted	No	No	-
TN	Alamo	Alamo Contaminated Ground Water	Final	No	No	50
TN	Arlington	Arlington Blending & Packaging	Final	No	No	39.03
TN	Chattanooga	Amnicola Dump	Deleted	No	No	-
TN	Chattanooga	Southside Chattanooga Lead	Final	No	No	50
TN	Chattanooga	Tennessee Products	Final	No	No	-
TN	Collierville	Carrier Air Conditioning Co.	Final	No	No	48.91
TN	Collierville	Smalley-Piper	Final	No	No	50
TN	Collierville	Walker Machine Products, Inc.	Final	No	No	50
TN	Copperhill	Copper Basin Mining District	Not NPL	Yes	No	-
TN	Cordova	National Fireworks	Not NPL	Yes	No	-
TN	Gallaway	Gallaway Pits	Deleted	No	No	-
TN	Harriman	Clinch River Corporation	Final	No	No	48.03
TN	Jackson	American Creosote Works, Inc. (Jackson Plant)	Final	No	No	35.22
TN	Jackson	ICG Iselin Railroad Yard	Deleted	No	No	-
TN	Knoxville	Smokey Mountain Smelters	Final	No	No	50
TN	Lawrenceburg	Murray-Ohio Dump	Final	No	No	46.44
TN	Lewisburg	Lewisburg Dump	Deleted	No	Yes	-
TN	Memphis	Former Custom Cleaners	Final	No	No	50
TN	Memphis	Illinois Central Railroad Company's Johnston Yard Superfund Site	Not NPL	Yes	Yes	-
TN	Memphis	Memphis Defense Depot (DLA)	Final	No	No	58.06
TN	Memphis	North Hollywood Dump	Deleted	No	No	-
TN	Memphis	Sixty One Industrial Park	Not NPL	Yes	No	-

St.	City/Area	Site Name	NPL[1] Status	SA Approach[2]	HEUC[3]	HRS Score[4]
TN	Milan	Milan Army Ammunition Plant	Final	No	No	58.15
TN	Moscow	Chemet Co.	Deleted	No	No	-
TN	Oak Ridge	Oak Ridge Reservation (USDOE)	Final	No	No	51.13
TN	Rossville	Ross Metals Inc.	Final	No	No	37.65
TN	Toone	Velsicol Chemical Corp. (Hardeman County)	Final	No	No	47.71
TN	Waynesboro	Mallory Capacitor Co.	Final	No	No	29.44
TN	Wrigley	Wrigley Charcoal Plant	Final	No	No	36.14
TX	Bell County	Rockwool Industries Inc.	Final	No	No	48
TX	Bridge City	Bailey Waste Disposal	Deleted	No	No	-
TX	Bridge City	Triangle Chemical Co.	Deleted	No	No	-
TX	Burnet	Main Street Ground Water Plume	Final	No	No	50
TX	Channelview	San Jacinto River Waste Pits	Final	No	No	50
TX	Conroe	Conroe Creosoting Company	Final	No	No	48
TX	Conroe	United Creosoting Co.	Final	No	No	37.29
TX	Corpus Christi	Brine Service Company	Final	No	No	50
TX	Crosby	French, Ltd.	Final	No	No	63.33
TX	Crosby	Sikes Disposal Pits	Final	No	No	61.62
TX	Crystal City	Crystal City Airport	Deleted	No	No	-
TX	Dallas	Lane Plating Works, Inc	Final	No	No	50
TX	Dallas	RSR Corp.	Final	No	No	-
TX	Deer Park	Patrick Bayou	Final	No	No	47.83
TX	Donna	Donna Reservoir and Canal System	Final	No	No	50
TX	Fort Worth	Air Force Plant #4 (General Dynamics)	Final	No	Yes	39.92
TX	Fort Worth	Pesses Chemical Co.	Deleted	No	No	-
TX	Freeport	Gulfco Marine Maintenance	Final	No	No	50
TX	Friendswood	Brio Refining, Inc.	Deleted	No	No	-
TX	Friendswood	Dixie Oil Processors, Inc.	Deleted	No	No	-
TX	Grand Prairie	Bio-Ecology Systems, Inc.	Deleted	No	No	-
TX	Grand Prairie	Delfasco Forge	Final	No	-	50
TX	Greenville	Old ESCO Manufacturing	Deleted	No	No	-
TX	Happy	North East 2nd Street (formerly Attebury Grain Storage Facility)	Final	No	No	32.33
TX	Hempstead	Sheridan Disposal Services	Final	No	No	30.16
TX	Highlands	Highlands Acid Pit	Final	No	No	37.77
TX	Houston	Crystal Chemical Co.	Final	No	No	60.9
TX	Houston	Geneva Industries/Fuhrmann Energy	Final	No	No	-
TX	Houston	Harris (Farley Street)	Deleted	No	No	-
TX	Houston	Jones Road Ground Water Plume	Final	No	No	46.5
TX	Houston	Many Diversified Interests, Inc.	Final	No	No	-
TX	Houston	North Cavalcade Street	Final	No	No	37.08
TX	Houston	Sol Lynn/Industrial Transformers	Final	No	No	39.65
TX	Houston	South Cavalcade Street	Final	No	No	38.69
TX	Ingleside	Falcon Refinery	Final	No	No	50
TX	Jasper	Hart Creosoting Company	Final	No	No	48
TX	Jasper	Jasper Creosoting Company Inc.	Final	No	No	50
TX	Jefferson County	State Marine of Port Arthur	Deleted	No	No	-
TX	Karnack	Longhorn Army Ammunition Plant	Final	No	No	39.83
TX	Kormit	Highway 18 Ground Water	Final	No	No	50
TX	La Marque	Motco, Inc.	Final	No	No	-
TX	Levelland	State Road 114 Ground Water Plume	Final	No	No	42.41
TX	Liberty	Petro-Chemical Systems, Inc. (Turtle Bayou)	Final	No	No	29.94
TX	Live Oak	Eldorado Chemical Co.,, Inc.	Final	No	No	38.85
TX	Longview	Garland Creosoting	Final	No	No	49.1
TX	Midland	Midessa Ground Water Plume	Final	No	No	50
TX	Midland	West County Road 112 Ground Water	Final	No	No	50
TX	Odessa	East 67th Street Ground Water Plume	Final	No	No	50
TX	Odessa	Odessa Chromium #1	Final	No	No	42.24
TX	Odessa	Odessa Chromium #2 (Andrews Highway)	Deleted	No	No	-
TX	Odessa	Sprague Road Ground Water Plume	Final	No	No	43.21

St.	City/Area	Site Name	NPL[1] Status	SA Approach[2]	HEUC[3]	HRS Score[4]
TX	Pantex Village	Pantex Plant (USDOE)	Final	No	No	51.22
TX	Pasadena	US Oil Recovery	Final	No	No	50
TX	Pelican Bay	Sandy Beach Road Ground Water Plume	Final	No	No	50
TX	Perryton	City of Perryton Well No. 2	Final	No	No	50
TX	Point Comfort	ALCOA (Point Comfort)/Lavaca Bay	Final	No	No	50
TX	Port Arthur	Palmer Barge Line	Deleted	No	No	-
TX	Port Neches	Star Lake Canal	Final	No	No	50
TX	San Antonio	Bandera Road Ground Water Plume	Final	No	No	50
TX	San Antonio	R & H Oil Company	Proposed	No	No	50
TX	San Antonio	River City Metal Finishing	Final	No	No	50
TX	Terrell	Van der Horst USA Corporation	Final	No	No	48
TX	Texarkana	Koppers Co., Inc. (Texarkana Plant)	Final	No	No	31.31
TX	Texarkana	Lone Star Army Ammunition Plant	Final	No	No	31.85
TX	Texarkana	Texarkana Wood Preserving Co.	Final	No	No	40.19
TX	Texas City	Malone Service Company, Inc.	Final	No	No	50
TX	Texas City	Tex-Tin Corp.	Final	No	No	-
TX	Waskom	Stewco, Inc.	Deleted	No	No	-
TX	Willow Park	Circle Court Ground Water Plume	Final	No	No	50
UT	Bountiful	Bountiful/Woods Cross 5th South PCE Plume	Final	No	No	50
UT	Bountiful	Intermountain Waste Oil Refinery	Final	No	No	50
UT	Copperton	Kennecott (South Zone)	Removed	Yes	No	-
UT	Eureka	Eureka Mills	Deleted	No	No	-
UT	Hill Afb	Hill Air Force Base	Final	No	No	49.94
UT	Magna	Kennecott (North Zone)	Proposed	No	No	59.18
UT	Midvale	Midvale Slag	Deleted	No	No	-
UT	Midvale	Sharon Steel Corp. (Midvale Tailings)	Deleted	No	No	-
UT	Monticello	Monticello Mill Tailings (USDOE)	Final	No	No	-
UT	Monticello	Monticello Radioactively Contaminated Properties	Deleted	No	No	-
UT	Murray City	Murray Smelter	Proposed	No	No	86.6
UT	Ogden	Ogden Defense Depot (DLA)	Final	No	No	45.1
UT	Park City	Richardson Flat Tailings	Proposed	No	No	39.13
UT	Salt Lake City	700 South 1600 East PCE Plume	Final	No	No	50
UT	Salt Lake City	Petrochem Recycling Corp./Ekotek, Inc.	Deleted	No	No	-
UT	Salt Lake City	Portland Cement (Kiln Dust 2 & 3)	Final	No	No	54.4
UT	Salt Lake City	Rose Park Sludge Pit	Deleted	No	No	-
UT	Salt Lake City	Utah Power & Light/American Barrel Co.	Final	No	No	37.93
UT	Salt Lake City	Wasatch Chemical Co. (Lot 6)	Final	No	No	49.91
UT	Sandy	Davenport and Flagstaff Smelters	Deleted	No	No	-
UT	Stockton	Jacobs Smelter	Final	No	No	-
UT	Tooele	International Smelting and Refining	Deleted	No	No	-
UT	Tooele	Tooele Army Depot (North Area)	Final	No	No	53.95
UT	Tooele County	U.S. Magnesium	Final	No	No	59.18
UT	Woods Cross/Bountiful	Five Points PCE Plume	Final	No	No	50
VA	Buckingham	Buckingham County Landfill	Final	No	No	40.7
VA	Chesapeake	St. Juliens Creek Annex (U.S. Navy)	Final	No	No	50
VA	Chesterfield County	C & R Battery Co., Inc.	Final	No	No	46.44
VA	Chesterfield County	Defense General Supply Center (DLA)	Final	No	No	33.85
VA	Chuckatuck	Saunders Supply Co.	Final	No	No	36.88
VA	Culpeper	Culpeper Wood Preservers, Inc.	Final	No	No	45.91
VA	Dahlgren	Naval Surface Warfare - Dahlgren	Final	No	No	50.03
VA	Farrington	H & H Inc., Burn Pit	Final	No	No	33.71
VA	Frederick County	Rhinehart Tire Fire Dump	Deleted	No	No	-
VA	Front Royal	Avtex Fibers, Inc.	Final	No	No	35.39
VA	Hampton	Langley Air Force Base/NASA Langley Research Center	Final	No	No	50
VA	Montross	Arrowhead Associates, Inc./Scovill Corp.	Final	No	No	37.15
VA	Newport News	Fort Eustis (US Army)	Final	No	No	50
VA	Newtown	Greenwood Chemical Co.	Final	No	No	53.17
VA	Norfolk	Norfolk Naval Base (Sewells Point Naval Complex)	Final	No	No	50
VA	Piney River	U.S. Titanium	Final	No	No	34.78

St.	City/Area	Site Name	NPL[1] Status	SA Approach[2]	HEUC[3]	HRS Score[4]
VA	Pittsylvania County	First Piedmont Corp. Rock Quarry (Route 719)	Final	No	No	30.16
VA	Portsmouth	Abex Corp.	Final	No	No	36.53
VA	Portsmouth	Atlantic Wood Industries, Inc.	Final	No	No	37.14
VA	Portsmouth	Norfolk Naval Shipyard	Final	No	No	50
VA	Portsmouth	Peck Iron and Metal	Final	No	No	48.52
VA	Quantico	Marine Corps Combat Development Command	Final	No	No	50
VA	Richmond	Rentokil, Inc. (Virginia Wood Preserving Division)	Final	No	No	-
VA	Roanoke	Matthews Electroplating	Deleted	No	No	-
VA	Salem	Dixie Caverns County Landfill	Deleted	No	No	-
VA	Saltville	Saltville Waste Disposal Ponds	Final	No	No	29.52
VA	Selma	Kim-Stan Landfill	Final	No	No	50
VA	Spotsylvania	L.A. Clarke & Son	Final	No	No	34.24
VA	Sterling	Hidden Lane Landfill	Final	No	No	50
VA	Suffolk	Former Nansemond Ordnance Depot	Final	No	No	-
VA	Suffolk	Suffolk City Landfill	Deleted	No	No	-
VA	Virginia Beach	Naval Amphibious Base Little Creek	Final	No	No	50
VA	York County	Chisman Creek	Final	No	No	47.19
VA	Yorktown	Naval Weapons Station - Yorktown	Final	No	No	50
VA	Yorktown	Naval Weapons Station Yorktown - Cheatham Annex	Final	No	No	49.27
VI	Christiansted	Island Chemical Corp./Virgin Islands Chemical Corp.	Deleted	No	No	-
VI	Tutu	Tutu Wellfield	Final	No	No	50
VT	Bennington	Bennington Municipal Sanitary Landfill	Final	No	No	49.07
VT	Bennington	Jard Company, Inc.	Final	No	No	58.31
VT	Bennington	Tansitor Electronics, Inc.	Deleted	No	No	-
VT	Burlington	Pine Street Canal	Final	No	No	-
VT	Corinth	Pike Hill Copper Mine	Final	No	No	50
VT	Lyndon	Darling Hill Dump	Deleted	No	No	-
VT	Lyndon	Parker Sanitary Landfill	Final	No	No	52.29
VT	Pownal	Pownal Tannery	Final	No	No	50
VT	Rockingham	BFI Sanitary Landfill (Rockingham)	Final	No	No	41.92
VT	Springfield	Old Springfield Landfill	Final	No	No	34.79
VT	Strafford	Elizabeth Mine	Final	No	No	50
VT	Vershire	Ely Copper Mine	Final	No	No	50
VT	Williston	Commerce Street Plume	Final	No	No	48.48
VT	Woodford	Burgess Brothers Landfill	Final	No	No	52.58
WA	Bainbridge Island	Wyckoff Co./Eagle Harbor	Final	No	No	32.55
WA	Bellingham	Oeser Co	Final	No	No	69.34
WA	Benton County	Hanford 100-Area (USDOE)	Final	No	No	-
WA	Benton County	Hanford 1100-Area (USDOE)	Deleted	No	No	-
WA	Benton County	Hanford 200-Area (USDOE)	Final	No	No	69.05
WA	Benton County	Hanford 300-Area (USDOE)	Final	No	No	65.23
WA	Bremerton	Bangor Ordnance Disposal (USNAVY)	Final	No	No	30.42
WA	Bremerton	Bremerton Gasworks	Final	No	No	50
WA	Bremerton	Puget Sound Naval Shipyard Complex	Final	No	No	50
WA	Brush Prairie	Toftdahl Drums	Deleted	No	No	-
WA	Centralia	Centralia Municipal Landfill	Final	No	No	36.36
WA	Chehalis	American Crossarm & Conduit Co.	Final	No	No	30.44
WA	Chehalis	Hamilton/Labree Roads Ground Water Contamination	Final	No	No	37.65
WA	Everson	Northwest Transformer	Deleted	No	No	-
WA	Everson	Northwest Transformer (South Harkness Street)	Deleted	No	No	-
WA	Freeman	Grain Handling Facility at Freeman	Final	No	No	50
WA	Indian Island	Port Hadlock Detachment (USNAVY)	Deleted	No	No	-
WA	Kent	Midway Landfill	Final	No	No	54.27
WA	Kent	Seattle Municipal Landfill (Kent Highlands)	Final	No	No	52.19
WA	Kent	Western Processing Co., Inc.	Final	No	No	58.63
WA	Keyport	Naval Undersea Warfare Station (4 Areas)	Final	No	No	33.6
WA	Kitsap County	Jackson Park Housing Complex (USNAVY)	Final	No	No	50
WA	Lakewood	Lakewood	Final	No	No	-

St.	City/Area	Site Name	NPL[1] Status	SA Approach[2]	HEUC[3]	HRS Score[4]
WA	Loomis	Silver Mountain Mine	Deleted	No	No	
WA	Manchester	Old Navy Dump/Manchester Laboratory (USEPA/NOAA)	Final	No	No	50
WA	Maple Valley	Queen City Farms	Final	No	No	34.38
WA	Marysville	Boeing Company Tulalip Test Site	Not NPL	Yes	No	-
WA	Marysville	Tulalip Landfill	Deleted	No	No	-
WA	Mead	Kaiser Aluminum (Mead Works)	Final	No	No	38.07
WA	Mica	Mica Landfill	Final	No	No	34.64
WA	Moses Lake	Moses Lake Wellfield Contamination	Final	No	No	50
WA	Neah Bay	Makah Reservation Warmhouse Beach Dump	Final	No	No	50
WA	North Bonneville	Hamilton Island Landfill (USA/COE)	Deleted	No	No	-
WA	Pasco	Pasco Sanitary Landfill	Final	No	No	44.46
WA	Pierce County	Hidden Valley Landfill (Thun Field)	Final	No	No	37.93
WA	Renton	Pacific Car & Foundry Co.	Final	No	No	42.33
WA	Renton	Quendall Terminals	Final	No	No	50
WA	Seattle	Harbor Island (Lead)	Final	No	No	-
WA	Seattle	Lockheed West Seattle	Final	No	No	50
WA	Seattle	Lower Duwamish Waterway	Final	No	No	50
WA	Seattle	Pacific Sound Resources	Final	No	No	70.71
WA	Silverdale	Bangor Naval Submarine Base	Final	No	No	55.91
WA	Spokane	Colbert Landfill	Final	No	No	41.59
WA	Spokane	Fairchild Air Force Base (4 Waste Areas)	Final	No	No	31.98
WA	Spokane	General Electric Co. (Spokane Shop)	Final	No	No	57.8
WA	Spokane	North Market Street	Final	No	No	32.61
WA	Spokane	Northside Landfill	Final	No	No	28.9
WA	Spokane	Old Inland Pit	Deleted	No	No	-
WA	Spokane	Spokane Junkyard/Associated Properties	Deleted	No	No	-
WA	Spokane County	Greenacres Landfill	Final	No	No	28.9
WA	Tacoma	American Lake Gardens/McChord AFB	Final	No	No	28.9
WA	Tacoma	Commencement Bay, Near Shore/Tide Flats	Final	No	No	-
WA	Tacoma	Commencement Bay, South Tacoma Channel	Final	No	No	-
WA	Tacoma	Fort Lewis (Landfill No. 5)	Deleted	No	No	-
WA	Tacoma	McChord Air Force Base (Wash Rack/Treatment Area)	Deleted	No	No	-
WA	Tillicum	Fort Lewis Logistics Center	Final	No	No	35.48
WA	Tumwater	Palermo Well Field Ground Water Contamination	Final	No	No	50
WA	Vancouver	ALCOA (Vancouver Smelter)	Deleted	No	No	-
WA	Vancouver	Bonneville Power Administration Ross Complex (USDOE)	Deleted	No	No	-
WA	Vancouver	Boomsnub/Airco	Final	No	No	-
WA	Vancouver	Frontier Hard Chrome, Inc.	Deleted	No	No	-
WA	Vancouver	Vancouver Water Station #1 Contamination	Deleted	No	No	-
WA	Vancouver	Vancouver Water Station #4 Contamination	Deleted	No	No	-
WA	Wellpinit	Midnite Mine	Final	No	No	50
WA	Whidbey Island	Naval Air Station, Whidbey Island (Ault Field)	Final	No	No	47.58
WA	Whidbey Island	Naval Air Station, Whidbey Island (Seaplane Base)	Deleted	No	No	-
WA	Yakima	FMC Corp. (Yakima)	Final	No	No	38.8
WA	Yakima	Pesticide Lab (Yakima)	Deleted	No	No	-
WA	Yakima	Yakima Plating Co.	Deleted	No	No	-
WI	Algoma	Algoma Municipal Landfill	Final	No	No	39.99
WI	Appleton	N.W. Mauthe Co., Inc.	Final	No	No	-
WI	Ashippun	Oconomowoc Electroplating Co., Inc.	Final	No	No	31.86
WI	Ashland	Ashland/Northern States Power Lakefront	Final	No	No	50
WI	Blooming Grove	Madison Metropolitan Sewerage District Lagoons	Final	No	No	32.65
WI	Brookfield	Master Disposal Service Landfill	Final	No	No	47.49
WI	Brookfield	Waste Management of Wisconsin (Brookfield Sanitary Landfill)	Final	No	No	28.9
WI	Caledonia	Hunts Disposal Landfill	Final	No	No	31.02
WI	Cedarburg	Amcast Industrial Corporation	Final	No	No	46.86
WI	Cedarburg	Cedar Creek	Not NPL	Yes	No	-
WI	Cleveland Township	Mid-State Disposal, Inc. Landfill	Final	No	No	35.23
WI	Daniels	Penta Wood Products	Final	No	No	50

St.	City/Area	Site Name	NPL[1] Status	SA Approach[2]	HEUC[3]	HRS Score[4]
WI	De Pere	Better Brite Plating Chrome & Zinc Shops	Final	No	No	48.91
WI	Delavan	Delavan Municipal Well #4	Final	No	No	28.9
WI	Dunn	City Disposal Corp. Landfill	Final	No	No	36.84
WI	Eau Claire	Eau Claire Municipal Well Field	Deleted	No	No	-
WI	Eau Claire	National Presto Industries, Inc.	Final	No	No	42.39
WI	Eau Claire	Waste Research & Reclamation Co.	Deleted	No	No	-
WI	Excelsior	Sauk County Landfill	Final	No	No	34.21
WI	Fond Du Lac County	Ripon City Landfill	Final	No	No	39.04
WI	Franklin	Fadrowski Drum Disposal	Deleted	No	No	-
WI	Franklin Township	Lemberger Transport & Recycling	Final	No	No	34.58
WI	Germantown	Omega Hills North Landfill	Deleted	No	No	-
WI	Green Bay	Fox River NRDA/PCB Releases	Proposed	No	No	50
WI	Green Bay	WPSC Green Bay MGP	Not NPL	Yes	No	-
WI	Harrison	Schmalz Dump	Final	No	No	48.92
WI	Janesville	Janesville Ash Beds	Final	No	No	57.9
WI	Janesville	Janesville Old Landfill	Final	No	No	57.93
WI	Kohler	Kohler Co. Landfill	Final	No	No	42.93
WI	La Prairie Township	Wheeler Pit	Deleted	No	No	-
WI	Manitowoc	WPSC Manitowoc MGP	Not NPL	Yes	No	-
WI	Marinette	WPSC Marinette MGP	Not NPL	Yes	No	-
WI	Medford	Scrap Processing Co., Inc.	Final	No	No	34.24
WI	Menomonee Falls	Lauer I Sanitary Landfill	Final	No	No	42.69
WI	Middleton	Refuse Hideaway Landfill	Final	No	No	34.67
WI	Milwaukee	Burnham Canal - Miller Compressing Company	Not NPL	Yes	No	-
WI	Milwaukee	Moss-American Co., Inc. (Kerr-McGee Oil Co.)	Final	No	No	32.14
WI	Milwaukee	Solvay Coke And Gas Company	Not NPL	Yes	No	-
WI	Muskego	Muskego Sanitary Landfill	Final	No	No	51.91
WI	Onalaska	Onalaska Municipal Landfill	Final	No	No	42.47
WI	Oshkosh	WPSC OshkoshMGP	Not NPL	Yes	No	-
WI	Sheboygan	Sheboygan Harbor & River	Final	No	No	33.79
WI	Sheboygan	WPSC Camp Marina MGP	Not NPL	Yes	No	-
WI	Sparta	Northern Engraving Co.	Deleted	No	No	-
WI	Spencer	Spickler Landfill	Final	No	No	44.24
WI	Stevens Point	WPSC Stevens Point	Not NPL	Yes	No	-
WI	Stoughton	Hagen Farm	Final	No	No	32.06
WI	Stoughton	Stoughton City Landfill	Final	No	No	35.79
WI	Tomah	Tomah Armory	Deleted	No	No	-
WI	Tomah	Tomah Fairgrounds	Deleted	No	No	-
WI	Tomah	Tomah Municipal Sanitary Landfill	Final	No	No	45.91
WI	Two Rivers	WPSC Two Rivers MGP	Not NPL	Yes	No	-
WI	Wausau	Wausau Ground Water Contamination	Final	No	No	28.91
WI	Whitelaw	Lemberger Landfill, Inc.	Final	No	No	34.07
WI	Williamstown	Hechimovich Sanitary Landfill	Final	No	No	47.91
WV	Clarksburg	North 25th Street Glass and Zinc	Final	No	No	48.03
WV	Fairmont	Big John Salvage - Hoult Road	Final	No	No	48.57
WV	Fairmont	Sharon Steel Corp (Fairmont Coke Works)	Final	No	No	57.08
WV	Follansbee	Follansbee	Deleted	No	No	-
WV	Leetown	Leetown Pesticide	Deleted	No	No	-
WV	Minden	Shaffer Equipment/arbuckle Creek Area	Final	No	No	50.54
WV	Mineral County	Allegany Ballistics Laboratory (USNAVY)	Final	No	No	50
WV	Morgantown	Ordnance Works Disposal Areas	Deleted	No	No	-
WV	Moundsville	Hanlin-Allied-Olin	Final	No	No	53.98
WV	Nitro	Fike Chemical, Inc.	Final	No	No	36.3
WV	Point Pleasant	West Virginia Ordnance (USARMY)	Final	No	No	-
WV	Ravenswood	Ravenswood PCE Ground Water Plume	Final	No	No	50
WV	Vienna	Vienna Tetrachloroethene	Final	No	No	50
WY	Cheyenne	F.E. Warren Air Force Base	Final	No	No	39.23
WY	Evansville	Mystery Bridge Rd/U.S. Highway 20	Final	No	No	-
WY	Laramie	Baxter/Union Pacific Tie Treating	Deleted	No	No	-

Notes: *(1) National Priorities List; (2) The Superfund alternative (SA) approach uses the same investigation and cleanup process and standards that are used for sites listed on the NPL. The SA approach is an alternative to listing a site on the NPL; it is not an alternative to Superfund or the Superfund process. The SA approach can potentially save the time and resources associated with listing a site on the NPL. As long as a PRP enters into an SA approach agreement with EPA, there is no need for EPA to list the site on the NPL (although the site qualifies for listing on the NPL). Currently, sites with SA approach agreements are a small subset of all Superfund cleanup agreements; (3) Human Exposure Under Control: This describes sites where contamination is present that could affect human health. This includes some sites where EPA has not yet begun cleanup. But it also includes sites where EPA has already done substantial cleanup work. For example, this includes sites where cleanup is partially complete but people may be exposed to contamination somewhere within a site's boundaries. At sites where EPA finds contamination that poses an imminent human health or environmental risk, EPA will use its Superfund removal authorities to address this risk and protect the public. This designation, which describes only 7 percent of sites, does not necessarily mean that people are being exposed, only that there is potential. An example of such a site would be one with lead-contaminated soil where EPA has cleaned up soil at several hundred residences, significantly reducing residents' exposure to lead in soil. But, if EPA is still cleaning up additional properties, the work is not yet complete and residents may be exposed. In this case, EPA would describe the site as Human Exposure Not Under Control; (4) Federal Register Hazard Rankings System (HRS) score. The HRS is a model that is used to evaluate the relative threats to human health and the environment posed by actual or potential releases of hazardous substances, pollutants, and contaminants. The HRS criteria take into account the population at risk, the hazard potential of the substances, as well as the potential for contamination of drinking water supplies, direct human contact, destruction of sensitive ecosystems, damage to natural resources affecting the human food chain, contamination of surface water used for recreation or potable water consumption, and contamination of ambient air. The higher the score, the higher the potential threat to human health or the environment. Any site scoring 28.50 or greater is eligible for the NPL.*

Source: *U.S. Environmental Protection Agency, Superfund Sites, July 2, 2019*

2017 ATSDR Substance Priority List

2017 Rank	Substance Name	Totals Points	CAS Number[1]
1	ARSENIC	1674	7440-38-2
2	LEAD	1531	7439-92-1
3	MERCURY	1458	7439-97-6
4	VINYL CHLORIDE	1358	75-01-4
5	POLYCHLORINATED BIPHENYLS	1345	1336-36-3
6	BENZENE	1329	71-43-2
7	CADMIUM	1320	7440-43-9
8	BENZO(A)PYRENE	1306	50-32-8
9	POLYCYCLIC AROMATIC HYDROCARBONS	1279	130498-29-2
10	BENZO(B)FLUORANTHENE	1251	205-99-2
11	CHLOROFORM	1203	67-66-3
12	AROCLOR 1260	1191	11096-82-5
13	DDT, P,P'-	1183	50-29-3
14	AROCLOR 1254	1172	11097-69-1
15	DIBENZO(A,H)ANTHRACENE	1156	53-70-3
16	TRICHLOROETHYLENE	1155	79-01-6
17	CHROMIUM, HEXAVALENT	1148	18540-29-9
18	DIELDRIN	1144	60-57-1
19	PHOSPHORUS, WHITE	1141	7723-14-0
20	HEXACHLOROBUTADIENE	1130	87-68-3
21	DDE, P,P'-	1127	72-55-9
22	CHLORDANE	1126	57-74-9
23	AROCLOR 1242	1126	53469-21-9
24	COAL TAR CREOSOTE	1124	8001-58-9
25	ALDRIN	1116	309-00-2
26	DDD, P,P'-	1114	72-54-8
27	AROCLOR 1248	1105	12672-29-6
28	HEPTACHLOR	1102	76-44-8
29	AROCLOR	1101	12767-79-2
30	BENZIDINE	1093	92-87-5
31	ACROLEIN	1090	107-02-8
32	TOXAPHENE	1089	8001-35-2
33	TETRACHLOROETHYLENE	1078	127-18-4
34	HEXACHLOROCYCLOHEXANE, GAMMA-	1076	58-89-9
35	CYANIDE	1071	57-12-5
36	HEXACHLOROCYCLOHEXANE, BETA-	1054	319-85-7
37	DISULFOTON	1049	298-04-4
38	BENZO(A)ANTHRACENE	1047	56-55-3
39	1,2-DIBROMOETHANE	1043	106-93-4
40	ENDRIN	1039	72-20-8
41	DIAZINON	1038	333-41-5
42	HEXACHLOROCYCLOHEXANE, DELTA-	1036	319-86-8
43	BERYLLIUM	1031	7440-41-7
44	ENDOSULFAN	1029	115-29-7
45	AROCLOR 1221	1028	11104-28-2
46	1,2-DIBROMO-3-CHLOROPROPANE	1027	96-12-8
47	HEPTACHLOR EPOXIDE	1022	1024-57-3
48	ENDOSULFAN, ALPHA	1019	959-98-8
49	CIS-CHLORDANE	1017	5103-71-9
50	CARBON TETRACHLORIDE	1014	56-23-5
51	COBALT	1013	7440-48-4
52	AROCLOR 1016	1012	12674-11-2
53	DDT, O,P'-	1009	789-02-6
54	PENTACHLOROPHENOL	1008	87-86-5
55	METHOXYCHLOR	1007	72-43-5

2017 Rank	Substance Name	Totals Points	CAS Number[1]
56	ENDOSULFAN SULFATE	1005	1031-07-8
57	NICKEL	996	7440-02-0
58	DI-N-BUTYL PHTHALATE	995	84-74-2
59	ENDRIN KETONE	993	53494-70-5
60	DIBROMOCHLOROPROPANE	984	67708-83-2
61	BENZO(K)FLUORANTHENE	970	207-08-9
62	TRANS-CHLORDANE	969	5103-74-2
63	ENDOSULFAN, BETA	968	33213-65-9
64	CHLORPYRIFOS	965	2921-88-2
65	XYLENES, TOTAL	964	1330-20-7
66	CHROMIUM(VI) TRIOXIDE	961	1333-82-0
67	AROCLOR 1232	959	11141-16-5
68	ENDRIN ALDEHYDE	959	7421-93-4
69	METHANE	952	74-82-8
70	3,3?-DICHLOROBENZIDINE	942	91-94-1
71	2-HEXANONE	941	591-78-6
72	2,3,7,8-TETRACHLORODIBENZO-P-DIOXIN	941	1746-01-6
73	BENZOFLUORANTHENE	937	56832-73-6
74	TOLUENE	917	108-88-3
75	ZINC	915	7440-66-6
76	PENTACHLOROBENZENE	907	608-93-5
77	DI(2-ETHYLHEXYL)PHTHALATE	906	117-81-7
78	CHROMIUM	895	7440-47-3
79	AROCLOR 1240	889	71328-89-7
80	2,4,6-TRINITROTOLUENE	879	118-96-7
81	NAPHTHALENE	877	91-20-3
82	1,1-DICHLOROETHENE	876	75-35-4
83	BROMODICHLOROETHANE	868	683-53-4
84	DDD, O,P'-	867	53-19-0
85	2,4,6-TRICHLOROPHENOL	867	88-06-2
86	BIS(2-CHLOROETHYL) ETHER	867	111-44-4
87	HYDRAZINE	862	302-01-2
88	METHYLENE CHLORIDE	860	75-09-2
89	2,4-DINITROPHENOL	859	51-28-5
90	4,4?-METHYLENEBIS(2-CHLOROANILINE)	859	101-14-4
91	1,2-DICHLOROETHANE	852	107-06-2
92	THIOCYANATE	847	302-04-5
93	HEXACHLOROBENZENE	844	118-74-1
94	ASBESTOS	841	1332-21-4
95	RDX (Cyclonite)	833	121-82-4
96	RADIUM-226	833	13982-63-3
97	URANIUM	832	7440-61-1
98	2,4-DINITROTOLUENE	832	121-14-2
99	ETHION	831	563-12-2
100	4,6-DINITRO-O-CRESOL	828	534-52-1
101	RADIUM	827	7440-14-4
102	THORIUM	824	7440-29-1
103	DIMETHYLARSINIC ACID	822	75-60-5
104	CHLORINE	821	7782-50-5
105	1,3,5-TRINITROBENZENE	820	99-35-4
106	RADON	818	10043-92-2
107	HEXACHLOROCYCLOHEXANE, ALPHA-	817	319-84-6
108	RADIUM-228	815	15262-20-1
109	THORIUM-230	813	14269-63-7
110	URANIUM-235	812	15117-96-1
111	THORIUM-228	810	14274-82-9
112	RADON-222	810	14859-67-7
113	URANIUM-234	809	13966-29-5
114	N-NITROSODI-N-PROPYLAMINE	808	621-64-7

2017 Rank	Substance Name	Totals Points	CAS Number[1]
115	COAL TARS	808	8007-45-2
116	METHYLMERCURY	808	22967-92-6
117	1,1,1-TRICHLOROETHANE	807	71-55-6
118	COPPER	807	7440-50-8
119	CHRYSOTILE ASBESTOS	806	12001-29-5
120	PLUTONIUM-239	806	15117-48-3
121	POLONIUM-210	805	13981-52-7
122	PLUTONIUM-238	805	13981-16-3
123	LEAD-210	805	14255-04-0
124	AMOSITE ASBESTOS	804	12172-73-5
124	PLUTONIUM	804	7/5/7440
124	STRONTIUM-90	804	10098-97-2
127	RADON-220	804	22481-48-7
128	CHLOROBENZENE	804	108-90-7
129	AMERICIUM-241	804	86954-36-1
130	HYDROGEN CYANIDE	803	74-90-8
131	AZINPHOS-METHYL	803	86-50-0
132	ETHYLBENZENE	802	100-41-4
133	CHLORDECONE	802	143-50-0
134	BARIUM	802	7440-39-3
135	NEPTUNIUM-237	802	13994-20-2
136	PLUTONIUM-240	801	14119-33-6
137	1,2,3-TRICHLOROBENZENE	801	87-61-6
138	FLUORANTHENE	800	206-44-0
139	S,S,S-TRIBUTYL PHOSPHOROTRITHIOATE	799	78-48-8
140	MANGANESE	798	7439-96-5
141	CHRYSENE	792	218-01-9
142	2,4,5-TRICHLOROPHENOL	792	95-95-4
143	PERFLUOROOCTANE SULFONIC ACID	788	1763-23-1
144	POLYBROMINATED BIPHENYLS	785	67774-32-7
145	DICOFOL	785	115-32-2
146	SELENIUM	776	7782-49-2
147	1,1,2,2-TETRACHLOROETHANE	776	79-34-5
148	PARATHION	774	56-38-2
149	HEPTACHLORODIBENZO-P-DIOXIN	774	37871-00-4
150	HEXACHLOROCYCLOHEXANE, TECHNICAL GRADE	774	608-73-1
151	TRICHLOROFLUOROETHANE	773	27154-33-2
152	BROMINE	771	7726-95-6
153	AROCLOR 1268	765	11100-14-4
154	1,3-BUTADIENE	762	106-99-0
155	PERFLUOROOCTANOIC ACID	758	335-67-1
156	HEPTACHLORODIBENZOFURAN	756	38998-75-3
157	TRIFLURALIN	755	1582-09-8
158	PERFLUOROHEXANESULFONIC ACID	749	355-46-4
159	1,2,3,4,6,7,8,9-OCTACHLORODIBENZOFURAN	743	39001-02-0
160	AMMONIA	742	7664-41-7
161	2-METHYLNAPHTHALENE	727	91-57-6
162	2,3,4,7,8-PENTACHLORODIBENZOFURAN	724	57117-31-4
163	1,4-DICHLOROBENZENE	724	106-46-7
164	1,1-DICHLOROETHANE	721	75-34-3
165	NALED	721	300-76-5
166	1,1,2-TRICHLOROETHANE	720	79-00-5
167	HEXACHLOROCYCLOPENTADIENE	719	77-47-4
168	1,2-DIPHENYLHYDRAZINE	718	122-66-7
169	PHORATE	716	298-02-2
170	TRICHLOROETHANE	713	25323-89-1
171	ACENAPHTHENE	710	83-32-9
172	TETRACHLOROBIPHENYL	710	26914-33-0

2017 Rank	Substance Name	Totals Points	CAS Number[1]
173	PALLADIUM	706	5/3/7440
174	OXYCHLORDANE	705	27304-13-8
175	CRESOL, PARA-	704	106-44-5
176	INDENO(1,2,3-CD)PYRENE	702	193-39-5
177	GAMMA-CHLORDENE	702	56641-38-4
178	TETRACHLOROPHENOL	699	25167-83-3
179	1,2-DICHLOROBENZENE	697	95-50-1
180	1,2-DICHLOROETHENE, TRANS-	691	156-60-5
181	CHLOROETHANE	687	75-00-3
182	P-XYLENE	687	106-42-3
183	ALUMINUM	687	7429-90-5
184	PHENOL	686	108-95-2
185	CARBON MONOXIDE	684	630-08-0
186	CARBON DISULFIDE	682	75-15-0
187	2,4-DIMETHYLPHENOL	680	105-67-9
188	DIBENZOFURAN	676	132-64-9
189	ACETONE	672	67-64-1
190	HEXACHLOROETHANE	671	67-72-1
191	BUTYL METHYL PHTHALATE	668	34006-76-3
192	CHLOROMETHANE	665	74-87-3
193	HEXACHLORODIBENZOFURAN	660	55684-94-1
194	BUTYL BENZYL PHTHALATE	658	85-68-7
195	HYDROGEN SULFIDE	658	6/4/7783
196	DICHLORVOS	656	62-73-7
197	DIBENZOFURANS, CHLORINATED	653	42934-53-2
198	CRESOL, ORTHO-	653	95-48-7
199	HEXACHLORODIBENZO-P-DIOXIN	652	34465-46-8
200	VANADIUM	650	7440-62-2
201	N-NITROSODIMETHYLAMINE	649	62-75-9
202	1,2,4-TRICHLOROBENZENE	647	120-82-1
203	PERFLUORONONANOIC ACID	647	375-95-1
204	ETHOPROP	644	13194-48-4
205	TETRACHLORODIBENZO-P-DIOXIN	641	41903-57-5
206	BROMOFORM	635	75-25-2
207	PENTACHLORODIBENZOFURAN	632	30402-15-4
208	1,3-DICHLOROBENZENE	628	541-73-1
209	PENTACHLORODIBENZO-P-DIOXIN	626	36088-22-9
210	N-NITROSODIPHENYLAMINE	625	86-30-6
211	2,4-DICHLOROPHENOL	619	120-83-2
212	2,3-DIMETHYLNAPHTHALENE	619	581-40-8
213	2,3,7,8-TETRACHLORODIBENZOFURAN	619	51207-31-9
214	1,4-DIOXANE	617	123-91-1
215	FLUORINE	613	7782-41-4
216	NITRITE	610	14797-65-0
217	CESIUM-137	610	10045-97-3
217	CHROMIC ACID	610	7738-94-5
219	2-BUTANONE	608	78-93-3
220	1,2-DICHLOROETHYLENE	608	540-59-0
221	POTASSIUM-40	608	13966-00-2
222	DINITROTOLUENE	607	25321-14-6
223	NITRATE	606	14797-55-8
224	FORMALDEHYDE	605	50-00-0
225	SILVER	605	7440-22-4
226	COAL TAR PITCH	605	65996-93-2
227	THORIUM-227	605	15623-47-9
228	ARSENIC ACID	604	7778-39-4
229	ARSENIC TRIOXIDE	604	1327-53-3
230	BENZOPYRENE	603	73467-76-2

2017 Rank	Substance Name	Totals Points	CAS Number[1]
231	CHLORDANE, TECHNICAL	602	12789-03-6
232	STROBANE	602	8001-50-1
233	4-AMINOBIPHENYL	602	92-67-1
233	PYRETHRUM	602	8003-34-7
235	ARSINE	602	7784-42-1
235	DIMETHOATE	602	60-51-5
237	BIS(CHLOROMETHYL) ETHER	602	542-88-1
237	CARBOPHENOTHION	602	786-19-6
239	ALPHA-CHLORDENE	601	56534-02-2
239	IODINE-131	601	10043-66-0
239	MERCURIC CHLORIDE	601	7487-94-7
239	SODIUM ARSENITE	601	7784-46-5
239	URANIUM-233	601	13968-55-3
244	ANTIMONY	601	7440-36-0
245	DIBROMOCHLOROMETHANE	601	124-48-1
246	CRESOLS	598	1319-77-3
247	DICHLOROBENZENE	596	25321-22-6
248	2,4-D	595	94-75-7
249	2-CHLOROPHENOL	591	95-57-8
250	BUTYLATE	591	2008-41-5
251	DIMETHYL FORMAMIDE	585	68-12-2
252	PHENANTHRENE	585	85-01-8
253	4-NITROPHENOL	580	100-02-7
254	DIURON	580	330-54-1
255	TETRACHLOROETHANE	577	25322-20-7
256	DICHLOROETHANE	568	1300-21-6
257	ETHYL ETHER	566	60-29-7
258	DIMETHYLANILINE	563	121-69-7
259	1,3-DICHLOROPROPENE, CIS-	561	10061-01-5
260	PYRENE	561	129-00-0
261	1,2,3,4,6,7,8-HEPTACHLORODIBENZO-P-DIOXIN	559	35822-46-9
262	PHOSPHINE	557	7803-51-2
263	TRICHLOROBENZENE	556	12002-48-1
264	2,6-DINITROTOLUENE	555	606-20-2
265	FLUORIDE ION	550	16984-48-8
266	PENTAERYTHRITOL TETRANITRATE	549	78-11-5
267	1,2,3,4,6,7,8-HEPTACHLORODIBENZOFURAN	549	67562-39-4
268	1,3-DICHLOROPROPENE, TRANS-	548	10061-02-6
269	ACRYLONITRILE	544	107-13-1
270	BIS(2-ETHYLHEXYL)ADIPATE	543	103-23-1
271	CARBAZOLE	541	86-74-8
272	2-CHLOROANILINE	539	95-51-2
273	METOLACHLOR	539	51218-45-2
274	1,2-DICHLOROETHENE, CIS-	539	156-59-2
275	1,2,3-TRICHLOROPROPANE	537	96-18-4

Notes: *Substances were assigned the same rank when two (or more) substances received equivalent total scores; (1) CAS Number = Chemical Abstracts Service registry number*

The Comprehensive Environmental Response, Compensation, and Liability Act (CERCLA) section 104 (i), as amended by the Superfund Amendments and Reauthorization Act (SARA), requires ATSDR and the EPA to prepare a list, in order of priority, of substances that are most commonly found at facilities on the National Priorities List (NPL) and which are determined to pose the most significant potential threat to human health due to their known or suspected toxicity and potential for human exposure at these NPL sites. This substance priority list is revised and published on a 2-year basis, with a yearly informal review and revision. Each substance on the list is a candidate to become the subject of a toxicological profile prepared by ATSDR. The listing algorithm prioritizes substances based on frequency of occurrence at NPL sites, toxicity, and potential for human exposure to the substances found at NPL sites. It should be noted that this priority list is not a list of "most toxic" substances, but rather a prioritization of substances based on a combination of their frequency, toxicity, and potential for human exposure at NPL sites. Thus, it is possible for substances with low toxicity but high NPL frequency of occurrence and exposure to be on this priority list. The objective of this priority list is to rank substances across all NPL hazardous waste sites to provide guidance in selecting which substances will be the subject of toxicological profiles prepared by ATSDR.

Source: *Center for Disease Control, Agency for Toxic Substances and Disease Registry, 2017 ATSDR Substance Priority List*

TRI On-site and Off-site Reported Disposed of or Otherwise Released (in pounds), for Facilities in All Industries, for All Chemicals, by State, U.S., 2017

State	Total On-site Disposal or Other Releases[1]	Total Off-site Disposal or Other Releases[2]	Total On- and Off-site Disposal or Other Releases
Alabama	62,270,109	15,039,981	77,310,090
Alaska	1,173,620,283	494,203	1,174,114,486
Arizona	76,334,953	1,232,144	77,567,098
Arkansas	28,962,967	3,022,526	31,985,493
California	19,645,929	6,618,717	26,264,647
Colorado	26,871,547	4,860,855	31,732,403
Connecticut	759,009	963,514	1,722,523
Delaware	4,586,103	344,921	4,931,025
District of Columbia	22,374	5,090	27,464
Florida	55,085,216	3,796,244	58,881,460
Georgia	45,408,825	2,912,956	48,321,781
Hawaii	2,834,986	227,006	3,061,992
Idaho	35,519,931	431,350	35,951,281
Illinois	64,499,002	44,252,516	108,751,518
Indiana	79,031,781	47,065,508	126,097,289
Iowa	27,262,017	6,985,263	34,247,280
Kansas	15,511,148	2,130,282	17,641,430
Kentucky	39,449,641	9,764,806	49,214,447
Louisiana	132,692,518	11,222,492	143,915,010
Maine	9,831,316	2,039,671	11,870,987
Maryland	3,702,668	1,341,375	5,044,044
Massachusetts	1,337,926	3,087,051	4,424,978
Michigan	48,085,009	44,662,769	92,747,778
Minnesota	18,442,409	4,592,642	23,035,051
Mississippi	62,091,707	3,887,880	65,979,587
Missouri	51,420,035	3,967,587	55,387,622
Montana	38,767,420	660,585	39,428,005
Nebraska	13,711,978	2,817,013	16,528,990
Nevada	392,828,707	4,914,261	397,742,968
New Hampshire	144,193	164,610	308,804
New Jersey	5,516,486	5,117,908	10,634,394
New Mexico	14,948,329	2,837,756	17,786,085
New York	10,061,529	2,700,938	12,762,468
North Carolina	39,330,576	12,777,396	52,107,972
North Dakota	25,818,637	6,258,104	32,076,741
Ohio	89,090,387	22,391,007	111,481,394
Oklahoma	27,616,428	2,497,025	30,113,453
Oregon	17,037,773	806,138	17,843,911
Pennsylvania	34,093,534	17,856,500	51,950,035
Rhode Island	191,519	181,315	372,834
South Carolina	26,720,419	6,213,790	32,934,208
South Dakota	6,076,639	330,510	6,407,149
Tennessee	69,608,613	12,700,343	82,308,956
Texas	182,717,184	19,517,763	202,234,947
Utah	302,558,301	1,540,082	304,098,383
Vermont	229,020	177,007	406,027
Virginia	30,788,769	3,679,762	34,468,531
Washington	26,162,905	5,417,353	31,580,258
West Virginia	22,726,954	7,414,537	30,141,492
Wisconsin	16,625,583	13,614,577	30,240,160
Wyoming	17,838,895	2,274,460	20,113,355
American Samoa	56,221	0	56,221
Guam	435,978	15	435,993
Northern Mariana Islands	19,158	360	19,518
Puerto Rico	1,421,047	222,401	1,643,448

State	Total On-site Disposal or Other Releases[1]	Total Off-site Disposal or Other Releases[2]	Total On- and Off-site Disposal or Other Releases
Virgin Islands	35,351	63	35,414
Total	3,498,457,946	380,032,931	3,878,490,877

Notes: *TRI = Toxic Release Inventory; Reporting year (RY) 2017 is the most recent TRI data available. Facilities reporting to TRI were required to submit RY 2017 data to EPA by July 1, 2018. TRI Explorer is using an updated data set (released to the public in April 2019). This dataset includes revisions for the years 1988 to 2017 processed by EPA, after the National Analysis Dataset was released. Revisions submitted to EPA after this time are not reflected in TRI Explorer reports.*

(1) On-site Disposal or Other Releases include Underground Injection to Class I Wells (Section 5.4.1), RCRA Subtitle C Landfills (5.5.1A), Other Landfills (5.5.1B), Fugitive or Non-point Air Emissions (5.1), Stack or Point Air Emissions (5.2), Surface Water Discharges (5.3), Underground Injection to Class II-V Wells (5.4.2), Land Treatment/Application Farming (5.5.2), RCRA Subtitle C Surface Impoundments (5.5.3A), Other Surface Impoundments (5.5.3B), and Other Land Disposal (5.5.4). Off-site Disposal or Other Releases include from Section 6.2 Class I Underground Injection Wells (M81), Class II-V Underground Injection Wells (M82, M71), RCRA Subtitle C Landfills (M65), Other Landfills (M64, M72), Storage Only (M10), Solidification/Stabilization - Metals and Metal Category Compounds only (M41 or M40), Wastewater Treatment (excluding POTWs) - Metals and Metal Category Compounds only (M62 or M61), RCRA Subtitle C Surface Impoundments (M66), Other Surface Impoundments (M67, M63), Land Treatment (M73), Other Land Disposal (M79), Other Off-site Management (M90), Transfers to Waste Broker - Disposal (M94, M91), and Unknown (M99) and, from Section 6.1 Transfers to POTWs (metals and metal category compounds only).

(2) Off-site disposal or other releases show only net off-site disposal or other releases, that is, off-site disposal or other releases transferred to other TRI facilities reporting such transfers as on-site disposal or other releases are not included to avoid double counting.

This report may not include all states in the US. A state may not be included in this report for two reasons: 1) there are no facilities reporting to TRI in the particular state; or 2) the facilities reporting to TRI in the particular state did not report to TRI for the user-specified selection criteria.

Users of TRI information should be aware that TRI data reflect releases and other waste management activities of chemicals, not whether (or to what degree) the public has been exposed to those chemicals. Release estimates alone are not sufficient to determine exposure or to calculate potential adverse effects on human health and the environment. TRI data, in conjunction with other information, can be used as a starting point in evaluating exposures that may result from releases and other waste management activities which involve toxic chemicals. The determination of potential risk depends upon many factors, including the toxicity of the chemical, the fate of the chemical, and the amount and duration of human or other exposure to the chemical after it is released.

Source: *U.S. Environmental Protection Agency, TRI Explorer, July 9, 2019*

TRI On-site and Off-site Reported Disposed of or Otherwise Released (in grams), for Facilities in All Industries, Dioxin and Dioxin-like Compounds, by State, U.S., 2017

State	Total On-site Disposal or Other Releases[1]	Total Off-site Disposal or Other Releases[2]	Total On- and Off-site Disposal or Other Releases
Alabama	179.897	94.375	274.272
Alaska	0.680	0.000	0.680
Arizona	18.061	36.790	54.851
Arkansas	52.388	7.069	59.457
California	11.760	62.234	73.994
Colorado	13.780	0.406	14.186
Connecticut	0.218	0.000	0.218
Delaware	3.007	0.098	3.105
Florida	48.944	0.710	49.654
Georgia	126.960	2.207	129.166
Hawaii	0.655	0.930	1.585
Idaho	7.044	8.100	15.144
Illinois	17.128	80.960	98.088
Indiana	183.651	328.941	512.592
Iowa	22.427	78.925	101.352
Kansas	4.403	21.808	26.211
Kentucky	119.661	3,350.470	3,470.131
Louisiana	135.000	581.164	716.164
Maine	5.208	1.884	7.092
Maryland	2.870	3.771	6.641
Massachusetts	0.863	0.000	0.863
Michigan	146.047	2,242.296	2,388.343
Minnesota	28.713	1,154.694	1,183.407
Mississippi	723.820	0.157	723.977
Missouri	37.821	0.000	37.821
Montana	6.921	2.270	9.191
Nebraska	3.602	4.540	8.142
Nevada	2.812	0.000	2.812
New Jersey	1.941	33.571	35.512
New Mexico	4.099	0.040	4.139
New York	9.203	4.243	13.445
North Carolina	93.260	2.902	96.162
North Dakota	17.924	0.000	17.924
Ohio	1,059.662	147.535	1,207.197
Oklahoma	34.812	43.060	77.872
Oregon	4.968	2.066	7.034
Pennsylvania	33.090	1.306	34.396
South Carolina	35.467	2.113	37.580
South Dakota	13.311	0.000	13.311
Tennessee	1,819.290	23.677	1,842.967
Texas	10,813.530	27,879.271	38,692.800
Utah	28,451.420	427.870	28,879.290
Virginia	14.449	13.739	28.188
Washington	18.989	106.958	125.947
West Virginia	16.646	32.593	49.239
Wisconsin	32.656	553.295	585.951
Wyoming	19.164	0.000	19.164
Guam	0.582	0.000	0.582
Puerto Rico	1.716	0.000	1.716
Virgin Islands	0.537	0.000	0.537
Total	44,401.054	37,339.038	81,740.091

Notes: *TRI = Toxic Release Inventory; Reporting year (RY) 2017 is the most recent TRI data available. Facilities reporting to TRI were required to submit RY 2017 data to EPA by July 1, 2018. TRI Explorer is using an updated data set (released to the public in April 2019). This dataset includes revisions for the years 1988 to 2017 processed by EPA, after the National Analysis Dataset was released. Revisions submitted to EPA after this time are not reflected in TRI Explorer reports.*

(1) On-site Disposal or Other Releases include Underground Injection to Class I Wells (Section 5.4.1), RCRA Subtitle C Landfills (5.5.1A), Other Landfills (5.5.1B), Fugitive or Non-point Air Emissions (5.1), Stack or Point Air Emissions (5.2), Surface Water Discharges (5.3), Underground Injection to Class II-V Wells (5.4.2), Land Treatment/Application Farming (5.5.2), RCRA Subtitle C Surface Impoundments (5.5.3A), Other Surface Impoundments (5.5.3B), and Other Land Disposal (5.5.4). Off-site Disposal or Other Releases include from Section 6.2 Class I Underground Injection Wells (M81), Class II-V Underground Injection Wells (M82, M71), RCRA Subtitle C Landfills (M65), Other Landfills (M64, M72), Storage Only (M10), Solidification/Stabilization - Metals and Metal Category Compounds only (M41 or M40), Wastewater Treatment (excluding POTWs) - Metals and Metal Category Compounds only (M62 or M61), RCRA Subtitle C Surface Impoundments (M66), Other Surface Impoundments (M67, M63), Land Treatment (M73), Other Land Disposal (M79), Other Off-site Management (M90), Transfers to Waste Broker - Disposal (M94, M91), and Unknown (M99) and, from Section 6.1 Transfers to POTWs (metals and metal category compounds only).

(2) Off-site disposal or other releases show only net off-site disposal or other releases, that is, off-site disposal or other releases transferred to other TRI facilities reporting such transfers as on-site disposal or other releases are not included to avoid double counting.

This report may not include all states in the US. A state may not be included in this report for two reasons: 1) there are no facilities reporting to TRI in the particular state; or 2) the facilities reporting to TRI in the particular state did not report to TRI for the user-specified selection criteria.

Users of TRI information should be aware that TRI data reflect releases and other waste management activities of chemicals, not whether (or to what degree) the public has been exposed to those chemicals. Release estimates alone are not sufficient to determine exposure or to calculate potential adverse effects on human health and the environment. TRI data, in conjunction with other information, can be used as a starting point in evaluating exposures that may result from releases and other waste management activities which involve toxic chemicals. The determination of potential risk depends upon many factors, including the toxicity of the chemical, the fate of the chemical, and the amount and duration of human or other exposure to the chemical after it is released.

***Source:** U.S. Environmental Protection Agency, TRI Explorer, July 9, 2019*

TRI On-site and Off-site Reported Disposed of or Otherwise Released (in pounds), for Facilities in All Industries, for All Chemicals, Top 75 Counties, 2017

Rank	County	State	Total On-site Disposal or Other Releases[1]	Total Off-site Disposal or Other Releases[2]	Total On- and Off-site Disposal or Other Releases
1	Northwest Arctic	Alaska	1,082,414,483	5	1,082,414,488
2	Salt Lake	Utah	268,582,572	161,630	268,744,202
3	Humboldt	Nevada	121,988,143	2,224	121,990,367
4	Eureka	Nevada	100,038,937	11,291	100,050,228
5	Lander	Nevada	66,860,251	6,506	66,866,757
6	Juneau	Alaska	60,673,875	143	60,674,018
7	Wayne	Michigan	15,064,413	41,193,739	56,258,153
8	Gila	Arizona	49,777,456	495,944	50,273,400
9	Elko	Nevada	43,367,085	388,814	43,755,899
10	Lake	Indiana	26,263,229	11,094,962	37,358,191
11	Brazoria	Texas	36,287,082	402,821	36,689,903
12	Harris	Texas	30,516,761	5,355,043	35,871,804
13	Escambia	Florida	31,552,135	110,491	31,662,625
14	Fairbanks North Star Boro	Alaska	30,272,255	366,623	30,638,878
15	Silver Bow	Montana	27,629,653	6	27,629,658
16	Mercer	North Dakota	14,586,983	11,991,714	26,578,697
17	White Pine	Nevada	26,387,197	33	26,387,230
18	Tooele	Utah	25,549,838	757,791	26,307,630
19	Ascension Parish	Louisiana	25,542,061	574,019	26,116,080
20	Peoria	Illinois	558,781	23,071,035	23,629,816
21	St Charles Parish	Louisiana	22,584,840	254,796	22,839,635
22	Washington	Illinois	20,354,674	0	20,354,674
23	Jefferson	Texas	13,041,386	6,557,060	19,598,446
24	Harrison	Mississippi	19,402,652	20,311	19,422,963
25	Nye	Nevada	17,930,114	86,510	18,016,623
26	Humphreys	Tennessee	17,312,726	172,036	17,484,762
27	Calcasieu Parish	Louisiana	17,025,560	341,393	17,366,953
28	Reynolds	Missouri	17,070,767	11,909	17,082,675
29	Monroe	Mississippi	16,643,327	220,103	16,863,430
30	Spencer	Indiana	14,392,970	1,024,031	15,417,001
31	Nueces	Texas	12,903,091	1,792,551	14,695,641
32	Jefferson Parish	Louisiana	11,841,252	2,322,755	14,164,007
33	Mobile	Alabama	4,224,110	9,335,070	13,559,181
34	Iron	Missouri	12,789,366	420,210	13,209,576
35	Calhoun	Texas	12,787,739	240,183	13,027,922
36	Sumter	Alabama	12,653,383	132,825	12,786,208
37	Carroll	Kentucky	7,100,911	5,659,831	12,760,742
38	Ouachita Parish	Louisiana	12,315,811	129	12,315,941
39	Allen	Ohio	11,706,116	447,613	12,153,728
40	Montgomery	Tennessee	11,919,160	157,987	12,077,147
41	Shoshone	Idaho	11,085,653	0	11,085,654
42	Posey	Indiana	1,935,614	9,065,014	11,000,628
43	Pershing	Nevada	10,959,672	19,908	10,979,580
44	Will	Illinois	8,780,124	1,607,522	10,387,646
45	Pend Oreille	Washington	10,224,124	1,081	10,225,204
46	Teller	Colorado	10,172,325	0	10,172,325
47	East Baton Rouge Parish	Louisiana	6,175,776	3,995,034	10,170,810
48	Iberville Parish	Louisiana	8,234,310	1,839,181	10,073,491
49	Marion	Indiana	167,443	9,903,726	10,071,170
50	Defiance	Ohio	9,735,774	178,278	9,914,052
51	Gilliam	Oregon	9,540,591	26,471	9,567,062
52	Montgomery	Virginia	9,281,476	278,577	9,560,053
53	Greenlee	Arizona	9,298,570	56,459	9,355,028
54	Allegheny	Pennsylvania	3,609,818	5,676,333	9,286,151
55	Galveston	Texas	8,867,584	230,697	9,098,281

Rank	County	State	Total On-site Disposal or Other Releases[1]	Total Off-site Disposal or Other Releases[2]	Total On- and Off-site Disposal or Other Releases
56	Marquette	Michigan	8,909,884	176,922	9,086,806
57	Gallia	Ohio	9,051,260	2,630	9,053,891
58	Cuyahoga	Ohio	5,480,089	3,476,411	8,956,499
59	Clark	Nevada	5,015,617	3,738,680	8,754,297
60	Cook	Illinois	2,767,999	5,759,570	8,527,569
61	Sandusky	Ohio	8,351,189	76,768	8,427,956
62	Rosebud	Montana	8,298,478	123,124	8,421,602
63	Los Angeles	California	3,314,244	4,924,659	8,238,902
64	Ashtabula	Ohio	7,675,283	79,753	7,755,035
65	Mccurtain	Oklahoma	7,474,361	1,204	7,475,565
66	Indiana	Pennsylvania	7,426,026	5,097	7,431,123
67	Jefferson	Alabama	4,595,188	2,737,809	7,332,997
68	Hutchinson	Texas	7,307,997	573	7,308,570
69	Harrison	West Virginia	7,107,164	2,349	7,109,513
70	San Juan	New Mexico	4,225,727	2,704,804	6,930,531
71	Shelby	Tennessee	3,512,486	3,348,527	6,861,012
72	Pima	Arizona	6,775,138	18,375	6,793,512
73	Richmond	Georgia	6,758,211	11,308	6,769,519
74	Caribou	Idaho	6,759,210	2,174	6,761,383
75	Macon	Illinois	4,432,424	2,148,168	6,580,592

Notes: *TRI = Toxic Release Inventory; Reporting year (RY) 2017 is the most recent TRI data available. Facilities reporting to TRI were required to submit RY 2017 data to EPA by July 1, 2018. TRI Explorer is using an updated data set (released to the public in April 2019). This dataset includes revisions for the years 1988 to 2017 processed by EPA, after the National Analysis Dataset was released. Revisions submitted to EPA after this time are not reflected in TRI Explorer reports.*

(1) On-site Disposal or Other Releases include Underground Injection to Class I Wells (Section 5.4.1), RCRA Subtitle C Landfills (5.5.1A), Other Landfills (5.5.1B), Fugitive or Non-point Air Emissions (5.1), Stack or Point Air Emissions (5.2), Surface Water Discharges (5.3), Underground Injection to Class II-V Wells (5.4.2), Land Treatment/Application Farming (5.5.2), RCRA Subtitle C Surface Impoundments (5.5.3A), Other Surface Impoundments (5.5.3B), and Other Land Disposal (5.5.4). Off-site Disposal or Other Releases include from Section 6.2 Class I Underground Injection Wells (M81), Class II-V Underground Injection Wells (M82, M71), RCRA Subtitle C Landfills (M65), Other Landfills (M64, M72), Storage Only (M10), Solidification/Stabilization - Metals and Metal Category Compounds only (M41 or M40), Wastewater Treatment (excluding POTWs) - Metals and Metal Category Compounds only (M62 or M61), RCRA Subtitle C Surface Impoundments (M66), Other Surface Impoundments (M67, M63), Land Treatment (M73), Other Land Disposal (M79), Other Off-site Management (M90), Transfers to Waste Broker - Disposal (M94, M91), and Unknown (M99) and, from Section 6.1 Transfers to POTWs (metals and metal category compounds only).

(2) Off-site disposal or other releases show only net off-site disposal or other releases, that is, off-site disposal or other releases transferred to other TRI facilities reporting such transfers as on-site disposal or other releases are not included to avoid double counting.

This report may not include all states in the US. A state may not be included in this report for two reasons: 1) there are no facilities reporting to TRI in the particular state; or 2) the facilities reporting to TRI in the particular state did not report to TRI for the user-specified selection criteria.

Users of TRI information should be aware that TRI data reflect releases and other waste management activities of chemicals, not whether (or to what degree) the public has been exposed to those chemicals. Release estimates alone are not sufficient to determine exposure or to calculate potential adverse effects on human health and the environment. TRI data, in conjunction with other information, can be used as a starting point in evaluating exposures that may result from releases and other waste management activities which involve toxic chemicals. The determination of potential risk depends upon many factors, including the toxicity of the chemical, the fate of the chemical, and the amount and duration of human or other exposure to the chemical after it is released.

Source: *U.S. Environmental Protection Agency, TRI Explorer, July 9, 2019*

TRI On-site and Off-site Reported Disposed of or Otherwise Released (in grams), for Facilities in All Industries, Dioxin and Dioxin-like Compounds, Top 75 Counties, 2017

Rank	County	State	Total On-site Disposal or Other Releases[1]	Total Off-site Disposal or Other Releases[2]	Total On- and Off-site Disposal or Other Releases
1	Tooele	Utah	28,441.314	411.620	28,852.934
2	Harris	Texas	14.690	27,781.187	27,795.878
3	Brazoria	Texas	6,098.030	11.130	6,109.160
4	Nueces	Texas	4,494.560	0.000	4,494.560
5	Marshall	Kentucky	20.971	3,340.574	3,361.545
6	Branch	Michigan	118.000	2,242.296	2,360.296
7	Humphreys	Tennessee	1,780.188	0.027	1,780.215
8	Dakota	Minnesota	12.182	1,154.275	1,166.457
9	Ashtabula	Ohio	1,016.479	0.000	1,016.479
10	Sheboygan	Wisconsin	6.798	542.541	549.339
11	San Patricio	Texas	5.306	410.748	416.054
12	Monroe	Mississippi	348.136	0.000	348.136
13	Allen	Indiana	10.014	325.160	335.174
14	Harrison	Mississippi	305.175	0.098	305.272
15	Calcasieu Parish	Louisiana	46.141	220.532	266.673
16	Ascension Parish	Louisiana	2.728	208.874	211.602
17	Iberville Parish	Louisiana	24.901	118.814	143.715
18	Tuscarawas	Ohio	6.668	129.690	136.358
19	Cass	Texas	122.926	0.000	122.926
20	Calhoun	Texas	5.902	85.298	91.200
21	Scott	Iowa	10.986	78.877	89.863
22	Pierce	Washington	1.086	82.260	83.346
23	Pike	Alabama	81.800	0.000	81.800
24	Porter	Indiana	76.675	0.000	76.675
25	Wabash	Indiana	68.030	0.000	68.030
26	Los Angeles	California	2.156	59.577	61.733
27	Catawba	North Carolina	58.670	0.000	58.670
28	Greene	Georgia	57.566	0.000	57.566
29	Butler	Kentucky	55.279	0.923	56.202
30	St Clair	Alabama	2.839	51.750	54.589
31	Kemper	Mississippi	52.180	0.000	52.180
32	East Baton Rouge Parish	Louisiana	38.493	7.671	46.164
33	Creek	Oklahoma	2.266	43.060	45.326
34	Peoria	Illinois	0.569	42.067	42.636
35	Maricopa	Arizona	5.283	36.790	42.073
36	Cook	Illinois	2.522	38.893	41.415
37	Etowah	Alabama	0.481	40.460	40.941
38	Orange	Texas	30.767	0.678	31.445
39	Cowlitz	Washington	6.352	24.008	30.360
40	Tuscaloosa	Alabama	29.709	0.000	29.709
41	St Charles Parish	Louisiana	6.400	21.404	27.804
42	Tyler	West Virginia	1.390	26.100	27.490
43	Mccurtain	Oklahoma	27.452	0.000	27.452
44	Carroll	Ohio	8.032	17.544	25.576
45	Linn	Kansas	0.220	21.750	21.970
46	Henderson	Kentucky	20.657	0.000	20.657
47	Escambia	Alabama	20.298	0.000	20.298
48	Jefferson	Arkansas	18.591	0.000	18.591
49	Weber	Utah	0.110	16.280	16.389
50	Bergen	New Jersey	0.000	15.799	15.799
51	Camden	New Jersey	1.321	14.380	15.701
52	Sullivan	Tennessee	14.927	0.033	14.960
53	Nassau	Florida	14.498	0.007	14.504
54	Mercer	North Dakota	13.811	0.000	13.811
55	York	South Carolina	13.620	0.000	13.620

Rank	County	State	Total On-site Disposal or Other Releases[1]	Total Off-site Disposal or Other Releases[2]	Total On- and Off-site Disposal or Other Releases
56	Bibb	Georgia	10.864	2.087	12.951
57	Fulton	Georgia	12.559	0.000	12.559
58	Ashley	Arkansas	12.160	0.000	12.160
59	Cleveland	Arkansas	8.199	3.856	12.055
60	Gallia	Ohio	11.687	0.000	11.687
61	Richmond	Georgia	11.296	0.060	11.356
62	Racine	Wisconsin	0.363	10.745	11.108
63	Blount	Tennessee	2.756	8.086	10.842
64	Yankton	South Dakota	10.696	0.000	10.696
65	Monroe	Michigan	10.343	0.000	10.343
66	Ashland	Wisconsin	9.858	0.000	9.858
67	Platte	Wyoming	9.364	0.000	9.364
68	Loudon	Tennessee	0.453	8.839	9.292
69	Pueblo	Colorado	9.257	0.000	9.257
70	Columbus	North Carolina	6.315	2.753	9.068
71	Isle Of Wight	Virginia	2.814	6.195	9.010
72	Brunswick	North Carolina	8.914	0.000	8.914
73	Schuylkill	Pennsylvania	7.801	0.862	8.662
74	Kootenai	Idaho	0.400	8.100	8.500
75	Apache	Arizona	8.417	0.000	8.417

Notes: *TRI = Toxic Release Inventory; Reporting year (RY) 2017 is the most recent TRI data available. Facilities reporting to TRI were required to submit RY 2017 data to EPA by July 1, 2018. TRI Explorer is using an updated data set (released to the public in April 2019). This dataset includes revisions for the years 1988 to 2017 processed by EPA, after the National Analysis Dataset was released. Revisions submitted to EPA after this time are not reflected in TRI Explorer reports.*

(1) On-site Disposal or Other Releases include Underground Injection to Class I Wells (Section 5.4.1), RCRA Subtitle C Landfills (5.5.1A), Other Landfills (5.5.1B), Fugitive or Non-point Air Emissions (5.1), Stack or Point Air Emissions (5.2), Surface Water Discharges (5.3), Underground Injection to Class II-V Wells (5.4.2), Land Treatment/Application Farming (5.5.2), RCRA Subtitle C Surface Impoundments (5.5.3A), Other Surface Impoundments (5.5.3B), and Other Land Disposal (5.5.4). Off-site Disposal or Other Releases include from Section 6.2 Class I Underground Injection Wells (M81), Class II-V Underground Injection Wells (M82, M71), RCRA Subtitle C Landfills (M65), Other Landfills (M64, M72), Storage Only (M10), Solidification/Stabilization - Metals and Metal Category Compounds only (M41 or M40), Wastewater Treatment (excluding POTWs) - Metals and Metal Category Compounds only (M62 or M61), RCRA Subtitle C Surface Impoundments (M66), Other Surface Impoundments (M67, M63), Land Treatment (M73), Other Land Disposal (M79), Other Off-site Management (M90), Transfers to Waste Broker - Disposal (M94, M91), and Unknown (M99) and, from Section 6.1 Transfers to POTWs (metals and metal category compounds only).

(2) Off-site disposal or other releases show only net off-site disposal or other releases, that is, off-site disposal or other releases transferred to other TRI facilities reporting such transfers as on-site disposal or other releases are not included to avoid double counting.

This report may not include all states in the US. A state may not be included in this report for two reasons: 1) there are no facilities reporting to TRI in the particular state; or 2) the facilities reporting to TRI in the particular state did not report to TRI for the user-specified selection criteria.

Users of TRI information should be aware that TRI data reflect releases and other waste management activities of chemicals, not whether (or to what degree) the public has been exposed to those chemicals. Release estimates alone are not sufficient to determine exposure or to calculate potential adverse effects on human health and the environment. TRI data, in conjunction with other information, can be used as a starting point in evaluating exposures that may result from releases and other waste management activities which involve toxic chemicals. The determination of potential risk depends upon many factors, including the toxicity of the chemical, the fate of the chemical, and the amount and duration of human or other exposure to the chemical after it is released.

Source: *U.S. Environmental Protection Agency, TRI Explorer, July 9, 2019*

TRI On-site and Off-site Reported Disposed of or Otherwise Released (in pounds), for Facilities in All Industries, for All Chemicals, Top 75 Zipcodes, 2017

Rank	Zip	City	State	Total On-site Disposal or Other Releases[1]	Total Off-site Disposal or Other Releases[2]	Total On- and Off-site Disposal or Other Releases
1	99752	Kotzebue	Alaska	1,082,414,483	5	1,082,414,488
2	84006	Bingham Canyon	Utah	234,372,667	391	234,373,058
3	89414	Golconda	Nevada	122,448,281	108	122,448,389
4	89822	Carlin	Nevada	107,084,521	384,791	107,469,311
5	89820	Battle Mountain	Nevada	66,860,251	21	66,860,272
6	99801	Juneau	Alaska	60,673,875	53	60,673,928
7	84044	Magna	Utah	33,306,284	4,954	33,311,238
8	89821	Crescent Valley	Nevada	31,345,712	0	31,345,712
9	85135	Hayden	Arizona	30,894,630	123	30,894,753
10	32533	Cantonment	Florida	30,878,358	9,387	30,887,745
11	77511	Alvin	Texas	30,404,456	1	30,404,457
12	59701	Butte	Montana	27,629,311	1	27,629,311
13	84029	Grantsville	Utah	25,552,601	469,895	26,022,496
14	46402	Gary	Indiana	24,298,333	911,500	25,209,833
15	48211	Detroit	Michigan	152,447	24,779,853	24,932,300
16	89319	Ruth	Nevada	23,563,694	0	23,563,694
17	99712	Fairbanks	Alaska	20,823,728	0	20,823,728
18	62257	Marissa	Illinois	20,331,435	0	20,331,435
19	65440	Boss	Missouri	19,501,253	242,848	19,744,101
20	39571	Pass Christian	Mississippi	19,314,946	1,188	19,316,134
21	70070	Luling	Louisiana	19,228,486	211	19,228,697
22	58523	Beulah	North Dakota	14,376,615	4,043,069	18,419,683
23	85532	Claypool	Arizona	17,875,495	483,071	18,358,566
24	39746	Hamilton	Mississippi	16,414,847	0	16,414,847
25	61615	Peoria	Illinois	2	16,356,111	16,356,113
26	37134	New Johnsonville	Tennessee	15,658,236	74	15,658,310
27	47635	Rockport	Indiana	14,381,108	1,024,031	15,405,139
28	70734	Geismar	Louisiana	14,500,108	253,036	14,753,144
29	77536	Deer Park	Texas	12,564,566	476,963	13,041,529
30	48111	Belleville	Michigan	12,841,165	77	12,841,242
31	35459	Emelle	Alabama	12,652,616	131,553	12,784,169
32	41045	Ghent	Kentucky	7,041,019	5,534,199	12,575,218
33	37040	Clarksville	Tennessee	11,918,866	157,987	12,076,853
34	70094	Westwego	Louisiana	11,821,544	68,422	11,889,965
35	45804	Lima	Ohio	11,639,713	243,034	11,882,747
36	89003	Beatty	Nevada	11,027,665	85,350	11,113,015
37	77979	Port Lavaca	Texas	10,824,176	207,499	11,031,675
38	47620	Mount Vernon	Indiana	1,935,614	9,065,013	11,000,627
39	70346	Donaldsonville	Louisiana	10,869,076	97,561	10,966,637
40	89419	Lovelock	Nevada	10,737,329	19,908	10,757,236
41	37660	Kingsport	Tennessee	5,530,921	5,192,219	10,723,140
42	70665	Sulphur	Louisiana	10,571,556	20,063	10,591,619
43	46312	East Chicago	Indiana	748,341	9,728,664	10,477,005
44	80860	Victor	Colorado	10,172,325	0	10,172,325
45	99153	Metaline Falls	Washington	9,990,648	570	9,991,218
46	43512	Defiance	Ohio	9,735,774	177,818	9,913,591
47	46231	Indianapolis	Indiana	12,809	9,723,579	9,736,388
48	97812	Arlington	Oregon	9,540,591	24,609	9,565,199
49	71280	Sterlington	Louisiana	9,535,345	96	9,535,441
50	85540	Morenci	Arizona	9,298,570	56,431	9,355,001
51	24141	Radford	Virginia	9,243,760	4,573	9,248,332
52	99737	Delta Junction	Alaska	9,226,306	9	9,226,315
53	45620	Cheshire	Ohio	9,051,240	2,630	9,053,871
54	77590	Texas City	Texas	8,863,462	163,290	9,026,752
55	49814	Champion	Michigan	8,586,188	430	8,586,618

Rank	Zip	City	State	Total On-site Disposal or Other Releases[1]	Total Off-site Disposal or Other Releases[2]	Total On- and Off-site Disposal or Other Releases
56	89015	Henderson	Nevada	4,816,147	3,737,158	8,553,305
57	59323	Colstrip	Montana	8,298,478	123,071	8,421,549
58	48120	Dearborn	Michigan	613,750	7,611,984	8,225,734
59	78380	Robstown	Texas	7,307,570	681,017	7,988,588
60	43464	Vickery	Ohio	7,659,617	15,072	7,674,689
61	44004	Ashtabula	Ohio	7,548,604	37,637	7,586,241
62	70805	Baton Rouge	Louisiana	4,226,201	3,323,704	7,549,905
63	26366	Haywood	West Virginia	7,087,685	2	7,087,687
64	61607	Peoria	Illinois	302,683	6,696,244	6,998,927
65	44105	Cleveland	Ohio	5,211,811	1,648,263	6,860,074
66	83276	Soda Springs	Idaho	6,759,210	2,111	6,761,321
67	89045	Round Mountain	Nevada	6,745,715	0	6,745,715
68	60436	Joliet	Illinois	6,716,784	24,475	6,741,259
69	70669	Westlake	Louisiana	6,412,477	255,379	6,667,855
70	70764	Plaquemine	Louisiana	6,322,913	151,620	6,474,533
71	71052	Mansfield	Louisiana	6,456,823	0	6,456,823
72	58530	Center	North Dakota	5,440,149	941,351	6,381,500
73	88252	Jal	New Mexico	6,370,967	0	6,370,967
74	83873	Wallace	Idaho	6,164,513	0	6,164,513
75	63633	Centerville	Missouri	6,120,410	3,900	6,124,310

Notes: *TRI = Toxic Release Inventory; Reporting year (RY) 2017 is the most recent TRI data available. Facilities reporting to TRI were required to submit RY 2017 data to EPA by July 1, 2018. TRI Explorer is using an updated data set (released to the public in April 2019). This dataset includes revisions for the years 1988 to 2017 processed by EPA, after the National Analysis Dataset was released. Revisions submitted to EPA after this time are not reflected in TRI Explorer reports.*

(1) On-site Disposal or Other Releases include Underground Injection to Class I Wells (Section 5.4.1), RCRA Subtitle C Landfills (5.5.1A), Other Landfills (5.5.1B), Fugitive or Non-point Air Emissions (5.1), Stack or Point Air Emissions (5.2), Surface Water Discharges (5.3), Underground Injection to Class II-V Wells (5.4.2), Land Treatment/Application Farming (5.5.2), RCRA Subtitle C Surface Impoundments (5.5.3A), Other Surface Impoundments (5.5.3B), and Other Land Disposal (5.5.4). Off-site Disposal or Other Releases include from Section 6.2 Class I Underground Injection Wells (M81), Class II-V Underground Injection Wells (M82, M71), RCRA Subtitle C Landfills (M65), Other Landfills (M64, M72), Storage Only (M10), Solidification/Stabilization - Metals and Metal Category Compounds only (M41 or M40), Wastewater Treatment (excluding POTWs) - Metals and Metal Category Compounds only (M62 or M61), RCRA Subtitle C Surface Impoundments (M66), Other Surface Impoundments (M67, M63), Land Treatment (M73), Other Land Disposal (M79), Other Off-site Management (M90), Transfers to Waste Broker - Disposal (M94, M91), and Unknown (M99) and, from Section 6.1 Transfers to POTWs (metals and metal category compounds only).

(2) Off-site disposal or other releases show only net off-site disposal or other releases, that is, off-site disposal or other releases transferred to other TRI facilities reporting such transfers as on-site disposal or other releases are not included to avoid double counting.

This report may not include all states in the US. A state may not be included in this report for two reasons: 1) there are no facilities reporting to TRI in the particular state; or 2) the facilities reporting to TRI in the particular state did not report to TRI for the user-specified selection criteria.

Users of TRI information should be aware that TRI data reflect releases and other waste management activities of chemicals, not whether (or to what degree) the public has been exposed to those chemicals. Release estimates alone are not sufficient to determine exposure or to calculate potential adverse effects on human health and the environment. TRI data, in conjunction with other information, can be used as a starting point in evaluating exposures that may result from releases and other waste management activities which involve toxic chemicals. The determination of potential risk depends upon many factors, including the toxicity of the chemical, the fate of the chemical, and the amount and duration of human or other exposure to the chemical after it is released.

Source: *U.S. Environmental Protection Agency, TRI Explorer, July 9, 2019*

TRI On-site and Off-site Reported Disposed of or Otherwise Released (in grams), for Facilities in All Industries, Dioxin and Dioxin-like Compounds, Top 75 Zipcodes, 2017

Rank	Zip	City	State	Total On-site Disposal or Other Releases[1]	Total Off-site Disposal or Other Releases[2]	Total On- and Off-site Disposal or Other Releases
1	84029	Grantsville	Utah	28,441.200	411.590	28,852.790
2	77571	La Porte	Texas	2.893	27,470.994	27,473.887
3	77541	Freeport	Texas	6,097.324	11.130	6,108.454
4	78380	Robstown	Texas	4,492.204	0.000	4,492.204
5	42029	Calvert City	Kentucky	20.971	3,340.574	3,361.545
6	49036	Coldwater	Michigan	118.000	2,242.296	2,360.296
7	37134	New Johnsonville	Tennessee	1,777.685	0.027	1,777.712
8	55068	Rosemount	Minnesota	11.493	1,154.275	1,165.768
9	44004	Ashtabula	Ohio	1,016.479	0.000	1,016.479
10	53081	Sheboygan	Wisconsin	6.798	542.541	549.339
11	39746	Hamilton	Mississippi	348.136	0.000	348.136
12	46774	New Haven	Indiana	10.014	325.160	335.174
13	39571	Pass Christian	Mississippi	305.175	0.098	305.272
14	77015	Houston	Texas	5.353	268.332	273.685
15	70669	Westlake	Louisiana	42.670	217.950	260.620
16	70734	Geismar	Louisiana	2.728	208.874	211.602
17	44683	Uhrichsville	Ohio	6.668	129.690	136.358
18	75572	Queen City	Texas	122.926	0.000	122.926
19	70764	Plaquemine	Louisiana	13.377	108.455	121.832
20	77978	Point Comfort	Texas	5.902	85.298	91.200
21	98421	Tacoma	Washington	1.086	82.260	83.346
22	52802	Davenport	Iowa	4.170	78.877	83.047
23	36079	Troy	Alabama	81.800	0.000	81.800
24	46304	Chesterton	Indiana	76.675	0.000	76.675
25	46992	Wabash	Indiana	68.030	0.000	68.030
26	91746	La Puente	California	0.164	59.577	59.741
27	30642	Greensboro	Georgia	57.566	0.000	57.566
28	28601	Hickory	North Carolina	56.969	0.000	56.969
29	42261	Morgantown	Kentucky	55.279	0.923	56.202
30	35987	Steele	Alabama	2.730	51.750	54.480
31	39358	Scooba	Mississippi	52.180	0.000	52.180
32	77536	Deer Park	Texas	4.460	41.861	46.322
33	74066	Sapulpa	Oklahoma	2.266	43.060	45.326
34	70805	Baton Rouge	Louisiana	37.635	7.671	45.306
35	61615	Peoria	Illinois	0.002	42.067	42.069
36	35903	Gadsden	Alabama	0.481	40.460	40.941
37	60411	Chicago Heights	Illinois	2.030	38.893	40.923
38	85338	Goodyear	Arizona	1.940	36.790	38.730
39	98632	Longview	Washington	6.352	24.008	30.360
40	35188	Woodstock	Alabama	29.548	0.000	29.548
41	77632	Orange	Texas	29.333	0.000	29.333
42	26146	Friendly	West Virginia	1.390	26.100	27.490
43	44657	Minerva	Ohio	8.032	17.544	25.576
44	66767	Prescott	Kansas	0.199	21.750	21.949
45	70765	Plaquemine	Louisiana	11.524	10.359	21.882
46	70079	Norco	Louisiana	0.603	19.570	20.172
47	42420	Henderson	Kentucky	19.995	0.000	19.995
48	74728	Broken Bow	Oklahoma	18.307	0.000	18.307
49	84404	Ogden	Utah	0.110	16.280	16.389
50	07407	Elmwood Park	New Jersey	0.000	15.799	15.799
51	08103	Camden	New Jersey	1.321	14.380	15.701
52	37660	Kingsport	Tennessee	14.927	0.033	14.960
53	36543	Huxford	Alabama	14.536	0.000	14.536
54	32034	Fernandina Beach	Florida	14.498	0.007	14.504
55	29704	Catawba	South Carolina	13.620	0.000	13.620

Rank	Zip	City	State	Total On-site Disposal or Other Releases[1]	Total Off-site Disposal or Other Releases[2]	Total On- and Off-site Disposal or Other Releases
56	31206	Macon	Georgia	10.864	2.087	12.951
57	30344	Atlanta	Georgia	12.559	0.000	12.559
58	71635	Crossett	Arkansas	12.160	0.000	12.160
59	71665	Rison	Arkansas	8.199	3.856	12.055
60	45620	Cheshire	Ohio	11.687	0.000	11.687
61	71602	White Hall	Arkansas	11.624	0.000	11.624
62	30906	Augusta	Georgia	11.290	0.002	11.292
63	37701	Alcoa	Tennessee	2.756	8.086	10.842
64	57078	Yankton	South Dakota	10.696	0.000	10.696
65	48161	Monroe	Michigan	10.343	0.000	10.343
66	54806	Ashland	Wisconsin	9.858	0.000	9.858
67	82201	Wheatland	Wyoming	9.364	0.000	9.364
68	37774	Loudon	Tennessee	0.453	8.839	9.292
69	74764	Valliant	Oklahoma	9.145	0.000	9.145
70	53177	Sturtevant	Wisconsin	0.363	8.758	9.121
71	28456	Riegelwood	North Carolina	6.315	2.753	9.068
72	23851	Franklin	Virginia	2.814	6.195	9.010
73	58523	Beulah	North Dakota	8.828	0.000	8.828
74	83854	Post Falls	Idaho	0.400	8.100	8.500
75	81004	Pueblo	Colorado	8.349	0.000	8.349

Notes: *TRI = Toxic Release Inventory; Reporting year (RY) 2017 is the most recent TRI data available. Facilities reporting to TRI were required to submit RY 2017 data to EPA by July 1, 2018. TRI Explorer is using an updated data set (released to the public in April 2019). This dataset includes revisions for the years 1988 to 2017 processed by EPA, after the National Analysis Dataset was released. Revisions submitted to EPA after this time are not reflected in TRI Explorer reports.*

(1) On-site Disposal or Other Releases include Underground Injection to Class I Wells (Section 5.4.1), RCRA Subtitle C Landfills (5.5.1A), Other Landfills (5.5.1B), Fugitive or Non-point Air Emissions (5.1), Stack or Point Air Emissions (5.2), Surface Water Discharges (5.3), Underground Injection to Class II-V Wells (5.4.2), Land Treatment/Application Farming (5.5.2), RCRA Subtitle C Surface Impoundments (5.5.3A), Other Surface Impoundments (5.5.3B), and Other Land Disposal (5.5.4). Off-site Disposal or Other Releases include from Section 6.2 Class I Underground Injection Wells (M81), Class II-V Underground Injection Wells (M82, M71), RCRA Subtitle C Landfills (M65), Other Landfills (M64, M72), Storage Only (M10), Solidification/Stabilization - Metals and Metal Category Compounds only (M41 or M40), Wastewater Treatment (excluding POTWs) - Metals and Metal Category Compounds only (M62 or M61), RCRA Subtitle C Surface Impoundments (M66), Other Surface Impoundments (M67, M63), Land Treatment (M73), Other Land Disposal (M79), Other Off-site Management (M90), Transfers to Waste Broker - Disposal (M94, M91), and Unknown (M99) and, from Section 6.1 Transfers to POTWs (metals and metal category compounds only).

(2) Off-site disposal or other releases show only net off-site disposal or other releases, that is, off-site disposal or other releases transferred to other TRI facilities reporting such transfers as on-site disposal or other releases are not included to avoid double counting.

This report may not include all states in the US. A state may not be included in this report for two reasons: 1) there are no facilities reporting to TRI in the particular state; or 2) the facilities reporting to TRI in the particular state did not report to TRI for the user-specified selection criteria.

Users of TRI information should be aware that TRI data reflect releases and other waste management activities of chemicals, not whether (or to what degree) the public has been exposed to those chemicals. Release estimates alone are not sufficient to determine exposure or to calculate potential adverse effects on human health and the environment. TRI data, in conjunction with other information, can be used as a starting point in evaluating exposures that may result from releases and other waste management activities which involve toxic chemicals. The determination of potential risk depends upon many factors, including the toxicity of the chemical, the fate of the chemical, and the amount and duration of human or other exposure to the chemical after it is released.

Source: *U.S. Environmental Protection Agency, TRI Explorer, July 9, 2019*

Advancing Sustainable Materials Management: 2015 Fact Sheet

Assessing Trends in Material Generation, Recycling, Composting, Combustion with Energy Recovery and Landfilling in the United States

July 2018

Source: *U.S. EPA, Advancing Sustainable Materials Management: 2015 Fact Sheet, July 2018*

Introduction

The U.S. Environmental Protection Agency (EPA) has collected and reported data on the generation and disposition of municipal solid waste (MSW) in the United States for more than 30 years. This information is used to measure the success of materials management programs across the country and to characterize the national waste stream. These facts and figures are based on the most recent information, which is from calendar year 2015.

In 2015, in the United States, approximately 262 million tons (U.S. short tons unless specified) of MSW were generated (*See* Figure 1). Of the MSW generated, approximately 68 million tons of MSW were recycled and 23 million tons of MSW were composted. Together, more than 91 million tons of MSW were recycled and composted, equivalent to a 34.7 percent recycling and composting rate (*See* Figure 2). In addition, more than 33 million tons of MSW (12.8 percent) were combusted with energy recovery. Finally, more than 137 million tons of MSW (52.5 percent) were landfilled (*See* Figure 3 and Table 1).

Information about waste generation and disposal is an important foundation for managing materials. Sustainably managing materials requires thinking beyond waste and instead focusing on the life cycle of a product, from the time it is produced, used, reused and ultimately recycled or discarded. This is known as Sustainable Materials Management (SMM). SMM refers to the use and reuse of materials in the most productive and sustainable way across their entire life cycle. SMM conserves resources, reduces waste and minimizes adverse environmental impacts from materials.

This report analyzes MSW trends in generation and management, materials and products, and economic indicators affecting MSW. It also includes a section on the generation of construction and demolition (C&D) debris, which is not a part of MSW, but comprises a significant portion of the non-hazardous solid waste stream.

Figure 1. MSW Generation Rates, 1960 to 2015

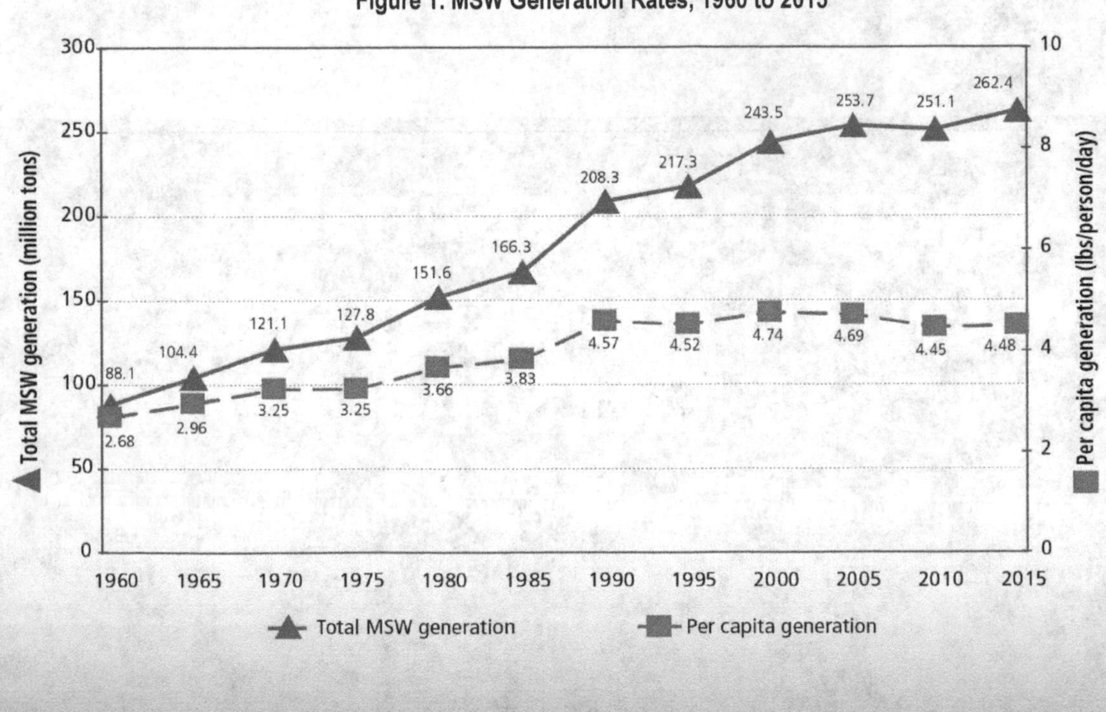

Source: *U.S. EPA, Advancing Sustainable Materials Management: 2015 Fact Sheet, July 2018*

Figure 2. MSW Recycling and Composting Rates, 1960 to 2015

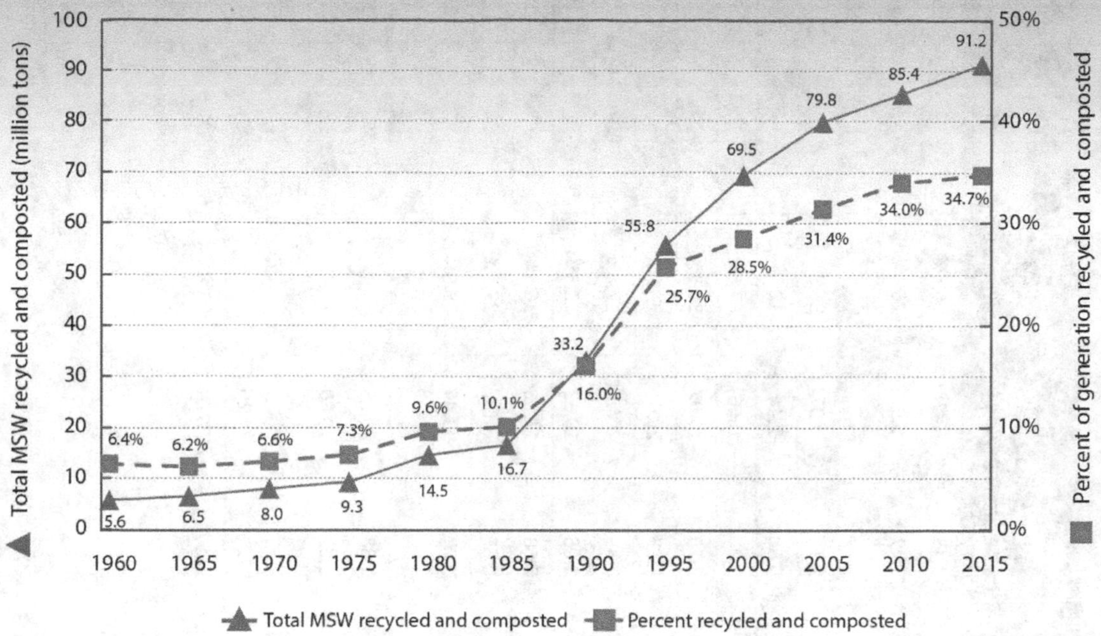

Total MSW recycled and composted (million tons)
Percent of generation recycled and composted
100
90
80
70
60
50
40
30
20
10
0
50%
40%
30%
20%
10%
0%
1960
1965
1970
1975
1980
1985
1990
1995
2000
2005
2010
2015
5.6
6.5
8.0
9.3
14.5
16.7
33.2
55.8
69.5
79.8
85.4
91.2
6.4%
6.2%
6.6%
7.3%
9.6%
10.1%
16.0%
25.7%
28.5%
31.4%
34.0%
34.7%
Total MSW recycled and composted
Percent recycled and composted

Figure 3. Management of MSW in the United States, 2015

Recycling
25.8%
Landfilling
52.5%
Composting
8.9%
Combustion with
Energy Recovery
12.8%

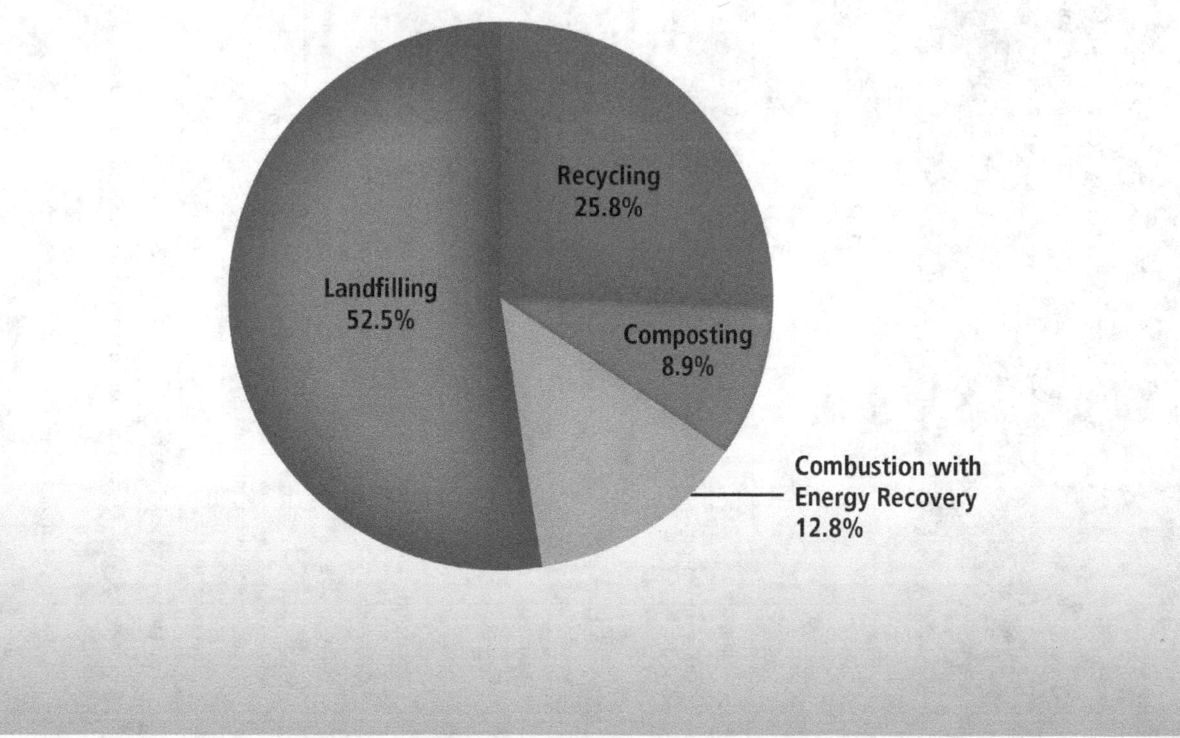

Source: *U.S. EPA, Advancing Sustainable Materials Management: 2015 Fact Sheet, July 2018*

Table 1. Generation, Recycling, Composting, Combustion with Energy Recovery and Landfilling of Materials in MSW, 2015*
(in millions of tons and percent of generation of each material)

Material	Weight Generated	Weight Recycled	Weight Composted	Weight Combusted with Energy Recovery	Weight Landfilled	Recycling as Percent of Generation	Composting as Percent of Generation	Combustion as Percent of Generation	Landfilling as Percent of Generation
Paper and paperboard	68.05	45.32	-	4.45	18.28	66.6%	-	6.5%	26.9%
Glass	11.47	3.03	-	1.47	6.97	26.4%	-	12.8%	60.8%
Metals									
Steel	18.17	6.06	-	2.14	9.97	33.3%	-	11.8%	54.9%
Aluminum	3.61	0.67	-	0.50	2.44	18.5%	-	13.9%	67.6%
Other nonferrous metals†	2.22	1.50	-	0.06	0.66	67.6%	-	2.7%	29.7%
Total metals	**24.00**	**8.23**	-	**2.70**	**13.07**	**34.3%**	-	11.2%	54.5%
Plastics	34.50	3.14	-	5.35	26.01	9.1%	-	15.5%	75.4%
Rubber and leather	8.48	1.51	-	2.49	4.48	17.8%	-	29.4%	52.8%
Textiles	16.03	2.45	-	3.05	10.53	15.3%	-	19.0%	65.7%
Wood	16.30	2.66	-	2.58	11.06	16.3%	-	15.8%	67.9%
Other materials	5.16	1.43	-	0.69	3.04	27.7%	-	13.4%	58.9%
Total materials in products	**183.99**	**67.77**	-	**22.78**	**93.44**	**36.8%**	-	**12.4%**	**50.8%**
Other wastes									
Food, other‡	39.73	-	2.10	7.38	30.25	-	5.3%	18.6%	76.1%
Yard trimmings	34.72	-	21.29	2.63	10.80	-	61.3%	7.6%	31.1%
Miscellaneous inorganic wastes	3.99	-	-	0.78	3.21	-	-	19.5%	80.5%
Total other wastes	**78.44**	-	**23.39**	**10.79**	**44.26**	-	**29.8%**	**13.8%**	**56.4%**
Total municipal solid waste	**262.43**	**67.77**	**23.39**	**33.57**	**137.70**	**25.8%**	**8.9%**	**12.8%**	**52.5%**

* Includes waste from residential, commercial and institutional sources.
† Includes lead from lead-acid batteries.
‡ Includes collection of other MSW organics for composting.

Details might not add to totals due to rounding.
Negligible = Less than 5,000 tons or 0.05 percent.
A dash in the table means that data are not available.

Source: *U.S. EPA, Advancing Sustainable Materials Management: 2015 Fact Sheet, July 2018*

Trends in Municipal Solid Waste

Our trash, or MSW, is comprised of various items consumers throw away. These items include packaging, food, yard trimmings, furniture, electronics, tires and appliances. MSW does not include industrial, hazardous or C&D waste. Sources of MSW include residential waste (including waste from multi-family housing) and waste from commercial and institutional locations, such as businesses, schools and hospitals.

Over the last few decades, the generation, recycling, composting, combustion with energy recovery and landfilling of MSW have changed substantially. Solid waste generation peaked at 4.74 pounds per person per day in 2000. However, the rate of 4.48 pounds per person per day in 2015 is slightly higher than the 2014 rate, which was 4.45 pounds per person per day (*See* Figure 1).

The combined recycling and composting rate increased from less than 10 percent of generated MSW in 1980 to 34.7 percent in 2015 (*See* Figure 2). Without including composting, recycling alone rose from 14.5 million tons (9.6 percent of MSW) in 1980 to 67.8 million tons (25.8 percent) in 2015. Composting was negligible in 1980, and it rose to 23.4 million tons in 2015 (8.9 percent; *see* Figure 3 and Table 2 for details).

Food

Nationally, the composting of food rose from 1.94 million tons in 2014 (5 percent of food) to 2.10 million tons in 2015 (5.3 percent of food).

Combustion with energy recovery was less than 2 percent of generation in 1980 (2.8 million tons). In 2015, more than 33.5 million tons (12.8 percent of MSW generated) were combusted with energy recovery (*See* Table 2).

Since 1990, the total amount of MSW going to landfills dropped by 7.6 million tons, from 145.3 million to 137.7 million tons in 2015 (*See* Table 2). The net per capita 2015 landfilling rate was 2.3 pounds per day, which was lower than the 3.2 per capita rate in 1990 (*See* Table 3).

Table 2. Generation, Recycling, Composting, Combustion with Energy Recovery and Landfilling of MSW, 1960 to 2015 (in millions of tons)

Activity	1960	1970	1980	1990	2000	2005	2010	2014	2015
Generation	88.1	121.1	151.6	208.3	243.5	253.7	251.1	259.0	262.4
Recycling	5.6	8.0	14.5	29.0	53.0	59.2	65.3	66.6	67.8
Composting*	neg.	neg.	neg.	4.2	16.5	20.6	20.2	23.0	23.4
Combustion with energy recovery†	0.0	0.5	2.8	29.8	33.7	31.7	29.3	33.2	33.5
Landfilling and other disposal‡	82.5	112.6	134.3	145.3	140.3	142.2	136.3	136.2	137.7

* Composting of yard trimmings, food and other MSW organic material. Does not include backyard composting.

† Includes combustion of MSW in mass burn or refuse-derived fuel form, and combustion with energy recovery of source separated materials in MSW (e.g., wood pallets, tire-derived fuel).

‡ Landfilling after recycling, composting and combustion with energy recovery. Includes combustion without energy recovery.

Details might not add to totals due to rounding.

neg. Negligible = less than 5,000 tons or 0.05 percent.

Source: *U.S. EPA, Advancing Sustainable Materials Management: 2015 Fact Sheet, July 2018*

Table 3. Generation, Recycling, Composting, Combustion with Energy Recovery and Landfilling of MSW, 1960 to 2015 (in pounds per person per day)

Activity	1960	1970	1980	1990	2000	2005	2010	2014	2015
Generation	2.7	3.3	3.7	4.6	4.7	4.7	4.4	4.4	4.5
Recycling	0.2	0.2	0.4	0.6	1.0	1.1	1.1	1.1	1.2
Composting*	neg.	neg.	neg.	0.1	0.3	0.4	0.4	0.4	0.4
Combustion with energy recovery†	0.0	neg.	0.1	0.7	0.7	0.6	0.5	0.6	0.6
Landfilling and other disposal‡	2.5	3.1	3.2	3.2	2.7	2.6	2.4	2.3	2.3
Population (In millions)	180.0	204.0	227.3	249.9	281.4	296.4	309.1	318.9	320.9

* Composting of yard trimmings, food, and other MSW organic material. Does not include backyard composting.

† Includes combustion of MSW in mass burn or refuse-derived fuel form, and combustion with energy recovery of source separated materials in MSW (e.g., wood pallets, tire-derived fuel).

‡ Landfilling after recycling, composting, and combustion with energy recovery. Includes combustion without energy recovery.

Details might not add to totals due to rounding.

neg. Negligible = less than 5,000 tons or 0.05 percent.

Analyzing MSW

EPA analyzes MSW by breaking down the data in two ways: by material or by product. Materials are made into products, which are ultimately reprocessed through recycling or composting, or managed by sending them to combustion with energy recovery facilities or landfills. Examples of materials that EPA tracks include paper and paperboard, plastics, metals, glass, rubber, leather, textiles, wood, food and yard trimmings. For a full list of materials, *see* Table 1.

Products are what people buy and handle, and they are manufactured out of the types of materials listed above. Product categories include containers and packaging, nondurable goods, durable goods, food and yard trimmings. Containers and packaging, such as milk cartons and plastic wrap, are assumed to be in use for a year or less; nondurable goods like newspaper and clothing are assumed to be in use for less than three years; and durable goods, such as furniture, are assumed to be in use for three or more years. Some products, such as appliances, may be made of more than one material. Information about products shows how consumers are using and discarding materials and offers strategies on how to maximize source reduction, recycling and composting of materials.

Materials in MSW

Table 1 and the following figures provide specific information about materials in municipal solid waste. Table 1 shows generation, recycling, composting, combustion with energy recovery and landfilling by material, by weight and percent of generation.

Source: *U.S. EPA, Advancing Sustainable Materials Management: 2015 Fact Sheet, July 2018*

Figure 4 below provides the breakdown of MSW generation by material. Paper and paperboard, and food continued to be the largest components of MSW generated. Paper and paperboard accounted for about 26 percent, while food accounted for 15 percent. Yard trimmings and plastics comprised about 13 percent each. The remaining amount of MSW generated consisted of rubber, leather, and textiles; metals; wood; glass and other materials.

Composting Collection Programs [1,2]

- About 3,860 community composting programs were documented in 2015—an increase from 3,227 in 2002.
- Food composting curbside collection programs served 3.8 million households in 2015. About 5.4 million households had access to drop-off food collection programs that year.

Figure 5 provides the breakdown of MSW recycling by material. Paper and paperboard was the largest component of MSW recycling, representing nearly 67 percent. Metals made up 12 percent of MSW recycled. The remaining amount of MSW recycled consisted of rubber, leather, and textiles; plastics; glass; wood and other materials.

Figure 6 provides the breakdown of MSW composting by material. Yard trimmings made up 91 percent of MSW composted. Food made up the remaining 9 percent of material composted.

Figure 7 provides the breakdown of MSW combustion with energy recovery.

Figure 8 provides the breakdown of MSW landfilling.

Figure 4. Total MSW Generation (by material), 2015
262 Million Tons

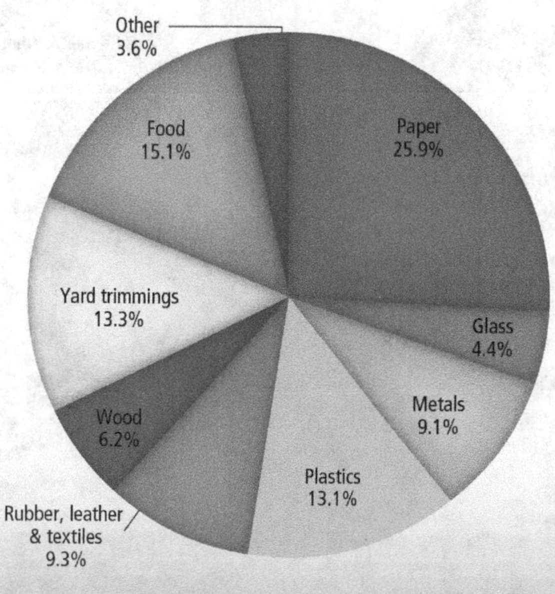

Source: *U.S. EPA, Advancing Sustainable Materials Management: 2015 Fact Sheet, July 2018*

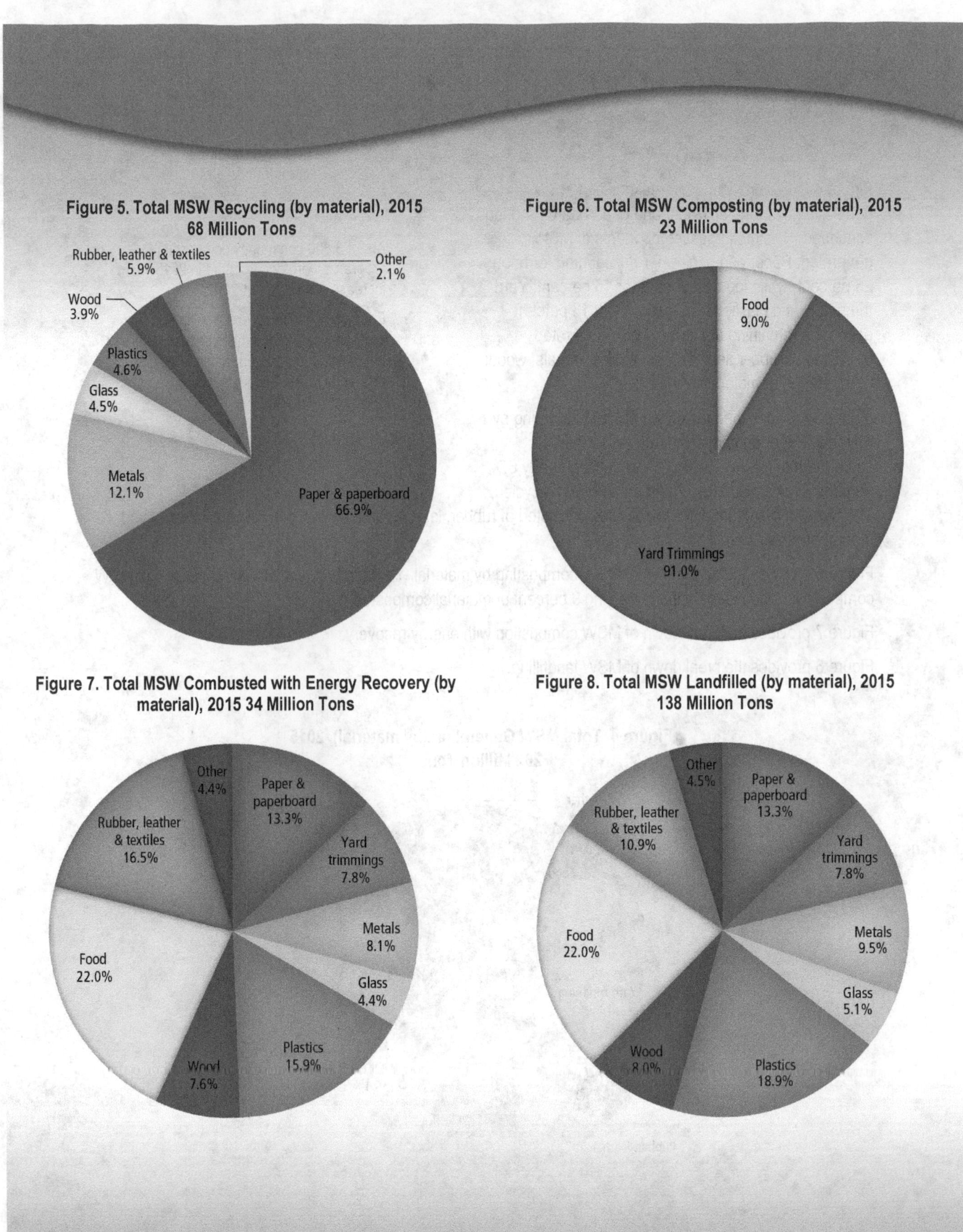

Source: *U.S. EPA, Advancing Sustainable Materials Management: 2015 Fact Sheet, July 2018*

Products in MSW

The following information provides the details of the products found in municipal solid waste. Table 4 shows generation, recycling, composting, combustion with energy recovery and landfilling by product category, weight and percent of generation. Figure 9 displays selected products with high recycling and composting rates.

Containers and packaging made up the largest portion of MSW generated at almost 78 million tons (29.7 percent). Nondurable and durable goods were more than 50 million tons each (about 20 percent for each). Food was 39.7 million tons (15.1 percent), yard trimmings were 34.7 million tons (13.2 percent), and other wastes were about four million tons (1.5 percent).

Containers and packaging was the product category with the highest recycling rate with approximately 53 percent of the generated materials recycled. Paper products, steel and aluminum were the most recycled materials by percentage in this category. The recycling of nondurable goods was approximately 31 percent. Paper products such as newspapers/mechanical papers were the most recycled nondurable goods. Newspapers/mechanical papers include newspapers, directories, inserts, as well as some advertisement and direct mail printing. Overall, about 19 percent of durable goods were recycled. With a 99 percent recycling rate, lead-acid batteries continued to be one of the most recycled products.

Yard trimmings was the product category with the highest composting rate at 61.3 percent. Food in MSW was composted at a rate of 5.3 percent.

Food was the product category with the highest rate of combustion with energy recovery with a rate of nearly 19 percent. Durable goods were combusted at a rate of nearly 16 percent and nondurables at a rate of nearly 14 percent. Containers and packaging, and yard trimmings were combusted at rates below 10 percent.

Food was the product category with the highest landfill rate at 76 percent. Durable goods followed with a landfill rate of 65 percent. Nondurable goods had the third highest landfill rate at 55 percent. Containers and packaging, and yard trimmings were the product categories with the lowest landfill rates at 38 percent and 31 percent, respectively.

Recycling Rates

Measured by percentage of generation, products with the highest recycling rates in 2015 were lead-acid batteries (99 percent), corrugated boxes (92.3 percent), steel cans (71.3 percent), newspapers/mechanical papers (71.2 percent), major appliances (61.7 percent), aluminum cans (54.9 percent), mixed paper (43.6 percent), tires (40.2 percent) and selected consumer electronics (39.8 percent). The 2015 composting rate for yard trimmings was 61.3 percent (*See* 2015 data tables).

Source: *U.S. EPA, Advancing Sustainable Materials Management: 2015 Fact Sheet, July 2018*

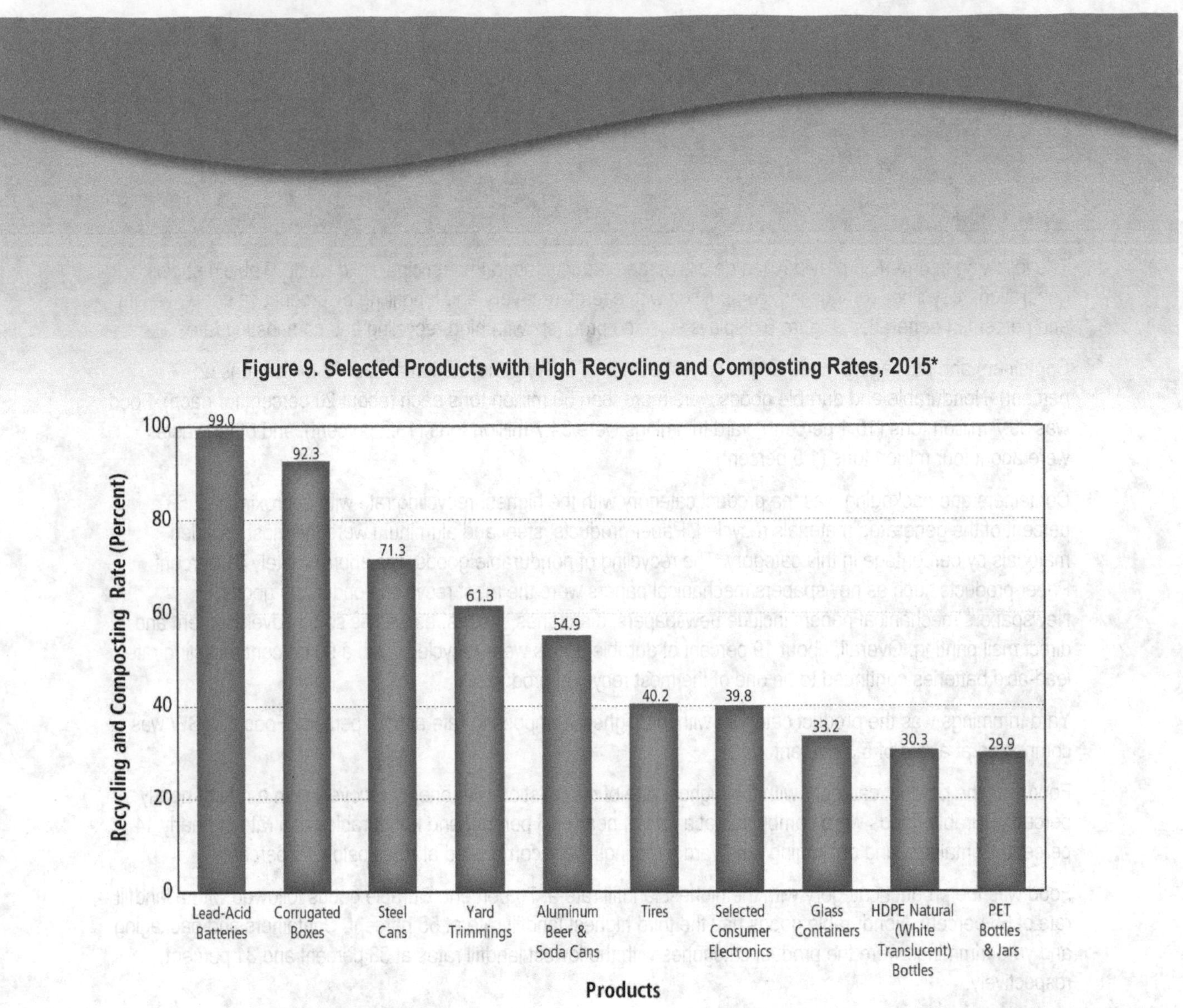

Source: *U.S. EPA, Advancing Sustainable Materials Management: 2015 Fact Sheet, July 2018*

Table 4. Generation, Recycling, Composting, Combustion with Energy Recovery and Landfilling of Products in MSW, 2015*
(in millions of tons and percent of generation of each product)

Products	Weight Generated	Weight Recycled	Weight Composted	Weight Combusted with Energy Recovery	Weight Landfilled	Recycling as Percent of Generation	Composting as Percent of Generation	Combustion as Percent of Generation	Landfilling as Percent of Generation
Durable goods									
Steel	15.95	4.44	-	2.02	9.49	27.8%	-	12.7%	59.5%
Aluminum	1.55	-	-	0.22	1.33	-	-	14.2%	85.8%
Other nonferrous metals†	2.22	1.50	-	0.06	0.66	67.6%	-	2.7%	29.7%
Glass	2.35	Negligible	-	0.27	2.08	Negligible	-	11.5%	88.5%
Plastics	12.50	0.83	-	1.49	10.18	6.6%	-	11.9%	81.5%
Rubber and leather	7.35	1.51	-	2.27	3.57	20.5%	-	30.9%	48.6%
Wood	6.48	Negligible	-	1.18	5.30	Negligible	-	18.2%	81.8%
Textiles	3.94	0.54	-	1.06	2.34	13.7%	-	26.9%	59.4%
Other materials	1.81	1.43	-	0.03	0.35	79.0%	-	1.7%	19.3%
Total durable goods	**54.15**	**10.25**	**-**	**8.60**	**35.30**	**18.9%**	**-**	**15.9%**	**65.2%**
Nondurable goods									
Paper and paperboard	28.12	14.12	-	2.74	11.26	50.2%	-	9.8%	40.0%
Plastics	7.32	0.16	-	1.40	5.76	2.2%	-	19.1%	78.7%
Rubber and leather	1.13	Negligible	-	0.22	0.91	Negligible	-	19.5%	80.5%
Textiles	11.77	1.91	-	1.93	7.93	16.2%	-	16.4%	67.4%
Other materials	3.58	Negligible	-	0.70	2.88	Negligible	-	19.6%	80.4%
Total nondurable goods	**51.92**	**16.19**	**-**	**6.99**	**28.74**	**31.2%**	**-**	**13.5%**	**55.3%**

(Continued on next page)

Source: *U.S. EPA, Advancing Sustainable Materials Management: 2015 Fact Sheet, July 2018*

Table 4. Generation, Recycling, Composting, Combustion with Energy Recovery and Landfilling of Products in MSW, 2015*
(in millions of tons and percent of generation of each product)

Products	Weight Generated	Weight Recycled	Weight Composted	Weight Combusted with Energy Recovery	Weight Landfilled	Recycling as Percent of Generation	Composting as Percent of Generation	Combustion as Percent of Generation	Landfilling as Percent of Generation
Containers and packaging									
Steel	2.22	1.62	-	0.12	0.48	73.0%	-	5.4%	21.6%
Aluminum	1.84	0.67	-	0.24	0.93	36.4%	-	13.0%	50.6%
Glass	9.12	3.03	-	1.20	4.89	33.2%	-	13.2%	53.6%
Paper and paperboard	39.92	31.20	-	1.71	7.01	78.2%	-	4.3%	17.5%
Plastics	14.68	2.15	-	2.46	10.07	14.6%	-	16.8%	68.6%
Wood	9.82	2.66	-	1.40	5.76	27.1%	-	14.3%	58.6%
Other materials	0.32	Negligible	-	0.06	0.26	Negligible	-	18.8%	81.2%
Total containers and packaging	**77.92**	**41.33**	**-**	**7.19**	**29.40**	**53.1%**	**-**	**9.2%**	**37.7%**
Other wastes									
Food, other‡	39.73	-	2.10	7.38	30.25	-	5.3%	18.6%	76.1%
Yard trimmings	34.72	-	21.29	2.63	10.80	-	61.3%	7.6%	31.1%
Miscellaneous inorganic wastes	3.99	-	-	0.78	3.21	-	-	19.5%	80.5%
Total other wastes	**78.44**	**-**	**23.39**	**10.79**	**44.26**	**-**	**29.8%**	**13.8%**	**56.4%**
Total municipal solid waste	**262.43**	**67.77**	**23.39**	**33.57**	**137.70**	**25.8%**	**8.9%**	**12.8%**	**52.5%**

* Includes waste from residential, commercial and institutional sources.

† Includes lead from lead-acid batteries.

‡ Includes collection of other MSW organics for composting.

Details might not add to totals due to rounding.

Negligible = less than 5,000 tons or 0.05 percent.

A dash in the table means that data are not available.

Source: *U.S. EPA, Advancing Sustainable Materials Management: 2015 Fact Sheet, July 2018*

Economic Indicators

The Benefits of Recycling

How our nation uses materials is fundamental to our economic and environmental future. Global competition for finite resources is expected to continue to increase. A more productive and less impactful use of materials helps our society remain economically competitive, contributes to our prosperity and protects the environment. By using waste materials as valuable raw materials, recycling creates jobs, builds more competitive manufacturing industries and significantly contributes to the U.S. economy.

EPA's 2001 Recycling Economic Information (REI) Study evaluated the number of recycling jobs, wages and tax revenue. The Agency updated the study with a 2016 REI Report[3] to increase the understanding of the economic implications of material reuse and recycling. The 2016 REI Report included updated information about the number of recycling jobs, wages and tax revenue (*See* Figure 10). The report showed that the recycling and reuse of materials creates jobs while also generating local and state tax revenues. The data from the most recent year available (2007) showed that in 2007, recycling and reuse activities in the United States accounted for:

- 757,000 jobs;
- $36.6 billion in wages; and
- $6.7 billion in tax revenues.

This equates to 1.57 jobs for every 1,000 tons of materials recycled. Construction and demolition debris provided the largest contribution to all three categories (jobs, wages and tax revenue), followed by ferrous metals and nonferrous metals, such as aluminum.

The 2016 REI Report used an updated analytical framework and a new Waste Input-Output methodology, which focused on the life cycle of materials. These refinements offered significant improvements over the original 2001 REI Study by providing a better definition of recycling and addressing double counting. This new methodology assists decision makers and researchers in more accurately estimating the economic benefits of recycling, and it creates a foundation upon which additional studies can be built.

Source: *U.S. EPA, Advancing Sustainable Materials Management: 2015 Fact Sheet, July 2018*

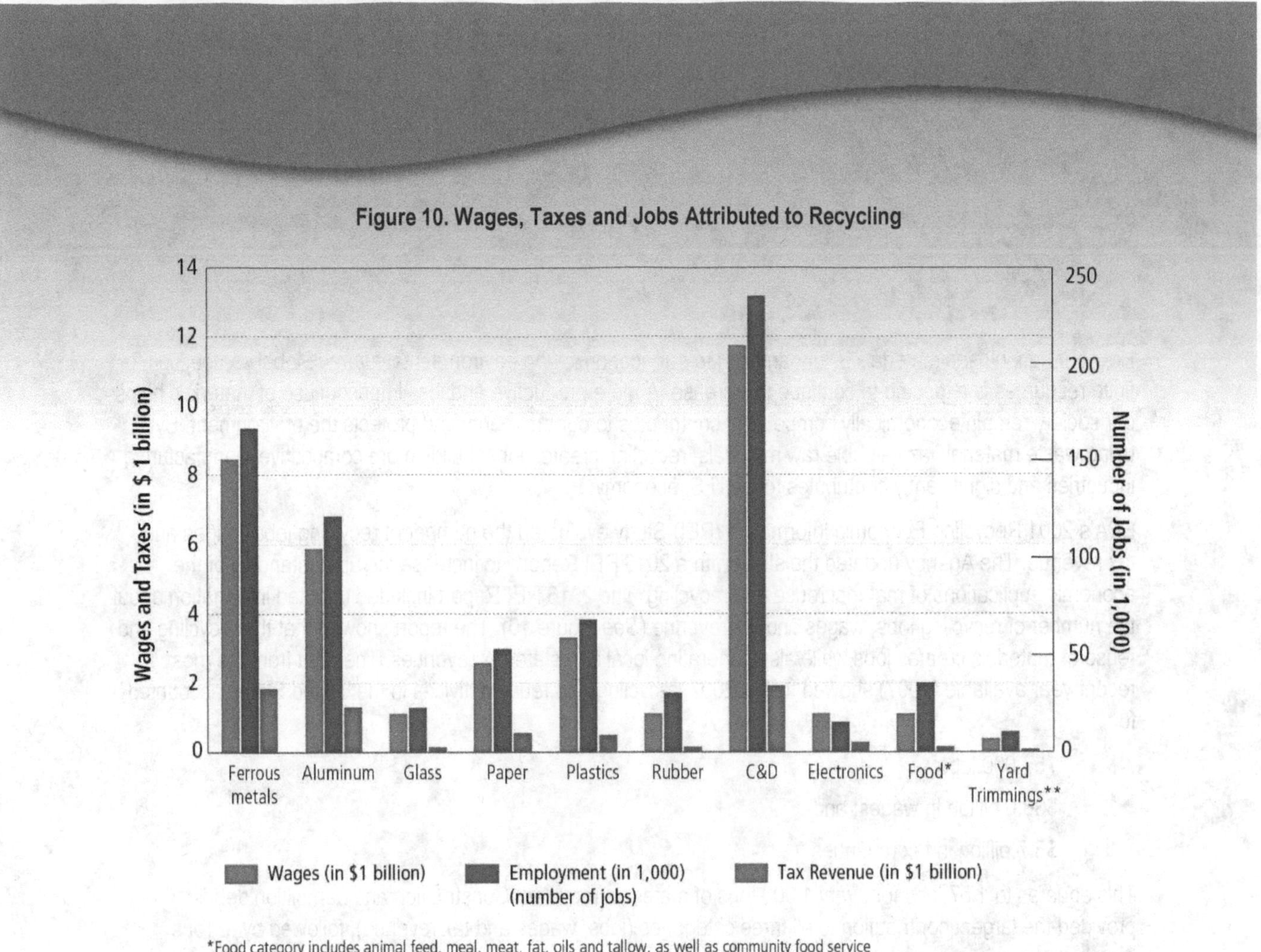

Recycled Commodity Values

Normalized to 2015, using the Consumer Price Index (CPI) from the Bureau of Labor Statistics to account for inflation, Figure 11 depicts the commodity values for high-density polyethylene (HDPE) natural bottles; polyethylene terephthalate (PET) clear bottles; aluminum used beverage cans (UBC); steel cans; old newspaper (ONP) (grade 6); old corrugated containers (OCC) (grade 11); paper stock (PS) (grade 1) soft mixed paper; and glass containers from 1990 to 2015.

Data were not available for ONP, metals, plastics and glass in 1997 and 1998. For plastics, glass and metals, there was a transition in data sources between 1996 and 1999 and between 2004 and 2005, so some of the change between years could be due to the methodology of the data source for capturing data.

Figure 11 shows the indexed values by year for the recycled commodities. It is indexed to allow commodity values with different metrics, such as dollars per ton, dollars per gross ton and dollars per short ton, to be shown on the same graph and to compare their relative rates of change. The indexed value indicates the change in value of the data since 1990, where one is equal to the value in 1990. For example, if for a given year the indexed value were two, then the commodity value for that year would be two times the 1990 value. In this case, if the 1990 value were 400, then the resulting year's value would be 800.

Source: *U.S. EPA, Advancing Sustainable Materials Management: 2015 Fact Sheet, July 2018*

Figure 11 shows similar trends across all commodities for indexed values. For example, values for plastics and papers spiked in 1995, and values for most commodities dipped in 2009 relative to their values in 1990. Additionally, many commodities, such as plastics and papers, also experienced a price spike in 2000, 2007 and 2011. In contrast, the indexed lines for glass (which represent an average of flint, amber and green glass container values), aluminum and steel cans appear to fluctuate less frequently.

Figure 11. Indexed Recycled Commodity Values by Year

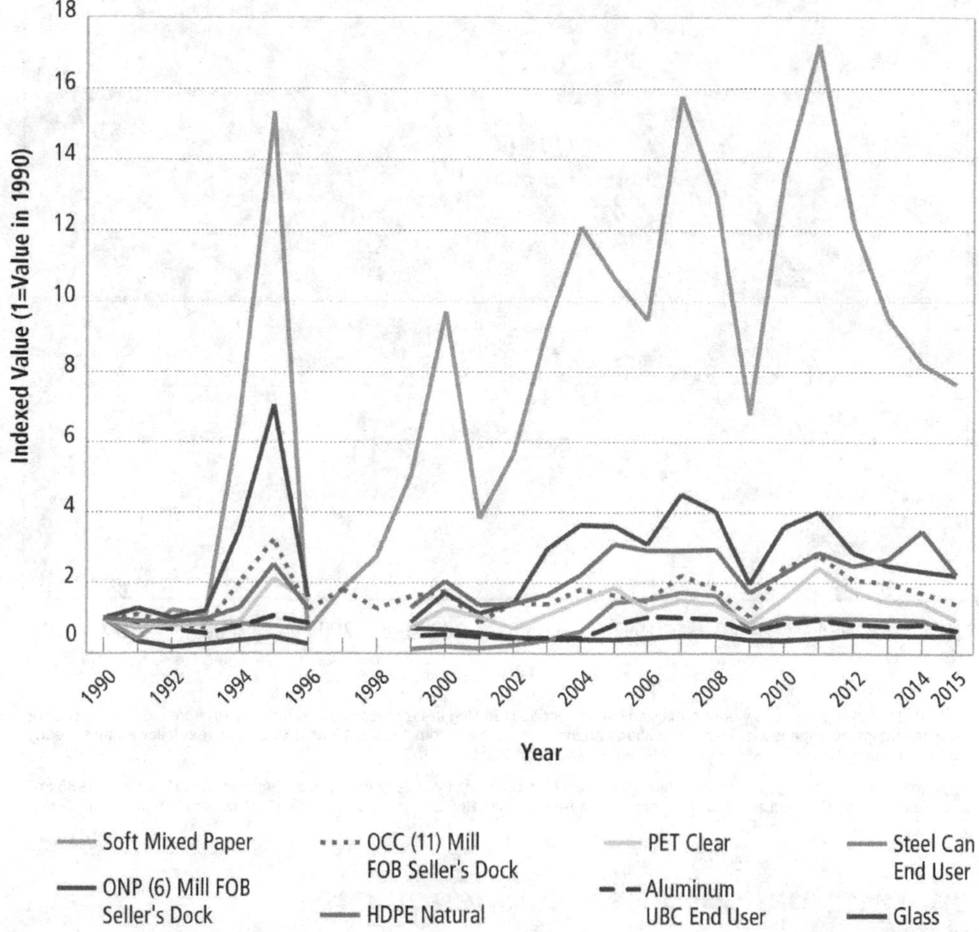

National mean annual commodity values were normalized to constant $2015 using the Consumer Price Index (CPI) from the Bureau of Labor Statistics to allow meaningful comparisons. 1990 has an indexed value of 1. Soft mixed paper consists of a clean, sorted mixture of various qualities of paper not limited as to type of fiber content. Prohibitive Materials may not exceed 1 percent. There are specific limits on the percent of contaminants allowed in soft mixed paper.

Source: Pulp & Paper Global Fact & Price Book, 2003-2004. Page 128. Paperloop, Inc. 2004.

Secondary Materials Pricing and Secondary Fiber Pricing. 2003-2015. Released September 2017. Available at http://www.recyclingmarkets.net/. Accessed September 2017.

1970 to 2004 historical data tabulated from weekly or monthly industry publications and averaged annually during the time periods shown. Publications included Waste Age Recycling Times, Waste News, Paper Recycler, Miller Freeman, Inc.

Source: *U.S. EPA, Advancing Sustainable Materials Management: 2015 Fact Sheet, July 2018*

Landfill Tipping Fees

From 1985 to 1995 there was a rapid rise in national landfill tipping fees, followed by a steady decrease from 1995 to 2004. Since 2004, there has been a slow and steady average increase of about one percent per year in landfill tipping fees (*See* Figure 12). The tipping fees are expressed in constant 2015 dollars.

Figure 12. National Landfill Tipping Fees, 1982-2015 ($2015 per ton)

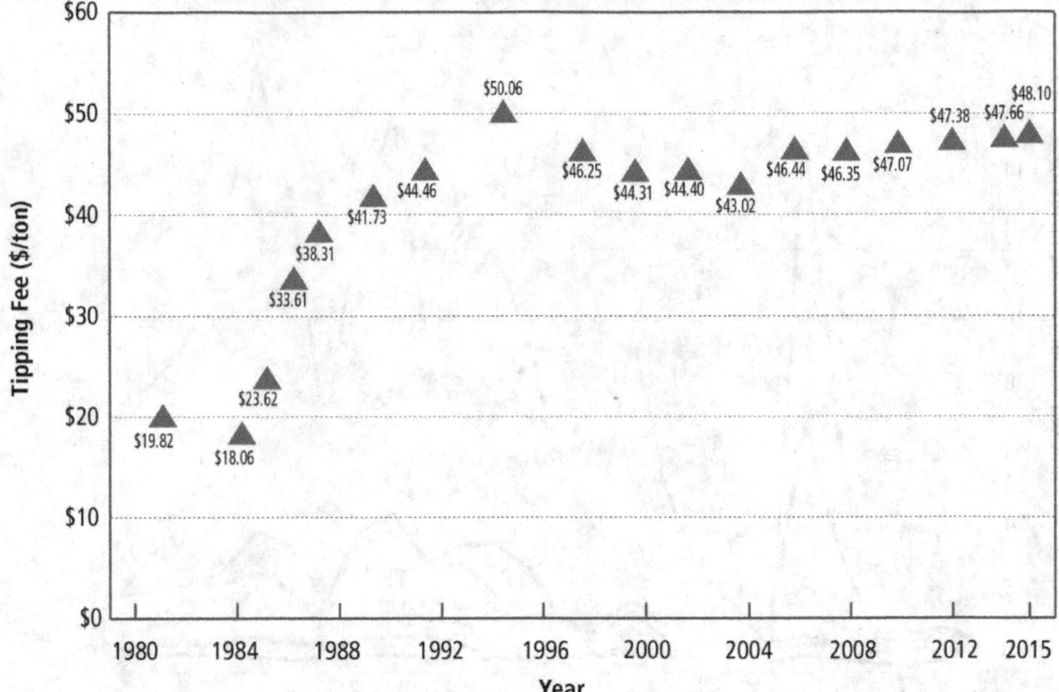

National mean annual landfill tipping fees were normalized to constant $2015 using the Consumer Price Index (CPI) from the Bureau of Labor Statistics to allow meaningful comparisons. This figure shows an average increase from 1985 to 1995 of $3.20 per year followed by a steady decrease of $0.78 per year followed by an increase of $0.46 per year from 2004 to 2015.

Source: National Solid Wastes Management Association (NSWMA) Municipal Solid Waste Landfill Facts. October 2011 (Data from 1985 to 2008). Waste Business Journal. "The Cost to Landfill MSW Continues to Rise Despite Soft Demand." July 11, 2017 (Data for 2010 to 2015).

MSW Generation and Household Spending

In the U.S., the change in the amount of MSW generated typically mirrors trends in how much money households spent on goods and services. Personal Consumer Expenditures (PCE) measure household spending on goods and services such as food, clothing, vehicles and recreation services. PCE is one of the four components of economic growth, along with government spending, private investments and net exports. As PCE is an indicator of the household consumption of goods and services, which make up nearly 70 percent of the gross domestic product (GDP), PCE has a stronger conceptual tie to MSW generation than the other three GDP components. PCE adjusted for inflation is referred to as real PCE. This metric is more useful in making comparisons over time because it normalizes the value of a dollar by considering how much a dollar could

Source: *U.S. EPA, Advancing Sustainable Materials Management: 2015 Fact Sheet, July 2018*

purchase in the past versus today. Figure 13 explores the relationship between MSW generated and real PCE since 1960.

Figure 13 is an indexed graph showing the relative changes in real PCE, MSW generated and MSW generated per capita over time. It is indexed to allow all three of these metrics to be shown on the same graph and to compare their relative rates of change since 1960. The indexed value indicates the change in the value of the data since 1960. For example, if for a given year the value were three, then the data value for that year would be three times the 1960 value. In this case, if the 1960 value were 200, then the resulting year's value would be 600. The 2015 MSW per capita generation indexed value is 1.7, which means MSW per capita generation has increased by 70 percent since 1960.

Figure 13 shows that real PCE has increased at a faster rate than MSW generation, and the disparity has become even more distinct since the mid-1990s. This metric indicates the amount of MSW generated per dollar spent is falling. In other words, the U.S. economy has been able to enjoy dramatic increases in household spending on consumer goods and services without the societal impact of similarly increasing MSW generation rates. This figure also shows that the MSW generated per capita leveled off in the early-to-mid 2000s.

Figure 13. Indexed MSW Generated and Real PCE over Time (1960-2015)

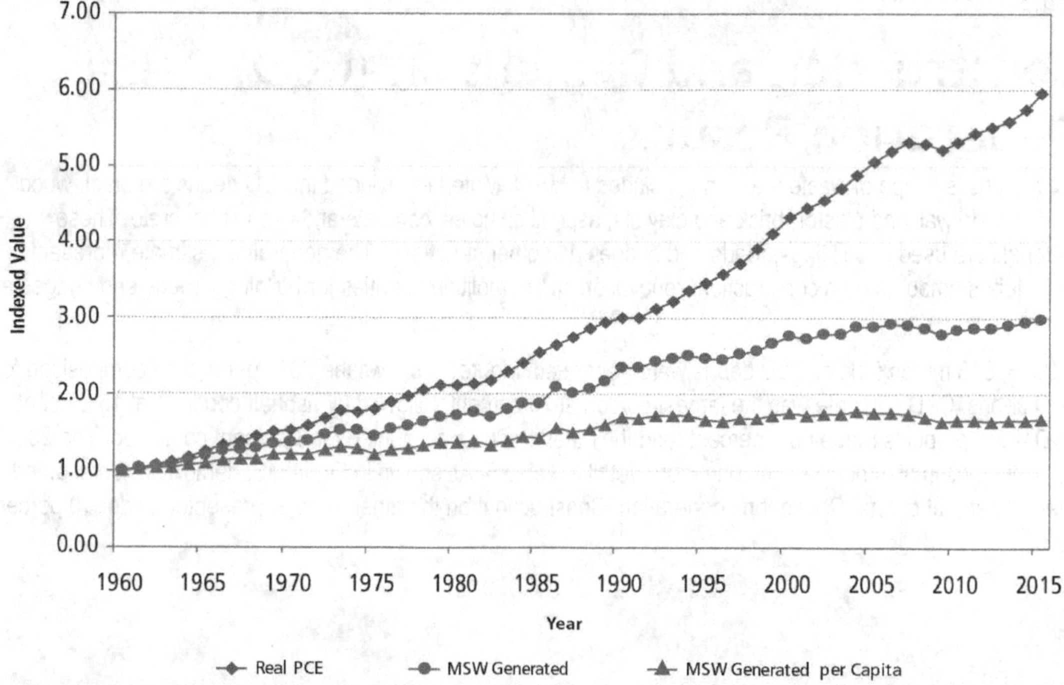

Source: *U.S. EPA, Advancing Sustainable Materials Management: 2015 Fact Sheet, July 2018*

MSW Methodology

The data summarized in this fact sheet characterizes the MSW stream as a whole by using a materials flow methodology that relies on a mass balance approach. EPA recognizes that there are several approaches to measuring material flows, such as by volume. To be consistent, EPA reports the quantities of materials in tons in the current fact sheet but will continue to explore options for alternative measurement quantifications to describe materials management in the United States.

EPA has consistently used materials flow analysis to allow for the comparison of data over the last three decades. EPA recognizes that this methodology differs from other methodologies that also estimate the generation of MSW and other waste data. EPA will continue to work with stakeholders to identify methodologies and additional publicly available data to improve our national understanding of materials flow in the United States.

Using data gathered from industry associations, businesses and government sources, such as the U.S. Department of Commerce and the U.S. Census Bureau, we estimate the weight in tons of all MSW materials and products generated, recycled, composted, combusted with energy recovery and landfilled. Other sources of data, such as waste characterizations and research reports performed by governments, industry or the press, supplement these data.

Construction and Demolition (C&D) Debris Generation Results

C&D debris is a type of waste that is not included in MSW. Materials included in C&D debris are steel, wood products, drywall and plaster, brick and clay tile, asphalt shingles, concrete and asphalt concrete. These materials are used in buildings, roads and bridges and other structures. The generation estimate represents C&D debris amounts from construction, renovation and demolition activities for buildings, roads and bridges and other structures.

In 2015, 548 million tons of C&D debris were generated. Figure 14 shows the 2015 generation composition for C&D debris. C&D concrete was the largest portion at 70 percent, followed by asphalt concrete at 15 percent. C&D wood products made up 7 percent, and the other products accounted for 8 percent combined. The 2015 generation estimates are presented in more detail in Table 5. As shown in Figure 15, demolition represented over 90 percent of total C&D debris generation. Construction, on the other hand, represented under 10 percent.

Source: *U.S. EPA, Advancing Sustainable Materials Management: 2015 Fact Sheet, July 2018*

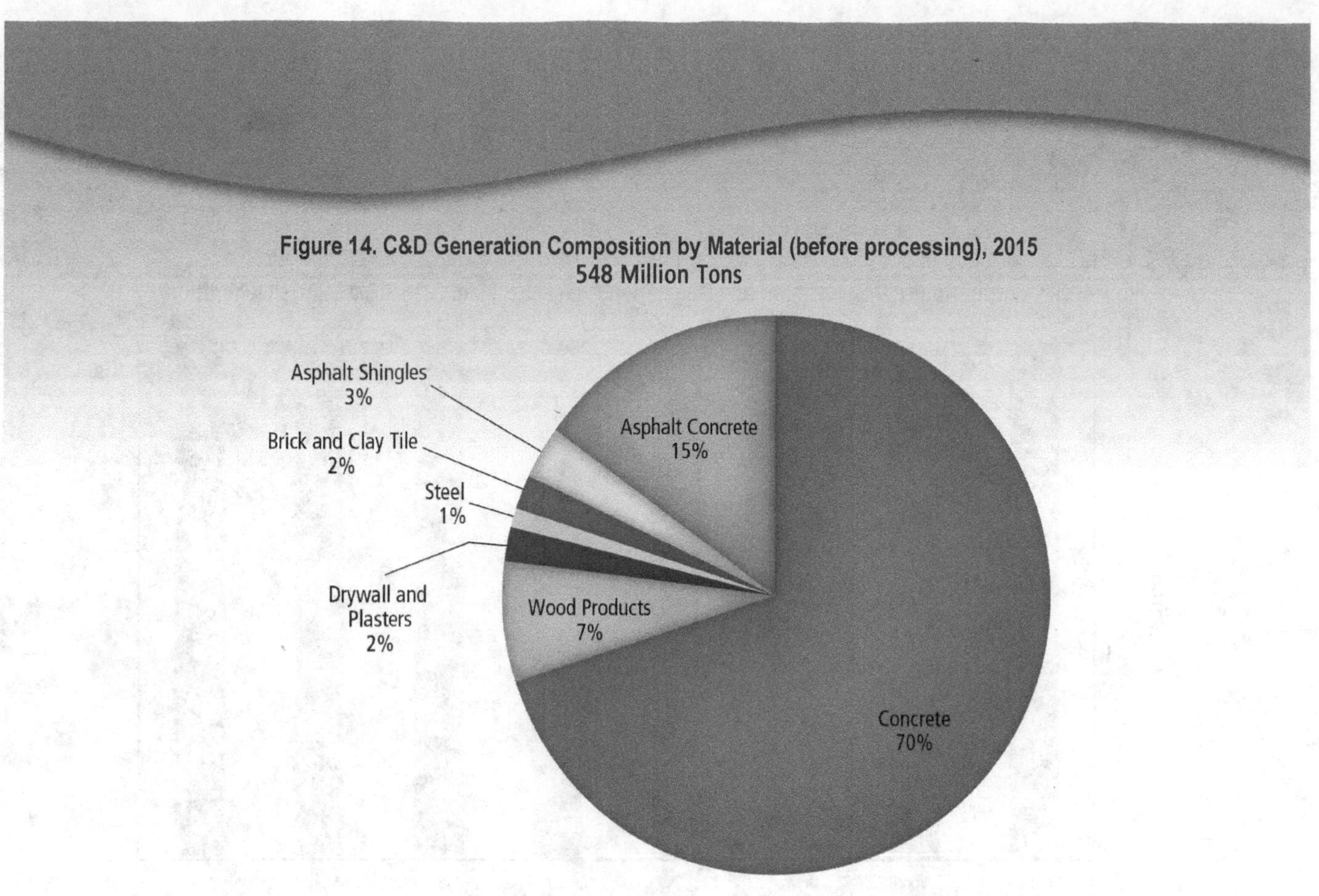

Figure 14. C&D Generation Composition by Material (before processing), 2015
548 Million Tons

Table 5. C&D Debris Generation by Material and Activity, 2015 (in millions of tons)

	Waste During Construction	Demolition Debris	Total C&D Debris
Concrete	23.1	358.7	381.8
Wood Products[1]	2.8	36.1	38.9
Drywall and Plasters	2.5	10.5	13.0
Steel[2]	0.0	4.5	4.5
Brick and Clay Tile	0.3	11.9	12.2
Asphalt Shingles	0.9	12.6	13.5
Asphalt Concrete	0.0	83.9	83.9
Total	**29.6**	**518.2**	**547.8**

1 Wood consumption in buildings also includes some lumber consumed for the construction of other structures. Data were not available to allocate lumber consumption for non-residential and unspecified uses between buildings and other structures except for railroad ties. Since non-residential buildings such as barns, warehouses and small commercial buildings are assumed to consume a greater amount of lumber than other structures, the amount of lumber for construction remaining after the amount for railroad ties is split out is included in the buildings source category.

2 Steel consumption in buildings also includes steel consumed for the construction of roads and bridges. Data were not available to allocate steel consumption across different sources, but buildings are assumed to consume the largest portion of steel for construction.

Source: *U.S. EPA, Advancing Sustainable Materials Management: 2015 Fact Sheet, July 2018*

Figure 15. Contribution of Construction and Demolition Phases to Total 2015 C&D Debris Generation

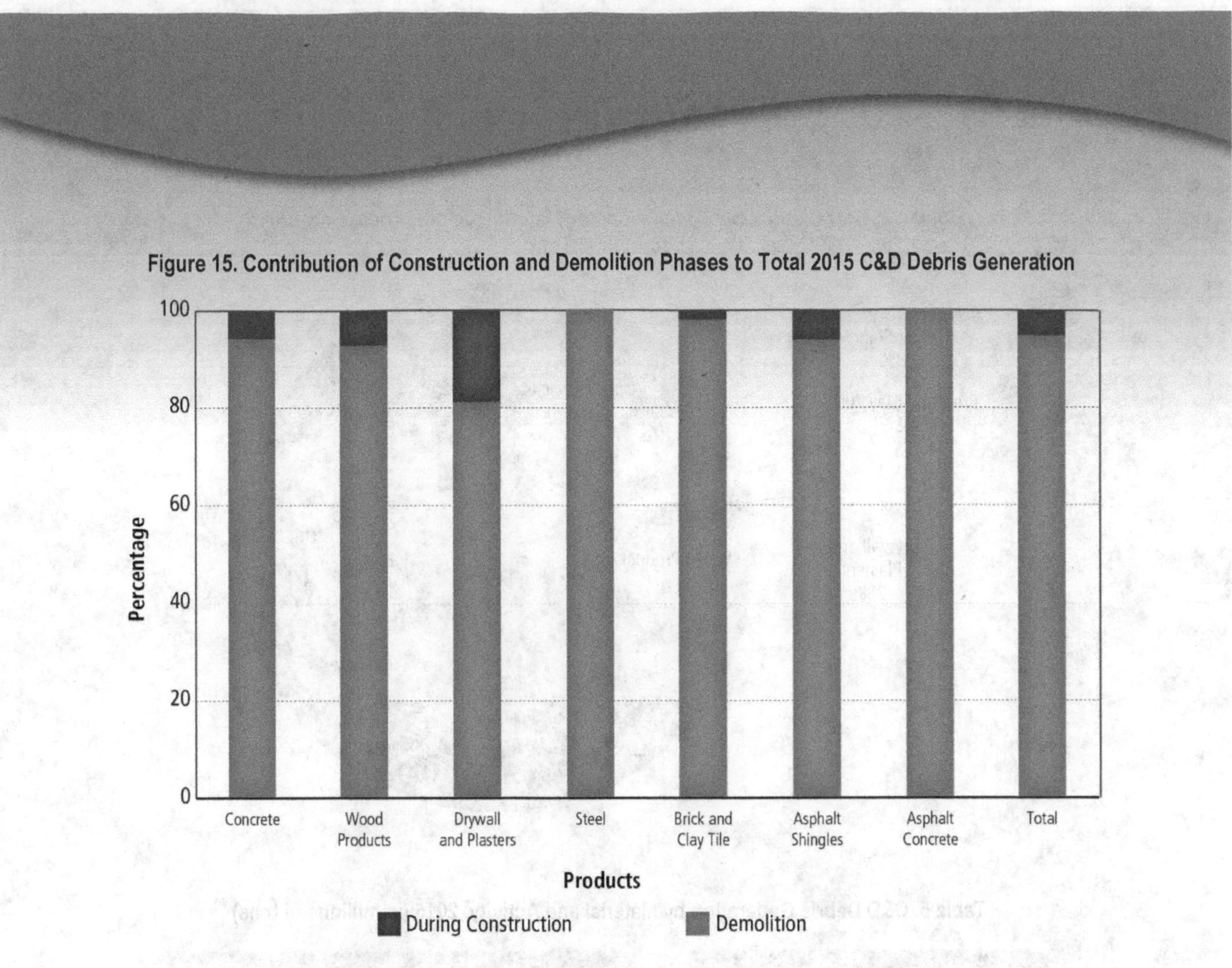

Table 6 displays the amount of C&D debris generation from buildings, roads and bridges and other structures for each material. The "other structures" category includes C&D debris generation estimates from communication, power, transportation, sewer and waste disposal, water supply, conservation and development and the manufacturing infrastructure. In 2015, roads and bridges contributed significantly more to C&D debris generation than buildings and other structures, and concrete made up the largest share of C&D debris generation for all three categories.

Source: U.S. EPA, Advancing Sustainable Materials Management: 2015 Fact Sheet, July 2018

Table 6. C&D Debris Generation by Source, 2015 (in millions of tons)

	Buildings	Roads and Bridges	Other
Concrete	88.4	158.4	135.0
Wood Products[1]	37.6	-	1.4
Drywall and Plasters	13.0	-	-
Steel[2]	4.5	-	-
Brick and Clay Tile	12.1	-	-
Asphalt Shingles	13.5	-	-
Asphalt Concrete	-	83.9	-
Total	**169.1**	**242.3**	**136.4**

[1] Wood consumption in buildings also includes some lumber consumed for the construction of other structures. Data were not available to allocate lumber consumption for non-residential and unspecified uses between buildings and other structures except for railroad ties. Since non-residential buildings such as barns, warehouses and small commercial buildings are assumed to consume a greater amount of lumber than other structures, the amount of lumber for construction remaining after the amount for railroad ties is split out is included in the buildings source category.

[2] Steel consumption in buildings also includes steel consumed for the construction of roads and bridges. Data were not available to allocate steel consumption across different sources, but buildings are assumed to consume the largest portion of steel for construction.

A dash in the table means that data are not available.

Thinking Beyond Waste

Measuring and understanding the data on MSW generation, recycling, composting, combustion with energy recovery and landfilling is an important foundation for knowing where these valuable resources are going. It is a starting point to figure out trends and ways to more efficiently use these resources and how to keep them in use. EPA is helping change the way our society views the materials and resources in solid waste by thinking beyond recycling, composting, combustion and landfilling. By going beyond the concept of "Reduce, Reuse, Recycle," EPA is employing a systemic approach to reduce material use and associated environmental impacts over the entire life cycle of materials through a process called Sustainable Materials Management (SMM). This process starts with the extraction of natural resources and material processing through product design and manufacturing, followed by the product use stage, then collection/processing, and lastly, end-of-life management. By examining how materials are used throughout their life cycle, an SMM approach seeks to use materials in the most productive way with an emphasis on using fewer materials and products, and reducing environmental impacts throughout the life cycle of a material. See https://www.epa.gov/smm for more information.

Source: *U.S. EPA, Advancing Sustainable Materials Management: 2015 Fact Sheet, July 2018*

Resources

The 2015 data tables and the summary of the MSW characterization methodology are available on the EPA website, along with information about waste reduction, recycling and sustainable materials management.

Please visit:

https://www.epa.gov/facts-and-figures-about-materials-waste-and-recycling

https://www.epa.gov/recycle

https://www.epa.gov/smm

Endnotes

1. Source for 2002 community composting program data: "The State of Garbage In America." Simmons, Phil, Scott M. Kaufman, and Nickolas J. Themelis. *BioCycle* 47, no. 4, p. 26 (2006). Source for 2015 data: Goldstein, N. 2017, "The State of Organics." *BioCycle*, October, p. 5, Table 2. Facilities composting yard trimmings, yard trimmings and food, and mixed organics. Excludes 740 facilities composting manure, biosolids, mixed MSW or not defined.
2. Sources for food composting collection programs: Streeter, V.; Platt B. 2017. Residential Food Waste Collection Access in the U.S. *BioCycle* December. Programs included are programs with startup dates in 2015 or earlier. Programs started in 2016 and 2017 are excluded. Programs with no startup date provided in the source document or identified through internet searches are also excluded.
3. US EPA. 2016. "Recycling Economic Information Report" (2016). https://www.epa.gov/smm/recycling-economic-information-rei-report.

Source: U.S. EPA, Advancing Sustainable Materials Management: 2015 Fact Sheet, July 2018

Advancing Sustainable Materials Management: 2015 Tables and Figures

Assessing Trends in Material Generation, Recycling, Composting, Combustion with Energy Recovery and Landfilling in the United States

July 2018

Source: *U.S. EPA, Advancing Sustainable Materials Management: 2015 Tables and Figures, July 2018*

Table 1. Materials Generated* in the Municipal Waste Stream, 1960 to 2015
(In thousands of tons and percent of total generation)

Materials	Thousands of Tons								
	1960	1970	1980	1990	2000	2005	2010	2014	2015
Paper and Paperboard	29,990	44,310	55,160	72,730	87,740	84,840	71,310	68,610	68,050
Glass	6,720	12,740	15,130	13,100	12,770	12,540	11,520	11,480	11,470
Metals									
Ferrous	10,300	12,360	12,620	12,640	14,150	15,210	16,920	17,880	18,170
Aluminum	340	800	1,730	2,810	3,190	3,330	3,510	3,530	3,610
Other Nonferrous	180	670	1,160	1,100	1,600	1,860	2,020	2,230	2,220
Total Metals	*10,820*	*13,830*	*15,510*	*16,550*	*18,940*	*20,400*	22,450	23,640	24,000
Plastics	390	2,900	6,830	17,130	25,550	29,380	31,400	33,390	34,500
Rubber and Leather	1,840	2,970	4,200	5,790	6,670	7,290	7,750	8,210	8,480
Textiles	1,760	2,040	2,530	5,810	9,480	11,510	13,220	15,240	16,030
Wood	3,030	3,720	7,010	12,210	13,570	14,790	15,710	16,120	16,300
Other **	70	770	2,520	3,190	4,000	4,290	4,710	5,120	5,160
Total Materials in Products	*54,620*	*83,280*	*108,890*	*146,510*	*178,720*	*185,040*	*178,070*	*181,810*	*183,990*
Other Wastes									
Food	12,200	12,800	13,000	23,860	30,700	32,930	35,740	38,670	39,730
Yard Trimmings	20,000	23,200	27,500	35,000	30,530	32,070	33,400	34,500	34,720
Miscellaneous Inorganic Wastes	1,300	1,780	2,250	2,900	3,500	3,690	3,840	3,970	3,990
Total Other Wastes	33,500	37,780	42,750	61,760	64,730	68,690	72,980	77,140	78,440
Total MSW Generated - Weight	88,120	121,060	151,640	208,270	243,450	253,730	251,050	258,950	262,430

Materials	Percent of Total Generation								
	1960	1970	1980	1990	2000	2005	2010	2014	2015
Paper and Paperboard	34.0%	36.6%	36.4%	34.9%	36.0%	33.4%	28.4%	26.5%	25.9%
Glass	7.6%	10.5%	10.0%	6.3%	5.2%	4.9%	4.6%	4.4%	4.4%
Metals									
Ferrous	11.7%	10.2%	8.3%	6.1%	5.8%	6.0%	6.7%	6.9%	6.9%
Aluminum	0.4%	0.7%	1.1%	1.3%	1.3%	1.3%	1.4%	1.4%	1.4%
Other Nonferrous	0.2%	0.6%	0.8%	0.5%	0.7%	0.7%	0.8%	0.8%	0.8%
Total Metals	*12.3%*	*11.4%*	*10.2%*	*7.9%*	*7.8%*	*8.0%*	*8.9%*	*9.1%*	9.1%
Plastics	0.4%	2.4%	4.5%	8.2%	10.5%	11.6%	12.5%	12.9%	13.1%
Rubber and Leather	2.1%	2.5%	2.8%	2.8%	2.7%	2.9%	3.1%	3.2%	3.2%
Textiles	2.0%	1.7%	1.7%	2.8%	3.9%	4.5%	5.3%	5.9%	6.1%
Wood	3.4%	3.1%	4.6%	5.9%	5.6%	5.8%	6.3%	6.2%	6.2%
Other **	0.1%	0.6%	1.7%	1.5%	1.6%	1.7%	1.9%	2.0%	2.1%
Total Materials in Products	62.0%	68.8%	71.8%	70.3%	73.4%	72.9%	70.9%	70.2%	70.1%
Other Wastes									
Food	13.8%	10.6%	8.6%	11.5%	12.6%	13.0%	14.2%	14.9%	15.1%
Yard Trimmings	22.7%	19.2%	18.1%	16.8%	12.5%	12.6%	13.3%	13.3%	13.3%
Miscellaneous Inorganic Wastes	1.5%	1.5%	1.5%	1.4%	1.4%	1.5%	1.5%	1.5%	1.5%
Total Other Wastes	38.0%	31.2%	28.2%	29.7%	26.6%	27.1%	29.1%	29.8%	29.9%
Total MSW Generated - %	100.0%	100.0%	100.0%	100.0%	100.0%	100.0%	100.0%	100.0%	100.0%

* Generation before materials recycling, composting, combustion with energy recovery or landfilling. Does not include construction & demolition debris, industrial process wastes or certain other wastes. Details may not add to totals due to rounding.

** Includes electrolytes in batteries and fluff pulp, feces and urine in disposable diapers.

Source: *U.S. EPA, Advancing Sustainable Materials Management: 2015 Tables and Figures, July 2018*

Table 2. Materials Recycled and Composted* in Municipal Solid Waste, 1960 to 2015

(In thousands of tons and percent of generation of each material)

Materials	Thousands of Tons								
	1960	1970	1980	1990	2000	2005	2010	2014	2015
Paper and Paperboard	5,080	6,770	11,740	20,230	37,560	41,960	44,570	44,400	45,320
Glass	100	160	750	2,630	2,880	2,590	3,130	2,990	3,030
Metals									
Ferrous	50	150	370	2,230	4,680	5,020	5,800	5,970	6,060
Aluminum	Neg.	10	310	1,010	860	690	680	710	670
Other Nonferrous	Neg.	320	540	730	1,060	1,280	1,440	1,550	1,500
Total Metals	*50*	*480*	*1,220*	*3,970*	*6,600*	*6,990*	7,920	*8,230*	*8,230*
Plastics	Neg.	Neg.	20	370	1,480	1,780	2,500	3,190	3,140
Rubber and Leather	330	250	130	370	820	1,050	1,440	1,440	1,510
Textiles	50	60	160	660	1,320	1,830	2,050	2,260	2,450
Wood	Neg.	Neg.	Neg.	130	1,370	1,830	2,280	2,570	2,660
Other **	Neg.	300	500	680	980	1,210	1,370	1,470	1,430
Total Materials in Products	5,610	8,020	14,520	29,040	53,010	59,240	65,260	66,550	67,770
Other Wastes									
Food^	Neg.	Neg.	Neg.	Neg.	680	690	970	1,940	2,100
Yard Trimmings	Neg.	Neg.	Neg.	4,200	15,770	19,860	19,200	21,080	21,290
Miscellaneous Inorganic Wastes	Neg.	Neg.	Neg.	Neg.	Neg.	Neg.	Neg.	Neg.	Neg.
Total Other Wastes	Neg.	Neg.	Neg.	4,200	16,450	20,550	20,170	23,020	23,390
Total MSW Recycled and Composted - Weight	5,610	8,020	14,520	33,240	69,460	79,790	85,430	89,570	91,160

Materials	Percent of Generation of Each Material								
	1960	1970	1980	1990	2000	2005	2010	2014	2015
Paper and Paperboard	16.9%	15.3%	21.3%	27.8%	42.8%	49.5%	62.5%	64.7%	66.6%
Glass	1.5%	1.3%	5.0%	20.1%	22.6%	20.7%	27.2%	26.0%	26.4%
Metals									
Ferrous	0.5%	1.2%	2.9%	17.6%	33.1%	33.0%	34.3%	33.4%	33.4%
Aluminum	Neg.	1.3%	17.9%	35.9%	27.0%	20.7%	19.4%	20.1%	18.6%
Other Nonferrous	Neg.	47.8%	46.6%	66.4%	66.3%	68.8%	71.3%	69.5%	67.6%
Total Metals	*0.5%*	*3.5%*	*7.9%*	*24.0%*	*34.8%*	*34.3%*	35.3%	*34.8%*	*34.3%*
Plastics	Neg.	Neg.	0.3%	2.2%	5.8%	6.1%	8.0%	9.6%	9.1%
Rubber and Leather	17.9%	8.4%	3.1%	6.4%	12.3%	14.4%	18.6%	17.5%	17.8%
Textiles	2.8%	2.9%	6.3%	11.4%	13.9%	15.9%	15.5%	14.8%	15.3%
Wood	Neg.	Neg.	Neg.	1.1%	10.1%	12.4%	14.5%	15.9%	16.3%
Other **	Neg.	39.0%	19.8%	21.3%	24.5%	28.2%	29.1%	28.7%	27.7%
Total Materials in Products	10.3%	9.6%	13.3%	19.8%	29.7%	32.0%	36.6%	36.6%	36.8%
Other Wastes									
Food^	Neg.	Neg.	Neg.	Neg.	2.2%	2.1%	2.7%	5.0%	5.3%
Yard Trimmings	Neg.	Neg.	Neg.	12.0%	51.7%	61.9%	57.5%	61.1%	61.3%
Miscellaneous Inorganic Wastes	Neg.	Neg.	Neg.	Neg.	Neg.	Neg.	Neg.	Neg.	Neg.
Total Other Wastes	Neg.	Neg.	Neg.	6.8%	25.4%	29.9%	27.6%	29.8%	29.8%
Total MSW Recycled and Composted - %	6.4%	6.6%	9.6%	16.0%	28.5%	31.4%	34.0%	34.6%	34.7%

* Recycling and composting of postconsumer wastes; does not include converting/fabrication scrap. Details may not add to totals due to rounding.

** Collection of electrolytes in batteries; probably not recycled.

Neg = Less than 5,000 tons or 0.05 percent.

^ Includes collection of other MSW organics for composting.

Source: *U.S. EPA, Advancing Sustainable Materials Management: 2015 Tables and Figures, July 2018*

Table 3. Materials Combusted with Energy Recovery* in the Municipal Waste Stream, 1960 to 2015

(In thousands of tons and percent of total combusted)

Materials	Thousands of Tons							
	1960	1970	1980	1990	2000	2005	2010	2014	2015
Paper and Paperboard		150	860	8,930	9,730	7,800	4,740	4,740	4,450
Glass		60	300	1,810	1,790	1,660	1,360	1,450	1,470
Metals									
Ferrous		60	250	1,690	1,610	1,640	1,810	2,030	2,140
Aluminum		0	30	300	390	410	440	470	500
Other Nonferrous		0	20	60	50	50	60	50	60
Total Metals		*60*	*300*	*2,050*	*2,050*	*2,100*	*2,310*	*2,550*	*2,700*
Plastics		0	140	2,980	4,120	4,330	4,530	5,010	5,350
Rubber and Leather		10	70	830	1,970	2,110	1,910	2,620	2,490
Textiles		10	50	880	1,880	2,110	2,270	3,020	3,050
Wood		10	150	2,080	2,290	2,270	2,310	2,540	2,580
Other **		0	30	410	540	510	540	670	690
Total Materials in Products		300	1,900	19,970	24,370	22,890	19,970	22,600	22,780
Other Wastes									
Food		50	260	4,060	5,820	5,870	6,150	7,200	7,380
Yard Trimmings		90	550	5,240	2,860	2,220	2,510	2,630	2,630
Miscellaneous Inorganic Wastes		10	50	490	680	670	680	780	780
Total Other Wastes		150	860	9,790	9,360	8,760	9,340	10,610	10,790
Total MSW Combusted - Weight		450	2,760	29,760	33,730	31,650	29,310	33,210	33,570
Materials	**Percent of Total Combusted**								
	1960	1970	1980	1990	2000	2005	2010	2014	2015
Paper and Paperboard		33.3%	31.2%	30.0%	28.8%	24.6%	16.2%	14.3%	13.3%
Glass		13.3%	10.9%	6.1%	5.3%	5.2%	4.6%	4.4%	4.4%
Metals									
Ferrous		13.3%	9.0%	5.7%	4.8%	5.2%	6.2%	6.1%	6.4%
Aluminum		0.0%	1.1%	1.0%	1.2%	1.3%	1.5%	1.4%	1.5%
Other Nonferrous		0.0%	0.7%	0.2%	0.1%	0.1%	0.2%	0.2%	0.2%
Total Metals		*13.3%*	*10.8%*	*6.9%*	*6.1%*	*6.6%*	*7.9%*	*7.7%*	*8.1%*
Plastics		Neg.	5.1%	10.0%	12.2%	13.7%	15.5%	15.1%	15.9%
Rubber and Leather		2.2%	2.5%	2.8%	5.9%	6.7%	6.5%	7.9%	7.4%
Textiles		2.2%	1.8%	2.9%	5.6%	6.7%	7.7%	9.1%	9.1%
Wood		2.2%	5.4%	7.0%	6.8%	7.2%	7.9%	7.6%	7.6%
Other **		Neg.	1.1%	1.4%	1.6%	1.6%	1.8%	2.0%	2.1%
Total Materials in Products		66.6%	68.8%	67.1%	72.3%	72.3%	68.1%	68.1%	67.9%
Other Wastes									
Food		11.1%	9.4%	13.6%	17.3%	18.5%	21.0%	21.7%	22.0%
Yard Trimmings		20.0%	20.0%	17.6%	8.5%	7.0%	8.6%	7.9%	7.8%
Miscellaneous Inorganic Wastes		2.3%	1.8%	1.7%	1.9%	2.1%	2.3%	2.3%	2.3%
Total Other Wastes		33.4%	31.2%	32.9%	27.7%	27.7%	31.9%	31.9%	32.1%
Total MSW Combusted with Energy Recovery- %		100.0%	100.0%	100.0%	100.0%	100.0%	100.0%	100.0%	100.0%

* Products and materials combusted with energy recovery estimated at percentage total MSW after recycling and composting. In 2015, 19.6 percent of MSW after recycling and composting was combusted with energy recovery except for major appliances, tires and lead-acid batteries (see Table 16). No combustion with energy recovery in 1960 (see Table 35). Does not include construction & demolition debris, industrial process wastes or certain other wastes. Details may not add to totals due to rounding.

** Includes electrolytes in batteries and fluff pulp, feces and urine in disposable diapers.

Source: U.S. EPA, *Advancing Sustainable Materials Management: 2015 Tables and Figures*, July 2018

Table 4. Materials Landfilled* in the Municipal Waste Stream, 1960 to 2015

(In thousands of tons and percent of total landfilled)

Materials	Thousands of Tons								
	1960	1970	1980	1990	2000	2005	2010	2014	2015
Paper and Paperboard	24,910	37,390	42,560	43,570	40,450	35,080	22,000	19,470	18,280
Glass	6,620	12,520	14,080	8,660	8,100	8,290	7,030	7,040	6,970
Metals									
Ferrous	10,250	12,150	12,000	8,720	7,860	8,550	9,310	9,880	9,970
Aluminum	340	790	1,390	1,500	1,940	2,230	2,390	2,350	2,440
Other Nonferrous	180	350	600	310	490	530	520	630	660
Total Metals	*10,770*	*13,290*	*13,990*	*10,530*	*10,290*	*11,310*	*12,220*	*12,860*	*13,070*
Plastics	390	2,900	6,670	13,780	19,950	23,270	24,370	25,190	26,010
Rubber and Leather	1,510	2,710	4,000	4,590	3,880	4,130	4,400	4,150	4,480
Textiles	1,710	1,970	2,320	4,270	6,280	7,570	8,900	9,960	10,530
Wood	3,030	3,710	6,860	10,000	9,910	10,690	11,120	11,010	11,060
Other **	70	470	1,990	2,100	2,480	2,570	2,800	2,980	3,040
Total Materials in Products	49,010	74,960	92,470	97,500	101,340	102,910	92,840	92,660	93,440
Other Wastes									
Food	12,200	12,750	12,740	19,800	24,200	26,370	28,620	29,530	30,250
Yard Trimmings	20,000	23,110	26,950	25,560	11,900	9,990	11,690	10,790	10,800
Miscellaneous Inorganic Wastes	1,300	1,770	2,200	2,410	2,820	3,020	3,160	3,190	3,210
Total Other Wastes	33,500	37,630	41,890	47,770	38,920	39,380	43,470	43,510	44,260
Total MSW Landfilled - Weight	82,510	112,590	134,360	145,270	140,260	142,290	136,310	136,170	137,700

Materials	Percent of Total Landfilled								
	1960	1970	1980	1990	2000	2005	2010	2014	2015
Paper and Paperboard	30.2%	33.2%	31.7%	30.0%	28.8%	24.7%	16.1%	14.3%	13.3%
Glass	8.0%	11.1%	10.5%	6.0%	5.8%	5.8%	5.1%	5.2%	5.1%
Metals									
Ferrous	12.4%	10.8%	8.9%	6.0%	5.6%	6.0%	6.8%	7.3%	7.2%
Aluminum	0.4%	0.7%	1.0%	1.0%	1.4%	1.6%	1.8%	1.7%	1.8%
Other Nonferrous	0.2%	0.3%	0.4%	0.2%	0.3%	0.3%	0.4%	0.5%	0.5%
Total Metals	*13.0%*	*11.8%*	*10.3%*	*7.2%*	*7.3%*	*7.9%*	*9.0%*	*9.5%*	*9.5%*
Plastics	0.5%	2.6%	5.0%	9.5%	14.2%	16.4%	17.9%	18.5%	18.9%
Rubber and Leather	1.8%	2.4%	3.0%	3.2%	2.8%	2.9%	3.2%	3.0%	3.3%
Textiles	2.1%	1.7%	1.7%	2.9%	4.5%	5.3%	6.5%	7.3%	7.6%
Wood	3.7%	3.3%	5.1%	6.9%	7.1%	7.5%	8.2%	8.1%	8.0%
Other **	0.1%	0.4%	1.5%	1.4%	1.8%	1.8%	2.1%	2.2%	2.2%
Total Materials in Products	59.4%	66.6%	68.8%	67.1%	72.3%	72.3%	68.1%	68.1%	67.9%
Other Wastes									
Food	14.8%	11.3%	9.5%	13.6%	17.3%	18.5%	21.0%	21.7%	22.0%
Yard Trimmings	24.2%	20.5%	20.1%	17.6%	8.5%	7.0%	8.6%	7.9%	7.8%
Miscellaneous Inorganic Wastes	1.6%	1.6%	1.6%	1.7%	1.9%	2.2%	2.3%	2.3%	2.3%
Total Other Wastes	40.6%	33.4%	31.2%	32.9%	27.7%	27.7%	31.9%	31.9%	32.1%
Total MSW Landfilled - %	100.0%	100.0%	100.0%	100.0%	100.0%	100.0%	100.0%	100.0%	100.0%

* Landfilling after recycling, composting and combustion with energy recovery. Does not include construction & demolition debris, industrial process wastes or certain other wastes. Details may not add to totals due to rounding.

** Includes electrolytes in batteries and fluff pulp, feces and urine in disposable diapers.

Source: U.S. EPA, *Advancing Sustainable Materials Management: 2015 Tables and Figures, July 2018*

Table 5. Paper and Paperboard Products In MSW, 2015
(In thousands of tons and percent of generation)

Product Category	Generation (Thousand tons)	Recycled (Thousand tons)	Recycled (Percent of generation)	Combusted with Energy Recovery (Thousand tons)	Landfilled (Thousand tons)
Nondurable Goods					
Newspapers/Mechanical Papers†	6,730	4,790	71.2%	380	1,560
Books	800				
Magazines	1,190				
Office-type Papers*	4,530				
Standard Mail**	4,050				
Other Commercial Printing	2,080				
Tissue Paper and Towels	3,680				
Paper Plates and Cups	1,360				
Other Nonpackaging Paper***	3,700				
Subtotal Nondurable Goods excluding Newspaper/Mechanical Papers§	21,390	9,330	43.6%	2,360	9,700
Total Paper and Paperboard Nondurable Goods	28,120	14,120	50.2%	2,740	11,260
Containers and Packaging					
Corrugated Boxes	31,330	28,930	92.3%	470	1,930
Gable Top/Aseptic Cartons‡	590				
Folding Cartons	5,380				
Other Paperboard Packaging	70				
Bags and Sacks	930				
Other Paper Packaging	1,620				
Subtotal Containers and Packaging excluding Corrugated Boxes§	8,590	2,270	26.4%	1,240	5,080
Total Paper and Paperboard Containers and Packaging	39,920	31,200	78.2%	1,710	7,010
Total Paper and Paperboard^	**68,040**	**45,320**	**66.6%**	**4,450**	**18,270**

† Starting in 2010, newsprint and groundwood inserts expanded to include directories and other mechanical papers previously counted as Other Commercial Printing.

* High-grade papers such as copy paper and printer paper; both residential and commercial.

** Formerly called Third Class Mail by the U.S. Postal Service.

*** Includes paper in games and novelties, cards, etc.

§ Valid default values for separating out paper and paperboard sub-categories for recycling, combustion with energy recovery and landfilling were not available.

‡ Includes milk, juice and other products packaged in gable top cartons and liquid food aseptic cartons.

^ Table 5 does not include 10,000 tons of paper used in durable goods (Table 1).

Neg. = Less than 5,000 tons or 0.05 percent.

Source: U.S. EPA, Advancing Sustainable Materials Management: 2015 Tables and Figures, July 2018

Table 6. Glass Products in MSW, 2015
(In thousands of tons and percent of generation)

Product Category	Generation	Recycled		Combusted with Energy Recovery	Landfilled
	(Thousand tons)	(Thousand tons)	(Percent of generation)	(Thousand tons)	(Thousand tons)
Durable Goods*	2,350	Neg.	Neg.	270	2,080
Containers and Packaging					
Beer and Soft Drink Bottles**	5,320	2,230	41.9%	610	2,480
Wine and Liquor Bottles	1,810	500	27.6%	260	1,050
Other Bottles and Jars	1,990	300	15.1%	330	1,360
Total Glass Containers	9,120	3,030	33.2%	1,200	4,890
Total Glass	**11,470**	**3,030**	**26.4%**	**1,470**	**6,970**

* Glass as a component of appliances, furniture, consumer electronics, etc.

** Includes carbonated drinks and non-carbonated water, teas, flavored drinks and ready-to-drink alcoholic coolers and cocktails.

Neg. = Less than 5,000 tons or 0.05 percent.

Details may not add to totals due to rounding.

Source: *U.S. EPA, Advancing Sustainable Materials Management: 2015 Tables and Figures, July 2018*

Table 7. Metal Products in MSW, 2015
(In thousands of tons and percent of generation)

Product Category	Generation	Recycled		Combusted with Energy Recovery	Landfilled
	(Thousand tons)	(Thousand tons)	(Percent of generation)	(Thousand tons)	(Thousand tons)
Durable Goods					
Ferrous Metals*	15,950	4,440	27.8%	2,020	9,490
Aluminum**	1,550	NA	NA	220	1,330
Lead†	1,520	1,500	98.7%		20
Other Nonferrous Metals‡	700	Neg.	Neg.	60	640
Total Metals in Durable Goods	**19,720**	**5,940**	**30.1%**	**2,300**	**11,480**
Nondurable Goods					
Aluminum	220	NA	NA	40	180
Containers and Packaging					
Steel					
Cans	1,740	1,240	71.3%	100	400
Other Steel Packaging	480	380	79.2%	20	80
Total Steel Packaging	**2,220**	**1,620**	**73.0%**	**120**	**480**
Aluminum					
Beer and Soft Drink Cans§	1,220	670	54.9%	110	440
Other Cans	130	NA	NA	30	100
Foil and Closures	490	NA	NA	100	390
Total Aluminum Packaging	**1,840**	**670**	**36.4%**	**240**	**930**
Total Metals in Containers and Packaging	**4,060**	**2,290**	**56.4%**	**360**	**1,410**
Total Metals	24,000	8,230	34.3%	2,700	13,070
Ferrous	18,170	6,060	33.4%	2,140	9,970
Aluminum	3,610	670	18.6%	500	2,440
Other nonferrous	2,220	1,500	67.6%	60	660

* Ferrous metals (iron and steel) in appliances, furniture, tires and miscellaneous durables.
** Aluminum in appliances, furniture and miscellaneous durables.
† Lead in lead-acid batteries.
‡ Other nonferrous metals in appliances and miscellaneous durables.
§ Aluminum can recycling does not include used beverage cans imported to produce new beverage cans.
NA = Not Available
Details may not add to totals due to rounding.

Source: *U.S. EPA, Advancing Sustainable Materials Management: 2015 Tables and Figures, July 2018*

Table 8. Plastics in Products In MSW, 2015
(In thousands of tons and percent of generation by resin)

Product Category	Generation	Recycled		Combusted with energy Recovery	Landfilled
	(Thousand tons)	(Thousand tons)	(Percent of generation)	(Thousand tons)	(Thousand tons)
Durable Goods					
PET	500				
HDPE	1,480				
PVC	200				
LDPE/LLDPE	1,940				
PP	4,250				
PS	760				
Other resins	3,370				
Total Plastics in Durable Goods	**12,500**	**830**	**6.6%**	**1,490**	**10,180**
Nondurable Goods‡					
Plastic Plates and Cups§					
LDPE/LLDPE	20				
PLA	20				
PP	160				
PS	850				
Subtotal Plastic Plates and Cups	1,050	Neg.	Neg.	210	840
Trash Bags					
HDPE	220				
LDPE/LLDPE	910				
Subtotal Trash Bags	1,130			220	910
All other nondurables*					
PET	680				
HDPE	560				
PVC	270				
LDPE/LLDPE	1,290				
PLA	30				
PP	1,490				
PS	200				
Other resins	620				
Subtotal All Other Nondurables	**5,140**	**160**	**3.1%**	**970**	**4,010**
Total Plastics in Nondurable Goods, by resin					
PET	680				
HDPE	780				
PVC	270				
LDPE/LLDPE	2,220				
PLA	50				
PP	1,650				
PS	1,050				
Other resins	620				
Total Plastics in Nondurable Goods	**7,320**	**160**	**2.2%**	**1,400**	**5,760**

Source: *U.S. EPA, Advancing Sustainable Materials Management: 2015 Tables and Figures, July 2018*

Table 8. Plastics in Products In MSW, 2015
(In thousands of tons and percent of generation by resin)

Product Category	Generation	Recycled		Combusted with energy Recovery	Landfilled
	(Thousand tons)	(Thousand tons)	(Percent of generation)	(Thousand tons)	(Thousand tons)
Plastic Containers & Packaging					
Bottles and Jars**					
PET	2,980	890	29.9%	410	1,680
Natural Bottles†					
HDPE	760	230	30.3%	100	430
Other plastic containers					
HDPE	1,540	340	22.1%		
PVC	20	Neg.			
LDPE/LLDPE	40	Neg.			
PP	250	20	8.0%		
PS	90	Neg.			
Subtotal Other Containers	**1,940**	**360**	**18.6%**	**310**	**1,270**
Bags, sacks, & wraps					
HDPE	730	40	5.5%		
PVC	60				
LDPE/LLDPE	2,610	490	18.8%		
PP	590				
PS	140				
Subtotal Bags, Sacks, & Wraps	**4,130**	**530**	**12.8%**	**710**	**2,890**
Other Plastics Packaging‡					
PET	940	50	5.3%		
HDPE	750	10	1.3%		
PVC	340	Neg.			
LDPE/LLDPE	1,120	Neg.			
PLA	10	Neg.			
PP	990	50	5.1%		
PS	330	30	9.1%		
Other resins	390	Neg.			
Subtotal Other Packaging	**4,870**	**140**	**2.9%**	**930**	**3,800**
Total Plastics in Containers & Packaging, by resin					
PET	3,920	940	24.0%		
HDPE	3,780	620	16.4%		
PVC	420	Neg.			
LDPE/LLDPE	3,770	490	13.0%		
PLA	10	Neg.			
PP	1,830	70	3.8%		
PS	560	30	5.4%		
Other resins	390	Neg.			
Total Plastics in Containers & Packaging	**14,680**	**2,150**	**14.6%**	**2,460**	**10,070**

Source: *U.S. EPA, Advancing Sustainable Materials Management: 2015 Tables and Figures, July 2018*

Table 8. Plastics in Products In MSW, 2015

(In thousands of tons and percent of generation by resin)

Product Category	Generation	Recycled		Combusted with energy Recovery	Landfilled
	(Thousand tons)	(Thousand tons)	(Percent of generation)	(Thousand tons)	(Thousand tons)
Total Plastics in MSW, by resin					
PET	5,100	940	18.4%		
HDPE	6,040	620	10.3%		
PVC	890	Neg.			
LDPE/LLDPE	7,930	490	6.2%		
PLA	60	Neg.			
PP	7,730	70	0.9%		
PS	2,370	30	1.3%		
Other resins	4,380	990	22.6%		
Total Plastics in MSW	**34,500**	**3,140**	**9.1%**	**5,350**	**26,010**

‡ Nondurable goods other than containers and packaging.

§ Due to source data aggregation, PET cups are included in "Other Plastic Packaging".

* All other nondurables include plastics in disposable diapers, clothing, footwear, etc.

** Injection stretch blow molded PET containers as identified in *Report on Postconsumer PET Container Recycling Activity in 2014*. National Association for PET Container Resources. Recycling includes caps, lids and other material collected with PET bottles and jars.

† White translucent homopolymer bottles as defined in the *2014 United States National Postconsumer Plastics Bottles Recycling Report*. American Chemistry Council and the Association of Postconsumer Plastic Recyclers.

Neg. = negligible, less than 5,000 tons

HDPE = High density polyethylene | PET = Polyethylene terephthalate | PS = Polystyrene
LDPE = Low density polyethylene | PP = Polypropylene | PVC = Polyvinyl chloride
LLDPE = Linear low density polyethylene | PLA = Polylactide

‡ Other plastic packaging includes coatings, closures, lids, PET cups, caps, clamshells, egg cartons, produce baskets, trays, shapes, loose fill, etc.

PP caps and lids recycled with PET bottles and jars are included in the recycling estimate for PET bottles and jars.

Other resins include commingled/undefined plastic packaging recycling.

Some detail of recycling by resin omitted due to lack of data.

Source: *U.S. EPA, Advancing Sustainable Materials Management: 2015 Tables and Figures, July 2018*

Table 9. Rubber and Leather Products In MSW, 2015
(In thousands of tons and percent of generation)

Product Category	Generation (Thousand tons)	Recycled (Thousand tons)	Recycled (Percent of generation)	Combusted with energy Recovery (Thousand tons)	Landfilled (Thousand tons)
Durable Goods					
Rubber in Tires*	3,750	1,510	40.3%	1,780	460
Other Durables**	3,600	Neg.	Neg.	490	3,110
Total Rubber & Leather Durable Goods	**7,350**	**1,510**	**20.5%**	**2,270**	**3,570**
Nondurable Goods					
Clothing and Footwear	860	Neg.	Neg.	170	690
Other Nondurables	270	Neg.	Neg.	50	220
Total Rubber & Leather Nondurable Goods	**1,130**	**Neg.**	**Neg.**	**220**	**910**
Total Rubber & Leather	8,480	1,510	17.8%	2,490	4,480

* Automobile and truck tires. Does not include other materials in tires.
** Includes carpets and rugs and other miscellaneous durables.
Neg. = Less than 5,000 tons or 0.05 percent.
Details may not add to totals due to rounding.

Source: *U.S. EPA, Advancing Sustainable Materials Management: 2015 Tables and Figures, July 2018*

Table 10. Products Generated* in the Municipal Waste Stream, 1960 to 2015
(In thousands of tons and percent of total generation)

Products	Thousands of Tons								
	1960	1970	1980	1990	2000	2005	2010	2014	2015
Durable Goods	9,920	14,660	21,800	29,810	38,870	45,060	49,350	53,040	54,150
(Detail in Table 14)									
Nondurable Goods	17,330	25,060	34,420	52,170	64,010	63,650	53,250	51,910	51,920
(Detail in Table 18)									
Containers and Packaging	27,370	43,560	52,670	64,530	75,840	76,330	75,470	76,860	77,920
Detail in Table 22)									
Total Product** Wastes	54,620	83,280	108,890	146,510	178,720	185,040	178,070	181,810	183,990
Other Wastes									
Food	12,200	12,800	13,000	23,860	30,700	32,930	35,740	38,670	39,730
Yard Trimmings	20,000	23,200	27,500	35,000	30,530	32,070	33,400	34,500	34,720
Miscellaneous Inorganic Wastes	1,300	1,780	2,250	2,900	3,500	3,690	3,840	3,970	3,990
Total Other Wastes	33,500	37,780	42,750	61,760	64,730	68,690	72,980	77,140	78,440
Total MSW Generated - Weight	88,120	121,060	151,640	208,270	243,450	253,730	251,050	258,950	262,430

Products	Percent of Total Generation								
	1960	1970	1980	1990	2000	2005	2010	2014	2015
Durable Goods	11.3%	12.1%	14.4%	14.3%	16.0%	17.8%	19.7%	20.5%	20.6%
(Detail in Table 14)									
Nondurable Goods	19.7%	20.7%	22.7%	25.0%	26.3%	25.1%	21.2%	20.0%	19.8%
(Detail in Table 18)									
Containers and Packaging	31.1%	36.0%	34.7%	31.0%	31.2%	30.1%	30.1%	29.7%	29.7%
(Detail in Table 23)									
Total Product** Wastes	62.0%	68.8%	71.8%	70.3%	73.4%	72.9%	70.9%	70.2%	70.1%
Other Wastes									
Food	13.8%	10.6%	8.6%	11.5%	12.6%	13.0%	14.2%	14.9%	15.1%
Yard Trimmings	22.7%	19.2%	18.1%	16.8%	12.5%	12.6%	13.3%	13.3%	13.2%
Miscellaneous Inorganic Wastes	1.5%	1.5%	1.5%	1.4%	1.4%	1.5%	1.5%	1.5%	1.5%
Total Other Wastes	38.0%	31.2%	28.2%	29.7%	26.6%	27.1%	29.1%	29.8%	29.9%
Total MSW Generated - %	100.0%	100.0%	100.0%	100.0%	100.0%	100.0%	100.0%	100.0%	100.0%

* Generation before materials recycling, composting, combustion with energy recovery or landfilling. Does not include construction & demolition debris, industrial process wastes or certain other wastes. Details may not add to totals due to rounding.

** Other than food products.

Source: *U.S. EPA, Advancing Sustainable Materials Management: 2015 Tables and Figures, July 2018*

Table 11. Products Recycled and Composted* in the Municipal Waste Stream, 1960 to 2015

(In thousands of tons and percent of generation of each product)

Products	Thousands of Tons								
	1960	1970	1980	1990	2000	2005	2010	2014	2015
Durable Goods	350	940	1,360	3,460	6,580	7,970	9,390	10,140	10,250
(Detail in Table 15)									
Nondurable Goods	2,390	3,730	4,670	8,800	17,560	19,770	19,190	16,820	16,190
(Detail in Table 19)									
Containers and Packaging	2,870	3,350	8,490	16,780	28,870	31,500	36,680	39,590	41,330
Detail in Table 24)									
Total Product** Wastes	5,610	8,020	14,520	29,040	53,010	59,240	65,260	66,550	67,770
Other Wastes									
Food^	Neg.	Neg.	Neg.	Neg.	680	690	970	1,940	2,100
Yard Trimmings	Neg.	Neg.	Neg.	4,200	15,770	19,860	19,200	21,080	21,290
Miscellaneous Inorganic Wastes	Neg.	Neg.	Neg.	Neg.	Neg.	Neg.	Neg.	Neg.	Neg.
Total Other Wastes	Neg.	Neg.	Neg.	4,200	16,450	20,550	20,170	23,020	23,390
Total MSW Recycled and Composted - Weight	5,610	8,020	14,520	33,240	69,460	79,790	85,430	89,570	91,160

Products	Percent of Total Generation								
	1960	1970	1980	1990	2000	2005	2010	2014	2015
Durable Goods	3.5%	6.4%	6.2%	11.6%	16.9%	17.7%	19.0%	19.1%	18.9%
(Detail in Table 15)									
Nondurable Goods	13.8%	14.9%	13.6%	16.9%	27.4%	31.1%	36.0%	32.4%	31.2%
(Detail in Table 19)									
Containers and Packaging	10.5%	7.7%	16.1%	26.0%	38.1%	41.3%	48.6%	51.5%	53.0%
(Detail in Table 25)									
Total Product** Wastes	10.3%	9.6%	13.3%	19.8%	29.7%	32.0%	36.6%	36.6%	36.8%
Other Wastes									
Food^	Neg.	Neg.	Neg.	Neg.	2.2%	2.1%	2.7%	5.0%	5.3%
Yard Trimmings	Neg.	Neg.	Neg.	12.0%	51.7%	61.9%	57.5%	61.1%	61.3%
Miscellaneous Inorganic Wastes	Neg.	Neg.	Neg.	Neg.	Neg.	Neg.	Neg.	Neg.	Neg.
Total Other Wastes	Neg.	Neg.	Neg.	6.8%	25.4%	29.9%	27.6%	29.8%	29.8%
Total MSW Recycled and Composted - %	6.4%	6.6%	9.6%	16.0%	28.5%	31.4%	34.0%	34.6%	34.7%

* Recycling and composting of postconsumer wastes; does not include converting/fabrication scrap. Details may not add to totals due to rounding.

** Other than food products.

^ Includes collection of other MSW organics for composting.

Neg. = Less than 5,000 tons or 0.05 percent.

Source: *U.S. EPA, Advancing Sustainable Materials Management: 2015 Tables and Figures, July 2018*

Table 12. Products Combusted with Energy Recovery* in the Municipal Waste Stream, 1960 to 2015

(In thousands of tons and percent of total combusted)

Products	Thousands of Tons								
	1960	1970	1980	1990	2000	2005	2010	2014	2015
Durable Goods		60	440	4,480	6,260	6,750	7,070	8,410	8,600
(Detail in Table 16)									
Nondurable Goods		90	580	7,380	9,000	7,980	6,030	6,880	6,990
(Detail in Table 20)									
Containers and Packaging		150	880	8,110	9,110	8,160	6,870	7,310	7,190
Detail in Table 26)									
Total Product** Wastes		300	1,900	19,970	24,370	22,890	19,970	22,600	22,780
Other Wastes									
Food		50	260	4,060	5,820	5,870	6,150	7,200	7,380
Yard Trimmings		90	550	5,240	2,860	2,220	2,510	2,630	2,630
Miscellaneous Inorganic Wastes		10	50	490	680	670	680	780	780
Total Other Wastes		150	860	9,790	9,360	8,760	9,340	10,610	10,790
Total MSW Combusted with Energy Recovery - Weight		450	2,760	29,760	33,730	31,650	29,310	33,210	33,570
Products	**Percent of Total Combusted**								
	1960	1970	1980	1990	2000	2005	2010	2014	2015
Durable Goods		13.3%	15.9%	15.1%	18.6%	21.3%	24.1%	25.4%	25.6%
(Detail in Table 16)									
Nondurable Goods		19.9%	21.0%	24.8%	26.7%	25.2%	20.6%	20.7%	20.9%
(Detail in Table 20)									
Containers and Packaging		33.3%	31.9%	27.3%	27.0%	25.8%	23.4%	22.0%	21.4%
(Detail in Table 27)									
Total Product** Wastes		66.6%	68.8%	67.1%	72.3%	72.3%	68.1%	68.1%	67.9%
Other Wastes									
Food		11.1%	9.4%	13.6%	17.3%	18.5%	21.0%	21.7%	22.0%
Yard Trimmings		20.0%	20.0%	17.6%	8.5%	7.0%	8.6%	7.9%	7.8%
Miscellaneous Inorganic Wastes		2.3%	1.8%	1.7%	1.9%	2.1%	2.3%	2.3%	2.3%
Total Other Wastes		33.4%	31.2%	32.9%	27.7%	27.7%	31.9%	31.9%	32.1%
Total MSW Combusted with Energy Recovery - %		100.0%	100.0%	100.0%	100.0%	100.0%	100.0%	100.0%	100.0%

* Products and materials combusted with energy recovery estimated at percentage total MSW after recycling and composting. In 2015, 19.6 percent of MSW after recycling and composting was combusted with energy recovery. Does not include construction & demolition debris, industrial process wastes or certain other wastes. Details may not add to totals due to rounding.

** Other than food products.

Neg. = Less than 5,000 tons or 0.05 percent.

Source: *U.S. EPA, Advancing Sustainable Materials Management: 2015 Tables and Figures, July 2018*

Table 13. Products Landfilled* in the Municipal Waste Stream, 1960 to 2015

(In thousands of tons and percent of total landfilled)

Products	Thousands of Tons								
	1960	1970	1980	1990	2000	2005	2010	2014	2015
Durable Goods	9,570	13,660	20,000	21,870	26,030	30,340	32,890	34,490	35,300
(Detail in Table 17									
Nondurable Goods	14,940	21,240	29,170	35,990	37,450	35,900	28,030	28,210	28,740
(Detail in Table 21)									
Containers and Packaging	24,500	40,060	43,300	39,640	37,860	36,670	31,920	29,960	29,400
Detail in Table 28)									
Total Product** Wastes	49,010	74,960	92,470	97,500	101,340	102,910	92,840	92,660	93,440
Other Wastes									
Food	12,200	12,750	12,740	19,800	24,200	26,370	28,620	29,530	30,250
Yard Trimmings	20,000	23,110	26,950	25,560	11,900	9,990	11,690	10,790	10,800
Miscellaneous Inorganic Wastes	1,300	1,770	2,200	2,410	2,820	3,020	3,160	3,190	3,210
Total Other Wastes	33,500	37,630	41,890	47,770	38,920	39,380	43,470	43,510	44,260
Total MSW Landfilled - Weight	82,510	112,590	134,360	145,270	140,260	142,290	136,310	136,170	137,700
Products	Percent of Total Landfilled								
	1960	1970	1980	1990	2000	2005	2010	2014	2015
Durable Goods	11.6%	12.1%	14.9%	15.0%	18.6%	21.3%	24.1%	25.4%	25.6%
(Detail in Table 17)									
Nondurable Goods	18.1%	18.9%	21.7%	24.8%	26.7%	25.2%	20.6%	20.7%	20.9%
(Detail in Table 21)									
Containers and Packaging	29.7%	35.6%	32.2%	27.3%	27.0%	25.8%	23.4%	22.0%	21.4%
(Detail in Table 29)									
Total Product** Wastes	59.4%	66.6%	68.8%	67.1%	72.3%	72.3%	68.1%	68.1%	67.9%
Other Wastes									
Food	14.8%	11.3%	9.5%	13.6%	17.3%	18.5%	21.0%	21.7%	22.0%
Yard Trimmings	24.2%	20.5%	20.1%	17.6%	8.5%	7.0%	8.6%	7.9%	7.8%
Miscellaneous Inorganic Wastes	1.6%	1.6%	1.6%	1.7%	1.9%	2.2%	2.3%	2.3%	2.3%
Total Other Wastes	40.6%	33.4%	31.2%	32.9%	27.7%	27.7%	31.9%	31.9%	32.1%
Total MSW Landfilled - %	100.0%	100.0%	100.0%	100.0%	100.0%	100.0%	100.0%	100.0%	100.0%

* Landfilling after recycling, composting and combustion with energy recovery. Does not include construction & demolition debris, industrial process wastes or certain other wastes. Details may not add to totals due to rounding.

** Other than food products.

Neg. = Less than 5,000 tons or 0.05 percent.

Source: *U.S. EPA, Advancing Sustainable Materials Management: 2015 Tables and Figures, July 2018*

Table 14. Products Generated* in the Municipal Waste Stream, 1960 to 2015 (With Detail On Durable Goods)

(In thousands of tons and percent of total generation)

Products	Thousands of Tons								
	1960	1970	1980	1990	2000	2005	2010	2014	2015
Durable Goods									
Major Appliances	1,630	2,170	2,950	3,310	3,640	3,610	4,020	4,650	4,860
Small Appliances**				460	1,040	1,180	1,830	1,960	1,960
Furniture and Furnishings	2,150	2,830	4,760	6,790	8,120	9,340	10,820	11,860	12,050
Carpets and Rugs**				1,660	2,460	2,960	3,720	3,730	3,630
Rubber Tires	1,120	1,890	2,720	3,610	4,930	4,910	5,130	5,560	5,840
Batteries, Lead-Acid	Neg.	820	1,490	1,510	2,280	2,750	3,020	3,230	3,130
Miscellaneous Durables									
Selected Consumer Electronics***					1,900	2,630	3,120	3,360	3,090
Other Miscellaneous Durables					14,500	17,680	17,690	18,690	19,590
Total Miscellaneous Durables	5,020	6,950	9,880	12,470	16,400	20,310	20,810	22,050	22,680
Total Durable Goods	9,920	14,660	21,800	29,810	38,870	45,060	49,350	53,040	54,150
Nondurable Goods	17,330	25,060	34,420	52,170	64,010	63,650	53,250	51,910	51,920
(Detail in Table 18)									
Containers and Packaging	27,370	43,560	52,670	64,530	75,840	76,330	75,470	76,860	77,920
(Detail in Table 22)									
Total Product Wastes†	54,620	83,280	108,890	146,510	178,720	185,040	178,070	181,810	183,990
Other Wastes									
Food	12,200	12,800	13,000	23,860	30,700	32,930	35,740	38,670	39,730
Yard Trimmings	20,000	23,200	27,500	35,000	30,530	32,070	33,400	34,500	34,720
Miscellaneous Inorganic Wastes	1,300	1,780	2,250	2,900	3,500	3,690	3,840	3,970	3,990
Total Other Wastes	33,500	37,780	42,750	61,760	64,730	68,690	72,980	77,140	78,440
Total MSW Generated - Weight	88,120	121,060	151,640	208,270	243,450	253,730	251,050	258,950	262,430
Products	**Percent of Total Generation**								
	1960	1970	1980	1990	2000	2005	2010	2014	2015
Durable Goods									
Major Appliances	1.8%	1.8%	1.9%	1.6%	1.5%	1.4%	1.6%	1.8%	1.8%
Small Appliances**				0.2%	0.4%	0.5%	0.7%	0.8%	0.7%
Furniture and Furnishings	2.4%	2.3%	3.1%	3.3%	3.3%	3.7%	4.3%	4.6%	4.6%
Carpets and Rugs**				0.8%	1.0%	1.2%	1.5%	1.5%	1.4%
Rubber Tires	1.3%	1.6%	1.8%	1.7%	2.0%	1.9%	2.0%	2.1%	2.2%
Batteries, Lead-Acid	Neg.	0.7%	1.0%	0.7%	0.9%	1.1%	1.2%	1.2%	1.2%
Miscellaneous Durables									
Selected Consumer Electronics***					0.8%	1.0%	1.2%	1.3%	1.2%
Other Miscellaneous Durables					6.0%	7.0%	7.0%	7.2%	7.5%
Total Miscellaneous Durables	5.7%	5.7%	6.5%	6.0%	6.7%	8.0%	8.3%	8.5%	8.7%
Total Durable Goods	11.3%	12.1%	14.4%	14.3%	16.0%	17.8%	19.7%	20.5%	20.6%
Nondurable Goods	19.7%	20.7%	22.7%	25.0%	26.3%	25.1%	21.2%	20.0%	19.8%
(Detail in Table 18)									
Containers and Packaging	31.1%	36.0%	34.7%	31.0%	31.2%	30.1%	30.1%	29.7%	29.7%
(Detail in Table 23)									
Total Product Wastes†	62.0%	68.8%	71.8%	70.3%	73.4%	72.9%	70.9%	70.2%	70.1%
Other Wastes									
Food	13.8%	10.6%	8.6%	11.5%	12.6%	13.0%	14.2%	14.9%	15.1%
Yard Trimmings	22.7%	19.2%	18.1%	16.8%	12.5%	12.6%	13.3%	13.4%	13.2%
Miscellaneous Inorganic Wastes	1.5%	1.5%	1.5%	1.4%	1.4%	1.5%	1.5%	1.5%	1.5%
Total Other Wastes	38.0%	31.2%	28.2%	29.7%	26.6%	27.1%	29.1%	29.8%	29.9%
Total MSW Generated - %	100.0%	100.0%	100.0%	100.0%	100.0%	100.0%	100.0%	100.0%	100.0%

* Generation before materials recycling, composting, combustion with energy recovery or landfilling. Does not include construction & demolition debris, industrial process wastes or certain other wastes. Details may not add to totals due to rounding.

** Not estimated separately prior to 1990. † Other than food products. Neg. = Less than 5,000 tons or 0.05 percent.

*** Not estimated separately prior to 2000.

Source: *U.S. EPA, Advancing Sustainable Materials Management: 2015 Tables and Figures, July 2018*

Table 15. Products Recycled and Composted* in the Municipal Waste Stream, 1960 to 2015 (With Detail On Durable Goods)

(In thousands of tons and percent of generation of each product)

Products	Thousands of Tons								
	1960	1970	1980	1990	2000	2005	2010	2014	2015
Durable Goods									
Major Appliances	10	50	130	1,070	2,000	2,420	2,610	2,710	3,000
Small Appliances**				10	20	20	120	120	120
Furniture and Furnishings	Neg.	Neg.	Neg.	Neg.	Neg.	Neg.	10	10	10
Carpets and Rugs**				Neg.	190	250	270	210	190
Rubber Tires	330	250	150	440	1,290	1,640	2,270	2,250	2,350
Batteries, Lead-Acid	Neg.	620	1,040	1,470	2,130	2,640	2,980	3,200	3,100
Miscellaneous Durables									
Selected Consumer Electronics***					190	360	650	1,400	1,230
Other Miscellaneous Durables					760	640	480	240	250
Total Miscellaneous Durables	10	20	40	470	950	1,000	1,130	1,640	1,480
Total Durable Goods	350	940	1,360	3,460	6,580	7,970	9,390	10,140	10,250
Nondurable Goods	2,390	3,730	4,670	8,800	17,560	19,770	19,190	16,820	16,190
(Detail in Table 19)									
Containers and Packaging	2,870	3,350	8,490	16,780	28,870	31,500	36,680	39,590	41,330
(Detail in Table 24)									
Total Product Wastes†	5,610	8,020	14,520	29,040	53,010	59,240	65,260	66,550	67,770
Other Wastes									
Food^	Neg.	Neg.	Neg.	Neg.	680	690	970	1,940	2,100
Yard Trimmings	Neg.	Neg.	Neg.	4,200	15,770	19,860	19,200	21,080	21,290
Miscellaneous Inorganic Wastes	Neg.	Neg.	Neg.	Neg.	Neg.	Neg.	Neg.	Neg.	Neg.
Total Other Wastes	Neg.	Neg.	Neg.	4,200	16,450	20,550	20,170	23,020	23,390
Total MSW Recycled and Composted - Weight	5,610	8,020	14,520	33,240	69,460	79,790	85,430	89,570	91,160

Products	Percent of Total Generation								
	1960	1970	1980	1990	2000	2005	2010	2014	2015
Durable Goods									
Major Appliances	0.6%	2.3%	4.4%	32.3%	54.9%	67.0%	64.9%	58.3%	61.7%
Small Appliances**				2.2%	1.9%	1.7%	6.6%	6.1%	6.1%
Furniture and Furnishings	Neg.	Neg.	Neg.	Neg.	Neg.	Neg.	0.1%	0.1%	0.1%
Carpets and Rugs**				Neg.	7.7%	8.4%	7.3%	5.6%	5.2%
Rubber Tires	29.5%	13.2%	5.5%	12.2%	26.2%	33.4%	44.2%	40.5%	40.2%
Batteries, Lead-Acid	Neg.	75.6%	69.8%	97.4%	93.4%	96.0%	98.7%	99.1%	99.0%
Miscellaneous Durables									
Selected Consumer Electronics***					10.0%	13.7%	20.8%	41.7%	39.8%
Other Miscellaneous Durables					5.2%	3.6%	2.7%	1.3%	1.3%
Total Miscellaneous Durables	0.2%	0.3%	0.4%	3.8%	5.8%	4.9%	5.4%	7.4%	6.5%
Total Durable Goods	3.5%	6.4%	6.2%	11.6%	16.9%	17.7%	19.0%	19.1%	18.9%
Nondurable Goods	13.8%	14.9%	13.6%	16.9%	27.4%	31.1%	36.0%	32.4%	31.2%
(Detail in Table 19)									
Containers and Packaging	10.5%	7.7%	16.1%	26.0%	38.1%	41.3%	48.6%	51.5%	53.0%
(Detail in Table 25)									
Total Product Wastes†	10.3%	9.6%	13.3%	19.8%	29.7%	32.0%	36.6%	36.6%	36.8%
Other Wastes									
Food^	Neg.	Neg.	Neg.	Neg.	2.2%	2.1%	2.7%	5.0%	5.3%
Yard Trimmings	Neg	Neg	Neg	12.0%	51.7%	61.9%	57.5%	61.1%	61.3%
Miscellaneous Inorganic Wastes	Neg.	Neg.	Neg.	Neg.	Neg.	Neg.	Neg.	Neg.	Neg.
Total Other Wastes	Neg.	Neg.	Neg.	6.8%	25.4%	29.9%	27.6%	29.8%	29.8%
Total MSW Recycled and Composted - %	6.4%	6.6%	9.6%	16.0%	28.5%	31.4%	34.0%	34.6%	34.7%

* Recycling and composting of postconsumer wastes; does not include converting/fabrication scrap. Details may not add to totals due to rounding.

** Not estimated separately prior to 1990. † Other than food products.

*** Not estimated separately prior to 2000.

^ Includes collection of other MSW organics for composting.

Neg. = Less than 5,000 tons or 0.05 percent.

Source: *U.S. EPA, Advancing Sustainable Materials Management: 2015 Tables and Figures, July 2018*

Table 16. Products Combusted with Energy Recovery* in the Municipal Waste Stream, 1960 to 2015 (With Detail On Durable Goods)

(In thousands of tons and percent of total combusted)

Products	Thousands of Tons								
	1960	1970	1980	1990	2000	2005	2010	2014	2015
Durable Goods									
Major Appliances±§		0	0	0	0	0	0	0	0
Small Appliances**				90	200	200	310	370	370
Furniture and Furnishings		Neg.	90	1,150	1,570	1,700	1,910	2,320	2,350
Carpets and Rugs**				290	440	490	610	690	670
Rubber Tires§		Neg.	30	400	2,260	2,390	2,000	3,080	2,780
Batteries, Lead-Acid±		0	0	0	0	0	0	0	0
Miscellaneous Durables									
Selected Consumer Electronics									
Other Miscellaneous Durables									
Total Miscellaneous Durables§		60	320	2,550	1,790	1,970	2,240	1,950	2,430
Total Durable Goods		60	440	4,480	6,260	6,750	7,070	8,410	8,600
Nondurable Goods		90	580	7,380	9,000	7,980	6,030	6,880	6,990
(Detail in Table 20)									
Containers and Packaging		150	880	8,110	9,110	8,160	6,870	7,310	7,190
(Detail in Table 26)									
Total Product Wastes†		300	1,900	19,970	24,370	22,890	19,970	22,600	22,780
Other Wastes									
Food		50	260	4,060	5,820	5,870	6,150	7,200	7,380
Yard Trimmings		90	550	5,240	2,860	2,220	2,510	2,630	2,630
Miscellaneous Inorganic Wastes		10	50	490	680	670	680	780	780
Total Other Wastes		150	860	9,790	9,360	8,760	9,340	10,610	10,790
Total MSW Combusted with Energy Recovery - Weight		450	2,760	29,760	33,730	31,650	29,310	33,210	33,570

Products	Percent of Total Combusted								
	1960	1970	1980	1990	2000	2005	2010	2014	2015
Durable Goods									
Major Appliances±§		0.0%	0.0%	0.0%	0.0%	0.0%	0.0%	0.0%	0.0%
Small Appliances**				0.3%	0.6%	0.6%	1.1%	1.1%	1.1%
Furniture and Furnishings		Neg.	3.3%	3.9%	4.7%	5.4%	6.5%	7.0%	7.0%
Carpets and Rugs**				1.0%	1.3%	1.5%	2.1%	2.1%	2.0%
Rubber Tires§		Neg.	1.1%	1.3%	6.7%	7.6%	6.8%	9.3%	8.3%
Batteries, Lead-Acid±		0.0%	0.0%	0.0%	0.0%	0.0%	0.0%	0.0%	0.0%
Miscellaneous Durables									
Selected Consumer Electronics									
Other Miscellaneous Durables									
Total Miscellaneous Durables§		13.3%	11.6%	8.6%	5.3%	6.2%	7.6%	5.9%	7.2%
Total Durable Goods		13.3%	15.9%	15.1%	18.6%	21.3%	24.1%	25.4%	25.6%
Nondurable Goods		19.9%	21.0%	24.8%	26.7%	25.2%	20.6%	20.7%	20.9%
(Detail in Table 20)									
Containers and Packaging		33.3%	31.9%	27.3%	27.0%	25.8%	23.4%	22.0%	21.4%
(Detail in Table 27)									
Total Product Wastes†		66.6%	68.8%	67.1%	72.3%	72.3%	68.1%	68.1%	67.9%

Source: *U.S. EPA, Advancing Sustainable Materials Management: 2015 Tables and Figures, July 2018*

Table 16. Products Combusted with Energy Recovery* in the Municipal Waste Stream, 1960 to 2014 (With Detail On Durable Goods)

(In thousands of tons and percent of total combusted)

Products	Percent of Total Combusted								
	1960	1970	1980	1990	2000	2005	2010	2014	2015
Other Wastes									
Food		11.1%	9.4%	13.6%	17.3%	18.5%	21.0%	21.7%	22.0%
Yard Trimmings		20.0%	20.0%	17.6%	8.5%	7.0%	8.6%	7.9%	7.8%
Miscellaneous Inorganic Wastes		2.3%	1.8%	1.7%	1.9%	2.1%	2.3%	2.3%	2.3%
Total Other Wastes		33.4%	31.2%	32.9%	27.7%	27.7%	31.9%	31.9%	32.1%
Total MSW Combusted with Energy Recovery - %		100.0%	100.0%	100.0%	100.0%	100.0%	100.0%	100.0%	100.0%

* Products and materials combusted with energy recovery estimated at percentage total MSW after recovery for recycling and composting. In 2015, 19.6 percent of MSW after recycling and composting was combusted with energy recovery except for major appliances, tires and lead-acid batteries. Does not include construction & demolition debris, industrial process wastes or certain other wastes. Details may not add to totals due to rounding.

** Not estimated separately prior to 1990.

† Other than food products.

§ Tires: tires to fuel based on industry percentage estimates applied to tire generation. *Total Miscellaneous Durables*: calculated as difference between total durable goods going to combustion and individual durable goods shown. The amounts of consumer electronics going to combustion with energy recovery are not available and are included in Total Miscellaneous Durables.

± Energy Recovery Council, 2016. Major appliances and lead-acid batteries are not accepted at waste-to-energy facilities.

Neg. = Less than 5,000 tons or 0.05 percent.

Source: *U.S. EPA, Advancing Sustainable Materials Management: 2015 Tables and Figures, July 2018*

Table 17. Products Landfilled* in the Municipal Waste Stream, 1960 to 2015 (With Detail On Durable Goods)

(In thousands of tons and percent of total landfilled)

Products	Thousands of Tons								
	1960	1970	1980	1990	2000	2005	2010	2014	2015
Durable Goods									
Major Appliances	1,620	2,120	2,820	2,240	1,640	1,190	1,410	1,940	1,860
Small Appliances**				360	820	960	1,400	1,470	1,470
Furniture and Furnishings	2,150	2,830	4,670	5,640	6,550	7,640	8,900	9,530	9,690
Carpets and Rugs**				1,370	1,830	2,220	2,840	2,830	2,770
Rubber Tires	790	1,640	2,540	2,770	1,380	880	860	230	710
Batteries, Lead-Acid		200	450	40	150	110	40	30	30
Miscellaneous Durables									
Selected Consumer Electronics***									
Other Miscellaneous Durables									
Total Miscellaneous Durables	5,010	6,870	9,520	9,450	13,660	17,340	17,440	18,460	18,770
Total Durable Goods	9,570	13,660	20,000	21,870	26,030	30,340	32,890	34,490	35,300
Nondurable Goods	14,940	21,240	29,170	35,990	37,450	35,900	28,030	28,210	28,740
(Detail in Table 21)									
Containers and Packaging	24,500	40,060	43,300	39,640	37,860	36,670	31,920	29,960	29,400
(Detail in Table 28)									
Total Product Wastes†	49,010	74,960	92,470	97,500	101,340	102,910	92,840	92,660	93,440
Other Wastes									
Food	12,200	12,750	12,740	19,800	24,200	26,370	28,620	29,530	30,250
Yard Trimmings	20,000	23,110	26,950	25,560	11,900	9,990	11,690	10,790	10,800
Miscellaneous Inorganic Wastes	1,300	1,770	2,200	2,410	2,820	3,020	3,160	3,190	3,210
Total Other Wastes	33,500	37,630	41,890	47,770	38,920	39,380	43,470	43,510	44,260
Total MSW Landfilled- Weight	82,510	112,590	134,360	145,270	140,260	142,290	136,310	136,170	137,700
Products	**Percent of Total Landfilled**								
	1960	1970	1980	1990	2000	2005	2010	2014	2015
Durable Goods									
Major Appliances	2.0%	1.9%	2.1%	1.5%	1.2%	0.8%	1.0%	1.4%	1.4%
Small Appliances**				0.2%	0.6%	0.7%	1.0%	1.1%	1.1%
Furniture and Furnishings	2.6%	2.5%	3.5%	3.9%	4.7%	5.4%	6.5%	7.0%	7.0%
Carpets and Rugs**				0.9%	1.3%	1.5%	2.1%	2.1%	2.0%
Rubber Tires	1.0%	1.5%	1.9%	1.9%	1.0%	0.6%	0.6%	0.2%	0.5%
Batteries, Lead-Acid	Neg.	0.2%	0.3%	0.1%	0.1%	0.1%	0.1%	Neg.	Neg.
Miscellaneous Durables									
Selected Consumer Electronics***									
Other Miscellaneous Durables									
Total Miscellaneous Durables	6.1%	6.1%	7.1%	6.5%	9.7%	12.2%	12.8%	13.6%	13.6%
Total Durable Goods	11.6%	12.1%	14.9%	15.0%	18.6%	21.3%	24.1%	25.4%	25.6%
Nondurable Goods	18.1%	18.9%	21.7%	24.8%	26.7%	25.2%	20.6%	20.7%	20.9%
(Detail in Table 21)									
Containers and Packaging	29.7%	35.6%	32.2%	27.3%	27.0%	25.8%	23.4%	22.0%	21.4%
(Detail in Table 29)									
Total Product Wastes†	59.4%	66.6%	68.8%	67.1%	72.3%	72.3%	68.1%	68.1%	67.9%
Other Wastes									
Food	14.8%	11.3%	9.5%	13.6%	17.3%	18.5%	21.0%	21.7%	22.0%
Yard Trimmings	24.2%	20.5%	20.1%	17.6%	8.5%	7.0%	8.6%	7.9%	7.8%
Miscellaneous Inorganic Wastes	1.6%	1.6%	1.6%	1.7%	1.9%	2.2%	2.3%	2.3%	2.3%
Total Other Wastes	40.6%	33.4%	31.2%	32.9%	27.7%	27.7%	31.9%	31.9%	32.1%
Total MSW Landfilled - %	100.0%	100.0%	100.0%	100.0%	100.0%	100.0%	100.0%	100.0%	100.0%

* Landfilling after recycling, composting and combustion with energy recovery. Details may not add to totals due to rounding.

** Not estimated separately prior to 1990.

*** The amount of consumer electronics going to combustion with energy recovery versus landfilling are not available. These products are included in Total Miscellaneous Durables.

† Other than food products.

Neg. = Less than 5,000 tons or 0.05 percent.

Source: *U.S. EPA, Advancing Sustainable Materials Management: 2015 Tables and Figures, July 2018*

Table 18. Products Generated* in the Municipal Waste Stream, 1960 to 2015 (With Detail on Nondurable Goods)

(In thousands of tons and percent of generation of each product)

Products	Thousands of Tons								
	1960	1970	1980	1990	2000	2005	2010	2014	2015
Durable Goods	9,920	14,660	21,800	29,810	38,870	45,060	49,350	53,040	54,150
(Detail in Table 14)									
Nondurable Goods									
Newspapers/Mechanical Papers†	7,110	9,510	11,050	13,430	14,790	12,790	9,880	7,620	6,730
Directories†**				610	680	660	-	-	-
Other Paper Nondurable Goods									
Books and Magazines	1,920	2,470	3,390						
Books**				970	1,240	1,100	990	830	800
Magazines**				2,830	2,230	2,580	1,590	1,260	1,190
Office-Type Papers***	1,520	2,650	4,000	6,410	7,420	6,620	5,260	4,530	4,530
Standard Mail§				3,820	5,570	5,830	4,340	4,050	4,050
Other Commercial Printing†	1,260	2,130	3,120	4,460	7,380	6,440	2,480	2,190	2,080
Tissue Paper and Towels	1,090	2,080	2,300	2,960	3,220	3,460	3,490	3,640	3,680
Paper Plates and Cups	270	420	630	650	960	1,160	1,350	1,380	1,360
Other Nonpackaging Paper	2,700	3,630	4,230	3,840	4,250	4,490	4,190	3,970	3,700
Total Other Paper Nondurable Goods							23,690	21,850	21,390
Disposable Diapers	Neg.	350	1,930	2,700	3,230	3,410	3,700	4,180	4,280
Plastic Plates and Cups§			190	650	870	930	890	1,020	1,050
Trash Bags**				780	850	1,060	980	1,000	1,130
Clothing and Footwear	1,360	1,620	2,170	4,010	6,470	7,890	9,100	11,170	11,940
Towels, Sheets and Pillowcases**				710	820	980	1,290	1,270	1,350
Other Miscellaneous Nondurables	100	200	1,410	3,340	4,030	4,250	3,720	3,800	4,050
Total Nondurable Goods	17,330	25,060	34,420	52,170	64,010	63,650	53,250	51,910	51,920
Containers and Packaging	27,370	43,560	52,670	64,530	75,840	76,330	75,470	76,860	77,920
(Detail in Table 22)									
Total Product Wastes‡	54,620	83,280	108,890	146,510	178,720	185,040	178,070	181,810	183,990
Other Wastes	33,500	37,780	42,750	61,760	64,730	68,690	72,980	77,140	78,440
Total MSW Generated - Weight	88,120	121,060	151,640	208,270	243,450	253,730	251,050	258,950	262,430

Products	Percent of Generation of Each Product								
	1960	1970	1980	1990	2000	2005	2010	2014	2015
Durable Goods	11.3%	12.1%	14.4%	14.3%	16.0%	17.8%	19.7%	20.5%	20.6%
(Detail in Table 14)									
Nondurable Goods									
Newspapers/Mechanical Papers†	8.1%	7.9%	7.3%	6.4%	6.1%	5.0%	3.9%	2.9%	2.6%
Directories†**				0.3%	0.3%	0.3%	-	-	-
Other Paper Nondurable Goods									
Books and Magazines	2.2%	2.0%	2.2%						
Books**				0.5%	0.5%	0.4%	0.4%	0.3%	0.3%
Magazines**				1.4%	0.9%	1.0%	0.6%	0.5%	0.5%
Office-Type Papers***	1.7%	2.2%	2.6%	3.1%	3.0%	2.6%	2.1%	1.8%	1.8%
Standard Mail§				1.8%	2.3%	2.3%	1.7%	1.6%	1.5%
Other Commercial Printing†	1.4%	1.8%	2.1%	2.1%	3.0%	2.5%	1.0%	0.8%	0.8%
Tissue Paper and Towels	1.2%	1.7%	1.5%	1.4%	1.3%	1.4%	1.4%	1.4%	1.4%
Paper Plates and Cups	0.3%	0.3%	0.4%	0.3%	0.4%	0.5%	0.5%	0.5%	0.5%
Other Nonpackaging Paper	3.1%	3.0%	2.8%	1.8%	1.7%	1.8%	1.7%	1.6%	1.5%
Total Other Paper Nondurable Goods							9.4%	8.5%	8.3%
Disposable Diapers	Neg.	0.3%	1.3%	1.3%	1.3%	1.3%	1.5%	1.6%	1.6%
Plastic Plates and Cups§			0.1%	0.3%	0.4%	0.4%	0.4%	0.4%	0.4%
Trash Bags**				0.4%	0.3%	0.4%	0.4%	0.4%	0.4%

Source: *U.S. EPA, Advancing Sustainable Materials Management: 2015 Tables and Figures, July 2018*

Table 18. Products Generated* in the Municipal Waste Stream, 1960 to 2015 (With Detail on Nondurable Goods)

(In thousands of tons and percent of generation of each product)

Products	Percent of Generation of Each Product								
	1960	1970	1980	1990	2000	2005	2010	2014	2015
Clothing and Footwear	1.5%	1.3%	1.4%	1.9%	2.7%	3.1%	3.6%	4.3%	4.5%
Towels, Sheets and Pillowcases**				0.3%	0.3%	0.4%	0.5%	0.5%	0.5%
Other Miscellaneous Nondurables	0.1%	0.2%	0.9%	1.6%	1.7%	1.7%	1.5%	1.5%	1.5%
Total Nondurables	19.7%	20.7%	22.7%	25.0%	26.3%	25.1%	21.2%	20.0%	19.8%
Containers and Packaging	31.1%	36.0%	34.7%	31.0%	31.2%	30.1%	30.1%	29.7%	29.7%
(Detail in Table 23)									
Total Product Wastes‡	62.0%	68.8%	71.8%	70.3%	73.4%	72.9%	70.9%	70.2%	70.1%
Other Wastes	38.0%	31.2%	28.2%	29.7%	26.6%	27.1%	29.1%	29.8%	29.9%
Total MSW Generated - %	100.0%	100.0%	100.0%	100.0%	100.0%	100.0%	100.0%	100.0%	100.0%

* Generation before materials recycling, composting, combustion with energy recovery or landfilling. Does not include construction & demolition debris, industrial process wastes or certain other wastes. Details may not add to totals due to rounding.

† Starting in 2010, newsprint and groundwood inserts expanded to include directories and other mechanical papers previously counted as Other Commercial Printing.

** Not estimated separately prior to 1990.

*** High-grade paper such as printer paper; generated in both commercial and residential sources.

§ Standard Mail: Not estimated separately prior to 1990. Formerly called Third Class Mail and Standard (A) Mail by the U.S. Postal Service.

§ Plastic Plates and Cups: Not estimated separately prior to 1980.

‡ Other than food products.

\- Detailed data not available.

Neg. = Less than 5,000 tons or 0.05 percent.

Source: *U.S. EPA, Advancing Sustainable Materials Management: 2015 Tables and Figures, July 2018*

Table 19. Products Recycled and Composted* in Municipal Solid Waste, 1960 to 2015 (With Detail on Nondurable Goods)

(In thousands of tons and percent of generation of each product)

Products	Thousands of Tons								
	1960	1970	1980	1990	2000	2005	2010	2014	2015
Durable Goods	350	940	1,360	3,460	6,580	7,970	9,390	10,140	10,250
(Detail in Table 15)									
Nondurable Goods									
Newspapers/Mechanical Papers†	1,820	2,250	3,020	5,110	8,720	9,360	7,070	5,200	4,790
Directories†**				50	120	120	-	-	-
Other Paper Nondurable Goods									
Books and Magazines	100	260	280						
Books**				100	240	270	-	-	-
Magazines**				300	710	960	-	-	-
Office-Type Papers***	250	710	870	1,700	4,090	4,110	-	-	-
Standard Mail§				200	1,830	2,090	-	-	-
Other Commercial Printing†	130	340	350	700	810	1,440	-	-	-
Tissue Paper and Towels	Neg.	Neg.	Neg.	Neg.	Neg.	Neg.	-	-	-
Paper Plates and Cups	Neg.	Neg.	Neg.	Neg.	Neg.	Neg.	-	-	-
Other Nonpackaging Paper	40	110	Neg.	Neg.	Neg.	Neg.	-	-	-
Total Other Paper Nondurable Goods							10,650	9,710	9,330
Disposable Diapers				Neg.	Neg.	Neg.	Neg.	Neg.	Neg.
Plastic Plates and Cups§			Neg.	Neg.	Neg.	Neg.	Neg.	Neg.	Neg.
Trash Bags**				Neg.	Neg.	Neg.	Neg.	Neg.	Neg.
Clothing and Footwear	50	60	150	520	900	1,250	1,250	1,540	1,690
Towels, Sheets and Pillowcases**				120	140	170	220	230	220
Other Miscellaneous Nondurables	Neg.	Neg.	Neg.	Neg.	Neg.	Neg.	Neg.	140	160
Total Nondurable Goods	2,390	3,730	4,670	8,800	17,560	19,770	19,190	16,820	16,190
Containers and Packaging	2,870	3,350	8,490	16,780	28,870	31,500	36,680	39,590	41,330
(Detail in Table 24)									
Total Product Wastes‡	5,610	8,020	14,520	29,040	53,010	59,240	65,260	66,550	67,770
Other Wastes	Neg.	Neg.	Neg.	4,200	16,450	20,550	20,170	23,020	23,390
Total MSW Recycled and Composted - Weight	5,610	8,020	14,520	33,240	69,460	79,790	85,430	89,570	91,160
Products	**Percent of Generation of Each Product**								
	1960	1970	1980	1990	2000	2005	2010	2014	2015
Durable Goods	3.5%	6.4%	6.2%	11.6%	16.9%	17.7%	19.0%	19.1%	18.9%
(Detail in Table 15)									
Nondurable Goods									
Newspapers/Mechanical Papers†	25.6%	23.7%	27.3%	38.0%	59.0%	73.2%	71.6%	68.2%	71.2%
Directories†**				8.2%	17.6%	18.2%	-	-	-
Other Paper Nondurable Goods									
Books and Magazines	5.2%	10.5%	8.3%						
Books**				10.3%	19.4%	24.5%	-	-	-
Magazines**				10.6%	31.8%	37.2%	-	-	-
Office-Type Papers***	16.4%	26.8%	21.8%	26.5%	55.1%	62.1%	-	-	-
Standard Mail§				5.2%	32.9%	35.8%	-	-	-
Other Commercial Printing†	10.3%	16.0%	11.2%	15.7%	11.0%	22.4%	-	-	-
Tissue Paper and Towels	Neg.	Neg.	Neg.	Neg.	Neg.	Neg.	-	-	-
Paper Plates and Cups	Neg.	Neg.	Neg.	Neg.	Neg.	Neg.	-	-	-
Other Nonpackaging Paper	1.5%	3.0%	Neg.	Neg.	Neg.	Neg.	-	-	-
Total Other Paper Nondurable Goods							45.0%	44.4%	43.6%

Source: *U.S. EPA, Advancing Sustainable Materials Management: 2015 Tables and Figures, July 2018*

Table 19. Products Recycled and Composted* in Municipal Solid Waste, 1960 to 2015
(With Detail on Nondurable Goods)
(In thousands of tons and percent of generation of each product)

Products	Percent of Generation of Each Product								
	1960	1970	1980	1990	2000	2005	2010	2014	2015
Disposable Diapers				Neg.	Neg.	Neg.	Neg.	Neg.	Neg.
Plastic Plates and Cups§			Neg.	Neg.	Neg.	Neg.	Neg.	Neg.	Neg.
Trash Bags**				Neg.	Neg.	Neg.	Neg.	Neg.	Neg.
Clothing and Footwear	Neg.	Neg.	Neg.	13.0%	13.9%	15.8%	13.7%	13.8%	14.2%
Towels, Sheets and Pillowcases**				16.9%	17.1%	17.3%	17.1%	18.1%	16.3%
Other Miscellaneous Nondurables	Neg.	Neg.	Neg.	Neg.	Neg.	Neg.	Neg.	3.7%	4.0%
Total Nondurables	13.8%	14.9%	13.6%	16.9%	27.4%	31.1%	36.0%	32.4%	31.2%
Containers and Packaging	10.5%	7.7%	16.1%	26.0%	38.1%	41.3%	48.6%	51.5%	53.0%
(Detail in Table 25)									
Total Product Wastes‡	10.3%	9.6%	13.3%	19.8%	29.7%	32.0%	36.6%	36.6%	36.8%
Other Wastes	Neg.	Neg.	Neg.	6.8%	25.4%	29.9%	27.6%	29.8%	29.8%
Total MSW Recycled and Composted - %	6.4%	6.6%	9.6%	16.0%	28.5%	31.4%	34.0%	34.6%	34.7%

* Recycling and composting of postconsumer wastes; does not include converting/fabrication scrap. Details may not add to totals due to rounding.

† Starting in 2010, newsprint and groundwood inserts expanded to include directories and other mechanical papers previously counted as Other Commercial Printing.

** Not estimated separately prior to 1990.

*** High-grade paper such as printer paper; generated in both commercial and residential sources.

§ Standard Mail: Not estimated separately prior to 1990. Formerly called Third Class Mail and Standard (A) Mail by the U.S. Postal Service.

§ Plastic Plates and Cups: Not estimated separately prior to 1980.

‡ Other than food products.

\- Detailed data not available.

Neg. = Less than 5,000 tons or 0.05 percent.

Source: *U.S. EPA, Advancing Sustainable Materials Management: 2015 Tables and Figures, July 2018*

Table 20. Products Combusted with Energy Recovery* in Municipal Solid Waste, 1960 to 2015 (With Detail on Nondurable Goods) (In thousands of tons and percent of total combusted)

Products	Thousands of Tons								
	1960	1970	1980	1990	2000	2005	2010	2014	2015
Durable Goods	0	60	440	4,480	6,260	6,750	7,070	8,410	8,600
(Detail in Table 16)									
Nondurable Goods									
Newspapers/Mechanical Papers†	0	30	160	1,420	1,180	620	500	470	380
Directories†**				100	110	100	-	-	-
Other Paper Nondurable Goods									
Books and Magazines	0	10	60						
Books**				150	190	150	-	-	-
Magazines**				430	290	290	-	-	-
Office-Type Papers***	0	10	60	800	650	460	-	-	-
Standard Mail§				620	730	680	-	-	-
Other Commercial Printing†	0	10	60	640	1,270	910	-	-	-
Tissue Paper and Towels	0	10	50	500	620	630	-	-	-
Paper Plates and Cups	0	Neg.	10	110	190	210	-	-	-
Other Nonpackaging Paper	0	10	80	650	820	820	-	-	-
Total Other Paper Nondurable Goods							2,310	2,380	2,360
Disposable Diapers		Neg.	30	460	630	620	650	820	840
Plastic Plates and Cups§			Neg.	110	170	170	160	200	210
Trash Bags**				130	160	190	170	200	220
Clothing and Footwear	0	10	50	590	1,080	1,210	1,390	1,890	2,010
Towels, Sheets and Pillowcases**				100	130	150	190	200	220
Other Miscellaneous Nondurables	0	Neg.	20	570	780	770	660	720	750
Total Nondurables	0	90	580	7,380	9,000	7,980	6,030	6,880	6,990
Containers and Packaging	0	150	880	8,110	9,110	8,160	6,870	7,310	7,190
(Detail in Table 26)									
Total Product Wastes‡	0	300	1,900	19,970	24,370	22,890	19,970	22,600	22,780
Other Wastes	0	150	860	9,790	9,360	8,760	9,340	10,610	10,790
Total MSW Combusted with Energy Recovery - Weight	0	450	2,760	29,760	33,730	31,650	29,310	33,210	33,570
Products	**Percent of Total Combusted**								
	1960	1970	1980	1990	2000	2005	2010	2014	2015
Durable Goods		13.3%	15.9%	15.1%	18.6%	21.3%	24.1%	25.4%	25.6%
(Detail in Table 16)									
Nondurable Goods									
Newspapers/Mechanical Papers†		6.7%	5.8%	4.8%	3.5%	2.0%	1.7%	1.4%	1.1%
Directories†**				0.3%	0.3%	0.3%	-	-	-
Other Paper Nondurable Goods									
Books and Magazines		2.2%	2.2%						
Books**				0.5%	0.6%	0.5%	-	-	-
Magazines**				1.4%	0.9%	0.9%	-	-	-
Office-Type Papers***		2.2%	2.2%	2.7%	1.8%	1.4%	-	-	-
Standard Mail§				2.1%	2.2%	2.1%	-	-	-
Other Commercial Printing†		2.2%	2.2%	2.2%	3.8%	2.9%	-	-	-

Source: *U.S. EPA, Advancing Sustainable Materials Management: 2015 Tables and Figures, July 2018*

Table 20. Products Combusted with Energy Recovery* in Municipal Solid Waste, 1960 to 2015 (With Detail on Nondurable Goods)

(In thousands of tons and percent of total combusted)

Products	Percent of Total Combusted								
	1960	1970	1980	1990	2000	2005	2010	2014	2015
Tissue Paper and Towels		2.2%	1.8%	1.7%	1.8%	2.0%	-	-	-
Paper Plates and Cups		Neg.	0.4%	0.4%	0.6%	0.7%	-	-	-
Other Nonpackaging Paper		2.2%	2.8%	2.2%	2.4%	2.6%	-	-	-
Total Other Paper Nondurable Goods							7.9%	7.2%	7.0%
Disposable Diapers		Neg.	1.1%	1.5%	1.9%	2.0%	2.2%	2.5%	2.5%
Plastic Plates and Cups§			Neg.	0.4%	0.5%	0.5%	0.5%	0.6%	0.6%
Trash Bags**				0.4%	0.5%	0.6%	0.6%	0.6%	0.7%
Clothing and Footwear		2.2%	1.8%	2.0%	3.2%	3.8%	4.7%	5.7%	6.0%
Towels, Sheets and Pillowcases**				0.3%	0.4%	0.5%	0.7%	0.6%	0.7%
Other Miscellaneous Nondurables		Neg.	0.7%	1.9%	2.3%	2.4%	2.3%	2.1%	2.3%
Total Nondurables		19.9%	21.0%	24.8%	26.7%	25.2%	20.6%	20.7%	20.9%
Containers and Packaging		33.3%	31.9%	27.3%	27.0%	25.8%	23.4%	22.0%	21.4%
(Detail in Table 27)									
Total Product Wastes‡		66.6%	68.8%	67.1%	72.3%	72.3%	68.1%	68.1%	67.9%
Other Wastes		33.4%	31.2%	32.9%	27.7%	27.7%	31.9%	31.9%	32.1%
Total MSW Combusted with Energy Recovery - %		100.0%	100.0%	100.0%	100.0%	100.0%	100.0%	100.0%	100.0%

* Products and materials combusted with energy recovery estimated at percentage total MSW after recovery for recycling and composting. In 2015, 19.6 percent of MSW after recycling and composting was combusted with energy recovery. Does not include construction & demolition debris, industrial process wastes or certain other wastes. Details may not add to totals due to rounding.

† Starting in 2010, newsprint and groundwood inserts expanded to include directories and other mechanical papers previously counted as Other Commercial Printing.

** Not estimated separately prior to 1990.

*** High-grade paper such as printer paper; generated in both commercial and residential sources.

§ Standard Mail: Not estimated separately prior to 1990. Formerly called Third Class Mail and Standard (A) Mail by the U.S. Postal Service.

§ Plastic Plates and Cups: Not estimated separately prior to 1980.

‡ Other than food products.

\- Detailed data not available.

Neg. = Less than 5,000 tons or 0.05 percent.

Source: *U.S. EPA, Advancing Sustainable Materials Management: 2015 Tables and Figures, July 2018*

Table 21. Products Landfilled* in Municipal Solid Waste, 1960 to 2015 (With Detail on Nondurable Goods)

(In thousands of tons and percent of total landfilled)

Products	Thousands of Tons								
	1960	1970	1980	1990	2000	2005	2010	2014	2015
Durable Goods	9,570	13,660	20,000	21,870	26,030	30,340	32,890	34,490	35,300
(Detail in Table 17)									
Nondurable Goods									
Newspapers/Mechanical Papers†	5,290	7,230	7,870	6,900	4,890	2,810	2,310	1,950	1,560
Directories†**				460	450	440	-	-	-
Other Paper Nondurable Goods									
Books and Magazines	1,820	2,200	3,050						
Books**				720	810	680	-	-	-
Magazines**				2,100	1,230	1,330	-	-	-
Office-Type Papers***	1,270	1,930	3,070	3,910	2,680	2,050	-	-	-
Standard Mail§				3,000	3,010	3,060	-	-	-
Other Commercial Printing†	1,130	1,780	2,710	3,120	5,300	4,090	-	-	-
Tissue Paper and Towels	1,090	2,070	2,250	2,460	2,600	2,830	-	-	-
Paper Plates and Cups	270	420	620	540	770	950	-	-	-
Other Nonpackaging Paper	2,660	3,510	4,150	3,190	3,430	3,670	-	-	-
Total Other Paper Nondurable Goods							10,730	9,760	9,700
Disposable Diapers		350	1,900	2,240	2,600	2,790	3,050	3,360	3,440
Plastic Plates and Cups§			190	540	700	760	730	820	840
Trash Bags**				650	690	870	810	800	910
Clothing and Footwear	1,310	1,550	1,970	2,900	4,490	5,430	6,460	7,740	8,240
Towels, Sheets and Pillowcases**				490	550	660	880	840	910
Other Miscellaneous Nondurables	100	200	1,390	2,770	3,250	3,480	3,060	2,940	3,140
Total Nondurables	14,940	21,240	29,170	35,990	37,450	35,900	28,030	28,210	28,740
Containers and Packaging	24,500	40,060	43,300	39,640	37,860	36,670	31,920	29,960	29,400
(Detail in Table 28)									
Total Product Wastes‡	49,010	74,960	92,470	97,500	101,340	102,910	92,840	92,660	93,440
Other Wastes	33,500	37,630	41,890	47,770	38,920	39,380	43,470	43,510	44,260
Total MSW Landfilled - Weight	82,510	112,590	134,360	145,270	140,260	142,290	136,310	136,170	137,700
Products	**Percent of Total Landfilled**								
	1960	1970	1980	1990	2000	2005	2010	2014	2015
Durable Goods	11.6%	12.1%	14.9%	15.1%	18.6%	21.3%	24.1%	25.4%	25.6%
(Detail in Table 17)									
Nondurable Goods									
Newspapers/Mechanical Papers†	6.4%	6.4%	5.9%	4.7%	3.5%	2.0%	1.7%	1.4%	1.1%
Directories†**				0.3%	0.3%	0.3%	-	-	-
Other Paper Nondurable Goods									
Books and Magazines	2.2%	2.0%	2.3%						
Books**				0.5%	0.6%	0.5%	-	-	-
Magazines**				1.4%	0.9%	0.9%	-	-	-
Office-Type Papers***	1.5%	1.7%	2.3%	2.7%	1.9%	1.4%	-	-	-
Standard Mail§				2.1%	2.1%	2.1%	-	-	-

Source: *U.S. EPA, Advancing Sustainable Materials Management: 2015 Tables and Figures, July 2018*

Table 21. Products Landfilled* in Municipal Solid Waste, 1960 to 2015 (With Detail on Nondurable Goods)

(In thousands of tons and percent of total landfilled)

Products	Percent of Total Landfilled								
	1960	1970	1980	1990	2000	2005	2010	2014	2015
Other Commercial Printing†	1.4%	1.6%	2.0%	2.1%	3.8%	2.9%	-	-	-
Tissue Paper and Towels	1.3%	1.8%	1.7%	1.7%	1.9%	2.0%	-	-	-
Paper Plates and Cups	0.3%	0.4%	0.5%	0.4%	0.5%	0.7%	-	-	-
Other Nonpackaging Paper	3.2%	3.1%	3.1%	2.2%	2.4%	2.6%	-	-	-
Total Other Paper Nondurable Goods							7.9%	7.2%	7.0%
Disposable Diapers	Neg.	0.3%	1.4%	1.5%	1.9%	2.0%	2.2%	2.5%	2.5%
Plastic Plates and Cups§			0.1%	0.4%	0.5%	0.5%	0.5%	0.6%	0.6%
Trash Bags**				0.4%	0.5%	0.6%	0.6%	0.6%	0.7%
Clothing and Footwear	1.6%	1.4%	1.5%	2.0%	3.2%	3.8%	4.7%	5.7%	6.0%
Towels, Sheets and Pillowcases**				0.3%	0.4%	0.5%	0.6%	0.6%	0.7%
Other Miscellaneous Nondurables	0.1%	0.2%	1.0%	1.9%	2.3%	2.4%	2.3%	2.1%	2.3%
Total Nondurables	18.1%	18.9%	21.7%	24.8%	26.7%	25.2%	20.6%	20.7%	20.9%
Containers and Packaging	29.7%	35.6%	32.2%	27.3%	27.0%	25.8%	23.4%	22.0%	21.4%
(Detail in Table 29)									
Total Product Wastes‡	59.4%	66.6%	68.8%	67.1%	72.3%	72.3%	68.1%	68.1%	67.9%
Other Wastes	40.6%	33.4%	31.2%	32.9%	27.7%	27.7%	31.9%	31.9%	32.1%
Total MSW Landfilled - %	100.0%	100.0%	100.0%	100.0%	100.0%	100.0%	100.0%	100.0%	100.0%

* Landfilling after recycling, composting and combustion with energy recovery. Does not include construction & demolition debris, industrial process wastes or certain other wastes. Details may not add to totals due to rounding.

† Starting in 2010, newsprint and groundwood inserts expanded to include directories and other mechanical papers previously counted as Other Commercial Printing.

** Not estimated separately prior to 1990.

*** High-grade paper such as printer paper; generated in both commercial and residential sources.

§ Standard Mail: Not estimated separately prior to 1990. Formerly called Third Class Mail and Standard (A) Mail by the U.S. Postal Service.

§ Plastic Plates and Cups: Not estimated separately prior to 1980.

‡ Other than food products.

\- Detailed data not available.

Neg. = Less than 5,000 tons or 0.05 percent.

Source: *U.S. EPA, Advancing Sustainable Materials Management: 2015 Tables and Figures, July 2018*

Table 22. Products Generated* in the Municipal Waste Stream, 1960 to 2015 (With Detail on Containers and Packaging)

(In thousands of tons)

Products	Thousands of Tons								
	1960	1970	1980	1990	2000	2005	2010	2014	2015
Durable Goods	9,920	14,660	21,800	29,810	38,870	45,060	49,350	53,040	54,150
(Detail in Table 14)									
Nondurable Goods	17,330	25,060	34,420	52,170	64,010	63,650	53,250	51,910	51,920
(Detail in Table 18)									
Containers and Packaging									
Glass Packaging									
Beer and Soft Drink Bottles**	1,400	5,580	6,740	5,640	5,710	6,540	5,670	5,370	5,320
Wine and Liquor Bottles	1,080	1,900	2,450	2,030	1,910	1,630	1,700	1,790	1,810
Other Bottles & Jars	3,710	4,440	4,780	4,160	3,420	2,290	1,990	2,040	1,990
Total Glass Packaging	6,190	11,920	13,970	11,830	11,040	10,460	9,360	*9,200*	*9,120*
Steel Packaging									
Beer and Soft Drink Cans	640	1,570	520	150	Neg.	Neg.	Neg.	Neg.	Neg.
Cans	3,760	3,540	2,850	2,540	2,630	2,130	2,300	1,850	1,740
Other Steel Packaging	260	270	240	200	240	240	440	510	480
Total Steel Packaging	4,660	5,380	3,610	2,890	2,870	2,370	2,740	*2,360*	*2,220*
Aluminum Packaging									
Beer and Soft Drink Cans	Neg.	100	850	1,550	1,520	1,450	1,370	1,250	1,220
Other Cans	Neg.	60	40	20	50	80	70	130	130
Foil and Closures	170	410	380	330	380	400	460	430	490
Total Aluminum Packaging	170	570	1,270	1,900	1,950	1,930	1,900	*1,810*	*1,840*
Paper & Paperboard Pkg									
Corrugated Boxes	7,330	12,760	17,080	24,010	30,210	30,930	29,050	30,490	31,330
Other Paper & Paperboard Pkg									
Gable Top/Aseptic Cartons‡			790	510	550	500	540	590	590
Folding Cartons			3,820	4,300	5,820	5,530	5,470	5,410	5,380
Other Paperboard Packaging	3,840	4,830	230	290	200	160	90	70	70
Bags and Sacks			3,380	2,440	1,490	1,120	1,040	880	930
Wrapping Papers			200	110	Neg.	Neg.	Neg.	Neg.	Neg.
Other Paper Packaging	2,940	3,810	850	1,020	1,670	1,400	1,490	1,690	1,620
Subtotal Other Paper & Paperboard Pkg	*6,780*	*8,640*	*9,270*	*8,670*	*9,730*	*8,710*	8,630	8,640	8,590
Total Paper & Board Pkg	14,110	21,400	26,350	32,680	39,940	39,640	37,680	39,130	39,920
Plastics Packaging									
PET Bottles and Jars			260	430	1,720	2,540	2,670	2,920	2,980
HDPE Natural Bottles			230	530	690	800	800	780	760
Other Containers	60	910	890	1,430	1,740	1,420	1,830	1,850	1,940
Bags and Sacks			390	940	1,650	1,640	770	-	-
Wraps			840	1,530	2,550	2,810	3,160	-	-
Subtotal Bags, Sacks, and Wraps			1,230	2,470	4,200	4,450	3,930	4,050	4,130
Other Plastics Packaging	60	1,180	790	2,040	2,840	3,210	4,450	4,720	4,870
Total Plastics Packaging	120	2,090	3,400	6,900	11,190	12,420	13,680	14,320	14,680
Other Packaging									
Wood Packaging	2,000	2,070	3,940	8,180	8,610	9,230	9,770	9,680	9,770
Other Misc. Packaging	120	130	130	150	240	280	340	360	370
Total Containers & Pkg	27,370	43,560	52,670	64,530	75,840	76,330	75,470	76,860	77,920
Total Product Wastes†	54,620	83,280	108,890	146,510	178,720	185,040	178,070	181,810	183,990
Other Wastes									
Food	12,200	12,800	13,000	23,860	30,700	32,930	35,740	38,670	39,730
Yard Trimmings	20,000	23,200	27,500	35,000	30,530	32,070	33,400	34,500	34,720
Miscellaneous Inorganic Wastes	1,300	1,780	2,250	2,900	3,500	3,690	3,840	3,970	3,990
Total Other Wastes	33,500	37,780	42,750	61,760	64,730	68,690	72,980	77,140	78,440
Total MSW Generated - Weight	88,120	121,060	151,640	208,270	243,450	253,730	251,050	258,950	262,430

* Generation before materials recycling, composting, combustion with energy recovery or landfilling. Details may not add to totals due to rounding.

** Includes carbonated drinks and non-carbonated water, teas, flavored drinks and ready-to-drink alcoholic coolers and cocktails.

‡ Includes milk, juice and other products packaged in gable top cartons and liquid food aseptic cartons.

† Other than food products. Neg. = Less than 5,000 tons or 0.05 percent. NA = Not Available - Detailed data not available.

Source: *U.S. EPA, Advancing Sustainable Materials Management: 2015 Tables and Figures, July 2018*

Table 23. Products Generated* in the Municipal Waste Stream, 1960 to 2015 (With Detail on Containers and Packaging)
(In percent of total generation)

Products	Percent of Total Generation								
	1960	1970	1980	1990	2000	2005	2010	2014	2015
Durable Goods	11.3%	12.1%	14.4%	14.3%	16.0%	17.8%	19.7%	20.5%	20.6%
(Detail in Table 14)									
Nondurable Goods	19.7%	20.7%	22.7%	25.0%	26.3%	25.1%	21.2%	20.0%	19.8%
(Detail in Table 18)									
Containers and Packaging									
Glass Packaging									
Beer and Soft Drink Bottles**	1.6%	4.6%	4.4%	2.7%	2.3%	2.6%	2.3%	2.1%	2.0%
Wine and Liquor Bottles	1.2%	1.6%	1.6%	1.0%	0.8%	0.6%	0.7%	0.7%	0.7%
Other Bottles & Jars	4.2%	3.7%	3.2%	2.0%	1.4%	0.9%	0.8%	0.8%	0.8%
Total Glass Packaging	7.0%	9.8%	9.2%	5.7%	4.5%	4.1%	3.7%	3.6%	3.5%
Steel Packaging									
Beer and Soft Drink Cans	0.7%	1.3%	0.3%	0.1%	Neg.	Neg.	Neg.	Neg.	Neg.
Cans	4.3%	2.9%	1.9%	1.2%	1.1%	0.8%	0.9%	0.7%	0.7%
Other Steel Packaging	0.3%	0.2%	0.2%	0.1%	0.1%	0.1%	0.2%	0.2%	0.2%
Total Steel Packaging	5.3%	4.4%	2.4%	1.4%	1.2%	0.9%	1.1%	*0.9%*	*0.9%*
Aluminum Packaging									
Beer and Soft Drink Cans	Neg.	0.1%	0.6%	0.7%	0.6%	0.6%	0.5%	0.5%	0.5%
Other Cans	Neg.	Neg.	Neg.	Neg.	Neg.	Neg.	0.03%	0.05%	0.05%
Foil and Closures	0.2%	0.3%	0.3%	0.2%	0.2%	0.2%	0.2%	0.2%	0.2%
Total Aluminum Packaging	0.2%	0.5%	0.8%	0.9%	0.8%	0.8%	0.8%	*0.8%*	*0.8%*
Paper & Paperboard Pkg									
Corrugated Boxes	8.3%	10.5%	11.3%	11.5%	12.4%	12.2%	11.6%	11.8%	11.9%
Other Paper & Paperboard Pkg									
Gable Top/Aseptic Cartons‡			0.5%	0.2%	0.2%	0.2%	0.2%	0.2%	0.2%
Folding Cartons			2.5%	2.1%	2.4%	2.2%	2.2%	2.1%	2.1%
Other Paperboard Packaging	4.4%	4.0%	0.2%	0.1%	0.1%	0.1%	0.0%	Neg.	Neg.
Bags and Sacks			2.2%	1.2%	0.6%	0.4%	0.4%	0.3%	0.4%
Wrapping Papers			0.1%	0.1%	Neg.	Neg.	Neg.	Neg.	Neg.
Other Paper Packaging	3.3%	3.1%	0.6%	0.5%	0.7%	0.6%	0.6%	0.7%	0.6%
Subtotal Other Paper & Paperboard Pkg							3.4%	3.3%	3.2%
Total Paper & Board Pkg	*16.0%*	*17.7%*	*17.4%*	*15.7%*	*16.4%*	*15.6%*	*15.0%*	*15.0%*	*15.1%*
Plastics Packaging									
PET Bottles and Jars			0.2%	0.2%	0.7%	1.0%	1.1%	1.1%	1.1%
HDPE Natural Bottles			0.2%	0.3%	0.3%	0.3%	0.3%	0.3%	0.3%
Other Containers	0.1%	0.8%	0.6%	0.7%	0.7%	0.6%	0.7%	0.7%	0.7%
Bags and Sacks			0.3%	0.5%	0.7%	0.6%	0.3%	-	-
Wraps			0.6%	0.7%	1.0%	1.1%	1.3%	-	-
Subtotal Bags, Sacks, and Wraps			*0.8%*	*1.2%*	*1.7%*	*1.8%*	*1.6%*	1.56%	1.6%
Other Plastics Packaging	0.1%	1.0%	0.5%	1.0%	1.2%	1.3%	1.8%	1.8%	1.8%
Total Plastics Packaging	0.1%	1.7%	2.2%	3.3%	4.6%	4.9%	5.4%	*5.5%*	*5.5%*
Other Packaging									
Wood Packaging	2.3%	1.7%	2.6%	3.9%	3.5%	3.6%	3.9%	3.7%	3.7%
Other Misc. Packaging	0.1%	0.1%	0.1%	0.1%	0.1%	0.1%	0.1%	0.1%	0.1%
Total Containers & Pkg	31.1%	36.0%	34.7%	31.0%	31.2%	30.1%	30.1%	29.7%	29.7%
Total Product Wastes†	62.0%	68.8%	71.8%	70.3%	73.4%	72.9%	70.9%	70.2%	70.1%
Other Wastes									
Food	13.8%	10.6%	8.6%	11.5%	12.6%	13.0%	14.2%	14.9%	15.1%
Yard Trimmings	22.7%	19.2%	18.1%	16.8%	12.5%	12.6%	13.3%	13.3%	13.3%
Miscellaneous Inorganic Wastes	1.5%	1.5%	1.5%	1.4%	1.4%	1.5%	1.5%	1.5%	1.5%
Total Other Wastes	38.0%	31.2%	28.2%	29.7%	26.6%	27.1%	29.1%	29.8%	29.9%
Total MSW Recycled and Composted - %	100.0%	100.0%	100.0%	100.0%	100.0%	100.0%	100.0%	100.0%	100.0%

* Generation before materials recycling, composting, combustion with energy recovery or landfilling. Details may not add to totals due to rounding.
** Includes carbonated drinks and non-carbonated water, teas, flavored drinks and ready-to-drink alcoholic coolers and cocktails.
‡ Includes milk, juice, and other products packaged in gable top cartons and liquid food aseptic cartons.
† Other than food products.
Neg. = Less than 5,000 tons or 0.05 percent.

Source: *U.S. EPA, Advancing Sustainable Materials Management: 2015 Tables and Figures, July 2018*

Table 24. Products Recycled and Composted* in Municipal Solid Waste, 1960 to 2015 (With Detail on Containers and Packaging)

(In thousands of tons)

Products	Thousands of Tons								
	1960	1970	1980	1990	2000	2005	2010	2014	2015
Durable Goods	350	940	1,360	3,460	6,580	7,970	9,390	10,140	10,250
(Detail in Table 15)									
Nondurable Goods	2,390	3,730	4,670	8,800	17,560	19,770	19,190	16,820	16,190
(Detail in Table 19)									
Containers and Packaging									
Glass Packaging									
Beer and Soft Drink Bottles**	90	140	730	1,890	1,530	2,000	2,350	2,120	2,230
Wine and Liquor Bottles	10	10	20	210	430	250	540	570	500
Other Bottles & Jars	Neg.	Neg.	Neg.	520	920	340	240	300	300
Total Glass Packaging	100	150	750	2,620	2,880	2,590	3,130	*2,990*	*3,030*
Steel Packaging									
Beer and Soft Drink Cans	10	20	50	40	Neg.	Neg.			
Cans	20	60	150	590	1,530	1,340	1,540	1,300	1,240
Other Steel Packaging	Neg.	Neg.	Neg.	60	160	160	350	410	380
Total Steel Packaging	30	80	200	690	1,690	1,500	1,890	*1,710*	*1,620*
Aluminum Packaging									
Beer and Soft Drink Cans	Neg.	10	320	990	830	650	680	710	670
Other Cans	Neg.	Neg.	Neg.	Neg.	Neg.	Neg.	NA	NA	NA
Foil and Closures	Neg.	Neg.	Neg.	20	30	40	NA	NA	NA
Total Aluminum Pkg	Neg.	10	320	1,010	860	690	680	*710*	*670*
Paper & Paperboard Pkg									
Corrugated Boxes	2,520	2,760	6,390	11,530	20,330	22,100	24,690	27,280	28,930
Other Paper & Paperboard Pkg									
Gable Top/Aseptic Cartons‡			Neg.	Neg.	Neg.	Neg.	-	-	-
Folding Cartons			520	340	410	1,190	-	-	-
Other Paperboard Packaging			Neg.	Neg.	Neg.	Neg.	-	-	-
Bags and Sacks			Neg.	200	300	320	-	-	-
Wrapping Papers			Neg.	Neg.	Neg.	Neg.	-	-	-
Other Paper Packaging	220	350	300	Neg.	Neg.	Neg.	-	-	-
Subtotal Other Paper & Paperboard Pkg							2,160	2,210	2,270
Total Paper & Board Pkg	2,740	3,110	7,210	12,070	21,040	23,610	26,850	*29,490*	*31,200*
Plastics Packaging									
PET Bottles and Jars			10	140	380	590	780	910	890
HDPE Natural Bottles			Neg.	20	210	230	220	230	230
Other Containers	Neg.	Neg.	Neg.	20	170	140	300	360	360
Bags and Sacks								-	-
Wraps								-	-
Subtotal Bags, Sacks, and Wraps			Neg.	60	180	230	450	500	530
Other Plastics Packaging	Neg.	Neg.	Neg.	20	90	90	100	120	140
Total Plastics Packaging	Neg.	Neg.	10	260	1,030	1,280	1,850	*2,120*	*2,150*
Other Packaging									
Wood Packaging	Neg.	Neg.	Neg.	130	1,370	1,830	2,280	2,570	2,660
Other Misc. Packaging	Neg.	Neg.	Neg.	Neg.	Neg.	Neg.	Neg.	Neg.	Neg.
Total Containers & Pkg	2,870	3,350	8,490	16,780	28,870	31,500	36,680	39,590	41,330
Total Product Wastes†	5,610	8,020	14,520	29,040	53,010	59,240	65,260	66,550	67,770

Source: *U.S. EPA, Advancing Sustainable Materials Management: 2015 Tables and Figures, July 2018*

Table 24. Products Recycled and Composted* in Municipal Solid Waste, 1960 to 2015 (With Detail on Containers and Packaging)

(In thousands of tons)

Products	Thousands of Tons								
	1960	1970	1980	1990	2000	2005	2010	2014	2015
Other Wastes									
Food^	Neg.	Neg.	Neg.	Neg.	680	690	970	1,940	2,100
Yard Trimmings	Neg.	Neg.	Neg.	4,200	15,770	19,860	19,200	21,080	21,290
Miscellaneous Inorganic Wastes	Neg.	Neg.	Neg.	Neg.	Neg.	Neg.	Neg.	Neg.	Neg.
Total Other Wastes	Neg.	Neg.	Neg.	4,200	16,450	20,550	20,170	23,020	23,390
Total MSW Recycled and Composted - Weight	5,610	8,020	14,520	33,240	69,460	79,790	85,430	89,570	91,160

* Recycling and composting of postconsumer wastes; does not include converting/fabrication scrap. Details may not add to totals due to rounding.
** Includes carbonated drinks and non-carbonated water, teas, flavored drinks and ready-to-drink alcoholic coolers and cocktails.
‡ Includes milk, juice and other products packaged in gable top cartons and liquid food aseptic cartons.
† Other than food products.
^ Includes collection of other MSW organics for composting.
Neg. = Less than 5,000 tons or 0.05 percent. NA = Not Available - Detailed data not available.

Source: *U.S. EPA, Advancing Sustainable Materials Management: 2015 Tables and Figures, July 2018*

Table 25. Products Recycled and Composted* in Municipal Solid Waste, 1960 to 2015 (With Detail on Containers and Packaging)

(In percent of generation of each product)

Products	Percent of Generation of Each Product								
	1960	1970	1980	1990	2000	2005	2010	2014	2015
Durable Goods	3.5%	6.4%	6.2%	11.6%	16.9%	17.7%	19.0%	19.1%	18.9%
(Detail in Table 15)									
Nondurable Goods	13.8%	14.9%	13.6%	16.9%	27.4%	31.1%	36.0%	32.4%	31.2%
(Detail in Table 19)									
Containers and Packaging									
Glass Packaging									
Beer and Soft Drink Bottles**	6.4%	2.5%	10.8%	33.5%	26.8%	30.6%	41.4%	39.5%	41.9%
Wine and Liquor Bottles	Neg.	Neg.	Neg.	10.3%	22.5%	15.3%	31.8%	31.8%	27.6%
Other Bottles & Jars	Neg.	Neg.	Neg.	12.5%	26.9%	14.8%	12.1%	14.7%	15.1%
Total Glass Packaging	1.6%	1.3%	5.4%	22.1%	26.1%	24.8%	33.4%	32.5%	33.2%
Steel Packaging									
Beer and Soft Drink Cans	1.6%	1.3%	9.6%	26.7%	Neg.	Neg.			
Cans	Neg.	1.7%	5.3%	23.2%	58.2%	62.9%	67.0%	70.3%	71.3%
Other Steel Packaging	Neg.	Neg.	Neg.	30.0%	66.7%	66.7%	79.5%	80.4%	79.2%
Total Steel Packaging	Neg.	1.5%	5.5%	23.9%	58.9%	63.3%	69.0%	72.5%	73.0%
Aluminum Packaging									
Beer and Soft Drink Cans	Neg.	10.0%	37.6%	63.9%	54.6%	44.8%	49.6%	56.8%	54.9%
Other Cans	Neg.	Neg.	Neg.	Neg.	Neg.	Neg.	NA	NA	NA
Foil and Closures	Neg.	Neg.	Neg.	6.1%	7.9%	10.0%	NA	NA	NA
Total Aluminum Pkg	Neg.	1.8%	25.2%	53.2%	44.1%	35.8%	35.8%	39.2%	36.4%
Paper & Paperboard Pkg									
Corrugated Boxes	34.4%	21.6%	37.4%	48.0%	67.3%	71.5%	85.0%	89.5%	92.3%
Other Paper & Paperboard Pkg									
Gable Top/Aseptic Cartons‡			Neg.	Neg.	Neg.	Neg.	-	-	-
Folding Cartons			Neg.	Neg.	7.0%	21.5%	-	-	-
Other Paperboard Packaging			Neg.	Neg.	Neg.	Neg.	-	-	-
Bags and Sacks			Neg.	Neg.	20.1%	28.6%	-	-	-
Wrapping Papers			Neg.	Neg.	Neg.	Neg.	-	-	-
Other Paper Packaging	7.5%	9.2%	35.3%	Neg.	Neg.	Neg.	-	-	-
Subtotal Other Paper & Paperboard Pkg							25.0%	25.6%	26.4%
Total Paper & Board Pkg‡	19.4%	14.5%	27.4%	36.9%	52.7%	59.6%	*71.3%*	*75.4%*	*78.2%*
Plastics Packaging									
PET Bottles and Jars			3.8%	32.6%	22.1%	23.2%	29.2%	31.2%	29.9%
HDPE Natural Bottles			Neg.	3.8%	30.4%	28.8%	27.5%	29.5%	30.3%
Other Containers	Neg.	Neg.	Neg.	1.4%	9.8%	9.9%	16.4%	19.5%	18.6%
Bags and Sacks									
Wraps									
Subtotal Bags, Sacks, and Wraps			Neg.	2.4%	4.3%	5.2%	11.5%	12.3%	12.8%
Other Plastics Packaging	Neg.	Neg.	Neg.	1.0%	3.2%	2.8%	2.2%	2.5%	2.9%
Total Plastics Packaging	Neg.	Neg.	Neg.	3.8%	9.2%	10.3%	*13.5%*	*14.8%*	*14.6%*
Other Packaging									
Wood Packaging	Neg.	Neg.	Neg.	1.6%	15.9%	19.8%	23.3%	26.5%	27.2%
Other Misc. Packaging	Neg.	Neg.	Neg.	Neg.	Neg.	Neg.	Neg.	Neg.	Neg.
Total Containers & Pkg	10.5%	7.7%	16.1%	26.0%	38.1%	41.3%	48.6%	51.5%	53.0%
Total Product Wastes†	10.3%	9.6%	13.3%	19.8%	29.7%	32.0%	36.6%	36.6%	36.8%

Source: *U.S. EPA, Advancing Sustainable Materials Management: 2015 Tables and Figures, July 2018*

Table 25. Products Recycled and Composted* in Municipal Solid Waste, 1960 to 2015
(With Detail on Containers and Packaging)
(In percent of generation of each product)

Products	Percent of Generation of Each Product								
	1960	1970	1980	1990	2000	2005	2010	2014	2015
Other Wastes									
Food^	Neg.	Neg.	Neg.	Neg.	2.2%	2.1%	2.7%	5.0%	5.3%
Yard Trimmings	Neg.	Neg.	Neg.	12.0%	51.7%	61.9%	57.5%	61.1%	61.3%
Miscellaneous Inorganic Wastes	Neg.	Neg.	Neg.	Neg.	Neg.	Neg.	Neg.	Neg.	Neg.
Total Other Wastes	Neg.	Neg.	Neg.	6.8%	25.4%	29.9%	27.6%	29.8%	29.8%
Total MSW Recycled and Composted - %	6.4%	6.6%	9.6%	16.0%	28.5%	31.4%	34.0%	34.6%	34.7%

* Recycling and composting of postconsumer wastes; does not include converting/fabrication scrap. Details may not add to totals due to rounding.
** Includes carbonated drinks and non-carbonated water, teas, flavored drinks and ready-to-drink alcoholic coolers and cocktails.
‡ Includes milk, juice and other products packaged in gable top cartons and liquid food aseptic cartons.
† Other than food products.
^ Includes collection of other MSW organics for composting.
Neg. = Less than 5,000 tons or 0.05 percent. NA = Not Available - Detailed data not available.

Source: *U.S. EPA, Advancing Sustainable Materials Management: 2015 Tables and Figures, July 2018*

Table 26. Products Combusted with Energy Recovery* in Municipal Solid Waste, 1960 to 2015 (With Detail on Containers and Packaging)

(In thousands of tons)

Products	Thousands of Tons								
	1960	1970	1980	1990	2000	2005	2010	2014	2015
Durable Goods	0	60	440	4,480	6,260	6,750	7,070	8,410	8,600
(Detail in Table 16)									
Nondurable Goods	0	90	580	7,380	9,000	7,980	6,030	6,880	6,990
(Detail in Table 20)									
Containers and Packaging									
Glass Packaging									
Beer and Soft Drink Bottles**	0	20	120	640	810	830	590	640	610
Wine and Liquor Bottles	0	10	50	310	290	250	210	240	260
Other Bottles & Jars	0	20	100	620	490	350	310	340	330
Total Glass Packaging	*0*	50	270	1,570	1,590	1,430	1,110	1,220	1,200
Steel Packaging									
Beer and Soft Drink Cans	0	10	10	20	Neg.	Neg.	Neg.	Neg.	Neg.
Cans	0	10	50	330	210	140	130	110	100
Other Steel Packaging	0	Neg.	Neg.	20	20	10	20	20	20
Total Steel Packaging	0	20	60	370	230	150	150	130	120
Aluminum Packaging									
Beer and Soft Drink Cans	0	Neg.	10	100	130	150	120	110	110
Other Cans	0	Neg.	Neg.	Neg.	10	10	10	30	30
Foil and Closures	0	Neg.	10	50	70	70	80	80	100
Total Aluminum Pkg	0	Neg.	20	150	210	230	210	220	240
Paper & Paperboard Pkg									
Corrugated Boxes	0	40	210	2,120	1,920	1,610	770	630	470
Other Paper & Paperboard Pkg									
Gable Top/Aseptic Cartons‡			20	90	110	90	-	-	-
Folding Cartons			70	670	1,050	790	-	-	-
Other Paperboard Packaging	0	20	Neg.	50	40	30	-	-	-
Bags and Sacks			70	380	230	150	-	-	-
Wrapping Papers			Neg.	20	Neg.	Neg.	-	-	-
Other Paper Packaging	0	10	10	170	320	250	-	-	-
Subtotal Other Paper & Paperboard Pkg							1,150	1,260	1,240
Total Paper & Board Pkg	*0*	*70*	*380*	*3,500*	*3,670*	*2,920*	*1,920*	*1,890*	*1,710*
Plastics Packaging									
PET Bottles and Jars			Neg.	50	260	350	330	390	410
HDPE Natural Bottles			Neg.	90	90	100	100	110	100
Other Containers	0	Neg.	20	240	300	230	270	290	310
Bags and Sacks									
Wraps									
Subtotal Bags, Sacks, and Wraps			30	410	780	770	620	700	710
Other Plastics Packaging	0	Neg.	20	340	530	570	770	900	930
Total Plastics Packaging	*0*	*Neg.*	*70*	*1,130*	*1,960*	*2,020*	*2,090*	*2,390*	*2,460*

Source: *U.S. EPA, Advancing Sustainable Materials Management: 2015 Tables and Figures, July 2018*

Table 26. Products Combusted with Energy Recovery* in Municipal Solid Waste, 1960 to 2015 (With Detail on Containers and Packaging)

(In thousands of tons)

Products	Thousands of Tons								
	1960	1970	1980	1990	2000	2005	2010	2014	2015
Other Packaging									
Wood Packaging	0	10	80	1,370	1,400	1,350	1,330	1,390	1,390
Other Misc. Packaging	0	Neg.	Neg.	20	50	60	60	70	70
Total Containers & Pkg	0	150	880	8,110	9,110	8,160	6,870	7,310	7,190
Total Product Wastes†	0	300	1,900	19,970	24,370	22,890	19,970	22,600	22,780
Other Wastes									
Food	0	50	260	4,060	5,820	5,870	6,150	7,200	7,380
Yard Trimmings	0	90	550	5,240	2,860	2,220	2,510	2,630	2,630
Miscellaneous Inorganic Wastes	0	10	50	490	680	670	680	780	780
Total Other Wastes	0	150	860	9,790	9,360	8,760	9,340	10,610	10,790
Total MSW Combusted with Energy Recovery - Weight	0	450	2,760	29,760	33,730	31,650	29,310	33,210	33,570

* Products and materials combusted with energy recovery estimated at percentage total MSW after recovery for recycling and composting. In 2015, 19.6 percent of MSW after recycling and composting was combusted with energy recovery. Details may not add to totals due to rounding.

** Includes carbonated drinks and non-carbonated water, teas, flavored drinks and ready-to-drink alcoholic coolers and cocktails.

‡ Includes milk, juice and other products packaged in gable top cartons and liquid food aseptic cartons.

† Other than food products.

Neg. = Less than 5,000 tons or 0.05 percent. NA = Not Available - Detailed data not available.

Source: U.S. EPA, *Advancing Sustainable Materials Management: 2015 Tables and Figures, July 2018*

Table 27. Products Combusted with Energy Recovery* in Municipal Solid Waste, 1960 to 2015 (With Detail on Containers and Packaging) (In percent of total combusted)

Products	Percent of Total Combusted								
	1960	1970	1980	1990	2000	2005	2010	2014	2015
Durable Goods		13.3%	15.9%	15.1%	18.6%	21.3%	24.1%	25.4%	25.6%
(Detail in Table 16)									
Nondurable Goods		19.9%	21.0%	24.8%	26.7%	25.2%	20.6%	20.7%	20.9%
(Detail in Table 20)									
Containers and Packaging									
Glass Packaging									
Beer and Soft Drink Bottles**		4.5%	4.3%	2.2%	2.4%	2.6%	2.0%	1.9%	1.8%
Wine and Liquor Bottles		2.2%	1.8%	1.0%	0.8%	0.8%	0.7%	0.7%	0.8%
Other Bottles & Jars		4.4%	3.6%	2.1%	1.5%	1.1%	1.1%	1.0%	1.0%
Total Glass Packaging		11.1%	9.8%	5.3%	4.7%	4.5%	3.8%	*3.6%*	*3.6%*
Steel Packaging									
Beer and Soft Drink Cans		2.2%	0.4%	0.1%	Neg.	Neg.	Neg.	Neg.	Neg.
Cans		2.2%	1.8%	1.1%	0.6%	0.5%	0.4%	0.3%	0.3%
Other Steel Packaging		Neg.	Neg.	0.1%	0.1%	0.0%	0.1%	0.1%	0.1%
Total Steel Packaging		4.4%	2.2%	1.2%	0.7%	0.5%	0.5%	*0.4%*	0.4%
Aluminum Packaging									
Beer and Soft Drink Cans		Neg.	0.4%	0.3%	0.4%	0.5%	0.4%	0.3%	0.3%
Other Cans		Neg.	Neg.	Neg.	Neg.	Neg.	Neg.	0.1%	0.1%
Foil and Closures		Neg.	0.4%	0.2%	0.2%	0.2%	0.3%	0.3%	0.3%
Total Aluminum Pkg		Neg.	0.7%	0.5%	0.6%	0.7%	0.7%	*0.7%*	0.7%
Paper & Paperboard Pkg									
Corrugated Boxes		8.9%	7.6%	7.1%	5.7%	5.1%	2.6%	1.9%	1.4%
Other Paper & Paperboard Pkg									
Gable Top/Aseptic Cartons‡			0.7%	0.3%	0.3%	0.3%	-	-	-
Folding Cartons			2.5%	2.3%	3.1%	2.5%	-	-	-
Other Paperboard Packaging		4.5%	Neg.	0.2%	0.1%	0.1%	-	-	-
Bags and Sacks			2.5%	1.3%	0.7%	0.4%	-	-	-
Wrapping Papers			Neg.	0.1%	Neg.	Neg.	-	-	-
Other Paper Packaging		2.2%	0.4%	0.6%	1.0%	0.8%	-	-	-
Subtotal Other Paper & Paperboard Pkg							3.9%	3.8%	3.7%
Total Paper & Board Pkg		15.6%	13.8%	11.8%	10.9%	9.2%	6.6%	*5.7%*	5.1%
Plastics Packaging									
PET Bottles and Jars			Neg.	0.2%	0.8%	1.1%	1.1%	1.2%	1.2%
HDPE Natural Bottles			Neg.	0.3%	0.3%	0.3%	0.4%	0.3%	0.3%
Other Containers		Neg.	0.7%	0.8%	0.9%	0.7%	0.9%	0.9%	0.9%
Bags and Sacks									
Wraps									
Subtotal Bags, Sacks, and Wraps			1.1%	1.4%	2.3%	2.4%	2.1%	2.1%	2.1%
Other Plastics Packaging		Neg.	0.7%	1.1%	1.5%	1.8%	2.6%	2.7%	2.8%
Total Plastics Packaging		Neg.	2.5%	3.8%	5.8%	6.4%	7.1%	*7.2%*	7.3%
Other Packaging									
Wood Packaging		2.2%	2.9%	4.6%	4.2%	4.3%	4.5%	4.2%	4.1%
Other Misc. Packaging		Neg.	Neg.	0.1%	0.1%	0.2%	0.2%	0.2%	0.2%
Total Containers & Pkg		33.3%	31.9%	27.3%	27.0%	25.8%	23.4%	22.0%	21.4%
Total Product Wastes†		66.6%	68.8%	67.1%	72.3%	72.3%	68.1%	68.1%	67.9%

Source: *U.S. EPA, Advancing Sustainable Materials Management: 2015 Tables and Figures, July 2018*

Table 27. Products Combusted with Energy Recovery* in Municipal Solid Waste, 1960 to 2015 (With Detail on Containers and Packaging) (In percent of total combusted)

Products	Percent of Total Combusted								
	1960	1970	1980	1990	2000	2005	2010	2014	2015
Other Wastes									
Food		11.1%	9.4%	13.6%	17.3%	18.5%	21.0%	21.7%	22.0%
Yard Trimmings		20.0%	20.0%	17.6%	8.5%	7.0%	8.6%	7.9%	7.8%
Miscellaneous Inorganic Wastes		2.3%	1.8%	1.7%	1.9%	2.1%	2.3%	2.3%	2.3%
Total Other Wastes		33.4%	31.2%	32.9%	27.7%	27.7%	31.9%	31.9%	32.1%
Total MSW Combusted with Energy Recovery - %		100.0%	100.0%	100.0%	100.0%	100.0%	100.0%	100.0%	100.0%

* Products and materials combusted with energy recovery estimated at percentage total MSW after recovery for recycling and composting. In 2015, 19.6 percent of MSW after recycling and composting was combusted with energy recovery. Details may not add to totals due to rounding.

** Includes carbonated drinks and non-carbonated water, teas, flavored drinks and ready-to-drink alcoholic coolers and cocktails.

‡ Includes milk, juice and other products packaged in gable top cartons and liquid food aseptic cartons.

† Other than food products.

Neg. = Less than 5,000 tons or 0.05 percent. NA = Not Available - Detailed data not available.

Source: *U.S. EPA, Advancing Sustainable Materials Management: 2015 Tables and Figures, July 2018*

Table 28. Products Landfilled* in Municipal Solid Waste, 1960 to 2015 (With Detail on Containers and Packaging) (In thousands of tons)

Products	Thousands of Tons								
	1960	1970	1980	1990	2000	2005	2010	2014	2015
Durable Goods	9,570	13,660	20,000	21,870	26,030	30,340	32,890	34,490	35,300
(Detail in Table 17)									
Nondurable Goods	14,940	21,240	29,170	35,990	37,450	35,900	28,030	28,210	28,740
(Detail in Table 21)									
Containers and Packaging									
Glass Packaging									
Beer and Soft Drink Bottles**	1,310	5,420	5,890	3,110	3,370	3,710	2,730	2,610	2,480
Wine and Liquor Bottles	1,070	1,880	2,380	1,510	1,190	1,130	950	980	1,050
Other Bottles & Jars	3,710	4,420	4,680	3,020	2,010	1,600	1,440	1,400	1,360
Total Glass Packaging	6,090	11,720	12,950	7,640	6,570	6,440	5,120	4,990	4,890
Steel Packaging									
Beer and Soft Drink Cans	630	1,540	460	90	Neg.	Neg.	Neg.	Neg.	Neg.
Cans	3,740	3,470	2,650	1,620	890	650	630	440	400
Other Steel Packaging	260	270	240	120	60	70	70	80	80
Total Steel Packaging	4,630	5,280	3,350	1,830	950	720	700	520	480
Aluminum Packaging									
Beer and Soft Drink Cans	Neg.	90	520	460	560	650	570	430	440
Other Cans	Neg.	60	40	20	40	70	60	100	100
Foil and Closures	170	410	370	260	280	290	380	350	390
Total Aluminum Pkg	170	560	930	740	880	1,010	1,010	880	930
Paper & Paperboard Pkg									
Corrugated Boxes	4,810	9,960	10,480	10,360	7,960	7,220	3,590	2,580	1,930
Other Paper & Paperboard Pkg									
Gable Top/Aseptic Cartons‡			770	420	440	410	-	-	-
Folding Cartons			3,230	3,290	4,360	3,550	-	-	-
Other Paperboard Packaging	3,840	4,810	230	240	160	130	-	-	-
Bags and Sacks			3,310	1,860	960	650	-	-	-
Wrapping Papers			200	90	Neg.	Neg.	-	-	-
Other Paper Packaging	2,720	3,450	540	850	1,350	1,150	-	-	-
Subtotal Other Paper & Paperboard Pkg							5,320	5,170	5,080
Total Paper & Board Pkg	11,370	18,220	18,760	17,110	15,230	13,110	8,910	7,750	7,010
Plastics Packaging									
PET Bottles and Jars			250	240	1,080	1,600	1,560	1,620	1,680
HDPE Natural Bottles			230	420	390	470	480	440	430
Other Containers	60	910	870	1,170	1,270	1,050	1,260	1,200	1,270
Bags and Sacks									
Wraps									
Subtotal Bags, Sacks, and Wraps			1,200	2,000	3,240	3,450	2,860	2,850	2,890
Other Plastics Packaging	60	1,180	770	1,680	2,220	2,550	3,580	3,700	3,800
Total Plastics Packaging	120	2,090	3,320	5,510	8,200	9,120	9,740	9,810	10,070
Other Packaging									
Wood Packaging	2,000	2,060	3,860	6,680	5,840	6,050	6,160	5,720	5,720
Other Misc. Packaging	120	130	130	130	190	220	280	290	300
Total Containers & Pkg	24,500	40,060	43,300	39,640	37,860	36,670	31,920	29,960	29,400
Total Product Wastes†	49,010	74,960	92,470	97,500	101,340	102,910	92,840	92,660	93,440
Other Wastes									
Food	12,200	12,750	12,740	19,800	24,200	26,370	28,620	29,530	30,250
Yard Trimmings	20,000	23,110	26,950	25,560	11,900	9,990	11,690	10,790	10,800
Miscellaneous Inorganic Wastes	1,300	1,770	2,200	2,410	2,820	3,020	3,160	3,190	3,210
Total Other Wastes	33,500	37,630	41,890	47,770	38,920	39,380	43,470	43,510	44,260
Total MSW Landfilled - Weight	82,510	112,590	134,360	145,270	140,260	142,290	136,310	136,170	137,700

* Landfilling after recycling, composting and combustion with energy recovery. Does not include construction & demolition debris, industrial process wastes or certain other wastes. Details may not add to totals due to rounding.

** Includes carbonated drinks and non-carbonated water, teas, flavored drinks and ready-to-drink alcoholic coolers and cocktails.

‡ Includes milk, juice and other products packaged in gable top cartons and liquid food aseptic cartons.

† Other than food products.

Neg. = Less than 5,000 tons or 0.05 percent. NA = Not Available - Detailed data not available.

Source: *U.S. EPA, Advancing Sustainable Materials Management: 2015 Tables and Figures, July 2018*

Table 29. Products Landfilled* in Municipal Solid Waste, 1960 to 2015 (With Detail on Containers and Packaging)

(In percent of total landfilled)

Products	Percent of Total Landfilled								
	1960	1970	1980	1990	2000	2005	2010	2014	2015
Durable Goods	11.6%	12.1%	14.9%	15.0%	18.6%	21.3%	24.1%	25.4%	25.6%
(Detail in Table 17)									
Nondurable Goods	18.1%	18.9%	21.7%	24.8%	26.7%	25.2%	20.6%	20.7%	20.9%
(Detail in Table 21)									
Containers and Packaging									
Glass Packaging									
Beer and Soft Drink Bottles**	1.6%	4.8%	4.4%	2.1%	2.4%	2.6%	2.0%	1.9%	1.8%
Wine and Liquor Bottles	1.3%	1.7%	1.8%	1.0%	0.8%	0.8%	0.7%	0.7%	0.8%
Other Bottles & Jars	4.5%	3.9%	3.5%	2.1%	1.5%	1.1%	1.1%	1.0%	1.0%
Total Glass Packaging	*7.4%*	*10.4%*	*9.6%*	*5.3%*	*4.7%*	*4.5%*	*3.8%*	*3.6%*	*3.6%*
Steel Packaging									
Beer and Soft Drink Cans	0.8%	1.4%	0.3%	0.1%	Neg.	Neg.	Neg.	Neg.	Neg.
Cans	4.5%	3.1%	2.0%	1.1%	0.6%	0.5%	0.5%	0.3%	0.3%
Other Steel Packaging	0.3%	0.2%	0.2%	0.1%	0.1%	0.0%	0.1%	0.1%	0.1%
Total Steel Packaging	*5.6%*	*4.7%*	*2.5%*	*1.3%*	*0.7%*	*0.5%*	*0.6%*	*0.4%*	*0.4%*
Aluminum Packaging									
Beer and Soft Drink Cans	Neg.	0.1%	0.4%	0.3%	0.4%	0.5%	0.4%	0.3%	0.3%
Other Cans	Neg.	0.1%	0.0%	0.0%	Neg.	Neg.	Neg.	0.1%	0.1%
Foil and Closures	0.2%	0.4%	0.3%	0.2%	0.2%	0.2%	0.3%	0.3%	0.3%
Total Aluminum Pkg	*0.2%*	*0.5%*	*0.7%*	*0.5%*	*0.6%*	*0.7%*	*0.7%*	*0.7%*	*0.7%*
Paper & Paperboard Pkg									
Corrugated Boxes	5.8%	8.8%	7.8%	7.1%	5.7%	5.1%	2.6%	1.9%	1.4%
Other Paper & Paperboard Pkg									
Gable Top/Aseptic Cartons‡			0.6%	0.3%	0.3%	0.3%	-	-	-
Folding Cartons			2.4%	2.3%	3.1%	2.5%	-	-	-
Other Paperboard Packaging	4.7%	4.3%	0.2%	0.2%	0.1%	0.1%	-	-	-
Bags and Sacks			2.5%	1.3%	0.7%	0.4%	-	-	-
Wrapping Papers			0.1%	0.1%	Neg.	Neg.	-	-	-
Other Paper Packaging	3.3%	3.1%	0.4%	0.6%	1.0%	0.8%	-	-	-
Subtotal Other Paper & Paperboard Pkg							3.9%	3.8%	3.7%
Total Paper & Board Pkg	*13.8%*	*16.2%*	*14.0%*	*11.8%*	*10.9%*	*9.2%*	*6.5%*	*5.7%*	*5.1%*
Plastics Packaging									
PET Bottles and Jars			0.2%	0.2%	0.8%	1.1%	1.1%	1.2%	1.2%
HDPE Natural Bottles			0.2%	0.3%	0.3%	0.3%	0.4%	0.3%	0.3%
Other Containers	0.1%	0.8%	0.6%	0.8%	0.9%	0.7%	0.9%	0.9%	0.9%
Bags and Sacks									
Wraps									
Subtotal Bags, Sacks, and Wraps			0.9%	1.4%	2.3%	2.4%	2.1%	2.1%	2.1%
Other Plastics Packaging	0.1%	1.0%	0.6%	1.2%	1.5%	1.8%	2.6%	2.7%	2.8%
Total Plastics Packaging	*0.1%*	*1.9%*	*2.5%*	*3.8%*	*5.8%*	*6.4%*	*7.1%*	*7.2%*	*7.3%*
Other Packaging									
Wood Packaging	2.4%	1.8%	2.9%	4.6%	4.2%	4.3%	4.5%	4.2%	4.1%
Other Misc. Packaging	0.1%	0.1%	0.1%	0.1%	0.1%	0.2%	0.2%	0.2%	0.2%
Total Containers & Pkg	29.7%	35.6%	32.2%	27.3%	27.0%	25.8%	23.4%	22.0%	21.4%
Total Product Wastes†	*59.4%*	*66.6%*	*68.8%*	*67.1%*	*72.3%*	*72.3%*	*68.1%*	*68.1%*	*67.9%*
Other Wastes									
Food	14.8%	11.3%	9.5%	13.6%	17.3%	18.5%	21.0%	21.7%	22.0%
Yard Trimmings	24.2%	20.5%	20.1%	17.6%	8.5%	7.0%	8.6%	7.9%	7.8%
Miscellaneous Inorganic Wastes	1.6%	1.6%	1.6%	1.7%	1.9%	2.2%	2.3%	2.3%	2.3%
Total Other Wastes	*40.6%*	*33.4%*	*31.2%*	*32.9%*	*27.7%*	*27.7%*	*31.9%*	*31.9%*	*32.1%*
Total MSW Landfilled - %	100.0%	100.0%	100.0%	100.0%	100.0%	100.0%	100.0%	100.0%	100.0%

* Landfilling after recycling, composting and combustion with energy recovery. Does not include construction & demolition debris, industrial process wastes or certain other wastes. Details may not add to totals due to rounding.

** Includes carbonated drinks and non-carbonated water, teas, flavored drinks and ready-to-drink alcoholic coolers and cocktails.

‡ Includes milk, juice and other products packaged in gable top cartons and liquid food aseptic cartons.

† Other than food products.

Neg. = Less than 5,000 tons or 0.05 percent. NA = Not Available - Detailed data not available.

Source: *U.S. EPA, Advancing Sustainable Materials Management: 2015 Tables and Figures, July 2018*

Table 30. Selected Examples of Source Reduction Practices

Source Reduction Practice	MSW Product Categories			
	Durable Goods	Nondurable Goods	Containers & Packaging	Organics (Wood, Yard Waste, Food, etc.)
Product or Packaging Redesign				
Materials reduction	▪ Downgauge metals in appliances ▪ Use fewer materials in electronics	▪ Use paperless purchase orders ▪ Use concentrated products	▪ Implement container lightweighting ▪ Use right size packaging ▪ Eliminate unnecessary layers of packaging ▪ Use refillable/reusable containers, including use of flexible pouches for refills for rigid containers	▪ Implement xeriscaping ▪ Use just in time ordering / inventory control ▪ Adjust menus to reduce frequently uneaten or wasted items
Materials substitution	▪ Use of composites in appliances and electronic circuitry		▪ Replace rigid or heavy packaging with lighter or more compact options, e.g., cereal in bags. coffee in brick packs ▪ Use life cycle data to choose material with lower lifecycle impact	
Lengthen product lifespan	▪ Use high mileage tires ▪ Design for upgrades (e.g., add computer memory or processing capacity, battery upgrades)	▪ Perform regular servicing ▪ Consider purchasing warranties to make repair more affordable ▪ Extend warranties	▪ Design for secondary use ▪ Use Reusable packaging	▪ Clearer label information on food expiration date ▪ Avoid spoilage by changing: – Packaging – Storage and transportation – Supply chain management
Consumer Practices				
	▪ Purchase long-lived products ▪ Perform regular servicing ▪ Perform repair ▪ Buy fewer items	▪ Perform repair ▪ Use duplex printing ▪ Share products ▪ Reduce unwanted mail ▪ Purchase concentrated products ▪ Buy fewer items	▪ Purchase products in bulk (less packaging) ▪ Use reusable bags and containers ▪ Buy fewer items	▪ Donate food ▪ Avoid spoilage by monitoring and tracking food and purchases and use ▪ Reduce over-purchasing ▪ Perform proper food storage and preparation ▪ Repurpose (e.g., older bread can be made into croutons) ▪ Do backyard composting ▪ Do vermi-composting ▪ Do grasscycling
Reuse				
By Design	▪ Document materials and methods for disassembly/ repair/reuse ▪ Use materials and systems that exhibit modularity, and standardization to facilitate reuse and repair – Minimize connections between parts and/or make connections more accessible for ease of repair and replacement of parts	▪ Use reusable shipping or mailing envelopes	▪ Use reusable pallets ▪ Use returnable secondary packaging ▪ Use reusable/refillable dispensers for cleaning products ▪ Use reusable service ware in food service ▪ Use durable reusable water bottles instead of disposable bottles	

Source: *U.S. EPA, Advancing Sustainable Materials Management: 2015 Tables and Figures, July 2018*

Table 30. Selected Examples of Source Reduction Practices

Source Reduction Practice	MSW Product Categories			
	Durable Goods	Nondurable Goods	Containers & Packaging	Organics (Wood, Yard Waste, Food, etc.)
	– Use mechanical connections with bolts and screws instead of glues, to facilitate repair – Minimize connections to increase ease of repair or part replacement – Provide adequate tolerances to allow for removal and replacement or repair of parts without affecting adjacent components			
Secondary	▪ Borrow or rent for temporary use ▪ Give to charity ▪ Buy or sell at garage sales	▪ Donate clothing, books ▪ Waste paper scratch pads	▪ Use reusable grocery sacks ▪ Reuse glass and plastic bottles and jars	

Source: *U.S. EPA, Advancing Sustainable Materials Management: 2015 Tables and Figures, July 2018*

Table 31. Households with Residential Food Collection Programs in the U.S., 2015

State	Curbside Households with Access	Drop-off Households with Access
Alaska		500
California	1,389,719	
Colorado	150,279	35,500
Connecticut		19,634
Illinois	16,355	
Iowa	44,430	
Maine		7,641
Maryland	18,225	
Massachusetts	35,769	348,448
Michigan	47,416	
Minnesota	141,517	1,030,371
New Jersey	9,158	
New York	790,090	3,153,535
North Carolina		452,000
Ohio	443	
Oregon	157,000	
Pennsylvania	3,600	
Texas	52,000	
Vermont	19,767	67,000
Virginia		20,000
Washington	957,688	253,622
Wisconsin	3,000	
Households with Access to Collection	**3,836,456**	**5,388,251**
Total U.S. Households	**116,926,305**	**116,926,305**
	3.3%	**4.6%**

Source: Streeter, V.; Platt B. 2017. Residential Food Waste Collection Access in the U.S. *BioCycle* December. Programs included in Table 31 are programs with startup dates in 2015 or earlier. Programs started in 2016 and 2017 are excluded. Programs with no startup date provided in the source document or identified through internet searches are also excluded.
U.S. Census Bureau. Selected Housing Characteristics 2011-2015 American Community Survey 5-Year Estimates DP04.

Source: *U.S. EPA, Advancing Sustainable Materials Management: 2015 Tables and Figures, July 2018*

Table 32. Material Recovery Facilities (MRF), 2015*

Region	Number	Estimated Throughput (tons per day)
NORTHEAST	139	23,546
SOUTH	168	25,402
MIDWEST	166	20,765
WEST	115	24,846
U.S. Total	588	94,559

*Number of facilities and throughput include bale and ship operations receiving fiber, mainly old corrugated cardboard (OCC), that bale and ship with no additional processing.

Source: Governmental Advisory Associates, Inc. Data provided May 2016.

Northeast: Connecticut, Maine, Massachusetts, New Hampshire, New Jersey, New York, Pennsylvania, Rhode Island, Vermont

South: Alabama, Arkansas, Delaware, District of Columbia, Florida, Georgia, Kentucky, Louisiana, Maryland, Mississippi, North Carolina, Oklahoma, South Carolina, Tennessee, Texas, Virginia, West Virginia

Midwest: Illinois, Indiana, Iowa, Kansas, Michigan, Minnesota, Missouri, Nebraska, North Dakota, Ohio, South Dakota, Wisconsin

West: Alaska, Arizona, California, Colorado, Hawaii, Idaho, Montana, Nevada, New Mexico, Oregon, Utah, Washington, Wyoming

Table 33. Municipal Waste-To-Energy Projects, 2015

Region	Number Operational	Design Capacity (tons per day)
NORTHEAST	37	43,995
SOUTH	19	32,194
MIDWEST	14	11,524
WEST	7	7,310
*U.S. Total**	77	95,023

*WTE includes mass burn, modular and refuse-derived fuel combustion facilities.

Source: "The 2016 ERC Directory of Waste-to-Energy Facilities." Energy Recovery Council (ERC). 2016.

Northeast: Connecticut, Maine, Massachusetts, New Hampshire, New Jersey, New York, Pennsylvania, Rhode Island, Vermont

South: Alabama, Arkansas, Delaware, District of Columbia, Florida, Georgia, Kentucky, Louisiana, Maryland, Mississippi, North Carolina, Oklahoma, South Carolina, Tennessee, Texas, Virginia, West Virginia

Midwest: Illinois, Indiana, Iowa, Kansas, Michigan, Minnesota, Missouri, Nebraska, North Dakota, Ohio, South Dakota, Wisconsin

West: Alaska, Arizona, California, Colorado, Hawaii, Idaho, Montana, Nevada, New Mexico, Oregon, Utah, Washington, Wyoming

Source: *U.S. EPA, Advancing Sustainable Materials Management: 2015 Tables and Figures, July 2018*

Table 34. Landfill Facilities, 2015

Region	Number of Landfills
NORTHEAST	120
SOUTH	624
MIDWEST	364
WEST	630
U.S. Total	1,738

Source: State environmental websites.

Northeast: Connecticut, Maine, Massachusetts, New Hampshire, New Jersey, New York, Pennsylvania, Rhode Island, Vermont

South: Alabama, Arkansas, Delaware, District of Columbia, Florida, Georgia, Kentucky, Louisiana, Maryland, Mississippi, North Carolina, Oklahoma, South Carolina, Tennessee, Texas, Virginia, West Virginia

Midwest: Illinois, Indiana, Iowa, Kansas, Michigan, Minnesota, Missouri, Nebraska, North Dakota, Ohio, South Dakota, Wisconsin

West: Alaska, Arizona, California, Colorado, Hawaii, Idaho, Montana, Nevada, New Mexico, Oregon, Utah, Washington, Wyoming

Source: *U.S. EPA, Advancing Sustainable Materials Management: 2015 Tables and Figures, July 2018*

Table 35. Generation, Recycling, Composting, Combustion with Energy Recovery and Landfilling of Municipal Solid Waste, 1960 to 2015

(In thousands of tons and percent of total generation)

	Thousands of Tons								
	1960	1970	1980	1990	2000	2005	2010	2014	2015
Generation	88,120	121,060	151,640	208,270	243,450	253,730	251,050	258,950	262,430
Recycling	5,610	8,020	14,520	29,040	53,010	59,240	65,260	66,550	67,770
Composting*	Neg.	Neg.	Neg.	4,200	16,450	20,550	20,170	23,020	23,390
Combustion with energy recovery**	0	450	2,760	29,760	33,730	31,650	29,310	33,210	33,570
Discards to landfill, other disposal†	82,510	112,590	134,360	145,270	140,260	142,290	136,310	136,170	137,700
	Pounds per Person per Day								
	1960	1970	1980	1990	2000	2005	2010	2014	2015
Generation	2.68	3.25	3.66	4.57	4.74	4.69	4.45	4.45	4.48
Recycling	0.17	0.22	0.35	0.64	1.03	1.10	1.16	1.14	1.16
Composting*	Neg.	Neg.	Neg.	0.09	0.32	0.38	0.36	0.40	0.40
Combustion with energy recovery**	0.00	0.01	0.07	0.65	0.66	0.59	0.52	0.57	0.57
Discards to landfill, other disposal†	2.51	3.02	3.24	3.19	2.73	2.62	2.41	2.34	2.35
Population (thousands)	179,979	203,984	227,255	249,907	281,422	296,410	309,051	318,857	320,897
	Percent of Total Generation								
	1960	1970	1980	1990	2000	2005	2010	2014	2015
Generation	100.0%	100.0%	100.0%	100.0%	100.0%	100.0%	100.0%	100.0%	100.0%
Recycling	6.4%	6.6%	9.6%	14.0%	21.8%	23.3%	26.0%	25.7%	25.8%
Composting*	Neg.	Neg.	Neg.	2.0%	6.7%	8.1%	8.0%	8.9%	8.9%
Combustion with energy recovery**	0.0%	0.3%	1.8%	14.2%	13.9%	12.5%	11.7%	12.8%	12.8%
Landfilling and other disposal†	93.6%	93.1%	88.6%	69.8%	57.6%	56.1%	54.3%	52.6%	52.5%

* Composting of yard trimmings, food and other MSW organic material. Does not include backyard composting.

** Includes combustion with energy recovery of MSW in mass burn or refuse-derived fuel form and combustion with energy recovery of source separated materials in MSW (e.g., wood pallets and tire-derived fuel). 2015 includes 30,270 MSW, 520 wood, and 2,780 tires (1,000 tons).

† Landfilling after recycling and composting minus combustion with energy recovery. Includes combustion without energy recovery.

Details may not add to totals due to rounding.

Source population: U.S. Census Bureau Population Division (NST-EST2016-01) December 2016.

Source: *U.S. EPA, Advancing Sustainable Materials Management: 2015 Tables and Figures, July 2018*

Figure 1. Municipal Solid Waste in the Universe of Subtitle D Wastes

Subtitle D Wastes

The Subtitle D Waste included in this report as Municipal Solid Waste (MSW), which includes:

- Containers and packaging such as soft drink bottles and corrugated boxes
- Durable goods such as furniture and appliances
- Nondurable goods such as newspapers, trash bags and clothing
- Other wastes such as food and yard trimmings.

Subtitle D Wastes not included as MSW in this report are:

- Municipal sludges
- Industrial nonhazardous process wastes
- Construction and demolition debris*
- Land clearing debris
- Transportation parts and equipment
- Agricultural wastes
- Oil and gas wastes
- Mining wastes
- Auto bodies
- Fats, grease and oils

*Construction and demolition debris is included in this report, but is outside of the scope of MSW.

Source: *U.S. EPA, Advancing Sustainable Materials Management: 2015 Tables and Figures, July 2018*

Figure 2. Definition of Terms

The materials flow methodology produces an estimate of total municipal solid waste (MSW) generation in the United States, by material categories and by product categories.

Generation refers to the weight of materials and products as they enter the waste management system from residential, commercial and institutional sources and before recycling, composting, combustion or landfilling take place. Preconsumer (industrial) scrap is not included in the generation estimate. Source reduction activities, such as backyard composting of yard trimmings, take place ahead of generation.

Source reduction as used in this report refers to activities that reduce the amount of wastes before they enter the municipal solid waste management system. Reuse is a source reduction activity involving the recovery or reapplication of a package, used product or material in a manner that retains its original form or identity. Reuse of products such as refillable glass bottles and reusable plastic food storage containers is considered to be source reduction, not recycling.

Recycling is defined as the recovery of useful materials, such as paper, glass, plastic and metals, from the MSW stream, along with the transformation of the materials, to make new products to reduce the amount of virgin raw materials needed to meet consumer demands.

Composting is the decomposition of organic materials by aerobic microorganisms. Composting facilities manage the amount of moisture and oxygen and mixture of organic materials for optimal composting conditions. The composting process emits heat, water vapor and biogenic carbon dioxide, reducing the raw organic materials in mass and volume to create compost.[1]

Combustion with energy recovery is often called "waste-to-energy," and as used in this report refers to confined and controlled burning with energy recovery, which not only decreases the volume of solid waste destined for landfills, but can also recover energy from the waste burning process.

Landfilling refers to the MSW remaining after recycling, composting and combustion with energy recovery. These materials presumably would be landfilled in a discrete area of land or excavation that receives household waste. Some MSW, however, is littered, stored or disposed onsite; or burned onsite, particularly in rural areas. There are no good estimates for these other disposal practices available, but the total amounts of MSW involved are assumed to be small.

For the analysis of municipal solid waste in this report, products are divided into three basic categories: durable goods, nondurable goods and containers and packaging. The durable goods and nondurable goods categories generally follow the definitions of the U.S. Department of Commerce.

Durable goods are those products that last three years or more. Products in this category include major and small appliances, furniture and furnishings, carpets and rugs, tires, lead-acid batteries, consumer electronics and other miscellaneous durables.

Nondurable goods are those products that last less than three years. Products in this category include newspapers, books, magazines, office papers, directories, mail, other commercial printing, tissue paper and towels, paper and plastic plates and cups, trash bags, disposable diapers, clothing and footwear, towels, sheets and pillowcases, other nonpackaging paper and other miscellaneous nondurables.

Containers and packaging are assumed to be discarded the same year the products they contain are purchased. Products in this category include bottles, containers, corrugated boxes, milk cartons, folding cartons, bags, sacks, and wraps, wood packaging and other miscellaneous packaging.

[1] Platt, B., Goldstein, N. 2014. State of Composting in the U.S. *BioCycle* 55(6): 19. http://www.biocycle.net/2014/07/16/state-of-composting-in-the-us/.

Source: *U.S. EPA, Advancing Sustainable Materials Management: 2015 Tables and Figures, July 2018*

Figure 3. Paper and Paperboard Products Generated in MSW, 2015

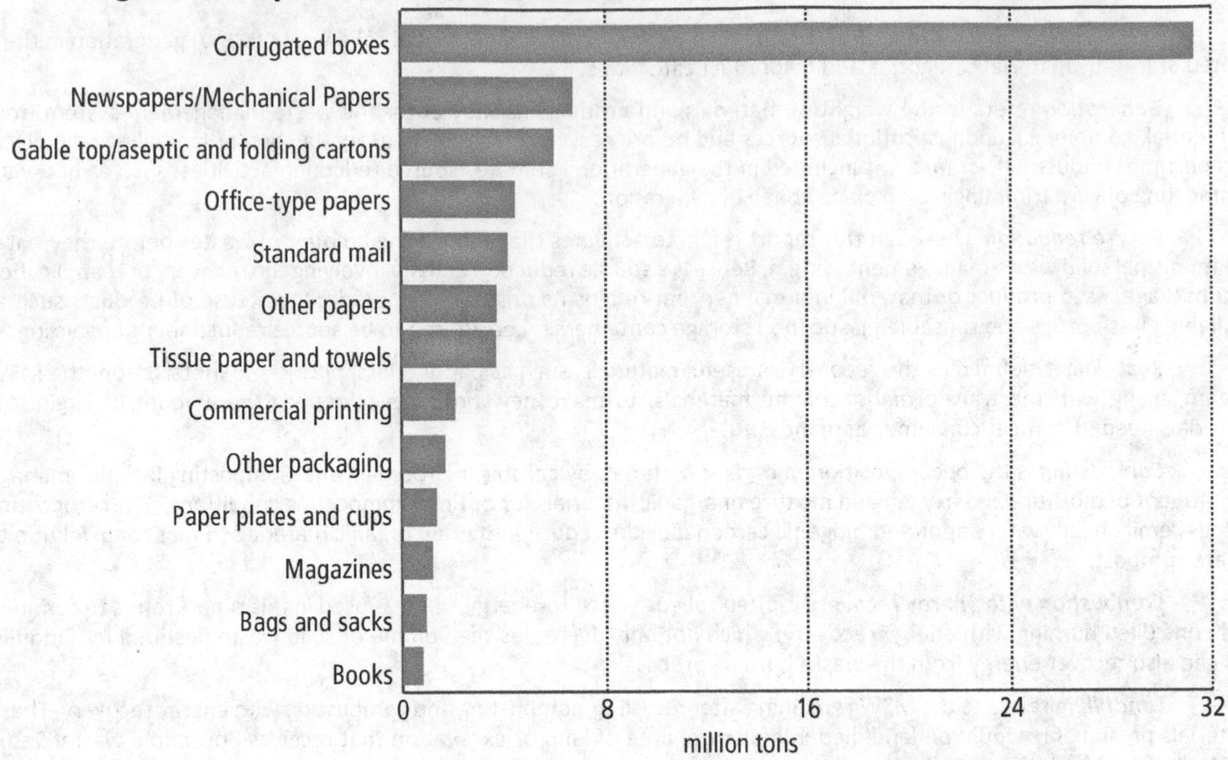

Corrugated boxes
Newspapers/Mechanical Papers
Gable top/aseptic and folding cartons
Office-type papers
Standard mail
Other papers
Tissue paper and towels
Commercial printing
Other packaging
Paper plates and cups
Magazines
Bags and sacks
Books
0 8 16 24 32
million tons

Figure 4. Paper and Paperboard Generation and Recycling, 1960 to 2015

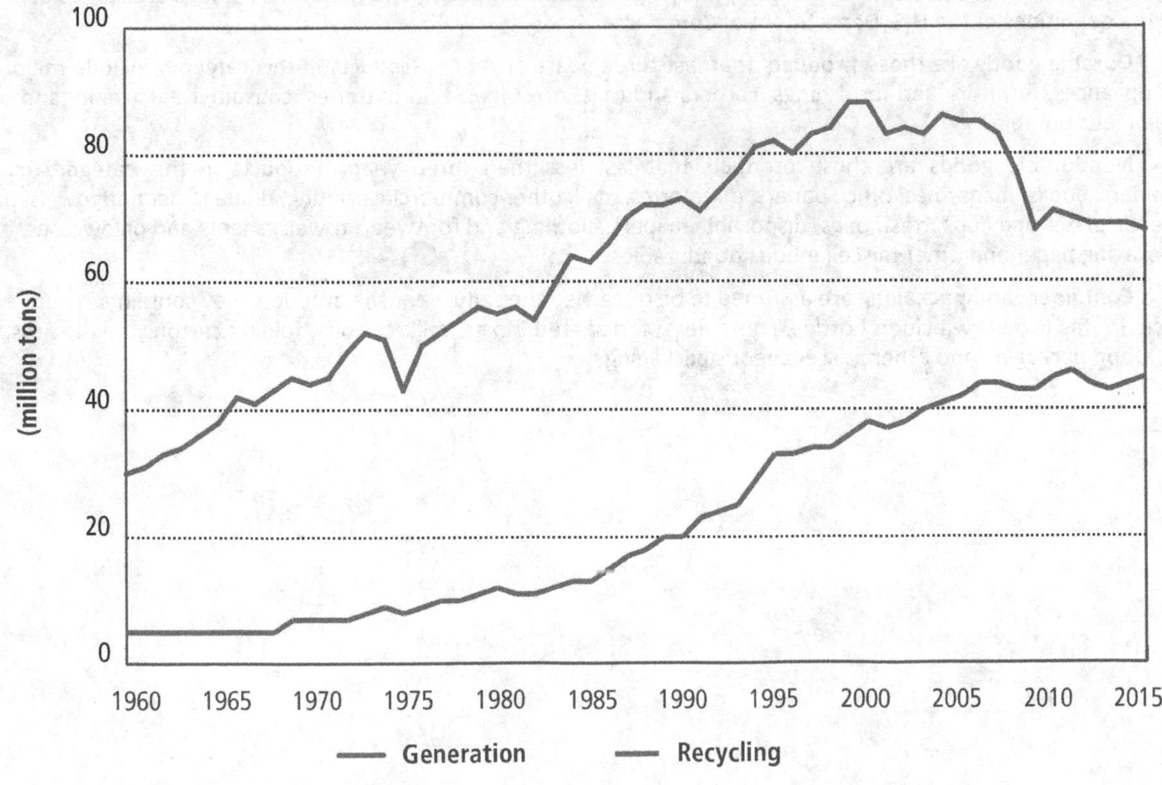

Source: *U.S. EPA, Advancing Sustainable Materials Management: 2015 Tables and Figures, July 2018*

Figure 5. Glass Products Generated in MSW, 2015

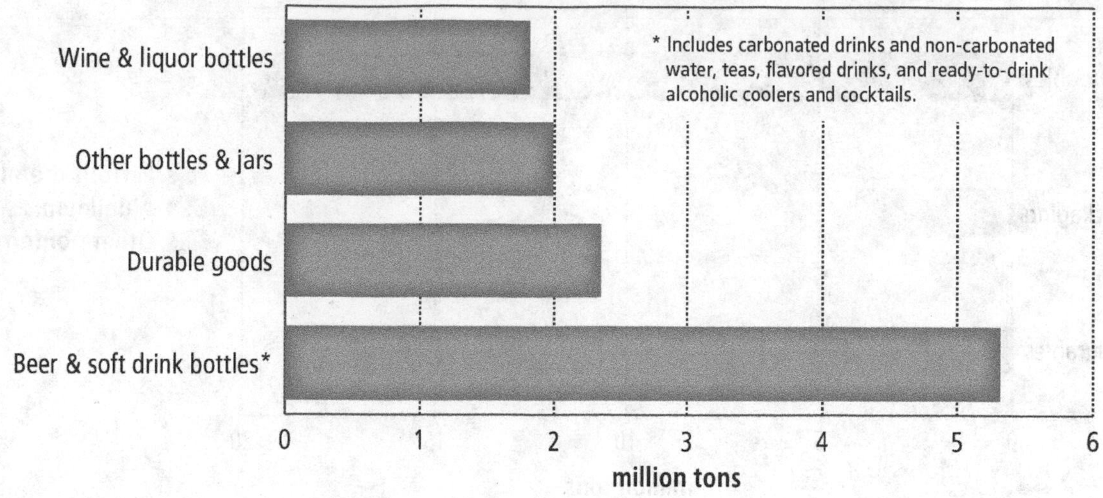

Wine & liquor bottles

Other bottles & jars

Durable goods

Beer & soft drink bottles*

0 1 2 3 4 5 6

million tons

* Includes carbonated drinks and non-carbonated water, teas, flavored drinks, and ready-to-drink alcoholic coolers and cocktails.

Figure 6. Glass Generation and Recycling, 1960 to 2015

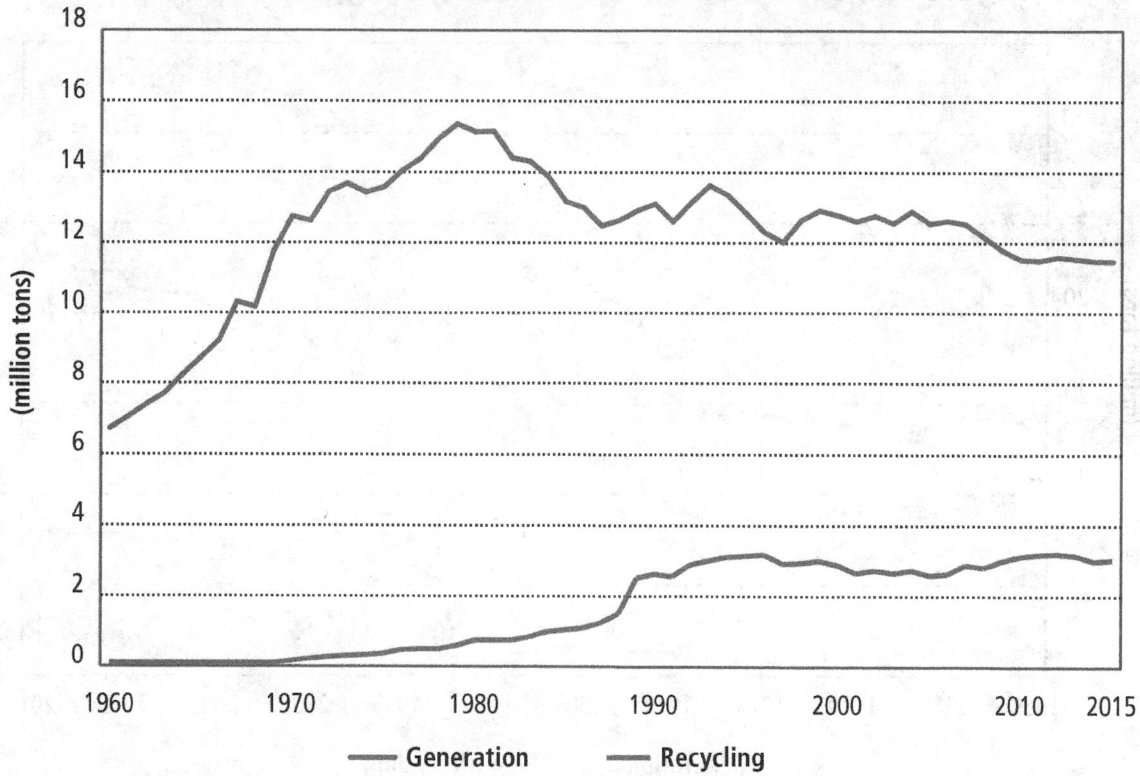

Source: *U.S. EPA, Advancing Sustainable Materials Management: 2015 Tables and Figures, July 2018*

Figure 7. Metal Products Generated in MSW, 2015

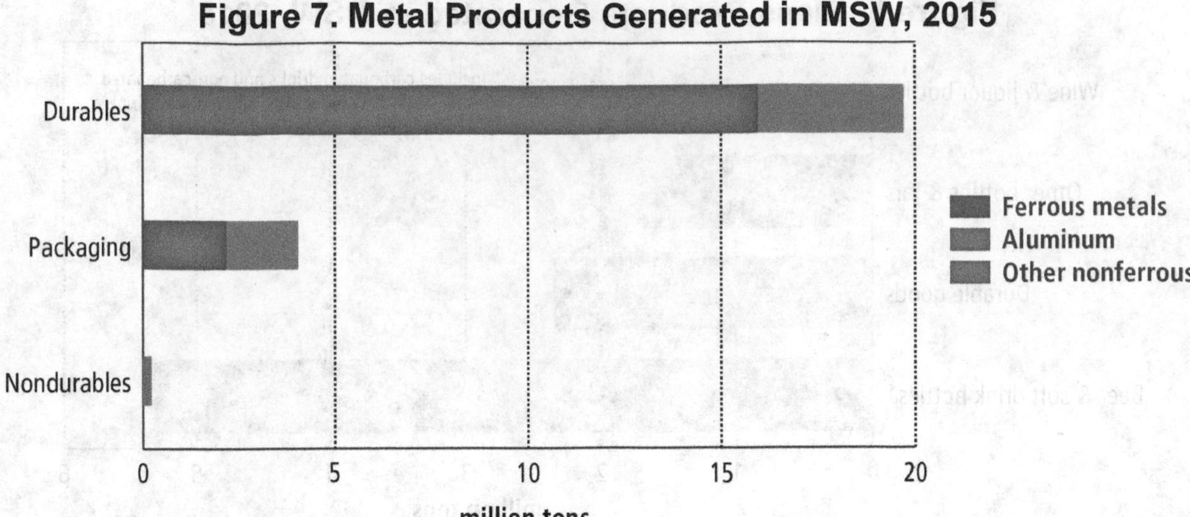

Figure 8. Metals Generation and Recycling, 1960 to 2015

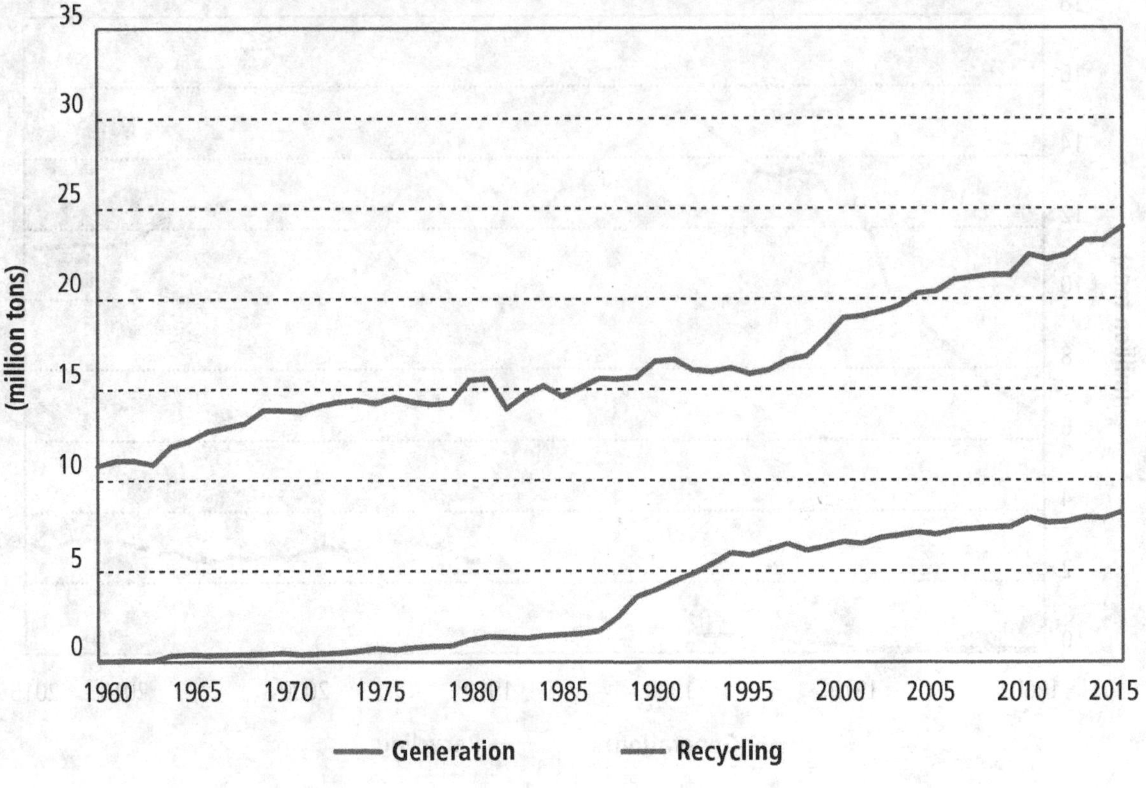

Source: *U.S. EPA, Advancing Sustainable Materials Management: 2015 Tables and Figures, July 2018*

Figure 9. Plastics Products Generated in MSW, 2015

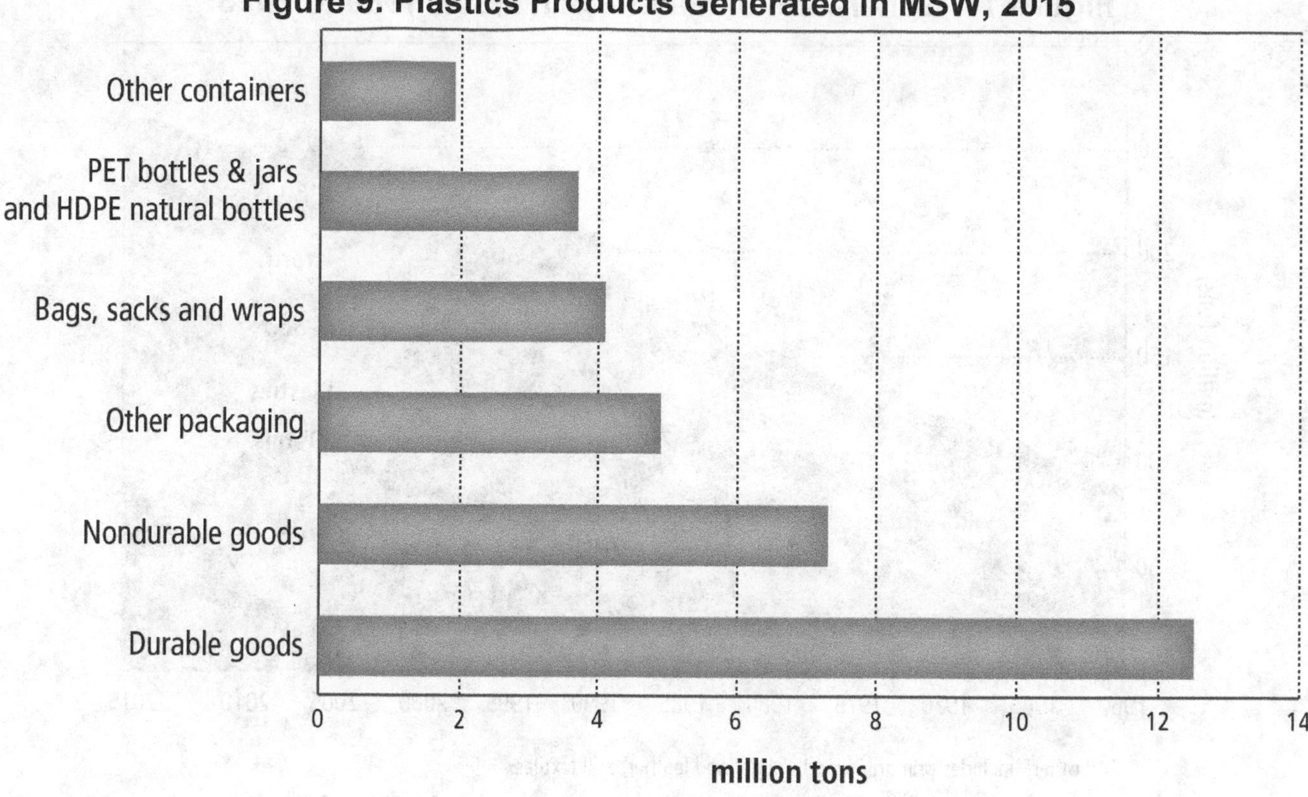

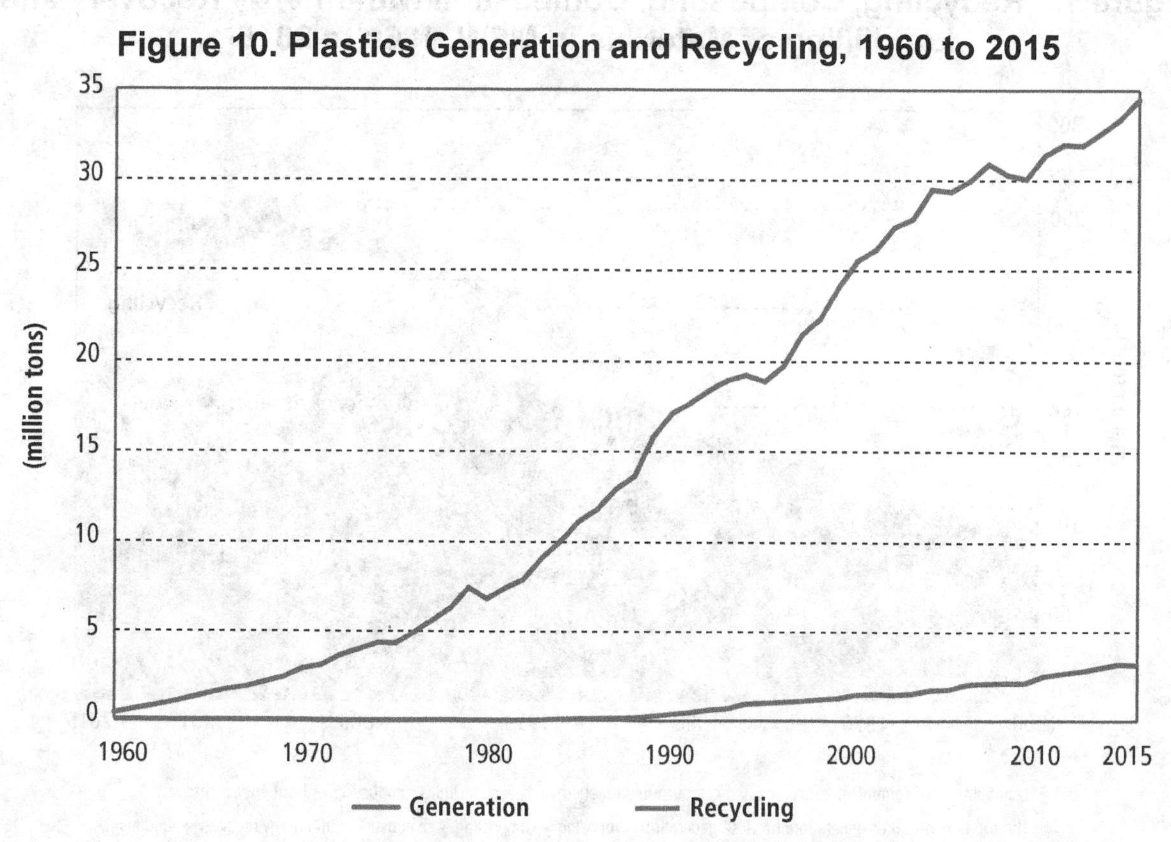

Source: *U.S. EPA, Advancing Sustainable Materials Management: 2015 Tables and Figures, July 2018*

Figure 11. Generation of Materials in MSW, 1960 to 2015

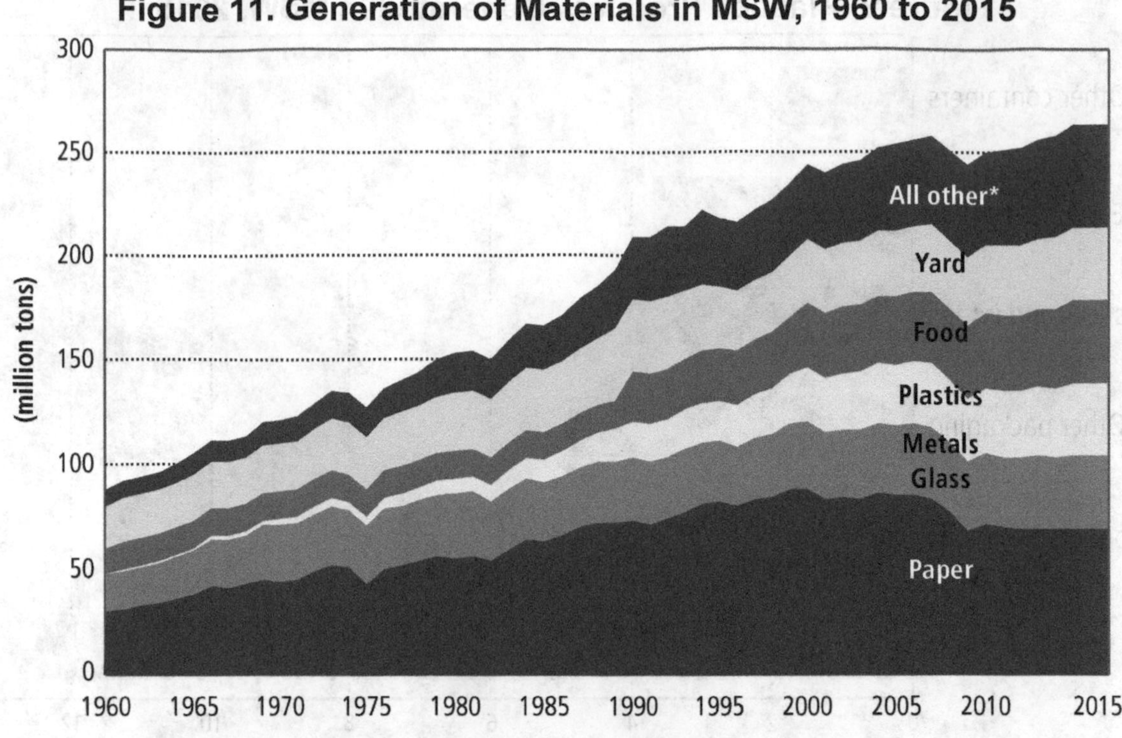

* "All other" includes primarily wood, rubber and leather, and textiles.

Figure 12. Recycling, Composting, Combustion with Energy Recovery and Landfilling of Materials in MSW, 1960 to 2015

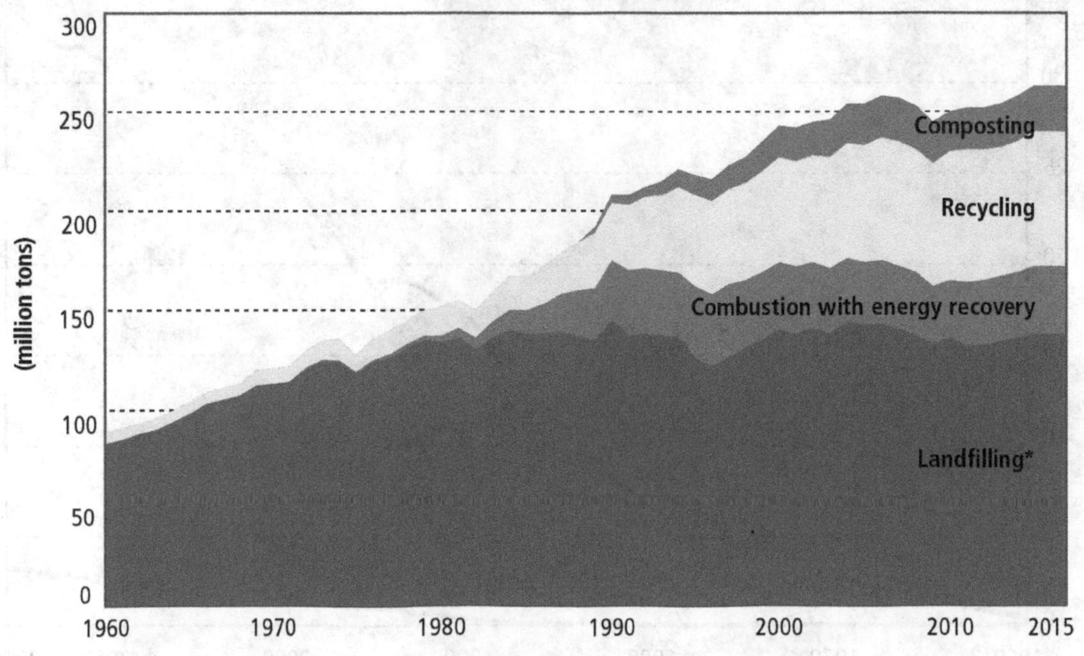

*Landfilling after composting, recycling and combustion with energy recovery. Includes combustion without energy recovery.

The top line measures generation, because generation = recycling + composting + combustion with energy recovery + landfilling.

Source: *U.S. EPA, Advancing Sustainable Materials Management: 2015 Tables and Figures, July 2018*

Figure 13. Materials Recycling and Composting in MSW,* 2015

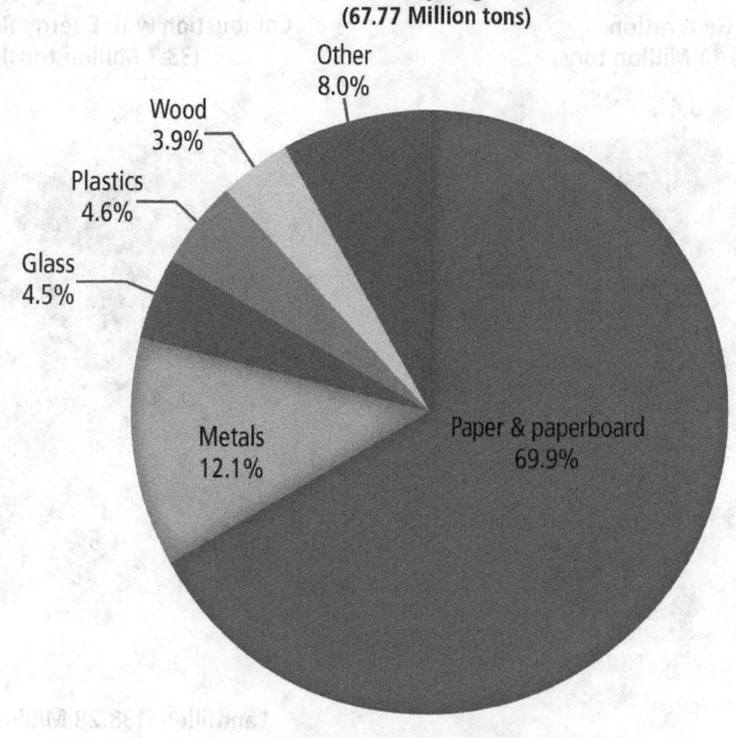

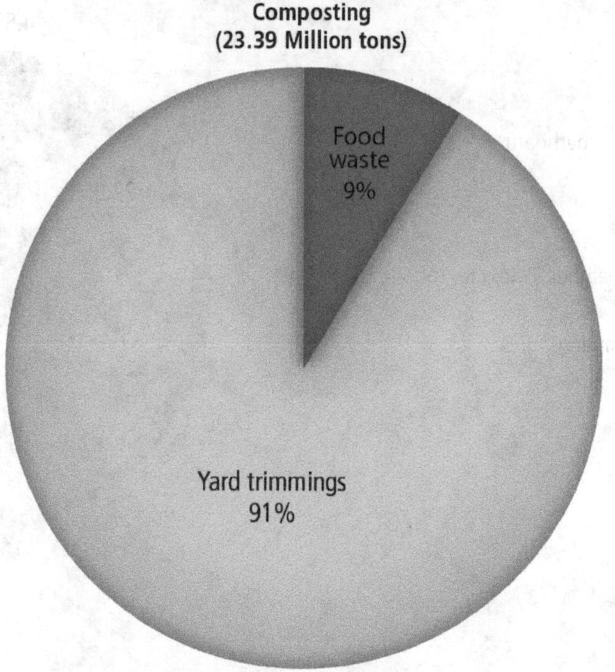

* In percent by weight of total recycling and composting

Source: *U.S. EPA, Advancing Sustainable Materials Management: 2015 Tables and Figures, July 2018*

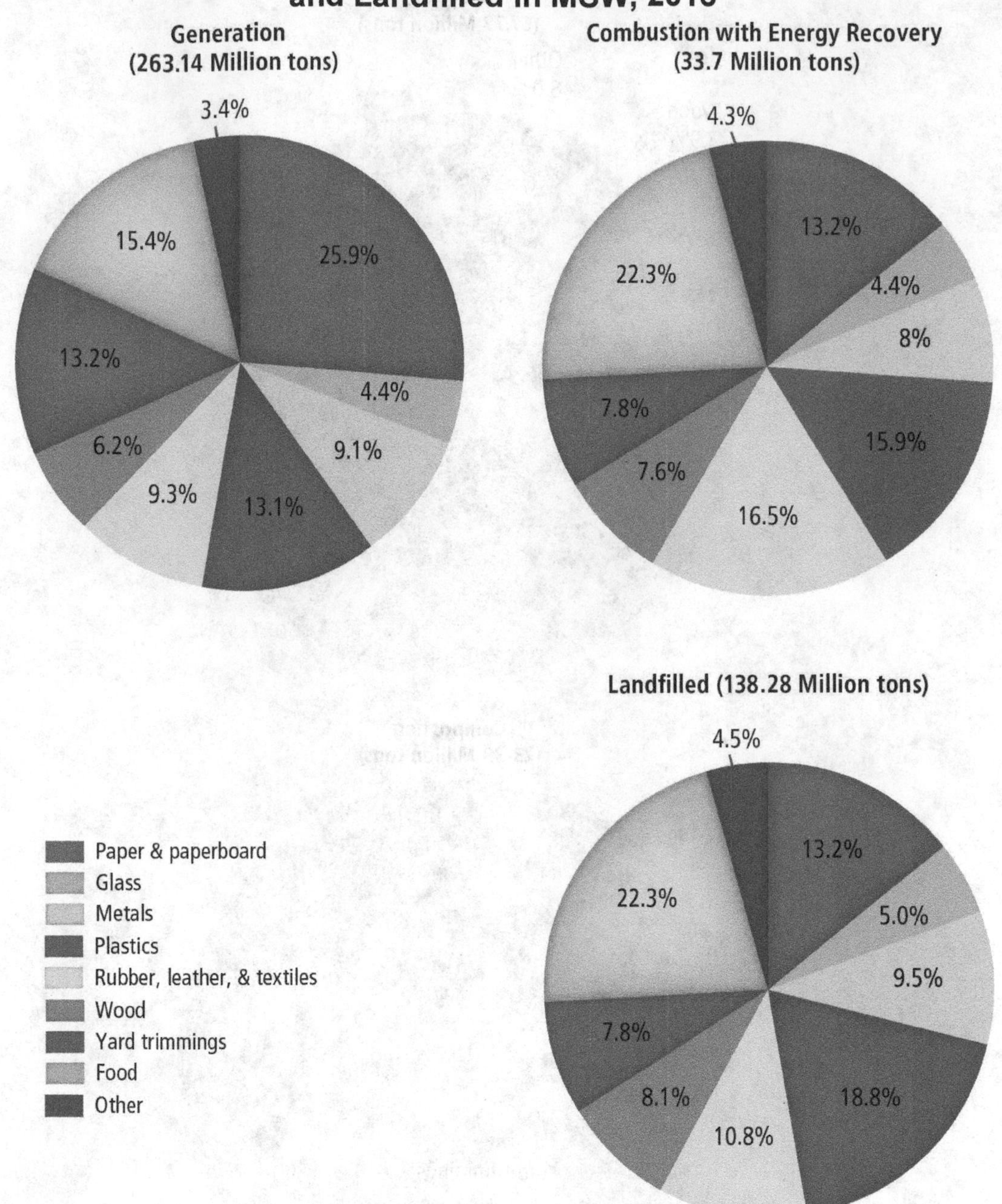

Source: *U.S. EPA, Advancing Sustainable Materials Management: 2015 Tables and Figures, July 2018*

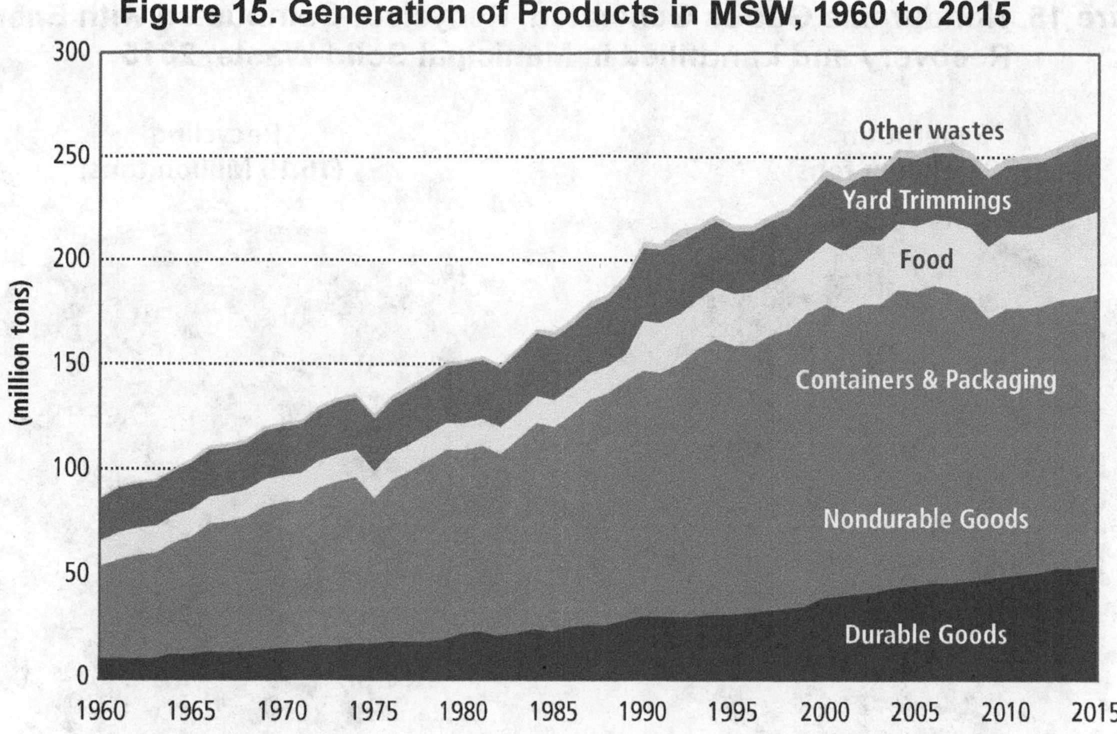

Source: *U.S. EPA, Advancing Sustainable Materials Management: 2015 Tables and Figures, July 2018*

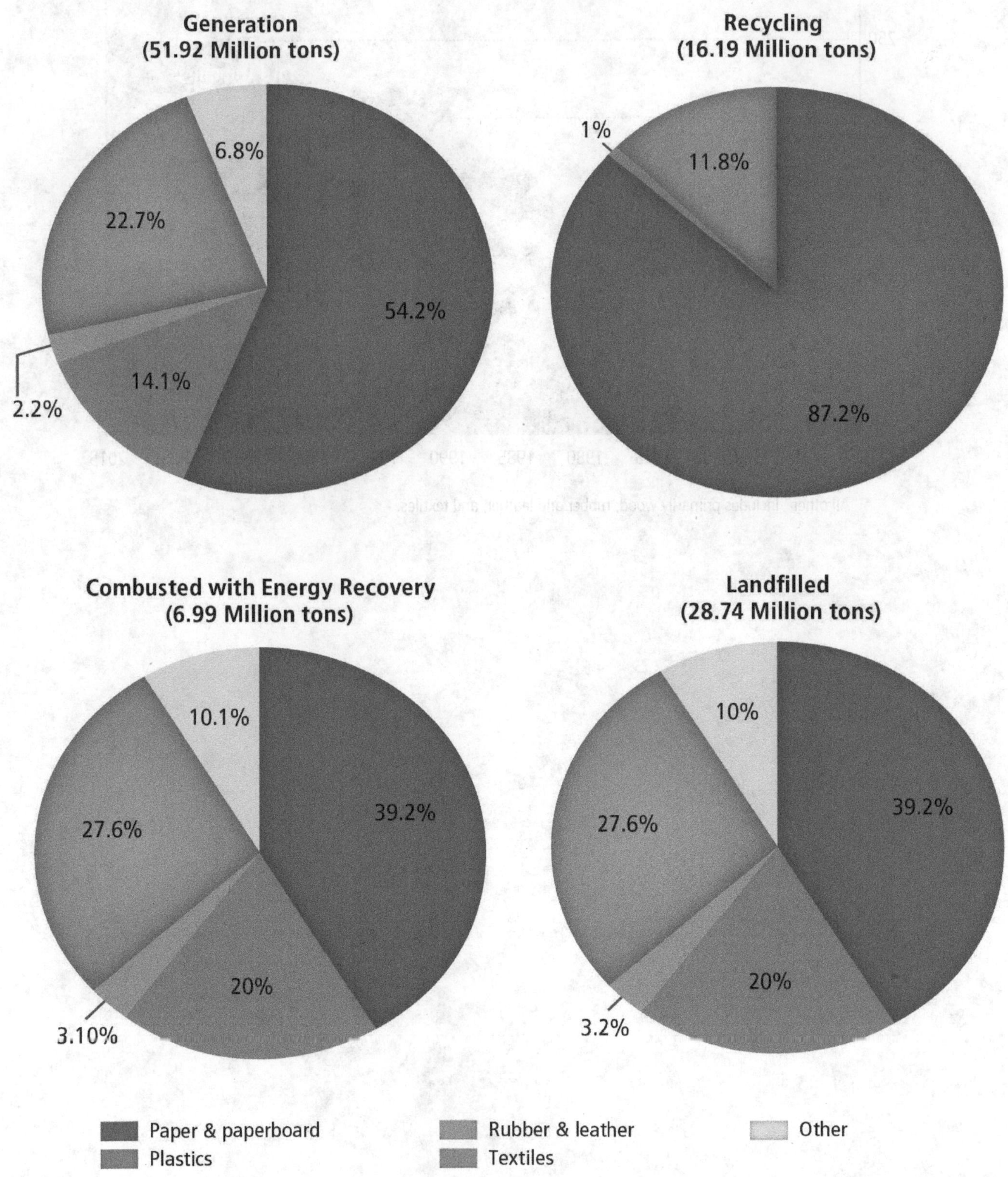

Source: U.S. EPA, Advancing Sustainable Materials Management: 2015 Tables and Figures, July 2018

Figure 17. Containers and Packaging Materials Generated, Recycled, Combusted with Energy Recovery and Landfilled in Municipal Solid Waste, 2015

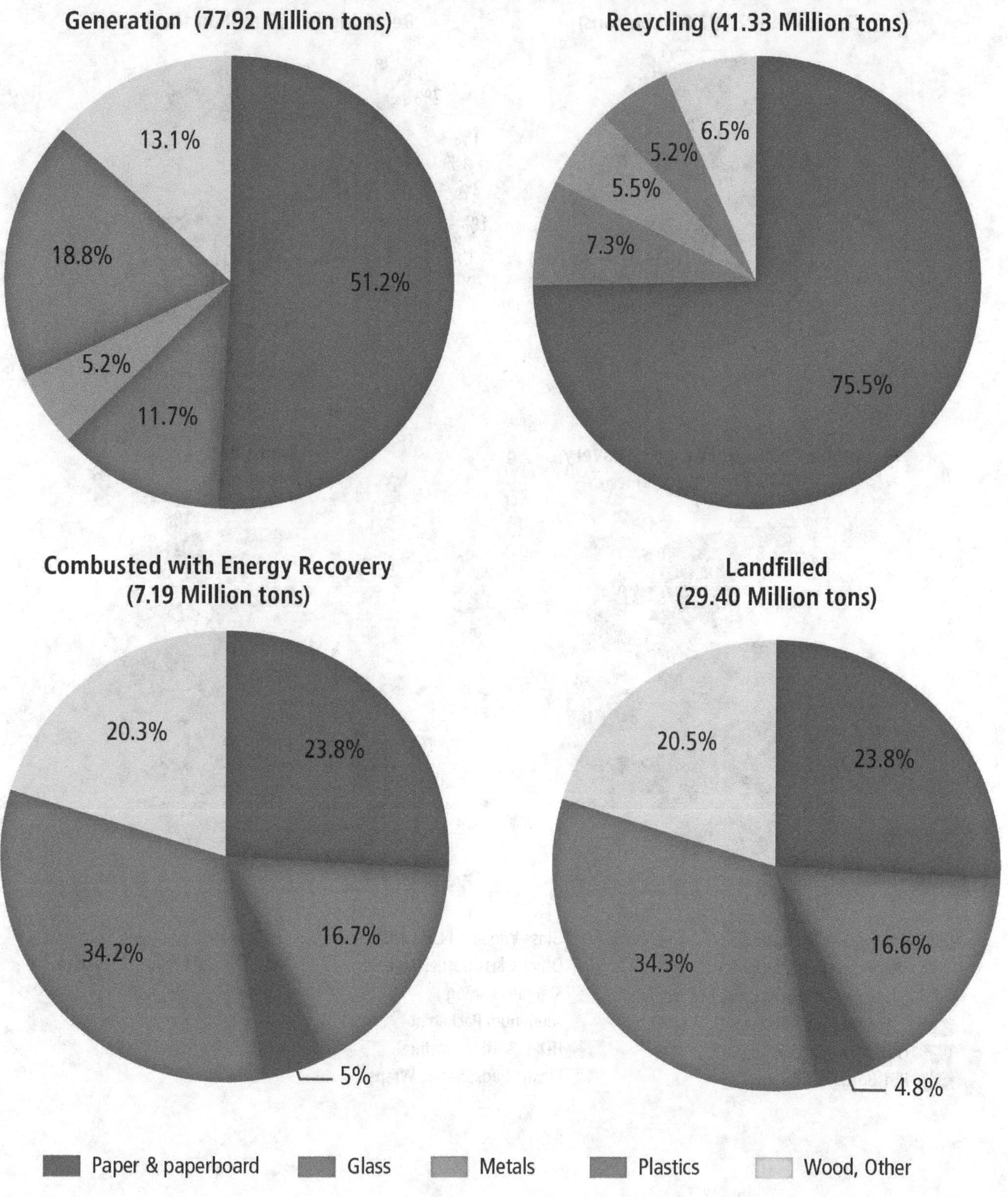

Source: *U.S. EPA, Advancing Sustainable Materials Management: 2015 Tables and Figures, July 2018*

Figure 18. Containers and Packaging Generated, Recycled, Combusted with Energy Recovery and Landfilled in Municipal Solid Waste, 2015

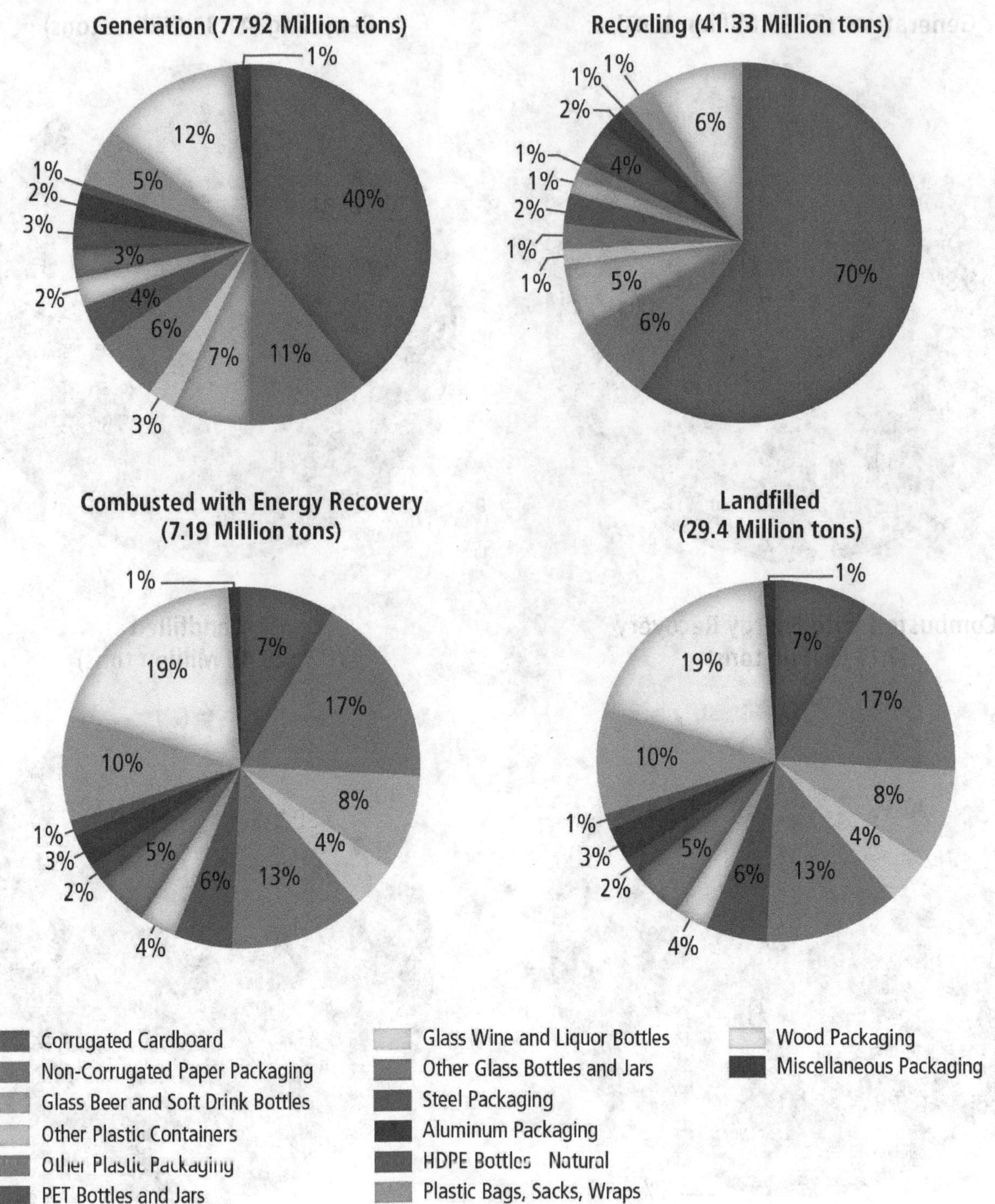

Source: *U.S. EPA, Advancing Sustainable Materials Management: 2015 Tables and Figures, July 2018*

Figure 19. Diagram of Solid Waste Management

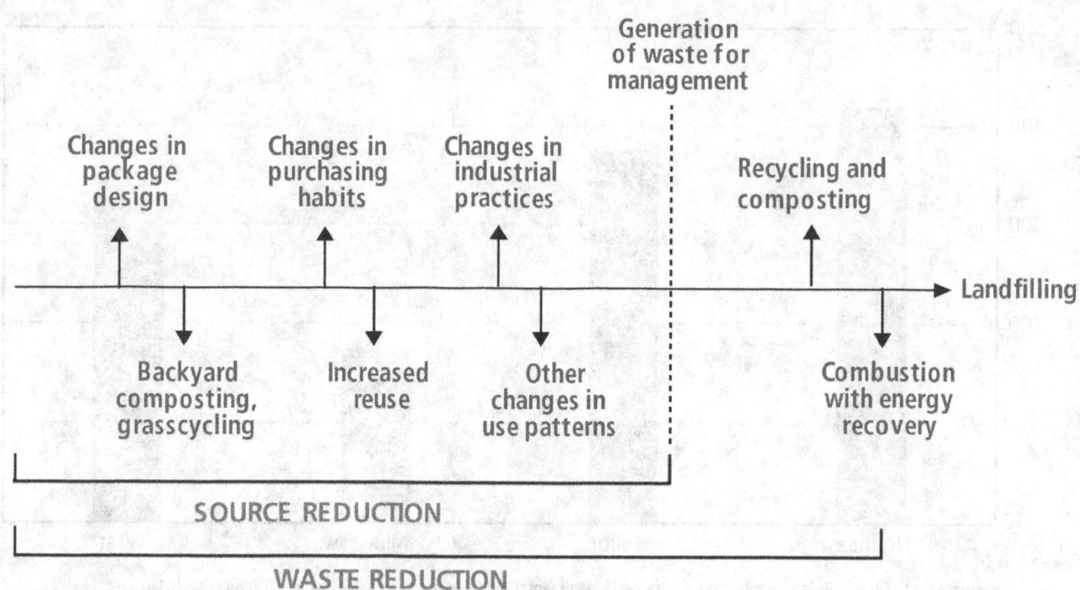

Figure 20. States with Bottle Deposit Rules

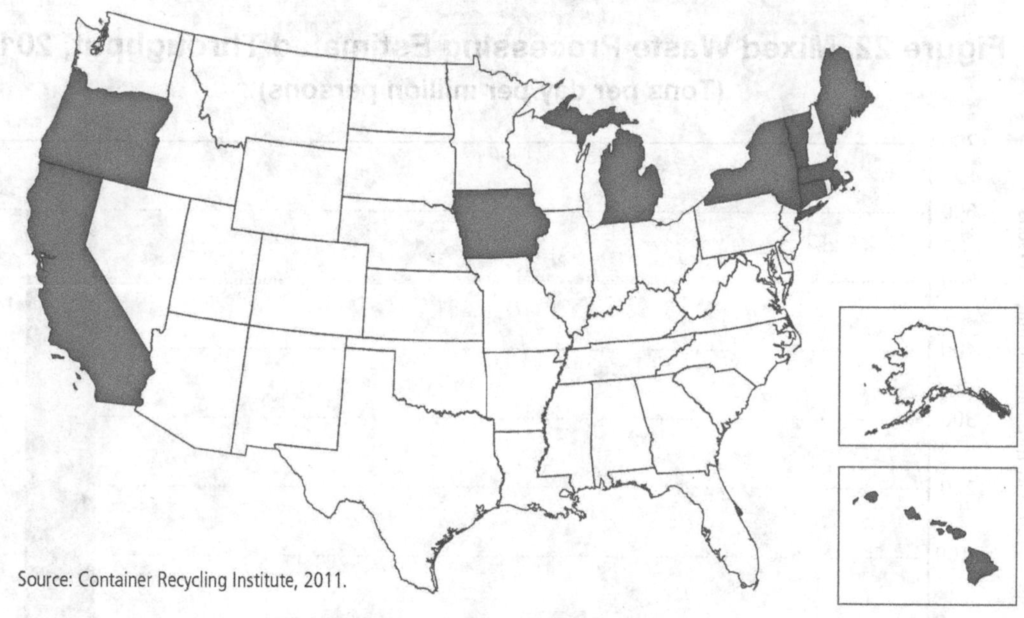

Source: *U.S. EPA, Advancing Sustainable Materials Management: 2015 Tables and Figures, July 2018*

Figure 21. Estimated MRF Throughput, 2015
(Tons per day per million persons)

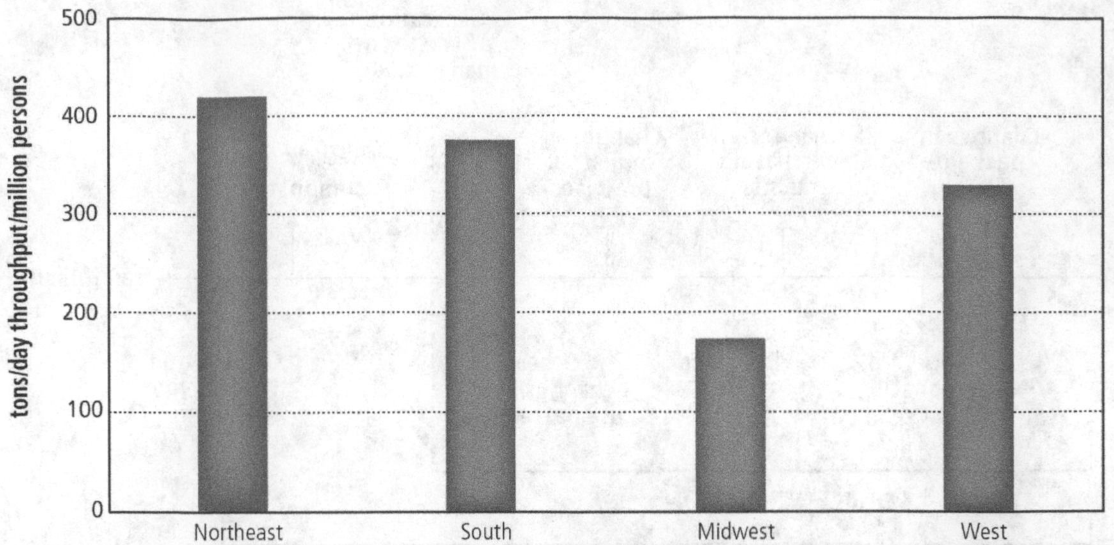

Source: U.S. Census Bureau population estimates; Governmental Advisory Associates, Inc. Data provided May 2016.

Northeast: Connecticut, Maine, Massachusetts, New Hampshire, New Jersey, New York, Pennsylvania, Rhode Island, Vermont

South: Alabama, Arkansas, Delaware, District of Columbia, Florida, Georgia, Kentucky, Louisiana, Maryland, Mississippi, North Carolina, Oklahoma, South Carolina, Tennessee, Texas, Virginia, West Virginia

Midwest: Illinois, Indiana, Iowa, Kansas, Michigan, Minnesota, Missouri, Nebraska, North Dakota, Ohio, South Dakota, Wisconsin

West: Alaska, Arizona, California, Colorado, Hawaii, Idaho, Montana, Nevada, New Mexico, Oregon, Utah, Washington, Wyoming

Figure 22. Mixed Waste Processing Estimated Throughput, 2015
(Tons per day per million persons)

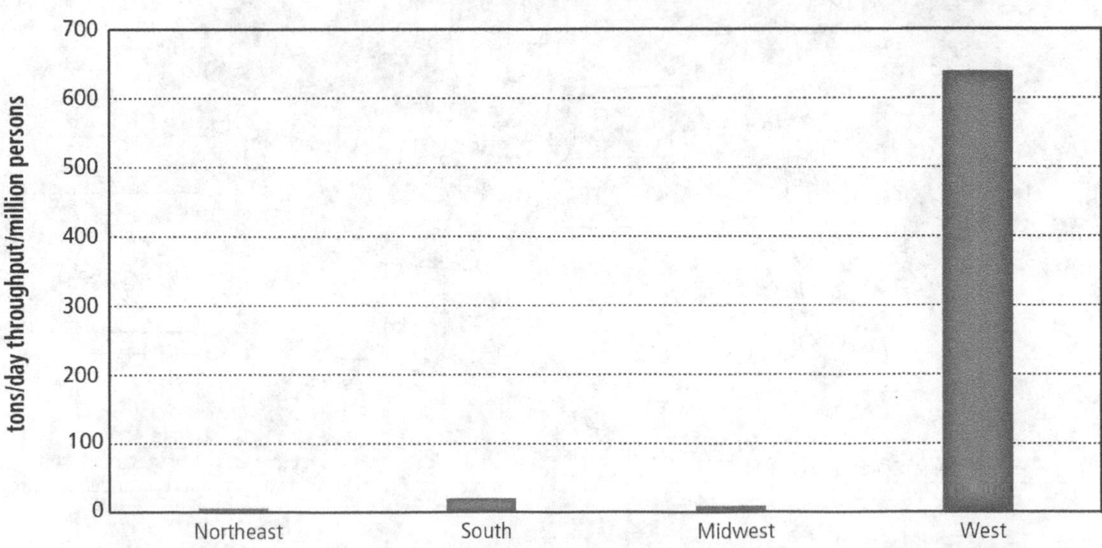

Source: U.S. Census Bureau population estimates; Governmental Advisory Associates, Inc. Data provided May 2016.

Northeast: Connecticut, Maine, Massachusetts, New Hampshire, New Jersey, New York, Pennsylvania, Rhode Island, Vermont

South: Alabama, Arkansas, Delaware, District of Columbia, Florida, Georgia, Kentucky, Louisiana, Maryland, Mississippi, North Carolina, Oklahoma, South Carolina, Tennessee, Texas, Virginia, West Virginia

Midwest: Illinois, Indiana, Iowa, Kansas, Michigan, Minnesota, Missouri, Nebraska, North Dakota, Ohio, South Dakota, Wisconsin

West: Alaska, Arizona, California, Colorado, Hawaii, Idaho, Montana, Nevada, New Mexico, Oregon, Utah, Washington, Wyoming

***Source:** U.S. EPA, Advancing Sustainable Materials Management: 2015 Tables and Figures, July 2018*

Figure 23. MSW Composting Capacity, 2015
(Capacity in tons per day per million persons)

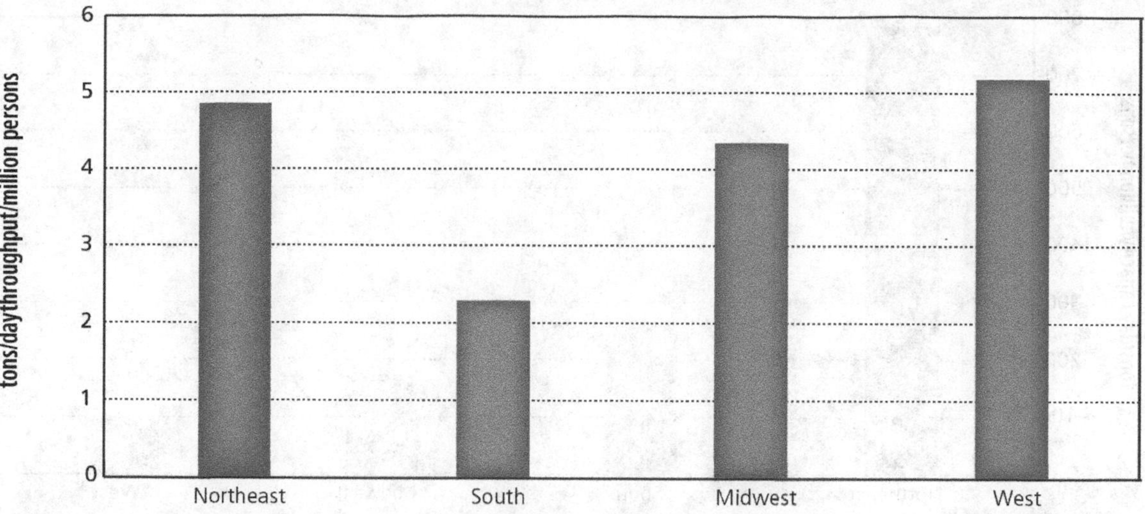

Source: U.S. Census Bureau; *BioCycle*, November 2011, *BioCycle* October 2017, Mariposa County, California and Medina County, Ohio websites.

Northeast: Connecticut, Maine, Massachusetts, New Hampshire, New Jersey, New York, Pennsylvania, Rhode Island, Vermont

South: Alabama, Arkansas, Delaware, District of Columbia, Florida, Georgia, Kentucky, Louisiana, Maryland, Mississippi, North Carolina, Oklahoma, South Carolina, Tennessee, Texas, Virginia, West Virginia

Midwest: Illinois, Indiana, Iowa, Kansas, Michigan, Minnesota, Missouri, Nebraska, North Dakota, Ohio, South Dakota, Wisconsin

West: Alaska, Arizona, California, Colorado, Hawaii, Idaho, Montana, Nevada, New Mexico, Oregon, Utah, Washington, Wyoming

Figure 24. Yard Trimmings Composting Facilities, 2015
(In number of facilities)

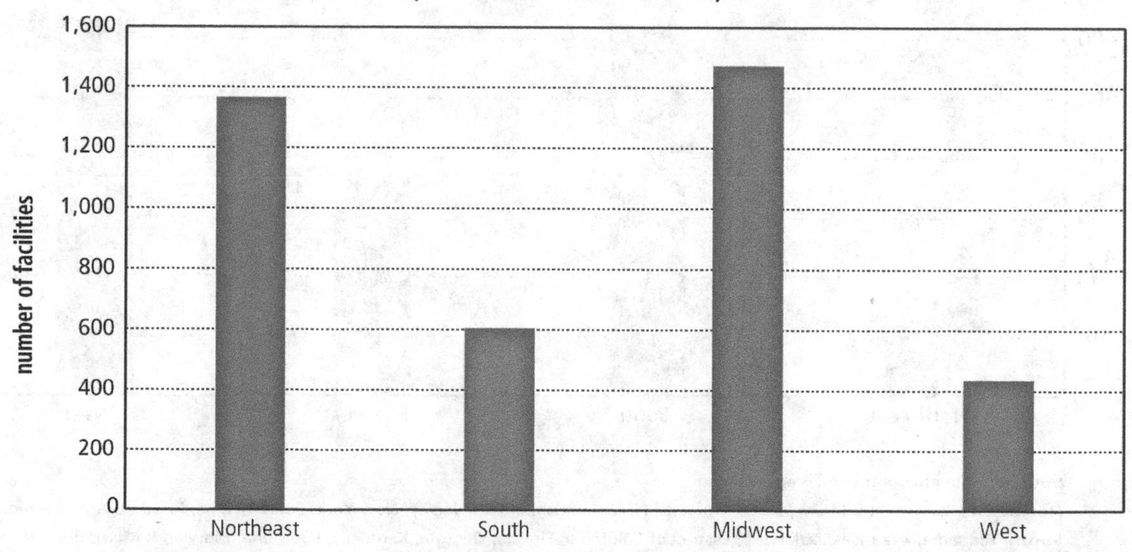

Source: Goldstein, N. "The State of Organics" *BioCycle*, October 2017.
Facilities composting yard trimmings, yard trimmings and food waste, and mixed organics. Excludes 740 facilities composting manure, biosolids, mixed MSW, or not defined.

Northeast: Connecticut, Maine, Massachusetts, New Hampshire, New Jersey, New York, Pennsylvania, Rhode Island, Vermont

South: Alabama, Arkansas, Delaware, District of Columbia, Florida, Georgia, Kentucky, Louisiana, Maryland, Mississippi, North Carolina, Oklahoma, South Carolina, Tennessee, Texas, Virginia, West Virginia

Midwest: Illinois, Indiana, Iowa, Kansas, Michigan, Minnesota, Missouri, Nebraska, North Dakota, Ohio, South Dakota, Wisconsin

West: Alaska, Arizona, California, Colorado, Hawaii, Idaho, Montana, Nevada, New Mexico, Oregon, Utah, Washington, Wyoming

***Source:** U.S. EPA, Advancing Sustainable Materials Management: 2015 Tables and Figures, July 2018*

Figure 25. Municipal Waste-To-Energy Capacity, 2015

(Capacity in tons per million persons)

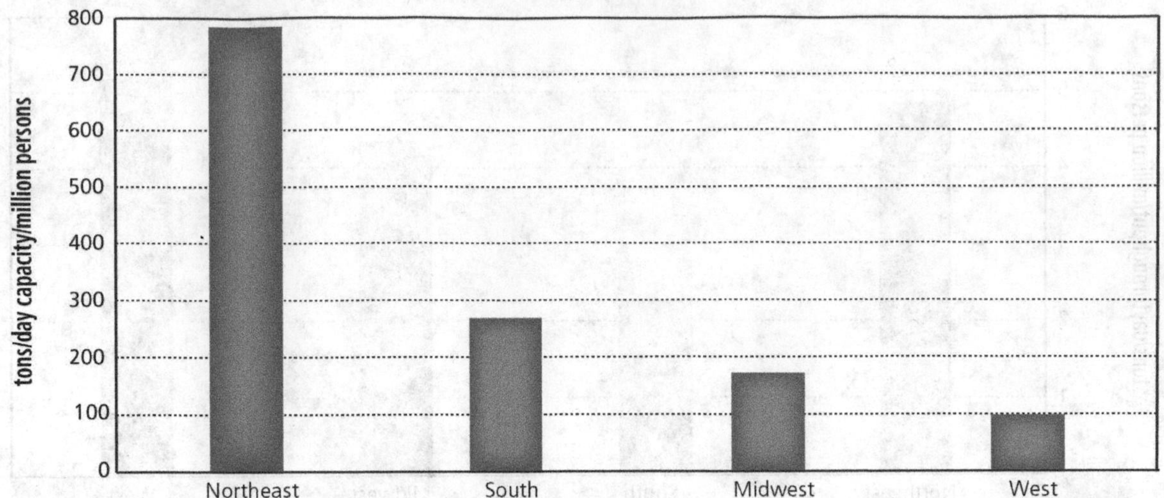

Source: U.S. Census Bureau population estimates; Energy Recovery Council (ERC). "The 2016 ERC Directory of Waste-to-Energy Facilities" 2016.

Northeast: Connecticut, Maine, Massachusetts, New Hampshire, New Jersey, New York, Pennsylvania, Rhode Island, Vermont

South: Alabama, Arkansas, Delaware, District of Columbia, Florida, Georgia, Kentucky, Louisiana, Maryland, Mississippi, North Carolina, Oklahoma, South Carolina, Tennessee, Texas, Virginia, West Virginia

Midwest: Illinois, Indiana, Iowa, Kansas, Michigan, Minnesota, Missouri, Nebraska, North Dakota, Ohio, South Dakota, Wisconsin

West: Alaska, Arizona, California, Colorado, Hawaii, Idaho, Montana, Nevada, New Mexico, Oregon, Utah, Washington, Wyoming

Figure 26. Number of Landfills in the U.S., 2015

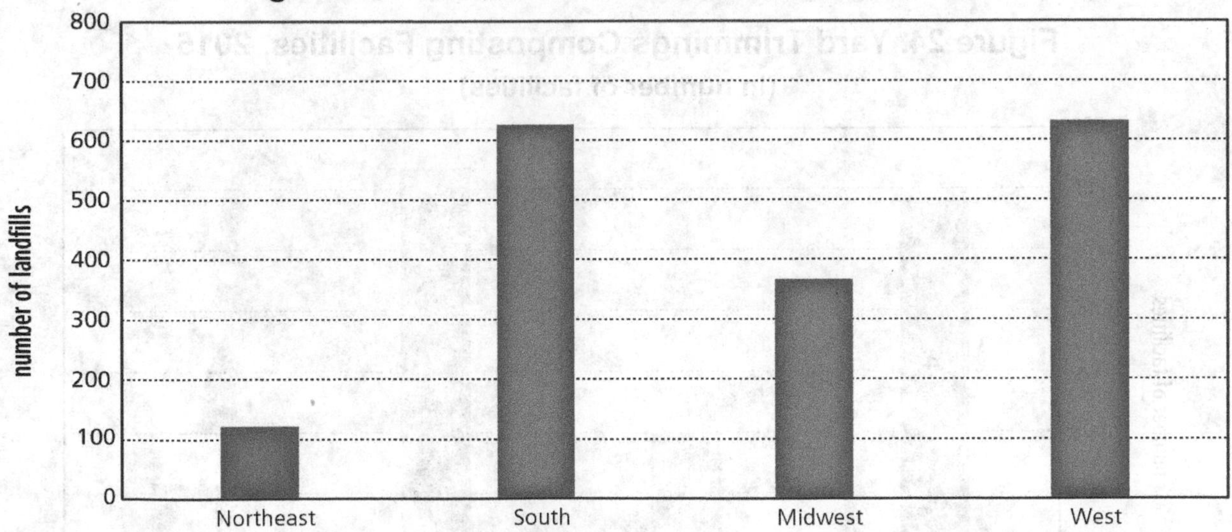

Source: State environmental websites.

Northeast: Connecticut, Maine, Massachusetts, New Hampshire, New Jersey, New York, Pennsylvania, Rhode Island, Vermont

South: Alabama, Arkansas, Delaware, District of Columbia, Florida, Georgia, Kentucky, Louisiana, Maryland, Mississippi, North Carolina, Oklahoma, South Carolina, Tennessee, Texas, Virginia, West Virginia

Midwest: Illinois, Indiana, Iowa, Kansas, Michigan, Minnesota, Missouri, Nebraska, North Dakota, Ohio, South Dakota, Wisconsin

West: Alaska, Arizona, California, Colorado, Hawaii, Idaho, Montana, Nevada, New Mexico, Oregon, Utah, Washington, Wyoming

***Source:** U.S. EPA, Advancing Sustainable Materials Management: 2015 Tables and Figures, July 2018*

1 Introduction

1.1 Purpose of Report

The U.S. Environmental Protection Agency (EPA) is responsible for regulating the production and use of pesticides in the United States under the Federal Insecticide, Fungicide, and Rodenticide Act (FIFRA) and the Federal Food, Drug, and Cosmetic Act (FFDCA). This report provides economic information on the U.S. sectors that produce and use pesticides covered by these federal regulatory statutes and programs. Economic profile information covers a variety of topics, particularly the pesticide market with respect to dollar values and quantities of active ingredient. The EPA Office of Pesticide Programs has issued such market reports since 1979 (EPA 1979). The intended audience of this document includes those entities seeking an overview of sales and usage in the pesticide industry, which may include federal and state agencies, researchers, academia, and the general public.

Neither EPA nor any other federal agency has a program devoted specifically to collecting information for the purpose of estimating the overall pesticide market in terms of dollars spent and quantities of active ingredients used on an annual basis. Therefore, this information must be compiled from external sources (see Data Sources). The data in this report represent approximate values rather than precise values with known statistical properties.

This report is intended only to present objective economic profile and trend information reflecting the best information available to EPA on pesticide sales and use. It does not interpret, offer conclusions, or make inferences about the data. Detailed analysis of causal factors or implications, such as potential impacts on human health, the environment, or the economy, falls beyond the scope of this report.

We caution the reader not to infer too much from changes in the amount of pesticides used from year to year. Changes in the amount of pesticides used are not necessarily correlated with changes in the level of pest control or changes in the human health and environmental risks associated with pesticide use. Yearly variation in pesticide sales may reflect for example, changes in survey methodology, changes in the price of pesticides, or the introduction and adoption of new pesticide/chemistries with associated higher prices. Similarly, yearly variation in pounds of pesticides applied may be influenced by factors such as survey methodology, pesticide pricing, increased usage of newer pesticide chemistries with similar toxicity at reduced application rates, or changes in application methodology (*e.g.,* seed treatment vs. post emergence applications).

1.2 Data Sources

The agency based its estimates of pesticide usage and expenditures on data from public and proprietary databases and market research reports that have met EPA requirements for environmental data as evidenced by their documented quality systems, including prescribed quality assurance and quality control activities to ensure the quality of the data (EPA 2008). Public data sources include several reports developed by the United States Department of Agriculture's National Agricultural Statistics Service (USDA/NASS). These publications cover a broad range of pesticide sales and usage information. The associated data quality measures for each report are published on the USDA/NASS website *(https://www.nass.usda.gov/Publications/Methodology_and_Data_Quality)*. Proprietary data sources include agricultural and non-agricultural pesticide survey data and research reports of pesticide usage statistics collected and sold by private market research firms. The survey methodology is documented in the firms' quality assurance documents, and results are deemed statistically valid by the Agency's standards. These data, produced by well-known organizations, also serve pesticide registrants and other private sector firms analysing the U.S. and world pesticide markets. The methods used by the various public and proprietary data sources vary from large statistically based grower/user samples or panels to use of more limited interview/survey approaches of growers, applicators, pesticide suppliers, and pest management consultants. No single source provides data on all use sites. Each source and its method were considered on their merits when judging the usefulness and relevance to making annual market estimates

Source: *U.S. EPA, Pesticide Industry Sales and Usage, 2008-2012 Market Estimate, Released 2017*

for this report. Comparisons across data sources were done where appropriate. Data presented in this report are merged, averaged, and rounded so that the presented information is not proprietary, business confidential, or trade secret.

It should be noted that additional pesticide usage may have occurred that is not included in this document because the available studies do not survey all sites (*e.g.*, small acreage crops). Furthermore, usage data on a particular site may be noted in data sources, but not quantified, because of small sample size or other factors. In these instances, usage data associated with the site are not reported in this document, and may therefore underestimate actual usage. Lack of reported usage data for a pesticide or use site does not imply zero usage.

This report presents data at both the producer and user levels. Producer level data are obtained by surveying companies that manufacture and formulate pesticides to determine the amount of pesticides sold in a given year in terms of dollars and pounds active ingredient (a.i.) by pesticide type (see Sections 2.1 and 3.1). User level data are obtained by surveying persons or businesses that purchase and apply pesticides, such as farmers, commercial pesticide applicators, and homeowners to determine the amount of pesticides applied in a given year in terms of dollars and pounds a.i. (see Sections 2.2 – 2.3, 3.2 – 3.7, and 4).

1.3 Scope of Report

This report profiles the U.S. pesticide industry, on an annual basis, for the years 2008-2012. Data were estimated using several different parameters (e.g., pesticide type, pesticide group, market sector) and appear in tabular form. The scope of the report is largely inclusive of the U.S. pesticide industry and includes data on expenditures (sales in dollars), volume (pounds applied), firms, individuals involved in production and use of pesticides, number of pesticides, and number of certified applicators, among other topics. Data on expenditures and sales are reported in nominal terms for the year indicated (*i.e.*, not adjusted or indexed for inflation). Data on pesticide usage are reported only as pounds applied and not acres treated. The report includes graphical representations of the data where useful for illustration purposes.

Following the Introduction (Section 1), Section 2 of the report summarizes world and U.S. pesticide expenditures, and Section 3 summarizes world and U.S. pesticide usage. Section 4 presents summary-level information on pesticide users and producers.

1.4 Data Reporting Changes

Since the last publication of this report (EPA 2011), there have been several changes in data sources and calculation methods used to derive the estimates of pesticide usage and expenditures. These changes were the result of discontinued private market research data sources and the availability of more current data that more accurately reflected pesticide sales and usage statistics for the reported timeframes.

The previous proprietary source of data for producer level expenditures on pesticides and pounds of pesticide applied in the world and U.S. markets has been discontinued and has been replaced with a new source. Thus, the grouping and trends in these data (Sections 2.1 and 3.1) may vary slightly from those reported in previous versions of this document.

Additionally, in previous versions of this report, some user level data were updated by calculating a percent change in the market and applying that percent change to the values presented in previous reports. In this report, no data are extrapolated with the exception of the 2009 Industrial/Commercial/ Government category values. Because of a lack of data, the 2009 values are an average of the 2012 and 2007 values for this category. All data presented are based on the best available estimates for each reported year. Not all of the included data sources for user level data report yearly; therefore, data are only reported for years for which data are available. Several studies used to determine the cost and quantity of non-agricultural pesticide use have also been discontinued. Therefore, in order to update this report, the

Source: *U.S. EPA, Pesticide Industry Sales and Usage, 2008-2012 Market Estimate, Released 2017*

values in these categories were calculated differently than in previous versions. In order to maintain continuity in the data, and to prevent the false appearance of changes in usage patterns, the values for 2005 and 2007 were recalculated using the same methods and sources used to update this report, and thus vary slightly from the values reported for these timeframes in previous versions of this publication.

Source: *U.S. EPA, Pesticide Industry Sales and Usage, 2008-2012 Market Estimate, Released 2017*

2 2008 - 2012 Sales

2.1 World and U.S. Pesticide Expenditures

World pesticide expenditures at the producer level totalled nearly $56 billion in 2012 (see Figure 2.1). Between 2008 and 2012, expenditures on herbicides consistently accounted for the largest portion of total expenditures in all years (approximately 45%), followed by expenditures on insecticides, fungicides, and other pesticides, respectively (see Table 2.1).

U.S. pesticide expenditures at the producer level totalled nearly $9 billion in 2012 (see Figure 2.1). Between 2008 and 2012, U.S. expenditures accounted for 18-16% of total world pesticide expenditures. Most recently, in 2012, U.S. expenditures accounted for 21% of world expenditures on herbicides (including plant growth regulators [PGRs]), 14% of world expenditures on insecticides, 10% of world expenditures on fungicides, and 23% of world expenditures on fumigants (Table 2.1). Figure 2.1 displays the distribution of pesticide expenditures by pesticide type in the U.S. and world markets. See Section 2.2 for a more detailed look at U.S. expenditures on pesticides from 2008 to 2012.

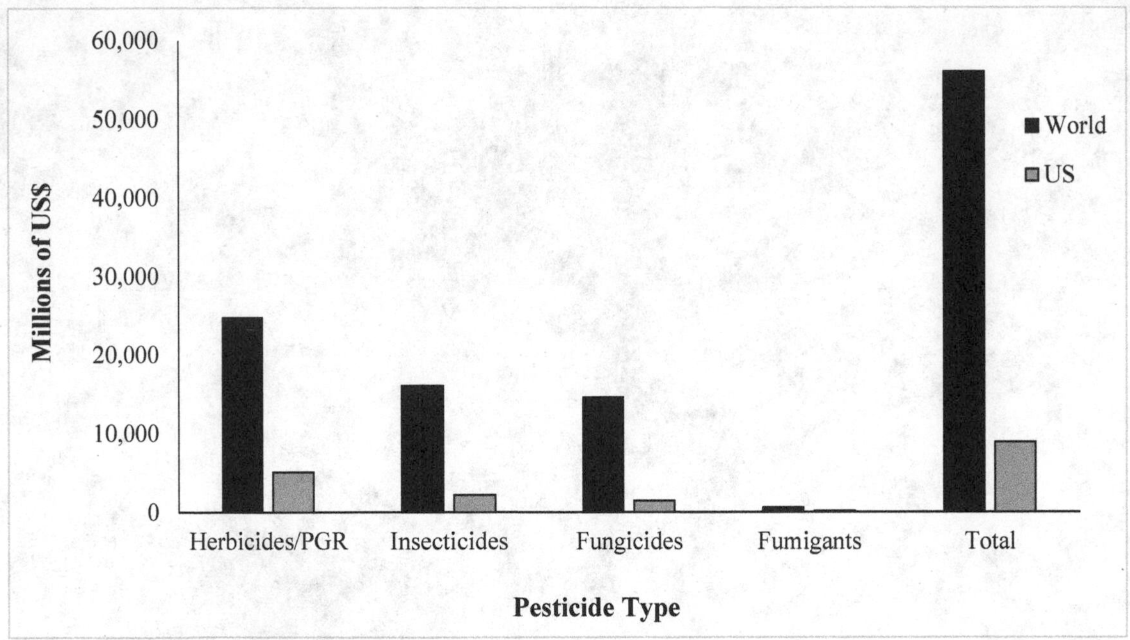

Figure 2.1. World and U.S. Pesticide Expenditures at Producer Level by Pesticide Type, 2012 Estimates

Source: Phillips McDougall, AgriService (2008-2012). (*http://phillipsmcdougall.co.uk/agriservice/*)

Source: *U.S. EPA, Pesticide Industry Sales and Usage, 2008-2012 Market Estimate, Released 2017*

Table 2.1. World and U.S. Pesticide Expenditures at the Producer Level by Pesticide Type, 2008 - 2012 Estimates

Year and Pesticide Type	World Market		U.S. Market		U.S. Percentage of World Market
	Millions of $	%	Millions of $	%	
2012					
Herbicides/PGR*	24,727	44	5,115	58	21
Insecticides	16,023	29	2,184	25	14
Fungicides	14,565	26	1,430	16	10
Fumigants	606	1	137	2	23
Total	55,921		8,866		16
2011					
Herbicides/PGR	23,322	44	4,904	58	21
Insecticides	15,055	28	2,125	25	14
Fungicides	13,898	26	1,348	16	10
Fumigants	554	1	145	2	26
Total	52,829		8,522		16
2010					
Herbicides/PGR	21,131	45	4,755	58	23
Insecticides	13,356	28	2,038	25	15
Fungicides	12,106	26	1,232	15	10
Fumigants	578	1	138	2	24
Total	47,171		8,163		17
2009					
Herbicides/PGR	21,376	46	5,058	59	24
Insecticides	12,382	27	2,009	23	16
Fungicides	11,692	25	1,166	14	10
Fumigants	557	1	122	1	22
Total	46,007		8,355		18
2008					
Herbicides/PGR	23,516	48	5,364	63	23
Insecticides	12,486	26	1,882	22	15
Fungicides	12,249	25	1,186	14	10
Fumigants	591	1	123	1	21
Total	48,842		8,555		18

Source: Phillips McDougall, AgriService (2008-2012). (http://phillipsmcdougall.co.uk/agriservice/)***Note:*** *Insecticide and fungicide values include seed treatment uses. Totals may not be exact due to rounding. Table data do not cover wood preservatives, specialty biocides, chlorine/hypochlorites, vertebrate pesticides or other chemicals used as pesticides (e.g., sulfur and petroleum oil).*

*PGR – Plant Growth Regulator

Source: *U.S. EPA, Pesticide Industry Sales and Usage, 2008-2012 Market Estimate, Released 2017*

2.2 User Expenditures on Conventional Pesticides in the United States

U.S. expenditures at the user level for conventional pesticides totalled nearly $14 billion in 2012 and nearly $13 billion in 2009 (see Figure 2.2 and Table 2.2). Conventional pesticides are defined here as all active ingredients other than biological pesticides and antimicrobial pesticides. Pesticides included in the estimates are herbicides (including PGRs), insecticides, fungicides, fumigants, sulfur and oils, and other pesticides. Other pesticides include chemicals that may be used as pesticides but are not primarily produced as pesticides for the agricultural market (*e.g.,* sulfuric acid and phosphoric acid), as well as rodenticides and repellents used in the home and industrial markets. The estimates exclude expenditures on wood preservatives and specialty biocides, which are discussed separately in section 3.7 of this report.

Increases in spending in the agricultural sector on all pesticide types, as well as increases in spending in the home and garden sector on insecticides, fungicides, and other pesticides, resulted in an overall increase in total pesticide expenditures in 2012. Expenditures in the agriculture sector accounted for approximately two-thirds of total pesticide expenditures in both 2012 and 2009. Within the agricultural sector, the majority of pesticide expenditures were on herbicides, which accounted for approximately 59% of the market in 2012 and 63% in 2009. In the remaining sectors, the majority of expenditures were on insecticides, which accounted for approximately 80% of expenditures in the home and garden sector and 50% of expenditures in the industrial/commercial/governmental sector in both 2009 and 2012 (see Table 2.2). Figure 2.2 displays the distribution of expenditures by pesticide type and sector in 2012.

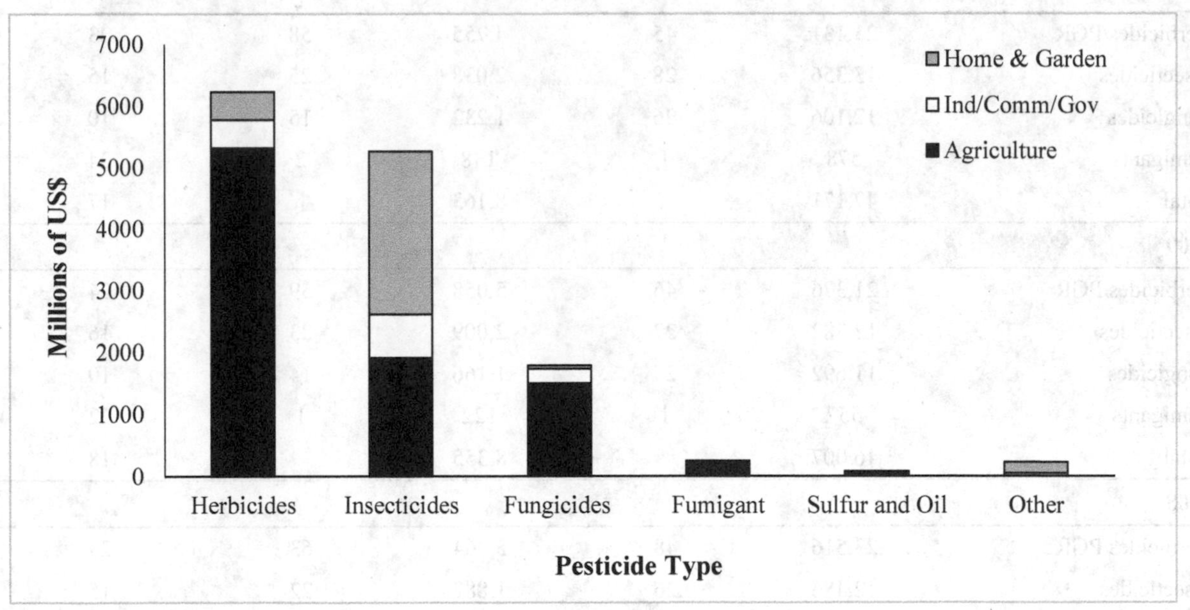

Figure 2.2. User Expenditures on Pesticides in the United States by Pesticide Type and Market Sector, 2012 Estimates

Sources: Agricultural Market Research Proprietary Data (2005-2012).
Non-Agricultural Market Research Proprietary Data (2005-2012)
USDA/NASS Quick Stats (*http://www.nass.usda.gov/Quick_Stats/*)

Source: *U.S. EPA, Pesticide Industry Sales and Usage, 2008-2012 Market Estimate, Released 2017*

Table 2.2. User Expenditures on Conventional Pesticides in the United States by Pesticide Type and Market Sector - 2012, 2009, 2007, and 2005 Estimates

Year and Market Sector	Herbicides/ PGR		Insecticides		Fungicides		Fumigant		Sulfur and Oil[1]		Other[2]		Total	
	Mil $	%	Mil $	%	Mil $	%	Mil $	%	Mil $	%	Mil $	%	Mil $	%
2012														
Agriculture[3]	5,313	85	1,909	36	1,499	84	245	100	82	100	7	3	9,055	66
Ind/Comm/Gov	460	7	700	13	230	13	—	—	—	—	40	18	1,430	10
Home & Garden	450	7	2,650	50	55	3	—	—	—	—	175	79	3,330	24
Total	6,223		5,259		1,784		245		82		222		13,815	
2009														
Agriculture[3]	5,192	85	1,618	34	1,128	79	229	100	70	100	4	2	8,241	64
Ind/Comm/Gov[4]	470	8	708	15	248	17	—	—	—	—	35	18	1,490	12
Home & Garden	475	8	2,500	52	50	4	—	—	—	—	155	80	3,180	25
Total	6,147		4,833		1,443		229		70		189		12,911	
2007*														
Agriculture[3]	4,135	82	1,428	31	820	73	227	100	66	100	6	4	6,682	59
Ind/Comm/Gov	480	10	715	15	265	23	—	—	—	—	30	20	1,490	13
Home & Garden	420	8	2,500	54	45	4	—	—	—	—	115	76	3,080	27
Total	5,035		4,643		1,130		227		66		151		11,252	
2005*														
Agriculture[3]	4,352	84	1,314	31	699	70	197	100	63	100	5	3	6,630	61
Ind/Comm/Gov	460	9	675	16	260	26	—	—	—	—	30	21	1,425	13
Home & Garden	395	8	2,200	53	40	4	—	—	—	—	109	76	2,744	25
Total	5,207		4,189		999		197		63		144		10,799	

Sources: Agricultural Market Research Proprietary Data (2005-2012).
Non-Agricultural Market Research Proprietary Data (2005-2012)
USDA/NASS Quick Stats (*http://www.nass.usda.gov/Quick_Stats/*)

Note: *Includes the cost of insecticides, herbicides, fungicides, and other pesticides, excluding the cost of custom application. Insecticide and fungicide values include seed treatment uses. Totals may not be exact due to rounding.*

1 "Sulfur and Oil" includes sulfur, petroleum distillate, and petroleum oil.

2 "Other" includes chemicals used as pesticides which are not primarily produced as pesticides for the agricultural market (e.g., sulfuric acid and phosphoric acid) as well as rodenticides and repellant use in the home and industrial markets. It does not cover specialty biocides or wood preservatives.

3 USDA/NASS data incorporated into agricultural expenditures to account for malathion expenditures in the Boll Weevil Eradication Program (BWEP).

4 Due to lack of data, the values presented for 2009 for the Industrial/Commercial/ Government category are an average of the 2012 and 2007 values. This value may over or underestimate actual 2009 usage, due to fluctuations in annual usage.

* Updated values for 2007 and 2005 presented for continuity. See Data Reporting Changes.

Source: *U.S. EPA, Pesticide Industry Sales and Usage, 2008-2012 Market Estimate, Released 2017*

2.3 Pesticide Farm Expenditures in the United States

Pesticides are a significant component of total farm production expenditures and an important element of farm budgeting and management. Farm expenditures includes the cost of pesticides (as reported in sections 2.1 and 2.2 of this report) as well as the cost of pesticide application. Based on available USDA/NASS Census of Agriculture data, which is published every five years, U.S. pesticide expenditures in 2007 and 2012 totalled 4.2% and 5% of total farm expenditures, respectively (see Table 2.3). Both farm expenditures and pesticide expenditures increased in 2012. Total farm production expenditures include all farm-related expenses. Pesticide expenses include insecticides, herbicides, fungicides, and other pesticides, including costs of custom application.

Table 2.3. Pesticide Farm Expenditures in the United States

Expenditure (Million $)	2012	2007
Total	$328,900	$241,000
Pesticides	$16,500	$10,000
Crop	$14,900	$8,900
Livestock	$1,600	$1,100
Pesticides as % of Total	5%	4.2%

Source: USDA/NASS. 2007 and 2012. Census of Agriculture: United States Summary and State Data, Volume 1, Part 51 (*"http://www.agcensus.usda.gov/Publications/2007 and* *http://www.agcensus.usda.gov/Publications/2012*).

Note: *Pesticide expenses include insecticides, herbicides, fungicides, and other pesticides, including cost of custom application.*

Source: *U.S. EPA, Pesticide Industry Sales and Usage, 2008-2012 Market Estimate, Released 2017*

3 2008 - 2012 Usage

3.1 World and U.S. Pesticide Usage

World pesticide usage at the producer level totalled nearly 6 billion pounds annually in both 2011 and 2012 (see Figure 3.1 and Table 3.1). Between 2008 and 2012, herbicides accounted for the largest portion of global usage (approximately 50% annually in all years), followed by fumigants, insecticides, and fungicides, respectively.

U.S. pesticide usage totalled over 1.1 billion pounds annually in both 2011 and 2012, with herbicides accounting for nearly 50% of total U.S. pesticide usage in 2011 and nearly 60% of usage in 2012 (see Table 3. 1). On average across all reported years (2008-2012), U.S. pesticide use accounted for approximately 23% of total pounds of pesticides applied, 25% of total pounds of herbicides applied, 43% of total pounds of fumigants applied, 12% of fungicides applied, and 6% of insecticides applied worldwide. Figure 3.1 displays the distribution of pounds of pesticides applied at the producer level by pesticide type in 2012. For a more detailed look at U.S. pesticide usage, see tables 3.2 through 3.7.

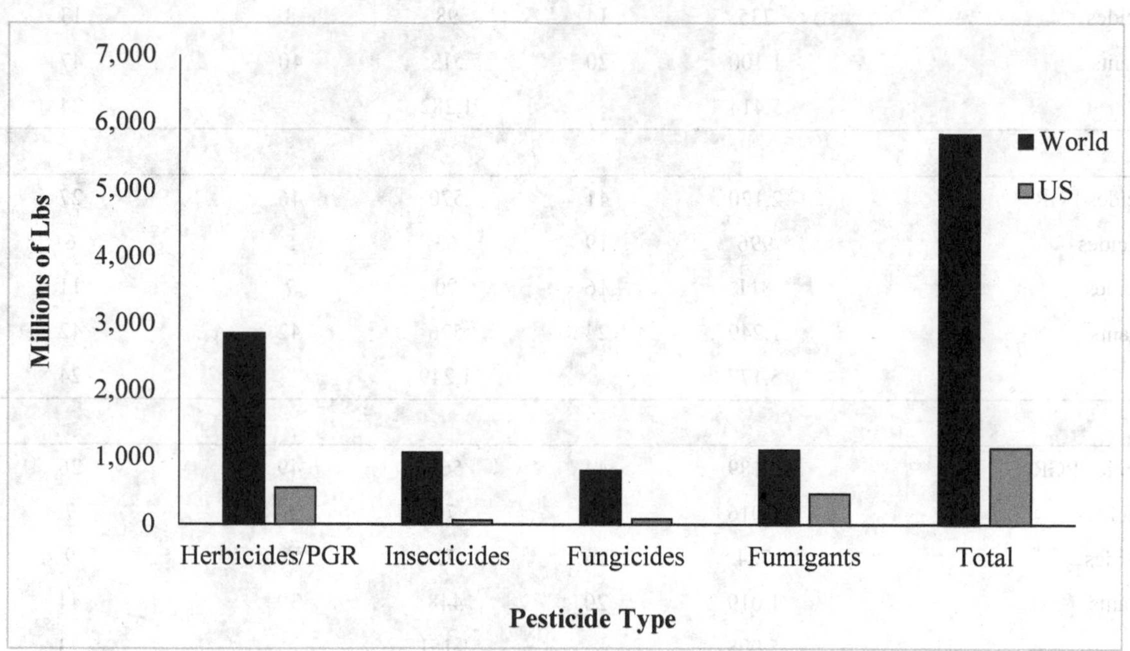

Figure 3.1. World and U.S. Pesticide Amounts of Active Ingredient at Producer Level by Pesticide Type, 2012 Estimates

Source: Phillips McDougall, AgriService, (2008-2012). (*http://phillipsmcdougall.co.uk/agriservice/*).

Source: *U.S. EPA, Pesticide Industry Sales and Usage, 2008-2012 Market Estimate, Released 2017*

Table 3.1. World and U.S. Amount of Pesticide Active Ingredient Used at the Producer Level by Pesticide Type 2008 - 2012 Estimates

Year and Pesticide Type	World Market		U.S. Market		U.S. Percentage of World Market
	Mil lbs	%	Mil lbs	%	
2012					
Herbicides/PGR	2,847	49	678	57	24
Insecticides	1,065	18	64	5	6
Fungicides	799	14	105	9	13
Fumigants	1,110	19	435	37	39
Total	5,821		1,182		20
2011					
Herbicides/PGR	2,508	46	609	48	24
Insecticides	1,070	20	62	5	6
Fungicides	735	14	98	8	13
Fumigants	1,100	20	513	40	47
Total	5,414		1,282		24
2010					
Herbicides/PGR	2,120	41	570	46	27
Insecticides	996	19	63	5	6
Fungicides	811	16	90	7	11
Fumigants	1,249	24	526	42	42
Total	5,177		1,249		24
2009					
Herbicides/PGR	2,189	44	560	49	26
Insecticides	1,016	20	70	6	7
Fungicides	784	16	72	6	9
Fumigants	1,019	20	448	39	44
Total	5,008		1,151		23
2008					
Herbicides/PGR	2,083	43	540	48	26
Insecticides	972	20	63	6	6
Fungicides	737	15	80	7	11
Fumigants	1,058	22	452	40	43
Total	4,850		1,135		23

Source: Phillips McDougall, AgriService, (2008-2012). (*http://phillipsmcdougall.co.uk/agriservice/*).

Note: *Insecticide and fungicide values include seed treatment uses. Totals may not be exact due to rounding. Table data do not cover wood preservatives, specialty biocides, chlorine/hypochlorites, vertebrate pesticides, or other chemicals used as pesticides (e.g., sulfur and petroleum oil).*

Source: *U.S. EPA, Pesticide Industry Sales and Usage, 2008-2012 Market Estimate, Released 2017*

3.2 Pesticide Usage in the United States: Conventional

Pesticide usage in the agricultural sector accounted for nearly 90% of the total pesticide usage between 2005 and 2012, with the two non-agricultural sectors (industry/commercial/government and home & garden) cumulatively accounting for the remaining percent of the total use in each year (see Figure 3.2 and Table 3.2). Usage in the agriculture sector also accounted for the majority of the total usage of each pesticide type. On average across all reported years (2008-2012), approximately 90% of herbicides, 85% of fungicides, 60% of insecticides, 100% of sulfur and oil, and approximately 60% of other pesticides applied in the U.S. were applied in the agricultural sector. Within all sectors, the majority of usage in 2012 was from herbicides, which accounted for approximately 62% of pesticides applied in the agricultural sector, 54% of pesticides applied in the professional sector, and 47% of pesticides applied in the home and garden sector. Figure 3.2 displays the distribution of usage by pesticide type and sector in 2012. Table 3.2 shows the breakout of conventional pesticide usage at the user level by pesticide type and market sector. Pesticide usage is reported as pounds applied and does not reflect acres treated.

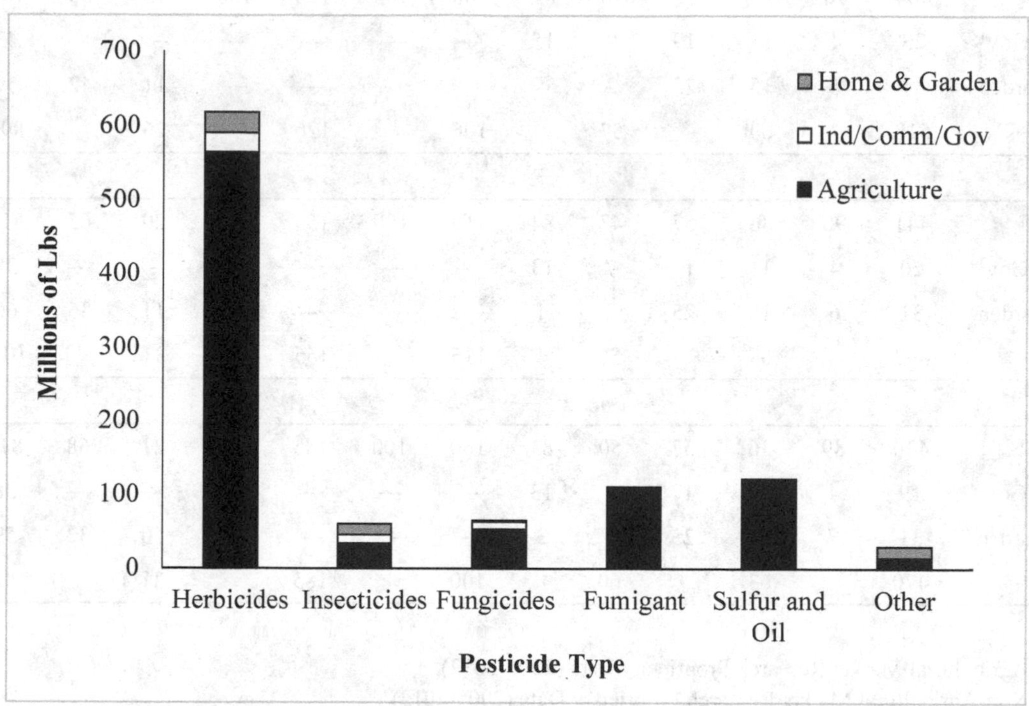

Figure 3.2. Conventional Pesticide Active Ingredient Usage in the United States by Pesticide Type and Market Sector, 2012 Estimates.

Sources: Agricultural Market Research Proprietary Data (2005-2012).
Non-Agricultural Market Research Proprietary Data (2005-2012)
USDA/NASS Quick Stats (*http://www.nass.usda.gov/Quick_Stats/*)

***Source:** U.S. EPA, Pesticide Industry Sales and Usage, 2008-2012 Market Estimate, Released 2017*

Table 3.2. Conventional Pesticide Active Ingredient Usage in the United States by Pesticide Type and Market Sector, 2012, 2009, 2007, and 2005 Estimates

Year and Market Sector	Herbicides/ PGR		Insecticides		Fungicides		Fumigant		Sulfur and Oil[1]		Other [2]		Total	
	Mil lbs	%	Mil lbs	%	Mil lbs	%	Mil lbs	%	Mil lbs	%	Mil lbs	%	Mil lbs	%
2012														
Agriculture[3]	564	91	34	57	53	82	111	100	122	100	15	50	899	89
Ind/Comm/Gov	26	4	12	20	10	15	—	—	—	—	—	—	48	5
Home & Garden	28	5	14	23	2	3	—	—	—	—	15	50	59	6
Total	618		60		65		111		122		30		1,006	
2009														
Agriculture[3]	464	90	33	55	46	81	106	100	126	100	15	58	790	89
Ind/Comm/Gov[4]	23	4	12	19	9	15	—	—	—	—	—	—	43	5
Home & Garden	31	6	15	25	2	4	—	—	—	—	11	42	59	7
Total	518		60		57		106		126		26		892	
2007*														
Agriculture[3]	441	90	36	57	47	84	115	100	155	100	20	65	814	89
Ind/Comm/Gov[3]	20	4	11	17	7	13	—	—	—	—	—	—	38	4
Home & Garden	31	6	16	25	2	4	—	—	—	—	11	35	60	7
Total	492		63		56		115		155		31		912	
2005*														
Agriculture[3]	420	89	36	57	50	83	100	100	185	100	21	68	812	89
Ind/Comm/Gov	19	4	11	17	8	13	—	—	—	—	—	—	38	4
Home & Garden	31	7	16	25	2	3	—	—	—	—	10	32	59	6
Total	470		63		60		100		185		31		909	

Sources: Agricultural Market Research Proprietary Data (2005-2012).
Non-Agricultural Market Research Proprietary Data (2005-2012)

USDA/NASS Quick Stats (*http://www.nass.usda.gov/Quick_Stats/*)

Note: *Insecticide and fungicide values include seed treatment uses. Totals may not be exact due to rounding.*

1 "Sulfur and Oil" includes sulfur, petroleum distillate, and petroleum oil.

2 "Other" includes chemicals used as pesticides which are not primarily produced as pesticides for the agricultural market (e.g., sulfuric acid and phosphoric acid) as well as rodenticides and repellant use in the home and industrial markets. It does not cover specialty biocides or wood preservatives.

3 USDA/NASS data incorporated into agricultural expenditures to account for malathion expenditures in the Boll Weevil Eradication Program (BWEP).

4 Due to lack of data, the values presented for 2009 are an average of the 2012 and 2007 values for the Industrial/Commercial/Government category. This value may over or underestimate actual 2009 usage, due to fluctuations in annual usage.

* Updated values for 2007 and 2005 presented for continuity. See Data Reporting Changes.

Source: *U.S. EPA, Pesticide Industry Sales and Usage, 2008-2012 Market Estimate, Released 2017*

3.3 Share of U.S. Conventional Pesticide Active Ingredient Usage in the Agricultural and Non-Agricultural Market Sectors

Table 3.3 shows the agricultural and non-agricultural market share of total conventional pesticides consumed in 2012, 2009, 2007, and 2005. The agricultural sector accounts for nearly 90% of the total amount of conventional pesticides used in all years.

Table 3.3. Share of U.S. Conventional Pesticide Active Ingredient Usage in the Agricultural and Non-Agricultural Market Sectors: 2012, 2009, 2007, and 2005 Estimates

Year	U. S.	Agricultural Market Sector		Non-Agricultural Market Sector	
	Mil lbs	Mil lbs	% of U.S.	Mil lbs	% of U.S.
2012	854	762	89	92	11
2009	735	649	88	86	12
2007*	726	639	88	87	12
2005*	693	606	87	87	13

Source: EPA estimates based on Table 3.2.

Note: *Table data excludes sulfur and oil, other chemicals used as pesticides (e.g., sulfuric acid and insect repellents), as well as wood preservatives, specialty biocides, and chlorine/hypochlorites.*

* Updated values for 2007 and 2005 presented for continuity.

3.4 Most Commonly Used Conventional Pesticide Active Ingredients in the U.S. Agricultural Market Sector

Table 3.4 shows the 25 most commonly used conventional pesticide active ingredients in the agricultural sector in 2012, and their ranking and usage range in selected earlier years. Glyphosate was the most used active ingredient in 2012 (270 million to 290 million pounds used), as it has been since 2001. Twelve of the top 25 active ingredients used in the agricultural sector in 2012 are herbicides; four are fungicides; two are insecticides; five are fumigants; and two are plant growth regulators. These rankings rely on the estimated pounds of conventional pesticides used in the agricultural sector, taken from public and proprietary databases. As noted previously, data only reflect pounds applied and not acres treated. Absence of a pesticide from this list should not be construed as lack of importance in agricultural crop production.

Source: *U.S. EPA, Pesticide Industry Sales and Usage, 2008-2012 Market Estimate, Released 2017*

Table 3.4. Most Commonly Used Conventional Pesticide Active Ingredients in the Agricultural Market Sector in 2012, and their Rankings and Usage Rate Range in 2012, 2009, 2007, and 2005 Estimates (Ranked by Range‡ in Millions of Pounds of Active Ingredient)

Active Ingredient	Type	2012		2009		2007*		2005*	
		Rank	Range	Rank	Range	Rank	Range	Rank	Range
Glyphosate	H	1	270-290	1	209-229	1	170-190	1	147-167
Atrazine	H	2	64-74	2	59-69	2	70-80	2	66-76
Metolachlor-S	H	3	34-44	6	24-34	4	27-37	5	25-35
Dichloropropene	Fum	4	32-42	4	27-37	6	24-34	4	28-38
2,4-D	H	5	30-40	5	24-34	7	22-32	7	21-31
Metam	Fum	6	30-40	3	30-40	3	48-58	3	36-46
Acetochlor	H	7	28-38	7	23-33	5	25-35	6	24-34
Metam Potassium	Fum	8	16-26	8	14-24	13	6-10	—	0-3
Chloropicrin	Fum	9	8-18	9	6-16	9	5-15	10	5-15
Chlorothalonil	F	10	6-16	11	6-10	12	6-10	13	6-10
Pendimethalin	H	11	6-16	10	6-16	10	6-10	9	5-15
Ethephon	PGR	12	7-11	12	6-10	11	6-10	11	7-11
Mancozeb	F	13	5-9	16	3-7	19	3-7	16	5-9
Chlorpyrifos	I	14	4-8	13	5-9	14	6-10	15	5-9
Metolachlor	H	15	4-8	22	1-5	—	0-4	—	0-3
Hydrated Lime	F	16	3-7	15	4-8	20	2-6	—	1-5
Propanil	H	17	3-7	17	3-7	18	3-7	18	3-7
Dicamba	H	18	3-7	25	1-5	—	1-5	22	1-5
Trifluralin	H	19	3-7	18	3-7	17	4-8	14	6-10
Decan-1-ol	PGR	20	3-7	—	1-5	—	1-5	—	0-4
Copper Hydroxide	F	21	3-7	20	2-6	15	5-9	12	7-11
Acephate	I	22	2-6	—	1-5	22	1-5	23	1-5
Paraquat	H	23	2-6	—	1-5	25	1-5	24	1-5
Methyl Bromide	Fum	24	2-6	14	5-9	8	8-18	8	9-19
Glufosinate	H	25	2-6	—	1-5	—	1-5	—	0-4

Sources: Agricultural Market Research Proprietary Data, (2007, 2009, and 2012).
USDA/NASS Quick Stats (*http://www.nass.usda.gov/Quick_Stats/*)

***Note:** This list is limited to conventional pesticides, and does not include sulfur, petroleum oil, and other chemicals used as pesticides (e.g., sulfuric acid and insect repellents), wood preservatives, specialty biocides, or chlorine/hypochlorites. H indicates herbicide; I, insecticide; Fum, fumigant; F, fungicide; and PGR, plant growth regulator. A dash (—) indicates that the pesticide was not one of the 25 most commonly used (pesticides) in the given year.*

‡ Values presented as a range to retain the proprietary nature of the data. Ranking based on actual values.
* Updated values for 2007 and 2005 presented for continuity.

***Source:** U.S. EPA, Pesticide Industry Sales and Usage, 2008-2012 Market Estimate, Released 2017*

3.5 Most Commonly Used Conventional Pesticide Active Ingredients in the U.S. Non-Agricultural Market Sector

Tables 3.5 and 3.6 show the 10 most commonly used conventional pesticide active ingredients in the two non-agricultural sectors (home & garden and industry/commercial/government) for 2012, and their rank and usage range in 2009. In 2012, six of the top 10 active ingredients used in the home and garden sector are herbicides, and four are insecticides. Five of the top 10 active ingredients used in the industry/commercial/government sector in 2012 are herbicides, one is a fungicide, and four are insecticides. Because some applicators apply pesticides in both markets, there may be some usage reported in one market that may have occurred in the other. The rankings are based on non-agricultural market research proprietary data and present the best available data.

Table 3.5. Most Commonly Used Conventional Pesticide Active Ingredients in the Home and Garden Market Sector in 2012, and their Rankings and Usage Rate Range in 2012, and 2009 Estimates (Ranked by Range‡ in Millions of Pounds of Active Ingredient)

Active Ingredient	Type	2012		2009	
		Rank	Range	Rank	Range
2,4-D	H	1	7-9	1	8-11
Glyphosate	H	2	4-6	2	5-8
*MCPP	H	3	2-4	4	4-6
Pendimethalin	H	4	2-4	5	3-5
Carbaryl	I	5	2-4	3	4-6
Acephate	I	6	1-3	10	<1
Permethrin and other pyrethroids	I	7	1-3	6	2-4
Dicamba	H	8	1-3	7	1-3
*MCPA	H	9	1-3	—	—
Malathion	I	10	1-3	6	2-4

Sources: Non-Agricultural Market Research Proprietary Data, (2012 and 2009).
USDA/NASS Quick Stats (*http://www.nass.usda.gov/Quick_Stats/*)

***Note:** H indicates herbicide, and I indicates insecticide. A dash (—) indicates that an estimate is not available.*

*MCPP - Methylchlorophenoxypropionic acid

*MCPA - 2-methyl-4-chlorophenoxyacetic acid

‡ Values presented as a range to retain the proprietary nature of the data. Ranking based on actual values.

***Source:** U.S. EPA, Pesticide Industry Sales and Usage, 2008-2012 Market Estimate, Released 2017*

Table 3.6. Most Commonly Used Conventional Pesticide Active Ingredients in the Industry/ Commercial/ Government Market Sector in 2012 and their Rankings and Usage Rate Range in 2012, and 2009 Estimates (Ranked by Range‡ in Millions of Pounds of Active Ingredient)

Active Ingredient	Type	2012		2009	
		Rank	Range	Rank	Range
Glyphosate	H	1	7-9	1	4-6
Chlorothalonil	F	2	5-7	3	2-4
2,4-D	H	3	4-6	2	3-5
Pendimethalin	H	4	2-4	4	1-3
Prodiamine	H	5	0-2	12	0-2
Sulfuryl fluoride	I	6	0-2	7	1-3
Acephate	I	7	0-2	13	0-2
Simazine	H	8	0-2	24	0-2
*Bti	I	9	0-2	43	0-2
Bifenthrin	I	10	0-2	34	0-2

Source: EPA estimates based on Non-Agricultural Market Research Proprietary Data (2012 and 2009).

***Note:** H indicates herbicide, I indicates insecticide, and F indicates fungicide.*

* *Bacillus thuringiensis serotype israelensis*
‡ *Values presented as a range to retain the proprietary nature of the data. Ranking based on actual values.*

3.6 Organophosphate Insecticides Usage in the United States

Since the passage of the Food Quality Protection Act (FQPA) in 1996, this class of conventional pesticides has been a primary focus of EPA reregistration and registration review activities. Table 3.7 compares usage of all active ingredients from 2000 to 2012 with all organophosphate (OP) insecticide usage over the same time period. This time period is displayed to provide a broad view of the decreasing trend in OP usage due in part to EPA action. OP insecticides with the most usage include acephate, chlorpyrifos, malathion, naled, phorate, dicrotophos, phosmet, dimethoate, terbufos, ethoprophos, and tetrachlorvinphos (see Table 3.8). For more information on the active ingredients included in this pesticide class and their registration status, refer to U.S. EPA's Office of Pesticide Programs Special Docket EPA-HQ-OPP-2007-0151 at *www.regulations.gov*.

The estimates of organophosphate insecticide usage rely on public and proprietary databases. The amount of OP insecticides used in the U.S. has declined more than 70% since 2000, from an estimated 70 million pounds to 20 million pounds in 2012 (see Table 3.8 and Figure 3.3). OP usage as a percentage of total insecticide use has decreased from 71% in 2000 to 33% in 2012. The decrease in OP usage reflects a shift in usage to other classes of pesticides (i.e., pyrethroids, neonicotinoids, and other new chemistries) because of the phasing out and use restrictions placed on OP insecticides as a result of pesticide registration review. The decrease also reflects reduced malathion usage due to the gradual completion of the Boll Weevil Eradication Program (BWEP).

***Source:** U.S. EPA, Pesticide Industry Sales and Usage, 2008-2012 Market Estimate, Released 2017*

Table 3.7. Organophosphate Insecticide Active Ingredients Usage in the United States All Market Sectors, 2000–2012 Estimates

Year	All Insecticides[1]	Organophosphate Insecticides	
	Mil lbs	Mil lbs	% of All Insecticides
2000	99	70	71
2001	102	54	53
2002	90	47	52
2003	84	41	48
2004	77	40	52
2005	69	33	48
2006	66	30	46
2007	64	27	42
2008	65	28	43
2009	60	23	38
2010	56	21	38
2011	56	22	39
2012	60	20	33

Source: Agricultural Market Research Proprietary Data (2000-2012).
Non-Agricultural Market Research Proprietary Data (2000-2012)
USDA/NASS Quick Stats (*http://www.nass.usda.gov/Quick_Stats/*)

[1] Table data only includes conventional insecticides.

Source: *U.S. EPA, Pesticide Industry Sales and Usage, 2008-2012 Market Estimate, Released 2017*

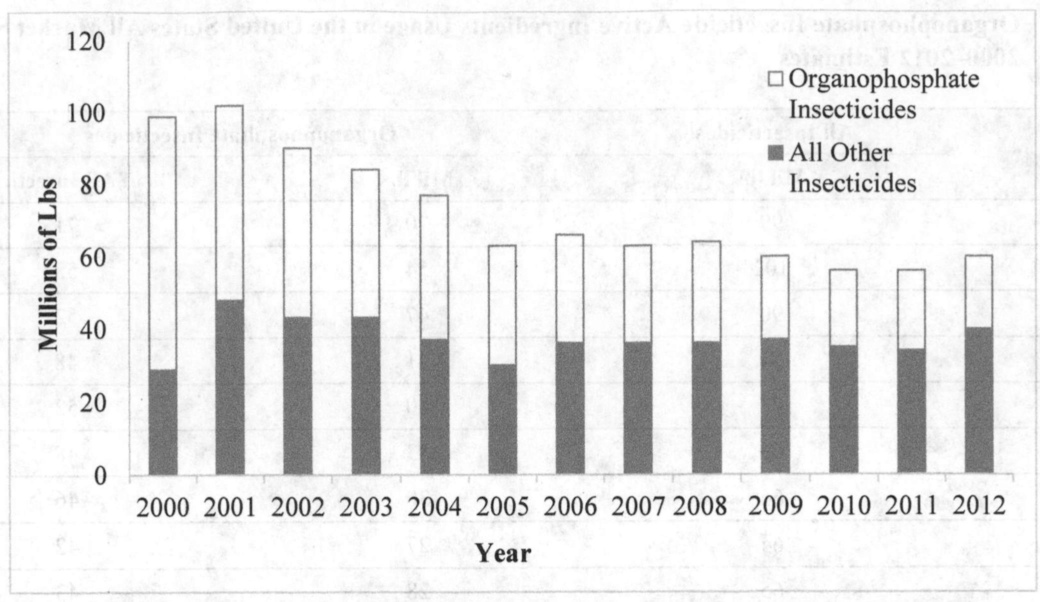

Figure 3.3. Total Amount of Organophosphate and All Other Insecticide Active Ingredients Usage in the United States in All Market Sectors, 2000–2012

Source: Agricultural Market Research Proprietary Data (2000-2012).
Non-Agricultural Market Research Proprietary Data (2000-2012)
USDA/NASS Quick Stats (*http://www.nass.usda.gov/Quick_Stats/*)

Table 3.8. Most Commonly Used Organophosphate Insecticide Active Ingredients, All Market Sectors, 2005, 2007, 2009, and 2012 Estimates (Ranked by Range in Millions of Pounds of Active Ingredient)

Active Ingredient	2012		2009		2007*		2005*	
	Rank	Range	Rank	Range	Rank	Range	Rank	Range
Chlorpyrifos	1	5-8	1	6-9	1	6-9	2	6-9
Acephate	2	5-8	2	3-6	3	3-6	3	3-5
Malathion	3	1-4	3	2-5	2	5-7	1	10-13
Naled	4	1-2	4	1-2	4	1-2	5	1-2
Phorate	5	1-2	6	<1	7	1-2	6	1-2
Dicrotophos	6	1-2	7	<1	5	1-2	7	1-2
Dimethoate	7	<1	8	<1	9	<1	9	<1
Terbufos	8	<1	9	<1	8	<1	—	—
Phosmet	9	<1	5	<1	6	1-2	4	1-3
Ethoprophos	10	<1	—	—	—	—	—	—

Source: Agricultural Market Research Proprietary Data (2005-2012).
Non-Agricultural Market Research Proprietary Data (2005-2012)
USDA/NASS Quick Stats (*http://www.nass.usda.gov/Quick_Stats/*)

Note: *A dash (—) indicates that the organophosphate pesticide was not one of the 10 most commonly used in the given year.*

* Updated values for 2007 and 2005 presented for continuity.

Source: *U.S. EPA, Pesticide Industry Sales and Usage, 2008-2012 Market Estimate, Released 2017*

3.7 Pesticide Usage in the United States: Specialty Biocides and Wood Preservatives

Table 3.9 shows the total amount of specialty biocides and wood preservatives by end-use market in the United States in 2012. Specialty biocides include water treatment chemicals (recreational and industrial), disinfectants and sanitizers, waterborne wood preservatives, and products for other uses such as use in adhesives, sealants, and leather. Water treatment chemicals accounted for most specialty biocide usage in 2012, approximately 50%, followed by waterborne wood preservatives, which account for approximately 35% of the total amount of specialty biocides usage.

Table 3.9. Specialty Biocides Used in the United States by End-Use Market, 2012 Estimates

Year and End Use Market	Total	
	Mil lbs	%
2012		
Recreational and Industrial Water Treatment[1]	285	47
Disinfectants and Sanitizers[2]	45	7
Other Specialty Biocides[3]	60	10
Waterborne Wood Preservatives	212	35
Total	602	100

Source: Kline & Company, Specialty Biocides, 2012

Note: *Totals may not be exact due to rounding.*

1 "Recreational and Industrial Water Treatment" does not include hypochlorite or chlorine use.

2 "Disinfectants and Sanitizers" includes industrial/institutional applications and household cleaning products, and does not include hypochlorite or chlorine use.

3 "Other Specialty Biocides" includes biocides for adhesives and sealants, leather, synthetic latex polymers, metalworking fluids, paints and coatings, petroleum products, plastics, mineral slurries, textiles, and antifoulants.

Source: *U.S. EPA, Pesticide Industry Sales and Usage, 2008-2012 Market Estimate, Released 2017*

4 Producers and Users

4.1 Pesticide Producers and Users in 2012

Table 4.1 lists 2012 estimates of the number of firms that are designated as pesticide producers, formulators, distributors, and establishments. Table 4.2 lists 2012 estimates of the number of exterminating and pest control firms and certified pesticide applicators. Table 4.3 lists 2012 estimates of farm land, acres harvested, and the number of farms using pesticides and fertilizers. Table 4.4 lists 2011 estimates of the number of households using pesticides.

Table 4.1. Number of U.S. Pesticide Producers, Formulators, and Distributors

Major Pesticide Producers	12
Other Pesticide Producers	100
Major Pesticide Formulators	120–150
Other Pesticide Formulators	1,550
Distributors	24,686
Establishments	42,160

Source: EPA Estimates

Note: *Entities may operate as both a producer and a formulator. This may result in the number of entities being overestimated.*

Table 4.2. Number of Exterminating and Pest Control Firms and Number of Certified Applicators

Exterminating and Pest Control Firms	23,413
Private[1] Certified Applicators	474,525
Commercial[2] Certified Applicators	425,086
Certified Applicators that Work for Federal Agencies	4,007

Sources: Kline & Company, Global Professional Pest Management Markets for Pesticides, 2012
Washington State University, Certification Plan and Reporting Database (CPARD), 2012
USDA, Office of Pest Management Policy (OPMP), Personal Communication, 2016

1 Private certified applicators refer primarily to farmers or other persons producing an agricultural commodity and using restricted-use pesticides (RUPs).

2 Commercial certified applicators refer to professional pesticide applicators.

Source: *U.S. EPA, Pesticide Industry Sales and Usage, 2008-2012 Market Estimate, Released 2017*

Table 4.3. Land in Farms, Land Harvested, Number of Farms, and Farms Using Pesticides

Land in Farms (acres)	915 million
Land in Production (acres)	390 million
Land Harvested (acres)	315 million
Total Number of Farms	2.109 million
Total Number of Farms with Cropland	1.552 million
Total Number of Farms with Harvested Cropland	1.289 million
Number of Farms Using Chemicals for:	
Insects on Crops/Hay	361,286
Nematodes	58,865
Diseases on Crops/Orchards	121,682
Weed/Grass/Brush	794,320
Defoliation/Fruit Thinning	53,200
Any or all of the above	999,806
Any or all of the above plus fertilizer	1,187,446

Source: USDA/NASS. 2012. Census of Agriculture: United States Summary and State Data, Volume 1, Part 51 (*http://www.agcensus.usda.gov/Publications/2012*).

Table 4.4. Number of U.S. Households Using Pesticides by Pesticide Type

Pesticide Type	Households
Insecticides	82 million
Fungicides	16 million
Herbicides	52 million
Repellents	57 million
Disinfectants	66 million
Any Pesticides	88 million

Sources: EPA estimates based on the 2012 Kline & Company study and 2010 U.S. Census Bureau population estimate

Source: *U.S. EPA, Pesticide Industry Sales and Usage, 2008-2012 Market Estimate, Released 2017*

5 Glossary

ACTIVE INGREDIENT (a.i.): The chemical or substance component of a pesticide product intended to kill, repel, attract, mitigate, or control a pest, or that acts as a plant growth regulator, desiccant, or nitrogen stabilizer. The remainder of a formulated pesticide product consists of one or more "inert ingredients" (*e.g.,* water, solvents, emulsifiers, surfactants, clay, and propellants), which are there for reasons other than pesticidal activity.

AGRICULTURAL SECTOR (OR MARKET): Pesticides applied by owner/operators and custom/commercial applicators to farms and facilities involved in the production of raw agricultural commodities, principally food, fiber, and tobacco; includes non-crop and post-harvest use as well as crop and field applications.

CERTIFIED APPLICATOR: A person who is authorized to apply "restricted-use" pesticides as a result of meeting requirements for certification under FIFRA-mandated programs. Applicator certification programs are conducted by states, territories, and tribes in accordance with national standards set by EPA. "Restricted-use pesticides" may be used only by or under the direct supervision of specially trained and certified applicators.

COMMERCIAL APPLICATOR: A person applying pesticides as part of a business, applying pesticides for hire, or applying pesticides as part of his or her job with another (not for hire) type of business, organization, or agency. Commercial applicators often are certified, but need to be so only if they apply restricted-use pesticides.

CONVENTIONAL PESTICIDES: Conventional pesticides are all active ingredients other than biological pesticides and antimicrobial pesticides. Conventional active ingredients are generally produced synthetically, *i.e.,* are synthetic chemicals that prevent, mitigate, destroy, or repel any pest; or that act as a plant growth regulator, desiccant, defoliant or nitrogen stabilizer.

ECONOMIC SECTORS (OR MARKETS): In this report, estimates of quantities used and user expenditures for pesticides are broken out separately for the three general economic user sectors (or markets) as follows: agriculture, industrial/commercial/governmental, and home and garden. These three sectors/markets are defined elsewhere in this glossary.

ESTABLISHMENT: The term "establishment" means any place where a pesticide or device or active ingredient used in producing a pesticide is produced, or held, for distribution or sale.

FDA: The U.S. Food and Drug Administration, a branch of the U.S. Department of Health and Human Services, is involved in regulation of pesticides in the United States, particularly in the enforcement of tolerances in food and feed products.

FFDCA: Federal Food, Drug, and Cosmetic Act, the law that controls pesticide residues in food and feed.

FIFRA: Federal Insecticide, Fungicide, and Rodenticide Act, the law that generally controls pesticide sale and use.

FQPA: The Food Quality Protection Act (FQPA) of 1996 amended the Federal Insecticide, Fungicide, and Rodenticide Act (FIFRA) and the Federal Food, Drug, and Cosmetic Act (FFDCA).

HOME AND GARDEN SECTOR (OR MARKET): Involves pesticides applied by homeowners to homes and gardens, including lawns and single and multiple unit housing. Does not include pesticides for home and garden applications by professional applicators.

INDUSTRIAL/COMMERCIAL/GOVERNMENTAL USER SECTOR (OR MARKET): Involves pesticides applied by professional applicators (by owners/operators/employees and custom/commercial applicators) to industrial, commercial, and governmental facilities, buildings, sites, and land, plus custom/commercial applications to homes and gardens, including lawns. May also be referred to as the "professional market" for pesticides.

Source: *U.S. EPA, Pesticide Industry Sales and Usage, 2008-2012 Market Estimate, Released 2017*

NON-AGRICULTURAL SECTORS: General term referring to a combination of the home and garden and industrial/ commercial/governmental sectors.

OTHER PESTICIDES: Chemicals registered as pesticides but that are produced and marketed mostly for other purposes (*i.e.,* multi-use chemicals). Notable examples are rodenticides, repellents, sulfur, petroleum products (*e.g.,* kerosene, oils, and distillates), salt, and sulfuric acid.

PESTICIDE: May be used to refer to an active ingredient (as defined above) or formulated pesticide product registered under FIFRA.

PESTICIDE USAGE: Refers to actual applications of pesticides, generally in terms of quantity applied or units treated.

PRIVATE APPLICATOR: A category of applicator certification for farmers and/or employees, such that they can legally apply restricted-use pesticides or supervise others doing so who are not certified.

PRODUCER LEVEL: Data covering companies that manufacture and formulate pesticides.

PROFESSIONAL MARKET: Sales of pesticides for application to industrial/commercial/governmental sector and to homes and gardens, by certified/commercial applicators.

PROPRIETARY DATA, AGRICULTURAL AND NON-AGRICULTURAL: Pesticide industry marketing research data that EPA purchases from private data research companies. These data are for EPA use only and cannot be divulged without vendor consent.

SPECIALTY BIOCIDES: Specialty biocides include biocides used for water treatment chemicals (recreational and industrial), disinfectants and sanitizers, waterborne wood preservatives, and products for other uses such as use in adhesives, sealants, and leather.

TOLERANCE: The maximum amount of a pesticide allowable in a food or feed product before it is considered adulterated, usually specified in parts per million.

USDA/NASS: The U.S. Department of Agriculture, National Agricultural Statistics Service. Publicly available data on U.S. agricultural pesticide use (www.nass.usda.gov).

USER LEVEL: Data covering persons or businesses that purchase and apply pesticides, such as farmers, commercial pesticide applicators, and homeowners.

WOOD PRESERVATIVES: Pesticide active ingredients intended to prevent wood degradation problems due to insects, fungal rot, or other pests.

Source: *U.S. EPA, Pesticide Industry Sales and Usage, 2008-2012 Market Estimate, Released 2017*

Occupational and Environmental Exposures Capable of Causing Illness

Common Name/Synonym	Primary Name	AOEC Code[1]	Use[2]	Asth-magen[3]	Asthma Detail[3]
1,1,1,2-Tetrafluoroethane	1,1,1,2-Tetrafluoroethane	190.156			
1,1,1-Trichloroethane	Methyl Chloroform	190.08	S		
1,1,2-Trichloroethane	1,1,2-Trichloroethane	190.12	S		
1,1-Azobisformamide	Azodicarbamide	260.18		Yes	Rs
1,2,3-Trihydroxybenzene	1,2,3-Trihydroxybenzene	180.06			
1,2,4-Benzenetricarboxylic Acid 1,2-Anhydride	Trimellitic Anhydride	151.03		Yes	Rs
1,2,4-Triazole-3-carboxamide	Ribavirin	321.32			
1,2,4-Trichlorobenzene	1,2,4-Trichlorobenzene	201.02			
1,2-benzenedicarboxaldehyde	Ortho-phthalaldehyde	120.10			R
1,2-Benzisothiazol-3(2H)one	Saccharin	320.38			R
1,2-Dibromoethane	Ethylene Dibromide	191.01	P		
1,2-Dichloroethane	Ethylene Dichloride	190.07	S		
1,2-Dichloroethylene	1,2-Dichloroethylene	190.06	S		
1,2-Dichloropropane	Propylene Dichloride	190.11	S		
1,2-Ethanediol	Ethylene Glycol	080.011			
1,3-Butylene Glycol	1,3-Butylene Glycol	080.04			
1,3-Dichloro-1,1,2,2,3-pentafluoropropane	1,3-Dichloro-1,1,2,2,3-pentafluoropropane	192.022			
1,3-Dichloro-2-Propanol	1,3-Dichloro-2-Propanol	190.17			
1,3-Dihydroxy-2-propanone	Dihydroxyacetone	130.08			
1,4-?-D-Glucan glucohydrolase	Amyloglucosidase	324.110		Yes	Rs
1,4-Benzenediamine	1,4-Benzenediamine	251.061			R
1,4-Dioxane	Dioxane	100.04	S		
1,5-Naphthylene Ester Isocyanic Acid	Naphthalene Diisocyanate	221.03		Yes	G
1,6-Diisocyanato-Hexane	Hexamethylene Diisocyanate	221.04		Yes	G
1,6-Hexanediamine	Hexamethylenediamine	232.10			R
1-Allyl-3-Methoxy-4-Hydroxybenzene	Eugenol	100.07		Yes	Rs
1-beta-D-ribofuranosyl-1H-1,2,4-triazole-3-carboxamide	Ribavirin	321.32			
1-Bromo-3-chloro-5,5-dimethylhydantoin	1-Bromo-3-chloro-5,5-dimethylhydantoin	191.04			R
1-bromopropane	Bromopropane	190.18			
1-Butanol	N-Butyl Alcohol	070.04	S		
1-Chloro-2,3-Epoxypropane	Epichlorohydrin	110.01			
1-Hydroxy-2-methoxybenzene	Guaiacol	100.09			
1-Methyl-2-Pyrrolidinone	1-Methyl-2-Pyrrolidinone	260.120			
1-Pentanol	Amyl Alcohol	070.02			
1-Propanol	Propyl Alcohol	070.08	S		
1-propyl bromide	Bromopropane	190.18			
1-Propyl Chloride	Chloropropane	190.05	S		
2,3,7,8-TCDD	2,3,7,8-Tetrachlorodibenzodioxin	200.041	P		
2,3,7,8-Tetrachlorodibenzodioxin	2,3,7,8-Tetrachlorodibenzodioxin	200.041	P		
2,4,5-T	2,4,5-T	200.011	P		
2,4,6-Trinitrophenol	Picric Acid	250.09			
2,4-D	2,4-D	200.012	P		
2,6-Dichlorobenzonitrile	2,6-Dichlorobenzonitrile	200.10	P		
2-Aminoethanol	Monoethanolamine	231.01		Yes	Rs
2-Aminopropane	Isopropylamine	230.03			
2-Butanone	Methyl Ethyl Ketone	130.03	S		
2-Butoxyethanol	2-Butoxyethanol	091.03	S		R
2-Chloroacetophenone	Mace	320.27			
2-Chloroethanol	Beta-Chloroethyl Alcohol	070.03			
2-Chloroethylphosphonic Acid	Ethephon	291.12	P		
2-Ethoxyethanol	Ethylene Glycol Monoethyl Ether	091.02	S		
2-Ethoxyethyl Acetate	2-Ethoxyethyl Acetate	141.05			
2-Ethylhexyl Nitrate	2-Ethylhexyl Nitrate	260.31			
2-Furanmethanol	Furfuryl Alcohol	070.090			R
2-Hydroxyethanethiol	Mercaptoethanol	310.04			

Common Name/Synonym	Primary Name	AOEC Code[1]	Use[2]	Asth-magen[3]	Asthma Detail[3]
2-Hydroxypropyl Acrylate	2-Hydroxypropyl Acrylate	142.09			
2-Methylpropane	Isobutane	060.04			
2-Naphthylamine	Beta-Naphthylamine	251.05			
2-Nitropropane	2-Nitropropane	260.141			
2-Oxetanone	Beta-Propiolactone	320.04			
2-Pentanone	Methyl Propyl Ketone	130.10			
2-Propanol	Isopropyl Alcohol	070.06	S		
2-Propanone	Acetone	130.01	S		
2-Propen-1-ol	Allyl Alcohol	070.01			
2-Propenal	Acrolein	120.02			
2-Thiocarbamide	2-Thiocarbamide	310.071			
3,3'-Dichlorobenzidene & Salts	3,3'-Dichlorobenzidene & Salts	250.13			
3,3-Dichloro-1,1,1,2,2-pentafluoropropane	3,3-Dichloro-1,1,1,2,2-pentafluoropropane	192.021			
3-Amino-5-mercapto-1,2,4-triazole	3-Amino-5-mercapto-1,2,4-triazole	260.30		Yes	Rs
3-Dimethylamino Propylamine	3-Dimethylamino Propylamine	232.05			R
3-DMAPA	3-Dimethylamino Propylamine	232.05			R
3-mercaptopropionate	3-mercaptopropionate	310.13			
3-mercaptopropionic Acid	3-mercaptopropionic Acid	310.12			
3-thiopropionic Acid	3-mercaptopropionic Acid	310.12			
4,4'-Methylenebis(2-Chloroaniline)	4,4'-Methylenebis(2-Chloroaniline)	250.03			
4,4-Aminodiphenyl	Benzidine	251.03			
4,4-Diaminodiphenylmethane	Methylenedianiline	250.16			
4-Hydroxyaniline	Para-Aminophenol	251.01			
4-Methyl-2-Pentanone	Methyl Isobutyl Ketone	130.04	S		
4-PC	4-Phenylcyclohexene	060.11			
4-Phenylcyclohexene	4-Phenylcyclohexene	060.11			
5-chloro-2-(2,4-dichlorohydroxy) phenol	5-chloro-2-(2,4-dichlorohydroxy) phenol	181.03		Yes	Rs
5-Nonanone	Butyl Ketone	130.06	S		
7 ACA	7-aminocephalosporanic acid	321.064			R
7-Amino-3-thiomethyl-3-cephalosporanic acid	7-Amino-3-thiomethyl-3-cephalosporanic acid	321.065			R
7-aminocephalosporanic acid	7-aminocephalosporanic acid	321.064			R
7CTD	Tosyalate dihydrate	321.069			R
7TACA	7-Amino-3-thiomethyl-3-cephalosporanic acid	321.065			R
8-Hydroxyquinoline	8-Hydroxyquinoline	250.02			
8-Quinolinol	8-Hydroxyquinoline	250.02			
90% Uncured methacrylate ester monomers	Optigard	142.13			
?-lactalbumin	?-lactalbumin	380.23		Yes	Rs
Abiruana	Pouteria glomerata	373.08		Yes	Rs
Abrasives, NOS	Abrasives, NOS	010.01			
ABS Copolymer	Acrylonitrile-Butadiene-Styrene Copolymer	270.29			R
Acacia	Gum Arabic	372.01		Yes	Rs
Acacia melanoxylon	Australian Blackwood	373.27		Yes	Rs
Acarian	Mites, NOS	382.13		Yes	G
Acephate	Acephate	291.11	P		R
Acetaldehyde	Acetaldehyde	120.01			
Acetamide	Acetamide	260.01			
Acetates, NOS	Acetates, NOS	141.00			
Acetic Acid	Glacial Acetic Acid	050.34		Yes	Rrs
Acetic Acid Ethyl Ester	Ethyl Acetate	141.03	S		
Acetic Anhydride	Acetic Anhydride	151.09			
Acetic Ether	Ethyl Acetate	141.03	S		
Acetic Oxide	Acetic Anhydride	151.09			
Acetone	Acetone	130.01	S		
Acetonitrile	Acetonitrile	210.01			
Acetophenone	Mace	320.27			
Acetylene	Acetylene	060.01			
Acetylene Dichloride	1,2-Dichloroethylene	190.06	S		
Acetylene Trichloride	Trichloroethylene	190.13	S		
Acid & Base Mixture	Acid & Base Mixture	050.33			

Common Name/Synonym	Primary Name	AOEC Code[1]	Use[2]	Asth-magen[3]	Asthma Detail[3]
Acid Solder	Acid Solder	050.26			
Acid Stripper	Acid Stripper	050.25			
Acids, Bases, Oxidizers, NOS	Acids, Bases, Oxidizers, NOS	050.00			
Acridine	Acridine	250.15			
Acrolein	Acrolein	120.02			
Acrylamide	Acrylamide	260.02			
Acrylate	Acrylic Monomer	142.01			
Acrylates, NOS	Acrylates, NOS	142.00			
Acrylic Acid	Acrylic Acid	150.08			R
Acrylic Acid Butyl Ester	Butyl Acrylate	142.02			R
Acrylic Acid Polymer	Acrylics	270.01			
Acrylic Acid, 1,1,1-(Trihydroxymethyl) Propane Triester	Trimethylolpropane Triacrylate	142.08			
Acrylic Acid, 2(Diethylamino)ethyl Ester	Diethylaminoethyl Acrylate	142.06			
Acrylic Acid, 2-Hydroxypropylester	2-Hydroxypropyl Acrylate	142.09			
Acrylic Aldehyde	Acrolein	120.02			
Acrylic Amide	Acrylamide	260.02			
Acrylic capstock pellets	Acrylic capstock pellets	270.43			
Acrylic Monomer	Acrylic Monomer	142.01			
Acrylic Resins	Acrylics	270.01			
Acrylics	Acrylics	270.01			
Acrylonitrile	Acrylonitrile	210.02			
Acrylonitrile-Butadiene-Styrene Copolymer	Acrylonitrile-Butadiene-Styrene Copolymer	270.29			
Acrylonitrile-Butadiene-Styrene-Polyvinyl Chloride	Acrylonitrile-Butadiene-Styrene-Polyvinyl Chloride	270.30			
Actibon	Activated Carbon	010.041			
Actinia equina	Actinia equina	381.21		Yes	Rs
Activated Carbon	Activated Carbon	010.041			
Activol	Para-Aminophenol	251.01			
Adding Machine	Keyboard Use	360.02			
Adhesive, Epoxy	Adhesive, Epoxy	110.06		Yes	G
Adhesive, NOS	Glues, NOS	320.110			
Aerosolized Pentamidine	Pentamidine	321.23			
Aflotoxins	Aflotoxins	391.091			
African Cherry	African Cherry	373.28		Yes	Rs
African Ebony	Ebony	373.20		Yes	Rs
African Maple, ayous, wawa, abeche, or samba	Triplochiton Scleroxylon	373.09		Yes	Rs
African Teak	Kejaat	373.12		Yes	Rs
African Zebrawood	Microberlinia brazzavillensis	373.13		Yes	Rs
Agent Orange	Agent Orange	200.010	P		
AIDS Exposure	HIV Exposure	390.08			
Air Bag Discharge Products	Air Bag Discharge Products	320.44			
Air Freshener	Air Freshener	320.42			
Air Pollutants, Indoor	Air Pollutants, Indoor	320.01			
Air Pollutants, Indoor, from Building Renovation	Indoor Air Pollutants from Building Renovation	320.33			
Air Pollutants, Outdoor	Air Pollutants, Outdoor	320.02			
Air Pressure, Changes	Air Pressure, Changes	350.07			
Albuterol Aerosol	Salbutamol	321.31		Yes	Rs
Alcalase	Bacillus Subtilis Enzymes	324.010		Yes	Rs
Alcohol	Ethanol	070.05	S		
Alcohols, NOS	Alcohols, NOS	070.00	S		
Aldehydes, NOS	Aldehydes, NOS	120.00			
Aldrin	Aldrin	280.01	P		
Alicyclic Hydrocarbons, NOS	Alicyclic Hydrocarbons, NOS	060.002			
Aliphatic Hydrocarbons, NOS	Aliphatic Hydrocarbons, NOS	060.001			
Alkyd Resins	Alkyd Resins	270.21			
Alkyl Dimethyl Benzyl Ammonium Chloride	Alkyl Dimethyl Benzyl Ammonium Chloride	322.3219		Yes	Rs
Alkylcyanoacrylates, NOS	Cyanoacrylates, NOS	142.07		Yes	Rs
Allyl Alcohol	Allyl Alcohol	070.01			
Allylguaiacol	Eugenol	100.07		Yes	Rs

Common Name/Synonym	Primary Name	AOEC Code[1]	Use[2]	Asthmagen[3]	Asthma Detail[3]
Almond Shell Dust (Prunus dulcis)	Almond Shell Dust (Prunus dulcis)	370.71		Yes	Rs
Alpha Amylase	Fungal Amylase	324.09		Yes	Rs
alpha Amylase (bacterial)	alpha Amylase (bacterial)	324.16		Yes	Rs
alpha Amylase (pancreatic)	alpha Amylase (pancreatic)	324.17		Yes	Rs
Alpha Lactalbumin	Alpha Lactalbumin	380.101		Yes	Rs
Alpha-Chlorotoluene	Benzyl Chloride	200.02			
Alpha-Naphthylamine	Alpha-Naphthylamine	251.04			
Alphitobius diaperinus	Alphitobius diaperinus	382.09			R
Alternaria	Alternaria	391.12		Yes	Rs
Alternaria Aleternata	Alternaria	391.12		Yes	Rs
Alternaria Alternata Toxin	Alternaria	391.12		Yes	Rs
Alternaria spp	Alternaria	391.12		Yes	Rs
Alumina	Aluminum Oxide	020.02		Yes	Rs
Aluminum	Aluminum	020.011		Yes	Rs
Aluminum Chloride	Aluminum Chloride	020.012		Yes	Rs
Aluminum Compounds	Aluminum Compounds	020.010		Yes	Rs
Aluminum Hydroxide	Aluminum Hydroxide	050.30			
Aluminum Oxide	Aluminum Oxide	020.02		Yes	Rs
Aluminum Oxide, Corundum	Aluminum Oxide, Corundum	020.021		Yes	Rs
Aluminum Phosphide	Aluminum Phosphide	040.31	P		
Amaranth	Amaranth	252.01			
AmBic	Ammonium bicarbonate	050.49			
Amino Acids, NOS	Amino Acids, NOS	250.19			
Amino Resins	Amino Resins	270.22			
Aminobenzene	Aniline	250.01			
Aminoethyl Ethanolamine	Aminoethyl Ethanolamine	231.03		Yes	Rs
Aminophen	Aniline	250.01			
Ammonia	Ammonium Hydroxide, NOS	322.07		Yes	Rrs
Ammonia Solution (10%)	Ammonia Solution (10%)	322.09		Yes	Rs
Ammonia Solution (29%)	Ammonia Solution (29%)	322.08		Yes	Rs
Ammonia Solution, NOS	Ammonium Hydroxide, NOS	322.07		Yes	Rrs
Ammonia, Household	Ammonia Solution (10%)	322.09		Yes	Rs
Ammonium bicarbonate	Ammonium bicarbonate	050.49			
Ammonium Bichromate	Ammonium Bichromate	022.02		Yes	Rs
Ammonium bifluoride	Ammonium bifluoride	040.34			
Ammonium Chloride	Ammonium Chloride	052.031			
Ammonium chloroplatinate	Ammonium Hexachloroplatinate (IV)	024.01		Yes	Rs
Ammonium Hexachloroplatinate (IV)	Ammonium Hexachloroplatinate (IV)	024.01		Yes	Rs
Ammonium hydrogen carbonate	Ammonium bicarbonate	050.49			
Ammonium Hydroxide, NOS	Ammonium Hydroxide, NOS	322.07		Yes	Rrs
Ammonium Persulfate	Ammonium Persulfate	052.04			
Ammonium Phosphate	Ammonium Phosphate	040.32	P		
Ammonium Salts	Ammonium Salts	052.030			
Ammonium Sulfate	Ammonium Sulfate	052.05			
Ampicillin	Ampicillin	321.041		Yes	G
Amprolium	Amprolium	321.11		Yes	Rs
AMT	3-Amino-5-mercapto-1,2,4-triazole	260.30		Yes	Rs
Amyl Acetate	Amyl Acetate	141.01			
Amyl Alcohol	Amyl Alcohol	070.02			
Amyl Nitrite	Amyl Nitrite	260.27			
Amylase and protease	Flaviastase	324.06		Yes	Rs
Amyloglucosidase	Amyloglucosidase	324.110		Yes	Rs
Ananase	Bromelain	324.07		Yes	Rs
Anesthetic Ethers, NOS	Anesthetic Ethers, NOS	190.155			R
Anesthetic Gases, Halogenated	Anesthetic Gases, Halogenated	190.154			R
Anesthetic Gases, NOS	Anesthetic Gases, NOS	320.03			
Angora wool	Angora wool	380.24		Yes	Rs
Anhydride, NOS	Anhydride, NOS	151.00			

Common Name/Synonym	Primary Name	AOEC Code[1]	Use[2]	Asth-magen[3]	Asthma Detail[3]
Anhydrous Ammonia	Anhydrous Ammonia	052.011		Yes	Rr
Aniline	Aniline	250.01			
Aniline Dyes, NOS	Aniline Dyes, NOS	251.00			
Animal Material, NOS	Animal Material, NOS	380.00			R
Animal Material, NOS (see specific animals)	Animal Material, NOS	380.00			R
Aningre (Tanganyika)	Aningre (Tanganyika)	373.10		Yes	Rs
Anisakis simplex	Anisakis simplex	382.26		Yes	Rs
Anthracene	Anthracene	161.01			
Antifreeze	Antifreeze	080.010			
Antigens, Animal	Antigens, Animal	380.01			
Antigens, Animal (see specific animals)	Antigens, Animal	380.01			
Antimony	Antimony	020.031			
Antimony Compounds	Antimony Compounds	020.030			
Antimony Hydride	Antimony Hydride	020.04			
Arabidopsis Thaliana	Arabidopsis Thaliana	370.52		Yes	Rs
Argan Powder	Argan Powder	370.81		Yes	Rs
Argon	Argon	040.01			
Arochlor	Polychlorinated Biphenyls	200.07			
Aromatic Hydrocarbons, NOS	Aromatic Hydrocarbons, NOS	160.00	S		
Aromatic Solvents, NOS	Aromatic Hydrocarbons, NOS	160.00	S		
Arsenic	Arsenic	020.051			
Arsenic Compounds	Arsenic Compounds	020.050			
Arsine	Arsine	020.06			
Arthropod, NOS	Insect, NOS	382.00			
Asbestos, Amosite	Asbestos, Amosite	010.021			
Asbestos, Chrysotile	Asbestos, Chrysotile	010.023			
Asbestos, Crocidolite	Asbestos, Crocidolite	010.024			
Asbestos, NOS	Asbestos, NOS	010.020			
Asbestos, Tremolite	Asbestos, Tremolite	010.025			
Ash, NOS	Ash, NOS	010.16			
Ashwood, Ash, American Ash, or White Ash	Fraxinus Americana	373.17		Yes	Rs
Aspergillus	Aspergillus	391.020			
Aspergillus Flavus	Aspergillus Flavus	391.021			
Aspergillus Fumigatus	Aspergillus Fumigatus	391.022			
Aspergillus Glaucus	Aspergillus Glaucus	391.023			
Aspergillus Niger	Aspergillus Niger	391.024			
Aspergillus Versicolor	Aspergillus Versicolor	391.025			
Asphalt	Asphalt	061.07			
Asphyxiant Gases, NOS	Asphyxiant Gases, NOS	040.25			
Assault, Physical	Assault, Physical	353.12			
Astral Oil	Astral Oil	061.032	S		
Atorvastatin powder	Atorvastatin powder	321.37			
Augmentin	Augmentin	321.044			
Auramine	Auramine	251.02			
Australian Blackwood	Australian Blackwood	373.27		Yes	RS
Australian Sheep Blowfly	Sheep Blowfly	382.12		Yes	Rs
Auto Accident	Motor Vehicle Accident	353.05			
Avian Material, NOS	Avian Material, NOS	380.16			
Ayruvedic Medications	Ayruvedic Medications	321.35			
Azabenzene	Pyridine	250.14			
Azine	Pyridine	250.14			
Aziridine	Ethylenimine	260.101			
Azo Compounds, NOS	Azo Compounds, NOS	252.00			
Azo Dyes, NOS	Azo Compounds, NOS	252.00			
Azobisformamide	Azodicarbamide	260.18		Yes	Rs
Azodicarbamide	Azodicarbamide	260.18		Yes	Rs
B-Galactosidase	Lactase	324.14			
B-Mercaptoethanol	Mercaptoethanol	310.04			
Baby's Breath	Baby's Breath	370.17		Yes	

Common Name/Synonym	Primary Name	AOEC Code[1]	Use[2]	Asth-magen[3]	Asthma Detail[3]
Bacillus lichenformis	Code added in error-no such code	324.012			
Bacillus Subtilis Enzymes	Bacillus Subtilis Enzymes	324.010		Yes	Rs
Bacillus Thurigiensis	Bacillus Thurigiensis	390.14	P		
Bacteria	Infectious Agents, NOS	390.070			
Balfourodendron Riedelianum	Pau Marfim	373.18		Yes	Rs
Baquacil	Polyhexamethylene Biguanide	260.29	P		
Barium	Barium	020.071			
Barium Compounds	Barium Compounds	020.070			
Barn Dust	Manure	380.02			
Barn Mite	Barn Mite	382.15		Yes	
Barometric Pressure, Changes	Air Pressure, Changes	350.07			
Bat Guano	Bat Guano	380.12		Yes	
Baygon	Propoxur	292.04	P		
BCDMH	1-Bromo-3-chloro-5,5-dimethylhydantoin	191.04			R
BCME	Bis Chloromethyl Ether	100.01			
Beadlet anemone	Actinia equina	381.21		Yes	Rs
Bee Moth	Galleria Mellonella	382.05		Yes	Rs
Bee Sting	Venom	380.05			
Bending	Posture, Body - Dynamic	362.03			
Benin Ebony	Ebony	373.20		Yes	Rs
Benlate Fungicide	Benomyl	260.03	P		
Benomyl	Benomyl	260.03	P		
Benzalkonium Chloride Quats in cleaning agents, NOS	Benzalkonium Chloride, NOS	322.321		Yes	Rs
Benzalkonium Chloride, NOS	Benzalkonium Chloride, NOS	322.321		Yes	Rs
Benzamide	N,N-diethyl-m-toluamide	260.26	P		
Benzene	Benzene	160.01	S		
Benzenediamine	Benzenediamine	251.060			R
Benzenediazonium Chloride	Diazonium Chloride	252.031		Yes	Rs
Benzidine	Benzidine	251.03			
Benzoic Acid	Benzoic Acid	150.02			
Benzol	Benzene	160.01	S		
Benzoyl Chloride	Benzoyl Chloride	200.09			
Benzoyl Peroxide	Benzoyl Peroxide	050.27			
Benzyl Chloride	Benzyl Chloride	200.02			
Benzyl-C10-16-alkyldimethyl, chlorides	Benzyl-C10-16-alkyldimethyl, chlorides	322.3211		Yes	Rs
Benzyl-C12-16-alkyldimethyl ammonium, chlorides	Benzyl-C12-16-alkyldimethyl ammonium, chlorides	322.3222		Yes	Rs
Benzyl-C12-18-alkyldimethyl ammonium, chlorides	Benzyl-C12-18-alkyldimethyl ammonium, chlorides	322.3221		Yes	Rs
Benzyl-C16-18-alkyldimethyl ammonium, chlorides	Benzyl-C16-18-alkyldimethyl ammonium, chlorides	322.3223		Yes	Rs
Benzyldimethylstearylammonium Chloride	Benzyldimethylstearylammonium Chloride	322.3215		Yes	Rs
Beryllium	Beryllium	020.081			
Beryllium Compounds	Beryllium Compounds	020.080			
Beta-Chloroethyl Alcohol	Beta-Chloroethyl Alcohol	070.03			
Beta-Galactosidase	Lactase	324.14			
Beta-glucanase	Beta-glucanase	324.22		Yes	Rs
Beta-Lactosidase	Lactase	324.14			
Beta-mercaptopropionic Acid	3-mercaptopropionic Acid	310.12			
Beta-Naphthylamine	Beta-Naphthylamine	251.05			
Beta-Propiolactone	Beta-Propiolactone	320.04			
Beta-thiopropionic Acid	3-mercaptopropionic Acid	310.12			
Bicarbonate of ammonia	Ammonium bicarbonate	050.49			
Bioaerosols	Microorganisms, NOS	390.00			
Bis 2-Chloroethyl Ether	Dichloroethyl Ether	100.03			
Bis Chloromethyl Ether	Bis Chloromethyl Ether	100.01			
Bis-2-Chloroethyl Sulfide	Mustard Gas	190.16			
Bismuth	Bismuth	020.091			
Bismuth Compounds	Bismuth Compounds	020.090			
Bisphenol A diglycidyl ether (BADGE)	Bisphenol A diglycidyl ether (BADGE)	110.08		Yes	Rs
Bitrex	Denatonium Benzoate	320.37			

Common Name/Synonym	Primary Name	AOEC Code[1]	Use[2]	Asth-magen[3]	Asthma Detail[3]
Black GR	Rifazol Black GR	325.08		Yes	Rs
Black Wattle	Australian Blackwood	373.27		Yes	Rs
Blackwood Acacia	Australian Blackwood	373.27		Yes	Rs
Blatella germanica (German cockroach)	Blatella germanica (German cockroach)	382.282		Yes	Rs
Bleach	Sodium Hypochlorite	322.10		Yes	Rs
Bleach plus Acid (mixture)	Bleach plus Acid (mixture)	322.11			R
Bleach plus Ammonia (Mixture)	Bleach plus Ammonia (Mixture)	322.12			R
Bleaching Powder	Calcium Hypochloride	322.13			
Blood Exposure (Unknown Infection Status)	Body Fluid Exposure (Unknown Infection Status)	390.16			
Bloodworm	Bloodworm	382.18			
Bodily Reaction	Bodily Reaction	360.07			
Body Fluid Exposure (Unknown Infection Status)	Body Fluid Exposure (Unknown Infection Status)	390.16			
Bombyx mori	Bombyx mori	382.01		Yes	Rs
Boric Acid	Boric Acid	020.101			
Boron	Boron	020.102			
Boron Compounds	Boron Compounds	020.100			
Boron Hydride	Diborane	020.11			
Borrelium Virus	Borrelium Virus	390.15			
Bovine Serum Albumin	Bovine Serum Albumin	380.13		Yes	Rs
BPL	Beta-Propiolactone	320.04			
Brass	Brass	020.43			
Brazil Ginseng	Brazil Ginseng	370.53		Yes	Rs
Brazilian Ginseng	Brazil Ginseng	370.53		Yes	Rs
Brazilian Rosewood	Palisandar	373.32		Yes	Rs
Brazilian walnut	Ipe	373.31		Yes	Rs
Brazing, NOS	Brazing, NOS	023.002			
Brick Oil	Creosote	180.01			
Brilliant Orange 3R	Rifazol Brilliant Orange 3R	325.07		Yes	Rs
Brilliant Yellow 160	Remazol Brilliant Yellow 4GL	325.27			R
Bromelain	Bromelain	324.07		Yes	Rs
Bromelin	Bromelain	324.07		Yes	Rs
Brominated Fluorocarbon	Brominated Fluorocarbon	192.03			
Brominated Pesticides, NOS	Brominated Pesticides, NOS	191.00	P		
Bromine	Bromine	030.01			
Bromomethane	Methyl Bromide	191.03	P		
Bromopropane	Bromopropane	190.18			
Bt	Bacillus Thurigiensis	390.14	P		
BTC 776	BTC 776	322.3218		Yes	Rs
BTC 927	BTC 927	322.3212		Yes	Rs
Buckwheat	Buckwheat	371.01		Yes	G
Building Renovation	Indoor Air Pollutants from Building Renovation	320.33			
Burning Fume	Welding, NOS	023.001			
Burnt Lime	Calcium Oxide	050.050			
Butadiene & Styrene	Butadiene & Styrene	271.01			
Butyl Acetate	Butyl Acetate	141.02	S		
Butyl Acrylate	Butyl Acrylate	142.02			R
Butyl Ketone	Butyl Ketone	130.06	S		
Butyl-Cellosolve	2-Butoxyethanol	091.03	S		R
C. Carnea	Chrysoperla Carnea	382.22			R
C.I. Pigment Red 48:1	Red BBN	325.22		Yes	Rs
C.I. Reactive Black 5	Remazol Black B	325.11			R
C.I. Reactive Blue 203	Remazol Marine Blue GG	325.24			R
C.I. Reactive Yellow 145	Rifafix Yellow 3 RN	325.06		Yes	Rs
C.I. Reactive Yellow 39	Lanasol Yellow 4G	325.09		Yes	Rs
Cabreuva	Cabreuva	373.23		Yes	Rs
Cacoon Seed	Cacoon Seed	370.32		Yes	Rs
Caddis Flies	Caddis Flies	382.27		Yes	Rs
Cadmium	Cadmium	020.121			

Common Name/Synonym	Primary Name	AOEC Code[1]	Use[2]	Asth-magen[3]	Asthma Detail[3]
Cadmium Compounds	Cadmium Compounds	020.120			
Cadmium Salts	Cadmium Salts	020.122			
Caesalpinia Echinata	Fernambouc	373.16			R
Calcium Bisulfite	Calcium Bisulfite	050.03			
Calcium Carbide	Calcium Carbide	050.36			
Calcium Carbonate	Calcium Carbonate	050.35			
Calcium Chloride	Calcium Chloride	041.01			
Calcium Cyanamide	Calcium Cyanamide	260.04			
Calcium Hypochloride	Calcium Hypochloride	322.13			
Calcium Oxide	Calcium Oxide	050.050			
Calcium Salts, NOS	Calcium Salts, NOS	040.02			
Calculator	Keyboard Use	360.02			
California Redwood	California Redwood	373.02		Yes	Rs
Camphor Oil	Camphor Oil	320.48			R
Cannabis dust (marijuana and hemp)	Cannabis dust (marijuana and hemp)	370.620		Yes	Rs
Cannabis smoke	Cannabis smoke	330.05		Yes	Rs
Capsicum	Capsicum	370.35			
Captafol	Captafol	320.081		Yes	Rs
Captan	Captan	260.05	P		
Car Accident	Motor Vehicle Accident	353.05			
Car Crash	Motor Vehicle Accident	353.05			
Carbamate Pesticides, NOS	Carbamate Pesticides, NOS	292.00	P		
Carbaryl	Carbaryl	292.02	P		
Carbazotic Acid	Picric Acid	250.09			
Carbinol	Methanol	070.07	S		
Carbolic Acid	Phenol	180.04			
Carbon Black	Carbon Black	010.042			
Carbon Dioxide	Carbon Dioxide	040.03			
Carbon Disulfide	Carbon Disulfide	310.01			
Carbon Monoxide	Carbon Monoxide	040.04			
Carbon Tetrachloride	Carbon Tetrachloride	190.01	S		
Carbonless Paper	Carbonless Paper	320.05			
Carbopol	Carbopol, NOS	270.36			
Carbopol, NOS	Carbopol, NOS	270.36			
Carborundum	Silicon Carbide	010.18			
Carene	Carene	060.21		Yes	Rs
Carmine	Carmine	320.24			
Carminic Acid	Carmine	320.24			
Carpet Dust	Carpet Dust	320.35			
Carpet Fibers	Carpet Dust	320.35			
Carrying	Lifting	361.02			
Casein	Casein	380.11		Yes	Rs
Cash Register Use	Keyboard Use	360.02			
Castanea denatata	Chestnut	373.30		Yes	Rs
Castor Bean	Castor Bean	370.13		Yes	
Cat	Cat	380.22		Yes	Rs
Catalysts, NOS	Enzymes, NOS	324.00			
Caught In or Between Objects	Caught In or Between Objects	353.10			
Caustic Soda	Sodium Hydroxide	050.18			
Caviuna	Palisandar	373.32		Yes	Rs
Ceclor	Ceclor	321.26			
Cedar of Lebanon	Cedar of Lebanon	373.03			R
Cedrus Libani	Cedar of Lebanon	373.03			R
Cefaclor	Ceclor	321.26			
Cefadroxil	Cefadroxil	321.061			R
Ceftazidine	Ceftazidine	321.062			R
Ceiba Pentandra Gaertner	Kapok	370.43		Yes	
Celery	Celery	370.011			
Cellosolve	Ethylene Glycol Monoethyl Ether	091.02	S		

Common Name/Synonym	Primary Name	AOEC Code[1]	Use[2]	Asth-magen[3]	Asthma Detail[3]
Cellulase	Cellulase	324.19		Yes	Rs
Cellulose	Cellulose	370.90		Yes	Rs
Cement Dust	Cement Dust	010.03			R
Central American Walnut	Juglans Olanchana	373.11		Yes	Rs
Cephalexin	Cephalexin	321.063			R
Cephalosporins	Cephalosporins	321.060			R
Ceratitis capitata	Ceratitis capitata	382.30		Yes	Rs
Cerium	Cerium	020.131			
Cerium Compounds	Cerium Compounds	020.130			
Cetalkonium Chloride	Cetalkonium Chloride	322.3217		Yes	Rs
Cetane	Cetane	061.10			
CFC	Chlorofluorocarbon, NOS	192.020			
Chamomile	Chamomile	370.54		Yes	Rs
Champignon flies	Champignon flies	382.29		Yes	Rs
Chan Ta Khien	Chengal	373.29		Yes	Rs
Chemical Dust, NOS	Chemicals, NOS	320.06			
Chemicals, NOS	Chemicals, NOS	320.06			
Chemicals, Unknown	Chemicals, NOS	320.06			
Chemotherapeutic Drugs	Chemotherapeutic Drugs	321.010			
Chengal	Chengal	373.29		Yes	Rs
Chestnut	Chestnut	373.30		Yes	Rs
Chi-Ngamat	Chengal	373.29		Yes	Rs
Chicken	Chicken	380.07		Yes	Rs
Chicory	Cichorium intybus	370.18		Yes	Rs
Chil-Perm CP-30	Chil-Perm CP-30	320.31	S		
Chironomidae thummi (the red midge)	Chironomidae thummi (the red midge)	382.31		Yes	Rs
Chloramide	Chloramine	030.09			R
Chloramine	Chloramine	030.09			R
Chloramine compounds, NOS	Chloramine compounds, NOS	030.090			
Chloramine T	Chloramine T	260.21		Yes	Rs
Chlorbenzol	Chlorobenzene	201.04	S		
Chlordane	Chlordane	280.02	P		
Chlorex	Dichloroethyl Ether	100.03			
Chlorhexidine	Chlorhexidine	200.08		Yes	Rs
Chlorimide	Dichloramine	030.10			R
Chlorinated Benzenes, NOS	Chlorinated Benzenes, NOS	201.00			
Chlorinated Dibenzodioxins	Chlorinated Dibenzodioxins	200.040			
Chlorinated Dibenzodioxins (except TCDD)	Chlorinated Dibenzodioxins	200.040	P		
Chlorinated Hydrocarbons, NOS	Chlorinated Hydrocarbons, NOS	190.00	S		
Chlorinated Naphthalene	Chlorinated Naphthalene	200.03			
Chlorinated Phenols, NOS	Chlorinated Phenols, NOS	181.00			
Chlorinated Solvents, NOS	Chlorinated Hydrocarbons, NOS	190.00	S		
Chlorine	Chlorine	030.02		Yes	Rrs
Chlorine Dioxide	Chlorine Dioxide	030.06			
Chlorine Trifluoride	Chlorine Trifluoride	030.05			
Chlorobenzene	Chlorobenzene	201.04	S		
Chlorobutadiene	Chloroprene	190.04			
Chlorodiphenyl	Polychlorinated Biphenyls	200.07			
Chloroethane	Chloroethane	190.02	S		
Chloroethene	Vinyl Chloride Monomer	190.14			
Chlorofluorocarbon, NOS	Chlorofluorocarbon, NOS	192.020			
Chloroform	Chloroform	190.03			
Chloromethyl Ether	Bis Chloromethyl Ether	100.01			
Chloromethyl Methyl Ether	Chloromethyl Methyl Ether	100.02			
Chlorophenoxy Herbicides, NOS	Chlorophenoxy Herbicides, NOS	200.11	P		
Chlorophora Excelsa	Iroko	373.05		Yes	Rs
Chloropicrin	Chloropicrin	260.06	P		
Chloroprene	Chloroprene	190.04			

Common Name/Synonym	Primary Name	AOEC Code[1]	Use[2]	Asth-magen[3]	Asthma Detail[3]
Chloropropane	Chloropropane	190.05	S		
Chlorothalonil	Chlorothalonil	210.03	P	Yes	Rs
Chlorous Acid	Chlorous Acid	030.07			
Chlorpyrifos	Chlorpyrifos	291.05	P		R
Chorella Algae	Chorella Algae	370.36		Yes	
Chromic Acid	Chromic Acid	022.04		Yes	Rs
Chromium Compounds	Chromium Compounds	020.140		Yes	Rs
Chromium Metal	Chromium Metal	020.141		Yes	Rs
Chromium, Hexavalent, NOS	Chromium, Hexavalent, NOS	022.00		Yes	Rs
Chromium, Not Hexavalent	Chromium, Not Hexavalent	020.142		Yes	Rs
Chrysonilia sitophilia	Chrysonilia sitophilia	390.111		Yes	Rs
Chrysoperla Carnea	Chrysoperla Carnea	382.22			R
Chymotrypsin	Chymotrypsin	324.20			R
Cibachrome Brilliant Scarlet 3R	Cibachrome Brilliant Scarlet 3R	325.03		Yes	Rs
Cichorium intybus	Cichorium intybus	370.18		Yes	Rs
Cidex	Glutaraldehyde	120.051		Yes	Rs
Cidex OPA	Ortho-phthalaldehyde	120.10			R
Cigarette Smoke	Cigarette Smoke	330.01			R
Cimetidine	Cimetidine	321.17		Yes	Rs
Cinnamene	Styrene	160.04	S	Yes	Rs
Cinnamic Aldehyde	Cinnamic Aldehyde	120.080			
Cinnamic Oil	Cinnamon Oil	120.089			
Cinnamomum Zeylanicum	Cinnamon	373.22			R
Cinnamon	Cinnamon	373.22			R
Citric Acid	Citric Acid	050.07			
Clams (Bivalvia class)	Clams (Bivalvia class)	381.10		Yes	Rs
Clandestine Drug laboratory	Methamphetamine Laboratory	320.40			
Clay	Clay	010.051			
Clay 347	Clay	010.051			
Clay, NOS	Clay, NOS	010.050			
Cleaner, Citric	Cleaner, Citric	322.36			
Cleaners, Abrasive	Cleaners, Abrasive	322.14			
Cleaners, Acid	Cleaners, Acid	322.15			
Cleaners, Carpet	Cleaners, Carpet	322.16			
Cleaners, Caustic (excluding Lye)	Cleaners, Caustic (excluding Lye)	322.17			
Cleaners, Detergent, NOS	Cleaners, Detergent, NOS	322.18			
Cleaners, Disinfectant, NOS	Cleaners, Disinfectant, NOS	322.19			
Cleaners, Drain	Cleaners, Drain	322.20			
Cleaners, Floor Stripping	Cleaners, Floor Stripping	322.21			
Cleaners, Graffiti Removing	Cleaners, Graffiti Removing	322.22	S		
Cleaners, Household, General Purpose	Cleaners, Household, General Purpose	322.04			
Cleaners, Laundry Soap/Detergent	Cleaners, Laundry Soap/Detergent	322.23			
Cleaners, Lye	Cleaners, Lye	322.24			
Cleaners, Oven	Cleaners, Oven	322.25			
Cleaners, Pine Oil	Cleaners, Pine Oil	322.26			
Cleaners, Solvent-Based	Cleaners, Solvent-Based	322.06	S		
Cleaners, Tile	Cleaners, Tile	322.27			
Cleaners, Toilet Bowl	Cleaners, Toilet Bowl	322.28			
Cleaners, Wallpaper	Cleaners, Wallpaper	322.29			
Cleaning Fluids, Photocopier	Cleaning Fluids, Photocopier	322.03			
Cleaning Fluids/Spot Removers	Cleaning Fluids/Spot Removers	322.30	S		
Cleaning Materials, NOS	Cleaning Materials, NOS	322.00			
Cleaning Mixtures (excluding Bleach plus Acid or Ammonia)	Cleaning Mixtures (excluding Bleach plus Acid or Ammonia)	322.31			
Clove Oil	Oil of Clove	160.06			
CMME	Chloromethyl Methyl Ether	100.02			
CO	Carbon Monoxide	040.04			
Coal	Coal	010.06			
Coal Naphtha	Benzene	160.01	S		

Common Name/Synonym	Primary Name	AOEC Code[1]	Use[2]	Asth-magen[3]	Asthma Detail[3]
Coal Tar	Polycyclic Aromatic Hydrocarbons, NOS	161.00			
Coal Tar Oil	Creosote	180.01			
Coating, Epoxy	Paint, Epoxy	110.05			
Cobalt	Cobalt	020.151		Yes	Rs
Cobalt Compounds	Cobalt Compounds	020.150		Yes	G
Cocabolla	Cocabolla	373.04			R
Cochlomyia hominovorax	Cochlomyia hominovorax	382.03		Yes	Rs
Cockroach	Cockroach	382.28		Yes	Rs
Cocoa	Cocoa Bean	370.47			
Cocoa Bean	Cocoa Bean	370.47			
Cocobolo	Cocabolla	373.04			R
Coconut	Coconut	370.009			
Codeine	Codeine	321.182		Yes	Rs
Coffee Bean	Coffee Bean	370.12		Yes	
Coke Oven Emissions	Polycyclic Aromatic Hydrocarbons, NOS	161.00			
Cold	Cold	350.02			
Colistin	Colistin	321.34		Yes	Rs
Collodion	Collodion	270.39			
Collodium	Collodion	270.39			
Colophony	Colophony	023.05		Yes	G
Color Index No. 0-16	Rifazol Brilliant Orange 3R	325.07		Yes	Rs
Color Index No. 0-20	Rifacion Orange HE 2G	325.05		Yes	Rs
Color Index No. BK-5	Rifazol Black GR	325.08		Yes	Rs
Colorado Potato Beetle	Leptinotarsa Decemlineata	382.23			R
Combustion Products, NOS	Smoke, NOS	330.03			
common greenbottle	Lucilia Caesar Larva	382.19		Yes	Rs
Computer Keyboard	Keyboard Use	360.02			
Computer Mouse Use	Keyboard Use	360.02			
Concrete, wet	Concrete, wet	010.24			
Contact Pressure	Contact Pressure	360.01			
Contaminated Well Water due to Hydrofracking	Contaminated Well Water due to Hydrofracking	170.10			
Coolants	Lubricants, NOS	320.14			
Copper	Copper	020.161			
Copper Compounds	Copper Compounds	020.160			
Copper Phthalocyanine	Copper Phthalocyanine	020.49			
Copper Sulfate	Copper Sulfate	020.51			
Copper Sulfate (Anhydrous)	Copper Sulfate	020.51			
Corn Dust	Corn Dust	370.51			
Corn Mint Oil	Corn Mint Oil	320.47			R
Corn Starch	Corn Starch	371.06			
Corrosive Preventative	Corrosive Preventative	060.23			
Cosmetics, NOS	Cosmetics, NOS	320.28			R
Cosmetology Chemicals, NOS	Cosmetics, NOS	320.28			R
Cotton Dust	Cotton Dust	370.02			
Coumarin	Coumarin	321.03			
Cow Dander	Cow Dander	380.041		Yes	
Crabs (Pleocyemata suborder)	Crabs (Pleocyemata suborder)	381.02		Yes	G
Crawfish (Cambaridae family)	Crawfish (Cambaridae family)	381.20			
Crayfish (Cambaridae family)	Crawfish (Cambaridae family)	381.20			
Creosote	Creosote	180.01			
Cresol	Cresol	180.02			
Cresylic Acid	Cresol	180.02			
Cricket	Cricket	382.04		Yes	
Crotonaldehyde	Crotonaldehyde	120.09			
CRT Radiation	Radiation, Electromagnetic	352.01			
Crude oil	Crude oil	170.04			
Cuprilinic Blue	Copper Phthalocyanine	020.49			
Cutting fluid, soy based	Cutting fluid, soy based	170.08			
Cutting Oils	Cutting Oils	170.01		Yes	G

Common Name/Synonym	Primary Name	AOEC Code[1]	Use[2]	Asth-magen[3]	Asthma Detail[3]
Cutting or Piercing Object, Except Blood-Contam. Sharps	Cutting or Piercing Object, Except Blood-Contam. Sharps	353.11			
Cuttlefish (Cephalopeda class)	Cuttlefish (Cephalopeda class)	381.06			R
Cyanides, NOS	Cyanides, NOS	211.00			
Cyanoacrylates, NOS	Cyanoacrylates, NOS	142.07		Yes	Rs
Cyanurotramide	Melamine	260.28			
Cyclohexane	Cyclohexane	060.14	S		
Cyclohexanediamine_(1,2-diaminocyclohexane)	Cyclohexanediamine_(1,2-diaminocyclohexane)	060.25			R
Cyclohexanone	Cyclohexanone	130.07	S		
Cyclohexylamine	Cyclohexylamine	230.06			
Cyclopentadiene	Cyclopentadiene	060.13			
Cyclophosphamide	Cyclophosphamide	321.29			
Cytoxan	Cyclophosphamide	321.29			
D-Limonene	D-Limonene	060.18	S		R
Dalbergia Nigra	Palisandar	373.32		Yes	Rs
Dalbergia Retusa	Cocabolla	373.04			R
Dander, Animal (NOS)	Dander, Animal (NOS)	380.040			
Daphnia	Daphnia	382.10			R
DCB	Dichlorobenzene	201.010	P		
DDT	DDT	280.03	P		
DEA (Diethanolamine)	Diethanolamine	231.041		Yes	Rs
DEA (Diethylaniline)	Diethylaniline	250.18			
DEET	N,N-diethyl-m-toluamide	260.26	P		
Degreaser, NOS	Degreaser, NOS	171.04			
Deicer-airplanes	Deicer-airplanes	080.05			
Denatonium Benzoate	Denatonium Benzoate	320.37			
Deodorizer, Aerosol	Air Freshener	320.42			
Dermasorb	Dimethyl Sulfoxide	310.14			
DHA	Dihydroxyacetone	130.08			
di-Halo	1-Bromo-3-chloro-5,5-dimethylhydantoin	191.04			R
Diacetyl	Diacetyl	130.09			
Diacetyl morphine	Diacetyl morphine	321.185		Yes	Rs
Dialkyl Methyl Benzyl Ammonium Chloride	Dialkyl Methyl Benzyl Ammonium Chloride	322.3213		Yes	Rs
Diamines, NOS	Diamines, NOS	233.00			
Diatomaceous Earth	Silica, Amorphous	010.12			
Diazinon	Diazinon	291.03	P		R
Diazomethane	Diazomethane	260.23			
Diazonium Chloride	Diazonium Chloride	252.031		Yes	Rs
Diazonium Salt, NOS	Diazonium Salt, NOS	252.030			R
Diazonium Tetrafluoroborate	Diazonium Tetrafluoroborate	252.032		Yes	Rs
Diborane	Diborane	020.11			
Dichlobenil	2,6-Dichlorobenzonitrile	200.10	P		
Dichloramine	Dichloramine	030.10			R
Dichlorobenzene	Dichlorobenzene	201.010	P		
Dichlorodiphenyltrichloroethane	DDT	280.03	P		
Dichloroethyl Ether	Dichloroethyl Ether	100.03			
Dichloromethane	Methylene Chloride	190.09	S		
Dichloromethyl Ether	Bis Chloromethyl Ether	100.01			
Dichlorosilane	Dichlorosilane	040.270			
Dichlorvos	Dichlorvos	291.10	P		R
Dicumyl-peroxide	Dicumyl-peroxide	050.141			
Didecyl Dimethyl Ammonium Chloride	Didecyl Dimethyl Ammonium Chloride	322.323		Yes	Rs
Dieldrin	Dieldrin	280.04	P		
Diesel Exhaust	Diesel Exhaust	331.01		Yes	Rrs
Diesel Fuel	Diesel Fuel	061.060	S		
Diesel Oil	Diesel Oil	061.061	S		
Diethanolamine	Diethanolamine	231.041		Yes	Rs
Diethyl Ether	Ethyl Ether	100.05			
Diethyl Formamide	Diethyl Formamide	260.24	S		

Common Name/Synonym	Primary Name	AOEC Code[1]	Use[2]	Asth-magen[3]	Asthma Detail[3]
Diethyl Silicate	Diethyl Silicate	140.02			
Diethyl Sulfate	Diethyl Sulfate	310.02			
Diethylamine	Diethylamine	230.02			
Diethylaminoethyl Acrylate	Diethylaminoethyl Acrylate	142.06			
Diethylaniline	Diethylaniline	250.18			
Diethylene Glycol	Diethylene Glycol	080.02			
Diethylenediamine	Piperazine	260.190		Yes	Rs
Diethylenetriamine	Diethylenetriamine	232.07			
Diethyltoluamide	N,N-diethyl-m-toluamide	260.26	P		
Difluoroethane	Difluoroethane	192.05			
Dihydroxyacetone	Dihydroxyacetone	130.08			
Diisocyanates, NOS	Diisocyanates, NOS	221.00		Yes	G
Dimethoate	Dimethoate	291.07	P		R
Dimethyl dicarbonate	Dimethyl dicarbonate	040.35			
Dimethyl Ethyl Benzyl Ammonium Chloride	Dimethyl Ethyl Benzyl Ammonium Chloride	322.3214		Yes	Rs
Dimethyl Ketone	Acetone	130.01	S		
Dimethyl Methane	Propane	060.20			
Dimethyl Sulfate	Dimethyl Sulfate	310.03			
Dimethyl Sulfide	Dimethyl Sulfide	165.01			
Dimethyl Sulfoxide	Dimethyl Sulfoxide	310.14			
Dimethylacetamide	N,N-Dimethylacetamide	260.07			
Dimethylamine	Dimethylamine	230.04			
Dimethylaminoethanol	Dimethylethanolamine	231.042		Yes	Rs
Dimethylbenzene	Xylene	160.03	S		
Dimethylethanolamine	Dimethylethanolamine	231.042		Yes	Rs
Dimethylhydrazine	Dimethylhydrazine	260.09			
Dinitro-o-Cresol	Dinitro-o-Cresol	250.06			
Dinitrobenzene	Dinitrobenzene	250.05			
Dinitrobenzol	Dinitrobenzene	250.05			
Dinitrol	Dinitro-o-Cresol	250.06			
Dinitrophenol	Dinitrophenol	250.12			
Dinitrotoluene	Dinitrotoluene	250.07			
Dinitrotoluol	Dinitrotoluene	250.07			
Dioctylphthalate	Dioctylphthalate	140.03			
Dioscorea Batatas	Dioscorea Batatas	370.39		Yes	
Diospyros Crassiflora	Ebony	373.20		Yes	Rs
Dioxane	Dioxane	100.04	S		
Dioxin	Chlorinated Dibenzodioxins	200.040			
Dipentene	Limonene	060.05	S		
Diphenylmethane Diisocyanate	Methylene Bisphenyl Diisocyanate	221.02		Yes	G
Dipropylene Glycol Methyl Ether	Dipropylene Glycol Methyl Ether	090.011	S		
Disinfectants, NOS	Disinfectants, NOS	050.28			
DMAC	N,N-Dimethylacetamide	260.07			
DMDC	Dimethyl dicarbonate	040.35			
DMF	N,N-Dimethylformamide	260.08	S		
DMN	N-Nitrosodimethylamine	240.01			
DMNA	N-Nitrosodimethylamine	240.01			
DMS	Dimethyl sulfide	165.01			
DMSO	Dimethyl Sulfoxide	310.14			
DNOC	Dinitro-o-Cresol	250.06			
DNT	Dinitrotoluene	250.07			
Dodecanedioic Acid	Dodecanedioic Acid	270.40		Yes	Rs
Dodecyl-dimethyl-benzylammonium Chloride	Dodecyl-dimethyl-benzylammonium Chloride	322.3216		Yes	Rs
Dodecylphenol	Dodecylphenol	180.08			
Drawing compound	Drawing compound	170.07			
Drilling mud, mineral oil based	Drilling mud, mineral oil based	168.02			
Drilling Mud, NOS	Drilling Mud, NOS	168.00			
Drilling mud, oil based NOS	Drilling mud, oil based NOS	168.04			

Common Name/Synonym	Primary Name	AOEC Code[1]	Use[2]	Asth-magen[3]	Asthma Detail[3]
Drilling mud, synthetic based	Drilling mud, synthetic based	168.05			
Drilling mud, vegetable oil based	Drilling mud, vegetable oil based	168.03			
Drilling mud, water based	Drilling mud, water based	168.01			
Drimaren Brilliant Blue K-BL	Drimaren Brilliant Blue K-BL	325.04		Yes	Rs
Drimaren Brilliant Yellow-K-3GL	Drimaren Brilliant Yellow K-3GL	325.02		Yes	Rs
Drimarene Brilliant Blue K-BL	Drimaren Brilliant Blue K-BL	325.04		Yes	Rs
Drimarene Brilliant Yellow K-3GL	Drimaren Brilliant Yellow K-3GL	325.02		Yes	Rs
Drosophila melanogaster	Drosophila melanogaster	382.07		Yes	Rs
Dry Air	Humidity, Low	350.04			
Dry Cleaning Fluid, NOS	Dry Cleaning Fluid, NOS	322.34	S		
Drywall Mud	Drywall Mud	010.23			
Dursban	Chlorpyrifos	291.05	P		R
Dust, NOS	Dust, NOS	010.00			
Dye Intermediates, NOS	Dyes, NOS	250.170			
Dyes, NOS	Dyes, NOS	250.170			
E-cigarette emissions	Electronic cigarette emissions	320.49			
E. Kuehniella	Ephestia Kuehniella	382.25		Yes	Rs
Eastern White Cedar	Eastern White Cedar	373.19		Yes	G
Ebony	Ebony	373.20		Yes	Rs
EDB	Ethylene Dibromide	191.01	P		
EDTA/Edetic Acid	Ethylenediamine Tetraacetic Acid	232.08			
EGBE	2-Butoxyethanol	091.03	S		R
EGEE	Ethylene Glycol Monoethyl Ether	091.02	S		
Egg Lysozyme	Lysozyme	324.08		Yes	Rs
Egg Protein	Egg Protein	380.06		Yes	G
EGME	Ethylene Glycol Monomethyl Ether	091.01	S		
Electrical Shock	Electrical Shock	353.01			
Electricity	Electrical Shock	353.01			
Electromagnetic Fields	Radiation, Electromagnetic	352.01			
Electronic cigarette emissions	Electronic cigarette emissions	320.49			
Electroplating Chemicals, NOS	Electroplating Chemicals, NOS	320.07			
ELF	Radiation, Electromagnetic	352.01			
Embalming fluid, NOS	Embalming fluid, NOS	120.20			
EMF	Radiation, Electromagnetic	352.01			
Enamel Thinner	Thinner	171.02	S		
endo-1,4-Xylanase (from Trichoderma viride)	endo-1,4-Xylanase (from Trichoderma viride)	324.122		Yes	Rs
Endotoxin	Endotoxin	391.13			
Endrin	Endrin	280.05	P		
Enflurane	Enflurane	190.151		Yes	Rs
Engine Exhaust	Engine Exhaust	331.02			
Engineered Stone Countertop Dust	Engineered Stone Dust	010.136			
Environmental electronic cigarette emissions	Electronic cigarette emissions	320.49			
Environmental Tobacco Smoke	Cigarette Smoke	330.01			R
Enzymes, NOS	Enzymes, NOS	324.00			
Ephestia Kuehniella	Ephestia Kuehniella	382.25		Yes	Rs
Epichlorohydrin	Epichlorohydrin	110.01			
Epigallocatechin gallate	Tea	370.14		Yes	Rs
EPO 60	EPO 60	232.06		Yes	Rs
Epoxies	Epoxy Resins	110.02		Yes	G
Epoxy Resin Hardeners	Epoxy Resins	110.02		Yes	G
Epoxy Resins	Epoxy Resins	110.02		Yes	G
Ergonomic Factors, NOS	Ergonomic Factors, NOS	360.00			
Esperase	Esperase	324.10		Yes	Rs
Estrogens	Estrogens	321.02			
Ethane Trichloride	1,1,2-Trichloroethane	190.12	S		
Ethanedioic Acid	Oxalic Acid	150.03			
Ethanol	Ethanol	070.05	S		
Ethanol Ethylene Diamine	Aminoethyl Ethanolamine	231.03		Yes	Rs
Ethanolamines, NOS	Ethanolamines, NOS	231.00		Yes	Rs

Common Name/Synonym	Primary Name	AOEC Code[1]	Use[2]	Asth-magen[3]	Asthma Detail[3]
Ethephon	Ethephon	291.12	P		
Ether	Ethyl Ether	100.05			
Ethidium Bromide	Ethidium Bromide	250.171			
Ethine	Acetylene	060.01			
Ethoxyethane	Ethyl Ether	100.05			
Ethyl 2-hydroxypropionate	Ethyl lactate	140.07			
Ethyl Acetate	Ethyl Acetate	141.03	S		
Ethyl acetone	Methyl Propyl Ketone	130.10			
Ethyl Acrylate	Ethyl Acrylate	142.05			
Ethyl Alcohol	Ethanol	070.05	S		
Ethyl Benzene	Ethyl Benzene	160.07	S		
Ethyl Chloride	Chloroethane	190.02	S		
Ethyl Ether	Ethyl Ether	100.05			
Ethyl lactate	Ethyl lactate	140.07			
Ethyl Methacrylate	Ethyl Methacrylate	142.03			R
Ethyl Methyl Ether	Ethyl Methyl Ether	100.06			
Ethyl Oxide	Ethyl Ether	100.05			
Ethyl Sulfate	Diethyl Sulfate	310.02			
Ethylene Chlorohydrin	Beta-Chloroethyl Alcohol	070.03			
Ethylene Dibromide	Ethylene Dibromide	191.01	P		
Ethylene Dichloride	Ethylene Dichloride	190.07	S		
Ethylene Glycol	Ethylene Glycol	080.011			
Ethylene Glycol Ethers, NOS	Ethylene Glycol Ethers, NOS	091.00	S		
Ethylene Glycol Monobutyl Ether	2-Butoxyethanol	091.03	S		R
Ethylene Glycol Monoethyl Ether	Ethylene Glycol Monoethyl Ether	091.02	S		
Ethylene Glycol Monomethyl Ether	Ethylene Glycol Monomethyl Ether	091.01	S		
Ethylene Oxide	Ethylene Oxide	110.03		Yes	Rr
Ethylenediamine	Ethylenediamine	232.01		Yes	Rs
Ethylenediamine Tetraacetic Acid	Ethylenediamine Tetraacetic Acid	232.08			
Ethylenimine	Ethylenimine	260.101			
Ethyne	Acetylene	060.01			
ETO	Ethylene Oxide	110.03		Yes	Rr
ETS	Cigarette Smoke	330.01			R
Eucalyptus Oil	Eucalyptus Oil	320.36			R
Eucalyptus Scent	Eucalyptus Oil	320.36			R
Eugenol	Eugenol	100.07		Yes	Rs
European Corn Borer	Ostrinia Nubilalis	382.24			R
Exercise	Exercise	360.06			
Exhaust, NOS	Exhaust, NOS	331.00			
Explosion	Explosion	353.02			
Extranase	Bromelain	324.07		Yes	Rs
Extremely Low Frequency Elctromagnetic Radiation	Radiation, Electromagnetic	352.01			
Fabric, NOS	Fabric, NOS	270.44			
Fall From Height	Fall, NOS	353.03			
Fall, NOS	Fall, NOS	353.03			
Fats	Oils, NOS	170.03			
FC 113	Trichlorotrifluoroethane	192.04			
FD&C Red No. 2	Amaranth	252.01			
Feldspar Dust	Feldspar Dust	010.131			
Fenamiphos	Nemacur	291.06	P		R
Fenthion	Fenthion	291.13	P	Yes	Rs
Fenugreek	Fenugreek	370.42		Yes	
Fernambouc	Fernambouc	373.16			R
Ferric Chloride	Ferric Chloride	020.201			
Fertilizers, NOS	Fertilizers, NOS	320.09			
Fiberglass	Fiberglass	010.091			
Fibrous Glass	Fiberglass	010.091			
Ficam	Ficam	292.03	P		

Common Name/Synonym	Primary Name	AOEC Code[1]	Use[2]	Asth-magen[3]	Asthma Detail[3]
Fingerprint Powder	Fingerprint Powder	320.34			
Fire Extinguisher Discharge	Fire Extinguisher Discharge	320.100			
Fire retardant	Halon	320.101			
Fish Feed	Fish Feed	381.09		Yes	R
Fixer	Photo Developing Chemicals, NOS	320.17			
Flaviastase	Flaviastase	324.06		Yes	Rs
Floor Finish	Floor Wax	322.35			
Floor Wax	Floor Wax	322.35			
Flour, NOS	Flour, NOS	371.00		Yes	G
Fluazinam	Fluazinam	320.082		Yes	Rs
Flumetsulam	N-(2,6-difluorophenyl)-5-methyl-(1,2,4) triazolo (1,5-a) pyrimidine-2-sulfonomide	320.131	P		
Fluorescent Lamp Phosphor	Fluorescent Lamp Phosphor	040.33			
Fluorine	Fluorine	030.03			R
Fluorocarbons, NOS	Fluorocarbons, NOS	192.00			
Fluosilicic Acid	Hydrofluosilicic Acid	050.44			
Fluxes, NOS	Fluxes, NOS	040.05			
Fly Ash	Fly Ash	010.07			
Forceful Movements, NOS	Forceful Movements, NOS	361.01			
Formaldehyde	Formaldehyde	120.03		Yes	G
Formalin	Formaldehyde	120.03		Yes	G
Formates, NOS	Formates, NOS	140.01			
Formic Acid	Formic Acid	150.01			
Fowl Mite	Fowl Mite	382.14		Yes	
Fraxinus Americana	Fraxinus Americana	373.17		Yes	Rs
Freesia	Freesia	370.30		Yes	
Freon, Heated	Freon, Heated	192.06		Yes	Rs
Freon, NOS	Freon, NOS	192.01			
Freon, Unheated	Freon, Unheated	192.07			
Frog	Frog	380.09		Yes	
Fruit Fly	Drosophila melanogaster	382.07		Yes	Rs
Fruit Juices	Fruit Juices	370.05			
Fulvin P/G	Griseofulvin	321.27			
Fumes, NOS	Smoke, NOS	330.03			
Fungal Amylase	Fungal Amylase	324.09		Yes	Rs
Fungal Amyloglucosidase	Amyloglucosidase	324.110		Yes	Rs
Fungal Hemicellulase	Fungal Hemicellulase	324.120		Yes	Rs
Fungi, NOS	Mold, NOS	391.01			R
Fungicide, NOS	Fungicide, NOS	320.08	P		
Furfural	Furfural	120.04			
Furfuryl Alcohol	Furfuryl Alcohol	070.090			R
Furfuryl alcohol mixed with a catalyst	Furfuryl alcohol mixed with a catalyst	070.092		Yes	Rs
Gabon Ebony	Ebony	373.20		Yes	Rs
Galleria Mellonella	Galleria Mellonella	382.05		Yes	Rs
Garlic Dust	Garlic Dust	370.21		Yes	
Garlon 4	Garlon 4	260.25	P		
Gas Metal Arc Welding on Uncoated Mild Steel	Gas Metal Arc Welding on Uncoated Mild Steel	023.07		Yes	Rs
Gasoline	Gasoline	061.04	S		
Gasoline Exhaust	Engine Exhaust	331.02			
Germanium	Germanium	020.171			
Germanium Compounds	Germanium Compounds	020.170			
Glacial Acetic Acid	Glacial Acetic Acid	050.34		Yes	Rrs
Glues, NOS	Glues, NOS	320.110			
Glutaraldehyde	Glutaraldehyde	120.051		Yes	Rs
Gluten	Gluten	371.02		Yes	G
Glyceryl Trinitrate	Nitroglycerin	261.01			
Glycol Compound and Benzyl Compound	Glycol Compound and Benzyl Compound	321.21		Yes	Rs
Glycol Ethers, NOS	Glycol Ethers, NOS	090.00	S		
Glycol Monoethyl Ether Acetate	2-Ethoxyethyl Acetate	141.05			

Common Name/Synonym	Primary Name	AOEC Code[1]	Use[2]	Asth-magen[3]	Asthma Detail[3]
Glyphosate	Glyphosate	320.132			
Gold	Gold	020.181			
Gold Compounds	Gold Compounds	020.180			
Gonystylus Bancanus	Gonystylus Bancanus	373.14		Yes	Rs
Grain Alcohol	Ethanol	070.05	S		
Grain Dust	Grain Dust	370.03		Yes	G
Grain Mite	Grain Mite	382.16		Yes	
Grain Parasite	Grain Mite	382.16		Yes	
Granite	Granite	011.01			
Granola, NOS	Granola, NOS	370.002			
Graphite	Graphite	010.08			
Grass Cuttings	Grass Cuttings	370.07			
Greases	Oils, NOS	170.03			
Greater wax moth	Galleria Mellonella	382.05		Yes	Rs
Green Beans	Green Beans	370.37		Yes	
Green Coffee Bean	Coffee Bean	370.12		Yes	G
Green Lacewing	Chrysoperla Carnea	382.22			R
Grinding Dust	Abrasives, NOS	010.01			
Gripping, Forceful	Gripping, Forceful	361.03			
Gris-PEG	Griseofulvin	321.27			
Grisactin-Ultra	Griseofulvin	321.27			
Griseofulvin	Griseofulvin	321.27			
Guaiacol	Guaiacol	100.09			
Guar	Guar	372.04		Yes	
Guayacan	Ipe	373.31		Yes	Rs
Guinea Pig Antigens	Guinea Pig Antigens	380.17		Yes	G
Gum Acacia	Gum Arabic	372.01		Yes	Rs
Gum Arabic	Gum Arabic	372.01		Yes	Rs
Gutta-percha	Gutta-percha	372.06		Yes	
Gypsophilia Paniculata	Baby's Breath	370.17		Yes	
Gypsum	Gypsum	010.171			
Gypsum, NOS	Gypsum, NOS	010.170			
H2S	Hydrogen Sulfide	040.06			
Habanolide	Habanolide	320.43			
Hair Products	Hair Products	320.12			
Hair Solutions	Hair Products	320.12			
Hair Spray	Hair Products	320.12			
Halon	Halon	320.101			
Halothane	Halothane	190.153			R
Halowax	Chlorinated Naphthalene	200.03			
Hand-Arm Posture	Posture, Upper Extremity	362.01			
Hand-Arm Vibration	Vibration, Regional	354.01			
Handroanthus excels	Ipe	373.31		Yes	Rs
Handwriting	Gripping, Forceful	361.03			
Haptachlorine	Heptachlor	280.08	P		
Hard Metal	Tungsten Compounds	020.52			
Hardwood, Tropical, NOS	Hardwood, Tropical, NOS	373.24			
Hay	Hay	370.08			
HBR	Hydrobromic Acid	050.09			
HCFC-225ca	3,3-Dichloro-1,1,1,2,2-pentafluoropropane	192.021			
HCFC-225cb	1,3-Dichloro-1,1,2,2,3-pentafluoropropane	192.022			
HCL	Hydrochloric Acid	050.10		Yes	Rr
HCN	Hydrogen Cyanide	211.01			
HDI	Hexamethylene Diisocyanate	221.04		Yes	G
HDI Prepolymers	Prepolymer of Hexamethylene diisocyanate	221.08		Yes	Rs
Heat	Heat	350.03			
Heat Shrink Wrapping	Heat Shrink Wrapping	326.02			R
Heated Electrostatic Polyester Paint	Polyethylene Terephthalate/Polybutylene Terephthalate	270.25		Yes	Rs

Common Name/Synonym	Primary Name	AOEC Code[1]	Use[2]	Asth-magen[3]	Asthma Detail[3]
Heated tape (140 C) containing dicumyl peroxide	Heated tape (140 C) containing dicumyl peroxide	050.142		Yes	Rs
Heavy Lifting	Lifting	361.02			
Heavy Metals, NOS	Heavy Metals, NOS	020.46			
Hemicellulase (from Aspergillus niger)	Hemicellulase (from Aspergillus niger)	324.121		Yes	Rs
Henna	Henna	370.27		Yes	
Hepatitis B	Hepatitis B	390.09			
Hepatitis C	Hepatitis C	390.12			
Heptachlor	Heptachlor	280.08	P		
Heptane	Heptane	060.03	S		
Herbal Tea, NOS	Herbal Tea, NOS	370.001			R
Herbicides, NOS	Herbicides, NOS	320.13	P		
Heroin	Diacetyl morphine	321.185		Yes	Rs
Hexachlorobenzene	Hexachlorobenzene	201.03	P		
Hexachlorophene	Hexachlorophene	181.02		Yes	Rs
Hexahydrophthalic Anhydride	Hexahydrophthalic Anhydride	151.08		Yes	Rs
Hexamethylene Diisocyanate	Hexamethylene Diisocyanate	221.04		Yes	G
Hexamethylenediamine	Hexamethylenediamine	232.10			R
Hexamethylenetetramine	Hexamethylenetetramine	232.02			R
Hexane	Hexane	060.02	S		
Hexone	Methyl Isobutyl Ketone	130.04	S		
Hexylene Glycol	Hexylene Glycol	080.03			
HF	Hydrofluoric Acid	050.11			
Hickory (Australian)	Australian Blackwood	373.27		Yes	Rs
High Force	Forceful Movements, NOS	361.01			
High Temperature	Heat	350.03			
Himic Anhydride	Himic Anhydride	151.07		Yes	Rs
Histoplasma Capsulatum	Histoplasma Capsulatum	390.03			
HIV Exposure	HIV Exposure	390.08			
Honeybee	Honeybee	382.08		Yes	
Hops	Hops	370.16		Yes	
Hot Liquid	Heat	350.03			
Hot Tub Fumes, NOS	Hot Tub Fumes, NOS	327.04			
Hoya	Sea Squirt (Halocynthia roretzi)	381.04			R
Humidity, High	Humidity, High	350.05			
Humidity, Low	Humidity, Low	350.04			
Hydralazine	Hydralazine	321.14		Yes	Rs
Hydrated Lime	Hydrated Lime	050.051			
Hydraulics	Lubricants, NOS	320.14			
Hydrazine	Hydrazine	260.110			
Hydrazine Derivatives	Hydrazine Derivatives	260.119			
Hydrazoic Acid	Hydrazoic Acid	050.08			
Hydrobromic Acid	Hydrobromic Acid	050.09			
Hydrocarbons, NOS	Hydrocarbons, NOS	170.00			
Hydrochloric Acid	Hydrochloric Acid	050.10		Yes	Rr
Hydrocodone	Hydrocodone	321.187		Yes	Rs
Hydrofluoric Acid	Hydrofluoric Acid	050.11			
Hydrofluosilicic Acid	Hydrofluosilicic Acid	050.44			
Hydrogen Bromide	Hydrobromic Acid	050.09			
Hydrogen Chloride	Hydrochloric Acid	050.10		Yes	Rr
Hydrogen Cyanide	Hydrogen Cyanide	211.01			
Hydrogen Fluoride	Hydrofluoric Acid	050.11			
Hydrogen gas	Hydrogen gas	040.36			
Hydrogen Peroxide	Hydrogen Peroxide	050.12			
Hydrogen Sulfate	Sulfuric Acid	050.24		Yes	Rr
Hydrogen Sulfide	Hydrogen Sulfide	040.06			
Hydroquinone	Hydroquinone	180.030			
Hydroxybenzene	Phenol	180.04			
Hypoxia	Hypoxia	353.04			

Common Name/Synonym	Primary Name	AOEC Code[1]	Use[2]	Asth-magen[3]	Asthma Detail[3]
ILA Soap	Cleaners, Solvent-Based	322.06	S		
Imbuia	Imbuia	373.26		Yes	Rs
Imidacloprid	Imidacloprid	320.451	P		
Imipenem	Imipenem	321.20			
Incense Smoke	Incense Smoke	330.07			
Incinerator Fume, NOS	Incinerator Fume, NOS	330.04			
Indium	Indium	020.191			
Indium Compounds	Indium Compounds	020.190			
Indoor Air Pollutants from Building Renovation	Indoor Air Pollutants from Building Renovation	320.33			
Infectious Agents, NOS	Infectious Agents, NOS	390.070			
Inflamen	Bromelain	324.07		Yes	Rs
Infrared Light	Infrared Light	352.05			
INH	Isonicotinic Acid Hydrazide	321.13		Yes	Rs
Inks containing 30% acrylic acid, 30% hydroxy-propanoic acid CAS# 79-33-4, 25% bronze po	Inks containing 30% acrylic acid, 30% hydroxy-propanoic acid CAS# 79-33-4, 25% bronze po	170.021		Yes	Rs
Inks, NOS	Inks, NOS	170.020			
Inorganic Acids, NOS	Acids, Bases, Oxidizers, NOS	050.00			
Inorganic Compounds, NOS	Inorganic Compounds, NOS	040.00			
Inorganic Dust, NOS	Dust, NOS	010.00			
Insect Bite, NOS	Insect Bite, NOS	382.21			
Insect, NOS	Insect, NOS	382.00			
Insecticides, NOS	Insecticides, NOS	320.450	P		
Iodine	Iodine	030.04			
Iodophors	Iodophors	322.05			
IPDI	Isophorone Diisocyanate	221.05		Yes	Rs
Ipe	Ipe	373.31		Yes	Rs
Ipecac	Ipecacuanha	321.16			R
Ipecacuanha	Ipecacuanha	321.16			R
IR	Infrared Light	352.05			
IR Light	Infrared Light	352.05			
Irgasan	5-chloro-2-(2,4-dichlorohydroxy) phenol	181.03		Yes	Rs
Iroko	Iroko	373.05		Yes	Rs
Iron	Iron	020.202			
Iron Compounds	Iron Compounds	020.200			
Irritant Gases, NOS	Irritant Gases, NOS	040.24			
Isoamyl Nitrite	Amyl Nitrite	260.27			
Isobutane	Isobutane	060.04			
Isocyanates, NOS	Isocyanates, NOS	220.00			
Isofenphos	Pyrfon	291.09	P		R
Isoflurane	Isoflurane	190.157		Yes	Rs
Isolyzer	Isolyzer	120.050		Yes	Rs
Isoniazid	Isonicotinic Acid Hydrazide	321.13		Yes	Rs
Isonicotinic Acid Hydrazide	Isonicotinic Acid Hydrazide	321.13		Yes	Rs
Isononanoyl Oxybenzene Sulfonate	Isononanoyl Oxybenzene Sulfonate	322.331			
Isooctane	Isooctane	060.12			
Isophorone diamine	Isophorone diamine	232.09			R
Isophorone Diisocyanate	Isophorone Diisocyanate	221.05		Yes	Rs
Isophthalic Acid Chloride	Isophthaloyl Chloride	200.05			
Isophthaloyl Chloride	Isophthaloyl Chloride	200.05			
Isopropanol	Isopropyl Alcohol	070.06	S		
Isopropyl Alcohol	Isopropyl Alcohol	070.06	S		
Isopropyl Nitrite	Isopropyl Nitrite	260.32			
Isopropylamine	Isopropylamine	230.03			
Jalapeno Pepper	Jalapeno Pepper	370.46			
Jet Exhaust	Jet Exhaust	331.03			
Jet Fuel	Jet Fuel	061.05	S		
Job Control	Stress	360.04			
Job Demand	Stress	360.04			
Joint replacement, elevated chromium	Joint replacement, elevated chromium	020.601			

Common Name/Synonym	Primary Name	AOEC Code[1]	Use[2]	Asth-magen[3]	Asthma Detail[3]
Joint replacement, elevated cobalt	Joint replacement, elevated cobalt	020.602			
Joint replacement, toxicity NOS	Joint replacement, toxicity NOS	020.600			
Juglans Olanchana	Juglans Olanchana	373.11		Yes	Rs
Kanechlor	Polychlorinated Biphenyls	200.07			
Kaolin	Clay	010.051			
Kapok	Kapok	370.43		Yes	
Karaya	Karaya	372.03		Yes	
Kejaat	Kejaat	373.12		Yes	Rs
Kerosene	Kerosene	061.031	S		
Kerosine	Kerosene	061.031	S		
Ketones, NOS	Ketones, NOS	130.00	S		
Kevlar	Poly (P-Phenylenediamine)	270.35			
Key Punching	Keyboard Use	360.02			
Keyboard and Mouse Use	Keyboard Use	360.02			
Keyboard Use	Keyboard Use	360.02			
Kiaat	Kejaat	373.12		Yes	Rs
Kneeling	Posture, Body - Static	362.02			
KOH	Potassium Hydroxide	050.17			
Kotibe	Kotibe	373.21			R
L. Caesar Larva	Lucilia Caesar Larva	382.19		Yes	Rs
L. Decemlineata	Leptinotarsa Decemlineata	382.23			R
Laboratory Animals, NOS (see specific animals)	Animal Material, NOS	380.00			R
Lacquer	Lacquer	171.07			
Lacquer Thinner	Thinner	171.02	S		
Lactase	Lactase	324.14			
lactic acid, ethyl ester	Ethyl lactate	140.07			
Lactoserum	Lactoserum	380.100		Yes	Rs
Lanasol Blue 3G	Lanasol Blue 3G	325.29			R
Lanasol Blue 3R	Lanasol Blue 3G	325.29			R
Lanasol Brown G	Lanasol Brown G	325.30			R
Lanasol Orange G	Lanasol Orange G	325.33			R
Lanasol Orange R	Lanasol Orange R	325.16			R
Lanasol Red 2G	Lanasol Red 2G	325.31			R
Lanasol Red 5B	Lanasol Red 5B	325.14			R
Lanasol Red B	Lanasol Red B	325.13			R
Lanasol Red G	Lanasol Red G	325.15			R
Lanasol Scarlet 2R	Lanasol Scarlet 2R	325.32			R
Lanasol Yellow 4G	Lanasol Yellow 4G	325.09		Yes	Rs
Lapacho	Ipe	373.31		Yes	Rs
Laser cutting, stainless	Laser cutting, stainless	023.011			
Lasers	Lasers	352.02			
Latex Gloves, NOS	Latex, Natural Rubber	270.02		Yes	G
Latex, Natural Rubber	Latex, Natural Rubber	270.02		Yes	G
Latex, Synthetic	Latex, Synthetic	270.030			
Lathyrus Sativus	Lathyrus Sativus	370.29		Yes	
Lauryl Dimethyl Benzyl Ammonium Chloride	Dodecyl-dimethyl-benzylammonium Chloride	322.3216		Yes	Rs
Leachate	Leachate	323.02			
Lead, Inorganic Compounds	Lead, Inorganic Compounds	020.210			
Lead, Metal	Lead, Metal	020.211			
Lead, Organic	Lead, Organic	020.221			
Lead, Organic Compounds	Lead, Organic Compounds	020.220			
Lead-based Paint	Lead-based Paint	020.212			
Leather Dust	Leather Dust	380.03			
Leptinotarsa Decemlineata	Leptinotarsa Decemlineata	382.23			R
Lesser Mealworm Beetle	Alphitobius diaperinus	382.09			R
Levafix Black 5-GA	Levafix Black 5-GA	325.18			R
Levafix Black EB	Remazol Black B	325.11			R
Levafix Black EG	Levafix Black EG	325.17			R

Common Name/Synonym	Primary Name	AOEC Code[1]	Use[2]	Asth-magen[3]	Asthma Detail[3]
Levafix Brilliant Blue K-BL	Drimaren Brilliant Blue K-BL	325.04		Yes	Rs
Levafix Brilliant Yellow E36	Levafix Brilliant Yellow E36	325.01		Yes	Rs
Levafix Golden Yellow E-3GA	Levafix Goldgelb E-3GA	325.20			R
Levafix Goldgelb E-3GA	Levafix Goldgelb E-3GA	325.20			R
Levafix Marinblau E-2BA	Levafix Marinblau E-2BA	325.19			R
Levafix Orange	Levafix Orange	325.12		Yes	Rs
Lifting	Lifting	361.02			
Lightning Powder	Fingerprint Powder	320.34			
Lightwood	Australian Blackwood	373.27		Yes	Rs
Lime	Calcium Oxide	050.050			
Lime Chloride	Calcium Hypochloride	322.13			
Limonene	Limonene	060.05	S		
Limonium Tataricum	Limonium Tataricum	370.38		Yes	
Lindane	Lindane	280.06	P		
Linseed Oil	Linseed Oil	060.15			
Linseed Oilcake	Linseed Oilcake	060.24		Yes	Rs
Lipase	Lipase	324.21		Yes	Rs
Lobster (Homarus and Nephrops genera)	Lobster (Homarus and Nephrops genera)	381.16		Yes	Rs
Local Vibration	Vibration, Regional	354.01			
Locust	Locust	382.02		Yes	
Losartan	Losartan	321.36			R
Low Temperature	Cold	350.02			
LPG	Propane	060.20			
Lubricants, NOS	Lubricants, NOS	320.14			
Lucilia Caesar Larva	Lucilia Caesar Larva	382.19		Yes	Rs
Lycopodium	Lycopodium	370.25		Yes	
Lye	Sodium Hydroxide	050.18			
Lysozyme	Lysozyme	324.08		Yes	Rs
m-Delphene	N,N-diethyl-m-toluamide	260.26	P		
Mace	Mace	320.27			
Magenta	Magenta	251.07			
Magnesium	Magnesium	020.231			
Magnesium Aluminum Silicate	Magnesium Aluminum Silicate	020.232			R
Magnesium Compounds	Magnesium Compounds	020.230			
Mahogany	Mahogany	373.07		Yes	Rs
Malathion	Malathion	291.01	P		R
Maleic Anhydride	Maleic Anhydride	151.02		Yes	Rs
Malt	Malt	370.56		Yes	Rs
Man-Made Mineral Fibers	Man-Made Mineral Fibers	010.092			
Man-Made Mineral Fibers, NOS	Man-Made Mineral Fibers, NOS	010.090			
Manganese	Manganese	020.241			
Manganese Compounds	Manganese Compounds	020.240			
Manure	Manure	380.02			
MAP	Ammonium Phosphate	040.32	P		
Marijuana dust	changed to 370.62	330.05			
Marijuana dust	Cannabis dust (marijuana and hemp)	370.620		Yes	Rs
Marijuana plant	Cannabis dust (marijuana and hemp)	370.620		Yes	Rs
Marijuana Smoke	Cannabis Smoke	330.05		Yes	Rs
Marinblau E-2BA	Levafix Marinblau E-2BA	325.19			R
Maxatase	Bacillus Subtilis Enzymes	324.010		Yes	Rs
MBK	Methyl N-Butyl Ketone	130.05	S		
MDA	Methylenedianiline	250.16			
MDI	Methylene Bisphenyl Diisocyanate	221.02		Yes	G
ME-MDA	4,4'-Methylenebis(2-Chloroaniline)	250.03			
Mechanical Pressure	Contact Pressure	360.01			
Med fly	Ceratitis capitata	382.30		Yes	Rs
Mediterranean flour moth	Ephestia Kuehniella	382.25		Yes	Rs
Mediterranean Fruit Fly	Ceratitis capitata	382.30		Yes	Rs

Common Name/Synonym	Primary Name	AOEC Code[1]	Use[2]	Asth-magen[3]	Asthma Detail[3]
MEK	Methyl Ethyl Ketone	130.03	S		
MEK Peroxide	MEK Peroxide	130.02			
Melamine	Melamine	260.28			
Menta Arvensis Piperadcens	Corn Mint Oil	320.47			R
Mental Factors	Stress	360.04			
Menthol	Menthol	370.61			R
Meongge	Sea Squirt (Halocynthia roretzi)	381.04			R
Mercaptans, NOS	Mercaptans, NOS	311.00			
Mercaptoethanol	Mercaptoethanol	310.04			
Mercaptopropionic Acid	3-mercaptopropionic Acid	310.12			
Mercuric Chloride	Mercuric Chloride	020.251			
Mercuric Salts	Mercuric Salts	020.252			
Mercury, Inorganic Compounds	Mercury, Inorganic Compounds	020.250			
Mercury, Organic	Mercury, Organic	020.261			
Mercury, Organic Compounds	Mercury, Organic Compounds	020.260			
Mesentericopeptidase	Esperase	324.10		Yes	Rs
Metal Carbonyls	Metal Carbonyls	020.44			
Metal Dust, NOS	Metal Dust, NOS	021.00			
Metal Fumes, NOS	Metal Fumes, NOS	020.00			
Metal Polish, Tarnish Remover, or Preventative	Metal Polish, Tarnish Remover, or Preventative	322.02			
Metal Working Fluids	Cutting Oils	170.01		Yes	G
Metallic Oxides, NOS	Metal Fumes, NOS	020.00			
Metals, NOS	Metals, NOS	020.47			
Metam Sodium	Sodium N-methyldithiocarbamate	292.01	P		
Methamidophos	Acephate	291.11	P		R
Methamphetamine Laboratory	Methamphetamine Laboratory	320.40			
Methane	Methane	060.06			
Methanol	Methanol	070.07	S		
Methaoxyethanol	Ethylene Glycol Monomethyl Ether	091.01	S		
Methoxychlor	Methoxychlor	280.07	P		
Methoxyflurane	Methoxyflurane	190.152			R
Methoxymethane	Ethyl Methyl Ether	100.06			
Methyl 2-Hydroxybenzoate Acrylate Acid	Methyl Salicylate	140.05			R
Methyl Alcohol	Methanol	070.07	S		
Methyl Blue	Methyl Blue	325.10		Yes	Rs
Methyl Bromide	Methyl Bromide	191.03	P		
Methyl Carbinol	Ethanol	070.05	S		
Methyl Cellosolve	Ethylene Glycol Monomethyl Ether	091.01	S		
Methyl Chloroform	Methyl Chloroform	190.08	S		
Methyl Dichlorosilane	Methyl Dichlorosilane	040.271			
Methyl Ester Isocyanic Acid	Methyl Isocyanate	220.01			
Methyl Ethyl Ketone	Methyl Ethyl Ketone	130.03	S		
Methyl Ethyl Ketone Peroxide	MEK Peroxide	130.02			
Methyl Isobutyl Ketone	Methyl Isobutyl Ketone	130.04	S		
Methyl Isocyanate	Methyl Isocyanate	220.01			
Methyl Isothiocyanate	Methyl Isothiocyanate	220.02	P		
Methyl Mercury due to Fish Consumption	Methyl Mercury, Organic	020.262			
Methyl Mercury, Organic	Methyl Mercury, Organic	020.262			
Methyl Methacrylate	Methyl Methacrylate	142.04		Yes	Rs
Methyl N-Butyl Ketone	Methyl N-Butyl Ketone	130.05	S		
Methyl Propyl Ketone	Methyl Propyl Ketone	130.10			
Methyl Pyrrolidone	Methyl Pyrrolidone	260.121			
Methyl Salicylate	Methyl Salicylate	140.05			R
Methyl Sulfoxide	Dimethyl Sulfoxide	310.14			
Methyl Tertiary Butyl Ether	Methyl Tertiary Butyl Ether	100.08			
Methyl Tetrahydrophthalic Anhydride	Methyl Tetrahydrophthalic Anhydride	151.05		Yes	Rs
Methyl-4-Isopropenyl Cyclohexene-1	Limonene	060.05	S		
Methylbenzene	Toluene	160.02	S		
Methylcatechol	Guaiacol	100.09			

Common Name/Synonym	Primary Name	AOEC Code[1]	Use[2]	Asthmagen[3]	Asthma Detail[3]
Methyldopa	Methyldopa	321.09		Yes	Rs
Methylene Bisphenyl Diisocyanate	Methylene Bisphenyl Diisocyanate	221.02		Yes	G
Methylene Chloride	Methylene Chloride	190.09	S		
Methylene Dichloride	Methylene Chloride	190.09	S		
Methylenedianiline	Methylenedianiline	250.16			
Methylphenol	Cresol	180.02			
Methylstyrene	Vinyl Toluene	160.08	S		
Methylthiomethane	Dimethyl sulfide	165.01			
Methylvinylbenzene	Vinyl Toluene	160.08	S		
Mexican Bean Weevil	Zabrotes subfasiatus	382.06		Yes	Rs
MGK 264	N-Octyl Bicycloheptene Dicarboximide	320.30	P		
MIBK	Methyl Isobutyl Ketone	130.04	S		
MIC	Methyl Isocyanate	220.01			
Mice	Mice	380.14		Yes	G
Micotil	Micotil	321.30			
Microberlinia brazzavillensis	Microberlinia brazzavillensis	373.13		Yes	Rs
Microorganisms, NOS	Microorganisms, NOS	390.00			
Mineral Naphtha	Benzene	160.01	S		
Mineral Oil	Mineral Oil	060.07			
Mineral Oil Mist	Mineral Oil	060.07			
Mineral Spirits	Petroleum Spirits	061.011	S		
Mineral Thinner	Naptha	061.012	S		
Mineral Turpentine	Naptha	061.012	S		
Mineral Wool	Rockwool	010.093			
MINT X Rodent repellant trash bags	MINT X Rodent repellant trash bags	320.50			R
Mites, NOS	Mites, NOS	382.13		Yes	G
Mitoxantrone	Mitoxantrone	321.011		Yes	Rs
Mixed DCB	Mixed DCB	201.011	P		
Mixture of Hydrogen Peroxide and Peroxyacetic Acid	Mixture of Hydrogen Peroxide and Peroxyacetic Acid	050.480		Yes	Rs
Mixture of Prepolymer of Polymethylene Polyphenylisocyanate (PPI) and 4,4'-Methylenediphen	Mixture of Prepolymer of Polymethylene Polyphenylisocyanate (PPI) and 4,4'-Methylenediphen	221.09		Yes	Rs
MMMF	Man-Made Mineral Fibers	010.092			
MMMF, NOS	Man-made Mineral Fibers, NOS	010.090			
MOCA	4,4'-Methylenebis(2-Chloroaniline)	250.03			
Moisture	Humidity, High	350.05			
Mold, NOS	Mold, NOS	391.01			R
Molybdenum	Molybdenum	020.271			
Molybdenum Compounds	Molybdenum Compounds	020.270			
Monoammonium Phosphate	Ammonium Phosphate	040.32	P		
Monobromomethane	Methyl Bromide	191.03	P		
Monochloroethane	Chloroethane	190.02	S		
Monochloroethylene	Vinyl Chloride Monomer	190.14			
Monoethanolamine	Monoethanolamine	231.01		Yes	Rs
Morphine	Morphine	321.181		Yes	Rs
Mosquito Bite	Insect Bite, NOS	382.21			
Motor Oil, Synthetic	Motor Oil, Synthetic	170.05			
Motor Vehicle Accident	Motor Vehicle Accident	353.05			
MPK	Methyl Propyl Ketone	130.10			
MTBE	Methyl Tertiary Butyl Ether	100.08			
Mubvamaropa	Kejaat	373.12		Yes	Rs
Mudgerabah	Australian Blackwood	373.27		Yes	Rs
Mukwa	Kejaat	373.12		Yes	Rs
Multiple Chemicals	Chemicals, NOS	320.06			
Multiple Solvents	Solvents, NOS	171.00	S		
Muramidase	Lysozyme	324.08		Yes	Rs
Muriatic Acid	Hydrochloric Acid	050.10		Yes	Rr
Mushrooms, NOS	Mushrooms, NOS	391.10			R
Mussels	Mussels	381.17			R

Common Name/Synonym	Primary Name	AOEC Code[1]	Use[2]	Asth-magen[3]	Asthma Detail[3]
Mustard Gas	Mustard Gas	190.16			
Mustargen	Mustargen HCL	321.28			
Mustargen HCL	Mustargen HCL	321.28			
Mycotoxins	Mycotoxins	391.090			
Mylar	Polyethylene Terephthalate	270.26			
Myrocarpus Fastigiatus	Cabreuva	373.23		Yes	Rs
N,N-diethyl-3-methyl-	N,N-diethyl-m-toluamide	260.26	P		
N,N-diethyl-m-toluamide	N,N-diethyl-m-toluamide	260.26	P		
N,N-Diethylethanamine	Triethylamine	230.05			
N,N-Dimethylacetamide	N,N-Dimethylacetamide	260.07			
N,N-Dimethylethanolamine	Dimethylethanolamine	231.042		Yes	Rs
N,N-Dimethylformamide	N,N-Dimethylformamide	260.08	S		
N,N-Dimethylnitrosamine	N-Nitrosodimethylamine	240.01			
N-(2,6-difluorophenyl)-5-methyl-(1,2,4) triazolo (1,5-a) pyrimidine-2-sulfonomide	N-(2,6-difluorophenyl)-5-methyl-(1,2,4) triazolo (1,5-a) pyrimidine-2-sulfonomide	320.131	P		
N-Amyl Acetate	Amyl Acetate	141.01			
N-Amyl Alcohol	Amyl Alcohol	070.02			
N-Butyl Acetate	Butyl Acetate	141.02	S		
N-Butyl Acrylate	Butyl Acrylate	142.02			R
N-Butyl Alcohol	N-Butyl Alcohol	070.04	S		
N-Butyl Mercaptan	N-Butyl Mercaptan	311.01			
N-Butylamine	N-Butylamine	230.01			
N-Chloropropane	Chloropropane	190.05	S		
N-Heptane	Heptane	060.03	S		
N-Hexane	Hexane	060.02	S		
N-Hexyl Acrylate	N-Hexyl Acrylate	142.12			
N-Methylmorpholine	N-Methylmorpholine	260.20			R
N-Nitrosodimethylamine	N-Nitrosodimethylamine	240.01			
N-Octyl Bicycloheptene Dicarboximide	N-Octyl Bicycloheptene Dicarboximide	320.30	P		
N-Pentane	Pentane	060.19	S		
N-Pentyl Acetate	Amyl Acetate	141.01			
n-propyl bromide	Bromopropane	190.18			
N2O	Nitrous Oxide	040.09			
NaClO	Sodium Hypochlorite	322.10		Yes	Rs
Nacre Dust	Nacre Dust	370.22			R
Nail Care Products	Nail Care Products	320.41			
NaOH	Sodium Hydroxide	050.18			
Naphtha	Naphtha	061.02	S		
Naphthalene	Naphthalene	160.05			
Naphthalene Diisocyanate	Naphthalene Diisocyanate	221.03		Yes	G
Naphthalin	Naphthalene	160.05			
Naptha	Naptha	061.012	S		
Natural Gas	Natural Gas	060.080			
Navy Blue HER	Navy Blue HER	325.21			R
NCR Paper	Carbonless Paper	320.05			
NDI	Naphthalene Diisocyanate	221.03		Yes	G
Nemacur	Nemacur	291.06	P		R
Neobalanocarpus heimii	Chengal	373.29		Yes	Rs
Neoprene	Neoprene	271.020			
Neosar	Cyclophosphamide	321.29			
Nerve Gas	Nerve Gas	291.04			
Nesorgordonia Papaverifera	Kotibe	373.21			R
Neurospora	Neurospora	390.11		Yes	Rs
New Carpet Odor	4-Phenylcyclohexene	060.11			
New Mexico range caterpillar	Hemileuca oliviae	382.20			R
New Mexico Range Moth Caterpillar	Hemileuca oliviae	382.20			R
Nickel	Nickel	020.281		Yes	Rs
Nickel Compounds	Nickel Compounds	020.280		Yes	Rs
Nicotine Sulfate	Nicotine Sulfate	260.13	P		

Common Name/Synonym	Primary Name	AOEC Code[1]	Use[2]	Asth-magen[3]	Asthma Detail[3]
Ninhydrin	Ninhydrin	320.25			
Nitramine	Tetryl	250.10			
Nitric Acid	Nitric Acid	050.13			
Nitric Oxide	Nitric Oxide	040.081			
Nitrobenzene	Nitrobenzene	250.04			
Nitrobenzol	Nitrobenzene	250.04			
Nitroethane	Nitroethane	260.142			
Nitrogen	Nitrogen	040.07			
Nitrogen chloride	Trichloramine	030.11		Yes	Rs
Nitrogen Dioxide	Nitrogen Dioxide	040.082			
Nitrogen Mustard Hydrochloride	Mustargen HCL	321.28			
Nitrogen Mustard, NOS	Nitrogen Mustard, NOS	050.061			
Nitrogen Oxide	Nitric Oxide	040.081			
Nitrogen Oxides, NOS	Nitrogen Oxides, NOS	040.080			
Nitroglycerin	Nitroglycerin	261.01			
Nitromethane	Nitromethane	260.143			
Nitroparaffins	Nitroparaffins	260.140			
Nitrophenol	Nitrophenol	250.11			
Nitrous Oxide	Nitrous Oxide	040.09			
NO	Nitric Oxide	040.081			
No. 1 Fuel Oil	Kerosene	061.031	S		
No. 2 Fuel Oil	No. 2 Fuel Oil	061.062	S		
NO2	Nitrogen Dioxide	040.082			
Noise	Noise	350.01			
Nonoxynol	Nonoxynol	320.461			
Nonylphenol polyethylene glycol ether	Nonylphenol polyethylene glycol ether	090.013			
Nuclear Reactor Release	Nuclear Reactor Release	351.02			
NuSpraylok	Glues, NOS	320.110			
Nylon	Nylon	270.17			
Nylon Flock	Nylon Flock	010.22			R
o-methoxyphenol	Guaiacol	100.09			
O. Nubilalis	Ostrinia Nubilalis	382.24			R
Oak	Quercus	373.06		Yes	Rs
Obuina	Palisandar	373.32		Yes	Rs
Octacide 264	N-Octyl Bicycloheptene Dicarboximide	320.30	P		
Octopus	Octopus	381.12		Yes	Rs
Odors	Odors	320.15			
Off gassing of fracking tanks	Off gassing of hydraulic fracturing holding tanks	170.09			
Off gassing of hydraulic fracturing holding tanks	Off gassing of hydraulic fracturing holding tanks	170.09			
Oil Dispersants, NOS	Oil Dispersants, NOS	320.193			
Oil Mist	Cutting Oils	170.01		Yes	G
Oil of Clove	Oil of Clove	160.06			
Oil of Mirbane	Nitrobenzene	250.04			
Oil of Wintergreen	Methyl Salicylate	140.05			R
Oil Orange SS	Oil Orange SS	252.02			
Oils, NOS	Oils, NOS	170.03			
Oils, Vegetable	Oils, Vegetable	370.34			
Omite	Propargite	310.060	P		
Omite Cr	Omite Cr	310.061	P		
OPA	Ortho-phthalaldehyde	120.10			R
Opiate Compounds	Opiate Compounds	321.180		Yes	Rs
Optigard	Optigard	142.13			
Orange 3R	Rifazol Brilliant Orange 3R	325.07		Yes	Rs
Orange HE 2G	Rifacion Orange HE 2G	325.05		Yes	Rs
Organic Chemicals, NOS	Hydrocarbons, NOS	170.00			
Organic Dusts, NOS	Organic Dusts, NOS	370.003			
Organic Phosphates, Nonpesticide	Organic Phosphates, Nonpesticide	300.00			
Organochlorine Insecticides, NOS	Organochlorine Pesticides, NOS	280.00	P		

Common Name/Synonym	Primary Name	AOEC Code[1]	Use[2]	Asth-magen[3]	Asthma Detail[3]
Organochlorine Pesticides, NOS	Organochlorine Pesticides, NOS	280.00	P		
Organophosphate Pesticides, NOS	Organophosphate Pesticides, NOS	291.00	P		R
Orthene	Acephate	291.11	P		R
Ortho-phthalaldehyde	Ortho-phthalaldehyde	120.10			R
Orthophenylphenol	Orthophenylphenol	180.07	P		R
Osmium	Osmium	020.291			
Osmium Compounds	Osmium Compounds	020.290			
Ostrinia Nubilalis	Ostrinia Nubilalis	382.24			R
Oxacyclohexedecen-2-one	Habanolide	320.43			
Oxalic Acid	Oxalic Acid	150.03			
Oxycide	Mixture of Hydrogen Peroxide and Peroxyacetic Acid	050.480		Yes	Rs
Oxycodone	Oxycodone	321.186		Yes	Rs
Oxygen Deficiency	Hypoxia	353.04			
Oxygen Propane Torch	Oxygen Propane Torch	023.012			
Oxygen, Liquid	Oxygen, Liquid	040.10			
Ozone	Ozone	040.11			
P-Dichlorobenzene	Dichlorobenzene	201.010	P		
P-Dihydroxybenzene	Hydroquinone	180.030			
P-Hydroxyphenol	Hydroquinone	180.030			
P-Mentha-1,8-Diene	Limonene	060.05	S		
PAH	Polycyclic Aromatic Hydrocarbons, NOS	161.00			
Paint Thinner	Thinner	171.02	S		
Paint, Acrylic	Acrylics	270.01			
Paint, Epoxy	Paint, Epoxy	110.05			
Paint, Latex	Paint, Latex	171.05			
Paint, NOS	Paint, NOS	171.01	S		
Paint, Oil-Based	Paint, Oil-Based	171.06			
Palisandar	Palisandar	373.32		Yes	Rs
Pancreatic amylase	alpha Amylase (pancreatic)	324.17		Yes	Rs
Pancreatin	Pancreatin	324.05		Yes	Rs
PAP	Para-Aminophenol	251.01			
Papain	Papain	324.03		Yes	Rs
Papaverine	Papaverine	321.184		Yes	Rs
Paper Dust	Paper Dust	370.010			
Paprika	Paprika	370.31		Yes	
Para-Aminophenol	Para-Aminophenol	251.01			
Paraffin	Paraffin	060.09			
Paraffin Oil	Mineral Oil	060.07			
Paraffin Wax	Paraffin	060.09			
Paraformaldehyde	Paraformaldehyde	120.06		Yes	G
Paraldehyde	Paraldehyde	120.07			
Paraquat	Paraquat	260.15	P		
Parasites, NOS	Parasites, NOS	382.17			
Parathion	Parathion	291.02	P		R
Pau Marfim	Pau Marfim	373.18		Yes	Rs
PCBs	Polychlorinated Biphenyls	200.07			
PCE	Perchlorethylene	190.10	S		
PCP	Pentachlorophenol	181.01			
PE, NOS	Polyethylene, NOS	270.06			
Pectin	Pectin	370.23		Yes	Rs
Pectinase	Pectinase	324.60		Yes	Rs
Penicillamine	Penicillamine	321.05		Yes	Rs
Penicillins	Penicillins	321.042		Yes	G
Penicillium	Penicillium	391.03		Yes	Rs
Pentachloronitrobenzene	Pentachloronitrobenzene	200.06	P		
Pentachlorophenol	Pentachlorophenol	181.01			
Pentaerythritol Tetrakis	3-mercaptopropionate	310.13			
Pentaerythritol Tetranitrate	Pentaerythritol Tetranitrate	261.02			

Common Name/Synonym	Primary Name	AOEC Code[1]	Use[2]	Asthmagen[3]	Asthma Detail[3]
Pentamidine	Pentamidine	321.23			
Pentane	Pentane	060.19	S		
Pepper Spray	Capsicum	370.35			
Peppermint (mentha piperita)	Menthol	370.61			R
Pepsin A	Pepsin A	324.040		Yes	G
Pepsin B (pig stomach)	Pepsin B (pig stomach)	324.041		Yes	Rs
Pepsin, NOS	Pepsin, NOS	324.04		Yes	G
Peptidase (from enterobacterium Serratia)	Peptidase (from enterobacterium Serratia)	324.18		Yes	Rs
Perc	Perchlorethylene	190.10	S		
Perchlorethylene	Perchlorethylene	190.10	S		
Perchlorobenzene Fungicide	Hexachlorobenzene	201.03	P		
Perchloroethylene	Perchlorethylene	190.10	S		
Perfume, NOS	Perfume, NOS	320.23			
Periplaneta americana (American cockroach)	Periplaneta americana (American cockroach)	382.281		Yes	Rs
Perlite	Perlite	010.15			
Peroxidase Catalyst	Peroxidase Catalyst	324.13			
Peroxide 2-Butanone	MEK Peroxide	130.02			
Peroxides	Peroxides	050.140			
Peroxyacetic Acid	Peroxyacetic Acid	050.42			R
Persulfate Salts	Persulfate Salts	040.26		Yes	G
Pesticides, NOS	Pesticides, NOS	320.16	P		
PETN	Pentaerythritol Tetranitrate	261.02			
Petrochemicals, NOS	Hydrocarbons, NOS	170.00			
Petrol	Gasoline	061.04	S		
Petrolatum Liquid	Mineral Oil	060.07			
Petroleum Distillates, NOS	Petroleum Fractions, NOS	061.00	S		
Petroleum Fractions, NOS	Petroleum Fractions, NOS	061.00	S		
Petroleum Naphtha	Naphtha	061.02	S		
Petroleum Spirits	Petroleum Spirits	061.011	S		
PFA	Polyfunctional aziridine	260.102		Yes	Rs
Pharmaceuticals, NOS	Pharmaceuticals, NOS	321.00			
Phenol	Phenol	180.04			
Phenol Formaldehyde Resin	Phenol Formaldehyde Resin	120.11		Yes	Rs
Phenolic Resins	Phenolics	270.04			
Phenolics	Phenolics	270.04			
Phenols, NOS	Phenols, NOS	180.00			
Phenyl Chloride	Chlorobenzene	201.04	S		
Phenylamine	Aniline	250.01			
Phenylene Diamine	Benzenediamine	251.060			R
Phenylglycine Acid Chloride	Phenylglycine Acid Chloride	321.07		Yes	Rs
Phenylmethane	Toluene	160.02	S		
Phosgene	Phosgene	040.12			
Phosphate Ester, NOS	Phosphate Ester, NOS	140.06			
Phosphine	Phosphine	040.13	P		
Phosphoric Acid	Phosphoric Acid	050.15			
Phosphorodithioic acid	Phosphorodithioic acid	291.15			
Phosphorodithoic acid	Phosphorodithoic acid	291.15			
Phosphorus Bromide	Phosphorus Bromide	050.32			
Phosphorus Pentasulfide	Phosphorus Pentasulfide	040.14			
Phosphorus Sulfide	Phosphorus Pentasulfide	040.14			
Phosphorus Tribromide	Phosphorus Bromide	050.32			
Phosphorus Trichloride	Phosphorus Trichloride	050.16			
Phostoxin	Aluminum Phosphide	040.31	P		
Photo Developer, Black & White	Photo Developer, Black & White	180.031			
Photo Developer, Color	Photo Developing Chemicals, NOS	320.17			
Photo Developing Chemicals, NOS	Photo Developing Chemicals, NOS	320.17			
Phthalate Ester	Phthalate Ester	140.04			
Phthalic Acid Anhydride	Phthalic Anhydride	151.01		Yes	Rs
Phthalic Aldehyde	Ortho-phthalaldehyde	120.10			R

Common Name/Synonym	Primary Name	AOEC Code[1]	Use[2]	Asthmagen[3]	Asthma Detail[3]
Phthalic Anhydride	Phthalic Anhydride	151.01		Yes	Rs
Phthaloyl Chloride	Isophthaloyl Chloride	200.05			
Physical Factors, NOS	Physical Factors, NOS	350.00			
Phytase	Phytase	324.23		Yes	Rs
Pianowood	Palisandar	373.32		Yes	Rs
Pickle Processing (Unknown Causal Agent)	Pickle Processing (Unknown Causal Agent)	326.01			
Picric Acid	Picric Acid	250.09			
Pig	Pig	380.08		Yes	
Pig stomach pepsin	New code 324.041	324.04			
Pigeon Droppings	Pigeon Droppings	380.21			
Pinching	Gripping, Forceful	361.03			
Pine Wood Dust	Pine Wood Dust	373.25			
Pinellia Ternata	Pinellia Ternata	370.40		Yes	
Piperacillin	Piperacillin	321.043		Yes	Rs
Piperazine	Piperazine	260.190		Yes	Rs
Piperazine Citrate	Piperazine Citrate	260.192		Yes	Rs
Piperazine Hydrochloride	Piperazine Hydrochloride	260.191		Yes	Rs
Piperonyl Butoxide	Piperonyl Butoxide	290.01	P		
Plant Material, NOS	Plant Material, NOS	370.004			
Plant Waste	Grass Cuttings	370.07			
Plasmopara	Plasmopara	391.05			
Plasmopara Viticola	Plasmopara	391.05			
Plaster	Plaster	010.10			
Plaster of Paris	Plaster of Paris	010.172			
Plastic Dust	Plastic Dust	010.143			
Plastic Smoke	Plastic Smoke	330.02			
Plasticizers	Plasticizers	270.13			
Plastics, NOS	Polymers, NOS	270.00			
Plastics, Pre-Polymer	Polymers, NOS	270.00			
Platinum	Platinum	020.301			
Platinum Compounds	Platinum Compounds	020.300			
Plexiglass	Polymethyl Methacrylate	142.11		Yes	Rs
Plexiglass Dust	New code is 142.11	270.18			
Plutonium	Plutonium	351.01			
PMMA	Polymethyl Methacrylate	142.11		Yes	Rs
PNA	Polycyclic Aromatic Hydrocarbons, NOS	161.00			
Poison Ivy	Poisonous Plants	370.06			
Poison Oak	Poisonous Plants	370.06			
Poison Sumac	Poisonous Plants	370.06			
Poisonous Plants	Poisonous Plants	370.06			
Pollen	Pollen	370.10			
Pollution from Acts of Terrorism/War	World Trade Center Pollution	320.39			
Poly (P-Phenylenediamine)	Poly (P-Phenylenediamine)	270.35			
Polyamide Fibers	Nylon Flock	010.22			R
Polyamine EPO 60	EPO 60	232.06		Yes	Rs
Polyamines, NOS	Polyamines, NOS	232.00			
Polybutadiene	Polybutadiene	270.42			
Polycarbamate	Polycarbamate	270.071			
Polychlorinated Biphenyls	Polychlorinated Biphenyls	200.07			
Polychlorobutadiene	Polychlorobutadiene	271.021			
Polychloroprene	Neoprene	271.020			
Polycyclic Aromatic Hydrocarbons, NOS	Polycyclic Aromatic Hydrocarbons, NOS	161.00			
Polydimethyl Siloxane	Polydimethyl Siloxane	270.031			
Polyester Resin	Polyester Resin	270.05			
Polyethylamine	Polyethylamine	230.07			
Polyethylene Glycol Stearates	Polyethylene Glycol Stearates	320.192			
Polyethylene Terephthalate	Polyethylene Terephthalate	270.26			
Polyethylene Terephthalate/Polybutylene Terephthalate	Polyethylene Terephthalate/Polybutylene Terephthalate	270.25		Yes	Rs

Common Name/Synonym	Primary Name	AOEC Code[1]	Use[2]	Asth-magen[3]	Asthma Detail[3]
Polyethylene, Heated	Polyethylene, Heated	270.31			R
Polyethylene, NOS	Polyethylene, NOS	270.06			
Polyethylene, Unheated	Polyethylene, Unheated	270.32			
Polyfunctional aziridine	Polyfunctional aziridine	260.102		Yes	Rs
Polyhexamethylene Biguanide	Polyhexamethylene Biguanide	260.29	P		
Polyimides	Polyimides	270.19			
Polymer Fume	Plastic Smoke	330.02			
Polymers, NOS	Polymers, NOS	270.00			
Polymethyl Methacrylate	Polymethyl Methacrylate	142.11		Yes	Rs
Polymethylene Polyphenylisocyanate	Polymethylene Polyphenylisocyanate	221.06		Yes	G
Polynuclear Aromatics	Polycyclic Aromatic Hydrocarbons, NOS	161.00			
Polypropylene, Heated	Polypropylene, Heated	270.33		Yes	Rs
Polypropylene, NOS	Polypropylene, NOS	270.24			
Polypropylene, Unheated	Polypropylene, Unheated	270.34			
Polystyrene	Polystyrene	270.20			
Polysulphide Polymer Adhesive	Polysulphide Polymer Adhesive	320.111			
Polytetrafluoroethylene	Polytetrafluoroethylene	270.12			
Polytetrafluoroethylene, Thermal Decomposition Products	Polytetrafluoroethylene, Thermal Decomposition Products	270.37			
Polyurethane	Polyurethane	270.079			
Polyurethane Coating	Polyurethane Coating	270.073			
Polyvinyl Alcohol	Polyvinyl Alcohol	270.08			
Polyvinyl Butyral Resins	Polyvinylbutyral	270.28			
Polyvinyl chloride (Fibrex)	Polyvinyl chloride (Fibrex)	270.093			
Polyvinyl Chloride (heated)	Polyvinyl Chloride (heated)	270.091		Yes	Rs
Polyvinyl Chloride (Non-heated)	Polyvinyl Chloride (Non-heated)	270.092		Yes	Rs
Polyvinyl Chloride Dust	Polyvinyl Chloride Dust	010.141			
Polyvinyl Chloride, Thermal Decomposition Products	Polyvinyl Chloride, Thermal Decomposition Products	270.38		Yes	Rs
Polyvinyl Pyrrolidone	Polyvinyl Pyrrolidone	270.14			
Polyvinylbutyral	Polyvinylbutyral	270.28			
Poppers	Amyl Nitrite	260.27			
Poppers	Isopropyl Nitrite	260.32			
Porcelain	Porcelain	010.11			
Portland Cement	Cement Dust	010.03			R
Posture, Body - Dynamic	Posture, Body - Dynamic	362.03			
Posture, Body - Static	Posture, Body - Static	362.02			
Posture, NOS	Posture, NOS	362.00			
Posture, Upper Extremity	Posture, Upper Extremity	362.01			
Potassium Aluminum Tetrafluoride (KALF4)	Potassium Aluminum Tetrafluoride (KALF4)	020.014		Yes	Rs
Potassium Bicarbonate	Potassium Bicarbonate	050.19			
Potassium Carbonate	Potassium Carbonate	050.41			
Potassium Chlorate	Potassium Chlorate	040.16			
Potassium Cyanide	Potassium Cyanide	211.02			
Potassium Dichromate	Potassium Dichromate	022.01			
Potassium Hydroxide	Potassium Hydroxide	050.17			
Potassium Nitrate	Potassium Nitrate	042.01			
Potassium Permanganate	Potassium Permanganate	050.39			
Potassium Salts, NOS	Potassium Salts, NOS	040.15			
Potroom exposures in primary aluminum production	Potroom exposures in primary aluminum production	020.013		Yes	Rs
Pouteria glomerata	Pouteria glomerata	373.08		Yes	Rs
Pouteria or Mukali	Aningre (Tanganyika)	373.10		Yes	Rs
Powdered baking ammonia	Ammonium bicarbonate	050.49			
PPI	Polymethylene Polyphenylisocyanate	221.06		Yes	G
Prawn	Prawn	381.03		Yes	G
Prepolymer of Hexamethylene diisocyanate	Prepolymer of Hexamethylene diisocyanate	221.08		Yes	Rs
Prepolymer of toluene diisocyanate	Prepolymer of toluene diisocyanate	221.07		Yes	Rs
Printing Chemicals, NOS	Printing Chemicals, NOS	320.29			
Producer Gas Residue	Polycyclic Aromatic Hydrocarbons, NOS	161.00			
Prolonged Position	Posture, Body - Static	362.02			

Common Name/Synonym	Primary Name	AOEC Code[1]	Use[2]	Asth-magen[3]	Asthma Detail[3]
Pronase	Pronase	324.24		Yes	Rs
Propane	Propane	060.20			
Propane Exhaust	Propane Exhaust	331.04			
Propanol	Isopropyl Alcohol	070.06	S		
Propargite	Propargite	310.060			
Propenamide	Acrylamide	260.02			
Propenenitrile	Acrylonitrile	210.02			
Propetamphos	Safrotin	291.08	P		R
Propionic Acid	Propionic Acid	310.15			
Propoxur	Propoxur	292.04	P		
Propyl Alcohol	Propyl Alcohol	070.08	S		
Propyl Hydride	Propane	060.20			
Propylene Dichloride	Propylene Dichloride	190.11	S		
Propylene Glycol Ethers	Propylene Glycol Ethers	090.012	S		
Propylene Oxide	Propylene Oxide	110.07			
Protease	Protease	324.011		Yes	Rs
Proteinase	Protease	324.011		Yes	Rs
Proteolytic Enzymes, NOS	Enzymes, NOS	324.00			
Protozoa Giardia	Protozoa Giardia	390.13			
Proventil	Salbutamol	321.31		Yes	Rs
Prunus africana	African Cherry	373.28		Yes	Rs
Psychological Factors	Stress	360.04			
Psyllium	Psyllium	321.08		Yes	Rs
Pteridine	Pteridine	250.20			
Pterocarpus Angolensis	Kejaat	373.12		Yes	Rs
PTFE	Polytetrafluoroethylene	270.12			
Pulling	Forceful Movements, NOS	361.01			
Pulp Mill Effluent	Pulp Mill Effluent	370.006			
Pushing	Forceful Movements, NOS	361.01			
PVA	Polyvinyl Alcohol	270.08			
PVC (heated)	Polyvinyl Chloride (heated)	270.091		Yes	Rs
PVC (Non-heated)	Polyvinyl Chloride (Non-heated)	270.092		Yes	Rs
PVC Dust	Polyvinyl Chloride Dust	010.141			
Pyrethrins	Pyrethrins	320.181	P		R
Pyrethroids	Pyrethroids	320.182	P		R
Pyrfon	Pyrfon	291.09	P		R
Pyridine	Pyridine	250.14			
Pyrogallic Acid	1,2,3-Trihydroxybenzene	180.06			
Pyrogallol	1,2,3-Trihydroxybenzene	180.06			
Pyromellitic Acid Dianhydride	Pyromellitic Dianhydride	151.04		Yes	Rs
Pyromellitic Dianhydride	Pyromellitic Dianhydride	151.04		Yes	Rs
Quartz Dust	Quartz Dust	010.132			
Quartz Surfacing Products	Engineered Stone Countertop Dust	010.136			
Quaternary Ammonium Compounds, NOS	Quaternary Ammonium Compounds, NOS	322.320			
Quercus	Quercus	373.06		Yes	Rs
Quicklime	Calcium Oxide	050.050			
Quillaja Bark	Quillaja Bark	373.15		Yes	Rs
Quinone	Quinone	180.05			
Rabbit Antigens	Rabbit Antigens	380.15		Yes	
Radiation, Electromagnetic	Radiation, Electromagnetic	352.01			
Radiation, Ionizing, NOS	Radiation, Ionizing, NOS	351.00			
Radiation, Microwave	Radiation, Microwave	352.03			
Radiation, Nonionizing, NOS	Radiation, Nonionizing, NOS	352.00			
Radiation, Ultraviolet	Radiation, Ultraviolet	352.04			
Radio Frequency Radiation	Radiation, Microwave	352.03			
Radiographic Fixative	Radiographic Fixative	320.32			R
Radioisotopes	Therapeutic Radiation	351.04			
Radon	Radon	351.03			
Ramin	Gonystylus Bancanus	373.14		Yes	Rs

Common Name/Synonym	Primary Name	AOEC Code[1]	Use[2]	Asth-magen[3]	Asthma Detail[3]
Raspberries	Fruit Juices	370.05			
Rat Antigens	Rat Antigens	380.18		Yes	G
Rat Feces	Rat Feces	380.20			
Reactice Red 78	Lanasol Scarlet 2R	325.32			R
Reactive Blue 114	Drimaren Brilliant Blue K-BL	325.04		Yes	Rs
Reactive Blue 171	Navy Blue HER	325.21			R
Reactive Blue 50	Lanasol Blue 3G	325.29			R
Reactive Brown 47	Lanasol Brown G	325.30			R
Reactive Dyes, NOS	Reactive Dyes, NOS	325.00			R
Reactive Orange 29	Lanasol Orange G	325.33			R
Reactive Orange 67	Levafix Goldgelb E-3GA	325.20			R
Reactive Orange 68	Lanasol Orange R	325.16			R
Reactive Orange 82	Remazol Brilliant Orange FR	325.26			R
Reactive Red 116	Lanasol Red 2G	325.31			R
Reactive Red 65	Lanasol Red B	325.13			R
Reactive Red 66	Lanasol Red 5B	325.14			R
Reactive Red 83	Lanasol Red G	325.15			R
Reactive Yellow 107	Remazol Gold Yellow RNL	325.25			R
Red BBN	Red BBN	325.22		Yes	Rs
Red HE 3B	Red HE 3B	325.23			R
Red Soft Coral (Dendronephthya nipponica)	Red Soft Coral (Dendronephthya nipponica)	381.05			R
Refined Petroleum Solvent	Refined Petroleum Solvent	061.013	S		
Refractory Ceramic Fiber	Refractory Ceramic Fiber	010.094			
Remazol Black B	Remazol Black B	325.11			R
Remazol Black GF	Remazol Black B	325.11			R
Remazol Black GR	Rifazol Black GR	325.08		Yes	Rs
Remazol Brilliant Orange 3R	Rifazol Brilliant Orange 3R	325.07		Yes	Rs
Remazol Brilliant Orange FR	Remazol Brilliant Orange FR	325.26			R
Remazol Brilliant Yellow 4GL	Remazol Brilliant Yellow 4GL	325.27			R
Remazol Gold Yellow RNL	Remazol Gold Yellow RNL	325.25			R
Remazol Marine Blue GG	Remazol Marine Blue GG	325.24			R
Remazol Navy Blue GG	Remazol Marine Blue GG	325.24			R
Rennet	Rennet	324.25		Yes	Rs
Repetitive Lifting	Lifting	361.02			
Repetitive Motion	Repetitive Motion	360.03			
Repetitive Trauma	Repetitive Motion	360.03			
Resin containing furfuryl alcohol	Resin containing furfuryl alcohol	070.091		Yes	Rs
Resin Systems, NOS	Resin Systems, NOS	270.150			
Resins, NOS	Resins, NOS	270.151			
Rhodium	Rhodium	020.53		Yes	Rs
Ribavirin	Ribavirin	321.32			
Rice Dust	Rice Dust	370.48		Yes	Rs
Rice Flour	Rice Flour	371.07			
Rifacion Orange HE 2G	Rifacion Orange HE 2G	325.05		Yes	Rs
Rifafix Yellow 3 RN	Rifafix Yellow 3 RN	325.06		Yes	Rs
Rifazol Black GR	Rifazol Black GR	325.08		Yes	Rs
Rifazol Brilliant Orange 3R	Rifazol Brilliant Orange 3R	325.07		Yes	Rs
Rizolipase	Lipase	324.21		Yes	Rs
Road Pitch	Asphalt	061.07			
Road Tar	Asphalt	061.07			
Rock, NOS	Rock, NOS	011.00			
Rockwool	Rockwool	010.093			
Roofing Tar	Asphalt	061.07			
Rose Hips	Rose Hips	370.19		Yes	
Rotating Shifts	Stress	360.04			
Round Up	Glyphosate	320.132			
Rubber Dust	Rubber Dust	010.142			
Rubber, NOS	Rubber, NOS	271.00			

Common Name/Synonym	Primary Name	AOEC Code[1]	Use[2]	Asth-magen[3]	Asthma Detail[3]
Rust Inhibitor	Rust Inhibitor	060.22			
Rye Dust	Rye Dust	370.49			
Rye Flour	Rye Flour	371.03		Yes	G
Saccharin	Saccharin	320.38			R
Safrotin	Safrotin	291.08	P		R
Salbutamol	Salbutamol	321.31		Yes	Rs
Salbutamol Intermediate	Glycol Compound and Benzyl Compound	321.21		Yes	Rs
Salicylate	Salicylic Acid	321.25			
Salicylic Acid	Salicylic Acid	321.25			
Sally Wattle	Australian Blackwood	373.27		Yes	Rs
Salmo salar	Salmon	381.13		Yes	Rs
Salmon	Salmon	381.13		Yes	Rs
SBR	Butadiene & Styrene	271.01			
Scallops (Pectinidae Family)	Scallops (Pectinidae Family)	381.18		Yes	Rs
Scopthalmus maximus	Turbot	381.14		Yes	Rs
Screw Worm Fly	Cochlomyia hominovorax	382.03		Yes	Rs
Scud Shrimp (Gammarus genus)	Scud Shrimp (Gammarus genus)	381.15		Yes	Rs
Sea Pineapple	Sea Squirt (Halocynthia roretzi)	381.04			R
Sea Squirt (Halocynthia roretzi)	Sea Squirt (Halocynthia roretzi)	381.04			R
Sec-Propyl Alcohol	Isopropyl Alcohol	070.06	S		
Selenium	Selenium	020.311			
Selenium Compounds	Selenium Compounds	020.310			
Senna	Senna Plant	321.19		Yes	Rs
Senna laxative	Senna laxative	321.191			R
Senna plant	Senna plant	321.19		Yes	Rs
Sequoia Sempervirens	California Redwood	373.02		Yes	Rs
Sericin	Sericin	370.26		Yes	Rs
Serralysin	Peptidase (from enterobacterium Serratia)	324.18		Yes	Rs
Sesame Seed Dust	Sesame Seed Dust	370.45			
Sevin	Carbaryl	292.02	P		
Sevoflurane	Sevoflurane	190.158		Yes	Rs
Sewage	Sewer Water	323.03			
Sewer Gas	Sewer Gas	040.061			
Sewer Water	Sewer Water	323.03			
Shale	Shale	061.08			
Shark Cartilage	Shark Cartilage	381.11			R
Sharps	HIV Exposure	390.08			
Sheep Blowfly	Sheep Blowfly	382.12		Yes	Rs
Shellfish	Shellfish	381.01			
shrimp meal (Artemia genus)	shrimp meal (Artemia genus)	381.070		Yes	Rs
Shrimp/Prawns (Decapoda order)	Shrimp/Prawns (Decapoda order)	381.071		Yes	Rs
Sick Building	Air Pollutants, Indoor	320.01			
Silage Microorganisms, NOS	Silage Microorganisms, NOS	391.11			
Silica Flour	Quartz Dust	010.132			
Silica Sand	Silica, Cystalline	010.133			
Silica, Amorphous	Silica, Amorphous	010.12			
Silica, Crystalline	Silica, Crystalline	010.133			
Silica, Crystalline, NOS	Silica, Crystalline, NOS	010.130			
Silica, Vitreous	Silica, Vitreous	010.135			
Silicon Carbide	Silicon Carbide	010.18			
Silicon Dioxide	Silica, Crystalline	010.133			
Silicone	Silicone	270.10			
Silicone Fluid	Silicone	270.10			
Silicone Rubber	Silicone	270.10			
Silkworm	Bombyx mori	382.01		Yes	Rs
Silkworm Larva	Bombyx mori	382.01		Yes	Rs
Siloxanes	Silicone	270.10			
Silver	Silver	020.321			

Common Name/Synonym	Primary Name	AOEC Code[1]	Use[2]	Asth-magen[3]	Asthma Detail[3]
Silver Compounds	Silver Compounds	020.320			
Silver Sulfate	Silver Sulfate	020.322			
Sitting	Posture, Body - Static	362.02			
Skin Contact	Contact Pressure	360.01			
Slime Mold	Slime Mold	391.06			
Slime Mold Dictyostelium Discoideum	Slime Mold	391.06			
Slip, Trip, or Fall on Same Level	Fall, NOS	353.03			
Smoke Inhalation	Smoke, NOS	330.03			
Smoke, Lead-Containing	Smoke, Lead-Containing	330.06			
Smoke, NOS	Smoke, NOS	330.03			
Snake Bite	Venom	380.05			
Snappers	Amyl Nitrite	260.27			
SO2	Sulfur Dioxide	040.201			
Soap, excluding Laundry Soap/Detergent	Soap, excluding Laundry Soap/Detergent	322.01			
Soapbark	Quillaja Bark	373.15		Yes	Rs
Soda Ash	Soda Ash	050.211			
Sodium Azide	Sodium Azide	211.04			
Sodium Benzoate	Sodium Benzoate	050.31			
Sodium Bisulfate	Sodium Bisulfate	050.40			
Sodium Bisulfite	Sodium Bisulfite	040.18			
Sodium Borohydride	Sodium Borohydride	040.29			
Sodium Carbonate	Sodium Carbonate	050.210			
Sodium Carboxymethyl Cellulose	Sodium Carboxymethyl Cellulose	270.11			
Sodium Caseinate	Casein	380.11		Yes	Rs
Sodium Chloride	Sodium Chloride	041.02			
Sodium Chlorite	Sodium Chlorite	030.08			
Sodium Cyanide	Sodium Cyanide	211.03			
Sodium Dichromate	Sodium Dichromate	022.03			
Sodium dioxide	Sodium dioxide	050.451			
Sodium dithionite	Sodium hydrosulfite	040.37			
Sodium hydrosulfite	Sodium hydrosulfite	040.37			
Sodium Hydroxide	Sodium Hydroxide	050.18			
Sodium Hypochlorite	Sodium Hypochlorite	322.10		Yes	Rs
Sodium Metabisulfite	Sodium Metabisulfite	040.28		Yes	Rs
Sodium Metasilicate	Sodium Metasilicate	050.22			
Sodium N-methyldithiocarbamate	Sodium N-methyldithiocarbamate	292.01	P		
Sodium Nitrate	Sodium Nitrate	042.02			
Sodium Oxide	Sodium Oxide	050.450			
Sodium Salts, NOS	Sodium Salts, NOS	040.17			
Sodium Silicate	Sodium Silicate	050.23			
Sodium Sulfide	Sodium Sulfide	040.19			
Sodium Sulfite	Sodium Bisulfite	040.18			
Sodium Tripolyphosphate	Sodium Tripolyphosphate	050.38			
Soldering flux (heated) Alkyl Aryl Polyether Alcohol/Polypropylene Glycol Mixt.	Soldering flux (heated) Alkyl Aryl Polyether Alcohol/Polypropylene Glycol	070.10		Yes	Rs
Soldering Flux (heated) Zinc Chloride/Ammonium Chloride	Soldering Flux (heated) Zinc Chloride/Ammonium Chloride	023.08		Yes	Rs
Soldering Flux, NOS	Soldering Flux, NOS	023.04			
Soldering, NOS	Soldering, NOS	023.10			
Soluble Halogenated Platinum Compounds, NOS	Soluble Halogenated Platinum Compounds, NOS	024.00		Yes	G
Solvent Naphtha	Naptha	061.012	S		
Solvents, NOS	Solvents, NOS	171.00	S		
Sour gas	Sour gas	060.081			
Soya Flour	Soya Flour	371.05		Yes	G
Soybean Lecithin	Soybean Lecithin	370.41		Yes	
Soybean Lectin	Soybean Lecithin	370.41		Yes	
Spider Bite	Insect Bite, NOS	382.21			
Spiramycin	Spiramycin	321.10		Yes	Rs
Spirits of Turpentine	Turpentine	060.10	S	Yes	Rs
Squid (Loligo vulgaris)	Squid (Loligo vulgaris)	381.19		Yes	Rs

Common Name/Synonym	Primary Name	AOEC Code[1]	Use[2]	Asth-magen[3]	Asthma Detail[3]
Stachybotrys	Stachybotrys	391.07			
Standing	Posture, Body - Static	362.02			
Staph Aureus	Staph Aureus	390.071			
Steam	Heat	350.03			
Stearic Acid	Stearic Acid	150.05			
Stibine	Antimony Hydride	020.04			
Stick Welding	Stick Welding	023.09			
Stoddard Solvent	Stoddard Solvent	061.014	S		
Stooping	Posture, Body - Dynamic	362.03			
Stress	Stress	360.04			
Stripper	Stripper	171.03	S		
Strontium	Strontium	020.501			
Strontium Compounds	Strontium Compounds	020.500			
Struck Against/Struck By Objects or Persons	Struck Against/Struck By Objects or Persons	353.09			
Struck by Falling Object	Struck by Falling Object	353.08			
Struck by Motor Vehicle (Road)	Struck by Motor Vehicle (Road)	353.06			
Struck by Vehicle or Equipment (Non-road)	Struck by Vehicle or Equipment (Non-road)	353.07			
Struck By/Against Object as Result of Fall	Fall, NOS	353.03			
Strychnine	Strychnine	260.16	P		
Styrene	Styrene	160.04	S	Yes	Rs
Styrene Monomer	Styrene	160.04	S	Yes	Rs
Styrene-Butadiene Copolymer	Butadiene & Styrene	271.01			
Styrene-Maleic Anhydride Polymer	Styrene-Maleic Anhydride Resin	270.23			
Styrene-Maleic Anhydride Resin	Styrene-Maleic Anhydride Resin	270.23			
Subtilisin	Bacillus Subtilis Enzymes	324.010			
Suffocation	Hypoxia	353.04			
Sulfites, NOS	Sulfites, NOS	310.10			
Sulfonates, NOS	Sulfonates, NOS	322.330			
Sulfur Chloride	Sulfur Chloride	040.22			
Sulfur Dioxide	Sulfur Dioxide	040.201			
Sulfur Gas	Sulfur Gas	040.21			
Sulfur Hydrocarbons, NOS	Sulfur Hydrocarbons, NOS	165.00			
Sulfur Monochloride	Sulfur Chloride	040.22			
Sulfur Oxides, NOS	Sulfur Oxides, NOS	040.200			
Sulfur, Elemental	Sulfur, Elemental	010.21	P		
Sulfuric Acid	Sulfuric Acid	050.24		Yes	Rr
Sulfuric Acid Diethyl Ester	Diethyl Sulfate	310.02			
Sulfuric Acid Dimethyl Ester	Dimethyl Sulfate	310.03			
Sunflower	Sunflower	370.20		Yes	
Surfactant-Specific amines	Surfactant-Specific amines	320.191		Yes	Rs
Surfactants, NOS	Surfactants, NOS	320.190			
Swietenia macrophylla	Mahogany	373.07		Yes	Rs
Takian Chan	Chengal	373.29		Yes	Rs
Takian Chantamaeo	Chengal	373.29		Yes	Rs
Talc	Talc	012.00			
Talc, Fibrous	Talc, Fibrous	012.01			
Talc, Nonasbestiform	Talc, Nonasbestiform	012.02			
Tall Oil, Crude	Tall Oil, Crude	110.041		Yes	Rs
Tall Oil, Fatty Acids	Tall Oil, Fatty Acids	110.043			R
Tall Oil, Rosin	Tall Oil, Rosin	110.042		Yes	Rs
Tannic Acid	Tannic Acid	150.06			
Tar Camphor	Naphthalene	160.05			
Tartaric Acid	Tartaric Acid	150.07			
Tasmanian Blackwood	Australian Blackwood	373.27		Yes	Rs
TCE	Trichloroethylene	190.13	S		
TDI	Toluene Diisocyanate	221.01		Yes	G
TDI Prepolymers	Prepolymer of toluene diisocyanate	221.07		Yes	Rs
Tea	Tea	370.14		Yes	Rs

Common Name/Synonym	Primary Name	AOEC Code[1]	Use[2]	Asth-magen[3]	Asthma Detail[3]
Tear Gas	Mace	320.27			
Teflon	Polytetrafluoroethylene	270.12			
Teflon, Thermal Decomposition Products	Polytetrafluoroethylene, Thermal Decomposition Products	270.37			
Tellurium	Tellurium	020.331			
Tellurium Compounds	Tellurium Compounds	020.330			
Tenebrio molitor (Mealworm beetle)	Tenebrio molitor (Mealworm beetle)	382.32		Yes	Rs
Terpene	Terpene	060.17	S		R
Terra Cotta	Terra Cotta	010.052			
Tetrachloro-Isophthalonitrile	Chlorothalonil	210.03	P	Yes	Rs
Tetrachloroethylene	Perchlorethylene	190.10	S		
Tetrachloromethane	Carbon Tetrachloride	190.01	S		
Tetrachlorophthalic Anhydride	Tetrachlorophthalic Anhydride	151.06		Yes	Rs
Tetracycline	Tetracycline	321.12		Yes	Rs
Tetraethyl Lead	Tetraethyl Lead	020.222			
Tetrahydrofuran	Tetrahydrofuran	060.16			
Tetramethrin	Tetramethrin	320.183	P	Yes	Rs
Tetrazene	Tetrazene	260.22		Yes	Rs
Tetryl	Tetryl	250.10			
Textile Dust, NOS	Textile Dust, NOS	320.22			
Thallium Compounds	Thallium Salts	040.23	P		
Thallium Salts	Thallium Salts	040.23	P		
Thapsia Garganica L	Thapsigargin	370.33			
Thapsigargin	Thapsigargin	370.33			
Theatrical Fog, Glycol-Based	Theatrical Fog, Glycol-Based	320.21			
Theatrical Fog, NOS	Theatrical Fog, NOS	320.20			
Thebaine	Thebaine	321.183		Yes	Rs
Theophylline	Theophylline	321.24			
Therapeutic Radiation	Therapeutic Radiation	351.04			
Thermal cutting of stainless steel	Thermal cutting of stainless steel	023.011			
Thermal Energy	Heat	350.03			
Thermophilic Actinomyces	Thermophilic Actinomyces	390.05			
Thiamine	Thiamine	370.60		Yes	Rs
Thinner	Thinner	171.02	S		
Thioglycol	Mercaptoethanol	310.04			
Thiophosphoric Anhydride	Phosphorus Pentasulfide	040.14			
Thiourea	Thiourea	310.070			
Thiram	Thiuram	310.08			
Thiuram	Thiuram	310.08			
Thorium	Thorium	020.341			
Thorium Compounds	Thorium Compounds	020.340			
THU	Thiourea	310.070			
Thuja Occidentalis	Eastern White Cedar	373.19		Yes	G
Thuja Plicata	Western Red Cedar	373.01		Yes	G
Thyme	Thyme	370.007		Yes	Rs
Thymol	Thymol	370.005			R
Thymus Vulgaris	Thyme	370.007		Yes	Rs
Tilmicosin Phosphate	Micotil	321.30			
Tin, Inorganic	Tin, Inorganic	020.351			
Tin, Inorganic Compounds	Tin, Inorganic Compounds	020.350			
Tin, Organic	Tin, Organic	020.361			R
Tin, Organic Compounds	Tin, Organic Compounds	020.360			R
Titanium	Titanium	020.481			
Titanium Compounds	Titanium Compounds	020.480			
TMA	Trimellitic Anhydride	151.03		Yes	Rs
TMPTA	Trimethylolpropane Triacrylate	142.08			
TNT	Trinitrotoluene	250.08			
Tobacco Leaf	Tobacco Leaf	370.15		Yes	G
Toluene	Toluene	160.02	S		
Toluene Diisocyanate	Toluene Diisocyanate	221.01		Yes	G

Common Name/Synonym	Primary Name	AOEC Code[1]	Use[2]	Asth-magen[3]	Asthma Detail[3]
Toluene-2,4-Diisocyanate	Toluene Diisocyanate	221.01		Yes	G
Toluol	Toluene	160.02	S		
Tomato	Tomato	370.55			R
Toner, Copier	Toner, Copier	010.040			
Tooth Enamel Dust	Tooth Enamel Dust	010.19			R
Tosyalate dihydrate	Tosyalate dihydrate	321.069			R
Tragacanth	Tragacanth	372.02		Yes	
Transmission Fluid	Lubricants, NOS	320.14			
Trauma, Acute, NOS	Trauma, Acute, NOS	353.00			
Traumanase	Bromelain	324.07		Yes	Rs
Trental	Trental	321.22			
Triazines, NOS	Triazines, NOS	260.17	P		
Tributyl Tin Oxide	Tributyl Tin Oxide	020.363	P	Yes	Rs
Trichloramine	Trichloramine	030.11		Yes	Rs
Trichloroacetic Acid	Trichloroacetic Acid	050.43			
Trichloroethylene	Trichloroethylene	190.13	S		
Trichloromethane	Chloroform	190.03			
Trichloronitromethane	Chloropicrin	260.06	P		
Trichlorotrifluoroethane	Trichlorotrifluoroethane	192.04			
Trichoderma	Trichoderma	391.08			
Trichoderma Koningii	Trichoderma	391.08			
Triclosan	5-chloro-2-(2,4-dichlorohydroxy) phenol	181.03		Yes	Rs
Tricresyl phosphate	Tricresyl phosphate	291.14			
Triethanolamine	Triethanolamine	231.02		Yes	Rs
Triethylamine	Triethylamine	230.05			
Triethylenetetramine	Triethylenetetramine	232.03		Yes	Rs
Trifluoroacetic Acid	Trifluoroacetic Acid	050.37			
Trifluorotrichloroethane	Trichlorotrifluoroethane	192.04			
Triglycidyl Isocyanurate	Triglycidyl Isocyanurate	270.41		Yes	Rs
Trimellitic Anhydride	Trimellitic Anhydride	151.03		Yes	Rs
Trimethylhexane-1,6-diamine/Isophorondiamine Mixture	Trimethylhexane-1,6-diamine/Isophorondiamine Mixture	232.04		Yes	Rs
Trimethylhexanediamine/Isophorondiamine Mixture	Trimethylhexane-1,6-diamine/Isophorondiamine Mixture	232.04		Yes	Rs
Trimethylolpropane Triacrylate	Trimethylolpropane Triacrylate	142.08			
Trimethylolpropane Triacrylate/2-Hydroxypropyl Acrylate	Trimethylolpropane Triacrylate/2-Hydroxypropyl Acrylate	142.10		Yes	Rs
Trinitroglycerin	Nitroglycerin	261.01			
Trinitrotoluene	Trinitrotoluene	250.08			
Trinitrotoluol	Trinitrotoluene	250.08			
Triplochiton Scleroxylon	Triplochiton Scleroxylon	373.09		Yes	Rs
Tris	Tris	300.01			
Tris 2,3-Dibromopropyl Phosphate	Tris	300.01			
Trisodium Phosphate	Trisodium Phosphate	050.20			
Trout	Trout	381.08		Yes	Rs
Trypsin	Trypsin	324.02		Yes	Rs
Tuberculosis	Tuberculosis	390.10			
Tungsten Carbide	Tungsten Carbide	020.37		Yes	Rs
Tungsten Carbide/Cobalt	Tungsten Carbide/Cobalt	020.451		Yes	Rs
Tungsten Compounds	Tungsten Compounds	020.52			
Turbot	Turbot	381.14		Yes	Rs
Turpentine	Turpentine	060.10	S	Yes	Rs
Twisting	Posture, Body - Dynamic	362.03			
Tylosin Tartrate	Tylosin Tartrate	321.15		Yes	Rs
Typewriter	Keyboard Use	360.02			
Typing	Keyboard Use	360.02			
Ultrasound	Ultrasound	350.06			
Unspecified Solvents	Solvents, NOS	171.00	S		
Upper Extremity Awkward Positions	Posture, Upper Extremity	362.01			
Uranium	Uranium	351.05			
Urea Formaldehyde	Urea Formaldehyde	270.160			R

Common Name/Synonym	Primary Name	AOEC Code[1]	Use[2]	Asth-magen[3]	Asthma Detail[3]
Urea Formaldehyde Resin	Urea Formaldehyde Resin	270.161		Yes	Rs
Urethane	Urethane	270.070			
Urethane Enamel Paint	Urethane Enamel Paint	270.072			
UV Light	Radiation, Ultraviolet	352.04			
UV Radiation	Radiation, Ultraviolet	352.04			
Vanadium	Vanadium	020.381			
Vanadium Compounds	Vanadium Compounds	020.380			
Vanadium Hydroxide Oxide Phosphate	Vanadium Hydroxide Oxide Phosphate	040.30			
Vancomycin	Vancomycin	321.33		Yes	Rs
Vapam	Sodium N-methyldithiocarbamate	292.01	P		
Vaping emissions	Electronic cigarette emissions	320.49			
Varethane Paint	Polyurethane Coating	270.073			
Varnish	Lacquer	171.07			
Varnish Makers' & Painters' Naphtha	Naptha	061.012	S		
Varsol	Naptha	061.012	S		
VDT Keyboard	Keyboard Use	360.02			
VDT Radiation	Radiation, Electromagnetic	352.01			
VDT Screen/Visual	VDT Screen/Visual	360.05			
VDT Typing	Keyboard Use	360.02			
Vegetable Dust	Vegetable Dust	370.04			
Vegetable Juices	Fruit Juices	370.05			
Velcorin	Dimethyl dicarbonate	040.35			
Venom	Venom	380.05			
Ventilation, Inadequate	Air Pollutants, Indoor	320.01			
Vermiculite	Vermiculite	010.20			
Vetch	Vicia Sativa	370.11		Yes	
Vibration, NOS	Vibration, NOS	354.00			
Vibration, Regional	Vibration, Regional	354.01			
Vibration, Whole Body	Vibration, Whole Body	354.02			
Vicia Sativa	Vicia Sativa	370.11		Yes	
Vinegar	Vinegar	050.46			R
Vinyl Acetate	Vinyl Acetate	141.04			
Vinyl Carbinol	Allyl Alcohol	070.01			
Vinyl Chloride Monomer	Vinyl Chloride Monomer	190.14			
Vinyl Cyanide	Acrylonitrile	210.02			
Vinyl Dust	Polyvinyl Chloride Dust	010.141			
Vinyl Fumes	Plastic Smoke	330.02			
Vinyl Monomer	Vinyl Chloride Monomer	190.14			
Vinyl Plastic Wrap	Vinyl Plastic Wrap	270.27			
Vinyl Toluene	Vinyl Toluene	160.08	S		
Vinyl Trichloride	1,1,2-Trichloroethane	190.12	S		
Vinyl, NOS	Vinyl, NOS	010.140			
Vinylbenzene	Styrene	160.04	S	Yes	Rs
Violence, Other than Physical Assault	Violence, Other than Physical Assault	353.13			
Violence, Physical Assault	Assault, Physical	353.12			
Virazole	Ribavirin	321.32			
Viruses	Infectious Agents, NOS	390.070			
VM & P Naphtha	Naptha	061.012	S		
VOC, NOS	Hydrocarbons, NOS	170.00			
Walking	Walking	360.08			
Waste water treatment chemicals	Waste water treatment chemicals	050.47			
Waste, Hazardous	Waste, Hazardous	323.01			
Waste, Hazardous Acid	Waste, Hazardous	323.01			
Waste, NOS	Waste, NOS	323.00			
Waste, Treated Human Sludge	Waste, Treated Human Sludge	323.04			
Water Chlorination Byproducts	Water Chlorination Byproducts	327.01			
Water Contamination, Inorganic	Water Contamination, Inorganic	327.02			
Water Contamination, NOS	Water Contamination, NOS	327.00			

Common Name/Synonym	Primary Name	AOEC Code[1]	Use[2]	Asth-magen[3]	Asthma Detail[3]
Water Contamination, Organic	Water Contamination, Organic	327.03			
Water Flea	Daphnia	382.10			R
Waxes, NOS	Waxes, NOS	170.06			
Weeping Fig	Weeping Fig	370.24		Yes	
Welding Freon	Freon, Heated	192.06		Yes	Rs
Welding Fume, Copper/Nickel	Welding Fume, Copper/Nickel	023.03			
Welding Fume, Galvanized Metal	Welding Fume, Galvanized Metal	023.06			
Welding Fume, Iron or Steel	Welding Fume, Iron or Steel	023.02			
Welding Fume, NOS	Welding Fume, NOS	023.000			
Welding Fume, Stainless Steel	Welding Fume, Stainless Steel	023.010		Yes	G
Welding, NOS	Welding, NOS	023.001			
West African Ebony	Ebony	373.20		Yes	Rs
Western Red Cedar	Western Red Cedar	373.01		Yes	G
Wet Weather	Humidity, High	350.05			
Wheat Dust	Wheat Dust	370.50			
Wheat Flour	Wheat Flour	371.04		Yes	G
White Oil	Mineral Oil	060.07			
White Spirits	Petroleum Spirits	061.011	S		
White Tar	Naphthalene	160.05			
Wild Teak	Kejaat	373.12		Yes	Rs
Wildfire smoke	Wildfire smoke	330.08			
Wood Alcohol	Methanol	070.07	S		
Wood Ash	Ash, NOS	010.16			
Wood Bark, NOS	Wood Dust, NOS	373.00			
Wood Dust, NOS	Wood Dust, NOS	373.00			
Wood Spirits	Methanol	070.07	S		
Wool Dust	Wool Dust	370.44			
Word Processing	Keyboard Use	360.02			
World Trade Center Dust	World Trade Center Pollution	320.39			
World Trade Center Pollution	World Trade Center Pollution	320.39			
X-Ray Developer	X-Ray Developer	180.032			
Xrays	Therapeutic Radiation	351.04			
Xylanase (from Thermomyces lanuginosis)	Xylanase (from Thermomyces lanuginosis)	324.123		Yes	Rs
Xylanase (Medical literature uses this as a synonym)	Fungal Hemicullulase	324.120		Yes	Rs
Xylene	Xylene	160.03	S		
Xylol	Xylene	160.03	S		
Yeast	Yeast	370.28			
Yellow 3 RN	Rifafix Yellow 3 RN	325.06		Yes	Rs
Yellow 3R	Yellow 3R	325.28			R
Yellow 4GL	Remazol Brilliant Yellow 4GL	325.27			R
Yellow GR	Yellow 3R	325.28			R
Zabrotes subfasiatus	Zabrotes subfasiatus	382.06		Yes	R
Zeolite	Zeolite	324.15			
Zinc	Zinc	020.391			R
Zinc Chloride	Zinc Chloride	020.40			
Zinc Compounds	Zinc Compounds	020.390			R
Zinc Oxide	Zinc Oxide	020.393		Yes	Rs
Zirconium	Zirconium	020.411			
Zirconium Compounds	Zirconium Compounds	020.410			

Note: *(1) Association of Occupational & Environmental Clinics code; (2) S=Solvent, P=Pesticide; (3) A supplemental designation for asthmagens (indicated by an "A") is included on the list. Formal criteria for the asthmagen designation were first established for sensitizer-induced asthma in 2002, and for irritant-induced asthma (Reactive Airways Dysfunction Syndrome (RADS) in 2008. These criteria were developed in collaboration with experts in occupational and pulmonary medicine. An * in the asthmagen designation field means that specific substances within this generic category meet the AOEC criteria for an asthmagen. There are many other specific substances within this category that have not been studied as to whether or not they cause asthma. Clinicians evaluating patients with exposure to other substances in this category should have a high level of suspicion that specific substances within this category that have not been studied may also cause asthma. Exposures designated with an "A" for asthmagen are further classified by which criteria they meet. Exposures reviewed and meeting criteria for sensitizer-induced asthma are designated "Rs"; those reviewed and meeting criteria for RADS are designated "Rr"; those reviewed and not meeting either set of criteria are designated "R". Should any exposures be reviewed and determined to meet both criteria they will be designated "Rrs". Substances that are generally accepted as asthmagens are designated "G". The Association of Occupational and Environmental Clinics (AOEC) Exposure Code List was first developed in 1994, for use by AOEC members in order to help systematically identify both existing and emerging occupational and environmental health concerns. The AOEC Exposure Code List includes a wide range of exposures including not only chemicals but exposures to metals, dusts, plants, animals etc. as well as physical hazards e.g. falls, lifting, repetitive strains, etc. Neither the AOEC exposure code list nor the asthmagen designations are considered an official document of any governmental agency.*
Source: *Association of Occupational & Environmental Clinics, July 9, 2019*

Serum Cotinine (1999 – 2010)

CAS Number 486-56-6

Metabolite of nicotine

Geometric mean and selected percentiles of serum concentrations (in ng/mL) for the ***non-smoking U.S. population from the National Health and Nutrition Examination Survey.

Categories (Survey Years)	Geometric Mean (95% conf. interval)	50th Percentile (95% conf. interval)	75th Percentile (95% conf. interval)	90th Percentile (95% conf. interval)	95th Percentile (95% conf. interval)	Sample Size
Total population (1999 - 2000)	*	.060 (<LOD-.080)	.240 (.190-.302)	1.02 (.770-1.28)	1.96 (1.60-2.62)	5999
Total population (2001 - 2002**)	.062 (.050-.077)	< LOD	.160 (.120-.220)	.930 (.740-1.17)	2.20 (1.83-2.44)	6819
Total population (2003 - 2004)	.071 (.057-.089)	.050 (.040-.070)	.210 (.140-.310)	.990 (.740-1.30)	2.17 (1.81-2.54)	6320
Total population (2005 - 2006)	.054 (.047-.061)	.040 (.030-.040)	.120 (.100-.150)	.630 (.460-.870)	1.47 (1.15-1.92)	6347
Total population (2007 - 2008)	.057 (.048-.068)	.040 (.030-.040)	.130 (.100-.180)	.760 (.550-1.09)	1.81 (1.45-2.43)	6197
Total population (2009 - 2010)	.041 (.037-.046)	.030 (.020-.030)	.070 (.070-.090)	.450 (.350-.580)	1.29 (1.04-1.61)	6678
Age 3-11 years (1999 - 2000)	.164 (.115-.234)	.110 (.066-.188)	.500 (.260-1.16)	1.88 (.997-3.44)	3.44 (1.42-4.79)	1174
Age 3-11 years (2001 - 2002**)	.110 (.076-.160)	.070 (<LOD-.130)	.570 (.310-1.00)	2.23 (1.63-2.78)	3.23 (2.53-4.01)	1415
Age 3-11 years (2003 - 2004)	.137 (.088-.213)	.120 (.060-.220)	.620 (.310-1.20)	2.04 (1.38-2.94)	3.35 (2.12-4.68)	1252
Age 3-11 years (2005 - 2006)	.078 (.062-.097)	.050 (.040-.070)	.220 (.160-.350)	1.22 (.880-1.82)	2.42 (1.63-3.46)	1296
Age 3-11 years (2007 - 2008)	.095 (.067-.136)	.060 (.040-.100)	.380 (.170-.840)	1.67 (1.10-2.54)	2.81 (2.26-3.54)	1337
Age 3-11 years (2009 - 2010)	.060 (.047-.075)	.040 (.030-.050)	.160 (.110-.250)	.920 (.560-1.58)	2.15 (1.35-3.00)	1355
Age 12-19 years (1999 - 2000)	.163 (.142-.187)	.110 (.080-.163)	.540 (.428-.660)	1.66 (1.50-1.95)	2.62 (2.09-3.39)	1773
Age 12-19 years (2001 - 2002**)	.086 (.059-.126)	.050 (<LOD-.110)	.350 (.190-.580)	1.53 (1.09-2.12)	3.12 (2.47-3.99)	1902
Age 12-19 years (2003 - 2004)	.110 (.087-.139)	.080 (.060-.120)	.510 (.350-.670)	1.55 (1.21-1.93)	2.68 (1.96-4.02)	1783
Age 12-19 years (2005 - 2006)	.074 (.060-.092)	.050 (.040-.060)	.230 (.150-.350)	1.16 (.860-1.69)	2.26 (1.69-2.72)	1714
Age 12-19 years (2007 - 2008)	.081 (.061-.106)	.050 (.030-.070)	.350 (.170-.550)	1.25 (.930-1.99)	2.54 (2.04-2.94)	934
Age 12-19 years (2009 - 2010)	.056 (.044-.072)	.030 (.020-.040)	.130 (.080-.230)	.980 (.510-1.80)	2.49 (1.31-3.65)	1042
Age 20+ years (1999 - 2000)	*	.050 (<LOD-.061)	.167 (.140-.193)	.630 (.533-.820)	1.50 (1.28-1.66)	3052
Age 20+ years (2001 - 2002**)	.052 (<LOD-.063)	< LOD	.110 (.090-.150)	.630 (.470-.790)	1.42 (1.14-1.89)	3502
Age 20+ years (2003 - 2004)	.058 (.047-.071)	.040 (.030-.050)	.140 (.100-.200)	.630 (.480-.840)	1.54 (1.26-1.92)	3285
Age 20+ years (2005 - 2006)	.047 (.042-.053)	.030 (.030-.040)	.100 (.080-.120)	.440 (.310-.620)	1.14 (.870-1.41)	3337
Age 20+ years (2007 - 2008)	.049 (.043-.057)	.030 (.030-.040)	.100 (.080-.120)	.490 (.390-.640)	1.37 (.970-1.70)	3926
Age 20+ years (2009 - 2010)	.037 (.034-.040)	.020 (.020-.030)	.070 (.060-.070)	.310 (.240-.390)	.990 (.700-1.24)	4281
Males (1999 - 2000)	.124 (.106-.145)	.080 (.060-.110)	.308 (.220-.410)	1.20 (.950-1.49)	2.39 (1.66-3.22)	2789
Males (2001 - 2002**)	.075 (.059-.094)	.050 (<LOD-.070)	.230 (.160-.320)	1.17 (.960-1.49)	2.44 (2.23-2.99)	3152
Males (2003 - 2004)	.087 (.070-.108)	.060 (.040-.080)	.280 (.190-.360)	1.23 (.910-1.68)	2.63 (2.09-3.19)	2937
Males (2005 - 2006)	.064 (.055-.074)	.040 (.040-.050)	.150 (.120-.190)	.720 (.550-1.07)	1.85 (1.42-2.24)	2922
Males (2007 - 2008)	.068 (.056-.081)	.040 (.040-.050)	.170 (.120-.240)	1.07 (.690-1.39)	2.52 (1.84-2.92)	2948
Males (2009 - 2010)	.046 (.042-.051)	.030 (.030-.030)	.080 (.070-.100)	.550 (.410-.700)	1.60 (1.19-2.38)	3181
Females (1999 - 2000)	*	< LOD	.180 (.148-.230)	.850 (.600-1.14)	1.85 (1.33-2.45)	3210
Females (2001 - 2002**)	.053 (<LOD-.066)	< LOD	.120 (.090-.180)	.710 (.540-.990)	1.77 (1.32-2.20)	3667
Females (2003 - 2004)	.060 (.047-.077)	.040 (.030-.060)	.160 (.110-.260)	.860 (.580-1.15)	1.76 (1.32-2.22)	3383
Females (2005 - 2006)	.047 (.040-.054)	.030 (.030-.040)	.100 (.070-.130)	.510 (.300-.830)	1.23 (1.04-1.52)	3425
Females (2007 - 2008)	.050 (.042-.059)	.030 (.030-.040)	.110 (.080-.150)	.630 (.400-.900)	1.40 (1.09-1.87)	3249
Females (2009 - 2010)	.037 (.033-.042)	.020 (.020-.030)	.070 (.050-.080)	.380 (.270-.570)	1.03 (.720-1.61)	3497

Limit of detection (LOD, see Data Analysis section) for Survey years 99-00, 01-02, 03-04, 05-06, 07-08, and 09-10 are 0.05, 0.05, 0.015, 0.015, 0.015, and 0.015, respectively.

< LOD means less than the limit of detection, which may vary for some chemicals by year and by individual sample.

* Not calculated: proportion of results below limit of detection was too high to provide a valid result.

**In the 2001-2002 survey period, 83% of measurements had an LOD of 0.015 ng/mL, and 17% had an LOD of 0.05 ng/mL.

***Non-smoking is defined as a serum cotinine concentration of 10 ng/mL or less.

Biomonitoring Summary: https://www.cdc.gov/biomonitoring/Cotinine_BiomonitoringSummary.html

Factsheet: https://www.cdc.gov/biomonitoring/Cotinine_FactSheet.html

Source: *Centers for Disease Control & Prevention, Fourth National Report on Human Exposure to Environmental Chemicals, Updated Tables, January 2019*

Serum Cotinine (1999 – 2010)

CAS Number 486-56-6

Metabolite of nicotine

Geometric mean and selected percentiles of serum concentrations (in ng/mL) for the ***non-smoking U.S. population from the National Health and Nutrition Examination Survey.

Categories (Survey Years)	Geometric Mean (95% conf. interval)	50th Percentile (95% conf. interval)	75th Percentile (95% conf. interval)	90th Percentile (95% conf. interval)	95th Percentile (95% conf. interval)	Sample Size
Mexican Americans (1999 - 2000)	*	< LOD	.140 (.110-.180)	.506 (.370-.726)	1.21 (.900-1.70)	2241
Mexican Americans (2001 - 2002**)	.060 (<LOD-.084)	< LOD	.160 (.080-.310)	.730 (.480-1.19)	2.12 (1.19-2.96)	1878
Mexican Americans (2003 - 2004)	.054 (.043-.068)	.030 (.020-.050)	.120 (.080-.180)	.690 (.430-1.00)	2.65 (1.87-3.57)	1707
Mexican Americans (2005 - 2006)	.047 (.038-.059)	.030 (.020-.040)	.100 (.070-.150)	.500 (.370-.730)	1.54 (.830-2.49)	1807
Mexican Americans (2007 - 2008)	.044 (.033-.057)	.030 (.020-.040)	.080 (.060-.120)	.480 (.290-.880)	1.59 (1.00-3.07)	1412
Mexican Americans (2009 - 2010)	.038 (.032-.045)	.020 (.020-.030)	.060 (.050-.080)	.360 (.230-.640)	1.35 (.710-2.25)	1615
Non-Hispanic blacks (1999 - 2000)	.175 (.153-.201)	.131 (.111-.150)	.505 (.400-.625)	1.43 (1.21-1.75)	2.34 (1.84-3.50)	1333
Non-Hispanic blacks (2001 - 2002**)	.164 (.137-.197)	.130 (.110-.160)	.580 (.450-.770)	1.77 (1.55-2.05)	3.15 (2.50-4.30)	1602
Non-Hispanic blacks (2003 - 2004)	.144 (.104-.198)	.120 (.080-.180)	.520 (.350-.770)	1.54 (1.20-2.14)	2.77 (2.18-3.54)	1704
Non-Hispanic blacks (2005 - 2006)	.114 (.085-.153)	.080 (.060-.120)	.440 (.240-.690)	1.42 (.900-2.03)	2.45 (1.70-3.70)	1630
Non-Hispanic blacks (2007 - 2008)	.094 (.079-.112)	.060 (.050-.090)	.320 (.250-.390)	1.19 (.980-1.46)	2.37 (1.75-2.88)	1244
Non-Hispanic blacks (2009 - 2010)	.095 (.074-.122)	.070 (.050-.090)	.320 (.210-.540)	1.33 (.900-2.05)	2.85 (1.97-3.60)	1129
Non-Hispanic whites (1999 - 2000)	*	.050 (<LOD-.073)	.216 (.154-.312)	.950 (.621-1.40)	1.92 (1.48-3.02)	1950
Non-Hispanic whites (2001 - 2002**)	.052 (<LOD-.068)	< LOD	.120 (.090-.180)	.800 (.570-1.11)	1.88 (1.48-2.30)	2847
Non-Hispanic whites (2003 - 2004)	.066 (.050-.087)	.040 (.030-.070)	.180 (.120-.300)	.920 (.620-1.32)	2.01 (1.70-2.49)	2500
Non-Hispanic whites (2005 - 2006)	.049 (.042-.056)	.030 (.030-.040)	.100 (.080-.130)	.530 (.330-.800)	1.27 (.980-1.62)	2404
Non-Hispanic whites (2007 - 2008)	.056 (.043-.073)	.040 (.030-.050)	.130 (.080-.240)	.750 (.440-1.27)	1.70 (1.24-2.54)	2485
Non-Hispanic whites (2009 - 2010)	.037 (.033-.043)	.020 (.020-.030)	.070 (.050-.080)	.350 (.240-.560)	1.06 (.780-1.60)	2743

Limit of detection (LOD, see Data Analysis section) for Survey years 99-00, 01-02, 03-04, 05-06, 07-08, and 09-10 are 0.05, 0.05, 0.015, 0.015, 0.015, and 0.015, respectively.

< LOD means less than the limit of detection, which may vary for some chemicals by year and by individual sample.

* Not calculated: proportion of results below limit of detection was too high to provide a valid result.

**In the 2001-2002 survey period, 83% of measurements had an LOD of 0.015 ng/mL, and 17% had an LOD of 0.05 ng/mL.

***Non-smoking is defined as a serum cotinine concentration of 10 ng/mL or less.

Biomonitoring Summary: https://www.cdc.gov/biomonitoring/Cotinine_BiomonitoringSummary.html

Factsheet: https://www.cdc.gov/biomonitoring/Cotinine_FactSheet.html

Source: *Centers for Disease Control & Prevention, Fourth National Report on Human Exposure to Environmental Chemicals, Updated Tables, January 2019*

Serum Cotinine (2011 – 2014)

CAS Number 486-56-6

Metabolite of nicotine

Geometric mean and selected percentiles of serum concentrations (in ng/mL) for the ***non-smoking U.S. population from the National Health and Nutrition Examination Survey.

Categories (Survey Years)	Geometric Mean (95% conf. interval)	50th Percentile (95% conf. interval)	75th Percentile (95% conf. interval)	90th Percentile (95% conf. interval)	95th Percentile (95% conf. interval)	Sample Size
Total population (2011 - 2012)	*	.020 (.018-.023)	.059 (.049-.072)	.356 (.263-.500)	1.30 (.882-1.60)	6108
Total population (2013 - 2014)	*	.017 (<LOD-.021)	.057 (.042-.082)	.388 (.246-.605)	1.53 (1.06-1.90)	6561
Age 3-11 years (2011 - 2012)	.058 (.045-.074)	.031 (.024-.045)	.172 (.100-.313)	1.02 (.627-1.94)	2.49 (1.56-3.36)	1348
Age 3-11 years (2013 - 2014)	.048 (.036-.065)	.021 (.015-.039)	.128 (.081-.239)	.962 (.471-1.70)	2.15 (1.44-3.33)	1445
Age 12-19 years (2011 - 2012)	.049 (.040-.061)	.025 (.020-.037)	.147 (.083-.235)	.711 (.520-1.06)	1.47 (1.05-2.29)	990
Age 12-19 years (2013 - 2014)	*	.023 (.016-.033)	.129 (.067-.246)	1.14 (.579-2.19)	2.87 (1.90-4.51)	1129
Age 20+ years (2011 - 2012)	*	.019 (.016-.020)	.047 (.040-.053)	.210 (.176-.263)	.835 (.566-1.38)	3770
Age 20+ years (2013 - 2014)	*	.016 (<LOD-.019)	.047 (.037-.061)	.244 (.149-.380)	.861 (.605-1.64)	3987
Males (2011 - 2012)	.041 (.037-.045)	.023 (.020-.026)	.076 (.065-.095)	.530 (.397-.715)	1.76 (1.35-2.42)	2903
Males (2013 - 2014)	*	.018 (.016-.024)	.068 (.049-.095)	.491 (.341-.743)	1.84 (1.35-2.41)	3063
Females (2011 - 2012)	*	.019 (.016-.021)	.048 (.040-.059)	.244 (.189-.314)	.819 (.572-1.31)	3205
Females (2013 - 2014)	*	.016 (<LOD-.020)	.049 (.036-.075)	.309 (.182-.482)	1.15 (.722-1.71)	3498
Mexican Americans (2011 - 2012)	.033 (.027-.042)	.021 (.016-.027)	.055 (.040-.081)	.230 (.106-.386)	.668 (.349-2.07)	886
Mexican Americans (2013 - 2014)	*	.016 (<LOD-.019)	.045 (.034-.056)	.144 (.104-.316)	.550 (.362-1.24)	1261
Non-Hispanic blacks (2011 - 2012)	.076 (.054-.107)	.045 (.032-.071)	.259 (.127-.513)	1.10 (.678-2.02)	2.86 (1.46-4.20)	1576
Non-Hispanic blacks (2013 - 2014)	.086 (.070-.106)	.052 (.041-.073)	.296 (.236-.394)	1.70 (1.26-2.16)	3.17 (2.50-3.97)	1297
Non-Hispanic whites (2011 - 2012)	*	.017 (<LOD-.020)	.048 (.039-.061)	.277 (.207-.363)	1.10 (.627-1.50)	1841
Non-Hispanic whites (2013 - 2014)	*	< LOD	.044 (.029-.075)	.287 (.137-.602)	1.09 (.687-1.84)	2309
All Hispanics (2011 - 2012)	.033 (.028-.040)	.021 (.017-.026)	.054 (.041-.074)	.233 (.123-.387)	.834 (.377-2.37)	1587
All Hispanics (2013 - 2014)	*	.017 (.015-.020)	.048 (.038-.060)	.239 (.140-.378)	.905 (.486-1.78)	1926
Asians (2011 - 2012)	.030 (.026-.035)	.023 (.020-.027)	.046 (.037-.058)	.123 (.083-.201)	.308 (.201-.594)	878
Asians (2013 - 2014)	.030 (.026-.036)	.021 (.017-.025)	.052 (.041-.063)	.140 (.091-.250)	.475 (.244-.841)	766

Limit of detection (LOD, see Data Analysis section) for Survey year 11-12 and 13-14 are 0.015 and 0.015, respectively.

< LOD means less than the limit of detection, which may vary for some chemicals by year and by individual sample.

***Non-smoking is defined as a serum cotinine concentration of 10 ng/mL or less.

*Not calculated: proportion of results below limit of detection was too high to provide a valid result.

Biomonitoring Summary: https://www.cdc.gov/biomonitoring/Cotinine_BiomonitoringSummary.html

Factsheet: https://www.cdc.gov/biomonitoring/Cotinine_FactSheet.html

Source: *Centers for Disease Control & Prevention, Fourth National Report on Human Exposure to Environmental Chemicals, Updated Tables, January 2019*

Serum Hydroxycotinine (2013 – 2014)

CAS Number 486-56-6

Metabolite of nicotine

Geometric mean and selected percentiles of serum concentrations (in ng/mL) for the ***non-smoking U.S. population from the National Health and Nutrition Examination Survey.

Categories (Survey Years)	Geometric Mean (95% conf. interval)	50th Percentile (95% conf. interval)	75th Percentile (95% conf. interval)	90th Percentile (95% conf. interval)	95th Percentile (95% conf. interval)	Sample Size
Total population (2013 - 2014)	*	< LOD	.023 (.018-.032)	.121 (.086-.232)	.553 (.425-.782)	6561
Age 3-11 years (2013 - 2014)	*	< LOD	.044 (.028-.070)	.314 (.161-.531)	.667 (.462-.984)	1445
Age 12-19 years (2013 - 2014)	*	< LOD	.038 (.020-.073)	.407 (.181-.662)	.848 (.447-1.39)	1129
Age 20+ years (2013 - 2014)	*	< LOD	.020 (.016-.025)	.088 (.063-.140)	.437 (.260-.744)	3987
Males (2013 - 2014)	*	< LOD	.024 (.018-.034)	.168 (.099-.286)	.673 (.489-.978)	3063
Females (2013 - 2014)	*	< LOD	.022 (.017-.030)	.095 (.070-.188)	.447 (.308-.677)	3498
Mexican Americans (2013 - 2014)	*	< LOD	< LOD	.058 (.038-.105)	.224 (.118-.437)	1261
Non-Hispanic blacks (2013 - 2014)	*	.015 (<LOD-.019)	.085 (.059-.116)	.476 (.314-.612)	.881 (.688-1.10)	1297
Non-Hispanic whites (2013 - 2014)	*	< LOD	.021 (.015-.033)	.095 (.066-.254)	.588 (.330-.896)	2309
All Hispanics (2013 - 2014)	*	< LOD	.015 (<LOD-.021)	.083 (.050-.141)	.378 (.192-.498)	1926
Asians (2013 - 2014)	*	< LOD	.015 (<LOD-.019)	.040 (.032-.051)	.115 (.052-.388)	766

Limit of detection (LOD, see Data Analysis section) for Survey year 13-14 is 0.015.

< LOD means less than the limit of detection, which may vary for some chemicals by year and by individual sample.

***Non-smoking is defined as a serum cotinine concentration of 10 ng/mL or less.

* Not calculated: proportion of results below limit of detection was too high to provide a valid result.

Biomonitoring Summary: https://www.cdc.gov/biomonitoring/Cotinine_BiomonitoringSummary.html

Factsheet: https://www.cdc.gov/biomonitoring/Cotinine_FactSheet.html

Source: *Centers for Disease Control & Prevention, Fourth National Report on Human Exposure to Environmental Chemicals, Updated Tables, January 2019*

Urinary NNAL (4-(methylnitrosamino)-1-(3-pyridyl)-1-butanol) (2007 – 2010)

CAS Number 76014-81-8

Metabolite of (4-(methylnitrosamino)-1-(3-pyridyl)-1-butanone) (NNK)

Geometric mean and selected percentiles of urine concentrations (in pg/mL) for the **non-smoking U.S. population from the National Health and Nutrition Examination Survey.

Categories (Survey Years)	Geometric Mean (95% conf. interval)	50th Percentile (95% conf. interval)	75th Percentile (95% conf. interval)	90th Percentile (95% conf. interval)	95th Percentile (95% conf. interval)	Sample Size
Total population (2007 - 2008)	*	< LOD	2.80 (2.20-3.70)	11.1 (8.80-14.4)	24.5 (18.0-30.4)	5212
Total population (2009 - 2010)	*	< LOD	1.90 (1.60-2.40)	7.30 (6.40-8.50)	16.7 (13.9-19.6)	6067
Age 6-11 years (2007 - 2008)	*	1.30 (.600-2.60)	8.50 (4.70-13.8)	31.4 (17.5-49.8)	60.6 (37.1-75.7)	875
Age 6-11 years (2009 - 2010)	*	.600 (<LOD-1.00)	3.10 (2.20-5.00)	15.5 (10.4-22.8)	29.3 (18.1-59.4)	937
Age 12-19 years (2007 - 2008)	*	1.20 (.600-2.10)	5.00 (3.80-9.20)	20.0 (11.9-27.5)	39.1 (20.6-60.9)	843
Age 12-19 years (2009 - 2010)	*	.900 (<LOD-1.50)	3.70 (2.70-5.20)	12.5 (6.90-25.5)	29.1 (13.9-51.4)	1004
Age 20+ years (2007 - 2008)	*	< LOD	2.10 (1.70-2.50)	8.20 (6.90-9.80)	16.6 (13.9-21.5)	3494
Age 20+ years (2009 - 2010)	*	< LOD	1.60 (1.30-1.90)	6.10 (5.10-6.90)	13.1 (10.7-15.8)	4126
Males (2007 - 2008)	*	< LOD	3.80 (3.00-4.50)	12.6 (10.6-15.0)	27.5 (18.9-38.1)	2463
Males (2009 - 2010)	*	< LOD	2.40 (1.90-3.00)	8.30 (7.20-9.90)	19.3 (15.2-22.5)	2903
Females (2007 - 2008)	*	< LOD	2.10 (1.50-2.90)	9.70 (7.10-13.6)	21.6 (16.6-28.0)	2749
Females (2009 - 2010)	*	< LOD	1.60 (1.30-1.90)	6.50 (4.70-8.80)	14.0 (10.7-19.0)	3164
Mexican Americans (2007 - 2008)	*	< LOD	2.00 (1.20-3.10)	6.90 (4.90-9.00)	13.9 (10.8-17.3)	1206
Mexican Americans (2009 - 2010)	*	< LOD	1.60 (1.20-2.20)	4.90 (3.70-7.00)	11.1 (5.70-18.4)	1476
Non-Hispanic blacks (2007 - 2008)	*	.800 (<LOD-1.90)	4.90 (3.60-6.30)	14.0 (11.6-17.2)	26.1 (18.5-33.2)	1057
Non-Hispanic blacks (2009 - 2010)	1.81 (1.30-2.54)	1.40 (<LOD-2.40)	5.90 (3.80-8.10)	18.9 (11.7-26.1)	34.0 (18.9-61.9)	1004
Non-Hispanic whites (2007 - 2008)	*	< LOD	2.80 (1.90-4.10)	11.9 (8.20-17.7)	27.5 (19.6-35.4)	2047
Non-Hispanic whites (2009 - 2010)	*	< LOD	1.80 (1.40-2.40)	6.80 (5.40-8.40)	15.2 (11.9-19.3)	2514

Limit of detection (LOD, see Data Analysis section) for Survey years 07-08 and 09-10 are 0.6 and 0.6 respectively.

< LOD means less than the limit of detection, which may vary for some chemicals by year and by individual sample.

* Not calculated: proportion of results below limit of detection was too high to provide a valid result.

**Non-smoking is defined as a serum cotinine concentration of 10 ng/mL or less.

Biomonitoring Summary: https://www.cdc.gov/biomonitoring/NNAL_BiomonitoringSummary.html

Factsheet: https://www.cdc.gov/biomonitoring/NNAL_FactSheet.html

Source: *Centers for Disease Control & Prevention, Fourth National Report on Human Exposure to Environmental Chemicals, Updated Tables, January 2019*

Urinary NNAL (4-(methylnitrosamino)-1-(3-pyridyl)-1-butanol) (2011 – 2012)

CAS Number 76014-81-8

Metabolite of (4-(methylnitrosamino)-1-(3-pyridyl)-1-butanone) (NNK)

Geometric mean and selected percentiles of urine concentrations (in pg/mL) for the **non-smoking U.S. population from the National Health and Nutrition Examination Survey.

Categories (Survey Years)	Geometric Mean (95% conf. interval)	50th Percentile (95% conf. interval)	75th Percentile (95% conf. interval)	90th Percentile (95% conf. interval)	95th Percentile (95% conf. interval)	Sample Size
Total population (2011 - 2012)	*	.800 (.700-.900)	2.30 (2.00-2.60)	7.40 (6.10-8.90)	15.7 (11.7-21.0)	5486
Age 6-11 years (2011 - 2012)	1.91 (1.57-2.32)	1.30 (1.10-1.70)	5.10 (3.80-7.30)	21.1 (11.5-31.9)	36.7 (20.1-60.2)	955
Age 12-19 years (2011 - 2012)	1.53 (1.35-1.73)	1.30 (1.10-1.40)	3.10 (2.20-4.30)	10.8 (7.60-14.4)	19.3 (13.2-27.0)	949
Age 20+ years (2011 - 2012)	*	.700 (.600-.900)	2.00 (1.80-2.20)	5.70 (4.80-6.80)	11.7 (10.0-14.9)	3582
Males (2011 - 2012)	1.32 (1.23-1.41)	1.00 (.900-1.10)	2.80 (2.40-3.10)	9.80 (7.60-11.2)	19.5 (13.5-26.4)	2616
Females (2011 - 2012)	*	.700 (.600-.800)	1.90 (1.70-2.20)	5.70 (4.60-7.20)	12.4 (9.00-18.5)	2870
Mexican Americans (2011 - 2012)	1.12 (.956-1.30)	.900 (.700-1.20)	1.90 (1.50-2.50)	5.30 (3.70-7.40)	9.50 (7.70-15.0)	775
Non-Hispanic blacks (2011 - 2012)	1.98 (1.57-2.48)	1.60 (1.30-2.10)	5.10 (3.30-8.70)	15.9 (9.40-28.8)	30.4 (18.5-46.7)	1393
Non-Hispanic whites (2011 - 2012)	*	.800 (.600-.900)	2.10 (1.80-2.40)	6.70 (5.30-8.50)	14.4 (11.4-20.4)	1679
Asians (2011 - 2012)	*	.600 (<LOD-.700)	1.20 (1.00-1.50)	2.80 (1.90-3.80)	5.00 (3.40-6.80)	814

Limit of detection (LOD, see Data Analysis section) for Survey year 11-12 is 0.6.

< LOD means less than the limit of detection, which may vary for some chemicals by year and by individual sample.

* Not calculated: proportion of results below limit of detection was too high to provide a valid result.

**Non-smoking is defined as a serum cotinine of 10 ng/mL or less.

Biomonitoring Summary: https://www.cdc.gov/biomonitoring/NNAL_BiomonitoringSummary.html

Factsheet: https://www.cdc.gov/biomonitoring/NNAL_FactSheet.html

Source: *Centers for Disease Control & Prevention, Fourth National Report on Human Exposure to Environmental Chemicals, Updated Tables, January 2019*

Urinary NNAL (4-(methylnitrosamino)-1-(3-pyridyl)-1-butanol) (creatinine corrected) (2007 – 2010)

CAS Number 76014-81-8

Metabolite of (4-(methylnitrosamino)-1-(3-pyridyl)-1-butanone) (NNK)

Geometric mean and selected percentiles of urine concentrations (in pg/mg of creatinine) for the **non-smoking U.S. population from the National Health and Nutrition Examination Survey.

Categories (Survey Years)	Geometric Mean (95% conf. interval)	50th Percentile (95% conf. interval)	75th Percentile (95% conf. interval)	90th Percentile (95% conf. interval)	95th Percentile (95% conf. interval)	Sample Size
Total population (2007 - 2008)	*	< LOD	2.79 (2.31-3.50)	10.3 (7.36-14.0)	20.5 (16.4-27.5)	5210
Total population (2009 - 2010)	*	< LOD	2.05 (1.88-2.28)	6.40 (5.71-7.41)	14.6 (11.5-17.3)	6066
Age 6-11 years (2007 - 2008)	*	2.15 (1.38-3.22)	10.7 (5.95-17.9)	38.3 (21.2-57.1)	60.9 (46.4-72.1)	875
Age 6-11 years (2009 - 2010)	*	1.19 (<LOD-1.52)	4.25 (2.88-6.37)	19.2 (11.0-28.8)	37.2 (22.9-53.0)	936
Age 12-19 years (2007 - 2008)	*	1.14 (.710-1.75)	4.40 (2.59-7.36)	14.2 (10.5-23.1)	29.2 (15.6-41.9)	841
Age 12-19 years (2009 - 2010)	*	1.05 (<LOD-1.26)	3.08 (1.96-4.37)	10.0 (6.02-15.2)	20.7 (12.3-30.2)	1004
Age 20+ years (2007 - 2008)	*	< LOD	2.34 (2.00-2.73)	6.82 (5.49-8.65)	15.1 (11.8-17.7)	3494
Age 20+ years (2009 - 2010)	*	< LOD	1.84 (1.71-2.00)	5.21 (4.57-6.07)	11.4 (8.42-14.1)	4126
Males (2007 - 2008)	*	< LOD	2.98 (2.39-3.71)	10.5 (7.57-12.9)	20.9 (15.7-29.0)	2462
Males (2009 - 2010)	*	< LOD	2.00 (1.86-2.25)	6.61 (6.00-7.83)	15.1 (11.7-19.8)	2902
Females (2007 - 2008)	*	< LOD	2.67 (2.14-3.37)	9.87 (6.79-14.9)	20.0 (15.7-27.9)	2748
Females (2009 - 2010)	*	< LOD	2.09 (1.82-2.36)	6.15 (4.88-8.21)	12.7 (9.26-17.3)	3164
Mexican Americans (2007 - 2008)	*	< LOD	2.16 (1.55-3.00)	5.91 (4.32-8.30)	13.3 (8.36-17.9)	1205
Mexican Americans (2009 - 2010)	*	< LOD	1.73 (1.36-2.11)	5.00 (3.72-6.84)	10.0 (6.79-14.7)	1476
Non-Hispanic blacks (2007 - 2008)	*	.960 (<LOD-1.42)	3.70 (2.50-5.31)	11.5 (9.18-14.2)	20.8 (14.5-28.8)	1056
Non-Hispanic blacks (2009 - 2010)	1.40 (.982-2.01)	1.21 (<LOD-2.06)	3.96 (2.78-5.99)	12.2 (7.29-20.3)	23.4 (14.3-35.4)	1003
Non-Hispanic whites (2007 - 2008)	*	< LOD	2.93 (2.22-4.00)	11.4 (7.22-17.1)	23.9 (17.1-32.0)	2047
Non-Hispanic whites (2009 - 2010)	*	< LOD	1.96 (1.82-2.15)	6.09 (5.00-7.83)	14.7 (10.0-18.2)	2514

< LOD means less than the limit of detection for the urine levels not corrected for creatinine.

* Not calculated: proportion of results below limit of detection was too high to provide a valid result.

**Non-smoking is defined as a serum cotinine concentration of 10 ng/mL or less.

Biomonitoring Summary: https://www.cdc.gov/biomonitoring/NNAL_BiomonitoringSummary.html

Factsheet: https://www.cdc.gov/biomonitoring/NNAL_FactSheet.html

Source: *Centers for Disease Control & Prevention, Fourth National Report on Human Exposure to Environmental Chemicals, Updated Tables, January 2019*

Urinary NNAL (4-(methylnitrosamino)-1-(3-pyridyl)-1-butanol) (creatinine corrected) (2011 – 2012)

CAS Number 76014-81-8

Metabolite of (4-(methylnitrosamino)-1-(3-pyridyl)-1-butanone) (NNK)

Geometric mean and selected percentiles of urine concentrations (in pg/mg of creatinine) for the **non-smoking U.S. population from the National Health and Nutrition Examination Survey.

Categories (Survey Years)	Geometric Mean (95% conf. interval)	50th Percentile (95% conf. interval)	75th Percentile (95% conf. interval)	90th Percentile (95% conf. interval)	95th Percentile (95% conf. interval)	Sample Size
Total population (2011 - 2012)	*	1.06 (1.00-1.14)	2.47 (2.14-2.72)	6.57 (5.24-8.25)	14.3 (11.7-18.4)	5483
Age 6-11 years (2011 - 2012)	2.57 (2.13-3.10)	1.91 (1.60-2.47)	5.93 (4.21-8.49)	23.5 (13.7-31.6)	39.1 (23.5-59.0)	954
Age 12-19 years (2011 - 2012)	1.45 (1.31-1.60)	1.14 (1.05-1.25)	3.40 (2.50-3.99)	9.14 (5.71-13.4)	18.4 (12.2-22.2)	949
Age 20+ years (2011 - 2012)	*	1.00 (.938-1.08)	2.12 (1.91-2.42)	5.00 (4.26-6.18)	10.5 (8.56-13.0)	3580
Males (2011 - 2012)	1.19 (1.10-1.29)	.984 (.909-1.05)	2.38 (2.08-2.68)	7.36 (5.60-9.33)	15.2 (11.5-21.4)	2615
Females (2011 - 2012)	*	1.18 (1.04-1.30)	2.48 (2.17-2.86)	5.67 (4.69-8.21)	13.5 (10.3-18.0)	2868
Mexican Americans (2011 - 2012)	1.15 (.985-1.35)	1.03 (.860-1.22)	1.94 (1.67-2.35)	4.72 (3.51-6.74)	9.93 (6.46-15.9)	775
Non-Hispanic blacks (2011 - 2012)	1.50 (1.18-1.91)	1.31 (1.02-1.63)	3.70 (2.36-6.09)	11.5 (6.69-19.0)	19.7 (11.5-33.7)	1392
Non-Hispanic whites (2011 - 2012)	*	1.04 (.984-1.14)	2.47 (2.06-2.79)	5.94 (5.14-7.72)	16.1 (11.5-18.9)	1677
Asians (2011 - 2012)	*	.972 (<LOD-1.17)	1.82 (1.56-2.24)	3.57 (2.86-4.79)	5.71 (4.29-8.57)	814

< LOD means less than the limit of detection for the urine levels not corrected for creatinine.
* Not calculated: proportion of results below limit of detection was too high to provide a valid result.
**Non-smoking is defined as a serum cotinine of 10 ng/mL or less.

Biomonitoring Summary: https://www.cdc.gov/biomonitoring/NNAL_BiomonitoringSummary.html

Factsheet: https://www.cdc.gov/biomonitoring/NNAL_FactSheet.html

Source: *Centers for Disease Control & Prevention, Fourth National Report on Human Exposure to Environmental Chemicals, Updated Tables, January 2019*

Urinary Bisphenol A (2003 – 2010)

CAS Number 80-05-7

Geometric mean and selected percentiles of urine concentrations (in µg/L) for the U.S. population from the National Health and Nutrition Examination Survey.

Categories (Survey Years)	Geometric Mean (95% conf. interval)	50th Percentile (95% conf. interval)	75th Percentile (95% conf. interval)	90th Percentile (95% conf. interval)	95th Percentile (95% conf. interval)	Sample Size
Total population (2003 - 2004)	2.64 (2.38-2.94)	2.80 (2.50-3.10)	5.50 (5.00-6.20)	10.6 (9.40-12.0)	16.0 (14.4-17.2)	2517
Total population (2005 - 2006)	1.90 (1.79-2.02)	2.00 (1.90-2.00)	3.70 (3.50-3.90)	7.00 (6.40-7.60)	11.5 (10.0-13.6)	2548
Total population (2007 - 2008)	2.08 (1.92-2.26)	2.10 (1.90-2.30)	4.10 (3.60-4.60)	7.70 (6.80-8.70)	13.0 (10.0-15.6)	2604
Total population (2009 - 2010)	1.83 (1.72-1.94)	1.90 (1.70-2.00)	3.50 (3.30-3.80)	6.60 (6.00-7.20)	9.60 (8.50-11.3)	2749
Age 6-11 years (2003 - 2004)	3.55 (2.95-4.29)	3.80 (2.70-5.00)	6.90 (6.00-8.30)	12.6 (9.50-15.1)	16.0 (11.5-23.3)	314
Age 6-11 years (2005 - 2006)	2.86 (2.52-3.24)	2.70 (2.30-2.90)	5.00 (4.40-5.80)	13.5 (9.30-16.8)	22.8 (13.6-34.6)	356
Age 6-11 years (2007 - 2008)	2.48 (2.21-2.77)	2.40 (1.90-3.00)	4.50 (3.70-5.50)	7.60 (6.30-9.50)	13.4 (8.80-17.8)	389
Age 6-11 years (2009 - 2010)	1.81 (1.55-2.10)	1.70 (1.50-2.00)	3.40 (3.00-4.00)	6.50 (4.30-9.70)	9.20 (6.50-15.1)	415
Age 12-19 years (2003 - 2004)	3.74 (3.31-4.22)	4.30 (3.60-4.60)	7.80 (6.50-9.00)	13.5 (11.8-15.2)	16.5 (15.2-20.9)	715
Age 12-19 years (2005 - 2006)	2.42 (2.18-2.68)	2.40 (2.10-2.70)	4.30 (3.90-5.20)	8.40 (6.50-10.8)	11.9 (10.7-14.8)	702
Age 12-19 years (2007 - 2008)	2.45 (2.14-2.80)	2.40 (2.10-2.60)	4.40 (3.60-5.50)	9.70 (7.30-11.9)	12.2 (9.70-19.0)	401
Age 12-19 years (2009 - 2010)	2.11 (1.86-2.40)	2.20 (1.90-2.40)	3.80 (3.20-4.50)	6.90 (4.70-10.8)	11.1 (6.90-21.0)	420
Age 20+ years (2003 - 2004)	2.41 (2.15-2.72)	2.60 (2.30-2.80)	5.10 (4.50-5.70)	9.50 (8.10-11.3)	15.2 (12.4-18.1)	1488
Age 20+ years (2005 - 2006)	1.75 (1.62-1.89)	1.80 (1.70-2.00)	3.40 (3.10-3.70)	6.40 (5.80-7.50)	10.7 (8.80-12.1)	1490
Age 20+ years (2007 - 2008)	1.99 (1.82-2.18)	2.00 (1.80-2.30)	3.90 (3.40-4.60)	7.40 (6.60-8.50)	13.2 (9.10-15.7)	1814
Age 20+ years (2009 - 2010)	1.79 (1.67-1.93)	1.80 (1.60-2.00)	3.50 (3.30-3.70)	6.50 (6.00-7.20)	9.60 (8.30-11.3)	1914
Males (2003 - 2004)	2.92 (2.63-3.24)	3.20 (2.70-3.60)	6.10 (5.40-6.60)	10.4 (9.50-11.6)	16.0 (12.7-17.6)	1229
Males (2005 - 2006)	2.09 (1.92-2.28)	2.10 (2.00-2.30)	3.70 (3.40-4.20)	7.70 (6.80-9.30)	12.8 (10.1-15.8)	1270
Males (2007 - 2008)	2.20 (2.01-2.41)	2.10 (1.90-2.40)	4.00 (3.60-4.70)	8.10 (6.70-9.70)	14.0 (8.70-20.8)	1294
Males (2009 - 2010)	1.94 (1.82-2.07)	1.90 (1.70-2.00)	3.70 (3.40-4.10)	6.90 (5.90-7.90)	10.9 (8.40-13.5)	1399
Females (2003 - 2004)	2.41 (2.11-2.75)	2.50 (2.20-2.80)	5.00 (4.20-6.20)	10.6 (8.70-12.5)	15.9 (13.5-20.1)	1288
Females (2005 - 2006)	1.74 (1.55-1.95)	1.80 (1.60-2.00)	3.70 (3.10-4.00)	6.20 (5.80-7.60)	10.4 (7.70-14.7)	1278
Females (2007 - 2008)	1.97 (1.80-2.16)	2.00 (1.80-2.20)	4.10 (3.60-4.60)	7.40 (6.80-8.20)	12.0 (9.60-14.1)	1310
Females (2009 - 2010)	1.73 (1.60-1.87)	1.80 (1.60-2.00)	3.40 (3.20-3.70)	6.50 (5.60-7.10)	9.20 (8.00-11.2)	1350
Mexican Americans (2003 - 2004)	2.58 (2.15-3.08)	2.60 (2.10-3.20)	5.20 (4.40-6.50)	9.90 (7.30-13.9)	15.4 (10.2-19.7)	613
Mexican Americans (2005 - 2006)	2.05 (1.75-2.40)	2.00 (1.70-2.40)	3.60 (3.00-4.20)	6.90 (5.40-10.1)	12.2 (8.00-15.6)	637
Mexican Americans (2007 - 2008)	2.09 (1.94-2.26)	2.00 (1.80-2.30)	3.80 (3.30-4.30)	7.10 (6.10-8.60)	11.7 (7.70-14.6)	531
Mexican Americans (2009 - 2010)	1.92 (1.69-2.19)	2.10 (1.80-2.30)	3.50 (3.10-4.10)	6.50 (5.20-7.50)	9.00 (6.90-16.2)	566
Non-Hispanic blacks (2003 - 2004)	4.24 (3.73-4.82)	4.30 (3.80-5.10)	8.20 (7.10-9.80)	14.2 (11.7-16.9)	20.6 (14.9-25.2)	652
Non-Hispanic blacks (2005 - 2006)	2.50 (2.25-2.77)	2.70 (2.30-3.00)	4.60 (4.00-5.00)	8.00 (6.80-9.30)	11.3 (8.90-14.2)	678
Non-Hispanic blacks (2007 - 2008)	2.66 (2.38-2.97)	2.80 (2.60-3.10)	5.40 (4.40-6.40)	9.10 (7.50-10.4)	13.3 (10.0-15.1)	597
Non-Hispanic blacks (2009 - 2010)	2.51 (2.22-2.83)	2.60 (2.30-3.00)	4.40 (3.80-5.00)	7.30 (6.10-8.80)	10.3 (7.90-13.6)	516
Non-Hispanic whites (2003 - 2004)	2.51 (2.26-2.79)	2.70 (2.50-3.00)	5.20 (4.70-5.80)	9.60 (8.30-10.9)	15.1 (12.6-16.7)	1092
Non-Hispanic whites (2005 - 2006)	1.76 (1.62-1.91)	1.80 (1.60-2.00)	3.50 (3.20-3.80)	6.80 (5.90-7.60)	11.0 (8.80-13.7)	1038
Non-Hispanic whites (2007 - 2008)	2.06 (1.87-2.27)	2.00 (1.80-2.30)	4.00 (3.40-4.70)	7.80 (6.70-8.90)	13.7 (9.80-16.1)	1077
Non-Hispanic whites (2009 - 2010)	1.73 (1.60-1.87)	1.70 (1.60-1.90)	3.40 (3.10-3.70)	6.40 (5.40-7.60)	9.20 (8.20-11.2)	1206

Limit of detection (LOD, see Data Analysis section) for Survey years 03-04, 05-06, 07-08 and 09-10 are 0.4, 0.4, 0.4, and 0.4 respectively.

Biomonitoring Summary: https://www.cdc.gov/biomonitoring/BisphenolA_BiomonitoringSummary.html

Factsheet: https://www.cdc.gov/biomonitoring/BisphenolA_FactSheet.html

Source: *Centers for Disease Control & Prevention, Fourth National Report on Human Exposure to Environmental Chemicals, Updated Tables, January 2019*

Urinary Bisphenol A (2011 – 2014)

CAS Number 80-05-7

Geometric mean and selected percentiles of urine concentrations (in µg/L) for the U.S. population from the National Health and Nutrition Examination Survey.

Categories (Survey Years)	Geometric Mean (95% conf. interval)	50th Percentile (95% conf. interval)	75th Percentile (95% conf. interval)	90th Percentile (95% conf. interval)	95th Percentile (95% conf. interval)	Sample Size
Total population (2011 - 2012)	1.51 (1.41-1.62)	1.40 (1.30-1.60)	3.00 (2.70-3.30)	5.60 (4.90-6.50)	9.40 (7.70-11.2)	2489
Total population (2013 - 2014)	1.28 (1.20-1.36)	1.30 (1.20-1.40)	2.50 (2.40-2.70)	4.90 (4.10-5.60)	7.70 (6.80-8.30)	2686
Age 6-11 years (2011 - 2012)	1.58 (1.41-1.78)	1.50 (1.30-1.70)	3.10 (2.60-3.50)	6.70 (5.10-8.00)	8.70 (6.20-21.4)	396
Age 6-11 years (2013 - 2014)	1.43 (1.30-1.59)	1.40 (1.30-1.60)	2.90 (2.30-3.40)	4.40 (4.10-5.20)	8.00 (5.20-10.2)	409
Age 12-19 years (2011 - 2012)	1.69 (1.42-2.00)	1.70 (1.30-2.10)	3.30 (2.80-4.00)	6.90 (4.80-7.90)	10.0 (7.10-13.0)	388
Age 12-19 years (2013 - 2014)	1.28 (1.16-1.41)	1.20 (1.10-1.40)	2.40 (1.90-2.70)	4.60 (3.30-5.20)	6.80 (5.20-8.10)	462
Age 20+ years (2011 - 2012)	1.48 (1.35-1.61)	1.40 (1.20-1.60)	2.90 (2.50-3.30)	5.40 (4.70-6.30)	9.30 (7.30-12.2)	1705
Age 20+ years (2013 - 2014)	1.26 (1.18-1.35)	1.30 (1.20-1.40)	2.50 (2.40-2.80)	4.90 (4.10-6.00)	7.80 (6.80-8.60)	1815
Males (2011 - 2012)	1.64 (1.49-1.81)	1.50 (1.40-1.70)	3.20 (2.70-3.70)	6.00 (5.00-7.70)	9.50 (7.80-11.2)	1259
Males (2013 - 2014)	1.43 (1.30-1.58)	1.40 (1.30-1.60)	2.80 (2.40-3.20)	5.30 (4.30-6.60)	8.30 (6.80-10.3)	1285
Females (2011 - 2012)	1.39 (1.25-1.55)	1.30 (1.20-1.50)	2.80 (2.40-3.20)	5.20 (4.30-6.30)	8.50 (6.50-13.4)	1230
Females (2013 - 2014)	1.15 (1.05-1.26)	1.20 (1.10-1.30)	2.30 (2.00-2.60)	4.20 (3.80-5.20)	7.20 (5.60-8.10)	1401
Mexican Americans (2011 - 2012)	1.45 (1.30-1.63)	1.40 (1.20-1.60)	2.80 (2.30-3.10)	5.00 (4.20-6.50)	7.70 (5.90-9.70)	316
Mexican Americans (2013 - 2014)	1.28 (1.06-1.53)	1.30 (1.00-1.70)	2.50 (2.10-2.80)	4.10 (3.50-4.90)	5.60 (4.60-7.30)	438
Non-Hispanic blacks (2011 - 2012)	2.12 (1.88-2.38)	2.00 (1.80-2.40)	4.10 (3.40-4.60)	7.10 (5.70-8.10)	11.4 (8.10-14.3)	665
Non-Hispanic blacks (2013 - 2014)	1.83 (1.62-2.07)	1.90 (1.50-2.20)	3.60 (3.20-4.10)	6.80 (5.70-7.80)	9.80 (7.70-12.9)	609
Non-Hispanic whites (2011 - 2012)	1.46 (1.34-1.58)	1.30 (1.20-1.50)	2.90 (2.50-3.20)	5.40 (4.60-6.60)	8.90 (6.90-13.4)	813
Non-Hispanic whites (2013 - 2014)	1.22 (1.13-1.31)	1.30 (1.10-1.40)	2.40 (2.20-2.70)	4.40 (3.90-5.90)	7.40 (6.40-8.30)	988
All Hispanics (2011 - 2012)	1.48 (1.25-1.74)	1.40 (1.20-1.70)	2.80 (2.20-3.40)	5.70 (4.20-7.30)	9.10 (6.50-14.1)	571
All Hispanics (2013 - 2014)	1.31 (1.18-1.46)	1.30 (1.10-1.50)	2.60 (2.20-2.80)	4.10 (3.70-4.70)	6.10 (4.90-7.50)	690
Asians (2011 - 2012)	1.03 (.863-1.23)	.900 (.800-1.10)	1.80 (1.50-2.20)	4.00 (2.40-6.40)	7.30 (3.90-11.9)	352
Asians (2013 - 2014)	.782 (.646-.948)	.800 (.700-.900)	1.40 (1.00-1.80)	2.40 (1.80-3.30)	3.60 (2.40-12.1)	289

Limit of detection (LOD, see Data Analysis section) for Survey years 11-12 and 13-14 are 0.4 and 0.2, respectively.

Biomonitoring Summary: https://www.cdc.gov/biomonitoring/BisphenolA_BiomonitoringSummary.html

Factsheet: https://www.cdc.gov/biomonitoring/BisphenolA_FactSheet.html

Source: *Centers for Disease Control & Prevention, Fourth National Report on Human Exposure to Environmental Chemicals, Updated Tables, January 2019*

Urinary Bisphenol A (creatinine corrected) (2003 – 2010)

CAS Number 80-05-7

Geometric mean and selected percentiles of urine concentrations (in µg/g of creatinine) for the U.S. population from the National Health and Nutrition Examination Survey.

Categories (Survey Years)	Geometric Mean (95% conf. interval)	50th Percentile (95% conf. interval)	75th Percentile (95% conf. interval)	90th Percentile (95% conf. interval)	95th Percentile (95% conf. interval)	Sample Size
Total population (2003 - 2004)	2.58 (2.36-2.82)	2.50 (2.31-2.80)	4.29 (3.88-4.75)	7.67 (6.62-8.66)	11.2 (9.78-12.4)	2514
Total population (2005 - 2006)	1.86 (1.79-1.92)	1.71 (1.64-1.79)	3.01 (2.86-3.20)	5.73 (5.29-6.36)	9.70 (8.31-10.9)	2548
Total population (2007 - 2008)	2.10 (1.95-2.25)	1.95 (1.84-2.03)	3.45 (3.02-3.83)	6.09 (5.10-7.45)	10.0 (7.48-13.2)	2604
Total population (2009 - 2010)	1.91 (1.79-2.04)	1.76 (1.67-1.84)	3.06 (2.80-3.33)	5.33 (4.68-6.06)	8.03 (6.94-10.0)	2749
Age 6-11 years (2003 - 2004)	4.32 (3.63-5.14)	4.29 (3.63-5.23)	7.14 (5.83-9.56)	12.2 (9.84-14.8)	15.7 (12.2-23.2)	314
Age 6-11 years (2005 - 2006)	3.14 (2.79-3.54)	2.80 (2.55-3.06)	5.04 (4.46-5.71)	15.6 (8.15-22.4)	24.6 (19.9-48.5)	356
Age 6-11 years (2007 - 2008)	3.05 (2.73-3.41)	2.69 (2.38-3.12)	5.06 (4.33-5.60)	11.9 (6.30-17.4)	20.8 (12.7-26.3)	389
Age 6-11 years (2009 - 2010)	2.36 (2.09-2.65)	2.18 (2.00-2.53)	3.70 (3.14-4.29)	5.97 (4.57-9.15)	9.57 (6.52-13.7)	415
Age 12-19 years (2003 - 2004)	2.80 (2.52-3.11)	2.74 (2.35-3.22)	4.74 (4.21-5.09)	7.79 (6.41-8.87)	11.8 (8.05-14.2)	713
Age 12-19 years (2005 - 2006)	1.80 (1.67-1.95)	1.65 (1.50-1.76)	2.73 (2.41-2.98)	5.71 (4.07-7.50)	8.52 (6.94-12.2)	702
Age 12-19 years (2007 - 2008)	1.90 (1.72-2.10)	1.69 (1.50-2.00)	2.94 (2.38-3.60)	5.10 (4.17-6.82)	7.72 (5.32-13.9)	401
Age 12-19 years (2009 - 2010)	1.70 (1.47-1.95)	1.60 (1.34-1.88)	2.63 (2.11-3.58)	4.47 (3.76-6.19)	6.71 (4.40-17.8)	420
Age 20+ years (2003 - 2004)	2.39 (2.17-2.64)	2.36 (2.15-2.59)	3.93 (3.44-4.33)	6.64 (5.97-7.74)	10.0 (9.01-11.4)	1487
Age 20+ years (2005 - 2006)	1.75 (1.67-1.84)	1.64 (1.56-1.75)	2.84 (2.67-3.08)	5.38 (4.89-5.87)	8.54 (7.58-9.77)	1490
Age 20+ years (2007 - 2008)	2.04 (1.90-2.20)	1.92 (1.79-2.03)	3.36 (2.91-3.78)	6.02 (4.88-7.48)	9.32 (7.48-12.1)	1814
Age 20+ years (2009 - 2010)	1.90 (1.76-2.05)	1.76 (1.66-1.84)	3.04 (2.76-3.24)	5.33 (4.67-6.11)	8.00 (6.97-10.0)	1914
Males (2003 - 2004)	2.38 (2.15-2.63)	2.31 (2.08-2.70)	4.19 (3.81-4.64)	7.10 (6.41-8.28)	9.94 (9.06-11.7)	1228
Males (2005 - 2006)	1.68 (1.57-1.80)	1.56 (1.45-1.64)	2.73 (2.43-3.14)	5.27 (4.64-6.04)	8.40 (6.81-11.4)	1270
Males (2007 - 2008)	1.85 (1.71-2.01)	1.77 (1.57-1.91)	2.97 (2.59-3.33)	5.41 (4.47-7.51)	9.52 (6.29-13.4)	1294
Males (2009 - 2010)	1.74 (1.62-1.87)	1.60 (1.48-1.72)	2.76 (2.53-2.96)	5.00 (4.16-5.86)	7.50 (6.22-9.00)	1399
Females (2003 - 2004)	2.78 (2.50-3.08)	2.68 (2.40-2.94)	4.41 (3.81-5.15)	7.93 (6.48-10.2)	12.4 (9.29-18.2)	1286
Females (2005 - 2006)	2.04 (1.95-2.14)	1.85 (1.76-2.02)	3.21 (2.98-3.39)	6.47 (5.51-7.50)	9.86 (8.62-11.8)	1278
Females (2007 - 2008)	2.36 (2.17-2.57)	2.14 (1.98-2.33)	3.77 (3.43-4.31)	6.67 (5.41-7.83)	10.5 (7.45-15.2)	1310
Females (2009 - 2010)	2.09 (1.92-2.27)	1.93 (1.80-2.15)	3.33 (2.94-3.84)	5.49 (4.87-6.74)	8.80 (6.47-12.5)	1350
Mexican Americans (2003 - 2004)	2.34 (2.02-2.71)	2.38 (2.00-2.65)	3.85 (3.24-4.55)	7.09 (5.00-9.04)	10.9 (8.50-14.3)	612
Mexican Americans (2005 - 2006)	1.84 (1.66-2.04)	1.62 (1.45-1.84)	2.99 (2.56-3.60)	6.00 (4.51-8.00)	10.3 (6.84-14.9)	637
Mexican Americans (2007 - 2008)	2.04 (1.86-2.24)	1.88 (1.72-2.11)	3.33 (2.96-3.95)	5.68 (5.05-6.59)	8.90 (6.30-11.8)	531
Mexican Americans (2009 - 2010)	1.91 (1.71-2.13)	1.76 (1.67-1.87)	3.13 (2.63-3.57)	5.51 (4.72-6.97)	8.71 (5.86-14.4)	566
Non-Hispanic blacks (2003 - 2004)	2.92 (2.58-3.32)	2.95 (2.51-3.27)	4.90 (4.07-6.13)	8.64 (7.53-9.63)	11.9 (10.2-13.3)	651
Non-Hispanic blacks (2005 - 2006)	1.76 (1.62-1.90)	1.68 (1.53-1.92)	2.82 (2.67-3.04)	4.56 (3.85-5.43)	6.81 (5.00-9.27)	678
Non-Hispanic blacks (2007 - 2008)	2.06 (1.91-2.23)	2.03 (1.83-2.25)	3.24 (2.86-3.78)	5.71 (5.15-6.54)	8.59 (6.54-10.9)	597
Non-Hispanic blacks (2009 - 2010)	1.82 (1.65-2.01)	1.70 (1.56-1.89)	2.90 (2.39-3.17)	4.94 (4.02-6.03)	6.74 (5.95-8.09)	516
Non-Hispanic whites (2003 - 2004)	2.58 (2.37-2.81)	2.55 (2.32-2.80)	4.30 (3.93-4.67)	7.58 (6.32-8.87)	11.0 (9.34-12.4)	1091
Non-Hispanic whites (2005 - 2006)	1.85 (1.75-1.96)	1.70 (1.60-1.82)	3.08 (2.78-3.31)	5.80 (5.13-6.72)	9.77 (7.87-11.5)	1038
Non-Hispanic whites (2007 - 2008)	2.15 (1.97-2.35)	1.97 (1.84-2.11)	3.50 (3.04-3.95)	6.44 (5.04-8.00)	10.9 (7.47-14.5)	1077
Non-Hispanic whites (2009 - 2010)	1.94 (1.79-2.10)	1.78 (1.67-1.92)	3.16 (2.80-3.59)	5.45 (4.67-6.94)	8.55 (6.73-10.0)	1206

Biomonitoring Summary: https://www.cdc.gov/biomonitoring/BisphenolA_BiomonitoringSummary.html

Factsheet: https://www.cdc.gov/biomonitoring/BisphenolA_FactSheet.html

Source: *Centers for Disease Control & Prevention, Fourth National Report on Human Exposure to Environmental Chemicals, Updated Tables, January 2019*

Urinary Bisphenol A (creatinine corrected) (2011 – 2014)

CAS Number 80-05-7

Geometric mean and selected percentiles of urine concentrations (in µg/g of creatinine) for the U.S. population from the National Health and Nutrition Examination Survey.

Categories (Survey Years)	**Geometric Mean** (95% conf. interval)	**50th Percentile** (95% conf. interval)	**75th Percentile** (95% conf. interval)	**90th Percentile** (95% conf. interval)	**95th Percentile** (95% conf. interval)	**Sample Size**
Total population (2011 - 2012)	1.72 (1.61-1.84)	1.58 (1.46-1.71)	2.86 (2.62-3.01)	4.62 (4.12-5.65)	8.24 (6.47-11.0)	2487
Total population (2013 - 2014)	1.28 (1.18-1.39)	1.21 (1.11-1.32)	2.12 (1.92-2.33)	3.88 (3.46-4.24)	5.09 (4.65-5.96)	2684
Age 6-11 years (2011 - 2012)	2.27 (1.97-2.62)	2.00 (1.78-2.16)	3.33 (2.93-3.75)	7.94 (4.71-12.4)	14.0 (6.45-47.5)	395
Age 6-11 years (2013 - 2014)	1.81 (1.68-1.96)	1.80 (1.52-2.03)	3.10 (2.63-3.46)	4.48 (4.00-4.96)	7.03 (5.00-9.92)	409
Age 12-19 years (2011 - 2012)	1.64 (1.44-1.87)	1.48 (1.13-1.98)	2.88 (2.21-3.23)	4.50 (3.37-8.16)	8.74 (3.57-18.4)	388
Age 12-19 years (2013 - 2014)	1.04 (.887-1.21)	.932 (.809-1.19)	1.71 (1.33-2.03)	2.69 (2.28-3.33)	3.99 (3.29-4.67)	462
Age 20+ years (2011 - 2012)	1.68 (1.57-1.80)	1.55 (1.43-1.68)	2.75 (2.54-3.00)	4.55 (4.00-5.39)	7.73 (5.73-10.0)	1704
Age 20+ years (2013 - 2014)	1.27 (1.16-1.39)	1.21 (1.11-1.30)	2.09 (1.90-2.31)	3.88 (3.33-4.37)	5.09 (4.58-5.97)	1813
Males (2011 - 2012)	1.54 (1.40-1.69)	1.37 (1.20-1.59)	2.55 (2.21-2.94)	4.38 (3.75-6.00)	8.24 (6.01-11.0)	1258
Males (2013 - 2014)	1.20 (1.11-1.31)	1.12 (.988-1.25)	1.95 (1.78-2.24)	3.75 (3.25-4.29)	4.91 (4.42-7.02)	1284
Females (2011 - 2012)	1.91 (1.76-2.08)	1.75 (1.57-1.97)	2.93 (2.73-3.24)	4.94 (4.27-6.24)	8.13 (6.00-11.1)	1229
Females (2013 - 2014)	1.36 (1.23-1.51)	1.28 (1.17-1.43)	2.25 (2.03-2.48)	3.94 (3.27-4.48)	5.18 (4.50-6.07)	1400
Mexican Americans (2011 - 2012)	1.64 (1.49-1.80)	1.46 (1.32-1.64)	2.70 (2.34-3.01)	4.50 (3.45-7.00)	7.37 (4.76-11.4)	316
Mexican Americans (2013 - 2014)	1.30 (1.16-1.45)	1.27 (1.05-1.57)	2.25 (1.97-2.50)	3.57 (3.04-3.98)	4.25 (3.93-4.83)	438
Non-Hispanic blacks (2011 - 2012)	1.65 (1.48-1.84)	1.50 (1.30-1.71)	2.63 (2.11-3.17)	4.82 (3.82-6.24)	7.23 (5.98-10.7)	665
Non-Hispanic blacks (2013 - 2014)	1.35 (1.25-1.46)	1.32 (1.13-1.46)	2.17 (1.96-2.35)	3.89 (3.24-4.27)	5.00 (4.40-6.01)	609
Non-Hispanic whites (2011 - 2012)	1.77 (1.64-1.92)	1.64 (1.49-1.78)	2.90 (2.65-3.08)	4.60 (4.05-6.00)	9.00 (6.11-12.3)	811
Non-Hispanic whites (2013 - 2014)	1.28 (1.14-1.44)	1.21 (1.06-1.38)	2.13 (1.85-2.42)	3.94 (3.33-4.56)	5.60 (4.65-6.53)	987
All Hispanics (2011 - 2012)	1.66 (1.44-1.90)	1.47 (1.28-1.70)	2.80 (2.39-3.14)	4.82 (3.67-7.00)	7.69 (5.76-9.62)	571
All Hispanics (2013 - 2014)	1.30 (1.19-1.43)	1.25 (1.09-1.42)	2.20 (1.92-2.47)	3.61 (3.13-3.98)	4.54 (4.03-4.89)	690
Asians (2011 - 2012)	1.38 (1.25-1.52)	1.32 (1.16-1.40)	2.11 (1.84-2.50)	4.04 (2.80-6.25)	7.42 (4.38-12.1)	352
Asians (2013 - 2014)	.990 (.847-1.16)	.918 (.778-1.05)	1.62 (1.39-1.97)	2.71 (2.09-4.00)	4.44 (2.71-10.0)	288

Biomonitoring Summary: https://www.cdc.gov/biomonitoring/BisphenolA_BiomonitoringSummary.html

Factsheet: https://www.cdc.gov/biomonitoring/BisphenolA_FactSheet.html

Source: *Centers for Disease Control & Prevention, Fourth National Report on Human Exposure to Environmental Chemicals, Updated Tables, January 2019*

Urinary Bisphenol F (2013 – 2014)

CAS Number 80-05-7

Geometric mean and selected percentiles of urine concentrations (in µg/L) for the U.S. population from the National Health and Nutrition Examination Survey.

Categories (Survey Years)	Geometric Mean (95% conf. interval)	50th Percentile (95% conf. interval)	75th Percentile (95% conf. interval)	90th Percentile (95% conf. interval)	95th Percentile (95% conf. interval)	Sample Size
Total population (2013 - 2014)	.532 (.460-.616)	.400 (.300-.500)	1.10 (.900-1.40)	4.00 (2.80-5.30)	9.80 (6.50-16.1)	2682
Age 6-11 years (2013 - 2014)	.421 (.343-.516)	.300 (.200-.400)	.900 (.600-1.30)	2.30 (1.50-3.30)	3.90 (3.00-6.10)	409
Age 12-19 years (2013 - 2014)	.567 (.458-.701)	.400 (.300-.600)	1.20 (1.00-1.50)	5.30 (2.50-8.40)	8.80 (6.50-18.7)	461
Age 20+ years (2013 - 2014)	.541 (.457-.641)	.400 (.300-.500)	1.20 (.900-1.50)	4.20 (2.60-6.30)	12.2 (6.00-21.4)	1812
Males (2013 - 2014)	.582 (.505-.671)	.400 (.400-.500)	1.20 (1.10-1.40)	5.10 (3.00-6.50)	12.4 (7.00-17.7)	1284
Females (2013 - 2014)	.489 (.401-.596)	.300 (.300-.500)	1.00 (.700-1.50)	3.30 (2.40-4.60)	8.90 (4.50-21.4)	1398
Mexican Americans (2013 - 2014)	*	.300 (<LOD-.400)	.600 (.400-1.10)	1.90 (1.00-5.10)	5.30 (1.90-14.9)	438
Non-Hispanic blacks (2013 - 2014)	.607 (.540-.683)	.400 (.400-.500)	1.30 (1.10-1.70)	5.40 (3.50-8.90)	14.6 (8.10-26.4)	608
Non-Hispanic whites (2013 - 2014)	.581 (.473-.713)	.400 (.300-.600)	1.30 (1.00-1.60)	4.30 (2.70-6.50)	12.4 (5.70-24.1)	987
All Hispanics (2013 - 2014)	*	.300 (.200-.400)	.700 (.500-1.10)	2.50 (1.40-5.90)	8.20 (4.10-18.0)	690
Asians (2013 - 2014)	*	< LOD	.400 (.300-.700)	1.10 (.600-2.00)	2.10 (1.10-7.00)	287

Limit of detection (LOD, see Data Analysis section) for Survey year 13-14 is 0.2.

< LOD means less than the limit of detection, which may vary for some chemicals by year and by individual sample.

* Not calculated: proportion of results below limit of detection was too high to provide a valid result.

Source: *Centers for Disease Control & Prevention, Fourth National Report on Human Exposure to Environmental Chemicals, Updated Tables, January 2019*

Urinary Bisphenol F (creatinine corrected) (2013 – 2014)

CAS Number 80-05-7

Geometric mean and selected percentiles of urine concentrations (in µg/g of creatinine) for the U.S. population from the National Health and Nutrition Examination Survey.

Categories (Survey Years)	Geometric Mean (95% conf. interval)	50th Percentile (95% conf. interval)	75th Percentile (95% conf. interval)	90th Percentile (95% conf. interval)	95th Percentile (95% conf. interval)	Sample Size
Total population (2013 - 2014)	.534 (.471-.606)	.444 (.385-.515)	1.07 (.899-1.21)	3.33 (2.39-4.76)	8.39 (5.90-12.0)	2680
Age 6-11 years (2013 - 2014)	.532 (.431-.656)	.452 (.360-.636)	1.19 (.798-1.74)	2.44 (1.91-3.49)	4.76 (3.48-10.0)	409
Age 12-19 years (2013 - 2014)	.460 (.365-.580)	.388 (.287-.474)	1.06 (.680-1.46)	3.23 (1.85-5.17)	8.80 (3.31-14.4)	461
Age 20+ years (2013 - 2014)	.546 (.479-.622)	.464 (.395-.526)	1.06 (.875-1.21)	3.40 (2.29-5.03)	8.75 (5.70-13.8)	1810
Males (2013 - 2014)	.489 (.426-.563)	.398 (.311-.492)	.994 (.783-1.16)	3.98 (2.63-5.17)	9.47 (6.81-13.8)	1283
Females (2013 - 2014)	.581 (.497-.678)	.494 (.421-.583)	1.11 (.896-1.40)	3.09 (2.11-4.10)	6.97 (3.89-14.1)	1397
Mexican Americans (2013 - 2014)	*	.308 (<LOD-.400)	.667 (.497-.875)	1.75 (.995-3.61)	4.22 (2.02-6.73)	438
Non-Hispanic blacks (2013 - 2014)	.449 (.392-.515)	.350 (.304-.389)	.980 (.758-1.27)	3.24 (2.37-4.67)	8.28 (4.67-12.1)	608
Non-Hispanic whites (2013 - 2014)	.611 (.515-.726)	.517 (.424-.612)	1.14 (.994-1.43)	3.89 (2.63-6.50)	10.8 (5.90-15.3)	986
All Hispanics (2013 - 2014)	*	.308 (.255-.395)	.698 (.526-.933)	2.02 (1.41-4.05)	5.56 (3.00-16.0)	690
Asians (2013 - 2014)	*	< LOD	.672 (.492-.843)	1.31 (.843-2.90)	2.00 (1.17-7.78)	286

< LOD means less than the limit of detection for the urine levels not corrected for creatinine.

* Not calculated: proportion of results below limit of detection was too high to provide a valid result.

Source: *Centers for Disease Control & Prevention, Fourth National Report on Human Exposure to Environmental Chemicals, Updated Tables, January 2019*

Urinary Bisphenol S (2013 – 2014)

CAS Number 80-05-7

Geometric mean and selected percentiles of urine concentrations (in µg/L) for the U.S. population from the National Health and Nutrition Examination Survey.

Categories (Survey Years)	Geometric Mean (95% conf. interval)	50th Percentile (95% conf. interval)	75th Percentile (95% conf. interval)	90th Percentile (95% conf. interval)	95th Percentile (95% conf. interval)	Sample Size
Total population (2013 - 2014)	.427 (.375-.487)	.400 (.300-.500)	.900 (.700-1.10)	2.10 (1.70-2.40)	3.60 (2.50-4.70)	2682
Age 6-11 years (2013 - 2014)	.351 (.306-.404)	.300 (.300-.400)	.700 (.500-.800)	1.40 (1.00-1.60)	2.10 (1.50-4.90)	409
Age 12-19 years (2013 - 2014)	.400 (.332-.482)	.400 (.300-.500)	.800 (.600-1.10)	1.80 (1.20-2.40)	3.20 (1.80-8.30)	461
Age 20+ years (2013 - 2014)	.441 (.381-.510)	.400 (.400-.500)	.900 (.800-1.10)	2.10 (1.80-2.50)	3.80 (2.60-4.60)	1812
Males (2013 - 2014)	.455 (.393-.527)	.400 (.400-.500)	.900 (.700-1.10)	2.30 (1.60-2.60)	3.90 (2.40-6.40)	1284
Females (2013 - 2014)	.403 (.343-.473)	.400 (.300-.500)	.900 (.700-1.10)	2.00 (1.50-2.30)	3.40 (2.40-4.60)	1398
Mexican Americans (2013 - 2014)	.498 (.381-.650)	.500 (.400-.600)	1.00 (.800-1.40)	2.10 (1.60-4.30)	4.90 (2.20-10.8)	438
Non-Hispanic blacks (2013 - 2014)	.636 (.537-.754)	.600 (.500-.700)	1.40 (1.20-1.70)	3.20 (2.10-4.80)	6.00 (3.50-9.50)	608
Non-Hispanic whites (2013 - 2014)	.383 (.334-.440)	.400 (.300-.400)	.800 (.600-.900)	1.90 (1.40-2.40)	3.00 (2.40-4.00)	987
All Hispanics (2013 - 2014)	.507 (.424-.606)	.500 (.400-.600)	1.00 (.800-1.30)	2.10 (1.70-3.30)	4.10 (2.60-6.40)	690
Asians (2013 - 2014)	.327 (.270-.397)	.300 (.300-.300)	.600 (.500-.900)	1.40 (1.00-2.70)	2.80 (1.60-6.50)	287

Limit of detection (LOD, see Data Analysis section) for Survey year 13-14 is 0.1.

Source: *Centers for Disease Control & Prevention, Fourth National Report on Human Exposure to Environmental Chemicals, Updated Tables, January 2019*

Urinary Bisphenol S (creatinine corrected) (2013 – 2014)

CAS Number 80-05-7

Geometric mean and selected percentiles of urine concentrations (in µg/g of creatinine) for the U.S. population from the National Health and Nutrition Examination Survey.

Categories (Survey Years)	Geometric Mean (95% conf. interval)	50th Percentile (95% conf. interval)	75th Percentile (95% conf. interval)	90th Percentile (95% conf. interval)	95th Percentile (95% conf. interval)	Sample Size
Total population (2013 - 2014)	.428 (.387-.474)	.380 (.352-.411)	.797 (.690-.903)	1.80 (1.49-2.10)	3.33 (2.60-4.68)	2680
Age 6-11 years (2013 - 2014)	.444 (.390-.505)	.405 (.345-.457)	.778 (.652-.938)	1.59 (1.14-2.27)	2.63 (2.05-4.93)	409
Age 12-19 years (2013 - 2014)	.325 (.287-.368)	.294 (.256-.331)	.588 (.500-.674)	1.31 (.886-1.88)	2.27 (1.33-4.58)	461
Age 20+ years (2013 - 2014)	.444 (.396-.498)	.389 (.357-.426)	.839 (.714-.960)	1.88 (1.56-2.22)	3.49 (2.71-4.91)	1810
Males (2013 - 2014)	.383 (.335-.437)	.333 (.299-.370)	.741 (.630-.851)	1.56 (1.33-1.93)	2.81 (1.88-4.76)	1283
Females (2013 - 2014)	.477 (.431-.529)	.417 (.385-.455)	.848 (.729-.986)	2.03 (1.67-2.60)	3.64 (2.97-5.20)	1397
Mexican Americans (2013 - 2014)	.507 (.410-.627)	.458 (.370-.549)	.962 (.722-1.25)	2.22 (1.30-5.42)	5.57 (2.26-14.9)	438
Non-Hispanic blacks (2013 - 2014)	.471 (.398-.557)	.414 (.336-.519)	.943 (.792-1.11)	2.10 (1.50-3.67)	4.11 (2.58-6.69)	608
Non-Hispanic whites (2013 - 2014)	.402 (.354-.457)	.357 (.316-.390)	.714 (.596-.864)	1.68 (1.38-1.95)	3.02 (2.20-4.58)	986
All Hispanics (2013 - 2014)	.503 (.435-.581)	.487 (.411-.538)	.909 (.756-1.09)	2.03 (1.53-2.78)	3.90 (2.80-5.75)	690
Asians (2013 - 2014)	.420 (.359-.492)	.389 (.357-.459)	.720 (.546-.938)	1.68 (.964-2.76)	2.76 (1.75-8.04)	286

Source: *Centers for Disease Control & Prevention, Fourth National Report on Human Exposure to Environmental Chemicals, Updated Tables, January 2019*

Urinary Triclosan (2003 – 2010)

CAS Number 3380-34-5

Geometric mean and selected percentiles of urine concentrations (in µg/L) for the U.S. population from the National Health and Nutrition Examination Survey.

Categories (Survey Years)	Geometric Mean (95% conf. interval)	50th Percentile (95% conf. interval)	75th Percentile (95% conf. interval)	90th Percentile (95% conf. interval)	95th Percentile (95% conf. interval)	Sample Size
Total population (2003 - 2004)	13.0 (11.6-14.6)	9.20 (7.90-10.9)	47.4 (38.2-58.4)	249 (188-304)	461 (383-522)	2517
Total population (2005 - 2006)	18.5 (16.1-21.3)	15.1 (11.8-18.5)	76.2 (57.9-97.6)	334 (279-402)	655 (573-739)	2548
Total population (2007 - 2008)	15.3 (13.5-17.4)	12.1 (10.2-13.8)	57.2 (46.1-65.9)	225 (176-288)	494 (371-615)	2604
Total population (2009 - 2010)	14.5 (12.6-16.6)	10.7 (8.80-12.6)	51.2 (39.4-67.7)	238 (200-284)	483 (398-569)	2749
Age 6-11 years (2003 - 2004)	8.16 (6.20-10.8)	6.00 (4.00-8.50)	20.7 (14.3-31.6)	123 (36.4-163)	157 (113-380)	314
Age 6-11 years (2005 - 2006)	12.8 (9.89-16.7)	10.3 (8.30-17.2)	35.4 (23.9-65.8)	97.6 (67.4-181)	246 (99.5-462)	356
Age 6-11 years (2007 - 2008)	11.8 (7.57-18.2)	9.80 (6.70-13.9)	27.7 (14.8-52.2)	98.5 (40.5-364)	296 (67.4-826)	389
Age 6-11 years (2009 - 2010)	10.9 (9.35-12.8)	9.90 (7.10-11.9)	28.3 (22.1-35.5)	95.5 (71.5-117)	200 (114-474)	415
Age 12-19 years (2003 - 2004)	14.5 (11.0-19.1)	10.3 (8.20-13.1)	39.0 (26.5-86.4)	304 (134-566)	655 (310-890)	715
Age 12-19 years (2005 - 2006)	18.8 (14.9-23.8)	15.4 (11.0-21.0)	67.5 (45.3-100)	330 (174-461)	566 (389-707)	702
Age 12-19 years (2007 - 2008)	18.2 (13.8-23.8)	13.8 (9.40-20.1)	63.2 (38.7-110)	296 (144-395)	401 (308-853)	401
Age 12-19 years (2009 - 2010)	11.7 (9.89-13.8)	8.80 (7.30-10.9)	30.2 (24.3-40.6)	165 (56.7-289)	301 (220-431)	420
Age 20+ years (2003 - 2004)	13.6 (12.0-15.3)	9.60 (8.20-11.5)	51.7 (39.6-65.7)	261 (198-317)	472 (406-522)	1488
Age 20+ years (2005 - 2006)	19.3 (16.4-22.6)	15.5 (11.8-19.4)	84.3 (61.0-114)	366 (289-462)	738 (583-864)	1490
Age 20+ years (2007 - 2008)	15.4 (13.7-17.3)	12.3 (10.1-14.4)	60.1 (48.5-69.0)	225 (185-286)	504 (378-573)	1814
Age 20+ years (2009 - 2010)	15.5 (12.9-18.5)	11.1 (8.60-14.2)	61.8 (41.8-86.0)	262 (214-327)	544 (415-621)	1914
Males (2003 - 2004)	16.2 (13.4-19.6)	11.7 (9.30-14.8)	84.9 (50.6-111)	317 (231-433)	574 (461-716)	1229
Males (2005 - 2006)	21.3 (17.6-25.7)	17.6 (11.9-23.2)	103 (69.9-143)	446 (366-488)	738 (601-873)	1270
Males (2007 - 2008)	15.2 (12.9-17.9)	12.3 (9.50-15.3)	60.6 (45.8-72.8)	236 (159-338)	467 (367-636)	1294
Males (2009 - 2010)	14.8 (12.7-17.4)	10.9 (8.60-13.3)	55.1 (40.4-77.5)	243 (214-295)	455 (327-600)	1399
Females (2003 - 2004)	10.6 (9.29-12.1)	7.60 (6.10-9.10)	33.2 (27.1-39.4)	144 (96.5-250)	380 (258-430)	1288
Females (2005 - 2006)	16.2 (13.9-18.8)	12.6 (10.1-15.6)	58.7 (41.5-81.9)	226 (169-304)	513 (310-773)	1278
Females (2007 - 2008)	15.5 (12.6-18.9)	12.0 (9.90-14.1)	52.1 (37.1-74.4)	210 (133-367)	504 (285-648)	1310
Females (2009 - 2010)	14.2 (12.0-16.8)	10.5 (8.70-12.6)	50.0 (34.4-63.8)	235 (149-302)	488 (332-661)	1350
Mexican Americans (2003 - 2004)	14.6 (10.6-20.1)	8.80 (5.40-17.5)	65.4 (32.8-127)	357 (225-456)	597 (372-992)	613
Mexican Americans (2005 - 2006)	26.7 (21.2-33.7)	18.7 (13.5-25.5)	196 (99.4-269)	668 (475-759)	866 (750-1180)	637
Mexican Americans (2007 - 2008)	17.1 (12.9-22.6)	11.8 (8.40-17.8)	67.4 (42.5-106)	358 (208-474)	556 (363-856)	531
Mexican Americans (2009 - 2010)	14.9 (12.2-18.3)	10.2 (8.20-12.8)	54.7 (33.3-86.5)	345 (260-494)	691 (443-1180)	566
Non-Hispanic blacks (2003 - 2004)	14.4 (11.4-18.2)	11.1 (8.70-16.1)	37.6 (30.2-58.0)	203 (87.5-341)	450 (254-750)	652
Non-Hispanic blacks (2005 - 2006)	17.3 (13.3-22.4)	14.0 (10.4-19.0)	59.2 (37.7-98.3)	258 (138-460)	541 (273-1190)	678
Non-Hispanic blacks (2007 - 2008)	13.7 (11.7-16.1)	11.3 (8.80-13.9)	41.4 (28.9-49.6)	150 (93.5-265)	480 (190-757)	597
Non-Hispanic blacks (2009 - 2010)	12.8 (10.8-15.0)	9.30 (7.70-11.7)	34.3 (24.0-44.6)	168 (88.4-263)	451 (202-959)	516
Non-Hispanic whites (2003 - 2004)	12.9 (11.2-14.9)	9.20 (7.40-11.0)	49.2 (37.8-63.4)	245 (163-334)	461 (383-527)	1092
Non-Hispanic whites (2005 - 2006)	17.5 (14.9-20.6)	15.1 (10.9-19.0)	74.3 (54.1-90.3)	288 (231-366)	569 (462-693)	1038
Non-Hispanic whites (2007 - 2008)	15.0 (12.6-17.7)	12.3 (9.80-14.5)	59.6 (41.9-73.4)	197 (147-266)	408 (296-537)	1077
Non-Hispanic whites (2009 - 2010)	14.0 (11.8-16.7)	10.5 (8.30-12.9)	51.7 (33.1-79.2)	216 (174-266)	431 (301-565)	1206

Limit of detection (LOD, see Data Analysis section) for Survey years 03-04, 05-06, 07-08 and 09-10 are 2.3, 2.3, 2.3, and 2.3 respectively.

Biomonitoring Summary: https://www.cdc.gov/biomonitoring/Triclosan_BiomonitoringSummary.html

Factsheet: https://www.cdc.gov/biomonitoring/Triclosan_FactSheet.html

Source: *Centers for Disease Control & Prevention, Fourth National Report on Human Exposure to Environmental Chemicals, Updated Tables, January 2019*

Urinary Triclosan (2011 – 2014)

CAS Number 3380-34-5

Geometric mean and selected percentiles of urine concentrations (in µg/L) for the U.S. population from the National Health and Nutrition Examination Survey.

Categories (Survey Years)	Geometric Mean (95% conf. interval)	50th Percentile (95% conf. interval)	75th Percentile (95% conf. interval)	90th Percentile (95% conf. interval)	95th Percentile (95% conf. interval)	Sample Size
Total population (2011 - 2012)	11.8 (10.6-13.1)	7.10 (6.10-7.90)	41.6 (30.2-59.5)	267 (207-332)	553 (429-722)	2489
Total population (2013 - 2014)	9.78 (9.01-10.6)	6.30 (5.70-7.20)	33.9 (29.1-39.1)	172 (138-208)	379 (324-431)	2686
Age 6-11 years (2011 - 2012)	7.18 (5.73-9.01)	5.00 (3.40-7.30)	17.2 (10.4-21.8)	77.6 (28.9-184)	184 (78.7-393)	396
Age 6-11 years (2013 - 2014)	8.24 (6.70-10.1)	6.10 (4.80-8.00)	22.9 (15.3-33.5)	73.8 (52.7-96.0)	124 (91.2-204)	409
Age 12-19 years (2011 - 2012)	10.1 (7.70-13.3)	5.80 (4.70-7.50)	25.5 (15.1-38.9)	156 (73.5-286)	489 (171-1550)	388
Age 12-19 years (2013 - 2014)	7.96 (6.81-9.31)	6.00 (4.80-7.40)	19.7 (15.4-25.3)	85.7 (37.2-183)	224 (122-325)	462
Age 20+ years (2011 - 2012)	12.7 (11.2-14.4)	7.60 (6.40-8.50)	57.4 (37.0-75.8)	298 (243-388)	594 (437-845)	1705
Age 20+ years (2013 - 2014)	10.3 (9.32-11.3)	6.40 (5.60-7.50)	39.3 (32.4-48.5)	203 (147-270)	420 (350-529)	1815
Males (2011 - 2012)	11.6 (10.1-13.1)	6.40 (5.30-7.50)	41.6 (28.1-58.7)	320 (211-388)	566 (392-722)	1259
Males (2013 - 2014)	9.95 (8.75-11.3)	6.40 (5.20-8.50)	34.7 (29.3-40.6)	172 (126-215)	372 (297-479)	1285
Females (2011 - 2012)	12.0 (10.2-14.0)	7.60 (6.20-8.60)	42.2 (25.7-75.8)	242 (188-286)	545 (380-855)	1230
Females (2013 - 2014)	9.63 (8.41-11.0)	6.20 (5.60-7.10)	31.7 (24.9-42.5)	173 (112-240)	384 (302-528)	1401
Mexican Americans (2011 - 2012)	12.6 (8.98-17.8)	7.20 (4.70-11.7)	47.6 (21.9-82.7)	411 (151-628)	628 (393-1250)	316
Mexican Americans (2013 - 2014)	8.65 (5.55-13.5)	5.20 (2.60-12.2)	31.9 (15.4-68.0)	191 (79.5-346)	488 (180-822)	438
Non-Hispanic blacks (2011 - 2012)	10.5 (9.08-12.2)	6.70 (5.70-8.40)	29.9 (22.4-40.0)	169 (106-278)	475 (278-718)	665
Non-Hispanic blacks (2013 - 2014)	8.34 (7.54-9.23)	5.50 (4.40-6.60)	24.9 (18.9-32.6)	145 (68.6-209)	304 (204-509)	609
Non-Hispanic whites (2011 - 2012)	11.7 (10.0-13.7)	7.00 (5.60-8.00)	44.6 (24.4-75.8)	248 (184-392)	552 (365-759)	813
Non-Hispanic whites (2013 - 2014)	10.0 (8.95-11.3)	6.40 (5.60-8.00)	34.7 (29.2-43.1)	148 (122-210)	350 (253-438)	988
All Hispanics (2011 - 2012)	13.4 (11.6-15.5)	7.50 (6.40-9.30)	48.3 (33.2-75.5)	411 (264-518)	861 (536-1040)	571
All Hispanics (2013 - 2014)	9.14 (6.95-12.0)	6.00 (3.70-9.50)	29.6 (17.9-44.3)	208 (131-325)	583 (325-737)	690
Asians (2011 - 2012)	11.7 (7.75-17.8)	7.30 (3.80-15.1)	42.9 (18.6-125)	274 (117-433)	453 (235-636)	352
Asians (2013 - 2014)	11.5 (9.24-14.3)	6.20 (4.30-9.10)	71.5 (25.2-121)	294 (212-428)	594 (384-740)	289

Limit of detection (LOD, see Data Analysis section) for Survey years 11-12 and 13-14 are 2.3 and 1.7, respectively.

Biomonitoring Summary: https://www.cdc.gov/biomonitoring/Triclosan_BiomonitoringSummary.html

Factsheet: https://www.cdc.gov/biomonitoring/Triclosan_FactSheet.html

Source: *Centers for Disease Control & Prevention, Fourth National Report on Human Exposure to Environmental Chemicals, Updated Tables, January 2019*

Urinary Triclosan (creatinine corrected) (2003 – 2010)

CAS Number 3380-34-5

Geometric mean and selected percentiles of urine concentrations (in µg/g of creatinine) for the U.S. population from the National Health and Nutrition Examination Survey.

Categories (Survey Years)	Geometric Mean (95% conf. interval)	50th Percentile (95% conf. interval)	75th Percentile (95% conf. interval)	90th Percentile (95% conf. interval)	95th Percentile (95% conf. interval)	Sample Size
Total population (2003 - 2004)	12.7 (11.5-14.1)	9.48 (8.22-10.4)	43.9 (33.8-60.6)	212 (172-241)	368 (294-463)	2514
Total population (2005 - 2006)	18.0 (16.0-20.3)	13.0 (11.5-16.1)	73.2 (57.3-91.6)	304 (240-364)	532 (434-674)	2548
Total population (2007 - 2008)	15.5 (13.7-17.5)	12.4 (10.6-14.2)	50.4 (40.2-59.8)	233 (171-300)	443 (330-559)	2604
Total population (2009 - 2010)	15.1 (13.2-17.4)	10.9 (9.41-12.4)	49.4 (37.0-67.3)	256 (191-322)	454 (352-557)	2749
Age 6-11 years (2003 - 2004)	9.93 (7.43-13.3)	7.55 (4.72-13.4)	25.1 (15.3-35.6)	116 (39.9-236)	236 (115-336)	314
Age 6-11 years (2005 - 2006)	14.1 (10.8-18.5)	13.5 (7.97-18.5)	38.6 (26.0-54.1)	108 (62.4-169)	241 (108-598)	356
Age 6-11 years (2007 - 2008)	14.5 (9.47-22.1)	13.0 (8.00-17.5)	33.1 (17.5-72.4)	132 (52.7-331)	331 (131-599)	389
Age 6-11 years (2009 - 2010)	14.2 (12.4-16.4)	12.0 (8.84-15.0)	37.1 (27.0-47.3)	129 (89.1-155)	300 (148-469)	415
Age 12-19 years (2003 - 2004)	10.9 (8.32-14.2)	7.45 (5.48-10.7)	31.8 (21.9-61.1)	193 (90.7-318)	356 (169-580)	713
Age 12-19 years (2005 - 2006)	14.0 (11.0-17.8)	11.1 (8.68-13.6)	51.0 (33.0-73.4)	193 (125-306)	385 (203-739)	702
Age 12-19 years (2007 - 2008)	14.1 (11.0-18.1)	11.0 (7.87-14.4)	50.2 (27.1-78.8)	206 (95.3-293)	378 (238-571)	401
Age 12-19 years (2009 - 2010)	9.38 (7.86-11.2)	7.71 (5.71-9.21)	23.2 (17.3-29.3)	153 (63.0-201)	247 (166-379)	420
Age 20+ years (2003 - 2004)	13.4 (12.0-15.1)	10.0 (8.89-11.4)	50.0 (36.0-73.8)	224 (186-272)	385 (308-506)	1487
Age 20+ years (2005 - 2006)	19.3 (16.9-22.0)	13.7 (11.6-17.0)	86.1 (64.0-109)	343 (262-411)	581 (440-718)	1490
Age 20+ years (2007 - 2008)	15.8 (14.0-17.8)	12.6 (10.7-14.5)	52.3 (43.8-64.6)	244 (186-309)	484 (336-568)	1814
Age 20+ years (2009 - 2010)	16.4 (13.7-19.6)	11.5 (9.63-14.8)	57.1 (38.4-80.2)	279 (202-364)	504 (372-601)	1914
Males (2003 - 2004)	13.2 (11.3-15.6)	9.21 (6.86-12.1)	73.1 (45.8-85.9)	237 (175-294)	384 (294-506)	1228
Males (2005 - 2006)	17.1 (14.1-20.7)	12.4 (10.0-18.5)	82.6 (58.2-109)	308 (232-368)	472 (355-721)	1270
Males (2007 - 2008)	12.8 (10.9-15.0)	10.0 (8.12-13.0)	45.7 (32.1-57.3)	191 (132-241)	330 (253-456)	1294
Males (2009 - 2010)	13.3 (11.3-15.7)	9.21 (7.40-11.7)	43.9 (33.5-67.4)	230 (178-276)	345 (276-429)	1399
Females (2003 - 2004)	12.2 (10.6-14.2)	9.54 (8.45-10.4)	32.3 (26.2-46.6)	182 (138-217)	336 (225-480)	1286
Females (2005 - 2006)	19.0 (16.1-22.6)	13.8 (11.7-16.7)	64.0 (47.6-89.8)	301 (209-434)	619 (418-898)	1278
Females (2007 - 2008)	18.5 (15.6-22.0)	14.4 (12.4-16.8)	55.3 (38.5-77.0)	300 (182-435)	571 (359-729)	1310
Females (2009 - 2010)	17.1 (14.6-20.1)	12.3 (10.7-14.8)	50.6 (37.0-71.3)	300 (187-422)	556 (422-668)	1350
Mexican Americans (2003 - 2004)	13.3 (9.38-18.8)	9.18 (5.45-13.9)	66.7 (28.8-112)	292 (151-432)	453 (263-1150)	612
Mexican Americans (2005 - 2006)	24.1 (19.3-29.9)	17.6 (13.3-22.8)	154 (96.4-242)	440 (379-601)	736 (601-818)	637
Mexican Americans (2007 - 2008)	16.6 (12.2-22.6)	12.6 (8.51-16.5)	60.1 (39.6-80.3)	325 (182-475)	637 (368-828)	531
Mexican Americans (2009 - 2010)	14.8 (12.1-18.2)	9.38 (7.63-12.4)	45.4 (32.2-110)	352 (244-458)	578 (402-737)	566
Non-Hispanic blacks (2003 - 2004)	9.94 (7.92-12.5)	7.74 (5.50-10.0)	30.2 (25.6-37.3)	132 (78.0-213)	260 (127-513)	651
Non-Hispanic blacks (2005 - 2006)	12.2 (9.47-15.6)	9.50 (7.64-11.8)	41.0 (23.3-77.4)	179 (106-243)	352 (203-674)	678
Non-Hispanic blacks (2007 - 2008)	10.6 (8.91-12.7)	8.34 (6.47-10.1)	28.6 (22.3-36.7)	120 (71.0-203)	266 (151-407)	597
Non-Hispanic blacks (2009 - 2010)	9.23 (7.62-11.2)	6.62 (5.63-8.18)	22.7 (16.9-29.1)	136 (63.6-240)	356 (180-689)	516
Non-Hispanic whites (2003 - 2004)	13.3 (11.6-15.1)	9.82 (8.11-11.5)	47.0 (34.3-67.7)	213 (160-272)	358 (276-480)	1091
Non-Hispanic whites (2005 - 2006)	18.4 (16.0-21.2)	13.5 (11.6-17.0)	73.4 (56.8-97.0)	282 (231-343)	472 (367-699)	1038
Non-Hispanic whites (2007 - 2008)	15.6 (13.1-18.7)	13.0 (10.7-14.8)	50.4 (35.9-65.9)	222 (129-303)	418 (262-586)	1077
Non-Hispanic whites (2009 - 2010)	15.8 (13.1-19.0)	11.4 (9.41-14.8)	52.0 (37.0-71.3)	242 (159-323)	410 (317-547)	1206

Biomonitoring Summary: https://www.cdc.gov/biomonitoring/Triclosan_BiomonitoringSummary.html

Factsheet: https://www.cdc.gov/biomonitoring/Triclosan_FactSheet.html

Source: *Centers for Disease Control & Prevention, Fourth National Report on Human Exposure to Environmental Chemicals, Updated Tables, January 2019*

Urinary Triclosan (creatinine corrected) (2011 – 2014)

CAS Number 3380-34-5

Geometric mean and selected percentiles of urine concentrations (in µg/g of creatinine) for the U.S. population from the National Health and Nutrition Examination Survey.

Categories (Survey Years)	Geometric Mean (95% conf. interval)	50th Percentile (95% conf. interval)	75th Percentile (95% conf. interval)	90th Percentile (95% conf. interval)	95th Percentile (95% conf. interval)	Sample Size
Total population (2011 - 2012)	13.4 (11.8-15.1)	8.39 (6.79-10.0)	49.3 (37.4-57.5)	309 (229-404)	642 (508-788)	2487
Total population (2013 - 2014)	9.83 (9.00-10.7)	6.90 (6.27-7.65)	29.9 (25.1-34.4)	173 (138-207)	358 (292-425)	2684
Age 6-11 years (2011 - 2012)	10.3 (8.18-12.9)	6.70 (5.62-9.06)	22.4 (16.3-31.7)	103 (54.5-153)	235 (113-333)	395
Age 6-11 years (2013 - 2014)	10.4 (8.61-12.6)	8.97 (6.62-11.5)	23.4 (18.4-36.1)	78.1 (57.0-125)	184 (81.2-268)	409
Age 12-19 years (2011 - 2012)	9.84 (7.85-12.4)	5.83 (4.95-7.23)	26.3 (19.0-37.8)	182 (65.0-399)	421 (182-647)	388
Age 12-19 years (2013 - 2014)	6.46 (5.24-7.96)	5.11 (4.39-5.93)	15.7 (10.0-21.8)	53.6 (33.2-105)	153 (102-289)	462
Age 20+ years (2011 - 2012)	14.4 (12.4-16.7)	9.06 (7.41-11.2)	54.3 (43.9-75.0)	364 (246-514)	660 (536-817)	1704
Age 20+ years (2013 - 2014)	10.4 (9.44-11.4)	7.17 (6.32-8.26)	34.4 (29.3-41.6)	202 (162-234)	408 (296-531)	1813
Males (2011 - 2012)	10.8 (9.49-12.2)	6.40 (5.24-8.53)	37.4 (26.8-49.4)	226 (153-309)	536 (311-656)	1258
Males (2013 - 2014)	8.36 (7.44-9.41)	5.74 (4.80-6.67)	26.7 (22.6-31.8)	143 (111-195)	296 (216-426)	1284
Females (2011 - 2012)	16.5 (13.8-19.6)	10.8 (8.44-12.7)	53.3 (44.2-75.0)	381 (273-539)	746 (614-900)	1229
Females (2013 - 2014)	11.5 (10.0-13.1)	8.08 (6.70-9.23)	34.4 (25.1-42.2)	205 (150-253)	419 (294-573)	1400
Mexican Americans (2011 - 2012)	14.2 (10.4-19.5)	8.29 (6.10-12.4)	62.5 (31.8-111)	399 (163-536)	536 (271-900)	316
Mexican Americans (2013 - 2014)	8.82 (5.50-14.1)	6.08 (3.08-13.4)	25.5 (15.9-61.3)	147 (68.8-340)	425 (142-659)	438
Non-Hispanic blacks (2011 - 2012)	8.18 (7.09-9.44)	5.52 (4.66-6.27)	21.5 (16.7-29.9)	130 (74.3-222)	365 (229-461)	665
Non-Hispanic blacks (2013 - 2014)	6.16 (5.30-7.15)	4.27 (3.52-4.93)	16.7 (12.7-21.3)	107 (66.1-125)	218 (116-284)	609
Non-Hispanic whites (2011 - 2012)	14.2 (12.1-16.7)	8.95 (6.79-11.7)	51.9 (39.1-69.1)	311 (180-569)	675 (508-817)	811
Non-Hispanic whites (2013 - 2014)	10.6 (9.78-11.5)	7.78 (6.67-9.09)	33.0 (26.4-40.2)	178 (128-215)	339 (247-420)	987
All Hispanics (2011 - 2012)	15.0 (13.0-17.3)	8.58 (6.52-11.4)	70.8 (40.8-98.6)	449 (320-514)	647 (506-913)	571
All Hispanics (2013 - 2014)	9.07 (6.64-12.4)	6.08 (3.75-11.0)	24.7 (17.0-55.6)	197 (114-322)	462 (322-619)	690
Asians (2011 - 2012)	15.7 (10.2-24.2)	10.5 (6.05-17.4)	51.8 (23.6-142)	333 (127-609)	575 (381-719)	352
Asians (2013 - 2014)	14.6 (11.5-18.6)	8.00 (5.74-13.3)	100 (39.3-151)	406 (247-528)	659 (419-917)	288

Biomonitoring Summary: https://www.cdc.gov/biomonitoring/Triclosan_BiomonitoringSummary.html

Factsheet: https://www.cdc.gov/biomonitoring/Triclosan_FactSheet.html

Source: *Centers for Disease Control & Prevention, Fourth National Report on Human Exposure to Environmental Chemicals, Updated Tables, January 2019*

Urinary Total Arsenic (2003 – 2010)

CAS Number 7440-38-2

Geometric mean and selected percentiles of urine concentrations (in µg /L) for the U.S. population from the National Health and Nutrition Examination Survey.

Categories (Survey Years)	Geometric Mean (95% conf. interval)	50th Percentile (95% conf. interval)	75th Percentile (95% conf. interval)	90th Percentile (95% conf. interval)	95th Percentile (95% conf. interval)	Sample Size
Total population (2003 - 2004)	8.30 (7.19-9.57)	7.70 (6.90-8.90)	16.0 (14.1-18.7)	37.4 (31.6-43.5)	65.4 (48.7-83.3)	2557
Total population (2005 - 2006)	9.29 (8.05-10.7)	8.65 (7.48-9.99)	17.1 (14.9-20.6)	41.1 (33.3-49.7)	66.7 (53.7-87.0)	2576
Total population (2007 - 2008)	8.10 (7.44-8.83)	7.49 (6.90-8.12)	14.9 (13.2-17.0)	33.3 (29.8-38.7)	50.8 (42.3-65.1)	2605
Total population (2009 - 2010)	9.28 (8.47-10.2)	8.15 (7.20-8.98)	18.0 (15.3-20.8)	44.6 (39.0-55.1)	85.6 (64.7-114)	2860
Age 6-11 years (2003 - 2004)	7.08 (5.66-8.84)	6.80 (5.90-7.70)	10.9 (8.90-14.2)	24.6 (13.8-61.8)	46.9 (17.5-178)	290
Age 6-11 years (2005 - 2006)	7.19 (5.81-8.90)	6.96 (5.32-8.88)	11.5 (9.19-16.0)	19.6 (13.1-51.5)	34.1 (19.6-58.5)	355
Age 6-11 years (2007 - 2008)	6.85 (5.98-7.83)	6.40 (5.74-7.23)	10.8 (9.75-12.3)	22.5 (16.9-34.7)	41.0 (21.1-52.8)	390
Age 6-11 years (2009 - 2010)	6.63 (5.74-7.66)	5.94 (5.14-7.19)	10.8 (9.37-12.5)	26.0 (18.2-33.4)	37.7 (27.8-65.6)	378
Age 12-19 years (2003 - 2004)	8.55 (7.34-9.97)	8.10 (6.80-9.40)	15.2 (12.2-17.8)	30.5 (23.1-40.4)	46.1 (32.9-62.5)	725
Age 12-19 years (2005 - 2006)	8.19 (6.87-9.77)	7.92 (6.37-9.50)	14.0 (11.6-18.1)	28.2 (22.9-32.9)	41.9 (32.7-48.0)	701
Age 12-19 years (2007 - 2008)	7.09 (6.17-8.14)	6.87 (5.88-7.86)	11.4 (9.41-13.7)	20.4 (16.1-26.6)	38.2 (21.6-53.3)	373
Age 12-19 years (2009 - 2010)	6.45 (5.58-7.47)	6.11 (5.26-6.89)	10.8 (8.59-13.7)	25.9 (16.2-32.9)	38.8 (27.8-55.1)	454
Age 20+ years (2003 - 2004)	8.41 (7.25-9.77)	7.90 (7.00-9.10)	17.0 (15.0-19.7)	40.5 (34.9-46.2)	66.2 (51.2-93.1)	1542
Age 20+ years (2005 - 2006)	9.76 (8.43-11.3)	9.12 (7.85-10.4)	18.9 (15.8-22.9)	44.2 (35.2-56.1)	71.4 (57.7-98.3)	1520
Age 20+ years (2007 - 2008)	8.43 (7.70-9.22)	7.94 (7.09-8.67)	16.2 (14.5-18.6)	35.2 (30.4-42.3)	59.0 (44.2-75.6)	1842
Age 20+ years (2009 - 2010)	10.2 (9.14-11.3)	8.75 (7.95-9.81)	20.4 (17.2-24.1)	52.1 (42.4-66.1)	93.1 (74.2-127)	2028
Males (2003 - 2004)	9.50 (8.34-10.8)	8.90 (7.70-9.80)	17.6 (15.2-20.1)	41.6 (32.5-52.8)	65.8 (48.7-95.4)	1281
Males (2005 - 2006)	10.1 (8.61-11.8)	8.95 (8.05-10.0)	18.3 (15.5-22.9)	40.8 (31.0-52.6)	63.7 (46.4-78.7)	1271
Males (2007 - 2008)	9.25 (8.28-10.3)	8.50 (7.37-9.53)	17.0 (14.6-19.4)	36.0 (32.1-44.2)	62.5 (44.3-84.6)	1318
Males (2009 - 2010)	10.1 (9.06-11.3)	8.80 (7.80-9.75)	20.4 (16.1-23.9)	47.4 (42.1-64.1)	89.1 (71.6-114)	1401
Females (2003 - 2004)	7.30 (6.02-8.84)	6.90 (5.90-8.30)	15.0 (11.3-19.5)	33.4 (26.5-41.7)	60.5 (40.8-77.1)	1276
Females (2005 - 2006)	8.60 (7.38-10.0)	8.18 (6.64-9.97)	15.9 (13.7-19.9)	41.5 (32.2-53.7)	72.6 (54.8-122)	1305
Females (2007 - 2008)	7.14 (6.51-7.82)	6.54 (6.09-7.14)	12.7 (11.6-14.4)	30.1 (26.0-34.0)	49.1 (40.1-57.5)	1287
Females (2009 - 2010)	8.55 (7.44-9.83)	7.63 (6.45-8.62)	15.8 (13.1-19.9)	41.5 (31.7-55.5)	81.5 (54.3-132)	1459
Mexican Americans (2003 - 2004)	9.29 (8.12-10.6)	9.20 (8.10-10.3)	16.2 (13.5-19.9)	34.4 (24.0-60.5)	68.2 (41.3-111)	618
Mexican Americans (2005 - 2006)	9.55 (8.54-10.7)	9.11 (7.99-10.3)	15.6 (14.0-17.1)	29.2 (21.4-56.8)	67.6 (41.7-81.4)	652
Mexican Americans (2007 - 2008)	8.98 (8.13-9.92)	8.84 (7.80-9.48)	15.4 (12.3-19.7)	35.2 (25.0-46.0)	53.0 (44.2-77.4)	510
Mexican Americans (2009 - 2010)	8.47 (7.30-9.84)	7.96 (6.87-9.08)	13.9 (11.3-17.7)	34.7 (25.0-53.2)	60.9 (49.3-78.7)	613
Non-Hispanic blacks (2003 - 2004)	11.6 (9.50-14.1)	10.4 (7.90-11.8)	21.5 (14.9-34.4)	43.5 (36.2-61.8)	78.0 (43.6-141)	722
Non-Hispanic blacks (2005 - 2006)	11.0 (8.60-14.0)	9.55 (6.99-13.3)	21.9 (14.9-28.9)	44.9 (31.1-71.4)	82.3 (49.2-164)	692
Non-Hispanic blacks (2007 - 2008)	10.5 (9.40-11.7)	9.21 (8.22-10.4)	18.4 (16.1-21.5)	42.4 (32.9-52.8)	65.6 (45.5-112)	585
Non-Hispanic blacks (2009 - 2010)	10.9 (9.46-12.5)	9.26 (7.70-11.4)	21.7 (17.6-24.2)	49.1 (32.2-81.7)	84.8 (51.3-174)	546
Non-Hispanic whites (2003 - 2004)	7.12 (6.13-8.27)	7.00 (6.10-7.90)	13.7 (11.3-15.8)	29.0 (22.6-35.9)	53.1 (38.4-65.6)	1074
Non-Hispanic whites (2005 - 2006)	8.66 (7.20-10.4)	8.05 (6.52-9.66)	16.3 (13.4-20.6)	40.8 (29.4-50.2)	58.5 (46.0-88.0)	1041
Non-Hispanic whites (2007 - 2008)	6.98 (6.31-7.71)	6.46 (5.93-7.29)	12.4 (11.3-14.3)	28.3 (21.6-32.6)	42.1 (32.3-50.0)	1088
Non-Hispanic whites (2009 - 2010)	8.18 (7.46-8.96)	7.24 (6.46-8.21)	14.8 (12.7-17.4)	38.9 (31.7-44.4)	66.3 (49.3-88.7)	1224

Limit of detection (LOD, see Data Analysis section) for Survey years 03-04, 05-06, 07-08 and 09-10 are 0.74, 0.74, 0.74, and 0.74 respectively.

Biomonitoring Summary: https://www.cdc.gov/biomonitoring/Arsenic_BiomonitoringSummary.html

Factsheet: https://www.cdc.gov/biomonitoring/Arsenic_FactSheet.html

Source: *Centers for Disease Control & Prevention, Fourth National Report on Human Exposure to Environmental Chemicals, Updated Tables, January 2019*

Urinary Total Arsenic (2011 – 2016)

CAS Number 7440-38-2

Geometric mean and selected percentiles of urine concentrations (in µg/L) for the U.S. population from the National Health and Nutrition Examination Survey.

Categories (Survey Years)	Geometric Mean (95% conf. interval)	50th Percentile (95% conf. interval)	75th Percentile (95% conf. interval)	90th Percentile (95% conf. interval)	95th Percentile (95% conf. interval)	Sample Size
Total population (2011 - 2012)	6.85 (5.85-8.02)	6.09 (5.22-7.12)	13.0 (10.9-16.6)	32.0 (25.9-39.0)	52.5 (41.9-66.2)	2504
Total population (2013 - 2014)	6.29 (5.58-7.08)	5.82 (5.10-6.69)	11.7 (10.5-13.2)	26.6 (23.7-30.1)	46.0 (37.5-56.1)	2662
Total population (2015 - 2016)	5.96 (5.53-6.43)	5.41 (4.92-5.84)	11.1 (9.91-12.2)	25.0 (20.8-30.0)	44.6 (35.7-53.8)	3061
Age 3-5 years (2015 - 2016)	4.05 (3.58-4.58)	3.72 (3.27-4.23)	6.67 (5.66-8.35)	12.8 (9.93-19.9)	22.4 (13.4-54.8)	486
Age 6-11 years (2011 - 2012)	6.02 (5.03-7.19)	5.50 (4.58-6.56)	10.5 (7.93-14.1)	30.1 (16.7-46.5)	53.0 (37.5-70.3)	399
Age 6-11 years (2013 - 2014)	5.21 (4.57-5.95)	4.78 (4.27-5.57)	8.79 (7.52-10.3)	17.1 (12.4-25.3)	29.0 (17.9-47.7)	402
Age 6-11 years (2015 - 2016)	4.89 (4.29-5.56)	4.51 (4.21-4.96)	7.59 (6.66-8.71)	15.7 (11.1-22.7)	28.9 (17.1-56.9)	379
Age 12-19 years (2011 - 2012)	6.01 (4.45-8.11)	5.26 (3.95-7.47)	10.9 (7.74-16.9)	25.9 (16.6-44.0)	44.0 (25.9-153)	390
Age 12-19 years (2013 - 2014)	5.79 (4.96-6.75)	5.33 (4.83-5.91)	9.40 (8.44-11.8)	22.0 (17.4-28.1)	44.1 (27.0-90.8)	451
Age 12-19 years (2015 - 2016)	5.00 (4.52-5.54)	4.75 (4.07-5.23)	8.78 (7.64-10.6)	17.1 (14.6-20.1)	29.8 (19.2-35.6)	402
Age 20+ years (2011 - 2012)	7.09 (6.03-8.33)	6.31 (5.32-7.45)	13.6 (11.3-18.3)	33.2 (26.7-39.5)	52.5 (41.9-77.3)	1715
Age 20+ years (2013 - 2014)	6.49 (5.72-7.36)	6.12 (5.22-7.06)	12.1 (10.9-14.2)	27.9 (24.1-32.1)	48.0 (37.5-57.5)	1809
Age 20+ years (2015 - 2016)	6.35 (5.88-6.84)	5.74 (5.15-6.59)	11.9 (10.7-13.7)	27.6 (23.5-33.2)	49.9 (38.9-59.9)	1794
Males (2011 - 2012)	7.69 (6.35-9.31)	6.84 (5.33-8.59)	15.4 (11.7-19.7)	33.5 (27.7-41.9)	56.5 (42.2-78.0)	1262
Males (2013 - 2014)	6.67 (5.97-7.46)	6.37 (5.68-7.12)	11.7 (10.8-13.0)	27.0 (22.3-32.5)	48.5 (33.3-57.5)	1316
Males (2015 - 2016)	6.54 (6.03-7.09)	5.66 (5.14-6.46)	11.3 (9.95-13.3)	26.7 (22.8-33.2)	49.9 (35.5-67.2)	1524
Females (2011 - 2012)	6.14 (5.22-7.22)	5.42 (4.79-6.25)	11.6 (9.85-13.7)	29.0 (22.5-38.2)	50.6 (37.5-79.8)	1242
Females (2013 - 2014)	5.94 (5.18-6.80)	5.38 (4.68-6.28)	11.2 (9.49-13.7)	26.0 (21.8-31.1)	43.6 (36.0-55.8)	1346
Females (2015 - 2016)	5.46 (4.89-6.10)	5.07 (4.50-5.65)	10.7 (9.14-12.1)	22.7 (17.6-29.5)	43.0 (32.1-51.1)	1537
Mexican Americans (2011 - 2012)	7.12 (5.73-8.84)	6.94 (5.34-8.70)	12.2 (9.84-16.5)	24.2 (18.4-35.7)	44.0 (23.8-70.3)	317
Mexican Americans (2013 - 2014)	5.73 (5.01-6.56)	5.64 (4.93-6.47)	9.19 (8.10-10.2)	17.5 (11.2-36.6)	36.6 (15.4-73.0)	453
Mexican Americans (2015 - 2016)	5.80 (5.30-6.35)	5.65 (5.15-6.17)	10.2 (8.62-11.3)	17.3 (14.6-22.8)	28.0 (18.8-54.7)	585
Non-Hispanic blacks (2011 - 2012)	9.31 (7.19-12.0)	8.18 (6.16-10.8)	17.9 (13.1-25.3)	46.8 (28.8-76.5)	82.1 (53.1-107)	669
Non-Hispanic blacks (2013 - 2014)	8.17 (6.87-9.72)	6.99 (6.01-8.20)	14.9 (10.9-18.2)	30.7 (25.5-38.2)	59.8 (40.0-79.0)	579
Non-Hispanic blacks (2015 - 2016)	7.89 (6.85-9.09)	7.00 (6.11-8.66)	15.5 (13.3-17.4)	31.2 (24.6-49.2)	62.7 (33.8-133)	671
Non-Hispanic whites (2011 - 2012)	5.89 (4.92-7.06)	5.08 (4.56-6.06)	10.8 (8.48-15.5)	26.3 (20.3-34.9)	43.2 (34.9-56.0)	820
Non-Hispanic whites (2013 - 2014)	5.67 (4.88-6.59)	5.30 (4.40-6.62)	11.0 (9.16-12.7)	22.4 (17.6-29.9)	39.0 (30.8-50.6)	985
Non-Hispanic whites (2015 - 2016)	5.17 (4.75-5.62)	4.64 (4.39-4.96)	9.61 (8.15-11.2)	20.4 (15.3-25.2)	36.1 (25.2-46.3)	924
All Hispanics (2011 - 2012)	7.62 (6.63-8.76)	7.32 (6.31-8.35)	13.7 (11.7-16.6)	25.8 (21.2-29.8)	45.6 (28.7-55.8)	573
All Hispanics (2013 - 2014)	6.16 (5.24-7.22)	5.93 (5.02-6.82)	10.4 (9.11-11.9)	20.2 (14.2-30.1)	37.5 (24.1-57.9)	701
All Hispanics (2015 - 2016)	6.38 (5.83-6.98)	5.94 (5.56-6.34)	11.1 (9.43-12.5)	22.9 (17.8-28.0)	40.6 (28.0-70.1)	982
Asians (2011 - 2012)	16.7 (14.7-18.9)	14.9 (12.8-19.0)	39.0 (33.2-44.8)	83.2 (61.4-108)	117 (88.4-145)	353
Asians (2013 - 2014)	12.1 (10.4-14.1)	11.5 (9.08-13.6)	30.8 (23.2-37.0)	70.7 (52.5-90.8)	126 (79.2-181)	292
Asians (2015 - 2016)	14.3 (11.6-17.7)	14.7 (10.9-17.9)	32.1 (21.2-47.4)	62.4 (50.5-85.5)	92.5 (65.7-127)	332

Limit of detection (LOD, see Data Analysis section) for Survey years 11-12, 13-14, and 15-16 are 1.25, 0.26, and 0.26, respectively.

Biomonitoring Summary: https://www.cdc.gov/biomonitoring/Arsenic_BiomonitoringSummary.html

Factsheet: https://www.cdc.gov/biomonitoring/Arsenic_FactSheet.html

Source: *Centers for Disease Control & Prevention, Fourth National Report on Human Exposure to Environmental Chemicals, Updated Tables, January 2019*

Urinary Total Arsenic (creatinine corrected) (2003 – 2010)

CAS Number 7440-38-2

Geometric mean and selected percentiles of urine concentrations (in µg /g of creatinine) for the U.S. population from the National Health and Nutrition Examination Survey.

Categories (Survey Years)	Geometric Mean (95% conf. interval)	50th Percentile (95% conf. interval)	75th Percentile (95% conf. interval)	90th Percentile (95% conf. interval)	95th Percentile (95% conf. interval)	Sample Size
Total population (2003 - 2004)	8.24 (7.07-9.59)	7.04 (5.93-8.51)	14.1 (11.6-17.2)	30.4 (26.0-38.7)	50.4 (40.3-64.5)	2557
Total population (2005 - 2006)	9.15 (7.93-10.6)	7.70 (6.55-8.98)	15.2 (11.7-19.4)	35.1 (26.5-44.7)	62.8 (44.7-85.0)	2576
Total population (2007 - 2008)	8.46 (7.78-9.21)	7.06 (6.56-7.74)	13.8 (12.5-15.2)	28.9 (24.2-36.7)	49.0 (38.8-70.5)	2605
Total population (2009 - 2010)	9.90 (9.06-10.8)	7.90 (6.98-8.97)	17.6 (15.4-20.2)	45.2 (36.6-53.3)	80.8 (60.5-94.4)	2860
Age 6-11 years (2003 - 2004)	8.25 (6.58-10.3)	7.18 (5.93-9.45)	11.7 (9.10-16.3)	22.2 (12.0-69.5)	40.1 (14.7-188)	290
Age 6-11 years (2005 - 2006)	8.88 (7.05-11.2)	7.87 (6.19-9.42)	11.8 (9.32-18.9)	24.5 (13.0-62.8)	45.4 (22.9-80.9)	355
Age 6-11 years (2007 - 2008)	8.87 (8.06-9.77)	7.53 (6.73-7.88)	13.4 (10.2-16.0)	26.7 (19.9-34.0)	37.2 (28.6-71.4)	390
Age 6-11 years (2009 - 2010)	8.97 (7.93-10.2)	7.42 (6.70-8.32)	11.0 (9.90-14.0)	33.5 (17.0-54.6)	60.8 (36.6-84.9)	378
Age 12-19 years (2003 - 2004)	6.11 (5.23-7.13)	5.06 (4.47-6.04)	9.66 (7.44-11.2)	17.8 (12.0-26.0)	27.8 (20.7-35.9)	725
Age 12-19 years (2005 - 2006)	6.30 (5.56-7.14)	5.19 (4.80-6.19)	9.62 (8.12-11.1)	19.4 (13.9-25.8)	28.0 (21.9-33.2)	701
Age 12-19 years (2007 - 2008)	5.50 (4.91-6.16)	4.96 (4.25-5.40)	7.69 (6.09-9.31)	16.8 (10.8-21.1)	22.5 (16.8-29.1)	373
Age 12-19 years (2009 - 2010)	6.06 (5.34-6.87)	4.95 (4.39-5.81)	9.18 (7.00-11.0)	19.2 (14.5-21.3)	28.4 (20.8-35.7)	454
Age 20+ years (2003 - 2004)	8.64 (7.38-10.1)	7.47 (6.20-9.01)	15.4 (12.7-18.8)	33.8 (27.3-41.2)	53.9 (45.4-64.5)	1542
Age 20+ years (2005 - 2006)	9.75 (8.46-11.2)	8.22 (6.98-9.75)	17.0 (12.8-21.3)	41.0 (29.6-52.5)	68.4 (52.8-89.7)	1520
Age 20+ years (2007 - 2008)	9.00 (8.20-9.88)	7.55 (6.79-8.53)	14.9 (13.1-17.1)	32.5 (25.8-41.0)	59.4 (41.0-86.2)	1842
Age 20+ years (2009 - 2010)	10.8 (9.71-12.0)	8.73 (7.69-9.71)	20.1 (16.5-24.2)	50.8 (40.5-59.7)	87.3 (70.0-105)	2028
Males (2003 - 2004)	8.00 (6.81-9.40)	6.75 (5.66-8.35)	13.7 (11.0-18.0)	28.7 (25.1-36.4)	45.6 (35.3-62.1)	1281
Males (2005 - 2006)	8.26 (7.09-9.63)	7.16 (5.87-8.54)	12.9 (10.2-18.0)	28.8 (22.9-36.3)	46.1 (35.1-66.5)	1271
Males (2007 - 2008)	8.30 (7.49-9.18)	6.79 (6.39-7.61)	13.2 (11.8-15.2)	28.9 (23.5-38.5)	47.7 (35.7-68.1)	1318
Males (2009 - 2010)	9.21 (8.55-9.93)	7.22 (6.43-8.67)	17.0 (14.9-18.6)	41.8 (35.4-47.9)	66.9 (52.0-81.5)	1401
Females (2003 - 2004)	8.47 (7.12-10.1)	7.33 (6.10-8.75)	14.4 (11.7-17.7)	32.3 (24.2-46.6)	58.4 (42.8-75.0)	1276
Females (2005 - 2006)	10.1 (8.72-11.7)	8.29 (7.23-9.87)	17.4 (13.0-21.4)	43.8 (29.2-61.5)	74.1 (55.0-96.2)	1305
Females (2007 - 2008)	8.63 (7.91-9.41)	7.13 (6.53-8.33)	14.1 (12.3-16.9)	27.9 (24.1-37.0)	51.4 (39.7-83.3)	1287
Females (2009 - 2010)	10.6 (9.36-12.0)	8.38 (7.40-9.41)	18.6 (14.9-23.9)	50.8 (35.1-72.9)	87.8 (66.8-109)	1459
Mexican Americans (2003 - 2004)	8.61 (7.33-10.1)	7.76 (6.30-9.44)	12.6 (10.2-15.9)	24.0 (17.7-34.8)	42.4 (24.8-62.4)	618
Mexican Americans (2005 - 2006)	8.98 (7.89-10.2)	7.48 (6.72-8.87)	12.8 (11.0-16.3)	28.1 (21.1-35.5)	49.1 (31.0-108)	652
Mexican Americans (2007 - 2008)	8.88 (7.71-10.2)	7.38 (6.51-8.63)	14.1 (10.6-17.8)	28.6 (22.5-35.3)	48.2 (31.1-75.7)	510
Mexican Americans (2009 - 2010)	8.88 (7.87-10.0)	7.62 (6.69-8.45)	13.2 (10.7-17.2)	31.4 (23.7-38.5)	49.8 (37.5-68.9)	613
Non-Hispanic blacks (2003 - 2004)	8.31 (6.99-9.88)	6.88 (5.66-8.41)	13.8 (11.5-17.0)	27.6 (17.9-56.0)	54.3 (27.5-120)	722
Non-Hispanic blacks (2005 - 2006)	7.96 (6.40-9.92)	6.48 (5.21-8.30)	13.4 (10.0-18.6)	32.5 (18.7-66.5)	71.4 (35.6-98.8)	692
Non-Hispanic blacks (2007 - 2008)	7.72 (6.98-8.54)	6.60 (6.01-7.56)	13.4 (11.5-15.4)	25.7 (22.1-30.0)	42.7 (31.4-60.3)	585
Non-Hispanic blacks (2009 - 2010)	8.67 (7.54-9.98)	7.26 (5.96-9.02)	15.6 (12.4-21.3)	38.7 (31.5-48.7)	63.9 (43.1-102)	546
Non-Hispanic whites (2003 - 2004)	7.50 (6.25-9.01)	6.32 (5.28-7.96)	12.5 (9.86-17.1)	26.8 (21.8-32.0)	40.0 (31.3-53.9)	1074
Non-Hispanic whites (2005 - 2006)	9.01 (7.57-10.7)	7.68 (6.18-9.56)	14.3 (11.1-20.8)	31.9 (24.1-46.1)	59.4 (37.9-96.2)	1041
Non-Hispanic whites (2007 - 2008)	7.82 (7.05-8.68)	6.72 (6.00-7.54)	12.5 (11.1-13.9)	24.6 (19.6-32.3)	43.1 (29.1-64.0)	1088
Non-Hispanic whites (2009 - 2010)	9.14 (8.35-10.0)	7.10 (6.43-8.06)	15.8 (13.7-18.4)	40.9 (30.4-50.8)	66.4 (50.9-90.0)	1224

Biomonitoring Summary: https://www.cdc.gov/biomonitoring/Arsenic_BiomonitoringSummary.html

Factsheet: https://www.cdc.gov/biomonitoring/Arsenic_FactSheet.html

Source: *Centers for Disease Control & Prevention, Fourth National Report on Human Exposure to Environmental Chemicals, Updated Tables, January 2019*

Urinary Total Arsenic (creatinine corrected) (2011 – 2016)

CAS Number 7440-38-2

Geometric mean and selected percentiles of urine concentrations (in µg/g of creatinine) for the U.S. population from the National Health and Nutrition Examination Survey.

Categories (Survey Years)	Geometric Mean (95% conf. interval)	50th Percentile (95% conf. interval)	75th Percentile (95% conf. interval)	90th Percentile (95% conf. interval)	95th Percentile (95% conf. interval)	Sample Size
Total population (2011 - 2012)	7.77 (6.85-8.81)	6.39 (5.57-7.24)	13.7 (11.5-16.5)	30.8 (24.6-38.6)	50.4 (38.2-70.1)	2502
Total population (2013 - 2014)	7.27 (6.62-7.99)	6.10 (5.39-6.88)	11.9 (10.5-13.5)	27.6 (23.8-32.8)	52.0 (43.5-60.9)	2661
Total population (2015 - 2016)	6.69 (6.32-7.08)	5.56 (5.32-5.85)	10.7 (9.74-11.5)	24.9 (20.1-30.0)	45.8 (32.0-65.3)	3058
Age 3-5 years (2015 - 2016)	9.31 (8.18-10.6)	8.27 (7.40-9.15)	12.5 (10.6-14.9)	21.1 (17.3-28.8)	40.9 (22.8-83.5)	485
Age 6-11 years (2011 - 2012)	8.63 (7.26-10.3)	6.87 (5.84-8.00)	12.3 (9.58-15.5)	27.7 (17.7-57.7)	91.2 (26.2-129)	398
Age 6-11 years (2013 - 2014)	7.78 (7.08-8.54)	6.91 (5.91-7.65)	12.5 (10.3-13.6)	17.7 (16.1-21.1)	29.9 (20.4-52.1)	402
Age 6-11 years (2015 - 2016)	6.93 (6.48-7.41)	6.09 (5.66-6.56)	9.53 (8.15-11.0)	18.2 (13.6-25.0)	28.1 (21.9-40.6)	379
Age 12-19 years (2011 - 2012)	5.75 (4.49-7.36)	4.69 (3.70-5.73)	8.73 (6.26-13.3)	22.1 (11.5-52.6)	34.9 (21.1-159)	390
Age 12-19 years (2013 - 2014)	5.24 (4.53-6.06)	4.21 (3.61-4.61)	7.92 (5.75-10.3)	17.6 (12.6-23.0)	30.5 (20.3-54.1)	451
Age 12-19 years (2015 - 2016)	4.67 (4.34-5.03)	3.94 (3.55-4.54)	7.09 (5.91-7.91)	14.7 (11.6-16.8)	22.3 (15.4-31.5)	402
Age 20+ years (2011 - 2012)	8.04 (7.07-9.14)	6.52 (5.88-7.69)	14.8 (12.1-18.8)	32.4 (25.2-39.8)	49.7 (38.2-70.1)	1714
Age 20+ years (2013 - 2014)	7.58 (6.87-8.36)	6.39 (5.66-7.29)	12.4 (10.9-14.7)	31.0 (26.0-37.9)	54.0 (47.9-66.1)	1808
Age 20+ years (2015 - 2016)	6.92 (6.51-7.35)	5.62 (5.27-5.95)	11.0 (10.3-12.5)	28.1 (21.9-33.6)	56.2 (36.5-74.6)	1792
Males (2011 - 2012)	7.20 (6.15-8.43)	6.13 (5.18-7.23)	12.5 (10.5-15.2)	28.3 (20.2-34.9)	50.4 (33.3-69.6)	1261
Males (2013 - 2014)	6.69 (6.07-7.38)	5.55 (4.96-6.26)	10.9 (9.50-12.5)	26.0 (19.5-30.6)	47.9 (36.5-55.3)	1315
Males (2015 - 2016)	6.21 (5.75-6.71)	5.23 (4.70-5.70)	9.81 (8.68-11.0)	22.3 (18.1-28.1)	43.3 (30.4-61.5)	1524
Females (2011 - 2012)	8.35 (7.40-9.42)	6.64 (6.12-7.37)	15.0 (12.2-19.1)	33.1 (26.1-41.4)	50.7 (39.8-79.0)	1241
Females (2013 - 2014)	7.88 (7.03-8.82)	6.67 (5.82-7.78)	13.1 (10.9-15.6)	31.3 (24.9-39.4)	54.1 (46.3-68.3)	1346
Females (2015 - 2016)	7.19 (6.54-7.89)	5.94 (5.47-6.40)	11.3 (9.96-13.8)	25.9 (20.0-33.4)	48.2 (31.5-71.1)	1534
Mexican Americans (2011 - 2012)	8.00 (6.85-9.36)	6.91 (6.07-7.98)	11.9 (9.05-14.6)	26.1 (16.7-39.4)	40.8 (24.0-70.1)	317
Mexican Americans (2013 - 2014)	6.54 (5.70-7.51)	5.83 (5.08-6.54)	8.97 (7.32-11.6)	17.1 (12.6-20.8)	29.2 (15.1-72.2)	453
Mexican Americans (2015 - 2016)	6.30 (5.77-6.88)	5.41 (5.14-5.91)	9.08 (7.94-10.8)	16.9 (13.8-20.2)	26.4 (19.5-41.2)	584
Non-Hispanic blacks (2011 - 2012)	7.24 (5.51-9.51)	5.83 (4.65-7.96)	13.5 (9.02-19.0)	28.8 (21.5-46.3)	55.4 (31.6-87.1)	669
Non-Hispanic blacks (2013 - 2014)	6.23 (5.25-7.39)	4.86 (4.24-6.22)	10.3 (8.03-13.4)	22.7 (17.8-29.1)	37.4 (25.8-70.5)	579
Non-Hispanic blacks (2015 - 2016)	6.28 (5.43-7.26)	5.21 (4.58-6.14)	11.1 (8.39-14.3)	26.5 (20.0-32.3)	41.2 (29.1-72.2)	669
Non-Hispanic whites (2011 - 2012)	7.13 (6.05-8.39)	5.72 (5.05-6.70)	12.4 (10.3-15.4)	28.4 (21.7-37.5)	46.5 (33.1-75.8)	818
Non-Hispanic whites (2013 - 2014)	7.01 (6.25-7.87)	5.87 (5.13-6.88)	11.6 (9.92-13.7)	27.5 (21.6-35.8)	49.5 (40.8-55.3)	984
Non-Hispanic whites (2015 - 2016)	6.09 (5.64-6.59)	5.14 (4.80-5.52)	9.30 (8.16-10.6)	19.9 (15.7-25.9)	33.8 (25.3-62.5)	924
All Hispanics (2011 - 2012)	8.53 (7.74-9.40)	7.60 (6.84-8.42)	12.8 (11.2-14.1)	25.3 (20.8-30.8)	37.5 (28.2-50.6)	573
All Hispanics (2013 - 2014)	6.87 (6.08-7.76)	6.26 (5.36-6.89)	10.3 (8.75-11.9)	18.7 (14.3-24.0)	28.7 (18.9-50.7)	701
All Hispanics (2015 - 2016)	7.19 (6.70-7.72)	6.05 (5.58-6.80)	11.0 (9.69-12.1)	20.8 (18.3-24.0)	39.5 (26.6-61.2)	981
Asians (2011 - 2012)	22.3 (19.1-26.1)	20.1 (16.3-25.2)	39.4 (32.2-61.0)	100 (73.2-129)	162 (114-202)	353
Asians (2013 - 2014)	19.0 (16.1-22.5)	15.2 (13.0-19.2)	41.9 (31.1-59.2)	95.0 (74.2-131)	137 (111-229)	292
Asians (2015 - 2016)	19.6 (15.9-24.1)	18.6 (13.9-25.4)	41.0 (30.9-47.6)	74.3 (51.3-113)	118 (73.7-173)	332

Biomonitoring Summary: https://www.cdc.gov/biomonitoring/Arsenic_BiomonitoringSummary.html

Factsheet: https://www.cdc.gov/biomonitoring/Arsenic_FactSheet.html

Source: *Centers for Disease Control & Prevention, Fourth National Report on Human Exposure to Environmental Chemicals, Updated Tables, January 2019*

Blood Lead (1999 – 2010)

CAS Number 7439-92-1

Geometric mean and selected percentiles of blood concentrations (in µg/dL) for the U.S. population from the National Health and Nutrition Examination Survey.

Categories (Survey Years)	Geometric Mean (95% conf. interval)	50th Percentile (95% conf. interval)	75th Percentile (95% conf. interval)	90th Percentile (95% conf. interval)	95th Percentile (95% conf. interval)	Sample Size
Total population (1999 - 2000)	1.66 (1.60-1.72)	1.60 (1.60-1.70)	2.50 (2.40-2.60)	3.80 (3.60-4.00)	5.00 (4.70-5.50)	7970
Total population (2001 - 2002)	1.45 (1.39-1.51)	1.40 (1.40-1.50)	2.20 (2.10-2.30)	3.40 (3.20-3.60)	4.50 (4.20-4.70)	8945
Total population (2003 - 2004)	1.43 (1.36-1.50)	1.40 (1.30-1.50)	2.10 (2.10-2.20)	3.20 (3.10-3.30)	4.20 (3.90-4.40)	8373
Total population (2005 - 2006)	1.29 (1.23-1.36)	1.27 (1.20-1.34)	2.01 (1.91-2.11)	3.05 (2.86-3.22)	3.91 (3.64-4.18)	8407
Total population (2007 - 2008)	1.27 (1.21-1.34)	1.22 (1.18-1.30)	1.90 (1.80-2.00)	2.80 (2.67-2.96)	3.70 (3.50-3.90)	8266
Total population (2009 - 2010)	1.12 (1.08-1.16)	1.07 (1.03-1.12)	1.70 (1.62-1.77)	2.58 (2.45-2.71)	3.34 (3.14-3.57)	8793
Age 1-5 years (1999 - 2000)	2.23 (1.96-2.53)	2.20 (1.90-2.50)	3.40 (2.80-3.90)	4.90 (4.00-6.60)	7.00 (6.10-8.30)	723
Age 1-5 years (2001 - 2002)	1.70 (1.55-1.87)	1.60 (1.50-1.80)	2.50 (2.20-2.90)	4.20 (3.50-5.20)	5.80 (4.70-6.90)	898
Age 1-5 years (2003 - 2004)	1.77 (1.60-1.95)	1.70 (1.50-1.90)	2.50 (2.30-2.80)	3.90 (3.30-4.60)	5.10 (4.10-6.60)	911
Age 1-5 years (2005 - 2006)	1.46 (1.36-1.57)	1.43 (1.34-1.55)	2.10 (1.97-2.20)	2.98 (2.72-3.32)	3.80 (3.49-4.54)	968
Age 1-5 years (2007 - 2008)	1.51 (1.37-1.66)	1.43 (1.30-1.60)	2.20 (1.98-2.31)	3.20 (2.65-3.85)	4.10 (3.40-5.19)	817
Age 1-5 years (2009 - 2010)	1.17 (1.08-1.26)	1.15 (1.03-1.27)	1.70 (1.50-1.87)	2.39 (2.08-2.65)	3.37 (2.63-4.11)	836
Age 6-11 years (1999 - 2000)	1.51 (1.36-1.66)	1.40 (1.30-1.60)	2.10 (1.80-2.50)	3.30 (2.80-3.80)	4.50 (3.40-6.20)	905
Age 6-11 years (2001 - 2002)	1.25 (1.14-1.36)	1.20 (1.00-1.30)	1.70 (1.60-2.00)	2.80 (2.50-3.10)	3.70 (3.00-4.70)	1044
Age 6-11 years (2003 - 2004)	1.25 (1.12-1.39)	1.20 (1.10-1.40)	1.80 (1.50-2.10)	2.60 (2.10-3.10)	3.30 (2.50-4.60)	856
Age 6-11 years (2005 - 2006)	1.02 (.948-1.10)	.970 (.890-1.01)	1.40 (1.28-1.55)	2.06 (1.80-2.72)	3.00 (2.26-3.81)	934
Age 6-11 years (2007 - 2008)	.988 (.914-1.07)	.960 (.880-1.07)	1.31 (1.22-1.49)	1.90 (1.70-2.11)	2.50 (2.10-2.88)	1011
Age 6-11 years (2009 - 2010)	.838 (.792-.887)	.810 (.740-.840)	1.13 (1.06-1.21)	1.64 (1.45-1.84)	2.01 (1.88-2.25)	1009
Age 12-19 years (1999 - 2000)	1.10 (1.04-1.17)	1.10 (1.00-1.20)	1.50 (1.40-1.70)	2.30 (2.10-2.40)	2.90 (2.70-3.00)	2135
Age 12-19 years (2001 - 2002)	.942 (.899-.986)	.900 (.900-1.00)	1.30 (1.20-1.40)	2.00 (1.90-2.10)	2.70 (2.40-2.90)	2231
Age 12-19 years (2003 - 2004)	.946 (.878-1.02)	.900 (.800-1.00)	1.30 (1.20-1.40)	1.90 (1.70-2.10)	2.60 (2.20-3.00)	2081
Age 12-19 years (2005 - 2006)	.797 (.746-.852)	.740 (.690-.790)	1.08 (.990-1.20)	1.69 (1.50-1.85)	2.23 (1.98-2.46)	1996
Age 12-19 years (2007 - 2008)	.800 (.744-.859)	.760 (.720-.820)	1.04 (.980-1.16)	1.50 (1.35-1.70)	1.90 (1.70-2.32)	1074
Age 12-19 years (2009 - 2010)	.680 (.636-.727)	.660 (.590-.700)	.910 (.840-.990)	1.29 (1.19-1.43)	1.72 (1.52-1.86)	1183
Age 20+ years (1999 - 2000)	1.75 (1.68-1.81)	1.70 (1.60-1.80)	2.60 (2.50-2.70)	3.90 (3.70-4.10)	5.20 (4.80-5.60)	4207
Age 20+ years (2001 - 2002)	1.56 (1.49-1.62)	1.60 (1.50-1.60)	2.30 (2.30-2.40)	3.60 (3.40-3.70)	4.60 (4.30-5.00)	4772
Age 20+ years (2003 - 2004)	1.52 (1.45-1.60)	1.50 (1.40-1.60)	2.30 (2.20-2.40)	3.30 (3.20-3.50)	4.30 (4.00-4.60)	4525
Age 20+ years (2005 - 2006)	1.41 (1.34-1.48)	1.41 (1.33-1.48)	2.17 (2.04-2.31)	3.22 (3.05-3.43)	4.12 (3.82-4.38)	4509
Age 20+ years (2007 - 2008)	1.38 (1.31-1.46)	1.34 (1.26-1.42)	2.06 (1.94-2.18)	3.00 (2.80-3.14)	3.90 (3.68-4.23)	5364
Age 20+ years (2009 - 2010)	1.23 (1.19-1.28)	1.20 (1.14-1.25)	1.85 (1.78-1.93)	2.77 (2.60-2.93)	3.57 (3.29-3.84)	5765

Limit of detection (LOD, see Data Analysis section) for Survey years 99-00, 01-02, 03-04, 05-06, 07-08, and 09-10 are 0.3, 0.3, 0.28, 0.25, 0.25, and 0.25 respectively.

Biomonitoring Summary: https://www.cdc.gov/biomonitoring/Lead_BiomonitoringSummary.html

Factsheet: https://www.cdc.gov/biomonitoring/Lead_FactSheet.html

Source: *Centers for Disease Control & Prevention, Fourth National Report on Human Exposure to Environmental Chemicals, Updated Tables, January 2019*

Blood Lead (1999 – 2010)

CAS Number 7439-92-1

Geometric mean and selected percentiles of blood concentrations (in µg/dL) for the U.S. population from the National Health and Nutrition Examination Survey.

Categories (Survey Years)	Geometric Mean (95% conf. interval)	50th Percentile (95% conf. interval)	75th Percentile (95% conf. interval)	90th Percentile (95% conf. interval)	95th Percentile (95% conf. interval)	Sample Size
Males (1999 - 2000)	2.01 (1.93-2.09)	1.90 (1.90-2.00)	2.90 (2.80-3.00)	4.50 (4.10-4.80)	6.00 (5.50-6.50)	3913
Males (2001 - 2002)	1.78 (1.71-1.86)	1.80 (1.70-1.80)	2.70 (2.50-2.80)	3.90 (3.80-4.10)	5.40 (5.00-5.50)	4339
Males (2003 - 2004)	1.69 (1.62-1.75)	1.60 (1.50-1.70)	2.50 (2.40-2.60)	3.70 (3.40-3.90)	4.80 (4.50-5.20)	4132
Males (2005 - 2006)	1.52 (1.42-1.62)	1.49 (1.41-1.58)	2.30 (2.12-2.51)	3.48 (3.20-3.75)	4.36 (4.04-4.76)	4092
Males (2007 - 2008)	1.47 (1.39-1.56)	1.40 (1.32-1.50)	2.17 (2.00-2.30)	3.21 (3.01-3.53)	4.41 (4.10-4.88)	4147
Males (2009 - 2010)	1.31 (1.25-1.36)	1.26 (1.20-1.32)	1.96 (1.89-2.03)	2.93 (2.72-3.15)	3.84 (3.54-4.39)	4366
Females (1999 - 2000)	1.37 (1.32-1.43)	1.30 (1.30-1.40)	2.00 (1.90-2.10)	3.10 (2.90-3.30)	4.00 (3.80-4.20)	4057
Females (2001 - 2002)	1.19 (1.14-1.25)	1.20 (1.10-1.20)	1.80 (1.70-1.90)	2.60 (2.50-2.80)	3.60 (3.10-4.00)	4606
Females (2003 - 2004)	1.22 (1.14-1.31)	1.20 (1.10-1.30)	1.80 (1.70-2.00)	2.70 (2.50-3.00)	3.50 (3.10-3.80)	4241
Females (2005 - 2006)	1.11 (1.05-1.17)	1.06 (.980-1.15)	1.73 (1.61-1.84)	2.59 (2.44-2.74)	3.25 (3.12-3.44)	4315
Females (2007 - 2008)	1.11 (1.06-1.16)	1.09 (1.00-1.14)	1.64 (1.54-1.74)	2.41 (2.35-2.50)	3.00 (2.81-3.20)	4119
Females (2009 - 2010)	.966 (.929-1.01)	.940 (.890-.970)	1.43 (1.36-1.53)	2.18 (2.08-2.30)	2.81 (2.63-2.93)	4427
Mexican Americans (1999 - 2000)	1.83 (1.75-1.91)	1.80 (1.70-1.90)	2.80 (2.60-2.90)	4.20 (3.90-4.60)	5.80 (5.10-6.60)	2742
Mexican Americans (2001 - 2002)	1.46 (1.34-1.60)	1.50 (1.30-1.60)	2.30 (2.10-2.60)	3.60 (3.40-4.20)	5.40 (4.40-6.70)	2268
Mexican Americans (2003 - 2004)	1.55 (1.43-1.69)	1.50 (1.40-1.60)	2.30 (2.10-2.50)	3.50 (2.90-4.20)	4.90 (3.90-6.40)	2085
Mexican Americans (2005 - 2006)	1.29 (1.21-1.38)	1.26 (1.15-1.36)	2.00 (1.87-2.20)	3.16 (2.79-3.58)	4.22 (3.47-5.36)	2236
Mexican Americans (2007 - 2008)	1.25 (1.15-1.36)	1.20 (1.10-1.31)	1.88 (1.70-2.06)	2.81 (2.60-3.20)	3.92 (3.20-5.00)	1712
Mexican Americans (2009 - 2010)	1.14 (1.03-1.28)	1.04 (.940-1.18)	1.76 (1.52-1.99)	2.93 (2.63-3.30)	3.92 (3.60-4.69)	1966
Non-Hispanic blacks (1999 - 2000)	1.87 (1.75-2.00)	1.80 (1.70-2.00)	2.80 (2.60-3.00)	4.30 (4.00-4.60)	5.70 (5.20-6.10)	1842
Non-Hispanic blacks (2001 - 2002)	1.65 (1.52-1.80)	1.60 (1.40-1.70)	2.60 (2.30-2.90)	4.20 (3.80-4.70)	5.80 (5.30-6.50)	2219
Non-Hispanic blacks (2003 - 2004)	1.69 (1.52-1.89)	1.60 (1.40-1.80)	2.60 (2.20-3.00)	4.10 (3.50-4.70)	5.30 (4.60-6.60)	2293
Non-Hispanic blacks (2005 - 2006)	1.39 (1.26-1.53)	1.31 (1.19-1.45)	2.16 (1.95-2.42)	3.48 (3.19-3.80)	4.65 (4.21-5.14)	2193
Non-Hispanic blacks (2007 - 2008)	1.39 (1.30-1.48)	1.30 (1.20-1.42)	2.10 (2.00-2.20)	3.22 (3.08-3.50)	4.50 (4.00-4.80)	1746
Non-Hispanic blacks (2009 - 2010)	1.24 (1.18-1.30)	1.19 (1.12-1.25)	1.87 (1.76-1.99)	2.90 (2.68-3.18)	3.86 (3.57-4.29)	1593
Non-Hispanic whites (1999 - 2000)	1.62 (1.55-1.69)	1.60 (1.50-1.70)	2.40 (2.30-2.50)	3.60 (3.40-3.90)	5.00 (4.40-5.70)	2716
Non-Hispanic whites (2001 - 2002)	1.43 (1.37-1.48)	1.40 (1.30-1.50)	2.20 (2.10-2.20)	3.20 (3.10-3.40)	4.20 (3.90-4.50)	3806
Non-Hispanic whites (2003 - 2004)	1.37 (1.32-1.43)	1.30 (1.30-1.40)	2.10 (2.00-2.10)	3.00 (2.80-3.20)	3.90 (3.60-4.30)	3478
Non-Hispanic whites (2005 - 2006)	1.28 (1.19-1.37)	1.27 (1.17-1.38)	1.97 (1.86-2.14)	2.99 (2.73-3.25)	3.82 (3.41-4.20)	3310
Non-Hispanic whites (2007 - 2008)	1.24 (1.16-1.33)	1.20 (1.10-1.30)	1.86 (1.72-2.00)	2.70 (2.54-2.90)	3.50 (3.20-3.89)	3461
Non-Hispanic whites (2009 - 2010)	1.10 (1.04-1.16)	1.07 (1.00-1.15)	1.67 (1.59-1.76)	2.49 (2.35-2.63)	3.14 (2.99-3.36)	3760

Limit of detection (LOD, see Data Analysis section) for Survey years 99-00, 01-02, 03-04, 05-06, 07-08, and 09-10 are 0.3, 0.3, 0.28, 0.25, 0.25, and 0.25 respectively.

Biomonitoring Summary: https://www.cdc.gov/biomonitoring/Lead_BiomonitoringSummary.html

Factsheet: https://www.cdc.gov/biomonitoring/Lead_FactSheet.html

Source: *Centers for Disease Control & Prevention, Fourth National Report on Human Exposure to Environmental Chemicals, Updated Tables, January 2019*

Blood Lead (2011 – 2016)

CAS Number 7439-92-1

Geometric mean and selected percentiles of blood concentrations (in µg/dL) for the U.S. population from the National Health and Nutrition Examination Survey.

Categories (Survey Years)	Geometric Mean (95% conf. interval)	50th Percentile (95% conf. interval)	75th Percentile (95% conf. interval)	90th Percentile (95% conf. interval)	95th Percentile (95% conf. interval)	Sample Size
Total population (2011 - 2012)	.973 (.916-1.04)	.930 (.880-.980)	1.52 (1.41-1.61)	2.38 (2.17-2.61)	3.16 (2.77-3.68)	7920
Total population (2013 - 2014)	.858 (.813-.906)	.830 (.780-.870)	1.32 (1.24-1.42)	2.10 (1.96-2.30)	2.81 (2.49-3.14)	5215
Total population (2015 - 2016)	.820 (.772-.872)	.780 (.740-.840)	1.32 (1.21-1.42)	2.14 (2.02-2.24)	2.75 (2.50-2.98)	4988
Age 1-5 years (2011 - 2012)	.970 (.877-1.07)	.950 (.870-1.04)	1.34 (1.20-1.65)	2.26 (1.88-2.65)	2.91 (2.41-3.83)	713
Age 1-5 years (2013 - 2014)	.782 (.705-.869)	.740 (.680-.800)	1.08 (.940-1.24)	1.58 (1.33-1.90)	2.24 (1.68-2.64)	818
Age 1-5 years (2015 - 2016)	.758 (.675-.850)	.690 (.610-.790)	1.10 (.950-1.32)	1.86 (1.50-2.65)	2.76 (1.94-3.81)	790
Age 6-11 years (2011 - 2012)	.681 (.623-.744)	.640 (.600-.700)	.930 (.820-1.05)	1.34 (1.14-1.60)	1.89 (1.36-2.94)	1048
Age 6-11 years (2013 - 2014)	.567 (.529-.607)	.530 (.500-.570)	.760 (.700-.820)	1.13 (1.01-1.23)	1.42 (1.21-1.83)	1075
Age 6-11 years (2015 - 2016)	.571 (.523-.623)	.550 (.510-.600)	.780 (.720-.830)	1.18 (.970-1.44)	1.59 (1.24-2.24)	1023
Age 12-19 years (2011 - 2012)	.554 (.511-.601)	.530 (.490-.570)	.740 (.660-.830)	1.09 (.960-1.19)	1.31 (1.16-1.65)	1129
Age 12-19 years (2013 - 2014)	.506 (.464-.551)	.460 (.420-.500)	.670 (.600-.750)	1.13 (.870-1.53)	1.69 (1.27-2.06)	627
Age 12-19 years (2015 - 2016)	.467 (.433-.504)	.450 (.410-.490)	.680 (.610-.730)	.930 (.820-1.03)	1.17 (.990-1.36)	565
Age 20+ years (2011 - 2012)	1.09 (1.03-1.16)	1.05 (1.00-1.12)	1.67 (1.56-1.79)	2.56 (2.33-2.77)	3.36 (2.98-3.93)	5030
Age 20+ years (2013 - 2014)	.967 (.921-1.02)	.940 (.900-.980)	1.45 (1.37-1.55)	2.26 (2.09-2.49)	3.03 (2.65-3.55)	2695
Age 20+ years (2015 - 2016)	.920 (.862-.982)	.880 (.810-.960)	1.46 (1.35-1.59)	2.30 (2.15-2.44)	2.89 (2.65-3.07)	2610
Males (2011 - 2012)	1.13 (1.06-1.21)	1.07 (1.01-1.14)	1.74 (1.63-1.88)	2.73 (2.48-3.01)	3.68 (3.18-4.22)	3968
Males (2013 - 2014)	.994 (.919-1.08)	.940 (.890-1.00)	1.48 (1.35-1.61)	2.41 (2.07-2.90)	3.47 (2.89-4.32)	2587
Males (2015 - 2016)	.921 (.864-.981)	.860 (.800-.930)	1.46 (1.33-1.60)	2.41 (2.18-2.62)	2.93 (2.75-3.26)	2488
Females (2011 - 2012)	.842 (.796-.890)	.820 (.780-.860)	1.30 (1.22-1.39)	1.98 (1.83-2.22)	2.59 (2.32-2.94)	3952
Females (2013 - 2014)	.746 (.715-.777)	.730 (.700-.760)	1.19 (1.11-1.28)	1.86 (1.69-2.02)	2.33 (2.24-2.42)	2628
Females (2015 - 2016)	.735 (.679-.795)	.720 (.650-.770)	1.16 (1.04-1.31)	1.88 (1.66-2.13)	2.39 (2.21-2.65)	2500
Mexican Americans (2011 - 2012)	.838 (.767-.916)	.780 (.690-.880)	1.27 (1.15-1.40)	2.05 (1.81-2.36)	3.06 (2.34-3.59)	1077
Mexican Americans (2013 - 2014)	.746 (.685-.813)	.690 (.650-.750)	1.17 (1.10-1.28)	1.88 (1.61-2.04)	2.38 (2.03-2.74)	969
Mexican Americans (2015 - 2016)	.704 (.659-.752)	.680 (.610-.730)	1.10 (.970-1.22)	1.77 (1.67-1.96)	2.39 (2.01-3.10)	994
Non-Hispanic blacks (2011 - 2012)	.998 (.947-1.05)	.910 (.850-.990)	1.53 (1.45-1.60)	2.58 (2.31-2.91)	3.72 (3.04-4.58)	2195
Non-Hispanic blacks (2013 - 2014)	.871 (.787-.963)	.830 (.720-.940)	1.39 (1.27-1.48)	2.17 (2.00-2.38)	3.03 (2.48-4.00)	1119
Non-Hispanic blacks (2015 - 2016)	.856 (.763-.962)	.790 (.700-.890)	1.32 (1.11-1.60)	2.19 (1.86-2.80)	3.11 (2.76-3.39)	1070
Non-Hispanic whites (2011 - 2012)	.993 (.914-1.08)	.960 (.880-1.03)	1.56 (1.40-1.73)	2.43 (2.11-2.74)	3.14 (2.67-3.85)	2493
Non-Hispanic whites (2013 - 2014)	.882 (.820-.950)	.870 (.800-.920)	1.34 (1.24-1.48)	2.20 (1.94-2.48)	2.97 (2.43-3.58)	1848
Non-Hispanic whites (2015 - 2016)	.835 (.774-.900)	.790 (.750-.860)	1.35 (1.23-1.49)	2.21 (2.03-2.36)	2.72 (2.39-2.98)	1511
All Hispanics (2011 - 2012)	.855 (.793-.922)	.820 (.750-.880)	1.27 (1.18-1.39)	2.00 (1.86-2.23)	2.84 (2.41-3.34)	1931
All Hispanics (2013 - 2014)	.742 (.695-.793)	.690 (.660-.730)	1.14 (1.08-1.24)	1.80 (1.62-1.99)	2.36 (2.03-2.72)	1481
All Hispanics (2015 - 2016)	.703 (.658-.750)	.670 (.620-.720)	1.10 (1.01-1.18)	1.73 (1.56-2.00)	2.39 (2.00-2.97)	1664
Asians (2011 - 2012)	1.15 (1.06-1.24)	1.14 (1.02-1.26)	1.70 (1.56-1.86)	2.56 (2.36-2.72)	3.28 (2.80-3.65)	1005
Asians (2013 - 2014)	1.01 (.923-1.11)	1.02 (.900-1.19)	1.48 (1.35-1.66)	2.25 (2.06-2.39)	2.67 (2.37-2.86)	510
Asians (2015 - 2016)	1.07 (.976-1.18)	1.08 (.920-1.20)	1.65 (1.47-1.96)	2.62 (2.11-2.92)	3.07 (2.76-3.49)	479

Limit of detection (LOD, see Data Analysis section) for Survey years 11-12, 13-14, and 15-16 are 0.25, 0.07, and 0.07 respectively.

Biomonitoring Summary: https://www.cdc.gov/biomonitoring/Lead_BiomonitoringSummary.html

Factsheet: https://www.cdc.gov/biomonitoring/Lead_FactSheet.html

Source: *Centers for Disease Control & Prevention, Fourth National Report on Human Exposure to Environmental Chemicals, Updated Tables, January 2019*

Urinary Lead (1999 – 2010)

CAS Number 7439-92-1

Geometric mean and selected percentiles of urine concentrations (in µg/L) for the U.S. population from the National Health and Nutrition Examination Survey.

Categories (Survey Years)	Geometric Mean (95% conf. interval)	50th Percentile (95% conf. interval)	75th Percentile (95% conf. interval)	90th Percentile (95% conf. interval)	95th Percentile (95% conf. interval)	Sample Size
Total population (1999 - 2000)	.766 (.708-.828)	.800 (.800-.900)	1.40 (1.30-1.50)	2.20 (2.00-2.30)	2.90 (2.60-3.30)	2465
Total population (2001 - 2002)	.677 (.637-.718)	.700 (.700-.800)	1.20 (1.20-1.30)	2.00 (1.90-2.20)	2.70 (2.50-2.80)	2690
Total population (2003 - 2004)	.636 (.595-.680)	.640 (.580-.690)	1.04 (.960-1.12)	1.73 (1.52-1.86)	2.29 (2.03-2.62)	2558
Total population (2005 - 2006)	.554 (.523-.587)	.570 (.540-.600)	.990 (.910-1.05)	1.58 (1.44-1.73)	2.14 (1.94-2.45)	2576
Total population (2007 - 2008)	.493 (.467-.520)	.500 (.470-.530)	.850 (.790-.910)	1.38 (1.23-1.58)	1.97 (1.75-2.17)	2627
Total population (2009 - 2010)	.458 (.441-.476)	.470 (.450-.480)	.790 (.750-.830)	1.24 (1.11-1.38)	1.65 (1.46-1.84)	2848
Age 6-11 years (1999 - 2000)	1.07 (.955-1.20)	1.10 (.900-1.30)	1.50 (1.40-1.70)	2.40 (1.80-3.10)	3.40 (2.40-5.00)	340
Age 6-11 years (2001 - 2002)	.753 (.661-.857)	.800 (.600-.900)	1.20 (1.10-1.40)	2.10 (1.60-2.40)	2.60 (2.10-3.70)	368
Age 6-11 years (2003 - 2004)	.795 (.671-.941)	.790 (.640-.900)	1.35 (.970-1.86)	2.27 (1.62-4.09)	3.33 (2.23-4.41)	290
Age 6-11 years (2005 - 2006)	.508 (.447-.579)	.510 (.440-.560)	.740 (.620-.980)	1.33 (1.00-1.86)	1.90 (1.33-2.60)	355
Age 6-11 years (2007 - 2008)	.494 (.411-.593)	.520 (.410-.590)	.790 (.660-.900)	1.23 (.980-1.73)	1.90 (1.51-2.18)	394
Age 6-11 years (2009 - 2010)	.443 (.399-.493)	.460 (.430-.490)	.710 (.630-.820)	1.09 (.880-1.33)	1.40 (1.06-1.82)	378
Age 12-19 years (1999 - 2000)	.659 (.579-.749)	.700 (.600-.800)	1.10 (.900-1.30)	1.80 (1.40-2.20)	2.20 (1.90-2.80)	719
Age 12-19 years (2001 - 2002)	.564 (.526-.605)	.600 (.500-.600)	1.00 (.800-1.10)	1.60 (1.40-1.70)	2.00 (1.80-2.40)	762
Age 12-19 years (2003 - 2004)	.604 (.553-.660)	.630 (.570-.680)	.920 (.810-1.02)	1.32 (1.14-1.80)	1.86 (1.44-2.29)	725
Age 12-19 years (2005 - 2006)	.472 (.421-.530)	.490 (.450-.540)	.780 (.710-.830)	1.19 (1.10-1.45)	1.65 (1.34-1.80)	701
Age 12-19 years (2007 - 2008)	.386 (.346-.431)	.380 (.350-.410)	.640 (.560-.720)	1.03 (.870-1.24)	1.38 (1.09-1.91)	376
Age 12-19 years (2009 - 2010)	.320 (.283-.361)	.320 (.270-.370)	.530 (.460-.630)	.830 (.710-1.10)	1.16 (.860-1.37)	451
Age 20+ years (1999 - 2000)	.752 (.691-.818)	.800 (.700-.900)	1.40 (1.30-1.50)	2.20 (2.00-2.40)	2.90 (2.60-3.30)	1406
Age 20+ years (2001 - 2002)	.688 (.641-.738)	.700 (.700-.800)	1.20 (1.20-1.30)	2.00 (1.90-2.30)	2.80 (2.50-2.90)	1560
Age 20+ years (2003 - 2004)	.625 (.579-.674)	.620 (.560-.700)	1.04 (.960-1.11)	1.70 (1.52-1.80)	2.21 (2.04-2.49)	1543
Age 20+ years (2005 - 2006)	.574 (.539-.612)	.600 (.560-.640)	1.02 (.970-1.13)	1.65 (1.53-1.81)	2.21 (1.99-2.57)	1520
Age 20+ years (2007 - 2008)	.512 (.485-.540)	.530 (.490-.560)	.900 (.820-.950)	1.49 (1.29-1.64)	2.01 (1.78-2.33)	1857
Age 20+ years (2009 - 2010)	.486 (.465-.507)	.490 (.470-.520)	.830 (.780-.880)	1.32 (1.16-1.46)	1.71 (1.52-2.03)	2019
Males (1999 - 2000)	.923 (.822-1.04)	.900 (.900-1.00)	1.60 (1.40-1.80)	2.50 (2.20-2.90)	3.40 (2.90-3.80)	1227
Males (2001 - 2002)	.808 (.757-.862)	.800 (.800-.900)	1.40 (1.30-1.50)	2.50 (2.20-2.70)	3.20 (2.90-3.50)	1335
Males (2003 - 2004)	.731 (.680-.785)	.730 (.680-.800)	1.17 (1.07-1.27)	2.03 (1.78-2.22)	2.66 (2.33-2.91)	1281
Males (2005 - 2006)	.672 (.638-.707)	.690 (.620-.760)	1.16 (1.04-1.28)	1.78 (1.60-2.00)	2.45 (2.00-2.97)	1271
Males (2007 - 2008)	.560 (.518-.606)	.570 (.530-.620)	.930 (.840-1.02)	1.63 (1.36-1.97)	2.30 (1.97-3.07)	1327
Males (2009 - 2010)	.527 (.491-.566)	.540 (.480-.580)	.880 (.820-.960)	1.41 (1.25-1.58)	1.83 (1.62-2.21)	1398
Females (1999 - 2000)	.642 (.589-.701)	.700 (.600-.800)	1.20 (1.10-1.30)	1.90 (1.60-2.20)	2.40 (2.10-3.00)	1238
Females (2001 - 2002)	.573 (.535-.613)	.600 (.600-.600)	1.10 (1.00-1.10)	1.60 (1.50-1.80)	2.20 (1.90-2.40)	1355
Females (2003 - 2004)	.558 (.506-.616)	.540 (.480-.620)	.920 (.820-1.04)	1.49 (1.24-1.75)	1.82 (1.59-2.30)	1277
Females (2005 - 2006)	.461 (.425-.499)	.460 (.430-.510)	.810 (.730-.880)	1.27 (1.17-1.46)	1.86 (1.54-2.17)	1305
Females (2007 - 2008)	.436 (.412-.461)	.430 (.400-.480)	.760 (.690-.830)	1.22 (1.05-1.34)	1.67 (1.44-1.81)	1300
Females (2009 - 2010)	.400 (.378-.424)	.420 (.390-.440)	.690 (.660-.740)	1.05 (.990-1.13)	1.42 (1.26-1.59)	1450

Limit of detection (LOD, see Data Analysis section) for Survey years 99-00, 01-02, 03-04, 05-06, 07-08, and 09-10 are 0.1, 0.1, 0.33, 0.1, 0.1, and 0.1 respectively.

Biomonitoring Summary: https://www.cdc.gov/biomonitoring/Lead_BiomonitoringSummary.html

Factsheet: https://www.cdc.gov/biomonitoring/Lead_FactSheet.html

Source: *Centers for Disease Control & Prevention, Fourth National Report on Human Exposure to Environmental Chemicals, Updated Tables, January 2019*

Urinary Lead (1999 – 2010)

CAS Number 7439-92-1

Geometric mean and selected percentiles of urine concentrations (in µg/L) for the U.S. population from the National Health and Nutrition Examination Survey.

Categories (Survey Years)	Geometric Mean (95% conf. interval)	50th Percentile (95% conf. interval)	75th Percentile (95% conf. interval)	90th Percentile (95% conf. interval)	95th Percentile (95% conf. interval)	Sample Size
Mexican Americans (1999 - 2000)	1.02 (.915-1.13)	1.10 (.900-1.20)	1.80 (1.60-1.90)	2.90 (2.50-3.40)	4.30 (3.10-5.40)	884
Mexican Americans (2001 - 2002)	.833 (.745-.931)	.900 (.700-1.00)	1.50 (1.20-1.70)	2.50 (2.00-2.90)	3.30 (2.70-3.80)	683
Mexican Americans (2003 - 2004)	.815 (.710-.935)	.840 (.700-.990)	1.31 (1.18-1.59)	2.19 (1.86-2.50)	2.66 (2.13-3.97)	618
Mexican Americans (2005 - 2006)	.729 (.653-.815)	.770 (.680-.860)	1.32 (1.15-1.59)	2.22 (1.81-2.64)	3.08 (2.50-4.03)	652
Mexican Americans (2007 - 2008)	.607 (.528-.698)	.610 (.530-.690)	.990 (.890-1.21)	1.76 (1.37-2.17)	2.29 (1.82-2.80)	515
Mexican Americans (2009 - 2010)	.546 (.483-.618)	.520 (.460-.580)	.930 (.800-1.09)	1.66 (1.34-1.89)	2.16 (1.80-2.87)	613
Non-Hispanic blacks (1999 - 2000)	1.11 (1.00-1.23)	1.10 (1.00-1.20)	1.90 (1.50-2.10)	3.00 (2.40-3.50)	4.20 (3.30-5.70)	568
Non-Hispanic blacks (2001 - 2002)	.940 (.833-1.06)	.900 (.800-1.00)	1.60 (1.30-1.80)	2.70 (2.10-3.40)	3.70 (2.90-4.80)	667
Non-Hispanic blacks (2003 - 2004)	.848 (.729-.986)	.850 (.710-1.00)	1.40 (1.10-1.72)	2.14 (1.78-2.64)	2.82 (2.31-3.89)	723
Non-Hispanic blacks (2005 - 2006)	.666 (.604-.734)	.660 (.590-.760)	1.09 (.980-1.18)	1.62 (1.42-1.85)	2.24 (1.65-2.90)	692
Non-Hispanic blacks (2007 - 2008)	.618 (.558-.685)	.620 (.560-.690)	1.01 (.920-1.13)	1.56 (1.38-1.90)	2.06 (1.88-2.60)	589
Non-Hispanic blacks (2009 - 2010)	.560 (.522-.601)	.550 (.490-.600)	.910 (.830-1.01)	1.53 (1.26-1.71)	1.96 (1.68-2.80)	544
Non-Hispanic whites (1999 - 2000)	.695 (.625-.773)	.700 (.700-.900)	1.30 (1.10-1.40)	2.00 (1.80-2.40)	2.70 (2.30-3.10)	822
Non-Hispanic whites (2001 - 2002)	.610 (.572-.651)	.700 (.600-.700)	1.10 (1.10-1.20)	1.90 (1.70-2.00)	2.40 (2.30-2.60)	1132
Non-Hispanic whites (2003 - 2004)	.591 (.556-.628)	.590 (.540-.650)	.960 (.910-.990)	1.52 (1.40-1.75)	2.14 (1.78-2.51)	1074
Non-Hispanic whites (2005 - 2006)	.520 (.477-.566)	.540 (.490-.580)	.950 (.820-1.05)	1.53 (1.30-1.76)	2.07 (1.78-2.45)	1041
Non-Hispanic whites (2007 - 2008)	.452 (.422-.485)	.460 (.430-.490)	.780 (.700-.880)	1.23 (1.03-1.50)	1.79 (1.58-1.97)	1095
Non-Hispanic whites (2009 - 2010)	.431 (.406-.458)	.450 (.410-.480)	.750 (.690-.820)	1.11 (1.05-1.24)	1.51 (1.39-1.67)	1225

Limit of detection (LOD, see Data Analysis section) for Survey years 99-00, 01-02, 03-04, 05-06, 07-08, and 09-10 are 0.1, 0.1, 0.33, 0.1, 0.1, and 0.1 respectively.

Biomonitoring Summary: https://www.cdc.gov/biomonitoring/Lead_BiomonitoringSummary.html

Factsheet: https://www.cdc.gov/biomonitoring/Lead_FactSheet.html

Source: *Centers for Disease Control & Prevention, Fourth National Report on Human Exposure to Environmental Chemicals, Updated Tables, January 2019*

Urinary Lead (2011 – 2016)

CAS Number 7439-92-1

Geometric mean and selected percentiles of urine concentrations (in µg/L) for the U.S. population from the National Health and Nutrition Examination Survey.

Categories (Survey Years)	Geometric Mean (95% conf. interval)	50th Percentile (95% conf. interval)	75th Percentile (95% conf. interval)	90th Percentile (95% conf. interval)	95th Percentile (95% conf. interval)	Sample Size
Total population (2011 - 2012)	.360 (.328-.396)	.370 (.340-.400)	.650 (.580-.720)	1.05 (.980-1.17)	1.49 (1.26-1.75)	2504
Total population (2013 - 2014)	.277 (.257-.298)	.290 (.270-.300)	.500 (.480-.530)	.840 (.780-.900)	1.17 (1.01-1.41)	2664
Total population (2015 - 2016)	.284 (.261-.308)	.290 (.260-.320)	.520 (.470-.570)	.960 (.860-1.02)	1.26 (1.13-1.44)	3061
Age 3-5 years (2015 - 2016)	.257 (.225-.292)	.230 (.210-.270)	.460 (.370-.560)	.870 (.710-1.09)	1.20 (.920-1.48)	486
Age 6-11 years (2011 - 2012)	.346 (.292-.410)	.370 (.300-.440)	.610 (.540-.770)	1.12 (.830-1.51)	1.54 (1.28-1.85)	399
Age 6-11 years (2013 - 2014)	.222 (.192-.258)	.240 (.200-.270)	.390 (.330-.450)	.630 (.560-.810)	.870 (.710-1.09)	402
Age 6-11 years (2015 - 2016)	.257 (.238-.276)	.250 (.230-.270)	.410 (.360-.480)	.680 (.580-.790)	.870 (.730-1.36)	379
Age 12-19 years (2011 - 2012)	.259 (.219-.305)	.260 (.220-.340)	.470 (.380-.530)	.720 (.540-.900)	.970 (.720-1.17)	390
Age 12-19 years (2013 - 2014)	.201 (.166-.245)	.220 (.190-.260)	.360 (.290-.440)	.550 (.450-.700)	.750 (.570-.880)	451
Age 12-19 years (2015 - 2016)	.196 (.183-.211)	.200 (.180-.220)	.340 (.300-.360)	.530 (.440-.650)	.730 (.580-1.12)	402
Age 20+ years (2011 - 2012)	.381 (.348-.416)	.390 (.360-.420)	.680 (.640-.730)	1.11 (1.01-1.21)	1.58 (1.28-1.90)	1715
Age 20+ years (2013 - 2014)	.297 (.280-.315)	.300 (.290-.320)	.540 (.510-.580)	.900 (.820-.980)	1.27 (1.08-1.55)	1811
Age 20+ years (2015 - 2016)	.304 (.276-.334)	.320 (.270-.360)	.570 (.510-.630)	1.01 (.950-1.08)	1.38 (1.18-1.51)	1794
Males (2011 - 2012)	.414 (.367-.466)	.420 (.380-.460)	.730 (.640-.800)	1.16 (.990-1.47)	1.73 (1.33-2.18)	1262
Males (2013 - 2014)	.315 (.295-.337)	.320 (.290-.340)	.580 (.520-.620)	.940 (.840-1.08)	1.48 (1.15-1.92)	1318
Males (2015 - 2016)	.313 (.285-.343)	.330 (.280-.380)	.590 (.540-.650)	1.02 (.900-1.08)	1.26 (1.11-1.49)	1524
Females (2011 - 2012)	.316 (.282-.355)	.320 (.290-.360)	.580 (.500-.660)	.970 (.830-1.14)	1.31 (1.15-1.41)	1242
Females (2013 - 2014)	.245 (.222-.269)	.260 (.240-.280)	.460 (.430-.480)	.720 (.670-.790)	1.00 (.870-1.16)	1346
Females (2015 - 2016)	.259 (.233-.288)	.260 (.230-.290)	.450 (.400-.530)	.880 (.730-.990)	1.26 (1.00-1.45)	1537
Mexican Americans (2011 - 2012)	.372 (.320-.431)	.380 (.320-.480)	.670 (.550-.780)	1.17 (.820-1.58)	1.67 (1.17-2.18)	317
Mexican Americans (2013 - 2014)	.277 (.240-.319)	.290 (.250-.320)	.480 (.440-.580)	.890 (.690-1.15)	1.21 (.930-1.97)	453
Mexican Americans (2015 - 2016)	.295 (.260-.335)	.290 (.260-.350)	.550 (.460-.590)	.960 (.810-1.16)	1.33 (1.10-1.99)	585
Non-Hispanic blacks (2011 - 2012)	.431 (.385-.483)	.440 (.370-.520)	.730 (.660-.830)	1.15 (1.00-1.39)	1.64 (1.39-1.87)	669
Non-Hispanic blacks (2013 - 2014)	.371 (.320-.429)	.380 (.310-.440)	.620 (.530-.730)	1.09 (.830-1.34)	1.45 (1.24-1.72)	581
Non-Hispanic blacks (2015 - 2016)	.340 (.298-.388)	.340 (.300-.380)	.620 (.490-.720)	1.01 (.820-1.19)	1.38 (1.09-1.65)	671
Non-Hispanic whites (2011 - 2012)	.346 (.311-.385)	.360 (.330-.390)	.610 (.540-.700)	1.02 (.920-1.16)	1.38 (1.14-1.85)	820
Non-Hispanic whites (2013 - 2014)	.267 (.245-.290)	.280 (.260-.300)	.500 (.450-.540)	.820 (.730-.920)	1.16 (.950-1.60)	985
Non-Hispanic whites (2015 - 2016)	.275 (.247-.305)	.270 (.230-.330)	.500 (.450-.570)	.930 (.790-1.03)	1.29 (1.08-1.52)	924
All Hispanics (2011 - 2012)	.372 (.327-.423)	.370 (.320-.420)	.670 (.590-.750)	1.15 (.950-1.31)	1.51 (1.18-2.13)	573
All Hispanics (2013 - 2014)	.270 (.239-.305)	.280 (.240-.320)	.480 (.440-.540)	.820 (.690-.930)	1.17 (.940-1.47)	701
All Hispanics (2015 - 2016)	.284 (.258-.312)	.280 (.260-.310)	.530 (.480-.560)	.930 (.850-1.04)	1.31 (1.18-1.50)	982
Asians (2011 - 2012)	.383 (.341-.429)	.380 (.350-.460)	.690 (.620-.790)	1.15 (.950-1.32)	1.38 (1.21-1.72)	353
Asians (2013 - 2014)	.257 (.230-.287)	.290 (.240-.350)	.470 (.410-.510)	.710 (.560-.790)	.890 (.750-.980)	292
Asians (2015 - 2016)	.292 (.264-.324)	.300 (.250-.360)	.570 (.460-.660)	.980 (.710-1.14)	1.14 (1.01-1.21)	332

Limit of detection (LOD, see Data Analysis section) for Survey years 11-12, 13-14, and 15-16 are 0.08, 0.03, and 0.03, respectively.

Biomonitoring Summary: https://www.cdc.gov/biomonitoring/Lead_BiomonitoringSummary.html

Factsheet: https://www.cdc.gov/biomonitoring/Lead_FactSheet.html

Source: *Centers for Disease Control & Prevention, Fourth National Report on Human Exposure to Environmental Chemicals, Updated Tables, January 2019*

Urinary Lead (creatinine corrected) (1999 – 2010)

CAS Number 7439-92-1

Geometric mean and selected percentiles of urine concentrations (in µg/g of creatinine) for the U.S. population from the National Health and Nutrition Examination Survey.

Categories (Survey Years)	Geometric Mean (95% conf. interval)	50th Percentile (95% conf. interval)	75th Percentile (95% conf. interval)	90th Percentile (95% conf. interval)	95th Percentile (95% conf. interval)	Sample Size
Total population (1999 - 2000)	.721 (.700-.742)	.701 (.677-.725)	1.11 (1.05-1.15)	1.70 (1.62-1.85)	2.38 (2.22-2.79)	2465
Total population (2001 - 2002)	.639 (.603-.677)	.635 (.588-.676)	1.03 (.963-1.08)	1.52 (1.43-1.61)	2.03 (1.89-2.22)	2689
Total population (2003 - 2004)	.632 (.603-.662)	.622 (.594-.655)	.979 (.920-1.03)	1.49 (1.33-1.64)	1.97 (1.73-2.26)	2558
Total population (2005 - 2006)	.546 (.520-.573)	.530 (.510-.560)	.860 (.810-.900)	1.27 (1.15-1.37)	1.71 (1.50-1.89)	2576
Total population (2007 - 2008)	.514 (.482-.548)	.500 (.460-.530)	.800 (.720-.880)	1.30 (1.23-1.42)	1.85 (1.73-1.96)	2627
Total population (2009 - 2010)	.488 (.466-.512)	.470 (.440-.500)	.760 (.710-.810)	1.16 (1.08-1.28)	1.53 (1.41-1.62)	2848
Age 6-11 years (1999 - 2000)	1.17 (.975-1.41)	1.06 (.918-1.22)	1.55 (1.22-1.97)	2.71 (1.67-4.66)	4.66 (1.97-18.0)	340
Age 6-11 years (2001 - 2002)	.918 (.841-1.00)	.870 (.800-.933)	1.27 (1.12-1.43)	2.33 (1.59-3.64)	3.64 (1.89-5.56)	368
Age 6-11 years (2003 - 2004)	.926 (.812-1.06)	.914 (.781-1.03)	1.45 (1.17-1.72)	2.14 (1.62-3.47)	3.47 (2.19-5.31)	290
Age 6-11 years (2005 - 2006)	.628 (.563-.701)	.590 (.530-.680)	.870 (.770-.940)	1.29 (1.03-1.82)	1.96 (1.32-2.42)	355
Age 6-11 years (2007 - 2008)	.643 (.543-.763)	.630 (.530-.730)	1.02 (.770-1.24)	1.50 (1.24-2.02)	2.04 (1.70-2.58)	394
Age 6-11 years (2009 - 2010)	.604 (.551-.662)	.580 (.520-.650)	.870 (.780-1.00)	1.32 (1.09-1.51)	1.60 (1.38-1.75)	378
Age 12-19 years (1999 - 2000)	.496 (.460-.535)	.469 (.408-.508)	.709 (.655-.828)	1.11 (.981-1.28)	1.65 (1.15-2.79)	719
Age 12-19 years (2001 - 2002)	.404 (.380-.428)	.375 (.342-.400)	.603 (.541-.702)	.990 (.882-1.18)	1.41 (1.07-1.63)	762
Age 12-19 years (2003 - 2004)	.432 (.404-.461)	.404 (.383-.436)	.623 (.551-.730)	.938 (.828-1.06)	1.23 (1.09-1.35)	725
Age 12-19 years (2005 - 2006)	.363 (.333-.395)	.340 (.310-.360)	.510 (.460-.600)	.800 (.690-.930)	1.07 (.940-1.23)	701
Age 12-19 years (2007 - 2008)	.302 (.270-.337)	.290 (.250-.340)	.430 (.400-.490)	.670 (.550-.790)	.900 (.700-1.09)	376
Age 12-19 years (2009 - 2010)	.299 (.273-.328)	.290 (.260-.320)	.420 (.370-.490)	.620 (.550-.760)	.880 (.740-1.01)	451
Age 20+ years (1999 - 2000)	.720 (.683-.758)	.712 (.667-.739)	1.10 (1.02-1.18)	1.69 (1.53-1.87)	2.31 (2.15-2.62)	1406
Age 20+ years (2001 - 2002)	.658 (.617-.703)	.652 (.608-.702)	1.05 (.992-1.11)	1.51 (1.40-1.61)	2.00 (1.85-2.19)	1559
Age 20+ years (2003 - 2004)	.641 (.606-.679)	.633 (.605-.670)	.988 (.917-1.04)	1.47 (1.28-1.63)	1.94 (1.72-2.12)	1543
Age 20+ years (2005 - 2006)	.573 (.548-.600)	.570 (.530-.600)	.890 (.850-.960)	1.32 (1.22-1.41)	1.77 (1.53-1.94)	1520
Age 20+ years (2007 - 2008)	.545 (.513-.579)	.530 (.490-.570)	.840 (.760-.910)	1.36 (1.27-1.49)	1.92 (1.78-2.08)	1857
Age 20+ years (2009 - 2010)	.514 (.489-.539)	.500 (.460-.530)	.790 (.730-.840)	1.22 (1.10-1.35)	1.57 (1.46-1.71)	2019
Males (1999 - 2000)	.720 (.679-.763)	.693 (.645-.734)	1.10 (.992-1.22)	1.68 (1.50-2.09)	2.43 (2.15-3.03)	1227
Males (2001 - 2002)	.639 (.607-.673)	.638 (.586-.686)	1.01 (.957-1.08)	1.55 (1.41-1.61)	2.06 (1.88-2.43)	1334
Males (2003 - 2004)	.615 (.588-.644)	.593 (.561-.639)	.914 (.862-.977)	1.44 (1.25-1.53)	2.00 (1.71-2.28)	1281
Males (2005 - 2006)	.551 (.522-.582)	.530 (.510-.580)	.830 (.770-.910)	1.25 (1.13-1.39)	1.77 (1.42-2.20)	1271
Males (2007 - 2008)	.501 (.471-.534)	.490 (.450-.530)	.750 (.700-.810)	1.29 (1.15-1.49)	1.88 (1.71-1.98)	1327
Males (2009 - 2010)	.481 (.458-.505)	.450 (.430-.490)	.740 (.690-.800)	1.15 (1.04-1.29)	1.56 (1.37-1.70)	1398
Females (1999 - 2000)	.722 (.681-.765)	.707 (.667-.746)	1.11 (1.05-1.18)	1.74 (1.50-2.02)	2.38 (2.03-2.88)	1238
Females (2001 - 2002)	.639 (.594-.688)	.625 (.571-.682)	1.03 (.946-1.11)	1.50 (1.39-1.61)	1.98 (1.85-2.15)	1355
Females (2003 - 2004)	.648 (.601-.698)	.649 (.604-.718)	1.03 (.938-1.10)	1.56 (1.34-1.73)	1.96 (1.72-2.20)	1277
Females (2005 - 2006)	.541 (.507-.577)	.530 (.500-.580)	.880 (.820-.940)	1.28 (1.12-1.41)	1.64 (1.38-1.91)	1305
Females (2007 - 2008)	.527 (.489-.568)	.500 (.470-.550)	.840 (.740-.960)	1.34 (1.23-1.47)	1.79 (1.56-2.08)	1300
Females (2009 - 2010)	.495 (.466-.526)	.480 (.450-.520)	.780 (.710-.830)	1.20 (1.08-1.32)	1.52 (1.39-1.62)	1450

Biomonitoring Summary: https://www.cdc.gov/biomonitoring/Lead_BiomonitoringSummary.html

Factsheet: https://www.cdc.gov/biomonitoring/Lead_FactSheet.html

Source: *Centers for Disease Control & Prevention, Fourth National Report on Human Exposure to Environmental Chemicals, Updated Tables, January 2019*

Urinary Lead (creatinine corrected) (1999 – 2010)

CAS Number 7439-92-1

Geometric mean and selected percentiles of urine concentrations (in µg/g of creatinine) for the U.S. population from the National Health and Nutrition Examination Survey.

Categories (Survey Years)	Geometric Mean (95% conf. interval)	50th Percentile (95% conf. interval)	75th Percentile (95% conf. interval)	90th Percentile (95% conf. interval)	95th Percentile (95% conf. interval)	Sample Size
Mexican Americans (1999 - 2000)	.940 (.876-1.01)	.887 (.796-1.03)	1.43 (1.37-1.58)	2.38 (2.08-2.77)	3.46 (2.78-4.18)	884
Mexican Americans (2001 - 2002)	.810 (.731-.898)	.774 (.702-.893)	1.29 (1.09-1.44)	2.05 (1.75-2.50)	2.78 (2.56-3.33)	682
Mexican Americans (2003 - 2004)	.755 (.681-.838)	.708 (.612-.851)	1.18 (1.09-1.31)	1.86 (1.50-2.26)	2.31 (1.98-2.92)	618
Mexican Americans (2005 - 2006)	.686 (.638-.737)	.680 (.620-.740)	1.00 (.930-1.13)	1.63 (1.39-1.88)	2.20 (1.77-3.20)	652
Mexican Americans (2007 - 2008)	.607 (.514-.717)	.590 (.500-.690)	.970 (.770-1.19)	1.56 (1.25-2.07)	2.20 (1.78-2.46)	515
Mexican Americans (2009 - 2010)	.573 (.526-.623)	.540 (.470-.610)	.950 (.780-1.06)	1.59 (1.41-1.82)	2.02 (1.82-2.40)	613
Non-Hispanic blacks (1999 - 2000)	.722 (.659-.790)	.671 (.583-.753)	1.11 (.988-1.20)	2.00 (1.56-2.51)	2.83 (2.20-3.88)	568
Non-Hispanic blacks (2001 - 2002)	.644 (.559-.742)	.608 (.510-.710)	.962 (.853-1.20)	1.79 (1.36-2.33)	2.75 (2.04-3.98)	667
Non-Hispanic blacks (2003 - 2004)	.609 (.529-.701)	.569 (.492-.698)	.900 (.793-1.03)	1.48 (1.11-1.97)	2.24 (1.65-2.88)	723
Non-Hispanic blacks (2005 - 2006)	.483 (.459-.508)	.470 (.440-.490)	.740 (.670-.820)	1.18 (1.06-1.29)	1.60 (1.37-1.85)	692
Non-Hispanic blacks (2007 - 2008)	.452 (.414-.492)	.440 (.400-.490)	.710 (.610-.780)	1.13 (.930-1.33)	1.57 (1.21-1.88)	589
Non-Hispanic blacks (2009 - 2010)	.444 (.417-.473)	.420 (.390-.470)	.680 (.600-.740)	1.07 (.940-1.18)	1.51 (1.18-1.65)	544
Non-Hispanic whites (1999 - 2000)	.696 (.668-.725)	.677 (.645-.718)	1.07 (.997-1.14)	1.66 (1.50-1.83)	2.31 (1.94-2.82)	822
Non-Hispanic whites (2001 - 2002)	.615 (.579-.654)	.621 (.571-.667)	1.00 (.933-1.07)	1.46 (1.37-1.52)	1.88 (1.62-2.03)	1132
Non-Hispanic whites (2003 - 2004)	.623 (.592-.655)	.618 (.587-.657)	.971 (.914-1.03)	1.44 (1.25-1.61)	1.85 (1.64-2.10)	1074
Non-Hispanic whites (2005 - 2006)	.541 (.500-.585)	.530 (.490-.580)	.850 (.790-.920)	1.24 (1.12-1.37)	1.62 (1.37-1.94)	1041
Non-Hispanic whites (2007 - 2008)	.506 (.466-.550)	.490 (.460-.540)	.790 (.700-.880)	1.27 (1.15-1.42)	1.81 (1.59-1.96)	1095
Non-Hispanic whites (2009 - 2010)	.482 (.448-.518)	.460 (.430-.500)	.740 (.690-.820)	1.15 (1.01-1.30)	1.46 (1.32-1.59)	1225

Biomonitoring Summary: https://www.cdc.gov/biomonitoring/Lead_BiomonitoringSummary.html

Factsheet: https://www.cdc.gov/biomonitoring/Lead_FactSheet.html

Source: *Centers for Disease Control & Prevention, Fourth National Report on Human Exposure to Environmental Chemicals, Updated Tables, January 2019*

Urinary Lead (creatinine corrected) (2011 – 2016)

CAS Number 7439-92-1

Geometric mean and selected percentiles of urine concentrations (in µg/g of creatinine) for the U.S. population from the National Health and Nutrition Examination Survey.

Categories (Survey Years)	Geometric Mean (95% conf. interval)	50th Percentile (95% conf. interval)	75th Percentile (95% conf. interval)	90th Percentile (95% conf. interval)	95th Percentile (95% conf. interval)	Sample Size
Total population (2011 - 2012)	.409 (.380-.440)	.396 (.374-.418)	.634 (.583-.675)	1.00 (.878-1.16)	1.51 (1.24-1.71)	2502
Total population (2013 - 2014)	.320 (.302-.339)	.313 (.294-.331)	.519 (.491-.554)	.823 (.756-.907)	1.16 (1.00-1.30)	2663
Total population (2015 - 2016)	.319 (.294-.346)	.302 (.279-.325)	.525 (.477-.560)	.870 (.766-.981)	1.13 (1.04-1.27)	3058
Age 3-5 years (2015 - 2016)	.590 (.532-.654)	.577 (.486-.658)	.897 (.783-1.07)	1.41 (1.13-1.89)	2.05 (1.50-2.69)	485
Age 6-11 years (2011 - 2012)	.494 (.430-.567)	.459 (.414-.529)	.708 (.559-.930)	1.18 (.884-1.56)	1.56 (1.12-2.22)	398
Age 6-11 years (2013 - 2014)	.331 (.297-.370)	.313 (.273-.370)	.500 (.452-.571)	.833 (.667-.938)	1.07 (.905-1.34)	402
Age 6-11 years (2015 - 2016)	.364 (.326-.406)	.329 (.278-.400)	.538 (.455-.642)	.857 (.714-1.05)	1.14 (.859-1.49)	379
Age 12-19 years (2011 - 2012)	.247 (.218-.281)	.224 (.206-.264)	.385 (.317-.429)	.541 (.440-.667)	.667 (.513-1.03)	390
Age 12-19 years (2013 - 2014)	.182 (.160-.208)	.169 (.142-.194)	.276 (.225-.330)	.457 (.339-.640)	.640 (.438-.908)	451
Age 12-19 years (2015 - 2016)	.183 (.166-.202)	.174 (.160-.194)	.260 (.226-.288)	.385 (.310-.521)	.538 (.392-.774)	402
Age 20+ years (2011 - 2012)	.433 (.402-.466)	.414 (.389-.437)	.660 (.619-.712)	1.05 (.929-1.22)	1.61 (1.28-1.87)	1714
Age 20+ years (2013 - 2014)	.346 (.331-.363)	.337 (.321-.353)	.554 (.505-.592)	.861 (.789-.935)	1.23 (1.04-1.46)	1810
Age 20+ years (2015 - 2016)	.331 (.303-.363)	.315 (.288-.350)	.541 (.492-.581)	.900 (.754-1.02)	1.14 (1.03-1.28)	1792
Males (2011 - 2012)	.388 (.346-.436)	.377 (.338-.418)	.590 (.524-.658)	.987 (.833-1.17)	1.51 (1.16-1.89)	1261
Males (2013 - 2014)	.315 (.293-.339)	.303 (.278-.327)	.486 (.440-.541)	.758 (.692-.913)	1.16 (.956-1.58)	1317
Males (2015 - 2016)	.297 (.269-.328)	.275 (.254-.309)	.500 (.422-.553)	.787 (.700-.923)	1.05 (.874-1.23)	1524
Females (2011 - 2012)	.430 (.405-.457)	.416 (.385-.444)	.667 (.626-.709)	1.03 (.905-1.21)	1.49 (1.21-1.71)	1241
Females (2013 - 2014)	.325 (.303-.348)	.325 (.308-.336)	.545 (.500-.580)	.864 (.785-.929)	1.18 (.970-1.33)	1346
Females (2015 - 2016)	.341 (.311-.374)	.324 (.300-.360)	.542 (.490-.608)	.941 (.780-1.13)	1.22 (1.09-1.37)	1534
Mexican Americans (2011 - 2012)	.418 (.370-.471)	.409 (.356-.462)	.667 (.598-.716)	1.05 (.822-1.25)	1.32 (1.16-1.54)	317
Mexican Americans (2013 - 2014)	.316 (.283-.352)	.319 (.278-.336)	.500 (.450-.589)	.845 (.720-1.04)	1.16 (.908-1.36)	453
Mexican Americans (2015 - 2016)	.323 (.288-.363)	.303 (.274-.331)	.510 (.423-.594)	.866 (.743-1.02)	1.21 (1.00-1.56)	584
Non-Hispanic blacks (2011 - 2012)	.335 (.301-.374)	.316 (.269-.357)	.529 (.464-.598)	.906 (.770-1.07)	1.34 (1.06-1.55)	669
Non-Hispanic blacks (2013 - 2014)	.282 (.251-.317)	.275 (.237-.316)	.455 (.398-.515)	.750 (.611-.920)	.977 (.836-1.21)	581
Non-Hispanic blacks (2015 - 2016)	.270 (.236-.309)	.252 (.218-.286)	.413 (.335-.516)	.750 (.561-.933)	1.06 (.857-1.16)	669
Non-Hispanic whites (2011 - 2012)	.419 (.378-.465)	.404 (.369-.439)	.642 (.559-.722)	.966 (.826-1.22)	1.62 (1.16-2.00)	818
Non-Hispanic whites (2013 - 2014)	.329 (.306-.353)	.317 (.293-.344)	.541 (.486-.589)	.860 (.750-.933)	1.23 (.983-1.60)	984
Non-Hispanic whites (2015 - 2016)	.324 (.293-.358)	.306 (.275-.348)	.538 (.484-.590)	.896 (.747-1.03)	1.14 (1.00-1.28)	924
All Hispanics (2011 - 2012)	.416 (.377-.460)	.401 (.366-.442)	.641 (.561-.694)	1.02 (.851-1.24)	1.40 (1.16-1.65)	573
All Hispanics (2013 - 2014)	.301 (.276-.328)	.307 (.269-.327)	.473 (.438-.508)	.795 (.667-.882)	1.07 (.882-1.24)	701
All Hispanics (2015 - 2016)	.321 (.294-.351)	.303 (.280-.324)	.510 (.453-.573)	.857 (.752-.980)	1.13 (1.00-1.41)	981
Asians (2011 - 2012)	.511 (.453-.577)	.512 (.440-.588)	.829 (.706-.980)	1.28 (1.05-1.57)	1.61 (1.40-2.22)	353
Asians (2013 - 2014)	.403 (.360-.451)	.417 (.342-.503)	.619 (.549-.708)	.929 (.767-1.03)	1.12 (.955-1.33)	292
Asians (2015 - 2016)	.399 (.353-.452)	.403 (.350-.464)	.647 (.524-.829)	.966 (.837-1.25)	1.34 (.935-1.69)	332

Biomonitoring Summary: https://www.cdc.gov/biomonitoring/Lead_BiomonitoringSummary.html

Factsheet: https://www.cdc.gov/biomonitoring/Lead_FactSheet.html

Source: *Centers for Disease Control & Prevention, Fourth National Report on Human Exposure to Environmental Chemicals, Updated Tables, January 2019*

Blood Total Mercury (2003 – 2010)

CAS Number 92786-62-4

Geometric mean and selected percentiles of blood concentrations (in µg/L) for the U.S. population from the National Health and Nutrition Examination Survey.

Categories (Survey Years)	Geometric Mean (95% conf. interval)	50th Percentile (95% conf. interval)	75th Percentile (95% conf. interval)	90th Percentile (95% conf. interval)	95th Percentile (95% conf. interval)	Sample Size
Total population (2003 - 2004)	.797 (.703-.903)	.800 (.700-.900)	1.70 (1.50-1.90)	3.30 (2.90-3.90)	4.90 (4.30-5.50)	8373
Total population (2005 - 2006)	.863 (.787-.946)	.830 (.760-.920)	1.66 (1.48-1.93)	3.20 (2.87-3.54)	4.64 (4.17-5.25)	8407
Total population (2007 - 2008)	.769 (.689-.859)	.740 (.660-.830)	1.48 (1.29-1.69)	2.95 (2.46-3.59)	4.64 (3.74-5.79)	8266
Total population (2009 - 2010)	.863 (.792-.941)	.790 (.730-.880)	1.68 (1.49-1.91)	3.43 (3.07-3.84)	5.13 (4.57-5.67)	8793
Age 1-5 years (2003 - 2004)	.326 (.285-.372)	.300 (.300-.300)	.500 (.500-.700)	1.00 (.800-1.60)	1.80 (1.30-2.50)	911
Age 1-5 years (2005 - 2006)	*	< LOD	.500 (.470-.550)	.940 (.820-1.24)	1.43 (1.25-1.59)	968
Age 1-5 years (2007 - 2008)	*	< LOD	.440 (.380-.540)	.830 (.620-1.12)	1.32 (.960-2.40)	817
Age 1-5 years (2009 - 2010)	*	< LOD	.490 (.430-.590)	.890 (.740-1.08)	1.30 (1.08-1.52)	836
Age 6-11 years (2003 - 2004)	.419 (.363-.484)	.400 (.400-.500)	.700 (.700-.900)	1.30 (1.00-1.60)	1.90 (1.40-3.50)	856
Age 6-11 years (2005 - 2006)	*	.410 (.330-.460)	.740 (.630-1.00)	1.43 (1.21-1.87)	2.34 (1.53-3.42)	934
Age 6-11 years (2007 - 2008)	*	.380 (.340-.440)	.700 (.600-.790)	1.21 (.970-1.36)	1.56 (1.34-1.80)	1011
Age 6-11 years (2009 - 2010)	*	.360 (<LOD-.400)	.670 (.590-.770)	1.22 (1.05-1.45)	1.88 (1.43-2.61)	1009
Age 12-19 years (2003 - 2004)	.490 (.418-.574)	.500 (.400-.600)	1.00 (.800-1.20)	1.80 (1.40-2.30)	2.60 (2.10-3.30)	2081
Age 12-19 years (2005 - 2006)	.513 (.461-.570)	.460 (.390-.530)	.850 (.740-1.04)	1.66 (1.31-1.98)	2.41 (2.12-2.90)	1996
Age 12-19 years (2007 - 2008)	.469 (.426-.516)	.440 (.390-.490)	.800 (.670-.970)	1.55 (1.30-1.72)	2.05 (1.77-2.34)	1074
Age 12-19 years (2009 - 2010)	.534 (.473-.602)	.450 (.370-.540)	.910 (.770-1.11)	2.04 (1.53-2.55)	3.01 (2.53-3.63)	1183
Age 20+ years (2003 - 2004)	.979 (.860-1.12)	1.00 (.800-1.10)	2.00 (1.70-2.30)	3.80 (3.20-4.40)	5.40 (4.60-6.70)	4525
Age 20+ years (2005 - 2006)	1.06 (.967-1.15)	1.03 (.930-1.15)	1.98 (1.73-2.22)	3.64 (3.33-4.01)	5.31 (4.82-5.67)	4509
Age 20+ years (2007 - 2008)	.944 (.833-1.07)	.890 (.780-1.03)	1.73 (1.47-2.09)	3.41 (2.82-4.17)	5.32 (4.32-6.72)	5364
Age 20+ years (2009 - 2010)	1.04 (.956-1.14)	.970 (.870-1.08)	2.00 (1.80-2.20)	3.96 (3.55-4.27)	5.75 (5.14-6.50)	5765
Males (2003 - 2004)	.814 (.714-.927)	.800 (.700-.900)	1.80 (1.50-2.00)	3.70 (3.20-4.30)	5.40 (4.60-6.50)	4132
Males (2005 - 2006)	.864 (.783-.954)	.810 (.720-.940)	1.69 (1.48-2.01)	3.30 (2.86-3.73)	4.83 (4.08-5.45)	4092
Males (2007 - 2008)	.809 (.709-.923)	.760 (.670-.850)	1.56 (1.31-1.81)	3.21 (2.72-4.06)	5.16 (4.12-6.97)	4147
Males (2009 - 2010)	.883 (.810-.962)	.790 (.730-.870)	1.75 (1.54-2.02)	3.84 (3.35-4.26)	5.65 (5.13-6.34)	4366
Females (2003 - 2004)	.781 (.689-.886)	.800 (.700-.900)	1.60 (1.40-1.80)	3.00 (2.50-3.50)	4.40 (3.60-5.30)	4241
Females (2005 - 2006)	.864 (.791-.943)	.850 (.770-.920)	1.63 (1.44-1.89)	3.09 (2.75-3.46)	4.51 (4.01-5.28)	4315
Females (2007 - 2008)	.748 (.677-.827)	.720 (.660-.810)	1.42 (1.24-1.60)	2.70 (2.27-3.27)	3.93 (3.17-5.16)	4119
Females (2009 - 2010)	.845 (.772-.924)	.800 (.720-.880)	1.61 (1.43-1.81)	3.13 (2.76-3.48)	4.43 (4.04-5.11)	4427
Mexican Americans (2003 - 2004)	.563 (.472-.672)	.600 (.500-.700)	1.00 (.800-1.30)	1.90 (1.60-2.40)	3.00 (2.20-3.80)	2085
Mexican Americans (2005 - 2006)	.597 (.524-.679)	.580 (.490-.670)	1.04 (.870-1.24)	1.70 (1.40-2.12)	2.58 (1.96-3.31)	2236
Mexican Americans (2007 - 2008)	.594 (.536-.658)	.580 (.520-.670)	1.03 (.900-1.17)	1.73 (1.49-2.04)	2.48 (2.10-2.91)	1712
Mexican Americans (2009 - 2010)	.613 (.571-.659)	.580 (.540-.630)	1.01 (.890-1.15)	1.63 (1.47-1.90)	2.45 (2.03-2.93)	1966
Non-Hispanic blacks (2003 - 2004)	.877 (.753-1.02)	.900 (.800-1.00)	1.60 (1.40-1.80)	3.00 (2.30-4.00)	4.40 (3.30-6.00)	2293
Non-Hispanic blacks (2005 - 2006)	.823 (.697-.972)	.800 (.670-.940)	1.50 (1.21-1.92)	2.72 (2.14-3.59)	4.09 (3.22-5.16)	2193
Non-Hispanic blacks (2007 - 2008)	.766 (.711-.825)	.780 (.710-.830)	1.32 (1.23-1.42)	2.25 (1.99-2.58)	3.42 (2.74-3.90)	1746
Non-Hispanic blacks (2009 - 2010)	.928 (.805-1.07)	.900 (.800-1.02)	1.67 (1.38-1.96)	2.93 (2.20-4.21)	4.56 (3.34-6.69)	1593
Non-Hispanic whites (2003 - 2004)	.776 (.655-.919)	.800 (.700-.900)	1.70 (1.40-2.00)	3.20 (2.60-3.90)	4.70 (4.00-5.60)	3478
Non-Hispanic whites (2005 - 2006)	.891 (.801-.992)	.870 (.770-1.00)	1.74 (1.50-2.10)	3.37 (2.88-3.76)	4.76 (4.18-5.37)	3310
Non-Hispanic whites (2007 - 2008)	.743 (.651-.847)	.720 (.620-.820)	1.43 (1.18-1.70)	2.79 (2.33-3.41)	4.18 (3.57-4.83)	3461
Non-Hispanic whites (2009 - 2010)	.856 (.766-.957)	.790 (.690-.920)	1.70 (1.46-1.98)	3.43 (2.94-3.94)	4.92 (4.30-5.65)	3760

Limit of detection (LOD, see Data Analysis section) for Survey years 03-04, 05-06, 07-08 and 09-10 are 0.2, 0.33, 0.33, and 0.33 respectively.

< LOD means less than the limit of detection, which may vary for some chemicals by year and by individual sample.

* Not calculated: proportion of results below limit of detection was too high to provide a valid result.

Biomonitoring Summary: https://www.cdc.gov/biomonitoring/Mercury_BiomonitoringSummary.html

Factsheet: https://www.cdc.gov/biomonitoring/Mercury_FactSheet.html

Source: *Centers for Disease Control & Prevention, Fourth National Report on Human Exposure to Environmental Chemicals, Updated Tables, January 2019*

Blood Total Mercury (2011 – 2016)

CAS Number 92786-62-4

Geometric mean and selected percentiles of blood concentrations (in µg/L) for the U.S. population from the National Health and Nutrition Examination Survey.

Categories (Survey Years)	Geometric Mean (95% conf. interval)	50th Percentile (95% conf. interval)	75th Percentile (95% conf. interval)	90th Percentile (95% conf. interval)	95th Percentile (95% conf. interval)	Sample Size
Total population (2011 - 2012)	.703 (.617-.801)	.640 (.580-.730)	1.38 (1.14-1.72)	2.87 (2.39-3.62)	4.40 (3.50-5.71)	7920
Total population (2013 - 2014)	.683 (.621-.751)	.620 (.540-.690)	1.29 (1.14-1.46)	2.65 (2.32-3.08)	4.36 (3.65-4.97)	5215
Total population (2015 - 2016)	.678 (.619-.743)	.600 (.540-.690)	1.26 (1.07-1.47)	2.55 (2.17-3.10)	4.25 (3.44-4.94)	4988
Age 1-5 years (2011 - 2012)	.262 (.237-.291)	.250 (.220-.270)	.390 (.340-.450)	.680 (.540-.880)	.990 (.790-1.21)	713
Age 1-5 years (2013 - 2014)	*	< LOD	.410 (.370-.450)	.810 (.710-.990)	1.21 (1.05-1.48)	818
Age 1-5 years (2015 - 2016)	*	< LOD	.380 (.340-.430)	.690 (.540-.830)	1.06 (.840-1.36)	790
Age 6-11 years (2011 - 2012)	.330 (.287-.379)	.320 (.280-.360)	.530 (.480-.600)	.930 (.780-1.20)	1.40 (1.02-2.17)	1048
Age 6-11 years (2013 - 2014)	*	.300 (<LOD-.360)	.570 (.470-.680)	1.12 (.980-1.36)	1.62 (1.38-2.19)	1075
Age 6-11 years (2015 - 2016)	*	.310 (.290-.340)	.480 (.430-.570)	.920 (.750-1.13)	1.33 (1.01-2.28)	1023
Age 12-19 years (2011 - 2012)	.411 (.355-.476)	.370 (.320-.450)	.680 (.590-.800)	1.32 (1.08-1.75)	2.25 (1.46-2.87)	1129
Age 12-19 years (2013 - 2014)	.412 (.367-.463)	.350 (.310-.420)	.630 (.530-.750)	1.20 (.900-1.67)	1.87 (1.30-2.38)	627
Age 12-19 years (2015 - 2016)	.395 (.356-.439)	.340 (.300-.370)	.590 (.470-.750)	1.00 (.850-1.35)	1.89 (1.02-3.34)	565
Age 20+ years (2011 - 2012)	.863 (.753-.990)	.790 (.690-.940)	1.68 (1.36-2.12)	3.35 (2.71-4.31)	5.02 (3.94-6.96)	5030
Age 20+ years (2013 - 2014)	.814 (.736-.900)	.740 (.650-.850)	1.54 (1.36-1.71)	3.08 (2.73-3.56)	4.88 (4.36-5.21)	2695
Age 20+ years (2015 - 2016)	.810 (.740-.886)	.740 (.660-.830)	1.47 (1.28-1.75)	2.86 (2.50-3.44)	4.66 (3.91-5.96)	2610
Males (2011 - 2012)	.712 (.623-.815)	.650 (.570-.730)	1.40 (1.17-1.72)	3.00 (2.44-3.91)	4.94 (3.50-6.79)	3968
Males (2013 - 2014)	.688 (.617-.767)	.620 (.530-.720)	1.30 (1.12-1.54)	2.76 (2.36-3.34)	4.52 (3.65-5.23)	2587
Males (2015 - 2016)	.679 (.621-.743)	.610 (.530-.700)	1.29 (1.06-1.60)	2.45 (2.06-3.31)	4.67 (3.77-5.39)	2488
Females (2011 - 2012)	.694 (.609-.791)	.640 (.580-.740)	1.36 (1.09-1.75)	2.81 (2.28-3.50)	4.03 (3.29-5.08)	3952
Females (2013 - 2014)	.678 (.617-.745)	.610 (.530-.700)	1.27 (1.14-1.42)	2.56 (2.17-3.08)	4.15 (3.37-4.93)	2628
Females (2015 - 2016)	.677 (.608-.754)	.600 (.530-.700)	1.23 (1.02-1.42)	2.57 (2.20-3.10)	3.95 (3.10-4.55)	2500
Mexican Americans (2011 - 2012)	.483 (.424-.550)	.480 (.400-.560)	.810 (.720-.900)	1.44 (1.16-1.63)	1.90 (1.57-2.19)	1077
Mexican Americans (2013 - 2014)	.487 (.433-.547)	.430 (.390-.510)	.760 (.690-.870)	1.41 (1.14-1.69)	1.98 (1.70-2.38)	969
Mexican Americans (2015 - 2016)	.540 (.522-.559)	.530 (.470-.570)	.840 (.790-.920)	1.41 (1.19-1.60)	1.81 (1.54-2.33)	994
Non-Hispanic blacks (2011 - 2012)	.679 (.542-.852)	.630 (.500-.790)	1.24 (.880-1.72)	2.45 (1.84-3.14)	3.80 (2.70-5.37)	2195
Non-Hispanic blacks (2013 - 2014)	.699 (.614-.796)	.650 (.570-.750)	1.20 (1.08-1.40)	2.30 (1.65-2.96)	3.34 (2.35-5.93)	1119
Non-Hispanic blacks (2015 - 2016)	.698 (.587-.829)	.630 (.510-.760)	1.21 (1.04-1.47)	2.49 (2.01-3.51)	4.51 (2.74-5.87)	1070
Non-Hispanic whites (2011 - 2012)	.688 (.582-.813)	.630 (.550-.750)	1.38 (1.09-1.82)	2.83 (2.18-3.82)	4.25 (3.02-6.24)	2493
Non-Hispanic whites (2013 - 2014)	.672 (.598-.755)	.620 (.520-.720)	1.30 (1.12-1.51)	2.61 (2.18-3.08)	4.15 (3.35-4.98)	1848
Non-Hispanic whites (2015 - 2016)	.638 (.563-.723)	.570 (.500-.670)	1.22 (.940-1.47)	2.29 (1.82-2.72)	3.95 (2.56-4.55)	1511
All Hispanics (2011 - 2012)	.612 (.527-.710)	.590 (.490-.700)	1.08 (.890-1.33)	1.96 (1.60-2.68)	3.03 (2.37-3.86)	1931
All Hispanics (2013 - 2014)	.551 (.486-.624)	.490 (.420-.580)	.910 (.820-1.10)	1.76 (1.44-2.12)	2.59 (2.06-3.14)	1481
All Hispanics (2015 - 2016)	.607 (.546-.675)	.570 (.520-.640)	1.00 (.870-1.17)	1.75 (1.38-2.33)	2.60 (1.85-3.25)	1664
Asians (2011 - 2012)	1.86 (1.58-2.19)	2.30 (1.84-2.64)	4.32 (3.71-5.21)	7.71 (6.38-8.79)	10.3 (8.85-12.0)	1005
Asians (2013 - 2014)	1.72 (1.46-2.03)	1.77 (1.42-2.26)	3.92 (3.35-4.55)	7.78 (6.39-9.16)	9.99 (9.16-13.7)	510
Asians (2015 - 2016)	1.73 (1.41-2.12)	2.03 (1.40-2.70)	4.21 (3.31-5.50)	7.66 (6.17-9.91)	11.3 (9.12-13.8)	479

Limit of detection (LOD, see Data Analysis section) for Survey years 11-12, 13-14, and 15-16 are 0.16, 0.28, and 0.28 respectively.

< LOD means less than the limit of detection, which may vary for some chemicals by year and by individual sample.

* Not calculated: proportion of results below limit of detection was too high to provide a valid result.

Biomonitoring Summary: https://www.cdc.gov/biomonitoring/Mercury_BiomonitoringSummary.html

Factsheet: https://www.cdc.gov/biomonitoring/Mercury_FactSheet.html

Source: *Centers for Disease Control & Prevention, Fourth National Report on Human Exposure to Environmental Chemicals, Updated Tables, January 2019*

Blood Inorganic Mercury (2003 – 2010)

CAS Number 92786-62-4

Geometric mean and selected percentiles of blood concentrations (in µg/L) for the U.S. population from the National Health and Nutrition Examination Survey.

Categories (Survey Years)	Geometric Mean (95% conf. interval)	50th Percentile (95% conf. interval)	75th Percentile (95% conf. interval)	90th Percentile (95% conf. interval)	95th Percentile (95% conf. interval)	Sample Size
Total population (2003 - 2004)	*	< LOD	< LOD	.600 (.500-.600)	.700 (.700-.700)	8147
Total population (2005 - 2006)	*	< LOD	< LOD	.540 (.500-.580)	.660 (.620-.710)	8371
Total population (2007 - 2008)	*	< LOD	.350 (<LOD-.370)	.520 (.500-.540)	.650 (.620-.690)	8162
Total population (2009 - 2010)	*	< LOD	< LOD	.390 (.360-.430)	.510 (.480-.570)	8733
Age 1-5 years (2003 - 2004)	*	< LOD	< LOD	< LOD	.500 (<LOD-.600)	792
Age 1-5 years (2005 - 2006)	*	< LOD	< LOD	.430 (<LOD-.470)	.510 (.430-.670)	948
Age 1-5 years (2007 - 2008)	*	< LOD	< LOD	.350 (<LOD-.450)	.500 (.410-.550)	726
Age 1-5 years (2009 - 2010)	*	< LOD	< LOD	< LOD	.360 (<LOD-.460)	789
Age 6-11 years (2003 - 2004)	*	< LOD	< LOD	< LOD	.600 (.500-.600)	842
Age 6-11 years (2005 - 2006)	*	< LOD	< LOD	.450 (<LOD-.520)	.560 (.470-.640)	932
Age 6-11 years (2007 - 2008)	*	< LOD	< LOD	.380 (.350-.410)	.470 (.420-.520)	1010
Age 6-11 years (2009 - 2010)	*	< LOD	< LOD	< LOD	.380 (.350-.440)	1006
Age 12-19 years (2003 - 2004)	*	< LOD	< LOD	.500 (<LOD-.500)	.600 (.500-.600)	2060
Age 12-19 years (2005 - 2006)	*	< LOD	< LOD	.430 (.410-.460)	.540 (.480-.590)	1984
Age 12-19 years (2007 - 2008)	*	< LOD	< LOD	.370 (<LOD-.400)	.480 (.410-.530)	1069
Age 12-19 years (2009 - 2010)	*	< LOD	< LOD	< LOD	.420 (.350-.500)	1184
Age 20+ years (2003 - 2004)	*	< LOD	< LOD	.600 (.500-.600)	.700 (.700-.800)	4453
Age 20+ years (2005 - 2006)	*	< LOD	< LOD	.570 (.530-.610)	.690 (.650-.750)	4507
Age 20+ years (2007 - 2008)	*	< LOD	.380 (.360-.390)	.550 (.530-.570)	.700 (.660-.730)	5357
Age 20+ years (2009 - 2010)	*	< LOD	< LOD	.420 (.390-.450)	.540 (.490-.600)	5754
Males (2003 - 2004)	*	< LOD	< LOD	.500 (.500-.600)	.600 (.600-.700)	4015
Males (2005 - 2006)	*	< LOD	< LOD	.480 (.450-.520)	.600 (.550-.640)	4076
Males (2007 - 2008)	*	< LOD	< LOD	.500 (.470-.520)	.600 (.570-.650)	4093
Males (2009 - 2010)	*	< LOD	< LOD	.370 (<LOD-.420)	.500 (.440-.560)	4336
Females (2003 - 2004)	*	< LOD	< LOD	.600 (.500-.600)	.700 (.700-.800)	4132
Females (2005 - 2006)	*	< LOD	< LOD	.580 (.550-.640)	.700 (.670-.780)	4295
Females (2007 - 2008)	*	< LOD	.380 (.360-.390)	.550 (.520-.570)	.700 (.670-.740)	4069
Females (2009 - 2010)	*	< LOD	< LOD	.410 (.380-.440)	.530 (.490-.600)	4397

Limit of detection (LOD, see Data Analysis section) for Survey years 03-04, 05-06, 07-08, and 09-10 are 0.42, 0.4, 0.35, and 0.35 respectively.

< LOD means less than the limit of detection, which may vary for some chemicals by year and by individual sample.

* Not calculated: proportion of results below limit of detection was too high to provide a valid result.

Biomonitoring Summary: https://www.cdc.gov/biomonitoring/Mercury_BiomonitoringSummary.html

Factsheet: https://www.cdc.gov/biomonitoring/Mercury_FactSheet.html

Source: *Centers for Disease Control & Prevention, Fourth National Report on Human Exposure to Environmental Chemicals, Updated Tables, January 2019*

Blood Inorganic Mercury (2003 – 2010)

CAS Number 92786-62-4

Geometric mean and selected percentiles of blood concentrations (in µg/L) for the U.S. population from the National Health and Nutrition Examination Survey.

Categories (Survey Years)	Geometric Mean (95% conf. interval)	50th Percentile (95% conf. interval)	75th Percentile (95% conf. interval)	90th Percentile (95% conf. interval)	95th Percentile (95% conf. interval)	Sample Size
Mexican Americans (2003 - 2004)	*	< LOD	< LOD	.500 (.500-.600)	.700 (.600-.800)	2007
Mexican Americans (2005 - 2006)	*	< LOD	< LOD	.530 (.470-.580)	.670 (.560-.830)	2224
Mexican Americans (2007 - 2008)	*	< LOD	< LOD	.430 (.400-.480)	.560 (.520-.610)	1685
Mexican Americans (2009 - 2010)	*	< LOD	< LOD	< LOD	.470 (.390-.530)	1947
Non-Hispanic blacks (2003 - 2004)	*	< LOD	< LOD	.600 (.500-.600)	.700 (.600-.800)	2240
Non-Hispanic blacks (2005 - 2006)	*	< LOD	< LOD	.530 (.470-.600)	.670 (.600-.760)	2183
Non-Hispanic blacks (2007 - 2008)	*	< LOD	< LOD	.490 (.450-.530)	.610 (.560-.650)	1729
Non-Hispanic blacks (2009 - 2010)	*	< LOD	< LOD	.370 (.350-.390)	.480 (.410-.530)	1580
Non-Hispanic whites (2003 - 2004)	*	< LOD	< LOD	.600 (.500-.600)	.700 (.600-.700)	3406
Non-Hispanic whites (2005 - 2006)	*	< LOD	< LOD	.540 (.500-.580)	.650 (.610-.710)	3298
Non-Hispanic whites (2007 - 2008)	*	< LOD	.360 (<LOD-.390)	.530 (.500-.550)	.660 (.620-.700)	3421
Non-Hispanic whites (2009 - 2010)	*	< LOD	< LOD	.410 (.370-.450)	.520 (.480-.590)	3739

Limit of detection (LOD, see Data Analysis section) for Survey years 03-04, 05-06, 07-08, and 09-10 are 0.42, 0.4, 0.35, and 0.35 respectively.

< LOD means less than the limit of detection, which may vary for some chemicals by year and by individual sample.

* Not calculated: proportion of results below limit of detection was too high to provide a valid result.

Biomonitoring Summary: https://www.cdc.gov/biomonitoring/Mercury_BiomonitoringSummary.html

Factsheet: https://www.cdc.gov/biomonitoring/Mercury_FactSheet.html

Source: Centers for Disease Control & Prevention, Fourth National Report on Human Exposure to Environmental Chemicals, Updated Tables, January 2019

Blood Inorganic Mercury (2011 – 2016)

CAS Number 92786-62-4

Geometric mean and selected percentiles of blood concentrations (in µg/L) for the U.S. population from the National Health and Nutrition Examination Survey.

Categories (Survey Years)	Geometric Mean (95% conf. interval)	50th Percentile (95% conf. interval)	75th Percentile (95% conf. interval)	90th Percentile (95% conf. interval)	95th Percentile (95% conf. interval)	Sample Size
Total population (2011 - 2012)	*	< LOD	< LOD	.440 (.390-.480)	.600 (.520-.680)	7841
Total population (2013 - 2014)	*	< LOD	< LOD	.410 (.380-.440)	.530 (.490-.570)	5175
Total population (2015 - 2016)	*	< LOD	< LOD	.350 (.300-.400)	.480 (.430-.530)	4938
Age 1-5 years (2011 - 2012)	*	< LOD	< LOD	< LOD	.280 (<LOD-.360)	657
Age 1-5 years (2013 - 2014)	*	< LOD	< LOD	< LOD	< LOD	779
Age 1-5 years (2015 - 2016)	*	< LOD	< LOD	< LOD	.270 (<LOD-.340)	749
Age 6-11 years (2011 - 2012)	*	< LOD	< LOD	.280 (<LOD-.320)	.360 (.290-.450)	1044
Age 6-11 years (2013 - 2014)	*	< LOD	< LOD	< LOD	.340 (<LOD-.420)	1074
Age 6-11 years (2015 - 2016)	*	< LOD	< LOD	< LOD	.330 (<LOD-.450)	1022
Age 12-19 years (2011 - 2012)	*	< LOD	< LOD	.280 (<LOD-.350)	.400 (.300-.540)	1121
Age 12-19 years (2013 - 2014)	*	< LOD	< LOD	< LOD	.360 (.290-.420)	627
Age 12-19 years (2015 - 2016)	*	< LOD	< LOD	< LOD	.400 (<LOD-.510)	565
Age 20+ years (2011 - 2012)	*	< LOD	.290 (.270-.310)	.470 (.420-.530)	.630 (.550-.760)	5019
Age 20+ years (2013 - 2014)	*	< LOD	.270 (<LOD-.300)	.440 (.410-.470)	.560 (.510-.660)	2695
Age 20+ years (2015 - 2016)	*	< LOD	< LOD	.380 (.330-.430)	.500 (.450-.560)	2602
Males (2011 - 2012)	*	< LOD	< LOD	.420 (.370-.480)	.600 (.490-.680)	3925
Males (2013 - 2014)	*	< LOD	< LOD	.400 (.340-.430)	.510 (.450-.560)	2570
Males (2015 - 2016)	*	< LOD	< LOD	.330 (.280-.400)	.430 (.400-.490)	2460
Females (2011 - 2012)	*	< LOD	.280 (<LOD-.300)	.450 (.390-.490)	.610 (.520-.700)	3916
Females (2013 - 2014)	*	< LOD	< LOD	.420 (.390-.450)	.550 (.510-.590)	2605
Females (2015 - 2016)	*	< LOD	< LOD	.370 (.320-.450)	.530 (.450-.620)	2478
Mexican Americans (2011 - 2012)	*	< LOD	< LOD	.390 (.330-.460)	.580 (.460-.710)	1058
Mexican Americans (2013 - 2014)	*	< LOD	< LOD	.380 (.330-.410)	.540 (.420-.640)	958
Mexican Americans (2015 - 2016)	*	< LOD	< LOD	.420 (.290-.600)	.560 (.430-.820)	988
Non-Hispanic blacks (2011 - 2012)	*	< LOD	< LOD	.410 (.370-.470)	.570 (.480-.670)	2170
Non-Hispanic blacks (2013 - 2014)	*	< LOD	< LOD	.380 (.330-.430)	.530 (.440-.630)	1110
Non-Hispanic blacks (2015 - 2016)	*	< LOD	< LOD	.330 (.270-.380)	.430 (.370-.490)	1058
Non-Hispanic whites (2011 - 2012)	*	< LOD	.270 (<LOD-.300)	.430 (.370-.490)	.590 (.480-.690)	2477
Non-Hispanic whites (2013 - 2014)	*	< LOD	< LOD	.420 (.360-.450)	.510 (.460-.570)	1835
Non-Hispanic whites (2015 - 2016)	*	< LOD	< LOD	.320 (.280-.400)	.460 (.400-.540)	1500
All Hispanics (2011 - 2012)	*	< LOD	< LOD	.430 (.370-.490)	.630 (.540-.760)	1902
All Hispanics (2013 - 2014)	*	< LOD	< LOD	.380 (.330-.410)	.540 (.440-.650)	1467
All Hispanics (2015 - 2016)	*	< LOD	< LOD	.380 (.300-.490)	.510 (.430-.650)	1648
Asians (2011 - 2012)	*	< LOD	.350 (.310-.390)	.550 (.500-.590)	.700 (.630-.760)	997
Asians (2013 - 2014)	*	< LOD	.330 (.270-.390)	.570 (.420-.680)	.750 (.580-1.10)	508
Asians (2015 - 2016)	*	< LOD	< LOD	.430 (.360-.540)	.600 (.470-.730)	473

Limit of detection (LOD, see Data Analysis section) for Survey years 11-12, 13-14, and 15-16 are 0.27, 0.27, and 0.27 respectively.

< LOD means less than the limit of detection, which may vary for some chemicals by year and by individual sample.

* Not calculated: proportion of results below limit of detection was too high to provide a valid result.

Biomonitoring Summary: https://www.cdc.gov/biomonitoring/Mercury_BiomonitoringSummary.html

Factsheet: https://www.cdc.gov/biomonitoring/Mercury_FactSheet.html

Source: *Centers for Disease Control & Prevention, Fourth National Report on Human Exposure to Environmental Chemicals, Updated Tables, January 2019*

Blood Ethyl Mercury (2011 – 2016)

CAS Number 92786-62-4

Geometric mean and selected percentiles of blood concentrations (in µg/L) for the U.S. population from the National Health and Nutrition Examination Survey.

Categories (Survey Years)	Geometric Mean (95% conf. interval)	50th Percentile (95% conf. interval)	75th Percentile (95% conf. interval)	90th Percentile (95% conf. interval)	95th Percentile (95% conf. interval)	Sample Size
Total population (2011 - 2012)	*	< LOD	< LOD	< LOD	< LOD	7841
Total population (2013 - 2014)	*	< LOD	< LOD	< LOD	< LOD	5175
Total population (2015 - 2016)	*	< LOD	< LOD	< LOD	< LOD	4936
Age 1-5 years (2011 - 2012)	*	< LOD	< LOD	< LOD	< LOD	657
Age 1-5 years (2013 - 2014)	*	< LOD	< LOD	< LOD	< LOD	779
Age 1-5 years (2015 - 2016)	*	< LOD	< LOD	< LOD	< LOD	749
Age 6-11 years (2011 - 2012)	*	< LOD	< LOD	< LOD	< LOD	1044
Age 6-11 years (2013 - 2014)	*	< LOD	< LOD	< LOD	< LOD	1074
Age 6-11 years (2015 - 2016)	*	< LOD	< LOD	< LOD	< LOD	1022
Age 12-19 years (2011 - 2012)	*	< LOD	< LOD	< LOD	< LOD	1121
Age 12-19 years (2013 - 2014)	*	< LOD	< LOD	< LOD	< LOD	627
Age 12-19 years (2015 - 2016)	*	< LOD	< LOD	< LOD	< LOD	565
Age 20+ years (2011 - 2012)	*	< LOD	< LOD	< LOD	< LOD	5019
Age 20+ years (2013 - 2014)	*	< LOD	< LOD	< LOD	< LOD	2695
Age 20+ years (2015 - 2016)	*	< LOD	< LOD	< LOD	< LOD	2600
Males (2011 - 2012)	*	< LOD	< LOD	< LOD	< LOD	3925
Males (2013 - 2014)	*	< LOD	< LOD	< LOD	< LOD	2570
Males (2015 - 2016)	*	< LOD	< LOD	< LOD	< LOD	2458
Females (2011 - 2012)	*	< LOD	< LOD	< LOD	< LOD	3916
Females (2013 - 2014)	*	< LOD	< LOD	< LOD	< LOD	2605
Females (2015 - 2016)	*	< LOD	< LOD	< LOD	< LOD	2478
Mexican Americans (2011 - 2012)	*	< LOD	< LOD	< LOD	< LOD	1058
Mexican Americans (2013 - 2014)	*	< LOD	< LOD	< LOD	< LOD	958
Mexican Americans (2015 - 2016)	*	< LOD	< LOD	< LOD	< LOD	988
Non-Hispanic blacks (2011 - 2012)	*	< LOD	< LOD	< LOD	< LOD	2170
Non-Hispanic blacks (2013 - 2014)	*	< LOD	< LOD	< LOD	< LOD	1110
Non-Hispanic blacks (2015 - 2016)	*	< LOD	< LOD	< LOD	< LOD	1057
Non-Hispanic whites (2011 - 2012)	*	< LOD	< LOD	< LOD	< LOD	2477
Non-Hispanic whites (2013 - 2014)	*	< LOD	< LOD	< LOD	< LOD	1835
Non-Hispanic whites (2015 - 2016)	*	< LOD	< LOD	< LOD	< LOD	1500
All Hispanics (2011 - 2012)	*	< LOD	< LOD	< LOD	< LOD	1902
All Hispanics (2013 - 2014)	*	< LOD	< LOD	< LOD	< LOD	1467
All Hispanics (2015 - 2016)	*	< LOD	< LOD	< LOD	< LOD	1647
Asians (2011 - 2012)	*	< LOD	< LOD	< LOD	.160 (<LOD-.280)	997
Asians (2013 - 2014)	*	< LOD	< LOD	< LOD	< LOD	508
Asians (2015 - 2016)	*	< LOD	< LOD	< LOD	< LOD	473

Limit of detection (LOD, see Data Analysis section) for Survey years 11-12, 13-14, and 15-16 are 0.16, 0.16, and 0.16 respectively.

< LOD means less than the limit of detection, which may vary for some chemicals by year and by individual sample.

* Not calculated: proportion of results below limit of detection was too high to provide a valid result.

Biomonitoring Summary: https://www.cdc.gov/biomonitoring/Mercury_BiomonitoringSummary.html

Factsheet: https://www.cdc.gov/biomonitoring/Mercury_FactSheet.html

Source: *Centers for Disease Control & Prevention, Fourth National Report on Human Exposure to Environmental Chemicals, Updated Tables, January 2019*

Blood Methyl Mercury (2011 – 2016)

CAS Number 92786-62-4

Geometric mean and selected percentiles of blood concentrations (in µg/L) for the U.S. population from the National Health and Nutrition Examination Survey.

Categories (Survey Years)	Geometric Mean (95% conf. interval)	50th Percentile (95% conf. interval)	75th Percentile (95% conf. interval)	90th Percentile (95% conf. interval)	95th Percentile (95% conf. interval)	Sample Size
Total population (2011 - 2012)	.498 (.423-.587)	.480 (.400-.570)	1.25 (.950-1.61)	2.81 (2.29-3.55)	4.43 (3.46-5.49)	7841
Total population (2013 - 2014)	.434 (.381-.495)	.420 (.340-.510)	1.09 (.940-1.27)	2.62 (2.18-3.04)	4.28 (3.74-4.93)	5175
Total population (2015 - 2016)	.413 (.361-.472)	.380 (.320-.490)	1.02 (.860-1.22)	2.30 (1.92-2.78)	3.92 (3.35-4.81)	4938
Age 1-5 years (2011 - 2012)	*	.140 (.120-.170)	.270 (.220-.350)	.540 (.420-.780)	.970 (.590-1.14)	657
Age 1-5 years (2013 - 2014)	*	< LOD	.260 (.230-.310)	.660 (.550-.810)	1.11 (.960-1.48)	779
Age 1-5 years (2015 - 2016)	*	< LOD	.200 (.170-.240)	.470 (.350-.630)	.830 (.590-1.21)	749
Age 6-11 years (2011 - 2012)	.209 (.182-.241)	.180 (.150-.220)	.400 (.330-.490)	.820 (.630-1.06)	1.34 (.940-1.84)	1044
Age 6-11 years (2013 - 2014)	*	.150 (<LOD-.200)	.380 (.280-.530)	.960 (.700-1.26)	1.58 (1.26-2.11)	1074
Age 6-11 years (2015 - 2016)	*	.140 (<LOD-.180)	.290 (.260-.340)	.730 (.530-.950)	1.11 (.870-1.91)	1022
Age 12-19 years (2011 - 2012)	.276 (.237-.322)	.270 (.210-.310)	.570 (.460-.670)	1.27 (.870-1.67)	2.15 (1.40-2.81)	1121
Age 12-19 years (2013 - 2014)	.233 (.202-.269)	.190 (.140-.260)	.480 (.380-.560)	1.02 (.730-1.60)	1.84 (1.20-2.57)	627
Age 12-19 years (2015 - 2016)	.212 (.180-.249)	.160 (.120-.220)	.420 (.310-.620)	.800 (.690-1.23)	1.81 (.800-3.14)	565
Age 20+ years (2011 - 2012)	.624 (.523-.746)	.610 (.500-.760)	1.53 (1.18-2.00)	3.28 (2.56-4.31)	4.97 (3.91-6.89)	5019
Age 20+ years (2013 - 2014)	.541 (.473-.618)	.540 (.450-.630)	1.32 (1.17-1.54)	3.05 (2.64-3.60)	4.92 (4.34-5.41)	2695
Age 20+ years (2015 - 2016)	.518 (.456-.588)	.530 (.420-.630)	1.23 (1.05-1.46)	2.59 (2.25-3.36)	4.42 (3.66-5.58)	2602
Males (2011 - 2012)	.509 (.433-.598)	.490 (.400-.590)	1.30 (.990-1.62)	2.84 (2.29-3.68)	4.77 (3.44-6.74)	3925
Males (2013 - 2014)	.448 (.390-.515)	.430 (.350-.530)	1.10 (.940-1.37)	2.67 (2.22-3.33)	4.44 (3.88-5.40)	2570
Males (2015 - 2016)	.429 (.379-.486)	.400 (.330-.520)	1.11 (.900-1.33)	2.24 (1.85-2.86)	4.42 (3.60-5.05)	2460
Females (2011 - 2012)	.489 (.413-.580)	.470 (.380-.560)	1.19 (.900-1.61)	2.72 (2.18-3.46)	3.99 (3.28-4.99)	3916
Females (2013 - 2014)	.422 (.367-.485)	.400 (.330-.490)	1.08 (.900-1.22)	2.46 (2.03-2.92)	3.91 (3.32-4.93)	2605
Females (2015 - 2016)	.399 (.338-.470)	.370 (.300-.470)	.950 (.760-1.18)	2.36 (1.91-2.81)	3.58 (2.92-4.24)	2478
Mexican Americans (2011 - 2012)	.320 (.264-.387)	.330 (.260-.410)	.610 (.500-.770)	1.23 (.920-1.40)	1.66 (1.33-2.06)	1058
Mexican Americans (2013 - 2014)	.276 (.239-.318)	.260 (.210-.310)	.540 (.440-.650)	1.06 (.770-1.43)	1.72 (1.27-2.34)	958
Mexican Americans (2015 - 2016)	.292 (.276-.309)	.290 (.260-.330)	.610 (.550-.690)	1.13 (.870-1.47)	1.54 (1.34-2.02)	988
Non-Hispanic blacks (2011 - 2012)	.517 (.392-.681)	.510 (.380-.660)	1.13 (.750-1.61)	2.37 (1.66-3.08)	3.63 (2.57-5.16)	2170
Non-Hispanic blacks (2013 - 2014)	.481 (.407-.569)	.460 (.370-.580)	1.03 (.900-1.22)	2.08 (1.55-2.72)	3.33 (2.15-5.12)	1110
Non-Hispanic blacks (2015 - 2016)	.461 (.376-.565)	.430 (.330-.580)	1.05 (.830-1.25)	2.34 (1.71-3.31)	4.08 (2.80-5.58)	1058
Non-Hispanic whites (2011 - 2012)	.478 (.392-.583)	.470 (.360-.580)	1.25 (.870-1.69)	2.76 (2.06-3.69)	4.24 (2.92-6.38)	2477
Non-Hispanic whites (2013 - 2014)	.420 (.357-.495)	.420 (.310-.530)	1.10 (.910-1.32)	2.62 (2.07-3.12)	4.01 (3.46-5.00)	1835
Non-Hispanic whites (2015 - 2016)	.380 (.319-.451)	.350 (.270-.490)	.960 (.750-1.22)	2.04 (1.55-2.51)	3.50 (2.32-4.49)	1500
All Hispanics (2011 - 2012)	.429 (.350-.525)	.420 (.340-.520)	.890 (.700-1.17)	1.81 (1.39-2.46)	2.94 (2.19-3.71)	1902
All Hispanics (2013 - 2014)	.326 (.278-.382)	.310 (.250-.350)	.680 (.580-.790)	1.50 (1.15-1.89)	2.34 (1.79-3.00)	1467
All Hispanics (2015 - 2016)	.353 (.305-.409)	.350 (.300-.390)	.760 (.630-.930)	1.53 (1.14-1.98)	2.26 (1.60-3.03)	1648
Asians (2011 - 2012)	1.58 (1.29-1.94)	2.16 (1.68-2.55)	4.35 (3.64-5.13)	7.57 (6.21-8.61)	10.5 (8.48-12.5)	997
Asians (2013 - 2014)	1.42 (1.16-1.74)	1.71 (1.17-2.07)	3.90 (3.31-4.54)	7.93 (6.42-9.21)	10.8 (9.57-13.6)	508
Asians (2015 - 2016)	1.37 (1.08-1.73)	1.85 (1.18-2.51)	3.80 (3.11-4.83)	7.52 (5.60-9.63)	11.0 (8.65-12.4)	473

Limit of detection (LOD, see Data Analysis section) for Survey years 11-12, 13-14, and 15-16 are 0.12, 0.12, and 0.12 respectively.

< LOD means less than the limit of detection, which may vary for some chemicals by year and by individual sample.

* Not calculated: proportion of results below limit of detection was too high to provide a valid result.

Biomonitoring Summary: https://www.cdc.gov/biomonitoring/Mercury_BiomonitoringSummary.html

Factsheet: https://www.cdc.gov/biomonitoring/Mercury_FactSheet.html

Source: *Centers for Disease Control & Prevention, Fourth National Report on Human Exposure to Environmental Chemicals, Updated Tables, January 2019*

Urinary Mercury (2003 – 2010)

CAS Number 92786-62-4

Geometric mean and selected percentiles of urine concentrations (in µg/L) for the U.S. population from the National Health and Nutrition Examination Survey.

Categories (Survey Years)	Geometric Mean (95% conf. interval)	50th Percentile (95% conf. interval)	75th Percentile (95% conf. interval)	90th Percentile (95% conf. interval)	95th Percentile (95% conf. interval)	Sample Size
Total population (2003 - 2004)	.447 (.406-.492)	.420 (.360-.480)	1.00 (.870-1.14)	2.08 (1.78-2.42)	3.19 (2.76-3.55)	2538
Total population (2005 - 2006)	.468 (.426-.514)	.460 (.410-.510)	1.03 (.900-1.12)	2.11 (1.88-2.36)	2.94 (2.58-3.26)	2578
Total population (2007 - 2008)	.443 (.408-.482)	.440 (.400-.470)	.880 (.760-1.00)	1.74 (1.62-1.96)	2.66 (2.29-3.08)	2634
Total population (2009 - 2010)	*	.400 (.360-.450)	.850 (.770-.910)	1.53 (1.30-1.81)	2.42 (2.07-2.72)	2865
Age 6-11 years (2003 - 2004)	.254 (.213-.304)	.200 (.160-.250)	.440 (.330-.580)	1.16 (.610-1.61)	1.96 (1.13-2.97)	287
Age 6-11 years (2005 - 2006)	.333 (.267-.416)	.320 (.250-.390)	.650 (.470-.840)	1.32 (.930-1.88)	2.18 (1.28-3.40)	355
Age 6-11 years (2007 - 2008)	.301 (.260-.347)	.290 (.230-.340)	.520 (.430-.620)	1.03 (.770-1.23)	1.87 (1.03-3.48)	398
Age 6-11 years (2009 - 2010)	*	.260 (.220-.320)	.510 (.430-.620)	1.03 (.730-1.31)	1.58 (1.18-1.88)	379
Age 12-19 years (2003 - 2004)	.358 (.313-.408)	.330 (.290-.370)	.700 (.530-.840)	1.60 (1.14-2.52)	2.93 (1.88-3.66)	722
Age 12-19 years (2005 - 2006)	.372 (.286-.486)	.350 (.270-.470)	.740 (.580-.920)	1.61 (.970-2.81)	2.59 (1.40-4.45)	703
Age 12-19 years (2007 - 2008)	.364 (.326-.406)	.380 (.320-.450)	.590 (.550-.650)	1.24 (.830-1.71)	1.82 (1.41-2.29)	375
Age 12-19 years (2009 - 2010)	*	.290 (.230-.360)	.530 (.470-.630)	1.09 (.890-1.31)	1.73 (1.28-2.31)	455
Age 20+ years (2003 - 2004)	.495 (.442-.555)	.480 (.410-.570)	1.12 (.930-1.29)	2.20 (1.85-2.65)	3.33 (2.76-3.88)	1529
Age 20+ years (2005 - 2006)	.505 (.468-.545)	.510 (.460-.560)	1.11 (1.04-1.16)	2.23 (1.97-2.50)	3.11 (2.64-3.37)	1520
Age 20+ years (2007 - 2008)	.477 (.435-.523)	.470 (.430-.520)	.970 (.850-1.10)	1.89 (1.69-2.20)	2.82 (2.33-3.56)	1861
Age 20+ years (2009 - 2010)	*	.450 (.390-.510)	.890 (.810-1.00)	1.66 (1.40-2.01)	2.53 (2.21-2.84)	2031
Males (2003 - 2004)	.433 (.405-.463)	.400 (.350-.460)	.940 (.840-1.05)	1.88 (1.63-2.18)	2.68 (2.34-3.05)	1266
Males (2005 - 2006)	.464 (.411-.523)	.450 (.400-.520)	.980 (.860-1.11)	2.03 (1.57-2.48)	3.00 (2.48-3.37)	1270
Males (2007 - 2008)	.457 (.417-.501)	.460 (.400-.520)	.880 (.780-1.01)	1.68 (1.53-1.77)	2.40 (2.11-2.76)	1326
Males (2009 - 2010)	*	.410 (.340-.480)	.860 (.750-.950)	1.46 (1.29-1.66)	2.21 (1.93-2.53)	1404
Females (2003 - 2004)	.460 (.396-.534)	.430 (.330-.530)	1.07 (.870-1.28)	2.26 (1.77-2.90)	3.54 (2.76-4.31)	1272
Females (2005 - 2006)	.472 (.424-.525)	.470 (.390-.550)	1.07 (.900-1.19)	2.14 (1.84-2.50)	2.89 (2.60-3.38)	1308
Females (2007 - 2008)	.431 (.388-.478)	.430 (.380-.460)	.870 (.710-1.05)	1.88 (1.55-2.38)	2.92 (2.27-4.17)	1308
Females (2009 - 2010)	*	.390 (.360-.450)	.840 (.730-.940)	1.61 (1.29-2.03)	2.61 (2.16-3.12)	1461
Mexican Americans (2003 - 2004)	.416 (.340-.509)	.360 (.280-.430)	.960 (.700-1.23)	2.19 (1.39-3.24)	3.16 (1.99-6.30)	619
Mexican Americans (2005 - 2006)	.451 (.369-.551)	.420 (.310-.560)	1.01 (.780-1.25)	2.22 (1.48-2.64)	3.00 (2.27-4.01)	651
Mexican Americans (2007 - 2008)	.409 (.349-.480)	.370 (.330-.450)	.780 (.700-.950)	1.82 (1.26-1.97)	2.55 (1.87-3.08)	514
Mexican Americans (2009 - 2010)	*	.350 (.280-.430)	.670 (.520-.890)	1.53 (1.06-1.84)	2.29 (1.81-2.76)	615
Non-Hispanic blacks (2003 - 2004)	.476 (.413-.549)	.430 (.360-.530)	.890 (.770-1.00)	1.96 (1.60-2.31)	3.09 (2.03-4.89)	713
Non-Hispanic blacks (2005 - 2006)	.453 (.384-.533)	.450 (.380-.550)	.890 (.710-1.13)	1.78 (1.34-2.29)	2.57 (2.21-3.15)	691
Non-Hispanic blacks (2007 - 2008)	.478 (.411-.556)	.460 (.380-.540)	.910 (.770-1.06)	1.85 (1.42-2.41)	2.76 (1.97-4.19)	589
Non-Hispanic blacks (2009 - 2010)	*	.410 (.340-.490)	.840 (.650-1.08)	1.66 (1.34-1.95)	2.64 (1.88-3.30)	546
Non-Hispanic whites (2003 - 2004)	.441 (.382-.509)	.420 (.330-.520)	1.01 (.840-1.23)	2.08 (1.67-2.46)	3.24 (2.67-3.60)	1066
Non-Hispanic whites (2005 - 2006)	.459 (.409-.513)	.440 (.400-.510)	1.00 (.860-1.12)	2.07 (1.77-2.40)	2.81 (2.47-3.37)	1044
Non-Hispanic whites (2007 - 2008)	.431 (.378-.493)	.430 (.380-.480)	.880 (.700-1.07)	1.71 (1.50-2.18)	2.70 (2.18-3.59)	1100
Non-Hispanic whites (2009 - 2010)	*	.390 (.330-.470)	.850 (.750-.950)	1.52 (1.26-2.01)	2.42 (1.93-2.85)	1225

Limit of detection (LOD, see Data Analysis section) for Survey years 03-04, 05-06, 07-08 and 09-10 are 0.14, 0.11, 0.08, and 0.08 respectively.

* Not calculated: proportion of results below limit of detection was too high to provide a valid result.

Biomonitoring Summary: https://www.cdc.gov/biomonitoring/Mercury_BiomonitoringSummary.html

Factsheet: https://www.cdc.gov/biomonitoring/Mercury_FactSheet.html

Source: *Centers for Disease Control & Prevention, Fourth National Report on Human Exposure to Environmental Chemicals, Updated Tables, January 2019*

Urinary Mercury (2011 – 2016)

CAS Number 92786-62-4

Geometric mean and selected percentiles of urine concentrations (in µg/L) for the U.S. population from the National Health and Nutrition Examination Survey.

Categories (Survey Years)	Geometric Mean (95% conf. interval)	50th Percentile (95% conf. interval)	75th Percentile (95% conf. interval)	90th Percentile (95% conf. interval)	95th Percentile (95% conf. interval)	Sample Size
Total population (2011 - 2012)	.324 (.285-.368)	.320 (.280-.370)	.660 (.580-.770)	1.37 (1.15-1.59)	1.83 (1.62-2.14)	2507
Total population (2013 - 2014)	.246 (.221-.273)	.200 (.170-.240)	.470 (.400-.570)	1.07 (.900-1.22)	1.64 (1.35-1.96)	2666
Total population (2015 - 2016)	*	< LOD	.280 (.250-.320)	.680 (.570-.780)	1.18 (.920-1.29)	3080
Age 3-5 years (2015 - 2016)	*	< LOD	< LOD	.160 (<LOD-.240)	.280 (.190-.510)	496
Age 6-11 years (2011 - 2012)	.241 (.206-.283)	.220 (.190-.270)	.450 (.390-.530)	.930 (.680-1.36)	1.37 (.990-2.03)	401
Age 6-11 years (2013 - 2014)	*	< LOD	.220 (.150-.310)	.560 (.340-.840)	.890 (.640-1.10)	401
Age 6-11 years (2015 - 2016)	*	< LOD	< LOD	.300 (.200-.380)	.520 (.360-.700)	380
Age 12-19 years (2011 - 2012)	.257 (.212-.312)	.270 (.220-.340)	.490 (.390-.600)	.840 (.650-1.24)	1.31 (.920-1.75)	390
Age 12-19 years (2013 - 2014)	*	< LOD	.240 (.200-.310)	.560 (.400-.860)	1.02 (.610-1.81)	452
Age 12-19 years (2015 - 2016)	*	< LOD	.130 (<LOD-.160)	.350 (.200-.470)	.610 (.380-1.14)	402
Age 20+ years (2011 - 2012)	.346 (.303-.396)	.340 (.290-.400)	.720 (.620-.850)	1.49 (1.20-1.67)	1.93 (1.67-2.29)	1716
Age 20+ years (2013 - 2014)	.274 (.246-.305)	.240 (.200-.280)	.540 (.450-.630)	1.16 (1.00-1.33)	1.76 (1.44-2.04)	1813
Age 20+ years (2015 - 2016)	*	.140 (.130-.150)	.340 (.310-.380)	.740 (.650-.890)	1.22 (.970-1.43)	1802
Males (2011 - 2012)	.342 (.293-.399)	.330 (.290-.380)	.670 (.580-.810)	1.34 (1.03-1.67)	1.91 (1.54-2.51)	1260
Males (2013 - 2014)	.243 (.219-.268)	.200 (.170-.220)	.480 (.390-.600)	1.07 (.840-1.33)	1.55 (1.28-1.96)	1319
Males (2015 - 2016)	*	< LOD	.280 (.230-.330)	.620 (.540-.710)	.900 (.760-1.18)	1533
Females (2011 - 2012)	.307 (.262-.360)	.300 (.250-.360)	.660 (.540-.770)	1.37 (1.17-1.54)	1.82 (1.54-2.14)	1247
Females (2013 - 2014)	.249 (.218-.284)	.210 (.170-.260)	.470 (.390-.570)	1.07 (.820-1.27)	1.75 (1.25-2.26)	1347
Females (2015 - 2016)	*	< LOD	.290 (.250-.350)	.730 (.570-.980)	1.27 (.940-1.88)	1547
Mexican Americans (2011 - 2012)	.301 (.261-.348)	.300 (.200-.400)	.620 (.510-.680)	1.25 (.910-1.53)	1.75 (1.32-2.25)	317
Mexican Americans (2013 - 2014)	.229 (.198-.265)	.160 (.150-.210)	.450 (.300-.620)	1.12 (.780-1.35)	1.47 (.970-2.38)	454
Mexican Americans (2015 - 2016)	*	< LOD	.230 (.170-.280)	.530 (.440-.640)	.900 (.650-1.22)	586
Non-Hispanic blacks (2011 - 2012)	.360 (.316-.410)	.360 (.320-.400)	.670 (.570-.800)	1.33 (1.06-1.60)	1.99 (1.48-3.06)	671
Non-Hispanic blacks (2013 - 2014)	.279 (.228-.340)	.250 (.190-.320)	.530 (.400-.690)	1.10 (.900-1.49)	1.82 (1.11-2.48)	580
Non-Hispanic blacks (2015 - 2016)	*	.140 (<LOD-.180)	.370 (.270-.510)	.800 (.620-1.19)	1.38 (.870-1.72)	676
Non-Hispanic whites (2011 - 2012)	.308 (.260-.365)	.290 (.260-.360)	.630 (.510-.810)	1.37 (1.09-1.64)	1.77 (1.49-2.14)	819
Non-Hispanic whites (2013 - 2014)	.240 (.211-.271)	.200 (.160-.230)	.460 (.370-.580)	1.06 (.840-1.24)	1.64 (1.24-2.04)	988
Non-Hispanic whites (2015 - 2016)	*	< LOD	.260 (.210-.330)	.700 (.480-.870)	1.18 (.860-1.40)	932
All Hispanics (2011 - 2012)	.330 (.299-.364)	.330 (.270-.390)	.680 (.610-.760)	1.30 (1.15-1.53)	1.98 (1.61-2.42)	574
All Hispanics (2013 - 2014)	.239 (.207-.276)	.180 (.150-.240)	.460 (.360-.620)	1.14 (.800-1.35)	1.57 (1.24-2.15)	702
All Hispanics (2015 - 2016)	*	< LOD	.260 (.210-.330)	.600 (.470-.740)	1.03 (.730-1.37)	986
Asians (2011 - 2012)	.430 (.351-.527)	.450 (.330-.580)	.910 (.750-1.12)	1.69 (1.31-2.06)	2.41 (1.77-3.53)	355
Asians (2013 - 2014)	.313 (.269-.363)	.270 (.220-.340)	.620 (.520-.710)	1.18 (.890-1.66)	1.78 (1.20-3.10)	291
Asians (2015 - 2016)	*	.180 (<LOD-.250)	.390 (.330-.510)	.720 (.610-.820)	.960 (.790-1.49)	333

Limit of detection (LOD, see Data Analysis section) for Survey years 11-12, 13-14, and 15-16 are 0.05, 0.13, and 0.13, respectively.

< LOD means less than the limit of detection, which may vary for some chemicals by year and by individual sample.

* Not calculated: proportion of results below limit of detection was too high to provide a valid result.

Biomonitoring Summary: https://www.cdc.gov/biomonitoring/Mercury_BiomonitoringSummary.html

Factsheet: https://www.cdc.gov/biomonitoring/Mercury_FactSheet.html

Source: *Centers for Disease Control & Prevention, Fourth National Report on Human Exposure to Environmental Chemicals, Updated Tables, January 2019*

Urinary Mercury (creatinine corrected) (2003 – 2010)

CAS Number 92786-62-4

Geometric mean and selected percentiles of urine concentrations (in µg/g of creatinine) for the U.S. population from the National Health and Nutrition Examination Survey.

Categories (Survey Years)	Geometric Mean (95% conf. interval)	50th Percentile (95% conf. interval)	75th Percentile (95% conf. interval)	90th Percentile (95% conf. interval)	95th Percentile (95% conf. interval)	Sample Size
Total population (2003 - 2004)	.443 (.404-.486)	.447 (.392-.498)	.909 (.785-1.00)	1.65 (1.40-1.86)	2.35 (1.88-2.85)	2537
Total population (2005 - 2006)	.460 (.414-.511)	.450 (.410-.510)	.870 (.790-1.00)	1.63 (1.44-1.75)	2.26 (2.12-2.50)	2578
Total population (2007 - 2008)	.462 (.425-.502)	.450 (.400-.490)	.820 (.750-.960)	1.57 (1.38-1.73)	2.32 (2.00-2.89)	2634
Total population (2009 - 2010)	*	.409 (.367-.459)	.793 (.691-.893)	1.43 (1.24-1.67)	2.09 (1.79-2.39)	2865
Age 6-11 years (2003 - 2004)	.297 (.246-.358)	.276 (.208-.347)	.485 (.391-.630)	1.25 (.667-1.79)	1.79 (1.11-2.61)	286
Age 6-11 years (2005 - 2006)	.411 (.323-.524)	.390 (.290-.500)	.710 (.510-.960)	1.30 (.990-2.12)	2.55 (1.38-3.50)	355
Age 6-11 years (2007 - 2008)	.393 (.351-.440)	.350 (.300-.440)	.630 (.540-.770)	1.15 (.860-1.50)	1.68 (1.18-2.99)	398
Age 6-11 years (2009 - 2010)	*	.357 (.306-.406)	.632 (.500-.750)	1.04 (.863-1.26)	1.62 (1.19-1.98)	379
Age 12-19 years (2003 - 2004)	.255 (.225-.289)	.217 (.196-.275)	.464 (.376-.535)	1.06 (.714-1.39)	1.67 (1.13-2.03)	722
Age 12-19 years (2005 - 2006)	.286 (.230-.356)	.260 (.200-.320)	.500 (.380-.660)	1.09 (.660-1.70)	1.76 (1.11-2.67)	703
Age 12-19 years (2007 - 2008)	.284 (.251-.320)	.280 (.230-.300)	.500 (.400-.550)	.890 (.620-1.08)	1.18 (.980-1.36)	375
Age 12-19 years (2009 - 2010)	*	.226 (.202-.287)	.481 (.429-.553)	.917 (.736-1.18)	1.41 (1.12-1.62)	455
Age 20+ years (2003 - 2004)	.508 (.455-.566)	.525 (.447-.616)	1.00 (.875-1.09)	1.76 (1.46-2.11)	2.54 (2.04-3.00)	1529
Age 20+ years (2005 - 2006)	.503 (.461-.549)	.510 (.470-.550)	.940 (.850-1.07)	1.69 (1.50-1.86)	2.31 (2.12-2.54)	1520
Age 20+ years (2007 - 2008)	.507 (.463-.555)	.500 (.450-.550)	.940 (.810-1.02)	1.69 (1.51-2.01)	2.56 (2.09-3.17)	1861
Age 20+ years (2009 - 2010)	*	.454 (.395-.517)	.861 (.731-.988)	1.51 (1.29-1.85)	2.15 (1.88-2.57)	2031
Males (2003 - 2004)	.365 (.333-.400)	.362 (.309-.417)	.696 (.620-.784)	1.31 (1.18-1.44)	1.87 (1.51-2.30)	1266
Males (2005 - 2006)	.380 (.336-.431)	.390 (.330-.440)	.740 (.600-.890)	1.27 (1.09-1.47)	1.73 (1.62-1.85)	1270
Males (2007 - 2008)	.408 (.374-.445)	.390 (.350-.450)	.730 (.650-.810)	1.22 (1.11-1.36)	1.69 (1.54-2.11)	1326
Males (2009 - 2010)	*	.337 (.298-.391)	.675 (.585-.802)	1.19 (1.06-1.29)	1.50 (1.33-1.78)	1404
Females (2003 - 2004)	.532 (.472-.599)	.545 (.455-.652)	1.06 (.969-1.21)	1.88 (1.64-2.30)	2.77 (2.12-3.56)	1271
Females (2005 - 2006)	.552 (.494-.617)	.540 (.490-.620)	1.09 (.850-1.27)	1.96 (1.72-2.14)	2.78 (2.35-3.17)	1308
Females (2007 - 2008)	.520 (.469-.576)	.490 (.460-.540)	.960 (.820-1.11)	1.92 (1.58-2.24)	2.83 (2.24-3.50)	1308
Females (2009 - 2010)	*	.475 (.423-.552)	.890 (.771-1.07)	1.81 (1.43-2.09)	2.57 (2.09-2.94)	1461
Mexican Americans (2003 - 2004)	.384 (.307-.480)	.365 (.280-.455)	.768 (.619-.990)	1.62 (1.23-2.16)	2.32 (1.78-4.01)	618
Mexican Americans (2005 - 2006)	.425 (.337-.536)	.400 (.310-.490)	.840 (.560-1.29)	1.82 (1.30-2.47)	2.63 (2.22-3.20)	651
Mexican Americans (2007 - 2008)	.409 (.350-.479)	.380 (.310-.480)	.790 (.690-.850)	1.55 (1.08-1.98)	2.03 (1.55-2.70)	514
Mexican Americans (2009 - 2010)	*	.333 (.272-.400)	.660 (.494-.861)	1.29 (1.02-1.54)	1.95 (1.52-2.89)	615
Non-Hispanic blacks (2003 - 2004)	.343 (.301-.391)	.306 (.265-.368)	.587 (.522-.687)	1.28 (.964-1.63)	2.13 (1.41-2.87)	713
Non-Hispanic blacks (2005 - 2006)	.328 (.285-.378)	.320 (.270-.370)	.610 (.470-.780)	1.15 (.930-1.40)	1.64 (1.29-1.96)	691
Non-Hispanic blacks (2007 - 2008)	.350 (.303-.404)	.330 (.280-.380)	.590 (.490-.690)	1.10 (.840-1.46)	1.85 (1.13-2.77)	589
Non-Hispanic blacks (2009 - 2010)	*	.317 (.259-.393)	.582 (.500-.659)	1.05 (.900-1.30)	1.55 (1.18-1.96)	546
Non-Hispanic whites (2003 - 2004)	.463 (.400-.537)	.476 (.385-.588)	.970 (.800-1.07)	1.67 (1.32-2.11)	2.40 (1.88-2.90)	1066
Non-Hispanic whites (2005 - 2006)	.475 (.426-.531)	.490 (.440-.540)	.890 (.820-1.02)	1.61 (1.42-1.75)	2.23 (1.98-2.50)	1044
Non-Hispanic whites (2007 - 2008)	.481 (.423-.546)	.480 (.390-.540)	.890 (.750-1.03)	1.58 (1.34-2.02)	2.49 (1.89-3.18)	1100
Non-Hispanic whites (2009 - 2010)	*	.434 (.370-.500)	.833 (.689-1.04)	1.50 (1.26-1.87)	2.12 (1.80-2.64)	1225

* Not calculated: proportion of results below limit of detection was too high to provide a valid result

Biomonitoring Summary: https://www.cdc.gov/biomonitoring/Mercury_BiomonitoringSummary.html

Factsheet: https://www.cdc.gov/biomonitoring/Mercury_FactSheet.html

Source: *Centers for Disease Control & Prevention, Fourth National Report on Human Exposure to Environmental Chemicals, Updated Tables, January 2019*

Urinary Mercury (creatinine corrected) (2011 – 2016)

CAS Number 92786-62-4

Geometric mean and selected percentiles of urine concentrations (in µg/g of creatinine) for the U.S. population from the National Health and Nutrition Examination Survey.

Categories (Survey Years)	Geometric Mean (95% conf. interval)	50th Percentile (95% conf. interval)	75th Percentile (95% conf. interval)	90th Percentile (95% conf. interval)	95th Percentile (95% conf. interval)	Sample Size
Total population (2011 - 2012)	.367 (.333-.405)	.353 (.306-.394)	.676 (.623-.754)	1.33 (1.13-1.50)	1.75 (1.49-2.32)	2505
Total population (2013 - 2014)	.283 (.260-.309)	.270 (.250-.290)	.571 (.511-.644)	1.20 (1.05-1.36)	1.61 (1.47-1.81)	2665
Total population (2015 - 2016)	*	< LOD	.356 (.318-.391)	.708 (.628-.817)	1.10 (.912-1.25)	3077
Age 3-5 years (2015 - 2016)	*	< LOD	< LOD	.667 (<LOD-.818)	.994 (.818-1.13)	495
Age 6-11 years (2011 - 2012)	.345 (.298-.398)	.306 (.276-.344)	.537 (.441-.613)	1.08 (.884-1.43)	1.62 (1.07-2.34)	400
Age 6-11 years (2013 - 2014)	*	< LOD	.429 (.310-.529)	.750 (.563-.897)	1.11 (.713-1.72)	401
Age 6-11 years (2015 - 2016)	*	< LOD	< LOD	.474 (.409-.529)	.643 (.500-1.00)	380
Age 12-19 years (2011 - 2012)	.246 (.219-.277)	.221 (.190-.269)	.405 (.368-.453)	.735 (.571-1.11)	1.21 (.742-1.49)	390
Age 12-19 years (2013 - 2014)	*	< LOD	.257 (.200-.281)	.580 (.391-.735)	.846 (.580-1.07)	452
Age 12-19 years (2015 - 2016)	*	< LOD	.194 (<LOD-.220)	.320 (.246-.568)	.650 (.385-.967)	402
Age 20+ years (2011 - 2012)	.393 (.351-.439)	.383 (.330-.437)	.750 (.673-.805)	1.38 (1.17-1.63)	1.95 (1.50-2.48)	1715
Age 20+ years (2013 - 2014)	.318 (.291-.349)	.304 (.281-.333)	.644 (.561-.741)	1.32 (1.13-1.47)	1.76 (1.50-1.88)	1812
Age 20+ years (2015 - 2016)	*	.198 (.184-.210)	.391 (.349-.449)	.776 (.692-.886)	1.15 (1.00-1.32)	1800
Males (2011 - 2012)	.320 (.278-.368)	.294 (.267-.358)	.558 (.478-.667)	1.11 (.791-1.44)	1.57 (1.21-2.00)	1259
Males (2013 - 2014)	.242 (.223-.263)	.231 (.206-.259)	.476 (.429-.542)	.902 (.779-1.11)	1.31 (1.13-1.49)	1318
Males (2015 - 2016)	*	< LOD	.274 (.246-.300)	.563 (.490-.628)	.818 (.705-.994)	1533
Females (2011 - 2012)	.418 (.374-.466)	.409 (.355-.453)	.800 (.706-.900)	1.46 (1.29-1.65)	2.00 (1.63-2.60)	1246
Females (2013 - 2014)	.330 (.297-.367)	.315 (.273-.356)	.692 (.600-.822)	1.44 (1.18-1.68)	1.83 (1.60-2.12)	1347
Females (2015 - 2016)	*	< LOD	.415 (.375-.473)	.875 (.750-1.00)	1.30 (1.06-1.86)	1544
Mexican Americans (2011 - 2012)	.339 (.288-.399)	.286 (.225-.393)	.641 (.433-.789)	1.17 (1.00-1.42)	1.70 (1.31-2.24)	317
Mexican Americans (2013 - 2014)	.261 (.231-.295)	.237 (.209-.273)	.516 (.409-.709)	1.04 (.810-1.48)	1.62 (1.11-2.55)	454
Mexican Americans (2015 - 2016)	*	< LOD	.283 (.236-.360)	.692 (.530-.810)	1.04 (.791-1.30)	585
Non-Hispanic blacks (2011 - 2012)	.280 (.245-.320)	.261 (.224-.294)	.467 (.411-.529)	.896 (.638-1.14)	1.43 (1.10-1.57)	671
Non-Hispanic blacks (2013 - 2014)	.211 (.169-.264)	.202 (.152-.269)	.409 (.333-.516)	.794 (.643-1.10)	1.34 (.880-1.52)	580
Non-Hispanic blacks (2015 - 2016)	*	.136 (<LOD-.163)	.303 (.237-.367)	.642 (.450-.848)	.901 (.695-1.18)	674
Non-Hispanic whites (2011 - 2012)	.372 (.323-.428)	.364 (.294-.433)	.700 (.619-.805)	1.35 (1.05-1.63)	1.75 (1.41-2.48)	817
Non-Hispanic whites (2013 - 2014)	.295 (.269-.323)	.278 (.257-.310)	.602 (.516-.689)	1.27 (1.08-1.45)	1.64 (1.46-1.82)	987
Non-Hispanic whites (2015 - 2016)	*	< LOD	.349 (.300-.400)	.708 (.563-.886)	1.10 (.827-1.32)	932
All Hispanics (2011 - 2012)	.369 (.342-.399)	.331 (.283-.384)	.674 (.612-.772)	1.24 (1.13-1.44)	1.86 (1.47-2.92)	574
All Hispanics (2013 - 2014)	.267 (.237-.300)	.237 (.214-.273)	.541 (.448-.634)	1.07 (.837-1.36)	1.61 (1.24-1.86)	702
All Hispanics (2015 - 2016)	*	< LOD	.348 (.284-.408)	.717 (.574-.917)	1.15 (.948-1.36)	985
Asians (2011 - 2012)	.577 (.473-.705)	.562 (.467-.700)	1.16 (.872-1.44)	1.82 (1.54-2.00)	2.29 (1.90-3.12)	355
Asians (2013 - 2014)	.488 (.422-.565)	.475 (.373-.600)	.917 (.779-1.06)	1.88 (1.35-2.19)	2.57 (1.88-4.24)	291
Asians (2015 - 2016)	*	.290 (<LOD-.375)	.594 (.457-.706)	1.02 (.808-1.22)	1.38 (1.11-1.80)	333

< LOD means less than the limit of detection for the urine levels not corrected for creatinine.

* Not calculated: proportion of results below limit of detection was too high to provide a valid result.

Biomonitoring Summary: https://www.cdc.gov/biomonitoring/Mercury_BiomonitoringSummary.html

Factsheet: https://www.cdc.gov/biomonitoring/Mercury_FactSheet.html

Source: *Centers for Disease Control & Prevention, Fourth National Report on Human Exposure to Environmental Chemicals, Updated Tables, January 2019*

Urinary Nitrate (2001 – 2010)

CAS Number 84145-82-4

Geometric mean and selected percentiles of urine concentrations (in mg/L) for the U.S. population from the National Health and Nutrition Examination Survey.

Categories (Survey Years)	Geometric Mean (95% conf. interval)	50th Percentile (95% conf. interval)	75th Percentile (95% conf. interval)	90th Percentile (95% conf. interval)	95th Percentile (95% conf. interval)	Sample Size
Total population (2001 - 2002)	48.2 (46.2-50.3)	49.0 (46.0-52.0)	78.0 (73.0-83.0)	100 (100-130)	140 (130-150)	1617
Total population (2005 - 2006)	42.7 (39.6-46.1)	47.8 (44.4-51.2)	74.6 (69.8-79.4)	108 (101-114)	133 (125-144)	7697
Total population (2007 - 2008)	46.3 (44.6-48.1)	50.3 (48.4-52.0)	76.0 (72.7-79.1)	110 (104-116)	138 (132-146)	7629
Total population (2009 - 2010)	40.7 (38.9-42.7)	43.3 (41.1-45.8)	68.7 (65.5-72.5)	98.5 (93.4-102)	126 (114-137)	2844
Age 6-11 years (2001 - 2002)	62.2 (53.8-71.8)	68.0 (58.0-79.0)	94.0 (84.0-100)	130 (100-160)	150 (120-380)	374
Age 6-11 years (2005 - 2006)	51.2 (47.4-55.4)	54.7 (51.9-58.2)	79.2 (72.8-87.2)	113 (101-128)	141 (120-158)	1054
Age 6-11 years (2007 - 2008)	55.2 (51.7-58.9)	60.2 (56.1-64.3)	84.5 (80.1-92.5)	117 (107-135)	149 (132-189)	1143
Age 6-11 years (2009 - 2010)	46.8 (43.2-50.6)	50.3 (45.5-58.2)	73.2 (70.2-79.1)	98.7 (86.7-112)	119 (98.0-186)	377
Age 12-19 years (2001 - 2002)	57.4 (53.5-61.6)	66.0 (60.0-69.0)	91.0 (86.0-95.0)	120 (100-130)	150 (130-160)	827
Age 12-19 years (2005 - 2006)	52.5 (48.5-56.8)	57.5 (52.3-62.6)	84.2 (79.9-88.4)	119 (111-124)	144 (129-153)	2106
Age 12-19 years (2007 - 2008)	55.5 (51.5-59.7)	56.8 (51.9-61.5)	84.1 (76.2-94.5)	119 (107-133)	144 (133-162)	1135
Age 12-19 years (2009 - 2010)	44.6 (41.0-48.4)	48.0 (43.3-54.9)	75.2 (70.0-79.4)	106 (91.6-119)	133 (106-163)	452
Age 20+ years (2001 - 2002)	45.4 (43.3-47.5)	49.0 (46.0-52.0)	78.0 (73.0-83.0)	100 (100-130)	140 (130-150)	1617
Age 20+ years (2005 - 2006)	40.5 (37.4-43.9)	45.0 (41.3-48.3)	71.7 (67.1-77.4)	105 (98.0-113)	129 (122-142)	4537
Age 20+ years (2007 - 2008)	44.2 (42.5-45.9)	48.1 (46.0-49.7)	73.2 (70.1-76.5)	107 (101-113)	135 (128-146)	5351
Age 20+ years (2009 - 2010)	39.6 (37.4-41.9)	42.3 (39.4-44.8)	66.4 (62.3-71.9)	97.2 (91.9-102)	124 (113-144)	2015
Males (2001 - 2002)	57.5 (54.6-60.6)	63.0 (59.0-67.0)	89.0 (83.0-94.0)	130 (100-140)	150 (140-170)	1335
Males (2005 - 2006)	48.4 (44.6-52.6)	52.7 (48.3-57.8)	79.4 (72.8-86.5)	110 (103-121)	136 (123-152)	3765
Males (2007 - 2008)	51.9 (49.9-54.1)	56.1 (53.8-58.0)	79.5 (75.7-83.5)	112 (105-119)	137 (131-149)	3839
Males (2009 - 2010)	44.9 (41.8-48.2)	46.0 (43.1-49.7)	73.3 (67.9-77.1)	105 (95.6-112)	133 (117-159)	1401
Females (2001 - 2002)	40.7 (38.4-43.2)	43.0 (41.0-48.0)	72.0 (68.0-76.0)	100 (98.0-120)	130 (120-150)	1483
Females (2005 - 2006)	37.9 (35.1-40.8)	42.0 (38.2-46.0)	69.2 (65.5-73.4)	104 (96.6-110)	130 (124-140)	3932
Females (2007 - 2008)	41.4 (39.3-43.7)	43.9 (41.5-46.3)	71.3 (67.5-74.8)	108 (99.8-115)	138 (132-149)	3790
Females (2009 - 2010)	37.1 (34.9-39.5)	40.3 (36.4-43.9)	65.9 (62.0-69.8)	92.2 (88.4-98.5)	117 (101-130)	1443
Mexican Americans (2001 - 2002)	53.2 (48.7-58.2)	59.0 (52.0-66.0)	84.0 (79.0-91.0)	120 (100-150)	160 (130-180)	707
Mexican Americans (2005 - 2006)	47.8 (44.7-51.2)	52.4 (49.9-56.2)	77.9 (75.1-83.1)	113 (104-120)	148 (133-156)	1972
Mexican Americans (2007 - 2008)	48.7 (45.0-52.6)	51.9 (47.4-56.7)	75.6 (69.7-81.3)	111 (100-122)	148 (127-164)	1505
Mexican Americans (2009 - 2010)	41.3 (39.3-43.5)	43.5 (41.2-46.4)	66.4 (61.0-73.9)	92.6 (86.5-99.7)	111 (94.4-132)	611
Non-Hispanic blacks (2001 - 2002)	53.8 (47.8-60.5)	58.0 (51.0-64.0)	84.0 (77.0-93.0)	120 (100-130)	140 (130-170)	680
Non-Hispanic blacks (2005 - 2006)	45.9 (42.1-50.0)	50.4 (46.6-54.9)	75.0 (68.8-80.8)	101 (95.3-110)	127 (114-148)	2078
Non-Hispanic blacks (2007 - 2008)	47.5 (45.0-50.3)	50.3 (48.6-52.5)	74.7 (71.9-77.3)	105 (97.1-116)	134 (125-150)	1707
Non-Hispanic blacks (2009 - 2010)	39.0 (36.5-41.7)	44.1 (41.6-46.3)	65.4 (61.5-69.6)	94.2 (86.6-101)	121 (101-141)	544
Non-Hispanic whites (2001 - 2002)	46.3 (44.1-48.6)	51.0 (47.0-53.0)	81.0 (78.0-85.0)	120 (100-130)	140 (130-150)	1228
Non-Hispanic whites (2005 - 2006)	41.2 (37.6-45.2)	46.2 (41.3-50.6)	73.3 (67.3-80.1)	107 (98.2-115)	129 (122-142)	3056
Non-Hispanic whites (2007 - 2008)	45.0 (42.7-47.5)	49.2 (46.1-52.6)	75.5 (70.5-80.0)	108 (101-116)	134 (128-140)	3190
Non-Hispanic whites (2009 - 2010)	39.8 (37.2-42.6)	42.1 (39.1-45.2)	68.4 (63.0-73.5)	95.6 (89.8-100)	119 (106-131)	1215

Limit of detection (LOD, see Data Analysis section) for Survey years 01-02, 05-06, 07-08, and 09-10 are 0.7, 0.7, 0.7, and 0.7 respectively.

Source: *Centers for Disease Control & Prevention, Fourth National Report on Human Exposure to Environmental Chemicals, Updated Tables, January 2019*

Urinary Nitrate (2011 – 2014)

CAS Number 84145-82-4

Geometric mean and selected percentiles of urine concentrations (in mg/L) for the U.S. population from the National Health and Nutrition Examination Survey.

Categories (Survey Years)	Geometric Mean (95% conf. interval)	50th Percentile (95% conf. interval)	75th Percentile (95% conf. interval)	90th Percentile (95% conf. interval)	95th Percentile (95% conf. interval)	Sample Size
Total population (2011 - 2012)	41.8 (39.7-44.1)	44.5 (42.3-47.2)	71.5 (68.1-76.4)	108 (99.3-116)	133 (119-156)	2467
Total population (2013 - 2014)	40.8 (38.8-42.9)	42.2 (39.6-45.7)	72.2 (67.8-78.7)	107 (101-112)	136 (123-151)	2644
Age 6-11 years (2011 - 2012)	47.4 (43.3-52.0)	54.1 (49.2-61.3)	78.6 (74.3-84.0)	99.8 (93.2-113)	121 (104-141)	394
Age 6-11 years (2013 - 2014)	44.7 (41.0-48.8)	47.3 (42.3-51.7)	79.2 (68.9-86.0)	119 (95.8-138)	151 (124-189)	398
Age 12-19 years (2011 - 2012)	43.3 (37.4-50.1)	50.4 (39.8-58.3)	71.5 (66.5-78.0)	107 (91.9-121)	135 (108-183)	384
Age 12-19 years (2013 - 2014)	46.5 (40.8-53.0)	51.1 (42.5-59.3)	83.4 (72.9-89.6)	112 (92.5-120)	122 (115-134)	449
Age 20+ years (2011 - 2012)	41.0 (38.7-43.5)	43.4 (40.8-46.2)	70.1 (66.1-75.7)	110 (98.7-117)	135 (117-164)	1689
Age 20+ years (2013 - 2014)	39.6 (37.6-41.8)	40.7 (38.2-44.1)	70.2 (64.2-76.1)	107 (101-111)	136 (120-153)	1797
Males (2011 - 2012)	46.9 (43.3-50.8)	48.4 (43.6-53.0)	76.2 (69.9-81.7)	114 (101-124)	150 (116-175)	1251
Males (2013 - 2014)	43.6 (40.1-47.4)	45.3 (41.0-50.6)	73.1 (64.3-83.5)	108 (99.8-113)	141 (118-157)	1313
Females (2011 - 2012)	37.4 (34.4-40.7)	41.2 (36.4-46.0)	67.9 (60.6-73.7)	101 (89.8-114)	120 (113-145)	1216
Females (2013 - 2014)	38.2 (36.1-40.5)	39.2 (37.5-41.7)	71.4 (67.8-74.8)	107 (99.8-112)	134 (120-141)	1331
Mexican Americans (2011 - 2012)	41.1 (36.9-45.8)	45.9 (40.4-51.3)	65.9 (61.8-70.9)	89.8 (78.4-108)	112 (89.8-159)	313
Mexican Americans (2013 - 2014)	42.0 (36.0-49.0)	45.3 (35.4-56.6)	72.0 (61.7-83.4)	111 (93.0-134)	136 (111-163)	451
Non-Hispanic blacks (2011 - 2012)	44.9 (41.5-48.6)	47.6 (41.6-52.3)	73.8 (67.8-79.8)	107 (97.1-117)	139 (116-150)	663
Non-Hispanic blacks (2013 - 2014)	46.4 (42.4-50.9)	50.0 (44.9-54.4)	73.6 (66.4-80.6)	105 (92.1-119)	135 (107-172)	574
Non-Hispanic whites (2011 - 2012)	41.0 (38.0-44.1)	43.6 (39.6-47.9)	71.9 (66.7-78.0)	110 (96.1-117)	132 (115-169)	810
Non-Hispanic whites (2013 - 2014)	39.3 (36.6-42.3)	40.2 (37.6-43.9)	71.9 (64.5-80.9)	107 (95.9-111)	128 (114-145)	976
All Hispanics (2011 - 2012)	41.0 (36.7-45.7)	44.4 (40.2-48.9)	67.2 (60.9-73.9)	95.3 (82.9-113)	120 (97.0-159)	566
All Hispanics (2013 - 2014)	41.1 (36.8-45.8)	44.4 (39.0-50.5)	70.0 (62.7-76.7)	107 (94.2-116)	138 (120-153)	699
Asians (2011 - 2012)	50.2 (43.7-57.6)	50.8 (45.8-57.5)	84.0 (72.1-91.9)	146 (121-171)	238 (142-380)	341
Asians (2013 - 2014)	44.4 (38.9-50.7)	45.2 (36.6-53.0)	91.6 (76.2-99.5)	150 (114-183)	189 (139-282)	291

Limit of detection (LOD, see Data Analysis section) for Survey year 11-12 and 13-14 are 0.7 and 0.7, respectively.

Source: *Centers for Disease Control & Prevention, Fourth National Report on Human Exposure to Environmental Chemicals, Updated Tables, January 2019*

Urinary Nitrate (creatinine corrected) (2001 – 2010)

CAS Number 84145-82-4

Geometric mean and selected percentiles of urine concentrations (in mg/g of creatinine) for the U.S. population from the National Health and Nutrition Examination Survey.

Categories (Survey Years)	Geometric Mean (95% conf. interval)	50th Percentile (95% conf. interval)	75th Percentile (95% conf. interval)	90th Percentile (95% conf. interval)	95th Percentile (95% conf. interval)	Sample Size
Total population (2001 - 2002)	49.8 (47.7-51.9)	46.9 (44.2-49.6)	63.8 (61.2-67.7)	90.9 (84.3-98.8)	120 (111-128)	1616
Total population (2005 - 2006)	42.6 (40.2-45.1)	42.4 (40.1-44.7)	59.7 (55.8-64.1)	85.5 (81.3-91.3)	113 (106-118)	7697
Total population (2007 - 2008)	47.7 (45.9-49.7)	46.0 (44.0-48.3)	66.5 (62.4-70.5)	98.0 (92.3-102)	127 (119-135)	7628
Total population (2009 - 2010)	43.7 (42.1-45.3)	42.3 (41.0-43.7)	60.2 (57.6-63.0)	88.5 (83.3-96.1)	115 (104-127)	2843
Age 6-11 years (2001 - 2002)	72.0 (66.1-78.4)	66.0 (62.6-70.4)	87.0 (80.2-97.7)	129 (96.5-144)	144 (130-235)	374
Age 6-11 years (2005 - 2006)	60.8 (57.4-64.5)	57.3 (53.6-60.6)	76.5 (70.9-82.1)	109 (95.0-123)	134 (121-164)	1054
Age 6-11 years (2007 - 2008)	70.2 (65.7-74.9)	65.9 (62.4-69.5)	89.0 (83.2-96.5)	128 (112-152)	173 (140-216)	1143
Age 6-11 years (2009 - 2010)	64.2 (58.8-70.0)	60.2 (56.3-63.3)	80.7 (68.9-96.1)	107 (96.1-124)	127 (105-202)	376
Age 12-19 years (2001 - 2002)	44.8 (43.4-46.2)	43.8 (42.6-45.0)	56.2 (52.2-59.7)	73.2 (65.2-85.1)	93.4 (79.0-104)	826
Age 12-19 years (2005 - 2006)	39.8 (37.8-41.9)	38.1 (36.3-40.3)	51.8 (47.7-56.0)	70.6 (63.1-78.8)	88.9 (79.4-103)	2106
Age 12-19 years (2007 - 2008)	43.4 (41.3-45.5)	40.5 (38.6-43.5)	56.0 (52.7-59.2)	76.6 (69.0-86.2)	98.0 (85.4-121)	1134
Age 12-19 years (2009 - 2010)	41.7 (39.3-44.4)	39.7 (38.3-41.7)	54.0 (48.4-57.4)	73.4 (61.0-86.1)	88.5 (71.0-117)	452
Age 20+ years (2001 - 2002)	48.3 (45.9-50.9)	46.9 (44.2-49.6)	63.8 (61.2-67.7)	90.9 (84.3-98.8)	120 (111-128)	1616
Age 20+ years (2005 - 2006)	41.4 (38.9-43.9)	41.0 (38.8-43.7)	58.6 (54.8-63.1)	85.3 (80.2-91.0)	111 (105-116)	4537
Age 20+ years (2007 - 2008)	46.5 (44.6-48.4)	44.7 (42.5-47.0)	65.0 (60.7-69.2)	96.1 (90.0-102)	125 (117-132)	5351
Age 20+ years (2009 - 2010)	42.2 (40.3-44.2)	41.0 (39.6-42.5)	58.6 (55.4-62.2)	87.7 (81.0-98.5)	116 (103-133)	2015
Males (2001 - 2002)	47.6 (44.7-50.7)	46.1 (43.4-48.7)	61.3 (58.0-64.5)	86.7 (77.1-97.3)	114 (97.3-125)	1335
Males (2005 - 2006)	40.1 (37.5-42.9)	39.5 (36.7-42.8)	55.3 (51.6-59.5)	77.2 (70.7-83.0)	95.9 (89.6-102)	3765
Males (2007 - 2008)	44.6 (42.8-46.6)	42.8 (40.7-45.1)	60.6 (58.1-64.4)	85.6 (81.1-91.3)	111 (101-121)	3839
Males (2009 - 2010)	41.0 (38.9-43.1)	39.1 (37.6-40.6)	54.6 (52.2-58.1)	83.3 (74.6-90.0)	103 (96.1-122)	1400
Females (2001 - 2002)	51.9 (49.9-54.1)	51.2 (48.4-53.0)	69.1 (66.7-71.2)	100 (91.7-111)	129 (118-140)	1481
Females (2005 - 2006)	45.1 (42.8-47.6)	45.0 (42.4-47.4)	64.4 (60.0-69.6)	96.8 (87.8-105)	128 (117-134)	3932
Females (2007 - 2008)	51.0 (48.9-53.2)	50.0 (47.5-52.7)	72.3 (67.8-76.8)	107 (101-116)	146 (129-163)	3789
Females (2009 - 2010)	46.5 (44.4-48.7)	46.5 (44.8-48.4)	64.2 (60.5-69.4)	96.6 (83.3-106)	121 (106-152)	1443
Mexican Americans (2001 - 2002)	50.9 (45.7-56.8)	48.1 (44.9-51.4)	67.4 (60.3-77.6)	97.3 (85.7-117)	135 (100-161)	707
Mexican Americans (2005 - 2006)	44.6 (42.6-46.7)	44.0 (42.2-45.3)	60.4 (58.1-62.9)	89.9 (82.0-95.4)	120 (111-128)	1972
Mexican Americans (2007 - 2008)	48.7 (45.1-52.7)	47.0 (43.5-50.5)	64.8 (59.7-69.9)	93.5 (88.9-101)	128 (108-156)	1505
Mexican Americans (2009 - 2010)	43.4 (40.5-46.5)	42.2 (39.7-45.9)	58.2 (54.7-61.3)	86.2 (77.1-92.5)	104 (90.8-122)	611
Non-Hispanic blacks (2001 - 2002)	38.7 (36.3-41.3)	38.0 (34.6-41.3)	53.5 (50.3-57.4)	70.3 (64.9-79.3)	91.7 (78.9-100)	679
Non-Hispanic blacks (2005 - 2006)	32.9 (30.9-35.0)	31.9 (29.8-34.1)	45.4 (41.5-49.6)	64.0 (60.1-68.0)	81.2 (75.3-89.6)	2078
Non-Hispanic blacks (2007 - 2008)	35.9 (34.2-37.7)	34.8 (33.3-36.6)	49.0 (44.8-53.6)	69.1 (63.5-77.4)	87.8 (78.1-97.4)	1706
Non-Hispanic blacks (2009 - 2010)	31.4 (28.9-34.0)	32.2 (29.7-34.5)	43.3 (40.8-47.3)	59.9 (54.8-69.7)	77.1 (62.2-98.3)	543
Non-Hispanic whites (2001 - 2002)	51.4 (49.4-53.4)	49.1 (46.9-51.5)	66.9 (64.2-69.4)	95.2 (87.7-100)	124 (115-132)	1227
Non-Hispanic whites (2005 - 2006)	43.7 (40.8-46.8)	43.9 (40.8-46.8)	61.4 (56.5-66.2)	85.5 (80.6-91.9)	110 (102-116)	3056
Non-Hispanic whites (2007 - 2008)	49.0 (46.7-51.4)	47.4 (44.9-50.5)	68.2 (63.3-73.1)	98.3 (91.2-105)	126 (118-135)	3190
Non-Hispanic whites (2009 - 2010)	44.7 (42.7-46.9)	43.8 (41.5-46.1)	62.0 (58.6-64.7)	87.7 (83.3-96.1)	106 (103-117)	1215

Source: *Centers for Disease Control & Prevention, Fourth National Report on Human Exposure to Environmental Chemicals, Updated Tables, January 2019*

Urinary Nitrate (creatinine corrected) (2011 – 2014)

CAS Number 84145-82-4

Geometric mean and selected percentiles of urine concentrations (in mg/g of creatinine) for the U.S. population from the National Health and Nutrition Examination Survey.

Categories (Survey Years)	Geometric Mean (95% conf. interval)	50th Percentile (95% conf. interval)	75th Percentile (95% conf. interval)	90th Percentile (95% conf. interval)	95th Percentile (95% conf. interval)	Sample Size
Total population (2011 - 2012)	47.8 (45.3-50.4)	46.0 (43.7-49.2)	67.4 (62.6-71.5)	103 (88.7-117)	137 (117-153)	2465
Total population (2013 - 2014)	47.2 (45.2-49.4)	46.3 (43.2-49.4)	66.2 (62.9-70.2)	97.3 (91.0-104)	123 (116-133)	2643
Age 6-11 years (2011 - 2012)	68.0 (63.3-73.1)	66.4 (60.9-68.7)	87.3 (81.2-95.6)	122 (110-132)	144 (124-156)	393
Age 6-11 years (2013 - 2014)	67.1 (62.3-72.2)	63.2 (59.4-67.1)	83.6 (72.4-95.2)	118 (99.1-145)	159 (110-230)	398
Age 12-19 years (2011 - 2012)	42.2 (39.6-44.9)	41.5 (38.7-43.8)	54.0 (51.2-57.7)	69.1 (63.6-77.1)	86.9 (69.1-104)	384
Age 12-19 years (2013 - 2014)	42.2 (39.7-44.8)	41.9 (37.2-44.7)	52.8 (47.9-58.1)	69.2 (61.0-82.0)	85.6 (72.6-107)	449
Age 20+ years (2011 - 2012)	46.8 (44.0-49.8)	44.9 (41.7-47.9)	66.8 (60.5-73.0)	105 (87.4-122)	142 (116-165)	1688
Age 20+ years (2013 - 2014)	46.3 (44.2-48.5)	45.2 (42.5-48.2)	66.0 (62.8-70.2)	97.4 (90.5-105)	123 (113-136)	1796
Males (2011 - 2012)	44.1 (41.8-46.6)	43.8 (40.8-45.9)	59.8 (57.0-62.4)	87.1 (76.9-98.4)	109 (98.4-120)	1250
Males (2013 - 2014)	43.7 (41.4-46.2)	42.5 (38.9-45.6)	59.8 (55.7-65.5)	84.0 (78.6-94.3)	110 (99.1-128)	1312
Females (2011 - 2012)	51.6 (47.9-55.5)	50.0 (45.8-54.0)	76.5 (68.9-85.1)	120 (98.1-143)	151 (132-170)	1215
Females (2013 - 2014)	50.9 (48.2-53.7)	50.5 (47.1-53.5)	71.6 (67.8-75.7)	107 (95.6-113)	135 (118-156)	1331
Mexican Americans (2011 - 2012)	46.4 (41.0-52.6)	43.6 (38.9-49.7)	62.4 (52.7-78.0)	86.4 (72.1-124)	110 (84.0-203)	313
Mexican Americans (2013 - 2014)	48.1 (43.4-53.2)	48.3 (46.0-50.9)	67.3 (62.1-72.0)	99.3 (83.0-116)	128 (100-169)	451
Non-Hispanic blacks (2011 - 2012)	35.0 (33.2-36.9)	34.3 (32.1-36.3)	47.5 (44.0-51.3)	69.2 (62.2-78.1)	89.3 (77.1-102)	663
Non-Hispanic blacks (2013 - 2014)	35.5 (33.4-37.8)	33.8 (32.0-35.9)	46.2 (43.5-49.7)	67.3 (60.4-75.0)	87.3 (76.6-95.6)	574
Non-Hispanic whites (2011 - 2012)	50.1 (47.2-53.2)	49.0 (45.7-52.3)	68.9 (63.8-79.4)	107 (91.1-129)	144 (121-154)	808
Non-Hispanic whites (2013 - 2014)	48.6 (46.3-50.9)	47.9 (44.8-51.4)	67.8 (62.9-72.5)	97.4 (89.5-105)	122 (109-136)	975
All Hispanics (2011 - 2012)	45.8 (42.4-49.5)	44.1 (41.7-46.2)	61.5 (55.4-69.3)	85.2 (78.5-95.6)	115 (86.4-159)	566
All Hispanics (2013 - 2014)	45.9 (43.1-48.9)	46.1 (43.1-48.3)	65.5 (61.0-68.6)	95.4 (85.0-105)	126 (105-137)	699
Asians (2011 - 2012)	67.2 (61.9-72.9)	62.9 (56.3-68.8)	106 (93.3-118)	178 (153-216)	247 (203-318)	341
Asians (2013 - 2014)	69.6 (62.2-78.0)	62.7 (52.5-76.8)	101 (85.2-132)	168 (140-194)	200 (173-261)	291

Source: *Centers for Disease Control & Prevention, Fourth National Report on Human Exposure to Environmental Chemicals, Updated Tables, January 2019*

UV Index for 58 U.S. Cities

City	State	Clear Sky UV Index					UV Index Forecast				
		Extreme	Very High	High	Moderate	Low	Extreme	Very High	High	Moderate	Low
Albuquerque	NM	107	80	42	104	30	69	99	45	108	42
Anchorage	AK	0	0	14	118	231	0	0	2	108	253
Atlanta	GA	57	119	52	115	20	7	119	54	102	81
Atlantic City	NJ	1	121	65	76	100	0	61	75	89	138
Baltimore	MD	3	123	62	77	98	0	66	70	87	140
Billings	MT	0	84	67	71	141	0	66	63	69	165
Bismarck	ND	0	68	75	69	151	0	41	58	99	165
Boise	ID	23	103	35	81	121	8	90	41	76	148
Boston	MA	0	101	64	78	120	0	47	69	82	165
Buffalo	NY	0	85	81	71	126	0	27	77	84	175
Burlington	VT	0	73	78	71	141	0	26	54	91	192
Charleston	SC	54	128	47	123	11	6	128	58	118	53
Charleston	WV	7	127	57	80	92	0	72	60	77	154
Cheyenne	WY	42	92	57	73	99	21	81	52	90	119
Chicago	IL	0	93	81	73	116	0	46	76	83	158
Cleveland	OH	0	99	77	73	114	0	44	69	89	161
Concord	NH	0	96	66	75	126	0	37	54	103	169
Dallas	TX	63	123	47	116	14	3	129	54	98	79
Denver	CO	50	97	50	86	80	25	89	55	97	97
Des Moines	IA	0	106	70	75	112	0	55	70	76	162
Detroit	MI	0	88	80	72	123	0	35	68	87	173
Dover	DE	1	124	63	76	99	0	62	69	87	145
Hartford	CT	0	105	70	73	115	0	48	67	84	164
Honolulu	HI	186	86	61	30	0	170	85	54	53	1
Houston	TX	101	110	46	106	0	19	149	40	106	49
Indianapolis	IN	5	120	59	79	100	0	59	71	84	149
Jackson	MS	70	119	48	119	7	10	128	48	104	73
Jacksonville	FL	90	109	46	118	0	39	127	55	115	27
Las Vegas	NV	67	94	49	103	50	18	124	51	107	63
Little Rock	AR	35	132	51	106	39	0	104	68	87	104
Los Angeles	CA	77	108	43	117	18	56	106	57	104	40
Louisville	KY	6	128	62	79	88	0	81	60	74	148
Memphis	TN	32	129	57	103	42	0	105	66	94	98
Miami	FL	144	90	59	70	0	98	102	63	96	4
Milwaukee	WI	0	83	84	70	126	0	36	76	87	164
Minneapolis	MN	0	75	78	70	140	0	31	56	87	189
Mobile	AL	95	109	44	115	0	41	125	49	119	29
New Orleans	LA	100	111	43	109	0	54	124	44	114	27
New York	NY	1	113	69	77	103	0	58	66	83	156
Norfolk	VA	11	136	50	91	75	0	95	72	84	112
Oklahoma City	OK	26	134	55	101	47	1	115	57	102	88
Omaha	NE	0	109	72	70	112	0	73	60	69	161
Philadelphia	PA	1	118	68	75	101	0	50	74	87	152
Phoenix	AZ	86	99	48	115	15	36	124	53	100	50
Pittsburgh	PA	2	115	68	74	104	0	54	63	76	170
Portland	ME	0	82	73	76	132	0	28	66	97	172
Portland	OR	1	82	61	76	143	0	67	42	51	203
Providence	RI	0	104	65	80	114	0	52	60	87	164
Raleigh	NC	17	138	52	99	57	0	105	53	106	99
Saint Louis	MO	5	130	58	81	89	0	88	63	69	143
Salt Lake City	UT	55	87	46	82	93	30	88	48	94	103
San Francisco	CA	25	114	62	96	66	4	121	51	83	104
San Juan	PR	212	97	54	0	0	183	98	69	13	0
Seattle	WA	0	68	68	78	149	0	45	56	68	194
Sioux Falls	SD	0	84	78	71	130	0	51	63	75	174

City	State	Clear Sky UV Index					UV Index Forecast				
		Extreme	Very High	High	Moderate	Low	Extreme	Very High	High	Moderate	Low
Tampa	FL	116	102	56	89	0	66	127	59	96	15
Washington	DC	4	124	60	79	96	0	73	65	90	135
Wichita	KS	15	126	60	91	71	0	100	49	96	118

Notes: *Figures are the number of days in each exposure category; The days may not add up to 365 due to missing data.*

The UV Index is a next day forecast of the amount of skin damaging UV radiation expected to reach the earth's surface at the time when the sun is highest in the sky (solar noon). The amount of UV radiation reaching the surface is primarily related to the elevation of the sun in the sky, the amount of ozone in the stratosphere, and the amount of clouds present. The UV Index can range from 0 (when it is night time) to 15 or 16 (in the tropics at high elevations under clear skies). UV radiation is greatest when the sun is highest in the sky and rapidly decreases as the sun approaches the horizon. The higher the UV Index, the greater the dose rate of skin damaging (and eye damaging) UV radiation. Consequently, the higher the UV Index, the smaller the time it takes before skin damage occurs.

Source: *NOAA, Climate Prediction Center, UV Index: Annual Time Series, 2017*

Acronyms & Abbreviations

A

A&I: Alternative and Innovative (Wastewater Treatment System)

AA: Accountable Area; Adverse Action; Advices of Allowance; Assistant Administrator; Associate Administrator; Atomic Absorption

AAEE: American Academy of Environmental Engineers

AANWR: Alaskan Arctic National Wildlife Refuge

AAP: Asbestos Action Program

AAPCO: American Association of Pesticide Control Officials

AARC: Alliance for Acid Rain Control

ABEL: EPA's computer model for analyzing a violator's ability to pay a civil penalty.

ABES: Alliance for Balanced Environmental Solutions

AC: Actual Commitment. Advisory Circular

A&C: Abatement and Control

ACA: American Conservation Association

ACBM: Asbestos-Containing Building Material

ACE: Alliance for Clean Energy

ACE: Any Credible Evidence

ACEEE: American Council for an Energy Efficient Economy

ACFM: Actual Cubic Feet Per Minute

ACL: Alternate Concentration Limit. Analytical Chemistry Laboratory

ACM: Asbestos-Containing Material

ACP: Agriculture Control Program (Water Quality Management); ACP: Air Carcinogen Policy

ACQUIRE: Aquatic Information Retrieval

ACQR: Air Quality Control Region

ACS: American Chemical Society

ACT: Action

ACTS: Asbestos Contractor Tracking System

ACWA: American Clean Water Association

ACWM: Asbestos-Containing Waste Material

ADABA: Acceptable Data Base

ADB: Applications Data Base

ADI: Acceptable Daily Intake

ADP: AHERA Designated Person; Automated Data Processing

ADQ: Audits of Data Quality

ADR: Alternate Dispute Resolution

ADSS: Air Data Screening System

ADT: Average Daily Traffic

AEA: Atomic Energy Act

AEC: Associate Enforcement Counsels

AEE: Alliance for Environmental Education

AEERL: Air and Energy Engineering Research Laboratory

AEM: Acoustic Emission Monitoring

AERE: Association of Environmental and Resource Economists

AES: Auger Electron Spectrometry

AFA: American Forestry Association

AFCA: Area Fuel Consumption Allocation

AFCEE: Air Force Center for Environmental Excellence

AFS: AIRS Facility Subsystem

AFUG: AIRS Facility Users Group

AH: Allowance Holders

AHERA: Asbestos Hazard Emergency Response Act

AHU: Air Handling Unit

AI: Active Ingredient

AIC: Active to Inert Conversion

AICUZ: Air Installation Compatible Use Zones

AID: Agency for International Development

AIHC: American Industrial Health Council

AIP: Auto Ignition Point

AIRMON: Atmospheric Integrated Research Monitoring Network

AIRS: Aerometric Information Retrieval System

AL: Acceptable Level

ALA: Delta-Aminolevulinic Acid

ALA-O: Delta-Aminolevulinic Acid Dehydrates

ALAPO: Association of Local Air Pollution Control Officers

ALARA: As Low As Reasonably Achievable

ALC: Application Limiting Constituent

ALJ: Administrative Law Judge

ALMS: Atomic Line Molecular Spectroscopy

ALR: Action Leakage Rate

AMBIENS: Atmospheric Mass Balance of Industrially Emitted and Natural Sulfur

AMOS: Air Management Oversight System

AMPS: Automatic Mapping and Planning System

AMSA: Association of Metropolitan Sewer Agencies

ANC: Acid Neutralizing Capacity

ANPR: Advance Notice of Proposed Rulemaking

ANRHRD: Air, Noise, & Radiation Health Research Division/ORD

ANSS: American Nature Study Society

AOAC: Association of Official Analytical Chemists

AOC: Abnormal Operating Conditions

AOD: Argon-Oxygen Decarbonization

AOML: Atlantic Oceanographic and Meteorological Laboratory

AP: Accounting Point

APA: Administrative Procedures Act

APCA: Air Pollution Control Association

APCD: Air Pollution Control District

APDS: Automated Procurement Documentation System

APHA: American Public Health Association

APRAC: Urban Diffusion Model for Carbon Monoxide from Motor Vehicle Traffic

APTI: Air Pollution Training Institute

APWA: American Public Works Association

AQ-7: Non-reactive Pollutant Modelling

AQCCT: Air-Quality Criteria and Control Techniques

AQCP: Air Quality Control Program

AQCR: Air-Quality Control Region

AQD: Air-Quality Digest

AQDHS: Air-Quality Data Handling System

AQDM: Air-Quality Display Model

AQMA: Air-Quality Maintenance Area

AQMD: Air Quality Management District

AQMP: Air-Quality Maintenance Plan; Air-Quality Management Plan

AQSM: Air-Quality Simulation Model

AQTAD: Air-Quality Technical Assistance Demonstration

AR: Administrative Record

A&R: Air and Radiation

ARA: Assistant Regional Administrator; Associate Regional Administrator

ARAC: Acid Rain Advisory Committee

ARAR: Applicable or Relevant and Appropriate Standards, Limitations, Criteria, and Requirements

ARB: Air Resources Board

ARC: Agency Ranking Committee

ARCC: American Rivers Conservation Council

ARCS: Alternative Remedial Contract Strategy

ARG: American Resources Group

ARIP: Accidental Release Information Program

ARL: Air Resources Laboratory

ARM: Air Resources Management

ARNEWS: Acid Rain National Early Warning Systems

ARO: Alternate Regulatory Option

ARRP: Acid Rain Research Program

ARRPA: Air Resources Regional Pollution Assessment Model

ARS: Agricultural Research Service

ARZ: Auto Restricted Zone

AS: Area Source

ASC: Area Source Category

ASDWA: Association of State Drinking Water Administrators

ASHAA: Asbestos in Schools Hazard Abatement Act

ASHRAE: American Society of Heating, Refrigerating, and Air-Conditioning Engineers

ASIWCPA: Association of State and Interstate Water Pollution Control Administrators

ASMDHS: Airshed Model Data Handling System

ASRL: Atmospheric Sciences Research Laboratory

AST: Advanced Secondary (Wastewater) Treatment

ASTHO: Association of State and Territorial Health Officers

ASTM: American Society for Testing and Materials

ASTSWMO: Association of State and Territorial Solid Waste Management Officials

AT: Advanced Treatment. Alpha Track Detection

ATERIS: Air Toxics Exposure and Risk Information System

ATS: Action Tracking System; Allowance Tracking System

ATSDR: Agency for Toxic Substances and Disease Registry

ATTF: Air Toxics Task Force

AUSM: Advanced Utility Simulation Model

A/WPR: Air/Water Pollution Report

AWRA: American Water Resources Association

AWT: Advanced Wastewater Treatment

AWWA: American Water Works Association

AWWARF: American Water Works Association Research Foundation.

B

BAA: Board of Assistance Appeals

BAC: Bioremediation Action Committee; Biotechnology Advisory Committee

BACM: Best Available Control Measures

BACT: Best Available Control Technology

BADT: Best Available Demonstrated Technology

BAF: Bioaccumulation Factor

BaP: Benzo(a)Pyrene

BAP: Benefits Analysis Program

BART: Best Available Retrofit Technology

BASIS: Battelle's Automated Search Information System

BAT: Best Available Technology

BATEA: Best Available Treatment Economically Achievable

BCT: Best Control Technology

BCPCT: Best Conventional Pollutant Control Technology

BDAT: Best Demonstrated Achievable Technology

BDCT: Best Demonstrated Control Technology

BDT: Best Demonstrated Technology

BEJ: Best Engineering Judgement. Best Expert Judgment

BF: Bonafide Notice of Intent to Manufacture or Import (IMD/OTS)

BID: Background Information Document. Buoyancy Induced Dispersion

BIOPLUME: Model to Predict the Maximum Extent of Existing Plumes

BMP: Best Management Practice(s)

BMR: Baseline Monitoring Report

BO: Budget Obligations

BOA: Basic Ordering Agreement (Contracts)

BOD: Biochemical Oxygen Demand. Biological Oxygen Demand

BOF: Basic Oxygen Furnace

BOP: Basic Oxygen Process

BOPF: Basic Oxygen Process Furnace

BOYSNC: Beginning of Year Significant Non-Compliers

BP: Boiling Point

BPJ: Best Professional Judgment

BPT: Best Practicable Technology. Pest Practicable Treatment

BPWTT: Best Practical Wastewater Treatment Technology

BRI: Building-Related Illness

BRS: Bibliographic Retrieval Service

BSI: British Standards Institute

BSO: Benzene Soluble Organics

BTZ: Below the Treatment Zone

BUN: Blood Urea Nitrogen

C

CA: Citizen Act. Competition Advocate. Cooperative Agreements. Corrective Action

CAA: Clean Air Act; Compliance Assurance Agreement

CAAA: Clean Air Act Amendments

CAER: Community Awareness and Emergency Response

CAFE: Corporate Average Fuel Economy

CAFO: Concentrated Animal Feedlot; Consent Agreement/Final Order

CAG: Carcinogenic Assessment Group

CAIR: Clean Air Interstate Rule: Comprehensive Assessment of Information Rule

CALINE: California Line Source Model

CAM: Compliance Assurance Monitoring rule; Compliance Assurance Monitoring

CAMP: Continuous Air Monitoring Program

CAN: Common Account Number

CAO: Corrective Action Order

CAP: Corrective Action Plan. Cost Allocation Procedure. Criteria Air Pollutant

CAPMoN: Canadian Air and Precipitation Monitoring Network

CAR: Corrective Action Report

CAS: Center for Automotive Safety; Chemical Abstract Service

CASAC: Clean Air Scientific Advisory Committee

CASLP: Conference on Alternative State and Local Practices

CASTNet: Clean Air Status and Trends Network

CATS: Corrective Action Tracking System

CAU: Carbon Adsorption Unit; Command Arithmetic Unit

CB: Continuous Bubbler

CBA: Chesapeake Bay Agreement. Cost Benefit Analysis

CBD: Central Business District

CBEP: Community Based Environmental Project

CBI: Compliance Biomonitoring Inspection; Confidential Business Information

CBOD: Carbonaceous Biochemical Oxygen Demand

CBP: Chesapeake Bay Program; County Business Patterns

CCA: Competition in Contracting Act

CCAA: Canadian Clean Air Act

CCAP: Center for Clean Air Policy; Climate Change Action Plan

CCEA: Conventional Combustion Environmental Assessment

CCHW: Citizens Clearinghouse for Hazardous Wastes

CCID: Confidential Chemicals Identification System

CCMS/NATO: Committee on Challenges of a Modern Society/North Atlantic Treaty Organization

CCP: Composite Correction Plan

CC/RTS: Chemical Collection/ Request Tracking System

CCTP: Clean Coal Technology Program

CD: Climatological Data

CDB: Consolidated Data Base

CDBA: Central Data Base Administrator

CDBG: Community Development Block Grant

CDD: Chlorinated dibenzo-p-dioxin

CDF: Chlorinated dibenzofuran

CDHS: Comprehensive Data Handling System

CDI: Case Development Inspection

CDM: Climatological Dispersion Model; Comprehensive Data Management

CDMQC: Climatological Dispersion Model with Calibration and Source Contribution

CDNS: Climatological Data National Summary

CDP: Census Designated Places

CDS: Compliance Data System

CE: Categorical Exclusion. Conditionally Exempt Generator

CEA: Cooperative Enforcement Agreement; Cost and Economic Assessment

CEAT: Contractor Evidence Audit Team

CEARC: Canadian Environmental Assessment Research Council

CEB: Chemical Element Balance

CEC: Commission for Environmental Cooperation

CECATS: CSB Existing Chemicals Assessment Tracking System

CEE: Center for Environmental Education

CEEM: Center for Energy and Environmental Management

CEI: Compliance Evaluation Inspection

CELRF: Canadian Environmental Law Research Foundation

CEM: Continuous Emission Monitoring

CEMS: Continuous Emission Monitoring System

CEPA: Canadian Environmental Protection Act

CEPP: Chemical Emergency Preparedness Plan

CEQ: Council on Environmental Quality

CERCLA: Comprehensive Environmental Response, Compensation, and Liability Act (1980)

CERCLIS: Comprehensive Environmental Response, Compensation, and Liability Information System

CERT: Certificate of Eligibility

CESQG: Conditionally Exempt Small Quantity Generator

CEST: Community Environmental Service Teams

CF: Conservation Foundation

CFC: Chlorofluorocarbons

CFM: Chlorofluoromethanes

CFR: Code of Federal Regulations

CHABA: Committee on Hearing and Bio-Acoustics

CHAMP: Community Health Air Monitoring Program

CHEMNET: Chemical Industry Emergency Mutual Aid Network

CHESS: Community Health and Environmental Surveillance System

CHIP: Chemical Hazard Information Profiles

CI: Compression Ignition. Confidence Interval

CIAQ: Council on Indoor Air Quality

CIBL: Convective Internal Boundary Layer

CICA: Competition in Contracting Act

CICIS: Chemicals in Commerce Information System

CIDRS: Cascade Impactor Data Reduction System

CIMI: Committee on Integrity and Management Improvement

CIS: Chemical Information System. Contracts Information System

CKD: Cement Kiln Dust

CKRC: Cement Kiln Recycling Coalition

CLC: Capacity Limiting Constituents

CLEANS: Clinical Laboratory for Evaluation and Assessment of Toxic Substances

CLEVER: Clinical Laboratory for Evaluation and Validation of Epidemiologic Research

CLF: Conservation Law Foundation

CLI: Consumer Labelling Initiative

CLIPS: Chemical List Index and Processing System

CLP: Contract Laboratory Program

CM: Corrective Measure

CMA: Chemical Manufacturers Association

CMB: Chemical Mass Balance

CME: Comprehensive Monitoring Evaluation

CMEL: Comprehensive Monitoring Evaluation Log

CMEP: Critical Mass Energy Project

CNG: Compressedd Natural Gas

COCO: Contractor-Owned/ Contractor-Operated

COD: Chemical Oxygen Demand

COH: Coefficient Of Haze

CPDA: Chemical Producers and Distributor Association

CPF: Carcinogenic Potency Factor

CPO: Certified Project Officer

CQA: Construction Quality Assurance

CR: Continuous Radon Monitoring

CROP: Consolidated Rules of Practice

CRP: Child-Resistant Packaging; Conservation Reserve Program

CRR: Center for Renewable Resources

CRSTER: Single Source Dispersion Model

CSCT: Committee for Site Characterization

CSGWPP: Comprehensive State Ground Water Protection Program

CSI: Common Sense Initiative; Compliance Sampling Inspection

CSIN: Chemical Substances Information Network

CSMA: Chemical Specialties Manufacturers Association

CSO: Combined Sewer Overflow

CSPA: Council of State Planning Agencies

CSRL: Center for the Study of Responsive Law

CTARC: Chemical Testing and Assessment Research Commission

CTG: Control Techniques Guidelines

CTSA: Cleaner TechnologiesSubstitutess Assessment

CV: Chemical Vocabulary

CVS: Constant Volume Sampler

CW: Continuous working-level monitoring

CWA: Clean Water Act (aka FWPCA)

CWAP: Clean Water Action Project

CWTC: Chemical Waste Transportation Council

CZMA: Coastal Zone Management Act

CZARA: Coastal Zone Management Act Reauthorization Amendments

D

DAPSS: Document and Personnel Security System (IMD)

DBP: Disinfection By-Product

DCI: Data Call-In

DCO: Delayed Compliance Order

DCO: Document Control Officer

DDT: DichloroDiphenylTrichloroethane

DERs: Data Evaluation Records

DES: Diethylstilbesterol

DfE: Design for the Environment

DI: Diagnostic Inspection

DMR: Discharge Monitoring Report

DNA: Deoxyribonucleic acid

DNAPL: Dense Non-Aqueous Phase Liquid

DO: Dissolved Oxygen

DOW: Defenders Of Wildlife

DPA: Deepwater Ports Act

DPD: Method of Measuring Chlorine Residual in Water

DQO: Data Quality Objective

DRE: Destruction and Removal Efficiency

DRES: Dietary Risk Evaluation System

DRMS: Defense Reutilization and Marketing Service

DRR: Data Review Record

DS: Dichotomous Sampler

DSAP: Data Self Auditing Program

DSCF: Dry Standard Cubic Feet

DSCM: Dry Standard Cubic Meter

DSS: Decision Support System; Domestic Sewage Study

DT: Detectors (radon) damaged or lost; Detention Time

DU: Decision Unit. Ducks Unlimited; Dobson Unit

DUC: Decision Unit Coordinator

DWEL: Drinking Water Equivalent Level

DWS: Drinking Water Standard

DWSRF: Drinking Water State Revolving Fund

E

EA: Endangerment Assessment; Enforcement Agreement; Environmental Action; Environmental Assessment;. Environmental Audit

EAF: Electric Arc Furnaces

EAG: Exposure Assessment Group

EAO: Emergency Administrative Order

EAP: Environmental Action Plan

EAR: Environmental Auditing Roundtable

EASI: Environmental Alliance for Senior Involvement

EB: Emissions Balancing

EC: Emulsifiable Concentrate; Environment Canada; Effective Concentration

ECA: Economic Community for Africa

ECAP: Employee Counselling and Assistance Program

ECD: Electron Capture Detector

ECHH: Electro-Catalytic Hyper-Heaters

ECHO: Enforcement and Compliance History Online

ECL: Environmental Chemical Laboratory

ECOS: Environmental Council of the States

ECR: Enforcement Case Review

ECRA: Economic Cleanup Responsibility Act

ED: Effective Dose

EDA: Emergency Declaration Area

EDB: Ethylene Dibromide

EDC: Ethylene Dichloride

EDD: Enforcement Decision Document

EDF: Environmental Defense Fund

EDRS: Enforcement Document Retrieval System

EDS: Electronic Data System; Energy Data System

EDTA: Ethylene Diamine Triacetic Acid

EDX: Electronic Data Exchange

EDZ: Emission Density Zoning

EEA: Energy and Environmental Analysis

EECs: Estimated Environmental Concentrations

EER: Excess Emission Report

EERL: Eastern Environmental Radiation Laboratory

EERU: Environmental Emergency Response Unit

EESI: Environment and Energy Study Institute

EESL: Environmental Ecological and Support Laboratory

EETFC: Environmental Effects, Transport, and Fate Committee

EF: Emission Factor

EFO: Equivalent Field Office

EFTC: European Fluorocarbon Technical Committee

EGR: Exhaust Gas Recirculation

EH: Redox Potential

EHC: Environmental Health Committee

EHS: Extremely Hazardous Substance

EI: Emissions Inventory

EIA: Environmental Impact Assessment. Economic Impact Assessment

EIL: Environmental Impairment Liability

EIR: Endangerment Information Report; Environmental Impact Report

EIS: Environmental Impact Statement; Environmental Inventory System

EIS/AS: Emissions Inventory System/Area Source

EIS/PS: Emissions Inventory System/Point Source

EJ: Environmental Justice

EKMA: Empirical Kinetic Modeling Approach

EL: Exposure Level

ELI: Environmental Law Institute

ELR: Environmental Law Reporter

EM: Electromagnetic Conductivity

EMAP: Environmental Mapping and Assessment Program

EMAS: Enforcement Management and Accountability System

EMR: Environmental Management Report

EMS: Enforcement Management System

EMSL: Environmental Monitoring Support Systems Laboratory

EMTS: Environmental Monitoring Testing Site; Exposure Monitoring Test Site

EnPA: Environmental Performance Agreement

EO: Ethylene Oxide

EOC: Emergency Operating Center

EOF: Emergency Operations Facility (RTP)

EOP: End Of Pipe

EOT: Emergency Operations Team

EP: Earth Protectors; Environmental Profile; End-use Product; Experimental Product; Extraction Procedure

EPAA: Environmental Programs Assistance Act

EPAAR: EPA Acquisition Regulations

EPCA: Energy Policy and Conservation Act

EPACT: Environmental Policy Act

EPACASR: EPA Chemical Activities Status Report

EPCRA: Emergency Planning and Community Right to Know Act

EPD: Emergency Planning District

EPI: Environmental Policy Institute

EPIC: Environmental Photographic Interpretation Center

EPNL: Effective Perceived Noise Level

EPRI: Electric Power Research Institute

EPTC: Extraction Procedure Toxicity Characteristic

EQIP: Environmental Quality Incentives Program

ER: Ecosystem Restoration; Electrical Resistivity

ERA: Economic Regulatory Agency

ERAMS: Environmental Radiation Ambient Monitoring System

ERC: Emergency Response Commission. Emissions Reduction Credit, Environmental Research Center

ERCS: Emergency Response Cleanup Services

ERDA: Energy Research and Development Administration

ERD&DAA: Environmental Research, Development and Demonstration Authorization Act

ERL: Environmental Research Laboratory

ERNS: Emergency Response Notification System

ERP: Enforcement Response Policy

ERT: Emergency Response Team

ERTAQ: ERT Air Quality Model

ES: Enforcement Strategy

ESA: Endangered Species Act. Environmentally Sensitive Area

ESC: Endangered Species Committee

ESCA: Electron Spectroscopy for Chemical Analysis

ESCAP: Economic and Social Commission for Asia and the Pacific

ESECA: Energy Supply and Environmental Coordination Act

ESH: Environmental Safety and Health

ESP: Electrostatic Precipitators

ET: Emissions Trading

ETI: Environmental Technology Initiative

ETP: Emissions Trading Policy

ETS: Emissions Tracking System; Environmental Tobacco Smoke

ETV: Environmental Technology Verification Program

EUP: End-Use Product; Experimental Use Permit

EWCC: Environmental Workforce Coordinating Committee

EXAMS: Exposure Analysis Modeling System

ExEx: Expected Exceedance

F

FACA: Federal Advisory Committee Act

FAN: Fixed Account Number

FATES: FIFRA and TSCA Enforcement System

FBC: Fluidized Bed Combustion

FCC: Fluid Catalytic Converter

FCCC: Framework Convention on Climate Change

FCCU: Fluid Catalytic Cracking Unit

FCO: Federal Coordinating Officer (in disaster areas); Forms Control Officer

FDF: Fundamentally Different Factors

FDL: Final Determination Letter

FDO: Fee Determination Official

FE: Fugitive Emissions

FEDS: Federal Energy Data System

FEFx: Forced Expiratory Flow

FEIS: Fugitive Emissions Information System

FEL: Frank Effect Level

FEPCA: Federal Environmental Pesticide Control Act; enacted as amendments to FIFRA.

FERC: Federal Energy Regulatory Commission

FES: Factor Evaluation System

FEV: Forced Expiratory Volume

FEV1: Forced Expiratory Volume—one second; Front End Volatility Index

FF: Federal Facilities

FFAR: Fuel and Fuel Additive Registration

FFDCA: Federal Food, Drug, and Cosmetic Act

FFEO: Federal Facilities Enforcement Office

FFF: Firm Financial Facility

FFFSG: Fossil-Fuel-Fired Steam Generator

FFIS: Federal Facilities Information System

FFP: Firm Fixed Price

FGD: Flue-Gas Desulfurization

FID: Flame Ionization Detector

FIFRA: Federal Insecticide, Fungicide, and Rodenticide Act

FIM: Friable Insulation Material

FINDS: Facility Index System

FIP: Final Implementation Plan

FIPS: Federal Information Procedures System

FIT: Field Investigation Team

FLETC: Federal Law Enforcement Training Center

FLM: Federal Land Manager

FLP: Flash Point

FLPMA: Federal Land Policy and Management Act

FMAP: Financial Management Assistance Project

F/M: Food to Microorganism Ratio

FML: Flexible Membrane Liner

FMP: Facility Management Plan

FMP: Financial Management Plan

FMS: Financial Management System

FMVCP: Federal Motor Vehicle Control Program

FOE: Friends Of the Earth

FOIA: Freedom Of Information Act

FOISD: Fiber Optic Isolated Spherical Dipole Antenna

FONSI: Finding Of No Significant Impact

FORAST: Forest Response to Anthropogenic Stress

FP: Fine Particulate

FPA: Federal Pesticide Act

FPAS: Foreign Purchase Acknowledgement Statements

FPD: Flame Photometric Detector

FPEIS: Fine Particulate Emissions Information System

FPM: Federal Personnel Manual

FPPA: Federal Pollution Prevention Act

FPR: Federal Procurement Regulation

FPRS: Federal Program Resources Statement; Formal Planning and Supporting System

FQPA: Food Quality Protection Act

FR: Federal Register. Final Rulemaking

FRA: Federal Register Act

FREDS: Flexible Regional Emissions Data System

FRES: Forest Range Environmental Study

FRM: Federal Reference Methods

FRN: Federal Register Notice. Final Rulemaking Notice

FRS: Formal Reporting System

FS: Feasibility Study

FSA: Food Security Act

FSS: Facility Status Sheet; Federal Supply Schedule

FTP: Federal Test Procedure (for motor vehicles)

FTS: File Transfer Service

FTTS: FIFRA/TSCA Tracking System

FUA: Fuel Use Act

FURS: Federal Underground Injection Control Reporting System

FVMP: Federal Visibility Monitoring Program

FWCA: Fish and Wildlife Coordination Act

FWPCA: Federal Water Pollution and Control Act (aka CWA). Federal Water Pollution and Control Administration

FY: Fiscal Year

G

GAAP: Generally Accepted Accounting Principles

GAC: Granular Activated Carbon

GACT: Granular Activated Carbon Treatment

GAW: Global Atmospheric Watch

GCC: Global Climate Convention

GC/MS: Gas Chromatograph/ Mass Spectograph

GCVTC: Grand Canyon Visibility Transport Commission

GCWR: Gross Combination Weight Rating

GDE: Generic Data Exemption

GEI: Geographic Enforcement Initiative

GEMI: Global Environmental Management Initiative

GEMS: Global Environmental Monitoring System; Graphical Exposure Modeling System

GEP: Good Engineering Practice

GFF: Glass Fiber Filter

GFO: Grant Funding Order

GFP: Government-Furnished Property

GICS: Grant Information and Control System

GIS: Geographic Information Systems; Global Indexing System

GLC: Gas Liquid Chromatography

GLERL: Great Lakes Environmental Research Laboratory

GLNPO: Great Lakes National Program Office

GLP: Good Laboratory Practices

GLWQA: Great Lakes Water Quality Agreement

GMCC: Global Monitoring for Climatic Change

G/MI: Grams per mile

GOCO: Government-Owned/ Contractor-Operated

GOGO: Government-Owned/ Government-Operated

GOP: General Operating Procedures

GOPO: Government-Owned/ Privately-Operated

GPAD: Gallons-per-acre per-day

GPG: Grams-per-Gallon

GPR: Ground-Penetrating Radar

GPRA: Government Performance and Results Act

GPS: Groundwater Protection Strategy

GR: Grab Radon Sampling

GRAS: Generally Recognized as Safe

GRCDA: Government Refuse Collection and Disposal Association

GRGL: Groundwater Residue Guidance Level

GT: Gas Turbine

GTN: Global Trend Network

GTR: Government Transportation Request

GVP: Gasoline Vapor Pressure

GVW: Gross Vehicle Weight

GVWR: Gross Vehicle Weight Rating

GW: Grab Working-Level Sampling. Groundwater

GWDR: Ground Water Disinfection Rule

GWM: Groundwater Monitoring

GWP: Global Warming Potential

GWPC: Ground Water Protection Council

GWPS: Groundwater Protection Standard; Groundwater Protection Strategy

H

HA: Health Advisory

HAD: Health Assessment Document

HAP: Hazardous Air Pollutant

HAPEMS: Hazardous Air Pollutant Enforcement Management System

HAPPS: Hazardous Air Pollutant Prioritization System

HATREMS: Hazardous and Trace Emissions System

HAZMAT: Hazardous Materials

HAZOP: Hazard and Operability Study

HBFC: Hydrobromofluorocarbon

HC: Hazardous Constituents; Hydrocarbon

HCCPD: Hexachlorocyclo-pentadiene

HCFC: Hydrochlorofluorocarbon

HCP: Hypothermal Coal Process

HDD: Heavy-Duty Diesel

HDDT: Heavy-duty Diesel Truck

HDDV: Heavy-Duty Diesel Vehicle

HDE: Heavy-Duty Engine

HDG: Heavy-Duty Gasoline-Powered Vehicle

HDGT: Heavy-Duty Gasoline Truck

HDGV: Heavy-Duty Gasoline Vehicle

HDPE: High Density Polyethylene

HDT: Highest Dose Tested in a study. Heavy-Duty Truck

HDV: Heavy-Duty Vehicle

HEAL: Human Exposure Assessment Location

HECC: House Energy and Commerce Committee

HEI: Health Effects Institute

HEM: Human Exposure Modeling

HEPA: High-Efficiency Particulate Air

HEPA: Highly Efficient Particulate Air Filter

HERS: Hyperion Energy Recovery System

HFC: Hydrofluorocarbon

HHDDV: Heavy Heavy-Duty Diesel Vehicle

HHE: Human Health and the Environment

HHV: Higher Heating Value

HI: Hazard Index

HI-VOL: High-Volume Sampler

HIWAY: A Line Source Model for Gaseous Pollutants

HLRW: High Level Radioactive Waste

HMIS: Hazardous Materials Information System

HMS: Highway Mobile Source

HMTA: Hazardous Materials Transportation Act

HMTR: Hazardous Materials Transportation Regulations

HOC: Halogenated Organic Carbons

HON: Hazardous Organic NESHAP

HOV: High-Occupancy Vehicle

HP: Horse Power

HPLC: High-Performance Liquid Chromatography

HPMS: Highway Performance Monitoring System

HPV: High Priority Violator

HQCDO: Headquarters Case Development Officer

HRS: Hazardous Ranking System

HRUP: High-Risk Urban Problem

HSDB: Hazardous Substance Data Base

HSL: Hazardous Substance List

HSWA: Hazardous and Solid Waste Amendments

HT: Hypothermally Treated

HTP: High Temperature and Pressure

HVAC: Heating, Ventilation, and Air-Conditioning system

HVIO: High Volume Industrial Organics

HW: Hazardous Waste

HWDMS: Hazardous Waste Data Management System

HWGTF: Hazardous Waste Groundwater Task Force; Hazardous Waste Groundwater Test Facility

HWIR: Hazardous Waste Identification Rule

HWLT: Hazardous Waste Land Treatment

HWM: Hazardous Waste Management

HWRTF: Hazardous Waste Restrictions Task Force

HWTC: Hazardous Waste Treatment Council

I

I/A: Innovative/Alternative

IA: Interagency Agreement

IAAC: Interagency Assessment Advisory Committee

IADN: Integrated Atmospheric Deposition Network

IAG: Interagency Agreement

IAP: Incentive Awards Program. Indoor Air Pollution

IAQ: Indoor Air Quality

IARC: International Agency for Research on Cancer

IATDB: Interim Air Toxics Data Base

IBSIN: Innovations in Building Sustainable Industries

IBT: Industrial Biotest Laboratory

IC: Internal Combustion

ICAIR: Interdisciplinary Planning and Information Research

ICAP: Inductively Coupled Argon Plasma

ICB: Information Collection Budget

ICBN: International Commission on the Biological Effects of Noise

ICCP: International Climate Change Partnership

ICE: Industrial Combustion Emissions Model. Internal Combustion Engine

ICP: Inductively Coupled Plasma

ICR: Information Collection Request

ICRE: Ignitability, Corrosivity, Reactivity, Extraction

ICRP: International Commission on Radiological Protection

ICRU: International Commission of Radiological Units and Measurements

ICS: Incident Command System. Institute for Chemical Studies; Intermittent Control Strategies.; Intermittent Control System

ICWM: Institute for Chemical Waste Management

IDEA: Integrated Data for Enforcement Analysis

IDLH: Immediately Dangerous to Life and Health

IEB: International Environment Bureau

IEMP: Integrated Environmental Management Project

IES: Institute for Environmental Studies

IFB: Invitation for Bid

IFCAM: Industrial Fuel Choice Analysis Model

IFCS: International Forum on Chemical Safety

IFIS: Industry File Information System

IFMS: Integrated Financial Management System

IFPP: Industrial Fugitive Process Particulate

IGCC: Integrated Gasification Combined Cycle

IGCI: Industrial Gas Cleaning Institute

IIS: Inflationary Impact Statement

IINERT: In-Place Inactivation and Natural Restoration Technologies

IJC: International Joint Commission (on Great Lakes)

I/M: Inspection/Maintenance

IMM: Intersection Midblock Model

IMPACT: Integrated Model of Plumes and Atmosphere in Complex Terrain

IMPROVE: Interagency Monitoring of Protected Visual Environment

INPUFF: Gaussian Puff Dispersion Model

INT: Intermittent

IOB: Iron Ore Beneficiation

IOU: Input/Output Unit

IPCS: International Program on Chemical Safety

IP: Inhalable Particles

IPM: Inhalable Particulate Matter. Integrated Pest Management

IPP: Implementation Planning Program. Integrated Plotting Package; Inter-media Priority Pollutant (document); Independent Power Producer

IPCC: Intergovernmental Panel on Climate Change

IPM: Integrated Pest Management

IRG: Interagency Review Group

IRLG: Interagency Regulatory Liaison Group (Composed of EPA, CPSC, FDA, and OSHA)

IRIS: Instructional Resources Information System. Integrated Risk Information System

IRM: Intermediate Remedial Measures

IRMC: Inter-Regulatory Risk Management Council

IRP: Installation Restoration Program

IRPTC: International Register of Potentially Toxic Chemicals

IRR: Institute of Resource Recovery

IRS: International Referral Systems

IS: Interim Status

ISAM: Indexed Sequential File Access Method

ISC: Industrial Source Complex

ISCL: Interim Status Compliance Letter

ISCLT: Industrial Source Complex Long Term Model

ISCST: Industrial Source Complex Short Term Model

ISD: Interim Status Document

ISE: Ion-specific electrode

ISMAP: Indirect Source Model for Air Pollution

ISO: International Organization for Standardization

ISPF: (IBM) Interactive System Productivity Facility

ISS: Interim Status Standards

ITC: Innovative Technology Council

ITC: Interagency Testing Committee

ITRC: Interstate Technology Regulatory Coordination

ITRD: Innovative Treatment Remediation Demonstration

IUP: Intended Use Plan

IUR: Inventory Update Rule

IWC: In-Stream Waste Concentration

IWS: Ionizing Wet Scrubber

J

JAPCA: Journal of Air Pollution Control Association

JCL: Job Control Language

JEC: Joint Economic Committee

JECFA: Joint Expert Committee of Food Additives

JEIOG: Joint Emissions Inventory Oversight Group

JLC: Justification for Limited Competition

JMPR: Joint Meeting on Pesticide Residues

JNCP: Justification for Non-Competitive Procurement

JOFOC: Justification for Other Than Full and Open Competition

JPA: Joint Permitting Agreement

JSD: Jackson Structured Design

JSP: Jackson Structured Programming

JTU: Jackson Turbidity Unit

L

LAA: Lead Agency Attorney

LADD: Lifetime Average Daily Dose; Lowest Acceptable Daily Dose

LAER: Lowest Achievable Emission Rate

LAI: Laboratory Audit Inspection

LAMP: Lake Acidification Mitigation Project

LC: Lethal Concentration. Liquid Chromatography

LCA: Life Cycle Assessment

LCD: Local Climatological Data

LCL: Lower Control Limit

LCM: Life Cycle Management

LCRS: Leachate Collection and Removal System

LD: Land Disposal. Light Duty

LD L0: The lowest dosage of a toxic substance that kills test organisms.

LDAR: Leak Detection and Repair

LDC: London Dumping Convention

LDCRS: Leachate Detection, Collection, and Removal System

LDD: Light-Duty Diesel

LDDT: Light-Duty Diesel Truck

LDDV: Light-Duty Diesel Vehicle

LDGT: Light-Duty Gasoline Truck

LDIP: Laboratory Data Integrity Program

LDR: Land Disposal Restrictions

LDRTF: Land Disposal Restrictions Task Force

LDS: Leak Detection System

LDT: Lowest Dose Tested. Light-Duty Truck

LDV: Light-Duty Vehicle

LEL: Lowest Effect Level. Lower Explosive Limit

LEP: Laboratory Evaluation Program

LEPC: Local Emergency Planning Committee

LERC: Local Emergency Response Committee

LEV: Low Emissions Vehicle

LFG: Landfill Gas

LFL: Lower Flammability Limit

LGR: Local Governments Reimbursement Program

LHDDV: Light Heavy-Duty Diesel Vehicle

LI: Langelier Index

LIDAR: Light Detection and Ranging

LIMB: Limestone-Injection Multi-Stage Burner

LLRW: Low Level Radioactive Waste

LMFBR: Liquid Metal Fast Breeder Reactor

LMOP: Landfill Methane Outreach Program

LNAPL: Light Non-Aqueous Phase Liquid

LOAEL: Lowest-Observed-Adverse-Effect-Level

LOD: Limit of Detection

LQER: Lesser Quantity Emission Rates

LQG: Large Quantity Generator

LRTAP: Long Range Transboundary Air Pollution

LUIS: Label Use Information System

M

MAC: Mobile Air Conditioner

MACT: Maximum Achievable Control Technology

MAPSIM: Mesoscale Air Pollution Simulation Model

MATC: Maximum Acceptable Toxic Concentration

MBAS: Methylene-Blue-Active Substances

MCL: Maximum Contaminant Level

MCLG: Maximum Contaminant Level Goal

MCS: Multiple Chemical Sensitivity

MDL: Method Detection Limit

MEC: Model Energy Code

MEI: Maximally (or most) Exposed Individual

MEP: Multiple Extraction Procedure

MHDDV: Medium Heavy-Duty Diesel Vehicle

MOBILE5A: Mobile Source Emission Factor Model

MOE: Margin Of Exposure

MOS: Margin of Safety

MP: Manufacturing-use Product; Melting Point

MPCA: Microbial Pest Control Agent

MPI: Maximum Permitted Intake

MPN: Maximum Possible Number

MPWC: Multiprocess Wet Cleaning

MRBMA: Mercury-Containing and Rechargeable Battery Management Act

MRF: Materials Recovery Facility

MRID: Master Record Identification number

MRL: Maximum-Residue Limit (Pesticide Tolerance)

MSW: Municipal Solid Waste

MTBE: Methyl tertiary butyl ether

MTD: Maximum Tolerated Dose

MUP: Manufacturing-Use Product

MUTA: Mutagenicity

MWC: Machine Wet Cleaning

N

NAA: Nonattainment Area

NAAEC: North American Agreement on Environmental Cooperation

NAAQS: National Ambient Air Quality Standards

NACA: National Agricultural Chemicals Association

NACEPT: National Advisory Council for Environmental Policy and Technology

NADP/NTN: National Atmospheric Deposition Program/National Trends Network

NAMS: National Air Monitoring Stations

NAPAP: National Acid Precipitation Assessment Program

NAPL: Non-Aqueous Phase Liquid

NAPS: National Air Pollution Surveillance

NARA: National Agrichemical Retailers Association

NARSTO: North American Research Strategy for Tropospheric Ozone

NAS: National Academy of Sciences

NASA: National Aeronautics and Space Administration

NASDA: National Association of State Departments of Agriculture

NCAMP: National Coalition Against the Misuse of Pesticides

NCEPI: National Center for Environmental Publications and Information

NCWS: Non-Community Water System

NEDS: National Emissions Data System

NEIC: National Enforcement Investigations Center

NEPA: National Environmental Policy Act

NEPI: National Environmental Policy Institute

NEPPS: National Environmental Performance Partnership System

NESHAP: National Emission Standard for Hazardous Air Pollutants

NIEHS: National Institute for Environmental Health Sciences

NETA: National Environmental Training Association

NFRAP: No Further Remedial Action Planned

NICT: National Incident Coordination Team

NIOSH: National Institute of Occupational Safety and Health

NIPDWR: National Interim Primary Drinking Water Regulations

NISAC: National Industrial Security Advisory Committee

NMHC: Nonmethane Hydrocarbons

NMOC: Non-Methane Organic Component

NMVOC: Non-methane Volatile Organic Chemicals

NO: Nitric Oxide

NOý: Nitrogen Dioxide

NOA: Notice of Arrival

NOAA: National Oceanographic and Atmospheric Agency

NOAC: Nature of Action Code

NOAEL: No Observable Adverse Effect Level

NOEL: No Observable Effect Level

NOIC: Notice of Intent to Cancel

NOIS: Notice of Intent to Suspend

N_2O: Nitrous Oxide

NOV: Notice of Violation

NO_x: Nitrogen Oxides

NORM: Naturally Occurring Radioactive Material

NPCA: National Pest Control Association

NPDES: National Pollutant Discharge Elimination System

NPHAP: National Pesticide Hazard Assessment Program

NPIRS: National Pesticide Information Retrieval System

NPMS: National Performance Measures Strategy

NPTN: National Pesticide Telecommunications Network

NRD: Natural Resource Damage

NRDC: Natural Resources Defense Council

NSDWR: National Secondary Drinking Water Regulations

NSEC: National System for Emergency Coordination

NSEP: National System for Emergency Preparedness

NSPS: New Source Performance Standards

NSR: New Source Review

NSR/PSD: National Source Review/Prevention of Significant Deterioration

NTI: National Toxics Inventory

NTIS: National Technical Information Service

NTNCWS: Non-Transient Non-Community Water System

NTP: National Toxicology Program

NTU: Nephlometric Turbidity Unit

O

O_3: Ozone

OAQPS: Office of Air Quality Planning and Standards

OCD: Offshore and Coastal Dispersion

ODP: Ozone-Depleting Potential

ODS: Ozone-Depleting Substances

OECA: Office of Enforcement and Compliance Assurance

OECD: Organization for Economic Cooperation and Development

OF: Optional Form

OI: Order for Information

OLC: Office of Legal Counsel

OLTS: On Line Tracking System

O&M: Operations and Maintenance

ORE: Office of Regulatory Enforcement

ORM: Other Regulated Material

ORP: Oxidation-Reduction Potential

OTAG: Ozone Transport Assessment Group

OTC: Ozone Transport Commission

OTIS: Online Tracking Information System

OTR: Ozone Transport Region

P

P2: Pollution Prevention

PAG: Pesticide Assignment Guidelines

PAH: Polynuclear Aromatic Hydrocarbons

PAI: Performance Audit Inspection (CWA); Pure Active Ingredient compound

PAM: Pesticide Analytical Manual

PAMS: Photochemical Assessment Monitoring Stations

PAT: Permit Assistance Team (RCRA)

PATS: Pesticide Action Tracking System; Pesticides Analytical Transport Solution

Pb: Lead

PBA: Preliminary Benefit Analysis (BEAD)

PCA: Principle Component Analysis

PCB: Polychlorinated Biphenyl

PCE: Perchloroethylene

PCM: Phase Contrast Microscopy

PCN: Policy Criteria Notice

PCO: Pest Control Operator

PCSD: President's Council on Sustainable Development

PDCI: Product Data Call-In

PFC: Perfluorated Carbon

PFCRA: Program Fraud Civil Remedies Act

PHC: Principal Hazardous Constituent

PHI: Pre-Harvest Interval

PHSA: Public Health Service Act

PI: Preliminary Injunction. Program Information

PIC: Products of Incomplete Combustion

PIGS: Pesticides in Groundwater Strategy

PIMS: Pesticide Incident Monitoring System

PIN: Pesticide Information Network

PIN: Procurement Information Notice

PIP: Public Involvement Program

PIPQUIC: Program Integration Project Queries Used in Interactive Command

PIRG: Public Interest Research Group

PIRT: Pretreatment Implementation Review Task Force

PIT: Permit Improvement Team

PITS: Project Information Tracking System

PLIRRA: Pollution Liability Insurance and Risk Retention Act

PLM: Polarized Light Microscopy

PLUVUE: Plume Visibility Model

PM: Particulate Matter

PMAS: Photochemical Assessment Monitoring Stations

$PM_{2.5}$: Particulate Matter Smaller than 2.5 Micrometers in Diameter

PM_{10}: Particulate Matter (nominally 10m and less)

PM_{15}: Particulate Matter (nominally 15m and less)

PMEL: Pacific Marine Environmental Laboratory

PMN: Premanufacture Notification

PMNF: Premanufacture Notification Form

PMR: Pollutant Mass Rate

PMR: Proportionate Mortality Ratio

PMRS: Performance Management and Recognition System

PMS: Program Management System

PNA: Polynuclear Aromatic Hydrocarbons

PO: Project Officer

POC: Point Of Compliance

POE: Point Of Exposure

POGO: Privately-Owned/ Government-Operated

POHC: Principal Organic Hazardous Constituent

POI: Point Of Interception

POLREP: Pollution Report

POM: Particulate Organic Matter. Polycyclic Organic Matter

POP: Persistent Organic Pollutant

POR: Program of Requirements

POTW: Publicly Owned Treatment Works

POV: Privately Owned Vehicle

PP: Program Planning

PPA: Planned Program Accomplishment

PPB: Parts Per Billion

PPE: Personal Protective Equipment

PPG: Performance Partnership Grant

PPIC: Pesticide Programs Information Center

PPIS: Pesticide Product Information System; Pollution Prevention Incentives for States

PPMAP: Power Planning Modeling Application Procedure

PPM/PPB: Parts per million/ parts per billion

PPSP: Power Plant Siting Program

PPT: Parts Per Trillion

PPTH: Parts Per Thousand

PQUA: Preliminary Quantitative Usage Analysis

PR: Pesticide Regulation Notice; Preliminary Review

PRA: Paperwork Reduction Act; Planned Regulatory Action

PRATS: Pesticides Regulatory Action Tracking System

PRC: Planning Research Corporation

PRI: Periodic Reinvestigation

PRM: Prevention Reference Manuals

PRN: Pesticide Registration Notice

PRP: Potentially Responsible Party

PRZM: Pesticide Root Zone Model

PS: Point Source

PSAM: Point Source Ambient Monitoring

PSC: Program Site Coordinator

PSD: Prevention of Significant Deterioration

PSES: Pretreatment Standards for Existing Sources

PSI: Pollutant Standards Index; Pounds Per Square Inch; Pressure Per Square Inch

PSIG: Pressure Per Square Inch Gauge

PSM: Point Source Monitoring

PSNS: Pretreatment Standards for New Sources

PSU: Primary Sampling Unit

PTDIS: Single Stack Meteorological Model in EPA UNAMAP Series

PTE: Potential to Emit

PTFE: Polytetrafluoroethylene (Teflon)

PTMAX: Single Stack Meteorological Model in EPA UNAMAP series

PTPLU: Point Source Gaussian Diffusion Model

PUC: Public Utility Commission

PV: Project Verification

PVC: Polyvinyl Chloride

PWB: Printed Wiring Board

PWS: Public Water Supply/ System

PWSS: Public Water Supply System

Q

QAC: Quality Assurance Coordinator

QA/QC: Quality Assistance/ Quality Control

QAMIS: Quality Assurance Management and Information System

QAO: Quality Assurance Officer

QAPP: Quality Assurance Program (or Project) Plan

QAT: Quality Action Team

QBTU: Quadrillion British Thermal Units

QC: Quality Control

QCA: Quiet Communities Act

QCI: Quality Control Index

QCP: Quiet Community Program

QL: Quantification Limit

QNCR: Quarterly Noncompliance Report

QUA: Qualitative Use Assessment

QUIPE: Quarterly Update for Inspector in Pesticide Enforcement

R

RA: Reasonable Alternative; Regulatory Alternatives; Regulatory Analysis; Remedial Action; Resource Allocation; Risk Analysis; Risk Assessment

RAATS: RCRA Administrate Action Tracking System

RAC: Radiation Advisory Committee. Raw Agricultural Commodity; Regional Asbestos Coordinator. Response Action Coordinator

RACM: Reasonably Available Control Measures

RACT: Reasonably Available Control Technology

RAD: Radiation Adsorbed Dose (unit of measurement of radiation absorbed by humans)

RADM: Random Walk Advection and Dispersion Model; Regional Acid Deposition Model

RAM: Urban Air Quality Model for Point and Area Source in EPA UNAMAP Series

RAMP: Rural Abandoned Mine Program

RAMS: Regional Air Monitoring System

RAP: Radon Action Program; Registration Assessment Panel; Remedial Accomplishment Plan; Response Action Plan

RAPS: Regional Air Pollution Study

RARG: Regulatory Analysis Review Group

RAS: Routine Analytical Service

RAT: Relative Accuracy Test

RB: Request for Bid

RBAC: Re-use Business Assistance Center

RBC: Red Blood Cell

RC: Responsibility Center

RCC: Radiation Coordinating Council

RCDO: Regional Case Development Officer

RCO: Regional Compliance Officer

RCP: Research Centers Program

RCRA: Resource Conservation and Recovery Act

RCRIS: Resource Conservation and Recovery Information System

RD/RA: Remedial Design/ Remedial Action

R&D: Research and Development

RD&D: Research, Development and Demonstration

RDF: Refuse-Derived Fuel

RDNA: Recombinant DNA

RDU: Regional Decision Units

RDV: Reference Dose Values

RE: Reasonable Efforts; Reportable Event

REAP: Regional Enforcement Activities Plan

REE: Rare Earth Elements

REEP: Review of Environmental Effects of Pollutants

RECLAIM: Regional Clean Air Initiatives Marker

RED: Reregistration Eligibility Decision Document

REDA: Recycling Economic Development Advocate

ReFIT: Reinvention for Innovative Technologies

REI: Restricted Entry Interval

REM: (Roentgen Equivalent Man)

REM/FIT: Remedial/Field Investigation Team

REMS: RCRA Enforcement Management System

REP: Reasonable Efforts Program

REPS: Regional Emissions Projection System

RESOLVE: Center for Environmental Conflict Resolution

RF: Response Factor

RFA: Regulatory Flexibility Act

RFB: Request for Bid

RfC: Reference Concentration

RFD: Reference Dose Values

RFI: Remedial Field Investigation

RFP: Reasonable Further Programs. Request for Proposal

RHRS: Revised Hazard Ranking System

RI: Reconnaissance Inspection

RI: Remedial Investigation

RIA: Regulatory Impact Analysis; Regulatory Impact Assessment

RIC: Radon Information Center

RICC: Retirement Information and Counseling Center

RICO: Racketeer Influenced and Corrupt Organizations Act

RI/FS: Remedial Investigation/ Feasibility Study

RIM: Regulatory Interpretation Memorandum

RIN: Regulatory Identifier Number

RIP: RCRA Implementation Plan

RISC: Regulatory Information Service Center

RJE: Remote Job Entry

RLL: Rapid and Large Leakage (Rate)

RMCL: Recommended Maximum Contaminant Level (this phrase being discontinued in favor of MCLG)

RMDHS: Regional Model Data Handling System

RMIS: Resources Management Information System

RMP: Risk Management Plan

RNA: Ribonucleic Acid

ROADCHEM: Roadway Version that Includes Chemical Reactions of BI, NO_2, and O_3

ROADWAY: A Model to Predict Pollutant Concentrations Near a Roadway

ROC: Record Of Communication

RODS: Records Of Decision System

ROG: Reactive Organic Gases

ROLLBACK: A Proportional Reduction Model

ROM: Regional Oxidant Model

ROMCOE: Rocky Mountain Center on Environment

ROP: Rate of Progress; Regional Oversight Policy

ROPA: Record Of Procurement Action

ROSA: Regional Ozone Study Area

RP: Radon Progeny Integrated Sampling. Respirable Particulates. Responsible Party

RPAR: Rebuttable Presumption Against Registration

RPM: Reactive Plume Model. Remedial Project Manager

RQ: Reportable Quantities

RRC: Regional Response Center

RRT: Regional Response Team; Requisite Remedial Technology

RS: Registration Standard

RSCC: Regional Sample Control Center

RSD: Risk-Specific Dose

RSE: Removal Site Evaluation

RTCM: Reasonable Transportation Control Measure

RTDF: Remediation Technologies Development Forum

RTDM: Rough Terrain Diffusion Model

RTECS: Registry of Toxic Effects of Chemical Substances

RTM: Regional Transport Model

RTP: Research Triangle Park

RUP: Restricted Use Pesticide

RVP: Reid Vapor Pressure

RWC: Residential Wood Combustion

S

S&A: Sampling and Analysis. Surveillance and Analysis

SAB: Science Advisory Board

SAC: Suspended and Cancelled Pesticides

SAEWG: Standing Air Emissions Work Group

SAIC: Special-Agents-In-Charge

SAIP: Systems Acquisition and Implementation Program

SAMI: Southern Appalachian Mountains Initiative

SAMWG: Standing Air Monitoring Work Group

SANE: Sulfur and Nitrogen Emissions

SANSS: Structure and Nomenclature Search System

SAP: Scientific Advisory Panel

SAR: Start Action Request. Structural Activity Relationship (of a qualitative assessment)

SARA: Superfund Amendments and Reauthorization Act of 1986

SAROAD: Storage and Retrieval Of Aerometric Data

SAS: Special Analytical Service. Statistical Analysis System

SASS: Source Assessment Sampling System

SAV: Submerged Aquatic Vegetation

SBC: Single Breath Cannister

SC: Sierra Club

SCAP: Superfund Consolidated Accomplishments Plan

SCBA: Self-Contained Breathing Apparatus

SCC: Source Classification Code

SCD/SWDC: Soil or Soil and Water Conservation District

SCFM: Standard Cubic Feet Per Minute

SCLDF: Sierra Club Legal Defense Fund

SCR: Selective Catalytic Reduction

SCRAM: State Consolidated RCRA Authorization Manual

SCRC: Superfund Community Relations Coordinator

SCS: Supplementary Control Strategy/System

SCSA: Soil Conservation Society of America

SCSP: Storm and Combined Sewer Program

SCW: Supercritical Water Oxidation

SDC: Systems Decision Plan

SDWA: Safe Drinking Water Act

SDWIS: Safe Drinking Water Information System

SBS: Sick Building Syndrome

SEA: State Enforcement Agreement

SEA: State/EPA Agreement

SEAM: Surface, Environment, and Mining

SEAS: Strategic Environmental Assessment System

SEDS: State Energy Data System

SEGIP: State Environmental Goals and Improvement Project

SEIA: Socioeconomic Impact Analysis

SEM: Standard Error of the Means

SEP: Standard Evaluation Procedures

SEP: Supplementary Environmental Project

SEPWC: Senate Environment and Public Works Committee

SERC: State Emergency Planning Commission

SES: Secondary Emissions Standard

SETAC: Society for Environmental Toxicology and Chemistry

SETS: Site Enforcement Tracking System

SF: Standard Form. Superfund

SFA: Spectral Flame Analyzers

SFDS: Sanitary Facility Data System

SFFAS: Superfund Financial Assessment System

SFIP: Sector Facility Indexing Project

SFIREG: State FIFRA Issues Research and Evaluation Group

SFS: State Funding Study

SHORTZ: Short Term Terrain Model

SHWL: Seasonal High Water Level

SI: International System of Units. Site Inspection. Surveillance Index. Spark Ignition

SIC: Standard Industrial Classification

SICEA: Steel Industry Compliance Extension Act

SIMS: Secondary Ion-Mass Spectrometry

SIP: State Implementation Plan

SITE: Superfund Innovative Technology Evaluation

SLAMS: State/Local Air Monitoring Station

SLN: Special Local Need

SLSM: Simple Line Source Model

SMART: Simple Maintenance of ARTS

SMCL: Secondary Maximum Contaminant Level

SMCRA: Surface Mining Control and Reclamation Act

SME: Subject Matter Expert

SMO: Sample Management Office

SMOA: Superfund Memorandum of Agreement

SMP: State Management Plan

SMR: Standardized Mortality Ratio

SMSA: Standard Metropolitan Statistical Area

SNA: System Network Architecture

SNAAQS: Secondary National Ambient Air Quality Standards

SNAP: Significant New Alternatives Project; Significant Noncompliance Action Program

SNARL: Suggested No Adverse Response Level

SNC: Significant Noncompliers

SNUR: Significant New Use Rule

SO_2: Sulfur Dioxide

SOC: Synthetic Organic Chemicals

SOCMI: Synthetic Organic Chemicals Manufacturing Industry

SOFC: Solid Oxide Fuel Cell

SOTDAT: Source Test Data

SOW: Scope Of Work

SPAR: Status of Permit Application Report

SPCC: Spill Prevention, Containment, and Countermeasure

SPE: Secondary Particulate Emissions

SPF: Structured Programming Facility

SPI: Strategic Planning Initiative

SPLMD: Soil-pore Liquid Monitoring Device

SPMS: Strategic Planning and Management System; Special Purpose Monitoring Stations

SPOC: Single Point Of Contact

SPS: State Permit System

SPSS: Statistical Package for the Social Sciences

SPUR: Software Package for Unique Reports

SQBE: Small Quantity Burner Exemption

SQG: Small Quantity Generator

SR: Special Review

SRAP: Superfund Remedial Accomplishment Plan

SRC: Solvent-Refined Coal

SRF: State Revolving Fund

SRM: Standard Reference Method

SRP: Special Review Procedure

SRR: Second Round Review. Submission Review Record

SRTS: Service Request Tracking System

SS: Settleable Solids. Superfund Surcharge. Suspended Solids

SSA: Sole Source Aquifer

SSAC: Soil Site Assimilated Capacity

SSC: State Superfund Contracts

SSD: Standards Support Document

SSEIS: Standard Support and Environmental Impact Statement; Stationary Source Emissions and Inventory System.

SSI: Size Selective Inlet

SSMS: Spark Source Mass Spectrometry

SSO: Sanitary Sewer Overflow; Source Selection Official

SSRP: Source Reduction Review Project

SSTS: Section Seven Tracking System

SSURO: Stop Sale, Use and Removal Order

STALAPCO: State and Local Air-Pollution Control Officials

STAPPA: State and Territorial Air Pollution

STAR: Stability Wind Rose. State Acid Rain Projects

STARS: Strategic Targeted Activities for Results System

STEL: Short Term Exposure Limit

STEM: Scanning Transmission-Electron Microscope

STN: Scientific and Technical Information Network

STORET: Storage and Retrieval of Water-Related Data

STP: Sewage Treatment Plant. Standard Temperature and Pressure

STTF: Small Town Task Force (EPA)

SUP: Standard Unit of Processing

SURE: Sulfate Regional Experiment Program

SV: Sampling Visit; Significant Violater

SW: Slow Wave

SWAP: Source Water Assessment Program

SWARF: Waste from Metal Grinding Process

SWC: Settlement With Conditions

SWDA: Solid Waste Disposal Act

SWIE: Southern Waste Information Exchange

SWMU: Solid Waste Management Unit

SWPA: Source Water Protection Area

SWQPPP: Source Water Quality Protection Partnership Petitions

SWTR: Surface Water Treatment Rule

SYSOP: Systems Operator

T

TAD: Technical Assistance Document

TAG: Technical Assistance Grant

TALMS: Tunable Atomic Line Molecular Spectroscopy

TAMS: Toxic Air Monitoring System

TAMTAC: Toxic Air Monitoring System Advisory Committee

TAP: Technical Assistance Program

TAPDS: Toxic Air Pollutant Data System

TAS: Tolerance Assessment System

TBT: Tributyltin

TC: Target Concentration. Technical Center. Toxicity Characteristics. Toxic Concentration:

TCDD: Dioxin (Tetrachlorodibenzo-p-dioxin)

TCDF: Tetrachlorodi-benzofurans

TCE: Trichloroethylene

TCF: Total Chlorine Free

TCLP: Total Concentrate Leachate Procedure. Toxicity Characteristic Leachate Procedure

TCM: Transportation Control Measure

TCP: Transportation Control Plan; Trichloropropane;

TCRI: Toxic Chemical Release Inventory

TD: Toxic Dose

TDS: Total Dissolved Solids

TEAM: Total Exposure Assessment Model

TEC: Technical Evaluation Committee

TED: Turtle Excluder Devices

TEG: Tetraethylene Glycol

TEGD: Technical Enforcement Guidance Document

TEL: Tetraethyl Lead

TEM: Texas Episodic Model

TEP: Typical End-use Product. Technical Evaluation Panel

TERA: TSCA Environmental Release Application

TES: Technical Enforcement Support

TEXIN: Texas Intersection Air Quality Model

TGO: Total Gross Output

TGAI: Technical Grade of the Active Ingredient

TGP: Technical Grade Product

THC: Total Hydrocarbons

THM: Trihalomethane

TI: Temporary Intermittent

TI: Therapeutic Index

TIBL: Thermal Internal Boundary Layer

TIC: Technical Information Coordinator. Tentatively Identified Compounds

TIM: Technical Information Manager

TIP: Technical Information Package

TIP: Transportation Improvement Program

TIS: Tolerance Index System

TISE: Take It Somewhere Else

TITC: Toxic Substance Control Act Interagency Testing Committee

TLV: Threshold Limit Value

TLV-C: TLV-Ceiling

TLV-STEL: TLV-Short Term Exposure Limit

TLV-TWA: TLV-Time Weighted Average

TMDL: Total Maximum Daily Limit; Total Maximum Daily Load

TMRC: Theoretical Maximum Residue Contribution

TNCWS: Transient Non-Community Water System

TNT: Trinitrotoluene

TO: Task Order

TOA: Trace Organic Analysis

TOC: Total Organic Carbon/ Compound

TOX: Tetradichloroxylene

TP: Technical Product; Total Particulates

TPC: Testing Priorities Committee

TPI: Technical Proposal Instructions

TPQ: Threshold Planning Quantity

TPSIS: Transportation Planning Support Information System

TPTH: Triphenyltinhydroxide

TPY: Tons Per Year

TQM: Total Quality Management

T-R: Transformer-Rectifier

TRC: Technical Review Committee

TRD: Technical Review Document

TRI: Toxic Release Inventory

TRIP: Toxic Release Inventory Program

TRIS: Toxic Chemical Release Inventory System

TRLN: Triangle Research Library Network

TRO: Temporary Restraining Order

TSA: Technical Systems Audit

TSCA: Toxic Substances Control Act

TSCATS: TSCA Test Submissions Database

TSCC: Toxic Substances Coordinating Committee

TSD: Technical Support Document

TSDF: Treatment, Storage, and Disposal Facility

TSDG: Toxic Substances Dialogue Group

TSI: Thermal System Insulation

TSM: Transportation System Management

TSO: Time Sharing Option

TSP: Total Suspended Particulates

TSS: Total Suspended (non-filterable) Solids

TTFA: Target Transformation Factor Analysis

TTHM: Total Trihalomethane

TTN: Technology Transfer Network

TTO: Total Toxic Organics

TTY: Teletypewriter

TVA: Tennessee Valley Authority

TVOC: Total Volatile Organic Compounds

TWA: Time Weighted Average

TWS: Transient Water System

TZ: Treatment Zone

U

UAC: User Advisory Committee

UAM: Urban Airshed Model

UAO: Unilateral Administrative Order

UAPSP: Utility Acid Precipitation Study Program

UAQI: Uniform Air Quality Index

UARG: Utility Air Regulatory Group

UCC: Ultra Clean Coal

UCCI: Urea-Formaldehyde Foam Insulation

UCL: Upper Control Limit

UDMH: Unsymmetrical Dimethyl Hydrazine

UEL: Upper Explosive Limit

UF: Uncertainty Factor

UFL: Upper Flammability Limit

ug/m^3: Micrograms Per Cubic Meter

UIC: Underground Injection Control

ULEV: Ultra Low Emission Vehicles

UMTRCA: Uranium Mill Tailings Radiation Control Act

UNAMAP: Users' Network for Applied Modeling of Air Pollution

UNECE: United Nations Economic Commission for Europe

UNEP: United Nations Environment Program

USC: Unified Soil Classification

USDA: United States Department of Agriculture

USDW: Underground Sources of Drinking Water

USFS: United States Forest Service

UST: Underground Storage Tank

UTM: Universal Transverse Mercator

UTP: Urban Transportation Planning

UV: Ultraviolet

UVA, UVB, UVC: Ultraviolet Radiation Bands

UZM: Unsaturated Zone Monitoring

V

VALLEY: Meteorological Model to Calculate Concentrations on Elevated Terrain

VCM: Vinyl Chloride Monomer

VCP: Voluntary Cleanup Program

VE: Visual Emissions

VEO: Visible Emission Observation

VHS: Vertical and Horizontal Spread Model

VHT: Vehicle-Hours of Travel

VISTTA: Visibility Impairment from Sulfur Transformation and Transport in the Atmosphere

VKT: Vehicle Kilometers Traveled

VMT: Vehicle Miles Traveled

VOC: Volatile Organic Compounds

VOS: Vehicle Operating Survey

VOST: Volatile Organic Sampling Train

VP: Vapor Pressure

VSD: Virtually Safe Dose

VSI: Visual Site Inspection

VSS: Volatile Suspended Solids

W

WA: Work Assignment

WADTF: Western Atmospheric Deposition Task Force

WAP: Waste Analysis Plan

WAVE: Water Alliances for Environmental Efficiency

WB: Wet Bulb

WCED: World Commission on Environment and Development

WDROP: Distribution Register of Organic Pollutants in Water

WENDB: Water Enforcement National Data Base

WERL: Water Engineering Research Laboratory

WET: Whole Effluent Toxicity test

WHO: World Health Organization

WHP: Wellhead Protection Program

WHPA: Wellhead Protection Area

WHWT: Water and Hazardous Waste Team

WICEM: World Industry Conference on Environmental Management

WL: Warning Letter; Working Level (radon measurement)

WLA/TMDL: Wasteload Allocation/Total Maximum Daily Load

WLM: Working Level Months

WMO: World Meteorological Organization

WP: Wettable Powder

WPCF: Water Pollution Control Federation

WQS: Water Quality Standard

WRC: Water Resources Council

WRDA: Water Resources Development Act

WRI: World Resources Institute

WS: Work Status

WSF: Water Soluble Fraction

WSRA: Wild and Scenic Rivers Act

WSTB: Water Sciences and Technology Board

WSTP: Wastewater Sewage Treatment Plant

WWEMA: Waste and Wastewater Equipment Manufacturers Association

WWF: World Wildlife Fund

WWTP: Wastewater Treatment Plant

WWTU: Wastewater Treatment Unit

Z

ZEV: Zero Emissions Vehicle

ZHE: Zero Headspace Extractor

ZOI: Zone Of Incorporation

ZRL: Zero Risk Level

***Note:** Some acronyms have more than one meaning. Multiple meanings are listed, separated by semi-colons.*

***Source:** U.S. Environmental Protection Agency, "Terms of Environment"*

Glossary of Environmental Terms

A

Abandoned Well: A well whose use has been permanently discontinued or which is in a state of such disrepair that it cannot be used for its intended purpose.

Abatement: Reducing the degree or intensity of, or eliminating, pollution.

Abatement Debris: Waste from remediation activities.

Absorbed Dose: In exposure assessment, the amount of a substance that penetrates an exposed organism's absorption barriers (e.g. skin, lung tissue, gastrointestinal tract) through physical or biological processes. The term is synonymous with internal dose.

Absorption: The uptake of water , other fluids, or dissolved chemicals by a cell or an organism (as tree roots absorb dissolved nutrients in soil.)

Absorption Barrier: Any of the exchange sites of the body that permit uptake of various substances at different rates (e.g. skin, lung tissue, and gastrointestinal-tract wall)

Accident Site: The location of an unexpected occurrence, failure or loss, either at a plant or along a transportation route, resulting in a release of hazardous materials.

Acclimatization: The physiological and behavioral adjustments of an organism to changes in its environment.

Acid: A corrosive solution with a pH less than 7.

Acid Aerosol: Acidic liquid or solid particles small enough to become airborne. High concentrations can irritate the lungs and have been associated with respiratory diseases like asthma.

Acid Deposition: A complex chemical and atmospheric phenomenon that occurs when emissions of sulfur and nitrogen compounds and other substances are transformed by chemical processes in the atmosphere, often far from the original sources, and then deposited on earth in either wet or dry form. The wet forms, popularly called "acid rain," can fall to earth as rain, snow, or fog. The dry forms are acidic gases or particulates.

Acid Mine Drainage: Drainage of water from areas that have been mined for coal or other mineral ores. The water has a low pH because of its contact with sulfur-bearing material and is harmful to aquatic organisms.

Acid Neutralizing Capacity: Measure of ability of a base (e.g. water or soil) to resist changes in pH.

Acid Rain: (See: acid deposition.)

Acidic: The condition of water or soil that contains a sufficient amount of acid substances to lower the pH below 7.0.

Action Levels: 1. Regulatory levels recommended by EPA for enforcement by FDA and USDA when pesticide residues occur in food or feed commodities for reasons other than the direct application of the pesticide. As opposed to "tolerances" which are established for residues occurring as a direct result of proper usage, action levels are set for inadvertent residues resulting from previous legal use or accidental contamination. 2. In the Superfund program, the existence of a contaminant concentration in the environment high enough to warrant action or trigger a response under SARA and the National Oil and Hazardous Substances Contingency Plan. The term is also used in other regulatory programs. (See: tolerances.)

Activated Carbon: A highly adsorbent form of carbon used to remove odors and toxic substances from liquid or gaseous emissions. In waste treatment, it is used to remove dissolved organic matter from waste drinking water. It is also used in motor vehicle evaporative control systems.

Activated Sludge: Product that results when primary effluent is mixed with bacteria-laden sludge and then agitated and aerated to promote biological treatment, speeding the breakdown of organic matter in raw sewage undergoing secondary waste treatment.

Activator: A chemical added to a pesticide to increase its activity.

Active Ingredient: In any pesticide product, the component that kills, or otherwise controls, target pests. Pesticides are regulated primarily on the basis of active ingredients.

Activity Plans: Written procedures in a school's asbestos-management plan that detail the steps a Local Education Agency (LEA) will follow in performing the initial and additional cleaning, operation and maintenance-program tasks; periodic surveillance; and reinspection required by the Asbestos Hazard Emergency Response Act (AHERA).

Acute Effect: An adverse effect on any living organism which results in severe symptoms that develop rapidly; symptoms often subside after the exposure stops.

Acute Exposure: A single exposure to a toxic substance which may result in severe biological harm or death. Acute exposures are usually characterized as lasting no longer than a day, as compared to longer, continuing exposure over a period of time.

Acute Toxicity: The ability of a substance to cause severe biological harm or death soon after a single exposure or dose. Also, any poisonous effect resulting from a single short-term exposure to a toxic substance. (See: chronic toxicity, toxicity.)

Adaptation: Changes in an organism's physiological structure or function or habits that allow it to survive in new surroundings.

Add-on Control Device: An air pollution control device such as carbon absorber or incinerator that reduces the pollution in an exhaust gas. The control device usually does not affect the process being controlled and thus is "add-on" technology, as opposed to a scheme to control pollution through altering the basic process itself.

Adequately Wet: Asbestos containing material that is sufficiently mixed or penetrated with liquid to prevent the release of particulates.

Administered Dose: In exposure assessment, the amount of a substance given to a test subject (human or animal) to determine dose-response relationships. Since exposure to chemicals is usually inadvertent, this quantity is often called potential dose.

Administrative Order: A legal document signed by EPA directing an individual, business, or other entity to take corrective action or refrain from an activity. It describes the violations and actions to be taken, and can be enforced in court. Such orders may be issued, for example, as a result of an administrative complaint whereby the respondent is ordered to pay a penalty for violations of a statute.

Administrative Order On Consent: A legal agreement signed by EPA and an individual, business, or other entity through which the violator agrees to pay for correction of violations, take the required corrective or cleanup actions, or refrain from an activity. It describes the actions to be taken, may be subject to a comment period, applies to civil actions, and can be enforced in court.

Administrative Procedures Act: A law that spells out procedures and requirements related to the promulgation of regulations.

Administrative Record: All documents which EPA considered or relied on in selecting the response action at a Superfund site, culminating in the record of decision for remedial action or, an action memorandum for removal actions.

Adsorption: Removal of a pollutant from air or water by collecting the pollutant on the surface of a solid material; e.g., an advanced method of treating waste in which activated carbon removes organic matter from waste-water.

Adulterants: Chemical impurities or substances that by law do not belong in a food, or pesticide.

Adulterated: 1. Any pesticide whose strength or purity falls below the quality stated on its label. 2. A food, feed, or product that contains illegal pesticide residues.

Advanced Treatment: A level of wastewater treatment more stringent than secondary treatment; requires an 85-percent reduction in conventional pollutant concentration or a significant reduction in non-conventional pollutants. Sometimes called tertiary treatment.

Advanced Wastewater Treatment: Any treatment of sewage that goes beyond the secondary or biological water treatment stage and includes the removal of nutrients such as phosphorus and nitrogen and a high percentage of suspended solids. (See primary, secondary treatment.)

Adverse Effects Data: FIFRA requires a pesticide registrant to submit data to EPA on any studies or other information regarding unreasonable adverse effects of a pesticide at any time after its registration.

Advisory: A non-regulatory document that communicates risk information to those who may have to make risk management decisions.

Aerated Lagoon: A holding and/or treatment pond that speeds up the natural process of biological decomposition of organic waste by stimulating the growth and activity of bacteria that degrade organic waste.

Aeration: A process which promotes biological degradation of organic matter in water. The process may be passive (as when waste is exposed to air), or active (as when a mixing or bubbling device introduces the air).

Aeration Tank: A chamber used to inject air into water.

Aerobic: Life or processes that require, or are not destroyed by, the presence of oxygen. (See: anaerobic.)

Aerobic Treatment: Process by which microbes decompose complex organic compounds in the presence of oxygen and use the liberated energy for reproduction and growth. (Such processes include extended aeration, trickling filtration, and rotating biological contactors.)

Aerosol: 1. Small droplets or particles suspended in the atmosphere, typically containing sulfur. They are usually emitted naturally (e.g. in volcanic eruptions) and as the result of anthropogenic (human) activities such as burning fossil fuels. 2. The pressurized gas used to propel substances out of a container.

Aerosol: A finely divided material suspended in air or other gaseous environment.

Affected Landfill: Under the Clean Air Act, landfills that meet criteria for capacity, age, and emissions rates set by the EPA. They are required to collect and combust their gas emissions.

Affected Public: 1.The people who live and/or work near a hazardous waste site. 2. The human population adversely impacted following exposure to a toxic pollutant in food, water, air, or soil.

Afterburner: In incinerator technology, a burner located so that the combustion gases are made to pass through its flame in order to remove smoke and odors. It may be attached to or be separated from the incinerator proper.

Age Tank: A tank used to store a chemical solution of known concentration for feed to a chemical feeder. Also called a day tank.

Agent: Any physical, chemical, or biological entity that can be harmful to an organism (synonymous with stressors.)

Agent Orange: A toxic herbicide and defoliant used in the Vietnam conflict, containing 2,4,5-trichlorophen-oxyacetic acid (2,4,5-T) and 2-4 dichlorophenoxyacetic acid (2,4-D) with trace amounts of dioxin.

Agricultural Pollution: Farming wastes, including runoff and leaching of pesticides and fertilizers; erosion and dust from plowing; improper disposal of animal manure and carcasses; crop residues, and debris.

Agricultural Waste: Poultry and livestock manure, and residual materials in liquid or solid form generated from the production and marketing of poultry, livestock or fur-bearing animals; also includes grain, vegetable, and fruit harvest residue.

Agroecosystem: Land used for crops, pasture, and livestock; the adjacent uncultivated land that supports other vegetation and wildlife; and the associated atmosphere, the underlying soils, groundwater, and drainage networks.

AHERA Designated Person (ADP): A person designated by a Local Education Agency to ensure that the AHERA requirements for asbestos management and abatement are properly implemented.

Air Binding: Situation where air enters the filter media and harms both the filtration and backwash processes.

Air Changes Per Hour (ACH): The movement of a volume of air in a given period of time; if a house has one air change per hour, it means that the air in the house will be replaced in a one-hour period.

Air Cleaning: Indoor-air quality-control strategy to remove various airborne particulates and/or gases from the air. Most common methods are particulate filtration, electrostatic precipitation, and gas sorption.

Air Contaminant: Any particulate matter, gas, or combination thereof, other than water vapor. (See: air pollutant.)

Air Curtain: A method of containing oil spills. Air bubbling through a perforated pipe causes an upward water flow that slows the spread of oil. It can also be used to stop fish from entering polluted water.

Air Exchange Rate: The rate at which outside air replaces indoor air in a given space.

Air Gap: Open vertical gap or empty space that separates drinking water supply to be protected from another water system in a treatment plant or other location. The open gap protects the drinking water from contamination by backflow or back siphonage.

Air Handling Unit: Equipment that includes a fan or blower, heating and/or cooling coils, regulator controls, condensate drain pans, and air filters.

Air Mass: A large volume of air with certain meteorological or polluted characteristics—e.g., a heat inversion or smogginess—while in one location. The characteristics can change as the air mass moves away.

Air Monitoring: (See: monitoring.)

Air/Oil Table: The surface between the vadose zone and ambient oil; the pressure of oil in the porous medium is equal to atmospheric pressure.

Air Padding: Pumping dry air into a container to assist with the withdrawal of liquid or to force a liquefied gas such as chlorine out of the container.

Air Permeability: Permeability of soil with respect to air. Important to the design of soil-gas surveys. Measured in darcys or centimeters-per-second.

Air Plenum: Any space used to convey air in a building, furnace, or structure. The space above a suspended ceiling is often used as an air plenum.

Air Pollutant: Any substance in air that could, in high enough concentration, harm man, other animals, vegetation, or material. Pollutants may include almost any natural or artificial composition of airborne matter capable of being airborne. They may be in the form of solid particles, liquid droplets, gases, or in combination thereof. Generally, they fall into two main groups: (1) those emitted directly from identifiable sources and (2) those produced in the air by interaction between two or more primary pollutants, or by reaction with normal atmospheric constituents, with or without photoactivation. Exclusive of pollen, fog, and dust, which are of natural origin, about 100 contaminants have been identified. Air pollutants are often grouped in categories for ease in classification; some of he categories are: solids, sulfur compounds, volatile organic chemicals, particulate matter, nitrogen compounds, oxygen compounds, halogen compounds, radioactive compound, and odors.

Air Pollution: The presence of contaminants or pollutant substances in the air that interfere with human health or welfare, or produce other harmful environmental effects.

Air Pollution Control Device: Mechanism or equipment that cleans emissions generated by a source (e.g. an incinerator, industrial smokestack, or an automobile exhaust system) by removing pollutants that would otherwise be released to the atmosphere.

Air Pollution Episode: A period of abnormally high concentration of air pollutants, often due to low winds and temperature inversion, that can cause illness and death. (See: episode, pollution.)

Air Quality Control Region:

Air Quality Criteria: The levels of pollution and lengths of exposure above which adverse health and welfare effects may occur.

Air Quality Standards: The level of pollutants prescribed by regulations that are not be exceeded during a given time in a defined area.

Air Sparging: Injecting air or oxygen into an aquifer to strip or flush volatile contaminants as air bubbles up through The ground water and is captured by a vapor extraction system.

Air Stripping: A treatment system that removes volatile organic compounds (VOCs) from contaminated ground water or surface water by forcing an airstream through the water and causing the compounds to evaporate.

Air Toxics: Any air pollutant for which a national ambient air quality standard (NAAQS) does not exist (i.e. excluding ozone, carbon monoxide, PM-10, sulfur dioxide, nitrogen oxide) that may reasonably be anticipated to cause cancer; respiratory, cardiovascular, or developmental effects; reproductive dysfunctions, neurological disorders, heritable gene mutations, or other serious or irreversible chronic or acute health effects in humans.

Airborne Particulates: Total suspended particulate matter found in the atmosphere as solid particles or liquid droplets. Chemical composition of particulates varies widely, depending on location and time of year. Sources of airborne particulates include: dust, emissions from industrial processes, combustion products from the burning of wood and coal, combustion products associated with motor vehicle or non-road engine exhausts, and reactions to gases in the atmosphere.

Airborne Release: Release of any pollutant into the air.

Alachlor: A herbicide, marketed under the trade name Lasso, used mainly to control weeds in corn and soybean fields.

Alar: Trade name for daminozide, a pesticide that makes apples redder, firmer, and less likely to drop off trees before growers are ready to pick them. It is also used to a lesser extent on peanuts, tart cherries, concord grapes, and other fruits.

Aldicarb: An insecticide sold under the trade name Temik. It is made from ethyl isocyanate.

Algae: Simple rootless plants that grow in sunlit waters in proportion to the amount of available nutrients. They can affect water quality adversely by lowering the dissolved oxygen in the water. They are food for fish and small aquatic animals.

Algal Blooms: Sudden spurts of algal growth, which can affect water quality adversely and indicate potentially hazardous changes in local water chemistry.

Algicide: Substance or chemical used specifically to kill or control algae.

Aliquot: A measured portion of a sample taken for analysis. One or more aliquots make up a sample. (See: duplicate.)

Alkaline: The condition of water or soil which contains a sufficient amount of alkali substance to raise the pH above 7.0.

Alkalinity: The capacity of bases to neutralize acids. An example is lime added to lakes to decrease acidity.

Allergen: A substance that causes an allergic reaction in individuals sensitive to it.

Alluvial: Relating to and/or sand deposited by flowing water.

Alternate Method: Any method of sampling and analyzing for an air or water pollutant that is not a reference or equivalent method but that has been demonstrated in specific cases-to EPA's satisfaction-to produce results adequate for compliance monitoring.

Alternative Compliance: A policy that allows facilities to choose among methods for achieving emission-reduction or risk-reduction instead of command-and control regulations that specify standards and how to meet them. Use of a theoretical emissions bubble over a facility to cap the amount of pollution emitted while allowing the company to choose where and how (within the facility) it complies.(See: bubble, emissions trading.)

Alternative Fuels: Substitutes for traditional liquid, oil-derived motor vehicle fuels like gasoline and diesel. Includes mixtures of alcohol-based fuels with gasoline, methanol, ethanol, compressed natural gas, and others.

Alternative Remedial Contract Strategy Contractors: Government contractors who provide project management and technical services to support remedial response activities at National Priorities List sites.

Ambient Air: Any unconfined portion of the atmosphere: open air, surrounding air.

Ambient Air Quality Standards: (See: Criteria Pollutants and National Ambient Air Quality Standards.)

Ambient Measurement: A measurement of the concentration of a substance or pollutant within the immediate environs of an organism; taken to relate it to the amount of possible exposure.

Ambient Medium: Material surrounding or contacting an organism (e.g. outdoor air, indoor air, water, or soil, through which chemicals or pollutants can reach the organism. (See: biological medium, environmental medium.)

Ambient Temperature: Temperature of the surrounding air or other medium.

Amprometric Titration: A way of measuring concentrations of certain substances in water using an electric current that flows during a chemical reaction.

Anaerobic: A life or process that occurs in, or is not destroyed by, the absence of oxygen.

Anaerobic Decomposition: Reduction of the net energy level and change in chemical composition of organic matter caused by microorganisms in an oxygen-free environment.

Animal Dander: Tiny scales of animal skin, a common indoor air pollutant.

Animal Studies: Investigations using animals as surrogates for humans with the expectation that the results are pertinent to humans.

Anisotropy: In hydrology, the conditions under which one or more hydraulic properties of an aquifer vary from a reference point.

Annular Space, Annulus: The space between two concentric tubes or casings, or between the casing and the borehole wall.

Antagonism: Interference or inhibition of the effect of one chemical by the action of another.

Antarctic "Ozone Hole": Refers to the seasonal depletion of ozone in the upper atmosphere above a large area of Antarctica. (See: Ozone Hole.)

Anti-Degradation Clause: Part of federal air quality and water quality requirements prohibiting deterioration where pollution levels are above the legal limit.

Anti-Microbial: An agent that kills microbes.

Applicable or Relevant and Appropriate Requirements (ARARs): Any state or federal statute that pertains to protection of human life and the environment in addressing specific conditions or use of a particular cleanup technology at a Superfund site,

Applied Dose: In exposure assessment, the amount of a substance in contact with the primary absorption boundaries of an organism (e.g. skin, lung tissue, gastrointestinal track) and available for absorption.

Aqueous: Something made up of water.

Aqueous Solubility: The maximum concentration of a chemical that will dissolve in pure water at a reference temperature.

Aquifer: An underground geological formation, or group of formations, containing water. Are sources of groundwater for wells and springs.

Aquifer Test: A test to determine hydraulic properties of an aquifer.

Aquitard: Geological formation that may contain groundwater but is not capable of transmitting significant quantities of it under normal hydraulic gradients. May function as confining bed.

Architectural Coatings: Coverings such as paint and roof tar that are used on exteriors of buildings.

Area of Review: In the UIC program, the area surrounding an injection well that is reviewed during the permitting process to determine if flow between aquifers will be induced by the injection operation.

Area Source: Any source of air pollution that is released over a relatively small area but which cannot be classified as a point source. Such sources may include vehicles and other small engines, small businesses and household activities, or biogenic sources such as a forest that releases hydrocarbons.

Aromatics: A type of hydrocarbon, such as benzene or toluene, with a specific type of ring structure. Aromatics are sometimes added to gasoline in order to increase octane. Some aromatics are toxic.

Arsenicals: Pesticides containing arsenic.

Artesian (Aquifer or Well): Water held under pressure in porous rock or soil confined by impermeable geological formations.

Asbestos: A mineral fiber that can pollute air or water and cause cancer or asbestosis when inhaled. EPA has banned or severely restricted its use in manufacturing and construction.

Asbestos Abatement: Procedures to control fiber release from asbestos-containing materials in a building or to remove them entirely, including removal, encapsulation, repair, enclosure, encasement, and operations and maintenance programs.

Asbestos Assessment: In the asbestos-in-schools program, the evaluation of the physical condition and potential for damage of all friable asbestos containing materials and thermal insulation systems.

Asbestos Program Manager: A building owner or designated representative who supervises all aspects of the facility asbestos management and control program.

Asbestos-Containing Waste Materials (ACWM): Mill tailings or any waste that contains commercial asbestos and is generated by a source covered by the Clean Air Act Asbestos NESHAPS.

Asbestosis: A disease associated with inhalation of asbestos fibers. The disease makes breathing progressively more difficult and can be fatal.

Ash: The mineral content of a product remaining after complete combustion.

Assay: A test for a specific chemical, microbe, or effect.

Assessment Endpoint: In ecological risk assessment, an explicit expression of the environmental value to be protected; includes both an ecological entity and specific attributed thereof. entity (e.g. salmon are a valued ecological entity; reproduction and population maintenance—the attribute—form an assessment endpoint.)

Assimilation: The ability of a body of water to purify itself of pollutants.

Assimilative Capacity: The capacity of a natural body of water to receive wastewaters or toxic materials without deleterious effects and without damage to aquatic life or humans who consume the water.

Association of Boards of Certification: An international organization representing boards which certify the operators of waterworks and wastewater facilities.

Attainment Area: An area considered to have air quality as good as or better than the national ambient air quality standards as defined in the Clean Air Act. An area may be an attainment area for one pollutant and a non-attainment area for others.

Attenuation: The process by which a compound is reduced in concentration over time, through absorption, adsorption, degradation, dilution, and/or transformation. an also be the decrease with distance of sight caused by attenuation of light by particulate pollution.

Attractant: A chemical or agent that lures insects or other pests by stimulating their sense of smell.

Attrition: Wearing or grinding down of a substance by friction. Dust from such processes contributes to air pollution.

Availability Session: Informal meeting at a public location where interested citizens can talk with EPA and state officials on a one-to-one basis.

Available Chlorine: A measure of the amount of chlorine available in chlorinated lime, hypochlorite compounds, and other materials used as a source of chlorine when compared with that of liquid or gaseous chlorines.

Avoided Cost: The cost a utility would incur to generate the next increment of electric capacity using its own resources; many landfill gas projects' buy back rates are based on avoided costs.

A-Scale Sound Level: A measurement of sound approximating the sensitivity of the human ear, used to note the intensity or annoyance level of sounds.

B

Back Pressure: A pressure that can cause water to backflow into the water supply when a user's waste water system is at a higher pressure than the public system.

Backflow/Back Siphonage: A reverse flow condition created by a difference in water pressures that causes water to flow back into the distribution pipes of a drinking water supply from any source other than the intended one.

Background Level: 1. The concentration of a substance in an environmental media (air, water, or soil) that occurs naturally or is not the result of human activities. 2. In exposure assessment the concentration of a substance in a defined control area, during a fixed period of time before, during, or after a data-gathering operation..

Backwashing: Reversing the flow of water back through the filter media to remove entrapped solids.

Backyard Composting: Diversion of organic food waste and yard trimmings from the municipal waste stream by composting hem in one's yard through controlled decomposition of organic matter by bacteria and fungi into a humus-like product. It is considered source reduction, not recycling, because the composted materials never enter the municipal waste stream.

Barrel Sampler: Open-ended steel tube used to collect soil samples.

BACT - Best Available Control Technology: An emission limitation based on the maximum degree of emission reduction (considering energy, environmental, and economic impacts) achievable through application of production processes and available methods, systems, and techniques. BACT does not permit emissions in excess of those allowed under any applicable Clean Air Act provisions. Use of the BACT concept is allowable on a case by case basis for major new or modified emissions sources in attainment areas and applies to each regulated pollutant.

Bacteria: (Singular: bacterium) Microscopic living organisms that can aid in pollution control by metabolizing organic matter in sewage, oil spills or other pollutants. However, bacteria in soil, water or air can also cause human, animal and plant health problems.

Bactericide: A pesticide used to control or destroy bacteria, typically in the home, schools, or hospitals.

Baffle: A flat board or plate, deflector, guide, or similar device constructed or placed in flowing water or slurry systems to cause more uniform flow velocities to absorb energy and to divert, guide, or agitate liquids.

Baffle Chamber: In incinerator design, a chamber designed to promote the settling of fly ash and coarse particulate matter by changing the direction and/or reducing the velocity of the gases produced by the combustion of the refuse or sludge.

Baghouse Filter: Large fabric bag, usually made of glass fibers, used to eliminate intermediate and large (greater than 20 PM in diameter) particles. This device operates like the bag of an electric vacuum cleaner, passing the air and smaller particles while entrapping the larger ones.

Bailer: A pipe with a valve at the lower end, used to remove slurry from the bottom or side of a well as it is being drilled, or to collect groundwater samples from wells or open boreholes. 2. A tube of varying length.

Baling: Compacting solid waste into blocks to reduce volume and simplify handling.

Ballistic Separator: A machine that sorts organic from inorganic matter for composting.

Band Application: The spreading of chemicals over, or next to, each row of plants in a field.

Banking: A system for recording qualified air emission reductions for later use in bubble, offset, or netting transactions. (See: emissions trading.)

Bar Screen: In wastewater treatment, a device used to remove large solids.

Barrier Coating(s): A layer of a material that obstructs or prevents passage of something through a surface that is to be protected; e.g., grout, caulk, or various sealing compounds; sometimes used with polyurethane membranes to prevent corrosion or oxidation of metal surfaces, chemical impacts on various materials, or, for example, to prevent radon infiltration through walls, cracks, or joints in a house.

Basal Application: In pesticides, the application of a chemical on plant stems or tree trunks just above the soil line.

Basalt: Consistent year-round energy use of a facility; also refers to the minimum amount of electricity supplied continually to a facility.

Bean Sheet: Common term for a pesticide data package record.

Bed Load: Sediment particles resting on or near the channel bottom that are pushed or rolled along by the flow of water.

BEN: EPA's computer model for analyzing a violator's economic gain from not complying with the law.

Bench-scale Tests: Laboratory testing of potential cleanup technologies (See: treatability studies.)

Benefit-Cost Analysis: An economic method for assessing the benefits and costs of achieving alternative health-based standards at given levels of health protection.

Benthic/Benthos: An organism that feeds on the sediment at the bottom of a water body such as an ocean, lake, or river.

Bentonite: A colloidal clay, expansible when moist, commonly used to provide a tight seal around a well casing.

Beryllium: An metal hazardous to human health when inhaled as an airborne pollutant. It is discharged by machine shops, ceramic and propellant plants, and foundries.

Best Available Control Measures (BACM): A term used to refer to the most effective measures (according to EPA guidance) for controlling small or dispersed particulates and other emissions from sources such as roadway dust, soot and ash from woodstoves and open burning of rush, timber, grasslands, or trash.

Best Available Control Technology (BACT): For any specific source, the currently available technology producing the greatest reduction of air pollutant emissions,taking into account energy, environmental, economic, and other costs.

Best Available Control Technology (BACT): The most stringent technology available for controlling emissions; major sources are required to use BACT, unless it can be demonstrated that it is not feasible for energy, environmental, or economic reasons.

Best Demonstrated Available Technology (BDAT): As identified by EPA, the most effective commercially available means of treating specific types of hazardous waste. The BDATs may change with advances in treatment technologies.

Best Management Practice (BMP): Methods that have been determined to be the most effective, practical means of preventing or reducing pollution from non-point sources.

Bimetal: Beverage containers with steel bodies and aluminum tops; handled differently from pure aluminum in recycling.

Bioaccumulants: Substances that increase in concentration in living organisms as they take in contaminated air, water, or food because the substances are very slowly metabolized or excreted. (See: biological magnification.)

Bioassay: A test to determine te relative strength of a substance by comparing its effect on a test organism with that of a standard preparation.

Bioavailability: Degree of ability to be absorbed and ready to interact in organism metabolism.

Biochemical Oxygen Demand (BOD): A measure of the amount of oxygen consumed in the biological processes that break down organic matter in water. The greater the BOD, the greater the degree of pollution.

Bioconcentration: The accumulation of a chemical in tissues of a fish or other organism to levels greater than in the surrounding medium.

Biodegradable: Capable of decomposing under natural conditions.

Biodiversity: Refers to the variety and variability among living organisms and the ecological complexes in which they occur. Diversity can be defined as the number of different items and their relative frequencies. For biological diversity, these items are organized at many levels, ranging from complete ecosystems to the biochemical structures that are the molecular basis of heredity. Thus, the term encompasses different ecosystems, species, and genes.

Biological Contaminants: Living organisms or derivates (e.g. viruses, bacteria, fungi, and mammal and bird antigens) that can cause harmful health effects when inhaled, swallowed, or otherwise taken into the body.

Biological Control: In pest control, the use of animals and organisms that eat or otherwise kill or out-compete pests.

Biological Integrity: The ability to support and maintain balanced, integrated, functionality in the natural habitat of a given region. Concept is applied primarily in drinking water management.

Biological Magnification: Refers to the process whereby certain substances such as pesticides or heavy metals move up the food chain, work their way into rivers or lakes, and are eaten by aquatic organisms such as fish, which in turn are eaten by large birds, animals or humans. The substances become concentrated in tissues or internal organs as they move up the chain. (See: bioaccumulants.)

Biological Measurement: A measurement taken in a biological medium. For exposure assessment, it is related to the measurement is taken to related it to the established internal dose of a compound.

Biological Medium: One of the major component of an organism; e.g. blood, fatty tissue, lymph nodes or breath, in which chemicals can be stored or transformed. (See: ambient medium, environmental medium.)

Biological Oxidation: Decomposition of complex organic materials by microorganisms. Occurs in self-purification of water bodies and in activated sludge wastewater treatment.

Biological Oxygen Demand (BOD): An indirect measure of the concentration of biologically degradable material present in organic wastes. It usually reflects the amount of oxygen consumed in five days by biological processes breaking down organic waste.

Biological pesticides: Certain microorganism, including bacteria, fungi, viruses, and protozoa that are effective in controlling pests. These agents usually do not have toxic effects on animals and people and do not leave toxic or persistent chemical residues in the environment.

Biological Stressors: Organisms accidentally or intentionally dropped into habitats in which they do not evolve naturally; e.g. gypsy moths, Dutch elm disease, certain types of algae, and bacteria.

Biological Treatment: A treatment technology that uses bacteria to consume organic waste.

Biologically Effective Dose: The amount of a deposited or absorbed compound reaching the cells or target sites where adverse effect occur, or where the chemical interacts with a membrane.

Biologicals: Vaccines, cultures and other preparations made from living organisms and their products, intended for use in diagnosing, immunizing, or treating humans or animals, or in related research.

Biomass: All of the living material in a given area; often refers to vegetation.

Biome: Entire community of living organisms in a single major ecological area. (See: biotic community.)

Biomonitoring: 1. The use of living organisms to test the suitability of effluents for discharge into receiving waters and to test the quality of such waters downstream from the discharge. 2. Analysis of blood, urine, tissues, etc. to measure chemical exposure in humans.

Bioremediation: Use of living organisms to clean up oil spills or remove other pollutants from soil, water, or wastewater; use of organisms such as non-harmful insects to remove agricultural pests or counteract diseases of trees, plants, and garden soil.

Biosensor: Analytical device comprising a biological recognition element (e.g. enzyme, receptor, DNA, antibody, or microorganism) in intimate contact with an electrochemical, optical, thermal, or acoustic signal transducer that together permit analyses of chemical properties or quantities. Shows potential development in some areas, including environmental monitoring.

Biosphere: The portion of Earth and its atmosphere that can support life.

Biostabilizer: A machine that converts solid waste into compost by grinding and aeration.

Biota: The animal and plant life of a given region.

Biotechnology: Techniques that use living organisms or parts of organisms to produce a variety of products (from medicines to industrial enzymes) to improve plants or animals or to develop microorganisms to remove toxics from bodies of water, or act as pesticides.

Biotic Community: A naturally occurring assemblage of plants and animals that live in the same environment and are mutually sustaining and interdependent. (See: biome.)

Biotransformation: Conversion of a substance into other compounds by organisms; includes biodegredation.

Blackwater: Water that contains animal, human, or food waste.

Blood Products: Any product derived from human blood, including but not limited to blood plasma, platelets, red or white corpuscles, and derived licensed products such as interferon.

Bloom: A proliferation of algae and/or higher aquatic plants in a body of water; often related to pollution, especially when pollutants accelerate growth.

BOD5: The amount of dissolved oxygen consumed in five days by biological processes breaking down organic matter.

Body Burden: The amount of a chemical stored in the body at a given time, especially a potential toxin in the body as the result of exposure.

Bog: A type of wetland that accumulates appreciable peat deposits. Bogs depend primarily on precipitation for their water source, and are usually acidic and rich in plant residue with a conspicuous mat of living green moss.

Boiler: A vessel designed to transfer heat produced by combustion or electric resistance to water. Boilers may provide hot water or steam.

Boom: 1. A floating device used to contain oil on a body of water. 2. A piece of equipment used to apply pesticides from a tractor or truck.

Borehole: Hole made with drilling equipment.

Botanical Pesticide: A pesticide whose active ingredient is a plant-produced chemical such as nicotine or strychnine. Also called a plant-derived pesticide.

Bottle Bill: Proposed or enacted legislation which requires a returnable deposit on beer or soda containers and provides for retail store or other redemption. Such legislation is designed to discourage use of throw-away containers.

Bottom Ash: The non-airborne combustion residue from burning pulverized coal in a boiler; the material which falls to the bottom of the boiler and is removed mechanically; a concentration of non-combustible materials, which may include toxics.

Bottom Land Hardwoods: Forested freshwater wetlands adjacent to rivers in the southeastern United States, especially valuable for wildlife breeding, nesting and habitat.

Bounding Estimate: An estimate of exposure, dose, or risk that is higher than that incurred by the person in the population with the currently highest exposure, dose, or risk. Bounding estimates are useful in developing statements that exposures, doses, or risks are not greater than an estimated value.

Brackish: Mixed fresh and salt water.

Breakpoint Chlorination: Addition of chlorine to water until the chlorine demand has been satisfied.

Breakthrough: A crack or break in a filter bed that allows the passage of floc or particulate matter through a filter; will cause an increase in filter effluent turbidity.

Breathing Zone: Area of air in which an organism inhales.

Brine Mud: Waste material, often associated with well-drilling or mining, composed of mineral salts or other inorganic compounds.

British Thermal Unit: Unit of heat energy equal to the amount of heat required to raise the temperature of one pound of water by one degree Fahrenheit at sea level.

Broadcast Application: The spreading of pesticides over an entire area.

Brownfields: Abandoned, idled, or under used industrial and commercial facilities/sites where expansion or redevelopment is complicated by real or perceived environmental contamination. They can be in urban, suburban, or rural areas. EPA's Brownfields initiative helps communities mitigate potential health risks and restore the economic viability of such areas or properties.

Bubble: A system under which existing emissions sources can propose alternate means to comply with a set of emissions limitations; under the bubble concept, sources can control more than required at one emission point where control costs are relatively low in return for a comparable relaxation of controls at a second emission point where costs are higher.

Bubble Policy: (See: emissions trading.)

Buffer: A solution or liquid whose chemical makeup is such that it minimizes changes in pH when acids or bases are added to it.

Buffer Strips: Strips of grass or other erosion-resisting vegetation between or below cultivated strips or fields.

Building Cooling Load: The hourly amount of heat that must be removed from a building to maintain indoor comfort (measured in British thermal units (Btus).

Building Envelope: The exterior surface of a building's construction—the walls, windows, floors, roof, and floor. Also called building shell.

Building Related Illness: Diagnosable illness whose cause and symptoms can be directly attributed to a specific pollutant source within a building (e.g. Legionnaire's disease, hypersensitivity, pneumonitis.) (See: sick building syndrome.)

Bulk Sample: A small portion (usually thumbnail size) of a suspect asbestos-containing building material collected by an asbestos inspector for laboratory analysis to determine asbestos content.

Bulky Waste: Large items of waste materials, such as appliances, furniture, large auto parts, trees, stumps.

Burial Ground (Graveyard): A disposal site for radioactive waste materials that uses earth or water as a shield.

Buy-Back Center: Facility where individuals or groups bring reyclables in return for payment.

By-product: Material, other than the principal product, generated as a consequence of an industrial process or as a breakdown product in a living system.

C

Cadmium (Cd): A heavy metal that accumulates in the environment.

Cancellation: Refers to Section 6 (b) of the Federal Insecticide, Fungicide and Rodenticide Act (FIFRA) which authorizes cancellation of a pesticide registration if unreasonable adverse effects to the environment and public health develop when a product is used according to widespread and commonly recognized practice, or if its labeling or other material required to be submitted does not comply with FIFRA provisions.

Cap: A layer of clay, or other impermeable material installed over the top of a closed landfill to prevent entry of rainwater and minimize leachate.

Capacity Assurance Plan: A statewide plan which supports a state's ability to manage the hazardous waste generated within its boundaries over a twenty year period.

Capillary Action: Movement of water through very small spaces due to molecular forces called capillary forces.

Capillary Fringe: The porous material just above the water table which may hold water by capillarity (a property of surface tension that draws water upwards) in the smaller void spaces.

Capillary Fringe: The zone above he water table within which the porous medium is saturated by water under less than atmospheric pressure.

Capture Efficiency: The fraction of organic vapors generated by a process that are directed to an abatement or recovery device.

Carbon Absorber: An add-on control device that uses activated carbon to absorb volatile organic compounds from a gas stream. (The VOCs are later recovered from the carbon.)

Carbon Adsorption: A treatment system that removes contaminants from ground water or surface water by forcing it through tanks containing activated carbon treated to attract the contaminants.

Carbon Monoxide (CO): A colorless, odorless, poisonous gas produced by incomplete fossil fuel combustion.

Carbon Tetrachloride (CC14): Compound consisting of one carbon atom ad four chlorine atoms, once widely used as a industrial raw material, as a solvent, and in the production of

CFCs. Use as a solvent ended when it was discovered to be carcinogenic.

Carboxyhemoglobin: Hemoglobin in which the iron is bound to carbon monoxide(CO) instead of oxygen.

Carcinogen: Any substance that can cause or aggravate cancer.

Carrier: 1.The inert liquid or solid material in a pesticide product that serves as a delivery vehicle for the active ingredient. Carriers do not have toxic properties of their own. 2. Any material or system that can facilitate the movement of a pollutant into the body or cells.

Carrying Capacity: 1. In recreation management, the amount of use a recreation area can sustain without loss of quality. 2. In wildlife management, the maximum number of animals an area can support during a given period.

CAS Registration Number: A number assigned by the Chemical Abstract Service to identify a chemical.

Case Study: A brief fact sheet providing risk, cost, and performance information on alternative methods and other pollution prevention ideas, compliance initiatives, voluntary efforts, etc.

Cask: A thick-walled container (usually lead) used to transport radioactive material. Also called a coffin.

Catalyst: A substance that changes the speed or yield of a chemical reaction without being consumed or chemically changed by the chemical reaction.

Catalytic Converter: An air pollution abatement device that removes pollutants from motor vehicle exhaust, either by oxidizing them into carbon dioxide and water or reducing them to nitrogen.

Catalytic Incinerator: A control device that oxidizes volatile organic compounds (VOCs) by using a catalyst to promote the combustion process. Catalytic incinerators require lower temperatures than conventional thermal incinerators, thus saving fuel and other costs.

Categorical Exclusion: A class of actions which either individually or cumulatively would not have a significant effect on the human environment and therefore would not require preparation of an environmental assessment or environmental impact statement under the National Environmental Policy Act (NEPA).

Categorical Pretreatment Standard: A technology-based effluent limitation for an industrial facility discharging into a municipal sewer system. Analogous in stringency to Best Availability Technology (BAT) for direct dischargers.

Cathodic Protection: A technique to prevent corrosion of a metal surface by making it the cathode of an electrochemical cell.

Cavitation: The formation and collapse of gas pockets or bubbles on the blade of an impeller or the gate of a valve; collapse of these pockets or bubbles drives water with such force that it can cause pitting of the gate or valve surface.

Cells: 1. In solid waste disposal, holes where waste is dumped, compacted, and covered with layers of dirt on a daily basis. 2. The smallest structural part of living matter capable of functioning as an independent unit.

Cementitious: Densely packed and nonfibrous friable materials.

Central Collection Point: Location were a generator of regulated medical waste consolidates wastes originally generated at various locations in his facility. The wastes are gathered together for treatment on-site or for transportation elsewhere for treatment and/or disposal. This term could also apply to community hazardous waste collections, industrial and other waste management systems.

Centrifugal Collector: A mechanical system using centrifugal force to remove aerosols from a gas stream or to remove water from sludge.

CERCLIS: The federal Comprehensive Environmental Response, Compensation, and Liability Information System is a database that includes all sites which have been nominated for investigation by the Superfund program.

Channelization: Straightening and deepening streams so water will move faster, a marsh-drainage tactic that can interfere with waste assimilation capacity, disturb fish and wildlife habitats, and aggravate flooding.

Characteristic: Any one of the four categories used in defining hazardous waste: ignitability, corrosivity, reactivity, and toxicity.

Characterization of Ecological Effects: Part of ecological risk assessment that evaluates ability of a stressor to cause adverse effects under given circumstances.

Characterization of Exposure: Portion of an ecological risk assessment that evaluates interaction of a stressor with one or more ecological entities.

Check-Valve Tubing Pump: Water sampling tool also referred to as a water Pump.

Chemical Case: For purposes of review and regulation, the grouping of chemically similar pesticide active ingredients (e.g. salts and esters of the same chemical) into chemical cases.

Chemical Compound: A distinct and pure substance formed by the union or two or more elements in definite proportion by weight.

Chemical Element: A fundamental substance comprising one kind of atom; the simplest form of matter.

Chemical Oxygen Demand (COD): A measure of the oxygen required to oxidize all compounds, both organic and inorganic, in water.

Chemical Stressors: Chemicals released to the environment through industrial waste, auto emissions, pesticides, and other human activity that can cause illnesses and even death in plants and animals.

Chemical Treatment: Any one of a variety of technologies that use chemicals or a variety of chemical processes to treat waste.

Chemnet: Mutual aid network of chemical shippers and contractors that assigns a contracted emergency response company to provide technical support if a representative of the firm whose chemicals are involved in an incident is not readily available.

Chemosterilant: A chemical that controls pests by preventing reproduction.

Chemtrec: The industry-sponsored Chemical Transportation Emergency Center; provides information and/or emergency assistance to emergency responders.

Child Resistant Packaging (CRP): Packaging that protects children or adults from injury or illness resulting from accidental contact with or ingestion of residential pesticides that meet or exceed specific toxicity levels. Required by FIFRA regulations. Term is also used for protective packaging of medicines.

Chiller: A device that generates a cold liquid that is circulated through an air-handling unit's cooling coil to cool the air supplied to the building.

Chilling Effect: The lowering of the Earth's temperature because of increased particles in the air blocking the sun's rays. (See: greenhouse effect.)

Chisel Plowing: Preparing croplands by using a special implement that avoids complete inversion of the soil as in conventional plowing. Chisel plowing can leave a protective cover or crops residues on the soil surface to help prevent erosion and improve filtration.

Chlorinated Hydrocarbons: 1. Chemicals containing only chlorine, carbon, and hydrogen. These include a class of persistent, broad-spectrum insecticides that linger in the environment and accumulate in the food chain. Among them are DDT, aldrin, dieldrin, heptachlor, chlordane, lindane, endrin, Mirex, hexachloride, and toxaphene. Other examples include TCE, used as an industrial solvent. 2. Any chlorinated organic compounds including chlorinated solvents such as dichloromethane, trichloromethylene, chloroform.

Chlorinated Solvent: An organic solvent containing chlorine atoms(e.g. methylene chloride and 1,1,1-trichloromethane). Uses of chlorinated solvents are include aerosol spray containers, in highway paint, and dry cleaning fluids.

Chlorination: The application of chlorine to drinking water, sewage, or industrial waste to disinfect or to oxidize undesirable compounds.

Chlorinator: A device that adds chlorine, in gas or liquid form, to water or sewage to kill infectious bacteria.

Chlorine-Contact Chamber: That part of a water treatment plant where effluent is disinfected by chlorine.

Chlorofluorocarbons (CFCs): A family of inert, nontoxic, and easily liquefied chemicals used in refrigeration, air conditioning, packaging, insulation, or as solvents and aerosol propellants. Because CFCs are not destroyed in the lower atmosphere they drift into the upper atmosphere where their chlorine components destroy ozone. (See: fluorocarbons.)

Chlorophenoxy: A class of herbicides that may be found in domestic water supplies and cause adverse health effects.

Chlorosis: Discoloration of normally green plant parts caused by disease, lack of nutrients, or various air pollutants.

Cholinesterase: An enzyme found in animals that regulates nerve impulses by the inhibition of acetylcholine. Cholinesterase inhibition is associated with a variety of acute symptoms such as nausea, vomiting, blurred vision, stomach cramps, and rapid heart rate.

Chromium: (See: heavy metals.)

Chronic Effect: An adverse effect on a human or animal in which symptoms recur frequently or develop slowly over a long period of time.

Chronic Exposure: Multiple exposures occurring over an extended period of time or over a significant fraction of an animal's or human's lifetime (Usually seven years to a lifetime.)

Chronic Toxicity: The capacity of a substance to cause long-term poisonous health effects in humans, animals, fish, and other organisms. (See: acute toxicity.)

Circle of Influence: The circular outer edge of a depression produced in the water table by the pumping of water from a well. (See: cone of depression.)

Cistern: Small tank or storage facility used to store water for a home or farm; often used to store rain water.

Clarification: Clearing action that occurs during wastewater treatment when solids settle out. This is often aided by centrifugal action and chemically induced coagulation in wastewater.

Clarifier: A tank in which solids settle to the bottom and are subsequently removed as sludge.

Class I Area: Under the Clean Air Act. a Class I area is one in which visibility is protected more stringently than under the national ambient air quality standards; includes national parks, wilderness areas, monuments, and other areas of special national and cultural significance.

Class I Substance: One of several groups of chemicals with an ozone depletion potential of 0.2 or higher, including CFCS, Halons, Carbon Tetrachloride, and Methyl Chloroform (listed in the Clean Air Act), and HBFCs and Ethyl Bromide (added by EPA regulations). (See: Global warming potential.)

Class II Substance: A substance with an ozone depletion potential of less than 0.2. All HCFCs are currently included in this classification. (See: Global warming potential.)

Clay Soil: Soil material containing more than 40 percent clay, less than 45 percent sand, and less than 40 percent silt.

Clean Coal Technology: Any technology not in widespread use prior to the Clean Air Act Amendments of 1990. This Act will achieve significant reductions in pollutants associated with the burning of coal.

Clean Fuels: Blends or substitutes for gasoline fuels, including compressed natural gas, methanol, ethanol, and liquified petroleum gas.

Cleaner Technologies Substitutes Assessment: A document that systematically evaluates the relative risk, performance, and cost trade-offs of technological alternatives; serves as a repository for all the technical data (including methodology and results) developed by a DfE or other pollution prevention or education project.

Cleanup: Actions taken to deal with a release or threat of release of a hazardous substance that could affect humans and/or the environment. The term "cleanup" is sometimes used interchangeably with the terms remedial action, removal action, response action, or corrective action.

Clear Cut: Harvesting all the trees in one area at one time, a practice that can encourage fast rainfall or snowmelt runoff, erosion, sedimentation of streams and lakes, and flooding, and destroys vital habitat.

Clear Well: A reservoir for storing filtered water of sufficient quantity to prevent the need to vary the filtration rate with variations in demand. Also used to provide chlorine contact time for disinfection.

Climate Change (also referred to as 'global climate change'): The term 'climate change' is sometimes used to refer to all forms of climatic inconsistency, but because the Earth's climate is never static, the term is more properly used to imply a significant change from one climatic condition to another. In some cases, 'climate change' has been used synonymously with the term, 'global warming'; scientists however, tend to use the term in the wider sense to also include natural changes in climate. (See: global warming.)

Cloning: In biotechnology, obtaining a group of genetically identical cells from a single cell; making identical copies of a gene.

Closed-Loop Recycling: Reclaiming or reusing wastewater for non-potable purposes in an enclosed process.

Closure: The procedure a landfill operator must follow when a landfill reaches its legal capacity for solid ceasing acceptance of solid waste and placing a cap on the landfill site.

Co-fire: Burning of two fuels in the same combustion unit; e.g., coal and natural gas, or oil and coal.

Coagulation: Clumping of particles in wastewater to settle out impurities, often induced by chemicals such as lime, alum, and iron salts.

Coal Cleaning Technology: A precombustion process by which coal is physically or chemically treated to remove some of its sulfur so as to reduce sulfur dioxide emissions.

Coal Gasification: Conversion of coal to a gaseous product by one of several available technologies.

Coastal Zone: Lands and waters adjacent to the coast that exert an influence on the uses of the sea and its ecology, or whose uses and ecology are affected by the sea.

Code of Federal Regulations (CFR): Document that codifies all rules of the executive departments and agencies of the federal government. It is divided into fifty volumes, known as titles. Title 40 of the CFR (referenced as 40 CFR) lists all environmental regulations.

Coefficient of Haze (COH): A measurement of visibility interference in the atmosphere.

Cogeneration: The consecutive generation of useful thermal and electric energy from the same fuel source.

Coke Oven: An industrial process which converts coal into coke, one of the basic materials used in blast furnaces for the conversion of iron ore into iron.

Cold Temperature CO: A standard for automobile emissions of carbon monoxide (CO) emissions to be met at a low temperature (i.e. 20 degrees Fahrenheit). Conventional automobile catalytic converters are not efficient in cold weather until they warm up.

Coliform Index: A rating of the purity of water based on a count of fecal bacteria.

Coliform Organism: Microorganisms found in the intestinal tract of humans and animals. Their presence in water indicates fecal pollution and potentially adverse contamination by pathogens.

Collector: Public or private hauler that collects nonhazardous waste and recyclable materials from residential, commercial, institutional and industrial sources. (See: hauler.)

Collector Sewers: Pipes used to collect and carry wastewater from individual sources to an interceptor sewer that will carry it to a treatment facility.

Colloids: Very small, finely divided solids (that do not dissolve) that remain dispersed in a liquid for a long time due to their small size and electrical charge.

Combined Sewer Overflows: Discharge of a mixture of storm water and domestic waste when the flow capacity of a sewer system is exceeded during rainstorms.

Combined Sewers: A sewer system that carries both sewage and storm-water runoff. Normally, its entire flow goes to a waste treatment plant, but during a heavy storm, the volume of water may be so great as to cause overflows of untreated mixtures of storm water and sewage into receiving waters. Storm-water runoff may also carry toxic chemicals from industrial areas or streets into the sewer system.

Combustion: 1. Burning, or rapid oxidation, accompanied by release of energy in the form of heat and light. 2. Refers to controlled burning of waste, in which heat chemically alters organic compounds, converting into stable inorganics such as carbon dioxide and water.

Combustion Chamber: The actual compartment where waste is burned in an incinerator.

Combustion Product: Substance produced during the burning or oxidation of a material.

Command Post: Facility located at a safe distance upwind from an accident site, where the on-scene coordinator, responders, and technical representatives make response decisions, deploy manpower and equipment, maintain liaison with news media, and handle communications.

Command-and-Control Regulations: Specific requirements prescribing how to comply with specific standards defining acceptable levels of pollution.

Comment Period: Time provided for the public to review and comment on a proposed EPA action or rulemaking after publication in the Federal Register.

Commercial Waste: All solid waste emanating from business establishments such as stores, markets, office buildings, restaurants, shopping centers, and theaters.

Commercial Waste Management Facility: A treatment, storage, disposal, or transfer facility which accepts waste from a variety of sources, as compared to a private facility which normally manages a limited waste stream generated by its own operations.

Commingled Recyclables: Mixed recyclables that are collected together.

Comminuter: A machine that shreds or pulverizes solids to make waste treatment easier.

Comminution: Mechanical shredding or pulverizing of waste. Used in both solid waste management and wastewater treatment.

Common Sense Initiative: Voluntary program to simplify environmental regulation to achieve cleaner, cheaper, smarter results, starting with six major industry sectors.

Community: In ecology, an assemblage of populations of different species within a specified location in space and time. Sometimes, a particular subgrouping may be specified, such as the fish community in a lake or the soil arthropod community in a forest.

Community Relations: The EPA effort to establish two-way communication with the public to create understanding of EPA programs and related actions, to ensure public input into decision-making processes related to affected communities, and to make certain that the Agency is aware of and responsive to public concerns. Specific community relations activities are required in relation to Superfund remedial actions.

Community Water System: A public water system which serves at least 15 service connections used by year-round residents or regularly serves at least 25 year-round residents.

Compact Fluorescent Lamp (CFL): Small fluorescent lamps used as more efficient alternatives to incandescent lighting. Also called PL, CFL, Twin-Tube, or BIAX lamps.

Compaction: Reduction of the bulk of solid waste by rolling and tamping.

Comparative Risk Assessment: Process that generally uses the judgement of experts to predict effects and set priorities among a wide range of environmental problems.

Complete Treatment: A method of treating water that consists of the addition of coagulant chemicals, flash mixing, coagulation-flocculation, sedimentation, and filtration. Also called conventional filtration.

Compliance Coal: Any coal that emits less than 1.2 pounds of sulfur dioxide per million Btu when burned. Also known as low sulfur coal.

Compliance Coating: A coating whose volatile organic compound content does not exceed that allowed by regulation.

Compliance Cycle: The 9-year calendar year cycle, beginning January 1, 1993, during which public water systems must monitor. Each cycle consists of three 3-year compliance periods.

Compliance Monitoring: Collection and evaluation of data, including self-monitoring reports, and verification to show whether pollutant concentrations and loads contained in permitted discharges are in compliance with the limits and conditions specified in the permit.

Compliance Schedule: A negotiated agreement between a pollution source and a government agency that specifies dates and procedures by which a source will reduce emissions and, thereby, comply with a regulation.

Composite Sample: A series of water samples taken over a given period of time and weighted by flow rate.

Compost: The relatively stable humus material that is produced from a composting process in which bacteria in soil mixed with garbage and degradable trash break down the mixture into organic fertilizer.

Composting: The controlled biological decomposition of organic material in the presence of air to form a humus-like material. Controlled methods of composting include mechanical mixing and aerating, ventilating the materials by dropping them through a vertical series of aerated chambers, or placing the compost in piles out in the open air and mixing it or turning it periodically.

Composting Facilities: 1. An offsite facility where the organic component of municipal solid waste is decomposed under controlled conditions; 2.an aerobic process in which organic materials are ground or shredded and then decomposed to humus in windrow piles or in mechanical digesters, drums, or similar enclosures.

Compressed Natural Gas (CNG): An alternative fuel for motor vehicles; considered one of the cleanest because of low hydrocarbon emissions and its vapors are relatively non-ozone producing. However, vehicles fueled with CNG do emit a significant quantity of nitrogen oxides.

Concentration: The relative amount of a substance mixed with another substance. An example is five ppm of carbon monoxide in air or 1 mg/l of iron in water.

Condensate: 1.Liquid formed when warm landfill gas cools as it travels through a collection system. 2. Water created by cooling steam or water vapor.

Condensate Return System: System that returns the heated water condensing within steam piping to the boiler and thus saves energy.

Conditional Registration: Under special circumstances, the Federal Insecticide, Fungicide, and Rodenticide Act (FIFRA) permits registration of pesticide products that is "conditional" upon the submission of additional data. These special circumstances include a finding by the EPA Administrator that a new product or use of an existing pesticide will not significantly increase the risk of unreasonable adverse effects. A product containing a new (previously unregistered) active ingredient may be conditionally registered only if the Administrator finds that such conditional registration is in the public interest, that a reasonable time for conducting the additional studies has not elapsed, and the use of the pesticide for the period of conditional registration will not present an unreasonable risk.

Conditionally Exempt Generators (CE): Persons or enterprises which produce less than 220 pounds of hazardous waste per month. Exempt from most regulation, they are required merely to determine whether their waste is hazardous, notify appropriate state or local agencies, and ship it by an authorized transporter to a permitted facility for proper disposal. (See : small quantity generator.)

Conductance: A rapid method of estimating the dissolved solids content of water supply by determining the capacity of a water sample to carry an electrical current. Conductivity is a measure of the ability of a solution to carry and electrical current.

Conductivity: A measure of the ability of a solution to carry an electrical current.

Cone of Depression: A depression in the water table that develops around a pumped well.

Cone of Influence: The depression, roughly conical in shape, produced in a water table by the pumping of water from a well.

Cone Penterometer Testing (CPT): A direct push system used to measure lithology based on soil penetration resistance. Sensors in the tip of the cone of the DP rod measure tip resistance and side-wall friction, transmitting electrical signals to digital processing equipment on the ground surface. (See: direct push.)

Confidential Business Information (CBI): Material that contains trade secrets or commercial or financial information that has been claimed as confidential by its source (e.g. a pesticide or new chemical formulation registrant). EPA has special procedures for handling such information.

Confidential Statement of Formula (CSF): A list of the ingredients in a new pesticide or chemical formulation. The list is submitted at the time for application for registration or change in formulation.

Confined Aquifer: An aquifer in which ground water is confined under pressure which is significantly greater than atmospheric pressure.

Confluent Growth: A continuous bacterial growth covering all or part of the filtration area of a membrane filter in which the bacteria colonies are not discrete.

Consent Decree: A legal document, approved by a judge, that formalizes an agreement reached between EPA and potentially responsible parties (PRPs) through which PRPs will conduct all or part of a cleanup action at a Superfund site; cease or correct actions or processes that are polluting the environment; or otherwise comply with EPA initiated regulatory enforcement actions to resolve the contamination at the Superfund site involved. The consent decree describes the actions PRPs will take and may be subject to a public comment period.

Conservation: Preserving and renewing, when possible, human and natural resources. The use, protection, and improvement of natural resources according to principles that will ensure their highest economic or social benefits.

Conservation Easement: Easement restricting a landowner to land uses that that are compatible with long-term conservation and environmental values.

Constituent(s) of Concern: Specific chemicals that are identified for evaluation in the site assessment process

Construction and Demolition Waste: Waste building materials, dredging materials, tree stumps, and rubble resulting from construction, remodeling, repair, and demolition of homes, commercial buildings and other structures and pavements. May contain lead, asbestos, or other hazardous substances.

Construction Ban: If, under the Clean Air Act, EPA disapproves an area's planning requirements for correcting nonattainment, EPA can ban the construction or modification of any major stationary source of the pollutant for which the area is in nonattainment.

Consumptive Water Use: Water removed from available supplies without return to a water resources system, e.g. water used in manufacturing, agriculture, and food preparation.

Contact Pesticide: A chemical that kills pests when it touches them, instead of by ingestion. Also, soil that contains the minute skeletons of certain algae that scratch and dehydrate waxy-coated insects.

Contaminant: Any physical, chemical, biological, or radiological substance or matter that has an adverse effect on air, water, or soil.

Contamination: Introduction into water, air, and soil of microorganisms, chemicals, toxic substances, wastes, or wastewater in a concentration that makes the medium unfit for its next intended use. Also applies to surfaces of objects, buildings, and various household and agricultural use products.

Contamination Source Inventory: An inventory of contaminant sources within delineated State Water-Protection Areas. Targets likely sources for further investigation.

Contingency Plan: A document setting out an organized, planned, and coordinated course of action to be followed in case of a fire, explosion, or other accident that releases toxic chemicals, hazardous waste, or radioactive materials that threaten human health or the environment. (See: National Oil and Hazardous Substances Contingency Plan.)

Continuous Discharge: A routine release to the environment that occurs without interruption, except for infrequent shutdowns for maintenance, process changes, etc.

Continuous Sample: A flow of water, waste or other material from a particular place in a plant to the location where samples are collected for testing. May be used to obtain grab or composite samples.

Contour Plowing: Soil tilling method that follows the shape of the land to discourage erosion.

Contour Strip Farming: A kind of contour farming in which row crops are planted in strips, between alternating strips of close-growing, erosion-resistant forage crops.

Contract Labs: Laboratories under contract to EPA, which analyze samples taken from waste, soil, air, and water or carry out research projects.

Control Technique Guidelines (CTG): EPA documents designed to assist state and local pollution authorities to achieve and maintain air quality standards for certain sources (e.g. organic emissions from solvent metal cleaning known as degreasing) through reasonably available control technologies (RACT).

Controlled Reaction: A chemical reaction under temperature and pressure conditions maintained within safe limits to produce a desired product or process.

Conventional Filtration: (See: complete treatment.)

Conventional Pollutants: Statutorily listed pollutants understood well by scientists. These may be in the form of organic waste, sediment, acid, bacteria, viruses, nutrients, oil and grease, or heat.

Conventional Site Assessment: Assessment in which most of the sample analysis and interpretation of data is completed off-site; process usually requires repeated mobilization of equipment and staff in order to fully determine the extent of contamination.

Conventional Systems: Systems that have been traditionally used to collect municipal wastewater in gravity sewers and convey it to a central primary or secondary treatment plant prior to discharge to surface waters.

Conventional Tilling: Tillage operations considered standard for a specific location and crop and that tend to bury the crop residues; usually considered as a base for determining the cost effectiveness of control practices.

Conveyance Loss: Water loss in pipes, channels, conduits, ditches by leakage or evaporation.

Cooling Electricity Use: Amount of electricity used to meet the building cooling load. (See: building cooling load.)

Cooling Tower: A structure that helps remove heat from water used as a coolant; e.g., in electric power generating plants.

Cooling Tower: Device which dissipates the heat from water-cooled systems by spraying the water through streams of rapidly moving air.

Cooperative Agreement: An assistance agreement whereby EPA transfers money, property, services or anything of value to a state, university, non-profit, or not-for-profit organization for the accomplishment of authorized activities or tasks.

Core: The uranium-containing heart of a nuclear reactor, where energy is released.

Core Program Cooperative Agreement: An assistance agreement whereby EPA supports states or tribal governments with funds to help defray the cost of non-item-specific administrative and training activities.

Corrective Action: EPA can require treatment, storage and disposal (TSDF) facilities handling hazardous waste to undertake corrective actions to clean up spills resulting from failure to follow hazardous waste management procedures or other mistakes. The process includes cleanup procedures designed to guide TSDFs toward in spills.

Corrosion: The dissolution and wearing away of metal caused by a chemical reaction such as between water and the pipes, chemicals touching a metal surface, or contact between two metals.

Corrosive: A chemical agent that reacts with the surface of a material causing it to deteriorate or wear away.

Cost/Benefit Analysis: A quantitative evaluation of the costs which would have incurred by implementing an environmental regulation versus the overall benefits to society of the proposed action.

Cost Recovery: A legal process by which potentially responsible parties who contributed to contamination at a Superfund site can be required to reimburse the Trust Fund for money spent during any cleanup actions by the federal government.

Cost Sharing: A publicly financed program through which society, as a beneficiary of environmental protection, shares part of the cost of pollution control with those who must actually install the controls. In Superfund, for example, the government may pay part of the cost of a cleanup action with those responsible for the pollution paying the major share.

Cost-Effective Alternative: An alternative control or corrective method identified after analysis as being the best available in terms of reliability, performance, and cost. Although costs are one important consideration, regulatory and compliance analysis does not require EPA to choose the least expensive alternative. For example, when selecting or approving a method for cleaning up a Superfund site, the Agency balances costs with the long-term effectiveness of the methods proposed and the potential danger posed by the site.

Cover Crop: A crop that provides temporary protection for delicate seedlings and/or provides a cover canopy for seasonal soil protection and improvement between normal crop production periods.

Cover Material: Soil used to cover compacted solid waste in a sanitary landfill.

Cradle-to-Grave or Manifest System: A procedure in which hazardous materials are identified and followed as they are produced, treated, transported, and disposed of by a series of permanent, linkable, descriptive documents (e.g. manifests). Commonly referred to as the cradle-to-grave system.

Criteria: Descriptive factors taken into account by EPA in setting standards for various pollutants. These factors are used to determine limits on allowable concentration levels, and to limit the number of violations per year. When issued by EPA, the criteria provide guidance to the states on how to establish their standards.

Criteria Pollutants: The 1970 amendments to the Clean Air Act required EPA to set National Ambient Air Quality Standards for certain pollutants known to be hazardous to human health. EPA has identified and set standards to protect human health and welfare for six pollutants: ozone, carbon monoxide, total suspended particulates, sulfur dioxide, lead, and nitrogen oxide. The term, "criteria pollutants" derives from the requirement that EPA must describe the characteristics and potential health and welfare effects of these pollutants. It is on the basis of these criteria that standards are set or revised.

Critical Effect: The first adverse effect, or its known precursor, that occurs as a dose rate increases. Designation is based on evaluation of overall database.

Crop Consumptive Use: The amount of water transpired during plant growth plus what evaporated from the soil surface and foliage in the crop area.

Crop Rotation: Planting a succession of different crops on the same land rea as opposed to planting the same crop time after time.

Cross Contamination: The movement of underground contaminants from one level or area to another due to invasive subsurface activities.

Cross-Connection: Any actual or potential connection between a drinking water system and an unapproved water supply or other source of contamination.

Crumb Rubber: Ground rubber fragments the size of sand or silt used in rubber or plastic products, or processed further into reclaimed rubber or asphalt products.

Cryptosporidium: A protozoan microbe associated with the disease cryptosporidiosis in man. The disease can be transmitted through ingestion of drinking water, person-to-person contact, or other pathways, and can cause acute diarrhea, abdominal pain, vomiting, fever, and can be fatal as it was in the Milwaukee episode.

Cubic Feet Per Minute (CFM): A measure of the volume of a substance flowing through air within a fixed period of time. With regard to indoor air, refers to the amount of air, in cubic feet, that is exchanged with outdoor air in a minute's time; i.e. the air exchange rate.

Cullet: Crushed glass.

Cultural Eutrophication: Increasing rate at which water bodies "die" by pollution from human activities.

Cultures and Stocks: Infectious agents and associated biologicals including cultures from medical and pathological laboratories; cultures and stocks of infectious agents from research and industrial laboratories; waste from the production of biologicals; discarded live and attenuated vaccines; and culture dishes and devices used to transfer, inoculate, and mix cultures. (See: regulated medical waste.)

Cumulative Ecological Risk Assessment: Consideration of the total ecological risk from multiple stressors to a given eco-zone.

Cumulative Exposure: The sum of exposures of an organism to a pollutant over a period of time.

Cumulative Working Level Months (CWLM): The sum of lifetime exposure to radon working levels expressed in total working level months.

Curb Stop: A water service shutoff valve located in a water service pipe near the curb and between the water main and the building.

Curbside Collection: Method of collecting recyclable materials at homes, community districts or businesses.

Cutie-Pie: An instrument used to measure radiation levels.

Cuttings: Spoils left by conventional drilling with hollow stem auger or rotary drilling equipment.

Cyclone Collector: A device that uses centrifugal force to remove large particles from polluted air.

D

Data Call-In: A part of the Office of Pesticide Programs (OPP) process of developing key required test data, especially on the long-term, chronic effects of existing pesticides, in advance of scheduled Registration Standard reviews. Data Call-In from manufacturers is an adjunct of the Registration Standards program intended to expedite re-registration.

Data Quality Objectives (DQOs): Qualitative and quantitative statements of the overall level of uncertainty that a decision-maker will accept in results or decisions based on environmental data. They provide the statistical framework for planning and managing environmental data operations consistent with user's needs.

Day Tank: Another name for deaerating tank. (See: age tank.)

DDT: The first chlorinated hydrocarbon insecticide chemical name: Dichloro-Diphenyl-Trichloroethane. It has a half-life of 15 years and can collect in fatty tissues of certain animals. EPA banned registration and interstate sale of DDT for virtually all but emergency uses in the United States in 1972 because of its persistence in the environment and accumulation in the food chain.

Dead End: The end of a water main which is not connected to other parts of the distribution system.

Deadmen: Anchors drilled or cemented into the ground to provide additional reactive mass for DP sampling rigs.

Glossary of Environmental Terms

Decant: To draw off the upper layer of liquid after the heaviest material (a solid or another liquid) has settled.

Decay Products: Degraded radioactive materials, often referred to as "daughters" or "progeny"; radon decay products of most concern from a public health standpoint are polonium-214 and polonium-218.

Dechlorination: Removal of chlorine from a substance.

Decomposition: The breakdown of matter by bacteria and fungi, changing the chemical makeup and physical appearance of materials.

Decontamination: Removal of harmful substances such as noxious chemicals, harmful bacteria or other organisms, or radioactive material from exposed individuals, rooms and furnishings in buildings, or the exterior environment.

Deep-Well Injection: Deposition of raw or treated, filtered hazardous waste by pumping it into deep wells, where it is contained in the pores of permeable subsurface rock.

Deflocculating Agent: A material added to a suspension to prevent settling.

Defluoridation: The removal of excess flouride in drinking water to prevent the staining of teeth.

Defoliant: An herbicide that removes leaves from trees and growing plants.

Degasification: A water treatment that removes dissolved gases from the water.

Degree-Day: A rough measure used to estimate the amount of heating required in a given area; is defined as the difference between the mean daily temperature and 65 degrees Fahrenheit. Degree-days are also calculated to estimate cooling requirements.

Delegated State: A state (or other governmental entity such as a tribal government) that has received authority to administer an environmental regulatory program in lieu of a federal counterpart. As used in connection with NPDES, UIC, and PWS programs, the term does not connote any transfer of federal authority to a state.

Delist: Use of the petition process to have a facility's toxic designation rescinded.

Demand-side Waste Management: Prices whereby consumers use purchasing decisions to communicate to product manufacturers that they prefer environmentally sound products packaged with the least amount of waste, made from recycled or recyclable materials, and containing no hazardous substances.

Demineralization: A treatment process that removes dissolved minerals from water.

Denitrification: The biological reduction of nitrate to nitrogen gas by denitrifying bacteria in soil.

Dense Non Aqueous Phase Liquid (DNAPL): Non-aqueous phase liquids such as chlorinated hydrocarbon solvents or petroleum fractions with a specific gravity greater than 1.0 that sink through the water column until they reach a confining layer. Because they are at the bottom of aquifers instead of floating on the water table, typical monitoring wells do not indicate their presence.

Density: A measure of how heavy a specific volume of a solid, liquid, or gas is in comparison to water. depending on the chemical.

Depletion Curve: In hydraulics, a graphical representation of water depletion from storage-stream channels, surface soil, and groundwater. A depletion curve can be drawn for base flow, direct runoff, or total flow.

Depressurization: A condition that occurs when the air pressure inside a structure is lower that the air pressure outdoors. Depressurization can occur when household appliances such as fireplaces or furnaces, that consume or exhaust house air, are not supplied with enough makeup air. Radon may be drawn into a house more rapidly under depressurized conditions.

Dermal Absorption/Penetration: Process by which a chemical penetrates the skin and enters the body as an internal dose.

Dermal Exposure: Contact between a chemical and the skin.

Dermal Toxicity: The ability of a pesticide or toxic chemical to poison people or animals by contact with the skin. (See: contact pesticide.)

DES: A synthetic estrogen, diethylstilbestrol is used as a growth stimulant in food animals. Residues in meat are thought to be carcinogenic.

Desalination: [Desalinization] (1) Removing salts from ocean or brackish water by using various technologies. (2) Removal of salts from soil by artificial means, usually leaching.

Desiccant: A chemical agent that absorbs moisture; some desiccants are capable of drying out plants or insects, causing death.

Design Capacity: The average daily flow that a treatment plant or other facility is designed to accommodate.

Design Value: The monitored reading used by EPA to determine an area's air quality status; e.g., for ozone, the fourth highest reading measured over the most recent three years is the design value.

Designated Pollutant: An air pollutant which is neither a criteria nor hazardous pollutant, as described in the Clean Air Act, but for which new source performance standards exist. The Clean Air Act does require states to control these pollutants, which include acid mist, total reduced sulfur (TRS), and fluorides.

Designated Uses: Those water uses identified in state water quality standards that must be achieved and maintained as required under the Clean Water Act. Uses can include cold water fisheries, public water supply, and irrigation.

Designer Bugs: Popular term for microbes developed through biotechnology that can degrade specific toxic chemicals at their source in toxic waste dumps or in ground water.

Destination Facility: The facility to which regulated medical waste is shipped for treatment and destruction, incineration, and/or disposal.

Destratification: Vertical mixing within a lake or reservoir to totally or partially eliminate separate layers of temperature, plant, or animal life.

Destroyed Medical Waste: Regulated medical waste that has been ruined, torn apart, or mutilated through thermal treatment, melting, shredding, grinding, tearing, or breaking, so that it is no longer generally recognized as medical waste, but has not yet been treated (excludes compacted regulated medical waste).

Destruction and Removal Efficiency (DRE): A percentage that represents the number of molecules of a compound removed or destroyed in an incinerator relative to the number of molecules entering the system (e.g. a DRE of 99.99 percent means that 9,999 molecules are destroyed for every 10,000 that enter; 99.99 percent is known as "four nines." For some pollutants, the RCRA removal requirement may be as stringent as "six nines").

Destruction Facility: A facility that destroys regulated medical waste.

Desulfurization: Removal of sulfur from fossil fuels to reduce pollution.

Detectable Leak Rate: The smallest leak (from a storage tank), expressed in terms of gallons- or liters-per-hour, that a test can reliably discern with a certain probability of detection or false alarm.

Detection Criterion: A predetermined rule to ascertain whether a tank is leaking or not. Most volumetric tests use a threshold value as the detection criterion. (See: volumetric tank tests.)

Detection Limit: The lowest concentration of a chemical that can reliably be distinguished from a zero concentration.

Detention Time: 1. The theoretical calculated time required for a small amount of water to pass through a tank at a given rate of flow. 2. The actual time that a small amount of water is in a settling basin, flocculating basin, or rapid-mix chamber. 3. In storage reservoirs, the length of time water will be held before being used.

Detergent: Synthetic washing agent that helps to remove dirt and oil. Some contain compounds which kill useful bacteria and encourage algae growth when they are in wastewater that reaches receiving waters.

Development Effects: Adverse effects such as altered growth, structural abnormality, functional deficiency, or death observed in a developing organism.

Dewater: 1. Remove or separate a portion of the water in a sludge or slurry to dry the sludge so it can be handled and disposed of. 2. Remove or drain the water from a tank or trench.

Diatomaceous Earth (Diatomite): A chalk-like material (fossilized diatoms) used to filter out solid waste in wastewater treatment plants; also used as an active ingredient in some powdered pesticides.

Diazinon: An insecticide. In 1986, EPA banned its use on open areas such as sod farms and golf courses because it posed a danger to migratory birds. The ban did not apply to agricultural, home lawn or commercial establishment uses.

Dibenzofurans: A group of organic compounds, some of which are toxic.

Dicofol: A pesticide used on citrus fruits.

Diffused Air: A type of aeration that forces oxygen into sewage by pumping air through perforated pipes inside a holding tank.

Diffusion: The movement of suspended or dissolved particles (or molecules) from a more concentrated to a less concentrated area. The process tends to distribute the particles or molecules more uniformly.

Digester: In wastewater treatment, a closed tank; in solid-waste conversion, a unit in which bacterial action is induced and accelerated in order to break down organic matter and establish the proper carbon to nitrogen ratio.

Digestion: The biochemical decomposition of organic matter, resulting in partial gasification, liquefaction, and mineralization of pollutants.

Dike: A low wall that can act as a barrier to prevent a spill from spreading.

Diluent: Any liquid or solid material used to dilute or carry an active ingredient.

Dilution Ratio: The relationship between the volume of water in a stream and the volume of incoming water. It affects the ability of the stream to assimilate waste.

Dimictic: Lakes and reservoirs that freeze over and normally go through two stratifications and two mixing cycles a year.

Dinocap: A fungicide used primarily by apple growers to control summer diseases. EPA proposed restrictions on its use in 1986 when laboratory tests found it caused birth defects in rabbits.

Dinoseb: A herbicide that is also used as a fungicide and insecticide. It was banned by EPA in 1986 because it posed the risk of birth defects and sterility.

Dioxin: Any of a family of compounds known chemically as dibenzo-p-dioxins. Concern about them arises from their potential toxicity as contaminants in commercial products. Tests on laboratory animals indicate that it is one of the more toxic anthropogenic (man-made) compounds.

Direct Discharger: A municipal or industrial facility which introduces pollution through a defined conveyance or system such as outlet pipes; a point source.

Direct Filtration: A method of treating water which consists of the addition of coagulent chemicals, flash mixing, coagulation, minimal flocculation, and filtration. Sedimentation is not uses.

Direct Push: Technology used for performing subsurface investigations by driving, pushing, and/or vibrating small-diameter hollow steel rods into the ground/ Also known as direct drive, drive point, or push technology.

Direct Runoff: Water that flows over the ground surface or through the ground directly into streams, rivers, and lakes.

Discharge: Flow of surface water in a stream or canal or the outflow of ground water from a flowing artesian well, ditch, or spring. Can also apply tp discharge of liquid effluent from a facility or to chemical emissions into the air through designated venting mechanisms.

Disinfectant: A chemical or physical process that kills pathogenic organisms in water, air, or on surfaces. Chlorine is often used to disinfect sewage treatment effluent, water supplies, wells, and swimming pools.

Disinfectant By-Product: A compound formed by the reaction of a disinfenctant such as chlorine with organic material in the water supply; a chemical byproduct of the disinfection process..

Disinfectant Time: The time it takes water to move from the point of disinfectant application (or the previous point of residual disinfectant measurement) to a point before or at the point where the residual disinfectant is measured. In pipelines, the time is calculated by dividing the internal volume of the pipe by he maximum hourly flow rate; within mixing basins and storage reservoirs it is determined by tracer studies of an equivalent demonstration.

Dispersant: A chemical agent used to break up concentrations of organic material such as spilled oil.

Displacement Savings: Saving realized by displacing purchases of natural gas or electricity from a local utility by using landfill gas for power and heat.

Disposables: Consumer products, other items, and packaging used once or a few times and discarded.

Disposal: Final placement or destruction of toxic, radioactive, or other wastes; surplus or banned pesticides or other chemicals; polluted soils; and drums containing hazardous materials from removal actions or accidental releases. Disposal may be accomplished through use of approved secure landfills, surface impoundments, land farming, deep-well injection, ocean dumping, or incineration.

Disposal Facilities: Repositories for solid waste, including landfills and combustors intended for permanent containment or destruction of waste materials. Excludes transfer stations and composting facilities.

Dissolved Oxygen (DO): The oxygen freely available in water, vital to fish and other aquatic life and for the prevention of odors. DO levels are considered a most important indicator of a water body's ability to support desirable aquatic life. Secondary and advanced waste treatment are generally designed to ensure adequate DO in waste-receiving waters.

Dissolved Solids: Disintegrated organic and inorganic material in water. Excessive amounts make water unfit to drink or use in industrial processes.

Distillation: The act of purifying liquids through boiling, so that the steam or gaseous vapors condense to a pure liquid. Pollutants and contaminants may remain in a concentrated residue.

Disturbance: Any event or series of events that disrupt ecosystem, community, or population structure and alters the physical environment.

Diversion: 1. Use of part of a stream flow as water supply. 2. A channel with a supporting ridge on the lower side constructed across a slope to divert water at a non-erosive velocity to sites where it can be used and disposed of.

Diversion Rate: The percentage of waste materials diverted from traditional disposal such as landfilling or incineration to be recycled, composted, or re-used.

DNA Hybridization: Use of a segment of DNA, called a DNA probe, to identify its complementary DNA; used to detect specific genes.

Dobson Unit (DU): Units of ozone level measurement. measurement of ozone levels. If, for example, 100 DU of ozone were brought to the earth's surface they would form a layer one millimeter thick. Ozone levels vary geographically, even in the absence of ozone depletion.

Domestic Application: Pesticide application in and around houses, office buildings, motels, and other living or working areas.(See: residential use.)

Dosage/Dose: 1. The actual quantity of a chemical administered to an organism or to which it is exposed. 2. The amount of a substance that reaches a specific tissue (e.g. the liver). 3. The amount of a substance available for interaction with metabolic processes after crossing the outer boundary of an organism. (See: absorbed dose, administered dose, applied dose, potential dose.)

Dose Equivalent: The product of the absorbed dose from ionizing radiation and such factors as account for biological differences due to the type of radiation and its distribution in the body in the body.

Dose Rate: In exposure assessment, dose per time unit (e.g. mg/day), sometimes also called dosage.

Dose Response: Shifts in toxicological responses of an individual (such as alterations in severity) or populations (such as alterations in incidence) that are related to changes in the dose of any given substance.

Dose Response Curve: Graphical representation of the relationship between the dose of a stressor and the biological response thereto.

Dose-Response Assessment: 1. Estimating the potency of a chemical. 2. In exposure assessment, the process of determining the relationship between the dose of a stressor and a specific biological response. 3. Evaluating the quantitative relationship between dose and toxicological responses.

Dose-Response Relationship: The quantitative relationship between the amount of exposure to a substance and the extent of toxic injury or disease produced.

Dosimeter: An instrument to measure dosage; many so-called dosimeters actually measure exposure rather than dosage. Dosimetry is the process or technology of measuring and/or estimating dosage.

DOT Reportable Quantity: The quantity of a substance specified in a U.S. Department of Transportation regulation that triggers labeling, packaging and other requirements related to shipping such substances.

Downgradient: The direction that groundwater flows; similar to "downstream" for surface water.

Downstream Processors: Industries dependent on crop production (e.g. canneries and food processors).

DP Hole: Hole in the ground made with DP equipment. (See: direct push.)

Draft: 1. The act of drawing or removing water from a tank or reservoir. 2. The water which is drawn or removed.

Draft Permit: A preliminary permit drafted and published by EPA; subject to public review and comment before final action on the application.

Drainage: Improving the productivity of agricultural land by removing excess water from the soil by such means as ditches or subsurface drainage tiles.

Drainage Basin: The area of land that drains water, sediment, and dissolved materials to a common outlet at some point along a stream channel.

Drainage Well: A well drilled to carry excess water off agricultural fields. Because they act as a funnel from the surface to the groundwater below. Drainage wells can contribute to groundwater pollution.

Drawdown: 1. The drop in the water table or level of water in the ground when water is being pumped from a well. 2. The amount of water used from a tank or reservoir. 3. The drop in the water level of a tank or reservoir.

Dredging: Removal of mud from the bottom of water bodies. This can disturb the ecosystem and causes silting that kills aquatic life. Dredging of contaminated muds can expose biota to heavy metals and other toxics. Dredging activities may be subject to regulation under Section 404 of the Clean Water Act.

Drilling Fluid: Fluid used to lubricate the bit and convey drill cuttings to the surface with rotary drilling equipment. Usually composed of bentonite slurry or muddy water. Can become contaminated, leading to cross contamination, and may require special disposal. Not used with DP methods

Drinking Water Equivalent Level: Protective level of exposure related to potentially non-carcinogenic effects of chemicals that are also known to cause cancer.

Drinking Water State Revolving Fund: The Fund provides capitalization grants to states to develop drinking water revolving loan funds to help finance system infrastructure improvements, assure source-water protection, enhance operation and management of drinking-water systems, and otherwise promote local water-system compliance and protection of public health.

Drive Casing: Heavy duty steel casing driven along with the sampling tool in cased DP systems. Keeps the hole open between sampling runs and is not removed until last sample has been collected.

Drive Point Profiler: An exposed groundwater DP system used to collect multiple depth-discrete groundwater samples. Ports in the tip of the probe connect to an internal stainless steel or teflon tube that extends to the surface. Samples are collected via suction or airlift methods. Deionized water is pumped down through the ports to prevent plugging while driving the tool to the next sampling depth.

Drop-off: Recyclable materials collection method in which individuals bring them to a designated collection site.

Dual-Phase Extraction: Active withdrawal of both liquid and gas phases from a well usually involving the use of a vacuum pump.

Dump: A site used to dispose of solid waste without environmental controls.

Duplicate: A second aliquot or sample that is treated the same as the original sample in order to determine the precision of the analytical method. (See: aliquot.)

Dustfall Jar: An open container used to collect large particles from the air for measurement and analysis.

Dynamometer. A device used to place a load on an engine and measure its performance.

Dystrophic Lakes: Acidic, shallow bodies of water that contain much humus and/or other organic matter; contain many plants but few fish.

E

Ecological Entity: In ecological risk assessment, a general term referring to a species, a group of species, an ecosystem function or characteristic, or a specific habitat or biome.

Ecological/Environmental Sustainability: Maintenance of ecosystem components and functions for future generations.

Ecological Exposure: Exposure of a non-human organism to a stressor.

Ecological Impact: The effect that a man-caused or natural activity has on living organisms and their non-living (abiotic) environment.

Ecological Indicator: A characteristic of an ecosystem that is related to, or derived from, a measure of biotic or abiotic variable, that can provide quantitative information on ecological structure and function. An indicator can contribute to a measure of integrity and sustainability.

Ecological Integrity: A living system exhibits integrity if, when subjected to disturbance, it sustains and organizes self-correcting ability to recover toward a biomass end-state that is normal for that system. End-states other than the pristine or naturally whole may be accepted as normal and good.

Ecological Risk Assessment: The application of a formal framework, analytical process, or model to estimate the effects of human actions(s) on a natural resource and to interpret the significance of those effects in light of the uncertainties identified in each component of the assessment process. Such analysis includes initial hazard identification, exposure and dose-response assessments, and risk characterization.

Ecology: The relationship of living things to one another and their environment, or the study of such relationships.

Economic Poisons: Chemicals used to control pests and to defoliate cash crops such as cotton.

Ecosphere: The "bio-bubble" that contains life on earth, in surface waters, and in the air. (See: biosphere.)

Ecosystem: The interacting system of a biological community and its non-living environmental surroundings.

Ecosystem Structure: Attributes related to the instantaneous physical state of an ecosystem; examples include species population density, species richness or evenness, and standing crop biomass.

Ecotone: A habitat created by the juxtaposition of distinctly different habitats; an edge habitat; or an ecological zone or boundary where two or more ecosystems meet.

Effluent: Wastewater—treated or untreated—that flows out of a treatment plant, sewer, or industrial outfall. Generally refers to wastes discharged into surface waters.

Effluent Guidelines: Technical EPA documents which set effluent limitations for given industries and pollutants.

Effluent Limitation: Restrictions established by a state or EPA on quantities, rates, and concentrations in wastewater discharges.

Effluent Standard: (See: effluent limitation.)

Ejector: A device used to disperse a chemical solution into water being treated.

Electrodialysis: A process that uses electrical current applied to permeable membranes to remove minerals from water. Often used to desalinize salty or brackish water.

Electromagnetic Geophysical Methods: Ways to measure subsurface conductivity via low-frequency electromagnetic induction.

Electrostatic Precipitator (ESP): A device that removes particles from a gas stream (smoke) after combustion occurs. The ESP imparts an electrical charge to the particles, causing them to adhere to metal plates inside the precipitator. Rapping on the plates causes the particles to fall into a hopper for disposal.

Eligible Costs: The construction costs for wastewater treatment works upon which EPA grants are based.

EMAP Data: Environmental monitoring data collected under the auspices of the Environmental Monitoring and Assessment Program. All EMAP data share the common attribute of being of known quality, having been collected in the context of explicit data quality objectives (DQOs) and a consistent quality assurance program.

Emergency and Hazardous Chemical Inventory: An annual report by facilities having one or more extremely hazardous substances or hazardous chemicals above certain weight limits.

Emergency (Chemical): A situation created by an accidental release or spill of hazardous chemicals that poses a threat to the safety of workers, residents, the environment, or property.

Emergency Episode: (See: air pollution episode.)

Emergency Exemption: Provision in FIFRA under which EPA can grant temporary exemption to a state or another federal agency to allow the use of a pesticide product not registered for that particular use. Such actions involve unanticipated and/or severe pest problems where there is not time or interest by a manufacturer to register the product for that use. (Registrants cannot apply for such exemptions.)

Emergency Removal Action: 1. Steps take to remove contaminated materials that pose imminent threats to local residents (e.g. removal of leaking drums or the excavation of explosive waste.) 2. The state record of such removals.

Emergency Response Values: Concentrations of chemicals, published by various groups, defining acceptable levels for short-term exposures in emergencies.

Emergency Suspension: Suspension of a pesticide product registration due to an imminent hazard. The action immediately halts distribution, sale, and sometimes actual use of the pesticide involved.

Emission: Pollution discharged into the atmosphere from smokestacks, other vents, and surface areas of commercial or industrial facilities; from residential chimneys; and from motor vehicle, locomotive, or aircraft exhausts.

Emission Cap: A limit designed to prevent projected growth in emissions from existing and future stationary sources from eroding any mandated reductions. Generally, such provisions require that any emission growth from facilities under the restrictions be offset by equivalent reductions at other facilities under the same cap. (See: emissions trading.)

Emission Factor: The relationship between the amount of pollution produced and the amount of raw material processed. For example, an emission factor for a blast furnace making iron would be the number of pounds of particulates per ton of raw materials.

Emission Inventory: A listing, by source, of the amount of air pollutants discharged into the atmosphere of a community; used to establish emission standards.

Emission Standard: The maximum amount of air polluting discharge legally allowed from a single source, mobile or stationary.

Emissions Trading: The creation of surplus emission reductions at certain stacks, vents or similar emissions sources and the use of this surplus to meet or redefine pollution requirements applicable to other emissions sources. This allows one source to increase emissions when another source reduces them, maintaining an overall constant emission level. Facilities that reduce emissions substantially may "bank" their "credits" or sell them to other facilities or industries.

Emulsifier: A chemical that aids in suspending one liquid in another. Usually an organic chemical in an aqueous solution.

Encapsulation: The treatment of asbestos-containing material with a liquid that covers the surface with a protective coating or embeds fibers in an adhesive matrix to prevent their release into the air.

Enclosure: Putting an airtight, impermeable, permanent barrier around asbestos-containing materials to prevent the release of asbestos fibers into the air.

End User: Consumer of products for the purpose of recycling. Excludes products for re-use or combustion for energy recovery.

End-of-the-pipe: Technologies such as scrubbers on smokestacks and catalytic convertors on automobile tailpipes that reduce emissions of pollutants after they have formed.

End-use Product: A pesticide formulation for field or other end use. The label has instructions for use or application to control pests or regulate plant growth. The term excludes products used to formulate other pesticide products.

Endangered Species: Animals, birds, fish, plants, or other living organisms threatened with extinction by anthropogenic (man-caused) or other natural changes in their environment. Requirements for declaring a species endangered are contained in the Endangered Species Act.

Endangerment Assessment: A study to determine the nature and extent of contamination at a site on the National Priorities List and the risks posed to public health or the environment. EPA or the state conducts the study when a legal action is to be taken to direct potentially responsible parties to clean up a site or pay for it. An endangerment assessment supplements a remedial investigation.

Endrin: A pesticide toxic to freshwater and marine aquatic life that produces adverse health effects in domestic water supplies.

Energy Management System: A control system capable of monitoring environmental and system loads and adjusting HVAC operations accordingly in order to conserve energy while maintaining comfort.

Energy Recovery: Obtaining energy from waste through a variety of processes (e.g. combustion).

Enforceable Requirements: Conditions or limitations in permits issued under the Clean Water Act Section 402 or 404 that, if violated, could result in the issuance of a compliance order or initiation of a civil or criminal action under federal or applicable state laws. If a permit has not been issued, the term includes any requirement which, in the Regional Administrator's judgement, would be included in the permit when issued. Where no permit applies, the term includes any requirement which the RA determines is necessary for the best practical waste treatment technology to meet applicable criteria.

Enforcement: EPA, state, or local legal actions to obtain compliance with environmental laws, rules, regulations, or agreements and/or obtain penalties or criminal sanctions for violations. Enforcement procedures may vary, depending on the requirements of different environmental laws and related implementing regulations. Under CERCLA, for example, EPA will seek to require potentially responsible parties to clean up a Superfund site, or pay for the cleanup, whereas under the Clean Air Act the Agency may invoke sanctions against cities failing to meet ambient air quality standards that could prevent certain types of construction or federal funding. In other situations, if investigations by EPA and state agencies uncover willful violations, criminal trials and penalties are sought.

Enforcement Decision Document (EDD): A document that provides an explanation to the public of EPA's selection of the cleanup alternative at enforcement sites on the National Priorities List. Similar to a Record of Decision.

Engineered Controls: Method of managing environmental and health risks by placing a barrier between the contamination and the rest of the site, thus limiting exposure pathways.

Enhanced Inspection and Maintenance (I&M): An improved automobile inspection and maintenance program—aimed at reducing automobile emissions—that contains, at a minimum, more vehicle types and model years, tighter inspection, and better management practices. It may also include annual computerized or centralized inspections, under-the-hood inspection—for signs of tampering with pollution control equipment—and increased repair waiver cost.

Enrichment: The addition of nutrients (e.g. nitrogen, phosphorus, carbon compounds) from sewage effluent or agricultural runoff to surface water, greatly increases the growth potential for algae and other aquatic plants.

Entrain: To trap bubbles in water either mechanically through turbulence or chemically through a reaction.

Environment: The sum of all external conditions affecting the life, development and survival of an organism.

Environmental Assessment: An environmental analysis prepared pursuant to the National Environmental Policy Act to determine whether a federal action would significantly affect the environment and thus require a more detailed environmental impact statement.

Environmental Audit: An independent assessment of the current status of a party's compliance with applicable environmental requirements or of a party's environmental compliance policies, practices, and controls.

Environmental/Ecological Risk: The potential for adverse effects on living organisms associated with pollution of the environment by effluents, emissions, wastes, or accidental chemical releases; energy use; or the depletion of natural resources.

Environmental Equity/Justice: Equal protection from environmental hazards for individuals, groups, or communities regardless of race, ethnicity, or economic status. This applies to the development, implementation, and enforcement of environmental laws, regulations, and policies, and implies that no population of people should be forced to shoulder a disproportionate share of negative environmental impacts of pollution or environmental hazard due to a lack of political or economic strength levels.

Environmental Exposure: Human exposure to pollutants originating from facility emissions. Threshold levels are not necessarily surpassed, but low-level chronic pollutant exposure is one of the most common forms of environmental exposure (See: threshold level).

Environmental Fate: The destiny of a chemical or biological pollutant after release into the environment.

Environmental Fate Data: Data that characterize a pesticide's fate in the ecosystem, considering factors that foster its degradation (light, water, microbes), pathways and resultant products.

Environmental Impact Statement: A document required of federal agencies by the National Environmental Policy Act for major projects or legislative proposals significantly affecting the environment. A tool for decision making, it describes the positive and negative effects of the undertaking and cites alternative actions.

Environmental Indicator: A measurement, statistic or value that provides a proximate gauge or evidence of the effects of environmental management programs or of the state or condition of the environment.

Environmental Justice: The fair treatment of people of all races, cultures, incomes, and educational levels with respect to the development and enforcement of environmental laws, regulations, and policies.

Environmental Lien: A charge, security, or encumbrance on a property's title to secure payment of cost or debt arising from response actions, cleanup, or other remediation of hazardous substances or petroleum products.

Environmental Medium: A major environmental category that surrounds or contacts humans, animals, plants, and other organisms (e.g. surface water, ground water, soil or air) and through which chemicals or pollutants move. (See: ambient medium, biological medium.)

Environmental Monitoring for Public Access and Community Tracking: Joint EPA, NOAA, and USGS program to provide timely and effective communication of environmental data and information through improved and updated technology solutions that support timely environmental monitoring reporting, interpreting, and use of the information for the benefit of the public. (See: real-time monitoring.)

Environmental Response Team: EPA experts located in Edison, N.J., and Cincinnati, OH, who can provide around-the-clock technical assistance to EPA regional offices and states during all types of hazardous waste site emergencies and spills of hazardous substances.

Environmental Site Assessment: The process of determining whether contamination is present on a parcel of real property.

Environmental Sustainability: Long-term maintenance of ecosystem components and functions for future generations.

Environmental Tobacco Smoke: Mixture of smoke from the burning end of a cigarette, pipe, or cigar and smoke exhaled by the smoker. (See: passive smoking/secondhand smoke.)

Epidemiology: Study of the distribution of disease, or other health-related states and events in human populations, as related to age, sex, occupation, ethnicity, and economic status in order to identify and alleviate health problems and promote better health.

Epilimnion: Upper waters of a thermally stratified lake subject to wind action.

Episode (Pollution): An air pollution incident in a given area caused by a concentration of atmospheric pollutants under meteorological conditions that may result in a significant increase in illnesses or deaths. May also describe water pollution events or hazardous material spills.

Equilibrium: In relation to radiation, the state at which the radioactivity of consecutive elements within a radioactive series is neither increasing nor decreasing.

Equivalent Method: Any method of sampling and analyzing for air pollution which has been demonstrated to the EPA Administrator's satisfaction to be, under specific conditions, an acceptable alternative to normally used reference methods.

Erosion: The wearing away of land surface by wind or water, intensified by land-clearing practices related to farming, residential or industrial development, road building, or logging.

Established Treatment Technologies: Technologies for which cost and performance data are readily available. (See: Innovative treatment technologies.)

Estimated Environmental Concentration: The estimated pesticide concentration in an ecosystem.

Estuary: Region of interaction between rivers and near-shore ocean waters, where tidal action and river flow mix fresh and salt water. Such areas include bays, mouths of rivers, salt marshes, and lagoons. These brackish water ecosystems shelter and feed marine life, birds, and wildlife. (See: wetlands.)

Ethanol: An alternative automotive fuel derived from grain and corn; usually blended with gasoline to form gasohol.

Ethylene Dibromide (EDB): A chemical used as an agricultural fumigant and in certain industrial processes. Extremely toxic and found to be a carcinogen in laboratory animals, EDB has been banned for most agricultural uses in the United States.

Eutrophic Lakes: Shallow, murky bodies of water with concentrations of plant nutrients causing excessive production of algae. (See: dystrophic lakes.)

Eutrophication: The slow aging process during which a lake, estuary, or bay evolves into a bog or marsh and eventually disappears. During the later stages of eutrophication the water body is choked by abundant plant life due to higher levels of nutritive compounds such as nitrogen and phosphorus. Human activities can accelerate the process.

Evaporation Ponds: Areas where sewage sludge is dumped and dried.

Evapotranspiration: The loss of water from the soil both by evaporation and by transpiration from the plants growing in the soil.

Exceedance: Violation of the pollutant levels permitted by environmental protection standards.

Exclusion: In the asbestos program, one of several situations that permit a Local Education Agency (LEA) to delete one or more of the items required by the Asbestos Hazard Emergency Response Act (AHERA); e.g. records of previous asbestos sample collection and analysis may be used by the accredited inspector in lieu of AHERA bulk sampling.

Exclusionary Ordinance: Zoning that excludes classes of persons or businesses from a particular neighborhood or area.

Exempt Solvent: Specific organic compounds not subject to requirements of regulation because they are deemed by EPA to be of negligible photochemical reactivity.

Exempted Aquifer: Underground bodies of water defined in the Underground Injection Control program as aquifers that are potential sources of drinking water though not being used as such, and thus exempted from regulations barring underground injection activities.

Exemption: A state (with primacy) may exempt a public water system from a requirement involving a Maximum Contaminant Level (MCL), treatment technique, or both, if the system cannot comply due to compelling economic or other factors, or because the system was in operation before the requirement or MCL was instituted; and the exemption will not create a public health risk. (See: variance.)

Exotic Species: A species that is not indigenous to a region.

Experimental Use Permit: Obtained by manufacturers for testing new pesticides or uses thereof whenever they conduct experimental field studies to support registration on 10 acres or more of land or one acre or more of water.

Experimental Use Permit: A permit granted by EPA that allows a producer to conduct tests of a new pesticide, product and/or use outside the laboratory. The testing is usually done on ten or more acres of land or water surface.

Explosive Limits: The amounts of vapor in the air that form explosive mixtures; limits are expressed as lower and upper limits and give the range of vapor concentrations in air that will explode if an ignition source is present.

Exports : In solid waste program, municipal solid waste and recyclables transported outside the state or locality where they originated.

Exposure: The amount of radiation or pollutant present in a given environment that represents a potential health threat to living organisms.

Exposure Assessment: Identifying the pathways by which toxicants may reach individuals, estimating how much of a chemical an individual is likely to be exposed to, and estimating the number likely to be exposed.

Exposure Concentration: The concentration of a chemical or other pollutant representing a health threat in a given environment.

Exposure Indicator: A characteristic of the environment measured to provide evidence of the occurrence or magnitude of a response indicator's exposure to a chemical or biological stress.

Exposure Level: The amount (concentration) of a chemical at the absorptive surfaces of an organism.

Exposure Pathway: The path from sources of pollutants via, soil, water, or food to man and other species or settings.

Exposure Route: The way a chemical or pollutant enters an organism after contact; i.e. by ingestion, inhalation, or dermal absorption.

Exposure-Response Relationship: The relationship between exposure level and the incidence of adverse effects.

Extraction Procedure (EP Toxic): Determining toxicity by a procedure which simulates leaching; if a certain concentration of a toxic substance can be leached from a waste, that waste is considered hazardous, i.e."EP Toxic."

Extraction Well: A discharge well used to remove groundwater or air.

Extremely Hazardous Substances: Any of 406 chemicals identified by EPA as toxic, and listed under SARA Title III. The list is subject to periodic revision.

F

Fabric Filter: A cloth device that catches dust particles from industrial emissions.

Facilities Plans: Plans and studies related to the construction of treatment works necessary to comply with the Clean Water Act or RCRA. A facilities plan investigates needs and provides information on the cost-effectiveness of alternatives, a recommended plan, an environmental assessment of the recommendations, and descriptions of the treatment works, costs, and a completion schedule.

Facility Emergency Coordinator: Representative of a facility covered by environmental law (e.g, a chemical plant) who participates in the emergency reporting process with the Local Emergency Planning Committee (LEPC).

Facultative Bacteria: Bacteria that can live under aerobic or anaerobic conditions.

Feasibility Study: 1. Analysis of the practicability of a proposal; e.g., a description and analysis of potential cleanup alternatives for a site such as one on the National Priorities List. The feasibility study usually recommends selection of a cost-effective alternative. It usually starts as soon as the remedial investigation is underway; together, they are commonly referred to as the "RI/FS". 2. A small-scale investigation of a problem to ascertain whether a proposed research approach is likely to provide useful data.

Fecal Coliform Bacteria: Bacteria found in the intestinal tracts of mammals. Their presence in water or sludge is an indicator of pollution and possible contamination by pathogens.

Federal Implementation Plan: Under current law, a federally implemented plan to achieve attainment of air quality standards, used when a state is unable to develop an adequate plan.

Federal Motor Vehicle Control Program: All federal actions aimed at controlling pollution from motor vehicles by such efforts as establishing and enforcing tailpipe and evaporative emission standards for new vehicles, testing methods development, and guidance to states operating inspection and maintenance programs. Federally designated area that is required to meet and maintain federal ambient air quality standards. May include nearby locations in the same state or nearby states that share common air pollution problems.

Feedlot: A confined area for the controlled feeding of animals. Tends to concentrate large amounts of animal waste that cannot be absorbed by the soil and, hence, may be carried to nearby streams or lakes by rainfall runoff.

Fen: A type of wetland that accumulates peat deposits. Fens are less acidic than bogs, deriving most of their water from groundwater rich in calcium and magnesium. (See: wetlands.)

Ferrous Metals: Magnetic metals derived from iron or steel; products made from ferrous metals include appliances, furniture, containers, and packaging like steel drums and barrels. Recycled products include processing tin/steel cans, strapping, and metals from appliances into new products.

FIFRA Pesticide Ingredient: An ingredient of a pesticide that must be registered with EPA under the Federal Insecticide, Fungicide, and Rodenticide Act. Products making pesticide claims must register under FIFRA and may be subject to labeling and use requirements.

Fill: Man-made deposits of natural soils or rock products and waste materials.

Filling: Depositing dirt, mud or other materials into aquatic areas to create more dry land, usually for agricultural or commercial development purposes, often with ruinous ecological consequences.

Filter Strip: Strip or area of vegetation used for removing sediment, organic matter, and other pollutants from runoff and wastewater.

Filtration: A treatment process, under the control of qualified operators, for removing solid (particulate) matter from water by means of porous media such as sand or a man-made filter; often used to remove particles that contain pathogens.

Financial Assurance for Closure: Documentation or proof that an owner or operator of a facility such as a landfill or other waste repository is capable of paying the projected costs of closing the facility and monitoring it afterwards as provided in RCRA regulations.

Finding of No Significant Impact: A document prepared by a federal agency showing why a proposed action would not have a significant impact on the environment and thus would not require preparation of an Environmental Impact Statement. An FNSI is based on the results of an environmental assessment.

Finished Water: Water is "finished" when it has passed through all the processes in a water treatment plant and is ready to be delivered to consumers.

First Draw: The water that comes out when a tap is first opened, likely to have the highest level of lead contamination from plumbing materials.

Fix a Sample: A sample is "fixed" in the field by adding chemicals that prevent water quality indicators of interest in the sample from changing before laboratory measurements are made.

Fixed-Location Monitoring: Sampling of an environmental or ambient medium for pollutant concentration at one location continuously or repeatedly.

Flammable: Any material that ignites easily and will burn rapidly.

Flare: A control device that burns hazardous materials to prevent their release into the environment; may operate continuously or intermittently, usually on top of a stack.

Flash Point: The lowest temperature at which evaporation of a substance produces sufficient vapor to form an ignitable mixture with air.

Floc: A clump of solids formed in sewage by biological or chemical action.

Flocculation: Process by which clumps of solids in water or sewage aggregate through biological or chemical action so they can be separated from water or sewage.

Floodplain: The flat or nearly flat land along a river or stream or in a tidal area that is covered by water during a flood.

Floor Sweep: Capture of heavier-than-air gases that collect at floor level.

Flow Rate: The rate, expressed in gallons -or liters-per-hour, at which a fluid escapes from a hole or fissure in a tank. Such measurements are also made of liquid waste, effluent, and surface water movement.

Flowable: Pesticide and other formulations in which the active ingredients are finely ground insoluble solids suspended in a liquid. They are mixed with water for application.

Flowmeter: A gauge indicating the velocity of wastewater moving through a treatment plant or of any liquid moving through various industrial processes.

Flue Gas: The air coming out of a chimney after combustion in the burner it is venting. It can include nitrogen oxides, carbon oxides, water vapor, sulfur oxides, particles and many chemical pollutants.

Flue Gas Desulfurization: A technology that employs a sorbent, usually lime or limestone, to remove sulfur dioxide from the gases produced by burning fossil fuels. Flue gas desulfurization is current state-of-the art technology for major SO_2 emitters, like power plants.

Fluidized: A mass of solid particles that is made to flow like a liquid by injection of water or gas is said to have been fluidized. In water treatment, a bed of filter media is fluidized by backwashing water through the filter.

Fluidized Bed Incinerator: An incinerator that uses a bed of hot sand or other granular material to transfer heat directly to waste. Used mainly for destroying municipal sludge.

Flume: A natural or man-made channel that diverts water.

Fluoridation: The addition of a chemical to increase the concentration of fluoride ions in drinking water to reduce the incidence of tooth decay.

Fluorides: Gaseous, solid, or dissolved compounds containing fluorine that result from industrial processes. Excessive amounts in food can lead to fluorosis.

Fluorocarbons (FCs): Any of a number of organic compounds analogous to hydrocarbons in which one or more hydrogen atoms are replaced by fluorine. Once used in the United States as a propellant for domestic aerosols, they are now found mainly in coolants and some industrial processes. FCs containing chlorine are called chlorofluorocarbons (CFCs). They are believed to be modifying the ozone layer in the stratosphere, thereby allowing more harmful solar radiation to reach the Earth's surface.

Flush: 1. To open a cold-water tap to clear out all the water which may have been sitting for a long time in the pipes. In new homes, to flush a system means to send large volumes of water gushing through the unused pipes to remove loose particles of solder and flux. 2. To force large amounts of water through a system to clean out piping or tubing, and storage or process tanks.

Flux: 1. A flowing or flow. 2. A substance used to help metals fuse together.

Fly Ash: Non-combustible residual particles expelled by flue gas.

Fogging: Applying a pesticide by rapidly heating the liquid chemical so that it forms very fine droplets that resemble smoke or fog. Used to destroy mosquitoes, black flies, and similar pests.

Food Chain: A sequence of organisms, each of which uses the next, lower member of the sequence as a food source.

Food Processing Waste: Food residues produced during agricultural and industrial operations.

Food Waste: Uneaten food and food preparation wastes from residences and commercial establishments such as grocery stores, restaurants, and produce stands, institutional cafeterias and kitchens, and industrial sources like employee lunchrooms.

Food Web: The feeding relationships by which energy and nutrients are transferred from one species to another.

Formaldehyde: A colorless, pungent, and irritating gas, CH20, used chiefly as a disinfectant and preservative and in synthesizing other compounds like resins.

Formulation: The substances comprising all active and inert ingredients in a pesticide.

Fossil Fuel: Fuel derived from ancient organic remains; e.g. peat, coal, crude oil, and natural gas.

Fracture: A break in a rock formation due to structural stresses; e.g. faults, shears, joints, and planes of fracture cleavage.

Free Product: A petroleum hydrocarbon in the liquid free or non aqueous phase. (See: non-aqueous phase liquid.)

Freeboard: 1. Vertical distance from the normal water surface to the top of a confining wall. 2. Vertical distance from the sand surface to the underside of a trough in a sand filter.

Fresh Water: Water that generally contains less than 1,000 milligrams-per-liter of dissolved solids.

Friable: Capable of being crumbled, pulverized, or reduced to powder by hand pressure.

Friable Asbestos: Any material containing more than one-percent asbestos, and that can be crumbled or reduced to powder by hand pressure. (May include previously non-friable material which becomes broken or damaged by mechanical force.)

Fuel Economy Standard: The Corporate Average Fuel Economy Standard (CAFE) effective in 1978. It enhanced the national fuel conservation effort imposing a miles-per-gallon floor for motor vehicles.

Fuel Efficiency: The proportion of energy released by fuel combustion that is converted into useful energy.

Fuel Switching: 1. A precombustion process whereby a low-sulfur coal is used in place of a higher sulfur coal in a power plant to reduce sulfur dioxide emissions. 2. Illegally using leaded gasoline in a motor vehicle designed to use only unleaded.

Fugitive Emissions: Emissions not caught by a capture system.

Fume: Tiny particles trapped in vapor in a gas stream.

Fumigant: A pesticide vaporized to kill pests. Used in buildings and greenhouses.

Functional Equivalent: Term used to describe EPA's decision-making process and its relationship to the environmental review conducted under the National Environmental Policy Act (NEPA). A review is considered functionally equivalent when it addresses the substantive components of a NEPA review.

Fungicide: Pesticides which are used to control, deter, or destroy fungi.

Fungistat: A chemical that keeps fungi from growing.

Fungus (Fungi): Molds, mildews, yeasts, mushrooms, and puffballs, a group of organisms lacking in chlorophyll (i.e. are not photosynthetic) and which are usually non-mobile, filamentous, and multicellular. Some grow in soil, others attach themselves to decaying trees and other plants whence they obtain nutrients. Some are pathogens, others stabilize sewage and digest composted waste.

Furrow Irrigation: Irrigation method in which water travels through the field by means of small channels between each groups of rows.

Future Liability: Refers to potentially responsible parties' obligations to pay for additional response activities beyond those specified in the Record of Decision or Consent Decree.

G

Game Fish: Species like trout, salmon, or bass, caught for sport. Many of them show more sensitivity to environmental change than "rough" fish.

Garbage: Animal and vegetable waste resulting from the handling, storage, sale, preparation, cooking, and serving of foods.

Gas Chromatograph/Mass Spectrometer: Instrument that identifies the molecular composition and concentrations of various chemicals in water and soil samples.

Gasahol: Mixture of gasoline and ethanol derived from fermented agricultural products containing at least nine percent ethanol. Gasohol emissions contain less carbon monoxide than those from gasoline.

Gasification: Conversion of solid material such as coal into a gas for use as a fuel.

Gasoline Volatility: The property of gasoline whereby it evaporates into a vapor. Gasoline vapor is a mixture of volatile organic compounds.

General Permit: A permit applicable to a class or category of dischargers.

General Reporting Facility: A facility having one or more hazardous chemicals above the 10,000 pound threshold for planning quantities. Such facilities must file MSDS and emergency inventory information with the SERC, LEPC, and local fire departments.

Generally Recognized as Safe (GRAS): Designation by the FDA that a chemical or substance (including certain pesticides) added to food is considered safe by experts, and so is exempted from the usual FFDCA food additive tolerance requirements.

Generator: 1. A facility or mobile source that emits pollutants into the air or releases hazardous waste into water or soil. 2. Any person, by site, whose act or process produces regulated medical waste or whose act first causes such waste to become subject to regulation. Where more than one person (e.g. doctors with separate medical practices) are located in the same building, each business entity is a separate generator.

Genetic Engineering: A process of inserting new genetic information into existing cells in order to modify a specific organism for the purpose of changing one of its characteristics.

Genotoxic: Damaging to DNA; pertaining to agents known to damage DNA.

Geographic Information System (GIS): A computer system designed for storing, manipulating, analyzing, and displaying data in a geographic context.

Geological Log: A detailed description of all underground features (depth, thickness, type of formation) discovered during the drilling of a well.

Geophysical Log: A record of the structure and composition of the earth encountered when drilling a well or similar type of test hold or boring.

Geothermal/Ground Source Heat Pump: These heat pumps are underground coils to transfer heat from the ground to the inside of a building. (See: heat pump; water source heat pump)

Germicide: Any compound that kills disease-causing microorganisms.

Giardia Lamblia: Protozoan in the feces of humans and animals that can cause severe gastrointestinal ailments. It is a common contaminant of surface waters.

Glass Containers: For recycling purposes, containers like bottles and jars for drinks, food, cosmetics and other products. When being recycled, container glass is generally separated into color categories for conversion into new containers, construction materials or fiberglass insulation.

Global Warming: An increase in the near surface temperature of the Earth. Global warming has occurred in the distant past as the result of natural influences, but the term is most often used to refer to the warming predicted to occur as a result of increased emissions of greenhouse gases. Scientists generally agree that the Earth's surface has warmed by about 1 degree Fahrenheit in the past 140 years. The Intergovernmental Panel on Climate Change (IPCC) recently concluded that increased concentrations of greenhouse gases are causing an increase in the Earth's surface temperature and that increased concentrations of sulfate aerosols have led to relative cooling in some regions, generally over and downwind of heavily industrialized areas. (See: climate change)

Global Warming Potential: The ratio of the warming caused by a substance to the warming caused by a similar mass of carbon dioxide. CFC-12, for example, has a GWP of 8,500, while water has a GWP of zero. (See: Class I Substance and Class II Substance.)

Glovebag: A polyethylene or polyvinyl chloride bag-like enclosure affixed around an asbestos-containing source (most often thermal system insulation) permitting the material to be removed while minimizing release of airborne fibers to the surrounding atmosphere.

Gooseneck: A portion of a water service connection between the distribution system water main and a meter. Sometimes called a pigtail.

Grab Sample: A single sample collected at a particular time and place that represents the composition of the water, air, or soil only at that time and place.

Grain Loading: The rate at which particles are emitted from a pollution source. Measurement is made by the number of grains per cubic foot of gas emitted.

Granular Activated Carbon Treatment: A filtering system often used in small water systems and individual homes to remove organics. Also used by municipal water treatment plantsd. GAC can be highly effective in lowering elevated levels of radon in water.

Grasscycling: Source reduction activities in which grass clippings are left on the lawn after mowing.

Grassed Waterway: Natural or constructed watercourse or outlet that is shaped or graded and established in suitable vegetation for the disposal of runoff water without erosion.

Gray Water: Domestic wastewater composed of wash water from kitchen, bathroom, and laundry sinks, tubs, and washers.

Greenhouse Effect: The warming of the Earth's atmosphere attributed to a buildup of carbon dioxide or other gases; some scientists think that this build-up allows the sun's rays to heat the Earth, while making the infra-red radiation atmosphere opaque to infra-red radiation, thereby preventing a counterbalancing loss of heat.

Greenhouse Gas: A gas, such as carbon dioxide or methane, which contributes to potential climate change.

Grinder Pump: A mechanical device that shreds solids and raises sewage to a higher elevation through pressure sewers.

Gross Alpha/Beta Particle Activity: The total radioactivity due to alpha or beta particle emissions as inferred from measurements on a dry sample.

Gross Power-Generation Potential: The installed power generation capacity that landfill gas can support.

Ground Cover: Plants grown to keep soil from eroding.

Ground Water: The supply of fresh water found beneath the Earth's surface, usually in aquifers, which supply wells and springs. Because ground water is a major source of drinking water, there is growing concern over contamination from leaching agricultural or industrial pollutants or leaking underground storage tanks.

Ground Water Under the Direct Influence (UDI) of Surface Water: Any water beneath the surface of the ground with: 1. significant occurence of insects or other microorganisms, algae, or large-diameter pathogens; 2. significant and relatively rapid shifts in water characteristics such as turbidity, temperature, conductivity, or pH which closely correlate to climatological or surface water conditions. Direct influence is determined for individual sources in accordance with criteria established by a state.

Ground-Penetrating Radar: A geophysical method that uses high frequency electromagnetic waves to obtain subsurface information.

Ground-Water Discharge: Ground water entering near coastal waters which has been contaminated by landfill leachate, deep well injection of hazardous wastes, septic tanks, etc.

Ground-Water Disinfection Rule: A 1996 amendment of the Safe Drinking Water Act requiring EPA to promulgate national primary drinking water regulations requiring disinfection as for all public water systems, including surface waters and ground water systems.

Gully Erosion: Severe erosion in which trenches are cut to a depth greater than 30 centimeters (a foot). Generally, ditches deep enough to cross with farm equipment are considered gullies.

H

Habitat: The place where a population (e.g. human, animal, plant, microorganism) lives and its surroundings, both living and non-living.

Habitat Indicator: A physical attribute of the environment measured to characterize conditions necessary to support an organism, population, or community in the absence of pollutants; e.g. salinity of estuarine waters or substrate type in streams or lakes.

Half-Life: 1. The time required for a pollutant to lose one-half of its original coconcentrationor example, the biochemical half-life of DDT in the environment is 15 years. 2. The time required for half of the atoms of a radioactive element to undergo self-transmutation or decay (half-life of radium is 1620 years). 3. The time required for the elimination of half a total dose from the body.

Halogen: A type of incandescent lamp with higher energy-efficiency that standard ones.

Halon: Bromine-containing compounds with long atmospheric lifetimes whose breakdown in the stratosphere causes depletion of ozone. Halons are used in firefighting.

Hammer Mill: A high-speed machine that uses hammers and cutters to crush, grind, chip, or shred solid waste.

Hard Water: Alkaline water containing dissolved salts that interfere with some industrial processes and prevent soap from sudsing.

Hauler: Garbage collection company that offers complete refuse removal service; many will also collect recyclables.

Hazard: 1. Potential for radiation, a chemical or other pollutant to cause human illness or injury. 2. In the pesticide program, the inherent toxicity of a compound. Hazard identification of a given substances is an informed judgment based on verifiable toxicity data from animal models or human studies.

Hazard Assessment: Evaluating the effects of a stressor or determining a margin of safety for an organism by comparing the concentration which causes toxic effects with an estimate of exposure to the organism.

Hazard Communication Standard: An OSHA regulation that requires chemical manufacturers, suppliers, and importers to assess the hazards of the chemicals that they make, supply, or import, and to inform employers, customers, and workers of these hazards through MSDS information.

Hazard Evaluation: A component of risk evaluation that involves gathering and evaluating data on the types of health injuries or diseases that may be produced by a chemical and on the conditions of exposure under which such health effects are produced.

Hazard Identification: Determining if a chemical or a microbe can cause adverse health effects in humans and what those effects might be.

Hazard Quotient: The ratio of estimated site-specific exposure to a single chemical from a site over a specified period to the estimated daily exposure level, at which no adverse health effects are likely to occur.

Hazard Ratio: A term used to compare an animal's daily dietary intake of a pesticide to its LD 50 value. A ratio greater than 1.0 indicates that the animal is likely to consume an a dose amount which would kill 50 percent of animals of the same species. (See: LD 50 /Lethal Dose.)

Hazardous Air Pollutants: Air pollutants which are not covered by ambient air quality standards but which, as defined in the Clean Air Act, may present a threat of adverse human health effects or adverse environmental effects.Such pollutants include asbestos, beryllium, mercury, benzene, coke oven emissions, radionuclides, and vinyl chloride.

Hazardous Chemical: An EPA designation for any hazardous material requiring an MSDS under OSHA's Hazard Communication Standard. Such substances are capable of producing fires and explosions or adverse health effects like cancer and dermatitis. Hazardous chemicals are distinct from hazardous waste.(See: Hazardous Waste.)

Hazardous Ranking System: The principal screening tool used by EPA to evaluate risks to public health and the environment associated with abandoned or uncontrolled hazardous waste sites. The HRS calculates a score based on the potential of hazardous substances spreading from the site through the air, surface water, or ground water, and on other factors such as density and proximity of human population. This score is the primary factor in deciding if the site should be on the National Priorities List and, if so, what ranking it should have compared to other sites on the list.

Hazardous Substance: 1. Any material that poses a threat to human health and/or the environment. Typical hazardous substances are toxic, corrosive, ignitable, explosive, or chemically reactive. 2. Any substance designated by EPA to be reported if a designated quantity of the substance is spilled in the waters of the United States or is otherwise released into the environment.

Hazardous Waste: By-products of society that can pose a substantial or potential hazard to human health or the environment when improperly managed. Possesses at least one of four characteristics (ignitability, corrosivity, reactivity, or toxicity), or appears on special EPA lists.

Hazardous Waste Landfill: An excavated or engineered site where hazardous waste is deposited and covered.

Hazardous Waste Minimization: Reducing the amount of toxicity or waste produced by a facility via source reduction or environmentally sound recycling.

Hazards Analysis: Procedures used to (1) identify potential sources of release of hazardous materials from fixed facilities or transportation accidents; (2) determine the vulnerability of a geographical area to a release of hazardous materials; and (3) compare hazards to determine which present greater or lesser risks to a community.

Hazards Identification: Providing information on which facilities have extremely hazardous substances, what those chemicals are, how much there is at each facility, how the chemicals are stored, and whether they are used at high temperatures.

Headspace: The vapor mixture trapped above a solid or liquid in a sealed vessel.

Health Advisory Level: A non-regulatory health-based reference level of chemical traces (usually in ppm) in drinking water at which there are no adverse health risks when ingested over various periods of time. Such levels are established for one day, 10 days, long-term and life-time exposure periods. They contain a wide margin of safety.

Health Assessment: An evaluation of available data on existing or potential risks to human health posed by a Superfund site. The Agency for Toxic Substances and Disease Registry (ATSDR) of the Department of Health and Human Services (DHHS) is required to perform such an assessment at every site on the National Priorities List.

Heat Island Effect: A "dome" of elevated temperatures over an urban area caused by structural and pavement heat fluxes, and pollutant emissions.

Heat Pump: An electric device with both heating and cooling capabilities. It extracts heat from one medium at a lower (the heat source) temperature and transfers it to another at a higher temperature (the heat sink), thereby cooling the first and warming the second. (See: geothermal, water source heat pump.)

Heavy Metals: Metallic elements with high atomic weights; (e.g. mercury, chromium, cadmium, arsenic, and lead); can damage living things at low concentrations and tend to accumulate in the food chain.

Heptachlor: An insecticide that was banned on some food products in 1975 and in all of them 1978. It was allowed for use in seed treatment until 1983. More recently it was found in milk and other dairy products in Arkansas and Missouri where dairy cattle were illegally fed treated seed.

Herbicide: A chemical pesticide designed to control or destroy plants, weeds, or grasses.

Herbivore: An animal that feeds on plants.

Heterotrophic Organisms: Species that are dependent on organic matter for food.

High End Exposure (dose) Estimate: An estimate of exposure, or dose level received anyone in a defined population that is greater than the 90th percentile of all individuals in that population, but less than the exposure at the highest percentile in that population. A high end risk descriptor is an estimate of the risk level for such individuals. Note that risk is based on a combination of exposure and susceptibility to the stressor.

High Intensity Discharge: A generic term for mercury vapor, metal halide, and high pressure sodium lamps and fixtures.

High-Density Polyethylene: A material used to make plastic bottles and other products that produces toxic fumes when burned.

High-Level Nuclear Waste Facility: Plant designed to handle disposal of used nuclear fuel, high-level radioactive waste, and plutonium waste.

High-Level Radioactive Waste (HLRW): Waste generated in core fuel of a nuclear reactor, found at nuclear reactors or by nuclear fuel reprocessing; is a serious threat to anyone who comes near the waste without shielding. (See: low-level radioactive waste.)

High-Line Jumpers: Pipes or hoses connected to fire hydrants and laid on top of the ground to provide emergency water service for an isolated portion of a distribution system.

High-Risk Community: A community located within the vicinity of numerous sites of facilities or other potential sources of envienvironmental exposure/health hazards which may result in high levels of exposure to contaminants or pollutants.

High-to-Low-Dose Extrapolation: The process of prediction of low exposure risk to humans and animals from the measured high-exposure-high-risk data involving laboratory animals.

Highest Dose Tested: The highest dose of a chemical or substance tested in a study.

Holding Pond: A pond or reservoir, usually made of earth, built to store polluted runoff.

Holding Time: The maximum amount of time a sample may be stored before analysis.

Hollow Stem Auger Drilling: Conventional drilling method that uses augurs to penetrate the soil. As the augers are rotated, soil cuttings are conveyed to the ground surface via augur spirals. DP tools can be used inside the hollow augers.

Homeowner Water System: Any water system which supplies piped water to a single residence.

Homogeneous Area: In accordance with Asbestos Hazard and Emergency Response Act (AHERA) definitions, an area of surfacing materials, thermal surface insulation, or miscellaneous material that is uniform in color and texture.

Hood Capture Efficiency: Ratio of the emissions captured by a hood and directed into a control or disposal device, expressed as a percent of all emissions.

Host: 1. In genetics, the organism, typically a bacterium, into which a gene from another organism is transplanted. 2. In medicine, an animal infected or parasitized by another organism.

Household Hazardous Waste: Hazardous products used and disposed of by residential as opposed to industrial consumers. Includes paints, stains, varnishes, solvents, pesticides, and other materials or products containing volatile chemicals that can catch fire, react or explode, or that are corrosive or toxic.

Household Waste (Domestic Waste): Solid waste, composed of garbage and rubbish, which normally originates in a private home or apartment house. Domestic waste may contain a significant amount of toxic or hazardous waste.

Human Equivalent Dose: A dose which, when administered to humans, produces an effect equal to that produced by a dose in animals.

Human Exposure Evaluation: Describing the nature and size of the population exposed to a substance and the magnitude and duration of their exposure.

Human Health Risk: The likelihood that a given exposure or series of exposures may have damaged or will damage the health of individuals.

Hydraulic Conductivity: The rate at which water can move through a permeable medium. (i.e. the coefficient of permeability.)

Hydraulic Gradient: In general, the direction of groundwater flow due to changes in the depth of the water table.

Hydrocarbons (HC): Chemical compounds that consist entirely of carbon and hydrogen.

Hydrogen Sulfide (H2S): Gas emitted during organic decomposition. Also a by-product of oil refining and burning. Smells like rotten eggs and, in heavy concentration, can kill or cause illness.

Hydrogeological Cycle: The natural process recycling water from the atmosphere down to (and through) the earth and back to the atmosphere again.

Hydrogeology: The geology of ground water, with particular emphasis on the chemistry and movement of water.

Hydrologic Cycle: Movement or exchange of water between the atmosphere and earth.

Hydrology: The science dealing with the properties, distribution, and circulation of water.

Hydrolysis: The decomposition of organic compounds by interaction with water.

Hydronic: A ventilation system using heated or cooled water pumped through a building.

Hydrophilic: Having a strong affinity for water.

Hydrophobic: Having a strong aversion for water.

Hydropneumatic: A water system, usually small, in which a water pump is automatically controlled by the pressure in a compressed air tank.

Hypersensitivity Diseases: Diseases characterized by allergic responses to pollutants; diseases most clearly associated with indoor air quality are asthma, rhinitis, and pneumonic hypersensitivity.

Hypolimnion: Bottom waters of a thermally stratified lake. The hypolimnion of a eutrophic lake is usually low or lacking in oxygen.

Hypoxia/Hypoxic Waters: Waters with dissolved oxygen concentrations of less than 2 ppm, the level generally accepted as the minimum required for most marine life to survive and reproduce.

I

Identification Code or EPA I.D. Number: The unique code assigned to each generator, transporter, and treatment, storage, or disposal facility by regulating agencies to facilitate identification and tracking of chemicals or hazardous waste.

Ignitable: Capable of burning or causing a fire.

IM240: A high-tech, transient dynamometer automobile emissions test that takes up to 240 seconds.

Imhoff Cone: A clear, cone-shaped container used to measure the volume of settleable solids in a specific volume of water.

Immediately Dangerous to Life and Health (IDLH): The maximum level to which a healthy individual can be exposed to a chemical for 30 minutes and escape without suffering irreversible health effects or impairing symptoms. Used as a "level of concern." (See: level of concern.)

Imminent Hazard: One that would likely result in unreasonable adverse effects on humans or the environment or risk unreasonable hazard to an endangered species during the time required for a pesticide registration cancellation proceeding.

Imminent Threat: A high probability that exposure is occurring.

Immiscibility: The inability of two or more substances or liquids to readily dissolve into one another, such as soil and water. Immiscibility The inability of two or more substances or liquids to readily dissolve into one another, such as soil and water.

Impermeable: Not easily penetrated. The property of a material or soil that does not allow, or allows only with great difficulty, the movement or passage of water.

Imports: Municipal solid waste and recyclables that have been transported to a state or locality for processing or final disposition (but that did not originate in that state or locality).

Impoundment: A body of water or sludge confined by a dam, dike, floodgate, or other barrier.

In Situ: In its original place; unmoved unexcavated; remaining at the site or in the subsurface.

In-Line Filtration: Pre-treattment method in which chemicals are mixed by the flowing water; commonly used in pressure filtration installations. Eliminates need for flocculation and sedimentation.

In-Situ Flushing: Introduction of large volumes of water, at times supplemented with cleaning compounds, into soil, waste, or ground water to flush hazardous contaminants from a site.

In-Situ Oxidation: Technology that oxidizes contaminants dissolved in ground water, converting them into insoluble compounds.

In-Situ Stripping: Treatment system that removes or "strips" volatile organic compounds from contaminated ground or surface water by forcing an airstream through the water and causing the compounds to evaporate.

In-Situ Vitrification: Technology that treats contaminated soil in place at extremely high temperatures, at or more than 3000 degrees Fahrenheit.

In Vitro: Testing or action outside an organism (e.g. inside a test tube or culture dish.)

In Vivo: Testing or action inside an organism.

Incident Command Post: A facility located at a safe distance from an emergency site, where the incident commander, key staff, and technical representatives can make decisions and deploy emergency manpower and equipment.

Incident Command System (ICS): The organizational arrangement wherein one person, normally the Fire Chief of the impacted district, is in charge of an integrated, comprehensive emergency response organization and the emergency incident site, backed by an Emergency Operations Center staff with resources, information, and advice.

Incineration: A treatment technology involving destruction of waste by controlled burning at high temperatures; e.g., burning sludge to remove the water and reduce the remaining residues to a safe, non-burnable ash that can be disposed of safely on land, in some waters, or in underground locations.

Incineration at Sea: Disposal of waste by burning at sea on specially-designed incinerator ships.

Incinerator: A furnace for burning waste under controlled conditions.

Incompatible Waste: A waste unsuitable for mixing with another waste or material because it may react to form a hazard.

Indemnification: In the pesticide program, legal requirement that EPA pay certain end-users, dealers, and distributors for the cost of stock on hand at the time a pesticide registration is suspended.

Indicator: In biology, any biological entity or processes, or community whose characteristics show the presence of specific environmental conditions. 2. In chemistry, a substance that shows a visible change, usually of color, at a desired point in a chemical reaction. 3.A device that indicates the result of a measurement; e.g. a pressure gauge or a moveable scale.

Indirect Discharge: Introduction of pollutants from a non-domestic source into a publicly owned waste-treatment system. Indirect dischargers can be commercial or industrial facilities whose wastes enter local sewers.

Indirect Source: Any facility or building, property, road or parking area that attracts motor vehicle traffic and, indirectly, causes pollution.

Indoor Air: The breathable air inside a habitable structure or conveyance.

Indoor Air Pollution: Chemical, physical, or biological contaminants in indoor air.

Indoor Climate: Temperature, humidity, lighting, air flow and noise levels in a habitable structure or conveyance. Indoor climate can affect indoor air pollution.

Industrial Pollution Prevention: Combination of industrial source reduction and toxic chemical use substitution.

Industrial Process Waste: Residues produced during manufacturing operations.

Industrial Sludge: Semi-liquid residue or slurry remaining from treatment of industrial water and wastewater.

Industrial Source Reduction: Practices that reduce the amount of any hazardous substance, pollutant, or contaminant entering any waste stream or otherwise released into the environment. Also reduces the threat to public health and the environment associated with such releases. Term includes equipment or technology modifications, substitution of raw materials, and improvements in housekeeping, maintenance, training or inventory control.

Industrial Waste: Unwanted materials from an industrial operation; may be liquid, sludge, solid, or hazardous waste.

Inert Ingredient: Pesticide components such as solvents, carriers, dispersants, and surfactants that are not active against target pests. Not all inert ingredients are innocuous.

Inertial Separator: A device that uses centrifugal force to separate waste particles.

Infectious Agent: Any organism, such as a pathogenic virus, parasite, or or bacterium, that is capable of invading body tissues, multiplying, and causing disease.

Infectious Waste: Hazardous waste capable of causing infections in humans, including: contaminated animal waste; human blood and blood products; isolation waste, pathological waste; and discarded sharps (needles, scalpels or broken medical instruments).

Infiltration: 1. The penetration of water through the ground surface into sub-surface soil or the penetration of water from the soil into sewer or other pipes through defective joints, connections, or manhole walls. 2. The technique of applying large volumes of waste water to land to penetrate the surface and percolate through the underlying soil. (See: percolation.)

Infiltration Gallery: A sub-surface groundwater collection system, typically shallow in depth, constructed with open-jointed or perforated pipes that discharge collected water into a watertight chamber from which the water is pumped to treatment facilities and into the distribution system. Usually located close to streams or ponds.

Infiltration Rate: The quantity of water that can enter the soil in a specified time interval.

Inflow: Entry of extraneous rain water into a sewer system from sources other than infiltration, such as basement drains, manholes, storm drains, and street washing.

Influent: Water, wastewater, or other liquid flowing into a reservoir, basin, or treatment plant.

Information Collection Request (ICR): A description of information to be gathered in connection with rules, proposed rules, surveys, and guidance documents that contain information-gathering requirements. The ICR describes what information is needed, why it is needed, how it will be collected, and how much collecting it will cost. The ICR is submitted by the EPA to the Office of Management and Budget (OMB) for approval.

Information File: In the Superfund program, a file that contains accurate, up-to-date documents on a Superfund site. The file is usually located in a public building (school, library, or city hall) convenient for local residents.

Inhalable Particles: All dust capable of entering the human respiratory tract.

Initial Compliance Period (Water): The first full three-year compliance period which begins at least 18 months after promulgation.

Injection Well: A well into which fluids are injected for purposes such as waste disposal, improving the recovery of crude oil, or solution mining.

Injection Zone: A geological formation receiving fluids through a well.

Innovative Technologies: New or inventive methods to treat effectively hazardous waste and reduce risks to human health and the environment.

Innovative Treatment Technologies: Technologies whose routine use is inhibited by lack of data on performance and cost. (See: Established treatment technologies.)

Inoculum: 1. Bacteria or fungi injected into compost to start biological action. 2. A medium containing organisms, usually bacteria or a virus, that is introduced into cultures or living organisms.

Inorganic Chemicals: Chemical substances of mineral origin, not of basically carbon structure.

Insecticide: A pesticide compound specifically used to kill or prevent the growth of insects.

Inspection and Maintenance (I/M): 1. Activities to ensure that vehicles' emission controls work properly. 2. Also applies to wastewater treatment plants and other anti-pollution facilities and processes.

Institutional Waste: Waste generated at institutions such as schools, libraries, hospitals, prisons, etc.

Instream Use: Water use taking place within a stream channel; e.g., hydro-electric power generation, navigation, water quality improvement, fish propagation, recreation.

Integrated Exposure Assessment: Cumulative summation (over time) of the magnitude of exposure to a toxic chemical in all media.

Integrated Pest Management (IPM): A mixture of chemical and other, non-pesticide, methods to control pests.

Integrated Waste Management: Using a variety of practices to handle municipal solid waste; can include source reduction, recycling, incineration, and landfilling.

Interceptor Sewers: Large sewer lines that, in a combined system, control the flow of sewage to the treatment plant. In a storm, they allow some of the sewage to flow directly into a receiving stream, thus keeping it from overflowing onto the streets. Also used in separate systems to collect the flows from main and trunk sewers and carry them to treatment points.

Interface: The common boundary between two substances such as a water and a solid, water and a gas, or two liquids such as water and oil.

Interfacial Tension: The strength of the film separating two immiscible fluids (e.g. oil and water) measured in dynes per, or millidynes per centimeter.

Interim (Permit) Status: Period during which treatment, storage and disposal facilities coming under RCRA in 1980 are temporarily permitted to operate while awaiting a permanent permit. Permits issued under these circumstances are usually called "Part A" or "Part B" permits.

Internal Dose: In exposure assessment, the amount of a substance penetrating the absorption barriers (e.g. skin, lung tissue, gastrointestinal tract) of an organism through either physical or biological processes. (See: absorbed dose)

Interstate Carrier Water Supply: A source of water for drinking and sanitary use on planes, buses, trains, and ships operating in more than one state. These sources are federally regulated.

Interstate Commerce Clause: A clause of the U.S. Constitution which reserves to the federal government the right to regulate the conduct of business across state lines. Under this clause, for example, the U.S. Supreme Court has ruled that states may not inequitably restrict the disposal of out-of-state wastes in their jurisdictions.

Interstate Waters: Waters that flow across or form part of state or international boundaries; e.g. the Great Lakes, the Mississippi River, or coastal waters.

Interstitial Monitoring: The continuous surveillance of the space between the walls of an underground storage tank.

Intrastate Product: Pesticide products once registered by states for sale and use only in the state. All intrastate products have been converted to full federal registration or canceled.

Inventory (TSCA): Inventory of chemicals produced pursuant to Section 8 (b) of the Toxic Substances Control Act.

Inversion: A layer of warm air that prevents the rise of cooling air and traps pollutants beneath it; can cause an air pollution episode.

Ion: An electrically charged atom or group of atoms.

Ion Exchange Treatment: A common water-softening method often found on a large scale at water purification plants that remove some organics and radium by adding calcium oxide or calcium hydroxide to increase the pH to a level where the metals will precipitate out.

Ionization Chamber: A device that measures the intensity of ionizing radiation.

Ionizing Radiation: Radiation that can strip electrons from atoms; e.g. alpha, beta, and gamma radiation.

IRIS: EPA's Integrated Risk Information System, an electronic data base containing the Agency's latest descriptive and quantitative regulatory information on chemical constituents.

Irradiated Food: Food subject to brief radioactivity, usually gamma rays, to kill insects, bacteria, and mold, and to permit storage without refrigeration.

Irradiation: Exposure to radiation of wavelengths shorter than those of visible light (gamma, x-ray, or ultra- violet), for medical purposes, to sterilize milk or other foodstuffs, or to induce polymerization of monomers or vulcanization of rubber.

Irreversible Effect: Effect characterized by the inability of the body to partially or fully repair injury caused by a toxic agent.

Irrigation: Applying water or wastewater to land areas to supply the water and nutrient needs of plants.

Irrigation Efficiency: The amount of water stored in the crop root zone compared to the amount of irrigation water applied.

Irrigation Return Flow: Surface and subsurface water which leaves the field following application of irrigation water.

Irritant: A substance that can cause irritation of the skin, eyes, or respiratory system. Effects may be acute from a single high level exposure, or chronic from repeated low-level exposures to such compounds as chlorine, nitrogen dioxide, and nitric acid.

Isoconcentration: More than one sample point exhibiting the same isolate concentration.

Isopleth: The line or area represented by an isoconcentration.

Isotope: A variation of an element that has the same atomic number of protons but a different weight because of the number of neutrons. Various isotopes of the same element may have different radioactive behaviors, some are highly unstable..

Isotropy: The condition in which the hydraulic or other properties of an aquifer are the same in all directions.

J

Jar Test: A laboratory procedure that simulates a water treatment plant's coagulation/flocculation units with differing chemical doses, mix speeds, and settling times to estimate the minimum or ideal coagulant dose required to achieve certain water quality goals.

Joint and Several Liability: Under CERCLA, this legal concept relates to the liability for Superfund site cleanup and other costs on the part of more than one potentially responsible party (i.e. if there were several owners or users of a site that became contaminated over the years, they could all be considered potentially liable for cleaning up the site.)

K

Karst: A geologic formation of irregular limestone deposits with sinks, underground streams, and caverns.

Kinetic Energy: Energy possessed by a moving object or water body.

Kinetic Rate Coefficient: A number that describes the rate at which a water constituent such as a biochemical oxygen demand or dissolved oxygen rises or falls, or at which an air pollutant reacts.

L

Laboratory Animal Studies: Investigations using animals as surrogates for humans.

Lagoon: 1. A shallow pond where sunlight, bacterial action, and oxygen work to purify wastewater; also used for storage of wastewater or spent nuclear fuel rods. 2. Shallow body of water, often separated from the sea by coral reefs or sandbars.

Land Application: Discharge of wastewater onto the ground for treatment or reuse. (See: irrigation.)

Land Ban: Phasing out of land disposal of most untreated hazardous wastes, as mandated by the 1984 RCRA amendments.

Land Disposal Restrictions: Rules that require hazardous wastes to be treated before disposal on land to destroy or immobilize hazardous constituents that might migrate into soil and ground water.

Land Farming (of Waste): A disposal process in which hazardous waste deposited on or in the soil is degraded naturally by microbes.

Landfills: 1. Sanitary landfills are disposal sites for non-hazardous solid wastes spread in layers, compacted to the smallest practical volume, and covered by material applied at the end of each operating day. 2. Secure chemical landfills are disposal sites for hazardous waste, selected and designed to minimize the chance of release of hazardous substances into the environment.

Landscape: The traits, patterns, and structure of a specific geographic area, including its biological composition, its physical environment, and its anthropogenic or social patterns. An area where interacting ecosystems are grouped and repeated in similar form.

Landscape Characterization: Documentation of the traits and patterns of the essential elements of the landscape.

Landscape Ecology: The study of the distribution patterns of communities and ecosystems, the ecological processes that affect those patterns, and changes in pattern and process over time.

Landscape Indicator: A measurement of the landscape, calculated from mapped or remotely sensed data, used to describe spatial patterns of land use and land cover across a geographic area. Landscape indicators may be useful as measures of certain kinds of environmental degradation such as forest fragmentation.

Langelier Index (LI): An index reflecting the equilibrium pH of a water with respect to calcium and alkalinity; used in stabilizing water to control both corrosion and scale deposition.

Large Quantity Generator: Person or facility generating more than 2200 pounds of hazardous waste per month. Such generators produce about 90 percent of the nation's hazardous waste, and are subject to all RCRA requirements.

Large Water System: A water system that services more than 50,000 customers.

Laser Induced Fluorescence: A method for measuring the relative amount of soil and/or groundwater with an in-situ sensor.

Latency: Time from the first exposure of a chemical until the appearance of a toxic effect.

Lateral Sewers: Pipes that run under city streets and receive the sewage from homes and businesses, as opposed to domestic feeders and main trunk lines.

Laundering Weir: Sedimention basin overflow weir.

LC 50/Lethal Concentration: Median level concentration, a standard measure of toxicity. It tells how much of a substance is needed to kill half of a group of experimental organisms in a given time. (See: LD 50.)

LD 50/ Lethal Dose: The dose of a toxicant or microbe that will kill 50 percent of the test organisms within a designated period. The lower the LD 50, the more toxic the compound.

Ldlo: Lethal dose low; the lowest dose in an animal study at which lethality occurs.

Leachate: Water that collects contaminants as it trickles through wastes, pesticides or fertilizers. Leaching may occur in farming areas, feedlots, and landfills, and may result in hazardous substances entering surface water, ground water, or soil.

Leachate Collection System: A system that gathers leachate and pumps it to the surface for treatment.

Leaching: The process by which soluble constituents are dissolved and filtered through the soil by a percolating fluid. (See: leachate.)

Lead (Pb): A heavy metal that is hazardous to health if breathed or swallowed. Its use in gasoline, paints, and plumbing compounds has been sharply restricted or eliminated by federal laws and regulations. (See: heavy metals.)

Lead Service Line: A service line made of lead which connects the water to the building inlet and any lead fitting connected to it.

Legionella: A genus of bacteria, some species of which have caused a type of pneumonia called Legionaires Disease.

Lethal Concentration 50: Also referred to as LC50, a concentration of a pollutant or effluent at which 50 percent of the test organisms die; a common measure of acute toxicity.

Lethal Dose 50: Also referred to as LD50, the dose of a toxicant that will kill 50 percent of test organisms within a designated period of time; the lower the LD 50, the more toxic the compound.

Level of Concern (LOC): The concentration in air of an extremely hazardous substance above which there may be serious immediate health effects to anyone exposed to it for short periods

Life Cycle of a Product: All stages of a product's development, from extraction of fuel for power to production, marketing, use, and disposal.

Lifetime Average Daily Dose: Figure for estimating excess lifetime cancer risk.

Lifetime Exposure: Total amount of exposure to a substance that a human would receive in a lifetime (usually assumed to be 70 years).

Lift: In a sanitary landfill, a compacted layer of solid waste and the top layer of cover material.

Lifting Station: (See: pumping station.)

Light Non-Aqueous Phase Liquid (LNAPL): A non-aqueous phase liquid with a specific gravity less than 1.0. Because the specific gravity of water is 1.0, most LNAPLs float on top of the water table. Most common petroleum hydrocarbon fuels and lubricating oils are LNAPLs.

Light-Emitting Diode: A long-lasting illumination technology used for exit signs which requires very little power

Limestone Scrubbing: Use of a limestone and water solution to remove gaseous stack-pipe sulfur before it reaches the atmosphere.

Limit of Detection (LOD): The minimum concentration of a substance being analyzed test that has a 99 percent probability of being identified.

Limited Degradation: An environmental policy permitting some degradation of natural systems but terminating at a level well beneath an established health standard.

Limiting Factor: A condition whose absence or excessive concentration, is incompatible with the needs or tolerance of a species or population and which may have a negative influence on their ability to thrive.

Limnology: The study of the physical, chemical, hydrological, and biological aspects of fresh water bodies.

Lindane: A pesticide that causes adverse health effects in domestic water supplies and is toxic to freshwater fish and aquatic life.

Liner: 1. A relatively impermeable barrier designed to keep leachate inside a landfill. Liner materials include plastic and dense clay. 2. An insert or sleeve for sewer pipes to prevent leakage or infiltration.

Lipid Solubility: The maximum concentration of a chemical that will dissolve in fatty substances. Lipid soluble substances are insoluble in water. They will very selectively disperse through the environment via uptake in living tissue.

Liquefaction: Changing a solid into a liquid.

Liquid Injection Incinerator: Commonly used system that relies on high pressure to prepare liquid wastes for incineration by breaking them up into tiny droplets to allow easier combustion.

List: Shorthand term for EPA list of violating facilities or firms debarred from obtaining government contracts because they violated certain sections of the Clean Air or Clean Water Acts. The list is maintained by The Office of Enforcement and Compliance Monitoring.

Listed Waste: Wastes listed as hazardous under RCRA but which have not been subjected to the Toxic Characteristics Listing Process because the dangers they present are considered self-evident.

Lithology: Mineralogy, grain size, texture, and other physical properties of granular soil, sediment, or rock.

Litter: 1. The highly visible portion of solid waste carelessly discarded outside the regular garbage and trash collection and disposal system. 2. leaves and twigs fallen from forest trees.

Littoral Zone: 1. That portion of a body of fresh water extending from the shoreline lakeward to the limit of occupancy of rooted plants. 2. A strip of land along the shoreline between the high and low water levels.

Local Education Agency (LEA): In the asbestos program, an educational agency at the local level that exists primarily to operate schools or to contract for educational services, including primary and secondary public and private schools. A single, unaffiliated school can be considered an LEA for AHERA purposes.

Local Emergency Planning Committee (LEPC): A committee appointed by the state emergency response commission, as required by SARA Title III, to formulate a comprehensive emergency plan for its jurisdiction.

Low Density Polyethylene (LOPE): Plastic material used for both rigid containers and plastic film applications.

Low Emissivity (low-E) Windows: New window technology that lowers the amount of energy loss through windows by inhibiting the transmission of radiant heat while still allowing sufficient light to pass through.

Low NO_x Burners: One of several combustion technologies used to reduce emissions of Nitrogen Oxides (NO_x.)

Low-Level Radioactive Waste (LLRW): Wastes less hazardous than most of those associated with a nuclear reactor; generated by hospitals, research laboratories, and certain industries. The Department of Energy, Nuclear Regulatory Commission, and EPA share responsibilities for managing them. (See: high-level radioactive wastes.)

Lower Detection Limit: The smallest signal above background noise an instrument can reliably detect.

Lower Explosive Limit (LEL): The concentration of a compound in air below which the mixture will not catch on fire.

Lowest Acceptable Daily Dose: The largest quantity of a chemical that will not cause a toxic effect, as determined by animal studies.

Lowest Achievable Emission Rate: Under the Clean Air Act, the rate of emissions that reflects (1) the most stringent emission limitation in the implementation plan of any state for such source unless the owner or operator demonstrates such limitations are not achievable; or (2) the most stringent emissions limitation achieved in practice, whichever is more stringent. A proposed new or modified source may not emit pollutants in excess of existing new source standards.

Lowest Observed Adverse Effect Level (LOAEL): The lowest level of a stressor that causes statistically and biologically significant differences in test samples as compared to other samples subjected to no stressor.

M

Macropores: Secondary soil features such as root holes or desiccation cracks that can create significant conduits for movement of NAPL and dissolved contaminants, or vapor-phase contaminants.

Magnetic Separation: Use of magnets to separate ferrous materials from mixed municipal waste stream.

Major Modification: This term is used to define modifications of major stationary sources of emissions with respect to Prevention of Significant Deterioration and New Source Review under the Clean Air Act.

Major Stationary Sources: Term used to determine the applicability of Prevention of Significant Deterioration and new source regulations. In a nonattainment area, any stationary pollutant source with potential to emit more than 100 tons per year is considered a major stationary source. In PSD areas the cutoff level may be either 100 or 250 tons, depending upon the source.

Majors: Larger publicly owned treatment works (POTWs) with flows equal to at least one million gallons per day (mgd) or servicing a population equivalent to 10,000 persons; certain other POTWs having significant water quality impacts. (See: minors.)

Man-Made (Anthropogenic) Beta Particle and Photon Emitters: All radionuclides emitting beta particles and/or photons listed in Maximum Permissible Body Burdens and Maximum Permissible Concentrations of Radonuclides in Air and Water for Occupational Exposure.

Management Plan: Under the Asbestos Hazard Emergency Response Act (AHERA), a document that each Local Education Agency is required to prepare, describing all activities planned and undertaken by a school to comply with AHERA regulations, including building inspections to identify asbestos-containing materials, response actions, and operations and maintenance programs to minimize the risk of exposure.

Managerial Controls: Methods of nonpoint source pollution control based on decisions about managing agricultural wastes or application times or rates for agrochemicals.

Mandatory Recycling: Programs which by law require consumers to separate trash so that some or all recyclable materials are recovered for recycling rather than going to landfills.

Manifest: A one-page form used by haulers transporting waste that lists EPA identification numbers, type and quantity of waste, the generator it originated from, the transporter that shipped it, and the storage or disposal facility to which it is being shipped. It includes copies for all participants in the shipping process.

Manifest System: Tracking of hazardous waste from "cradle-to-grave" (generation through disposal) with accompanying documents known as manifests.(See: cradle to grave.)

Manual Separation: Hand sorting of recyclable or compostable materials in waste.

Manufacturer's Formulation: A list of substances or component parts as described by the maker of a coating, pesticide, or other product containing chemicals or other substances.

Manufacturing Use Product: Any product intended (labeled) for formulation or repackaging into other pesticide products.

Margin of Safety: Maximum amount of exposure producing no measurable effect in animals (or studied humans) divided by the actual amount of human exposure in a population.

Margin of Exposure (MOE): The ratio of the no-observed adverse-effect-level to the estimated exposure dose.

Marine Sanitation Device: Any equipment or process installed on board a vessel to receive, retain, treat, or discharge sewage.

Marsh: A type of wetland that does not accumulate appreciable peat deposits and is dominated by herbaceous vegetation. Marshes may be either fresh or saltwater, tidal or non-tidal. (See: wetlands.)

Material Category: In the asbestos program, broad classification of materials into thermal surfacing insulation, surfacing material, and miscellaneous material.

Material Safety Data Sheet (MSDS): A compilation of information required under the OSHA Communication Standard on the identity of hazardous chemicals, health, and physical hazards, exposure limits, and precautions. Section 311 of SARA requires facilities to submit MSDSs under certain circumstances.

Material Type: Classification of suspect material by its specific use or application; e.g., pipe insulation, fireproofing, and floor tile.

Materials Recovery Facility (MRF): A facility that processes residentially collected mixed recyclables into new products available for market.

Maximally (or Most) Exposed Individual: The person with the highest exposure in a given population.

Maximum Acceptable Toxic Concentration: For a given ecological effects test, the range (or geometric mean) between the No Observable Adverse Effect Level and the Lowest Observable Adverse Effects Level.

Maximum Available Control Technology (MACT): The emission standard for sources of air pollution requiring the maximum reduction of hazardous emissions, taking cost and feasibility into account. Under the Clean Air Act Amendments of 1990, the MACT must not be less than the average emission level achieved by controls on the best performing 12 percent of existing sources, by category of industrial and utility sources.

Maximum Contaminant Level: The maximum permissible level of a contaminant in water delivered to any user of a public system. MCLs are enforceable standards.

Maximum Contaminant Level Goal (MCLG): Under the Safe Drinking Water Act, a non-enforceable concentration of a drinking water contaminant, set at the level at which no known or anticipated adverse effects on human health occur and which allows an adequate safety margin. The MCLG is usually the starting point for determining the regulated Maximum Contaminant Level. (See: maximum contaminant level.)

Maximum Exposure Range: Estimate of exposure or dose level received by an individual in a defined population that is greater than the 98th percentile dose for all individuals in that population, but less than the exposure level received by the person receiving the highest exposure level.

Maximum Residue Level: Comparable to a U.S. tolerance level, the Maximum Residue Level the enforceable limit on food pesticide levels in some countries. Levels are set by the Codex Alimentarius Commission, a United Nations agency managed and funded jointly by the World Health Organization and the Food and Agriculture Organization.

Maximum Tolerated Dose: The maximum dose that an animal species can tolerate for a major portion of its lifetime without significant impairment or toxic effect other than carcinogenicity.

Measure of Effect/ Measurement Endpoint: A measurable characteristic of ecological entity that can be related to an assessment endpoint; e.g. a laboratory test for eight species meeting certain requirements may serve as a measure of effect for an assessment endpoint, such as survival of fish, aquatic, invertebrate or algal species under acute exposure.

Measure of Exposure: A measurable characteristic of a stressor (such as the specific amount of mercury in a body of water) used to help quantify the exposure of an ecological entity or individual organism.

Mechanical Aeration: Use of mechanical energy to inject air into water to cause a waste stream to absorb oxygen.

Mechanical Separation: Using mechanical means to separate waste into various components.

Mechanical Turbulence: Random irregularities of fluid motion in air caused by buildings or other nonthermal, processes.

Media: Specific environments—air, water, soil—which are the subject of regulatory concern and activities.

Medical Surveillance: A periodic comprehensive review of a worker's health status; acceptable elements of such surveillance program are listed in the Occupational Safety and Health Administration standards for asbestos.

Medical Waste: Any solid waste generated in the diagnosis, treatment, or immunization of human beings or animals, in research pertaining thereto, or in the production or testing of biologicals, excluding hazardous waste identified or listed under 40 CFR Part 261 or any household waste as defined in 40 CFR Sub-section 261.4 (b)(1).

Medium-size Water System: A water system that serves 3,300 to 50,000 customers.

Meniscus: The curved top of a column of liquid in a small tube.

Mercury (Hg): Heavy metal that can accumulate in the environment and is highly toxic if breathed or swallowed. (See:heavy metals.)

Mesotrophic: Reservoirs and lakes which contain moderate quantities of nutrients and are moderately productive in terms of aquatic animal and plant life.

Metabolites: Any substances produced by biological processes, such as those from pesticides.

Metalimnion: The middle layer of a thermally stratified lake or reservoir. In this layer there is a rapid decrease in temperature with depth. Also called thermocline.

Methane: A colorless, nonpoisonous, flammable gas created by anaerobic decomposition of organic compounds. A major component of natural gas used in the home.

Methanol: An alcohol that can be used as an alternative fuel or as a gasoline additive. It is less volatile than gasoline; when blended with gasoline it lowers the carbon monoxide emissions but increases hydrocarbon emissions. Used as pure fuel, its emissions are less ozone-forming than those from gasoline. Poisonous to humans and animals if ingested.

Glossary of Environmental Terms

Method 18: An EPA test method which uses gas chromatographic techniques to measure the concentration of volatile organic compounds in a gas stream.

Method 24: An EPA reference method to determine density, water content and total volatile content (water and VOC) of coatings.

Method 25: An EPA reference method to determine the VOC concentration in a gas stream.

Method Detection Limit (MDL): See limit of detection.

Methoxychlor: Pesticide that causes adverse health effects in domestic water supplies and is toxic to freshwater and marine aquatic life.

Methyl Orange Alkalinity: A measure of the total alkalinity in a water sample in which the color of methyl orange reflects the change in level.

Microbial Growth: The amplification or multiplication of microorganisms such as bacteria, algae, diatoms, plankton, and fungi.

Microbial Pesticide: A microorganism that is used to kill a pest, but is of minimum toxicity to humans.

Microclimate: 1. Localized climate conditions within an urban area or neighborhood. 2. The climate around a tree or shrub or a stand of trees.

Microenvironmental Method: A method for sequentially assessing exposure for a series of microenvironments that can be approximated by constant concentrations of a stressor.

Microenvironments: Well-defined surroundings such as the home, office, or kitchen that can be treated as uniform in terms of stressor concentration.

Million-Gallons Per Day (MGD): A measure of water flow.

Minimization: A comprehensive program to minimize or eliminate wastes, usually applied to wastes at their point of origin. (See: waste minimization.)

Mining of an Aquifer: Withdrawal over a period of time of ground water that exceeds the rate of recharge of the aquifer.

Mining Waste: Residues resulting from the extraction of raw materials from the earth.

Minor Source: New emissions sources or modifications to existing emissions sources that do not exceed NAAQS emission levels.

Minors: Publicly owned treatment works with flows less than 1 million gallons per day. (See: majors.)

Miscellaneous ACM: Interior asbestos-containing building material or structural components, members or fixtures, such as floor and ceiling tiles; does not include surfacing materials or thermal system insulation.

Miscellaneous Materials: Interior building materials on structural components, such as floor or ceiling tiles.

Miscible Liquids: Two or more liquids that can be mixed and will remain mixed under normal conditions.

Missed Detection: The situation that occurs when a test indicates that a tank is "tight" when in fact it is leaking.

Mist: Liquid particles measuring 40 to 500 micrometers (pm), are formed by condensation of vapor. By comparison, fog particles are smaller than 40 micrometers (pm).

Mitigation: Measures taken to reduce adverse impacts on the environment.

Mixed Funding: Settlements in which potentially responsible parties and EPA share the cost of a response action.

Mixed Glass: Recovered container glass not sorted into categories (e.g. color, grade).

Mixed Liquor: A mixture of activated sludge and water containing organic matter undergoing activated sludge treatment in an aeration tank.

Mixed Metals: Recovered metals not sorted into categories such as aluminum, tin, or steel cans or ferrous or non-ferrous metals.

Mixed Municipal Waste: Solid waste that has not been sorted into specific categories (such as plastic, glass, yard trimmings, etc.)

Mixed Paper: Recovered paper not sorted into categories such as old magazines, old newspapers, old corrugated boxes, etc.

Mixed Plastic: Recovered plastic unsorted by category.

Mobile Incinerator Systems: Hazardous waste incinerators that can be transported from one site to another.

Mobile Source: Any non-stationary source of air pollution such as cars, trucks, motorcycles, buses, airplanes, and locomotives.

Model Plant: A hypothetical plant design used for developing economic, environmental, and energy impact analyses as support for regulations or regulatory guidelines; first step in exploring the economic impact of a potential NSPS.

Modified Bin Method: Way of calculating the required heating or cooling for a building based on determining how much energy the system would use if outdoor temperatures were within a certain temperature interval and then multiplying the energy use by the time the temperature interval typically occurs.

Modified Source: The enlargement of a major stationary pollutant sources is often referred to as modification, implying that more emissions will occur.

Moisture Content: 1.The amount of water lost from soil upon drying to a constant weight, expressed as the weight per unit of dry soil or as the volume of water per unit bulk volume of the soil. For a fully saturated medium, moisture content indicates the porosity. 2. Water equivalent of snow on the ground; an indicator of snowmelt flood potential.

Molecule: The smallest division of a compound that still retains or exhibits all the properties of the substance.

Molten Salt Reactor: A thermal treatment unit that rapidly heats waste in a heat-conducting fluid bath of carbonate salt.

Monitoring: Periodic or continuous surveillance or testing to determine the level of compliance with statutory requirements and/or pollutant levels in various media or in humans, plants, and animals.

Monitoring Well: 1. A well used to obtain water quality samples or measure groundwater levels. 2. A well drilled at a hazardous waste management facility or Superfund site to collect ground-water samples for the purpose of physical, chemical, or biological analysis to determine the amounts, types, and distribution of contaminants in the groundwater beneath the site.

Monoclonal Antibodies (Also called MABs and MCAs): 1. Man-made (anthropogenic) clones of a molecule, produced in quantity for medical or research purposes. 2. Molecules of living organisms that selectively find and attach to other molecules to which their structure conforms exactly. This could also apply to equivalent activity by chemical molecules.

Monomictic: Lakes and reservoirs which are relatively deep, do not freeze over during winter, and undergo a single stratification and mixing cycle during the year (usually in the fall).

Montreal Protocol: Treaty, signed in 1987, governs stratospheric ozone protection and research, and the production and use of ozone-depleting substances. It provides for the end of production of ozone-depleting substances such as CFCS. Under the Protocol, various research groups continue to assess the ozone layer. The Multilateral Fund provides resources to developing nations to promote the transition to ozone-safe technologies.

Moratorium: During the negotiation process, a period of 60 to 90 days during which EPA and potentially responsible parties may reach settlement but no site response activities can be conducted.

Morbidity: Rate of disease incidence.

Mortality: Death rate.

Most Probable Number: An estimate of microbial density per unit volume of water sample, based on probability theory.

Muck Soils: Earth made from decaying plant materials.

Mudballs: Round material that forms in filters and gradually increases in size when not removed by backwashing.

Mulch: A layer of material (wood chips, straw, leaves, etc.) placed around plants to hold moisture, prevent weed growth, and enrich or sterilize the soil.

Multi-Media Approach: Joint approach to several environmental media, such as air, water, and land.

Multiple Chemical Sensitivity: A diagnostic label for people who suffer multi-system illnesses as a result of contact with, or proximity to, a variety of airborne agents and other substances.

Multiple Use: Use of land for more than one purpose; e.g., grazing of livestock, watershed and wildlife protection, recreation, and timber production. Also applies to use of bodies of water for recreational purposes, fishing, and water supply.

Multistage Remote Sensing: A strategy for landscape characterization that involves gathering and analyzing information at several geographic scales, ranging from generalized levels of detail at the national level through high levels of detail at the local scale.

Municipal Discharge: Discharge of effluent from waste water treatment plants which receive waste water from households, commercial establishments, and industries in the coastal drainage basin. Combined sewer/separate storm overflows are included in this category.

Municipal Sewage: Wastes (mostly liquid) originating from a community; may be composed of domestic wastewaters and/or industrial discharges.

Municipal Sludge: Semi-liquid residue remaining from the treatment of municipal water and wastewater.

Municipal Solid Waste: Common garbage or trash generated by industries, businesses, institutions, and homes.

Mutagen/Mutagenicity: An agent that causes a permanent genetic change in a cell other than that which occurs during normal growth. Mutagenicity is the capacity of a chemical or physical agent to cause such permanent changes.

N

National Ambient Air Quality Standards (NAAQS): Standards established by EPA that apply for outdoor air throughout the country. (See: criteria pollutants, state implementation plans, emissions trading.)

National Emissions Standards for Hazardous Air Pollutants (NESHAPS): Emissions standards set by EPA for an air pollutant not covered by NAAQS that may cause an increase in fatalities or in serious, irreversible, or incapacitating illness. Primary standards are designed to protect human health, secondary standards to protect public welfare (e.g. building facades, visibility, crops, and domestic animals).

National Environmental Performance Partnership Agreements: System that allows states to assume greater responsibility for environmental programs based on their relative ability to execute them.

National Estuary Program: A program established under the Clean Water Act Amendments of 1987 to develop and implement conservation and management plans for protecting estuaries and restoring and maintaining their chemical, physical, and biological integrity, as well as controlling point and nonpoint pollution sources.

National Municipal Plan: A policy created in 1984 by EPA and the states in 1984 to bring all publicly owned treatment works (POTWs) into compliance with Clean Water Act requirements.

National Oil and Hazardous Substances Contingency Plan (NOHSCP/NCP): The federal regulation that guides determination of the sites to be corrected under both the Superfund program and the program to prevent or control spills into surface waters or elsewhere.

National Pollutant Discharge Elimination System (NPDES): A provision of the Clean Water Act which prohibits discharge of pollutants into waters of the United States unless a special permit is issued by EPA, a state, or, where delegated, a tribal government on an Indian reservation.

National Priorities List (NPL): EPA's list of the most serious uncontrolled or abandoned hazardous waste sites identified for possible long-term remedial action under Superfund. The list is based primarily on the score a site receives from the Hazard Ranking System. EPA is required to update the NPL at least once a year. A site must be on the NPL to receive money from the Trust Fund for remedial action.

National Response Center: The federal operations center that receives notifications of all releases of oil and hazardous substances into the environment; open 24 hours a day, is operated by the U.S. Coast Guard, which evaluates all reports and notifies the appropriate agency.

National Response Team (NRT): Representatives of 13 federal agencies that, as a team, coordinate federal responses to nationally significant incidents of pollution—an oil spill, a major chemical release, or a - superfund response action—and provide advice and technical assistance to the responding agency(ies) before and during a response action.

National Secondary Drinking Water Regulations: Commonly referred to as NSDWRs.

Navigable Waters: Traditionally, waters sufficiently deep and wide for navigation by all, or specified vessels; such waters in the United States come under federal jurisdiction and are protected by certain provisions of the Clean Water Act.

Necrosis: Death of plant or animal cells or tissues. In plants, necrosis can discolor stems or leaves or kill a plant entirely.

Negotiations (Under Superfund): After potentially responsible parties are identified for a site, EPA coordinates with them to reach a settlement that will result in the PRP paying for or conducting the cleanup under EPA supervision. If negotiations fail, EPA can order the PRP to conduct the cleanup or EPA can pay for the cleanup using Superfund monies and then sue to recover the costs.

Nematocide: A chemical agent which is destructive to nematodes.

Nephelometric: Method of of measuring turbidity in a water sample by passing light through the sample and measuring the amount of the light that is deflected.

Netting: A concept in which all emissions sources in the same area that owned or controlled by a single company are treated as one large source, thereby allowing flexibility in controlling individual sources in order to meet a single emissions standard. (See: bubble.)

Neutralization: Decreasing the acidity or alkalinity of a substance by adding alkaline or acidic materials, respectively.

New Source: Any stationary source built or modified after publication of final or proposed regulations that prescribe a given standard of performance.

New Source Performance Standards (NSPS): Uniform national EPA air emission and water effluent standards which limit the amount of pollution allowed from new sources or from modified existing sources.

New Source Review (NSR): A Clean Air Act requirement that State Implementation Plans must include a permit review that applies to the construction and operation of new and modified stationary sources in nonattainment areas to ensure attainment of national ambient air quality standards.

Nitrate: A compound containing nitrogen that can exist in the atmosphere or as a dissolved gas in water and which can have harmful effects on humans and animals. Nitrates in water can cause severe illness in infants and domestic animals. A plant nutrient and inorganic fertilizer, nitrate is found in septic systems, animal feed lots, agricultural fertilizers, manure, industrial waste waters, sanitary landfills, and garbage dumps.

Nitric Oxide (NO): A gas formed by combustion under high temperature and high pressure in an internal combustion engine; it is converted by sunlight and photochemical processes in ambient air to nitrogen oxide. NO is a precursor of ground-level ozone pollution, or smog..

Nitrification: The process whereby ammonia in wastewater is oxidized to nitrite and then to nitrate by bacterial or chemical reactions.

Nitrilotriacetic Acid (NTA): A compound now replacing phosphates in detergents.

Nitrite: 1. An intermediate in the process of nitrification. 2. Nitrous oxide salts used in food preservation.

Nitrogen Dioxide (NO_2): The result of nitric oxide combining with oxygen in the atmosphere; major component of photochemical smog.

Nitrogen Oxide (NO_x): The result of photochemical reactions of nitric oxide in ambient air; major component of photochemical smog. Product of combustion from transportation and stationary sources and a major contributor to the formation of ozone in the troposphere and to acid deposition.

Nitrogenous Wastes: Animal or vegetable residues that contain significant amounts of nitrogen.

Nitrophenols: Synthetic organopesticides containing carbon, hydrogen, nitrogen, and oxygen.

No Further Remedial Action Planned: Determination made by EPA following a preliminary assessment that a site does not pose a significant risk and so requires no further activity under CERCLA.

No Observable Adverse Effect Level (NOAEL): An exposure level at which there are no statistically or biologically significant increases in the frequency or severity of adverse effects between the exposed population and its appropriate control; some effects may be produced at this level, but they are not considered as adverse, or as precurors to adverse effects. In an experiment with several NOAELs, the regulatory focus is primarily on the highest one, leading to the common usage of the term NOAEL as the highest exposure without adverse effects.

No Till: Planting crops without prior seedbed preparation, into an existing cover crop, sod, or crop residues, and eliminating subsequent tillage operations.

No-Observed-Effect-Level (NOEL): Exposure level at which there are no statistically or biological significant differences in the frequency or severity of any effect in the exposed or control populations.

Noble Metal: Chemically inactive metal such as gold; does not corrode easily.

Noise: Product-level or product-volume changes occurring during a test that are not related to a leak but may be mistaken for one.

Non-Aqueous Phase Liquid (NAPL): Contaminants that remain undiluted as the original bulk liquid in the subsurface, e.g. spilled oil. (See: fee product.)

Non-Attainment Area: Area that does not meet one or more of the National Ambient Air Quality Standards for the criteria pollutants designated in the Clean Air Act.

Non-Binding Allocations of Responsibility (NBAR): A process for EPA to propose a way for potentially responsible parties to allocate costs among themselves.

Non-Community Water System: A public water system that is not a community water system; e.g. the water supply at a camp site or national park.

Non-Compliance Coal: Any coal that emits greater than 3.0 pounds of sulfur dioxide per million BTU when burned. Also known as high-sulfur coal.

Non-Contact Cooling Water: Water used for cooling which does not come into direct contact with any raw material, product, byproduct, or waste.

Non-Conventional Pollutant: Any pollutant not statutorily listed or which is poorly understood by the scientific community.

Non-Degradation: An environmental policy which disallows any lowering of naturally occurring quality regardless of preestablished health standards.

Non-Ferrous Metals: Nonmagnetic metals such as aluminum, lead, and copper. Products made all or in part from such metals include containers, packaging, appliances, furniture, electronic equipment and aluminum foil.

Non-ionizing Electromagnetic Radiation: 1. Radiation that does not change the structure of atoms but does heat tissue and may cause harmful biological effects. 2. Microwaves, radio waves, and low-frequency electromagnetic fields from high-voltage transmission lines.

Non-Methane Hydrocarbon (NMHC): The sum of all hydrocarbon air pollutants except methane; significant precursors to ozone formation.

Non-Methane Organic Gases (NMOG): The sum of all organic air pollutants. Excluding methane; they account for aldehydes, ketones, alcohols, and other pollutants that are not hydrocarbons but are precursors of ozone.

Non-Point Sources: Diffuse pollution sources (i.e. without a single point of origin or not introduced into a receiving stream from a specific outlet). The pollutants are generally carried off the land by storm water. Common non-point sources are agriculture, forestry, urban, mining, construction, dams, channels, land disposal, saltwater intrusion, and city streets.

Non-potable: Water that is unsafe or unpalatable to drink because it contains pollutants, contaminants, minerals, or infective agents.

Non-Road Emissions: Pollutants emitted by combustion engines on farm and construction equipment, gasoline-powered lawn and garden equipment, and power boats and outboard motors.

Non-Transient Non-Community Water System: A public water system that regularly serves at least 25 of the same non-resident persons per day for more than six months per year.

Nondischarging Treatment Plant: A treatment plant that does not discharge treated wastewater into any stream or river. Most are pond systems that dispose of the total flow they receive by means of evaporation or percolation to groundwater, or facilities that dispose of their effluent by recycling or reuse (e.g. spray irrigation or groundwater discharge).

Nonfriable Asbestos-Containing Materials: Any material containing more than one percent asbestos (as determined by Polarized Light Microscopy) that, when dry, cannot be crumbled, pulverized, or reduced to powder by hand pressure.

Nonhazardous Industrial Waste: Industrial process waste in wastewater not considered municipal solid waste or hazardous waste under RARA.

Notice of Deficiency: An EPA request to a facility owner or operator requesting additional information before a preliminary decision on a permit application can be made.

Notice of Intent to Cancel: Notification sent to registrants when EPA decides to cancel registration of a product containing a pesticide.

Notice of Intent to Deny: Notification by EPA of its preliminary intent to deny a permit application.

Notice of Intent to Suspend: Notification sent to a pesticide registrant when EPA decides to suspend product sale and distribution because of failure to submit requested data in a timely and/or acceptable manner, or because of imminent hazard. (See: emergency suspension.)

Nuclear Reactors and Support Facilities: Uranium mills, commercial power reactors, fuel reprocessing plants, and uranium enrichment facilities.

Nuclear Winter: Prediction by some scientists that smoke and debris rising from massive fires of a nuclear war could block sunlight for weeks or months, cooling the earth's surface and producing climate changes that could, for example, negatively affect world agricultural and weather patterns.

Nuclide: An atom characterized by the number of protons, neturons, and energy in the nucleus.

Nutrient: Any substance assimilated by living things that promotes growth. The term is generally applied to nitrogen and phosphorus in wastewater, but is also applied to other essential and trace elements.

Nutrient Pollution: Contamination of water resources by excessive inputs of nutrients. In surface waters, excess algal production is a major concern.

O

Ocean Discharge Waiver: A variance from Clean Water Act requirements for discharges into marine waters.

Odor Threshold: The minimum odor of a water or air sample that can just be detected after successive dilutions with odorless water. Also called threshold odor.

OECD Guidelines: Testing guidelines prepared by the Organization of Economic and Cooperative Development of the United Nations. They assist in preparation of protocols for studies of toxicology, environmental fate, etc.

Off-Site Facility: A hazardous waste treatment, storage or disposal area that is located away from the generating site.

Office Paper: High grade papers such as copier paper, computer printout, and stationary almost entirely made of uncoated chemical pulp, although some ground wood is used. Such waste is also generated in homes, schools, and elsewhere.

Offsets: A concept whereby emissions from proposed new or modified stationary sources are balanced by reductions from existing sources to stabilize total emissions. (See: bubble, emissions trading, netting)

Offstream Use: Water withdrawn from surface or groundwater sources for use at another place.

Oil and Gas Waste: Gas and oil drilling muds, oil production brines, and other waste associated with exploration for, development and production of crude oil or natural gas.

Oil Desulfurization: Widely used precombustion method for reducing sulfur dioxide emissions from oil-burning power plants. The oil is treated with hydrogen, which removes some of the sulfur by forming hydrogen sulfide gas.

Oil Fingerprinting: A method that identifies sources of oil and allows spills to be traced to their source.

Oil Spill: An accidental or intentional discharge of oil which reaches bodies of water. Can be controlled by chemical dispersion, combustion, mechanical containment, and/or adsorption. Spills from tanks and pipelines can also occur away from water bodies, contaminating the soil, getting into sewer systems and threatening underground water sources.

Oligotrophic Lakes: Deep clear lakes with few nutrients, little organic matter and a high dissolved-oxygen level.

On-Scene Coordinator (OSC): The predesignated EPA, Coast Guard, or Department of Defense official who coordinates and directs Superfund removal actions or Clean Water Act oil- or hazardous-spill response actions.

On-Site Facility: A hazardous waste treatment, storage or disposal area that is located on the generating site.

Onboard Controls: Devices placed on vehicles to capture gasoline vapor during refueling and route it to the engines when the vehicle is starting so that it can be efficiently burned.

Onconogenicity: The capacity to induce cancer.

One-hit Model: A mathematical model based on the biological theory that a single "hit" of some minimum critical amount of a carcinogen at a cellular target such as DNA can start an irreversible series events leading to a tumor.

Opacity: The amount of light obscured by particulate pollution in the air; clear window glass has zero opacity, a brick wall is 100 percent opaque. Opacity is an indicator of changes in performance of particulate control systems.

Open Burning: Uncontrolled fires in an open dump.

Open Dump: An uncovered site used for disposal of waste without environmental controls. (See: dump.)

Operable Unit: Term for each of a number of separate activities undertaken as part of a Superfund site cleanup. A typical operable unit would be removal of drums and tanks from the surface of a site.

Operating Conditions: Conditions specified in a RCRA permit that dictate how an incinerator must operate as it burns different waste types. A trial burn is used to identify operating conditions needed to meet specified performance standards.

Operation and Maintenance: 1. Activities conducted after a Superfund site action is completed to ensure that the action is effective. 2. Actions taken after construction to ensure that facilities constructed to treat waste water will be properly operated and maintained to achieve normative efficiency levels and prescribed effluent limitations in an optimum manner. 3. On-going asbestos management plan in a school or other public building, including regular inspections, various methods of maintaining asbestos in place, and removal when necessary.

Operator Certification: Certification of operators of community and nontransient noncommunity water systems, asbestos specialists, pesticide applicators, hazardous waste transporter, and other such specialists as required by the EPA or a state agency implementing an EPA-approved environmental regulatory program.

Optimal Corrosion Control Treatment: An erosion control treatment that minimizes the lead and copper concentrations at users' taps while also ensuring that the treatment does not cause the water system to violate any national primary drinking water regulations.

Oral Toxicity: Ability of a pesticide to cause injury when ingested.

Organic: 1. Referring to or derived from living organisms. 2. In chemistry, any compound containing carbon.

Organic Chemicals/Compounds: Naturally occuring (animal or plant-produced or synthetic) substances containing mainly carbon, hydrogen, nitrogen, and oxygen.

Organic Matter: Carbonaceous waste contained in plant or animal matter and originating from domestic or industrial sources

Organism: Any form of animal or plant life.

Organophosphates: Pesticides that contain phosphorus; short-lived, but some can be toxic when first applied.

Organophyllic: A substance that easily combines with organic compounds.

Organotins: Chemical compounds used in anti-foulant paints to protect the hulls of boats and ships, buoys, and pilings from marine organisms such as barnacles.

Original AHERA Inspection/Original Inspection/Inspection: Examination of school buildings arranged by Local Education Agencies to identify asbestos-containing-materials, evaluate their condition, and take samples of materials suspected to contain asbestos; performed by EPA-accredited inspectors.

Original Generation Point: Where regulated medical or other material first becomes waste.

Osmosis: The passage of a liquid from a weak solution to a more concentrated solution across a semipermeable membrane that allows passage of the solvent (water) but not the dissolved solids.

Other Ferrous Metals: Recyclable metals from strapping, furniture, and metal found in tires and consumer electronics but does not include metals found in construction materials or cars, locomotives, and ships. (See: ferrous metals.)

Other Glass: Recyclable glass from furniture, appliances, and consumer electronics. Does not include glass from transportation products (cars trucks or shipping containers) and construction or demolition debris. (See: glass.)

Other Nonferrous Metals: Recyclable nonferrous metals such as lead, copper, and zinc from appliances, consumer electronics, and nonpackaging aluminum products. Does not include nonferrous metals from industrial applications and construction and demolition debris. (See: nonferrous metals.)

Other Paper: For Recyclable paper from books, third-class mail, commercial printing, paper towels, plates and cups; and other nonpackaging paper such as posters, photographic papers, cards and games, milk cartons, folding boxes, bags, wrapping paper, and paperboard. Does not include wrapping paper or shipping cartons.

Other Plastics: Recyclable plastic from appliances, eating utensils, plates, containers, toys, and various kinds of equipment. Does not include heavy-duty plastics such as yielding materials.

Other Solid Waste: Recyclable nonhazardous solid wastes, other than municipal solid waste, covered under Subtitle D of RARA. (See: solid waste.)

Other Wood: Recyclable wood from furniture, consumer electronics cabinets, and other nonpackaging wood products. Does not include lumber and tree stumps recovered from construction and demolition activities, and industrial process waste such as shavings and sawdust.

Outdoor Air Supply: Air brought into a building from outside.

Outfall: The place where effluent is discharged into receiving waters.

Overburden: Rock and soil cleared away before mining.

Overdraft: The pumping of water from a groundwater basin or aquifer in excess of the supply flowing into the basin; results in a depletion or "mining" of the groundwater in the basin. (See: groundwater mining)

Overfire Air: Air forced into the top of an incinerator or boiler to fan the flames.

Overflow Rate: One of the guidelines for design of the settling tanks and clarifers in a treatment plant; used by plant operators to determine if tanks and clarifiers are over or under-used.

Overland Flow: A land application technique that cleanses waste water by allowing it to flow over a sloped surface. As the water flows over the surface, contaminants are absorbed and the water is collected at the bottom of the slope for reuse.

Oversized Regulated Medical Waste: Medical waste that is too large for plastic bags or standard containers.

Overturn: One complete cycle of top to bottom mixing of previously stratified water masses. This phenomenon may occur in spring or fall, or after storms, and results in uniformity of chemical and physical properties of water at all depths.

Oxidant: A collective term for some of the primary constituents of photochemical smog.

Oxidation Pond: A man-made (anthropogenic) body of water in which waste is consumed by bacteria, used most frequently with other waste-treatment processes; a sewage lagoon.

Oxidation: The chemical addition of oxygen to break down pollutants or organizac waste; e.g., destruction of chemicals such as cyanides, phenols, and organic sulfur compounds in sewage by bacterial and chemical means.

Oxidation-Reduction Potential: The electric potential required to transfer electrons from one compound or element (the oxidant) to another compound (the reductant); used as a qualitative measure of the state of oxidation in water treatment systems.

Oxygenated Fuels: Gasoline which has been blended with alcohols or ethers that contain oxygen in order to reduce carbon monoxide and other emissions.

Oxygenated Solvent: An organic solvent containing oxygen as part of the molecular structure. Alcohols and ketones are oxygenated compounds often used as paint solvents.

Ozonation/Ozonator: Application of ozone to water for disinfection or for taste and odor control. The ozonator is the device that does this.

Ozone (O_3): Found in two layers of the atmosphere, the stratosphere and the troposphere. In the stratosphere (the atmospheric layer 7 to 10 miles or more above the earth's surface) ozone is a natural form of oxygen that provides a protective layer shielding the earth from ultraviolet radiation.In the troposphere (the layer extending up 7 to 10 miles from the earth's surface), ozone is a chemical oxidant and major component of photochemical smog. It can seriously impair the respiratory system and is one of the most wide- spread of all the criteria pollutants for which the Clean Air Act required EPA to set standards. Ozone in the troposphere is produced through complex chemical reactions of nitrogen oxides, which are among the primary pollutants emitted by combustion sources; hydrocarbons, released into the atmosphere through the combustion, handling and processing of petroleum products; and sunlight.

Ozone Depletion: Destruction of the stratospheric ozone layer which shields the earth from ultraviolet radiation harmful to life. This destruction of ozone is caused by the breakdown of certain chlorine and/or bromine containing compounds (chlorofluorocarbons or halons), which break down when they reach the stratosphere and then catalytically destroy ozone molecules.

Ozone Hole: A thinning break in the stratospheric ozone layer. Designation of amount of such depletion as an "ozone hole" is made when the detected amount of depletion exceeds fifty percent. Seasonal ozone holes have been observed over both the Antarctic and Arctic regions, part of Canada, and the extreme northeastern United States.

Ozone Layer: The protective layer in the atmosphere, about 15 miles above the ground, that absorbs some of the sun's ultraviolet rays, thereby reducing the amount of potentially harmful radiation that reaches the earth's surface.

P

Packaging: The assembly of one or more containers and any other components necessary to ensure minimum compliance with a program's storage and shipment packaging requirements. Also, the containers, etc. involved.

Packed Bed Scrubber: An air pollution control device in which emissions pass through alkaline water to neutralize hydrogen chloride gas.

Packed Tower: A pollution control device that forces dirty air through a tower packed with crushed rock or wood chips while liquid is sprayed over the packing material. The pollutants in the air stream either dissolve or chemically react with the liquid.

Packer: An inflatable gland, or balloon, used to create a temporary seal in a borehole, probe hole, well, or drive casing. It is made of rubber or non-reactive materials.

Palatable Water: Water, at a desirable temperature, that is free from objectionable tastes, odors, colors, and turbidity.

Pandemic: A widespread epidemic throughout an area, nation or the world.

Paper: In the recycling business, refers to products and materials, including newspapers, magazines, office papers, corrugated containers, bags and some paperboard packaging that can be recycled into new paper products.

Paper Processor/Plastics Processor: Intermediate facility where recovered paper or plastic products and materials are sorted, decontaminated, and prepared for final recycling.

Parameter: A variable, measurable property whose value is a determinant of the characteristics of a system; e.g. temperature, pressure, and density are parameters of the atmosphere.

Paraquat: A standard herbicide used to kill various types of crops, including marijuana. Causes lung damage if smoke from the crop is inhaled..

Parshall Flume: Device used to measure the flow of water in an open channel.

Part A Permit, Part B Permit: (See: Interim Permit Status.)

Participation Rate: Portion of population participating in a recycling program.

Particle Count: Results of a microscopic examination of treated water with a special "particle counter" that classifies suspended particles by number and size.

Particulate Loading: The mass of particulates per unit volume of air or water.

Particulates: 1. Fine liquid or solid particles such as dust, smoke, mist, fumes, or smog, found in air or emissions. 2. Very small solids suspended in water; they can vary in size, shape, density and electrical charge and can be gathered together by coagulation and flocculation.

Partition Coefficient: Measure of the sorption phenomenon, whereby a pesticide is divided between the soil and water phase; also referred to as adsorption partition coefficient.

Parts Per Billion (ppb)/Parts Per Million (ppm): Units commonly used to express contamination ratios, as in establishing the maximum permissible amount of a contaminant in water, land, or air.

Passive Smoking/Secondhand Smoke: Inhalation of others' tobacco smoke.

Passive Treatment Walls: Technology in which a chemical reaction takes place when contaminated ground water comes in contact with a barrier such as limestone or a wall containing iron filings.

Pathogens: Microorganisms (e.g., bacteria, viruses, or parasites) that can cause disease in humans, animals and plants.

Pathway: The physical course a chemical or pollutant takes from its source to the exposed organism.

Pay-As-You-Throw/Unit-Based Pricing: Systems under which residents pay for municipal waste management and disposal services by weight or volume collected, not a fixed fee.

Peak Electricity Demand: The maximum electricity used to meet the cooling load of a building or buildings in a given area.

Peak Levels: Levels of airborne pollutant contaminants much higher than average or occurring for short periods of time in response to sudden releases.

Percent Saturatiuon: The amount of a substance that is dissolved in a solution compared to the amount that could be dissolved in it.

Perched Water: Zone of unpressurized water held above the water table by impermeable rock or sediment.

Percolating Water: Water that passes through rocks or soil under the force of gravity.

Percolation: 1. The movement of water downward and radially through subsurface soil layers, usually continuing downward to ground water. Can also involve upward movement of water. 2. Slow seepage of water through a filter.

Performance Bond: Cash or securities deposited before a landfill operating permit is issued, which are held to ensure that all requirements for operating ad subsequently closing the landfill are faithful performed. The money is returned to the owner after proper closure of the landfill is completed. If contamination or other problems appear at any time during operation, or upon closure, and are not addressed, the owner must forfeit all or part of the bond which is then used to cover clean-up costs.

Performance Data (For Incinerators): Information collected, during a trial burn, on concentrations of designated organic compounds and pollutants found in incinerator emissions. Data analysis must show that the incinerator meets performance standards under operating conditions specified in the RCRA permit. (See: trial burn; performance standards.)

Performance Standards: 1. Regulatory requirements limiting the concentrations of designated organic compounds, particulate matter, and hydrogen chloride in emissions from incinerators. 2. Operating standards established by EPA for various permitted pollution control systems, asbestos inspections, and various program operations and maintenance requirements.

Periphyton: Microscopic underwater plants and animals that are firmly attached to solid surfaces such as rocks, logs, and pilings.

Permeability: The rate at which liquids pass through soil or other materials in a specified direction.

Permissible Dose: The dose of a chemical that may be received by an individual without the expectation of a significantly harmful result.

Permissible Exposure Limit: Also referred to as PEL, federal limits for workplace exposure to contaminants as established by OSHA.

Permit: An authorization, license, or equivalent control document issued by EPA or an approved state agency to implement the requirements of an environmental regulation; e.g. a permit to operate a wastewater treatment plant or to operate a facility that may generate harmful emissions.

Persistence: Refers to the length of time a compound stays in the environment, once introduced. A compound may persist for less than a second or indefinitely.

Persistent Pesticides: Pesticides that do not break down chemically or break down very slowly and remain in the environment after a growing season.

Personal Air Samples: Air samples taken with a pump that is directly attached to the worker with the collecting filter and cassette placed in the worker's breathing zone (required under OSHA asbestos standards and EPA worker protection rule).

Personal Measurement: A measurement collected from an individual's immediate environment.

Personal Protective Equipment: Clothing and equipment worn by pesticide mixers, loaders and applicators and re-entry workers, hazmat emergency responders, workers cleaning up Superfund sites, et. al., which is worn to reduce their exposure to potentially hazardous chemicals and other pollutants.

Pest: An insect, rodent, nematode, fungus, weed or other form of terrestrial or aquatic plant or animal life that is injurious to health or the environment.

Pest Control Operator: Person or company that applies pesticides as a business (e.g. exterminator); usually describes household services, not agricultural applications.

Pesticide: Substances or mixture there of intended for preventing, destroying, repelling, or mitigating any pest. Also, any substance or mixture intended for use as a plant regulator, defoliant, or desiccant.

Pesticide Regulation Notice: Formal notice to pesticide registrants about important changes in regulatory policy, procedures, regulations.

Pesticide Tolerance: The amount of pesticide residue allowed by law to remain in or on a harvested crop. EPA sets these levels well below the point where the compounds might be harmful to consumers.

PETE (Polyethylene Terepthalate): Thermoplastic material used in plastic soft drink and rigid containers.

Petroleum: Crude oil or any fraction thereof that is liquid under normal conditions of temperature and pressure. The term includes petroleum-based substances comprising a complex blend of hydrocarbons derived from crude oil through the process of separation, conversion, upgrading, and finishing, such as motor fuel, jet oil, lubricants, petroleum solvents, and used oil.

Petroleum Derivatives: Chemicals formed when gasoline breaks down in contact with ground water.

pH: An expression of the intensity of the basic or acid condition of a liquid; may range from 0 to 14, where 0 is the most acid and 7 is neutral. Natural waters usually have a pH between 6.5 and 8.5.

Pharmacokinetics: The study of the way that drugs move through the body after they are swallowed or injected.

Phenolphthalein Alkalinity: The alkalinity in a water sample measured by the amount of standard acid needed to lower the pH to a level of 8.3 as indicated by the change of color of the phenolphthalein from pink to clear.

Phenols: Organic compounds that are byproducts of petroleum refining, tanning, and textile, dye, and resin manufacturing. Low concentrations cause taste and odor problems in water; higher concentrations can kill aquatic life and humans.

Phosphates: Certain chemical compounds containing phosphorus.

Phosphogypsum Piles (Stacks): Principal byproduct generated in production of phosphoric acid from phosphate rock. These piles may generate radioactive radon gas.

Phosphorus: An essential chemical food element that can contribute to the eutrophication of lakes and other water bodies. Increased phosphorus levels result from discharge of phosphorus-containing materials into surface waters.

Phosphorus Plants: Facilities using electric furnaces to produce elemental phosphorous for commercial use, such as high grade phosphoric acid, phosphate-based detergent, and organic chemicals use.

Photochemical Oxidants: Air pollutants formed by the action of sunlight on oxides of nitrogen and hydrocarbons.

Photochemical Smog: Air pollution caused by chemical reactions of various pollutants emitted from different sources. (See: photochemical oxidants.)

Photosynthesis: The manufacture by plants of carbohydrates and oxygen from carbon dioxide mediated by chlorophyll in the presence of sunlight.

Physical and Chemical Treatment: Processes generally used in large-scale wastewater treatment facilities. Physical processes may include air-stripping or filtration. Chemical treatment includes coagulation, chlorination, or ozonation. The term can also refer to treatment of toxic materials in surface and ground waters, oil spills, and some methods of dealing with hazardous materials on or in the ground.

Phytoplankton: That portion of the plankton community comprised of tiny plants; e.g. algae, diatoms.

Phytoremediation: Low-cost remediation option for sites with widely dispersed contamination at low concentrations.

Phytotoxic: Harmful to plants.

Phytotreatment: The cultivation of specialized plants that absorb specific contaminants from the soil through their roots or foliage. This reduces the concentration of contaminants in the soil, but incorporates them into biomasses that may be released back into the environment when the plant dies or is harvested.

Picocuries Per Liter pCi/L): A unit of measure for levels of radon gas; becquerels per cubic meter is metric equivalent.

Piezometer: A nonpumping well, generally of small diameter, for measuring the elevation of a water table.

Pilot Tests: Testing a cleanup technology under actual site conditions to identify potential problems prior to full-scale implementation.

Plankton: Tiny plants and animals that live in water.

Plasma Arc Reactors: devices that use an electric arc to thermally decompose organic and inorganic materials at ultra-high temperatures into gases and a vitrified slag residue. A plasma arc reactor can operate as any of the following:

- integral component of chemical, fuel, or electricty production systems, processing high or medium value organic compounds into a synthetic gas used as a fuel

- materials recovery device, processing scrap to recover metal from the slag
- destruction or incineration system, processing waste materials into slag and gases ignited inside of a secondary combustion chamber that follows the reactor

Plasmid: A circular piece of DNA that exists apart from the chromosome and replicates independently of it. Bacterial plasmids carry information that renders the bacteria resistant to antibiotics. Plasmids are often used in genetic engineering to carry desired genes into organisms.

Plastics: Non-metallic chemoreactive compounds molded into rigid or pliable construction materials, fabrics, etc.

Plate Tower Scrubber: An air pollution control device that neutralizes hydrogen chloride gas by bubbling alkaline water through holes in a series of metal plates.

Plug Flow: Type of flow the occurs in tanks, basins, or reactors when a slug of water moves through without ever dispersing or mixing with the rest of the water flowing through.

Plugging: Act or process of stopping the flow of water, oil, or gas into or out of a formation through a borehole or well penetrating that formation.

Plume: 1. A visible or measurable discharge of a contaminant from a given point of origin. Can be visible or thermal in water, or visible in the air as, for example, a plume of smoke. 2 The area of radiation leaking from a damaged reactor. 3. Area downwind within which a release could be dangerous for those exposed to leaking fumes.

Plutonium: A radioactive metallic element chemically similar to uranium.

PM-10/PM-2.5: PM 10 is measure of particles in the atmosphere with a diameter of less than ten or equal to a nominal 10 micrometers. PM-2.5 is a measure of smaller particles in the air. PM-10 has been the pollutant particulate level standard against which EPA has been measuring Clean Air Act compliance. On the basis of newer scientific findings, the Agency is considering regulations that will make PM-2.5 the new "standard".

Pneumoconiosis: Health conditions characterized by permanent deposition of substantial amounts of particulate matter in the lungs and by the tissue reaction to its presence; can range from relatively harmless forms of sclerosis to the destructive fibrotic effect of silicosis.

Point Source: A stationary location or fixed facility from which pollutants are discharged; any single identifiable source of pollution; e.g. a pipe, ditch, ship, ore pit, factory smokestack.

Point-of-Contact Measurement of Exposure: Estimating exposure by measuring concentrations over time (while the exposure is taking place) at or near the place where it is occurring.

Point-of-Disinfectant Application: The point where disinfectant is applied and water downstream of that point is not subject to recontamination by surface water runoff.

Point-of-Use Treatment Device: Treatment device applied to a single tap to reduce contaminants in the drinking water at the one faucet.

Pollen: The fertilizing element of flowering plants; background air pollutant.

Pollutant: Generally, any substance introduced into the environment that adversely affects the usefulness of a resource or the health of humans, animals, or ecosystems..

Pollutant Pathways: Avenues for distribution of pollutants. In most buildings, for example, HVAC systems are the primary pathways although all building components can interact to affect how air movement distributes pollutants.

Pollutant Standard Index (PSI): Indicator of one or more pollutants that may be used to inform the public about the potential for adverse health effects from air pollution in major cities.

Pollution: Generally, the presence of a substance in the environment that because of its chemical composition or quantity prevents the functioning of natural processes and produces undesirable environmental and health effects.Under the Clean Water Act, for example, the term has been defined as the man-made or man-induced alteration of the physical, biological, chemical, and radiological integrity of water and other media.

Pollution Prevention: 1. Identifying areas, processes, and activities which create excessive waste products or pollutants in order to reduce or prevent them through, alteration, or eliminating a process. Such activities, consistent with the Pollution Prevention Act of 1990, are conducted across all EPA programs and can involve cooperative efforts with such agencies as the Departments of Agriculture and Energy. 2. EPA has initiated a number of voluntary programs in which industrial, or commercial or "partners" join with EPA in promoting activities that conserve energy, conserve and protect water supply, reduce emissions or find ways of utilizing them as energy resources, and reduce the waste stream. Among these are: Agstar, to reduce methane emissions through manure management. Climate Wise, to lower industrial greenhouse-gas emissions and energy costs. Coalbed Methane Outreach, to boost methane recovery at coal mines. Design for the Environment, to foster including environmental considerations in product design and processes. Energy Star programs, to promote energy efficiency in commercial and residential buildings, office equipment, transformers, computers, office equipment, and home appliances. Environmental Accounting, to help businesses identify environmental costs and factor them into management decision making. Green Chemistry, to promote and recognize cost-effective breakthroughs in chemistry that prevent pollution. Green Lights, to spread the use of energy-efficient lighting technologies. Indoor Environments, to reduce risks from indoor-air pollution. Landfill Methane Outreach, to develop landfill gas-to-energy projects. Natural Gas Star, to reduce methane emissions from the natural gas industry. Ruminant Livestock Methane, to reduce methane emissions from ruminant livestock. Transportation Partners, to reduce carbon dioxide emissions from the transportation sector. Voluntary Aluminum Industrial Partnership, to reduce perfluorocarbon emissions from the primary aluminum industry. WAVE, to promote efficient water use in the lodging industry. Wastewi$e, to reduce business-generated solid waste through prevention, reuse, and recycling. (See: Common Sense Initiative and Project XL.)

Polychlorinated Biphenyls: A group of toxic, persistent chemicals used in electrical transformers and capacitors for insulating purposes, and in gas pipeline systems as lubricant. The sale and new use of these chemicals, also known as PCBs, were banned by law in 1979.

Portal-of-Entry Effect: A local effect produced in the tissue or organ of first contact between a toxicant and the biological system.

Polonium: A radioactive element that occurs in pitchblende and other uranium-containing ores.

Polyelectrolytes: Synthetic chemicals that help solids to clump during sewage treatment.

Polymer: A natural or synthetic chemical structure where two or more like molecules are joined to form a more complex molecular structure (e.g. polyethylene in plastic).

Polyvinyl Chloride (PVC): A tough, environmentally indestructible plastic that releases hydrochloric acid when burned.

Population: A group of interbreeding organisms occupying a particular space; the number of humans or other living creatures in a designated area.

Population at Risk: A population subgroup that is more likely to be exposed to a chemical, or is more sensitive to the chemical, than is the general population.

Porosity: Degree to which soil, gravel, sediment, or rock is permeated with pores or cavities through which water or air can move.

Post-Chlorination: Addition of chlorine to plant effluent for disinfectant purposes after the effluent has been treated.

Post-Closure: The time period following the shutdown of a waste management or manufacturing facility; for monitoring purposes, often considered to be 30 years.

Post-Consumer Materials/Waste: Recovered materials that are diverted from municipal solid waste for the purpose of collection, recycling, and disposition.

Post-Consumer Recycling: Use of materials generated from residential and consumer waste for new or similar purposes; e.g. converting wastepaper from offices into corrugated boxes or newsprint.

Potable Water: Water that is safe for drinking and cooking.

Potential Dose: The amount of a compound contained in material swallowed, breathed, or applied to the skin.

Potentially Responsible Party (PRP): Any individual or company—including owners, operators, transporters or generators—potentially responsible for, or contributing to a spill or other contamination at a Superfund site. Whenever possible, through administrative and legal actions, EPA requires PRPs to clean up hazardous sites they have contaminated.

Potentiation: The ability of one chemical to increase the effect of another chemical.

Potentiometric Surface: The surface to which water in an aquifer can rise by hydrostatic pressure.

Precautionary Principle: When information about potential risks is incomplete, basing decisions about the best ways to manage or reduce risks on a preference for avoiding unnecessary health risks instead of on unnecessary economic expenditures.

Pre-Consumer Materials/Waste: Materials generated in manufacturing and converting processes such as manufacturing scrap and trimmings and cuttings. Includes print overruns, overissue publications, and obsolete inventories.

Pre-Harvest Interval: The time between the last pesticide application and harvest of the treated crops.

Prechlorination: The addition of chlorine at the headworks of a treatment plant prior to other treatment processes. Done mainly for disinfection and control of tastes, odors, and aquatic growths, and to aid in coagulation and settling,

Precipitate: A substance separated from a solution or suspension by chemical or physical change.

Precipitation: Removal of hazardous solids from liquid waste to permit safe disposal; removal of particles from airborne emissions as in rain (e.g. acid precipitation).

Precipitator: Pollution control device that collects particles from an air stream.

Precursor: In photochemistry, a compound antecedent to a pollutant. For example, volatile organic compounds (VOCs) and nitric oxides of nitrogen react in sunlight to form ozone or other photochemical oxidants. As such, VOCs and oxides of nitrogen are precursors.

Preliminary Assessment: The process of collecting and reviewing available information about a known or suspected waste site or release.

Prescriptive: Water rights which are acquired by diverting water and putting it to use in accordance with specified procedures; e.g. filing a request with a state agency to use unused water in a stream, river, or lake.

Pressed Wood Products: Materials used in building and furniture construction that are made from wood veneers, particles, or fibers bonded together with an adhesive under heat and pressure.

Pressure Sewers: A system of pipes in which water, wastewater, or other liquid is pumped to a higher elevation.

Pressure, Static: In flowing air, the total pressure minus velocity pressure, pushing equally in all directions.

Pressure, Total: In flowing air, the sum of the static and velocity pressures.

Pressure, Velocity: In flowing air, the pressure due to velocity and density of air.

Pretreatment: Processes used to reduce, eliminate, or alter the nature of wastewater pollutants from non-domestic sources before they are discharged into publicly owned treatment works (POTWs).

Prevalent Level Samples: Air samples taken under normal conditions (also known as ambient background samples).

Prevalent Levels: Levels of airborne contaminant occurring under normal conditions.

Prevention of Significant Deterioration (PSD): EPA program in which state and/or federal permits are required in order to restrict emissions from new or modified sources in places where air quality already meets or exceeds primary and secondary ambient air quality standards.

Primacy: Having the primary responsibility for administering and enforcing regulations.

Primary Drinking Water Regulation: Applies to public water systems and specifies a contaminant level, which, in the judgment of the EPA Administrator, will not adversely affect human health.

Primary Effect: An effect where the stressor acts directly on the ecological component of interest, not on other parts of the ecosystem. (See: secondary effect.)

Primary Standards: National ambient air quality standards designed to protect human health with an adequate margin for safety. (See: National Ambient Air Quality Standards, secondary standards.)

Primary Treatment: First stage of wastewater treatment in which solids are removed by screening and settling.

Primary Waste Treatment: First steps in wastewater treatment; screens and sedimentation tanks are used to remove most materials that float or will settle. Primary treatment removes about 30 percent of carbonaceous biochemical oxygen demand from domestic sewage.

Principal Organic Hazardous Constituents (POHCs): Hazardous compounds monitored during an incinerator's trial burn, selected for high concentration in the waste feed and difficulty of combustion.

Prions: Microscopic particles made of protein that can cause disease.

Prior Appropriation: A doctrine of water law that allocates the rights to use water on a first-come, first-served basis.

Probability of Detection : The likelihood, expressed as a percentage, that a test method will correctly identify a leaking tank.

Process Variable: A physical or chemical quantity which is usually measured and controlled in the operation of a water treatment plant or industrial plant.

Process Verification: Verifying that process raw materials, water usage, waste treatment processes, production rate and other facts relative to quantity and quality of pollutants contained in discharges are substantially described in the permit application and the issued permit.

Process Wastewater: Any water that comes into contact with any raw material, product, byproduct, or waste.

Process Weight: Total weight of all materials, including fuel, used in a manufacturing process; used to calculate the allowable particulate emission rate.

Producers: Plants that perform photosynthesis and provide food to consumers.

Product Level: The level of a product in a storage tank.

Product Water: Water that has passed through a water treatment plant and is ready to be delivered to consumers.

Products of Incomplete Combustion (PICs): Organic compounds formed by combustion. Usually generated in small amounts and sometimes toxic, PICs are heat-altered versions of the original material fed into the incinerator (e.g. charcoal is a P.I.C. from burning wood).

Project XL: An EPA initiative to give states and the regulated community the flexibility to develop comprehensive strategies as alternatives to multiple current regulatory requirements in order to exceed compliance and increase overall environmental benefits.

Propellant: Liquid in a self-pressurized pesticide product that expels the active ingredient from its container.

Proportionate Mortality Ratio (PMR): The number of deaths from a specific cause in a specific period of time per 100 deaths from all causes in the same time period.

Proposed Plan: A plan for a site cleanup that is available to the public for comment.

Proteins: Complex nitrogenous organic compounds of high molecular weight made of amino acids; essential for growth and repair of animal tissue. Many, but not all, proteins are enzymes.

Protocol: A series of formal steps for conducting a test.

Protoplast: A membrane-bound cell from which the outer wall has been partially or completely removed. The term often is applied to plant cells.

Protozoa: One-celled animals that are larger and more complex than bacteria. May cause disease.

Public Comment Period: The time allowed for the public to express its views and concerns regarding an action by EPA (e.g. a Federal Register Notice of proposed rule-making, a public notice of a draft permit, or a Notice of Intent to Deny).

Public Health Approach: Regulatory and voluntary focus on effective and feasible risk management actions at the national and community level to reduce human exposures and risks, with priority given to reducing exposures with the biggest impacts in terms of the number affected and severity of effect.

Public Health Context: The incidence, prevalence, and severity of diseases in communities or populations and the factors that account for them, including infections, exposure to pollutants, and other exposures or activities.

Public Hearing: A formal meeting wherein EPA officials hear the public's views and concerns about an EPA action or proposal. EPA is required to consider such comments when evaluating its actions. Public hearings must be held upon request during the public comment period.

Public Notice: 1. Notification by EPA informing the public of Agency actions such as the issuance of a draft permit or scheduling of a hearing. EPA is required to ensure proper public notice, including publication in newspapers and broadcast over radio and television stations. 2. In the safe drinking water program, water suppliers are required to publish and broadcast notices when pollution problems are discovered.

Public Water System: A system that provides piped water for human consumption to at least 15 service connections or regularly serves 25 individuals.

Publicly Owned Treatment Works (POTWs): A waste-treatment works owned by a state, unit of local government, or Indian tribe, usually designed to treat domestic wastewaters.

Pumping Station: Mechanical device installed in sewer or water system or other liquid-carrying pipelines to move the liquids to a higher level.

Pumping Test: A test conducted to determine aquifer or well characteristics.

Purging: Removing stagnant air or water from sampling zone or equipment prior to sample collection.

Putrefaction: Biological decomposition of organic matter; associated with anaerobic conditions.

Putrescible: Able to rot quickly enough to cause odors and attract flies.

Pyrolysis: Decomposition of a chemical by extreme heat.

Q

Qualitative Use Assessment: Report summarizing the major uses of a pesticide including percentage of crop treated, and amount of pesticide used on a site.

Quality Assurance/Quality Control: A system of procedures, checks, audits, and corrective actions to ensure that all EPA research design and performance, environmental monitoring and sampling, and other technical and reporting activities are of the highest achievable quality.

Quench Tank: A water-filled tank used to cool incinerator residues or hot materials during industrial processes.

R

Radiation: Transmission of energy though space or any medium. Also known as radiant energy.

Radiation Standards: Regulations that set maximum exposure limits for protection of the public from radioactive materials.

Radio Frequency Radiation: (See non-ionizing electromagnetic radiation.)

Radioactive Decay: Spontaneous change in an atom by emission of of charged particles and/or gamma rays; also known as radioactive disintegration and radioactivity.

Radioactive Substances: Substances that emit ionizing radiation.

Radioactive Waste: Any waste that emits energy as rays, waves, streams or energetic particles. Radioactive materials are often mixed with hazardous waste, from nuclear reactors, research institutions, or hospitals.

Radioisotopes: Chemical variants of radioactive elements with potentially oncogenic, teratogenic, and mutagenic effects on the human body.

Radionuclide: Radioactive particle, man-made (anthropogenic) or natural, with a distinct atomic weight number. Can have a long life as soil or water pollutant.

Radius of Vulnerability Zone: The maximum distance from the point of release of a hazardous substance in which the airborne concentration could reach the level of concern under specified weather conditions.

Radius of Influence: 1. The radial distance from the center of a wellbore to the point where there is no lowering of the water table or potentiometric surface (the edge of the cone of depression); 2. the radial distance from an extraction well that has adequate air flow for effective removal of contaminants when a vacuum is applied to the extraction well.

Radon: A colorless naturally occurring, radioactive, inert gas formed by radioactive decay of radium atoms in soil or rocks.

Radon Daughters/Radon Progeny: Short-lived radioactive decay products of radon that decay into longer-lived lead isotopes that can attach themselves to airborne dust and other particles and, if inhaled, damage the linings of the lungs.

Radon Decay Products: A term used to refer collectively to the immediate products of the radon decay chain. These include Po-218, Pb-214, Bi-214, and Po-214, which have an average combined half-life of about 30 minutes.

Rainbow Report: Comprehensive document giving the status of all pesticides now or ever in registration or special reviews. Known as the "rainbow report" because chapters are printed on different colors of paper.

Rasp: A machine that grinds waste into a manageable material and helps prevent odor.

Raw Agricultural Commodity: An unprocessed human food or animal feed crop (e.g., raw carrots, apples, corn, or eggs.)

Raw Sewage: Untreated wastewater and its contents.

Raw Water: Intake water prior to any treatment or use.

Re-entry: (In indoor air program) Refers to air exhausted from a building that is immediately brought back into the system through the air intake and other openings.

Reactivity: Refers to those hazardous wastes that are normally unstable and readily undergo violent chemical change but do not explode.

Reaeration: Introduction of air into the lower layers of a reservoir. As the air bubbles form and rise through the water, the oxygen dissolves into the water and replenishes the dissolved oxygen. The rising bubbles also cause the lower waters to rise to the surface where they take on oxygen from the atmosphere.

Real-Time Monitoring: Monitoring and measuring environmental developments with technology and communications systems that provide time-relevant information to the public in an easily understood format people can use in day-to-day decision-making about their health and the environment.

Reasonable Further Progress: Annual incremental reductions in air pollutant emissions as reflected in a State Implementation Plan that EPA deems sufficient to provide for the attainment of the applicable national ambient air quality standards by the statutory deadline.

Reasonable Maximum Exposure: The maximum exposure reasonably expected to occur in a population.

Reasonable Worst Case: An estimate of the individual dose, exposure, or risk level received by an individual in a defined population that is greater than the 90th percentile but less than that received by anyone in the 98th percentile in the same population.

Reasonably Available Control Measures (RACM): A broadly defined term referring to technological and other measures for pollution control.

Reasonably Available Control Technology (RACT): Control technology that is reasonably available, and both technologically and economically feasible. Usually applied to existing sources in nonattainment areas; in most cases is less stringent than new source performance standards.

Recarbonization: Process in which carbon dioxide is bubbled into water being treated to lower the pH.

Receiving Waters: A river, lake, ocean, stream or other watercourse into which wastewater or treated effluent is discharged.

Receptor: Ecological entity exposed to a stressor.

Recharge: The process by which water is added to a zone of saturation, usually by percolation from the soil surface; e.g., the recharge of an aquifer.

Recharge Area: A land area in which water reaches the zone of saturation from surface infiltration, e.g., where rainwater soaks through the earth to reach an aquifer.

Recharge Rate: The quantity of water per unit of time that replenishes or refills an aquifer.

Reclamation: (In recycling) Restoration of materials found in the waste stream to a beneficial use which may be for purposes other than the original use.

Recombinant Bacteria: A microorganism whose genetic makeup has been altered by deliberate introduction of new genetic elements. The offspring of these altered bacteria also contain these new genetic elements; i.e. they "breed true."

Recombinant DNA: The new DNA that is formed by combining pieces of DNA from different organisms or cells.

Recommended Maximum Contaminant Level (RMCL): The maximum level of a contaminant in drinking water at which no known or anticipated adverse effect on human health would occur, and that includes an adequate margin of safety. Recommended levels are nonenforceable health goals. (See: maximum contaminant level.)

Reconstructed Source: Facility in which components are replaced to such an extent that the fixed capital cost of the new components exceeds 50 percent of the capital cost of constructing a comparable brand-new facility. New-source performance standards may be applied to sources reconstructed after the proposal of the standard if it is technologically and economically feasible to meet the standards.

Reconstruction of Dose: Estimating exposure after it has occurred by using evidence within an organism such as chemical levels in tissue or fluids.

Record of Decision (ROD): A public document that explains which cleanup alternative(s) will be used at National Priorities List sites where, under CERCLA, Trust Funds pay for the cleanup.

Recovery Rate: Percentage of usable recycled materials that have been removed from the total amount of municipal solid waste generated in a specific area or by a specific business.

Recycle/Reuse: Minimizing waste generation by recovering and reprocessing usable products that might otherwise become waste (.i.e. recycling of aluminum cans, paper, and bottles, etc.).

Recycling and Reuse Business Assistance Centers: Located in state solid-waste or economic-development agencies, these centers provide recycling businesses with customized and targeted assistance.

Recycling Economic Development Advocates: Individuals hired by state or tribal economic development offices to focus financial, marketing, and permitting resources on creating recycling businesses.

Recycling Mill: Facility where recovered materials are remanufactured into new products.

Recycling Technical Assistance Partnership National Network: A national information-sharing resource designed to help businesses and manufacturers increase their use of recovered materials.

Red Bag Waste: (See: infectious waste.)

Red Border: An EPA document undergoing review before being submitted for final management decision-making.

Red Tide: A proliferation of a marine plankton toxic and often fatal to fish, perhaps stimulated by the addition of nutrients. A tide can be red, green, or brown, depending on the coloration of the plankton.

Redemption Program: Program in which consumers are monetarily compensated for the collection of recyclable materials, generally through prepaid deposits or taxes on beverage containers. In some states or localities legislation has enacted redemption programs to help prevent roadside litter. (See: bottle bill.)

Reduction: The addition of hydrogen, removal of oxygen, or addition of electrons to an element or compound.

Reentry Interval: The period of time immediately following the application of a pesticide during which unprotected workers should not enter a field.

Reference Dose (RfD): The RfD is a numerical estimate of a daily oral exposure to the human population, including sensitive subgroups such as children, that is not likely to cause harmful effects during a lifetime. RfDs are generally used for health effects that are thought to have a threshold or low dose limit for producing effects.

Reformulated Gasoline: Gasoline with a different composition from conventional gasoline (e.g., lower aromatics content) that cuts air pollutants.

Refueling Emissions: Emissions released during vehicle re-fueling.

Refuse: (See: solid waste.)

Refuse Reclamation: Conversion of solid waste into useful products; e.g., composting organic wastes to make soil conditioners or separating aluminum and other metals for recycling.

Regeneration: Manipulation of cells to cause them to develop into whole plants.

Regional Response Team (RRT): Representatives of federal, local, and state agencies who may assist in coordination of activities at the request of the On-Scene Coordinator before and during a significant pollution incident such as an oil spill, major chemical release, or Superfund response.

Registrant: Any manufacturer or formulator who obtains registration for a pesticide active ingredient or product.

Registration: Formal listing with EPA of a new pesticide before it can be sold or distributed. Under the Federal Insecticide, Fungicide, and Rodenticide Act, EPA is responsible for registration (pre-market licensing) of pesticides on the basis of data demonstrating no unreasonable adverse effects on human health or the environment when applied according to approved label directions.

Registration Standards: Published documents which include summary reviews of the data available on a pesticide's active ingredient, data gaps, and the Agency's existing regulatory position on the pesticide.

Regulated Asbestos-Containing Material (RACM): Friable asbestos material or nonfriable ACM that will be or has been subjected to sanding, grinding, cutting, or abrading or has crumbled, or been pulverized or reduced to powder in the course of demolition or renovation operations.

Regulated Medical Waste: Under the Medical Waste Tracking Act of 1988, any solid waste generated in the diagnosis, treatment, or immunization of human beings or animals, in research pertaining thereto, or in the production or testing of biologicals. Included are cultures and stocks of infectious agents; human blood and blood products; human pathological body wastes from surgery and autopsy; contaminated animal carcasses from medical research; waste from patients with communicable diseases; and all used sharp implements, such as needles and scalpels, and certain unused sharps. (See: treated medical waste; untreated medical waste; destroyed medical waste.)

Relative Ecological Sustainability: Ability of an ecosystem to maintain relative ecological integrity indefinitely.

Relative Permeability: The permeability of a rock to gas, NAIL, or water, when any two or more are present.

Relative Risk Assessment: Estimating the risks associated with different stressors or management actions.

Release: Any spilling, leaking, pumping, pouring, emitting, emptying, discharging, injecting, escaping, leaching, dumping, or disposing into the environment of a hazardous or toxic chemical or extremely hazardous substance.

Remedial Action (RA): The actual construction or implementation phase of a Superfund site cleanup that follows remedial design.

Remedial Design: A phase of remedial action that follows the remedial investigation/feasibility study and includes development of engineering drawings and specifications for a site cleanup.

Remedial Investigation: An in-depth study designed to gather data needed to determine the nature and extent of contamination at a Superfund site; establish site cleanup criteria; identify preliminary alternatives for remedial action; and support technical and cost analyses of alternatives. The remedial investigation is usually done with the feasibility study. Together they are usually referred to as the "RI/FS".

Remedial Project Manager (RPM): The EPA or state official responsible for overseeing on-site remedial action.

Remedial Response: Long-term action that stops or substantially reduces a release or threat of a release of hazardous substances that is serious but not an immediate threat to public health.

Remediation: 1. Cleanup or other methods used to remove or contain a toxic spill or hazardous materials from a Superfund site; 2. for the Asbestos Hazard Emergency Response program, abatement methods including evaluation, repair, enclosure, encapsulation, or removal of greater than 3 linear feet or square feet of asbestos-containing materials from a building.

Remote Sensing: The collection and interpretation of information about an object without physical contact with the object; e.g., satellite imaging, aerial photography, and open path measurements.

Removal Action: Short-term immediate actions taken to address releases of hazardous substances that require expedited response. (See: cleanup.)

Renewable Energy Production Incentive (REPI): Incentive established by the Energy Policy Act available to renewable energy power projects owned by a state or local government or nonprofit electric cooperative.

Repeat Compliance Period: Any subsequent compliance period after the initial one.

Reportable Quantity (RQ): Quantity of a hazardous substance that triggers reports under CERCLA. If a substance exceeds its RQ, the release must be reported to the National Response Center, the SERC, and community emergency coordinators for areas likely to be affected.

Repowering: Rebuilding and replacing major components of a power plant instead of building a new one.

Representative Sample: A portion of material or water that is as nearly identical in content and consistency as possible to that in the larger body of material or water being sampled.

Reregistration: The reevaluation and relicensing of existing pesticides originally registered prior to current scientific and regulatory standards. EPA reregisters pesticides through its Registration Standards Program

Reserve Capacity: Extra treatment capacity built into solid waste and wastewater treatment plants and interceptor sewers to accommodate flow increases due to future population growth.

Reservoir: Any natural or artificial holding area used to store, regulate, or control water.

Residential Use: Pesticide application in and around houses, office buildings, apartment buildings, motels, and other living or working areas.

Residential Waste: Waste generated in single and multi-family homes, including newspapers, clothing, disposable tableware, food packaging, cans, bottles, food scraps, and yard trimmings other than those that are diverted to backyard composting. (See: Household hazardous waste.)

Residual: Amount of a pollutant remaining in the environment after a natural or technological process has taken place; e.g., the sludge remaining after initial wastewater treatment, or particulates remaining in air after it passes through a scrubbing or other process.

Residual Risk: The extent of health risk from air pollutants remaining after application of the Maximum Achievable Control Technology (MACT).

Residual Saturation: Saturation level below which fluid drainage will not occur.

Residue: The dry solids remaining after the evaporation of a sample of water or sludge.

Resistance: For plants and animals, the ability to withstand poor environmental conditions or attacks by chemicals or disease. May be inborn or acquired.

Resource Recovery: The process of obtaining matter or energy from materials formerly discarded.

Response Action: 1. Generic term for actions taken in response to actual or potential health-threatening environmental events such as spills, sudden releases, and asbestos abatement/management problems. 2. A CERCLA-authorized action involving either a short-term removal action or a long-term removal response. This may include but is not limited to: removing hazardous materials from a site to an EPA-approved hazardous waste facility for treatment, containment or treating the waste on-site, identifying and removing the sources of ground-water contamination and halting further migration of contaminants. 3. Any of the following actions taken in school buildings in response to AHERA to reduce the risk of exposure to asbestos: removal, encapsulation, enclosure, repair, and operations and maintenance. (See: cleanup.)

Responsiveness Summary: A summary of oral and/or written public comments received by EPA during a comment period on key EPA documents, and EPA's response to those comments.

Restoration: Measures taken to return a site to pre-violation conditions.

Restricted Entry Interval: The time after a pesticide application during which entry into the treated area is restricted.

Restricted Use: A pesticide may be classified (under FIFRA regulations) for restricted use if it requires special handling because of its toxicity, and, if so, it may be applied only by trained, certified applicators or those under their direct supervision.

Restriction Enzymes: Enzymes that recognize specific regions of a long DNA molecule and cut it at those points.

Retrofit: Addition of a pollution control device on an existing facility without making major changes to the generating plant. Also called backfit.

Reuse: Using a product or component of municipal solid waste in its original form more than once; e.g., refilling a glass bottle that has been returned or using a coffee can to hold nuts and bolts.

Reverse Osmosis: A treatment process used in water systems by adding pressure to force water through a semi-permeable membrane. Reverse osmosis removes most drinking water contaminants. Also used in wastewater treatment. Large-scale reverse osmosis plants are being developed.

Reversible Effect: An effect which is not permanent; especially adverse effects which diminish when exposure to a toxic chemical stops.

Ribonucleic Acid (RNA): A molecule that carries the genetic message from DNA to a cellular protein-producing mechanism.

Rill: A small channel eroded into the soil by surface runoff; can be easily smoothed out or obliterated by normal tillage.

Ringlemann Chart: A series of shaded illustrations used to measure the opacity of air pollution emissions, ranging from light grey through black; used to set and enforce emissions standards.

Riparian Habitat: Areas adjacent to rivers and streams with a differing density, diversity, and productivity of plant and animal species relative to nearby uplands.

Riparian Rights: Entitlement of a land owner to certain uses of water on or bordering the property, including the right to prevent diversion or misuse of upstream waters. Generally a matter of state law.

Risk: A measure of the probability that damage to life, health, property, and/or the environment will occur as a result of a given hazard.

Risk (Adverse) for Endangered Species: Risk to aquatic species if anticipated pesticide residue levels equal one-fifth of LD10 or one-tenth of LC50; risk to terrestrial species if anticipated pesticide residue levels equal one-fifth of LC10 or one-tenth of LC50.

Risk Assessment: Qualitative and quantitative evaluation of the risk posed to human health and/or the environment by the actual or potential presence and/or use of specific pollutants.

Risk Characterization: The last phase of the risk assessment process that estimates the potential for adverse health or ecological effects to occur from exposure to a stressor and evaluates the uncertainty involved.

Risk Communication: The exchange of information about health or environmental risks among risk assessors and managers, the general public, news media, interest groups, etc.

Risk Estimate: A description of the probability that organisms exposed to a specific dose of a chemical or other pollutant will develop an adverse response, e.g., cancer.

Risk Factor: Characteristics (e.g., race, sex, age, obesity) or variables (e.g., smoking, occupational exposure level) associated with increased probability of a toxic effect.

Risk for Non-Endangered Species: Risk to species if anticipated pesticide residue levels are equal to or greater than LC50.

Risk Management: The process of evaluating and selecting alternative regulatory and non-regulatory responses to risk. The selection process necessarily requires the consideration of legal, economic, and behavioral factors.

Risk-based Targeting: The direction of resources to those areas that have been identified as having the highest potential or actual adverse effect on human health and/or the environment.

Risk-Specific Dose: The dose associated with a specified risk level.

River Basin: The land area drained by a river and its tributaries.

Rodenticide: A chemical or agent used to destroy rats or other rodent pests, or to prevent them from damaging food, crops, etc.

Rotary Kiln Incinerator: An incinerator with a rotating combustion chamber that keeps waste moving, thereby allowing it to vaporize for easier burning.

Rough Fish: Fish not prized for sport or eating, such as gar and suckers. Most are more tolerant of changing environmental conditions than are game or food species.

Route of Exposure: The avenue by which a chemical comes into contact with an organism, e.g., inhalation, ingestion, dermal contact, injection.

Rubbish: Solid waste, excluding food waste and ashes, from homes, institutions, and workplaces.

Run-Off: That part of precipitation, snow melt, or irrigation water that runs off the land into streams or other surface-water. It can carry pollutants from the air and land into receiving waters.

Running Losses: Evaporation of motor vehicle fuel from the fuel tank while the vehicle is in use.

S

Sacrifical Anode: An easily corroded material deliberately installed in a pipe or intake to give it up (sacrifice it) to corrosion while the rest of the water supply facility remains relatively corrosion-free.

Safe: Condition of exposure under which there is a practical certainty that no harm will result to exposed individuals.

Safe Water: Water that does not contain harmful bacteria, toxic materials, or chemicals, and is considered safe for drinking even if it may have taste, odor, color, and certain mineral problems.

Safe Yield: The annual amount of water that can be taken from a source of supply over a period of years without depleting that source beyond its ability to be replenished naturally in "wet years."

Safener: A chemical added to a pesticide to keep it from injuring plants.

Salinity: The percentage of salt in water.

Salt Water Intrusion: The invasion of fresh surface or ground water by salt water. If it comes from the ocean it may be called sea water intrusion.

Salts: Minerals that water picks up as it passes through the air, over and under the ground, or from households and industry.

Salvage: The utilization of waste materials.

Sampling Frequency: The interval between the collection of successive samples.

Sanctions: Actions taken by the federal government for failure to provide or implement a State Implementation Plan (SIP). Such action may include withholding of highway funds and a ban on construction of new sources of potential pollution.

Sand Filters: Devices that remove some suspended solids from sewage. Air and bacteria decompose additional wastes filtering through the sand so that cleaner water drains from the bed.

Sanitary Landfill: (See: landfills.)

Sanitary Sewers: Underground pipes that carry off only domestic or industrial waste, not storm water.

Sanitary Survey: An on-site review of the water sources, facilities, equipment, operation and maintenance of a public water system to evaluate the adequacy of those elements for producing and distributing safe drinking water.

Sanitary Water (Also known as gray water): Water discharged from sinks, showers, kitchens, or other non-industrial operations, but not from commodes.

Sanitation: Control of physical factors in the human environment that could harm development, health, or survival.

Saprolite: A soft, clay-rich, thoroughly decomposed rock formed in place by chemical weathering of igneous or metamorphic rock. Forms in humid, tropical, or subtropical climates.

Saprophytes: Organisms living on dead or decaying organic matter that help natural decomposition of organic matter in water.

Saturated Zone: The area below the water table where all open spaces are filled with water under pressure equal to or greater than that of the atmosphere.

Saturation: The condition of a liquid when it has taken into solution the maximum possible quantity of a given substance at a given temperature and pressure.

Science Advisory Board (SAB): A group of external scientists who advise EPA on science and policy.

Scrap: Materials discarded from manufacturing operations that may be suitable for reprocessing.

Scrap Metal Processor: Intermediate operating facility where recovered metal is sorted, cleaned of contaminants, and prepared for recycling.

Screening: Use of screens to remove coarse floating and suspended solids from sewage.

Screening Risk Assessment: A risk assessment performed with few data and many assumptions to identify exposures that should be evaluated more carefully for potential risk.

Scrubber: An air pollution device that uses a spray of water or reactant or a dry process to trap pollutants in emissions.

Secondary Drinking Water Regulations: Non-enforceable regulations applying to public water systems and specifying the maximum contamination levels that, in the judgment of EPA, are required to protect the public welfare. These regulations apply to any contaminants that may adversely affect the odor or appearance of such water and consequently may cause people served by the system to discontinue its use.

Secondary Effect: Action of a stressor on supporting components of the ecosystem, which in turn impact the ecological component of concern. (See: primary effect.)

Secondary Materials: Materials that have been manufactured and used at least once and are to be used again.

Secondary Standards: National ambient air quality standards designed to protect welfare, including effects on soils, water, crops, vegetation, man-made (anthropogenic) materials, animals, wildlife, weather, visibility, and climate; damage to property; transportation hazards; economic values, and personal comfort and well-being.

Secondary Treatment: The second step in most publicly owned waste treatment systems in which bacteria consume the organic parts of the waste. It is accomplished by bringing together waste, bacteria, and oxygen in trickling filters or in the activated sludge process. This treatment removes floating and settleable solids and about 90 percent of the oxygen-demanding substances and suspended solids. Disinfection is the final stage of secondary treatment. (See: primary, tertiary treatment.)

Secure Chemical Landfill: (See:landfills.)

Secure Maximum Contaminant Level: Maximum permissible level of a contaminant in water delivered to the free flowing outlet of the ultimate user, or of contamination resulting from corrosion of piping and plumbing caused by water quality.

Glossary of Environmental Terms

Sediment: Topsoil, sand, and minerals washed from the land into water, usually after rain or snow melt.

Sediment Yield: The quantity of sediment arriving at a specific location.

Sedimentation: Letting solids settle out of wastewater by gravity during treatment.

Sedimentation Tanks: Wastewater tanks in which floating wastes are skimmed off and settled solids are removed for disposal.

Sediments: Soil, sand, and minerals washed from land into water, usually after rain. They pile up in reservoirs, rivers and harbors, destroying fish and wildlife habitat, and clouding the water so that sunlight cannot reach aquatic plants. Careless farming, mining, and building activities will expose sediment materials, allowing them to wash off the land after rainfall.

Seed Protectant: A chemical applied before planting to protect seeds and seedlings from disease or insects.

Seepage: Percolation of water through the soil from unlined canals, ditches, laterals, watercourses, or water storage facilities.

Selective Pesticide: A chemical designed to affect only certain types of pests, leaving other plants and animals unharmed.

Semi-Confined Aquifer: An aquifer partially confined by soil layers of low permeability through which recharge and discharge can still occur.

Semivolatile Organic Compounds: Organic compounds that volatilize slowly at standard temperature (20 degrees C and 1 atm pressure).

Senescence: The aging process. Sometimes used to describe lakes or other bodies of water in advanced stages of eutrophication. Also used to describe plants and animals.

Septic System: An on-site system designed to treat and dispose of domestic sewage. A typical septic system consists of tank that receives waste from a residence or business and a system of tile lines or a pit for disposal of the liquid effluent (sludge) that remains after decomposition of the solids by bacteria in the tank and must be pumped out periodically.

Septic Tank: An underground storage tank for wastes from homes not connected to a sewer line. Waste goes directly from the home to the tank. (See: septic system.)

Service Connector: The pipe that carries tap water from a public water main to a building.

Service Line Sample: A one-liter sample of water that has been standing for at least 6 hours in a service pipeline and is collected according to federal regulations.

Service Pipe: The pipeline extending from the water main to the building served or to the consumer's system.

Set-Back: Setting a thermometer to a lower temperature when the building is unoccupied to reduce consumption of heating energy. Also refers to setting the thermometer to a higher temperature during unoccupied periods in the cooling season.

Settleable Solids: Material heavy enough to sink to the bottom of a wastewater treatment tank.

Settling Chamber: A series of screens placed in the way of flue gases to slow the stream of air, thus helping gravity to pull particles into a collection device.

Settling Tank: A holding area for wastewater, where heavier particles sink to the bottom for removal and disposal.

7Q10: Seven-day, consecutive low flow with a ten year return frequency; the lowest stream flow for seven consecutive days that would be expected to occur once in ten years.

Sewage: The waste and wastewater produced by residential and commercial sources and discharged into sewers.

Sewage Lagoon: (See: lagoon.)

Sewage Sludge: Sludge produced at a Publicly Owned Treatment Works, the disposal of which is regulated under the Clean Water Act.

Sewer: A channel or conduit that carries wastewater and storm-water runoff from the source to a treatment plant or receiving stream. "Sanitary" sewers carry household, industrial, and commercial waste. "Storm" sewers carry runoff from rain or snow. "Combined" sewers handle both.

Sewerage: The entire system of sewage collection, treatment, and disposal.

Shading Coefficient: The amount of the sun's heat transmitted through a given window compared with that of a standard 1/8- inch-thick single pane of glass under the same conditions.

Sharps: Hypodermic needles, syringes (with or without the attached needle), Pasteur pipettes, scalpel blades, blood vials, needles with attached tubing, and culture dishes used in animal or human patient care or treatment, or in medical, research or industrial laboratories. Also included are other types of broken or unbroken glassware that were in contact with infectious agents, such as used slides and cover slips, and unused hypodermic and suture needles, syringes, and scalpel blades.

Shock Load: The arrival at a water treatment plant of raw water containing unusual amounts of algae, colloidal matter. color, suspended solids, turbidity, or other pollutants.

Short-Circuiting: When some of the water in tanks or basins flows faster than the rest; may result in shorter contact, reaction, or settling times than calculated or presumed.

Sick Building Syndrome: Building whose occupants experience acute health and/or comfort effects that appear to be linked to time spent therein, but where no specific illness or cause can be identified. Complaints may be localized in a particular room or zone, or may spread throughout the building. (See: building-related illness.)

Signal: The volume or product-level change produced by a leak in a tank.

Signal Words: The words used on a pesticide label—Danger, Warning, Caution—to indicate level of toxicity.

Significant Deterioration: Pollution resulting from a new source in previously "clean" areas. (See: prevention of significant deterioration.)

Significant Municipal Facilities: Those publicly owned sewage treatment plants that discharge a million gallons per day or more and are therefore considered by states to have the potential to substantially affect the quality of receiving waters.

Significant Non-Compliance: (See significant violations.)

Significant Potential Source of Contamination: A facility or activity that stores, uses, or produces compounds with potential for significant contaminating impact if released into the source water of a public water supply.

Significant Violations: Violations by point source dischargers of sufficient magnitude or duration to be a regulatory priority.

Silt: Sedimentary materials composed of fine or intermediate-sized mineral particles.

Silviculture: Management of forest land for timber.

Single-Breath Canister: Small one-liter canister designed to capture a single breath. Used in air pollutant ingestion research.

Sink: Place in the environment where a compound or material collects.

Sinking: Controlling oil spills by using an agent to trap the oil and sink it to the bottom of the body of water where the agent and the oil are biodegraded.

SIP Call: EPA action requiring a state to resubmit all or part of its State Implementation Plan to demonstrate attainment of the require national ambient air quality standards within the statutory deadline. A SIP Revision is a revision of a SIP altered at the request of EPA or on a state's initiative. (See: State Implementation Plan.)

Site: An area or place within the jurisdiction of the EPA and/or a state.

Site Assessment Program: A means of evaluating hazardous waste sites through preliminary assessments and site inspections to develop a Hazard Ranking System score.

Site Inspection: The collection of information from a Superfund site to determine the extent and severity of hazards posed by the site. It follows and is more extensive than a preliminary assessment. The purpose is to gather information necessary to score the site, using the Hazard Ranking System, and to determine if it presents an immediate threat requiring prompt removal.

Site Safety Plan: A crucial element in all removal actions, it includes information on equipment being used, precautions to be taken, and steps to take in the event of an on-site emergency.

Siting: The process of choosing a location for a facility.

Skimming: Using a machine to remove oil or scum from the surface of the water.

Slow Sand Filtration: Passage of raw water through a bed of sand at low velocity, resulting in substantial removal of chemical and biological contaminants.

Sludge: A semi-solid residue from any of a number of air or water treatment processes; can be a hazardous waste.

Sludge Digester: Tank in which complex organic substances like sewage sludges are biologically dredged. During these reactions, energy is released and much of the sewage is converted to methane, carbon dioxide, and water.

Slurry: A watery mixture of insoluble matter resulting from some pollution control techniques.

Small Quantity Generator (SQG-sometimes referred to as "Squeegee"): Persons or enterprises that produce 220-2200 pounds per month of hazardous waste; they are required to keep more records than conditionally exempt generators. The largest category of hazardous waste generators, SQGs, include automotive shops, dry cleaners, photographic developers, and many other small businesses. (See: conditionally exempt generators.)

Smelter: A facility that melts or fuses ore, often with an accompanying chemical change, to separate its metal content. Emissions cause pollution. "Smelting" is the process involved.

Smog: Air pollution typically associated with oxidants. (See: photochemical smog.)

Smoke: Particles suspended in air after incomplete combustion.

Soft Detergents: Cleaning agents that break down in nature.

Soft Water: Any water that does not contain a significant amount of dissolved minerals such as salts of calcium or magnesium.

Soil Adsorption Field: A sub-surface area containing a trench or bed with clean stones and a system of piping through which treated sewage may seep into the surrounding soil for further treatment and disposal.

Soil and Water Conservation Practices: Control measures consisting of managerial, vegetative, and structural practices to reduce the loss of soil and water.

Soil Conditioner: An organic material like humus or compost that helps soil absorb water, build a bacterial community, and take up mineral nutrients.

Soil Erodibility: An indicator of a soil's susceptibility to raindrop impact, runoff, and other erosive processes.

Soil Gas: Gaseous elements and compounds in the small spaces between particles of the earth and soil. Such gases can be moved or driven out under pressure.

Soil Moisture: The water contained in the pore space of the unsaturated zone.

Soil Sterilant: A chemical that temporarily or permanently prevents the growth of all plants and animals,

Solder: Metallic compound used to seal joints between pipes. Until recently, most solder contained 50 percent lead. Use of solder containing more than 0.2 percent lead in pipes carrying drinking water is now prohibited.

Sole-Source Aquifer: An aquifer that supplies 50-percent or more of the drinking water of an area.

Solid Waste: Non-liquid, non-soluble materials ranging from municipal garbage to industrial wastes that contain complex and sometimes hazardous substances. Solid wastes also include sewage sludge, agricultural refuse, demolition wastes, and mining residues. Technically, solid waste also refers to liquids and gases in containers.

Solid Waste Disposal: The final placement of refuse that is not salvaged or recycled.

Solid Waste Management: Supervised handling of waste materials from their source through recovery processes to disposal.

Solidification and Stabilization: Removal of wastewater from a waste or changing it chemically to make it less permeable and susceptible to transport by water.

Solubility: The amount of mass of a compound that will dissolve in a unit volume of solution. Aqueous Solubility is the maximum concentration of a chemical that will dissolve in pure water at a reference temperature.

Soot: Carbon dust formed by incomplete combustion.

Sorption: The action of soaking up or attracting substances; process used in many pollution control systems.

Source Area: The location of liquid hydrocarbons or the zone of highest soil or groundwater concentrations, or both, of the chemical of concern.

Source Characterization Measurements: Measurements made to estimate the rate of release of pollutants into the environment from a source such as an incinerator, landfill, etc.

Source Reduction: Reducing the amount of materials entering the waste stream from a specific source by redesigning products or patterns of production or consumption (e.g., using returnable beverage containers). Synonymous with waste reduction.

Source Separation: Segregating various wastes at the point of generation (e.g., separation of paper, metal and glass from other wastes to make recycling simpler and more efficient).

Source-Water Protection Area: The area delineated by a state for a Public Water Supply or including numerous such suppliers, whether the source is ground water or surface water or both.

Sparge or Sparging: Injection of air below the water table to strip dissolved volatile organic compounds and/or oxygenate ground water to facilitate aerobic biodegradation of organic compounds.

Special Local-Needs Registration: Registration of a pesticide product by a state agency for a specific use that is not federally registered. However, the active ingredient must be federally registered for other uses. The special use is specific to that state and is often minor, thus may not warrant the additional cost of a full federal registration process. SLN registration cannot be issued for new active ingredients, food-use active ingredients without tolerances, or for a canceled registration. The products cannot be shipped across state lines.

Special Review: Formerly known as Rebuttable Presumption Against Registration (RPAR), this is the regulatory process through which existing pesticides suspected of posing unreasonable risks to human health, non-target organisms, or the environment are referred for review by EPA. Such review requires an intensive risk/benefit analysis with opportunity for public comment. If risk is found to outweigh social and economic benefits, regulatory actions can be initiated, ranging from label revisions and use-restriction to cancellation or suspended registration.

Special Waste: Items such as household hazardous waste, bulky wastes (refrigerators, pieces of furniture, etc.) tires, and used oil.

Species: 1. A reproductively isolated aggregate of interbreeding organisms having common attributes and usually designated by a common name.2. An organism belonging to belonging to such a category.

Specific Conductance: Rapid method of estimating the dissolved solid content of a water supply by testing its capacity to carry an electrical current.

Specific Yield: The amount of water a unit volume of saturated permeable rock will yield when drained by gravity.

Spill Prevention, Containment, and Countermeasures Plan (SPCP): Plan covering the release of hazardous substances as defined in the Clean Water Act.

Spoil: Dirt or rock removed from its original location—destroying the composition of the soil in the process—as in strip-mining, dredging, or construction.

Sprawl: Unplanned development of open land.

Spray Tower Scrubber: A device that sprays alkaline water into a chamber where acid gases are present to aid in neutralizing the gas.

Spring: Ground water seeping out of the earth where the water table intersects the ground surface.

Spring Melt/Thaw: The process whereby warm temperatures melt winter snow and ice. Because various forms of acid deposition may have been stored in the frozen water, the melt can result in abnormally large amounts of acidity entering streams and rivers, sometimes causing fish kills.

Stabilization: Conversion of the active organic matter in sludge into inert, harmless material.

Stabilization Ponds: (See: lagoon.)

Stable Air: A motionless mass of air that holds, instead of dispersing, pollutants.

Stack: A chimney, smokestack, or vertical pipe that discharges used air.

Stack Effect: Air, as in a chimney, that moves upward because it is warmer than the ambient atmosphere.

Stack Effect: Flow of air resulting from warm air rising, creating a positive pressure area at the top of a building and negative pressure area at the bottom. This effect can overpower the mechanical system and disrupt building ventilation and air circulation.

Stack Gas: (See: flue gas.)

Stage II Controls: Systems placed on service station gasoline pumps to control and capture gasoline vapors during refuelling.

Stagnation: Lack of motion in a mass of air or water that holds pollutants in place.

Stakeholder: Any organization, governmental entity, or individual that has a stake in or may be impacted by a given approach to environmental regulation, pollution prevention, energy conservation, etc.

Standard Industrial Classification Code: Also known as SIC Codes, a method of grouping industries with similar products or services and assigning codes to these groups.

Standard Sample: The part of finished drinking water that is examined for the presence of coliform bacteria.

Standards: Norms that impose limits on the amount of pollutants or emissions produced. EPA establishes minimum standards, but states are allowed to be stricter.

Start of a Response Action: The point in time when there is a guarantee or set-aside of funding by EPA, other federal agencies, states or Principal Responsible Parties in order to begin response actions at a Superfund site.

State Emergency Response Commission (SERC): Commission appointed by each state governor according to the requirements of SARA Title III. The SERCs designate emergency planning districts, appoint local emergency planning committees, and supervise and coordinate their activities.

State Environmental Goals and Indication Project: Program to assist state environmental agencies by providing technical and financial assistance in the development of environmental goals and indicators.

State Implementation Plans (SIP): EPA approved state plans for the establishment, regulation, and enforcement of air pollution standards.

State Management Plan: Under FIFRA, a state management plan required by EPA to allow states, tribes, and U.S. territories the flexibility to design and implement ways to protect ground water from the use of certain pesticides.

Static Water Depth: The vertical distance from the centerline of the pump discharge down to the surface level of the free pool while no water is being drawn from the pool or water table.

Static Water Level: 1. Elevation or level of the water table in a well when the pump is not operating. 2. The level or elevation to which water would rise in a tube connected to an artesian aquifer or basin in a conduit under pressure.

Stationary Source: A fixed-site producer of pollution, mainly power plants and other facilities using industrial combustion processes. (See: point source.)

Sterilization: The removal or destruction of all microorganisms, including pathogenic and other bacteria, vegetative forms, and spores.

Sterilizer: One of three groups of anti-microbials registered by EPA for public health uses. EPA considers an antimicrobial to be a sterilizer when it destroys or eliminates all forms of bacteria, viruses, and fungi and their spores. Because spores are considered the most difficult form of microorganism to destroy, EPA considers the term sporicide to be synonymous with sterilizer.

Storage: Temporary holding of waste pending treatment or disposal, as in containers, tanks, waste piles, and surface impoundments.

Storm Sewer: A system of pipes (separate from sanitary sewers) that carries water runoff from buildings and land surfaces.

Stratification: Separating into layers.

Stratigraphy: Study of the formation, composition, and sequence of sediments, whether consolidated or not.

Stratosphere: The portion of the atmosphere 10-to-25 miles above the earth's surface.

Stressors: Physical, chemical, or biological entities that can induce adverse effects on ecosystems or human health.

Strip-Cropping: Growing crops in a systematic arrangement of strips or bands that serve as barriers to wind and water erosion.

Strip-Mining: A process that uses machines to scrape soil or rock away from mineral deposits just under the earth's surface.

Structural Deformation: Distortion in walls of a tank after liquid has been added or removed.

Subchronic: Of intermediate duration, usually used to describe studies or periods of exposure lasting between 5 and 90 days.

Subchronic Exposure: Multiple or continuous exposures lasting for approximately ten percent of an experimental species lifetime, usually over a three-month period.

Submerged Aquatic Vegetation: Vegetation that lives at or below the water surface; an important habitat for young fish and other aquatic organisms.

Subwatershed: Topographic perimeter of the catchment area of a stream tributary.

Sulfur Dioxide (SO_2): A pungent, colorless, gasformed primarily by the combustion of fossil fuels; becomes a pollutant when present in large amounts.

Sump: A pit or tank that catches liquid runoff for drainage or disposal.

Superchlorination: Chlorination with doses that are deliberately selected to produce water free of combined residuals so large as to require dechlorination.

Supercritical Water: A type of thermal treatment using moderate temperatures and high pressures to enhance the ability of water to break down large organic molecules into smaller, less toxic ones. Oxygen injected during this process combines with simple organic compounds to form carbon dioxide and water.

Superfund: The program operated under the legislative authority of CERCLA and SARA that funds and carries out EPA solid waste emergency and long-term removal and remedial activities. These activities include establishing the National Priorities List, investigating sites for inclusion on the list, determining their priority, and conducting and/or supervising cleanup and other remedial actions.

Superfund Innovative Technology Evaluation (SITE) Program: EPA program to promote development and use of innovative treatment and site characterization technologies in Superfund site cleanups.

Supplemental Registration: An arrangement whereby a registrant licenses another company to market its pesticide product under the second company's registration.

Supplier of Water: Any person who owns or operates a public water supply.

Surface Impoundment: Treatment, storage, or disposal of liquid hazardous wastes in ponds.

Surface Runoff: Precipitation, snow melt, or irrigation water in excess of what can infiltrate the soil surface and be stored in small surface depressions; a major transporter of non-point source pollutants in rivers, streams, and lakes..

Surface Uranium Mines: Strip mining operations for removal of uranium-bearing ore.

Surface Water: All water naturally open to the atmosphere (rivers, lakes, reservoirs, ponds, streams, impoundments, seas, estuaries, etc.)

Surface-Water Treatment Rule: Rule that specifies maximum contaminant level goals for Giardia lamblia, viruses, and Legionella and promulgates filtration and disinfection requirements for public water systems using surface-water or ground-water sources under the direct influence of surface water. The regulations also specify water quality, treatment, and watershed protection criteria under which filtration may be avoided.

Surfacing ACM: Asbestos-containing material that is sprayed or troweled on or otherwise applied to surfaces, such as acoustical plaster on ceilings and fireproofing materials on structural members.

Surfacing Material: Material sprayed or troweled onto structural members (beams, columns, or decking) for fire protection; or on ceilings or walls for fireproofing, acoustical or decorative purposes. Includes textured plaster, and other textured wall and ceiling surfaces.

Surfactant: A detergent compound that promotes lathering.

Surrogate Data: Data from studies of test organisms or a test substance that are used to estimate the characteristics or effects on another organism or substance.

Surveillance System: A series of monitoring devices designed to check on environmental conditions.

Susceptibility Analysis: An analysis to determine whether a Public Water Supply is subject to significant pollution from known potential sources.

Suspect Material: Building material suspected of containing asbestos; e.g., surfacing material, floor tile, ceiling tile, thermal system insulation.

Suspended Loads: Specific sediment particles maintained in the water column by turbulence and carried with the flow of water.

Suspended Solids: Small particles of solid pollutants that float on the surface of, or are suspended in, sewage or other liquids. They resist removal by conventional means.

Suspension: Suspending the use of a pesticide when EPA deems it necessary to prevent an imminent hazard resulting from its continued use. An emergency suspension takes effect immediately; under an ordinary suspension a registrant can request a hearing before the suspension goes into effect. Such a hearing process might take six months.

Suspension Culture: Cells growing in a liquid nutrient medium.

Swamp: A type of wetland dominated by woody vegetation but without appreciable peat deposits. Swamps may be fresh or salt water and tidal or non-tidal. (See: wetlands.)

Synergism: An interaction of two or more chemicals that results in an effect greater than the sum of their separate effects.

Synthetic Organic Chemicals (SOCs): Man-made (anthropogenic) organic chemicals. Some SOCs are volatile; others tend to stay dissolved in water instead of evaporating.

System With a Single Service Connection: A system that supplies drinking water to consumers via a single service line.

Systemic Pesticide: A chemical absorbed by an organism that interacts with the organism and makes the organism toxic to pests.

T

Tail Water: The runoff of irrigation water from the lower end of an irrigated field.

Tailings: Residue of raw material or waste separated out during the processing of crops or mineral ores.

Tailpipe Standards: Emissions limitations applicable to mobile source engine exhausts.

Tampering: Adjusting, negating, or removing pollution control equipment on a motor vehicle.

Technical Assistance Grant (TAG): As part of the Superfund program, Technical Assistance Grants of up to $50,000 are provided to citizens' groups to obtain assistance in interpreting information related to clean-ups at Superfund sites or those proposed for the National Priorities List. Grants are used by such groups to hire technical advisors to help them understand the site-related technical information for the duration of response activities.

Technical-Grade Active Ingredient (TGA): A pesticide chemical in pure form as it is manufactured prior to being formulated into an end-use product (e.g. wettable powders, granules, emulsifiable concentrates). Registered manufactured products composed of such chemicals are known as Technical Grade Products.

Technology-Based Limitations: Industry-specific effluent limitations based on best available preventive technology applied to a discharge when it will not cause a violation of water quality standards at low stream flows. Usually applied to discharges into large rivers.

Technology-Based Standards: Industry-specific effluent limitations applicable to direct and indirect sources which are developed on a category-by-category basis using statutory factors, not including water-quality effects.

Teratogen: A substance capable of causing birth defects.

Teratogenesis: The introduction of nonhereditary birth defects in a developing fetus by exogenous factors such as physical or chemical agents acting in the womb to interfere with normal embryonic development.

Terracing: Dikes built along the contour of sloping farm land that hold runoff and sediment to reduce erosion.

Tertiary Treatment: Advanced cleaning of wastewater that goes beyond the secondary or biological stage, removing nutrients such as phosphorus, nitrogen, and most BOD and suspended solids.

Theoretical Maximum Residue Contribution: The theoretical maximum amount of a pesticide in the daily diet of an average person. It assumes that the diet is composed of all food items for which there are tolerance-level residues of the pesticide. The TMRC is expressed as milligrams of pesticide/kilograms of body weight/day.

Therapeutic Index: The ratio of the dose required to produce toxic or lethal effects to the dose required to produce nonadverse or therapeutic response.

Thermal Pollution: Discharge of heated water from industrial processes that can kill or injure aquatic organisms.

Thermal Stratification: The formation of layers of different temperatures in a lake or reservoir.

Thermal System Insulation (TSI): Asbestos-containing material applied to pipes, fittings, boilers, breeching, tanks, ducts, or other interior structural components to prevent heat loss or gain or water condensation.

Thermal Treatment: Use of elevated temperatures to treat hazardous wastes. (See: incineration; pyrolysis.)

Thermocline: The middle layer of a thermally stratified lake or reservoir. In this layer, there is a rapid decrease in temperatures in a lake or reservoir.

Threshold: The lowest dose of a chemical at which a specified measurable effect is observed and below which it is not observed.

Threshold: The dose or exposure level below which a significant adverse effect is not expected.

Threshold Level: Time-weighted average pollutant concentration values, exposure beyond which is likely to adversely affect human health. (See: environmental exposure)

Threshold Limit Value (TLV): The concentration of an airborne substance to which an average person can be repeatedly exposed without adverse effects. TLVs may be expressed in three ways: (1) TLV-TWA—Time weighted average, based on an allowable exposure averaged over a normal 8-hour workday or 40-hour work- week; (2) TLV-STEL—Short-term exposure limit or maximum concentration for a brief specified period of time, depending on a specific chemical (TWA must still be met); and (3) TLV-C—Ceiling Exposure Limit or maximum exposure concentration not to be exceeded under any circumstances. (TWA must still be met.)

Threshold Odor: (See: Odor threshold)

Threshold Planning Quantity: A quantity designated for each chemical on the list of extremely hazardous substances that triggers notification by facilities to the State Emergency Response Commission that such facilities are subject to emergency planning requirements under SARA Title III.

Thropic Levels: A functional classification of species that is based on feeding relationships (e.g. generally aquatic and terrestrial green plants comprise the first thropic level, and herbivores comprise the second.)

Tidal Marsh: Low, flat marshlands traversed by channels and tidal hollows, subject to tidal inundation; normally, the only vegetation present is salt-tolerant bushes and grasses. (See: wetlands.)

Tillage: Plowing, seedbed preparation, and cultivation practices.

Time-weighted Average (TWA): In air sampling, the average air concentration of contaminants during a given period.

Tire Processor: Intermediate operating facility where recovered tires are processed in preparation for recycling.

Tires: As used in recycling, passenger car and truck tires (excludes airplane, bus, motorcycle and special service military, agricultural, off-the-road and-slow speed industrial tires). Car and truck tires are recycled into rubber products such as trash cans, storage containers, rubberized asphalt or used whole for playground and reef construction.

Tolerance Petition: A formal request to establish a new tolerance or modify an existing one.

Tolerances: Permissible residue levels for pesticides in raw agricultural produce and processed foods. Whenever a pesticide is registered for use on a food or a feed crop, a tolerance (or exemption from the tolerance requirement) must be established. EPA establishes the tolerance levels, which are enforced by the Food and Drug Administration and the Department of Agriculture.

Tonnage: The amount of waste that a landfill accepts, usually expressed in tons per month. The rate at which a landfill accepts waste is limited by the landfill's permit.

Topography: The physical features of a surface area including relative elevations and the position of natural and man-made (anthropogenic) features.

Total Dissolved Phosphorous: The total phosphorous content of all material that will pass through a filter, which is determined as orthophosphate without prior digestion or hydrolysis. Also called soluble P. or ortho P.

Total Dissolved Solids (TDS): All material that passes the standard glass river filter; now called total filtrable residue. Term is used to reflect salinity.

Total Petroleum Hydrocarbons (TPH): Measure of the concentration or mass of petroleum hydrocarbon constituents present in a given amount of soil or water. The word "total" is a misnomer—few, if any, of the procedures for quantifying hydrocarbons can measure all of them in a given sample. Volatile ones are usually lost in the process and not quantified and non-petroleum hydrocarbons sometimes appear in the analysis.

Total Recovered Petroleum Hydrocarbon: A method for measuring petroleum hydrocarbons in samples of soil or water.

Total Suspended Particles (TSP): A method of monitoring airborne particulate matter by total weight.

Total Suspended Solids (TSS): A measure of the suspended solids in wastewater, effluent, or water bodies, determined by tests for "total suspended non-filterable solids." (See: suspended solids.)

Toxaphene: Chemical that causes adverse health effects in domestic water supplies and is toxic to fresh water and marine aquatic life.

Toxic Chemical: Any chemical listed in EPA rules as "Toxic Chemicals Subject to Section 313 of the Emergency Planning and Community Right-to-Know Act of 1986."

Toxic Chemical Release Form: Information form required of facilities that manufacture, process, or use (in quantities above a specific amount) chemicals listed under SARA Title III.

Toxic Chemical Use Substitution: Replacing toxic chemicals with less harmful chemicals in industrial processes.

Toxic Cloud: Airborne plume of gases, vapors, fumes, or aerosols containing toxic materials.

Toxic Concentration: The concentration at which a substance produces a toxic effect.

Toxic Dose: The dose level at which a substance produces a toxic effect.

Toxic Pollutants: Materials that cause death, disease, or birth defects in organisms that ingest or absorb them. The quantities and exposures necessary to cause these effects can vary widely.

Toxic Release Inventory: Database of toxic releases in the United States compiled from SARA Title III Section 313 reports.

Toxic Substance: A chemical or mixture that may present an unreasonable risk of injury to health or the environment.

Toxic Waste: A waste that can produce injury if inhaled, swallowed, or absorbed through the skin.

Toxicant: A harmful substance or agent that may injure an exposed organism.

Toxicity: The degree to which a substance or mixture of substances can harm humans or animals. Acute toxicity involves harmful effects in an organism through a single or short-term exposure. Chronic toxicity is the ability of a substance or mixture of substances to cause harmful effects over an extended period, usually upon repeated or continuous exposure sometimes lasting for the entire life of the exposed organism. Subchronic toxicity is the ability of the substance to cause effects for more than one year but less than the lifetime of the exposed organism.

Toxicity Assessment: Characterization of the toxicological properties and effects of a chemical, with special emphasis on establishment of dose-response characteristics.

Toxicity Testing: Biological testing (usually with an invertebrate, fish, or small mammal) to determine the adverse effects of a compound or effluent.

Toxicological Profile: An examination, summary, and interpretation of a hazardous substance to determine levels of exposure and associated health effects.

Transboundary Pollutants: Air pollution that travels from one jurisdiction to another, often crossing state or international boundaries. Also applies to water pollution.

Transfer Station: Facility where solid waste is transferred from collection vehicles to larger trucks or rail cars for longer distance transport.

Transient Water System: A non-community water system that does not serve 25 of the same nonresidents per day for more than six months per year.

Transmission Lines: Pipelines that transport raw water from its source to a water treatment plant, then to the distribution grid system.

Transmissivity: The ability of an aquifer to transmit water.

Transpiration: The process by which water vapor is lost to the atmosphere from living plants. The term can also be applied to the quantity of water thus dissipated.

Transportation Control Measures (TCMs): Steps taken by a locality to reduce vehicular emission and improve air quality by reducing or changing the flow of traffic; e.g. bus and HOV lanes, carpooling and other forms of ride-shairing, public transit, bicycle lanes.

Transporter: Hauling firm that picks up properly packaged and labeled hazardous waste from generators and transports it to designated facilities for treatment, storage, or disposal. Transporters are subject to EPA and DOT hazardous waste regulations.

Trash: Material considered worthless or offensive that is thrown away. Generally defined as dry waste material, but in common usage it is a synonym for garbage, rubbish, or refuse.

Trash-to-Energy Plan: Burning trash to produce energy.

Treatability Studies: Tests of potential cleanup technologies conducted in a laboratory (See: bench-scale tests.)

Treated Regulated Medical Waste: Medical waste treated to substantially reduce or eliminate its pathogenicity, but that has not yet been destroyed.

Treated Wastewater: Wastewater that has been subjected to one or more physical, chemical, and biological processes to reduce its potential of being health hazard.

Treatment: (1) Any method, technique, or process designed to remove solids and/or pollutants from solid waste, waste-streams, effluents, and air emissions. (2) Methods used to change the biological character or composition of any regulated medical waste so as to substantially reduce or eliminate its potential for causing disease.

Treatment Plant: A structure built to treat wastewater before discharging it into the environment.

Treatment, Storage, and Disposal Facility: Site where a hazardous substance is treated, stored, or disposed of. TSD facilities are regulated by EPA and states under RCRA.

Tremie: Device used to place concrete or grout under water.

Trial Burn: An incinerator test in which emissions are monitored for the presence of specific organic compounds, particulates, and hydrogen chloride.

Trichloroethylene (TCE): A stable, low boiling-point colorless liquid, toxic if inhaled. Used as a solvent or metal degreasing agent, and in other industrial applications.

Trickle Irrigation: Method in which water drips to the soil from perforated tubes or emitters.

Trickling Filter: A coarse treatment system in which wastewater is trickled over a bed of stones or other material covered with bacteria that break down the organic waste and produce clean water.

Trihalomethane (THM): One of a family of organic compounds named as derivative of methane. THMs are generally by-products of chlorination of drinking water that contains organic material.

Troposhpere: The layer of the atmosphere closest to the earth's surface.

Trust Fund (CERCLA): A fund set up under the Comprehensive Environmental Response, Compensation and Liability Act (CERCLA) to help pay for cleanup of hazardous waste sites and for legal action to force those responsible for the sites to clean them up.

Tube Settler: Device using bundles of tubes to let solids in water settle to the bottom for removal by conventional sludge collection means; sometimes used in sedimentation basins and clarifiers to improve particle removal.

Tuberculation: Development or formation of small mounds of corrosion products on the inside of iron pipe. These tubercules roughen the inside of the pipe, increasing its resistance to water flow.

Tundra: A type of treeless ecosystem dominated by lichens, mosses, grasses, and woody plants. Tundra is found at high latitudes (arctic tundra) and high altitudes (alpine tundra). Arctic tundra is underlain by permafrost and is usually water saturated. (See: wetlands.)

Turbidimeter: A device that measures the cloudiness of suspended solids in a liquid; a measure of the quantity of suspended solids.

Turbidity: 1. Haziness in air caused by the presence of particles and pollutants. 2. A cloudy condition in water due to suspended silt or organic matter.

U

Ultra Clean Coal (UCC): Coal that is washed, ground into fine particles, then chemically treated to remove sulfur, ash, silicone, and other substances; usually briquetted and coated with a sealant made from coal.

Ultraviolet Rays: Radiation from the sun that can be useful or potentially harmful. UV rays from one part of the spectrum (UV-A) enhance plant life. UV rays from other parts of the spectrum (UV-B) can cause skin cancer or other tissue damage. The ozone layer in the atmosphere partly shields us from ultraviolet rays reaching the earth's surface.

Uncertainty Factor: One of several factors used in calculating the reference dose from experimental data. UFs are intended to account for (1) the variation in sensitivity among humans; (2) the uncertainty in extrapolating animal data to humans; (3) the uncertainty in extrapolating data obtained in a study that covers less than the full life of the exposed animal or human; and (4) the uncertainty in using LOAEL data rather than NOAEL data.

Unconfined Aquifer: An aquifer containing water that is not under pressure; the water level in a well is the same as the water table outside the well.

Underground Injection Control (UIC): The program under the Safe Drinking Water Act that regulates the use of wells to pump fluids into the ground.

Underground Injection Wells: Steel- and concrete-encased shafts into which hazardous waste is deposited by force and under pressure.

Underground Sources of Drinking Water: Aquifers currently being used as a source of drinking water or those capable of supplying a public water system. They have a total dissolved solids content of 10,000 milligrams per liter or less, and are not "exempted aquifers." (See: exempted aquifer.)

Underground Storage Tank (UST): A tank located at least partially underground and designed to hold gasoline or other petroleum products or chemicals.

Unreasonable Risk: Under the Federal Insecticide, Fungicide, and Rodenticide Act (FIFRA), "unreasonable adverse effects" means any unreasonable risk to man or the environment, taking into account the medical, economic, social, and environmental costs and benefits of any pesticide.

Unsaturated Zone: The area above the water table where soil pores are not fully saturated, although some water may be present.

Upper Detection Limit: The largest concentration that an instrument can reliably detect.

Uranium Mill Tailings Piles: Former uranium ore processing sites that contain leftover radioactive materials (wastes), including radium and unrecovered uranium.

Uranium Mill-Tailings Waste Piles: Licensed active mills with tailings piles and evaporation ponds created by acid or alkaline leaching processes.

Urban Runoff: Storm water from city streets and adjacent domestic or commercial properties that carries pollutants of various kinds into the sewer systems and receiving waters.

Urea-Formaldehyde Foam Insulation: A material once used to conserve energy by sealing crawl spaces, attics, etc.; no longer used because emissions were found to be a health hazard.

Use Cluster: A set of competing chemicals, processes, and/or technologies that can substitute for one another in performing a particular function.

Used Oil: Spent motor oil from passenger cars and trucks collected at specified locations for recycling (not included in the category of municipal solid waste).

User Fee: Fee collected from only those persons who use a particular service, as compared to one collected from the public in general.

Utility Load: The total electricity demand for a utility district.

V

Vadose Zone: The zone between land surface and the water table within which the moisture content is less than saturation (except in the capillary fringe) and pressure is less than atmospheric. Soil pore space also typically contains air or other gases. The capillary fringe is included in the vadose zone. (See: Unsaturated Zone.)

Valued Environmental Attributes/Components: Those aspects(components/processes/functions) of ecosystems, human health, and environmental welfare considered to be important and potentially at risk from human activity or natural hazards. Similar to the term "valued environmental components" used in environmental impact assessment.

Vapor: The gas given off by substances that are solids or liquids at ordinary atmospheric pressure and temperatures.

Vapor Capture System: Any combination of hoods and ventilation system that captures or contains organic vapors so they may be directed to an abatement or recovery device.

Vapor Dispersion: The movement of vapor clouds in air due to wind, thermal action, gravity spreading, and mixing.

Vapor Plumes: Flue gases visible because they contain water droplets.

Vapor Pressure: A measure of a substance's propensity to evaporate, vapor pressure is the force per unit area exerted by vapor in an equilibrium state with surroundings at a given pressure. It increases exponentially with an increase in temperature. A relative measure of chemical volatility, vapor pressure is used to calculate water partition coefficients and volatilization rate constants.

Vapor Recovery System: A system by which the volatile gases from gasoline are captured instead of being released into the atmosphere.

Variance: Government permission for a delay or exception in the application of a given law, ordinance, or regulation.

Vector: 1. An organism, often an insect or rodent, that carries disease. 2. Plasmids, viruses, or bacteria used to transport genes into a host cell. A gene is placed in the vector; the vector then "infects" the bacterium.

Vegetative Controls: Non-point source pollution control practices that involve vegetative cover to reduce erosion and minimize loss of pollutants.

Vehicle Miles Travelled (VMT): A measure of the extent of motor vehicle operation; the total number of vehicle miles travelled within a specific geographic area over a given period of time.

Ventilation Rate: The rate at which indoor air enters and leaves a building. Expressed as the number of changes of outdoor air per unit of time (air changes per hour (ACH), or the rate at which a volume of outdoor air enters in cubic feet per minute (CFM).

Ventilation/Suction: The act of admitting fresh air into a space in order to replace stale or contaminated air; achieved by blowing air into the space. Similarly, suction represents the admission of fresh air into an interior space by lowering the pressure outside of the space, thereby drawing the contaminated air outward.

Venturi Scrubbers: Air pollution control devices that use water to remove particulate matter from emissions.

Vinyl Chloride: A chemical compound, used in producing some plastics, that is believed to be oncogenic.

Virgin Materials: Resources extracted from nature in their raw form, such as timber or metal ore.

Viscosity: The molecular friction within a fluid that produces flow resistance.

Volatile: Any substance that evaporates readily.

Volatile Liquids: Liquids which easily vaporize or evaporate at room temperature.

Volatile Organic Compound (VOC): Any organic compound that participates in atmospheric photochemical reactions except those designated by EPA as having negligible photochemical reactivity.

Volatile Solids: Those solids in water or other liquids that are lost on ignition of the dry solids at 550ø centigrade.

Volatile Synthetic Organic Chemicals: Chemicals that tend to volatilize or evaporate.

Volume Reduction: Processing waste materials to decrease the amount of space they occupy, usually by compacting, shredding, incineration, or composting.

Volumetric Tank Test: One of several tests to determine the physical integrity of a storage tank; the volume of fluid in the tank is measured directly or calculated from product-level changes. A marked drop in volume indicates a leak.

Vulnerability Analysis: Assessment of elements in the community that are susceptible to damage if hazardous materials are released.

Vulnerable Zone: An area over which the airborne concentration of a chemical accidentally released could reach the level of concern.

W

Waste: 1. Unwanted materials left over from a manufacturing process. 2. Refuse from places of human or animal habitation.

Waste Characterization: Identification of chemical and microbiological constituents of a waste material.

Waste Exchange: Arrangement in which companies exchange their wastes for the benefit of both parties.

Waste Feed: The continuous or intermittent flow of wastes into an incinerator.

Waste Generation: The weight or volume of materials and products that enter the waste stream before recycling, composting, landfilling, or combustion takes place. Also can represent the amount of waste generated by a given source or category of sources.

Waste Load Allocation: 1. The maximum load of pollutants each discharger of waste is allowed to release into a particular waterway. Discharge limits are usually required for each specific water quality criterion being, or expected to be, violated. 2. The portion of a stream's total assimilative capacity assigned to an individual discharge.

Waste Minimization: Measures or techniques that reduce the amount of wastes generated during industrial production processes; term is also applied to recycling and other efforts to reduce the amount of waste going into the waste stream.

Waste Piles: Non-containerized, lined or unlined accumulations of solid, nonflowing waste.

Waste Reduction: Using source reduction, recycling, or composting to prevent or reduce waste generation.

Waste Stream: The total flow of solid waste from homes, businesses, institutions, and manufacturing plants that is recycled, burned, or disposed of in landfills, or segments thereof such as the "residential waste stream" or the "recyclable waste stream."

Waste Treatment Lagoon: Impoundment made by excavation or earth fill for biological treatment of wastewater.

Waste Treatment Plant: A facility containing a series of tanks, screens, filters and other processes by which pollutants are removed from water.

Waste Treatment Stream: The continuous movement of waste from generator to treater and disposer.

Waste-Heat Recovery: Recovering heat discharged as a byproduct of one process to provide heat needed by a second process.

Waste-to-Energy Facility/Municipal-Waste Combustor: Facility where recovered municipal solid waste is converted into a usable form of energy, usually via combustion.

Wastewater: The spent or used water from a home, community, farm, or industry that contains dissolved or suspended matter.Water Pollution: The presence in water of enough harmful or objectionable material to damage the water's quality.

Wastewater Infrastructure: The plan or network for the collection, treatment, and disposal of sewage in a community. The level of treatment will depend on the size of the community, the type of discharge, and/or the designated use of the receiving water.

Wastewater Operations and Maintenance: Actions taken after construction to ensure that facilities constructed to treat wastewater will be operated, maintained, and managed to reach prescribed effluent levels in an optimum manner.

Wastewater Treatment Plan: A facility containing a series of tanks, screens, filters, and other processes by which pollutants are removed from water. Most treatments include chlorination to attain safe drinking water standards.

Water Purveyor: A public utility, mutual water company, county water district, or municipality that delivers drinking water to customers.

Water Quality Criteria: Levels of water quality expected to render a body of water suitable for its designated use. Criteria are based on specific levels of pollutants that would make the water harmful if used for drinking, swimming, farming, fish production, or industrial processes.

Water Quality Standards: State-adopted and EPA-approved ambient standards for water bodies. The standards prescribe the use of the water body and establish the water quality criteria that must be met to protect designated uses.

Water Quality-Based Limitations: Effluent limitations applied to dischargers when mere technology-based limitations would cause violations of water quality standards. Usually applied to discharges into small streams.

Water Quality-Based Permit: A permit with an effluent limit more stringent than one based on technology performance. Such limits may be necessary to protect the designated use of receiving waters (e.g. recreation, irrigation, industry or water supply).

Water Solubility: The maximum possible concentration of a chemical compound dissolved in water. If a substance is water soluble it can very readily disperse through the environment.

Water Storage Pond: An impound for liquid wastes designed to accomplish some degree of biochemical treatment.

Water Supplier: One who owns or operates a public water system.

Water Supply System: The collection, treatment, storage, and distribution of potable water from source to consumer.

Water Table: The level of groundwater.

Water Treatment Lagoon: An impound for liquid wastes designed to accomplish some degree of biochemical treatment.

Water Well: An excavation where the intended use is for location, acquisition, development, or artificial recharge of ground water.

Water-Soluble Packaging: Packaging that dissolves in water; used to reduce exposure risks to pesticide mixers and loaders.

Water-Source Heat Pump: Heat pump that uses wells or heat exchangers to transfer heat from water to the inside of a building. Most such units use ground water. (See: groundsource heat pump; heat pump.)

Waterborne Disease Outbreak: The significant occurence of acute illness associated with drinking water from a public water system that is deficient in treatment, as determined by appropriate local or state agencies.

Watershed: The land area that drains into a stream; the watershed for a major river may encompass a number of smaller watersheds that ultimately combine at a common point.

Watershed Approach: A coordinated framework for environmental management that focuses public and private efforts on the highest priority problems within hydrologically-defined geographic areas taking into consideration both ground and surface water flow.

Watershed Area: A topographic area within a line drawn connecting the highest points uphill of a drinking waterintake into which overland flow drains.

Weight of Scientific Evidence: Considerations in assessing the interpretation of published information about toxicity—quality of testing methods, size and power of study design, consistency of results across studies, and biological plausibility of exposure-response relationships and statistical associations.

Weir: 1. A wall or plate placed in an open channel to measure the flow of water. 2. A wall or obstruction used to control flow from settling tanks and clarifiers to ensure a uniform flow rate and avoid short-circuiting. (See: short-circuiting.)

Well: A bored, drilled, or driven shaft, or a dug hole whose depth is greater than the largest surface dimension and whose purpose is to reach underground water supplies or oil, or to store or bury fluids below ground.

Well Field: Area containing one or more wells that produce usable amounts of water or oil.

Well Injection: The subsurface emplacement of fluids into a well.

Well Monitoring: Measurement by on-site instruments or laboratory methods of well water quality.

Well Plug: A watertight, gastight seal installed in a bore hole or well to prevent movement of fluids.

Well Point: A hollow vertical tube, rod, or pipe terminating in a perforated pointed shoe and fitted with a fine-mesh screen.

Wellhead Protection Area: A protected surface and subsurface zone surrounding a well or well field supplying a public water system to keep contaminants from reaching the well water.

Wetlands: An area that is saturated by surface or ground water with vegetation adapted for life under those soil conditions, as swamps, bogs, fens, marshes, and estuaries.

Wettability: The relative degree to which a fluid will spread into or coat a solid surface in the presence of other immiscible fluids.

Wettable Powder: Dry formulation that must be mixed with water or other liquid before it is applied.

Wheeling: The transmission of electricity owned by one entity through the facilities owned by another (usually a utility).

Whole-Effluent-Toxicity Tests: Tests to determine the toxicity levels of the total effluent from a single source as opposed to a series of tests for individual contaminants.

Wildlife Refuge: An area designated for the protection of wild animals, within which hunting and fishing are either prohibited or strictly controlled.

Wire-to-Wire Efficiency: The efficiency of a pump and motor together.

Wood Packaging: Wood products such as pallets, crates, and barrels.

Wood Treatment Facility: An industrial facility that treats lumber and other wood products for outdoor use. The process employs chromated copper arsenate, which is regulated as a hazardous material.

Wood-Burning-Stove Pollution: Air pollution caused by emissions of particulate matter, carbon monoxide, total suspended particulates, and polycyclic organic matter from wood-burning stoves.

Working Level (WL): A unit of measure for documenting exposure to radon decay products, the so-called "daughters." One working level is equal to approximately 200 picocuries per liter.

Working Level Month (WLM): A unit of measure used to determine cumulative exposure to radon.

Xenobiota: Any biotum displaced from its normal habitat; a chemical foreign to a biological system.

Yard Waste: The part of solid waste composed of grass clippings, leaves, twigs, branches, and other garden refuse.

Yellow-Boy: Iron oxide flocculant (clumps of solids in waste or water); usually observed as orange-yellow deposits in surface streams with excess iron content. (See: floc, flocculation.)

Yield: The quantity of water (expressed as a rate of flow or total quantity per year) that can be collected for a given use from surface or groundwater sources.

Z

Zero Air: Atmospheric air purified to contain less than 0.1 ppm total hydrocarbons.

Zooplankton: Small (often microscopic) free-floating aquatic plants or animals.

Zone of Saturation: The layer beneath the surface of the land containing openings that may fill with water.

Source: *U.S. Environmental Protection Agency, "Terms of Environment"*

A

Entry Name Index

Entry Name Index

B

Entry Name Index

C

Entry Name Index

Entry Name Index

D

E

Entry Name Index

F

G

H

I

Entry Name Index

L

Entry Name Index

N

P

Q

R

S

Entry Name Index

X

Y

Z

Alabama

Alaska

Arizona

Arkansas

California

Colorado

Connecticut

Delaware

District of Columbia

Florida

Georgia

Hawaii

Idaho

Illinois

Indiana

Iowa

Kansas

Kentucky

Louisiana

Maine

Maryland

Massachusetts

Michigan

Minnesota

Mississippi

Missouri

Montana

Nebraska

Nevada

New Hampshire

New Jersey

New Mexico

New York

North Carolina

North Dakota

Ohio

Oklahoma

Oregon

Pennsylvania

Rhode Island

South Carolina

South Dakota

Tennessee

Texas

Utah

Vermont

Virginia

Washington

West Virginia

Wisconsin

Wyoming

Arctic ecology

Arid regions

Asbestos

Atmospheric sciences

Biology-Ecology

Biomass energy

Biotechnology

Biotic communities (*See also*: Plant communities)

Botanical ecology

Buildings, Environmental engineering of

Chemical toxicology

Children's environmental health

Coastal engineering (*See also*: Coastal zone management)

Coastal zone management (*See also*: Coastal engineering)

Coasts (*See also*: Coastal engineering)

Conservation of natural resources

Coral reef ecology

Dolphins

Drinking water

Ecological preserves

Ecology (*See also*: Conservation of natural resources)

Electricity

Elephants

Endangered species, Animals

Subject Index

Environmental design

Environmental economics (*See also:* Energy economics)

Environmental education

Environmental engineering (*See also:* Environmental design)

Environmental ethics

Environmental finances

Environmental health (*See also:* Air pollution)

Environmental impact analysis

Environmental monitoring

Environmental policy

Environmental protection

Environmental quality

Environmental sciences

Estuaries

Fertilizers

Subject Index

Fire ecology

Fish feeding and feeds

Fish habitat

Fish populations

Fish reproduction and growth

Fisheries

Fishery management

Fishery policy

Fishes

Food science and technology

Forest ecology

Forest management (*See also*: Fire ecology)

Forests and forestry (*See also*: National forests)

Fuels
(*See also*: Biomass energy)

Geographic information systems

Geothermal resources

Glaciology

Global warming

Great Lakes

Groundwater

Habitat, Ecology

Hazardous substances

Hazardous waste

Hazardous waste management

Human ecology
(*See also*: Conservation of natural resources)

Subject Index

Hydrocarbons

Hydrogen as fuel

Hydrology

Industrial hygiene

Industrial safety

Inhalation toxicology

Lake renewal

Lakes

Land use (*See also*: Agricultural conservation)

Land use and development

Law, Environmental (*See also*: Acid rain; Air pollution)

Litter (Trash)

Livestock

Marine biology (*See also*: Marine ecology)

Marine ecology (*See also*: Coral reef ecology)

Marine engineering

Marine industries (*See also*: Marine resources)

Marine mammals (*See also*: Dolphins; Whales)

Marine pollution

Marine resources

Marine sciences

Maritime law

Materials testing

Mines and mineral resources

Mountain ecology

Municipal waste

National forests (*See also*: Forests and forestry)

National parks and reserves (*See also*: Parks)

Natural products

Natural resources

Natural resources development

Subject Index

Pollution
(*See also*: Air pollution)

Pollution control

Pollution, Environmental effects of

Population

Prairie ecology

Public awareness/information programs

Pulp and paper technology

Radiation effects

Radioactive pollution (*See also*: Radioactive wastes)

Radioactive wastes (*See also*: Hazardous waste management)

Radon

Rain forest

Recreation areas

Recycling (*See also*: Energy conservation)

Renewable energy sources (*See also*: Solar energy, Wind energy)

Renewable natural resources

Reservoirs (*See also*: Water resources)

Risk

Rivers (*See also*: Estuaries; Water pollution; Watersheds)

Salmon

Sand dune ecology

Sanitary engineering (*See also*: Pollution; Water resources)

Sedimentation and deposition

Sewage sludge

Soil conservation

Soil pollution

Solar energy

Solid waste

Solid waste management

Speleology

Sustainable agriculture

Technology and the environment

Thermal energy

Tourism and recreation

Toxicology

Trails

Tropical ecology
(*See also*: Ecology, Tropical)

Tropical forestry

Underground storage

Urban wildlife

Vegetation mapping

Waste disposal

Waste management

Waste products (*See also*: Recycling [Waste, etc.])

Waste treatment

Wastewater treatment

Water conservation (*See also*: Water quality control)

Water pollution (*See also*: Acid rain)

Water quality (*See also*: Water pollution; Water quality control)

Water quality control (*See also*: Water reclamation)

Water reclamation (*See also*: Water use)

Water resources (*See also*: Groundwater; Reservoirs)

Water treatment (*See also*: Water reclamation)

Water use (*See also*: Water reclamation)

Waterfowl

Watersheds

Wetlands (*See also*: Estuaries)

Whales

Wilderness area

Wildlife (*See also*: Animal ecology; Wildlife management)

Wildlife management

Wind energy

2019 Title List

Visit **www.GreyHouse.com** for Product Information, Table of Contents, and Sample Pages.

General Reference

America's College Museums
American Environmental Leaders: From Colonial Times to the Present
Encyclopedia of African-American Writing
Encyclopedia of Constitutional Amendments
Encyclopedia of Human Rights and the United States
Encyclopedia of Invasions & Conquests
Encyclopedia of Prisoners of War & Internment
Encyclopedia of Religion & Law in America
Encyclopedia of Rural America
Encyclopedia of the Continental Congress
Encyclopedia of the United States Cabinet, 1789-2010
Encyclopedia of War Journalism
Encyclopedia of Warrior Peoples & Fighting Groups
The Environmental Debate: A Documentary History
The Evolution Wars: A Guide to the Debates
From Suffrage to the Senate: America's Political Women
Gun Debate: An Encyclopedia of Gun Rights & Gun Control in the U.S.
Opinions throughout History: National Security vs. Civil and Privacy Rights
Opinions throughout History: Immigration
Opinions throughout History: Drug Use & Abuse
Opinions throughout History: Gender: Roles & Rights
Opinions throughout History: The Environment
Opinions throughout History: Social Media Issues
Opinions throughout History: The Death Penalty
Opinions throughout History: Voters' Rights
Political Corruption in America
Privacy Rights in the Digital Age
The Religious Right: A Reference Handbook
Speakers of the House of Representatives, 1789-2009
This is Who We Were: 1880-1900
This is Who We Were: A Companion to the 1940 Census
This is Who We Were: In Colonial America
This is Who We Were: In the 1900s
This is Who We Were: In the 1910s
This is Who We Were: In the 1920s
This is Who We Were: In the 1940s
This is Who We Were: In the 1950s
This is Who We Were: In the 1960s
This is Who We Were: In the 1970s
This is Who We Were: In the 1980s
This is Who We Were: In the 1990s
This is Who We Were: In the 2000s
U.S. Land & Natural Resource Policy
The Value of a Dollar 1600-1865: Colonial Era to the Civil War
The Value of a Dollar: 1860-2019
Working Americans 1880-1999 Vol. I: The Working Class
Working Americans 1880-1999 Vol. II: The Middle Class
Working Americans 1880-1999 Vol. III: The Upper Class
Working Americans 1880-1999 Vol. IV: Their Children
Working Americans 1880-2015 Vol. V: Americans At War
Working Americans 1880-2005 Vol. VI: Women at Work
Working Americans 1880-2006 Vol. VII: Social Movements
Working Americans 1880-2007 Vol. VIII: Immigrants
Working Americans 1770-1869 Vol. IX: Revolutionary War to the Civil War
Working Americans 1880-2009 Vol. X: Sports & Recreation
Working Americans 1880-2010 Vol. XI: Inventors & Entrepreneurs
Working Americans 1880-2011 Vol. XII: Our History through Music
Working Americans 1880-2012 Vol. XIII: Education & Educators
Working Americans 1880-2016 Vol. XIV: Industry Through the Ages
Working Americans 1880-2017 Vol. XV: Politics & Politicians
World Cultural Leaders of the 20th & 21st Centuries

Education Information

Charter School Movement
The Comparative Guide to American Elementary & Secondary Schools
Complete Learning Disabilities Resource Guide
Educators Resource Guide
Special Education: A Reference Book for Policy and Curriculum Development

Health Information

Comparative Guide to American Hospitals
Complete Resource Guide for Pediatric Disorders
Complete Resource Guide for People with Chronic Illness
Complete Resource Guide for People with Disabilities
Complete Mental Health Resource Guide
Diabetes in America: Analysis of an Epidemic
Guide to Health Care Group Purchasing Organizations
Guide to U.S. HMO's & PPO's
Medical Device Market Place
Older Americans Information Resource

Business Information

Complete Television, Radio & Cable Industry Guide
Business Information Resources
Directory of Mail Order Catalogs
Guide to Venture Capital & Private Equity Firms
Environmental Resource Handbook
Financial Literacy Starter Kit
Food & Beverage Market Place
The Grey House Homeland Security Directory
The Grey House Performing Arts Industry Guide
The Grey House Safety & Security Directory
Hudson's Washington News Media Contacts Directory
New York State Directory
Sports Market Place

Statistics & Demographics

American Tally
America's Top-Rated Cities
America's Top-Rated Smaller Cities
Ancestry & Ethnicity in America
The Asian Databook
The Comparative Guide to American Suburbs
The Hispanic Databook
Nations of the World
Profiles of America
"Profiles of" Series - State Handbooks
Weather America

Financial Ratings Series

Financial Literacy Basics
TheStreet Ratings' Ultimate Guided Tour of Stock Investing
Weiss Ratings' Investment Research Guide to Bond & Money Market Mutual Funds
Weiss Ratings' Investment Research Guide to Stocks
Weiss Ratings' Investment Research Guide to Exchange-Traded Funds
Weiss Ratings' Investment Research Guide to Stock Mutual Funds
Weiss Ratings' Consumer Guides
Weiss Ratings' Financial Literary Basic Guides
Weiss Ratings' Guide to Banks
Weiss Ratings' Guide to Credit Unions
Weiss Ratings' Guide to Health Insurers
Weiss Ratings' Guide to Life & Annuity Insurers
Weiss Ratings' Guide to Property & Casualty Insurers

Bowker's Books In Print® Titles

American Book Publishing Record® Annual
American Book Publishing Record® Monthly
Books In Print®
Books In Print® Supplement
Books Out Loud™
Bowker's Complete Video Directory™
Children's Books In Print®
El-Hi Textbooks & Serials In Print®
Forthcoming Books®
Law Books & Serials In Print™
Medical & Health Care Books In Print™
Publishers, Distributors & Wholesalers of the US™
Subject Guide to Books In Print®
Subject Guide to Children's Books In Print®

2019 Title List

Visit www.GreyHouse.com for Product Information, Table of Contents, and Sample Pages.

Canadian General Reference

Associations Canada
Canadian Almanac & Directory
Canadian Environmental Resource Guide
Canadian Parliamentary Guide
Canadian Venture Capital & Private Equity Firms
Canadian Who's Who
Financial Post Bonds
Financial Post Directory of Directors
Financial Post Equities
Financial Post Survey
Financial Services Canada
Government Canada
Health Guide Canada
The History of Canada
Libraries Canada
Major Canadian Cities

2019 Title List

Visit www.SalemPress.com for Product Information, Table of Contents, and Sample Pages.

Science, Careers & Mathematics

Ancient Creatures
Applied Science
Applied Science: Engineering & Mathematics
Applied Science: Science & Medicine
Applied Science: Technology
Biomes and Ecosystems
Careers in the Arts: Fine, Performing & Visual
Careers in Building Construction
Careers in Business
Careers in Chemistry
Careers in Communications & Media
Careers in Environment & Conservation
Careers in Financial Services
Careers in Green Energy
Careers in Healthcare
Careers in Hospitality & Tourism
Careers in Human Services
Careers in Law, Criminal Justice & Emergency Services
Careers in Manufacturing
Careers in Nursing
Careers Outdoors
Careers Overseas
Careers in Physics
Careers in Protective Services
Careers in Psychology
Careers in Sales, Insurance & Real Estate
Careers in Science & Engineering
Careers in Social Media
Careers in Sports & Fitness
Careers in Sports Medicine & Training
Careers in Technology Services & Equipment Repair
Careers in Transportation
Computer Technology Innovators
Contemporary Biographies in Business
Contemporary Biographies in Chemistry
Contemporary Biographies in Communications & Media
Contemporary Biographies in Environment & Conservation
Contemporary Biographies in Healthcare
Contemporary Biographies in Hospitality & Tourism
Contemporary Biographies in Law & Criminal Justice
Contemporary Biographies in Physics
Earth Science
Earth Science: Earth Materials & Resources
Earth Science: Earth's Surface and History
Earth Science: Physics & Chemistry of the Earth
Earth Science: Weather, Water & Atmosphere
Encyclopedia of Energy
Encyclopedia of Environmental Issues
Encyclopedia of Environmental Issues: Atmosphere and Air Pollution
Encyclopedia of Environmental Issues: Ecology and Ecosystems
Encyclopedia of Environmental Issues: Energy and Energy Use
Encyclopedia of Environmental Issues: Policy and Activism
Encyclopedia of Environmental Issues: Preservation/Wilderness Issues
Encyclopedia of Environmental Issues: Water and Water Pollution
Encyclopedia of Global Resources
Encyclopedia of Global Warming
Encyclopedia of Mathematics & Society
Encyclopedia of Mathematics & Society: Engineering, Tech, Medicine
Encyclopedia of Mathematics & Society: Great Mathematicians
Encyclopedia of Mathematics & Society: Math & Social Sciences
Encyclopedia of Mathematics & Society: Math Development/Concepts
Encyclopedia of Mathematics & Society: Math in Culture & Society
Encyclopedia of Mathematics & Society: Space, Science, Environment
Encyclopedia of the Ancient World
Forensic Science
Geography Basics
Internet Innovators
Inventions and Inventors
Magill's Encyclopedia of Science: Animal Life
Magill's Encyclopedia of Science: Plant life
Notable Natural Disasters
Principles of Artificial Intelligence & Robotics
Principles of Astronomy
Principles of Biology
Principles of Biotechnology
Principles of Business: Accounting
Principles of Business: Economics
Principles of Business: Entrepreneurship
Principles of Business: Finance
Principles of Business: Globalization
Principles of Business: Leadership
Principles of Business: Management
Principles of Business: Marketing
Principles of Chemistry
Principles of Climatology
Principles of Ecology
Principles of Modern Agriculture
Principles of Pharmacology
Principles of Physical Science
Principles of Physics
Principles of Programming & Coding
Principles of Research Methods
Principles of Sociology: Group Relationships & Behavior
Principles of Sociology: Personal Relationships & Behavior
Principles of Sociology: Societal Issues & Behavior
Principles of Sustainability
Science and Scientists
Solar System
Solar System: Great Astronomers
Solar System: Study of the Universe
Solar System: The Inner Planets
Solar System: The Moon and Other Small Bodies
Solar System: The Outer Planets
Solar System: The Sun and Other Stars
USA in Space
World Geography

Literature

American Ethnic Writers
Classics of Science Fiction & Fantasy Literature
Critical Approaches to Literature
Critical Insights: Authors
Critical Insights: Film
Critical Insights: Literary Collection Bundles
Critical Insights: Themes
Critical Insights: Works
Critical Survey of Drama
Critical Survey of Graphic Novels: Heroes & Superheroes
Critical Survey of Graphic Novels: History, Theme & Technique
Critical Survey of Graphic Novels: Independents/Underground Classics
Critical Survey of Graphic Novels: Manga
Critical Survey of Long Fiction
Critical Survey of Mystery & Detective Fiction
Critical Survey of Mythology and Folklore: Gods & Goddesses
Critical Survey of Mythology and Folklore: Heroes & Heroines
Critical Survey of Mythology and Folklore: Love, Sexuality & Desire
Critical Survey of Mythology and Folklore: World Mythology
Critical Survey of Poetry
Critical Survey of Poetry: American Poets
Critical Survey of Poetry: British, Irish & Commonwealth Poets
Critical Survey of Poetry: Cumulative Index
Critical Survey of Poetry: European Poets
Critical Survey of Poetry: Topical Essays
Critical Survey of Poetry: World Poets
Critical Survey of Science Fiction & Fantasy Literature
Critical Survey of Shakespeare's Plays
Critical Survey of Shakespeare's Sonnets
Critical Survey of Short Fiction
Critical Survey of Short Fiction: American Writers
Critical Survey of Short Fiction: British, Irish, Commonwealth Writers
Critical Survey of Short Fiction: Cumulative Index
Critical Survey of Short Fiction: European Writers
Critical Survey of Short Fiction: Topical Essays

2019 Title List

Visit **www.SalemPress.com** for Product Information, Table of Contents, and Sample Pages.

Critical Survey of Short Fiction: World Writers
Critical Survey of World Literature
Critical Survey of Young Adult Literature
Cyclopedia of Literary Characters
Cyclopedia of Literary Places
Holocaust Literature
Introduction to Literary Context: American Poetry of the 20th Century
Introduction to Literary Context: American Post-Modernist Novels
Introduction to Literary Context: American Short Fiction
Introduction to Literary Context: English Literature
Introduction to Literary Context: Plays
Introduction to Literary Context: World Literature
Magill's Literary Annual
Magill's Survey of American Literature
Magill's Survey of World Literature
Masterplots
Masterplots, 2002-2018 Supplement
Masterplots II: African American Literature
Masterplots II: American Fiction Series
Masterplots II: British & Commonwealth Fiction Series
Masterplots II: Christian Literature
Masterplots II: Drama Series
Masterplots II: Juvenile & Young Adult Literature, Supplement
Masterplots II: Nonfiction Series
Masterplots II: Poetry Series
Masterplots II: Short Story Series
Masterplots II: Women's Literature Series
Notable African American Writers
Notable American Novelists
Notable Playwrights
Notable Poets
Novels into Film: Adaptations & Interpretation
Recommended Reading: 600 Classics Reviewed
Short Story Writers

History and Social Science

The 1910s in America
The 2000s in America
50 States
African American History
Agriculture in History
American First Ladies
American Heroes
American Indian Culture
American Indian History
American Indian Tribes
American Presidents
American Villains
America's Historic Sites
Ancient Greece
The Bill of Rights
The Civil Rights Movement
The Cold War
Countries: Their Wars & Conflicts: A World Survey
Countries, Peoples & Cultures
Countries, Peoples & Cultures: Central & South America
Countries, Peoples & Cultures: Central, South & Southeast Asia
Countries, Peoples & Cultures: East & South Africa
Countries, Peoples & Cultures: East Asia & the Pacific
Countries, Peoples & Cultures: Eastern Europe
Countries, Peoples & Cultures: Middle East & North Africa
Countries, Peoples & Cultures: North America & the Caribbean
Countries, Peoples & Cultures: West & Central Africa
Countries, Peoples & Cultures: Western Europe
Defining Documents: American Revolution
The Criminal Justice System
Defining Documents: American West
Defining Documents: Ancient World
Defining Documents: Asia
Defining Documents: Business Ethics
Defining Documents: Capital Punishment
Defining Documents: Civil Rights
Defining Documents: Civil War
Defining Documents: Court Cases
Defining Documents: Dissent & Protest
Defining Documents: Emergence of Modern America
Defining Documents: Exploration & Colonial America
Defining Documents: The Free Press
Defining Documents: The Gun Debate
Defining Documents: Immigration & Immigrant Communities
Defining Documents: The Legacy of 9/11
Defining Documents: LGBTQ+
Defining Documents: Manifest Destiny
Defining Documents: Middle Ages
Defining Documents: Middle East
Defining Documents: Nationalism & Populism
Defining Documents: Native Americans
Defining Documents: Political Campaigns, Candidates & Debates
Defining Documents: Postwar 1940s
Defining Documents: Prison Reform
Defining Documents: Reconstruction
Defining Documents: Renaissance & Early Modern Era
Defining Documents: Secrets, Leaks & Scandals
Defining Documents: Slavery
Defining Documents: Supreme Court Decisions
Defining Documents: 1920s
Defining Documents: 1930s
Defining Documents: 1950s
Defining Documents: 1960s
Defining Documents: 1970s
Defining Documents: The 17th Century
Defining Documents: The 18th Century
Defining Documents: The 19th Century
Defining Documents: The 20th Century: 1900-1950
Defining Documents: Vietnam War
Defining Documents: Women's Rights
Defining Documents: World War I
Defining Documents: World War II
Education Today
The Eighties in America
Encyclopedia of American Immigration
Encyclopedia of Flight
Encyclopedia of the Ancient World
Ethics: Questions & Morality of Human Actions
Fashion Innovators
The Fifties in America
The Forties in America
Great Athletes
Great Athletes: Baseball
Great Athletes: Basketball
Great Athletes: Boxing & Soccer
Great Athletes: Cumulative Index
Great Athletes: Football
Great Athletes: Golf & Tennis
Great Athletes: Olympics
Great Athletes: Racing & Individual Sports
Great Contemporary Athletes
Great Events from History: 17th Century
Great Events from History: 18th Century
Great Events from History: 19th Century
Great Events from History: 20th Century (1901-1940)
Great Events from History: 20th Century (1941-1970)
Great Events from History: 20th Century (1971-2000)
Great Events from History: 21st Century (2000-2016)
Great Events from History: African American History
Great Events from History: Cumulative Indexes
Great Events from History: Human Rights
Great Events from History: LGBTQ Events
Great Events from History: Middle Ages
Great Events from History: Modern Scandals
Great Events from History: Secrets, Leaks & Scandals
Great Events from History: Renaissance & Early Modern Era
Great Lives from History: 17th Century
Great Lives from History: 18th Century

 SALEM PRESS

2019 Title List

Visit **www.SalemPress.com** for Product Information, Table of Contents, and Sample Pages.

Great Lives from History: 19th Century
Great Lives from History: 20th Century
Great Lives from History: 21st Century (2000-2017)
Great Lives from History: American Heroes
Great Lives from History: American Women
Great Lives from History: Ancient World
Great Lives from History: Asian & Pacific Islander Americans
Great Lives from History: Cumulative Indexes
Great Lives from History: Incredibly Wealthy
Great Lives from History: Inventors & Inventions
Great Lives from History: Jewish Americans
Great Lives from History: Latinos
Great Lives from History: Renaissance & Early Modern Era
Great Lives from History: Scientists & Science
Historical Encyclopedia of American Business
Issues in U.S. Immigration
Magill's Guide to Military History
Milestone Documents in African American History
Milestone Documents in American History
Milestone Documents in World History
Milestone Documents of American Leaders
Milestone Documents of World Religions
Music Innovators
Musicians & Composers 20th Century
The Nineties in America
The Seventies in America
The Sixties in America
Sociology Today
Survey of American Industry and Careers
The Thirties in America
The Twenties in America
United States at War
U.S. Court Cases
U.S. Government Leaders
U.S. Laws, Acts, and Treaties
U.S. Legal System
U.S. Supreme Court
Weapons and Warfare
World Conflicts: Asia and the Middle East

Health

Addictions, Substance Abuse & Alcoholism
Adolescent Health & Wellness
Aging
Cancer
Complementary & Alternative Medicine
Community & Family Health Issues
Genetics & Inherited Conditions
Infectious Diseases & Conditions
Magill's Medical Guide
Nutrition
Psychology & Behavioral Health
Psychology Basics
Women's Health

2019 Title List

Visit **www.HWWilsonInPrint.com** for Product Information, Table of Contents and Sample Pages.

Current Biography
Current Biography Cumulative Index 1946-2013
Current Biography Monthly Magazine
Current Biography Yearbook: 2003
Current Biography Yearbook: 2004
Current Biography Yearbook: 2005
Current Biography Yearbook: 2006
Current Biography Yearbook: 2007
Current Biography Yearbook: 2008
Current Biography Yearbook: 2009
Current Biography Yearbook: 2010
Current Biography Yearbook: 2011
Current Biography Yearbook: 2012
Current Biography Yearbook: 2013
Current Biography Yearbook: 2014
Current Biography Yearbook: 2015
Current Biography Yearbook: 2016
Current Biography Yearbook: 2017
Current Biography Yearbook: 2018

Core Collections
Children's Core Collection
Fiction Core Collection
Graphic Novels Core Collection
Middle & Junior High School Core
Public Library Core Collection: Nonfiction
Senior High Core Collection
Young Adult Fiction Core Collection

The Reference Shelf
Affordable Housing
Aging in America
Alternative Facts: Post Truth & the Information War
The American Dream
American Military Presence Overseas
The Arab Spring
Artificial Intelligence
The Brain
The Business of Food
Campaign Trends & Election Law
Conspiracy Theories
Democracy Evolving
The Digital Age
Dinosaurs
Embracing New Paradigms in Education
Faith & Science
Families: Traditional and New Structures
The Future of U.S. Economic Relations: Mexico, Cuba, and Venezuela
Global Climate Change
Graphic Novels and Comic Books
Guns in America
Immigration
Immigration in the U.S.
Internet Abuses & Privacy Rights
Internet Safety
LGBTQ in the 21st Century
Marijuana Reform
New Frontiers in Space
The News and its Future
The Paranormal
Politics of the Ocean
Prescription Drug Abuse
Racial Tension in a "Postracial" Age
Reality Television
Representative American Speeches: 2008-2009
Representative American Speeches: 2009-2010
Representative American Speeches: 2010-2011
Representative American Speeches: 2011-2012
Representative American Speeches: 2012-2013
Representative American Speeches: 2013-2014
Representative American Speeches: 2014-2015
Representative American Speeches: 2015-2016
Representative American Speeches: 2016-2017
Representative American Speeches: 2017-2018
Representative American Speeches: 2018-2019
Rethinking Work
Revisiting Gender
Robotics
Russia
Social Networking
Social Services for the Poor
The South China Seas Conflict
Space Exploration & Development
Sports in America
The Supreme Court
The Transformation of American Cities
The Two Koreas
U.S. Infrastructure
U.S. National Debate Topic: Educational Reform
U.S. National Debate Topic: Surveillance
U.S. National Debate Topic: The Ocean
U.S. National Debate Topic: Transportation Infrastructure
Whistleblowers

Readers' Guide
Abridged Readers' Guide to Periodical Literature
Readers' Guide to Periodical Literature

Indexes
Index to Legal Periodicals & Books
Short Story Index
Book Review Digest

Sears List
Sears List of Subject Headings
Sears: Lista de Encabezamientos de Materia

Facts About Series
Facts About American Immigration
Facts About China
Facts About the 20th Century
Facts About the Presidents
Facts About the World's Languages

Nobel Prize Winners
Nobel Prize Winners: 1901-1986
Nobel Prize Winners: 1987-1991
Nobel Prize Winners: 1992-1996
Nobel Prize Winners: 1997-2001
Nobel Prize Winners: 2002-2018

World Authors
World Authors: 1995-2000
World Authors: 2000-2005

Famous First Facts
Famous First Facts
Famous First Facts About American Politics
Famous First Facts About Sports
Famous First Facts About the Environment
Famous First Facts: International Edition

American Book of Days
The American Book of Days
The International Book of Days

Monographs
American Game Changers
American Reformers

 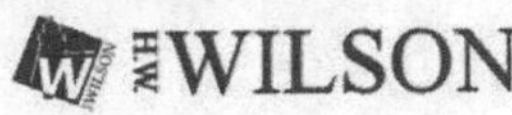

2019 Title List

Visit **www.HWWilsonInPrint.com** for Product Information, Table of Contents and Sample Pages.

The Barnhart Dictionary of Etymology
Celebrate the World
Guide to the Ancient World
Indexing from A to Z
Nobel Prize Winners
The Poetry Break
Radical Change: Books for Youth in a Digital Age
Speeches of American Presidents

Wilson Chronology
Wilson Chronology of Asia and the Pacific
Wilson Chronology of Human Rights
Wilson Chronology of Ideas
Wilson Chronology of the Arts
Wilson Chronology of the World's Religions
Wilson Chronology of Women's Achievements

Grey House Publishing | Salem Press | H.W. Wilson | 4919 Route, 22 PO Box 56, Amenia NY 12501-0056